THE FAMINE IMMIGRANTS

Lists of Irish Immigrants
Arriving at the Port of New York,
1846-1851

Illustrated London News

Irish emigrants leaving home—the priest's blessing.

THE FAMINE IMMIGRANTS

Lists of Irish Immigrants Arriving at the Port of New York, 1846-1851

Ira A. Glazier
Editor

Michael Tepper
Associate Editor

Volume V
October 1849-May 1850

Baltimore
GENEALOGICAL PUBLISHING CO., INC.
1985

Genealogical Publishing Co., Inc.
Baltimore, Maryland

Library of Congress Catalogue Card Number 83-80078
International Standard Book Number 0-8063-1123-1
Made in the United States of America

Foreword

The fifth volume of *The Famine Immigrants* contains a chronological list of over 60,000 Irish passengers who arrived at the port of New York between October 1849 and May 1850. The passenger lists, as in the preceding volumes, are arranged by ship and date of arrival and contain information on name, age, sex, occupation, and family relationships when noted in the manifests.

Although emigration moderated in 1848, a new wave unleashed by the harvest failure of 1848 pushed annual migration figures to over 200,000 in 1849 and 1850. A detailed analysis of the timing and magnitude of these flows and changes in their structure and composition will be undertaken when all the manifests have been published.

Once again, we would like to express our appreciation to the students and staff at the Temple University—Balch Institute Center for Immigration Research whose collective efforts have made this work possible.

I.A.G.

KEY

passenger

sex

age

occupation

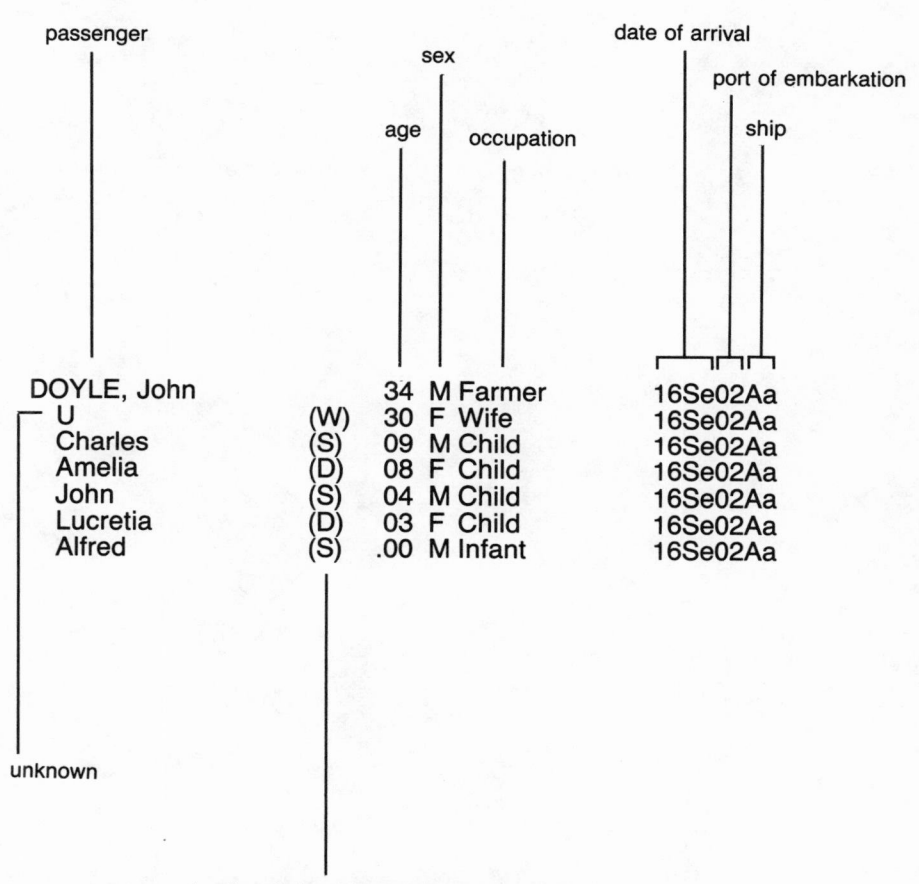

date of arrival

port of embarkation

ship

DOYLE, John		34	M	Farmer	16Se02Aa
U	(W)	30	F	Wife	16Se02Aa
Charles	(S)	09	M	Child	16Se02Aa
Amelia	(D)	08	F	Child	16Se02Aa
John	(S)	04	M	Child	16Se02Aa
Lucretia	(D)	03	F	Child	16Se02Aa
Alfred	(S)	.00	M	Infant	16Se02Aa

unknown

family relationship (wife, son, daughter)

Also *A* aunt; *B* brother; *C* cousin; *F* stepdaughter; *G* stepson; *H* husband; *L* in-law; *M* mother; *N* niece/nephew; *O* widow/widower; *P* father; *R* relative; *T* sister; *Y* grandparent; *Z* grandchild.

LIST OF SHIPS
With Code Letters

AA COLUMBINE
AB ENTERPRIZE
AC NASCONOMO
AD HANNAH-THORNTON
AE MOUNTAINEER
AF ARAB
AG CANADA
AH COLUMBUS
AI DROMAHAIR
AJ VICTORIA
AK MINNESOTA
AL ROSE
AM BROTHERS
AN HOTTINGUER
AO GREAT-WESTERN
AP MINERVA
AQ ZELPHA-P.BROWN
AR DEWITT-CLINTON
AS MONTREAL
AT ROSCIUS
AU LONDON
AV ATLANTIC
AW CORNELIA
AX GUY-MANNERING
AY HINDOSTAN
AZ YORKSHIRE
BA MADISON
BB ASHBURTON
BC SARAH-MARIA
BD FALCON
BE DUCHESS-OF-KENT
BF MARGARET-EVANS
BG NIAGARA
BH EFFINGHAM
BI CHARLOTTE-HARRISON
BJ WARRIOR
BK METEOR
BL MONTEZUMA
BM CONSTELLATION
BN GERTRUDE
BO KATE
BP BRITISH-QUEEN
BQ CHAOS
BR SARDINIA
BS MORTIMER-LIVINGSTON
BT IVANHOE
BU ST.GEORGE
BV ALBERT
BW MARGARET
BX LIVERPOOL
BY MARIA
BZ LADY-OF-THE-LAKE
CA ADIRONDACK
CB RAPPAHANOCK
CC DEVONSHIRE
CD SIDDONS
CE HOUGHTON
CF GENERAL-SCOTT
CG AMERICA
CH DENMARK
CI MARIA
CJ CORA-LINN
CK CORSAIR
CL AMERICAN-EAGLE
CM JAVA
CN INDIAN-QUEEN
CO WM.H.HARBECK
CP JOSEPHINE
CQ HARMONIA
CR MEDOMACK
CS WATERLOO
CT MARMION
CU L.Z.
CV DEBORAH
CW PATRICK-HENRY
CX NEW-YORK
CY WESTMINSTER
CZ ADMIRAL
DA ABEONA
DB CENTURION
DC JANE-GOWDIE
DD PHILADELPHIA
DE JANET
DF HIBERNIA
DG QUEEN-OF-THE-WEST
DH OREGON
DI WISCONSIN
DJ LADY-MILTON
DK ALBION
DL CONSTITUTION
DM CAMBRIDGE
DN SHERIDAN
DO SOUTHAMPTON
DP JOHN-R.SKIDDY
DQ J.Z.
DR YORKTOWN
DS OHIO
DT ANDREW-FOSTER
DU BROOKSBY
DV LADY-HOBART
DW GARRICK
DY OXFORD
DZ ST.PATRICK
EA JAS.H.SHEPHERD
EB SIR-WM.MOLESWORTH
EC NEW-WORLD
ED A.Z.
EE HYNDEFORD
EF IRWIN
EG VANDALIA
EH FIDELIA
EI SARAH
EJ ANN-KENNY
EK JOHN-MARSHALL
EL CIRCASSIAN
EM HEATHER-BELL
EN ROBERT-SCURFIELD
EO LIBERTY
EP JANE-BLACK
EQ SHANNON
ER WEST-POINT
ES SILAS-GREENMAN
ET IDA-KISS
EU SARAH-PARKER
EV NAOMI
EW JAMES-DRAKE
EX ANN-HARLEY
EY IOWA
EZ CATHERINE
FA HENDRIK-HUDSON
FB ALBERT-GALLATIN
FC EMPIRE-STATE
FD ISAAC-WRIGHT
FE EUROPA
FF MT.STUART-ELPHINSTON
FG EXCELSIOR
FH SIR-HENRY-POTTINGER
FI DEVONIA
FJ SWITZERLAND
FK COLUMBIA
FL BRYAN-ABBS
FM JAMESTOWN
FN ABERDEEN
FO JOHN-CURRIER
FP KATE-HUNTER
FQ DAVID-CANNON
FR BRANT
FS JACOB-A.WESTERVELT
FT COROMANDEL
FU RHEIN
FV GENERAL-WASHINGTON
FW JAMES-WRIGHT
FX ELIZA-HELEN
FY SAMUEL-CAMPBELL
FZ COLONIST
GA ROSANNA
GB EMPIRE-CITY
GC WASHINGTON
GD TICONDEROGA
GE STAR-OF-THE-WEST
GF NISIDI-STEWART
GG VANGUARD
GH PRINCETON
GI BELLOND
GJ INDUSTRY
GK MARY-RUSSELL
GL MARY-MORRIS
GM CITY-OF-GLASGOW
GN JOHN-HANCOCK
GO MONMOUTH
GP MISSISSIPPI
GQ JOHN-HAMILTON
GR HENRY
GS LADY-COLEBROOKE
GT ADAM-CARR
GU EMIGRANT
GV ATLAS
GW DANUBE
GX CLARENCE
GZ KATHLEEN
HA ISAAC-WEBB
HB WAVE
HC WM.D.SEWELL
HD MANHATTAN
HE WABAN
HF ASHLAND
HG GLADIATOR
HH CORNELIA
HI NEW-HAMPSHIRE
HJ HAITI
HK CELESTE
HL ELIZA
HM CAMBRIA
HN EDWARD
HO UNDINE
HP LETITIA-HYNE
HQ GIPSEY
HR ROLLA
HS DUKE
HT FOREST-QUEEN
HU RIVERDALE
HV INDEPENDENCE
HW FLORA
HX HENRY-WOODS
HY JAMES-FAGAN
HZ CHINA
IA ANNIE
IB NORWAY
IC WOLFVILLE
ID FRANCONIA

IE QUEEN
IF AFGHAN
IG WALHOLDING
IH ADONIA
II HESPERUS
IK EUGENIA
IL ABBY-LAND
IM MARCHIONESS-OF-BUTE
IN NEPTUNIS
IO KATE-HOWE
IP WILLIAM-RATHBONE
IQ WATTROW
IR TYNE
IS WATERFORD
IT EL-DORADO
IU ORONOCO
IV ANNONDALE
IW SIR-HARRY-SMITH
IX ANNA-MARIA
IY CHARLES-CROOKER
IZ NESTORIAN
JA FANNY
JB COSMO
JC SOLWAY
JD MASONIC
JE ANNA-TIFT
JF DELAWARE
JG GRACE-MCNEA
JH HELENA
JI FORESTAL
JJ ELIZABETH
JK LIVING-AGE
JL OPHELIA
JM HUGUENOT
JN DOWNES
JO AMULET
JP MARY-WARD
JQ ANN-MOORE
JR ATALANTA
JS AMBASSADRESS
JT WARREN
JU ROSS
JV M.HAWES
JW DEVON
JX PRINCESS-VICTORY
JY ACME
JZ ELIZA-ANN
KA ALERT
KB HANNAH-KERR
KC HIGHLAND-MARY
KD CHARLES-RICHARD
KE DESMAHAGAN
KF HARLEQUIN
KG WESTERN-WORLD
KH MARTHA-WARD
KI FINANCIER
KJ POLLY
KK ADLER
KL GEORGE
KM POLYNESIA
KN ACADIA
KO WILLIAM
KP SCOTLAND
KQ NANCY
KR ODESSA
KS MARY-HALE
KT HERCULES
KU MARTHA-KINSMAN
KV EUPHEMIA

Ports of Embarkation
With Code Numbers

01 LONDONDERRY
02 LIVERPOOL
03 HAVRE
04 NEWRY
05 DUBLIN
06 LONDON
07 ST.JOHNS, N.B.
08 HALIFAX
09 SLIGO
10 LIMERICK
11 ST.JOHNS, N.F.
12 LIVERPOOL AND HALIFAX
13 BERMUDA AND ST.THOMAS
14 LONDON AND PORTSMOUTH
15 PLYMOUTH
16 PENZANCE
17 BELFAST
18 CORK
19 GREENOCK
20 MALAGA, GIBRALTAR
21 GLASGOW
22 BERMUDA
23 CHAGRES AND JAMAICA
24 ST.KITTS
25 ST.THOMAS AND BERMUDA
26 GLOUCESTER
27 VERA CRUZ
28 SAVANILLA
29 NEWCASTLE
30 PORT-AU-PRINCE
31 CARDIFF
32 HAVANA
33 DEMERARA
34 BRISTOL
35 WATERFORD
36 CHAGRES AND KINGSTON
37 DEMERARA AND TURK'S ISLAND
38 ELEUTHERA
39 AMBERLAND, NOVA SCOTIA
40 HAMILTON, BERMUDA
41 GLASGOW AND GREENOCK
42 GALWAY
43 ST.JOHNS, P.R.
44 HULL
45 NEWPORT, WALES
46 FAYAL
47 CHAGRES AND HAVANA
48 ST.KITES(?)
49 FALMOUTH
50 ST.MARTINS
51 ST.THOMAS
52 WINDSOR
53 YARMOUTH, N.S.
54 SANTO DOMINGO
55 CORK AND CARDIFF
56 MADEIRA
57 WEXFORD

List of Occupations
With Code Letters

AGRC	AGRICULTURIST
ASSTENGR	ASSISTANT ENGINEER
AY-OFF	ARMY OFFICER
BACMCHT	BACON MERCHANT
BOMKR	BONNET MAKER
BRF	BRASS FOUNDER
BT-SHMK	BOOT-SHOEMAKER
BTLMKR	BOTTLE MAKER
CAGT	COMMERCIAL AGENT
CBTMKR	CABINET MAKER
CCHBLDR	COACH BUILDER
CLCP	CALICO PRINTER
CRDPTR	CARD PRINTER
CST	CORSET-STAY MAKER
CTLDLR	CATTLE DEALER
CTNSP	COTTON SPINNER
CVER	CIVIL ENGINEER
CVR-GLDR	CARVER-GILDER
D-FMR	DAUGHTER OF FARMER
ENGD	ENGINE DRIVER
ENGFTR	ENGINE FITTER
ENGR-MLWR	ENGINEER-MILLWRIGHT
EWD	EARTHENWARE DEALER
FLABR	FARM LABORER
FSVNT	FARM SERVANT
FWKR	FACTORY WORKER
GDNR	GARDENER, GROWER
HRSDLR	HORSE DEALER
IMKR	INSTRUMENT MAKER
IRNMLDR	IRON MOULDER
LAD	LAUNDRY WORKER
LDGHKPR	LODGINGHOUSE KEEPER
LDSTWT	LAND STEWARD
LMNFTR	LEATHER MANUFACTURER
LNBL	LINEN BLEACHER
LNMNFTR	LINEN MANUFACTURER
LRFH	LEATHER FINISHER
MEDST	MEDICAL STUDENT
MMRNR	MASTER MARINER
MTLDLR	METAL DEALER
NVOF	NAVY OFFICER
PLTWKR	PLATE WORKER
PPHGR	PAPER HANGER
PPSTR	PAPER STAINER
PROF-MUS	PROFESSOR OF MUSIC
PWLWVR	POWERLOOM WEAVER
RGD	RAILWAY GUARD
RRCTTR	RAILWAY CONTRACTOR
SCHM	SCHOOL MASTER
SCHMS	SCHOOL MISTRESS
SDLMKR	SADDLE MAKER
SGNS	SHIP'S SURGEON
SHPC	SHIP'S CARPENTER
SPDMKR	SPINDLE MAKER
STCTR	STONE CUTTER
STKW	STOCKING WEAVER
TALCH	TALLOW CHANDLER
TBCMNFTR	TOBACCO MANUFACTURER
TIPWKR	TINPLATE WORKER
W-FMR	WIFE OF FARMER
W-LABR	WIFE OF LABORER
WI	WIDOW/WIDOWER
WMCHT	WINE MERCHANT

THE FAMINE IMMIGRANTS

Lists of Irish Immigrants
Arriving at the Port of New York,
1846-1851

COLUMBINE 02 OCTOBER 1849

From London And Portsmouth

NAMES OF PASSENGERS	AGE	SEX	OCCUPATIONS	DATE PORT SHIP
CHANCY, Thos.	20	M	Unknown	020c14Aa
ABRAHAM, Wm.	30	M	Unknown	020c14Aa
Ann	30	F	Unknown	020c14Aa
Wm.G.	2	M	Child	020c14Aa
Ansel	.00	M	Infant	020c14Aa
GARROD, John	36	M	Unknown	020c14Aa
Amelia	29	F	Unknown	020c14Aa
Joseph	9	M	Child	020c14Aa
Elizabeth	5	F	Child	020c14Aa
Emma	.00	F	Infant	020c14Aa
PETIT, Robt.	32	M	Unknown	020c14Aa
Elizabeth	22	F	Unknown	020c14Aa
G.	4	U	Child	020c14Aa
Fredk.	1	M	Child	020c14Aa
BOYCES, Wm.	27	M	Unknown	020c14Aa
Margaret	23	F	Unknown	020c14Aa
Wm.	2	M	Child	020c14Aa
Charles	.00	M	Infant	020c14Aa
GRINBER, Anna	26	F	Unknown	020c14Aa
Anna	12	F	Unknown	020c14Aa
Henry	9	M	Child	020c14Aa
Sophia	8	F	Child	020c14Aa
Joseph	7	M	Child	020c14Aa
Wm.	6	M	Child	020c14Aa
COURTY, Thos.	26	M	Unknown	020c14Aa
WALLIS, Michael	27	M	Unknown	020c14Aa
Harriet	24	F	Unknown	020c14Aa
RICH, Zac.	35	M	Unknown	020c14Aa
Flora	32	F	Unknown	020c14Aa
Jasper	19	M	Unknown	020c14Aa
Wm.	12	M	Unknown	020c14Aa
Flora	10	F	Unknown	020c14Aa
Leveeden	8	U	Child	020c14Aa
Alfred	6	M	Child	020c14Aa
Edwin	5	M	Child	020c14Aa
BICKESTER, John	31	M	Unknown	020c14Aa
PEACOCK, John	20	M	Unknown	020c14Aa
TEMPLAR, Wm.	32	M	Unknown	020c14Aa
Sarah	31	F	Unknown	020c14Aa
Emma	11	F	Unknown	020c14Aa
Sarah-Ann	9	F	Child	020c14Aa
Elizabeth	7	F	Child	020c14Aa
Ellen	4	F	Child	020c14Aa
BOYCE, William	35	M	Unknown	020c14Aa
D.Mary	29	F	Unknown	020c14Aa
John	.00	M	Infant	020c14Aa
ADDY, Thos.	22	M	Unknown	020c14Aa
SMITH, Thos.	19	M	Unknown	020c14Aa
RELSALL, Wm.	18	M	Unknown	020c14Aa
DONAHUE, Humphrey	26	M	Unknown	020c14Aa
Mary	26	F	Unknown	020c14Aa
SCULINGER, John	23	M	Unknown	020c14Aa
RELLE, Frederic	24	M	Unknown	020c14Aa
RATRAS, Henry	20	M	Unknown	020c14Aa
BARFORD, Charles	20	M	Unknown	020c14Aa
GREEN, Marie-Ann	25	F	Unknown	020c14Aa
Mary-Ann	3	F	Child	020c14Aa
Emma	1	F	Child	020c14Aa
WATTS, Caroline	30	F	Unknown	020c14Aa
WEST, Erwin	29	M	Unknown	020c14Aa
SIDDALL, Jas.	37	M	Unknown	020c14Aa
Whoda	31	U	Unknown	020c14Aa
Ellen	5	F	Child	020c14Aa
RAICE, Sarah	26	F	Unknown	020c14Aa
Elizabeth	.00	F	Infant	020c14Aa
COBB, Ann	60	F	Unknown	020c14Aa
OBRIAN, Patrick	40	M	Unknown	020c14Aa
Margaret	40	F	Unknown	020c14Aa
Ellen	9	F	Child	020c14Aa
Mary	6	F	Child	020c14Aa
Margaret	4	F	Child	020c14Aa
Bridget	2	F	Child	020c14Aa
Mary	30	F	Unknown	020c14Aa
CALLINAN, John	35	M	Unknown	020c14Aa
TAYLOR, Wm.	24	M	Unknown	020c14Aa
HOWARD, Julia	27	F	Unknown	020c14Aa
TILBY, Emma	21	F	Unknown	020c14Aa
RUSSEL, Walter	28	M	Unknown	020c14Aa
Mary	28	F	Unknown	020c14Aa
WELSCH, Thos.	29	M	Unknown	020c14Aa
Elizabeth	27	F	Unknown	020c14Aa
Ann	.00	F	Infant	020c14Aa
BECK, Matthew	24	M	Unknown	020c14Aa
Hickle--, Simon	27	M	Unknown	020c14Aa
PALMER, Theresa	22	F	Unknown	020c14Aa
MEDLER, Maria	34	F	Unknown	020c14Aa
Mary-Ann	9	F	Child	020c14Aa
Thos.	1	M	Child	020c14Aa
BALL, Wm.Beagle	35	M	Unknown	020c14Aa
Wm.Henry	13	M	Unknown	020c14Aa
MINERS, Saml.	39	M	Unknown	020c14Aa
Sidwell	24	U	Unknown	020c14Aa
Eliza-Jane	1	F	Child	020c14Aa
DYERS, Susannah	24	F	Unknown	020c14Aa
TELLER, Ann	31	F	Unknown	020c14Aa
Caroline	6	F	Child	020c14Aa
Eliza-Ann	4	F	Child	020c14Aa
Ellen	3	F	Child	020c14Aa
LANGDON, Wm.Tucker	31	M	Unknown	020c14Aa
Elizabeth	33	F	Unknown	020c14Aa
CULNO, John	24	M	Unknown	020c14Aa
Mathew	18	M	Unknown	020c14Aa
JAY, Richd.	19	M	Unknown	020c14Aa
FRANCTON, Louis	24	M	Unknown	020c14Aa
BASSETT, John	28	M	Unknown	020c14Aa
Catherine	28	F	Unknown	020c14Aa
COLLINS, Austin	24	M	Unknown	020c14Aa
RICHARDS, Anne	30	F	Unknown	020c14Aa
Joseph	9	M	Child	020c14Aa
Elizabeth-Anne	7	F	Child	020c14Aa
MITCHEL, Mary-Jane	18	F	Unknown	020c14Aa
Wm.	16	M	Unknown	020c14Aa
Joseph	13	M	Unknown	020c14Aa
Edwin	8	M	Child	020c14Aa
Ellen	6	F	Child	020c14Aa
Charles	4	M	Child	020c14Aa
HAVEN, Joel	65	M	Unknown	020c14Aa
Fanny	27	F	Unknown	020c14Aa
Moses	9	M	Child	020c14Aa
WARD, U-Mrs.	38	F	Unknown	020c14Aa
U-Miss	24	F	Unknown	020c14Aa
BASSETT, Elizabeth-Jan Died-At-Sea	1	F	Child	020c14Aa
MITCHEL, Joseph Died-At-Sea	44	M	Unknown	020c14Aa
Mary-Ann Died-At-Sea	45	F	Unknown	020c14Aa
John Died-At-Sea	20	M	Unknown	020c14Aa
George Died-At-Sea	10	M	Unknown	020c14Aa
PERCIVAL, Fanny Died-At-Sea	.00	F	Infant	020c14Aa
MENKE, Abraham Died-At-Sea	36	M	Unknown	020c14Aa
BUCKHARDT, George Died-At-Sea	38	M	Unknown	020c14Aa
FRANK, Herman Died-At-Sea	2	M	Child	020c14Aa

NAMES OF PASSENGERS	AGE	SEX	OCCUPATIONS	DATE PORT SHIP
MILLS, Wm.	25	M	Unknown	020c14Aa
Died-At-Sea				
FISHER, Wm.F.A.	39	M	Unknown	020c14Aa
Died-At-Sea				

ENTERPRIZE 03 OCTOBER 1849

From Liverpool

NAMES OF PASSENGERS	AGE	SEX	OCCUPATIONS	DATE PORT SHIP
QUIRK, Michael	22	M	Laborer	030c02Ab
Julia	18	F	Unknown	030c02Ab
Julia	17	F	Unknown	030c02Ab
COOPER, Fenwick	24	M	Unknown	030c02Ab
Mary	24	F	Unknown	030c02Ab
Mary	20	F	Unknown	030c02Ab
BOLTON, Robert	24	M	Unknown	030c02Ab
Ann	24	F	Unknown	030c02Ab
RUNDLE, John	24	M	Unknown	030c02Ab
U-Mrs.	23	F	Unknown	030c02Ab
Robert	.00	M	Infant	030c02Ab
COLL, Robert	29	M	Unknown	030c02Ab
SWYNE, Thomas	32	M	Unknown	030c02Ab
MCCARTNEY, John	24	M	Unknown	030c02Ab
Grace	20	F	Unknown	030c02Ab
FULLERTON, U-Mrs.	40	F	Unknown	030c02Ab
Elizabeth	12	F	Unknown	030c02Ab
Robert	9	M	Child	030c02Ab
Died-At-Sea				
Benjamin	5	M	Child	030c02Ab
KENEDY, Mark	22	M	Unknown	030c02Ab
Patrick	18	M	Unknown	030c02Ab
DEVINE, Ann	21	F	Unknown	030c02Ab
SALISBURY, Samuel	24	M	Unknown	030c02Ab
Catherine	23	F	Unknown	030c02Ab
Francis	22	M	Unknown	030c02Ab
KENAHAN, Barbara	24	F	Unknown	030c02Ab
George	.06	M	Infant	030c02Ab
CASSON, Ann	22	F	Unknown	030c02Ab
KELLY, James	23	M	Unknown	030c02Ab
JONES, William	23	M	Unknown	030c02Ab
COONEY, John	24	M	Unknown	030c02Ab
Margaret	20	F	Unknown	030c02Ab
COCHRAN, Sarah	20	F	Unknown	030c02Ab
HALL, Ellen	18	F	Unknown	030c02Ab
MURPHY, Michael	50	M	Unknown	030c02Ab
Mary	48	F	Unknown	030c02Ab
TIGHE, Mary	3	F	Child	030c02Ab
Mary-Ann	1	F	Child	030c02Ab
MCNALLY, Michael	22	M	Unknown	030c02Ab
MESERS, U-Mrs.	30	F	Unknown	030c02Ab
Eliza	18	F	Unknown	030c02Ab
Wm.	16	M	Unknown	030c02Ab
WALKER, Thomas	20	M	Unknown	030c02Ab
STOKES, Wm.	40	M	Unknown	030c02Ab
MOORE, John	32	M	Unknown	030c02Ab
U-Mrs.	30	F	Unknown	030c02Ab
DOYLE, John	21	M	Unknown	030c02Ab
BURNS, Mary-Ann	12	F	Unknown	030c02Ab
James	8	M	Child	030c02Ab
EGAN, Ann	20	F	Unknown	030c02Ab
FLYNNE, Michael	20	M	Unknown	030c02Ab
CAREY, Thomas	25	M	Unknown	030c02Ab
Mary	25	F	Unknown	030c02Ab
MEANLY, David	42	M	Unknown	030c02Ab
James	21	M	Unknown	030c02Ab
Michael	19	M	Unknown	030c02Ab
Ellen	17	F	Unknown	030c02Ab
NADDY, Leonard	40	M	Unknown	030c02Ab
DILLON, Catherine	20	F	Unknown	030c02Ab

NAMES OF PASSENGERS	AGE	SEX	OCCUPATIONS	DATE PORT SHIP
SMITH, Owen	31	M	Unknown	030c02Ab
MURPHY, Wm.	19	M	Unknown	030c02Ab
MIHONY, Thomas	16	M	Unknown	030c02Ab
BURKE, Catherine	24	F	Unknown	030c02Ab
Mary	.00	F	Infant	030c02Ab
CORRIGAN, Edward	21	M	Unknown	030c02Ab
SCOLLAN, James	19	M	Unknown	030c02Ab
CARROLL, James	24	M	Unknown	030c02Ab
MCMULLEN, Christn.	24	M	Unknown	030c02Ab
SHERIDAN, Maria	22	F	Unknown	030c02Ab
MOORE, Robert	20	M	Unknown	030c02Ab
HEANEY, John	23	M	Unknown	030c02Ab
BAXTER, Philip	20	M	Unknown	030c02Ab
TEAYNOR, Pat	45	M	Unknown	030c02Ab
U-Mrs.	40	F	Unknown	030c02Ab
Bridget	17	F	Unknown	030c02Ab
DAULTON, Mathew	30	M	Unknown	030c02Ab
Mary	30	F	Unknown	030c02Ab
Catherine	10	F	Unknown	030c02Ab
Bridget	2	F	Child	030c02Ab
LANGTON, Amos	18	M	Unknown	030c02Ab
CONNOR, Timothy	26	M	Unknown	030c02Ab
BROWNE, Thomas	19	M	Unknown	030c02Ab
CORBY, Abby	40	F	Unknown	030c02Ab
Mary	20	F	Unknown	030c02Ab
LACY, John	35	M	Unknown	030c02Ab
FOLEY, Patrick	24	M	Unknown	030c02Ab
MORAN, Michael	21	M	Unknown	030c02Ab
KING, Bridget	20	F	Unknown	030c02Ab
ONEILL, U-Mrs.	30	F	Unknown	030c02Ab
MURPHY, Luke	32	M	Unknown	030c02Ab
Catherine	30	F	Unknown	030c02Ab
Catherine	5	F	Child	030c02Ab
Died-At-Sea				
Philip	4	M	Child	030c02Ab
Thomas	2	M	Unknown	030c02Ab
John	.00	M	Infant	030c02Ab
KELLY, Rose	16	F	Unknown	030c02Ab
MCLOUGHLEN, Pat	30	M	Unknown	030c02Ab
MILLIKEN, Joseph	20	M	Unknown	030c02Ab
ENSOR, Thomas	21	M	Unknown	030c02Ab
Elizabeth	20	F	Unknown	030c02Ab
KIRKUP, Anthony	27	M	Unknown	030c02Ab
Sarah	26	F	Unknown	030c02Ab
Rachel	.05	F	Infant	030c02Ab
CONNOR, David	60	M	Unknown	030c02Ab
Julia	55	F	Unknown	030c02Ab
William	32	M	Unknown	030c02Ab
John	24	M	Unknown	030c02Ab
SULLIVAN, James	46	M	Unknown	030c02Ab
Margaret	40	F	Unknown	030c02Ab
Bartholomeu	25	M	Unknown	030c02Ab
James	20	M	Unknown	030c02Ab
Julian	16	M	Unknown	030c02Ab
David	14	M	Unknown	030c02Ab
Roger	12	M	Unknown	030c02Ab
Honora	8	F	Child	030c02Ab
Eliza	6	F	Child	030c02Ab
John	4	M	Child	030c02Ab
Cath.	.06	F	Infant	030c02Ab
John	40	M	Unknown	030c02Ab
Johanah	36	F	Unknown	030c02Ab
James	11	M	Unknown	030c02Ab
Jeremiah	9	M	Child	030c02Ab
Mary	7	F	Child	030c02Ab
Julian	5	F	Child	030c02Ab
Margaret	4	F	Child	030c02Ab
Bartholomeu	.06	M	Infant	030c02Ab
DOWNEY, Patrick	30	M	Unknown	030c02Ab
Died-At-Sea				
Margaret	36	F	Unknown	030c02Ab
John	.06	M	Infant	030c02Ab
John	25	M	Unknown	030c02Ab
CORNELL, John	30	M	Unknown	030c02Ab
RATIGAN, Bridget	20	F	Unknown	030c02Ab

NAMES OF PASSENGERS	AGE	SEX	OCCUPATIONS	DATE PORT SHIP
LINSKY, Judy	35	F	Unknown	030c02Ab
Thomas	6	M	Child	030c02Ab
CAVANAGH, James	22	M	Unknown	030c02Ab
CONLAN, John	23	M	Unknown	030c02Ab
Ann	21	F	Unknown	030c02Ab
HIGGINS, Rose	18	F	Unknown	030c02Ab
MORAN, Pat	19	M	Laborer	030c02Ab
Margaret	17	F	Unknown	030c02Ab
QUINN, Margaret	18	F	Unknown	030c02Ab
BROWN, Mary	18	F	Unknown	030c02Ab
REYNOLDS, Letitia	20	F	Unknown	030c02Ab
DUGAN, Margaret	35	F	Unknown	030c02Ab
LINSKY, Nathanial	30	M	Unknown	030c02Ab
Died-At-Sea				
Martin	3	M	Child	030c02Ab
MINAN, Biddy	25	F	Unknown	030c02Ab
KILDEA, Ann	20	F	Unknown	030c02Ab
Biddy	25	F	Unknown	030c02Ab
WILSON, Thomas	20	M	Unknown	030c02Ab
NUGENT, Wm.	40	M	Unknown	030c02Ab
U-Mrs.	34	F	Unknown	030c02Ab
Mary	10	M	Unknown	030c02Ab
Margaret	8	F	Child	030c02Ab
SHIELDS, Cath.	20	F	Unknown	030c02Ab
CLARKE, Pat	20	M	Unknown	030c02Ab
Cath.	28	F	Unknown	030c02Ab
Ann	.06	F	Infant	030c02Ab
CORCORAN, Thomas	20	M	Unknown	030c02Ab
MCLYDE, Francis	20	M	Unknown	030c02Ab
CARNE, Bridget	35	F	Unknown	030c02Ab
HICKSON, Bridget	29	F	Unknown	030c02Ab
CANN, Wm.	16	M	Unknown	030c02Ab
Cath.	15	F	Unknown	030c02Ab
CRAIG, Jas.	30	M	Unknown	030c02Ab
MCCOLLOCH, Mary	23	F	Unknown	030c02Ab
TROTTER, Darcus	22	F	Unknown	030c02Ab
KENEDY, Catherine	32	F	Unknown	030c02Ab
Died-At-Sea				
BIGGS, Teresa	20	F	Unknown	030c02Ab
POWELL, Robert	22	M	Unknown	030c02Ab
Mary	20	F	Unknown	030c02Ab
CONNELL, Michael	25	M	Unknown	030c02Ab
SULLIVAN, Catherine	18	F	Unknown	030c02Ab
Mary	15	F	Unknown	030c02Ab
Ellen	30	F	Unknown	030c02Ab
CONNOR, Bridget	20	F	Unknown	030c02Ab
RUSSELL, John	35	M	Unknown	030c02Ab
Theresa	35	F	Unknown	030c02Ab
Mary	30	F	Unknown	030c02Ab
GILES, Michael	30	M	Unknown	030c02Ab
MCCOY, Mary	27	F	Unknown	030c02Ab
U	.06	F	Infant	030c02Ab
REILLY, Peter	20	M	Infant	030c02Ab
NEVILLE, Margaret	18	F	Unknown	030c02Ab
MOLONY, C.	40	M	Unknown	030c02Ab
Garrett	11	M	Unknown	030c02Ab
Ellen	11	F	Unknown	030c02Ab
Ellen	9	F	Child	030c02Ab
Kate	5	F	Child	030c02Ab
Johanna	.10	F	Infant	030c02Ab
DONAGHUE, Mary	24	F	Unknown	030c02Ab
John	5	M	Child	030c02Ab
Michael	3	M	Child	030c02Ab
Nancy	.00	F	Infant	030c02Ab
Died-At-Sea				
ONEILL, Catherine	20	F	Unknown	030c02Ab
HYNES, Pat	22	M	Unknown	030c02Ab
ROURKE, Pat	28	M	Unknown	030c02Ab
MULLILLY, Margaret	21	F	Unknown	030c02Ab
Michael	21	M	Unknown	030c02Ab
BIGGS, Mary	26	F	Unknown	030c02Ab
Elizh.	20	F	Unknown	030c02Ab
Thos.John	.06	M	Infant	030c02Ab
BRENNAN, Celia	20	F	Unknown	030c02Ab
CAIN, Biddy	14	F	Unknown	030c02Ab

NAMES OF PASSENGERS	AGE	SEX	OCCUPATIONS	DATE PORT SHIP
BLACK, John	53	M	Unknown	030c02Ab
Charlotte	40	F	Unknown	030c02Ab
Harriett	19	F	Unknown	030c02Ab
James	22	M	Unknown	030c02Ab
Samuel	15	M	Unknown	030c02Ab
Jane	13	F	Unknown	030c02Ab
NOWLAN, Mary	25	F	Unknown	030c02Ab
BRIGGS, John	15	M	Unknown	030c02Ab
FEELY, Catherine	19	F	Unknown	030c02Ab
BIRRELL, Margaret	17	F	Unknown	030c02Ab
Catherine	15	F	Unknown	030c02Ab
COWAN, Margaret	16	F	Unknown	030c02Ab
SMITH, Ann	30	F	Unknown	030c02Ab
Elizabeth	10	F	Unknown	030c02Ab
Mary-Jane	8	F	Unknown	030c02Ab
Isabella	6	F	Child	030c02Ab
Martha	4	F	Child	030c02Ab
Ann	.10	F	Infant	030c02Ab
HARTNETT, Michael	33	M	Unknown	030c02Ab
MCGUIRE, Elizabeth	21	F	Unknown	030c02Ab
TAAFE, Mary	25	F	Unknown	030c02Ab
SAVILLE, Mary	21	F	Unknown	030c02Ab
CURRY, Mary-Ann	19	F	Unknown	030c02Ab
PINDABLE, W.	45	M	Unknown	030c02Ab
Died-At-Sea				
Margaret	9	F	Child	030c02Ab
SCANLON, Margaret	60	F	Unknown	030c02Ab
SMALL, Danl.	26	M	Unknown	030c02Ab
John	4	M	Child	030c02Ab
NEEDHAM, Osten	24	M	Unknown	030c02Ab
MACK, Mary	26	F	Unknown	030c02Ab
BRADLY, Patrick	24	M	Unknown	030c02Ab
Died-At-Sea				
QUICK, Thos.	22	M	Unknown	030c02Ab
CARSON, Francis	24	M	Lawyer	030c02Ab

NASCONOMO 03 OCTOBER 1849

From Liverpool

NAMES OF PASSENGERS	AGE	SEX	OCCUPATIONS	DATE PORT SHIP
MURRAY, Eliza	30	F	Spinster	030c02Ac
NEWMAN, Mary	20	F	Spinster	030c02Ac
Ellen	11	F	Spinster	030c02Ac
COLLINS, Anne	20	F	Spinster	030c02Ac
James	11	M	None	030c02Ac
Mary-Ann	3	F	Child	030c02Ac
GALLENTY, Rosa	32	F	Unknown	030c02Ac
RYLY, Ellen	11	F	None	030c02Ac
Hugh	10	M	None	030c02Ac
Mary	8	F	Child	030c02Ac
HINDS, Martin	14	M	None	030c02Ac
Jno.	11	M	None	030c02Ac
DALTON, James	30	M	Laborer	030c02Ac
DOYLE, Mike	30	M	Laborer	030c02Ac
PARTLAN, Rose	11	F	Spinster	030c02Ac
Anne	9	F	Child	030c02Ac
KENT, Mike	30	M	Laborer	030c02Ac
MALEY, Bridget	32	F	Spinster	030c02Ac
Mary	27	F	Spinster	030c02Ac
Anne	34	F	Spinster	030c02Ac
Mary	10	F	None	030c02Ac
Bridget	6	F	Child	030c02Ac
Catherine	3	F	Child	030c02Ac
Anne	6	F	Child	030c02Ac
CUNNINGHAM, Ellen	14	F	Servant	030c02Ac
MCNULTY, Mary	28	F	Servant	030c02Ac
Anne	17	F	Servant	030c02Ac
Mary	13	F	Servant	030c02Ac
Margaret	12	F	Servant	030c02Ac

NAMES OF PASSENGERS	AGE	SEX	OCCUPATIONS	DATE PORT SHIP
MCNULTY, James	10	M	Laborer	030c02Ac
Peter	8	M	Child	030c02Ac
KEASE, Eliza	45	F	Servant	030c02Ac
DUFFY, Anne	40	F	Servant	030c02Ac
DUNN, Mary	16	F	Servant	030c02Ac
Mary	20	F	Servant	030c02Ac
Mary	10	F	None	030c02Ac
Thomas	9	M	Child	030c02Ac
QUILLAN, James	85	M	Laborer	030c02Ac
BAIG, Charles	24	M	Laborer	030c02Ac
DUNN, Moses	13	M	Laborer	030c02Ac
MALONE, M.	27	M	Laborer	030c02Ac
MCVIE, Pat	32	M	Laborer	030c02Ac
Mathew	27	M	Laborer	030c02Ac
Ellen	23	F	Servant	030c02Ac
Francis	6	M	Child	030c02Ac
Margaret	3	F	Child	030c02Ac
DAISY, Peter	30	M	Laborer	030c02Ac
MERING, Catherine	30	F	Servant	030c02Ac
Jno.	10	M	Laborer	030c02Ac
Pat	3	M	Child	030c02Ac
CANNON, Peter	16	M	Laborer	030c02Ac
CRUISE, Honora	26	F	Servant	030c02Ac
Jeane	9	F	Child	030c02Ac
Mary	5	F	Child	030c02Ac
MURPHY, Jane	16	F	Servant	030c02Ac
GRIMES, Harry	12	M	None	030c02Ac
ODONNELL, James	30	F	Laborer	030c02Ac
EGAN, Mary	10	F	Servant	030c02Ac
Eliza	4	F	Child	030c02Ac
HANLEY, Hugh	38	M	Servant	030c02Ac
Catherine	30	F	Servant	030c02Ac
Bridget	12	F	Servant	030c02Ac
Michael	10	M	Laborer	030c02Ac
Rose	7	F	Child	030c02Ac
Pat	12	M	Laborer	030c02Ac
John	2	M	Child	030c02Ac
Mike	4	M	Child	030c02Ac
SMITH, Phil	30	M	Laborer	030c02Ac
Mary	27	F	Servant	030c02Ac
Bridget	4	F	Child	030c02Ac
Lawrence	26	M	Laborer	030c02Ac
KEEF, Ellen	20	M	Servant	030c02Ac
TOOL, Edward	22	M	Laborer	030c02Ac
RUBNANN, Ann	20	F	Servant	030c02Ac
HEULLER, U	28	M	Laborer	030c02Ac
Mary	20	F	Servant	030c02Ac
Jno.	31	M	Laborer	030c02Ac
George	10	M	Laborer	030c02Ac
Margaret	10	F	Servant	030c02Ac
MCCONNEL, Mary	22	M	Servant	030c02Ac
FITZPATRICK, Eliza	18	M	Servant	030c02Ac
MOORE, Samuel	25	M	Laborer	030c02Ac
BIRMINGHAM, Wm.	35	M	Laborer	030c02Ac
FOLEY, Jesey	40	M	Laborer	030c02Ac
KELLY, Robert-H.	18	M	Laborer	030c02Ac
EGAN, Samuel	35	M	Laborer	030c02Ac
Julia	31	F	Servant	030c02Ac
Ellen	8	F	Child	030c02Ac
Honora	6	F	Child	030c02Ac
Pat	3	M	Child	030c02Ac
HOLLAND, Helen	10	F	Unknown	030c02Ac
CONNOR, Jas.	20	M	Laborer	030c02Ac
Ellen	18	F	Servant	030c02Ac
KENNEDY, Peter	35	M	Laborer	030c02Ac
Catherine	20	F	Servant	030c02Ac
MORIARTY, Edwd.	21	M	Laborer	030c02Ac
GARRY, James	28	M	Laborer	030c02Ac
KEEFE, Mary	20	F	Servant	030c02Ac
CASEY, Cath.	17	F	Servant	030c02Ac
KEEFE, James	28	M	Laborer	030c02Ac
OLEARY, Mary	13	F	Servant	030c02Ac
MOLLAN, Mary	30	F	Servant	030c02Ac
BARRY, Andy	30	M	Laborer	030c02Ac
CASEY, Mary	20	F	Servant	030c02Ac

NAMES OF PASSENGERS	AGE	SEX	OCCUPATIONS	DATE PORT SHIP
ORYAN, Julia	20	F	Servant	030c02Ac
LOVE, Jno.	60	M	Laborer	030c02Ac
SHEPPARD, Ed.	30	M	Laborer	030c02Ac
SULLIVAN, Jerry	29	M	Laborer	030c02Ac
Joanna	28	F	Servant	030c02Ac
Jerry	7	M	Child	030c02Ac
Terry	5	M	Child	030c02Ac
Dan	2	M	Child	030c02Ac
HECTORY, Thos.	36	M	Laborer	030c02Ac
NEILL, Jno.	40	M	Laborer	030c02Ac
BROWN, Thos.	35	M	Laborer	030c02Ac
Thos.	13	M	None	030c02Ac
Mary	15	F	Servant	030c02Ac
DUGGAN, Cath.	32	F	Servant	030c02Ac
JAFFNEY, Jno.	35	M	Laborer	030c02Ac
Mary	30	F	Servant	030c02Ac
Cecilia	20	F	Servant	030c02Ac
MULVEY, Cath.	30	F	Servant	030c02Ac
COLLINS, Margt.	25	F	Servant	030c02Ac
COSTIAN, Thos.	22	M	Laborer	030c02Ac
QUALL, Fred.	22	M	Laborer	030c02Ac
NAULTON, Cath.	30	F	Servant	030c02Ac
MCLEARY, Hugh	45	M	Laborer	030c02Ac
Mary	50	F	Servant	030c02Ac
MITCHELL, Susan	20	F	Servant	030c02Ac
Thomas	18	M	Laborer	030c02Ac
Honor	16	F	Servant	030c02Ac
MCKENNA, Margt.	18	F	Servant	030c02Ac
FARRELL, Thos.	25	M	Laborer	030c02Ac
Charles	30	M	Laborer	030c02Ac
MALONEY, Jerry	20	M	Laborer	030c02Ac
CONNER, Pat	30	M	Laborer	030c02Ac
CALENDEN, Jno.	25	M	Laborer	030c02Ac
CONNELL, Mich.	28	M	Laborer	030c02Ac
STACK, Pat	30	M	Laborer	030c02Ac
MOLLAN, Jno.	40	M	Laborer	030c02Ac
CONNELL, Ellen	28	F	Servant	030c02Ac
PANETT, Cath.	30	F	Servant	030c02Ac
KEEFE, Mike	22	M	Laborer	030c02Ac
James	28	M	Laborer	030c02Ac
KELLY, Martha	30	F	Servant	030c02Ac
MULLEN, Wm.	28	M	Laborer	030c02Ac
Mike	24	M	Laborer	030c02Ac
FLOOD, Peter	30	M	Laborer	030c02Ac
James	30	M	Laborer	030c02Ac
Julia	8	F	Child	030c02Ac
Mary	5	F	Child	030c02Ac
Pat	2	M	Child	030c02Ac
ENNIS, Wm.	30	M	Laborer	030c02Ac
REYNOLDS, Bernard	40	M	Laborer	030c02Ac
KEMBLE, James	28	M	Laborer	030c02Ac
QUERWIN, Bridget	40	F	Servant	030c02Ac
Mary	2	F	Child	030c02Ac
Pat	1	M	Child	030c02Ac
KELLY, Norbetr	18	M	Laborer	030c02Ac
Jane	17	F	Servant	030c02Ac
GRAY, Pat	30	M	Laborer	030c02Ac
Mary	17	F	Servant	030c02Ac
SEFF, Pat	22	M	Laborer	030c02Ac
COFFER, Moses	28	M	Laborer	030c02Ac
BALLARD, Ellen	20	F	Servant	030c02Ac
DUNN, Edw.	25	M	Laborer	030c02Ac
Jno.	28	M	Laborer	030c02Ac
CARR, Jno.	26	M	Laborer	030c02Ac
MCQUINAN, Pat	40	M	Laborer	030c02Ac
MCQUAID, Margaret	30	F	Servant	030c02Ac
GRANT, Bridget	45	F	Servant	030c02Ac
George	20	M	Laborer	030c02Ac
Francis	30	M	Laborer	030c02Ac
KAYS, Mary	27	F	Servant	030c02Ac
Jas.	60	M	Laborer	030c02Ac
GRADY, George	78	M	Laborer	030c02Ac
CAREY, Mary	70	F	Servant	030c02Ac
HACEY, S.	60	M	Laborer	030c02Ac
HUGHES, Ellen	18	F	Servant	030c02Ac

NAMES OF PASSENGERS	AGE	SEX	OCCUPATIONS	DATE PORT SHIP
MALONE, Bridget	16	F	Servant	030c02Ac
MCDONALD, Ben	22	M	Laborer	030c02Ac
CARROL, Magt.	18	F	Servant	030c02Ac
MCCAY, Cath.	20	F	Servant	030c02Ac
LARDNER, Judith	3	F	Child	030c02Ac
MCFORAN, Rose	15	F	Servant	030c02Ac
Jno.	25	M	Laborer	030c02Ac
Francis	20	M	Laborer	030c02Ac
CULLEN, James	20	M	Laborer	030c02Ac
REGNERY, James	25	M	Laborer	030c02Ac
MCDONALD, Buck	32	M	Laborer	030c02Ac
CRONE, Readey	18	M	Laborer	030c02Ac
MCDONALD, Mary	2	F	Child	030c02Ac
POWER, Jno.	45	M	Laborer	030c02Ac
REEDY, Mary	30	F	Servant	030c02Ac
CARTY, Jno.	22	M	Laborer	030c02Ac
MCVIE, Cath.	22	F	Servant	030c02Ac
GALLAGHER, Thos.	60	M	Laborer	030c02Ac
Eliza	21	F	Servant	030c02Ac
BOYD, James	23	M	Laborer	030c02Ac
Pat	2	M	Child	030c02Ac
GEOGAN, Pat	18	M	Laborer	030c02Ac
MCEON, Eliza	25	F	Servant	030c02Ac
GORMAN, Bridget	13	F	Servant	030c02Ac
NEMARA, Jno.	24	M	Laborer	030c02Ac
SYRAN, Thos.	30	M	Laborer	030c02Ac
ONEAL, Mich.	60	M	Laborer	030c02Ac
BRETT, Pat	75	M	Laborer	030c02Ac
MURPHY, Bridget	20	F	Servant	030c02Ac
KELLY, David	30	M	Laborer	030c02Ac
BELTON, Jno.	35	M	Laborer	030c02Ac
Eliz.	27	F	Unknown	030c02Ac
Thos.	29	M	Cchbldr	030c02Ac
Fanny-Stevenson	7	F	Child	030c02Ac
Helen	5	F	Child	030c02Ac
John-Jeremy	3	M	Child	030c02Ac
PHILIPS, Wm.	44	M	Shoemaker	030c02Ac
WALKER, Martha	34	F	Unknown	030c02Ac
Thos.	33	M	Laborer	030c02Ac
PHILIPS, John	32	M	Shoemaker	030c02Ac
GRUFF, Wm.	24	M	Shoemaker	030c02Ac
GREGG, Margt.	22	F	Shoemaker	030c02Ac
ROBINSON, Mary-Ann	27	F	Unknown	030c02Ac
FOULDS, Wm.	40	M	Shoemaker	030c02Ac
Emily-Brget.	28	F	Unknown	030c02Ac
Wm.Jos.Thompson	4	M	Child	030c02Ac
Helen-Davis	.11	F	Infant	030c02Ac
DAVIES, Theresa-James	18	F	Unknown	030c02Ac

HANNAH-THORNTON 02 OCTOBER 1849

From Londonderry

NAMES OF PASSENGERS	AGE	SEX	OCCUPATIONS	DATE PORT SHIP
BROWN, Robert	20	M	Unknown	020c01Ad
Saml.	21	M	Unknown	020c01Ad
DOOGAN, Jno.	25	M	Unknown	020c01Ad
MCDERMOTT, J.	21	M	Unknown	020c01Ad
MCGOLRICK, Mary	40	F	Unknown	020c01Ad
LAGAN, Mary	54	F	Unknown	020c01Ad
NELSON, Margt.	32	F	Unknown	020c01Ad
NILSON, Thos.	9	M	Child	020c01Ad
Anne-Jane	5	F	Child	020c01Ad
George	2	M	Child	020c01Ad
Kitty	13	F	Unknown	020c01Ad
ARBUCKLE, Mary-Ann	20	F	Unknown	020c01Ad
MCCAFFERTY, Henry	18	M	Unknown	020c01Ad
OHARA, William	20	M	Unknown	020c01Ad
DONAGHY, James	20	M	Unknown	020c01Ad
COYLE, Dennis	60	M	Unknown	020c01Ad
COYLE, Margery	24	F	Unknown	020c01Ad
MAGEE, Mary	20	F	Unknown	020c01Ad
James	10	M	Unknown	020c01Ad
Jno.	6	M	Child	020c01Ad
PEACELY, Saml.	26	M	Unknown	020c01Ad
COLTON, Anne	53	F	Unknown	020c01Ad
BRYSON, Ellen	20	F	Unknown	020c01Ad
LOVE, John	60	M	Unknown	020c01Ad
GARDNER, Saml.	18	F	Unknown	020c01Ad
CULLIAN, Hugh	30	M	Unknown	020c01Ad
MCNABB, Nancy	20	F	Unknown	020c01Ad
SMITH, Susan	38	F	Unknown	020c01Ad
Eliza	16	F	Unknown	020c01Ad
ONEILL, Jno.	32	M	Unknown	020c01Ad
MCMASTER, James	23	M	Unknown	020c01Ad
John	18	M	Unknown	020c01Ad
CHEATLY, Anne	28	F	Unknown	020c01Ad
MCKANE, Isabella	20	F	Unknown	020c01Ad
Nancy	18	F	Unknown	020c01Ad
IRWIN, Richd.	42	M	Unknown	020c01Ad
U (W)	40	F	Unknown	020c01Ad
PATER, Isabella	18	F	Unknown	020c01Ad
IRWIN, Wm.	13	M	Unknown	020c01Ad
Fanny	10	F	Unknown	020c01Ad
Catherine	8	F	Child	020c01Ad
Mary	6	F	Child	020c01Ad
Margt.	4	F	Child	020c01Ad
Jane	2	F	Child	020c01Ad
KEANE, Alexander	18	M	Unknown	020c01Ad
Ellen	28	F	Unknown	020c01Ad
MCBRIDE, Chas.	17	M	Unknown	020c01Ad
QUINN, Biddy	40	F	Unknown	020c01Ad
Catherine	21	F	Unknown	020c01Ad
Edward	20	M	Unknown	020c01Ad
COX, Susannah	17	F	Unknown	020c01Ad
COYLE, Cathe.	61	F	Unknown	020c01Ad
MCDERMOTT, Anthy.	15	M	Unknown	020c01Ad
MCCAFFILL, Michl.	35	M	Unknown	020c01Ad
Betty	30	F	Unknown	020c01Ad
Mary-Ann	8	F	Child	020c01Ad
Sarah	6	F	Child	020c01Ad
Margt.	4	F	Child	020c01Ad
Patt	2	M	Child	020c01Ad
BRADLY, Michl.	30	M	Unknown	020c01Ad
CARSON, Isabella	21	F	Unknown	020c01Ad
HAMILTON, Sam.	20	F	Unknown	020c01Ad
Eliza	18	F	Unknown	020c01Ad
IRVINE, Matilda	20	F	Unknown	020c01Ad
Eliza	18	F	Unknown	020c01Ad
Eliza	18	F	Unknown	020c01Ad
JOHNSTON, Elizabeth	40	F	Unknown	020c01Ad
Elizabeth	14	F	Unknown	020c01Ad
U	11	M	Unknown	020c01Ad
Robt.	2	M	Child	020c01Ad
STEVENSON, Cathe.	35	F	Unknown	020c01Ad
Mary	6	F	Child	020c01Ad
MCARTHUR, Sarah	30	F	Unknown	020c01Ad
MCGEE, Sarah-A.	30	F	Unknown	020c01Ad
Cathe.	5	F	Child	020c01Ad
DUDDY, Isabella	19	F	Unknown	020c01Ad
RODGERS, Jane	35	F	Unknown	020c01Ad
MCKNIGHT, Jas.	30	M	Unknown	020c01Ad
Jane	32	F	Unknown	020c01Ad
Ellen	32	F	Unknown	020c01Ad
E.Jane	9	F	Child	020c01Ad
Margt.	7	F	Child	020c01Ad
Nancy	5	F	Child	020c01Ad
Alexander	2	M	Child	020c01Ad
PARKERTON, Alex.	45	M	Unknown	020c01Ad
MULLEN, Michl.	40	M	Unknown	020c01Ad
HOLLOS, Edwd.	25	M	Unknown	020c01Ad
Eliza	22	F	Unknown	020c01Ad
JYFFE, John-Jas.	25	M	Unknown	020c01Ad
MCCULLOUGH, Mary	26	F	Unknown	020c01Ad
Cathe.	22	F	Unknown	020c01Ad

NAMES OF PASSENGERS	AGE	SEX	OCCUPATIONS	DATE PORT SHIP
MCCULLOUGH, Biddy	23	F	Unknown	020c01Ad
GREEN, Ellen	20	F	Unknown	020c01Ad
JAMES, John	36	M	Unknown	020c01Ad
U (W)	24	F	Unknown	020c01Ad
LYON, Mathew	28	M	Unknown	020c01Ad
U (W)	26	F	Unknown	020c01Ad
Robt.	3	M	Child	020c01Ad
James	2	M	Child	020c01Ad
MCCOOK, Ellen	18	F	Unknown	020c01Ad
KILPATRICK, Saml.	26	M	Unknown	020c01Ad
FOWLER, Rob.	17	M	Unknown	020c01Ad
SWAN, Isabella	20	F	Unknown	020c01Ad
HUTCHINSON, Thos.	37	M	Unknown	020c01Ad
James	12	M	Unknown	020c01Ad
John	4	M	Child	020c01Ad
MORRISON, Wm.	44	M	Unknown	020c01Ad
Nancy	42	F	Unknown	020c01Ad
Martha	13	F	Unknown	020c01Ad
John	11	M	Unknown	020c01Ad
James	10	M	Unknown	020c01Ad
Charles	9	M	Child	020c01Ad
Danl.	2	M	Child	020c01Ad
Mary-Ann	1	F	Child	020c01Ad
Eliza-Margt.	6	F	Child	020c01Ad
Sarah-Jane	8	F	Child	020c01Ad
Wm.	.03	M	Infant	020c01Ad
MCANIVISTON, Margt.	27	F	Unknown	020c01Ad
KELLY, Sally	20	F	Unknown	020c01Ad
CUNNINGHAM, Eliza	24	F	Unknown	020c01Ad
LAIRD, John	26	M	Unknown	020c01Ad
KEARNEY, Wm.	35	M	Unknown	020c01Ad
LEACH, Joseph	16	M	Unknown	020c01Ad
GALBRAITH, Isabella	30	F	Unknown	020c01Ad
HYNDMAN, Joseph	18	M	Unknown	020c01Ad
MURRAY, James	18	M	Unknown	020c01Ad
Isabella	13	F	Unknown	020c01Ad
MCGINTY, Mary-Ann	16	F	Unknown	020c01Ad
BRADLY, Patt	30	M	Unknown	020c01Ad
REEVE, J.	24	M	Unknown	020c01Ad
MCGOWAN, Bridget	18	F	Unknown	020c01Ad
BROWN, Hannah	16	F	Unknown	020c01Ad
COCHRAN, Joseph	55	M	Unknown	020c01Ad
U (W)	30	F	Unknown	020c01Ad
CASEY, U-Mrs.	34	F	Unknown	020c01Ad
Cathe.	20	F	Unknown	020c01Ad
Mary-Jane	18	F	Unknown	020c01Ad
WOODS, Andw.	21	M	Unknown	020c01Ad
SMITH, Andw.	16	M	Unknown	020c01Ad
KILPATRICK, Geo.C.	21	M	Unknown	020c01Ad
ARMSTRONG, Chas.	30	M	Unknown	020c01Ad
MOORE, Acheson	19	M	Unknown	020c01Ad

DROMAHAIR 03 OCTOBER 1849

From Sligo

NAMES OF PASSENGERS	AGE	SEX	OCCUPATIONS	DATE PORT SHIP
BEGLANE, Ann	22	F	Spinster	030c09Ai
DREW, Jno.	50	M	Farmer	030c09Ai
Ellen	30	F	Matron	030c09Ai
MCDERMOTT, Bridget	18	F	Spinster	030c09Ai
Jane	14	F	Spinster	030c09Ai
HARGADON, Pat	22	M	Farmer	030c09Ai
HAALY, Jno.	14	M	None	030c09Ai
Thomas	50	M	Farmer	030c09Ai
QUIN, Bridget	16	F	Spinster	030c09Ai
DOWN, Jas.	21	M	Spinner	030c09Ai
OBRIEN, Terence	21	M	Farmer	030c09Ai
CAIN, Margaret	19	F	Spinster	030c09Ai
QUIN, Margaret	16	F	Spinster	030c09Ai
ENNIG, Thomas	30	M	Farmer	030c09Ai
Bessy	25	F	Wife	030c09Ai
DOWNERS, Margaret	30	F	Spinster	030c09Ai
WALKER, Mary	20	F	Spinster	030c09Ai
HART, Henry	22	M	Farmer	030c09Ai
STEWART, Bridget	40	F	Matron	030c09Ai
SHAW, Jas.	19	M	Servant	030c09Ai
KILLGALLEN, Mary	20	F	Spinster	030c09Ai
MAHON, Bridget	13	F	Spinster	030c09Ai
MCMURRAY, Maria	18	F	Spinster	030c09Ai
FEENEY, Maria	8	F	Child	030c09Ai
Jas.	6	M	Child	030c09Ai
MCDONOUGH, Jane	18	F	Spinster	030c09Ai
SMITH, Eliza	19	F	Spinster	030c09Ai
BUDERY, Jno.	30	M	Farmer	030c09Ai
MCLOUGHLIN, Catherine	18	F	Spinster	030c09Ai
BUDERY, Ann	28	F	Wife	030c09Ai
Jno.	.00	M	Infant	030c09Ai
DOLANY, Mich.	18	M	Spinner	030c09Ai
Catherine	16	F	Spinster	030c09Ai
HYLAND, Jane	18	F	Spinster	030c09Ai
FLANAGAN, Ellen	25	F	Spinster	030c09Ai
LAUREAN, Ellen	17	F	Spinster	030c09Ai
JENKS, Jno.	9	M	Child	030c09Ai
ROGERS, Ellen	10	F	Unknown	030c09Ai
CASEY, Catherine	14	F	Spinster	030c09Ai
HENRY, Pat	35	M	Farmer	030c09Ai
Mary	24	F	Spinster	030c09Ai
KILLCULLEN, Mack	20	M	Farmer	030c09Ai
NEARY, Peter	16	M	Farmer	030c09Ai
EARLY, Mary	17	F	Spinster	030c09Ai
Jane	19	F	Spinster	030c09Ai
BEGLANE, James	60	M	Farmer	030c09Ai
Mary	26	F	Spinster	030c09Ai
LAUNG, Mary	45	F	Matron	030c09Ai
TRUMBLE, Thomas	21	M	Yeoman	030c09Ai
SHARKEY, Jno.	21	M	Farmer	030c09Ai
WALLS, Jno.	18	M	Farmer	030c09Ai
GALECK, Andrew	33	M	Farmer	030c09Ai
Mary	25	F	Spinster	030c09Ai
Mary	5	F	Child	030c09Ai
William	.04	M	Infant	030c09Ai
MCDONOGH, U	39	M	Farmer	030c09Ai
Jno.	50	M	Farmer	030c09Ai
Morgan	17	M	Farmer	030c09Ai
CORCORAN, M.	21	M	Farmer	030c09Ai
COYNE, Jno.	26	M	Farmer	030c09Ai
CURREN, Bess	13	F	Unknown	030c09Ai
Jno.	5	M	Child	030c09Ai
CLARK, Ann	19	F	Spinster	030c09Ai
Winfred	21	M	Spinster	030c09Ai
CAVANAUGH, Thomas	15	M	Farmer	030c09Ai
TUNNEY, Mary	8	F	Child	030c09Ai
DOWANS, Mary	18	F	Spinster	030c09Ai
SHERIDAN, Ellen	19	F	Spinster	030c09Ai
BURNETT, Mary	18	F	Spinster	030c09Ai
REDDICAN, Jno.	22	M	Laborer	030c09Ai
WATSON, William	14	M	Farmer	030c09Ai
GIBBNY, Jane	26	F	Spinster	030c09Ai
BURK, Bridget	36	F	Matron	030c09Ai
Jno.	30	M	Yeoman	030c09Ai
Mary	17	F	Spinster	030c09Ai
Bessy	9	F	Child	030c09Ai
Mary	5	F	Child	030c09Ai
NOLAN, Jno.	23	M	Farmer	030c09Ai
PHILLIPS, Biddy	22	F	Spinster	030c09Ai
CARROLL, Ann	19	F	Spinster	030c09Ai
GALLAGHER, Pat	24	M	Farmer	030c09Ai
Ann	20	F	Wife	030c09Ai
Mary	20	F	Spinster	030c09Ai
Honora	20	F	Spinster	030c09Ai
CAWLEY, Mary	18	F	Spinster	030c09Ai
William	20	M	Farmer	030c09Ai
Catherine	16	F	Spinster	030c09Ai
TAAFFE, Alley	30	F	Matron	030c09Ai

NAMES OF PASSENGERS	AGE	SEX	OCCUPATIONS	DATE PORT SHIP
TAAFFE, Jane	25	F	Spinster	030c09Ai
NEARY, James	30	M	Unknown	030c09Ai
MUCHNUG, Charlotte	50	F	Matron	030c09Ai
Charlotte	18	F	Spinster	030c09Ai
GADDES, Ann	20	F	Spinster	030c09Ai
SWEETMARY, Mary	22	F	Spinster	030c09Ai
BURNETT, Jane	18	F	Spinster	030c09Ai
THEHARY, Ellen	18	F	Spinster	030c09Ai
Mary	14	F	Spinster	030c09Ai
TUNNEY, Catherine	12	F	Unknown	030c09Ai
GOVERANY, Francis	36	M	Farmer	030c09Ai
Honora	32	F	Matron	030c09Ai
Ann	17	F	Unknown	030c09Ai
Thomas	14	M	Unknown	030c09Ai
MCGEE, Winfred	11	M	Unknown	030c09Ai
HANNEY, Jno.	22	M	Farmer	030c09Ai
DEISHANY, James	30	M	Shopkeeper	030c09Ai
HEALY, Ellen	30	F	Spinster	030c09Ai
CURRAN, Ann	10	F	Unknown	030c09Ai
MCKINY, Isaac	23	M	Unknown	030c09Ai
JOHNSTON, William	19	M	Unknown	030c09Ai
PARKS, Thomas	23	M	Unknown	030c09Ai
GIBBNY, Louisa	43	F	Unknown	030c09Ai
Michl.	17	M	Unknown	030c09Ai
Jas.	13	M	Unknown	030c09Ai
Benjamin	11	M	Unknown	030c09Ai

MOUNTAINEER 03 OCTOBER 1849

From Penzance

NAMES OF PASSENGERS	AGE	SEX	OCCUPATIONS	DATE PORT SHIP
THOMAS, Henry	23	M	Miner	030c16Ae
Elizabeth	24	F	Unknown	030c16Ae
U	.00	M	Infant	030c16Ae
BUCKETT, James	56	M	Unknown	030c16Ae
Hannah	55	F	Unknown	030c16Ae
James	25	M	Unknown	030c16Ae
Elizabeth	20	F	Unknown	030c16Ae
Samuel	10	M	Unknown	030c16Ae
GIRARD, John	24	M	Farmer	030c16Ae
RALPH, Sally	45	F	Unknown	030c16Ae
Honor	23	F	Unknown	030c16Ae
Amelia	16	F	Unknown	030c16Ae
Sally	21	F	Unknown	030c16Ae
Betsy	11	F	Unknown	030c16Ae
Po--LASE, Elizabeth	31	F	Unknown	030c16Ae
Thomas	6	M	Child	030c16Ae
U	.00	F	Infant	030c16Ae
NANCARVIS, John	43	M	Unknown	030c16Ae
STEVENS, Wm.	60	M	Unknown	030c16Ae
Ann	60	F	Unknown	030c16Ae
Elizabeth	25	F	Unknown	030c16Ae
WHITE, Eleanor	51	F	Unknown	030c16Ae
Jno.Morgan	20	M	Unknown	030c16Ae
Eleanor	17	F	Unknown	030c16Ae
Edmund	9	M	Child	030c16Ae
Mathew	7	M	Child	030c16Ae
Charles	13	M	Unknown	030c16Ae
WATERS, Edward	27	M	Unknown	030c16Ae
GILBERT, Wm.	41	M	Unknown	030c16Ae
LANER, Richd.	30	M	Unknown	030c16Ae
EVANS, James	28	M	Mason	030c16Ae
Eliz.	23	F	Unknown	030c16Ae
DUNCAN, Ann	40	F	Unknown	030c16Ae
Ann	8	F	Child	030c16Ae
Grace	8	F	Child	030c16Ae
JEFFERY, Jane	39	F	Unknown	030c16Ae
Emily	11	F	Unknown	030c16Ae
Eliza-Jane	8	F	Child	030c16Ae

NAMES OF PASSENGERS	AGE	SEX	OCCUPATIONS	DATE PORT SHIP
JEFFERY, Mary	4	F	Child	030c16Ae
U	.00	F	Infant	030c16Ae
SMITH, Mark	23	M	Unknown	030c16Ae
HICKS, Mary	21	F	Unknown	030c16Ae
BLIGHT, U	26	M	Miner	030c16Ae
Mary	28	F	Unknown	030c16Ae
Barke--, Th.Saml.	17	M	Unknown	030c16Ae
Ann	23	F	Unknown	030c16Ae
Elizabeth-Ann	29	F	Unknown	030c16Ae
U, U	00	F	Unknown	030c16Ae
Margaret	4	F	Child	030c16Ae
Frances	2	F	Child	030c16Ae
JAMES, Wm.	24	M	Unknown	030c16Ae
THOMAS, Benjamin	34	M	Farmer	030c16Ae
Jane	23	F	Unknown	030c16Ae
ROCK, Mary-Ann	28	F	Unknown	030c16Ae
U	.00	F	Infant	030c16Ae
Anthony	27	M	Unknown	030c16Ae
DOWNING, Christian	27	M	Unknown	030c16Ae
Wm.Jno.	6	M	Child	030c16Ae
Thos.	2	M	Child	030c16Ae
James	19	M	Unknown	030c16Ae
Hannah	31	F	Unknown	030c16Ae
Wm.	20	M	Unknown	030c16Ae
Zachariah	7	M	Child	030c16Ae
HICKS, Jane	25	F	Unknown	030c16Ae
Margt.	3	F	Child	030c16Ae
WALL, Elizabeth	31	F	Unknown	030c16Ae
HOSKING, Thos.	11	M	Unknown	030c16Ae
WALL, Jane	7	F	Child	030c16Ae
Jas.	5	M	Child	030c16Ae
Wm.	3	M	Child	030c16Ae
BOYES, John	23	M	Carpenter	030c16Ae
HOCKING, Sally	28	F	Unknown	030c16Ae
John	6	M	Child	030c16Ae
Geo.	5	M	Child	030c16Ae
U	.00	M	Infant	030c16Ae
Wm.	30	M	Unknown	030c16Ae
Jane	30	F	Unknown	030c16Ae
Nanny	5	F	Child	030c16Ae
Mary	3	F	Child	030c16Ae
U	.00	M	Infant	030c16Ae
OLDS, Hannah	39	F	Unknown	030c16Ae
Elizabeth	22	F	Unknown	030c16Ae
Mary	20	F	Unknown	030c16Ae
Mary	14	F	Unknown	030c16Ae
Grace	13	F	Unknown	030c16Ae
Wm.	12	M	Unknown	030c16Ae
Cathe.	9	F	Child	030c16Ae
Fanny	8	F	Child	030c16Ae
Samuel	3	M	Child	030c16Ae
U	.00	M	Infant	030c16Ae
TWILL, Hannah	12	F	Unknown	030c16Ae
Richd.	11	F	Unknown	030c16Ae
Jno.	10	M	Unknown	030c16Ae
ODGERS, John	24	M	Unknown	030c16Ae
WILLIAMS, John	33	M	Unknown	030c16Ae
John	16	M	Unknown	030c16Ae
RALPH, Jane	27	F	Unknown	030c16Ae
JOHNS, Samuel	22	M	Unknown	030c16Ae
ROWE, Edmund	22	M	Unknown	030c16Ae
HARVEY, Grace	23	F	Unknown	030c16Ae
TAYLOR, Elizabeth	30	F	Unknown	030c16Ae
Mary-Eliza	7	F	Child	030c16Ae
John	4	M	Child	030c16Ae
U	.00	F	Infant	030c16Ae
Margery	25	F	Unknown	030c16Ae
WILLIAMS, Elizabeth	23	F	Unknown	030c16Ae
Henry	9	M	Child	030c16Ae
Joseph	7	M	Child	030c16Ae
TEAGUE, Alice	47	F	Unknown	030c16Ae
John	17	M	Unknown	030c16Ae
Alice	13	F	Unknown	030c16Ae
Henry	12	M	Unknown	030c16Ae
Prudence	11	F	Unknown	030c16Ae

NAMES OF PASSENGERS	AGE	SEX	OCCUPATIONS	DATE PORT SHIP
TEAGUE, Elizabeth-Ann	8	F	Child	030c16Ae
Louisa	6	F	Child	030c16Ae
WHITE, James	23	M	Unknown	030c16Ae
GILL, Thos.	23	M	Unknown	030c16Ae
MOYLE, John	24	M	Unknown	030c16Ae
HODGE, James	29	M	Unknown	030c16Ae
ROWE, Richard	24	M	Unknown	030c16Ae
PHILLIPS, John	30	M	Unknown	030c16Ae
BARNETT, Elizabeth	24	F	Unknown	030c16Ae
MATHEWS, Clarinda	50	F	Unknown	030c16Ae
Wm.	21	M	Unknown	030c16Ae
Thos.	25	M	Unknown	030c16Ae
EUSTICE, Christian	48	M	Unknown	030c16Ae
Wm.	15	M	Unknown	030c16Ae
Jas.	13	M	Unknown	030c16Ae
Thos.Henry	3	M	Child	030c16Ae
LAITY, Mary	47	F	Unknown	030c16Ae
Wm.	18	M	Unknown	030c16Ae
Richard	25	M	Unknown	030c16Ae
Henry	11	M	Unknown	030c16Ae
Marianne	19	F	Unknown	030c16Ae
MOON, Wm.	30	M	Unknown	030c16Ae
GILBERT, Lucy	30	F	Unknown	030c16Ae
Wm.	6	M	Child	030c16Ae
John	5	M	Child	030c16Ae
WREN, Edward	20	M	Unknown	030c16Ae
HORKIN, John	20	M	Unknown	030c16Ae
Wm.	14	M	Unknown	030c16Ae

CANADA 04 OCTOBER 1849

From Liverpool And Halifax

NAMES OF PASSENGERS	AGE	SEX	OCCUPATIONS	DATE PORT SHIP
GALLWAY, R.	30	M	Army	040c12Ag
PHILLIP, W.	21	M	Merchant	040c12Ag
DOUGLAS, C.	21	M	Army	040c12Ag
BLACKBURROW, J.	50	M	None	040c12Ag
M.	40	F	None	040c12Ag
M.	20	F	None	040c12Ag
ARTHUR, Alexr.	38	M	Merchant	040c12Ag
C.	26	F	None	040c12Ag
Alexr.	2	M	Child	040c12Ag
B.	1	F	Child	040c12Ag
WILSON, Jane	28	F	None	040c12Ag
Fredk.	5	M	Child	040c12Ag
WICKHAM, J.	30	F	None	040c12Ag
H.L.	3	F	Child	040c12Ag
A.M.	1	F	Child	040c12Ag
TOKER, Mary	40	F	None	040c12Ag
Mary	12	F	None	040c12Ag
Clara	10	F	None	040c12Ag
MAYWOOD, C.A.	30	M	Merchant	040c12Ag
ANDERSON, W.	51	M	Merchant	040c12Ag
HOLFORD, James	60	M	Banker	040c12Ag
PAUL, James	29	M	None	040c12Ag
BUTTERFIELD, R.	31	M	Merchant	040c12Ag
GORE, Henry	22	M	Army	040c12Ag
BAILEY, Wm.	20	M	Farmer	040c12Ag
RISBY, J.S.	30	M	Engineer	040c12Ag
LLOYD, Jno.	40	M	Gdnr	040c12Ag
BAMING, C.	21	M	Mechanic	040c12Ag
ROBINSON, C.W.	24	M	Merchant	040c12Ag
GRANT, P.	31	M	Merchant	040c12Ag
CARTER, D.	20	M	Merchant	040c12Ag
SMITH, M.	41	F	Servant	040c12Ag
KITTLE, Susan	22	F	Servant	040c12Ag
HARRIS, Mary	26	F	Servant	040c12Ag
AITKEN, Gordon	20	M	Servant	040c12Ag

VICTORIA 06 OCTOBER 1849

From St.JOHNS,N.B.

NAMES OF PASSENGERS	AGE	SEX	OCCUPATIONS	DATE PORT SHIP
CILINAN, Helen	22	F	Unknown	060c07Aj

ARAB 06 OCTOBER 1849

From Belfast

NAMES OF PASSENGERS	AGE	SEX	OCCUPATIONS	DATE PORT SHIP
TURRISON, William	44	M	Laborer	060c17Af
Hannah	40	F	Laborer	060c17Af
William	17	M	Laborer	060c17Af
Thomas	23	M	Laborer	060c17Af
Mary	16	F	Laborer	060c17Af
BRADLEY, Mary	17	F	Laborer	060c17Af
ONEILL, Eliza	20	F	Laborer	060c17Af
SLOAN, Eliza	20	F	Laborer	060c17Af
MOFFAT, Cath.	20	F	Laborer	060c17Af
KANE, Mary	25	F	Laborer	060c17Af
MCFEBRIDGE, Geo.	26	M	Laborer	060c17Af
MEGUIRE, Peggy	20	F	Laborer	060c17Af
REDMOND, Biddy	26	F	Laborer	060c17Af
KENNEDY, Margt.	40	F	Laborer	060c17Af
Margt.	13	F	Laborer	060c17Af
TRAVERS, William	25	M	Laborer	060c17Af
KANE, Thomas	18	M	Laborer	060c17Af
GRAHAM, Eliza	20	F	Laborer	060c17Af
MCCOLLOUGH, Ann	21	F	Laborer	060c17Af
GRAHAM, Martha	21	F	Laborer	060c17Af
MCCOLLOUGH, John	27	M	Laborer	060c17Af
Mary	25	F	Laborer	060c17Af
Ann	22	F	Laborer	060c17Af
Mary	.00	F	Infant	060c17Af
MCDOWELL, Jane	40	F	Laborer	060c17Af
Ellen	17	F	Laborer	060c17Af
BRADLEY, James	18	M	Laborer	060c17Af
BRYSON, Mary	40	F	Laborer	060c17Af
NETTLESON, Robt.	35	M	Laborer	060c17Af
Sarah	35	F	Laborer	060c17Af
Eliza	7	F	Child	060c17Af
Richd.	5	M	Child	060c17Af
Sarah	4	F	Child	060c17Af
WALKER, Eliza	32	F	Laborer	060c17Af
James	7	M	Child	060c17Af
Isabella	5	F	Child	060c17Af
Ellen	4	F	Child	060c17Af
Margt.	.00	F	Infant	060c17Af
Alex	13	M	Laborer	060c17Af
MULLIKIN, Edwd.	20	M	Laborer	060c17Af
MULLEN, Isabella	20	F	Laborer	060c17Af
GREEN, Phoebus	17	M	Laborer	060c17Af
MCNULTY, John	26	M	Laborer	060c17Af
LEVI, Wm.	13	M	Laborer	060c17Af
MCDONALD, Mary	18	F	Laborer	060c17Af
PURVIS, Margt.	30	F	Laborer	060c17Af
Mary	16	F	Laborer	060c17Af
James	13	M	Laborer	060c17Af
Henry	11	M	Laborer	060c17Af
Margt.	10	F	Laborer	060c17Af
John	8	M	Child	060c17Af
Eliza	6	F	Child	060c17Af
Saml.	.00	M	Infant	060c17Af

NAMES OF PASSENGERS	AGE	SEX	OCCUPATIONS	DATE PORT SHIP
DUFFY, Thos.	30	M	Laborer	060c17Af
TATE, Esther	36	F	Laborer	060c17Af
Saml.	6	M	Child	060c17Af
Mathew	4	M	Child	060c17Af
Isabella	2	F	Child	060c17Af
ROBINS, Jane	30	F	Laborer	060c17Af
Mary	4	F	Child	060c17Af
Robt.	.00	M	Infant	060c17Af
DIMONS, Reilly	38	M	Laborer	060c17Af
Eliza	24	F	Laborer	060c17Af
Magt.	5	F	Child	060c17Af
COYLE, Rose-Ann	19	F	Laborer	060c17Af
Susan	.00	F	Infant	060c17Af
THOMPSON, James	30	M	Laborer	060c17Af
HITTRICK, Freely	32	M	Laborer	060c17Af
NULTY, Pat	30	M	Laborer	060c17Af
Eliza	22	F	Laborer	060c17Af
Jane	.00	F	Infant	060c17Af
ONEILL, Michl.	20	M	Laborer	060c17Af
MCCURRY, John	20	M	Laborer	060c17Af
FARRELL, James	35	M	Laborer	060c17Af
MCHAGGENY, Robt.	30	M	Laborer	060c17Af
JOYCE, John	40	M	Laborer	060c17Af
James	17	M	Laborer	060c17Af
Margt.	15	F	Laborer	060c17Af
Saml.	13	M	Laborer	060c17Af
MCHAGGARD, Charlotte	11	F	Laborer	060c17Af
James	9	M	Child	060c17Af
KENNEDY, Pat	45	M	Laborer	060c17Af
LEHAN, Edwd.	33	M	Laborer	060c17Af
GRAHAM, Eliza	18	F	Laborer	060c17Af
MCGAIR, Sarah	45	F	Laborer	060c17Af
Jane	23	F	Laborer	060c17Af
James	15	M	Laborer	060c17Af
MCAPEEL, John	13	M	Laborer	060c17Af
DOLZELL, Ellen	26	F	Laborer	060c17Af
James	1	M	Child	060c17Af
William	2	M	Child	060c17Af
Agnes	.00	F	Infant	060c17Af
MONTGOMERY, Jon.	36	M	Laborer	060c17Af
MCKILLOP, Mary	35	F	Laborer	060c17Af
Sarah	16	F	Laborer	060c17Af
WHITEFORD, Margt.	19	F	Laborer	060c17Af
Jane	21	F	Laborer	060c17Af
Joseph	.00	M	Infant	060c17Af
HUNTER, Thos.	17	M	Laborer	060c17Af
MCENLLEY, John	21	M	Laborer	060c17Af
PATTON, Eliza	50	F	Laborer	060c17Af
JENKINS, Ann	30	F	Laborer	060c17Af
CAMPBELL, Margt.	30	F	Laborer	060c17Af
Margt.	40	F	Laborer	060c17Af
William	7	M	Child	060c17Af
MCCORMICK, John	20	M	Laborer	060c17Af
HAMSON, William	20	M	Laborer	060c17Af
MCCOVERY, Eliza	30	F	Laborer	060c17Af
HAMSON, Ellen	20	F	Laborer	060c17Af
SMITH, Jane	29	F	Laborer	060c17Af
DWIRE, Cathe.	19	F	Laborer	060c17Af
MCCORMICK, A.	25	M	Laborer	060c17Af
HODGSON, Isaac	68	M	Laborer	060c17Af
Cathe.	50	F	Laborer	060c17Af
Jane	19	F	Laborer	060c17Af
John	14	M	Laborer	060c17Af
Wm.	12	M	Laborer	060c17Af
John	19	M	Laborer	060c17Af
RITCHIE, James	30	M	Laborer	060c17Af
HARLON, Marcus	15	M	Laborer	060c17Af
MCKEAG, Isaac	30	M	Laborer	060c17Af
Jane	26	F	Laborer	060c17Af
James	3	M	Child	060c17Af
Mary	2	F	Child	060c17Af
Sarah	.00	F	Infant	060c17Af
MCCERT, Peter	40	M	Laborer	060c17Af
HAGAN, Mary-Jane	20	F	Laborer	060c17Af
MCCUSKAR, Cathe.	20	F	Laborer	060c17Af

NAMES OF PASSENGERS	AGE	SEX	OCCUPATIONS	DATE PORT SHIP
SEILSON, Elizt.	20	F	Laborer	060c17Af
Fras.	.00	M	Infant	060c17Af
Died-At-Sea				
MAGENNIS, Cathe.	20	F	Laborer	060c17Af
Mary-A.	.00	F	Infant	060c17Af
BARCLAY, John	50	M	Laborer	060c17Af
Susan	50	F	Laborer	060c17Af
MCALEER, David	30	M	Laborer	060c17Af
Mary	28	F	Laborer	060c17Af
Cath.	7	F	Child	060c17Af
John	5	M	Child	060c17Af
Patk.	3	M	Child	060c17Af
MEHAN, Rob.	30	M	Laborer	060c17Af

COLUMBUS 08 OCTOBER 1849

From Liverpool

NAMES OF PASSENGERS	AGE	SEX	OCCUPATIONS	DATE PORT SHIP
DEVLIN, Patrick	29	M	Laborer	080c02Ah
GORMLEY, Julia	17	F	None	080c02Ah
Kate	15	F	None	080c02Ah
MCDONAGH, Dominick	20	M	Laborer	080c02Ah
MALLON, Biddy	40	F	None	080c02Ah
BRENGAN, Cathe.	23	F	None	080c02Ah
TAAFFE, Henry-Edmd.	24	M	Laborer	080c02Ah
Sarah-Louisa	20	F	None	080c02Ah
Died-At-Sea				
TAYLOR, Eliza	13	F	None	080c02Ah
Thos.	2	M	Child	080c02Ah
RYAN, Edwd.	16	M	Laborer	080c02Ah
DORAN, Martha	28	F	None	080c02Ah
Saml.	3	M	Child	080c02Ah
Mary	.00	F	Infant	080c02Ah
KELLY, Pat	38	M	Laborer	080c02Ah
Mary	30	F	None	080c02Ah
Willm.	10	M	None	080c02Ah
John	6	M	Child	080c02Ah
Mary	2	F	Child	080c02Ah
KILKENNEY, Barbara	12	F	None	080c02Ah
TAAFFE, Marmaduke	1	M	Child	080c02Ah
Died-At-Sea				
Henry-Edmd.	.00	M	Infant	080c02Ah
ANSLEY, Susan	30	F	None	080c02Ah
George	9	M	Child	080c02Ah
Thos.	5	M	Child	080c02Ah
Hannah	1	F	Child	080c02Ah
Died-At-Sea				
YOUNG, John	16	M	Laborer	080c02Ah
Thos.	28	M	Laborer	080c02Ah
HIGGINS, Ann	19	F	None	080c02Ah
Maria	18	F	None	080c02Ah
FARRELL, Ann	18	F	None	080c02Ah
KELLY, John	3	M	Child	080c02Ah
MCENERY, Mary	40	F	None	080c02Ah
Ellen	16	F	None	080c02Ah
LAWLER, Patrick	19	M	Laborer	080c02Ah
PURCELL, Jeffrey	20	M	Laborer	080c02Ah
MAHER, Michl.	30	M	Laborer	080c02Ah
MCDONGHAN, John	45	M	Laborer	080c02Ah
John	15	M	Laborer	080c02Ah
Alexr.	13	M	Laborer	080c02Ah
Mary	11	F	None	080c02Ah
Cathe.	9	F	Child	080c02Ah
DONOUGH, Morris	30	M	Laborer	080c02Ah
HORAN, Michl.	20	M	Laborer	080c02Ah
HAFFARTY, Timothy	50	M	Laborer	080c02Ah
MULLEN, Bridgt.	18	F	None	080c02Ah
KEMPSEY, Bridgt.	12	F	None	080c02Ah
KENNEDY, U	50	F	Wi	080c02Ah

NAMES OF PASSENGERS	AGE	SEX	OCCUPATIONS	DATE PORT SHIP
KENNA, Pat	19	M	Laborer	080c02Ah
GLANCY, Bridgt.	16	F	None	080c02Ah
TRAINER, Mary	36	F	None	080c02Ah
Died-At-Sea				
PALMER, Susan	34	F	None	080c02Ah
Edwd.	9	M	Child	080c02Ah
Ann	6	F	Child	080c02Ah
Maria	3	F	Child	080c02Ah
Died-At-Sea				
LYNCH, Mathew	23	M	Laborer	080c02Ah
Ann	20	F	None	080c02Ah
TIERNEY, Cathe.	12	F	None	080c02Ah
MOYNAGH, Margret	17	F	None	080c02Ah
BROWN, Mary	19	F	None	080c02Ah
WARD, Josh.	50	M	Laborer	080c02Ah
U (W)	45	F	None	080c02Ah
SUMMERELL, U-Mrs.	40	F	None	080c02Ah
Thomas	22	M	Laborer	080c02Ah
CORBETT, U-Mrs.	40	F	None	080c02Ah
KELLY, U	40	F	None	080c02Ah
KANE, Ann	40	F	None	080c02Ah
MCCORMICK, Willm.	37	M	Laborer	080c02Ah
Mary	26	F	None	080c02Ah
Pat	11	M	None	080c02Ah
Mary	9	F	Child	080c02Ah
Cathe.	7	F	Child	080c02Ah
Willm.	3	M	Child	080c02Ah
FITZGERRALD, Margt.	25	F	None	080c02Ah
GRANT, Cathe.	40	F	None	080c02Ah
Cathe.	10	F	None	080c02Ah
FARREN, Michl.	22	M	Laborer	080c02Ah
MURRAY, Pat	16	M	Laborer	080c02Ah
KENNEDY, Ellen	17	F	None	080c02Ah
HANDY, Biddy	30	F	None	080c02Ah
FALLON, Ann	22	F	None	080c02Ah
MIDGLEY, Edwd.	24	M	Laborer	080c02Ah
Elesia	21	F	None	080c02Ah
HINDS, Alexr.	19	M	Laborer	080c02Ah
BAINES, Chas.	24	M	Laborer	080c02Ah
SHEPPARD, Willm.	25	M	Laborer	080c02Ah
BATES, Matilda	24	F	None	080c02Ah
COLLINS, Mary	19	F	None	080c02Ah
FARRELL, Johannah	30	F	None	080c02Ah
Patrick	8	M	Child	080c02Ah
Bridgt.	22	F	None	080c02Ah
ROCHE, Mary	12	F	None	080c02Ah
Willm.	9	M	Child	080c02Ah
HENRY, Mary	21	F	None	080c02Ah
BARRY, Bridgt.	23	F	None	080c02Ah
Mary	21	F	None	080c02Ah
Garrett	19	M	Laborer	080c02Ah
BONDRAN, James	00	M	Laborer	080c02Ah
Ellen	00	F	None	080c02Ah
Michl.	10	M	None	080c02Ah
COWLEY, Dennis	00	M	None	080c02Ah
GRIFFIN, Daniel	26	M	Laborer	080c02Ah
Patrick	9	M	Child	080c02Ah
Luke	6	M	Child	080c02Ah
SHANNESSY, John	23	M	Laborer	080c02Ah
DILLON, Biddy	23	F	None	080c02Ah
CLANCY, Mary	50	F	None	080c02Ah
Honora	20	F	None	080c02Ah
Ellen	14	F	None	080c02Ah
Mary	4	F	Child	080c02Ah
CONNELL, John	19	M	Laborer	080c02Ah
DUNN, Thos.	36	M	Laborer	080c02Ah
Died-At-Sea				
Ann	36	F	None	080c02Ah
Edwd.	12	M	None	080c02Ah
Thos.	10	M	None	080c02Ah
Willm.	7	M	Child	080c02Ah
Josh.	4	M	Child	080c02Ah
John	1	M	Child	080c02Ah
GREGORY, Elizh.	30	F	None	080c02Ah
FURMGAN, Daniel	55	M	Laborer	080c02Ah
Died-At-Sea				
Johanna	48	F	None	080c02Ah
Died-At-Sea				
Mary	22	F	None	080c02Ah
John	20	M	Laborer	080c02Ah
Died-At-Sea				
Kelly	16	M	Laborer	080c02Ah
Judy	7	F	Child	080c02Ah
CONNOR, John	00	M	None	080c02Ah
Died-At-Sea				
Kelly	25	M	Laborer	080c02Ah
FOLEY, John	50	M	Laborer	080c02Ah
Died-At-Sea				
Ellen	52	F	None	080c02Ah
Died-At-Sea				
Derby	18	M	Laborer	080c02Ah
Ellen	21	F	None	080c02Ah
Died-At-Sea				
John	21	M	Laborer	080c02Ah
Died-At-Sea				
Patrick	16	M	Laborer	080c02Ah
Mary	24	F	None	080c02Ah
Johanna	11	F	None	080c02Ah
Died-At-Sea				
Julia	8	F	Child	080c02Ah
SULLIMAN, John	30	M	Laborer	080c02Ah
Ellen	30	F	None	080c02Ah
SULLIVAN, Patrick	27	M	Laborer	080c02Ah
SMITH, Margt.	23	F	None	080c02Ah
Nancy	25	F	None	080c02Ah
Daniel	25	M	Laborer	080c02Ah
MCDENEHRY, Dennis	60	M	Laborer	080c02Ah
Johanna	50	F	None	080c02Ah
Mathew	21	M	Laborer	080c02Ah
Mary	23	F	None	080c02Ah
Daniel	19	M	Laborer	080c02Ah
John	17	M	Laborer	080c02Ah
Biddy	15	F	None	080c02Ah
Michl.	11	M	None	080c02Ah
Died-At-Sea				
Alice	7	F	Child	080c02Ah
Dennis	10	M	None	080c02Ah
Thaddy	3	M	Child	080c02Ah
CLEARY, Mathw.	50	M	Laborer	080c02Ah
Mary	45	F	None	080c02Ah
Judy	20	F	None	080c02Ah
Darcy	18	F	None	080c02Ah
John	16	M	Laborer	080c02Ah
Patrick	13	M	None	080c02Ah
Daniel	4	M	Child	080c02Ah
Johanna	6	F	Child	080c02Ah
CASEY, John	56	M	Laborer	080c02Ah
Barbara	17	F	None	080c02Ah
Johanna	18	F	None	080c02Ah
Rosanna	16	F	None	080c02Ah
Michl.	13	M	None	080c02Ah
SULLIVAN, Mary	26	F	None	080c02Ah
OCONNELL, Danl.	45	M	Laborer	080c02Ah
SULLIVAN, John	.04	M	Infant	080c02Ah
Died-At-Sea				
OCONNELL, Margt.	35	F	None	080c02Ah
Danl.	15	M	Laborer	080c02Ah
John	13	M	None	080c02Ah
Jerry	10	M	None	080c02Ah
Died-At-Sea				
Mary	9	F	Child	080c02Ah
Johanna	8	F	Child	080c02Ah
Peggy	5	F	Child	080c02Ah
LENEHAN, Mary	20	F	None	080c02Ah
Ann	50	F	None	080c02Ah
Kate	9	F	Child	080c02Ah
Ellen	7	F	Child	080c02Ah
KEEFFA, Margt.	50	F	None	080c02Ah
Nancy	23	F	None	080c02Ah

NAMES OF PASSENGERS	AGE	SEX	OCCUPATIONS	DATE PORT SHIP
KEEFFA, Johanna	21	F	None	080c02Ah
Eugene	17	M	None	080c02Ah
Jane	13	F	None	080c02Ah
LEARY, Conner	55	M	Laborer	080c02Ah
Ellen	50	F	None	080c02Ah
Johanna	20	F	None	080c02Ah
John	18	M	Laborer	080c02Ah
Ellen	16	F	None	080c02Ah
Mathew	13	M	None	080c02Ah
Died-At-Sea				
Jerry	7	M	Child	080c02Ah
Peggy	5	F	Child	080c02Ah
DALY, Daniel	50	M	Laborer	080c02Ah
Margt.	50	F	None	080c02Ah
John	26	M	Laborer	080c02Ah
Judy	20	F	None	080c02Ah
Margt.	19	F	None	080c02Ah
Bessy	25	F	None	080c02Ah
GALVIN, John	30	M	Laborer	080c02Ah
Peggy	30	F	None	080c02Ah
Thadde	30	M	Laborer	080c02Ah
Biddy	4	F	None	080c02Ah
Patrick	2	M	None	080c02Ah
MCCARTHY, Margt.	00	F	None	080c02Ah
CLERNE, Timothy	42	M	Laborer	080c02Ah
Mary	42	F	None	080c02Ah
Daniel	13	M	None	080c02Ah
Nelly	10	F	None	080c02Ah
Mick	8	M	Child	080c02Ah
Thadde	5	M	Child	080c02Ah
Cornelius	3	M	Child	080c02Ah
DENEHY, Dennis	50	M	Laborer	080c02Ah
Johanna	49	F	None	080c02Ah
Mary	19	F	None	080c02Ah
Daniel	17	M	Laborer	080c02Ah
Cornelius	15	M	Laborer	080c02Ah
Mick	13	M	Laborer	080c02Ah
Dennis	7	M	Child	080c02Ah
Mathew	5	M	Child	080c02Ah
MITCHELL, Mary	13	F	None	080c02Ah
MCARDIFF, Dennis	28	M	Laborer	080c02Ah
Johanna	24	F	None	080c02Ah
Michael	22	M	Laborer	080c02Ah
Robt.	17	M	Laborer	080c02Ah
TOBIN, Richd.	40	M	Laborer	080c02Ah
Mary	35	F	None	080c02Ah
James	2	M	Child	080c02Ah
Mary	7	F	Child	080c02Ah
BURKE, Chas.	23	M	Laborer	080c02Ah
OSULLIVAN, Mary	27	F	None	080c02Ah
KELLEHER, Daniel	29	M	Laborer	080c02Ah
Kelly	26	M	Laborer	080c02Ah
John	36	M	Laborer	080c02Ah
Mary	21	F	None	080c02Ah
Thade	2	M	Child	080c02Ah
Kelly	3	M	Child	080c02Ah
LYON, Mick	24	M	Laborer	080c02Ah
Died-At-Sea				
Daniel	21	M	Laborer	080c02Ah
Ellen	20	F	None	080c02Ah
OCONNELL, Pat	50	M	Laborer	080c02Ah
Ellen	44	F	None	080c02Ah
Died-At-Sea				
Mary	22	F	None	080c02Ah
Phillip	19	M	Laborer	080c02Ah
Danl.	16	M	Laborer	080c02Ah
Judy	15	F	None	080c02Ah
John	13	M	None	080c02Ah
Margt.	7	F	Child	080c02Ah
Johanna	4	F	Child	080c02Ah
CORBETT, Johanna	20	F	None	080c02Ah
DENNY, Anastasia	20	F	None	080c02Ah
KELLAN, Danl.	31	M	Laborer	080c02Ah
PRICE, E.	30	M	Laborer	080c02Ah
Elizh.	33	F	None	080c02Ah
PRICE, Betsy	7	F	Child	080c02Ah
CARNEY, Martin	30	M	Laborer	080c02Ah
MATTISON, John	27	M	Laborer	080c02Ah
U (W)	24	F	None	080c02Ah
GAGAHAN, Patk.	20	M	Laborer	080c02Ah
CARROLL, Hugh	18	M	Laborer	080c02Ah
FOX, Esther	20	F	None	080c02Ah
John	9	M	Child	080c02Ah
Thomas	7	M	Child	080c02Ah
Bernard	5	M	Child	080c02Ah
SEAMARK, George	27	M	Laborer	080c02Ah
BELLARS, John	30	M	Laborer	080c02Ah
MADDY, Ann	30	F	None	080c02Ah
Jane	20	F	None	080c02Ah
GRANTON, Peter	36	M	Laborer	080c02Ah
Died-At-Sea				
KETTS, Francis	17	M	Laborer	080c02Ah
DONOHOE, Ellen	20	F	None	080c02Ah
Bernan	11	M	None	080c02Ah
MAHRE, Michl.	40	M	Laborer	080c02Ah
Norry	9	M	Child	080c02Ah
MARA, John	27	M	Laborer	080c02Ah
BARRY, Mathew	20	M	Laborer	080c02Ah
MURPHY, Pat	35	M	Laborer	080c02Ah
BRANNER, Martin	32	M	Laborer	080c02Ah
BRENNAN, Ann	25	F	None	080c02Ah
MULLANY, Pat	27	M	Laborer	080c02Ah
MCGUIRE, John	35	M	Laborer	080c02Ah
MCKEY, John	12	M	Unknown	080c02Ah
Ann	9	F	Child	080c02Ah
Cathe.	5	F	Child	080c02Ah
John	.00	M	Infant	080c02Ah
SMITH, Eleanor	40	F	None	080c02Ah
Cathe.	18	F	None	080c02Ah
Mary	2	F	Child	080c02Ah
DOUGHERTY, Alice	25	F	None	080c02Ah
Thos.	4	M	Child	080c02Ah
Bridgt.	2	F	Child	080c02Ah
Mary-A.	.00	F	Infant	080c02Ah
FARLEY, Phoebe	50	F	None	080c02Ah
PAYNE, John	30	M	Laborer	080c02Ah
Elizh.	25	F	None	080c02Ah
George	1	M	Child	080c02Ah
PHILLIPS, Thos.	23	M	Laborer	080c02Ah
Mary	21	F	None	080c02Ah
Willm.	.00	M	Infant	080c02Ah
MCGUIRE, Mary	20	F	None	080c02Ah
BRADLEY, John	42	M	Laborer	080c02Ah
DAWSON, John	28	M	Laborer	080c02Ah
KELLY, Margt.	13	F	None	080c02Ah
CANNON, Thos.	60	M	Laborer	080c02Ah
Bridgt.	4	F	Child	080c02Ah
QUINN, Bridgt.	28	F	None	080c02Ah
James	8	M	Child	080c02Ah
Thos.	2	M	Child	080c02Ah
FAGAN, Robt.	26	M	Laborer	080c02Ah
BURKE, Patk.	14	M	Laborer	080c02Ah
Mary	21	F	None	080c02Ah
KIMBERLY, Mary-A.	30	F	None	080c02Ah
Mary-A.	6	F	Child	080c02Ah
KENEDY, Willm.	30	M	Laborer	080c02Ah
GALLAGHER, Bridget	32	F	None	080c02Ah
John	17	M	Laborer	080c02Ah
REILLY, Ann	18	F	None	080c02Ah
CALLEN, Ann	9	F	Child	080c02Ah
CROSSMAN, Alice	6	F	Child	080c02Ah
Mary	13	F	None	080c02Ah
GORMAN, Cathe.	40	F	None	080c02Ah
HOROHO, James	23	M	Laborer	080c02Ah
RILEY, Owen	30	M	Laborer	080c02Ah
Died-At-Sea				
DUNLOP, Mary-A.	24	F	None	080c02Ah
Elizh.	22	F	None	080c02Ah
Margt.Jane	20	F	None	080c02Ah
DALY, John	24	M	Laborer	080c02Ah

NAMES OF PASSENGERS	AGE	SEX	OCCUPATIONS	DATE PORT SHIP
KING, Jane	20	F	None	080c02Ah
Died-At-Sea				
Willm.	.00	M	Infant	080c02Ah
Died-At-Sea				
NORRIS, Wm.	20	M	Laborer	080c02Ah
MILNES, Josh.	39	M	Laborer	080c02Ah
MAHER, Mary	22	F	None	080c02Ah
HENRY, Patrick	31	M	Laborer	080c02Ah
FLYNN, Chas.	14	M	Laborer	080c02Ah
Patk.	11	M	None	080c02Ah
JOHNSTONE, Sarah	16	F	None	080c02Ah
GALLAGHER, Cathe.	16	F	None	080c02Ah
James	12	M	None	080c02Ah
MCKEE, James	18	M	Laborer	080c02Ah
HILDRETH, H.R.	17	M	Laborer	080c02Ah
MCCABE, Thomas	29	M	Laborer	080c02Ah
DOYLE, Maria	9	F	Child	080c02Ah
FEGAN, Catherine	00	F	None	080c02Ah
William	00	M	None	080c02Ah
H--E, James	25	M	Laborer	080c02Ah
DEMPHEY, Catherine	30	F	None	080c02Ah
Patrick	22	M	Laborer	080c02Ah
MCKINLEY, Charles	26	M	Laborer	080c02Ah
MINAGH, Mary	22	F	None	080c02Ah
MAILEY, Ann	28	F	None	080c02Ah
John	3	M	Child	080c02Ah
GRIMES, Mathew	30	M	Laborer	080c02Ah
Mary	25	F	None	080c02Ah
Julia	22	F	None	080c02Ah
MAY, John	30	M	Laborer	080c02Ah
Mary	22	F	None	080c02Ah
WALL, Margret	30	F	None	080c02Ah
KEEAN, Mary	28	F	None	080c02Ah
Patrick	20	M	Laborer	080c02Ah
HANAGAN, Mary	16	F	None	080c02Ah
RYAN, Patrick	25	M	Laborer	080c02Ah
MANNON, Eliza	17	F	None	080c02Ah
MCCABE, Joseph	20	M	Laborer	080c02Ah
BRACEY, Brinell	19	M	Laborer	080c02Ah
MCKEY, John	12	M	Laborer	080c02Ah

MINNESOTA 08 OCTOBER 1849

From Liverpool

NAMES OF PASSENGERS	AGE	SEX	OCCUPATIONS	DATE PORT SHIP
COLLINS, Richard	28	M	Clerk	080c02Ak
Margt.	24	F	Unknown	080c02Ak
Wm.Richard	.01	M	Infant	080c02Ak
HURLEY, Cathr.	26	F	Unknown	080c02Ak
GORMAN, Michael	26	M	Laborer	080c02Ak
WARD, Thomas	24	M	Laborer	080c02Ak
Anne	22	F	Unknown	080c02Ak
John	.01	M	Infant	080c02Ak
James	16	M	Unknown	080c02Ak
DOWD, Cathr.	17	F	Unknown	080c02Ak
SMITH, Cathr.	18	F	Unknown	080c02Ak
FITZGERALD, Pat.	22	M	Laborer	080c02Ak
MCELVOY, U-Mrs.	40	F	Unknown	080c02Ak
Wm.	14	M	Unknown	080c02Ak
MURPHY, John	27	M	Laborer	080c02Ak
Lawrence	30	M	Laborer	080c02Ak
Mary	22	F	Unknown	080c02Ak
Eliza	19	F	Unknown	080c02Ak
Cathr.	17	F	Unknown	080c02Ak
CARROLL, Pat	24	M	Mechanic	080c02Ak
RYAN, Thos.	24	M	Laborer	080c02Ak
Phil.	22	M	Laborer	080c02Ak
DOWNEY, Wm.	30	M	Farmer	080c02Ak
Mary	30	F	Unknown	080c02Ak
HOGAN, Susan	26	F	Unknown	080c02Ak
HEGARTY, Danl.	26	M	Mechanic	080c02Ak
CUDDY, Ann	20	F	Unknown	080c02Ak
BOORDEN, Cathr.	25	F	Unknown	080c02Ak
ROONEY, Ann	20	F	Unknown	080c02Ak
FAULKNER, Diana	28	F	Unknown	080c02Ak
James	9	M	Child	080c02Ak
George	7	M	Child	080c02Ak
Eliza	4	F	Child	080c02Ak
COSKORAN, Thos.	28	M	Laborer	080c02Ak
FARRELL, Julia	21	F	Unknown	080c02Ak
CLEARY, Winefred	16	F	Unknown	080c02Ak
Mary	17	F	Unknown	080c02Ak
Maria	7	F	Child	080c02Ak
Patrick	3	M	Child	080c02Ak
ELLIS, James	30	M	Mechanic	080c02Ak
Margt.	28	F	Unknown	080c02Ak
Walter	35	M	Mechanic	080c02Ak
Catherine	25	F	Unknown	080c02Ak
Catherine	10	F	Unknown	080c02Ak
James	4	M	Child	080c02Ak
Thomas	8	M	Child	080c02Ak
HIGHLANDS, James	31	M	Laborer	080c02Ak
BRACK, Wm.	25	M	Laborer	080c02Ak
Patrick	25	M	Laborer	080c02Ak
STRONG, John	20	M	Laborer	080c02Ak
JAMES, Thomas	21	M	Laborer	080c02Ak
MOONE, Wm.	30	M	Laborer	080c02Ak
MCSHERY, John	30	M	Laborer	080c02Ak
QUINN, John	28	M	Laborer	080c02Ak
KERIGAN, Rose	18	F	Unknown	080c02Ak
MADDEN, Edwd.	46	M	Farmer	080c02Ak
Pat	22	M	Farmer	080c02Ak
Cath.	23	F	Unknown	080c02Ak
Ann	22	F	Unknown	080c02Ak
John	10	M	Unknown	080c02Ak
Michl.	8	M	Child	080c02Ak
Patrick	4	M	Child	080c02Ak
COYLE, James	18	M	Laborer	080c02Ak
COLEMAN, Patrick	22	M	Farmer	080c02Ak
Bridget	18	F	Unknown	080c02Ak
Mary	50	F	Unknown	080c02Ak
LOWRY, Peter	27	M	Laborer	080c02Ak
Margt.	26	F	Unknown	080c02Ak
Maria	.01	F	Infant	080c02Ak
BURKE, Denis	30	M	Laborer	080c02Ak
KENEDY, Honora	23	F	Unknown	080c02Ak
ROURKE, Margt.	20	F	Unknown	080c02Ak
DEGAN, Cathr.	14	F	Unknown	080c02Ak
CASSIDY, Andw.	28	M	Laborer	080c02Ak
DUNN, Margt.	21	F	Unknown	080c02Ak
ELLY, Elisabeth	22	F	Unknown	080c02Ak
CARYLAN, Elizabeth	18	F	Unknown	080c02Ak
MOONEY, Eliza	26	F	Unknown	080c02Ak
Ann	10	F	Unknown	080c02Ak
Richd.	9	M	Child	080c02Ak
COLIHAN, Mat	21	M	Laborer	080c02Ak
KELLY, Francis	18	F	Unknown	080c02Ak
SUTTON, Thos.	45	M	Laborer	080c02Ak
Saml.	19	M	Laborer	080c02Ak
Adam	11	M	Laborer	080c02Ak
COE, Cathr.	23	F	Unknown	080c02Ak
U	.00	F	Infant	080c02Ak
MATTHEWS, Robert	25	M	Laborer	080c02Ak
HEGGARTY, Dennis	18	M	Laborer	080c02Ak
LOWRY, Pat	21	M	Laborer	080c02Ak
BULGER, Pat.	24	M	Laborer	080c02Ak
HANNAN, John	30	M	Laborer	080c02Ak
MCGUANE, Thos.	26	M	Farmer	080c02Ak
Bridget	20	F	Unknown	080c02Ak
BROGAN, Margt.	20	F	Unknown	080c02Ak
MCGUANE, Mary	20	F	Unknown	080c02Ak
BROGAN, Ann	21	F	Unknown	080c02Ak
CARTHY, Bridget	23	F	Unknown	080c02Ak
DEA, Maurice	18	M	Laborer	080c02Ak

NAMES OF PASSENGERS	AGE	SEX	OCCUPATIONS	DATE PORT SHIP
MALONEY, Mary	18	F	Unknown	080c02Ak
CARRIG, Stephen	20	M	Laborer	080c02Ak
MCNAMARA, Michl.	43	M	Laborer	080c02Ak
Mary	43	F	Unknown	080c02Ak
MAHER, Michl.	26	M	Mechanic	080c02Ak
Daniel	22	M	Mechanic	080c02Ak
MCGEANE, Jno.	25	M	Laborer	080c02Ak
Margt.	24	F	Unknown	080c02Ak
FLANAGAN, James	30	M	Farmer	080c02Ak
Jane	25	F	Unknown	080c02Ak
Mary	2	F	Child	080c02Ak
Christopher	1	M	Child	080c02Ak
Mary	54	F	Unknown	080c02Ak
WADE, Cathr.	16	F	Unknown	080c02Ak
KELLY, Bridget	18	F	Unknown	080c02Ak
COSTELLO, Ellen	19	F	Unknown	080c02Ak
QUINN, Judith	19	F	Unknown	080c02Ak
CLEMENTS, Mary-Ann	25	F	Unknown	080c02Ak
Biddy	6	F	Child	080c02Ak
Anthony	4	M	Child	080c02Ak
BURTON, Joseph	22	M	Laborer	080c02Ak
CASH, Ann	22	F	Unknown	080c02Ak
CARNEY, Michael	20	M	Laborer	080c02Ak
HARNARAN, Thos.	28	M	Laborer	080c02Ak
Biddy	30	F	Unknown	080c02Ak
SULLIVAN, Thomas	26	M	Laborer	080c02Ak
GALLIGHER, Bridget	30	F	Unknown	080c02Ak
Margt.	2	F	Child	080c02Ak
COLEMAN, Rebecca	25	F	Unknown	080c02Ak
Elizabeth	2	F	Child	080c02Ak
SANDERSON, Jane	5	F	Child	080c02Ak
COLEMAN, Mary	25	F	Unknown	080c02Ak
KELLY, Bernard	38	M	Laborer	080c02Ak
DAGGAN, James	23	M	Laborer	080c02Ak
GALLAGHER, Wm.	35	M	Farmer	080c02Ak
Jas.	18	M	Farmer	080c02Ak
MCCALL, Mary	25	F	Unknown	080c02Ak
BYRNE, Kitty	30	F	Unknown	080c02Ak
KELLY, Mary	19	F	Unknown	080c02Ak
Eliza	18	F	Unknown	080c02Ak
CAMPBELL, Elisa	19	F	Unknown	080c02Ak
REILLY, James	18	M	Laborer	080c02Ak
GLEESON, John	24	M	Laborer	080c02Ak
James	25	M	Laborer	080c02Ak
MEE, Wm.	26	M	Laborer	080c02Ak
MITCHAEL, U-Mrs.	34	F	Unknown	080c02Ak
Wm.	20	M	Laborer	080c02Ak
SMITH, Anne	22	F	Unknown	080c02Ak
Biddy	4	F	Child	080c02Ak
MCGUIRE, Bryan	30	M	Farmer	080c02Ak
Mary	30	F	Unknown	080c02Ak
Margt.	1	F	Child	080c02Ak
Ellen	.01	F	Infant	080c02Ak
CUDDY, Mary	20	F	Unknown	080c02Ak
Ellen	19	F	Unknown	080c02Ak
LAMB, George	20	M	Laborer	080c02Ak
HARTNETT, Michael	33	M	Mechanic	080c02Ak
DUFFY, Mary	64	F	Unknown	080c02Ak

ROSE 08 OCTOBER 1849

From St.JOHNS,N.F.

NAMES OF PASSENGERS	AGE	SEX	OCCUPATIONS	DATE PORT SHIP
CONWAY, Thomas	39	M	Laborer	080c11Al
Mary	40	F	Unknown	080c11Al
John	12	M	Unknown	080c11Al
Patrick	8	M	Child	080c11Al
Mary	6	F	Child	080c11Al
Bridget	3	F	Child	080c11Al
NOWLAN, Bridget	26	F	Unknown	080c11Al
NOWLAND, Thos.	1	M	Child	080c11Al
Catharine	16	F	Unknown	080c11Al

BROTHERS 08 OCTOBER 1849

From Newry

NAMES OF PASSENGERS	AGE	SEX	OCCUPATIONS	DATE PORT SHIP
MCLEAN, Wm.Rev.	50	M	Clergyman	080c04Am
Fanny	20	F	Lady	080c04Am
DOWNEY, Mary	34	F	Unknown	080c04Am
KIERSANS, Mary-Ann	12	F	Unknown	080c04Am
Michael	16	M	Clerk	080c04Am
BRADY, Jane	26	F	Governess	080c04Am
HORNER, Catherine	34	F	Lady	080c04Am
MAGUINESS, Rose	25	F	Spinster	080c04Am
HENDERSON, Mary	14	F	Spinster	080c04Am
OWENS, James	50	M	Farmer	080c04Am
Michael	19	M	Relative	080c04Am
Thomas	16	M	Relative	080c04Am
Mary	14	F	Relative	080c04Am
James	12	M	Relative	080c04Am
Patt	10	M	Relative	080c04Am
Peter	6	M	Child	080c04Am
SLOAN, Agnes	16	F	Spinster	080c04Am
Alexander (B)	11	M	Relative	080c04Am
Samuel (B)	9	M	Child	080c04Am
SEMPLE, James	22	M	Shoemaker	080c04Am
Margaret	20	F	Wife	080c04Am
Mary-Ann	.00	F	Infant	080c04Am
LOUGHRAN, James	21	M	Currier	080c04Am
COULTER, Margaret	23	F	Spinster	080c04Am
TOYHANIS, Richard	14	M	Carpenter	080c04Am
MCGERRITY, Catherine	18	F	Spinster	080c04Am
RAMSEY, John	18	M	Millwright	080c04Am
BOLTON, Eliza	18	F	Spinster	080c04Am
SMITH, Sarah	40	F	Spinster	080c04Am
Mary	15	F	Relative	080c04Am
John	13	M	Relative	080c04Am
Margaret	10	F	Relative	080c04Am
William	9	M	Child	080c04Am
COLE, Elizabeth	26	F	Spinster	080c04Am
HANLON, Margaret	25	F	Spinster	080c04Am
FOWLER, Richard	32	M	Coach Maker	080c04Am
BRAMTEN, John	22	M	Architect	080c04Am
CONVERY, Eliza-Jane	22	M	Spinster	080c04Am
MCDONALD, Arthur	24	M	Painter	080c04Am
LOWDEN, Samuel	43	M	Smith	080c04Am
Sarah	42	F	Wife	080c04Am
Mary-Jane	17	F	Relative	080c04Am
Samuel	13	F	Relative	080c04Am
Frances	11	F	Relative	080c04Am
William	9	M	Child	080c04Am
Alexander	4	M	Child	080c04Am
MCKIBBEN, Henry	34	M	Mechanic	080c04Am
Ellen	32	F	Wife	080c04Am
DICKSON, Rebecca	20	F	Spinster	080c04Am
Margaret	22	F	Spinster	080c04Am
MCILRATH, John	45	M	Farmer	080c04Am
Thomas	15	M	Relative	080c04Am
Margaret	17	F	Relative	080c04Am
MCDONNELL, Bridget	19	F	Spinster	080c04Am
ROONEY, Margaret	28	F	Spinster	080c04Am
SMALL, Mary	21	F	Spinster	080c04Am
Michael	22	M	Cbtmkr	080c04Am
BYRNES, John	13	M	Unknown	080c04Am
COFFEY, Isaac	20	M	Locksmith	080c04Am
CAMBERS, William	17	M	Baker	080c04Am
HILLAN, Margaret	15	F	Spinster	080c04Am

NAMES OF PASSENGERS	AGE	SEX	OCCUPATIONS	DATE PORT SHIP
CONNOLLY, Peter	21	M	Miller	080c04Am
LENNON, Anne	23	F	Spinster	080c04Am
MCCARTNEY, Margaret	15	F	Spinster	080c04Am
MALONE, Susan	20	F	Spinster	080c04Am
Mary	15	F	Spinster	080c04Am
Catherine	17	F	Spinster	080c04Am
HAYES, Anne	22	F	Spinster	080c04Am
KENNEDY, John	24	M	Farmer	080c04Am
Jane	21	F	Wife	080c04Am
VALLELLY, John	39	M	Spdmkr	080c04Am
MCGIVERN, Alice	13	F	Spinster	080c04Am
SHILLIDAY, Sarah	24	F	Spinster	080c04Am
ROBB, Eliza	20	F	Spinster	080c04Am
James	.00	M	Infant	080c04Am
FEGAN, Mary	45	F	Wi	080c04Am
Catherine	20	F	Daughter	080c04Am
GORDON, Sarah	23	F	Spinster	080c04Am
Robert	.00	M	Infant	080c04Am
SMITH, Anne	30	F	Wi	080c04Am
James (S)	3	M	Child	080c04Am
John (S)	.00	M	Infant	080c04Am
MCCONNELL, Isabella	24	F	Spinster	080c04Am
CONNOLLY, Bridget	22	F	Dressmaker	080c04Am
BRENNAN, Patrick	19	M	Saddler	080c04Am
FINNIGAN, Margaret	55	F	Wife	080c04Am
Ann	18	F	Daughter	080c04Am
Mary	25	F	Daughter	080c04Am
FLANIGAN, John	24	M	Carpenter	080c04Am
BENNETT, Nancy	18	F	Spinster	080c04Am
DABSELL, Margaret	25	F	Spinster	080c04Am
Mary-Jane	2	F	Child	080c04Am
James	.00	M	Infant	080c04Am
TURNER, James	14	M	Shoemaker	080c04Am
Elizabeth	17	F	Sister	080c04Am
GOLLOGLY, James	48	M	Farmer	080c04Am
Ellen	18	F	Relative	080c04Am
Mary-Ann	16	F	Relative	080c04Am
Susan	12	F	Relative	080c04Am
NEARY, Denis	28	M	Sawer	080c04Am
Mary	30	F	Wife	080c04Am
BARRETT, Bernard	21	M	Smith	080c04Am
MONAGHAN, James	28	M	Mason	080c04Am
WEIR, Jane	28	F	Spinster	080c04Am
BOYLE, Thomas	40	M	Shoemaker	080c04Am
WILLIAMSON, Andrew	15	M	Unknown	080c04Am
MERRSERS, Mary	36	F	Spinster	080c04Am
MADDEN, Patrick	18	M	Baker	080c04Am
GALLAGHER, Edward	25	M	Coppersmith	080c04Am
MURRAY, Biddy	12	F	Unknown	080c04Am
Peggy	18	F	Spinster	080c04Am
QUINN, Catherine	30	F	Spinster	080c04Am
SMITH, Edward	40	M	Carpenter	080c04Am

HOTTINGUER 09 OCTOBER 1849

From Liverpool

NAMES OF PASSENGERS	AGE	SEX	OCCUPATIONS	DATE PORT SHIP
TAYLOR, Robert	44	M	Farmer	090c02An
DOWLIN, Daniel	40	M	Physician	090c02An
Ellen	40	F	Unknown	090c02An
Martin	6	M	Child	090c02An
Mary	5	F	Child	090c02An
Died-At-Sea				
Andrew	1	M	Child	090c02An
CUNNIFFE, Catherine	20	F	Unknown	090c02An
OFLYNN, James	36	M	Merchant	090c02An
Maria	30	F	Unknown	090c02An
Edward	11	M	Unknown	090c02An
Sarah-Ann	2	F	Child	090c02An
OFLYNN, Martha	10	F	Unknown	090c02An
Honor	15	F	Unknown	090c02An
GAHEGAN, Catherine	17	F	Unknown	090c02An
Margaret	20	F	Unknown	090c02An
Bridget	16	F	Unknown	090c02An
MURPHY, Margaret	25	F	Unknown	090c02An
DALY, Bridget	36	F	Unknown	090c02An
Clara	30	F	Unknown	090c02An
Elisha	23	F	Unknown	090c02An
Ellen	20	F	Unknown	090c02An
WALSH, Mary	17	F	Unknown	090c02An
Elisha	13	F	Unknown	090c02An
LYNCH, Maurice	22	M	Laborer	090c02An
Michael	5	M	Child	090c02An
MAKERLAND, John	22	M	Unknown	090c02An
COSS, Thomas	30	M	Unknown	090c02An
Honor	40	F	Unknown	090c02An
Daniel	21	M	Unknown	090c02An
Julia	8	F	Child	090c02An
BROOK, Mary	20	F	Unknown	090c02An
DUNN, Catherine	22	F	Unknown	090c02An
LINICHEN, Cornelius	35	M	Unknown	090c02An
QUIN, Catherine	15	F	Dressmaker	090c02An
MCKENNA, Eliza	35	F	Dressmaker	090c02An
Mary	16	F	Dressmaker	090c02An
Thomas	12	M	Unknown	090c02An
Eliza	6	F	Child	090c02An
John	10	M	Unknown	090c02An
Margaret	5	F	Child	090c02An
HANNCHIN, Biddy	19	F	Unknown	090c02An
RICKENS, Mary-Ann	17	F	Dressmaker	090c02An
CONOLEY, Sarah	21	F	Dressmaker	090c02An
BURN, Andrew	18	M	Laborer	090c02An
BERRIGAN, Catherine	19	F	Servant	090c02An
Mary	16	F	Servant	090c02An
Martin	18	M	Laborer	090c02An
ELKINS, Bridget	20	F	Unknown	090c02An
ELLIS, Mary	28	F	Unknown	090c02An
QUIN, Mary	24	F	Unknown	090c02An
Bridget	15	F	Unknown	090c02An
AGAN, Mary	16	F	Unknown	090c02An
FLINN, Betty	16	F	Unknown	090c02An
JONES, Samuel	50	M	Steward	090c02An
CUPPAGE, Thomas	23	M	Farmer	090c02An
GREESON, Joseph	24	M	Unknown	090c02An
WALSH, Pat	16	M	Unknown	090c02An
CURRIN, Hannah	17	F	Unknown	090c02An
OWEN, Thomas	23	M	Sailor	090c02An
Bridget	24	F	Unknown	090c02An
LEE, Catherine	50	F	Unknown	090c02An
Bernard	19	M	Unknown	090c02An
Catherine	11	F	Unknown	090c02An
CORRIGAN, Ann	30	F	Unknown	090c02An
John	20	M	Unknown	090c02An
RENNELS, Pat	11	M	Unknown	090c02An
Terence	9	M	Child	090c02An
Charles	7	M	Child	090c02An
Ann	1	F	Child	090c02An
QUIN, Mary-Ann	20	F	Unknown	090c02An
FAILEY, Mary	20	F	Unknown	090c02An
MCCUSKEY, Mary	6	F	Child	090c02An
RENNELS, Catherine	35	F	Unknown	090c02An
CASEY, Rose	18	F	Unknown	090c02An
STAPLETON, Catherine	20	F	Servant	090c02An
HAMELTON, Bridget	9	F	Child	090c02An
KERRY, Edward	22	M	Ploughman	090c02An
HAMELTON, John	10	M	Unknown	090c02An
Ellen	30	F	Unknown	090c02An
MCCARTY, George	21	M	Unknown	090c02An
HAYES, Margaret	30	F	Unknown	090c02An
MALLACHY, Pat	24	M	Unknown	090c02An
John	16	M	Unknown	090c02An
ALLCACH, Margaret	30	F	Unknown	090c02An
GONNAN, Sarah	19	F	Seamstress	090c02An
HAYES, Margaret	6	F	Child	090c02An

NAMES OF PASSENGERS	AGE	SEX	OCCUPATIONS	DATE PORT SHIP
KELLY, Pat	40	M	Unknown	090c02An
CORREGAN, Ann	3	F	Child	090c02An
BROPHY, Daniel	20	M	Unknown	090c02An
Died-At-Sea				
BOWE, Lucy	17	F	Unknown	090c02An
WELCH, Barney	30	M	Unknown	090c02An
DOYLE, Peter	34	M	Shoemaker	090c02An
HENELY, Patrick	23	M	Unknown	090c02An
MEGHAN, Pat	25	M	Unknown	090c02An
MARKEY, Mary	25	F	Unknown	090c02An
GELLANDIS, Eliza	19	F	Unknown	090c02An
CORREGAN, Thomas	5	M	Child	090c02An
Ann	3	F	Child	090c02An
Died-At-Sea				
MARKEY, Bessy	1	F	Child	090c02An
CANLIN, Gerry	15	M	Unknown	090c02An
SULLIVAN, Pat	18	M	Unknown	090c02An
MCMAHON, Mary	21	F	Dressmaker	090c02An
HANDELON, Mary	10	F	Unknown	090c02An
Catherine	20	F	Unknown	090c02An
MCMAHON, Margaret	19	F	Unknown	090c02An
HANDELON, Michael	12	M	Unknown	090c02An
LYNCH, Ann	25	F	Servant	090c02An
KEGAN, Thomas	15	M	Unknown	090c02An
HALLOW, Peggy	30	F	Unknown	090c02An
CRANE, Pat.	25	M	Tailor	090c02An
PANDON, Michael	20	M	Unknown	090c02An
CAHILL, Ann	21	F	Unknown	090c02An
Ann	20	F	Unknown	090c02An
Joseph	21	M	Unknown	090c02An
MCBRIDE, Mary	30	F	Unknown	090c02An
Died-At-Sea				
MCGOVAN, Peter	3	M	Child	090c02An
James	2	M	Child	090c02An
MAHON, Ann	18	F	Servant	090c02An
CARROLL, Edward	20	M	Mason	090c02An
FANNING, Charles	23	M	Unknown	090c02An
DUNN, Robert	23	M	Weaver	090c02An
DONLEY, Pat	24	M	Laborer	090c02An
MCMANUS, Bentley	12	M	Unknown	090c02An
KILLIGAN, Ebby	21	F	Dressmaker	090c02An
KARLY, Honnorah	14	F	Unknown	090c02An
KERBEY, Ebby	14	F	Unknown	090c02An
Michael	55	M	Unknown	090c02An
Died-At-Sea				
John	16	M	Unknown	090c02An
James	24	M	Unknown	090c02An
BREEN, Mary	19	F	Unknown	090c02An
Pennela	18	F	Unknown	090c02An
BURN, Lawrence	45	M	Laborer	090c02An
John	20	M	Unknown	090c02An
Richard	16	M	Unknown	090c02An
Lawrence	15	M	Unknown	090c02An
Michael	12	M	Unknown	090c02An
Catherine	10	F	Unknown	090c02An
HOGAN, Pat	28	M	Carpenter	090c02An
FLINN, Pat	28	M	Unknown	090c02An
Thomas	38	M	Unknown	090c02An
Bridget	20	F	Unknown	090c02An
HAND, James	30	M	Unknown	090c02An
CORRAN, John	30	M	Unknown	090c02An
MALONAY, John	20	M	Laborer	090c02An
DOOLAN, Maurice	20	M	Unknown	090c02An
LEIGHE, James	20	M	Unknown	090c02An
SHEY, Ellen	17	F	Unknown	090c02An
MALONEY, John	20	M	Laborer	090c02An
SULLIVAN, Patrick	27	M	Unknown	090c02An
STACK, Mary	18	F	Unknown	090c02An
PEARCE, Thomas	23	M	Laborer	090c02An
SHEY, Mary	17	F	Unknown	090c02An
COLBERT, John	24	M	Unknown	090c02An
HOLMES, Michael	25	M	Unknown	090c02An
MCGONDER, James	22	M	Unknown	090c02An
MCKENNA, David	24	M	Unknown	090c02An
John	16	M	Unknown	090c02An

NAMES OF PASSENGERS	AGE	SEX	OCCUPATIONS	DATE PORT SHIP
MCKENNA, Esey	14	F	Unknown	090c02An
GOULD, William	24	M	Unknown	090c02An
Robert	22	M	Unknown	090c02An
Catherine	20	F	Unknown	090c02An
HEARLEY, Michael	24	M	Unknown	090c02An
REDY, Morris	30	M	Unknown	090c02An
MURRAY, John	28	M	Engineer	090c02An
Mary-Ann	19	F	Unknown	090c02An
DOYLE, Johannah	20	F	Unknown	090c02An
FITZGERALD, Catherine	23	F	Unknown	090c02An
HOGAN, Pat.	40	M	Unknown	090c02An
Mary-Ann	36	F	Unknown	090c02An
Mary	28	F	Unknown	090c02An
KELLY, Ann	20	F	Unknown	090c02An
HOGAN, William-M.	10	M	Unknown	090c02An
Catherine	7	F	Child	090c02An
Mary	5	F	Child	090c02An
John	1	M	Child	090c02An
TURNEY, Pat	30	M	Unknown	090c02An
STACK, Edward	20	U	Unknown	090c02An
FLINN, William	25	M	Unknown	090c02An
MURPHY, Pat	32	M	Unknown	090c02An
SHANDLON, Michael	20	M	Laborer	090c02An
MCKENNY, Michael	20	M	Laborer	090c02An
FITZGERALD, Mary	40	F	Unknown	090c02An
BROWN, Catherine	40	F	Unknown	090c02An
Pat	26	M	Unknown	090c02An
HARNOTT, Margeret	18	F	Unknown	090c02An
FLINN, Johannah	29	F	Unknown	090c02An
CORTAIN, Catherine	4	F	Child	090c02An
Germiah	2	F	Child	090c02An
KELLY, Pat.	30	M	Unknown	090c02An
Bridget	30	F	Unknown	090c02An
MURPHY, Kate	20	F	Unknown	090c02An
DOOLEY, Ann	20	F	Unknown	090c02An
SMITH, Rose	24	F	Dressmaker	090c02An
CLARK, Margeret	20	F	Unknown	090c02An
MCGEE, Michael	20	M	Unknown	090c02An
DOHERTY, Mary	50	F	Unknown	090c02An
John	22	M	Unknown	090c02An
Bernerd	20	M	Unknown	090c02An
Mary	15	F	Unknown	090c02An
Catherine	12	F	Unknown	090c02An
ROACH, Bridget	17	F	Unknown	090c02An
Patrick	7	M	Child	090c02An
GALVAN, Mary	18	F	Dairymaid	090c02An
DONOHOE, Bridget	19	F	Unknown	090c02An
MARSHALL, James	20	M	Weaver	090c02An
SERRY, Thomas	22	M	Herd	090c02An
DONOHOE, Pat	20	M	Unknown	090c02An
KING, James	20	M	Unknown	090c02An
LACKEY, Edmond	27	M	Unknown	090c02An
Thomas	7	M	Child	090c02An
GLEESON, Owen	30	M	Unknown	090c02An
LACKEY, Bridget	11	F	Unknown	090c02An
FLANNERY, Mary	30	F	Unknown	090c02An
Pat	7	M	Child	090c02An
William	5	M	Child	090c02An
CAHILL, Margeret	19	F	Unknown	090c02An
ADAMS, William	40	M	Servant	090c02An
Sophia	36	U	Servant	090c02An
Henry	16	M	Laborer	090c02An
William	14	M	Unknown	090c02An
HARYALAN, Eliza	22	F	Unknown	090c02An
LEONARD, Pat.	29	M	Unknown	090c02An
CORREGAN, John	7	M	Child	090c02An
Died-At-Sea				
MARKEY, John	1	M	Child	090c02An

GREAT-WESTERN 10 OCTOBER 1849

From Bermuda And St.Thomas

NAMES OF PASSENGERS	AGE	SEX	OCCUPATIONS	DATE PORT SHIP
TAYLOR, W.R.N.	25	M	Army	100c13Ao
GIBBONS, Wm.Barton	48	M	Planter	100c13Ao
Ann-M.H.	24	F	None	100c13Ao
Fredk.Fitzroy	7	M	Child	100c13Ao
Mary-Louise	3	F	Child	100c13Ao
KELLY, Anne	20	F	Servant	100c13Ao

ZELPHA-P.BROWN 10 OCTOBER 1849

From Dublin

NAMES OF PASSENGERS	AGE	SEX	OCCUPATIONS	DATE PORT SHIP
ROURKE, Thomas	22	M	Tailor	100c05Aq
MARSH, Ann	20	F	Dressmaker	100c05Aq
MCDONOUGH, Edwd.	25	M	Tailor	100c05Aq
DONOHOE, John	30	M	Tailor	100c05Aq
Margt.	19	F	Milliner	100c05Aq
BUCKLEY, Mary	23	F	Boot Closer	100c05Aq
TAYLOR, Mary	19	F	Glover	100c05Aq
FETHERSTON, Michl.	22	M	Brf	100c05Aq
BENTLEY, Ann	25	F	Housekeeper	100c05Aq
CONNOR, John	30	M	Stone Mason	100c05Aq
PRESTON, Bridget	26	F	Servant	100c05Aq
U	.00	F	Infant	100c05Aq
LYONS, F.Mrs.	40	F	Unknown	100c05Aq
HALPIN, C.	23	M	Dressmaker	100c05Aq
U	.00	F	Infant	100c05Aq
LYONS, U	.00	F	Infant	100c05Aq
MARTIN, Wm.	26	M	Cbtmkr	100c05Aq
Hannah	23	F	Matron	100c05Aq
Eliza	40	F	Matron	100c05Aq
Henry	13	M	None	100c05Aq
Eliza	10	F	None	100c05Aq
Emily	7	F	Child	100c05Aq
MARRA, Jas.	28	M	Laborer	100c05Aq
Thomas	30	M	Laborer	100c05Aq
BOULGER, Patrick	30	M	Tailor	100c05Aq
Ann	29	F	Matron	100c05Aq
Thomas	6	M	Child	100c05Aq
COLLINS, Ann	26	F	Dressmaker	100c05Aq
U	.00	F	Infant	100c05Aq
TAYLOR, Ann	12	F	Servant	100c05Aq
BRANEN, Bridget	27	F	Servant	100c05Aq
JUDGE, Jas.	50	M	Farmer	100c05Aq
Wm.	30	M	Laborer	100c05Aq
Patrick	21	M	Laborer	100c05Aq
BRYAN, Patrick	20	M	Laborer	100c05Aq
JUDGE, Ellen	14	F	Servant	100c05Aq
Clara	12	F	Servant	100c05Aq
James	10	M	Servant	100c05Aq
Ann	6	F	Child	100c05Aq
Maria	4	M	Child	100c05Aq
REDDY, U-Mrs.	34	F	Matron	100c05Aq
CARTER, Ann	18	F	Servant	100c05Aq
REDDY, Ann	12	F	Servant	100c05Aq
Catharine	10	F	Servant	100c05Aq
Patrick	8	M	Child	100c05Aq
Thomas	5	M	Child	100c05Aq
BRADY, Alice	30	F	Servant	100c05Aq
Thomas	9	M	Child	100c05Aq
BRADY, U	.00	M	Infant	100c05Aq
DOYLE, William	25	M	Baker	100c05Aq
BYRNE, Bridget	25	F	Servant	100c05Aq
KELLY, Thomas	13	M	Bookbinder	100c05Aq
FULLAM, Ann	6	F	Child	100c05Aq
HUTCHISON, George	22	M	Painter	100c05Aq
VANCE, Joseph	16	M	Clerk	100c05Aq
CONDEN, Isabella	11	F	Servant	100c05Aq
CONNER, Jane	26	F	Servant	100c05Aq
MCKENNA, James	25	M	Weaver	100c05Aq
Jane	30	F	Matron	100c05Aq
James	15	M	Weaver	100c05Aq
Cathn.	11	F	Servant	100c05Aq
Ally	9	F	Child	100c05Aq
Mary	7	F	Child	100c05Aq
Patrick	5	M	Child	100c05Aq
MULVEY, Ellen	16	F	Servant	100c05Aq
FETHERSTON, U-Mrs.	23	F	Dressmaker	100c05Aq
U	.00	F	Infant	100c05Aq
CALLAGHAN, Mary	30	F	Matron	100c05Aq
Patrick	11	M	Laborer	100c05Aq
U	.00	M	Infant	100c05Aq
HART, Edward	40	M	Farmer	100c05Aq
U (W)	40	F	Matron	100c05Aq
U	7	F	Child	100c05Aq
U	6	F	Child	100c05Aq
U	6	F	Child	100c05Aq
PHELAN, Margaret	25	F	Servant	100c05Aq
LEONARD, Alice	25	F	Servant	100c05Aq
HAVERTY, Bridget	16	F	Servant	100c05Aq
KELLY, U	50	F	Wi	100c05Aq
Ann	10	F	None	100c05Aq
Fenton	8	F	Child	100c05Aq
Michael	3	M	Child	100c05Aq
CALLAGHAN, Catharine	20	F	Servant	100c05Aq
MCDONALD, Mary	20	F	Servant	100c05Aq
COLLINS, Jane	54	F	Dressmaker	100c05Aq
BUTLER, Thos.	15	M	Laborer	100c05Aq
William	10	M	None	100c05Aq
John	8	M	Child	100c05Aq
LANCER, Chas.	22	M	Tailor	100c05Aq
FITZPATRICK, Mary	16	F	Servant	100c05Aq
Laurence	11	M	Laborer	100c05Aq
KEEGAN, Mary	25	F	Servant	100c05Aq
BROPHY, Edward	40	M	Stctr	100c05Aq
DALY, Thomas	20	M	Servant	100c05Aq
BRACKEN, Mary	20	F	Servant	100c05Aq
PHELAN, Margaret	20	F	Servant	100c05Aq
FITZPATRICK, Jas.	20	M	Laborer	100c05Aq
CONNOLLY, John	20	M	Laborer	100c05Aq
SPIER, Margt.	17	F	Servant	100c05Aq
GAFFNEY, John	7	M	Child	100c05Aq
WHEELIHAN, Joseph	12	M	Laborer	100c05Aq
DONNELLY, James	28	M	Servant	100c05Aq
ABBOTT, Henry	15	M	Laborer	100c05Aq
Benjamin	15	M	Laborer	100c05Aq
REILLY, Catharine	18	F	None	100c05Aq
ANDREW, Mary-Ann	40	F	None	100c05Aq
CORCORAN, Johanna	27	F	None	100c05Aq
Ellen	24	F	None	100c05Aq
FARRELL, Andrew	40	M	Farmer	100c05Aq
Mary (W)	23	F	None	100c05Aq
MCCORMICK, Mary	25	F	Matron	100c05Aq
Bridget	5	F	Child	100c05Aq
Mary	2	F	Child	100c05Aq
U	.00	F	Infant	100c05Aq
FITZGERALD, Jas.	23	M	Unknown	100c05Aq
FLANNEHAN, Bridget	40	F	Matron	100c05Aq
LEE, Eliza	23	F	Servant	100c05Aq
Mary-Jane	20	F	Servant	100c05Aq
MCCABE, Patrick	23	M	Laborer	100c05Aq
KING, Bessey	20	F	Dressmaker	100c05Aq
WISTENAN, John	40	M	Cook	100c05Aq
MCGARRY, Michael	4	M	Child	100c05Aq
MCKENNA, Thomas	.00	M	Infant	100c05Aq

NAMES OF PASSENGERS	AGE	SEX	OCCUPATIONS	DATE PORT SHIP
CALLAGHAN, Sally	7	F	Child	100c05Aq
John	5	M	Child	100c05Aq
GAFFNEY, Ellen	50	F	Matron	100c05Aq
FITZGERALD, Mary	40	F	Matron	100c05Aq
FIELDING, U-Dr.	23	M	Unknown	100c05Aq
DAVIS, U	20	F	Unknown	100c05Aq
WARD, John	40	M	Unknown	100c05Aq
Jane-Mrs.	37	F	Unknown	100c05Aq
Henry	.00	M	Infant	100c05Aq
Harriet	.00	F	Infant	100c05Aq
LEPLEA, Ellen	17	F	Unknown	100c05Aq
CURRY, Martin	22	M	Unknown	100c05Aq
WARD, William	7	M	Child	100c05Aq

CORNELIA 11 OCTOBER 1849

From Liverpool

NAMES OF PASSENGERS	AGE	SEX	OCCUPATIONS	DATE PORT SHIP
GAMBLE, A.	32	M	Merchant	110c02Aw
Isabella	31	F	None	110c02Aw
Annie-Eliza	5	F	Child	110c02Aw
Louisa-A.J.	4	F	Child	110c02Aw
Edith-J.	3	F	Child	110c02Aw
MAGRANE, Mary	45	F	Servant	110c02Aw
FENNELLY, Richard	50	M	Merchant	110c02Aw
Margaret	45	F	None	110c02Aw
William	28	M	Merchant	110c02Aw
John-J.	26	M	Merchant	110c02Aw
Bridget	20	F	Unknown	110c02Aw
Margaret	18	F	Unknown	110c02Aw
Alice	18	F	Unknown	110c02Aw
Sarah	14	F	Unknown	110c02Aw
POWER, James-Revd.	34	M	Minister	110c02Aw
ARCHDALE, George	19	M	Clerk	110c02Aw
KEARNEY, Patrick	50	M	Engineer	110c02Aw
Sophia	45	F	None	110c02Aw
Ann	15	F	None	110c02Aw
Sophia	15	F	None	110c02Aw
Mary	10	F	None	110c02Aw
Kate	6	F	Child	110c02Aw
James	3	M	Child	110c02Aw
William	2	M	Child	110c02Aw
WRIGHT, Jeannette	21	F	None	110c02Aw
FIELD, Hannah	60	F	None	110c02Aw
LINDEN, Fidelia	25	F	None	110c02Aw
ROWAN, Ann-Jane	21	F	None	110c02Aw
MANUS, William	21	M	Clerk	110c02Aw
GARVEY, Ellen	30	F	None	110c02Aw
RICH, Thomas	10	M	None	110c02Aw
MARSTON, Ann	20	F	None	110c02Aw
Cath.	16	F	None	110c02Aw
WATTERS, Eliza	20	F	None	110c02Aw
KENNEDY, Mary	20	F	None	110c02Aw
DONOVAN, James	21	M	Farmer	110c02Aw
ROGERS, Joseph	21	M	Farmer	110c02Aw
KENNEDY, Thos.	20	M	Farmer	110c02Aw
Died-At-Sea				
HOWELL, John	45	M	Laborer	110c02Aw
Wm.	9	M	Child	110c02Aw
Edwd.	7	M	Child	110c02Aw
FORD, Bridget	29	F	None	110c02Aw
HARRINGTON, Ann	40	F	None	110c02Aw
MCCORMICK, Mary	14	F	None	110c02Aw
WILSON, Mary	22	F	None	110c02Aw
HOWELL, Jane	36	F	None	110c02Aw
Margaret	3	F	Child	110c02Aw
George	1	F	Child	110c02Aw
Pat	22	M	Laborer	110c02Aw
MCCORMICK, Jas.	16	M	Laborer	110c02Aw
HOWELL, John	5	M	Child	110c02Aw
MCGURK, Thomas	5	M	Child	110c02Aw
GIELAN, Ellen	24	F	None	110c02Aw
MORRIS, Eliza	19	F	None	110c02Aw
CLARK, Mary	26	F	None	110c02Aw
CURTIS, Hugh	27	M	Laborer	110c02Aw
Hugh-Jr.	2	M	Child	110c02Aw
Bridget	1	F	Child	110c02Aw
FARREL, Edmund	36	M	Laborer	110c02Aw
Died-At-Sea				
Cath.	28	F	None	110c02Aw
STAUNTON, Tim.	17	M	Laborer	110c02Aw
POWER, Pat	22	M	Laborer	110c02Aw
MACNAMARA, Jas.	30	M	Laborer	110c02Aw
Mary	35	F	None	110c02Aw
HACHRON, William	23	M	Laborer	110c02Aw
Mary	21	F	None	110c02Aw
MCKEAN, Cath.	20	F	None	110c02Aw
Judy	15	F	None	110c02Aw
Ann	1	F	Child	110c02Aw
DOYLE, Bridget	21	F	None	110c02Aw
KANE, Eliza	20	F	None	110c02Aw
FAGAN, Mary	14	F	None	110c02Aw
Rose	12	F	None	110c02Aw
WARD, Margaret	35	F	None	110c02Aw
Thomas	.00	M	Infant	110c02Aw
Born-At-Sea				
Biddy	15	F	None	110c02Aw
Mary	13	F	None	110c02Aw
OSWALD, Robert	54	M	Clerk	110c02Aw
Mary	50	F	None	110c02Aw
Hester	16	F	None	110c02Aw
Matilda	12	F	None	110c02Aw
William	10	M	None	110c02Aw
SLING, Grace	64	F	None	110c02Aw
HUGHES, Pat	25	M	Laborer	110c02Aw
Mary	20	F	None	110c02Aw
Died-At-Sea				
Edward	20	M	None	110c02Aw
Died-At-Sea				
KANE, Margaret	18	F	None	110c02Aw
HALLEY, Margaret	8	F	Child	110c02Aw
CAREY, Biddy	18	F	None	110c02Aw
Ann	17	F	None	110c02Aw
Nelly	50	F	None	110c02Aw
Nelly	10	F	None	110c02Aw
John	12	M	None	110c02Aw
CALLAHAN, Pat	26	M	Laborer	110c02Aw
John	24	M	Laborer	110c02Aw
CASEY, John	20	M	Laborer	110c02Aw
TAYLER, Eliza	17	F	None	110c02Aw
HAMILTON, Matilda	21	F	None	110c02Aw
FOX, Mary	16	F	None	110c02Aw
JACKSON, Eliza	20	F	None	110c02Aw
GILLGAN, Susan	16	F	None	110c02Aw
JACKSON, Tom	5	M	Child	110c02Aw
CURRAN, Francis	30	M	Laborer	110c02Aw
TACTON, William	20	M	Laborer	110c02Aw
MCCORMICK, Thos.	20	M	Laborer	110c02Aw
FITZGERALD, Ellen	20	F	None	110c02Aw
SMALLINS, Margaret	10	F	None	110c02Aw
SEED, Henry	33	M	Laborer	110c02Aw
CLEARY, Pat	25	M	Laborer	110c02Aw
KEATING, Sarah	22	F	None	110c02Aw
DELANY, Mary	40	F	None	110c02Aw
Honora	12	F	None	110c02Aw
TENDER, Jane	40	F	None	110c02Aw
Josephine	12	F	None	110c02Aw
Cath.	22	F	None	110c02Aw
James	14	M	None	110c02Aw
NICHOLS, Wm.	20	M	Miner	110c02Aw
CONNOLLY, Nelly	23	F	None	110c02Aw
Biddy	13	F	None	110c02Aw
MULLAY, Jane	14	F	None	110c02Aw

NAMES OF PASSENGERS	AGE	SEX	OCCUPATIONS	DATE PORT SHIP
CONNOLLY, James	25	M	Laborer	110c02Aw
Died-At-Sea				
CONNOLLY, Thomas	15	M	Laborer	110c02Aw
KONLEY, James	42	M	Laborer	110c02Aw
CONNOLLY, Tim.	50	M	Laborer	110c02Aw
Died-At-Sea				
Mary	50	F	None	110c02Aw
Tim.	9	M	Child	110c02Aw
Cath.	7	F	Child	110c02Aw
Pat	19	M	Laborer	110c02Aw
BURKE, Peter	22	M	Laborer	110c02Aw
CARROLL, John	22	M	Laborer	110c02Aw
BURKE, Mary	17	F	None	110c02Aw
CONNOLLY, Ellen	30	F	None	110c02Aw
Margaret	9	F	Child	110c02Aw
MADDEN, John	48	M	Laborer	110c02Aw
STRAHAN, Henry	26	M	Laborer	110c02Aw
COSEN, John	18	M	Baker	110c02Aw
SHINDRAGAN, Barry	37	M	Laborer	110c02Aw
MORAN, Pat	20	M	Laborer	110c02Aw
CONESTAN, Pat	40	M	Laborer	110c02Aw
Died-At-Sea				
NOLAN, Pat	30	M	Laborer	110c02Aw
Died-At-Sea				
LACEY, James	16	M	Laborer	110c02Aw
William	10	M	None	110c02Aw
Biddy	13	F	None	110c02Aw
ANDERSEN, Eliza	20	F	None	110c02Aw
LACY, Martha	43	F	None	110c02Aw
HENDERSON, George	.3	M	None	110c02Aw
SHERRY, Mary	25	F	None	110c02Aw
CALLAHAN, Cath.	40	F	None	110c02Aw
LENAGHAN, Cath.	20	F	None	110c02Aw
ROGAN, Hannah	20	F	None	110c02Aw
HANES, Mich.	40	M	Carpenter	110c02Aw
KANE, Hugh	16	M	Laborer	110c02Aw
MULANY, Neill	35	M	Laborer	110c02Aw
DONNELLY, Mary	18	F	None	110c02Aw
MORAN, Mary	18	F	None	110c02Aw
GIOIN, Bridget	19	F	None	110c02Aw
WELCH, James	18	M	Laborer	110c02Aw
Thomas	24	M	Laborer	110c02Aw
Margaret	24	F	None	110c02Aw
CALAHAN, Pat	8	M	Child	110c02Aw
Julia	7	F	Child	110c02Aw
DUFFEY, Maria	18	F	None	110c02Aw
Margaret	17	F	None	110c02Aw
KENNEY, Ellen	15	F	None	110c02Aw
WELSH, John	20	M	Laborer	110c02Aw
FLAHERTY, Tom	22	M	Laborer	110c02Aw
KENNEY, Tom	22	M	Laborer	110c02Aw
HARTIGAN, Thomas	25	M	Laborer	110c02Aw
RILEY, Owen	20	M	Clerk	110c02Aw
FLEMING, Alice	34	F	None	110c02Aw
Ann-Jane	6	F	Child	110c02Aw
BRADY, Thos.	40	M	Laborer	110c02Aw
Cath.	20	F	None	110c02Aw
Margaret	49	F	None	110c02Aw
Died-At-Sea				
James	11	M	None	110c02Aw
John	10	M	None	110c02Aw
Susan	18	F	None	110c02Aw
RILEY, Eliza	14	F	None	110c02Aw
BRENNAN, Cath.	13	F	None	110c02Aw
Bridget	5	F	Child	110c02Aw
Died-At-Sea				
YOUNG, Cath.	30	F	None	110c02Aw
TATE, Rob.	6	M	Child	110c02Aw
John	35	M	None	110c02Aw
Died-At-Sea				
Eliza	34	F	None	110c02Aw
Died-At-Sea				
Elizabeth	10	F	None	110c02Aw
James	14	M	None	110c02Aw
MEHAN, Martin	30	M	Laborer	110c02Aw

NAMES OF PASSENGERS	AGE	SEX	OCCUPATIONS	DATE PORT SHIP
TUHEY, Cornelius	20	M	Laborer	110c02Aw
TATE, Latimer	40	M	Sawer	110c02Aw
MORGAN, Mary	35	F	None	110c02Aw
John	13	M	None	110c02Aw
Peggy	11	F	None	110c02Aw
Cath.	9	F	Child	110c02Aw
Nancy	4	F	Child	110c02Aw
Ellen	5	F	Child	110c02Aw
SMART, Robert	25	M	Blacksmith	110c02Aw
BOYD, John	18	M	Laborer	110c02Aw
PATTERSON, John	16	M	Laborer	110c02Aw
REED, Joseph	16	M	Laborer	110c02Aw
BURNS, John	24	M	Laborer	110c02Aw
MULDOWNEY, Mich.	24	M	Laborer	110c02Aw
MCLAUGHLIN, Mich.	24	M	Laborer	110c02Aw
CONNOLLY, Mary	20	F	None	110c02Aw
Peggy	18	F	None	110c02Aw
HAYES, David	26	M	None	110c02Aw
Bridget	24	F	None	110c02Aw
Cath.	22	F	None	110c02Aw
DAGER, George	25	M	None	110c02Aw
Died-At-Sea				
MULLAN, Ellen	4	F	Child	110c02Aw
Died-At-Sea				
BRADY, Francis	36	M	Laborer	110c02Aw
Died-At-Sea				
CONNOLLY, Mary	18	F	Laborer	110c02Aw

GUY-MANNERING 12 OCTOBER 1849

From Liverpool

NAMES OF PASSENGERS	AGE	SEX	OCCUPATIONS	DATE PORT SHIP
LUDGATE, John	28	M	Farmer	120c02Ax
Patrick	26	M	Farmer	120c02Ax
Michael	14	M	Unknown	120c02Ax
Catherine	24	F	Unknown	120c02Ax
Fanney	8	F	Child	120c02Ax
Thomas	4	M	Child	120c02Ax
Queen	.00	F	Infant	120c02Ax
TURPEY, Martin	20	M	Clerk	120c02Ax
Maria	18	F	Unknown	120c02Ax
Bridget	16	F	Unknown	120c02Ax
CAVANEY, Anne	20	F	Unknown	120c02Ax
MURPHY, Charles	30	M	Shopkeeper	120c02Ax
Maria	26	F	Unknown	120c02Ax
ONEILL, Terence	60	M	Merchant	120c02Ax
John	24	M	Law Student	120c02Ax
BARRON, Richard	56	M	Farmer	120c02Ax
Anne	50	F	Unknown	120c02Ax
Judith	21	F	Unknown	120c02Ax
Mary	22	F	Unknown	120c02Ax
Richard	15	M	Unknown	120c02Ax
Margaret	25	F	Unknown	120c02Ax
MCGREGOR, Mary-Anne	18	F	Dressmaker	120c02Ax
Eliza	16	F	Dressmaker	120c02Ax
MARTIN, Thomas	33	[illegible]	[illegible]erk	120c02Ax
Clare	25	[illegible]	[illegible]known	120c02Ax
Joseph	7	[illegible]	Child	120c02Ax
Francis	5	F	Child	120c02Ax
William	2	M	Child	120c02Ax
Eliza	.00	F	Infant	120c02Ax
FINN, Mary-Anne	14	F	Servant	120c02Ax
HAMER, George	18	M	Miller	120c02Ax
BRIGAN, Robert	24	M	Servant	120c02Ax
SAVAGE, Patrick	24	M	Laborer	120c02Ax
DALEY, James	24	M	Laborer	120c02Ax
REARDON, Patrick	40	M	Schm	120c02Ax
Catherine	40	F	Unknown	120c02Ax
HYLAND, Thomas	30	M	Mason	120c02Ax

NAMES OF PASSENGERS	AGE	SEX	OCCUPATIONS	DATE PORT SHIP
WOODLOCK, John	38	M	Gdnr	120c02Ax
MCCORMICK, William	20	M	Farmer	120c02Ax
CLOYNE, Bridget	20	F	Servant	120c02Ax
OSHAUGNESSEY, Martha	24	F	Unknown	120c02Ax
FARRELL, George	28	M	Laborer	120c02Ax
MCKINEY, James	28	M	Laborer	120c02Ax
LARKIN, John	28	M	Laborer	120c02Ax
DAILEY, James	25	M	Farmer	120c02Ax
RUSSELL, Ellen	21	F	Unknown	120c02Ax
MALONEY, Mary	30	F	Unknown	120c02Ax
BARRY, John	10	M	Unknown	120c02Ax
Died-At-Sea				
Bridget	8	F	Child	120c02Ax
Died-At-Sea				
MULVANY, Richard	28	M	Laborer	120c02Ax
OSHAUGNESSEY, Johanna	20	F	Servant	120c02Ax
Died-At-Sea				
HAVERTY, Michael	19	M	Servant	120c02Ax
ROACH, Catherine	19	F	Servant	120c02Ax
MALONE, Henry	30	M	Carpenter	120c02Ax
Margaret	25	F	Unknown	120c02Ax
MCCALLON, Catherine	24	F	Unknown	120c02Ax
Mary	.00	F	Infant	120c02Ax
BRODEGAN, John	14	M	Unknown	120c02Ax
Died-At-Sea				
MCNAMARA, James	22	M	Servant	120c02Ax
SMITH, James	44	M	Farmer	120c02Ax
Susan	16	F	Unknown	120c02Ax
Wilhelmina	11	F	Unknown	120c02Ax
HARRIGAN, John	24	M	Farmer	120c02Ax
QUINN, William	20	M	Shopkeeper	120c02Ax
DIGNAN, Michael	24	M	Laborer	120c02Ax
BYRNE, Anne	21	F	Servant	120c02Ax
ONEILL, Patrick	24	M	Coach Maker	120c02Ax
SHEELEY, Michael	24	M	Gdnr	120c02Ax
NOONAN, Margaret	26	F	Unknown	120c02Ax
NEILL, Thomas	21	F	Unknown	120c02Ax
LYNCH, Bridget	30	F	Unknown	120c02Ax
HOMECAN, Patk.	25	M	Unknown	120c02Ax
Winifred	18	M	Unknown	120c02Ax
FITZPATRICK, John	23	M	Draper	120c02Ax
Frederick	21	M	Draper	120c02Ax
Caroline	16	F	Unknown	120c02Ax
Arabella	40	F	Unknown	120c02Ax
RYAN, John	20	M	Servant	120c02Ax
BRETT, Pierce	50	M	Farmer	120c02Ax
Died-At-Sea				
BIRT, Johana	45	F	Unknown	120c02Ax
Bridget	20	F	Unknown	120c02Ax
Catherine	19	F	Unknown	120c02Ax
Michael	17	M	Unknown	120c02Ax
Thomas	16	M	Unknown	120c02Ax
Geoffrey	14	M	Unknown	120c02Ax
RYAN, Thomas	21	M	Unknown	120c02Ax
MURPHY, Johanna	22	F	Shoemaker	120c02Ax
Honora	22	F	Shoemaker	120c02Ax
HYDE, Daniel	20	F	Shoemaker	120c02Ax
MACKEN, James	22	M	Laborer	120c02Ax
CLARKE, Lawrence	22	M	Laborer	120c02Ax
Mary	20	F	Unknown	120c02Ax
Died-At-Sea				
CLIFFORD, Patrick	20	M	Laborer	120c02Ax
CONNERY, William	40	M	Laborer	120c02Ax
Jane	41	F	Unknown	120c02Ax
Mary	16	F	Unknown	120c02Ax
Margaret	13	F	Unknown	120c02Ax
Thomas	12	M	Unknown	120c02Ax
Mary	6	F	Child	120c02Ax
Catherine	6	F	Child	120c02Ax
Honora	4	F	Child	120c02Ax
Bridget	2	F	Child	120c02Ax
KEVILL, George	45	M	Maurer	120c02Ax
Mary-Ann	24	F	Unknown	120c02Ax
Caroline	22	F	Unknown	120c02Ax
Eliza	22	F	Unknown	120c02Ax
KEVILL, Harriet	14	F	Unknown	120c02Ax
Henry	9	M	Child	120c02Ax
John	7	M	Child	120c02Ax
Sophia	6	F	Child	120c02Ax
COTTERALL, John	25	M	Laborer	120c02Ax
COONEY, Thomas	22	M	Laborer	120c02Ax
NOONAN, Ellen	17	F	Unknown	120c02Ax
ONEILL, Thomas	22	M	Laborer	120c02Ax
QUINLAHAN, Maria	23	F	Unknown	120c02Ax
HUBHIS, Ellen	17	F	Unknown	120c02Ax
COLLINS, Timothy	20	M	Unknown	120c02Ax
Mary	48	F	Unknown	120c02Ax
Patrick	8	M	Child	120c02Ax
GRADY, John	40	M	Unknown	120c02Ax
NEENAN, Robert	38	M	Laborer	120c02Ax
Johanna	28	F	Unknown	120c02Ax
William	24	M	Unknown	120c02Ax
William	7	M	Child	120c02Ax
Mary	9	F	Child	120c02Ax
Johanna	5	F	Child	120c02Ax
Ellen	3	F	Child	120c02Ax
BLAKE, Thomas	21	M	Laborer	120c02Ax
FITZGERALD, Barton	21	M	Laborer	120c02Ax
MARTIN, Hugh	26	M	Farmer	120c02Ax
FLOOD, Thomas	20	M	Farmer	120c02Ax
CLARKE, Michael	30	M	Laborer	120c02Ax
Biddy	25	F	Laborer	120c02Ax
Patrick	9	M	Child	120c02Ax
MCGEE, Mary	50	F	Servant	120c02Ax
Mary	24	F	Servant	120c02Ax
MERAN, Mary	40	F	Unknown	120c02Ax
Owen	10	M	Unknown	120c02Ax
BRAN, Bridget	23	F	Servant	120c02Ax
Margaret	18	F	Servant	120c02Ax
MCNAMARA, Biddy	30	F	Servant	120c02Ax
DUNNE, Luke	26	M	Laborer	120c02Ax
MCDERMOT, Thomas	25	M	Laborer	120c02Ax
HUNNE, James	18	M	Laborer	120c02Ax
MCQUADE, Christ.	22	F	Servant	120c02Ax
ARMSTRONG, Irwin	25	M	Servant	120c02Ax
Eliza	25	F	Servant	120c02Ax
Andrew	1	M	Child	120c02Ax
Died-At-Sea				
KEONE, Margt.	20	F	Unknown	120c02Ax
MCNAMARA, Patrick	21	M	Laborer	120c02Ax
FALLON, Ellen	60	F	Servant	120c02Ax
Margaret	17	F	Servant	120c02Ax
Nappy	12	F	Servant	120c02Ax
Patrick	2	M	Child	120c02Ax
MCEVOY, Ann	20	F	Servant	120c02Ax
WHELAN, Anne	24	F	Servant	120c02Ax
GOODWIN, Patrick	35	M	Laborer	120c02Ax
Thomas	9	M	Child	120c02Ax
MCGUIRK, Anne	18	F	Unknown	120c02Ax
DOWD, Anne	18	F	Servant	120c02Ax
HUGHES, Anne	35	F	Unknown	120c02Ax
Judy	12	F	Servant	120c02Ax
Honora	10	F	Servant	120c02Ax
HOGAN, William	21	M	Laborer	120c02Ax
HAUGH, Martin	14	M	Unknown	120c02Ax
Catherine	20	F	Laborer	120c02Ax
GLEESON, Margt.	18	F	Laborer	120c02Ax
FALLON, Daniel	23	F	Laborer	120c02Ax
HANLON, James	23	M	Laborer	120c02Ax
Francis	22	M	Laborer	120c02Ax
MARA, Cathr.	22	F	Laborer	120c02Ax
HORKEN, Bridget	25	F	Servant	120c02Ax
Died-At-Sea				
LEO, Thomas	25	M	Laborer	120c02Ax
HANNAN, Margt.	26	F	Unknown	120c02Ax
William	34	M	Unknown	120c02Ax
FORD, William	21	M	Unknown	120c02Ax
HOWARD, Margt.	24	F	Servant	120c02Ax
DUNNE, Mary	26	F	Servant	120c02Ax
TRACEY, Winney	21	F	Servant	120c02Ax

NAMES OF PASSENGERS	AGE	SEX	OCCUPATIONS	DATE PORT SHIP
GOULD, Catherine	20	F	Servant	120c02Ax
SHANKFORD, Honora	50	F	Servant	120c02Ax
Died-At-Sea				
John	11	M	Servant	120c02Ax
MCGOWAN, Patt	25	M	Servant	120c02Ax
Ellen	35	F	Servant	120c02Ax
Bell	14	F	Servant	120c02Ax
John	26	M	Servant	120c02Ax
Catherine	25	F	Servant	120c02Ax
HAZELTON, Maria	30	F	Servant	120c02Ax
Margt.	14	F	Servant	120c02Ax
Martha	6	F	Child	120c02Ax
Charlotte	3	F	Child	120c02Ax
LENNY, Mary-Ann	16	F	Servant	120c02Ax
DEVLEN, Rose	22	F	Servant	120c02Ax
Rebecca	.00	F	Infant	120c02Ax
GAVIN, Mary	30	F	Servant	120c02Ax
Mary	16	F	Servant	120c02Ax
MCDERMOT, Rose	15	F	Servant	120c02Ax
CONWAY, Ellen	30	F	Servant	120c02Ax
Michael	.00	M	Infant	120c02Ax
QUIRK, Thomas	28	M	Laborer	120c02Ax
Ellen	24	F	Unknown	120c02Ax
MCBURNEY, John	16	F	Unknown	120c02Ax
HOVENDEN, Sarah	50	F	Unknown	120c02Ax
Robert	21	M	Shoemaker	120c02Ax
Dora	15	F	Unknown	120c02Ax
Grace	11	F	Unknown	120c02Ax
Susan-Jane	9	F	Child	120c02Ax
Thomas	7	M	Child	120c02Ax
BOURKE, Patrick	22	M	Tailor	120c02Ax
MAHER, William	22	M	Carpenter	120c02Ax
Catherine	20	F	Unknown	120c02Ax
DUNN, John	24	M	Shoemaker	120c02Ax
Margt.	18	F	Unknown	120c02Ax
FARRELL, John	27	M	Farmer	120c02Ax
STOREY, Catherine	20	F	Servant	120c02Ax
BRACKEN, Joseph	22	M	Engineer	120c02Ax
FRAYNE, Lawrence	30	M	Farmer	120c02Ax
Mary	26	F	Unknown	120c02Ax
Francis	6	M	Child	120c02Ax
Dennis	5	M	Child	120c02Ax
Susan	3	F	Child	120c02Ax
Mary	1	F	Child	120c02Ax
Anne	.00	F	Infant	120c02Ax
KANE, Catherine	21	F	Unknown	120c02Ax
CASSIDY, Felix	28	M	Farmer	120c02Ax
DOWNES, Eliza	21	F	Unknown	120c02Ax
DOLAN, James	20	M	Laborer	120c02Ax
MCGOWAN, Bridget	36	F	Servant	120c02Ax
ROCHE, David	40	M	Laborer	120c02Ax
James	20	M	Laborer	120c02Ax
Thomas	16	M	Laborer	120c02Ax
QUINN, John	26	M	Laborer	120c02Ax
John	24	M	Laborer	120c02Ax
DOWD, John	25	M	Laborer	120c02Ax
ASHE, William	25	M	Weaver	120c02Ax
Margaret	17	F	Unknown	120c02Ax
MCNALLEY, James	23	F	Weaver	120c02Ax
DUFFY, James	18	M	Laborer	120c02Ax
Alicia	22	F	Unknown	120c02Ax
Patrick	15	M	Laborer	120c02Ax
MCGUIRE, Mary	33	F	Servant	120c02Ax
Ellen	10	F	Servant	120c02Ax
LYNCH, Thomas	43	M	Servant	120c02Ax
DUNNE, Mary	26	F	Servant	120c02Ax
HANLON, John	25	M	Laborer	120c02Ax
WALSH, Edward	18	M	Tailor	120c02Ax
LYNCH, Peter	37	M	Laborer	120c02Ax
CLARK, Patt	20	M	Laborer	120c02Ax
RUSSELL, Mary	20	F	Laborer	120c02Ax
CALLAHAN, Jane	21	F	Servant	120c02Ax
LONG, Mary	25	F	Servant	120c02Ax
DALY, Cath.	26	F	Servant	120c02Ax
Margt.	15	F	Servant	120c02Ax

NAMES OF PASSENGERS	AGE	SEX	OCCUPATIONS	DATE PORT SHIP
DALY, John	11	M	Unknown	120c02Ax
Kate	8	F	Child	120c02Ax
COLGAN, Patt	46	M	Laborer	120c02Ax
SAVAGE, Mary	13	F	Unknown	120c02Ax
James	12	M	Unknown	120c02Ax
MORAN, Ann	40	F	Servant	120c02Ax
Patrick	21	M	Laborer	120c02Ax
Hugh	19	M	Laborer	120c02Ax
Frank	13	M	Laborer	120c02Ax
Arthur	9	M	Child	120c02Ax
Mary	5	F	Child	120c02Ax
John	.00	M	Infant	120c02Ax
Died-At-Sea				
FANNING, Peter	26	M	Laborer	120c02Ax
Died-At-Sea				
GILMORE, Patt	26	M	Laborer	120c02Ax
CHANCE, Eliza	30	F	Servant	120c02Ax
Anne	10	F	Unknown	120c02Ax
MCGOVERN, Peter	25	M	Laborer	120c02Ax
GAHERN, Joseph	24	M	Engineer	120c02Ax
CAIN, Mry	20	F	Servant	120c02Ax
BOHAN, John	11	M	Unknown	120c02Ax
Ellen	8	F	Child	120c02Ax
BOLAND, Bridget	50	F	Servant	120c02Ax
Anne	8	F	Child	120c02Ax
FARRELL, Mary	15	F	Servant	120c02Ax
EGAN, Owen	34	M	Laborer	120c02Ax
MULCAHY, Michael	21	M	Baker	120c02Ax
NOONAN, William	20	M	Baker	120c02Ax
NASH, Honora	30	F	Servant	120c02Ax
ROCHE, Mary	50	F	Servant	120c02Ax
Catherine	17	F	Servant	120c02Ax
Mary	14	F	Unknown	120c02Ax
Anne	11	F	Unknown	120c02Ax
John	8	M	Child	120c02Ax
GARVEY, John	15	M	Laborer	120c02Ax
Patk.	17	M	Laborer	120c02Ax
CODY, Ellen	17	F	Servant	120c02Ax
ROONEY, Margaret	22	F	Servant	120c02Ax
MEEHAN, Susan	18	F	Servant	120c02Ax
HICKEY, Mary	20	F	Servant	120c02Ax
FARRELL, Catherine	18	F	Servant	120c02Ax
BOLAND, Edward	40	M	Carpenter	120c02Ax
Anne	20	F	Servant	120c02Ax
POWELL, Mary	21	F	Servant	120c02Ax
CONWAY, John	16	M	Laborer	120c02Ax
MAHONEY, James	30	M	Laborer	120c02Ax
James	1	M	Child	120c02Ax
SULLIVAN, Mich.	19	M	Servant	120c02Ax
LINEHAN, Mary	20	F	Servant	120c02Ax
BYRNE, Thomas	21	M	Laborer	120c02Ax
CARTY, Michael	21	M	Laborer	120c02Ax
WYNNE, Patk.	28	M	Laborer	120c02Ax
MCFYE, Honora	40	F	Servant	120c02Ax
Bridget	18	F	Unknown	120c02Ax
Honora	11	F	Unknown	120c02Ax
CUSSACK, John	22	M	Laborer	120c02Ax
FAKY, Domenick	22	M	Laborer	120c02Ax
DILLON, Anne	40	F	Servant	120c02Ax
IGOE, Thomas	13	M	Unknown	120c02Ax
DILLON, John	50	M	Laborer	120c02Ax
TAYLOR, Edward	12	M	Unknown	120c02Ax
MAYHAN, Martin	30	M	Laborer	120c02Ax
Mary	9	F	Child	120c02Ax
REYNOLDS, Thomas	21	M	Laborer	120c02Ax
MCGUINESS, Phillip	27	M	Laborer	120c02Ax
Anne	24	F	Unknown	120c02Ax
GORRIGAN, Peter	21	M	Laborer	120c02Ax
HUGHES, Anne	21	F	Servant	120c02Ax
MULVANEY, John	25	M	Laborer	120c02Ax
CURRAN, Edward	30	M	Laborer	120c02Ax
LOUNDS, Thomas	17	M	Laborer	120c02Ax
Frank	15	M	Laborer	120c02Ax
Bess	13	F	Unknown	120c02Ax
BARRY, Michael	20	M	Laborer	120c02Ax

NAMES OF PASSENGERS	AGE	SEX	OCCUPATIONS	DATE PORT SHIP
BARRY, Bernard	20	M	Laborer	120c02Ax
GIBBON, Mary	30	F	Servant	120c02Ax
DOWD, Thomas	25	M	Laborer	120c02Ax
Mary	30	F	Servant	120c02Ax
FARRELL, John	21	M	Laborer	120c02Ax
Peter	11	M	Unknown	120c02Ax
FOX, Catherine	25	F	Unknown	120c02Ax
Mary	23	F	Unknown	120c02Ax
HYNES, Patk.	22	M	Unknown	120c02Ax
Bridget	20	F	Unknown	120c02Ax
CASSIDY, Bernard	30	M	Laborer	120c02Ax
Cath.	28	F	Unknown	120c02Ax
Anne	.00	F	Infant	120c02Ax
MCGORRIN, Bridget	18	F	Servant	120c02Ax
LUNNY, Cathr.	16	F	Servant	120c02Ax
NESMITH, James	14	M	Servant	120c02Ax
KEHOE, Anne	18	F	Servant	120c02Ax
HOGAN, William	22	M	Laborer	120c02Ax
Daniel	22	M	Laborer	120c02Ax
MCGOVERN, John	24	M	Laborer	120c02Ax
Jane	22	F	Laborer	120c02Ax
KEEGAN, Thomas	20	M	Laborer	120c02Ax
FITZPATRICK, Peter	26	M	Laborer	120c02Ax
KEEGAN, John	33	M	Laborer	120c02Ax
Mary	25	F	Unknown	120c02Ax
John	8	M	Child	120c02Ax
Elizth.	4	F	Child	120c02Ax
Michael	2	M	Child	120c02Ax
MCGRATH, Christ.	40	M	Laborer	120c02Ax
BRADY, Owen	21	M	Laborer	120c02Ax
MCCARTY, Judith	18	F	Servant	120c02Ax
FARRELL, Patk.	24	M	Laborer	120c02Ax
REGAN, Jane	23	F	Servant	120c02Ax
MCNEIVE, Ann	19	F	Servant	120c02Ax
LENAHAN, Peter	30	M	Laborer	120c02Ax
Catherine	17	F	Servant	120c02Ax
John	8	M	Child	120c02Ax
HALLORAN, Jane	21	F	Servant	120c02Ax
HIGGINS, Honora	21	F	Servant	120c02Ax
FOX, Patk.	27	M	Cooper	120c02Ax
ODONNELL, Jane	20	F	Servant	120c02Ax
GIBBIN, Ann-Jane	23	F	Servant	120c02Ax
MCEVOY, Biddy	18	F	Servant	120c02Ax
CHERRY, Moses	22	M	Laborer	120c02Ax
Catherine	21	F	Unknown	120c02Ax
STEVENSON, John	20	M	Laborer	120c02Ax
James	18	M	Shoemaker	120c02Ax
DOUGLAS, James	20	M	Shoemaker	120c02Ax
CAHILL, James	35	M	Laborer	120c02Ax
Biddy	30	F	Unknown	120c02Ax
Died-At-Sea				
Biddy	.00	F	Infant	120c02Ax
FOX, John	24	M	Tailor	120c02Ax
Michael	6	M	Child	120c02Ax
ONEILL, Mary	7	F	Child	120c02Ax
Peter	4	M	Child	120c02Ax
COSTELLO, Catherine	20	F	Servant	120c02Ax
HYNES, Bridget	20	F	Servant	120c02Ax
JUDGE, Thomas	18	M	Laborer	120c02Ax
BREMAN, Cathe.	21	F	Servant	120c02Ax
DOWLING, Mary	24	F	Servant	120c02Ax
Bridgt.	23	F	Servant	120c02Ax
WHEELAN, Patk.	23	M	Laborer	120c02Ax
KERWIN, Joseph	22	M	Smith	120c02Ax
KERLEY, Stephen	33	M	Currier	120c02Ax
FOWLEY, Bernard	60	M	Unknown	120c02Ax
CONNOR, Ann	18	F	Servant	120c02Ax
MCCLELLAND, Jno.	30	M	Farmer	120c02Ax
Jane	28	F	Unknown	120c02Ax
MCGUIRE, Cathe.	48	F	Unknown	120c02Ax
Died-At-Sea				
CONNOLLY, Cath.	13	F	Unknown	120c02Ax
HARRINGTON, Pat	7	M	Child	120c02Ax
FORRESTER, Peter	36	M	Miner	120c02Ax
Edward	18	M	Unknown	120c02Ax

NAMES OF PASSENGERS	AGE	SEX	OCCUPATIONS	DATE PORT SHIP
CORCORAN, And.	26	M	Unknown	120c02Ax
Ann	28	F	Unknown	120c02Ax
Wm.	18	M	Unknown	120c02Ax
MORONEY, Thomas	20	M	Laborer	120c02Ax
Died-At-Sea				
LONEGAN, Michl.	22	M	Laborer	120c02Ax
CONNERTON, Willm.	21	M	Laborer	120c02Ax
BAKER, George	35	M	Student	120c02Ax
WELSH, Margt.	19	F	Servant	120c02Ax
LEARY, Honora	20	F	Servant	120c02Ax
TUCKER, John	60	M	Laborer	120c02Ax
Died-At-Sea				
Ann	50	F	Unknown	120c02Ax
Cath.	17	F	Unknown	120c02Ax
Joseph	13	M	Unknown	120c02Ax
LYNE, Corns.	26	M	Laborer	120c02Ax
SULLIVAN, Danl.	26	M	Laborer	120c02Ax
Died-At-Sea				
DWYER, Honora	25	F	Servant	120c02Ax
GRIFFITH, Elizth.	24	F	Servant	120c02Ax
GARYHAN, John	23	M	Laborer	120c02Ax
LYNCH, Christn.	25	M	Carpenter	120c02Ax
COSTELLO, John	18	M	Laborer	120c02Ax
Michl.	16	M	Laborer	120c02Ax
KELLY, U-Mrs.	26	F	Unknown	120c02Ax
James	4	M	Child	120c02Ax
WOLFE, William	20	M	Laborer	120c02Ax
GILLON, Mary	30	F	Servant	120c02Ax
MCDERMOTT, Cath.	20	F	Servant	120c02Ax
Died-At-Sea				
QUINN, Winfred	20	F	Servant	120c02Ax
Died-At-Sea				
MARKEY, John	25	F	Servant	120c02Ax
Died-At-Sea				
RACHEL, Susan	16	F	Servant	120c02Ax
LARKIN, Anne	20	F	Servant	120c02Ax
Died-At-Sea				
SHIELS, Cath.	28	F	Unknown	120c02Ax
RYAN, Michl.	7	M	Child	120c02Ax
FLANNIGAN, James	25	M	Laborer	120c02Ax
HANNELLY, Celia	25	F	Servant	120c02Ax
Bridgt.	11	F	Unknown	120c02Ax
Sally	.00	F	Infant	120c02Ax
BOWDEN, Miles	18	M	Sailor	120c02Ax
MULVIHILL, Letitia	20	F	Milliner	120c02Ax
COADY, Alley	20	F	Servant	120c02Ax
FITZSIMMONS, Rose	16	F	Servant	120c02Ax
Cathe.	14	F	Servant	120c02Ax
LYONS, Margery	30	F	Servant	120c02Ax

MINERVA 15 OCTOBER 1849

From Halifax

NAMES OF PASSENGERS	AGE	SEX	OCCUPATIONS	DATE PORT SHIP
CRAMER, Joseph	20	M	Physician	150c08Ap
MCNEIL, Ann	8	F	Child	150c08Ap
BUGRIE, U-Miss	22	F	Unknown	150c08Ap
MURPHY, Emma	8	F	Child	150c08Ap

DEWITT-CLINTON 15 OCTOBER 1849

From Liverpool

NAMES OF PASSENGERS	AGE	SEX	OCCUPATIONS	DATE PORT SHIP
DOLAN, Kieran	23	M	Farmer	150c02Ar
PENDER, Patrick	23	M	Unknown	150c02Ar
DOLAN, John	26	M	Unknown	150c02Ar
GRAY, Andrew	24	M	Unknown	150c02Ar
MALONEY, Sarah	24	F	Servant	150c02Ar
KELLY, Mary	18	F	Servant	150c02Ar
Bridget	14	F	Servant	150c02Ar
SWEENEY, Ellen	18	F	Servant	150c02Ar
BENTLEY, Ellen	40	F	Servant	150c02Ar
HALLIDAY, Thomas	25	M	Mechanic	150c02Ar
REGAN, Michl.	30	M	Unknown	150c02Ar
MCDONNELL, Peter	24	M	Unknown	150c02Ar
SCOTT, Saml.	50	M	Unknown	150c02Ar
Isabella	50	F	Unknown	150c02Ar
Samuel	18	M	Unknown	150c02Ar
Isabella	13	F	Unknown	150c02Ar
Thomas	11	M	Unknown	150c02Ar
Killan	9	M	Child	150c02Ar
Mary-Ann	7	F	Child	150c02Ar
BELL, Saml.	22	M	Unknown	150c02Ar
BEATTY, William	30	M	Unknown	150c02Ar
MCCORRIN, Cath.	30	F	Unknown	150c02Ar
RIDLEY, Robert	30	M	Unknown	150c02Ar
Mary	30	F	Unknown	150c02Ar
Esther	8	F	Child	150c02Ar
George	6	M	Child	150c02Ar
Hugh	3	M	Child	150c02Ar
Susannah	.04	F	Infant	150c02Ar
SHERIDAN, James	26	M	Farmer	150c02Ar
Margaret	24	F	Unknown	150c02Ar
MITCHELL, John	22	M	Unknown	150c02Ar
ROWLAND, William	22	M	Unknown	150c02Ar
POLLARD, Nicholas	24	M	Unknown	150c02Ar
SULLIVAN, Corns.	22	M	Unknown	150c02Ar
KENNEDY, Daniel	22	M	Unknown	150c02Ar
CRONIN, Ellen	26	F	Unknown	150c02Ar
Mary	6	F	Child	150c02Ar
Peggy Died-At-Sea	.00	F	Infant	150c02Ar
FLEMING, Thomas	46	M	Unknown	150c02Ar
Ellen	46	F	Unknown	150c02Ar
David	18	M	Unknown	150c02Ar
Mary	12	F	Unknown	150c02Ar
Kitty	11	F	Unknown	150c02Ar
John	8	M	Child	150c02Ar
CONNERS, John	30	M	Unknown	150c02Ar
Johana	20	F	Unknown	150c02Ar
John	.08	M	Infant	150c02Ar
CASEY, Thomas	31	M	Unknown	150c02Ar
CALLAGHAN, Edward	40	M	Unknown	150c02Ar
BREEN, Jeremiah	22	M	Unknown	150c02Ar
Patrick	28	M	Unknown	150c02Ar
HURLEHEY, William	22	M	Farmer	150c02Ar
CALLAGHAN, Mary	30	F	Farmer	150c02Ar
BRODERICK, Bessy	21	F	Farmer	150c02Ar
SULLIVAN, John	29	M	Unknown	150c02Ar
HAGAN, Pat	23	M	Unknown	150c02Ar
Ellen	21	F	Unknown	150c02Ar
Ann	20	F	Unknown	150c02Ar
SEIRLE, Wm.	25	M	Unknown	150c02Ar
QUIGLEY, John	20	M	Unknown	150c02Ar
GORMAN, Margt.	22	F	Unknown	150c02Ar
Ann	20	F	Unknown	150c02Ar
GORDON, Eliza	22	F	Unknown	150c02Ar
ROSBORO, Robert	24	M	Unknown	150c02Ar
FITZPATRICK, Stephen	20	M	Unknown	150c02Ar
OCONNELL, John	22	M	Unknown	150c02Ar
Eliza	22	F	Unknown	150c02Ar
GALVIN, John	24	M	Unknown	150c02Ar
CASEY, Thomas	24	M	Unknown	150c02Ar
ENRIGHT, Michl.	20	M	Unknown	150c02Ar
BOLAND, John	18	M	Unknown	150c02Ar
Eliza	14	F	Unknown	150c02Ar
ODONNELL, John	18	M	Unknown	150c02Ar
COSTELLO, Pat	20	M	Unknown	150c02Ar
CUSHION, Michl.	30	M	Unknown	150c02Ar
LENIHAN, Honora	36	F	Unknown	150c02Ar
KANOVAN, Pat	30	M	Unknown	150c02Ar
SMITH, Rob	18	M	Unknown	150c02Ar
DAVIES, Robert	20	M	Unknown	150c02Ar
REILLY, Bern.	20	M	Unknown	150c02Ar
NEILAND, John	17	M	Unknown	150c02Ar
Bridget	11	F	Unknown	150c02Ar
Pat	9	M	Child	150c02Ar
GILLESPIE, Faby	22	F	Unknown	150c02Ar
CORCORAN, Margt.	42	F	Unknown	150c02Ar
DOCKRALL, Jno.	12	M	Unknown	150c02Ar
MCCULLEN, Eliza	18	F	Unknown	150c02Ar
MORRISSEN, Kate	18	F	Unknown	150c02Ar
PARKE, John	28	M	Unknown	150c02Ar
PANER, Chas.	23	M	Unknown	150c02Ar
HARRIS, Jane	22	F	Unknown	150c02Ar
WHITE, John	19	M	Merchant	150c02Ar
TUMMASEY, James	28	M	Farmer	150c02Ar
FLYNN, Alice	38	F	Unknown	150c02Ar
Johanah	23	F	Unknown	150c02Ar
MURTAGH, Cath.	21	F	Unknown	150c02Ar
POCKRIDGE, Mark	29	M	Unknown	150c02Ar
U-Mrs.	25	F	Unknown	150c02Ar
TRODDEN, Ellen	17	F	Unknown	150c02Ar
Thomas	1	M	Child	150c02Ar
Sarah	10	F	Unknown	150c02Ar
MCNEME, Barney	25	M	Unknown	150c02Ar
FLEMING, George	25	M	Unknown	150c02Ar
MOLLOY, John	23	M	Unknown	150c02Ar
BLITH, Mick	20	M	Unknown	150c02Ar
NAUGHTON, John	30	M	Unknown	150c02Ar
Winney	18	F	Unknown	150c02Ar
MCDONNELL, Luke	40	M	Unknown	150c02Ar
BRENNAN, James	21	M	Unknown	150c02Ar
MAHER, George	29	M	Unknown	150c02Ar
LEA, Cath.	20	F	Unknown	150c02Ar
REILLY, Margt.	28	F	Unknown	150c02Ar
CRONER, J.	20	U	Unknown	150c02Ar
MURRAY, Cath.	30	F	Unknown	150c02Ar
Bridget	8	F	Child	150c02Ar
KANE, Pat	24	M	Unknown	150c02Ar
Bridget	20	F	Unknown	150c02Ar
Cath.	18	F	Unknown	150c02Ar
Mick	15	M	Unknown	150c02Ar
James	11	M	Unknown	150c02Ar
Sarah	6	F	Child	150c02Ar
HEALEY, Pat	60	M	Unknown	150c02Ar
HUTTON, Elizt.	24	F	Unknown	150c02Ar
Ellen	23	F	Unknown	150c02Ar
GORMAN, Thomas	25	M	Unknown	150c02Ar
U-Mrs.	25	F	Unknown	150c02Ar
MOLLOY, Edward	25	M	Unknown	150c02Ar
CLARKE, Thomas	26	M	Unknown	150c02Ar
DAVIES, Robert	18	M	Unknown	150c02Ar
MCCAULEY, Michl.	25	M	Unknown	150c02Ar
DOLAN, Michl.	22	M	Unknown	150c02Ar
Lawrence	30	M	Unknown	150c02Ar
ROCHE, Ann	17	F	Unknown	150c02Ar
CURRAN, Ellen	20	F	Unknown	150c02Ar
HUNT, Bridget	24	F	Unknown	150c02Ar
MCGEE, Cath.	30	F	Unknown	150c02Ar
FARRELL, Ann	00	F	Unknown	150c02Ar
MURPHY, Morris	21	M	Unknown	150c02Ar
MCGOVERN, John	23	M	Unknown	150c02Ar

NAMES OF PASSENGERS		AGE	SEX	OCCUPATIONS	DATE PORT SHIP
ROACH, Thomas		21	M	Unknown	150c02Ar
READY, Michael		19	M	Unknown	150c02Ar

MONTREAL 15 OCTOBER 1849

From Limerick

NAMES OF PASSENGERS		AGE	SEX	OCCUPATIONS	DATE PORT SHIP
CARROLL, Patt		25	M	Farmer	150c10As
COLEMAN, Patt		25	M	Cooper	150c10As
OLOUGHLAN, Patt		20	M	Farmer	150c10As
Donough		26	M	Farmer	150c10As
Jeremiah		30	M	Farmer	150c10As
Bryan		21	M	Farmer	150c10As
STORINS, Frank		22	M	Laborer	150c10As
Margt.		17	F	Spinster	150c10As
RYAN, James		14	M	Servant	150c10As
Margt.		17	F	Servant	150c10As
CASEY, Patrick		24	M	Laborer	150c10As
CONNOLL, Jas.		30	M	Farmer	150c10As
Honora	(W)	30	F	Wife	150c10As
Cath.		10	F	Unknown	150c10As
Mary		4	F	Child	150c10As
DEE, James		16	M	Laborer	150c10As
GALAGHER, Mary		50	F	Matron	150c10As
MOORE, Edmd.		40	M	Farmer	150c10As
Ellen	(W)	30	F	Wife	150c10As
Margt.		10	F	Unknown	150c10As
James		4	M	Child	150c10As
John		.10	M	Infant	150c10As
KIRBY, Susan		20	F	Spinster	150c10As
Margt.		.11	F	Infant	150c10As
Mary		21	F	Wife	150c10As
Margt.		19	F	Servant	150c10As
LES, William		25	M	Laborer	150c10As
MULVIHILL, Jas.		48	M	Farmer	150c10As
Honora	(W)	48	F	Wife	150c10As
Danl.		23	M	Farmer	150c10As
Honora		22	F	Spinster	150c10As
John		19	M	Laborer	150c10As
Patt		17	M	Laborer	150c10As
Denis		12	M	Laborer	150c10As
Margt.		26	F	Spinster	150c10As
RIORDAN, John		24	M	Laborer	150c10As
MCMAHON, Corns.		30	M	Laborer	150c10As
Anne		16	F	Spinster	150c10As
DOHERTY, Philip		25	M	Farmer	150c10As
REARDON, Ellen		16	F	Spinster	150c10As
FLAHANAN, Jas.		25	M	Farmer	150c10As
SCANLON, Ellen		20	F	Spinster	150c10As
BRANDON, John		22	M	Farmer	150c10As
MULGRAVE, Bridget		22	F	Servant	150c10As
HARTIGAN, John		13	M	Unknown	150c10As
Cathn.		18	F	Spinster	150c10As
KINAN, John		34	M	Laborer	150c10As
LINAHAN, Margt.		16	F	Spinster	150c10As
Bridget		14	F	Servant	150c10As
NOLAN, Michl.		25	M	Farmer	150c10As
Bridget		22	F	Wife	150c10As
Cathn.		42	F	Matron	150c10As
FRAWLEY, Cathn.		20	F	Spinster	150c10As
NOLAN, Mary		.10	F	Infant	150c10As
Died-At-Sea					
RONAN, John		30	M	Laborer	150c10As
Mary		25	F	Spinster	150c10As
SHRAHEN, Nancy		30	F	Servant	150c10As
CONNOLL, Michl.		24	M	Farmer	150c10As
Fredk.		22	M	Farmer	150c10As
Margt.		15	F	Spinster	150c10As
Cathr.		12	F	Unknown	150c10As

NAMES OF PASSENGERS		AGE	SEX	OCCUPATIONS	DATE PORT SHIP
LINAHAN, Patrick		16	M	Laborer	150c10As
Bridget		16	F	Spinster	150c10As
Honora		13	F	Unknown	150c10As
CULHAIN, John		20	M	Farmer	150c10As
BOURKE, Thos.		29	M	Farmer	150c10As
Anne		26	F	Spinster	150c10As
COLLINS, Ellen		20	F	Unknown	150c10As
JACKSON, Ellen		35	F	Matron	150c10As
CONNERS, Thos.		43	M	Laborer	150c10As
LYNCH, Patt		25	M	Laborer	150c10As
LEDDIN, Patt		18	M	Laborer	150c10As
LYNCH, Bridget		20	F	Spinster	150c10As
TRACY, Cathn.		24	F	Spinster	150c10As
MEEHAN, Patt		24	M	Laborer	150c10As
REEDY, Mary		23	F	Spinster	150c10As
DILLON, Thos.		30	M	Laborer	150c10As
DEAN, Johanne		30	F	Spinster	150c10As
SHEAHEN, Ellen		12	F	Unknown	150c10As
CUDDIHY, Michl.		24	M	Laborer	150c10As
SHANAHAN, Bridget		30	F	Spinster	150c10As
ODEAN, Bridget		30	F	Spinster	150c10As
DWYER, Michl.		20	M	Laborer	150c10As
GABBETT, Mary		19	F	Spinster	150c10As
FLYNN, Bridget		45	F	Matron	150c10As
BOURKE, Ann		22	F	Spinster	150c10As
FITZGERALD, Garret		49	M	Farmer	150c10As
Mary		22	F	Spinster	150c10As
MCINIRY, Mary		21	F	Spinster	150c10As
MULVIHILL, Patrick		12	M	Unknown	150c10As
Nancy		8	F	Child	150c10As
HOGAN, William		22	M	Farmer	150c10As
Bridget	(W)	22	F	Wife	150c10As
MULVIHILL, Connor		26	M	Laborer	150c10As
CONNORS, Cathn.		28	F	Spinster	150c10As
Cathn.		12	F	Unknown	150c10As
KIRNON, Mary		53	F	Matron	150c10As
HETHERMAN, Johana		22	F	Spinster	150c10As
COLLOSSY, Mary		22	F	Spinster	150c10As
BONAN, Bridget		45	F	Matron	150c10As
HANNAN, Eliza		18	F	Spinster	150c10As
HOULAHAN, James		24	M	Laborer	150c10As
MCCARTHY, Mary		24	F	Spinster	150c10As
SPAIGHT, Edmd.		16	M	Laborer	150c10As
Mary		40	F	Matron	150c10As
LYONS, Danl.		20	M	Laborer	150c10As
MCMAHON, Jas.		22	M	Laborer	150c10As
MEANY, Mary		15	F	Spinster	150c10As
TOLSON, John		21	M	Laborer	150c10As
LEWIS, Margt.		27	F	Matron	150c10As
REEDY, Mary		21	F	Servant	150c10As
QUIRK, Johana		26	F	Spinster	150c10As
SHEAHEN, Margt.		14	F	Spinster	150c10As
Mary		10	F	Unknown	150c10As
Honora		12	F	Unknown	150c10As
OBRIAN, John		30	M	Laborer	150c10As
LYNCH, Thos.		14	M	Laborer	150c10As
MCMAHON, Honora		47	F	Matron	150c10As
Honora		18	F	Spinster	150c10As
Margt.		25	F	Spinster	150c10As
MADIGAN, Mray		25	F	Spinster	150c10As
MULVIHILL, Thos.		22	M	Laborer	150c10As
FLAHANAN, Mary		20	F	Spinster	150c10As
CARTY, Cathn.		30	F	Spinster	150c10As
DONOHAN, Patrick		26	M	Laborer	150c10As
MORAN, John		13	M	Unknown	150c10As
Bridget		13	F	Unknown	150c10As
GLEESON, Ellen		22	F	Spinster	150c10As
Cathr.		2	F	Child	150c10As
REEDY, John		40	M	Laborer	150c10As
Bridget		25	F	Spinster	150c10As
TALTY, Cathr.		30	F	Matron	150c10As
Bridget		10	F	Unknown	150c10As
John		3	M	Child	150c10As
Winny		6	F	Child	150c10As
Jas.		.11	M	Infant	150c10As

NAMES OF PASSENGERS	AGE	SEX	OCCUPATIONS	DATE PORT SHIP
WALLIS, Mary	24	F	Spinster	150c10As
BARRETT, Alice	17	F	Spinster	150c10As
KELLY, Cathn.	10	F	Unknown	150c10As
CASEY, Michl.	3	M	Child	150c10As
KENRICK, Cathr.	20	F	Spinster	150c10As
Mary	3	F	Child	150c10As
MCINERY, Allice	46	F	Matron	150c10As
Anne	25	F	Spinster	150c10As
Mary	13	F	Unknown	150c10As
Thos.	7	M	Child	150c10As
BREEN, Mary	22	F	Spinster	150c10As
MOORE, Margt.	24	F	Wife	150c10As
Saml.	26	M	Farmer	150c10As
MORAN, John	25	M	Laborer	150c10As
BARRETT, John	24	M	Laborer	150c10As
RYAN, Mary	19	F	Spinster	150c10As
MADIGAN, Mary	23	F	Spinster	150c10As
SCANLAN, Bridget	15	F	Spinster	150c10As
CONNORS, Timth.	28	M	Laborer	150c10As
MULVIHILL, John	35	M	Laborer	150c10As
Bridget	18	F	Spinster	150c10As
FITZGERALD, Patt	22	M	Laborer	150c10As
MOORE, Johanna	17	F	Spinster	150c10As
CUNNINGHAM, Mary	20	F	Spinster	150c10As
CONNELLS, Patt.	35	M	Laborer	150c10As
CONNELLY, John	28	M	Laborer	150c10As
NEILLES, Timth.	30	M	Laborer	150c10As
MCMAHON, Patt.	18	M	Laborer	150c10As
ENRIGHT, Margt.	22	F	Spinster	150c10As
COONEY, Jas.	17	M	Laborer	150c10As
MEEHAN, Ed.	45	M	Laborer	150c10As
Michl.	12	M	Unknown	150c10As
PARKER, Anne	26	F	Matron	150c10As
BANBURY, Patt	20	M	Teacher	150c10As
TALLY, Honora	24	F	Spinster	150c10As
WAREN, Anne	19	F	Matron	150c10As
FLYNN, Margt.	24	F	Spinster	150c10As
Eliza	20	F	Spinster	150c10As
LEWIS, Maria	.04	F	Infant	150c10As
HILLS, Arundel	51	M	Gentleman	150c10As
BARRY, John	14	M	Gentleman	150c10As
OLOUGHLAN, Michl.	21	M	Gentleman	150c10As
BURKE, Mary	45	F	Matron	150c10As
MCCUTCHEN, Rebecca	40	F	Matron	150c10As
Cathn.	24	F	Spinster	150c10As
Eliza	22	F	Spinster	150c10As
Rebecca	17	F	Spinster	150c10As
ODRISCOL, Anne	3	F	Child	150c10As
MEEHAN, Michl.	25	M	Laborer	150c10As

LONDON 15 OCTOBER 1849

From London

NAMES OF PASSENGERS	AGE	SEX	OCCUPATIONS	DATE PORT SHIP
MIDDLETON, Robt.	18	M	Unknown	150c06Au
CAMPBELL, Margaret	37	F	Unknown	150c06Au
Jane	19	F	Unknown	150c06Au
Minnie	7	F	Child	150c06Au
Donata	6	F	Child	150c06Au
PRINGLE, James-E.	33	M	Mechanic	150c06Au
LANHAN, Geo.	35	M	Builder	150c06Au
Louisa	34	F	Unknown	150c06Au
Mary-Ann	10	F	Unknown	150c06Au
Henry	8	M	Child	150c06Au
Robt.	7	M	Child	150c06Au
Emma	.00	F	Infant	150c06Au
LACOCQUE, Wm.	21	M	Unknown	150c06Au
ALDRIDGE, Francis	38	M	Unknown	150c06Au
BURTON, Robt.	28	M	Hairdresser	150c06Au
JOHNSON, Wm.	35	M	Unknown	150c06Au
SMITH, Wm.	49	M	Cooper	150c06Au
REEVES, Wm.	32	M	Laborer	150c06Au
OCONNER, Thomas	32	M	Unknown	150c06Au

ROSCIUS 16 OCTOBER 1849

From Liverpool

NAMES OF PASSENGERS	AGE	SEX	OCCUPATIONS	DATE PORT SHIP
DEADMAN, Arthur-W.	33	M	Farmer	160c02At
Jane-M.	28	F	Unknown	160c02At
Edwd.A.	3	M	Child	160c02At
Catherine-N.	.10	F	Infant	160c02At
FORBES, John-A.	10	M	Unknown	160c02At
Robert-R.	7	M	Child	160c02At
PADLEY, Chas.	26	M	Unknown	160c02At
ROBINSON, Alicia-Isabe	58	F	Lady	160c02At
RAYNES, Robert-J.	26	M	Soldier	160c02At
SWEENEY, John	22	M	Surgeon	160c02At
TRAYNOR, Jane	17	F	Lady'S Maid	160c02At
BARRATT, Chas.	36	M	Cutler	160c02At
Elizabeth	36	F	Unknown	160c02At
BLAKE, Juliana	28	F	Unknown	160c02At
BONDIDEAR, Catherine	55	F	Cst	160c02At
Johanna	22	F	Cst	160c02At
Sarah	12	F	Cst	160c02At
Stephen	17	M	Tailor	160c02At
BRADY, Thomas	18	M	Grocer	160c02At
John	28	M	Grocer	160c02At
CAMPBELL, Ann	27	F	Spinster	160c02At
COOK, Catherine	60	F	Unknown	160c02At
DARWIN, Edward	30	M	Painter	160c02At
Mary	32	F	Unknown	160c02At
HOCKING, Alexander	25	M	Carpenter	160c02At
Sarah	28	F	Unknown	160c02At
MCARTHUR, Jeanette	62	F	Unknown	160c02At
NICHOLAS, James	24	M	Unknown	160c02At
PERIGO, Ann	25	F	Servant	160c02At
WEBSTER, Henry	18	M	Clerk	160c02At
WEAVER, George	22	M	Sculptor	160c02At
Jane	24	F	Unknown	160c02At
WHITE, Catherine	20	F	Unknown	160c02At
YAPP, James	56	M	Wheelwright	160c02At
Ann	50	F	Unknown	160c02At
Mary	23	F	Unknown	160c02At
James-Jun-.	26	M	Wheelwright	160c02At
George	15	M	Wheelwright	160c02At
ASHTON, James	30	M	Wire Worker	160c02At
Elizabeth	24	F	Unknown	160c02At
BARNETT, Eliza	21	F	Unknown	160c02At
BARTLE, Martin	13	M	Unknown	160c02At
Margaret	26	F	Unknown	160c02At
BENTLEY, Biddy	23	F	Unknown	160c02At
BELCHER, Catherine	19	F	Servant	160c02At
BOHAN, John	16	M	Laborer	160c02At
BLOOMFIELD, Hessy	17	F	Unknown	160c02At
BLACK, Ann	14	F	Unknown	160c02At
BRADEY, Patrick	33	M	Laborer	160c02At
Eliza	25	F	Unknown	160c02At
Catherine	28	F	Unknown	160c02At
Mary	2	F	Child	160c02At
Mary	16	F	Unknown	160c02At
BRADLEY, Mary	15	F	Unknown	160c02At
Mary	17	F	Unknown	160c02At
BRUCKAN, James	22	M	Stctr	160c02At
BURNS, Edward	28	M	Laborer	160c02At
BURN, Ann	26	F	Unknown	160c02At
Ellen	14	F	Unknown	160c02At
Eliza	11	F	Unknown	160c02At

NAMES OF PASSENGERS	AGE	SEX	OCCUPATIONS	DATE PORT SHIP
BURN, John	5	M	Child	160c02At
Mary	3	F	Child	160c02At
BURNS, Ann	19	F	Servant	160c02At
BURN, Mary	27	F	Unknown	160c02At
BURK, Biddy	60	F	Unknown	160c02At
BULLEN, Mary-Ann	24	F	Dressmaker	160c02At
BUCHANON, John	35	M	Gdnr	160c02At
CASEY, Sarah	40	F	Unknown	160c02At
CARTY, Christopher	24	M	Blacksmith	160c02At
Died-At-Sea				
Catherine	28	F	Unknown	160c02At
CASSIDY, John	24	M	Butcher	160c02At
Ellen	24	F	Unknown	160c02At
CALLAGHAN, Michael	20	M	Baker	160c02At
CLARK, Michael	26	M	Laborer	160c02At
Mary	16	F	Servant	160c02At
Bridget	28	F	Unknown	160c02At
Mary	7	F	Child	160c02At
Rosa	5	F	Child	160c02At
Thomas	.10	M	Infant	160c02At
Patrick	25	M	Laborer	160c02At
CALLAGHAN, Catherine	28	F	Unknown	160c02At
CLARK, Ja.W.	33	M	Compositor	160c02At
CORTLAND, Thomas	30	M	Cord Winder	160c02At
COCKRAN, John	17	M	Weaver	160c02At
CONNOLLY, Patrick	18	M	Carpenter	160c02At
COOS, John	14	M	Servant	160c02At
Kim	11	F	Unknown	160c02At
COOLAGHAN, Bridget	20	F	Servant	160c02At
CONNOR, Mary	22	F	Unknown	160c02At
COSGROVE, Mary	21	F	Unknown	160c02At
CANNON, Mary	18	F	Unknown	160c02At
COONEY, Hannah	14	F	Unknown	160c02At
CONLIN, Ann	27	F	Unknown	160c02At
Ann	2	F	Child	160c02At
CRAWFORD, George	48	M	Farmer	160c02At
Barbara	45	F	Unknown	160c02At
Eliza	19	F	Unknown	160c02At
Alexander	17	M	Unknown	160c02At
Rosa	12	F	Unknown	160c02At
Willm.R.	6	M	Child	160c02At
Jane	4	F	Child	160c02At
CREAN, John	18	M	Tailor	160c02At
CRONAN, Ellen	18	F	Unknown	160c02At
Ann	17	F	Unknown	160c02At
Catherine	20	F	Unknown	160c02At
Mary	6	F	Child	160c02At
Bridget	5	F	Child	160c02At
CREEGAN, William	20	M	Unknown	160c02At
CREIGHTON, Judith	2	F	Child	160c02At
CURLEY, James	16	M	Tailor	160c02At
Hugh	17	M	Laborer	160c02At
Peter	14	M	Unknown	160c02At
Martin	19	M	Laborer	160c02At
CHAMBERS, James	30	M	Laborer	160c02At
DAVIS, Thomas	25	M	Laborer	160c02At
DAWSON, William	21	M	Laborer	160c02At
DAY, Mary	20	F	Unknown	160c02At
DERANGER, Thomas	26	M	Laborer	160c02At
DESMOND, Daniel	22	M	Laborer	160c02At
DEVON, Patrick	40	M	Laborer	160c02At
DARNLEY, Jane	18	F	Dressmaker	160c02At
DENIN, Bridget	18	F	Unknown	160c02At
DOLAN, Michael	26	M	Laborer	160c02At
Michael	36	M	Laborer	160c02At
Martin	12	M	Unknown	160c02At
Thomas	18	M	Laborer	160c02At
John	16	M	Laborer	160c02At
DOWNEY, Thomas	18	M	Laborer	160c02At
DOYLE, Hugh	19	M	Laborer	160c02At
James	13	M	Laborer	160c02At
Mary	24	F	Unknown	160c02At
Agnes	7	F	Child	160c02At
Martin	10	M	Unknown	160c02At
Kate	2	F	Child	160c02At

NAMES OF PASSENGERS	AGE	SEX	OCCUPATIONS	DATE PORT SHIP
DOYD, Francis	20	M	Unknown	160c02At
Ann	45	F	Unknown	160c02At
DONOVAN, Catherine	35	F	Servant	160c02At
Henry	6	M	Child	160c02At
M.A.	15	F	Unknown	160c02At
DOOLEY, Mary-Ann	20	F	Unknown	160c02At
DONNOLLY, Alice	17	F	Unknown	160c02At
DUGAN, Margaret	24	F	Servant	160c02At
DURNIN, Phillip	19	M	Laborer	160c02At
DUNN, William	20	M	Laborer	160c02At
Thomas	11	M	Laborer	160c02At
Alice	20	F	Unknown	160c02At
DUNNAN, Mary	16	F	Unknown	160c02At
DURNIN, Betty	26	F	Unknown	160c02At
DUGGIN, Rachael	19	F	Unknown	160c02At
ELLISON, Richard	60	M	Unknown	160c02At
Mary	60	F	Unknown	160c02At
EGAN, Mary	16	F	Unknown	160c02At
ENGLISH, Mary	17	F	Unknown	160c02At
EDWARDS, Richard	30	M	Tailor	160c02At
Jane	28	F	Unknown	160c02At
FAGAN, John	26	M	Laborer	160c02At
FIELDSAND, Ann	26	F	Unknown	160c02At
Rose-A.	12	F	Unknown	160c02At
Joshua	9	M	Child	160c02At
Mary	8	F	Child	160c02At
Elizabeth	2	F	Child	160c02At
Emma	15	F	Unknown	160c02At
FLANNIGAN, Patrick	23	M	Laborer	160c02At
FORD, Mary	19	F	Servant	160c02At
James	19	M	Servant	160c02At
FOLEY, Patrick	30	M	Laborer	160c02At
GALLAGHAN, Michael	30	M	Laborer	160c02At
GAGHAN, Sarah	20	F	Servant	160c02At
Ellen	21	F	Servant	160c02At
GILMORE, Patrick	20	M	Storekeeper	160c02At
Alice	25	F	Unknown	160c02At
James	3	M	Child	160c02At
GILL, Thomas	53	M	Farmer	160c02At
GILMARTIN, Ann	10	F	Unknown	160c02At
GILLAN, Owen	22	M	Laborer	160c02At
GILLESPIE, Ann	30	M	Laborer	160c02At
Sally	7	F	Child	160c02At
Mary	4	F	Child	160c02At
Frances	2	F	Child	160c02At
Alice	.06	F	Infant	160c02At
GILMARTIN, Thomas	12	M	Unknown	160c02At
Mary	8	F	Child	160c02At
GLYNN, John	25	M	Laborer	160c02At
GOSS, James	27	M	Weaver	160c02At
GOODMAN, Lawrence	22	M	Butcher	160c02At
GORDON, Dennis	15	M	Servant	160c02At
Elizabeth	50	F	Unknown	160c02At
GORAL, Catherine	28	F	Unknown	160c02At
John	3	M	Child	160c02At
GRANT, Patrick	24	M	Unknown	160c02At
Michael	23	M	Groom	160c02At
GRADY, Catherine	20	F	Unknown	160c02At
GREANEY, Eliza	24	F	Servant	160c02At
GROGAN, Mary	22	F	Servant	160c02At
Maria	16	F	Servant	160c02At
GREAREY, John	60	M	Servant	160c02At
GREANEY, William	5	M	Child	160c02At
Mary	2	F	Child	160c02At
GRINEY, William	22	M	Laborer	160c02At
GRIFFIN, John	25	M	Laborer	160c02At
HARRIS, Mary	20	F	Servant	160c02At
HANLEY, William	19	M	Laborer	160c02At
HARDCASTLE, Ann	31	F	Unknown	160c02At
Thomas	7	M	Child	160c02At
Joseph	10	M	Unknown	160c02At
HANNIGAN, James	50	M	Laborer	160c02At
HENRY, Jane	19	F	Unknown	160c02At
Nancy	22	F	Servant	160c02At

NAMES OF PASSENGERS	AGE	SEX	OCCUPATIONS	DATE PORT SHIP
HANLIN, Michael	36	M	Hatter	160c02At
Died-At-Sea				
HOILISON, Robt.	17	M	Laborer	160c02At
HORTON, Eliza	22	F	Unknown	160c02At
HOWARD, Patrick	25	M	Laborer	160c02At
HUGHES, Mary	32	F	Unknown	160c02At
James	40	M	Laborer	160c02At
John	14	M	Unknown	160c02At
Died-At-Sea				
Francis	47	M	Farmer	160c02At
James	12	M	Unknown	160c02At
IRVIN, James	35	M	Laborer	160c02At
JOHNSON, William	45	M	Unknown	160c02At
Harriet	38	F	Unknown	160c02At
Died-At-Sea				
Edward	11	M	Unknown	160c02At
James	9	M	Child	160c02At
Willm.Hy.	7	M	Child	160c02At
Richard	5	M	Child	160c02At
Alfred	2	M	Child	160c02At
Elizabeth	.05	F	Infant	160c02At
JONES, William	35	M	Unknown	160c02At
KANE, Mary	18	F	Unknown	160c02At
KEAN, Isabella	17	F	Unknown	160c02At
KELLY, Sarah	35	F	Unknown	160c02At
William	3	M	Child	160c02At
Thomas	.11	M	Infant	160c02At
Mary	18	F	Unknown	160c02At
Catherine	22	F	Unknown	160c02At
KEEGAN, Daniel	30	M	Laborer	160c02At
KENNEDY, Margaret	23	F	Unknown	160c02At
John	22	M	Laborer	160c02At
KILLAN, Johanna	24	F	Servant	160c02At
KILGAY, Ann	20	F	Unknown	160c02At
KILDOCK, Mary-Ann	28	F	Servant	160c02At
KILGAN, Biddy	35	M	Servant	160c02At
KING, Patrick	27	M	Shoemaker	160c02At
KINSHELLA, Biddy	5	F	Child	160c02At
KIRWIN, Mary	40	F	Unknown	160c02At
Ellen	7	F	Child	160c02At
Judy	6	F	Child	160c02At
Peter	26	M	Groom	160c02At
KNOX, William	9	M	Child	160c02At
LARKIN, Michael	18	M	Laborer	160c02At
LEACH, Ann	40	F	Unknown	160c02At
LEONARD, Dennis	27	M	Bricklayer	160c02At
MCCABE, Biddy	19	F	Dressmaker	160c02At
MCCANN, Martin	20	M	Laborer	160c02At
MCCOY, John	14	M	Servant	160c02At
MCDONOUGH, Patrick	20	M	Laborer	160c02At
MCGAVAN, Michael	30	M	Laborer	160c02At
MCGARATTY, Catherine	40	F	Unknown	160c02At
MCGARRATTY, Chas.	9	M	Child	160c02At
John	4	M	Child	160c02At
Mary	.02	F	Infant	160c02At
MCGINN, James	20	M	Laborer	160c02At
MCGRAPH, Bridget	17	F	Unknown	160c02At
MCGRAIN, Michael	30	M	Laborer	160c02At
MCGRIFFY, Michael	22	M	Laborer	160c02At
MCGUIRE, Teddy	23	M	Laborer	160c02At
MCMARAH, James	30	M	Surveyor	160c02At
Norah	22	F	Unknown	160c02At
Margaret	.11	F	Infant	160c02At
MCMAHON, Ann	21	F	Unknown	160c02At
MCMANNAGH, Margaret	18	F	Unknown	160c02At
MCMANNUS, Ann	14	F	Unknown	160c02At
MCLOSKEY, Mary	17	F	Servant	160c02At
MCNICHOLAS, John	22	M	Laborer	160c02At
MCSHERRY, Ann	21	F	Unknown	160c02At
MADDEN, Ellen	20	F	Servant	160c02At
William	17	M	Laborer	160c02At
MANGIN, Eliza	18	F	Unknown	160c02At
MAHON, Patrick	20	M	Laborer	160c02At
MALONEY, Kate	17	F	Servant	160c02At
MANEARY, Rose-Ann	21	F	Servant	160c02At

NAMES OF PASSENGERS	AGE	SEX	OCCUPATIONS	DATE PORT SHIP
MARTIN, John	20	M	Baker	160c02At
Biddy	40	F	Unknown	160c02At
John	11	M	Unknown	160c02At
Henry	8	M	Child	160c02At
MEEHAN, Thomas	29	M	Laborer	160c02At
Michael	32	M	Cbtmkr	160c02At
Norah	28	F	Unknown	160c02At
Joseph	4	M	Child	160c02At
Owen	1	M	Child	160c02At
Mary	.03	F	Infant	160c02At
MORAN, Mary	19	F	Servant	160c02At
James	30	M	Grinder	160c02At
Bridget	27	F	Unknown	160c02At
Mary-Ann	8	F	Child	160c02At
James	6	M	Child	160c02At
Win.	.11	U	Infant	160c02At
Edmund	20	M	Farmer	160c02At
Thomas	24	M	Laborer	160c02At
MORRIS, Thomas	30	M	Laborer	160c02At
MULANEY, Pat.	25	M	Laborer	160c02At
MULLIN, Michael	48	M	Laborer	160c02At
Pat	16	M	Laborer	160c02At
Bessy	16	F	Unknown	160c02At
Catherine	18	F	Unknown	160c02At
MULHALL, James	13	M	Unknown	160c02At
Eliza	40	F	Unknown	160c02At
Mich.	11	M	Unknown	160c02At
Margaret	9	F	Child	160c02At
CRAWFORD, Annie	8	F	Child	160c02At
DOYLE, Ann	16	F	Unknown	160c02At
HICKY, James	27	M	Laborer	160c02At
LARKIN, Owen	16	M	Farmer	160c02At
Michael	16	M	Laborer	160c02At

ATLANTIC 16 OCTOBER 1849

From Havre

NAMES OF PASSENGERS	AGE	SEX	OCCUPATIONS	DATE PORT SHIP
OREILLY, George	17	M	Gentleman	160c03Av

HINDOSTAN 17 OCTOBER 1849

From Liverpool

NAMES OF PASSENGERS	AGE	SEX	OCCUPATIONS	DATE PORT SHIP
GARVEY, Philip	23	M	Blacksmith	170c02Ay
MCMAHON, Edward	56	M	Farmer	170c02Ay
Rose	55	F	Unknown	170c02Ay
Pat	30	M	Farmer	170c02Ay
Edwd.	20	M	Farmer	170c02Ay
Hugh	18	M	Farmer	170c02Ay
Philip	17	M	Farmer	170c02Ay
Eliza	14	F	Unknown	170c02Ay
Mary	13	F	Unknown	170c02Ay
John	10	M	Farmer	170c02Ay
MURPHY, Jerem.	20	M	Tailor	170c02Ay
NELLY, James	27	M	Unknown	170c02Ay
CROWLEY, Margt.	30	F	Unknown	170c02Ay
FADDEN, Robt.	37	M	Gdnr	170c02Ay
SULLIVAN, John	40	M	Laborer	170c02Ay
Johana	11	F	Unknown	170c02Ay
John	7	M	Child	170c02Ay
James	3	M	Child	170c02Ay
DUNDERDALE, Margt.	53	F	Unknown	170c02Ay

NAMES OF PASSENGERS	AGE	SEX	OCCUPATIONS	DATE PORT SHIP
MARTINS, Mich	22	M	Tailor	170c02Ay
MAXWELL, Robt.	28	M	Blacksmith	170c02Ay
George	20	M	Blacksmith	170c02Ay
CONNOLLY, Edward	25	M	Shoemaker	170c02Ay
FAGAN, Peter	20	M	Stone Mason	170c02Ay
SHIELDS, John	20	M	Blacksmith	170c02Ay
HOTCHKISS, George	27	M	Engftr	170c02Ay
LINDSAY, Isabel	30	F	Unknown	170c02Ay
Jane	8	F	Child	170c02Ay
Arthur	6	M	Child	170c02Ay
LEE, John	22	M	Shoemaker	170c02Ay
ATCHESON, George	24	M	Clerk	170c02Ay
ONEILL, John	26	M	Laborer	170c02Ay
NOLAN, Michl.	21	M	Laborer	170c02Ay
KILLEN, Edwd.	30	M	Porter	170c02Ay
SMITH, Pat	41	M	Butcher	170c02Ay
Anne	39	F	Unknown	170c02Ay
Cathr.	12	F	Unknown	170c02Ay
LARKIN, James	29	M	Miller	170c02Ay
Anne	23	F	Unknown	170c02Ay
DUNNE, Bryan	21	M	Laborer	170c02Ay
ANDREWS, Wm.	35	M	Laborer	170c02Ay
MCGURK, Wm.	25	M	Laborer	170c02Ay
DAILEY, Bart	23	M	Porter	170c02Ay
POWELL, George	32	M	Porter	170c02Ay
Winifred	25	M	Porter	170c02Ay
Anne	22	F	Unknown	170c02Ay
John	7	M	Child	170c02Ay
MATTHEWS, James	27	M	Baker	170c02Ay
HANSBAND, Saml.	36	M	Blacksmith	170c02Ay
Harriet	34	F	Unknown	170c02Ay
James	17	M	Blacksmith	170c02Ay
Thos.	15	M	Unknown	170c02Ay
Wm.	13	M	Unknown	170c02Ay
Wm.	10	M	Unknown	170c02Ay
Samuel	9	M	Child	170c02Ay
Arthur	8	M	Child	170c02Ay
James	7	M	Child	170c02Ay
BURGESS, John	35	M	Tailor	170c02Ay
NEWTON, Wm.	49	M	Wheelwright	170c02Ay
John	48	M	Whitesmith	170c02Ay
Sarah	27	F	Unknown	170c02Ay
Anne	23	F	Unknown	170c02Ay
John	21	M	Unknown	170c02Ay
Mary	18	F	Unknown	170c02Ay
Charles	11	M	Unknown	170c02Ay
Eliza	9	F	Child	170c02Ay
MCCABE, Peter	40	M	Unknown	170c02Ay
Died-At-Sea				
RYAN, John	34	M	Unknown	170c02Ay
Died-At-Sea				
POWER, Michael	8	M	Child	170c02Ay
Died-At-Sea				
FADDIN, Mary	40	F	Unknown	170c02Ay
Died-At-Sea				
OSBORN, James	7	M	Child	170c02Ay
Died-At-Sea				
NEWTON, Wm.	5	M	Child	170c02Ay
Died-At-Sea				
HARRIS, U	00	M	Unknown	170c02Ay
U-Mrs.	00	F	Unknown	170c02Ay
FISSINGTON, U	00	M	Unknown	170c02Ay
U-Mrs.	00	F	Unknown	170c02Ay
READ, U	00	M	Unknown	170c02Ay
U-Mrs.	00	F	Unknown	170c02Ay
BONEY, U	00	M	Unknown	170c02Ay

YORKSHIRE 17 OCTOBER 1849

From Liverpool

NAMES OF PASSENGERS	AGE	SEX	OCCUPATIONS	DATE PORT SHIP
SHEA, Mary	24	F	Servant	170c02Az
LENNON, Mathew	24	M	Laborer	170c02Az
Catherine	23	F	Laborer	170c02Az
Margaret	12	F	Laborer	170c02Az
QUIGLEY, Mary	50	F	Servant	170c02Az
Thomas	6	M	Child	170c02Az
MCSWEENEY, William	50	M	Farmer	170c02Az
Mary	40	F	Farmer	170c02Az
William	25	M	Farmer	170c02Az
John	22	M	Farmer	170c02Az
Maria	17	F	Farmer	170c02Az
Ellen	14	F	Farmer	170c02Az
LEAHY, Biddy	20	F	Servant	170c02Az
Mary	5	F	Child	170c02Az
MCSWEENEY, Kate	12	F	Servant	170c02Az
FOOKS, Margaret	18	F	Servant	170c02Az
Died-At-Sea				
CORVELL, Robert	25	M	Laborer	170c02Az
SLUTTERY, Edward	24	M	Laborer	170c02Az
Mary	40	F	Servant	170c02Az
SULLIVAN, Michael	4	M	Child	170c02Az
MULLARY, Michael	28	M	Laborer	170c02Az
Mary	26	F	Laborer	170c02Az
Patrick	4	M	Child	170c02Az
Biddy	3	F	Child	170c02Az
SCANLAN, Mary	16	F	Servant	170c02Az
GALVIN, Patrick	22	M	Laborer	170c02Az
TYGOOD, Francis	26	M	Laborer	170c02Az
Ellen	24	F	Laborer	170c02Az
SCANLAN, Daniel	24	M	Laborer	170c02Az
Mary	23	F	Laborer	170c02Az
SULLIVAN, Terry	20	M	Laborer	170c02Az
Nancy	21	F	Laborer	170c02Az
U	.00	U	Infant	170c02Az
John	20	M	Laborer	170c02Az
ENWRIGHT, Hannah	30	F	Servant	170c02Az
U	.00	U	Infant	170c02Az
SHEAHAN, Eliza	19	F	Servant	170c02Az
ANGLIN, Darly	55	M	Farmer	170c02Az
Kate	40	F	Farmer	170c02Az
U	.00	U	Infant	170c02Az
Kate	13	F	Farmer	170c02Az
Honora	9	F	Child	170c02Az
Edward	8	M	Child	170c02Az
HICKEY, Ellen	30	F	Servant	170c02Az
LIDDY, John	26	M	Laborer	170c02Az
Honor	21	F	Laborer	170c02Az
CLINE, Mary	24	F	Servant	170c02Az
KELLY, Thomas	24	M	Laborer	170c02Az
FLANNAGAN, Sally	28	F	Servant	170c02Az
BATTON, Michael	22	M	Laborer	170c02Az
DUGAN, Mary	18	F	Dressmaker	170c02Az
St.LEDGER, Daniel	18	M	Laborer	170c02Az
COOLEY, Michael	18	M	Laborer	170c02Az
SHEA, Martin	22	M	Laborer	170c02Az
LYNCH, Biddy	60	F	Servant	170c02Az
Mary	24	F	Servant	170c02Az
U	.00	U	Infant	170c02Az
Mary	17	F	Servant	170c02Az
Mary	2	F	Child	170c02Az
COFFEY, Jane	26	F	Servant	170c02Az
Michael	8	M	Child	170c02Az
Andrew	6	M	Child	170c02Az
CORNELL, Maurice	24	M	Laborer	170c02Az
SHEA, John	22	M	Laborer	170c02Az

NAMES OF PASSENGERS	AGE	SEX	OCCUPATIONS	DATE PORT SHIP
MCMAHON, Mary	18	F	Servant	170c02Az
SHEA, Margaret	14	F	Servant	170c02Az
Judy	22	F	Servant	170c02Az
U	.00	U	Infant	170c02Az
Ellen	30	F	Servant	170c02Az
CONNOR, Catherine	34	F	Servant	170c02Az
ROURKE, Eliza	26	F	Servant	170c02Az
CONNOR, Anna	18	F	Servant	170c02Az
DEMPSEY, Patrick	19	M	Laborer	170c02Az
LAWLER, Eliza	17	F	Servant	170c02Az
HAYES, Mary	12	F	Servant	170c02Az
Catherine	8	F	Child	170c02Az
SEXTON, Mary	19	F	Servant	170c02Az
CONNOR, Catherine	28	F	Servant	170c02Az
DWYER, Catherine	18	F	Servant	170c02Az
RUSSEL, Dennis	40	M	Laborer	170c02Az
Johanna	15	F	Servant	170c02Az
SEXTON, David	12	M	Laborer	170c02Az
DOYLL, Michael	16	M	Laborer	170c02Az
MALONY, John	50	M	Laborer	170c02Az
Patrick	30	M	Laborer	170c02Az
NICHOL, Mary	30	F	Servant	170c02Az
DWYER, Cornelius	45	M	Farmer	170c02Az
Bridget	38	F	Farmer	170c02Az
Honora	16	F	Farmer	170c02Az
Mary	14	F	Farmer	170c02Az
Edward	12	M	Farmer	170c02Az
John	11	M	Farmer	170c02Az
Bridget	9	F	Child	170c02Az
Cornelius	7	M	Child	170c02Az
Patrick	5	M	Child	170c02Az
Johanna	3	F	Child	170c02Az
Margaret	19	F	Farmer	170c02Az
MAGRATH, Thomas	35	M	Laborer	170c02Az
MOORE, Thomas	19	M	Laborer	170c02Az
Mary	18	F	Servant	170c02Az
Biddy	12	F	Servant	170c02Az
TOONEY, Patrick	25	M	Laborer	170c02Az
MCDONALD, Ellen	23	F	Servant	170c02Az
LUCUS, Biddy	26	F	Servant	170c02Az
GALLIGAN, Thomas	23	M	Laborer	170c02Az
Biddy	48	F	Servant	170c02Az
James	8	M	Child	170c02Az
Nancy	23	F	Child	170c02Az
CUNNINGHAM, John	28	M	Laborer	170c02Az
Mary	30	F	Laborer	170c02Az
U	.00	U	Infant	170c02Az
CARTER, William	26	M	Farmer	170c02Az
Catherine	22	F	Farmer	170c02Az
Jane	54	F	Farmer	170c02Az
Richard	4	M	Child	170c02Az
BARROW, John	18	M	Servant	170c02Az
LOVELACE, Sarah	22	F	Servant	170c02Az
MAHER, Jane	16	F	Dressmaker	170c02Az
Eliza	25	F	Dressmaker	170c02Az
RAMSEY, Margaret	18	F	Servant	170c02Az
MCGERALD, Patrick	24	M	Laborer	170c02Az
Michael	26	M	Laborer	170c02Az
SHEA, Margaret	50	F	Servant	170c02Az
U	.00	U	Infant	170c02Az
FITZMAURICE, Mary	16	F	Servant	170c02Az
MURPHY, Johanna	24	F	Servant	170c02Az
RYAN, Margaret	28	F	Servant	170c02Az
U	.00	U	Infant	170c02Az
HANLOW, Margaret	20	F	Servant	170c02Az
OCONNOR, Mary	40	F	Servant	170c02Az
Edward	9	M	Child	170c02Az
John	4	M	Child	170c02Az
ONEIL, Bridget	13	F	Child	170c02Az
Nancy	8	F	Child	170c02Az
John	4	M	Child	170c02Az
RILEY, Ellen	20	F	Servant	170c02Az
BAILLY, Bernard	25	M	Laborer	170c02Az
CONLAN, Mary	30	F	Servant	170c02Az
GALLIGAN, Catherine	16	F	Servant	170c02Az

NAMES OF PASSENGERS	AGE	SEX	OCCUPATIONS	DATE PORT SHIP
GRAY, Mary	40	F	Servant	170c02Az
REILLY, Margaret	43	F	Servant	170c02Az
John	14	M	Servant	170c02Az
Lawrence	10	M	Servant	170c02Az
Mary	12	F	Servant	170c02Az
SHEHAN, Thomas	15	M	Laborer	170c02Az
CARNEY, Mary	19	F	Servant	170c02Az
GORMAN, Julia	20	F	Servant	170c02Az
MCDONALD, Margaret	63	F	Servant	170c02Az
U	.00	U	Infant	170c02Az
CARRAHER, Margaret	60	F	Infant	170c02Az
MCDONALD, Mary	3	F	Child	170c02Az
HUGHES, Mary-Ann	21	F	Servant	170c02Az
TAFFEE, Catherine	15	F	Servant	170c02Az
CONROY, Betsey	15	F	Servant	170c02Az
HALLY, John	16	M	Laborer	170c02Az
MCCANN, Francis	16	M	Laborer	170c02Az
CONNELLY, Rose	50	F	Servant	170c02Az
CALLAHAN, Mary	12	F	Servant	170c02Az
Anna	8	F	Child	170c02Az
LYNCH, John-C.	30	M	Farmer	170c02Az
Ellen	28	F	Farmer	170c02Az
U	.00	U	Infant	170c02Az
REDMUND, Catherine	26	F	Servant	170c02Az
BALLEVIN, Mary	30	F	Servant	170c02Az
BRADY, Rose	16	F	Servant	170c02Az
FLYNN, Catherine	46	F	Servant	170c02Az
CARR, Anna	14	F	Servant	170c02Az
Alexander	12	M	Servant	170c02Az
Margaret	5	F	Child	170c02Az
CAFFREY, Pattrick	20	M	Laborer	170c02Az
CARR, Betsy	3	F	Child	170c02Az
OBRIEN, Dennis	30	M	Laborer	170c02Az
MURPHEY, James	28	M	Mason	170c02Az
Bridget	24	F	Mason	170c02Az
RIELEY, Patrick	22	M	Smith	170c02Az
DONOHUE, Mary	19	F	Servant	170c02Az
MURPHEY, Dennis	20	M	Carpenter	170c02Az
DALY, Mary-Ann	18	F	Dressmaker	170c02Az
WARD, Edward	21	M	Laborer	170c02Az
WHELON, William	47	M	Farmer	170c02Az
DORWIN, Julia	40	F	Servant	170c02Az
U	.00	U	Infant	170c02Az
Patrick	10	M	Servant	170c02Az
HOWARD, Lawrence	35	M	Laborer	170c02Az
William	2	M	Child	170c02Az
U	.00	U	Infant	170c02Az
BROWN, John	27	M	Laborer	170c02Az
LEWIS, Anna	26	F	Servant	170c02Az
FARROLL, Patrick	19	M	Laborer	170c02Az
WRIGHT, Sally	12	F	Servant	170c02Az
EDGEWORTH, Margaret	25	F	Servant	170c02Az
WARD, Mary	28	F	Servant	170c02Az
Frances	12	F	Servant	170c02Az
Patrick	10	M	Child	170c02Az
Michael	7	M	Child	170c02Az
Issabella	5	F	Child	170c02Az
Mary	3	F	Child	170c02Az
DOUGHERTY, Catherine	18	F	Servant	170c02Az
MORAN, Edward	25	M	Laborer	170c02Az
SHEVELIN, Charles	20	M	Laborer	170c02Az
HILL, Robert	18	M	Tailor	170c02Az
MCNALLY, Rose	17	F	Servant	170c02Az
ALLEN, Biddy	28	F	Servant	170c02Az
MURPHY, Michael	27	M	Farmer	170c02Az
John	56	M	Farmer	170c02Az
SHEREDAN, John	22	M	Cbtmkr	170c02Az
GRACE, Catherine	20	F	Servant	170c02Az
SENNOT, Mary	24	F	Servant	170c02Az
FITZPATRICK, Dennis	44	M	Laborer	170c02Az
Mary-Anna	24	F	Servant	170c02Az
Mary-A.	58	F	Servant	170c02Az
Bridget	7	F	Child	170c02Az
Edmund	19	M	Servant	170c02Az
WHELON, Thomas	21	M	Laborer	170c02Az

NAMES OF PASSENGERS	AGE	SEX	OCCUPATIONS	DATE PORT SHIP
COLLINS, Simon	22	M	Cooper	170c02Az
CAMPTON, Judy	24	F	Servant	170c02Az
FAWLIS, Margaret	36	F	Servant	170c02Az
John	18	M	Laborer	170c02Az
HOGAN, Benjamin	35	M	Farmer	170c02Az
Margaret	30	F	Farmer	170c02Az
U	.00	U	Infant	170c02Az
Jane	5	F	Child	170c02Az
Margaret	3	F	Child	170c02Az
LYONS, Joseph	25	M	Farmer	170c02Az
CUNNINGHAM, Jane	20	F	Servant	170c02Az
SHEAHAN, James	23	M	Laborer	170c02Az
Cornelius	20	M	Laborer	170c02Az
REILLY, Catherine	23	F	Servant	170c02Az
SHANNAHAN, Timothy	26	M	Bootmaker	170c02Az
Mary	24	F	Bootmaker	170c02Az
MCCARTHY, Florence	20	M	Laborer	170c02Az
Ellen	20	F	Servant	170c02Az
DARLEY, John	25	M	Laborer	170c02Az
CULRANE, Dennis	47	M	Laborer	170c02Az
SULLIVAN, Johanna	18	F	Servant	170c02Az
KANE, Patrick	21	M	Laborer	170c02Az
Luke	19	M	Laborer	170c02Az
LEARY, James	26	M	Laborer	170c02Az
Mary	22	F	Laborer	170c02Az
KEANE, Margaret	26	F	Servant	170c02Az
COLLINS, James	24	M	Laborer	170c02Az
LEARY, Dennis	25	M	Laborer	170c02Az
TANGREY, Michael	26	M	Laborer	170c02Az
COTTER, Mary	19	F	Servant	170c02Az
CLIFFORD, Catherine	26	F	Servant	170c02Az
Dennis	3	M	Child	170c02Az
Timothy	2	M	Child	170c02Az
GILK, John	25	M	Laborer	170c02Az
HANNAHAN, John	30	M	Engineer	170c02Az
MCDONALD, James	52	M	Farmer	170c02Az
PURCELL, William	16	M	Cart Maker	170c02Az
BRIDGET, John	22	M	Laborer	170c02Az
PERCIVAL, Arthur	26	M	Farmer	170c02Az
BURKE, Patrick	28	M	Farmer	170c02Az
HIGGINS, James	22	M	Laborer	170c02Az
CONNOR, Thomas	35	M	Laborer	170c02Az
JORDAN, Margaret	18	F	Servant	170c02Az
KEAN, Patrick	26	M	Laborer	170c02Az
FITZGERALD, Joseph	19	M	Laborer	170c02Az
MCCARTHY, Anthony	30	M	Laborer	170c02Az
CONNOR, Thomas	22	M	Laborer	170c02Az
GALLAGHAN, Biddy	20	F	Servant	170c02Az
GRANT, Nancy	25	F	Servant	170c02Az
Martin	35	M	Laborer	170c02Az
DANKEY, Joseph	36	M	Laborer	170c02Az
Johanna	29	F	Laborer	170c02Az
Michael	2	M	Child	170c02Az
HALLINAN, Patrick	20	M	Laborer	170c02Az
LENAN, Michael	23	M	Laborer	170c02Az
MURPHY, Michael	40	M	Laborer	170c02Az
Ellen	12	F	Laborer	170c02Az
BLACKHALL, Mathew	25	M	Laborer	170c02Az
SHEAHAN, Mary	20	F	Servant	170c02Az
LYNCH, Biddy	20	F	Servant	170c02Az
FEIGH, Mary	20	F	Servant	170c02Az
MAHONY, Michael	30	M	Laborer	170c02Az
CONNELL, John	20	M	Laborer	170c02Az
CARROLL, Nancy	20	F	Servant	170c02Az
SOMERS, Ellen	20	F	Servant	170c02Az
ROURKE, Margaret	20	F	Servant	170c02Az
LYNCH, Rose	17	F	Servant	170c02Az
LOGAN, Hugh	62	M	Merchant	170c02Az
Mary	20	F	Servant	170c02Az
MORAN, Thomas	24	M	Laborer	170c02Az
KELLY, Edward	26	M	Mason	170c02Az
MCLEER, Ellen	21	F	Servant	170c02Az
DRENEN, Letitia	18	F	Servant	170c02Az
MCKEAN, Bridget	22	F	Servant	170c02Az
ROGERS, Catherine	3	F	Servant	170c02Az

NAMES OF PASSENGERS	AGE	SEX	OCCUPATIONS	DATE PORT SHIP
CASEY, William	50	M	Crdprt	170c02Az
Bridget	30	F	Crdprt	170c02Az
U	.00	U	Infant	170c02Az
Thomas	10	M	Crdprt	170c02Az
James	8	M	Child	170c02Az
Anty.	6	M	Child	170c02Az
Margaret	2	F	Child	170c02Az
BRADY, Catherine	18	F	Servant	170c02Az
REILLY, Bernard	21	M	Laborer	170c02Az
MINTEN, Henry	30	M	Shoemaker	170c02Az
Eliza	26	F	Shoemaker	170c02Az
CORRIGAN, Bridget	50	F	Servant	170c02Az
Patrick	24	M	Laborer	170c02Az
NOONAN, Dennis	10	M	Laborer	170c02Az
Bridget	35	F	Servant	170c02Az
JENNINGS, Winnifred	17	M	Laborer	170c02Az
COLLINS, Mary	24	F	Servant	170c02Az
U	.00	U	Infant	170c02Az
BRYAN, Jane	50	F	Servant	170c02Az
James	8	M	Child	170c02Az
William	6	M	Child	170c02Az
Samuel	4	M	Child	170c02Az
COUGHLAN, Ellen	30	F	Servant	170c02Az
U	.00	U	Infant	170c02Az
John	00	M	None	170c02Az
THORNTON, Anna	4	F	Child	170c02Az
TIERNEY, James	20	M	Baker	170c02Az
COLELOUGH, Abraham	18	M	Wheelwright	170c02Az
Mary	50	F	Wheelwright	170c02Az
DWYER, Eliza	19	F	Dressmaker	170c02Az
MCDERMOT, Mary	24	F	Servant	170c02Az
FITZPATRICK, Catherine	24	F	Servant	170c02Az
GALLAGHER, Mary	20	F	Servant	170c02Az
MAHAN, Thomas	20	M	Laborer	170c02Az
QUINN, Ann	25	F	Servant	170c02Az
SHEAHAN, Eliza	20	F	Servant	170c02Az
MORAN, Patrick	26	M	Laborer	170c02Az
FAGAN, Rose	28	F	Servant	170c02Az
SHEA, Bridget	18	F	Servant	170c02Az
CORMICK, Catherine	14	F	Servant	170c02Az
CORNEY, Ellen	20	F	Servant	170c02Az
EGAN, Patrick	5	M	Child	170c02Az
NOON, Catherine	19	F	Servant	170c02Az
DONOHUE, Sarah	40	F	Servant	170c02Az
CUMMINGS, Catherine	26	F	Servant	170c02Az
ENWRIGHT, Mary	24	F	Servant	170c02Az
GOEKIN, Catherine	18	F	Servant	170c02Az
LAWLER, Eliza	16	F	None	170c02Az
REILLY, William	26	M	Laborer	170c02Az
COLLINS, Cornelius	35	M	Laborer	170c02Az
BRUSHNAHAN, Patrick	11	M	Farmer	170c02Az
Bridget	9	F	Child	170c02Az
Ellen	7	F	Child	170c02Az
Julia	5	F	Child	170c02Az
KIETCH, Harry	18	M	Clerk	170c02Az
MCROBERTS, Jackson	27	M	Mercer	170c02Az
WHELON, Mary	30	F	Servant	170c02Az
MARKEY, Martha	24	F	Dressmaker	170c02Az
CRUISE, Thomas	34	M	Laborer	170c02Az
Francis	10	M	Laborer	170c02Az
RIENNAN, Maria	24	F	Dressmaker	170c02Az
NORRY, Michael	19	M	Laborer	170c02Az
TIERNEY, Thomas	40	M	Cooper	170c02Az
Rose	20	F	Servant	170c02Az
BURKE, Catherine	18	F	Servant	170c02Az
HANERNARD, Maria	19	F	Servant	170c02Az
SULLIVAN, Thomas	40	M	Slater	170c02Az
Bridget	17	F	Servant	170c02Az
Peggy	20	F	Servant	170c02Az
THORNTON, Eliza	26	F	Laborer	170c02Az
Mary	6	F	Child	170c02Az

MADISON 17 OCTOBER 1849

From Newcastle

NAMES OF PASSENGERS	AGE	SEX	OCCUPATIONS	DATE PORT SHIP
NESBIT, Gibbert	36	M	Tailor	170c29Ba
ALLAN, Wm.	33	M	Tailor	170c29Ba
John	12	M	None	170c29Ba
SMITH, Thomas	40	M	Farmer	170c29Ba
Thomas-G.	2	M	Child	170c29Ba
Elizabeth-D.	35	F	Unknown	170c29Ba
Elizabeth	8	F	Child	170c29Ba
Sarah-Ann	6	F	Child	170c29Ba
Dinah	.02	F	Infant	170c29Ba

ASHBURTON 18 OCTOBER 1849

From Liverpool

NAMES OF PASSENGERS	AGE	SEX	OCCUPATIONS	DATE PORT SHIP
HIGGINS, Charles	38	M	Surgeon	180c02Bb
Anne-E.	25	F	None	180c02Bb
Charles	14	M	None	180c02Bb
Edmond	12	M	None	180c02Bb
William-H.	10	M	None	180c02Bb
Anne	7	F	Child	180c02Bb
Robert	5	M	Child	180c02Bb
Henry	3	M	Child	180c02Bb
NICHOLSON, Elizabeth	28	F	None	180c02Bb
CURELL, John	35	M	Gentleman	180c02Bb
Isabel	20	F	None	180c02Bb
PARR, Ellen	45	F	None	180c02Bb
Alice	16	F	None	180c02Bb
PATON, Janet	22	F	None	180c02Bb
MCCABE, Bridget	20	F	None	180c02Bb
DAVIS, David	30	M	None	180c02Bb
Mary	30	F	None	180c02Bb
ADAMS, Ann	9	F	Child	180c02Bb
BYRNE, Charles	34	M	Laborer	180c02Bb
ATKINS, Thos.	17	M	None	180c02Bb
Mary	19	F	None	180c02Bb
GARRETT, Robert	34	M	Laborer	180c02Bb
WALLACE, Margaret-A.	22	F	None	180c02Bb
MURPHY, Mary	20	F	None	180c02Bb
VALLALLY, Ann	16	F	None	180c02Bb
GLOVER, James	19	M	Farmer	180c02Bb
CLARKE, Joseph	21	M	Weaver	180c02Bb
MAGINNIS, Mary	38	F	None	180c02Bb
Jane	9	F	Child	180c02Bb
Ann	7	F	Child	180c02Bb
Bell	4	F	Child	180c02Bb
PURSELL, Michael	25	M	None	180c02Bb
FITZSIMMONS, James	20	M	Laborer	180c02Bb
Thos.	6	M	Child	180c02Bb
BRADY, Patk.	8	M	Child	180c02Bb
BEAKY, William	19	M	Laborer	180c02Bb
DINGWALL, Alex	29	M	Farmer	180c02Bb
GRAY, Patk.	20	M	Laborer	180c02Bb
CONNOR, Catherine	20	F	None	180c02Bb
MATHEWS, Catherine	25	F	None	180c02Bb
DOWLING, Elizabeth	23	F	None	180c02Bb
RILEY, Margeret	16	F	None	180c02Bb
MANN, William	28	M	Farmer	180c02Bb
Catherine	28	F	None	180c02Bb
BRIDE, Ellen	28	F	None	180c02Bb
SMITH, Owen	25	M	Weaver	180c02Bb
HOARE, Bridget	18	F	None	180c02Bb
SMITH, John	20	M	None	180c02Bb
Richd.	40	M	Hrsm	180c02Bb
John	16	M	None	180c02Bb
CORMICK, Michael	25	M	Clerk	180c02Bb
Ellen	23	F	None	180c02Bb
William	4	M	Child	180c02Bb
Michael	2	M	Child	180c02Bb
CARROLL, Margeret	25	F	None	180c02Bb
FITZSIMMONS, Catherine	24	F	None	180c02Bb
TALFRIE, Edwd.	35	M	Laborer	180c02Bb
MOTTEL, Morris	24	M	Carpenter	180c02Bb
RYAN, Johanna	21	F	None	180c02Bb
Mary-F.	24	F	None	180c02Bb
NELSON, Edwd.	22	M	Laborer	180c02Bb
SCANLIN, James	38	M	Laborer	180c02Bb
GILLANS, John	40	M	Laborer	180c02Bb
CONNOR, James	20	M	Laborer	180c02Bb
CUMMING, George	22	M	Laborer	180c02Bb
SCOTT, William	25	M	Laborer	180c02Bb
PATON, Elizabeth	20	F	None	180c02Bb
YOUNG, William-E.	20	M	Gentleman	180c02Bb
VICKERS, John-L.	20	M	Gentleman	180c02Bb
DORAN, Ellen	35	F	None	180c02Bb
CAMPBELL, Elizabeth	40	F	None	180c02Bb
CORNWALL, John	23	M	Clerk	180c02Bb
Mary-Anne	20	F	None	180c02Bb
CONNOR, Francis	53	M	Laborer	180c02Bb
Anne	50	F	None	180c02Bb
Charles	24	M	Laborer	180c02Bb
COOKE, Fanny	26	F	None	180c02Bb
LEIR, Thos.	31	M	Painter	180c02Bb
Anne	29	F	Painter	180c02Bb
Richard	26	M	Laborer	180c02Bb
Francis	6	M	Child	180c02Bb
Mary-Anne	4	F	Child	180c02Bb
Louisa	2	F	Child	180c02Bb
Sarah	.10	F	Infant	180c02Bb
MCDONNELL, Elisa	28	F	None	180c02Bb
Elisa	.10	F	Infant	180c02Bb
LEADER, Mary	40	F	None	180c02Bb
John	30	M	Laborer	180c02Bb
KELLY, James	45	M	Laborer	180c02Bb
MCELERLEY, Mary	26	F	None	180c02Bb
MCMEHAN, Biddy	20	F	None	180c02Bb
SULLIVAN, Peter	20	M	Laborer	180c02Bb
KANE, Hugh	50	M	Farmer	180c02Bb
Letitia	50	F	None	180c02Bb
Mary	22	F	None	180c02Bb
Jane	20	F	None	180c02Bb
Letitia	18	F	None	180c02Bb
Charles	20	M	Farmer	180c02Bb
Hugh	9	M	Child	180c02Bb
Alexander	8	M	Child	180c02Bb
MCKEOWN, Robt.	30	M	Tailor	180c02Bb
Robt.	18	M	Tailor	180c02Bb
Elizabeth	30	F	None	180c02Bb
Maria	17	F	None	180c02Bb
GETTY, Jane	28	F	None	180c02Bb
BLAKELY, Sally	18	F	None	180c02Bb
MCMULLEN, Sally	18	F	None	180c02Bb
MCCABE, John	50	M	None	180c02Bb
Died-At-Sea				
Jane	49	F	None	180c02Bb
Died-At-Sea				
Jane	40	F	None	180c02Bb
SIMPSON, Ben.	16	M	Weaver	180c02Bb
HANNAH, Saml.	23	M	Laborer	180c02Bb
Elisa	1	F	Child	180c02Bb
GETTY, Robt.	20	M	Laborer	180c02Bb
MCNULTY, Nancy	20	F	None	180c02Bb
ORR, Jane	25	F	None	180c02Bb
SMITH, Edwd.	40	M	Laborer	180c02Bb
COCHRANE, Alexander	22	M	Farmer	180c02Bb

NAMES OF PASSENGERS	AGE	SEX	OCCUPATIONS	DATE PORT SHIP
WALLACE, James	20	M	Laborer	180c02Bb
MCLAUGHLIN, Thos.	25	M	Laborer	180c02Bb
Edwd.	50	M	Laborer	180c02Bb
HORULY, Thos.	27	M	Laborer	180c02Bb
DALY, James	20	M	Laborer	180c02Bb
WELDS, Jane	20	F	None	180c02Bb
William	16	M	Laborer	180c02Bb
HAMELL, Patk.	25	M	Laborer	180c02Bb
CONLON, Peter	27	M	Gdnr	180c02Bb
MURRY, Patt	23	M	Laborer	180c02Bb
GOOGARTY, Mary	8	F	Child	180c02Bb
HUGHES, Letitia	50	F	None	180c02Bb
Joseph	21	M	Laborer	180c02Bb
MAGUIRE, Anne	30	F	None	180c02Bb
MCLEIR, Rosy	30	F	None	180c02Bb
CRAWFORD, Thos.	46	M	Laborer	180c02Bb
Saml.	16	M	Carpenter	180c02Bb
SIMPSON, Allen	23	M	Carpenter	180c02Bb
MCBRIDE, Mary	20	F	None	180c02Bb
HITCHEN, Anne	30	F	None	180c02Bb
Elizabeth	2	F	Child	180c02Bb
Harriett	.10	F	Infant	180c02Bb
SNOWDON, Jane	36	F	None	180c02Bb
HOWIE, John	30	M	Laborer	180c02Bb
KANE, John	30	M	Laborer	180c02Bb
Hugh	20	M	Laborer	180c02Bb
LAWLOR, Henry	22	M	Carpenter	180c02Bb
MORRIS, William-G.	39	M	Miller	180c02Bb
Charlotte	29	F	None	180c02Bb
Emma	5	F	Child	180c02Bb
William	1	M	Child	180c02Bb
Francis	60	M	Laborer	180c02Bb
Francis	30	M	Laborer	180c02Bb
James	28	M	Wheelwright	180c02Bb
Mary	25	F	None	180c02Bb
William	3	M	Child	180c02Bb
James	1	M	Child	180c02Bb
CARROLL, Henry	31	M	Laborer	180c02Bb
Sarah	26	F	None	180c02Bb
George	6	M	Child	180c02Bb
FRENCH, Charles	19	M	Laborer	180c02Bb
BOLIN, Sabina	12	F	None	180c02Bb
PAYNE, William	22	M	Laborer	180c02Bb
OSBORNE, Harry	20	M	Laborer	180c02Bb
HICKNEY, Harry	27	M	Laborer	180c02Bb
MAGOTT, James	19	M	Laborer	180c02Bb
CUMMINS, George	17	M	Servant	180c02Bb
WHITE, Thos.	23	M	Carpenter	180c02Bb
Lucy	23	F	None	180c02Bb
Betsy	18	F	None	180c02Bb
Edwd.	.09	M	Infant	180c02Bb
BURKE, John	40	M	Tailor	180c02Bb
CURTIS, Thos.	29	M	Laborer	180c02Bb
Jane	27	F	None	180c02Bb
SLOAN, James	30	M	Laborer	180c02Bb
CONNOR, Thos.	25	M	Laborer	180c02Bb
CURTIS, Patt	18	M	Laborer	180c02Bb
PUNTNEY, John	40	M	Laborer	180c02Bb
ECKFORD, Peter	25	M	Engineer	180c02Bb
BRADLEY, James	50	M	Laborer	180c02Bb
KILLEN, Patk.	15	M	Laborer	180c02Bb
MORAN, Sicily	30	M	Laborer	180c02Bb
Ellen	4	F	Child	180c02Bb
Patk.	.08	M	Infant	180c02Bb
CAVANAGH, Mary	25	F	None	180c02Bb
BERRY, Mary	13	F	None	180c02Bb
KEOGH, Edmond	23	M	Laborer	180c02Bb
RYAN, Danl.	30	M	Laborer	180c02Bb
Thos.	22	M	Laborer	180c02Bb
Margt.	25	F	None	180c02Bb
CLAFFY, Mary	20	F	None	180c02Bb
PAYNE, Stephen	25	M	Laborer	180c02Bb
ACTON, John	26	M	Laborer	180c02Bb
BALL, Thos.	46	M	Bookmaker	180c02Bb
Nancy	36	F	None	180c02Bb

NAMES OF PASSENGERS	AGE	SEX	OCCUPATIONS	DATE PORT SHIP
BALL, John	13	M	None	180c02Bb
James	13	M	None	180c02Bb
Alice	11	F	None	180c02Bb
Danl.	9	M	Child	180c02Bb
Mary-Anne	6	F	Child	180c02Bb
Phebe	.08	F	Infant	180c02Bb
TYRRELL, Francis	30	M	Laborer	180c02Bb
MCCLELLAND, George	22	M	Laborer	180c02Bb
Matilda	24	F	None	180c02Bb
INGRUSLEY, Margt.	20	F	None	180c02Bb
Margt.	10	F	None	180c02Bb
FLANAGAN, Charles	20	M	Laborer	180c02Bb
Dominick	25	M	Laborer	180c02Bb
DILLON, Patk.	20	M	Laborer	180c02Bb
CONNOR, Margt.	20	F	None	180c02Bb
MANGAN, Patk.	20	M	Laborer	180c02Bb
MYLES, Anne	50	F	None	180c02Bb
PLUNKETT, Anne	30	F	None	180c02Bb
MULLEN, Cath.	22	F	None	180c02Bb
MYLES, James	12	M	None	180c02Bb
MCMANUS, Biddy	20	F	None	180c02Bb
DUFFY, Betty	12	F	None	180c02Bb
MCMAHON, Biddy	20	F	None	180c02Bb
BEATTIE, Sarah	20	F	None	180c02Bb
ANDREWS, John	65	M	Farmer	180c02Bb
Elizabeth	56	F	None	180c02Bb
Margt.	20	F	None	180c02Bb
Martha	18	F	None	180c02Bb
WOODS, Peter	22	M	Builder	180c02Bb
Mary	27	F	None	180c02Bb
TWAMLEY, William	40	M	Laborer	180c02Bb
Anne	45	F	None	180c02Bb
Anne	30	F	None	180c02Bb
FISHER, Joseph	26	M	Matchmaker	180c02Bb
HOWLEY, Cath.	21	F	None	180c02Bb
WILLIS, Susan	20	F	None	180c02Bb
Cath.	18	F	None	180c02Bb
ROBINSON, William	34	M	Laborer	180c02Bb
BAXTER, John	20	M	Laborer	180c02Bb
BURNSIDE, Margt.	20	F	None	180c02Bb
LENNON, Biddy	15	F	None	180c02Bb
Arthur	13	M	None	180c02Bb
CASEY, Susan	26	F	None	180c02Bb
William	22	M	Laborer	180c02Bb
Mary-Anne	20	F	None	180c02Bb
CARROLL, Bridget	21	F	None	180c02Bb
MCBRIDE, Con	12	M	None	180c02Bb
RYAN, Mary	12	F	None	180c02Bb
KING, James	20	M	Laborer	180c02Bb
KANE, Patk.	22	M	Laborer	180c02Bb
DORAN, David	18	M	Laborer	180c02Bb
MANIX, Johana	32	F	None	180c02Bb
Mary	6	F	Child	180c02Bb
Patk.	10	M	None	180c02Bb
Susan	4	F	Child	180c02Bb
Ann	1	F	Child	180c02Bb
Died-At-Sea				
HAYNES, William	26	M	Laborer	180c02Bb
BRUCE, William	26	M	Laborer	180c02Bb
Bridget	25	F	None	180c02Bb
RILLEY, Ellen	25	F	None	180c02Bb
BRUCE, Mary-Jane	.00	F	Infant	180c02Bb
DUFFY, Ellen	26	F	None	180c02Bb
DUGAN, Patk.	11	M	None	180c02Bb
MURPHY, Ellen	5	F	Child	180c02Bb
MCANN, Owen	20	M	Laborer	180c02Bb
William	26	M	Laborer	180c02Bb
HASSET, John	34	M	None	180c02Bb
SWIFT, John	24	M	Cutler	180c02Bb
CHAPMAN, Henry	22	M	Cutler	180c02Bb
FAGAN, Ann	30	F	None	180c02Bb
William	2	M	Child	180c02Bb
Mary-Ann	.00	F	Infant	180c02Bb
SLATTERY, Thomas	40	M	Laborer	180c02Bb
Mary	40	F	None	180c02Bb

NAMES OF PASSENGERS	AGE	SEX	OCCUPATIONS	DATE PORT SHIP
MCKNIGHT, Mary	27	M	Weaver	180c02Bb
FITZPATRICK, James	24	M	Laborer	180c02Bb
WALLACE, U-Mrs.	25	F	None	180c02Bb
HOBB, Robt.	23	M	Laborer	180c02Bb
DYER, John	26	M	Laborer	180c02Bb
JOHNSTON, Rebecca	28	F	None	180c02Bb
William-John	2	M	Child	180c02Bb
HAMES, Michael	60	M	Victualler	180c02Bb
Michael	35	M	Butler	180c02Bb
Robert	20	M	Butler	180c02Bb
Mary	22	F	None	180c02Bb
Margeret	17	F	None	180c02Bb
CANTWELL, James	24	M	Miller	180c02Bb
MCGLAUGHLAN, James	25	M	None	180c02Bb
HOGAN, Francis	26	M	Laborer	180c02Bb
OBRIAN, John	20	M	Engineer	180c02Bb
DARBY, Catherine	19	F	None	180c02Bb
FALLON, Sally	40	F	None	180c02Bb
Tady	9	M	Child	180c02Bb
Pat	8	M	Child	180c02Bb
Margeret	7	F	Child	180c02Bb
Michael	5	M	Child	180c02Bb
Mary	2	F	Child	180c02Bb
HARDGRAM, Eliza	55	F	None	180c02Bb
Died-At-Sea				
Benjm.	7	M	Child	180c02Bb
Thos.	3	M	Child	180c02Bb
SHANLEY, Jane	22	F	None	180c02Bb
HARDGRAN, Michael	22	M	Laborer	180c02Bb
Mary	17	F	None	180c02Bb
HOURIGHAN, John	18	M	Laborer	180c02Bb
Jude	13	F	None	180c02Bb
CARROLL, John	28	M	Laborer	180c02Bb
LYONS, Wm.	30	F	None	180c02Bb
ROCHFORD, Bridget	20	F	None	180c02Bb
LYONS, Ann	3	F	Child	180c02Bb
Francis	2	M	Child	180c02Bb
John	.06	M	Infant	180c02Bb
CUMMINS, Patk.	40	M	Carpenter	180c02Bb
Johana	17	F	None	180c02Bb
FAHY, Bessy	20	F	None	180c02Bb
NEVILLE, Mary	21	F	None	180c02Bb
LIDDY, Thomas	37	M	Laborer	180c02Bb
Judy	32	F	None	180c02Bb
Margeret	13	F	None	180c02Bb
Bridget	11	F	None	180c02Bb
Mary	10	F	None	180c02Bb
John	9	M	Child	180c02Bb
Ann	.08	F	Infant	180c02Bb
BURNS, William	25	M	Laborer	180c02Bb
Bridget	11	F	None	180c02Bb
Mary	9	F	Child	180c02Bb
Died-At-Sea				
TIERNEY, Ellen	22	F	None	180c02Bb
RILEY, Mary	45	F	None	180c02Bb
Mary	20	F	None	180c02Bb
CONOLLY, Catherine	25	F	None	180c02Bb
Mary	20	F	None	180c02Bb
BUTTERFIELD, Martin	37	M	Laborer	180c02Bb
Jane	35	F	None	180c02Bb
Elizabeth	13	F	None	180c02Bb
John	12	M	None	180c02Bb
Francis	10	M	None	180c02Bb
William	3	M	Child	180c02Bb
Joseph	.08	M	Infant	180c02Bb
Mary-Jane	7	F	Child	180c02Bb
Sarah-Jane	5	F	Child	180c02Bb
THOMSON, George	25	M	Smith	180c02Bb
MURPHY, John	40	M	Laborer	180c02Bb
Mary	30	F	None	180c02Bb
Helen	6	F	Child	180c02Bb
Michael	4	M	Child	180c02Bb
OBRIAN, Mary	27	F	None	180c02Bb
DOYLE, Ann	20	F	None	180c02Bb
OBRIEN, John	25	M	Laborer	180c02Bb

NAMES OF PASSENGERS	AGE	SEX	OCCUPATIONS	DATE PORT SHIP
BRADLEY, Patk.	25	M	Laborer	180c02Bb
Mary	27	F	None	180c02Bb
MCSWEENY, Bridget	24	F	None	180c02Bb
DALY, Thos.	50	M	Farmer	180c02Bb
Bridget	13	F	None	180c02Bb
Judith	11	F	None	180c02Bb
CUNNIFF, Mary	35	F	None	180c02Bb
Ellen	10	F	None	180c02Bb
Christopher	6	M	Child	180c02Bb
Mary	1	F	Child	180c02Bb
Thos.	.10	M	Infant	180c02Bb
MCADAM, John	21	M	Laborer	180c02Bb
DUGAN, Bridget	35	F	None	180c02Bb
Mary-Ann	12	F	None	180c02Bb
Hugh	10	M	None	180c02Bb
Henry	7	M	Child	180c02Bb
Susan	4	F	Child	180c02Bb
John	2	M	Child	180c02Bb
MCGREEVY, Catherine	30	F	None	180c02Bb
AVERAL, Richd.	20	M	Laborer	180c02Bb
MILLAR, Adam	19	M	Laborer	180c02Bb
SCOTT, Jeanette	50	F	None	180c02Bb
RUTHERFORD, John	30	M	Mason	180c02Bb
TIMONEY, John	28	M	Laborer	180c02Bb
Isabela	20	F	None	180c02Bb
MCNULTY, Catherine	20	F	None	180c02Bb
MUNNEY, Thos.	35	M	Farmer	180c02Bb
SMITH, Mary	16	F	None	180c02Bb
ODONNELL, Margeret	30	F	None	180c02Bb
Patk.	9	M	Child	180c02Bb
Robt.	4	M	Child	180c02Bb
Died-At-Sea				
GODFREY, John	30	M	Laborer	180c02Bb
U (W)	30	F	None	180c02Bb
SEDON, Patk.	26	M	Laborer	180c02Bb
KANE, Patk.	12	M	None	180c02Bb
Mathew	10	M	None	180c02Bb
SCOTT, George	22	M	Laborer	180c02Bb
Thomas	20	M	Laborer	180c02Bb
BIRGAN, Thomas	21	M	Laborer	180c02Bb
MAHONY, Margeret	28	F	None	180c02Bb
HILLBAINS, Joseph	24	M	Laborer	180c02Bb
COOK, James	31	M	Farmer	180c02Bb
U (W)	26	F	None	180c02Bb
KILLEY, Margeret	30	F	None	180c02Bb
Mary	20	F	None	180c02Bb
Mary	4	F	Child	180c02Bb
HAGERTY, Catherine	28	F	None	180c02Bb
Susan	.08	F	Infant	180c02Bb
HAW, Charles	23	M	Farmer	180c02Bb
U (W)	22	F	None	180c02Bb
ROBINSON, George	28	M	Laborer	180c02Bb
THISTLEWORTH, John	30	M	None	180c02Bb
RODGERS, Lydia	30	F	None	180c02Bb
George	6	M	Child	180c02Bb
Louisa	5	F	Child	180c02Bb
Eliza	.09	F	Infant	180c02Bb
PIGGIT, John	26	M	Farmer	180c02Bb
ROBINSON, John	28	M	Mason	180c02Bb
Robt.	21	M	Mason	180c02Bb
PEACOCK, Charles	28	M	Molder	180c02Bb
Philis	28	F	None	180c02Bb
CAMPBELL, Robt.	40	M	Laborer	180c02Bb
SERGENTSON, Eubank	42	M	Painter	180c02Bb
BEATIE, Catherine	70	F	None	180c02Bb
REINES, William	29	M	None	180c02Bb
James	4	M	Child	180c02Bb
William	2	M	Child	180c02Bb
CONROY, U	25	F	None	180c02Bb
MCSLANDIN, James	25	M	None	180c02Bb
PURSELL, Michael	30	M	Laborer	180c02Bb
HEANEY, James	30	M	Laborer	180c02Bb
MCGARRY, Thos.	25	M	Laborer	180c02Bb
CANTWELL, John	12	M	None	180c02Bb
ONEIL, John	30	M	None	180c02Bb

NAMES OF PASSENGERS	AGE	SEX	OCCUPATIONS	DATE PORT SHIP
LINCH, Patrick	26	M	None	180c02Bb

ENTERPRIZE 18 OCTOBER 1849

From Dublin

NAMES OF PASSENGERS	AGE	SEX	OCCUPATIONS	DATE PORT SHIP
FLETCHER, Sarah	20	F	Unknown	180c05Ab
CUNNINGHAM, David	20	M	Unknown	180c05Ab
BRANGAN, Bridget	24	F	Unknown	180c05Ab
MONK, Ann	30	F	Unknown	180c05Ab
Margt.	20	F	Unknown	180c05Ab
DUFFY, Margt.	22	F	Unknown	180c05Ab
GUDDING, Richard	10	M	Unknown	180c05Ab
COWLEY, Ann	15	F	Unknown	180c05Ab
MOLLONY, U-Mrs.	50	F	Unknown	180c05Ab
U	21	F	Unknown	180c05Ab
En--, Maria	22	F	Unknown	180c05Ab
Mcd--, Patrick	30	M	Unknown	180c05Ab
U (W)	28	F	Unknown	180c05Ab
LYNCH, John	16	M	Unknown	180c05Ab
Margt.	20	F	Unknown	180c05Ab
SHELBY, James	15	M	Unknown	180c05Ab
Michael	13	M	Unknown	180c05Ab
PATTERSON, U-Mrs.	30	F	Unknown	180c05Ab
Thos.	13	M	Unknown	180c05Ab
Bridget	12	F	Unknown	180c05Ab
DOYLE, Thomas	40	M	Unknown	180c05Ab
U (W)	45	F	Unknown	180c05Ab
Patt	20	M	Unknown	180c05Ab
James	15	M	Unknown	180c05Ab
CAVANAGH, Thomas	22	M	Unknown	180c05Ab
BRANIGAN, Cather.	24	F	Unknown	180c05Ab
HUSSEY, U-Mrs.	00	F	Unknown	180c05Ab
Patt	7	M	Child	180c05Ab
RODERICK, U-Mrs.	40	F	Unknown	180c05Ab
Bess	20	F	Unknown	180c05Ab
DUGAN, John	25	M	Unknown	180c05Ab
BYRNE, Cristy	30	M	Unknown	180c05Ab
Thomas	9	M	Child	180c05Ab
HOLMES, Richard	26	M	Unknown	180c05Ab
U (W)	25	F	Unknown	180c05Ab
Mal--, Ann	00	F	Unknown	180c05Ab
Judith	15	F	Unknown	180c05Ab
David	12	M	Unknown	180c05Ab
Died-At-Sea				
Mary	9	F	Child	180c05Ab
Cather.	7	F	Child	180c05Ab
Ellen	5	F	Child	180c05Ab
Michael	.00	M	Infant	180c05Ab
MALONE, Larance	5	M	Child	180c05Ab
U-Mrs.	45	F	Unknown	180c05Ab
Bridget	22	F	Unknown	180c05Ab
Kate	20	F	Unknown	180c05Ab
Ann	13	F	Unknown	180c05Ab
James	18	M	Unknown	180c05Ab
Michael	16	M	Unknown	180c05Ab
Murly	.00	M	Infant	180c05Ab
COSGROVE, R.	28	M	Unknown	180c05Ab
DAYLE, U	26	M	Unknown	180c05Ab
HALEY, U	20	M	Unknown	180c05Ab
DEVANY, Patt	23	M	Unknown	180c05Ab
JORDAN, John	20	M	Unknown	180c05Ab
LOWERY, Fran.	36	M	Unknown	180c05Ab
Mary	23	F	Unknown	180c05Ab
John	2	M	Child	180c05Ab
Eliza	.00	F	Infant	180c05Ab
BOWES, Honora	45	F	Unknown	180c05Ab
Margret	13	F	Unknown	180c05Ab
Patt	.00	M	Infant	180c05Ab
BYRNE, U-Mrs.	24	F	Unknown	180c05Ab
GREHAM, Michael	21	M	Unknown	180c05Ab
SEALEY, U-Mrs.	22	F	Unknown	180c05Ab
OBRYAN, U	20	M	Unknown	180c05Ab
BRADY, U	26	M	Unknown	180c05Ab
Eluca	24	F	Unknown	180c05Ab
KERNAN, Ann	20	F	Unknown	180c05Ab
Pare--, Mary	20	F	Unknown	180c05Ab
Sarah	19	F	Unknown	180c05Ab
CRANY, Lawrence	25	M	Unknown	180c05Ab
MASON, Rebecca	24	F	Unknown	180c05Ab
BERRY, Ellen	24	F	Unknown	180c05Ab
NOLAN, Ellen	22	F	Unknown	180c05Ab
BERRY, Terry	20	M	Unknown	180c05Ab
HALL, U-Mrs.	23	F	Unknown	180c05Ab
WILLIS, William	12	M	Unknown	180c05Ab
LYNCH, Thomas	26	M	Unknown	180c05Ab
U (W)	23	F	Unknown	180c05Ab
Margret	4	F	Child	180c05Ab
LANGAN, James	24	M	Unknown	180c05Ab
MULHALL, Cather.	25	F	Unknown	180c05Ab
IRWIN, U	27	M	Unknown	180c05Ab
FITZHARRAY, William	55	M	Unknown	180c05Ab
Jane	50	F	Unknown	180c05Ab
Mary	25	F	Unknown	180c05Ab
La--L	22	M	Unknown	180c05Ab
Lach--	20	M	Unknown	180c05Ab
Ellen	17	F	Unknown	180c05Ab
KEATING, Ned	60	M	Unknown	180c05Ab
Catherine	18	F	Unknown	180c05Ab
Arthur	13	M	Unknown	180c05Ab
CLEMENTS, W.	50	M	Unknown	180c05Ab
Mary	45	F	Unknown	180c05Ab
Died-At-Sea				
KERSHAW, Sarah	20	F	Unknown	180c05Ab
JAMES, Margret	20	F	Unknown	180c05Ab
BACON, Bridget	25	F	Unknown	180c05Ab
KAVAUGH, James	20	M	Unknown	180c05Ab
FOWERY, Wm.	22	M	Unknown	180c05Ab
SMITH, Ellen	17	F	Unknown	180c05Ab
Matt	16	M	Unknown	180c05Ab
THOMAS, U	30	M	Unknown	180c05Ab
U (W)	26	F	Unknown	180c05Ab
MORRIS, Joseph	20	M	Unknown	180c05Ab
Frances	16	F	Unknown	180c05Ab
HOLMES, Allen	25	F	Unknown	180c05Ab
Marto--, William	12	M	Unknown	180c05Ab
CLARK, Bridget	21	F	Unknown	180c05Ab
DOYLE, Kate	20	F	Unknown	180c05Ab
CANNAN, Bridget	23	F	Unknown	180c05Ab
DORAN, Biddy	26	F	Unknown	180c05Ab
KELLY, William	21	M	Unknown	180c05Ab
CONNERY, Michael	21	M	Unknown	180c05Ab
MITCHELL, Michael	20	M	Unknown	180c05Ab
WALSH, John	2	M	Child	180c05Ab
BUCKLEY, W.J.	50	M	Unknown	180c05Ab
Matt	23	M	Unknown	180c05Ab
Mary	28	F	Unknown	180c05Ab
Michael	21	F	Unknown	180c05Ab
Matt	18	F	Unknown	180c05Ab
William	16	M	Unknown	180c05Ab
Eliza	14	F	Unknown	180c05Ab
Ann	12	F	Unknown	180c05Ab
CONLEY, John	26	M	Unknown	180c05Ab
FANDY, B.	22	M	Unknown	180c05Ab
CARBEL, William-C.	13	M	Unknown	180c05Ab
HAND, U	30	M	Unknown	180c05Ab
CARROLL, Mary	50	F	Unknown	180c05Ab
Margret	13	F	Unknown	180c05Ab
FOLEY, U-Mrs.	27	F	Unknown	180c05Ab
Mary	5	F	Child	180c05Ab
Cather.	.00	F	Infant	180c05Ab
ROCK, Hugh	21	M	Unknown	180c05Ab
BARRY, James	32	M	Unknown	180c05Ab
JORDAN, T.	26	F	Unknown	180c05Ab

NAMES OF PASSENGERS	AGE	SEX	OCCUPATIONS	DATE PORT SHIP
MCALESTER, Cather.	22	F	Unknown	180c05Ab
EGAN, S.	22	M	Unknown	180c05Ab
Mary	20	F	Unknown	180c05Ab
Cather.	16	F	Unknown	180c05Ab
MCEVOY, Eliza	22	F	Unknown	180c05Ab
Mary	19	F	Unknown	180c05Ab
MCCAFFREY, John	25	M	Unknown	180c05Ab
Elizabeth	00	F	Unknown	180c05Ab
Died-At-Sea				
COFFEY, U	27	M	Unknown	180c05Ab
Died-At-Sea				
U (W)	26	F	Unknown	180c05Ab
Eliza	2	F	Child	180c05Ab
Mary-Ann	.00	F	Infant	180c05Ab
Mary	50	F	Unknown	180c05Ab
Eliza	20	F	Unknown	180c05Ab
James	28	M	Unknown	180c05Ab
Cristy	25	M	Unknown	180c05Ab
Patt	23	M	Unknown	180c05Ab
MCMULLEN, James	46	M	Unknown	180c05Ab
MAYSON, William	16	M	Unknown	180c05Ab
FOLEY, U	24	M	Unknown	180c05Ab
LYNCH, James	25	M	Unknown	180c05Ab
COLLINS, Alley	40	F	Unknown	180c05Ab
Martin	13	M	Unknown	180c05Ab
Cather.	20	F	Unknown	180c05Ab
Joseph	10	M	Unknown	180c05Ab
Peter	10	M	Unknown	180c05Ab
Died-At-Sea				
Biddy	8	F	Child	180c05Ab
Stephan	5	M	Child	180c05Ab
Michael	3	M	Child	180c05Ab
HENRY, Cather.	20	F	Unknown	180c05Ab
MANNY, Mary	20	F	Unknown	180c05Ab
MORAN, Cath.	20	F	Unknown	180c05Ab
BENN, Selia	20	F	Unknown	180c05Ab
HUNT, U	20	F	Unknown	180c05Ab
GAY, Ed.	20	M	Unknown	180c05Ab
WALSH, U	25	M	Unknown	180c05Ab
U (W)	23	F	Unknown	180c05Ab
John	3	M	Child	180c05Ab
Julia	.00	F	Infant	180c05Ab
USHER, John	25	M	Unknown	180c05Ab

SARAH-MARIA 19 OCTOBER 1849

From Sligo

NAMES OF PASSENGERS	AGE	SEX	OCCUPATIONS	DATE PORT SHIP
GORDON, Mary	30	F	Spinster	190c09Bc
REGAN, Honora	19	F	Spinster	190c09Bc
GILHOOLEY, Catherine	18	F	Spinster	190c09Bc
BURNETT, Jane	20	F	Spinster	190c09Bc
DOHERTY, Jane	20	F	Matron	190c09Bc
Eliza	.00	F	Infant	190c09Bc
MAGUIRE, Matty	30	F	Matron	190c09Bc
Thomas	10	M	None	190c09Bc
Michael	8	M	Child	190c09Bc
Terence	4	M	Child	190c09Bc
GARVEN, Pat	24	M	Farmer	190c09Bc
CULLEN, Bridget	24	F	Spinster	190c09Bc
HOPE, Jno.	32	M	Farmer	190c09Bc
MIDDLETON, Mary	40	F	Matron	190c09Bc
Jane	20	F	Spinster	190c09Bc
Thomas	21	M	Farmer	190c09Bc
CLANCEY, Mary	19	F	Spinster	190c09Bc
Biddy	17	F	Spinster	190c09Bc
MCGUIRE, Frank	21	M	Farmer	190c09Bc
CLENTON, Honora	10	F	None	190c09Bc
Bernard	8	M	Child	190c09Bc
TRAVERSE, Catherine	20	F	Spinster	190c09Bc
FAHANY, Catherine	19	F	Spinster	190c09Bc
CARR, Thomas	22	M	Farmer	190c09Bc
KEEGAN, Catherine	20	F	Spinster	190c09Bc
CONROY, Bridget	14	F	Spinster	190c09Bc
Peggy	10	F	Spinster	190c09Bc
BARNEY, Elizabeth	21	F	Spinster	190c09Bc
WALSH, Henry	9	M	Child	190c09Bc
SMITH, William	19	M	Laborer	190c09Bc
MEHAN, Peter	28	M	Laborer	190c09Bc
FOY, Winey	19	F	Spinster	190c09Bc
CLANREY, Margaret	18	F	Spinster	190c09Bc
Walter	12	M	Laborer	190c09Bc
KROLAHIN, Jas.	24	M	Block Maker	190c09Bc
GELHOOLY, Rose	23	F	Wife	190c09Bc
Died-At-Sea				
FLYN, Catherine	.10	F	Infant	190c09Bc
OCONNOR, Dormas	22	F	Spinster	190c09Bc
MILDORN, Margaret	19	F	Spinster	190c09Bc
William	29	M	Mason	190c09Bc
KROLAHAN, Maria	30	F	Matron	190c09Bc
Jno.	10	M	None	190c09Bc
OHARA, Mary	19	F	Spinster	190c09Bc
CAMPBELL, James	30	M	Farmer	190c09Bc
FLYNN, James	20	M	Farmer	190c09Bc
VERNON, William	17	M	None	190c09Bc
CALLAN, Henry	19	M	Laborer	190c09Bc
MCNULTY, Michael	70	M	Laborer	190c09Bc
SWEENEY, Catherine	18	F	Spinster	190c09Bc
Mary	17	F	Spinster	190c09Bc
KROLAHAN, Mary	28	F	Matron	190c09Bc
Jane	.00	F	Infant	190c09Bc
Margaret	7	F	Child	190c09Bc
Mary	5	F	Child	190c09Bc
FIENY, Bridget	19	F	Spinster	190c09Bc
Catherine	17	F	Spinster	190c09Bc
GILGAN, Ann	19	F	Spinster	190c09Bc
HART, Michael	31	M	Farmer	190c09Bc
MEHAN, William	40	M	Farmer	190c09Bc
RORKE, Beezy	20	F	Spinster	190c09Bc
MCNORRA, Pat	21	M	Farmer	190c09Bc
MCGREENY, Jno.	20	M	Farmer	190c09Bc
Margaret	19	F	Wife	190c09Bc
ROONEY, Thomas	38	M	Farmer	190c09Bc
Jane	36	F	Wife	190c09Bc
Joseph	.09	M	Infant	190c09Bc
Catherine	5	F	Child	190c09Bc
Simon	40	M	None	190c09Bc
REED, Jane	19	F	Wi	190c09Bc
Thomas	10	M	None	190c09Bc
Robt.	45	M	None	190c09Bc
Joseph	28	M	None	190c09Bc
Sarah	29	F	Wi	190c09Bc
CULLEN, Anthony	20	M	Farmer	190c09Bc
James	19	M	Farmer	190c09Bc
CAREY, Charlotte	18	F	Spinster	190c09Bc
Jane	19	F	Spinster	190c09Bc
COSGROVE, Ann	17	F	Spinster	190c09Bc

MORTIMER-LIVINGSTON 19 OCTOBER 1849

From Liverpool

NAMES OF PASSENGERS	AGE	SEX	OCCUPATIONS	DATE PORT SHIP
DUNN, Mary	27	F	Farmer	190c02Bs
BARNBROOK, Joseph	27	M	Unknown	190c02Bs
WOODS, Jane	40	F	Unknown	190c02Bs
SULLIVAN, Cathe.	35	F	Unknown	190c02Bs
WOODS, Patrk.	9	M	Child	190c02Bs
Margt.	7	F	Child	190c02Bs

NAMES OF PASSENGERS	AGE	SEX	OCCUPATIONS	DATE PORT SHIP
WOODS, Cathe.	4	F	Child	190c02Bs
Bridget	2	F	Child	190c02Bs
GILBERT, Geo.	26	M	Unknown	190c02Bs
Jane	28	F	Unknown	190c02Bs
BUCKSTON, Fredk.S.	26	M	Unknown	190c02Bs
BROODY, Cathe.	22	F	Unknown	190c02Bs
GOIN, George	22	M	Unknown	190c02Bs
JONES, Mary-Ann	29	F	Unknown	190c02Bs
BISHOP, Saml.	25	M	Unknown	190c02Bs
FALLON, Elizh.	41	F	Unknown	190c02Bs
Martin	8	M	Child	190c02Bs
Edwd.	4	M	Child	190c02Bs
RYAN, Michl.	25	M	Unknown	190c02Bs
KENNEDY, Thos.	21	M	Unknown	190c02Bs
QUIGLEY, Michl.	20	M	Unknown	190c02Bs
HICKEY, Thos.	22	M	Unknown	190c02Bs
QUIGLEY, John	23	M	Unknown	190c02Bs
GLASHON, Jeremiah	27	M	Unknown	190c02Bs
BOYLE, Michl.	15	M	Unknown	190c02Bs
WALSH, Honora	28	F	Unknown	190c02Bs
John	4	M	Child	190c02Bs
Jas.	2	M	Child	190c02Bs
Michl.	.00	M	Infant	190c02Bs
CREED, Bridgt.	19	F	Unknown	190c02Bs
WALSH, Mary	17	F	Unknown	190c02Bs
KERR, Wm.	30	M	Unknown	190c02Bs
Elzh.	30	F	Unknown	190c02Bs
Wm.	9	M	Child	190c02Bs
Sarah	7	F	Child	190c02Bs
FELLIN, Jas.	21	M	Unknown	190c02Bs
MCCONNELL, Peter	22	M	Unknown	190c02Bs
MCVAY, Felix	20	M	Unknown	190c02Bs
HAYES, Ellen	25	F	Unknown	190c02Bs
LYNCH, Ann	30	F	Unknown	190c02Bs
Cathe.	4	F	Child	190c02Bs
Fanny	3	F	Child	190c02Bs
Jno.	.00	M	Infant	190c02Bs
COSGROVE, Jno.	42	M	Unknown	190c02Bs
POWERS, Geo.	37	M	Unknown	190c02Bs
HUNT, Wm.	30	M	Unknown	190c02Bs
Sabina	26	F	Unknown	190c02Bs
CULLEN, Corns.	23	M	Unknown	190c02Bs
Michl.	21	M	Unknown	190c02Bs
Jas.	23	M	Unknown	190c02Bs
Cathe.	30	F	Unknown	190c02Bs
Rebecca	.00	F	Infant	190c02Bs
Timothy	13	M	Unknown	190c02Bs
Michl.	7	M	Child	190c02Bs
Jno.	5	M	Child	190c02Bs
HENNESSY, Danl.	26	M	Unknown	190c02Bs
MCCARTY, Dennis Died-At-Sea	80	M	Unknown	190c02Bs
Anorah	70	F	Unknown	190c02Bs
Felix	28	M	Unknown	190c02Bs
Mary	26	F	Unknown	190c02Bs
Bridgt.	25	F	Unknown	190c02Bs
Dennis	23	M	Unknown	190c02Bs
Wm.	22	M	Unknown	190c02Bs
Eugene	20	M	Unknown	190c02Bs
Jas.	10	M	Unknown	190c02Bs
BRENNAN, Mary	70	F	Unknown	190c02Bs
SHEA, Mary	25	F	Unknown	190c02Bs
KENNY, Mary	26	F	Unknown	190c02Bs
SHEA, Mary	24	F	Unknown	190c02Bs
GRAHAM, Michl.	20	M	Unknown	190c02Bs
QUIGLEY, Andw.	30	M	Unknown	190c02Bs
Jas.	8	M	Child	190c02Bs
Judy	25	F	Unknown	190c02Bs
Cathe.	9	F	Child	190c02Bs
Mary	3	F	Child	190c02Bs
CONCANNON, Patrk.	20	M	Unknown	190c02Bs
REYNOLDS, Wm.	36	M	Unknown	190c02Bs
Elizh.	50	F	Unknown	190c02Bs
Margt.	20	F	Unknown	190c02Bs
Elizh.	16	F	Unknown	190c02Bs
HEALY, Cathe.	26	F	Unknown	190c02Bs
DUGGAN, Wm.	30	F	Unknown	190c02Bs
MAHON, Jno.	20	F	Unknown	190c02Bs
MCCORMIC, Dennis	30	M	Unknown	190c02Bs
FOX, Honora	40	F	Unknown	190c02Bs
GREEN, Jas.	24	M	Unknown	190c02Bs
MCCUE, Patrk.	34	M	Unknown	190c02Bs
HOBSWORTH, Saml.	20	M	Unknown	190c02Bs
FOX, Mary	.00	F	Infant	190c02Bs
MCCULL, Wm.	36	M	Unknown	190c02Bs
MEHAN, Margt.	23	F	Unknown	190c02Bs
MEAD, Bridget	20	F	Unknown	190c02Bs
Margt.	18	F	Unknown	190c02Bs
Ann	16	F	Unknown	190c02Bs
MOLONEY, Hannah	19	F	Unknown	190c02Bs
Wm.	15	M	Unknown	190c02Bs
Patrk.	13	M	Unknown	190c02Bs
Ann	5	F	Child	190c02Bs
RUSSELL, Jas.	40	M	Unknown	190c02Bs
BORTHENY, Wm.	31	M	Unknown	190c02Bs
SHUDY, Jno.	35	M	Unknown	190c02Bs
MCKINNEY, Thos.	24	M	Unknown	190c02Bs
MCCOSORT, Michl.	22	M	Unknown	190c02Bs
MASKEY, Lawrence	24	M	Unknown	190c02Bs
BLAKE, Thos.	15	M	Unknown	190c02Bs
Eliza	21	F	Unknown	190c02Bs
JENNINGS, A.	19	M	Unknown	190c02Bs
KELLY, Margt.	60	F	Unknown	190c02Bs
SWIFT, Margt.	27	F	Unknown	190c02Bs
Rosanna	7	F	Child	190c02Bs
Elizh.	4	F	Child	190c02Bs
Mary	.00	F	Infant	190c02Bs
MCDANIEL, Mary	28	F	Unknown	190c02Bs
Wm.	2	M	Child	190c02Bs
Jermh.	.00	M	Infant	190c02Bs
Danl.	32	M	Unknown	190c02Bs
LAMB, Mary	17	F	Unknown	190c02Bs
Maria	19	F	Unknown	190c02Bs
KELLY, Honora	22	F	Unknown	190c02Bs
TYNE, Julia	20	F	Unknown	190c02Bs
Eliza	18	F	Unknown	190c02Bs
FLANNARY, Patrk.	20	M	Unknown	190c02Bs
Jane	19	F	Unknown	190c02Bs
JOHNSON, Saml.	25	M	Unknown	190c02Bs
RILEY, Mary	27	F	Unknown	190c02Bs
John	14	M	Unknown	190c02Bs
Cathe.	12	F	Unknown	190c02Bs
Pat	10	M	Unknown	190c02Bs
Mary	5	F	Child	190c02Bs
SHEEREN, Patrk.	20	M	Unknown	190c02Bs
ORILEY, Farrel	20	M	Unknown	190c02Bs
REAGAN, Mathw.	28	M	Unknown	190c02Bs
PRESTON, Mary	19	F	Unknown	190c02Bs
HEALY, Cathe. Died-At-Sea	55	F	Unknown	190c02Bs
Jno.	15	M	Unknown	190c02Bs
HESLEY, Martin	11	M	Unknown	190c02Bs
Margt.	8	F	Child	190c02Bs
Mary	4	F	Child	190c02Bs
BYRNE, Mary	40	F	Unknown	190c02Bs
KOUGH, Patrk.	27	M	Unknown	190c02Bs
MURPHY, Dennis Died-At-Sea	55	M	Unknown	190c02Bs
Mary Died-At-Sea	30	F	Unknown	190c02Bs
Jno. Died-At-Sea	1	M	Child	190c02Bs
Jno. Died-At-Sea	23	M	Unknown	190c02Bs
Danl.	21	M	Unknown	190c02Bs
Dennis	9	M	Child	190c02Bs
Nora	5	F	Child	190c02Bs
Tim	3	M	Child	190c02Bs
Johannah	15	F	Unknown	190c02Bs
CLARKE, Jno.	27	M	Unknown	190c02Bs

NAMES OF PASSENGERS	AGE	SEX	OCCUPATIONS	DATE PORT SHIP
LALLY, Martin	30	M	Unknown	190c02Bs
BATES, Stephen	34	M	Unknown	190c02Bs
Elizh.	34	F	Unknown	190c02Bs
Thos.	8	M	Child	190c02Bs
Stephen-Jr.	6	M	Child	190c02Bs
Died-At-Sea				
Joseph	4	M	Child	190c02Bs
Danl.	1	M	Child	190c02Bs
Elizh.	.00	F	Infant	190c02Bs
RATHBONE, Jno.	30	M	Unknown	190c02Bs
PARKS, Mary	30	F	Unknown	190c02Bs
Elizh.	8	F	Child	190c02Bs
HARRIS, Ann	48	F	Unknown	190c02Bs
CULLEN, Caroline	22	F	Unknown	190c02Bs
HARRIS, Abrhm.	11	M	Unknown	190c02Bs
Thos.	10	M	Unknown	190c02Bs
Sarah	9	F	Child	190c02Bs
MCGLOUGHLIN, Jno.	33	M	Unknown	190c02Bs
MAY, Susan	23	F	Unknown	190c02Bs
Cathe.	34	F	Unknown	190c02Bs
Jno.	27	M	Unknown	190c02Bs
LEE, Thos.	19	M	Unknown	190c02Bs
KENT, Jas.	20	M	Unknown	190c02Bs
STEWART, Wm.	20	M	Unknown	190c02Bs
BANG, Jacob	20	M	Unknown	190c02Bs
COSTALLO, Wm.	39	M	Unknown	190c02Bs
MCCARTY, Danl.	26	M	Unknown	190c02Bs
CAVIN, Mary	15	F	Unknown	190c02Bs
Jno.	11	M	Unknown	190c02Bs
FINAN, Margt.	22	F	Unknown	190c02Bs
FLANAGAN, Bridget	20	F	Unknown	190c02Bs
DAVINE, Thos.	21	M	Unknown	190c02Bs
TRACY, Ann	18	F	Unknown	190c02Bs
MOOLEY, Bridget	17	F	Unknown	190c02Bs
MCGUIRE, Mary	12	F	Unknown	190c02Bs
FARREL, Bridget	19	F	Unknown	190c02Bs
LARKIN, Mary	14	F	Unknown	190c02Bs
MURRAY, Margt.	25	F	Unknown	190c02Bs
John	2	M	Child	190c02Bs
KOUGH, Mary	25	F	Unknown	190c02Bs
HEANY, Thos.	17	M	Unknown	190c02Bs
CANE, Matilda	25	F	Unknown	190c02Bs
MURPHY, Bridgt.	26	F	Unknown	190c02Bs
CANE, Eliza	4	F	Child	190c02Bs
Michl.	2	M	Child	190c02Bs
SHINE, Michl.	18	M	Unknown	190c02Bs
MARTIN, Hugh	13	M	Unknown	190c02Bs
BLAIR, Jas.	54	M	Unknown	190c02Bs
Mary	52	F	Unknown	190c02Bs
Ruth	19	F	Unknown	190c02Bs
Elizh.	16	F	Unknown	190c02Bs
Mary-Ann	10	F	Unknown	190c02Bs
Sarah	8	F	Child	190c02Bs
Matilda	6	F	Child	190c02Bs
Danl.	13	M	Unknown	190c02Bs
HARRISON, Thos.	24	M	Unknown	190c02Bs
COCKRAN, Patrk.	60	M	Unknown	190c02Bs
Michl.	29	M	Unknown	190c02Bs
HOLLAND, Phillip	14	M	Unknown	190c02Bs
RODGERS, Jno.	48	M	Unknown	190c02Bs
SULLIVAN, Mary	29	F	Unknown	190c02Bs
POWER, Thos.	21	M	Unknown	190c02Bs
CHADD, Thos.	18	M	Unknown	190c02Bs
HIGGINS, Jno.	31	M	Unknown	190c02Bs
KAUGHTON, Mary	24	F	Unknown	190c02Bs
CHADD, Jonathan	25	M	Unknown	190c02Bs
Died-At-Sea				
KELLET, Chas.	19	M	Unknown	190c02Bs
HANLAN, Geo.	49	M	Unknown	190c02Bs
Geo.Jr.	20	M	Unknown	190c02Bs
Died-At-Sea				
LYONS, Ellen	40	F	Unknown	190c02Bs
CROGAN, Cathe.	40	F	Unknown	190c02Bs
QUIN, Mary	30	F	Unknown	190c02Bs
Anne	.00	F	Infant	190c02Bs

NAMES OF PASSENGERS	AGE	SEX	OCCUPATIONS	DATE PORT SHIP
MCGUIRE, Jas.	26	M	Unknown	190c02Bs
MOLAHAN, Pat	17	M	Unknown	190c02Bs
Mary	18	F	Unknown	190c02Bs
MCCORMIC, Ellen	20	F	Unknown	190c02Bs
HAND, Mary	19	F	Unknown	190c02Bs
MCCABE, Cathe.	28	F	Unknown	190c02Bs
DELAHANSTY, Ann	21	F	Unknown	190c02Bs
ELKSTONE, Paul	26	M	Unknown	190c02Bs
KILLELIE, Ann	20	F	Unknown	190c02Bs
Rose	18	F	Unknown	190c02Bs
SHANNEHAN, Johanna	30	F	Unknown	190c02Bs
Mary	12	F	Unknown	190c02Bs
Honora	10	F	Unknown	190c02Bs
John	6	M	Child	190c02Bs
Corns.	4	M	Child	190c02Bs
Ellen	9	F	Child	190c02Bs
CARROLL, Peggy	17	F	None	190c02Bs
GLEESON, Cathe.	20	F	None	190c02Bs
Cathe.	8	F	Child	190c02Bs
COLLINS, Owen	32	M	Unknown	190c02Bs
DUNDASS, Hugh	60	M	Unknown	190c02Bs
Lucy	20	F	Unknown	190c02Bs
GILDEN, Bridget	45	F	Unknown	190c02Bs
MCNELLY, Patrk.	47	F	Unknown	190c02Bs
R.-Mrs.	40	F	Unknown	190c02Bs
Rodger	20	M	Unknown	190c02Bs
John	14	M	Unknown	190c02Bs
Michl.	18	M	Unknown	190c02Bs
Rose	4	M	Child	190c02Bs
MONTGOMERY, Ellen	20	F	Unknown	190c02Bs
COLEMAN, Jane	20	F	Unknown	190c02Bs
CRANE, Wm.	31	M	Unknown	190c02Bs
Ann	28	F	Unknown	190c02Bs
Bridget	20	F	Unknown	190c02Bs
DICKINSON, David	38	M	Unknown	190c02Bs
WIRES, Mary	50	F	Unknown	190c02Bs
Jas.	15	M	Unknown	190c02Bs
NUGENT, Christian	19	F	Unknown	190c02Bs
MARSHALL, Bridgt.	19	F	Unknown	190c02Bs
KILCANNON, Wm.	20	M	Unknown	190c02Bs
JEFFERS, Wm.	21	M	Unknown	190c02Bs
MUNRO, Mary	18	F	Unknown	190c02Bs
KILROY, John	48	M	Unknown	190c02Bs
JUDGE, Dominic	40	M	Unknown	190c02Bs
Died-At-Sea				
HEMMENWAY, Jno.	21	M	Unknown	190c02Bs
KANE, Ellen	20	F	Unknown	190c02Bs
Ellen	18	F	Unknown	190c02Bs
GOODWIN, Saml.	31	M	Unknown	190c02Bs
MCAULEY, Margt.	25	F	Unknown	190c02Bs
GILBERT, Geo.	26	M	Artist	190c02Bs
U (W)	28	F	Unknown	190c02Bs
CARY, U-Mrs.	24	F	Unknown	190c02Bs
ADAMS, G.C.	24	M	Student	190c02Bs

MARGARET-EVANS 19 OCTOBER 1849

From London

NAMES OF PASSENGERS	AGE	SEX	OCCUPATIONS	DATE PORT SHIP
DACEY, Ann	28	F	Unknown	190c06Bf
OKEATH, Mary	30	F	Unknown	190c06Bf
John	10	M	Unknown	190c06Bf
HOWARD, Martin	22	M	Laborer	190c06Bf
HANRAHN, Mary-Ann	24	F	Unknown	190c06Bf
CARROL, Bridget	23	F	Unknown	190c06Bf
Elizabeth	21	F	Unknown	190c06Bf
SHEPHERD, Ellen	28	F	Unknown	190c06Bf
Catherine	20	F	Unknown	190c06Bf
SLATER, Patrick	38	M	Carpenter	190c06Bf

NAMES OF PASSENGERS	AGE	SEX	OCCUPATIONS	DATE PORT SHIP
OBRIEN, Catherine	48	F	Unknown	190c06Bf
Mary	18	F	Servant	190c06Bf
Edward	12	M	Unknown	190c06Bf
Ellen	9	F	Child	190c06Bf
TWOOMAY, William	28	M	Laborer	190c06Bf
MURPHY, John	23	M	Laborer	190c06Bf
REED, Daniel	20	M	Laborer	190c06Bf
KELLY, Cornelius	30	M	Shoemaker	190c06Bf
MCKAY, Julia	35	F	Unknown	190c06Bf
REED, Margaret	27	F	Unknown	190c06Bf
GRADY, Mary	23	F	Unknown	190c06Bf
HAYDEN, John	32	M	Bootmaker	190c06Bf
CLARK, Alice	18	F	Unknown	190c06Bf
KELLY, Mary	52	F	Unknown	190c06Bf
Joseph	22	M	Laborer	190c06Bf
James	20	M	Laborer	190c06Bf
Patrick	18	M	Laborer	190c06Bf
Jane	16	F	Servant	190c06Bf
William	9	M	Child	190c06Bf
HUTCHINSON, Hugh	35	M	Laborer	190c06Bf
Mary	32	F	Unknown	190c06Bf
Samuel	11	M	Unknown	190c06Bf
Jane	8	F	Child	190c06Bf
William	6	M	Child	190c06Bf
Eliza	2	F	Child	190c06Bf
Mary	12	F	Unknown	190c06Bf
TUCKER, James	26	M	Laborer	190c06Bf

IVANHOE 19 OCTOBER 1849

From Liverpool

NAMES OF PASSENGERS	AGE	SEX	OCCUPATIONS	DATE PORT SHIP
HUGHES, Francis	30	M	Soap Maker	190c02Bt
MCARDLE, Jno.	26	M	Laborer	190c02Bt
MOORE, Thomas	25	M	Carpenter	190c02Bt
SMITH, Margaret	16	F	Unknown	190c02Bt
James	14	M	Unknown	190c02Bt
John	11	M	Unknown	190c02Bt
Mary	2	F	Child	190c02Bt
KELLY, Mary	20	F	Unknown	190c02Bt
Celina	19	F	Unknown	190c02Bt
CONNOLLY, Thomas	20	M	Laborer	190c02Bt
Rose	18	F	Unknown	190c02Bt
DUFFY, Peter	10	M	Unknown	190c02Bt
Thomas	8	M	Child	190c02Bt
WARD, Anne	10	F	Unknown	190c02Bt
MOORE, Thomas	34	M	Carpenter	190c02Bt
Anne	27	F	Unknown	190c02Bt
Richard	7	M	Child	190c02Bt
Anne	3	F	Child	190c02Bt
Rose	.00	F	Infant	190c02Bt
Thomas	12	M	Unknown	190c02Bt
John	11	M	Unknown	190c02Bt
KELLY, Anne	21	F	Spinster	190c02Bt
MULDOON, Cathn.	19	F	Spinster	190c02Bt
PHEALY, William	20	M	Laborer	190c02Bt
HARMON, Edmond	24	M	Laborer	190c02Bt
MAHONEY, Patk.	30	M	Laborer	190c02Bt
CARROLL, Morris	23	M	Laborer	190c02Bt
MORIARTY, Garrett	24	M	Laborer	190c02Bt
STACK, Julia	21	F	Spinster	190c02Bt
KENNA, Julia	20	F	Spinster	190c02Bt
DRURY, Johannah	23	F	Spinster	190c02Bt
HALPEN, Bridget	24	F	Spinster	190c02Bt
BYRNE, James	35	M	Laborer	190c02Bt
Mary	30	F	Laborer	190c02Bt
Thomas	5	M	Child	190c02Bt
Edward	3	M	Child	190c02Bt
Anne	30	F	Spinster	190c02Bt

NAMES OF PASSENGERS	AGE	SEX	OCCUPATIONS	DATE PORT SHIP
BELL, Maria	30	F	Spinster	190c02Bt
Mary-Ann	13	F	Spinster	190c02Bt
MCKEOWN, Margt.	25	F	Spinster	190c02Bt
BUCKLY, John	36	M	Farmer	190c02Bt
U-Mrs.	35	F	Unknown	190c02Bt
Honora	15	F	Unknown	190c02Bt
Margaret	13	F	Unknown	190c02Bt
Jeremiah	11	M	Unknown	190c02Bt
Edmond	9	M	Child	190c02Bt
Catherine	6	F	Child	190c02Bt
Sarah	3	F	Child	190c02Bt
John	1	M	Child	190c02Bt
BRADY, Thos.	19	M	Laborer	190c02Bt
WILLIS, Thos.	18	M	Laborer	190c02Bt
REILLY, Margaret	50	F	Unknown	190c02Bt
BEGG, Richard	40	M	Tailor	190c02Bt
DUNNE, Thomas	21	M	Laborer	190c02Bt
CROUGH, Ellen	20	F	Unknown	190c02Bt
TYNAN, Mary	22	F	Unknown	190c02Bt
DUNE, Mary	.00	F	Infant	190c02Bt
SPLAIN, Mary	35	F	Unknown	190c02Bt
Ony	12	F	Unknown	190c02Bt
William	10	M	Unknown	190c02Bt
Michael	8	M	Child	190c02Bt
Patrick	6	M	Child	190c02Bt
SWEENEY, Michael	38	M	Unknown	190c02Bt
Mary	34	F	Unknown	190c02Bt
Thomas	9	M	Child	190c02Bt
Ellen	4	F	Child	190c02Bt
Anty	.00	M	Infant	190c02Bt
CAMPION, Patk.	48	M	Laborer	190c02Bt
ROURKE, James	30	M	Laborer	190c02Bt
MAHON, Patrick	48	M	Laborer	190c02Bt
BYRNE, Patk.	22	M	Laborer	190c02Bt
MURTAGH, Mary	27	F	Spinster	190c02Bt
COX, Patrick	35	M	Laborer	190c02Bt
Mary	26	F	Unknown	190c02Bt
KENNY, John	11	M	Laborer	190c02Bt
SUMMERS, John	23	M	Mason	190c02Bt
Mary	23	F	Unknown	190c02Bt
William	.00	M	Infant	190c02Bt
ADDY, Jane	25	F	Unknown	190c02Bt
Edward	11	M	Unknown	190c02Bt
George	9	M	Child	190c02Bt
Bridget	7	F	Child	190c02Bt
Matthew	5	M	Child	190c02Bt
Julia	3	F	Child	190c02Bt
John	1	M	Child	190c02Bt
CLARKE, Mary	22	F	Servant	190c02Bt
ROLAND, Mary	26	F	Unknown	190c02Bt
Cathn.	7	F	Child	190c02Bt
Michael	.00	M	Infant	190c02Bt
REILLY, Bridget	24	F	Unknown	190c02Bt
BREEN, Mary	21	F	Unknown	190c02Bt
MCGUIRE, Cathn.	13	F	Unknown	190c02Bt
MAHONY, Francis	20	M	Seaman	190c02Bt
SHARPE, Philip	22	M	Laborer	190c02Bt
OLIVER, Mary-Mrs.	40	F	Unknown	190c02Bt
Jno.	8	M	Child	190c02Bt
Thomas	6	M	Child	190c02Bt
William	2	M	Child	190c02Bt
Margt.	20	F	Unknown	190c02Bt
BRIDE, Bridgt.	22	F	Spinster	190c02Bt
MURPHY, Patt	22	M	Laborer	190c02Bt
Cathn.	4	F	Child	190c02Bt
BAYNE, Michael	22	M	Laborer	190c02Bt
Chas.	18	M	Laborer	190c02Bt
Peter	22	M	Laborer	190c02Bt
MAHON, Michl.	20	M	Laborer	190c02Bt
PATON, Ellen-Maria	20	F	Spinster	190c02Bt
KAVANAH, Mary	22	F	Spinster	190c02Bt
COX, Michl.	26	M	Laborer	190c02Bt
ROCHE, Mathew	21	M	Laborer	190c02Bt
DORAN, Margt.	22	F	Servant	190c02Bt
Cathn.	20	F	Servant	190c02Bt

NAMES OF PASSENGERS	AGE	SEX	OCCUPATIONS	DATE PORT SHIP
DORRY, Betsy	24	F	Unknown	190c02Bt
NOONAN, Bridget	28	F	Unknown	190c02Bt
STEPHENSON, Jane	22	F	Unknown	190c02Bt
BROWN, Eliza	19	F	Unknown	190c02Bt
Matilda	21	F	Unknown	190c02Bt
MCLEAN, George	30	M	Teacher	190c02Bt
U-Mrs.	30	F	Teacher	190c02Bt
MURPHY, Michael	34	M	Laborer	190c02Bt
U-Mrs.	24	F	Unknown	190c02Bt
WICKHAM, Thos.	26	M	Laborer	190c02Bt
MCGURGAM, Ellen	20	F	Unknown	190c02Bt
DEVLIN, Mary	20	F	Unknown	190c02Bt
KEENAHAN, John	21	M	Clerk	190c02Bt
CARTY, David	22	M	Laborer	190c02Bt
DUNNE, James	21	M	Laborer	190c02Bt
HICKS, James	19	M	Boot Closer	190c02Bt
BLAKE, John	37	M	Laborer	190c02Bt
PATTON, Ellen	25	F	Laborer	190c02Bt
WAUGHAN, John	24	M	Farmer	190c02Bt
CONNOR, Danl.	23	M	Farmer	190c02Bt
Bridgt.	23	F	Unknown	190c02Bt
CAUGHTON, Mary	22	F	Unknown	190c02Bt
Ellen	21	F	Unknown	190c02Bt
BARRY, Margt.	30	F	Unknown	190c02Bt
Honora	12	F	Unknown	190c02Bt
Michael	10	M	Unknown	190c02Bt
REED, John	10	M	Unknown	190c02Bt
Mary-Anne	.11	F	Infant	190c02Bt
JONES, Thos.	28	M	Farmer	190c02Bt
FOGARTY, Patt	24	M	Farmer	190c02Bt
HAYES, Dennis	21	M	Laborer	190c02Bt
QUADE, Patk.	11	M	Unknown	190c02Bt
HOWETT, Sarah	28	F	Unknown	190c02Bt
William	6	M	Child	190c02Bt
Moses	4	M	Child	190c02Bt
Mary-Anne	2	F	Child	190c02Bt
U	.10	U	Infant	190c02Bt
JORDAN, Phillip	20	M	Unknown	190c02Bt
TOBIN, Mary	24	F	Unknown	190c02Bt
SULLIVAN, Jno.	28	M	Shoemaker	190c02Bt
Judy	24	F	Unknown	190c02Bt
James	10	M	Unknown	190c02Bt
Eugene	1	M	Child	190c02Bt
COONEY, Mary	26	F	Unknown	190c02Bt
STANTON, Cathn.	26	F	Unknown	190c02Bt
SULLIVAN, Mary	19	F	Unknown	190c02Bt
MURPHY, Mary	20	F	Unknown	190c02Bt
MAHONEY, Mary	24	F	Unknown	190c02Bt
BURLEY, Ann	24	F	Unknown	190c02Bt
BARRY, James	28	M	Laborer	190c02Bt
FLYNNE, Timothy	50	M	Smith	190c02Bt
Ellen	49	F	Unknown	190c02Bt
Dennis	21	M	Unknown	190c02Bt
Thomas	19	M	Unknown	190c02Bt
Eliza	21	F	Unknown	190c02Bt
Catherine	13	F	Unknown	190c02Bt
SLATTERY, William	40	M	Laborer	190c02Bt
John	5	M	Child	190c02Bt
RITCARDSON, William	17	M	Laborer	190c02Bt
SLATTERY, Honora	35	F	Unknown	190c02Bt
CARNY, Mary	40	F	Unknown	190c02Bt
LEARY, Ellen	20	F	Unknown	190c02Bt
SLATTERY, Andw.	32	M	Laborer	190c02Bt
Judy	37	F	Unknown	190c02Bt
Mary	35	F	Unknown	190c02Bt
LEARY, John	24	M	Laborer	190c02Bt
Judy	20	F	Unknown	190c02Bt
CORMELL, Judy	20	F	Unknown	190c02Bt
REID, Ellen	40	F	Unknown	190c02Bt
Michl.	12	M	Unknown	190c02Bt
James	10	M	Unknown	190c02Bt
BRIEN, Mary	20	F	Unknown	190c02Bt
DRAKE, Bridgt.	20	F	Unknown	190c02Bt
RICE, Edmd.	18	M	Laborer	190c02Bt
MCSWEENY, Owen	25	M	Laborer	190c02Bt
GAINOR, Honora	24	F	Unknown	190c02Bt
MURPHY, Mary	24	F	Unknown	190c02Bt
MCQUIN, Patk.	40	M	Unknown	190c02Bt
RYAN, Mary	24	F	Laborer	190c02Bt
WHITE, Judy	24	F	Unknown	190c02Bt
Patt	8	M	Child	190c02Bt
COONEY, Saml.	30	M	Stone Mason	190c02Bt
ROCHE, Jno.	22	M	Laborer	190c02Bt
Danl.	9	M	Child	190c02Bt
Ellen	13	F	Unknown	190c02Bt
CROWLEY, Thomas	20	M	Weaver	190c02Bt
GONCHER, Jno.	19	M	Laborer	190c02Bt
BYRNE, Mary	18	F	Unknown	190c02Bt
James	25	M	Laborer	190c02Bt
KELLEY, Jno.	18	M	Laborer	190c02Bt
NOWLAND, Mary	25	F	Unknown	190c02Bt
KEARNEY, Eliza	17	F	Unknown	190c02Bt
GAFFNEY, Cathn.	30	F	Unknown	190c02Bt
GEOUGH, John	22	M	Laborer	190c02Bt
ELLIS, John	34	M	Laborer	190c02Bt
GRIMES, William	22	M	Laborer	190c02Bt
FINNEGAN, Wm.	20	M	Stone Mason	190c02Bt
BEGELY, Patk.	40	M	Laborer	190c02Bt
Gilley	16	M	Unknown	190c02Bt
Susan	13	F	Unknown	190c02Bt
Dennis	11	M	Unknown	190c02Bt
Mary	30	F	Unknown	190c02Bt
Shela	20	F	Unknown	190c02Bt
Patt	2	M	Child	190c02Bt
MCDERMOTT, John	21	M	Laborer	190c02Bt
MORAN, Margt.	18	F	Unknown	190c02Bt
EARLY, Mary	17	F	Unknown	190c02Bt
DUNLEVY, Bridget	22	F	Unknown	190c02Bt
MALONE, Edmond	18	M	Laborer	190c02Bt
CONNORS, William	25	M	Laborer	190c02Bt
ABBOTT, Jas.	25	M	Tinsmith	190c02Bt
WAUGH, Edwd.	18	M	Student	190c02Bt
WINTER, Charlotte	30	F	Unknown	190c02Bt
Richd.	.09	M	Infant	190c02Bt
MCGOWAN, Eliza	20	F	Unknown	190c02Bt
Eliza	.11	F	Infant	190c02Bt
Cul--, Anne	23	F	Unknown	190c02Bt
CUMMINGS, Jno.	24	M	Laborer	190c02Bt
COCHRAN, Mary	17	F	Unknown	190c02Bt
FRAULY, Eliza	15	F	Unknown	190c02Bt
ODEA, Worry	20	M	Unknown	190c02Bt
WALSH, Patt	22	M	Laborer	190c02Bt
OBRIEN, Patt	46	M	Laborer	190c02Bt
OCONNELL, Ellen	25	F	Unknown	190c02Bt
OHALLORAN, Michl.	24	M	Laborer	190c02Bt
STAPLETON, Ellen	27	F	Unknown	190c02Bt
DRISCOLL, Margret	25	F	Unknown	190c02Bt
Ellen	12	F	Unknown	190c02Bt
Thomas	4	M	Child	190c02Bt
COOPER, Margt.	16	F	Unknown	190c02Bt
HARMON, Michl.	25	M	Laborer	190c02Bt
INGLESLY, Judith	50	F	Unknown	190c02Bt
MCPEAKE, Cath.	42	F	Unknown	190c02Bt
MARTIN, Jno.	22	M	Unknown	190c02Bt
DROWDE, Thos.	23	M	Unknown	190c02Bt
DUNNE, Chas.	25	M	Unknown	190c02Bt
MCELROY, Owen	26	M	Unknown	190c02Bt
KEARNS, John	35	M	Unknown	190c02Bt
Margaret	2	F	Child	190c02Bt
MOORE, Thomas	6	M	Laborer	190c02Bt
DRURY, Johanna	23	F	Unknown	190c02Bt
REILY, Margt.	15	F	Unknown	190c02Bt
SLATTERY, William	22	M	Unknown	190c02Bt
MCGILL, John	35	M	Unknown	190c02Bt

NAMES OF PASSENGERS		AGE	SEX	OCCUPATIONS	DATE PORT SHIP

NIAGARA 20 OCTOBER 1849

From Liverpool

NAMES OF PASSENGERS		AGE	SEX	OCCUPATIONS	DATE PORT SHIP
DYER, Leon		48	M	Priest	200c02Bg
PUGH, Rd.		38	M	Priest	200c02Bg
DWYER, J.P.O.-Revd.		29	M	Priest	200c02Bg

DUCHESS-OF-KENT 22 OCTOBER 1849

From Liverpool

NAMES OF PASSENGERS		AGE	SEX	OCCUPATIONS	DATE PORT SHIP
IRVINE, Janet		30	F	Unknown	220c02Be
John-B.		13	M	Unknown	220c02Be
PARLANE, John-B.		44	M	Ctnsp	220c02Be
Margt.		80	F	Unknown	220c02Be
STEVENS, Elzth.		21	F	Unknown	220c02Be
MCFARLANE, Janet		33	F	Dressmaker	220c02Be
GALLOWAY, Isabella		27	F	Dressmaker	220c02Be
GRAHAM, Margt.		50	F	Unknown	220c02Be
Margt.		13	F	Unknown	220c02Be
MCMILLAN, David		23	M	Laborer	220c02Be
REYNOLDS, Jas.		24	M	Laborer	220c02Be
MCLEUGH, Jas.		23	M	Laborer	220c02Be
MCNAB, Saml.		26	M	Blacksmith	220c02Be
LOGAN, U-Mrs.		50	F	Unknown	220c02Be
MURRAY, Andw.		28	M	Tailor	220c02Be
CARLISLE, Hugh		22	M	Mason	220c02Be
MILLER, U-Mrs.		35	F	None	220c02Be
Jno.		13	M	None	220c02Be
Jas.		10	M	None	220c02Be
TOD, H.		50	M	Farmer	220c02Be
Christiana		25	F	Wife	220c02Be

FALCON 22 OCTOBER 1849

From HAMILTON, Bermuda

NAMES OF PASSENGERS		AGE	SEX	OCCUPATIONS	DATE PORT SHIP
WHITNEY, F.W.		30	M	Merchant	220c40Bd
U	(W)	28	F	Lady	220c40Bd
Henry		5	M	Child	220c40Bd
E.		3	F	Child	220c40Bd
F.		2	F	Child	220c40Bd
U, Florinda		17	F	Servant	220c40Bd

METEOR 22 OCTOBER 1849

From Liverpool

NAMES OF PASSENGERS		AGE	SEX	OCCUPATIONS	DATE PORT SHIP
CASEY, Patt		35	M	Laborer	220c02Bk
FITZGIBBON, Rchd.		38	M	Laborer	220c02Bk
SWEENY, Ellen		30	F	None	220c02Bk
DALEY, Willm.		20	M	Laborer	220c02Bk
MAHEY, Honora		24	F	None	220c02Bk
CALLAHAN, Jno.		21	M	Laborer	220c02Bk
Ellen		23	F	None	220c02Bk
MURPHY, Louisa		20	F	None	220c02Bk
MAHEY, Margt.		12	F	None	220c02Bk
MORRIS, Maria		17	F	None	220c02Bk
U		.00	U	Infant	220c02Bk
Born-At-Sea					
MCGRATH, Thos.		18	M	Laborer	220c02Bk
HOLLOHAN, Margt.		18	F	None	220c02Bk
SHEA, Thos.		20	M	Laborer	220c02Bk
GRADY, Heny.		14	M	Laborer	220c02Bk
MURPHY, Mary		22	F	Laborer	220c02Bk
Catherine		15	F	None	220c02Bk
MCANALLY, Willm.		20	M	Laborer	220c02Bk
TRAFFETT, Jno.		25	M	Laborer	220c02Bk
U	(W)	25	F	None	220c02Bk
Ellen		.00	F	Infant	220c02Bk
Died-At-Sea					
James		24	M	None	220c02Bk
GOODWIN, M.		40	U	Laborer	220c02Bk
GOLDING, Mchl.		20	M	Laborer	220c02Bk
WALSH, Mary		50	F	Laborer	220c02Bk
BERNS, Winny		20	U	Laborer	220c02Bk
HOWARD, Jas.		15	M	Laborer	220c02Bk
PARKER, Margt.		28	F	Laborer	220c02Bk
Henry		28	M	Laborer	220c02Bk
Ann		4	F	Child	220c02Bk
James		2	M	Child	220c02Bk
Sarah		.00	F	Infant	220c02Bk
MASTERTON, Bridget		20	F	Laborer	220c02Bk
DYER, Rchd.		25	M	Laborer	220c02Bk
Annie		16	F	Laborer	220c02Bk
CALLERY, Ann		45	F	Laborer	220c02Bk
MCNAMARA, Catherine		40	F	Laborer	220c02Bk
Thos.		15	M	Laborer	220c02Bk
Bridget		13	F	Laborer	220c02Bk
Catherine		11	F	Laborer	220c02Bk
Ann		9	F	Child	220c02Bk
Jno.		7	M	Child	220c02Bk
Mchl.		5	M	Child	220c02Bk
Margaret		3	F	Child	220c02Bk
QUINLON, Annie		26	F	Laborer	220c02Bk
HAY, Pat		20	M	Laborer	220c02Bk
MCNAMARA, Bridget		25	F	Laborer	220c02Bk
Tim		4	M	Child	220c02Bk
MCCAULEY, F.		22	U	Laborer	220c02Bk
KELLY, Edwd.		21	M	Laborer	220c02Bk
CARROLL, Biddy		30	F	Laborer	220c02Bk
CONDON, Mary		30	F	Laborer	220c02Bk
MURPHY, Dennis		25	M	Laborer	220c02Bk
MCMAHON, Mary		16	F	Laborer	220c02Bk
Annie		18	F	Laborer	220c02Bk
Margt.		13	F	Laborer	220c02Bk
COOLAHAN, Ellen		30	F	Laborer	220c02Bk
Pat		8	M	Child	220c02Bk
Jno.		6	M	Child	220c02Bk
Mchl.		.00	M	Infant	220c02Bk
WHELAN, Annie		50	F	Laborer	220c02Bk
CASSIDY, Mchl.		45	M	Laborer	220c02Bk
Died-At-Sea					
Ellen		35	F	Laborer	220c02Bk
SHEEHAN, Ellen		15	F	Laborer	220c02Bk
MAGEE, Pat		19	M	Laborer	220c02Bk
MULLARY, Thos.		18	M	Laborer	220c02Bk
ADAMSON, Jas.		18	M	Laborer	220c02Bk
BUCKLEY, Honora		25	F	Laborer	220c02Bk
SHEEHAN, Mary		2	F	Child	220c02Bk
DRISCOLL, Bridget		21	F	Laborer	220c02Bk
HODGIN, Jno.		20	M	Laborer	220c02Bk
WARD, Kerin		20	M	Laborer	220c02Bk
EVENSON, Allen		28	M	Laborer	220c02Bk
GERRY, Catherine		40	F	Laborer	220c02Bk

NAMES OF PASSENGERS	AGE	SEX	OCCUPATIONS	DATE PORT SHIP
GERRY, Pat	10	M	Laborer	220c02Bk
Elias	8	M	Child	220c02Bk
CROWLEY, Catherine	8	F	Child	220c02Bk
Jno.	6	M	Child	220c02Bk
Thos.	.00	M	Infant	220c02Bk
LOGHLEN, Jas.	20	M	Laborer	220c02Bk
SMITH, Jno.	20	M	Laborer	220c02Bk
MCDERNOT, Mchl.	20	M	Laborer	220c02Bk
SCOTT, Mchl.	22	M	Laborer	220c02Bk
GOGAN, Wm.	25	M	Laborer	220c02Bk
Bridget	23	F	Laborer	220c02Bk
MONAHAN, Mchl.	24	M	Laborer	220c02Bk
CASSEL, Pat	20	M	Laborer	220c02Bk
Biddy	22	F	Laborer	220c02Bk
SHEA, Johanna	30	F	Laborer	220c02Bk
Margaret	30	F	Laborer	220c02Bk
Honora	8	F	Child	220c02Bk
FLEMING, Pat	24	M	Laborer	220c02Bk
FEHN, Nchlas.	24	M	Laborer	220c02Bk
LICKEY, James	25	M	Laborer	220c02Bk
Mary	22	F	Laborer	220c02Bk
Eliza	.00	F	Infant	220c02Bk
FLEMING, Mary	30	F	Laborer	220c02Bk
Walter	3	M	Child	220c02Bk
Kate	.00	F	Infant	220c02Bk
FLYNN, Fanny	28	F	Laborer	220c02Bk
Kate	3	F	Child	220c02Bk
KENNAY, Water	20	M	Laborer	220c02Bk
Thos.	18	M	Laborer	220c02Bk
Ellen	16	F	Laborer	220c02Bk
DUNCAN, Thos.	23	F	Laborer	220c02Bk
CHALMERS, Wm.B.	30	M	Laborer	220c02Bk
CROWLEY, Thos.	25	M	Laborer	220c02Bk
CLUFF, Maria	60	F	Laborer	220c02Bk
HUGHES, Annie	20	F	Laborer	220c02Bk
MCCANN, Sally	20	F	Laborer	220c02Bk
JOHNSON, Mary	20	F	Laborer	220c02Bk
MOLYNEUX, Saml.	30	M	Laborer	220c02Bk
BOWLES, Mary	20	F	Laborer	220c02Bk
LIVINGSTONE, James	20	M	Laborer	220c02Bk
CAMPBELL, Wm.	19	M	Laborer	220c02Bk
Mary	16	F	Laborer	220c02Bk
MULLIGAN, Saml.	25	M	Laborer	220c02Bk
MORTON, Jane	20	F	Laborer	220c02Bk
MONTGOMERY, Jno.	25	M	Laborer	220c02Bk
GIBSON, Christ.	25	M	Laborer	220c02Bk
ROGERS, Pat	28	M	Laborer	220c02Bk
ODONNELL, Jno.	25	M	Laborer	220c02Bk
U (W)	25	F	Laborer	220c02Bk
Catherine	12	F	Laborer	220c02Bk
Wm.	.00	M	Infant	220c02Bk
WHELAN, Peter	23	M	Laborer	220c02Bk
LOGHLEN, Dennis	28	M	Laborer	220c02Bk
Matt	17	M	Laborer	220c02Bk
CONDON, Ellen	25	F	Laborer	220c02Bk
Wm.	20	M	Laborer	220c02Bk
MALONEY, Margt.	4	F	Child	220c02Bk
CONDON, Bridget	.00	F	Infant	220c02Bk
MCNAMARA, Biddy	30	F	Laborer	220c02Bk
Hannah	12	F	Laborer	220c02Bk
Thos.	11	M	Laborer	220c02Bk
Bridget	8	F	Child	220c02Bk
NOLAN, Biddy	30	F	Laborer	220c02Bk
DELOUPHEY, Pat	19	M	Laborer	220c02Bk
Margt.	22	F	Laborer	220c02Bk
MULLIGAN, Honora	26	F	Laborer	220c02Bk
Pat	.00	M	Infant	220c02Bk
MAHONEY, Jno.	50	M	Laborer	220c02Bk
Biddy	35	F	Laborer	220c02Bk
Kate	5	F	Child	220c02Bk
MEHAN, Jno.	19	M	Laborer	220c02Bk
KELLY, Bryan	18	M	Laborer	220c02Bk
MCBRYDE, Margt.	20	F	Laborer	220c02Bk
DEVINE, Jno.	22	M	Laborer	220c02Bk
KANE, Lawrence	24	M	Laborer	220c02Bk

NAMES OF PASSENGERS	AGE	SEX	OCCUPATIONS	DATE PORT SHIP
QUICK, Jeremiah	32	M	Laborer	220c02Bk
Mary	32	F	Laborer	220c02Bk
RYAN, Catherine	36	F	Laborer	220c02Bk
Bridget	16	F	Laborer	220c02Bk
Mary	12	F	Laborer	220c02Bk
Stephen	10	M	Laborer	220c02Bk
Margaret	8	F	Child	220c02Bk
NAGLE, Pat	21	M	Laborer	220c02Bk
Ann	40	F	Laborer	220c02Bk
CUSHON, Elizabeth	16	F	Laborer	220c02Bk
DARCY, Jno.	23	M	Laborer	220c02Bk
COWAN, Jas.	21	M	Laborer	220c02Bk
CURTIS, Hugh	30	M	Laborer	220c02Bk
CROWLEY, Ellen	30	F	Laborer	220c02Bk
GERRY, Jno.	5	M	Child	220c02Bk
Mary	6	F	Child	220c02Bk
Edwd.	4	M	Child	220c02Bk
Kate	.00	F	Infant	220c02Bk
BURKE, Jno.	23	M	Laborer	220c02Bk
CLARY, Dennis	36	M	Laborer	220c02Bk
Mary	30	F	Laborer	220c02Bk
Mary	.00	F	Infant	220c02Bk
MEEHAN, Mchl.	30	M	Laborer	220c02Bk
BULGIN, Bridget	35	F	Laborer	220c02Bk
Stephen	9	M	Child	220c02Bk
Johanna	7	F	Child	220c02Bk
Peter	4	M	Child	220c02Bk
DOWNEY, Ann	40	F	Laborer	220c02Bk
RYAN, Catherine	25	F	Laborer	220c02Bk
WALSH, James	12	M	Laborer	220c02Bk
RYAN, Bridget	6	F	Child	220c02Bk
Jno.	4	M	Child	220c02Bk
Ellen	.00	F	Infant	220c02Bk
BYRNE, Mary	35	F	Laborer	220c02Bk
Jno.	.00	M	Infant	220c02Bk
MULICK, Jas.	35	M	Laborer	220c02Bk
Margt.	30	F	Laborer	220c02Bk
Bernard	9	M	Child	220c02Bk
Mary	6	F	Child	220c02Bk
EARLY, Ellen	30	F	Laborer	220c02Bk
James	.00	M	Infant	220c02Bk
QUIRK, Andrew Died-At-Sea	5	M	Child	220c02Bk
Bridget Died-At-Sea	.00	F	Infant	220c02Bk
CROWLEY, E. Died-At-Sea	2	U	Child	220c02Bk
SHEA, C. Died-At-Sea	4	U	Child	220c02Bk

WARRIOR 22 OCTOBER 1849

From Belfast

NAMES OF PASSENGERS	AGE	SEX	OCCUPATIONS	DATE PORT SHIP
HODGSON, Eliza	40	F	Farmer	220c17Bj
Ann-Jane	24	F	Unknown	220c17Bj
ALEESE, Rose-W.	18	F	Unknown	220c17Bj
Margt.	7	F	Child	220c17Bj
MARSHALL, Margt.	18	F	Unknown	220c17Bj
MARTIN, John	25	M	Unknown	220c17Bj
John	40	M	Unknown	220c17Bj
Mary	35	F	Unknown	220c17Bj
Mary	16	F	Unknown	220c17Bj
MCDERMON, John	20	M	Unknown	220c17Bj
Jane	20	F	Unknown	220c17Bj
MURRAY, Jane	14	F	Unknown	220c17Bj
MCFRUSTY, Rose	15	F	Unknown	220c17Bj
OCONNOR, Mary	27	F	Unknown	220c17Bj
HAMELTON, Sarah	40	F	Unknown	220c17Bj

NAMES OF PASSENGERS	AGE	SEX	OCCUPATIONS	DATE PORT SHIP
HAMELTON, Rebecca	22	F	Unknown	220c17Bj
James	17	M	Unknown	220c17Bj
MARTON, Cath.	35	F	Unknown	220c17Bj
DONAHOE, Ellen	7	F	Child	220c17Bj
ROBERTS, Richd.	21	M	Unknown	220c17Bj
ASHMORE, Mathew	20	M	Unknown	220c17Bj
ARMSTRONG, Jas.	22	M	Unknown	220c17Bj
Margaret	21	F	Unknown	220c17Bj
Sarah	.00	F	Infant	220c17Bj
CARL, Robert	35	M	Unknown	220c17Bj
Ellen	25	F	Unknown	220c17Bj
James	12	M	Unknown	220c17Bj
Joseph	5	M	Child	220c17Bj
Robert	7	M	Child	220c17Bj
Ellen	6	F	Child	220c17Bj
Andrew	3	M	Child	220c17Bj
William	.00	M	Infant	220c17Bj
STEWART, Ann	40	F	Unknown	220c17Bj
Sarah	45	F	Unknown	220c17Bj
MARTON, Margaret	25	F	Unknown	220c17Bj
OHARA, John	20	M	Unknown	220c17Bj
William	18	M	Unknown	220c17Bj
MCGAFFIN, Mary	17	F	Unknown	220c17Bj
MCGACHAN, Ann	17	F	Unknown	220c17Bj
MAHOOD, Andrew	20	M	Unknown	220c17Bj
MACDONALD, Selma	30	F	Unknown	220c17Bj
THOMPSON, Robert	26	M	Unknown	220c17Bj
Ellenor	60	F	Unknown	220c17Bj
ROBINSON, Eliza-J.	8	F	Child	220c17Bj
CANERON, Margaret-A.	30	F	Unknown	220c17Bj
MCCLURCAN, Ann	20	F	Unknown	220c17Bj
BRATTY, James	25	M	Unknown	220c17Bj
CASSIDY, Mary-Ann	17	F	Unknown	220c17Bj
CRAIG, Margaret	20	F	Unknown	220c17Bj
CLARK, Thomas	20	M	Unknown	220c17Bj
ROGAN, Sally	35	F	Unknown	220c17Bj
Margaret	7	F	Child	220c17Bj
Edward	34	M	Unknown	220c17Bj
Ann	3	F	Child	220c17Bj
Charles	.00	M	Infant	220c17Bj
MONAGHAN, James	50	M	Unknown	220c17Bj
MCKENNAN, Catherine	16	F	Unknown	220c17Bj
MCCOURT, Arthur	37	M	Unknown	220c17Bj
FREMAN, John	22	M	Unknown	220c17Bj
BARNETT, Samuel	23	F	Unknown	220c17Bj
Eliza-Jane	20	F	Unknown	220c17Bj
William	.00	M	Infant	220c17Bj
GANBEL, Sarah	21	F	Unknown	220c17Bj
Margaret	24	F	Unknown	220c17Bj
Ann	.00	F	Infant	220c17Bj
MCLARE, Mary	2	F	Child	220c17Bj
MORGAN, Ann	20	F	Unknown	220c17Bj
CLARK, John	28	M	Unknown	220c17Bj
Bridget	26	F	Unknown	220c17Bj
William	.00	M	Infant	220c17Bj
LAMB, Robert	20	M	Unknown	220c17Bj
GILMORE, Ann	18	F	Unknown	220c17Bj
BELL, Elizabeth	18	F	Unknown	220c17Bj
DELARGEY, Edward	25	M	Unknown	220c17Bj
CARROL, John	23	M	Unknown	220c17Bj
COWAN, John	23	M	Unknown	220c17Bj
LEEDIVED, David	28	M	Unknown	220c17Bj
CARLETON, U-Mr.	37	M	Unknown	220c17Bj
U-Mrs.	37	F	Matron	220c17Bj
Abige.	13	F	Unknown	220c17Bj
DIWER, John	55	M	Unknown	220c17Bj
MCDERMOTT, Frak.	21	M	Unknown	220c17Bj
BURN, Andrew	26	M	Unknown	220c17Bj
Eliza	26	F	Unknown	220c17Bj
HAMELTON, Robt.	35	M	Unknown	220c17Bj
Elizabeth	50	F	Unknown	220c17Bj
Margaret	22	M	Unknown	220c17Bj
DONAHOE, Margaret	30	F	Unknown	220c17Bj

VICTORIA 22 OCTOBER 1849

From London

NAMES OF PASSENGERS	AGE	SEX	OCCUPATIONS	DATE PORT SHIP
MILES, Rosalia	27	F	Dressmaker	220c06Aj
KNOWLAND, Bridget	28	F	Dressmaker	220c06Aj
GOOD, John	31	M	Ppstr	220c06Aj
Jane	35	F	Unknown	220c06Aj
Fanny	8	F	Child	220c06Aj
Jane	6	F	Child	220c06Aj
Eliza	4	F	Child	220c06Aj
Morrice	.00	M	Infant	220c06Aj
William	35	M	Unknown	220c06Aj
John	8	M	Child	220c06Aj
Robert	7	M	Child	220c06Aj
Peggy	35	F	Unknown	220c06Aj
MCCULLOUGH, William	23	M	Tailor	220c06Aj
LEARY, Winfred	25	U	Servant	220c06Aj
PADGETT, John	27	M	Bootmaker	220c06Aj
SHEREDIN, Redman	29	M	Laborer	220c06Aj
SAXTON, William	33	M	Laborer	220c06Aj
Bridget (W)	26	F	Unknown	220c06Aj
U	3	U	Child	220c06Aj
U	.00	U	Infant	220c06Aj
CONNOR, Nancy	30	F	Dressmaker	220c06Aj
Mary (D)	2	F	Child	220c06Aj
KEATH, Catherine	24	F	Servant	220c06Aj
BRYAN, Ellen	25	F	Servant	220c06Aj
TURVEY, Eliza	22	F	Servant	220c06Aj
CONOLLY, Morris	30	M	Bricklayer	220c06Aj
MITCHEL, William	17	M	Laborer	220c06Aj
MACKLIN, David	23	M	Laborer	220c06Aj
MALANEY, Mary	44	F	Servant	220c06Aj
MELANY, Mary	44	F	Servant	220c06Aj
William	9	M	Child	220c06Aj
Cecelia	7	F	Child	220c06Aj
Margaret	5	F	Child	220c06Aj
LARRIGAN, Patrick	22	M	Servant	220c06Aj
CRAWLEY, Daniel	32	M	Laborer	220c06Aj

EFFINGHAM 22 OCTOBER 1849

From Cork

NAMES OF PASSENGERS	AGE	SEX	OCCUPATIONS	DATE PORT SHIP
BEAZLEY, Jane	24	F	Laborer	220c18Bh
Ann	20	F	Unknown	220c18Bh
BURCH, John	17	M	Unknown	220c18Bh
BARRY, John	28	M	Unknown	220c18Bh
Ellen	24	F	Unknown	220c18Bh
Margt.	5	F	Child	220c18Bh
Patt	10	M	Unknown	220c18Bh
MORRISSY, Batty	30	F	Unknown	220c18Bh
HIGGINS, Michl.	18	M	Unknown	220c18Bh
MORRISSY, Denis	4	M	Child	220c18Bh
BURKE, Mary	24	M	Unknown	220c18Bh
MURPHY, Mary	20	F	Unknown	220c18Bh
BUCKLEY, David	20	M	Unknown	220c18Bh
BARRY, Mary	17	F	Unknown	220c18Bh
BUCKLEY, Jerry	24	M	Unknown	220c18Bh
SHEELLY, Patt	30	M	Unknown	220c18Bh
DUNNE, Patt	20	M	Unknown	220c18Bh
HENNESSY, Ellen	20	F	Unknown	220c18Bh
QUINLAN, Wm.	.06	M	Infant	220c18Bh

NAMES OF PASSENGERS	AGE	SEX	OCCUPATIONS	DATE PORT SHIP
RYAN, Mary	30	F	Unknown	220c18Bh
Tim	20	M	Unknown	220c18Bh
LEANE, James	22	M	Unknown	220c18Bh
Johanah	20	F	Unknown	220c18Bh
EGAN, Maria	30	F	Unknown	220c18Bh
John	13	M	Unknown	220c18Bh
David	6	M	Child	220c18Bh
COGAN, Mary	20	F	Unknown	220c18Bh
SHEA, Kitty	20	F	Unknown	220c18Bh
BEAZLY, Elydi	20	F	Unknown	220c18Bh
SHINICK, Patt	24	M	Unknown	220c18Bh
COUGHLAN, Garrett	20	M	Unknown	220c18Bh
John	20	M	Unknown	220c18Bh
HOROGAN, Bess	24	F	Unknown	220c18Bh
SMIDDY, John	20	M	Unknown	220c18Bh
DOOLING, Ellen	20	F	Unknown	220c18Bh
Norry	20	F	Unknown	220c18Bh
HARRINGTON, Kitty	20	F	Unknown	220c18Bh
U	.05	U	Infant	220c18Bh
KILNANE, U-Mr.	20	M	Unknown	220c18Bh
U-Mrs.	20	F	Unknown	220c18Bh
REARDON, Owen	50	M	Unknown	220c18Bh
Mary	40	F	Unknown	220c18Bh
Peggy	20	F	Unknown	220c18Bh
MANNING, Ellen	20	F	Unknown	220c18Bh
MOORE, Anthony	20	M	Unknown	220c18Bh
SHEA, John	24	M	Unknown	220c18Bh
SHANNAHAN, Margt.	20	F	Unknown	220c18Bh
Julia	18	F	Unknown	220c18Bh
SULLIVAN, James	50	M	Unknown	220c18Bh
Norry	50	F	Unknown	220c18Bh
Thomas	16	M	Unknown	220c18Bh
SHEEHAN, Catherine	20	F	Unknown	220c18Bh
CONNOR, Catherine	20	F	Unknown	220c18Bh
SHEEHY, Biddy	20	F	Unknown	220c18Bh
MCEGAN, Mary	20	F	Unknown	220c18Bh
FITZGERALD, Dan	25	M	Unknown	220c18Bh
Ellen	40	F	Unknown	220c18Bh
Ellen	12	F	Unknown	220c18Bh
Johannah	10	F	Unknown	220c18Bh
Kate	8	F	Child	220c18Bh
Eliza	2	F	Child	220c18Bh
SHEA, Ellen	35	F	Unknown	220c18Bh
Norry	20	F	Unknown	220c18Bh
Paddy	20	M	Unknown	220c18Bh
John	7	M	Child	220c18Bh
Ellen	30	F	Unknown	220c18Bh
SEARS, Nancy	20	F	Unknown	220c18Bh
JOHNSON, Johanah	13	F	Unknown	220c18Bh
LOVETT, Mary	30	F	Unknown	220c18Bh
Biddy	8	F	Child	220c18Bh
Catherine	4	F	Child	220c18Bh
BRIEN, Norry	26	F	Unknown	220c18Bh
SULLIVAN, Ellen	20	F	Unknown	220c18Bh
FINNERTY, Ellen	20	F	Unknown	220c18Bh
Michl.	24	M	Unknown	220c18Bh
Mary	2	F	Child	220c18Bh
CONNELL, Patrick	40	M	Unknown	220c18Bh
GEHIN, Patt	10	M	Unknown	220c18Bh
SHEA, Ellen	12	F	Unknown	220c18Bh
Dan	8	M	Child	220c18Bh
MURPHY, Mary	13	F	Unknown	220c18Bh
Biddy	10	F	Unknown	220c18Bh
MANNING, Johanah	26	F	Unknown	220c18Bh
Mary	8	F	Child	220c18Bh
SULLIVAN, Patt	30	M	Unknown	220c18Bh
CURRANE, Peggy	25	F	Unknown	220c18Bh
SULLIVAN, Kate	20	F	Unknown	220c18Bh
SCANLON, Ellen	20	F	Unknown	220c18Bh
SULLIVAN, John	25	M	Unknown	220c18Bh
HIGGINS, Michl.	20	M	Unknown	220c18Bh
FITZGERALD, Danl.	12	M	Unknown	220c18Bh
MORRIARTY, Maurice	12	M	Unknown	220c18Bh
Danl.	14	M	Unknown	220c18Bh
SHEA, Johanah	20	F	Unknown	220c18Bh

NAMES OF PASSENGERS	AGE	SEX	OCCUPATIONS	DATE PORT SHIP
CONNELL, Nell	20	F	Unknown	220c18Bh
SEARS, Mary	23	F	Unknown	220c18Bh
Mary	2	F	Child	220c18Bh
MORIARTY, Ellen	30	F	Child	220c18Bh
Maurice	00	M	Unknown	220c18Bh
CONNOR, Mary	40	F	Unknown	220c18Bh
SHEA, Mary	40	F	Unknown	220c18Bh
John	7	M	Child	220c18Bh
Maurice	3	M	Child	220c18Bh
Thos.	8	M	Child	220c18Bh
KENNEDY, Mary	40	F	Unknown	220c18Bh
Biddy	9	F	Child	220c18Bh
Michl.	6	M	Child	220c18Bh
FITZGERALD, Michl.	20	M	Unknown	220c18Bh
HAARE, Johannah	20	F	Unknown	220c18Bh
Michl.	.09	M	Infant	220c18Bh
ROURKE, Thos.	13	M	Unknown	220c18Bh
BARRY, James	40	M	Unknown	220c18Bh
Julia	40	F	Unknown	220c18Bh
Ellen	6	F	Child	220c18Bh
Ellen	40	F	Unknown	220c18Bh
Margt.	10	F	Unknown	220c18Bh
Thomas	8	M	Child	220c18Bh
CUNNINGHAM, Abygal	20	F	Unknown	220c18Bh
NEIL, Johannah	18	F	Unknown	220c18Bh
SULLIVAN, Mark	10	M	Unknown	220c18Bh
LEARY, John	14	M	Unknown	220c18Bh
SAVAGE, Bessy	40	F	Unknown	220c18Bh
Mutty	7	M	Child	220c18Bh
DONOVAN, John	13	M	Unknown	220c18Bh
SWORDS, Robert	20	M	Unknown	220c18Bh
NEIL, Richard	40	M	Unknown	220c18Bh
Bridget	40	F	Unknown	220c18Bh
Margt.	20	F	Unknown	220c18Bh
Ellen	25	F	Unknown	220c18Bh
Mary	18	F	Unknown	220c18Bh
Patrick	16	M	Unknown	220c18Bh
Batt	13	M	Unknown	220c18Bh
Norry	12	F	Unknown	220c18Bh
Biddy	11	F	Unknown	220c18Bh
Johanna	6	F	Child	220c18Bh
John	4	M	Child	220c18Bh
MOORE, Mary	20	F	Unknown	220c18Bh
SCANNELL, Mary	20	F	Unknown	220c18Bh
MULCAHY, Catherine	20	F	Unknown	220c18Bh
QUINLAN, Margt.	20	F	Unknown	220c18Bh
William	5	M	Child	220c18Bh
FITZMAURICE, Eliza.	20	F	Unknown	220c18Bh
HEALY, Ellen	20	F	Unknown	220c18Bh
KENNEDY, Ellen	32	F	Unknown	220c18Bh
DALY, Catherine	22	F	Unknown	220c18Bh
KEEFFE, Mary	30	F	Unknown	220c18Bh
Denis	7	M	Child	220c18Bh
SHINE, Mary	25	F	Unknown	220c18Bh
CORMCODY, Mary	20	F	Unknown	220c18Bh
DOYLE, John	22	M	Unknown	220c18Bh
Mary	20	F	Unknown	220c18Bh
SULLIVAN, Mary	20	F	Unknown	220c18Bh
CARROLL, Patrick	20	M	Unknown	220c18Bh
HURLEY, John	20	M	Unknown	220c18Bh
LYONS, Charles	20	M	Unknown	220c18Bh
KELLCHER, Andrew	20	M	Unknown	220c18Bh
MORTEL, Alice	22	F	Unknown	220c18Bh
SLATTERY, Ellen	20	F	Unknown	220c18Bh
MORTELL, Patt	3	M	Child	220c18Bh
DENBY, Kitty	25	F	Unknown	220c18Bh
Denis	20	M	Unknown	220c18Bh
Mary	6	F	Child	220c18Bh
MORIARTY, Kate	20	F	Unknown	220c18Bh
SULLIVAN, Michl.	20	M	Unknown	220c18Bh
CONNORS, John	24	M	Unknown	220c18Bh
SWEENY, Ellen	30	F	Unknown	220c18Bh
SANDY, Ellen	25	F	Unknown	220c18Bh
LUCY, Mary	24	F	Unknown	220c18Bh
Bessy	10	F	Unknown	220c18Bh

NAMES OF PASSENGERS	AGE	SEX	OCCUPATIONS	DATE PORT SHIP
KINNIRY, John	30	M	Unknown	220c18Bh
AMBROSE, Norry	20	F	Unknown	220c18Bh
COPPINGER, U-Mrs.	40	F	Unknown	220c18Bh
OLIFFE, U-Mrs.	20	F	Unknown	220c18Bh
Mary	2	F	Child	220c18Bh
MENDAL, Eliza	20	F	Unknown	220c18Bh
MCNAMARA, Mary	20	F	Unknown	220c18Bh
MCAULIFFE, Ellen	20	F	Unknown	220c18Bh
HEGARTY, Alice	40	F	Unknown	220c18Bh
MCCANN, Mary	20	F	Unknown	220c18Bh
GALWAY, Mary	20	F	Unknown	220c18Bh
COLLINS, Ellen	20	F	Unknown	220c18Bh
Timothy	22	M	Unknown	220c18Bh
BURCHILL, James	40	M	Unknown	220c18Bh
Anne	40	F	Unknown	220c18Bh
CALLIGHAN, Catherine	30	F	Unknown	220c18Bh
MCNAMARA, Richd.	35	M	Unknown	220c18Bh
MURPHY, Dan	24	M	Unknown	220c18Bh
OLDHAM, Rich	18	M	Unknown	220c18Bh
BRODERICK, Mary	20	F	Unknown	220c18Bh
PHELAN, Peggy	20	F	Unknown	220c18Bh
SULLIVAN, Mary	20	F	Unknown	220c18Bh
OLDHAM, Michl.	20	M	Unknown	220c18Bh
CARROLL, Mary	26	F	Unknown	220c18Bh
FITZGERALD, Tho.	20	M	Unknown	220c18Bh
CALLAGHAN, Patt	20	M	Unknown	220c18Bh
BURGESS, Ellen	20	F	Unknown	220c18Bh
MURPHY, Mary	30	F	Unknown	220c18Bh
Ellen	.03	F	Infant	220c18Bh
CARROLL, Jane	40	F	Unknown	220c18Bh
Maurice	15	M	Unknown	220c18Bh
Jane	10	F	Unknown	220c18Bh
Mary	8	F	Child	220c18Bh
Timothy	6	M	Child	220c18Bh
Stephen	2	M	Child	220c18Bh
LEAHY, Catherine	24	F	Unknown	220c18Bh
BOYCE, Timothy	26	M	Unknown	220c18Bh
DESMOND, Judy	20	F	Unknown	220c18Bh
LINEHAN, Mary	20	F	Unknown	220c18Bh
SCOTT, Susan	20	F	Unknown	220c18Bh
SPILLANE, Margt.	40	F	Unknown	220c18Bh
John	12	M	Unknown	220c18Bh
Edward	10	M	Unknown	220c18Bh
David	20	M	Unknown	220c18Bh
LINEHAN, John	20	M	Unknown	220c18Bh
SWEETMAN, John	24	M	Unknown	220c18Bh
Rebecca	20	F	Unknown	220c18Bh
William	3	M	Child	220c18Bh
Rebecca	.00	F	Infant	220c18Bh
Mary-Anne	20	F	Unknown	220c18Bh
TOBIN, Margt.	20	F	Unknown	220c18Bh
CARY, Margt.	20	F	Unknown	220c18Bh
FITZGERALD, Mary	20	F	Unknown	220c18Bh
WALKER, Saml.	30	M	Unknown	220c18Bh
SULLIVAN, Mary	30	F	Unknown	220c18Bh
Owen	3	M	Child	220c18Bh
BURKETT, John	20	M	Unknown	220c18Bh
ARNOLD, Abigal	20	F	Unknown	220c18Bh
FAME, Norry	40	F	Unknown	220c18Bh
Ellen	12	F	Unknown	220c18Bh
Mary-Ann	10	F	Unknown	220c18Bh
Jane	8	F	Child	220c18Bh
BARRY, Michl.	30	M	Unknown	220c18Bh
COAKLEY, Patt	20	M	Unknown	220c18Bh
SINGLETON, Patt	20	M	Unknown	220c18Bh
DANLEY, Michl.	30	M	Unknown	220c18Bh
DESMOND, Catherine	20	F	Unknown	220c18Bh
MOORE, John	18	M	Unknown	220c18Bh
LEAHY, Mary	14	F	Unknown	220c18Bh
CONDON, James	7	M	Child	220c18Bh
Ellen	5	F	Child	220c18Bh
SHOSE, Peggy	20	F	Unknown	220c18Bh
SULLIVAN, Mary	20	F	Unknown	220c18Bh
Cath.	20	F	Unknown	220c18Bh
DELANY, Margt.	20	F	Unknown	220c18Bh

NAMES OF PASSENGERS	AGE	SEX	OCCUPATIONS	DATE PORT SHIP
MAGNER, Michl.	20	M	Unknown	220c18Bh
BRIDE, Mary	30	F	Unknown	220c18Bh
Jerry	20	F	Unknown	220c18Bh
Ellen	18	F	Unknown	220c18Bh
Mary	15	F	Unknown	220c18Bh
COLBERT, Patt	20	M	Unknown	220c18Bh
MORGAN, Henry	18	M	Unknown	220c18Bh
MANLY, Mary	20	F	Unknown	220c18Bh
LYONS, Margt.	20	F	Unknown	220c18Bh
BARRY, James	12	M	Unknown	220c18Bh
BRIEN, Patrick	22	M	Unknown	220c18Bh
FENNESSY, John	19	M	Unknown	220c18Bh
SEALS, John	30	M	Unknown	220c18Bh
U-Mrs.	28	F	Unknown	220c18Bh
FORREST, U-Mr.	25	M	Unknown	220c18Bh
U-Mrs.	20	F	Unknown	220c18Bh
SLORACH, Alex.	20	M	Unknown	220c18Bh
COLLINS, U-Miss	20	F	Unknown	220c18Bh
U-Miss	18	F	Unknown	220c18Bh
U-Mr.	14	M	Unknown	220c18Bh
MORROGH, Edw.	18	M	Unknown	220c18Bh

CONSTELLATION 24 OCTOBER 1849

From Liverpool

NAMES OF PASSENGERS	AGE	SEX	OCCUPATIONS	DATE PORT SHIP
JACKSON, Wm.	40	M	Clerk	240c02Bm
James	22	M	Clerk	240c02Bm
DAVENPORT, James	21	M	Blacksmith	240c02Bm
NUTTLE, John	22	M	Collier	240c02Bm
PRENTY, Michl.	20	M	Laborer	240c02Bm
NATHAN, Henry	28	M	Laborer	240c02Bm
EAGLE, Solomon	34	M	Farmer	240c02Bm
Ellen	34	F	Unknown	240c02Bm
LAWLER, Mary	17	F	Unknown	240c02Bm
EAGLE, Ann	10	F	Unknown	240c02Bm
Charlotte	8	F	Child	240c02Bm
Josephine	6	F	Child	240c02Bm
Mildert	4	M	Child	240c02Bm
Solomon	1	M	Child	240c02Bm
Jane-Letitia	.03	F	Infant	240c02Bm
RYAN, Patrick	27	M	Laborer	240c02Bm
James	17	M	Laborer	240c02Bm
GANNON, Bridget	26	F	Unknown	240c02Bm
Honora	.06	F	Infant	240c02Bm
MULLENHILL, Maria	24	F	Unknown	240c02Bm
Margt.	25	F	Unknown	240c02Bm
FARRELL, Ann	24	F	Unknown	240c02Bm
DAKER, Hannah	31	F	Unknown	240c02Bm
Ralph	5	M	Child	240c02Bm
John-Thos.	4	M	Child	240c02Bm
Alfred	2	M	Child	240c02Bm
Walter	.05	M	Infant	240c02Bm
KAY, Wm.	50	M	Innkeeper	240c02Bm
Thomas	18	M	Innkeeper	240c02Bm
GARDNER, John	26	M	Laborer	240c02Bm
Bridget	22	F	Unknown	240c02Bm
MURPHY, Cathn.	30	F	Unknown	240c02Bm
Margt.	.08	F	Infant	240c02Bm
BAKER, Ann	28	F	Unknown	240c02Bm
Harriet	4	F	Child	240c02Bm
John	.06	M	Infant	240c02Bm
WATSON, Mary	50	F	Unknown	240c02Bm
Mary	17	F	Unknown	240c02Bm
Jane	14	F	Unknown	240c02Bm
Nancy	9	F	Child	240c02Bm
Elizth.	7	F	Child	240c02Bm
Robert	5	M	Child	240c02Bm
Patrick	18	M	Unknown	240c02Bm

NAMES OF PASSENGERS	AGE	SEX	OCCUPATIONS	DATE PORT SHIP
HASLIN, Ellen	24	F	Unknown	240c02Bm
Mary	24	F	Unknown	240c02Bm
John	5	M	Child	240c02Bm
BARNES, Mary	20	F	Unknown	240c02Bm
MCCONN, Cathn.	20	F	Unknown	240c02Bm
COOK, George	28	M	Farmer	240c02Bm
Elizth.	28	F	Unknown	240c02Bm
William	7	M	Child	240c02Bm
BUTTON, George	33	M	Unknown	240c02Bm
William	23	M	Unknown	240c02Bm
U-Mrs.	50	F	Unknown	240c02Bm
MILES, John	20	M	Cooper	240c02Bm
STEWART, Robert	24	M	Ctnsp	240c02Bm
OWEN, Griffith	24	M	Joiner	240c02Bm
JONES, Thos.	22	M	Joiner	240c02Bm
GROLINS, Wm.	16	M	Farmer	240c02Bm
MURPHY, Wm.	19	M	Farmer	240c02Bm
HUNTER, George	40	M	Traveller	240c02Bm
WILEY, Samuel	27	M	Hatter	240c02Bm
Elizth.	26	F	Unknown	240c02Bm
MULVANY, John	21	M	Baker	240c02Bm
PERRIN, George	63	M	Farmer	240c02Bm
Elizth.	49	F	Unknown	240c02Bm
Jane	23	F	Unknown	240c02Bm
Betsy	22	F	Unknown	240c02Bm
James	20	M	Unknown	240c02Bm
George	18	M	Unknown	240c02Bm
John	15	M	Unknown	240c02Bm
William	12	M	Unknown	240c02Bm
Mary	10	F	Unknown	240c02Bm
Ann	8	F	Child	240c02Bm
SHIELDS, Betsy	24	F	Unknown	240c02Bm
SIDDONS, Mary	26	U	Unknown	240c02Bm
Alfred	.06	M	Infant	240c02Bm
CADY, John	35	M	Laborer	240c02Bm
RYAN, Margt.	25	F	Unknown	240c02Bm
CONNER, Thos.	35	M	Laborer	240c02Bm
Maria	23	F	Unknown	240c02Bm
MCARTHUR, Robert	19	M	Unknown	240c02Bm
KENNEHAN, Joseph	36	M	Engr-Mlwr	240c02Bm
Janett	36	F	Unknown	240c02Bm
MCARTHUR, Janett	12	F	Unknown	240c02Bm
Mary	13	F	Unknown	240c02Bm
KINGHORN, Janett	19	F	Unknown	240c02Bm
HUTCHINSON, Wm.	16	M	Unknown	240c02Bm
Jas.	5	M	Child	240c02Bm
SEYTHROP, Wm.	19	M	Unknown	240c02Bm
ROSS, Eliz.	14	F	Unknown	240c02Bm
MALONEY, John	19	M	Laborer	240c02Bm
SAMPSON, Ann	21	F	Laborer	240c02Bm
BLACK, John	40	M	Cooper	240c02Bm
Mary-Ann	35	F	Unknown	240c02Bm
KIRIVAN, James	18	M	Laborer	240c02Bm
HANLEY, Fanny	18	F	Unknown	240c02Bm
WASHINGTON, Ellen	8	F	Child	240c02Bm
HOWEN, Elizth.	20	F	Unknown	240c02Bm
SMITH, Ellen	25	F	Unknown	240c02Bm
JOHNSTON, Wm.	33	M	Chemist	240c02Bm
Sarah	25	F	Unknown	240c02Bm
Sarah	14	F	Unknown	240c02Bm
Jervis	25	M	Clerk	240c02Bm
Wm.	.03	M	Infant	240c02Bm
MATHEWS, Jane	28	F	Unknown	240c02Bm
DICKSON, Charles	30	M	Unknown	240c02Bm
Fanny	28	F	Unknown	240c02Bm
COOK, Wm.	26	M	Farmer	240c02Bm
Sarah	26	F	Unknown	240c02Bm
BULGER, Edd.	40	M	Laborer	240c02Bm
OBRIEN, Mary	25	F	Unknown	240c02Bm
CLARKE, Michl.	30	M	Laborer	240c02Bm
Thos.	20	M	Laborer	240c02Bm
IGOE, Patrick	27	M	Laborer	240c02Bm
DUNN, John	21	M	Laborer	240c02Bm
TERLEY, Wm.	32	M	Laborer	240c02Bm
Elizth.	33	F	Unknown	240c02Bm
TERLEY, Chas.	3	M	Child	240c02Bm
William	1	M	Child	240c02Bm
BURCH, Thomas	42	M	Laborer	240c02Bm
Mary	36	F	Unknown	240c02Bm
Saml.	7	M	Child	240c02Bm
Selina	4	F	Child	240c02Bm
SEAR, George	24	M	Unknown	240c02Bm
CROSHIE, James	30	M	Coachman	240c02Bm
MCDONALD, James	29	M	Laborer	240c02Bm
Michl.	26	M	Laborer	240c02Bm
Ann	32	F	Unknown	240c02Bm
Michl.	.05	M	Infant	240c02Bm
James	2	M	Child	240c02Bm
THORNTON, James	29	M	Laborer	240c02Bm
KNOCK, George	28	M	Laborer	240c02Bm
Edd.	36	M	Laborer	240c02Bm
FARRELL, Mary	21	F	Unknown	240c02Bm
MCKEATON, Ellen	18	F	Unknown	240c02Bm
BOYLAN, James	18	M	Laborer	240c02Bm
ENGLEBY, Wm.	28	M	Farmer	240c02Bm
BARBER, John	23	M	Rrcttr	240c02Bm
HOWAN, Benjn.	19	M	Farmer	240c02Bm
BRIKER, Mary	30	F	Unknown	240c02Bm
John	6	M	Child	240c02Bm
NICKLE, Thomas	27	M	Laborer	240c02Bm
BURKE, John	35	M	Laborer	240c02Bm
Sally	27	F	Unknown	240c02Bm
RAY, Wm.	46	M	Unknown	240c02Bm
Robt.	17	M	Unknown	240c02Bm
HEATON, Wm.	20	M	Farmer	240c02Bm
CONSIDINE, Ellen	20	F	Unknown	240c02Bm
TOOGER, John	26	M	Unknown	240c02Bm
BURRALL, Thos.	20	M	Ctnsp	240c02Bm
BOWHAN, Patrick	32	M	Laborer	240c02Bm
WRIGHT, Naomi	36	F	Unknown	240c02Bm
George	18	M	Unknown	240c02Bm
Chas.	15	F	Unknown	240c02Bm
Saml.	13	F	Unknown	240c02Bm
Wm.	11	F	Unknown	240c02Bm
John	10	F	Unknown	240c02Bm
Mary	9	F	Child	240c02Bm
METCALF, Ann	27	F	Unknown	240c02Bm
WYNN, Mary	26	F	Unknown	240c02Bm
METCALF, John	6	M	Child	240c02Bm
Martha	4	F	Child	240c02Bm
Joseph	1	M	Child	240c02Bm
WYNN, Thos.	3	M	Child	240c02Bm
METCALF, Edd.	.06	M	Infant	240c02Bm
NOWLAN, Cathn.	40	F	Unknown	240c02Bm
Cathn.	5	F	Child	240c02Bm
HALE, Mary-Ann	26	F	Unknown	240c02Bm
George	9	M	Child	240c02Bm
GRANT, Jos.	28	M	Baker	240c02Bm
Sarah	20	F	Unknown	240c02Bm
HERTIN, James	22	M	Farmer	240c02Bm
JOHNSTON, John	28	M	Farmer	240c02Bm
BURLEY, Thos.	24	M	Farmer	240c02Bm
JOHNSTON, Thomas	24	M	Farmer	240c02Bm
SIVARY, Wm.	42	M	Unknown	240c02Bm
HACKETT, James	30	M	Unknown	240c02Bm
GREEN, Bernd.	44	M	Tailor	240c02Bm
Elizth.	40	F	Unknown	240c02Bm
Terence	17	M	Tailor	240c02Bm
James	12	M	Unknown	240c02Bm
Denis	3	M	Child	240c02Bm
ROONEY, Brian	34	M	Laborer	240c02Bm
SHERRY, John	26	M	Laborer	240c02Bm
QUINN, Mary	10	F	Unknown	240c02Bm
James	8	M	Child	240c02Bm
MCNANCY, Margt.	30	F	Unknown	240c02Bm
ROGERS, John	28	M	Laborer	240c02Bm
Eliza	30	F	Unknown	240c02Bm
Mary	20	F	Unknown	240c02Bm
HACKNEY, Ellen	25	F	Milliner	240c02Bm
NAOLI, Michael	16	M	Unknown	240c02Bm

NAMES OF PASSENGERS	AGE	SEX	OCCUPATIONS	DATE PORT SHIP
HACKETT, Laurence	40	M	Laborer	240c02Bm
Ann	36	F	Unknown	240c02Bm
John	20	M	Unknown	240c02Bm
Laurce.	18	M	Unknown	240c02Bm
Ann	9	F	Child	240c02Bm
Bridget	26	F	Unknown	240c02Bm
John	6	M	Child	240c02Bm
Maria	4	F	Child	240c02Bm
Patrick	.06	M	Infant	240c02Bm
Cathn.	.06	F	Infant	240c02Bm
ELLIOTT, Bridget	19	F	Unknown	240c02Bm
Bridget	16	F	Unknown	240c02Bm
MCGILL, Samuel	23	M	Laborer	240c02Bm
LYNCH, Ann	24	F	Unknown	240c02Bm
BRIGGS, Saml.	24	M	Miner	240c02Bm
Mary-Ann	23	F	Unknown	240c02Bm
HENNESSY, John	23	M	Laborer	240c02Bm
WILSON, Saml.	23	M	Brick Maker	240c02Bm
BELL, Thos.	34	M	Wheelwright	240c02Bm
Mary	30	F	Unknown	240c02Bm
Charlotte	6	F	Child	240c02Bm
William	4	M	Child	240c02Bm
Thomas	3	M	Child	240c02Bm
John	1	M	Child	240c02Bm
George	21	M	Wheelwright	240c02Bm
COOGAN, Mary	24	F	Unknown	240c02Bm
ROTHERFORD, Robert	40	M	Stkw	240c02Bm
RICHARD, David	44	M	Grocer	240c02Bm
WATSON, Thomas	30	M	Farmer	240c02Bm
NAILOR, Wm.	39	M	Mpol	240c02Bm
COURKIN, Andw.	30	M	Laborer	240c02Bm
Margt.	28	F	Unknown	240c02Bm
LENNAN, Ann	19	F	Unknown	240c02Bm
COOK, Ann	15	F	Unknown	240c02Bm
MOORE, John	53	M	Unknown	240c02Bm
Elizth.	43	F	Unknown	240c02Bm
Elizth.	10	F	Unknown	240c02Bm
CORR, Mary-Ann	18	F	Unknown	240c02Bm
DONNELLY, Patrick	19	M	Laborer	240c02Bm
AMBROSE, Mary	20	F	Unknown	240c02Bm
CONNOR, Johanna	17	F	Unknown	240c02Bm
MANNY, Wm.	33	M	Laborer	240c02Bm
Betsy	22	F	Unknown	240c02Bm
KEARNEY, Cathn.	24	F	Unknown	240c02Bm
LEONARD, James	28	M	Unknown	240c02Bm
Sarah	20	F	Unknown	240c02Bm
SMITH, Catherine	18	F	Unknown	240c02Bm
BRAMAN, John	35	M	Unknown	240c02Bm
GAMBLE, John-R.	28	M	Merchant	240c02Bm
BROWN, Jane	37	F	Unknown	240c02Bm
Robt.	11	M	Unknown	240c02Bm
John	9	M	Child	240c02Bm
James	5	M	Child	240c02Bm
Margt.	3	F	Child	240c02Bm
Mary-Ann	.05	F	Infant	240c02Bm
GARTLAND, John	40	M	Laborer	240c02Bm
Thomas	20	M	Unknown	240c02Bm
Mary	18	F	Unknown	240c02Bm
FINIGAN, Nancy	12	F	Unknown	240c02Bm
CLARKE, Peter	20	M	Laborer	240c02Bm
Cathn.	20	F	Unknown	240c02Bm
MCGUIRE, Frank	25	M	Laborer	240c02Bm
MALLY, Cathne.	22	F	Unknown	240c02Bm
GARLAN, Ann	18	F	Unknown	240c02Bm
PENNINGTON, Edd.	24	M	Frplh	240c02Bm
BERGEN, Henry	24	M	Cbtmkr	240c02Bm
Sarah-Ann	24	F	Unknown	240c02Bm
SHULAN, Patrick	22	M	Blacksmith	240c02Bm
MCDONALD, Luke	25	M	Laborer	240c02Bm
MURNEY, John	13	M	Laborer	240c02Bm
Patrick	12	M	Laborer	240c02Bm
MCMULLAN, James	28	M	Unknown	240c02Bm
Patrick	26	M	Unknown	240c02Bm
CRINAM, Bridget	00	F	Unknown	240c02Bm
PLUNKETT, Sarah	00	F	Unknown	240c02Bm
COWAN, Jane	00	F	Unknown	240c02Bm
MCMULLEN, Thos.	00	M	Laborer	240c02Bm
MCDONALD, Eliza	00	F	Unknown	240c02Bm
MILLS, Sarah	00	F	Dressmaker	240c02Bm
Maria-Ann	4	F	Child	240c02Bm
Thomas	.05	M	Infant	240c02Bm
MIHAN, Patrick	00	M	Laborer	240c02Bm
HIGGINS, Jas.	00	M	Laborer	240c02Bm
MURRAN, Bernd.	8	M	Child	240c02Bm
EARLY, Ann	22	F	Laborer	240c02Bm
HALLIDAY, Andrew	24	M	Whitesmith	240c02Bm
JONES, U-Mrs.	24	F	Unknown	240c02Bm
BRANT, Wm.	22	M	Gdnr	240c02Bm
BASSETT, Wm.	19	M	Paper Maker	240c02Bm
GORMAN, Michl.	24	M	Laborer	240c02Bm
SKEVINGTON, Richd.	24	M	Laborer	240c02Bm
BURAN, Danl.	35	M	Laborer	240c02Bm
DRENNAN, John	55	M	Laborer	240c02Bm
CASTERDINE, Wm.	24	M	Watchmaker	240c02Bm
STORAN, Bridget	20	F	Unknown	240c02Bm
FAHY, Mary	18	F	Unknown	240c02Bm
CORCORAN, Patrick	24	M	Laborer	240c02Bm
Mary	20	F	Laborer	240c02Bm
MCGUINESS, Bessy	18	F	Unknown	240c02Bm
FLYNN, Bridget	20	F	Unknown	240c02Bm
MALONE, Ann	40	F	Unknown	240c02Bm
HARVEY, Cathn.	40	F	Unknown	240c02Bm
HALLORAN, James	40	M	Laborer	240c02Bm
Cathn.	38	F	Unknown	240c02Bm
John	12	M	Unknown	240c02Bm
Mary	11	F	Unknown	240c02Bm
Ellen	10	F	Unknown	240c02Bm
Michl.	8	M	Child	240c02Bm
Cathne.	6	F	Child	240c02Bm
FALLON, John	4	M	Child	240c02Bm
Margaret	2	F	Child	240c02Bm
Thomas	.08	M	Infant	240c02Bm
LORIGAN, John	25	M	Unknown	240c02Bm
BRYAN, Ellen	21	F	Unknown	240c02Bm
MONAGHAN, Terence	24	M	Laborer	240c02Bm
Ann	20	F	Unknown	240c02Bm
MCDONOUGH, Mick	28	M	Laborer	240c02Bm
KELLY, Bridget	17	F	Unknown	240c02Bm
MCCANNAN, John	30	M	Laborer	240c02Bm
Susan	35	F	Unknown	240c02Bm
Susan	7	F	Child	240c02Bm
Sarah	5	F	Child	240c02Bm
HOME, James	58	M	Laborer	240c02Bm
OLIVER, John	20	M	Farmer	240c02Bm
Jane	20	F	Unknown	240c02Bm
Ellen	.03	F	Infant	240c02Bm
MCAUDRY, Sarah	33	F	Unknown	240c02Bm
Agnes	9	F	Child	240c02Bm
Sarah	7	F	Child	240c02Bm
James	5	M	Child	240c02Bm
Susan	3	F	Child	240c02Bm
REILLY, Honora	20	F	Unknown	240c02Bm
BRIAN, Michl.	28	M	Laborer	240c02Bm
CONOLLY, Eliza	22	F	Unknown	240c02Bm
Constantine	5	M	Child	240c02Bm
John	3	M	Child	240c02Bm
SMITH, Margaret	16	F	Unknown	240c02Bm
CONNOVAN, Margaret	13	F	Unknown	240c02Bm
James	11	M	Laborer	240c02Bm
John	9	M	Child	240c02Bm
Alice	4	F	Child	240c02Bm
MURPHY, Alice	13	F	Unknown	240c02Bm
CONOLLY, Margt.	14	F	Unknown	240c02Bm
COSGROVE, M.	32	M	Unknown	240c02Bm
H.	20	M	Unknown	240c02Bm
Francis	15	M	Unknown	240c02Bm
Nancy	20	F	Unknown	240c02Bm
Cathne.	12	F	Unknown	240c02Bm
KELLY, Sarah	14	F	Unknown	240c02Bm
CARR, Edward	22	M	Laborer	240c02Bm

NAMES OF PASSENGERS	AGE	SEX	OCCUPATIONS	DATE PORT SHIP
CARR, Bridget	20	F	Unknown	240c02Bm
Julia	9	F	Child	240c02Bm
MADDEN, Lawrence	45	M	Laborer	240c02Bm
Biddy	46	F	Unknown	240c02Bm
Thomas	18	M	Unknown	240c02Bm
Mary	16	F	Unknown	240c02Bm
CULLEN, Thomas	45	M	Laborer	240c02Bm
Alice	40	F	Unknown	240c02Bm
NOSHUR, John	30	M	Collier	240c02Bm
CAINES, Rebecca	20	F	Unknown	240c02Bm
HANNA, Alexr.	40	M	Laborer	240c02Bm
MCKEENE, Betty	18	F	Unknown	240c02Bm
COOKE, Stephen	21	M	Unknown	240c02Bm
WOODS, Mary	15	F	Unknown	240c02Bm
SMITH, Benjn.	13	M	Unknown	240c02Bm
MCGUINESS, Patrick	30	M	Unknown	240c02Bm
Mary	20	F	Unknown	240c02Bm
MCBREARTY, Wm.	30	M	Unknown	240c02Bm
GRACE, Mary	18	F	Unknown	240c02Bm
Ann	16	F	Unknown	240c02Bm
REILLY, Thomas	30	M	Laborer	240c02Bm
Mary	25	F	Unknown	240c02Bm
Patrick	.04	M	Infant	240c02Bm
Margt.	24	F	Unknown	240c02Bm
Margt.	20	F	Unknown	240c02Bm
FINNEGAN, Ann	18	F	Unknown	240c02Bm
MARTIN, Thos.	24	M	Laborer	240c02Bm
Cathne.	20	F	Unknown	240c02Bm
MCGUIRE, Barney	30	M	Unknown	240c02Bm
DOBBYN, James	25	M	Gdnr	240c02Bm
Eliza	18	F	Unknown	240c02Bm
MURRAY, Patrick	21	M	Laborer	240c02Bm
Cathne.	26	F	Unknown	240c02Bm
MITCHELL, Honora	25	F	Unknown	240c02Bm
DAILY, Cathne.	30	F	Unknown	240c02Bm
Mary	5	F	Child	240c02Bm
MCGRATH, Patrick	27	M	Unknown	240c02Bm
CONNOLLY, Michl.	19	M	Laborer	240c02Bm
BOUGH, Francis	21	M	Laborer	240c02Bm
SMITH, Peter	18	M	Unknown	240c02Bm
LYNCH, Ann	19	F	Unknown	240c02Bm
OBRIEN, Rosanna	40	F	Unknown	240c02Bm
Hugh	12	M	Unknown	240c02Bm
James	10	M	Unknown	240c02Bm
Bridget	8	F	Child	240c02Bm
John	5	M	Child	240c02Bm
MINNIS, Sarah	18	F	Unknown	240c02Bm
Cathne.	15	F	Unknown	240c02Bm
MULHOLEN, Peter	16	M	Unknown	240c02Bm
KELLY, Cathne.	20	F	Unknown	240c02Bm
Pat.	25	M	Unknown	240c02Bm
KANE, Pat.	30	M	Laborer	240c02Bm
Judy	25	F	Unknown	240c02Bm
Mary	10	F	Unknown	240c02Bm
Patrick	8	M	Child	240c02Bm
John	6	M	Child	240c02Bm
OLDHAM, John	16	M	Unknown	240c02Bm
HICKEY, Owen	24	M	Laborer	240c02Bm
MULVANY, Bridget	40	F	Unknown	240c02Bm
Patrick	12	M	Unknown	240c02Bm
Mary	10	F	Unknown	240c02Bm
James	8	M	Child	240c02Bm
Ann	4	F	Child	240c02Bm
John	2	M	Child	240c02Bm
HADY, U-Mrs.	34	F	Unknown	240c02Bm
Martha	10	F	Unknown	240c02Bm
Hannah	2	F	Child	240c02Bm
Thomas	.08	F	Infant	240c02Bm
STODDART, Julia	25	F	Unknown	240c02Bm
George	2	M	Child	240c02Bm
MADDEN, Michl.	25	M	Laborer	240c02Bm
GLENMAN, Mary	19	F	Unknown	240c02Bm
MCGUIRE, Mary	20	F	Unknown	240c02Bm
MCFARLANE, Elizth.	22	F	Unknown	240c02Bm
CROGIN, Elizth.	18	F	Unknown	240c02Bm
PRIN, Mary	22	F	Unknown	240c02Bm
QUINCY, Cathne.	12	F	Unknown	240c02Bm
RUSSELL, Terence	20	M	Laborer	240c02Bm
ONEILL, Bridget	19	F	Laborer	240c02Bm
QUINN, Isabella	40	F	Unknown	240c02Bm
CLEMENTS, Thomas	43	M	Surveyor	240c02Bm
GANNON, Michl.	30	M	Laborer	240c02Bm
Ellen	40	F	Unknown	240c02Bm
BIRTWELL, A.	00	M	Saddler	240c02Bm
TOHER, Wm.	33	M	Laborer	240c02Bm
CUNNINGHAM, Pat	30	M	Laborer	240c02Bm
KAYS, Pat	18	M	Laborer	240c02Bm
KENNY, Michl.	15	M	Unknown	240c02Bm
COODY, Mary	46	F	Unknown	240c02Bm
Edward	20	M	Unknown	240c02Bm
Ellen	18	F	Unknown	240c02Bm
Cathne.	16	F	Unknown	240c02Bm
Pierce	9	M	Child	240c02Bm
Bridget	6	F	Child	240c02Bm
Michael	4	M	Child	240c02Bm
MCDONNELL, John	14	M	Unknown	240c02Bm
JONES, Saml.	55	M	Unknown	240c02Bm
Alexander	25	M	Unknown	240c02Bm
Bridget	56	F	Unknown	240c02Bm
KELLY, Richd.	21	M	Medst	240c02Bm
CORRIGAN, Robt.	20	M	Unknown	240c02Bm
Eliza	22	F	Unknown	240c02Bm
Ann	13	F	Unknown	240c02Bm
Sarah	11	F	Unknown	240c02Bm
HARRINGTON, Martin	21	M	Unknown	240c02Bm
Michl.	19	M	Unknown	240c02Bm
Eliza	16	F	Unknown	240c02Bm
KENNEDY, Wm.	45	M	Farmer	240c02Bm
Ann	38	F	Unknown	240c02Bm
Michl.	11	M	Unknown	240c02Bm
Patrick	10	M	Unknown	240c02Bm
Martin	8	M	Child	240c02Bm
Margt.	4	F	Child	240c02Bm
NEWLIN, Chas.	23	M	Laborer	240c02Bm
MADDEN, John	19	M	Unknown	240c02Bm
FAHY, Cathne.	20	F	Unknown	240c02Bm
MALONY, Margt.	18	F	Unknown	240c02Bm
LYNCH, James	19	M	Laborer	240c02Bm
LONG, Margt.	30	F	Unknown	240c02Bm
Peggy	9	F	Child	240c02Bm
Patrick	7	M	Child	240c02Bm
Johanna	3	F	Child	240c02Bm
TALTY, Bridget	20	F	Unknown	240c02Bm
Peter	18	M	Unknown	240c02Bm
Ellen	13	F	Unknown	240c02Bm
KELLY, Honora	50	F	Unknown	240c02Bm
Bridget	16	F	Unknown	240c02Bm
Patrick	40	M	Laborer	240c02Bm
Margt.	30	F	Unknown	240c02Bm
Michl.	9	M	Child	240c02Bm
Peter	7	M	Child	240c02Bm
Sarah	.05	F	Infant	240c02Bm
BARRY, Sarah	25	F	Unknown	240c02Bm
HOLDEN, Ellenor	50	F	Unknown	240c02Bm
Cathne.	17	F	Unknown	240c02Bm
Francis	10	M	Unknown	240c02Bm
DEIGHAN, Thomas	19	M	Unknown	240c02Bm
Cathne.	19	F	Unknown	240c02Bm
CLARKE, Cathne.	40	F	Unknown	240c02Bm
Herbert	11	M	Unknown	240c02Bm
KENNY, John	35	M	Laborer	240c02Bm
DEMPSEY, Margt.	24	F	Unknown	240c02Bm
ROTHERHAM, Mary-Ann	18	F	Unknown	240c02Bm
John	12	M	Unknown	240c02Bm
Edd.	8	M	Child	240c02Bm
DEMPSEY, Ellen	28	F	Unknown	240c02Bm
MCINERNY, Connor	45	M	Unknown	240c02Bm
Mary	13	F	Unknown	240c02Bm
Judy	12	F	Unknown	240c02Bm
BERNFIELD, Nancy	16	F	Unknown	240c02Bm

NAMES OF PASSENGERS	AGE	SEX	OCCUPATIONS	DATE PORT SHIP
WILLIAMS, Giles	30	M	Laborer	240c02Bm
Cathne.	25	F	Unknown	240c02Bm
GRIFFIN, David	22	M	Laborer	240c02Bm
HINCHERY, Eliza	27	F	Unknown	240c02Bm
MAHER, Mary	34	F	Unknown	240c02Bm
KELLY, Robt.	20	M	Laborer	240c02Bm
Margt.	21	F	Laborer	240c02Bm
BENNETT, Edward	21	M	Laborer	240c02Bm
LINHAM, Patrick	35	M	Laborer	240c02Bm
TEMORY, James	23	M	Laborer	240c02Bm
MCDERMOTT, Patrick	20	M	Laborer	240c02Bm
OROURKE, Michl.	20	M	Tailor	240c02Bm
MORT, Betty	25	F	Unknown	240c02Bm
KENDRICK, John	54	M	Weaver	240c02Bm
MCGLONE, Danl.	22	M	Unknown	240c02Bm
TELTON, Henry	21	M	Painter	240c02Bm
TURNER, James	31	M	Ctnsp	240c02Bm
Mary-Ann	27	F	Unknown	240c02Bm
Sarah	5	F	Child	240c02Bm
CATOR, Wm.	23	M	Unknown	240c02Bm
TAYLOR, Isaiah	18	M	Miner	240c02Bm
HUGHES, John	30	M	Bleacher	240c02Bm
Eliza	25	F	Unknown	240c02Bm
Eliza	.05	F	Infant	240c02Bm
MCILWAIN, Hugh	24	M	Unknown	240c02Bm
Sarah	24	F	Unknown	240c02Bm
WALLS, Jane	22	F	Unknown	240c02Bm
James	35	M	Laborer	240c02Bm
DOAL, George	19	M	Unknown	240c02Bm
MCNICHOLL, Mary	20	F	Unknown	240c02Bm
CAMLIN, Eliza	20	F	Unknown	240c02Bm
CAMPBELL, Eliza	30	F	Unknown	240c02Bm
Wm.	16	M	Clerk	240c02Bm
James	14	M	Unknown	240c02Bm
Sarah	11	F	Unknown	240c02Bm
Eliza	9	M	Child	240c02Bm
John	7	M	Child	240c02Bm
Thomas	4	M	Child	240c02Bm
Jane	3	F	Child	240c02Bm
Washington	.05	M	Infant	240c02Bm
KEILT, Eliza	19	F	Unknown	240c02Bm
HILLY, Sally	27	F	Unknown	240c02Bm
MCNICHOLL, Miles	50	M	Unknown	240c02Bm
CONWAY, John	9	M	Child	240c02Bm
FITZPATRICK, Michl.	20	M	Laborer	240c02Bm
Peggy	11	F	Unknown	240c02Bm
FORBES, Wm.	27	M	Engineer	240c02Bm
BARNETT, Michl.	60	M	Laborer	240c02Bm
Bridget	48	F	Unknown	240c02Bm
BARRETT, John	19	M	Laborer	240c02Bm
Ellen	13	F	Unknown	240c02Bm
Robert	10	M	Unknown	240c02Bm
Cathne.	4	M	Child	240c02Bm
DONOHOE, Bridget	40	F	Unknown	240c02Bm
Patrick	13	M	Unknown	240c02Bm
Mary	10	F	Unknown	240c02Bm
BRAZELL, Mary	20	F	Unknown	240c02Bm
WALLACE, Mary	20	F	Unknown	240c02Bm
CONNERY, Mick	18	M	Laborer	240c02Bm
OBRIEN, Patr.	22	M	Laborer	240c02Bm
MULLANE, Patr.	18	M	Unknown	240c02Bm
Ellen	17	F	Unknown	240c02Bm
FARRELL, Eliza	20	F	Unknown	240c02Bm
JONNY, James	22	M	Laborer	240c02Bm
MALONEY, Patrick	46	M	Laborer	240c02Bm
Mary	30	F	Unknown	240c02Bm
CONWAY, James	40	M	Unknown	240c02Bm
Bridget	16	F	Unknown	240c02Bm
Patrick	13	M	Laborer	240c02Bm
Cathne.	11	F	Unknown	240c02Bm
Ellen	8	F	Child	240c02Bm
Mary	6	F	Child	240c02Bm
HEALY, John	26	M	Laborer	240c02Bm
ODONNELL, R.	22	M	Laborer	240c02Bm
MCKENNA, Wm.	22	M	Clerk	240c02Bm

NAMES OF PASSENGERS	AGE	SEX	OCCUPATIONS	DATE PORT SHIP
MCKENNA, Randall	19	M	Clerk	240c02Bm
NICKSON, R.	33	M	Unknown	240c02Bm
Mary	30	F	Unknown	240c02Bm
John	4	M	Child	240c02Bm
Cathne.	.06	F	Infant	240c02Bm
HENRY, Hugh	25	M	Laborer	240c02Bm
CAMPBELL, Margaret	25	F	Unknown	240c02Bm
DONNELLY, Margaret	25	F	Unknown	240c02Bm
Johanna	20	F	Unknown	240c02Bm
MONAGHAN, Danl.	22	M	Laborer	240c02Bm
Honor	25	F	Unknown	240c02Bm
HARTY, James	20	M	Laborer	240c02Bm
MORIARTY, M.	7	M	Child	240c02Bm
Johanna	6	F	Child	240c02Bm
Johanna	25	F	Unknown	240c02Bm
CONNOR, Ellenor	40	F	Unknown	240c02Bm
Margt.	11	F	Unknown	240c02Bm
Mary	7	F	Child	240c02Bm
James	2	M	Child	240c02Bm
MOORE, Bridget	20	F	Unknown	240c02Bm
SMITH, James	27	M	Unknown	240c02Bm
STOCKDALE, William	20	M	Unknown	240c02Bm
CORBETT, Letitia	18	F	Unknown	240c02Bm
SANDERSON, J.	18	F	Unknown	240c02Bm
ODONNELL, Mick	30	M	Unknown	240c02Bm
Ellen	30	F	Unknown	240c02Bm
PURCELL, Cathne.	24	F	Unknown	240c02Bm
FARRELL, Bridget	22	F	Unknown	240c02Bm
CONLON, Mary	18	F	Unknown	240c02Bm
MCCANN, Cathne.	17	F	Unknown	240c02Bm
CANNON, P.	21	M	Unknown	240c02Bm
GAINOR, Bessie	25	F	Unknown	240c02Bm
HOPKINS, Cathne.	21	F	Unknown	240c02Bm
MCKENNA, Margt.	23	F	Unknown	240c02Bm
William	1	M	Child	240c02Bm
CUDDY, F.	16	M	Laborer	240c02Bm
WHITTY, Elizth.	29	F	Unknown	240c02Bm
William	8	M	Child	240c02Bm
Ann	4	F	Child	240c02Bm
Jessica	2	F	Child	240c02Bm
TOWNSEND, Joseph	22	M	Machinist	240c02Bm
MULLOON, Edward	44	M	Laborer	240c02Bm
MULLONEY, Patrick	40	M	Unknown	240c02Bm
Mary	20	F	Unknown	240c02Bm
James	12	M	Unknown	240c02Bm
Ann	.06	F	Infant	240c02Bm
GRAHAM, Peter	00	M	Unknown	240c02Bm
EMMETT, Cathne.	20	F	Unknown	240c02Bm
MARSHALL, Wm.	28	M	Unknown	240c02Bm
OHERN, Ellen	30	F	Unknown	240c02Bm
Pat.	8	M	Child	240c02Bm
QUINN, Mary	20	F	Unknown	240c02Bm
JAURY, James	20	M	Unknown	240c02Bm
ONEILL, Ann	16	F	Unknown	240c02Bm
Bridget	13	F	Unknown	240c02Bm
MULAHY, Mary	22	F	Unknown	240c02Bm
WALSH, James	20	M	Laborer	240c02Bm
BAINE, Ellen	20	F	Unknown	240c02Bm
BIRD, Mary	20	F	Unknown	240c02Bm
OBIERNE, Sally	21	F	Unknown	240c02Bm
Mary	23	F	Unknown	240c02Bm
DILLON, Margaret	20	F	Unknown	240c02Bm
CONSIDINE, Bridget	20	F	Unknown	240c02Bm
MORRISEY, Cathne.	27	F	Unknown	240c02Bm
QUINN, N.	13	M	Unknown	240c02Bm
Ellen	11	F	Unknown	240c02Bm
Martin	7	M	Child	240c02Bm
OHANLON, P.	20	M	Trade Man	240c02Bm
LEDIN, John	21	M	Laborer	240c02Bm
GILLIGAN, Wm.	15	M	Unknown	240c02Bm
Johanna	35	F	Unknown	240c02Bm
Ellen	13	F	Unknown	240c02Bm
Brady	11	M	Unknown	240c02Bm
Mary	9	F	Child	240c02Bm
Margt.	3	F	Child	240c02Bm

NAMES OF PASSENGERS	AGE	SEX	OCCUPATIONS	DATE PORT SHIP
GILLIGAN, Richd.	.05	M	Infant	240c02Bm
MURRAY, Richard	20	M	Laborer	240c02Bm
KEARNEY, H.	60	M	Laborer	240c02Bm
HANLY, Mary	32	F	Unknown	240c02Bm
Maria	10	F	Unknown	240c02Bm
Edd.	10	M	Unknown	240c02Bm
William	8	M	Child	240c02Bm
John	6	M	Child	240c02Bm
Thomas	4	M	Child	240c02Bm
James	4	M	Child	240c02Bm
Honor	.06	F	Infant	240c02Bm
Rose	20	F	Unknown	240c02Bm
Mary	25	F	Unknown	240c02Bm
DOOLAN, Richd.	60	M	Laborer	240c02Bm
MURRAY, Patrick	16	M	Unknown	240c02Bm
BROWN, Benjn.	23	M	Laborer	240c02Bm
LANIGAN, Mick	25	M	Unknown	240c02Bm
WHITE, Michl.	12	M	Unknown	240c02Bm
JINNY, John	24	M	Unknown	240c02Bm
DALY, James	20	M	Unknown	240c02Bm
FARRELL, Patrick	40	M	Unknown	240c02Bm
DEVINE, Mary	6	F	Child	240c02Bm
Edd.	12	M	Unknown	240c02Bm
DIGAN, Edd.	58	M	Unknown	240c02Bm
U (W)	58	F	Unknown	240c02Bm
Danl.	23	M	Unknown	240c02Bm
Winifred	20	F	Unknown	240c02Bm
Mathew	18	M	Unknown	240c02Bm
Martin	13	M	Unknown	240c02Bm
GALLAHER, Patrick	26	M	Laborer	240c02Bm
LENNON, Michl.	40	M	Unknown	240c02Bm
U (W)	26	F	Unknown	240c02Bm
James	4	M	Child	240c02Bm
Edward	.04	M	Infant	240c02Bm
BRADY, James	30	M	Unknown	240c02Bm
BOODLE, Robert	17	M	Unknown	240c02Bm
MCGRANE, Margt.	40	F	Unknown	240c02Bm
Peter	25	M	Unknown	240c02Bm
Thomas	20	M	Unknown	240c02Bm
Terence	11	M	Unknown	240c02Bm
Owen	6	M	Child	240c02Bm
Elizth.	9	F	Child	240c02Bm
CORCORAN, James	30	M	Laborer	240c02Bm
HOPKINS, Margt.	20	F	Unknown	240c02Bm
HANLEY, Ellen	15	F	Unknown	240c02Bm
GEOGHAN, James	40	M	Farmer	240c02Bm
Mary	30	F	Unknown	240c02Bm
Mary-Ann	20	F	Unknown	240c02Bm
FITZPATRICK, Cathne.	40	F	Unknown	240c02Bm
Patrick	14	M	Unknown	240c02Bm
Mary	11	F	Unknown	240c02Bm
Richd.	9	M	Child	240c02Bm
GANNON, Ann	16	F	Unknown	240c02Bm
HART, Mary	4	F	Child	240c02Bm
MADDEN, Mary	14	F	Unknown	240c02Bm
DUNN, Mary	24	F	Unknown	240c02Bm
SMITH, Mary	35	F	Unknown	240c02Bm
John	35	M	Laborer	240c02Bm
Martha	35	F	Unknown	240c02Bm
Margt.	35	F	Unknown	240c02Bm
Mary	35	F	Unknown	240c02Bm
Thomas	35	M	Unknown	240c02Bm
MURPHY, Terence	50	M	Unknown	240c02Bm
Ellen	16	F	Unknown	240c02Bm
GRIMES, Ann	19	F	Unknown	240c02Bm
HAMILL, Ally	40	F	Unknown	240c02Bm
Terence	6	M	Child	240c02Bm
Mary	4	F	Child	240c02Bm
Patrick	2	M	Child	240c02Bm
DOYLE, John	50	M	Laborer	240c02Bm
U (W)	30	F	Unknown	240c02Bm
John	4	M	Child	240c02Bm
CONOLLY, Alice	36	F	Unknown	240c02Bm
John	4	M	Child	240c02Bm
FITZGERALD, Cathne.	26	F	Unknown	240c02Bm
FITZGERALD, Cornls.	10	M	Unknown	240c02Bm
John	8	M	Child	240c02Bm
Thomas	6	M	Child	240c02Bm
BYNAM, Margt.	32	F	Unknown	240c02Bm
Martha	14	F	Unknown	240c02Bm
Edward	10	M	Unknown	240c02Bm
Jane	5	F	Child	240c02Bm
FEIRY, Keiran	12	M	Unknown	240c02Bm
COONEY, Bridget	18	F	Unknown	240c02Bm
CLIFFORD, John	11	M	Unknown	240c02Bm
MCDERMOTT, Margaret	24	F	Unknown	240c02Bm
CORRIGAN, Bridget	8	F	Child	240c02Bm
Honor	6	F	Child	240c02Bm
MARSHALL, Thomas	30	M	Laborer	240c02Bm
WOGAN, Rose	20	F	Unknown	240c02Bm
MARSHALL, Mary	13	F	Unknown	240c02Bm
Michl.	11	M	Unknown	240c02Bm
James	9	M	Child	240c02Bm
Ellen	7	F	Child	240c02Bm
Patrick	5	M	Child	240c02Bm
MAUNEN, Mary	14	F	Unknown	240c02Bm
FOLEY, Maurice	20	M	Unknown	240c02Bm
Johanna	5	F	Child	240c02Bm
QUINN, Michl.	15	M	Unknown	240c02Bm
Mary	24	F	Unknown	240c02Bm
Michl.	.06	M	Infant	240c02Bm
DUNN, Sarah	15	F	Unknown	240c02Bm
Thomas	13	M	Unknown	240c02Bm
James	8	M	Child	240c02Bm
Michael	11	M	Unknown	240c02Bm
COLE, Charles	16	M	Unknown	240c02Bm
Maurice	10	M	Unknown	240c02Bm
MCCANN, Betty	18	F	Unknown	240c02Bm
HORAN, Keiran	11	M	Unknown	240c02Bm
REAG, Mary	30	F	Unknown	240c02Bm
HEARN, John	30	M	Laborer	240c02Bm
BELL, Wm.	13	M	Unknown	240c02Bm
MCVALTER, George	36	M	Cooper	240c02Bm
Mary	26	F	Unknown	240c02Bm
Courtney	9	M	Child	240c02Bm
John	7	M	Child	240c02Bm
Mary	4	F	Child	240c02Bm
Elizth.	1	F	Child	240c02Bm
SAGE, Courtney	39	M	Cooper	240c02Bm
IRVING, Wm.	20	M	Laborer	240c02Bm
CARTNEY, Michl.	20	M	Laborer	240c02Bm
WARREN, John	30	M	Unknown	240c02Bm
Margt.	30	F	Unknown	240c02Bm
LYNCH, Michael	20	M	Unknown	240c02Bm
MCNAMARA, Wm.	30	M	Laborer	240c02Bm
QUILLAN, Patrick	18	M	Unknown	240c02Bm
CRONAN, Mary	11	F	Unknown	240c02Bm
DIXON, Margt.	30	M	Unknown	240c02Bm
Michl.	8	M	Child	240c02Bm
Willm.	5	M	Child	240c02Bm
Ellen	4	F	Child	240c02Bm
DOLAN, John	33	M	Unknown	240c02Bm
ONEILL, John	18	M	Blacksmith	240c02Bm
Michl.	17	M	Blacksmith	240c02Bm
COLLAN, Michl.	18	M	Laborer	240c02Bm
JONES, Mary	37	F	Unknown	240c02Bm
Sarah	14	F	Unknown	240c02Bm
John	7	M	Child	240c02Bm
STEPHENS, Kate	20	F	Unknown	240c02Bm
GUY, Mat.	30	M	Laborer	240c02Bm
HOLLAND, Cathne.	24	F	Unknown	240c02Bm
Wm.	6	M	Child	240c02Bm
MCMAHON, Patrick	7	M	Child	240c02Bm
GRAY, Mary	00	F	Unknown	240c02Bm
Ellen	00	F	Unknown	240c02Bm
SCALLY, James	00	M	Unknown	240c02Bm
Michl.	00	M	Unknown	240c02Bm
HORSFIELD, Ann	00	F	Unknown	240c02Bm
Elizth.	00	F	Unknown	240c02Bm
Edwd.	00	M	Unknown	240c02Bm

NAMES OF PASSENGERS	AGE	SEX	OCCUPATIONS	DATE PORT SHIP
HORSFIELD, Hannah	00	F	Unknown	240c02Bm
Rachel	3	F	Child	240c02Bm
MCCORT, Margt.	00	F	Unknown	240c02Bm
Ann	13	F	Unknown	240c02Bm
Patrick	11	M	Unknown	240c02Bm
Francis	5	M	Child	240c02Bm
U-Mrs.	00	F	Unknown	240c02Bm
MCQUADE, Margt.	14	F	Unknown	240c02Bm
Jane	7	F	Child	240c02Bm
Edwd.	4	M	Child	240c02Bm
ONEILL, Mary	00	F	Unknown	240c02Bm
SHERIDAN, Rose	00	F	Unknown	240c02Bm
MCKENSIE, George	00	M	Servant	240c02Bm
FOX, Patrick	00	M	Laborer	240c02Bm
Michael	00	M	Unknown	240c02Bm
MONAHAN, Mary	19	F	Unknown	240c02Bm
GILL, George	50	M	Farmer	240c02Bm
Jane	50	F	Unknown	240c02Bm
Ann	17	F	Unknown	240c02Bm
Hannah	12	F	Unknown	240c02Bm
Thomas	8	M	Child	240c02Bm
COOKES, Thomas	25	M	Farmer	240c02Bm
HODWAY, Benjn.	40	M	Farmer	240c02Bm
Eliza	35	F	Unknown	240c02Bm
James	4	M	Child	240c02Bm
DAVISON, Mary	30	F	Unknown	240c02Bm
BURRELL, Henry	28	M	Goldsmith	240c02Bm
Jane	30	F	Unknown	240c02Bm
William	1	M	Child	240c02Bm
CALDWELL, Henry	20	M	Surveyor	240c02Bm
DAVISON, Wm.	30	M	Rrcttr	240c02Bm
Mary	31	F	Unknown	240c02Bm
George	3	M	Child	240c02Bm
ARMSTRONG, James	39	M	Rrcttr	240c02Bm
Alice	39	F	Unknown	240c02Bm
Elizth.	7	F	Child	240c02Bm
Alice	2	F	Child	240c02Bm
John	.05	M	Infant	240c02Bm
PURCELL, Peter	27	M	Unknown	240c02Bm
MOOLEY, Patrick	00	M	Unknown	240c02Bm
Died-At-Sea				
ROE, Jas.	00	M	Unknown	240c02Bm
Died-At-Sea				
MOLEY, Ann	00	F	Unknown	240c02Bm
Died-At-Sea				
BARRETT, James	7	M	Child	240c02Bm

MONTEZUMA 29 OCTOBER 1849

From Liverpool

NAMES OF PASSENGERS	AGE	SEX	OCCUPATIONS	DATE PORT SHIP
PRINELABM, Nora	30	F	Servant	290c02Bl
Margt.	.00	F	Infant	290c02Bl
QUINLAN, Mary	35	F	Servant	290c02Bl
SMITH, Ann	50	F	Servant	290c02Bl
Died-At-Sea				
Cath.	18	F	Servant	290c02Bl
CUNNINGHAM, Mary	14	F	Servant	290c02Bl
Rose	12	F	Servant	290c02Bl
DUNN, Bridgt.	27	F	Servant	290c02Bl
DORAN, Nancy	18	F	Servant	290c02Bl
SMITH, Ann	20	F	Servant	290c02Bl
CAREY, Mary	35	F	Wife	290c02Bl
Jane	.00	F	Infant	290c02Bl
Died-At-Sea				
Ann	10	F	Unknown	290c02Bl
Bridgt.	8	F	Child	290c02Bl
Mary	6	F	Child	290c02Bl
Luke	3	M	Child	290c02Bl
CONNOR, Nancy	30	F	Servant	290c02Bl
BONE, Ellen	8	F	Child	290c02Bl
Mary	5	F	Child	290c02Bl
U	.00	F	Infant	290c02Bl
MITCHELL, Eliza	22	F	Seamstress	290c02Bl
CAHALLER, Michl.	20	M	Laborer	290c02Bl
MCDERMOTT, Cath.	50	F	Servant	290c02Bl
LUMBERT, Eliza	22	F	Servant	290c02Bl
HENESSY, Wm.	40	M	Farmer	290c02Bl
Joanna	10	F	Unknown	290c02Bl
Tho.	6	M	Child	290c02Bl
Jno.	3	M	Child	290c02Bl
RYAN, Tho.	14	M	Laborer	290c02Bl
PENNEN, Ann	22	F	Servant	290c02Bl
KELLY, Mary	6	F	Child	290c02Bl
Bridgt.	8	F	Child	290c02Bl
LOWE, Bridget	30	F	Servant	290c02Bl
Jane	22	F	Servant	290c02Bl
JUDGE, Eliz.	20	F	Servant	290c02Bl
BRADY, Eliza	40	F	Mtmkr	290c02Bl
FITZGERALD, Pat	26	M	Laborer	290c02Bl
COWAN, Cathn.	18	F	Servant	290c02Bl
PINELLY, Bridgt.	30	F	Servant	290c02Bl
Jas.	7	M	Child	290c02Bl
Bridgt.	4	F	Child	290c02Bl
Wm.	3	M	Child	290c02Bl
RIDDAN, Mary	38	F	Servant	290c02Bl
COYLE, Bessy	19	F	Servant	290c02Bl
BROCK, Tho.	4	M	Child	290c02Bl
PAGAN, Ann	19	F	Servant	290c02Bl
Bessy	17	F	Servant	290c02Bl
DOYLE, Wm.	30	M	Servant	290c02Bl
Pat	7	M	Child	290c02Bl
Hines	5	M	Child	290c02Bl
WOODS, Peter	60	M	Farmer	290c02Bl
Jno.Jr.	16	M	Shoemaker	290c02Bl
FAGAN, Ann	40	F	Servant	290c02Bl
Margt.	11	F	Unknown	290c02Bl
Mary	8	F	Child	290c02Bl
Leah	6	F	Child	290c02Bl
Jno.	4	M	Child	290c02Bl
MCDERMITT, Martin	44	M	Laborer	290c02Bl
RITCHIE, Jane	20	F	Laborer	290c02Bl
Alex	12	M	Laborer	290c02Bl
GELLISPIE, Jno.	17	M	Laborer	290c02Bl
Ann	24	F	Servant	290c02Bl
THOMPSON, Cathn.	21	F	Servant	290c02Bl
MURPHY, Martin	2	M	Child	290c02Bl
PLENNING, Julia	20	F	Servant	290c02Bl
BAMBRICK, Ann	17	F	Servant	290c02Bl
COX, Bridget	22	F	Dressmaker	290c02Bl
MILEY, Mary	18	F	Servant	290c02Bl
LYNCH, Bridget	18	F	Servant	290c02Bl
Jno	16	M	Servant	290c02Bl
HAND, Mary	15	F	Servant	290c02Bl
Bridgt.	14	F	Servant	290c02Bl
FLYNN, Mary	45	F	Servant	290c02Bl
Mary	30	F	Servant	290c02Bl
Bridgt.	25	F	Servant	290c02Bl
Mary	.00	F	Infant	290c02Bl
Wm.	5	M	Child	290c02Bl
Jas	1	M	Child	290c02Bl
VERDEN, Jane	25	F	Laborer	290c02Bl
LAWLER, Jno.	25	M	Laborer	290c02Bl
MCDOOL, Fore	27	M	Laborer	290c02Bl
Peter	17	M	Laborer	290c02Bl
STRUTE, Ellen	24	F	Servant	290c02Bl
Margt.	3	F	Child	290c02Bl
MCMAHON, P.	22	M	Laborer	290c02Bl
BEDDORES, Sarah	27	F	Servant	290c02Bl
Geo.	4	M	Child	290c02Bl
Died-At-Sea				
Jas.	2	M	Child	290c02Bl
Died-At-Sea				
BARY, Margt.	35	F	Servant	290c02Bl

NAMES OF PASSENGERS	AGE	SEX	OCCUPATIONS	DATE PORT SHIP
BRISLANE, Edwd.	4	M	Child	290c02BI
Died-At-Sea				
Mary	6	F	Child	290c02BI
CASSY, Ellen	5	F	Child	290c02BI
LYNES, Jno.	21	M	Laborer	290c02BI
MINTHEN, Jas.	20	M	Laborer	290c02BI
SMITH, Pat	10	M	Laborer	290c02BI
Mary	7	F	Child	290c02BI
GUY, Eliza	25	F	Servant	290c02BI
Mary-A.	6	F	Child	290c02BI
Eliza	3	F	Child	290c02BI
Sarah	.00	F	Infant	290c02BI
Died-At-Sea				
LEDGWICK, Jas.	30	M	Farmer	290c02BI
BYRNS, Sarah	28	F	Wife	290c02BI
Sarah	2	F	Child	290c02BI
Wm.	.00	M	Infant	290c02BI
KERWAN, Wm.	24	M	Laborer	290c02BI
Bridgt.	20	F	Wife	290c02BI
MULLAGAN, Ann	20	F	Laborer	290c02BI
RIELLY, Ellen	25	F	Servant	290c02BI
MURPHY, Michl.	30	M	Servant	290c02BI
MULDOON, Jas.	18	M	Servant	290c02BI
Michl.	18	M	Servant	290c02BI
Pat	12	M	Servant	290c02BI
CONVEL, Jno.	30	M	Laborer	290c02BI
DOYLE, Wm.	25	M	Laborer	290c02BI
ONIELLE, Ellen	21	F	Servant	290c02BI
MERGAN, Margt.	21	F	Servant	290c02BI
MCMAHON, Hines	13	M	Servant	290c02BI
GORMAN, Michl.	17	M	Servant	290c02BI
LAHEY, Wm.	13	M	Laborer	290c02BI
KEARNS, Ann	26	F	Servant	290c02BI
NEWELL, Jane	13	F	Servant	290c02BI
Jane	11	F	Unknown	290c02BI
Emily	8	F	Child	290c02BI
Mar	5	F	Child	290c02BI
SCOLES, Jno.	27	M	Laborer	290c02BI
FINGLE, Mary	2	F	Child	290c02BI
BAKER, Wm.	23	M	Laborer	290c02BI
Jas.	4	M	Child	290c02BI
MAXWELL, Eliza	29	F	Servant	290c02BI
SMITH, Mary-A.	27	F	Servant	290c02BI
Dan	2	M	Child	290c02BI
CALLAGHAN, Tho.	25	M	Laborer	290c02BI
MCCORMICK, Michl.	21	M	Laborer	290c02BI
KENNEDY, Cathn.	21	F	Servant	290c02BI
BUTLER, Tho.	20	M	Servant	290c02BI
SAYE, Mary	18	F	Servant	290c02BI
MULLANEY, Dan	19	M	Laborer	290c02BI
SHENDAN, Bridgt.	18	F	Laborer	290c02BI
HUGHES, Mary	17	M	Servant	290c02BI
SAYE, Michl.	14	M	Servant	290c02BI
KEEFE, And.	36	M	Servant	290c02BI
U-Mrs.	26	F	Unknown	290c02BI
Bridgt.	2	F	Child	290c02BI
Jon.	.00	F	Infant	290c02BI
DARLY, Eliza	24	F	Servant	290c02BI
Mary	20	F	Servant	290c02BI
MCKERNAN, Robt.	24	M	Laborer	290c02BI
Eliza	34	F	Unknown	290c02BI
Geo.	4	M	Child	290c02BI
David	2	M	Child	290c02BI
MCNEW, Jas.	21	M	Shopman	290c02BI
CALLAGHAN, Ellen	46	F	Servant	290c02BI
ATKINSON, Maria	24	F	Servant	290c02BI
MULLEN, Bryon	20	M	Laborer	290c02BI
Ann	45	F	Laborer	290c02BI
OCONNER, Dan	10	M	Unknown	290c02BI
BERGIN, Eliza	18	F	Servant	290c02BI
BLANCHARD, Jno.	25	M	Servant	290c02BI
MAKER, U-Mr.	40	M	Servant	290c02BI
MALLON, Margt.	20	F	Servant	290c02BI
GEE, Martha	25	F	Wife	290c02BI
Died-At-Sea				

NAMES OF PASSENGERS	AGE	SEX	OCCUPATIONS	DATE PORT SHIP
GEE, Wm.	22	M	Unknown	290c02BI
Jas.	17	M	Unknown	290c02BI
JONES, Mary	25	F	Unknown	290c02BI
HAYE, Betty	15	F	Servant	290c02BI
Betty	16	F	Servant	290c02BI
Robt.	14	M	Unknown	290c02BI
RILEY, Tho.	20	M	Laborer	290c02BI
MEEHAN, Ellen	20	F	Servant	290c02BI
QUINN, Jas.	18	M	Servant	290c02BI
MOORE, Betty	30	F	Servant	290c02BI
MCCURDY, Jas.	50	M	Servant	290c02BI
FITZGERALD, Michl.	20	M	Farmer	290c02BI
HERTER, Jas.	34	M	Farmer	290c02BI
HORAN, Pat	18	M	Farmer	290c02BI
CARTELLE, Jno.	40	M	Farmer	290c02BI
BRENNAN, Bridgt.	30	F	Servant	290c02BI
KELLY, Mary	18	F	Servant	290c02BI
KILGAN, Jas.	25	M	Servant	290c02BI
MURRAY, Mary	22	F	Servant	290c02BI
Mary	20	F	Servant	290c02BI
Cathn.	18	F	Servant	290c02BI
JOHNSTON, Tho.	50	M	Laborer	290c02BI
Ann	45	F	Servant	290c02BI
Martha	22	F	Servant	290c02BI
Richd.	19	M	Servant	290c02BI
Robt.	15	M	Servant	290c02BI
Jane	20	F	Servant	290c02BI
Wm.	9	M	Child	290c02BI
Ann	7	F	Child	290c02BI
Fanny	5	F	Child	290c02BI
Betsy	5	F	Child	290c02BI
MOSS, Wm.	32	M	Farmer	290c02BI
Jane	8	F	Child	290c02BI
Wm.	5	M	Child	290c02BI
Cathn.	.00	F	Infant	290c02BI
Died-At-Sea				
DWYRE, Jno.	26	M	Laborer	290c02BI
Bridgt.	25	F	Servant	290c02BI
Mary	25	F	Wife	290c02BI
Mary	27	F	Servant	290c02BI
Henry	.00	M	Infant	290c02BI
Ann	.00	F	Infant	290c02BI
HACKETT, Jno.	23	M	Laborer	290c02BI
WARD, Cathn.	20	F	Laborer	290c02BI
MCBRIE, Chas.	23	M	Laborer	290c02BI
MADDEN, Bridgt.	40	F	Servant	290c02BI
Cathn.	10	F	Servant	290c02BI
ATKIN, Wm.	38	M	Servant	290c02BI
CUDDEN, Margt.	20	F	Servant	290c02BI
FELL, Elenor	20	F	Servant	290c02BI
KELLY, Mary	22	F	Servant	290c02BI
RYAN, Mary	45	F	Servant	290c02BI
Tho.	11	M	Unknown	290c02BI
WILLIS, Jno.	33	M	Laborer	290c02BI
Jane	35	F	Laborer	290c02BI
Died-At-Sea				
Jno.	9	M	Child	290c02BI
MCANANY, Ann	13	F	Unknown	290c02BI
CASEY, Lanry	35	F	Servant	290c02BI
MURTEN, Wm.	45	M	Servant	290c02BI
HIGGINS, Mary	30	F	Servant	290c02BI
GRALEY, Mary	30	F	Servant	290c02BI
GRADY, Kitty	20	F	Servant	290c02BI
SMITH, Margt.	17	F	Servant	290c02BI
CONNELL, Tho.	25	M	Shoemaker	290c02BI
HUMPHRYS, Betty	30	F	Wife	290c02BI
Wm.	.00	M	Infant	290c02BI
SWEENEY, Ann	20	F	Servant	290c02BI
Bridgt.	18	F	Servant	290c02BI
CASSIDY, Mary	25	F	Servant	290c02BI
Margt.	23	F	Servant	290c02BI
LASHER, Maria	18	F	Servant	290c02BI
RIELLY, Tho.	19	M	Laborer	290c02BI
KELLY, Chas.	20	M	Laborer	290c02BI
Mary	24	F	Servant	290c02BI

NAMES OF PASSENGERS	AGE	SEX	OCCUPATIONS	DATE PORT SHIP
KELLY, Cathn.	18	F	Servant	290c02BI
Mary	16	F	Servant	290c02BI
BULTOOLY, Cathn.	20	F	Servant	290c02BI
VERDON, Alice	25	F	Servant	290c02BI
KELLY, Pat	24	M	Laborer	290c02BI
Cathn.	17	F	Servant	290c02BI
MUNNAY, Pat	26	M	Servant	290c02BI
HANNON, Michl.	35	M	Servant	290c02BI
Sarah	28	F	Servant	290c02BI
Jane	6	F	Child	290c02BI
HERK, Jno.	35	M	Laborer	290c02BI
Mary	30	F	Unknown	290c02BI
CLERKEN, Mary	30	F	Servant	290c02BI
Bridgt.	13	F	Servant	290c02BI
MCENROE, Mary	18	F	Servant	290c02BI
CANTY, Wm.	36	M	Servant	290c02BI
LYNCH, Peter	30	M	Laborer	290c02BI
MORAN, Ellen	24	F	Servant	290c02BI
ANDERSON, Robt.	21	M	Servant	290c02BI
KILBRIDGE, Tho.	21	M	Digger	290c02BI
TOOL, Cathn.	24	F	Servant	290c02BI
DOOLEY, Margt.	26	F	Servant	290c02BI
GORMAN, Jas.	24	M	Farmer	290c02BI
Ellen	28	F	Unknown	290c02BI
Cathn.	.00	F	Infant	290c02BI
Keeran	2	M	Child	290c02BI
BINN, Margt.	60	F	Servant	290c02BI
Fra.	22	M	Servant	290c02BI
Bridgt.	26	F	Servant	290c02BI
DARCY, Jane	26	F	Servant	290c02BI
MUNANG, Mary	60	F	Unknown	290c02BI
MCCANN, Mary	4	F	Child	290c02BI
Michl.	2	M	Child	290c02BI
HICKEY, Cathn.	15	F	Unknown	290c02BI
Edwd.	14	M	Unknown	290c02BI
RYAN, Cathn.	20	F	Servant	290c02BI
REERAN, Tho.	20	M	Laborer	290c02BI
DONOHUE, Farrel	35	M	Farmer	290c02BI
Pat	13	M	Farmer	290c02BI
Michl.	10	M	Farmer	290c02BI
Mary	9	F	Child	290c02BI
Berri	4	M	Child	290c02BI
FLINN, Mary	18	F	Servant	290c02BI
LARKIN, Michl.	18	M	Servant	290c02BI
CASEY, Mary	20	F	Servant	290c02BI
REILLY, Ann	18	F	Servant	290c02BI
MORHEN, Bridgt.	14	F	Servant	290c02BI
FEENY, Sarah	11	F	Unknown	290c02BI
Farely	12	M	Unknown	290c02BI
FINNEGAN, Cathn.	36	F	Servant	290c02BI
Rose	9	F	Child	290c02BI
Jas.	7	M	Child	290c02BI
GALLAGHER, Honor	20	F	Laborer	290c02BI
Bridgt.	.00	F	Infant	290c02BI
TOOLE, Bridgt.	16	F	Servant	290c02BI
HYNDS, Ann	17	F	Servant	290c02BI
SIMS, Jno.	24	M	Servant	290c02BI
Deborah	60	F	Servant	290c02BI
Died-At-Sea				
CRONIN, Ellen	30	F	Servant	290c02BI
Died-At-Sea				
Jno.	.00	M	Infant	290c02BI
Died-At-Sea				
Margt.	.00	F	Infant	290c02BI
Died-At-Sea				
DALTON, Peter	29	M	Laborer	290c02BI
U	26	F	Unknown	290c02BI
Wm.	.00	M	Infant	290c02BI
MILLER, Tho.	43	M	Servant	290c02BI
Anna	40	F	Servant	290c02BI
Eliza	11	F	Unknown	290c02BI
Mercy	9	F	Child	290c02BI
MCDONNELL, Michl.	30	M	Laborer	290c02BI
RON, Robt.	35	M	Servant	290c02BI
CASEY, Pat	30	M	Servant	290c02BI

NAMES OF PASSENGERS	AGE	SEX	OCCUPATIONS	DATE PORT SHIP
MCDONNELL, U-Mrs.	26	F	Servant	290c02BI
MALE, Solo	25	M	Laborer	290c02BI
Sarah	25	F	Servant	290c02BI
THORN, Wm.	45	M	Farmer	290c02BI
U-Mrs	45	F	Unknown	290c02BI
Eliza	21	F	Unknown	290c02BI
Martha	21	F	Unknown	290c02BI
Jno.	20	M	Unknown	290c02BI
Mary	19	F	Unknown	290c02BI
Jane	17	F	Unknown	290c02BI
Lucy	14	F	Unknown	290c02BI
HILLOP, Mary	30	F	Servant	290c02BI
Jane	2	F	Child	290c02BI
HAGAN, Michl.	40	M	Laborer	290c02BI
EDGEWORTH, Anna	17	F	Servant	290c02BI
LANGHLAN, Pat	27	M	Servant	290c02BI
ANDERSON, Jno.	15	M	Unknown	290c02BI
MYERS, Pat	15	M	Unknown	290c02BI
Mary	13	F	Unknown	290c02BI
BRYON, Jno.	20	M	Servant	290c02BI
DOONER, Jno.	25	M	Servant	290c02BI
HENESSY, Ann	8	F	Child	290c02BI
CASSIDY, Mary	00	F	Unknown	290c02BI
Died-At-Sea				
FINLAY, Wm.	00	M	Unknown	290c02BI
Died-At-Sea				
BRADY, Cath.	00	F	Unknown	290c02BI
Died-At-Sea				
FEGAN, Teressa	00	F	Unknown	290c02BI
Died-At-Sea				
TAYLER, Jos.	00	M	Unknown	290c02BI
Died-At-Sea				
MCKERINON, David	00	M	Unknown	290c02BI
Died-At-Sea				
CARLTON, Jos.	00	M	Unknown	290c02BI
Died-At-Sea				
BOWERS, Mary	00	F	Unknown	290c02BI
Died-At-Sea				
BURNS, Wm.	00	M	Unknown	290c02BI
Died-At-Sea				
MURPHY, Marie	00	F	Unknown	290c02BI
Died-At-Sea				

KATE 29 OCTOBER 1849

From Liverpool

NAMES OF PASSENGERS		AGE	SEX	OCCUPATIONS	DATE PORT SHIP
HUGHS, Edwd.		45	M	Weaver	290c02Bo
Ann		11	F	None	290c02Bo
FAGAN, Bernard		20	M	Farmer	290c02Bo
Thos.		3	M	Child	290c02Bo
KELLY, Bernard		22	M	Blacksmith	290c02Bo
MCARTHY, Pat		21	M	Tailor	290c02Bo
MCCABE, James		40	M	Coachman	290c02Bo
U	(W)	35	F	None	290c02Bo
Edward		16	M	None	290c02Bo
Mary		6	F	Child	290c02Bo
MCFARLAN, Kitty		26	F	Servant	290c02Bo
Michael		.06	M	Infant	290c02Bo
DOYLE, Cath.		16	F	Servant	290c02Bo
ROGERS, Pat		24	M	Laborer	290c02Bo
HANEY, John		39	M	Engineer	290c02Bo
U	(W)	30	F	None	290c02Bo
Nicolas		12	M	None	290c02Bo
Thomas		10	M	None	290c02Bo
John		2	M	Child	290c02Bo
Peter		.03	M	Infant	290c02Bo
QUINN, Eliza		19	F	Servant	290c02Bo
Rosanna		16	F	Servant	290c02Bo

NAMES OF PASSENGERS	AGE	SEX	OCCUPATIONS	DATE PORT SHIP
DOYLE, Margaret	17	F	Servant	290c02Bo
WARD, Margaret	18	F	Servant	290c02Bo
FEELY, Edwd.	25	M	Laborer	290c02Bo
CARTY, Cathn.	7	F	Child	290c02Bo
FARREL, John	23	M	Laborer	290c02Bo
FLINN, Thos.	9	M	Child	290c02Bo
LYNCH, Cathn.	28	F	Servant	290c02Bo
EGAN, James	11	M	None	290c02Bo
Matilda	8	F	Child	290c02Bo
MAHON, Mich.	20	M	Farmer	290c02Bo
CAREY, Thos.	18	M	Farmer	290c02Bo
KEDEN, Edwd.	21	M	Farmer	290c02Bo
CUNNINGHAM, Eliza	6	F	Child	290c02Bo
Andrew	.10	M	Infant	290c02Bo
SULIVAN, Hanora	23	F	Servant	290c02Bo
Cathn.	3	F	Child	290c02Bo
CALMAN, Essie	19	F	Servant	290c02Bo
MURPHY, Eliza	20	F	Bomkr	290c02Bo
BRANNAN, Mary	19	F	Servant	290c02Bo
MANION, Mary	20	F	Servant	290c02Bo
BRIAN, James	22	M	Stone Mason	290c02Bo
CALLAGHAN, Hanora	30	F	Servant	290c02Bo
Michl.	13	M	None	290c02Bo
John	9	M	Child	290c02Bo
James	6	M	Child	290c02Bo
Mary	4	F	Child	290c02Bo
BRIAN, John	34	M	Laborer	290c02Bo
BREW, Hugh	20	M	Laborer	290c02Bo
KENNY, Edwd.	25	M	Blacksmith	290c02Bo
DONAVAN, John	21	M	Laborer	290c02Bo
CUNNIN, John	20	M	Laborer	290c02Bo
FARREL, Margret	21	F	Servant	290c02Bo
SOMERS, John	40	M	Laborer	290c02Bo
CROHAN, Margret	20	F	Dressmaker	290c02Bo
WHITE, Mary	19	F	Cook	290c02Bo
LILLEY, Geo.	14	M	None	290c02Bo
SPALLAN, Sally	63	F	Nurse	290c02Bo
Mary	30	F	Servant	290c02Bo
William	9	M	Child	290c02Bo
Michael	5	M	Child	290c02Bo
John	3	M	Child	290c02Bo
BRADY, Ellen	22	F	Servant	290c02Bo
FAGAN, Mary	19	F	Servant	290c02Bo
MARKY, Pat	19	M	Laborer	290c02Bo
FAGAN, Peter	17	M	Laborer	290c02Bo
FIBBAN, John	40	M	Laborer	290c02Bo
RIDLEY, Ellen	20	F	Dressmaker	290c02Bo
MCALISTER, Pat	11	M	None	290c02Bo
Jane	6	F	Child	290c02Bo
Dora	4	F	Child	290c02Bo
FENTON, Dan.	16	M	Servant	290c02Bo
MANION, Mary	19	F	Servant	290c02Bo
COGLAN, Martin	30	M	Shoemaker	290c02Bo
Thomas	4	M	Child	290c02Bo
Cath.	.10	F	Infant	290c02Bo
ROACH, James	29	M	Excavator	290c02Bo
CUNNINGHAM, Mch.	29	M	Excavator	290c02Bo
DEVLIN, Cath.	18	F	Stay Maker	290c02Bo
CARLIN, Jane	20	F	Stay Maker	290c02Bo
DANLAN, John	16	M	None	290c02Bo
HOWARD, Thos.	23	M	Scribe	290c02Bo
DUNN, Bridget	26	F	Servant	290c02Bo
Essie	.06	F	Infant	290c02Bo
Died-At-Sea				
KELLY, John	22	M	Laborer	290c02Bo
MADDEN, Mich.	20	M	Laborer	290c02Bo
SULIVAN, Cath.	25	F	Servant	290c02Bo
Mary	3	F	Child	290c02Bo
Died-At-Sea				
Peter	.11	M	Infant	290c02Bo
LANG, Mich.	18	M	Laborer	290c02Bo
TAMPAY, Mary	30	F	Servant	290c02Bo
Patrick	7	M	Child	290c02Bo
Margaret	5	F	Child	290c02Bo
OHANNIN, Wm.	27	M	Shoemaker	290c02Bo

NAMES OF PASSENGERS	AGE	SEX	OCCUPATIONS	DATE PORT SHIP
BYRNE, Ellen	21	F	Servant	290c02Bo
Eliza	19	F	Servant	290c02Bo
GRIFFEN, John	27	M	Laborer	290c02Bo
TRIG, James	15	M	Brush Maker	290c02Bo
MAURISSEY, John	22	M	Laborer	290c02Bo
Mary	20	F	Servant	290c02Bo
CANWAY, James	21	M	Saw Maker	290c02Bo
SAWELLE, Edwd.	22	M	Farmer	290c02Bo
RADY, Wm.	57	M	Farmer	290c02Bo
Died-At-Sea				
Thady	70	M	Farmer	290c02Bo
Died-At-Sea				
Mary	57	F	None	290c02Bo
Timothy	23	M	Farmer	290c02Bo
Mary	20	F	None	290c02Bo
Bridget	18	F	None	290c02Bo
Rosa	16	F	None	290c02Bo
William	14	M	None	290c02Bo
Fanny	12	F	None	290c02Bo
Ellen	11	F	None	290c02Bo
Joseph	9	M	Child	290c02Bo
Ann	7	F	Child	290c02Bo
Patrick	5	M	Child	290c02Bo
DWYRE, Ann	18	F	Servant	290c02Bo
Maria	16	F	Servant	290c02Bo
Martin	13	M	None	290c02Bo
Died-At-Sea				
Teresa	8	F	Child	290c02Bo
Martha	12	F	None	290c02Bo
James	5	M	Child	290c02Bo
GIBBON, Mch.	21	M	Laborer	290c02Bo
HENEVAN, Peter	28	M	Laborer	290c02Bo
CAMPBELL, James	18	M	Laborer	290c02Bo
Bessie	16	F	Servant	290c02Bo
CORHEN, John	21	M	Laborer	290c02Bo
WARD, Martin	24	M	Laborer	290c02Bo
Walter	2	M	Child	290c02Bo
Bridget	.06	F	Infant	290c02Bo
Died-At-Sea				
MANIASKY, Johanna	24	F	Servant	290c02Bo
Mary	28	F	Servant	290c02Bo
CANNER, Elizabeth	17	F	Dressmaker	290c02Bo
MULKAHY, Cath.	20	F	Servant	290c02Bo
Thos.	33	M	Laborer	290c02Bo
DAGNELL, Rose	17	F	Servant	290c02Bo
Died-At-Sea				
MCGUIRE, Mary	30	F	Servant	290c02Bo
James	11	M	None	290c02Bo
Died-At-Sea				
Mary	9	F	Child	290c02Bo
Died-At-Sea				
Rosa	7	F	Child	290c02Bo
Died-At-Sea				
CANWAY, Margret	20	F	Servant	290c02Bo
HARDMAN, Bridget	18	F	Servant	290c02Bo
KIRWAN, Margret	18	F	Servant	290c02Bo
FREGUSON, Alex.	22	M	Engineer	290c02Bo
RAFFERTY, Cath.	30	F	Servant	290c02Bo
Hugh	19	M	Laborer	290c02Bo
FOX, Judy	24	F	Servant	290c02Bo
MITCHELL, Anne	20	F	Servant	290c02Bo
Mary	33	F	Servant	290c02Bo
Catherine	7	F	Child	290c02Bo
Mary	17	F	Servant	290c02Bo

GERTRUDE 30 OCTOBER 1849

From Liverpool

NAMES OF PASSENGERS	AGE	SEX	OCCUPATIONS	DATE PORT SHIP
HOGAN, Thos.	55	M	Farmer	300c02Bn
Eliza	55	F	Unknown	300c02Bn
Mary	23	F	Unknown	300c02Bn
Eliza	3	F	Child	300c02Bn
John	1	M	Child	300c02Bn
SULLIVAN, Dennis	22	M	Unknown	300c02Bn
CORBIT, Ann	47	F	Unknown	300c02Bn
Pat	12	M	Unknown	300c02Bn
CROGAN, Martin	30	M	Unknown	300c02Bn
Mary	25	F	Unknown	300c02Bn
MORAY, John	46	M	Unknown	300c02Bn
Thomas	25	M	Unknown	300c02Bn
Mary	20	F	Unknown	300c02Bn
Betty	22	F	Unknown	300c02Bn
SULLIVAN, Wm.	40	M	Unknown	300c02Bn
Ellen	36	F	Unknown	300c02Bn
Mary	18	F	Unknown	300c02Bn
Eugene	12	M	Unknown	300c02Bn
GILLMAN, Henry	17	M	Unknown	300c02Bn
Patrick	7	M	Child	300c02Bn
COLLINS, John	25	M	Unknown	300c02Bn
HANNAHAN, Peter	20	M	Unknown	300c02Bn
DOWLEY, Jane	20	M	Unknown	300c02Bn
LARKIN, Jim	20	M	Unknown	300c02Bn
DORAN, Mick	18	M	Unknown	300c02Bn
HOGAN, Mary	28	F	Unknown	300c02Bn
HARRA, Bridget	25	F	Unknown	300c02Bn
Ann	8	F	Child	300c02Bn
Mike	2	M	Child	300c02Bn
CONWAY, Wm.	40	M	Unknown	300c02Bn
JOHNSTON, Robt.	22	M	Unknown	300c02Bn
FOSBROOK, Wm.	60	M	Farmer	300c02Bn
PARK, Henrietta	21	F	Unknown	300c02Bn
CLARK, Robt.	20	M	Unknown	300c02Bn
GROGAN, Henry	22	M	Unknown	300c02Bn
CASTIGAN, Maria	18	F	Unknown	300c02Bn
MCCAN, Catherine	20	F	Unknown	300c02Bn
CHAMBERS, Judy	17	F	Unknown	300c02Bn
SHENDON, James	18	M	Unknown	300c02Bn
MILLER, Christy	18	F	Unknown	300c02Bn
MCFILEY, James	13	M	Unknown	300c02Bn
AVERY, Pat-W.	25	M	Unknown	300c02Bn
MCGOVEN, Jane	40	M	Unknown	300c02Bn
Bridget	11	F	Unknown	300c02Bn
James	6	M	Child	300c02Bn
MILLER, Bess	20	F	Unknown	300c02Bn
LYNCH, George	23	M	Unknown	300c02Bn
LEWIS, Harris	24	M	Unknown	300c02Bn
MOLLOY, Wm.	30	M	Unknown	300c02Bn
Ann	23	F	Unknown	300c02Bn
Mary	2	F	Child	300c02Bn
COGHLAN, Thos.	24	M	Unknown	300c02Bn
CANTWEL, Pat	48	M	Unknown	300c02Bn
POWER, Alice	30	F	Unknown	300c02Bn
CARTER, Mary	30	F	Unknown	300c02Bn
Peter	.00	M	Infant	300c02Bn
Died-At-Sea				
REILLY, Pat	13	M	Farmer	300c02Bn
DRYAN, John	25	M	Unknown	300c02Bn
Mary	25	F	Unknown	300c02Bn
Betty	25	F	Unknown	300c02Bn
MCNEVIN, Pat	23	M	Unknown	300c02Bn
BALGER, John	20	M	Unknown	300c02Bn
BALLEN, Owen-W.	22	M	Unknown	300c02Bn
FLYNN, David	32	M	Unknown	300c02Bn
FLYNN, Catherine	28	F	Unknown	300c02Bn
John	5	M	Child	300c02Bn
Catherine	3	F	Child	300c02Bn
Peter	.00	M	Infant	300c02Bn
RYAN, Nancy	35	F	Unknown	300c02Bn
Died-At-Sea				
Peter	6	M	Child	300c02Bn
Samuel	3	M	Child	300c02Bn
Kate	1	F	Child	300c02Bn
CUSACK, Pat	20	M	Unknown	300c02Bn
LEARY, John	21	M	Unknown	300c02Bn
Michael	45	M	Unknown	300c02Bn
FITZGERALD, Thos.	20	M	Unknown	300c02Bn
Mary	22	F	Unknown	300c02Bn
SHEAHAN, Mary	24	F	Unknown	300c02Bn
MADIGAN, John	23	M	Unknown	300c02Bn
Mary	20	F	Unknown	300c02Bn
MUNGAVIN, Pat	12	M	Unknown	300c02Bn
MADGAN, Howard	15	F	Unknown	300c02Bn
Avire	18	F	Unknown	300c02Bn
SHAYHAN, Maurice	25	M	Unknown	300c02Bn
Died-At-Sea				
Mary	24	F	Unknown	300c02Bn
Died-At-Sea				
WATSON, Mary-W.	22	F	Unknown	300c02Bn
CAVANAGH, Darby	30	M	Unknown	300c02Bn
MALONEY, Mary	15	F	Unknown	300c02Bn
Pat	13	M	Unknown	300c02Bn
DELLON, Ellen	30	F	Unknown	300c02Bn
CONAN, Margt.	19	F	Unknown	300c02Bn
TURPLEY, Pat	38	M	Unknown	300c02Bn
Con.	27	M	Unknown	300c02Bn
Mary	20	F	Unknown	300c02Bn
MALLOON, Pat	40	M	Unknown	300c02Bn
BLAKE, Jno.	24	M	Unknown	300c02Bn
NOWLAN, Margt.	24	F	Unknown	300c02Bn
MCLEAN, Margt.	40	F	Unknown	300c02Bn
Mary-Anna	18	F	Unknown	300c02Bn
Margt.	13	F	Unknown	300c02Bn
Mary	11	F	Unknown	300c02Bn
Elizabeth	9	F	Child	300c02Bn
Alexander	7	M	Child	300c02Bn
CREIGHTON, Pat	46	M	Unknown	300c02Bn
U-Mrs.	45	F	Unknown	300c02Bn
Ellen	20	F	Unknown	300c02Bn
ROTHERAM, James	50	M	Unknown	300c02Bn
Died-At-Sea				
Mary	25	F	Unknown	300c02Bn
RYAN, Michael	24	M	Unknown	300c02Bn
Margt.	24	F	Unknown	300c02Bn
Jamie	.00	F	Infant	300c02Bn
COOK, James	32	M	Unknown	300c02Bn
HARVEY, Margt.	50	M	Unknown	300c02Bn
ONEIL, Henry	36	M	Unknown	300c02Bn
Elizabeth	36	F	Unknown	300c02Bn
SHEDY, Wm.	30	M	Unknown	300c02Bn
Saml.	2	M	Child	300c02Bn
Johanna	.00	F	Infant	300c02Bn
HOWEL, Nicholas	32	M	Unknown	300c02Bn
HAMILTON, Ann	10	F	Unknown	300c02Bn
Maria	3	F	Child	300c02Bn
HOGAN, Michael	22	M	Unknown	300c02Bn
Ann	25	F	Unknown	300c02Bn
Margt.	19	F	Unknown	300c02Bn
Catherine	27	F	Unknown	300c02Bn
HAND, James	18	M	Unknown	300c02Bn
GOURT, James	25	M	Unknown	300c02Bn
SPRAT, Catherine	17	F	Unknown	300c02Bn
Bridget	34	F	Unknown	300c02Bn
SLATTERY, Thos.	50	M	Unknown	300c02Bn
Johanna	30	F	Unknown	300c02Bn
James	16	M	Unknown	300c02Bn
Michel	13	M	Unknown	300c02Bn
Alice	11	F	Unknown	300c02Bn
Thos.	8	M	Child	300c02Bn

NAMES OF PASSENGERS	AGE	SEX	OCCUPATIONS	DATE PORT SHIP
SLATTERY, Wm.	5	M	Child	300c02Bn
Mary	3	F	Child	300c02Bn
Died-At-Sea				
Johanna	21	F	Unknown	300c02Bn
Pat	.00	M	Infant	300c02Bn
DONOVAN, Johanna	2	F	Child	300c02Bn
Catherine	21	F	Unknown	300c02Bn
BYRNE, Catherine	18	F	Unknown	300c02Bn
Mary	7	F	Child	300c02Bn
CANNON, Pat	2	M	Child	300c02Bn
MCCABE, John	27	M	Unknown	300c02Bn
GELRIDGE, Jim	29	M	Unknown	300c02Bn
MCQUIS, Francis	18	M	Unknown	300c02Bn
TULLY, Mary	20	F	Unknown	300c02Bn
CASEY, Mary	28	F	Unknown	300c02Bn
GILLMAN, Catherine	25	F	Unknown	300c02Bn
DALEY, Eliza	18	F	Unknown	300c02Bn
HAYES, Wm.	30	M	Unknown	300c02Bn
MCGUIRE, James	17	M	Unknown	300c02Bn
OBREEN, Mike	24	M	Unknown	300c02Bn
Died-At-Sea				
CANNON, Thos.	40	M	Unknown	300c02Bn
U-Mrs.	30	F	Unknown	300c02Bn
RILEY, Robt.	30	M	Unknown	300c02Bn
CONOLY, Ann	18	F	Unknown	300c02Bn
CAROL, Mary	20	F	Unknown	300c02Bn
MARTIN, Mary	20	F	Unknown	300c02Bn
CONNOR, Thos.	10	M	Unknown	300c02Bn
Bridget	7	F	Child	300c02Bn
Peter	.00	M	Infant	300c02Bn
BOWLAN, Bridget	23	F	Unknown	300c02Bn
DELANY, U-Mrs.	18	F	Unknown	300c02Bn
FURGUSON, Ellen	19	F	Unknown	300c02Bn
Matilda	20	F	Unknown	300c02Bn
OAKS, Matilda	22	F	Unknown	300c02Bn
FEDGAN, James	22	M	Unknown	300c02Bn
MULLIGAN, Ellen	20	F	Unknown	300c02Bn
Mary	19	F	Unknown	300c02Bn
WALSH, Biddy	17	F	Unknown	300c02Bn
MCDONNEL, Pat	26	M	Unknown	300c02Bn
MCSHENY, Pat	26	M	Unknown	300c02Bn
FARNEY, Henry	20	M	Unknown	300c02Bn
MCDONNEL, Thos.	33	M	Unknown	300c02Bn
Mary	30	F	Unknown	300c02Bn
John	7	M	Child	300c02Bn
Died-At-Sea				
Thos.	5	M	Child	300c02Bn
James	2	M	Child	300c02Bn
Mary	.00	F	Infant	300c02Bn
Died-At-Sea				
SHANAHAN, Catherine	20	F	Unknown	300c02Bn
LARKIN, James	22	M	Unknown	300c02Bn
MORAN, Catherine	25	F	Unknown	300c02Bn
Owen	22	M	Unknown	300c02Bn
James	7	M	Child	300c02Bn
John	5	M	Child	300c02Bn
HISK, Mary	45	F	Child	300c02Bn
James	20	M	Unknown	300c02Bn
John	10	M	Unknown	300c02Bn
HUSE, Biddy	24	F	Unknown	300c02Bn
Michael	.00	M	Infant	300c02Bn
MCANDREW, Biddy	21	F	Unknown	300c02Bn
Pat	45	M	Unknown	300c02Bn
MACKEY, Sally	20	F	Unknown	300c02Bn
LIVARTY, John	25	M	Unknown	300c02Bn
U-Mrs.	25	F	Unknown	300c02Bn
KELLEY, Thos.	26	M	Unknown	300c02Bn
Peggy	16	F	Unknown	300c02Bn
James	14	M	Unknown	300c02Bn
Anne	21	F	Unknown	300c02Bn
Jane	10	F	Unknown	300c02Bn
DOE, Charles	21	M	Unknown	300c02Bn
PIXTON, Thos.	25	M	Unknown	300c02Bn
CALLAGHAN, James	20	M	Unknown	300c02Bn
RYAN, James	21	M	Unknown	300c02Bn
RYAN, Thomas	19	M	Unknown	300c02Bn
Died-At-Sea				
LANNCEY, Daniel	20	M	Unknown	300c02Bn
MCLAUGHLIN, Betty	20	F	Unknown	300c02Bn
RATTAN, Wm.	30	M	Unknown	300c02Bn
DEAN, John	23	M	Unknown	300c02Bn
MCMICHAEL, Wm.	59	M	Unknown	300c02Bn
Cath.	50	F	Unknown	300c02Bn
Maria	20	F	Unknown	300c02Bn
William	16	M	Unknown	300c02Bn
James	11	M	Unknown	300c02Bn
TULLY, John	19	M	Unknown	300c02Bn
LOWAN, Mary	36	F	Unknown	300c02Bn
MCCABE, Judy	30	F	Unknown	300c02Bn
GILLAN, Wm.	26	M	Unknown	300c02Bn
MCCABE, Biddy	25	F	Unknown	300c02Bn
HANLEY, Edward	19	M	Unknown	300c02Bn
U-Mrs.	19	F	Unknown	300c02Bn
GLEASON, Julia	26	F	Unknown	300c02Bn
BRADY, Mary	20	F	Unknown	300c02Bn
CARROLL, Thos.	28	M	Unknown	300c02Bn
MCGOWAN, U	24	F	Unknown	300c02Bn
MCLURIA, Jane	20	F	Unknown	300c02Bn
NESBIT, Catherine	30	F	Unknown	300c02Bn
CARR, Biddy	60	F	Unknown	300c02Bn
HAMILTON, Isaac	40	M	Unknown	300c02Bn
Rebecca	20	F	Unknown	300c02Bn
THORPE, Pat	25	M	Unknown	300c02Bn
Died-At-Sea				
Margt.	25	F	Unknown	300c02Bn
Jim	60	M	Unknown	300c02Bn
Died-At-Sea				
MORE, John	30	M	Unknown	300c02Bn
Died-At-Sea				
THORPE, Eliza	.00	F	Infant	300c02Bn
KERR, Sarah	37	F	Unknown	300c02Bn
MCKEON, Dennis	40	M	Unknown	300c02Bn
Mick	16	M	Unknown	300c02Bn
HEALY, Mary	22	F	Unknown	300c02Bn
CROSIER, Wm.	21	M	Unknown	300c02Bn
MATTNELL, Ann	26	F	Unknown	300c02Bn
Hannah	3	F	Child	300c02Bn
BRADY, Pat	21	M	Unknown	300c02Bn
James	21	M	Unknown	300c02Bn
HIMMEL, Thos.	18	M	Unknown	300c02Bn
GALWAY, Richard	00	M	Unknown	300c02Bn
DEVIN, Joseph-L.	00	M	Unknown	300c02Bn
HEALY, Mary-Ann	00	F	Unknown	300c02Bn

BRITISH-QUEEN 30 OCTOBER 1849

From Dublin

NAMES OF PASSENGERS	AGE	SEX	OCCUPATIONS	DATE PORT SHIP
RYAN, Michael	54	M	Farmer	300c05Bp
Anne	42	F	Matron	300c05Bp
Mary-Ann	20	F	Spinster	300c05Bp
Patrick	18	M	Laborer	300c05Bp
Catherine	16	F	Spinster	300c05Bp
Timothy	.11	M	Infant	300c05Bp
ROURKE, William	40	M	Farmer	300c05Bp
Catherine	22	F	Spinster	300c05Bp
Ann	20	F	Spinster	300c05Bp
Margeret	18	F	Spinster	300c05Bp
Mary-Ann	16	F	Spinster	300c05Bp
Bridget	14	F	Spinster	300c05Bp
James	.11	M	Infant	300c05Bp
WATSON, Wm.	19	M	Paper Maker	300c05Bp
CONNERS, Thomas	20	M	Carpenter	300c05Bp
CLANEY, John	54	M	Stctr	300c05Bp

NAMES OF PASSENGERS		AGE	SEX	OCCUPATIONS	DATE PORT SHIP
CLANEY, Jane	(W)	50	F	None	300c05Bp
Bridget		10	F	None	300c05Bp
Margaret		7	F	Child	300c05Bp
Jane		.06	F	Infant	300c05Bp
GILL, Patrick		20	M	Stctr	300c05Bp
MCGUIRE, Rose		25	F	Spinster	300c05Bp
BEATTY, Moore		24	M	Laborer	300c05Bp
GITTIGAN, James		21	M	Laborer	300c05Bp
RYAN, Anne		28	F	Spinster	300c05Bp
ROACH, Henry		50	M	Farmer	300c05Bp
Margaret	(W)	40	F	None	300c05Bp
Bridget		16	F	Relative	300c05Bp
Ed.		14	M	Relative	300c05Bp
Mary		12	F	Relative	300c05Bp
Thomas		8	M	Relative	300c05Bp
Henry		.06	M	Infant	300c05Bp
MCCANN, Owen		27	M	Laborer	300c05Bp
FLANNEGAN, Mary		39	F	Matron	300c05Bp
Patrick		12	M	Relative	300c05Bp
Bernard		10	M	Relative	300c05Bp
Bridget		4	F	Child	300c05Bp
James		.03	M	Infant	300c05Bp
DEVINE, Catherine		31	F	Matron	300c05Bp
Luke		7	M	Child	300c05Bp
James		5	M	Child	300c05Bp
Margaret		3	F	Child	300c05Bp
Garrett		.05	M	Infant	300c05Bp
WYNNE, Richard		26	M	Laborer	300c05Bp
BIRD, Ellen		19	F	Spinster	300c05Bp
MCCORMICK, Mary		18	F	Spinster	300c05Bp
MCDONOUGH, Jno.		29	M	Laborer	300c05Bp
KNOWLES, William		20	M	Laborer	300c05Bp
BAILEY, Eliza		25	F	Spinster	300c05Bp
MURPHY, Jeriga		23	F	Spinster	300c05Bp
WEST, Simon		20	M	Paper Maker	300c05Bp
REILLY, Phillip		28	M	Carver	300c05Bp
BUTLER, Edward		40	M	Laborer	300c05Bp
Thomas		30	M	Laborer	300c05Bp
Bridget		40	F	Matron	300c05Bp
KELLY, Mathew		30	M	Laborer	300c05Bp
Mary		30	F	Matron	300c05Bp
FREEBURNE, Hannah		18	F	Spinster	300c05Bp
KEANE, Patrick		19	M	Laborer	300c05Bp
MAHON, Mary-Ann		22	F	Matron	300c05Bp
Margaret		20	F	Spinster	300c05Bp
DOONAN, Anne		24	F	Spinster	300c05Bp
ANDERSON, James		26	M	Laborer	300c05Bp
DUFFY, Mary		21	F	Spinster	300c05Bp
VAUGHAN, Mary		25	F	Spinster	300c05Bp
MCGOWAN, Peter		27	M	Smith	300c05Bp
CARROLL, James		28	M	Laborer	300c05Bp
MCCARTHY, Mary		14	F	Spinster	300c05Bp
DODD, Michael		30	M	Upholsterer	300c05Bp
Ursula	(W)	20	F	None	300c05Bp
Thomas		.04	M	Infant	300c05Bp
MCELEVY, James		41	M	Laborer	300c05Bp
HARLAN, Henry		17	M	Shoemaker	300c05Bp
HEENEY, Thos.		50	M	Laborer	300c05Bp
Maria	(W)	42	F	None	300c05Bp
Thomas		11	M	None	300c05Bp
LAWLER, Anne		21	F	Spinster	300c05Bp
ROBERTS, Jno.		32	M	Laborer	300c05Bp
Mary	(W)	25	F	None	300c05Bp
BUCKLEY, Eliza		23	F	Spinster	300c05Bp
DOYLE, Ellen		20	F	Spinster	300c05Bp
MOORE, Mary-Jane		20	F	Spinster	300c05Bp
QUINN, Patrick		34	M	Farmer	300c05Bp
Sarah	(W)	37	F	None	300c05Bp
John		7	M	Child	300c05Bp
SCAL, Margaret		24	F	Spinster	300c05Bp
DEVORE, Edward		24	M	Weaver	300c05Bp
RILLEY, James		19	M	Smith	300c05Bp
MALLIN, Ann		24	F	Spinster	300c05Bp
BRADY, Michael		25	M	Laborer	300c05Bp
SULLIVAN, John		24	M	Laborer	300c05Bp

NAMES OF PASSENGERS		AGE	SEX	OCCUPATIONS	DATE PORT SHIP
WILL, Jane		26	F	Spinster	300c05Bp
REILLY, Anne		26	F	Spinster	300c05Bp
GALLAGHER, Bernard		50	M	Clerk	300c05Bp
Ann	(W)	40	F	None	300c05Bp
John		18	M	Laborer	300c05Bp
Rosana		17	F	None	300c05Bp
William		12	M	None	300c05Bp
Eliza		7	F	Child	300c05Bp
Dennis		5	M	Child	300c05Bp
Anne-Marie		4	F	Child	300c05Bp
Mary-Zerega		3	F	Child	300c05Bp
Bernard		.10	M	Infant	300c05Bp
DOWD, Ann		19	F	Spinster	300c05Bp
Catherine		17	F	Spinster	300c05Bp
COX, John		34	M	Sawer	300c05Bp
JONES, Thomas		59	M	Laborer	300c05Bp
John		18	M	Laborer	300c05Bp
MCCALLA, Patrick		18	M	Laborer	300c05Bp
BATES, Jane		38	F	Matron	300c05Bp
Ann		12	F	Relative	300c05Bp
Mary-Jane		10	F	Relative	300c05Bp
Robert-Francis		5	M	Child	300c05Bp
Martha		.03	F	Infant	300c05Bp
BLACK, William		36	M	Tailor	300c05Bp
WHITE, Patrick		23	M	Laborer	300c05Bp
ROCK, John		22	M	Laborer	300c05Bp
COGAN, Nicholas		22	M	Laborer	300c05Bp
QUINN, James		28	M	Laborer	300c05Bp
WHITLEY, Mary-Ann		28	F	Matron	300c05Bp
Susan		8	F	Child	300c05Bp
Mary-Ann		3	F	Child	300c05Bp
Elizabeth		.10	F	Infant	300c05Bp
MARTIN, Margaret		15	F	Spinster	300c05Bp
LYNCH, Richard		38	M	Laborer	300c05Bp
Ann	(W)	30	F	None	300c05Bp
Edward		6	M	Child	300c05Bp
Edward		4	M	Child	300c05Bp
Francis		3	M	Child	300c05Bp
Mary-Ann		.02	F	Infant	300c05Bp
VAUGH, George		31	M	Dyer	300c05Bp
Margaret	(W)	29	F	None	300c05Bp
Mary-Jane		9	F	Child	300c05Bp
Wm.		3	M	Child	300c05Bp
George		.10	M	Infant	300c05Bp
SHORT, Wm.		20	M	Shoemaker	300c05Bp
BURKE, Robert		18	M	Laborer	300c05Bp
PARK, Leonard		30	M	Farmer	300c05Bp
Mary		55	F	Matron	300c05Bp
Marjory		26	F	Spinster	300c05Bp
Margaret		24	F	Spinster	300c05Bp
Jane		20	F	Spinster	300c05Bp
KEOGH, Bridget		48	F	Matron	300c05Bp
Martha		23	F	Spinster	300c05Bp
Peter		21	M	Laborer	300c05Bp
Mary		.11	F	Infant	300c05Bp
CAMPBELL, Phillip		25	M	Laborer	300c05Bp
BROWN, Margaret		19	F	Spinster	300c05Bp
SAUNDERS, William		60	M	Shoemaker	300c05Bp
George		27	M	Shoemaker	300c05Bp
Ann		26	F	Spinster	300c05Bp
Ann		55	F	Matron	300c05Bp
Marcella		18	F	Spinster	300c05Bp
James		20	M	Shoemaker	300c05Bp
WHITE, Richard		30	M	Laborer	300c05Bp
Alice		.07	F	Infant	300c05Bp
CORMICK, William		20	M	Laborer	300c05Bp
MCARDLE, Patrick		22	M	Chemist	300c05Bp
Bernard		20	M	Chemist	300c05Bp
BISSIT, Patrick		20	M	Laborer	300c05Bp
SEVERTMAN, Richard		25	M	Laborer	300c05Bp
JOHN, Patrick		23	M	Laborer	300c05Bp
SCULLY, Thomas		20	M	Laborer	300c05Bp
John		26	M	Laborer	300c05Bp
KELLY, Mary		23	F	Spinster	300c05Bp
Ann		20	F	Spinster	300c05Bp

NAMES OF PASSENGERS	AGE	SEX	OCCUPATIONS	DATE PORT SHIP
KELLY, Bridget	17	F	Spinster	300c05Bp
MCCANN, Patrick	30	M	Spinner	300c05Bp
CARROLL, Francis	21	M	Cbtmkr	300c05Bp
DEAKIN, Patrick	26	M	Laborer	300c05Bp
CURLEY, Bridget	50	F	Matron	300c05Bp
Patrick	20	M	Relative	300c05Bp
Catherine	16	F	Relative	300c05Bp
Jane	14	F	Relative	300c05Bp
Ann	.10	F	Infant	300c05Bp
POWER, Francis	30	M	Laborer	300c05Bp
Bridget (W)	30	F	None	300c05Bp
Patrick	7	M	Child	300c05Bp
John	6	M	Child	300c05Bp
Johanna	5	F	Child	300c05Bp
Catherine	.04	F	Infant	300c05Bp
CAHILL, Ann	23	F	Spinster	300c05Bp
MAHONY, Sylvester	19	M	Laborer	300c05Bp
BULGER, Mat	36	M	Laborer	300c05Bp
BLAINFIELD, Nicholas	30	M	Laborer	300c05Bp
MACKEY, James	28	M	Butcher	300c05Bp
Mary-Ann (W)	20	F	None	300c05Bp
MOLLARD, Mary-Ann	24	F	Spinster	300c05Bp
JACKSON, Francis	27	M	Hatter	300c05Bp
THOMPSON, Mary	21	F	Spinster	300c05Bp
SCOTT, Ann	20	F	Spinster	300c05Bp
Michael	14	M	Laborer	300c05Bp
NEILL, Margaret	19	F	Spinster	300c05Bp
QUIGLEY, John	46	M	Farmer	300c05Bp
Pat	22	M	Farmer	300c05Bp
Valentine	20	M	Farmer	300c05Bp
HAMMOND, Margaret	25	F	Matron	300c05Bp
James	.03	M	Infant	300c05Bp
REILLY, Patrick	20	M	Laborer	300c05Bp
GALLAGHER, Thomas	20	M	Laborer	300c05Bp
DEVANEY, John	20	M	Laborer	300c05Bp
KEIRNN, Patrick	19	M	Sawer	300c05Bp
GALLAGHER, Mary	25	F	Matron	300c05Bp
Thomas	.10	M	Infant	300c05Bp
CLARKE, William	15	M	Laborer	300c05Bp
KEIRNY, George	22	M	Silversmith	300c05Bp
CONQUEST, Christopher	24	M	Silversmith	300c05Bp
FARRELL, Ma.	16	F	Spinster	300c05Bp
KEEVAINE, Patrick	23	M	Shoemaker	300c05Bp
WARD, Robert	18	M	Shoemaker	300c05Bp
GILL, Catherine	18	F	Spinster	300c05Bp
DEVINE, Catherine	10	F	None	300c05Bp
MURPHY, Catherine	18	F	Spinster	300c05Bp
CREAD, Ann	21	F	Spinster	300c05Bp
BERRICE, Terrence	24	M	Laborer	300c05Bp
HIGGINS, Catherine	52	F	Matron	300c05Bp
John	24	M	Relative	300c05Bp
Bridget	22	F	Relative	300c05Bp
Patrick	18	M	Relative	300c05Bp
Thos.	16	M	Relative	300c05Bp
Michael	14	M	Relative	300c05Bp
Joseph	13	M	Relative	300c05Bp
Margaret	22	F	Relative	300c05Bp
Mary	.11	F	Infant	300c05Bp
WHITE, Thomas	21	M	Laborer	300c05Bp
WATKINS, Patrick	28	M	Laborer	300c05Bp
LOFFEN, Joseph	30	M	Merchant	300c05Bp
BADGE, Frances	28	F	Spinster	300c05Bp
WALLACE, Eliza	20	F	Spinster	300c05Bp
KENNA, Patrick	22	M	Clerk	300c05Bp
Lawrence	17	M	Clerk	300c05Bp
MAGUIRE, Elizabeth	50	F	Matron	300c05Bp
William	30	M	Relative	300c05Bp
Eliza	14	F	Relative	300c05Bp
Margaret	8	F	Child	300c05Bp
NEILL, James	30	M	Farmer	300c05Bp
LANEGAN, Philip	27	M	Farmer	300c05Bp
CATTON, Mary-Ann	24	F	Spinster	300c05Bp
MORAN, Mary	23	F	Matron	300c05Bp
OCONNOR, Margaret	20	F	Spinster	300c05Bp
MCDONOUGH, Michael	22	M	Merchant	300c05Bp

SARDINIA 31 OCTOBER 1849

From Liverpool

NAMES OF PASSENGERS	AGE	SEX	OCCUPATIONS	DATE PORT SHIP
GRAHAM, Patt	26	M	Laborer	310c02Br
MANNION, Ann	18	F	Servant	310c02Br
WHITE, Ellen	20	F	Servant	310c02Br
COLEMAN, Mary	3	F	Child	310c02Br
BLACK, Rosey	18	F	None	310c02Br
DANER, James	30	M	Laborer	310c02Br
JUDGE, Patt	28	M	Laborer	310c02Br
DOUGHERTY, Elizh.	12	F	Servant	310c02Br
HOPKINS, Bridgt.	51	F	Servant	310c02Br
Willm.	8	M	Child	310c02Br
CANNON, Thos.	2	M	Child	310c02Br
BYRNE, Mary	20	F	None	310c02Br
Sally	18	F	None	310c02Br
KELLY, John	18	M	Potter	310c02Br
GROGAN, Mary-A.	18	F	Servant	310c02Br
CONNOR, John	17	M	None	310c02Br
FALLON, Cathe.	20	F	None	310c02Br
WARD, Patt	19	M	Laborer	310c02Br
NOONAN, Mary	50	F	None	310c02Br
Patt	25	M	Laborer	310c02Br
TATE, Mary	20	F	Laborer	310c02Br
Thomas	16	M	Laborer	310c02Br
KELLY, Mary	40	F	Laborer	310c02Br
James	11	M	None	310c02Br
Margt.	10	F	None	310c02Br
BYRNE, Patt	15	M	None	310c02Br
CAMPBELL, Margt.	70	F	None	310c02Br
Margt.	26	F	Dressmaker	310c02Br
MCGUIRK, Patt	39	M	Laborer	310c02Br
DONOHUE, Rose	21	F	Servant	310c02Br
MCMAHON, Alice	20	F	Servant	310c02Br
HANLEY, Patrick	19	M	Laborer	310c02Br
KILROY, Patt	18	M	Laborer	310c02Br
Cathe.	15	F	None	310c02Br
HANLEY, Mary	30	F	Servant	310c02Br
MURPHY, Mary	29	F	Servant	310c02Br
KELLY, Margt.	16	F	Servant	310c02Br
Cathe.	14	F	Servant	310c02Br
SMITH, James	20	M	Laborer	310c02Br
MCGUIRE, Patt	43	M	Laborer	310c02Br
Mary	39	F	None	310c02Br
Danl.	30	M	Laborer	310c02Br
Margt.	11	F	None	310c02Br
Mary	10	F	None	310c02Br
CAIN, Martin	15	M	None	310c02Br
MCCONNAN, Ellen	20	F	Servant	310c02Br
COTTEN, James	33	M	Carpenter	310c02Br
CANNON, Elizh.	18	F	Servant	310c02Br
ROONEY, Nancy	16	F	Servant	310c02Br
KELLY, Chas.	11	M	None	310c02Br
CAMPBELL, James	31	M	Mason	310c02Br
Elizh.	23	F	None	310c02Br
Jane	.00	F	Infant	310c02Br
KELLY, Michl.	2	M	Child	310c02Br
Mary	.00	F	Infant	310c02Br
RYAN, Patt	17	M	Laborer	310c02Br
HOGAN, Ann	20	F	Servant	310c02Br
GERMEN, Mary-A.	20	F	Dressmaker	310c02Br
SHANNON, Eliza	18	F	Servant	310c02Br
Thos.	16	M	None	310c02Br
CONNOR, Benjn.	24	M	Laborer	310c02Br
HARRALD, James	18	M	Laborer	310c02Br
CONNOR, Eliza	24	F	Servant	310c02Br
Mary	.00	F	Infant	310c02Br
COLWELL, Mary	20	F	Servant	310c02Br

NAMES OF PASSENGERS	AGE	SEX	OCCUPATIONS	DATE PORT SHIP
GAFFREY, Andrew	30	M	Laborer	310c02Br
James	8	M	Child	310c02Br
Ann	6	F	Child	310c02Br
KILKENNY, Bridgt.	11	F	Servant	310c02Br
Cathe.	9	F	Child	310c02Br
FARRELL, Patt	17	M	Laborer	310c02Br
Cathe.	14	F	None	310c02Br
DWYER, Mary-King	26	F	Servant	310c02Br
Michl.	3	M	Child	310c02Br
Patt	.00	M	Infant	310c02Br
MARRION, Daniel	42	M	Laborer	310c02Br
Mary	38	F	None	310c02Br
Bridget	18	F	None	310c02Br
Willm.	14	M	None	310c02Br
HANALAN, Elizh.	18	F	Servant	310c02Br
Eliza	12	F	Servant	310c02Br
Julia	9	F	Child	310c02Br
James	6	M	Child	310c02Br
Mary	3	F	Child	310c02Br
KELLY, Mary	20	F	Servant	310c02Br
CONLON, Mary-A.	21	F	Servant	310c02Br
FLANAGAN, Jane	21	F	Servant	310c02Br
CASSIDY, Michl.	21	M	Servant	310c02Br
BEHAN, Mary	17	F	Servant	310c02Br
SHERIDAN, U	35	F	Wi	310c02Br
MONAGHAN, Patt	21	M	Brick Maker	310c02Br
SHARKEY, John	20	M	Laborer	310c02Br
MCMAINS, Hugh	24	M	Farmer	310c02Br
MCCLINTOCK, John	20	M	Laborer	310c02Br
SCOTT, James	20	M	Laborer	310c02Br
MULHALL, Margt.	45	F	Servant	310c02Br
Esther	18	F	Servant	310c02Br
Mary	16	F	Servant	310c02Br
Margt.	11	F	None	310c02Br
Sarah-Ann	5	F	Child	310c02Br
CRAGAN, Francis	19	M	Wool Comber	310c02Br
TYNAN, Patt	22	M	Wool Comber	310c02Br
FIELD, Mary	50	F	Servant	310c02Br
FREELY, Austin	21	M	Farmer	310c02Br
REILLY, Austin	60	M	Farmer	310c02Br
Tim	17	M	Farmer	310c02Br
CRAIGNULL, Jane	30	F	Servant	310c02Br
HACKETT, James	36	M	Laborer	310c02Br
Bridgt.	34	F	None	310c02Br
Mary	9	F	Child	310c02Br
James	7	M	Child	310c02Br
Rosey	5	F	Child	310c02Br
John	2	M	Child	310c02Br
Christopher	.00	M	Infant	310c02Br
OSHEA, Henry	26	M	Laborer	310c02Br
MCGAHAN, Bridgt.	26	F	Servant	310c02Br
MCKEE, Margt.	30	F	Servant	310c02Br
BREEN, Margt.	18	F	Servant	310c02Br
DELANEY, Mary-A.	22	F	Servant	310c02Br
RUSSELL, John	24	M	Laborer	310c02Br
CARR, Michl.	25	M	Tailor	310c02Br
PRICE, Edwd.	13	M	Servant	310c02Br
MCGUIRE, Phillip	20	M	Laborer	310c02Br
SCOTT, Saml.	40	M	Farmer	310c02Br
Elizh.	26	F	None	310c02Br
Henry	20	M	None	310c02Br
ARMSTRONG, Willm.	20	M	None	310c02Br
SCOTT, Eliza	11	F	None	310c02Br
Willm.	10	M	None	310c02Br
Edwd.John	8	M	Child	310c02Br
Mary-Jane	5	F	Child	310c02Br
Robt.Henry	.00	M	Infant	310c02Br
Died-At-Sea				
DOUGHERTY, John	12	M	Servant	310c02Br
Peter	6	M	Child	310c02Br
Margt.	8	F	Child	310c02Br
BURNS, Julia	14	F	None	310c02Br
CLARKE, Cathe.	20	F	Servant	310c02Br
TRAINER, Margt.	8	F	Child	310c02Br
STAINTON, Cathe.	14	F	Dressmaker	310c02Br

NAMES OF PASSENGERS	AGE	SEX	OCCUPATIONS	DATE PORT SHIP
MCDONNELL, Mary	14	F	Servant	310c02Br
Bridgt.	15	F	Servant	310c02Br
COLLINS, Cathe.	21	F	Servant	310c02Br
Thos.	2	M	Child	310c02Br
BOYLE, Mary	50	F	Spinner	310c02Br
John	20	M	Spinner	310c02Br
SEXTON, Patt	24	M	Laborer	310c02Br
DAVERSON, Biddy	46	F	Servant	310c02Br
James	3	M	Child	310c02Br
STOCKPOOL, Patt	44	M	Laborer	310c02Br
LAWLER, Ann	21	F	Servant	310c02Br
MCKUE, Mary	30	F	Servant	310c02Br
Betsy	8	F	Child	310c02Br
DOWNES, John	21	M	Laborer	310c02Br
Cathe.	15	F	None	310c02Br
BURNS, Patt	40	M	Farmer	310c02Br
WALL, John	40	M	Farmer	310c02Br
REILLY, Bernard	20	M	Laborer	310c02Br
Ann	18	F	None	310c02Br
MULSTEY, Margt.	20	F	Servant	310c02Br
TUMMINS, Celia	20	F	Servant	310c02Br
HENRY, Thos.	35	M	Laborer	310c02Br
Susannah	34	F	None	310c02Br
Margt.Jane	9	F	Child	310c02Br
STEPHENSON, John	25	M	Laborer	310c02Br
Eliza	20	F	None	310c02Br
DALY, Ellen	56	F	Servant	310c02Br
Thos.	17	M	None	310c02Br
Cathe.	12	F	None	310c02Br
GALLAGHER, Daniel	52	M	Laborer	310c02Br
Peter	16	M	None	310c02Br
Mary	14	F	None	310c02Br
HOGAN, Margt.	24	F	Servant	310c02Br
WARD, Ann	30	F	Servant	310c02Br
BROWNE, Cathe.	26	F	Servant	310c02Br
James	3	M	Child	310c02Br
MURPHY, John	50	M	Ham Curer	310c02Br
SMYLIE, John	50	M	Ham Curer	310c02Br
DONNELLY, Edwd.	56	M	Ham Curer	310c02Br
Mary	18	F	None	310c02Br
MCELROY, John	37	M	None	310c02Br
MCBRIAN, John	42	M	None	310c02Br
LOCKLAN, Willm.	47	M	None	310c02Br
MURPHY, Thos.	13	M	None	310c02Br
CAIN, Robt.	18	M	Cooper	310c02Br
BLAINEY, John	40	M	Shoemaker	310c02Br
Ann	40	F	None	310c02Br
Daniel	17	M	None	310c02Br
John	14	M	None	310c02Br
Ann	11	F	None	310c02Br
James	8	M	Child	310c02Br
Thos.	8	M	Child	310c02Br
BUCKLEY, Mary	19	F	Servant	310c02Br
DUFFEY, Patt	24	M	Tailor	310c02Br
HURLEY, Patt	21	M	Laborer	310c02Br
Cathe.	35	F	None	310c02Br
CAREW, Elizh.	10	F	None	310c02Br
Ellen-Jane	9	F	Child	310c02Br
Mary	7	F	Child	310c02Br
Kate	5	F	Child	310c02Br
Sarah	4	F	Child	310c02Br
Ann	1	F	Child	310c02Br
CAMPBELL, Elizh.	.00	F	Infant	310c02Br
Born-At-Sea				

CHARLOTTE-HARRISON 31 OCTOBER 1849

From Greenock

NAMES OF PASSENGERS	AGE	SEX	OCCUPATIONS	DATE PORT SHIP
GORDON, William	32	M	Unknown	31Oc19Bi
CUMMING, James	30	M	Laborer	31Oc19Bi
BARR, Neil	23	M	Molder	31Oc19Bi
CAMERON, Alex.	39	M	Blacksmith	31Oc19Bi
SMITH, Andrew	41	M	Laborer	31Oc19Bi
Margaret	30	F	Unknown	31Oc19Bi
Agnes	6	F	Child	31Oc19Bi
Andrew	2	M	Child	31Oc19Bi
MCKENZIE, Mary	38	F	Unknown	31Oc19Bi
Janet	12	F	Unknown	31Oc19Bi
John	10	M	Unknown	31Oc19Bi
Margaret	6	F	Child	31Oc19Bi
Mary	3	F	Child	31Oc19Bi
DAVIDSON, Thos.	25	M	Laborer	31Oc19Bi
DUFFY, Mary	28	F	Servant	31Oc19Bi
MCINTIRE, W.	25	M	Joiner	31Oc19Bi
GALLAHER, Michael	25	M	Joiner	31Oc19Bi
WHITEFORD, David	23	M	Laborer	31Oc19Bi
Janet	23	F	Unknown	31Oc19Bi
John	4	M	Child	31Oc19Bi
Hugh	2	M	Child	31Oc19Bi
Eliza	.01	F	Infant	31Oc19Bi
CLEMENT, Anderson	23	M	Laborer	31Oc19Bi
Margaret	23	F	Unknown	31Oc19Bi
David	2	M	Child	31Oc19Bi
MCGIBBON, James	25	M	Laborer	31Oc19Bi
MCGAVEY, Hannah	20	F	Servant	31Oc19Bi
COULON, Jane	20	F	Servant	31Oc19Bi
OHALE, Mary-A.	20	F	Servant	31Oc19Bi
AGNEW, Thos.	20	M	Laborer	31Oc19Bi
RAE, Jane	67	F	Unknown	31Oc19Bi
Margaret	24	F	Servant	31Oc19Bi
DOWNIE, Andrew	24	M	Laborer	31Oc19Bi
Mary	20	F	Unknown	31Oc19Bi
CARRUTHERS, Jane	30	F	Unknown	31Oc19Bi
Margaret	.10	F	Infant	31Oc19Bi
FALCONER, Robert	20	M	Smith	31Oc19Bi
DONNELLY, Thomas	20	M	Laborer	31Oc19Bi
GIBSON, James	26	M	Carpenter	31Oc19Bi
Jane	26	F	Unknown	31Oc19Bi
Ann	3	F	Child	31Oc19Bi
Jane	.10	F	Infant	31Oc19Bi
BRUCE, James	50	M	Carpenter	31Oc19Bi
Jane	50	F	Unknown	31Oc19Bi
Jane	20	F	Servant	31Oc19Bi
Margaret	18	F	Servant	31Oc19Bi
Mary	16	F	Servant	31Oc19Bi
DAVIDSON, John	49	M	Farmer	31Oc19Bi
OBRYAN, Dennis	30	M	Laborer	31Oc19Bi
BRYDEN, Bryan	28	M	Laborer	31Oc19Bi
DAVIDSON, Betsy	31	F	Servant	31Oc19Bi

CHAOS 31 OCTOBER 1849

From Liverpool

NAMES OF PASSENGERS	AGE	SEX	OCCUPATIONS	DATE PORT SHIP
QUIN, Thomas	24	M	Laborer	31Oc02Bq
BROWN, James	15	M	Laborer	31Oc02Bq
Mary	16	F	Unknown	31Oc02Bq
BURK, Patk.	16	M	Laborer	31Oc02Bq
Cathn.	17	F	Unknown	31Oc02Bq
DOYLE, Letty	22	F	Unknown	31Oc02Bq
HARRIS, Wm.	25	M	Laborer	31Oc02Bq
HENNESY, Edmund	22	M	Laborer	31Oc02Bq
Mary	16	F	Unknown	31Oc02Bq
CAREW, Margt.	7	F	Child	31Oc02Bq
Ellen	6	F	Child	31Oc02Bq
MULVANY, Mary	18	F	Unknown	31Oc02Bq
CONSTANTINE, Timothy	14	M	Laborer	31Oc02Bq
TURBUTT, Mary-Ann	12	F	Unknown	31Oc02Bq
CUNNINGHAM, Henry	27	M	Laborer	31Oc02Bq
READY, Margt.	30	F	Unknown	31Oc02Bq
EGAN, John	6	M	Child	31Oc02Bq
ANGLIN, Mary	20	F	Unknown	31Oc02Bq
DEASY, Maria	16	F	Unknown	31Oc02Bq
OBRIAN, Cathn.	19	F	Unknown	31Oc02Bq
DOYLE, Cathn.	17	F	Unknown	31Oc02Bq
Ann	15	F	Unknown	31Oc02Bq
MCVEADY, Patk.	19	M	Laborer	31Oc02Bq
Honor	20	F	Unknown	31Oc02Bq
MCLOUGHLIN, John	30	M	Laborer	31Oc02Bq
Julia	20	F	Unknown	31Oc02Bq
Martin	12	M	Laborer	31Oc02Bq
KELLY, Mary	19	F	Unknown	31Oc02Bq
NUGENT, Mary	20	F	Unknown	31Oc02Bq
CONWAY, Mary	19	F	Unknown	31Oc02Bq
MCIVE, Margt.	30	F	Unknown	31Oc02Bq

ST.GEORGE 01 NOVEMBER 1849

From Liverpool

NAMES OF PASSENGERS	AGE	SEX	OCCUPATIONS	DATE PORT SHIP
FITZGERALD, John	25	M	Laborer	01No02Bu
CROW, Ann	28	F	Unknown	01No02Bu
CROWE, James	22	M	Laborer	01No02Bu
KANE, John	25	M	Laborer	01No02Bu
Died-At-Sea				
FLANAGAN, Pat	27	M	Laborer	01No02Bu
GRIFFIN, Margaret	24	F	Unknown	01No02Bu
DARBY, Catharine	18	F	Unknown	01No02Bu
FLANEGAN, Mike	20	M	Laborer	01No02Bu
KELLY, Ellen	16	F	Unknown	01No02Bu
KENNEY, Julia	21	F	Unknown	01No02Bu
KIRKADY, Thomas	24	M	Laborer	01No02Bu
FLANAGAN, Bridget	17	F	Unknown	01No02Bu
KENNEY, Danl.	9	M	Child	01No02Bu
KERKADY, Eliza	24	F	Unknown	01No02Bu
MCQUE, John	21	M	Laborer	01No02Bu
MEHAN, Thomas	18	M	Laborer	01No02Bu
SHEA, Bridget	16	F	Unknown	01No02Bu
MAY, Catharine	13	F	Unknown	01No02Bu
MCGORKIN, Sarah	30	F	Unknown	01No02Bu
Mary	10	F	Unknown	01No02Bu
Died-At-Sea				
Nancy	5	F	Child	01No02Bu
John	3	M	Child	01No02Bu
James	.00	M	Infant	01No02Bu
WATSON, Nancy	36	F	Unknown	01No02Bu
Matty	14	F	Unknown	01No02Bu
Robert	12	M	Unknown	01No02Bu
John	10	M	Unknown	01No02Bu
William	10	M	Unknown	01No02Bu
Eliza	7	F	Child	01No02Bu
James	4	M	Child	01No02Bu
MOORE, Ellen	20	F	Unknown	01No02Bu
PATTEN, Mary	48	F	Unknown	01No02Bu
Rosanna	12	F	Unknown	01No02Bu
Mary	10	F	Unknown	01No02Bu

NAMES OF PASSENGERS	AGE	SEX	OCCUPATIONS	DATE PORT SHIP
PATTEN, John	8	M	Child	01No02Bu
FLANRY, Margaret	22	F	Unknown	01No02Bu
CARLISLE, John	36	M	Blacksmith	01No02Bu
LESTER, Thomas	18	M	Laborer	01No02Bu
GALLORYONDY, Ellen	34	F	Unknown	01No02Bu
John	11	M	Unknown	01No02Bu
Pat	9	M	Child	01No02Bu
CALAHAN, Julia	30	F	Unknown	01No02Bu
BRUCE, Ann	10	F	Unknown	01No02Bu
Mary	8	F	Child	01No02Bu
Died-At-Sea				
CARTEY, Andrew	14	M	Unknown	01No02Bu
Mary	11	F	Unknown	01No02Bu
JENKINS, Thomas	18	M	Shoemaker	01No02Bu
KENEDY, David	28	M	Farmer	01No02Bu
Mary	21	F	Unknown	01No02Bu
MCCLARY, Isacc	19	M	Laborer	01No02Bu
MANNIN, Ann	18	F	Unknown	01No02Bu
Bridget	18	F	Milliner	01No02Bu
FRASER, Ann	19	F	Milliner	01No02Bu
PHILLIPS, John	20	M	Laborer	01No02Bu
DONNELLY, Pat	20	M	Laborer	01No02Bu
MARSHALL, Robert	40	M	Farmer	01No02Bu
RILEY, Catharine	17	F	Unknown	01No02Bu
Rose	15	F	Unknown	01No02Bu
TURNEY, Ann	13	F	Unknown	01No02Bu
HARTY, Margaret	12	F	Unknown	01No02Bu
NEIL, John	50	M	Farmer	01No02Bu
LALOR, Edward	25	M	Laborer	01No02Bu
Ann	27	F	Unknown	01No02Bu
Died-At-Sea				
Margaret	.00	F	Infant	01No02Bu
Died-At-Sea				
SHANNON, Mary	31	F	Unknown	01No02Bu
Margaret	10	F	Unknown	01No02Bu
Bridget	8	F	Child	01No02Bu
Ann	5	F	Child	01No02Bu
CLARK, Hugh	10	M	Laborer	01No02Bu
Mary	8	F	Child	01No02Bu
MONAHAN, Ann	17	F	Unknown	01No02Bu
TONHAN, Catharine	20	F	Unknown	01No02Bu
MCKENNA, James	25	M	Laborer	01No02Bu
BIRD, Mary	30	F	Unknown	01No02Bu
Susan	7	F	Child	01No02Bu
Jane	5	F	Child	01No02Bu
Mary	3	F	Child	01No02Bu
Elisha	.00	M	Infant	01No02Bu
SINCLAIR, Harriet	20	F	Unknown	01No02Bu
WHELAN, Eliza	18	F	Unknown	01No02Bu
LALOR, Margaret	18	F	Unknown	01No02Bu
Died-At-Sea				
KELLY, Catharine	20	F	Unknown	01No02Bu
MALONE, Bridget	33	F	Unknown	01No02Bu
CHAMBERLAIN, Catherine	26	F	Milliner	01No02Bu
John	21	M	Laborer	01No02Bu
MALONE, Danl.	23	M	Machinist	01No02Bu
KIRBY, John	22	M	Mason	01No02Bu
MCCARTY, Mary	22	F	Unknown	01No02Bu
TOBIN, Margaret	22	F	Unknown	01No02Bu
BARRY, Mary	17	F	Unknown	01No02Bu
TRACY, Mary	20	F	Unknown	01No02Bu
RYAN, Mary	25	F	Unknown	01No02Bu
BURK, Richard	40	M	Farmer	01No02Bu
Judy	25	F	Unknown	01No02Bu
BARRY, David	19	M	Laborer	01No02Bu
TRACY, Mary	60	F	Unknown	01No02Bu
BRENNAN, Pat	20	M	Laborer	01No02Bu
LUBY, Michael	21	M	Laborer	01No02Bu
John	24	M	Laborer	01No02Bu
WELSH, Betsey	20	F	Unknown	01No02Bu
MCNARNY, Mary	16	F	Unknown	01No02Bu
LENAHAN, Mary	20	F	Unknown	01No02Bu
GAFFNEY, Catharine	18	F	Unknown	01No02Bu
MULLIGAN, Ellen	20	F	Unknown	01No02Bu
HASLOP, Thomas	29	M	Laborer	01No02Bu

NAMES OF PASSENGERS	AGE	SEX	OCCUPATIONS	DATE PORT SHIP
HASLOP, James	9	M	Child	01No02Bu
CAFFREY, Bernard	15	M	Unknown	01No02Bu
MCNARTNY, Perine	35	M	Unknown	01No02Bu
LENON, John	25	M	Unknown	01No02Bu
DRISCOLL, Margaret	14	F	Unknown	01No02Bu
Ellen	12	F	Unknown	01No02Bu
LENON, Rose	38	F	Unknown	01No02Bu
MCGUIRE, Michael	28	M	Laborer	01No02Bu
TROY, John	25	M	Laborer	01No02Bu
BRADLY, Pat	22	M	Laborer	01No02Bu
Bridget	27	F	Laborer	01No02Bu
GIBBON, Betsey	18	F	Unknown	01No02Bu
WELSH, Thomas	21	M	Laborer	01No02Bu
QUIGLY, Mary-Ann	20	F	Child	01No02Bu
CONOLLY, Ellen	20	F	Child	01No02Bu
AGAN, Dan	20	M	Laborer	01No02Bu
SHEVLAN, Dennis	15	M	Unknown	01No02Bu
John	13	M	Unknown	01No02Bu
James	10	M	Unknown	01No02Bu
Ann	8	F	Child	01No02Bu
Mary	5	F	Child	01No02Bu
RIDDLE, Mary	22	F	Unknown	01No02Bu
Catharine	.00	F	Infant	01No02Bu
BERGAN, Eliza	16	F	Unknown	01No02Bu
CHAPMAN, Mary	40	F	Unknown	01No02Bu
Eliza	16	F	Unknown	01No02Bu
Margaret	14	F	Unknown	01No02Bu
John	12	M	Unknown	01No02Bu
James	12	M	Unknown	01No02Bu
Henry	10	M	Unknown	01No02Bu
William	7	M	Child	01No02Bu
Died-At-Sea				
Robert	4	M	Child	01No02Bu
Died-At-Sea				
KELLY, Rosanna	40	F	Servant	01No02Bu
Died-At-Sea				
Rosanna	16	F	Servant	01No02Bu
Died-At-Sea				
James	14	M	Unknown	01No02Bu
Margaret	10	F	Unknown	01No02Bu
LYNCH, Michael	30	M	Laborer	01No02Bu
WELSH, John	18	M	Laborer	01No02Bu
MOUNTAN, Margaret	30	F	Unknown	01No02Bu
George	4	M	Child	01No02Bu
Mary	.00	F	Infant	01No02Bu
HARE, Susan	24	F	Unknown	01No02Bu
GOGGIN, Ellen	15	F	Unknown	01No02Bu
ALLEN, Catharine	25	F	Unknown	01No02Bu
NEWSMAN, Margaret	22	F	Unknown	01No02Bu
CARNEY, Cathrine	16	F	Unknown	01No02Bu
WOLF, Thomas	24	M	Unknown	01No02Bu
FITZGERALD, James	19	M	Laborer	01No02Bu
MURPHY, John	27	M	Blacksmith	01No02Bu
Ellen	30	F	Servant	01No02Bu
Tim	27	M	Servant	01No02Bu
KAIN, Ellen	23	F	Servant	01No02Bu
COLEMAN, Catharine	60	F	Servant	01No02Bu
BURNS, Hannah	24	F	Servant	01No02Bu
John	4	M	Child	01No02Bu
ONEIL, Mary	35	F	Unknown	01No02Bu
John	11	M	Unknown	01No02Bu
Jeremiah	6	M	Child	01No02Bu
MCGRATH, Catharine	36	F	Unknown	01No02Bu
Margaret	25	F	Unknown	01No02Bu
Pat	50	M	Laborer	01No02Bu
Mary	50	F	Unknown	01No02Bu
Margaret	.00	F	Infant	01No02Bu
HANLEY, James	22	M	Laborer	01No02Bu
CULLEN, Pat	26	M	Laborer	01No02Bu
CARROLL, John	14	M	Laborer	01No02Bu
DUNN, John	28	M	Laborer	01No02Bu
SHANKLAND, Christopher	9	M	Child	01No02Bu
SHANNON, James	21	M	Unknown	01No02Bu
KELLY, James	35	M	Unknown	01No02Bu
WALSH, Maria	15	F	Unknown	01No02Bu

NAMES OF PASSENGERS	AGE	SEX	OCCUPATIONS	DATE PORT SHIP
BERGEN, Mary	25	F	Unknown	01No02Bu
MORAN, Ann	15	F	Unknown	01No02Bu
WELSH, Ann	10	F	Unknown	01No02Bu
FOSSETT, Robert	30	M	Laborer	01No02Bu
HAZARD, Richard	20	M	Laborer	01No02Bu
BRADY, John	17	M	Laborer	01No02Bu
Mary	15	F	Unknown	01No02Bu
TURNER, James	30	M	Shoemaker	01No02Bu
Catharine	41	F	Unknown	01No02Bu
BRADY, Bridget	50	F	Unknown	01No02Bu
BURNS, Mary	16	F	Unknown	01No02Bu
MURPHY, Margaret	16	F	Unknown	01No02Bu
TRYRE, Bridget	19	F	Unknown	01No02Bu
LANE, Honora	39	F	Unknown	01No02Bu
Con.	4	M	Child	01No02Bu
CULBERT, William	28	M	Tailor	01No02Bu
SULLIVAN, John	21	M	Laborer	01No02Bu
WILD, Mary	30	F	Unknown	01No02Bu
PITTS, Alex	40	M	Laborer	01No02Bu
CLONEY, Mary	23	F	Unknown	01No02Bu
TERNERY, Phillip	23	M	Unknown	01No02Bu
BURK, John	24	M	Farmer	01No02Bu
OBRIEN, Danl.	19	M	Laborer	01No02Bu
HENNESEY, Morris	17	M	Laborer	01No02Bu
PHELAN, Bridget	21	F	Unknown	01No02Bu
Ellen	23	F	Unknown	01No02Bu
MURPHY, Morris	20	M	Laborer	01No02Bu
MCCORMICK, John	20	M	Cbtmkr	01No02Bu
COLLINS, Morris	35	M	Carpenter	01No02Bu
COGAN, Mary	21	F	Unknown	01No02Bu
JOYCE, Bridget	19	F	Unknown	01No02Bu
HOLLAND, Catharine	19	F	Unknown	01No02Bu
Died-At-Sea				
KEENAN, Betsey	6	F	Child	01No02Bu
DOLAN, John	19	M	Laborer	01No02Bu
COSTIGAN, John	35	M	Laborer	01No02Bu
DUNN, Charles	12	M	Unknown	01No02Bu
MAYER, Betsey	20	F	Unknown	01No02Bu
KELLY, Margaret	20	F	Unknown	01No02Bu
SPROAL, Mary	28	F	Unknown	01No02Bu
LALORS, Catharine	25	F	Milliner	01No02Bu
SPROAL, Andrew	22	M	Laborer	01No02Bu
SHULTZ, Betsey	25	F	Unknown	01No02Bu
CAMPBELL, Arthur	16	M	Laborer	01No02Bu
DEVLIN, Susan	30	F	Unknown	01No02Bu
FLANAGAN, Bridget	22	F	Unknown	01No02Bu
BROSNEHANS, Darby	29	M	Laborer	01No02Bu
MURDOUGH, Susan	19	F	Unknown	01No02Bu
BOON, Honora	14	F	Unknown	01No02Bu
Honora	30	F	Unknown	01No02Bu
Betsey	12	F	Unknown	01No02Bu
Danl.	9	M	Child	01No02Bu
Con.	5	M	Child	01No02Bu
Catharine	.00	F	Infant	01No02Bu
CURTAIN, Michael	28	M	Laborer	01No02Bu
Bridget	26	F	Unknown	01No02Bu
John	.00	M	Infant	01No02Bu
Died-At-Sea				
William	.00	M	Infant	01No02Bu
Died-At-Sea				
MCCLEAN, Sarah-A.	11	F	Unknown	01No02Bu
Died-At-Sea				
Margaret-J.	9	F	Child	01No02Bu
RILEY, Pat	22	M	Laborer	01No02Bu
REGAN, Pat	32	M	Laborer	01No02Bu
CURTAIN, Dennis	19	M	Laborer	01No02Bu
MORA, Danl.	30	M	Laborer	01No02Bu
HOLLAND, John	40	M	Laborer	01No02Bu
MCCLEAN, Martha	40	F	Laborer	01No02Bu
KERIGAN, Danl.	30	M	Laborer	01No02Bu
MCLAUGHLIN, Mary	20	F	Servant	01No02Bu
CALLOHAN, Lucy	18	F	Unknown	01No02Bu
FITZGERALD, Ellen	20	F	Unknown	01No02Bu
KELLY, Mary	20	F	Unknown	01No02Bu
LEONS, James	26	M	Laborer	01No02Bu

NAMES OF PASSENGERS	AGE	SEX	OCCUPATIONS	DATE PORT SHIP
MULLY, Mary	30	F	Unknown	01No02Bu
Died-At-Sea				
WHELAN, Ann	30	F	Unknown	01No02Bu
GALLAGER, Mary	23	F	Unknown	01No02Bu
JUDGE, James	24	M	Laborer	01No02Bu
Died-At-Sea				
LEINTOT, Edward	20	M	Laborer	01No02Bu
MCDONALD, Bridget	30	F	Unknown	01No02Bu
MCGRATH, Eliza	10	F	Unknown	01No02Bu
George	8	M	Child	01No02Bu
John	50	M	Mason	01No02Bu
Ellen	25	F	Unknown	01No02Bu
Jane	18	F	Unknown	01No02Bu
Ellen	12	F	Unknown	01No02Bu
WELSH, Bridget	20	F	Unknown	01No02Bu
FOTEY, William	21	M	Unknown	01No02Bu
KANE, John	23	M	Laborer	01No02Bu
WELSH, Mike	16	M	Unknown	01No02Bu
THORNTON, James	21	M	Laborer	01No02Bu
William	7	M	Child	01No02Bu
Margaret	5	F	Child	01No02Bu
David	3	M	Child	01No02Bu
CAMPBELL, Phebe	28	F	Unknown	01No02Bu
CAUGHLIN, Michael	21	M	Laborer	01No02Bu
GANNON, Michael	21	M	Laborer	01No02Bu
KENNAN, Ann	16	F	Unknown	01No02Bu
MURPHY, Mary	20	F	Unknown	01No02Bu
KEARNEY, Charles	21	M	Laborer	01No02Bu
SULLIVAN, Rose	16	F	Unknown	01No02Bu
FENNEY, Thomas	21	M	Mason	01No02Bu
HOPPERS, Michael	23	M	Laborer	01No02Bu
MCINTYRE, Pat	21	M	Weaver	01No02Bu
BRIGHS, Sarah	30	F	Unknown	01No02Bu
Samuel	8	M	Child	01No02Bu
Margaret	6	F	Child	01No02Bu
Elizabeth	5	F	Child	01No02Bu
HUGHS, William	20	M	Laborer	01No02Bu
CASSADY, Ellen	19	F	Unknown	01No02Bu
BROWN, Bridget	22	F	Unknown	01No02Bu
DONOVAN, Ellen	18	F	Unknown	01No02Bu
DAWES, Bridget	24	F	Unknown	01No02Bu
RUTTER, Fran.	47	M	Silversmith	01No02Bu
Samuel	8	M	Child	01No02Bu
Rueben	14	M	Unknown	01No02Bu
DORATHY, John	28	M	Unknown	01No02Bu
Mary	27	F	Unknown	01No02Bu
HACKETT, Mary	30	F	Unknown	01No02Bu
MORRIS, Daniel	25	M	Engineer	01No02Bu
WRIGHT, Jane	24	F	Unknown	01No02Bu
Eliza-Jane	.00	F	Infant	01No02Bu
MURPHY, Michael	28	M	Farmer	01No02Bu
Mary	22	F	Unknown	01No02Bu
Daniel	26	M	Farmer	01No02Bu
CARTY, Ann	23	F	Unknown	01No02Bu
GALLAHAR, Rose	16	F	Unknown	01No02Bu
Ann	22	F	Unknown	01No02Bu
MCCORMICK, Catharine	44	F	Unknown	01No02Bu
HART, John	8	M	Child	01No02Bu
WINKLE, Mary	20	F	Unknown	01No02Bu
RENEY, James	45	M	Mmrnr	01No02Bu
HOLLAND, Bridget	25	F	Unknown	01No02Bu

ALBERT 02 NOVEMBER 1849

From St.JOHNS,N.B.

NAMES OF PASSENGERS	AGE	SEX	OCCUPATIONS	DATE PORT SHIP
WHALEN, Patrick	35	M	Farmer	02No07Bv

MARGARET 02 NOVEMBER 1849

From Glasgow

NAMES OF PASSENGERS	AGE	SEX	OCCUPATIONS	DATE PORT SHIP
CLARK, U-Mrs.	23	F	Wife	02No21Bw
Robert	2	M	Child	02No21Bw
Thomas	.00	M	Infant	02No21Bw
KELLS, U-Mrs.	24	F	Wife	02No21Bw
Joseph	.00	M	Infant	02No21Bw
HIGGINS, Thomas	29	M	Laborer	02No21Bw
Margaret	3	F	Child	02No21Bw
JEFFREY, Edward	32	M	Tailor	02No21Bw
MILLER, Alexander	40	M	Merchant	02No21Bw
LOUGHERY, Philip	20	M	Farmer	02No21Bw
Mary	22	F	Weaver	02No21Bw
KANE, Katharine	26	F	Spinster	02No21Bw
Jane	6	F	Child	02No21Bw
Sarah-Ann	4	F	Child	02No21Bw
Mary	2	F	Child	02No21Bw
KEVIN, Ann-Jane	30	F	Spinster	02No21Bw
Elisabeth	6	F	Child	02No21Bw
George	4	M	Child	02No21Bw
John	.00	M	Infant	02No21Bw
RICE, Jane	32	F	Spinster	02No21Bw
Mary	9	F	Child	02No21Bw
WHYTE, William	50	M	Farmer	02No21Bw
Sarah-Ann	47	F	Wife	02No21Bw
Elisabeth	22	F	Spinster	02No21Bw
Mary-Ann	19	F	Spinster	02No21Bw
Sarah-Ann-Jane	11	F	Unknown	02No21Bw
Susan	9	F	Child	02No21Bw
Isabella	7	F	Child	02No21Bw
Ruth	5	F	Child	02No21Bw
William-George	.00	M	Infant	02No21Bw
STEWART, Rebecca	38	F	Spinster	02No21Bw
Robert	10	M	Unknown	02No21Bw
John-Thomas	6	M	Child	02No21Bw
Jane	4	F	Child	02No21Bw
Rebecca	2	F	Child	02No21Bw
William	.00	M	Infant	02No21Bw
WHYTE, John	14	M	Laborer	02No21Bw
THOMSON, Wm.	40	M	Farmer	02No21Bw
HAMILTON, Eliza	30	F	Spinster	02No21Bw
CROSSET, Margaret	25	F	Servant	02No21Bw
THOMSON, Jane	16	F	Servant	02No21Bw
Rose	7	F	Child	02No21Bw
John	6	M	Child	02No21Bw
MCPEAK, Patrick	36	M	Farmer	02No21Bw
Sarah	31	F	Wife	02No21Bw
COBURN, Elisabeth	38	F	Servant	02No21Bw
DEVINE, Bridget	23	F	Wife	02No21Bw
Mary	3	F	Child	02No21Bw
Mary	.00	M	Infant	02No21Bw
KING, Henry	23	M	Laborer	02No21Bw
COURTENAY, Joshua	25	M	Laborer	02No21Bw
SOMERVILLE, John	20	M	Farmer	02No21Bw
Jane	22	F	Spinster	02No21Bw
MCKINLAY, John	26	M	Farmer	02No21Bw
VALLALEY, Margaret	34	F	Servant	02No21Bw
HART, Elisabeth	25	F	Servant	02No21Bw
HIGGINS, Owen	20	M	Farmer	02No21Bw

DEVONSHIRE 03 NOVEMBER 1849

From London

NAMES OF PASSENGERS	AGE	SEX	OCCUPATIONS	DATE PORT SHIP
HAMILTON, Thomas-W.	20	M	Journalist	03No06Cc

MARIA 05 NOVEMBER 1849

From Belfast

NAMES OF PASSENGERS	AGE	SEX	OCCUPATIONS	DATE PORT SHIP
SHARPE, Samuel	17	M	Farmer	05No17By
JENKINS, John	15	M	Unknown	05No17By
BEATTIE, James	40	M	Unknown	05No17By
Janie	40	F	Unknown	05No17By
Ann	12	F	Unknown	05No17By
George	10	M	Unknown	05No17By
Sarah	8	F	Child	05No17By
Wm.L.	6	M	Child	05No17By
Nancy	.00	F	Infant	05No17By
William	24	M	Unknown	05No17By
Thomas	23	M	Unknown	05No17By
Ellen	26	M	Unknown	05No17By
YOUNG, Nancy	20	F	Unknown	05No17By
OLIVER, Ellen	20	F	Unknown	05No17By
HAGAN, Pat	25	M	Unknown	05No17By
BOLE, John	23	M	Unknown	05No17By
HARRINGTON, William	40	M	Unknown	05No17By
Sarah	35	F	Unknown	05No17By
Sarah	19	F	Unknown	05No17By
Mary	13	F	Unknown	05No17By
Isabella	4	F	Child	05No17By
FARRELL, Mary	40	F	Unknown	05No17By
Thomas	11	M	Unknown	05No17By
NUGENT, Isabella	19	F	Unknown	05No17By
Isabella	21	F	Unknown	05No17By
ROGERS, Biddy	19	F	Unknown	05No17By
MCCLOUD, Eliza	45	F	Unknown	05No17By
William	16	M	Unknown	05No17By
U	14	U	Unknown	05No17By
Gregg	12	M	Unknown	05No17By
Joseph	10	M	Unknown	05No17By
WATERS, Margt.	16	F	Unknown	05No17By
RITCHIE, James	21	M	Unknown	05No17By
Mary	20	F	Unknown	05No17By
GRAHAM, Biddy	20	F	Unknown	05No17By
WILSON, Thomas	18	M	Unknown	05No17By
WOOD, M.	18	U	Unknown	05No17By
PHILLIPS, Thomas	18	M	Unknown	05No17By
BOLE, James	28	M	Unknown	05No17By
ANDREWS, Thomas	50	M	Unknown	05No17By
SAMPSON, John	20	M	Unknown	05No17By
GLASS, Thomas	50	M	Unknown	05No17By
Sarah	50	F	Unknown	05No17By
BORLAND, Mary	24	F	Unknown	05No17By
MARSHALL, Mary	25	F	Unknown	05No17By
H.	20	U	Unknown	05No17By
CORDY, John	28	M	Unknown	05No17By
Eliza	25	F	Unknown	05No17By
REID, Mary	20	F	Unknown	05No17By
PATTERSON, Elicia	23	F	Unknown	05No17By
SMITH, Elicia	22	F	Unknown	05No17By
Eliza	17	F	Unknown	05No17By
Thomas	.00	M	Infant	05No17By

NAMES OF PASSENGERS		AGE	SEX	OCCUPATIONS	DATE PORT SHIP
HANNAN, Mary		19	F	Unknown	05No17By
U, Rachel		21	F	Unknown	05No17By
STONE, George		22	M	Unknown	05No17By
Isabella		20	F	Unknown	05No17By
William		7	M	Child	05No17By
GLENHONE, Henry		40	M	Unknown	05No17By
BROWN, Rebecca		35	F	Unknown	05No17By
Betty		16	F	Unknown	05No17By
Margt.		13	F	Unknown	05No17By
Anne		10	F	Unknown	05No17By
David		2	M	Child	05No17By
Nathanl.		.00	M	Infant	05No17By
STONE, John		20	M	Unknown	05No17By
Thomas		19	M	Unknown	05No17By
LAVERTY, Mary		25	F	Unknown	05No17By
Michael		2	M	Child	05No17By
MCDONNELL, Stewart		28	M	Unknown	05No17By
WILSON, William		23	M	Unknown	05No17By
HENSON, John		25	M	Unknown	05No17By
GAMBLE, Mary		26	F	Unknown	05No17By
Rachel		24	F	Unknown	05No17By
MCDANIEL, Jane		26	F	Unknown	05No17By
GIL--, James		30	M	Unknown	05No17By
MACKEY, Leticia		35	F	Unknown	05No17By
John		10	M	Unknown	05No17By
William		8	M	Child	05No17By
Thomas		6	M	Child	05No17By
Margt.		3	F	Child	05No17By
James		.00	M	Infant	05No17By
LEE, Francis		25	M	Unknown	05No17By
Daniel		20	M	Unknown	05No17By
Margt.		18	F	Unknown	05No17By
Bernard		15	M	Unknown	05No17By
KANE, Martha		25	F	Unknown	05No17By
DUNCAN, Jane		20	F	Unknown	05No17By
STEWART, Joseph-G.		25	M	Unknown	05No17By
DONAGHER, John		29	M	Unknown	05No17By
MABINE, James		16	M	Unknown	05No17By
HAMMOND, Martha		20	F	Unknown	05No17By
Alice		18	F	Unknown	05No17By
MOON, Margt.		60	F	Unknown	05No17By
Samuel		30	M	Unknown	05No17By
Robert		27	M	Unknown	05No17By
Sarah		26	F	Unknown	05No17By
Ellen		17	F	Unknown	05No17By
Maria		13	F	Unknown	05No17By
David		1	M	Child	05No17By
ALLEN, Ben		25	M	Unknown	05No17By
MIDDLEDORY, John		18	M	Unknown	05No17By
LARKIN, Francis		26	M	Unknown	05No17By
SMITH, Eliza		25	F	Unknown	05No17By
STEN, James		21	M	Unknown	05No17By
LOWRY, Savage		23	M	Unknown	05No17By

INDIAN-QUEEN 05 NOVEMBER 1849

From London

NAMES OF PASSENGERS		AGE	SEX	OCCUPATIONS	DATE PORT SHIP
PARKER, W.		30	M	Unknown	05No06Cn
DRINAN, Thos.		14	M	None	05No06Cn
CRISP, Mary-Ann		41	F	Wife	05No06Cn
Frederick	(S)	15	M	None	05No06Cn
Fanny	(D)	13	F	None	05No06Cn
Cath.	(D)	12	F	None	05No06Cn
Anna-Maria	(D)	11	F	None	05No06Cn
James	(S)	5	M	Child	05No06Cn
Robt.	(S)	12	M	None	05No06Cn
Died-At-Sea					
CAMPBELL, Arthur		22	M	Painter	05No06Cn
SMITH, Wm.		35	M	Carpenter	05No06Cn
Mary-Ann	(W)	29	F	None	05No06Cn
William	(S)	8	M	Child	05No06Cn
Emma	(D)	6	F	Child	05No06Cn
MCINTOSH, Agnes		17	F	Clerk	05No06Cn
PUMBELL, Wm.		20	M	Tailor	05No06Cn
Thomas		18	M	Tailor	05No06Cn
RICHARDS, Edward		19	M	Jeweller	05No06Cn
HOLNESS, John		41	M	Farmer	05No06Cn
Elizabeth	(W)	39	F	None	05No06Cn
Wm.	(S)	16	M	None	05No06Cn
Lucy	(D)	10	F	None	05No06Cn
Thomas	(S)	6	M	Child	05No06Cn
LYNCH, Tim.		38	M	Shoemaker	05No06Cn
Margt.	(W)	30	F	None	05No06Cn
Margt.	(D)	5	F	Child	05No06Cn
Ann	(D)	4	F	Child	05No06Cn
Thomas	(S)	2	M	Child	05No06Cn
CALAGHAN, Cath.		20	F	Servant	05No06Cn
BRILLARD, Fred.		38	M	Unknown	05No06Cn
DODD, Wm.		43	M	Tailor	05No06Cn
KIDD, Al.		29	M	Pphgr	05No06Cn
LUCAS, Wm.		36	M	Bookbinder	05No06Cn
SMITH, Chs.		25	M	Cooper	05No06Cn
Eliza	(W)	24	F	None	05No06Cn
PARRY, John		45	M	Shoemaker	05No06Cn
MILWARD, John		36	M	Painter	05No06Cn
BAILEY, Wm.		23	M	Laborer	05No06Cn
FITZGERALD, Geo.		33	M	Molder	05No06Cn
Eliza	(W)	30	F	None	05No06Cn
Fanny	(D)	9	F	Child	05No06Cn
Emilia	(D)	4	F	Child	05No06Cn
Elizabeth	(D)	.09	F	Infant	05No06Cn
DOWLING, Wm.		30	M	Tailor	05No06Cn
Betsey	(W)	30	F	None	05No06Cn
Leonard	(S)	5	M	Child	05No06Cn
Ebenezer	(S)	2	M	Child	05No06Cn
Elizabeth		.09	F	Infant	05No06Cn
ROHILL, Mary		44	F	Servant	05No06Cn
OCONNELL, Lucy		15	F	None	05No06Cn
PEARSON, Alfred		27	M	Tailor	05No06Cn
BURGESS, Sarah		56	F	Shoe Binder	05No06Cn
Elizabeth	(D)	18	F	None	05No06Cn
ONEIL, Michl.		29	M	Bootmaker	05No06Cn
Ellen	(W)	26	F	None	05No06Cn
HALLOWAY, Thomas		56	M	Farmer	05No06Cn
DRISCOLL, Ellen		50	F	Servant	05No06Cn
Henry	(S)	5	M	Child	05No06Cn
ANDERSON, John		34	M	Bootmaker	05No06Cn
MARSON, Chs.		31	M	Carpenter	05No06Cn
Eliza	(W)	28	F	None	05No06Cn
RING, Michl.		32	M	Laborer	05No06Cn
CLARK, Mary		25	F	Unknown	05No06Cn
JONES, Charlotte		40	F	Wi	05No06Cn
JORDAN, John		24	M	Laborer	05No06Cn
AUSTIN, Geo.		38	M	Tailor	05No06Cn
Mary	(W)	36	F	None	05No06Cn
Sarah	(D)	13	F	None	05No06Cn
Elizabeth	(D)	8	F	Child	05No06Cn
Anna	(D)	2	F	Child	05No06Cn
Edwd.John	(S)	11	M	None	05No06Cn
SNIDERLY, Wm.		31	M	Gastronomer	05No06Cn
Louisa	(W)	26	F	None	05No06Cn
MODE, Ellen		52	F	Tailor	05No06Cn
John	(S)	10	M	None	05No06Cn

LIVERPOOL 10 NOVEMBER 1849

From Liverpool

NAMES OF PASSENGERS	AGE	SEX	OCCUPATIONS	DATE PORT SHIP
TRAVERS, John-N.	23	M	Gentleman	10No02Bx
Elizabeth	21	F	Lady	10No02Bx
FAY, Maria	00	F	Nurse	10No02Bx
EGAN, James	28	M	Cord Winder	10No02Bx
Eliza	.00	F	Infant	10No02Bx
Wm.	6	M	Child	10No02Bx
MCGUINESS, Ellen	17	F	Servant	10No02Bx
REYNOLDS, Mgt.	30	F	Servant	10No02Bx
James	8	M	Child	10No02Bx
Maria	6	F	Child	10No02Bx
GOUGH, Mary	31	F	Servant	10No02Bx
FAY, Mary	12	F	Servant	10No02Bx
COOLEY, Mich	22	M	Laborer	10No02Bx
Died-At-Sea				
Pat	25	M	Laborer	10No02Bx
GILLIEN, Peter	18	M	Laborer	10No02Bx
Mgt.	19	F	Laborer	10No02Bx
RIELY, John	54	F	Laborer	10No02Bx
Ann (W)	50	F	Wife	10No02Bx
Cath.	9	F	Child	10No02Bx
Peter	7	M	Child	10No02Bx
OHARA, Peter	35	M	Unknown	10No02Bx
Honora	29	F	Servant	10No02Bx
DUFFY, Mary	15	F	Servant	10No02Bx
MCDERMOTT, Hon.	60	F	Servant	10No02Bx
DAILY, Ann	21	F	Servant	10No02Bx
HEFFRAN, John	16	M	Laborer	10No02Bx
Sarah	12	F	Servant	10No02Bx
Wm.	10	M	Servant	10No02Bx
Betsy	6	F	Child	10No02Bx
Barny	4	M	Child	10No02Bx
DUFFY, Pat	20	M	Laborer	10No02Bx
Mich	20	M	Laborer	10No02Bx
Died-At-Sea				
OHARA, Eliza	23	F	Servant	10No02Bx
Wm.	21	M	Laborer	10No02Bx
DOHERTY, Eliza	20	F	Laborer	10No02Bx
OHARA, Mich	18	F	Laborer	10No02Bx
ROUNDREE, Rose	30	F	Wife	10No02Bx
Cath.	4	F	Child	10No02Bx
Died-At-Sea				
SHERIDAN, Bgt.	18	F	Servant	10No02Bx
Betsy	11	F	Servant	10No02Bx
Ellen	9	F	Child	10No02Bx
MCNALLY, Bgt.	19	F	Laborer	10No02Bx
John	11	M	Servant	10No02Bx
STONE, Mich	26	M	Servant	10No02Bx
FARLEY, Bryan	60	M	Keeper	10No02Bx
Bgt.	50	F	Keeper	10No02Bx
Mgt.	11	F	Keeper	10No02Bx
John	9	M	Child	10No02Bx
HARTY, Cath.	28	F	Servant	10No02Bx
Owen	11	M	Servant	10No02Bx
James	7	M	Child	10No02Bx
MURRAY, Wm.	25	M	Laborer	10No02Bx
Mary	60	F	Laborer	10No02Bx
WHITE, Martin	23	M	Laborer	10No02Bx
Died-At-Sea				
KILLIHAN, Sally	27	F	Servant	10No02Bx
CONNOLLY, Cath.	18	F	Servant	10No02Bx
THORNTON, Byran	30	F	Servant	10No02Bx
CONNOLLY, John	23	M	Carpenter	10No02Bx
DONOHUE, Mary	21	F	Servant	10No02Bx
Bgt.	17	F	Servant	10No02Bx
Ann	12	F	Servant	10No02Bx

NAMES OF PASSENGERS	AGE	SEX	OCCUPATIONS	DATE PORT SHIP
DONOHUE, James	10	M	Servant	10No02Bx
BOUGH, Pat	21	M	Laborer	10No02Bx
VAUGHAN, Mgt.	19	F	Servant	10No02Bx
FARRELL, Bgt.	5	F	Child	10No02Bx
JOHNSTONE, Sarah	20	F	Servant	10No02Bx
BUCKLEY, Thos.	32	M	Servant	10No02Bx
SULLIVAN, Eliza	25	F	Servant	10No02Bx
KAVANAH, John	18	M	Laborer	10No02Bx
CONNOLLY, Cath.	21	F	Servant	10No02Bx
Ann	19	F	Servant	10No02Bx
MURPHY, Mgt.	30	F	Servant	10No02Bx
Mary	12	F	Servant	10No02Bx
DOYLE, Mary	18	F	Servant	10No02Bx
MCGUINESS, Ann	19	F	Servant	10No02Bx
REYNOLDS, Jane	2	F	Child	10No02Bx
SMITH, Mary	25	F	Servant	10No02Bx
DOONY, Mgt.	20	F	Servant	10No02Bx
RESPIRE, Mgt.	20	F	Servant	10No02Bx
SMITH, James	26	M	Carpenter	10No02Bx
KELLY, John	30	M	Laborer	10No02Bx
Ann	25	F	Unknown	10No02Bx
James	4	M	Child	10No02Bx
Mary	3	F	Child	10No02Bx
John	.00	M	Infant	10No02Bx
DARBY, Mary	17	F	Unknown	10No02Bx
MCCUE, Benj.	18	M	Unknown	10No02Bx
JONES, Bgt.	18	F	Servant	10No02Bx
Mary	20	F	Unknown	10No02Bx
BARRY, Richd.	21	M	Carpenter	10No02Bx
JOHNSTONE, John	18	M	Laborer	10No02Bx
HARRIS, Ann	30	F	Servant	10No02Bx
Ann	10	F	Servant	10No02Bx
Thos.	8	M	Child	10No02Bx
Mgt.	4	F	Child	10No02Bx
Jane	.00	F	Infant	10No02Bx
Died-At-Sea				
GOHERTY, Mary	20	F	Servant	10No02Bx
ONEIL, John	34	M	Laborer	10No02Bx
LANE, Ann	21	F	Servant	10No02Bx
Mary	18	F	Servant	10No02Bx
DOHERTY, Mary	16	F	Servant	10No02Bx
HARTNET, Jullen	21	M	Laborer	10No02Bx
KIEF, Danl.	23	M	Laborer	10No02Bx
Frank	22	M	Laborer	10No02Bx
MOORE, Mary	20	F	Servant	10No02Bx
Kate.	20	F	Servant	10No02Bx
MCGILL, Henry	25	M	Laborer	10No02Bx
Jane	22	F	Laborer	10No02Bx
RILEY, Peter	30	M	Laborer	10No02Bx
CONNOR, Danl.	26	M	Laborer	10No02Bx
Eliza	18	F	Servant	10No02Bx
COLLIER, Paul	38	M	Laborer	10No02Bx
MURPHY, John	38	M	Laborer	10No02Bx
LOGAN, Mary	27	F	Servant	10No02Bx
Ann	4	F	Child	10No02Bx
Thos.	2	M	Child	10No02Bx
DEVINE, Thos.	21	M	Servant	10No02Bx
Sarah	18	F	Servant	10No02Bx
CAHILL, John	24	M	Laborer	10No02Bx
GILL, Michl.	40	M	Laborer	10No02Bx
Pat	16	M	Laborer	10No02Bx
HERHLY, Geo.	45	M	Laborer	10No02Bx
Johan	44	M	Laborer	10No02Bx
Mary	20	F	Laborer	10No02Bx
Thos.	16	F	Laborer	10No02Bx
Patk.	13	M	Laborer	10No02Bx
Johan	2	M	Child	10No02Bx
HARRINGTON, Thomas	26	M	Laborer	10No02Bx
CONNOR, Mary	20	F	Servant	10No02Bx
KELHAN, Mary	20	F	Servant	10No02Bx
NORRIS, Richd.	25	M	Laborer	10No02Bx
BROWN, Pat	20	M	Laborer	10No02Bx
Died-At-Sea				
DALLY, Mary	60	F	Wife	10No02Bx
Ann	15	F	Wife	10No02Bx

NAMES OF PASSENGERS	AGE	SEX	OCCUPATIONS	DATE PORT SHIP
DALLY, Thos.	15	M	Unknown	10No02Bx
DUFFY, John	35	M	Unknown	10No02Bx
HARTNETT, Larry	45	M	Piper	10No02Bx
LANGORAN, John	26	M	Laborer	10No02Bx
BEGLEY, Jane	15	M	Laborer	10No02Bx
Betsey	11	F	Unknown	10No02Bx
William	9	M	Child	10No02Bx
HICKEY, Margt.	24	F	Unknown	10No02Bx
SHAY, Pat	21	M	Unknown	10No02Bx
KILLRAIN, Morris	22	M	Unknown	10No02Bx
Mich	33	M	Unknown	10No02Bx
Died-At-Sea				
Bridget	28	F	Wife	10No02Bx
James	3	M	Child	10No02Bx
Morris	.00	M	Infant	10No02Bx
MALONEY, Michl.	36	M	Laborer	10No02Bx
William	23	M	Laborer	10No02Bx
CRONAN, Joseph	21	M	Laborer	10No02Bx
COLLINS, Dennis	24	M	Laborer	10No02Bx
GALLAGHER, Murty	30	M	Laborer	10No02Bx
Ellen	26	F	Servant	10No02Bx
LYONS, Thos.	20	M	Unknown	10No02Bx
SULLIVAN, Pat	32	M	Farmer	10No02Bx
Julia	26	F	Wife	10No02Bx
Mary	7	F	Child	10No02Bx
John	3	M	Child	10No02Bx
Robt.	.00	M	Infant	10No02Bx
MURPHY, Eliza	30	F	Servant	10No02Bx
WALSH, Katl.	16	F	Servant	10No02Bx
REIDON, Ellen	20	F	Servant	10No02Bx
DUNFORD, John	18	M	Laborer	10No02Bx
DALEY, Mary	20	F	Servant	10No02Bx
LINSEY, Martha	18	F	Wife	10No02Bx
Jane	40	F	Unknown	10No02Bx
Sarah	9	F	Child	10No02Bx
LINDSEY, Eliza	7	F	Child	10No02Bx
Norah	5	F	Child	10No02Bx
Esther	3	F	Child	10No02Bx
HUGHES, Mary	24	F	Servant	10No02Bx
Died-At-Sea				
HAYES, John	21	M	Laborer	10No02Bx
PUWER, Thos.	30	M	Laborer	10No02Bx
John	11	M	Laborer	10No02Bx
LARRY, Pat	20	M	Laborer	10No02Bx
DEVILLEN, Pat	26	M	Laborer	10No02Bx
John	25	M	Laborer	10No02Bx
James	30	M	Laborer	10No02Bx
Edmond	22	M	Unknown	10No02Bx
Mary	22	F	Unknown	10No02Bx
Edmd.	9	M	Child	10No02Bx
QUIRK, John	30	M	Unknown	10No02Bx
CUDHY, Patk.	24	M	Unknown	10No02Bx
QUINN, Thos.	28	F	Servant	10No02Bx
BLEWITT, Katl.	16	F	Servant	10No02Bx
MCGOUGHLIN, Sarah	19	F	Milliner	10No02Bx
MURRAY, Bridgt.	30	F	Servant	10No02Bx
QINLAN, Edwd.	24	M	Laborer	10No02Bx
Katl.	60	F	Unknown	10No02Bx
CASTELLOW, John	50	M	Unknown	10No02Bx
WARD, Mich	20	M	Unknown	10No02Bx
WOLF, Rich	32	M	Unknown	10No02Bx
Mary	30	F	Unknown	10No02Bx
Margt.	8	F	Child	10No02Bx
Richd.	6	M	Child	10No02Bx
Johan	4	M	Child	10No02Bx
Michl.	2	M	Child	10No02Bx
FRANCIS, Robt.	44	M	Unknown	10No02Bx
Ellen	40	F	Wife	10No02Bx
Julia	13	F	Unknown	10No02Bx
DORAN, Johan	16	M	Servant	10No02Bx
WELLIGAN, Dennis	36	M	Laborer	10No02Bx
HAGGETT, Fanny	20	F	Servant	10No02Bx
ROLLINSON, James	60	M	Farmer	10No02Bx
Mary-Ann	50	F	Wife	10No02Bx
Richd.	25	M	Unknown	10No02Bx
ROLLINSON, Isabella	18	F	Unknown	10No02Bx
Harriet	13	F	Unknown	10No02Bx
Kate	10	F	Unknown	10No02Bx
Johan	8	M	Child	10No02Bx
WILSON, Ellen	13	F	Servant	10No02Bx
Ann	12	F	Servant	10No02Bx
HAYES, Fanny	18	F	Wife	10No02Bx
Alice	3	F	Child	10No02Bx
Fanny	.00	F	Infant	10No02Bx
BARRY, John	35	M	Laborer	10No02Bx
Died-At-Sea				
Margt.	30	F	Wife	10No02Bx
SMITH, Bridget	13	F	Unknown	10No02Bx
MORRIS, Mary	18	F	Unknown	10No02Bx
LYONS, John	20	M	Laborer	10No02Bx
Brig.	15	F	Servant	10No02Bx
PALDEN, Mich	25	M	Laborer	10No02Bx
DILLON, Kate	20	F	Servant	10No02Bx
NEWCOMBE, Brig.	18	F	Servant	10No02Bx
FARRELL, Katl.	35	F	Wife	10No02Bx
Mich	8	M	Child	10No02Bx
Martin	6	M	Child	10No02Bx
Robt.	4	M	Child	10No02Bx
GRIMES, Patk.	28	M	Laborer	10No02Bx
MCCUE, Mary	25	F	Servant	10No02Bx
MCEVOY, Cath.	25	F	Servant	10No02Bx
HUNT, Bridgt.	38	F	Servant	10No02Bx
BARRATT, Cath.	28	F	Servant	10No02Bx
PADDEN, Cath.	28	F	Wife	10No02Bx
Anty.	.00	M	Infant	10No02Bx
MURPHY, Jane	27	F	Servant	10No02Bx
LYONS, Deb.	18	F	Servant	10No02Bx
KANE, Ellen	12	F	Servant	10No02Bx
MCGRAIN, Pat	22	M	Laborer	10No02Bx
BURNS, Danl.	40	M	Unknown	10No02Bx
Michl.	30	M	Unknown	10No02Bx
CARROL, Pat	31	M	Unknown	10No02Bx
KELLY, Peter	34	M	Unknown	10No02Bx
RUPER, Cathl.	18	F	Servant	10No02Bx
MURPHY, Ellen	13	F	Unknown	10No02Bx
Died-At-Sea				
RALCHELLY, Ellen	12	F	Unknown	10No02Bx
KEGAN, Willm.	24	M	Laborer	10No02Bx
CLONAN, Kernan	45	M	Laborer	10No02Bx
Lucy	35	F	Wife	10No02Bx
Bridget	12	F	Unknown	10No02Bx
Rose	9	F	Child	10No02Bx
Lucy	6	F	Child	10No02Bx
Eliza	3	F	Child	10No02Bx
Ann	.00	F	Infant	10No02Bx
CARROLL, Peggy	34	F	Servant	10No02Bx
CUNIFF, John	30	M	Laborer	10No02Bx
MAGRATH, Thos.	25	M	Unknown	10No02Bx
FLEMING, Thos.	25	M	Unknown	10No02Bx
Mary	24	F	Servant	10No02Bx
HOWLY, Maria	16	F	Unknown	10No02Bx
Rosa	14	F	Unknown	10No02Bx
OURLAND, Ellen	20	F	Servant	10No02Bx
HIDE, John	20	M	Unknown	10No02Bx
MATTHEWS, Ann	24	F	Unknown	10No02Bx
BURKE, Benj.	26	M	Laborer	10No02Bx
TWIGG, Nancy	20	F	Servant	10No02Bx
James	14	M	Unknown	10No02Bx
CULVERSON, Thos.	19	M	Unknown	10No02Bx
MOORHOUSE, John	30	M	Unknown	10No02Bx
HEFFRAN, Mary	8	F	Child	10No02Bx
MURPHEY, Mgt.	17	F	Unknown	10No02Bx
DOYLE, Cathn.	17	F	Unknown	10No02Bx
GWINEY, Bridgt.	20	F	Unknown	10No02Bx
FLAHAFF, Hon.	20	F	Servant	10No02Bx
MANTY, Anty.	19	M	Baker	10No02Bx
PAYNE, Richd.	37	M	Baker	10No02Bx
Thos.	10	M	Baker	10No02Bx
DUNN, Rose	18	F	Servant	10No02Bx
HARTY, Mgt.	40	F	Unknown	10No02Bx

NAMES OF PASSENGERS	AGE	SEX	OCCUPATIONS	DATE PORT SHIP
HARTY, Thos.	11	M	Unknown	10No02Bx
Mary	9	F	Child	10No02Bx
Wm.	3	M	Child	10No02Bx
Mgt.	.00	F	Infant	10No02Bx
DONOHUE, Wm.	22	M	Tailor	10No02Bx
GOMERTY, Mary	18	F	Servant	10No02Bx
Died-At-Sea				
FITZGIBBON, Pat	22	M	Laborer	10No02Bx
SHANNON, Mich	26	M	Laborer	10No02Bx
REARDON, John	26	M	Laborer	10No02Bx
QUIRK, Mary	30	F	Unknown	10No02Bx
WOLFE, Pat	30	M	Laborer	10No02Bx
Died-At-Sea				
MALORE, John	18	M	Laborer	10No02Bx
BARRATT, Sarah	20	F	Servant	10No02Bx
ROWAN, Biddy	22	F	Servant	10No02Bx
SIMONS, Biddy	50	F	Unknown	10No02Bx
TRACY, John	20	F	Unknown	10No02Bx
James	17	M	Unknown	10No02Bx
Bgt.	30	F	Unknown	10No02Bx
Eliza	19	F	Unknown	10No02Bx
Jane	2	F	Child	10No02Bx
Died-At-Sea				
GOODE, Biddy	48	F	Unknown	10No02Bx
Pat	21	M	Laborer	10No02Bx
MATHEWS, Eliza	16	F	Unknown	10No02Bx
KELLY, Mary	20	F	Unknown	10No02Bx
LYONS, John	34	M	Unknown	10No02Bx
DUNN, James	30	M	Unknown	10No02Bx
Died-At-Sea				
MCCLINE, Matty	16	F	Servant	10No02Bx
KILBY, Ann	16	F	Wife	10No02Bx
Mary	.00	F	Infant	10No02Bx
RILEY, Biddy	22	F	Servant	10No02Bx
CAFFREY, Cath.	17	F	Servant	10No02Bx
Mgt.	17	F	Servant	10No02Bx
FRENNAN, Wm.	24	M	Laborer	10No02Bx
GRACE, Mich	20	M	Laborer	10No02Bx
SCANLON, Pat	25	M	Laborer	10No02Bx
HESSIAN, Thos.	30	M	Unknown	10No02Bx
TALEY, Wm.	29	M	Unknown	10No02Bx
FARREL, Biddy	32	F	Wife	10No02Bx
Thos.	12	M	Unknown	10No02Bx
Mary	11	F	Unknown	10No02Bx
Died-At-Sea				
Mgt.	8	F	Child	10No02Bx
Mich.	6	M	Child	10No02Bx
DONELEY, Mary	16	F	Servant	10No02Bx
CONN, Biddy	18	F	Servant	10No02Bx
CANTWELL, Eliza	26	F	Wife	10No02Bx
Jane	10	F	Unknown	10No02Bx
Died-At-Sea				
John	7	M	Child	10No02Bx
Ellen	5	F	Child	10No02Bx
MURPHY, Pat	13	M	Unknown	10No02Bx
MCGEE, Cath.	12	F	Servant	10No02Bx
Mary	8	F	Child	10No02Bx
HEFFERAN, Mary	30	F	Wife	10No02Bx
KILGALLON, Mary	20	F	Servant	10No02Bx

SIDDONS 12 NOVEMBER 1849

From Liverpool

NAMES OF PASSENGERS	AGE	SEX	OCCUPATIONS	DATE PORT SHIP
TOMB, Daniel	21	M	Clerk	12No02Cd
Jane	23	F	Unknown	12No02Cd
BLACKBURN, Christr.	28	M	Farmer	12No02Cd
Annie	45	F	Unknown	12No02Cd
Mary	26	F	Unknown	12No02Cd
BLACKBURN, Margaret	20	F	Unknown	12No02Cd
Jane	16	F	Unknown	12No02Cd
WALKER, Henry	40	M	Storekeeper	12No02Cd
MCELWEE, Wm.	25	M	Laborer	12No02Cd
BOOTH, Eliza	25	F	Unknown	12No02Cd
LAVIN, John	50	M	Laborer	12No02Cd
Mary	40	F	Unknown	12No02Cd
John	25	M	Laborer	12No02Cd
Samuel	23	M	Laborer	12No02Cd
THOMPSON, James	25	M	Laborer	12No02Cd
Margaret	30	F	Unknown	12No02Cd
COURTNEY, Sarah	25	F	Unknown	12No02Cd
CAMLIN, John	52	M	Laborer	12No02Cd
William	3	M	Laborer	12No02Cd
FALLON, Thomas	25	M	Laborer	12No02Cd
Bridget	23	F	Unknown	12No02Cd
COOLOHAN, Frank	16	M	Laborer	12No02Cd
HEDIAN, Michl.	40	M	Laborer	12No02Cd
Sarah	36	F	Laborer	12No02Cd
KELLY, Robert	40	M	Laborer	12No02Cd
DARRARD, Pat	16	M	Laborer	12No02Cd
KELLY, John	28	M	Laborer	12No02Cd
DONOHOE, Michl.	25	M	Laborer	12No02Cd
CONNOR, Thomas	31	M	Laborer	12No02Cd
BOLLARD, Nichls.	42	M	Laborer	12No02Cd
Wm.	13	M	Laborer	12No02Cd
John	7	M	Child	12No02Cd
Richard	2	M	Child	12No02Cd
Mary	33	F	Unknown	12No02Cd
Ellen	11	F	Unknown	12No02Cd
Fanny	9	F	Child	12No02Cd
Eliza	3	F	Child	12No02Cd
Jane	.04	F	Infant	12No02Cd
FREEMAN, Richard	30	M	Laborer	12No02Cd
HAYNES, John	27	M	Laborer	12No02Cd
CARROLL, John	36	M	Laborer	12No02Cd
FALLON, Michl.	27	M	Laborer	12No02Cd
BERRY, Wm.	22	M	Laborer	12No02Cd
LANKIN, Andw.	25	M	Laborer	12No02Cd
KEENA, Garret	24	M	Laborer	12No02Cd
PATTERSON, Eliza	23	F	Unknown	12No02Cd
Eliza	3	F	Child	12No02Cd
HARLOT, Biddy	43	F	Unknown	12No02Cd
CONNOR, Edward	14	M	Laborer	12No02Cd
Andrew	12	M	Laborer	12No02Cd
SHANE, Michael	30	M	Laborer	12No02Cd
NORRAYS, John	29	M	Laborer	12No02Cd
REILLY, George	18	M	Laborer	12No02Cd
DUGGAN, Denis	23	M	Laborer	12No02Cd
FLYNNE, Pat	20	M	Bootmaker	12No02Cd
Bess	21	F	Unknown	12No02Cd
CALLAGHAN, Tim	23	M	Laborer	12No02Cd
SPILLANE, Mary	6	F	Child	12No02Cd
Margt.	7	F	Unknown	12No02Cd
CONNOR, Daniel	30	M	Farmer	12No02Cd
Mary	23	F	Unknown	12No02Cd
John	3	M	Child	12No02Cd
Pat	1	M	Child	12No02Cd
DWYER, Jane	16	F	Unknown	12No02Cd
LACEY, John	20	M	Laborer	12No02Cd
RYAN, Mick	30	M	Laborer	12No02Cd
HEDIAN, Anthoney	20	M	Laborer	12No02Cd
Anne	3	F	Child	12No02Cd
CORKORAN, Biddy	30	F	Unknown	12No02Cd
LOFTUS, John	30	M	Carpenter	12No02Cd
MURRAY, William	19	M	Laborer	12No02Cd
HEIFERMAN, Connor	32	M	Laborer	12No02Cd
HANLY, James	28	M	Laborer	12No02Cd
HALFPENNY, Pat	31	M	Laborer	12No02Cd
MCKEON, John	29	M	Laborer	12No02Cd
Winefred	25	F	Unknown	12No02Cd
Mary	3	F	Child	12No02Cd
Jane	.06	F	Infant	12No02Cd
CAIN, Pat	25	M	Laborer	12No02Cd
WHELAN, Anthony	26	M	Laborer	12No02Cd

NAMES OF PASSENGERS	AGE	SEX	OCCUPATIONS	DATE PORT SHIP
WHELAN, Mary	8	F	Child	12No02Cd
DUFFY, Law.	27	M	Laborer	12No02Cd
MCCAN, Thomas	27	M	Laborer	12No02Cd
CALLEN, Margt.	23	F	Unknown	12No02Cd
Patk.	12	M	Unknown	12No02Cd
CARROLL, Owen	23	M	Laborer	12No02Cd
MCKEONE, John	20	M	Laborer	12No02Cd
COURY, Michl.	44	M	Laborer	12No02Cd
Margt.	34	F	Unknown	12No02Cd
Ann	12	F	Laborer	12No02Cd
Margt.	5	F	Child	12No02Cd
DREW, James	37	M	Laborer	12No02Cd
DOUGLASS, Eliza	26	F	Unknown	12No02Cd
Jane	2	F	Child	12No02Cd
LEONARD, Biddy	20	F	Laborer	12No02Cd
MANNING, James	24	M	Laborer	12No02Cd
RUNNER, Thomas	23	M	Laborer	12No02Cd
KING, John	25	M	Laborer	12No02Cd
DERBY, Anne	22	F	Unknown	12No02Cd
MCPHERSON, Robt.	30	M	Laborer	12No02Cd
BRODERICK, Nichls.	39	M	Laborer	12No02Cd
SHERIDAN, William	25	M	Laborer	12No02Cd
Alley	22	F	Unknown	12No02Cd
Biddy	24	F	Unknown	12No02Cd
KELLY, Ellen	29	F	Unknown	12No02Cd
Mary	13	F	Unknown	12No02Cd
John	12	M	Unknown	12No02Cd
Julia	10	F	Unknown	12No02Cd
Pat	9	M	Child	12No02Cd
Biddy	8	F	Child	12No02Cd
James	2	M	Child	12No02Cd
BURK, John	29	M	Smith	12No02Cd
Abbey	26	F	Unknown	12No02Cd
SHARPE, Robt.	20	M	Laborer	12No02Cd
Benjamin	29	M	Laborer	12No02Cd
DALY, Pat	13	M	Laborer	12No02Cd
MCCABBE, Judy	22	F	Unknown	12No02Cd
NULTY, Rose	25	F	Unknown	12No02Cd
Margt.	22	F	Unknown	12No02Cd
QUIGLY, John	28	M	Laborer	12No02Cd
Anne	20	F	Unknown	12No02Cd
Anne	.03	F	Infant	12No02Cd
REILLY, Charles	36	M	Smith	12No02Cd
LEDDANE, Ellen	25	F	Unknown	12No02Cd
CURTIN, Ellen	25	F	Unknown	12No02Cd
Pat	3	M	Child	12No02Cd
DEVEREUX, Thomas	40	M	Tinsmith	12No02Cd
CAROLIN, John	18	M	Laborer	12No02Cd
BOURKE, Martin	22	M	Laborer	12No02Cd
BARING, Biddy	22	F	Unknown	12No02Cd
RUNNERS, Anne	21	F	Unknown	12No02Cd
MURPHY, Mary	20	F	Unknown	12No02Cd
COSTELLO, Betty	18	F	Unknown	12No02Cd
KELLY, Pat	10	M	Laborer	12No02Cd
FIERNAN, Ellen	23	F	Unknown	12No02Cd
SEATON, Margt.	15	F	Unknown	12No02Cd
GIBBONS, Eliza	14	F	Unknown	12No02Cd
John	12	M	Unknown	12No02Cd
Sarah	7	F	Child	12No02Cd
Mary	6	F	Child	12No02Cd
HANLON, Mary	22	F	Unknown	12No02Cd
BECKET, Mary	22	F	Unknown	12No02Cd
BORE, Ellen	25	F	Unknown	12No02Cd
Mary	23	F	Unknown	12No02Cd
GRIFFITH, Jane	18	F	Unknown	12No02Cd
LITT, Pat	20	M	Laborer	12No02Cd
HAYES, Margt.	22	F	Unknown	12No02Cd
NULTY, Mat	25	M	Laborer	12No02Cd
Rose	20	F	Unknown	12No02Cd
COONEY, Luke	60	M	Carpenter	12No02Cd
Mary	52	F	Unknown	12No02Cd
Maria	20	F	Unknown	12No02Cd
COURY, John	24	M	Mason	12No02Cd
MCCABE, Cathn.	21	F	Unknown	12No02Cd
Mary	.06	F	Infant	12No02Cd
BOYDE, Thos.	21	M	Laborer	12No02Cd
WARD, Mick	27	M	Pensioner	12No02Cd
Died-At-Sea				
DORAN, Mick	20	M	Pensioner	12No02Cd
WILSON, Pat	25	M	Pensioner	12No02Cd
Mary	46	F	Unknown	12No02Cd
Thomas	14	M	Pensioner	12No02Cd
Nicholas	11	M	Pensioner	12No02Cd
William	9	M	Child	12No02Cd
James	6	M	Child	12No02Cd
Mary	4	F	Child	12No02Cd
DEN, Ellen	40	F	Unknown	12No02Cd
MCGRATH, Edward	26	M	Pensioner	12No02Cd
OBRIEN, Eliza	26	F	Unknown	12No02Cd
KELLY, Sabina	20	F	Unknown	12No02Cd
CLABBY, Eliza	21	F	Unknown	12No02Cd
QUNTIN, Arthur	43	M	Laborer	12No02Cd
Hanah	56	F	Unknown	12No02Cd
Margt.	13	F	Unknown	12No02Cd
William	11	M	Laborer	12No02Cd
Hanah	9	F	Child	12No02Cd
Hanah	28	F	Unknown	12No02Cd
KENEDY, Ellen	20	F	Unknown	12No02Cd
MURRAY, John	24	M	Laborer	12No02Cd
CREDDY, Mary	24	F	Unknown	12No02Cd
HENRY, Sarah	26	F	Unknown	12No02Cd
FERGUSON, Isabella	19	F	Unknown	12No02Cd
Margt.	18	F	Unknown	12No02Cd
ONEILL, Alicia	17	F	Unknown	12No02Cd
HEALY, Tim	40	M	Laborer	12No02Cd
HOGAN, Margt.	27	F	Unknown	12No02Cd
Martin	.02	M	Infant	12No02Cd
DEVEREUX, Lucy	20	F	Unknown	12No02Cd
KEANE, Anne	22	F	Unknown	12No02Cd
SUMMERS, Anthony	40	M	Unknown	12No02Cd
TWEEDY, Rose	70	F	Unknown	12No02Cd
MCCABE, Baniel	22	M	Laborer	12No02Cd
EASTON, James	33	M	Engineer	12No02Cd
Mary	29	F	Unknown	12No02Cd
Thos.	11	M	Unknown	12No02Cd
Catherine	2	F	Child	12No02Cd
FORDE, John	52	M	Laborer	12No02Cd
Catherine	48	F	Unknown	12No02Cd
BORE, John	18	M	Laborer	12No02Cd
QURKE, Ann	19	F	Unknown	12No02Cd
CLIFFORD, Michl.	21	M	Laborer	12No02Cd
REIDE, Cath.	11	F	Unknown	12No02Cd
SEUNLON, Cath.	23	F	Unknown	12No02Cd
CURRAN, Mary	27	F	Unknown	12No02Cd
BIGGY, Margt.	54	F	Unknown	12No02Cd
GIBBONS, Pat	17	M	Laborer	12No02Cd
BIGGY, John	68	M	Laborer	12No02Cd
WILSON, Pat	24	M	Laborer	12No02Cd
COYNE, Wm.	20	M	Laborer	12No02Cd
DARDIS, John	30	M	Laborer	12No02Cd
THOMPSON, Jane	28	F	Laborer	12No02Cd
GRADY, Eliza	20	F	Unknown	12No02Cd
SIMCOX, Bidy	20	F	Unknown	12No02Cd
CASEY, Pat	22	M	Laborer	12No02Cd
DALY, Lan.	20	M	Laborer	12No02Cd
HUGHES, Danl.	27	M	Laborer	12No02Cd
Mary	25	F	Unknown	12No02Cd
WALSH, Biddy	20	F	Unknown	12No02Cd
SWORDS, Anne	17	F	Unknown	12No02Cd
CONNOLLY, James	22	M	Servant	12No02Cd
DUNN, Thos.	20	M	Unknown	12No02Cd
CLERK, Wm.	22	M	Laborer	12No02Cd
CUNNINGHAM, Mick.	21	M	Laborer	12No02Cd
REILLY, Terance	21	M	Laborer	12No02Cd
LOFTUS, Thos.	21	M	Laborer	12No02Cd
MORAN, Thos.	21	M	Laborer	12No02Cd
Pat	26	M	Laborer	12No02Cd
KELLY, John	28	M	Laborer	12No02Cd
WILSON, John	23	M	Laborer	12No02Cd
MCCARTHY, Michl.	26	M	Servant	12No02Cd

NAMES OF PASSENGERS	AGE	SEX	OCCUPATIONS	DATE PORT SHIP
CARSON, James	22	M	Laborer	12No02Cd
MCKENNAN, Anthony	26	M	Laborer	12No02Cd
SMITH, Anne	20	F	Unknown	12No02Cd
MOONEY, Judy	18	F	Unknown	12No02Cd
LLOYDE, Frank	23	M	Laborer	12No02Cd
Ellen	10	F	Unknown	12No02Cd
BURNS, Catherine	13	F	Unknown	12No02Cd
CRASBIE, Eliza	11	F	Unknown	12No02Cd
DILLON, Cathn.	21	F	Unknown	12No02Cd
HALLIGAN, Thomas	22	M	Laborer	12No02Cd
DAVID, John	23	M	Laborer	12No02Cd
THOMPSON, James	19	M	Laborer	12No02Cd
Ellen	16	F	Unknown	12No02Cd
BUTLER, Walter	30	M	Laborer	12No02Cd
CONNOLLY, Mary	26	F	Unknown	12No02Cd
Catherine	30	F	Unknown	12No02Cd
MULCAHEY, Cathn.	21	F	Unknown	12No02Cd
CONNELLY, Michl.	60	M	Laborer	12No02Cd
BYRON, Cathn.	20	F	Unknown	12No02Cd
KILROE, Pat	70	M	Laborer	12No02Cd
FEENEY, Michl.	25	M	Laborer	12No02Cd
MURRAY, Pat	22	M	Laborer	12No02Cd
KILROE, Cathn.	20	F	Laborer	12No02Cd
DONNELLY, Pat	18	M	Laborer	12No02Cd
Cathn.	20	F	Unknown	12No02Cd
JONES, Biddy	20	F	Unknown	12No02Cd
CREGONS, Ellen	22	F	Unknown	12No02Cd
CONNOR, William	27	M	Unknown	12No02Cd
GRIFFEN, Biddy	21	F	Unknown	12No02Cd
GAFFNEY, Pat	40	M	Tailor	12No02Cd
FINLAY, Judy	19	F	Tailor	12No02Cd
REILLY, James	21	M	Laborer	12No02Cd
CULLIGAN, Lawr.	23	M	Mason	12No02Cd
DAWSON, Caroline	22	F	Dressmaker	12No02Cd
MCCHRISTEE, Anne	19	F	Unknown	12No02Cd
MCNEIFF, Barney	21	M	Laborer	12No02Cd
John	60	M	Laborer	12No02Cd
Rose	55	F	Unknown	12No02Cd
Catherine	14	F	Unknown	12No02Cd
RYAN, Mark	30	M	Laborer	12No02Cd
ARCHER, Jane	44	F	Unknown	12No02Cd
Wm.	16	M	Laborer	12No02Cd
Jane	12	F	Unknown	12No02Cd
KING, Mary	20	F	Unknown	12No02Cd
CLERKE, Esther	22	F	Unknown	12No02Cd
Jane	62	F	Unknown	12No02Cd
BERRY, Anne	36	F	Unknown	12No02Cd
Honor	12	F	Unknown	12No02Cd
Samuel	10	M	Laborer	12No02Cd
WALSH, Michl.	38	M	Laborer	12No02Cd
REORDAN, James	21	M	Laborer	12No02Cd
MAHER, Ellen	22	F	Laborer	12No02Cd
DEMPSTER, Mary	17	F	Unknown	12No02Cd
CARROLL, Margt.	18	F	Unknown	12No02Cd
WALSH, Pat	22	M	Laborer	12No02Cd
BARDEN, William	29	M	Laborer	12No02Cd
MCNIFF, Honor	17	F	Laborer	12No02Cd
CONROY, Ellen	23	F	Unknown	12No02Cd
CALLAGHAN, Hanah	18	F	Laborer	12No02Cd
HAMILTON, William	35	M	Laborer	12No02Cd
Bess	34	F	Unknown	12No02Cd
Philip	.03	M	Infant	12No02Cd
CRAWLEY, Margt.	20	F	Unknown	12No02Cd
Margt.	50	F	Unknown	12No02Cd
KENNY, Dora	16	F	Unknown	12No02Cd
Margt.	40	F	Unknown	12No02Cd
Margt.	11	F	Unknown	12No02Cd
Susan	7	F	Child	12No02Cd
Michael	5	M	Child	12No02Cd
Kate	.09	F	Infant	12No02Cd
POWELL, Cathn.	25	F	Unknown	12No02Cd
Norah	8	F	Child	12No02Cd
Thomas	7	M	Child	12No02Cd
FOX, Owen	18	M	Laborer	12No02Cd
SHERIDAN, Lawr.	25	M	Laborer	12No02Cd
SHERIDAN, Anne	16	F	Unknown	12No02Cd
MULDOON, Mary	20	F	Unknown	12No02Cd
Julia	16	F	Unknown	12No02Cd
CONAUGTY, Biddy	20	F	Laborer	12No02Cd
CRAVEN, Margt.	20	F	Unknown	12No02Cd
Agnus	20	F	Unknown	12No02Cd
HEALY, Catherine	18	F	Unknown	12No02Cd
GRIMES, Mary	30	F	Unknown	12No02Cd
DUFFEY, Bridget	30	F	Unknown	12No02Cd
SHERNY, Mary	18	F	Unknown	12No02Cd
HICKEY, James	28	M	Laborer	12No02Cd
John	22	M	Laborer	12No02Cd
Margt.	22	F	Unknown	12No02Cd
COULON, Michl.	26	M	Laborer	12No02Cd
BURKE, William	36	M	Clerk	12No02Cd
KENT, Robt.	30	M	Laborer	12No02Cd
Anne	21	F	Unknown	12No02Cd
TOOHER, Thos.	25	M	Laborer	12No02Cd
DREW, William	23	M	Laborer	12No02Cd
MORRISS, Thomas	25	M	Laborer	12No02Cd
Anne	12	F	Unknown	12No02Cd
Bridget	7	F	Child	12No02Cd
KILHOOLEY, Peter	33	M	Unknown	12No02Cd
WALSH, Margt.	32	F	Unknown	12No02Cd
GRANT, Mary	15	F	Unknown	12No02Cd
Margt.	45	F	Unknown	12No02Cd
MCNEIFFE, Peter	52	M	Laborer	12No02Cd

ADIRONDACK 12 NOVEMBER 1849

From Liverpool

MURRAY, Michael	24	M	Laborer	12No02Ca
Bridget	11	F	None	12No02Ca
Margaret	8	F	Child	12No02Ca
Rose	7	F	Child	12No02Ca
John	4	M	Child	12No02Ca
MATTHEWS, John	20	M	Laborer	12No02Ca
James	14	M	None	12No02Ca
CONNOR, Catharine	28	F	None	12No02Ca
Richd.	6	M	Child	12No02Ca
Elise	4	F	Child	12No02Ca
John	2	M	Child	12No02Ca
OBRIEN, Mathew	24	M	None	12No02Ca
SHERRAN, Bridget	35	F	None	12No02Ca
Sally	7	F	Child	12No02Ca
Ellen	5	F	Child	12No02Ca
Mary	2	F	Child	12No02Ca
FLOOD, Catherine	40	F	None	12No02Ca
Ann	11	F	None	12No02Ca
James	9	M	Child	12No02Ca
MURRAY, Marianne Died-At-Sea	22	F	None	12No02Ca
Catharine	21	F	None	12No02Ca
MCCOY, Johanne	26	F	None	12No02Ca
Ellen	7	F	Child	12No02Ca
HARGRAVES, Ellen	28	F	None	12No02Ca
Joseph	2	M	Child	12No02Ca
SMITH, Mary	23	F	None	12No02Ca
SCALY, Charles	24	M	Unknown	12No02Ca
KENNEY, Mic.	16	M	Farmer	12No02Ca
MCDOWELL, Ben.	27	M	Irnmldr	12No02Ca
ASKEW, Thos.	30	M	Farmer	12No02Ca

LADY-OF-THE-LAKE 12 NOVEMBER 1849

From Bermuda

NAMES OF PASSENGERS	AGE	SEX	OCCUPATIONS	DATE PORT SHIP
HICK, John	28	M	Tailor	12No22Bz

RAPPAHANOCK 12 NOVEMBER 1849

From Liverpool

NAMES OF PASSENGERS	AGE	SEX	OCCUPATIONS	DATE PORT SHIP
NOLAN, Pat	50	M	Laborer	12No02Cb
Alice	20	F	Servant	12No02Cb
Mary	18	F	Servant	12No02Cb
KELLY, Brid.	30	F	Servant	12No02Cb
Ann	9	F	Child	12No02Cb
Jane	7	F	Child	12No02Cb
Cath.	5	F	Child	12No02Cb
STANTON, John	20	M	Laborer	12No02Cb
WARD, Brid.	50	F	Servant	12No02Cb
Brid.	18	F	Servant	12No02Cb
MEALY, Mary	20	F	Servant	12No02Cb
FITZPATRICK, Dan	18	M	Laborer	12No02Cb
BUTLER, Thos.	28	M	Laborer	12No02Cb
GAVAN, Pat	32	M	Laborer	12No02Cb
FARRELL, Thos.	33	M	Laborer	12No02Cb
SPILANE, Dan	00	M	Laborer	12No02Cb
Dan	15	M	Laborer	12No02Cb
Jno.	19	M	Laborer	12No02Cb
Pat	13	M	Laborer	12No02Cb
Brid.	50	F	Servant	12No02Cb
HALLIHAN, Mary	20	F	Servant	12No02Cb
DONOHUE, Mich.	20	M	Laborer	12No02Cb
GALVIN, Ellen	22	F	Servant	12No02Cb
MAHONY, Cath.	22	F	Servant	12No02Cb
EARLY, Bryan	34	M	Laborer	12No02Cb
COWLEY, Pat	19	M	Laborer	12No02Cb
Peter	17	M	Laborer	12No02Cb
MCILLINNY, Mich.	19	M	Laborer	12No02Cb
COLLINS, Ellen	42	F	Servant	12No02Cb
Martin	11	M	Laborer	12No02Cb
Mary	5	F	Child	12No02Cb
SCULLY, Thos.	47	M	Laborer	12No02Cb
MADDEN, Wm.	18	M	Laborer	12No02Cb
CRUMLEY, John	14	M	Laborer	12No02Cb
FOX, Margt.	40	F	Servant	12No02Cb
Jas.	20	M	Laborer	12No02Cb
Wm.	11	M	Laborer	12No02Cb
John	9	M	Child	12No02Cb
Edward	7	M	Child	12No02Cb
James	22	M	Laborer	12No02Cb
FITZGIBBON, Honor	17	M	Laborer	12No02Cb
HASSETT, James	22	M	Laborer	12No02Cb
Cath.	50	F	Servant	12No02Cb
Died-At-Sea				
Ellen	16	F	Servant	12No02Cb
John	6	M	Child	12No02Cb
Brid.	2	F	Child	12No02Cb
Cath.	4	F	Child	12No02Cb
REGAN, Ann	28	F	Servant	12No02Cb
Ann	.00	F	Infant	12No02Cb
DONOHUE, Ellen	55	F	Servant	12No02Cb
Brid.	26	F	Servant	12No02Cb
Ann	17	F	Servant	12No02Cb

NAMES OF PASSENGERS	AGE	SEX	OCCUPATIONS	DATE PORT SHIP
MURPHY, Margt.	40	F	Servant	12No02Cb
Jas.	7	M	Child	12No02Cb
Died-At-Sea				
HIGGERTY, Mary	40	F	Servant	12No02Cb
Mary	14	F	Servant	12No02Cb
Nelly	11	F	Servant	12No02Cb
Jere	9	F	Child	12No02Cb
Margt.	7	F	Child	12No02Cb
Kitty	3	F	Child	12No02Cb
RADLEY, Thos.	30	M	Unknown	12No02Cb
DOOGAN, Brid.	18	F	Unknown	12No02Cb
OCONNOR, John	20	M	Unknown	12No02Cb
Margt.	22	F	Unknown	12No02Cb
CANNON, Margt.	32	F	Unknown	12No02Cb
John	10	M	Unknown	12No02Cb
Rosan	8	F	Child	12No02Cb
Mary	6	F	Child	12No02Cb
MCCLUSKEY, Ellen	18	F	Servant	12No02Cb
KELLY, John	22	M	Laborer	12No02Cb
Brid.	22	F	Servant	12No02Cb
SLATTERY, Wm.	20	M	Laborer	12No02Cb
DUDY, Brid.	20	F	Servant	12No02Cb
KEEFE, Cath.	20	F	Servant	12No02Cb
Honor	18	M	Laborer	12No02Cb
LEDDY, Mary	50	F	Servant	12No02Cb
Honor	12	M	Laborer	12No02Cb
Mary	6	F	Child	12No02Cb
Michl.	4	M	Child	12No02Cb
OBRIAN, John	27	M	Laborer	12No02Cb
CROOK, Margt.	40	F	Servant	12No02Cb
CAROLIN, Margt.	20	F	Servant	12No02Cb
DOYLE, Alex	35	M	Laborer	12No02Cb
MCHUGH, Margt.	12	F	Servant	12No02Cb
MILLS, John	30	M	Laborer	12No02Cb
FRAME, Brid.	20	F	Servant	12No02Cb
Margt.	5	F	Child	12No02Cb
Hugh	7	M	Child	12No02Cb
MCGUIRE, Ann	14	F	Servant	12No02Cb
CUDDY, Mary	4	F	Child	12No02Cb
MATHEWS, John	25	M	Laborer	12No02Cb
Margt.	23	F	Servant	12No02Cb
MURPHY, Judy	20	F	Servant	12No02Cb
Thos.	.00	M	Infant	12No02Cb
MCKEON, James	15	M	Laborer	12No02Cb
MCCABE, Mary	25	F	Servant	12No02Cb
CONNOR, James	25	M	Laborer	12No02Cb
MILLER, Eliz.	50	F	Servant	12No02Cb
Thomas	25	M	Laborer	12No02Cb
Robt.	9	M	Child	12No02Cb
Ben	11	M	Laborer	12No02Cb
DEMPSEY, Ann	16	F	Servant	12No02Cb
RUDDY, Cath.	28	F	Servant	12No02Cb
ENGLISH, James	26	M	Laborer	12No02Cb
DIXON, Mary-A.	27	F	Servant	12No02Cb
HEWITT, Sarah	14	F	Servant	12No02Cb
Margt.	11	F	Servant	12No02Cb
NEAL, Brid.	18	F	Servant	12No02Cb
BRADY, Margt.	30	F	Servant	12No02Cb
Bryan	2	M	Child	12No02Cb
Died-At-Sea				
DELANY, Pat	28	M	Laborer	12No02Cb
LOOBY, Step.	20	M	Laborer	12No02Cb
MEADE, Ann	17	F	Servant	12No02Cb
LENAHAN, Stephen	7	M	Child	12No02Cb
Pat	5	M	Child	12No02Cb
MCCLUSKY, Jas.	30	M	Laborer	12No02Cb
LEVY, Thomas	45	M	Laborer	12No02Cb
Thomas	10	M	Laborer	12No02Cb
CONALLY, Jane	30	F	Laborer	12No02Cb
Brid.	15	F	Servant	12No02Cb
James	5	M	Child	12No02Cb
DOYLE, Mary	30	F	Servant	12No02Cb
CONNOUGHTON, Maria	18	F	Servant	12No02Cb
CARR, Margt.	40	F	Servant	12No02Cb
Eliza	11	F	Servant	12No02Cb

NAMES OF PASSENGERS	AGE	SEX	OCCUPATIONS	DATE PORT SHIP
CARR, Robt.	9	M	Child	12No02Cb
Lan.	7	M	Child	12No02Cb
James	2	M	Child	12No02Cb
KELBY, Mary	24	F	Servant	12No02Cb
MADDEN, Margt.	9	F	Child	12No02Cb
MCNAMARA, Brid.	24	F	Servant	12No02Cb
GILLENAN, Brid.	15	F	Servant	12No02Cb
PATTEN, Jas.	21	M	Servant	12No02Cb
WHELAN, Pat	55	M	Servant	12No02Cb
Fra.	20	F	Servant	12No02Cb
Cath.	7	F	Child	12No02Cb
KELLY, Pat	25	M	Laborer	12No02Cb
SEDGWICK, Mich.	38	M	Laborer	12No02Cb
Ellen	14	F	Servant	12No02Cb
DUFFY, Brid.	17	F	Servant	12No02Cb
MEARLY, Brid.	25	F	Servant	12No02Cb
GALLAGHER, John	6	M	Child	12No02Cb
EMMETT, Alex-Andrew	24	M	Servant	12No02Cb
SULIVAN, John	22	M	Servant	12No02Cb
OBRIAN, Mary	19	M	Servant	12No02Cb
MOLLY, Thos.	19	M	Laborer	12No02Cb
SMITH, Thos.	13	M	Laborer	12No02Cb
BRADY, Mary	35	F	Dressmaker	12No02Cb
GILLESPIE, John	40	M	Cooper	12No02Cb
MELLRAN, Margt.	50	F	Servant	12No02Cb
Mary-A.	10	F	None	12No02Cb
HUSSEY, Mary	10	F	None	12No02Cb
MELLRAN, Hannah	8	F	Child	12No02Cb
Ellen	4	F	Child	12No02Cb
MALOWNEY, Jas.	20	M	Laborer	12No02Cb
Brid.	20	F	Servant	12No02Cb
COLLIER, Eliza	40	F	Servant	12No02Cb
Eliza	7	F	Child	12No02Cb
OBRIAN, Margt.	22	F	Servant	12No02Cb
KELLY, Mick	40	M	Laborer	12No02Cb
KEARNS, Pat	27	M	Laborer	12No02Cb
DOWLIN, Lan	28	M	Laborer	12No02Cb
Fra.	28	M	Servant	12No02Cb
Pat	12	M	None	12No02Cb
MCCAFFREY, Pat	18	M	Laborer	12No02Cb
FARLEY, Cath.	20	F	Servant	12No02Cb
HAND, Mary	20	F	Servant	12No02Cb
MACKEHAL, Mary	22	F	Servant	12No02Cb
DIGGINS, Julia	30	F	Servant	12No02Cb
FORD, Wm.	21	M	Laborer	12No02Cb
DOHERTY, Mat.	28	M	Laborer	12No02Cb
Died-At-Sea				
SINNAN, Cath.	35	F	Servant	12No02Cb
Mick	40	M	Laborer	12No02Cb
Sarah	18	F	Servant	12No02Cb
CUNNINGHAM, Pat	30	M	Laborer	12No02Cb
CLOY, Mat	30	M	Laborer	12No02Cb
TAYLER, Peter	25	M	Laborer	12No02Cb
MCBRIDE, Thos.	20	M	Laborer	12No02Cb
FORD, Thos.	24	M	Laborer	12No02Cb
FARRELLY, Judy	23	F	Servant	12No02Cb
John	3	M	Child	12No02Cb
Cath.	.00	F	Infant	12No02Cb
Died-At-Sea				
CROTTY, Margt.	26	F	Servant	12No02Cb
COODY, Margt.	17	F	Servant	12No02Cb
GANNON, Thos.	30	M	Laborer	12No02Cb
CUFFE, Lucy	35	F	Servant	12No02Cb
Mick	5	M	Child	12No02Cb
Pat	.00	M	Infant	12No02Cb
HALL, Mick	15	M	Laborer	12No02Cb
Julia	18	F	Servant	12No02Cb
CORBETT, Cath.	18	F	Servant	12No02Cb
ROGAN, Ellen	40	F	Servant	12No02Cb
Margt.	20	F	Servant	12No02Cb
Bird	5	F	Child	12No02Cb
Cath.	3	F	Child	12No02Cb
KENNEDY, Mich.	26	M	Laborer	12No02Cb
TRACY, James	18	M	Laborer	12No02Cb
KILLRIDE, Pat	26	M	Laborer	12No02Cb

NAMES OF PASSENGERS	AGE	SEX	OCCUPATIONS	DATE PORT SHIP
DUNN, Thomas	28	M	Laborer	12No02Cb
Julia	23	F	Servant	12No02Cb
Pat	.00	M	Infant	12No02Cb
Died-At-Sea				
MOORE, Thomas	33	M	Laborer	12No02Cb
Mary-A.	33	F	Servant	12No02Cb
Mary-A.	6	F	Child	12No02Cb
Dan	5	M	Child	12No02Cb
Jno.	2	M	Child	12No02Cb
Thos.	.00	M	Infant	12No02Cb
Died-At-Sea				
Margt.	27	F	Servant	12No02Cb
CONNELL, Cath.	20	F	Servant	12No02Cb
HORLEY, Pat	15	M	Laborer	12No02Cb
GARVIN, John	22	M	Laborer	12No02Cb
DAY, Mick	23	M	Laborer	12No02Cb
MURPHY, Mary	17	F	Servant	12No02Cb
DALAHANTY, Dan	40	M	Laborer	12No02Cb
RYAN, Quin	24	M	Laborer	12No02Cb
HEANEY, Geo.	27	M	Laborer	12No02Cb
TYRRELL, Brid.	20	F	Servant	12No02Cb
WELSH, Judy	30	F	Servant	12No02Cb
Edmond	.00	M	Infant	12No02Cb
Died-At-Sea				
MCGOWAN, Barney	22	M	Laborer	12No02Cb
Mary	22	F	Servant	12No02Cb
CARR, Ann	29	F	Servant	12No02Cb
WELSH, Mary	9	F	Child	12No02Cb
CARR, Andrew	8	M	Child	12No02Cb
Ann	5	F	Child	12No02Cb
Mary	10	F	None	12No02Cb
Martha	.00	F	Infant	12No02Cb
HAYES, Morgan	38	M	Laborer	12No02Cb
U (W)	32	F	Servant	12No02Cb
Cath.	7	F	Child	12No02Cb
John	15	M	Laborer	12No02Cb
Brid.	6	F	Child	12No02Cb
Pat	2	M	Child	12No02Cb
Ellen	.00	F	Infant	12No02Cb
Thomas	4	M	Child	12No02Cb
KEAN, Ellen	18	F	Servant	12No02Cb
BURNS, John	16	M	Laborer	12No02Cb
OBRIEN, Tim	40	M	Laborer	12No02Cb
Wn.	40	F	Servant	12No02Cb
Wm.	7	M	Child	12No02Cb
Mary	3	F	Child	12No02Cb
Ellen	.00	F	Infant	12No02Cb
MCGRATH, Mick	28	M	Laborer	12No02Cb
MURPHY, Cath.	20	F	Servant	12No02Cb
WELCH, Nancy	20	F	Servant	12No02Cb
DELANY, Pat	18	M	Laborer	12No02Cb
MORRIS, Martin	19	M	Laborer	12No02Cb
FREELY, John	28	M	Laborer	12No02Cb
TOOMEY, Pat	60	M	Laborer	12No02Cb
JONES, Mary	40	F	Servant	12No02Cb
CAHILL, Mary	20	F	Servant	12No02Cb
STAKEHAM, Maria	13	F	Servant	12No02Cb
ROCK, Brid.	18	F	Servant	12No02Cb
BRENNAN, Ann	28	F	Servant	12No02Cb
RYAN, Pat	24	M	Laborer	12No02Cb
FARRON, Wm.	22	M	Laborer	12No02Cb
BUSK, John	22	M	Laborer	12No02Cb
Cath.	20	F	Servant	12No02Cb
CAMPBELL, Mary	13	F	Servant	12No02Cb
SARMLEY, Ellen	19	F	Servant	12No02Cb
Mary	16	F	Servant	12No02Cb
MYSON, Mick	21	M	Laborer	12No02Cb
PURCELL, James	20	M	Laborer	12No02Cb
KENNEDY, John	18	M	Laborer	12No02Cb
CLARKE, Cath.	15	F	Servant	12No02Cb
DELMAGE, Geo.	21	M	Laborer	12No02Cb
MCGUIRE, Bessy	50	F	Servant	12No02Cb
BOYLE, Mary	20	F	Servant	12No02Cb
MCGUIRE, Sally	15	F	Servant	12No02Cb
Wm.	9	M	Child	12No02Cb

NAMES OF PASSENGERS	AGE	SEX	OCCUPATIONS	DATE PORT SHIP
BOYLE, Cath.	22	F	Servant	12No02Cb
Margt.	.00	F	Infant	12No02Cb
FARRELL, Brid.	20	F	Servant	12No02Cb
Mich.	12	M	Laborer	12No02Cb
CUSHING, Lou.	29	M	Laborer	12No02Cb
FORRESTER, Mary	26	F	Servant	12No02Cb
MARK, James	30	M	Laborer	12No02Cb
MCGUIRE, Connell	50	M	Laborer	12No02Cb
MAHON, James	35	M	Laborer	12No02Cb
KELLY, Wm.	22	M	Laborer	12No02Cb
HABBITTS, F.	35	M	Laborer	12No02Cb
CLARK, Geo.	30	M	Laborer	12No02Cb
COSTELLO, Ann	20	F	Servant	12No02Cb
MURPHY, Mick	20	M	Laborer	12No02Cb
GARLAND, Lee	35	M	Laborer	12No02Cb
CONELLY, Brid.	18	F	Servant	12No02Cb
Rose	17	F	Servant	12No02Cb
LAMB, Margt.	18	F	Servant	12No02Cb
Ellen	17	F	Servant	12No02Cb
DYER, Mick	18	M	Laborer	12No02Cb
Cath.	40	F	Servant	12No02Cb
Cath.	4	F	Child	12No02Cb
Edward	6	M	Child	12No02Cb
TETHER, Sarah	28	F	Servant	12No02Cb
Jane	.00	F	Infant	12No02Cb
BURDEN, Geo.	3	M	Child	12No02Cb
FOY, Pat	26	M	Laborer	12No02Cb
Benj.	24	M	Laborer	12No02Cb
LIPSIT, Hugh	28	M	Unknown	12No02Cb
Ann	25	F	Servant	12No02Cb
KELLY, Julia	22	F	Servant	12No02Cb
CLANNEY, Mary	19	F	Servant	12No02Cb
SHERLOCK, Thomas	40	M	Laborer	12No02Cb
RAHILLY, Brid.	18	F	Servant	12No02Cb
GILMOUR, Mary	18	F	Servant	12No02Cb
BERRY, John	40	M	Laborer	12No02Cb
Mary	36	F	Servant	12No02Cb
Martha	17	F	Servant	12No02Cb
MCANDREWS, Owen	36	M	Laborer	12No02Cb
GRAZIER, Geo.	27	M	Laborer	12No02Cb
Jno.	25	M	Laborer	12No02Cb
James	22	M	Laborer	12No02Cb
MCCUMMINS, Hugh	40	M	Laborer	12No02Cb
Jno.	14	M	Laborer	12No02Cb
ENNIS, Wm.	25	M	Laborer	12No02Cb
DONOHUE, Fra.	55	M	Servant	12No02Cb
Died-At-Sea				
CURTAIN, Jas.	30	M	Laborer	12No02Cb
Sarah	30	F	Servant	12No02Cb
TUCKER, Ellen	25	F	Servant	12No02Cb
MULLEN, Jas.	18	M	Laborer	12No02Cb
WOODS, Mary	20	F	Servant	12No02Cb
MCGARTY, Ann	23	F	Servant	12No02Cb
Cath.	23	F	Servant	12No02Cb
MONELLY, Fra.	29	F	Servant	12No02Cb
DOOLAN, Jas.	20	M	Laborer	12No02Cb
Ann	20	F	Servant	12No02Cb
SHANLEY, Mick	24	M	Laborer	12No02Cb
Fra.	22	F	Servant	12No02Cb
U	.00	U	Infant	12No02Cb
Born-At-Sea				
Margt.	20	F	Servant	12No02Cb
Cath.	21	F	Servant	12No02Cb
Eliza	21	F	Servant	12No02Cb
U, Mary	13	F	Servant	12No02Cb
KERNAN, Char.	19	F	Servant	12No02Cb
STEPHENSON, Ann	22	F	Servant	12No02Cb
SMITH, Wm.	20	M	Laborer	12No02Cb
BOOTH, Rebec.	20	F	Servant	12No02Cb
KILLINGBECK, Mark	24	M	Laborer	12No02Cb
Richd.	20	M	Laborer	12No02Cb
WALSH, John	36	M	Laborer	12No02Cb
Ben	30	M	Laborer	12No02Cb
LIPSEY, John	18	M	Laborer	12No02Cb
Thos.	19	M	Laborer	12No02Cb

NAMES OF PASSENGERS	AGE	SEX	OCCUPATIONS	DATE PORT SHIP
LIPSEY, Margt.	12	F	Servant	12No02Cb
MANCELY, Wm.	35	M	Laborer	12No02Cb
Mick	4	M	Child	12No02Cb
KEELAN, Mick	20	M	Laborer	12No02Cb
CASEY, Edward	36	M	Laborer	12No02Cb
MCCARTLEY, Brid.	17	F	Servant	12No02Cb
REILLY, Mary	40	F	Servant	12No02Cb
Ellen	15	F	Servant	12No02Cb
Brid.	10	F	None	12No02Cb
Ann	6	F	Child	12No02Cb
Margt.	4	F	Child	12No02Cb
KEYS, Fanny	41	F	Servant	12No02Cb
Thos.	11	M	Laborer	12No02Cb
Wm.	10	M	Laborer	12No02Cb
Jas.	7	M	Child	12No02Cb
Mary	5	F	Child	12No02Cb
Pat	3	M	Child	12No02Cb
KENNY, Mary	45	F	Servant	12No02Cb
Mich.	12	M	None	12No02Cb
Brid.	6	F	Child	12No02Cb
RUDDIN, Cath.	30	F	Servant	12No02Cb
MCAVOY, Mary	35	F	Servant	12No02Cb
NEILAN, Ann	18	F	Servant	12No02Cb
LEONARD, John	50	M	Laborer	12No02Cb
BREEN, Margt.	17	F	Servant	12No02Cb
MULLIGAN, Wm.	21	M	Laborer	12No02Cb
EGAN, Mary	35	F	Servant	12No02Cb
Mich.	10	M	None	12No02Cb
Brid.	8	F	Child	12No02Cb
Pat	3	M	Child	12No02Cb
Maria	.00	F	Infant	12No02Cb
JONES, Henry	28	M	Laborer	12No02Cb
Matilda	19	F	Servant	12No02Cb
Sophia	17	F	Servant	12No02Cb
OWEN, Mary	20	F	Servant	12No02Cb
HUMPHRIES, Fanny	18	F	Servant	12No02Cb
WHALIN, Pat	20	M	Laborer	12No02Cb
COGHILL, John	41	M	Laborer	12No02Cb
Eliz.	37	F	Servant	12No02Cb
Ellen	8	F	Child	12No02Cb
OWEN, Mich.	18	M	Laborer	12No02Cb
CAMPBELL, Edwd.	27	M	Laborer	12No02Cb
MORGAN, Terence	25	M	Laborer	12No02Cb
MISSELEY, Will.	38	M	Laborer	12No02Cb
BOURKE, Jno.	20	M	Laborer	12No02Cb
FARGUSSON, Wm.	40	M	Laborer	12No02Cb
Wm.	18	M	Laborer	12No02Cb
MURDOCK, John	50	M	Laborer	12No02Cb
John	27	M	Laborer	12No02Cb
MCBRYAN, John	24	M	Laborer	12No02Cb
COLEMAN, Cath.	24	F	Servant	12No02Cb
LAFFAN, Mary	22	F	Servant	12No02Cb
BURKE, Wm.	60	M	Laborer	12No02Cb
Wm.	32	M	Laborer	12No02Cb
JULIAN, James	26	M	Laborer	12No02Cb
MALLON, Edward	31	M	Laborer	12No02Cb
CONOLLY, Mick	18	M	Laborer	12No02Cb
BOYLAN, Ann	20	F	Servant	12No02Cb
Ellen	19	F	Servant	12No02Cb
QUINN, And.	7	M	Child	12No02Cb
DEVINE, Mary	45	F	Servant	12No02Cb
Edward	13	M	Laborer	12No02Cb
William	10	M	None	12No02Cb
ROY, Betty	20	F	Servant	12No02Cb
LYNCH, Margt.	20	F	Servant	12No02Cb
MAURRY, Thomas	20	M	Laborer	12No02Cb
FINNERTY, Pat	20	M	Laborer	12No02Cb
FINEGAN, Ann	20	F	Servant	12No02Cb
MORGAN, Th.	22	M	Laborer	12No02Cb
BYRNE, Mary	16	F	Servant	12No02Cb
GOVEN, James	20	M	Laborer	12No02Cb
MULVEY, Pat.	18	M	Laborer	12No02Cb
COLWELL, Michl.	20	M	Laborer	12No02Cb
HAYES, Johanna	20	F	Servant	12No02Cb

HOUGHTON 13 NOVEMBER 1849

From Liverpool

NAMES OF PASSENGERS		AGE	SEX	OCCUPATIONS	DATE PORT SHIP
GREEN, Mary		14	F	Servant	13No02Ce
CATTON, Catharine		16	F	Servant	13No02Ce
SMITH, Thos.		48	M	Butcher	13No02Ce
Ellen		48	F	None	13No02Ce
NAHAN, Johan.		20	F	Servant	13No02Ce
BARNEY, Margt.		22	F	Servant	13No02Ce
OBRYAN, Mary		28	F	Servant	13No02Ce
QUADE, James		18	M	Laborer	13No02Ce
GRIFFIN, Jeremiah		56	M	Farmer	13No02Ce
Mary		40	F	None	13No02Ce
Died-At-Sea					
David		17	M	None	13No02Ce
Ellen		13	F	None	13No02Ce
Terry		12	M	None	13No02Ce
Far.		10	M	None	13No02Ce
Mary		8	F	Child	13No02Ce
Bid.		6	F	Child	13No02Ce
Died-At-Sea					
Margt.		3	F	Child	13No02Ce
Johan.		.00	F	Infant	13No02Ce
John		50	M	Farmer	13No02Ce
Sarah		40	F	None	13No02Ce
Sarah		.00	F	Infant	13No02Ce
David		7	M	Child	13No02Ce
Her.		14	F	None	13No02Ce
Margt.		4	F	Child	13No02Ce
Conn		3	M	Child	13No02Ce
Catherine		11	F	None	13No02Ce
BROWN, Johan.		18	F	None	13No02Ce
MCANNATY, De.		23	M	Laborer	13No02Ce
LAVRELL, Michael		23	M	Laborer	13No02Ce
MCGRAGH, Eliz.		18	F	Servant	13No02Ce
MORRICE, Thos.		22	M	Mason	13No02Ce
Dennis		18	M	None	13No02Ce
Brid.		17	F	None	13No02Ce
MORTON, James		18	M	None	13No02Ce
MCGRATH, Michael		50	M	Farmer	13No02Ce
Ellen		10	F	None	13No02Ce
WARD, Ann		20	F	Tailor	13No02Ce
HOWARD, Dennis		50	M	Laborer	13No02Ce
Ally		24	F	None	13No02Ce
DONAHUE, Catharine		19	F	Tailor	13No02Ce
KENELLY, Mary		25	F	Tailor	13No02Ce
Pat		2	M	Child	13No02Ce
CONOUGH, Pat		32	M	Laborer	13No02Ce
KELLY, Pat		40	M	Laborer	13No02Ce
CORONHAN, John		26	M	Carpenter	13No02Ce
Mary	(W)	24	F	None	13No02Ce
Died-At-Sea					
Thomas	(S)	.00	M	Infant	13No02Ce
Died-At-Sea					
SHEA, Ned		22	M	Laborer	13No02Ce
KEEGAN, Mary		24	F	Servant	13No02Ce
GILL, Catharine		20	F	Servant	13No02Ce
HEWS, Betty		24	F	Servant	13No02Ce
DOOLAN, Joseph		28	M	Laborer	13No02Ce
HOWARD, Michael		28	M	Laborer	13No02Ce
MCKUEN, James		28	M	Laborer	13No02Ce
FERRISS, Miranda		25	F	Milliner	13No02Ce
CUNNINGHAM, Ellen		23	F	Milliner	13No02Ce
DALY, H.		50	F	Servant	13No02Ce
Michael		16	M	None	13No02Ce
BABBOT, Briget		4	F	Child	13No02Ce
CORR, John		22	M	Laborer	13No02Ce
REILLY, Ann		20	F	None	13No02Ce
FALLAN, Pat		20	M	Carpenter	13No02Ce
Bernard		17	M	Laborer	13No02Ce
HEFFRAN, Brid.		27	F	Servant	13No02Ce
DEMMINS, Ellen		23	F	Servant	13No02Ce
WHITE, Brid.		20	F	Servant	13No02Ce
FINNIN, Andrew		20	M	Laborer	13No02Ce
Catharine		13	F	Servant	13No02Ce
KELLY, Ma.		20	F	Servant	13No02Ce
FLANAGAN, Michael		20	M	Laborer	13No02Ce
TORRY, Martin		17	M	Laborer	13No02Ce
HAWKES, George		28	M	Laborer	13No02Ce
Henry		11	M	Laborer	13No02Ce
BRYAN, Ellen		25	F	Tailor	13No02Ce
Mich.	(S)	6	M	Child	13No02Ce
SMITH, Francis		24	M	Laborer	13No02Ce
DONNELLY, Margt.		20	F	Servant	13No02Ce
Mary		16	F	Servant	13No02Ce
GANIN, Rose		17	F	Servant	13No02Ce
CARBY, Brid.		32	F	Milliner	13No02Ce
BRENNAN, Catherine		11	F	Servant	13No02Ce
FALLON, Rose		7	F	Child	13No02Ce
MARTIN, Mary		40	F	Servant	13No02Ce
Ann		11	F	None	13No02Ce
Brid.		3	F	Child	13No02Ce
Maria		6	F	Child	13No02Ce
ALLEN, Eliza		25	F	Milliner	13No02Ce
LEONARD, John		17	M	Unknown	13No02Ce
BRYAN, John		17	M	Laborer	13No02Ce
Sarah		28	F	Laborer	13No02Ce
Catharine		14	F	Laborer	13No02Ce
Mary		12	F	Laborer	13No02Ce
BRENNAN, Joshua		18	M	Laborer	13No02Ce
SIKES, David		32	M	Shoemaker	13No02Ce
WALCH, Lawrence		23	M	Laborer	13No02Ce
Mary	(W)	21	F	None	13No02Ce
MILLS, Francis		24	M	Laborer	13No02Ce
CATTON, Wm.		24	M	Laborer	13No02Ce
LENAHAN, Andrew		22	M	Laborer	13No02Ce
ANEAX, Thos.		30	M	Laborer	13No02Ce
DEARY, Ann		50	F	Laborer	13No02Ce
Ann		22	F	Laborer	13No02Ce
Eliza		.00	F	Infant	13No02Ce
LARRY, Wilm.		36	M	Laborer	13No02Ce
MOUNTAIN, Robert		23	M	Laborer	13No02Ce
WALLACE, John		30	M	Laborer	13No02Ce
PARKER, Michael		25	M	Laborer	13No02Ce
HANRETY, John		30	M	Laborer	13No02Ce
WALCH, Mary		22	F	Servant	13No02Ce
Margt.		18	F	Servant	13No02Ce
MARTIN, Barth.		28	M	Shoemaker	13No02Ce
HARMON, Mary		18	F	Tailor	13No02Ce
DUNN, Brid.		20	F	Tailor	13No02Ce
KENNY, Brid.		18	F	Tailor	13No02Ce
BRASNOHAN, Terry		35	M	Laborer	13No02Ce
Mary		25	F	None	13No02Ce
Johanah		23	F	None	13No02Ce
MCDONNELL, Michael		25	M	Shoemaker	13No02Ce
Mary		26	F	None	13No02Ce
Ellen		13	F	None	13No02Ce
Jane		7	F	Child	13No02Ce
Margt.		5	F	Child	13No02Ce
LINCH, Mary		21	F	Servant	13No02Ce
Brid.		19	F	Servant	13No02Ce
KELLY, Davy		23	M	Laborer	13No02Ce
SULIVAN, John		41	M	Carpenter	13No02Ce
K--FICH, Thos.		60	M	Farmer	13No02Ce
Catharine		50	F	None	13No02Ce
Mary		30	F	None	13No02Ce
Michael		27	M	None	13No02Ce
Wm.		25	M	None	13No02Ce
Margt.		23	F	None	13No02Ce
Catherine		21	F	None	13No02Ce
Thomas		19	M	None	13No02Ce
Ellen		17	F	None	13No02Ce
Bessy		15	F	None	13No02Ce

NAMES OF PASSENGERS	AGE	SEX	OCCUPATIONS	DATE PORT SHIP
K--FICH, Johan.	9	F	Child	13No02Ce
J.	12	M	None	13No02Ce
NELSON, Thomas	34	M	Carpenter	13No02Ce
CONNOR, Mary	19	F	Spinner	13No02Ce
ROACH, Wm.	30	M	Farmer	13No02Ce
Mary (W)	28	F	None	13No02Ce
KENELLY, David	50	M	Laborer	13No02Ce
DOOLAN, Bryan	24	M	Laborer	13No02Ce
MADDEN, Michael	24	M	Laborer	13No02Ce
Died-At-Sea				
COLLER, Moses	26	M	Laborer	13No02Ce
MARTIN, John	40	M	Laborer	13No02Ce
Marcella	26	F	Laborer	13No02Ce
Pat	6	M	Child	13No02Ce
Jno.	4	M	Child	13No02Ce
Thomas	2	M	Child	13No02Ce
Benjamin	.00	M	Infant	13No02Ce
FALLEN, Thomas	20	M	Laborer	13No02Ce
GORDON, David	28	M	Laborer	13No02Ce
Percy	26	F	Shoemaker	13No02Ce
MORAN, James	30	M	Laborer	13No02Ce
AGAN, James	28	M	Laborer	13No02Ce
BINDERVILLE, Mary	20	F	Servant	13No02Ce
SHERIDAN, James	25	M	Tailor	13No02Ce
Died-At-Sea				
MURPHY, James	40	M	Bleacher	13No02Ce
QUINDAN, Morrice	22	M	Farmer	13No02Ce
SCANLAN, John	24	M	Laborer	13No02Ce
Pat	22	M	Laborer	13No02Ce
MCPARLIN, Catharine	30	M	Laborer	13No02Ce
MAHAN, Peter	11	M	Laborer	13No02Ce
BOYLE, Frank	9	M	Child	13No02Ce
TOOLY, Judy	32	F	Laborer	13No02Ce
Darby	12	M	Laborer	13No02Ce
Mary	.00	F	Infant	13No02Ce
Margt.	10	F	None	13No02Ce
MCHIGAN, Honora	30	F	Servant	13No02Ce
Julia	7	F	Child	13No02Ce
MCCATRY, Thomas	35	M	Laborer	13No02Ce
BRODRICK, Dan.	10	M	Laborer	13No02Ce
WHELAN, Ann	17	F	Tailor	13No02Ce
GARRY, Mathew	26	M	Laborer	13No02Ce
Catharine	18	F	Laborer	13No02Ce
RENAN, Ann	12	F	Laborer	13No02Ce
Pat	10	M	Laborer	13No02Ce
DRISCOLL, Mary	25	F	Milliner	13No02Ce
DONERAN, Johan.	8	F	Child	13No02Ce
HARKIN, Thomas	26	M	Painter	13No02Ce
MCGRATH, Brid.	17	F	Servant	13No02Ce
LEDDY, Brid.	16	F	Servant	13No02Ce
CUSACK, John	16	M	Laborer	13No02Ce
Farrell	11	M	Laborer	13No02Ce
COLLINS, Mary	36	F	Laborer	13No02Ce
DUFFY, John	16	M	Laborer	13No02Ce
Catharine	11	F	Laborer	13No02Ce
CARRALL, Mary	35	F	Laborer	13No02Ce
James	11	M	Laborer	13No02Ce
Thomas	9	M	Child	13No02Ce
Ann	3	F	Child	13No02Ce
Pat	2	M	Child	13No02Ce
Died-At-Sea				
MCDONAGH, Brid.	15	F	Laborer	13No02Ce
FAHY, Mary	7	F	Child	13No02Ce
KENEDY, Mary	24	F	Milliner	13No02Ce
Margt.	23	F	Milliner	13No02Ce
SHELLY, Martin	31	M	Laborer	13No02Ce
RATHCAN, Mary	18	F	Laborer	13No02Ce
KING, Michael	18	M	Servant	13No02Ce
MILLIN, Andrew	27	M	Miner	13No02Ce
Died-At-Sea				
John	22	M	Miner	13No02Ce
S.	24	M	Miner	13No02Ce
BYRNE, Morgan	27	M	Miner	13No02Ce
Catharine	33	F	None	13No02Ce
Died-At-Sea				
KELLY, John	26	M	Miner	13No02Ce
KEARY, Wm.	28	M	Miner	13No02Ce
DOWLING, Peter	26	M	Miner	13No02Ce
CHAMPION, Timothy	19	M	Laborer	13No02Ce
LARKIN, Pat	20	M	Laborer	13No02Ce
DOYLE, Ann	18	F	Servant	13No02Ce
BYRNES, Mary	20	F	Servant	13No02Ce
HADDER, John	30	M	Laborer	13No02Ce
Catharine	27	M	Laborer	13No02Ce
FEENY, Michael	35	M	Laborer	13No02Ce
BRADY, Mary	22	F	Servant	13No02Ce
BOYLE, Pat	22	M	Laborer	13No02Ce
HEANY, James	19	M	Laborer	13No02Ce
MCMASTERS, George	35	M	Laborer	13No02Ce
MORAN, Margt.	19	F	Servant	13No02Ce
FOLEY, Hiram	24	M	Tailor	13No02Ce
Daniel	20	M	Tailor	13No02Ce
KENELY, Michael	40	M	Laborer	13No02Ce
Michael	11	M	Laborer	13No02Ce
Ellen	15	F	None	13No02Ce
Died-At-Sea				
HARISON, Pat	40	M	Laborer	13No02Ce
REILLY, Julia	18	F	Dressmaker	13No02Ce
CONNERS, Simon	50	M	Farmer	13No02Ce
Pat	19	M	Farmer	13No02Ce
John	30	M	Farmer	13No02Ce
Died-At-Sea				
Mary	30	F	None	13No02Ce
MALOMPHY, David	40	M	Laborer	13No02Ce
J.	45	F	None	13No02Ce
Mary	15	F	None	13No02Ce
BARNEY, Mary	23	F	None	13No02Ce
CONDAN, Johan.	23	F	None	13No02Ce
RICE, Homer	23	M	Farmer	13No02Ce
BARRY, John	11	M	None	13No02Ce
SULIVAN, Michael	40	M	Farmer	13No02Ce
Honora	30	F	None	13No02Ce
Wm.	5	M	Child	13No02Ce
HUDSON, Ann	45	F	Servant	13No02Ce
L.	10	M	None	13No02Ce
MARCHAL, Robert	40	M	Laborer	13No02Ce
CURRAN, Hugh	28	M	Laborer	13No02Ce
MULLANY, Thomas	18	M	Laborer	13No02Ce
REELY, James	21	M	Laborer	13No02Ce
KISHAL, John	40	M	Laborer	13No02Ce
BANKS, Michael	22	M	Tinsmith	13No02Ce
Briged	16	F	None	13No02Ce
MCKERNAN, Brid.	22	F	Servant	13No02Ce
Died-At-Sea				
DOONAN, Ann	15	F	Servant	13No02Ce
PRICE, Margt.	17	F	Dressmaker	13No02Ce
CONLAN, Mary	40	F	Laborer	13No02Ce
Died-At-Sea				
Maria	15	F	Laborer	13No02Ce
Died-At-Sea				
Thos.	20	M	Laborer	13No02Ce
Died-At-Sea				
MURRAY, Mary	14	F	Laborer	13No02Ce
STACK, Joseph	22	M	Priest	13No02Ce
MULVARY, M.Revd.	35	M	Priest	13No02Ce
DUN, Joseph	24	M	Farmer	13No02Ce
MCNAMARA, Catharine	19	F	Dressmaker	13No02Ce
GOTT, Daniel	24	M	Laborer	13No02Ce
PEAL, Joseph	18	M	Laborer	13No02Ce
HARTY, Ellen	17	F	Servant	13No02Ce
BRANNAN, Brid.	4	F	Child	13No02Ce
HAY, Mary	22	F	Servant	13No02Ce
MCKERNAN, Mary	13	F	Servant	13No02Ce
LINES, Winny	17	F	None	13No02Ce
WEALY, Ann	8	F	Child	13No02Ce
KEARNS, Rose	18	F	None	13No02Ce
MCMAHAN, Allice	50	F	None	13No02Ce
Allice	16	F	None	13No02Ce
Mary	14	F	None	13No02Ce
Catharine	8	F	Child	13No02Ce

NAMES OF PASSENGERS	AGE	SEX	OCCUPATIONS	DATE PORT SHIP
LEARY, Brid.	30	F	None	13No02Ce
ALLEN, Ellen	30	F	None	13No02Ce
Robert	7	M	Child	13No02Ce
Thos.	4	M	Child	13No02Ce
MCDONALD, John	27	M	Miner	13No02Ce
Wm.	23	M	Miner	13No02Ce
Catharine	21	F	None	13No02Ce
BRUTHIE, John	20	M	Miner	13No02Ce
OBRYAN, James	18	M	Laborer	13No02Ce
LAHEY, Maurice	24	M	Laborer	13No02Ce
LAWLESS, Mary	18	F	Servant	13No02Ce
CARNEY, Richard	19	M	Laborer	13No02Ce
CONNELL, Cathn.	22	F	Servant	13No02Ce
WYNE, Hugh	35	M	Laborer	13No02Ce
HEALY, Michael	38	M	Teacher	13No02Ce
RAYNOLS, Thomas	24	M	Laborer	13No02Ce
CARTER, Ellen	28	F	Dressmaker	13No02Ce
RAFERTY, Martin	36	M	Laborer	13No02Ce

GENERAL-SCOTT 14 NOVEMBER 1849

From Dublin

NAMES OF PASSENGERS	AGE	SEX	OCCUPATIONS	DATE PORT SHIP
DAYLEY, U-Mrs.	40	F	Laborer	14No05Cf
John	22	M	Laborer	14No05Cf
Catherine	20	F	Lady	14No05Cf
CASEY, Daniel	20	M	Laborer	14No05Cf
MURPHY, Maurice	30	M	Mechanic	14No05Cf
BANNON, Nancy	19	F	Lady	14No05Cf
HODGES, Catherine	30	F	Lady	14No05Cf
CONNER, Wm.	20	M	Mechanic	14No05Cf
Elizabeth	19	F	Lady	14No05Cf
WALSH, Mary	20	F	Lady	14No05Cf
DUGAN, Mary	20	F	Lady	14No05Cf
Bridget	20	F	Lady	14No05Cf
FINN, Mary	26	F	Lady	14No05Cf
John	30	M	Accountant	14No05Cf
Thomas	30	M	Accountant	14No05Cf
Caroline	3	F	Child	14No05Cf
ARDEN, Mary	18	F	Lady	14No05Cf
DOWLING, Edmond	22	M	Farmer	14No05Cf
COLLINS, Johanna	26	F	Lady	14No05Cf
Abbey	30	F	Lady	14No05Cf
HONARAHN, Margt.	26	F	Lady	14No05Cf
Thomas	10	M	Mechanic	14No05Cf
Daniel	8	M	Child	14No05Cf
SHEINAN, Danl.	8	M	Child	14No05Cf
BYRNE, Ellen	12	F	Lady	14No05Cf
Jane	20	F	Lady	14No05Cf
NEVIN, Catherine	18	F	Lady	14No05Cf
KING, Andrew	22	M	Farmer	14No05Cf
FITZPATRICK, Mat	22	M	Farmer	14No05Cf
SHELTON, Richd.	22	M	Farmer	14No05Cf
Margaret	22	F	Lady	14No05Cf
CULLIN, Wm.	24	M	Laborer	14No05Cf
CONLLEN, James	22	M	Laborer	14No05Cf
MASSEY, U-Mrs.	40	F	Lady	14No05Cf
Jno.	19	M	Gentleman	14No05Cf
FARRELL, Mary	40	F	Lady	14No05Cf
Ann	20	F	Lady	14No05Cf
WILLS, Ann	20	F	Lady	14No05Cf
MORAN, Danl.	20	M	Mechanic	14No05Cf
CONNER, Ann	20	F	Lady	14No05Cf
FEHAN, Ann	22	F	Lady	14No05Cf
LYONS, Catherine	20	F	Lady	14No05Cf
WILSON, John	27	M	Laborer	14No05Cf
U-Mrs.	22	F	Lady	14No05Cf
FARRELL, John	16	M	Mechanic	14No05Cf
Peter	15	M	Mechanic	14No05Cf

NAMES OF PASSENGERS	AGE	SEX	OCCUPATIONS	DATE PORT SHIP
FARRELL, Joseph	20	M	Mechanic	14No05Cf
Ossey	21	M	Mechanic	14No05Cf
Rose	10	F	Lady	14No05Cf
Anne	8	F	Child	14No05Cf
FLYNN, Mary	20	F	Lady	14No05Cf
James	28	M	Laborer	14No05Cf
KELLY, Joseph	20	M	Laborer	14No05Cf
MEHAUGTON, U-Mrs.	20	F	Lady	14No05Cf
Mary	36	F	Lady	14No05Cf
MURRAY, Rose	20	F	Lady	14No05Cf
MOORE, U-Mrs.	26	F	Lady	14No05Cf
U-Miss	27	F	Lady	14No05Cf
U-Miss	10	F	Lady	14No05Cf
GOLLION, Wm.	40	M	Farmer	14No05Cf
Mary	24	F	Lady	14No05Cf
John	9	M	Child	14No05Cf
Mary	4	F	Child	14No05Cf
Catherine	4	F	Child	14No05Cf
SCOTT, John	24	M	Mechanic	14No05Cf
TRACY, Margt.	21	F	Lady	14No05Cf
Ann	50	F	Lady	14No05Cf
HELFORD, Catherine	45	F	Lady	14No05Cf
COSTELLO, John	45	M	Laborer	14No05Cf
Anty	17	F	Lady	14No05Cf
Michael	15	M	Mechanic	14No05Cf
Mary	10	F	Unknown	14No05Cf
James	8	M	Child	14No05Cf
ANDERSON, Michael	20	M	Mechanic	14No05Cf
OBRIEN, Thos.	22	M	Mechanic	14No05Cf
ROURKE, Joseph	22	M	Mechanic	14No05Cf
John	20	M	Mechanic	14No05Cf
GILLS, U-Mrs.	24	F	Lady	14No05Cf
KENNELLY, Martin	24	M	Farmer	14No05Cf
Catherine	28	F	Lady	14No05Cf
BYRAN, Mary	20	F	Lady	14No05Cf
MAHAN, U-Mrs.	26	F	Lady	14No05Cf
BYRNE, M.A.	20	F	Lady	14No05Cf
FARREL, Ellen	18	F	Lady	14No05Cf
LEONARD, Anne	17	F	Lady	14No05Cf
DOYLE, Margret	30	F	Lady	14No05Cf
KENNEDY, Bridget	20	F	Lady	14No05Cf
MORAN, Thomas	25	M	Mechanic	14No05Cf
MCFIDY, John	16	M	Mechanic	14No05Cf
COGAN, Julia	24	F	Lady	14No05Cf
Mary	22	F	Lady	14No05Cf
Bridget	20	F	Lady	14No05Cf
KENNEDY, Neill	20	M	Mechanic	14No05Cf
FANNIN, Mary	20	F	Lady	14No05Cf
MITCHELL, Martha	15	F	Lady	14No05Cf
MURTAH, John	16	M	Farmer	14No05Cf
Ellen	20	F	Lady	14No05Cf
LEGGETT, John	20	M	Accountant	14No05Cf
FITZPATRICK, Patrick	24	M	Farmer	14No05Cf
KANE, John	20	M	Farmer	14No05Cf
MORGAN, Peter	24	M	Farmer	14No05Cf
KELMA, James	22	M	Farmer	14No05Cf
Mat	20	M	Mechanic	14No05Cf
HAYES, Wm.	20	M	Mechanic	14No05Cf
MANSON, Frederick	20	M	Mechanic	14No05Cf
U-Mrs.	38	F	Lady	14No05Cf
JACKSON, John	24	M	Merchant	14No05Cf
HOGAN, Jno.	24	M	Merchant	14No05Cf
MAYHANY, U-Miss	22	F	Lady	14No05Cf
STRONG, John	40	M	Merchant	14No05Cf
BRUCE, U-Miss	20	F	Lady	14No05Cf
FENLY, U-Mrs.	25	F	Lady	14No05Cf
Robt.	3	M	Child	14No05Cf

DENMARK 14 NOVEMBER 1849

From Liverpool

NAMES OF PASSENGERS	AGE	SEX	OCCUPATIONS	DATE PORT SHIP
MCVERRY, Thomas	30	M	Mechanic	14No02Ch
TOOLE, Patrick	36	M	Laborer	14No02Ch
Anne	36	F	None	14No02Ch
Peter	30	M	None	14No02Ch
Patrick	5	M	Child	14No02Ch
Thomas	3	M	Child	14No02Ch
Betsey	.00	F	Infant	14No02Ch
FALLAN, Catherine	17	F	Laborer	14No02Ch
KELLY, Mary	20	F	None	14No02Ch
HALLEY, Anne	40	F	None	14No02Ch
Bridget	12	F	None	14No02Ch
Patrick	7	M	Child	14No02Ch
Charles	5	M	Child	14No02Ch
Thomas	4	M	Child	14No02Ch
LAREN, Thomas	24	M	None	14No02Ch
CAREY, Catharine	36	F	None	14No02Ch
Bridget	5	F	Child	14No02Ch
Denis	4	M	Child	14No02Ch
KELLY, Mary	25	F	None	14No02Ch
RODICAN, Anne	17	F	None	14No02Ch
MCRAN, Mary	15	F	None	14No02Ch
Michael	5	M	Child	14No02Ch
KAVANAGH, Ellen	18	F	None	14No02Ch
MCTAGUE, Bridget	18	F	None	14No02Ch
SHEA, Michael	26	M	None	14No02Ch
HACKETT, Mary	18	F	None	14No02Ch
CONNORS, Mary	20	F	None	14No02Ch
HARTIGAN, Sally	50	F	None	14No02Ch
Catharine	17	F	None	14No02Ch
Johanna	14	F	None	14No02Ch
John	16	M	None	14No02Ch
BUCANNON, Thomas	50	M	None	14No02Ch
Mary	50	F	None	14No02Ch
Mary	18	F	None	14No02Ch
Michael	15	M	None	14No02Ch
WALSH, Anne	30	F	None	14No02Ch
HARAN, Johanna	20	F	None	14No02Ch
CHILDE, Mary	18	F	None	14No02Ch
KENON, Henry	11	M	None	14No02Ch

MARGARET 16 NOVEMBER 1849

From Belfast

NAMES OF PASSENGERS	AGE	SEX	OCCUPATIONS	DATE PORT SHIP
MOWKINGRY, William	20	M	Unknown	16No17Bw
Sophia	20	F	Unknown	16No17Bw
Sarah	18	F	Unknown	16No17Bw
WELLS, Sarah	25	F	Unknown	16No17Bw
Eliza	3	F	Child	16No17Bw
ARMSTRONG, Mary	35	F	Unknown	16No17Bw
Jane	12	F	Unknown	16No17Bw
Thomas	10	M	Unknown	16No17Bw
John	8	M	Child	16No17Bw
Lewisia	5	F	Child	16No17Bw
William	3	M	Child	16No17Bw
Robert	.00	M	Infant	16No17Bw
WILSON, Stewart	25	M	Unknown	16No17Bw
ROBINSON, Susanah	25	F	Unknown	16No17Bw
Stewart	20	M	Unknown	16No17Bw
BI----, Anne	24	F	Unknown	16No17Bw
Thomas	.00	M	Infant	16No17Bw
WOODWARD, Eliza	25	F	Unknown	16No17Bw
ORR, James	50	M	Unknown	16No17Bw
Margaret	50	F	Unknown	16No17Bw
HUGHES, Ann	24	F	Unknown	16No17Bw
MELVILLE, Jane	60	F	Unknown	16No17Bw
Ellen	21	F	Unknown	16No17Bw
Henry	19	M	Unknown	16No17Bw
DOAK, Hugh	30	M	Unknown	16No17Bw
Jane	28	F	Unknown	16No17Bw
Matilda	10	F	Unknown	16No17Bw
Margaret	2	F	Child	16No17Bw
Mary	.00	F	Infant	16No17Bw
BROWN, Jane	20	F	Unknown	16No17Bw
Mary	17	F	Unknown	16No17Bw
BODAN, Jane	19	F	Unknown	16No17Bw
Ann	17	F	Unknown	16No17Bw
PALMER, Catharine	30	F	Unknown	16No17Bw
Eliza	7	F	Child	16No17Bw
MCATAGGART, Michael	25	M	Unknown	16No17Bw
Sarah	25	F	Unknown	16No17Bw
Margaret	2	F	Child	16No17Bw
John	.00	M	Infant	16No17Bw
MCGEE, Catharine	30	F	Unknown	16No17Bw
BURNS, Martha	32	F	Unknown	16No17Bw
William	10	M	Unknown	16No17Bw
Margaret	7	F	Child	16No17Bw
Matilda	5	F	Child	16No17Bw
John	.00	M	Infant	16No17Bw
MCDADE, William	35	M	Unknown	16No17Bw
RONEY, James	19	M	Unknown	16No17Bw
Reno-, Sally	25	F	Unknown	16No17Bw
MCCREA, Margaret	40	F	Unknown	16No17Bw
Eliza	11	F	Unknown	16No17Bw
James	9	M	Child	16No17Bw
Ann	7	F	Child	16No17Bw
MCCLEMENTS, Thomas	21	M	Unknown	16No17Bw
Margret	20	F	Unknown	16No17Bw
PETTICREW, Eliza	55	F	Unknown	16No17Bw
Absolam	30	M	Unknown	16No17Bw
Margaret	28	F	Unknown	16No17Bw
Alexander	30	M	Unknown	16No17Bw
Marshall	22	M	Unknown	16No17Bw
DONALDSON, James	20	M	Unknown	16No17Bw
JAMESON, Jane	25	F	Unknown	16No17Bw
James	21	M	Unknown	16No17Bw
Mary	4	F	Child	16No17Bw
John	2	M	Child	16No17Bw
NELSON, William	25	M	Unknown	16No17Bw
BAMMER, Eliza	21	F	Unknown	16No17Bw
HENDERSON, Sarah	21	F	Unknown	16No17Bw
Eliza	19	F	Unknown	16No17Bw
GRIFFIN, Catharine	26	F	Unknown	16No17Bw
Henry	4	M	Child	16No17Bw
John	.00	M	Infant	16No17Bw
GRAHAM, William	17	M	Unknown	16No17Bw
LAPPAN, James	18	M	Unknown	16No17Bw
DORAN, Ellen	20	F	Unknown	16No17Bw
MCGONGHAL, James	22	M	Unknown	16No17Bw
MAGGINNIS, Sarah	20	F	Unknown	16No17Bw
GORMAN, Eliza	35	F	Unknown	16No17Bw
James	4	M	Child	16No17Bw
MCCULLOUGH, Ann	16	F	Unknown	16No17Bw
Patrick	12	M	Unknown	16No17Bw
WILSON, Noble	30	U	Unknown	16No17Bw
SPEARS, William	25	M	Unknown	16No17Bw
LEVELIN, John	22	M	Unknown	16No17Bw
Bessy	19	F	Unknown	16No17Bw
MCCLEMENTS, Margaret	13	F	Unknown	16No17Bw
MCCONNELL, Francis	17	M	Unknown	16No17Bw
STEVENSON, James	30	M	Unknown	16No17Bw
SERVICE, Robert	22	M	Unknown	16No17Bw
MCBRIDE, William	34	M	Unknown	16No17Bw
Mary	22	F	Unknown	16No17Bw

NAMES OF PASSENGERS	AGE	SEX	OCCUPATIONS	DATE PORT SHIP
MCBRIDE, Margaret	5	F	Child	16No17Bw
Robert	.00	M	Infant	16No17Bw
MCKINSTRY, Eliza	28	F	Unknown	16No17Bw
THOMPSON, James	37	M	Unknown	16No17Bw
Ann	30	F	Unknown	16No17Bw
Mary	10	F	Unknown	16No17Bw
Ester	9	F	Child	16No17Bw
Robert	7	M	Child	16No17Bw
WATT, Robert	30	M	Unknown	16No17Bw
Mary	30	F	Unknown	16No17Bw
John	10	M	Unknown	16No17Bw
James	3	M	Child	16No17Bw
Robert	.00	M	Infant	16No17Bw
CLARK, David-C.	30	M	Unknown	16No17Bw
HACKET, Eliza	63	F	Unknown	16No17Bw
William	37	M	Unknown	16No17Bw
Ann	26	F	Unknown	16No17Bw
Jane	23	F	Unknown	16No17Bw
Eliza	21	F	Unknown	16No17Bw
HIGGINBOTTOM, Fanny	20	F	Unknown	16No17Bw
FULTON, Thos.	30	M	Unknown	16No17Bw
DUFFIN, William	20	M	Unknown	16No17Bw
CARNS, William	35	M	Unknown	16No17Bw
CAMBELL, George	30	M	Unknown	16No17Bw
Jane	20	F	Unknown	16No17Bw
Daniel	.00	M	Infant	16No17Bw
MILLER, William	35	M	Unknown	16No17Bw
ALEXANDER, George	19	M	Unknown	16No17Bw
COWAN, William	19	M	Unknown	16No17Bw
BATHURST, William	22	M	Unknown	16No17Bw
PREBLE, Eliza	18	F	Unknown	16No17Bw
SERVICE, John	25	M	Unknown	16No17Bw
HOUSTON, Alexander	26	M	Unknown	16No17Bw
THORNTON, Jane	25	F	Unknown	16No17Bw
CARSON, Mary	50	F	Unknown	16No17Bw
Robert	21	M	Unknown	16No17Bw
GILLESPIE, Susanna	17	F	Unknown	16No17Bw
MCCRICKARD, Sarah	21	F	Unknown	16No17Bw
RORKE, John	20	M	Unknown	16No17Bw
LAVERTY, Barnard	20	M	Unknown	16No17Bw
Catharine	25	F	Unknown	16No17Bw
NEVIN, Margaret	17	F	Unknown	16No17Bw
EWANT, William	21	M	Unknown	16No17Bw

AMERICA 17 NOVEMBER 1849

From Liverpool

REDMOND, W.S.	32	M	Merchant	17No02Cg
LACKSON, John	45	M	Merchant	17No02Cg

CORA-LINN 19 NOVEMBER 1849

From Glasgow

NAMES OF PASSENGERS	AGE	SEX	OCCUPATIONS	DATE PORT SHIP
MORRIS, Philip	23	M	Laborer	19No21Cj
DIVINN, John	21	M	Laborer	19No21Cj
MCCLUSKY, Patrick	35	M	Laborer	19No21Cj
MOONEY, Cathrne.	50	F	Unknown	19No21Cj
Nancy	20	F	Unknown	19No21Cj
Margaret	13	F	Unknown	19No21Cj
Patrick	12	M	Unknown	19No21Cj
Hugh	11	M	Unknown	19No21Cj
MOONEY, Catherine	4	F	Child	19No21Cj
CAPPRI, Peter	34	M	Laborer	19No21Cj
Bissy	35	F	Unknown	19No21Cj
COMMILAN, Michl.	22	M	Laborer	19No21Cj
CAPPRI, George	12	M	Laborer	19No21Cj
HARKINS, Edward	40	M	Laborer	19No21Cj
MYNER, William	25	M	Laborer	19No21Cj
CONOLY, Peter	20	M	Laborer	19No21Cj
CAINES, Patrick	20	M	Laborer	19No21Cj
LYNCH, James	20	M	Laborer	19No21Cj
COYLE, Hugh	25	M	Laborer	19No21Cj
CURRAN, Jane	23	F	Servant	19No21Cj
RATHAY, Mary	30	F	Unknown	19No21Cj
SLOANE, Hugh	29	M	Blacksmith	19No21Cj
GRATTAN, John	24	M	Blacksmith	19No21Cj
GALATIN, Thomas	26	M	Laborer	19No21Cj
ODONNEL, Peter	22	M	Laborer	19No21Cj
JOHNSTON, Wm.	24	M	Laborer	19No21Cj
Mary	45	F	Unknown	19No21Cj
Jane	15	F	Unknown	19No21Cj
CULLEN, Bridget	19	F	Servant	19No21Cj
FISHER, John	22	M	Blacksmith	19No21Cj
MCKAY, Isabella	24	F	Unknown	19No21Cj
Mary-Ann	17	F	Unknown	19No21Cj
Robt.	3	M	Child	19No21Cj
James	1	M	Child	19No21Cj
ISLES, Robert	38	M	Tailor	19No21Cj
MCKAY, William	15	M	Unknown	19No21Cj
MCKENSIE, Mary	36	F	Unknown	19No21Cj
BEALE, Ellen	21	F	Unknown	19No21Cj

MARIA 19 NOVEMBER 1849

From MALAGA, Gibraltar

MICKLE, U-Miss	28	F	None	19No20Cl

COLUMBUS 21 NOVEMBER 1849

From Liverpool

GELDEN, Anne	24	F	Unknown	21No02Ah
COLE, James-W.	20	M	Unknown	21No02Ah
BURKE, Edwd.	19	M	Unknown	21No02Ah
Bridget	11	F	Unknown	21No02Ah
WHITE, Pierce	21	M	Unknown	21No02Ah
SHEERAN, Catherine	26	F	Unknown	21No02Ah
KELLY, Owen	17	M	Unknown	21No02Ah
SHAUNESSY, Mary	18	F	Unknown	21No02Ah
FOHEY, Ellen	19	F	Unknown	21No02Ah
Patrick	11	M	Unknown	21No02Ah
DAWLON, John	19	M	Unknown	21No02Ah
MCKENNOT, Bridget	20	F	Unknown	21No02Ah
MOONEY, Jane	16	F	Unknown	21No02Ah
DONNLIS, Henry-W.	17	M	Unknown	21No02Ah
RYAN, Catherine	21	F	Unknown	21No02Ah
DOWLAN, Francis	21	M	Unknown	21No02Ah
Jules	19	M	Unknown	21No02Ah
MEEGAN, Hugh	19	M	Unknown	21No02Ah
PHILBORN, John	21	M	Unknown	21No02Ah
BELFORD, Joseph	17	M	Unknown	21No02Ah
MURRAY, Jane-M.	26	F	Unknown	21No02Ah
DUFFEY, Anne	22	F	Unknown	21No02Ah

NAMES OF PASSENGERS	AGE	SEX	OCCUPATIONS	DATE PORT SHIP
MCGUIRE, Ellen	18	F	Unknown	21No02Ah
MCGRUYON, Isabela	22	F	Unknown	21No02Ah
RODGERS, Dawson	24	M	Unknown	21No02Ah
DONALDSON, U-Mrs.	26	F	Unknown	21No02Ah
U	.00	U	Infant	21No02Ah
Robert	6	M	Child	21No02Ah
AULD, Jacob	00	M	Unknown	21No02Ah
RENSHAW, Ellen	00	F	Unknown	21No02Ah
STOREY, D.	00	U	Unknown	21No02Ah
FARRELY, Marg.	19	F	Unknown	21No02Ah
MCCOFFREY, Owen	29	M	Unknown	21No02Ah
MCCAFFREY, Hugh	27	M	Unknown	21No02Ah
William	27	M	Unknown	21No02Ah
U	.00	U	Infant	21No02Ah
LENAGHORE, Catherine	19	F	Unknown	21No02Ah
Elonor	17	F	Unknown	21No02Ah
CALLAGHAN, Mich	21	M	Unknown	21No02Ah
WYNNE, Robert	6	M	Child	21No02Ah
SULLIVAN, Ellen	19	F	Unknown	21No02Ah
Jeremiah	18	M	Unknown	21No02Ah
John	12	M	Unknown	21No02Ah
FITZPATRICK, Anne	00	F	Unknown	21No02Ah
ONEIL, John	00	M	Unknown	21No02Ah
FITZPATRICK, Thomas	00	M	Unknown	21No02Ah
MCELROY, Rose	40	F	Unknown	21No02Ah
U	.00	U	Infant	21No02Ah
Alice	3	F	Child	21No02Ah
STUGAL, Mich	19	M	Unknown	21No02Ah
Michl.	13	M	Unknown	21No02Ah
HYSEN, Bridget	11	F	Unknown	21No02Ah
MCNAMARRA, John	19	M	Unknown	21No02Ah
CONNELL, Patrick	26	M	Unknown	21No02Ah
Mary	34	F	Unknown	21No02Ah
John	32	M	Unknown	21No02Ah
COURNAY, Mary	19	F	Unknown	21No02Ah
DENAHOE, Thomas	24	M	Unknown	21No02Ah
Anne	20	F	Unknown	21No02Ah
SMYTH, Margt.	19	F	Unknown	21No02Ah
HEALY, Mary	17	F	Unknown	21No02Ah
MOHOER, Rose	21	F	Unknown	21No02Ah
Bridget	17	F	Unknown	21No02Ah
SHANNON, John	36	M	Unknown	21No02Ah
Peggy	34	F	Unknown	21No02Ah
Patrick	12	M	Unknown	21No02Ah
Peter	8	M	Child	21No02Ah
Bridgt.	11	F	Unknown	21No02Ah
Mary	9	F	Child	21No02Ah
John	4	M	Child	21No02Ah
Julie	12	F	Unknown	21No02Ah
MOGHANE, Fanny	19	F	Unknown	21No02Ah
MCALLEN, Owen	26	M	Unknown	21No02Ah
FOX, Catherine	13	F	Unknown	21No02Ah
KING, Mary	19	F	Unknown	21No02Ah
MCCANEL, Eliza	17	F	Unknown	21No02Ah
SIMPSON, Martha	20	F	Unknown	21No02Ah
RUSSELL, John	17	M	Unknown	21No02Ah
BROWN, Joseph	19	M	Unknown	21No02Ah
DONAHENY, Ellen	16	F	Unknown	21No02Ah
HARWEY, Margt.	14	F	Unknown	21No02Ah
MCCALE, Pat	18	M	Unknown	21No02Ah
LENOHAN, Mich	17	M	Unknown	21No02Ah
DAILY, Cath.	29	F	Unknown	21No02Ah
U	.00	U	Infant	21No02Ah
Malvin	7	M	Child	21No02Ah
Bryan	7	M	Child	21No02Ah
Julie	10	F	Unknown	21No02Ah
BARTY, Margt.W.	21	F	Unknown	21No02Ah
SHIELDS, Sophia	17	F	Unknown	21No02Ah
NEIL, Bridgt.	19	F	Unknown	21No02Ah
HARRIGAN, Mary	23	F	Unknown	21No02Ah
Mary-Anne	11	F	Unknown	21No02Ah
CAMPBELL, John	22	M	Unknown	21No02Ah
SMYTH, Anne	36	F	Unknown	21No02Ah
Patrick	37	M	Unknown	21No02Ah
Catherine	11	F	Unknown	21No02Ah
SMYTH, Anne	8	F	Child	21No02Ah
John	4	M	Child	21No02Ah
James	2	M	Child	21No02Ah
RILLEY, Mary	19	F	Unknown	21No02Ah
BRODY, Peter	22	M	Unknown	21No02Ah
Rose	20	F	Unknown	21No02Ah
John	12	M	Unknown	21No02Ah
FARRELL, Jerm.	26	M	Unknown	21No02Ah
COFFREY, Bridgt.	24	F	Unknown	21No02Ah
DONLON, Anne	26	F	Unknown	21No02Ah
Mary	18	F	Unknown	21No02Ah
Becky	17	F	Unknown	21No02Ah
DOYLE, Owen	17	M	Unknown	21No02Ah
SCOLLY, Bernard	60	M	Unknown	21No02Ah
MCKEON, Hugh	26	M	Unknown	21No02Ah
John	27	M	Unknown	21No02Ah
Timothy	20	M	Unknown	21No02Ah
Anne	13	F	Unknown	21No02Ah
Patrick	19	M	Unknown	21No02Ah
Catherine	6	F	Child	21No02Ah
Ellen	11	F	Unknown	21No02Ah
OBRIEN, Anne	30	F	Unknown	21No02Ah
Francis	9	M	Child	21No02Ah
Mary	11	F	Unknown	21No02Ah
Mary	26	F	Unknown	21No02Ah
Mary	20	F	Unknown	21No02Ah
James	11	M	Unknown	21No02Ah
Beddy	8	U	Child	21No02Ah
Jane	6	F	Child	21No02Ah
Christopher	3	M	Child	21No02Ah
SMYTH, Jane	22	F	Unknown	21No02Ah
U	.00	U	Infant	21No02Ah
John	5	M	Child	21No02Ah
James	4	M	Child	21No02Ah
NELSON, Margt.	16	F	Unknown	21No02Ah
YOUNG, Mary	29	F	Unknown	21No02Ah
Lucy	12	F	Unknown	21No02Ah
Margareth	10	F	Unknown	21No02Ah
William	8	M	Child	21No02Ah
WALKER, Catherine	29	F	Unknown	21No02Ah
U	.00	U	Infant	21No02Ah
REILEY, B.	26	U	Unknown	21No02Ah
MEEHAN, Margt.	30	F	Unknown	21No02Ah
U	.00	U	Infant	21No02Ah
KIERNAN, Biddy	20	F	Unknown	21No02Ah
HUGHES, Mary	19	F	Unknown	21No02Ah
RULEY, W.	30	U	Unknown	21No02Ah
U	.00	U	Infant	21No02Ah
Catherine	8	F	Child	21No02Ah
Anne	4	F	Child	21No02Ah
Patrick	2	M	Child	21No02Ah
MEEHAN, Mall.	19	U	Unknown	21No02Ah
FEEGAN, Mary	19	F	Unknown	21No02Ah
MONGHAN, Catherine	12	F	Unknown	21No02Ah
Richard	10	M	Unknown	21No02Ah
Bridget	7	F	Child	21No02Ah
MCKENNEY, John	26	M	Unknown	21No02Ah
GARVEY, John	21	M	Unknown	21No02Ah
CONWAY, Bridgt.	21	F	Unknown	21No02Ah
MCCAFFREY, John	20	M	Unknown	21No02Ah
Mary	17	F	Unknown	21No02Ah
KENEDY, Mich	18	M	Unknown	21No02Ah
MCHUGH, Bridgt.	16	F	Unknown	21No02Ah
Sarah	7	F	Child	21No02Ah
MURRAY, Catherine	9	F	Child	21No02Ah
HARAHON, Bridgt.	19	F	Unknown	21No02Ah
James	5	M	Child	21No02Ah
BATES, M.A.	26	U	Unknown	21No02Ah
U	.00	U	Infant	21No02Ah
U-Miss	13	F	Unknown	21No02Ah
John	8	M	Child	21No02Ah
CONNOR, Anne	19	F	Unknown	21No02Ah
BOLAND, Mich	21	M	Unknown	21No02Ah
MCQUADE, John	19	M	Unknown	21No02Ah
LAUREL, Mich.	27	M	Unknown	21No02Ah

NAMES OF PASSENGERS	AGE	SEX	OCCUPATIONS	DATE PORT SHIP
LAUREL, Catherine	21	F	Unknown	21No02Ah
Patrick	19	M	Unknown	21No02Ah
Bridgt.	12	F	Unknown	21No02Ah
Peter	24	M	Unknown	21No02Ah
HEIGHTON, Margt.	19	F	Unknown	21No02Ah
BATES, Benjamin	21	M	Unknown	21No02Ah
William	18	M	Unknown	21No02Ah
PIERSON, Sarah	23	F	Unknown	21No02Ah
HARRY, Elizabeth	30	F	Unknown	21No02Ah
U	.00	U	Infant	21No02Ah
PENDERGAST, Joseph	21	M	Unknown	21No02Ah
Anne	11	F	Unknown	21No02Ah
GARTLAND, Julia	17	F	Unknown	21No02Ah
HIGGINS, Nancy	19	F	Unknown	21No02Ah
Mary	21	F	Unknown	21No02Ah
U	.00	U	Infant	21No02Ah
OBRIEN, Hugh	19	M	Unknown	21No02Ah
FLEMMING, Bridgt.	22	F	Unknown	21No02Ah
FOX, Owen	21	M	Unknown	21No02Ah
Rose	20	F	Unknown	21No02Ah
Mary	19	F	Unknown	21No02Ah
James	18	M	Unknown	21No02Ah
KENNEY, Betsey	21	F	Unknown	21No02Ah
CONNOR, Julia	17	F	Unknown	21No02Ah
MOHERE, Sally	21	F	Unknown	21No02Ah
BROPHY, Mary	20	F	Unknown	21No02Ah
CASSEDY, Margt.	17	F	Unknown	21No02Ah
John	9	M	Child	21No02Ah
Mary	7	F	Child	21No02Ah
Anne	5	F	Child	21No02Ah
Bridgt.	2	F	Child	21No02Ah
DERMOTH, Eliza-W.	29	F	Unknown	21No02Ah
U	.00	U	Infant	21No02Ah
Margt.	9	F	Child	21No02Ah
John	5	M	Child	21No02Ah
MCNEIL, James	30	M	Unknown	21No02Ah
DURIN, Cathr.	26	F	Unknown	21No02Ah
DWYER, Mary	27	F	Unknown	21No02Ah
COSHELL, Julia	27	F	Unknown	21No02Ah
HUGHES, Henry	29	M	Unknown	21No02Ah
Bridgt.	24	F	Unknown	21No02Ah
HAMILTON, Mary	19	F	Unknown	21No02Ah
CONNOR, U-Mrs.	27	F	Unknown	21No02Ah
Ryan	11	M	Unknown	21No02Ah
CONLON, Rose	18	F	Unknown	21No02Ah
WHITE, Anne	21	F	Unknown	21No02Ah
CARROLL, Thomas	21	M	Unknown	21No02Ah
MCDANIELS, Thomas	21	M	Unknown	21No02Ah
ARMSTRONG, Anne	27	F	Unknown	21No02Ah
William	5	M	Child	21No02Ah
John	3	M	Child	21No02Ah
COX, John	17	M	Unknown	21No02Ah
HURT, Patr.	27	M	Unknown	21No02Ah
TAGUE, Man.	17	M	Unknown	21No02Ah
ONEIL, M.	49	M	Unknown	21No02Ah
Patr.	19	M	Unknown	21No02Ah
William	13	M	Unknown	21No02Ah
Ellen	19	F	Unknown	21No02Ah
Catherine	17	F	Unknown	21No02Ah
Eliza	12	F	Unknown	21No02Ah
CLANCY, Cath.	36	F	Unknown	21No02Ah
U	.00	U	Infant	21No02Ah
RYAN, Cath.	17	F	Unknown	21No02Ah
HUGH, U-Mrs.	33	F	Unknown	21No02Ah
U	.00	U	Infant	21No02Ah
U	9	U	Child	21No02Ah
U	7	U	Child	21No02Ah
U	5	U	Child	21No02Ah
FITZWORTH, Thomas	18	M	Unknown	21No02Ah
FOX, Patrick	21	M	Unknown	21No02Ah
RICE, Ellen	27	F	Unknown	21No02Ah
HUNT, Ellen	21	F	Unknown	21No02Ah
STEPHENSON, Patrick	24	M	Unknown	21No02Ah
HUGHES, John	27	M	Unknown	21No02Ah
Mary	24	F	Unknown	21No02Ah
Died-At-Sea				
John	6	M	Child	21No02Ah
BURKE, John	21	M	Unknown	21No02Ah
QUINN, Barth.	29	M	Unknown	21No02Ah
RYAN, Margt.	24	F	Unknown	21No02Ah
U	.00	U	Infant	21No02Ah
HERRYTH, Patr.	24	M	Unknown	21No02Ah
NASH, Honor.	28	F	Unknown	21No02Ah
STROWLEY, Mich	20	M	Unknown	21No02Ah
HEALY, Nancy	22	F	Unknown	21No02Ah
GRACE, Beddy	40	U	Unknown	21No02Ah
Mary	6	F	Child	21No02Ah
Patr.	3	M	Child	21No02Ah
Biddy	7	F	Child	21No02Ah
FITZGERALD, James	30	M	Unknown	21No02Ah
HICKEY, Ellen	35	F	Unknown	21No02Ah
OBRIEN, Jerm.	35	M	Unknown	21No02Ah
George	31	M	Unknown	21No02Ah
U	.00	U	Infant	21No02Ah
Robert	9	M	Child	21No02Ah
Edward	12	M	Unknown	21No02Ah
George	6	M	Child	21No02Ah
Julia	11	F	Unknown	21No02Ah
LYNCH, John	20	M	Unknown	21No02Ah
COLEMAN, Honor	35	F	Unknown	21No02Ah
BURKE, John	22	M	Unknown	21No02Ah
Patr.	20	M	Unknown	21No02Ah
LYNCH, John	16	M	Unknown	21No02Ah
LURKEY, Mich.	18	M	Unknown	21No02Ah
HOGAN, Margt.	20	F	Unknown	21No02Ah
QUINN, Nancy	13	F	Unknown	21No02Ah
WALSH, Patr.	24	M	Unknown	21No02Ah
Lawrence	27	M	Unknown	21No02Ah
Honor	24	F	Unknown	21No02Ah
U	.00	U	Infant	21No02Ah
MCHUMMER, Patr.	22	M	Unknown	21No02Ah
MCGRATH, Patr.	35	M	Unknown	21No02Ah
DOUTHERTY, James	24	M	Unknown	21No02Ah
QUALON, Mary	22	F	Unknown	21No02Ah
MINAHAN, John	20	M	Unknown	21No02Ah
RILEY, Mary-A.	20	F	Unknown	21No02Ah
FARRELL, Ellen	20	F	Unknown	21No02Ah
BRICK, Mich	22	M	Unknown	21No02Ah
Mary	19	F	Unknown	21No02Ah
LEYTON, Honor	18	F	Unknown	21No02Ah
STICKEY, Mary	13	F	Unknown	21No02Ah
MCDONNELL, Rich	20	M	Unknown	21No02Ah
NAUGHTON, John	40	M	Unknown	21No02Ah
Biddy	35	F	Unknown	21No02Ah
Mary	12	F	Unknown	21No02Ah
CALEDGHORN, Patr.	18	M	Unknown	21No02Ah
RYAN, Mary	12	F	Unknown	21No02Ah
MCDONNELL, Thomas	30	M	Unknown	21No02Ah
Mary	25	F	Unknown	21No02Ah
Patr.	23	M	Unknown	21No02Ah
Thomas	8	M	Child	21No02Ah
James	7	M	Child	21No02Ah
DOERMER, John	36	M	Unknown	21No02Ah
SWIFT, Honor	32	F	Unknown	21No02Ah
MURRAY, Biddy	13	F	Unknown	21No02Ah
U	.00	U	Infant	21No02Ah
COPPRESS, Mich	25	M	Unknown	21No02Ah
LYNCH, Margt.	19	F	Unknown	21No02Ah
MORRAN, Biddy	20	F	Unknown	21No02Ah
SULLMAN, Mary	34	F	Unknown	21No02Ah
U	.00	U	Infant	21No02Ah
Mary	9	F	Child	21No02Ah
Honor	7	F	Child	21No02Ah
HOLMES, Ellen	14	F	Unknown	21No02Ah
Margaret	12	F	Unknown	21No02Ah
BARRELS, Patr.	24	M	Unknown	21No02Ah
SULLAVAN, Cath.	21	F	Unknown	21No02Ah
MEADE, Patr.	27	M	Unknown	21No02Ah
MULCARNE, Mich.	20	M	Unknown	21No02Ah

NAMES OF PASSENGERS	AGE	SEX	OCCUPATIONS	DATE PORT SHIP
HUMPRIES, Julia	40	F	Unknown	21No02Ah
U	.00	U	Infant	21No02Ah
John	3	M	Child	21No02Ah
OBRIEN, Patr.	14	M	Unknown	21No02Ah
BRODY, Anne	20	F	Unknown	21No02Ah
TUDD, U-Mrs.	36	F	Unknown	21No02Ah
U	.00	U	Infant	21No02Ah
Joseph	6	M	Child	21No02Ah
Henry	4	M	Child	21No02Ah
VALERTY, Eliza	19	F	Unknown	21No02Ah
BREEN, Mary	4	F	Child	21No02Ah
REDNAGH, Roddy	20	M	Unknown	21No02Ah
Mary	24	F	Unknown	21No02Ah
MAIR, Anne	19	F	Unknown	21No02Ah
MCNEIL, Fanny	6	F	Child	21No02Ah
John	4	M	Child	21No02Ah
KNIGHT, Patr.	22	M	Unknown	21No02Ah
Edmond	20	M	Unknown	21No02Ah
Bridgt.	19	F	Unknown	21No02Ah
KENDRICK, Anne	24	F	Unknown	21No02Ah
WALSH, Mary	21	F	Unknown	21No02Ah
STANTON, John	29	M	Unknown	21No02Ah
SLYNN, John	21	M	Unknown	21No02Ah
COSEY, Belly	19	U	Unknown	21No02Ah
ROBERTS, U-Mrs.	22	F	Unknown	21No02Ah
STOTT, Mary	21	F	Unknown	21No02Ah
U	.00	U	Infant	21No02Ah
EDWARDS, Anne	24	F	Unknown	21No02Ah
BANTZ, Caroline	21	F	Unknown	21No02Ah
EDMONDSON, John	29	M	Unknown	21No02Ah
U-Mrs.	24	F	Unknown	21No02Ah
John	21	M	Unknown	21No02Ah
Thomas	19	M	Unknown	21No02Ah
Joseph	10	M	Unknown	21No02Ah
HODGESON, Joseph	22	M	Unknown	21No02Ah
CALLONER, James	21	M	Unknown	21No02Ah
OCONNOR, John	19	M	Unknown	21No02Ah
OBRIEN, Bridgt.	12	F	Unknown	21No02Ah
FLOOD, Thomas	19	M	Unknown	21No02Ah
Margt.	6	F	Child	21No02Ah
BRADY, Bridgt.	12	F	Unknown	21No02Ah
MONTGOMERY, Cate	27	F	Unknown	21No02Ah
RENNAN, Mary	19	F	Unknown	21No02Ah
CARTY, Owen	21	M	Unknown	21No02Ah
HACKET, Ellen	17	F	Unknown	21No02Ah
KANE, Catherine	29	F	Unknown	21No02Ah
LITHERSTEN, Anne	17	F	Unknown	21No02Ah
KELLY, John	24	M	Unknown	21No02Ah
MCGREY, Hugh	20	M	Unknown	21No02Ah
JULIAN, Thomas	21	M	Unknown	21No02Ah
MCKENNA, Mich	16	M	Unknown	21No02Ah
FITZPATRICK, Mary	20	F	Unknown	21No02Ah
QUILANN, Mary	20	F	Unknown	21No02Ah
MCKENNA, Mary	24	F	Unknown	21No02Ah
CULLENAY, Rose	21	F	Unknown	21No02Ah
RILEY, Catherin	27	F	Unknown	21No02Ah
Mary	4	F	Child	21No02Ah
Ellen	20	F	Unknown	21No02Ah
FITZPATRICK, Honor	00	F	Unknown	21No02Ah
JORDAN, Edward	21	M	Unknown	21No02Ah
MORE, Ellen	21	F	Unknown	21No02Ah
John	27	M	Unknown	21No02Ah
LAUGHT, Cathr.W.	19	F	Unknown	21No02Ah
MARTIN, William	21	M	Unknown	21No02Ah
BOWMAN, George	27	M	Unknown	21No02Ah
DOYLE, James	27	M	Unknown	21No02Ah
Thomas	21	M	Unknown	21No02Ah
Thomas	19	M	Unknown	21No02Ah
Julie	17	F	Unknown	21No02Ah
RILEY, Peter	19	M	Unknown	21No02Ah
FOX, Mary	20	F	Unknown	21No02Ah
OBRIEN, Margt.	26	F	Unknown	21No02Ah
Mary	12	F	Unknown	21No02Ah
Martha	6	F	Child	21No02Ah
HENSTON, George	20	M	Unknown	21No02Ah

NAMES OF PASSENGERS	AGE	SEX	OCCUPATIONS	DATE PORT SHIP
MAROON, Francis	19	M	Unknown	21No02Ah
Mary	20	F	Unknown	21No02Ah
Anne	21	F	Unknown	21No02Ah
Catherine	16	F	Unknown	21No02Ah
REDEOR, Alice	19	F	Unknown	21No02Ah
COUNNON, Ellen	20	F	Unknown	21No02Ah
MORGAN, U-Mrs.	24	F	Unknown	21No02Ah
HARMON, Marg.	7	F	Child	21No02Ah
GANNON, U-Mrs.	27	F	Unknown	21No02Ah
U	.00	U	Infant	21No02Ah
SAWLOR, Anne	17	F	Unknown	21No02Ah
FLEET, U-Mrs.	00	F	Unknown	21No02Ah
Susan	00	F	Unknown	21No02Ah
OLANDY, Robt.Gray	00	M	Servant	21No02Ah
BEATY, Andrew	00	M	Unknown	21No02Ah
LEWIS, M.	00	M	Clergyman	21No02Ah
PERRY, U-Miss	00	F	Unknown	21No02Ah
KANELS, Peter-Anth.	00	M	Unknown	21No02Ah
PATCHELL, John	00	M	Unknown	21No02Ah
LARRAGHAN, Mich	00	M	Unknown	21No02Ah
HUGHES, Margt.	00	F	Unknown	21No02Ah
Died-At-Sea				
SULLIVAN, Mary	00	F	Unknown	21No02Ah
Died-At-Sea				
DONDON, Ely	00	U	Unknown	21No02Ah
Died-At-Sea				
Cath.	00	F	Unknown	21No02Ah
Died-At-Sea				
HAROE, James-D.	19	M	Unknown	21No02Ah

WM.H.HARBECK 26 NOVEMBER 1849

From Liverpool

NAMES OF PASSENGERS	AGE	SEX	OCCUPATIONS	DATE PORT SHIP
BOOTH, Sarah	23	F	Unknown	26No02Co
James	5	M	Child	26No02Co
Mary-Ann	3	F	Child	26No02Co
Emerelda	.00	F	Infant	26No02Co
NAYLOR, Elizabeth	25	F	Unknown	26No02Co
James	6	M	Child	26No02Co
Mary	4	F	Child	26No02Co
John	3	M	Child	26No02Co
Sarah-Ann	1	F	Child	26No02Co
TOOLE, Mary	20	F	Unknown	26No02Co
Mary	6	F	Child	26No02Co
Patrick	4	M	Child	26No02Co
ASPINNALL, Robt.	72	M	Unknown	26No02Co
Alice	67	F	Unknown	26No02Co
Barnabas	17	M	Unknown	26No02Co
WATERHOURE, Ellen	23	F	Unknown	26No02Co
Sarah	3	F	Child	26No02Co
John	2	M	Child	26No02Co
HACKETT, James	30	M	Unknown	26No02Co
CLAREBUT, Gaiuis	22	M	Unknown	26No02Co
MURRAY, John	22	M	Unknown	26No02Co
KELLY, Ann	22	F	Unknown	26No02Co
FURY, Mark	25	M	Unknown	26No02Co
MORTON, Wm.	23	M	Unknown	26No02Co
LEDDY, Mary	40	F	Unknown	26No02Co
Mary	12	F	Unknown	26No02Co
Thomas	8	M	Child	26No02Co
GABAREN, Margt.	19	F	Unknown	26No02Co
REILLY, Bridgt.	12	F	Unknown	26No02Co
FERAN, Samuel	18	M	Unknown	26No02Co
George	13	M	Unknown	26No02Co
Elizabeth	40	F	Unknown	26No02Co
CASHIN, Michl.	29	M	Unknown	26No02Co
HYNES, Wm.	28	M	Unknown	26No02Co
COONAN, John	24	M	Unknown	26No02Co

NAMES OF PASSENGERS	AGE	SEX	OCCUPATIONS	DATE PORT SHIP
KENEDY, Ellen	21	F	Unknown	26No02Co
Bridget	25	F	Unknown	26No02Co
SCULLY, Ellen	21	F	Unknown	26No02Co
LENNON, Patk.	20	M	Unknown	26No02Co
Rose	23	F	Unknown	26No02Co
REILLY, Rose	22	F	Unknown	26No02Co
CARELTTON, Cath.	25	F	Unknown	26No02Co
HOLLAND, Sarah	20	F	Unknown	26No02Co
Mary	18	F	Unknown	26No02Co
DUNN, Hannah	20	F	Unknown	26No02Co
MULHALL, John	30	M	Unknown	26No02Co
FINN, Michl.	36	M	Unknown	26No02Co
ROGERS, George	56	M	Unknown	26No02Co
Mary	25	F	Unknown	26No02Co
Sarah	21	F	Unknown	26No02Co
Robt.	19	M	Unknown	26No02Co
MURPHY, Patt	22	M	Unknown	26No02Co
TYE, Patk.	24	M	Unknown	26No02Co
HOGGINSON, Eliza	19	F	Unknown	26No02Co
ANDELL, John	34	M	Unknown	26No02Co
Eliza	35	F	Unknown	26No02Co
Martha	9	F	Child	26No02Co
Christina	6	F	Child	26No02Co
Eliza	4	F	Child	26No02Co
Joseph	2	M	Child	26No02Co
James	.00	M	Infant	26No02Co
MARTIN, Robt.	21	M	Unknown	26No02Co
MOORE, Mary	18	F	Unknown	26No02Co
MAHARDY, Samuel	30	M	Unknown	26No02Co
U-Mrs.	22	F	Unknown	26No02Co
Mary-Jane	1	F	Child	26No02Co
MCKENNA, Margt.	45	F	Unknown	26No02Co
HANLON, James	25	M	Unknown	26No02Co
DELANY, John	60	M	Unknown	26No02Co
TULLY, Mary	30	F	Unknown	26No02Co
Patk.	13	M	Unknown	26No02Co
REILLY, Margt.	30	F	Unknown	26No02Co
Hugh	5	M	Child	26No02Co
WATSON, Matty	22	M	Unknown	26No02Co
POWER, Danl.	20	M	Unknown	26No02Co
EYRE, Edmund	23	M	Unknown	26No02Co
Mary	25	M	Unknown	26No02Co
SMITH, George	23	M	Unknown	26No02Co
WILSON, Wm.	24	M	Unknown	26No02Co
HART, Patk.	21	M	Unknown	26No02Co
GRADY, Mary	24	F	Unknown	26No02Co
QUIRK, Pat	18	M	Unknown	26No02Co
James	16	M	Unknown	26No02Co
Margaret	14	F	Unknown	26No02Co
COOP, Wm.	21	M	Unknown	26No02Co
Emma	21	F	Unknown	26No02Co
LUKE, Wm.	35	M	Unknown	26No02Co
Anna-Mrs.	33	F	Unknown	26No02Co
MARTIN, Ellen	40	F	Unknown	26No02Co
Patk.	18	M	Unknown	26No02Co
Wm.	12	M	Unknown	26No02Co
Biddy	10	F	Unknown	26No02Co
BRABAZIN, Edward	34	M	Unknown	26No02Co
Hannah	34	F	Unknown	26No02Co
SHAW, Benjamin	37	M	Unknown	26No02Co
REILLY, John	21	M	Unknown	26No02Co
COLLIER, Saml.	35	M	Unknown	26No02Co
GRAHAM, George	25	M	Unknown	26No02Co
WHITE, John	28	M	Unknown	26No02Co
GUINN, Ann	29	F	Unknown	26No02Co
SMITH, Joseph	27	M	Unknown	26No02Co
HOBBS, Wm.	25	M	Unknown	26No02Co
KELLY, Edward	35	M	Unknown	26No02Co
WHITE, Patk.	24	M	Unknown	26No02Co
SMIRE, Maria	35	F	Unknown	26No02Co
BLACK, Margt.	12	F	Unknown	26No02Co
Elizabeth	20	F	Unknown	26No02Co
ALLEN, Gabriel	24	M	Unknown	26No02Co
BARDSLEY, John	26	M	Unknown	26No02Co
GRIFFITHS, John	24	M	Unknown	26No02Co

NAMES OF PASSENGERS	AGE	SEX	OCCUPATIONS	DATE PORT SHIP
WALL, Joseph	27	M	Unknown	26No02Co
CALKEN, James	30	M	Unknown	26No02Co
USHER, James	30	M	Unknown	26No02Co
DILLON, Peter	30	M	Unknown	26No02Co
BOWDEN, Ann	20	F	Unknown	26No02Co
MCANALLY, Peter	13	M	Unknown	26No02Co
WHITE, Richd.	21	M	Unknown	26No02Co
MARTIN, John	22	M	Unknown	26No02Co
BLACKMORE, Joseph	19	M	Unknown	26No02Co
GORMAN, Gabr.	50	F	Unknown	26No02Co
MERRIOT, Robt.	35	M	Unknown	26No02Co
HAMAVAN, Frank	28	M	Unknown	26No02Co
DUNNE, Thomas	24	M	Unknown	26No02Co
Mary	15	F	Unknown	26No02Co
DWYER, John	24	M	Unknown	26No02Co
Ellen	30	F	Unknown	26No02Co
CLAYTON, John	50	M	Unknown	26No02Co
HORTOP, Wm.	36	M	Unknown	26No02Co
RICHARDSON, John	30	M	Unknown	26No02Co
LAKE, John	36	M	Unknown	26No02Co
Elizabeth	32	F	Unknown	26No02Co
Alfred	.00	M	Infant	26No02Co
PARRENDER, Lydia	16	F	Unknown	26No02Co
FAIRWEATHER, Wm.	33	M	Unknown	26No02Co
Mary	27	F	Unknown	26No02Co
Mary	50	F	Unknown	26No02Co
Samuel	50	M	Unknown	26No02Co
Anne	4	F	Child	26No02Co
NAYLOR, Benjamin	18	M	Unknown	26No02Co
COLEMAN, Michl.	32	M	Unknown	26No02Co
Anne-Mrs.	30	F	Unknown	26No02Co
John	5	M	Child	26No02Co
ROUFT, Joseph	27	M	Unknown	26No02Co
KOURER, Jacob	32	M	Unknown	26No02Co
Elize	30	F	Unknown	26No02Co
RICHARDS, Sarah	42	F	Unknown	26No02Co
Wm.	20	M	Unknown	26No02Co
Thomas	14	M	Unknown	26No02Co
Mary	11	F	Unknown	26No02Co
George	7	M	Child	26No02Co
Died-At-Sea				
GRADY, Lawrence	30	M	Unknown	26No02Co
Bridget	20	F	Unknown	26No02Co
MOLLOY, Thomas	16	M	Unknown	26No02Co
DIXEN, Michl.	20	M	Unknown	26No02Co
Mary	12	F	Unknown	26No02Co
MCQUADE, Owen	65	M	Unknown	26No02Co
Mary	60	F	Unknown	26No02Co
John	24	M	Unknown	26No02Co
GREENE, Joseph	27	M	Unknown	26No02Co
MCGOVERN, Bridget	21	F	Unknown	26No02Co
BARRETT, Richd.	30	M	Unknown	26No02Co
MCCARLTRY, Cath.	13	F	Unknown	26No02Co
MCHALL, Natty	20	F	Unknown	26No02Co
BROWNE, Honora	12	F	Unknown	26No02Co
SMITH, Andy	55	M	Unknown	26No02Co
OCONNELL, Elizabeth	17	F	Unknown	26No02Co
HART, Cormack	23	M	Unknown	26No02Co
COFFEE, Johann	12	F	Unknown	26No02Co
COWLEY, James	60	M	Unknown	26No02Co
Patrick	30	M	Unknown	26No02Co
PHILLIPS, Bridget	22	F	Unknown	26No02Co
FAINN, Mary	30	F	Unknown	26No02Co
Sarah	7	F	Child	26No02Co
John	3	M	Child	26No02Co
Patrick	.00	M	Infant	26No02Co
FLAHERTY, Patrick	28	M	Unknown	26No02Co
MURPHY, John	18	M	Unknown	26No02Co
Maria	16	F	Unknown	26No02Co
EDMISTIN, John	17	M	Unknown	26No02Co
Eliza	13	F	Unknown	26No02Co
Charlotte	9	F	Child	26No02Co
James	6	M	Child	26No02Co
Mary-Anne	3	F	Child	26No02Co
HENRY, Charlotte	17	F	Unknown	26No02Co

NAMES OF PASSENGERS	AGE	SEX	OCCUPATIONS	DATE PORT SHIP
BREE, Mary	40	F	Unknown	26No02Co
WHITE, Ellen	25	F	Unknown	26No02Co
MCCARTHY, Cath.	20	F	Unknown	26No02Co
WOOD, Owen	55	M	Unknown	26No02Co
Cath.	17	F	Unknown	26No02Co
LEE, Bridget	25	F	Unknown	26No02Co
Ann-Jane	.00	F	Infant	26No02Co
FARRELL, Stephen	21	M	Unknown	26No02Co
KEARNS, Thomas	21	M	Unknown	26No02Co
CONNOLLY, Anne	30	F	Unknown	26No02Co
FARRELL, Ellen	18	F	Unknown	26No02Co
WARD, Cath.	11	F	Unknown	26No02Co
RYAN, Denis	20	M	Unknown	26No02Co
WOOD, George	28	M	Unknown	26No02Co
JACKSON, Joseph	38	M	Unknown	26No02Co
QUINN, Rich.	45	M	Unknown	26No02Co
Wm.	55	M	Unknown	26No02Co
LAWRENCE, Luke	49	M	Unknown	26No02Co
Mary	47	F	Unknown	26No02Co
Mary-Ann	14	F	Unknown	26No02Co
Susanna	12	F	Unknown	26No02Co
Sarah-Jane	16	F	Unknown	26No02Co
DORAN, John	30	M	Unknown	26No02Co
GILHOOLEY, Wm.	15	M	Unknown	26No02Co
Elizabeth	13	F	Unknown	26No02Co
REGAN, David	20	M	Unknown	26No02Co
HARNON, Michl.	23	M	Unknown	26No02Co
CONNERS, James	25	M	Unknown	26No02Co
OKEEFE, Danl.	35	M	Unknown	26No02Co
GRIFFIN, Mary	22	F	Unknown	26No02Co
DWYER, Hanah	20	F	Unknown	26No02Co
FOLEY, Mary	20	F	Unknown	26No02Co
SUGRUE, Julius	18	M	Unknown	26No02Co
COFFEY, R.	23	M	Unknown	26No02Co
Daniel	30	M	Unknown	26No02Co
FOLEY, Patt	25	M	Unknown	26No02Co
CONNELL, Julia	26	F	Unknown	26No02Co
BARRY, Ellen	23	F	Unknown	26No02Co
MCAULIFFE, John	28	M	Unknown	26No02Co
SULLIVAN, Patt	17	M	Unknown	26No02Co
POWER, John	27	M	Unknown	26No02Co
MURPHY, Jerry	27	M	Unknown	26No02Co
MCAULIFFE, Mary	26	F	Unknown	26No02Co
BUCKLEY, Ellen	26	F	Unknown	26No02Co
HEALEY, Mary	18	F	Unknown	26No02Co
GOULD, Ulysses	25	M	Unknown	26No02Co
Margt.	22	F	Unknown	26No02Co
Robt.	.00	M	Infant	26No02Co
RIORDON, Danl.	26	M	Unknown	26No02Co
MACK, Wm.	30	M	Unknown	26No02Co
Thomas	23	M	Unknown	26No02Co
Bridget	22	F	Unknown	26No02Co
OCONNELL, Danl.	27	M	Unknown	26No02Co
WED, John	30	M	Unknown	26No02Co
Nelly	30	F	Unknown	26No02Co
Mary	30	F	Unknown	26No02Co
WALSH, Michl.	23	M	Unknown	26No02Co
Mary	30	F	Unknown	26No02Co
Kate	2	F	Child	26No02Co
COUGHLAN, Jade	23	M	Unknown	26No02Co
CONNELL, James	22	M	Unknown	26No02Co
Michl.	20	M	Unknown	26No02Co
SWEENEY, Mary	20	F	Unknown	26No02Co
DUNCAN, John	35	M	Unknown	26No02Co
Wm.	54	M	Unknown	26No02Co
GREENE, Edmund	40	M	Unknown	26No02Co
DONOVAN, Mary	53	F	Unknown	26No02Co
CASEY, Margt.	21	F	Unknown	26No02Co
COLTER, Mary	22	F	Unknown	26No02Co
LUDDY, Thomas	25	M	Unknown	26No02Co
ODONNELL, Mary	25	F	Unknown	26No02Co
BARRY, Michl.	30	M	Unknown	26No02Co
Mary	20	F	Unknown	26No02Co
MURPHY, Michl.	20	M	Unknown	26No02Co
COLEMAN, George	25	M	Unknown	26No02Co

NAMES OF PASSENGERS	AGE	SEX	OCCUPATIONS	DATE PORT SHIP
MAHONEY, John	15	M	Unknown	26No02Co
BUCKLEY, Honora	15	F	Unknown	26No02Co
NEENAN, Ellen	19	F	Unknown	26No02Co
HALLERY, John	35	M	Unknown	26No02Co
Mary	35	F	Unknown	26No02Co
Patrick	9	M	Child	26No02Co
DOWNEY, Honora	22	F	Unknown	26No02Co
MURPHY, Edmond	30	M	Unknown	26No02Co
Honora	20	F	Unknown	26No02Co
GAVAN, John	21	M	Unknown	26No02Co
GALLAHER, Edmond	23	M	Unknown	26No02Co
FARRELLY, Lawrence	28	M	Unknown	26No02Co
Rosina	25	F	Unknown	26No02Co
CARR, James	32	M	Unknown	26No02Co
OBRIEN, Thomas	26	M	Unknown	26No02Co
RYAN, Patk.	30	M	Unknown	26No02Co
CLEARY, Martha	22	F	Unknown	26No02Co
KELDEA, Cath.	28	F	Unknown	26No02Co
Michl.	3	M	Child	26No02Co
COMERFORD, Michl.	25	M	Unknown	26No02Co
BYRNE, John	22	M	Unknown	26No02Co
PENDER, Alice	24	F	Unknown	26No02Co
TIERNEY, Bridget	12	F	Unknown	26No02Co
RYAN, Lawrence	30	M	Unknown	26No02Co
DOYLE, Patk.	25	M	Unknown	26No02Co
ANGLAM, Cath.	20	F	Unknown	26No02Co
Ellen	18	F	Unknown	26No02Co
MCNAMARA, Thos.	12	M	Unknown	26No02Co
Mary	26	F	Unknown	26No02Co
BOURKE, Hannah	40	F	Unknown	26No02Co
John	21	M	Unknown	26No02Co
Thomas	18	M	Unknown	26No02Co
Eliza	15	F	Unknown	26No02Co
Mary-Anne	13	F	Unknown	26No02Co
Cath.	9	F	Child	26No02Co
Hannah	9	F	Child	26No02Co
MAYNE, Richd.	27	M	Unknown	26No02Co
HAYES, Wm.	27	M	Unknown	26No02Co
WALSH, W.	42	M	Laborer	26No02Co
Cath.	35	F	Unknown	26No02Co
Patk.	13	M	Unknown	26No02Co
Edmond	11	M	Unknown	26No02Co
John	9	M	Child	26No02Co
Bridget	4	F	Child	26No02Co
Cath.	16	F	Unknown	26No02Co
Margt.	16	F	Unknown	26No02Co
Margt.	20	F	Unknown	26No02Co
BOURKE, Jeoffry	20	M	Unknown	26No02Co
HOURICAN, James	58	M	Unknown	26No02Co
Mary	58	F	Unknown	26No02Co
Mary	35	F	Unknown	26No02Co
Michl.	4	M	Child	26No02Co
WINNERS, Cath.	60	F	Unknown	26No02Co
NEELIGAN, Ellen	15	F	Unknown	26No02Co
PHILLIPS, Margt.	30	F	Unknown	26No02Co
Alexander	10	M	Unknown	26No02Co
John	8	M	Child	26No02Co
RYAN, Ellen	21	F	Unknown	26No02Co
Eliza	25	F	Unknown	26No02Co
VAUGHAN, Mary	20	F	Unknown	26No02Co
Patk.	.00	M	Infant	26No02Co
KELLY, Ellen	20	F	Unknown	26No02Co
LYNCH, Wm.	26	M	Unknown	26No02Co
John	22	M	Unknown	26No02Co
Alice	16	F	Unknown	26No02Co
James	15	M	Unknown	26No02Co
SPILLANE, Honora	34	F	Unknown	26No02Co
Denis	4	M	Child	26No02Co
LEO, Mary	30	F	Unknown	26No02Co
John	5	M	Child	26No02Co
CARROLL, Ellen	14	F	Unknown	26No02Co
MEEHAN, Cath.	9	F	Child	26No02Co
HAWKINS, Winifred	20	F	Unknown	26No02Co
Peter	5	M	Child	26No02Co
Stephen	3	M	Child	26No02Co

NAMES OF PASSENGERS	AGE	SEX	OCCUPATIONS	DATE PORT SHIP
COLEMAN, Michl.	11	M	Unknown	26No02Co
GANNON, Patk.	16	M	Unknown	26No02Co
NEILSON, Ann	16	F	Unknown	26No02Co
MURPHY, Margt.	18	F	Unknown	26No02Co
GRAY, Clement	35	M	Unknown	26No02Co
GARRIGAN, Michl.	13	M	Unknown	26No02Co
Ellen	11	F	Unknown	26No02Co
DUGGAN, Bridget	18	F	Unknown	26No02Co
Mary	20	F	Unknown	26No02Co
DONNELLY, Bridget	18	F	Unknown	26No02Co
DRISCOLL, James	30	M	Unknown	26No02Co

AMERICAN-EAGLE 26 NOVEMBER 1849

From London

NAMES OF PASSENGERS	AGE	SEX	OCCUPATIONS	DATE PORT SHIP
DONOVAN, Mary	30	F	Unknown	26No06Cl
Catherine	22	F	Unknown	26No06Cl
KELLY, Batt	22	M	Laborer	26No06Cl
Ellen	36	F	Unknown	26No06Cl
COLEMAN, John	38	M	Laborer	26No06Cl

CORSAIR 27 NOVEMBER 1849

From Bermuda

NAMES OF PASSENGERS	AGE	SEX	OCCUPATIONS	DATE PORT SHIP
ORMON, Joseph	30	M	Carpenter	27No22Ck
CHENEY, Charles	35	M	Mason	27No22Ck
EMBERSON, H.	45	M	Mason	27No22Ck
BISHOP, Richd.	30	M	Shoemaker	27No22Ck
EVERITT, John	25	M	Farmer	27No22Ck
EVANS, James-E.	19	M	Clerk	27No22Ck

JAVA 28 NOVEMBER 1849

From Liverpool

NAMES OF PASSENGERS	AGE	SEX	OCCUPATIONS	DATE PORT SHIP
GILBERT, Eliza	47	F	Servant	28No02Cm
HEWART, Wm.	50	M	Laborer	28No02Cm
GILBERT, M.	11	M	Laborer	28No02Cm
Henry	10	M	Laborer	28No02Cm
Frances	9	F	Child	28No02Cm
Benjamin	7	M	Child	28No02Cm
Margaret	6	F	Servant	28No02Cm
Ann	2	F	Servant	28No02Cm
CONNELL, Mary	30	F	Servant	28No02Cm
AHERN, Johanna	17	F	Servant	28No02Cm
TANGUENY, Ellen	21	F	Servant	28No02Cm
LONG, John	21	M	Laborer	28No02Cm
LYONS, Francis	21	M	Laborer	28No02Cm
MARTIN, Wm.S.	30	M	Laborer	28No02Cm
DAVIS, John	30	M	Laborer	28No02Cm
QUANLAN, Wm.	7	M	Child	28No02Cm
CORNEY, Ann	18	F	Servant	28No02Cm
OBRIEN, James	26	M	Laborer	28No02Cm
Mathe	26	F	Servant	28No02Cm
U	.00	U	Infant	28No02Cm

NAMES OF PASSENGERS	AGE	SEX	OCCUPATIONS	DATE PORT SHIP
PARK, John	14	M	Laborer	28No02Cm
Patrick	11	M	Laborer	28No02Cm
GALLAGHER, John	14	M	Laborer	28No02Cm
Sarah	16	F	Servant	28No02Cm
MCELROY, A.	35	M	Laborer	28No02Cm
DARCY, M.	00	M	Laborer	28No02Cm
FOX, G.W.	00	M	Laborer	28No02Cm
Ellen	00	F	Servant	28No02Cm
DANIEL, Henry	00	M	Laborer	28No02Cm
James	8	M	Child	28No02Cm
Susanne	6	F	Child	28No02Cm
JAMS, Charles	8	M	Child	28No02Cm
FOX, Ellen	4	F	Child	28No02Cm
Richd.	11	M	Laborer	28No02Cm
Edward	10	M	Laborer	28No02Cm
EDINGTIN, Jos.	30	M	Laborer	28No02Cm
LENNINGHAM, T.	30	M	Laborer	28No02Cm
HOY, T.	50	M	Laborer	28No02Cm
Clinshame	20	M	Laborer	28No02Cm
Jane	17	F	Servant	28No02Cm
James	5	M	Child	28No02Cm
HASTIE, Adam	24	M	Laborer	28No02Cm
RIER, Mary	22	F	Servant	28No02Cm
LOUGH, R.	25	M	Laborer	28No02Cm
DUFFY, C.	24	M	Laborer	28No02Cm
Bridg.	44	F	Servant	28No02Cm
Alice	16	F	Servant	28No02Cm
Susan	13	F	Servant	28No02Cm
Bridget	10	F	Servant	28No02Cm
Michl.	7	M	Child	28No02Cm
Eliza	5	F	Child	28No02Cm
Johanna	3	F	Child	28No02Cm
MCKENZIE, M.A.	16	F	Servant	28No02Cm
Daniel	14	M	Laborer	28No02Cm
ROSS, Johanna	21	F	Servant	28No02Cm
BUTLER, John	21	M	Laborer	28No02Cm
Ellen	11	F	Servant	28No02Cm
SCOTT, John	24	M	Laborer	28No02Cm
Eliza	27	F	Servant	28No02Cm
CUSKEY, Mich	22	M	Laborer	28No02Cm
HUMPHRY, Walter	60	M	Laborer	28No02Cm
Ann	54	F	Servant	28No02Cm
Elzth.	24	F	Servant	28No02Cm
HENRY, Wm.	22	M	Laborer	28No02Cm
Sampson	20	M	Laborer	28No02Cm
Frances	16	F	Servant	28No02Cm
Catherine	14	F	Servant	28No02Cm
GREEN, Jane	34	F	Servant	28No02Cm
James	8	M	Child	28No02Cm
Mary	4	F	Child	28No02Cm
DENTON, Edwd.	20	M	Laborer	28No02Cm
Ellen	18	F	Servant	28No02Cm
Mary	20	F	Servant	28No02Cm
MORLIN, Ann	30	F	Servant	28No02Cm
U	.00	U	Infant	28No02Cm
Ann	11	F	Servant	28No02Cm
Pat	8	M	Child	28No02Cm
Martha	6	F	Child	28No02Cm
Peter	4	M	Child	28No02Cm
HANAHAN, T.	21	M	Laborer	28No02Cm
ELLIS, Wm.	34	M	Laborer	28No02Cm
U-Mrs.	22	F	Lady	28No02Cm
Richard	3	M	Child	28No02Cm
WHELAN, R.	45	M	Laborer	28No02Cm
KEARRY, Jas.	30	M	Laborer	28No02Cm
SMITH, Ann	30	F	Servant	28No02Cm
Michl.	5	M	Child	28No02Cm
Ann	3	F	Child	28No02Cm
COYLE, Rose	50	F	Servant	28No02Cm
Mary	8	F	Child	28No02Cm
CULLEN, Michl.	35	M	Laborer	28No02Cm
Catherine	13	F	Servant	28No02Cm
PURSAIL, John	25	M	Laborer	28No02Cm
Harriet	23	F	Servant	28No02Cm
BERNE, Michl.	21	M	Laborer	28No02Cm

NAMES OF PASSENGERS	AGE	SEX	OCCUPATIONS	DATE PORT SHIP
GARTLAND, Julia	17	F	Servant	28No02Cm
COGAN, Mary	18	F	Servant	28No02Cm
Stephen	5	M	Child	28No02Cm
SWEENY, Pat	22	M	Laborer	28No02Cm
Ann	24	F	Servant	28No02Cm
John	12	M	Laborer	28No02Cm
KILNERRY, Ann	21	F	Servant	28No02Cm
QUIN, Tim	34	M	Laborer	28No02Cm
Chas.	10	M	Laborer	28No02Cm
HARRINGTON, Cm.	8	M	Child	28No02Cm
Mary	6	F	Child	28No02Cm
John	4	M	Child	28No02Cm
RODY, Betty	30	F	Servant	28No02Cm
U	.00	U	Infant	28No02Cm
MCGOVERN, John	34	M	Laborer	28No02Cm
Pat	6	M	Child	28No02Cm
MAHON, Mary	18	F	Servant	28No02Cm
DORAN, Pat	20	M	Laborer	28No02Cm
Bridget	20	F	Servant	28No02Cm
JENKINS, C.W.	24	M	Laborer	28No02Cm
Elizth.	20	F	Servant	28No02Cm
E.Geo.	24	F	Servant	28No02Cm
W.Geo.	18	F	Servant	28No02Cm
SMITH, Mary	18	F	Servant	28No02Cm
JENKINS, Mary	10	F	Servant	28No02Cm
Eliz.	8	F	Child	28No02Cm
Wm.	6	M	Child	28No02Cm
Cath.	4	F	Child	28No02Cm
James	2	F	Child	28No02Cm
Richard	2	M	Child	28No02Cm
PATERSON, John	25	M	Laborer	28No02Cm
CONDSONE, Jas.	25	M	Laborer	28No02Cm
Alice	25	F	Servant	28No02Cm
DUFFY, Frances	19	F	Servant	28No02Cm
Sarah	18	F	Servant	28No02Cm
WALTERS, Mary	23	F	Servant	28No02Cm
Maria	8	F	Child	28No02Cm
Joseph	4	M	Child	28No02Cm
RHODA, Mary	3	F	Child	28No02Cm
BURKE, John	22	M	Laborer	28No02Cm
QUINN, B.	23	M	Laborer	28No02Cm
BENNETT, Ed.	19	M	Laborer	28No02Cm
Honora	10	F	Servant	28No02Cm
CORRALL, Julia	30	F	Servant	28No02Cm
Margt.	20	F	Servant	28No02Cm
Patt	30	M	Laborer	28No02Cm
COFFEE, Michl.	19	M	Laborer	28No02Cm
MCCALEE, Cath.	18	F	Servant	28No02Cm
MCVIGO, John	19	F	Laborer	28No02Cm
Patt	10	F	Laborer	28No02Cm
CASSIDY, Mary	28	F	Servant	28No02Cm
Cath.	12	F	Servant	28No02Cm
WARDE, Mary	35	F	Servant	28No02Cm
Bridget	13	F	Servant	28No02Cm
Nancy	11	F	Servant	28No02Cm
Ann	9	F	Child	28No02Cm
Hugh	7	M	Child	28No02Cm
John	5	M	Child	28No02Cm
Rose	1	F	Child	28No02Cm
Eliza	16	F	Servant	28No02Cm
BYFORD, Peter	22	M	Laborer	28No02Cm
KENNEDY, Eliza	30	F	Servant	28No02Cm
Michl.	32	M	Laborer	28No02Cm
Mary	23	F	Servant	28No02Cm
MCCLIFF, M.	30	M	Laborer	28No02Cm
DUNGAN, Mary	35	F	Servant	28No02Cm
Luke	10	M	Laborer	28No02Cm
John	8	M	Child	28No02Cm
James	11	M	Laborer	28No02Cm
ROURKE, Cath.	20	F	Servant	28No02Cm
OBRIEN, Q.	17	M	Laborer	28No02Cm
HIGGINBOTTOM, E.	42	M	Laborer	28No02Cm
TAYLOR, M.	23	M	Laborer	28No02Cm
Bessy	20	F	Servant	28No02Cm
Ann	14	F	Servant	28No02Cm
TAYLOR, James	12	M	Laborer	28No02Cm
Ann	5	F	Child	28No02Cm
MARTINE, Nancy	37	F	Servant	28No02Cm
Mary-Ann	2	F	Child	28No02Cm
RANSON, Ann	35	F	Servant	28No02Cm
Edmd.	00	M	Laborer	28No02Cm
RALLIGAN, B.	20	M	Laborer	28No02Cm
RANSON, E.	37	F	Servant	28No02Cm
U	.00	U	Infant	28No02Cm
Wm.	11	M	Laborer	28No02Cm
BOURKE, Wm.	21	M	Laborer	28No02Cm
PEGGETT, E.	30	M	Laborer	28No02Cm
Mary	11	F	Servant	28No02Cm
WREN, Eliza	28	F	Servant	28No02Cm
CARNEY, Thomas	11	M	Laborer	28No02Cm
Eliza	8	F	Child	28No02Cm
WYNN, Wm.	22	M	Laborer	28No02Cm
GILBERT, U	.00	U	Infant	28No02Cm

JOSEPHINE 30 NOVEMBER 1849

From Belfast

NAMES OF PASSENGERS	AGE	SEX	OCCUPATIONS	DATE PORT SHIP
MAHOD, Robert	23	M	Farmer	30No17Cp
OHARE, Aliza	18	F	Servant	30No17Cp
MAGEE, William	19	M	Farmer	30No17Cp
MAULISCH, William	35	M	Farmer	30No17Cp
GILMORE, Sam	20	M	Farmer	30No17Cp
KENE, Joe	25	M	Farmer	30No17Cp
STRICKLAND, James	22	M	Farmer	30No17Cp
PATRICK, Mary	21	F	Servant	30No17Cp
MACDONALL, H.	35	M	Farmer	30No17Cp
COFFE, Rose	25	F	None	30No17Cp
KILIAN, Margaret	17	F	None	30No17Cp
MANELLEY, John	25	M	Farmer	30No17Cp
CONWAY, Ann	25	F	Servant	30No17Cp
Ann	.01	F	Infant	30No17Cp
CANEERE, James	32	M	Farmer	30No17Cp
Ann (W)	36	F	None	30No17Cp
CAMPBEL, Suley	40	F	None	30No17Cp
KINNEERE, Eliza	10	F	None	30No17Cp
Ellen	8	F	Child	30No17Cp
William	6	M	Child	30No17Cp
Margaret	2	F	Child	30No17Cp
Alexander	3	M	Child	30No17Cp
Sarah	.01	F	Infant	30No17Cp
DONNE, Mary	35	F	Seamstress	30No17Cp
ASHTON, W.	40	M	Farmer	30No17Cp
HUMPHREY, Eliza	18	F	Seamstress	30No17Cp
MCNELEY, Betty	40	F	Wife	30No17Cp
Ann-Jane	8	F	Child	30No17Cp
Henry	4	M	Child	30No17Cp
John	3	M	Child	30No17Cp
Died-At-Sea				
WILSON, W.	30	M	Seaman	30No17Cp
MCCONNEL, Alexander	18	M	Servant	30No17Cp
NANGEY, Sarah	22	F	Servant	30No17Cp
KILAND, Rob.	23	M	Farmer	30No17Cp
MURPHEY, Pat	58	M	Farmer	30No17Cp
Ellen (W)	54	F	None	30No17Cp
Ellen	13	F	None	30No17Cp
Elizabeth	11	F	None	30No17Cp
Nancy	9	F	Child	30No17Cp
Mary	7	F	Child	30No17Cp
GILESPIE, Andrew	25	M	Servant	30No17Cp
WILLEY, John	17	M	Servant	30No17Cp
U, Ann-Jane	50	F	Wife	30No17Cp
WICKS, Mary	36	F	Wife	30No17Cp
James	14	M	None	30No17Cp

NAMES OF PASSENGERS		AGE	SEX	OCCUPATIONS	DATE PORT SHIP
MORESON, Jane		35	F	Wife	30No17Cp
Mary		14	F	None	30No17Cp
Andrew		12	M	None	30No17Cp
Samuel		7	M	Child	30No17Cp
Isabella		5	F	Child	30No17Cp
William		3	M	Child	30No17Cp
Ann		.10	F	Infant	30No17Cp
WISH, James		27	M	Farmer	30No17Cp
MUSHGRAVE, Nancy		30	F	Seamstress	30No17Cp
HOLMS, James		25	M	Mechanic	30No17Cp
COATS, Robt.		34	M	Mechanic	30No17Cp
Rebeca	(W)	28	F	None	30No17Cp
Robt.		3	M	Child	30No17Cp
Sarah		.09	F	Infant	30No17Cp
MACOAVEY, James		25	M	Farmer	30No17Cp
Ellen	(W)	24	F	None	30No17Cp
Mary		.08	F	Infant	30No17Cp
Died-At-Sea					
STERRGIHE, John		22	M	Farmer	30No17Cp
CAMBEL, John		23	M	Farmer	30No17Cp
Pruden.	(W)	30	F	None	30No17Cp
Samuel		.07	M	Infant	30No17Cp
FINLEY, John		20	M	Farmer	30No17Cp
Mary	(W)	18	F	None	30No17Cp
KNIPE, Thomas		40	M	Farmer	30No17Cp
Sarah	(W)	38	F	None	30No17Cp
Sarah		14	F	None	30No17Cp
John		13	M	None	30No17Cp
Anne		10	F	None	30No17Cp
Mary		7	F	Child	30No17Cp
Thomas		4	M	Child	30No17Cp
OBRIEN, M.		40	F	Seamstress	30No17Cp
MCDONALD, Pat		40	M	Farmer	30No17Cp
Bessey		16	F	Servant	30No17Cp
John		13	M	Child	30No17Cp
MADILL, Wil.		18	M	Laborer	30No17Cp
MCGLIME, Mary		25	F	Servant	30No17Cp
John		.00	M	Infant	30No17Cp
KINGSBOROUGH, John		34	M	Teamster	30No17Cp
John		13	M	None	30No17Cp
Ben		6	M	Child	30No17Cp
Elizabeth		3	F	Child	30No17Cp
HAILIARD, Robt.		21	M	Laborer	30No17Cp
Henry		23	M	Laborer	30No17Cp
HEGEN, Margaret		20	F	Seamstress	30No17Cp
BOYD, Ann		20	F	Seamstress	30No17Cp
PATRICK, Mary		21	F	Seamstress	30No17Cp
BAHER, Jane		21	F	Seamstress	30No17Cp
WETTERSHEAD, W.		37	M	Farmer	30No17Cp
Bessey		.03	F	Infant	30No17Cp
ADAMS, Mary		40	F	Wife	30No17Cp
Charlot		17	F	Seamstress	30No17Cp
E.Jane		12	F	None	30No17Cp
Magt.		11	F	None	30No17Cp
Alsander		9	M	Child	30No17Cp
Mary		6	F	Child	30No17Cp
Isabella		4	F	Child	30No17Cp
BASETT, John		25	M	Farmer	30No17Cp
ROBERTS, Samuel		16	M	Farmer	30No17Cp
NELWOOD, Joseph		18	M	Servant	30No17Cp
HARVEY, Sarah		16	F	Servant	30No17Cp
Mary-Ann		18	F	Servant	30No17Cp
KILLEY, Mary		50	F	Wife	30No17Cp
GAREN, Bessey		40	F	Wife	30No17Cp
John		14	M	None	30No17Cp
Eliza		11	F	None	30No17Cp
Frances		6	F	Child	30No17Cp
Mary-Anne		4	F	Child	30No17Cp
Teresa		2	F	Child	30No17Cp
Pat		13	M	None	30No17Cp
Joseph		11	M	None	30No17Cp
PEARSON, John		60	M	Farmer	30No17Cp
MCCLOUNE, Margt.		44	F	Wife	30No17Cp
MCCORMICK, Eliza		22	F	Seamstress	30No17Cp
MCCANNEY, Bessey		22	F	Seamstress	30No17Cp

NAMES OF PASSENGERS		AGE	SEX	OCCUPATIONS	DATE PORT SHIP
HASTEY, J.		39	M	Servant	30No17Cp
CANICK, P.		25	F	Seamstress	30No17Cp
COLWORTH, John-C.		21	M	Servant	30No17Cp
ADAMS, Mary-Ann		34	F	Wife	30No17Cp
Jane		.01	F	Infant	30No17Cp
MURPHEY, John		20	M	Farmer	30No17Cp
Jane	(W)	20	F	None	30No17Cp
MCCRIGHT, Jane		18	F	Servant	30No17Cp
GALAGHER, James		23	M	Farmer	30No17Cp
COX, Robt.		25	M	Farmer	30No17Cp
Rachel	(W)	21	F	None	30No17Cp
SIMINGTON, Pat		13	M	None	30No17Cp
John		15	M	None	30No17Cp
WILSON, A.		19	M	Servant	30No17Cp
MCMULLIN, Cat.		30	F	Wife	30No17Cp
MCERLIN, Cat.		39	F	Wife	30No17Cp
John		14	M	None	30No17Cp
Peter		12	M	None	30No17Cp
Died-At-Sea					
Pat		10	M	None	30No17Cp
Rose		8	F	Child	30No17Cp
F.		4	M	Child	30No17Cp
Mary		6	F	Child	30No17Cp
Died-At-Sea					
Daniel		2	M	Child	30No17Cp
Died-At-Sea					
CONNER, Anne		36	F	Seamstress	30No17Cp
MCCORMICK, John		22	M	Farmer	30No17Cp
RURK, Lettey		17	F	Servant	30No17Cp
EMBISLEY, M.		20	F	Servant	30No17Cp
MCCANNE, Mich.		50	M	Farmer	30No17Cp
Susan		23	F	Servant	30No17Cp
Mary		21	F	Servant	30No17Cp
Magt.		19	F	Servant	30No17Cp
LAGAN, Pat		24	M	Farmer	30No17Cp
Mich.		21	M	Farmer	30No17Cp
MCSHANE, Wm.		22	M	Farmer	30No17Cp
DOWNING, Mary		50	F	Wife	30No17Cp
John		20	M	Servant	30No17Cp
Mary-Anne		15	F	None	30No17Cp
Catherine		13	F	None	30No17Cp
MCCONNELL, H.		25	M	Laborer	30No17Cp
MCKIESH, Ellen		18	F	Servant	30No17Cp
CONER, Andrew		45	M	Servant	30No17Cp
DYHSON, Mary		28	F	Servant	30No17Cp
KILING, Richd.		35	M	Farmer	30No17Cp
Charlot	(W)	35	F	None	30No17Cp
SHULE, Jane		30	F	Wife	30No17Cp
Rose		3	F	Child	30No17Cp
MCCORMICK, Agnes		21	F	Seamstress	30No17Cp
PILLAR, Alex.		40	M	Farmer	30No17Cp
MCCONEY, H.		26	M	Farmer	30No17Cp
SCOTT, Magt.		22	F	Servant	30No17Cp
Thomas		.01	M	Infant	30No17Cp
CARNER, Hugh		24	M	Farmer	30No17Cp
MAGEE, John		14	M	None	30No17Cp
William		12	M	None	30No17Cp
MULLIN, Margt.		18	F	None	30No17Cp
MCCLIUNE, Sarah		18	F	Servant	30No17Cp
WILSON, Susan		25	F	Servant	30No17Cp
MCCRANE, Rose		21	F	Servant	30No17Cp
CLARKE, Hamtn.		27	M	Farmer	30No17Cp
BLEACH, Magt.		27	F	Servant	30No17Cp
CLOSE, Wm.		8	M	Child	30No17Cp
NELSON, Susan		30	F	Schms	30No17Cp
LEAHY, John		75	M	Farmer	30No17Cp
Magt.	(W)	68	F	None	30No17Cp
Saml.		35	M	Farmer	30No17Cp
Rose	(W)	30	F	None	30No17Cp
Thomas		11	M	None	30No17Cp
Magt.		9	F	Child	30No17Cp
Sam.		3	M	Child	30No17Cp
Robt.		.06	M	Infant	30No17Cp
MCCRELEY, John		24	M	Farmer	30No17Cp
Mary	(W)	30	F	None	30No17Cp

NAMES OF PASSENGERS	AGE	SEX	OCCUPATIONS	DATE PORT SHIP
MCCRELEY, Sally	.04	F	Infant	30No17Cp
MACNEREY, John	20	M	Seaman	30No17Cp
EILER, Sam	18	M	Servant	30No17Cp
Wm.	21	M	Servant	30No17Cp
FAILES, Magt.	19	F	Servant	30No17Cp
MADISON, L.	20	M	Servant	30No17Cp
Campell	19	M	Servant	30No17Cp
HUNTER, F.	15	M	Farmer	30No17Cp
INGERAM, A.	20	M	Farmer	30No17Cp
FLEMING, Pat	21	M	Farmer	30No17Cp
MONEY, John	16	M	Farmer	30No17Cp
MCMINTRY, Robt.	24	M	Farmer	30No17Cp
MEEREY, F.	18	M	Sailor	30No17Cp
RICE, John	19	M	Sailor	30No17Cp
DAVIS, W.	30	M	Clerk	30No17Cp
MCCRIGHT, W.	19	M	Gentleman	30No17Cp
BOYD, H.C.	22	M	Gentleman	30No17Cp
C.	21	M	Gentleman	30No17Cp
STOWARD, U-Capt.	37	M	Unknown	30No17Cp
MURPHY, John	25	M	Unknown	30No17Cp
JOSSRON, James	39	M	Unknown	30No17Cp
HIGON, James	50	M	Unknown	30No17Cp
Mary	52	F	Unknown	30No17Cp

NO RECORD OF SHIP

From Glasgow

NAMES OF PASSENGERS	AGE	SEX	OCCUPATIONS	DATE PORT SHIP
QUIGLEY, Michael	18	M	Laborer	30No21
GORGAN, John	28	M	Laborer	30No21
Bridget	13	F	Unknown	30No21
CASGROVE, Barnaby	20	M	Laborer	30No21
CONNELLY, Betsey	20	F	Unknown	30No21
MULVY, Patric	20	M	Unknown	30No21
MCKENZIE, U-Miss	00	F	Unknown	30No21
CHURCHILL, Francis	00	F	Unknown	30No21
Lucy	00	F	Unknown	30No21
BUCKBURN, U-Miss	00	F	Unknown	30No21
WILSON, U-Mrs.	00	F	Unknown	30No21
BOYL, U-Mrs.	00	F	Unknown	30No21
U-Miss	00	F	Unknown	30No21
U	00	M	Unknown	30No21

MEDOMACK 01 DECEMBER 1849

From Liverpool

NAMES OF PASSENGERS	AGE	SEX	OCCUPATIONS	DATE PORT SHIP
TAYLOR, John	45	M	Laborer	01De02Cr
Mary	40	F	Unknown	01De02Cr
LATCHAN, Richd.	30	M	Unknown	01De02Cr
TURNER, Jas.	23	M	Unknown	01De02Cr
Elizh.	26	F	Unknown	01De02Cr
WHITTLE, Richd.	60	M	Unknown	01De02Cr
Ann	52	F	Unknown	01De02Cr
Died-At-Sea				
Mary-A.	9	F	Child	01De02Cr
HANNON, Pat	18	M	Unknown	01De02Cr
VIRGIN, Asmith	37	F	Unknown	01De02Cr
Died-At-Sea				
Joseph	13	M	Unknown	01De02Cr
Died-At-Sea				
Jane	10	F	Unknown	01De02Cr
Hannah	9	F	Child	01De02Cr

NAMES OF PASSENGERS	AGE	SEX	OCCUPATIONS	DATE PORT SHIP
VIRGIN, Susan	7	F	Child	01De02Cr
MAGALL, Elizh.	13	F	Unknown	01De02Cr
Died-At-Sea				
LYNCH, Ann	38	F	Unknown	01De02Cr
Died-At-Sea				
Mary	10	F	Unknown	01De02Cr
Died-At-Sea				
Ellen	7	F	Child	01De02Cr
Rose	3	F	Child	01De02Cr
Died-At-Sea				
James	6	M	Child	01De02Cr
SWEENEY, Bridget	30	F	Unknown	01De02Cr
Mary	12	F	Unknown	01De02Cr
Ellen	7	F	Child	01De02Cr
Pat	3	M	Child	01De02Cr
BATCHELOR, Joe	24	M	Unknown	01De02Cr
Peter	26	M	Unknown	01De02Cr
Died-At-Sea				
Ann	25	F	Unknown	01De02Cr
Peter	.00	M	Infant	01De02Cr
Abm.	28	M	Unknown	01De02Cr
PITHJEN, Chrisn.	35	M	Unknown	01De02Cr
Sarah	28	F	Unknown	01De02Cr
PARADISE, Jas.	26	M	Unknown	01De02Cr
JORDEN, Jas.	50	M	Unknown	01De02Cr
Died-At-Sea				
Esther	45	F	Unknown	01De02C
Esther	15	F	Unknown	01De02C
Jas.	5	M	Child	01De02C
Mary-A.	.00	F	Infant	01De02Cr
ARTHUR, Wm.	31	M	Unknown	01De02C
Died-At-Sea				
PEARSON, Wm.	22	M	Unknown	01De02C
KEVONS, Wm.	27	M	Unknown	01De02C
Elizh.	28	F	Unknown	01De02C
ATKINS, Jas.	30	M	Unknown	01De02C
Susan	28	F	Unknown	01De02C
Fanny	2	F	Child	01De02C
Isabella	.00	F	Infant	01De02C
HIRDSON, George	19	M	Unknown	01De02C
OXLEY, Jas.	22	M	Unknown	01De02C
WARREN, Jas.	36	M	Unknown	01De02C
Sarah	29	F	Unknown	01De02C
BARNWELL, Mary	15	F	Unknown	01De02C
ROBERTS, Robt.	30	M	Unknown	01De02C
WELSH, Michl.	25	M	Unknown	01De02C
Honora	22	F	Unknown	01De02C
SOMSVILLE, Wm.	30	M	Unknown	01De02C
MCCARTHY, John	24	M	Unknown	01De02C
Ellen	21	F	Unknown	01De02C
Michl.	20	M	Unknown	01De02C
KILLHAN, Johanna	20	F	Unknown	01De02C
LILLISH, Wm.	24	M	Unknown	01De02C
PURCELL, Kane	21	U	Unknown	01De02C
BAGGOTT, Corns.	30	M	Unknown	01De02C
BYRNE, Barny	25	M	Unknown	01De02C
SANDERSON, Robt.	45	M	Unknown	01De02C
Died-At-Sea				
Ellen	40	F	Unknown	01De02C
Eliza	9	F	Child	01De02C
THOMPSON, Thos.	40	M	Unknown	01De02C
HASSEN, John	52	M	Unknown	01De02C
Died-At-Sea				
BELL, Jane	39	F	Unknown	01De02C
Robt.	11	M	None	01De02C
Margt.	9	F	Child	01De02C
Sarah	4	F	Child	01De02C
BURNS, Michl.	27	M	Unknown	01De02C
CARTY, Jas.	25	M	Unknown	01De02C
COCHRANE, Mary	17	F	Unknown	01De02C
AHERN, Johanna	29	F	Unknown	01De02C
LEHAM, Ellen	12	F	Unknown	01De02C
C--DY, John	14	M	Unknown	01De02C
U, Mary	7	F	Child	01De02C
CRONNIN, Mary	60	F	Unknown	01De02C

NAMES OF PASSENGERS	AGE	SEX	OCCUPATIONS	DATE PORT SHIP
SHEEHAN, Corns.	30	M	Unknown	01De02Cr
LEHAN, Mary	12	F	Unknown	01De02Cr
CONNOR, Dennis	16	M	Unknown	01De02Cr
BRANNIN, Bridget	40	F	Unknown	01De02Cr
BARRETT, Margt.	30	F	Unknown	01De02Cr
Mary	4	F	Child	01De02Cr
Chrisn.	2	M	Child	01De02Cr
Died-At-Sea				
STOKES, Mary	19	F	Unknown	01De02Cr
Stephen	14	M	Unknown	01De02Cr
Wm.	12	M	Unknown	01De02Cr
MONAGHAN, Mary	24	F	Unknown	01De02Cr
Jane	14	F	Unknown	01De02Cr
GREEN, Betsy	28	F	Unknown	01De02Cr
WINS, Betsy	20	F	Unknown	01De02Cr
KING, Richd.	60	M	Unknown	01De02Cr
Mary	45	F	Unknown	01De02Cr
Richd.	12	M	Unknown	01De02Cr
NEHON, Henry	33	M	Unknown	01De02Cr
GRENNON, Jas.	24	M	Unknown	01De02Cr
PARKINSON, John	23	M	Unknown	01De02Cr
PILKINTON, Wm.	24	M	Unknown	01De02Cr
LEAHOM, Pat	21	M	Unknown	01De02Cr
CARTY, Teddy	25	M	Unknown	01De02Cr
CONNELL, Mary	50	F	Unknown	01De02Cr
Died-At-Sea				
Margt.	20	F	Unknown	01De02Cr
Died-At-Sea				
Cath.	18	F	Unknown	01De02Cr
Daniel	15	M	Unknown	01De02Cr
LYNCH, Pat	21	M	Unknown	01De02Cr
CONWAY, Pat	23	M	Unknown	01De02Cr
Cath.	22	F	Unknown	01De02Cr
CORBETT, Winifred	20	F	Unknown	01De02Cr
CLEARY, Ann	26	F	Unknown	01De02Cr
MCMAHA, Johanna	30	F	Unknown	01De02Cr
QUINLAN, Thos.	7	M	Child	01De02Cr
QUAILY, Bridget	24	F	Unknown	01De02Cr
HOGAN, Ann	25	F	Unknown	01De02Cr
SCANLAN, Jane	17	F	Unknown	01De02Cr
TOUHY, Margt.	25	F	Unknown	01De02Cr
HENNESSY, Dennis	25	M	Unknown	01De02Cr
JONES, Jas.	30	M	Unknown	01De02Cr
STACK, Michl.	30	M	Unknown	01De02Cr
CUNNINGHAM, Thos.	40	M	Unknown	01De02Cr
HOGAN, Thos.	12	M	Unknown	01De02Cr
MCNAMARA, Margt.	23	F	Unknown	01De02Cr
RODGERS, Mary	30	F	Unknown	01De02Cr
Andw.	11	M	Unknown	01De02Cr
Michl.	.00	M	Infant	01De02Cr
HICKEY, Cath.	15	F	Unknown	01De02Cr
CULLINAN, John	22	M	Unknown	01De02Cr
Cath.	20	F	Unknown	01De02Cr
LYNCH, Mary	22	F	Unknown	01De02Cr
BEHAN, Cath.	26	F	Unknown	01De02Cr
CONDON, John	22	M	Unknown	01De02Cr
CORBETT, Bridgt.	18	F	Unknown	01De02Cr
QUALLY, Mary	30	F	Unknown	01De02Cr
Died-At-Sea				
John	7	M	Child	01De02Cr
BURN, Richd.	30	M	Unknown	01De02Cr
MAHONY, Michl.	20	M	Unknown	01De02Cr
Ellen	18	F	Unknown	01De02Cr
ONEILL, Bridgt.	20	F	Unknown	01De02Cr
NEVILLE, Reddy	24	M	Unknown	01De02Cr
MCMAHON, Bridgt.	20	F	Unknown	01De02Cr
FLAHERTY, Cath.	30	F	Unknown	01De02Cr
Died-At-Sea				
Bridgt.	5	F	Child	01De02Cr
CONNING, Ellen	17	F	Unknown	01De02Cr
RUSSELL, Honora	20	F	Unknown	01De02Cr
HALLANAN, Susanna	19	F	Unknown	01De02Cr
MEHAN, Mary	18	F	Unknown	01De02Cr
LANNIN, Jas.	20	M	Unknown	01De02Cr
MCCANTY, Fanny	20	F	Unknown	01De02Cr

NAMES OF PASSENGERS	AGE	SEX	OCCUPATIONS	DATE PORT SHIP
HARDWICK, Wm.	30	M	Unknown	01De02Cr
MAHER, John	45	M	Unknown	01De02Cr
U (W)	40	F	Unknown	01De02Cr
Timothy	30	M	Unknown	01De02Cr
Bridgt.	7	F	Child	01De02Cr
Honora	6	F	Child	01De02Cr
Margt.	3	F	Child	01De02Cr
GRIMES, Margt.	18	F	Unknown	01De02Cr
DANIEL, Ellen	20	F	Unknown	01De02Cr
RYAN, Mary	25	F	Unknown	01De02Cr
MAHER, John	20	M	Unknown	01De02Cr
RYAN, Michl.	.00	M	Infant	01De02Cr
Died-At-Sea				
HENLAN, Chas.	19	M	Unknown	01De02Cr
HOLTRIP, Ludwig	20	M	Unknown	01De02Cr
CHRISTIE, Ruben-G.	20	M	Unknown	01De02Cr
CARNEY, Mary	25	F	Unknown	01De02Cr
LAWLERS, Richd.	20	M	Unknown	01De02Cr
Ann	19	F	Unknown	01De02Cr
BOLAND, Ann	19	F	Unknown	01De02Cr
MCAVOY, Mary	23	F	Unknown	01De02Cr
FITZPATRICK, Margt.	20	F	Unknown	01De02Cr
MCKENNA, John	25	M	Unknown	01De02Cr
HUGHES, Wm.	30	M	Unknown	01De02Cr
CLARKE, Mary	23	F	Unknown	01De02Cr
GOLDEN, Hannah	24	F	Unknown	01De02Cr
BAXTER, John	40	M	Unknown	01De02Cr
Margt.	10	F	Unknown	01De02Cr
Eliza	5	F	Child	01De02Cr
Pat	2	M	Child	01De02Cr
PLUNKETT, Thos.	20	M	Laborer	01De02Cr
HOY, Owen	25	M	Unknown	01De02Cr
Thos.	19	M	Unknown	01De02Cr
Ann	16	F	Unknown	01De02Cr
MCCABE, Mary	56	F	Unknown	01De02Cr
FITZGERALD, Armstatia	23	M	Unknown	01De02Cr
GUYNAN, Chas.	18	M	Unknown	01De02Cr
HINES, Cath.	30	F	Unknown	01De02Cr
CONLEY, Bridgt.	35	F	Unknown	01De02Cr
FITZPATRICK, Edwd.	19	M	Unknown	01De02Cr
COOKE, Bridgt.	16	F	Unknown	01De02Cr
Jas.	4	M	Child	01De02Cr
CARNEY, Mary	5	F	Child	01De02Cr
Cath.	3	F	Child	01De02Cr
John	.00	M	Infant	01De02Cr
Died-At-Sea				
DELANEY, Bridgt.	15	F	Unknown	01De02Cr
Died-At-Sea				
WHEATON, Mary-Quigley	30	F	Unknown	01De02Cr
Died-At-Sea				
ARNOLD, Robt.	70	M	Unknown	01De02Cr
Died-At-Sea				
REILLY, Maria	11	F	Unknown	01De02Cr
KENNY, Bridgt.	18	F	Unknown	01De02Cr
JORDON, Wommick	23	F	Unknown	01De02Cr
MCDERMOTT, Wommick	30	F	Unknown	01De02Cr
Cath.	26	F	Unknown	01De02Cr
Celia	20	F	Unknown	01De02Cr
NEALE, Mary	30	F	Unknown	01De02Cr
Alfred	.00	M	Infant	01De02Cr
TAYLOR, Job	24	M	Unknown	01De02Cr
Ann-Mrs.	48	F	Unknown	01De02Cr
Died-At-Sea				
Emely	14	F	Unknown	01De02Cr
COMBES, Mary	28	F	Unknown	01De02Cr
DUCK, Jane	22	F	Unknown	01De02Cr
Died-At-Sea				
TALLY, Wm.	12	M	Unknown	01De02Cr
Richd.	8	M	Child	01De02Cr
ALLISON, Wm.	32	M	Unknown	01De02Cr
Charlotte	35	F	Unknown	01De02Cr
Joseph	4	M	Child	01De02Cr
John	2	M	Child	01De02Cr
DAWSON, George	25	M	Unknown	01De02Cr

NAMES OF PASSENGERS	AGE	SEX	OCCUPATIONS	DATE PORT SHIP
Elizh.	26	F	Unknown	01De02Cr
Died-At-Sea				
DAWSON, Edwin	.00	M	Infant	01De02Cr
Died-At-Sea				
SYKES, Mark	26	M	Unknown	01De02Cr
Died-At-Sea				
KEEN, Martha	33	F	Unknown	01De02Cr
Mary-A.	10	F	Unknown	01De02Cr
Joseph	7	M	Child	01De02Cr
Fanny	5	F	Child	01De02Cr
SINNAN, Thos.	40	M	Unknown	01De02Cr
Mary	8	F	Child	01De02Cr
Pat	6	M	Child	01De02Cr
MCCORMICK, John	22	M	Unknown	01De02Cr
RODGERS, Ann	00	F	Unknown	01De02Cr
Edwd.	00	M	Unknown	01De02Cr
Henry	00	M	Unknown	01De02Cr
BUTLER, Sarah	00	F	Unknown	01De02Cr
OREILLY, Ann-P.	00	F	Unknown	01De02Cr
Hannah-Marie	00	F	Unknown	01De02Cr
DOOGAN, Mary	00	F	Unknown	01De02Cr

WATERLOO 03 DECEMBER 1849

From Liverpool

NAMES OF PASSENGERS	AGE	SEX	OCCUPATIONS	DATE PORT SHIP
MOLONY, W.F.Revd.	53	M	Unknown	03De02Cs
YOUNG, Wm.	19	M	Clerk	03De02Cs
SMYTH, Mary	26	F	None	03De02Cs
Mary-Ann	22	F	None	03De02Cs
HOGAN, Wm.	26	M	Farmer	03De02Cs
GYLES, Robt.Ross	27	M	Farmer	03De02Cs
BRANAGAN, John	42	M	Farmer	03De02Cs
JONES, Robert	55	M	Farmer	03De02Cs
NEWITT, William	24	M	Farmer	03De02Cs
MORRIS, Eliza	26	F	None	03De02Cs
HALEY, Ann	21	F	None	03De02Cs
HUNT, Pat	13	M	Laborer	03De02Cs
SPRING, Ann	24	F	None	03De02Cs
SHERIDAN, Richd.	24	M	Carpenter	03De02Cs
Ann	22	F	Unknown	03De02Cs
Pat	3	M	Child	03De02Cs
Margt.	.00	F	Infant	03De02Cs
SWAN, Thomas	34	M	Farmer	03De02Cs
Rose	30	F	Unknown	03De02Cs
Mary	16	F	Unknown	03De02Cs
Thos.	8	M	Child	03De02Cs
Eliza	6	F	Child	03De02Cs
MCGUINNESS, Margt.	25	F	None	03De02Cs
WALSH, Richd.	20	M	Clerk	03De02Cs
WILKINS, Marthw.	18	M	Laborer	03De02Cs
DUNN, Pat	20	M	Laborer	03De02Cs
BRADY, Terence	45	M	Farmer	03De02Cs
Ann	30	F	Unknown	03De02Cs
MCKEEVER, Bridget	21	F	None	03De02Cs
Judith	24	F	None	03De02Cs
MULLEN, Mary	25	F	None	03De02Cs
MCKENNA, Mary	30	F	None	03De02Cs
Kate	6	F	Child	03De02Cs
MEARA, Martin	21	M	Laborer	03De02Cs
KELLY, Wm.	22	M	Joiner	03De02Cs
Eliza	20	F	Unknown	03De02Cs
Ann	17	F	Unknown	03De02Cs
DELANY, Judy	17	F	Unknown	03De02Cs
MOORE, Mary	19	F	Unknown	03De02Cs
LACY, Mary	18	F	Unknown	03De02Cs
TOKER, Maria	17	F	Unknown	03De02Cs
KINSHELLA, Susan	20	F	Unknown	03De02Cs
FOLEY, John	27	M	Laborer	03De02Cs

NAMES OF PASSENGERS	AGE	SEX	OCCUPATIONS	DATE PORT SHIP
GRAY, Philip	20	M	Laborer	03De02Cs
DUFFY, John	60	M	Farmer	03De02Cs
Winifred	16	F	Unknown	03De02Cs
SHELLY, Paddy	12	M	Unknown	03De02Cs
BARRETT, Mary	26	F	None	03De02Cs
MULLIGAN, John	20	M	Laborer	03De02Cs
WALSH, Margt.	22	F	None	03De02Cs
CREEMY, Danl.	30	M	Farmer	03De02Cs
ROURKE, James	28	M	Farmer	03De02Cs
CREEMY, Margt.	55	F	None	03De02Cs
ROURKE, Ann	26	F	None	03De02Cs
Thos.	2	M	Child	03De02Cs
Mary	.00	F	Infant	03De02Cs
FULLEST, John	30	M	Saddler	03De02Cs
DONEGAN, Michl.	20	M	Laborer	03De02Cs
SWEENY, James	21	M	Laborer	03De02Cs
NANCY, Cathne.	23	F	None	03De02Cs
MOORE, Mary	20	F	None	03De02Cs
RYDER, Elizth.	20	F	None	03De02Cs
MULREY, Bridget	18	F	None	03De02Cs
LUBY, U-Mrs.	24	F	None	03De02Cs
Ann	.00	F	Infant	03De02Cs
MCDONNELL, Alexr.	30	M	Laborer	03De02Cs
MARKEY, James	37	M	Laborer	03De02Cs
PELLINGTON, Cathne.	18	F	Unknown	03De02Cs
LOONEY, Pat	23	M	Laborer	03De02Cs
CASEY, Judith	20	F	Unknown	03De02Cs
CREW, Margt.	30	F	Unknown	03De02Cs
BRIEN, John	35	M	Laborer	03De02Cs
QUIN, Sophia	25	F	None	03De02Cs
RAY, Joseph	20	M	Weaver	03De02Cs
MOORE, Saml.	21	M	Farmer	03De02Cs
MCENTER, James	16	M	None	03De02Cs
Mary	17	F	Unknown	03De02Cs
PARKIN, Mary	25	F	Unknown	03De02Cs
FITZGIBBONS, Wm.	18	M	Laborer	03De02Cs
RYAN, John	23	M	Laborer	03De02Cs
Pat	26	M	Laborer	03De02Cs
DUFFY, Sarah	15	F	Unknown	03De02Cs
Pat	11	M	Unknown	03De02Cs
ALLEN, Mary-Ann	30	F	None	03De02Cs
DWYER, John	25	M	Laborer	03De02Cs
ARMSTRONG, Henry	20	M	Clerk	03De02Cs
MCCLUNY, John	50	M	Laborer	03De02Cs
MCCANN, Cathn.	14	F	Unknown	03De02Cs
Pat	15	M	Unknown	03De02Cs
Mick	13	M	Unknown	03De02Cs
Elizth.	11	F	Unknown	03De02Cs
RYAN, Eliza	29	F	Unknown	03De02Cs
SHELTON, John	26	M	Laborer	03De02Cs
Cathne.	26	F	Unknown	03De02Cs
CUSHEN, Elizth.	22	F	Unknown	03De02Cs
Mary	24	F	Unknown	03De02Cs
QUIN, George	40	M	Dealer	03De02Cs
MCKEE, A.	19	M	Clerk	03De02Cs
HUGHES, John	14	M	Unknown	03De02Cs
ARCHER, Anty	23	F	Unknown	03De02Cs
Cathne.	22	F	Unknown	03De02Cs
KILBRIDE, John	25	M	Laborer	03De02Cs
PARLAN, Wm.	26	M	Shoemaker	03De02Cs
KILBRIDE, Michl.	22	M	Laborer	03De02Cs
BLAIR, John	20	M	Farmer	03De02Cs
MAHER, Wm.	22	M	Laborer	03De02Cs
Ann	18	F	Unknown	03De02Cs
CARLESON, James	50	M	Farmer	03De02Cs
Ellen	50	F	Unknown	03De02Cs
Eliza	23	F	Unknown	03De02Cs
James	19	M	Unknown	03De02Cs
John	16	M	Unknown	03De02Cs
Harriette	13	F	Unknown	03De02Cs
PRICE, Richd.	28	M	Farmer	03De02Cs
Mary	25	F	Unknown	03De02Cs
David	24	M	Farmer	03De02Cs
Chas.	4	M	Child	03De02Cs
James	3	M	Child	03De02Cs

NAMES OF PASSENGERS	AGE	SEX	OCCUPATIONS	DATE PORT SHIP
PRICE, David	.00	M	Infant	03De02Cs
MULEY, Mary	40	F	None	03De02Cs
Michl.	13	M	Unknown	03De02Cs
Cathne.	11	F	Unknown	03De02Cs
Mary	9	F	Child	03De02Cs
James	2	M	Child	03De02Cs
KERNEY, Bridget	26	F	None	03De02Cs
BAKER, John	21	M	Laborer	03De02Cs
MURTHA, Pat	13	M	Unknown	03De02Cs
BIGNAL, Ann	20	F	Unknown	03De02Cs
BRADDOCK, John	27	M	Laborer	03De02Cs
COSTELLO, Michl.	60	M	Laborer	03De02Cs
CAMPBELL, George	21	M	Laborer	03De02Cs
MORRISON, Margt.Jane	22	F	Unknown	03De02Cs
MADDEN, Wm.	25	M	Miller	03De02Cs
FARRELL, Cathn.	50	F	None	03De02Cs
Cathne.	17	F	Unknown	03De02Cs
HARRINGTON, Bridget	13	F	Unknown	03De02Cs
DALEY, Hugh	20	M	Farmer	03De02Cs
Bridget	18	F	None	03De02Cs
BROWN, Archd.	19	M	Cooper	03De02Cs
Mary	19	F	Unknown	03De02Cs
CUMMINS, Margt.	18	F	Unknown	03De02Cs
ANDERSON, Thos.	30	M	Farmer	03De02Cs
MCKEIG, Wm.	23	M	Weaver	03De02Cs
Wm.	.00	M	Infant	03De02Cs
DONELLAN, John	18	M	Servant	03De02Cs
SHEA, Martin	40	M	Butcher	03De02Cs
James	15	M	Unknown	03De02Cs
CONNERS, Cathne.	26	F	None	03De02Cs
CONDER, Wm.	14	M	Unknown	03De02Cs
James	11	M	Unknown	03De02Cs
Bridget	8	F	Child	03De02Cs
MCCANN, Henry	43	M	Laborer	03De02Cs
Mary	35	F	Unknown	03De02Cs
Isabella	5	F	Child	03De02Cs
OBRIEN, Michl.	24	M	Laborer	03De02Cs
James	20	M	Laborer	03De02Cs
Kennedy	22	M	Laborer	03De02Cs
COSTIGAN, Edwd.	26	M	Laborer	03De02Cs
Cathne.	20	F	Unknown	03De02Cs
RAMSEY, Mary-Ann	30	F	Unknown	03De02Cs
Ralph	.00	M	Infant	03De02Cs
KEEGAN, John	22	M	Laborer	03De02Cs
Ann	20	F	Unknown	03De02Cs
COLLINS, Pat	26	M	Laborer	03De02Cs
Cathne.	24	F	Unknown	03De02Cs
TOOMEY, Danl.	26	M	Laborer	03De02Cs
BRYAN, James	22	M	Laborer	03De02Cs
EGAN, Pat	27	M	Butcher	03De02Cs
HEALY, Pat	29	M	Dyer	03De02Cs
BOWLAN, Margt.	30	F	None	03De02Cs
DUNN, Ann	45	F	None	03De02Cs
Fanny	18	F	Unknown	03De02Cs
Andy	9	M	Child	03De02Cs
Kate	5	F	Child	03De02Cs
MCGINNIS, Edwd.	20	M	Unknown	03De02Cs
WILLS, John	20	M	Laborer	03De02Cs
RICE, Hugh	32	M	Farmer	03De02Cs
Rose	22	F	Unknown	03De02Cs
Mary	10	F	Unknown	03De02Cs
Pat	8	M	Child	03De02Cs
MCGUIN, James	32	M	Farmer	03De02Cs
Mary	32	F	Unknown	03De02Cs
CARROLL, Thos.	18	M	Shop Boy	03De02Cs
MCDONNELL, Judy	35	F	None	03De02Cs
Margt.	.00	F	Infant	03De02Cs
DUNCAN, Cathne.	26	F	Unknown	03De02Cs
Bernard	.00	M	Infant	03De02Cs
SMITH, Cathne.	12	F	Unknown	03De02Cs
TAMINY, Ellen	16	F	Unknown	03De02Cs
KELLY, Ann	18	F	Unknown	03De02Cs
MCMANUS, Sarah	16	F	Unknown	03De02Cs
LARNEY, John	36	M	Butcher	03De02Cs
Bridget	44	F	Unknown	03De02Cs

NAMES OF PASSENGERS	AGE	SEX	OCCUPATIONS	DATE PORT SHIP
LARNEY, John	16	M	Unknown	03De02Cs
CURRAN, John	25	M	Laborer	03De02Cs
REILLY, Patk.	20	M	Laborer	03De02Cs
Ann	24	F	Unknown	03De02Cs
CARR, John	20	M	Laborer	03De02Cs
BRICE, John	20	M	Laborer	03De02Cs
ROWLEY, Bridget	25	F	None	03De02Cs
LENARD, Luke	2	M	Laborer	03De02Cs
KENNEDY, Patk.	21	M	Blacksmith	03De02Cs
GALLAGHER, Sally	18	F	None	03De02Cs
KENNY, Margt.	18	F	Unknown	03De02Cs
Owney	16	M	Unknown	03De02Cs
FITZPATRICK, John	20	M	Laborer	03De02Cs
TELFORD, Susan	20	F	Unknown	03De02Cs
Jno.Hy.	.00	M	Infant	03De02Cs
DUFFY, Ellen	34	F	None	03De02Cs
BRACKENS, Biddy	50	F	None	03De02Cs
GOKEN, Mary	23	F	None	03De02Cs
COONEY, Mary	40	F	None	03De02Cs
RYAN, Thos.	22	M	Keeper	03De02Cs
BRADY, Patk.	24	M	Laborer	03De02Cs
GAYNEY, Ann	19	F	Unknown	03De02Cs
Susan	9	F	Child	03De02Cs
Michl.	7	M	Child	03De02Cs
HUTCHINSON, Michl.	40	M	Laborer	03De02Cs
BRADY, Maria	26	F	None	03De02Cs
John	.00	M	Infant	03De02Cs
FITZPATRICK, Pat	18	M	Unknown	03De02Cs
KELLY, Lawrence	12	M	Unknown	03De02Cs
KILLEN, John-S.	19	M	Unknown	03De02Cs
CORNELL, John	35	M	Laborer	03De02Cs
David	7	M	Child	03De02Cs
RYAN, Danl.	22	M	Laborer	03De02Cs
KELLY, Bridget	30	F	None	03De02Cs
WEBB, John	20	M	Unknown	03De02Cs
CARROLL, Thos.	35	M	Laborer	03De02Cs
Margt.	30	F	Unknown	03De02Cs
FEENEY, Margt.	23	F	Unknown	03De02Cs
DARRAGH, John	24	M	Trade Man	03De02Cs
TRACEY, Mary	26	F	None	03De02Cs
Thos.	.00	M	Infant	03De02Cs
CURTIN, Thos.	24	M	Laborer	03De02Cs
GRANGER, Frank	40	M	Laborer	03De02Cs
DILLON, Richd.	30	M	Farmer	03De02Cs
Margt.	35	F	Unknown	03De02Cs
HINCHEY, Mary	20	F	Unknown	03De02Cs
MCCABE, Pat	14	M	Unknown	03De02Cs
Ann	16	F	Unknown	03De02Cs
FEENEY, Martin	23	M	Laborer	03De02Cs
OBOYLE, Sarah	15	F	Unknown	03De02Cs
COMMONS, Cathne.	20	F	Unknown	03De02Cs
MCCAFFREY, Hannah	54	F	None	03De02Cs
Mary	23	F	Unknown	03De02Cs
Patrick	17	M	Unknown	03De02Cs
MCILROY, Ellen	22	F	Unknown	03De02Cs
Francis	10	M	Unknown	03De02Cs
James	12	M	Unknown	03De02Cs
Philip	3	M	Child	03De02Cs
ROGERS, Cathne.	27	F	None	03De02Cs
John	19	M	Unknown	03De02Cs
SEWAN, Mary	18	F	Unknown	03De02Cs
CUNNINGHAM, Mary	11	F	Unknown	03De02Cs
Margt.	9	F	Child	03De02Cs
James	4	M	Child	03De02Cs
DAGUAN, Bridget	20	F	Unknown	03De02Cs
GILLEN, Bridget	3	F	Child	03De02Cs
FLYNN, Bridget	19	F	Unknown	03De02Cs
Cathne.	17	F	Unknown	03De02Cs
TRELFORD, George	22	M	Laborer	03De02Cs
SAVAGE, Bernd.	22	M	Laborer	03De02Cs
Elizth.L.	19	F	Unknown	03De02Cs
BOARDMAN, Joseph	22	M	Laborer	03De02Cs
GILMEY, Cathne.	40	F	None	03De02Cs
Cathne.	10	F	Unknown	03De02Cs
Ellen	8	F	Child	03De02Cs

NAMES OF PASSENGERS	AGE	SEX	OCCUPATIONS	DATE PORT SHIP
GILMEY, Margt.	3	F	Child	03De02Cs
PARRAH, Susan	40	F	None	03De02Cs
Patrick	11	M	Unknown	03De02Cs
Thomas	8	M	Child	03De02Cs
Rose	34	F	Unknown	03De02Cs
Rose	.00	F	Infant	03De02Cs
CARRIHA, Rose	60	F	Unknown	03De02Cs
Elizth.	30	F	Unknown	03De02Cs
MALONEY, Edwd.	38	M	Laborer	03De02Cs
JONES, Margt.	28	F	Unknown	03De02Cs
KINDER, Fredk.	17	M	Unknown	03De02Cs
Wm.	13	M	Unknown	03De02Cs
Jane	11	F	Unknown	03De02Cs
Robt.	7	M	Child	03De02Cs
DICKSON, Willm.	26	M	Laborer	03De02Cs
MCCANE, Charlotte	40	F	None	03De02Cs
LYNCH, Mary	50	F	Unknown	03De02Cs
CURRY, Pate	35	M	Laborer	03De02Cs
RODGERS, Jno.	21	M	Laborer	03De02Cs
MCKEIGH, Hester	21	F	Unknown	03De02Cs
DUNN, Isabella	00	F	Unknown	03De02Cs
Rose	00	F	Unknown	03De02Cs
Shep---, Patk.	00	M	Unknown	03De02Cs
MCCORMICK, Christ.	18	M	Laborer	03De02Cs

L.Z. 03 DECEMBER 1849

From Liverpool

NAMES OF PASSENGERS	AGE	SEX	OCCUPATIONS	DATE PORT SHIP
CASSADY, Mary	30	F	Spinster	03De02Cu
Catharine	12	F	Spinster	03De02Cu
Phillipp	2	M	Child	03De02Cu
JUDGE, Ann	50	F	Lad	03De02Cu
Margt.	20	F	Lad	03De02Cu
Bessey	23	F	Lad	03De02Cu
Joseph	16	M	Laborer	03De02Cu
John	13	M	Laborer	03De02Cu
Nana	11	F	Laborer	03De02Cu
Charles	9	M	Child	03De02Cu
Henry	6	M	Child	03De02Cu
SULLIVAN, Mary	40	F	Bblk	03De02Cu
Rose	16	F	Bblk	03De02Cu
KELLEY, Niri	16	F	Bblk	03De02Cu
DOOLEY, Michael	24	M	Laborer	03De02Cu
TOBIN, Michael	25	M	Laborer	03De02Cu
KEATING, Thomas	24	M	Laborer	03De02Cu
BURKE, Pat	36	M	Laborer	03De02Cu
CONDOR, Michael	25	M	Laborer	03De02Cu
HAYES, Bridget	20	F	Servant	03De02Cu
RYAN, Mary	18	F	Servant	03De02Cu
CADDY, Ellen	25	F	Servant	03De02Cu
KELLEY, Thomas	30	M	Weaver	03De02Cu
Ellen	35	F	Weaver	03De02Cu
Mary	40	F	Weaver	03De02Cu
Died-At-Sea				
KERNE, Mary	7	F	Child	03De02Cu
TRAINOR, Bridget	25	F	Servant	03De02Cu
MORAN, Catharine	20	F	Servant	03De02Cu
MCCULLOCK, Magt.	18	F	Servant	03De02Cu
MCANULTY, James	18	M	Laborer	03De02Cu
MCKAY, Rose	18	F	Servant	03De02Cu
COLLONS, Magt.	21	F	Servant	03De02Cu
DAILY, Rosa	28	F	Servant	03De02Cu
Mary	24	F	Servant	03De02Cu
CALLAGAN, Michael	50	M	Laborer	03De02Cu
Michael	20	M	Laborer	03De02Cu
Mary	21	F	Servant	03De02Cu
COONEY, Luke	20	M	Laborer	03De02Cu
FLYNN, Pat	20	M	Farmer	03De02Cu

NAMES OF PASSENGERS	AGE	SEX	OCCUPATIONS	DATE PORT SHIP
FLYNN, Pat	27	M	Farmer	03De02Cu
Eliza	29	F	Servant	03De02Cu
MAURY, Ann	50	F	Seamstress	03De02Cu
HOOD, Ann	20	F	Seamstress	03De02Cu
MCGAUCHSON, Mary	18	F	Servant	03De02Cu
Catharine	5	F	Child	03De02Cu
WARD, Elizabeth	16	F	Servant	03De02Cu
MULOOY, Hannah	19	F	Servant	03De02Cu
Mary	18	F	Servant	03De02Cu
MALY, Pat	19	M	Laborer	03De02Cu
Mary	18	F	Servant	03De02Cu
BURNE, Michael	25	M	Farmer	03De02Cu
WELCH, Jane	20	F	Servant	03De02Cu
LANEY, Pat	20	M	Laborer	03De02Cu
SULLIVAN, William	48	M	Farmer	03De02Cu
Mary	34	F	Seamstress	03De02Cu
James	20	M	Laborer	03De02Cu
Catharine	18	F	Servant	03De02Cu
Deborah	12	F	Servant	03De02Cu
Ann	10	F	Servant	03De02Cu
Daniel	8	M	Child	03De02Cu
Bessey	.00	F	Infant	03De02Cu
CONNER, James	30	M	Miner	03De02Cu
Bridget	25	F	Servant	03De02Cu
Kate	22	F	Servant	03De02Cu
FALVEY, Mark	18	M	Farmer	03De02Cu
DUNN, Pat	27	M	Laborer	03De02Cu
BATTLE, Margt.	50	F	Seamstress	03De02Cu
Pat	27	M	Laborer	03De02Cu
James	2	M	Child	03De02Cu
MURPHEY, Ann	30	F	Servant	03De02Cu
HOGAN, Michael	22	M	Laborer	03De02Cu
Mary	20	F	Servant	03De02Cu
FLANNING, Martin	35	M	Laborer	03De02Cu
Died-At-Sea				
MAHEN, Mary	20	F	Servant	03De02Cu
Catharine	22	F	Servant	03De02Cu
HOGAN, Mary	25	F	Servant	03De02Cu
Thomas	9	M	Child	03De02Cu
Mary	3	F	Child	03De02Cu
DUNN, Catharine	21	F	Mtmkr	03De02Cu
CONNER, Mary	26	F	Servant	03De02Cu
Nancy	5	F	Child	03De02Cu
Catharine	4	F	Child	03De02Cu
Mary	.00	F	Infant	03De02Cu
MCMAHON, Catharine	20	F	Servant	03De02Cu
CAVANAGH, Pat	20	M	Laborer	03De02Cu
PATTRATH, Robert	29	M	Laborer	03De02Cu
Ellen	27	F	Servant	03De02Cu
GALBRATH, Amelia	6	F	Child	03De02Cu
Robert	4	M	Child	03De02Cu
Eliza	2	F	Child	03De02Cu
William	.00	M	Infant	03De02Cu
MORAN, Mary-A.	20	F	Spinster	03De02Cu
MCLOUGHLIN, Michael	25	M	Farmer	03De02Cu
GUNNER, Bridget	20	F	Servant	03De02Cu
RANN, Pat	26	M	Unknown	03De02Cu
MAHER, John	25	M	Unknown	03De02Cu
DYER, John	30	M	Unknown	03De02Cu
Pat	19	M	Unknown	03De02Cu
LONEGAN, Bridget	30	F	Seamstress	03De02Cu
DONLEY, Mary-A.	14	F	Seamstress	03De02Cu
LONEGAN, Catharine	11	F	Seamstress	03De02Cu
FARLEY, Bridget	30	F	Seamstress	03De02Cu
CASSADY, Pat	36	M	Laborer	03De02Cu
DOOLY, Michael	22	M	Laborer	03De02Cu
MATNER, William	50	M	Farmer	03De02Cu
Samuel	20	M	Farmer	03De02Cu
RYAN, John	35	M	Farmer	03De02Cu
KEALEY, Thomas	21	M	Farmer	03De02Cu
TOONEY, Pat	20	M	Farmer	03De02Cu
NOONAN, Pat	22	M	Farmer	03De02Cu
MADDEN, Mary	24	F	Dressmaker	03De02Cu
DUFFAN, Mary	22	F	Bomkr	03De02Cu
BOURTH, Jane	28	F	Bomkr	03De02Cu

NAMES OF PASSENGERS	AGE	SEX	OCCUPATIONS	DATE PORT SHIP
BYRON, Ann	21	F	Bomkr	03De02Cu
FITZPATRICK, Mary	40	F	Lad	03De02Cu
Betty	15	F	Lad	03De02Cu
Paul	14	M	Laborer	03De02Cu
John	8	M	Child	03De02Cu
CAIN, Thomas	28	M	Watchmaker	03De02Cu
MURPHY, Ann	30	F	Servant	03De02Cu
MCGARTY, Daniel	30	M	Laborer	03De02Cu
MCCUNAN, John	35	M	Laborer	03De02Cu
BURKE, Pat	28	M	Laborer	03De02Cu
Ellen	27	F	Servant	03De02Cu
Bridgt.	.00	F	Infant	03De02Cu
MILLIGAN, Tarance	22	M	Servant	03De02Cu
MCBRIDE, Ann	50	F	Seamstress	03De02Cu
Francis	18	F	Seamstress	03De02Cu
FARRELL, Elizabeth	23	F	Servant	03De02Cu
FOX, Joseph	20	M	Farmer	03De02Cu
DOUGHERTY, Catherine	17	F	Servant	03De02Cu
Unity	15	F	Servant	03De02Cu
KEENAN, John	20	M	Clerk	03De02Cu
LANG, Walter	28	M	Clerk	03De02Cu
KELLEY, Bartle	50	M	Laborer	03De02Cu
Ann	50	F	Lad	03De02Cu
Bridget	12	F	Lad	03De02Cu
HOGANS, Owen	30	M	Farmer	03De02Cu
LONGLIN, Ann	24	F	Servant	03De02Cu
DOOLEY, Mary	22	F	Servant	03De02Cu
DONOVAN, Magt.	25	F	Servant	03De02Cu
SWEENY, Catharine	15	F	Servant	03De02Cu
BRENNAN, Alice	30	F	Servant	03De02Cu
SHEA, John	3	M	Child	03De02Cu
BRIEN, John	15	M	Servant	03De02Cu
AHERN, Catharine	14	F	Servant	03De02Cu
NOBLE, Mary-A.	24	F	Servant	03De02Cu
Magt.	22	F	Servant	03De02Cu
MCCARTY, Daniel	23	M	Laborer	03De02Cu
David	2	M	Child	03De02Cu
Catharine	8	F	Child	03De02Cu
CRANNEY, Catherine	15	F	Servant	03De02Cu
Bridget	13	F	Servant	03De02Cu
RILEY, Mary	40	F	Seamstress	03De02Cu
Eliza	11	F	Seamstress	03De02Cu
Ann	7	F	Child	03De02Cu
Joseph	5	M	Child	03De02Cu
FARRELL, Thomas	18	M	Farmer	03De02Cu
Ann	16	F	Servant	03De02Cu
DELANY, Pat	22	M	Laborer	03De02Cu
Magt.	17	F	Servant	03De02Cu
LARKIN, Michael	18	M	Laborer	03De02Cu
MCLOUGHLIN, William	26	M	Laborer	03De02Cu
MCGRADE, Rose	50	F	Lad	03De02Cu
Catharine	26	F	Lad	03De02Cu
Mary	21	F	Lad	03De02Cu
Mary	2	F	Child	03De02Cu
KING, John	50	M	Farmer	03De02Cu
John	7	M	Child	03De02Cu
FEENY, Bridget	40	F	Seamstress	03De02Cu
Pat	15	M	Laborer	03De02Cu
Ann	10	F	Laborer	03De02Cu
MCHINES, Daniel	11	M	Laborer	03De02Cu
LANG, Susan	16	F	Servant	03De02Cu
James	16	M	Laborer	03De02Cu
Peter	13	M	Laborer	03De02Cu
DONNELL, Hugh	25	M	Farmer	03De02Cu
MCMANNUS, Magt.	12	F	Farmer	03De02Cu
James	10	M	Farmer	03De02Cu
Susan	8	F	Child	03De02Cu
Sally	6	F	Child	03De02Cu
DOYLE, Ann	21	F	Dressmaker	03De02Cu
CUNNINGHAM, Mary	25	F	Dressmaker	03De02Cu
BLASELL, Ellen	40	F	Dressmaker	03De02Cu
John	19	M	Laborer	03De02Cu
John	4	M	Child	03De02Cu
Mary	9	F	Child	03De02Cu
MCHANNA, William	40	M	Farmer	03De02Cu
MCHANNA, Catharine	20	F	Servant	03De02Cu
Hugh	36	M	Farmer	03De02Cu
PENDERGAST, Bridget	28	F	Seamstress	03De02Cu
Catharine	24	F	Seamstress	03De02Cu
MCNAMARA, Catharine	29	F	Servant	03De02Cu
MCGUIRE, Pat	18	M	Laborer	03De02Cu
REGAN, Catharine	35	F	Servant	03De02Cu
William	9	M	Child	03De02Cu
MCINERY, Thomas	14	M	Laborer	03De02Cu
REGAN, John	7	M	Child	03De02Cu
Michael	2	M	Child	03De02Cu
RYAN, Thomas	7	M	Child	03De02Cu
John	18	M	Laborer	03De02Cu
Mary	19	F	Servant	03De02Cu
HUGHLAHAN, Joseph	24	M	Farmer	03De02Cu
Ellen	22	F	Servant	03De02Cu
Mary	.00	F	Infant	03De02Cu
MCMAHEN, Ellen	18	F	Servant	03De02Cu
CARTY, Thomas	22	M	Laborer	03De02Cu
William	22	M	Laborer	03De02Cu
MCCAULEY, Pat	20	M	Laborer	03De02Cu
REA, James	44	M	Laborer	03De02Cu
Jane	33	F	Dressmaker	03De02Cu
MCALEEN, Margt.	28	F	Servant	03De02Cu
CAREY, John	30	M	Laborer	03De02Cu
Mary	25	F	Servant	03De02Cu
AGAN, Thomas	21	M	Laborer	03De02Cu
BEACH, James	31	M	Silversmith	03De02Cu
Ann	31	F	Bomkr	03De02Cu
MCAULP, John	40	M	Laborer	03De02Cu
BRADY, Peter	35	M	Laborer	03De02Cu
WALCH, Pat	51	M	Laborer	03De02Cu
Catharine	21	F	Servant	03De02Cu
Magt.	18	F	Servant	03De02Cu
Mary	24	F	Servant	03De02Cu
Eliza	22	F	Servant	03De02Cu
BLAKE, Sarah	12	F	Servant	03De02Cu
BARNEY, Mary	20	F	Servant	03De02Cu
CLONREY, U-Mrs.	50	F	Seamstress	03De02Cu
Jane	24	F	Seamstress	03De02Cu
Eliza	20	F	Seamstress	03De02Cu
Thomas	16	M	Laborer	03De02Cu
John	14	M	Laborer	03De02Cu
Robert	11	M	Laborer	03De02Cu
James	8	M	Child	03De02Cu
CLONRAY, Pat	56	M	Laborer	03De02Cu
U-Mrs.	53	F	Spinster	03De02Cu
Edward	32	M	Laborer	03De02Cu
Ellen	29	F	Servant	03De02Cu
Pat	26	M	Laborer	03De02Cu
James	26	M	Laborer	03De02Cu
CLONSEY, Margaret	21	F	Servant	03De02Cu
Betty	18	F	Servant	03De02Cu
Mary	15	F	Servant	03De02Cu
Catharine	12	F	Servant	03De02Cu
SMITH, Ana	19	F	Dressmaker	03De02Cu
CLOWEY, William	35	M	Farmer	03De02Cu
GREGG, Robert	18	M	Farmer	03De02Cu
DEWPREY, James	25	M	Farmer	03De02Cu
NEWMAN, Rosey	28	F	Servant	03De02Cu
DRISCOLL, Johan	27	F	Dressmaker	03De02Cu
MURPHY, Margt.	23	F	Dressmaker	03De02Cu
BRANNAN, Pat	28	M	Laborer	03De02Cu
Magt.	27	F	Servant	03De02Cu

MARMION 04 DECEMBER 1849

From Liverpool

NAMES OF PASSENGERS	AGE	SEX	OCCUPATIONS	DATE PORT
DUFFEY, Margaret	30	F	Servant	04De02Ct
MOONEY, Phillip	11	M	None	04De02Ct
CONNEALY, James	56	M	Laborer	04De02Ct
Bridget	50	F	None	04De02Ct
Catherine	16	F	Servant	04De02Ct
Michael	20	M	Servant	04De02Ct
Ann	14	F	None	04De02Ct
Margaret	11	F	None	04De02Ct
REILLY, Catherine	24	F	Servant	04De02Ct
CONNEALY, James	24	M	Laborer	04De02Ct
Margaret	22	F	None	04De02Ct
Patrick	.00	M	Infant	04De02Ct
MELANY, James	28	M	Laborer	04De02Ct
BOHAN, Ann	30	F	Servant	04De02Ct
Matthew	.00	M	Infant	04De02Ct
Died-At-Sea				
BYRNES, James	30	M	Laborer	04De02Ct
BAILEY, James	20	M	Laborer	04De02Ct
DOYLE, Mary	20	F	Servant	04De02Ct
MCLOUGHLAN, Patt	60	M	Laborer	04De02Ct
Mary	56	F	None	04De02Ct
John	22	M	Laborer	04De02Ct
Mary	5	F	Child	04De02Ct
FINNERTY, William	18	M	Laborer	04De02Ct
MAHONY, Bridget	25	F	None	04De02Ct
ROBINSON, James	19	M	Laborer	04De02Ct
KELLY, Thos.	22	M	Laborer	04De02Ct
Margaret	20	F	None	04De02Ct
FITZMORRIS, Mary	18	F	Servant	04De02Ct
MCELROY, Cathe.	26	F	None	04De02Ct
Mary	.00	F	Infant	04De02Ct
Daniel	3	M	Child	04De02Ct
MURPHY, Arthur	21	M	Laborer	04De02Ct
Mary	25	F	Servant	04De02Ct
Bridget	18	F	Servant	04De02Ct
OHARE, Mary	16	F	Servant	04De02Ct
MCNAMEE, Danl.	22	M	Laborer	04De02Ct
HOLLAND, William	46	M	Pwlwvr	04De02Ct
MCMANUS, John	48	M	Laborer	04De02Ct
DOUGLAS, Elizabeth	20	F	Servant	04De02Ct
Harriett	17	F	Servant	04De02Ct
Sarah	14	F	Servant	04De02Ct
BELL, Alice	20	F	Servant	04De02Ct
FLETCHER, Alexander	34	M	Laborer	04De02Ct
Margaret	24	F	Servant	04De02Ct
DOWNEY, Geo.	50	M	Farmer	04De02Ct
James	20	M	Shoemaker	04De02Ct
DEVINS, John	18	M	Grocer	04De02Ct
CAHILL, Michael	21	M	Laborer	04De02Ct
CAIN, Mary	21	F	None	04De02Ct
FARRELL, Mary	22	F	None	04De02Ct
NICHOLLS, John	19	M	Laborer	04De02Ct
WOODS, Martha	20	M	Laborer	04De02Ct
Martha	.00	F	Infant	04De02Ct
Died-At-Sea				
RUTH, Patrick	46	M	Miller	04De02Ct
MACKAY, Patrick	17	M	Miller	04De02Ct
MCKENNA, Michael	25	M	Coppersmith	04De02Ct
BYRNE, Daniel	30	M	Farmer	04De02Ct
HOGAN, William	10	M	None	04De02Ct
CONNEALY, Ellen	30	F	None	04De02Ct
James	11	M	None	04De02Ct
Patrick	8	M	Child	04De02Ct
Jane	4	F	Child	04De02Ct
FOLEY, John	30	M	None	04De02Ct
Died-At-Sea				
COLLINS, Francis	36	M	Farmer	04De02Ct
CAREY, Judy	28	F	None	04De02Ct
IRETON, Anne	32	F	None	04De02Ct
Jane	12	F	None	04De02Ct
William	.00	M	Infant	04De02Ct
MYLETT, Patrick	25	M	Tailor	04De02Ct
KENNEY, Thos.	22	M	Laborer	04De02Ct
COLEMAN, Ellen	24	F	Servant	04De02Ct
KEARNEY, Mary	26	F	Servant	04De02Ct
SWEENEY, Cath.	32	F	None	04De02Ct
Cath.	11	F	None	04De02Ct
Margaret	9	F	Child	04De02Ct
Mary	7	F	Child	04De02Ct
Bridget	2	F	Child	04De02Ct
CLEARY, Patrick	25	M	Laborer	04De02Ct
Honora	25	F	None	04De02Ct
James	3	M	Child	04De02Ct
William	.00	M	Infant	04De02Ct
JOHNSTON, David	28	M	Bt-Shmk	04De02Ct
FLYNN, Cathe.	25	F	Servant	04De02Ct
HYNES, William	20	M	Servant	04De02Ct
Cathe.	19	F	None	04De02Ct
Bridget	.00	F	Infant	04De02Ct
MCLOUGHLAN, Rose	30	F	Servant	04De02Ct
RAFFERTY, Bridget	20	F	Servant	04De02Ct
HANRAHAN, Ellen	26	F	Servant	04De02Ct
COLGAN, Maria	24	F	Servant	04De02Ct
TORPY, Martin	3	M	Child	04De02Ct
JOHNSTON, Samuel	24	M	Laborer	04De02Ct
DONAHY, John	24	M	Laborer	04De02Ct
STRINGER, Robert	24	M	Laborer	04De02Ct
MCCAITNEY, Patrick	29	M	Carpenter	04De02Ct
BRANNON, James	20	M	Laborer	04De02Ct
CROSS, James	28	M	Laborer	04De02Ct
Mary	26	F	None	04De02Ct
Ellen	2	F	Child	04De02Ct
Bridget	.00	F	Infant	04De02Ct
DOOLEY, Patrick	24	M	Laborer	04De02Ct
DARCEY, Mary	22	F	Laborer	04De02Ct
John	7	M	Child	04De02Ct
BURKE, Catherine	30	F	None	04De02Ct
Rebecca	13	F	None	04De02Ct
CASSIN, Edmund	28	M	Laborer	04De02Ct
BYRNE, John	25	M	Farmer	04De02Ct
WALSH, John	56	M	Laborer	04De02Ct
Eliza	18	F	None	04De02Ct
MOONEY, James	30	M	Ctldlr	04De02Ct
Eliza	28	F	None	04De02Ct
BYRNE, Alice	30	F	None	04De02Ct
BUCKLEY, Mary	24	F	Servant	04De02Ct
CREED, Francis	22	M	Servant	04De02Ct
John	26	M	Servant	04De02Ct
COLLINS, Michael	21	M	Baker	04De02Ct
Honora	16	F	None	04De02Ct
CLARKE, Cathe.	21	F	Servant	04De02Ct
Bridget	24	F	Servant	04De02Ct
HOLLAND, Martha	21	F	Servant	04De02Ct
BABBY, Mary	21	F	Servant	04De02Ct
JOYCE, Michael	40	M	Unknown	04De02Ct
MCGOVERN, Patt	21	M	Sawer	04De02Ct
James	25	M	Weaver	04De02Ct
Francis	19	M	Laborer	04De02Ct
MURPHY, Jane	20	F	Seamstress	04De02Ct
GILROY, John	23	M	Laborer	04De02Ct
Biddy	22	F	Servant	04De02Ct
DENNAN, John	26	M	Laborer	04De02Ct
CAROLAN, Michael	30	M	Weaver	04De02Ct
BAIDEN, Betty	35	F	None	04De02Ct
Owen	17	M	Laborer	04De02Ct
Anne	15	F	None	04De02Ct
Julia	13	F	None	04De02Ct
Bryan	11	M	None	04De02Ct
PAGE, Samuel	25	M	Traveller	04De02Ct

NAMES OF PASSENGERS	AGE	SEX	OCCUPATIONS	DATE PORT SHIP
JOYCE, Cather.	20	F	None	04De02Ct
KENNEDY, John	37	M	Paper Maker	04De02Ct
PIGOTT, Patrick	35	M	Laborer	04De02Ct
MEEHAN, James	30	M	Laborer	04De02Ct
RYAN, Timothy	25	M	Shoemaker	04De02Ct
MADDEN, Thos.	40	M	Laborer	04De02Ct
Judy	30	F	None	04De02Ct
Bridget	3	F	Child	04De02Ct
Patrick	.00	M	Infant	04De02Ct
HARPER, Alex.	27	M	Carpenter	04De02Ct
MAXWELL, John	36	M	Mason	04De02Ct
Eliza	30	F	None	04De02Ct
Benjamin	8	M	Child	04De02Ct
NOOMAN, Joseph	18	M	Laborer	04De02Ct
KENNEDY, John	26	M	Laborer	04De02Ct
RICE, Bessey	16	F	Servant	04De02Ct
HEALY, James	24	M	Laborer	04De02Ct
DENNIN, Julia	23	F	Servant	04De02Ct
COSTELLO, Cathe.	35	F	Servant	04De02Ct
Mary	8	F	Child	04De02Ct
ROCHE, William	30	M	Laborer	04De02Ct
John	40	M	Laborer	04De02Ct
KIRBY, Edmund	25	M	Laborer	04De02Ct
HAYES, Ellen	20	F	Nurse Maid	04De02Ct
TIERNEY, Luke	18	M	Laborer	04De02Ct
JORDAN, Austin	20	M	Blacksmith	04De02Ct
MURRAY, Patrick	27	M	Laborer	04De02Ct
FARRELL, Garrett	25	M	Laborer	04De02Ct
HENESSY, Mary	26	F	None	04De02Ct
BURKE, Michael	30	M	Laborer	04De02Ct
COLLINS, Ellen	36	F	None	04De02Ct
Mary	14	F	None	04De02Ct
Bridget	10	F	None	04De02Ct
ODEA, John	37	M	Laborer	04De02Ct
NUNAN, John	30	M	Laborer	04De02Ct
Bridget	30	F	None	04De02Ct
MCQUADE, Patk.	25	M	Laborer	04De02Ct
RYAN, Mary	30	F	None	04De02Ct
Mary	24	F	None	04De02Ct
Mathew	8	M	Child	04De02Ct
DWYER, Thos.	22	M	Laborer	04De02Ct
Cathe.	20	F	Servant	04De02Ct
HENRY, Barbara	28	F	Dressmaker	04De02Ct
HESTER, Margt.	27	F	House Maid	04De02Ct
Sarah	19	F	Servant	04De02Ct
CONNELLY, Thos.	27	M	Tailor	04De02Ct
HIGGINS, James	20	M	Laborer	04De02Ct
FEASE, Bridget	20	F	Servant	04De02Ct
ROONEY, Bridget	19	F	Servant	04De02Ct
CAVANNAH, Ellen	21	F	Servant	04De02Ct
DESMOND, Cathe.	26	F	Servant	04De02Ct
Mary	24	F	Servant	04De02Ct
KEEGAN, Eliza	19	F	Laborer	04De02Ct
John	21	M	Laborer	04De02Ct
MCDERMIT, Mary	19	F	Servant	04De02Ct
TUNNEY, John	30	M	Peddler	04De02Ct
Mary	.00	F	Infant	04De02Ct
ROGERS, John	19	M	Laborer	04De02Ct
CARROLL, Michael	21	M	Mason	04De02Ct
FLANNAGAN, Thos.	20	M	Laborer	04De02Ct
FORMSY, Margt.	23	F	None	04De02Ct
MCCONGHREY, Ellen	21	F	Servant	04De02Ct
DOGHERTY, Cornelius	60	M	Laborer	04De02Ct
Ellen	24	F	None	04De02Ct
HALLERON, Willm.	21	M	Laborer	04De02Ct
SHIELS, Arthur	16	M	Laborer	04De02Ct
John	14	M	Laborer	04De02Ct
WISELEY, John	54	M	Laborer	04De02Ct
Ann	54	F	None	04De02Ct
Patrick	12	M	None	04De02Ct
LYNCH, Mary	30	F	None	04De02Ct
Cathe.	12	F	None	04De02Ct
Owen	8	M	Child	04De02Ct
John	5	M	Child	04De02Ct
Biddy	4	F	Child	04De02Ct

NAMES OF PASSENGERS	AGE	SEX	OCCUPATIONS	DATE PORT SHIP
LYNCH, Ann	.00	F	Infant	04De02Ct
OBRIEN, Margaret	30	F	None	04De02Ct
Michael	11	M	None	04De02Ct
Catherine	9	F	Child	04De02Ct
Ann	6	F	Child	04De02Ct
John	3	M	Child	04De02Ct
KELLY, Ann	35	F	None	04De02Ct
Peter	14	M	None	04De02Ct
Bernard	10	M	None	04De02Ct
Mary	12	F	None	04De02Ct
Margaret	8	F	Child	04De02Ct
Catherine	4	F	Child	04De02Ct
Ann	.00	F	Infant	04De02Ct
FITZGERALD, Johanna	24	F	None	04De02Ct
Julia-Malone	.00	F	Infant	04De02Ct
KIRRANE, John	16	M	Laborer	04De02Ct
Mary	11	F	None	04De02Ct
CONBOY, Mary	16	F	Servant	04De02Ct
John	14	M	Servant	04De02Ct
Thomas	13	M	None	04De02Ct
MELENEY, Margaret	15	F	None	04De02Ct
Cicely	11	F	None	04De02Ct
HARVEY, Catherine	35	F	None	04De02Ct
KEENAN, Eliza	15	F	None	04De02Ct
Sarah	11	F	None	04De02Ct
John	7	M	Child	04De02Ct
Thomas	3	M	Child	04De02Ct
CHARLES, Margaret	40	F	None	04De02Ct
Mary	11	F	None	04De02Ct
Ann	9	F	Child	04De02Ct
Cecily	6	F	Child	04De02Ct
Peter	4	M	Child	04De02Ct
Margaret	.00	F	Infant	04De02Ct
MCGUIRE, Bridget	11	F	None	04De02Ct
Anna	7	F	Child	04De02Ct
James	12	M	None	04De02Ct
Ann	10	F	None	04De02Ct
Catherine	8	F	Child	04De02Ct
Mary	6	F	Child	04De02Ct
BOHEN, Margaret	18	F	None	04De02Ct
William	14	M	None	04De02Ct
MCDONNELL, Anthony	16	M	Servant	04De02Ct
CONNOLLY, Mary	32	F	None	04De02Ct
Wm.	9	M	Child	04De02Ct
Mary	8	F	Child	04De02Ct
Patrick	6	M	Child	04De02Ct
Catherine	7	F	Child	04De02Ct
Michael	.00	M	Infant	04De02Ct
MCGOVERN, John	21	M	Laborer	04De02Ct
Rose	19	F	None	04De02Ct
Michael	9	M	Child	04De02Ct
Rose-Ann	7	F	Child	04De02Ct
GIBBONS, Sarah	40	F	None	04De02Ct
Betty	7	F	Child	04De02Ct
MOORE, Bridget	43	F	None	04De02Ct
Patrick	19	M	Laborer	04De02Ct
James	17	M	Laborer	04De02Ct
Mary	13	F	None	04De02Ct
Bridget	11	F	None	04De02Ct
Michael	7	M	Child	04De02Ct
Peter	9	M	Child	04De02Ct
NICHOLS, Margaret	15	F	None	04De02Ct
MARRON, Thomas	34	M	Laborer	04De02Ct
TORPAY, Patt	32	M	Laborer	04De02Ct
Bridget	30	F	None	04De02Ct
MONOHAN, John	8	M	Child	04De02Ct
HOLLAND, James	21	M	Laborer	04De02Ct
Mary	8	F	Child	04De02Ct
CLARKE, Alice	40	F	None	04De02Ct
Peter	12	M	None	04De02Ct
James	10	M	None	04De02Ct
Mary	7	F	Child	04De02Ct
Ellen	3	F	Child	04De02Ct
KILFOYLE, Patrick	35	M	Laborer	04De02Ct
Bridget	6	F	Child	04De02Ct

NAMES OF PASSENGERS		AGE	SEX	OCCUPATIONS	DATE PORT SHIP
NUTLY, Ann		50	F	None	04De02Ct
AHEARN, William		17	M	Laborer	04De02Ct
MALONE, Catharine		13	F	None	04De02Ct
Johanna		10	F	None	04De02Ct
TUNNEY, Mary		26	F	None	04De02Ct

DEBORAH 04 DECEMBER 1849

From Liverpool

NAMES OF PASSENGERS		AGE	SEX	OCCUPATIONS	DATE PORT SHIP
MORAN, Bridget		20	F	Spinster	04De02Cv
OCONNEL, Thos.		20	M	Laborer	04De02Cv
SLATTERY, Bridget		18	F	Spinster	04De02Cv
NIXON, E.		42	M	Laborer	04De02Cv
GALLICH, Ann		18	F	Wife	04De02Cv
FARRELL, Mick		18	M	Laborer	04De02Cv
LYNCH, Christ.		18	M	Laborer	04De02Cv
SMITH, Anne		40	F	Spinster	04De02Cv
FARRELL, Ellen		14	F	Spinster	04De02Cv
Edward	(S)	8	M	Child	04De02Cv
LACY, Thos.		5	M	Child	04De02Cv
Will		3	M	Child	04De02Cv
Kitty		.00	F	Infant	04De02Cv
AMES, Nancy		4	F	Child	04De02Cv
Catharine		.00	F	Infant	04De02Cv
QUIN, Mary		19	F	Spinster	04De02Cv
CUNNINGHAM, Patk.		20	M	Laborer	04De02Cv
QUIN, John		20	M	Laborer	04De02Cv
DUNNE, Thos.		50	M	Laborer	04De02Cv
Denis		21	M	Laborer	04De02Cv
MCLONGSTAN, Tedy		40	M	Laborer	04De02Cv
John		20	M	Laborer	04De02Cv
COLIGAN, Magt.		19	F	Spinster	04De02Cv
CLARK, Cathe.		30	F	Spinster	04De02Cv
Bridget		12	F	Spinster	04De02Cv
John	(S)	10	M	None	04De02Cv
HUME, Nancy		.00	F	Infant	04De02Cv
LAIN, John		29	M	Laborer	04De02Cv
Peggy		19	F	Wife	04De02Cv
RYAN, Peggy		30	F	Wife	04De02Cv
Patt	(S)	6	M	Child	04De02Cv
James	(S)	.00	M	Infant	04De02Cv
RIDLEY, Abbey		18	F	Wife	04De02Cv
MCKENNA, John		23	M	Laborer	04De02Cv
HOGAN, Eliza		40	F	Wife	04De02Cv
Magt.		10	F	Spinster	04De02Cv
Ann		.00	F	Infant	04De02Cv
Eliza		13	F	None	04De02Cv
SULLEY, Ellen		19	F	None	04De02Cv
NORRIS, George		40	M	Laborer	04De02Cv
HANEY, Denis		29	M	Laborer	04De02Cv
SHEA, John		25	M	Laborer	04De02Cv
BLAKE, Patt		20	M	Laborer	04De02Cv
BUSHOLAN, Dan		25	M	Laborer	04De02Cv
QUASE, Nancy		24	F	Wife	04De02Cv
MCMANUS, David		9	M	Child	04De02Cv
ROCHE, Patt		25	M	Laborer	04De02Cv
OBRIEN, Dennis		19	M	Laborer	04De02Cv
HICKEY, Mick		21	M	Laborer	04De02Cv
HOGAN, Mary		21	F	Spinster	04De02Cv
MANERY, Thos.		36	M	Laborer	04De02Cv
LYDDEY, Cath.		24	F	Wife	04De02Cv
Andrew	(S)	4	M	Child	04De02Cv
Pat	(S)	.00	M	Infant	04De02Cv
HEATNEY, Simon		22	M	Laborer	04De02Cv
CROALEY, John		30	M	Laborer	04De02Cv
DOWNEY, James		.00	M	Infant	04De02Cv
REDDY, Peter	(S)	5	M	Child	04De02Cv
Ellen	(D)	.00	F	Infant	04De02Cv
GRIFFIN, Mick		27	M	Laborer	04De02Cv
HOGAN, Jane		17	F	Spinster	04De02Cv
MORRIS, John		21	M	Laborer	04De02Cv
FLAGHERTY, Bridget		17	F	Spinster	04De02Cv
FITZGERALD, Mick		24	M	Laborer	04De02Cv
HURT, Anne		48	F	Spinster	04De02Cv
Johannah		18	F	Spinster	04De02Cv
FLANEY, Magt.		68	F	Wife	04De02Cv
HARMAN, Ellen		27	F	Wife	04De02Cv
DUFFY, Cathe.		24	F	Wife	04De02Cv
HANAN, Jas.		4	M	Child	04De02Cv
Thomas		.00	M	Infant	04De02Cv
SMITH, Henry		20	M	Laborer	04De02Cv
FISHER, Helen		20	F	Spinster	04De02Cv
MCLOUGHAN, Joseph		24	M	Laborer	04De02Cv
SHANNON, Robt.		29	M	Laborer	04De02Cv
FITZGERALD, Will		40	M	Laborer	04De02Cv
Honora	(W)	40	F	None	04De02Cv
BROWN, Bridget		24	F	Spinster	04De02Cv
Bridget		18	F	Spinster	04De02Cv
Catharine		15	F	Spinster	04De02Cv
Nancy		12	F	Spinster	04De02Cv
KELLY, Mary		25	F	Spinster	04De02Cv
REYNOLDS, Mary		17	F	Spinster	04De02Cv
MCCLEAN, Thomas		20	M	Laborer	04De02Cv
MCENARY, Pat		20	M	Laborer	04De02Cv
MCCLEAN, Elizabeth		25	F	Spinster	04De02Cv
HOGAN, Will		18	M	Laborer	04De02Cv
KELLY, Mary		25	F	Spinster	04De02Cv
MEADOWS, Bessy		15	F	Spinster	04De02Cv
NOOLAN, Thomas		36	M	Laborer	04De02Cv
GINTY, Cath.		30	F	Spinster	04De02Cv
Bernard		12	M	Laborer	04De02Cv
Andrew		10	M	None	04De02Cv
Francis		5	M	Child	04De02Cv
Catherine		.00	F	Infant	04De02Cv
CALLAGHAN, Margaret		26	F	Spinster	04De02Cv
John		17	M	None	04De02Cv
GRIFFIN, Mick		40	M	Laborer	04De02Cv
MADDEN, Magt.		20	F	Spinster	04De02Cv
CONNOR, Maria		15	F	Spinster	04De02Cv
HEANEN, Mick		20	M	Laborer	04De02Cv
SHEPARD, Honora		25	F	Spinster	04De02Cv
Will	(S)	.00	M	Infant	04De02Cv
KIRRION, Hannah		30	F	Spinster	04De02Cv
KENNA, Edith		16	F	Spinster	04De02Cv
LOVE, Mick		18	M	Laborer	04De02Cv
MURPHY, Danl.		25	M	Laborer	04De02Cv
Magt.		23	F	Spinster	04De02Cv
Mich.		13	F	None	04De02Cv
RYAN, James		12	M	None	04De02Cv
LITTLE, Jonathan		33	M	Laborer	04De02Cv
Ellen	(W)	40	F	None	04De02Cv
Mary	(D)	8	F	None	04De02Cv
Mary	(D)	.00	F	Infant	04De02Cv
Jno.		26	M	None	04De02Cv
MATTHEWS, Bryan		20	M	Laborer	04De02Cv
Magt.	(W)	20	F	None	04De02Cv
REYNOLDS, Ellen		20	F	Spinster	04De02Cv
LANSTRITH, Cath.		25	F	Spinster	04De02Cv
HYLAND, Magt.		27	F	Spinster	04De02Cv
DUNN, Brigt.		34	F	Spinster	04De02Cv
BUNKER, James		20	M	Laborer	04De02Cv
CONNELLAN, John		32	M	Laborer	04De02Cv
Mary	(W)	30	F	None	04De02Cv
Pat		15	M	Laborer	04De02Cv
Mich.		11	M	None	04De02Cv
Cath.		7	F	Child	04De02Cv
KENNEDY, Eleanor		30	F	Spinster	04De02Cv
DONOHUE, Mary		40	M	Laborer	04De02Cv
Cathe.	(W)	36	F	None	04De02Cv
Bridget	(D)	15	F	None	04De02Cv
Homer	(S)	13	M	None	04De02Cv
Jno.	(S)	11	M	None	04De02Cv
James	(S)	.00	M	Infant	04De02Cv

NAMES OF PASSENGERS		AGE	SEX	OCCUPATIONS	DATE PORT SHIP
CONNELLAN, Mary		24	F	Wife	04De02Cv
Ha.		16	F	None	04De02Cv
Magt.		12	F	None	04De02Cv
Cath.		.00	F	Infant	04De02Cv
CUSACK, Mary		30	F	Spinster	04De02Cv
Mary	(D)	.00	F	Infant	04De02Cv
MAKIN, Peter		21	M	Laborer	04De02Cv
QUIGLEY, Biddy		25	F	Wife	04De02Cv
MCANAN, Biddy		16	F	Spinster	04De02Cv
WALSH, W.		27	M	Laborer	04De02Cv
Laura		.00	F	Infant	04De02Cv
FITZGERALD, Ellen		27	F	Wife	04De02Cv
Anna	(D)	.00	F	Infant	04De02Cv
GORALEY, Hugh		21	M	Laborer	04De02Cv
MCENTEE, James		12	M	Laborer	04De02Cv
WARD, Sally		50	F	Wife	04De02Cv
Pat	(S)	12	M	None	04De02Cv
GANNEY, Jno.		22	M	Laborer	04De02Cv
CRONIN, Mary		26	F	Spinster	04De02Cv
Ellen		.00	F	Infant	04De02Cv
GILMAN, Hannah		18	F	Spinster	04De02Cv
TAYLOR, Ann		50	F	Wife	04De02Cv
Wm.	(S)	19	M	None	04De02Cv
Henry	(S)	.00	M	Infant	04De02Cv
BUTTERANT, Thomas	(S)	13	M	None	04De02Cv
COONEY, Dennis		.00	M	Infant	04De02Cv
MCCLILAN, Mary		7	F	Child	04De02Cv

PATRICK-HENRY 05 DECEMBER 1849

From Liverpool

NAMES OF PASSENGERS		AGE	SEX	OCCUPATIONS	DATE PORT SHIP
PROPLEY, Margt.		24	F	Milliner	05De02Cw
Mary-Ann		20	F	Milliner	05De02Cw
MURPHY, Fanny		20	F	Milliner	05De02Cw
DUNN, Mary		20	F	Domestic	05De02Cw
FARRALL, Patrick		24	M	Laborer	05De02Cw
LYNCH, Richard		24	M	Farmer	05De02Cw
Peter		40	M	Farmer	05De02Cw
Burtle		28	M	Farmer	05De02Cw
DALEY, Patrick		27	M	Laborer	05De02Cw
GRIMES, Judith		50	F	Domestic	05De02Cw
Mary		14	F	Domestic	05De02Cw
Alice		20	F	Domestic	05De02Cw
LINCH, Judith		50	F	Domestic	05De02Cw
Ann		16	F	Domestic	05De02Cw
MCGEE, Alice		15	F	Domestic	05De02Cw
CAROLIN, U		15	F	Domestic	05De02Cw
DARGIN, Jane		20	F	None	05De02Cw
Peter		19	M	Farmer	05De02Cw
Ellen		30	F	None	05De02Cw
Richard		22	M	None	05De02Cw
James		25	M	None	05De02Cw
John		11	M	None	05De02Cw
Mad.		8	M	Child	05De02Cw
Edward		2	M	Child	05De02Cw
Rose		6	F	Child	05De02Cw
MCGUIRE, Dennis		20	M	Laborer	05De02Cw
Mary		8	F	Child	05De02Cw
Eliza		7	F	Child	05De02Cw
HAGAN, James		30	M	Laborer	05De02Cw
LYNCH, Garrett		30	M	Farmer	05De02Cw
James		10	M	None	05De02Cw
Thos.		7	M	Child	05De02Cw
Patrick		5	M	Child	05De02Cw
DALEY, Ann		18	F	Domestic	05De02Cw
MCCORMICK, Thos.		30	M	Laborer	05De02Cw
Cathe.		30	F	None	05De02Cw
Willm.		5	M	Child	05De02Cw
MCCORMICK, John		2	M	Child	05De02Cw
Catharine Died-At-Sea		.00	F	Infant	05De02Cw
MULHALL, Bridget		7	F	Child	05De02Cw
MULLEN, Cathe.		20	F	None	05De02Cw
RATIGAN, Peter		28	M	Laborer	05De02Cw
MOFFATT, Sarah		30	F	Boot Closer	05De02Cw
James		11	M	None	05De02Cw
OHARA, James		28	M	Groom	05De02Cw
DILLON, James		24	M	Coachman	05De02Cw
CARROLL, Thos.		24	M	Farmer	05De02Cw
Rose		22	F	None	05De02Cw
DUFFY, Judith		22	F	Domestic	05De02Cw
CARROLL, John Died-At-Sea		.00	M	Infant	05De02Cw
KELLY, Lawrence		20	M	Laborer	05De02Cw
STOUT, Willm.		26	M	Laborer	05De02Cw
Harriet		25	F	Domestic	05De02Cw
CRISPIN, John		30	M	Laborer	05De02Cw
Frances		33	F	None	05De02Cw
BURNSIDE, Rose		50	F	Housekeeper	05De02Cw
Ann		20	F	Milliner	05De02Cw
MILEN, John		60	M	Butler	05De02Cw
EGAN, Mary		21	F	Domestic	05De02Cw
GRINDER, Mary		25	F	Domestic	05De02Cw
WALSH, Mathew		34	M	Laborer	05De02Cw
Mary		27	F	None	05De02Cw
SWARDS, Peter		27	M	Laborer	05De02Cw
LEE, Cathe.		26	F	Dressmaker	05De02Cw
Cathe.		21	F	Dressmaker	05De02Cw
Cathe.		4	F	Child	05De02Cw
Robert		.00	M	Infant	05De02Cw
CONNOR, Willm.		40	M	Laborer	05De02Cw
CASEY, Nichs.		27	M	Laborer	05De02Cw
MURPHY, Mary-A.		19	F	Domestic	05De02Cw
DILLON, Garrett		25	M	Laborer	05De02Cw
CORCORAN, Bridget		24	F	Domestic	05De02Cw
KENNEDY, Hugh		46	M	Laborer	05De02Cw
BYRNES, Chrs.		46	M	Laborer	05De02Cw
FARRALL, Thos.		26	M	Laborer	05De02Cw
Henry		24	M	Laborer	05De02Cw
Peter		22	M	Laborer	05De02Cw
Joseph		21	M	Laborer	05De02Cw
BRENNAN, Ed.		57	M	Farmer	05De02Cw
Mary		52	F	None	05De02Cw
John		32	M	None	05De02Cw
Ann		30	F	None	05De02Cw
Bridget		16	F	None	05De02Cw
Michael		28	M	None	05De02Cw
Matthew		14	M	None	05De02Cw
Thomas		11	M	None	05De02Cw
EGAN, John		46	M	Laborer	05De02Cw
SMITH, Willm.		39	M	Farmer	05De02Cw
John		12	M	None	05De02Cw
Edward		9	M	Child	05De02Cw
Ellen		39	F	None	05De02Cw
Eliza		11	F	None	05De02Cw
Sophia-S.		7	F	Child	05De02Cw
NOWLANS, Bridget		24	F	Milliner	05De02Cw
BYRNES, F.		32	M	Farmer	05De02Cw
Bridget		40	M	Boot Closer	05De02Cw
QUIN, Biddy		25	F	Housekeeper	05De02Cw
SHAUGHESSY, Johanna		50	F	Housekeeper	05De02Cw
Mary		20	F	Domestic	05De02Cw
Catharine		18	F	Domestic	05De02Cw
Patrick		16	M	None	05De02Cw
Thomas		14	M	None	05De02Cw
Johanna		12	F	None	05De02Cw
Margaret		5	F	Child	05De02Cw
John		10	M	None	05De02Cw
Michael		3	M	Child	05De02Cw
SHEEHAN, Pat		20	M	Farmer	05De02Cw
COMERFARD, Margt.		45	F	None	05De02Cw
Edwd.		26	F	None	05De02Cw
DUNN, Mary		20	F	Domestic	05De02Cw

NAMES OF PASSENGERS	AGE	SEX	OCCUPATIONS	DATE PORT SHIP
DELANY, Johanna	20	F	Domestic	05De02Cw
Cathe.	17	F	Domestic	05De02Cw
Laurence	4	M	Child	05De02Cw
CATTLETON, Michael	18	M	None	05De02Cw
KENNY, Pat	30	M	Blacksmith	05De02Cw
MCGACHY, Anty.	20	M	Laborer	05De02Cw
MULLEN, Charles	28	M	Laborer	05De02Cw
EANES, Mary	50	F	Domestic	05De02Cw
DYMES, Ellen	26	F	Domestic	05De02Cw
John	4	M	Child	05De02Cw
MCLOUGHLIN, Pat	30	M	Laborer	05De02Cw
MAHONY, Martin	25	M	Shoemaker	05De02Cw
Margaret	21	F	None	05De02Cw
SLATTERY, Mary	17	F	Domestic	05De02Cw
BRODERICK, Margt.	22	F	Domestic	05De02Cw
Bridget	14	F	None	05De02Cw
CONNAUGHTON, Pat	19	M	Laborer	05De02Cw
MULDOWNY, John	1	M	Child	05De02Cw
CARTHILL, Michael	35	M	Laborer	05De02Cw
HALLERAN, Thos.	20	M	Laborer	05De02Cw
Darby	19	M	None	05De02Cw
MCMAHON, Thos.	20	M	None	05De02Cw
Bridget	45	F	Housekeeper	05De02Cw
HICKEY, Ann	13	F	Domestic	05De02Cw
MCNANTY, Hannah	22	F	None	05De02Cw
JUDGE, Brian	32	M	Miller	05De02Cw
Mary	27	F	None	05De02Cw
Margt.	1	F	Child	05De02Cw
Bernard	7	M	Child	05De02Cw
Michael	5	M	Child	05De02Cw
MEHAS, Mich.	2	M	Child	05De02Cw
Peter	.00	M	Infant	05De02Cw
KANE, John	20	M	None	05De02Cw
KELLY, Thos.	25	M	Laborer	05De02Cw
Mary	25	F	Domestic	05De02Cw
Sally	17	F	None	05De02Cw
Charlotte	24	F	None	05De02Cw
CONLEY, John	25	M	Laborer	05De02Cw
CASSIDY, Mary	20	F	Domestic	05De02Cw
RYAN, Luke	23	M	None	05De02Cw
Ellen	24	F	None	05De02Cw
Patrick	3	M	Child	05De02Cw
John	5	M	Child	05De02Cw
Mary	.00	F	Infant	05De02Cw
OHAGAN, John	20	M	None	05De02Cw
CAREY, Margt.	27	F	Dressmaker	05De02Cw
DOWLAN, Mich.	29	M	Laborer	05De02Cw
KELLY, Mich.	26	M	None	05De02Cw
CARRALL, James	50	M	None	05De02Cw
WATERSON, Willm.	31	M	None	05De02Cw
SHAME, Ann	12	F	Domestic	05De02Cw
MCKEOWN, Mary	40	F	Housekeeper	05De02Cw
John	3	M	Child	05De02Cw
Bessy	19	F	Housekeeper	05De02Cw
BEATTY, Michael	60	M	Domestic	05De02Cw
CAHILL, Rose	6	F	Child	05De02Cw
MONGAN, Thos.	40	M	Laborer	05De02Cw
MCMAHON, Cathe.	30	F	Tailor	05De02Cw
Mary	4	F	Child	05De02Cw
Edmond Died-At-Sea	.00	M	Infant	05De02Cw
MULCAN, Mary	27	F	Domestic	05De02Cw
Johanna	30	F	None	05De02Cw
SULLIVAN, John	30	M	None	05De02Cw
BURNES, Pat	20	M	Laborer	05De02Cw
CARTEY, Bridget	42	F	Domestic	05De02Cw
Mary-Jane	20	F	None	05De02Cw
Cathe.	7	F	Child	05De02Cw
TRIMBLE, Ann	20	F	None	05De02Cw
WRIGHT, Francis	35	M	Laborer	05De02Cw
CALWELL, Patrick	20	M	Groom	05De02Cw
RILEY, Lawrence	20	M	Laborer	05De02Cw
FIRMGAN, Bernard	22	M	None	05De02Cw
ALLEN, John	22	M	None	05De02Cw
MCAULIFFE, Johanna	23	F	Dressmaker	05De02Cw

NAMES OF PASSENGERS	AGE	SEX	OCCUPATIONS	DATE PORT SHIP
MCAULIFFE, Eliza	22	F	None	05De02Cw
Patrick	50	M	Blacksmith	05De02Cw
GERARTY, John	40	M	Laborer	05De02Cw
Bridget	35	F	Domestic	05De02Cw
James	12	M	Laborer	05De02Cw
Pat	10	M	None	05De02Cw
John	7	M	Child	05De02Cw
William	4	M	Child	05De02Cw
Mary	.00	F	Infant	05De02Cw
FLYNN, Cathe.	17	F	Domestic	05De02Cw
TURLEY, Winnifred	27	F	None	05De02Cw
KENNY, Cathe.	20	F	None	05De02Cw
GAFFNY, John	22	M	Tailor	05De02Cw
WALSH, Elisa	21	F	Dressmaker	05De02Cw
GIBBEN, Richd.	19	M	Laborer	05De02Cw
KENNEDY, Thos.	35	M	Laborer	05De02Cw
COSTELLO, Thos.	47	M	Blacksmith	05De02Cw
Cathe.	35	F	None	05De02Cw
KELLY, Julia	35	F	Domestic	05De02Cw
DUMPHEY, Willm.	34	M	Laborer	05De02Cw
Ann	33	F	None	05De02Cw
Bridget	.00	F	Infant	05De02Cw
MURPHY, Cathe.	40	F	Domestic	05De02Cw
Bridget	45	F	Domestic	05De02Cw
AYWARD, Mary	1	F	Child	05De02Cw
Bridgett	.00	F	Infant	05De02Cw
TURNEY, Laurence	42	M	Farmer	05De02Cw
Bridget	50	M	None	05De02Cw
Michael	19	M	Laborer	05De02Cw
John	17	M	None	05De02Cw
Cathe.	15	F	None	05De02Cw
KEATING, Pat	20	M	None	05De02Cw
Margt.	27	F	Domestic	05De02Cw
BRADLEY, Margt.	25	F	None	05De02Cw
BRENNAN, Mick	30	M	Tailor	05De02Cw
Bridget	30	F	Domestic	05De02Cw
QUIN, John	23	M	Laborer	05De02Cw
Elisa	13	F	Domestic	05De02Cw
CONNAR, Peter	17	M	Laborer	05De02Cw
ROACH, Honora	17	F	Domestic	05De02Cw
DOWD, Michael	7	M	Child	05De02Cw
Cathe.	30	F	None	05De02Cw
NOONAN, Ellen	25	F	None	05De02Cw
John	28	M	Farmer	05De02Cw
Mary	25	F	None	05De02Cw
David	26	M	None	05De02Cw
Anthony	27	M	None	05De02Cw
Pat	28	M	None	05De02Cw
Mary	29	M	None	05De02Cw
Catharine	9	F	Child	05De02Cw
HILAND, John	27	M	Laborer	05De02Cw
DOYLE, Danl.	35	M	None	05De02Cw
BYRNES, Willm.	35	M	Laborer	05De02Cw
Esther	30	F	None	05De02Cw
REILLY, Thos.	12	M	None	05De02Cw
MATHEWS, Julia	17	F	Domestic	05De02Cw
QUILLANE, Judith	11	F	None	05De02Cw
JOHNSTON, Mary	13	F	None	05De02Cw
STONE, Ann	9	F	Child	05De02Cw
Martin	7	M	Child	05De02Cw
Judy	3	F	Child	05De02Cw
KELLY, Julia	18	F	Housekeeper	05De02Cw
DARAS, Terence	15	M	Laborer	05De02Cw
MCCONNELL, M.J.	27	M	Farmer	05De02Cw
Jane	25	F	None	05De02Cw
GARNON, Pat	20	M	Shoemaker	05De02Cw
WATSON, John	30	M	Laborer	05De02Cw
Margaret	3	M	Child	05De02Cw
ODONNELL, Rose	40	F	Wife	05De02Cw
Pat	17	M	Laborer	05De02Cw
James	15	M	Laborer	05De02Cw
Biddy	20	F	Domestic	05De02Cw
ROONEY, Eugene	25	M	Laborer	05De02Cw
Margaret	23	F	Domestic	05De02Cw
QUIN, Mary	18	F	None	05De02Cw

NAMES OF PASSENGERS	AGE	SEX	OCCUPATIONS	DATE PORT SHIP
HILL, John	20	M	Laborer	05De02Cw
CASTY, John	30	M	Laborer	05De02Cw
FLOOD, Anthony	30	M	None	05De02Cw
CARLETT, Margaret	24	F	Domestic	05De02Cw
SIZE, Cathe.	24	F	None	05De02Cw
HUGHES, Mary	25	F	None	05De02Cw
COONEY, Bridget	18	F	None	05De02Cw
CARLETT, Peggy	14	F	None	05De02Cw
HOWARD, Nancy	00	F	Dressmaker	05De02Cw
Martha	1	F	Child	05De02Cw
RALPH, Margaret	20	F	Domestic	05De02Cw
Joseph	9	M	Child	05De02Cw
DOYLE, John	20	M	Laborer	05De02Cw
LYNCH, Pat	22	M	Laborer	05De02Cw
REHILLY, Eugene	30	M	Laborer	05De02Cw
G.	25	F	Domestic	05De02Cw
Norry	22	F	None	05De02Cw
BRENNAN, Mary	19	F	None	05De02Cw
SLACK, Mary	23	F	None	05De02Cw
FOGARTY, Judy	22	F	None	05De02Cw
REHILLY, Julia	26	F	None	05De02Cw
CHRISTIAN, John	7	M	Child	05De02Cw
Cathe.	5	F	Child	05De02Cw
PATTON, Jane	30	F	None	05De02Cw
RANKIN, U	30	M	Merchant	05De02Cw

ADMIRAL 06 DECEMBER 1849

From Liverpool

NAMES OF PASSENGERS	AGE	SEX	OCCUPATIONS	DATE PORT SHIP
FALLIS, Ann	43	F	Wife	06De02Cz
Stephen	16	M	None	06De02Cz
Margaret	12	F	None	06De02Cz
WILLIAMS, Ann	40	F	Wife	06De02Cz
Edward	13	M	None	06De02Cz
Mary-Ann	9	F	Child	06De02Cz
Catharine	3	F	Child	06De02Cz
FARRELL, Bridget Died-At-Sea	13	F	Servant	06De02Cz
DONNELLY, Elizabeth	35	F	Wife	06De02Cz
Andrew	6	M	Child	06De02Cz
Michael	.00	M	Infant	06De02Cz
CORBET, Larry	26	M	Laborer	06De02Cz
MULLIGAN, James	30	M	Butcher	06De02Cz
MADDEN, Bridget	20	F	Servant	06De02Cz
KEEGAN, Michael	40	M	Laborer	06De02Cz
MCGUIRE, James	25	M	Laborer	06De02Cz
GRAY, Bridget	20	F	Servant	06De02Cz
ROCK, Catharine	19	F	Servant	06De02Cz
LAWLER, Michael	27	M	Laborer	06De02Cz
Johana	20	F	Servant	06De02Cz
MURPHY, Michael	26	M	Laborer	06De02Cz
LUTTRELL, John	21	M	Farmer	06De02Cz
FARRELL, John	22	M	Bookkeeper	06De02Cz
FORRESTER, Jane	40	F	Wife	06De02Cz
Samuel	8	M	Child	06De02Cz
SKILTON, Susan	22	F	Servant	06De02Cz
MCCARNEY, Michael	20	M	Ostler	06De02Cz
MCGRATH, Terrence	22	M	Laborer	06De02Cz
CONNER, Timothy	22	M	Laborer	06De02Cz
GILGAN, Patrick	18	M	Laborer	06De02Cz
FINAGAN, Michael	40	M	Laborer	06De02Cz
KIVALA, John	50	M	Laborer	06De02Cz
MCKENZIE, Ann	28	F	Cook	06De02Cz
MCCOLUM, Thomas	27	M	Farmer	06De02Cz
Matilda	25	F	None	06De02Cz
Sarah-Ann	3	F	Child	06De02Cz
Elizabeth-Jane	.00	F	Infant	06De02Cz
GIBBONS, James	22	M	Stone Mason	06De02Cz
GIBBONS, Maria	21	F	Stone Mason	06De02Cz
BUCKLEY, Patrick	40	M	Groom	06De02Cz
Ellen	30	F	Servant	06De02Cz
SULLIVAN, Margaret	50	F	None	06De02Cz
BUCKLEY, Timothy	11	M	None	06De02Cz
Margaret	10	F	None	06De02Cz
Bridget	8	F	Child	06De02Cz
Catharine	6	F	Child	06De02Cz
Patrick	3	M	Child	06De02Cz
David	.00	M	Infant	06De02Cz
MURPHY, Eliza	20	F	Servant	06De02Cz
CONLY, Jane	20	F	Servant	06De02Cz
LOUGHLEED, James	25	M	Fsvnt	06De02Cz
Mary	30	F	Servant	06De02Cz
CONLAN, Bridget	20	F	House Maid	06De02Cz
CRONAN, Carn.	23	M	Laborer	06De02Cz
LENRY, Johana	30	F	Servant	06De02Cz
JOYCE, Peter	25	M	Laborer	06De02Cz
Sally	30	F	None	06De02Cz
KEW, George	16	M	Flabr	06De02Cz
OFLAHERTY, John	22	M	Flabr	06De02Cz
HEALEY, Patt	18	M	Laborer	06De02Cz
CONLAN, John	30	M	Laborer	06De02Cz
Margaret	30	F	None	06De02Cz
Ann	40	F	None	06De02Cz
Mary	13	F	None	06De02Cz
James	11	M	None	06De02Cz
Mary	3	F	Child	06De02Cz
Catharine Died-At-Sea	.00	F	Infant	06De02Cz
ONEAL, Catharine	17	F	Servant	06De02Cz
Mary	25	F	Servant	06De02Cz
JOHNSTON, Bridget	20	F	Servant	06De02Cz
GRIFFIN, Andrew	61	M	Weaver	06De02Cz
Margaret	50	F	None	06De02Cz
John	33	M	Laborer	06De02Cz
John	27	M	Laborer	06De02Cz
Andrew	20	M	Laborer	06De02Cz
Honor	17	F	None	06De02Cz
HORN, Philip	20	M	Laborer	06De02Cz
GAY, Mathew	40	M	Laborer	06De02Cz
Ann	30	F	None	06De02Cz
Sarah	70	F	None	06De02Cz
Lucinda	20	F	Servant	06De02Cz
GILLMOUR, James	20	M	Laborer	06De02Cz
Saml.	18	M	Laborer	06De02Cz
MURRAY, Elizabeth	30	F	Wife	06De02Cz
Thomas	11	M	None	06De02Cz
Maria	9	F	Child	06De02Cz
Elizabeth	5	F	Child	06De02Cz
MONOGHAN, John	15	M	None	06De02Cz
Michael	11	M	None	06De02Cz
MULLANY, Ann	20	F	Servant	06De02Cz
WILKIN, John	33	M	Farmer	06De02Cz
Elizbth.	43	F	None	06De02Cz
Andrew	19	M	None	06De02Cz
John	17	M	None	06De02Cz
Thos.	13	M	None	06De02Cz
David	11	M	None	06De02Cz
LEONARD, John	18	M	Laborer	06De02Cz
Mary	12	F	None	06De02Cz
WHOLOHAN, John	20	M	Laborer	06De02Cz
Margaret	19	F	Servant	06De02Cz
LOUGHNAR, Jane	00	F	Wife	06De02Cz
Michael	.00	M	Infant	06De02Cz
CONLAN, Patrick	00	M	Unknown	06De02Cz
James	00	M	Unknown	06De02Cz
GORMLY, Patrick	20	M	Laborer	06De02Cz
DUNN, Anthonia	30	F	Lady'S Maid	06De02Cz
WHALAN, Judy	21	F	Servant	06De02Cz
DARGTHY, Catharine	20	F	Servant	06De02Cz
QUILTY, James	21	M	Laborer	06De02Cz
MADAGAN, Patrick	30	M	Laborer	06De02Cz
DONOHUE, Benjamin	30	M	Laborer	06De02Cz
Mary	24	F	None	06De02Cz

NAMES OF PASSENGERS	AGE	SEX	OCCUPATIONS	DATE PORT SHIP
SHEEHAN, Johan	35	M	Laborer	06De02Cz
BUCKLEY, Michael	20	M	Laborer	06De02Cz
KILHAUL, Michael	25	M	Surveyor	06De02Cz
DOYLE, Catharine	18	F	Servant	06De02Cz
BUCKLEY, Mary	25	F	Servant	06De02Cz
BROWN, Daniel	26	M	Laborer	06De02Cz
COGHTER, Bridget	35	F	Wife	06De02Cz
John	10	M	None	06De02Cz
Patrick	3	M	Child	06De02Cz
James	.00	M	Infant	06De02Cz
KINSELLO, Timothy	40	M	Flabr	06De02Cz
Mary	35	F	None	06De02Cz
Ellen	16	F	None	06De02Cz
Bridget	12	F	None	06De02Cz
Ann	10	F	None	06De02Cz
Michael	8	M	Child	06De02Cz
Betty	6	F	Child	06De02Cz
Thomas	.00	M	Infant	06De02Cz
MCDONNELL, James	30	M	Flabr	06De02Cz
GROGAN, Thomas	30	M	Flabr	06De02Cz
MCTYMER, Thomas	40	M	Shopkeeper	06De02Cz
KEHOE, Lazarus	27	M	Attorney	06De02Cz
KELLY, Thomas	26	M	Laborer	06De02Cz
Patrick	18	M	Laborer	06De02Cz
Hugh	19	M	Laborer	06De02Cz
MONOGHAN, Mary	29	F	Wife	06De02Cz
RYAN, William	26	M	Flabr	06De02Cz
Bridget	26	F	Servant	06De02Cz
QUINLAN, Patrick	35	M	Laborer	06De02Cz
MARA, John	19	M	Laborer	06De02Cz
Michael	18	M	Laborer	06De02Cz
POOLE, Mathew	22	M	Laborer	06De02Cz
CALLAM, James	25	M	Laborer	06De02Cz
REILY, Patrick	22	M	Shipwright	06De02Cz
WHALAN, James	19	M	Laborer	06De02Cz
QUILLEN, James	40	M	Laborer	06De02Cz
ROGAN, Mary	20	F	Servant	06De02Cz
LARKIN, Kernan	26	M	Laborer	06De02Cz
HORTAGE, William	13	M	Laborer	06De02Cz
FITZPATRICK, Philip	21	M	Laborer	06De02Cz
Mary	15	F	None	06De02Cz
DONLIN, Bridget	11	F	None	06De02Cz
Mary	9	F	Child	06De02Cz
CUNLIFFE, Thos.	40	M	Laborer	06De02Cz
BURKE, Oliver	50	M	Laborer	06De02Cz
Ellen	35	F	None	06De02Cz
WALSH, Agnes	20	F	Servant	06De02Cz
COSTELLO, Michael	35	M	Laborer	06De02Cz
CONWAY, Catharine	18	F	Servant	06De02Cz
William	5	M	Child	06De02Cz
BIGLAN, Margaret	50	F	Wife	06De02Cz
Timothy	16	M	None	06De02Cz
Patrick	11	M	None	06De02Cz
William	9	M	Child	06De02Cz
Owen	7	M	Child	06De02Cz
Maria	5	F	Child	06De02Cz
IRWIN, Bridget	16	F	Dressmaker	06De02Cz
Thomas	12	M	None	06De02Cz
DESMONE, Hannah	32	F	Wife	06De02Cz
MONOGHAN, Hugh	14	M	None	06De02Cz
DONOHUE, Timothy	22	M	Laborer	06De02Cz
Ellen	3	F	Child	06De02Cz
Catharine	70	F	None	06De02Cz
HEALEY, John	21	M	Laborer	06De02Cz
Michael	12	M	None	06De02Cz
Mark	14	M	None	06De02Cz
ONEAL, Honora	23	F	Servant	06De02Cz
Patrick	14	M	None	06De02Cz
Bridget	11	F	None	06De02Cz
KEARNS, Catharine	22	F	Servant	06De02Cz
MUNROE, Patrick	20	M	Laborer	06De02Cz
MAHER, Honor	22	F	Servant	06De02Cz
CRONIN, Isabella	26	F	Servant	06De02Cz
MCMAHON, Catharine	25	F	Servant	06De02Cz
SCREENAN, Rose	20	F	Servant	06De02Cz

NAMES OF PASSENGERS	AGE	SEX	OCCUPATIONS	DATE PORT SHIP
HUGHES, Catharine	20	F	Servant	06De02Cz
LYNAN, Garrett	28	M	Laborer	06De02Cz
MORAN, Wm.	48	M	Farmer	06De02Cz
Richard	18	M	None	06De02Cz
CLARKE, Henry	22	M	Ostler	06De02Cz
Margaret	22	F	None	06De02Cz
Ann	.00	F	Infant	06De02Cz
QUIGLEY, Catharine	24	F	Servant	06De02Cz
Judith	20	F	Servant	06De02Cz
COSTELLO, William	50	M	Farmer	06De02Cz
Margaret	14	F	None	06De02Cz
HARGADEN, Charles	25	M	Pvmt	06De02Cz
GLEESON, John	25	M	Laborer	06De02Cz
Michael	19	M	Laborer	06De02Cz
Ann	27	F	None	06De02Cz
John	00	M	Unknown	06De02Cz
Margaret	.00	F	Infant	06De02Cz
Bridget	.00	F	Infant	06De02Cz
MEAGHER, Thomas	27	M	Laborer	06De02Cz
Sally	28	F	None	06De02Cz
BROPHY, Patrick	35	M	Laborer	06De02Cz
MELAMPY, Philip	35	M	Laborer	06De02Cz
COLLISON, James	23	M	Laborer	06De02Cz
SHANAHAN, Nancy	26	F	Servant	06De02Cz
SHORE, Thos.	30	M	Bootmaker	06De02Cz
BANNON, Judy	50	F	None	06De02Cz
John	17	M	Laborer	06De02Cz
KENNEDY, Sally	25	F	Servant	06De02Cz
Betty	15	F	Servant	06De02Cz
MCMUNN, Maria	28	F	Wife	06De02Cz
Mary	.00	F	Infant	06De02Cz
NAVAN, Peter	48	M	Farmer	06De02Cz
GAFNEY, Patrick	16	M	Spinner	06De02Cz
CASSIDY, Law.	25	M	Butler	06De02Cz
John	22	M	Stctr	06De02Cz
Ann	24	F	Servant	06De02Cz
DAILY, Ellen	23	F	Servant	06De02Cz
Catharine	20	F	Servant	06De02Cz
FINNERTY, Redman	22	M	Laborer	06De02Cz
BYRNE, Julia	18	F	Servant	06De02Cz
Mary	16	F	Servant	06De02Cz
GLENDEN, Mary	20	F	Servant	06De02Cz
Eliza	18	F	Servant	06De02Cz
BYRNES, Maria	19	F	Servant	06De02Cz
CURLY, Mary	40	F	Unknown	06De02Cz
Mary	20	F	None	06De02Cz
MARTIN, Bernard	21	M	Laborer	06De02Cz
KELLY, Edward	26	M	Laborer	06De02Cz
PHEVLIN, Mary	18	F	Servant	06De02Cz
GARRY, Ann	20	F	Servant	06De02Cz
WHALAN, Ann	00	F	Daughter	06De02Cz
BRENNAN, Ann	22	F	Servant	06De02Cz
NOLAN, John	36	M	Laborer	06De02Cz
AMOOTY, Matthew	16	M	Laborer	06De02Cz
William	9	M	Child	06De02Cz
DUFFY, James	35	M	Laborer	06De02Cz
BRYAN, Patrick	45	M	Laborer	06De02Cz
CRIMLEY, John	19	M	Tipwkr	06De02Cz
MURPHY, Mary	20	F	Servant	06De02Cz
Bridget	18	F	Servant	06De02Cz
SHERIDAN, Rose	18	F	Servant	06De02Cz
OCONNOR, Margt.	50	F	Unknown	06De02Cz
HART, Mary	17	F	Servant	06De02Cz
CONNERTY, Michael	16	M	Laborer	06De02Cz
MCCAHILL, John	20	M	Laborer	06De02Cz
Julia	12	F	None	06De02Cz
Thomas	7	M	Child	06De02Cz
Ann	12	F	None	06De02Cz
MCCABE, Hugh	20	M	Laborer	06De02Cz
GIBNEY, Margaret	20	F	Servant	06De02Cz
LOCKHART, William	30	M	Shoemaker	06De02Cz
Sarah	18	F	Dressmaker	06De02Cz
LINDY, Daniel	44	M	Laborer	06De02Cz
Mary	45	F	None	06De02Cz
SMITH, William	28	M	Gdnr	06De02Cz

NAMES OF PASSENGERS	AGE	SEX	OCCUPATIONS	DATE PORT SHIP

MINERVA 06 DECEMBER 1849

From Halifax

NAMES OF PASSENGERS	AGE	SEX	OCCUPATIONS	DATE PORT SHIP
COOTH, Wm.	24	M	Gentleman	06De08Ap
COLBERT, Wm.	28	M	Laborer	06De08Ap
MOONEY, R.	24	M	Cooper	06De08Ap
WARD, U-Mrs.	36	F	Unknown	06De08Ap

ABEONA 07 DECEMBER 1849

From Liverpool

NAMES OF PASSENGERS	AGE	SEX	OCCUPATIONS	DATE PORT SHIP
COLLINS, Mary	36	F	Mangler	07De02Da
Elizabeth	8	F	Child	07De02Da
DALEY, Maria	17	F	Servant	07De02Da
BUTLER, Bridget	20	F	Servant	07De02Da
BUCKLY, Mary	22	F	Spinster	07De02Da
KELLY, Margaret	18	F	Spinster	07De02Da
KENAN, John	25	M	Laborer	07De02Da
Mary-Ann	.08	F	Infant	07De02Da
SMITH, Anne	14	F	Spinster	07De02Da
Bridget	10	F	Spinster	07De02Da
Andrew	5	M	Child	07De02Da
Edward	3	M	Child	07De02Da
Mary	17	F	Spinster	07De02Da
Sarah	20	F	Spinster	07De02Da
RYLER, Conner	55	M	Farmer	07De02Da
MCGOVEN, John	21	M	Laborer	07De02Da
MCGUIRE, Hugh	16	M	Laborer	07De02Da
MCALOON, Ellen	16	F	Spinster	07De02Da
MCGUIRE, Margaret	16	F	Spinster	07De02Da
Mary	19	F	Spinster	07De02Da
HUDSON, Susan	20	F	Spinster	07De02Da
BAXTER, Catherine	18	F	Spinster	07De02Da
DUFFY, Patrick	40	M	Laborer	07De02Da
Mary	30	F	Servant	07De02Da
EGAN, Michael	9	M	Child	07De02Da
DUFFY, Bridget	1	F	Child	07De02Da
BOYLE, Margaret	24	F	None	07De02Da
HANLEY, Margaret	30	F	Servant	07De02Da
Judy	.06	F	Infant	07De02Da
Died-At-Sea				
CONNER, Patrick	20	M	Servant	07De02Da
Ann	12	F	Servant	07De02Da
FINN, Mary	18	F	Spinster	07De02Da
CAULIFFE, Bridget	18	F	Servant	07De02Da
CARLIN, Ellen	20	F	Servant	07De02Da
TREMBLE, Michael	18	M	Laborer	07De02Da
BRADLY, Catherine	40	F	Unknown	07De02Da
Mary	29	F	Servant	07De02Da
John	5	M	Child	07De02Da
Catherine	3	F	Child	07De02Da
Ellen	.09	F	Infant	07De02Da
DUFFY, John	20	M	Farmer	07De02Da
NEILAND, Patrick	26	M	Farmer	07De02Da
DEGNAN, Peter	16	M	Laborer	07De02Da
Ann	20	F	Spinster	07De02Da
GOVIN, Mary	20	F	Spinster	07De02Da
ENNIS, John	20	M	Laborer	07De02Da
James	15	M	Laborer	07De02Da
DONLAND, Mathew	30	M	Farmer	07De02Da
Ellen	30	F	None	07De02Da
DONLAND, Mary	9	F	Child	07De02Da
John	5	M	Child	07De02Da
Ellen	.11	F	Infant	07De02Da
NICHOLL, Robert	50	M	Carter	07De02Da
Sally	50	F	Spinster	07De02Da
BOYLE, Francis	4	M	Child	07De02Da
NICHOLL, Arthur	10	M	Carter	07De02Da
Matilda	12	F	Spinster	07De02Da
KEYS, U	13	F	Spinster	07De02Da
Thomas	8	M	Child	07De02Da
WILSON, Mary	23	F	Servant	07De02Da
PARK, A.	20	F	Servant	07De02Da
MCVAUGH, Ann	40	F	Servant	07De02Da
REWIN, Mary	20	F	Servant	07De02Da
DEGMAN, Mary	20	F	Servant	07De02Da
RODDY, James	22	M	Blacksmith	07De02Da
John	12	M	None	07De02Da
Honora	10	F	Spinster	07De02Da
Mary	7	F	Child	07De02Da
KENEDY, Arthur	22	M	Farmer	07De02Da
MCARDLE, John	24	M	Laborer	07De02Da
MURPHY, Bridget	20	F	Servant	07De02Da
LAUGHLIN, Michael	22	M	Laborer	07De02Da
Rebecca	22	F	Servant	07De02Da
James	3	M	Child	07De02Da
Died-At-Sea				
HOMEN, John	25	M	Laborer	07De02Da
HOOLAHAN, Patrick	25	M	Laborer	07De02Da
CUNNINGHAM, Mary	25	F	Servant	07De02Da
FARREL, Bryan	40	M	Weaver	07De02Da
DONELAND, Peter	7	M	Child	07De02Da
BOYLE, Andrew	6	M	Child	07De02Da
FARREL, Margret	4	F	Child	07De02Da
Patrick	10	M	None	07De02Da
A.	8	F	Child	07De02Da
Ellen	6	F	Child	07De02Da
WILSON, Mary	60	F	Wi	07De02Da
Francis	22	M	Spinner	07De02Da
KELLY, Maria	32	F	None	07De02Da
MCCONNIE, Bridget	27	F	None	07De02Da
KELLEY, Ann	.07	F	Infant	07De02Da
SHEELY, Timothy	22	M	Laborer	07De02Da
Mary-Ann	21	F	Servant	07De02Da
SULIVAN, John	40	M	Miner	07De02Da
SHEELAND, Edward	26	M	Laborer	07De02Da
Mary	30	F	Servant	07De02Da
MALON, Phillip	26	M	Laborer	07De02Da
CALLESTEN, Mary	20	F	Servant	07De02Da
MCARDLE, James	25	M	Laborer	07De02Da
RYAN, Thomas	40	M	Farmer	07De02Da
Johanna	13	F	Servant	07De02Da
CREIGHTON, Thomas	18	M	Tailor	07De02Da
ARMSTRONG, Ellen	18	F	Spinster	07De02Da
MOORE, Amabella	18	F	Spinster	07De02Da
RYAN, Catherine	12	F	Spinster	07De02Da
RODDY, Ellen	40	F	Servant	07De02Da
HALFPENNY, Mary	20	F	Servant	07De02Da
THOMPSON, William	26	M	Farmer	07De02Da
MAY, William	20	M	Farmer	07De02Da
CONCANNON, Patrick	22	M	Blacksmith	07De02Da
MURPHY, Patrick	40	M	Farmer	07De02Da
Ann	20	F	Spinster	07De02Da
Mary	18	F	Spinster	07De02Da
James	14	M	Farmer	07De02Da
CONWAY, Mary	16	F	Spinster	07De02Da
WARD, Leary	25	M	Fidlr	07De02Da
Margaret	20	F	Servant	07De02Da
BOYLE, Ann	20	F	Servant	07De02Da
DOVAN, Bridget	16	F	Servant	07De02Da
MCMAHON, Margaret	20	F	Spinster	07De02Da
FITZMAURICE, Margaret	19	F	Nurse	07De02Da
ARNOLD, Michael	20	M	Laborer	07De02Da
CALLAGHAN, Rose	27	F	Dressmaker	07De02Da
MCENAMY, Bridget	20	F	Dressmaker	07De02Da
BOYLAND, Bridget	18	F	Spinster	07De02Da

NAMES OF PASSENGERS	AGE	SEX	OCCUPATIONS	DATE PORT SHIP
BALLAM, John	30	M	Tailor	07De02Da
KENAN, Mary	18	F	Servant	07De02Da
CONNOLLY, Patrick	28	M	Tailor	07De02Da
HANNAH, Rose	23	F	Spinster	07De02Da
CONNOLLY, Betsy	24	F	Spinster	07De02Da
GUNN, Andrew	30	M	Farmer	07De02Da
FARREL, Catherine	20	F	Spinster	07De02Da
ONEIL, Catherine	35	F	Servant	07De02Da
HERON, Patrick	30	M	Farmer	07De02Da
Thomas	28	M	Farmer	07De02Da
KENT, James	24	M	Farmer	07De02Da
KINNEY, Michael	28	M	Porter	07De02Da
KEALY, Edward	26	M	Jobber	07De02Da
DILLON, Sarah	45	F	Nurse	07De02Da
MONAN, Catherine	18	F	Spinster	07De02Da
MAYHU, Mary	48	F	Spinster	07De02Da
BYRNE, Bridget	19	F	Dressmaker	07De02Da
GREEN, Winfred	19	M	Servant	07De02Da
MCGUIRE, Francis	20	M	Laborer	07De02Da
MCDONAL, Ellen	19	F	Servant	07De02Da
FORY, Margaret	19	F	Servant	07De02Da
MCDONALD, George	20	M	Laborer	07De02Da
HAYES, Honora	28	F	Spinster	07De02Da
Anastatia	23	F	Spinster	07De02Da
Roddy	14	M	Farmer	07De02Da
John	13	M	Farmer	07De02Da
CLANCY, John	50	M	Laborer	07De02Da
Honora	.04	F	Infant	07De02Da
KEHOE, James	21	M	Laborer	07De02Da
BYRNES, Mary	22	F	Servant	07De02Da
MORLAND, John	28	M	Servant	07De02Da
EUSTIC, Catherine	20	F	Servant	07De02Da
WRIGHT, Alexander	20	M	Farmer	07De02Da
HUMPHRY, Michael	25	M	Farmer	07De02Da
GORGAN, Robert	25	M	Farmer	07De02Da
MCCARTHY, Brandy	22	F	Seamstress	07De02Da
BOYLE, James	25	M	Cooper	07De02Da
CONNOR, James	31	M	Tailor	07De02Da
Honora	27	F	Servant	07De02Da
CREIGHTON, Dennis	31	M	Laborer	07De02Da
READY, John	25	M	Bricklayer	07De02Da
Ann	24	F	Dressmaker	07De02Da
TEERANAN, Robert	23	M	Farmer	07De02Da
LEEMAN, Mary	23	F	Wife	07De02Da
STRONG, John	30	M	Farmer	07De02Da
Margaret (W)	30	F	None	07De02Da
KENEDY, Honora	40	F	Servant	07De02Da
DOBSON, Mary	18	F	Spinster	07De02Da
HANCHEON, Nicholas	27	M	Laborer	07De02Da
YOUNG, Thomas	20	M	Cooper	07De02Da
FAHAL, John	26	M	Blacksmith	07De02Da
MCCORMIC, Michael	25	M	Laborer	07De02Da
WELSH, Patrick	36	M	Laborer	07De02Da
SHOOTIN, Thomas	26	M	Farmer	07De02Da
TOOLE, James	46	M	Paper Maker	07De02Da
RYAN, James	30	M	Laborer	07De02Da
DEMODY, Thomas	20	M	Laborer	07De02Da
PURCELL, Phillip	25	M	Laborer	07De02Da
BURK, David	20	M	Carpenter	07De02Da
MCGUIRE, John	19	M	Laborer	07De02Da
CONNER, Dennis	24	M	Laborer	07De02Da
HAND, John	23	M	Laborer	07De02Da
HARY, Ann	19	F	Dressmaker	07De02Da
MCAVORY, Bridget	21	F	Servant	07De02Da
BOWLAND, Mary	20	F	Spinster	07De02Da
CONNERY, Judey	20	F	Servant	07De02Da
RYAN, Michael	20	M	Laborer	07De02Da
KENEDEY, Thomas	30	M	Steward	07De02Da
TRACEY, Ellen	25	F	Servant	07De02Da
MCALROY, Catherine	23	F	Servant	07De02Da
CONNER, John	20	M	Tailor	07De02Da
Eliza	10	F	Servant	07De02Da
HAMMOND, John	23	M	Laborer	07De02Da
HOYE, Margaret	18	F	Servant	07De02Da
MCKAY, Henry	30	M	Iron Monger	07De02Da
MCWIGGINS, James	50	M	Laborer	07De02Da
Bryan	23	M	Laborer	07De02Da
Patrick	18	M	Servant	07De02Da
MCWIGGANS, Ann	50	F	Servant	07De02Da
MCWIGGAN, Mary	24	F	Servant	07De02Da
Rose	22	F	Servant	07De02Da
MINGIN, Bridge	20	F	Servant	07De02Da
DOONAN, Catherine	30	F	Servant	07De02Da
Mary	6	F	Child	07De02Da
Bridget	4	F	Child	07De02Da
BRADLY, William	18	M	Laborer	07De02Da
REID, Mary	26	F	Servant	07De02Da
Rebecca	3	F	Child	07De02Da
Thomas	2	M	Child	07De02Da
MAHER, Paul	21	M	Servant	07De02Da
CALLAGAN, Margaret	30	F	Servant	07De02Da
HAGAN, Alic	22	F	Servant	07De02Da
MCWIGGAN, Ann	26	F	Servant	07De02Da
KEATING, John	23	M	Laborer	07De02Da
CALLAGHAN, John	3	M	Child	07De02Da
CALLAGAN, Mary	.07	F	Infant	07De02Da
Mary	20	F	Spinster	07De02Da
CAUGHLIN, Mary	21	F	Spinster	07De02Da
MORRISON, Bridget	21	F	Spinster	07De02Da
BLACK, John	20	M	Carpenter	07De02Da
Michael	18	M	Laborer	07De02Da
Margaret	21	F	Spinster	07De02Da
Ellen	15	F	Spinster	07De02Da
Catherine	.06	F	Infant	07De02Da
MEAGHER, Bridget	21	F	Spinster	07De02Da
Ann	18	F	Spinster	07De02Da
COMMEFORD, Margaret	21	F	Spinster	07De02Da
SMITH, James	35	M	Farmer	07De02Da
DALEY, Patrick	18	M	Butcher	07De02Da
MCLAUGHLIN, Michael	21	M	Surveyor	07De02Da
Ellen	14	F	Servant	07De02Da
Thomas	11	M	Servant	07De02Da
DEVINE, Anthony	36	M	Laborer	07De02Da
SMITH, Thomas	20	M	Unknown	07De02Da
DELISH, William	18	M	Farmer	07De02Da
SEDWIC, John	10	M	Servant	07De02Da
BYRNES, Patrick	18	M	Ostler	07De02Da
GREENAN, Ann	20	F	Servant	07De02Da
HYNAN, James	28	M	Laborer	07De02Da
ENNIS, Thomas	15	M	Servant	07De02Da
HAMILL, Ann	18	F	Spinster	07De02Da
FARREL, Thomas	25	M	Blacksmith	07De02Da
Catherine	25	F	Servant	07De02Da
Bridget	.06	F	Infant	07De02Da
STEPTES, Mervin	20	F	Servant	07De02Da
RYAN, Bridget	20	F	Servant	07De02Da
SWINGSTON, John	30	M	Weaver	07De02Da
CONNELLY, David	20	M	Laborer	07De02Da
Dennis	20	M	Laborer	07De02Da
GALLAGHAN, Conner	26	M	Laborer	07De02Da
OCONNER, Timothy	30	M	Servant	07De02Da
MEHONG, Honora	16	F	Servant	07De02Da
FITZGERRALD, Ellen	35	F	Servant	07De02Da
John	9	M	Child	07De02Da
SHEAN, Daniel	25	M	Servant	07De02Da
FARRELL, Edward	30	M	Mason	07De02Da
Ellen	35	F	Servant	07De02Da
Thomas	3	M	Child	07De02Da
Michael	.02	M	Infant	07De02Da
CASSEY, Thomas	26	M	Servant	07De02Da
SHEDDY, Ellen	19	F	Servant	07De02Da
MORRIGAN, Bridget	25	F	Servant	07De02Da
HENESEY, Honora	25	F	Servant	07De02Da
Thomas	18	M	Servant	07De02Da
RYLEY, Thomas	20	M	Servant	07De02Da
Cathe.	18	F	Servant	07De02Da
YORE, Catherine	28	F	Unknown	07De02Da
Catherine	50	F	Unknown	07De02Da
Peter	2	M	Child	07De02Da
BYRNE, John	40	M	None	07De02Da

NAMES OF PASSENGERS	AGE	SEX	OCCUPATIONS	DATE PORT SHIP
BYRNES, Ann	30	F	Servant	07De02Da
Ann	18	F	Servant	07De02Da
MCCORMIC, James	20	M	Servant	07De02Da
MARTIN, Thomas	17	M	Servant	07De02Da
FARRELL, Catherine	20	F	Servant	07De02Da
BRANDON, James	50	M	Servant	07De02Da
Jane	40	F	Servant	07De02Da
Francis	12	M	Servant	07De02Da
John	9	M	Child	07De02Da
ARMSTRONG, Eliza	40	F	Servant	07De02Da
Margaret Died-At-Sea	35	F	Servant	07De02Da
DUNHOL, James	22	M	Grocer	07De02Da
MCCABE, James	20	M	Farmer	07De02Da
DONOHOL, Mary	20	F	Servant	07De02Da
WHEELAN, Catherine	22	F	Servant	07De02Da
Judy	30	F	Servant	07De02Da
SMITH, Margaret	20	F	Servant	07De02Da
WELSH, Mary	20	F	Servant	07De02Da
SMITH, Andrew	12	M	Servant	07De02Da
Thomas	9	M	Child	07De02Da
CANNANGS, Patrick	28	M	Laborer	07De02Da
Judith	20	F	Servant	07De02Da
BUTLERS, Alice	28	F	Servant	07De02Da
KENNA, Bridget	24	F	Servant	07De02Da
MCDONALD, Mary	20	F	Servant	07De02Da
BIRNES, John	21	M	Shoemaker	07De02Da
MCCORMICK, Ann	18	F	Servant	07De02Da
FLANHAURY, Mary	20	F	Servant	07De02Da
MCALOON, Margaret	16	F	Servant	07De02Da
BYRNES, Mary	5	F	Child	07De02Da
MCGOW, John	20	M	Servant	07De02Da

WESTMINSTER 10 DECEMBER 1849

From London

NAMES OF PASSENGERS	AGE	SEX	OCCUPATIONS	DATE PORT SHIP
RILEY, Mary	32	F	Unknown	10De06Cy
Bridget	7	F	Child	10De06Cy
Stephen	4	M	Child	10De06Cy
Cath.	1	F	Child	10De06Cy
CAREY, Margaret	23	F	Unknown	10De06Cy
Sarah	20	F	Unknown	10De06Cy
FLYNN, Peter	30	M	Laborer	10De06Cy
RATAGAN, Margaret	39	F	Unknown	10De06Cy
Bridget	13	F	Unknown	10De06Cy
Cath.	11	F	Unknown	10De06Cy
Wm.	7	M	Child	10De06Cy
Sarah	5	F	Child	10De06Cy
Mary-A.	2	F	Child	10De06Cy
RYAN, Mary	45	F	Unknown	10De06Cy
OHARA, Cath.	32	F	Unknown	10De06Cy
Mary-A.	9	F	Child	10De06Cy
HEWLETT, Geo.	30	M	Unknown	10De06Cy
Eliza	30	F	Unknown	10De06Cy
William	8	M	Child	10De06Cy
Geo	6	M	Child	10De06Cy
Louisa	4	F	Child	10De06Cy
Florence	3	F	Child	10De06Cy
PARKEMAN, Mary-Ann	22	F	Unknown	10De06Cy
BURNS, James	22	M	Mariner	10De06Cy

GREAT-WESTERN 10 DECEMBER 1849

From Bermuda And St.Thomas

NAMES OF PASSENGERS	AGE	SEX	OCCUPATIONS	DATE PORT SHIP
CHAMBERS, James	35	M	Merchant	10De13Ao
GIBB, George	16	M	Student	10De13Ao
WINNARD, Wm.	26	M	Tinsmith	10De13Ao
WATTS, Robt.	31	M	Stone Mason	10De13Ao
ROFE, Wm.	28	M	Laborer	10De13Ao
SMART, Andw.	26	M	Stone Mason	10De13Ao
KNOTT, John	30	M	Carpenter	10De13Ao
WADDANS, Wm.	30	M	Baker	10De13Ao
LEWIS, Hugh	31	M	Sawer	10De13Ao
CHURCHLEY, Wm.	44	M	Laborer	10De13Ao

CENTURION 12 DECEMBER 1849

From Liverpool

NAMES OF PASSENGERS	AGE	SEX	OCCUPATIONS	DATE PORT SHIP
WALSH, Thos.	25	M	Farmer	12De02Db
Julia	26	F	Unknown	12De02Db
MURPHY, Ellen	20	F	Unknown	12De02Db
WILKINSON, Jas.	28	M	Unknown	12De02Db
DONNELLY, D.	20	M	Unknown	12De02Db
WILKINSON, Margt.	20	F	Unknown	12De02Db
KILMARTIN, Ellen	22	F	Unknown	12De02Db
MCKENEY, Ed.	24	M	Unknown	12De02Db
WILKINSON, Wm.	20	M	Unknown	12De02Db
SHEA, Pat.	36	M	Unknown	12De02Db
LUMBARD, Mary	53	F	Unknown	12De02Db
Johan.	50	F	Unknown	12De02Db
Rich	25	M	Unknown	12De02Db
Pat	18	M	Unknown	12De02Db
WILKINSON, Ellen	18	F	Unknown	12De02Db
HENNESSEY, Mary	60	F	Unknown	12De02Db
WALSH, Ellen	21	F	Unknown	12De02Db
DILLARIE, Jerry	18	F	Unknown	12De02Db
Pet	15	M	Unknown	12De02Db
HAYES, Wm.	40	M	Unknown	12De02Db
Mary	40	F	Unknown	12De02Db
Cath.	13	F	Unknown	12De02Db
Eliza	12	F	Unknown	12De02Db
Ellen	11	F	Unknown	12De02Db
COLLINS, Corn.	17	M	Unknown	12De02Db
SWEENEY, Thos.	25	M	Unknown	12De02Db
SHEEHAN, John	26	M	Unknown	12De02Db
BUCKLEY, Tim	30	M	Unknown	12De02Db
ROURKE, John	22	M	Unknown	12De02Db
Geo.	18	M	Unknown	12De02Db
Eliza	22	F	Unknown	12De02Db
DILLON, Mary	20	F	Unknown	12De02Db
SHEEHAN, Ellen	40	F	Unknown	12De02Db
Corn.	11	M	Unknown	12De02Db
Margt.	8	F	Child	12De02Db
Mary	6	F	Child	12De02Db
Pat	3	M	Child	12De02Db
Ben	.06	M	Infant	12De02Db
FITZGERRALD, Mick	22	M	Unknown	12De02Db
Bridget	10	F	Unknown	12De02Db
Jerry	8	M	Child	12De02Db
CURTIN, Eliza	32	F	Unknown	12De02Db
Jas.	3	M	Child	12De02Db
Dan	35	M	Unknown	12De02Db

NAMES OF PASSENGERS	AGE	SEX	OCCUPATIONS	DATE PORT SHIP
CURTIN, David	.03	M	Infant	12De02Db
KEEFE, Jim	30	M	Unknown	12De02Db
CALLIGAN, John	25	M	Unknown	12De02Db
FALVY, Mary	28	F	Unknown	12De02Db
Jerry	26	M	Unknown	12De02Db
SULLIVAN, Margt.	50	F	Unknown	12De02Db
SHEA, Dennis	5	M	Child	12De02Db
Mary	3	F	Child	12De02Db
LEARY, Pat	27	M	Unknown	12De02Db
Ellen	35	F	Unknown	12De02Db
Mary	19	F	Unknown	12De02Db
Deborah	7	F	Child	12De02Db
SULLIVAN, Honor	24	F	Unknown	12De02Db
Jerry	20	F	Unknown	12De02Db
CRONAN, Mary	20	F	Unknown	12De02Db
SULLIVAN, Dan	40	M	Unknown	12De02Db
LEARY, Dennis	32	M	Unknown	12De02Db
JERRITT, Ed	30	M	Unknown	12De02Db
OKEEFE, Mary	20	F	Unknown	12De02Db
Harriet	16	F	Unknown	12De02Db
CRONIN, Phil	19	M	Unknown	12De02Db
FITZGERALD, Mick	14	M	Unknown	12De02Db
AHERN, Pat	20	M	Unknown	12De02Db
NAGLE, Eliza	34	F	Unknown	12De02Db
KEEFE, Pat	19	M	Unknown	12De02Db
ROCHE, Wm.	27	M	Unknown	12De02Db
PRISCOLL, Honor	30	F	Unknown	12De02Db
FITZPATRICK, Mary	20	F	Unknown	12De02Db
FITZGERALD, Mary	19	F	Unknown	12De02Db
Mary	60	F	Unknown	12De02Db
SULLIVAN, Johanna	40	F	Unknown	12De02Db
Mary	9	F	Child	12De02Db
Owen	5	M	Child	12De02Db
John	.03	M	Infant	12De02Db
GEHAN, Nelly	18	F	Unknown	12De02Db
Jerry	20	M	Unknown	12De02Db
AHERN, Cath.	20	F	Unknown	12De02Db
LONG, Eliza	40	F	Unknown	12De02Db
John	8	M	Child	12De02Db
Jas.	4	M	Child	12De02Db
DUNN, Pat	50	M	Unknown	12De02Db
HOLAHAN, Dan	40	M	Unknown	12De02Db
KIRVANE, Jas.	25	M	Unknown	12De02Db
CONNER, John	16	M	Unknown	12De02Db
BARRETT, Cath.	50	F	Unknown	12De02Db
John	16	M	Unknown	12De02Db
CONNER, Nancy	40	F	Unknown	12De02Db
GRIFFIN, Ellen	50	F	Unknown	12De02Db
Thos.	15	M	Unknown	12De02Db
GARARTY, Ellen	30	F	Unknown	12De02Db
Pat	8	M	Child	12De02Db
Eliza	5	F	Child	12De02Db
KILKELLAN, Dan	20	M	Unknown	12De02Db
FLAHINE, John	24	F	Unknown	12De02Db
Honor	15	F	Unknown	12De02Db
SULLIVAN, Mick	30	M	Unknown	12De02Db
MORAN, Pat	30	M	Unknown	12De02Db
JULIAN, Honor	30	F	Unknown	12De02Db
WALSH, Johanna	16	F	Unknown	12De02Db
NEIL, Margt.	20	F	Unknown	12De02Db
GRIFFIN, Cath.	19	F	Unknown	12De02Db
KENNEY, Tho.	26	M	Unknown	12De02Db
GRADY, Mick	25	M	Unknown	12De02Db
ROCHE, Jno.	23	M	Unknown	12De02Db
HOLBERT, Eliza	24	F	Unknown	12De02Db
GILLAN, B.	50	F	Unknown	12De02Db
Mary	14	F	Unknown	12De02Db
Wm.	10	M	Unknown	12De02Db
RADY, Margt.	20	F	Unknown	12De02Db
SHERLOCK, Jas.	13	M	Unknown	12De02Db
Ann	11	F	Unknown	12De02Db
COLLINS, R.	15	M	Unknown	12De02Db
HARNETT, Johan	30	M	Unknown	12De02Db
LYNCH, Harriet	30	F	Unknown	12De02Db
KING, Bryan	40	M	Unknown	12De02Db

NAMES OF PASSENGERS	AGE	SEX	OCCUPATIONS	DATE PORT SHIP
KING, Julia	44	F	Unknown	12De02Db
DUKE, Jas.	35	M	Unknown	12De02Db
Jas.	12	M	Unknown	12De02Db
MULLOY, Peter	18	M	Unknown	12De02Db
REYNOLDS, Ann	18	F	Unknown	12De02Db
Ann	18	F	Unknown	12De02Db
Mary	26	F	Unknown	12De02Db
MCAWEENEY, Thos.	3	M	Child	12De02Db
Frank	2	M	Child	12De02Db
MURPHY, Dennis	28	M	Unknown	12De02Db
Cath.	26	F	Unknown	12De02Db
Johanna	20	F	Unknown	12De02Db
Ellen	5	F	Child	12De02Db
Honor	.06	F	Infant	12De02Db
Mary	.06	F	Infant	12De02Db
DOWNEY, Mary	20	F	Unknown	12De02Db
KEEGAN, Pat	48	M	Unknown	12De02Db
Mary	30	F	Unknown	12De02Db
Margt.	14	F	Unknown	12De02Db
Brid.	11	F	Unknown	12De02Db
Cath.	9	F	Child	12De02Db
Maria	7	F	Child	12De02Db
Ann	5	F	Child	12De02Db
Pat	.09	M	Infant	12De02Db
HORAN, Pat	20	M	Unknown	12De02Db
HUNT, John	53	M	Unknown	12De02Db
Mary	45	F	Unknown	12De02Db
Rich	30	M	Unknown	12De02Db
Thos.	15	M	Unknown	12De02Db
Wm.	13	M	Unknown	12De02Db
Ann	11	F	Unknown	12De02Db
Saml.	9	M	Child	12De02Db
Robt.	7	M	Child	12De02Db
Eliza	5	F	Child	12De02Db
Henry	3	F	Child	12De02Db
Sarah	2	F	Child	12De02Db
Fanny	.03	F	Infant	12De02Db
Died-At-Sea				
PARSONS, John	21	M	Unknown	12De02Db
DALEY, Robt.	18	M	Unknown	12De02Db
TRACY, Dennis	32	M	Unknown	12De02Db
Cath.	41	F	Unknown	12De02Db
CONNERS, Brid.	20	F	Unknown	12De02Db
Mary	28	F	Unknown	12De02Db
KANE, Mary	20	F	Unknown	12De02Db
GARRIGAN, Ann	40	F	Unknown	12De02Db
Mick	35	M	Unknown	12De02Db
Mat	20	M	Unknown	12De02Db
Ann	18	F	Unknown	12De02Db
Brid.	16	F	Unknown	12De02Db
Brid.	18	F	Unknown	12De02Db
Mary	8	F	Child	12De02Db
Mat	.03	M	Infant	12De02Db
BAILEY, Alex	49	M	Unknown	12De02Db
U-Mrs.	40	F	Unknown	12De02Db
Henry	13	M	Unknown	12De02Db
Alex	12	M	Unknown	12De02Db
BETTRIDGE, John	43	M	Unknown	12De02Db
U-Mrs.	44	F	Unknown	12De02Db
John	18	M	Unknown	12De02Db
George	15	M	Unknown	12De02Db
Robt.	13	M	Unknown	12De02Db
Alf.	3	M	Child	12De02Db
Sarah	10	F	Unknown	12De02Db
Emily	8	F	Child	12De02Db
FINCHARD, Jas.	23	M	Unknown	12De02Db
BRYAN, Jas.	39	M	Unknown	12De02Db
Ann	39	F	Unknown	12De02Db
Bartley	.06	M	Infant	12De02Db
Died-At-Sea				
Bartley	18	M	Unknown	12De02Db
DORAN, John	43	M	Unknown	12De02Db
Cath.	30	F	Unknown	12De02Db
Wm.	1	M	Child	12De02Db
Died-At-Sea				

NAMES OF PASSENGERS	AGE	SEX	OCCUPATIONS	DATE PORT SHIP
WATERS, John	12	M	Unknown	12De02Db
WALSH, Mary	22	F	Unknown	12De02Db
Brid.	19	F	Unknown	12De02Db
HART, Margt.	22	F	Unknown	12De02Db
HAYES, Rose	17	F	Unknown	12De02Db
COLEMAN, U-Mrs.	25	F	Unknown	12De02Db
CARNEY, Kevin	35	F	Unknown	12De02Db
GIBBONS, Chas.	30	M	Unknown	12De02Db
Tim	28	M	Unknown	12De02Db
Thos.	21	M	Unknown	12De02Db
Cath.	30	F	Unknown	12De02Db
Jane	26	F	Unknown	12De02Db
Cath.	29	F	Unknown	12De02Db
DARQUIS, Julia	30	F	Unknown	12De02Db
DWYER, John	22	M	Unknown	12De02Db
HALL, John	22	M	Unknown	12De02Db
Ellen	20	F	Unknown	12De02Db
MAHON, Cath.	21	F	Unknown	12De02Db
Cath.	22	F	Unknown	12De02Db
FOLEY, Honor	20	F	Unknown	12De02Db
LEARY, Sue	23	F	Unknown	12De02Db
IRELAND, Judy	30	F	Unknown	12De02Db
Mary-Ann	15	F	Unknown	12De02Db
John	11	M	Unknown	12De02Db
Ellen	8	F	Child	12De02Db
Eliza	6	F	Child	12De02Db
Richard	3	M	Child	12De02Db
Julia	.06	F	Infant	12De02Db
HOWARD, Ellen	7	F	Child	12De02Db
BRYAN, Jas.	20	M	Unknown	12De02Db
LARKIN, Jas.	19	M	Unknown	12De02Db
MCCANNA, Peter	20	M	Unknown	12De02Db
Cath.	15	F	Unknown	12De02Db
CABBER, Pat	30	M	Unknown	12De02Db
Pat	20	M	Unknown	12De02Db
St.GEORGE, Mary	30	F	Unknown	12De02Db
TOGAN, Jas.	17	M	Unknown	12De02Db
KELLEY, Margt.	22	F	Unknown	12De02Db
Eliza	20	F	Unknown	12De02Db
TAYLOR, Peter	27	M	Unknown	12De02Db
Thos.	21	M	Unknown	12De02Db
BARROWS, H.	23	M	Unknown	12De02Db
GULLIVER, Rich	40	U	Unknown	12De02Db
U-Mrs.	35	F	Unknown	12De02Db
Margt.	6	F	Child	12De02Db
CUNNINGHAM, Jane	20	F	Unknown	12De02Db
CARLEY, Pat	25	M	Unknown	12De02Db
WARD, Brid.	18	F	Unknown	12De02Db
CUSACK, Pat	23	M	Unknown	12De02Db
U-Mrs.	18	F	Unknown	12De02Db
Mary	15	F	Unknown	12De02Db
MALLOY, Brid.	21	F	Unknown	12De02Db
Peter	18	M	Unknown	12De02Db
LOVELL, Mick	20	M	Unknown	12De02Db
Mary	18	F	Unknown	12De02Db
MANGAN, Pat	19	M	Unknown	12De02Db
BURKE, John	22	M	Unknown	12De02Db
FLYNN, Morris	24	M	Unknown	12De02Db
U-Mrs.	24	F	Unknown	12De02Db
John	5	M	Child	12De02Db
Mick	.03	M	Infant	12De02Db
MCKENNA, Jas.	50	M	Unknown	12De02Db
Arthur	15	M	Unknown	12De02Db
Ann	13	F	Unknown	12De02Db
Pat	12	M	Unknown	12De02Db
Mary	7	F	Child	12De02Db
WILSON, John	32	M	Unknown	12De02Db
U-Mrs.	24	F	Unknown	12De02Db
OCONNER, Mat.	20	M	Unknown	12De02Db
SWEYR, John	40	M	Unknown	12De02Db
FOGARTY, Mick	60	M	Unknown	12De02Db
Jas.	13	M	Unknown	12De02Db
Cath.	18	F	Unknown	12De02Db
And.	11	M	Unknown	12De02Db
Died-At-Sea				
LAWLER, Jas.	37	M	Unknown	12De02Db
HENDERSON, Ellen	30	F	Unknown	12De02Db
DAYLEY, Jas.	50	M	Unknown	12De02Db
Brid.	30	F	Unknown	12De02Db
Mary	10	F	Unknown	12De02Db
Cath.	8	F	Child	12De02Db
Ellen	6	F	Child	12De02Db
Mthos.	4	M	Child	12De02Db
Chas.	.06	M	Infant	12De02Db
GRANT, H.	24	M	Unknown	12De02Db
FOGARTY, Mick	35	M	Unknown	12De02Db
WALSH, Rich	30	M	Unknown	12De02Db
Jas.	18	M	Unknown	12De02Db
SHEA, Phil	34	M	Unknown	12De02Db
KENNEY, Margt.	25	F	Unknown	12De02Db
DOWNEY, Rich	20	M	Unknown	12De02Db
DRENNAN, Margt.	13	F	Unknown	12De02Db
FLANNIGAN, Wm.	20	M	Unknown	12De02Db
Lew.	18	M	Unknown	12De02Db
LENAHAN, Margt.	20	F	Unknown	12De02Db
RYAN, Ann	20	F	Unknown	12De02Db
GRACE, Mick	45	M	Unknown	12De02Db
Mary-Ann	14	F	Unknown	12De02Db
John	11	M	Unknown	12De02Db
MANGAN, Wm.	40	M	Unknown	12De02Db
DOYLE, Eliza	19	F	Unknown	12De02Db
MILDOON, Brid.	19	F	Unknown	12De02Db
LEDWITH, Marcella	21	F	Unknown	12De02Db
DALTON, Julia	18	F	Unknown	12De02Db
BREEN, Phil.	17	M	Unknown	12De02Db
Mich.	13	M	Unknown	12De02Db
Died-At-Sea				
Alley	9	F	Child	12De02Db
CALLAGAN, Michael	18	M	Unknown	12De02Db
DUGGAN, Margt.	18	F	Unknown	12De02Db
HENNESSEY, Honor	20	F	Unknown	12De02Db
COTTRELL, Sarah	50	F	Unknown	12De02Db
CAMPBELL, John	20	M	Unknown	12De02Db
DUKE, John	18	M	Unknown	12De02Db
GIBBONS, Ben.	21	M	Unknown	12De02Db
CREAN, Jas.	20	M	Unknown	12De02Db
WILDE, Jas.	46	M	Unknown	12De02Db
HOLBROOK, Jas.	24	M	Unknown	12De02Db
HERAN, U-Mrs.	40	F	Unknown	12De02Db
MCDOWEL, U	15	F	Unknown	12De02Db
LUCKLIN, U-Mrs.	20	F	Unknown	12De02Db
ARMSTRONG, Wm.	25	M	Unknown	12De02Db
Jane	20	F	Unknown	12De02Db
W.	.03	M	Infant	12De02Db
WALSH, Thos.	25	M	Farmer	12De02Db
Julia	26	F	Unknown	12De02Db
MURPHY, Ellen	20	F	Unknown	12De02Db
WILKINSON, Jas.	28	M	Unknown	12De02Db
DONNELLY, D.	20	M	Unknown	12De02Db
WILKINSON, Margt.	20	F	Unknown	12De02Db
KILMARTIN, Ellen	22	F	Unknown	12De02Db
MCKENEY, Ed.	24	M	Unknown	12De02Db
WILKINSON, Wm.	20	M	Unknown	12De02Db
SHEA, Pat.	36	M	Unknown	12De02Db
LUMBARD, Mary	53	F	Unknown	12De02Db
Johan.	50	F	Unknown	12De02Db
Rich	25	M	Unknown	12De02Db
Pat	18	M	Unknown	12De02Db
WILKINSON, Ellen	18	F	Unknown	12De02Db
HENNESSEY, Mary	60	F	Unknown	12De02Db
WALSH, Ellen	21	F	Unknown	12De02Db
DILLARIE, Jerry	18	F	Unknown	12De02Db
Pet	15	M	Unknown	12De02Db
HAYES, Wm.	40	M	Unknown	12De02Db
Mary	40	F	Unknown	12De02Db
Cath.	13	F	Unknown	12De02Db
Eliza	12	F	Unknown	12De02Db
Ellen	11	F	Unknown	12De02Db
COLLINS, Corn.	17	M	Unknown	12De02Db
SWEENEY, Thos.	25	M	Unknown	12De02Db

NAMES OF PASSENGERS	AGE	SEX	OCCUPATIONS	DATE PORT SHIP
SHEEHAN, John	26	M	Unknown	12De02Db
BUCKLEY, Tim	30	M	Unknown	12De02Db
ROURKE, John	22	M	Unknown	12De02Db
Geo.	18	M	Unknown	12De02Db
Eliza	22	F	Unknown	12De02Db
DILLON, Mary	20	F	Unknown	12De02Db
SHEEHAN, Ellen	40	F	Unknown	12De02Db
Corn.	11	M	Unknown	12De02Db
Margt.	8	F	Child	12De02Db
Mary	6	F	Child	12De02Db
Pat	3	M	Child	12De02Db
Ben	.06	M	Infant	12De02Db
FITZGERRALD, Mick	22	M	Unknown	12De02Db
Bridget	10	F	Unknown	12De02Db
Jerry	8	M	Child	12De02Db
CURTIN, Eliza	32	F	Unknown	12De02Db
Jas.	3	M	Child	12De02Db
Dan	35	M	Unknown	12De02Db
David	.03	M	Infant	12De02Db
KEEFE, Jim	30	M	Unknown	12De02Db
CALLIGAN, John	25	M	Unknown	12De02Db
FALVY, Mary	28	F	Unknown	12De02Db
Jerry	26	M	Unknown	12De02Db
SULLIVAN, Margt.	50	F	Unknown	12De02Db
SHEA, Dennis	5	M	Child	12De02Db
Mary	3	F	Child	12De02Db
LEARY, Pat	27	M	Unknown	12De02Db
Ellen	35	F	Unknown	12De02Db
Mary	19	F	Unknown	12De02Db
Deborah	7	F	Child	12De02Db
SULLIVAN, Honor	24	F	Unknown	12De02Db
Jerry	20	F	Unknown	12De02Db
CRONAN, Mary	20	F	Unknown	12De02Db
SULLIVAN, Dan	40	M	Unknown	12De02Db
LEARY, Dennis	32	M	Unknown	12De02Db
JERRITT, Ed	30	M	Unknown	12De02Db
OKEEFE, Mary	20	F	Unknown	12De02Db
Harriet	16	F	Unknown	12De02Db
CRONIN, Phil	19	M	Unknown	12De02Db
FITZGERALD, Mick	14	M	Unknown	12De02Db
AHERN, Pat	20	M	Unknown	12De02Db
NAGLE, Eliza	34	F	Unknown	12De02Db
KEEFE, Pat	19	M	Unknown	12De02Db
ROCHE, Wm.	27	M	Unknown	12De02Db
PRISCOLL, Honor	30	F	Unknown	12De02Db
FITZPATRICK, Mary	20	F	Unknown	12De02Db
FITZGERALD, Mary	19	F	Unknown	12De02Db
Mary	60	F	Unknown	12De02Db
SULLIVAN, Johanna	40	F	Unknown	12De02Db
Mary	9	F	Child	12De02Db
Owen	5	M	Child	12De02Db
John	.03	M	Infant	12De02Db
GEHAN, Nelly	18	F	Unknown	12De02Db
Jerry	20	M	Unknown	12De02Db
AHERN, Cath.	20	F	Unknown	12De02Db
LONG, Eliza	40	F	Unknown	12De02Db
John	8	M	Child	12De02Db
Jas.	4	M	Child	12De02Db
DUNN, Pat	50	M	Unknown	12De02Db
HOLAHAN, Dan	40	M	Unknown	12De02Db
KIRVANE, Jas.	25	M	Unknown	12De02Db
CONNER, John	16	M	Unknown	12De02Db
BARRETT, Cath.	50	F	Unknown	12De02Db
John	16	M	Unknown	12De02Db
CONNER, Nancy	40	F	Unknown	12De02Db
GRIFFIN, Ellen	50	F	Unknown	12De02Db
Thos.	15	M	Unknown	12De02Db
GARARTY, Ellen	30	F	Unknown	12De02Db
Pat	8	M	Child	12De02Db
Eliza	5	F	Child	12De02Db
KILKELLAN, Dan	20	M	Unknown	12De02Db
FLAHINE, John	24	F	Unknown	12De02Db
Honor	15	F	Unknown	12De02Db
SULLIVAN, Mick	30	M	Unknown	12De02Db
MORAN, Pat	30	M	Unknown	12De02Db
JULIAN, Honor	30	F	Unknown	12De02Db
WALSH, Johanna	16	F	Unknown	12De02Db
NEIL, Margt.	20	F	Unknown	12De02Db
GRIFFIN, Cath.	19	F	Unknown	12De02Db
KENNEY, Tho.	26	M	Unknown	12De02Db
GRADY, Mick	25	M	Unknown	12De02Db
ROCHE, Jno.	23	M	Unknown	12De02Db
HOLBERT, Eliza	24	F	Unknown	12De02Db
GILLAN, B.	50	F	Unknown	12De02Db
Mary	14	F	Unknown	12De02Db
Wm.	10	M	Unknown	12De02Db
RADY, Margt.	20	F	Unknown	12De02Db
SHERLOCK, Jas.	13	M	Unknown	12De02Db
Ann	11	F	Unknown	12De02Db
COLLINS, R.	15	M	Unknown	12De02Db
HARNETT, Johan	30	M	Unknown	12De02Db
LYNCH, Harriet	30	F	Unknown	12De02Db
KING, Bryan	40	M	Unknown	12De02Db
Julia	44	F	Unknown	12De02Db
DUKE, Jas.	35	M	Unknown	12De02Db
Jas.	12	M	Unknown	12De02Db
MULLOY, Peter	18	M	Unknown	12De02Db
REYNOLDS, Ann	18	F	Unknown	12De02Db
Ann	18	F	Unknown	12De02Db
Mary	26	F	Unknown	12De02Db
MCAWEENEY, Thos.	3	M	Child	12De02Db
Frank	2	M	Child	12De02Db
MURPHY, Dennis	28	M	Unknown	12De02Db
Cath.	26	F	Unknown	12De02Db
Johanna	20	F	Unknown	12De02Db
Ellen	5	F	Child	12De02Db
Honor	.06	F	Infant	12De02Db
Mary	.06	F	Infant	12De02Db
DOWNEY, Mary	20	F	Unknown	12De02Db
KEEGAN, Pat	48	M	Unknown	12De02Db
Mary	30	F	Unknown	12De02Db
Margt.	14	F	Unknown	12De02Db
Brid.	11	F	Unknown	12De02Db
Cath.	9	F	Child	12De02Db
Maria	7	F	Child	12De02Db
Ann	5	F	Child	12De02Db
Pat	.09	M	Infant	12De02Db
HORAN, Pat	20	M	Unknown	12De02Db
HUNT, John	53	M	Unknown	12De02Db
Mary	45	F	Unknown	12De02Db
Rich	30	M	Unknown	12De02Db
Thos.	15	M	Unknown	12De02Db
Wm.	13	M	Unknown	12De02Db
Ann	11	F	Unknown	12De02Db
Saml.	9	M	Child	12De02Db
Robt.	7	M	Child	12De02Db
Eliza	5	F	Child	12De02Db
Henry	3	F	Child	12De02Db
Sarah	2	F	Child	12De02Db
Fanny Died-At-Sea	.03	F	Infant	12De02Db
PARSONS, John	21	M	Unknown	12De02Db
DALEY, Robt.	18	M	Unknown	12De02Db
TRACY, Dennis	32	M	Unknown	12De02Db
Cath.	41	F	Unknown	12De02Db
CONNERS, Brid.	20	F	Unknown	12De02Db
Mary	28	F	Unknown	12De02Db
KANE, Mary	20	F	Unknown	12De02Db
GARRIGAN, Ann	40	F	Unknown	12De02Db
Mick	35	M	Unknown	12De02Db
Mat	20	M	Unknown	12De02Db
Ann	18	F	Unknown	12De02Db
Brid.	16	F	Unknown	12De02Db
Brid.	18	F	Unknown	12De02Db
Mary	8	F	Child	12De02Db
Mat	.03	M	Infant	12De02Db
BAILEY, Alex	49	M	Unknown	12De02Db
U-Mrs.	40	F	Unknown	12De02Db
Henry	13	M	Unknown	12De02Db
Alex	12	M	Unknown	12De02Db

NAMES OF PASSENGERS	AGE	SEX	OCCUPATIONS	DATE PORT SHIP
BETTRIDGE, John	43	M	Unknown	12De02Db
U-Mrs.	44	F	Unknown	12De02Db
John	18	M	Unknown	12De02Db
George	15	M	Unknown	12De02Db
Robt.	13	M	Unknown	12De02Db
Alf.	3	M	Child	12De02Db
Sarah	10	F	Unknown	12De02Db
Emily	8	F	Child	12De02Db
FINCHARD, Jas.	23	M	Unknown	12De02Db
BRYAN, Jas.	39	M	Unknown	12De02Db
Ann	39	F	Unknown	12De02Db
Bartley	.06	M	Infant	12De02Db
Died-At-Sea				
Bartley	18	M	Unknown	12De02Db
DORAN, John	43	M	Unknown	12De02Db
Cath.	30	F	Unknown	12De02Db
Wm.	1	M	Child	12De02Db
Died-At-Sea				
WATERS, John	12	M	Unknown	12De02Db
WALSH, Mary	22	F	Unknown	12De02Db
Brid.	19	F	Unknown	12De02Db
HART, Margt.	22	F	Unknown	12De02Db
HAYES, Rose	17	F	Unknown	12De02Db
COLEMAN, U-Mrs.	25	F	Unknown	12De02Db
CARNEY, Kevin	35	F	Unknown	12De02Db
GIBBONS, Chas.	30	M	Unknown	12De02Db
Tim	28	M	Unknown	12De02Db
Thos.	21	M	Unknown	12De02Db
Cath.	30	F	Unknown	12De02Db
Jane	26	F	Unknown	12De02Db
Cath.	29	F	Unknown	12De02Db
DARQUIS, Julia	30	F	Unknown	12De02Db
DWYER, John	22	M	Unknown	12De02Db
HALL, John	22	M	Unknown	12De02Db
Ellen	20	F	Unknown	12De02Db
MAHON, Cath.	21	F	Unknown	12De02Db
Cath.	22	F	Unknown	12De02Db
FOLEY, Honor	20	F	Unknown	12De02Db
LEARY, Sue	23	F	Unknown	12De02Db
IRELAND, Judy	30	F	Unknown	12De02Db
Mary-Ann	15	F	Unknown	12De02Db
John	11	M	Unknown	12De02Db
Ellen	8	F	Child	12De02Db
Eliza	6	F	Child	12De02Db
Richard	3	M	Child	12De02Db
Julia	.06	F	Infant	12De02Db
HOWARD, Ellen	7	F	Child	12De02Db
BRYAN, Jas.	20	M	Unknown	12De02Db
LARKIN, Jas.	19	M	Unknown	12De02Db
MCCANNA, Peter	20	M	Unknown	12De02Db
Cath.	15	F	Unknown	12De02Db
CABBER, Pat	30	M	Unknown	12De02Db
Pat	20	M	Unknown	12De02Db
St.GEORGE, Mary	30	F	Unknown	12De02Db
TOGAN, Jas.	17	M	Unknown	12De02Db
KELLEY, Margt.	22	F	Unknown	12De02Db
Eliza	20	F	Unknown	12De02Db
TAYLOR, Peter	27	M	Unknown	12De02Db
Thos.	21	M	Unknown	12De02Db
BARROWS, H.	23	M	Unknown	12De02Db
GULLIVER, Rich	40	U	Unknown	12De02Db
U-Mrs.	35	F	Unknown	12De02Db
Margt.	6	F	Child	12De02Db
CUNNINGHAM, Jane	20	F	Unknown	12De02Db
CARLEY, Pat	25	M	Unknown	12De02Db
WARD, Brid.	18	F	Unknown	12De02Db
CUSACK, Pat	23	M	Unknown	12De02Db
U-Mrs.	18	F	Unknown	12De02Db
Mary	15	F	Unknown	12De02Db
MALLOY, Brid.	21	F	Unknown	12De02Db
Peter	18	M	Unknown	12De02Db
LOVELL, Mick	20	M	Unknown	12De02Db
Mary	18	F	Unknown	12De02Db
MANGAN, Pat	19	M	Unknown	12De02Db
BURKE, John	22	M	Unknown	12De02Db

NAMES OF PASSENGERS	AGE	SEX	OCCUPATIONS	DATE PORT SHIP
FLYNN, Morris	24	M	Unknown	12De02Db
U-Mrs.	24	F	Unknown	12De02Db
John	5	M	Child	12De02Db
Mick	.03	M	Infant	12De02Db
MCKENNA, Jas.	50	M	Unknown	12De02Db
Arthur	15	M	Unknown	12De02Db
Ann	13	F	Unknown	12De02Db
Pat	12	M	Unknown	12De02Db
Mary	7	F	Child	12De02Db
WILSON, John	32	M	Unknown	12De02Db
U-Mrs.	24	F	Unknown	12De02Db
OCONNER, Mat.	20	M	Unknown	12De02Db
SWEYR, John	40	M	Unknown	12De02Db
FOGARTY, Mick	60	M	Unknown	12De02Db
Jas.	13	M	Unknown	12De02Db
Cath.	18	F	Unknown	12De02Db
And.	11	M	Unknown	12De02Db
Died-At-Sea				
LAWLER, Jas.	37	M	Unknown	12De02Db
HENDERSON, Ellen	30	F	Unknown	12De02Db
DAYLEY, Jas.	50	M	Unknown	12De02Db
Brid.	30	F	Unknown	12De02Db
Mary	10	F	Unknown	12De02Db
Cath.	8	F	Child	12De02Db
Ellen	6	F	Child	12De02Db
Mthos.	4	M	Child	12De02Db
Chas.	.06	M	Infant	12De02Db
GRANT, H.	24	M	Unknown	12De02Db
FOGARTY, Mick	35	M	Unknown	12De02Db
WALSH, Rich	30	M	Unknown	12De02Db
Jas.	18	M	Unknown	12De02Db
SHEA, Phil	34	M	Unknown	12De02Db
KENNEY, Margt.	25	F	Unknown	12De02Db
DOWNEY, Rich	20	M	Unknown	12De02Db
DRENNAN, Margt.	13	F	Unknown	12De02Db
FLANNIGAN, Wm.	20	M	Unknown	12De02Db
Lew.	18	M	Unknown	12De02Db
LENAHAN, Margt.	20	F	Unknown	12De02Db
RYAN, Ann	20	F	Unknown	12De02Db
GRACE, Mick	45	M	Unknown	12De02Db
Mary-Ann	14	F	Unknown	12De02Db
John	11	M	Unknown	12De02Db
MANGAN, Wm.	40	M	Unknown	12De02Db
DOYLE, Eliza	19	F	Unknown	12De02Db
MILDOON, Brid.	19	F	Unknown	12De02Db
LEDWITH, Marcella	21	F	Unknown	12De02Db
DALTON, Julia	18	F	Unknown	12De02Db
BREEN, Phil.	17	M	Unknown	12De02Db
Mich.	13	M	Unknown	12De02Db
Died-At-Sea				
Alley	9	F	Child	12De02Db
CALLAGAN, Michael	18	M	Unknown	12De02Db
DUGGAN, Margt.	18	F	Unknown	12De02Db
HENNESSEY, Honor	20	F	Unknown	12De02Db
COTTRELL, Sarah	50	F	Unknown	12De02Db
CAMPBELL, John	20	M	Unknown	12De02Db
DUKE, John	18	M	Unknown	12De02Db
GIBBONS, Ben.	21	M	Unknown	12De02Db
CREAN, Jas.	20	M	Unknown	12De02Db
WILDE, Jas.	46	M	Unknown	12De02Db
HOLBROOK, Jas.	24	M	Unknown	12De02Db
HERAN, U-Mrs.	40	F	Unknown	12De02Db
MCDOWEL, U	15	F	Unknown	12De02Db
LUCKLIN, U-Mrs.	20	F	Unknown	12De02Db
ARMSTRONG, Wm.	25	M	Unknown	12De02Db
Jane	20	F	Unknown	12De02Db
W.	.03	M	Infant	12De02Db

QUEEN-OF-THE-WEST 17 DECEMBER 1849

From Liverpool

NAMES OF PASSENGERS	AGE	SEX	OCCUPATIONS	DATE PORT SHIP
CREAMER, Mary	18	F	Servant	17De02Dg
MCCUDDEN, Las.	50	F	Spinster	17De02Dg
Wm.	28	M	Farmer	17De02Dg
Cath.	24	F	Farmer	17De02Dg
Eliza	7	F	Child	17De02Dg
LITTLE, Rose	20	F	Farmer	17De02Dg
SHEERIN, Ann	18	F	Unknown	17De02Dg
DRURY, Winn.	4	F	Child	17De02Dg
Cath.	3	F	Child	17De02Dg
MOORE, Charles	30	M	Laborer	17De02Dg
KEAN, Mich	40	M	Laborer	17De02Dg
John	16	M	Laborer	17De02Dg
Mary	9	F	Child	17De02Dg
GILLESPIE, Margt.	18	F	Servant	17De02Dg
READY, Pat	20	M	Laborer	17De02Dg
RAYWOOD, Thos.	60	M	Carpenter	17De02Dg
Ellen	50	F	Carpenter	17De02Dg
Thos.	17	M	Carpenter	17De02Dg
Ellen	10	F	Carpenter	17De02Dg
Richd.	11	M	Carpenter	17De02Dg
Jas.	8	M	Child	17De02Dg
Henry	6	M	Child	17De02Dg
BEE, Mary	34	F	Carpenter	17De02Dg
Michael	.00	M	Infant	17De02Dg
MURPHY, John	22	M	Laborer	17De02Dg
Died-At-Sea				
READY, Cath.	20	F	Spinster	17De02Dg
BOGART, Mary	60	F	None	17De02Dg
MCNULTY, Jane	18	F	Unknown	17De02Dg
Wm.	14	M	Unknown	17De02Dg
DANLANCY, Hannah	20	F	Spinster	17De02Dg
SULLIVAN, Ann	10	F	None	17De02Dg
LOOLEY, Pat	23	M	Unknown	17De02Dg
Bridg.	20	F	Laborer	17De02Dg
Julia	18	F	Laborer	17De02Dg
COOGAN, Ann	18	F	Servant	17De02Dg
MCLAUGHLIN, Dennis	14	M	Servant	17De02Dg
CALLAGHAN, Ann	20	F	Unknown	17De02Dg
Maria	14	F	Spinster	17De02Dg
Rose	12	F	Spinster	17De02Dg
KIRNAN, John	25	M	Laborer	17De02Dg
FARRELL, John	18	M	Laborer	17De02Dg
GAFFEY, Pat	19	M	Laborer	17De02Dg
HUGHES, Mary	16	F	Servant	17De02Dg
MCNAMARA, Wm.	20	M	Laborer	17De02Dg
KELLEY, John	30	M	Blacksmith	17De02Dg
POWELL, John	30	M	Farmer	17De02Dg
REYNOLDS, Simon	9	M	Child	17De02Dg
KELLY, Polly	21	F	Lad	17De02Dg
MCELROY, Cath.	30	F	None	17De02Dg
John	.00	M	Infant	17De02Dg
Pat	11	M	None	17De02Dg
Hugh	9	M	Child	17De02Dg
Mary-A.	7	F	Child	17De02Dg
Charles	4	M	Child	17De02Dg
LANDRIGAN, Bridg.	22	F	Dressmaker	17De02Dg
KIRWAN, Ann	18	F	Spinster	17De02Dg
RAFERTY, Mary	9	F	Child	17De02Dg
Thos.	7	M	Child	17De02Dg
Margt.	5	F	Child	17De02Dg
Jno.	3	M	Child	17De02Dg
MALLOY, Maria	19	F	Spinster	17De02Dg
QUINN, Alice	18	F	Spinster	17De02Dg
BRODRICK, Alice	17	F	Wife	17De02Dg
Thos.	16	M	Unknown	17De02Dg
BRODRICK, Mary	40	F	Unknown	17De02Dg
Jno.	10	M	Unknown	17De02Dg
Margt.	8	F	Child	17De02Dg
Pat	5	M	Child	17De02Dg
Luke	3	M	Child	17De02Dg
BRENNAN, Ann	16	F	Spinster	17De02Dg
SHORTY, Mick	10	M	Unknown	17De02Dg
NELSON, Jno.	25	M	Laborer	17De02Dg
LOBIN, Jno.	4	M	Child	17De02Dg
LANCEY, Thos.	23	M	Laborer	17De02Dg
QUIRK, Wm.	27	M	Laborer	17De02Dg
DINAN, Ellen	28	F	Spinster	17De02Dg
Dan	.00	M	Infant	17De02Dg
CARR, Eliza	18	F	Servant	17De02Dg
STRACHAN, Rose	50	F	None	17De02Dg
Jno.	20	M	None	17De02Dg
Robt.	11	M	None	17De02Dg
MCCARVELL, Cath.	30	F	Servant	17De02Dg
MCINTEE, Mary	12	F	None	17De02Dg
Margt.	10	F	None	17De02Dg
HAYES, Ellen	60	F	None	17De02Dg
Jas.	16	F	None	17De02Dg
Michl.	13	F	None	17De02Dg
QUINLAN, Margt.	40	F	None	17De02Dg
HENNISLEY, Margt.	18	F	None	17De02Dg
Ellen	9	F	Child	17De02Dg
Bridg.	7	F	Child	17De02Dg
Pat	5	M	Child	17De02Dg
DALY, Michl.	19	M	Laborer	17De02Dg
CONWAY, Anty.	45	M	Farmer	17De02Dg
Bridg.	12	F	None	17De02Dg
Ann	9	F	Child	17De02Dg
FLANIGAN, Cath.	24	F	None	17De02Dg
Pat	2	M	Child	17De02Dg
Cath.	.00	F	Infant	17De02Dg
MCLEENY, Mary	18	F	Servant	17De02Dg
CONROY, Mich.	22	M	Laborer	17De02Dg
GILLILANA, Wm.	20	M	Laborer	17De02Dg
Pag	14	F	None	17De02Dg
Las.	18	F	None	17De02Dg
Margt.	10	F	None	17De02Dg
PIGOTT, Bridg.	20	F	Servant	17De02Dg
Mary	18	F	Servant	17De02Dg
GAVIGNAN, Bridg.	20	F	Spinster	17De02Dg
BRADY, Judy	19	F	None	17De02Dg
BOYLAN, Jas.	45	M	Stone Mason	17De02Dg
Margt.	45	F	None	17De02Dg
Mary	16	F	None	17De02Dg
Cath.	15	F	None	17De02Dg
KENNETT, Thos.	58	M	Laborer	17De02Dg
FARRELL, Ellen	19	F	Servant	17De02Dg
DOWNEY, Susan	18	F	None	17De02Dg
BYRNES, Ann	33	F	None	17De02Dg
Jno.	2	M	Child	17De02Dg
Michl.	.00	M	Infant	17De02Dg
FORREST, Margt.	27	F	Servant	17De02Dg
DOOLING, Ann	18	F	None	17De02Dg
BROPHY, Jno.	12	M	None	17De02Dg
MURPHY, Johan	30	M	None	17De02Dg
Johan	.00	M	Infant	17De02Dg
MULLHOLLAND, Ann	24	F	Servant	17De02Dg
CAFFREY, Peter	19	M	Laborer	17De02Dg
SHEENEY, Eliza	17	F	None	17De02Dg
Johan	14	M	None	17De02Dg
BARTON, Dan	15	M	Laborer	17De02Dg
BYRNE, Jas.	25	M	Farmer	17De02Dg
LESKEY, John	26	M	Laborer	17De02Dg
HOWARDON, Mary	36	M	None	17De02Dg
Wm.	36	M	Laborer	17De02Dg
Adam	7	M	Child	17De02Dg
FOLEY, Cath.	20	F	None	17De02Dg
BUCKLEY, Mary	20	F	Servant	17De02Dg
BRYAN, Mary	20	F	Servant	17De02Dg
MCCARTY, Tim	30	M	Laborer	17De02Dg
SKERRY, Eliza	21	F	None	17De02Dg

NAMES OF PASSENGERS	AGE	SEX	OCCUPATIONS	DATE PORT SHIP
SULLIVAN, Johan	26	F	None	17De02Dg
OCONNELL, Michl.	18	M	Laborer	17De02Dg
COLBERT, Mary	32	F	Spinster	17De02Dg
SWEENEY, Thos.	18	M	Laborer	17De02Dg
BERNARD, Mary	40	F	None	17De02Dg
Thos.	8	M	Child	17De02Dg
Jno.	4	M	Child	17De02Dg
Died-At-Sea				
HORAN, John	3	M	Child	17De02Dg
KELLEY, Pat	10	M	None	17De02Dg
MALONEY, Wm.	19	M	Laborer	17De02Dg
MONAGHAN, Dan	26	M	Laborer	17De02Dg
Ann	24	F	None	17De02Dg
LOWE, Michl.	21	M	Laborer	17De02Dg
LANG, U-Mrs.	38	F	None	17De02Dg
Michl.	17	M	None	17De02Dg
Bessy	15	M	None	17De02Dg
JONES, Robt.	16	M	Surveyor	17De02Dg
RALEIGH, Jas.	26	M	Surveyor	17De02Dg
REILLY, Thos.	31	M	Laborer	17De02Dg
Mary	32	F	None	17De02Dg
MURRANA, Pat	50	M	Farmer	17De02Dg
U-Mrs.	40	F	None	17De02Dg
Michl.	15	M	None	17De02Dg
Bridg.	9	F	Child	17De02Dg
Thos.	6	M	Child	17De02Dg
U	45	F	Wi	17De02Dg
Pat	20	M	None	17De02Dg
Margt.	14	F	None	17De02Dg
MORTON, Bridgt.	40	F	None	17De02Dg
Mary	16	F	None	17De02Dg
Bridget	14	F	None	17De02Dg
Thos.	12	M	None	17De02Dg
RYAN, Godfrey	25	M	Clerk	17De02Dg
CLINTON, Richd.	40	M	Farmer	17De02Dg
LAWLESS, Richd.	25	M	Farmer	17De02Dg
Alice	19	F	None	17De02Dg
CREAMER, Owen	25	M	Laborer	17De02Dg
LEDDY, Mary	18	F	Spinster	17De02Dg
CANNON, Mary	18	F	Spinster	17De02Dg
CANLOW, Pat	22	M	None	17De02Dg
Mary	20	F	None	17De02Dg
Bridg.	20	F	None	17De02Dg
CUNNINGHAM, Michl.	22	M	Laborer	17De02Dg
MURPHY, Mat	40	F	Laborer	17De02Dg
PRICE, Jas.	36	M	Laborer	17De02Dg
FLYNN, Margt.	20	F	None	17De02Dg
SHERIDAN, Margt.	20	F	None	17De02Dg
CORR, Mary	30	F	None	17De02Dg
Andrew	6	M	Child	17De02Dg
Owen	3	M	Child	17De02Dg
SMITH, Ellen	15	F	None	17De02Dg
ROACH, Maurice	32	M	Smith	17De02Dg
FITZPATRICK, Jas.	38	M	Laborer	17De02Dg
DUNN, Michl.	32	M	Laborer	17De02Dg
U-Mrs.	31	F	Unknown	17De02Dg
Michl.	8	M	Child	17De02Dg
Cornelius	.00	M	Infant	17De02Dg
JACKSON, Cath.	21	F	None	17De02Dg
KANE, Margt.	21	F	None	17De02Dg
POWELL, Mary	34	M	None	17De02Dg
Hannah	10	F	Unknown	17De02Dg
Margt.	6	F	Child	17De02Dg
Maurice	4	M	Child	17De02Dg
Evan	.00	M	Infant	17De02Dg
MORGAN, Sarah	20	F	None	17De02Dg
COPELAND, Ralph	35	M	Laborer	17De02Dg
CRUMLEY, Dennis	22	M	Farmer	17De02Dg
Cath.	22	F	Unknown	17De02Dg
MARLESS, Nelly	22	F	None	17De02Dg
ODONNELL, Anty.	22	M	Laborer	17De02Dg
SHERLIN, Cath.	20	F	None	17De02Dg
BANNOW, Pat	20	M	Laborer	17De02Dg
RYAN, Mary	18	F	None	17De02Dg
Margt.	19	F	None	17De02Dg

NAMES OF PASSENGERS	AGE	SEX	OCCUPATIONS	DATE PORT SHIP
TOOLE, Ted	25	M	Laborer	17De02Dg
LYONS, John	22	M	Laborer	17De02Dg
BAAGGS, Barbara	13	F	None	17De02Dg
LAUGHLIN, Thos.	25	M	Laborer	17De02Dg
FOLEY, John	19	M	Laborer	17De02Dg
MURPHY, Wm.	27	M	Laborer	17De02Dg
BODEN, Margt.	28	F	None	17De02Dg
WELSH, Martin	20	M	None	17De02Dg
Bridg.	18	F	None	17De02Dg
Judy	17	F	None	17De02Dg
WILLIAMSON, Geo.	24	M	Shopkeeper	17De02Dg
Thos.	12	M	None	17De02Dg
DAILY, Cath.	19	F	Servant	17De02Dg
FAGAN, Cath.	27	F	None	17De02Dg
Margt.	2	F	Child	17De02Dg
Mary	.00	F	Infant	17De02Dg
HUGHS, Cath.	18	F	None	17De02Dg
FURNISH, Edwd.	21	M	None	17De02Dg
KELLEY, Dan	28	M	Servant	17De02Dg
Ellen	21	F	None	17De02Dg
HANNAH, Thos.	21	M	Servant	17De02Dg
CLARK, John	25	M	Farmer	17De02Dg
FLORA, Ann	22	F	None	17De02Dg
CANAVAN, Pat	18	M	Laborer	17De02Dg
CARTER, Alex	28	M	Engineer	17De02Dg
U-Mrs.	24	F	None	17De02Dg
Agnes	3	F	Child	17De02Dg
JONES, Robt.	44	M	Farmer	17De02Dg
DWANE, Law.	27	M	Laborer	17De02Dg
HOOLEY, Bridg.	32	F	None	17De02Dg
Pat	6	M	Child	17De02Dg
GARNEY, Thos.	3	M	Child	17De02Dg
Mat.	2	M	Child	17De02Dg
MCGUIRE, Mary	22	F	Spinster	17De02Dg
ROONEY, John	18	M	Laborer	17De02Dg
COULOGH, Edwd.	35	M	Laborer	17De02Dg
MURPHY, Margt.	18	F	Servant	17De02Dg
KATING, U-Miss	26	F	None	17De02Dg
CULLEN, Ellen	21	F	None	17De02Dg
Honor	20	F	None	17De02Dg
Eliza	18	F	None	17De02Dg
OCONNOR, Mary	22	F	None	17De02Dg
OLEARY, John	23	M	Farmer	17De02Dg
Cons.	21	M	None	17De02Dg
CALOPY, John	20	M	Farmer	17De02Dg
CONNELL, B.	15	U	None	17De02Dg
FOLEY, John	19	M	Laborer	17De02Dg
MULIEL, Ellen	21	F	None	17De02Dg
CUMMING, Mary	22	F	None	17De02Dg
WHITE, Bridgt.	22	F	None	17De02Dg
GLEESON, Michl.	26	M	Laborer	17De02Dg
JONES, Chas.	37	M	Farmer	17De02Dg
CORBERRY, Jno.	27	M	Farmer	17De02Dg
Jane	22	F	None	17De02Dg
MCGOEY, Bartlet	35	M	Farmer	17De02Dg
Margt.	40	F	None	17De02Dg
CARROLL, Thos.	25	M	Farmer	17De02Dg
Mary	25	F	None	17De02Dg
Jas.	4	M	Child	17De02Dg
Cath.	3	F	Child	17De02Dg
CORMICK, Pat	24	M	Farmer	17De02Dg
LEARY, Dan	19	M	Farmer	17De02Dg
COOK, Jas.	25	M	Farmer	17De02Dg
Rose	21	F	None	17De02Dg
LYNCH, Peter	19	M	Farmer	17De02Dg
DEMPSEY, Simon	19	M	Farmer	17De02Dg
FITZSIMMONS, Jno.	30	M	Farmer	17De02Dg
WINTERS, Pat	20	M	Farmer	17De02Dg
HANNAWAY, Jas.	30	M	Laborer	17De02Dg
Pat	25	M	None	17De02Dg
CANN, Michl.	40	M	Laborer	17De02Dg
GUMAN, Honor	35	F	None	17De02Dg
Thos.	15	M	None	17De02Dg
CALAHAN, Martin	10	M	Laborer	17De02Dg
BENNETT, Mary	30	F	None	17De02Dg

NAMES OF PASSENGERS	AGE	SEX	OCCUPATIONS	DATE PORT SHIP
BENNETT, Margt.	.00	F	Infant	17De02Dg
MCGRAGH, Jas.	26	M	Shoemaker	17De02Dg
AGAN, Thos.	30	M	Laborer	17De02Dg
Judy	26	F	None	17De02Dg
Cath.	29	F	None	17De02Dg
FRAMEY, John	30	M	Laborer	17De02Dg
WELSH, Jas.	30	M	Farmer	17De02Dg
Margt.	28	F	None	17De02Dg
John	8	M	Child	17De02Dg
Mary	6	F	Child	17De02Dg
Edwd.	3	M	Child	17De02Dg
MCDONALD, Margt.	28	F	Servant	17De02Dg
COGHLIN, John	30	M	Farmer	17De02Dg
Ellen	28	F	None	17De02Dg
Wm.	.00	M	Infant	17De02Dg
U	50	F	Wi	17De02Dg
Wm.	24	M	None	17De02Dg
MURPHY, Mary	25	F	None	17De02Dg
DONAGHAN, Conl.	24	M	Laborer	17De02Dg
KEIGHAN, Wia.	37	F	None	17De02Dg
Mary	3	F	Child	17De02Dg
Wm.	.00	M	Infant	17De02Dg
CURRY, Wm.	28	M	Farmer	17De02Dg
U-Mrs.	23	F	None	17De02Dg
Pat	3	M	Child	17De02Dg
Ann	.00	F	Infant	17De02Dg
KENEDY, Johan	21	M	Servant	17De02Dg
GLEESON, Mich.	33	M	Servant	17De02Dg
MCCORMICK, E.	32	M	Farmer	17De02Dg
U-Mrs.	21	F	None	17De02Dg
DILLON, Bridgt.	22	F	None	17De02Dg
FOOLEY, Jas.	20	M	Laborer	17De02Dg
SINNOTT, Ann	18	F	Servant	17De02Dg
Ellen	24	F	Servant	17De02Dg
GASNEY, Peter	22	M	Laborer	17De02Dg
MAXWELL, Pat	30	M	Laborer	17De02Dg
COSTELLO, Mary	30	F	None	17De02Dg
Thos.	20	M	None	17De02Dg
MCBRIDE, Mary	28	F	None	17De02Dg
RUSSELL, Eliza	20	F	Servant	17De02Dg
MCLEE, Margt.	19	F	Upholsterer	17De02Dg
ATKINSON, Thos.	40	M	None	17De02Dg
CUNNINGHAM, Dan	16	M	None	17De02Dg
Died-At-Sea				
FLOOD, Cath.	22	M	None	17De02Dg
Died-At-Sea				
Betsey	.00	F	Infant	17De02Dg
MCNIGHT, Wm.	17	F	None	17De02Dg
DAVIN, Cath.	20	F	Servant	17De02Dg
LINNIHAN, Wm.	28	M	Laborer	17De02Dg
Dennis	28	M	Laborer	17De02Dg
WELSH, Mary	20	F	Servant	17De02Dg
WHONOHAN, Dennis	20	M	Laborer	17De02Dg
GARVEY, Wm.	28	M	Laborer	17De02Dg
MCGUIRE, Mat.	35	M	Farmer	17De02Dg
Mary	40	F	None	17De02Dg
John	7	M	Child	17De02Dg
Jane	5	F	Child	17De02Dg
Wm.	3	M	Child	17De02Dg
Jas.	.00	M	Infant	17De02Dg
LYSAGHT, Wm.	20	M	Clerk	17De02Dg
Mary	40	F	None	17De02Dg
ROACH, Ellen	18	F	None	17De02Dg
ROHAN, Conl.	32	M	Laborer	17De02Dg
Bridg.	60	F	Unknown	17De02Dg
Mich.	20	M	Unknown	17De02Dg
Ellen	13	F	Unknown	17De02Dg
NEWELL, Ann	20	F	Servant	17De02Dg
Jno.	.00	M	Infant	17De02Dg
NOLAN, Mary	30	F	None	17De02Dg
KEEFE, Arthur	11	M	None	17De02Dg
MATTHEWS, Ellen	12	F	None	17De02Dg
GRADY, Johan	20	M	None	17De02Dg
GRACE, Eliza	20	F	None	17De02Dg
Margt.	20	F	None	17De02Dg

NAMES OF PASSENGERS	AGE	SEX	OCCUPATIONS	DATE PORT SHIP
CONNELLY, Mich.	19	M	Laborer	17De02Dg
GAVNEY, Pat	30	M	Laborer	17De02Dg
TAYLOR, Robt.	25	M	Farmer	17De02Dg
U-Mrs.	24	F	None	17De02Dg
John	4	M	Child	17De02Dg
Felicia	.00	F	Infant	17De02Dg
DWYNE, Ellen	20	F	Servant	17De02Dg
WALSH, Robt.	32	M	Laborer	17De02Dg
Margt.	23	F	None	17De02Dg
BRENNAN, Hugh	33	M	Laborer	17De02Dg
Francis	22	M	None	17De02Dg
RYAN, Thos.	9	M	Child	17De02Dg
Cath.	7	F	Child	17De02Dg
MURPHY, Peter	21	M	Laborer	17De02Dg
KELLEY, Mary	40	F	None	17De02Dg
Peggy	28	F	None	17De02Dg
Jno.	18	M	None	17De02Dg
Bridg.	7	F	Child	17De02Dg
Ann	10	F	None	17De02Dg
Honor	8	F	Child	17De02Dg
Conl.	.00	M	Infant	17De02Dg
SYMS, George	00	M	Gentleman	17De02Dg
SHILL, John	00	M	Clergyman	17De02Dg
NICHOLL, Robert	00	M	Gentleman	17De02Dg

NEW-YORK 18 DECEMBER 1849

From Liverpool

NAMES OF PASSENGERS	AGE	SEX	OCCUPATIONS	DATE PORT SHIP
HYLAND, Honora	16	F	Spinster	18De02Cx
William	30	M	Laborer	18De02Cx
MCDERMOTT, Jane	50	F	Laborer	18De02Cx
Jane	24	F	Spinster	18De02Cx
Cathne.	9	F	Child	18De02Cx
CULKIN, Anne	6	F	Child	18De02Cx
HARKIN, John	26	M	Laborer	18De02Cx
NUGENT, Thomas	30	M	Unknown	18De02Cx
Margret	22	F	Unknown	18De02Cx
Ellen	20	F	Spinster	18De02Cx
Alicia	18	F	Unknown	18De02Cx
Michael	12	M	Unknown	18De02Cx
HARRINGTON, Mary	15	F	Spinster	18De02Cx
DONOVAN, Mary	20	F	Spinster	18De02Cx
MOORE, Cathn.	38	F	Spinster	18De02Cx
ALCOCK, Thomas	30	M	Laborer	18De02Cx
NIELY, Cathn.	24	F	Spinster	18De02Cx
JOHNSON, Arthur	26	M	Laborer	18De02Cx
OBRIEN, Francis	27	M	Laborer	18De02Cx
Margt.	24	F	Spinster	18De02Cx
NULLY, Bridgt.	20	F	Spinster	18De02Cx
COLLINS, Anne	21	F	Spinster	18De02Cx
Thomas	13	M	Spinster	18De02Cx
TROY, James	26	M	Laborer	18De02Cx
SHEADY, Mary	20	F	Spinster	18De02Cx
Ellen	3	F	Child	18De02Cx
John	8	M	Child	18De02Cx
Peter	1	M	Child	18De02Cx
SHORT, Mary	12	F	Spinster	18De02Cx
HEDRAN, James	24	M	Laborer	18De02Cx
John	30	M	Laborer	18De02Cx
RIELY, Cornelius	18	M	Laborer	18De02Cx
PATTERSON, David	18	M	Laborer	18De02Cx
CASEY, Mary	20	F	Spinster	18De02Cx
Anne	24	F	Spinster	18De02Cx
Thomas	26	M	Laborer	18De02Cx
MOONEY, Edward	36	M	Laborer	18De02Cx
Thomas	19	M	Laborer	18De02Cx
Margaret	26	F	Spinster	18De02Cx
JOHNSON, Thos.	35	M	Laborer	18De02Cx

NAMES OF PASSENGERS	AGE	SEX	OCCUPATIONS	DATE PORT SHIP
REED, Robt.	20	M	Laborer	18De02Cx
MULLIGAN, Bridgt.	13	F	Laborer	18De02Cx
CARR, Mary	21	F	Spinster	18De02Cx
FAILER, Thos.	20	M	Laborer	18De02Cx
MCGANN, Patk.	20	M	Laborer	18De02Cx
HURLEY, Denis	18	M	Laborer	18De02Cx
GOUGH, James	29	M	Laborer	18De02Cx
BURK, Mary	30	F	Laborer	18De02Cx
Cathne.	21	F	Spinster	18De02Cx
Bridgt.	3	F	Child	18De02Cx
MURPHY, Betty	20	F	Spinster	18De02Cx
DAVIS, Peter	42	M	Laborer	18De02Cx
Mary	40	F	Laborer	18De02Cx
Eliza	15	F	Spinster	18De02Cx
Mary	13	F	Spinster	18De02Cx
James	10	M	Spinster	18De02Cx
Elizabeth	7	F	Child	18De02Cx
John	3	M	Child	18De02Cx
GRUNDY, Suzan	22	F	Spinster	18De02Cx
Willm.	.10	M	Infant	18De02Cx
BANTHERAN, Mary	20	F	Spinster	18De02Cx
MCCABE, Anne	30	F	Spinster	18De02Cx
HAVIRTY, Jane	18	F	Spinster	18De02Cx
COFFEE, James	20	M	Laborer	18De02Cx
KEVINAN, Christy	18	M	Laborer	18De02Cx
OBRIEN, James	40	M	Laborer	18De02Cx
Mary	24	F	Spinster	18De02Cx
CUNNINGHAM, Thomas	5	M	Child	18De02Cx
Daniel	4	M	Child	18De02Cx
Mary	3	F	Child	18De02Cx
GRAHAM, Bridgt.	20	F	Spinster	18De02Cx
KENNEDY, Sarah	17	F	Spinster	18De02Cx
DUNN, Elizabeth	25	F	Spinster	18De02Cx
KELLY, Mary	17	F	Spinster	18De02Cx
CLARKE, Margt.	45	F	Spinster	18De02Cx
Thomas	25	M	Laborer	18De02Cx
KERRIGAN, Patk.	10	M	Laborer	18De02Cx
KELLY, Cathne.	8	F	Child	18De02Cx
BEATY, Cathne.	28	F	Spinster	18De02Cx
Patk.	31	M	Laborer	18De02Cx
FEGAN, Anne	17	F	Spinster	18De02Cx
OWENS, Peter	27	M	Laborer	18De02Cx
HARRINGTON, Mary	19	F	Spinster	18De02Cx
SHEELY, Danl.	32	M	Laborer	18De02Cx
WYMER, Mary	28	F	Spinster	18De02Cx
Thos.	30	M	Laborer	18De02Cx
HAY, Elizabeth	18	F	Spinster	18De02Cx
CALLAHAN, Mary	24	F	Spinster	18De02Cx
FITZPATRICK, Suzan	18	F	Spinster	18De02Cx
MINGAN, Mary	13	F	Spinster	18De02Cx
TIERMAN, Eliza	13	F	Spinster	18De02Cx
KELLEY, Margt.	22	F	Spinster	18De02Cx
GIBBINS, Mary-J.	40	F	Spinster	18De02Cx
Mary	6	F	Child	18De02Cx
Ellen	4	F	Child	18De02Cx
DAVITT, Mary	24	F	Spinster	18De02Cx
Honora	4	F	Child	18De02Cx
BURKE, John	24	M	Laborer	18De02Cx
MCKENNA, Cathe.	24	F	Spinster	18De02Cx
HOPKINS, Rose	20	F	Spinster	18De02Cx
OBRIEN, Thomas	38	M	Laborer	18De02Cx
GANNON, Thos.	20	M	Laborer	18De02Cx
WALSH, James	36	M	Laborer	18De02Cx
NOONAN, Edward	20	M	Laborer	18De02Cx
John	35	M	Laborer	18De02Cx
DOYLE, Anne	30	F	Laborer	18De02Cx
Anne	12	F	Laborer	18De02Cx
Michael	5	M	Child	18De02Cx
John	7	M	Child	18De02Cx
Luke	3	M	Child	18De02Cx
MULLY, Thomas	42	M	Laborer	18De02Cx
CASEY, Mary	28	F	Laborer	18De02Cx
U	.07	F	Infant	18De02Cx
Mary	6	F	Child	18De02Cx
Cathne.	4	F	Child	18De02Cx

NAMES OF PASSENGERS	AGE	SEX	OCCUPATIONS	DATE PORT SHIP
GREY, Rose-Ann	17	F	Spinster	18De02Cx
DENNANGE, Rose	9	F	Child	18De02Cx
HARGEDON, John	28	M	Laborer	18De02Cx
MANNION, Michael	13	M	Laborer	18De02Cx
DALY, Bridgt.	26	F	Laborer	18De02Cx
Ellen	9	F	Child	18De02Cx
Jane	7	F	Child	18De02Cx
HALE, Anne	20	F	Spinster	18De02Cx
CRANE, Thomas	21	M	Laborer	18De02Cx
SAPLE, Johanah	35	F	Laborer	18De02Cx
Anne	11	F	Laborer	18De02Cx
John	9	M	Child	18De02Cx
Michl.	7	M	Child	18De02Cx
James	5	M	Child	18De02Cx
David	2	M	Child	18De02Cx
ABION, John	40	M	Mechanic	18De02Cx
COLLINS, Cathe.	30	F	Unknown	18De02Cx
Michl.	4	M	Child	18De02Cx
BRYAN, Ellen	28	F	Unknown	18De02Cx
Daniel	1	M	Child	18De02Cx
OLEARY, Cornls.	13	M	Mechanic	18De02Cx
John	16	M	Laborer	18De02Cx
COYLE, Thos.	60	M	Laborer	18De02Cx
Cathe.	60	F	Laborer	18De02Cx
Judith	18	F	Spinster	18De02Cx
Peter	15	M	Spinster	18De02Cx
HEARNE, Margt.	20	F	Spinster	18De02Cx
FOX, Bridgt.	18	F	Spinster	18De02Cx
MCGUIRE, Cathe.	30	F	Spinster	18De02Cx
SHEA, Julia	30	F	Spinster	18De02Cx
SULLIVAN, Mary	18	F	Spinster	18De02Cx
DESMOND, Mary	30	F	Spinster	18De02Cx
Mary	4	F	Child	18De02Cx
Andrew	3	M	Child	18De02Cx
SPILLANE, Nelly	22	F	Spinster	18De02Cx
CALLAHAN, Barbara	7	F	Child	18De02Cx
MOLONE, Patk.	22	M	Laborer	18De02Cx
Sarah	19	F	Spinster	18De02Cx
LEARY, Julia	28	F	Spinster	18De02Cx
MCALOON, Bridgt.	34	F	Spinster	18De02Cx
U	.10	F	Infant	18De02Cx
Peter	10	M	Unknown	18De02Cx
Patrick	8	M	Child	18De02Cx
Mary	6	F	Child	18De02Cx
Eliza	4	F	Child	18De02Cx
Biddy	2	F	Child	18De02Cx
LYNCH, Mary	36	F	Spinster	18De02Cx
SMITH, Phillip	40	M	Laborer	18De02Cx
John	12	M	Laborer	18De02Cx
REED, Margt.	61	F	Spinster	18De02Cx
LAPPIN, Patk.	20	M	Laborer	18De02Cx
MURTY, Margt.	48	F	Laborer	18De02Cx
James	16	M	Laborer	18De02Cx
Eliza	15	F	Spinster	18De02Cx
NEWINAN, Pheebe	18	F	Spinster	18De02Cx
JUDGE, Anne	30	F	Spinster	18De02Cx
LONGHEEN, Jane	30	F	Spinster	18De02Cx
U	.04	U	Infant	18De02Cx
Eliza	3	F	Child	18De02Cx
CREA, John	20	M	Laborer	18De02Cx
James	14	M	Laborer	18De02Cx
BRENNAN, Rebecca	40	F	Laborer	18De02Cx
U	.05	M	Infant	18De02Cx
Rebecca	10	F	Laborer	18De02Cx
John	8	M	Child	18De02Cx
Catherine	4	F	Child	18De02Cx
WYNN, Arthur	33	M	Laborer	18De02Cx
BRADY, James	41	M	Laborer	18De02Cx
MALLEY, Michl.	18	M	Laborer	18De02Cx
QUINN, Mary	27	F	Spinster	18De02Cx
MCGRATH, Celia	51	F	Spinster	18De02Cx
MULDOWNEY, Mary	18	F	Spinster	18De02Cx
MORON, John	40	M	Laborer	18De02Cx
Charles	18	M	Laborer	18De02Cx
CAUFIELD, Bridgt.	26	F	Spinster	18De02Cx

NAMES OF PASSENGERS	AGE	SEX	OCCUPATIONS	DATE PORT SHIP
CURLEY, Sabina	50	F	Spinster	18De02Cx
John	24	M	Laborer	18De02Cx
Thos.	17	M	Laborer	18De02Cx
Maria	12	F	Laborer	18De02Cx
MCGRANN, Ellen	27	F	Spinster	18De02Cx
CONNEN, Willm.	12	M	Spinster	18De02Cx
DAVIS, Elizabeth	31	F	Spinster	18De02Cx
Arthur	8	M	Child	18De02Cx
John	5	M	Child	18De02Cx
James	2	M	Child	18De02Cx
DUGGAN, Michl.	40	M	Farmer	18De02Cx
Bridgt.	40	F	Farmer	18De02Cx
Cathe.	20	F	Spinster	18De02Cx
Maria	18	F	Spinster	18De02Cx
Charlotte	10	F	Spinster	18De02Cx
James	16	M	Laborer	18De02Cx
MCGRATH, John	24	M	Laborer	18De02Cx
BEALE, Francis	23	M	Laborer	18De02Cx
VINCENT, Sidney	30	M	Laborer	18De02Cx
DODD, Willm.	28	M	Accountant	18De02Cx
ROGERS, Ellen	20	F	Spinster	18De02Cx
Anne	16	F	Spinster	18De02Cx
MCDONOUGH, Annie	31	F	Spinster	18De02Cx
CUNNINGHAM, Margt.	33	F	Spinster	18De02Cx
MCGALNEY, Sarah	18	F	Spinster	18De02Cx
Ellen	22	F	Spinster	18De02Cx
U	.07	F	Infant	18De02Cx
SMITH, Alexr.	40	M	Farmer	18De02Cx
MARKIN, John	19	M	Laborer	18De02Cx
MCCABE, Patk.	13	M	Laborer	18De02Cx
YOUNG, Willm.	46	M	Laborer	18De02Cx
Mary	47	F	Laborer	18De02Cx
Thomas	21	M	Laborer	18De02Cx
James	19	M	Laborer	18De02Cx
Bridgt.	17	F	Spinster	18De02Cx
MULADY, James	36	M	Laborer	18De02Cx
FARRELL, Cathe.	18	F	Spinster	18De02Cx
RYAN, Cathe.	17	F	Spinster	18De02Cx
Mary	12	F	Spinster	18De02Cx
DOOLY, Bridgt.	36	F	Spinster	18De02Cx
FEGAN, Christo.	23	M	Laborer	18De02Cx
Lawrence	35	M	Laborer	18De02Cx
MCLEAN, John	16	M	Laborer	18De02Cx
COMISKY, Mary	25	F	Spinster	18De02Cx
KEARNS, Ellen	27	F	Spinster	18De02Cx
U	.03	F	Infant	18De02Cx
CONNELL, Elizabeth	16	F	Spinster	18De02Cx
CAFFREY, James	22	M	Laborer	18De02Cx
Bridgt.	20	F	Spinster	18De02Cx
BUCKLEY, David	22	M	Laborer	18De02Cx
WILLIS, John	34	M	Laborer	18De02Cx
HEFFERMAN, Ellen	30	F	Spinster	18De02Cx
CLERK, John	24	M	Laborer	18De02Cx
BYRNE, Owen	17	M	Laborer	18De02Cx
MARTIN, Mary	19	F	Spinster	18De02Cx
FENNULLY, Mary	21	F	Spinster	18De02Cx
CAVANNY, Peggy	18	F	Spinster	18De02Cx
COYLE, James	25	M	Laborer	18De02Cx
MULVERHILL, Barney	26	M	Laborer	18De02Cx
MAGOWAN, Anne	20	F	Spinster	18De02Cx
BRATT, Judy	20	F	Spinster	18De02Cx
HAGERTY, James	24	M	Laborer	18De02Cx
LANGAN, James	25	M	Laborer	18De02Cx
GRIMES, Peter	21	M	Laborer	18De02Cx
DUFFY, Frank	28	M	Laborer	18De02Cx
DALY, John	21	M	Laborer	18De02Cx
BRYAN, Emily	23	F	Spinster	18De02Cx
LUNEY, Michl.	50	M	Laborer	18De02Cx
Mary	48	F	Laborer	18De02Cx
Kate	18	F	Spinster	18De02Cx
SHANNON, Ellen	18	F	Spinster	18De02Cx
Biddy	12	F	Spinster	18De02Cx
Amity	60	F	Spinster	18De02Cx
Biddy	50	F	Spinster	18De02Cx
Nancy	17	F	Spinster	18De02Cx
SHANNON, Patrick	13	M	Spinster	18De02Cx
Biddy	9	F	Child	18De02Cx
COLLINS, Maurice	28	M	Laborer	18De02Cx
Michael	22	M	Laborer	18De02Cx
MERRISY, Biddy	33	F	Unknown	18De02Cx
MCNAMARA, Biddy	23	F	Unknown	18De02Cx
MCCREA, Walter	22	M	Laborer	18De02Cx
William	7	M	Child	18De02Cx
Sarah	9	F	Child	18De02Cx
MCNAMARA, Honerah	18	F	Spinster	18De02Cx
FISH, James	28	M	Laborer	18De02Cx
RICE, Michl.	28	M	Laborer	18De02Cx
FISH, Anne	28	F	Laborer	18De02Cx
Willm.	7	M	Child	18De02Cx
Julia	4	F	Child	18De02Cx
James	2	M	Child	18De02Cx
FITZPATRICK, John	34	M	Laborer	18De02Cx
SMITH, John	24	M	Laborer	18De02Cx
James	18	M	Laborer	18De02Cx
Maria	13	F	Spinster	18De02Cx
REYNOLDS, Thos.	21	M	Laborer	18De02Cx
Ellen	22	F	Spinster	18De02Cx
MCMANUS, Michl.	30	M	Laborer	18De02Cx
BYRNES, Mary	26	F	Spinster	18De02Cx
RYAN, Mary	3	F	Child	18De02Cx
KEENAN, Mary	42	F	Spinster	18De02Cx
RYAN, John	48	M	Laborer	18De02Cx
CHAMBERS, Thomas	50	M	Laborer	18De02Cx
MEARA, Danl.	24	M	Laborer	18De02Cx
FLEMING, Anne	20	F	Spinster	18De02Cx
BEGLEY, Honora	60	F	Spinster	18De02Cx
Nancy	48	F	Spinster	18De02Cx
CLINTON, Thos.	40	M	Laborer	18De02Cx
LARNEY, Thos.	40	M	Laborer	18De02Cx
LIDDY, Biddy	24	F	Laborer	18De02Cx
U	.04	F	Infant	18De02Cx
GILLIGAN, Cathe.	34	F	Spinster	18De02Cx
MCGUIRE, Michl.	20	M	Laborer	18De02Cx
Patrick	6	M	Child	18De02Cx
MURPHY, Edward	22	M	Laborer	18De02Cx
WALSH, Mary	21	F	Spinster	18De02Cx
MCKENNA, Owen	40	M	Laborer	18De02Cx
PARTLAND, Suzan	18	F	Spinster	18De02Cx
MCKENNA, Bridgt.	24	F	Spinster	18De02Cx
MCAVER, Cathe.	20	F	Spinster	18De02Cx
GILL, Anne	28	F	Spinster	18De02Cx
FARRELL, Michl.	40	M	Laborer	18De02Cx
U-Mrs.	30	F	Laborer	18De02Cx
U	.07	F	Infant	18De02Cx
Mary	10	F	Laborer	18De02Cx
Louisa	6	F	Child	18De02Cx
Michl.	8	M	Child	18De02Cx
Harriett	4	F	Child	18De02Cx
Jane	2	F	Child	18De02Cx
JOHNSON, Henry	18	M	Laborer	18De02Cx
MCDERMOTT, Mary-A.	12	F	Laborer	18De02Cx
INGLEBY, Isabella	40	F	Laborer	18De02Cx
U	.05	F	Infant	18De02Cx
Mary-Anne	3	F	Child	18De02Cx
OSBORNE, Thos.	26	M	Laborer	18De02Cx
NUIFFE, Mary	31	F	Laborer	18De02Cx
U	.08	F	Infant	18De02Cx
Edward	4	M	Child	18De02Cx
HARINGHBY, Anne	41	F	Spinster	18De02Cx
NEALE, Mark	36	M	Laborer	18De02Cx
BIRD, David	20	M	Laborer	18De02Cx
HURLEY, Danl.	28	M	Laborer	18De02Cx
KELLY, Mary	21	F	Spinster	18De02Cx
HALAM, John	34	M	Laborer	18De02Cx
SHANNON, Mary-A.	19	F	Spinster	18De02Cx
MCKEE, Thos.	28	M	Mechanic	18De02Cx
RICHARDSON, Saml.G.	31	M	Mechanic	18De02Cx
Aunie	29	F	Mechanic	18De02Cx
FENNING, Patk.	21	M	Laborer	18De02Cx
DUNDAR, Cathe.	19	F	Spinster	18De02Cx

NAMES OF PASSENGERS	AGE	SEX	OCCUPATIONS	DATE PORT SHIP

JANE-GOWDIE 18 DECEMBER 1849

From London

LANNET, John	39	M	Farmer	18De06Dc
HANDLER, Thomas	27	M	Mechanic	18De06Dc
HANDLY, Elizabeth	27	F	Unknown	18De06Dc
RHODES, James	51	M	Mechanic	18De06Dc
Harriet	40	F	Unknown	18De06Dc
Mary	17	F	Unknown	18De06Dc
HEARNEY, Timothy	19	M	Laborer	18De06Dc
DAVIS, James	45	M	Laborer	18De06Dc
BRITCHER, John	30	M	Laborer	18De06Dc
CARSEY, Timothy	23	M	Laborer	18De06Dc
Cathering	6	F	Child	18De06Dc
HITCHINGS, Rob.	21	M	Laborer	18De06Dc
PEARCE, John	22	M	Laborer	18De06Dc
GOLDBERG, Gutav	25	M	Laborer	18De06Dc
DENONE, William	40	M	Laborer	18De06Dc

HIBERNIA 18 DECEMBER 1849

From Liverpool

JACKSON, J.A.	20	M	Gentleman	18De02Df
FITZGERALD, W.J.	33	M	Gentleman	18De02Df
TRIMBLE, Thos.	39	M	Gentleman	18De02Df
DEWAR, S.	28	M	Merchant	18De02Df
MCKINSTRY, S.	20	M	Merchant	18De02Df

OREGON 19 DECEMBER 1849

From Liverpool

SKEELS, Biddy	25	F	Laborer	19De02Dh
BURNS, Mary	25	F	Unknown	19De02Dh
GERAGHTY, Rose	30	F	Unknown	19De02Dh
MAGUIRE, Hugh	35	M	Unknown	19De02Dh
Mary	30	F	Unknown	19De02Dh
HANLY, Mary	30	F	Unknown	19De02Dh
HOPKINS, Biddy	15	F	Unknown	19De02Dh
John	45	M	Unknown	19De02Dh
Mary	35	F	Unknown	19De02Dh
John	.00	M	Infant	19De02Dh
FITZGERALD, John	20	M	Unknown	19De02Dh
Kate	18	F	Unknown	19De02Dh
Norry	16	M	Unknown	19De02Dh
Margaret	13	F	Unknown	19De02Dh
CONNOR, John	40	M	Unknown	19De02Dh
Biddy	30	F	Unknown	19De02Dh
Pat	10	M	Unknown	19De02Dh
KIRK, Jane	17	F	Unknown	19De02Dh
MCMANNS, Catherine	17	F	Unknown	19De02Dh
MALONE, Mick	20	M	Unknown	19De02Dh
EARLY, James	20	M	Unknown	19De02Dh
CONNOR, Andy	25	M	Unknown	19De02Dh
MURRAY, Angus	24	M	Unknown	19De02Dh
MALLFY, Mary	24	F	Unknown	19De02Dh
TAYLOR, John	55	M	Unknown	19De02Dh
Ann	52	F	Unknown	19De02Dh
John	22	M	Unknown	19De02Dh
Frank	19	M	Unknown	19De02Dh
Robert	14	M	Unknown	19De02Dh
Richard	12	M	Unknown	19De02Dh
Henry	10	M	Unknown	19De02Dh
Mary-Jane	9	F	Child	19De02Dh
MCMANNS, Pat	22	M	Unknown	19De02Dh
HEASE, Margaret	40	F	Unknown	19De02Dh
DONAVAN, Patt	20	M	Unknown	19De02Dh
LACY, Margaret	28	F	Unknown	19De02Dh
MCCAUL, Catherine	16	F	Unknown	19De02Dh
HORNE, Thomas	19	M	Unknown	19De02Dh
MCDONALD, Pat	20	M	Unknown	19De02Dh
REILLY, John	60	M	Unknown	19De02Dh
Catherine	25	F	Unknown	19De02Dh
Ann	27	F	Unknown	19De02Dh
CALLIN, Jan	30	M	Unknown	19De02Dh
CAMBELL, Thomas	30	M	Unknown	19De02Dh
CARROLL, Peter	25	M	Unknown	19De02Dh
FALLS, Margaret	22	F	Unknown	19De02Dh
DODDS, James	21	M	Unknown	19De02Dh
REILLY, Alexander	22	M	Unknown	19De02Dh
BOYD, Mary	33	F	Unknown	19De02Dh
Saml.	10	M	Unknown	19De02Dh
Elisth.Jane	8	F	Child	19De02Dh
Margaret	6	F	Child	19De02Dh
Robert	2	M	Child	19De02Dh
Agnes	.00	F	Infant	19De02Dh
REARDON, Mary-Ann	22	F	Unknown	19De02Dh
Margaret	20	F	Unknown	19De02Dh
SMITH, Mary-Ann	30	F	Unknown	19De02Dh
Thomas	5	M	Child	19De02Dh
George	2	M	Child	19De02Dh
CUTHBERT, Benjamin	24	M	Unknown	19De02Dh
FARROW, Martin	44	M	Unknown	19De02Dh
Gabin	41	M	Unknown	19De02Dh
John	18	M	Unknown	19De02Dh
Thomas	16	M	Unknown	19De02Dh
Emma	12	F	Unknown	19De02Dh
Asher	10	M	Unknown	19De02Dh
Jessie	8	M	Child	19De02Dh
Lucy	6	F	Child	19De02Dh
Asher	26	M	Unknown	19De02Dh
PENN, Reuben	23	M	Unknown	19De02Dh
SILIERS, Robert	17	M	Unknown	19De02Dh
CARRENTHERS, John-Gale	36	M	Unknown	19De02Dh
Sarah	36	F	Unknown	19De02Dh
Angeline	11	F	Unknown	19De02Dh
Charles	7	M	Child	19De02Dh
Jane	5	F	Child	19De02Dh
Charles	3	M	Child	19De02Dh
CAPPELL, Wm.	32	M	Sawer	19De02Dh

JANET 20 DECEMBER 1849

From Newry

PATTERSON, Robert	20	M	Carpenter	20De04De
Mary	22	F	Unknown	20De04De
MCKENNA, Biddy	30	F	Unknown	20De04De
Sarah	7	F	Child	20De04De
Jane	4	F	Child	20De04De
John	3	M	Child	20De04De
DUNCAN, Nancy	25	F	Spinster	20De04De
HENING, Eliza	30	F	Unknown	20De04De
Samuel-B.	.00	M	Infant	20De04De

NAMES OF PASSENGERS	AGE	SEX	OCCUPATIONS	DATE PORT SHIP
KELLY, John	16	M	Shoemaker	20De04De
CLESDALE, Alex	30	M	Smith	20De04De
BEATTY, Robert	30	M	Saddler	20De04De
Margaret	30	F	Wife	20De04De
Eliza	7	F	Child	20De04De
Nancy	3	F	Child	20De04De
John	.00	M	Infant	20De04De
DEVLIN, Patrick	25	M	Merchant	20De04De
Sarah	25	F	Sister	20De04De
WILSON, John	16	M	Locksmith	20De04De
BRANNON, Thomas	20	M	Weaver	20De04De
GRAHAM, Margaret	24	F	Spinster	20De04De
Catharine	18	F	Unknown	20De04De
HANLON, John	50	M	Carpenter	20De04De
John	15	M	Unknown	20De04De
Bridget	18	F	Spinster	20De04De
HEALY, James	20	M	Smith	20De04De
Jane	20	F	Wife	20De04De
BEATTY, Elizabeth	.00	F	Infant	20De04De
THOMPSON, Samuel	28	M	Watchmaker	20De04De
MCCULLOUGH, Ann	20	F	Dressmaker	20De04De
WILSON, Sarah	21	F	Unknown	20De04De
SCOTT, Letetia	20	F	Unknown	20De04De
BOZO, Robert	21	M	Millwright	20De04De
SWEENY, Ann	20	F	Spinster	20De04De
MCKEE, Joseph	87	M	Laborer	20De04De
Died-At-Sea				
BOYLE, Mary	30	F	Unknown	20De04De
Margaret	25	F	Unknown	20De04De
Michael	6	M	Child	20De04De
Margt.	4	F	Child	20De04De
Margt.	.00	F	Infant	20De04De
DONNELLY, Mary	15	F	Spinster	20De04De
GARLAND, Mary-Ann	25	F	Wi	20De04De
Henry	5	M	Child	20De04De
John	2	M	Child	20De04De
DELANEY, John	24	M	Farmer	20De04De
MORROW, James	24	M	Farmer	20De04De
Elizabeth	24	F	Wife	20De04De
MILLER, Mary	22	F	Spinster	20De04De
FRIER, Mary	17	F	Spinster	20De04De
EWART, Ann	20	F	Spinster	20De04De
HUME, George	20	M	Saddler	20De04De
HUNTER, Hamilton	18	M	Unknown	20De04De
MCGUIRE, Sally	23	F	Unknown	20De04De
WATERS, James	27	M	Baker	20De04De
Elizabeth	27	F	Wife	20De04De
Ellen	33	F	Unknown	20De04De
Thomas	2	M	Child	20De04De
Richard	.00	M	Infant	20De04De
SARSFIELD, Tho.	26	M	Mechanic	20De04De
Mary	25	F	Unknown	20De04De
Mary	.00	F	Infant	20De04De
QUIN, Judith	20	F	Unknown	20De04De
STEWART, Thomas	20	M	Smith	20De04De
CROTHERS, Mary	25	F	Spinster	20De04De
MOORE, Ann	26	F	Unknown	20De04De
GILLESPIE, Robert	21	M	Clock Maker	20De04De
Eliza	18	F	Wife	20De04De
John	15	M	Unknown	20De04De
MCGUFFIN, James	40	M	Farmer	20De04De
Margt	35	F	Wife	20De04De
Henry	17	M	Unknown	20De04De
Nancy	15	F	Unknown	20De04De
Eliz.Margt.	12	F	Unknown	20De04De
Sarah	10	F	Unknown	20De04De
James	8	M	Child	20De04De
John	6	M	Child	20De04De
BARDON, John	20	M	Laborer	20De04De
CLARKE, James	20	M	Tailor	20De04De
Thomas	19	M	Slater	20De04De
BROWNLOW, Richd.	19	M	Mason	20De04De
LOVETS, John	20	M	Shoemaker	20De04De
KEAN, Bridgt.	19	F	Spinster	20De04De
Eliza	23	F	Spinster	20De04De
WRIGHT, Thomas	27	M	Brush Maker	20De04De
Cath.Jane	25	F	Wife	20De04De
Thomas-J.	5	M	Child	20De04De
Charlotte	1	F	Child	20De04De
WILSON, Ruth	56	F	Laborer	20De04De
HYNES, John	25	M	Unknown	20De04De
Mary	19	F	Unknown	20De04De
Ellen	17	F	Unknown	20De04De
MCKENNA, Felix	20	M	Unknown	20De04De
Cath.	20	F	Unknown	20De04De
Elizabeth	.00	F	Infant	20De04De
Died-At-Sea				
GALWAY, John	20	M	Unknown	20De04De
TREANOR, Hugh	25	M	Unknown	20De04De
WHITE, Ann	20	F	Unknown	20De04De
James	20	M	Unknown	20De04De
ADAMS, Jane	23	F	Wi	20De04De
Elizabeth	.00	F	Infant	20De04De
WALLACH, Hugh	35	M	Farmer	20De04De
Agnes	30	F	Wife	20De04De
John	14	M	Shoemaker	20De04De
Joseph	13	M	Unknown	20De04De
Ann	6	F	Child	20De04De
Hugh	5	M	Child	20De04De
NEILL, Jane	25	F	Unknown	20De04De
MCFARLAND, John	25	M	Laborer	20De04De
Michl.	25	M	Unknown	20De04De
DOBBIN, Bridget	20	F	Spinster	20De04De
MCFARLAND, Betty	25	F	Unknown	20De04De
WHITE, U	.00	M	Infant	20De04De
Born-At-Sea				
HARSHAW, John	25	M	Unknown	20De04De
James	23	M	Unknown	20De04De
MCCLUSKEY, Ann	25	F	Unknown	20De04De

EMPIRE-STATE 26 DECEMBER 1849

From Chagres And Jamaica

NAMES OF PASSENGERS	AGE	SEX	OCCUPATIONS	DATE PORT SHIP
MCLANE, Patrick	31	M	Miner	26De23Fc

PHILADELPHIA 31 DECEMBER 1849

From Liverpool

NAMES OF PASSENGERS	AGE	SEX	OCCUPATIONS	DATE PORT SHIP
DIXON, Robert	22	M	Unknown	31De02Dd
QUIGLEY, Jno.	30	M	Unknown	31De02Dd
Margaret	27	F	Unknown	31De02Dd
Mary	.00	F	Infant	31De02Dd
CAHILL, Mary	27	F	Unknown	31De02Dd
Edward	9	M	Child	31De02Dd
John	7	M	Child	31De02Dd
Pat	5	M	Child	31De02Dd
CLEAR, Judy	25	F	Unknown	31De02Dd
WARD, Sarah	26	F	Unknown	31De02Dd
CLEARY, Jno.	23	M	Unknown	31De02Dd
Wm.	20	M	Unknown	31De02Dd
LOGAN, Jas.	29	M	Unknown	31De02Dd
Nancy	25	F	Unknown	31De02Dd
Rose	3	F	Child	31De02Dd
HARR, Catharine	20	F	Unknown	31De02Dd
John	20	M	Unknown	31De02Dd
DROGER, Mary	45	F	Unknown	31De02Dd

NAMES OF PASSENGERS	AGE	SEX	OCCUPATIONS	DATE PORT SHIP
RUSH, Honora	18	F	Unknown	31De02Dd
MCGRADE, Austin	50	M	Unknown	31De02Dd
Chas.	25	M	Unknown	31De02Dd
Peter	23	M	Unknown	31De02Dd
Felix	21	M	Unknown	31De02Dd
Bridget	17	F	Unknown	31De02Dd
SMITH, Farrell	23	M	Unknown	31De02Dd
WALTON, Jas.	39	M	Unknown	31De02Dd
FRANK, John	20	M	Unknown	31De02Dd
LAWLOR, John	20	M	Unknown	31De02Dd
MCCONNELL, Henry	21	M	Unknown	31De02Dd
DOLAN, Michael	20	M	Unknown	31De02Dd
WILKINSON, Thos.	25	M	Unknown	31De02Dd
SHEEHY, Cath.	26	F	Unknown	31De02Dd
MCGRATT, Bridget	17	F	Unknown	31De02Dd
Mary	10	F	Unknown	31De02Dd
Edward	8	M	Child	31De02Dd
Margaret	6	F	Child	31De02Dd
SHEALEY, Michael	10	M	Child	31De02Dd
MCCUNIE, James-Orr	35	M	Unknown	31De02Dd
DANIEL, Thos.	20	M	Unknown	31De02Dd
TOOLE, Patrick	30	M	Unknown	31De02Dd
U-Mrs.	28	F	Unknown	31De02Dd
MOOLAN, Jas.	30	M	Unknown	31De02Dd
Bridget	25	F	Unknown	31De02Dd
CARNEY, Michael	25	M	Unknown	31De02Dd
Ellen	25	F	Unknown	31De02Dd
CARROLL, Wm.	30	M	Unknown	31De02Dd
LYONS, Michael	20	M	Unknown	31De02Dd
WALSH, Thos.	30	M	Unknown	31De02Dd
Biddy	22	F	Unknown	31De02Dd
FLYNN, John	20	M	Unknown	31De02Dd
Mary	19	F	Unknown	31De02Dd
BLAKE, Margt.	20	F	Unknown	31De02Dd
LYNCH, John	22	M	Unknown	31De02Dd
CARTIN, Michael	21	M	Unknown	31De02Dd
Pat	20	M	Unknown	31De02Dd
Margt.	16	F	Unknown	31De02Dd
MCDONNELL, Ellen	21	F	Unknown	31De02Dd
FALLON, Mary	30	F	Unknown	31De02Dd
Ann	10	F	Unknown	31De02Dd
Pat	7	M	Child	31De02Dd
CARR, John	30	M	Unknown	31De02Dd
FINEGAN, Mary	20	F	Unknown	31De02Dd
FOGHARTY, Bridgt.	19	F	Unknown	31De02Dd
KEARNS, Mary	18	F	Unknown	31De02Dd
MAHON, Jas.	10	M	Unknown	31De02Dd
MCANALLY, Jas.	25	M	Unknown	31De02Dd
Cath.	22	F	Unknown	31De02Dd
MCCONNELL, Pat	15	M	Unknown	31De02Dd
COONEY, John	20	M	Unknown	31De02Dd
CAMPBELL, Pat	19	M	Unknown	31De02Dd
STEVENSON, Joseph	23	M	Unknown	31De02Dd
Kitty	30	F	Unknown	31De02Dd
KENNEDY, Winefred	30	M	Unknown	31De02Dd
KILFOYLE, Judy	25	F	Unknown	31De02Dd
MONA, Margt.	25	F	Unknown	31De02Dd
LONG, Mary	20	F	Unknown	31De02Dd
KELLY, Mary	18	F	Unknown	31De02Dd
CONNOR, Mary	20	F	Unknown	31De02Dd
MONAGHAN, John	25	M	Unknown	31De02Dd
MCQUAID, Hannah	21	F	Unknown	31De02Dd
MULLOCKILL, John	26	M	Unknown	31De02Dd
KINAGH, Biddy	20	F	Unknown	31De02Dd
FILITON, Russel	29	M	Unknown	31De02Dd
BROWN, Richard	24	M	Unknown	31De02Dd
ROWE, Wm.	21	M	Unknown	31De02Dd
BLACK, Joseph	30	M	Unknown	31De02Dd
FLYNNE, Mary	47	F	Unknown	31De02Dd
MCGLINN, Jane	25	F	Unknown	31De02Dd
MCKEOWN, Edward	20	M	Unknown	31De02Dd
RIELY, Mary	20	F	Unknown	31De02Dd
RUTHERFORD, Thos.	50	M	Unknown	31De02Dd
Jane	50	F	Unknown	31De02Dd
Allen	27	M	Unknown	31De02Dd

NAMES OF PASSENGERS	AGE	SEX	OCCUPATIONS	DATE PORT SHIP
RUTHERFORD, Mary-Anne	25	F	Unknown	31De02Dd
Eliza	23	F	Unknown	31De02Dd
Robt.	18	M	Unknown	31De02Dd
Mgt.Jane	16	F	Unknown	31De02Dd
George	11	M	Unknown	31De02Dd
BRYAN, John	35	M	Unknown	31De02Dd
Cath.	24	F	Unknown	31De02Dd
Bridgit-G.	2	F	Child	31De02Dd
Jane	.00	F	Infant	31De02Dd
DODD, John	50	M	Unknown	31De02Dd
John	20	M	Unknown	31De02Dd
Martha	18	F	Unknown	31De02Dd
LATTER, Thos.	20	M	Unknown	31De02Dd
LEONARD, Henry	61	M	Unknown	31De02Dd
Sarah	58	F	Unknown	31De02Dd
Susan	27	F	Unknown	31De02Dd
Eliza	24	F	Unknown	31De02Dd
Caroline	19	F	Unknown	31De02Dd
HART, Mick	22	M	Unknown	31De02Dd
Ellen	12	F	Unknown	31De02Dd
Margt.	10	F	Unknown	31De02Dd
RYAN, Mary	30	F	Unknown	31De02Dd
Bessy	9	F	Child	31De02Dd
Thos.	7	F	Child	31De02Dd
Anne	4	F	Child	31De02Dd
Fras.	2	M	Child	31De02Dd
MORROW, Pat	13	M	Unknown	31De02Dd
Margt.	11	F	Unknown	31De02Dd
MALINEY, John	20	M	Unknown	31De02Dd
Mary	22	F	Unknown	31De02Dd
MORVILL, Mary	26	F	Unknown	31De02Dd
HAMILL, Pat	21	M	Unknown	31De02Dd
FLYNNE, Jas.	18	M	Unknown	31De02Dd
ARMSTRONG, Mary	20	F	Unknown	31De02Dd
RYAN, Julia	30	F	Unknown	31De02Dd
MCKENNA, John	13	M	Unknown	31De02Dd
HIGGENBOTTOM, Wm.	24	M	Unknown	31De02Dd
HAMILL, Jas.	24	M	Unknown	31De02Dd
MOORE, Sam	16	M	Unknown	31De02Dd
MCDONOUGH, Bernard	20	M	Unknown	31De02Dd
HALPIN, Pat	17	M	Unknown	31De02Dd
INGLOW, Edmund	40	M	Unknown	31De02Dd
REID, Phillip	24	M	Unknown	31De02Dd
CUNNINGHAM, Mary	18	F	Unknown	31De02Dd
WALSH, Catharine	22	F	Unknown	31De02Dd
HAYES, Biddy	19	F	Unknown	31De02Dd
KEARNEY, Ellen	40	F	Unknown	31De02Dd
QUINN, Pat	35	M	Unknown	31De02Dd
Michael	30	M	Unknown	31De02Dd
Biddy	28	F	Unknown	31De02Dd
CONNOLLY, Jas.	35	M	Unknown	31De02Dd
Margt.	30	F	Unknown	31De02Dd
BYRNE, Jas.	50	M	Unknown	31De02Dd
MCLAUGHLIN, Peggy	20	F	Unknown	31De02Dd
MULHOLLAND, Wm.	20	M	Unknown	31De02Dd
MCANDREW, Wm.	24	M	Unknown	31De02Dd
MCDONALD, Jas.	18	M	Unknown	31De02Dd
Biddy	16	F	Unknown	31De02Dd
WYNN, U-Mrs.	54	F	Unknown	31De02Dd
Jas.	20	M	Unknown	31De02Dd
Robert	17	M	Unknown	31De02Dd
Harriet	13	F	Unknown	31De02Dd
Holand	10	M	Unknown	31De02Dd
David	7	M	Child	31De02Dd
DONOVAN, Mick	20	M	Unknown	31De02Dd
SHEEHAN, John	20	M	Unknown	31De02Dd
DULY, Mary	22	F	Unknown	31De02Dd
CONNELL, Ellen	22	F	Unknown	31De02Dd
CONNOR, Matt	21	M	Unknown	31De02Dd
BURRELL, Mgt.	20	F	Unknown	31De02Dd
MCCARTHY, Ellen	21	F	Unknown	31De02Dd
IRWINE, Cath.	20	F	Unknown	31De02Dd
Mary	19	F	Unknown	31De02Dd
DALY, Maria	21	F	Unknown	31De02Dd
BENNETT, Mick	24	M	Unknown	31De02Dd

NAMES OF PASSENGERS	AGE	SEX	OCCUPATIONS	DATE PORT SHIP
BENNETT, Edward	20	M	Unknown	31De02Dd
Julia	22	F	Unknown	31De02Dd
DALY, Dan	18	M	Unknown	31De02Dd
Dennis	12	M	Unknown	31De02Dd
BUCKLEY, Owen	30	M	Unknown	31De02Dd
GOSNELL, Wm.	21	M	Unknown	31De02Dd
SCANNELL, Mick	21	M	Unknown	31De02Dd
DONOVAN, Dan	24	M	Unknown	31De02Dd
CARRY, John	35	M	Unknown	31De02Dd
Anne	32	F	Unknown	31De02Dd
John	7	M	Child	31De02Dd
Pat	5	M	Child	31De02Dd
MALONEY, Walt	27	M	Unknown	31De02Dd
MOLOY, Pat	13	M	Unknown	31De02Dd
MULONY, John	20	M	Unknown	31De02Dd
RILEY, Ellen	35	F	Unknown	31De02Dd
HASTIN, Mary-A.	21	F	Unknown	31De02Dd
HOLMS, Robert	28	M	Unknown	31De02Dd
HART, Wm.	27	M	Unknown	31De02Dd
Margt.	27	F	Unknown	31De02Dd
Cath.	3	F	Child	31De02Dd
GATELY, Mary	20	F	Unknown	31De02Dd
Margt.	18	F	Unknown	31De02Dd
BRADRISS, Mary	19	F	Unknown	31De02Dd
ROURKE, Cath.	20	F	Unknown	31De02Dd
HEALY, Wm.	25	M	Unknown	31De02Dd
Margt.	22	F	Unknown	31De02Dd
Pat	18	M	Unknown	31De02Dd
CONNOR, Thos.	20	M	Unknown	31De02Dd
FITZGERALD, Richd.	18	M	Unknown	31De02Dd
DOWD, Owen	40	M	Unknown	31De02Dd
NOLAN, Thos.	35	M	Unknown	31De02Dd
DILLON, Bett	38	F	Unknown	31De02Dd
Joan	38	F	Unknown	31De02Dd
CONNOR, Mick	38	M	Unknown	31De02Dd
John	20	M	Unknown	31De02Dd
TEARNY, Denis	20	M	Unknown	31De02Dd
RIAN, Thos.	25	M	Unknown	31De02Dd
Henry	23	M	Unknown	31De02Dd
Cath.	19	F	Unknown	31De02Dd
FALEY, John	30	M	Unknown	31De02Dd
JONES, Thos.	22	M	Unknown	31De02Dd
MURPHY, Philip	55	M	Unknown	31De02Dd
Ellen	40	F	Unknown	31De02Dd
Philip	19	M	Unknown	31De02Dd
Maria	16	F	Unknown	31De02Dd
Cath.	13	F	Unknown	31De02Dd
Jane	11	F	Unknown	31De02Dd
Ellen	9	F	Child	31De02Dd
Joseph	7	M	Child	31De02Dd
James	4	M	Child	31De02Dd
CONRAN, Mary	20	F	Unknown	31De02Dd
Anne	18	F	Unknown	31De02Dd
WARD, Honora	30	F	Unknown	31De02Dd
Anne	6	F	Child	31De02Dd
Daniel	4	M	Child	31De02Dd
DALY, Bett	18	F	Unknown	31De02Dd
HUIRN, Dan	25	M	Unknown	31De02Dd
Mick	18	M	Unknown	31De02Dd
BLAKE, Wm.	50	M	Unknown	31De02Dd
Mary	40	F	Unknown	31De02Dd
Mary	12	F	Unknown	31De02Dd
Pat	11	M	Unknown	31De02Dd
John	9	M	Child	31De02Dd
Mary	7	F	Child	31De02Dd
Wm.	.00	M	Infant	31De02Dd
Ellen	6	F	Child	31De02Dd
Bess	4	F	Child	31De02Dd
Deb	5	F	Child	31De02Dd
MCCARTNEY, Johanna	18	F	Unknown	31De02Dd
BARRETT, Jas.	18	M	Unknown	31De02Dd
SKINER, Mary	20	F	Unknown	31De02Dd
HUIRN, Conner	24	M	Unknown	31De02Dd
Mick	21	M	Unknown	31De02Dd
WALSH, Jno.	25	M	Unknown	31De02Dd
WALSH, Johanna	25	F	Unknown	31De02Dd
Pat	27	M	Unknown	31De02Dd
HOULAHAN, Denis	18	M	Unknown	31De02Dd
MCCARTHY, Tim	17	M	Unknown	31De02Dd
ODONOGHIN, John	25	M	Unknown	31De02Dd
MARK, John	28	M	Unknown	31De02Dd
Denis	19	M	Unknown	31De02Dd
Kate	30	F	Unknown	31De02Dd
DONOVAN, John	24	M	Unknown	31De02Dd
MUSSIN, Thos.	50	M	Unknown	31De02Dd
Jane	50	F	Unknown	31De02Dd
Mathew	16	M	Unknown	31De02Dd
John	13	M	Unknown	31De02Dd
HIGGINS, Eliza	50	F	Unknown	31De02Dd
Sarah	60	F	Unknown	31De02Dd
Jas.	16	M	Unknown	31De02Dd
George	12	M	Unknown	31De02Dd
DOLAN, Harriet	20	F	Unknown	31De02Dd
Martin	.00	M	Infant	31De02Dd
Anne	6	F	Child	31De02Dd
MALONE, Cath.	13	F	Unknown	31De02Dd
Johanna	12	F	Unknown	31De02Dd
HARKIGAN, Cath.	17	F	Unknown	31De02Dd
HIGGINS, Mary	17	F	Unknown	31De02Dd
DUNNE, Mary	9	F	Child	31De02Dd
TORY, Ellen	21	F	Unknown	31De02Dd
FLYMORE, Sarah	21	F	Unknown	31De02Dd
Maria	3	F	Child	31De02Dd
LAWSON, Rachael	22	F	Unknown	31De02Dd
Hannah	5	F	Child	31De02Dd
PHILM, Levinia	56	F	Unknown	31De02Dd
MOORE, John-Henry	13	M	Unknown	31De02Dd
David	11	M	Unknown	31De02Dd
ROZANNE, Cath.	11	F	Unknown	31De02Dd
CUCKROWN, Bridget	40	F	Unknown	31De02Dd
Pat	13	M	Unknown	31De02Dd
RILEY, Cath.	18	F	Unknown	31De02Dd
John	11	M	Unknown	31De02Dd
Ellen	9	F	Child	31De02Dd
FITZSIMMONS, Mary	21	F	Unknown	31De02Dd
George	8	M	Child	31De02Dd
POWERS, John	22	M	Unknown	31De02Dd
COLEMAN, Mary	34	F	Unknown	31De02Dd
Martin	15	M	Unknown	31De02Dd
Anne	10	F	Unknown	31De02Dd
Jane	7	F	Child	31De02Dd
Maria	4	F	Child	31De02Dd
MURTAGH, Mary	19	F	Unknown	31De02Dd
CHERRY, Eliza	30	F	Unknown	31De02Dd
Sarah	15	F	Unknown	31De02Dd
John	11	M	Unknown	31De02Dd
James	9	M	Child	31De02Dd
Henry	2	M	Child	31De02Dd
MCCALE, Henry	30	M	Unknown	31De02Dd
MCGUIRE, John	11	M	Unknown	31De02Dd
GREGAN, James Died-At-Sea	53	M	Unknown	31De02Dd
HUBBROLIN, Mary Died-At-Sea	.00	F	Infant	31De02Dd
GLANCY, Thos. Died-At-Sea	50	M	Unknown	31De02Dd
POST, Mary Died-At-Sea	.00	F	Infant	31De02Dd
MAHER, Michael Died-At-Sea	26	M	Unknown	31De02Dd
SHIRLY, Honora Died-At-Sea	20	F	Unknown	31De02Dd
FLANOY, Maria Died-At-Sea	2	F	Child	31De02Dd
WYNNE, Jas. Died-At-Sea	54	M	Unknown	31De02Dd
MURPHY, Pat Died-At-Sea	24	M	Unknown	31De02Dd
LAWSON, John Died-At-Sea	.00	M	Infant	31De02Dd

NAMES OF PASSENGERS	AGE	SEX	OCCUPATIONS	DATE PORT SHIP
DIXON, Mary	30	F	Unknown	31De02Dd
Died-At-Sea				
FITZSIMON, Robt.	6	M	Child	31De02Dd
Died-At-Sea				
CLEMARD, John	.00	M	Infant	31De02Dd
Died-At-Sea				
CAULFIELD, Francis	14	M	Unknown	31De02Dd
Cath.	14	F	Unknown	31De02Dd
LYNCH, Mary	26	F	Unknown	31De02Dd
SULLIVAN, Margt.	28	F	Unknown	31De02Dd
DIXON, Alex.	.00	M	Infant	31De02Dd
Died-At-Sea				
Mary	3	F	Child	31De02Dd
FITZPATRICK, Pat	21	M	Unknown	31De02Dd
HOWARD, Andrew	35	M	Unknown	31De02Dd
Margt.	12	F	Unknown	31De02Dd
OLDHAM, Harriett	28	F	Unknown	31De02Dd
Fredk.	3	M	Child	31De02Dd
Sarah	.00	F	Infant	31De02Dd
LOUGHLIN, Martin	25	M	Unknown	31De02Dd
GRENNAN, John	30	M	Unknown	31De02Dd
GANLEY, Jno.	24	M	Unknown	31De02Dd
PALMER, Martin	22	M	Unknown	31De02Dd
SPENCE, Chas.	25	M	Unknown	31De02Dd
CRAWFORD, Isaac	52	M	Unknown	31De02Dd
Mary	50	F	Unknown	31De02Dd
Isaac	24	M	Unknown	31De02Dd
LOAKE, M.	49	M	Unknown	31De02Dd
FLANAGAN, Michael	26	M	Unknown	31De02Dd
FANIAN, John	18	M	Unknown	31De02Dd
DARROCK, Ann	20	F	Unknown	31De02Dd
GREANY, Mary	26	F	Unknown	31De02Dd
Michael	.00	M	Infant	31De02Dd
FIELDING, Edmund	26	M	Unknown	31De02Dd
CONNELL, Nicholas	30	M	Unknown	31De02Dd
DONNELLY, Bridget	25	F	Unknown	31De02Dd
CANLIFF, Jas.	28	M	Unknown	31De02Dd
PARRY, John	18	M	Unknown	31De02Dd
BRADY, Pat	20	M	Unknown	31De02Dd
Margaret	18	F	Unknown	31De02Dd
Daniel	12	M	Unknown	31De02Dd
KELLY, Ellen	18	F	Unknown	31De02Dd
MCNAUGHTON, Charles	44	M	Unknown	31De02Dd
Thos.	20	M	Unknown	31De02Dd
Chas.	19	M	Unknown	31De02Dd
Ellen	17	F	Unknown	31De02Dd
FLANAGAN, June	20	F	Unknown	31De02Dd
Celia	18	F	Unknown	31De02Dd
CELLOVLEY, Ann	19	F	Unknown	31De02Dd
BURTON, John	35	M	Unknown	31De02Dd
Ellen	23	F	Unknown	31De02Dd
FAHEY, Bryan	21	M	Unknown	31De02Dd
GURRY, Mary	18	F	Unknown	31De02Dd
DOYLE, Martin	12	M	Unknown	31De02Dd
MEEHAN, Bridget	22	F	Unknown	31De02Dd
MAHER, Bridget	41	F	Unknown	31De02Dd
GORMAN, John	30	M	Unknown	31De02Dd
WHELAN, Mary	25	F	Unknown	31De02Dd
MANSON, Rose	13	F	Unknown	31De02Dd
Michael	17	M	Unknown	31De02Dd
GODROGER, Catharine	18	F	Unknown	31De02Dd
HART, Mary	24	F	Unknown	31De02Dd
MCGRATH, Cath.	22	F	Unknown	31De02Dd
CHALMERS, Wm.	40	M	Unknown	31De02Dd
U-Mrs.	40	F	Unknown	31De02Dd
Alex.	44	M	Unknown	31De02Dd
CARROLL, Elisha	19	F	Unknown	31De02Dd
MATHEWS, Peter	19	M	Unknown	31De02Dd
KERR, Bridget	19	M	Unknown	31De02Dd
rMEAHER, John	40	M	Unknown	31De02Dd
Eliza	37	F	Unknown	31De02Dd
Cath.	.00	F	Infant	31De02Dd
Martin	25	M	Unknown	31De02Dd
POWELL, George	24	M	Unknown	31De02Dd
Thos.	22	M	Unknown	31De02Dd

NAMES OF PASSENGERS	AGE	SEX	OCCUPATIONS	DATE PORT SHIP
POWELL, Margaret	26	F	Unknown	31De02Dd
RYAN, Michael	19	M	Unknown	31De02Dd
TURNPAIN, Jas.	22	M	Unknown	31De02Dd
COFFY, Michael	20	M	Unknown	31De02Dd
Winifred	13	M	Unknown	31De02Dd
Mary	11	F	Unknown	31De02Dd
RYAN, Anne	20	F	Unknown	31De02Dd
LONG, Thos.	23	M	Unknown	31De02Dd
SMALLEN, Hugh	30	M	Unknown	31De02Dd
Anne	22	F	Unknown	31De02Dd
MCANALLY, U-Mrs.	27	F	Unknown	31De02Dd
Cath.	7	F	Child	31De02Dd
COLLINS, Christopher	30	M	Unknown	31De02Dd
CALLAHAN, Pat	25	F	Unknown	31De02Dd
Mary	25	F	Unknown	31De02Dd
Jas.	.00	M	Infant	31De02Dd
Jas.	20	M	Unknown	31De02Dd
Francis	16	M	Unknown	31De02Dd
DUNCAN, Samuel	30	M	Unknown	31De02Dd
RUFF, Betty	22	F	Unknown	31De02Dd
KELLY, Cath.	20	F	Unknown	31De02Dd
PAGE, Michael	40	M	Unknown	31De02Dd
CLARKE, Newton	36	M	Unknown	31De02Dd
HINRAHAN, Bridget	26	F	Unknown	31De02Dd
BURKE, Bridget	24	F	Unknown	31De02Dd
MACK, Patrick	29	M	Unknown	31De02Dd
Anne	.00	F	Infant	31De02Dd
Mary	20	F	Unknown	31De02Dd
MCMAHON, Mary	19	F	Unknown	31De02Dd
FLEMING, Morris	20	M	Unknown	31De02Dd
Ellen	25	F	Unknown	31De02Dd
WALSH, Mary	20	F	Unknown	31De02Dd
Bess	12	F	Unknown	31De02Dd
HUBBERLIN, Mary	26	F	Unknown	31De02Dd
John	4	M	Child	31De02Dd
Michael	2	M	Child	31De02Dd
GAUL, Bridget	19	F	Unknown	31De02Dd
BROWN, Honora	24	F	Unknown	31De02Dd
ANDERSON, Jas.	31	M	Unknown	31De02Dd
MCCONEL, Jas.	17	M	Unknown	31De02Dd
MURTAGH, John	56	M	Unknown	31De02Dd
Jane	21	F	Unknown	31De02Dd
MUIR, John-D.	24	M	Unknown	31De02Dd
MADDEN, Pat	26	M	Unknown	31De02Dd
CONLON, John	23	M	Unknown	31De02Dd
OWENS, Michael	21	M	Unknown	31De02Dd
KILLARHEY, John	55	M	Unknown	31De02Dd
Margt.	20	F	Unknown	31De02Dd
Wm.	11	M	Unknown	31De02Dd
Timothy	9	M	Child	31De02Dd
John	4	M	Child	31De02Dd
DROMONDY, Thos.	40	M	Unknown	31De02Dd
DODDS, Jno.	22	M	Unknown	31De02Dd
QUINN, Mary	24	F	Unknown	31De02Dd
Cath.	.00	F	Infant	31De02Dd
MORROW, Pat	21	M	Unknown	31De02Dd
U-Mrs.	20	F	Unknown	31De02Dd
Mary	.00	F	Infant	31De02Dd
LARKIN, Jas.	40	M	Unknown	31De02Dd
Margt.	18	F	Unknown	31De02Dd
RAFFERTY, Biddy	40	F	Unknown	31De02Dd
Hugh	4	M	Child	31De02Dd
TIERNEY, Owen	25	M	Unknown	31De02Dd
CONNOR, Patk.	22	M	Unknown	31De02Dd
MURRELL, George	32	M	Unknown	31De02Dd
Eliza	30	F	Unknown	31De02Dd
Sam.	11	M	Unknown	31De02Dd
June	9	F	Child	31De02Dd
Wm.	5	M	Child	31De02Dd
Margt.	3	F	Child	31De02Dd
John	2	M	Child	31De02Dd
FARRELL, Richd.	27	M	Unknown	31De02Dd
MONEGANT, Jeremiah	24	M	Unknown	31De02Dd
CROWLY, Mary	23	M	Unknown	31De02Dd
MCDONALD, Peter	20	M	Unknown	31De02Dd

NAMES OF PASSENGERS	AGE	SEX	OCCUPATIONS	DATE PORT SHIP
MCDONALD, Pat	18	M	Unknown	31De02Dd
LAWLESS, Nancy	53	F	Unknown	31De02Dd
Honora	20	F	Unknown	31De02Dd
STATIERY, Michael	40	M	Unknown	31De02Dd
CAROLAN, Pat	25	M	Unknown	31De02Dd
DONAVAN, Peter	12	M	Unknown	31De02Dd
KERLAN, John	30	M	Unknown	31De02Dd
OBRIEN, Thos.	18	M	Unknown	31De02Dd
Cath.	20	F	Unknown	31De02Dd
MULTY, George	20	M	Unknown	31De02Dd
Rose	30	F	Unknown	31De02Dd
Ed.	9	M	Child	31De02Dd
John	7	M	Child	31De02Dd
Pat	5	M	Child	31De02Dd
Thos.	.00	M	Infant	31De02Dd
LAGGY, Thos.	30	M	Unknown	31De02Dd
Margt.	30	F	Unknown	31De02Dd
DOBBIN, Henry	30	M	Unknown	31De02Dd
MAY, Anthony	17	M	Unknown	31De02Dd
MORLEY, Robert	27	M	Unknown	31De02Dd
HANRY, Anne	40	F	Unknown	31De02Dd
ALLEN, John	25	M	Unknown	31De02Dd
STEVENS, Mary	16	F	Unknown	31De02Dd
BRENAN, Thos.	23	M	Unknown	31De02Dd
Ellen	13	F	Unknown	31De02Dd
MULLONEY, Margt.	22	F	Unknown	31De02Dd
Anne	23	F	Unknown	31De02Dd
Margt.	12	F	Unknown	31De02Dd
STEVENS, Thos.	20	M	Unknown	31De02Dd
RICHARDSON, Jane	35	F	Unknown	31De02Dd
Robert	16	M	Unknown	31De02Dd
David	7	M	Child	31De02Dd
Eliza	5	F	Child	31De02Dd
RYAN, Jas.	12	M	Child	31De02Dd
OBRIEN, Johanna	45	F	Unknown	31De02Dd
BRADY, Mary	30	F	Unknown	31De02Dd
CLARK, Michael	16	M	Unknown	31De02Dd
MORAN, Mary	7	F	Child	31De02Dd
KEARNEY, Michael	26	M	Unknown	31De02Dd
CAULFIELD, Bart.	40	M	Unknown	31De02Dd
Eliza	17	F	Unknown	31De02Dd
Mary	12	F	Unknown	31De02Dd
MURRAY, Mary	17	F	Unknown	31De02Dd
Margt.	13	F	Unknown	31De02Dd
SMITH, Mary	19	F	Unknown	31De02Dd
GALLIVAN, Cath.	24	F	Unknown	31De02Dd
PORT, Sarah	25	F	Unknown	31De02Dd
Mary	25	F	Unknown	31De02Dd
FEGAN, Thos.	21	M	Unknown	31De02Dd
GROGAN, John	18	M	Unknown	31De02Dd
CRAFFERY, Jas.	21	M	Unknown	31De02Dd
SMITH, Ellen	13	F	Unknown	31De02Dd
KERR, Lydia-Mary	13	F	Unknown	31De02Dd
Jas.	11	M	Unknown	31De02Dd
John	9	M	Child	31De02Dd
Mary	7	F	Child	31De02Dd
MAHON, Eliza	25	F	Unknown	31De02Dd
GARITY, Mary	20	F	Unknown	31De02Dd
FINLAND, Christopher	23	M	Unknown	31De02Dd
TIGHE, Bridget	21	F	Unknown	31De02Dd
Susanna	1	F	Child	31De02Dd
QUIGLEY, Michael	22	M	Unknown	31De02Dd
MURPHY, Margaret	21	F	Unknown	31De02Dd
MCCABE, Alexander	30	M	Unknown	31De02Dd
CADDEN, Michael	30	M	Unknown	31De02Dd
LARMAN, Jas.	30	M	Unknown	31De02Dd
Ann	28	F	Unknown	31De02Dd
Cath.	1	F	Child	31De02Dd
MORGAN, Jas.	25	M	Unknown	31De02Dd
Mary	24	F	Unknown	31De02Dd
CUNINGHAM, Henry	25	M	Unknown	31De02Dd
TIGH, Catharine	40	F	Unknown	31De02Dd
MCLAUGHLIN, Rose	20	F	Unknown	31De02Dd
TIGHE, Martin	11	M	Unknown	31De02Dd
Ellen	10	F	Unknown	31De02Dd
TIGHE, Anne	8	F	Child	31De02Dd
HIGGINS, Ellen	20	F	Unknown	31De02Dd
Honora	18	F	Unknown	31De02Dd
RIELLY, John	37	M	Unknown	31De02Dd
MAGEE, Richard	30	M	Unknown	31De02Dd
Jane	24	F	Unknown	31De02Dd
CLEGG, Henry	22	M	Unknown	31De02Dd
DOUGHERTY, Pat	20	M	Unknown	31De02Dd
BYRNE, Mary	20	F	Unknown	31De02Dd
Biddy	18	F	Unknown	31De02Dd
IRWIN, Wm.	34	M	Unknown	31De02Dd
Honora	26	F	Unknown	31De02Dd
GRAHAM, Honora	21	F	Unknown	31De02Dd
DAN, Catharine	38	F	Unknown	31De02Dd
John	18	M	Unknown	31De02Dd
Mary	19	F	Unknown	31De02Dd
Catharine	17	F	Unknown	31De02Dd
FALKNERR, Elina	40	F	Unknown	31De02Dd
Jane	12	F	Unknown	31De02Dd
Mary	8	F	Child	31De02Dd
MARTIN, James	11	M	Unknown	31De02Dd
NEVILLE, David	9	M	Child	31De02Dd
RAMSBOTTOM, John	49	M	Unknown	31De02Dd
Ellen	49	F	Unknown	31De02Dd
Maria	9	F	Child	31De02Dd
Elizabeth	7	F	Child	31De02Dd
PLATT, Alice	26	F	Unknown	31De02Dd
Minerva	6	F	Child	31De02Dd
Maria	3	F	Child	31De02Dd
Euclid	2	M	Child	31De02Dd
MURRAY, Owen	40	M	Unknown	31De02Dd
Jane	32	F	Unknown	31De02Dd
Jane	14	F	Unknown	31De02Dd
Nicholas	11	M	Unknown	31De02Dd
Thomas	7	M	Child	31De02Dd
Catharine	5	F	Child	31De02Dd

WISCONSIN 02 JANUARY 1850

From Liverpool

NAMES OF PASSENGERS	AGE	SEX	OCCUPATIONS	DATE PORT SHIP
BURNS, James	18	M	Laborer	02Ja02Di
POWERS, Mary	20	F	Servant	02Ja02Di
Cathe.	20	F	Servant	02Ja02Di
HAYES, Andy	20	M	Laborer	02Ja02Di
MAPOTHER, Dillen	18	M	Engineer	02Ja02Di
REILLY, Mary	40	F	Unknown	02Ja02Di
Christr.	6	M	Child	02Ja02Di
Patt	4	M	Child	02Ja02Di
SMITH, Farrell	20	M	Laborer	02Ja02Di
KELLY, Mary	24	F	Servant	02Ja02Di
FARNEY, Patt	30	M	Laborer	02Ja02Di
MUNEALISS, Mary	20	F	Dressmaker	02Ja02Di
DONAGHEY, Edwd.	21	M	Laborer	02Ja02Di
Ellen	4	F	Child	02Ja02Di
GILLAN, Edwd.	22	M	Dyer	02Ja02Di
Cathe.	22	F	Servant	02Ja02Di
MELANE, Rose	60	F	Unknown	02Ja02Di
Margt.	19	F	Dressmaker	02Ja02Di
FOX, Bridgt.	21	F	Servant	02Ja02Di
MCANANY, Rebecca-Ann	20	F	Dressmaker	02Ja02Di
GULCH, Francis	20	M	Laborer	02Ja02Di
OLEVNEY, Patt	23	M	Irnmldr	02Ja02Di
MURRAY, Terrence	35	M	Laborer	02Ja02Di
REILLY, Patt	25	M	Laborer	02Ja02Di
BENNY, Bridgt.	25	F	Servant	02Ja02Di
FINNIGAN, Bessy	18	F	Servant	02Ja02Di
FITZPATRICK, John	26	M	Weaver	02Ja02Di
CURRIGAN, Elizth.	23	F	Servant	02Ja02Di

NAMES OF PASSENGERS	AGE	SEX	OCCUPATIONS	DATE PORT SHIP
CULLEN, Ann	30	F	Servant	02Ja02Di
BOURKE, Patt	20	M	Laborer	02Ja02Di
BROWNE, Bridgt.	23	F	Dressmaker	02Ja02Di
LOUGHIN, Cathe.	20	F	Servant	02Ja02Di
WALKER, Rowley	18	M	Unknown	02Ja02Di
Margt.	13	F	Unknown	02Ja02Di
Hannah	11	F	Unknown	02Ja02Di
James	9	M	Child	02Ja02Di
Eliza	5	F	Child	02Ja02Di
Margt.	44	F	Unknown	02Ja02Di
Fredk.	48	M	Unknown	02Ja02Di
HUGHES, Ann	32	F	Unknown	02Ja02Di
Kenrick	3	M	Child	02Ja02Di
John	.00	M	Infant	02Ja02Di
WILLIAMS, Margt.	40	F	Unknown	02Ja02Di
Mary-A.	14	F	Servant	02Ja02Di
MONAGHAN, Patt	25	M	Farmer	02Ja02Di
MCCLOUGHIN, John	25	M	Laborer	02Ja02Di
TUMILLY, Hugh	23	M	Laborer	02Ja02Di
RICHARDSON, George	18	M	Laborer	02Ja02Di
MCDERMOTT, Mary	20	F	Servant	02Ja02Di
WATSON, Thomas	25	M	Tinsmith	02Ja02Di
Hinera	22	F	Unknown	02Ja02Di
WHITE, Jeremiah	20	M	Laborer	02Ja02Di
MURPHY, Bridgt.	18	F	Servant	02Ja02Di
DEVIN, Thomas	21	M	Laborer	02Ja02Di
OHANNER, Cathe.	18	F	Servant	02Ja02Di
Margt.	17	F	Servant	02Ja02Di
MCELMEAL, Alice	35	F	Spinner	02Ja02Di
John	12	M	Unknown	02Ja02Di
Hugh	9	M	Child	02Ja02Di
Mary	7	F	Child	02Ja02Di
Rose	3	F	Child	02Ja02Di
Patt	.00	M	Infant	02Ja02Di
MCQUADE, Cathe.	19	F	Servant	02Ja02Di
John	15	M	Shoemaker	02Ja02Di
Mary	12	F	Unknown	02Ja02Di
Edwd.	10	M	Unknown	02Ja02Di
CORMODY, John	21	M	Laborer	02Ja02Di
Mary	20	F	Unknown	02Ja02Di
RYAN, Peggy	17	F	Servant	02Ja02Di
CORMODY, Jane	.00	F	Infant	02Ja02Di
MCCARTY, Margt.	30	F	Servant	02Ja02Di
DORAN, James	23	M	Laborer	02Ja02Di
HARNETT, Elizth.	11	F	Unknown	02Ja02Di
HEATON, Bridgt.	20	F	Servant	02Ja02Di
MARA, Margt.	25	F	Servant	02Ja02Di
ENGLISH, Michl.	22	M	Shoemaker	02Ja02Di
THINNTON, Patt	20	M	Laborer	02Ja02Di
Ann	18	F	Servant	02Ja02Di
BROWNE, Edwd.	25	M	Laborer	02Ja02Di
ENRIGHT, Michl.	20	M	Laborer	02Ja02Di
REYNOLDS, Patt	18	M	Laborer	02Ja02Di
Mary	20	F	Servant	02Ja02Di
WHALEN, Mary	21	F	Servant	02Ja02Di
HARRICK, Ann	20	F	Servant	02Ja02Di
SMITH, Andw.	35	M	Laborer	02Ja02Di
James	33	M	Laborer	02Ja02Di
KENNEDY, Bernd.	30	M	Laborer	02Ja02Di
Mary	30	F	Dressmaker	02Ja02Di
Bernd.	.00	M	Infant	02Ja02Di
SHORT, Michl.	30	M	Laborer	02Ja02Di
Bridgt.	30	F	Dressmaker	02Ja02Di
CANNANE, Michl.	40	M	Gdnr	02Ja02Di
BRETT, John	20	M	Butcher	02Ja02Di
SHAW, Forbus	22	M	Laborer	02Ja02Di
CARR, Patt	22	M	Laborer	02Ja02Di
KEIGAN, John	15	M	Laborer	02Ja02Di
Ellen	16	F	Dressmaker	02Ja02Di
MCENTYRE, Margt.	17	F	Servant	02Ja02Di
GILL, Rose	17	F	Servant	02Ja02Di
LAWLER, Patt	30	M	Miller	02Ja02Di
FLYNN, James	23	M	Laborer	02Ja02Di
FARMER, Elizth.	21	F	Servant	02Ja02Di
COSGROVE, Patt	24	M	Laborer	02Ja02Di
MCCAFFREY, Isabella	50	F	Unknown	02Ja02Di
John	11	M	Unknown	02Ja02Di
Isabella	9	F	Child	02Ja02Di
NEENAN, Honora	12	F	Unknown	02Ja02Di
Ellen	9	F	Child	02Ja02Di
MCCABE, John	18	M	Laborer	02Ja02Di
WELSH, John	35	M	Coppersmith	02Ja02Di
Michl.	16	M	Shpc	02Ja02Di
MURPHY, John	45	M	Shpc	02Ja02Di
Mary	45	F	Unknown	02Ja02Di
Margt.	11	F	Unknown	02Ja02Di
Ellen	9	F	Child	02Ja02Di
FLINN, Ann	22	F	Servant	02Ja02Di
SHERDEN, Cathe.	24	F	Servant	02Ja02Di
ODONNELL, Hugh	32	M	Laborer	02Ja02Di
Patt	7	M	Child	02Ja02Di
Margt.	16	F	Unknown	02Ja02Di
Ellen	14	F	Unknown	02Ja02Di
FARLEY, Judy	20	F	Servant	02Ja02Di
Mary	19	F	Servant	02Ja02Di
MCGRATH, Peter	30	M	Farmer	02Ja02Di
COYLE, Barney	25	M	Laborer	02Ja02Di
Mick	28	M	Laborer	02Ja02Di
Patt	20	M	Laborer	02Ja02Di
Margt.	40	F	Unknown	02Ja02Di
ALLWAYAND, David	28	M	Laborer	02Ja02Di
KEATING, Jane	35	F	Unknown	02Ja02Di
Susan	10	F	Unknown	02Ja02Di
Michl.	7	M	Child	02Ja02Di
Simon	2	M	Child	02Ja02Di
SKELLY, John	31	M	Clerk	02Ja02Di
KEARNEY, Cathe.	24	F	Servant	02Ja02Di
ROWEN, Jane	22	F	Servant	02Ja02Di
CONNELL, Patt	19	M	Laborer	02Ja02Di
Bridget	18	F	Weaver	02Ja02Di
CROSSAN, Margt.	20	F	Servant	02Ja02Di
TARNY, Margt.	30	F	Servant	02Ja02Di
CURTEN, John	32	M	Laborer	02Ja02Di
Dennis	34	M	Laborer	02Ja02Di
SULLIVAN, Timothy	30	M	Laborer	02Ja02Di
LASLEY, Edwd.	30	M	Laborer	02Ja02Di
Francis	8	M	Child	02Ja02Di
Mary	6	F	Child	02Ja02Di
Bridget	4	F	Child	02Ja02Di
GEARY, Pat	35	M	Laborer	02Ja02Di
DUGGAN, John	20	M	Laborer	02Ja02Di
POWER, John	37	M	Laborer	02Ja02Di
IRVIN, John	20	M	Laborer	02Ja02Di
CONOLLY, Michl.	20	M	Laborer	02Ja02Di
GEARY, Amelia	20	F	Servant	02Ja02Di
HURLEY, Michl.	11	M	Unknown	02Ja02Di
Willm.	10	M	Unknown	02Ja02Di
Joseph	7	M	Child	02Ja02Di
GARRY, Danl.	3	M	Child	02Ja02Di
Wm.	.00	M	Infant	02Ja02Di
HAYDEN, Agnes	17	F	Unknown	02Ja02Di
Cathe.	13	F	Unknown	02Ja02Di
Margt.	5	F	Child	02Ja02Di
KING, Bridget	40	F	Unknown	02Ja02Di
Michl.	4	M	Child	02Ja02Di
REILLY, Owen	37	M	Carpenter	02Ja02Di
Margt.	37	F	Unknown	02Ja02Di
Edwd.	9	M	Child	02Ja02Di
Bridget	27	F	Servant	02Ja02Di
Cathe.	24	F	Servant	02Ja02Di
OBRIEN, Pat	32	M	Farmer	02Ja02Di
Cathe.	32	F	Unknown	02Ja02Di
Mary	29	F	Unknown	02Ja02Di
Maria	7	F	Child	02Ja02Di
LYONS, John	18	M	Unknown	02Ja02Di
CAFFREY, Pat	24	M	Laborer	02Ja02Di
MALONEY, Mary	20	F	Servant	02Ja02Di
LAWLEY, Ellen	12	F	Servant	02Ja02Di
Bridget	11	F	Servant	02Ja02Di
REILLY, James	40	M	Weaver	02Ja02Di

NAMES OF PASSENGERS	AGE	SEX	OCCUPATIONS	DATE PORT SHIP
TRACEY, John	44	M	Laborer	02Ja02Di
Mary	42	F	Unknown	02Ja02Di
John	25	M	Laborer	02Ja02Di
Ellen	18	F	Servant	02Ja02Di
HALYCAN, Bryan	47	M	Laborer	02Ja02Di
Michl.	17	M	Laborer	02Ja02Di
Bridget	14	F	Servant	02Ja02Di
Mary	12	F	Servant	02Ja02Di
Cathn.	10	F	Servant	02Ja02Di
Bernard	8	M	Child	02Ja02Di
RILEY, Thos.	35	M	Laborer	02Ja02Di
SMITH, Mary	35	F	Servant	02Ja02Di
Eliza	4	F	Child	02Ja02Di
Bridget	33	F	Unknown	02Ja02Di
LEE, Fergus	34	M	Laborer	02Ja02Di
DOOHTY, Mary	19	F	Servant	02Ja02Di
GRAY, Francis	20	M	Merchant	02Ja02Di
BYRNE, Bernard	16	M	Laborer	02Ja02Di
SIMPSON, Andrew	35	M	Farmer	02Ja02Di
Martha	45	F	Unknown	02Ja02Di
Robt.	11	M	Unknown	02Ja02Di
FITZGERALD, James	25	M	Cooper	02Ja02Di

LADY-MILTON 02 JANUARY 1850

From Dublin

NAMES OF PASSENGERS	AGE	SEX	OCCUPATIONS	DATE PORT SHIP
HUSSEY, Margaret	40	F	Unknown	02Ja05Dj
Thomas	13	M	Unknown	02Ja05Dj
RAFTEN, James	36	M	Unknown	02Ja05Dj
GRIFFIN, Henry	24	M	Unknown	02Ja05Dj
BRENNAN, Sarah	20	F	Unknown	02Ja05Dj
MOORE, John	22	M	Unknown	02Ja05Dj
TRACY, Margaret	15	F	Unknown	02Ja05Dj
Peggy	10	F	Unknown	02Ja05Dj
Dan	14	M	Unknown	02Ja05Dj
Thomas	12	M	Unknown	02Ja05Dj
FEHELY, Cath.	20	F	Unknown	02Ja05Dj
CLARKE, Miriam	18	F	Unknown	02Ja05Dj
CARTER, Ellen	22	F	Unknown	02Ja05Dj
REGAN, Julie	20	F	Unknown	02Ja05Dj
MCCARLY, Dennis	20	M	Unknown	02Ja05Dj
ROHERY, Thomas	26	M	Unknown	02Ja05Dj
John	40	M	Unknown	02Ja05Dj
Richard	30	M	Unknown	02Ja05Dj
DEMPSEY, U-Mrs.	25	F	Spinster	02Ja05Dj
KENNA, Wm.	26	M	Unknown	02Ja05Dj
Ellen	20	F	Unknown	02Ja05Dj
KENSELLA, Wm.	20	M	Unknown	02Ja05Dj
HANDY, Mary	30	F	Unknown	02Ja05Dj
Frank	36	M	Unknown	02Ja05Dj
KEENAN, John	13	M	Unknown	02Ja05Dj
DOWLING, John	21	M	Unknown	02Ja05Dj
U-Mrs.	40	F	Unknown	02Ja05Dj
Catherine	40	F	Unknown	02Ja05Dj
Elizabeth	19	F	Unknown	02Ja05Dj
James	18	M	Unknown	02Ja05Dj
Matthew	16	M	Unknown	02Ja05Dj
Ellen	11	F	Unknown	02Ja05Dj
Thomas	9	M	Unknown	02Ja05Dj
Joseph	7	M	Child	02Ja05Dj
John	5	M	Child	02Ja05Dj
HALPIN, Ellen	40	F	Unknown	02Ja05Dj
KING, M.	20	F	Unknown	02Ja05Dj
STANFIELD, Peter	26	M	Laborer	02Ja05Dj
U-Mrs.	24	F	Unknown	02Ja05Dj
BYRNE, U-Mrs.	36	F	Unknown	02Ja05Dj
Mary	20	F	Unknown	02Ja05Dj
DOOGAN, Mary	30	F	Unknown	02Ja05Dj
MALONE, U-Mrs.	36	F	Unknown	02Ja05Dj
Wm.	40	M	Unknown	02Ja05Dj
BOONE, Wm.	19	M	Unknown	02Ja05Dj
Martin	20	M	Unknown	02Ja05Dj
B.	20	U	Unknown	02Ja05Dj
KEALY, Mary	24	F	Unknown	02Ja05Dj
Sher--, Susan	00	F	Unknown	02Ja05Dj
Thomas	3	M	Child	02Ja05Dj
Susan	.00	F	Infant	02Ja05Dj
HANLEY, John	20	M	Unknown	02Ja05Dj
KIRMAN, Mark	40	M	Unknown	02Ja05Dj
U-Mrs.	40	F	Unknown	02Ja05Dj
Dennis	24	M	Unknown	02Ja05Dj
Darby	20	M	Unknown	02Ja05Dj
Ellen	17	F	Unknown	02Ja05Dj
James	15	M	Unknown	02Ja05Dj
Mark	13	M	Unknown	02Ja05Dj
Rose	11	F	Unknown	02Ja05Dj
Anty	24	F	Unknown	02Ja05Dj
Rose	1	F	Infant	02Ja05Dj
Eliza	.00	F	Infant	02Ja05Dj
BRACKLIN, Eliza	24	F	Unknown	02Ja05Dj
Eliza	4	F	Child	02Ja05Dj
James	2	M	Child	02Ja05Dj
Patrick	.00	M	Infant	02Ja05Dj
HORAN, Honor	14	F	Unknown	02Ja05Dj
QUINN, Thomas	24	M	Unknown	02Ja05Dj
Anne	20	F	Unknown	02Ja05Dj
HYLAND, Anne	15	F	Unknown	02Ja05Dj
Catherine	30	F	Unknown	02Ja05Dj
CASEY, Ellen	19	F	Unknown	02Ja05Dj
MALONE, Mick	20	M	Unknown	02Ja05Dj
HAVERHAN, Marcella Died-At-Sea	40	F	Unknown	02Ja05Dj
Catherine	15	F	Unknown	02Ja05Dj
ABBOTT, Wm.	26	M	Unknown	02Ja05Dj
HAVERHAN, Catherine	20	F	Unknown	02Ja05Dj
FARNHAN, James	24	M	Unknown	02Ja05Dj
Judith	30	F	Unknown	02Ja05Dj
MARTIN, Edw.	20	M	Unknown	02Ja05Dj
CLEAR, Wm.	20	M	Unknown	02Ja05Dj
ROE, Anne	20	F	Unknown	C2Ja05Dj
WALL, Essey	20	F	Unknown	02Ja05Dj
LABOR, Cath.	20	F	Unknown	02Ja05Dj
ENGLISH, Walter	40	M	Unknown	02Ja05Dj
Ellen	45	F	Unknown	02Ja05Dj
Ellenore	24	F	Unknown	02Ja05Dj
Ruth	21	F	Unknown	02Ja05Dj
John	17	M	Unknown	02Ja05Dj
Michael	14	M	Unknown	02Ja05Dj
Mary	13	F	Unknown	02Ja05Dj
Wm.	8	M	Child	02Ja05Dj
Margt.	26	F	Unknown	02Ja05Dj
DWYER, Mary	7	F	Child	02Ja05Dj
WHEELAN, Daniel	36	M	Unknown	02Ja05Dj
Judith	32	F	Unknown	02Ja05Dj
Mary	13	F	Unknown	02Ja05Dj
Eliza	12	F	Unknown	02Ja05Dj
Biddy	10	F	Unknown	02Ja05Dj
Juliee	8	F	Child	02Ja05Dj
Mick	6	M	Child	02Ja05Dj
Philip	4	M	Child	02Ja05Dj
Ellen	2	F	Child	02Ja05Dj
Anne	.00	F	Infant	02Ja05Dj
CARROLL, Eliza	20	F	Unknown	02Ja05Dj
MILTON, Thomas	36	M	Unknown	02Ja05Dj
Ann	15	F	Unknown	02Ja05Dj
Anty	21	F	Unknown	02Ja05Dj
Merry	12	F	Unknown	02Ja05Dj
Eney	30	U	Unknown	02Ja05Dj
Anne	27	F	Unknown	02Ja05Dj
Margt.	.00	F	Infant	02Ja05Dj
S--, U-Miss	20	F	Unknown	02Ja05Dj
BURKE, Mick	28	M	Unknown	02Ja05Dj
Francis	26	M	Unknown	02Ja05Dj

NAMES OF PASSENGERS	AGE	SEX	OCCUPATIONS	DATE PORT SHIP
BURKE, Margt.	26	F	Unknown	02Ja05Dj
Catherine	.00	F	Infant	02Ja05Dj
Anne	8	F	Child	02Ja05Dj
Patrick	.00	M	Infant	02Ja05Dj
MURPHY, Mick	24	M	Unknown	02Ja05Dj
James	22	M	Unknown	02Ja05Dj
KENNA, Wm.	30	M	Unknown	02Ja05Dj
Margt.	27	F	Unknown	02Ja05Dj
Catherine	7	F	Child	02Ja05Dj
Mary	5	F	Child	02Ja05Dj
Michael	2	M	Child	02Ja05Dj
CAUFIELD, John	17	M	Unknown	02Ja05Dj
BUTLER, John	13	M	Unknown	02Ja05Dj
KEOGH, John	24	M	Unknown	02Ja05Dj
Ellen	26	F	Unknown	02Ja05Dj
DOYLE, Andrew	28	M	Unknown	02Ja05Dj
Garnett	28	M	Unknown	02Ja05Dj
NOWLAN, Michael	18	M	Unknown	02Ja05Dj
DOYLE, Cath.	28	F	Unknown	02Ja05Dj
NOWLAN, Ellen	19	F	Unknown	02Ja05Dj
Johanna	20	F	Unknown	02Ja05Dj
Daniel	.00	M	Infant	02Ja05Dj
MOORE, John	27	M	Unknown	02Ja05Dj
DUNN, Robt.	25	M	Unknown	02Ja05Dj
CROWE, Ellen	25	F	Unknown	02Ja05Dj
SHORTALL, Anne	20	F	Unknown	02Ja05Dj
MOORE, John	21	M	Unknown	02Ja05Dj
GORMAN, Mary	21	F	Unknown	02Ja05Dj
RUDD, Wm.	39	M	Unknown	02Ja05Dj
Anne	35	F	Unknown	02Ja05Dj
Mary	18	F	Unknown	02Ja05Dj
Elicia	15	F	Unknown	02Ja05Dj
Robt.	13	M	Unknown	02Ja05Dj
Janee	11	F	Unknown	02Ja05Dj
Cath.	.00	F	Infant	02Ja05Dj
Gordon	20	M	Unknown	02Ja05Dj
MURPHY, Anne	20	F	Unknown	02Ja05Dj
LYNCH, Michael	18	M	Unknown	02Ja05Dj
MCQUILLEN, James	25	M	Unknown	02Ja05Dj
Mary	26	F	Unknown	02Ja05Dj
BRIGGS, Francis	20	M	Unknown	02Ja05Dj
CRUM, Rich.	20	M	Unknown	02Ja05Dj
BRADY, Margaret	20	F	Unknown	02Ja05Dj
Rose	20	F	Unknown	02Ja05Dj
FEEHY, Catherine	19	F	Unknown	02Ja05Dj
Biddy	30	F	Unknown	02Ja05Dj
LARKIN, Harriet	3	F	Child	02Ja05Dj
Patk.	20	M	Unknown	02Ja05Dj
MONAHAN, Patk.	28	M	Unknown	02Ja05Dj
BYRNE, Chatherine	20	F	Unknown	02Ja05Dj
BARRETT, Eliza	20	F	Unknown	02Ja05Dj
MCQUIRE, Ellen	20	F	Unknown	02Ja05Dj
MULLEN, Robt.	22	M	Unknown	02Ja05Dj
GROGHAN, John	22	M	Unknown	02Ja05Dj
ROCHE, Martin	22	M	Unknown	02Ja05Dj
GROGHAN, Anne	23	F	Unknown	02Ja05Dj
Mary	23	F	Unknown	02Ja05Dj
Anne	20	F	Unknown	02Ja05Dj
John	30	M	Unknown	02Ja05Dj
RODE, James	30	M	Unknown	02Ja05Dj
FLANNAGAN, Michael	32	M	Unknown	02Ja05Dj
MITCHELL, Wm.	13	M	Unknown	02Ja05Dj
GLAZENBROOK, Wm.	13	M	Unknown	02Ja05Dj
Thos.	11	M	Unknown	02Ja05Dj
MURPHY, James	9	M	Unknown	02Ja05Dj
Patk.	00	M	Unknown	02Ja05Dj
Mary	00	F	Unknown	02Ja05Dj
KEEGAN, James	24	M	Unknown	02Ja05Dj
GIBNEY, Margt.	20	F	Unknown	02Ja05Dj
Margt.	18	F	Unknown	02Ja05Dj
FLINN, Biddy	30	F	Unknown	02Ja05Dj
BYRNE, Philip	48	M	Unknown	02Ja05Dj
DOYLE, Cath.	30	F	Unknown	02Ja05Dj
Maria	20	F	Unknown	02Ja05Dj
FARRELL, U-Mrs.	30	F	Unknown	02Ja05Dj

NAMES OF PASSENGERS	AGE	SEX	OCCUPATIONS	DATE PORT SHIP
FARRELL, Mary	10	F	Unknown	02Ja05Dj
CARROLL, Matthew	20	M	Unknown	02Ja05Dj
WHEELAN, Pat	30	M	Unknown	02Ja05Dj
Margt.	30	F	Unknown	02Ja05Dj
NOWLAN, Elizabeth	36	F	Unknown	02Ja05Dj
Pat.	2	M	Child	02Ja05Dj
Honor	3	F	Child	02Ja05Dj
Catherine	7	F	Child	02Ja05Dj
Elizabeth	9	F	Child	02Ja05Dj
Pelicie	9	F	Child	02Ja05Dj
LEARY, Dennis	12	M	Unknown	02Ja05Dj
Biddy	26	F	Unknown	02Ja05Dj
COATES, Anne	24	F	Unknown	02Ja05Dj
HOPKINS, Margt.	20	F	Unknown	02Ja05Dj
MOONEY, Wm.	20	M	Unknown	02Ja05Dj
CAREY, Margt.	30	F	Unknown	02Ja05Dj
FLOOD, U-Mrs.	30	F	Unknown	02Ja05Dj
Pat.	3	M	Child	02Ja05Dj
Mary	.00	F	Infant	02Ja05Dj
BURKE, Mary	40	F	Unknown	02Ja05Dj
WHEELAN, John	26	M	Unknown	02Ja05Dj
Betty	24	F	Unknown	02Ja05Dj
FENNELL, Mary	20	F	Unknown	02Ja05Dj
PHILLIPS, Matthew	20	M	Unknown	02Ja05Dj
KELLY, Thos.	40	M	Unknown	02Ja05Dj
CRONEY, Patrick	28	M	Unknown	02Ja05Dj
U-Mrs.	26	F	Unknown	02Ja05Dj
MOONEY, Patrick	20	M	Unknown	02Ja05Dj
ROONEY, Edward	40	M	Unknown	02Ja05Dj
James	10	M	Unknown	02Ja05Dj
Michl.	14	M	Unknown	02Ja05Dj
CAREY, Margaret	20	F	Unknown	02Ja05Dj
SHEA, John	42	M	Unknown	02Ja05Dj
Ellen	20	F	Unknown	02Ja05Dj
MCCARTER, Edward	21	M	Unknown	02Ja05Dj
MUDGE, Richd.	00	M	Physician	02Ja05Dj
CRUM, John	00	M	Physician	02Ja05Dj
LORD, Michl.	00	M	Physician	02Ja05Dj
LANDER, Henry	25	M	Unknown	02Ja05Dj

ALBION 03 JANUARY 1850

From Galway

NAMES OF PASSENGERS	AGE	SEX	OCCUPATIONS	DATE PORT SHIP
BRENDERGAT, Bridget	14	F	Unknown	03Ja42Dk
CONCOUM, Bridget	.00	F	Infant	03Ja42Dk
MOLLOY, Martin	20	M	Unknown	03Ja42Dk
COUGHLAN, May	25	F	Unknown	03Ja42Dk
Michl.	35	M	Unknown	03Ja42Dk
Bridget	3	F	Child	03Ja42Dk
John	.00	M	Infant	03Ja42Dk
NEHILL, Jas.	20	M	Unknown	03Ja42Dk
DEMPSEY, Bridget	20	F	Unknown	03Ja42Dk
OLOUGHLIN, Ann	45	F	Unknown	03Ja42Dk
FLINN, Cathn.	20	F	Unknown	03Ja42Dk
Cecila	18	F	Unknown	03Ja42Dk
OLOUGHLIN, May	20	F	Unknown	03Ja42Dk
ROUGHAN, Tady	18	M	Unknown	03Ja42Dk
GREENE, John	24	M	Unknown	03Ja42Dk
KENNEDY, Honor	20	F	Unknown	03Ja42Dk
EGAN, Bridget	20	F	Unknown	03Ja42Dk
HAYNES, James	40	M	Unknown	03Ja42Dk
Bridget	22	F	Unknown	03Ja42Dk
LEE, John	18	F	Unknown	03Ja42Dk
KELLY, Michl.	38	M	Unknown	03Ja42Dk
SHAUGHENSY, Honor	22	F	Unknown	03Ja42Dk
Mary	24	F	Unknown	03Ja42Dk
Peter	.00	M	Infant	03Ja42Dk
ERWIN, Biddy	22	F	Unknown	03Ja42Dk

NAMES OF PASSENGERS	AGE	SEX	OCCUPATIONS	DATE PORT SHIP
FINNIGAN, Honor	22	F	Unknown	03Ja42Dk
HAVERTY, Ann	18	F	Unknown	03Ja42Dk
Bridget	20	F	Unknown	03Ja42Dk
BEEGAN, Catherine	35	F	Unknown	03Ja42Dk
LEACHE, Sebina	15	F	Unknown	03Ja42Dk
Bridget	16	F	Unknown	03Ja42Dk
MALSA, Thos.	21	M	Unknown	03Ja42Dk
CELEHAN, Magt.	24	F	Unknown	03Ja42Dk
EGAN, Biddy	17	F	Unknown	03Ja42Dk
THALOR, Martin	24	M	Unknown	03Ja42Dk
May	19	F	Unknown	03Ja42Dk
James	.00	M	Infant	03Ja42Dk
CONNOR, Thos.	26	M	Unknown	03Ja42Dk
FOLEY, Honor	25	F	Unknown	03Ja42Dk
DUANE, Ellen	46	F	Unknown	03Ja42Dk
Biddy	20	F	Unknown	03Ja42Dk
BURK, Michl.	25	M	Unknown	03Ja42Dk
MEANY, Mary	50	F	Unknown	03Ja42Dk
Andrew	20	M	Unknown	03Ja42Dk
Pat	.00	M	Infant	03Ja42Dk
NOONE, Michl.	24	M	Unknown	03Ja42Dk
REVILL, Thos.	25	M	Unknown	03Ja42Dk
DONOLAN, Martin	28	M	Unknown	03Ja42Dk
FARRELL, Catherine	30	F	Unknown	03Ja42Dk
OGRADY, Jas.	24	M	Unknown	03Ja42Dk
Edmond	22	M	Unknown	03Ja42Dk
BROWN, Michl.	21	M	Unknown	03Ja42Dk
Ann	18	F	Unknown	03Ja42Dk
Ellen	16	F	Unknown	03Ja42Dk
RUANE, Nancy	19	F	Unknown	03Ja42Dk
Cather.	17	F	Unknown	03Ja42Dk
Nancy	18	F	Unknown	03Ja42Dk
Sally	17	F	Unknown	03Ja42Dk
COSTELLO, Peggy	18	F	Unknown	03Ja42Dk
Mary	16	F	Unknown	03Ja42Dk
KAWLEY, Bridget	21	F	Unknown	03Ja42Dk
ODEA, John	40	M	Unknown	03Ja42Dk
Mary	30	F	Unknown	03Ja42Dk
Mary	3	F	Child	03Ja42Dk
Kitty	.00	F	Infant	03Ja42Dk
SLATERY, Kitty	34	F	Unknown	03Ja42Dk
Biddy	6	F	Child	03Ja42Dk
Mary	.00	F	Infant	03Ja42Dk
SULLIVAN, Mary	50	F	Unknown	03Ja42Dk
Bridget	16	F	Unknown	03Ja42Dk
Ellen	13	F	Unknown	03Ja42Dk
FALLON, Martin	20	M	Unknown	03Ja42Dk
Honor	24	F	Unknown	03Ja42Dk
TANNAN, Mary	22	F	Unknown	03Ja42Dk
FARRELL, Kitty	24	F	Unknown	03Ja42Dk
SWIFT, Ann	18	F	Unknown	03Ja42Dk
ODONNELL, Francis	26	M	Unknown	03Ja42Dk
MCNAMARA, Cathn.	28	F	Unknown	03Ja42Dk
ROGAN, Ellen	30	F	Unknown	03Ja42Dk
COUGHLAN, Mary	26	F	Unknown	03Ja42Dk
KEOUGH, James	20	M	Unknown	03Ja42Dk
KELLY, Biddy	33	F	Unknown	03Ja42Dk
Margt.	.00	F	Infant	03Ja42Dk
MALONE, Mary	22	F	Unknown	03Ja42Dk
MAROONEY, John	44	M	Unknown	03Ja42Dk
CLEARY, Cathn.	19	F	Unknown	03Ja42Dk
FLINN, John	32	M	Unknown	03Ja42Dk
MCMAHON, John	20	M	Unknown	03Ja42Dk
Bridget	20	F	Unknown	03Ja42Dk
CRAWLEY, Honor	20	F	Unknown	03Ja42Dk
KENNAN, Mary	30	F	Unknown	03Ja42Dk
MCGUANE, John	22	M	Unknown	03Ja42Dk
Ann	12	F	Unknown	03Ja42Dk
MCCORMICK, Mary	24	F	Unknown	03Ja42Dk
LEE, Judath	22	F	Unknown	03Ja42Dk
Ellen	26	F	Unknown	03Ja42Dk
DILLON, Cella	28	F	Unknown	03Ja42Dk
JOYCE, Sarah	25	F	Unknown	03Ja42Dk
RYAN, Nay	30	F	Unknown	03Ja42Dk
REYNOLDS, Bridget	16	F	Unknown	03Ja42Dk

NAMES OF PASSENGERS	AGE	SEX	OCCUPATIONS	DATE PORT SHIP
KELLY, Bridget	20	F	Unknown	03Ja42Dk
GARVEY, Pat	18	M	Unknown	03Ja42Dk
Mary	35	F	Unknown	03Ja42Dk
CUNNINGHAM, Margt.	20	F	Unknown	03Ja42Dk
GIBBON, Pat	35	M	Unknown	03Ja42Dk
KENNEDY, Mary	24	F	Unknown	03Ja42Dk
MOONEY, Daniel	27	M	Unknown	03Ja42Dk
Peirce	24	M	Unknown	03Ja42Dk
GIBBONS, Ellen	27	F	Unknown	03Ja42Dk
KEAN, Bridget	16	F	Unknown	03Ja42Dk
BLAKE, Ann	21	F	Unknown	03Ja42Dk
HONAN, Johanna	19	F	Unknown	03Ja42Dk
THALOR, Mary	21	F	Unknown	03Ja42Dk
GORMAN, Ann	18	F	Unknown	03Ja42Dk
HOSTY, Margt.	40	F	Unknown	03Ja42Dk
MOONEY, John	18	M	Unknown	03Ja42Dk
DEVENEY, Eliza	18	F	Unknown	03Ja42Dk
ODWYER, Cor.	20	M	Unknown	03Ja42Dk
MCDONNELL, Pat	22	M	Unknown	03Ja42Dk
COFFEE, Dennis	25	M	Unknown	03Ja42Dk
Michl.	24	M	Unknown	03Ja42Dk
COSTELLO, John	13	M	Unknown	03Ja42Dk
SULLIVAN, Mich.	12	M	Unknown	03Ja42Dk
COMMONS, Wm.	8	M	Child	03Ja42Dk
DUANE, Honor	16	F	Unknown	03Ja42Dk
KELLY, Cathn.	6	F	Child	03Ja42Dk
John	5	M	Child	03Ja42Dk
MOLLOY, Larry	6	M	Child	03Ja42Dk
REYNOLDS, Thos.	14	M	Unknown	03Ja42Dk
TYRONE, Michl.	18	M	Unknown	03Ja42Dk
HEALY, Martin	16	M	Unknown	03Ja42Dk
KEANE, Pat	22	M	Unknown	03Ja42Dk
James	23	M	Unknown	03Ja42Dk
MULLENS, Mick	24	M	Unknown	03Ja42Dk
DUANE, Bridget	23	F	Unknown	03Ja42Dk
LEE, Betty	19	F	Unknown	03Ja42Dk
LAFFY, Mary	23	F	Unknown	03Ja42Dk
ONEILL, Janie	22	F	Unknown	03Ja42Dk
DWYER, Biddy	18	F	Unknown	03Ja42Dk
KELLY, Margt.	20	F	Unknown	03Ja42Dk
ONEILL, James	28	M	Unknown	03Ja42Dk
ODWYER, Jerry	15	M	Unknown	03Ja42Dk
MEALA, Pat	27	M	Unknown	03Ja42Dk
FEENAGHTY, Mich.	20	M	Unknown	03Ja42Dk

ALBERT-GALLATIN 09 JANUARY 1850

From Liverpool

NAMES OF PASSENGERS	AGE	SEX	OCCUPATIONS	DATE PORT SHIP
HARMAN, Anthony	21	M	Shoemaker	09Ja02Fb
SHERIDAN, Judith	30	F	Unknown	09Ja02Fb
BYRNES, Mary	20	F	Unknown	09Ja02Fb
NOWLAN, Martin	20	M	Laborer	09Ja02Fb
WARD, George	14	M	Unknown	09Ja02Fb
SILLERY, Chas.	55	M	Laborer	09Ja02Fb
Chas.	28	M	Laborer	09Ja02Fb
Judith	26	F	Unknown	09Ja02Fb
Biddy	3	F	Child	09Ja02Fb
John	.00	M	Infant	09Ja02Fb
MURRAY, Thos.	35	M	Laborer	09Ja02Fb
LYNCH, Mary	20	F	Unknown	09Ja02Fb
SMITH, Pat	45	M	Laborer	09Ja02Fb
MONTGOMERY, Robt.	00	M	Tailor	09Ja02Fb
MANY, Edwd.	50	M	Laborer	09Ja02Fb
Ellen	40	F	Unknown	09Ja02Fb
John	13	M	Unknown	09Ja02Fb
Edmund	11	M	Unknown	09Ja02Fb
Mary	9	F	Child	09Ja02Fb
Cathr.	6	M	Child	09Ja02Fb

NAMES OF PASSENGERS	AGE	SEX	OCCUPATIONS	DATE PORT SHIP
CUMMINGS, Mary	55	F	Unknown	09Ja02Fb
LEON, Pat	40	M	Farmer	09Ja02Fb
GALLAGAN, Margt.	18	F	Unknown	09Ja02Fb
SHEA, Bridget	25	F	Unknown	09Ja02Fb
HEWITT, John	24	M	Shoemaker	09Ja02Fb
TAYLOR, Benjm.	26	M	Laborer	09Ja02Fb
DOYLE, James	19	M	Laborer	09Ja02Fb
HARE, Thos.	20	M	Laborer	09Ja02Fb
Mary	20	F	Unknown	09Ja02Fb
John	.00	M	Infant	09Ja02Fb
ALWELL, Ellen	20	F	Unknown	09Ja02Fb
SHIELLS, Ann	12	F	Unknown	09Ja02Fb
BRADY, Michl.	35	M	Laborer	09Ja02Fb
SMITH, Cathn.	30	F	Unknown	09Ja02Fb
FITZPATRICK, Alice	20	F	Unknown	09Ja02Fb
Mary	30	F	Unknown	09Ja02Fb
Died-At-Sea				
LARRY, Owen	20	M	Blacksmith	09Ja02Fb
CONOLLY, Pat	20	M	Laborer	09Ja02Fb
GREYSON, George	30	M	Laborer	09Ja02Fb
TEARNY, John	25	M	Laborer	09Ja02Fb
MEALY, Jas.	55	M	Tailor	09Ja02Fb
Ann	50	F	Unknown	09Ja02Fb
MCGRATH, James	3	M	Child	09Ja02Fb
Died-At-Sea				
CONNOR, Mick	22	M	Laborer	09Ja02Fb
Cathn.	22	F	Unknown	09Ja02Fb
John	.00	M	Infant	09Ja02Fb
MURROUGH, James	21	M	Blacksmith	09Ja02Fb
TOOHEY, Ellen	35	F	Unknown	09Ja02Fb
Mick	9	M	Child	09Ja02Fb
Bessey	7	F	Child	09Ja02Fb
Mary	5	F	Child	09Ja02Fb
John	3	M	Child	09Ja02Fb
Died-At-Sea				
MOORE, Robert	26	M	Carpenter	09Ja02Fb
FORSYTH, Walter	32	M	Carpenter	09Ja02Fb
Cathn.	30	F	Unknown	09Ja02Fb
Archibald	.00	M	Infant	09Ja02Fb
Died-At-Sea				
DRUMORE, Ann	3	F	Child	09Ja02Fb
MCCALL, Euphenia	28	F	Unknown	09Ja02Fb
Died-At-Sea				
Flora	60	F	Unknown	09Ja02Fb
Died-At-Sea				
JAMES, Thos.	30	M	Laborer	09Ja02Fb
Rachel	30	F	Unknown	09Ja02Fb
Elizabeth	1	F	Child	09Ja02Fb
Mary-Ann	.00	F	Infant	09Ja02Fb
MORRIS, Paddy	30	M	Tailor	09Ja02Fb
MAHON, Margt.	30	F	Unknown	09Ja02Fb
PATTERSON, John	30	M	Blacksmith	09Ja02Fb
Eliza	26	F	Unknown	09Ja02Fb
PARRY, Cathn.	24	F	Unknown	09Ja02Fb
PATTERSON, Elizabeth	4	F	Child	09Ja02Fb
Robert	1	M	Child	09Ja02Fb
James	.00	M	Infant	09Ja02Fb
DERIVAN, Biddy	25	F	Unknown	09Ja02Fb
GARRITY, Ann	20	F	Unknown	09Ja02Fb
Mary	18	F	Unknown	09Ja02Fb
MCDONNOUGH, M.	30	M	Farmer	09Ja02Fb
GOULDING, John	20	M	Laborer	09Ja02Fb
CAMBELL, Edwd.	22	M	Shoemaker	09Ja02Fb
BURK, Joseph	40	M	Laborer	09Ja02Fb
MORROW, John	17	M	Laborer	09Ja02Fb
AHEARN, Jas.	20	M	Laborer	09Ja02Fb
MAHON, Jas.	20	M	Laborer	09Ja02Fb
Cathn.	17	F	Unknown	09Ja02Fb
COLEMAN, Mary	18	F	Unknown	09Ja02Fb
CARROLL, Thos.	36	M	Farmer	09Ja02Fb
Johanna	21	F	Unknown	09Ja02Fb
BAYNAL, Thos.	22	M	Laborer	09Ja02Fb
LAWSON, Robt.	20	M	Laborer	09Ja02Fb
SMITH, Owen	30	M	Blacksmith	09Ja02Fb
Thomas	4	M	Child	09Ja02Fb

NAMES OF PASSENGERS	AGE	SEX	OCCUPATIONS	DATE PORT SHIP
SMITH, James	1	M	Child	09Ja02Fb
U	.00	U	Infant	09Ja02Fb
BORVEL, Henry	28	M	Farmer	09Ja02Fb
GILLIGAN, Pat	24	M	Laborer	09Ja02Fb
Mary	24	F	Unknown	09Ja02Fb
KERWIN, Bridget	20	F	Unknown	09Ja02Fb
Died-At-Sea				
MCGAHAN, Jas.	30	M	Shoemaker	09Ja02Fb
MCNANCY, Rose	30	F	Unknown	09Ja02Fb
CURTIS, Pat	20	M	Laborer	09Ja02Fb
HENRY, Jas.	27	M	Tailor	09Ja02Fb
Pat	19	M	Laborer	09Ja02Fb
Sarah	20	F	Unknown	09Ja02Fb
ROE, John	40	M	Farmer	09Ja02Fb
Pat	17	M	Laborer	09Ja02Fb
GIBSON, Daniel	24	M	Laborer	09Ja02Fb
ZIMMERINE, Jacob	23	M	Laborer	09Ja02Fb
COUSINS, Thos.	24	M	Laborer	09Ja02Fb
HALFPENNY, Ann	40	F	Unknown	09Ja02Fb
John	26	M	Laborer	09Ja02Fb
Thomas	23	M	Laborer	09Ja02Fb
Pat	19	M	Laborer	09Ja02Fb
Died-At-Sea				
COCKRAN, Mick	38	M	Laborer	09Ja02Fb
SAVAGE, Robert	19	M	Laborer	09Ja02Fb
Cathn.	40	F	Unknown	09Ja02Fb
DOLAN, Ann	22	F	Unknown	09Ja02Fb
BRADY, James	22	M	Laborer	09Ja02Fb
MCGRAYLE, John	34	M	Farmer	09Ja02Fb
Bridget	26	F	Unknown	09Ja02Fb
Honor	.00	M	Infant	09Ja02Fb
GORMAN, Nicholas	30	M	Laborer	09Ja02Fb
Mary	30	F	Unknown	09Ja02Fb
Nichls.	5	M	Child	09Ja02Fb
Elizabeth	1	F	Child	09Ja02Fb
Died-At-Sea				
KIERNAN, Jane	22	F	Unknown	09Ja02Fb
Pat	20	M	Laborer	09Ja02Fb
NOWLAN, Andrew	30	M	Tailor	09Ja02Fb
BROWN, Mick	25	M	Laborer	09Ja02Fb
MCGORVAN, Mary	27	F	Unknown	09Ja02Fb
LAWLOR, Cathrn.	13	F	Unknown	09Ja02Fb
HIGGINS, Jas.	25	M	Laborer	09Ja02Fb
FITZPATRICK, John	29	M	Laborer	09Ja02Fb
Julia	27	F	Unknown	09Ja02Fb
ALEXANDER, Wm.	30	M	Shoemaker	09Ja02Fb
HALLOCK, Edward	18	M	Laborer	09Ja02Fb
MCBRIDE, Mary	9	F	Child	09Ja02Fb
Bridget	7	F	Child	09Ja02Fb
Died-At-Sea				
PRIOR, Ann	15	F	Unknown	09Ja02Fb
CAULFIELD, Margt.	26	F	Unknown	09Ja02Fb
FITZGERALD, Cath.	4	F	Child	09Ja02Fb
CAVANNAH, Ann	26	F	Child	09Ja02Fb
Mary	3	F	Child	09Ja02Fb
MARTIN, Pat	30	M	Laborer	09Ja02Fb
Died-At-Sea				
DERVIN, John	25	M	Farmer	09Ja02Fb
NORMAN, James	4	M	Child	09Ja02Fb
MCCARTHY, Chas.	15	M	Unknown	09Ja02Fb
MURRAY, Allen	16	M	Unknown	09Ja02Fb
DORAN, Eliza	50	F	Unknown	09Ja02Fb
Eliza	20	F	Unknown	09Ja02Fb
Johanna	18	F	Unknown	09Ja02Fb
Margt.	12	F	Unknown	09Ja02Fb
Cathn.	10	F	Unknown	09Ja02Fb
MCDONALD, Pat	15	M	Unknown	09Ja02Fb
MCGARRET, Owen	40	M	Shoemaker	09Ja02Fb
Cath.	40	F	Unknown	09Ja02Fb
Nancy	16	F	Unknown	09Ja02Fb
LAWLOR, Thos.	19	M	Laborer	09Ja02Fb
MCCORMICK, Mary	20	F	Unknown	09Ja02Fb
MCELHEINE, Cath.	16	F	Unknown	09Ja02Fb
FURY, James	25	M	Farmer	09Ja02Fb
MARTIN, John	13	M	Farmer	09Ja02Fb

NAMES OF PASSENGERS	AGE	SEX	OCCUPATIONS	DATE PORT SHIP
PROCTOR, Mary-Ann	8	F	Child	09Ja02Fb
NEAL, Bridget	19	F	Unknown	09Ja02Fb
DEARMODY, James	25	M	Laborer	09Ja02Fb
MURPHY, John	26	M	Laborer	09Ja02Fb
Died-At-Sea				
FEASON, Patrick	30	M	Tailor	09Ja02Fb
TOHIN, John	50	M	Laborer	09Ja02Fb
FLYNN, Margaret	27	F	Unknown	09Ja02Fb
BRADLEY, Allan	21	M	Unknown	09Ja02Fb
ARMSTRONG, Fras.	54	M	Laborer	09Ja02Fb
Died-At-Sea				
Ann	50	F	Unknown	09Ja02Fb
Mary-Ann	16	F	Unknown	09Ja02Fb
Margt.	13	F	Unknown	09Ja02Fb
Eliza	8	F	Child	09Ja02Fb
BROWN, James	30	M	Farmer	09Ja02Fb
WREN, Richard	20	M	Laborer	09Ja02Fb
GERAGHTY, Pat	40	M	Laborer	09Ja02Fb
Mary	35	F	Unknown	09Ja02Fb
Ann	15	F	Unknown	09Ja02Fb
Pat	8	M	Child	09Ja02Fb
James	.00	M	Infant	09Ja02Fb
Died-At-Sea				
RUSH, John	33	M	Laborer	09Ja02Fb
Ann	34	F	Unknown	09Ja02Fb
Died-At-Sea				
Pat	3	M	Child	09Ja02Fb
MCDONOUGH, Jas.	25	M	Farmer	09Ja02Fb
Bridget	15	F	Unknown	09Ja02Fb
MANGAN, Ellen	20	F	Unknown	09Ja02Fb
Died-At-Sea				
GLEOMAN, Pat	13	M	Unknown	09Ja02Fb
FAHY, Mary	20	F	Unknown	09Ja02Fb
DALY, Mick	21	M	Laborer	09Ja02Fb
Cath.	19	F	Unknown	09Ja02Fb
CONNORS, Bridget	20	F	Unknown	09Ja02Fb
TARPEY, Bridget	25	F	Unknown	09Ja02Fb
WREN, Wm.	35	M	Tailor	09Ja02Fb
Perry	21	M	Laborer	09Ja02Fb
GAMMON, Edward	21	M	Laborer	09Ja02Fb
WREN, Ellen	19	F	Unknown	09Ja02Fb
Cathn.	15	F	Unknown	09Ja02Fb
William	8	M	Child	09Ja02Fb
Nichs.	6	M	Child	09Ja02Fb
DORDIS, Judith	40	F	Unknown	09Ja02Fb
Mary	18	F	Unknown	09Ja02Fb
BRENNAN, Bridget	6	F	Child	09Ja02Fb
Rose	18	F	Unknown	09Ja02Fb
COSTELLO, Cath.	00	F	Unknown	09Ja02Fb
MOSELY, Jas.	32	M	Laborer	09Ja02Fb
HANSON, Rose	18	F	Unknown	09Ja02Fb
MAINE, John	50	M	Laborer	09Ja02Fb
Mary-Ann	50	F	Unknown	09Ja02Fb
Margt.Ann	10	F	Unknown	09Ja02Fb
RUXTON, John	17	M	Laborer	09Ja02Fb
MCKEOWN, Michl.	30	M	Laborer	09Ja02Fb
MAHAR, Jeremiah	45	M	Laborer	09Ja02Fb
Mary	40	F	Unknown	09Ja02Fb
Died-At-Sea				
Fanny	9	F	Child	09Ja02Fb
OBRIEN, Maurice	13	M	Unknown	09Ja02Fb
NEARY, James	43	M	Laborer	09Ja02Fb
Bridget	33	F	Unknown	09Ja02Fb
Thos.	13	M	Unknown	09Ja02Fb
Paul	2	M	Child	09Ja02Fb
James	12	M	Unknown	09Ja02Fb
SHANNON, John	39	M	Farmer	09Ja02Fb
MULLIGAN, John,	24	M	Tailor	09Ja02Fb
FITZGERALD, Cathn.	40	F	Unknown	09Ja02Fb
Joseph	20	M	Laborer	09Ja02Fb
Mary	18	F	Unknown	09Ja02Fb
Cathn.	1	F	Child	09Ja02Fb
Ann	12	F	Unknown	09Ja02Fb
BRASSIL, Cathn.	18	F	Unknown	09Ja02Fb
OBRIEN, Michl.	22	M	Laborer	09Ja02Fb

NAMES OF PASSENGERS	AGE	SEX	OCCUPATIONS	DATE PORT SHIP
OBRIEN, Pat	26	M	Laborer	09Ja02Fb
CARLETT, Pat	22	M	Laborer	09Ja02Fb
TAFT, Wm.	24	M	Farmer	09Ja02Fb
Margt.E.	25	F	Unknown	09Ja02Fb
Charlotte	2	F	Child	09Ja02Fb
George	.00	M	Infant	09Ja02Fb
COFFEY, Margt.	35	F	Unknown	09Ja02Fb
Died-At-Sea				
Cathrn.	11	F	Unknown	09Ja02Fb
John	4	M	Child	09Ja02Fb
Mary	.00	F	Infant	09Ja02Fb
Died-At-Sea				
PARKASAN, Kieram	35	M	Farmer	09Ja02Fb
Mary	29	F	Unknown	09Ja02Fb
Died-At-Sea				
Edward	4	M	Child	09Ja02Fb
James	.00	M	Infant	09Ja02Fb
REDMOND, Thomas	26	M	Tailor	09Ja02Fb
Margt.	22	F	Unknown	09Ja02Fb
Sarah	.00	F	Infant	09Ja02Fb
FLANNAGAN, John	21	M	Tailor	09Ja02Fb
Bridget	18	F	Unknown	09Ja02Fb
Margt.	.00	F	Infant	09Ja02Fb
PETERS, Michl.	26	M	Laborer	09Ja02Fb
Mary	26	F	Unknown	09Ja02Fb
CONRON, Silvester	24	M	Laborer	09Ja02Fb
SHILL, Edward	26	M	Farmer	09Ja02Fb
HUTCHESON, Saml.	38	M	Laborer	09Ja02Fb
WHITE, Wm.	32	M	Laborer	09Ja02Fb
BRANNAN, Peter	18	M	Laborer	09Ja02Fb
NUGENT, Ellen	30	F	Unknown	09Ja02Fb
Mary	8	F	Child	09Ja02Fb
Fanny	4	F	Child	09Ja02Fb
John	2	M	Child	09Ja02Fb
Died-At-Sea				
Nicholas	.00	M	Infant	09Ja02Fb
Died-At-Sea				
BRADY, Thos.	25	M	Shoemaker	09Ja02Fb
U-Mrs.	19	F	Unknown	09Ja02Fb
REYNOLDS, Owen	25	M	Farmer	09Ja02Fb
RILEY, Cathn.	20	F	Unknown	09Ja02Fb
FARREL, Cathn.	18	F	Unknown	09Ja02Fb
Bridget	18	F	Unknown	09Ja02Fb
LISH, Wm.	8	M	Child	09Ja02Fb
NOLAN, Michl.	32	M	Blacksmith	09Ja02Fb
Bridget	23	F	Unknown	09Ja02Fb
HART, Patk.	18	M	Unknown	09Ja02Fb
TURBUT, Margt.	22	F	Unknown	09Ja02Fb
TUOMAN, Cathn.	30	F	Unknown	09Ja02Fb
Thomas	6	M	Child	09Ja02Fb
Bridget	4	F	Child	09Ja02Fb
Died-At-Sea				
QUIN, Celia	19	F	Unknown	09Ja02Fb
CUNNINGHAM, Bridget	30	F	Unknown	09Ja02Fb
Patrick	13	M	Unknown	09Ja02Fb
WALPOLE, Thos.	21	M	Blacksmith	09Ja02Fb
FLOOD, Cathn.	24	F	Unknown	09Ja02Fb
COHETT, Mick	13	M	Unknown	09Ja02Fb
MCERROY, Michl.	12	M	Unknown	09Ja02Fb
HELLEY, Mary	13	F	Unknown	09Ja02Fb
DOOGAN, Michl.	24	M	Laborer	09Ja02Fb
HEALEY, Thos.	24	M	Laborer	09Ja02Fb
ROSS, Robt.	20	M	Laborer	09Ja02Fb
DURAN, Mary	50	F	Unknown	09Ja02Fb
Rose	25	F	Unknown	09Ja02Fb
Eliza	23	F	Unknown	09Ja02Fb
Mary	21	F	Unknown	09Ja02Fb
KELLY, Jas.	32	M	Farmer	09Ja02Fb
Eliza	34	F	Unknown	09Ja02Fb
Cathn.	8	F	Child	09Ja02Fb
James	3	M	Child	09Ja02Fb
Henry	.00	M	Infant	09Ja02Fb
MEE, Jane	50	F	Unknown	09Ja02Fb
Mary	24	F	Unknown	09Ja02Fb
FLOOD, Francis	22	M	Farmer	09Ja02Fb

NAMES OF PASSENGERS	AGE	SEX	OCCUPATIONS	DATE PORT SHIP
MEE, John	28	M	Laborer	09Ja02Fb
William	26	M	Laborer	09Ja02Fb
RAHILL, Owen	22	M	Laborer	09Ja02Fb
John	20	M	Laborer	09Ja02Fb
Died-At-Sea				
Mary	18	F	Unknown	09Ja02Fb
REILLY, Mary	20	F	Unknown	09Ja02Fb
CLARKE, Ann	12	F	Unknown	09Ja02Fb
Died-At-Sea				
BRADY, Pat	40	M	Laborer	09Ja02Fb
Died-At-Sea				
Mary	36	F	Unknown	09Ja02Fb
Bernard	8	M	Child	09Ja02Fb
Ann	6	F	Child	09Ja02Fb
Cathn.	.00	F	Infant	09Ja02Fb
GAVAN, Biddy	50	F	Unknown	09Ja02Fb
Died-At-Sea				
James	28	M	Laborer	09Ja02Fb
Devan	21	M	Laborer	09Ja02Fb
Pat	19	M	Laborer	09Ja02Fb
Mary	15	F	Unknown	09Ja02Fb
U, Jos.	12	M	Unknown	09Ja02Fb
BOILAN, Michl.	21	M	Tailor	09Ja02Fb
Died-At-Sea				
GIBBONS, Mary	30	F	Unknown	09Ja02Fb
Ellen	20	F	Unknown	09Ja02Fb
RYAN, Ellen	18	F	Unknown	09Ja02Fb
Tuie	18	M	Laborer	09Ja02Fb
BRIEN, Nicholas	23	M	Farmer	09Ja02Fb
FINAN, Pat	24	M	Laborer	09Ja02Fb
Mick	18	M	Laborer	09Ja02Fb
Ellen	50	F	Unknown	09Ja02Fb
WHITE, Mary	50	F	Unknown	09Ja02Fb
FINAN, Mary	30	F	Unknown	09Ja02Fb
Pat	4	M	Child	09Ja02Fb
MCFADDEN, Mick	40	M	Shoemaker	09Ja02Fb
Ellen	22	F	Unknown	09Ja02Fb
SWEENEY, Mick	8	M	Child	09Ja02Fb
SHERRAN, Bernard	26	M	Laborer	09Ja02Fb
MCGUIRE, Barny	20	M	Laborer	09Ja02Fb
SURAN, Mary	20	F	Unknown	09Ja02Fb
LUKE, Thos.	25	M	Farmer	09Ja02Fb
James	20	M	Laborer	09Ja02Fb
DUFFY, Cathn.	40	F	Unknown	09Ja02Fb
Cathn.	12	F	Unknown	09Ja02Fb
RILEY, Thomas	60	M	Farmer	09Ja02Fb
FITZPATRICK, Honora	26	F	Unknown	09Ja02Fb
Died-At-Sea				
Peter	20	M	Unknown	09Ja02Fb
Michl.	50	M	Laborer	09Ja02Fb
Honora	20	F	Unknown	09Ja02Fb
Died-At-Sea				
Connor	2	M	Child	09Ja02Fb
Died-At-Sea				
HERDMAN, John	31	M	Laborer	09Ja02Fb
CUNNINGHAM, Alexander	22	M	Tailor	09Ja02Fb
HEYLOR, John	29	M	Laborer	09Ja02Fb
HERROR, Martin	40	M	Laborer	09Ja02Fb
PRIOR, Ann	24	F	Unknown	09Ja02Fb
COAKLEY, Thomas	38	M	Blacksmith	09Ja02Fb
CARTEY, Michl.	48	M	Laborer	09Ja02Fb
Edward	10	M	Unknown	09Ja02Fb
DEVILIN, Thomas	22	M	Farmer	09Ja02Fb
MONAGHAN, Betty	21	F	Unknown	09Ja02Fb
Owen	21	M	Laborer	09Ja02Fb
KERNAN, James	30	M	Laborer	09Ja02Fb
Ann	30	F	Unknown	09Ja02Fb
Pat	3	M	Child	09Ja02Fb
Eliza	.00	F	Infant	09Ja02Fb
Bren---, John	00	M	Unknown	09Ja02Fb
Thomas	19	M	Laborer	09Ja02Fb
Edward	18	M	Laborer	09Ja02Fb
Margaret	26	F	Unknown	09Ja02Fb
Cathn.	1	F	Child	09Ja02Fb
HEYNAN, Maria	19	F	Unknown	09Ja02Fb
LEE, Michl.	13	M	Laborer	09Ja02Fb
HOGAN, Owen	29	M	Laborer	09Ja02Fb
MCQUAID, Edward	40	M	Blacksmith	09Ja02Fb
Died-At-Sea				
Biddy	36	F	Unknown	09Ja02Fb
Sarah	7	F	Child	09Ja02Fb
Thomas	.00	M	Infant	09Ja02Fb
CLARKE, Irwan	50	M	Laborer	09Ja02Fb
Died-At-Sea				

CAMBRIDGE 09 JANUARY 1850

From Liverpool

NAMES OF PASSENGERS	AGE	SEX	OCCUPATIONS	DATE PORT SHIP
DROUGHT, Robert	22	M	Carpenter	09Ja02Dm
Matilda	18	F	None	09Ja02Dm
DUNNE, Anne	18	F	Servant	09Ja02Dm
FALLON, Patrick	17	M	None	09Ja02Dm
MILADY, James	30	M	Clerk	09Ja02Dm
CASEY, Patk.	20	M	Clerk	09Ja02Dm
James	14	M	Clerk	09Ja02Dm
OCONNELL, Patrick	23	M	Victualler	09Ja02Dm
EGAN, Michl.	35	M	Laborer	09Ja02Dm
MCINROO, Henry	35	M	Gdnr	09Ja02Dm
MAJOR, Thos.	22	M	Clerk	09Ja02Dm
CASEY, Michl.	26	M	Laborer	09Ja02Dm
BERRY, John	40	M	Clerk	09Ja02Dm
MCDONALD, Alex.	24	M	Blacksmith	09Ja02Dm
HOWE, Timothy	19	M	Clerk	09Ja02Dm
GILLAN, Bridget	19	F	Servant	09Ja02Dm
MCADDEN, John	15	M	Servant	09Ja02Dm
MARTIN, Anne	23	F	Servant	09Ja02Dm
Patk.	4	M	Child	09Ja02Dm
PENDER, Bridget	24	F	Servant	09Ja02Dm
MURPHY, Andrew	50	M	Farmer	09Ja02Dm
Mary-Ann	26	F	Servant	09Ja02Dm
James	24	M	Farmer	09Ja02Dm
Richard	2	M	Child	09Ja02Dm
ROE, James	23	M	Laborer	09Ja02Dm
DOYLE, Bridget	24	F	Servant	09Ja02Dm
REILLY, Mary-Ann	17	F	Servant	09Ja02Dm
DOLAN, Cathn.	30	F	Servant	09Ja02Dm
CAROLAN, Judith	16	F	Servant	09Ja02Dm
JORDAN, Cathn.	14	F	Servant	09Ja02Dm
DOLAN, John	8	M	Child	09Ja02Dm
Thos.	6	M	Child	09Ja02Dm
James	3	M	Child	09Ja02Dm
FITZSIMONS, Garret	26	M	Clerk	09Ja02Dm
Bridgt.	25	F	Servant	09Ja02Dm
GANNON, Anne	30	F	Servant	09Ja02Dm
KEEGAN, Anne	26	F	None	09Ja02Dm
Edwd.	7	M	Child	09Ja02Dm
James	5	M	Child	09Ja02Dm
SIMPSON, James	12	M	None	09Ja02Dm
CAROLAN, Mary	38	F	None	09Ja02Dm
Honora	7	F	Child	09Ja02Dm
Mary	6	F	Child	09Ja02Dm
Bridgt.	2	F	Child	09Ja02Dm
GAVIN, Bridgt.	18	F	Servant	09Ja02Dm
BREDON, Peter	18	M	Clerk	09Ja02Dm
Mary	16	F	Servant	09Ja02Dm
BLAKE, John	19	M	Laborer	09Ja02Dm
KELEREE, Brian	19	M	Laborer	09Ja02Dm
NOONAN, Cornelius	19	M	Miller	09Ja02Dm
HEALY, Maurice	19	M	Tailor	09Ja02Dm
CLEAR, Margt.	18	F	Servant	09Ja02Dm
Mary	7	F	Child	09Ja02Dm
James	3	M	Child	09Ja02Dm
DELAHOE, Brian	40	M	Laborer	09Ja02Dm

NAMES OF PASSENGERS	A G E	S E X	OCCUPATIONS	DATE PORT SHIP
WALL, Bridget	20	F	Servant	09Ja02Dm
Mary	7	F	Child	09Ja02Dm
Joseph	20	M	Laborer	09Ja02Dm
CORMACK, Patk.	22	M	Laborer	09Ja02Dm
KIRMAN, Mary-Ann	20	F	Servant	09Ja02Dm
SAVAGE, Eliza	18	F	Servant	09Ja02Dm
BUTLER, Judith	18	F	Servant	09Ja02Dm
LEAMY, Patk.	27	M	Laborer	09Ja02Dm
TOBIN, Patk.	25	M	Laborer	09Ja02Dm
LONDREGAN, David	25	M	Laborer	09Ja02Dm
MACKEY, Thos.	30	M	Farmer	09Ja02Dm
Ann	14	F	Servant	09Ja02Dm
Mary	23	F	None	09Ja02Dm
MURPHY, Sibby	50	F	None	09Ja02Dm
Patk.	18	M	Clerk	09Ja02Dm
Henry	16	M	None	09Ja02Dm
MCADAM, Cathe.	48	F	None	09Ja02Dm
Died-At-Sea				
Cathe.	14	F	Servant	09Ja02Dm
James	16	M	Servant	09Ja02Dm
Michl.	8	M	Child	09Ja02Dm
Edwd.	10	M	None	09Ja02Dm
BROWN, Mary	20	F	Servant	09Ja02Dm
CUNNINGHAM, John	30	M	Ploughman	09Ja02Dm
WHELAN, Daniel	25	M	Carpenter	09Ja02Dm
DAUGHAN, Daniel	20	M	Laborer	09Ja02Dm
COYNE, Joseph	30	M	Laborer	09Ja02Dm
Anne	28	F	None	09Ja02Dm
Patrick	7	M	Child	09Ja02Dm
Died-At-Sea				
MURPHY, John	67	M	Laborer	09Ja02Dm
MCDONALD, Magt.	17	F	Servant	09Ja02Dm
HARLAND, James	8	M	Child	09Ja02Dm
Bridget	10	F	None	09Ja02Dm
CHRISTIE, Sarah	17	F	Servant	09Ja02Dm
MCEVOY, Michl.	14	M	None	09Ja02Dm
FAY, Ellen	33	F	None	09Ja02Dm
MCGOMERIL, Cicely	42	F	None	09Ja02Dm
Anne	14	F	None	09Ja02Dm
John	18	M	None	09Ja02Dm
Patk.	10	M	None	09Ja02Dm
Michl.	8	M	Child	09Ja02Dm
Neale	7	M	Child	09Ja02Dm
DOGHERTY, John	20	M	Laborer	09Ja02Dm
FAY, Danl.	40	M	Blacksmith	09Ja02Dm
TRAYNOR, Patk.	22	M	Laborer	09Ja02Dm
SHERRY, Ellen	50	F	None	09Ja02Dm
Rosannah	18	F	None	09Ja02Dm
LAWLER, James	12	M	None	09Ja02Dm
KIERNAN, Michl.	15	M	Laborer	09Ja02Dm
Mary-Anne	20	F	Servant	09Ja02Dm
FORAN, John	56	M	Laborer	09Ja02Dm
LAWLER, Anne	22	F	Servant	09Ja02Dm
MCSORLY, Cath.	37	F	Servant	09Ja02Dm
MARTIN, Ellen	28	F	Servant	09Ja02Dm
GILL, Mary	25	F	Servant	09Ja02Dm
CONCANNON, Mary	18	F	Servant	09Ja02Dm
Pat	12	M	None	09Ja02Dm
Anne	10	F	None	09Ja02Dm
DOYLE, Cathn.	25	F	None	09Ja02Dm
KERR, Mary	24	F	None	09Ja02Dm
Patk.	30	M	None	09Ja02Dm
CAHILL, Patk.	40	M	Laborer	09Ja02Dm
COURTNEY, Brian	60	M	Mason	09Ja02Dm
WATSON, John	15	M	Servant	09Ja02Dm
CAFFREY, Hugh	8	M	Child	09Ja02Dm
Alicia	45	F	None	09Ja02Dm
U	11	U	None	09Ja02Dm
Margt.	10	F	None	09Ja02Dm
RYAN, Dennis	26	M	Laborer	09Ja02Dm
TENNY, James	15	M	Laborer	09Ja02Dm
SHARKEY, Edwd.	30	M	Laborer	09Ja02Dm
MCGRATH, Timothy	22	M	Tailor	09Ja02Dm
CAHILL, Anne	22	F	Servant	09Ja02Dm
BRIAN, Mary	18	F	Servant	09Ja02Dm
BRIAN, Cathe.	14	F	Servant	09Ja02Dm
COURTNEY, Ellen	8	F	Child	09Ja02Dm
HUTTON, Patk.	25	M	Shoemaker	09Ja02Dm
May	20	F	None	09Ja02Dm
Henry	1	M	Child	09Ja02Dm
CAROLAN, Eliza	19	F	Servant	09Ja02Dm
BOLGER, Margt.	20	F	None	09Ja02Dm
HANDIBOW, John	19	M	Laborer	09Ja02Dm
KELLY, James	40	M	Laborer	09Ja02Dm
HANDIBOW, Anne	17	F	Servant	09Ja02Dm
BRANNIGAN, Bridgt.	23	F	Servant	09Ja02Dm
BOYLAN, Arthur	16	M	Servant	09Ja02Dm
KELLY, Mary	23	F	Servant	09Ja02Dm
Cathn.	27	F	Servant	09Ja02Dm
DELANY, Dennis	38	M	Laborer	09Ja02Dm
Eliz.	40	F	None	09Ja02Dm
Mary	11	F	None	09Ja02Dm
Bridgt.	7	F	Child	09Ja02Dm
Daniel	1	M	Child	09Ja02Dm
DWYER, Anne	15	F	Servant	09Ja02Dm
Cathe.	20	F	Servant	09Ja02Dm
Bridgt.	17	F	None	09Ja02Dm
RYAN, Winifred	22	F	None	09Ja02Dm
BURKE, Norry	30	F	None	09Ja02Dm
Judy	7	F	Child	09Ja02Dm
Ellen	5	F	Child	09Ja02Dm
Margt.	3	F	Child	09Ja02Dm
Michl.	12	M	None	09Ja02Dm
Wm.	11	M	None	09Ja02Dm
Richd.	6	M	Child	09Ja02Dm
DWYER, John	20	M	Laborer	09Ja02Dm
MAGUIRE, John	25	M	Laborer	09Ja02Dm
MCCLARE, Patk.	16	M	Weaver	09Ja02Dm
HANNAN, Rosannah	24	F	Servant	09Ja02Dm
QUIN, Robert	12	M	None	09Ja02Dm
Edwd.	10	M	None	09Ja02Dm
HANNAN, John	20	M	Clerk	09Ja02Dm
BUCKLEY, Michl.	20	M	Laborer	09Ja02Dm
CAGNEY, Cathn.	22	F	None	09Ja02Dm
GREGAN, Thos.	10	M	None	09Ja02Dm
Math.	1	M	Child	09Ja02Dm
KELLY, Mary	57	F	Servant	09Ja02Dm
John	16	M	Servant	09Ja02Dm
Mary	18	F	Servant	09Ja02Dm
FOLEY, John	7	M	Child	09Ja02Dm
BRECKNICK, James	30	M	Carpenter	09Ja02Dm
Michl.	17	M	Laborer	09Ja02Dm
Patk.	20	M	Laborer	09Ja02Dm
MITCHELL, Mary	30	F	None	09Ja02Dm
Patk.	20	M	None	09Ja02Dm
Sarah	4	F	Child	09Ja02Dm
MURRAY, Cathn.	20	F	None	09Ja02Dm
John	10	M	None	09Ja02Dm
James	25	M	None	09Ja02Dm
Bridgt.	1	F	Child	09Ja02Dm
FOX, Cathn.	60	F	None	09Ja02Dm
Jas.	72	M	None	09Ja02Dm
Margt.	13	F	None	09Ja02Dm
Michl.	3	M	Child	09Ja02Dm
CARROLL, Patk.	25	M	Laborer	09Ja02Dm
FOX, Thos.	23	M	Laborer	09Ja02Dm
James	17	M	Laborer	09Ja02Dm
CONCANNON, Mary	18	F	None	09Ja02Dm
HOGAN, Michl.	21	F	None	09Ja02Dm
TOBIN, Bridgt.	20	F	None	09Ja02Dm
FOX, Cath.	21	F	None	09Ja02Dm
CONWAY, Winny	23	F	Servant	09Ja02Dm
MORAN, Andrew	28	M	Laborer	09Ja02Dm
Cathn.	26	F	None	09Ja02Dm
FARRELL, Christina	20	F	Servant	09Ja02Dm
FOX, Bridgt.	7	F	Child	09Ja02Dm
SEARY, Mary	29	F	None	09Ja02Dm
DALY, Timy.	21	M	Blacksmith	09Ja02Dm
COONEY, Michl.	32	M	Millwright	09Ja02Dm
OBRIEN, Mary	50	F	None	09Ja02Dm

NAMES OF PASSENGERS	AGE	SEX	OCCUPATIONS	DATE PORT SHIP
OBRIEN, Thos.	13	M	None	09Ja02Dm
John	10	M	None	09Ja02Dm
MADDEN, Thos.	7	M	Child	09Ja02Dm
Died-At-Sea				
CRAWFORD, John	50	M	None	09Ja02Dm
Cathn.	50	F	None	09Ja02Dm
Mary	11	F	None	09Ja02Dm
CORR, Eliza	18	F	Servant	09Ja02Dm
CONOLLY, Patt	20	M	None	09Ja02Dm
James	14	M	None	09Ja02Dm
Lawrence	10	M	None	09Ja02Dm
MURPHY, Anestice	64	F	None	09Ja02Dm
Died-At-Sea				
CAROLAN, Bridgt.	3	F	Child	09Ja02Dm
Died-At-Sea				
MULLAN, Betty	26	F	None	09Ja02Dm
Died-At-Sea				
MAGEE, James	27	M	None	09Ja02Dm
Died-At-Sea				
Kavanaugh-GREGAN, Mary	7	F	Child	09Ja02Dm
Died-At-Sea				
Mary	35	F	None	09Ja02Dm
Died-At-Sea				
COMAGHTON, Michl.	26	M	None	09Ja02Dm
Died-At-Sea				
MULLIGAN, Patt	26	M	None	09Ja02Dm
Died-At-Sea				
MADDEN, Mary	24	F	None	09Ja02Dm
Died-At-Sea				
James	25	M	None	09Ja02Dm
Died-At-Sea				

CONSTITUTION 09 JANUARY 1850

From Liverpool

NAMES OF PASSENGERS	AGE	SEX	OCCUPATIONS	DATE PORT SHIP
James	35	M	Laborer	09Ja02Dl
Johan	33	F	Unknown	09Ja02Dl
FORD, Ellen	25	F	Unknown	09Ja02Dl
IGOE, Julia	16	F	Unknown	09Ja02Dl
ABERNETHY, Eliza	16	F	Unknown	09Ja02Dl
HILTON, John	50	M	Frngmr	09Ja02Dl
Isaac	30	M	Frngmr	09Ja02Dl
POPE, Leonard	22	M	Laborer	09Ja02Dl
GRAY, John	22	M	Laborer	09Ja02Dl
DOOLD, Edmd.	30	M	Laborer	09Ja02Dl
WALSH, Mich	20	M	Laborer	09Ja02Dl
GORDEN, Cath.	30	F	Laborer	09Ja02Dl
FLAM, Thos.	17	M	Laborer	09Ja02Dl
CLEGG, Sam	21	M	Farmer	09Ja02Dl
Ann	21	F	Farmer	09Ja02Dl
PEPPER, Eliza	19	F	Servant	09Ja02Dl
Fia	14	F	Servant	09Ja02Dl
CARTER, Bessy	23	F	Servant	09Ja02Dl
VAUGHN, U-Mrs.	35	F	Shoemaker	09Ja02Dl
ALEIM, Mary	25	F	Shoemaker	09Ja02Dl
MAUGAN, Mary	18	F	Shoemaker	09Ja02Dl
HEATHERINGTON, Eliza	23	F	Shoemaker	09Ja02Dl
ARMSTRONG, John	21	M	Shoemaker	09Ja02Dl
Eliza	15	F	Shoemaker	09Ja02Dl
Henry	8	M	Child	09Ja02Dl
LYNCH, John	28	M	Laborer	09Ja02Dl
Ann	40	F	Laborer	09Ja02Dl
DALY, Pat	18	M	Smith	09Ja02Dl
FANELL, Mary	15	F	Servant	09Ja02Dl
DIVINE, Cecily	55	F	Servant	09Ja02Dl
Mary	2	F	Child	09Ja02Dl
Thos.	13	M	Servant	09Ja02Dl
Jno.	10	M	Servant	09Ja02Dl
DIVINE, Jas.	8	M	Child	09Ja02Dl
Wm.	5	M	Child	09Ja02Dl
Jas.	18	M	Servant	09Ja02Dl
ABSON, Jas.	27	M	Servant	09Ja02Dl
DALTON, Donck	27	M	Servant	09Ja02Dl
Mary	17	F	Servant	09Ja02Dl
CRIEGHTON, Mick	45	M	Servant	09Ja02Dl
ROWAN, Jas.	24	M	Gdnr	09Ja02Dl
WHITEHEAD, Jas.	43	M	Laborer	09Ja02Dl
MCGINNES, Jas.	16	M	Laborer	09Ja02Dl
Mary	14	F	Laborer	09Ja02Dl
ONIEL, Thos.	24	M	Laborer	09Ja02Dl
Hugh	21	M	Laborer	09Ja02Dl
Mary-A.	18	F	Laborer	09Ja02Dl
U-Mrs.	60	F	Laborer	09Ja02Dl
RONAN, Mick	40	M	Laborer	09Ja02Dl
MCDOWELL, Jas.	18	M	Laborer	09Ja02Dl
MCLAUGHLIN, Ann	16	F	Laborer	09Ja02Dl
Mary	15	F	Laborer	09Ja02Dl
MCKONE, Jno.	35	M	Laborer	09Ja02Dl
HARMAN, Jas.	53	M	Laborer	09Ja02Dl
Mary	30	F	Laborer	09Ja02Dl
CONNY, Margt.	55	F	Laborer	09Ja02Dl
Isaac	22	M	Laborer	09Ja02Dl
Margt.	20	F	Laborer	09Ja02Dl
SMITH, Mary-J.	20	F	Laborer	09Ja02Dl
Jno.	14	M	Laborer	09Ja02Dl
TONER, Bridget	25	F	Laborer	09Ja02Dl
COTTON, Rich	18	M	Laborer	09Ja02Dl
MCNAMARA, Jno.	27	M	Laborer	09Ja02Dl
MCCARTHY, Chas.	30	M	Laborer	09Ja02Dl
CURTIN, Mary	40	F	Laborer	09Ja02Dl
KIELEY, Johan	11	F	Laborer	09Ja02Dl
Mary	8	F	Child	09Ja02Dl
Michael	6	M	Child	09Ja02Dl
NUGENT, Thos.	20	M	Laborer	09Ja02Dl
Mick	9	M	Child	09Ja02Dl
Eliza	21	F	Laborer	09Ja02Dl
MAXWELL, Cath.	22	F	Laborer	09Ja02Dl
MORAN, Jane	45	F	Laborer	09Ja02Dl
Edwd.	45	M	Laborer	09Ja02Dl
LYNANE, Peter	45	M	Laborer	09Ja02Dl
Sam	20	M	Laborer	09Ja02Dl
Ony	13	M	Laborer	09Ja02Dl
CONNELL, Peter	12	M	Laborer	09Ja02Dl
QUINN, Pat	45	M	Laborer	09Ja02Dl
PHILLIPS, Jno.	15	M	Laborer	09Ja02Dl
QUIN, Henry	17	F	Laborer	09Ja02Dl
OCONNELL, Pat	12	M	Laborer	09Ja02Dl
POWER, John	28	M	Laborer	09Ja02Dl
SCOLLY, Ellen	12	F	Laborer	09Ja02Dl
DONNOVAN, Ellen	8	F	Child	09Ja02Dl
GRETTEN, Eliza	17	F	Laborer	09Ja02Dl
FONQUE, Fanny	24	F	Laborer	09Ja02Dl
Wm.	3	M	Child	09Ja02Dl
MURTAGH, Margt.	20	F	Laborer	09Ja02Dl
KEEFE, Ellen	30	F	Laborer	09Ja02Dl
FAGAN, Cath.	20	F	Laborer	09Ja02Dl
SPAIN, Thos.	28	M	Laborer	09Ja02Dl
SHANLEY, Pat	25	M	Laborer	09Ja02Dl
DONOHOE, Law.	20	M	Laborer	09Ja02Dl
CARROLL, Jane	21	F	Laborer	09Ja02Dl
HAREY, John	30	M	Laborer	09Ja02Dl
BONLAND, Jno.	40	M	Laborer	09Ja02Dl
Mary	12	F	Laborer	09Ja02Dl
MALONEY, Thos.	45	M	Laborer	09Ja02Dl
Telfira	11	F	Laborer	09Ja02Dl
Dora	8	F	Child	09Ja02Dl
Edmd.	6	M	Child	09Ja02Dl
TALCUTT, Thos.	31	M	Laborer	09Ja02Dl
WHITE, Thos.	21	M	Laborer	09Ja02Dl
Mary	23	F	Laborer	09Ja02Dl
Cath.	15	F	Laborer	09Ja02Dl
DOYLE, Etty	30	F	Laborer	09Ja02Dl
ROWE, Joshua	18	M	Laborer	09Ja02Dl

NAMES OF PASSENGERS	AGE	SEX	OCCUPATIONS	DATE PORT SHIP
DALTON, Law.	30	M	Laborer	09Ja02DI
LAWSON, Wm.	50	M	Laborer	09Ja02DI
CONLIN, Phil	21	M	Laborer	09Ja02DI
FINALLY, Kearn	32	M	Shopkeeper	09Ja02DI
Martin	8	M	Child	09Ja02DI
Ellen	33	F	Laborer	09Ja02DI
Nancy	30	F	Laborer	09Ja02DI
U-Mrs.	50	F	Laborer	09Ja02DI
Margt.	5	F	Child	09Ja02DI
BRENNAN, Pat	40	M	Laborer	09Ja02DI
WHALAN, Jno.	40	M	Laborer	09Ja02DI
DUFFY, Cath.	30	F	Laborer	09Ja02DI
Kearn	18	M	Laborer	09Ja02DI
Bud	10	M	Laborer	09Ja02DI
ROWKE, Mary	35	F	Laborer	09Ja02DI
Bud	9	M	Child	09Ja02DI
Bernd.	5	M	Child	09Ja02DI
DUFFY, Dan	21	M	Laborer	09Ja02DI
Bud	20	M	Laborer	09Ja02DI
ALMOND, David	23	M	Laborer	09Ja02DI
Betsey	21	F	Laborer	09Ja02DI
KELLY, Henry	22	M	Laborer	09Ja02DI
FARRELL, Jas.	40	M	Laborer	09Ja02DI
JACKSON, Jas.	24	M	Laborer	09Ja02DI
MCLAUGHLIN, Thos.	21	M	Laborer	09Ja02DI
Jas.	20	M	Laborer	09Ja02DI
LYONS, Peter	19	M	Laborer	09Ja02DI
DOWLING, Mary	26	F	Laborer	09Ja02DI
MATTHEWS, Bridget	50	F	Laborer	09Ja02DI
David	20	M	Laborer	09Ja02DI
Martin	15	M	Laborer	09Ja02DI
MURPHY, B.	20	M	Laborer	09Ja02DI
REILLY, Bridget	20	F	Laborer	09Ja02DI
FARRELL, Mary	30	F	Laborer	09Ja02DI
Cath.	22	F	Laborer	09Ja02DI
Rosan	6	F	Child	09Ja02DI
Matthew	9	M	Child	09Ja02DI
FREEMAN, Micky	40	M	Laborer	09Ja02DI
WHALAN, Ann	20	F	Laborer	09Ja02DI
MCGUIRE, Jno.	25	M	Laborer	09Ja02DI
LYNCH, Giles	47	M	Shoemaker	09Ja02DI
Jno.	45	M	Shoemaker	09Ja02DI
Wm.	26	M	Shoemaker	09Ja02DI
Mary	37	F	Shoemaker	09Ja02DI
APPLETON, Jas.	36	M	Laborer	09Ja02DI
HINTER, Pat	25	M	Laborer	09Ja02DI
COLMAN, Mick	24	M	Laborer	09Ja02DI
Ann	22	F	Laborer	09Ja02DI
LANVIN, Mat	25	M	Laborer	09Ja02DI
Wm.	00	M	Laborer	09Ja02DI
GRAY, Pat	18	M	Laborer	09Ja02DI
CLUFFREY, Micky	20	M	Laborer	09Ja02DI
Margt.	18	F	Laborer	09Ja02DI
MULLANY, Pat	22	M	Laborer	09Ja02DI
HINES, Bud	22	M	Laborer	09Ja02DI
MCDERMOTT, Mick	22	M	Laborer	09Ja02DI
Ellen	22	F	Laborer	09Ja02DI
HOWARD, Robt.	30	M	Laborer	09Ja02DI
U-Mrs.	32	F	Laborer	09Ja02DI
DUNN, Edmd.	60	M	Laborer	09Ja02DI
Jno.	25	M	Laborer	09Ja02DI
Edmund	22	M	Laborer	09Ja02DI
Pat	19	M	Laborer	09Ja02DI
MALONE, Jane	40	F	Laborer	09Ja02DI
MURPHY, Thos.	22	M	Laborer	09Ja02DI
DONOHOE, Cath.	30	F	Laborer	09Ja02DI
MCLAUGHLIN, Ann	18	F	Laborer	09Ja02DI
MURPHY, Wm.	32	M	Laborer	09Ja02DI
SHIRTALL, Jas.	25	M	Laborer	09Ja02DI
WHELAN, O.	30	M	Laborer	09Ja02DI
KILPATRICK, Jno.	40	M	Laborer	09Ja02DI
CUNY, Mary	16	F	Laborer	09Ja02DI
LONGHREY, Jno.	23	M	Laborer	09Ja02DI
Mary	20	F	Laborer	09Ja02DI
BRADLEY, Jas.	45	M	Laborer	09Ja02DI

NAMES OF PASSENGERS	AGE	SEX	OCCUPATIONS	DATE PORT SHIP
GRIER, Martha	20	F	Laborer	09Ja02DI
DANSEN, Jas.	48	M	Laborer	09Ja02DI
BONER, Edwd.	41	M	Laborer	09Ja02DI
SULLY, Mary	40	F	Laborer	09Ja02DI
HARKIN, Jno.	33	M	Laborer	09Ja02DI
MANNING, Jno.	45	M	Laborer	09Ja02DI
GARVEY, Andw.	15	M	Laborer	09Ja02DI
STOKES, Thos.	35	M	Laborer	09Ja02DI
Ann	30	F	Laborer	09Ja02DI
Mary-Anne	12	F	Laborer	09Ja02DI
Rose	8	F	Child	09Ja02DI
Margt.	6	F	Child	09Ja02DI
LEE, Mary	18	F	Laborer	09Ja02DI
MCGINNIS, Mary	21	F	Laborer	09Ja02DI
HOOD, Nat	24	M	Laborer	09Ja02DI
BREWER, Pat	22	M	Laborer	09Ja02DI
HARKIN, Nancy	20	F	Laborer	09Ja02DI
Bud	18	M	Laborer	09Ja02DI
BELL, Jno.	34	M	Laborer	09Ja02DI
MCCARTHY, Pat	38	M	Laborer	09Ja02DI
MCGINNES, Neal	25	M	Laborer	09Ja02DI
Robt.	18	M	Laborer	09Ja02DI
GILGAN, Jno.	30	M	Laborer	09Ja02DI
MITCHELL, Wm.	13	M	Laborer	09Ja02DI
Cath.	30	F	Laborer	09Ja02DI
DWYRE, Bess	34	F	Laborer	09Ja02DI
COLLOGHAN, Pat	30	M	Laborer	09Ja02DI
GRIFFITH, Edmund	32	M	Laborer	09Ja02DI
EGAN, Mick	30	M	Laborer	09Ja02DI
KEARNE, Wm.	21	M	Laborer	09Ja02DI
MCLAUGHLIN, Pat	35	M	Laborer	09Ja02DI
RILEY, Pat	20	M	Laborer	09Ja02DI
BURTON, Jno.	25	M	Laborer	09Ja02DI
Jas.	23	M	Laborer	09Ja02DI
Cath.	21	F	Laborer	09Ja02DI
DOWLASS, Cath.	23	F	Laborer	09Ja02DI
MCALLEN, Jno.	32	M	Laborer	09Ja02DI
BOYD, Cath.	20	F	Laborer	09Ja02DI
Mary	18	F	Laborer	09Ja02DI
Ellen	12	F	Laborer	09Ja02DI
MCHUGH, Cath.	15	F	Laborer	09Ja02DI
LEGRAVE, Rose	20	F	Laborer	09Ja02DI
AHEARN, Cath.	25	F	Farmer	09Ja02DI
Jno.	4	M	Child	09Ja02DI
M.	46	M	Farmer	09Ja02DI
SHOONAN, Marcus	28	M	Servant	09Ja02DI
HUTTON, Arch.	19	M	Unknown	09Ja02DI
Jno.	13	M	Unknown	09Ja02DI
FLANAGAN, Brid.	19	F	Unknown	09Ja02DI
DOOLING, Bird	18	M	Unknown	09Ja02DI
DEVANY, Mary	20	F	Unknown	09Ja02DI
MAHER, Jno.	30	M	Unknown	09Ja02DI
Mary	45	F	Unknown	09Ja02DI
Jas.	10	M	Unknown	09Ja02DI
Pat	8	M	Child	09Ja02DI
Bud	6	M	Child	09Ja02DI
BRODERICK, Mans	50	M	Unknown	09Ja02DI
Cath.	18	F	Unknown	09Ja02DI
KAIN, Bird	30	M	Unknown	09Ja02DI
Margt.	32	F	Unknown	09Ja02DI
PINDER, Jno.	40	M	Unknown	09Ja02DI
MULLEN, Mick	40	M	Unknown	09Ja02DI
Hannah	3	F	Child	09Ja02DI
PHALEN, Pat	22	M	Unknown	09Ja02DI
DRILLEN, Martin	25	M	Unknown	09Ja02DI
GIBBON, Jno.	32	M	Unknown	09Ja02DI
MCAVOY, Mary	18	F	Unknown	09Ja02DI
BAKER, Cond.	22	M	Unknown	09Ja02DI
LYNCH, Joe	20	M	Unknown	09Ja02DI
MCGRATH, Mary	20	F	Unknown	09Ja02DI
Ann	17	F	Unknown	09Ja02DI
MUAN, Cornelius	19	M	Unknown	09Ja02DI
THOMPSON, Jas.	24	M	Unknown	09Ja02DI
JACKSON, Jno.	30	M	Unknown	09Ja02DI
U-Mrs.	26	F	Unknown	09Ja02DI

SOUTHAMPTON 09 JANUARY 1850

From London

NAMES OF PASSENGERS	AGE	SEX	OCCUPATIONS	DATE PORT SHIP
STREATFIELD, Wm.G.	25	M	Gentleman	09Ja06Do
Laura	25	F	Lady	09Ja06Do
CLARK, Emma	14	F	Lady	09Ja06Do
Ann	9	F	Child	09Ja06Do
YOUNG, Allen	22	M	Gentleman	09Ja06Do
TALBOTT, Mary	69	F	Lady	09Ja06Do
Martha	37	F	Lady	09Ja06Do
George-F.	17	M	Agent	09Ja06Do
BRITTON, Manley	29	M	Grocer	09Ja06Do
SAMUELS, Rachel	10	F	None	09Ja06Do
Adelaide	8	F	Child	09Ja06Do
Juliett	5	F	Child	09Ja06Do
KERR, James	23	M	None	09Ja06Do
HUGHES, James	33	M	None	09Ja06Do
WRIGHT, Thos.	27	M	Laborer	09Ja06Do
GLINCH, John	21	M	Laborer	09Ja06Do
BARNETT, Mark	29	M	Clothier	09Ja06Do
Augustus	21	M	Clothier	09Ja06Do
BENNETT, Alice	.00	F	Infant	09Ja06Do
Sally	.00	F	Infant	09Ja06Do
COHEN, F.	29	M	Laborer	09Ja06Do
BUCKNALL, George	15	M	Laborer	09Ja06Do
HOOK, George	18	M	Laborer	09Ja06Do
HYAMS, James	45	M	Laborer	09Ja06Do
Sarah	39	F	Laborer	09Ja06Do
Rose	18	F	None	09Ja06Do
John	2	M	Child	09Ja06Do
Rosa	.00	F	Infant	09Ja06Do
BATTY, Ths.	19	M	Farmer	09Ja06Do
MOCKETT, Bill	40	M	Farmer	09Ja06Do
Mary	40	F	None	09Ja06Do
Richd.	11	M	None	09Ja06Do
John	9	M	Child	09Ja06Do
Eliza	3	F	Child	09Ja06Do
JEFFREY, John	14	M	Clerk	09Ja06Do
Johnson	19	M	Clerk	09Ja06Do
HOBBS, James	38	M	Clerk	09Ja06Do
Sarah	38	F	None	09Ja06Do
GROOM, Francis-L.	22	M	Unknown	09Ja06Do
Elizabeth	22	F	None	09Ja06Do
PRICE, Benj.	36	M	Laborer	09Ja06Do
SHEPHERD, Elizth.	32	F	None	09Ja06Do
Saml.	11	M	None	09Ja06Do
Mary	9	F	Child	09Ja06Do
Ths.	6	M	Child	09Ja06Do
George	3	M	Child	09Ja06Do
Ann	.00	F	Infant	09Ja06Do
TORPFORD, Wm.	32	M	Unknown	09Ja06Do

SHERIDAN 09 JANUARY 1850

From Liverpool

NAMES OF PASSENGERS	AGE	SEX	OCCUPATIONS	DATE PORT SHIP
MANNING, Fredrick	40	M	Unknown	09Ja02Dn
GOORSON, Henry	15	M	Unknown	09Ja02Dn
HILL, Wm.	30	M	Farmer	09Ja02Dn
Mary-Ann	21	F	Unknown	09Ja02Dn
WALSH, Cathne.	26	F	Servant	09Ja02Dn
WARD, Pat	50	M	Laborer	09Ja02Dn
WARD, Mary	50	F	Laborer	09Ja02Dn
Mary	18	F	Laborer	09Ja02Dn
John	26	M	Unknown	09Ja02Dn
MCBRIDE, John	24	M	Laborer	09Ja02Dn
SHUKEY, Michl.	22	M	Laborer	09Ja02Dn
FARLEY, Ann	18	F	Laborer	09Ja02Dn
MCCABE, Margt.	10	F	Laborer	09Ja02Dn
KEELAN, Cathn.	18	F	Laborer	09Ja02Dn
CAHILL, Michl.	22	M	Laborer	09Ja02Dn
DAILEY, Philip	22	M	Laborer	09Ja02Dn
MURPHY, John	30	M	Laborer	09Ja02Dn
Cath.	24	F	Unknown	09Ja02Dn
John	.00	M	Infant	09Ja02Dn
WELSH, Alexr.	15	M	Laborer	09Ja02Dn
BOWEN, Eliza	16	F	Laborer	09Ja02Dn
LAWLER, Margt.	18	F	Servant	09Ja02Dn
BARRY, Celia	13	F	Servant	09Ja02Dn
KELLY, Michl.	26	M	Laborer	09Ja02Dn
U-Mrs.	20	F	Laborer	09Ja02Dn
MARTIN, John	45	M	Laborer	09Ja02Dn
Ann	20	F	Laborer	09Ja02Dn
Maria	16	F	Laborer	09Ja02Dn
SMITH, Mary	22	F	Servant	09Ja02Dn
BROWN, Mary	20	F	Servant	09Ja02Dn
MCCABE, Thos.	45	M	Laborer	09Ja02Dn
FITZPATRICK, Joseph	19	M	Laborer	09Ja02Dn
SHIELDS, Thos.	19	M	Laborer	09Ja02Dn
GORDON, Wm.	14	M	Laborer	09Ja02Dn
Michl.	12	M	Laborer	09Ja02Dn
MANGAN, Biddy	30	F	Laborer	09Ja02Dn
Mary	.00	F	Infant	09Ja02Dn
MCSHERRY, Michl.	24	M	Laborer	09Ja02Dn
MILLER, Jas.	27	M	Laborer	09Ja02Dn
Wm.	28	M	Laborer	09Ja02Dn
Agnes	31	F	Laborer	09Ja02Dn
Mary	28	F	Laborer	09Ja02Dn
Mary	17	F	Laborer	09Ja02Dn
Christ.	.00	M	Infant	09Ja02Dn
GILSEMAN, Jas.	18	M	Laborer	09Ja02Dn
SHORT, Mary	20	F	Servant	09Ja02Dn
Biddy	22	F	Servant	09Ja02Dn
MURPHY, Elestia	18	F	Servant	09Ja02Dn
MONTAGH, Honor	35	F	Servant	09Ja02Dn
BURNE, Pat	40	M	Servant	09Ja02Dn
Patt	20	M	Servant	09Ja02Dn
HEARNY, Michl.	20	M	Servant	09Ja02Dn
CONLAN, Pat	20	M	Servant	09Ja02Dn
Rose	20	F	Servant	09Ja02Dn
Mary	18	F	Servant	09Ja02Dn
CROSS, Thos.	30	M	Servant	09Ja02Dn
Wm.	32	M	Servant	09Ja02Dn
Mary	32	F	Servant	09Ja02Dn
Wm.	7	M	Child	09Ja02Dn
CREELY, David	19	M	Laborer	09Ja02Dn
FILLINGHAM, Isaac	24	M	Joiner	09Ja02Dn
DONOHOE, Bridt.	24	F	Servant	09Ja02Dn
Bridt.	18	F	Servant	09Ja02Dn
CONOLLY, Francis	50	M	Joiner	09Ja02Dn
Ann	50	F	Unknown	09Ja02Dn
Mary	20	F	Unknown	09Ja02Dn
Patk.	16	M	Joiner	09Ja02Dn
Terence	13	M	Joiner	09Ja02Dn
HUGHES, Cathn.	16	F	Servant	09Ja02Dn
PLUNKETT, Jas.	20	M	Laborer	09Ja02Dn
CONNOLLY, Owen	44	M	Laborer	09Ja02Dn
WALSH, Mary	35	F	Servant	09Ja02Dn
Bridt.	12	F	Unknown	09Ja02Dn
Ann	7	F	Child	09Ja02Dn
Margt.	.00	F	Infant	09Ja02Dn
MCGREGAN, John	40	M	Laborer	09Ja02Dn
Mary	34	F	Laborer	09Ja02Dn
Patt	12	M	Laborer	09Ja02Dn
Mary	9	F	Child	09Ja02Dn
Elva	7	F	Child	09Ja02Dn
Ellen	.00	F	Infant	09Ja02Dn

NAMES OF PASSENGERS	AGE	SEX	OCCUPATIONS	DATE PORT SHIP
HUGHES, Peter	30	M	Joiner	09Ja02Dn
KENAN, Terry	27	M	Blacksmith	09Ja02Dn
HUGHES, John	25	M	Farmer	09Ja02Dn
DRESDEN, Clements	26	F	Housewife	09Ja02Dn
DOGHERTY, Mary	40	F	Unknown	09Ja02Dn
Ellen	13	F	Unknown	09Ja02Dn
Isabella	12	F	Unknown	09Ja02Dn
Hugh	10	M	Unknown	09Ja02Dn
Thos.	6	M	Child	09Ja02Dn
Eliza	2	F	Child	09Ja02Dn
GOFFNEY, Thos.	40	M	Laborer	09Ja02Dn
TULTY, Peter	45	M	Laborer	09Ja02Dn
Johanna	40	F	Unknown	09Ja02Dn
Michl.	20	M	Unknown	09Ja02Dn
Hugh	13	M	Unknown	09Ja02Dn
Mary	9	F	Child	09Ja02Dn
ONEILL, Patt	40	M	Laborer	09Ja02Dn
STACK, Jas.	20	M	Laborer	09Ja02Dn
TULTY, Mary	20	F	Housekeeper	09Ja02Dn
Mary	6	F	Child	09Ja02Dn
Margt.	25	F	Unknown	09Ja02Dn
Johanna	.00	F	Infant	09Ja02Dn
GRANT, Peter	16	M	Farmer	09Ja02Dn
LOGAN, Alice	16	F	Servant	09Ja02Dn
LANGAN, Pat	23	M	Laborer	09Ja02Dn
CAHILL, John	55	M	Gdnr	09Ja02Dn
LYNCH, Cathn.	12	F	Servant	09Ja02Dn
JONES, Jas.	25	M	Tailor	09Ja02Dn
GLANCY, Cathn.	25	F	Unknown	09Ja02Dn
Margt.	24	F	Unknown	09Ja02Dn
BRIEN, Jane	39	F	Housekeeper	09Ja02Dn
Eliza	.00	F	Infant	09Ja02Dn
John	11	M	Unknown	09Ja02Dn
Ann-Jane	9	F	Child	09Ja02Dn
Mary	7	F	Child	09Ja02Dn
Matt	5	M	Child	09Ja02Dn
Robert	3	M	Child	09Ja02Dn
BRADY, Cathr.	20	F	Servant	09Ja02Dn
OBRIEN, Biddy	18	F	Laborer	09Ja02Dn
Thos.	16	M	Laborer	09Ja02Dn
REILLY, Cathr.	20	F	Servant	09Ja02Dn
TEDDY, Mary	7	F	Child	09Ja02Dn
DUFFY, John	13	M	Unknown	09Ja02Dn
REILLY, Sally	20	F	Unknown	09Ja02Dn
WALDRON, Ann	20	F	Servant	09Ja02Dn
COYLE, Ellen	30	F	Servant	09Ja02Dn
CONROY, Peter	25	M	Grocer	09Ja02Dn
CURREN, Mary	28	F	Servant	09Ja02Dn
Meddy	3	F	Child	09Ja02Dn
Norry	.00	F	Infant	09Ja02Dn
HERBERT, Pat	30	M	Clerk	09Ja02Dn
Died-At-Sea				
SHEA, Danl.	23	M	Laborer	09Ja02Dn
CUNNINGHAM, Judy	30	F	Housewife	09Ja02Dn
Thos.	6	M	Child	09Ja02Dn
HERBERT, John	20	M	Shoemaker	09Ja02Dn
COLLINS, Bridgt.	21	F	Servant	09Ja02Dn
Michl.	18	M	Unknown	09Ja02Dn
FRANLEY, Morgan	22	M	Unknown	09Ja02Dn
KELLY, Mary	13	F	Unknown	09Ja02Dn
FOX, Mary	18	F	Unknown	09Ja02Dn
SULLIVAN, Paul	40	M	Farmer	09Ja02Dn
Maria	36	F	Unknown	09Ja02Dn
Thos.	10	M	Unknown	09Ja02Dn
Bridt.	8	F	Child	09Ja02Dn
Michl.	6	M	Child	09Ja02Dn
Ann	3	F	Child	09Ja02Dn
ATKINS, Bridt.	30	F	Unknown	09Ja02Dn
BROWN, Thos.	16	M	Laborer	09Ja02Dn
Philip	13	M	Unknown	09Ja02Dn
Ann	10	F	Unknown	09Ja02Dn
Patk.	5	M	Child	09Ja02Dn
FINN, John	21	M	Unknown	09Ja02Dn
CLARK, Cathn.	16	F	Servant	09Ja02Dn
CARROLL, Patt	18	M	Laborer	09Ja02Dn
PHELAN, Cathn.	22	F	Unknown	09Ja02Dn
JACKSON, Wm.	24	M	Unknown	09Ja02Dn
Wm.	15	M	Unknown	09Ja02Dn
LOURY, Jas.	12	M	Unknown	09Ja02Dn
CARNEY, Ann	22	F	Unknown	09Ja02Dn
DIGNAN, Rose	17	F	Unknown	09Ja02Dn
FALKEN, Ellen	6	F	Child	09Ja02Dn
MCCANN, Ann	26	F	Servant	09Ja02Dn
MCGUNGHORY, Jas.	28	M	Laborer	09Ja02Dn
Mary	8	F	Child	09Ja02Dn
John	6	M	Child	09Ja02Dn
MCCANN, Jas.	38	M	Laborer	09Ja02Dn
Died-At-Sea				
EGAN, Jas.	42	M	Laborer	09Ja02Dn
WALSH, Eliza	20	F	Unknown	09Ja02Dn
LACEY, Mary	10	F	Servant	09Ja02Dn
Edwd.	8	M	Child	09Ja02Dn
MCCARTY, John	22	M	Laborer	09Ja02Dn
CAREY, Geo.	23	M	Joiner	09Ja02Dn
MULLEN, Patt	26	M	Laborer	09Ja02Dn
Ann	20	F	Unknown	09Ja02Dn
REILLY, Bridgt.	25	F	Unknown	09Ja02Dn
BACON, Thos.	38	F	Unknown	09Ja02Dn
CAHILL, Laurence	27	M	Servant	09Ja02Dn
MULGAN, Thos.	20	M	Laborer	09Ja02Dn
Jane	19	F	Unknown	09Ja02Dn
HOGAN, Hugh	20	F	Unknown	09Ja02Dn
HARDY, Thos.	30	M	Laborer	09Ja02Dn
WOLF, Charles	27	M	Tailor	09Ja02Dn
Elizth.	25	F	Unknown	09Ja02Dn
Thos.	5	M	Child	09Ja02Dn
PALMER, John	21	M	Chemist	09Ja02Dn
KERR, Geo.	43	M	Farmer	09Ja02Dn
Ann	40	F	Unknown	09Ja02Dn
DICKINSON, Wm.	25	M	Laborer	09Ja02Dn
KERR, Richd.	19	M	Farmer	09Ja02Dn
Thos.	14	M	Farmer	09Ja02Dn
Bella	16	F	Unknown	09Ja02Dn
Wm.	14	M	Unknown	09Ja02Dn
CAMPBELL, John	40	M	Unknown	09Ja02Dn
STEVENSON, Thos.	20	M	Laborer	09Ja02Dn
KIRK, U-Mrs.	50	F	Unknown	09Ja02Dn
MCBENNETT, Bernard	12	M	Laborer	09Ja02Dn
TINN, John	24	M	Carpenter	09Ja02Dn
Ann	19	F	Unknown	09Ja02Dn
HORAN, Wm.	18	M	Laborer	09Ja02Dn
CORBITT, Richd.	19	M	Painter	09Ja02Dn
FOX, Mary	16	F	Servant	09Ja02Dn
Bridgt.	13	F	Unknown	09Ja02Dn
Mary	12	F	Unknown	09Ja02Dn
MULLIGAN, Cathn.	28	F	Unknown	09Ja02Dn
Patk.	30	M	Laborer	09Ja02Dn
Jas.	11	M	Laborer	09Ja02Dn
Bridt.	9	F	Child	09Ja02Dn
Michl.	7	M	Child	09Ja02Dn
Bernard	5	M	Child	09Ja02Dn
BOYLAN, Bryan	38	M	Laborer	09Ja02Dn
Mary	38	F	Unknown	09Ja02Dn
REILLY, Francis	24	M	Butcher	09Ja02Dn
STUCK, Cathn.	27	F	Servant	09Ja02Dn
MORAN, Cathn.	20	F	Servant	09Ja02Dn
MADDEN, Jeremiah	7	M	Child	09Ja02Dn
DUFFEY, John	27	M	Unknown	09Ja02Dn
KILLMAN, John	19	M	Servant	09Ja02Dn
TRAINER, Cathr.	21	F	Servant	09Ja02Dn
MCMULLEN, Pat	21	M	Laborer	09Ja02Dn
HENDERSON, Geo.	24	M	Farmer	09Ja02Dn
Malina	20	F	Farmer	09Ja02Dn
Martha	18	F	Farmer	09Ja02Dn
Robert	13	M	Farmer	09Ja02Dn
Wm.	12	M	Farmer	09Ja02Dn
OBRIEN, Jas.	19	M	Laborer	09Ja02Dn
MARA, Wm.	26	M	Laborer	09Ja02Dn
Cathn.	20	F	Servant	09Ja02Dn

NAMES OF PASSENGERS	AGE	SEX	OCCUPATIONS	DATE PORT SHIP
Margt.	1	F	Child	09Ja02Dn
Died-At-Sea				
REARDEN, David	20	M	Laborer	09Ja02Dn
FITZPATRICK, Cathn.	21	F	Servant	09Ja02Dn
HALPIN, Thos.	13	M	Laborer	09Ja02Dn
Ann	11	F	Laborer	09Ja02Dn
Michl.	5	M	Child	09Ja02Dn
John	2	M	Child	09Ja02Dn
Mary	6	F	Child	09Ja02Dn
HAND, Michl.	50	M	Laborer	09Ja02Dn
Mary	36	F	Laborer	09Ja02Dn
Peter	20	M	Laborer	09Ja02Dn
Mary	14	F	Laborer	09Ja02Dn
Jane	11	F	Laborer	09Ja02Dn
Bridgt.	9	F	Child	09Ja02Dn
Phill.	7	M	Child	09Ja02Dn
Margt.	5	M	Child	09Ja02Dn
COWLAN, Jas.	22	M	Laborer	09Ja02Dn
Bernard	18	M	Laborer	09Ja02Dn
Bessey	16	M	Laborer	09Ja02Dn
COLEMAN, Barney	23	M	Laborer	09Ja02Dn
FARRY, Sarah	26	F	Servant	09Ja02Dn
QUINN, Bridgt.	25	F	Housewife	09Ja02Dn
Bridgt.	2	F	Child	09Ja02Dn
Nicholas	.00	M	Infant	09Ja02Dn
Died-At-Sea				
BROPHY, Thos.	40	M	Farmer	09Ja02Dn
Margt.	35	F	Farmer	09Ja02Dn
Patt	7	M	Child	09Ja02Dn
John	5	M	Child	09Ja02Dn
Patt	3	M	Child	09Ja02Dn
MCGLINN, Patt	25	M	Laborer	09Ja02Dn
Cathn.	18	F	Laborer	09Ja02Dn
Bridgt.	.00	F	Infant	09Ja02Dn
DOLAN, John	50	M	Laborer	09Ja02Dn
Bridgt.	40	F	Laborer	09Ja02Dn
MCGLINN, Bridgt.	20	F	Servant	09Ja02Dn
LYONS, Thos.	25	M	Servant	09Ja02Dn
Bridgt.	26	F	Servant	09Ja02Dn
John	.00	M	Infant	09Ja02Dn
GRIFFITHS, Wm.	22	M	Unknown	09Ja02Dn
FOX, Jas.	30	M	Hatter	09Ja02Dn
MCEVROY, Anthony	18	M	Hatter	09Ja02Dn
PHELAN, Pat	23	M	Cooper	09Ja02Dn
WILSON, John	26	M	Gdnr	09Ja02Dn
LAWRENCE, Henry	22	M	Coachman	09Ja02Dn
CAMPION, John	23	M	Laborer	09Ja02Dn
SKAHAN, Michl.	23	M	Laborer	09Ja02Dn
Margt.	22	F	Laborer	09Ja02Dn
MCDONNALD, Margt.	50	F	Housewife	09Ja02Dn
Margt.	25	F	Housewife	09Ja02Dn
MCCUE, Jas.	20	M	Unknown	09Ja02Dn
ARMSTRONG, Andrew	30	M	Laborer	09Ja02Dn
LOGAN, Jas.	23	M	Laborer	09Ja02Dn
THOMPSON, Richd.	30	M	Farmer	09Ja02Dn
Fanny	30	F	Farmer	09Ja02Dn
MCKEOWN, Margt.	28	F	Servant	09Ja02Dn
THOMPSON, Richd.	10	M	Farmer	09Ja02Dn
Wm.	8	M	Child	09Ja02Dn
John	.00	M	Infant	09Ja02Dn
CLARKE, John	30	M	Laborer	09Ja02Dn
Jas.	32	M	Laborer	09Ja02Dn
Eliza-Jane	30	F	Laborer	09Ja02Dn
Wm.John	.00	M	Infant	09Ja02Dn
BOYD, David	21	M	Laborer	09Ja02Dn
DYNES, Richd.	20	M	Laborer	09Ja02Dn
DONAGHY, Patt	24	M	Laborer	09Ja02Dn
HANLIN, John	26	M	Laborer	09Ja02Dn
MAGUIRE, Ann	25	F	Laborer	09Ja02Dn
James	.00	M	Infant	09Ja02Dn
HYNAN, John	20	M	Laborer	09Ja02Dn
JONES, Kitty	23	F	Housewife	09Ja02Dn
Mary	20	F	Housewife	09Ja02Dn
Roger	10	M	Unknown	09Ja02Dn
Patt	8	M	Child	09Ja02Dn
RYAN, Judy	25	F	Servant	09Ja02Dn
LAHY, Mary	30	F	Unknown	09Ja02Dn
Michl.	11	M	Unknown	09Ja02Dn
Bridgt.	10	F	Unknown	09Ja02Dn
DWYER, John	40	M	Laborer	09Ja02Dn
Mary	30	F	Laborer	09Ja02Dn
MULCAHY, Patt	28	M	Laborer	09Ja02Dn
Johanna	26	F	Laborer	09Ja02Dn
RIELEY, Bessy	20	F	Laborer	09Ja02Dn
COOK, Margt.	16	F	Servant	09Ja02Dn
ELLIOTT, U-Miss	20	F	Unknown	09Ja02Dn
ROCHE, Jas.	40	M	Farmer	09Ja02Dn
HOGAN, Maurice	40	M	Farmer	09Ja02Dn
BROSMAN, Corns.	24	M	Farmer	09Ja02Dn
MAHONY, John	27	M	Laborer	09Ja02Dn
Johanna	22	F	Laborer	09Ja02Dn
Dennis	3	M	Child	09Ja02Dn
COGLAN, Michl.	27	M	Unknown	09Ja02Dn
Margt.	21	F	Unknown	09Ja02Dn
GALLAVAN, Humphrey	40	M	Laborer	09Ja02Dn
Eliza	30	F	Unknown	09Ja02Dn
REDDY, Morris	24	M	Laborer	09Ja02Dn
WALSH, John	35	M	Laborer	09Ja02Dn
HIGGINS, Morris	35	M	Laborer	09Ja02Dn
LENANE, Julia	16	F	Servant	09Ja02Dn
Bridt.	14	F	Servant	09Ja02Dn
DALY, Mary	30	F	Servant	09Ja02Dn
Nelly	25	F	Servant	09Ja02Dn
NEILL, Ellen	23	F	Servant	09Ja02Dn
SPILMAN, Kitty	20	F	Servant	09Ja02Dn
HICKEY, Biddy	25	F	Servant	09Ja02Dn
CULLINANE, Dennis	13	M	Unknown	09Ja02Dn
John	12	M	Unknown	09Ja02Dn
BREENE, David	9	M	Child	09Ja02Dn
Timmy	6	M	Child	09Ja02Dn
Mary	6	F	Child	09Ja02Dn
SPILLMAN, Mary	25	F	Unknown	09Ja02Dn
MATHEWS, Edwd.	25	M	Nail Maker	09Ja02Dn
John	19	M	Unknown	09Ja02Dn
CLARKE, Ann	19	F	Unknown	09Ja02Dn
LYNCH, Bridt.	30	F	Unknown	09Ja02Dn
Judy	22	F	Unknown	09Ja02Dn
Archd.	.00	M	Infant	09Ja02Dn
SULLIVAN, Mary	30	F	Unknown	09Ja02Dn
Jas.	8	M	Child	09Ja02Dn
John	6	M	Child	09Ja02Dn
Tur---, Emma	28	F	Farmer	09Ja02Dn
Harriet	20	F	Farmer	09Ja02Dn
PALMER, Isaac	30	M	Farmer	09Ja02Dn
Elizth.	32	F	Farmer	09Ja02Dn
HELPIN, Thos.	40	M	Farmer	09Ja02Dn
RINGLEY, Richd.	34	M	Shoemaker	09Ja02Dn
HALPIN, Jane	30	F	Unknown	09Ja02Dn
Elizth.	.00	F	Infant	09Ja02Dn
KIRK, Joel	40	M	Farmer	09Ja02Dn
Henry	34	M	Farmer	09Ja02Dn
MORRIS, John	00	M	Farmer	09Ja02Dn
MCDERMOTT, Pat	22	M	Farmer	09Ja02Dn
GRAY, Bernard	3	M	Child	09Ja02Dn
RUSSELL, Charles	20	M	Unknown	09Ja02Dn
GOODWIN, Margt.	20	F	Unknown	09Ja02Dn
Died-At-Sea				
Cathr.	00	F	Unknown	09Ja02Dn
QUINN, John	20	M	Tailor	09Ja02Dn
POWER, Edwd.	21	M	Laborer	09Ja02Dn
HOGAN, John	23	M	Laborer	09Ja02Dn
BESSEY, John	26	M	Laborer	09Ja02Dn

JOHN-R.SKIDDY 09 JANUARY 1850

From Liverpool

NAMES OF PASSENGERS	AGE	SEX	OCCUPATIONS	DATE PORT SHIP
MCKEON, Margt.	24	F	Unknown	09Ja02Dp
BOYLE, Mary	17	F	Unknown	09Ja02Dp
Mary	22	F	Unknown	09Ja02Dp
REILLY, Mary	17	F	Unknown	09Ja02Dp
COSTELLO, Alicia	29	F	Unknown	09Ja02Dp
Margt.	25	F	Unknown	09Ja02Dp
MCCANN, Margt.	20	F	Unknown	09Ja02Dp
WHELAN, Julia	28	F	Unknown	09Ja02Dp
MONK, Fanny	20	F	Unknown	09Ja02Dp
RYAN, John	40	M	Farmer	09Ja02Dp
MARTIN, Cathne.	35	F	Unknown	09Ja02Dp
KELLY, Ellen	21	F	Unknown	09Ja02Dp
Died-At-Sea				
MARTIN, John	12	M	Unknown	09Ja02Dp
Bridget	10	F	Unknown	09Ja02Dp
Thos.	8	M	Child	09Ja02Dp
James	4	M	Child	09Ja02Dp
Wm.	4	M	Child	09Ja02Dp
Henry	1	M	Child	09Ja02Dp
GLEESON, Judith	25	F	Unknown	09Ja02Dp
MOONEY, Cathne.	8	F	Child	09Ja02Dp
John	5	M	Child	09Ja02Dp
HAYWARD, Rose	39	F	Unknown	09Ja02Dp
Elizh.	26	F	Unknown	09Ja02Dp
Edwd.	11	M	Unknown	09Ja02Dp
Wm.	6	M	Child	09Ja02Dp
Arthur	4	M	Child	09Ja02Dp
STURY, Christ.H.	34	M	Unknown	09Ja02Dp
Mary-J.	14	F	Unknown	09Ja02Dp
TOMMANEY, Edwr.	35	M	Unknown	09Ja02Dp
Mary	40	F	Unknown	09Ja02Dp
CCX, Mary	40	F	Unknown	09Ja02Dp
John	14	M	Unknown	09Ja02Dp
Cathne.	14	F	Unknown	09Ja02Dp
Ellen	12	F	Unknown	09Ja02Dp
Michl.	9	M	Child	09Ja02Dp
COOLAHAN, Mary	30	F	Unknown	09Ja02Dp
MAGIN, Patk.	29	M	Unknown	09Ja02Dp
Margt.	29	F	Unknown	09Ja02Dp
LENEHAN, James	50	M	Unknown	09Ja02Dp
LENAHAN, Elizh.	50	F	Unknown	09Ja02Dp
Matilda	24	F	Unknown	09Ja02Dp
James	1	M	Child	09Ja02Dp
MULRENNY, James	50	M	Unknown	09Ja02Dp
Betty	45	F	Unknown	09Ja02Dp
Bridget	20	F	Unknown	09Ja02Dp
Anty	15	F	Unknown	09Ja02Dp
John	20	M	Laborer	09Ja02Dp
Judith	1	F	Child	09Ja02Dp
SHAW, Michl.	22	M	Unknown	09Ja02Dp
LYNCH, John	26	M	Unknown	09Ja02Dp
MCCANN, John	21	M	Unknown	09Ja02Dp
HARNEY, Bridget	18	F	Unknown	09Ja02Dp
FLATTERY, Winniford	16	F	Unknown	09Ja02Dp
BOYS, Anne	20	F	Unknown	09Ja02Dp
Elizh.	25	F	Unknown	09Ja02Dp
SMITH, Anne	16	F	Unknown	09Ja02Dp
FINLAY, Mary	50	F	Unknown	09Ja02Dp
RYAN, Mary	35	F	Unknown	09Ja02Dp
NORTON, Denis	26	M	Unknown	09Ja02Dp
CARDEN, John	20	M	Unknown	09Ja02Dp
ARMSTRONG, William	15	M	Unknown	09Ja02Dp
Mary-A.	19	F	Unknown	09Ja02Dp
Isabella	17	F	Unknown	09Ja02Dp
LYON, Michl.	20	M	Unknown	09Ja02Dp
HARRINGTON, Mary	21	F	Unknown	09Ja02Dp
MOONEY, Berd.	20	M	Unknown	09Ja02Dp
Mary	16	F	Unknown	09Ja02Dp
AIRLEY, John	20	M	Unknown	09Ja02Dp
MULLIGAN, Cathne.	16	F	Unknown	09Ja02Dp
DONNELLY, Edwd.	20	M	Unknown	09Ja02Dp
HARVEY, James	20	M	Unknown	09Ja02Dp
NEAL, Kyran	50	M	Unknown	09Ja02Dp
Margt.	20	F	Unknown	09Ja02Dp
Anty	17	F	Unknown	09Ja02Dp
Pat	11	M	Unknown	09Ja02Dp
Pierce	22	M	Unknown	09Ja02Dp
NOLAN, John	18	M	Unknown	09Ja02Dp
KEEFE, Judith	22	F	Unknown	09Ja02Dp
ROSS, James	22	M	Unknown	09Ja02Dp
FARRELL, John	28	M	Unknown	09Ja02Dp
Pat	12	M	Unknown	09Ja02Dp
ROONEY, Margt.	18	F	Unknown	09Ja02Dp
KEAN, Martha	13	F	Unknown	09Ja02Dp
John	11	M	Unknown	09Ja02Dp
Michael	9	M	Child	09Ja02Dp
James	7	M	Child	09Ja02Dp
Edwd.	5	M	Child	09Ja02Dp
Cathne.	3	F	Child	09Ja02Dp
Anne	2	F	Child	09Ja02Dp
FLYNN, Bridget	21	F	Unknown	09Ja02Dp
ONEIL, Mary	20	F	Unknown	09Ja02Dp
RYAN, Margt.	25	F	Unknown	09Ja02Dp
Peter	15	M	Unknown	09Ja02Dp
Laurence	14	M	Unknown	09Ja02Dp
DUFFY, Anne	21	F	Unknown	09Ja02Dp
GREEN, Mary	21	F	Unknown	09Ja02Dp
DOLAN, John	14	M	Laborer	09Ja02Dp
Honor	12	F	Unknown	09Ja02Dp
HEFFERNAN, Betty	16	F	Unknown	09Ja02Dp
DOLAN, Pat	20	M	Unknown	09Ja02Dp
Margt.	6	F	Child	09Ja02Dp
GORE, Judith	30	F	Unknown	09Ja02Dp
MITCHELL, Thom.	30	M	Unknown	09Ja02Dp
Jane	30	F	Unknown	09Ja02Dp
Maria	17	F	Unknown	09Ja02Dp
James	10	M	Unknown	09Ja02Dp
George	1	M	Child	09Ja02Dp
HAWKS, Garret	20	M	Unknown	09Ja02Dp
Cathne.	19	F	Unknown	09Ja02Dp
WYNNE, Anne	15	F	Unknown	09Ja02Dp
SMITH, Anne	14	F	Unknown	09Ja02Dp
MURPHY, James	26	M	Unknown	09Ja02Dp
BURKE, John	30	M	Unknown	09Ja02Dp
Bridget	26	F	Unknown	09Ja02Dp
SHEERY, James	30	M	Unknown	09Ja02Dp
WALSH, Honora	20	F	Unknown	09Ja02Dp
BARNETT, Cathne.	18	F	Unknown	09Ja02Dp
FITZSIMMONS, Thom.	21	M	Unknown	09Ja02Dp
Cathne.	28	F	Unknown	09Ja02Dp
FANNON, Moran	24	M	Unknown	09Ja02Dp
POWER, James	15	M	Unknown	09Ja02Dp
MAHONEY, John	19	M	Unknown	09Ja02Dp
WALSH, Ellen	27	F	Unknown	09Ja02Dp
LENNARD, Julia	34	F	Unknown	09Ja02Dp
KILTY, James	24	M	Unknown	09Ja02Dp
LENAHAN, John	12	M	Unknown	09Ja02Dp
James	10	M	Unknown	09Ja02Dp
Tim	7	M	Child	09Ja02Dp
Cathne.	17	F	Unknown	09Ja02Dp
Mary-A.	2	F	Child	09Ja02Dp
MOONEY, Pat	28	M	Unknown	09Ja02Dp
William	3	M	Child	09Ja02Dp
MOTLEY, Mary	11	F	Unknown	09Ja02Dp
CORBETT, William	26	M	Unknown	09Ja02Dp
CUDDY, Michl.	19	M	Unknown	09Ja02Dp
SMITH, John	50	M	Unknown	09Ja02Dp
James	9	M	Child	09Ja02Dp
Pat	7	M	Child	09Ja02Dp
REIRDON, Honora	25	F	Unknown	09Ja02Dp

NAMES OF PASSENGERS	AGE	SEX	OCCUPATIONS	DATE PORT SHIP
REIRDON, Honora	60	F	Unknown	09Ja02Dp
Pat	3	M	Child	09Ja02Dp
COSTELLO, Wm.	35	M	Unknown	09Ja02Dp
Mary	30	F	Unknown	09Ja02Dp
Pat	7	M	Child	09Ja02Dp
Tim	5	M	Child	09Ja02Dp
Anne	3	F	Child	09Ja02Dp
Wm.	1	M	Child	09Ja02Dp
WALSH, Peter	35	M	Unknown	09Ja02Dp
Anty	25	F	Unknown	09Ja02Dp
Alice	7	F	Child	09Ja02Dp
Died-At-Sea				
Anty	6	F	Child	09Ja02Dp
Peggy	4	F	Child	09Ja02Dp
John	2	M	Child	09Ja02Dp
PHILIPS, Mathew	44	M	Unknown	09Ja02Dp
Rose	34	F	Unknown	09Ja02Dp
Michael	4	M	Child	09Ja02Dp
MURPHY, John	30	M	Unknown	09Ja02Dp
FLYNN, Thom.	19	M	Unknown	09Ja02Dp
BRENNAN, Michl.	30	M	Unknown	09Ja02Dp
DOLAN, Mary	30	F	Unknown	09Ja02Dp
MOORE, Margt.	30	F	Unknown	09Ja02Dp
PURCELL, Thom.	16	M	Unknown	09Ja02Dp
BRENNAN, Wm.	7	M	Child	09Ja02Dp
PURCELL, James	9	M	Child	09Ja02Dp
Michl.	16	M	Unknown	09Ja02Dp
WALSH, Richd.	60	M	Unknown	09Ja02Dp
Mary	54	F	Unknown	09Ja02Dp
Honora	20	F	Unknown	09Ja02Dp
Richd.	15	M	Unknown	09Ja02Dp
Johanna	13	F	Unknown	09Ja02Dp
John	12	M	Unknown	09Ja02Dp
Mary	20	F	Unknown	09Ja02Dp
CRONAN, Jerry	22	M	Unknown	09Ja02Dp
KEEFE, Fanny	50	F	Unknown	09Ja02Dp
Pat	13	M	Unknown	09Ja02Dp
Mary	9	F	Child	09Ja02Dp
NOON, Betty	50	F	Unknown	09Ja02Dp
MURPHY, Michl.	30	M	Unknown	09Ja02Dp
ROACH, Wm.	32	M	Unknown	09Ja02Dp
CARROL, Pat	21	M	Unknown	09Ja02Dp
DOYLE, Sally	27	F	Unknown	09Ja02Dp
John	5	M	Child	09Ja02Dp
Cathne.	1	F	Child	09Ja02Dp
LENAHAN, John	20	M	Unknown	09Ja02Dp
Mary	17	F	Unknown	09Ja02Dp
FLYNN, Peter	40	M	Unknown	09Ja02Dp
BARTON, Mary	56	F	Unknown	09Ja02Dp
John	38	M	Unknown	09Ja02Dp
Mary	21	F	Unknown	09Ja02Dp
James	4	M	Child	09Ja02Dp
FEE, Hannah	18	F	Unknown	09Ja02Dp
WHELAHAN, Anne	21	F	Unknown	09Ja02Dp
REILLY, Mary	19	F	Unknown	09Ja02Dp
CONNELL, Mary	60	F	Unknown	09Ja02Dp
Died-At-Sea				
Phil	3	M	Child	09Ja02Dp
MAHON, John	13	M	Unknown	09Ja02Dp
Margt.	35	F	Unknown	09Ja02Dp
Judith	14	F	Unknown	09Ja02Dp
CONNIFF, Michl.	9	M	Child	09Ja02Dp
Mary	30	F	Unknown	09Ja02Dp
John	6	M	Child	09Ja02Dp
Eliza	2	F	Child	09Ja02Dp
LEE, Thom.	20	M	Unknown	09Ja02Dp
LENAHAN, Michl.	19	M	Unknown	09Ja02Dp
Cathne.	16	F	Unknown	09Ja02Dp
NANCY, Ellen	30	F	Unknown	09Ja02Dp
LUCY, Honora	50	F	Unknown	09Ja02Dp
Bridget	6	F	Child	09Ja02Dp
COLLINS, John	30	M	Unknown	09Ja02Dp
BRYAN, Margt.	17	F	Unknown	09Ja02Dp
Denis	30	M	Unknown	09Ja02Dp
ASHE, James	60	M	Unknown	09Ja02Dp

NAMES OF PASSENGERS	AGE	SEX	OCCUPATIONS	DATE PORT SHIP
HALPIN, John	12	M	Unknown	09Ja02Dp
Died-At-Sea				
Margt.	10	F	Unknown	09Ja02Dp
Judith	9	F	Child	09Ja02Dp
Kate	7	F	Child	09Ja02Dp
Christ.	6	M	Child	09Ja02Dp
Pat	2	M	Child	09Ja02Dp
DOWDALL, Edwd.	12	M	Unknown	09Ja02Dp
PHILIP, Bryan	15	M	Unknown	09Ja02Dp
HANLY, Honora	22	F	Unknown	09Ja02Dp
DAVIS, William	25	M	Unknown	09Ja02Dp
CARROL, Agnes	22	F	Unknown	09Ja02Dp
LOLLY, Margt.	50	F	Unknown	09Ja02Dp
PURCELL, Michl	12	M	Unknown	09Ja02Dp
COOPER, U	.00	F	Infant	09Ja02Dp
Born-At-Sea				
U, U	00	U	Unknown	09Ja02Dp
Died-At-Sea				
U	00	U	Unknown	09Ja02Dp
Died-At-Sea				
U	00	U	Unknown	09Ja02Dp
Died-At-Sea				
U	00	U	Unknown	09Ja02Dp
Died-At-Sea				
U	00	U	Unknown	09Ja02Dp
Died-At-Sea				
U	00	U	Unknown	09Ja02Dp
Died-At-Sea				
U	00	U	Unknown	09Ja02Dp
Died-At-Sea				
U	00	U	Unknown	09Ja02Dp
Died-At-Sea				
U	00	U	Unknown	09Ja02Dp
Died-At-Sea				
U	00	U	Unknown	09Ja02Dp
Died-At-Sea				
U	00	U	Unknown	09Ja02Dp
Died-At-Sea				
U	00	U	Unknown	09Ja02Dp
Died-At-Sea				
U	00	U	Unknown	09Ja02Dp
Died-At-Sea				
U	00	U	Unknown	09Ja02Dp
Died-At-Sea				
U	00	U	Unknown	09Ja02Dp
Died-At-Sea				
U	00	U	Unknown	09Ja02Dp
Died-At-Sea				
U	00	U	Unknown	09Ja02Dp
Died-At-Sea				

J.Z. 10 JANUARY 1850

From Liverpool

NAMES OF PASSENGERS	AGE	SEX	OCCUPATIONS	DATE PORT SHIP
VALLERY, Ann	30	F	Servant	10Ja02Dq
IGOE, Brid.	14	F	Milliner	10Ja02Dq
Edwd.	12	M	None	10Ja02Dq
Fanny	9	F	Child	10Ja02Dq
QUIGLEY, Honor	20	F	Servant	10Ja02Dq
Mary	22	F	None	10Ja02Dq
HANLEY, Jno.	55	M	None	10Ja02Dq
Tho.	7	M	Child	10Ja02Dq
Pat	.09	M	Infant	10Ja02Dq
Died-At-Sea				
KELLY, Mary	50	F	None	10Ja02Dq
Pat	9	M	Child	10Ja02Dq
CRONAN, Margt.	12	F	None	10Ja02Dq
MEEHAN, Ann	30	F	Farmer	10Ja02Dq

NAMES OF PASSENGERS	AGE	SEX	OCCUPATIONS	DATE PORT SHIP
MEEHAN, Mary	10	F	None	10Ja02Dq
Jno.	7	M	Child	10Ja02Dq
Martin	3	M	Child	10Ja02Dq
Pat	.11	M	Infant	10Ja02Dq
CALLAHAN, Jno.	32	M	Laborer	10Ja02Dq
Mary	32	F	None	10Ja02Dq
TIERNAN, Tho.	9	M	Child	10Ja02Dq
Darby	7	M	Child	10Ja02Dq
LARKIN, Jno.	17	M	Farmer	10Ja02Dq
REILLY, Michl.	38	M	Laborer	10Ja02Dq
MAGUIRE, Brid.	28	F	None	10Ja02Dq
FLYNN, Ann	18	F	None	10Ja02Dq
Maria	14	F	None	10Ja02Dq
DEVINE, Mary	5	F	Child	10Ja02Dq
Ann	3	F	Child	10Ja02Dq
DONOHUE, Eliz.	15	F	None	10Ja02Dq
GREEN, Jas.	10	M	None	10Ja02Dq
MCCABE, Owen	55	M	None	10Ja02Dq
John	20	M	None	10Ja02Dq
MCKENNON, Terence	18	M	Smith	10Ja02Dq
DEVINE, Cath.	20	F	Servant	10Ja02Dq
DOLAN, Peter	19	M	None	10Ja02Dq
Mich.	13	M	None	10Ja02Dq
MORAN, Ann	50	F	None	10Ja02Dq
Died-At-Sea				
Mary	35	F	None	10Ja02Dq
Wm.	.09	M	Infant	10Ja02Dq
Died-At-Sea				
CONWAY, Rich.	60	M	Laborer	10Ja02Dq
BYERS, Ann-J.	30	F	None	10Ja02Dq
Fra.	9	F	Child	10Ja02Dq
John	5	M	Child	10Ja02Dq
Wm.	.11	M	Infant	10Ja02Dq
Died-At-Sea				
MERRICK, Mary	21	F	Servant	10Ja02Dq
KELLY, Mary	22	F	None	10Ja02Dq
GREENLAW, Isab.	20	F	None	10Ja02Dq
COULTER, Margt.	13	F	Washer	10Ja02Dq
Isab.	11	F	None	10Ja02Dq
Jane	6	F	Child	10Ja02Dq
WADDICK, Mary	60	F	None	10Ja02Dq
Ann	26	F	None	10Ja02Dq
BROPHY, John	14	M	None	10Ja02Dq
DEAN, Mary	13	F	None	10Ja02Dq
John	9	M	Child	10Ja02Dq
Ann	5	F	Child	10Ja02Dq
CONER, Maria	16	F	Servant	10Ja02Dq
PURCELL, Brid.	16	F	None	10Ja02Dq
Mary	12	F	None	10Ja02Dq
LEARD, Jane	30	F	None	10Ja02Dq
John	8	M	Child	10Ja02Dq
Henry	6	M	Child	10Ja02Dq
Jane	.10	F	Infant	10Ja02Dq
Died-At-Sea				
RYAN, Wm.	14	M	None	10Ja02Dq
MCLOUGHLIN, Dan	30	M	None	10Ja02Dq
Margt.	25	F	Servant	10Ja02Dq
BRENNON, Wm.	25	M	Farmer	10Ja02Dq
Mary	24	F	None	10Ja02Dq
BURKE, Wm.	30	M	Laborer	10Ja02Dq
NANISY, Ellen	4	F	Child	10Ja02Dq
LAVERTY, Bryan	18	M	None	10Ja02Dq
DUFFY, John	50	M	Baker	10Ja02Dq
Brid.	40	F	None	10Ja02Dq
Cath.	21	F	None	10Ja02Dq
Maria	19	F	None	10Ja02Dq
GLENON, Brid.	14	F	Washer	10Ja02Dq
KENNEDY, Hugh	24	M	Laborer	10Ja02Dq
TRACY, Brid.	21	F	None	10Ja02Dq
BRIDGEMAN, Pat	20	M	None	10Ja02Dq
DUNLAP, Sanderson	20	M	None	10Ja02Dq
Mary	30	F	None	10Ja02Dq
Hugh	15	M	None	10Ja02Dq
WALSH, Mich.	14	M	None	10Ja02Dq
Mary	17	F	None	10Ja02Dq

NAMES OF PASSENGERS	AGE	SEX	OCCUPATIONS	DATE PORT SHIP
WALSH, Cath.	30	F	None	10Ja02Dq
Mary	30	F	None	10Ja02Dq
Tho.	12	M	None	10Ja02Dq
Pat	.09	M	Infant	10Ja02Dq
Died-At-Sea				
BRYAN, Brid.	24	F	None	10Ja02Dq
DOYLE, Jno.	60	M	None	10Ja02Dq
Thos.	22	M	None	10Ja02Dq
Jos.	19	M	Laborer	10Ja02Dq
Jas.	18	M	Laborer	10Ja02Dq
Sarah	19	F	None	10Ja02Dq
WHALEN, Margt.	22	F	None	10Ja02Dq
TONER, Fra.	26	F	None	10Ja02Dq
DOOLEY, Mick	19	M	Servant	10Ja02Dq
MCGUIRE, B.	18	M	Servant	10Ja02Dq
MCGAUGHAM, Jane	18	F	None	10Ja02Dq
MCCANN, Mary	40	F	None	10Ja02Dq
Betty	10	F	None	10Ja02Dq
CONELLY, Judy	35	F	None	10Ja02Dq
HASHEN, Milly	17	F	None	10Ja02Dq
GREENWOOD, Eliz.	48	F	None	10Ja02Dq
THORNTON, John	14	M	None	10Ja02Dq
GREGSON, Mary	28	F	None	10Ja02Dq
Betty	2	F	Child	10Ja02Dq
CORCORAN, M.	35	M	None	10Ja02Dq
Cath.	28	F	None	10Ja02Dq
Maria	.09	F	Infant	10Ja02Dq
NEAL, Eliz.	20	F	Servant	10Ja02Dq
Jas.	.10	M	Infant	10Ja02Dq
MEEHAN, U-Mrs.	26	F	Washer	10Ja02Dq
John	.08	M	Infant	10Ja02Dq
Died-At-Sea				
MCSHEY, Mary	20	F	Laborer	10Ja02Dq
CONNLEY, John	18	M	None	10Ja02Dq
NOTT, Brid.	45	F	Farmer	10Ja02Dq
Brid.	20	F	None	10Ja02Dq
Jas.	19	M	None	10Ja02Dq
Margt.	15	F	None	10Ja02Dq
Michl.	10	M	None	10Ja02Dq
Pat	.11	M	Infant	10Ja02Dq
Margt.	16	F	None	10Ja02Dq
Fra.	14	F	None	10Ja02Dq
Hubert	8	M	Child	10Ja02Dq
HUGHES, Mick	18	M	None	10Ja02Dq
MCKENNA, Brid.	30	F	None	10Ja02Dq
ANDREWS, Henry	18	M	None	10Ja02Dq
GARVIN, Matt	35	M	None	10Ja02Dq
Cath.	32	F	None	10Ja02Dq
Mary	8	F	Child	10Ja02Dq
Conner	4	M	Child	10Ja02Dq
Matt	.08	M	Infant	10Ja02Dq
Died-At-Sea				
John	23	M	None	10Ja02Dq
Michl.	21	M	None	10Ja02Dq
John	27	M	None	10Ja02Dq
Ellen	24	F	None	10Ja02Dq
WHALEN, Dennis	25	M	None	10Ja02Dq
Rick	23	M	Smith	10Ja02Dq
GALAGAN, Mary	24	F	Seamstress	10Ja02Dq
MULLEN, Brid.	23	F	Seamstress	10Ja02Dq
LYDON, Martin	36	M	Laborer	10Ja02Dq
Sarah	30	F	None	10Ja02Dq
Pat	2	M	Child	10Ja02Dq
Mary	22	F	None	10Ja02Dq
CARROLL, Margt.	30	F	None	10Ja02Dq
CAVANAGH, Mick	20	M	None	10Ja02Dq
MCDERMOTT, Mary	20	F	None	10Ja02Dq
KELLY, Mick	31	M	None	10Ja02Dq
Sarah	30	F	None	10Ja02Dq
Margt.	31	F	None	10Ja02Dq
Rich.	12	M	None	10Ja02Dq
Jas.	9	M	Child	10Ja02Dq
Lucy	6	F	Child	10Ja02Dq
Tho.	3	M	Child	10Ja02Dq
Isabel	.11	F	Infant	10Ja02Dq

NAMES OF PASSENGERS	AGE	SEX	OCCUPATIONS	DATE PORT SHIP
CHAMBERS, Geo.	25	M	Blacksmith	10Ja02Dq
SPIRE, Ann	18	F	Washer	10Ja02Dq
JORDAN, Ann	18	F	Washer	10Ja02Dq
RAMSDEN, Sam	23	M	Laborer	10Ja02Dq
FELTEN, Jas.	26	M	Laborer	10Ja02Dq
BRADEN, Ann	30	F	Servant	10Ja02Dq
RYAN, Honor	20	F	None	10Ja02Dq
FALY, Mary	19	F	None	10Ja02Dq
MURLING, John	20	M	Laborer	10Ja02Dq
SULLIVAN, Dan	20	M	None	10Ja02Dq
MYERS, John	24	M	None	10Ja02Dq
Mary	24	F	None	10Ja02Dq
DAMAGH, J.	21	M	Laborer	10Ja02Dq
Wm.	16	M	None	10Ja02Dq
CONNAL, Brid.	20	F	None	10Ja02Dq
CUSHMAN, Morris	30	M	None	10Ja02Dq
Ellen	25	F	None	10Ja02Dq
Mary	34	F	None	10Ja02Dq
Mary	6	F	Child	10Ja02Dq
Michl.	4	M	Child	10Ja02Dq
Pat	.10	M	Infant	10Ja02Dq
MURPHY, Terence	40	M	None	10Ja02Dq
REILLY, Jas.	18	M	Laborer	10Ja02Dq
MCCANNA, Pat	20	M	None	10Ja02Dq
BRENNAN, Michl.	46	M	Farmer	10Ja02Dq
Ellen	44	F	None	10Ja02Dq
Mick	22	M	None	10Ja02Dq
Anty.	18	F	None	10Ja02Dq
Brid.	15	F	None	10Ja02Dq
Cath.	13	F	None	10Ja02Dq
Ellen	11	F	None	10Ja02Dq
John	9	M	Child	10Ja02Dq
Ann	7	F	Child	10Ja02Dq
Martin	4	M	Child	10Ja02Dq
Eliza	2	F	Child	10Ja02Dq
Margt.	.11	F	Infant	10Ja02Dq
Pat	25	M	None	10Ja02Dq
MCDERMOTT, Eliza	44	F	Farmer	10Ja02Dq
Pat	50	M	None	10Ja02Dq
Ann	25	F	None	10Ja02Dq
Con.	.09	M	Infant	10Ja02Dq
Died-At-Sea				
KILLRIDGE, Eliza	26	F	Servant	10Ja02Dq
BORDEN, Martha	20	F	None	10Ja02Dq
MCDERMOTT, Ann	30	F	Servant	10Ja02Dq
FALLON, Pat	20	M	Laborer	10Ja02Dq
Pat	20	M	None	10Ja02Dq
Mary	16	F	Servant	10Ja02Dq
BROUGHAM, Michl.	27	M	Laborer	10Ja02Dq
COYLE, Mary	20	F	None	10Ja02Dq
BARRY, Jas.	18	M	None	10Ja02Dq
KENNEDY, Brid.	21	F	None	10Ja02Dq
Jas.	.09	M	Infant	10Ja02Dq
Ellen	30	F	None	10Ja02Dq
Jas.	.09	M	Infant	10Ja02Dq
Died-At-Sea				
SALE, Pat	25	M	Laborer	10Ja02Dq
GILL, Pat	30	M	None	10Ja02Dq
MARTIN, Maria	10	F	None	10Ja02Dq
DEMPSEY, Sarah	24	F	None	10Ja02Dq
Ellen	22	F	None	10Ja02Dq
Paul	21	M	None	10Ja02Dq
KEENAN, Mary	52	F	None	10Ja02Dq
RYAN, Cath.	20	F	None	10Ja02Dq
Julia	26	F	None	10Ja02Dq
DUNN, Phill.	12	M	Blacksmith	10Ja02Dq
RYAN, Martin	30	M	None	10Ja02Dq
KEATING, Robt.	19	M	None	10Ja02Dq
JORDAN, Ann	18	F	Servant	10Ja02Dq
BATTERSBY, Wm.	45	M	Farmer	10Ja02Dq
Mary	35	F	None	10Ja02Dq
Ellen	13	F	None	10Ja02Dq
Hannah	10	F	None	10Ja02Dq
Mary	7	F	Child	10Ja02Dq
John	4	M	Child	10Ja02Dq
BATTERSBY, Margt.	2	F	Child	10Ja02Dq
Mich.	20	M	Laborer	10Ja02Dq
BARRY, Mary	30	F	None	10Ja02Dq
Margt.	40	F	None	10Ja02Dq
AHERN, Margt.	18	F	None	10Ja02Dq
CUMMINS, Pat	30	M	Servant	10Ja02Dq
COGLAN, Margt.	13	F	None	10Ja02Dq
ONEAL, Wm.	32	M	None	10Ja02Dq
REYNOLDS, Brid.	20	F	None	10Ja02Dq
TRELLEN, Isaac	36	M	None	10Ja02Dq
GOODMAN, Naman	21	M	None	10Ja02Dq
NEAL, Bryan	18	M	None	10Ja02Dq
Cath.	20	F	None	10Ja02Dq
EAGIN, John	22	M	Laborer	10Ja02Dq
MCCULLOGH, R.	24	M	Servant	10Ja02Dq
John	17	M	None	10Ja02Dq
JUDGE, Sarah	20	F	None	10Ja02Dq
MCKEE, Nancy	21	F	None	10Ja02Dq
SULLIVAN, Jas.	33	M	None	10Ja02Dq
RAWSON, Thos.	25	M	None	10Ja02Dq
BOYLE, Roger	16	M	None	10Ja02Dq
JUDGE, John	16	M	Servant	10Ja02Dq

OHIO 10 JANUARY 1850

From Glasgow

BOYD, David	31	M	Blacksmith	10Ja21Ds
CANNON, James	22	M	Laborer	10Ja21Ds
HIMOND, Eliza	26	F	Unknown	10Ja21Ds
Robert	3	M	Child	10Ja21Ds
John-J.	.05	M	Infant	10Ja21Ds
SULLIVAN, Dennis	27	M	Laborer	10Ja21Ds
QUINLIVEN, Thomas	29	M	Unknown	10Ja21Ds
James	23	M	Unknown	10Ja21Ds
CARRAN, Ellen	50	F	Unknown	10Ja21Ds
Ann	12	F	Unknown	10Ja21Ds
PEARCE, Eliza	20	F	Unknown	10Ja21Ds
ELLIOT, William	29	M	Laborer	10Ja21Ds
CAMPBELL, Letitia	39	F	Unknown	10Ja21Ds
CARSON, Elizabeth	60	F	Unknown	10Ja21Ds
Mary	25	F	Unknown	10Ja21Ds
John	25	M	Farmer	10Ja21Ds
Lawrence	25	M	Unknown	10Ja21Ds
Thomas-C.	25	M	Unknown	10Ja21Ds
LONG, John	30	M	Unknown	10Ja21Ds
HALLIGAN, William	30	M	Unknown	10Ja21Ds
CARSON, Martha-C.	25	F	Unknown	10Ja21Ds
Elizabeth	7	F	Child	10Ja21Ds
Ann	5	F	Child	10Ja21Ds
Francis	2	M	Child	10Ja21Ds
U	.11	U	Infant	10Ja21Ds
MCNALLY, Felix	17	M	Clerk	10Ja21Ds
MARTIN, Martha	13	F	Unknown	10Ja21Ds
MCCANN, James	17	M	Farmer	10Ja21Ds

IDA-KISS 10 JANUARY 1850

From NEWPORT, Wales

KAMERER, Joseph	26	M	Matchmaker	10Ja45Et
Elizabeth	25	F	Unknown	10Ja45Et
BAILEY, John	33	M	Laborer	10Ja45Et

NAMES OF PASSENGERS	AGE	SEX	OCCUPATIONS	DATE PORT SHIP
CRAWFORD, James	27	M	Butcher	10Ja45Et
SIMMONS, John	25	M	Carpenter	10Ja45Et
FRANKAND, Thomas	19	M	Plumber	10Ja45Et
WRIGHT, James	38	M	Bookseller	10Ja45Et
EADES, John	34	M	Farmer	10Ja45Et
TREGASKIS, Sarah	18	F	Unknown	10Ja45Et
WRIGHT, Ann	27	F	Unknown	10Ja45Et
FETTERS, Charlotte	19	F	Unknown	10Ja45Et
WRIGHT, William	6	M	Child	10Ja45Et
Ann	.00	F	Infant	10Ja45Et
WELDSMITH, Elisabeth	45	F	Infant	10Ja45Et
PETERS, Charles	24	M	Farmer	10Ja45Et
SOANES, Thomas	34	M	Author	10Ja45Et
MAY, Stephen	32	M	Butcher	10Ja45Et
SESBOURNE, Philas	40	M	Unknown	10Ja45Et
Luisa	28	F	Unknown	10Ja45Et
John	11	M	Unknown	10Ja45Et
Alethia	10	F	Unknown	10Ja45Et
Isabel	9	F	Child	10Ja45Et
Theophilus	7	M	Child	10Ja45Et
Bertha	4	F	Child	10Ja45Et
LEDA, Alfred	25	M	Mmrnr	10Ja45Et
BONTLDS, Samuel	26	M	Carpenter	10Ja45Et
BURTON, Emma	15	F	Unknown	10Ja45Et
Rosanna	16	F	Unknown	10Ja45Et
John	11	M	Unknown	10Ja45Et
William	8	M	Child	10Ja45Et
Thomas	5	M	Child	10Ja45Et
TODD, Hanah	27	F	Unknown	10Ja45Et
Mary	8	F	Child	10Ja45Et
Margaret	5	F	Child	10Ja45Et
Hanah	.00	F	Infant	10Ja45Et
BLACKBURN, Mark	39	M	Unknown	10Ja45Et
Martha	40	F	Unknown	10Ja45Et
James	15	M	Unknown	10Ja45Et
Martha	8	F	Child	10Ja45Et
Mark	5	M	Child	10Ja45Et
Jane	1	F	Child	10Ja45Et
James	31	M	Unknown	10Ja45Et
SIMMONS, Hannah	54	F	Unknown	10Ja45Et
Robert	21	M	Unknown	10Ja45Et
William	19	M	Hatter	10Ja45Et
Ann	16	F	Unknown	10Ja45Et
HOLLISTON, Theophilus	26	M	Hatter	10Ja45Et
DABSON, Jane	35	F	Unknown	10Ja45Et
Jane	10	F	Unknown	10Ja45Et
EDWARDS, Isaac	21	M	Turner	10Ja45Et
SAVAGE, Joseph	40	M	Laborer	10Ja45Et
Ann	40	F	Unknown	10Ja45Et
Robert	16	M	Unknown	10Ja45Et
Fanny	14	F	Unknown	10Ja45Et
Lucy	7	F	Child	10Ja45Et
Albert	4	M	Child	10Ja45Et
HOSKINS, Elisabeth	43	F	Unknown	10Ja45Et
William	17	M	Laborer	10Ja45Et
Guillinia	11	F	Unknown	10Ja45Et
Charles	5	M	Child	10Ja45Et
Elisa.	2	F	Child	10Ja45Et
TAYLOR, Anderson	17	M	Cutter	10Ja45Et
Alfred	22	M	Unknown	10Ja45Et
Hester	23	F	Unknown	10Ja45Et
HACKIN, Richard	32	M	Shoemaker	10Ja45Et
MORTIMER, Barnabus	25	M	Laborer	10Ja45Et
Jane	26	F	Unknown	10Ja45Et
Simeon	21	M	Unknown	10Ja45Et
Sarah	22	F	Unknown	10Ja45Et
William	.00	M	Infant	10Ja45Et
BULL, John	21	M	Laborer	10Ja45Et
MAHLER, Dioderick	21	M	Sugar Maker	10Ja45Et
Cashina-Elisbth.	26	F	Unknown	10Ja45Et
HENRY, John	.00	M	Infant	10Ja45Et
DIXON, William	36	M	Tailor	10Ja45Et
Ann	36	F	Unknown	10Ja45Et
Jesse	16	F	Tailor	10Ja45Et
Emma	14	F	Unknown	10Ja45Et
DIXON, Henry	11	M	Unknown	10Ja45Et
Elisabeth	10	F	Unknown	10Ja45Et
Usina	9	F	Child	10Ja45Et
Jacob	8	M	Child	10Ja45Et
John	4	M	Child	10Ja45Et
Alfred	1	M	Child	10Ja45Et
CHURCH, George	28	M	Unknown	10Ja45Et
Anne	28	F	Laborer	10Ja45Et
George	3	M	Child	10Ja45Et
Augusta	1	M	Child	10Ja45Et
FADDEN, Charles	26	M	Carpenter	10Ja45Et
Mary-Ann	28	F	Unknown	10Ja45Et
Mary	1	F	Child	10Ja45Et
GEORGE, William	24	M	Carpenter	10Ja45Et
Ann	49	F	Unknown	10Ja45Et
Elisabeth	22	F	Unknown	10Ja45Et
Ann	20	F	Unknown	10Ja45Et
Mary	16	F	Unknown	10Ja45Et
Emma	11	F	Unknown	10Ja45Et
Lousia	9	F	Child	10Ja45Et
Hanah	8	F	Child	10Ja45Et
FROST, William	30	M	Mariner	10Ja45Et
GREEN, Edward	23	M	Tailor	10Ja45Et
WATERS, Henry	40	M	Farmer	10Ja45Et
OAKLEY, Mary	20	F	Unknown	10Ja45Et
EDWARDS, Thomas	24	M	Turner	10Ja45Et

YORKTOWN 10 JANUARY 1850

From London

NAMES OF PASSENGERS	AGE	SEX	OCCUPATIONS	DATE PORT SHIP
COOK, Cornelius	24	M	Butcher	10Ja06Dr
PEEK, George	28	M	Clerk	10Ja06Dr
HUTTON, Thomas	43	M	Unknown	10Ja06Dr
ELLIOT, Alexander	20	M	Farmer	10Ja06Dr
JOHNSON, C.G.	24	M	Clerk	10Ja06Dr
FOAT, Daniel	24	M	Unknown	10Ja06Dr
STEPHENS, Daniel	37	M	Unknown	10Ja06Dr
RUSS, James	50	M	Baker	10Ja06Dr
George	47	M	Unknown	10Ja06Dr
Walter	17	M	Unknown	10Ja06Dr
Barbaray	15	M	Unknown	10Ja06Dr
Frank	11	M	Unknown	10Ja06Dr
CUSICK, Mary	20	F	Servant	10Ja06Dr
MACNAMARA, Jane	25	F	Servant	10Ja06Dr
James	29	M	Servant	10Ja06Dr
Ann	11	F	Servant	10Ja06Dr
Nora	6	F	Child	10Ja06Dr
DIAS, Sarah	40	F	Servant	10Ja06Dr
Maria	11	F	Servant	10Ja06Dr
Rosetta	7	F	Child	10Ja06Dr
Adelaide	20	F	Servant	10Ja06Dr
Wileme	17	F	Servant	10Ja06Dr
Eliza	4	F	Child	10Ja06Dr
STEPHENS, William	26	M	Clerk	10Ja06Dr
JOHNSON, Patrick	27	M	Tailor	10Ja06Dr
HARRIS, James	28	M	Hatter	10Ja06Dr
Eliza	25	F	Hatter	10Ja06Dr
James	3	M	Child	10Ja06Dr
Ann	.06	F	Infant	10Ja06Dr
HANEFORD, Richard	22	M	Hatter	10Ja06Dr
LEE, Anna	38	F	Clerk	10Ja06Dr
William	10	M	Clerk	10Ja06Dr
Eliza	7	F	Child	10Ja06Dr
Edward	5	M	Child	10Ja06Dr
Caroline	2	F	Child	10Ja06Dr
SHEARS, Harriet	21	F	Seamstress	10Ja06Dr
THOMKINSON, John	30	M	Smith	10Ja06Dr
STORAN, Alexander	30	M	Piano Maker	10Ja06Dr

NAMES OF PASSENGERS	AGE	SEX	OCCUPATIONS	DATE PORT SHIP
EVINS, John	29	M	Cigar Maker	10Ja06Dr
FOSSEE, Samuel	20	M	Farmer	10Ja06Dr
Maria	34	F	Farmer	10Ja06Dr
Thos.	8	M	Child	10Ja06Dr
William	10	M	Unknown	10Ja06Dr
James	6	M	Child	10Ja06Dr
Esther	4	F	Child	10Ja06Dr
CLUNK, William	20	M	Laborer	10Ja06Dr
Hariett	20	F	Servant	10Ja06Dr
BURN, William	20	M	Clerk	10Ja06Dr
PARKS, Samuel	17	M	Clerk	10Ja06Dr
GOLDSMITH, Barbary	20	M	Milliner	10Ja06Dr
KOHLER, Ellen	22	F	Unknown	10Ja06Dr
TAILER, William	45	M	Farmer	10Ja06Dr
ADAMS, Richard	26	M	Farmer	10Ja06Dr
Pheobe	24	F	Unknown	10Ja06Dr
Richard	7	M	Child	10Ja06Dr
Ann	.08	F	Infant	10Ja06Dr
MOSS, John	29	M	Carpenter	10Ja06Dr
Henry	22	M	Farmer	10Ja06Dr
BAKER, Charles	21	M	Farmer	10Ja06Dr
GLUCK, John	53	M	Farmer	10Ja06Dr
SMITH, Thos.	24	M	Farmer	10Ja06Dr
SPIRE, Phillip	21	M	Farmer	10Ja06Dr
HENRY, Richard	21	M	Unknown	10Ja06Dr
RUSSELL, James	38	M	Engineer	10Ja06Dr
JONNES, Edward	14	M	Engineer	10Ja06Dr
BENNETT, Thomas	27	M	Seaman	10Ja06Dr

ANDREW-FOSTER 11 JANUARY 1850

From Liverpool

NAMES OF PASSENGERS	AGE	SEX	OCCUPATIONS	DATE PORT SHIP
RIERDON, Nicholas	24	M	Unknown	11Ja02Dt
DELLAWAY, Cath.D.	45	F	Laborer	11Ja02Dt
Died-At-Sea				
TRAFFOR, Ann	20	F	Unknown	11Ja02Dt
MONESSEY, James	25	M	Laborer	11Ja02Dt
CONLAN, Patrick	22	M	Laborer	11Ja02Dt
PENDER, Mick	35	M	Laborer	11Ja02Dt
GALLAGHER, James	25	M	Laborer	11Ja02Dt
DOOLEY, Patrick	20	M	Laborer	11Ja02Dt
RAFFERTY, Cath.	20	F	Unknown	11Ja02Dt
LYNCH, Bridget	16	F	Unknown	11Ja02Dt
CONNOR, Patrick	27	M	Laborer	11Ja02Dt
CAMPBELL, Margaret	20	F	Unknown	11Ja02Dt
LENOX, James	60	M	Laborer	11Ja02Dt
COYLE, Mary-J.	25	F	Unknown	11Ja02Dt
Edwd.	50	M	Laborer	11Ja02Dt
Mary	49	F	Unknown	11Ja02Dt
James	18	M	Laborer	11Ja02Dt
KELLY, Joseph	40	M	Laborer	11Ja02Dt
Mary	12	F	Unknown	11Ja02Dt
CAHILL, Mick	37	M	Laborer	11Ja02Dt
WARD, James	30	M	Laborer	11Ja02Dt
LAHEY, Thomas	40	M	Laborer	11Ja02Dt
MITCHELL, Mike	23	M	Laborer	11Ja02Dt
CALLAHAN, Martin	21	M	Laborer	11Ja02Dt
WELSH, Patrick	28	M	Laborer	11Ja02Dt
Ellen	26	F	Unknown	11Ja02Dt
Mary-E.	5	F	Child	11Ja02Dt
WAUGHTON, Mary-E.	31	F	Unknown	11Ja02Dt
WELSH, Thomas	3	M	Child	11Ja02Dt
MCCARTHY, Ellen	34	F	Unknown	11Ja02Dt
Ellen	17	F	Unknown	11Ja02Dt
Dennis	.09	M	Infant	11Ja02Dt
MORRIS, John	22	M	Laborer	11Ja02Dt
RYAN, Mick	12	M	Laborer	11Ja02Dt
MURPHY, Thaddy	25	M	Laborer	11Ja02Dt

NAMES OF PASSENGERS	AGE	SEX	OCCUPATIONS	DATE PORT SHIP
BRADLEY, Mary	32	F	Unknown	11Ja02Dt
HOOLAHAN, Ann	28	F	Unknown	11Ja02Dt
Julia	21	F	Unknown	11Ja02Dt
Jane	20	F	Unknown	11Ja02Dt
SULLIVAN, Julia	15	F	Unknown	11Ja02Dt
SEXTON, Honor	22	F	Unknown	11Ja02Dt
BARRET, John	38	M	Unknown	11Ja02Dt
MONAGHAN, Humphrey	22	M	Laborer	11Ja02Dt
KEANE, Ellen	18	F	Unknown	11Ja02Dt
CONNOR, Bridget	16	F	Unknown	11Ja02Dt
CARMODY, Maurice	26	M	Laborer	11Ja02Dt
BARRY, Arthur	28	M	Laborer	11Ja02Dt
Julia	26	F	Unknown	11Ja02Dt
James	.00	M	Infant	11Ja02Dt
SULLIVAN, Cath.	19	F	Unknown	11Ja02Dt
MURPHY, John	24	M	Laborer	11Ja02Dt
Alexander	26	M	Laborer	11Ja02Dt
MCCARTHY, Richd.	19	M	Laborer	11Ja02Dt
CONNOR, Patrick	27	M	Laborer	11Ja02Dt
Tim	24	M	Laborer	11Ja02Dt
Mary	26	F	Unknown	11Ja02Dt
U	.00	U	Infant	11Ja02Dt
Born-At-Sea				
DERMONY, Mary	27	F	Unknown	11Ja02Dt
TYNAM, Patrick	46	M	Laborer	11Ja02Dt
DOYLE, Garret	44	M	Laborer	11Ja02Dt
RYAN, Margaret	26	F	Unknown	11Ja02Dt
DORMAND, Johanna	24	F	Unknown	11Ja02Dt
HOLDEN, Anthony	25	M	Laborer	11Ja02Dt
COGHLAN, Edward	25	M	Shoemaker	11Ja02Dt
MCCABE, Betty	22	F	Unknown	11Ja02Dt
BRYNE, Johanna	17	F	Unknown	11Ja02Dt
RILEY, John	25	M	Laborer	11Ja02Dt
DOBIN, Alexander	21	M	Laborer	11Ja02Dt
BARR, John	40	M	Laborer	11Ja02Dt
HERFORD, Daniel	17	M	Laborer	11Ja02Dt
LIFLEY, George	25	M	Laborer	11Ja02Dt
UPTON, William	23	M	Laborer	11Ja02Dt
TOOLE, John	18	M	Laborer	11Ja02Dt
Mary	13	F	Unknown	11Ja02Dt
NUTLEY, John	21	M	Laborer	11Ja02Dt
BRICK, William	51	M	Laborer	11Ja02Dt
RYAN, James	34	M	Laborer	11Ja02Dt
CASSAC, Patrick	30	M	Laborer	11Ja02Dt
Thos.	22	M	Laborer	11Ja02Dt
HOYLAN, Mary	20	F	Unknown	11Ja02Dt
MULLEN, Thos.	19	M	Laborer	11Ja02Dt
POWELL, Mary	22	F	Unknown	11Ja02Dt
CASSACK, Honard	13	F	Unknown	11Ja02Dt
Michl.	12	M	Unknown	11Ja02Dt
NELIGAN, Jessie	30	F	Unknown	11Ja02Dt
SCANLON, Dennis	32	M	Laborer	11Ja02Dt
NELIGAN, Francis	27	F	Unknown	11Ja02Dt
FITZMAURICE, Henry	30	M	Laborer	11Ja02Dt
FERRERTY, Rodger	26	M	Laborer	11Ja02Dt
NOLAN, Thomas	26	M	Laborer	11Ja02Dt
NELIGAN, Francis	27	F	Unknown	11Ja02Dt
MCDONNELL, Tim	26	M	Laborer	11Ja02Dt
GORMAN, Bridget	20	F	Unknown	11Ja02Dt
FLYNN, Thos.	22	M	Laborer	11Ja02Dt
CONNELL, Pat	20	M	Laborer	11Ja02Dt
Jno.	20	M	Laborer	11Ja02Dt
GORMAN, Mary	22	F	Unknown	11Ja02Dt
WARD, Mary	18	F	Unknown	11Ja02Dt
RILEY, Cathe.	30	F	Unknown	11Ja02Dt
Ann	.00	F	Infant	11Ja02Dt
FOLEY, Wm.	31	M	Laborer	11Ja02Dt
ODARE, Jno.	20	M	Laborer	11Ja02Dt
FOX, Wm.	60	M	Laborer	11Ja02Dt
Mary	50	F	Unknown	11Ja02Dt
Marg.	31	F	Unknown	11Ja02Dt
Wm.	12	M	Unknown	11Ja02Dt
Jno.	8	M	Child	11Ja02Dt
Cathe.	2	F	Child	11Ja02Dt
KELLY, Jno.	21	M	Laborer	11Ja02Dt

NAMES OF PASSENGERS	AGE	SEX	OCCUPATIONS	DATE PORT SHIP
KELLY, Ann	19	F	Unknown	11Ja02D+
FITZPATRICK, Darty	20	M	Laborer	11Ja02D+
DOYEN, Mary	28	F	Unknown	11Ja02D+
Maria	4	F	Child	11Ja02D+
Cathe.	2	F	Child	11Ja02D+
EMSTOCK, Jno.	30	M	Laborer	11Ja02D+
Ann	30	F	Unknown	11Ja02D+
Elizabeth	14	F	Unknown	11Ja02D+
Fannie	12	F	Unknown	11Ja02D+
Mary-Anne	16	F	Unknown	11Ja02D+
Thos.	10	M	Laborer	11Ja02D+
Hannah	6	F	Child	11Ja02D+
Joseph	5	M	Child	11Ja02D+
FRENNAN, Ben.	24	M	Laborer	11Ja02D+
SHEAN, Mary	20	F	Unknown	11Ja02D+
Ellen	20	F	Unknown	11Ja02D+
Florence	3	F	Child	11Ja02D+
Died-At-Sea				
MACK, Pat	32	M	Laborer	11Ja02D+
Died-At-Sea				
QUINN, Jno.	28	M	Laborer	11Ja02D+
MCNAMARA, Pat	32	M	Laborer	11Ja02D+
Mary	28	F	Unknown	11Ja02D+
Thos.	3	M	Child	11Ja02D+
CLANNERY, Thos.	30	M	Laborer	11Ja02D+
Judy	30	F	Unknown	11Ja02D+
Jno.	5	M	Child	11Ja02D+
Mick	3	M	Child	11Ja02D+
Mary	.00	F	Infant	11Ja02D+
MCNAMARA, Mary	60	F	Unknown	11Ja02D+
Pat	5	M	Child	11Ja02D+
Mary	3	F	Child	11Ja02D+
TORFORY, Margaret	18	F	Unknown	11Ja02D+
MCNAMARA, Mic	42	M	Laborer	11Ja02D+
BRAMER, M.	27	F	Unknown	11Ja02D+
BRADLEY, Thos.	12	M	Laborer	11Ja02D+
HENNEY, Terrence	25	M	Laborer	11Ja02D+
Ellen	20	F	Unknown	11Ja02D+
DORLAN, Mick	23	M	Laborer	11Ja02D+
FLUCK, Chas.	22	M	Laborer	11Ja02D+
PEACOCK, Elizabeth	25	F	Unknown	11Ja02D+
Jabez	8	M	Child	11Ja02D+
KELLY, Wm.	30	M	Laborer	11Ja02D+
STRINGER, Ann	26	F	Unknown	11Ja02D+
Ann	23	F	Unknown	11Ja02D+
DAWSEN, Mary	35	F	Unknown	11Ja02D+
MCINRIE, Owen	40	M	Laborer	11Ja02D+
KELLY, Pat	31	M	Laborer	11Ja02D+
WOOD, Mick	28	M	Laborer	11Ja02D+
Mary	25	F	Laborer	11Ja02D+
Mary	.00	F	Infant	11Ja02D+
MAHON, Mick	34	M	Laborer	11Ja02D+
DOUGHERTY, Edwd.	25	M	Laborer	11Ja02D+
Mary	18	F	Unknown	11Ja02D+
NEIL, Bridget	20	F	Unknown	11Ja02D+
REYNOLDS, Peter	19	M	Laborer	11Ja02D+
MCDERMOTT, Ann	16	F	Unknown	11Ja02D+
MANION, Mary	14	F	Unknown	11Ja02D+
EDWARDS, Edwd.	30	M	Laborer	11Ja02D+
OBRIEN, Mary	30	F	Unknown	11Ja02D+
HAND, Ann	20	F	Unknown	11Ja02D+
CONELLY, Mary	22	F	Unknown	11Ja02D+
Jno.	10	M	Unknown	11Ja02D+
Francis	8	M	Child	11Ja02D+
Julia	5	F	Child	11Ja02D+
FOX, Daniel	22	M	Laborer	11Ja02D+
CALION, Philip	46	M	Laborer	11Ja02D+
Cathe.	50	F	Unknown	11Ja02D+
Jno.	23	M	Laborer	11Ja02D+
Daniel	21	M	Laborer	11Ja02D+
Mary	19	F	Unknown	11Ja02D+
Pat	17	M	Unknown	11Ja02D+
Cathe.	14	F	Unknown	11Ja02D+
Johanna	13	F	Unknown	11Ja02D+
Richd.	11	M	Unknown	11Ja02D+
CALION, Phillip	9	M	Child	11Ja02D+
Mick	6	M	Child	11Ja02D+
Ann	3	F	Child	11Ja02D+
Cathe.	20	F	Unknown	11Ja02D+
MORAN, Ann	30	F	Unknown	11Ja02D+
Bridget	10	F	Unknown	11Ja02D+
Died-At-Sea				
Mary	7	F	Child	11Ja02D+
George	4	M	Child	11Ja02D+
WALCH, Richd.	20	M	Laborer	11Ja02D+
EDGAR, Mary	14	F	Unknown	11Ja02D+
MOORE, Biddy	30	F	Unknown	11Ja02D+
WAILOR, Wm.	40	M	Laborer	11Ja02D+
Ellen	13	F	Unknown	11Ja02D+
Died-At-Sea				
Cathe.	11	F	Unknown	11Ja02D+
Margt.	9	F	Child	11Ja02D+
Jane	1	F	Child	11Ja02D+
FARREL, Pat	27	M	Laborer	11Ja02D+
MILLER, Eliza	36	F	Unknown	11Ja02D+
PHELAN, Sarah	40	F	Unknown	11Ja02D+
MILLER, Sarah	8	F	Child	11Ja02D+
Maurice	5	M	Child	11Ja02D+
Wm.	3	M	Child	11Ja02D+
MARPHTON, Ann	15	F	Unknown	11Ja02D+
WARD, Pat	18	M	Laborer	11Ja02D+
MARER, Thos.	25	M	Laborer	11Ja02D+
WILMOT, Wm.	26	M	Laborer	11Ja02D+
BESNUT, Ben.	20	M	Laborer	11Ja02D+
James	18	M	Laborer	11Ja02D+
MCANNIS, Jno.	24	M	Laborer	11Ja02D+
SMITH, Bridget	50	F	Unknown	11Ja02D+
Jno.	16	M	Unknown	11Ja02D+
Robt.	12	M	Unknown	11Ja02D+
James	9	M	Child	11Ja02D+
Edward	5	M	Child	11Ja02D+
Ann	9	F	Child	11Ja02D+
USHER, Richd.	30	M	Laborer	11Ja02D+
Bridget	10	F	Unknown	11Ja02D+
Pat	8	M	Child	11Ja02D+
Cathe.	6	F	Child	11Ja02D+
COOLEY, Anne	4	F	Child	11Ja02D+
MARCH, Peter	24	M	Laborer	11Ja02D+
BRENNON, Cathe.	18	F	Unknown	11Ja02D+
Bridget	12	F	Unknown	11Ja02D+
COOPER, Daniel	22	M	Unknown	11Ja02D+
DELAHUNTY, Mick	35	M	Laborer	11Ja02D+
CAMFORD, Jno.	26	M	Laborer	11Ja02D+
Cath.	30	F	Unknown	11Ja02D+
KIRWAN, Pat	27	M	Laborer	11Ja02D+
WALSH, David	28	M	Laborer	11Ja02D+
FITZPATRICK, Mary	20	F	Unknown	11Ja02D+
JOHNSON, Thos.	35	M	Laborer	11Ja02D+
Mary	28	F	Unknown	11Ja02D+
Marg.	7	F	Child	11Ja02D+
Jno.	4	M	Child	11Ja02D+
Ellen	.09	F	Infant	11Ja02D+
BOWES, Ann	30	F	Unknown	11Ja02D+
COGHLAN, Judy	18	F	Unknown	11Ja02D+
CADOR, Alex	34	M	Laborer	11Ja02D+
MCINTYRE, James	30	M	Laborer	11Ja02D+
MORAN, Bridget	18	F	Unknown	11Ja02D+
FORRESTER, Mary-A.	25	F	Unknown	11Ja02D+
MCCASHIN, Hugh	28	M	Laborer	11Ja02D+
GALLAGHAN, Jno.	25	M	Laborer	11Ja02D+
MCCALLAGH, Arthur	45	M	Laborer	11Ja02D+
FITZPATRICK, Jno.	25	M	Laborer	11Ja02D+
Mary	25	F	Unknown	11Ja02D+
Ann	25	F	Unknown	11Ja02D+
MCINTYRE, Miles	16	M	Laborer	11Ja02D+
GARRET, Mary	30	F	Unknown	11Ja02D+
Bridget	3	F	Child	11Ja02D+
Bernard	4	M	Child	11Ja02D+
MURPHY, Bitty	30	F	Unknown	11Ja02D+
DUGGIN, James	18	M	Laborer	11Ja02D+

NAMES OF PASSENGERS	AGE	SEX	OCCUPATIONS	DATE PORT SHIP
DAVY, Jno.	30	M	Laborer	11Ja02Dt
DURGER, Eliza	50	F	Unknown	11Ja02Dt
Ann	22	F	Unknown	11Ja02Dt
SMITH, Cath.	21	F	Unknown	11Ja02Dt
FLOOD, Maurice	25	M	Laborer	11Ja02Dt
CASHEL, Thos.	26	M	Laborer	11Ja02Dt
Julia	26	F	Unknown	11Ja02Dt
Cathe.	.00	F	Infant	11Ja02Dt
Died-At-Sea				
COLLINS, Mick	21	M	Laborer	11Ja02Dt
CASHELL, Thos.	20	M	Laborer	11Ja02Dt
HANNAHAN, Thos.	20	M	Laborer	11Ja02Dt
CASKLO, James	25	M	Laborer	11Ja02Dt
SMITH, Eliza	16	F	Unknown	11Ja02Dt
WALTERS, Ann	6	F	Child	11Ja02Dt
Elizabeth	3	F	Child	11Ja02Dt
GROOM, Eliza	32	F	Unknown	11Ja02Dt
Edmund	11	M	Unknown	11Ja02Dt
Alfred	8	M	Child	11Ja02Dt
Jno.	6	M	Child	11Ja02Dt
Cathe.	4	F	Child	11Ja02Dt
CLANCY, Peter	21	M	Laborer	11Ja02Dt
WALTERS, Sarah	11	F	Unknown	11Ja02Dt
COGHLAN, Jno.	24	M	Laborer	11Ja02Dt
WALKER, Mary	19	F	Unknown	11Ja02Dt
LYNCH, Jno.	29	M	Unknown	11Ja02Dt
CONLEY, Mary	40	F	Unknown	11Ja02Dt
FARREL, Bernard	30	M	Laborer	11Ja02Dt
Ann	20	F	Unknown	11Ja02Dt
Ann	10	F	Unknown	11Ja02Dt
Cath.	8	F	Child	11Ja02Dt
Mary	6	F	Child	11Ja02Dt
Died-At-Sea				
Kieran	4	F	Child	11Ja02Dt
Francis	2	F	Child	11Ja02Dt
MALONE, James	27	M	Laborer	11Ja02Dt
MCNULLY, H.	30	M	Laborer	11Ja02Dt
Mary	9	F	Child	11Ja02Dt
MALEY, Ellen	25	F	Unknown	11Ja02Dt
H.	15	F	Unknown	11Ja02Dt
GIBBONS, Wm.	9	M	Child	11Ja02Dt
WALSH, John	20	M	Laborer	11Ja02Dt
DONER, James	20	M	Laborer	11Ja02Dt
HENNEFRY, Michl.	21	M	Laborer	11Ja02Dt
DEVANE, Cathe.	19	F	Unknown	11Ja02Dt
KITARD, Keran	30	M	Laborer	11Ja02Dt
Thos.	6	M	Child	11Ja02Dt
HUMPHRY, Cath.	25	F	Unknown	11Ja02Dt
CORNIELA, Johanna	20	F	Unknown	11Ja02Dt
FLAKRY, Patrick	25	M	Laborer	11Ja02Dt
Edmund	22	M	Laborer	11Ja02Dt
SHENAN, Edmd.	28	M	Laborer	11Ja02Dt
DEAN, Jno.	47	M	Laborer	11Ja02Dt
Wm.	12	M	Laborer	11Ja02Dt
Edmd.	4	M	Laborer	11Ja02Dt
ROE, Susan	35	F	Unknown	11Ja02Dt
MCGUIRE, Ann	30	F	Unknown	11Ja02Dt
RYAN, Jno.	27	M	Laborer	11Ja02Dt
Win	27	F	Unknown	11Ja02Dt
LACEY, Pat	22	M	Laborer	11Ja02Dt
HUMPHRY, Dennis	27	M	Laborer	11Ja02Dt
BOORMAN, Noah	23	M	Laborer	11Ja02Dt
HAMELOW, Bridgt.	15	F	Unknown	11Ja02Dt
GOLDSMITH, Hannah	21	F	Unknown	11Ja02Dt
SCALLEY, Dennis	40	M	Laborer	11Ja02Dt
KIRSICK, Peggy	15	F	Unknown	11Ja02Dt
MAHER, Mary	47	F	Unknown	11Ja02Dt
KENNAGE, Jas.	28	M	Laborer	11Ja02Dt
VAUGHAN, Mary	24	F	Unknown	11Ja02Dt
MOORE, Bryan	20	M	Laborer	11Ja02Dt
JONES, Sam	25	M	Laborer	11Ja02Dt
DOWNING, Geo.	24	M	Laborer	11Ja02Dt
AGNEW, Pat	35	M	Laborer	11Ja02Dt
MIRKEY, Mick	25	M	Laborer	11Ja02Dt
Edwd.	40	M	Laborer	11Ja02Dt

NAMES OF PASSENGERS	AGE	SEX	OCCUPATIONS	DATE PORT SHIP
BRENNAN, Peter	42	M	Laborer	11Ja02Dt
TRAVIS, Ann	20	F	Unknown	11Ja02Dt
Pat	6	M	Child	11Ja02Dt
MURPHY, Pat	28	M	Laborer	11Ja02Dt
U-Mrs.	28	F	Unknown	11Ja02Dt
Michael	.00	M	Infant	11Ja02Dt
BYNER, Geo.	21	M	Laborer	11Ja02Dt
BOYLAN, Bernard	20	M	Laborer	11Ja02Dt
BASK, Mary	20	F	Unknown	11Ja02Dt
Ann	20	F	Unknown	11Ja02Dt
CAREY, Daniel	26	M	Laborer	11Ja02Dt
U-Mrs.	22	F	Unknown	11Ja02Dt
HARUL, Jno.	45	M	Laborer	11Ja02Dt
Cath.	18	F	Unknown	11Ja02Dt
MCGUIN, Sally	46	F	Unknown	11Ja02Dt
MCMAHON, Nancy	21	F	Unknown	11Ja02Dt
SMITH, Francis	20	F	Unknown	11Ja02Dt
Jno.	22	M	Laborer	11Ja02Dt
HARPER, Kit	20	M	Laborer	11Ja02Dt
MARKEY, Michl.	23	M	Laborer	11Ja02Dt
STUART, Jno.	40	M	Laborer	11Ja02Dt
BRENNAN, Michl.	21	M	Laborer	11Ja02Dt
MOUNTAIN, Dennis	40	M	Laborer	11Ja02Dt
CARROL, Margt.	20	F	Unknown	11Ja02Dt
CUMMINS, Wm.	35	M	Laborer	11Ja02Dt
Jno.	30	M	Laborer	11Ja02Dt
Thomas	28	M	Laborer	11Ja02Dt
Johanna	26	F	Unknown	11Ja02Dt
SLATTER, Martin	25	M	Laborer	11Ja02Dt
FLANNAGAN, Jno.	25	M	Laborer	11Ja02Dt
GLASHAN, Michl.	24	M	Laborer	11Ja02Dt
HEPPERMAN, Margt.	19	F	Unknown	11Ja02Dt
QUINLAN, Winnifred	40	F	Unknown	11Ja02Dt
Patrick	12	M	Laborer	11Ja02Dt
COMERFORD, Wm.	40	M	Laborer	11Ja02Dt
RODGERS, Jno.	48	M	Laborer	11Ja02Dt
CLARK, Thos.	21	M	Laborer	11Ja02Dt
FLYNN, Jno.	20	M	Laborer	11Ja02Dt
DEMFRY, U-Mrs.	40	F	Laborer	11Ja02Dt
CASSIDY, Cath.	25	F	Unknown	11Ja02Dt
TATE, Jno.	30	M	Laborer	11Ja02Dt
DOOLEY, Wm.	26	M	Laborer	11Ja02Dt
Thos.	35	M	Laborer	11Ja02Dt
Dan	20	M	Laborer	11Ja02Dt
CORSAIR, Alex	24	M	Laborer	11Ja02Dt
U-Mrs.	22	F	Unknown	11Ja02Dt
Esther	.07	F	Infant	11Ja02Dt
Died-At-Sea				
CASSOCK, James	19	M	Unknown	11Ja02Dt
U-Mrs.	19	F	Unknown	11Ja02Dt
MCKNIGHT, Ellen	20	F	Unknown	11Ja02Dt
CASSOCK, Martin	1	M	Child	11Ja02Dt
MCCLISTER, Jno.	23	M	Laborer	11Ja02Dt
OMARA, Dennis	27	M	Laborer	11Ja02Dt
Thos.	20	M	Laborer	11Ja02Dt
MURPHY, Barnard	35	M	Laborer	11Ja02Dt
RILEY, Dennis	18	M	Laborer	11Ja02Dt
BURLEY, Michl.	25	M	Laborer	11Ja02Dt
Maria	24	F	Unknown	11Ja02Dt
Maria	.06	F	Infant	11Ja02Dt
KEIGHRIN, Mary	44	F	Unknown	11Ja02Dt
Winnefred	9	F	Child	11Ja02Dt
OBRIEN, Mary	19	F	Unknown	11Ja02Dt
Mary	.11	F	Infant	11Ja02Dt
Pat	9	M	Child	11Ja02Dt
Chas.	7	M	Child	11Ja02Dt
Bridget	4	F	Child	11Ja02Dt
EMERSON, Wm.	18	M	Laborer	11Ja02Dt
Geo.	16	M	Laborer	11Ja02Dt
DUFFY, Cath.	18	F	Unknown	11Ja02Dt
MENNA, Dan	20	M	Laborer	11Ja02Dt
CASSIDY, Ellen	20	F	Unknown	11Ja02Dt
BROMAN, Jno.	25	M	Laborer	11Ja02Dt
U-Mrs.	21	F	Unknown	11Ja02Dt
Lewis	.10	M	Infant	11Ja02Dt

NAMES OF PASSENGERS	AGE	SEX	OCCUPATIONS	DATE PORT SHIP
KELLY, Cath.	22	F	Unknown	11Ja02Dt
CONNELL, Jno.	16	M	Laborer	11Ja02Dt
Elizabeth	22	F	Unknown	11Ja02Dt
DWYER, Ellen	50	F	Unknown	11Ja02Dt
Margt.	12	F	Unknown	11Ja02Dt
QUIDAR, Fletcher	32	M	Laborer	11Ja02Dt
Saml.	2	M	Child	11Ja02Dt
Herman	.11	M	Infant	11Ja02Dt
DENT, Margt.	50	F	Unknown	11Ja02Dt
Jno.	21	M	Laborer	11Ja02Dt
Joseph	15	M	Laborer	11Ja02Dt
Jonathan	13	M	Laborer	11Ja02Dt
Robt.	10	M	Laborer	11Ja02Dt
Esther	22	F	Unknown	11Ja02Dt
COWARD, Andy	21	M	Laborer	11Ja02Dt
U-Mrs.	20	F	Unknown	11Ja02Dt
Thos.	.00	M	Infant	11Ja02Dt
MAHER, Edwd.	15	M	Unknown	11Ja02Dt
Cathe.	14	F	Unknown	11Ja02Dt
Michl.	12	M	Unknown	11Ja02Dt
Wm.	10	M	Unknown	11Ja02Dt
Pat	8	M	Child	11Ja02Dt
Mary	6	F	Child	11Ja02Dt
MURPHY, Ann	40	F	Unknown	11Ja02Dt
Pat	13	M	Unknown	11Ja02Dt
TRAVERS, Michl.	22	M	Laborer	11Ja02Dt
GARRETTY, Cath.	24	F	Unknown	11Ja02Dt
Mary	.09	F	Infant	11Ja02Dt
MCBENNETT, Jno.	18	M	Laborer	11Ja02Dt
KING, Elizabeth	21	F	Unknown	11Ja02Dt
MCGUIRE, Pat	35	M	Laborer	11Ja02Dt
OBRIEN, Wm.	20	M	Laborer	11Ja02Dt
Pat	20	M	Laborer	11Ja02Dt
LYNCH, Cath.	45	F	Unknown	11Ja02Dt
SULLIVAN, Joseph	21	M	Laborer	11Ja02Dt
EWING, Elizab.	20	F	Unknown	11Ja02Dt
MCSORLEY, Peter	14	M	Laborer	11Ja02Dt
Pat	18	M	Laborer	11Ja02Dt
FADDEN, Thos.	11	M	Laborer	11Ja02Dt
FAGAN, Mary	20	F	Unknown	11Ja02Dt
MOORE, Ann	20	F	Unknown	11Ja02Dt
DALTON, Pat	22	M	Laborer	11Ja02Dt
MALONE, James	20	M	Laborer	11Ja02Dt
SHERIDAN, Ellen	15	F	Unknown	11Ja02Dt
WARD, Cath.	28	F	Unknown	11Ja02Dt
FARREL, Lifford	30	M	Laborer	11Ja02Dt
COSTELLO, Joseph	35	M	Laborer	11Ja02Dt
MCGUIRE, Pat	20	M	Laborer	11Ja02Dt
USHER, Mick	17	M	Laborer	11Ja02Dt
MATHEWS, Michael	21	M	Unknown	11Ja02Dt
DENBY, Patrick	14	M	Unknown	11Ja02Dt

LADY-HOBART 12 JANUARY 1850

From Liverpool

NAMES OF PASSENGERS	AGE	SEX	OCCUPATIONS	DATE PORT SHIP
DAY, John	35	M	Farmer	12Ja02Dv
Jane (W)	27	F	Wife	12Ja02Dv
Helen	20	F	Servant	12Ja02Dv
John	5	M	Child	12Ja02Dv
Thomas	3	M	Child	12Ja02Dv
Ellen	.00	F	Infant	12Ja02Dv
DONAHUE, Peggy	25	F	Servant	12Ja02Dv
DONNELL, Mary	19	F	Servant	12Ja02Dv
Judy	21	F	Servant	12Ja02Dv
GRIFFIN, Bridget	24	F	Servant	12Ja02Dv
DONNELL, Peggy	22	F	Servant	12Ja02Dv
GALLAHAR, Mary	30	F	Wi	12Ja02Dv
James	10	M	Relative	12Ja02Dv
MORREN, Mary	22	F	Servant	12Ja02Dv
HICKEY, Patrick	40	M	Farmer	12Ja02Dv
Catherine (W)	40	F	Wife	12Ja02Dv
Michael	16	M	Relative	12Ja02Dv
Edward	14	M	Relative	12Ja02Dv
William	10	M	Relative	12Ja02Dv
Mary	8	F	Child	12Ja02Dv
John	4	M	Child	12Ja02Dv
Patk.	.00	M	Infant	12Ja02Dv
GRIFFIN, Thos.	17	M	Laborer	12Ja02Dv
Marty	11	F	None	12Ja02Dv
Edward	9	M	Child	12Ja02Dv
BURNE, Michael	21	M	Tailor	12Ja02Dv
HENWICK, Thos.	24	M	Laborer	12Ja02Dv
STOKES, Chas	27	M	Laborer	12Ja02Dv
REDMOND, Owen	21	M	Laborer	12Ja02Dv
FREENAN, Daniel	46	M	Blacksmith	12Ja02Dv
Catherine (W)	46	F	Wife	12Ja02Dv
Mary	9	F	Child	12Ja02Dv
TUOMY, Timothy	26	M	Laborer	12Ja02Dv
Julia (W)	19	F	Wife	12Ja02Dv
HARRINGTON, James	19	M	Upholsterer	12Ja02Dv
Margaret (W)	19	F	Wife	12Ja02Dv
Johanna	.00	F	Infant	12Ja02Dv
TOULEY, Margaret	18	F	Servant	12Ja02Dv
Mary	20	F	Servant	12Ja02Dv
CONNELL, David	20	M	Laborer	12Ja02Dv
WRIGHT, Margaret-Q. (W)	22	F	Wife	12Ja02Dv
BRYAN, Patrick	32	M	Laborer	12Ja02Dv
Mary (W)	28	F	Wife	12Ja02Dv
Joseph	5	M	Child	12Ja02Dv
KEARNY, Bridget	7	F	Child	12Ja02Dv
CORCORAN, William	16	M	None	12Ja02Dv
OHENEM, Margaret	3	F	Child	12Ja02Dv
ENGLISH, Alice	24	F	Servant	12Ja02Dv
A.Hobart-Trowbridge	.00	M	Infant	12Ja02Dv
LINCH, Mary-Ann	27	F	Dressmaker	12Ja02Dv
CLARK, Catherine	24	F	Dressmaker	12Ja02Dv
OBRIAN, Ann	9	F	Child	12Ja02Dv
Margaret	7	F	Child	12Ja02Dv
OCONNOR, Banes	23	M	Printer	12Ja02Dv
KEEFE, Mary	23	F	Spinster	12Ja02Dv
WHITE, Margaret	22	F	Spinster	12Ja02Dv
MAHER, Helen	21	F	Dressmaker	12Ja02Dv
BUTLER, William	21	M	Shoemaker	12Ja02Dv
MCNAMARA, John	40	M	Laborer	12Ja02Dv
LUCUS, Helen	30	F	Spinster	12Ja02Dv
MUNIM, Thos.	18	M	Laborer	12Ja02Dv
BUNNAR, Pat	25	M	Laborer	12Ja02Dv
GRANNAN, Pat	17	M	Laborer	12Ja02Dv
GATELY, Bridget	18	F	Servant	12Ja02Dv
FALLAN, Edward	30	M	Laborer	12Ja02Dv
Mary (W)	28	F	Wife	12Ja02Dv
Bridget	4	F	Child	12Ja02Dv
Mary	.00	F	Infant	12Ja02Dv
LENNON, Michael	20	M	Laborer	12Ja02Dv
DONAHUE, Joe-O.	26	M	Laborer	12Ja02Dv
GATELY, Pat	49	M	Laborer	12Ja02Dv
BAIN, Mary	20	F	Spinster	12Ja02Dv
GATELY, Catherine	14	F	None	12Ja02Dv
Honor	12	M	None	12Ja02Dv
GLENN, William	28	M	Laborer	12Ja02Dv
DALY, Martin	30	M	Laborer	12Ja02Dv
MANING, Lusan	20	F	Servant	12Ja02Dv
TURNER, Anne	40	F	Wife	12Ja02Dv
Mary	5	F	Child	12Ja02Dv
FITZGERALD, Nancy	30	F	Servant	12Ja02Dv
HEALY, Mary	52	F	Servant	12Ja02Dv
LOFTUS, Mary	28	F	Wife	12Ja02Dv
ONEILL, Ellen	46	F	Wife	12Ja02Dv
HYTES, Thos.	23	M	Carpenter	12Ja02Dv
Ann (W)	23	F	Wife	12Ja02Dv
HYDE, Eliza	18	F	Servant	12Ja02Dv
GATLANS, John	20	M	Laborer	12Ja02Dv
ROGEN, Jane	28	F	Laborer	12Ja02Dv

NAMES OF PASSENGERS		AGE	SEX	OCCUPATIONS	DATE PORT SHIP
FLOTS, Betsy		40	F	Spinster	12Ja02Dv
GLYNN, Bridget		24	F	Servant	12Ja02Dv
OBRIEN, Martin		30	M	Shepherd	12Ja02Dv
Margaret	(W)	23	F	Wife	12Ja02Dv
Julia		.00	F	Infant	12Ja02Dv
WALSH, Michael		18	M	Laborer	12Ja02Dv
NOLAN, Letty		35	F	Wife	12Ja02Dv
Hannah		15	F	Unknown	12Ja02Dv
Helen		4	F	Child	12Ja02Dv
BAGGAN, Owen		18	M	Laborer	12Ja02Dv
SHERMAN, Patrick		19	M	Laborer	12Ja02Dv
JORDAN, Kitty		30	F	Wife	12Ja02Dv
Ann		6	F	Child	12Ja02Dv
CONDON, John		50	M	Courier	12Ja02Dv
Helen	(W)	50	F	Wife	12Ja02Dv
Daniel		15	M	Unknown	12Ja02Dv
WALSH, Mary		20	F	Servant	12Ja02Dv
YOUNG, Catherine		18	F	Servant	12Ja02Dv
BUCKLY, Catherine		23	F	Servant	12Ja02Dv
CALTER, Mary		20	F	Servant	12Ja02Dv
LULLIAN, Margaret		18	F	Servant	12Ja02Dv
LEHNAN, Patrick		20	M	Laborer	12Ja02Dv
Kitty		21	F	Servant	12Ja02Dv
PAYNE, Mary		18	F	Servant	12Ja02Dv
HERAN, Thos.		30	M	Laborer	12Ja02Dv
Eleanor	(W)	30	F	Wife	12Ja02Dv
Patrick		3	M	Child	12Ja02Dv
DOROD, Dennis		23	M	Laborer	12Ja02Dv
ELLWORTH, Christopher		25	M	Laborer	12Ja02Dv
Bridget		18	F	Laborer	12Ja02Dv
Mary		28	F	Servant	12Ja02Dv
BOLEN, Maria		18	F	Servant	12Ja02Dv
KEILLY, Pat		26	M	Laborer	12Ja02Dv
FIGAN, Pat		24	M	Laborer	12Ja02Dv
CAULFIELD, Thedy		21	M	Laborer	12Ja02Dv
Patrick		27	M	Laborer	12Ja02Dv
Catherine	(W)	28	F	Wife	12Ja02Dv
Michael		.00	M	Infant	12Ja02Dv
Christopher		3	M	Child	12Ja02Dv
GLANERY, Francis		18	M	Laborer	12Ja02Dv
Mary		60	F	Wi	12Ja02Dv
MADON, Maria		8	F	Child	12Ja02Dv
BROWN, Mich.		30	M	Laborer	12Ja02Dv
J.		20	M	Laborer	12Ja02Dv
Michael		30	M	Laborer	12Ja02Dv
Peter		18	M	Laborer	12Ja02Dv
BIRD, Betsey		38	F	Wife	12Ja02Dv
Simon		12	M	Unknown	12Ja02Dv
Luke		7	M	Child	12Ja02Dv
Ann		21	F	Spinster	12Ja02Dv
CARTIGAN, Pat		36	M	Laborer	12Ja02Dv
CAGE, William		25	M	Weaver	12Ja02Dv
PURCELL, Philip		21	M	Laborer	12Ja02Dv
DALTON, Mary		3	F	Child	12Ja02Dv
Marge		20	F	Servant	12Ja02Dv
ONEILL, Margaret		22	F	Spinster	12Ja02Dv
NORRIS, Bridget		30	F	Wife	12Ja02Dv
John		5	M	Child	12Ja02Dv
Margaret		3	F	Child	12Ja02Dv
FOX, Bridget		30	F	Wife	12Ja02Dv
Ellen		6	F	Child	12Ja02Dv
Bridget		.00	F	Infant	12Ja02Dv
LEALY, Jane		19	F	Servant	12Ja02Dv
HOPKINS, Maria		10	F	Unknown	12Ja02Dv
Catherine		8	F	Child	12Ja02Dv
HAGARTY, Owen		20	M	Laborer	12Ja02Dv
HART, Bridget		11	F	Unknown	12Ja02Dv
CASEY, Michael		25	M	Laborer	12Ja02Dv
MCGUIRE, Bridget		20	F	Servant	12Ja02Dv
H.		.00	U	Infant	12Ja02Dv
DALTON, Mary		36	F	Wife	12Ja02Dv
Bridget		36	F	Wife	12Ja02Dv
Mathew		10	M	Unknown	12Ja02Dv
Bridget		.00	F	Infant	12Ja02Dv
BURKE, James		20	M	Carter	12Ja02Dv

NAMES OF PASSENGERS		AGE	SEX	OCCUPATIONS	DATE PORT SHIP
BURKE, Bridget		19	F	Servant	12Ja02Dv
Johanna		18	F	Servant	12Ja02Dv
CINDON, Mihol		24	M	Laborer	12Ja02Dv
HEARNEY, Patrick		60	M	Laborer	12Ja02Dv
Bridget	(W)	50	F	Wife	12Ja02Dv
Margaret		17	F	Spinster	12Ja02Dv
Eliza		15	F	Spinster	12Ja02Dv
Patrick		20	M	Laborer	12Ja02Dv
CAPPEL, Mary		18	F	Spinster	12Ja02Dv
Honor		13	F	Unknown	12Ja02Dv
John		10	M	Unknown	12Ja02Dv
Mauruce		7	M	Child	12Ja02Dv
Catherine		3	F	Child	12Ja02Dv
WILSON, Mary		40	F	Wife	12Ja02Dv
John		12	M	Unknown	12Ja02Dv
CARTY, Ann		35	F	Wife	12Ja02Dv
MURPHY, Margret		17	F	Servant	12Ja02Dv
KEARNEY, Thos.		50	M	Laborer	12Ja02Dv
Ellen	(W)	52	F	Wife	12Ja02Dv
MCDERMOT, Bridget		17	F	Servant	12Ja02Dv
BURNS, Eliza		35	F	Wife	12Ja02Dv
Mary		8	F	Child	12Ja02Dv
Ann		6	F	Child	12Ja02Dv
Patrick		4	M	Child	12Ja02Dv
Patrick		35	M	Fsvnt	12Ja02Dv
FOWLEY, Jeremiah		45	M	Farmer	12Ja02Dv
Julia	(W)	33	F	Wife	12Ja02Dv
Honora		8	F	Child	12Ja02Dv
Catherine		6	F	Child	12Ja02Dv
Daniel		4	M	Child	12Ja02Dv
Michael		2	M	Child	12Ja02Dv
WALSH, John		20	M	Laborer	12Ja02Dv
GAVIN, Catherine		44	F	Wi	12Ja02Dv
Michael		22	M	Laborer	12Ja02Dv
CANNON, Peggy		20	F	Spinster	12Ja02Dv
GAVIN, Margaret		20	F	Spinster	12Ja02Dv
BRIN, William		25	M	Laborer	12Ja02Dv
EGAN, Ann		28	F	Wife	12Ja02Dv
Mary		4	F	Child	12Ja02Dv
HAGAN, John		24	M	Laborer	12Ja02Dv
Margaret		22	F	Dressmaker	12Ja02Dv
RABBIT, John		28	M	Laborer	12Ja02Dv
LAFFIN, John		22	M	Coachman	12Ja02Dv
GODKIN, Jane		25	F	Servant	12Ja02Dv
DOUGLASS, Mary		48	F	Wife	12Ja02Dv
John		22	M	Laborer	12Ja02Dv
WHELAN, Ann		22	F	Wife	12Ja02Dv
Mary		2	F	Child	12Ja02Dv
RAFFERTY, Rossanne		21	F	Reeler	12Ja02Dv
Thomas		.00	M	Infant	12Ja02Dv
BELE, William		19	M	Clerk	12Ja02Dv
KEAN, Michael		33	M	Asstengr	12Ja02Dv
Francis	(W)	30	F	Wife	12Ja02Dv
Margaret		11	F	Unknown	12Ja02Dv
Patrick		10	M	Unknown	12Ja02Dv
William		7	M	Child	12Ja02Dv
Ann-Maria		6	F	Child	12Ja02Dv
John		3	M	Child	12Ja02Dv
Michael		.00	M	Infant	12Ja02Dv
FANNY, William		33	M	Laborer	12Ja02Dv
Mary		32	F	Laborer	12Ja02Dv
Elizabeth		8	F	Child	12Ja02Dv
Jason		5	M	Child	12Ja02Dv
WALLACE, Robert		21	M	Laborer	12Ja02Dv
Sarah		18	F	Servant	12Ja02Dv
HUGHES, Ann		18	F	Servant	12Ja02Dv
DEANY, Patrick		18	M	Laborer	12Ja02Dv
CARTIGEN, John		21	M	Fsvnt	12Ja02Dv
GALLAGHER, Ann		30	F	Wife	12Ja02Dv
James		7	M	Child	12Ja02Dv
John		5	M	Child	12Ja02Dv
CONNOR, Mary		50	F	Wi	12Ja02Dv
Thos.		19	M	Laborer	12Ja02Dv
Martin		17	M	Laborer	12Ja02Dv
Margaret		12	F	Unknown	12Ja02Dv

NAMES OF PASSENGERS	AGE	SEX	OCCUPATIONS	DATE PORT SHIP
CONNOR, Cecily	7	F	Child	12Ja02Dv
MORNE, Cecily	40	F	Wife	12Ja02Dv
Michael	18	M	Laborer	12Ja02Dv
Thos.	14	M	Unknown	12Ja02Dv
Patrick	12	M	Unknown	12Ja02Dv
John	10	M	Unknown	12Ja02Dv
Edward	8	M	Child	12Ja02Dv
Bernard	6	M	Child	12Ja02Dv
Celia	2	F	Child	12Ja02Dv
LYNCH, Catherine	22	F	Wife	12Ja02Dv
Maria	2	F	Child	12Ja02Dv
DONNOR, Thos.	40	M	Laborer	12Ja02Dv
REID, Honor	20	M	Servant	12Ja02Dv
RICHARD, Thos.	30	M	Laborer	12Ja02Dv
CUNNINGHAM, Edward	27	M	Servant	12Ja02Dv
HIGGINS, Catharine	17	F	Servant	12Ja02Dv
DOWNE, Mary	18	F	Servant	12Ja02Dv
GIB, John	24	M	Tailor	12Ja02Dv
CUINANE, John	27	M	Laborer	12Ja02Dv
MCGRAPH, John	23	M	Laborer	12Ja02Dv
MCGUIRE, Ann	22	F	Servant	12Ja02Dv
KEEFE, John	27	M	Gdnr	12Ja02Dv
MCCARTY, James	21	M	Unknown	12Ja02Dv
Died-At-Sea				
MCDERMOT, Honora	20	F	Unknown	12Ja02Dv
Died-At-Sea				
U, U	.00	U	Infant	12Ja02Dv
Died-At-Sea				
U	.00	U	Infant	12Ja02Dv
Died-At-Sea				
KIRBY, Mary-Ann	21	F	Unknown	12Ja02Dv
Walter	55	M	Shopkeeper	12Ja02Dv
HICKEY, James	12	M	Relative	12Ja02Dv

JAS.H.SHEPHERD 12 JANUARY 1850

From Liverpool

NAMES OF PASSENGERS	AGE	SEX	OCCUPATIONS	DATE PORT SHIP
FAY, Pat	28	M	Piper	12Ja02Ea
U (W)	26	F	None	12Ja02Ea
Pat	.00	M	Infant	12Ja02Ea
CLENN, John	30	M	Laborer	12Ja02Ea
Brdgt.	26	F	None	12Ja02Ea
John	5	M	Child	12Ja02Ea
Pat	4	M	Child	12Ja02Ea
Cath.	2	F	Child	12Ja02Ea
Died-At-Sea				
Dan	14	M	None	12Ja02Ea
Mgt.	20	F	None	12Ja02Ea
HISSEN, Michl.	40	M	None	12Ja02Ea
Mary	50	F	None	12Ja02Ea
SCULLY, Brdt.	30	F	None	12Ja02Ea
Margt.	18	F	None	12Ja02Ea
Mary	.00	F	Infant	12Ja02Ea
CLARKE, Brdgt.	19	F	Servant	12Ja02Ea
Pat	13	M	None	12Ja02Ea
THOMPSON, Edwd.	25	M	None	12Ja02Ea
Mary	21	F	None	12Ja02Ea
LARKIN, Peter	30	M	Cobbler	12Ja02Ea
Abby	25	F	None	12Ja02Ea
Mary	10	F	None	12Ja02Ea
Nancy	8	F	Child	12Ja02Ea
Abby	3	F	Child	12Ja02Ea
Bernard	.00	M	Infant	12Ja02Ea
Brd.	19	F	None	12Ja02Ea
LYMAN, Thos.	66	M	Farmer	12Ja02Ea
U (W)	60	F	None	12Ja02Ea
Oney	16	U	None	12Ja02Ea
Mary	16	F	None	12Ja02Ea
LYMAN, Cath.	13	F	None	12Ja02Ea
Bernard	11	M	None	12Ja02Ea
James	10	M	None	12Ja02Ea
Wm.	8	M	Child	12Ja02Ea
Mgt.	6	F	Child	12Ja02Ea
Brdgt.	3	F	Child	12Ja02Ea
Thos.	.00	M	Infant	12Ja02Ea
COXLY, Wm.	21	M	Laborer	12Ja02Ea
DOLAN, Thos.	23	M	Laborer	12Ja02Ea
U (W)	23	F	Laborer	12Ja02Ea
Pat	4	M	Child	12Ja02Ea
Ann	2	F	Child	12Ja02Ea
Cath.	40	F	None	12Ja02Ea
Nancy	16	F	None	12Ja02Ea
MANGAN, John	26	M	Laborer	12Ja02Ea
MARTIN, James	35	M	Laborer	12Ja02Ea
Mary	38	F	None	12Ja02Ea
Mary	11	F	None	12Ja02Ea
James	13	M	None	12Ja02Ea
Allice	.00	F	Infant	12Ja02Ea
KENNEDY, James	25	M	Blacksmith	12Ja02Ea
Michl.	20	M	None	12Ja02Ea
MEHAM, John	40	M	Farmer	12Ja02Ea
Pat	20	M	None	12Ja02Ea
Ann	18	F	None	12Ja02Ea
MCDERMOT, Cath.	18	F	Servant	12Ja02Ea
SMITH, Arthur	40	M	Blacksmith	12Ja02Ea
CUMING, Allex	20	M	Laborer	12Ja02Ea
BROWN, Mary	26	F	Servant	12Ja02Ea
HEAD, Honor	20	F	None	12Ja02Ea
HENRY, Brdgt.	20	F	None	12Ja02Ea
FENNERTY, Cath.	20	F	None	12Ja02Ea
LANE, Richd.	35	M	Farmer	12Ja02Ea
GRANT, John	30	M	Laborer	12Ja02Ea
OHARE, James	28	M	Ostler	12Ja02Ea
SMITH, Michl.	35	M	Farmer	12Ja02Ea
Rose	18	F	None	12Ja02Ea
Michl.	19	M	None	12Ja02Ea
HAYLAN, John	20	M	None	12Ja02Ea
LOGAN, Phil.	19	M	None	12Ja02Ea
TULLEY, Michl.	25	M	None	12Ja02Ea
RILEY, Mgt.	18	F	None	12Ja02Ea
HIGGINS, Brdgt.	30	F	None	12Ja02Ea
KEARNE, Mary	25	F	Servant	12Ja02Ea
GARAGON, Judy	45	F	None	12Ja02Ea
DONAGAN, Peter	23	M	Laborer	12Ja02Ea
DOGHERTY, Thos.	40	M	Weaver	12Ja02Ea
CULBERTON, Albert	5	M	Child	12Ja02Ea
MCKENNA, Pat	11	M	None	12Ja02Ea
Ann	11	F	None	12Ja02Ea
Michl.	8	M	Child	12Ja02Ea
Anna	13	F	None	12Ja02Ea
John	12	M	None	12Ja02Ea
QUINN, Brdgt.	20	F	Servant	12Ja02Ea
Brdgt.	8	F	Child	12Ja02Ea
LOODEN, An.	45	U	None	12Ja02Ea
Thos.	00	M	None	12Ja02Ea
Dan	9	M	Child	12Ja02Ea
Dennis	7	M	Child	12Ja02Ea
Mary	3	F	Child	12Ja02Ea
CASTELLO, Cath.	30	F	None	12Ja02Ea
Nancy	5	F	Child	12Ja02Ea
U	2	M	Child	12Ja02Ea
ANDERSON, Mary	19	F	Servant	12Ja02Ea
Pat	14	M	None	12Ja02Ea
CARROL, Cath.	17	F	Servant	12Ja02Ea
MALONY, Mary	9	F	Child	12Ja02Ea
CULBERTON, Jane	30	F	None	12Ja02Ea
John	7	M	Child	12Ja02Ea
MCCABE, Cath.	22	F	Servant	12Ja02Ea
John	6	M	Child	12Ja02Ea
BRAHENY, Thos.	18	M	Laborer	12Ja02Ea
Eliza	11	F	None	12Ja02Ea
TRACY, John	58	M	Laborer	12Ja02Ea
Peggy	40	F	None	12Ja02Ea

NAMES OF PASSENGERS		AGE	SEX	OCCUPATIONS	DATE PORT SHIP
TRACY, Michl.		.00	M	Infant	12Ja02Ea
CONNOR, Mary		32	F	None	12Ja02Ea
DONNEGAN, Mary		24	F	None	12Ja02Ea
HIGGINS, Sarah		46	F	None	12Ja02Ea
Mark		7	M	Child	12Ja02Ea
BRADLY, Thos.		20	M	Laborer	12Ja02Ea
HALEY, James		27	M	Laborer	12Ja02Ea
Mary		25	F	None	12Ja02Ea
Cath.		25	F	None	12Ja02Ea
REYNOLDS, James		50	M	Baker	12Ja02Ea
DUFFEE, Bernd.		15	M	None	12Ja02Ea
OCONNOR, Mary		15	F	None	12Ja02Ea
MULLAN, Michl.		40	M	Butcher	12Ja02Ea
U	(W)	33	F	None	12Ja02Ea
HENERY, Mary		24	F	Servant	12Ja02Ea
FLUREN, John		22	M	Laborer	12Ja02Ea
BREAGLE, John		26	M	Laborer	12Ja02Ea
Michl.		20	M	None	12Ja02Ea
Pat		25	M	None	12Ja02Ea
DABLY, James		26	M	None	12Ja02Ea
DYER, Thos.		36	M	Farmer	12Ja02Ea
Mary		36	F	None	12Ja02Ea
MULLALY, Maurice		30	M	Laborer	12Ja02Ea
BROUGHILL, Larry		20	M	None	12Ja02Ea
MORAN, Michl.		25	M	Laborer	12Ja02Ea
HATTERY, Mgt.		38	F	None	12Ja02Ea
John		13	M	None	12Ja02Ea
Ellen		5	F	Child	12Ja02Ea
Michl.		4	M	Child	12Ja02Ea
SHEELY, Ann		27	F	Cook	12Ja02Ea
Brdgt.		21	F	None	12Ja02Ea
MORTON, Mary		19	F	Servant	12Ja02Ea
CONWAY, David		28	M	Laborer	12Ja02Ea
CONDRON, Mary		40	F	None	12Ja02Ea
NESBIT, Wm.		16	M	Laborer	12Ja02Ea
WILSON, G.		28	M	Laborer	12Ja02Ea
Betsy		22	F	None	12Ja02Ea
Mgt.		4	F	Child	12Ja02Ea
Maria		2	F	Child	12Ja02Ea
Hugh		.00	M	Infant	12Ja02Ea
DAVIS, Henry		40	M	Farmer	12Ja02Ea
Sarah		30	F	None	12Ja02Ea
Joseph		19	M	None	12Ja02Ea
Thos.		12	M	None	12Ja02Ea
Mary-J.		11	F	None	12Ja02Ea
Geo.		8	M	Child	12Ja02Ea
Henry		4	M	Child	12Ja02Ea
Eliza		3	F	Child	12Ja02Ea
Mgt.		.00	F	Infant	12Ja02Ea
KILLEY, Pat		20	M	Laborer	12Ja02Ea
DORAN, Jas.		24	M	Carpenter	12Ja02Ea
Ellinor		20	F	None	12Ja02Ea
QUINN, Cath.		35	F	None	12Ja02Ea
MOLONY, Peter		18	M	Laborer	12Ja02Ea
James		38	M	None	12Ja02Ea
CONWAY, John		27	M	Laborer	12Ja02Ea
Mary		25	F	None	12Ja02Ea
CONNELLY, Mgt.		31	F	None	12Ja02Ea
LOFTUSS, Ann		25	F	None	12Ja02Ea
Pat		.00	M	Infant	12Ja02Ea
QUANAN, Daily		51	M	Farmer	12Ja02Ea
Michl.		20	M	Farmer	12Ja02Ea
MEREDITH, Henry		23	F	None	12Ja02Ea
Cath.		22	F	None	12Ja02Ea
BERRY, James		25	M	Laborer	12Ja02Ea
COLEMAN, Geo.		16	M	None	12Ja02Ea
Ann		14	F	None	12Ja02Ea
Betsey		16	F	None	12Ja02Ea
CONNER, Anty.		13	F	None	12Ja02Ea
Sarah		12	F	None	12Ja02Ea
BRAMMINGTON, Martin		18	M	Laborer	12Ja02Ea
Pat		21	M	None	12Ja02Ea
MCCLEAN, Pat		19	M	Laborer	12Ja02Ea
KING, Chas.		20	M	Laborer	12Ja02Ea
RYAN, Rose		17	F	None	12Ja02Ea

NAMES OF PASSENGERS	AGE	SEX	OCCUPATIONS	DATE PORT SHIP
QUILAN, Mary	35	F	None	12Ja02Ea
DEVINE, Ann	20	F	Laborer	12Ja02Ea
MULLIGAN, Pat	20	M	None	12Ja02Ea
MCCARRICK, Jas.	20	M	None	12Ja02Ea
LANEY, Wm.	20	M	Carpenter	12Ja02Ea
SPOUSER, Wm.	24	M	Laborer	12Ja02Ea
COUNA, Brdgt.	20	F	None	12Ja02Ea
WHALEN, John	36	M	Gunsmith	12Ja02Ea
SULLERAN, Anty	26	F	None	12Ja02Ea
James	3	M	Child	12Ja02Ea
John	.00	M	Infant	12Ja02Ea
TENLLY, Pat	28	M	Laborer	12Ja02Ea
John	20	M	None	12Ja02Ea
Cath.	24	F	None	12Ja02Ea
CLARKE, Mary	18	F	None	12Ja02Ea
QUALAN, Cath.	16	F	None	12Ja02Ea
MCKNIGHT, Robt.	24	M	Laborer	12Ja02Ea
MANN, Dan	35	M	Laborer	12Ja02Ea
RICKSON, Mary-A.	25	F	None	12Ja02Ea
CLARKE, John	20	M	Tailor	12Ja02Ea
MCGAUGHLIN, Wm.	30	M	Laborer	12Ja02Ea
SMITH, James	20	M	None	12Ja02Ea
MULLEN, Wm.	25	M	None	12Ja02Ea

BROOKSBY 12 JANUARY 1850

From Glasgow

MCLAUCHLAN, Michael	28	M	Laborer	12Ja21Du
QUIGLEY, William	50	M	Laborer	12Ja21Du
Ann	45	F	Relative	12Ja21Du
William	11	M	Relative	12Ja21Du
George	9	M	Relative	12Ja21Du
Margt.	9	F	Relative	12Ja21Du
John	5	M	Relative	12Ja21Du
ATKINSON, Ann-Jane	27	F	None	12Ja21Du
BENE, Mary	35	F	None	12Ja21Du
Francis	6	M	Child	12Ja21Du
Patrick	4	M	Child	12Ja21Du
FALLON, Peter	27	M	Laborer	12Ja21Du
MCCORMICK, Pat	21	M	Laborer	12Ja21Du
WALKER, David	20	M	Laborer	12Ja21Du
SWEENIE, John	53	M	Laborer	12Ja21Du
Margery	53	F	Relative	12Ja21Du
Elizth.	17	F	Relative	12Ja21Du
Agnes	15	F	Relative	12Ja21Du
WILSON, David	64	M	Laborer	12Ja21Du
SCOTT, Andw.	24	M	Laborer	12Ja21Du
CAMPBELL, Elizth.	21	F	None	12Ja21Du
GUNNING, John	21	M	Laborer	12Ja21Du
ROBERTSON, Robt.	21	M	Laborer	12Ja21Du
MITCHELL, Margt.	22	F	None	12Ja21Du
JAMIESON, Joseph	45	M	Farmer	12Ja21Du
Mary	42	F	Relative	12Ja21Du
Eliza	10	F	Relative	12Ja21Du
Agnes	8	F	Relative	12Ja21Du
WALKER, Catharine	19	F	Spinster	12Ja21Du
HIGGINS, Mary-Ann	23	F	Spinster	12Ja21Du
Francis	13	M	None	12Ja21Du
MCBRIDE, Ann	25	F	Spinster	12Ja21Du
SCULHON, Susan	45	F	None	12Ja21Du
Mary	20	F	None	12Ja21Du
Ann	15	F	None	12Ja21Du
Wm.	12	M	None	12Ja21Du
Robt.	10	M	None	12Ja21Du
Henry	7	M	Child	12Ja21Du
Jane	5	F	Child	12Ja21Du
BURNS, Matilda	36	F	None	12Ja21Du
Samuel	12	M	None	12Ja21Du

NAMES OF PASSENGERS	AGE	SEX	OCCUPATIONS	DATE PORT SHIP
BURNS, Harriett	8	F	Child	12Ja21Du
George	6	M	Child	12Ja21Du
Eliza-Jane	3	F	Child	12Ja21Du
MCCUTCHEON, John	45	M	Laborer	12Ja21Du
Effy	40	F	None	12Ja21Du
Jane	12	F	None	12Ja21Du
Margt.	10	F	None	12Ja21Du
Isabella	8	F	Child	12Ja21Du
Ann	6	F	Child	12Ja21Du
Joseph	4	M	Child	12Ja21Du
Rebecca	.09	F	Infant	12Ja21Du
MCCOSTELL, Pat	34	M	Laborer	12Ja21Du
HIGGINS, Ann	22	F	None	12Ja21Du
U	.09	F	Infant	12Ja21Du
MCMASTER, George	25	M	Laborer	12Ja21Du
KELLY, John	32	M	Laborer	12Ja21Du
Ellis	21	M	None	12Ja21Du
Hugh	.07	M	Infant	12Ja21Du
ELLIOTT, William	48	M	Farmer	12Ja21Du
Rosanna	46	F	None	12Ja21Du
Lancelot	20	M	None	12Ja21Du
Isabella	16	F	None	12Ja21Du
George	12	M	None	12Ja21Du
Rosanna	7	F	Child	12Ja21Du
REILLY, James	25	M	Laborer	12Ja21Du
BAIRD, James-Mrs.	30	F	None	12Ja21Du
John	6	M	Child	12Ja21Du
Sarah	.11	F	Infant	12Ja21Du
LATH, Alexr.	14	M	Laborer	12Ja21Du
BROWN, Geo.	19	M	Laborer	12Ja21Du
WALKER, Geo.	22	M	Laborer	12Ja21Du
FERGUSON, Alexr.	19	M	Laborer	12Ja21Du
Barbara	11	F	None	12Ja21Du
MCTAGGART, Jas.	30	M	Laborer	12Ja21Du
Jane	25	F	None	12Ja21Du
John	5	M	Child	12Ja21Du
Cathe.	.09	F	Infant	12Ja21Du
CURRIE, Jas.	21	M	Laborer	12Ja21Du
TONNER, Frank	35	M	Laborer	12Ja21Du
BARTON, John	20	M	Laborer	12Ja21Du
AITKIN, Jas.	70	M	Laborer	12Ja21Du
Cath.	50	F	None	12Ja21Du
Susan	20	F	None	12Ja21Du
Ann	18	F	None	12Ja21Du
MCCALLY, Jas.	55	M	Laborer	12Ja21Du
Mary	50	F	None	12Ja21Du
Cath.	14	F	None	12Ja21Du
Bridget	11	F	None	12Ja21Du
BROLLY, Unity	53	F	None	12Ja21Du
Sarah	12	F	None	12Ja21Du
MORE, Mary	32	F	None	12Ja21Du
Susan	11	F	None	12Ja21Du
John	9	M	Child	12Ja21Du
Ellen	7	F	Child	12Ja21Du
Wm.	5	M	Child	12Ja21Du
Joseph	3	M	Child	12Ja21Du
Isabella	.08	F	Infant	12Ja21Du
MCFARLANE, Jane	40	F	None	12Ja21Du
Wm.	10	M	None	12Ja21Du
John	7	M	Child	12Ja21Du
Geo.	4	M	Child	12Ja21Du
James	2	M	Child	12Ja21Du
MCGUIN, Sarah	25	F	None	12Ja21Du
MCWILLIAMS, Michael	25	M	Laborer	12Ja21Du
HALY, James	30	M	Laborer	12Ja21Du
BURDEN, William	22	M	Laborer	12Ja21Du
HARPER, Daniel	22	M	Laborer	12Ja21Du
MCKAY, Thos.	22	M	Laborer	12Ja21Du
MURRY, Agnes-Mrs.	39	F	None	12Ja21Du
Agnes	13	F	None	12Ja21Du
HETHERINGTON, Jas.	24	M	Laborer	12Ja21Du
ROBERTSON, Jas.	21	M	Laborer	12Ja21Du
MCINTYRE, John	28	M	Laborer	12Ja21Du
WILSON, Elizth.	30	F	None	12Ja21Du
Ann-Jane	5	F	Child	12Ja21Du
WILSON, Margt.	2	F	Child	12Ja21Du
FARREN, Wm.	67	M	Laborer	12Ja21Du
MCCARRON, John	32	M	None	12Ja21Du
MCEWAN, Jane-Mrs.	32	F	None	12Ja21Du
Margt.	9	F	Child	12Ja21Du
Jas.	7	M	Child	12Ja21Du
ODONNELL, Cath.	28	F	Spinster	12Ja21Du
HIGH, Wm.	29	M	Merchant	12Ja21Du
JORDIN, David	20	M	Laborer	12Ja21Du
DONAGHY, Jas.	45	M	Laborer	12Ja21Du
MCBRERTY, Ann	35	F	None	12Ja21Du
Jessie	9	F	Child	12Ja21Du
Michael	6	M	Child	12Ja21Du
LEPPER, Cathe.	26	F	Spinster	12Ja21Du
MCCALLY, Eliza	38	F	Spinster	12Ja21Du
HENNESSY, Ann	18	F	Spinster	12Ja21Du
BOWELS, Henry	20	M	Laborer	12Ja21Du
HARPER, Wm.	17	M	Laborer	12Ja21Du
BROADLY, Wm.	22	M	Laborer	12Ja21Du
KELLY, Jas.	30	M	Laborer	12Ja21Du
LAPIN, Mary	30	F	Laborer	12Ja21Du

GARRICK 12 JANUARY 1850

From Liverpool

NAMES OF PASSENGERS	AGE	SEX	OCCUPATIONS	DATE PORT SHIP
CARR, Charles	20	M	Laborer	12Ja02Dw
Teddy	18	M	Shoemaker	12Ja02Dw
Mary	60	F	Lad	12Ja02Dw
James	8	M	Child	12Ja02Dw
Ann	6	F	Child	12Ja02Dw
MCINTOSH, Cath.	25	F	Lad	12Ja02Dw
MCCLUTCHY, James	13	M	Miner	12Ja02Dw
BELL, Biddy	50	F	Lad	12Ja02Dw
MURPHY, Cath.	40	F	Lad	12Ja02Dw
LAFFERTY, Ellen	22	F	Lad	12Ja02Dw
TEAN, John-Jas.	14	M	Laborer	12Ja02Dw
MCQUADE, Cath.	17	F	Lad	12Ja02Dw
MARRION, Thos.	20	M	Laborer	12Ja02Dw
MILAN, Pat	31	M	Laborer	12Ja02Dw
FITZPATRICK, Mary	11	F	Unknown	12Ja02Dw
BURKE, Mick	25	M	Laborer	12Ja02Dw
KEEFFE, Cath.	20	F	Lad	12Ja02Dw
DOLAN, John	17	M	Miner	12Ja02Dw
Eliza	11	F	Unknown	12Ja02Dw
CARROLL, Cecilia	3	F	Child	12Ja02Dw
MCINTAGART, Pat	22	M	Laborer	12Ja02Dw
HEARLY, Mary	19	F	Servant	12Ja02Dw
John	17	M	Servant	12Ja02Dw
MOORE, Helena	10	F	Unknown	12Ja02Dw
CAWLEY, John	45	M	Mason	12Ja02Dw
Aisty	30	F	Unknown	12Ja02Dw
HEART, Edwd.	24	M	Mason	12Ja02Dw
MARTIN, Ann	24	F	Servant	12Ja02Dw
CREILLY, Bernd.	36	M	Laborer	12Ja02Dw
GIBBONS, Miles	40	M	Laborer	12Ja02Dw
WALSH, Bridgt.	17	F	Lad	12Ja02Dw
MCCORMICK, Pat	45	M	Laborer	12Ja02Dw
DURKON, John	27	M	Laborer	12Ja02Dw
Mary	18	F	Servant	12Ja02Dw
LOFTEN, Anna	60	F	Servant	12Ja02Dw
OHARA, Pat	7	M	Child	12Ja02Dw
ALLEN, Robt.	28	M	Laborer	12Ja02Dw
MCCARTY, Thomas	34	M	Laborer	12Ja02Dw
REILLY, Mary	19	F	Servant	12Ja02Dw
CONNELL, Pat	30	M	Laborer	12Ja02Dw
TIERNEY, Pat	35	M	Laborer	12Ja02Dw
PIGOTT, Robt.	28	M	Laborer	12Ja02Dw
REED, Absolem	16	M	Laborer	12Ja02Dw

NAMES OF PASSENGERS	AGE	SEX	OCCUPATIONS	DATE PORT SHIP
LYNCH, Thomas	30	M	Blacksmith	12Ja02Dw
Mary	47	F	Unknown	12Ja02Dw
Owen	18	M	Blacksmith	12Ja02Dw
Biddy	16	F	Servant	12Ja02Dw
Michl.	15	M	Laborer	12Ja02Dw
Margt.	13	F	Unknown	12Ja02Dw
Mary	11	F	Unknown	12Ja02Dw
Ann	9	F	Child	12Ja02Dw
John	7	M	Child	12Ja02Dw
FARLEY, James	20	M	Laborer	12Ja02Dw
GILLOCK, Peter	18	M	Laborer	12Ja02Dw
LESTER, Richd.	44	M	Clerk	12Ja02Dw
BIGGIN, Fras.	3	M	Child	12Ja02Dw
Cath.	5	F	Child	12Ja02Dw
Biddy	.00	F	Infant	12Ja02Dw
Mary	30	F	Lad	12Ja02Dw
Pat	25	M	Laborer	12Ja02Dw
Peter	21	M	Laborer	12Ja02Dw
Ellen	24	F	Servant	12Ja02Dw
MCKIBBEN, Joseph	22	M	Laborer	12Ja02Dw
DENNY, Jane	29	F	Lad	12Ja02Dw
Sarah	.00	F	Infant	12Ja02Dw
Alexr.	5	M	Child	12Ja02Dw
CALLAGHAN, John	18	M	Laborer	12Ja02Dw
DAMERAS, Wm.	25	M	Laborer	12Ja02Dw
JONES, Owen	42	M	Mason	12Ja02Dw
Bridt.	18	F	Servant	12Ja02Dw
Mary	3	F	Child	12Ja02Dw
GARAHTY, Sarah	22	F	Unknown	12Ja02Dw
John	.00	M	Infant	12Ja02Dw
KINSELLA, Wm.	31	M	Blacksmith	12Ja02Dw
NOLAN, James	40	M	Laborer	12Ja02Dw
Biddy	30	F	Unknown	12Ja02Dw
Ellen	13	F	Unknown	12Ja02Dw
Michl.	9	M	Child	12Ja02Dw
Margt.	7	F	Child	12Ja02Dw
Bridgt.	5	F	Child	12Ja02Dw
Wm.	4	M	Child	12Ja02Dw
Pat	3	M	Child	12Ja02Dw
Kitty	.00	F	Infant	12Ja02Dw
Michael	25	M	Domestic	12Ja02Dw
DAVIS, Bridt.	50	F	Lad	12Ja02Dw
LONRIGAN, Thomas	4	M	Child	12Ja02Dw
PLUNKETT, Wini	35	M	Laborer	12Ja02Dw
Thos.	12	M	Unknown	12Ja02Dw
Wini	10	M	Unknown	12Ja02Dw
Ellen	8	F	Child	12Ja02Dw
Mary	37	F	Unknown	12Ja02Dw
John	5	M	Child	12Ja02Dw
Margt.	23	F	Unknown	12Ja02Dw
KINGSLEY, John	21	M	Laborer	12Ja02Dw
DISKIN, Fibi	18	F	Spinner	12Ja02Dw
BURKE, Jer.	35	M	Farmer	12Ja02Dw
Thos.	28	M	Farmer	12Ja02Dw
James	42	M	Farmer	12Ja02Dw
Ann	37	F	Unknown	12Ja02Dw
Thos.	3	M	Child	12Ja02Dw
Mary	.00	F	Infant	12Ja02Dw
ROONEY, John	20	M	Laborer	12Ja02Dw
MAHON, John	16	M	Laborer	12Ja02Dw
CONWAY, Thos.	20	M	Laborer	12Ja02Dw
BARKE, Julia	21	F	Servant	12Ja02Dw
SMITH, Edwd.	23	M	Laborer	12Ja02Dw
MOORE, Bernd.	20	M	Laborer	12Ja02Dw
KELLY, Patk.	20	M	Farmer	12Ja02Dw
MOORE, Fis.	40	M	Farmer	12Ja02Dw
Joseph	20	M	Farmer	12Ja02Dw
Peter	10	M	Unknown	12Ja02Dw
Susan	5	F	Child	12Ja02Dw
MALLEN, James	24	M	Laborer	12Ja02Dw
BYRNE, Oliver	22	M	Laborer	12Ja02Dw
MURPHY, Eliz.	23	F	Lad	12Ja02Dw
CASSIDY, James	19	M	Laborer	12Ja02Dw
LEONARD, John	65	M	Laborer	12Ja02Dw
Jane	50	F	Unknown	12Ja02Dw

NAMES OF PASSENGERS	AGE	SEX	OCCUPATIONS	DATE PORT SHIP
LEONARD, Cath.	26	F	Servant	12Ja02Dw
Mary	24	F	Servant	12Ja02Dw
Mary	1	F	Child	12Ja02Dw
Pat	20	M	Laborer	12Ja02Dw
Rich	17	M	Laborer	12Ja02Dw
Jane	13	F	Servant	12Ja02Dw
Ann	11	F	Unknown	12Ja02Dw
BYRNE, Mary	18	F	Servant	12Ja02Dw
Ann	16	F	Servant	12Ja02Dw
REILLY, O.	40	M	Miller	12Ja02Dw
ROBERSON, Margt.	20	F	Servant	12Ja02Dw
POWER, Mary	36	F	Lad	12Ja02Dw
John	9	M	Child	12Ja02Dw
Thomas	6	M	Child	12Ja02Dw
SMITH, Mary	45	F	Lad	12Ja02Dw
Ellen	9	F	Child	12Ja02Dw
Bridt.	30	F	Lad	12Ja02Dw
Jane	6	F	Child	12Ja02Dw
DUFFY, Pat	22	M	Carpenter	12Ja02Dw
James	15	M	Carpenter	12Ja02Dw
Rose	20	F	Unknown	12Ja02Dw
DUNHALTY, Tom	25	M	Laborer	12Ja02Dw
MURRY, John	10	M	Laborer	12Ja02Dw
DARCEY, James	32	M	Laborer	12Ja02Dw
ROURKE, Cath.	30	F	Lad	12Ja02Dw
Marten	2	M	Child	12Ja02Dw
Mick	1	M	Child	12Ja02Dw
CARROLL, James	49	M	Farmer	12Ja02Dw
EGAN, Ellen	25	F	Servant	12Ja02Dw
HERAGHTY, Martin	25	M	Laborer	12Ja02Dw
CONNLY, Cath.	32	F	Unknown	12Ja02Dw
Jane	9	F	Child	12Ja02Dw
MADDEN, Biddy	19	F	Servant	12Ja02Dw
NEAL, Mary	19	F	Dressmaker	12Ja02Dw
FARRELL, Biddy	20	F	Servant	12Ja02Dw
KELLY, Robt.	40	M	Farmer	12Ja02Dw
Biddy	36	F	Unknown	12Ja02Dw
Ann	16	F	Unknown	12Ja02Dw
Edwd.	18	M	Unknown	12Ja02Dw
Robt.	15	M	Unknown	12Ja02Dw
Pat	10	M	Unknown	12Ja02Dw
Bernd.	9	M	Child	12Ja02Dw
MCSHEAN, Jno.	20	M	Laborer	12Ja02Dw
COFFEY, Jno.	55	M	Laborer	12Ja02Dw
Died-At-Sea				
Cath.	18	F	Servant	12Ja02Dw
John	11	M	Unknown	12Ja02Dw
KILKENNY, Edwd.	38	M	Laborer	12Ja02Dw
FLYNN, Henry	38	M	Laborer	12Ja02Dw
KILKENNY, Maria	10	F	Unknown	12Ja02Dw
Bill	8	F	Child	12Ja02Dw
Torn	7	M	Child	12Ja02Dw
KING, Alice	18	F	Servant	12Ja02Dw
SMITH, Mick	30	M	Laborer	12Ja02Dw
Cath.	25	F	Unknown	12Ja02Dw
FARRON, James	36	M	Cbtmkr	12Ja02Dw
Margt.	33	F	Unknown	12Ja02Dw
KEEF, Richd.	26	M	Laborer	12Ja02Dw
PLUNKETT, James	23	M	Laborer	12Ja02Dw
REYNOLDS, Peter	36	M	Laborer	12Ja02Dw
NOLAN, Mary	29	F	Lad	12Ja02Dw
Mary	2	F	Child	12Ja02Dw
HANNON, Brid.	15	F	Servant	12Ja02Dw
NAVAN, Brid.	18	F	Servant	12Ja02Dw
REILLY, Bernd.	20	M	Baker	12Ja02Dw
KENNEDY, Margt.	18	F	Servant	12Ja02Dw
CALLIVAN, Cath.	21	F	Dressmaker	12Ja02Dw
GRANT, Neil	20	M	Laborer	12Ja02Dw
Cath.	14	F	Servant	12Ja02Dw
Cath.	14	F	Servant	12Ja02Dw
REILLY, Hugh	30	M	Gdnr	12Ja02Dw
KANE, Mick	20	M	Ploughman	12Ja02Dw
QUINN, John	20	M	Farmer	12Ja02Dw
Eleanor	20	F	Unknown	12Ja02Dw
PHELAN, Dennis	25	M	Laborer	12Ja02Dw

NAMES OF PASSENGERS	AGE	SEX	OCCUPATIONS	DATE PORT SHIP
PHELAN, Frances	18	F	Servant	12Ja02Dw
PHEELS, George	14	F	Servant	12Ja02Dw
Margt.	18	F	Servant	12Ja02Dw
MURRAY, John	29	M	Mason	12Ja02Dw
CALAGHAN, Mick	19	M	Laborer	12Ja02Dw
Cath.	22	F	Servant	12Ja02Dw
Bridt.	14	F	Servant	12Ja02Dw
Edwd.	13	M	Servant	12Ja02Dw
MCCANN, Mick	20	M	Laborer	12Ja02Dw
Margt.	18	F	Servant	12Ja02Dw
MCDERMOTT, Jas.	30	M	Laborer	12Ja02Dw
RYAN, John	40	M	Laborer	12Ja02Dw
CARY, Cath.	20	F	Servant	12Ja02Dw
LYNE, Honor	22	F	Servant	12Ja02Dw
FINNIGAN, Mary	20	F	Milliner	12Ja02Dw
CONWAY, Bud	30	F	Lad	12Ja02Dw
John	11	M	Unknown	12Ja02Dw
Pat	9	M	Child	12Ja02Dw
Mary	5	F	Child	12Ja02Dw
JONES, John	42	M	Farmer	12Ja02Dw
SAVAGE, Henry	35	M	Laborer	12Ja02Dw
CONROY, Ellen	25	F	Milliner	12Ja02Dw
Mary	.00	F	Infant	12Ja02Dw
EDGAR, Saml.	30	M	Mason	12Ja02Dw
KIERNAN, James	28	M	Laborer	12Ja02Dw
REILLY, James	29	M	Laborer	12Ja02Dw
BRADY, Pat	39	M	Laborer	12Ja02Dw
Rose	40	F	Servant	12Ja02Dw
Cath.	19	F	Servant	12Ja02Dw
Margt.	20	F	Servant	12Ja02Dw
MORRIS, Sarah	40	F	Unknown	12Ja02Dw
Thos.	20	M	Laborer	12Ja02Dw
James	15	M	Laborer	12Ja02Dw
Brid.	11	F	Unknown	12Ja02Dw
Ann	9	F	Child	12Ja02Dw
Wm.	7	M	Child	12Ja02Dw
Jane	7	F	Child	12Ja02Dw
Sarah	6	F	Child	12Ja02Dw
Owen	.00	M	Infant	12Ja02Dw
Rose	3	F	Child	12Ja02Dw
Died-At-Sea				
DUFFY, Betty	12	F	Unknown	12Ja02Dw
Susan	10	F	Unknown	12Ja02Dw
MOORE, Maria	20	F	Servant	12Ja02Dw
RYAN, Jas.	20	M	Laborer	12Ja02Dw
Wm.	19	M	Laborer	12Ja02Dw
REILLY, Cath.	17	F	Servant	12Ja02Dw
RYAN, Ellen	17	F	Servant	12Ja02Dw
Peggy	17	F	Servant	12Ja02Dw
MURRAY, James	22	M	Laborer	12Ja02Dw
TRACEY, Lawl.	27	M	Laborer	12Ja02Dw
HAYES, Mary	30	F	Lad	12Ja02Dw
Ellen	6	F	Child	12Ja02Dw
Mary	3	F	Child	12Ja02Dw
Jane	.00	F	Infant	12Ja02Dw
SMITH, Andrew	30	M	Pouterer	12Ja02Dw
DUNN, Pat	24	M	Clerk	12Ja02Dw
BRYAN, Ann	25	F	Servant	12Ja02Dw
MULLIN, Brid.	20	F	Servant	12Ja02Dw
CASSON, Alice	18	F	Servant	12Ja02Dw
MAHONY, Jno.	20	M	Laborer	12Ja02Dw
WHALEN, Ann	20	F	Servant	12Ja02Dw
DEANER, Cathe.	20	F	Unknown	12Ja02Dw
DWYER, Michl.	26	M	Laborer	12Ja02Dw
MILAN, Ellen	18	F	Servant	12Ja02Dw
MULLIGAN, Mary	18	F	Servant	12Ja02Dw
GARAGHTY, U	.00	M	Infant	12Ja02Dw
Born-At-Sea				

OXFORD 12 JANUARY 1850

From Liverpool

NAMES OF PASSENGERS	AGE	SEX	OCCUPATIONS	DATE PORT SHIP
MARTIN, Patrick	30	M	Laborer	12Ja02Dy
SLATTERLY, John	10	M	Laborer	12Ja02Dy
BOYLE, Edward	25	M	Laborer	12Ja02Dy
Died-At-Sea				
MCBRIDE, Ann	24	F	Servant	12Ja02Dy
Ann	.10	F	Infant	12Ja02Dy
COSTELLO, Michael	28	M	Laborer	12Ja02Dy
KENNY, Bridget	17	F	Servant	12Ja02Dy
CLOONAN, John	27	M	Laborer	12Ja02Dy
CASSIDY, Bridget	40	F	Servant	12Ja02Dy
Bridget	.09	F	Infant	12Ja02Dy
Julia	14	F	None	12Ja02Dy
CLARK, Julia	11	F	None	12Ja02Dy
CASSIDY, Patrick	12	M	Laborer	12Ja02Dy
James	9	M	Child	12Ja02Dy
Margaret	10	F	None	12Ja02Dy
John	5	M	Child	12Ja02Dy
Owen	5	M	Child	12Ja02Dy
Ann	.11	F	Infant	12Ja02Dy
SULLIVAN, Mary	19	F	Servant	12Ja02Dy
COSTELLO, James	18	M	Laborer	12Ja02Dy
Bridget	20	F	None	12Ja02Dy
MCGARRY, Catherine	28	F	Servant	12Ja02Dy
Thomas	6	M	Child	12Ja02Dy
HENNEBURY, Michael	20	M	Laborer	12Ja02Dy
GRAHAM, Hugh	25	M	Laborer	12Ja02Dy
HANLEY, Patrick	23	M	Laborer	12Ja02Dy
FLANNAGAN, Michael	27	M	Laborer	12Ja02Dy
CRONIN, Mary	18	F	Servant	12Ja02Dy
BARRY, Patrick	30	M	Laborer	12Ja02Dy
Catherine	28	F	Servant	12Ja02Dy
Garrett	14	M	Servant	12Ja02Dy
Michael	.08	M	Infant	12Ja02Dy
KEEFFE, Sarah	62	F	Servant	12Ja02Dy
Anthony	25	M	Servant	12Ja02Dy
Honora	19	F	Servant	12Ja02Dy
Mary	17	F	Servant	12Ja02Dy
BRADY, Bridget	25	F	Servant	12Ja02Dy
Ann	20	F	Servant	12Ja02Dy
ROGERS, Catherine	30	F	Servant	12Ja02Dy
John	2	M	Child	12Ja02Dy
Michael	.06	M	Infant	12Ja02Dy
MINAHAN, Ellen	35	F	None	12Ja02Dy
CODY, James	25	M	Laborer	12Ja02Dy
GORMAN, John	10	M	Laborer	12Ja02Dy
William	8	M	Child	12Ja02Dy
Mary	5	F	Child	12Ja02Dy
TIGHE, Peter	20	M	Laborer	12Ja02Dy
Bridget	13	F	Laborer	12Ja02Dy
TOMMON, Catherine	20	F	Servant	12Ja02Dy
COLLINS, Bridget	28	F	Servant	12Ja02Dy
Bridget	6	F	Child	12Ja02Dy
John	4	M	Child	12Ja02Dy
Ann	2	F	Child	12Ja02Dy
Died-At-Sea				
Thomas	.09	M	Infant	12Ja02Dy
Died-At-Sea				
BRENNAN, Johanna	30	F	Servant	12Ja02Dy
Catherine	4	F	Child	12Ja02Dy
Honora	10	F	Servant	12Ja02Dy
CANLON, James	19	M	Tailor	12Ja02Dy
BURNS, John	30	M	Laborer	12Ja02Dy
Garrett	2	M	Child	12Ja02Dy
Died-At-Sea				
MURNANE, Bridget	26	F	Servant	12Ja02Dy

NAMES OF PASSENGERS	AGE	SEX	OCCUPATIONS	DATE PORT SHIP
MONOHAN, James	35	M	Laborer	12Ja02Dy
OBRIEN, Bridget	20	F	Servant	12Ja02Dy
KELLY, Bridget	20	F	Servant	12Ja02Dy
LENEHAN, Mary	30	F	Servant	12Ja02Dy
KENNEY, Patrick	5	M	Child	12Ja02Dy
SMITH, Catherine	50	F	Servant	12Ja02Dy
STEVENSON, Sidney	30	M	Laborer	12Ja02Dy
Catherine	6	F	Child	12Ja02Dy
Ann	4	F	Child	12Ja02Dy
Died-At-Sea				
Thomas	.10	M	Infant	12Ja02Dy
SMITH, Catherine	44	F	Servant	12Ja02Dy
James	14	M	Servant	12Ja02Dy
Susan	12	F	Servant	12Ja02Dy
Michael	10	M	Servant	12Ja02Dy
Rose	.08	F	Infant	12Ja02Dy
CAVANAGH, James	15	M	Laborer	12Ja02Dy
MCANULTY, Peter	18	M	Laborer	12Ja02Dy
Catherine	16	F	Servant	12Ja02Dy
MCKNIGHT, Isabel	19	F	Servant	12Ja02Dy
SANDERSON, Mary-J.	15	F	Servant	12Ja02Dy
COSTELLO, Bridget	30	F	Servant	12Ja02Dy
Margaret	7	F	Child	12Ja02Dy
DAY, Thomas	3	M	Child	12Ja02Dy
KELLY, David	14	M	Servant	12Ja02Dy
Ellen	9	F	Child	12Ja02Dy
COSTELLO, John	17	M	Tailor	12Ja02Dy
REYNOLDS, John	19	M	Tailor	12Ja02Dy
KELLY, Michael	16	M	Tailor	12Ja02Dy
Patrick	14	M	Laborer	12Ja02Dy
SLATER, Martha	30	F	Servant	12Ja02Dy
William	4	M	Child	12Ja02Dy
GRAHAM, Rose	20	F	Servant	12Ja02Dy
FLYNN, Catherine	19	F	Servant	12Ja02Dy
Catherine	5	F	Child	12Ja02Dy
PHELAN, Catherine	15	F	Servant	12Ja02Dy
WALSH, Julia	17	F	Servant	12Ja02Dy
CLARKE, Bridget	20	F	Servant	12Ja02Dy
WARD, Ann	16	F	Servant	12Ja02Dy
BURKE, Johanna	20	F	Servant	12Ja02Dy
MOORE, Martha	15	F	Servant	12Ja02Dy
RIALTY, Catherine	30	F	Servant	12Ja02Dy
Daniel	8	M	Child	12Ja02Dy
John	5	M	Child	12Ja02Dy
Margaret	.11	F	Infant	12Ja02Dy
HART, Mary	23	F	Servant	12Ja02Dy
HORAN, Dominick	30	M	Servant	12Ja02Dy
BERGEN, Mary	70	F	Servant	12Ja02Dy
MCCANN, Ann	24	F	Servant	12Ja02Dy
Michael	4	M	Child	12Ja02Dy
Patrick	2	M	Child	12Ja02Dy
RIELLY, Bridget	27	F	Servant	12Ja02Dy
Peter	3	M	Child	12Ja02Dy
John	.11	M	Infant	12Ja02Dy
Died-At-Sea				
HENRY, Edward	30	M	Laborer	12Ja02Dy
Charles	20	M	Laborer	12Ja02Dy
EARLY, Ellen	16	F	Servant	12Ja02Dy
KEOGAN, Catherine	18	F	Servant	12Ja02Dy
Julia	15	F	Servant	12Ja02Dy
MURPHY, James	23	M	Laborer	12Ja02Dy
Mary	25	F	Servant	12Ja02Dy
DONAHOE, William	14	M	Servant	12Ja02Dy
EGAN, John	30	M	Laborer	12Ja02Dy
PHELAN, Eliza	30	F	Servant	12Ja02Dy
William	.09	M	Infant	12Ja02Dy
GRAHAM, Patrick	30	M	Laborer	12Ja02Dy
NESTOR, Michael	22	M	Laborer	12Ja02Dy
HUGHES, Bridget	18	F	Laborer	12Ja02Dy
HALEY, Catherine	25	F	Servant	12Ja02Dy
BURNS, Richard	28	M	Laborer	12Ja02Dy
Mary	28	F	Servant	12Ja02Dy
MCCREAT, Johanna	23	F	Servant	12Ja02Dy
MAHER, Mary	20	F	Servant	12Ja02Dy
BURNS, Edward	3	M	Child	12Ja02Dy

NAMES OF PASSENGERS	AGE	SEX	OCCUPATIONS	DATE PORT SHIP
CRAIG, Matilda	20	F	Servant	12Ja02Dy
CUDDY, Margaret	34	F	Servant	12Ja02Dy
Ellen	13	F	Servant	12Ja02Dy
Michael	11	M	Servant	12Ja02Dy
Judy	7	F	Child	12Ja02Dy
James	3	M	Child	12Ja02Dy
Died-At-Sea				
CONLON, Charles	21	M	Laborer	12Ja02Dy
RYAN, Patrick	21	M	Laborer	12Ja02Dy
Bridget	18	F	Laborer	12Ja02Dy
Catherine	14	F	Laborer	12Ja02Dy
PILLION, Mary	24	F	Laborer	12Ja02Dy
KIRWAN, Mary	46	F	Laborer	12Ja02Dy
SHAW, Bessy	25	F	Laborer	12Ja02Dy
BEASLEY, Elizabeth	35	F	Laborer	12Ja02Dy
Mary	8	F	Child	12Ja02Dy
WEEKS, Mary	50	F	Servant	12Ja02Dy
GILL, Jane	24	F	Servant	12Ja02Dy
Jonathan	3	M	Child	12Ja02Dy
Mary-Ann	.09	F	Infant	12Ja02Dy
SHERIDAN, Mary	40	F	Servant	12Ja02Dy
Ann	18	F	Servant	12Ja02Dy
ONEAL, Edward	20	M	Laborer	12Ja02Dy
BEVANS, William	28	M	Laborer	12Ja02Dy
CARTHY, Samuel	8	M	Child	12Ja02Dy
Honora	7	F	Child	12Ja02Dy
Timothy	5	M	Child	12Ja02Dy
ELLIOTT, John	15	M	Laborer	12Ja02Dy
MURRAY, James	30	M	Laborer	12Ja02Dy
Ann	30	F	Laborer	12Ja02Dy
John	11	M	Laborer	12Ja02Dy
Margaret-Ann	9	F	Child	12Ja02Dy
Michael	7	M	Child	12Ja02Dy
Thomas	4	M	Child	12Ja02Dy
James	.11	M	Infant	12Ja02Dy
MORRIS, John	25	M	Laborer	12Ja02Dy
MCANANY, Ann	30	F	Servant	12Ja02Dy
John	7	M	Child	12Ja02Dy
GREER, Mary	20	F	Servant	12Ja02Dy
ROONEY, James	14	M	Laborer	12Ja02Dy
Ann	10	F	Servant	12Ja02Dy
Honora	7	F	Child	12Ja02Dy
COGGIN, Bartholomew	17	M	Laborer	12Ja02Dy
SMYTH, Michael	21	M	Laborer	12Ja02Dy
GERAGHTY, Ann	26	F	Servant	12Ja02Dy
BYRNE, Lawrence	14	M	Laborer	12Ja02Dy
BEHAN, Eliza	40	F	Servant	12Ja02Dy
Bridget	11	F	Servant	12Ja02Dy
Patrick	7	M	Child	12Ja02Dy
Catherine	4	F	Child	12Ja02Dy
Eliza	.10	F	Infant	12Ja02Dy
Died-At-Sea				
Mary	13	F	Servant	12Ja02Dy
BOURELL, Edward	25	M	Laborer	12Ja02Dy
CAVANAGH, Ellen	21	F	Servant	12Ja02Dy
FLYNN, Kieran	23	M	Laborer	12Ja02Dy
Sarah	14	F	Servant	12Ja02Dy
CARROLL, James	22	M	Laborer	12Ja02Dy
James	3	M	Child	12Ja02Dy
MURRAY, Biddy	20	F	Servant	12Ja02Dy
Ellen	50	F	Servant	12Ja02Dy
Ann	18	F	Servant	12Ja02Dy
Rose	15	F	Servant	12Ja02Dy
James	13	M	Servant	12Ja02Dy
COMISKEY, Mary	40	F	Servant	12Ja02Dy
Patrick	10	M	Servant	12Ja02Dy
Ann	12	F	Servant	12Ja02Dy
COYLE, Patrick	25	M	Servant	12Ja02Dy
Ann	18	F	Servant	12Ja02Dy
BAXTER, James	22	M	Laborer	12Ja02Dy
LYNCH, Ellen	20	F	Servant	12Ja02Dy
BAKER, James	28	M	Laborer	12Ja02Dy
GUINEN, Bernard	25	M	Laborer	12Ja02Dy
Mary	19	F	Servant	12Ja02Dy
BRADY, Patrick	33	M	Laborer	12Ja02Dy

NAMES OF PASSENGERS	AGE	SEX	OCCUPATIONS	DATE PORT SHIP
GUNN, John	40	M	Laborer	12Ja02Dy
WATERS, Mary	18	F	Servant	12Ja02Dy
JOYCE, Mary	22	F	Servant	12Ja02Dy
HOBAN, Bridget	18	F	Servant	12Ja02Dy
Catherine	20	F	Servant	12Ja02Dy
CHRISTIAN, Thomas	44	M	Laborer	12Ja02Dy
KELLY, Bryan	25	M	Laborer	12Ja02Dy
Mary	17	F	Servant	12Ja02Dy
SHERIDAN, Mary	20	F	Servant	12Ja02Dy
SENIOR, Sarah	22	F	Servant	12Ja02Dy
Emma	.11	F	Infant	12Ja02Dy
BARKER, Benjamin	11	M	Servant	12Ja02Dy
MCCARTHY, Thomas	25	M	Laborer	12Ja02Dy
BARLOW, George	54	M	Laborer	12Ja02Dy
DANTON, Mary	13	F	Servant	12Ja02Dy

ST.PATRICK 12 JANUARY 1850

From Liverpool

NAMES OF PASSENGERS	AGE	SEX	OCCUPATIONS	DATE PORT SHIP
BYRNE, Mary	34	F	Spinster	12Ja02Dz
Catherine	22	F	Spinster	12Ja02Dz
Died-At-Sea				
Margaret	20	F	Spinster	12Ja02Dz
Died-At-Sea				
OBRIEN, James	48	M	Laborer	12Ja02Dz
MADDEN, Thomas	28	M	Laborer	12Ja02Dz
Edmund	18	M	Laborer	12Ja02Dz
Thomas	16	M	Laborer	12Ja02Dz
Catherine	20	F	Spinster	12Ja02Dz
CONNERTON, Bridget	3	F	Child	12Ja02Dz
HARDIMAN, Patk.	32	M	Laborer	12Ja02Dz
Sarah	50	F	Wife	12Ja02Dz
KELLY, Patk.	19	M	Laborer	12Ja02Dz
CLARKE, Bridget	18	F	Spinster	12Ja02Dz
KENNY, Bridget	7	F	Child	12Ja02Dz
SULLIVAN, Bridget	26	F	Spinster	12Ja02Dz
Mary	5	F	Child	12Ja02Dz
Michael	2	M	Child	12Ja02Dz
Bridget	.00	F	Infant	12Ja02Dz
MADDEN, Mary	30	F	Wife	12Ja02Dz
Catherine	8	F	Child	12Ja02Dz
Mary	.00	F	Infant	12Ja02Dz
KEARNEY, Mary	50	F	Wife	12Ja02Dz
William	24	M	Laborer	12Ja02Dz
Michael	24	M	Laborer	12Ja02Dz
MAHER, William	22	M	Laborer	12Ja02Dz
MCINERY, George	20	M	Laborer	12Ja02Dz
KEOUGH, Patk.	24	M	Laborer	12Ja02Dz
RIDDY, Bridget	25	F	Wife	12Ja02Dz
Catherine	3	F	Child	12Ja02Dz
Tamessa	.00	F	Infant	12Ja02Dz
WHALEN, Wm.	19	M	Laborer	12Ja02Dz
Died-At-Sea				
Ellen	20	F	Spinster	12Ja02Dz
James	26	M	Laborer	12Ja02Dz
Mary	24	F	Spinster	12Ja02Dz
Mary	5	F	Child	12Ja02Dz
Bridget	3	F	Child	12Ja02Dz
RYAN, Catherine	20	F	Spinster	12Ja02Dz
OBRIEN, Anthony	29	M	Laborer	12Ja02Dz
KELLY, Margaret	18	F	Spinster	12Ja02Dz
CONNELL, Wm.	22	M	Laborer	12Ja02Dz
TOBIN, Wm.	27	M	Laborer	12Ja02Dz
Margaret	18	F	Spinster	12Ja02Dz
CALLAGHAN, Pearce	18	M	Laborer	12Ja02Dz
BRETT, Michl.	40	M	Laborer	12Ja02Dz
Ellen	30	F	Wife	12Ja02Dz
Edward	8	M	Child	12Ja02Dz
BRETT, Patk.	2	M	Child	12Ja02Dz
WELSH, Margaret	20	F	Spinster	12Ja02Dz
KEHOE, Michael	20	M	Laborer	12Ja02Dz
MCGOULNACK, Cathn.	20	F	Spinster	12Ja02Dz
BAR, John	40	M	Law Student	12Ja02Dz
KOGAN, Timth.	23	M	Shoemaker	12Ja02Dz
Winnifred	19	F	Spinster	12Ja02Dz
BRENNAN, Michl.	27	M	Laborer	12Ja02Dz
STAFFORD, John	21	M	Laborer	12Ja02Dz
MEGAN, Bridget	22	F	Spinster	12Ja02Dz
HICKEY, Dolly	30	F	Wi	12Ja02Dz
CORCORAN, James	27	M	Laborer	12Ja02Dz
DEWITT, Charles	40	M	Laborer	12Ja02Dz
Judy	35	F	Wife	12Ja02Dz
Michl.	5	M	Child	12Ja02Dz
Patk.	.00	M	Infant	12Ja02Dz
Died-At-Sea				
Mary	.00	F	Infant	12Ja02Dz
RAY, David	27	M	Farmer	12Ja02Dz
DEAGAN, John	32	M	Laborer	12Ja02Dz
Bridget	4	F	Child	12Ja02Dz
HOLLY, Patk.	30	M	Laborer	12Ja02Dz
QUIN, Stephen	23	M	Shoemaker	12Ja02Dz
CALLAGHAN, Ally	31	F	Spinster	12Ja02Dz
DOLAN, Catherine	36	F	Spinster	12Ja02Dz
BRENNAN, Mary	36	F	Wife	12Ja02Dz
William	.00	M	Infant	12Ja02Dz
MATHEWS, Patk.	50	M	Farmer	12Ja02Dz
Betty	10	F	Spinster	12Ja02Dz
KENNEY, David	35	M	Shoemaker	12Ja02Dz
COGAN, Pat	26	M	Laborer	12Ja02Dz
REGAN, Owen	43	M	Laborer	12Ja02Dz
Mary	40	F	Wife	12Ja02Dz
Elisabeth	.00	F	Infant	12Ja02Dz
Mary	35	F	Wife	12Ja02Dz
Catherine	10	F	Unknown	12Ja02Dz
Ellen	1	F	Child	12Ja02Dz
SWINNEY, Morgan	38	M	Laborer	12Ja02Dz
LEARY, David	23	M	Laborer	12Ja02Dz
DOOLAN, James	24	M	Laborer	12Ja02Dz
Mick	6	M	Child	12Ja02Dz
Bartle	4	M	Child	12Ja02Dz
Mary	20	F	Spinster	12Ja02Dz
LONG, John	40	M	Laborer	12Ja02Dz
James	9	M	Child	12Ja02Dz
Joseph	7	M	Child	12Ja02Dz
Mary	5	F	Child	12Ja02Dz
CONNOR, Bryan	26	M	Laborer	12Ja02Dz
KENNA, Margaret	25	F	Spinster	12Ja02Dz
GRACE, William	19	M	Grocer	12Ja02Dz
QUINN, Mary	20	F	Spinster	12Ja02Dz
DWYER, Dennis	35	M	Laborer	12Ja02Dz
Mick	24	M	Laborer	12Ja02Dz
BUTTLER, Michael	38	M	Laborer	12Ja02Dz
Eliza	21	F	Wife	12Ja02Dz
MULLEN, Mary	20	F	Spinster	12Ja02Dz
CASSIDY, Owen	50	M	Grocer	12Ja02Dz
MCCABE, Ellen	28	F	Wife	12Ja02Dz
KENNA, Ann	31	F	Wife	12Ja02Dz
MCCABE, U	.00	U	Infant	12Ja02Dz
KENNA, U	.00	U	Infant	12Ja02Dz
Martin	8	M	Child	12Ja02Dz
Essey	6	M	Child	12Ja02Dz
RICE, Peter	13	M	Laborer	12Ja02Dz
KENT, Bartlett	42	M	Farmer	12Ja02Dz
Ann	16	F	Spinster	12Ja02Dz
Francis	11	M	Unknown	12Ja02Dz
Sarah	10	F	Unknown	12Ja02Dz
GRIFFITHS, William	24	M	Clerk	12Ja02Dz
WELSH, George	40	M	Laborer	12Ja02Dz
U-Mrs.	35	F	Wife	12Ja02Dz
James	7	M	Child	12Ja02Dz
Edward	5	M	Child	12Ja02Dz
TYRRELL, Henry	25	M	Laborer	12Ja02Dz
PURDEN, Edward	30	M	Laborer	12Ja02Dz

NAMES OF PASSENGERS	AGE	SEX	OCCUPATIONS	DATE PORT SHIP
SULLIVAN, Ellen	30	F	Wife	12Ja02Dz
KEVANNA, Catherine	35	F	Wife	12Ja02Dz
SULLIVAN, Mary	6	F	Child	12Ja02Dz
SKIDDY, Edward	30	M	Laborer	12Ja02Dz
HICKEY, Ellen	32	F	Spinster	12Ja02Dz
POWER, David	26	M	Laborer	12Ja02Dz
CORWIN, Mary	19	F	Spinster	12Ja02Dz
Samuel	17	M	Laborer	12Ja02Dz
Michael	4	M	Child	12Ja02Dz
MARTIN, John	35	M	Laborer	12Ja02Dz
MAGEE, Michael	22	M	Laborer	12Ja02Dz
QUINN, Catherine	21	F	Wife	12Ja02Dz
SWEENEY, Catherine	24	F	Wife	12Ja02Dz
LYONS, Julia	46	F	Spinster	12Ja02Dz
Timothy	16	M	Laborer	12Ja02Dz
MCGENTY, Margaret	30	F	Wife	12Ja02Dz
John	24	M	Laborer	12Ja02Dz
Michael	16	M	Laborer	12Ja02Dz
LONG, Nicholas	23	M	Shoemaker	12Ja02Dz
MULLERNEY, Catherine	20	F	Wife	12Ja02Dz
HALLINAN, Judy	16	F	Spinster	12Ja02Dz
MAHER, Margaret	39	F	Wife	12Ja02Dz
Lawrence	10	M	Unknown	12Ja02Dz
Joseph	5	M	Child	12Ja02Dz
HAND, Fanny	17	F	Spinster	12Ja02Dz
KELLY, Ellen	20	F	Spinster	12Ja02Dz
Etty	19	F	Spinster	12Ja02Dz
WARD, Ellen	19	F	Spinster	12Ja02Dz
KENNA, Christopher	35	M	Laborer	12Ja02Dz
William	25	M	Laborer	12Ja02Dz
LAWLER, Samuel	21	M	Laborer	12Ja02Dz
MCADDER, Daniel	25	M	Laborer	12Ja02Dz
MCEVOY, Mary	19	F	Spinster	12Ja02Dz
CONNELL, Patrick	19	M	Carpenter	12Ja02Dz
CUNNINGHAM, Mick	9	M	Child	12Ja02Dz
Ann	8	F	Child	12Ja02Dz
TIBBY, John	15	M	Unknown	12Ja02Dz
ENGLISH, Hugh	44	M	Weaver	12Ja02Dz
Eliza	40	F	Wife	12Ja02Dz
Charles	32	M	Weaver	12Ja02Dz
Jane	12	F	Unknown	12Ja02Dz
Ann	9	F	Child	12Ja02Dz
Emily	6	F	Child	12Ja02Dz
KEAGHERY, Mary	21	F	Spinster	12Ja02Dz
CASS, Catherine	60	F	Wi	12Ja02Dz
COSTELLO, Ellen	40	F	Wi	12Ja02Dz
Catherine	12	F	Unknown	12Ja02Dz
Patrick	12	M	Unknown	12Ja02Dz
William	5	M	Child	12Ja02Dz
BEATY, Mary-Jane	18	F	Spinster	12Ja02Dz
MCCOOLE, Margaret	14	F	Spinster	12Ja02Dz
DEVINE, Michael	9	M	Child	12Ja02Dz
Patrick	18	M	Laborer	12Ja02Dz
MOLLOY, Hannah	15	F	Spinster	12Ja02Dz
Elisha	17	F	Spinster	12Ja02Dz
MAHAN, Mary	27	F	Wife	12Ja02Dz
Catherine	2	F	Child	12Ja02Dz
Died-At-Sea				
FLOOD, John	23	M	Laborer	12Ja02Dz
Margaret	19	F	Spinster	12Ja02Dz
Bridget	11	F	Unknown	12Ja02Dz
KENNA, Thomas	11	M	Laborer	12Ja02Dz
LOUGHLAN, U-Mrs.	30	F	Wife	12Ja02Dz
Patrick	11	M	Unknown	12Ja02Dz
Mary	6	F	Child	12Ja02Dz
Margaret	3	F	Child	12Ja02Dz
Rose	.00	F	Infant	12Ja02Dz
DEVINE, Ann	23	F	Spinster	12Ja02Dz
DELENAY, James	26	M	Laborer	12Ja02Dz
U-Mrs.	23	F	Wife	12Ja02Dz
GRIFFITH, Patrick	18	M	Laborer	12Ja02Dz
PATTERSON, Cathe.	25	F	Spinster	12Ja02Dz
GUFFY, James	22	M	Laborer	12Ja02Dz
MCMEE, Cathn.	23	F	Spinster	12Ja02Dz
RIBBIN, Mick	18	M	Laborer	12Ja02Dz

NAMES OF PASSENGERS	AGE	SEX	OCCUPATIONS	DATE PORT SHIP
BRENNA, Maria	2	F	Child	12Ja02Dz
DOYLE, Mick	18	M	Laborer	12Ja02Dz
Catherine	28	F	Spinster	12Ja02Dz
Samuel	11	M	Unknown	12Ja02Dz
Edward	6	M	Child	12Ja02Dz
Anastasia	3	F	Child	12Ja02Dz
MCCORMICK, Elizth.	56	F	Wi	12Ja02Dz
RYAN, Mick	54	M	Farmer	12Ja02Dz
Mary	55	F	Wife	12Ja02Dz
Catherine	22	F	Spinster	12Ja02Dz
Ellen	21	F	Spinster	12Ja02Dz
John	18	M	Laborer	12Ja02Dz
Bridget	16	F	Spinster	12Ja02Dz
Margaret	13	F	Spinster	12Ja02Dz
James	11	M	Unknown	12Ja02Dz
Ann	10	F	Unknown	12Ja02Dz
Mary-Ann	9	F	Child	12Ja02Dz
Michael	8	M	Child	12Ja02Dz
MCINTYRE, Patrick	18	M	Laborer	12Ja02Dz
Mary	20	F	Sister	12Ja02Dz
Catherine	4	F	Child	12Ja02Dz
EUSTACE, John	24	M	Laborer	12Ja02Dz
BRADLEY, Betsey	19	F	Spinster	12Ja02Dz
Catherine	4	F	Child	12Ja02Dz
FOLEY, Mick	38	M	Blacksmith	12Ja02Dz
Judy	20	F	Wife	12Ja02Dz
LAWLER, Margaret	24	F	Spinster	12Ja02Dz
HAND, Richard	20	M	Laborer	12Ja02Dz
DOWD, Patrick	30	M	Laborer	12Ja02Dz
MALONEY, Arthur	20	M	Laborer	12Ja02Dz
HARRICOTT, Samuel	21	M	Laborer	12Ja02Dz
MCCASHLAN, U-Mrs.	26	F	Wife	12Ja02Dz
Mick	.00	M	Infant	12Ja02Dz
HAND, Catherine	33	F	Wi	12Ja02Dz
CONROY, Elisa	40	F	Spinster	12Ja02Dz
John	29	M	Laborer	12Ja02Dz
CAMPBELL, Catharine	55	F	Wi	12Ja02Dz
John	21	M	Laborer	12Ja02Dz
Mary	18	F	Spinster	12Ja02Dz
SCULLY, Denny	27	M	Laborer	12Ja02Dz
MALONE, Mary	26	F	Spinster	12Ja02Dz
MURPHY, Pat	27	M	Laborer	12Ja02Dz
Stephen	22	M	Laborer	12Ja02Dz
Catherine	20	F	Spinster	12Ja02Dz
Thomas	12	M	Unknown	12Ja02Dz
MCCAHEY, Alice	31	F	Wife	12Ja02Dz
Rose	10	F	Unknown	12Ja02Dz
Mick	8	M	Child	12Ja02Dz
Ann	.00	F	Infant	12Ja02Dz
MCINTYRE, James	27	M	Laborer	12Ja02Dz
BEGLEY, Ann	20	F	Spinster	12Ja02Dz
MCSHANE, Bridget	30	F	Spinster	12Ja02Dz
KING, Richard	33	M	Gdnr	12Ja02Dz
U-Mrs.	28	F	Wife	12Ja02Dz
MURPHY, Ann	22	F	Spinster	12Ja02Dz
Biddy	18	F	Spinster	12Ja02Dz
MULLIGAN, Mary	15	F	Spinster	12Ja02Dz
GALLIGAN, James	14	M	Unknown	12Ja02Dz
Patrick	11	M	Unknown	12Ja02Dz
FOX, Michl.	20	M	Unknown	12Ja02Dz
MOSSISS, George	36	M	Laborer	12Ja02Dz
MCGOWN, Bridget	44	F	Wi	12Ja02Dz
Francis	10	M	Unknown	12Ja02Dz
Mary	11	F	Unknown	12Ja02Dz
Bridget	7	F	Child	12Ja02Dz
CARROLL, John	18	M	Laborer	12Ja02Dz
LOFTUS, Andrew	45	M	Laborer	12Ja02Dz
SHEA, Rose	36	F	Wife	12Ja02Dz
John	28	M	Laborer	12Ja02Dz
Mary	7	F	Child	12Ja02Dz
Cath.	3	F	Child	12Ja02Dz
GAFRAN, John	18	M	Servant	12Ja02Dz
MCGOWAN, Honour	50	F	Wi	12Ja02Dz
DONELY, Cathn.	20	F	Spinster	12Ja02Dz
MEGAN, Rosanna	14	F	Spinster	12Ja02Dz

NAMES OF PASSENGERS	AGE	SEX	OCCUPATIONS	DATE PORT SHIP
PETERS, Ann	30	F	Wi	12Ja02Dz
CROFTON, Martin	28	M	Farmer	12Ja02Dz
MCKAY, James	26	M	Saddler	12Ja02Dz
MINCHAN, Joseph	00	M	Unknown	12Ja02Dz
U-Mrs.	00	F	Unknown	12Ja02Dz
JOHNSTON, U-Dr.	00	M	Sgns	12Ja02Dz

DAVID-CANNON 14 JANUARY 1850

From Liverpool

NAMES OF PASSENGERS	AGE	SEX	OCCUPATIONS	DATE PORT SHIP
BARRY, Eugene	45	M	Farmer	14Ja02Fq
Michl.	21	M	Unknown	14Ja02Fq
Johana	40	F	Unknown	14Ja02Fq
Margt.	18	F	Spinster	14Ja02Fq
Eliza	19	F	Spinster	14Ja02Fq
Mary-Ann	16	F	Spinster	14Ja02Fq
Hannah	12	F	Spinster	14Ja02Fq
James	9	M	Child	14Ja02Fq
Honora	18	F	Spinster	14Ja02Fq
CONNELLY, Pat	35	M	Laborer	14Ja02Fq
Margt.	28	F	Laborer	14Ja02Fq
Mary	11	F	Laborer	14Ja02Fq
Margt.	9	F	Child	14Ja02Fq
Edw.	6	M	Child	14Ja02Fq
Swime--, Rose	25	F	Laborer	14Ja02Fq
Harris	2	M	Child	14Ja02Fq
Rose	.00	F	Infant	14Ja02Fq
ASHER, Harner	22	M	Unknown	14Ja02Fq
Hannah	21	F	Unknown	14Ja02Fq
JONES, Richd.	68	M	Farmer	14Ja02Fq
Henry	35	M	Farmer	14Ja02Fq
Llewellyn	38	M	Farmer	14Ja02Fq
David	22	M	Farmer	14Ja02Fq
MACKSON, Emmanuel	30	M	Farmer	14Ja02Fq
BELCHER, Thos.	40	M	Laborer	14Ja02Fq
BLOCK, Alexr.	26	M	Unknown	14Ja02Fq
GLASIER, Ann	25	F	Wife	14Ja02Fq
FARRELL, John	23	M	Laborer	14Ja02Fq
NOWLAN, Margt.	21	F	Laborer	14Ja02Fq
Elizth.	18	F	Laborer	14Ja02Fq
Pat	4	M	Child	14Ja02Fq
Mary-Ann	5	F	Child	14Ja02Fq
FAMATHERLY, Geo.	45	M	Laborer	14Ja02Fq
DAVIS, John	20	M	Laborer	14Ja02Fq
HUSTON, James	21	M	Laborer	14Ja02Fq
JOHNSTON, John	47	M	Laborer	14Ja02Fq
CAVANAGH, John	50	M	Laborer	14Ja02Fq
John	20	M	Laborer	14Ja02Fq
HARPER, Cathen.	22	F	Laborer	14Ja02Fq
Edwd.	23	M	Laborer	14Ja02Fq
SHERIFF, Thos.	31	M	Laborer	14Ja02Fq
KELLY, Joseph	21	M	Laborer	14Ja02Fq
Eliza	47	F	Wife	14Ja02Fq
Eliza	17	F	Wife	14Ja02Fq
HEADON, Cath.	21	F	Wife	14Ja02Fq
Mary	10	F	Child	14Ja02Fq
HASTON, Darby	23	M	Unknown	14Ja02Fq
ODONOUGH, Ellen	22	F	Wife	14Ja02Fq
DEVELIN, Mary	50	F	Unknown	14Ja02Fq
GILL, Elizth.	25	F	Unknown	14Ja02Fq
CAMPBELL, Wm.	23	M	Farmer	14Ja02Fq
Mary	17	F	Farmer	14Ja02Fq
SULLIVAN, Mick	23	M	Farmer	14Ja02Fq
ELLIS, Nicholas	24	M	Farmer	14Ja02Fq
MUNDAY, Robt.	24	M	Farmer	14Ja02Fq
HUGHING, Wm.	21	M	Farmer	14Ja02Fq
SULLIVAN, Jane	20	F	Spinster	14Ja02Fq
BODEL, John	21	M	Laborer	14Ja02Fq
FOSTER, Margt.	20	F	Unknown	14Ja02Fq
HARVEY, Peter	21	M	Unknown	14Ja02Fq
Mary	21	F	Spinster	14Ja02Fq
KIDNEY, Geoe.	24	M	Unknown	14Ja02Fq
SAND, Mary-Jane	16	F	Spinster	14Ja02Fq
MCGUIRE, Rose	20	F	Spinster	14Ja02Fq
CORRIGAN, Mary	20	F	Spinster	14Ja02Fq
MAGIN, Sarah	31	F	Spinster	14Ja02Fq
Martha	9	F	Child	14Ja02Fq
Died-At-Sea				
Mary	9	F	Child	14Ja02Fq
Bridget	7	F	Child	14Ja02Fq
Sarah	.00	F	Infant	14Ja02Fq
REILLY, Biddy	40	F	Spinster	14Ja02Fq
MURPHY, Mary	27	F	Spinster	14Ja02Fq
CROWE, John	24	M	Laborer	14Ja02Fq
CARROLL, John	20	M	Unknown	14Ja02Fq
CASSIDY, James	18	M	Unknown	14Ja02Fq
FINNEGAN, James	16	M	Unknown	14Ja02Fq
FINN, Ellen	36	F	Wife	14Ja02Fq
Mary	25	F	Unknown	14Ja02Fq
MAGUIRE, Maria	22	F	Unknown	14Ja02Fq
HOAR, Edwd.	20	M	Laborer	14Ja02Fq
LEDDY, Peter	32	M	Laborer	14Ja02Fq
DEMPSEY, Patk.	27	M	Laborer	14Ja02Fq
MACKEY, John	29	M	Laborer	14Ja02Fq
MCKENNA, James	50	M	Laborer	14Ja02Fq
WOODS, James	20	M	Laborer	14Ja02Fq
FAHEY, Timy.	23	M	Laborer	14Ja02Fq
KELLY, John	24	M	Laborer	14Ja02Fq
John	33	M	Laborer	14Ja02Fq
MURPHY, Lawrence	35	M	Laborer	14Ja02Fq
MCKEOWN, Ellen	16	F	Spinster	14Ja02Fq
Jane	10	F	Unknown	14Ja02Fq
John	23	M	Farmer	14Ja02Fq
BEATTY, Christy	22	M	Unknown	14Ja02Fq
Margt.	34	F	Unknown	14Ja02Fq
PHILLIPS, John	34	M	Unknown	14Ja02Fq
Michl.	12	M	Unknown	14Ja02Fq
Bridget	32	F	Wife	14Ja02Fq
Pat	10	M	Child	14Ja02Fq
Rosey	8	F	Child	14Ja02Fq
Thomas	3	M	Child	14Ja02Fq
VERDON, Jane	20	F	Spinster	14Ja02Fq
CURRAN, Mary	27	F	Unknown	14Ja02Fq
BARTY, Mary	18	F	Unknown	14Ja02Fq
KIRK, John	20	M	Laborer	14Ja02Fq
DICKEY, Alexr.	30	F	Wife	14Ja02Fq
Jane	30	F	Unknown	14Ja02Fq
Nathnl.	7	M	Child	14Ja02Fq
Jas.	.00	M	Infant	14Ja02Fq
LECKEY, Betty	14	F	Unknown	14Ja02Fq
DOUGHERTY, Jas.	21	M	Laborer	14Ja02Fq
MARA, John	21	M	Unknown	14Ja02Fq
KEANES, Nancy	35	F	Spinster	14Ja02Fq
Dan	4	M	Child	14Ja02Fq
James	.00	M	Infant	14Ja02Fq
BURKE, Mary	23	F	Spinster	14Ja02Fq
Nancy	18	F	Spinster	14Ja02Fq
KEEGAN, Bridgt.	50	F	Spinster	14Ja02Fq
Charles	18	M	Unknown	14Ja02Fq
Mary	16	F	Spinster	14Ja02Fq
Ann	11	F	Unknown	14Ja02Fq
REYNOLDS, Mick	70	M	Laborer	14Ja02Fq
Betty	56	F	Laborer	14Ja02Fq
Denis	27	M	Laborer	14Ja02Fq
Betty	18	F	Laborer	14Ja02Fq
Bridgt.	25	F	Laborer	14Ja02Fq
Eliza	9	F	Child	14Ja02Fq
CORMICK, Ellen	10	F	Laborer	14Ja02Fq
CARTEY, Mary	50	F	Laborer	14Ja02Fq
Michl.	25	M	Laborer	14Ja02Fq
Ann	4	F	Child	14Ja02Fq
SHEPHERD, Mary	18	F	Laborer	14Ja02Fq
MEANY, Edwd.	13	M	Unknown	14Ja02Fq

NAMES OF PASSENGERS	AGE	SEX	OCCUPATIONS	DATE PORT SHIP
MEANY, Bridgt.	20	F	Spinster	14Ja02Fq
CURRAN, Mary	16	F	Unknown	14Ja02Fq
John	12	M	Unknown	14Ja02Fq
FLAVAHAN, Dennis	30	M	Farmer	14Ja02Fq
PEACOCK, Geoe.	30	M	Farmer	14Ja02Fq
Margt.	19	F	Farmer	14Ja02Fq
KING, Rose	50	F	Farmer	14Ja02Fq
Bridgt.	22	F	Farmer	14Ja02Fq
Cathn.	20	F	Farmer	14Ja02Fq
Lawn.	18	M	Farmer	14Ja02Fq
Mary	14	F	Spinster	14Ja02Fq
Sarah	12	F	Unknown	14Ja02Fq
Bernard	10	M	Unknown	14Ja02Fq
CUMMINS, John	32	M	Laborer	14Ja02Fq
Mary	7	F	Child	14Ja02Fq
Mary	4	F	Child	14Ja02Fq
Johana	3	F	Child	14Ja02Fq
Mary	28	F	Laborer	14Ja02Fq
John	.00	M	Infant	14Ja02Fq
Margt.	12	F	Unknown	14Ja02Fq
Johana	4	F	Child	14Ja02Fq
David	35	M	Laborer	14Ja02Fq
Thomas	6	M	Child	14Ja02Fq
Ellen	8	F	Child	14Ja02Fq
Mary	36	F	Laborer	14Ja02Fq
Margt.	9	F	Child	14Ja02Fq
John	7	M	Child	14Ja02Fq
Margt.	21	F	Wife	14Ja02Fq
WILSON, Peter	21	M	Laborer	14Ja02Fq
CONNOR, Jas.	50	M	Laborer	14Ja02Fq
Janet	48	F	Laborer	14Ja02Fq
Peter	24	M	Laborer	14Ja02Fq
RYAN, John	20	M	Laborer	14Ja02Fq
HAYS, Thomas	26	M	Laborer	14Ja02Fq
MCNAMARA, Jas.	22	M	Unknown	14Ja02Fq
HAYS, Julia	21	F	Spinster	14Ja02Fq
DEVINE, Margt.	26	F	Unknown	14Ja02Fq
FULTON, John	22	M	Laborer	14Ja02Fq
MCARTNEY, Geoe.	22	M	Laborer	14Ja02Fq
BARRY, John	41	M	Laborer	14Ja02Fq
GORMAN, Thos.	25	M	Laborer	14Ja02Fq
BURN, Mary	16	F	Spinster	14Ja02Fq
Cath.	17	F	Unknown	14Ja02Fq
CORMICK, Thomas	60	M	Farmer	14Ja02Fq
William	12	M	Unknown	14Ja02Fq
Judith	13	F	Unknown	14Ja02Fq
Anty.	30	M	Unknown	14Ja02Fq
WALSH, Biddy	40	F	Unknown	14Ja02Fq
DAYSLEY, John	26	M	Laborer	14Ja02Fq
DEVITT, Edw.	20	M	Laborer	14Ja02Fq
CHRISTY, Martin	21	M	Laborer	14Ja02Fq
FLEMING, James	21	M	Laborer	14Ja02Fq
DUNLOP, Bessey	21	F	Spinster	14Ja02Fq
GALLAGHER, Richd.	25	M	Laborer	14Ja02Fq
BURKE, Wm.	24	M	Laborer	14Ja02Fq
DOUGHERTY, Thos.	30	M	Laborer	14Ja02Fq
COUGHLIN, Wm.	18	M	Laborer	14Ja02Fq
MEALIN, Michl.	28	M	Laborer	14Ja02Fq
PATTERSON, Edwd.	18	M	Laborer	14Ja02Fq
FITZPATRICK, Benjn.	25	M	Laborer	14Ja02Fq
Hannah	25	F	Wife	14Ja02Fq
Robert	20	M	Farmer	14Ja02Fq
BURGESS, Thomas	18	M	Unknown	14Ja02Fq
CROWE, Astin	27	M	Shoemaker	14Ja02Fq
MADIGAN, Martin	20	M	Laborer	14Ja02Fq
DAY, John	20	M	Laborer	14Ja02Fq
KEYDON, Michl.	33	M	Laborer	14Ja02Fq
QUIN, Michl.	38	M	Laborer	14Ja02Fq
LILLES, Ellen	22	F	Spinster	14Ja02Fq
MADDIN, John	21	M	Laborer	14Ja02Fq
Michl.	20	M	Unknown	14Ja02Fq
Hannah	20	F	Wife	14Ja02Fq
CROSIER, James	19	M	Carpenter	14Ja02Fq
Martha	20	F	Wife	14Ja02Fq
MALONE, Mary	27	F	Unknown	14Ja02Fq

NAMES OF PASSENGERS	AGE	SEX	OCCUPATIONS	DATE PORT SHIP
DUFFY, James	40	M	Farmer	14Ja02Fq
IRWIN, Thos.	18	M	Farmer	14Ja02Fq
OWENS, Michl.	26	M	Farmer	14Ja02Fq
Margt.	20	F	Farmer	14Ja02Fq
CONNOR, Michl.	24	M	Farmer	14Ja02Fq
FILAN, Patk.	14	M	Laborer	14Ja02Fq
MURPHY, Patk.	18	M	Unknown	14Ja02Fq
MANEY, Pat	77	M	Unknown	14Ja02Fq
Margt.	60	F	Wife	14Ja02Fq
Bryan	19	M	Laborer	14Ja02Fq
Margt.	17	F	Laborer	14Ja02Fq
QUICK, Andrew	23	M	Laborer	14Ja02Fq
BROUTH, John	40	M	Laborer	14Ja02Fq
MCANEENY, James	77	M	Laborer	14Ja02Fq
Thos.	34	M	Laborer	14Ja02Fq
Hugh	32	M	Laborer	14Ja02Fq
John	4	M	Child	14Ja02Fq
SULLIVAN, Owen	27	M	Laborer	14Ja02Fq
MCFARNEY, Jas.	21	M	Laborer	14Ja02Fq
DOWD, Winney	16	F	Spinster	14Ja02Fq
CLISDALE, Wm.	57	M	Farmer	14Ja02Fq
John	23	M	Unknown	14Ja02Fq
Ann	56	F	Wife	14Ja02Fq
Mary-A.	16	F	Unknown	14Ja02Fq
Matilda	14	F	Unknown	14Ja02Fq
Esther	11	F	Unknown	14Ja02Fq
WALLIS, Martha	21	F	Unknown	14Ja02Fq
Sarah	18	F	Unknown	14Ja02Fq
LEECH, Martha	14	F	Unknown	14Ja02Fq
TERRY, Wm.	40	M	Laborer	14Ja02Fq
EDWARDS, Thos.	31	M	Laborer	14Ja02Fq
FARRELL, Pat	27	M	Laborer	14Ja02Fq
FOGARTY, Mat	31	M	Laborer	14Ja02Fq
FOYLE, Bridgt.	20	F	Laborer	14Ja02Fq
MARKEY, Michl.	26	M	Laborer	14Ja02Fq
CARR, Danl.	24	M	Laborer	14Ja02Fq
GIBBONS, Edwd.	24	M	Laborer	14Ja02Fq
HOLAGHAN, Wm.	24	M	Laborer	14Ja02Fq
DUGLAN, Thos.	24	M	Laborer	14Ja02Fq
SHARPE, James	30	M	Laborer	14Ja02Fq
Isabella	24	F	Wife	14Ja02Fq
Ann	.00	F	Infant	14Ja02Fq
BENNETT, Anna	50	F	Unknown	14Ja02Fq
Ellen	35	F	Unknown	14Ja02Fq
Ellen	17	F	Unknown	14Ja02Fq
Kate	18	F	Unknown	14Ja02Fq
Wm.	12	M	None	14Ja02Fq
Johana	15	F	Spinster	14Ja02Fq
Margt.	17	F	Spinster	14Ja02Fq
MCAULIFF, Ellen	17	F	Spinster	14Ja02Fq
BROWNE, Kate	10	F	Unknown	14Ja02Fq
MURPHY, Cath.	18	F	Spinster	14Ja02Fq
QUINLAN, Biddy	35	F	Wife	14Ja02Fq
DELANEY, Sarah	30	M	Unknown	14Ja02Fq
PRATT, John	15	M	Laborer	14Ja02Fq
COLLINS, Michl.	18	M	Laborer	14Ja02Fq
Willm.	20	M	Laborer	14Ja02Fq
SULLIVAN, John	21	M	Laborer	14Ja02Fq
FLANNIGAN, John	20	M	Laborer	14Ja02Fq
MANN, John	24	M	Laborer	14Ja02Fq
Margt.	21	F	Wife	14Ja02Fq
DONOGHUE, Hannah	21	F	Wife	14Ja02Fq
SWEENEY, Margt.	22	F	Wife	14Ja02Fq
Mary	20	F	Wife	14Ja02Fq
MCGEERY, Sarah	60	F	Wife	14Ja02Fq
Sarah	16	F	Unknown	14Ja02Fq
Ann	14	F	Unknown	14Ja02Fq
MCMENOMY, Hugh	20	M	Laborer	14Ja02Fq
Bridgt.	17	F	Spinster	14Ja02Fq
Barra-BARRY, Johana	26	F	Spinster	14Ja02Fq
Patk.	.00	M	Infant	14Ja02Fq
GREANY, Pat	26	M	Laborer	14Ja02Fq
DELANEY, Michl.	26	M	Laborer	14Ja02Fq
MALONEY, Martin	20	M	Laborer	14Ja02Fq
HICKEY, John	30	M	Laborer	14Ja02Fq

NAMES OF PASSENGERS	AGE	SEX	OCCUPATIONS	DATE PORT SHIP
HICKEY, John	20	M	Laborer	14Ja02Fq
MCAVOY, Michl.	30	M	Laborer	14Ja02Fq
SMITH, Hugh	26	M	Laborer	14Ja02Fq
GORMAN, Margt.	32	F	Spinster	14Ja02Fq
SMITH, Margt.	25	F	Unknown	14Ja02Fq
NOON, Peter	30	M	Laborer	14Ja02Fq
James	4	M	Child	14Ja02Fq
Ann	30	F	Wife	14Ja02Fq
Peter	8	M	Child	14Ja02Fq
Mary	6	M	Child	14Ja02Fq
Ann	.00	F	Infant	14Ja02Fq
HORAN, John	3	M	Child	14Ja02Fq
Ann	.00	F	Infant	14Ja02Fq
MCMAHON, Danl.	24	M	Laborer	14Ja02Fq
LEAHY, Michl.	20	M	Laborer	14Ja02Fq
BELLINGER, Michl.	50	M	Laborer	14Ja02Fq
CORBITT, Dennis	28	M	Laborer	14Ja02Fq
MURPHY, Cornl.	25	M	Laborer	14Ja02Fq
Cath.	24	F	Wife	14Ja02Fq
STOCK, Mary	20	F	Spinster	14Ja02Fq
MORIARTY, Honor	30	F	Unknown	14Ja02Fq
STEVENSON, Thomas	30	M	Farmer	14Ja02Fq
MCGOWAN, James	30	M	Farmer	14Ja02Fq
COX, John	36	M	Farmer	14Ja02Fq
MAHON, Pat	18	M	Farmer	14Ja02Fq
WHALIN, Francis	18	M	Laborer	14Ja02Fq
KING, Owen	66	M	Unknown	14Ja02Fq
Margt.	21	F	Unknown	14Ja02Fq
MALEY, Margt.	21	F	Unknown	14Ja02Fq
NOLAN, Judith	30	F	Unknown	14Ja02Fq
ARMSTRONG, Jane	21	F	Unknown	14Ja02Fq
JOICE, John	24	M	Farmer	14Ja02Fq
Mary	24	F	Wife	14Ja02Fq
MCNULTY, Chas.	50	M	Laborer	14Ja02Fq
Mary	50	F	Unknown	14Ja02Fq
Pat	17	M	Unknown	14Ja02Fq
John	14	M	None	14Ja02Fq
Isabella	12	F	None	14Ja02Fq
Mary	8	F	Child	14Ja02Fq
BURN, Miles	14	M	None	14Ja02Fq
Peter	16	M	Laborer	14Ja02Fq
SAVAGE, Robt.	30	M	Unknown	14Ja02Fq
Margt.	8	F	Child	14Ja02Fq
Lizzy	7	F	Child	14Ja02Fq
MALLIN, John	20	M	Laborer	14Ja02Fq
Ann	25	F	Wife	14Ja02Fq
MALONEY, Pat	25	M	Farmer	14Ja02Fq
HALLORAN, John	25	M	Farmer	14Ja02Fq
DUNWORTH, Michl.	18	M	Farmer	14Ja02Fq
KEATING, Wm.	28	M	Farmer	14Ja02Fq
MCELROY, Cath.	7	F	Child	14Ja02Fq
DUFFY, Hugh	26	M	Laborer	14Ja02Fq
Anne	25	F	Wife	14Ja02Fq
Francis	6	M	Child	14Ja02Fq
Kate	2	F	Child	14Ja02Fq
Peter	.00	M	Infant	14Ja02Fq
Betty	26	F	Unknown	14Ja02Fq
MOONEY, Ellen	26	F	Unknown	14Ja02Fq
Margt.	16	F	Unknown	14Ja02Fq
COLLIN, Rose	23	F	Unknown	14Ja02Fq
SMITH, Mary	22	F	Unknown	14Ja02Fq
FLYNN, Honor	26	F	Unknown	14Ja02Fq
Peggy	18	F	Unknown	14Ja02Fq
CARLIN, James	22	M	Laborer	14Ja02Fq
LOUGHLIN, Pat	40	M	Unknown	14Ja02Fq
Kate	25	F	Wife	14Ja02Fq
John	.00	M	Infant	14Ja02Fq
EGAN, Martin	27	M	Laborer	14Ja02Fq
SILK, Thos.	20	M	Laborer	14Ja02Fq
GORMAN, Thos.	20	M	Laborer	14Ja02Fq
ANSBORO, Martin	20	M	Laborer	14Ja02Fq
GODFREY, Wm.	20	M	Laborer	14Ja02Fq
STABLETON, John	50	M	Laborer	14Ja02Fq
Michl.	20	M	Unknown	14Ja02Fq
Judy	20	F	Wife	14Ja02Fq
PURCELL, John	21	M	Farmer	14Ja02F
MCNALLY, Peter	20	M	Farmer	14Ja02F
John	19	M	Farmer	14Ja02F
SCAHILL, Michl.	25	M	Farmer	14Ja02F
HAYS, Denis	25	M	Farmer	14Ja02F
SCANLIN, Pat	21	M	Farmer	14Ja02F
GREENAN, James	25	M	Farmer	14Ja02F
Peter	18	M	Farmer	14Ja02F
WALSH, Michl.	28	M	Farmer	14Ja02F
MEEHAN, Wm.	25	M	Farmer	14Ja02F
DEVITT, Bridgt.	50	F	Wife	14Ja02F
GARVEY, John	22	M	Laborer	14Ja02F
Mary	20	F	Wife	14Ja02F
CONWAY, John	19	M	Laborer	14Ja02F
Bridgt.	17	F	Laborer	14Ja02F
COYLE, Phil	40	M	Laborer	14Ja02F
Mary	14	F	Laborer	14Ja02F
GLANCEY, Honora	50	F	Laborer	14Ja02F
Bridgt.	46	F	Laborer	14Ja02F
John	.00	M	Infant	14Ja02F
Bridget	4	F	Child	14Ja02F
LEAHEY, John	30	M	Farmer	14Ja02F
HIGGINS, John	51	M	Farmer	14Ja02F
HEFFERMAN, Wm.	19	M	Farmer	14Ja02F
COLBERT, Mary	25	F	Wife	14Ja02F
CARROLL, Cath.	20	F	Wife	14Ja02F
MURPHY, Johana	22	F	Wife	14Ja02F
HEFFERMAN, Kate	20	F	Wife	14Ja02F
DONNELLY, Nelly	20	F	Wife	14Ja02F
ONEAL, Michl.	56	M	Laborer	14Ja02F
Mary	30	F	Wife	14Ja02F
Ellen	2	F	Child	14Ja02F
Margt.	.00	F	Infant	14Ja02F
Died-At-Sea				
SMITH, John	22	M	Farmer	14Ja02F
DOWNEY, Timy.	22	M	Unknown	14Ja02F
Bridgt.	20	F	Spinster	14Ja02F
GRACE, Cath.	30	F	Spinster	14Ja02F
KELLY, Esther	26	F	Spinster	14Ja02F
SHERLOCK, Pat	25	M	Laborer	14Ja02F
DORAN, Michl.	26	M	Laborer	14Ja02F
CLERKIN, D.	27	F	Spinster	14Ja02F
Mary	22	F	Spinster	14Ja02F
CUSTOTON, Thos.	30	M	Laborer	14Ja02F
GAVAN, Eliza	24	F	Unknown	14Ja02F
BEHAN, Edmond	27	M	Unknown	14Ja02F
RYAN, Margt.	38	F	Unknown	14Ja02F
Ellen	12	F	Unknown	14Ja02F
Cath.	10	F	Unknown	14Ja02F
Edward	5	M	Child	14Ja02F
Belon-GORMAN, Margt.	27	F	Unknown	14Ja02F
Thomas	3	M	Child	14Ja02F
Margt.	.00	F	Infant	14Ja02F
Born-At-Sea				
FITZGERALD, David	22	M	Unknown	14Ja02F
DUFFY, Sarah	18	F	Unknown	14Ja02F
Owen	20	M	Unknown	14Ja02F
FLEMMING, Jas.	28	M	Unknown	14Ja02F
TIERNEY, Chas.	24	M	Unknown	14Ja02F
Michl.	20	M	Unknown	14Ja02F
CONWAY, Thos.	18	M	Unknown	14Ja02F
CONNOVAN, Wm.	12	M	Unknown	14Ja02F
BROWN, Anne	26	F	Unknown	14Ja02F
TIERNEY, Margt.	35	F	Unknown	14Ja02F
QUIGLEY, Thomas	25	M	Unknown	14Ja02F
KELLY, Cathe.	22	M	Unknown	14Ja02F
DWYER, Jas.	40	M	Unknown	14Ja02F
Michl.	18	M	Unknown	14Ja02F
BREEN, Johana	28	F	Unknown	14Ja02F
DWYER, Honora	40	F	Unknown	14Ja02F
CARBILT, Bess	28	F	Unknown	14Ja02F
COLLY, Thos.	24	M	Unknown	14Ja02F
MELTY, Ann	18	F	Unknown	14Ja02F
TUCKER, Margt.	30	F	Unknown	14Ja02F
Wm.	3	M	Child	14Ja02F

NAMES OF PASSENGERS	AGE	SEX	OCCUPATIONS	DATE PORT SHIP
TUCKER, Bridgt.	.00	F	Infant	14Ja02Fq
WALSH, Mary	26	F	Unknown	14Ja02Fq
Lyons-LYNDS, Michl.	22	M	Unknown	14Ja02Fq
EGAN, Martin	25	M	Unknown	14Ja02Fq
MARTIN, Pat	21	M	Unknown	14Ja02Fq
Betty	16	F	Unknown	14Ja02Fq
Cathe.	14	F	Unknown	14Ja02Fq
HOGAN, Thomas	15	M	Unknown	14Ja02Fq
Margt.	50	F	Unknown	14Ja02Fq
CONROY, Stephen	25	M	Unknown	14Ja02Fq
Died-At-Sea				
Hegan-KEAGAN, Nancy	12	F	Unknown	14Ja02Fq
HYNES, Bridgt.	10	F	Unknown	14Ja02Fq
WHITE, Lawrence	7	M	Child	14Ja02Fq
MALONEY, Michl.	23	M	Unknown	14Ja02Fq
QUIN, Jas.	35	M	Unknown	14Ja02Fq
MCMAHON, Jas.	19	M	Unknown	14Ja02Fq
MAGUIRE, Thos.	34	M	Unknown	14Ja02Fq
MCMAHON, Jas.-Or-Cathe	19	U	Unknown	14Ja02Fq
Bridgt.	4	F	Child	14Ja02Fq
Francis	2	M	Child	14Ja02Fq
Pat	.00	M	Infant	14Ja02Fq
POWER, Pat	36	M	Laborer	14Ja02Fq
Ann	30	F	Wife	14Ja02Fq
Francis	27	M	Unknown	14Ja02Fq
Ann	7	F	Child	14Ja02Fq
Thomas	3	M	Child	14Ja02Fq
Cathe.	2	F	Child	14Ja02Fq
Ellen	.00	F	Infant	14Ja02Fq
Died-At-Sea				
Bridgt.	5	F	Child	14Ja02Fq
Died-At-Sea				
FINNESY, John	31	M	Farmer	14Ja02Fq
BUTLER, Michl.	22	M	Farmer	14Ja02Fq
REILLY, Jas.	28	M	Farmer	14Ja02Fq
Bridget	24	F	Wife	14Ja02Fq
Michl.	21	M	Laborer	14Ja02Fq
Mary	18	F	Spinster	14Ja02Fq
Pat	5	M	Child	14Ja02Fq
Michl.	.00	M	Infant	14Ja02Fq
MARTIN, Chas.	40	M	Farmer	14Ja02Fq
Bernd.	11	M	Farmer	14Ja02Fq
FINNEGAN, Jas.	21	M	Farmer	14Ja02Fq
KELLY, John	40	M	Farmer	14Ja02Fq
Hannah	20	F	Wife	14Ja02Fq
Bridgt.	25	F	Unknown	14Ja02Fq
SILK, Ann	35	F	Unknown	14Ja02Fq
WOODE, Francis	30	M	Laborer	14Ja02Fq
Jas.	25	M	Laborer	14Ja02Fq
BURN, Moses	38	M	Laborer	14Ja02Fq
Margt.	30	F	Wife	14Ja02Fq
Kate	25	F	Unknown	14Ja02Fq
STIMSON, John	25	M	Laborer	14Ja02Fq
BRYAN, Miles	23	M	Unknown	14Ja02Fq
MURPHY, Kate	25	F	Spinster	14Ja02Fq
Ellen	24	F	Spinster	14Ja02Fq
REDMOND, Cathe.	18	F	Spinster	14Ja02Fq
DODDY, Denny	19	M	Laborer	14Ja02Fq
Cathe.	20	F	Unknown	14Ja02Fq
CONDRON, Thos.	20	M	Unknown	14Ja02Fq
BAGAN, Ellen	20	F	Wife	14Ja02Fq
Rosey	18	F	Unknown	14Ja02Fq
HETHERMAN, Jas.	37	M	Farmer	14Ja02Fq
Ellen	30	F	Wife	14Ja02Fq
Cathe.	30	F	Wife	14Ja02Fq
QUIN, Edmond	4	M	Child	14Ja02Fq
MOLLOY, Mary	20	F	Unknown	14Ja02Fq
JOICE, Henry	23	M	Farmer	14Ja02Fq
WALSH, John	23	M	Laborer	14Ja02Fq
TIERNEY, John	24	M	Unknown	14Ja02Fq
MALEY, Jas.	22	M	Unknown	14Ja02Fq
HIGGINS, Kate	20	F	Servant	14Ja02Fq
CONNOR, Brid.	20	F	Unknown	14Ja02Fq
SULLIVAN, Mary	35	F	Wife	14Ja02Fq
James	9	M	Child	14Ja02Fq

NAMES OF PASSENGERS	AGE	SEX	OCCUPATIONS	DATE PORT SHIP
SULLIVAN, John	.00	M	Infant	14Ja02Fq
FINN, Honora	19	F	Spinster	14Ja02Fq
Mary	.00	F	Infant	14Ja02Fq
WHITE, Ann	22	F	Spinster	14Ja02Fq
COOGAN, Ann	50	F	Spinster	14Ja02Fq
Denis	18	M	Laborer	14Ja02Fq
Cathe.	17	F	Wife	14Ja02Fq
Esther	13	F	None	14Ja02Fq
FARLEY, Phil	30	M	Farmer	14Ja02Fq
KEARNEY, Thos.	22	M	Unknown	14Ja02Fq
Margt.	21	F	Wife	14Ja02Fq
Cathe.	30	F	Wife	14Ja02Fq
MURRAY, Bridgt.	40	F	Wife	14Ja02Fq
BEATTY, Margt.	24	F	Wife	14Ja02Fq
Christy	24	M	Laborer	14Ja02Fq
Thomas	.00	M	Infant	14Ja02Fq
Died-At-Sea				
HACKETT, Judith	50	F	Wife	14Ja02Fq
Danl.	30	M	Unknown	14Ja02Fq
Margt.	25	F	Unknown	14Ja02Fq
Ellen	18	F	Unknown	14Ja02Fq
Wm.	14	M	Laborer	14Ja02Fq
EGAN, Thos.	25	M	Laborer	14Ja02Fq
BYRNE, James	24	M	Unknown	14Ja02Fq
DUNN, Betty	29	F	Wife	14Ja02Fq
Belle	10	F	Unknown	14Ja02Fq
John	.00	M	Infant	14Ja02Fq
Died-At-Sea				
ALLEN, James	28	M	Laborer	14Ja02Fq
Jane	22	F	Wife	14Ja02Fq
WILSON, Martha	21	F	Unknown	14Ja02Fq
MCGAHAN, John	21	M	Laborer	14Ja02Fq
BALIFF, Thomas	19	M	Laborer	14Ja02Fq
GAFFIN, Michl.	19	M	Laborer	14Ja02Fq
NESBITT, S.	20	M	Laborer	14Ja02Fq
TULLY, Alice	35	F	Laborer	14Ja02Fq
CONNOR, Pat	23	M	Laborer	14Ja02Fq
HANIFY, Michl.	40	M	Laborer	14Ja02Fq
KEATING, Patk.	21	M	Laborer	14Ja02Fq
Wm.	19	M	Laborer	14Ja02Fq
Bridgt.	11	F	None	14Ja02Fq
DUNN, John	25	M	Farmer	14Ja02Fq
DOUGLAS, Thos.	26	M	Unknown	14Ja02Fq
MEANESS, Wm.	22	M	Farmer	14Ja02Fq
DWYER, Danl.	20	M	Farmer	14Ja02Fq
HENRATTY, Barney	30	M	Farmer	14Ja02Fq
COAKLEY, Abram	20	M	Farmer	14Ja02Fq
SOUTHERLAND, John	22	M	Farmer	14Ja02Fq
DUNLEACH, Cathe.	28	F	Servant	14Ja02Fq
LEMMON, Josh.	28	M	Laborer	14Ja02Fq
FITZPATRICK, Hugh	21	M	Laborer	14Ja02Fq
MANGAN, Thos.	27	M	Laborer	14Ja02Fq
TOOLE, John	34	M	Laborer	14Ja02Fq
EGAN, Thos.	16	M	Laborer	14Ja02Fq
ONEAL, Ellen	30	F	Wife	14Ja02Fq
EGAN, Bridgt.	20	F	Unknown	14Ja02Fq
RAFFERTY, Michl.	18	M	Laborer	14Ja02Fq
MARSHALL, Josh.	30	M	Unknown	14Ja02Fq
SHERIDAN, John	17	M	Unknown	14Ja02Fq
DOOGAN, Margt.	30	F	Laborer	14Ja02Fq
Mary	9	F	Child	14Ja02Fq
Pat	7	M	Child	14Ja02Fq
John	.00	M	Infant	14Ja02Fq
SHANNON, Thos.	28	M	Farmer	14Ja02Fq
HIGGINS, Jno.	29	M	Unknown	14Ja02Fq
Ellen	30	F	Wife	14Ja02Fq
Ellen	.00	F	Infant	14Ja02Fq
REILLY, Bessy	12	F	Unknown	14Ja02Fq
NOLAN, John	30	M	Laborer	14Ja02Fq
SWEENY, Michl.	26	M	Laborer	14Ja02Fq
MCCONNELL, Owen	26	M	Laborer	14Ja02Fq
MCGEE, Pat	26	M	Laborer	14Ja02Fq
LUCAS, Hugh	22	M	Laborer	14Ja02Fq
LAMB, Barbara	18	F	Servant	14Ja02Fq
CHRISTOPHER, Julia	20	F	Unknown	14Ja02Fq

NAMES OF PASSENGERS	AGE	SEX	OCCUPATIONS	DATE PORT SHIP
CHRISTOPHER, John	8	M	Child	14Ja02Fq
MCCREAN, Cathe.	17	F	Spinster	14Ja02Fq
GORMAN, Judy	26	F	Unknown	14Ja02Fq
DARCEY, Cath	7	F	Child	14Ja02Fq
ABBA, Ann	31	F	Wife	14Ja02Fq
Eliza	12	F	None	14Ja02Fq
Ellen	8	F	Child	14Ja02Fq
Christr.	6	M	Child	14Ja02Fq
Jane	.00	F	Infant	14Ja02Fq
WOOD, Orange	24	M	Laborer	14Ja02Fq
FLANNAGAN, Ellen	.00	F	Infant	14Ja02Fq
Died-At-Sea				
Mcguinn-QUIN, Sarah	.00	F	Infant	14Ja02Fq
Born-At-Sea				
COLBERT, Bridget	10	F	None	14Ja02Fq
COLLINS, Bridgt.	18	F	Unknown	14Ja02Fq
REILLY, Jas.	19	M	Unknown	14Ja02Fq
SULLIVAN, Josh.	36	M	Unknown	14Ja02Fq
DOOGAN, Ellen	8	F	Child	14Ja02Fq
GRAY, Jane	25	F	Unknown	14Ja02Fq
MCGRATH, Margt.	20	F	Unknown	14Ja02Fq
BELCHEY, U-Capt.	18	M	Unknown	14Ja02Fq

EMPIRE-STATE 14 JANUARY 1850

From Liverpool

NAMES OF PASSENGERS	AGE	SEX	OCCUPATIONS	DATE PORT SHIP
MELVIN, Mary	60	F	Wi	14Ja02Fc
Mary	18	F	Spinster	14Ja02Fc
ARMSTRONG, Andrew	24	M	Surgeon	14Ja02Fc
W.Ed.	22	M	Unknown	14Ja02Fc
MCLAUGHLIN, Michl.	16	M	Laborer	14Ja02Fc
FINNAN, Timth.	11	M	Laborer	14Ja02Fc
FOX, Wm.	30	M	Laborer	14Ja02Fc
HEFFREN, Walter	26	M	Mason	14Ja02Fc
MOHAN, James	36	M	Mason	14Ja02Fc
Thos.	10	M	Mason	14Ja02Fc
SMITH, Michl.	20	M	Carpenter	14Ja02Fc
Mathw.	17	M	Carpenter	14Ja02Fc
Terence	12	M	Carpenter	14Ja02Fc
DENNIN, Hugh	18	M	Tinman	14Ja02Fc
HIGGINS, Lloyd	18	M	Tinman	14Ja02Fc
CONARTY, Cathe.	16	F	Spinster	14Ja02Fc
CAVANAGH, Bernd.	35	M	Mason	14Ja02Fc
Mary	28	F	Mason	14Ja02Fc
Margt.	20	F	Unknown	14Ja02Fc
Biddy	.00	F	Infant	14Ja02Fc
BRADY, Alice	28	F	Unknown	14Ja02Fc
Ann	.00	F	Infant	14Ja02Fc
Bridgt.	20	F	Spinster	14Ja02Fc
REILLY, Margt.	38	F	Wi	14Ja02Fc
Ann	15	F	Unknown	14Ja02Fc
Edwd.	13	M	Unknown	14Ja02Fc
Mary	9	F	Child	14Ja02Fc
Terrence	6	M	Child	14Ja02Fc
LENAGHAN, Patt	19	M	Mason	14Ja02Fc
MCDONALD, Cathe.	36	F	Seamstress	14Ja02Fc
Hugh	12	M	Unknown	14Ja02Fc
Peter	7	M	Child	14Ja02Fc
Margt.	3	F	Child	14Ja02Fc
GANNELL, U	60	F	Wi	14Ja02Fc
Robt.	32	M	Mason	14Ja02Fc
COCHRANE, Thos.	22	M	Mason	14Ja02Fc
Julia	24	F	Unknown	14Ja02Fc
CUTLER, Mary	28	F	Spinster	14Ja02Fc
Ellen	19	F	Spinster	14Ja02Fc
CONNELL, Peter	21	M	Carpenter	14Ja02Fc
CULLIGAN, Bridgt.	14	F	Spinster	14Ja02Fc
MCDANIEL, Michl.	20	M	Laborer	14Ja02Fc
MCDONNELL, Francis	27	M	Laborer	14Ja02Fc
COGINS, Mary	6	F	Child	14Ja02Fc
SHARKEY, John	20	M	Turf Cutter	14Ja02Fc
CONNER, Owen	25	M	Turf Cutter	14Ja02Fc
Bridgt.	22	F	Unknown	14Ja02Fc
TULLY, Bridgt.	20	F	Spinster	14Ja02Fc
CULLIN, Ellen	10	F	Spinster	14Ja02Fc
FLANNAGAN, Patt	16	M	Mason	14Ja02Fc
EAGAN, Edwd.	21	M	Mason	14Ja02Fc
MULDOWNEY, Patt	20	M	Mason	14Ja02Fc
Cathe.	16	F	Spinster	14Ja02Fc
CREIGHTON, Hannah	40	F	Wi	14Ja02Fc
Darby	16	M	Laborer	14Ja02Fc
RATTIGAN, Daniel	45	M	Laborer	14Ja02Fc
Mary	22	F	Laborer	14Ja02Fc
Patt	20	M	Unknown	14Ja02Fc
Peter	18	M	Laborer	14Ja02Fc
ROURKE, Peter	18	M	Mason	14Ja02Fc
GATELY, John	20	M	Mason	14Ja02Fc
CULLEN, Eliza	10	F	Unknown	14Ja02Fc
MCGRATH, Ann	40	F	Wi	14Ja02Fc
Michl.	20	M	Carpenter	14Ja02Fc
Cathe.	14	F	Unknown	14Ja02Fc
Dan	11	M	Unknown	14Ja02Fc
Barnd.	9	M	Child	14Ja02Fc
Bridgt.	6	F	Child	14Ja02Fc
Peter	4	M	Child	14Ja02Fc
Handy	.00	M	Infant	14Ja02Fc
TUTE, Thomas	13	M	Laborer	14Ja02Fc
Patt	11	M	Laborer	14Ja02Fc
BRADY, Bridgt.	10	F	Unknown	14Ja02Fc
CLARKE, Michl.	17	M	Laborer	14Ja02Fc
BIRCH, U-Mrs.	35	F	Seamstress	14Ja02Fc
KENNY, Ann	40	F	Servant	14Ja02Fc
BIRCH, John-Wm.	.00	M	Infant	14Ja02Fc
FOX, John	30	M	Laborer	14Ja02Fc
James	24	M	Laborer	14Ja02Fc
DALY, Michl.	50	M	Laborer	14Ja02Fc
SMITH, Ellen	29	F	Spinster	14Ja02Fc
MCGOLRICK, Bernd.	26	M	Mason	14Ja02Fc
MITCHELL, Matilda	20	F	Spinster	14Ja02Fc
MCNAMARA, John	27	M	Carpenter	14Ja02Fc
Eliza	26	F	Unknown	14Ja02Fc
BASTOW, Alice	35	F	Wi	14Ja02Fc
James	11	M	Unknown	14Ja02Fc
BASTON, Hannah	3	F	Child	14Ja02Fc
HOLDEN, Jane	34	F	Weaver	14Ja02Fc
Rosana	12	F	Weaver	14Ja02Fc
Patt	9	M	Child	14Ja02Fc
Elizth.	7	F	Child	14Ja02Fc
Jane	4	F	Child	14Ja02Fc
Thos.	.00	M	Infant	14Ja02Fc
SCOTT, Hannah	40	F	Wi	14Ja02Fc
LYNCH, Margt.	13	F	Unknown	14Ja02Fc
FAY, Benjam.	20	M	Mason	14Ja02Fc
Bridgt.	10	F	Unknown	14Ja02Fc
MCCAME, Rose	40	F	Wi	14Ja02Fc
Stephen	7	M	Child	14Ja02Fc
FEEHELY, Mary	20	F	Spinster	14Ja02Fc
MCDOUGH, Sarah	19	F	Spinster	14Ja02Fc
LAWLESS, Ann	15	F	Spinster	14Ja02Fc
CURRINGTON, Mary	19	F	Spinster	14Ja02Fc
SMITH, Patt	40	M	Laborer	14Ja02Fc
James	25	M	Laborer	14Ja02Fc
Cathe.	20	F	Spinster	14Ja02Fc
REILLY, Bridgt.	20	F	Spinster	14Ja02Fc
SMITH, Peter	.00	M	Infant	14Ja02Fc
WITHERS, Margt.	20	F	Servant	14Ja02Fc
SMITH, Margt.	20	F	Servant	14Ja02Fc
Bridgt.	20	F	Servant	14Ja02Fc
Francis	30	M	Mason	14Ja02Fc
Thomas	26	M	Mason	14Ja02Fc
REILLY, John	25	M	Mason	14Ja02Fc
HAND, Ann	30	F	Spinster	14Ja02Fc
RUDDEN, Ann	26	F	Spinster	14Ja02Fc

NAMES OF PASSENGERS	AGE	SEX	OCCUPATIONS	DATE PORT SHIP
MCENTIRE, Sally	20	F	Spinster	14Ja02Fc
RUDDEN, Margt.	.00	F	Infant	14Ja02Fc
GORDON, John	28	M	Carpenter	14Ja02Fc
WAND, Hugh	18	M	Mason	14Ja02Fc
COONEY, Hannah	40	F	Wi	14Ja02Fc
Patt	12	M	Unknown	14Ja02Fc
CONNELL, Ellen	25	F	Spinster	14Ja02Fc
SMITH, Cathe.	18	F	Spinster	14Ja02Fc
FITZSIMMONS, Margt.	18	F	Spinster	14Ja02Fc
HEALY, Ann	18	F	Spinster	14Ja02Fc
BARTLEY, Bridgt.	30	F	Spinster	14Ja02Fc
MURPHY, Michl	25	M	Tinman	14Ja02Fc
Jane	22	F	Unknown	14Ja02Fc
REILLY, Chas.	21	M	Mason	14Ja02Fc
Rose	20	F	Unknown	14Ja02Fc
DALY, Henry	18	M	Carpenter	14Ja02Fc
COONEY, Patt	30	M	Carpenter	14Ja02Fc
MATHEWS, Mary	28	F	Spinster	14Ja02Fc
LYNCH, Rose	17	F	Spinster	14Ja02Fc
REILLY, Owen	20	M	Mason	14Ja02Fc
FITZSIMMONS, Ally	24	F	Spinster	14Ja02Fc
Patt	40	M	Carpenter	14Ja02Fc
REILLY, John	20	M	Carpenter	14Ja02Fc
RODGERS, Patt	30	M	Carpenter	14Ja02Fc
MCCORMICK, Bridgt.	46	F	Wi	14Ja02Fc
Died-At-Sea				
Bridgt.	16	F	Unknown	14Ja02Fc
Peter	17	M	Mason	14Ja02Fc
FLOOD, John	20	M	Mason	14Ja02Fc
REILLY, Patt	18	M	Laborer	14Ja02Fc
Margt.	20	F	Spinster	14Ja02Fc
BRADY, Mary	18	F	Spinster	14Ja02Fc
CORCORAN, Thos.	21	M	Carpenter	14Ja02Fc
Mary	25	F	Unknown	14Ja02Fc
Ann	23	F	Unknown	14Ja02Fc
Ellen	19	F	Unknown	14Ja02Fc
GIRVIN, Anthy.	48	M	Laborer	14Ja02Fc
Thomas	28	M	Laborer	14Ja02Fc
BURKE, John	28	M	Laborer	14Ja02Fc
Mary	22	F	Spinster	14Ja02Fc
GIRVIN, Mary	22	F	Spinster	14Ja02Fc
HAFFARAN, John	28	M	Carpenter	14Ja02Fc
NEAL, Hugh	28	M	Carpenter	14Ja02Fc
Mary	22	F	Spinster	14Ja02Fc
BYRNE, John	30	M	Laborer	14Ja02Fc
Ann	28	F	Unknown	14Ja02Fc
DUGGAN, Michl.	20	M	Mason	14Ja02Fc
SHERIDAN, James	60	M	Laborer	14Ja02Fc
Cathe.	50	F	Unknown	14Ja02Fc
James	18	M	Unknown	14Ja02Fc
GILL, Jane	40	F	Spinster	14Ja02Fc
GOODMAN, James	30	M	Carpenter	14Ja02Fc
KEARY, Patt	40	M	Mason	14Ja02Fc
GROGAN, Wm.	22	M	Mason	14Ja02Fc
MCDONALD, Patt	22	M	Mason	14Ja02Fc
CAREY, Cathe.	40	F	Wi	14Ja02Fc
Mary	17	F	Unknown	14Ja02Fc
Patt	15	M	Unknown	14Ja02Fc
QUINN, Bridgt.	18	F	Spinster	14Ja02Fc
MCDERMOTT, Wm.	20	M	Carpenter	14Ja02Fc
DRURY, Peter	20	M	Carpenter	14Ja02Fc
PEMEFEATHER, Michl.	40	M	Mason	14Ja02Fc
Edwd.	12	M	Mason	14Ja02Fc
HAYES, John	18	M	Laborer	14Ja02Fc
MALONE, Ann	40	F	Spinster	14Ja02Fc
KEEGAN, Cathe.	23	F	Spinster	14Ja02Fc
MAHONY, John	30	M	Turf Cutter	14Ja02Fc
Ellen	25	F	Turf Cutter	14Ja02Fc
DUFFY, Peter	16	M	Laborer	14Ja02Fc
Rose	18	F	Spinster	14Ja02Fc
Mary	15	F	Spinster	14Ja02Fc
NEAL, Mary	14	F	Spinster	14Ja02Fc
CONNER, Lucy	6	F	Child	14Ja02Fc
KELLY, Judy	20	F	Spinster	14Ja02Fc
QUIGLY, Thos.	23	M	Mason	14Ja02Fc

NAMES OF PASSENGERS	AGE	SEX	OCCUPATIONS	DATE PORT SHIP
ARMSTRONG, Lawrence	20	M	Mason	14Ja02Fc
Patt	25	M	Mason	14Ja02Fc
PIGEN, Cathe.	23	F	Seamstress	14Ja02Fc
Edwd.	.00	M	Infant	14Ja02Fc
Died-At-Sea				
CUNNIAN, Mary	50	F	Wi	14Ja02Fc
KELLY, Honora	18	F	Spinster	14Ja02Fc
GANNEN, Rose	17	F	Spinster	14Ja02Fc
QUINN, Michl.	16	M	Laborer	14Ja02Fc
BYRNE, Cathe.	20	F	Spinster	14Ja02Fc
RILEY, Ann	11	F	Spinster	14Ja02Fc
Margt.	9	F	Child	14Ja02Fc
Wm.	6	M	Child	14Ja02Fc
Mary	17	F	Spinster	14Ja02Fc
WOODS, Mary	18	F	Spinster	14Ja02Fc
DUNN, Dennis	41	M	Farmer	14Ja02Fc
CROOK, John	23	M	Farmer	14Ja02Fc
Margt.	11	F	Unknown	14Ja02Fc
OBRIEN, Ann	20	F	Spinster	14Ja02Fc
MULLIGAN, Cathe.	20	F	Spinster	14Ja02Fc
SHIELDS, John	20	M	Mason	14Ja02Fc
CASSIDAY, Bridgt.	26	F	Spinster	14Ja02Fc
SHIELDS, Francis	23	M	Carpenter	14Ja02Fc
JOYCE, John	40	M	Carpenter	14Ja02Fc
BURKE, Richd.	40	M	Carpenter	14Ja02Fc
JOYCE, Mary	20	F	Spinster	14Ja02Fc
Michl.	12	M	Laborer	14Ja02Fc
LINGIN, Ann	32	F	Wi	14Ja02Fc
John	5	M	Child	14Ja02Fc
DOWNERRY, James	20	M	Carpenter	14Ja02Fc
Mary	18	F	Unknown	14Ja02Fc
MULHOLLAND, Christ.	20	M	Mason	14Ja02Fc
MATHEWS, Cathe.	18	F	Spinster	14Ja02Fc
BRUSNIHAN, Timy.	26	M	Laborer	14Ja02Fc
MCCORMICK, Bridgt.	12	F	Unknown	14Ja02Fc
HEFFERNAN, Thos.	26	M	Carpenter	14Ja02Fc
KEHOE, Walter	40	M	Painter	14Ja02Fc
KENNEDY, Bridgt.	45	F	Wi	14Ja02Fc
James	13	M	Unknown	14Ja02Fc
Thos.	5	M	Child	14Ja02Fc
KEATING, Cathne.	25	F	Spinster	14Ja02Fc
ARMSTRONG, Robt.	17	M	Mason	14Ja02Fc
MORRISON, James	25	M	Mason	14Ja02Fc
LANELY, Mary	16	F	Spinster	14Ja02Fc
FLYNN, Helen	18	F	Spinster	14Ja02Fc
Owen	15	M	Laborer	14Ja02Fc
JOHNSTONE, James	26	M	Carpenter	14Ja02Fc
MCCUSHIN, Patt	22	M	Turf Cutter	14Ja02Fc
WOLF, Cathe.	20	F	Spinster	14Ja02Fc
CENTLEY, Wm.	29	M	Mason	14Ja02Fc
MAHER, Mary	25	F	Spinster	14Ja02Fc
Thomas	12	M	Unknown	14Ja02Fc
MACKAY, Patt	28	M	Carpenter	14Ja02Fc
TIERNAY, Peter	10	M	Unknown	14Ja02Fc
CASSIDAY, Margt.	20	F	Spinster	14Ja02Fc
MURPHY, Phillip	15	M	Mason	14Ja02Fc
CURRAGAN, James	24	M	Laborer	14Ja02Fc
MCGOVRIN, James	18	M	Laborer	14Ja02Fc
LOAHY, Thos.	25	M	Laborer	14Ja02Fc
Ann	21	F	Spinster	14Ja02Fc
CLUBERAN, Fanny	23	F	Spinster	14Ja02Fc
KEOGH, Bridgt.	11	F	Spinster	14Ja02Fc
CARTLEY, Wm.	29	M	Carpenter	14Ja02Fc
GALVIN, Ann	32	F	Wi	14Ja02Fc
John	9	M	Child	14Ja02Fc
Michl.	7	M	Child	14Ja02Fc
WELSH, Patt	30	M	Mason	14Ja02Fc
HEMINGWAY, Hannah	22	F	Spinster	14Ja02Fc
DILLEN, Mary	26	F	Spinster	14Ja02Fc
Thomas	.00	M	Infant	14Ja02Fc
Died-At-Sea				
DOYLE, Bridgt.	17	F	Unknown	14Ja02Fc
Mary	9	F	Child	14Ja02Fc
RYAN, Wm.	30	M	Carpenter	14Ja02Fc
SHERIDAN, Cathe.	40	F	Wi	14Ja02Fc

NAMES OF PASSENGERS	AGE	SEX	OCCUPATIONS	DATE PORT SHIP
SHERIDAN, Charles	17	M	Unknown	14Ja02Fc
John	12	M	Unknown	14Ja02Fc
Peter	10	M	Unknown	14Ja02Fc
BAKLEY, Sarah	20	F	Spinster	14Ja02Fc
KELLY, Thomas	28	M	Mason	14Ja02Fc
Rosana	20	F	Spinster	14Ja02Fc
HERAN, Bridgt.	20	F	Spinster	14Ja02Fc
WAYLAN, Bridgt.	20	F	Spinster	14Ja02Fc
MACKAY, Winifred	23	F	Spinster	14Ja02Fc
WATSON, Thomas	32	M	Mason	14Ja02Fc
Isabella	2	F	Child	14Ja02Fc
Thomas	5	M	Child	14Ja02Fc
Eliza	3	F	Child	14Ja02Fc
John	.00	M	Infant	14Ja02Fc
WHITE, Esther	45	F	Spinster	14Ja02Fc
James	25	M	Carpenter	14Ja02Fc
Jane	18	F	Spinster	14Ja02Fc
Thomas	16	M	Laborer	14Ja02Fc
Samuel	13	M	Laborer	14Ja02Fc
Washington	11	M	Laborer	14Ja02Fc
WOODS, Moses	8	M	Child	14Ja02Fc
COLE, Elizabeth	28	F	Spinster	14Ja02Fc
BROWN, John-W.	31	M	Blacksmith	14Ja02Fc
FYNAN, Mary	24	F	Spinster	14Ja02Fc
SAAFE, William	6	M	Child	14Ja02Fc
MAY, Richard	25	M	Painter	14Ja02Fc
Elizabeth	25	F	Spinster	14Ja02Fc
Joseph	18	M	Laborer	14Ja02Fc
DENAGH, John-W.	25	M	Laborer	14Ja02Fc
BRADY, Pat	35	M	Laborer	14Ja02Fc
MCGROYAN, Peter	21	M	Laborer	14Ja02Fc
CLERKEY, Owen	21	M	Laborer	14Ja02Fc
BOONEY, Michael	22	M	Tailor	14Ja02Fc
REYNOLDS, Pat	25	M	Mason	14Ja02Fc
ADAMS, Mary	19	F	Spinster	14Ja02Fc
Bessy	6	F	Child	14Ja02Fc
POPHAM, James	60	M	Farmer	14Ja02Fc
PLOW, Michael	36	M	Farmer	14Ja02Fc
MCGUIRE, Dennis	55	M	Farmer	14Ja02Fc
Died-At-Sea				
Dennis	14	M	Unknown	14Ja02Fc
James	32	M	Laborer	14Ja02Fc
PLUNKETT, Ann	15	F	Spinster	14Ja02Fc
GOODMAN, Bridget	38	F	Servant	14Ja02Fc
Ann	16	F	Servant	14Ja02Fc
LYNOUGH, John	18	M	Servant	14Ja02Fc
COOK, Ann	18	F	Spinster	14Ja02Fc
RYDER, Ellen	27	F	Wi	14Ja02Fc
COLEMAN, Bridget	50	F	Seamstress	14Ja02Fc
MAHONY, Mary	17	F	Servant	14Ja02Fc
CORRIGAN, Mary	24	F	Servant	14Ja02Fc
MARTIN, Margt.	15	F	Unknown	14Ja02Fc
SHILCOCK, Harry	37	M	Painter	14Ja02Fc
CORBITT, James	50	M	Farmer	14Ja02Fc
Bridget	50	F	Wife	14Ja02Fc
WALKER, James	30	M	Carpenter	14Ja02Fc
PICKETS, Mary	17	F	Unknown	14Ja02Fc
WILSON, Ellen	20	F	Unknown	14Ja02Fc
Martha	.00	F	Infant	14Ja02Fc
Alice	.00	F	Infant	14Ja02Fc
BRAWLEY, Mary	19	F	Servant	14Ja02Fc
John	15	M	Servant	14Ja02Fc
KANE, James	20	M	Shoemaker	14Ja02Fc
Mary	6	F	Child	14Ja02Fc
ONEIL, Patrick	18	M	Laborer	14Ja02Fc
FOWLER, Mary	20	F	Servant	14Ja02Fc
ANGLIM, Daniel	55	M	Laborer	14Ja02Fc
William	22	M	Laborer	14Ja02Fc
Biddy	55	F	Servant	14Ja02Fc
Patrick	15	M	Laborer	14Ja02Fc
Kitty	19	F	Servant	14Ja02Fc
CONNOR, Johanna	30	F	Servant	14Ja02Fc
DOYLE, Martin	10	M	Unknown	14Ja02Fc
DOOLAN, Bridget	16	F	Servant	14Ja02Fc
MILLAR, James	32	M	Laborer	14Ja02Fc

NAMES OF PASSENGERS	AGE	SEX	OCCUPATIONS	DATE PORT SHIP
GRAHAM, Joseph	20	M	Laborer	14Ja02Fc
KENNY, Joseph	24	M	Servant	14Ja02Fc
GILL, Thomas	25	M	Servant	14Ja02Fc
Ann	20	F	Servant	14Ja02Fc
Bridget	18	F	Servant	14Ja02Fc
FLANAGAN, Patrick	16	M	Laborer	14Ja02Fc
GILLIGAN, Mick	19	M	Laborer	14Ja02Fc
BRADY, Catherine	16	F	Servant	14Ja02Fc
MOORE, John	17	M	Servant	14Ja02Fc
FAGAN, Frank	26	M	Laborer	14Ja02Fc
REILLY, James	22	M	Laborer	14Ja02Fc
CONNERLY, James	25	M	Laborer	14Ja02Fc
KERMAN, Bridget	17	F	Servant	14Ja02Fc
Catherine	12	F	Unknown	14Ja02Fc
KIERMAN, John	30	M	Mason	14Ja02Fc
DOFFE, Christopher	14	M	Servant	14Ja02Fc
CROMER, Catherine	12	F	Unknown	14Ja02Fc
SMITH, Margaret	32	F	Servant	14Ja02Fc
CONNSKY, James	35	M	Laborer	14Ja02Fc
U-Mrs.	27	F	Unknown	14Ja02Fc
U	.00	U	Infant	14Ja02Fc
Bridget	3	F	Child	14Ja02Fc
GRIM, John	25	M	Laborer	14Ja02Fc
Ally	21	F	Unknown	14Ja02Fc
U	.00	U	Infant	14Ja02Fc
Elizabeth	50	F	Seamstress	14Ja02Fc
Connor	18	F	Servant	14Ja02Fc
Hugh	17	M	Laborer	14Ja02Fc
Ann	16	F	Servant	14Ja02Fc
James	13	M	Unknown	14Ja02Fc
Mary	10	F	Unknown	14Ja02Fc
Charles	9	M	Child	14Ja02Fc
MACKIN, John	35	M	Blacksmith	14Ja02Fc
FOX, Bridget	40	F	Seamstress	14Ja02Fc
Mary	6	F	Child	14Ja02Fc
MCDONNELL, John	44	M	Mason	14Ja02Fc
James	17	M	Servant	14Ja02Fc
Edward	11	M	Servant	14Ja02Fc
DWYER, Thomas	30	M	Laborer	14Ja02Fc
FITZPATRICK, William	32	M	Laborer	14Ja02Fc
RYAN, Dennis	21	M	Baker	14Ja02Fc
CLERK, Margret	32	F	Servant	14Ja02Fc
Ann	5	F	Child	14Ja02Fc
DARLEY, Walker	35	M	Mason	14Ja02Fc
LYONS, Joseph	25	M	Mason	14Ja02Fc
FORSTER, Peter	30	M	Servant	14Ja02Fc
KELLY, James	42	M	Laborer	14Ja02Fc
HUGH, Mathew	16	M	Servant	14Ja02Fc
HAYS, Margaret	29	F	Servant	14Ja02Fc
RIDLY, Michael	9	M	Child	14Ja02Fc
DUFFY, Frank	17	M	Servant	14Ja02Fc
DONLAN, Michael	8	M	Child	14Ja02Fc
CAUFIELD, Patrick	51	M	Mason	14Ja02Fc
Henry	17	F	Servant	14Ja02Fc
Michael	10	M	Unknown	14Ja02Fc
FEGAN, Mary	30	F	Seamstress	14Ja02Fc
Patrick	29	M	Mason	14Ja02Fc
Peter	11	M	Unknown	14Ja02Fc
Andy	10	M	Unknown	14Ja02Fc
James	8	M	Child	14Ja02Fc
CORMICK, Patrick	45	M	Carpenter	14Ja02Fc
SHERSY, Catherine	16	F	Servant	14Ja02Fc
GARREY, Bridget	30	F	Servant	14Ja02Fc
Mary	26	F	Servant	14Ja02Fc
CORDY, Ellen	24	F	Servant	14Ja02Fc
BRADY, John	69	M	Laborer	14Ja02Fc
Mary	15	F	Unknown	14Ja02Fc
HANLON, Michael	23	M	Servant	14Ja02Fc
CAHILL, Mary	2	F	Child	14Ja02Fc
BROWN, John	26	M	Laborer	14Ja02Fc
COREY, James	18	M	Servant	14Ja02Fc
Ellen	25	F	Servant	14Ja02Fc
DOWLING, Margaret	20	F	Servant	14Ja02Fc
BELL, Ann	39	F	Servant	14Ja02Fc
U	.00	U	Infant	14Ja02Fc

NAMES OF PASSENGERS	AGE	SEX	OCCUPATIONS	DATE PORT SHIP
BELL, Patrick	13	M	Unknown	14Ja02Fc
Mary	9	F	Child	14Ja02Fc
Ann	10	F	Unknown	14Ja02Fc
Jane	6	F	Child	14Ja02Fc
FITZGIBBON, Kate	16	F	Unknown	14Ja02Fc
PINELL, Catherine	24	F	Seamstress	14Ja02Fc
MURRAY, Rose	35	F	Servant	14Ja02Fc
Andrew	18	M	Servant	14Ja02Fc
Ann	14	F	Servant	14Ja02Fc
James	10	M	Servant	14Ja02Fc
Edward	8	M	Child	14Ja02Fc
REYNOLDS, Patrick	14	M	Servant	14Ja02Fc
DOYLE, Rose	17	F	Servant	14Ja02Fc
KILLOWER, Bridget	13	F	Servant	14Ja02Fc
SPELLMAN, Mary	19	F	Servant	14Ja02Fc
MCCANN, Rose	18	F	Servant	14Ja02Fc
Rose	10	F	Servant	14Ja02Fc
REILLY, John	28	M	Laborer	14Ja02Fc
BRANLIN, Margaret	19	F	Servant	14Ja02Fc
HARNICON, Catherine	50	F	Servant	14Ja02Fc
HOGE, John	40	M	Laborer	14Ja02Fc
MCNAMARA, Catherine	8	F	Child	14Ja02Fc
Bridget	6	F	Child	14Ja02Fc
LONG, Catherine	27	F	Seamstress	14Ja02Fc
SHERLY, John	18	M	Servant	14Ja02Fc
GANCHY, Ann	22	F	Servant	14Ja02Fc
KEARS, Michael	16	M	Servant	14Ja02Fc
MARTIN, Bridget	17	F	Servant	14Ja02Fc
REILLY, Margaret	19	F	Servant	14Ja02Fc
BARRON, Catherine	16	F	Servant	14Ja02Fc
TOOLEY, Bridget	6	F	Child	14Ja02Fc
HARNELL, Patrick	25	M	Laborer	14Ja02Fc
DAVIS, Martin	20	M	Laborer	14Ja02Fc
WYNNE, Margaret	45	F	Servant	14Ja02Fc
Patrick	18	M	Laborer	14Ja02Fc
Domenick	19	M	Laborer	14Ja02Fc
Mary	11	F	Unknown	14Ja02Fc
Bridget	8	F	Child	14Ja02Fc
Ellen	6	F	Child	14Ja02Fc
John	4	M	Child	14Ja02Fc
Mary	35	F	Servant	14Ja02Fc
Patrick	12	M	Unknown	14Ja02Fc
Margaret	8	F	Child	14Ja02Fc
Ellen	5	F	Child	14Ja02Fc
Bessy	2	F	Child	14Ja02Fc
ALMESTY, Mary-Ann	26	F	Seamstress	14Ja02Fc
Susan	11	F	Unknown	14Ja02Fc
Jean	9	F	Child	14Ja02Fc
Thomas	7	M	Child	14Ja02Fc
BRENNAN, Catherine	45	F	Servant	14Ja02Fc
Patrick	17	M	Laborer	14Ja02Fc
Thomas	14	M	Laborer	14Ja02Fc
Sarah	11	F	Unknown	14Ja02Fc
Fanny	8	F	Child	14Ja02Fc
GILLISPIE, Sarah	70	F	Seamstress	14Ja02Fc
MCGLOUR, Ally	22	F	Servant	14Ja02Fc
PARKS, Margaret	11	F	Unknown	14Ja02Fc
DONLIN, Nick	3	M	Child	14Ja02Fc
Ann	20	F	Servant	14Ja02Fc
PARKS, Charles	9	M	Child	14Ja02Fc
PATTERSON, John	30	M	Laborer	14Ja02Fc
MCLOUGHLIN, John	18	M	Laborer	14Ja02Fc
Margaret	22	F	Servant	14Ja02Fc
PAUL, James	16	M	Laborer	14Ja02Fc
MAGUINN, Ellen	24	F	Servant	14Ja02Fc
Catherine	6	F	Child	14Ja02Fc
Patrick	4	M	Child	14Ja02Fc
TRAMER, Mary	30	F	Servant	14Ja02Fc
MCKENNA, Ann	11	F	Unknown	14Ja02Fc
CARNIFF, Michael	13	M	Unknown	14Ja02Fc
BEATY, Edward	16	M	Unknown	14Ja02Fc
ONEAL, Mary	20	F	Servant	14Ja02Fc
GRIMES, Rose	9	F	Child	14Ja02Fc
DOOLEY, Rose	17	F	Servant	14Ja02Fc
MCNALLY, Ann	16	F	Servant	14Ja02Fc
MCNALLY, Owen	8	M	Child	14Ja02Fc
Sarah	5	F	Child	14Ja02Fc
LIDDY, John	15	M	Unknown	14Ja02Fc
Thomas	11	M	Unknown	14Ja02Fc
SHERRY, Catherine	60	F	Seamstress	14Ja02Fc
COONEY, Thomas	17	M	Laborer	14Ja02Fc
MALONE, Sarah	18	F	Servant	14Ja02Fc
MCELLION, Rachael	19	F	Servant	14Ja02Fc
HAND, Julia	18	F	Servant	14Ja02Fc
Catherine	19	F	Servant	14Ja02Fc
COLLINS, Thomas	20	M	Laborer	14Ja02Fc
Mathew	28	M	Laborer	14Ja02Fc
CORCORAN, Arnold	11	M	Unknown	14Ja02Fc
CRANSTON, Rose	30	F	Servant	14Ja02Fc
U Died-At-Sea	.00	U	Infant	14Ja02Fc
James	14	M	Unknown	14Ja02Fc
Mary	7	F	Child	14Ja02Fc
Sarah	6	F	Child	14Ja02Fc
William	2	M	Child	14Ja02Fc
SPRIGHT, John	10	M	Unknown	14Ja02Fc
MCGINNESS, Margaret	30	F	Servant	14Ja02Fc
MCCAFFERY, Ann	26	F	Servant	14Ja02Fc
MOGOGERTY, Michael	11	M	Unknown	14Ja02Fc
MURPHY, Julia	40	F	Servant	14Ja02Fc
Nancy	14	F	Servant	14Ja02Fc
BANACK, Robert	20	M	Servant	14Ja02Fc
LYON, John	11	M	Servant	14Ja02Fc
DALY, Catherine	23	F	Servant	14Ja02Fc
MCENTIRE, Thomas	16	M	Servant	14Ja02Fc
John	20	M	Servant	14Ja02Fc
MCGRIER, Catherine	20	F	Servant	14Ja02Fc
DOYLE, Eliza	24	F	Servant	14Ja02Fc
Eliza	20	F	Servant	14Ja02Fc
James	6	M	Child	14Ja02Fc
MELIN, Bridget	20	F	Servant	14Ja02Fc
SHAW, Hannah	21	F	Servant	14Ja02Fc
Charlotte	4	F	Child	14Ja02Fc
Amelia	2	F	Child	14Ja02Fc
CAHILL, John	24	M	Laborer	14Ja02Fc
Mary	24	F	Servant	14Ja02Fc
Patrick	10	M	Unknown	14Ja02Fc
SULLIVAN, Mary	30	F	Servant	14Ja02Fc
Edward	10	M	Unknown	14Ja02Fc
Catherine	8	F	Child	14Ja02Fc
Thomas	6	M	Child	14Ja02Fc
CONNSKY, U	.00	U	Infant	14Ja02Fc
Ally	.00	F	Infant	14Ja02Fc
NORTHEART, Ann-B.	30	F	Lady	14Ja02Fc
VANCE, William-J.	26	M	Barrister	14Ja02Fc

NO RECORD OF SHIP

From Liverpool

ROBERTS, David-J.	28	M	Farmer	14Ja02
DOVE, Joseph	19	M	Laborer	14Ja02
ALENDALE, Alexr.	39	M	Paper Maker	14Ja02
Amelia	30	F	None	14Ja02
Rebecca	7	F	Child	14Ja02
HALFPENNY, Patt	40	M	Laborer	14Ja02
Bridgt.	20	F	Laborer	14Ja02
STANFIELD, Richd.	45	M	Tinker	14Ja02
Willm.	24	M	Tinker	14Ja02
NELSON, Ellenor	20	F	Spinster	14Ja02
Ann	18	F	Spinster	14Ja02
RILEY, Bridgt.	20	F	Spinster	14Ja02
GALLAGHER, Ann	20	F	Spinster	14Ja02
CURR, Bridgt.	23	F	Spinster	14Ja02

NAMES OF PASSENGERS	AGE	SEX	OCCUPATIONS	DATE PORT SHIP
CAMP, Jane	20	F	Spinster	14Ja02
FITZPATRICK, Owen	26	M	Brick Maker	14Ja02
Catherine	20	F	Brick Maker	14Ja02
Sarah	11	F	Brick Maker	14Ja02
CRINOG, Thomas	21	M	Laborer	14Ja02
JONES, Wm.	20	M	Laborer	14Ja02
COSGROVE, Thomas	28	M	Laborer	14Ja02
John	17	M	Laborer	14Ja02
CAHIRR, Pat	30	M	Mason	14Ja02
Mary	30	F	Mason	14Ja02
Catherine	8	F	Child	14Ja02
Rody	6	F	Child	14Ja02
Mary	.11	F	Infant	14Ja02
Mccai--, Mary	16	F	Servant	14Ja02
LOUGHEN, John	65	M	Laborer	14Ja02
Saml.	30	M	Laborer	14Ja02
Martha	23	F	Laborer	14Ja02
Margaret	19	F	Laborer	14Ja02
MOORE, Robert	21	M	Carpenter	14Ja02
GREHAM, Wm.	21	M	Mason	14Ja02
DUNWOODY, Wm.	21	M	Mason	14Ja02
JOHNSTONE, Saml.	41	M	Cork Cutter	14Ja02
John	21	M	Cork Cutter	14Ja02
MCCONNELL, Rosey	20	F	Spinster	14Ja02
KANE, Patt	30	M	Laborer	14Ja02
MCCONNELL, Kiron	19	M	Servant	14Ja02
KANE, Ann	20	F	Servant	14Ja02
DELAHAN, Ann	21	F	Spinster	14Ja02
DAGNON, Bridget	21	F	Spinster	14Ja02
BRANNEN, Paul	30	M	Tinker	14Ja02
MCDERMOTT, Owen	22	M	Carpenter	14Ja02
MALEY, Elisa	19	F	Spinster	14Ja02
Margaret	17	F	Spinster	14Ja02
MCMICHALS, Bridget	17	F	Spinster	14Ja02
James	18	M	Spinner	14Ja02
SIMONS, Bridget	20	F	Spinster	14Ja02
Mary	50	F	Spinster	14Ja02
MCMAHON, Michel	19	M	Laborer	14Ja02
JORDAN, Chas.	31	M	Laborer	14Ja02
SHEA, Patt	49	M	Laborer	14Ja02
Died-At-Sea				
Martha	20	F	Spinster	14Ja02
Died-At-Sea				
John	18	M	Unknown	14Ja02
Margaret	16	F	Spinster	14Ja02
Patt	12	M	Unknown	14Ja02
Bridget	12	F	Spinster	14Ja02
RAIN, John	27	M	Mason	14Ja02
Died-At-Sea				
TEARNEY, Ann	59	F	Wi	14Ja02
John	15	M	Laborer	14Ja02
Catherine	11	F	Laborer	14Ja02
DAGNON, Wm.	21	M	Laborer	14Ja02
James	30	M	Laborer	14Ja02
Owen	17	M	Laborer	14Ja02
CHAMETY, Mary	18	F	Spinster	14Ja02
MCDENOUGH, Wm.	20	M	Laborer	14Ja02
r Bridget	20	F	Laborer	14Ja02
LALLY, Ann	15	F	Spinster	14Ja02
MCKEIN, Charlotte	21	F	Spinster	14Ja02
GLEASON, Ellen	20	F	Spinster	14Ja02
CALLION, Patt	30	M	Laborer	14Ja02
SANDLER, John	44	M	Tinman	14Ja02
John	13	M	Tinman	14Ja02
Chris.	11	M	Tinman	14Ja02
DEAREY, Phillip	30	M	Laborer	14Ja02
QUINN, Patt	36	M	Mason	14Ja02
HEDGELLY, Jacob	25	M	Sailor	14Ja02
Hen., Henry	42	M	Mason	14Ja02
Mary	12	F	Mason	14Ja02
John	3	M	Child	14Ja02
SHEAN, Wm.	23	M	Laborer	14Ja02
SMITH, Ann	22	F	Spinster	14Ja02
COSSGOODE, Elizabeth	20	F	Spinster	14Ja02
Sm., Sarah	20	F	Spinster	14Ja02
REILLY, Ann	21	F	Spinster	14Ja02
MULREADY, Patt	46	M	Tinker	14Ja02
Catherine	30	F	Tinker	14Ja02
Mary	27	F	Tinker	14Ja02
DALEY, Henry	20	M	Unknown	14Ja02
JOHNSON, Bridget	19	F	Servant	14Ja02
Elizabeth	17	F	Servant	14Ja02
OBYNS, Morgan	19	M	Mason	14Ja02
FABLIN, Margaret	19	F	Unknown	14Ja02
SYRIL, Jane	25	F	Draper	14Ja02
Ann	22	F	Spinster	14Ja02
CANING, Thomas	20	M	Laborer	14Ja02
FITZGERALD, Michle.	32	M	Mason	14Ja02
Mary	35	F	Mason	14Ja02
Ellen	30	F	Mason	14Ja02
Died-At-Sea				
KELLY, Judy	60	F	Wi	14Ja02
REILLY, Christopher	30	M	Unknown	14Ja02
COYLE, Sally	30	F	Spinster	14Ja02
KENRY, Patrick	50	M	Laborer	14Ja02
KENNY, Cath.	30	F	Laborer	14Ja02
Mary	9	F	Child	14Ja02
Ann	4	F	Child	14Ja02
Patt.	1	M	Child	14Ja02
LYND, Eliza	20	F	Spinster	14Ja02
Robt.	12	M	Spinster	14Ja02
William	12	M	Spinster	14Ja02
FINEGAN, Bridget	27	F	Spinster	14Ja02
FEILA, Marg.	15	F	Spinster	14Ja02
KENON, Bridget	15	F	Spinster	14Ja02
CLARKE, Cath.	35	F	Wi	14Ja02
Barney	13	M	Unknown	14Ja02
Ellen	12	F	Unknown	14Ja02
Johny	7	M	Child	14Ja02
Pattr.	3	M	Child	14Ja02
CALLUELL, Joseph	32	M	Laborer	14Ja02
CONORE, Mary	30	F	Laborer	14Ja02
Honora	10	F	Unknown	14Ja02
Mary	8	F	Child	14Ja02
Michael	7	M	Child	14Ja02
Owen	4	M	Child	14Ja02
BUTLER, Thomas	19	M	Mason	14Ja02
MEHENY, Bridget	20	F	Spinster	14Ja02
OBRIEN, Michael	17	M	Laborer	14Ja02
WHEELAN, Michael	12	M	Laborer	14Ja02
QUIN, Ann	20	F	Servant	14Ja02
FARRELL, Margaret	24	F	Servant	14Ja02
BRADLEY, Margaret	21	F	Servant	14Ja02
GALLIGAN, Mary	25	F	Servant	14Ja02
HERLEHY, Johana	20	F	Servant	14Ja02
DICKSON, James	30	M	Laborer	14Ja02
KERWOOD, Sarah	30	F	Laborer	14Ja02
William	1	M	Child	14Ja02
John	.00	M	Infant	14Ja02
BERTON, Thomas	30	M	Unknown	14Ja02
MULLOY, Patt.	28	M	Unknown	14Ja02
HUGHES, John	20	M	Builder	14Ja02
Cath.	20	F	Unknown	14Ja02
GREEN, Mary	22	F	Unknown	14Ja02
Abraham	10	M	Unknown	14Ja02
Mary	.00	F	Infant	14Ja02
MCCARTY, Michael	50	M	Mason	14Ja02
MURPHY, Richd.	22	M	Mason	14Ja02
U-Mrs.	22	F	Unknown	14Ja02
MCCREHAM, Michael	30	M	Carpenter	14Ja02
Mary	27	F	Unknown	14Ja02
Eugene	9	M	Child	14Ja02
DOOLIN, Edwin	20	M	Unknown	14Ja02
James	18	M	Laborer	14Ja02
POWER, Mary	20	F	Unknown	14Ja02
DEE, Mary	35	F	Unknown	14Ja02
MCCARTY, Johana	28	F	Unknown	14Ja02
MURPHY, Thomas	1	M	Child	14Ja02
SUPPLE, Thomas	27	M	Laborer	14Ja02
WHALAN, Rodger	35	M	Laborer	14Ja02

NAMES OF PASSENGERS	AGE	SEX	OCCUPATIONS	DATE PORT SHIP
RABBITT, Thomas	30	M	Laborer	14Ja02
LAHERT, Patt.	20	M	Laborer	14Ja02
CLEARY, Johann	25	F	Spinster	14Ja02
TAYLOR, Ellen	25	F	Spinster	14Ja02
CONAN, Elish	33	U	Wi	14Ja02
Mary	11	F	Unknown	14Ja02
Margt.	5	F	Child	14Ja02
Jane	3	F	Child	14Ja02
MCCORMICK, Sally	18	F	Spinster	14Ja02
CANDY, Bridget	20	F	Spinster	14Ja02
Mary	22	F	Unknown	14Ja02
MONTGOMERY, James	21	M	Mason	14Ja02
FINEGAN, Julia	13	F	Mason	14Ja02
KORANE, Michael	30	M	Mason	14Ja02
BROWNE, Patt.	36	M	Mason	14Ja02
WADDER, Jannett	28	F	Servant	14Ja02
John	9	M	Child	14Ja02
MURRAY, Ann	21	F	Spinster	14Ja02
BYRNE, Marget.	28	F	Wi	14Ja02
Rose	14	F	Unknown	14Ja02
Brigt.	10	F	Unknown	14Ja02
John	.00	M	Infant	14Ja02
GLASS, John	40	M	Tinker	14Ja02
JOHNSTONE, Robt.	24	M	Tinker	14Ja02
MORRISSON, John	22	M	Tinker	14Ja02
John	20	M	Tinker	14Ja02
GLASS, Wilson	18	M	Tinker	14Ja02
John	12	M	Tinker	14Ja02
LAND, Fanny	19	F	Spinster	14Ja02
Margaret	16	F	Spinster	14Ja02
FLANNIGAN, Cath.	19	F	Spinster	14Ja02
KELLENEN, Cath.	17	F	Spinster	14Ja02
Ann	15	F	Unknown	14Ja02
DERAN, Bridgett	17	F	Spinster	14Ja02
COLLIN, Thomas	24	M	Carpenter	14Ja02
KINKAN, Michael	20	M	Carpenter	14Ja02
CLINGAN, James	27	M	Mason	14Ja02
Died-At-Sea				
Leticia	11	F	Mason	14Ja02
RODMAN, Mary	20	F	Spinster	14Ja02
MEANY, Ann	35	F	Dressmaker	14Ja02
John	9	M	Child	14Ja02
Thomas	6	M	Child	14Ja02
BENAN, Theresa	21	F	Servant	14Ja02
GRESSON, Mary	21	F	Servant	14Ja02
BELLINGTON, Robt.	26	M	Laborer	14Ja02
KURMAN, Christ.	28	M	Laborer	14Ja02
MCCARVEE, Mary	23	F	Farmer	14Ja02
DEAKIN, Thomas	21	M	Farmer	14Ja02
CATLLEN, Ann	35	F	Seamstress	14Ja02
Joseph	8	M	Child	14Ja02
Eleanor	3	F	Child	14Ja02
Henry	5	M	Child	14Ja02
Benj.	.00	M	Infant	14Ja02
KEYWORTH, Grace	21	F	Seamstress	14Ja02
MAHONE, Mary	20	F	Unknown	14Ja02
KAMPSON, Allan	30	M	Farmer	14Ja02
John	5	M	Child	14Ja02
Thomas	.00	M	Infant	14Ja02
BARRETT, Mary	22	F	Servant	14Ja02
FLAMEY, Margaret	22	F	Servant	14Ja02
RIDDINAN, Margaret	25	F	Servant	14Ja02
Cath.	4	F	Child	14Ja02
CUNNINGHAM, Patt.	25	M	Laborer	14Ja02
Ellen	10	F	Laborer	14Ja02
GRIFFITH, John	22	M	Laborer	14Ja02
MORAN, Thomas	19	M	Mason	14Ja02
MCDONOUGH, Wm.	40	M	Carpenter	14Ja02
CALLAGAHN, Mary	60	F	Wi	14Ja02
CAIRNY, Cath.	25	F	Spinster	14Ja02
MULLIGAN, Bridgt.	40	F	Spinster	14Ja02
DONOVAN, Mary	24	F	Spinster	14Ja02
JONES, Eliza	18	F	Spinster	14Ja02
REDDY, James	37	M	Blacksmith	14Ja02
DOYLE, Michael	28	M	Laborer	14Ja02
HOLLANDER, George	20	M	Mason	14Ja02
MCCARTY, Mary	20	F	Spinster	14Ja02
HACKETT, Pat.	50	M	Farmer	14Ja02
Patt.	21	M	Farmer	14Ja02
Arthur	15	M	Farmer	14Ja02
Kitty	10	F	Farmer	14Ja02
Rose	55	F	Farmer	14Ja02
MCCARROLL, John	41	M	Farmer	14Ja02
QUINN, Patt.	40	M	Laborer	14Ja02
WAITTS, John	19	M	Carpenter	14Ja02
PIERCE, Hugh	16	M	Carpenter	14Ja02
Cath.	20	F	Unknown	14Ja02
GOODHAN, Thomas	40	M	Locksmith	14Ja02
CROMEN, Phillip	30	M	Laborer	14Ja02
Mary	27	F	Laborer	14Ja02
RYLEY, Ann	19	F	Spinster	14Ja02
CAHIRN, John	30	M	Laborer	14Ja02
DOIL, Maria	18	F	Spinster	14Ja02
FLYNN, James	27	M	Laborer	14Ja02

SARAH-PARKER 14 JANUARY 1850

From Newry

NAMES OF PASSENGERS	AGE	SEX	OCCUPATIONS	DATE PORT SHIP
MURPHY, John	30	M	Laborer	14Ja04Eu
Anne	25	F	Wife	14Ja04Eu
Mary	2	F	Child	14Ja04Eu
Peter	1	M	Child	14Ja04Eu
Died-At-Sea				
LONGHRAN, James	21	M	Laborer	14Ja04Eu
MALLON, Daniel	21	M	Laborer	14Ja04Eu
KILPATRICK, Eliza	50	F	Wi	14Ja04Eu
James	22	M	Relative	14Ja04Eu
Rebecca	17	F	Relative	14Ja04Eu
Eliza	15	F	Relative	14Ja04Eu
DUFFY, Mary	18	F	Spinster	14Ja04Eu
Bridget	13	F	Spinster	14Ja04Eu
CONAN, Bernard	40	M	Laborer	14Ja04Eu
KANE, Andrew	20	M	Carpenter	14Ja04Eu
Catherine	20	F	Wife	14Ja04Eu
ONEILL, Ellen	22	F	Spinster	14Ja04Eu
MCIVER, Patrick	19	M	Carpenter	14Ja04Eu
KIERNAN, Anne	30	F	Wi	14Ja04Eu
James	3	M	Child	14Ja04Eu
Mary	1	F	Child	14Ja04Eu
Died-At-Sea				
GUN, Felix	35	M	Tailor	14Ja04Eu
KERR, Mary	21	F	Wife	14Ja04Eu
Peter	1	M	Child	14Ja04Eu
Died-At-Sea				
CHAPMAN, Anne	30	F	Spinster	14Ja04Eu
Margaret	30	F	Spinster	14Ja04Eu
Maria	16	F	Spinster	14Ja04Eu
MCCLEAN, Anne	13	F	Spinster	14Ja04Eu
MCGAVEY, Francis	60	M	Farmer	14Ja04Eu
DOHERTY, Bernard	20	M	Mason	14Ja04Eu
FLANAGAN, Patrick	20	M	Carpenter	14Ja04Eu
FITZPATRICK, Sarah	18	F	Spinster	14Ja04Eu
TRENN, Elizabeth	18	F	Spinster	14Ja04Eu
DOWNEY, Anne	20	F	Spinster	14Ja04Eu
Charlotte	18	F	Spinster	14Ja04Eu
CONVERY, Hannah	18	F	Spinster	14Ja04Eu
BELL, James	18	M	Shoemaker	14Ja04Eu
TATE, Joseph	45	M	Farmer	14Ja04Eu
Jane	35	F	Wife	14Ja04Eu
Eliza-Ann	16	F	Relative	14Ja04Eu
Arthur	12	M	Relative	14Ja04Eu
Joseph	10	M	Relative	14Ja04Eu
Saml.	8	M	Child	14Ja04Eu

NAMES OF PASSENGERS	AGE	SEX	OCCUPATIONS	DATE PORT SHIP
TATE, Sally	6	F	Child	14Ja04Eu
Margt.	4	F	Child	14Ja04Eu
BRADY, Edwd.	20	M	Laborer	14Ja04Eu
MCKEOWN, Agnes	25	F	Spinster	14Ja04Eu
WARD, Anne	13	F	Spinster	14Ja04Eu
TRONTON, Maria	40	F	Spinster	14Ja04Eu
DUDGEN, James	27	M	Laborer	14Ja04Eu
MORROW, Robert	22	M	Laborer	14Ja04Eu
William	50	M	Laborer	14Ja04Eu
CAMPBELL, Saml.	13	M	Laborer	14Ja04Eu
MOON, Denis	18	M	Laborer	14Ja04Eu
MORROW, Thomas	26	M	Laborer	14Ja04Eu
BOYLE, Anne	20	F	Spinster	14Ja04Eu
HAMILTON, Andrew	18	M	Smith	14Ja04Eu
MCQUADE, John	40	M	Farmer	14Ja04Eu
FOLEY, Wm.	20	M	Farmer	14Ja04Eu
MCQUADE, Anne	25	F	Spinster	14Ja04Eu
Anne	40	F	Spinster	14Ja04Eu
MOORE, Patrick	20	M	Tailor	14Ja04Eu
BRADY, Willm.	24	M	Shoemaker	14Ja04Eu
Sarah-Anne	20	F	Spinster	14Ja04Eu
HAWTHORNE, Samuel	29	M	Farmer	14Ja04Eu
Mary-Anne	29	F	Wife	14Ja04Eu
James	3	M	Child	14Ja04Eu
Agnes	2	F	Child	14Ja04Eu
William-John	1	M	Child	14Ja04Eu
Died-At-Sea				
CONLAN, John	25	M	Laborer	14Ja04Eu
OHEAR, Margt.	18	F	Spinster	14Ja04Eu
CAMPBELL, Rob.	20	M	Weaver	14Ja04Eu
FLANAGAN, Sarah	20	F	Spinster	14Ja04Eu
MULHOLLAND, Ellen	20	F	Spinster	14Ja04Eu
SMITH, Bridget	20	F	Spinster	14Ja04Eu
PRICE, Jane	20	F	Spinster	14Ja04Eu
HAMILTON, Mary-Jane	20	F	Spinster	14Ja04Eu
HEANY, Anne	20	F	Spinster	14Ja04Eu
Cathe.	18	F	Spinster	14Ja04Eu
MCCOY, Margt.	22	F	Wi	14Ja04Eu
Owen	3	M	Child	14Ja04Eu
Margt.	1	F	Child	14Ja04Eu
Died-At-Sea				
LIDDY, Daniel	45	M	Farmer	14Ja04Eu
Cathe.	45	F	Wife	14Ja04Eu
Terence	19	M	Unknown	14Ja04Eu
Catherine	12	F	Unknown	14Ja04Eu
Eliza	10	F	Unknown	14Ja04Eu
COYLE, Owen	18	M	Farmer	14Ja04Eu
BLACK, Danl.	45	M	Farmer	14Ja04Eu
HOLLYWOOD, Peter	35	M	Farmer	14Ja04Eu
Ellen	25	F	Relative	14Ja04Eu
Cathe.	2	F	Child	14Ja04Eu
Owen	1	M	Child	14Ja04Eu
Died-At-Sea				
BLACK, Michl.	18	M	Laborer	14Ja04Eu
MCCANN, Cathn.	20	F	Spinster	14Ja04Eu
Biddy	20	F	Spinster	14Ja04Eu
ADAMS, Robert	20	M	Farmer	14Ja04Eu
Sarah	20	F	Wife	14Ja04Eu
Elizabeth	3	F	Child	14Ja04Eu
Mary-Jane	1	F	Child	14Ja04Eu
Died-At-Sea				
LARY, James	50	M	Farmer	14Ja04Eu
John	11	M	Farmer	14Ja04Eu
WRIGHT, Cathe.	20	F	Spinster	14Ja04Eu
DONALDSON, Jane	20	F	Spinster	14Ja04Eu
HOLLAND, Thomas	30	M	Laborer	14Ja04Eu
CAMPBELL, Francis	40	M	Laborer	14Ja04Eu
Christina	30	F	Wife	14Ja04Eu
KELLY, John	40	M	Farmer	14Ja04Eu
Margt.	30	F	Wife	14Ja04Eu
William	10	M	Relative	14Ja04Eu
John	8	M	Child	14Ja04Eu
James	5	M	Child	14Ja04Eu
Margt.	2	F	Child	14Ja04Eu

NAMES OF PASSENGERS	AGE	SEX	OCCUPATIONS	DATE PORT SHIP
Thomas	1	M	Child	14Ja04Eu
Died-At-Sea				
MATTHEWS, Mary	20	F	Unknown	14Ja04Eu
GINNIS, Gerald	28	M	Farmer	14Ja04Eu
Margt.	28	F	Wife	14Ja04Eu
Alexr.	9	M	Child	14Ja04Eu
Sarah	4	F	Child	14Ja04Eu
Maria-Jane	2	F	Child	14Ja04Eu
Margt.Horne	1	F	Child	14Ja04Eu
Died-At-Sea				
LOUGHRAN, Rose	22	F	Spinster	14Ja04Eu
MCGINETY, Cathe.	20	F	Spinster	14Ja04Eu
MOONEY, Edwd.	28	M	Farmer	14Ja04Eu
Mary	28	F	Wife	14Ja04Eu
Margt.	11	F	Relative	14Ja04Eu
Maria	4	F	Child	14Ja04Eu
Sarah-Ann	1	F	Child	14Ja04Eu
Died-At-Sea				
Lucinda	1	F	Child	14Ja04Eu
Died-At-Sea				
CADOR, Charles	20	M	Carpenter	14Ja04Eu
MCMANUS, Margt.	21	F	Spinster	14Ja04Eu
GRIMES, Mary	13	F	Spinster	14Ja04Eu
CORRIGAN, John	20	M	Laborer	14Ja04Eu
DALY, John	20	M	Laborer	14Ja04Eu
SYRINGTON, George	50	M	Laborer	14Ja04Eu
Margt.	40	F	Laborer	14Ja04Eu
John	25	M	Laborer	14Ja04Eu
James	23	M	Shoemaker	14Ja04Eu
PARKS, Robert	20	M	Painter	14Ja04Eu
Jane	24	F	Baker	14Ja04Eu
MULLIGAN, John	21	M	Laborer	14Ja04Eu
BROWN, George	22	M	Laborer	14Ja04Eu
WILLIAMS, Henry	21	M	Mariner	14Ja04Eu
MCCLENCHY, Simon	50	M	Carpenter	14Ja04Eu
Betty-Ann	24	F	Relative	14Ja04Eu
George	28	M	Relative	14Ja04Eu
John	26	M	Relative	14Ja04Eu
Adam	18	M	Relative	14Ja04Eu
Charles	22	M	Relative	14Ja04Eu
William	16	M	Relative	14Ja04Eu
Maria	13	F	Relative	14Ja04Eu

A.Z. 14 JANUARY 1850

From Liverpool

NAMES OF PASSENGERS	AGE	SEX	OCCUPATIONS	DATE PORT SHIP
CARTY, John-H.	45	M	Trader	14Ja02Ed
GORMAN, Dealy	20	M	Laborer	14Ja02Ed
SULLIVAN, Mary	20	F	Servant	14Ja02Ed
Catherine	16	F	Servant	14Ja02Ed
Nancy	20	F	Servant	14Ja02Ed
FURLONG, Martin	28	M	Laborer	14Ja02Ed
ADAMS, Alice	26	F	Servant	14Ja02Ed
Eliza	8	F	Child	14Ja02Ed
Sarah	3	F	Child	14Ja02Ed
George	.00	M	Infant	14Ja02Ed
PIGOT, Mary	17	F	Servant	14Ja02Ed
JOHNSTON, Richd.	15	M	None	14Ja02Ed
FAGAN, Peter	15	M	Laborer	14Ja02Ed
Ann	20	F	Servant	14Ja02Ed
MCKENNON, Ann	4	F	Child	14Ja02Ed
Edwd.	2	M	Child	14Ja02Ed
KEENAN, Michl.	33	M	Carpenter	14Ja02Ed
Sarah	60	F	None	14Ja02Ed
HANTON, Ann	12	F	None	14Ja02Ed
Thoms.	10	M	None	14Ja02Ed
John	7	M	Child	14Ja02Ed
RYAN, Nancy	20	F	Servant	14Ja02Ed

NAMES OF PASSENGERS	AGE	SEX	OCCUPATIONS	DATE PORT SHIP
CASEY, Mary	24	F	Servant	14Ja02Ed
MCMAHON, Ann	23	F	Servant	14Ja02Ed
CARROLL, Mary	21	F	Servant	14Ja02Ed
REILY, Phill.	14	M	Servant	14Ja02Ed
Thoms.	10	M	Servant	14Ja02Ed
MCCAHILL, Fra.	48	M	Laborer	14Ja02Ed
Michl.	11	M	Laborer	14Ja02Ed
John	8	M	Child	14Ja02Ed
Ann	6	F	Child	14Ja02Ed
FOLEY, Eliza	50	F	Servant	14Ja02Ed
Thoms.	4	M	Child	14Ja02Ed
MCDANIEL, Peter	22	M	Laborer	14Ja02Ed
FERMEY, Mary	5	F	Child	14Ja02Ed
FORNLEY, Jane	17	F	Servant	14Ja02Ed
CREIGHTON, John	34	M	Laborer	14Ja02Ed
Bridt.	24	F	Wife	14Ja02Ed
ATKINSON, Margt.	30	F	Servant	14Ja02Ed
John	11	M	Relative	14Ja02Ed
William	8	M	Child	14Ja02Ed
Maria	5	F	Child	14Ja02Ed
LYONS, Cath.	17	F	Dressmaker	14Ja02Ed
BUCKLEY, Steven	21	M	Servant	14Ja02Ed
HARTNETT, Mary	20	F	Servant	14Ja02Ed
SHAUGNASSY, Ellen	20	F	Servant	14Ja02Ed
KELLY, Bridgt.	20	F	Servant	14Ja02Ed
HARLEY, Michl.	10	M	Servant	14Ja02Ed
FOUGHLAN, Bridgt.	28	F	Servant	14Ja02Ed
Michl.	7	M	Child	14Ja02Ed
Edwd.	9	M	Child	14Ja02Ed
George	5	M	Child	14Ja02Ed
GOOD, John	12	M	Unknown	14Ja02Ed
GOFF, Sarah	60	F	Unknown	14Ja02Ed
Mary	20	F	Unknown	14Ja02Ed
MARLOW, Margt.	16	F	Unknown	14Ja02Ed
RILEY, Thoms.	40	M	Laborer	14Ja02Ed
Mary	38	F	Relative	14Ja02Ed
John	20	M	Relative	14Ja02Ed
Mary	18	F	Relative	14Ja02Ed
Cath.	16	F	Relative	14Ja02Ed
Pat	15	M	Relative	14Ja02Ed
Ann	11	F	Relative	14Ja02Ed
Ellen	9	F	Child	14Ja02Ed
Thoms.	7	M	Child	14Ja02Ed
Rose	14	F	Relative	14Ja02Ed
Hugh	6	M	Child	14Ja02Ed
Bridt.	.10	F	Infant	14Ja02Ed
MCBRIAN, Pat	20	M	Laborer	14Ja02Ed
CALLIGAN, Peter	43	M	Laborer	14Ja02Ed
MURPHY, Thoms.	20	M	Laborer	14Ja02Ed
CUNNINGHAM, Pat	35	M	Laborer	14Ja02Ed
Susan	25	F	Wife	14Ja02Ed
MCANERNY, John	28	M	Grocer	14Ja02Ed
Rose	24	F	Sister	14Ja02Ed
DUFFY, Edwd.	25	M	Laborer	14Ja02Ed
WELSH, Ann	20	F	Servant	14Ja02Ed
KEATING, John	24	M	Laborer	14Ja02Ed
MCNICHOLLASS, John	24	M	Laborer	14Ja02Ed
MCKULLOCH, Allice	22	F	Servant	14Ja02Ed
MURPHEY, James	38	M	Laborer	14Ja02Ed
CLARK, Hugh	18	M	Laborer	14Ja02Ed
Sarah	45	F	Mother	14Ja02Ed
MCDANIEL, Bridt.	18	F	Servant	14Ja02Ed
SPENCE, Sean	36	M	Farmer	14Ja02Ed
U-Mrs.	34	F	Wife	14Ja02Ed
CAMPBELL, Thoms.	21	M	Farmer	14Ja02Ed
DORAN, Benj.	25	M	Laborer	14Ja02Ed
FLINN, Terance	21	M	Laborer	14Ja02Ed
Ann	24	F	Sister	14Ja02Ed
BRADY, Bridt.	21	F	Servant	14Ja02Ed
FARRELL, Margt.	40	F	Servant	14Ja02Ed
CARRIGAN, Mary	17	F	Servant	14Ja02Ed
Cath.	11	F	Servant	14Ja02Ed
TULLY, Pat	35	M	Laborer	14Ja02Ed
SMITH, Hugh	40	M	Carpenter	14Ja02Ed
Died-At-Sea				
MCCORAN, Ellen	50	F	Relative	14Ja02Ed
CARROLL, John	40	M	Laborer	14Ja02Ed
Agnes	32	F	Relative	14Ja02Ed
Thoms.	13	M	Relative	14Ja02Ed
John	10	M	Relative	14Ja02Ed
Ann	8	F	Child	14Ja02Ed
John	.10	M	Infant	14Ja02Ed
MURPHEY, Charles	40	M	Unknown	14Ja02Ed
SYGNETT, Pat	18	M	Laborer	14Ja02Ed
Ann	22	F	Relative	14Ja02Ed
Mary	24	F	Relative	14Ja02Ed
MILLS, Thoms.	17	M	Laborer	14Ja02Ed
MCGORAN, John	34	M	Laborer	14Ja02Ed
LYNCH, Pat	22	M	Laborer	14Ja02Ed
CAVANAGH, John	26	M	Laborer	14Ja02Ed
COX, Cath.	40	F	Relative	14Ja02Ed
Cath.	18	F	Relative	14Ja02Ed
Wini	16	M	Relative	14Ja02Ed
Edwd.	13	M	Relative	14Ja02Ed
Thom.	9	M	Child	14Ja02Ed
RYAN, Tere.	13	M	Unknown	14Ja02Ed
John	12	M	Unknown	14Ja02Ed
Pat	12	M	Unknown	14Ja02Ed
Dan	8	M	Child	14Ja02Ed
Mary	13	F	Unknown	14Ja02Ed
Honor	3	F	Child	14Ja02Ed
KELLY, John	25	M	Unknown	14Ja02Ed
SIMPSON, George	17	M	Clerk	14Ja02Ed
MCLOCKLAN, Michl.	33	M	Laborer	14Ja02Ed
SLAVAN, Ann	30	F	Relative	14Ja02Ed
MARTIN, Mary	18	F	Servant	14Ja02Ed
PATTEN, M.	18	M	Laborer	14Ja02Ed
MALONE, John	35	M	Laborer	14Ja02Ed
MOORE, James	22	M	Laborer	14Ja02Ed
ALLEN, W.M.	25	M	Laborer	14Ja02Ed
CAVANAGH, Mary	20	F	Servant	14Ja02Ed
BRADY, Mary	22	F	Servant	14Ja02Ed
MAHON, Margt.	24	F	Servant	14Ja02Ed
DOLAN, Eliza	19	F	Unknown	14Ja02Ed
COLLINS, James	24	M	Laborer	14Ja02Ed
MCCAVLAN, Jane	25	F	Servant	14Ja02Ed
HYNES, Michl.	18	M	Laborer	14Ja02Ed
GRIFFIN, Michl.	38	M	Laborer	14Ja02Ed
BRENAN, Thomas	20	M	Laborer	14Ja02Ed
CARR, Mary	45	F	Unknown	14Ja02Ed
Alice	36	F	Relative	14Ja02Ed
Richd.	7	M	Child	14Ja02Ed
Susan	5	F	Child	14Ja02Ed
Hugh	3	M	Child	14Ja02Ed
MULLIGAN, Michl.	19	M	Laborer	14Ja02Ed
DOUGLESS, John	24	M	Laborer	14Ja02Ed
QUINLAN, Denis	20	M	Unknown	14Ja02Ed
MCKAY, John	30	M	Relative	14Ja02Ed
Nancy	30	F	Relative	14Ja02Ed
Hannah	30	F	Relative	14Ja02Ed
Susan	12	F	Relative	14Ja02Ed
Pat	30	M	Relative	14Ja02Ed
Anty.	.10	M	Infant	14Ja02Ed
GALLIGAN, Willm.	30	M	Laborer	14Ja02Ed
MOFFATT, Wm.	29	M	Laborer	14Ja02Ed
VIRTUE, Alexr.	38	M	Laborer	14Ja02Ed
FALLAN, Ann	24	F	Servant	14Ja02Ed
Edwd.	.10	M	Infant	14Ja02Ed
MADDEN, Allen	18	M	Farmer	14Ja02Ed
CAVANAGH, Fra	22	M	Laborer	14Ja02Ed
KENAN, Pat	28	M	Laborer	14Ja02Ed
Cath.	24	F	Relative	14Ja02Ed
COOGAN, Bridt.	20	F	Relative	14Ja02Ed
LYONS, James	20	M	Laborer	14Ja02Ed
CONNELL, Bridt.	25	F	Servant	14Ja02Ed
James (S)	8	M	Child	14Ja02Ed
FARMAY, Mary	30	F	Servant	14Ja02Ed
ROCKLINGTON, Betsey	29	F	Laborer	14Ja02Ed
Thomas	30	M	Relative	14Ja02Ed
John	5	M	Child	14Ja02Ed

NAMES OF PASSENGERS	AGE	SEX	OCCUPATIONS	DATE PORT SHIP
ROCKLINGTON, Margt.	.10	F	Infant	14Ja02Ed
BRADY, Margt.	35	F	Relative	14Ja02Ed
FAULKNER, Thoms.	20	M	Laborer	14Ja02Ed
SEVINS, Henry	20	M	Carpenter	14Ja02Ed
RYAN, Margt.	56	F	Servant	14Ja02Ed
MAURICE, Ellen	17	F	Unknown	14Ja02Ed
KEIFE, Timm	21	M	Laborer	14Ja02Ed
Rose	18	M	Unknown	14Ja02Ed
OHERN, Wm.	50	M	Baker	14Ja02Ed
MCCORMICK, Mary	30	F	Relative	14Ja02Ed
Edwd.	7	M	Child	14Ja02Ed
Pat	3	M	Child	14Ja02Ed
Pat	.10	M	Infant	14Ja02Ed
Died-At-Sea				
HAYS, John	35	M	Laborer	14Ja02Ed
CONDORAN, James	25	M	Carpenter	14Ja02Ed
Mary	24	F	Wife	14Ja02Ed
BURK, Bridgt.	30	F	Servant	14Ja02Ed
MCHOMERD, Margt.	30	F	Unknown	14Ja02Ed
STANLEY, Pat	30	M	Shoemaker	14Ja02Ed
Pat (S)	3	M	Child	14Ja02Ed
HEALY, John	40	M	Laborer	14Ja02Ed
HAYS, Pat	22	M	Laborer	14Ja02Ed
James	20	M	Unknown	14Ja02Ed
LYNCH, John	21	M	Unknown	14Ja02Ed
CAVANAGH, John	30	M	Carpenter	14Ja02Ed
STALPIN, James	32	M	Laborer	14Ja02Ed
DUGAN, Martin	18	M	Laborer	14Ja02Ed
MORRIS, James	25	M	Unknown	14Ja02Ed
Cath.	25	F	Relative	14Ja02Ed
Ellen	50	F	Unknown	14Ja02Ed
MOORE, Pat	15	M	Laborer	14Ja02Ed
MORRISON, Cath.	54	F	Relative	14Ja02Ed
HAMMILL, Pat	19	M	Laborer	14Ja02Ed
GRAHAM, Edwd.	21	M	Laborer	14Ja02Ed
MCGELLAN, James	25	M	Unknown	14Ja02Ed
STANLEY, Mary	22	F	Servant	14Ja02Ed
GANNON, Bart	11	M	Relative	14Ja02Ed
REYNOLDS, Pat	25	M	Laborer	14Ja02Ed
FITZPATRICK, Eliza	25	F	Servant	14Ja02Ed
HYNES, Ann	19	F	Unknown	14Ja02Ed
QUIN, Ann	20	F	Unknown	14Ja02Ed
FLANAGAN, John	41	M	Laborer	14Ja02Ed
James (S)	8	M	Child	14Ja02Ed
Thoms. (S)	4	M	Child	14Ja02Ed
MCFARLOW, Michl.	35	M	Laborer	14Ja02Ed
DURKIN, Mae	28	F	Unknown	14Ja02Ed
MCAVOY, Cath.	26	F	Servant	14Ja02Ed
GRAY, Allice	18	F	Servant	14Ja02Ed
CAHILL, Bridt.	20	F	Servant	14Ja02Ed
MCCALL, Mary	24	F	Servant	14Ja02Ed
MCGORMAN, Owen	24	M	Laborer	14Ja02Ed
WARD, Michl.M.	30	M	Laborer	14Ja02Ed
Fanny	12	F	Relative	14Ja02Ed
John	8	M	Child	14Ja02Ed
MCKAY, John	.11	M	Infant	14Ja02Ed

NEW-WORLD 15 JANUARY 1850

From Liverpool

NAMES OF PASSENGERS	AGE	SEX	OCCUPATIONS	DATE PORT SHIP
MORRIS, William	30	M	Tailor	15Ja02Ec
MCMAHON, Peter	49	M	Farmer	15Ja02Ec
Ann	49	F	Wife	15Ja02Ec
Mary	22	F	Daughter	15Ja02Ec
Bridgett	20	F	Daughter	15Ja02Ec
Catharine	16	F	Daughter	15Ja02Ec
Jane	12	F	Daughter	15Ja02Ec
Anthony	10	M	Son	15Ja02Ec
MCMAHON, Bessy	8	F	Child	15Ja02Ec
Rose	27	F	Servant	15Ja02Ec
James	.00	M	Infant	15Ja02Ec
RILEY, Mick	50	M	Laborer	15Ja02Ec
Margt.	22	F	Servant	15Ja02Ec
Phillip	18	M	Laborer	15Ja02Ec
Ellenor	16	F	Servant	15Ja02Ec
GINTY, Catherine	16	F	Servant	15Ja02Ec
DICKSON, John	22	M	Seaman	15Ja02Ec
KELLY, Pat	54	M	Farmer	15Ja02Ec
Thomas	21	M	Farmer	15Ja02Ec
DUNN, Owen	19	M	Farmer	15Ja02Ec
KELLY, Mary	20	F	Servant	15Ja02Ec
Ann	17	F	Servant	15Ja02Ec
Bridget	15	F	Servant	15Ja02Ec
Michl.	23	M	Laborer	15Ja02Ec
JENNINGS, John	27	M	Mason	15Ja02Ec
ARMSTRONG, Margt.	48	F	Wife	15Ja02Ec
DUGAN, Farrel	24	M	Farmer	15Ja02Ec
DELANEY, John	35	M	Farmer	15Ja02Ec
KELLY, Michl.	25	M	Laborer	15Ja02Ec
Elizth.	26	F	Wife	15Ja02Ec
MCGAW, Pat	40	M	Mason	15Ja02Ec
Margt.	40	F	Wife	15Ja02Ec
Margt.	18	F	Servant	15Ja02Ec
Peter	13	F	Servant	15Ja02Ec
Wm.	9	M	Child	15Ja02Ec
James	3	M	Child	15Ja02Ec
WHELAN, Peter	26	M	Farmer	15Ja02Ec
KELLY, John	22	M	Stoker	15Ja02Ec
HAISLET, John	27	M	Farmer	15Ja02Ec
DONALDSON, John	38	M	Farmer	15Ja02Ec
Mary	29	F	Wife	15Ja02Ec
Hugh	8	M	Child	15Ja02Ec
Jane	6	F	Child	15Ja02Ec
Jane	40	F	Unknown	15Ja02Ec
HOGAN, Catherine	22	F	Servant	15Ja02Ec
Maria	16	F	Servant	15Ja02Ec
MURPHY, John	21	M	Laborer	15Ja02Ec
Michael	20	M	Laborer	15Ja02Ec
MARKAY, Thos.	21	M	Shoemaker	15Ja02Ec
Maria	21	F	Wife	15Ja02Ec
CALLAGHAN, James	25	M	Laborer	15Ja02Ec
Mary	25	F	Wife	15Ja02Ec
MCCULLOUGH, Thos.	17	M	Laborer	15Ja02Ec
MCKILLIN, Mary	35	F	Wife	15Ja02Ec
REID, Robt.	43	M	Laborer	15Ja02Ec
RIDDLE, Flanning	38	M	Laborer	15Ja02Ec
MCCORMICK, Mary	14	F	Servant	15Ja02Ec
MALONE, Cather.	19	F	Servant	15Ja02Ec
HEILAN, Ellen	30	F	Servant	15Ja02Ec
HALPIN, Ellen	14	F	Servant	15Ja02Ec
KEIFF, Margt.	28	F	Servant	15Ja02Ec
MULAGHAN, Thos.	20	M	Laborer	15Ja02Ec
CARDIFF, Harriet	18	F	Wife	15Ja02Ec
ROCHE, James	40	M	Farmer	15Ja02Ec
MALONE, Bridget	21	F	Servant	15Ja02Ec
HOPKINS, Royer	40	M	Farmer	15Ja02Ec
FITZGERALD, John	21	M	Laborer	15Ja02Ec
KENNEDY, Mary	25	F	Servant	15Ja02Ec
GIBEREY, Cather.	19	F	Servant	15Ja02Ec
ROURKE, Pat	26	M	Stone Mason	15Ja02Ec
DONNILAN, Andrew	26	M	Farmer	15Ja02Ec
Margt.	17	F	Servant	15Ja02Ec
MCNAMARA, Honora	13	F	Servant	15Ja02Ec
WHITE, Bridget	12	F	Servant	15Ja02Ec
MULROONEY, John	28	M	Farmer	15Ja02Ec
Bridget	18	F	Servant	15Ja02Ec
MCGUIRE, John	19	M	Farmer	15Ja02Ec
KING, James	16	M	Laborer	15Ja02Ec
Pat	20	F	Laborer	15Ja02Ec
Cathn.	17	F	Servant	15Ja02Ec
BRADY, Judith	30	F	Servant	15Ja02Ec
Mary-Anne	20	F	Servant	15Ja02Ec
Bridget	20	F	Servant	15Ja02Ec

NAMES OF PASSENGERS	AGE	SEX	OCCUPATIONS	DATE PORT SHIP
BRADY, Thos.Keogh	14	M	Unknown	15Ja02Ec
John	13	M	Unknown	15Ja02Ec
Margt.	12	F	Unknown	15Ja02Ec
Barney	11	M	Unknown	15Ja02Ec
James	9	M	Child	15Ja02Ec
Pat	6	M	Child	15Ja02Ec
HURLBURT, William	21	M	Laborer	15Ja02Ec
KENRICK, William	22	M	Laborer	15Ja02Ec
WALSH, James	26	M	Laborer	15Ja02Ec
Mary	24	F	Wife	15Ja02Ec
Margt.	11	F	Servant	15Ja02Ec
Bridgt.	4	F	Child	15Ja02Ec
James	2	M	Child	15Ja02Ec
WALLACE, William	23	M	Farmer	15Ja02Ec
HINCHEY, Sarah	40	F	Wife	15Ja02Ec
TORPY, John	4	M	Child	15Ja02Ec
GALLOWAY, Robt.	16	M	Printer	15Ja02Ec
DOWDE, Mary	22	F	Servant	15Ja02Ec
BOHAN, Cathn.	11	F	Servant	15Ja02Ec
MCGARTY, Cathn.	15	F	Servant	15Ja02Ec
Ellen	11	F	Servant	15Ja02Ec
MCENESSLEY, Nancy	25	F	Wife	15Ja02Ec
KELLY, Margt.	5	F	Child	15Ja02Ec
FEENEY, Ann	20	F	Servant	15Ja02Ec
KELLY, Ann	4	F	Child	15Ja02Ec
KAIN, Michl.	23	M	Laborer	15Ja02Ec
JACKSON, Bridget	48	F	Wife	15Ja02Ec
BOWDEN, William-Jr.	28	M	Farmer	15Ja02Ec
CLARK, Michl.	45	M	Laborer	15Ja02Ec
Maragt.	42	F	Wife	15Ja02Ec
Mary	12	F	Unknown	15Ja02Ec
John	10	M	Unknown	15Ja02Ec
Bridget	6	F	Child	15Ja02Ec
MARSAY, John	30	M	Tailor	15Ja02Ec
CARLOTT, John	30	M	Laborer	15Ja02Ec
DALY, Thos.	30	M	Farmer	15Ja02Ec
KELLY, Ann	18	F	Servant	15Ja02Ec
MALONE, Mary	35	F	Wife	15Ja02Ec
MANY, Ellenor	35	F	Wife	15Ja02Ec
Sam	7	M	Child	15Ja02Ec
KELLY, William	22	M	Farmer	15Ja02Ec
FLOOD, Margt.	20	F	Servant	15Ja02Ec
GEOGHEYAN, John	20	M	Laborer	15Ja02Ec
DOWD, John	16	M	Laborer	15Ja02Ec
WESTFIELD, Wm.	17	M	Laborer	15Ja02Ec
Jemima	16	F	Servant	15Ja02Ec
Robt.	12	M	Unknown	15Ja02Ec
Wm.Allen	10	M	Unknown	15Ja02Ec
ROBINSON, Thos.	12	M	Unknown	15Ja02Ec
Mathew	10	M	Unknown	15Ja02Ec
JACKSON, Wm.	23	M	Joiner	15Ja02Ec
BEAUMONT, Andrew	25	M	Mason	15Ja02Ec
Mary	21	F	Wife	15Ja02Ec
Nancy	1	F	Child	15Ja02Ec
PATTERSON, Robert	24	M	Weaver	15Ja02Ec
CARR, Patrick	35	M	Laborer	15Ja02Ec
HARNEY, John	36	M	Farmer	15Ja02Ec
Eliza	36	F	Wife	15Ja02Ec
Ann-Jane	12	F	Unknown	15Ja02Ec
Prudence	10	F	Unknown	15Ja02Ec
Saml.John	9	M	Child	15Ja02Ec
James	4	M	Child	15Ja02Ec
Eliza	.00	F	Infant	15Ja02Ec
BARNEY, Mick	27	M	Farmer	15Ja02Ec
KILMARTIN, Margt.	25	F	Servant	15Ja02Ec
Mary	19	F	Servant	15Ja02Ec
KELLY, Mick	18	M	Laborer	15Ja02Ec
Mary	20	F	Servant	15Ja02Ec
FITZPATRICK, Thos.	44	M	Farmer	15Ja02Ec
MINTAGH, Thos.	17	M	Laborer	15Ja02Ec
MCENTIN, Pat	26	M	Laborer	15Ja02Ec
MURPHY, Rose	19	F	Wife	15Ja02Ec
Wm.	22	M	Physician	15Ja02Ec
LYNE, E.M.	34	M	Gentleman	15Ja02Ec
Jane	22	F	Wife	15Ja02Ec
MCCOLLUND, John	28	M	Laborer	15Ja02Ec
SHIEL, Thos.	20	M	Laborer	15Ja02Ec
DOYLE, Mary	40	F	Wife	15Ja02Ec
Cornelius	18	M	Laborer	15Ja02Ec
Eliza	13	F	Unknown	15Ja02Ec
Margt.	9	F	Child	15Ja02Ec
Anne	6	F	Child	15Ja02Ec
Mary	4	F	Child	15Ja02Ec
JACKSON, John	14	M	None	15Ja02Ec
Ellen	11	F	None	15Ja02Ec
Joseph	9	M	Child	15Ja02Ec
Thomas	7	M	Child	15Ja02Ec

ENTERPRIZE 15 JANUARY 1850

From Liverpool

NAMES OF PASSENGERS	AGE	SEX	OCCUPATIONS	DATE PORT SHIP
BURKE, Patrick	65	M	Farmer	15Ja02Ab
Mary	60	F	Farmer	15Ja02Ab
Maria	20	F	Farmer	15Ja02Ab
TOWERS, John	28	M	Farmer	15Ja02Ab
James	14	M	Farmer	15Ja02Ab
FARRELL, Michael	32	M	Laborer	15Ja02Ab
CONLAN, Margaret	18	F	Seamstress	15Ja02Ab
BRYAN, Patrick	24	M	Laborer	15Ja02Ab
CRANE, Margaret	24	F	Seamstress	15Ja02Ab
John	25	M	Laborer	15Ja02Ab
Mary	24	F	Seamstress	15Ja02Ab
MCKEOWN, Mary	35	F	Seamstress	15Ja02Ab
Bartholw.	11	M	Servant	15Ja02Ab
Ann	12	F	Servant	15Ja02Ab
Catherine	2	F	Child	15Ja02Ab
Margaret	7	F	Child	15Ja02Ab
GILOOLY, Martin	35	M	Farmer	15Ja02Ab
DOWD, John	40	M	Farmer	15Ja02Ab
SHEA, Patrick	50	M	Farmer	15Ja02Ab
RATIGAN, Patrick	23	M	Farmer	15Ja02Ab
Mary	20	F	Farmer	15Ja02Ab
Ann	18	F	Farmer	15Ja02Ab
John	8	M	Child	15Ja02Ab
KELLY, John	12	M	Farmer	15Ja02Ab
Margaret	9	F	Child	15Ja02Ab
GLYNN, Catherine	24	F	Seamstress	15Ja02Ab
GAVIGAN, Maria	22	F	Servant	15Ja02Ab
MULOOLY, Elisabeth	18	F	Servant	15Ja02Ab
DAY, James	50	M	Laborer	15Ja02Ab
Sarah	50	F	Laborer	15Ja02Ab
John	21	M	Laborer	15Ja02Ab
MCCURDY, Thomas	21	M	Laborer	15Ja02Ab
WARD, Patrick	26	M	Farmer	15Ja02Ab
Francis	24	M	Farmer	15Ja02Ab
CARNEY, Joseph	38	M	Laborer	15Ja02Ab
Catherine	30	F	Laborer	15Ja02Ab
MULLEN, Thomas	22	M	Laborer	15Ja02Ab
HARKEN, Mary	25	F	Servant	15Ja02Ab
Daniel	12	M	Laborer	15Ja02Ab
James	10	M	Laborer	15Ja02Ab
DEVINE, Hannah	17	F	Servant	15Ja02Ab
MORRIS, Thomas	45	M	Farmer	15Ja02Ab
Thomas	20	M	Farmer	15Ja02Ab
MALOWNEY, Thomas	26	M	Farmer	15Ja02Ab
HENESSY, Bridget	50	F	Farmer	15Ja02Ab
Mary	26	F	Farmer	15Ja02Ab
Margaret	16	F	Farmer	15Ja02Ab
Ann	12	F	Farmer	15Ja02Ab
Patrick	18	M	Farmer	15Ja02Ab
Neil	20	M	Farmer	15Ja02Ab
FITZGERALD, Bridget	19	F	Servant	15Ja02Ab
WHELAN, Rose	30	F	Servant	15Ja02Ab

NAMES OF PASSENGERS	AGE	SEX	OCCUPATIONS	DATE PORT SHIP
MURRAY, Frances	50	F	Servant	15Ja02Ab
Wm.	50	M	Servant	15Ja02Ab
John	23	M	Laborer	15Ja02Ab
HARTLEY, John	45	M	Laborer	15Ja02Ab
HEALY, Mathew	30	M	Laborer	15Ja02Ab
GARRY, Joseph	22	M	Laborer	15Ja02Ab
ALLEN, Wm.	30	M	Laborer	15Ja02Ab
ROSE, James	31	M	Laborer	15Ja02Ab
HEALY, Ann	30	F	Seamstress	15Ja02Ab
GARLICK, Betty	28	F	Seamstress	15Ja02Ab
Jane	25	F	Seamstress	15Ja02Ab
HEALY, Jane	8	F	Child	15Ja02Ab
John	6	M	Child	15Ja02Ab
William	2	M	Child	15Ja02Ab
MCGINNES, Mary	14	F	Servant	15Ja02Ab
BYRNE, Peter	22	M	Servant	15Ja02Ab
Biddy	20	F	Servant	15Ja02Ab
KENEDY, Ellen	25	F	Servant	15Ja02Ab
MCHUGH, Neil	60	M	Servant	15Ja02Ab
NEILAN, Maria	30	F	Servant	15Ja02Ab
Thomas	.00	M	Infant	15Ja02Ab
GILDEA, James	26	M	Servant	15Ja02Ab
Thomas	23	M	Servant	15Ja02Ab
Mary	23	F	Servant	15Ja02Ab
Catherine	17	F	Servant	15Ja02Ab
HORAN, Edward	45	M	Servant	15Ja02Ab
GILHOOLY, Biddy	30	F	Seamstress	15Ja02Ab
ROWLEY, Cathe.	20	F	Seamstress	15Ja02Ab
LYNCH, Thomas	22	M	Laborer	15Ja02Ab
FISHER, Robert	40	M	Laborer	15Ja02Ab
John	5	M	Child	15Ja02Ab
ROHILL, Michael	26	M	Laborer	15Ja02Ab
DUFFY, Mary	40	F	Laborer	15Ja02Ab
Mary	19	F	Laborer	15Ja02Ab
Margaret	17	F	Laborer	15Ja02Ab
WINKLE, Ellen	30	F	Laborer	15Ja02Ab
Henry	10	M	Laborer	15Ja02Ab
Bridget	7	F	Child	15Ja02Ab
MCNAMARA, Denis	30	M	Farmer	15Ja02Ab
FLOOD, Martha	10	F	Farmer	15Ja02Ab
CLANCY, Cathe.	20	F	Servant	15Ja02Ab
CAVANAGH, James	17	M	Servant	15Ja02Ab
Mary	19	F	Servant	15Ja02Ab
CURLY, Feargus	17	M	Servant	15Ja02Ab
MCGANN, Thomas	24	M	Laborer	15Ja02Ab
GAMON, Pat	20	M	Laborer	15Ja02Ab
NEWMAN, Pat	20	M	Farmer	15Ja02Ab
Winifred	16	F	Farmer	15Ja02Ab
Hannah	14	F	Farmer	15Ja02Ab
William	11	M	Farmer	15Ja02Ab
Timothy	9	M	Child	15Ja02Ab
John	7	M	Child	15Ja02Ab
RYAN, Pat	38	M	Child	15Ja02Ab
WALSH, Philip	27	M	Laborer	15Ja02Ab
ENGLISH, Dennis	21	M	Laborer	15Ja02Ab
CAVANAGH, Cathe.	39	F	Laborer	15Ja02Ab
Patrick	20	M	Laborer	15Ja02Ab
WHITE, Michael	35	M	Laborer	15Ja02Ab
KEEFE, Pat	35	M	Laborer	15Ja02Ab
RYAN, Margaret	55	F	Farmer	15Ja02Ab
Winifred	24	F	Farmer	15Ja02Ab
Margaret	4	F	Child	15Ja02Ab
Mary	3	F	Child	15Ja02Ab
Elisa	40	F	Farmer	15Ja02Ab
FOLEY, James	40	M	Laborer	15Ja02Ab
Mary	20	F	Laborer	15Ja02Ab
HILL, Martin	38	M	Laborer	15Ja02Ab
GARLICK, Owen	30	M	Laborer	15Ja02Ab
HEALY, Mary	20	F	Servant	15Ja02Ab
JORDAN, Richard	29	M	Servant	15Ja02Ab
CARROLL, Ann	18	F	Servant	15Ja02Ab
Jane	15	F	Servant	15Ja02Ab
WISEMAN, Robert	28	M	Servant	15Ja02Ab
MCGUINNESS, John	40	M	Servant	15Ja02Ab
CLARY, John	30	M	Servant	15Ja02Ab

NAMES OF PASSENGERS	AGE	SEX	OCCUPATIONS	DATE PORT SHIP
CLARK, James	25	M	Servant	15Ja02Ab
Catherine	50	F	Servant	15Ja02Ab
Mary	20	F	Servant	15Ja02Ab
THOMPSON, Mary-Ann	28	F	Seamstress	15Ja02Ab
KIRK, Bell	50	F	Farmer	15Ja02Ab
John	28	M	Farmer	15Ja02Ab
Jane	26	F	Farmer	15Ja02Ab
Richard	24	M	Farmer	15Ja02Ab
Samuel	22	M	Farmer	15Ja02Ab
George	20	M	Farmer	15Ja02Ab
Bessy	17	F	Farmer	15Ja02Ab
Martha	15	F	Farmer	15Ja02Ab
Isabella	13	F	Farmer	15Ja02Ab
William	9	M	Child	15Ja02Ab
SMITH, Mary	20	F	Servant	15Ja02Ab
KIERNAN, John	40	M	Farmer	15Ja02Ab
Alice	35	F	Farmer	15Ja02Ab
Ellen	10	F	Farmer	15Ja02Ab
James	4	M	Child	15Ja02Ab
Mary	24	F	Farmer	15Ja02Ab
Catherine	.00	F	Infant	15Ja02Ab
Born-At-Sea				
KENIFICK, Wm.	28	M	Farmer	15Ja02Ab
REILLY, Mary	16	F	Servant	15Ja02Ab
Cath.	12	F	Servant	15Ja02Ab
Ann	10	F	Servant	15Ja02Ab
RYAN, Mary	20	F	Servant	15Ja02Ab
Ann	8	F	Child	15Ja02Ab
PURDY, Bessy	19	F	Servant	15Ja02Ab
SWEENY, Denis	30	M	Laborer	15Ja02Ab
DONAHOE, Johanna	21	M	Laborer	15Ja02Ab
NOONAN, Timothy	40	M	Laborer	15Ja02Ab
John	12	M	Laborer	15Ja02Ab
MCANLIFFE, Daniel	40	M	Laborer	15Ja02Ab
Mary	40	F	Laborer	15Ja02Ab
GALVIN, Catherine	40	F	Farmer	15Ja02Ab
David	18	M	Farmer	15Ja02Ab
Nancy	15	F	Farmer	15Ja02Ab
Mary	10	F	Farmer	15Ja02Ab
John	4	M	Child	15Ja02Ab
QUINLAN, David	30	M	Farmer	15Ja02Ab
DONOVAN, Timothy	12	M	Laborer	15Ja02Ab
BUCKLEY, Michael	20	M	Laborer	15Ja02Ab
Bridget	20	F	Laborer	15Ja02Ab
MOORE, Henry	12	M	Laborer	15Ja02Ab
CARROLL, Patrick	32	M	Laborer	15Ja02Ab
Jeremiah	20	M	Servant	15Ja02Ab
RING, Honorah	20	F	Servant	15Ja02Ab
CONNELL, Ellen	20	F	Seamstress	15Ja02Ab
GALVIN, Johanna	20	F	Seamstress	15Ja02Ab
DAVIS, Mary	23	F	Seamstress	15Ja02Ab
Catherine	.00	F	Infant	15Ja02Ab
Born-At-Sea				
HART, Patrick	20	M	Laborer	15Ja02Ab
MULLIGAN, Ann	15	F	Laborer	15Ja02Ab
Margaret	11	F	Laborer	15Ja02Ab
William	9	M	Child	15Ja02Ab
Ellen	5	F	Child	15Ja02Ab
MEGEHEY, Rebecca	17	F	Servant	15Ja02Ab
Mary	12	F	Servant	15Ja02Ab
KELLY, Bridget	18	F	Servant	15Ja02Ab
DONOHOE, Celia	17	F	Servant	15Ja02Ab
Bridget	6	F	Child	15Ja02Ab
GANNON, Patrick	16	M	Laborer	15Ja02Ab
Joseph	20	M	Laborer	15Ja02Ab
SWEENY, James	11	M	Laborer	15Ja02Ab
BODDY, William	13	M	Laborer	15Ja02Ab
TYLER, John	29	M	Farmer	15Ja02Ab
U-Mrs.	26	F	Farmer	15Ja02Ab
William	9	M	Child	15Ja02Ab
John	7	M	Child	15Ja02Ab
Samuel	3	M	Child	15Ja02Ab
Eli	1	M	Child	15Ja02Ab
MCCABE, John	20	M	Farmer	15Ja02Ab
Mary	16	F	Farmer	15Ja02Ab

NAMES OF PASSENGERS	AGE	SEX	OCCUPATIONS	DATE PORT SHIP
GRANT, Michael	24	M	Servant	15Ja02Ab
DONELLY, Catherine	17	F	Servant	15Ja02Ab

IVANHOE 15 JANUARY 1850

From Liverpool

NAMES OF PASSENGERS	AGE	SEX	OCCUPATIONS	DATE PORT SHIP
SHANNON, Con	35	M	Farmer	15Ja02Bt
Betty	35	F	None	15Ja02Bt
Mary	15	F	None	15Ja02Bt
Michael	13	M	None	15Ja02Bt
John	7	M	Child	15Ja02Bt
Thomas	.10	M	Infant	15Ja02Bt
CARNEY, Kate	30	F	None	15Ja02Bt
KINE, Catharine	23	F	None	15Ja02Bt
MIHEN, Mary	25	F	None	15Ja02Bt
SHANNON, Thomas	35	M	Farmer	15Ja02Bt
Norie	30	F	None	15Ja02Bt
James	13	M	None	15Ja02Bt
Michael	11	M	None	15Ja02Bt
Thomas	5	M	Child	15Ja02Bt
Daniel	.10	M	Infant	15Ja02Bt
Judy	.11	F	Infant	15Ja02Bt
DEVARN, Margaret	28	F	None	15Ja02Bt
DANIELS, Mary	12	F	None	15Ja02Bt
William	7	M	Child	15Ja02Bt
CLARY, H.	23	F	None	15Ja02Bt
KINE, Patrick	40	M	None	15Ja02Bt
WINE, Edmond	30	M	None	15Ja02Bt
POWER, James	30	M	None	15Ja02Bt
MAGEE, Patrick	20	M	None	15Ja02Bt
MURPHY, Bose	18	F	None	15Ja02Bt
NOCTIN, Patrick	25	M	None	15Ja02Bt
CASEY, Denis	19	M	None	15Ja02Bt
Ellen	50	F	None	15Ja02Bt
MALONY, Catharine	30	F	None	15Ja02Bt
BYRNS, James-Jr.	55	M	None	15Ja02Bt
Mathew	29	M	None	15Ja02Bt
BRADY, Patrick	23	M	None	15Ja02Bt
KEOGHAN, John	19	M	None	15Ja02Bt
MALIN, Henry	32	M	None	15Ja02Bt
BRADY, Mary	30	F	None	15Ja02Bt
Rose	20	F	None	15Ja02Bt
KEOGHAN, Ann	15	F	None	15Ja02Bt
FAGAN, James	35	M	None	15Ja02Bt
Ann	35	F	None	15Ja02Bt
Ann	4	F	Child	15Ja02Bt
KERNAN, Mary	40	F	None	15Ja02Bt
Rose	16	F	None	15Ja02Bt
Ann	12	F	None	15Ja02Bt
Peter	10	M	None	15Ja02Bt
Patrick	30	M	Laborer	15Ja02Bt
Judy	26	F	None	15Ja02Bt
Patrick	.09	M	Infant	15Ja02Bt
HART, Henry	36	M	Laborer	15Ja02Bt
Bridget	22	F	Laborer	15Ja02Bt
COYLE, John	24	M	Laborer	15Ja02Bt
MCGIVENY, Henry	40	M	Laborer	15Ja02Bt
Rose	20	M	Laborer	15Ja02Bt
Henry-Jr.	18	M	Laborer	15Ja02Bt
Mary	14	F	Laborer	15Ja02Bt
MCNAMARA, Bernan	40	F	Laborer	15Ja02Bt
WALSH, Mary	40	M	Laborer	15Ja02Bt
Ellen	17	F	Laborer	15Ja02Bt
Thomas	15	M	Laborer	15Ja02Bt
Patrick	13	M	Laborer	15Ja02Bt
Hugh	3	M	Child	15Ja02Bt
John	9	M	Child	15Ja02Bt
GRIFFETHS, Anthony	30	M	Weaver	15Ja02Bt
GRIFFETHS, Mary-Kiley	36	F	Weaver	15Ja02Bt
Catharine	13	F	Weaver	15Ja02Bt
Patrick	11	M	Weaver	15Ja02Bt
Philip	9	M	Child	15Ja02Bt
Michael	6	M	Child	15Ja02Bt
FASLEY, Mary	65	F	Weaver	15Ja02Bt
MCNAMARA, Daniel	12	M	Laborer	15Ja02Bt
Ann	32	F	Laborer	15Ja02Bt
JOHNSON, Thomas	35	M	Laborer	15Ja02Bt
SLOAN, James	24	M	Laborer	15Ja02Bt
MCQUID, Patrick	55	M	Laborer	15Ja02Bt
Mary	21	F	Laborer	15Ja02Bt
Catharine	19	F	Laborer	15Ja02Bt
CRONIN, Patrick	28	M	Laborer	15Ja02Bt
DOHERTY, John	26	M	Laborer	15Ja02Bt
ENGLISH, James	27	M	Laborer	15Ja02Bt
BYAN, Timothy	29	M	Laborer	15Ja02Bt
DOHERTY, Ann	25	F	Laborer	15Ja02Bt
Bridget	23	F	Laborer	15Ja02Bt
RYAN, Ann	22	F	Laborer	15Ja02Bt
TIERNEY, Mark	26	M	Laborer	15Ja02Bt
Patrick	21	M	Laborer	15Ja02Bt
LAY, John	24	M	Laborer	15Ja02Bt
Mary	26	F	Laborer	15Ja02Bt
RICE, Michael	50	M	Laborer	15Ja02Bt
TRACEY, Ann	50	F	Laborer	15Ja02Bt
Mary	11	F	Laborer	15Ja02Bt
BRYAN, Ann	30	F	Laborer	15Ja02Bt
LOWRY, Ann	30	F	Laborer	15Ja02Bt
BRYAN, Timothy	2	M	Child	15Ja02Bt
TRACEY, Thomas	20	M	Laborer	15Ja02Bt
HOPKINS, James	29	M	Laborer	15Ja02Bt
RAGAN, Luke	21	M	Laborer	15Ja02Bt
LARKIN, Frank	36	M	Laborer	15Ja02Bt
DALY, Patrick	29	M	Laborer	15Ja02Bt
NOONAN, Bridget	21	F	Laborer	15Ja02Bt
LOWRY, Nancy	20	F	Laborer	15Ja02Bt
ROOT, Ann	30	F	Laborer	15Ja02Bt
CAMEL, Ann	18	F	Laborer	15Ja02Bt
CORNLY, Peter	20	M	Laborer	15Ja02Bt
Mary	18	F	Laborer	15Ja02Bt
CONGLY, Mary	18	F	Laborer	15Ja02Bt
MCCLANE, Mary	20	F	Laborer	15Ja02Bt
BURR, Catharine	20	F	Laborer	15Ja02Bt
MCCONE, Bridget	3	F	Child	15Ja02Bt
BURR, Ann	4	F	Child	15Ja02Bt
QUINEFFE, Ann	20	F	None	15Ja02Bt
KILY, Mary	20	F	None	15Ja02Bt
MALONY, Ann	18	F	None	15Ja02Bt
HAGARTY, Johanna	17	F	None	15Ja02Bt
Daniel	14	M	None	15Ja02Bt
John	15	M	None	15Ja02Bt
Mary	8	F	Child	15Ja02Bt
CRANE, Michael	24	M	Blacksmith	15Ja02Bt
HAGARTY, Margauld	6	F	Child	15Ja02Bt
HALY, Cornelius	17	M	Laborer	15Ja02Bt
LANTY, Eliza	25	F	Laborer	15Ja02Bt
SCOTT, James	31	M	Laborer	15Ja02Bt
Mary	26	F	Laborer	15Ja02Bt
Thomas	5	M	Child	15Ja02Bt
KINLAN, Owen	24	M	Laborer	15Ja02Bt
CAWAN, William	31	M	Laborer	15Ja02Bt
BEENAN, Ann	22	F	Laborer	15Ja02Bt
Bridget	26	F	Laborer	15Ja02Bt
DONAHOE, Bridget	22	F	Laborer	15Ja02Bt
CALLIGAN, Rosa	20	F	Laborer	15Ja02Bt
KEELY, Mary	22	F	Laborer	15Ja02Bt
ROGERS, Patrick	9	M	Child	15Ja02Bt
COYLE, John	30	M	Laborer	15Ja02Bt
Catherine	25	F	Laborer	15Ja02Bt
Ann	.00	F	Infant	15Ja02Bt
FITZPATRICK, Rose	50	F	None	15Ja02Bt
Ann	22	F	None	15Ja02Bt
Hugh	20	M	None	15Ja02Bt
Farrell	18	M	None	15Ja02Bt

NAMES OF PASSENGERS	AGE	SEX	OCCUPATIONS	DATE PORT SHIP
COYLE, Lawrance	25	M	None	15Ja02Bt
MACKINROW, Thomas	24	M	None	15Ja02Bt
SHARKLY, Mary	40	F	None	15Ja02Bt
KELLY, Mary	19	F	None	15Ja02Bt
CARDEN, Peter	20	M	None	15Ja02Bt
BOYLE, Owen	40	M	None	15Ja02Bt
Patrick	40	M	None	15Ja02Bt
MCDONALD, John	20	M	None	15Ja02Bt
MCNERNY, Ann	40	F	None	15Ja02Bt
Henry	11	M	None	15Ja02Bt
Ellen	2	F	Child	15Ja02Bt
Died-At-Sea				
MEHAN, Catharine	16	F	Laborer	15Ja02Bt
MULLIGAN, Catharine	19	F	Laborer	15Ja02Bt
BASSETT, Ellen	22	F	Laborer	15Ja02Bt
COGAN, Michael	40	M	Laborer	15Ja02Bt
James	40	M	None	15Ja02Bt
MAHEN, John	36	M	Farmer	15Ja02Bt
Ellen	40	F	Laborer	15Ja02Bt
Grace	13	F	Laborer	15Ja02Bt
Bridget	3	F	Child	15Ja02Bt
PLUNKET, Patrick	15	M	Laborer	15Ja02Bt
John	19	M	Laborer	15Ja02Bt
SWEENY, James	19	M	Laborer	15Ja02Bt
KINSELLY, Edward	40	M	Laborer	15Ja02Bt
Ann	30	F	Laborer	15Ja02Bt
Mary	.00	F	Infant	15Ja02Bt
Catherine	70	F	Laborer	15Ja02Bt
KELLY, Catherine	24	F	Laborer	15Ja02Bt
ROACH, Daniel	21	M	Laborer	15Ja02Bt
Thomas	22	M	Laborer	15Ja02Bt
FLANNAN, Michael	25	M	Laborer	15Ja02Bt
Mary	26	F	Laborer	15Ja02Bt
HOWREGAN, Judy	16	F	Laborer	15Ja02Bt
John	14	M	Laborer	15Ja02Bt
FORELY, Mary	25	F	Laborer	15Ja02Bt
QUINLIVIN, John	20	M	Laborer	15Ja02Bt
Edward	50	M	Laborer	15Ja02Bt
Edward	23	M	Laborer	15Ja02Bt
HENNISY, Patrick	30	M	Laborer	15Ja02Bt
FLOAR, Patrick	28	M	Laborer	15Ja02Bt
LINES, Patrick	30	M	Laborer	15Ja02Bt
MCKOWN, William	20	M	Laborer	15Ja02Bt
LINCH, Patrick	14	M	Laborer	15Ja02Bt
Judy	10	F	Laborer	15Ja02Bt
SULLIVAN, Ann	20	F	Laborer	15Ja02Bt
HANLY, Mary	25	F	Laborer	15Ja02Bt
DUNN, Bridget	26	F	Laborer	15Ja02Bt
Daniel	3	M	Child	15Ja02Bt
William	.00	M	Infant	15Ja02Bt
JONES, Catharine	25	F	Laborer	15Ja02Bt
TIMMONS, Patrick	21	M	Laborer	15Ja02Bt
WARDLEY, John	22	M	Laborer	15Ja02Bt
Lavinia	20	F	Laborer	15Ja02Bt
BESEGAN, William	21	M	Laborer	15Ja02Bt
ODONNEL, James	35	M	Laborer	15Ja02Bt
MAHAN, James	34	M	Laborer	15Ja02Bt
HOGAN, Michael	35	M	Laborer	15Ja02Bt
MAHAN, Bridget	30	F	Laborer	15Ja02Bt
DONOHOE, Patrick	50	M	Laborer	15Ja02Bt
Ann	48	F	Laborer	15Ja02Bt
Patrick	19	M	Laborer	15Ja02Bt
Margaret	15	F	Laborer	15Ja02Bt
Daniel	13	M	Laborer	15Ja02Bt
Michael	11	M	Laborer	15Ja02Bt
John	9	M	Child	15Ja02Bt
LINCH, Thomas	19	M	Laborer	15Ja02Bt
SMITH, Michael	75	M	Laborer	15Ja02Bt
Philip	19	M	Laborer	15Ja02Bt
BIRD, Patrick	15	M	Laborer	15Ja02Bt
Terence	13	M	Laborer	15Ja02Bt
CLARK, Patrick	22	M	Laborer	15Ja02Bt
Margaret	21	F	None	15Ja02Bt
MCDONALD, Joseph	23	M	Baker	15Ja02Bt
Alice	19	F	None	15Ja02Bt
RILEY, Michael	24	M	Laborer	15Ja02Bt
BASSETT, Andrew	22	M	Laborer	15Ja02Bt
GAGIN, Ann	24	F	Laborer	15Ja02Bt
SWIFT, Rose	15	F	Laborer	15Ja02Bt
DOYLE, Catharine	27	F	Laborer	15Ja02Bt
DELANEY, Daniel	27	M	Laborer	15Ja02Bt
KINE, Thomas	26	M	Laborer	15Ja02Bt
SWEENY, Owen	27	M	Laborer	15Ja02Bt
CASEDY, Patrick	30	M	Laborer	15Ja02Bt
KINE, Mary	26	F	Laborer	15Ja02Bt
SWEENY, Mary	32	F	Laborer	15Ja02Bt
CASIDY, Mary	29	F	Laborer	15Ja02Bt
FLANAGAN, Ally	28	F	Laborer	15Ja02Bt
Margaret	18	F	Laborer	15Ja02Bt
SHANLIN, Judith	25	F	Laborer	15Ja02Bt
FLANNAGAN, Andre	24	M	Laborer	15Ja02Bt
Michael	55	M	Laborer	15Ja02Bt
Michael	17	M	Laborer	15Ja02Bt
Thomas	40	M	Laborer	15Ja02Bt
KANE, Sally	52	F	Laborer	15Ja02Bt
Rosy	16	F	Laborer	15Ja02Bt
Bridget	14	F	Laborer	15Ja02Bt
James	9	M	Child	15Ja02Bt
Nancy	7	F	Child	15Ja02Bt
KINNEY, Bridget	18	F	Laborer	15Ja02Bt
NORWOOD, James	25	M	Laborer	15Ja02Bt
NASH, James	30	M	Laborer	15Ja02Bt
COAFAY, Philip	40	M	Laborer	15Ja02Bt
Catharine	30	F	Laborer	15Ja02Bt
Bridget	4	F	Child	15Ja02Bt
Mary	.00	F	Infant	15Ja02Bt
GRAHAM, Jane	10	F	Laborer	15Ja02Bt
CARBARG, Alice	25	F	Laborer	15Ja02Bt
OBRIEN, Thomas	28	M	Coachman	15Ja02Bt
WALCH, John	20	M	Farmer	15Ja02Bt
HOBIN, Patrick	25	M	Laborer	15Ja02Bt
GALLAGHER, Owen	27	M	Laborer	15Ja02Bt
BYLAN, Edward	19	M	Laborer	15Ja02Bt
B.	17	M	Laborer	15Ja02Bt
MONAHAN, Margaret	20	F	Laborer	15Ja02Bt
BYLAN, Margaret	18	F	Laborer	15Ja02Bt
LYNCH, Mary	36	F	Laborer	15Ja02Bt
Mary	12	F	Laborer	15Ja02Bt
MCLOCHLIN, Margaret	20	F	Laborer	15Ja02Bt
MCCADE, Mary	18	F	Laborer	15Ja02Bt
COLLIER, Nicholas	23	M	Printer	15Ja02Bt
William	29	M	Printer	15Ja02Bt
BOSMAN, David	29	M	Mason	15Ja02Bt
BAGAN, James	50	M	Mason	15Ja02Bt
Sarah-Ann	8	F	Child	15Ja02Bt
CRENA, Ellen	17	F	None	15Ja02Bt
BAKER, Alice	60	F	None	15Ja02Bt
BIGGINS, John	18	M	None	15Ja02Bt
KEEDIN, Michael	20	M	Laborer	15Ja02Bt
DALY, Bridget	25	F	Laborer	15Ja02Bt
KELLY, Mary	22	F	Laborer	15Ja02Bt
MCKAY, Bridget	23	F	Laborer	15Ja02Bt
DALEY, Alice	.00	F	Infant	15Ja02Bt
BROCK, Judy	44	F	Laborer	15Ja02Bt
John	19	M	Laborer	15Ja02Bt
Catharine	16	M	Laborer	15Ja02Bt
Eliza	14	F	Tailor	15Ja02Bt
Marsale	11	F	Laborer	15Ja02Bt
Francis	9	M	Child	15Ja02Bt
Bridget	7	F	Child	15Ja02Bt
Lawrence	7	M	Child	15Ja02Bt
Joseph	.00	M	Infant	15Ja02Bt
HUGHES, Margaret	19	F	Laborer	15Ja02Bt
DEVINE, Mary	20	F	Laborer	15Ja02Bt
ODONNELL, Ann	17	F	Laborer	15Ja02Bt
BYRNS, Bridget	18	F	Laborer	15Ja02Bt
REILY, Thomas	26	M	Laborer	15Ja02Bt
Mary	20	F	Laborer	15Ja02Bt
LEARY, John	26	M	Tailor	15Ja02Bt
Mary	24	F	Tailor	15Ja02Bt

NAMES OF PASSENGERS	AGE	SEX	OCCUPATIONS	DATE PORT SHIP
BRADLY, Joseph	33	M	Tailor	15Ja02Bt
GORDON, James	22	M	Laborer	15Ja02Bt
POWER, Thomas	23	M	Baker	15Ja02Bt
KILFILE, William	18	M	Laborer	15Ja02Bt
HOWAGAN, Rosey	18	F	None	15Ja02Bt
Catharine	20	F	None	15Ja02Bt
DONOHOE, Mary	18	F	None	15Ja02Bt
LEE, John	21	M	None	15Ja02Bt
WALSH, Martin	40	M	Laborer	15Ja02Bt
LINCH, Thomas	15	M	Laborer	15Ja02Bt
BRENIN, Daniel	20	M	Laborer	15Ja02Bt
NOLAN, Dennis	20	M	Seaman	15Ja02Bt
HOWLEGAN, U Born-At-Sea	.00	U	Infant	15Ja02Bt

HYNDEFORD 15 JANUARY 1850

From Glasgow

NAMES OF PASSENGERS	AGE	SEX	OCCUPATIONS	DATE PORT SHIP
WILSON, Jas.	26	M	Engineer	15Ja21Ee
GLASS, Wm.	40	M	Laborer	15Ja21Ee
MCGALLOWAY, Jno.	15	M	Laborer	15Ja21Ee
QUINN, Michl.	25	M	Laborer	15Ja21Ee
MCLEAVY, Saml.	39	M	Laborer	15Ja21Ee
PATTERSON, George	23	M	Laborer	15Ja21Ee
Matilda	25	F	Spinster	15Ja21Ee
REYNOLD, Edwd.	30	M	Laborer	15Ja21Ee
KENNY, Ann	50	F	Wife	15Ja21Ee
QUINN, Sarah	35	F	Wife	15Ja21Ee
Marge	15	F	Relative	15Ja21Ee
Patk.	4	M	Child	15Ja21Ee
Hannah	2	F	Child	15Ja21Ee
DOCHERTY, Jno.	17	M	Laborer	15Ja21Ee
HARVEY, Robt.	40	M	Laborer	15Ja21Ee
BROWN, Jas.	27	M	Laborer	15Ja21Ee
U (W)	25	F	Wife	15Ja21Ee
Marge	16	F	Relative	15Ja21Ee
ARRAN, Julia	15	F	Relative	15Ja21Ee
DAVIDSON, Elizth.	38	F	Wife	15Ja21Ee
James	18	M	Relative	15Ja21Ee
Ann	10	F	Relative	15Ja21Ee
Agness	8	F	Child	15Ja21Ee
Ellen	6	F	Child	15Ja21Ee
BRANNAGEN, Peter	40	M	Laborer	15Ja21Ee
WILSON, Jno.	37	M	Laborer	15Ja21Ee
BOYLE, James	21	M	Laborer	15Ja21Ee
MURRAY, James	19	M	Laborer	15Ja21Ee
WALTERS, Jane	28	F	Wife	15Ja21Ee
Jane	1	F	Child	15Ja21Ee
MARTEN, Wm.	19	M	Laborer	15Ja21Ee
MCMULLEN, Margt.	17	F	Spinster	15Ja21Ee
HART, Hugh	33	M	Laborer	15Ja21Ee
WILSON, Mary	34	F	Wife	15Ja21Ee
QUINN, Catherine	7	F	Child	15Ja21Ee
WILSON, Mary	11	F	Unknown	15Ja21Ee
Marge	6	F	Child	15Ja21Ee
Catherine	.05	F	Infant	15Ja21Ee
DEAS, Robert	36	M	Unknown	15Ja21Ee

SARAH 15 JANUARY 1850

From Fayal

NAMES OF PASSENGERS	AGE	SEX	OCCUPATIONS	DATE PORT SHIP
MCCOY, Pat	60	M	Farmer	15Ja46EI
Ann	25	F	Unknown	15Ja46EI
Margt.	23	F	Unknown	15Ja46EI
Jno.	20	M	Unknown	15Ja46EI
Bridgt.	12	F	Unknown	15Ja46EI
BURNS, Peter	15	F	Unknown	15Ja46EI
BARRY, Hannah	19	F	Unknown	15Ja46EI
OBRIEN, Ellen	17	F	Laborer	15Ja46EI
WYMB, Rose	40	F	Unknown	15Ja46EI
Oney	19	M	Unknown	15Ja46EI
CRAWFORD, Cath.	50	F	Unknown	15Ja46EI
BURNS, John	40	M	Unknown	15Ja46EI
CURRAN, John	22	M	Unknown	15Ja46EI
FOLEY, Thomas	30	M	Unknown	15Ja46EI
NEWMAN, Rose	10	F	Unknown	15Ja46EI
FOLEY, Michl.	28	M	Unknown	15Ja46EI
CRAWFORD, Jno.	13	M	Unknown	15Ja46EI
WHITE, Michl.	24	M	Unknown	15Ja46EI
DALEY, Pat	20	M	Unknown	15Ja46EI
OHAIR, James	35	M	Unknown	15Ja46EI
HENRIGHT, Pat	25	M	Unknown	15Ja46EI
SLATERY, Denis	20	M	Unknown	15Ja46EI
EAGAN, Dennis	29	M	Unknown	15Ja46EI
CARAGAR, Pat	40	M	Unknown	15Ja46EI
BEATY, Henry	26	M	Unknown	15Ja46EI
COYLE, Owen	30	M	Farmer	15Ja46EI
HUTCHER, Jno.	26	M	Unknown	15Ja46EI
CRAWFORD, Susan	10	F	Unknown	15Ja46EI
BURNS, Edwd.	26	M	Unknown	15Ja46EI
Hannah	23	F	Unknown	15Ja46EI
CUSGULL, Bridgt.	20	F	Unknown	15Ja46EI
MULVEY, Jas.	10	M	Unknown	15Ja46EI
CAYNE, Jno.	16	M	Unknown	15Ja46EI
SCOTT, Joseph	20	M	Unknown	15Ja46EI
DIAMOND, Robt.	22	M	Unknown	15Ja46EI
Jas.	21	M	Unknown	15Ja46EI
Eliza	19	F	Unknown	15Ja46EI
MULVEY, Margt.	50	F	Unknown	15Ja46EI
HENNESSY, Johanna	20	F	Unknown	15Ja46EI
WARD, Cath.	19	F	Unknown	15Ja46EI
WALL, Cath.	21	F	Unknown	15Ja46EI
HOOGAN, Ellen	18	F	Unknown	15Ja46EI
Alice	17	F	Unknown	15Ja46EI
CANAGH, Bridgt.	20	F	Unknown	15Ja46EI
RADY, Cath.	19	F	Unknown	15Ja46EI
ODONALD, Margt.Shea	30	F	Unknown	15Ja46EI
LULE, Mary	30	F	Unknown	15Ja46EI
LYONS, Mary	18	F	Unknown	15Ja46EI
Johanna	16	F	Unknown	15Ja46EI
DAVIS, Mary	8	F	Child	15Ja46EI
MATTHEWS, Betty	20	F	Unknown	15Ja46EI
MADDEN, Mary	21	F	Unknown	15Ja46EI
GORAN, Bridgt.	19	F	Unknown	15Ja46EI
CROGAN, Ellen	9	F	Child	15Ja46EI
CRONAGAR, John	6	M	Child	15Ja46EI
DOWD, Ellen	30	F	Unknown	15Ja46EI
MURPHY, Eliza	50	F	Unknown	15Ja46EI
MALANY, Mary	18	F	Unknown	15Ja46EI
MADDEN, Mary	18	F	Unknown	15Ja46EI
CARNEY, Bridgt.	19	F	Unknown	15Ja46EI
COYLE, Cath.	19	F	Unknown	15Ja46EI
Mary	20	F	Unknown	15Ja46EI
SHIELDS, Mary-J.	18	F	Unknown	15Ja46EI
Ann	10	F	Unknown	15Ja46EI
MONAGAN, Mary	18	F	Unknown	15Ja46EI

NAMES OF PASSENGERS	AGE	SEX	OCCUPATIONS	DATE PORT SHIP
EVANS, Mary	20	F	Unknown	15Ja46Ei
Jno.	30	M	Unknown	15Ja46Ei
Pat	26	M	Unknown	15Ja46Ei
CAFFERTY, Owen	18	M	Unknown	15Ja46Ei
ONEIL, Richd.	30	M	Unknown	15Ja46Ei
Eliza	29	F	Unknown	15Ja46Ei
Eliza	9	F	Child	15Ja46Ei
Arthur	6	M	Child	15Ja46Ei
Jane	5	F	Child	15Ja46Ei
DONNEL, Ellen	50	F	Unknown	15Ja46Ei
DONOHUE, Ellen	30	F	Unknown	15Ja46Ei
OHARE, Cath.	20	F	Unknown	15Ja46Ei
MICHELMY, Eliza	20	F	Unknown	15Ja46Ei
HARRY, Mary	20	F	Unknown	15Ja46Ei
BRITTON, Cath.	30	F	Unknown	15Ja46Ei
GREATH, Bridgt.	29	F	Unknown	15Ja46Ei
BURNS, Mary	24	F	Unknown	15Ja46Ei
MULCANY, Eliza	18	F	Unknown	15Ja46Ei
CANAGH, Bridgt.	23	F	Unknown	15Ja46Ei
FORD, Mary	21	F	Unknown	15Ja46Ei
HEALEY, Cath.	20	F	Unknown	15Ja46Ei
FITZGERALD, Mary	23	F	Unknown	15Ja46Ei
Ann	22	F	Unknown	15Ja46Ei
MCNULTY, Edwd.	22	F	Unknown	15Ja46Ei
CRAWFORD, Andrew	20	F	Unknown	15Ja46Ei
ODONALD, Jno.	20	F	Unknown	15Ja46Ei
FOLY, Thos.	18	M	Unknown	15Ja46Ei
Barney	10	M	Unknown	15Ja46Ei
Bridgt.	50	F	Unknown	15Ja46Ei
Barney	50	M	Unknown	15Ja46Ei
Jas.	12	M	Unknown	15Ja46Ei
Pat	2	M	Child	15Ja46Ei
Mary	3	F	Child	15Ja46Ei
HUGHES, Mary	11	F	Unknown	15Ja46Ei
Wm.	21	M	Unknown	15Ja46Ei
MCREIGH, Thos.	33	M	Unknown	15Ja46Ei
WEDDELLE, Wm.	25	M	Unknown	15Ja46Ei
RAMSDILL, Jno.	26	M	Unknown	15Ja46Ei
COHREGIN, Thos.	20	M	Unknown	15Ja46Ei
CLARK, Michl.	36	M	Unknown	15Ja46Ei
WELSH, Jno.	25	M	Unknown	15Ja46Ei
DALY, Jas.	50	M	Unknown	15Ja46Ei
CARTEN, Bartel	12	M	Unknown	15Ja46Ei
LYONS, Dennis	50	M	Unknown	15Ja46Ei
WELDRON, Thos.	16	M	Unknown	15Ja46Ei
GRIFFIN, Michl.	26	M	Unknown	15Ja46Ei
MOREAN, Jno.	12	M	Unknown	15Ja46Ei
LANDER, Jno.	13	M	Unknown	15Ja46Ei
ROSSETY, Miles	30	M	Unknown	15Ja46Ei
FLEMERY, Thos.	18	M	Unknown	15Ja46Ei
MURPHY, Owen	18	M	Unknown	15Ja46Ei
Pat	16	M	Unknown	15Ja46Ei
NEIL, Edwd.	26	M	Unknown	15Ja46Ei
RODGERS, Thos.	22	M	Unknown	15Ja46Ei
BARRY, Jas.	20	M	Unknown	15Ja46Ei
MULEY, Bridgt.	12	F	Unknown	15Ja46Ei
Margt.	14	F	Unknown	15Ja46Ei
MCQUEENY, Bridgt.	12	F	Unknown	15Ja46Ei
Ann	10	F	Unknown	15Ja46Ei
RODGERS, Barney	24	F	Unknown	15Ja46Ei
Margt.	50	F	Unknown	15Ja46Ei
Pat	13	M	Unknown	15Ja46Ei
Betty	16	F	Unknown	15Ja46Ei
Alice	12	F	Unknown	15Ja46Ei
BARRY, Mary	40	F	Unknown	15Ja46Ei
Pat	17	M	Unknown	15Ja46Ei
Jno.	15	M	Unknown	15Ja46Ei
Thos.	12	M	Unknown	15Ja46Ei
Edwd.	10	M	Unknown	15Ja46Ei
Cath.	7	F	Child	15Ja46Ei
Mary	13	F	Unknown	15Ja46Ei
KIRBY, Mary	27	F	Unknown	15Ja46Ei
Johannah	21	F	Unknown	15Ja46Ei
WEBB, Mary	20	F	Unknown	15Ja46Ei
LILLIES, Mary	13	F	Unknown	15Ja46Ei
KENT, Jas.	50	M	Unknown	15Ja46Ei
STAFFORD, Jno.	20	M	Unknown	15Ja46Ei
HIBB, Edwd.	24	M	Unknown	15Ja46Ei
LAWDER, Jno.	30	M	Unknown	15Ja46Ei
WATTS, Benj.	40	M	Unknown	15Ja46Ei
PARKER, Jno.	40	M	Unknown	15Ja46Ei
Mary	29	F	Unknown	15Ja46Ei
Herbert	15	M	Unknown	15Ja46Ei
Sarah	12	F	Unknown	15Ja46Ei
Mary-Ann	8	F	Child	15Ja46Ei
Jno.	7	M	Child	15Ja46Ei
KELLON, Joseph	38	M	Unknown	15Ja46Ei
Eliza	39	F	Unknown	15Ja46Ei
Eliza	26	F	Unknown	15Ja46Ei
Henry	11	M	Unknown	15Ja46Ei
Edwd.	8	M	Child	15Ja46Ei
Phillip	.00	M	Infant	15Ja46Ei
CHARLES, Thos.	31	M	Unknown	15Ja46Ei
Eliza	31	F	Unknown	15Ja46Ei
Larrnie	8	U	Child	15Ja46Ei
Antorie	4	U	Child	15Ja46Ei
Wesley	2	M	Child	15Ja46Ei
Luther	.00	M	Infant	15Ja46Ei
JACKSON, Charlotte	22	F	Unknown	15Ja46Ei
Wm.	44	M	Unknown	15Ja46Ei
ROBERTS, Geo.	36	M	Unknown	15Ja46Ei
Ellen	35	F	Unknown	15Ja46Ei
WATT, Jno.	46	M	Unknown	15Ja46Ei
PECK, Carrington	49	M	Unknown	15Ja46Ei
Francis	48	M	Unknown	15Ja46Ei
CHAPMAN, Martha	2	F	Child	15Ja46Ei
BOWMAN, Wm.	23	M	Unknown	15Ja46Ei
Emma	25	F	Unknown	15Ja46Ei
SELWAY, Jno.	32	M	Unknown	15Ja46Ei
Jane	30	F	Unknown	15Ja46Ei
HEBB, Martha	26	F	Unknown	15Ja46Ei
HASLAM, Margt.	50	F	Unknown	15Ja46Ei
Ann	13	F	Unknown	15Ja46Ei
SHEEN, Thos.	40	M	Unknown	15Ja46Ei
Margt.	43	F	Unknown	15Ja46Ei
GLINE, Bridget	20	F	Unknown	15Ja46Ei
TAYLOR, Ann	23	F	Unknown	15Ja46Ei
Wattson	.00	M	Infant	15Ja46Ei
BLACKWELL, Eliza	40	F	Unknown	15Ja46Ei
BAILEY, Mary	22	F	Unknown	15Ja46Ei
BARTLEY, Ellen	19	F	Unknown	15Ja46Ei
LOWNS, Eliza	22	F	Unknown	15Ja46Ei
VESAY, Medden	20	M	Unknown	15Ja46Ei
FARLEY, Michl.	44	M	Unknown	15Ja46Ei
JONE, Matthew	20	M	Unknown	15Ja46Ei
HELEY, Jeremiah	21	M	Unknown	15Ja46Ei
ELLIS, John	51	M	Unknown	15Ja46Ei
Sophia Died-At-Sea	45	F	Unknown	15Ja46Ei
Joseph	25	M	Unknown	15Ja46Ei
Hannah	16	F	Unknown	15Ja46Ei
Eliza	13	F	Unknown	15Ja46Ei
Mary-Ann	11	F	Unknown	15Ja46Ei
MAWEY, Pat	21	M	Unknown	15Ja46Ei
BANNON, Pat	23	M	Unknown	15Ja46Ei
ALEXANDER, Ellen	21	F	Unknown	15Ja46Ei
MCGUIRE, Mary	20	M	Unknown	15Ja46Ei
BERRY, Ellen	18	F	Unknown	15Ja46Ei
BROGAN, Mary	30	F	Unknown	15Ja46Ei
CARLIN, Bridget	12	F	Unknown	15Ja46Ei
TULLEY, Jno.	40	M	Unknown	15Ja46Ei
Mary	43	F	Unknown	15Ja46Ei
DEAN, Nancey Died-At-Sea	40	F	Unknown	15Ja46Ei
NICHLOR, Mary	21	F	Unknown	15Ja46Ei
DYSON, Esther	40	F	Unknown	15Ja46Ei
Francis	13	M	Unknown	15Ja46Ei
Joseph	10	M	Unknown	15Ja46Ei
MEREDITH, John	30	M	Unknown	15Ja46Ei
Maria	28	F	Unknown	15Ja46Ei

NAMES OF PASSENGERS	AGE	SEX	OCCUPATIONS	DATE PORT SHIP
MEREDITH, Mary	4	F	Child	15Ja46Ei
SMITH, Betty	20	F	Unknown	15Ja46Ei
Jas.	11	M	Unknown	15Ja46Ei
DELANEY, Jas.	28	M	Unknown	15Ja46Ei
Thos.	30	M	Unknown	15Ja46Ei
SHANNON, Denis	9	M	Child	15Ja46Ei
TRACEY, Danl.	10	M	Unknown	15Ja46Ei
HARDMAN, Wm.	10	M	Unknown	15Ja46Ei
TRONEY, Eliza	29	F	Unknown	15Ja46Ei
MCHIBBIN, Sarah	30	F	Unknown	15Ja46Ei
MORRISON, Betty	26	F	Unknown	15Ja46Ei
CASEY, Bridgt.	28	F	Unknown	15Ja46Ei
Jas.	.00	M	Infant	15Ja46Ei
TEENEY, Cath.	20	F	Unknown	15Ja46Ei
WEDLOCK, Mary	22	F	Unknown	15Ja46Ei
CULLIN, Cath.	19	F	Unknown	15Ja46Ei
DELANY, Margt.	20	F	Unknown	15Ja46Ei
Ellen	18	F	Unknown	15Ja46Ei
MOREAN, Susan	19	F	Unknown	15Ja46Ei
MCCORT, Margt.	20	F	Unknown	15Ja46Ei
SMITH, Cath.	12	F	Unknown	15Ja46Ei
MOREAN, Martha	21	F	Unknown	15Ja46Ei
CAIN, Ann	16	F	Unknown	15Ja46Ei
SMITH, Mor.	50	M	Unknown	15Ja46Ei
Jno.	27	M	Unknown	15Ja46Ei
DAWSON, Jas.	19	M	Unknown	15Ja46Ei
PALMER, Thos.	26	M	Unknown	15Ja46Ei
VERITY, Jno.	25	M	Unknown	15Ja46Ei
HORNER, Mary	60	F	Unknown	15Ja46Ei
LAMNEY, Isabella	20	F	Unknown	15Ja46Ei
Sarah	6	F	Child	15Ja46Ei
HAMILTON, Christopher	25	M	Unknown	15Ja46Ei
HUTCHISON, Robt.	11	M	Unknown	15Ja46Ei
MITCHELL, Pat	60	M	Unknown	15Ja46Ei
Bridgt.	56	F	Unknown	15Ja46Ei
CRANE, Andrew	24	M	Unknown	15Ja46Ei
CODDY, Jno.	19	M	Unknown	15Ja46Ei
SCULLY, Danl.	19	M	Unknown	15Ja46Ei
DOLAN, Pat	26	M	Unknown	15Ja46Ei
Mary	25	F	Unknown	15Ja46Ei
Mary	20	F	Unknown	15Ja46Ei
TRACEY, Ellen	23	F	Unknown	15Ja46Ei
LOGAN, Mary	22	F	Unknown	15Ja46Ei
BROWN, Edwd.	27	M	Unknown	15Ja46Ei
Ann	26	F	Unknown	15Ja46Ei
Michl.	.00	M	Infant	15Ja46Ei
Died-At-Sea				
Bridgt.	19	F	Unknown	15Ja46Ei
LINING, Mary	9	F	Child	15Ja46Ei
James	3	M	Child	15Ja46Ei
COYLE, Cath.	20	F	Unknown	15Ja46Ei
CAIN, Pat	31	M	Unknown	15Ja46Ei
Margt.	26	F	Unknown	15Ja46Ei
Ann	6	F	Child	15Ja46Ei
Dennis	3	M	Child	15Ja46Ei
TRANER, Michl.	30	M	Unknown	15Ja46Ei
Ellen	28	F	Unknown	15Ja46Ei
Thos.	.00	M	Infant	15Ja46Ei
DOWNEY, Pat	31	M	Unknown	15Ja46Ei
GORMAN, Edwd.	26	M	Unknown	15Ja46Ei
MANING, Bridgt.	38	F	Unknown	15Ja46Ei
MANSFIELD, Ellen	50	F	Unknown	15Ja46Ei
Bridgt.	15	F	Unknown	15Ja46Ei
MCALISTER, Cath.	12	F	Unknown	15Ja46Ei
LATHY, Betty	21	F	Unknown	15Ja46Ei
OGAN, Michl.	28	M	Unknown	15Ja46Ei
KELLY, Joseph	27	M	Unknown	15Ja46Ei
FARREL, Molachy	18	M	Unknown	15Ja46Ei
WEBB, Thos.	24	M	Unknown	15Ja46Ei
SULLIVAN, Martin	24	M	Unknown	15Ja46Ei
MOARE, Ellen	50	F	Unknown	15Ja46Ei
Jeremiah	16	F	Unknown	15Ja46Ei
Nicholas	12	F	Unknown	15Ja46Ei
Edmond	9	M	Child	15Ja46Ei
Hugh	6	M	Child	15Ja46Ei

NAMES OF PASSENGERS	AGE	SEX	OCCUPATIONS	DATE PORT SHIP
BEATTY, Martin	27	M	Unknown	15Ja46Ei
Jane-Ann	26	F	Unknown	15Ja46Ei
HENRY, Wm.	5	M	Child	15Ja46Ei
Eliza	3	F	Child	15Ja46Ei
Mary	.00	F	Infant	15Ja46Ei
MURPHY, Margt.	60	F	Unknown	15Ja46Ei
Wm.	20	M	Unknown	15Ja46Ei
Thos.	16	M	Unknown	15Ja46Ei
HEAGAN, Cath.	24	F	Unknown	15Ja46Ei
MCDONALD, Cath.	18	F	Unknown	15Ja46Ei
RUDDY, Pat	22	M	Unknown	15Ja46Ei
NULTY, Stephen	20	M	Unknown	15Ja46Ei
FARLEY, Pat	20	M	Unknown	15Ja46Ei
HAYES, Pat	21	M	Unknown	15Ja46Ei
SCANLAN, Pat	16	M	Unknown	15Ja46Ei
GERRITTY, Thos.	38	M	Unknown	15Ja46Ei
Hannah	30	F	Unknown	15Ja46Ei
Thos.	9	M	Child	15Ja46Ei
EVANS, Wm.	40	M	Unknown	15Ja46Ei
Richd.	16	M	Unknown	15Ja46Ei
SMITH, Mary	21	F	Unknown	15Ja46Ei
RIELY, Margt.	21	F	Unknown	15Ja46Ei
Margt.	18	F	Unknown	15Ja46Ei
MARTIN, Mary	18	F	Unknown	15Ja46Ei
BREADY, Cath.	19	F	Unknown	15Ja46Ei
BUCKLEY, Margt.	22	F	Unknown	15Ja46Ei
Martin	6	M	Child	15Ja46Ei
Jno.	5	M	Child	15Ja46Ei
KENNEDY, Mary	20	F	Unknown	15Ja46Ei
KIDD, Wm.	9	M	Child	15Ja46Ei
GLEANY, Mary	30	F	Unknown	15Ja46Ei
Anora	25	F	Unknown	15Ja46Ei
MCBRIDE, Isabela	20	F	Unknown	15Ja46Ei
BOYLAN, Judy	19	F	Unknown	15Ja46Ei
LYNCH, Mary	23	F	Unknown	15Ja46Ei
Ann	20	F	Unknown	15Ja46Ei
Cath.	12	F	Unknown	15Ja46Ei
Bridgt.	19	F	Unknown	15Ja46Ei
CURRIN, Mary	20	F	Unknown	15Ja46Ei
CLARK, Bridgt.	50	F	Unknown	15Ja46Ei
Ellen	19	F	Unknown	15Ja46Ei
BURNE, Ann	19	F	Unknown	15Ja46Ei
MULVEY, Peter	12	M	Unknown	15Ja46Ei
CONNOR, Ann	35	F	Unknown	15Ja46Ei
Mary	12	F	Unknown	15Ja46Ei
Margt.	11	F	Unknown	15Ja46Ei
COLE, Mary	19	F	Unknown	15Ja46Ei
MCQUADE, Mary	25	F	Unknown	15Ja46Ei
Pat	4	M	Child	15Ja46Ei
COUGHLAN, Michl.	23	M	Unknown	15Ja46Ei
HANEVIN, James	30	M	Unknown	15Ja46Ei
GILANAN, Henry	23	M	Unknown	15Ja46Ei
GARGAN, Mary	6	F	Child	15Ja46Ei
BURNS, Ann	8	F	Child	15Ja46Ei
ALLEN, Jno.	24	M	Unknown	15Ja46Ei
BURNS, Ellen	10	F	Unknown	15Ja46Ei
U, U	.00	U	Infant	15Ja46Ei
U	.00	U	Infant	15Ja46Ei

SIR-WM.MOLESWORTH 16 JANUARY 1850

From St.Thomas And Bermuda

NAMES OF PASSENGERS	AGE	SEX	OCCUPATIONS	DATE PORT SHIP
WELCH, Ellen	30	F	Unknown	16Ja25Eb
DIMAN, Kitty	30	F	Unknown	16Ja25Eb
QUIRK, Timothy	24	M	Unknown	16Ja25Eb
BOYDEN, Pat	24	M	Unknown	16Ja25Eb
SULLIVAN, Tim	24	M	Unknown	16Ja25Eb
MURPHY, Thos.	20	M	Unknown	16Ja25Eb

NAMES OF PASSENGERS	AGE	SEX	OCCUPATIONS	DATE PORT SHIP
MURPHY, Agnes	18	F	Unknown	16Ja25Eb
SULLIVAN, Nancy	20	F	Unknown	16Ja25Eb
KENNEDY, Mary	40	F	Unknown	16Ja25Eb
Ellen	11	F	Unknown	16Ja25Eb
Peggy	8	F	Child	16Ja25Eb
Mary	5	F	Child	16Ja25Eb
Tommy	3	M	Child	16Ja25Eb
Arrey	.06	M	Infant	16Ja25Eb
SULLIVAN, Mary	40	F	Unknown	16Ja25Eb
Wm.	13	M	Unknown	16Ja25Eb
Margt.	10	F	Unknown	16Ja25Eb
Bess	8	F	Child	16Ja25Eb
Mary	6	F	Child	16Ja25Eb
Lewis	.04	M	Infant	16Ja25Eb
CODY, Wm.	57	M	Unknown	16Ja25Eb
John	19	M	Unknown	16Ja25Eb
Pat	17	M	Unknown	16Ja25Eb
KEFFER, Arthur	.02	M	Infant	16Ja25Eb
MURPHY, Mic	30	M	Unknown	16Ja25Eb
Johanna	25	F	Unknown	16Ja25Eb
Margt.	4	F	Child	16Ja25Eb
Wm.	.06	M	Infant	16Ja25Eb
TOUMAY, Bridget	21	F	Unknown	16Ja25Eb
LYONS, Johanna	20	F	Unknown	16Ja25Eb
CLAFFERS, Mary	20	F	Unknown	16Ja25Eb
HENNESSY, Jas.	20	M	Unknown	16Ja25Eb
Mary	40	F	Unknown	16Ja25Eb
Mary	2	F	Child	16Ja25Eb
Ellen	.06	F	Infant	16Ja25Eb
HURLEY, Ellen	10	F	Unknown	16Ja25Eb
HARTRUTT, Ellen	20	F	Unknown	16Ja25Eb
LEARY, Cathe.	20	F	Unknown	16Ja25Eb
WALCH, Richd.	20	M	Unknown	16Ja25Eb
Mary	20	F	Unknown	16Ja25Eb
TUCKER, Arry	20	M	Unknown	16Ja25Eb
James	6	M	Child	16Ja25Eb
SULLIVAN, Johanna	20	F	Unknown	16Ja25Eb
WALCH, John	24	M	Unknown	16Ja25Eb
RHYS, John	20	M	Unknown	16Ja25Eb
MORRISARY, Nancy	30	F	Unknown	16Ja25Eb
Jeremiah	2	M	Child	16Ja25Eb
HEALY, Mary	30	F	Unknown	16Ja25Eb
DONOHUE, Dennis	30	M	Unknown	16Ja25Eb
Betty	30	F	Unknown	16Ja25Eb
Ellen	7	F	Child	16Ja25Eb
Mary	.03	F	Infant	16Ja25Eb
Dennis	20	M	Unknown	16Ja25Eb
Silvester	20	M	Unknown	16Ja25Eb
Mary	30	F	Unknown	16Ja25Eb
Silvester	16	M	Unknown	16Ja25Eb
Dennis	12	F	Unknown	16Ja25Eb
Hannah	9	F	Child	16Ja25Eb
Mary	7	F	Child	16Ja25Eb
Peggy	6	F	Child	16Ja25Eb
Bridget	.06	F	Infant	16Ja25Eb
HEALY, John	12	M	Unknown	16Ja25Eb
MURPHY, Paddy	20	M	Unknown	16Ja25Eb
FITZPATRICK, Billy	20	M	Unknown	16Ja25Eb
CRUM, M.N.	20	M	Unknown	16Ja25Eb
SHEEHAN, Danl.	20	M	Unknown	16Ja25Eb
BYRNES, Darby	40	M	Unknown	16Ja25Eb
Wm.	12	M	Unknown	16Ja25Eb
John	10	M	Unknown	16Ja25Eb
Mary	9	F	Child	16Ja25Eb
HARLEY, Mary	22	F	Unknown	16Ja25Eb
Bess	20	F	Unknown	16Ja25Eb
RICHLEY, Richd.	20	M	Unknown	16Ja25Eb
LINEHAN, Timothy	25	M	Unknown	16Ja25Eb
ARTHUR, Mincy	40	M	Unknown	16Ja25Eb
Matt	12	M	Unknown	16Ja25Eb
CULVERSEN, Mich.	26	M	Unknown	16Ja25Eb
TIMMS, Mich.	28	M	Unknown	16Ja25Eb
GRIFFIN, Jane	20	F	Unknown	16Ja25Eb
HAMOGAN, John	35	M	Unknown	16Ja25Eb
Ellen	30	F	Unknown	16Ja25Eb
HAMOGAN, David	16	M	Unknown	16Ja25Eb
Mary	18	F	Unknown	16Ja25Eb
Nory	.06	F	Infant	16Ja25Eb
MCALLEN, Ennis	30	M	Infant	16Ja25Eb
LYNCH, Mgt.	30	F	Infant	16Ja25Eb
John	10	M	Infant	16Ja25Eb
Julia	8	F	Child	16Ja25Eb
Danl.	2	M	Child	16Ja25Eb
Ellen	.05	F	Infant	16Ja25Eb
FLYNN, Julia	20	F	Unknown	16Ja25Eb
CURRIE, Cathe.	20	F	Unknown	16Ja25Eb
CALLAGAN, Cath.	20	F	Unknown	16Ja25Eb
WALCH, Mat	20	M	Unknown	16Ja25Eb
MAHONEY, Jerry	24	M	Unknown	16Ja25Eb
SHEBEEN, John	24	M	Unknown	16Ja25Eb
SHATTERY, Ellen	16	F	Unknown	16Ja25Eb
SIMMONDS, Jas.	20	M	Unknown	16Ja25Eb
MULLACHY, Thos.	20	M	Unknown	16Ja25Eb
KINNERY, Ellen	20	F	Unknown	16Ja25Eb
NEIR, John	35	M	Unknown	16Ja25Eb
Joanna	30	F	Unknown	16Ja25Eb
James	8	F	Child	16Ja25Eb
Thos.	6	M	Child	16Ja25Eb
Mary	4	F	Child	16Ja25Eb
Felix	.06	M	Infant	16Ja25Eb
LONG, Cathe.	30	F	Unknown	16Ja25Eb
Mary	20	F	Unknown	16Ja25Eb
Thos.	22	M	Unknown	16Ja25Eb
WALLACE, Julia	20	F	Unknown	16Ja25Eb
FITZGERALD, Eliza	30	F	Unknown	16Ja25Eb
Mary	2	F	Child	16Ja25Eb
Kitty	7	F	Child	16Ja25Eb
Pat	.11	M	Infant	16Ja25Eb
CASTILLO, John	20	M	Unknown	16Ja25Eb
SULLIVAN, Mary	35	F	Unknown	16Ja25Eb
Pat	6	M	Child	16Ja25Eb
Jerry	4	F	Child	16Ja25Eb
SHIELDS, Hannah	30	F	Unknown	16Ja25Eb
Mary	12	F	Unknown	16Ja25Eb
LYONS, Mary	18	F	Unknown	16Ja25Eb
Cathe.	16	F	Unknown	16Ja25Eb
MALONEY, Cathe.	20	F	Unknown	16Ja25Eb
MCDONALD, Hannah	30	F	Unknown	16Ja25Eb
COLLINS, Ann	19	F	Unknown	16Ja25Eb
GREEN, Mary	20	F	Unknown	16Ja25Eb
Tommy	22	M	Unknown	16Ja25Eb
MURPHY, Manance	26	M	Unknown	16Ja25Eb
COLLINS, Daniel	25	M	Unknown	16Ja25Eb
MULACHY, Julia	20	F	Unknown	16Ja25Eb
HOGARD, Betty	20	F	Unknown	16Ja25Eb
Mary	11	F	Unknown	16Ja25Eb
ONEILL, Mary	20	F	Unknown	16Ja25Eb
WELCH, Mary	20	F	Unknown	16Ja25Eb
COLLINS, Bridget	20	F	Unknown	16Ja25Eb
MCGARTHY, John	20	M	Unknown	16Ja25Eb
LEANE, Pat	20	M	Unknown	16Ja25Eb
DRISCOLL, Cathe.	20	F	Unknown	16Ja25Eb
SULLIVAN, Pat	30	M	Unknown	16Ja25Eb
Jerry	30	M	Unknown	16Ja25Eb
Jerry	13	M	Unknown	16Ja25Eb
Eugene	25	M	Unknown	16Ja25Eb
Bridget	20	F	Unknown	16Ja25Eb
SLYNE, Dennis	40	M	Unknown	16Ja25Eb
Ellen	40	F	Unknown	16Ja25Eb
James	12	M	Unknown	16Ja25Eb
John	10	M	Unknown	16Ja25Eb
REGAN, Pat	21	M	Unknown	16Ja25Eb
Margt.	18	F	Unknown	16Ja25Eb
SLYNE, Thos.	.08	M	Infant	16Ja25Eb
BARRY, Betsy	24	F	Unknown	16Ja25Eb
FORD, Mary	30	F	Unknown	16Ja25Eb
RYAN, Johanna	40	F	Unknown	16Ja25Eb
Bassey	10	F	Unknown	16Ja25Eb
Wm.	7	M	Child	16Ja25Eb
MOLAN, Mary	25	F	Unknown	16Ja25Eb

NAMES OF PASSENGERS	AGE	SEX	OCCUPATIONS	DATE PORT SHIP
SULLIVAN, John	40	M	Unknown	16Ja25Eb
Johanna	40	F	Unknown	16Ja25Eb
Jas.	12	M	Unknown	16Ja25Eb
Mary	5	F	Child	16Ja25Eb
KENNEDY, Mary	13	F	Unknown	16Ja25Eb
MARTIN, Mary	13	F	Unknown	16Ja25Eb
Pat	12	M	Unknown	16Ja25Eb
KENNEDY, Margt.	35	F	Unknown	16Ja25Eb
John	10	M	Unknown	16Ja25Eb
Kitty	3	F	Child	16Ja25Eb
Ellen	.09	F	Infant	16Ja25Eb
KELLIGAN, John	13	M	Unknown	16Ja25Eb
CORRAN, John	25	M	Unknown	16Ja25Eb
DONOGHUE, Mary	20	F	Unknown	16Ja25Eb
CROWLY, Corry	20	M	Unknown	16Ja25Eb
ONEILL, Cathe.	26	F	Unknown	16Ja25Eb
John	9	M	Child	16Ja25Eb
Nelly	7	F	Child	16Ja25Eb
Tom	3	M	Child	16Ja25Eb
Jas.	.10	M	Infant	16Ja25Eb
MCCARTHY, Mgt.	50	F	Unknown	16Ja25Eb
DOWD, Corry	22	M	Unknown	16Ja25Eb
MCCARTHY, Mgt.	30	F	Unknown	16Ja25Eb
GALLAGHER, Kitty	13	F	Unknown	16Ja25Eb
Silvester	7	M	Child	16Ja25Eb
EVANS, Mary	30	F	Unknown	16Ja25Eb
Wm.	6	M	Child	16Ja25Eb
Jeremiah	2	M	Child	16Ja25Eb
MACHEM, Mic	30	M	Unknown	16Ja25Eb
ALLEN, Thos.	20	M	Unknown	16Ja25Eb
SULLIVAN, Jerry	24	M	Unknown	16Ja25Eb
GORMAN, Danl.	20	M	Unknown	16Ja25Eb
SHEBEEN, Mary	22	F	Unknown	16Ja25Eb
Danl.	2	M	Child	16Ja25Eb
KEFFER, Wm.	20	M	Unknown	16Ja25Eb
CANE, John	24	M	Unknown	16Ja25Eb

FIDELIA 17 JANUARY 1850

From Liverpool

NAMES OF PASSENGERS	AGE	SEX	OCCUPATIONS	DATE PORT SHIP
CONNOR, Bernard	38	M	Farmer	17Ja02Eh
Martin	33	M	Farmer	17Ja02Eh
CARR, Thomas	36	M	Farmer	17Ja02Eh
MANSFIELD, Priscilla	23	F	Milliner	17Ja02Eh
CUMMING, James	14	M	Unknown	17Ja02Eh
John	11	M	Unknown	17Ja02Eh
MCHUGH, John	28	M	Clerk	17Ja02Eh
BOWEN, Ellen	45	F	Unknown	17Ja02Eh
MCDERMOTT, Michl.	20	M	Clerk	17Ja02Eh
MULHERN, Dennis	38	M	Minister	17Ja02Eh
Elizabeth	17	F	Unknown	17Ja02Eh
Jane	37	F	Unknown	17Ja02Eh
Robt.John	16	M	Unknown	17Ja02Eh
William	14	M	Unknown	17Ja02Eh
Daniel	13	M	Unknown	17Ja02Eh
Ann	11	F	Unknown	17Ja02Eh
James	8	M	Child	17Ja02Eh
Vesey	4	F	Child	17Ja02Eh
Harriet	.00	F	Infant	17Ja02Eh
MCKIM, Ann	23	F	Unknown	17Ja02Eh
Elizabeth	50	F	Unknown	17Ja02Eh
Elizabeth	26	F	Unknown	17Ja02Eh
MIDDLETON, Elizabeth	9	F	Child	17Ja02Eh
BRADSHAW, William	30	M	Schm	17Ja02Eh
HOGAN, John	14	M	Unknown	17Ja02Eh
REILLY, Christopher	25	M	Laborer	17Ja02Eh
Elizabeth	20	F	Unknown	17Ja02Eh
WELDOW, Honoria	20	F	Unknown	17Ja02Eh
MCQUAID, Terence	35	M	Laborer	17Ja02Eh
Biddy	10	F	Unknown	17Ja02Eh
Patrick	6	M	Child	17Ja02Eh
MCCANN, Patrick	20	M	Laborer	17Ja02Eh
TRAINOR, Ellen	18	F	Servant	17Ja02Eh
MCHUGH, Patrick	17	M	Laborer	17Ja02Eh
Mary	10	F	Unknown	17Ja02Eh
MCCORMICK, Jane	19	F	Unknown	17Ja02Eh
James	55	M	Unknown	17Ja02Eh
Mary	53	F	Unknown	17Ja02Eh
CALLAHAN, Johanna	22	F	Milliner	17Ja02Eh
Julia	14	F	Unknown	17Ja02Eh
Patrick	18	M	Laborer	17Ja02Eh
Mary	18	F	Unknown	17Ja02Eh
Terence	.00	M	Infant	17Ja02Eh
GALLAGHER, Mary	40	F	Unknown	17Ja02Eh
Mary	26	F	Unknown	17Ja02Eh
Ann	6	F	Child	17Ja02Eh
James	.00	M	Infant	17Ja02Eh
FITZSIMON, Cath.	10	F	Unknown	17Ja02Eh
WRIGHT, Bridget	35	F	Unknown	17Ja02Eh
Catherine	35	F	Unknown	17Ja02Eh
Julia	8	F	Child	17Ja02Eh
Martha	8	F	Child	17Ja02Eh
John	5	M	Child	17Ja02Eh
ACHISON, William	22	M	Laborer	17Ja02Eh
Margaret	20	F	Unknown	17Ja02Eh
MCCONNOR, Michael	30	M	Hairdresser	17Ja02Eh
Antony	20	M	Laborer	17Ja02Eh
Bernard	20	M	Laborer	17Ja02Eh
Jane	18	F	Milliner	17Ja02Eh
Catherine	16	F	Unknown	17Ja02Eh
DOUGHERTY, Patrick	26	M	Laborer	17Ja02Eh
BRADY, Charles	20	M	Laborer	17Ja02Eh
CONNACHAN, Martin	22	M	Laborer	17Ja02Eh
MURPHY, Hugh	26	M	Laborer	17Ja02Eh
MCCOURT, Mary	25	F	Spinner	17Ja02Eh
MIDDLETON, Susan	25	F	Milliner	17Ja02Eh
EGAN, John	21	M	Laborer	17Ja02Eh
KELLY, Thomas	70	M	Laborer	17Ja02Eh
HEFFRON, Patrick	35	M	Laborer	17Ja02Eh
Mary	30	F	Unknown	17Ja02Eh
Catherine	.00	F	Infant	17Ja02Eh
GLYNN, Anne	20	F	Servant	17Ja02Eh
MCGUIRE, Mary	10	F	Unknown	17Ja02Eh
TOLL, Alice	20	F	Servant	17Ja02Eh
HIGGINS, James	35	M	Mason	17Ja02Eh
TRIMBLE, James	35	M	Sawer	17Ja02Eh
HIGGINS, John	18	M	Blacksmith	17Ja02Eh
MCSHAW, Patrick	16	M	Servant	17Ja02Eh
KILMURRY, Peter	21	M	Laborer	17Ja02Eh
FAGAN, Patrick	27	M	Laborer	17Ja02Eh
SWEENEY, Patrick	20	M	Laborer	17Ja02Eh
OAKLEY, Patrick	35	M	Laborer	17Ja02Eh
CHAMLEY, Thomas	28	M	Clerk	17Ja02Eh
MORAN, John	29	M	Laborer	17Ja02Eh
DALY, Charles	10	M	Unknown	17Ja02Eh
GROGAN, John	29	M	Laborer	17Ja02Eh
TRIMBLE, Biddy	18	F	Servant	17Ja02Eh
Winifred	27	F	Unknown	17Ja02Eh
MCSHEEHAN, Catherine	14	F	Unknown	17Ja02Eh
Nancy	5	F	Child	17Ja02Eh
MCKEOW, Margaret	15	F	Unknown	17Ja02Eh
BELL, William	22	M	Farmer	17Ja02Eh
OAKELEY, William	30	M	Laborer	17Ja02Eh
Nancy	30	F	Unknown	17Ja02Eh
Catherine	8	F	Child	17Ja02Eh
Maria	8	F	Child	17Ja02Eh
SLONEY, Margaret	26	F	Servant	17Ja02Eh
MOHAM, Mary	24	F	Unknown	17Ja02Eh
GRAVEL, Mary	22	F	Servant	17Ja02Eh
GEHAN, Michael	26	M	Laborer	17Ja02Eh
BENMOM, John	36	M	Laborer	17Ja02Eh
MARTIN, Mary	45	F	Unknown	17Ja02Eh
Eliza	12	F	Unknown	17Ja02Eh

NAMES OF PASSENGERS	AGE	SEX	OCCUPATIONS	DATE PORT SHIP
MARTIN, Elizabeth	11	F	Unknown	17Ja02Eh
Patrick	8	M	Child	17Ja02Eh
BURKE, Mary	28	F	Unknown	17Ja02Eh
Ann	21	F	Unknown	17Ja02Eh
Thomas	21	M	Laborer	17Ja02Eh
Walker	.00	M	Infant	17Ja02Eh
EVEY, Bridget	29	F	Unknown	17Ja02Eh
John	3	M	Child	17Ja02Eh
Thomas	5	M	Child	17Ja02Eh
GALLAGHER, Mary	31	F	Unknown	17Ja02Eh
Catherine	.00	F	Infant	17Ja02Eh
DEVINE, Mary	17	F	Servant	17Ja02Eh
MCCARTT, Ann	25	F	Servant	17Ja02Eh
DALTON, Bridget	12	F	Unknown	17Ja02Eh
Martin	9	M	Child	17Ja02Eh
Winifred	49	F	Unknown	17Ja02Eh
BARRY, Catherine	38	F	Unknown	17Ja02Eh
QUINN, Ann	30	F	Unknown	17Ja02Eh
LOFTUS, Patrick	50	M	Mason	17Ja02Eh
Anthony	18	M	Blacksmith	17Ja02Eh
Catherine	14	F	Unknown	17Ja02Eh
Thomas	12	M	Unknown	17Ja02Eh
Mary	10	F	Unknown	17Ja02Eh
Biddy	20	F	Unknown	17Ja02Eh
FLAHERTY, Mary	23	F	Milliner	17Ja02Eh
MALOY, Rose	17	F	Unknown	17Ja02Eh
MCCARTT, Sarah	23	F	Unknown	17Ja02Eh
MCMAKEN, Ann	22	F	Unknown	17Ja02Eh
LYNCH, John	35	M	Farmer	17Ja02Eh
DOLAN, Richard	20	M	Laborer	17Ja02Eh
FOGARTY, Kennedy	27	M	Laborer	17Ja02Eh
DELANY, Thomas	20	M	Shoemaker	17Ja02Eh
SHORTLER, Patrick	23	M	Laborer	17Ja02Eh
DUNN, Mark	20	M	Laborer	17Ja02Eh
REDDICAN, Peter	14	M	Unknown	17Ja02Eh
EGAN, John	20	M	Laborer	17Ja02Eh
DOYLE, Miles	16	M	Unknown	17Ja02Eh
CARSON, Mary	35	F	Unknown	17Ja02Eh
MOLANY, Mary	40	F	Unknown	17Ja02Eh
Thomas	4	M	Child	17Ja02Eh
Catherine	6	F	Child	17Ja02Eh
Alice	8	F	Child	17Ja02Eh
MCHUGH, Patrick	25	M	Laborer	17Ja02Eh
Catherine	22	F	Unknown	17Ja02Eh
Michael	3	M	Child	17Ja02Eh
James	.00	M	Infant	17Ja02Eh
PARK, Isaac	22	M	Cbtmkr	17Ja02Eh
WILKIN, Thomas	22	M	Laborer	17Ja02Eh
KIERNAN, Edward	19	M	Laborer	17Ja02Eh
SHEEHAN, Dennis	20	M	Laborer	17Ja02Eh
BRYANT, Daniel	17	M	Laborer	17Ja02Eh
GALLAGHER, Patrick	21	M	Laborer	17Ja02Eh
GRIMES, Catherine	40	F	Unknown	17Ja02Eh
Mary	15	F	Unknown	17Ja02Eh
Thomas	9	M	Child	17Ja02Eh
Catherine	7	F	Child	17Ja02Eh
William	5	M	Child	17Ja02Eh
Francis	3	M	Child	17Ja02Eh
FAY, Anne	64	F	Unknown	17Ja02Eh
Mary	24	F	Servant	17Ja02Eh
FOLEY, Mary	17	F	Servant	17Ja02Eh
HOGAN, Thomas	35	M	Laborer	17Ja02Eh
MCCARTHY, Justin	22	M	Laborer	17Ja02Eh
CARTHY, Mary	19	F	Unknown	17Ja02Eh
Catherine	13	F	Unknown	17Ja02Eh
Michael	11	M	Unknown	17Ja02Eh
MEAGHER, Alice	19	F	Servant	17Ja02Eh
COGHLAN, Nancy	16	F	Unknown	17Ja02Eh
DOLAN, Mary	20	F	Unknown	17Ja02Eh
HOAR, Ellen	22	F	Unknown	17Ja02Eh
MEE, John	22	M	Laborer	17Ja02Eh
MCGREIG, Alice	23	F	Unknown	17Ja02Eh
CREILLY, Catherine	21	F	Servant	17Ja02Eh
CAHILL, Patrick	33	M	Laborer	17Ja02Eh
DUFFY, Thomas	20	M	Laborer	17Ja02Eh
CUNWISKY, John	22	M	Laborer	17Ja02Eh
CAVE, John	22	M	Laborer	17Ja02Eh
MILLER, Nancy	20	F	Servant	17Ja02Eh
MALONE, Judy	17	F	Unknown	17Ja02Eh
SLATTERY, Daniel	36	M	Laborer	17Ja02Eh
Ellen	35	F	Unknown	17Ja02Eh
KERRIGAN, John	13	M	Unknown	17Ja02Eh
MALONEY, Mary	18	F	Unknown	17Ja02Eh
SULLIVAN, Michael	30	M	Laborer	17Ja02Eh
Catherine	28	F	Unknown	17Ja02Eh
QUINN, Charles	23	M	Farmer	17Ja02Eh
Jane	9	F	Child	17Ja02Eh
RODEN, Anne	18	F	Unknown	17Ja02Eh
Rose	15	F	Unknown	17Ja02Eh
MCGHEE, Ann	24	F	Servant	17Ja02Eh
CONLAN, Bridget	14	F	Unknown	17Ja02Eh
MCMANUS, Mary	16	F	Unknown	17Ja02Eh
KEOUGH, Ann	20	F	Servant	17Ja02Eh
COR, Catherine	16	F	Unknown	17Ja02Eh
GORMAN, Catherine	18	F	Servant	17Ja02Eh
BRADY, Patrick	30	M	Laborer	17Ja02Eh
Anne	28	F	Unknown	17Ja02Eh
Peter	.00	M	Infant	17Ja02Eh
LYNCH, John	18	M	Laborer	17Ja02Eh
Judy	13	F	Unknown	17Ja02Eh
COYLE, Peter	15	M	Unknown	17Ja02Eh
DOUGHERTY, Owen	28	M	Laborer	17Ja02Eh
DOLAN, Patrick	17	M	Laborer	17Ja02Eh
RICHIE, Peter	49	M	Weaver	17Ja02Eh
Isabella	44	F	Unknown	17Ja02Eh
Mary-Ann	18	F	Unknown	17Ja02Eh
Sarah-Jane	16	F	Unknown	17Ja02Eh
John	14	M	Unknown	17Ja02Eh
Peter	12	M	Unknown	17Ja02Eh
Patrick	10	M	Unknown	17Ja02Eh
Biddy	8	F	Child	17Ja02Eh
John	36	M	Laborer	17Ja02Eh
Sarah	28	F	Unknown	17Ja02Eh
John	12	M	Unknown	17Ja02Eh
Michael	8	M	Child	17Ja02Eh
Mary	6	F	Child	17Ja02Eh
Ann-Jane	3	F	Child	17Ja02Eh
Peter	.00	M	Infant	17Ja02Eh
ROURKE, Catherine	30	F	Unknown	17Ja02Eh
Ann	8	F	Child	17Ja02Eh
Catherine	6	F	Child	17Ja02Eh
BAXTER, Hugh	36	M	Laborer	17Ja02Eh
WALLACE, Bridget	22	F	Servant	17Ja02Eh
MCKEON, Mary	33	F	Unknown	17Ja02Eh
Catherine	6	F	Child	17Ja02Eh
Maria	2	F	Child	17Ja02Eh
FAUGHANAN, Edward	45	M	Laborer	17Ja02Eh
Nancy	45	F	Unknown	17Ja02Eh
Ann	14	F	Unknown	17Ja02Eh
Catherine	12	F	Unknown	17Ja02Eh
Edward	8	M	Child	17Ja02Eh
HUGHES, Mary	18	F	Servant	17Ja02Eh
MCEBRADDEN, Thomas	19	M	Laborer	17Ja02Eh
DONOHO, James	12	M	Unknown	17Ja02Eh
Arthur	10	M	Unknown	17Ja02Eh
ROURKE, Anthony	15	M	Unknown	17Ja02Eh
CONLAN, Peter	25	M	Laborer	17Ja02Eh
CLANCEY, Mary	16	F	Unknown	17Ja02Eh
DOOHEY, Catherine	18	F	Unknown	17Ja02Eh
KELLY, Malachi	22	M	Laborer	17Ja02Eh
CONWAY, Peter	7	M	Child	17Ja02Eh
Mary	6	F	Child	17Ja02Eh
GALLAGHER, Ann	24	F	Servant	17Ja02Eh
FLANNEGAN, Ann	13	F	Unknown	17Ja02Eh
DUNN, Mary	15	F	Servant	17Ja02Eh
Michael	12	M	Unknown	17Ja02Eh
Mary	9	F	Child	17Ja02Eh
DOYLE, Miles	17	M	Laborer	17Ja02Eh
DODD, Beth	25	F	Servant	17Ja02Eh
MOONEY, John	50	M	Laborer	17Ja02Eh

NAMES OF PASSENGERS	AGE	SEX	OCCUPATIONS	DATE PORT SHIP
MOONEY, Patrick	18	M	Laborer	17Ja02Eh
Michael	14	M	Unknown	17Ja02Eh
Thomas	12	M	Unknown	17Ja02Eh
John	7	M	Child	17Ja02Eh
Mary	20	F	Unknown	17Ja02Eh
Bridget	16	F	Unknown	17Ja02Eh
Margaret	15	F	Unknown	17Ja02Eh
Winifred	13	F	Unknown	17Ja02Eh

VANDALIA 17 JANUARY 1850

From Liverpool

NAMES OF PASSENGERS	AGE	SEX	OCCUPATIONS	DATE PORT SHIP
FINNEGAN, Mary	35	F	Spinster	17Ja02Eg
CAHILL, Bridget	14	F	Spinster	17Ja02Eg
GAFFNEY, Mary	9	F	Child	17Ja02Eg
EDDINGTON, Elizabeth	22	F	Spinster	17Ja02Eg
BATTRY, Allice	26	F	Matron	17Ja02Eg
Emma	3	F	Child	17Ja02Eg
Jane	.10	F	Infant	17Ja02Eg
RYAN, Daniel	20	M	Laborer	17Ja02Eg
FLANNERY, Peggy	20	F	Nurse	17Ja02Eg
KENNEDY, Peggy	22	F	Nurse	17Ja02Eg
KANE, Martin	23	M	Laborer	17Ja02Eg
MURPHY, Catharine	17	F	Spinster	17Ja02Eg
DUNN, Kearn	24	M	Laborer	17Ja02Eg
MAHER, Sally	23	F	Matron	17Ja02Eg
HEANAHON, Michael	27	M	Laborer	17Ja02Eg
WELSH, John	25	M	Laborer	17Ja02Eg
COLEMAN, Patt	26	M	Laborer	17Ja02Eg
SHERIDAN, Margaret	40	F	Nurse	17Ja02Eg
Thomas	12	M	Laborer	17Ja02Eg
Catharine	10	F	Laborer	17Ja02Eg
Brien	8	M	Child	17Ja02Eg
CUNNINGHAM, Michael	30	M	Laborer	17Ja02Eg
Margaret	10	F	Unknown	17Ja02Eg
MCCANN, Peter	23	M	Laborer	17Ja02Eg
Mary	22	F	Spinster	17Ja02Eg
SUTLIFFE, Ann	27	F	Spinster	17Ja02Eg
COOLEY, Mary	20	F	Spinster	17Ja02Eg
Catharine	27	F	Spinster	17Ja02Eg
BRODDEY, Bridget	27	F	Spinster	17Ja02Eg
DOYLE, John	40	M	Laborer	17Ja02Eg
DONAGHUE, Mary	25	F	Spinster	17Ja02Eg
CONNOR, John	35	M	Laborer	17Ja02Eg
Ann	30	F	Wife	17Ja02Eg
Biddy	4	F	Child	17Ja02Eg
Ann	2	F	Child	17Ja02Eg
Patt	.00	M	Infant	17Ja02Eg
CAIN, Peggy	19	F	Spinster	17Ja02Eg
DOUGHERTY, John	25	M	Laborer	17Ja02Eg
CULLEN, Ellen	23	F	Spinster	17Ja02Eg
RATTIGAN, Patt	22	M	Laborer	17Ja02Eg
Ann	11	F	Spinster	17Ja02Eg
HERRON, Mary	40	F	Nurse	17Ja02Eg
REGAN, Daniel	32	M	Laborer	17Ja02Eg
U (W)	30	F	Wife	17Ja02Eg
John	.00	M	Infant	17Ja02Eg
Died-At-Sea				
MURPHY, Cornelius	60	M	Laborer	17Ja02Eg
U-Mrs.	50	F	Laborer	17Ja02Eg
Mary-Ann	.11	F	Infant	17Ja02Eg
Barthw.	24	M	Laborer	17Ja02Eg
Patrick	22	M	Laborer	17Ja02Eg
BYRNES, Mary	18	F	Spinster	17Ja02Eg
SALLY, Mary	18	F	Spinster	17Ja02Eg
KELLY, Rose	16	F	Spinster	17Ja02Eg
Bridget	40	F	Spinster	17Ja02Eg
MEARMLTY, Peggy	20	F	Spinster	17Ja02Eg
SHERIDAN, Peggy	20	F	Spinster	17Ja02Eg
LEWIS, William	59	M	Laborer	17Ja02Eg
David	28	M	Laborer	17Ja02Eg
FARRELL, Patrick	21	M	Laborer	17Ja02Eg
MCCABE, Beranrd	22	M	Laborer	17Ja02Eg
MULLEN, John	26	M	Laborer	17Ja02Eg
FITZPATRICK, Biddy	18	F	Spinster	17Ja02Eg
HART, Patt	18	M	Laborer	17Ja02Eg
BAMBRICK, Thomas	40	M	Laborer	17Ja02Eg
Judy	15	F	Spinster	17Ja02Eg
BRENNAN, Kate	16	F	Spinster	17Ja02Eg
HANLON, Jane	23	F	Spinster	17Ja02Eg
MAHER, William	21	M	Laborer	17Ja02Eg
HARRIGAN, Patt	24	M	Laborer	17Ja02Eg
Peter	22	M	Laborer	17Ja02Eg
Mary	20	F	Spinster	17Ja02Eg
MULLEN, Peter	25	M	Laborer	17Ja02Eg
Allice	25	F	Spinster	17Ja02Eg
RILEY, Michael	40	M	Laborer	17Ja02Eg
HARRIGAN, Ann	19	F	Spinster	17Ja02Eg
James	.00	M	Infant	17Ja02Eg
MULLEN, Edward	.00	M	Infant	17Ja02Eg
MULLIGAN, Nancy	28	F	Spinster	17Ja02Eg
Pat	.00	M	Infant	17Ja02Eg
Peter	21	M	Laborer	17Ja02Eg
HANNELL, Adam	22	M	Laborer	17Ja02Eg
CORCORAN, Martha	48	F	Nurse	17Ja02Eg
MCCAW, John	24	M	Laborer	17Ja02Eg
MORISAY, John	20	M	Laborer	17Ja02Eg
CORBETT, John	25	M	Laborer	17Ja02Eg
HEFFEREN, Mary	20	F	Spinster	17Ja02Eg
CUDDYHA, Michael	40	M	Laborer	17Ja02Eg
Edward	22	M	Laborer	17Ja02Eg
Mary	20	F	Spinster	17Ja02Eg
REDDY, Michael	22	M	Laborer	17Ja02Eg
HAW, Catharine	54	F	Nurse	17Ja02Eg
Catharine	18	F	Nurse	17Ja02Eg
MANSFIELD, Mary	42	F	Nurse	17Ja02Eg
John	13	M	Unknown	17Ja02Eg
Michael	9	M	Child	17Ja02Eg
Mary	4	F	Child	17Ja02Eg
MCSWIGGIN, Mary	50	F	Nurse	17Ja02Eg
BYRNES, Mary	29	F	Nurse	17Ja02Eg
Mark	8	M	Child	17Ja02Eg
Ellen	5	F	Child	17Ja02Eg
Catharine	.00	F	Infant	17Ja02Eg
MULLIGAN, Peter	22	M	Laborer	17Ja02Eg
HYMES, Rose	19	F	Spinster	17Ja02Eg
MCGUIRE, John	18	M	Laborer	17Ja02Eg
Ann	22	F	Spinster	17Ja02Eg
FLYNNE, John	16	M	Laborer	17Ja02Eg
GIBSON, Richard	25	M	Laborer	17Ja02Eg
MCGUIRE, Owen	22	M	Laborer	17Ja02Eg
U-Mrs.	27	F	Nurse	17Ja02Eg
MULLIGAN, Catharine	30	F	Nurse	17Ja02Eg
James	5	M	Child	17Ja02Eg
Bridget	.00	F	Infant	17Ja02Eg
MOAN, Patt	26	M	Laborer	17Ja02Eg
MURPHY, James	36	M	Laborer	17Ja02Eg
MCMAHON, Patt	26	M	Laborer	17Ja02Eg
WOODS, Patt	29	M	Laborer	17Ja02Eg
MCMAHON, Cal	29	M	Laborer	17Ja02Eg
U-Mrs.	28	F	Nurse	17Ja02Eg
Anthony	3	M	Child	17Ja02Eg
Mary	.00	F	Infant	17Ja02Eg
WOODS, Nancy	25	F	Spinster	17Ja02Eg
MYERS, Biddy	25	F	Spinster	17Ja02Eg
KIDD, Watson	40	M	Laborer	17Ja02Eg
COSS, Michael	21	M	Laborer	17Ja02Eg
Margaret	16	F	Spinster	17Ja02Eg
FLYNN, Patt	18	M	Laborer	17Ja02Eg
Thomas	4	M	Child	17Ja02Eg
Jane	11	F	Spinster	17Ja02Eg
BURKE, John	23	M	Laborer	17Ja02Eg
SWEENEY, Edmund	18	M	Laborer	17Ja02Eg

NAMES OF PASSENGERS	AGE	SEX	OCCUPATIONS	DATE PORT SHIP
SWEENEY, Bridget	13	F	Spinster	17Ja02Eg
PHAER, Jane	40	F	Nurse	17Ja02Eg
Ann	25	F	Nurse	17Ja02Eg
Robert	11	M	Laborer	17Ja02Eg
BERRIGAN, Peirce	35	M	Laborer	17Ja02Eg
U-Mrs.	25	F	Nurse	17Ja02Eg
Catharine	12	F	Spinster	17Ja02Eg
Edward	8	M	Child	17Ja02Eg
GRIMES, Lindley	48	M	Laborer	17Ja02Eg
U-Mrs.	46	F	Matron	17Ja02Eg
JACKSON, Benjamin	25	M	Laborer	17Ja02Eg
GRIMES, Benjamin	11	M	Laborer	17Ja02Eg
Richard	9	M	Child	17Ja02Eg
Thomas	6	M	Child	17Ja02Eg
WILLSON, Archibald	40	M	Laborer	17Ja02Eg
Grace	40	F	Nurse	17Ja02Eg
Thomas	13	M	Unknown	17Ja02Eg
Martha	11	F	Unknown	17Ja02Eg
Archie	9	M	Child	17Ja02Eg
Samuel	7	M	Child	17Ja02Eg
MURRAY, Martha	24	F	Spinster	17Ja02Eg
CORCORAN, Ann	18	F	Spinster	17Ja02Eg
CONNELLY, Caterine	38	F	Nurse	17Ja02Eg
Mary	9	F	Child	17Ja02Eg
Ann	7	F	Child	17Ja02Eg
Catharine	5	F	Child	17Ja02Eg
SMITH, Jane	16	F	Spinster	17Ja02Eg
GAFFNEY, Catharine	11	F	Spinster	17Ja02Eg
Thomas	9	M	Child	17Ja02Eg
CRUGAN, Mary	11	F	Unknown	17Ja02Eg
MCCORTIE, Mary	35	F	Matron	17Ja02Eg
Dennis	8	M	Child	17Ja02Eg
James	6	M	Child	17Ja02Eg
Margaret	4	F	Child	17Ja02Eg
Patrick	2	M	Child	17Ja02Eg
U	.00	U	Infant	17Ja02Eg
Born-At-Sea				
GARROW, Margaret	22	F	Spinster	17Ja02Eg
BURNSEY, Mary	21	F	Spinster	17Ja02Eg

COROMANDEL 18 JANUARY 1849

From Liverpool

NAMES OF PASSENGERS	AGE	SEX	OCCUPATIONS	DATE PORT SHIP
REYNOLDS, Mary	50	F	Laborer	18Ja02Ft
Bartholomew	20	M	Unknown	18Ja02Ft
Margaret	17	F	Unknown	18Ja02Ft
Margaret	14	F	Unknown	18Ja02Ft
Winefred	11	F	Unknown	18Ja02Ft
Peter	.00	M	Infant	18Ja02Ft
Maria	12	F	Unknown	18Ja02Ft
Bernard	5	M	Child	18Ja02Ft
Mary	12	F	Unknown	18Ja02Ft
Michael	20	M	Unknown	18Ja02Ft
CULLIN, Bridget	22	F	Unknown	18Ja02Ft
GLANEY, Cathrn.	20	F	Unknown	18Ja02Ft
MORAN, Ann	18	F	Unknown	18Ja02Ft
GLANEY, Pat	4	M	Child	18Ja02Ft
William	2	M	Child	18Ja02Ft
MCCONNELL, Pat	24	M	Unknown	18Ja02Ft
MCGOWAN, Owen	18	M	Unknown	18Ja02Ft
KELLEY, James	15	M	Unknown	18Ja02Ft
FAULKNER, Mary	30	F	Unknown	18Ja02Ft
MCGOVERN, Bridget	30	F	Unknown	18Ja02Ft
Cathrn.	10	F	Unknown	18Ja02Ft
Mary	12	F	Unknown	18Ja02Ft
DOLAN, John	20	M	Unknown	18Ja02Ft
MCGOMLIE, Phil	20	M	Unknown	18Ja02Ft
DORAN, Chas.	30	M	Unknown	18Ja02Ft
DORAN, Bridget	10	F	Unknown	18Ja02Ft
Catherine	4	F	Child	18Ja02Ft
Ann	40	F	Unknown	18Ja02Ft
John	.00	M	Infant	18Ja02Ft
Honoria	.00	F	Infant	18Ja02Ft
CORMACK, Thos.	50	M	Unknown	18Ja02Ft
Mary	46	F	Unknown	18Ja02Ft
Eliza	19	F	Unknown	18Ja02Ft
Pat	28	M	Unknown	18Ja02Ft
Hugh	21	M	Unknown	18Ja02Ft
CORMICK, Pat	.00	M	Infant	18Ja02Ft
COYLE, John	22	M	Unknown	18Ja02Ft
Ellen	22	F	Unknown	18Ja02Ft
Betsey	14	F	Unknown	18Ja02Ft
MCMAHON, Phil	51	M	Unknown	18Ja02Ft
Bridget	45	F	Unknown	18Ja02Ft
Ellen	12	F	Unknown	18Ja02Ft
James	9	M	Child	18Ja02Ft
Philip-Jr.	6	M	Child	18Ja02Ft
Jane	3	F	Child	18Ja02Ft
MULLOY, Jas.	30	M	Unknown	18Ja02Ft
KELLEY, Pat	50	M	Unknown	18Ja02Ft
COFFEE, Pat	30	F	Unknown	18Ja02Ft
Margt.	26	F	Unknown	18Ja02Ft
Mary	.00	F	Infant	18Ja02Ft
FITZGERALD, Pat	23	M	Unknown	18Ja02Ft
Anna	20	F	Unknown	18Ja02Ft
COUGHLIN, Pat	18	M	Unknown	18Ja02Ft
FITZGERALD, Norry	18	U	Unknown	18Ja02Ft
Kate	5	F	Child	18Ja02Ft
BURNS, Cathrn.	40	F	Child	18Ja02Ft
Owen	13	M	Child	18Ja02Ft
Terence	11	M	Unknown	18Ja02Ft
Bernard	9	M	Child	18Ja02Ft
Ellen	7	F	Child	18Ja02Ft
Honoria	5	F	Child	18Ja02Ft
Mary-Ann	3	F	Child	18Ja02Ft
Cath.	.00	F	Infant	18Ja02Ft
NEALON, John	12	M	Unknown	18Ja02Ft
Thos.	9	M	Child	18Ja02Ft
CORCORAN, Jno.	32	M	Unknown	18Ja02Ft
Ann	24	F	Unknown	18Ja02Ft
Honoria	40	F	Unknown	18Ja02Ft
Pat	2	M	Child	18Ja02Ft
ROWAN, Jas.	18	M	Unknown	18Ja02Ft
SCANLON, Jno.	22	M	Unknown	18Ja02Ft
HOREZ, U-Mrs.	26	F	Unknown	18Ja02Ft
Margt.	4	F	Child	18Ja02Ft
SLUTERY, Jas.	19	M	Unknown	18Ja02Ft
Bridget	20	F	Unknown	18Ja02Ft
MEEHAN, Patrick	26	M	Unknown	18Ja02Ft
NEILL, Jas.	26	M	Unknown	18Ja02Ft
COREY, Wm.	50	M	Unknown	18Ja02Ft
Elenor	40	F	Unknown	18Ja02Ft
Michael	11	M	Unknown	18Ja02Ft
Thos.	10	M	Unknown	18Ja02Ft
Mary	9	F	Child	18Ja02Ft
David	8	M	Child	18Ja02Ft
Jas.	6	M	Child	18Ja02Ft
Margaret	2	F	Child	18Ja02Ft
Pat	.00	M	Infant	18Ja02Ft
SULIVAN, Pat	23	M	Unknown	18Ja02Ft
BYMER, Mary	21	F	Unknown	18Ja02Ft
REDMOND, John	17	M	Unknown	18Ja02Ft
CANEY, Ann	25	F	Unknown	18Ja02Ft
Owen	5	M	Child	18Ja02Ft
Patrick	3	M	Child	18Ja02Ft
Mary	.00	F	Infant	18Ja02Ft
John	28	M	Unknown	18Ja02Ft
MCCABE, Jas.	6	M	Child	18Ja02Ft
Mary	4	F	Child	18Ja02Ft
KELLEY, John	4	M	Unknown	18Ja02Ft
THOMPSON, Wm.	26	M	Unknown	18Ja02Ft
Jane	20	F	Unknown	18Ja02Ft
TAYLOR, Ann	21	F	Unknown	18Ja02Ft

NAMES OF PASSENGERS	AGE	SEX	OCCUPATIONS	DATE PORT SHIP
FITZPATRICK, Hannah	40	F	Unknown	18Ja02Ft
Pat	11	M	Unknown	18Ja02Ft
Essy	5	F	Child	18Ja02Ft
Ann	3	F	Child	18Ja02Ft
MCALVIN, Ally	40	F	Unknown	18Ja02Ft
Mary	15	F	Unknown	18Ja02Ft
William	11	M	Unknown	18Ja02Ft
Ann	9	F	Child	18Ja02Ft
Ellen	7	F	Child	18Ja02Ft
Peter	5	M	Child	18Ja02Ft
Margaret	2	F	Child	18Ja02Ft
SANGLEY, John	35	M	Unknown	18Ja02Ft
DWYER, John	35	M	Unknown	18Ja02Ft
HACKETT, Bridget	22	F	Unknown	18Ja02Ft
GARDNER, Ann	17	F	Unknown	18Ja02Ft
MCINTIRE, Terence	32	M	Unknown	18Ja02Ft
Cath.	22	F	Unknown	18Ja02Ft
REEDENS, Ann	22	F	Unknown	18Ja02Ft
Susanna	20	F	Unknown	18Ja02Ft
MCMAHON, Fanny	16	F	Unknown	18Ja02Ft
COSTELLOE, Ann	25	F	Unknown	18Ja02Ft
HOY, Martin	50	M	Unknown	18Ja02Ft
Bernard	24	M	Unknown	18Ja02Ft
Michael	20	M	Unknown	18Ja02Ft
ONIEL, Geo.	20	M	Unknown	18Ja02Ft
Ann	20	F	Unknown	18Ja02Ft
Thos.	17	M	Unknown	18Ja02Ft
FOY, Honora	18	F	Unknown	18Ja02Ft
MCINTIRE, Margt.	17	F	Unknown	18Ja02Ft
FOY, Margt.	25	F	Unknown	18Ja02Ft
MCINTIRE, Mary	38	F	Unknown	18Ja02Ft
CONBOY, Cath.	36	F	Unknown	18Ja02Ft
Mich	10	M	Unknown	18Ja02Ft
Ann	8	F	Child	18Ja02Ft
Ed	2	M	Child	18Ja02Ft
JAAFFE, Cath.	18	F	Unknown	18Ja02Ft
MCNALLY, Pat	42	M	Unknown	18Ja02Ft
SHAUGHNESY, Mary	22	F	Unknown	18Ja02Ft
MURPHY, Honora	22	F	Unknown	18Ja02Ft
COTLIN, Bridget	40	F	Unknown	18Ja02Ft
Bridget	9	F	Child	18Ja02Ft
Mary	8	F	Child	18Ja02Ft
Michael	7	M	Child	18Ja02Ft
Cath.	4	F	Child	18Ja02Ft
Ann	2	F	Child	18Ja02Ft
Bess.	.00	F	Infant	18Ja02Ft
HALSEY, Bridget	10	F	Unknown	18Ja02Ft
SHAUGHNESY, Ed	22	M	Unknown	18Ja02Ft
KEENAN, Bridget	8	F	Child	18Ja02Ft
FEALY, Bridget	18	F	Unknown	18Ja02Ft
REILY, Mary	22	F	Unknown	18Ja02Ft
TAYLOR, Ann	20	F	Unknown	18Ja02Ft
MONAHAN, Ed	20	M	Unknown	18Ja02Ft
SULEVAN, John	19	M	Unknown	18Ja02Ft
MCNALLY, Pat	19	M	Unknown	18Ja02Ft
SPILLANE, Mary	35	M	Unknown	18Ja02Ft
Norry	5	U	Unknown	18Ja02Ft
SULIVAN, Dan	15	M	Unknown	18Ja02Ft
Ann	19	F	Unknown	18Ja02Ft
CONNER, Margt.	20	F	Unknown	18Ja02Ft
BARKER, Bridget	40	F	Unknown	18Ja02Ft
Leonard	19	M	Unknown	18Ja02Ft
James	9	M	Child	18Ja02Ft
Will	9	M	Child	18Ja02Ft
Ellen	6	F	Child	18Ja02Ft
Mary	4	F	Child	18Ja02Ft
BRODERICK, Mary	19	F	Unknown	18Ja02Ft
ASMOND, Jno.	19	M	Unknown	18Ja02Ft
ROACH, Michael	20	M	Unknown	18Ja02Ft
BRODERICK, Chas.	18	M	Unknown	18Ja02Ft
WALSH, Jas.	24	M	Unknown	18Ja02Ft
FLUDDY, Susanna	32	F	Unknown	18Ja02Ft
Cath.	16	F	Unknown	18Ja02Ft
Philip	11	M	Unknown	18Ja02Ft
DUFFY, Mary	18	F	Unknown	18Ja02Ft

NAMES OF PASSENGERS	AGE	SEX	OCCUPATIONS	DATE PORT SHIP
MCARDLE, Mary	18	F	Unknown	18Ja02Ft
MCELLEER, Jas.	19	M	Unknown	18Ja02Ft
WALKER, Mary-Ann	35	F	Unknown	18Ja02Ft
Jas.	7	M	Child	18Ja02Ft
Chas.	5	M	Child	18Ja02Ft
Elizabeth	.00	F	Infant	18Ja02Ft
MAHEN, Elizabeth	9	F	Child	18Ja02Ft
Bridget	6	F	Child	18Ja02Ft
CLEARRY, Pat	50	M	Unknown	18Ja02Ft
BRENAN, Johanna	23	F	Unknown	18Ja02Ft
BUTLER, John	7	M	Child	18Ja02Ft
POWER, Nancy	3	F	Child	18Ja02Ft
HASTINGS, Philip	44	M	Unknown	18Ja02Ft
Cath.	40	F	Unknown	18Ja02Ft
Mary	17	F	Unknown	18Ja02Ft
Michael	13	M	Unknown	18Ja02Ft
Bridget	11	F	Unknown	18Ja02Ft
John	9	M	Child	18Ja02Ft
Cath.	.00	F	Infant	18Ja02Ft
NEILL, Margt.	23	F	Unknown	18Ja02Ft
Alley	16	F	Unknown	18Ja02Ft
CARNEY, Bridget	33	F	Unknown	18Ja02Ft
CURRAN, Michael	17	M	Unknown	18Ja02Ft
OBRIEN, Cath.	48	F	Unknown	18Ja02Ft
Honora	11	F	Unknown	18Ja02Ft
Ann	10	F	Unknown	18Ja02Ft
Jas.	7	M	Child	18Ja02Ft
Luke	5	M	Child	18Ja02Ft
Pat	3	M	Child	18Ja02Ft
BROWN, Matilda	23	F	Unknown	18Ja02Ft
DILLON, Jas.	50	U	Unknown	18Ja02Ft
Rachael	50	F	Unknown	18Ja02Ft
SULIVAN, Julia	40	F	Unknown	18Ja02Ft
SEARY, Pat	13	M	Unknown	18Ja02Ft
SULIVAN, Mary	9	F	Child	18Ja02Ft
John	7	M	Child	18Ja02Ft
Daniel	5	M	Child	18Ja02Ft
COUGHLAN, Dennis	40	M	Unknown	18Ja02Ft
Cath.	33	F	Unknown	18Ja02Ft
MCAULIFFE, Cath.	20	F	Unknown	18Ja02Ft
CORNELL, Jas.	35	M	Unknown	18Ja02Ft
Wm.	15	M	Unknown	18Ja02Ft
GUING, Benj.	14	M	Unknown	18Ja02Ft
Abby	8	F	Child	18Ja02Ft
MURPHY, Constance	29	F	Unknown	18Ja02Ft
MOORE, Michael	35	M	Unknown	18Ja02Ft
BARRY, David	23	M	Unknown	18Ja02Ft
MCAULIFFE, J.	36	M	Unknown	18Ja02Ft
Julia	35	F	Unknown	18Ja02Ft
Kitty	6	F	Child	18Ja02Ft
Johanna	3	F	Child	18Ja02Ft
Daniel	.00	M	Infant	18Ja02Ft
DREW, Honora	.00	F	Infant	18Ja02Ft
Mary	25	F	Unknown	18Ja02Ft
MORRESSEY, Jas.	25	M	Unknown	18Ja02Ft
DWYER, Pat	22	M	Unknown	18Ja02Ft
Judith	24	F	Unknown	18Ja02Ft
Grace	21	F	Unknown	18Ja02Ft
HALL, Bridget	40	F	Unknown	18Ja02Ft
Mary	40	F	Unknown	18Ja02Ft
Johanna	30	F	Unknown	18Ja02Ft
Cath.	15	F	Unknown	18Ja02Ft
Ellen	12	F	Unknown	18Ja02Ft
Ed	8	M	Child	18Ja02Ft
Pat	7	M	Child	18Ja02Ft
RYAN, Mich	19	M	Unknown	18Ja02Ft
Jno.	25	M	Unknown	18Ja02Ft
MCDERMOTT, Peter	35	M	Unknown	18Ja02Ft
Pat	12	M	Unknown	18Ja02Ft
Laurence	10	M	Unknown	18Ja02Ft
Cath.	7	F	Child	18Ja02Ft
KELLEY, Thos.	38	M	Unknown	18Ja02Ft
MULLEN, Owen	19	M	Unknown	18Ja02Ft
RIDGE, Jas.	32	M	Unknown	18Ja02Ft
KENEDY, Anthony	39	M	Unknown	18Ja02Ft

NAMES OF PASSENGERS	AGE	SEX	OCCUPATIONS	DATE PORT SHIP
KENEDY, Bridget	30	F	Unknown	18Ja02Ft
Mary	11	F	Unknown	18Ja02Ft
Ellen	9	F	Child	18Ja02Ft
Cath.	5	F	Child	18Ja02Ft
Emmy	2	F	Child	18Ja02Ft
Martin	.00	M	Infant	18Ja02Ft
TREACY, Mary	55	F	Unknown	18Ja02Ft
Margt.	22	F	Unknown	18Ja02Ft
Jerry	24	M	Unknown	18Ja02Ft
Margt.	12	F	Unknown	18Ja02Ft
KNIGHT, Jane	3	F	Child	18Ja02Ft
MAHER, Cath.	35	F	Unknown	18Ja02Ft
CALLAGHAN, Ellen	35	F	Unknown	18Ja02Ft
Malachi	3	M	Child	18Ja02Ft
KEENE, Margt.	17	F	Unknown	18Ja02Ft
Mary	11	F	Unknown	18Ja02Ft
HANLY, Biddy	30	F	Unknown	18Ja02Ft
John	3	M	Child	18Ja02Ft
BRADY, Jas.	20	M	Unknown	18Ja02Ft
KERWIN, Johanna	20	F	Unknown	18Ja02Ft
CALLAGHAN, Wm.	10	M	Unknown	18Ja02Ft
Pat	8	M	Child	18Ja02Ft
Bridget	4	F	Child	18Ja02Ft
LANIGAN, Tim	29	M	Unknown	18Ja02Ft
Ann	29	F	Unknown	18Ja02Ft
Cath.	4	F	Child	18Ja02Ft
Tim	2	M	Child	18Ja02Ft
John	.00	M	Infant	18Ja02Ft
BROUGHTEN, Mat	25	M	Unknown	18Ja02Ft
CREMING, Geo.	26	M	Unknown	18Ja02Ft
HICKEY, Wm.	15	M	Unknown	18Ja02Ft
Tim	11	M	Unknown	18Ja02Ft
HAYES, Cath.	26	F	Unknown	18Ja02Ft
HULEY, Dan	30	M	Unknown	18Ja02Ft
Michael	28	M	Unknown	18Ja02Ft
Mary	26	F	Unknown	18Ja02Ft
Brien	2	M	Child	18Ja02Ft
WALLACE, Thos.	31	M	Unknown	18Ja02Ft
Winefred	20	F	Unknown	18Ja02Ft
MEE, Celia	20	F	Unknown	18Ja02Ft
HAGGERTY, Bridget	21	F	Unknown	18Ja02Ft
OWENS, Bridget	19	F	Unknown	18Ja02Ft
PETTIT, Peter	20	M	Unknown	18Ja02Ft
ONIEL, Owen	25	M	Unknown	18Ja02Ft
MCBRIDE, Ellen	25	F	Unknown	18Ja02Ft
MAHON, Margt.	13	F	Unknown	18Ja02Ft
Mary	35	F	Unknown	18Ja02Ft
FLANAGAN, Ann	36	F	Unknown	18Ja02Ft
Edward	11	M	Unknown	18Ja02Ft
Catherine	9	F	Child	18Ja02Ft
Peter	8	M	Child	18Ja02Ft
Augustin	6	M	Child	18Ja02Ft
CONNER, Catherine	19	F	Unknown	18Ja02Ft
DILLON, John	23	M	Unknown	18Ja02Ft
Wm.	19	M	Unknown	18Ja02Ft
Allen	17	M	Unknown	18Ja02Ft
KENNEDY, Daniel	50	M	Unknown	18Ja02Ft
Grace	48	F	Unknown	18Ja02Ft
John	23	M	Unknown	18Ja02Ft
Mary	22	F	Unknown	18Ja02Ft
Catherine	20	F	Unknown	18Ja02Ft
Judith	18	F	Unknown	18Ja02Ft
Bridget	15	F	Unknown	18Ja02Ft
Garnes	12	M	Unknown	18Ja02Ft
Ann	9	F	Child	18Ja02Ft
DOHERTY, Maurice	46	M	Unknown	18Ja02Ft
CROWE, Thomas	32	M	Unknown	18Ja02Ft
MCCARTY, John	5	M	Child	18Ja02Ft
Jem.	21	M	Unknown	18Ja02Ft
Elizabeth	18	F	Unknown	18Ja02Ft
KEANE, Denis	30	M	Unknown	18Ja02Ft
Ellen	20	F	Unknown	18Ja02Ft
Judith	9	F	Child	18Ja02Ft
Denis	4	M	Child	18Ja02Ft
Ann	.00	F	Infant	18Ja02Ft
DOHERTY, John	20	M	Unknown	18Ja02Ft
CEVAN, Margaret	27	F	Unknown	18Ja02Ft
Margaret	13	F	Unknown	18Ja02Ft
Denis	11	M	Unknown	18Ja02Ft
CORCORAN, Michael	.00	M	Infant	18Ja02Ft

JOHN-MARSHALL 18 JANUARY 1850

From London

NAMES OF PASSENGERS	AGE	SEX	OCCUPATIONS	DATE PORT SHIP
MCTENNAN, Bridget	60	F	Unknown	18Ja06Ek
DALY, Ellen	24	F	Unknown	18Ja06Ek
Robt.	2	M	Child	18Ja06Ek
MORRIS, John	58	M	Gdnr	18Ja06Ek

ANN-KENNY 18 JANUARY 1850

From Liverpool

NAMES OF PASSENGERS	AGE	SEX	OCCUPATIONS	DATE PORT SHIP
MURRAY, Thomas	21	M	Laborer	18Ja02Ej
U-Mrs.	21	F	Unknown	18Ja02Ej
MULLIGAN, Ann	21	F	Unknown	18Ja02Ej
MURRAY, Ann	.00	F	Infant	18Ja02Ej
BYRON, James	19	M	Unknown	18Ja02Ej
BRADY, Robert	23	M	Unknown	18Ja02Ej
BARNS, Ann	50	F	Unknown	18Ja02Ej
Ann	20	F	Unknown	18Ja02Ej
James	15	M	Unknown	18Ja02Ej
Patrick	15	M	Unknown	18Ja02Ej
Michael	12	M	Unknown	18Ja02Ej
Rosey	8	F	Child	18Ja02Ej
CAFFREN, Charles	20	M	Unknown	18Ja02Ej
MARTIN, William	18	M	Unknown	18Ja02Ej
CUSBEEN, H.G.	18	M	Unknown	18Ja02Ej
MCVOY, Thomas	40	M	Unknown	18Ja02Ej
Cathe.	40	F	Unknown	18Ja02Ej
Fanny	16	F	Unknown	18Ja02Ej
Mary	15	F	Unknown	18Ja02Ej
Larry	13	M	Unknown	18Ja02Ej
Thomas	12	M	Unknown	18Ja02Ej
Joseph	5	M	Child	18Ja02Ej
DUNN, Lawrence	30	M	Unknown	18Ja02Ej
Mary	14	F	Unknown	18Ja02Ej
FALLEN, Biddy	23	F	Unknown	18Ja02Ej
KENNEDY, Biddy	20	F	Unknown	18Ja02Ej
BROWN, James	25	M	Unknown	18Ja02Ej
TAYLER, Robt.	24	M	Unknown	18Ja02Ej
KENNY, John	18	M	Unknown	18Ja02Ej
ELIZA, Michl.	18	M	Unknown	18Ja02Ej
HOGAN, Biddy	35	F	Unknown	18Ja02Ej
Patk.	12	M	Unknown	18Ja02Ej
Cathe.	8	F	Child	18Ja02Ej
Dennis	5	M	Child	18Ja02Ej
JOHNSIN, Nancy	35	F	Unknown	18Ja02Ej
CLARK, John	27	M	Unknown	18Ja02Ej
STEPHENSON, Mary	30	F	Unknown	18Ja02Ej
Emma	9	F	Child	18Ja02Ej
Henry	.00	M	Infant	18Ja02Ej
Jas.	9	M	Child	18Ja02Ej
Mathew	7	M	Child	18Ja02Ej
POWER, Patk.	28	M	Unknown	18Ja02Ej
WARD, Walsh	23	M	Unknown	18Ja02Ej
WILSON, Thomas	32	M	Unknown	18Ja02Ej

NAMES OF PASSENGERS	AGE	SEX	OCCUPATIONS	DATE PORT SHIP
ERINS, Mary	34	F	Unknown	18Ja02Ej
Kitty	34	F	Unknown	18Ja02Ej
James	15	M	Unknown	18Ja02Ej
James	.00	M	Infant	18Ja02Ej
KILROY, Emma	13	F	Unknown	18Ja02Ej
HAYMAND, Christian	31	M	Unknown	18Ja02Ej
Ann	30	F	Unknown	18Ja02Ej
FYGENHAM, Christian	31	F	Unknown	18Ja02Ej
FLEMING, Richard	35	M	Unknown	18Ja02Ej
Kitty	30	F	Unknown	18Ja02Ej
Patrick	7	M	Child	18Ja02Ej
Andrew	5	M	Child	18Ja02Ej
Eliza	2	F	Child	18Ja02Ej
U	.00	M	Infant	18Ja02Ej
BRENAN, Cathe.	20	F	Unknown	18Ja02Ej
DORSEY, James	33	M	Unknown	18Ja02Ej
MAHEN, Thomas	22	M	Unknown	18Ja02Ej
Honor	21	F	Unknown	18Ja02Ej
KENNEDY, Margt.	20	F	Unknown	18Ja02Ej
ROBINSON, Margt.	22	F	Unknown	18Ja02Ej
MCFADDEN, Biddy	35	F	Unknown	18Ja02Ej
SMITH, Mary	17	F	Unknown	18Ja02Ej
BENSON, Mary	28	F	Unknown	18Ja02Ej
HOYE, Martin	50	M	Unknown	18Ja02Ej
Michl.	17	M	Unknown	18Ja02Ej
Martin	25	M	Unknown	18Ja02Ej
HARTS, Ann	25	F	Unknown	18Ja02Ej
CONNOLLY, Thos.	24	M	Unknown	18Ja02Ej
BRIEN, Bridgt.	26	F	Unknown	18Ja02Ej
MURPHY, William	20	M	Unknown	18Ja02Ej
CARROLL, John	30	M	Unknown	18Ja02Ej
DAGERSBY, R.	26	M	Unknown	18Ja02Ej
CULLEN, Michl.	25	M	Unknown	18Ja02Ej
BYRNE, Thos.	23	M	Unknown	18Ja02Ej
BURK, Martin	21	M	Unknown	18Ja02Ej
Patrick	17	M	Unknown	18Ja02Ej
Bridgt.	15	F	Unknown	18Ja02Ej
BYRNE, Mary	18	F	Unknown	18Ja02Ej
MORAN, Mary	30	F	Unknown	18Ja02Ej
Pat	12	M	Unknown	18Ja02Ej
Bridgt.	10	F	Unknown	18Ja02Ej
James	3	M	Child	18Ja02Ej
SHERRIDAN, Mary	20	F	Unknown	18Ja02Ej
GIBBONS, Mary	23	F	Unknown	18Ja02Ej
CONWAY, Thos.	23	M	Unknown	18Ja02Ej
HERREN, John	27	M	Unknown	18Ja02Ej
DANNAL, John	40	M	Unknown	18Ja02Ej
OBRIEN, Michl.	19	M	Laborer	18Ja02Ej
FENNEY, Mary	20	F	Unknown	18Ja02Ej
OBRIEN, William	25	M	Unknown	18Ja02Ej
BLANCHEN, Mary	25	F	Unknown	18Ja02Ej
Margt.	23	F	Unknown	18Ja02Ej
Ellen	21	F	Unknown	18Ja02Ej
Cathe.	19	F	Unknown	18Ja02Ej
CARRIGAN, Biddy	50	F	Unknown	18Ja02Ej
James	17	M	Unknown	18Ja02Ej
Bridget	4	F	Child	18Ja02Ej
Mary	13	F	Unknown	18Ja02Ej
Died-At-Sea				
Patrick	8	M	Child	18Ja02Ej
Jno.	9	M	Child	18Ja02Ej
CASSIDY, John	37	M	Unknown	18Ja02Ej
Mary	37	F	Unknown	18Ja02Ej
Bridget	12	F	Unknown	18Ja02Ej
Mary	10	F	Unknown	18Ja02Ej
Ann	8	F	Child	18Ja02Ej
Ellen	4	F	Child	18Ja02Ej
John	.00	M	Infant	18Ja02Ej
CAULFELT, Michl.	20	M	Unknown	18Ja02Ej
Margt.	19	F	Unknown	18Ja02Ej
MCGRATH, James	20	M	Unknown	18Ja02Ej
CAUFELT, Philip	20	M	Unknown	18Ja02Ej
OBRIEN, Denis	14	M	Unknown	18Ja02Ej
CARNEY, Patrick	20	M	Unknown	18Ja02Ej
ALLEY, Ellen	18	F	Unknown	18Ja02Ej

NAMES OF PASSENGERS	AGE	SEX	OCCUPATIONS	DATE PORT SHIP
LYNCH, John	30	M	Unknown	18Ja02Ej
LEE, Henry	27	M	Unknown	18Ja02Ej
RYAN, Terence	50	M	Unknown	18Ja02Ej
Judy	56	F	Unknown	18Ja02Ej
John	59	M	Unknown	18Ja02Ej
Honor	21	F	Unknown	18Ja02Ej
Ellen	19	F	Unknown	18Ja02Ej
Timothy	13	M	Unknown	18Ja02Ej
Mary	17	F	Unknown	18Ja02Ej
STOKES, William	26	M	Unknown	18Ja02Ej
James	21	M	Unknown	18Ja02Ej
GANS, George	55	M	Unknown	18Ja02Ej
John	24	M	Unknown	18Ja02Ej
Susan	28	F	Unknown	18Ja02Ej
George	20	M	Unknown	18Ja02Ej
Margt.	25	F	Unknown	18Ja02Ej
MERA, Patk.	35	M	Unknown	18Ja02Ej
KELLY, Patk.	19	M	Unknown	18Ja02Ej
COLLINS, Biddy	40	F	Unknown	18Ja02Ej
Biddy	9	F	Child	18Ja02Ej
Mary	8	F	Child	18Ja02Ej
Michl.	7	M	Child	18Ja02Ej
Cathe.	4	F	Child	18Ja02Ej
Ann	2	F	Child	18Ja02Ej
Rose	.00	F	Infant	18Ja02Ej
FAGAN, Michl.	35	M	Unknown	18Ja02Ej
Patk.	23	M	Unknown	18Ja02Ej
STARKEY, Nancy	22	F	Unknown	18Ja02Ej
BRYAN, Ellen	28	F	Unknown	18Ja02Ej
Michl.	3	M	Child	18Ja02Ej
FARRELL, Margt.	18	F	Unknown	18Ja02Ej
HUGHES, Mary	18	F	Unknown	18Ja02Ej
CLARKE, Jas.	42	M	Unknown	18Ja02Ej
Patk.	17	M	Unknown	18Ja02Ej
Bridgt.	13	F	Unknown	18Ja02Ej
DUFFEY, Cathe.	34	F	Unknown	18Ja02Ej
Mary	16	F	Unknown	18Ja02Ej
Ann	13	F	Unknown	18Ja02Ej
Bridget	11	F	Unknown	18Ja02Ej
Alice	9	F	Child	18Ja02Ej
Patk.	7	M	Child	18Ja02Ej
TURNER, John	55	M	Unknown	18Ja02Ej
Jas.	13	M	Unknown	18Ja02Ej
Rosey	9	F	Child	18Ja02Ej
Patrick	5	M	Child	18Ja02Ej
Ann	18	F	Unknown	18Ja02Ej
BLONDALL, Thos.	35	M	Unknown	18Ja02Ej
HUGHES, Michl.	27	M	Unknown	18Ja02Ej
WOODS, Biddy	50	F	Unknown	18Ja02Ej
BURNS, Bridget	30	F	Unknown	18Ja02Ej
RESLAND, Ellen	30	F	Unknown	18Ja02Ej
Eliza	7	F	Child	18Ja02Ej
MCGANNIS, Elizt.	16	F	Unknown	18Ja02Ej
MURRAY, Mary	24	F	Unknown	18Ja02Ej
FITZGERALD, Cathe.	25	F	Unknown	18Ja02Ej
MCALLON, Bridget	20	F	Unknown	18Ja02Ej
Elizth.	7	F	Child	18Ja02Ej
CONNERY, James	30	M	Unknown	18Ja02Ej
KING, Julia	22	F	Unknown	18Ja02Ej
LYNCH, U-Mrs.	45	F	Unknown	18Ja02Ej
FYGENHAM, U	.00	U	Infant	18Ja02Ej

HEATHER-BELL 20 JANUARY 1850

From Limerick

NAMES OF PASSENGERS	AGE	SEX	OCCUPATIONS	DATE PORT SHIP
RYAN, Saml.	20	M	Laborer	20Ja10Em
DENAHAN, Michl.	30	M	Unknown	20Ja10Em
Thady	26	M	Unknown	20Ja10Em

NAMES OF PASSENGERS	AGE	SEX	OCCUPATIONS	DATE PORT SHIP
BURKE, Thomas	25	M	Unknown	20Ja10Em
RYALL, John	45	M	Unknown	20Ja10Em
Mary	21	F	Unknown	20Ja10Em
Mary	17	F	Unknown	20Ja10Em
COLLINS, James	20	M	Unknown	20Ja10Em
NEWMAN, Ellen	30	F	Unknown	20Ja10Em
John	25	M	Unknown	20Ja10Em
Thomas	14	M	Unknown	20Ja10Em
John	12	M	Unknown	20Ja10Em
Richard	11	M	Unknown	20Ja10Em
William	9	M	Child	20Ja10Em
Michael	5	M	Child	20Ja10Em
FLYNN, Richard	46	M	Unknown	20Ja10Em
MALONEY, John	25	M	Unknown	20Ja10Em
DALY, Mary	20	F	Unknown	20Ja10Em
WINEGAN, Mary	20	F	Unknown	20Ja10Em
BURKE, Thomas	30	M	Unknown	20Ja10Em
CONNRAY, Conner	25	M	Unknown	20Ja10Em
MALONE, Mathew	24	M	Unknown	20Ja10Em
Patrick	24	M	Unknown	20Ja10Em
CONWAY, Parry	24	M	Unknown	20Ja10Em
ODONNELL, Cath.	17	F	Unknown	20Ja10Em
SHAUGNESSEY, Mary	24	F	Unknown	20Ja10Em
Morgan	30	M	Unknown	20Ja10Em
Connor	.00	M	Infant	20Ja10Em
BROWNE, Johanna	14	F	Unknown	20Ja10Em
Daniel	20	M	Unknown	20Ja10Em
SHAUGNESSEY, Mary	50	F	Unknown	20Ja10Em
Dennis	20	M	Unknown	20Ja10Em
David	7	M	Child	20Ja10Em
Margt.	6	F	Child	20Ja10Em
Bridget	20	F	Unknown	20Ja10Em
Thomas	21	M	Unknown	20Ja10Em
LANCE, Honor	23	F	Unknown	20Ja10Em
FANNY, Bridget	20	F	Unknown	20Ja10Em
BURKE, James	31	M	Unknown	20Ja10Em
John	5	M	Child	20Ja10Em
MANN, Michael	30	M	Unknown	20Ja10Em
KELLY, Ellen	23	F	Unknown	20Ja10Em
OBURNY, James	25	M	Unknown	20Ja10Em
HEARN, James	25	M	Unknown	20Ja10Em
Edmund	16	M	Unknown	20Ja10Em
Johana	22	F	Unknown	20Ja10Em
GRADY, John	25	M	Unknown	20Ja10Em
CRUMP, William	40	M	Unknown	20Ja10Em
Mary	40	F	Unknown	20Ja10Em
Ellen	30	F	Unknown	20Ja10Em
ONEIL, Patt	30	M	Unknown	20Ja10Em
CUMMINGS, Margt.	.00	F	Infant	20Ja10Em
SHANAHAN, Alice	20	F	Unknown	20Ja10Em
DUGGAN, Mary	9	F	Child	20Ja10Em
LYSTON, Margt.	19	F	Unknown	20Ja10Em
KENNY, John	11	M	Unknown	20Ja10Em
LEARY, Michl.	22	M	Unknown	20Ja10Em
CROWLER, Hannah	19	F	Unknown	20Ja10Em
Edmund	35	M	Unknown	20Ja10Em
Ellen	35	F	Unknown	20Ja10Em
Michael	20	M	Unknown	20Ja10Em
MCDONNORY, Joseph	40	M	Unknown	20Ja10Em
KEEHAN, John	44	M	Unknown	20Ja10Em
FITZGERALD, Mary	30	F	Unknown	20Ja10Em
GRADY, Michl.	30	M	Unknown	20Ja10Em
Cath.	31	F	Unknown	20Ja10Em
Mary	25	F	Unknown	20Ja10Em
Margt.	22	F	Unknown	20Ja10Em
Patrick	6	M	Child	20Ja10Em
Margt.	.00	F	Infant	20Ja10Em
DILLON, Hanah	27	F	Unknown	20Ja10Em
NEWMAN, Johana	16	F	Unknown	20Ja10Em
Margt.	24	F	Unknown	20Ja10Em
ONEIL, Mary	20	F	Unknown	20Ja10Em
WALSH, Ellen	20	F	Unknown	20Ja10Em
QUITTY, Bridgt.	20	F	Unknown	20Ja10Em
TRACY, Bessy	30	F	Unknown	20Ja10Em
Judy	.00	F	Infant	20Ja10Em

NAMES OF PASSENGERS	AGE	SEX	OCCUPATIONS	DATE PORT SHIP
CONSIKORN, Cath.	34	F	Unknown	20Ja10Em
John	5	M	Child	20Ja10Em
Patt	.00	M	Infant	20Ja10Em
CORBETT, Margt.	25	F	Unknown	20Ja10Em
Mary	.00	F	Infant	20Ja10Em
GLEESON, Mary	18	F	Unknown	20Ja10Em
MULBERRY, Mary	24	F	Unknown	20Ja10Em
MUGGSY, Jary	19	U	Unknown	20Ja10Em
BROWN, James	34	M	Unknown	20Ja10Em
HURLEY, Bridget	19	F	Unknown	20Ja10Em
CALLAHAN, Wm.	25	M	Unknown	20Ja10Em
CAULFIELD, John	35	M	Unknown	20Ja10Em
GRADY, Margt.	20	F	Unknown	20Ja10Em
LYNES, Mathew	23	M	Unknown	20Ja10Em
CONNELL, Nancy	17	F	Unknown	20Ja10Em
Kate	.00	F	Infant	20Ja10Em
Patt	.00	M	Infant	20Ja10Em
EDGAR, Michl.	30	M	Unknown	20Ja10Em
Bridgt.	25	F	Unknown	20Ja10Em
Kate	4	F	Child	20Ja10Em
CASEY, Anne	30	F	Unknown	20Ja10Em
John	6	M	Child	20Ja10Em
Johanne	5	F	Child	20Ja10Em
James	.00	M	Infant	20Ja10Em
DUGAN, Patt	30	M	Unknown	20Ja10Em
ONEIL, John	30	M	Unknown	20Ja10Em
Mary	25	F	Unknown	20Ja10Em
Bridgt.	4	F	Child	20Ja10Em
Cath.	.00	F	Infant	20Ja10Em
SHIELDS, Johanne	20	F	Unknown	20Ja10Em
DUGGAN, James	18	M	Unknown	20Ja10Em
DALY, Cath.	25	F	Unknown	20Ja10Em
CONNROY, Michael	34	M	Unknown	20Ja10Em
KENNEDY, Daniel	26	M	Unknown	20Ja10Em
OBRIEN, James	50	M	Unknown	20Ja10Em
Margt.	43	F	Unknown	20Ja10Em
Jeremiah	17	M	Unknown	20Ja10Em
William	12	M	Unknown	20Ja10Em
Mary	.00	F	Infant	20Ja10Em
STOKES, Mary	22	F	Unknown	20Ja10Em
GOMIER, Michael	28	M	Unknown	20Ja10Em
Eliza	27	F	Unknown	20Ja10Em
MULLEN, Michael	25	M	Unknown	20Ja10Em
BURKE, Patt	26	M	Unknown	20Ja10Em
Thomas	22	M	Unknown	20Ja10Em
HUNNINGTON, Mary-Anne	18	F	Unknown	20Ja10Em
RYAN, Hannah	20	F	Unknown	20Ja10Em
REYS, Richard	25	M	Unknown	20Ja10Em
Catharine	25	F	Unknown	20Ja10Em
Edward	19	M	Unknown	20Ja10Em
William	.00	M	Infant	20Ja10Em
HANON, Charles	21	M	Unknown	20Ja10Em
Ellen	23	F	Unknown	20Ja10Em
BENNAN, Timothy	20	F	Unknown	20Ja10Em
ALLEN, Mathew	20	M	Unknown	20Ja10Em
HENRY, Mary	21	F	Unknown	20Ja10Em
HICKEY, Margt.	35	F	Unknown	20Ja10Em
Michl.	20	M	Unknown	20Ja10Em
SHIELDS, Thomas	30	M	Unknown	20Ja10Em

ROBERT-SCURFIELD 21 JANUARY 1849

From Limerick

NAMES OF PASSENGERS	AGE	SEX	OCCUPATIONS	DATE PORT SHIP
CORTLE, William	25	M	Tailor	21Ja10En
CORNY, Margt.	30	F	Servant	21Ja10En
BLEAD, Dennis	20	M	Laborer	21Ja10En
GRADY, Kate	24	F	Spinster	21Ja10En
Ellen	22	F	Spinster	21Ja10En

NAMES OF PASSENGERS		AGE	SEX	OCCUPATIONS	DATE PORT SHIP
GRADY, Bridget		20	F	Spinster	21Ja10En
MUROGUE, Bridget		23	F	Spinster	21Ja10En
Ellen		21	F	Spinster	21Ja10En
MCGRATH, Mary		22	F	Spinster	21Ja10En
BOURK, Walter		26	M	Smith	21Ja10En
SCOTT, Patt		22	M	Farmer	21Ja10En
MCTREEHENY, Morgan		48	M	Farmer	21Ja10En
Kate	(W)	41	F	None	21Ja10En
Michl.	(S)	24	M	None	21Ja10En
Denis	(S)	21	M	None	21Ja10En
Catherine	(D)	19	F	None	21Ja10En
Bridget	(D)	17	F	None	21Ja10En
Maria	(D)	13	F	None	21Ja10En
Margt.	(D)	12	F	None	21Ja10En
Catherine	(D)	11	F	None	21Ja10En
Eliza	(D)	6	F	Child	21Ja10En
Susan	(D)	3	F	Child	21Ja10En
KELLY, Charles		21	M	Farmer	21Ja10En
Bridget	(W)	21	F	None	21Ja10En
MCTREEHENY, Eliza		18	F	Spinster	21Ja10En
KELLY, Mary		.09	F	Infant	21Ja10En
RYAN, John		26	M	Farmer	21Ja10En
WELSH, Pat		26	M	Farmer	21Ja10En
John		20	M	Farmer	21Ja10En
HOGAN, Kate		20	F	Spinster	21Ja10En
Ann		19	F	Spinster	21Ja10En
SLATTERY, Ml.		18	M	Laborer	21Ja10En
C.		16	M	Laborer	21Ja10En
Denis		13	M	Laborer	21Ja10En
MCGRATH, Bid		24	F	Spinster	21Ja10En
MCNAMARA, Ed.		30	M	Laborer	21Ja10En
Ellen	(W)	30	F	None	21Ja10En
Eugene	(S)	11	M	None	21Ja10En
Ann	(D)	9	F	Child	21Ja10En
CORNY, Mary		10	F	Spinster	21Ja10En
QUINN, Patt		30	M	Farmer	21Ja10En
ANGLIM, Thady		24	M	Farmer	21Ja10En
WALL, Maurice		24	M	Farmer	21Ja10En
GRIFFIN, Richd.		20	M	Farmer	21Ja10En
DUNAVAN, Thos.		20	M	Farmer	21Ja10En
MANGAN, Bridget		20	F	Spinster	21Ja10En
SCOTT, Wm.		20	M	Laborer	21Ja10En
WELCH, Honora		25	F	Spinster	21Ja10En
HARLEY, Mary		30	F	Spinster	21Ja10En
Cath.		3	F	Child	21Ja10En
FALL, Michl.		18	M	Laborer	21Ja10En
DUNOVAN, Michl.		40	M	Farmer	21Ja10En
Johanna	(W)	30	F	None	21Ja10En
Bridget		11	F	None	21Ja10En
Ml.	(S)	3	M	Child	21Ja10En
Margt.		.05	F	Infant	21Ja10En
COLLINS, Thos.		32	M	Farmer	21Ja10En
CRONIN, James		20	M	Farmer	21Ja10En
CONDEN, Kate		16	F	Spinster	21Ja10En
HERNS, James		20	M	Servant	21Ja10En
RIEDY, John		26	M	Servant	21Ja10En
MCNAMARA, Kate		20	F	Spinster	21Ja10En
OCONNOR, Betsy		26	F	Spinster	21Ja10En
Margt.		20	F	Spinster	21Ja10En
John		21	M	Servant	21Ja10En
FLINN, Danl.		28	M	Farmer	21Ja10En
DONELLAN, Sarah		35	F	Farmer	21Ja10En
FLINN, Thos.		21	M	Farmer	21Ja10En
LISTON, Edward		44	M	Farmer	21Ja10En
Mary		18	F	None	21Ja10En
RYAN, Martin		10	M	Servant	21Ja10En
BUCKLEY, Ann		19	F	Spinster	21Ja10En
GOULDING, Terry		21	M	Farmer	21Ja10En
FLAHERTY, Kate		20	F	Spinster	21Ja10En
DOOLY, Margt.		23	F	Spinster	21Ja10En
MALVIHILL, Kate		24	F	Spinster	21Ja10En
DELANY, Wm.		40	M	Laborer	21Ja10En
FINUCANE, John		22	M	Farmer	21Ja10En
Kate	(W)	20	F	None	21Ja10En
MOORE, John		22	M	Farmer	21Ja10En
MOORE, Johanna	(W)	19	F	None	21Ja10En
CONLON, Ann		22	F	Spinster	21Ja10En
FLAHERTY, Johanna		12	F	Spinster	21Ja10En
MOYLAN, Ellen		22	F	Spinster	21Ja10En
QUAID, Peter		30	M	Farmer	21Ja10En
RYAN, Wm.		33	M	Farmer	21Ja10En
Catherine	(W)	25	F	None	21Ja10En
John		3	M	Child	21Ja10En
FOLEY, Catherine		30	F	Farmer	21Ja10En
John	(S)	4	M	Child	21Ja10En
BROWN, Mary		22	F	Spinster	21Ja10En
FRAWLEY, Thos.		25	M	Farmer	21Ja10En
SHAUGHNESSY, Ellen		25	F	Spinster	21Ja10En
Michl.		3	M	Child	21Ja10En
CARROLL, John		22	M	Farmer	21Ja10En
MCALISTONN, Kate		18	F	Spinster	21Ja10En
MCJOHERNY, Wm.		18	M	Farmer	21Ja10En
D.		22	M	Farmer	21Ja10En
ANHELLY, Dennis		20	M	Farmer	21Ja10En
MURPHY, Timothy		36	M	Farmer	21Ja10En
CONOLLY, Michl.		28	M	Farmer	21Ja10En
HENESSY, Ann		26	F	Farmer	21Ja10En
MCMAHON, Martin		24	M	Farmer	21Ja10En
ONEILL, Nancy		25	F	Spinster	21Ja10En
CONNELL, Mary		20	F	Spinster	21Ja10En
HENNESSY, Pat		22	M	Farmer	21Ja10En
John		24	M	Farmer	21Ja10En
Mary		26	F	Spinster	21Ja10En
MACK, Eliza		20	F	Spinster	21Ja10En
F.		20	M	None	21Ja10En

NAOMI 23 JANUARY 1850

From Liverpool

NAMES OF PASSENGERS		AGE	SEX	OCCUPATIONS	DATE PORT SHIP
DONNELLY, Hugh		36	M	Carpenter	23Ja02Ev
DONNETT, Mary		26	F	Matron	23Ja02Ev
MURPHY, James		35	M	Carpenter	23Ja02Ev
Johanna		28	F	Matron	23Ja02Ev
Ann		2	F	Child	23Ja02Ev
Johanna		.00	F	Infant	23Ja02Ev
REYNOLDS, John		13	M	Unknown	23Ja02Ev
AINSBORO, Patt.		30	M	Tailor	23Ja02Ev
CUNIGAN, Pattk.		30	M	Tailor	23Ja02Ev
GANNON, James		26	M	Tailor	23Ja02Ev
MCKUSCAR, Cath.		40	F	Matron	23Ja02Ev
John		9	M	Child	23Ja02Ev
Edward		7	M	Child	23Ja02Ev
Owen		2	M	Child	23Ja02Ev
MCCUSCAN, John		.00	M	Infant	23Ja02Ev
MAHER, Biddy		18	F	Servant	23Ja02Ev
DONOHENY, James		14	M	Laborer	23Ja02Ev
PHELAN, Martin		12	M	Laborer	23Ja02Ev
KELLY, Catharine		30	F	Matron	23Ja02Ev
MURRAY, Bridget		18	F	Unknown	23Ja02Ev
KELLEY, Bridget		9	F	Child	23Ja02Ev
CURLEY, Michael		30	M	Joiner	23Ja02Ev
LARKIN, Mary		55	F	Matron	23Ja02Ev
Ann		8	F	Child	23Ja02Ev
MONOHAN, Thos.		32	M	Tinker	23Ja02Ev
Bridget		26	F	Unknown	23Ja02Ev
LEWIS, Sam		40	M	Laborer	23Ja02Ev
Wm.		13	M	None	23Ja02Ev
CUNNINGHAM, Patrick		28	M	Joiner	23Ja02Ev
DOCEY, Cath.		47	F	Matron	23Ja02Ev
LUNNEY, Mary		13	F	None	23Ja02Ev
LARKIN, John		6	M	Child	23Ja02Ev
DOCEY, Wm.		22	M	Laborer	23Ja02Ev
Mary		19	F	Laborer	23Ja02Ev

NAMES OF PASSENGERS	AGE	SEX	OCCUPATIONS	DATE PORT SHIP
DOCEY, Patk.	15	M	Laborer	23Ja02Ev
Margt.	13	F	Laborer	23Ja02Ev
John	11	M	Laborer	23Ja02Ev
Ellen	9	F	Child	23Ja02Ev
Michael	7	M	Child	23Ja02Ev
KENSELLA, Martin	22	M	Tailor	23Ja02Ev
MCDANIEL, Biddy	30	F	Servant	23Ja02Ev
GAHARETY, Honor	30	F	Servant	23Ja02Ev
MCDANIEL, Ellen	16	F	Servant	23Ja02Ev
John	.00	M	Infant	23Ja02Ev
MOONEY, Michael	20	M	Farmer	23Ja02Ev
FITZGERALD, David	20	M	Laborer	23Ja02Ev
MALONEY, Patk.	35	M	Joiner	23Ja02Ev
KELLY, John	22	M	Laborer	23Ja02Ev
TEAS, Judy	20	F	Servant	23Ja02Ev
GRACE, Margt.	50	F	Servant	23Ja02Ev
NOLAN, Michael	12	M	Laborer	23Ja02Ev
QUINLAN, Patt	35	M	Laborer	23Ja02Ev
Mary	35	F	Laborer	23Ja02Ev
MAHER, Patt	47	M	Farmer	23Ja02Ev
Judy	40	F	Farmer	23Ja02Ev
Wm.	14	M	Farmer	23Ja02Ev
James	13	M	Farmer	23Ja02Ev
Mary	11	F	Farmer	23Ja02Ev
Catharine	9	F	Child	23Ja02Ev
Richd.	7	M	Child	23Ja02Ev
Thos.	5	M	Child	23Ja02Ev
PENNEY, Thos.	2	M	Child	23Ja02Ev
MAHER, Judy	.00	F	Infant	23Ja02Ev
PURCELL, Mary	40	F	Servant	23Ja02Ev
CAVANNAH, Mary	22	F	Servant	23Ja02Ev
Judy	13	F	Servant	23Ja02Ev
GILDEA, Thos.	20	M	Laborer	23Ja02Ev
PHELAN, Johanna	20	F	Servant	23Ja02Ev
HENNESEY, Thos.	7	M	Child	23Ja02Ev
Cath.	5	F	Child	23Ja02Ev
LOCHADEN, John	30	M	Laborer	23Ja02Ev
PHARLEY, Philip	22	M	Laborer	23Ja02Ev
Margt.	15	F	Servant	23Ja02Ev
CASSIDY, Patt	30	M	Laborer	23Ja02Ev
BRADY, James	28	M	Laborer	23Ja02Ev
MOLLOY, John	28	M	Tinker	23Ja02Ev
Mary	23	F	Unknown	23Ja02Ev
HILL, John	36	M	Laborer	23Ja02Ev
CORBETT, Bridget	23	F	Servant	23Ja02Ev
FAY, Martin	22	M	Laborer	23Ja02Ev
CARROLL, Mary	20	F	Servant	23Ja02Ev
DONOGAN. Edward	50	M	Laborer	23Ja02Ev
RILEY, Biddy	30	F	Servant	23Ja02Ev
Bridgt.	9	F	Child	23Ja02Ev
Patk.	.00	M	Infant	23Ja02Ev
NOLAN, Ellen	17	F	Servant	23Ja02Ev
MULLEN, Lebina	26	F	Farmer	23Ja02Ev
Patt	2	M	Child	23Ja02Ev
John	.00	M	Infant	23Ja02Ev
GALLAHER, Owen	28	M	Laborer	23Ja02Ev
LATIMORE, John	20	M	Laborer	23Ja02Ev
Jane	18	F	Laborer	23Ja02Ev
HETHERTON, Peter	18	M	Laborer	23Ja02Ev
Rose	11	F	Servant	23Ja02Ev
BIKER, John	26	M	Carpenter	23Ja02Ev
CURRAN, Bridget	20	F	Servant	23Ja02Ev
RIGNEY, Eliza	20	F	Servant	23Ja02Ev
SPROUL, Franics	30	M	Farmer	23Ja02Ev
Margt.	26	F	Farmer	23Ja02Ev
John	4	M	Child	23Ja02Ev
Francis	.00	M	Infant	23Ja02Ev
MANNING, Winfred	40	F	Farmer	23Ja02Ev
COOKE, Edward	20	M	Laborer	23Ja02Ev
BAITEN, John	22	M	Laborer	23Ja02Ev
LEWIS, James	23	M	Laborer	23Ja02Ev
BYRNE, Michael	22	M	Laborer	23Ja02Ev
DARCEY, Michael	20	M	Laborer	23Ja02Ev
BANNEY, Thomas	21	M	Laborer	23Ja02Ev
CASSIDY, Barney	18	M	Laborer	23Ja02Ev

NAMES OF PASSENGERS	AGE	SEX	OCCUPATIONS	DATE PORT SHIP
DUFFY, Mary-A.	13	F	Servant	23Ja02Ev
DANIEL, William	20	M	Laborer	23Ja02Ev
Abbey	18	F	Servant	23Ja02Ev
Julia	18	F	Servant	23Ja02Ev
MCCONNELL, Arthur	23	M	Laborer	23Ja02Ev
RYAN, Thos.	20	M	Laborer	23Ja02Ev
TRACEY, Biddy	26	F	Servant	23Ja02Ev
Mary	21	F	Servant	23Ja02Ev
MCEVOY, Denis	21	M	Laborer	23Ja02Ev
Mary	20	F	Laborer	23Ja02Ev
MADGRAVE, Denis	50	M	Laborer	23Ja02Ev
Denis	20	M	Laborer	23Ja02Ev
LAVERTY, Cath.	17	F	Servant	23Ja02Ev
CALLIGAN, Martin	46	M	Laborer	23Ja02Ev
Ann	40	F	Laborer	23Ja02Ev
Matthew	12	M	Laborer	23Ja02Ev
Matilda	10	F	Laborer	23Ja02Ev
Mary	5	F	Child	23Ja02Ev
MCDONNELL, Bridt.	21	F	Servant	23Ja02Ev
MCCABE, Barney	30	M	Laborer	23Ja02Ev
Owen	18	M	Laborer	23Ja02Ev
GILLIVAN, Francis	21	M	Laborer	23Ja02Ev
MORRISSON, Richd.	23	M	Laborer	23Ja02Ev
PONDER, Benj.	23	M	Laborer	23Ja02Ev
KELLEY, Cath.	40	F	Servant	23Ja02Ev
Mary	15	F	Servant	23Ja02Ev
Cath.	12	F	Servant	23Ja02Ev
Margt.	7	F	Child	23Ja02Ev
WILSON, John	30	M	Laborer	23Ja02Ev
William	54	M	Laborer	23Ja02Ev
Patk.	20	M	Laborer	23Ja02Ev
Ann	17	F	Laborer	23Ja02Ev
FINN, Mark	20	M	Laborer	23Ja02Ev
FITZGIBBON, Edward	37	M	Laborer	23Ja02Ev
ENGLISH, Abram	30	M	Laborer	23Ja02Ev
KEOUGH, Wm.	18	M	Laborer	23Ja02Ev
NORTON, Mary	30	F	Servant	23Ja02Ev
Thos.	8	M	Child	23Ja02Ev
Mary	.00	F	Infant	23Ja02Ev
Died-At-Sea				
REILLEY, Barney	35	M	Laborer	23Ja02E
CLARK, Thos.	40	M	Laborer	23Ja02E
Ann	30	F	Laborer	23Ja02E
Ann	.00	F	Infant	23Ja02E
MCNAMARRA, Peter	34	M	Laborer	23Ja02E
John	22	M	Laborer	23Ja02E
TIERNEY, Eliza	22	F	Servant	23Ja02E
Winfred	15	F	Servant	23Ja02E
EARLEY, Michael	40	M	Laborer	23Ja02E
CLANEY, Patt	25	M	Laborer	23Ja02E
EARLEY, Ann	40	F	Servant	23Ja02E
ONEILL, Michael	40	M	Farmer	23Ja02E
Peggy	35	F	Farmer	23Ja02E
Mary	14	F	Farmer	23Ja02E
Patt	20	M	Farmer	23Ja02E
MAHON, Phillip	20	M	Laborer	23Ja02E
MCNAMMARA, Benjn.	40	M	Laborer	23Ja02E
REILLY, Michael	10	M	Laborer	23Ja02E
Judy	8	F	Child	23Ja02E
GAHAN, Eliza	21	F	Servant	23Ja02E
Thos	4	M	Servant	23Ja02E
PIGOTT, Wm.	30	M	Laborer	23Ja02E
KEEFFE, Mary	30	F	Farmer	23Ja02E
Eliza	7	F	Child	23Ja02E
John	5	M	Child	23Ja02E
Honor	3	F	Child	23Ja02E
Died-At-Sea				
KENNEDY, Timothy	23	M	Laborer	23Ja02E
BRADEY, Michael	20	M	Laborer	23Ja02E
MURPHY, Peter	20	M	Laborer	23Ja02E
TRACEY, Michael	30	M	Laborer	23Ja02E
FARMON, Thos.	22	M	Laborer	23Ja02E
NOONE, John	25	M	Laborer	23Ja02E
Patt	10	M	Laborer	23Ja02E
Margt.	8	F	Child	23Ja02E

NAMES OF PASSENGERS	AGE	SEX	OCCUPATIONS	DATE PORT SHIP
SULLIVAN, Patt	40	M	Laborer	23Ja02Ev
Norra	40	F	Laborer	23Ja02Ev
Timothy	10	M	Laborer	23Ja02Ev
Cornelius	10	M	Child	23Ja02Ev
Bridgt.	24	F	Servant	23Ja02Ev
CONNELLY, Lane	20	F	Servant	23Ja02Ev
NICHOLSON, Thos.	28	M	Laborer	23Ja02Ev
DALEY, Thos.	32	M	Laborer	23Ja02Ev
RYAN, Susan	20	F	Servant	23Ja02Ev
MCCAUL, James	40	M	Laborer	23Ja02Ev
STANTOM, Patt	25	M	Laborer	23Ja02Ev
MCLAUGHLIN, Mary Died-At-Sea	30	F	Servant	23Ja02Ev
DORCEY, Onney	30	F	Servant	23Ja02Ev
Michael	7	M	Child	23Ja02Ev
KINNELLY, Edward	17	M	Laborer	23Ja02Ev
MURPHY, James	21	M	Laborer	23Ja02Ev
Bridgt.	17	F	Servant	23Ja02Ev
RYAN, Cath.	18	F	Servant	23Ja02Ev
Ally	16	F	Servant	23Ja02Ev
DUNLAN, Wm.	28	M	Laborer	23Ja02Ev
QUINLAN, James	21	M	Laborer	23Ja02Ev
Richard	19	M	Laborer	23Ja02Ev
MANNOY, Margt.	18	F	Servant	23Ja02Ev
LALLY, Margt.	20	F	Servant	23Ja02Ev
BRANIGAN, Michael	22	M	Laborer	23Ja02Ev
MCEVOY, Ann	20	F	Servant	23Ja02Ev
KEAN, Martin	23	M	Laborer	23Ja02Ev
BRANIGAN, Denis	24	M	Laborer	23Ja02Ev
MCFANNAN, Peter	26	M	Laborer	23Ja02Ev
DIGNAN, Margt.	40	F	Farmer	23Ja02Ev
Cath.	13	F	Farmer	23Ja02Ev
Margt.	11	F	Farmer	23Ja02Ev
Mary	8	F	Child	23Ja02Ev
NOONE, Mary	30	F	Servant	23Ja02Ev
KEARY, Anthony	22	M	Laborer	23Ja02Ev
Mary	20	F	Laborer	23Ja02Ev
THOMPSON, Wm.	25	M	Laborer	23Ja02Ev
MORAN, Wm.	26	M	Laborer	23Ja02Ev
Ellen	18	F	Laborer	23Ja02Ev
Susan	2	F	Child	23Ja02Ev
James	18	M	Laborer	23Ja02Ev
MCGOREE, James	40	M	Laborer	23Ja02Ev
Pattk.	15	M	Laborer	23Ja02Ev
TRAYMORE, Michael	17	M	Laborer	23Ja02Ev
LEONARD, James	40	M	Laborer	23Ja02Ev
GREAVES, George	20	M	Laborer	23Ja02Ev
GOUGH, Thomas	18	M	Laborer	23Ja02Ev
COLLINS, Wm.	21	M	Laborer	23Ja02Ev
RENNOHON, Michael	42	M	Laborer	23Ja02Ev
MCEVOY, Mary	14	F	Servant	23Ja02Ev
DONNELLY, John	33	M	Joiner	23Ja02Ev

JANE-BLACK 28 JANUARY 1850

From Limerick

NAMES OF PASSENGERS	AGE	SEX	OCCUPATIONS	DATE PORT SHIP
MALONEY, Mary	30	F	Laborer	28Ja10Ep
Martin	2	M	Child	28Ja10Ep
Michl.	.00	M	Infant	28Ja10Ep
MORGAN, Patt	35	M	Unknown	28Ja10Ep
Biddy	30	F	Unknown	28Ja10Ep
BOLAND, Biddy	23	F	Unknown	28Ja10Ep
TIERNEY, Patt	32	M	Unknown	28Ja10Ep
Eliza	23	F	Unknown	28Ja10Ep
CARROLL, Oliver	9	M	Child	28Ja10Ep
James	7	M	Child	28Ja10Ep
GUNMANDEL, Margt.	20	F	Unknown	28Ja10Ep
NEEDLEY, Edward	29	M	Unknown	28Ja10Ep
SHEEHON, Con.	20	M	Unknown	28Ja10Ep
MAHONEY, Mary	17	F	Unknown	28Ja10Ep
COHDENEA, J.	12	M	Unknown	28Ja10Ep
CORDAUGH, Maurice	24	M	Unknown	28Ja10Ep
CONDEN, John	26	M	Unknown	28Ja10Ep
Cath.	26	F	Unknown	28Ja10Ep
Mary	2	F	Child	28Ja10Ep
LEAHY, Mary	19	F	Unknown	28Ja10Ep
Biddy	26	F	Unknown	28Ja10Ep
RYAN, John	30	M	Unknown	28Ja10Ep
CALKINS, William	20	M	Unknown	28Ja10Ep
Johanna	30	F	Unknown	28Ja10Ep
MCMAHON, Michl.	50	M	Unknown	28Ja10Ep
Mary	45	F	Unknown	28Ja10Ep
Thomas	12	M	Unknown	28Ja10Ep
John	10	M	Unknown	28Ja10Ep
Mary	5	F	Unknown	28Ja10Ep
DONNELL, Thomas	40	M	Unknown	28Ja10Ep
CONNELL, Biddy	12	F	Unknown	28Ja10Ep
WEED, Biddy	20	F	Unknown	28Ja10Ep
Ellen	25	F	Unknown	28Ja10Ep
GLEESON, John	26	M	Unknown	28Ja10Ep
BURNS, James	25	M	Unknown	28Ja10Ep
Biddy	20	F	Unknown	28Ja10Ep
ALLEN, John	24	M	Unknown	28Ja10Ep
KEARNEY, Michl.	40	M	Unknown	28Ja10Ep
Michl.	19	M	Unknown	28Ja10Ep
HOKLETON, Michl.	30	M	Unknown	28Ja10Ep
CONSEDINE, James	21	M	Laborer	28Ja10Ep
CASEY, Thomas	35	M	Unknown	28Ja10Ep
KEANE, Mary	21	F	Unknown	28Ja10Ep
COSGRAVE, John	25	M	Unknown	28Ja10Ep
DEA, Michl.	25	M	Unknown	28Ja10Ep
CORBETT, Mary	19	F	Unknown	28Ja10Ep
RIORDEN, Johana	25	F	Unknown	28Ja10Ep
BRIEN, John	30	M	Unknown	28Ja10Ep
ODONNELL, Patt	20	M	Unknown	28Ja10Ep
KEVIN, Michl.	22	M	Unknown	28Ja10Ep
HILL, Michl.	18	M	Unknown	28Ja10Ep
SCANLIN, Biddy	20	F	Unknown	28Ja10Ep
LASSY, Barth.	21	M	Unknown	28Ja10Ep
Bridgt.	18	F	Unknown	28Ja10Ep
MCKIRGE, John	25	M	Unknown	28Ja10Ep
FAHY, Thomas	25	M	Unknown	28Ja10Ep
MCGRATH, James	20	M	Unknown	28Ja10Ep
FLANAGAN, Thomas	39	M	Unknown	28Ja10Ep
MCGRATH, Patt	19	M	Unknown	28Ja10Ep
MCNAMARA, Biddy	32	F	Unknown	28Ja10Ep
Patt	4	M	Child	28Ja10Ep
Nancy	.00	F	Infant	28Ja10Ep
FINNEN, Thomas	45	M	Unknown	28Ja10Ep
DUGGAN, Mandy	35	M	Unknown	28Ja10Ep
DAFFY, John	35	M	Unknown	28Ja10Ep
OCONNOR, Mary	24	F	Unknown	28Ja10Ep
FLYNN, Cath.	21	F	Unknown	28Ja10Ep
SHEAHAN, John	28	M	Unknown	28Ja10Ep
SCANLIN, Patt	20	M	Unknown	28Ja10Ep
RYAN, Michl.	20	M	Unknown	28Ja10Ep
LYNCH, Timothy	24	M	Unknown	28Ja10Ep
FINLEY, Eliza	15	F	Unknown	28Ja10Ep
OBRIEN, James	26	M	Unknown	28Ja10Ep
HOGAN, Ellen	19	F	Unknown	28Ja10Ep
BULL, Daniel	24	M	Unknown	28Ja10Ep
RYAN, Hann	30	U	Unknown	28Ja10Ep
HAYES, Margt.	50	F	Unknown	28Ja10Ep
Patt	23	M	Unknown	28Ja10Ep
Thomas	21	M	Unknown	28Ja10Ep
H.John	19	M	Unknown	28Ja10Ep
James	17	M	Unknown	28Ja10Ep
Margt.	15	F	Unknown	28Ja10Ep
Johanna	13	F	Unknown	28Ja10Ep
WALSH, Darby	50	M	Unknown	28Ja10Ep
Alley	48	F	Unknown	28Ja10Ep
Patt	17	M	Unknown	28Ja10Ep
Margt.	15	F	Unknown	28Ja10Ep

NAMES OF PASSENGERS	AGE	SEX	OCCUPATIONS	DATE PORT SHIP
WALSH, Mary	13	F	Unknown	28Ja10Ep
Johana	10	F	Unknown	28Ja10Ep
Jeremiah	9	M	Child	28Ja10Ep
Bridget	4	F	Child	28Ja10Ep
SHEAHON, John	35	M	Laborer	28Ja10Ep
BUCKLEY, Conor	30	F	Unknown	28Ja10Ep
Biddy	11	F	Unknown	28Ja10Ep
HAYES, Roger	40	M	Unknown	28Ja10Ep
MITCHELL, John	21	M	Unknown	28Ja10Ep
Hannah	21	F	Unknown	28Ja10Ep
MCNANNON, Mary	25	F	Unknown	28Ja10Ep
THOMPSON, William	22	M	Unknown	28Ja10Ep
George	26	M	Unknown	28Ja10Ep
BUDYMAN, Thomas	24	M	Unknown	28Ja10Ep
OCONNOR, Michl.	22	M	Unknown	28Ja10Ep
Bridgt.	21	F	Unknown	28Ja10Ep
HOWE, Thomas	23	M	Unknown	28Ja10Ep
BOURKE, Michl.	45	M	Unknown	28Ja10Ep
Ellen	40	F	Unknown	28Ja10Ep
Mary	14	F	Unknown	28Ja10Ep
CONNELL, Jane	24	F	Unknown	28Ja10Ep
Bridgt.	27	F	Unknown	28Ja10Ep
FITZPATRICK, Mary	30	F	Unknown	28Ja10Ep
Michl.	5	M	Child	28Ja10Ep
MCMAHON, Thos.	20	M	Unknown	28Ja10Ep
WALL, James	16	M	Unknown	28Ja10Ep
KIRBY, Michl.	25	M	Unknown	28Ja10Ep
Edward	30	M	Unknown	28Ja10Ep
ROUGHEN, Edmund	25	M	Unknown	28Ja10Ep
HEANEY, L.	30	M	Unknown	28Ja10Ep
Biddy	22	F	Unknown	28Ja10Ep
Cath.	24	F	Unknown	28Ja10Ep
MCDONNELL, John	24	M	Unknown	28Ja10Ep
LEONARD, Jane	50	F	Unknown	28Ja10Ep
John	17	M	Unknown	28Ja10Ep
Michl.	13	M	Unknown	28Ja10Ep
Peter	9	M	Child	28Ja10Ep
MCNAMARA, Margt.	34	F	Unknown	28Ja10Ep
BANNWELL, Patt	40	M	Unknown	28Ja10Ep
Richard	20	M	Unknown	28Ja10Ep
MORGAN, Johana	20	F	Unknown	28Ja10Ep
HOGAN, James	56	M	Unknown	28Ja10Ep
Nancy	56	F	Unknown	28Ja10Ep
John	14	M	Unknown	28Ja10Ep
James	12	M	Unknown	28Ja10Ep
Mary	11	F	Unknown	28Ja10Ep
Kate	10	F	Unknown	28Ja10Ep
BRADSHAW, George	24	M	Unknown	28Ja10Ep
KARNEY, Kate	13	F	Unknown	28Ja10Ep
Biddy	10	F	Unknown	28Ja10Ep
Margt.	13	F	Unknown	28Ja10Ep
SULLIVAN, Ren	35	M	Unknown	28Ja10Ep
Edward	34	M	Unknown	28Ja10Ep
FITZGERALD, John	22	M	Unknown	28Ja10Ep
LYNCH, Patt	20	M	Laborer	28Ja10Ep
Thomas	16	M	Unknown	28Ja10Ep
John	13	M	Unknown	28Ja10Ep
HENNER, Peggy	30	M	Unknown	28Ja10Ep
Timothy	9	M	Child	28Ja10Ep
William	.00	M	Infant	28Ja10Ep
HINLEY, Nancy	23	F	Unknown	28Ja10Ep
COONEY, Mary	46	F	Unknown	28Ja10Ep
COLLINS, Michl.	30	M	Unknown	28Ja10Ep
John	35	M	Unknown	28Ja10Ep
KENNEY, James	40	M	Unknown	28Ja10Ep
COLLINS, Thomas	30	M	Unknown	28Ja10Ep
CONNERS, Martin	24	M	Unknown	28Ja10Ep
RYAN, John	25	M	Unknown	28Ja10Ep
TUOHY, Mary	22	F	Unknown	28Ja10Ep
LEARTY, James	20	M	Unknown	28Ja10Ep
MOORE, John	26	M	Unknown	28Ja10Ep
Mary	26	F	Unknown	28Ja10Ep
Mary	20	F	Unknown	28Ja10Ep
Michl.	.00	M	Infant	28Ja10Ep
CONWAY, Martin	26	M	Unknown	28Ja10Ep
CONWAY, Bridgt.	26	F	Unknown	28Ja10Ep
Mary	11	F	Unknown	28Ja10Ep
Biddy	4	F	Child	28Ja10Ep
Nancy	3	F	Child	28Ja10Ep
Michl.	9	M	Child	28Ja10Ep
ADAMS, John	20	M	Unknown	28Ja10Ep
MORRIS, Michl.	30	M	Unknown	28Ja10Ep
MULLIGAN, Mary	22	F	Unknown	28Ja10Ep
HOGAN, Anne	6	F	Child	28Ja10Ep
Johanna	6	F	Child	28Ja10Ep
William	.00	M	Infant	28Ja10Ep
KENEDY, James	25	M	Unknown	28Ja10Ep
CONNOR, John	40	M	Unknown	28Ja10Ep
Jane	35	F	Unknown	28Ja10Ep
Eliza	12	F	Unknown	28Ja10Ep
Jane	.00	F	Infant	28Ja10Ep
OSHADY, George	26	M	Unknown	28Ja10Ep
SHANNON, Patt	40	M	Unknown	28Ja10Ep
MCNAMARA, Mary	22	F	Unknown	28Ja10Ep
KEANE, Biddy	20	F	Unknown	28Ja10Ep
GLEESON, James	20	M	Unknown	28Ja10Ep
LEONARD, Anne	26	F	Unknown	28Ja10Ep
BOURKE, Patt	20	M	Unknown	28Ja10Ep
CROWNEY, James	30	M	Unknown	28Ja10Ep
MALONEY, Biddy	20	F	Unknown	28Ja10Ep
MCCARTHY, Eugene	20	M	Unknown	28Ja10Ep
RYAN, John	30	M	Unknown	28Ja10Ep
William	30	M	Unknown	28Ja10Ep
OBRIEN, Anne	24	F	Unknown	28Ja10Ep
HARTIGAN, Johann	25	F	Laborer	28Ja10Ep
BARNY, David	22	M	Unknown	28Ja10Ep
LYNCH, Michl.	22	M	Unknown	28Ja10Ep
RYAN, Cath.	24	F	Unknown	28Ja10Ep
Judy	42	F	Unknown	28Ja10Ep
MOYLAN, Cath.	40	F	Unknown	28Ja10Ep
Ellen	11	F	Unknown	28Ja10Ep
Thomas	3	M	Child	28Ja10Ep
ODONNELL, Patt	24	M	Unknown	28Ja10Ep
MOLONEY, Michl.	30	M	Unknown	28Ja10Ep
MACK, Biddy	25	F	Unknown	28Ja10Ep
RYAN, Cath.	14	F	Unknown	28Ja10Ep
Anne	12	F	Unknown	28Ja10Ep
POTTER, John	20	M	Unknown	28Ja10Ep
CORBETT, Thos.	33	M	Unknown	28Ja10Ep
Harriet	29	F	Unknown	28Ja10Ep
Honora	9	F	Child	28Ja10Ep
Eliza	2	F	Child	28Ja10Ep
David	.00	M	Infant	28Ja10Ep
HARRINGTON, Michl.	28	M	Unknown	28Ja10Ep
BENNETT, William	46	M	Unknown	28Ja10Ep
HOGAN, John	30	M	Unknown	28Ja10Ep
MULLENS, James	22	M	Unknown	28Ja10Ep
John	24	M	Unknown	28Ja10Ep
HUNNINGTON, Mary	34	F	Unknown	28Ja10Ep
BOURKE, James	20	M	Unknown	28Ja10Ep
KELLY, John	60	M	Unknown	28Ja10Ep
Patt	30	M	Unknown	28Ja10Ep
Peggy	12	F	Unknown	28Ja10Ep
Johanna	2	F	Child	28Ja10Ep
Mary	.00	F	Infant	28Ja10Ep
REEDY, Michl.	20	M	Unknown	28Ja10Ep
CORKERAN, Roger	22	M	Unknown	28Ja10Ep
BROWN, Simon	29	M	Unknown	28Ja10Ep
MOORE, Mary	40	F	Unknown	28Ja10Ep
Ellen	14	F	Unknown	28Ja10Ep
John	17	M	Unknown	28Ja10Ep
FLAHERTY, Judy	40	F	Unknown	28Ja10Ep
Mary	18	F	Unknown	28Ja10Ep
Margt.	16	F	Unknown	28Ja10Ep
MCCARTHY, Johanna	30	F	Unknown	28Ja10Ep
FOX, Mary	29	F	Unknown	28Ja10Ep
LYONS, Mary	29	F	Unknown	28Ja10Ep
HEALY, Margt.	24	F	Unknown	28Ja10Ep
RILEY, Margt.	30	F	Unknown	28Ja10Ep
RYAN, Mary	29	F	Unknown	28Ja10Ep

NAMES OF PASSENGERS	AGE	SEX	OCCUPATIONS	DATE PORT SHIP
SHAUGNESSEY, Michl.	30	M	Unknown	28Ja10Ep
MULLENS, John	23	M	Unknown	28Ja10Ep
HENNESSY, Patt	60	M	Unknown	28Ja10Ep
Bridgt.	25	F	Unknown	28Ja10Ep
HYNES, Bessy	18	F	Unknown	28Ja10Ep
FOLEY, John	31	M	Laborer	28Ja10Ep
RUSS, Con.	30	M	Laborer	28Ja10Ep
HEALY, Nancy	45	F	Laborer	28Ja10Ep

EUROPA 11 FEBRUARY 1850

From Liverpool

NAMES OF PASSENGERS	AGE	SEX	OCCUPATIONS	DATE PORT SHIP
WHITE, U	26	M	Gentleman	11Fe02Fe
BRYNS, U-Miss	24	F	Unknown	11Fe02Fe
FIERGUS, W.	20	F	Unknown	11Fe02Fe

LIBERTY 11 FEBRUARY 1850

From Glasgow

NAMES OF PASSENGERS	AGE	SEX	OCCUPATIONS	DATE PORT SHIP
HAGGERTY, Ellen	30	F	Unknown	11Fe21Eo
Mary	8	F	Child	11Fe21Eo
Ellen	3	F	Child	11Fe21Eo
Rose	20	F	Unknown	11Fe21Eo
Anthony	.07	M	Infant	11Fe21Eo
Patrick	2	M	Child	11Fe21Eo
CASSEY, Catherine	23	F	Unknown	11Fe21Eo
DUNCAN, David	28	M	Spinner	11Fe21Eo
HARDY, Michael	23	M	Mason	11Fe21Eo
LOFT, Thomas	25	M	Unknown	11Fe21Eo
HALL, Thomas	30	M	Unknown	11Fe21Eo

WEST-POINT 13 FEBRUARY 1850

From Liverpool

NAMES OF PASSENGERS	AGE	SEX	OCCUPATIONS	DATE PORT SHIP
DODD, William	30	M	Farmer	13Fe02Er
U (W)	24	F	None	13Fe02Er
NOWLAN, U-Mrs.	26	F	None	13Fe02Er
Mary-Ann	.00	F	Infant	13Fe02Er
MAGUIRE, Eliza	24	F	Servant	13Fe02Er
FAGAN, Bridget	24	F	Servant	13Fe02Er
CURRANS, Denis	27	M	Farmer	13Fe02Er
Margaret	22	F	None	13Fe02Er
MCLAUGHLIN, John	32	M	Farmer	13Fe02Er
ROURKE, Michael	19	M	Laborer	13Fe02Er
CROUGHWELL, Julia	45	F	None	13Fe02Er
Mary	12	F	None	13Fe02Er
Julia	5	F	Child	13Fe02Er
Ann	4	F	Child	13Fe02Er
Margaret	3	F	Child	13Fe02Er
RILEY, Bridget	35	F	None	13Fe02Er
Bridget	16	F	None	13Fe02Er
Margaret	11	F	None	13Fe02Er
Mary	10	F	None	13Fe02Er
James	8	M	Child	13Fe02Er
RILEY, Ann	4	F	Child	13Fe02Er
Catherine	2	F	Child	13Fe02Er
Bridget	15	F	None	13Fe02Er
BOYLE, Margaret	35	F	None	13Fe02Er
MURPHY, Margaret	24	F	Servant	13Fe02Er
RILEY, Peter	20	M	Laborer	13Fe02Er
KEENAN, Charles	21	M	Laborer	13Fe02Er
POWELL, Michael	20	M	Laborer	13Fe02Er
COAL, William	37	M	Gdnr	13Fe02Er
RYAN, Ellen	19	F	Servant	13Fe02Er
GLYNN, John	20	M	Laborer	13Fe02Er
LAMB, Bartley	19	M	Laborer	13Fe02Er
GRIMES, John	35	M	Laborer	13Fe02Er
DWYRE, Alice	43	F	None	13Fe02Er
Michael	25	M	None	13Fe02Er
David	23	M	None	13Fe02Er
Mary	21	F	None	13Fe02Er
FOLEY, James	30	M	None	13Fe02Er
Mary	22	F	None	13Fe02Er
Peggy	.00	F	Infant	13Fe02Er
HEFRON, James	40	M	Laborer	13Fe02Er
FITZGERALD, John	42	M	Laborer	13Fe02Er
RAIL, Simon	48	M	Laborer	13Fe02Er
DARLEY, Peter	23	M	Shepherd	13Fe02Er
KEATING, Peter	30	M	Smith	13Fe02Er
U (W)	30	F	None	13Fe02Er
Jane	6	F	Child	13Fe02Er
Edward	3	M	Child	13Fe02Er
KENNY, Bridget	60	F	None	13Fe02Er
HOGAN, James	20	M	Laborer	13Fe02Er
Bridget	25	F	None	13Fe02Er
Owen	16	M	None	13Fe02Er
Mary	15	F	None	13Fe02Er
RYAN, Patrick	22	M	Laborer	13Fe02Er
WHITE, Eliza	35	F	None	13Fe02Er
James	12	M	None	13Fe02Er
Eliza-Jane	14	F	None	13Fe02Er
Isabella	11	F	None	13Fe02Er
ROBINSON, Rachel	9	F	Child	13Fe02Er
Charlotte	4	F	Child	13Fe02Er
OTOOL, Morgan	16	M	Laborer	13Fe02Er
CORMICK, John	36	M	Smith	13Fe02Er
QUINN, John	20	M	Laborer	13Fe02Er
DONNELLY, Mary	40	F	Paper Maker	13Fe02Er
James	17	M	Paper Maker	13Fe02Er
Patrick	20	M	Paper Maker	13Fe02Er
Mary-Ann	11	F	Paper Maker	13Fe02Er
Betsey	18	F	Paper Maker	13Fe02Er
CONNAUGHTON, Mary	18	F	Servant	13Fe02Er
OWENS, Morris	57	M	Laborer	13Fe02Er
Catherine	30	F	None	13Fe02Er
Pat	19	M	None	13Fe02Er
Michael	15	M	None	13Fe02Er
KEENAN, Rose	16	F	Servant	13Fe02Er
HINCH, Thomas	21	M	Laborer	13Fe02Er
SHEARES, John	40	M	Laborer	13Fe02Er
Pat	18	M	Laborer	13Fe02Er
TRACEY, Thomas	30	M	Laborer	13Fe02Er
SCULLY, Mary	25	F	None	13Fe02Er
Bridget	13	F	None	13Fe02Er
Richard	16	M	None	13Fe02Er
GLASHY, Bridget	18	F	None	13Fe02Er
John	.00	M	Infant	13Fe02Er
LEIGH, Thomas	20	M	Laborer	13Fe02Er
CLEARY, Thomas	30	M	Laborer	13Fe02Er
KINNEY, Ellen	35	F	Servant	13Fe02Er
GILL, John	25	M	Laborer	13Fe02Er
U, John	.00	M	Infant	13Fe02Er
Bridget	27	F	Weaver	13Fe02Er
Catherine	23	F	Weaver	13Fe02Er
Margt.	18	F	Weaver	13Fe02Er
Mary	15	F	Weaver	13Fe02Er
Ann	14	F	Weaver	13Fe02Er
Theresa	7	F	Child	13Fe02Er
Eliza	10	F	None	13Fe02Er

NAMES OF PASSENGERS	AGE	SEX	OCCUPATIONS	DATE PORT SHIP
U, John	20	M	Weaver	13Fe02Er
Rose	12	F	None	13Fe02Er
WOODS, Margaret	21	F	Servant	13Fe02Er
Margt.	22	F	Servant	13Fe02Er
CONROY, John	18	M	Laborer	13Fe02Er
SHAUGHNESSY, John	5	M	Child	13Fe02Er
JENNINGS, Margaret	23	F	Servant	13Fe02Er
COMINGS, Patrick	5	M	Child	13Fe02Er
Michael	4	M	Child	13Fe02Er
LOCKWIN, Cath.A.	14	F	Servant	13Fe02Er
RILEY, Margaret	40	F	Servant	13Fe02Er
Ann	.00	F	Infant	13Fe02Er
Mary	11	F	None	13Fe02Er
Michael	9	M	Child	13Fe02Er
Ellen	7	F	Child	13Fe02Er
Margaret	4	F	Child	13Fe02Er
POWELL, Patrick	25	M	Laborer	13Fe02Er
HEANY, Daniel	17	M	Mason	13Fe02Er
MCMURROUGH, Patrick	4	M	Child	13Fe02Er
Mary	18	F	Servant	13Fe02Er
DUNN, Eliza	40	F	Servant	13Fe02Er
Thomas	12	M	Servant	13Fe02Er
Eliza	9	F	Child	13Fe02Er
John	7	M	Child	13Fe02Er
Mary-Ann	5	F	Child	13Fe02Er
J.	3	M	Child	13Fe02Er
RICHARDSON, Moses	45	M	Smith	13Fe02Er
Martha	60	F	None	13Fe02Er
CLARKE, John	40	M	Laborer	13Fe02Er
MCGOFF, John	10	M	None	13Fe02Er
Patrick	8	M	Child	13Fe02Er
KEENAN, Sarah	19	F	Servant	13Fe02Er
Mary	16	F	Servant	13Fe02Er
FINNEGAN, Michael	23	M	Laborer	13Fe02Er
Patrick	25	M	Laborer	13Fe02Er
BARRY, John	36	M	Mason	13Fe02Er
ELWOOD, James	21	M	Laborer	13Fe02Er
Johanna	18	F	Servant	13Fe02Er

ROSCIUS 15 FEBRUARY 1850

From Liverpool

NAMES OF PASSENGERS	AGE	SEX	OCCUPATIONS	DATE PORT SHIP
DEE, Pat	21	M	Laborer	15Fe02At
Bryan	18	M	Laborer	15Fe02At
CONNELL, Michael	22	M	Laborer	15Fe02At
Mary	20	F	None	15Fe02At
Michael	25	M	Laborer	15Fe02At
Eliza	17	F	Servant	15Fe02At
TYRRAL, Henry	50	M	Laborer	15Fe02At
Bridget	40	M	Laborer	15Fe02At
Bridget	13	F	Servant	15Fe02At
John	12	M	None	15Fe02At
HORAM, Thomas	28	M	Laborer	15Fe02At
COURTENAY, James	22	M	Nailer	15Fe02At
BRENNAN, John	26	M	Laborer	15Fe02At
CONNOR, Garrett	25	M	Laborer	15Fe02At
KELLY, Mary	30	F	Servant	15Fe02At
MCDONOUGH, Jane	23	F	Servant	15Fe02At
KELLY, Paul	4	M	Child	15Fe02At
John	10	M	None	15Fe02At
FRANCES, Catharine	23	F	Servant	15Fe02At
MURPHY, Winifred	24	F	Dressmaker	15Fe02At
DURPHIN, William	25	M	Laborer	15Fe02At
Vesta	21	F	None	15Fe02At
Mary	18	F	Servant	15Fe02At
MAGRATH, Catharine	22	F	Dressmaker	15Fe02At
Alice	15	F	Servant	15Fe02At
KELLY, Simon	17	M	Tailor	15Fe02At

NAMES OF PASSENGERS	AGE	SEX	OCCUPATIONS	DATE PORT SHIP
MCNEARNY, Francis	30	M	Tinker	15Fe02At
John	35	M	Laborer	15Fe02At
Nancy	11	F	Servant	15Fe02At
Catharine	25	F	None	15Fe02At
Pat	9	M	Child	15Fe02At
Hugh	3	M	Child	15Fe02At
Catharine	10	F	None	15Fe02At
REILLY, Mary	30	F	Dressmaker	15Fe02At
SMITH, Michael	35	M	Laborer	15Fe02At
Catharine	40	F	None	15Fe02At
ROACH, Bridget	19	F	Servant	15Fe02At
Edward	11	M	None	15Fe02At
CASSERLY, Jane	30	F	Servant	15Fe02At
James	18	M	Laborer	15Fe02At
BRASSON, Jane	27	F	Dressmaker	15Fe02At
Catherine	7	F	Child	15Fe02At
Mary	4	F	Child	15Fe02At
SHANLY, James	42	M	Laborer	15Fe02At
MCGARVON, Maria	11	F	None	15Fe02At
KERNAN, Peter	20	M	Nailer	15Fe02At
CALLIVAN, Ann	28	F	Servant	15Fe02At
COURNAY, Bridget	6	F	Child	15Fe02At
GAUGHAN, Michael	44	M	Laborer	15Fe02At
DUNN, Henry	18	M	Laborer	15Fe02At
LAWLESS, William	17	M	Laborer	15Fe02At
CONLON, Philip	40	M	Laborer	15Fe02At
MAHON, Mary	24	F	Dressmaker	15Fe02At
CONNEL, James	22	M	Laborer	15Fe02At
MULDOON, William	22	M	Laborer	15Fe02At
Catherine	19	F	None	15Fe02At
GOULDING, James	18	M	Laborer	15Fe02At
GALLAGHAN, Philip	35	M	Laborer	15Fe02At
Ann	30	M	None	15Fe02At
GORMAN, Patrick	18	M	Laborer	15Fe02At
Catharine	15	F	None	15Fe02At
DUFFY, Bridget	16	F	None	15Fe02At
GLASS, Margaret	19	F	Dressmaker	15Fe02At
Mary	16	F	None	15Fe02At
DOOLAN, Mary	17	F	Dressmaker	15Fe02At
PIKE, Ann	9	F	Child	15Fe02At
Julia	7	F	Child	15Fe02At
MONAGHAN, Nancy	20	F	Servant	15Fe02At
WELSH, Michael	21	M	Laborer	15Fe02At
GEARY, Thomas	27	M	Laborer	15Fe02At
MAGRATH, John	23	M	Laborer	15Fe02At
Judy	20	F	None	15Fe02At
CONLON, John	24	M	Laborer	15Fe02At
James	22	M	Laborer	15Fe02At
Catharine	13	F	None	15Fe02At
Ellen	16	F	None	15Fe02At
WALL, Walter	30	M	Laborer	15Fe02At
DOLAN, Nancy	30	F	Dressmaker	15Fe02At
COCHLIN, William	25	M	Laborer	15Fe02At
William	2	M	Child	15Fe02At
KILLIAN, Bridget	18	F	Dressmaker	15Fe02At
MCCOOK, Thomas	25	M	Laborer	15Fe02At
ROSS, Mary	18	F	Servant	15Fe02At
SCANLAN, Ellen	35	F	Wife	15Fe02At
Johanna	8	F	Child	15Fe02At
Patrick	5	M	Child	15Fe02At
Mary	4	F	Child	15Fe02At
DALY, Michael	25	M	Laborer	15Fe02At
DONOVAN, Bartholomew	23	M	Laborer	15Fe02At
Peter	14	M	Laborer	15Fe02At
SLOAN, Margaret	40	F	Wife	15Fe02At
James	15	M	None	15Fe02At
John	12	M	None	15Fe02At
Robert	7	M	Child	15Fe02At
Margaret	4	F	Child	15Fe02At
MANLY, Michael	25	M	Laborer	15Fe02At
Mary	20	F	None	15Fe02At
BURNS, John	23	M	Laborer	15Fe02At
FLINN, Judy	23	F	Dressmaker	15Fe02At
DOLEY, James	27	M	Laborer	15Fe02At
ACKROYD, William	46	M	Weaver	15Fe02At

NAMES OF PASSENGERS	AGE	SEX	OCCUPATIONS	DATE PORT SHIP
CARNON, Laurence	50	M	Laborer	15Fe02At
Margaret	18	F	None	15Fe02At
Andrew	14	M	None	15Fe02At
Jane	12	F	None	15Fe02At
DOWKER, Edward	55	M	Laborer	15Fe02At
Ellen	55	F	None	15Fe02At
Eliza	18	F	None	15Fe02At
Susan	14	F	None	15Fe02At
ROGERS, Maria	17	F	Dressmaker	15Fe02At
CUMMINS, Michael	17	M	Laborer	15Fe02At
MCDONNEL, Peter	18	M	Shoemaker	15Fe02At
CUFF, Michael	21	M	Laborer	15Fe02At
Martin	18	M	Laborer	15Fe02At
WEIR, Dora	16	F	Dressmaker	15Fe02At
CLAPPIT, Sarah	18	F	Servant	15Fe02At
SCULLY, Michael	20	M	Laborer	15Fe02At
REEFF, Bridget	40	F	Wife	15Fe02At
Maria	13	F	None	15Fe02At
Thomas	11	M	None	15Fe02At
Honora	6	F	Child	15Fe02At
Patrick	5	M	Child	15Fe02At
James	3	M	Child	15Fe02At
Elizabeth	.04	F	Infant	15Fe02At
BURNS, Paul	26	M	Laborer	15Fe02At
NOLAN, Pat	24	M	Laborer	15Fe02At
REYNOLDS, Mary	30	F	Servant	15Fe02At
GATELY, Michael	28	M	Laborer	15Fe02At
Luke	16	M	Laborer	15Fe02At
MANXWELL, Amy	18	F	Dressmaker	15Fe02At
MURTOUGH, Catharine	18	F	Servant	15Fe02At
GILL, Catharine	21	F	Milliner	15Fe02At
MALONE, James	32	M	Laborer	15Fe02At
RYAN, Mary	16	F	Servant	15Fe02At
Michael	12	M	Laborer	15Fe02At
ROBINS, Jane	25	F	Servant	15Fe02At
DICKS, Pat	21	M	Laborer	15Fe02At
PRIOR, Bridget	22	F	Dressmaker	15Fe02At
FITZSIMONS, Ann	37	F	Wife	15Fe02At
John	10	M	None	15Fe02At
Ellen	18	F	Servant	15Fe02At
Thomas	5	M	Child	15Fe02At
LYNCH, Ann	17	F	Servant	15Fe02At
BRACKEN, Mary	18	F	Dressmaker	15Fe02At
ODONNEL, Darby	21	M	Laborer	15Fe02At
BARRY, Mary	10	F	None	15Fe02At
James	4	M	Child	15Fe02At
CROW, John	25	M	Laborer	15Fe02At
KIRVAN, Pat	17	M	Laborer	15Fe02At
Ann	11	F	None	15Fe02At
DOLAN, Bridget	18	F	Milliner	15Fe02At
DUNN, Edward	36	M	Laborer	15Fe02At
Mary	34	F	None	15Fe02At
Anthony	11	M	None	15Fe02At
Lawrence	9	M	Child	15Fe02At
Sally	7	F	Child	15Fe02At
Catharine	4	F	Child	15Fe02At
Margaret	.02	F	Infant	15Fe02At
DONELLY, John	20	M	Laborer	15Fe02At
BIRD, James	30	M	Laborer	15Fe02At
SWEENY, Owen	26	M	Laborer	15Fe02At
THOMPSON, George	28	M	Laborer	15Fe02At
MOONEY, Patrick	22	M	Tailor	15Fe02At
MCNALLY, Andrew	22	M	Painter	15Fe02At
GRATH, Harriet	21	F	Dressmaker	15Fe02At
James	5	M	Child	15Fe02At
ANNESLEY, Robert	28	M	Draper	15Fe02At
Jane	28	F	None	15Fe02At
MCDAVIS, Mary	25	F	Dressmaker	15Fe02At
MCGROOTY, Constantine	30	M	Baker	15Fe02At
Ellen	30	F	None	15Fe02At
Bridget	33	F	None	15Fe02At
Margaret	5	F	Child	15Fe02At
Mary	3	F	Child	15Fe02At
Michael	1	M	Child	15Fe02At
KELLY, Ann	21	F	Milliner	15Fe02At
SEMMAN, Ann	40	F	None	15Fe02At
HAZARD, Pat	20	M	Laborer	15Fe02At
HAVERON, Mary	25	F	Servant	15Fe02At
TRYAN, Joseph	24	M	Painter	15Fe02At
Ann	23	F	None	15Fe02At
BOLTON, Robert	30	M	Mariner	15Fe02At
CAVANAGH, Felix	34	M	Carpenter	15Fe02At
Margaret	27	F	None	15Fe02At
Edward	22	M	None	15Fe02At
Eliza	18	F	None	15Fe02At
YAIL, Henry	24	M	Laborer	15Fe02At
MCGOVEN, Biddy	23	F	Servant	15Fe02At
BOGG, Catharine	22	F	Servant	15Fe02At
Eliza	6	F	Child	15Fe02At
HORE, Ann	20	F	Servant	15Fe02At
GAUGHAN, Michael	26	M	Laborer	15Fe02At
MURPHY, James	45	M	Laborer	15Fe02At
SHERIDAN, Pat	18	M	Laborer	15Fe02At
MCKABER, James	18	M	Laborer	15Fe02At
WELSH, Thomas	40	M	Laborer	15Fe02At

MONTEZUMA 16 FEBRUARY 1850

From Demerara

NAMES OF PASSENGERS	AGE	SEX	OCCUPATIONS	DATE PORT SHIP
NORTON, P.	32	M	Merchant	16Fe33Bl
MCKIE, Alexander	40	M	None	16Fe33Bl

LONDON 18 FEBRUARY 1850

From London

NAMES OF PASSENGERS	AGE	SEX	OCCUPATIONS	DATE PORT SHIP
CAGER, Edward	21	M	None	18Fe06Au
Jane	20	F	Unknown	18Fe06Au
MOXON, James	30	M	Unknown	18Fe06Au
Lydia	24	F	Unknown	18Fe06Au
BEARD, Jos.	23	M	Unknown	18Fe06Au
HUTCHINSON, Wm.	18	M	Unknown	18Fe06Au
MUNN, John	48	M	Unknown	18Fe06Au
Harriet	45	F	Unknown	18Fe06Au
Harriet	15	F	Unknown	18Fe06Au
George	13	M	Unknown	18Fe06Au
YOUNG, Thos.	25	M	Unknown	18Fe06Au
Elizabeth	25	F	Unknown	18Fe06Au
Elizabeth	7	F	Child	18Fe06Au
Sarah	4	F	Child	18Fe06Au
Emily	3	F	Child	18Fe06Au
Ellen	.06	F	Infant	18Fe06Au
WALSH, Catharine	20	F	Unknown	18Fe06Au
Mary	1	F	Child	18Fe06Au
MUNN, U Born-At-Sea	.00	F	Infant	18Fe06Au

SHANNON 20 FEBRUARY 1850

From Liverpool

NAMES OF PASSENGERS	AGE	SEX	OCCUPATIONS	DATE PORT SHIP
FAHY, Ellen	41	F	Laborer	20Fe02Eq
John	16	M	Unknown	20Fe02Eq
Ann	13	F	Unknown	20Fe02Eq
Mary	11	F	Unknown	20Fe02Eq
Bridget	8	F	Child	20Fe02Eq
Cathe.	5	F	Child	20Fe02Eq
Richard	2	M	Child	20Fe02Eq
MORRIS, William	24	M	Unknown	20Fe02Eq
BRIERE, Martin	30	M	Unknown	20Fe02Eq
ROONEY, John	22	M	Unknown	20Fe02Eq
DUFFY, Patrick	26	M	Unknown	20Fe02Eq
Mary	50	F	Unknown	20Fe02Eq
John	20	M	Unknown	20Fe02Eq
FOLEY, John	21	M	Unknown	20Fe02Eq
Maurice	30	M	Unknown	20Fe02Eq
BAILY, James	30	M	Unknown	20Fe02Eq
CONDDEM, Pat	25	M	Unknown	20Fe02Eq
Margt.	35	F	Unknown	20Fe02Eq
Dennis	11	M	Unknown	20Fe02Eq
John	9	M	Child	20Fe02Eq
Margt.	7	F	Child	20Fe02Eq
DUFFY, Simon	16	M	Laborer	20Fe02Eq
Margaret	12	F	Unknown	20Fe02Eq
Mary	9	F	Child	20Fe02Eq
BRENNAN, Cathe.	15	F	Unknown	20Fe02Eq
NAUGHTON, Rose	23	F	Unknown	20Fe02Eq
GARAN, Domk.	20	M	Unknown	20Fe02Eq
DORR, Sally	30	F	Unknown	20Fe02Eq
Mary	6	F	Child	20Fe02Eq
Bridget	4	F	Child	20Fe02Eq
Patrick	12	M	Unknown	20Fe02Eq
NAUGHTON, Mary	30	F	Unknown	20Fe02Eq
MAXWELL, Bridget	17	F	Unknown	20Fe02Eq
HEARY, Bernard	29	M	Unknown	20Fe02Eq
GRIFFIN, Dennis	18	M	Unknown	20Fe02Eq
JOHNSON, William	28	M	Unknown	20Fe02Eq
Antonietta	25	F	Unknown	20Fe02Eq
William	.00	M	Infant	20Fe02Eq
WALSH, Lawrence	30	M	Unknown	20Fe02Eq
KEATING, Pat	30	M	Unknown	20Fe02Eq
Biddy	27	F	Unknown	20Fe02Eq
James	.00	M	Infant	20Fe02Eq
NAUGHTON, Thos.	30	M	Unknown	20Fe02Eq
ENGLESH, Cathr.	20	F	Unknown	20Fe02Eq
BARRY, Cathe.	20	F	Unknown	20Fe02Eq
PURCELL, Michl.	22	M	Unknown	20Fe02Eq
CAHILL, Mary	27	F	Unknown	20Fe02Eq
CONY, Ellen	22	F	Unknown	20Fe02Eq
CUDAHY, Mary	24	F	Unknown	20Fe02Eq
DESPAN, Edward	26	M	Unknown	20Fe02Eq
CLARKE, James	49	M	Unknown	20Fe02Eq
SLOAN. Jas.Mrs.	37	F	Unknown	20Fe02Eq
John	8	M	Child	20Fe02Eq
LENEGAN, Bridget	40	F	Unknown	20Fe02Eq
Johanna	20	F	Unknown	20Fe02Eq
Ellen	13	F	Unknown	20Fe02Eq
Honora	12	F	Unknown	20Fe02Eq
Mary	10	F	Unknown	20Fe02Eq
Edward	16	M	Unknown	20Fe02Eq
John	7	M	Child	20Fe02Eq
Thomas	5	M	Child	20Fe02Eq
FEELEY, James	28	M	Unknown	20Fe02Eq
FOLEY, Michl.	21	M	Unknown	20Fe02Eq
Patrick	21	M	Unknown	20Fe02Eq
CONDDEM, Patrick	5	M	Child	20Fe02Eq

NAMES OF PASSENGERS	AGE	SEX	OCCUPATIONS	DATE PORT SHIP
CONDDEM, Mary	.00	F	Infant	20Fe02Eq
LANE, John	27	M	Unknown	20Fe02Eq
Ellen	27	F	Unknown	20Fe02Eq
Owen	.00	M	Infant	20Fe02Eq
KANE, Thomas	45	M	Unknown	20Fe02Eq
Bridget	35	F	Unknown	20Fe02Eq
Margt.	12	F	Unknown	20Fe02Eq
LEARY, Cathe.	18	F	Unknown	20Fe02Eq
DALY, Jeremiah	30	M	Unknown	20Fe02Eq
Ellen	30	F	Unknown	20Fe02Eq
Thomas	1	M	Child	20Fe02Eq
CORBETT, Cornelius	20	M	Unknown	20Fe02Eq
DALY, Honora	20	F	Unknown	20Fe02Eq
DONOHOE, Danl.	45	M	Laborer	20Fe02Eq
CAHILL, Pat	50	M	Unknown	20Fe02Eq
Mary	40	F	Unknown	20Fe02Eq
Darby	7	M	Child	20Fe02Eq
Patrick	6	M	Child	20Fe02Eq
Lawrence	5	M	Child	20Fe02Eq
KENERY, Mary	20	F	Unknown	20Fe02Eq
CASEY, Mary	20	F	Unknown	20Fe02Eq
COLLINS, Cathe.	19	F	Unknown	20Fe02Eq
COUGHLAN, Thos.	21	M	Unknown	20Fe02Eq
BRIEN, Mary	21	F	Unknown	20Fe02Eq
CROWLEY, Daniel	29	M	Unknown	20Fe02Eq
MCCARTHY, John	27	M	Unknown	20Fe02Eq
SPILLANE, Maurice	54	M	Unknown	20Fe02Eq
Ellen	52	F	Unknown	20Fe02Eq
John	32	M	Unknown	20Fe02Eq
Michl.	29	M	Unknown	20Fe02Eq
Ellen	23	F	Unknown	20Fe02Eq
Maurice	20	M	Unknown	20Fe02Eq
Patrick	18	M	Unknown	20Fe02Eq
Cathe.	13	F	Unknown	20Fe02Eq
Ann	11	F	Unknown	20Fe02Eq
Cathe.	24	F	Unknown	20Fe02Eq
SPELLANE, John	28	M	Unknown	20Fe02Eq
CROWLEY, John	26	M	Unknown	20Fe02Eq
CRONIN, Pat	22	M	Unknown	20Fe02Eq
SHEILS, Andrew	18	M	Unknown	20Fe02Eq
COSSIN, Ellen	22	F	Unknown	20Fe02Eq
John	2	M	Child	20Fe02Eq
COYLE, Ellen	22	F	Unknown	20Fe02Eq
MCENROE, Rose	20	F	Unknown	20Fe02Eq
REGAN, Martin	20	M	Unknown	20Fe02Eq
SCHOOLS, William	50	M	Unknown	20Fe02Eq
Richard	20	M	Unknown	20Fe02Eq
Daria	11	F	Unknown	20Fe02Eq
Sarah	21	F	Unknown	20Fe02Eq
Bess	15	F	Unknown	20Fe02Eq
William	30	M	Unknown	20Fe02Eq
William	5	M	Child	20Fe02Eq
MONTGOMERY, Thomas	50	M	Unknown	20Fe02Eq
U-Mrs.	46	F	Unknown	20Fe02Eq
James	22	M	Unknown	20Fe02Eq
Thomas	18	M	Unknown	20Fe02Eq
HAMILTON, Sandy	29	F	Unknown	20Fe02Eq
MCDONNELL, Cathe.	40	F	Unknown	20Fe02Eq
REILLY, Thomas	28	M	Unknown	20Fe02Eq
Mary	25	F	Unknown	20Fe02Eq
Cathe.	20	F	Unknown	20Fe02Eq
KEENAN, James	30	M	Unknown	20Fe02Eq
MCDOWAL, Rich.	30	M	Unknown	20Fe02Eq
Mary-A.	26	F	Unknown	20Fe02Eq
Ann	7	F	Child	20Fe02Eq
Mary	5	F	Child	20Fe02Eq
Jane	3	F	Child	20Fe02Eq
William	.00	M	Infant	20Fe02Eq
KILROY, John	20	M	Unknown	20Fe02Eq
Eliza	12	F	Unknown	20Fe02Eq
ARMSTRONG, Geo.	20	M	Laborer	20Fe02Eq
JOHNSON, Isabella	22	F	Unknown	20Fe02Eq
WATERS, Mary	10	F	Unknown	20Fe02Eq
Ann	7	F	Child	20Fe02Eq
RIDLY, Margt.	60	F	Unknown	20Fe02Eq

NAMES OF PASSENGERS	AGE	SEX	OCCUPATIONS	DATE PORT SHIP
NEIL, Mary	50	F	Unknown	20Fe02Eq
Maria	20	F	Unknown	20Fe02Eq
Patrick	17	M	Unknown	20Fe02Eq
James	11	M	Unknown	20Fe02Eq
Bridget	9	F	Child	20Fe02Eq
LYNCH, Moses	24	M	Unknown	20Fe02Eq
John	18	M	Unknown	20Fe02Eq
Cath.	22	F	Unknown	20Fe02Eq
MORRISSEY, Pat	18	M	Unknown	20Fe02Eq
WALSH, Biddy	30	F	Unknown	20Fe02Eq
Honora	.00	F	Infant	20Fe02Eq
MORRIS, Lawrence	24	M	Unknown	20Fe02Eq
CONDON, Thos.	20	M	Unknown	20Fe02Eq
KEENAN, Thos.	27	M	Unknown	20Fe02Eq
MACK, Edwd.	34	M	Unknown	20Fe02Eq
Mary	30	F	Unknown	20Fe02Eq
ONEILL, John	84	M	Unknown	20Fe02Eq
WALLACE, James	50	M	Unknown	20Fe02Eq
U-Mrs.	40	F	Unknown	20Fe02Eq
Andrew	19	M	Unknown	20Fe02Eq
Samuel	15	M	Unknown	20Fe02Eq
Sarah	13	F	Unknown	20Fe02Eq
Eliza	11	F	Unknown	20Fe02Eq
James	9	M	Child	20Fe02Eq
John	7	M	Child	20Fe02Eq
Isabella	5	F	Child	20Fe02Eq
Oliver	3	M	Child	20Fe02Eq
William	.00	M	Infant	20Fe02Eq
BRYNE, Robt.	25	M	Unknown	20Fe02Eq
RAWLINS, Chas.	40	M	Unknown	20Fe02Eq
TOHILL, John	26	M	Unknown	20Fe02Eq
CONLAN, Andrew	31	M	Unknown	20Fe02Eq
Ann	31	F	Unknown	20Fe02Eq
Pat	9	M	Child	20Fe02Eq
Mary	7	F	Child	20Fe02Eq
James	3	M	Child	20Fe02Eq
Bridget	.00	F	Infant	20Fe02Eq
MULLIGAN, Rose	10	F	Unknown	20Fe02Eq
FITZPATRICK, Alise	40	F	Unknown	20Fe02Eq
Bridget	6	F	Child	20Fe02Eq
John	4	M	Child	20Fe02Eq
Bernard	2	M	Child	20Fe02Eq
Thomas	.00	M	Infant	20Fe02Eq
QUINAN, Cath.	12	F	Unknown	20Fe02Eq
HASEY, John	30	M	Unknown	20Fe02Eq
Michl.	25	M	Unknown	20Fe02Eq
Patrick	18	M	Unknown	20Fe02Eq
SMITH, Bridget	20	F	Unknown	20Fe02Eq
REILLY, Mary	20	F	Unknown	20Fe02Eq
CAFFREY, Bernard	16	M	Unknown	20Fe02Eq
VICTORY, Thomas	17	M	Unknown	20Fe02Eq
Bess	19	F	Unknown	20Fe02Eq
John	40	M	Unknown	20Fe02Eq
SMITH, Pat	19	M	Unknown	20Fe02Eq
Margt.	20	F	Unknown	20Fe02Eq
REILLY, James	27	M	Unknown	20Fe02Eq
KEALEHER, John	27	M	Unknown	20Fe02Eq
CASEY, Danl.	27	M	Unknown	20Fe02Eq
SULLIVAN, Ellen	50	F	Unknown	20Fe02Eq
Julia	22	F	Unknown	20Fe02Eq
James	13	M	Unknown	20Fe02Eq
Timothy	11	M	Unknown	20Fe02Eq
Ellen	4	F	Unknown	20Fe02Eq
CONLON, Margt.	16	F	Unknown	20Fe02Eq
MOORE, Pat	18	M	Unknown	20Fe02Eq
WALSH, Ellen	20	F	Unknown	20Fe02Eq
HENESEY, Ellen	20	F	Unknown	20Fe02Eq
CONWELL, James	20	M	Unknown	20Fe02Eq
Margt.	20	F	Unknown	20Fe02Eq
BROWNE, Mary	25	F	Unknown	20Fe02Eq
OWENS, William	30	M	Unknown	20Fe02Eq
MCCABE, Thomas	30	M	Unknown	20Fe02Eq
KINAHAN, John	22	M	Unknown	20Fe02Eq
TONE, John	30	M	Unknown	20Fe02Eq
FARY, Mary	22	F	Unknown	20Fe02Eq

NAMES OF PASSENGERS	AGE	SEX	OCCUPATIONS	DATE PORT SHIP
EDGAN, Peggy	32	F	Unknown	20Fe02Eq
HOLLAND, Elizt.	30	F	Unknown	20Fe02Eq
Margaret	6	F	Child	20Fe02Eq
Richard	4	M	Child	20Fe02Eq
DOWD, Honora	20	F	Unknown	20Fe02Eq
James	22	M	Unknown	20Fe02Eq
BREHANY, Peter	20	M	Unknown	20Fe02Eq
MURRAY, John	19	M	Unknown	20Fe02Eq
SALLER, Matilda	36	F	Laborer	20Fe02Eq
Emma	13	F	Unknown	20Fe02Eq
MALONE, John	21	M	Unknown	20Fe02Eq
Ann	22	F	Unknown	20Fe02Eq
NEWLAN, Pat	40	M	Unknown	20Fe02Eq
MCBRIDE, Pat	21	M	Unknown	20Fe02Eq
Mary	28	F	Unknown	20Fe02Eq
James	8	M	Child	20Fe02Eq
Cath.	6	F	Child	20Fe02Eq
Margt.	4	F	Child	20Fe02Eq
Mary	.00	F	Infant	20Fe02Eq
HUME, E.	50	U	Unknown	20Fe02Eq
M.	16	U	Unknown	20Fe02Eq
John	11	M	Unknown	20Fe02Eq
TOOLE, Biddy	25	F	Unknown	20Fe02Eq
John	4	M	Child	20Fe02Eq
WALSH, Thomas	26	M	Unknown	20Fe02Eq
SALT, Henry	25	M	Unknown	20Fe02Eq
MULLIGAN, Sam	40	M	Unknown	20Fe02Eq
Cath.	13	F	Unknown	20Fe02Eq
John	6	M	Child	20Fe02Eq
BYRNE, John	21	M	Unknown	20Fe02Eq
DOODY, Mary	35	F	Unknown	20Fe02Eq
Daria	12	F	Unknown	20Fe02Eq
Mary	7	F	Child	20Fe02Eq
CONNOR, Edwd.	30	M	Unknown	20Fe02Eq
MULLEN, Michl.	48	M	Unknown	20Fe02Eq
Ann	31	F	Unknown	20Fe02Eq
MITCHELL, Peter	32	M	Unknown	20Fe02Eq
Margt.	22	F	Unknown	20Fe02Eq
Died-At-Sea				
COHEN, Patk.	30	M	Unknown	20Fe02Eq
Cathe.	35	F	Unknown	20Fe02Eq
Mary-A.	.00	F	Infant	20Fe02Eq
AUSTIN, Jas.	20	M	Unknown	20Fe02Eq
Henry	22	M	Unknown	20Fe02Eq
Mary	21	F	Unknown	20Fe02Eq
NAVIN, Honora	19	F	Unknown	20Fe02Eq
Margt.	19	F	Unknown	20Fe02Eq
BRODRICK, Sarah	14	F	Unknown	20Fe02Eq
BYLAN, Rose	30	F	Unknown	20Fe02Eq
TULLY, Mathew	30	M	Unknown	20Fe02Eq
Mary	30	F	Unknown	20Fe02Eq
CASSIDY, Jas.	25	M	Unknown	20Fe02Eq
Eliza	26	F	Unknown	20Fe02Eq
Patrick	.00	M	Infant	20Fe02Eq
HALPEN, William	23	M	Unknown	20Fe02Eq
Patrick	22	M	Unknown	20Fe02Eq
Bryan	17	M	Unknown	20Fe02Eq
Nicholas	13	M	Laborer	20Fe02Eq
Thos.	24	M	Unknown	20Fe02Eq
Mary	26	F	Unknown	20Fe02Eq
BEDDEN, Geo.	32	M	Unknown	20Fe02Eq
BALL, Thos.	26	M	Unknown	20Fe02Eq
Mary-A.	28	F	Unknown	20Fe02Eq
HEENLEHY, John	18	M	Unknown	20Fe02Eq
LEAHY, Joseph	27	M	Unknown	20Fe02Eq
KELLY, Richd.	40	M	Unknown	20Fe02Eq
JOHNSON, Wm.	25	M	Unknown	20Fe02Eq
MATHEWS, Wm.	21	M	Unknown	20Fe02Eq
BARRY, Martha	18	F	Unknown	20Fe02Eq
Michl.	40	M	Unknown	20Fe02Eq
MCDONNELL, Felix	10	M	Unknown	20Fe02Eq
CLARKE, Owen	23	M	Unknown	20Fe02Eq
DUFFY, Eliza	16	F	Unknown	20Fe02Eq
FERRIGAN, Rose	23	F	Unknown	20Fe02Eq
REILY, James	60	M	Unknown	20Fe02Eq

NAMES OF PASSENGERS	AGE	SEX	OCCUPATIONS	DATE PORT SHIP
REILY, Philis	20	F	Unknown	20Fe02Eq
BELL, Wm.	24	M	Unknown	20Fe02Eq
CRUMBLE, Chr.	20	M	Unknown	20Fe02Eq
FEGAN, Thos.	20	M	Unknown	20Fe02Eq
ARNOLD, Kate	20	F	Unknown	20Fe02Eq
HICKEY, Ellen	20	F	Laborer	20Fe02Eq
HURLEY, Alice	21	F	Unknown	20Fe02Eq
MOLAN, James	46	M	Unknown	20Fe02Eq
DONOHOE, Bernard	24	M	Unknown	20Fe02Eq
Mary	64	F	Unknown	20Fe02Eq
Margt.	18	F	Unknown	20Fe02Eq
DUNNE, Ellen	24	F	Unknown	20Fe02Eq
GARYBRAN, Mary	30	F	Unknown	20Fe02Eq
Antony	9	M	Child	20Fe02Eq
COSGROVE, Pat	23	M	Unknown	20Fe02Eq
TIERNAN, Robt.	34	M	Unknown	20Fe02Eq
Cathe.	22	F	Unknown	20Fe02Eq
DUNNE, Patrick	23	M	Unknown	20Fe02Eq
HYNES, Justin	20	M	Unknown	20Fe02Eq
WHELAN, James	19	M	Unknown	20Fe02Eq
NICHOLS, John	21	M	Unknown	20Fe02Eq
HESLIN, Cath.	25	F	Unknown	20Fe02Eq
DALY, Owen	29	M	Unknown	20Fe02Eq
Ellen	20	F	Unknown	20Fe02Eq
FEENEY, Francis	18	M	Unknown	20Fe02Eq
MCKEOWN, U-Mrs.	23	F	Unknown	20Fe02Eq
BYRNE, Thomas	50	M	Unknown	20Fe02Eq
Eliza	20	F	Unknown	20Fe02Eq
Rose	17	F	Unknown	20Fe02Eq
John	13	M	Unknown	20Fe02Eq
George	11	M	Unknown	20Fe02Eq
WILLIAMS, Phil	42	M	Unknown	20Fe02Eq
WHELAN, Michl.	23	M	Unknown	20Fe02Eq
Margt.	23	F	Unknown	20Fe02Eq
HARINGTON, Thos.	40	M	Unknown	20Fe02Eq
Herman	11	M	Unknown	20Fe02Eq
Edwin	28	M	Unknown	20Fe02Eq
HOYLE, Phineas	20	M	Unknown	20Fe02Eq
WRIGHT, George	24	M	Unknown	20Fe02Eq
William	13	M	Unknown	20Fe02Eq
GRIFFEN, Mary	23	F	Unknown	20Fe02Eq
Patrick	22	M	Unknown	20Fe02Eq
Edward	11	M	Unknown	20Fe02Eq
MAHONEY, James	24	M	Unknown	20Fe02Eq
GORMAN, Mochl.	30	M	Unknown	20Fe02Eq
Mary	27	F	Unknown	20Fe02Eq
BERNFIELD, Luke	24	M	Unknown	20Fe02Eq
SCANLAN, James	30	M	Unknown	20Fe02Eq
Mary	17	F	Unknown	20Fe02Eq
MUTTALL, William	23	M	Unknown	20Fe02Eq
VAUGHAN, Thomas	30	M	Unknown	20Fe02Eq
FAIRLY, Alex	22	M	Unknown	20Fe02Eq
TRAINOR, Pat	30	M	Unknown	20Fe02Eq
Ann	25	F	Unknown	20Fe02Eq
Bridget	3	F	Child	20Fe02Eq
Paul	.00	M	Infant	20Fe02Eq
CASS, Ann	28	F	Unknown	20Fe02Eq
John	6	M	Child	20Fe02Eq
SCHOFFIELD, John	25	M	Unknown	20Fe02Eq
Esther	26	F	Unknown	20Fe02Eq
MITCHIE, Henry	22	M	Unknown	20Fe02Eq
NEILL, James	17	M	Laborer	20Fe02Eq
LENNON, Mich.	26	M	Unknown	20Fe02Eq
SANDERS, Thomas	26	M	Unknown	20Fe02Eq
Mary	26	F	Unknown	20Fe02Eq
LANEGAN, Matthew	38	M	Unknown	20Fe02Eq
ONEILL, Mary	26	F	Unknown	20Fe02Eq
MOHIDE, Matty	34	M	Unknown	20Fe02Eq
TEBARN, James	30	M	Unknown	20Fe02Eq
GIBBONS, James	40	M	Unknown	20Fe02Eq
PASSER, Sarah	40	F	Unknown	20Fe02Eq
Thomas	13	M	Unknown	20Fe02Eq
William	11	M	Unknown	20Fe02Eq
BOUGHLAN, William	25	M	Unknown	20Fe02Eq
WOODMAN, Frances	22	M	Unknown	20Fe02Eq

NAMES OF PASSENGERS	AGE	SEX	OCCUPATIONS	DATE PORT SHIP
LANCASTER, John	39	M	Unknown	20Fe02Eq
RECKER, Wm.	29	M	Unknown	20Fe02Eq
AUDLIN, Edwd.	22	M	Unknown	20Fe02Eq
BROOKS, William	2	M	Child	20Fe02Eq
Bessy	.00	F	Infant	20Fe02Eq
U-Mrs.	27	F	Unknown	20Fe02Eq
ADAMS, Eliza	15	F	Unknown	20Fe02Eq
BROWN, John	32	M	Unknown	20Fe02Eq
U-Mrs.	32	F	Unknown	20Fe02Eq
BLAYLOCH, Josep	25	M	Unknown	20Fe02Eq
Mary-A.	22	F	Unknown	20Fe02Eq
JONES, Arther	26	M	Unknown	20Fe02Eq
U-Mrs.	25	F	Unknown	20Fe02Eq
Jane	4	F	Child	20Fe02Eq
John	2	M	Child	20Fe02Eq
Fanny	.00	F	Infant	20Fe02Eq
ONEIL, Math.	23	M	Unknown	20Fe02Eq
A.	34	F	Unknown	20Fe02Eq
MONARTS, U	22	F	Unknown	20Fe02Eq
U	17	F	Unknown	20Fe02Eq
WOOD, U-Mrs.	30	F	Unknown	20Fe02Eq
U	00	F	Child	20Fe02Eq
FILSON, J.	50	M	Unknown	20Fe02Eq
J.	25	U	Unknown	20Fe02Eq
MURPHY, Path.	00	M	Unknown	20Fe02Eq
LUDLAM, Jos.	00	M	Unknown	20Fe02Eq
FRAHAN, Mary	23	F	Unknown	20Fe02Eq
KIERNAN, Mary	18	F	Unknown	20Fe02Eq

YORKSHIRE 21 FEBRUARY 1850

From Liverpool

NAMES OF PASSENGERS	AGE	SEX	OCCUPATIONS	DATE PORT SHIP
MAHER, Honer	20	F	Spinster	21Fe02Az
Ellen	10	F	Spinster	21Fe02Az
CONNLY, Wm.	25	M	Laborer	21Fe02Az
Rose	23	F	Laborer	21Fe02Az
Eliza	1	F	Child	21Fe02Az
MEEHENE, Richd.	18	M	Laborer	21Fe02Az
HOUGHTON, Wm.	40	M	Laborer	21Fe02Az
DEVO, Jno.	10	M	Laborer	21Fe02Az
Derrick	9	M	Child	21Fe02Az
LYNCH, Mary	10	F	Unknown	21Fe02Az
LENAHAN, Jno.	9	M	Child	21Fe02Az
BRADLY, Henry	20	M	Laborer	21Fe02Az
Margt.	18	F	Laborer	21Fe02Az
MULORY, Pat	25	M	Laborer	21Fe02Az
DOHERTY, Cathn.	19	F	Laborer	21Fe02Az
QUIG, Elenor	9	F	Child	21Fe02Az
BEATTY, Mary	23	F	Laborer	21Fe02Az
KELLY, Brid.	35	F	Spinster	21Fe02Az
Kate	.00	F	Infant	21Fe02Az
Jno.	6	M	Child	21Fe02Az
KENNEDY, Maria	19	F	Spinster	21Fe02Az
GALLAGHER, Pat	14	M	Spinster	21Fe02Az
Brien	12	M	Spinster	21Fe02Az
STEEN, Wm.	45	M	Mason	21Fe02Az
Jno.	26	M	Mason	21Fe02Az
Jas.	23	M	Mason	21Fe02Az
Wm.	21	M	Mason	21Fe02Az
Ann	22	F	Mason	21Fe02Az
Peter	11	M	Mason	21Fe02Az
Geo.	8	M	Child	21Fe02Az
Wilson	3	M	Child	21Fe02Az
MURPHY, Biddy	22	F	Laborer	21Fe02Az
CROWLY, Dennis	21	M	Laborer	21Fe02Az
Danl.	21	M	Laborer	21Fe02Az
CLARK, Luke	24	M	Laborer	21Fe02Az
MCDOWELL, Pat	40	M	Laborer	21Fe02Az

NAMES OF PASSENGERS	AGE	SEX	OCCUPATIONS	DATE PORT SHIP
MCDOWELL, Jno.	15	M	Laborer	21Fe02Az
Mary	12	F	Laborer	21Fe02Az
Thos.	10	M	Laborer	21Fe02Az
Pat	8	M	Child	21Fe02Az
FOX, Thos.	20	M	Laborer	21Fe02Az
QUINAN, Jno.	25	M	Laborer	21Fe02Az
SHAHAN, Brid.	30	F	Laborer	21Fe02Az
Dan	2	M	Child	21Fe02Az
Ann	3	F	Child	21Fe02Az
Ellen	.00	F	Infant	21Fe02Az
SLATTERY, Mary	28	F	Laborer	21Fe02Az
Ann	8	F	Child	21Fe02Az
Wm.	6	M	Child	21Fe02Az
RYAN, Jane	24	F	Spinster	21Fe02Az
MCCABE, Thos.	19	M	Unknown	21Fe02Az
Francis	14	M	Unknown	21Fe02Az
MCCONWELL, Jno.	20	M	Unknown	21Fe02Az
Michl.	18	M	Unknown	21Fe02Az
JOHNSTON, Jno.	15	M	Laborer	21Fe02Az
MONAGHAN, Thos.	22	M	Laborer	21Fe02Az
BILLINGTON, Wm.	28	M	Laborer	21Fe02Az
NIEL, Jno.	25	M	Laborer	21Fe02Az
KEHERY, Thos.	25	M	Laborer	21Fe02Az
KELLY, Edwd.	21	M	Laborer	21Fe02Az
DERRY, Firoence	23	F	Laborer	21Fe02Az
TRACY, Wm.	35	M	Shoemaker	21Fe02Az
KELLY, Roger	18	M	Laborer	21Fe02Az
rWHEELEN, Jno.	35	M	Laborer	21Fe02Az
FEENEY, Thos.	18	M	Laborer	21Fe02Az
CONNELL, Rose	22	F	Laborer	21Fe02Az
HUGHES, Mary-A.	20	F	Laborer	21Fe02Az
COLLON, Cathn.	21	F	Laborer	21Fe02Az
TIERNEY, Mary	22	F	Laborer	21Fe02Az
OLDHAM, Richd.	20	M	Laborer	21Fe02Az
HIGHLAND, Wm.	30	M	Farmer	21Fe02Az
Quin	28	M	Farmer	21Fe02Az
Michl.	24	M	Farmer	21Fe02Az
Pat	22	M	Farmer	21Fe02Az
Ester	20	F	Farmer	21Fe02Az
Judy	22	F	Farmer	21Fe02Az
Jane	10	F	Farmer	21Fe02Az
MULHOLD, Eliza	20	F	Laborer	21Fe02Az
BYRNE, Wm.	25	M	Laborer	21Fe02Az
Ellen	26	F	Laborer	21Fe02Az
Ann	20	F	Laborer	21Fe02Az
Ellen	16	F	Laborer	21Fe02Az
MORAN, Jno.	24	M	Laborer	21Fe02Az
CONNELLY, And.	30	M	Laborer	21Fe02Az
QUIGLEY, Ann	20	F	Laborer	21Fe02Az
BURK, Eliza	18	F	Laborer	21Fe02Az
PAREY, U-Mrs.	17	F	Saddler	21Fe02Az
Mary	22	F	Saddler	21Fe02Az
CROWLY, Denis	35	M	Saddler	21Fe02Az
CLARK, Luke	40	M	Saddler	21Fe02Az
FRAE, Rose	20	F	Saddler	21Fe02Az
ONEILL, Cathn.	30	F	Saddler	21Fe02Az
WHALEN, Jno.	12	M	Saddler	21Fe02Az
Margt.	10	F	Saddler	21Fe02Az
KEEGAN, Honora	20	F	Saddler	21Fe02Az
Michl.	15	M	Saddler	21Fe02Az
FINKLESTEN, Jacob	17	M	Barber	21Fe02Az
CODY, Ellen	35	F	None	21Fe02Az
Mary	16	F	None	21Fe02Az
SCOTT, Robt.	23	M	None	21Fe02Az
Alex	48	M	Clerk	21Fe02Az
HANNY, Jno.	20	M	Clerk	21Fe02Az
DOUGHTY, Michl.	24	M	Laborer	21Fe02Az
U-Mrs.	24	F	Laborer	21Fe02Az
SHAUGNESSEY, Pat	28	M	Laborer	21Fe02Az
Ann	20	F	Laborer	21Fe02Az
QUININ, Jno.	22	M	Laborer	21Fe02Az
SMITH, U-Mrs.	20	F	Laborer	21Fe02Az
BUZOO, Eliza	23	F	Laborer	21Fe02Az
Jas.	.00	M	Infant	21Fe02Az
KEELING, Wm.	37	M	Laborer	21Fe02Az

NAMES OF PASSENGERS	AGE	SEX	OCCUPATIONS	DATE PORT SHIP
KEELING, U-Mrs.	45	F	Laborer	21Fe02Az
Cath.	13	F	Laborer	21Fe02Az
Jos.	4	M	Child	21Fe02Az
Martha	8	F	Child	21Fe02Az
Wm.	3	M	Child	21Fe02Az
MATHEWS, Anty	28	M	Laborer	21Fe02Az
ROCHE, Moris	24	M	Laborer	21Fe02Az
RYAN, Mary	26	F	Binder	21Fe02Az
QUININ, Ann	24	F	Servant	21Fe02Az
MCIREE, Eliza	20	F	Servant	21Fe02Az
Jno.	30	M	Servant	21Fe02Az
Edwd.	18	M	Servant	21Fe02Az
Alex.	13	M	Servant	21Fe02Az
WHIGAL, Charlet.	25	F	None	21Fe02Az
LIGHTFOOT, Wm.	7	M	Child	21Fe02Az
IRVING, U-Mrs.	18	F	Laborer	21Fe02Az
FREEL, Rose	30	F	Laborer	21Fe02Az
Paul	2	M	Child	21Fe02Az
MCMAHON, Richd.	12	M	Engineer	21Fe02Az
Ann	9	F	Child	21Fe02Az
SWEENEY, Maria	20	F	Laborer	21Fe02Az
FLEMING, Michl.	24	M	Laborer	21Fe02Az
BRYEN, Michl.	20	M	Laborer	21Fe02Az
MACK, Pat	24	M	Laborer	21Fe02Az
Onny	23	M	Laborer	21Fe02Az
BRATIER, Michl.	25	M	Laborer	21Fe02Az
WOODWARD, Richd.	30	M	Clerk	21Fe02Az
LALLY, Jno.	19	M	Laborer	21Fe02Az
FOX, Roger	40	M	Laborer	21Fe02Az
Michl.	16	M	Laborer	21Fe02Az
MCCARLANE, Jno.	25	M	Baker	21Fe02Az
Ellen	22	F	Laborer	21Fe02Az
SHEA, Ellen	22	F	Laborer	21Fe02Az
ONEILL, Jno.	3	M	Child	21Fe02Az
ROSS, Mary	18	F	Laborer	21Fe02Az
WALSH, U-Mrs.	45	F	Laborer	21Fe02Az
U-Miss	20	F	Laborer	21Fe02Az
Pat	7	M	Child	21Fe02Az
BEAUMONT, Jas.	22	M	Weaver	21Fe02Az
HOLMES, Anna	25	F	Laborer	21Fe02Az
BOLAND, Jas.	35	M	Laborer	21Fe02Az
SWEENEY, Denis	30	M	Laborer	21Fe02Az
WHITE, Pat	22	M	Laborer	21Fe02Az
SHAUGNESSEY, Cathn.	18	F	Laborer	21Fe02Az
OBRIAN, Mary	40	F	Laborer	21Fe02Az
Ellen	14	F	Laborer	21Fe02Az
Dan	12	M	Laborer	21Fe02Az
Jere.	10	M	Laborer	21Fe02Az
Peggy	8	F	Child	21Fe02Az
Michl.	4	M	Child	21Fe02Az
HUGHES, Cathn.	35	F	Laborer	21Fe02Az
Francis	1	M	Child	21Fe02Az
Cathn.	3	F	Child	21Fe02Az
BRANAGAN, Jno.	23	M	Laborer	21Fe02Az
DUFFY, Mary	18	F	Laborer	21Fe02Az
STEPHENSON, Isabella	21	F	Spinster	21Fe02Az
LANCELET, Jas.	25	M	Jeweller	21Fe02Az
BRAILY, Jas.	18	M	Weaver	21Fe02Az
FLETCHER, Jas.	14	M	Wire Worker	21Fe02Az
MURPHY, Michl.	22	M	Laborer	21Fe02Az
CORNING, U-Mrs.	32	F	Laborer	21Fe02Az
Alice	6	F	Child	21Fe02Az
Owen	3	M	Child	21Fe02Az
Mary-A.	2	F	Child	21Fe02Az
DURINN, Thos.	24	M	Laborer	21Fe02Az
HALFPENNY, Thos.	22	M	Laborer	21Fe02Az
HAND, Nath.	20	M	Laborer	21Fe02Az
Jane	18	F	Laborer	21Fe02Az
PITCHERD, Cathn.	40	F	Laborer	21Fe02Az
Brady	10	F	Laborer	21Fe02Az

NAMES OF PASSENGERS	AGE	SEX	OCCUPATIONS	DATE PORT SHIP

JAMES-DRAKE 25 FEBRUARY 1850

From Liverpool

NAMES OF PASSENGERS	AGE	SEX	OCCUPATIONS	DATE PORT SHIP
HOGAN, Bridget	12	F	None	25Fe02Ew
CARROLL, Ellen	20	F	None	25Fe02Ew
RYAN, Catharine	20	F	None	25Fe02Ew
Margaret	.11	F	Infant	25Fe02Ew
DONNALLEY, Rosanna	28	F	None	25Fe02Ew
John	.05	M	Infant	25Fe02Ew
Thomas	5	M	Child	25Fe02Ew
CONNORS, James	23	M	Laborer	25Fe02Ew
John	20	M	Laborer	25Fe02Ew
Catharine	40	F	None	25Fe02Ew
Ellen	15	F	None	25Fe02Ew
Mary	13	F	None	25Fe02Ew
FOLEY, John	18	M	Laborer	25Fe02Ew
LAHERTY, Honora	18	F	None	25Fe02Ew
HENRY, Patrick	24	M	Laborer	25Fe02Ew
C---, John	29	M	Laborer	25Fe02Ew
MCDOOLE, James	27	M	Laborer	25Fe02Ew
MORGAN, Henry	20	M	Mechanic	25Fe02Ew
LAKEY, Catharine	20	F	None	25Fe02Ew
BRADLEY, John	18	M	Laborer	25Fe02Ew
COREY, Mary	28	F	None	25Fe02Ew
Margaret	18	F	None	25Fe02Ew
GREEN, Johanna	27	F	None	25Fe02Ew
EGAN, Margaret	22	F	None	25Fe02Ew
COLE, Catharine	17	F	None	25Fe02Ew
ROWLAN, Honora	19	F	None	25Fe02Ew
KENT, Sarah	24	F	None	25Fe02Ew
MALONEY, Honor	30	F	None	25Fe02Ew
Michael	.08	M	Infant	25Fe02Ew
HONEGAN, Margaret	21	F	None	25Fe02Ew
HANNEN, Ann	20	F	None	25Fe02Ew
CAMMING, Margaret	16	F	None	25Fe02Ew
SELKIRK, Bridget	40	F	None	25Fe02Ew
TAYLOR, Ellen	30	F	None	25Fe02Ew
SHIELDS, Ann	18	F	None	25Fe02Ew
WHEELAN, Bridget	20	F	None	25Fe02Ew
RYAN, Eliza	23	F	None	25Fe02Ew
MORRISON, Patrick	20	M	Mechanic	25Fe02Ew
MCGRATH, Bridget	30	F	None	25Fe02Ew
MURRAY, Eliza	18	F	None	25Fe02Ew
OBRIEN, Mary	18	F	None	25Fe02Ew
FLAHERTY, Honora	23	F	None	25Fe02Ew
DOHENY, Johanna	18	F	None	25Fe02Ew
REDETON, Mary	22	F	None	25Fe02Ew
HANNAN, Mary	33	F	None	25Fe02Ew
Patrick	3	M	Child	25Fe02Ew
John	.10	M	Infant	25Fe02Ew
MCCORMICK, Ann	34	F	None	25Fe02Ew
Julia	12	F	None	25Fe02Ew
John	8	M	Child	25Fe02Ew
Ann	5	F	Child	25Fe02Ew
Mary	.11	F	Infant	25Fe02Ew
MALONEY, Bridget	30	F	None	25Fe02Ew
CAHILL, James	22	M	Laborer	25Fe02Ew
OCONNELL, Julia	18	F	None	25Fe02Ew
TAHY, Honora	19	F	None	25Fe02Ew
RESSANE, Catharine	24	F	None	25Fe02Ew
HENRY, Patrick	20	M	Laborer	25Fe02Ew
BLAKE, Ellen	20	F	None	25Fe02Ew
MCKEON, John	35	M	Laborer	25Fe02Ew
Patrick	26	M	Laborer	25Fe02Ew
James	14	M	Laborer	25Fe02Ew
Mary	15	F	None	25Fe02Ew
CARROLL, Rose	26	F	None	25Fe02Ew
Anne	.11	F	Infant	25Fe02Ew
BREEN, Michael	24	M	Mechanic	25Fe02Ew
NEILL, John	42	M	Mechanic	25Fe02Ew
Sarah	33	F	None	25Fe02Ew
Died-At-Sea				
CROWNES, Margaret	30	F	None	25Fe02Ew
Bridget	.05	F	Infant	25Fe02Ew
Died-At-Sea				
Betsey	5	F	Child	25Fe02Ew
James	7	M	Child	25Fe02Ew
MCNAMARA, Timothy	22	M	Laborer	25Fe02Ew
CLINKE, Daniel	30	M	Mechanic	25Fe02Ew
HEANKE, William	27	M	Mechanic	25Fe02Ew
GLANEY, John	24	M	Mechanic	25Fe02Ew
BREEN, Anne	20	F	None	25Fe02Ew
MALLONEY, John	22	M	Laborer	25Fe02Ew
CATTON, Mary	30	F	None	25Fe02Ew
Charles	.05	M	Infant	25Fe02Ew
BRACKEN, Bridget	44	F	None	25Fe02Ew
Joseph	8	M	Child	25Fe02Ew
William	.05	M	Infant	25Fe02Ew
CORMICK, John	17	M	Laborer	25Fe02Ew
Mary	12	F	None	25Fe02Ew

SILAS-GREENMAN 22 FEBRUARY 1850

From Liverpool

NAMES OF PASSENGERS	AGE	SEX	OCCUPATIONS	DATE PORT SHIP
FARRELL, Mary-Ann	30	F	Unknown	22Fe02Es
Richard	9	M	Child	22Fe02Es
Mary	7	F	Child	22Fe02Es
John	3	M	Child	22Fe02Es
Andrew	.00	M	Infant	22Fe02Es
GLERMAN, U	40	M	Unknown	22Fe02Es
SHEEHAN, Ellen	30	F	Unknown	22Fe02Es
Cornelius	7	M	Child	22Fe02Es
Timothy	4	M	Child	22Fe02Es
NUTLY, Mary	20	F	Unknown	22Fe02Es
BARTLEY, Mary	20	F	Unknown	22Fe02Es
CONROY, James	20	M	Unknown	22Fe02Es
Eliza	18	F	Unknown	22Fe02Es
Maria	16	F	Unknown	22Fe02Es
Jane	22	F	Unknown	22Fe02Es
Catherine	24	F	Unknown	22Fe02Es
Catherine	21	F	Unknown	22Fe02Es
SWEENEY, John	60	M	Unknown	22Fe02Es
CONNOR, John	20	M	Unknown	22Fe02Es
MOORE, Thomas	30	M	Unknown	22Fe02Es
David	25	M	Unknown	22Fe02Es
John	22	M	Unknown	22Fe02Es
Sarah-Ann	20	F	Unknown	22Fe02Es
BEALEY, Charles	23	M	Unknown	22Fe02Es
RUSH, John	21	M	Unknown	22Fe02Es
Mary	20	F	Unknown	22Fe02Es
DONNELLY, Patt	30	M	Unknown	22Fe02Es
DOUGLAS, Geo.	34	M	Unknown	22Fe02Es
EVANS, Edward	22	M	Unknown	22Fe02Es
CRONIN, Thomas	60	M	Unknown	22Fe02Es
WALSH, Betsey	19	F	Unknown	22Fe02Es
DROYER, Mary	20	F	Unknown	22Fe02Es
LINDE, Margt.	30	F	Unknown	22Fe02Es
FEGAN, Betty	18	F	Unknown	22Fe02Es
MANNAHAN, Mary	20	F	Unknown	22Fe02Es
Edward	8	M	Child	22Fe02Es
MOLAN, Johana	30	F	Unknown	22Fe02Es
William	16	M	Unknown	22Fe02Es
WALSH, John	23	M	Unknown	22Fe02Es
BARRAY, Wm.	24	M	Unknown	22Fe02Es
CASCHPOLE, C.G.	27	M	Unknown	22Fe02Es
BRIER, Wm.P.	27	M	Unknown	22Fe02Es

NAMES OF PASSENGERS	AGE	SEX	OCCUPATIONS	DATE PORT SHIP
BOMAN, James	26	M	Unknown	22Fe02Es
AIREY, Henry	22	M	Unknown	22Fe02Es
BURKE, David	27	M	Unknown	22Fe02Es
MARTIN, Mary	40	F	Unknown	22Fe02Es
Catherine	18	F	Unknown	22Fe02Es
Ellen	13	F	Unknown	22Fe02Es
Michl.	11	M	Unknown	22Fe02Es
John	8	M	Child	22Fe02Es
Mary	7	F	Child	22Fe02Es
CARSTLE, John	35	M	Unknown	22Fe02Es
HEALEY, Dan	29	M	Unknown	22Fe02Es
U-Mrs.	26	F	Unknown	22Fe02Es
KINGSTON, John	40	M	Unknown	22Fe02Es
MALONEY, John	35	M	Unknown	22Fe02Es
Bridget	30	F	Unknown	22Fe02Es
Thomas	9	M	Child	22Fe02Es
Richard	7	M	Child	22Fe02Es
Danl.	2	M	Child	22Fe02Es
Bridget	.00	F	Infant	22Fe02Es
POWELL, James	22	M	Unknown	22Fe02Es
Mary	23	F	Unknown	22Fe02Es
MCDERMOTT, Mary	27	F	Unknown	22Fe02Es
FINN, Feargus	35	M	Unknown	22Fe02Es
TOLLISS, John	31	M	Unknown	22Fe02Es
Anna	28	F	Unknown	22Fe02Es
Sarah	8	F	Child	22Fe02Es
John	6	M	Child	22Fe02Es
Myran	4	F	Child	22Fe02Es
Robert	2	M	Child	22Fe02Es
DODD, James	17	M	Unknown	22Fe02Es
FLOCKSON, Wm.	33	M	Unknown	22Fe02Es
LANGFORD, Geo.	41	M	Unknown	22Fe02Es
BRINAN, Charles	29	M	Unknown	22Fe02Es
Emma	23	F	Unknown	22Fe02Es
Fanny	3	F	Child	22Fe02Es
Charles	2	F	Child	22Fe02Es
Harriet	.00	F	Infant	22Fe02Es
BURKE, Mary	30	F	Unknown	22Fe02Es
James	8	M	Child	22Fe02Es
Margt.	6	F	Child	22Fe02Es
DIXON, John	42	M	Unknown	22Fe02Es
DICKINSON, Denis	36	M	Unknown	22Fe02Es
MCCABE, Patt	30	M	Unknown	22Fe02Es
Mary	28	F	Unknown	22Fe02Es
Cathe.	.00	F	Infant	22Fe02Es
MUSNER, Fredk.	21	M	Unknown	22Fe02Es
CLEARY, Kody	36	M	Unknown	22Fe02Es
Ellen	26	F	Unknown	22Fe02Es
Winefred	6	M	Child	22Fe02Es
Essey	4	F	Child	22Fe02Es
Patrick	.00	M	Infant	22Fe02Es
WHELAN, Martin	50	M	Unknown	22Fe02Es
MARTIN, Matilda	14	F	Unknown	22Fe02Es
Mary	50	F	Unknown	22Fe02Es
HAIG, Ben.	30	M	Unknown	22Fe02Es
Anne	25	F	Unknown	22Fe02Es
DONOHUE, Anne	18	F	Unknown	22Fe02Es
CAIRNS, Bernd.	20	M	Unknown	22Fe02Es
BALE, Hy	22	M	Unknown	22Fe02Es
CASSIDY, Patt	40	M	Unknown	22Fe02Es
PLUMBTREE, Elijah	21	M	Unknown	22Fe02Es
OBRIAN, Hy	26	M	Unknown	22Fe02Es
DAY, Francis	21	M	Unknown	22Fe02Es
FRAZIER, James	24	M	Unknown	22Fe02Es
MINT, Anne	26	F	Unknown	22Fe02Es
CARTWRIGHT, John	22	M	Unknown	22Fe02Es
MEENEY, Patt	40	M	Unknown	22Fe02Es
SMITH, Wm.	35	M	Unknown	22Fe02Es
Isabella	30	F	Unknown	22Fe02Es
Susannah	45	F	Unknown	22Fe02Es
John	3	M	Child	22Fe02Es
William	.00	M	Infant	22Fe02Es
PATTEN, John	19	M	Unknown	22Fe02Es
James	19	M	Unknown	22Fe02Es
Daniel	24	M	Unknown	22Fe02Es

NAMES OF PASSENGERS	AGE	SEX	OCCUPATIONS	DATE PORT SHIP
SLATTERY, John	45	M	Unknown	22Fe02Es
Mary	40	F	Unknown	22Fe02Es
Michael	18	M	Unknown	22Fe02Es
DONOHUE, Timthy.	22	M	Unknown	22Fe02Es
MARA, Johanna	15	F	Unknown	22Fe02Es
SLATTERY, Timthy.	23	M	Unknown	22Fe02Es
WALSH, James	20	M	Unknown	22Fe02Es
MOONEY, James	20	M	Unknown	22Fe02Es
ALLEN, James	23	M	Unknown	22Fe02Es
FAULKNER, Anne	18	F	Unknown	22Fe02Es
CURRY, Mary	25	F	Unknown	22Fe02Es
CONLAN, James	24	M	Unknown	22Fe02Es
DUFFY, James	20	M	Unknown	22Fe02Es
FOGARTY, John	46	M	Unknown	22Fe02Es
AGNEW, Andrew	61	M	Unknown	22Fe02Es
U-Mrs.	58	F	Unknown	22Fe02Es
James	30	M	Unknown	22Fe02Es
Sally	24	F	Unknown	22Fe02Es
Robert	22	M	Unknown	22Fe02Es
Anne	20	F	Unknown	22Fe02Es
Margaret	18	F	Unknown	22Fe02Es
Andrew	16	M	Unknown	22Fe02Es
RITCHIE, David	35	M	Unknown	22Fe02Es
Jane	30	F	Unknown	22Fe02Es
Anne	2	F	Child	22Fe02Es
Sarah-Jane	.00	F	Infant	22Fe02Es
Bessy	30	F	Unknown	22Fe02Es
ALLEN, Margaret	20	F	Unknown	22Fe02Es
STEWART, Thomas	30	M	Unknown	22Fe02Es
Catherine	30	F	Unknown	22Fe02Es
William	3	M	Child	22Fe02Es
Samuel	1	M	Child	22Fe02Es
CONNOR, James	20	M	Unknown	22Fe02Es
LUCAS, Alexander	45	M	Unknown	22Fe02Es
STEWART, Alexander	21	M	Unknown	22Fe02Es
LUCAS, Margaret	47	F	Unknown	22Fe02Es
STEWART, Janet	19	F	Unknown	22Fe02Es
KELLY, Hugh	34	F	Unknown	22Fe02Es
KING, John	28	M	Unknown	22Fe02Es
KEATING, Patt	30	M	Unknown	22Fe02Es
Honora	25	F	Unknown	22Fe02Es
DAVIS, Mathew	25	M	Unknown	22Fe02Es
DUSON, Richard	18	M	Unknown	22Fe02Es
HICKS, Robert	20	M	Unknown	22Fe02Es
Eliza	20	F	Unknown	22Fe02Es
GIBSON, Jane	20	F	Unknown	22Fe02Es
TUTOR, Joseph	25	M	Unknown	22Fe02Es
Mary	25	F	Unknown	22Fe02Es
Thomas	25	M	Unknown	22Fe02Es
MCANENY, Berd.	15	M	Unknown	22Fe02Es
Patrick	13	M	Unknown	22Fe02Es
CLARK, Lawrence	24	M	Unknown	22Fe02Es
THOMPSON, Henry	16	M	Unknown	22Fe02Es
BUCHANAN, John	20	M	Unknown	22Fe02Es
Eliza-Mrs.	20	F	Unknown	22Fe02Es
Isabella	22	F	Unknown	22Fe02Es
BYRNE, James	30	M	Unknown	22Fe02Es
BARRY, Edmund	30	M	Unknown	22Fe02Es
CLERKEN, Danl.	12	M	Unknown	22Fe02Es
DONNELLY, Ellen	25	F	Unknown	22Fe02Es
COX, Ann	11	F	Unknown	22Fe02Es
KENNY, Bridget	15	F	Unknown	22Fe02Es
Winefred	13	M	Unknown	22Fe02Es
FITZSIMONS, Mary	50	F	Unknown	22Fe02Es
Catherine	24	F	Unknown	22Fe02Es
Bridget	11	F	Unknown	22Fe02Es
BARRY, Francis	26	M	Unknown	22Fe02Es
Anne	26	F	Unknown	22Fe02Es
Mathew	2	M	Child	22Fe02Es
Mary	.00	F	Infant	22Fe02Es
SMITH, William Died-At-Sea	1	M	Child	22Fe02Es
MULONEY, Bridget Died-At-Sea	1	F	Child	22Fe02Es

NAMES OF PASSENGERS	AGE	SEX	OCCUPATIONS	DATE PORT SHIP
MURRAY, Patrick	1	M	Child	22Fe02Es
Died-At-Sea				
RITCHER, Sarah-Ann	1	F	Child	22Fe02Es
Died-At-Sea				
SWEENY, John	65	M	Unknown	22Fe02Es
Died-At-Sea				
BRINNEN, Harriet	1	F	Child	22Fe02Es
Died-At-Sea				
TURTEES, Henry-John	00	M	Unknown	22Fe02Es

CATHERINE 22 FEBRUARY 1850

From Liverpool

NAMES OF PASSENGERS	AGE	SEX	OCCUPATIONS	DATE PORT SHIP
DUNN, Mary	45	F	Wi	22Fe02Ez
Mary	18	F	Relative	22Fe02Ez
Andrew	12	M	Relative	22Fe02Ez
Philip	.00	M	Infant	22Fe02Ez
BURT, Jno.	20	M	Laborer	22Fe02Ez
RILEY, Mick	40	M	Farmer	22Fe02Ez
James	13	M	Farmer	22Fe02Ez
COOLEY, Elizabeth	20	F	Spinster	22Fe02Ez
GANIGAN, Margaret	12	F	Spinster	22Fe02Ez
HALTIN, Pat	30	M	Laborer	22Fe02Ez
HILTON, James	25	M	Laborer	22Fe02Ez
MCMAHON, Bryan	15	M	Farmer	22Fe02Ez
Mary-Ann	23	F	Relative	22Fe02Ez
Catharine	21	F	Relative	22Fe02Ez
Pat	19	M	Relative	22Fe02Ez
Johannah	13	F	Relative	22Fe02Ez
Betsey	11	F	Relative	22Fe02Ez
Margaret	9	F	Child	22Fe02Ez
Sarah	7	F	Child	22Fe02Ez
Mick	5	M	Child	22Fe02Ez
PHILIN, Martin	27	M	Laborer	22Fe02Ez
DOYLE, Margaret	20	F	Spinster	22Fe02Ez
DUNN, Jno.	35	M	Farmer	22Fe02Ez
Margaret	35	F	Relative	22Fe02Ez
Margaret	18	F	Relative	22Fe02Ez
CORCORAN, Pat	23	M	Farmer	22Fe02Ez
COONEY, Jno.	23	M	Farmer	22Fe02Ez
OBRIEN, Danl.	26	M	Farmer	22Fe02Ez
Catharine	24	F	Relative	22Fe02Ez
John	4	M	Child	22Fe02Ez
Ellen	.00	F	Infant	22Fe02Ez
Larry	.00	M	Infant	22Fe02Ez
TRACEY, Esther	23	F	Spinster	22Fe02Ez
KEGAN, Margaret	35	F	Spinster	22Fe02Ez
ELLEN, David	34	M	Laborer	22Fe02Ez
CUNAN, Margaret	25	F	Spinster	22Fe02Ez
Peggy	19	F	Spinster	22Fe02Ez
COLLINS, Jno.	31	M	Laborer	22Fe02Ez
HEATLEY, Thos.	24	M	Laborer	22Fe02Ez
KEARNEY, Edwd.	30	M	Laborer	22Fe02Ez
GOLDERT, Bridget	26	F	Spinster	22Fe02Ez
Margery	20	F	Spinster	22Fe02Ez
RILEY, Pat	13	M	Laborer	22Fe02Ez
RYAN, Mick	35	M	Farmer	22Fe02Ez
Pat	6	M	Child	22Fe02Ez
Mary	.00	F	Infant	22Fe02Ez
ARMSTRONG, Wm.	25	M	Farmer	22Fe02Ez
BROUGHAM, John	22	M	Farmer	22Fe02Ez
MCGRAGH, James	19	M	Farmer	22Fe02Ez
KELLY, Pat	55	M	Farmer	22Fe02Ez
James	12	M	Laborer	22Fe02Ez
DONALDSON, Thos.	27	M	Laborer	22Fe02Ez
CORCORAN, John	35	M	Laborer	22Fe02Ez
MAHER, John	23	M	Laborer	22Fe02Ez
WILLIAMSON, Wm.	32	M	Farmer	22Fe02Ez

NAMES OF PASSENGERS	AGE	SEX	OCCUPATIONS	DATE PORT SHIP
WILLIAMSON, Sarah	30	F	Relative	22Fe02Ez
Jerminia	34	F	Relative	22Fe02Ez
Eliza	3	F	Child	22Fe02Ez
Mary	.00	F	Infant	22Fe02Ez
FARRELL, Lawrence	30	M	Laborer	22Fe02Ez
GILHURST, Pat	23	M	Farmer	22Fe02Ez
Catharine	19	F	Wife	22Fe02Ez
KILFRY, Margaret	45	F	Wi	22Fe02Ez
John	19	M	Relative	22Fe02Ez
Pat	17	M	Relative	22Fe02Ez
Mick	15	M	Relative	22Fe02Ez
Mary	13	F	Relative	22Fe02Ez
Margaret	6	F	Child	22Fe02Ez
Thomas	4	M	Child	22Fe02Ez
Died-At-Sea				
Ann	3	F	Child	22Fe02Ez
Died-At-Sea				
CUKERAN, Pat	30	M	Farmer	22Fe02Ez
MCMAHON, Margt.	40	F	Farmer	22Fe02Ez
William	16	M	Relative	22Fe02Ez
Arthur	14	M	Relative	22Fe02Ez
John	12	M	Relative	22Fe02Ez
Eliza	8	F	Child	22Fe02Ez
Biddy	19	F	Relative	22Fe02Ez
Edward	20	M	Relative	22Fe02Ez
CLARKE, Pat	20	M	Laborer	22Fe02Ez
KELLY, Margt.	19	F	Spinster	22Fe02Ez
CALDWELL, Alice	40	F	Wi	22Fe02Ez
James	15	M	Relative	22Fe02Ez
Eliza	9	F	Child	22Fe02Ez
COGGINS, John	20	M	Laborer	22Fe02Ez
Died-At-Sea				
DENIANS, James	22	M	Laborer	22Fe02Ez
NEILY, Wm.	26	M	Laborer	22Fe02Ez
Chas.	22	M	Laborer	22Fe02Ez
CARROLL, Michl.	50	M	Farmer	22Fe02Ez
Ann	40	F	Wife	22Fe02Ez
MAHER, Cathe.	16	F	Relative	22Fe02Ez
Mary	13	F	Relative	22Fe02Ez
Rody	11	M	Relative	22Fe02Ez
Pat	9	M	Child	22Fe02Ez
Bridget	7	F	Child	22Fe02Ez
Catharine	5	F	Child	22Fe02Ez
Mick	3	M	Child	22Fe02Ez
Johannah	.00	F	Infant	22Fe02Ez
MURPHY, Jno.	20	M	Laborer	22Fe02Ez
KING, Mick	55	M	Farmer	22Fe02Ez
Mary	50	F	Relative	22Fe02Ez
James	17	M	Relative	22Fe02Ez
OWENS, Mick	40	M	Farmer	22Fe02Ez
HART, Ann	15	F	Spinster	22Fe02Ez
ODONNELL, Mary	16	F	Spinster	22Fe02Ez
REID, Bridget	18	F	Spinster	22Fe02Ez
CUNAN, Cathe.	18	F	Spinster	22Fe02Ez
Aly	16	F	Spinster	22Fe02Ez
FEEHAN, Pat	24	M	Farmer	22Fe02Ez
Ann	20	F	Wife	22Fe02Ez
CULLEN, Thomas	39	M	Laborer	22Fe02Ez
BYRNE, Sarah	31	F	Spinster	22Fe02Ez
James	6	M	Child	22Fe02Ez
CRAMEY, James	24	M	Laborer	22Fe02Ez
CANNING, Joseph	22	M	Laborer	22Fe02Ez
WALSH, John	40	M	Farmer	22Fe02Ez
George	18	M	Relative	22Fe02Ez
Mary	38	F	Relative	22Fe02Ez
Ellen	16	F	Relative	22Fe02Ez
MCDONNELL, John	25	M	Laborer	22Fe02Ez
CARROLEY, Pat	25	M	Laborer	22Fe02Ez
CARROLL, Mary	40	F	Wi	22Fe02Ez
Mary	17	F	Relative	22Fe02Ez
James	13	M	Relative	22Fe02Ez
DOCKERY, J.H.	36	M	Laborer	22Fe02Ez
BRYAN, Ben.	20	M	Laborer	22Fe02Ez
RYAN, John	40	M	Farmer	22Fe02Ez
U-Mrs.	36	F	Relative	22Fe02Ez

NAMES OF PASSENGERS	AGE	SEX	OCCUPATIONS	DATE PORT SHIP
RYAN, William	13	M	Relative	22Fe02Ez
Thomas	11	M	Relative	22Fe02Ez
Pat	9	M	Child	22Fe02Ez
Mary	7	F	Child	22Fe02Ez
Daniel	6	M	Child	22Fe02Ez
Johannah	4	F	Child	22Fe02Ez
Catharine	.00	F	Infant	22Fe02Ez
BOYLE, John	30	M	Laborer	22Fe02Ez
COLLINS, Peter	23	M	Laborer	22Fe02Ez
MCDONNELL, John	22	M	Farmer	22Fe02Ez
MCGARY, Denis	22	M	Farmer	22Fe02Ez
BREMAN, Luke	20	M	Farmer	22Fe02Ez
CUNIGHAM, Henry	42	M	Farmer	22Fe02Ez
MCDOUGH, Anne	24	F	Spinster	22Fe02Ez
CAWLEY, John	40	M	Farmer	22Fe02Ez
U-Mrs.	32	F	Relative	22Fe02Ez
Eliza	22	F	Relative	22Fe02Ez
Thomas	9	M	Child	22Fe02Ez
John	.00	M	Infant	22Fe02Ez
Mary	4	F	Child	22Fe02Ez
BURNE, John	25	M	Farmer	22Fe02Ez
Catharine	25	F	Relative	22Fe02Ez
Miles	6	M	Child	22Fe02Ez
Lawrence	3	M	Child	22Fe02Ez
Patt	.00	M	Infant	22Fe02Ez
SHEA, Pat	40	M	Laborer	22Fe02Ez
KELLY, Pat	35	M	Laborer	22Fe02Ez
BRADY, Phill	25	M	Laborer	22Fe02Ez
HENNESSEY, Thomas	35	M	Farmer	22Fe02Ez
Sarah	16	F	Relative	22Fe02Ez
Robert	13	M	Relative	22Fe02Ez
Daniel	11	M	Relative	22Fe02Ez
DUSSE, John	30	M	Farmer	22Fe02Ez
U-Mrs.	30	F	Relative	22Fe02Ez
Anne	6	F	Child	22Fe02Ez
Edward	3	M	Child	22Fe02Ez
Michael	.00	M	Infant	22Fe02Ez
QUIRK, John	30	M	Farmer	22Fe02Ez
CADDLECHY, Pat	26	M	Farmer	22Fe02Ez
U-Mrs.	26	F	Relative	22Fe02Ez
Maria	.00	F	Infant	22Fe02Ez
Thomas	24	M	Laborer	22Fe02Ez
CORKIN, Will.	20	M	Laborer	22Fe02Ez
MOORE, Bridget	24	F	Spinster	22Fe02Ez
MCCAFFERY, John	26	M	Farmer	22Fe02Ez
MCGUINE, James	26	M	Farmer	22Fe02Ez
William	20	M	Farmer	22Fe02Ez
DUFFY, Anne	25	F	Spinster	22Fe02Ez
WHILY, Biddy	25	F	Spinster	22Fe02Ez
FINN, Johannah	24	F	Spinster	22Fe02Ez
EGAN, James	18	M	Laborer	22Fe02Ez
LYONS, Margaret	18	F	Laborer	22Fe02Ez
MARTIN, Dominick	30	M	Laborer	22Fe02Ez
SCOFFER, Rodger	50	M	Farmer	22Fe02Ez
Julia	15	F	Relative	22Fe02Ez
Jerry	14	M	Relative	22Fe02Ez
Johannah	30	F	Relative	22Fe02Ez
DONOVAN, Corns.	36	M	Farmer	22Fe02Ez
Margaret	36	F	Relative	22Fe02Ez
Mary	11	F	Relative	22Fe02Ez
RYANS, Thos.	26	M	Farmer	22Fe02Ez
Catharine	26	F	Wife	22Fe02Ez
HAMILL, John	26	M	Relative	22Fe02Ez
BERRY, Mick	22	M	Relative	22Fe02Ez
HEALY, Will	22	M	Relative	22Fe02Ez
James	22	M	Relative	22Fe02Ez
DOYLE, Robt.	24	M	Relative	22Fe02Ez
John	30	M	Relative	22Fe02Ez
DUNN, Anne	20	F	Spinster	22Fe02Ez
DOGHERTY, Thos.	33	M	Laborer	22Fe02Ez
CLARK, Owen	20	M	Laborer	22Fe02Ez
LAMB, Dennis	20	M	Farmer	22Fe02Ez
DOONERY, Denis	20	M	Farmer	22Fe02Ez
WHELAN, Pat	35	M	Farmer	22Fe02Ez
KING, John	24	M	Farmer	22Fe02Ez

NAMES OF PASSENGERS	AGE	SEX	OCCUPATIONS	DATE PORT SHIP
DUNN, Eliza	23	F	Spinster	22Fe02Ez
FINNEGAN, Pat	35	M	Farmer	22Fe02Ez
Mick	27	M	Farmer	22Fe02Ez
James	23	M	Farmer	22Fe02Ez
BARNES, Mick	22	M	Farmer	22Fe02Ez
Anne	25	F	Wife	22Fe02Ez
CONNER, Mick	50	M	Farmer	22Fe02Ez
Mary	50	F	Wife	22Fe02Ez
GRAHAM, John	20	M	Farmer	22Fe02Ez
GUINNESS, John	26	M	Farmer	22Fe02Ez
Anne	22	F	Wife	22Fe02Ez
FOX, Rose	20	F	Spinster	22Fe02Ez
Anne	16	F	Spinster	22Fe02Ez
MURRAY, John	20	M	Laborer	22Fe02Ez
NANSELL, Guy	24	M	Laborer	22Fe02Ez
MCEMARY, Matthew	45	M	Farmer	22Fe02Ez
Biddy	8	F	Child	22Fe02Ez
Bernd.	6	M	Child	22Fe02Ez
GALLICK, Pat	20	M	Laborer	22Fe02Ez
CARROLL, Michl.	45	M	Farmer	22Fe02Ez
Margaret	45	F	Relative	22Fe02Ez
Cisley	15	F	Relative	22Fe02Ez
John Died-At-Sea	13	M	Relative	22Fe02Ez
Mary	10	F	Relative	22Fe02Ez
Margaret	8	F	Child	22Fe02Ez
Catharine Died-At-Sea	7	F	Child	22Fe02Ez
CARNEY, John	50	M	Farmer	22Fe02Ez
Wm.	19	M	Relative	22Fe02Ez
Pat	17	M	Relative	22Fe02Ez
Bridget	16	F	Relative	22Fe02Ez
Catharine	15	F	Relative	22Fe02Ez
CONNEL, James	15	M	Farmer	22Fe02Ez
CUNNINGHAM, Pat	46	M	Farmer	22Fe02Ez
Mary	46	F	Relative	22Fe02Ez
Mary	17	F	Relative	22Fe02Ez
Pat	15	M	Relative	22Fe02Ez
Margaret	15	F	Relative	22Fe02Ez
Edward	11	M	Relative	22Fe02Ez
John	6	M	Child	22Fe02Ez
Michl.	4	M	Child	22Fe02Ez
Bridget	.00	F	Infant	22Fe02Ez
DINNIN, Pat	20	M	Farmer	22Fe02Ez
MCCABE, Bridget	20	F	Spinster	22Fe02Ez
GRAHAM, Mick	23	M	Farmer	22Fe02Ez

HENDRIK-HUDSON 22 FEBRUARY 1850

From London

BURRUSS, John	29	M	Mariner	22Fe06Fa

ISAAC-WRIGHT 23 FEBRUARY 1850

From Liverpool

BANNON, Bridget	20	F	Servant	23Fe02Fd
MCLOUGHLIN, Honor	38	F	Servant	23Fe02Fd
Michl.	10	M	Servant	23Fe02Fd
Pat	12	M	Servant	23Fe02Fd
MURPHY, Cath.	18	F	Seamstress	23Fe02Fd
John	9	M	Child	23Fe02Fd

NAMES OF PASSENGERS	AGE	SEX	OCCUPATIONS	DATE PORT SHIP
MCTIGHE, Pat	23	M	Servant	23Fe02Fd
Mary	22	F	Servant	23Fe02Fd
Died-At-Sea				
Mary	1	F	Child	23Fe02Fd
DUFFY, U-Mrs.	40	F	Housekeeper	23Fe02Fd
Margt.	25	F	Dressmaker	23Fe02Fd
Daniel	20	M	Laborer	23Fe02Fd
Died-At-Sea				
Edwd.	18	M	Laborer	23Fe02Fd
B.	16	U	Laborer	23Fe02Fd
Michl.	14	M	Laborer	23Fe02Fd
Stephen	10	M	Laborer	23Fe02Fd
Maria	2	F	Child	23Fe02Fd
RAFFERTY, Mary	32	F	Servant	23Fe02Fd
Rose	8	F	Child	23Fe02Fd
Brid.	2	F	Child	23Fe02Fd
Hugh	6	M	Child	23Fe02Fd
BROPHY, Anne	28	F	Seamstress	23Fe02Fd
Wm.	.00	M	Infant	23Fe02Fd
Mary	6	F	Child	23Fe02Fd
Eliza	4	F	Child	23Fe02Fd
Kate	3	F	Child	23Fe02Fd
DUNNE, Margt.	40	M	Milliner	23Fe02Fd
BIRMINGHAM, Bridget	26	F	Servant	23Fe02Fd
Died-At-Sea				
John	.00	M	Infant	23Fe02Fd
Died-At-Sea				
Ellen	2	F	Child	23Fe02Fd
Died-At-Sea				
MCEVOY, Thos.	45	M	Laborer	23Fe02Fd
MCANANY, Francis	7	M	Child	23Fe02Fd
Cath.	10	F	Laborer	23Fe02Fd
CARROLL, Thos.	50	M	Clerk	23Fe02Fd
Mary	8	F	Child	23Fe02Fd
GALLAGHER, Pat	30	M	Servant	23Fe02Fd
Maria	7	F	Child	23Fe02Fd
Brid.	5	F	Child	23Fe02Fd
Cath.	3	F	Child	23Fe02Fd
DEMPSY, Anne	21	F	Stay Maker	23Fe02Fd
DOWD, Eliza	60	F	Servant	23Fe02Fd
DELANY, Bessy	11	F	Servant	23Fe02Fd
Brid.	9	F	Child	23Fe02Fd
MCCABE, Brid.	19	F	Servant	23Fe02Fd
ROURKE, Brid.	17	F	Servant	23Fe02Fd
CONNOR, Jim	16	M	Laborer	23Fe02Fd
MCARDLE, Francis	20	M	Laborer	23Fe02Fd
Susan	10	F	Laborer	23Fe02Fd
EGAN, U-Mrs.	40	F	Cap Maker	23Fe02Fd
Pat	7	M	Child	23Fe02Fd
Brid.	9	F	Child	23Fe02Fd
Mary	11	F	Unknown	23Fe02Fd
FARMER, Anne	25	F	Servant	23Fe02Fd
Henry	23	M	Laborer	23Fe02Fd
BEIRNE, John	11	M	Laborer	23Fe02Fd
Died-At-Sea				
FEE, Geo.	40	M	Mechanic	23Fe02Fd
Eliza	30	F	Mechanic	23Fe02Fd
Mary-S.	5	F	Child	23Fe02Fd
James	4	M	Child	23Fe02Fd
Wm.	1	M	Child	23Fe02Fd
Died-At-Sea				
KELLY, Margt.	25	F	Bomkr	23Fe02Fd
HEALY, Mary	14	F	Bomkr	23Fe02Fd
LINGAM, David	70	M	Farmer	23Fe02Fd
Brid.	55	F	Housekeeper	23Fe02Fd
John	24	M	Laborer	23Fe02Fd
Nancy	18	F	Laborer	23Fe02Fd
Nat.	14	M	Laborer	23Fe02Fd
Brid.	22	F	Laborer	23Fe02Fd
Died-At-Sea				
Ellen	20	F	Laborer	23Fe02Fd
Eliza	12	F	Laborer	23Fe02Fd
WALLACE, Cath.	26	F	Servant	23Fe02Fd
CLEAR, Eliza	25	F	Servant	23Fe02Fd
WALSH, David	21	M	Mason	23Fe02Fd
ODONNELL, Michl.	52	M	Carpenter	23Fe02Fd
QUILTY, Eliza	22	F	Servant	23Fe02Fd
Died-At-Sea				
FLINN, Margt.	27	F	Milliner	23Fe02Fd
HASSETT, Owen	25	M	Comb Maker	23Fe02Fd
WALSH, Margt.	28	F	Servant	23Fe02Fd
CASSEY, Johan	39	F	Servant	23Fe02Fd
Michl.	21	M	Smith	23Fe02Fd
Brid.	18	F	Unknown	23Fe02Fd
GEAMY, Pat	28	M	Stctr	23Fe02Fd
Died-At-Sea				
Jim	26	M	Bricklayer	23Fe02Fd
HIGGINS, Thos.	22	M	Mason	23Fe02Fd
CONNOR, Magt.	18	F	Unknown	23Fe02Fd
SCOTT, John	24	M	Cfnmk	23Fe02Fd
LEONARD, Hugh	33	M	Printer	23Fe02Fd
MCCORMICK, Mary	18	F	Milliner	23Fe02Fd
BLAKE, John	23	M	Engraver	23Fe02Fd
Emma	10	F	Unknown	23Fe02Fd
OBRIEN, Edwd.	23	M	Laborer	23Fe02Fd
GIBBONS, Brid.	50	F	Housekeeper	23Fe02Fd
Cath.	25	F	Servant	23Fe02Fd
Wini	6	F	Child	23Fe02Fd
Brid.	2	F	Child	23Fe02Fd
Died-At-Sea				
BEATTY, Ellen	40	F	Servant	23Fe02Fd
Died-At-Sea				
Michl.	8	M	Child	23Fe02Fd
Mary	10	F	Unknown	23Fe02Fd
ROWAN, Brid.	16	F	Unknown	23Fe02Fd
Pat	10	M	Unknown	23Fe02Fd
KELLY, Anne	6	F	Child	23Fe02Fd
Mary	3	F	Child	23Fe02Fd
MEEHAN, Cath.	16	F	Unknown	23Fe02Fd
NEAL, Eliza	38	F	Cap Maker	23Fe02Fd
Died-At-Sea				
Charles	1	M	Child	23Fe02Fd
Died-At-Sea				
MCMANUS, Anne	20	F	Tailor	23Fe02Fd
KEENAN, Thos.	24	M	Compositor	23Fe02Fd
CASEY, Ellen	25	F	Servant	23Fe02Fd
Johan	25	F	Servant	23Fe02Fd
ROCK, K.	21	M	Laborer	23Fe02Fd
Mary	2	F	Child	23Fe02Fd
Died-At-Sea				
Edwd.	31	M	Laborer	23Fe02Fd
Betty	25	F	Servant	23Fe02Fd
MAGUIRE, Phil.	19	M	Brguskr	23Fe02Fd
KELLY, Ellen	19	F	Dressmaker	23Fe02Fd
CLERKEN, Ellen	21	F	Dressmaker	23Fe02Fd
Brid.	3	F	Child	23Fe02Fd
WILSON, Margt.	52	F	Servant	23Fe02Fd
Henry	53	M	Unknown	23Fe02Fd
Mary	21	F	Unknown	23Fe02Fd
Geo.	19	M	Tailor	23Fe02Fd
Jas.	17	M	Tailor	23Fe02Fd
Thos.	15	M	Tailor	23Fe02Fd
Geo.	19	M	Tailor	23Fe02Fd
Jas.	17	M	Tailor	23Fe02Fd
Thos.	18	M	Tailor	23Fe02Fd
Wm.	12	M	Tailor	23Fe02Fd
Sarah	9	F	Child	23Fe02Fd
DOGHERTY, Patt	25	M	Joiner	23Fe02Fd
CAVESTON, Margt.	35	F	Servant	23Fe02Fd
Mary	10	F	Unknown	23Fe02Fd
John	9	M	Child	23Fe02Fd
Michl.	.00	M	Infant	23Fe02Fd
Died-At-Sea				
FALLON, Julia	21	F	Lady'S Maid	23Fe02Fd
MATTHEWS, Jas.	30	M	Printer	23Fe02Fd
Ellen	26	F	Unknown	23Fe02Fd
Died-At-Sea				
MCCANN, Margt.	21	F	Servant	23Fe02Fd
OBRIEN, Mary	21	F	Milliner	23Fe02Fd
FARLEY, Jas.	30	M	Joiner	23Fe02Fd

NAMES OF PASSENGERS	AGE	SEX	OCCUPATIONS	DATE PORT SHIP
MONAGHAN, Nabby	26	F	Servant	23Fe02Fd
Mary	.00	F	Infant	23Fe02Fd
Died-At-Sea				
MCCORMICK, Patt	30	M	Stone Mason	23Fe02Fd
KING, Owen	35	M	Laborer	23Fe02Fd
AYLWARD, Patt	33	M	Weaver	23Fe02Fd
FEE, Eliza	21	F	Servant	23Fe02Fd
SMIKE, Pat	30	M	Laborer	23Fe02Fd
Honor	20	F	Servant	23Fe02Fd
Mick	20	M	Laborer	23Fe02Fd
HUSTON, Jas.	20	M	Designer	23Fe02Fd
GIBBONS, Michl.	23	M	Carpenter	23Fe02Fd
GILMORE, Thos.	30	M	Smith	23Fe02Fd
BURKE, Pat	25	M	Clerk	23Fe02Fd
Joan	22	F	Unknown	23Fe02Fd
CARBERRY, Peter	50	M	Printer	23Fe02Fd

MARGARET-EVANS 23 FEBRUARY 1850

From London

NAMES OF PASSENGERS	AGE	SEX	OCCUPATIONS	DATE PORT SHIP
HERRING, Thos.	30	M	Laborer	23Fe06Bf
CLARKE, Margaret	50	F	Unknown	23Fe06Bf
Bridget	14	F	Unknown	23Fe06Bf
Ann	12	F	Unknown	23Fe06Bf
Michael	8	M	Child	23Fe06Bf
MAHONY, Ann	30	F	Unknown	23Fe06Bf
Catherine	11	F	Unknown	23Fe06Bf
WELTON, John	35	M	Laborer	23Fe06Bf
Mary	14	F	Unknown	23Fe06Bf
DORRINGTON, Michael	35	M	Nailer	23Fe06Bf

MT.STUART-ELPHINSTON 25 FEBRUARY 1850

From Glasgow

NAMES OF PASSENGERS	AGE	SEX	OCCUPATIONS	DATE PORT SHIP
KELLY, Margt.	60	F	None	25Fe21Ff
John	20	M	Laborer	25Fe21Ff
HAUGHY, Jane	20	F	None	25Fe21Ff
SMITH, Margt.	20	F	None	25Fe21Ff
PARK, Robt.	18	M	Druggist	25Fe21Ff
ONEIL, James	32	M	Farmer	25Fe21Ff
Hannah	50	F	None	25Fe21Ff
Elizabeth	30	F	None	25Fe21Ff
Daniel	12	M	None	25Fe21Ff
James	10	M	None	25Fe21Ff
Bernard	8	M	Child	25Fe21Ff
Patrick	5	M	Child	25Fe21Ff
HUGHES, Owen	13	M	None	25Fe21Ff
John	15	M	None	25Fe21Ff
GARTLAND, James	30	M	Farmer	25Fe21Ff
MURRAY, Catherine	26	F	Unknown	25Fe21Ff
Chas.	1	M	Child	25Fe21Ff
BROOM, Catherine	28	F	None	25Fe21Ff
Jane	7	F	Child	25Fe21Ff
Ann	4	F	Child	25Fe21Ff
James	2	M	Child	25Fe21Ff

ANN-HARLEY 25 FEBRUARY 1850

From Glasgow

NAMES OF PASSENGERS	AGE	SEX	OCCUPATIONS	DATE PORT SHIP
DONNELLY, Richard	20	M	Farmer	25Fe21Ex

DEWITT-CLINTON 25 FEBRUARY 1850

From Liverpool

NAMES OF PASSENGERS	AGE	SEX	OCCUPATIONS	DATE PORT SHIP
QUINN, Thomas	28	M	Laborer	25Fe02Ar
CURTIN, Daniel	22	M	Laborer	25Fe02Ar
Honora	28	F	Laborer	25Fe02Ar
John	3	M	Child	25Fe02Ar
James	.00	M	Infant	25Fe02Ar
MCNAMARA, Daniel	22	M	Unknown	25Fe02Ar
SHEVLIN, Thomas	35	M	Unknown	25Fe02Ar
CONNOLLY, Ellen	20	F	Seamstress	25Fe02Ar
Ann	16	F	Seamstress	25Fe02Ar
FITZGERALD, Mary	21	F	Seamstress	25Fe02Ar
FENNELL, John	29	M	Laborer	25Fe02Ar
Mary	30	F	Laborer	25Fe02Ar
James	3	M	Child	25Fe02Ar
Ann	.00	F	Infant	25Fe02Ar
CASHION, Owen	35	M	Farmer	25Fe02Ar
Lawrence	40	M	Farmer	25Fe02Ar
AHEIRN, John	20	M	Laborer	25Fe02Ar
CASHILL, Lawrence	12	M	Laborer	25Fe02Ar
DONNELLAN, John	25	M	Farmer	25Fe02Ar
NATTEN, Christina	21	F	Laborer	25Fe02Ar
CASLEN, Mary	34	F	Laborer	25Fe02Ar
Sally	13	F	Laborer	25Fe02Ar
Patrick	7	M	Child	25Fe02Ar
John	1	M	Child	25Fe02Ar
MCDONNELL, Pat	49	M	Laborer	25Fe02Ar
Bridget	48	F	Laborer	25Fe02Ar
Peter	20	M	Laborer	25Fe02Ar
Patrick	18	M	Laborer	25Fe02Ar
Mary	16	F	Laborer	25Fe02Ar
Thomas	13	M	Laborer	25Fe02Ar
Bridget	11	F	Laborer	25Fe02Ar
Christopher	9	M	Child	25Fe02Ar
Bessy	4	F	Child	25Fe02Ar
FINNAN, Bridget	14	F	Laborer	25Fe02Ar
DWYER, Edmund	25	M	Laborer	25Fe02Ar
Thomas	21	M	Laborer	25Fe02Ar
KERWICK, Edward	22	M	Laborer	25Fe02Ar
SLATTERY, Edmund	22	M	Laborer	25Fe02Ar
Died-At-Sea				
FARNELL, Ann	20	F	Laborer	25Fe02Ar
GUCKIAN, James	26	M	Farmer	25Fe02Ar
MCGRATH, Thomas	23	M	Laborer	25Fe02Ar
CODY, Pierce	39	M	Laborer	25Fe02Ar
Bridget	34	F	Laborer	25Fe02Ar
Bridget	6	F	Child	25Fe02Ar
John	3	M	Child	25Fe02Ar
Patrick	.00	M	Infant	25Fe02Ar
FITZSIMON, Patrick	19	M	Farmer	25Fe02Ar
MCKAY, Catherine	21	F	Seamstress	25Fe02Ar
WHELAN, John	21	M	Tinker	25Fe02Ar
LYONS, Luke	23	M	Farmer	25Fe02Ar
LAMB, Bridget	35	F	Farmer	25Fe02Ar
Simon	6	M	Child	25Fe02Ar

NAMES OF PASSENGERS	AGE	SEX	OCCUPATIONS	DATE PORT SHIP
MCCAFFREY, Susan	40	F	Farmer	25Fe02Ar
Edward	21	M	Farmer	25Fe02Ar
Bridget	18	F	Farmer	25Fe02Ar
John	13	M	Farmer	25Fe02Ar
KELLY, Patrick	40	M	Farmer	25Fe02Ar
CARTY, John	30	M	Farmer	25Fe02Ar
WHELAN, Bridget	20	F	Farmer	25Fe02Ar
MCKINNY, John	21	M	Farmer	25Fe02Ar
COSTELLA, Edward	26	M	Farmer	25Fe02Ar
BRACKEN, Jas.	20	M	Farmer	25Fe02Ar
CONLAN, Pat	20	M	Farmer	25Fe02Ar
Ann	20	F	Farmer	25Fe02Ar
Margaret	17	F	Farmer	25Fe02Ar
COYNE, Mary	20	F	Seamstress	25Fe02Ar
MCTEAGUE, Matthew	50	M	Laborer	25Fe02Ar
DURKIN, Sibby	35	F	Farmer	25Fe02Ar
GAVIGAN, Pat	19	M	Farmer	25Fe02Ar
KELLY, John	25	M	Farmer	25Fe02Ar
PARTLAND, Bryan	19	M	Farmer	25Fe02Ar
Jane	20	F	Farmer	25Fe02Ar
FLEMING, Jerrold	24	M	Laborer	25Fe02Ar
Mary	32	F	Laborer	25Fe02Ar
DUNNE, Mary	24	F	Seamstress	25Fe02Ar
Patrick	11	M	Laborer	25Fe02Ar
PHELAN, Michael	28	M	Laborer	25Fe02Ar
CARROLL, Bridget	20	F	Seamstress	25Fe02Ar
HENSON, John	28	M	Farmer	25Fe02Ar
DUNLEARY, James	45	M	Farmer	25Fe02Ar
TIERNAN, John	20	M	Farmer	25Fe02Ar
FEGAN, James	23	M	Farmer	25Fe02Ar
Mary	18	F	Farmer	25Fe02Ar
MORAN, Honora	19	F	Farmer	25Fe02Ar
FEE, Samuel	26	M	Farmer	25Fe02Ar
Rossanah-Mrs.	26	F	Farmer	25Fe02Ar
Maria	24	F	Farmer	25Fe02Ar
Maria	1	F	Child	25Fe02Ar
LAVIN, Bernard	30	M	Child	25Fe02Ar
DAVIN, Patrick	36	M	Farmer	25Fe02Ar
Bridget	24	F	Farmer	25Fe02Ar
MOLLOY, Pat	25	M	Farmer	25Fe02Ar
Ellen	24	F	Farmer	25Fe02Ar
MCDONOUGH, Mary	17	F	Farmer	25Fe02Ar
MCGALE, John	24	M	Shoemaker	25Fe02Ar
SHEVLIN, Patrick	30	M	Shoemaker	25Fe02Ar
STONE, Samuel	35	M	Farmer	25Fe02Ar
GLENNAN, James	21	M	Farmer	25Fe02Ar
MCGAVERN, Joseph	45	M	Farmer	25Fe02Ar
GARTY, Rose-Miss	24	F	Seamstress	25Fe02Ar
WARD, James	18	M	Laborer	25Fe02Ar
CUSACK, Bernard	22	M	Laborer	25Fe02Ar
KENNY, Owen	40	M	Farmer	25Fe02Ar
John	24	M	Farmer	25Fe02Ar
Rose	18	F	Farmer	25Fe02Ar
Mary	16	F	Farmer	25Fe02Ar
MCANALLY, Thomas	26	M	Laborer	25Fe02Ar
DURKIN, James	30	M	Laborer	25Fe02Ar
FAHEY, Thomas	23	M	Laborer	25Fe02Ar
BOYLAN, Pat	25	M	Laborer	25Fe02Ar
Mary	25	F	Laborer	25Fe02Ar
Mary-Ann	.00	F	Infant	25Fe02Ar
MCINTEER, Catherine	18	F	Seamstress	25Fe02Ar
BOYLAN, William	18	M	Laborer	25Fe02Ar
GORMLEY, Ann	45	F	Farmer	25Fe02Ar
DOW, Wm.	22	M	Joiner	25Fe02Ar
HOGAN, Margaret	40	F	Farmer	25Fe02Ar
Bridget	10	F	Farmer	25Fe02Ar
Rody	4	F	Child	25Fe02Ar
FARRELL, Michael	25	M	Farmer	25Fe02Ar
COFFEY, Bridget	20	F	Farmer	25Fe02Ar
Catherine	24	F	Farmer	25Fe02Ar
RYAN, Margaret	24	F	Seamstress	25Fe02Ar
GLYNNE, Pat	40	M	Farmer	25Fe02Ar
TOOLE, Michael	35	M	Farmer	25Fe02Ar
MURTAGH, Margaret	26	F	Farmer	25Fe02Ar
Mary	10	F	Farmer	25Fe02Ar
MURTAGH, Elisa	16	F	Farmer	25Fe02Ar
Mary	15	F	Farmer	25Fe02Ar
DIGNAN, Lawrence	18	M	Farmer	25Fe02Ar
MICHALL, James	14	M	Farmer	25Fe02Ar
BRODERICK, Betty	24	F	Farmer	25Fe02Ar
LANCE, Margaret	40	F	Farmer	25Fe02Ar
Bridget	30	F	Farmer	25Fe02Ar
Peter	9	M	Child	25Fe02Ar
Anastatia	.00	F	Infant	25Fe02Ar
HYNES, John	21	M	Farmer	25Fe02Ar
HANLEY, Judy	40	F	Farmer	25Fe02Ar
Ellen	11	F	Farmer	25Fe02Ar
Mary	9	F	Child	25Fe02Ar
DONOHUE, Daniel	19	M	Farmer	25Fe02Ar
ROURKE, Margt.	24	F	Farmer	25Fe02Ar
CONNOR, Cath.	18	F	Farmer	25Fe02Ar
Norry	4	M	Child	25Fe02Ar
Margaret	20	F	Farmer	25Fe02Ar
KEEFE, Bridget	20	F	Farmer	25Fe02Ar
DEVITT, Ellen	24	F	Farmer	25Fe02Ar
STOAKES, Elisa	26	F	Farmer	25Fe02Ar
Johanna	18	F	Farmer	25Fe02Ar
KELLY, Pat	46	M	Farmer	25Fe02Ar
MURPHY, Daniel	22	M	Laborer	25Fe02Ar
Bernard	22	M	Laborer	25Fe02Ar
REILLY, James	22	M	Laborer	25Fe02Ar
Charles	22	M	Laborer	25Fe02Ar
MOYNAHAN, Ellen	13	F	Laborer	25Fe02Ar
Francis	21	F	Laborer	25Fe02Ar
Maurice	11	M	Laborer	25Fe02Ar
CESS, Richard	20	M	Laborer	25Fe02Ar
MCENTEGGART, Pat	28	M	Farmer	25Fe02Ar
Mary	26	F	Farmer	25Fe02Ar
Cath.	6	F	Child	25Fe02Ar
Bridget	4	F	Child	25Fe02Ar
Mary	.00	F	Infant	25Fe02Ar
Died-At-Sea				
Owen	18	M	Farmer	25Fe02Ar
Patk.	14	M	Farmer	25Fe02Ar
Bridget	12	F	Farmer	25Fe02Ar
CARROLL, Cath.	24	F	Farmer	25Fe02Ar
KERR, Rose	20	F	Farmer	25Fe02Ar
LEAHY, Mary-Mrs.	40	F	Farmer	25Fe02Ar
Elisa	15	F	Farmer	25Fe02Ar
Dennis	13	M	Farmer	25Fe02Ar
John	12	M	Farmer	25Fe02Ar
Pat	7	M	Child	25Fe02Ar
Francis	4	M	Child	25Fe02Ar
DALANEY, Sarah	18	F	Farmer	25Fe02Ar
Margaret	16	F	Farmer	25Fe02Ar
LARKIN, Thomas	26	M	Farmer	25Fe02Ar
FALLS, Cath.	40	F	Farmer	25Fe02Ar
MCGOWAN, Owen	60	M	Farmer	25Fe02Ar
Pat	25	M	Farmer	25Fe02Ar
Owen	12	M	Farmer	25Fe02Ar
Catherine	50	F	Farmer	25Fe02Ar
CRAWLEY, Mary	18	F	Farmer	25Fe02Ar
NARAN, Mary	15	F	Farmer	25Fe02Ar
ROCK, James	25	M	Farmer	25Fe02Ar
CRAWLEY, John	22	M	Farmer	25Fe02Ar
MCGRATH, Bridget	35	F	Farmer	25Fe02Ar
Pat	12	M	Farmer	25Fe02Ar
James	10	M	Farmer	25Fe02Ar
Catherine	5	F	Child	25Fe02Ar
NANON, Hugh	39	M	Laborer	25Fe02Ar
GIBLIN, Edward	23	M	Laborer	25Fe02Ar
KEENAN, U-Mrs.	28	F	Seamstress	25Fe02Ar
PHILIPS, Mich.	20	M	Farmer	25Fe02Ar
MCGARRY, Mich.	30	M	Farmer	25Fe02Ar
Maria-Mrs.	30	F	Farmer	25Fe02Ar
Ann	.00	F	Infant	25Fe02Ar
QUINCY, Keirnan	25	M	Farmer	25Fe02Ar
WHITE, Mary-Mrs.	22	F	Farmer	25Fe02Ar
William	.00	M	Infant	25Fe02Ar
DELANEY, Andrew	25	M	Farmer	25Fe02Ar

NAMES OF PASSENGERS	AGE	SEX	OCCUPATIONS	DATE PORT SHIP
OBRIEN, Winney	32	F	Seamstress	25Fe02Ar
MCCARTHY, Jerry	20	M	Laborer	25Fe02Ar
LARGEY, John	50	M	Laborer	25Fe02Ar
Kitty-Mrs.	50	F	Laborer	25Fe02Ar
Owen	14	M	Laborer	25Fe02Ar
Pat	6	M	Child	25Fe02Ar
William	4	M	Child	25Fe02Ar
CORBITT, John	25	M	Laborer	25Fe02Ar
MARA, Stephen	20	M	Laborer	25Fe02Ar
KELLY, Thomas	30	M	Farmer	25Fe02Ar
LYDEN, Christy	35	M	Farmer	25Fe02Ar
NAUGHTEN, John	30	M	Farmer	25Fe02Ar
KELLY, Bridget	24	F	Farmer	25Fe02Ar
Peggy	18	F	Farmer	25Fe02Ar
GOLDING, Mich.	30	M	Farmer	25Fe02Ar
GLYNNE, Mark	30	M	Laborer	25Fe02Ar
Michael	25	M	Laborer	25Fe02Ar
DONLAN, Anthony	30	M	Laborer	25Fe02Ar
LALLY, Anthony	30	M	Laborer	25Fe02Ar
Mary	25	F	Laborer	25Fe02Ar
DEVINES, Bridget	20	F	Seamstress	25Fe02Ar
SALLY, Sally	2	F	Child	25Fe02Ar
Edmund Died-At-Sea	.00	M	Infant	25Fe02Ar
Catherine	2	F	Child	25Fe02Ar
HEUES, Mich.	50	M	Laborer	25Fe02Ar
MCCONNELL, Robert	48	M	Laborer	25Fe02Ar
PURDY, Bessy	19	F	Seamstress	25Fe02Ar
EGAN, James	33	M	Farmer	25Fe02Ar
LAWLER, John	25	M	Farmer	25Fe02Ar
Michael	22	M	Farmer	25Fe02Ar
Thomas	36	M	Farmer	25Fe02Ar
Ellen	35	F	Farmer	25Fe02Ar
Christy	3	M	Child	25Fe02Ar
John	.00	M	Infant	25Fe02Ar
CORRY, Michael	30	M	Farmer	25Fe02Ar
BRADY, Sarah	30	F	Farmer	25Fe02Ar
KEOUGH, Lawrence	20	M	Farmer	25Fe02Ar
BYRNE, Wm.	25	M	Farmer	25Fe02Ar
Bridget	20	F	Farmer	25Fe02Ar
SULLIVAN, John	28	M	Farmer	25Fe02Ar
Abby-Mrs.	28	F	Farmer	25Fe02Ar
Elisa	.00	F	Infant	25Fe02Ar
MCCARTHY, Mary	18	F	Seamstress	25Fe02Ar
MCKENNA, Felix	17	M	Laborer	25Fe02Ar
Mary	6	F	Child	25Fe02Ar
MCANALLY, Thomas	26	M	Laborer	25Fe02Ar
DURKIN, James	30	M	Laborer	25Fe02Ar
FAHEY, Thomas	23	M	Tinker	25Fe02Ar
KELLY, John	30	M	Farmer	25Fe02Ar
Mary	60	F	Farmer	25Fe02Ar
Pat	15	M	Farmer	25Fe02Ar
BIGHAM, John	24	M	Farmer	25Fe02Ar
Mary	22	F	Farmer	25Fe02Ar
MCELRATH, James	22	M	Farmer	25Fe02Ar
GLENNAN, Ellen	20	F	Seamstress	25Fe02Ar
FLYNNE, James	24	M	Laborer	25Fe02Ar
MCMANUS, Michael	60	M	Farmer	25Fe02Ar
KELLY, Pat	60	M	Farmer	25Fe02Ar
Bridgett	19	F	Farmer	25Fe02Ar
MURPHY, Antony	60	M	Blacksmith	25Fe02Ar
Catherine	60	F	Unknown	25Fe02Ar
Eliza	18	F	Unknown	25Fe02Ar
MCCABE, William	18	M	Mariner	25Fe02Ar
SCOLLON, James	31	M	Mechanic	25Fe02Ar

COLUMBUS 25 FEBRUARY 1850

From Liverpool

NAMES OF PASSENGERS	AGE	SEX	OCCUPATIONS	DATE PORT SHIP
LUNELY, Margt.	35	F	Unknown	25Fe02Ah
John	12	M	Unknown	25Fe02Ah
Elizth.	8	F	Child	25Fe02Ah
Margt.	10	F	Unknown	25Fe02Ah
CAVANAGH, John	18	M	Laborer	25Fe02Ah
SHEEHAN, Corns.	18	M	Laborer	25Fe02Ah
ROOK, Michl.	50	M	Unknown	25Fe02Ah
Michl.	11	M	Unknown	25Fe02Ah
John	20	M	Unknown	25Fe02Ah
RYAN, Willm.	45	M	Unknown	25Fe02Ah
U-Mrs.	33	F	Unknown	25Fe02Ah
Bridgt.	12	F	Unknown	25Fe02Ah
Edwd.	10	M	Unknown	25Fe02Ah
Simon	8	M	Child	25Fe02Ah
Wm.	7	M	Child	25Fe02Ah
Mary	5	F	Child	25Fe02Ah
Cathe.	.00	F	Infant	25Fe02Ah
Richd.	28	M	Laborer	25Fe02Ah
Ally	28	M	Laborer	25Fe02Ah
Patt	28	M	Laborer	25Fe02Ah
Bridgt.	2	F	Child	25Fe02Ah
Mary	.00	F	Infant	25Fe02Ah
QUINLAN, Patt	25	M	Laborer	25Fe02Ah
Mary	24	F	Unknown	25Fe02Ah
Mathw.	3	M	Child	25Fe02Ah
RYAN, John	40	M	Laborer	25Fe02Ah
SLATTERY, Thos.	30	M	Laborer	25Fe02Ah
CALLEN, Thos.	25	M	Farmer	25Fe02Ah
MCCALE, Francis	25	M	Laborer	25Fe02Ah
REILLY, Thomas	30	M	Laborer	25Fe02Ah
MORRISS, Peter	61	M	Laborer	25Fe02Ah
SHAUGHNESS, Alice	14	F	Unknown	25Fe02Ah
CLARK, James	18	M	Laborer	25Fe02Ah
KELLY, Michl.	44	M	Mason	25Fe02Ah
DUNN, James	30	M	Laborer	25Fe02Ah
Julia	20	F	Unknown	25Fe02Ah
Maria	25	F	Unknown	25Fe02Ah
DEAN, Edwd.	40	M	Laborer	25Fe02Ah
MCDONOUGH, Michl.	40	M	Laborer	25Fe02Ah
FITZPATRICK, Ellen	22	F	Unknown	25Fe02Ah
BOYLAN, Mary	16	F	Unknown	25Fe02Ah
DONLAN, Eliza	22	F	Unknown	25Fe02Ah
BOWS, Letitia	22	F	Unknown	25Fe02Ah
Robt.	12	M	Unknown	25Fe02Ah
John	7	M	Child	25Fe02Ah
David	3	M	Child	25Fe02Ah
ROSMAN, James	22	M	Unknown	25Fe02Ah
CURREN, Thos.	25	M	Unknown	25Fe02Ah
HEALEY, James	21	M	Unknown	25Fe02Ah
GILMARTIN, James	10	M	Unknown	25Fe02Ah
CAIN, Hugh	13	M	Unknown	25Fe02Ah
HAGAN, Margt.	22	F	Unknown	25Fe02Ah
OBRIEN, Nichls.	51	M	Unknown	25Fe02Ah
MCCUE, Bridgt.	12	F	Unknown	25Fe02Ah
DOYLE, Ann	40	F	Unknown	25Fe02Ah
Patt	17	M	Laborer	25Fe02Ah
GREENWOOD, Mary	18	F	Unknown	25Fe02Ah
MOARN, Betsy	30	F	Unknown	25Fe02Ah
SHENELLEN, Margt.	20	F	Unknown	25Fe02Ah
COSTELOEW, Ellen	26	F	Unknown	25Fe02Ah
MCADAM, Patt	37	M	Laborer	25Fe02Ah
Mary	35	F	Unknown	25Fe02Ah
Ally	13	M	Unknown	25Fe02Ah
Ann	11	F	Unknown	25Fe02Ah
Cathe.	9	F	Child	25Fe02Ah

NAMES OF PASSENGERS	AGE	SEX	OCCUPATIONS	DATE PORT SHIP
MCADAM, Bridgt.	7	F	Child	25Fe02Ah
Edwd.	5	M	Child	25Fe02Ah
Mary	3	F	Child	25Fe02Ah
MCMAHER, Michl.	37	M	Laborer	25Fe02Ah
Elizth.	38	F	Unknown	25Fe02Ah
James	12	M	Unknown	25Fe02Ah
Cathe.	10	F	Unknown	25Fe02Ah
Mary	8	F	Child	25Fe02Ah
Ann	4	F	Child	25Fe02Ah
Rose	11	F	Unknown	25Fe02Ah
Bridgt.	2	F	Child	25Fe02Ah
Michl.	.00	M	Infant	25Fe02Ah
DUFFY, Cathe.	35	F	Unknown	25Fe02Ah
Rose	12	F	Unknown	25Fe02Ah
Eleaner	10	F	Unknown	25Fe02Ah
Cathe.	6	F	Child	25Fe02Ah
John	4	M	Child	25Fe02Ah
CASSICK, Ann	40	F	Unknown	25Fe02Ah
OSBORNE, John	45	M	Unknown	25Fe02Ah
Mary	45	F	Unknown	25Fe02Ah
Charles	13	M	Unknown	25Fe02Ah
KING, Michl.	30	M	Laborer	25Fe02Ah
MARA, John	50	M	Farmer	25Fe02Ah
Patt	21	M	Farmer	25Fe02Ah
John	19	M	Unknown	25Fe02Ah
Biddy	11	F	Unknown	25Fe02Ah
Thomas	9	M	Child	25Fe02Ah
WILSON, Willm.	38	M	Farmer	25Fe02Ah
James	17	M	Unknown	25Fe02Ah
Eliza	15	F	Unknown	25Fe02Ah
Thomas	12	M	Unknown	25Fe02Ah
MCQUADE, John	23	M	Farmer	25Fe02Ah
Bessy	21	F	Unknown	25Fe02Ah
MCKAY, Peter	40	M	Farmer	25Fe02Ah
Michl.	20	M	Unknown	25Fe02Ah
Pierce	19	M	Unknown	25Fe02Ah
Peter	17	M	Unknown	25Fe02Ah
CLARK, Thomas	20	M	Laborer	25Fe02Ah
MCKAY, Annie	12	F	Unknown	25Fe02Ah
DOHANY, Johanna	24	F	Unknown	25Fe02Ah
DOOLEY, Patt	25	M	Farmer	25Fe02Ah
NEAIN, Robt.	36	M	Coachman	25Fe02Ah
STENEY, Francis	25	M	Farmer	25Fe02Ah
MCDONALD, Mary	24	F	Unknown	25Fe02Ah
BECK, Sarah	30	F	Unknown	25Fe02Ah
George	4	M	Child	25Fe02Ah
Thomas	.00	M	Infant	25Fe02Ah
Eliza	23	F	Unknown	25Fe02Ah
CLARK, Hugh	18	M	Laborer	25Fe02Ah
FITZSIMMONS, Dermot	20	M	Unknown	25Fe02Ah
LAWLER, Peter	18	M	Unknown	25Fe02Ah
DUFF, Patt	30	M	Unknown	25Fe02Ah
Died-At-Sea				
FARLEY, Judy	30	F	Unknown	25Fe02Ah
Phillip	6	M	Child	25Fe02Ah
Bernd.	2	M	Child	25Fe02Ah
Cathe.	.00	F	Infant	25Fe02Ah
SHENDEN, Michl.	30	M	Laborer	25Fe02Ah
KILCLINE, Andw.	22	M	Laborer	25Fe02Ah
FITZGERALD, Michl.	21	M	Blacksmith	25Fe02Ah
SCOTT, Thomas	35	M	Farmer	25Fe02Ah
RYAN, John	28	M	Laborer	25Fe02Ah
HUGHES, Arthur	20	M	Laborer	25Fe02Ah
ALYLLWAND, John	30	M	Laborer	25Fe02Ah
CONNOR, Kate	1	F	Child	25Fe02Ah
Died-At-Sea				
MOORE, Nancy	23	F	Unknown	25Fe02Ah
CAIN, Morriss	25	M	Laborer	25Fe02Ah
Nancy	28	F	Unknown	25Fe02Ah
James	.00	M	Infant	25Fe02Ah
Died-At-Sea				
HEGARTY, Conner	53	M	Laborer	25Fe02Ah
HALLERAN, Cathe.	19	F	Unknown	25Fe02Ah
Margt.	13	F	Unknown	25Fe02Ah
HEGARTY, John	13	M	Unknown	25Fe02Ah
FOLEY, Ann	21	F	Unknown	25Fe02Ah
NOLAN, Margt.	11	F	Unknown	25Fe02Ah
Michl.	13	M	Unknown	25Fe02Ah
BYRNES, Owen	24	M	Laborer	25Fe02Ah
Cathe.	28	F	Unknown	25Fe02Ah
CLARKE, Cathe.	34	F	Unknown	25Fe02Ah
Mary	16	F	Unknown	25Fe02Ah
James	.00	M	Infant	25Fe02Ah
MAHER, Bridgt.	20	F	Unknown	25Fe02Ah
DOOLAN, Mary	.00	F	Infant	25Fe02Ah
SMITH, Bridgt.	14	F	Unknown	25Fe02Ah
FARLEY, Mary	7	F	Child	25Fe02Ah
ROONEY, Mary	35	F	Unknown	25Fe02Ah
RICHARDSON, Richd.	38	M	Clerk	25Fe02Ah
Harriett	32	F	Unknown	25Fe02Ah
George	4	M	Child	25Fe02Ah
Jane	2	F	Child	25Fe02Ah
WISE, Dennis	27	M	Laborer	25Fe02Ah
James	9	M	Child	25Fe02Ah
Margt.	7	F	Child	25Fe02Ah
HARRINGTON, Bridgt.	23	F	Unknown	25Fe02Ah
CARBERRY, Cathe.	25	F	Unknown	25Fe02Ah
Margt.	22	F	Unknown	25Fe02Ah
Cathe.	11	F	Unknown	25Fe02Ah
John	9	M	Child	25Fe02Ah
MINICK, Martin	37	M	Unknown	25Fe02Ah
CAMPBELL, Mary	32	F	Unknown	25Fe02Ah
RIBNEY, Bridgt.	28	F	Unknown	25Fe02Ah
HACKETT, John	35	M	Unknown	25Fe02Ah
CONNER, John	40	M	Farmer	25Fe02Ah
Judith	26	F	Unknown	25Fe02Ah
Margt.	24	F	Unknown	25Fe02Ah
QUINN, Lucy	21	F	Unknown	25Fe02Ah
CONROY, John	37	M	Laborer	25Fe02Ah
BACON, Mary	25	F	Unknown	25Fe02Ah
CONNER, Michl.	1	M	Child	25Fe02Ah
Died-At-Sea				
Luke	30	M	Farmer	25Fe02Ah
Ellen	28	F	Unknown	25Fe02Ah
Essy	9	F	Child	25Fe02Ah
Sally	11	F	Unknown	25Fe02Ah
Mary	7	F	Child	25Fe02Ah
Patt	4	M	Child	25Fe02Ah
Chas.	2	M	Child	25Fe02Ah
Bernd.	30	M	Unknown	25Fe02Ah
FLANNIGAN, James	42	M	Clerk	25Fe02Ah
OLOUGHLIN, James	37	M	Unknown	25Fe02Ah
MARSHALL, George	28	M	Laborer	25Fe02Ah
CARTINE, Willm.	22	M	Farmer	25Fe02Ah
Dennis	11	M	Unknown	25Fe02Ah
DOOLAN, James	35	M	Unknown	25Fe02Ah
U-Mrs.	33	F	Unknown	25Fe02Ah
KEEGAN, Cathe.	11	F	Unknown	25Fe02Ah
LANE, Patt	30	M	Unknown	25Fe02Ah
Mary	20	F	Unknown	25Fe02Ah
FOWLER, Bridgt.	21	F	Unknown	25Fe02Ah
MOONAN, Bridgt.	25	F	Unknown	25Fe02Ah
Mary	2	F	Child	25Fe02Ah
LAHEY, Mary	28	F	Unknown	25Fe02Ah
EARLE, Dennis	28	M	Laborer	25Fe02Ah
U-Mrs.	39	F	Unknown	25Fe02Ah
WOOD, Mary	25	F	Unknown	25Fe02Ah
EARLE, Mary	4	F	Child	25Fe02Ah
Cath.	2	F	Child	25Fe02Ah
ROONEY, Mary	1	F	Child	25Fe02Ah
CALDWELL, John	37	M	Sugblr	25Fe02Ah
CURIATT, James	42	M	Laborer	25Fe02Ah
NEAL, Edwd.	45	M	Laborer	25Fe02Ah
CASEY, Michl.	27	M	Laborer	25Fe02Ah
BYRNES, Cathe.	32	F	Unknown	25Fe02Ah
KANE, Anne	28	F	Unknown	25Fe02Ah
COUGHLIN, Patt	30	M	Laborer	25Fe02Ah
Ellen	8	F	Child	25Fe02Ah
Wm.	7	M	Child	25Fe02Ah
KEEFFE, John	28	M	Laborer	25Fe02Ah

NAMES OF PASSENGERS	AGE	SEX	OCCUPATIONS	DATE PORT SHIP
KEEFFE, Patt	26	M	Laborer	25Fe02Ah
BEEKHAM, Patt	32	M	Laborer	25Fe02Ah
Margt.	28	F	Unknown	25Fe02Ah
BYRNE, Michl.	25	M	Laborer	25Fe02Ah
HEFFERAN, Mary	29	F	Unknown	25Fe02Ah
John	6	M	Child	25Fe02Ah
HENESSY, Cathe.	23	F	Unknown	25Fe02Ah
AMBROSE, Norry	27	F	Unknown	25Fe02Ah
BRADY, John	33	M	Unknown	25Fe02Ah
U-Mrs.	35	F	Unknown	25Fe02Ah
Mary	31	F	Unknown	25Fe02Ah
Margt.	11	F	Unknown	25Fe02Ah
Ann	9	F	Child	25Fe02Ah
John	4	M	Child	25Fe02Ah
Phillip	6	M	Child	25Fe02Ah
CONNOLLY, Edwd.	42	M	Farmer	25Fe02Ah
U-Mrs.	40	F	Unknown	25Fe02Ah
Mary	10	F	Unknown	25Fe02Ah
Bridgt.	8	F	Child	25Fe02Ah
MOONEY, Margt.	27	F	Unknown	25Fe02Ah
RYANS, Mary	32	F	Unknown	25Fe02Ah
CULLEN, Cathe.	35	F	Unknown	25Fe02Ah
DEMPSEY, Cathe.	34	F	Unknown	25Fe02Ah
Cathe.	8	F	Child	25Fe02Ah
Bridgt.	9	F	Child	25Fe02Ah
MCCABE, Cathe.	10	F	Unknown	25Fe02Ah
REILLY, Ann	28	F	Unknown	25Fe02Ah
Charles	8	M	Child	25Fe02Ah
Mathw.	7	M	Child	25Fe02Ah
Mary	5	F	Child	25Fe02Ah
BOYLAN, Patt	27	M	Laborer	25Fe02Ah
MCGRASS, Willm.	38	M	Gdnr	25Fe02Ah
U-Mrs.	35	F	Unknown	25Fe02Ah
BREEN, Wm.	27	M	Unknown	25Fe02Ah
U-Mrs.	29	F	Unknown	25Fe02Ah
Mary	4	F	Child	25Fe02Ah
Michl.	3	M	Child	25Fe02Ah
KELLY, Margt.	25	F	Unknown	25Fe02Ah
Mary	11	F	Unknown	25Fe02Ah
Lawrence	9	M	Child	25Fe02Ah
John	6	M	Child	25Fe02Ah
Margt.	2	F	Child	25Fe02Ah
QUILT, Nancy	27	F	Unknown	25Fe02Ah
FERBECK, Newman	45	M	Unknown	25Fe02Ah
BYRNE, John	33	M	Unknown	25Fe02Ah
Bridgt.	31	F	Unknown	25Fe02Ah
DELAHUNTY, Margt.	25	F	Unknown	25Fe02Ah
Thomas	11	M	Unknown	25Fe02Ah
Michl.	10	M	Unknown	25Fe02Ah
John	9	M	Child	25Fe02Ah
RYAN, Thomas	28	M	Unknown	25Fe02Ah
Timothy	32	M	Unknown	25Fe02Ah
DELAHUNTY, Judy	32	F	Unknown	25Fe02Ah
Margt.	28	F	Unknown	25Fe02Ah
REILLY, Edwd.	41	M	Unknown	25Fe02Ah
LANE, Dennis	1	M	Child	25Fe02Ah
EARLE, Bridget	2	F	Child	25Fe02Ah
KANE, Patt	2	M	Child	25Fe02Ah
HEFFERAN, Bridget	1	F	Child	25Fe02Ah
CONOLLY, Catherine	3	F	Child	25Fe02Ah
REILLY, Biddy	.08	F	Infant	25Fe02Ah
MCEROSS, Catherine	1	F	Child	25Fe02Ah
Died-At-Sea				
BREEN, William	.11	M	Infant	25Fe02Ah
MARTIN, James	32	M	Carpenter	25Fe02Ah
U-Mrs.	30	F	Unknown	25Fe02Ah
Dennis	.09	M	Infant	25Fe02Ah
Thomas	3	M	Child	25Fe02Ah
MOONEY, Patt	32	M	Unknown	25Fe02Ah
Thomas	29	M	Unknown	25Fe02Ah
SCANLON, Bridget	37	F	Unknown	25Fe02Ah
CONLON, Garrett	25	M	Unknown	25Fe02Ah
MARA, Issabella	11	F	Unknown	25Fe02Ah
Joseph	8	M	Child	25Fe02Ah
Michael	8	M	Child	25Fe02Ah

NAMES OF PASSENGERS	AGE	SEX	OCCUPATIONS	DATE PORT SHIP
MARA, Bridget	5	F	Child	25Fe02Ah
Ann	4	F	Child	25Fe02Ah
NOLAN, Michael	32	M	Unknown	25Fe02Ah
MOLANEY, Bridget	27	F	Unknown	25Fe02Ah
GAHEY, Mary	25	F	Unknown	25Fe02Ah
DROUT, Mary	25	F	Unknown	25Fe02Ah
LYNCH, James	27	M	Laborer	25Fe02Ah
Catherine	25	F	Unknown	25Fe02Ah
Catherine	3	F	Child	25Fe02Ah
KENNEDY, James	37	M	Unknown	25Fe02Ah
SHAUGHNESSY, Patt	42	M	Unknown	25Fe02Ah
DAY, James	25	M	Stone Mason	25Fe02Ah
KANE, John	33	M	Laborer	25Fe02Ah
DUNN, Daniel	27	M	Laborer	25Fe02Ah
WARD, William	25	M	Laborer	25Fe02Ah
READMAN, William	32	M	Unknown	25Fe02Ah
WARD, John	37	M	Unknown	25Fe02Ah
DOWNEY, James	35	M	Unknown	25Fe02Ah
TRACEY, Catherine	33	F	Unknown	25Fe02Ah
MASEY, Thomas	27	M	Unknown	25Fe02Ah
MURRY, Mary	32	F	Unknown	25Fe02Ah
MCCABE, James	25	M	Unknown	25Fe02Ah
LYNCH, Matthew	18	M	Unknown	25Fe02Ah
WARD, Catherine	15	F	Unknown	25Fe02Ah
RIGNEY, Patt	32	M	Unknown	25Fe02Ah
Ann	28	F	Unknown	25Fe02Ah
DUNN, John	35	M	Unknown	25Fe02Ah
NEALS, James	35	M	Unknown	25Fe02Ah
Thomas	33	M	Unknown	25Fe02Ah
Johan	25	M	Unknown	25Fe02Ah
Ann	24	F	Unknown	25Fe02Ah
Bridget	21	F	Unknown	25Fe02Ah
CALLAGHAN, Mary	25	F	Unknown	25Fe02Ah
Mary	6	F	Child	25Fe02Ah
AHERN, Michael	52	M	Farmer	25Fe02Ah
Margt.	13	F	Unknown	25Fe02Ah
RYAN, Connor	34	M	Unknown	25Fe02Ah
Kate	37	F	Unknown	25Fe02Ah
Thomas	18	M	Unknown	25Fe02Ah
Michael	15	M	Unknown	25Fe02Ah
Jerry	10	M	Unknown	25Fe02Ah
Ellen	10	F	Unknown	25Fe02Ah
ARMSTRONG, Thomas	20	M	Cbtmkr	25Fe02Ah
LORD, Ellen	30	F	Unknown	25Fe02Ah
KANE, Margt.	18	F	Unknown	25Fe02Ah
Elizabeth	15	F	Unknown	25Fe02Ah
Mary	11	F	Unknown	25Fe02Ah
Patt	7	M	Child	25Fe02Ah
Ann	4	F	Child	25Fe02Ah
Margt.	.08	F	Infant	25Fe02Ah
MYLLAN, Rose	21	F	Unknown	25Fe02Ah
Patt	11	M	Unknown	25Fe02Ah
FLANAGAN, Bridget	23	F	Unknown	25Fe02Ah
Mary	4	F	Child	25Fe02Ah
MCINTERE, Margt.	29	F	Unknown	25Fe02Ah
TIE, Ann	32	F	Unknown	25Fe02Ah
LALLY, Catherine	28	F	Unknown	25Fe02Ah
Patt	4	M	Child	25Fe02Ah
Michael	3	M	Child	25Fe02Ah
MCMAHON, Thom.	37	M	Weaver	25Fe02Ah
LYNCH, Mary	18	F	Unknown	25Fe02Ah
GALLAGHER, Ann	27	F	Unknown	25Fe02Ah
ABRAHAM, John	29	M	Unknown	25Fe02Ah
Stephen	8	M	Child	25Fe02Ah
Thomas	3	M	Child	25Fe02Ah
WILLIAMSON, Matilda	32	F	Unknown	25Fe02Ah
Mary	12	F	Unknown	25Fe02Ah
MAHAN, Eleanor-Bridget	27	F	Unknown	25Fe02Ah
ROONEY, Bridget	19	F	Unknown	25Fe02Ah
Mary	11	F	Unknown	25Fe02Ah
MALONE, Sarah	25	F	Unknown	25Fe02Ah
HANNIGAN, John	29	M	Shoemaker	25Fe02Ah
HICKEY, Matthew	32	M	Unknown	25Fe02Ah
BOUCHER, Mary-Ann	27	F	Unknown	25Fe02Ah
MARSHALL, Margt.	32	F	Unknown	25Fe02Ah

NAMES OF PASSENGERS	AGE	SEX	OCCUPATIONS	DATE PORT SHIP
DALTON, Ellen	27	F	Unknown	25Fe02Ah
DUNN, Patt	35	M	Unknown	25Fe02Ah
OBRIEN, John	26	M	Unknown	25Fe02Ah
OGRADY, Martin	22	M	Unknown	25Fe02Ah
MICHAELSON, John	25	M	Unknown	25Fe02Ah
CONN, Patt	33	M	Unknown	25Fe02Ah
COLLY, Phil.	20	M	Unknown	25Fe02Ah
BRADEY, Mary	16	F	Unknown	25Fe02Ah
MCMANN, Bridget	12	F	Unknown	25Fe02Ah
MAHEAN, Mary	17	F	Unknown	25Fe02Ah
WALSH, Catherine	24	F	Unknown	25Fe02Ah
BRADY, Bridget	33	F	Laborer	25Fe02Ah

SIR-HENRY-POTTINGER 01 MARCH 1850

From Belfast

NAMES OF PASSENGERS	AGE	SEX	OCCUPATIONS	DATE PORT SHIP
IRWIN, Samuel	27	M	Laborer	01Mr17Fh
Jane	20	F	Unknown	01Mr17Fh
Rebecca	20	F	Unknown	01Mr17Fh
SLOAN, Eliza	18	F	Unknown	01Mr17Fh
LAFFERTY, Eliza	46	F	Unknown	01Mr17Fh
John	13	M	Unknown	01Mr17Fh
RICHNOR, Jane	18	F	Unknown	01Mr17Fh
GONNELL, Jane	18	F	Unknown	01Mr17Fh
MCKING, William	30	M	Unknown	01Mr17Fh
Mary	30	F	Unknown	01Mr17Fh
James	20	M	Unknown	01Mr17Fh
Magt.	16	F	Unknown	01Mr17Fh
Robert	12	M	Unknown	01Mr17Fh
Hugh	8	M	Child	01Mr17Fh
LYLE, Willm.	21	M	Unknown	01Mr17Fh
WISNER, Andrew	19	M	Unknown	01Mr17Fh
BUCKMAN, John	22	M	Unknown	01Mr17Fh
COULTER, William	34	M	Unknown	01Mr17Fh
Jane	28	F	Unknown	01Mr17Fh
Mary	7	F	Child	01Mr17Fh
Doreathea	5	F	Child	01Mr17Fh
William	2	M	Child	01Mr17Fh
CROZIER, William	20	M	Unknown	01Mr17Fh
KANE, John	19	M	Unknown	01Mr17Fh
QUINN, Eliza	25	F	Unknown	01Mr17Fh
FEGAN, Cath.	23	F	Unknown	01Mr17Fh
REID, Margt.	60	F	Unknown	01Mr17Fh
Mary	56	F	Unknown	01Mr17Fh
HETHINGTON, Ann	12	F	Unknown	01Mr17Fh
PATTERSON, Ben	22	M	Unknown	01Mr17Fh
GUNEA, Darcus	40	M	Unknown	01Mr17Fh
Jane	31	F	Unknown	01Mr17Fh
GALLAGHER, Sarah	18	F	Unknown	01Mr17Fh
MCKELVEY, Saml.	18	M	Unknown	01Mr17Fh
STEWART, James	35	M	Unknown	01Mr17Fh
CRASEN, William	25	M	Unknown	01Mr17Fh
COURTNEY, James	36	M	Unknown	01Mr17Fh
ROMNEY, Teddy	16	M	Unknown	01Mr17Fh
FENNY, James	20	M	Unknown	01Mr17Fh
NOBLE, Margt.	20	F	Unknown	01Mr17Fh
MCCUSKER, James	30	M	Unknown	01Mr17Fh
KENEDY, William	52	M	Unknown	01Mr17Fh
Eliza	30	F	Unknown	01Mr17Fh
James	20	M	Unknown	01Mr17Fh
SCOTT, Jane	25	F	Unknown	01Mr17Fh
ENRITT, Mary	25	F	Unknown	01Mr17Fh
KENEDY, Eliza-Jane	19	F	Unknown	01Mr17Fh
Joseph	7	M	Child	01Mr17Fh
Mary	6	F	Child	01Mr17Fh
William	4	M	Child	01Mr17Fh
David	.00	M	Infant	01Mr17Fh
SCULLION, Paul	21	M	Unknown	01Mr17Fh
WILLIS, Samuel	25	M	Unknown	01Mr17Fh
MCTEAGH, Pat	19	M	Unknown	01Mr17Fh
QUIGLEY, Eliza	30	F	Unknown	01Mr17Fh
ONEILL, David	18	M	Unknown	01Mr17Fh
MCTEAGH, Mary	19	F	Unknown	01Mr17Fh
MURPHY, Nelly-A.	28	F	Unknown	01Mr17Fh
DUNLAP, Samuel	26	M	Unknown	01Mr17Fh
WILSON, James	24	M	Unknown	01Mr17Fh
MOORE, Richard	26	M	Unknown	01Mr17Fh
HUGHES, Edward	26	M	Unknown	01Mr17Fh
ROBINSON, Archy	20	M	Unknown	01Mr17Fh
Isabella	18	F	Unknown	01Mr17Fh
MCCARNEY, Ann	35	F	Unknown	01Mr17Fh
Cath.	12	F	Unknown	01Mr17Fh
CAVANAGH, Dennis	20	M	Unknown	01Mr17Fh
Cath.	18	F	Unknown	01Mr17Fh
CALLAGHAN, Charles	40	M	Unknown	01Mr17Fh
DONNELLY, Pat	35	M	Unknown	01Mr17Fh
OLAUGHLIN, Pat	32	M	Unknown	01Mr17Fh
BARKLEY, Alex.	22	M	Unknown	01Mr17Fh
Sophia	19	F	Unknown	01Mr17Fh
DUKE, Saml.	20	M	Unknown	01Mr17Fh
DOLLY, Jane	20	F	Unknown	01Mr17Fh
REORIN, John	25	M	Unknown	01Mr17Fh
FITZSIMONS, James	28	M	Unknown	01Mr17Fh
HAGAN, Hugh	25	M	Unknown	01Mr17Fh
DUFFY, Pat	20	M	Unknown	01Mr17Fh
BEATHEL, John	40	M	Unknown	01Mr17Fh
Mary	25	F	Unknown	01Mr17Fh
Martha	23	F	Unknown	01Mr17Fh
Joseph	28	M	Unknown	01Mr17Fh
Mary	22	F	Unknown	01Mr17Fh
Peggy	18	F	Unknown	01Mr17Fh
Jane	.00	F	Infant	01Mr17Fh
MCLAUGHLIN, James	28	M	Unknown	01Mr17Fh
James	20	M	Unknown	01Mr17Fh
ONEIL, James	16	M	Unknown	01Mr17Fh
ARMSTRONG, Mary	24	F	Unknown	01Mr17Fh
MAGHERY, Pat	21	M	Unknown	01Mr17Fh
GANNON, Willm.	25	M	Unknown	01Mr17Fh
BOYLAN, Patr.	13	M	Unknown	01Mr17Fh
MOORE, William	40	M	Unknown	01Mr17Fh
Margt.	40	F	Unknown	01Mr17Fh
Margt.	17	F	Unknown	01Mr17Fh
Martha	15	F	Unknown	01Mr17Fh
Robert	13	M	Unknown	01Mr17Fh
Mathew	11	M	Unknown	01Mr17Fh
James	9	M	Child	01Mr17Fh
William	9	M	Child	01Mr17Fh
Thomas	4	M	Child	01Mr17Fh
Jane	2	F	Child	01Mr17Fh
Margt.	.00	F	Infant	01Mr17Fh
DUNN, Pat	28	M	Unknown	01Mr17Fh
FREANON, Pat	20	M	Unknown	01Mr17Fh
WOOD, Alex.	22	M	Unknown	01Mr17Fh
Arthur	20	M	Unknown	01Mr17Fh
KERR, Mary	22	F	Unknown	01Mr17Fh
KANE, Pat	29	M	Unknown	01Mr17Fh
REARDON, William	44	M	Unknown	01Mr17Fh
Fanny	28	F	Unknown	01Mr17Fh
Ann-Jane	.00	F	Infant	01Mr17Fh
HALLIDAY, Robt.	21	M	Unknown	01Mr17Fh
ALEXANDER, George	25	M	Unknown	01Mr17Fh
Jane	25	F	Unknown	01Mr17Fh
William	3	M	Child	01Mr17Fh
COULTER, William	14	M	Laborer	01Mr17Fh
BREEN, Anne	25	F	Unknown	01Mr17Fh
DILLON, Ellen	24	F	Unknown	01Mr17Fh
Ellen	7	F	Child	01Mr17Fh
HUGHES, Beranrd	19	M	Unknown	01Mr17Fh
KELLY, Robert	16	M	Unknown	01Mr17Fh
MAGUIRE, James	21	M	Unknown	01Mr17Fh
Francis	17	M	Unknown	01Mr17Fh
Mary	24	F	Unknown	01Mr17Fh
HALLIDAY, Jessy	20	M	Unknown	01Mr17Fh

NAMES OF PASSENGERS	AGE	SEX	OCCUPATIONS	DATE PORT SHIP
YOUNG, James	20	M	Unknown	01Mr17Fh
MCGLANAGHAN, Eliza	19	F	Unknown	01Mr17Fh
BLACKBORN, Wm.	40	M	Unknown	01Mr17Fh
Saml.	40	M	Unknown	01Mr17Fh
Matilda	16	F	Unknown	01Mr17Fh
Mara	17	F	Unknown	01Mr17Fh
Sarah	13	F	Unknown	01Mr17Fh
DUNLOP, John	50	M	Unknown	01Mr17Fh
Racheal	50	F	Unknown	01Mr17Fh
James	17	M	Unknown	01Mr17Fh
Joseph	11	M	Unknown	01Mr17Fh
Jenyman	9	U	Child	01Mr17Fh
ANDERSON, Wm.	30	M	Unknown	01Mr17Fh
Martha	30	F	Unknown	01Mr17Fh
Jane	10	F	Unknown	01Mr17Fh
Sarah	.00	F	Infant	01Mr17Fh
ONEIL, Wm.	30	M	Unknown	01Mr17Fh
MILLS, Eliza	22	F	Unknown	01Mr17Fh
Wm.John	.00	M	Infant	01Mr17Fh
CONNELLY, Patt	30	M	Unknown	01Mr17Fh
WILSON, Martha	49	F	Unknown	01Mr17Fh
MCDOWELL, Wm.	20	M	Unknown	01Mr17Fh
HUGHES, James	40	M	Unknown	01Mr17Fh
Patt	19	M	Unknown	01Mr17Fh
FERRIS, Allen	19	M	Unknown	01Mr17Fh
Ellen	18	F	Unknown	01Mr17Fh
RICE, John	21	M	Unknown	01Mr17Fh
CONNELY, Margt.	17	F	Unknown	01Mr17Fh
SHERRARD, William	20	M	Unknown	01Mr17Fh
ATKINSON, Henry	20	M	Unknown	01Mr17Fh
LINNETT, Michael	28	M	Unknown	01Mr17Fh
HENRY, John	18	M	Unknown	01Mr17Fh
MCKANE, Biddy	47	F	Unknown	01Mr17Fh
Anne	12	F	Unknown	01Mr17Fh
Mary	7	F	Child	01Mr17Fh
MCQUAID, Michael	11	M	Unknown	01Mr17Fh
Bernard	9	M	Child	01Mr17Fh
James	2	M	Child	01Mr17Fh
BELL, John	20	M	Unknown	01Mr17Fh
Jane	26	F	Unknown	01Mr17Fh
TAGGART, Patt	20	M	Unknown	01Mr17Fh
SKEFFINGTON, Bernard	20	M	Unknown	01Mr17Fh
MCKEA, Neal	25	M	Unknown	01Mr17Fh
HUGHES, Ann	20	F	Unknown	01Mr17Fh
THOMSON, Thomas	25	M	Unknown	01Mr17Fh
KIRKPATRICK, Nancy	30	F	Unknown	01Mr17Fh
Betty	4	F	Child	01Mr17Fh
Sarah	2	F	Child	01Mr17Fh
NEIL, William	21	M	Unknown	01Mr17Fh
Bella	11	F	Unknown	01Mr17Fh
FIELDING, Samuel	35	M	Unknown	01Mr17Fh
HOLMES, Joseph	25	M	Unknown	01Mr17Fh

IOWA 01 MARCH 1850

From Glasgow

NAMES OF PASSENGERS	AGE	SEX	OCCUPATIONS	DATE PORT SHIP
MOORE, James	24	M	Farmer	01Mr21Ey
Christina	24	F	Unknown	01Mr21Ey
Elizabeth	1	F	Child	01Mr21Ey
BUCK, Margarie	12	F	Unknown	01Mr21Ey
MCAULAY, Mary	34	F	Unknown	01Mr21Ey
Matilda	12	F	Unknown	01Mr21Ey
James	10	M	Unknown	01Mr21Ey
Margaret	7	F	Child	01Mr21Ey
John	2	M	Child	01Mr21Ey
RILLEY, Anthoney	21	M	Laborer	01Mr21Ey
Thomas	24	M	Laborer	01Mr21Ey
CAMPBELL, Patrick	33	M	Laborer	01Mr21Ey
CRAYTON, Thomas	36	M	Laborer	01Mr21Ey
WANERY, John	24	M	Laborer	01Mr21Ey
MCALLISTER, James	00	M	Speculator	01Mr21Ey

ST.GEORGE 01 MARCH 1850

From Liverpool

NAMES OF PASSENGERS	AGE	SEX	OCCUPATIONS	DATE PORT SHIP
NEICE, James	21	M	Cooper	01Mr02Bu
RONAN, Phillip	22	M	Laborer	01Mr02Bu
FERMAN, Patrick	22	M	Laborer	01Mr02Bu
Ann	19	F	Servant	01Mr02Bu
BRYAN, Bridget	19	F	Servant	01Mr02Bu
RILEY, Ann	19	F	Servant	01Mr02Bu
DOYLE, John	30	M	Mason	01Mr02Bu
LILY, John	24	M	Laborer	01Mr02Bu
Arthur	26	M	Laborer	01Mr02Bu
FOOTE, John	26	M	Laborer	01Mr02Bu
Lawrence	19	M	Laborer	01Mr02Bu
HAMMOND, Anthony	30	M	Laborer	01Mr02Bu
KENNEDY, Eliza	21	F	Servant	01Mr02Bu
Ellen	19	F	Servant	01Mr02Bu
Micheal	13	M	Unknown	01Mr02Bu
BRENAN, James	22	M	Baker	01Mr02Bu
CURRAN, James	24	M	Laborer	01Mr02Bu
MALONE, James	20	M	Baker	01Mr02Bu
Pat	25	M	Clerk	01Mr02Bu
GRACEY, Ann	23	F	Servant	01Mr02Bu
WHELAN, John	23	M	Laborer	01Mr02Bu
DOYLE, Edward	14	M	Unknown	01Mr02Bu
HEALY, Patrick	50	M	Unknown	01Mr02Bu
MCBARTH, Ellen	22	F	Unknown	01Mr02Bu
Robert	11	M	Unknown	01Mr02Bu
Sarah-J.	8	F	Child	01Mr02Bu
Rachel	7	F	Child	01Mr02Bu
James	4	M	Child	01Mr02Bu
BELLEW, Jane	20	F	Servant	01Mr02Bu
CARROLL, Cathe.	25	F	Servant	01Mr02Bu
DELHANTY, Judy	20	F	Servant	01Mr02Bu
KENEDY, Danl.	45	M	Miner	01Mr02Bu
Mary	12	F	Unknown	01Mr02Bu
CULLEN, John	22	M	Laborer	01Mr02Bu
SHUBOTTOM, James	25	M	Laborer	01Mr02Bu
STEVENS, Jermina	21	F	Milliner	01Mr02Bu
WHELAN, Judy	22	F	Servant	01Mr02Bu
Jeremiah	10	M	Unknown	01Mr02Bu
Micheal	8	M	Child	01Mr02Bu
HILL, James	35	M	Laborer	01Mr02Bu
GIVEN, Robert	35	M	Shoemaker	01Mr02Bu
WHITE, John	22	M	Shoemaker	01Mr02Bu
NICOLL, John	16	M	Unknown	01Mr02Bu
WHITE, Eliza	22	F	Unknown	01Mr02Bu
Nancy	12	F	Unknown	01Mr02Bu
WILLIAMS, Martha	21	F	Milliner	01Mr02Bu
WOODS, William	19	M	Butcher	01Mr02Bu
BURKES, Jim	34	M	Laborer	01Mr02Bu
BROUGHAN, Pat	21	M	Laborer	01Mr02Bu
QUARRY, William	20	M	Laborer	01Mr02Bu
James	23	M	Laborer	01Mr02Bu
DELANY, Edward	23	M	Laborer	01Mr02Bu
ROSEBOUGH, Robt.	25	M	Farmer	01Mr02Bu
MANALLY, Pat	17	M	Laborer	01Mr02Bu
COX, Tim	16	M	Laborer	01Mr02Bu
MAHER, Micheal	22	M	Laborer	01Mr02Bu
HOGAN, John	23	M	Laborer	01Mr02Bu
PARKINSON, Mary	18	F	Servant	01Mr02Bu
DONNELLY, Edward	26	M	Laborer	01Mr02Bu
Eliza	23	F	Unknown	01Mr02Bu
Ann	.00	F	Infant	01Mr02Bu

NAMES OF PASSENGERS	AGE	SEX	OCCUPATIONS	DATE PORT SHIP
MCDONNEL, Dan	26	M	Laborer	01Mr02Bu
HICKEY, Margaret	48	F	Unknown	01Mr02Bu
James	18	M	Servant	01Mr02Bu
KELLY, Mary	17	F	Unknown	01Mr02Bu
Ann	7	F	Child	01Mr02Bu
HUNTER, Andrew	19	M	Laborer	01Mr02Bu
DENMAN, Susan	40	F	Unknown	01Mr02Bu
Edward	13	M	Unknown	01Mr02Bu
Judy	11	F	Unknown	01Mr02Bu
Patrick	8	M	Child	01Mr02Bu
Margaret	8	F	Child	01Mr02Bu
Peter	6	F	Child	01Mr02Bu
MCCABE, Mary	40	F	Unknown	01Mr02Bu
GEGAN, Jane	35	F	Unknown	01Mr02Bu
Mary	11	F	Unknown	01Mr02Bu
FEY, Mike	23	M	Unknown	01Mr02Bu
MCSHERRY, Wm.	25	M	Laborer	01Mr02Bu
GREY, Julia	22	F	Unknown	01Mr02Bu
MORAN, Patrick	23	M	Weaver	01Mr02Bu
SULLIVAN, John	35	M	Mariner	01Mr02Bu
JOYCE, Ann	19	F	Milliner	01Mr02Bu
MURRAY, Ellen	18	F	Servant	01Mr02Bu
Ann	20	F	Servant	01Mr02Bu
FARRALL, Patrick	36	M	Laborer	01Mr02Bu
Catharine	34	F	Unknown	01Mr02Bu
Edward	.00	M	Infant	01Mr02Bu
FOLEY, Johanna	17	F	Milliner	01Mr02Bu
CROTTY, Julia	24	F	Servant	01Mr02Bu
FOLEY, Jeremiah	25	M	Laborer	01Mr02Bu
HERLELY, John	30	M	Laborer	01Mr02Bu
GORMAN, John	40	M	Farmer	01Mr02Bu
Mary	34	F	Unknown	01Mr02Bu
Catharine	12	F	Unknown	01Mr02Bu
John	10	M	Unknown	01Mr02Bu
Catharine	7	F	Child	01Mr02Bu
James	.00	M	Infant	01Mr02Bu
Died-At-Sea				
Peter	5	M	Child	01Mr02Bu
FOLY, Dan	26	M	Laborer	01Mr02Bu
PHILLIPS, Mary	38	F	Unknown	01Mr02Bu
Joseph	6	M	Child	01Mr02Bu
Catharine	4	F	Child	01Mr02Bu
FLANAGAN, Mary	18	F	Servant	01Mr02Bu
CLAIR, Phillip	25	M	Plumber	01Mr02Bu
CONNERS, Dan	36	M	Laborer	01Mr02Bu
KELLY, Pat	30	M	Laborer	01Mr02Bu
BARNES, Wm	22	M	Laborer	01Mr02Bu
QUINLAN, Bridget	18	F	Servant	01Mr02Bu
CARROT, Bridget	18	F	Servant	01Mr02Bu
LARKINS, Pat	28	M	Laborer	01Mr02Bu
John	30	M	Laborer	01Mr02Bu
Died-At-Sea				
DUFFY, Bridget	20	F	Servant	01Mr02Bu
RIELLY, Mary	15	F	Servant	01Mr02Bu
FARRALL, Honora	18	F	Servant	01Mr02Bu
RIELLY, Bridget	16	F	Servant	01Mr02Bu
Phillip	14	M	Unknown	01Mr02Bu
Mary	14	F	Unknown	01Mr02Bu
GILLIGAN, Mary	18	F	Servant	01Mr02Bu
Mary	25	F	Servant	01Mr02Bu
SMITH, Mary	16	F	Servant	01Mr02Bu
MCCOURTH, John	20	M	Laborer	01Mr02Bu
Martha	60	F	Unknown	01Mr02Bu
Ann	58	F	Unknown	01Mr02Bu
Dennis	29	M	Laborer	01Mr02Bu
GLYN, Martin	28	M	Laborer	01Mr02Bu
GODFREY, Mike	28	M	Laborer	01Mr02Bu
Cato	30	M	Laborer	01Mr02Bu
KILMARTIN, John	20	M	Unknown	01Mr02Bu
Mary	40	F	Servant	01Mr02Bu
LAWSON, John	40	M	Carpenter	01Mr02Bu
FOGARTY, Thomas	40	M	Laborer	01Mr02Bu
Mary	40	F	Unknown	01Mr02Bu
William	21	M	Unknown	01Mr02Bu
Danl.	21	M	Butcher	01Mr02Bu

NAMES OF PASSENGERS	AGE	SEX	OCCUPATIONS	DATE PORT SHIP
RYAN, Patrick	40	M	Gdnr	01Mr02Bu
COSTAGAN, Pat	17	M	Laborer	01Mr02Bu
Thomas	40	M	Laborer	01Mr02Bu
FERNAN, Luke	28	M	Laborer	01Mr02Bu
QUIN, Catharine	18	F	Servant	01Mr02Bu
FARRALL, Cato	18	M	Laborer	01Mr02Bu
DAWD, Catharine	18	F	Servant	01Mr02Bu
RODGERS, Ann	17	F	Servant	01Mr02Bu
GRILLY, John	22	M	Unknown	01Mr02Bu
FINARTY, Martin	36	M	Laborer	01Mr02Bu
KELLY, John	22	M	Miner	01Mr02Bu
JONES, John	40	M	Laborer	01Mr02Bu
Bridget	18	F	Servant	01Mr02Bu
MCDONALD, Pat	18	M	Laborer	01Mr02Bu
LARKINS, Cathe.	60	F	Unknown	01Mr02Bu
Martin	21	M	Tailor	01Mr02Bu
Patrick	23	M	Laborer	01Mr02Bu
John	25	M	Laborer	01Mr02Bu
Patrick	19	M	Laborer	01Mr02Bu
MANGIN, Martin	24	M	Laborer	01Mr02Bu
WELSH, Mike	25	M	Laborer	01Mr02Bu
HECKEY, Patrick	25	M	Laborer	01Mr02Bu
LARKIN, Mary	19	F	Servant	01Mr02Bu
QUIN, Bridget	19	F	Servant	01Mr02Bu
HANAHON, Mary	19	F	Servant	01Mr02Bu
RUGAN, John	24	M	Laborer	01Mr02Bu
KELLY, Thomas	30	M	Laborer	01Mr02Bu
CAVANAH, Martin	23	M	Laborer	01Mr02Bu
COLLIN, William	28	M	Seaman	01Mr02Bu
Mary-Ann	23	F	Sailor	01Mr02Bu
OROURKE, John	22	M	Clerk	01Mr02Bu
HECKEY, Catharine	18	F	Servant	01Mr02Bu

BRYAN-ABBS 07 MARCH 1850

From Limerick

NAMES OF PASSENGERS	AGE	SEX	OCCUPATIONS	DATE PORT SHIP
SLATTERY, John	25	M	Laborer	07Mr10Fl
MORRISEY, Dan	30	M	Laborer	07Mr10Fl
Mary	30	F	Laborer	07Mr10Fl
CAHILL, Mary	18	F	Laborer	07Mr10Fl
DREW, Denis	24	M	Laborer	07Mr10Fl
Dan	23	M	Laborer	07Mr10Fl
CARROLL, Thos.	18	M	Laborer	07Mr10Fl
Mary	13	F	Laborer	07Mr10Fl
John	11	M	Laborer	07Mr10Fl
Biddy	30	F	Laborer	07Mr10Fl
DREW, Mary	35	F	Laborer	07Mr10Fl
HAYNES, William	25	M	Laborer	07Mr10Fl
HAYES, Hannah	20	F	Laborer	07Mr10Fl
MORRISEY, Johanna	20	F	Laborer	07Mr10Fl
HAYES, Hannah	20	F	Laborer	07Mr10Fl
SHEEHAN, Mich.	25	M	Laborer	07Mr10Fl
Cath.	21	F	Laborer	07Mr10Fl
BRAZIL, Mary	40	F	Laborer	07Mr10Fl
Mary	5	F	Child	07Mr10Fl
Michl.	2	M	Child	07Mr10Fl
ROURKE, Patt	24	M	Laborer	07Mr10Fl
BIGLEY, Mary	40	F	Laborer	07Mr10Fl
Jane	25	F	Laborer	07Mr10Fl
HASSETT, Patt	25	M	Laborer	07Mr10Fl
Biddey	22	F	Laborer	07Mr10Fl
HEALEY, Eliza	20	F	Laborer	07Mr10Fl
MORRAN, Johanna	21	F	Laborer	07Mr10Fl
Conor	.00	M	Infant	07Mr10Fl
BYRNE, Joseph	18	M	Laborer	07Mr10Fl
QUADE, Mary	36	F	Laborer	07Mr10Fl
Johanna	3	F	Child	07Mr10Fl
John	.00	M	Infant	07Mr10Fl

NAMES OF PASSENGERS	AGE	SEX	OCCUPATIONS	DATE PORT SHIP
FARRELL, Betty	30	F	Laborer	07Mr10FI
Mary	8	F	Child	07Mr10FI
Maurice	4	M	Child	07Mr10FI
Biddy	2	F	Child	07Mr10FI
ODEA, Cath.	22	F	Laborer	07Mr10FI
HOGAN, Honor	40	F	Laborer	07Mr10FI
Thos.	9	M	Child	07Mr10FI
JACKSON, William	25	M	Laborer	07Mr10FI
MCHUGHES, Cecillia	20	F	Laborer	07Mr10FI
PURCELL, Ellen	18	F	Laborer	07Mr10FI
Thos.	17	M	Laborer	07Mr10FI
John	15	M	Laborer	07Mr10FI
Mary	11	F	Laborer	07Mr10FI
rNULTY, Abby	30	F	Laborer	07Mr10FI
Joseph	2	M	Child	07Mr10FI
John	.00	M	Infant	07Mr10FI
Denis	4	M	Child	07Mr10FI
HOGAN, James	20	M	Laborer	07Mr10FI
Marg.	15	F	Laborer	07Mr10FI
JOHNSON, Anne	13	F	Laborer	07Mr10FI
OBRIEN, Mary	19	F	Laborer	07Mr10FI
ONEIL, James	20	M	Laborer	07Mr10FI
MALONEY, Cath.	19	F	Laborer	07Mr10FI
OKEARNY, Mary	20	F	Laborer	07Mr10FI
OBRIEN, Mary	20	F	Laborer	07Mr10FI
MULLINS, Mary	20	F	Laborer	07Mr10FI
Honor	18	F	Laborer	07Mr10FI
SWEENEY, Miley	24	M	Laborer	07Mr10FI
Anne	34	F	Laborer	07Mr10FI
Thos.	18	M	Laborer	07Mr10FI
Ally	6	F	Child	07Mr10FI
Michl.	4	M	Child	07Mr10FI
John	2	M	Child	07Mr10FI
QUIRK, Judy	52	F	Laborer	07Mr10FI
Mary	16	F	Laborer	07Mr10FI
Edward	14	M	Laborer	07Mr10FI
Michl.	10	M	Laborer	07Mr10FI
Timothy	10	M	Laborer	07Mr10FI
FORRESTAL, Patt	21	M	Laborer	07Mr10FI
Mary	20	F	Laborer	07Mr10FI
Winny	16	F	Laborer	07Mr10FI
Cath.	10	F	Laborer	07Mr10FI
MOLONEY, Cath.	17	F	Laborer	07Mr10FI
Ellen	15	F	Laborer	07Mr10FI
Thos.	11	M	Laborer	07Mr10FI
Stephen	7	M	Child	07Mr10FI
Mary	20	F	Laborer	07Mr10FI
Peter	20	M	Laborer	07Mr10FI
GEARY, David	35	M	Laborer	07Mr10FI
Ellen	27	F	Laborer	07Mr10FI
Hannah	7	F	Child	07Mr10FI
David	.00	M	Infant	07Mr10FI
MCMANUS, Margt.	22	F	Laborer	07Mr10FI
KELLY, John	34	M	Laborer	07Mr10FI
MALONEY, Mary	21	F	Laborer	07Mr10FI
BROYLE, James	.00	M	Infant	07Mr10FI
OKEAFE, Patt	25	M	Laborer	07Mr10FI
GLEESON, Johanna	25	F	Laborer	07Mr10FI
OBRIEN, Tom	20	M	Laborer	07Mr10FI
COLLAMAN, Mary	20	F	Laborer	07Mr10FI
Ellen	18	F	Laborer	07Mr10FI
OLAUGHLIN, Bridgt.	19	F	Laborer	07Mr10FI
DARCY, John	40	M	Laborer	07Mr10FI
HAYS, Mary	24	F	Laborer	07Mr10FI
SHEEHAN, John	34	M	Laborer	07Mr10FI
Patt	3	M	Child	07Mr10FI
Mary	.00	F	Infant	07Mr10FI
DALEY, Honor	24	F	Laborer	07Mr10FI
DUNN, Honor	23	F	Laborer	07Mr10FI
OBRIEN, James	36	M	Laborer	07Mr10FI
Dennis	30	M	Laborer	07Mr10FI
Mary	25	F	Laborer	07Mr10FI
Dan	6	M	Child	07Mr10FI
James	4	M	Child	07Mr10FI
John	2	M	Child	07Mr10FI
OBRIEN, Richard	.00	M	Infant	07Mr10FI
KILMARTIN, Biddy	36	F	Laborer	07Mr10FI
CONNOR, Anne	46	F	Laborer	07Mr10FI
WELSH, Honor	30	F	Laborer	07Mr10FI
FREEMAN, Mary	26	F	Laborer	07Mr10FI
HYNES, John	20	M	Laborer	07Mr10FI
ROUGHAN, Ellen	24	F	Laborer	07Mr10FI
DEVITT, Patt	22	M	Laborer	07Mr10FI
HONEGAN, William	23	M	Laborer	07Mr10FI
RYAN, Dan	23	M	Laborer	07Mr10FI
Mag.	34	F	Laborer	07Mr10FI
Thos.	4	M	Child	07Mr10FI
COFFEE, Michl.	30	M	Unknown	07Mr10FI
BOLAND, Michl.	22	M	Unknown	07Mr10FI
GOREY, Biddy	34	F	Unknown	07Mr10FI
John	30	M	Unknown	07Mr10FI
MCMAHON, Thos.	20	M	Unknown	07Mr10FI
GRIFFIN, Thos.	21	M	Unknown	07Mr10FI
BYNE, Darby-R.	44	M	Unknown	07Mr10FI

CONSTELLATION 08 MARCH 1850

From Liverpool

NAMES OF PASSENGERS	AGE	SEX	OCCUPATIONS	DATE PORT SHIP
GILL, Thomas	30	M	Importer	08Mr02Bm
Edward	23	M	Importer	08Mr02Bm
MCINTOSH, John	20	M	Mason	08Mr02Bm
HAYDEN, Ellenor	22	F	None	08Mr02Bm
FARRELL, James	24	M	Glass Maker	08Mr02Bm
BROWN, William	35	M	Draper	08Mr02Bm
CASS, John	30	M	Laborer	08Mr02Bm
MONROE, John	25	M	Laborer	08Mr02Bm
HAYDEN, Cath.	18	F	Laborer	08Mr02Bm
MILNER, Maria	20	F	Unknown	08Mr02Bm
MORRISSY, Margt.	40	F	Unknown	08Mr02Bm
Ellen	20	F	Unknown	08Mr02Bm
Catherine	22	F	Servant	08Mr02Bm
Edward	26	M	Laborer	08Mr02Bm
Egbert	20	M	Laborer	08Mr02Bm
Roger	20	M	Laborer	08Mr02Bm
John	21	M	Laborer	08Mr02Bm
Jerry	12	M	Unknown	08Mr02Bm
Thomas	11	M	Unknown	08Mr02Bm
NOONAN, Dennis	25	M	Laborer	08Mr02Bm
MARSHALL, Jane	30	F	Unknown	08Mr02Bm
CLARK, Jane	30	F	Unknown	08Mr02Bm
GAHAZEN, Winny	24	F	Unknown	08Mr02Bm
MURPHY, William	40	M	Unknown	08Mr02Bm
GAHAGAN, Catherine	26	F	Unknown	08Mr02Bm
GAHAZEN, Fanny	20	F	Unknown	08Mr02Bm
KILDAYS, Catherine	7	F	Child	08Mr02Bm
Mary	6	F	Child	08Mr02Bm
MURPHY, William	14	M	Merchant	08Mr02Bm
Ann	13	F	Unknown	08Mr02Bm
Harriett	11	F	Unknown	08Mr02Bm
Margt.	9	F	Child	08Mr02Bm
Thomas	6	F	Child	08Mr02Bm
Hetra	4	F	Child	08Mr02Bm
Charlott	3	F	Child	08Mr02Bm
Amelia	.00	F	Infant	08Mr02Bm
SCOTT, Ellen	17	F	Unknown	08Mr02Bm
FISHER, Margt.	16	F	Unknown	08Mr02Bm
Thomas	14	M	Unknown	08Mr02Bm
Ellen	12	F	Unknown	08Mr02Bm
MULLOWNY, Mick	22	M	Laborer	08Mr02Bm
Mary	21	F	Unknown	08Mr02Bm
HALLAN, Edward	22	M	Laborer	08Mr02Bm
HENRY, John	24	M	Servant	08Mr02Bm
MILLS, John	18	M	Servant	08Mr02Bm

NAMES OF PASSENGERS	AGE	SEX	OCCUPATIONS	DATE PORT SHIP
MCCLANE, Anne	50	F	Unknown	08Mr02Bm
Margt.	23	F	Unknown	08Mr02Bm
Rachel	24	F	Unknown	08Mr02Bm
William	20	M	Laborer	08Mr02Bm
Samuel	15	M	Laborer	08Mr02Bm
Alex	25	M	Farmer	08Mr02Bm
HIRN, John	22	M	Laborer	08Mr02Bm
MADDOCK, Bridget	25	F	Unknown	08Mr02Bm
MADDEN, Mary	25	F	Unknown	08Mr02Bm
DUGAN, Mary	30	F	Unknown	08Mr02Bm
MAHON, Patk.	25	M	Laborer	08Mr02Bm
KELLY, U-Mrs.	28	F	Unknown	08Mr02Bm
WIRE, John	17	M	Laborer	08Mr02Bm
BEDDOW, Benjn.	31	M	Brick Maker	08Mr02Bm
CURRAN, Robert	30	M	Laborer	08Mr02Bm
QUINN, Darby	25	M	Laborer	08Mr02Bm
OTES, Michl.	30	M	Laborer	08Mr02Bm
ROULSTON, Samuel	25	M	Farmer	08Mr02Bm
DUFFAS, Peter	20	M	Laborer	08Mr02Bm
BUCKLEY, Jermh.	22	M	Draper	08Mr02Bm
DARRAGH, Charles	34	M	Laborer	08Mr02Bm
WILSON, Peter	25	M	Laborer	08Mr02Bm
LINSEY, Smuel.	24	M	Coach Maker	08Mr02Bm
LINSLEY, William	25	M	Unknown	08Mr02Bm
MORAN, John	35	M	Laborer	08Mr02Bm
FLANAGAN, John	30	M	Laborer	08Mr02Bm
REO, John	20	M	Laborer	08Mr02Bm
MCNAMARA, Patk.	20	M	Laborer	08Mr02Bm
ROWAN, Mary	20	F	Laborer	08Mr02Bm
Biddy	13	F	Laborer	08Mr02Bm
Ann	17	F	Laborer	08Mr02Bm
BARRAH, John	20	M	Laborer	08Mr02Bm
Jane	17	F	Unknown	08Mr02Bm
Thomas	13	M	Unknown	08Mr02Bm
LEONARD, Pat	40	M	Unknown	08Mr02Bm
Ann	18	F	Unknown	08Mr02Bm
James	18	M	Unknown	08Mr02Bm
MURRY, Michl.	18	M	Unknown	08Mr02Bm
Cath.	29	F	Unknown	08Mr02Bm
BRENNAN, Ann	33	F	Unknown	08Mr02Bm
MULLAN, Cath.	30	F	Unknown	08Mr02Bm
Biddy	33	F	Unknown	08Mr02Bm
GOVERN, Malachi	18	M	Unknown	08Mr02Bm
Michael	20	M	Unknown	08Mr02Bm
Patk.	21	M	Unknown	08Mr02Bm
DAY, Francis	21	M	Unknown	08Mr02Bm
MCHUGH, Edward	22	M	Unknown	08Mr02Bm
Mary	23	M	Unknown	08Mr02Bm
Mary	.00	F	Infant	08Mr02Bm
RYDER, Judith	20	F	Unknown	08Mr02Bm
Rose	18	F	Unknown	08Mr02Bm
LAUGHLIN, Mary	20	F	Unknown	08Mr02Bm
MURPHY, Humphry	27	M	Laborer	08Mr02Bm
LENHAN, John	20	M	Unknown	08Mr02Bm
Mat	20	M	Unknown	08Mr02Bm
MURPHY, Mary	20	F	Unknown	08Mr02Bm
DOUGHERTY, Pat	26	F	Unknown	08Mr02Bm
MCMAHAN, Danl.	30	M	Unknown	08Mr02Bm
DOUGHERTY, Unity	00	M	Unknown	08Mr02Bm
BAKER, Saml.	26	M	Unknown	08Mr02Bm
U-Mrs.	20	F	Unknown	08Mr02Bm
BOHAN, Mary	53	F	Unknown	08Mr02Bm
Elizabeth	16	F	Unknown	08Mr02Bm
DAILY, Terence	30	M	Unknown	08Mr02Bm
CULLEN, James	22	M	Unknown	08Mr02Bm
GILLOONY, Thomas	25	M	Mason	08Mr02Bm
Cath.	20	F	Unknown	08Mr02Bm
QUIRK, John	25	M	Carpenter	08Mr02Bm
LAUGHLIN, John	26	M	Mason	08Mr02Bm
RALEIGH, Richd.	35	M	Baker	08Mr02Bm
Ann	33	F	Unknown	08Mr02Bm
Mary-Ann	8	F	Child	08Mr02Bm
Mich.	7	M	Child	08Mr02Bm
MULLER, Patk.	40	M	Laborer	08Mr02Bm
Cath.	40	F	Unknown	08Mr02Bm
MULLER, James	13	M	Unknown	08Mr02Bm
Pat	12	M	Unknown	08Mr02Bm
Thos.	9	M	Child	08Mr02Bm
Peggy	7	F	Child	08Mr02Bm
MCAVOY, Thos.	23	M	Laborer	08Mr02Bm
CARROLL, Danl.	30	M	Laborer	08Mr02Bm
EAGAN, Thos.	35	M	Laborer	08Mr02Bm
DALEY, Kirry	40	M	Laborer	08Mr02Bm
LANSON, James	20	M	Laborer	08Mr02Bm
BALGEN, William	22	M	Laborer	08Mr02Bm
BROPHY, Pat	56	M	Weaver	08Mr02Bm
CONROY, John	36	M	Laborer	08Mr02Bm
James	30	M	Laborer	08Mr02Bm
KELLY, John	23	M	Laborer	08Mr02Bm
COTRICK, Judy	45	F	Unknown	08Mr02Bm
BRENNAN, Cath.	19	F	Unknown	08Mr02Bm
DOWD, Pat	26	M	Laborer	08Mr02Bm
MCGRATH, Pat	25	M	Laborer	08Mr02Bm
FAIRLEY, James	24	M	Laborer	08Mr02Bm
RAGAN, Johan	32	M	Laborer	08Mr02Bm
Eliz.	6	F	Child	08Mr02Bm
Wm.	3	M	Child	08Mr02Bm
ROBERTS, Johan	17	M	Unknown	08Mr02Bm
HICKEY, Maria	35	F	Unknown	08Mr02Bm
COREY, Cath.	19	F	Unknown	08Mr02Bm
WATERS, Mary-Ann	11	F	Unknown	08Mr02Bm
Cath.	8	F	Child	08Mr02Bm
KENNEY, Mary	22	F	Unknown	08Mr02Bm
MCCARTY, Mary	23	F	Unknown	08Mr02Bm
LYNCH, Mary	11	F	Unknown	08Mr02Bm
BYRNE, Cath.	18	F	Unknown	08Mr02Bm
TULLY, Thos.	40	M	Unknown	08Mr02Bm
Ellen	12	F	Unknown	08Mr02Bm
John	18	M	Unknown	08Mr02Bm
CAVANAGH, James	32	M	Unknown	08Mr02Bm
Mary-Ann	26	F	Unknown	08Mr02Bm
Mary-Ann	8	F	Child	08Mr02Bm
Cath.	6	F	Child	08Mr02Bm
John	4	M	Child	08Mr02Bm
Eliza	2	F	Child	08Mr02Bm
Died-At-Sea				
MARA, Thos.	25	M	Laborer	08Mr02Bm
RYAN, John	25	M	Laborer	08Mr02Bm
Edward	22	M	Laborer	08Mr02Bm
GIBBONS, Michl.	22	M	Laborer	08Mr02Bm
MARA, Mary	22	F	Unknown	08Mr02Bm
HIGGINS, Biddy	20	F	Unknown	08Mr02Bm
HINCKY, Mary	18	F	Unknown	08Mr02Bm
CALLARAN, Kitty	34	F	Unknown	08Mr02Bm
MARON, Mary	22	F	Unknown	08Mr02Bm
GLEESON, Thos.	25	M	Unknown	08Mr02Bm
BROWN, Mick	30	M	Unknown	08Mr02Bm
BRYAN, Mich.	28	M	Unknown	08Mr02Bm
RYAN, Michl.	40	M	Unknown	08Mr02Bm
MARRION, Thos.	17	M	Laborer	08Mr02Bm
DARKER, George	18	M	Laborer	08Mr02Bm
BRAY, John	22	M	Laborer	08Mr02Bm
WELDON, John	30	M	Laborer	08Mr02Bm
FLANAGAN, James	22	M	Laborer	08Mr02Bm
MURPHY, Mary	20	F	Unknown	08Mr02Bm
DWYER, Cath.	40	F	Unknown	08Mr02Bm
MCLAUGHLIN, Delia	10	F	Unknown	08Mr02Bm
GEOFFREY, Cath.	18	F	Unknown	08Mr02Bm
LATIMER, Will	18	M	Laborer	08Mr02Bm
James	14	M	Laborer	08Mr02Bm
FLANAGAN, Cormick	25	M	Laborer	08Mr02Bm
QUIGLEY, James	20	M	Laborer	08Mr02Bm
MURPHY, Eliza	28	F	Unknown	08Mr02Bm
Thos.	10	M	Unknown	08Mr02Bm
John	8	M	Child	08Mr02Bm
Wm.	6	M	Child	08Mr02Bm
FAUGHY, Thos.	23	M	Laborer	08Mr02Bm
BRYAN, Cornelius	25	M	Laborer	08Mr02Bm
CONNELL, John	35	M	Laborer	08Mr02Bm
GUCKER, John	23	M	Laborer	08Mr02Bm

NAMES OF PASSENGERS	AGE	SEX	OCCUPATIONS	DATE PORT SHIP
GUCKER, William	24	M	Laborer	08Mr02Bm
RYAN, John	20	M	Laborer	08Mr02Bm
GARNERON, Thos.	15	M	Unknown	08Mr02Bm
MCGRAIL, Pat	30	M	Laborer	08Mr02Bm
Cath.	30	F	Unknown	08Mr02Bm
Cath.	5	F	Child	08Mr02Bm
Patk.	.00	M	Infant	08Mr02Bm
Died-At-Sea				
SYMMES, Julia	15	F	Unknown	08Mr02Bm
FLOOD, Ann	21	F	Unknown	08Mr02Bm
KELLEY, Mary	18	F	Unknown	08Mr02Bm
DUFFEY, Pat	40	M	Laborer	08Mr02Bm
ONEIL, Jno.	25	M	Laborer	08Mr02Bm
STOREY, Pat	24	M	Laborer	08Mr02Bm
WOODS, Jos.	10	M	Laborer	08Mr02Bm
Rose	22	F	Unknown	08Mr02Bm
HUNDRETTY, Cath.	18	F	Unknown	08Mr02Bm
HAGERTY, Ann	30	F	Unknown	08Mr02Bm
CONROY, Margt.	22	F	Unknown	08Mr02Bm
HUNTER, Thos.	28	M	Farmer	08Mr02Bm
Ann	28	F	Unknown	08Mr02Bm
ROBINSON, Jos.	22	M	Laborer	08Mr02Bm
SCOFIELD, James	37	M	Laborer	08Mr02Bm
DAVY, Wm.	35	M	Laborer	08Mr02Bm
Winifred	35	F	Unknown	08Mr02Bm
CRARY, Jno.	12	M	Unknown	08Mr02Bm
COLLINS, Robt.	35	M	Farmer	08Mr02Bm
DUFFY, Thos.	36	M	Farmer	08Mr02Bm
FAHY, Wm.	21	M	Laborer	08Mr02Bm
Frank	26	M	Laborer	08Mr02Bm
MAROONEY, Martin	45	M	Laborer	08Mr02Bm
RILEY, Chris	45	M	Laborer	08Mr02Bm
WHALEN, Dennis	20	M	Laborer	08Mr02Bm
Ann	17	F	Unknown	08Mr02Bm
MCALLEN, Mary-Ann	25	F	Laborer	08Mr02Bm
HILLIAR, Thos.	29	M	Laborer	08Mr02Bm
KELLY, Pat	24	M	Laborer	08Mr02Bm
DOOGAN, Mich.	20	M	Laborer	08Mr02Bm
HURLEY, Jno.	25	M	Laborer	08Mr02Bm
BENNETT, Margt.	22	F	Unknown	08Mr02Bm
LEONARD, Sarah	20	F	Unknown	08Mr02Bm
CARRINGTON, Pat	23	M	Laborer	08Mr02Bm
Bridget	21	F	Unknown	08Mr02Bm
STOREY, Barnard	18	M	Laborer	08Mr02Bm
James	16	M	Laborer	08Mr02Bm
HENRY, Mary	30	F	Unknown	08Mr02Bm
Mary	.00	F	Infant	08Mr02Bm
GARNON, Mary	15	F	Unknown	08Mr02Bm
Julia	13	F	Unknown	08Mr02Bm
CODY, James	22	M	Unknown	08Mr02Bm
Allen	20	M	Unknown	08Mr02Bm
LEE, Jno.	9	M	Child	08Mr02Bm
GRIFFIN, Wm.	45	M	Unknown	08Mr02Bm
ELLWOOD, Pat	22	M	Unknown	08Mr02Bm
KELLY, Ann	30	F	Unknown	08Mr02Bm
Jno.	9	M	Child	08Mr02Bm
Mick	7	M	Child	08Mr02Bm
Bernard	5	M	Child	08Mr02Bm
SPARROW, Edward	20	M	Unknown	08Mr02Bm
MCMURRAN, Dan	23	M	Unknown	08Mr02Bm
CARROLL, John	20	M	Laborer	08Mr02Bm
MCGOVERN, Jas.	20	M	Laborer	08Mr02Bm
CORRIGAN, Pat	45	M	Laborer	08Mr02Bm
Cath.	33	F	Unknown	08Mr02Bm
Ann	15	F	Unknown	08Mr02Bm
James	10	M	Unknown	08Mr02Bm
Chris	7	M	Child	08Mr02Bm
Rosamond	2	F	Child	08Mr02Bm
DUGAN, Francis	49	M	Laborer	08Mr02Bm
U-Mrs.	40	F	Unknown	08Mr02Bm
Francis-Jr.	20	M	Unknown	08Mr02Bm
James	15	M	Unknown	08Mr02Bm
Margt.	13	F	Unknown	08Mr02Bm
Pat	11	M	Unknown	08Mr02Bm
Mich.	9	M	Child	08Mr02Bm

NAMES OF PASSENGERS	AGE	SEX	OCCUPATIONS	DATE PORT SHIP
DUGAN, Thos.	6	M	Child	08Mr02Bm
Joseph	5	M	Child	08Mr02Bm
Edward	4	M	Child	08Mr02Bm
Biddy	2	F	Child	08Mr02Bm
Lawrence	.00	M	Infant	08Mr02Bm
HOGAN, Cath.	20	F	Unknown	08Mr02Bm
ROBINSON, Geo.	50	M	Unknown	08Mr02Bm
WARD, Jno.	25	M	Unknown	08Mr02Bm
Mary	45	F	Unknown	08Mr02Bm
MOONY, Ann	24	F	Unknown	08Mr02Bm
KENNEDY, Mary	62	F	Unknown	08Mr02Bm
DUFF, Edw.	18	M	Laborer	08Mr02Bm
James	15	M	Unknown	08Mr02Bm
William	15	M	Unknown	08Mr02Bm
Harriett	20	F	Unknown	08Mr02Bm
FANAGAN, Wm.	37	M	Laborer	08Mr02Bm
REYNOLDS, James	23	M	Laborer	08Mr02Bm
Bridget	20	F	Unknown	08Mr02Bm
Michael	12	M	Unknown	08Mr02Bm
DORAN, Pat	30	M	Laborer	08Mr02Bm
MORRISSY, Jno.	25	M	Laborer	08Mr02Bm
Dennis	13	M	Unknown	08Mr02Bm
TARNEY, Michl.	13	M	Unknown	08Mr02Bm
CLAFFIN, Thos.	40	M	Laborer	08Mr02Bm
Thos.	16	M	Unknown	08Mr02Bm
JONES, Henry	24	M	Pntr-Gzr	08Mr02Bm
REYNOLDS, Wm.	25	M	Laborer	08Mr02Bm
U-Mrs.	25	F	Unknown	08Mr02Bm
FOX, Saml.	22	M	Laborer	08Mr02Bm
REYNOLDS, Sarah	3	F	Child	08Mr02Bm
Mary	8	F	Child	08Mr02Bm
CONROY, Teddy	18	M	Laborer	08Mr02Bm

JAMESTOWN 11 MARCH 1850

From Liverpool

NAMES OF PASSENGERS	AGE	SEX	OCCUPATIONS	DATE PORT SHIP
OSBORN, Frederick-John	27	M	Cver	11Mr02Fm
Henrietta-E.	20	F	Lady	11Mr02Fm
KINNIEL, Jas.	50	M	Physician	11Mr02Fm
LONG, Francis	30	M	Physician	11Mr02Fm
PIERCY, Samuel	30	M	Modeler	11Mr02Fm
RYAN, Jason	16	M	Unknown	11Mr02Fm
HOOLEHAN, John	20	M	Laborer	11Mr02Fm
FITZPATRICK, Martin	25	M	Laborer	11Mr02Fm
CONNOR, Daniel	35	M	Laborer	11Mr02Fm
Carolina (W)	26	F	Wife	11Mr02Fm
Mary	9	F	Child	11Mr02Fm
Carolina	7	F	Child	11Mr02Fm
John	5	M	Child	11Mr02Fm
Patk.	2	M	Child	11Mr02Fm
LEONARD, Peter	35	M	Laborer	11Mr02Fm
Bridget (W)	30	F	Wife	11Mr02Fm
Mary	.00	F	Infant	11Mr02Fm
WALSH, Jas.	19	M	Laborer	11Mr02Fm
KEENE, Patk.	25	M	Farmer	11Mr02Fm
MOLLOY, John	34	M	Farmer	11Mr02Fm
SALLY, Shanas	24	M	Laborer	11Mr02Fm
GRIBBIN, John	24	M	Laborer	11Mr02Fm
DWYER, Wm.	19	M	Farmer	11Mr02Fm
James	21	M	Laborer	11Mr02Fm
SMITH, Timothy	21	M	Laborer	11Mr02Fm
GILLICUDDY, Mary	18	F	Servant	11Mr02Fm
Ellen	30	F	Wife	11Mr02Fm
Biddy	9	F	Child	11Mr02Fm
Jery	3	U	Child	11Mr02Fm
Ellen	.00	F	Infant	11Mr02Fm
KEATING, Wm.	43	M	Carpenter	11Mr02Fm
Mary (W)	25	F	Wife	11Mr02Fm

NAMES OF PASSENGERS		AGE	SEX	OCCUPATIONS	DATE PORT SHIP
KELLEY, John		24	M	Farmer	11Mr02Fm
MECHAN, Cath.		22	F	Wife	11Mr02Fm
Patk.		.00	M	Infant	11Mr02Fm
Mary		22	F	Servant	11Mr02Fm
DERMONDY, Jas.		21	M	Farmer	11Mr02Fm
John		27	M	Laborer	11Mr02Fm
BUTLER, John		26	M	Laborer	11Mr02Fm
CONNELL, Jas.		20	M	Laborer	11Mr02Fm
SHEVLIN, Bridget		30	F	Servant	11Mr02Fm
ROGAN, Margt.		30	F	Servant	11Mr02Fm
QUINN, Cath.		30	F	Servant	11Mr02Fm
GERETY, Cath.		17	F	Servant	11Mr02Fm
HICKEY, Jas.		23	M	Carpenter	11Mr02Fm
Mary		20	F	Servant	11Mr02Fm
LEONARD, Ellen		18	F	Servant	11Mr02Fm
REDDY, Patk.		26	M	Farmer	11Mr02Fm
Mary-Anne		24	F	Servant	11Mr02Fm
Jane		21	F	Servant	11Mr02Fm
FITZSIMMONS, James		24	M	Laborer	11Mr02Fm
Bridget		20	F	Servant	11Mr02Fm
HANDY, Mary		20	F	Servant	11Mr02Fm
KEENAN, Mary		20	F	Servant	11Mr02Fm
MCGINN, Jas.		35	M	Laborer	11Mr02Fm
Jas.		20	M	Laborer	11Mr02Fm
DOWD, Charles		35	M	Laborer	11Mr02Fm
Died-At-Sea					
GARATY, Jas.		28	M	Laborer	11Mr02Fm
DOOLAN, Michael		22	M	Laborer	11Mr02Fm
REYNOLDS, Jane		22	F	Servant	11Mr02Fm
Cath.		20	F	Servant	11Mr02Fm
KILROLY, Ellen		14	F	Servant	11Mr02Fm
RYAN, William		25	M	Laborer	11Mr02Fm
LONG, Robt.		22	M	Laborer	11Mr02Fm
MORETON, Anne		24	F	Servant	11Mr02Fm
LYNCH, Thomas		45	M	Laborer	11Mr02Fm
Rose	(W)	40	F	Wife	11Mr02Fm
Bridget		12	F	Servant	11Mr02Fm
Ellen		7	F	Child	11Mr02Fm
BOURKE, Anne		17	F	Servant	11Mr02Fm
HODGINS, Thos.		34	M	Laborer	11Mr02Fm
Fanny	(W)	24	F	Wife	11Mr02Fm
BRADY, Philip		27	M	Smith	11Mr02Fm
HOWARD, John		21	M	Cbtmkr	11Mr02Fm
CADELER, James		24	M	Farmer	11Mr02Fm
BRADY, Edward		50	M	Laborer	11Mr02Fm
Eliza		18	F	Servant	11Mr02Fm
MARTIN, Owen		24	M	Laborer	11Mr02Fm
LYNCH, Margaret		22	F	Servant	11Mr02Fm
GERATY, Michael		30	M	Servant	11Mr02Fm
TIERNEY, Mary		20	F	Servant	11Mr02Fm
CONNOLLY, John		24	M	Carpenter	11Mr02Fm
MURRAY, Bridget		20	F	Servant	11Mr02Fm
MCANENY, Patrick		22	M	Butcher	11Mr02Fm
DUFFY, John		30	M	Laborer	11Mr02Fm
Patrick		20	M	Laborer	11Mr02Fm
DUNNE, James		22	M	Clerk	11Mr02Fm
BRIEN, Stephen		21	M	Baker	11Mr02Fm
PURTILL, Cath.		20	F	Servant	11Mr02Fm
BANNIGAN, Bernard		23	M	Laborer	11Mr02Fm
James		18	M	Laborer	11Mr02Fm
WARE, Anthony		21	M	Laborer	11Mr02Fm
CAROLAN, Biddy		17	F	Servant	11Mr02Fm
DALY, John		25	M	Laborer	11Mr02Fm
Mary	(W)	23	F	Wife	11Mr02Fm
REYNOLDS, Bridget		35	F	Wi	11Mr02Fm
Anne		14	F	Servant	11Mr02Fm
SKELTON, John		28	M	Farmer	11Mr02Fm
Sarah-Anne		24	F	Servant	11Mr02Fm
DALTON, John		36	M	Laborer	11Mr02Fm
MANGAN, Michael		30	M	Farmer	11Mr02Fm
HYLANDS, Charlotte		24	F	Servant	11Mr02Fm
BERGEN, Bridget		24	F	Servant	11Mr02Fm
KING, Peter		38	M	Farmer	11Mr02Fm
Anne	(W)	38	F	Wife	11Mr02Fm
Patrick		5	M	Child	11Mr02Fm
KING, Margaret		2	F	Child	11Mr02Fm
Michael		.00	M	Infant	11Mr02Fm
MCFADDEN, Margaret		22	F	Servant	11Mr02Fm
CLARK, Margaret		20	F	Wife	11Mr02Fm
KING, Cath.		38	F	Wi	11Mr02Fm
Margaret		10	F	Unknown	11Mr02Fm
ARCHIBOLD, John		30	M	Laborer	11Mr02Fm
Margaret	(W)	28	F	Wife	11Mr02Fm
Bridget		3	F	Unknown	11Mr02Fm
Thomas		.00	M	Infant	11Mr02Fm
MALONY, Thos.		21	M	Laborer	11Mr02Fm
BRADY, Bridget		24	F	Servant	11Mr02Fm
MEE, James		24	M	Cord Cutter	11Mr02Fm
DUFFY, Martin		22	M	Farmer	11Mr02Fm
Biddy		20	F	Servant	11Mr02Fm
Cathren		18	F	Servant	11Mr02Fm
EGAN, Peter		21	M	Laborer	11Mr02Fm
LAW, John		26	M	Laborer	11Mr02Fm
James		30	M	Laborer	11Mr02Fm
Jane	(W)	25	F	Wife	11Mr02Fm
Patrick		.00	M	Infant	11Mr02Fm
DONOUGH, Mary		24	M	Servant	11Mr02Fm
MCANALLY, M.		12	F	Servant	11Mr02Fm
Owen		11	M	Unknown	11Mr02Fm
Letty		8	F	Child	11Mr02Fm
BEVAN, Bissie		22	F	Servant	11Mr02Fm
BYRNE, Edward		33	M	Laborer	11Mr02Fm
CALIHAN, Philip		33	M	Sailor	11Mr02Fm
Alice		18	F	Servant	11Mr02Fm
Judith		18	F	Servant	11Mr02Fm
PORTER, John		18	M	Laborer	11Mr02Fm
MAHER, Mathew		30	M	Laborer	11Mr02Fm
CUMMINS, John		24	M	Gdnr	11Mr02Fm
HAGDEN, Michael		30	M	Blacksmith	11Mr02Fm
MCCRUM, James		50	M	Laborer	11Mr02Fm
Wm.		19	M	Carpenter	11Mr02Fm
OBRIEN, John		26	M	Laborer	11Mr02Fm
FORD, Edward		24	M	Laborer	11Mr02Fm
Bridget		22	F	Servant	11Mr02Fm
Thos.		20	M	Laborer	11Mr02Fm
DUNNE, Edmond		19	M	Laborer	11Mr02Fm
CLEARY, Edward		24	M	Laborer	11Mr02Fm
PARKINS, James		24	M	Servant	11Mr02Fm
OHARA, Bridget		25	F	Wife	11Mr02Fm
DONALLY, Patrick		44	M	Laborer	11Mr02Fm
Rose	(W)	31	F	Wife	11Mr02Fm
Patrick		13	M	Unknown	11Mr02Fm
Mary		1	F	Child	11Mr02Fm
GOOLY, John		21	M	Laborer	11Mr02Fm
KELLY, Dorah		20	F	Servant	11Mr02Fm
ELWOOD, Michael		36	M	Mason	11Mr02Fm
Margaret	(W)	26	F	Wife	11Mr02Fm
Nicholas		36	M	Unknown	11Mr02Fm
Julia		3	F	Child	11Mr02Fm
Mary-Anne		.00	F	Infant	11Mr02Fm
HOGAN, Michael		21	M	Laborer	11Mr02Fm
GARRIT, John		30	M	Laborer	11Mr02Fm
MAKIN, Bridget		26	F	Servant	11Mr02Fm
BOYLE, Alexander		28	M	Laborer	11Mr02Fm
Susan	(W)	23	F	Wife	11Mr02Fm
Peter		.00	M	Infant	11Mr02Fm
Died-At-Sea					
KANE, Isabella		24	F	Servant	11Mr02Fm
BRADLY, John		23	M	Farmer	11Mr02Fm
SHANAHAN, John		27	M	Laborer	11Mr02Fm
SMALL, Thos.		30	M	Laborer	11Mr02Fm
FOX, Philip		35	M	Laborer	11Mr02Fm
Mary	(W)	30	F	Wife	11Mr02Fm
DEARY, Bridget		34	F	Servant	11Mr02Fm
OMARRA, Ellen		22	F	Servant	11Mr02Fm
SEXTON, Margaret		24	F	Servant	11Mr02Fm
CONSIDINE, Michael		45	M	Laborer	11Mr02Fm
OBRIEN, Thos.		34	M	Laborer	11Mr02Fm
Patrick		32	M	Laborer	11Mr02Fm
DOWNS, Michael		7	M	Child	11Mr02Fm

NAMES OF PASSENGERS		AGE	SEX	OCCUPATIONS	DATE PORT SHIP
DOWNS, Thos.		5	M	Child	11Mr02Fm
James		3	M	Child	11Mr02Fm
COLLINS, James		20	M	Laborer	11Mr02Fm
LEYDEN, John		35	M	Laborer	11Mr02Fm
Daniel		22	M	Laborer	11Mr02Fm
Patrick		24	M	Laborer	11Mr02Fm
BURN, John		40	M	Laborer	11Mr02Fm
FAHEY, Margaret		25	F	Servant	11Mr02Fm
Cath.		24	F	Servant	11Mr02Fm
MAHER, Patrick		18	M	Laborer	11Mr02Fm
FAY, Bryan		30	M	Laborer	11Mr02Fm
Sally	(W)	22	F	Wife	11Mr02Fm
JOHNSON, James		20	M	Joiner	11Mr02Fm
DARCY, Mary		26	F	Wife	11Mr02Fm
CROWLEY, Cath.		34	F	Wife	11Mr02Fm
MATHEWS, Peter		40	M	Laborer	11Mr02Fm
Alice		20	F	Servant	11Mr02Fm
FEGAN, Anne		20	F	Servant	11Mr02Fm
BOYD, Hannah		30	F	Wife	11Mr02Fm
BENNETT, Lucy		22	F	Wife	11Mr02Fm
RIELLY, Mathew		33	M	Laborer	11Mr02Fm
Anne		26	F	Servant	11Mr02Fm
Anne		42	F	Wi	11Mr02Fm
Jane		12	F	Servant	11Mr02Fm
FINLEY, Judith		14	F	Servant	11Mr02Fm
WELESON, Thos.		26	M	Laborer	11Mr02Fm
MCMAHON, Mary		34	F	Wi	11Mr02Fm
CONNOLLY, Thos.		40	M	Laborer	11Mr02Fm
Anne		25	F	Servant	11Mr02Fm
Patrick		28	M	Servant	11Mr02Fm
MOYNEHAN, Cath.		20	F	Servant	11Mr02Fm
FINLEY, Thos.		25	M	Carpenter	11Mr02Fm
Eliza	(W)	25	F	Wife	11Mr02Fm
CAMPBELL, John		50	M	Laborer	11Mr02Fm
FLYNN, James		24	M	Laborer	11Mr02Fm
SMITH, Cath.		27	F	Wife	11Mr02Fm
OBRIEN, William		22	M	Clerk	11Mr02Fm
MADDEN, Patrick		40	M	Laborer	11Mr02Fm
Mary		18	F	Servant	11Mr02Fm
Honorah		16	F	Servant	11Mr02Fm
MARTIN, Andrew		16	M	Laborer	11Mr02Fm
LARKIN, Martin		17	M	Laborer	11Mr02Fm
MCSHANE, Sarah		30	F	Servant	11Mr02Fm
LYNCH, Richard		20	M	Laborer	11Mr02Fm
MCCORMACK, Honorah		35	F	Wife	11Mr02Fm
COOK, Peter		24	M	Laborer	11Mr02Fm
HUSS, Mary		23	F	Servant	11Mr02Fm
MCGRATH, John		23	M	Laborer	11Mr02Fm
CASSAN, John		18	M	Weaver	11Mr02Fm
KINCILLA, Bridget		24	F	Wife	11Mr02Fm
STAFFORD, John		20	M	Plasterer	11Mr02Fm
MORAN, James		22	M	Plasterer	11Mr02Fm
GEDDES, Samuel		36	M	Laborer	11Mr02Fm
Elizabeth	(W)	36	F	Wife	11Mr02Fm
Mary		16	F	Servant	11Mr02Fm
Betty		13	F	Servant	11Mr02Fm
William		11	M	Servant	11Mr02Fm
Robert		9	M	Child	11Mr02Fm
Anne		7	F	Child	11Mr02Fm
Margaret		.00	F	Infant	11Mr02Fm
Anne		22	F	Unknown	11Mr02Fm
John		21	M	Laborer	11Mr02Fm
HICKEY, Michael		30	M	Farmer	11Mr02Fm
Anstice		26	F	Servant	11Mr02Fm
Ellen		9	F	Child	11Mr02Fm
Judith		22	F	Wife	11Mr02Fm
GAYNOR, Bartholimew		21	M	Laborer	11Mr02Fm
Eliza		19	F	Servant	11Mr02Fm
HALFERDY, James		30	M	Clerk	11Mr02Fm
RYAN, Francis		40	M	Lawyer	11Mr02Fm
AYERS, Daniel		24	M	Laborer	11Mr02Fm
GRACE, James		23	M	Farmer	11Mr02Fm
Michael		23	M	Farmer	11Mr02Fm
Honorah		20	F	Servant	11Mr02Fm
MCBRIDE, Rosina		19	F	Servant	11Mr02Fm

NAMES OF PASSENGERS		AGE	SEX	OCCUPATIONS	DATE PORT SHIP
HANLY, Patrick		50	M	Mason	11Mr02Fm
Peggy	(W)	46	F	Wife	11Mr02Fm
John		13	M	Unknown	11Mr02Fm
Patrick		10	M	Unknown	11Mr02Fm
Mary		7	F	Child	11Mr02Fm
Bridget		2	F	Child	11Mr02Fm
ROURKE, James		32	M	Mason	11Mr02Fm
Dolly		23	F	Servant	11Mr02Fm
KENNEDY, Michael		30	M	Laborer	11Mr02Fm
Sarah		26	F	Servant	11Mr02Fm
FAY, Peter		52	M	Laborer	11Mr02Fm
BYRNE, Michael		50	M	Laborer	11Mr02Fm
John		13	M	Laborer	11Mr02Fm
KNOX, John		21	M	Laborer	11Mr02Fm
JORDAN, Cath.		21	F	Servant	11Mr02Fm
Mary-Jane		19	F	Servant	11Mr02Fm
Eliza		13	F	Servant	11Mr02Fm
HANNON, Patrick		20	M	Cbtmkr	11Mr02Fm
WILSON, John		24	M	Joiner	11Mr02Fm
MCCUIN, Arthur		33	M	Laborer	11Mr02Fm
MCALOON, Rose		22	F	Servant	11Mr02Fm
Ellen		20	F	Wife	11Mr02Fm
BOHAN, Richard		30	M	Cordwainer	11Mr02Fm
Jane	(W)	24	F	Wife	11Mr02Fm
MCCONNELL, Maria		14	F	Servant	11Mr02Fm
ONEIL, Thos.		25	M	Farmer	11Mr02Fm
BROPHY, Cath.		18	F	Servant	11Mr02Fm
OWENS, Bartholemew		26	M	Laborer	11Mr02Fm
COLLINS, Dennis		24	M	Laborer	11Mr02Fm
RICHARDSON, Mathew		20	M	Laborer	11Mr02Fm
HAYES, Mary		20	F	Wife	11Mr02Fm
GAFFNEY, Cath.		18	F	Servant	11Mr02Fm
NIXON, Rebecca		46	F	Wi	11Mr02Fm
MCGUIRE, Mary		10	F	Servant	11Mr02Fm
ORIELLY, Mine		18	F	Servant	11Mr02Fm
WARE, Mary		20	F	Servant	11Mr02Fm
Ellen		19	F	Servant	11Mr02Fm
RUSSELL, John		30	M	Clerk	11Mr02Fm
Sarah	(W)	20	F	Wife	11Mr02Fm
CARROLL, James		58	M	Steward	11Mr02Fm
Sarah	(W)	56	F	Wife	11Mr02Fm
OGRADY, Ellen	(W)	22	F	Wife	11Mr02Fm
Mary-Anne		8	F	Child	11Mr02Fm
James		34	M	Laborer	11Mr02Fm
Jeremiah		22	M	Draper	11Mr02Fm
GAVIN, James		6	M	Child	11Mr02Fm
Margaret		4	F	Child	11Mr02Fm
Julia		2	F	Child	11Mr02Fm
Cornelius		32	M	Farmer	11Mr02Fm
Mary	(W)	22	F	Wife	11Mr02Fm
Judith		2	F	Child	11Mr02Fm
CLEARY, Hannah		48	F	Unknown	11Mr02Fm
Margaret		14	F	Servant	11Mr02Fm
Cath.		12	F	Servant	11Mr02Fm
James		4	M	Child	11Mr02Fm
CORCORAN, Patrick		30	M	Laborer	11Mr02Fm
CAVANNAH, Betty		23	F	Servant	11Mr02Fm
CLEARY, Judy		2	F	Child	11Mr02Fm
FLARRHERTY, Anne		25	F	Servant	11Mr02Fm

MONTEZUMA 11 MARCH 1850

From Liverpool

NAMES OF PASSENGERS		AGE	SEX	OCCUPATIONS	DATE PORT SHIP
CARNEY, James		22	M	Laborer	11Mr02Bl
MCGRATH, John		12	M	Unknown	11Mr02Bl
GAGGAN, Andy		21	M	Laborer	11Mr02Bl
Catherine		17	F	Unknown	11Mr02Bl
WARD, Mary		17	F	Unknown	11Mr02Bl

NAMES OF PASSENGERS	AGE	SEX	OCCUPATIONS	DATE PORT SHIP
FOLEY, Johanna	29	F	Unknown	11Mr02BI
MALLOY, Thomas	52	M	Laborer	11Mr02BI
U-Mrs.	40	F	Unknown	11Mr02BI
Patrick	21	M	Laborer	11Mr02BI
Mary	17	F	Unknown	11Mr02BI
Catherine	15	F	Unknown	11Mr02BI
James	12	M	Unknown	11Mr02BI
Ann	7	F	Child	11Mr02BI
HARRINGTON, Catherine	18	F	Unknown	11Mr02BI
Johannah	20	F	Unknown	11Mr02BI
DONOVAN, John	24	M	Laborer	11Mr02BI
HENNESSY, Margaret	20	F	Unknown	11Mr02BI
Eliza	13	F	Unknown	11Mr02BI
SULLIVAN, James	40	M	Laborer	11Mr02BI
CONNOR, Edward	18	M	Laborer	11Mr02BI
LYNCH, John	30	M	Laborer	11Mr02BI
KELLAHEN, Johannah	17	F	Unknown	11Mr02BI
ALLEN, John	19	M	Laborer	11Mr02BI
TURNER, George	27	M	Laborer	11Mr02BI
HOWLAND, William	27	M	Unknown	11Mr02BI
DOSKEY, John	48	M	Laborer	11Mr02BI
Mary	32	F	Unknown	11Mr02BI
REILLY, Mary	20	F	Servant	11Mr02BI
DEVON, Catherine	25	F	Servant	11Mr02BI
OBRIEN, Morris	19	M	Laborer	11Mr02BI
MONAGHAN, James	14	M	Unknown	11Mr02BI
Mary	13	F	Unknown	11Mr02BI
GRADY, James	21	M	Laborer	11Mr02BI
CARROLL, Catherine	30	F	Unknown	11Mr02BI
U	.00	U	Infant	11Mr02BI
WILSON, Sarah	26	F	Servant	11Mr02BI
Emma	4	F	Child	11Mr02BI
MCMANNERY, Mary	16	F	Servant	11Mr02BI
BERNIE, Fanny	21	F	Servant	11Mr02BI
SMITH, Barthy	51	M	Laborer	11Mr02BI
Rose	13	F	Unknown	11Mr02BI
LYNCH, Catherine	60	F	Unknown	11Mr02BI
Margaret	19	F	Servant	11Mr02BI
Catherine	17	F	Servant	11Mr02BI
GALLAHER, Honora	15	F	Servant	11Mr02BI
SHEEHAN, Cornelius	27	M	Laborer	11Mr02BI
HAMMELL, Margeret	6	F	Child	11Mr02BI
MCGINAN, Alice	15	F	Unknown	11Mr02BI
KENNEY, Patrick	33	M	Laborer	11Mr02BI
HORAN, Henrietta	29	F	None	11Mr02BI
CASIN, Ann	16	F	Servant	11Mr02BI
LEARY, Ann	23	F	Servant	11Mr02BI
KELLY, Honor	27	F	Servant	11Mr02BI
HOUGH, Betty	25	F	Servant	11Mr02BI
DOONAN, Daniel	20	M	Laborer	11Mr02BI
Michael	19	M	Laborer	11Mr02BI
CAMPAN, Judith	18	F	Servant	11Mr02BI
FITZGIBBON, James	30	M	Laborer	11Mr02BI
SHEARMAN, John	17	M	Laborer	11Mr02BI
LEARY, John	21	M	Laborer	11Mr02BI
GANNON, Bernard	20	M	Laborer	11Mr02BI
CONNALLY, Edward	18	M	Laborer	11Mr02BI
TURMAN, Peter	10	M	Unknown	11Mr02BI
Ann	28	F	Servant	11Mr02BI
MCGACHER, John	18	M	Laborer	11Mr02BI
LEWARTH, Samuel	20	M	Laborer	11Mr02BI
NEARY, Dennis	20	M	Laborer	11Mr02BI
COFF, Judy	18	F	Servant	11Mr02BI
MEEGHAN, Patrick	20	M	Laborer	11Mr02BI
CANLEY, Nancy	30	F	Servant	11Mr02BI
DORKES, Peggy	22	F	Servant	11Mr02BI
CONNELLY, Dennis	20	M	Laborer	11Mr02BI
SMITH, Robert	22	M	Laborer	11Mr02BI
JOHNSON, Samuel	22	M	Laborer	11Mr02BI
GRIFFES, Thomas	12	M	Laborer	11Mr02BI
CASLOW, Rose	20	F	Servant	11Mr02BI
SMITH, Phillip	18	M	Laborer	11Mr02BI
Mary	20	F	Servant	11Mr02BI
OAKLEY, Ann	26	F	Unknown	11Mr02BI
Richard	9	M	Child	11Mr02BI

NAMES OF PASSENGERS	AGE	SEX	OCCUPATIONS	DATE PORT SHIP
OAKLEY, Thomas	7	M	Child	11Mr02BI
HAWLEY, Ellen	20	F	Servant	11Mr02BI
KEOHOE, William	18	M	Laborer	11Mr02BI
SCANLAN, John	33	M	Laborer	11Mr02BI
LYNCH, Alicia	34	F	Servant	11Mr02BI
Daniel	30	M	Laborer	11Mr02BI
NEAGLE, Garrett	47	M	Laborer	11Mr02BI
NEVILLE, Bridget	24	F	Servant	11Mr02BI
CRONAN, Cornelius	10	M	Unknown	11Mr02BI
REILLY, Mathew	30	M	Laborer	11Mr02BI
Mary	20	F	Servant	11Mr02BI
KEEGAN, Ellen	30	F	Servant	11Mr02BI
John	2	M	Child	11Mr02BI
TAFFEY, Bridget	26	F	Servant	11Mr02BI
MALLOY, Thomas	4	M	Child	11Mr02BI
MCDARBY, James	24	M	Laborer	11Mr02BI
DOHERTY, Bridget	28	F	Servant	11Mr02BI
Mary	30	F	Unknown	11Mr02BI
U	.00	U	Infant	11Mr02BI
GAHERTY, Mary	30	F	Unknown	11Mr02BI
Ann	18	F	Unknown	11Mr02BI
HAYHURST, Edward	25	M	Laborer	11Mr02BI
Catherine	24	F	Unknown	11Mr02BI
U	.00	U	Infant	11Mr02BI
William	3	M	Child	11Mr02BI
CAGARIN, Bridget	23	F	Servant	11Mr02BI
WINNE, Michael	25	M	Laborer	11Mr02BI
DURNALON, Julia	26	F	Unknown	11Mr02BI
Amos	3	M	Child	11Mr02BI
Mary	5	F	Child	11Mr02BI
TRAVIS, Owen	25	M	Laborer	11Mr02BI
Margaret	14	F	Unknown	11Mr02BI
John	15	M	Unknown	11Mr02BI
Margaret	19	F	Servant	11Mr02BI
KILIVRE, John	21	M	Laborer	11Mr02BI
William	28	M	Laborer	11Mr02BI
DALEY, Michael	30	M	Laborer	11Mr02BI
SHEA, John	36	M	Laborer	11Mr02BI
WHITE, Michael	30	M	Laborer	11Mr02BI
BUCKLEY, Jeremiah	30	M	Laborer	11Mr02BI
Elizabeth	9	F	Child	11Mr02BI
William	8	M	Child	11Mr02BI
CONNOR, Ann	32	F	Servant	11Mr02BI
Died-At-Sea				
Ellen	14	F	Unknown	11Mr02BI
DEAN, Frederick	29	M	Laborer	11Mr02BI
ACKERS, Patrick	21	M	Laborer	11Mr02BI
Ann	14	F	Laborer	11Mr02BI
MCKENNA, Ann	32	F	Servant	11Mr02BI
FITZGIBBON, John	50	M	Laborer	11Mr02BI
HOGAN, Edmond	22	M	Laborer	11Mr02BI
CAVANAGH, Thomas	21	M	Laborer	11Mr02BI
KELLY, Hugh	35	M	Laborer	11Mr02BI
CREEGAN, John	30	M	Laborer	11Mr02BI
Bridget	17	F	Servant	11Mr02BI
MULDSON, Mary	30	F	Servant	11Mr02BI
Winfred	13	F	Unknown	11Mr02BI
Bridget	12	F	Unknown	11Mr02BI
Patrick	9	M	Child	11Mr02BI
SMITH, Michael	49	M	Laborer	11Mr02BI
Catherine	49	F	Unknown	11Mr02BI
Mathew	18	M	Laborer	11Mr02BI
Margaret	16	F	Unknown	11Mr02BI
Michael	12	M	Unknown	11Mr02BI
Christy	7	M	Child	11Mr02BI
Peter	7	M	Child	11Mr02BI
CARNEY, Honora	16	F	Servant	11Mr02BI
FOX, James	30	M	Laborer	11Mr02BI
RUSSELL, James	18	M	Laborer	11Mr02BI
HOGAN, Michael	15	M	Unknown	11Mr02BI
CONLAN, Mary	52	F	Unknown	11Mr02BI
FAVE, Edmond	30	M	Laborer	11Mr02BI
Margeret	28	F	Unknown	11Mr02BI
BUTLER, Ann	17	F	Servant	11Mr02BI
FINE, Anty	25	M	Laborer	11Mr02BI

NAMES OF PASSENGERS	AGE	SEX	OCCUPATIONS	DATE PORT SHIP
HILL, George	42	M	Laborer	11Mr02BI
MCDONNELL, William	18	M	Laborer	11Mr02BI
DOYLE, John	22	M	Laborer	11Mr02BI
Eliza	20	F	Unknown	11Mr02BI
DARDES, Bridget	14	F	Unknown	11Mr02BI
Thomas	13	M	Unknown	11Mr02BI
LAYCOCK, Mary	20	F	Servant	11Mr02BI
FARRELL, Mary	33	F	Servant	11Mr02BI
Patrick	3	M	Child	11Mr02BI
Mary	6	F	Child	11Mr02BI
KEARNS, Patrick	22	M	Laborer	11Mr02BI
STJOHN, Johannah	27	F	Unknown	11Mr02BI
U	.00	U	Infant	11Mr02BI
St.JOHN, John	6	M	Child	11Mr02BI
STJOHN, Edmund	4	M	Child	11Mr02BI
CONNELL, Mary	50	F	Unknown	11Mr02BI
Ellen	10	F	Unknown	11Mr02BI
James	9	M	Child	11Mr02BI
Judith	5	F	Child	11Mr02BI
SULLIVAN, Bartholomew	18	M	Unknown	11Mr02BI
Jeremiah	31	M	Laborer	11Mr02BI
Margaret	20	F	Servant	11Mr02BI
AHERN, Catherine	34	F	Servant	11Mr02BI
Michael	10	M	Unknown	11Mr02BI
Ann	8	F	Child	11Mr02BI
Daniel	2	M	Child	11Mr02BI
rCASEY, Nanny	16	F	Servant	11Mr02BI
CALLAGHAN, John	30	M	Laborer	11Mr02BI
Peggy	32	F	Unknown	11Mr02BI
Judy	7	F	Child	11Mr02BI
Michael	5	M	Child	11Mr02BI
CUDDY, John	23	M	Laborer	11Mr02BI
Michael	21	M	Laborer	11Mr02BI
DWYER, Margaret	35	F	Unknown	11Mr02BI
John	11	M	Unknown	11Mr02BI
LYNAN, Mary	35	F	Unknown	11Mr02BI
FLINN, U-Mrs.	35	F	Unknown	11Mr02BI
Mary	11	F	Unknown	11Mr02BI
Margaret	9	F	Child	11Mr02BI
WALSH, Michael	17	M	Unknown	11Mr02BI
William	14	M	Unknown	11Mr02BI
SMITH, Catherine	15	F	Unknown	11Mr02BI
HOEY, James	35	M	Laborer	11Mr02BI
D-Ns---, Catherine	19	F	Unknown	11Mr02BI
FARRELL, Michael	24	M	Laborer	11Mr02BI
Ann	19	F	Unknown	11Mr02BI
LYONS, Ann	25	F	Unknown	11Mr02BI
LOUNAN, Ann	24	F	Unknown	11Mr02BI
MORAN, Patrick	25	M	Laborer	11Mr02BI
KELLY, Rose	45	F	Unknown	11Mr02BI
NEAL, Rose	20	F	Unknown	11Mr02BI
KENNALLY, Catherine	23	F	Unknown	11Mr02BI
SMITH, Bridget	16	F	Unknown	11Mr02BI
LAMB, Lawrence	62	M	Laborer	11Mr02BI
REILLY, Catherine	20	F	Unknown	11Mr02BI
SULLIVAN, Thomas	26	M	Laborer	11Mr02BI
KING, Thomas	20	M	Laborer	11Mr02BI
WICKS, Mary	22	F	Unknown	11Mr02BI
BENNINGHAM, John	40	M	Laborer	11Mr02BI
Ann	26	F	Unknown	11Mr02BI
U	.00	U	Infant	11Mr02BI
SHORAN, Ann	19	F	Unknown	11Mr02BI
DELANEY, Patrick	18	M	Laborer	11Mr02BI
BRIAN, Christopher	22	M	Laborer	11Mr02BI
LEARY, Catherine	19	F	Unknown	11Mr02BI
MCHUGH, James	22	M	Laborer	11Mr02BI
FEA, Phebe	22	F	Unknown	11Mr02BI
William	15	M	Unknown	11Mr02BI
BRYAN, Dennis	21	M	Laborer	11Mr02BI
MURPHY, James	30	M	Laborer	11Mr02BI
COFFEE, Ann	35	F	Unknown	11Mr02BI
U	.00	U	Infant	11Mr02BI
Michael	24	M	Laborer	11Mr02BI
Mary	20	F	Unknown	11Mr02BI
Hannah	18	F	Unknown	11Mr02BI

NAMES OF PASSENGERS	AGE	SEX	OCCUPATIONS	DATE PORT SHIP
COFFEE, Ann	12	F	Unknown	11Mr02BI
DONOHUE, Patrick	24	M	Laborer	11Mr02BI
DUNN, Mathew	28	M	Laborer	11Mr02BI
DOLAN, Edward	35	M	Laborer	11Mr02BI
COOK, Ann	16	F	Unknown	11Mr02BI
FARRELL, Mary-Ann	26	F	Unknown	11Mr02BI
Elizabeth	18	F	Unknown	11Mr02BI
Thomas	22	M	Laborer	11Mr02BI
Patrick	12	M	Unknown	11Mr02BI
DONAHUE, Owen	18	M	Laborer	11Mr02BI
BRADY, Michael	22	M	Laborer	11Mr02BI
REILLY, Hugh	24	M	Laborer	11Mr02BI
MOLLOY, Bridget	30	F	Unknown	11Mr02BI
SMITH, John	20	M	Cooper	11Mr02BI
MORAN, Patrick	26	M	Laborer	11Mr02BI
WALLACE, Edward	25	M	Laborer	11Mr02BI
Rose	18	F	Unknown	11Mr02BI
Walla--, Julia	16	F	Unknown	11Mr02BI
CONNETH, John	18	M	Laborer	11Mr02BI
FITZSIMMONS, John	18	M	Unknown	11Mr02BI
Jane	16	F	Unknown	11Mr02BI
COLEMAN, Bridget	30	F	Unknown	11Mr02BI
WYNN, Catherine	18	F	Unknown	11Mr02BI
FALLON, John	28	M	Laborer	11Mr02BI
ONEAL, John	21	M	Laborer	11Mr02BI
Bernard	7	M	Child	11Mr02BI
MCGINNIS, Hugh	18	M	Laborer	11Mr02BI
John	16	M	Unknown	11Mr02BI
MEHAN, James	24	M	Laborer	11Mr02BI
John	20	M	Laborer	11Mr02BI
Ann	16	F	Unknown	11Mr02BI
MCCORMICK, Patrick	28	M	Laborer	11Mr02BI
Rose	23	F	Unknown	11Mr02BI
CONALLY, Sarah	18	F	Unknown	11Mr02BI
MEHAN, Peter	18	M	Laborer	11Mr02BI
MCDONNELL, John	30	M	Doctor	11Mr02BI
U-Mrs.	25	F	Unknown	11Mr02BI
U	.00	U	Infant	11Mr02BI
PLUNKETT, Elizabeth	26	F	Unknown	11Mr02BI
MCDONNELL, Catherine	14	F	Unknown	11Mr02BI
REILLY, Thomas	21	M	Laborer	11Mr02BI
BARKER, George	26	M	Laborer	11Mr02BI
U-Mrs.	20	F	Unknown	11Mr02BI
QUINN, Henry	30	M	Laborer	11Mr02BI
Michael	27	M	Laborer	11Mr02BI
James	25	M	Laborer	11Mr02BI
Patrick	21	M	Laborer	11Mr02BI
Mary	23	F	Unknown	11Mr02BI
Catherine	15	F	Unknown	11Mr02BI
ELLIS, John	35	M	Laborer	11Mr02BI
MORLAND, John	21	M	Farmer	11Mr02BI
CLARK, Bridget	18	F	Unknown	11Mr02BI
MORIS, Patrick	21	M	Laborer	11Mr02BI
WELCH, Thomas	21	M	Laborer	11Mr02BI
KENT, Randell	44	M	Publican	11Mr02BI
Eliza	34	F	Unknown	11Mr02BI
Eliza	18	F	Unknown	11Mr02BI
Ann	14	F	Unknown	11Mr02BI
Priscilla	11	F	Unknown	11Mr02BI
William	8	M	Child	11Mr02BI
Randell	6	M	Child	11Mr02BI
Susan	5	F	Child	11Mr02BI
WEIS, Joseph	19	M	Laborer	11Mr02BI
TRAVIS, Mary	14	F	Unknown	11Mr02BI
PILLAN, Francis	30	M	Laborer	11Mr02BI
COFFEE, Margert-A.	19	F	Servant	11Mr02BI
Susan	16	F	Servant	11Mr02BI
Ellen	14	F	Unknown	11Mr02BI
REILLY, Peter	20	M	Laborer	11Mr02BI
Edward	14	M	Unknown	11Mr02BI
MCKEINNAN, Mary	30	F	Servant	11Mr02BI
Margeret	6	F	Child	11Mr02BI
Catherine	12	F	Unknown	11Mr02BI
CONELLY, Mary	35	F	Unknown	11Mr02BI
Ellen	23	F	Servant	11Mr02BI

NAMES OF PASSENGERS	AGE	SEX	OCCUPATIONS	DATE PORT SHIP
CONELLY, Bernard	16	M	Unknown	11Mr02Bl
FARREL, Bridget	25	F	Unknown	11Mr02Bl
DOONER, Patrick	21	M	Laborer	11Mr02Bl
Ellen	15	F	Unknown	11Mr02Bl
MCNAMEE, Peter	19	M	Laborer	11Mr02Bl
DALTON, Martin	19	M	Unknown	11Mr02Bl
TEOLEN, Catherine	30	F	Servant	11Mr02Bl
COFFEE, Martin	24	M	Laborer	11Mr02Bl
KEGAN, Micheal	30	M	Laborer	11Mr02Bl
CALLAGAN, Henry	24	M	Laborer	11Mr02Bl
FAY, Micheal	18	M	Laborer	11Mr02Bl
COURTNEY, Patrick	35	M	Laborer	11Mr02Bl
MCDERMOT, Edward	20	M	Laborer	11Mr02Bl
SOMERS, Peter	35	M	Laborer	11Mr02Bl
CORMICK, Rose	35	F	Unknown	11Mr02Bl
REILLY, Margeret	16	F	Servant	11Mr02Bl
Thomas	10	M	Unknown	11Mr02Bl
John	19	M	Unknown	11Mr02Bl
GAFNEY, Edward	30	M	Laborer	11Mr02Bl
U-Mrs.	38	F	Unknown	11Mr02Bl
U	.00	U	Infant	11Mr02Bl
Peter	2	M	Child	11Mr02Bl
TOBEN, Catherine	16	F	Servant	11Mr02Bl
CONNOR, Keran	33	M	Laborer	11Mr02Bl
U-Mrs.	30	F	Unknown	11Mr02Bl
James	7	M	Child	11Mr02Bl
Ann	26	F	Unknown	11Mr02Bl
TYRE, Bridget	20	F	Servant	11Mr02Bl
DADLEY, John	40	M	Laborer	11Mr02Bl
Bridget	40	F	Unknown	11Mr02Bl
Catherine	18	F	Unknown	11Mr02Bl
Bridget	16	F	Servant	11Mr02Bl
Ann	14	F	Unknown	11Mr02Bl
Micheal	12	M	Unknown	11Mr02Bl
Margaret	10	F	Unknown	11Mr02Bl
Rose	8	F	Child	11Mr02Bl
John	6	M	Child	11Mr02Bl
DOOLEY, John	28	M	Unknown	11Mr02Bl
Eliza	28	F	Unknown	11Mr02Bl
Susan	16	F	Unknown	11Mr02Bl
CUMMIN, Phillip	50	M	Unknown	11Mr02Bl
Luke	30	M	Unknown	11Mr02Bl
HOGAN, James	21	M	Unknown	11Mr02Bl

EXCELSIOR 12 MARCH 1850

From Liverpool

NAMES OF PASSENGERS	AGE	SEX	OCCUPATIONS	DATE PORT SHIP
SMITH, B.	00	M	Servant	12Mr02Fg
John	35	M	Gardener	12Mr02Fg
Mary	35	F	Gardener	12Mr02Fg
MCGARVY, Mary	24	F	Servant	12Mr02Fg
MCFOLEY, Peter	26	M	Farmer	12Mr02Fg
Rosey	21	F	Farmer	12Mr02Fg
Sally	19	F	Farmer	12Mr02Fg
MCCUSKEN, Mary	21	F	Servant	12Mr02Fg
CLARK, Jeremiah	22	M	Baker	12Mr02Fg
MURPHY, John	20	M	Farmer	12Mr02Fg
GUTTERY, George	20	M	Servant	12Mr02Fg
DORAN, Terrence	20	M	Servant	12Mr02Fg
BLAKE, John	20	M	Servant	12Mr02Fg
DUNN, Ann	40	F	Wi	12Mr02Fg
COUGHLIN, Patt	30	M	Servant	12Mr02Fg
Cathe.	25	F	Servant	12Mr02Fg
HOGAN, Ellen	18	F	Unknown	12Mr02Fg
COUGHLIN, John	1	M	Child	12Mr02Fg
MCMAHON, Mary	20	F	Servant	12Mr02Fg
Bridgt.	18	F	Servant	12Mr02Fg
MARTIN, John	35	M	Carpenter	12Mr02Fg
MCDONOUGH, Patt	27	M	Laborer	12Mr02Fg
GALLAGHER, Patt	24	M	Laborer	12Mr02Fg
DOLAN, Thomas	24	M	Tailor	12Mr02Fg
Margt.	20	F	Tailor	12Mr02Fg
Eliza	18	F	Tailor	12Mr02Fg
COYLE, Thomas	18	M	Tailor	12Mr02Fg
FEENEY, Darby	25	M	Tailor	12Mr02Fg
RATTIGAN, James	27	M	Tailor	12Mr02Fg
REILLY, Bridgt.	15	F	Servant	12Mr02Fg
MCCANN, Thomas	37	M	Laborer	12Mr02Fg
Elizh.	24	F	Laborer	12Mr02Fg
Mary	.00	F	Infant	12Mr02Fg
FAY, Patt	32	M	Laborer	12Mr02Fg
REILLY, Cathe.	20	F	Servant	12Mr02Fg
SMITH, Cathe.	20	F	Servant	12Mr02Fg
MCGUIRE, Charles	51	M	Farmer	12Mr02Fg
GAFFNEY, John	25	M	Laborer	12Mr02Fg
MCKEOWN, Rose	31	F	Wife	12Mr02Fg
Ann	8	F	Child	12Mr02Fg
Thos.	5	M	Child	12Mr02Fg
Rose	3	F	Child	12Mr02Fg
Elizh.	.00	F	Infant	12Mr02Fg
RYAN, James	17	M	Servant	12Mr02Fg
HENNY, Mary	20	F	Servant	12Mr02Fg
HOGAN, Mary	20	F	Servant	12Mr02Fg
ONEAL, Eliza	22	F	Servant	12Mr02Fg
CONNOLLY, Betsy	30	F	Servant	12Mr02Fg
Mary	8	F	Child	12Mr02Fg
PEAKLEY, Susan	21	F	Servant	12Mr02Fg
HAYNES, Timothy	20	M	Laborer	12Mr02Fg
HOPKINS, George	18	M	Servant	12Mr02Fg
KEATING, Cathe.	32	F	Servant	12Mr02Fg
John	13	M	Servant	12Mr02Fg
Ann	11	F	Servant	12Mr02Fg
BRAKAN, Cathe.	22	F	Servant	12Mr02Fg
STEPHENS, Mary	20	F	Servant	12Mr02Fg
CREATIN, Ellen	29	F	Servant	12Mr02Fg
GILCHRIST, Eliza.	19	F	Servant	12Mr02Fg
DUNSDIN, Ann	19	F	Servant	12Mr02Fg
CASEY, Mary	20	F	Servant	12Mr02Fg
HALLMAN, Winfd.	30	F	Servant	12Mr02Fg
James	14	M	Servant	12Mr02Fg
RYAN, Michl.	19	M	Laborer	12Mr02Fg
KINLEY, Margt.	19	F	Servant	12Mr02Fg
WILLIAMS, Cathe.	40	F	Servant	12Mr02Fg
REILLY, Margt.	20	F	Servant	12Mr02Fg
CARTLEY, Patt	18	M	Laborer	12Mr02Fg
OCONNELL, Hannah	18	F	Servant	12Mr02Fg
FAHY, Sarah	40	F	Servant	12Mr02Fg
MCBRIERTY, Mary	36	F	Wife	12Mr02Fg
James	.00	M	Infant	12Mr02Fg
FAHY, Hannah	13	F	Servant	12Mr02Fg
Bridgt.	9	F	Child	12Mr02Fg
BERAINE, Bridgt.	20	F	Servant	12Mr02Fg
HARLYNE, Bridgt.	23	F	Servant	12Mr02Fg
GILMORE, James	30	M	Servant	12Mr02Fg
SWEENEY, Cathe.	15	F	Servant	12Mr02Fg
DWYRE, Wm.	23	M	Farmer	12Mr02Fg
CAIN, Patt	15	M	Farmer	12Mr02Fg
SULLIVAN, Honora	24	F	Servant	12Mr02Fg
LANE, Cathe.	33	F	Servant	12Mr02Fg
KINNER, Ann	18	F	Servant	12Mr02Fg
HOLLAND, John	36	M	Farmer	12Mr02Fg
Ann	33	F	Farmer	12Mr02Fg
Cathe.	12	F	Farmer	12Mr02Fg
Thomas	10	M	Farmer	12Mr02Fg
Patt	7	F	Child	12Mr02Fg
John	4	M	Child	12Mr02Fg
Sally	17	F	Farmer	12Mr02Fg
Mary	18	F	Farmer	12Mr02Fg
DUFFY, Mary-A.	21	F	Milliner	12Mr02Fg
LOUGHLEY, Wm.	25	M	Tailor	12Mr02Fg
MARTIN, Patt	40	M	Farmer	12Mr02Fg
HUSSEY, John	26	M	Clerk	12Mr02Fg
FULHAM, Jane	36	F	Servant	12Mr02Fg

NAMES OF PASSENGERS	AGE	SEX	OCCUPATIONS	DATE PORT SHIP
RYAN, Simon	32	M	Tailor	12Mr02Fg
John	28	M	Tailor	12Mr02Fg
NAUGHTON, Mary	21	F	Bookbinder	12Mr02Fg
SAVAGE, Mary	20	F	Servant	12Mr02Fg
MOLENEY, James	22	M	Servant	12Mr02Fg
CONNOLLY, Bridgt.	20	F	Servant	12Mr02Fg
CRIMMIN, John	35	M	Laborer	12Mr02Fg
LONG, Barthm.	30	M	Laborer	12Mr02Fg
Mary	30	F	Servant	12Mr02Fg
David	26	M	Servant	12Mr02Fg
Margt.	26	F	Servant	12Mr02Fg
Jenny	6	F	Child	12Mr02Fg
Ellen	.00	F	Infant	12Mr02Fg
HARRINGTON, Mary	19	F	Servant	12Mr02Fg
CONNOR, Mary	44	F	Servant	12Mr02Fg
Mary	8	F	Child	12Mr02Fg
DOHERTY, Phillip	28	M	Servant	12Mr02Fg
Mary	23	F	Servant	12Mr02Fg
HICKEY, Daniel	28	M	Servant	12Mr02Fg
U-Mrs.	25	F	Servant	12Mr02Fg
Michl.	6	M	Child	12Mr02Fg
LITTLE, James	36	M	Smith	12Mr02Fg
HENNESEY, Timothy	55	M	Clerk	12Mr02Fg
CARMODY, Michl.	20	M	Laborer	12Mr02Fg
OWENS, Cathe.	30	F	Wife	12Mr02Fg
Mary	13	F	None	12Mr02Fg
Cathe.	3	F	Child	12Mr02Fg
COONEY, Patt	13	M	Servant	12Mr02Fg
Cathe.	11	F	Servant	12Mr02Fg
KELLY, Mary	19	F	Servant	12Mr02Fg
STEPHENS, Thomas	28	M	Shoemaker	12Mr02Fg
Maria	19	F	Shoemaker	12Mr02Fg
LORACHAN, Richd.	28	M	Laborer	12Mr02Fg
MCEWER, Cathe.	26	F	Servant	12Mr02Fg
DALY, Mick	13	M	Tailor	12Mr02Fg
Joseph	11	M	Tailor	12Mr02Fg
MURRAY, Maria	00	F	Servant	12Mr02Fg
MARTINS, Mary	00	F	Servant	12Mr02Fg
TREACY, Jerry	24	M	Servant	12Mr02Fg
HANGAN, Dennis	45	M	Farmer	12Mr02Fg
Dennis	24	M	Farmer	12Mr02Fg
Timothy	14	M	Farmer	12Mr02Fg
Mary-A.	15	F	Farmer	12Mr02Fg
Johanna	17	F	Farmer	12Mr02Fg
Cathe.	15	F	Farmer	12Mr02Fg
Thomas	13	M	Farmer	12Mr02Fg
Mary	11	F	Farmer	12Mr02Fg
Julia	17	F	Farmer	12Mr02Fg
Timothy	35	M	Farmer	12Mr02Fg
CONNELL, Hannah	22	F	Servant	12Mr02Fg
TOBIN, Gregery	30	M	Servant	12Mr02Fg
DONOGHOE, Bridgt.	36	F	Wife	12Mr02Fg
Sally	11	F	None	12Mr02Fg
Peter	9	M	Child	12Mr02Fg
Rosey	8	F	Child	12Mr02Fg
Patt	4	M	Child	12Mr02Fg
Cathe. Died-At-Sea	.00	F	Infant	12Mr02Fg
MCGILVIE, John	29	M	Baker	12Mr02Fg
MURRAY, Nancy	40	F	Wi	12Mr02Fg
Cathe.	16	F	None	12Mr02Fg
Patt	18	M	Servant	12Mr02Fg
DAWSON, Daniel	44	M	Stone Mason	12Mr02Fg
PENSY, Ellen	21	F	Dressmaker	12Mr02Fg
BRANNIN, Owen	30	M	Farmer	12Mr02Fg
BARNS, Michl.	32	M	Laborer	12Mr02Fg
FOLEY, Nancy	17	F	Servant	12Mr02Fg
ATKINSON, Robt.	25	M	Farmer	12Mr02Fg
Caroline	22	F	Farmer	12Mr02Fg
Eliza	.00	F	Infant	12Mr02Fg
KILCRAIN, Bgh.	17	F	Servant	12Mr02Fg
REYNOLDS, Ann	17	F	Servant	12Mr02Fg
CUSICK, John	15	M	Servant	12Mr02Fg
CONNELL, Bgh.	21	F	Servant	12Mr02Fg
DONOGHOE, John	4	M	Child	12Mr02Fg
REILLY, Ellen	13	F	Servant	12Mr02Fg

ASHBURTON 12 MARCH 1850

From Liverpool

NAMES OF PASSENGERS	AGE	SEX	OCCUPATIONS	DATE PORT SHIP
CROSS, Sarah	40	F	Laborer	12Mr02Bb
Sarah	21	F	Laborer	12Mr02Bb
John	8	M	Child	12Mr02Bb
John	.00	M	Infant	12Mr02Bb
KERR, John	20	M	Weaver	12Mr02Bb
FITZGERALD, Mary	21	F	Laborer	12Mr02Bb
Ann	9	F	Child	12Mr02Bb
Thos.	7	M	Child	12Mr02Bb
Edward	.00	M	Infant	12Mr02Bb
MAYNE, James	38	M	Miner	12Mr02Bb
HUSTEN, Wm.	26	M	Laborer	12Mr02Bb
Hannah	26	F	Laborer	12Mr02Bb
Joseph	.00	M	Infant	12Mr02Bb
WILLIAMSON, Saml.	25	M	Carpenter	12Mr02Bb
Eliza	22	F	Unknown	12Mr02Bb
Ann	2	F	Child	12Mr02Bb
Fanny	.00	F	Infant	12Mr02Bb
DALEY, Ann	17	M	Laborer	12Mr02Bb
BURKE, Honora	27	F	Unknown	12Mr02Bb
KELLEY, John	40	M	Unknown	12Mr02Bb
NEAL, Michl.B.	19	M	Baker	12Mr02Bb
LYON, James	20	M	Smith	12Mr02Bb
HALL, Wm.	22	M	Laborer	12Mr02Bb
VICTOR, Hugh	26	M	Unknown	12Mr02Bb
WALSH, Hugh	16	M	Shoemaker	12Mr02Bb
Ann	15	F	Unknown	12Mr02Bb
FENNELLY, Danl.	20	M	Laborer	12Mr02Bb
Mary	50	F	Laborer	12Mr02Bb
Margaret	18	F	Laborer	12Mr02Bb
Mary	16	F	Laborer	12Mr02Bb
Ellen	10	F	Laborer	12Mr02Bb
MOORE, Bridget	21	F	Laborer	12Mr02Bb
MENAN, Mary	38	F	Laborer	12Mr02Bb
Mary	13	F	Laborer	12Mr02Bb
Thos.	11	M	Laborer	12Mr02Bb
Wm.	1	M	Child	12Mr02Bb
DENNING, Wm.	29	M	Laborer	12Mr02Bb
MCKEON, Andrew	28	M	Laborer	12Mr02Bb
REILLY, Hugh	22	M	Laborer	12Mr02Bb
HAND, Pat	18	M	Laborer	12Mr02Bb
Ann	20	F	Laborer	12Mr02Bb
HYANS, Patrick	20	M	Laborer	12Mr02Bb
Lawrence	23	M	Laborer	12Mr02Bb
MATHEW, Phillip	21	M	Laborer	12Mr02Bb
CONNOR, Michl.	40	M	Farmer	12Mr02Bb
CUGAN, Bridget	17	F	Farmer	12Mr02Bb
MCGUINE, Thos.	20	M	Laborer	12Mr02Bb
John	17	M	Cooper	12Mr02Bb
Bridget	14	F	Cooper	12Mr02Bb
MCCARTHEY, Wm.	22	M	Laborer	12Mr02Bb
KERR, Wm.	23	M	Laborer	12Mr02Bb
Mary	21	F	Laborer	12Mr02Bb
CHRISTIE, John	22	M	Farmer	12Mr02Bb
HORNER, Ann	30	F	Laborer	12Mr02Bb
Ann	28	F	Laborer	12Mr02Bb
MCBRIDE, Margt.	35	F	Laborer	12Mr02Bb
Mathew	10	M	Laborer	12Mr02Bb
RYAN, John	18	M	Laborer	12Mr02Bb
NOLAN, Thos.	21	M	Victualler	12Mr02Bb
John	29	M	Victualler	12Mr02Bb
HONON, Eliza	19	F	Laborer	12Mr02Bb
CLEARY, Mary	20	F	Laborer	12Mr02Bb
CONELY, Cathn.	21	F	Laborer	12Mr02Bb

NAMES OF PASSENGERS	AGE	SEX	OCCUPATIONS	DATE PORT SHIP
TIGH, Mary	18	F	Laborer	12Mr02Bb
FRAN, Pat	20	M	Laborer	12Mr02Bb
MCNALLY, Pat	21	M	Laborer	12Mr02Bb
REILLY, Ann	18	F	Dressmaker	12Mr02Bb
Judith	20	F	Dressmaker	12Mr02Bb
DUNN, Dennis	25	M	Laborer	12Mr02Bb
FINNALL, John	41	M	Farmer	12Mr02Bb
BROWN, Saml.	24	M	Farmer	12Mr02Bb
ROACH, Jas.	30	M	Farmer	12Mr02Bb
Pat	32	M	Tinker	12Mr02Bb
DONOHUE, Betsey	21	F	Laborer	12Mr02Bb
Ellen	19	F	Laborer	12Mr02Bb
HEYDEN, Margt.	16	F	Laborer	12Mr02Bb
BREWSTHER, Ed.	22	M	Gdnr	12Mr02Bb
Bridget	20	F	Gdnr	12Mr02Bb
QUIN, Mary	20	F	Laborer	12Mr02Bb
SUMMERS, James	25	M	Laborer	12Mr02Bb
MAHER, Michl.	25	M	Laborer	12Mr02Bb
CURTIS, Michl.	40	M	Laborer	12Mr02Bb
BYRNE, Arthur	21	M	Laborer	12Mr02Bb
PICKETT, Thos.	20	M	Laborer	12Mr02Bb
MAHON, Byron	40	M	Laborer	12Mr02Bb
LEE, Elizabeth	25	F	Laborer	12Mr02Bb
JOHNSTON, John	31	M	Plasterer	12Mr02Bb
DOYLE, John	26	M	Laborer	12Mr02Bb
DELANEY, Betty	21	F	Laborer	12Mr02Bb
SMITH, Eliza	30	F	Laborer	12Mr02Bb
SEXTON, John	20	M	Smith	12Mr02Bb
Ann	22	F	Smith	12Mr02Bb
Ann	23	F	Smith	12Mr02Bb
Mary	16	F	Laborer	12Mr02Bb
Terence	14	M	Laborer	12Mr02Bb
CLARKE, Pat	18	M	Laborer	12Mr02Bb
MCCARTHY, Michl.	20	M	Laborer	12Mr02Bb
FINN, Thos.	24	M	Laborer	12Mr02Bb
Died-At-Sea				
MCMAHON, Henry	20	M	Laborer	12Mr02Bb
GILMORE, John	18	M	Laborer	12Mr02Bb
WILLIAM, John	13	M	Laborer	12Mr02Bb
WATTS, Geo.	17	M	Plasterer	12Mr02Bb
MCGAHAGAN, Jas.	23	M	Laborer	12Mr02Bb
Christ.	20	M	Laborer	12Mr02Bb
Cathn.	16	F	Laborer	12Mr02Bb
Peter	9	M	Child	12Mr02Bb
Margaret	8	F	Child	12Mr02Bb
MALEY, Jos.	45	M	Laborer	12Mr02Bb
Mary	40	F	Laborer	12Mr02Bb
Martha	10	F	Laborer	12Mr02Bb
Biddy	8	F	Child	12Mr02Bb
John	7	M	Child	12Mr02Bb
MCKENNA, Mary	20	F	Laborer	12Mr02Bb
COX, Wm.	40	M	Shoemaker	12Mr02Bb
Ann	36	F	Laborer	12Mr02Bb
Patk.	9	M	Child	12Mr02Bb
DEVINE, Ann	7	F	Child	12Mr02Bb
KEVELAN, James	17	M	Laborer	12Mr02Bb
DALEY, Michl.	23	M	Laborer	12Mr02Bb
COSSACK, Burthe	20	M	Laborer	12Mr02Bb
FLANAGAN, Michl.	35	M	Laborer	12Mr02Bb
Cathn.	25	F	Laborer	12Mr02Bb
MCNANE, Mary	55	F	Laborer	12Mr02Bb
MURPHY, Bridgt.	55	F	Laborer	12Mr02Bb
John	22	M	Laborer	12Mr02Bb
Biddy	15	F	Laborer	12Mr02Bb
Betsy	13	F	Laborer	12Mr02Bb
MCNAME, Peter	7	M	Child	12Mr02Bb
TROY, Pat	23	M	Child	12Mr02Bb
STONE, Robt.	30	M	Weaver	12Mr02Bb
STEPHENS, Richd.	25	M	Weaver	12Mr02Bb
TAYLOR, Arthur	32	M	Weaver	12Mr02Bb
HANNAH, James	35	M	Farmer	12Mr02Bb
WHELAN, Wm.	20	M	Farmer	12Mr02Bb
PILE, John	40	M	Smith	12Mr02Bb
MCCALIN, John	43	M	Laborer	12Mr02Bb
BENNETT, Thos.	25	M	Farmer	12Mr02Bb
HIGGINS, Thos.	22	M	Farmer	12Mr02Bb
BYRNES, Bridgt.	40	F	Laborer	12Mr02Bb
Anthy.	12	M	Laborer	12Mr02Bb
Mary	10	F	Laborer	12Mr02Bb
MARTIN, Michl.	38	M	Laborer	12Mr02Bb
KELLY, Martin	32	M	Laborer	12Mr02Bb
MARTIN, Jas.	13	M	Laborer	12Mr02Bb
MALONEY, Michl.	24	M	Laborer	12Mr02Bb
THOMAS, Phillip	24	M	Laborer	12Mr02Bb
Margaret	18	F	Laborer	12Mr02Bb
LOUGHLIN, Ellen	20	F	Laborer	12Mr02Bb
HEWETT, Olivia	26	F	Dressmaker	12Mr02Bb
Susan	8	F	Child	12Mr02Bb
COSTELLO, Thos.	52	M	Farmer	12Mr02Bb
Thos.	22	M	Farmer	12Mr02Bb
Terence	20	M	Farmer	12Mr02Bb
John	18	M	Farmer	12Mr02Bb
Ellen	16	F	Farmer	12Mr02Bb
CONNER, Maria	22	F	Laborer	12Mr02Bb
Terence	16	M	Laborer	12Mr02Bb
Honora	23	F	Laborer	12Mr02Bb
DALTON, Bridget	42	F	Laborer	12Mr02Bb
MONAGAN, Ann	23	F	Servant	12Mr02Bb
Julia	17	F	Laborer	12Mr02Bb
Ed.	18	M	Laborer	12Mr02Bb
HOSEY, Ann	40	F	Laborer	12Mr02Bb
STEVANS, Jas.	28	M	Laborer	12Mr02Bb
Sophia	28	F	Laborer	12Mr02Bb
HANNAH, John	20	M	Laborer	12Mr02Bb
Mary-Ann	18	F	Laborer	12Mr02Bb
Ellen	15	F	Laborer	12Mr02Bb
CANAHER, Hugh	27	M	Groom	12Mr02Bb
Michl.	20	M	Laborer	12Mr02Bb
Bridget	16	F	Laborer	12Mr02Bb
MCARDLE, Owen	30	M	Groom	12Mr02Bb
MEHAN, Ann	16	F	Unknown	12Mr02Bb
MCCALA, Rosey	26	F	Laborer	12Mr02Bb
CONNELLY, Cath.	29	F	Laborer	12Mr02Bb
MOORSHEND, Ann	28	F	Laborer	12Mr02Bb
MOORHEAD, Francis	28	F	Laborer	12Mr02Bb
MCCALEE, John	36	M	Laborer	12Mr02Bb
CLARKE, Thos.	21	M	Laborer	12Mr02Bb
MCAULIFFE, Richd.	30	M	Laborer	12Mr02Bb
Chas.	23	M	Laborer	12Mr02Bb
Cathn.	24	F	Laborer	12Mr02Bb
Timothy	8	M	Child	12Mr02Bb
John	6	M	Child	12Mr02Bb
Cathn.	.00	F	Infant	12Mr02Bb
MCKENNA, James	47	M	Laborer	12Mr02Bb
Rosa-Mrs.	40	F	Laborer	12Mr02Bb
James	12	M	Laborer	12Mr02Bb
CANAHER, Ann	20	F	Laborer	12Mr02Bb
REILLY, Joseph	30	M	Farmer	12Mr02Bb
Mary-Ann	26	F	Farmer	12Mr02Bb
Ellen	.00	F	Infant	12Mr02Bb
Thomas	23	M	Farmer	12Mr02Bb
Charles	18	M	Farmer	12Mr02Bb
John	17	M	Farmer	12Mr02Bb
Jane	27	F	Farmer	12Mr02Bb
Ellen	20	F	Farmer	12Mr02Bb
Fanny	13	F	Farmer	12Mr02Bb
Wm.	10	M	Farmer	12Mr02Bb
Thomas	6	M	Child	12Mr02Bb
FARLEY, John	12	M	Laborer	12Mr02Bb
GLUMON, Michl.	20	M	Laborer	12Mr02Bb
BROWN, Michl.	24	M	Laborer	12Mr02Bb
CLANCY, Richd.	21	M	Laborer	12Mr02Bb
DRITIGG, Margt.	20	F	Laborer	12Mr02Bb
FLEMING, Margt.	20	F	Laborer	12Mr02Bb
MANNING, Cathn.	25	F	Laborer	12Mr02Bb
Corns.	.00	M	Infant	12Mr02Bb
BRANAGAN, Dennis	40	M	Accountant	12Mr02Bb
COMONS, Wm.	30	M	Laborer	12Mr02Bb
FORD, Julia	22	F	Laborer	12Mr02Bb
Mary	24	F	Laborer	12Mr02Bb

NAMES OF PASSENGERS	AGE	SEX	OCCUPATIONS	DATE PORT SHIP
FORD, Michl.	.00	M	Infant	12Mr02Bb
BARKENWELL, John	20	M	Laborer	12Mr02Bb
Richd.	22	M	Laborer	12Mr02Bb
James	11	M	Laborer	12Mr02Bb
MORAN, Danl.	20	M	Laborer	12Mr02Bb
DOYLE, Ann	25	F	Laborer	12Mr02Bb
COSGRIEF, Margt.	19	F	Laborer	12Mr02Bb
FLANAGAN, John	30	M	Laborer	12Mr02Bb
Elizbth.	31	F	Laborer	12Mr02Bb
SMITH, Eliza	31	F	Laborer	12Mr02Bb
DOWNEY, Judith	29	F	Laborer	12Mr02Bb
HOFFIN, Thos.	23	M	Farmer	12Mr02Bb
CLIFTON, John	22	M	Farmer	12Mr02Bb
JOHNSTONE, Robt.	19	M	Farmer	12Mr02Bb
WARD, Michl.	14	M	Laborer	12Mr02Bb
CODY, Bridget	46	F	Laborer	12Mr02Bb
Mary	18	F	Laborer	12Mr02Bb
ODONNELL, Bridget	30	F	Laborer	12Mr02Bb
Mary	19	F	Laborer	12Mr02Bb
Ellen	6	F	Child	12Mr02Bb
KELLEY, Timothy	20	M	Farmer	12Mr02Bb
FARRELL, Thos.	21	M	Laborer	12Mr02Bb
CONDEN, James	38	M	Laborer	12Mr02Bb
Mary	30	F	Laborer	12Mr02Bb
Michl.	39	F	Laborer	12Mr02Bb
WALSH, Mick	38	F	Laborer	12Mr02Bb
Mick	26	F	Laborer	12Mr02Bb
John	20	F	Laborer	12Mr02Bb
John	.00	M	Infant	12Mr02Bb
FAHEY, John	35	M	Laborer	12Mr02Bb
Cathn.	30	F	Laborer	12Mr02Bb
Bridgt.	5	F	Child	12Mr02Bb
Tim	.00	M	Infant	12Mr02Bb
HALORAN, Martin	13	M	Laborer	12Mr02Bb
QUINLAN, John	28	M	Laborer	12Mr02Bb
CARROLL, Mary	28	F	Laborer	12Mr02Bb
Mary	.00	F	Infant	12Mr02Bb
BURNES, Ed.	17	M	Laborer	12Mr02Bb
BLEAHAN, Mary	16	F	Laborer	12Mr02Bb
OBRIEN, Mary	50	F	Laborer	12Mr02Bb
John	16	M	Laborer	12Mr02Bb
CLEARY, Wm.	3	M	Child	12Mr02Bb
WALLACE, Mary	40	F	Laborer	12Mr02Bb
Richd.	12	M	Laborer	12Mr02Bb
Mary	10	F	Laborer	12Mr02Bb
MCCONAGHY, Mary	35	F	Laborer	12Mr02Bb
John	10	M	Laborer	12Mr02Bb
Bernard	8	M	Child	12Mr02Bb
BURKE, Patk.	17	M	Laborer	12Mr02Bb
Ellen	19	F	Laborer	12Mr02Bb
GEGAN, Patk.	20	M	Laborer	12Mr02Bb
Ed.	18	M	Laborer	12Mr02Bb
CANN, Elizabeth	27	F	Laborer	12Mr02Bb
John	7	M	Child	12Mr02Bb
Stephan	2	F	Child	12Mr02Bb
FLOCTON, Thos.	15	M	Laborer	12Mr02Bb
BOYLE, Michl.	10	M	Laborer	12Mr02Bb
SHEN, Ellen	13	F	Servant	12Mr02Bb
FRAY, Cathn.	12	F	Servant	12Mr02Bb
BRADLY, Margt.	50	F	Servant	12Mr02Bb
Jane	20	F	Servant	12Mr02Bb
BALDWIN, John	28	M	Servant	12Mr02Bb
HALLORAN, Dennis	28	M	Servant	12Mr02Bb
KELLY, James	17	M	Servant	12Mr02Bb
COLLINS, Johanna	16	F	Servant	12Mr02Bb
THOMAS, Joseph	26	M	Cvr-Gldr	12Mr02Bb
Emily	26	F	Cvr-Gldr	12Mr02Bb
Mary	2	F	Child	12Mr02Bb
Elizabeth	.00	F	Infant	12Mr02Bb
GRIGSON, Wm.	23	M	Smith	12Mr02Bb
WHITELY, Joseph	32	M	Carpenter	12Mr02Bb
Elizbth.	28	F	Carpenter	12Mr02Bb
Mary	26	F	Dressmaker	12Mr02Bb
Martha	21	F	Dressmaker	12Mr02Bb
Ann	24	F	Cook	12Mr02Bb
ROSE, Wm.	28	M	Engineer	12Mr02Bb
PHILLIPS, Mary	51	F	Laborer	12Mr02Bb
MURRAY, Michl.	20	M	Laborer	12Mr02Bb
LEARY, Michl.	35	M	Laborer	12Mr02Bb
Alice	36	F	Laborer	12Mr02Bb
Alice	22	F	Laborer	12Mr02Bb
Patk.	19	M	Laborer	12Mr02Bb
KENNEDY, James	39	M	Laborer	12Mr02Bb
CARNEY, Michl.	30	M	Laborer	12Mr02Bb
Died-At-Sea				
BURKE, Ann	23	F	Laborer	12Mr02Bb
TREUMAN, Mary-Mrs.	40	F	Laborer	12Mr02Bb
Augustus	13	M	Laborer	12Mr02Bb
Byron	10	M	Laborer	12Mr02Bb
Fegan	6	M	Child	12Mr02Bb
Ada	3	F	Child	12Mr02Bb
Isabela	2	F	Child	12Mr02Bb
RICE, Peter	40	M	Unknown	12Mr02Bb
HOLLAND, James	21	M	Unknown	12Mr02Bb
HENDERSON, Eliza	18	F	Laborer	12Mr02Bb
MCCOWEN, Danl.	23	M	Unknown	12Mr02Bb
CONNER, John	20	M	Laborer	12Mr02Bb
DOHERTY, W.H.	45	M	Clergyman	12Mr02Bb
Marieanna	40	F	Unknown	12Mr02Bb
Isabella	9	F	Child	12Mr02Bb
Marieannna	8	F	Child	12Mr02Bb
Robt.	6	M	Child	12Mr02Bb
Emily-J.	.00	F	Infant	12Mr02Bb
EDGE, Mather-L.	25	M	Gentleman	12Mr02Bb
SWALES, John-B.	29	M	Gentleman	12Mr02Bb
ODONNELL, John-P.	40	M	Gentleman	12Mr02Bb
Thos.S.	31	M	Gentleman	12Mr02Bb
MCNEICE, Saml.L.	23	M	Gentleman	12Mr02Bb

SWITZERLAND 13 MARCH 1850

From London

NAMES OF PASSENGERS	AGE	SEX	OCCUPATIONS	DATE PORT SHIP
GLUM, Michael	31	M	Laborer	13Mr06Fj
MCCARTY, John	30	M	Laborer	13Mr06Fj
GLEASON, Patrick	32	M	Smith	13Mr06Fj
JONES, William	44	M	Lrfh	13Mr06Fj

ABERDEEN 13 MARCH 1850

From Liverpool

NAMES OF PASSENGERS	AGE	SEX	OCCUPATIONS	DATE PORT SHIP
FITZGERALD, Robt.	30	M	Farmer	13Mr02Fn
TOBIN, Grace	25	F	Servant	13Mr02Fn
HORAN, Ann	16	F	Servant	13Mr02Fn
CARROLL, Pat	28	M	Laborer	13Mr02Fn
FITZPATRICK, Dennis	20	M	Mechanic	13Mr02Fn
MILAN, Peter	28	M	Laborer	13Mr02Fn
ROURKE, John	30	M	Laborer	13Mr02Fn
LYONS, Daniel	30	M	Laborer	13Mr02Fn
RYAN, James	20	M	Farmer	13Mr02Fn
BYRNE, Andrew	19	M	Laborer	13Mr02Fn
RUSSEL, Patrick	21	M	Laborer	13Mr02Fn
COONEY, Martin	40	M	Laborer	13Mr02Fn
SMITH, James	24	M	Laborer	13Mr02Fn
CLAN, Darby	16	M	Laborer	13Mr02Fn
CONNOLLY, Mary	20	F	Laborer	13Mr02Fn
HILLEN, Michael	28	M	Laborer	13Mr02Fn

NAMES OF PASSENGERS		AGE	SEX	OCCUPATIONS	DATE PORT SHIP
GANALIN, John		24	M	Laborer	13Mr02Fn
Patt		22	M	Laborer	13Mr02Fn
RAFFERTY, James		19	M	Laborer	13Mr02Fn
FLANNERY, Margaret		30	F	Laborer	13Mr02Fn
CATON, Mary		28	F	Laborer	13Mr02Fn
MADDEN, Catherine		16	F	Laborer	13Mr02Fn
HOBBINS, Catherine		12	F	Laborer	13Mr02Fn
DOLAN, Mary-Ann		15	F	Laborer	13Mr02Fn
FRASEY, Bridget		16	F	Laborer	13Mr02Fn
FROCTON, Thomas		28	M	Laborer	13Mr02Fn
Bridget		20	F	Wife	13Mr02Fn
MORRISON, Michael		26	M	Laborer	13Mr02Fn
CLARK, John		26	M	Laborer	13Mr02Fn
KERNAN, Catherine		20	F	Laborer	13Mr02Fn
HUGHES, Patrick		50	M	Laborer	13Mr02Fn
Owen		20	M	Laborer	13Mr02Fn
Patrick		16	M	Laborer	13Mr02Fn
Margaret		11	F	Laborer	13Mr02Fn
MURPHY, Pat		26	M	Laborer	13Mr02Fn
MURRAY, Bridget		20	F	Laborer	13Mr02Fn
MAHONY, John		37	M	Laborer	13Mr02Fn
OGRADY, Henry		24	M	Laborer	13Mr02Fn
FAGAN, John		23	M	Laborer	13Mr02Fn
James		18	M	Laborer	13Mr02Fn
MALONE, William		24	M	Laborer	13Mr02Fn
KAVANNAH, Mathew		26	M	Laborer	13Mr02Fn
NEILL, Pat		24	M	Laborer	13Mr02Fn
LYNCH, Pat		24	M	Laborer	13Mr02Fn
DONNEGAN, Peter		28	M	Laborer	13Mr02Fn
Bridget		25	F	Wife	13Mr02Fn
SMITH, Catherine		50	F	Unknown	13Mr02Fn
Died-At-Sea					
LEDDY, Pat		24	M	Laborer	13Mr02Fn
HANNESY, Thos.		16	M	Laborer	13Mr02Fn
BYRNE, Martin		35	M	Laborer	13Mr02Fn
FORD, Biddy		26	F	Laborer	13Mr02Fn
MCMULLEN, Lucinda		22	F	Laborer	13Mr02Fn
COCKRANE, Robt.		26	M	Laborer	13Mr02Fn
SMITH, John		25	M	Laborer	13Mr02Fn
HIGGINS, Michael		19	M	Laborer	13Mr02Fn
MCCARTHY, Chesty		25	M	Laborer	13Mr02Fn
Dennis		17	M	Laborer	13Mr02Fn
WALSH, Edward		18	M	Laborer	13Mr02Fn
DWYER, Anthony		26	M	Laborer	13Mr02Fn
HICKY, Catherine		20	F	Laborer	13Mr02Fn
SLATTERLY, James		35	M	Laborer	13Mr02Fn
Ellen	(W)	35	F	Wife	13Mr02Fn
CLANCY, Catherine		34	F	Unknown	13Mr02Fn
MCGIVNY, Peter		18	M	Laborer	13Mr02Fn
FINNEGAN, Mary		25	F	Laborer	13Mr02Fn
RICHARDSON, John		20	M	Laborer	13Mr02Fn
Mary		20	F	Wife	13Mr02Fn
Anne	(D)	9	F	Child	13Mr02Fn
Michael	(S)	2	M	Child	13Mr02Fn
John	(S)	.00	M	Infant	13Mr02Fn
Michael		20	M	Laborer	13Mr02Fn
Margaret		18	F	Laborer	13Mr02Fn
CAIN, May		14	F	Laborer	13Mr02Fn
DEVIN, John		19	M	Mechanic	13Mr02Fn
LAFFY, Festus		24	M	Laborer	13Mr02Fn
HENSON, Michael		44	M	Mechanic	13Mr02Fn
HANDY, Pat		21	M	Laborer	13Mr02Fn
FOGARTY, Pat		23	M	Laborer	13Mr02Fn
Michael		24	M	Laborer	13Mr02Fn
MEEHAN, James		23	M	Laborer	13Mr02Fn
HARRIS, Richard		21	M	Laborer	13Mr02Fn
BYRNE, Michael		19	M	Laborer	13Mr02Fn
BRADY, John		26	M	Laborer	13Mr02Fn
BANDY, James		28	M	Laborer	13Mr02Fn
Mary		20	F	Laborer	13Mr02Fn
FARRELL, Timothy		22	M	Mechanic	13Mr02Fn
Thos.		20	M	Student	13Mr02Fn
HYLAND, Margaret		25	F	Laborer	13Mr02Fn
SMITH, Edward		20	M	Farmer	13Mr02Fn
George		21	M	Farmer	13Mr02Fn

NAMES OF PASSENGERS		AGE	SEX	OCCUPATIONS	DATE PORT SHIP
CUMMINS, Peter		10	M	Unknown	13Mr02Fn
James		8	M	Child	13Mr02Fn
Catherine		6	F	Sister	13Mr02Fn
ENNIS, John		28	M	Laborer	13Mr02Fn
Mary		22	F	Wife	13Mr02Fn
James	(S)	.00	M	Infant	13Mr02Fn
SAPHAM, Michael		35	M	Laborer	13Mr02Fn
SKELLY, John		19	M	Laborer	13Mr02Fn
MCMAHON, Thomas		21	M	Laborer	13Mr02Fn
MANNIN, John		24	M	Laborer	13Mr02Fn
CONROY, John		24	M	Laborer	13Mr02Fn
Elizabeth	(W)	22	F	Wife	13Mr02Fn
ONELL, James	(W)	34	M	Laborer	13Mr02Fn
FEENY, Bridget	(W)	38	F	Unknown	13Mr02Fn
HAMILL, Pat		16	M	Laborer	13Mr02Fn
MCARDLE, Bridget		17	F	Laborer	13Mr02Fn
GRAHAM, Susan		18	F	Laborer	13Mr02Fn
GAFFRY, Michael		50	M	Laborer	13Mr02Fn
Rose	(W)	50	F	Wife	13Mr02Fn
Thomas	(S)	25	M	Unknown	13Mr02Fn
Mary	(D)	20	F	Unknown	13Mr02Fn
Rose	(D)	10	F	Unknown	13Mr02Fn
FOLY, John		47	M	Laborer	13Mr02Fn
Mary	(D)	16	F	Unknown	13Mr02Fn
William	(S)	13	M	Unknown	13Mr02Fn
MCLEDDY, Pat		38	M	Laborer	13Mr02Fn
Mary	(W)	34	F	Wife	13Mr02Fn
Mary	(D)	12	F	Unknown	13Mr02Fn
Owen	(S)	10	M	Unknown	13Mr02Fn
Elizabeth	(D)	6	F	Child	13Mr02Fn
Margaret	(D)	3	F	Child	13Mr02Fn
Marcella	(D)	.00	F	Infant	13Mr02Fn
CULLEN, Michael		50	M	Victualler	13Mr02Fn
KENNEDY, Mary		25	M	Laborer	13Mr02Fn
Mary	(D)	11	F	Unknown	13Mr02Fn
RELLY, William		24	M	Laborer	13Mr02Fn
Bridget		24	F	Wife	13Mr02Fn
KINGSBURY, John		25	M	Laborer	13Mr02Fn
James		20	M	Laborer	13Mr02Fn
Mary-Anne		18	F	Laborer	13Mr02Fn
ALLEN, Mary		18	F	Laborer	13Mr02Fn
SKIFFINGTON, Pat		21	M	Mechanic	13Mr02Fn
TRAINOR, John		28	M	Laborer	13Mr02Fn
RIELLY, Mary		15	F	Unknown	13Mr02Fn
Bernard		12	F	Unknown	13Mr02Fn
Edward		10	M	Unknown	13Mr02Fn
BOYLAND, Charles		24	M	Mechanic	13Mr02Fn
MARTIN, Mathew		20	M	Miner	13Mr02Fn
CASEY, Pat		17	M	Laborer	13Mr02Fn
Catherine		15	F	Sister	13Mr02Fn
HILL, Anne		26	F	Servant	13Mr02Fn
REID, James		50	M	Laborer	13Mr02Fn
KELLY, John		22	M	Laborer	13Mr02Fn
FLANNAGAN, William		20	M	Laborer	13Mr02Fn
Mary		18	F	Sister	13Mr02Fn
JOICE, Martin		21	M	Laborer	13Mr02Fn
Mary		40	F	Unknown	13Mr02Fn
Mary		20	F	Sister	13Mr02Fn
Mary		9	F	Child	13Mr02Fn
MCANELLY, James		60	M	Unknown	13Mr02Fn
Died-At-Sea					
Francis		27	M	Laborer	13Mr02Fn
Thomas		20	M	Laborer	13Mr02Fn
Mary		16	F	Laborer	13Mr02Fn
Francis		5	M	Child	13Mr02Fn
DAILY, John		19	M	Laborer	13Mr02Fn
CONNOLLY, Henry		24	M	Mariner	13Mr02Fn
HARRIS, William		21	M	Mariner	13Mr02Fn
CONNOLLY, Mary		22	F	Wife	13Mr02Fn
HARRIS, Betty		17	F	Laborer	13Mr02Fn
Anne		18	F	Laborer	13Mr02Fn
CRAWFORD, Eliza		16	F	Laborer	13Mr02Fn
David		50	M	Laborer	13Mr02Fn
Mary	(W)	50	F	Wife	13Mr02Fn
Elizabeth	(D)	16	F	Daughter	13Mr02Fn

NAMES OF PASSENGERS		AGE	SEX	OCCUPATIONS	DATE PORT SHIP
CRAWFORD, Susan	(D)	17	F	Daughter	13Mr02Fn
William	(S)	25	M	Son	13Mr02Fn
HART, Peter		21	M	Laborer	13Mr02Fn
MORGAN, John		20	M	Laborer	13Mr02Fn
COSGROVE, Anthony		20	M	Laborer	13Mr02Fn
MERRY, Dominick		25	M	Laborer	13Mr02Fn
HUGHES, James		25	M	Laborer	13Mr02Fn
FLYNN, Cornelius		28	M	Mechanic	13Mr02Fn
HYNES, William		38	M	Laborer	13Mr02Fn
KELLY, Charles		20	M	Laborer	13Mr02Fn
William		11	M	Brother	13Mr02Fn
BRENNAN, Joseph		28	M	Mechanic	13Mr02Fn
FANNAN, Marcella		26	F	Laborer	13Mr02Fn
PINION, James		21	M	Mechanic	13Mr02Fn
LYNCHAN, Edward		22	M	Laborer	13Mr02Fn
FENNETY, Edward		32	M	Laborer	13Mr02Fn
MILLS, James		23	M	Laborer	13Mr02Fn
KELLY, Peter		30	M	Mechanic	13Mr02Fn
Catherine		24	F	Wife	13Mr02Fn
r Margaret	(D)	.00	F	Infant	13Mr02Fn
CUMMINS, Honora		16	F	Mechanic	13Mr02Fn
KENNEDY, Edward		23	M	Mechanic	13Mr02Fn
KELLY, Thomas		19	M	Mechanic	13Mr02Fn
DOWD, James		18	M	Laborer	13Mr02Fn
HART, Michael		14	M	Laborer	13Mr02Fn
SMITH, Pat		18	M	Laborer	13Mr02Fn
HAGAN, James		21	M	Laborer	13Mr02Fn
CONNER, Daniel		22	M	Laborer	13Mr02Fn
DILLON, Richard		27	M	Laborer	13Mr02Fn
CONDON, Eliza		13	M	Laborer	13Mr02Fn
THOMPSON, Wm.H.		31	M	Merchant	13Mr02Fn
GRAY, Daniel		40	M	Unknown	13Mr02Fn
Died-At-Sea					
IVORY, Daniel		18	M	Laborer	13Mr02Fn
Margaret		16	F	Sister	13Mr02Fn
COLLINS, Thomas		20	M	Laborer	13Mr02Fn
CONDON, Margaret		20	F	Laborer	13Mr02Fn
SWEENY, Thomas		13	M	Laborer	13Mr02Fn
MARTIN, John		30	M	Teacher	13Mr02Fn
MCCRUM, Saml.		26	M	Laborer	13Mr02Fn
DOOLY, Margaret		30	F	Laborer	13Mr02Fn
MCCRUM, Agnes		40	F	Unknown	13Mr02Fn
Robt.		19	M	Laborer	13Mr02Fn
John		13	M	Laborer	13Mr02Fn
Hugh		12	M	Laborer	13Mr02Fn
Johanna		11	F	Sister	13Mr02Fn
QUIRK, Mary	(C)	21	F	Cousin	13Mr02Fn
ANDERSON, Thos.		21	M	Laborer	13Mr02Fn
Bella-Jane		19	F	Wife	13Mr02Fn
WRIGHT, James		30	M	Mechanic	13Mr02Fn
ONEILL, Cath.		30	F	Mechanic	13Mr02Fn
KEEFE, Mary		17	F	Laborer	13Mr02Fn
COFFY, Bessy		18	F	Laborer	13Mr02Fn
CULLEY, Mathew		50	M	Laborer	13Mr02Fn
DELANY, Essey		20	F	Laborer	13Mr02Fn
SAWLOR, Bridget		25	F	Laborer	13Mr02Fn
MCLAUGHLON, Bridget		19	F	Laborer	13Mr02Fn
MAHAN, Maria		30	F	Laborer	13Mr02Fn
CULLEY, Michael		18	M	Laborer	13Mr02Fn
BLASSET, Jane		19	F	Laborer	13Mr02Fn
GARRATY, James		21	M	Laborer	13Mr02Fn
Mary	(W)	19	F	Wife	13Mr02Fn
DILLON, Cath.		52	F	Laborer	13Mr02Fn
Ellen	(D)	14	F	Daughter	13Mr02Fn
Elizabeth		8	F	Child	13Mr02Fn
Jane		7	F	Child	13Mr02Fn
DELANY, Dennis		60	M	Laborer	13Mr02Fn
Margaret	(W)	55	F	Wife	13Mr02Fn
Patrick	(S)	21	M	Son	13Mr02Fn
Esther	(D)	00	F	Daughter	13Mr02Fn
DOOLY, John		21	M	Laborer	13Mr02Fn
MCCABE, Cath.		20	F	Laborer	13Mr02Fn
DOOLY, Danl.		20	M	Laborer	13Mr02Fn
KILLILAN, Rose		33	F	Laborer	13Mr02Fn
Rose-Ann		11	F	Daughter	13Mr02Fn
KILLILAN, Henry	(S)	9	M	Child	13Mr02Fn
Mary-Anne	(D)	7	F	Child	13Mr02Fn
Eliza	(D)	6	F	Child	13Mr02Fn
John	(S)	2	M	Child	13Mr02Fn
Edward	(S)	.00	M	Infant	13Mr02Fn
HORGAN, John		35	M	Laborer	13Mr02Fn
Mary	(W)	33	F	Wife	13Mr02Fn
Margaret		30	F	Sister	13Mr02Fn
Timothy	(S)	6	M	Child	13Mr02Fn
Ellen	(D)	4	F	Child	13Mr02Fn
HOYTON, Mary		66	F	Laborer	13Mr02Fn
Richard		27	M	Mechanic	13Mr02Fn
Patrick	(N)	10	M	Nephew	13Mr02Fn
Edward	(N)	8	M	Child	13Mr02Fn
Thomas	(N)	6	M	Child	13Mr02Fn
William	(N)	4	M	Child	13Mr02Fn
PRIOR, Edward		25	M	Mechanic	13Mr02Fn
Marcella		26	F	Sister	13Mr02Fn
MCARDLE, Wm.		10	M	Unknown	13Mr02Fn
CONNOR, Pat		18	M	Laborer	13Mr02Fn
Honora	(T)	9	F	Child	13Mr02Fn

GERTRUDE 15 MARCH 1850

From Liverpool

NAMES OF PASSENGERS		AGE	SEX	OCCUPATIONS	DATE PORT SHIP
PAGE, Peter		33	M	Farmer	15Mr02Bn
THOMPSON, James		23	M	Unknown	15Mr02Bn
PAYTON, Mary		19	F	Unknown	15Mr02Bn
GALLAHAN, Bridget		20	F	Unknown	15Mr02Bn
DEVINE, Bridget		12	F	Unknown	15Mr02Bn
HICKEY, Thos.		28	M	Unknown	15Mr02Bn
Cath.		22	F	Unknown	15Mr02Bn
Margt.		.00	F	Infant	15Mr02Bn
RYAN, Margt.		24	F	Unknown	15Mr02Bn
ARMSTRONG, Saml.		50	M	Unknown	15Mr02Bn
Ann		45	F	Unknown	15Mr02Bn
Noble		16	M	Unknown	15Mr02Bn
Henry		11	M	Unknown	15Mr02Bn
PENDEGRASS, Mick		30	M	Unknown	15Mr02Bn
HOGAN, Anthony		30	M	Unknown	15Mr02Bn
Mary		40	F	Unknown	15Mr02Bn
Mary		25	F	Unknown	15Mr02Bn
Kate		12	F	Unknown	15Mr02Bn
Honora		10	F	Unknown	15Mr02Bn
Mick		2	M	Child	15Mr02Bn
Matt		.00	M	Infant	15Mr02Bn
CUNNINGHAM, Kate		36	F	Unknown	15Mr02Bn
Biddy		6	F	Child	15Mr02Bn
MCCRAKEN, Hugh		24	M	Unknown	15Mr02Bn
MITCHEL, Biddy		30	F	Unknown	15Mr02Bn
FALLAN, George		19	M	Unknown	15Mr02Bn
FANNELL, Mick		28	M	Unknown	15Mr02Bn
Ellen		25	F	Unknown	15Mr02Bn
Mary		4	F	Child	15Mr02Bn
Margt.		3	F	Child	15Mr02Bn
Thos.		.00	M	Infant	15Mr02Bn
MCQUARY, Mary		25	F	Unknown	15Mr02Bn
CUNNINGHAM, Ann		55	F	Unknown	15Mr02Bn
Rosey		20	F	Unknown	15Mr02Bn
Johanna		.00	F	Infant	15Mr02Bn
TORNEY, James		25	M	Unknown	15Mr02Bn
HORNY, Noah		24	M	Unknown	15Mr02Bn
PORTER, James		12	M	Unknown	15Mr02Bn
JEFFERS, Charles		38	M	Unknown	15Mr02Bn
Harriet		15	F	Unknown	15Mr02Bn
Emma		14	F	Unknown	15Mr02Bn
Thomas		12	M	Unknown	15Mr02Bn
Mary		9	F	Child	15Mr02Bn

NAMES OF PASSENGERS	AGE	SEX	OCCUPATIONS	DATE PORT SHIP
JEFFERS, Eliza	7	F	Child	15Mr02Bn
KELTON, Isaac	19	M	Unknown	15Mr02Bn
ALSOP, Edwd.	18	M	Unknown	15Mr02Bn
LOTT, Charles	31	M	Unknown	15Mr02Bn
Hannah	28	F	Unknown	15Mr02Bn
Eliza	7	F	Child	15Mr02Bn
Elisia	5	F	Child	15Mr02Bn
John	1	M	Child	15Mr02Bn
FRESTON, Richard	33	M	Unknown	15Mr02Bn
Mary	35	F	Unknown	15Mr02Bn
Elisabeth	10	F	Unknown	15Mr02Bn
James-L.	42	M	Unknown	15Mr02Bn
PARTRIGE, U	22	M	Unknown	15Mr02Bn
Sarah	22	F	Unknown	15Mr02Bn
WRIGHT, James	18	M	Unknown	15Mr02Bn
GILBERT, Jerry	19	M	Unknown	15Mr02Bn
OLSIEN, Pat	25	M	Unknown	15Mr02Bn
Mone	00	F	Unknown	15Mr02Bn
BRANNIN, Thos.	25	M	Unknown	15Mr02Bn
James	24	M	Unknown	15Mr02Bn
Betsey	22	F	Unknown	15Mr02Bn
HICKEY, Biddy	30	F	Unknown	15Mr02Bn
KELLY, Henry	22	M	Unknown	15Mr02Bn
CORBETT, Thos.	30	M	Unknown	15Mr02Bn
CLARKE, Bryan	20	M	Unknown	15Mr02Bn
Ellen	17	F	Unknown	15Mr02Bn
MCCIBBIN, James	20	M	Unknown	15Mr02Bn
BUNVAN, James	18	M	Unknown	15Mr02Bn
DOHERTY, Thos.	40	M	Unknown	15Mr02Bn
CORIE, Mick	40	M	Unknown	15Mr02Bn
SALMON, Eliza	27	F	Unknown	15Mr02Bn
Thos.	9	M	Child	15Mr02Bn
John	7	M	Child	15Mr02Bn
CLARKE, John	34	M	Unknown	15Mr02Bn
HAMILTON, Andrew	40	M	Unknown	15Mr02Bn
BURKE, Mike	30	M	Unknown	15Mr02Bn
CRONAN, Dan	24	M	Unknown	15Mr02Bn
CURTIS, Mary	19	F	Unknown	15Mr02Bn
BURKE, Margt.	20	F	Unknown	15Mr02Bn
BANNICK, Susan	18	F	Unknown	15Mr02Bn
Catherine	12	F	Unknown	15Mr02Bn
HALPIN, James	22	M	Unknown	15Mr02Bn
RALPH, Joseph	21	M	Unknown	15Mr02Bn
CHRISTIAN, M.	28	M	Unknown	15Mr02Bn
Harriet	26	F	Unknown	15Mr02Bn
PIGOT, Pat	16	M	Unknown	15Mr02Bn
MULLIN, James	40	M	Unknown	15Mr02Bn
DAGNAL, James	30	M	Unknown	15Mr02Bn
CONWAY, Mick	23	M	Unknown	15Mr02Bn
DAGNAL, Pat	27	M	Unknown	15Mr02Bn
OLSIEN, Daniel	28	M	Unknown	15Mr02Bn
GARATTY, Thos.	22	M	Unknown	15Mr02Bn
NALLY, Thos.	19	M	Unknown	15Mr02Bn
Catherine	12	F	Unknown	15Mr02Bn
DUNN, James	25	M	Unknown	15Mr02Bn
LORYMAN, Mary-A.	31	F	Unknown	15Mr02Bn
JONES, James	20	M	Unknown	15Mr02Bn
Mary	34	F	Unknown	15Mr02Bn
Sarah	4	F	Child	15Mr02Bn
Wm.	.00	M	Infant	15Mr02Bn
HOGAN, Thos.	40	M	Unknown	15Mr02Bn
Died-At-Sea				
MULLIN, Pat	24	M	Unknown	15Mr02Bn
MCDERMOT, Edwd.	20	M	Unknown	15Mr02Bn
DUNN, Thos.	22	M	Unknown	15Mr02Bn
STEWART, Wm.	20	M	Unknown	15Mr02Bn
BOYLSON, James	30	M	Unknown	15Mr02Bn
HOGAN, James	21	M	Unknown	15Mr02Bn
SULLIVAN, Pat	14	M	Unknown	15Mr02Bn
Biddy	16	F	Unknown	15Mr02Bn
DWIRE, Mary	20	F	Unknown	15Mr02Bn
MCGRATH, Dennis	25	M	Unknown	15Mr02Bn
SWEENY, Miles	26	M	Unknown	15Mr02Bn
DONOKEN, Denis	30	M	Unknown	15Mr02Bn
CLARKE, Ellen	50	F	Unknown	15Mr02Bn
CLARKE, Pat	25	M	Unknown	15Mr02Bn
Mary	24	F	Unknown	15Mr02Bn
ROBINSON, Jane	27	F	Unknown	15Mr02Bn
Francis	15	M	Unknown	15Mr02Bn
SULLIVAN, Johanna	36	F	Unknown	15Mr02Bn
Jerry	12	M	Unknown	15Mr02Bn
MCCORMACK, Dennis	25	M	Unknown	15Mr02Bn
Jane	21	F	Unknown	15Mr02Bn
MCAULIFF, Mary	24	F	Unknown	15Mr02Bn
HINES, Pat	45	M	Unknown	15Mr02Bn
Cath.	45	F	Unknown	15Mr02Bn
Mary	9	F	Child	15Mr02Bn
Charles	7	M	Child	15Mr02Bn
Pat	5	M	Child	15Mr02Bn
HAULEY, Elisabeth	22	F	Unknown	15Mr02Bn
MORNINGTON, Ellen	12	F	Unknown	15Mr02Bn
BULGER, James	22	M	Unknown	15Mr02Bn
Cath.	24	F	Unknown	15Mr02Bn
LANEL, Bridget	20	F	Unknown	15Mr02Bn
BULGER, Phil.	6	M	Child	15Mr02Bn
Pat	3	M	Child	15Mr02Bn
Mary	.00	F	Infant	15Mr02Bn
REILLY, John	50	M	Unknown	15Mr02Bn
Pat	18	M	Unknown	15Mr02Bn
James	15	M	Unknown	15Mr02Bn
BOYLE, Mary	20	F	Unknown	15Mr02Bn
Mary	23	F	Unknown	15Mr02Bn
RYANS, John	38	M	Unknown	15Mr02Bn
Died-At-Sea				
Margt.	23	F	Unknown	15Mr02Bn
Mack	20	M	Unknown	15Mr02Bn
KEAREY, Ellen	32	F	Unknown	15Mr02Bn
Thos.	27	M	Unknown	15Mr02Bn
Catherine	.00	F	Infant	15Mr02Bn
Died-At-Sea				
RANSON, Biddy	17	F	Unknown	15Mr02Bn
GELS, Peter	18	M	Unknown	15Mr02Bn
FLINN, Thos.	15	M	Unknown	15Mr02Bn
Nancy	13	F	Unknown	15Mr02Bn
COLEHOUSE, Henry	49	M	Unknown	15Mr02Bn
BRIEN, Wm.	24	M	Unknown	15Mr02Bn
FITZPATRICK, Dennis	21	M	Unknown	15Mr02Bn
James	22	M	Unknown	15Mr02Bn
Mary	22	F	Unknown	15Mr02Bn
CLARK, James	20	M	Unknown	15Mr02Bn
ROBINSON, Sarah	30	F	Unknown	15Mr02Bn
MCMAHON, Anthony	70	M	Unknown	15Mr02Bn
John	35	M	Unknown	15Mr02Bn
Owen	25	M	Unknown	15Mr02Bn
Anthony	11	M	Unknown	15Mr02Bn
Cath.	10	F	Unknown	15Mr02Bn
Peter	9	M	Child	15Mr02Bn
Rose	6	F	Child	15Mr02Bn
Mary	4	F	Child	15Mr02Bn
Hugh	.00	M	Infant	15Mr02Bn
LEARY, Maurice	24	M	Unknown	15Mr02Bn
HEALY, Judy	23	F	Unknown	15Mr02Bn
CASEY, Pat	24	M	Unknown	15Mr02Bn
GLAVIN, Pat	24	M	Unknown	15Mr02Bn
SHEHAN, Jim	24	M	Unknown	15Mr02Bn
CAROLL, Jim	18	M	Unknown	15Mr02Bn
Mick	24	M	Unknown	15Mr02Bn
Maria	23	F	Unknown	15Mr02Bn
SULLIVAN, Johanna	30	F	Unknown	15Mr02Bn
John	30	M	Unknown	15Mr02Bn
Eliza	25	F	Unknown	15Mr02Bn
Stephen	5	M	Child	15Mr02Bn
Mary	3	F	Child	15Mr02Bn
James	.00	M	Infant	15Mr02Bn
HALING, Mary	18	F	Unknown	15Mr02Bn
ONEIL, Biddy	25	F	Unknown	15Mr02Bn
SHEA, Thos.	25	M	Unknown	15Mr02Bn
Julia	16	F	Unknown	15Mr02Bn
Dennis	.00	M	Infant	15Mr02Bn
CASEY, Mary	12	F	Unknown	15Mr02Bn

NAMES OF PASSENGERS	AGE	SEX	OCCUPATIONS	DATE PORT SHIP
ANDERSON, John	20	M	Unknown	15Mr02Bn
MCDONALD, James	45	M	Unknown	15Mr02Bn
Rose	27	F	Unknown	15Mr02Bn
Mary-Ann	.00	F	Infant	15Mr02Bn
MURPHY, Cath.	30	F	Unknown	15Mr02Bn
SWEENEY, Mary	19	F	Unknown	15Mr02Bn
HANNARY, Wm.	42	M	Unknown	15Mr02Bn
Mary	36	F	Unknown	15Mr02Bn
George	14	M	Unknown	15Mr02Bn
Wm.	13	M	Unknown	15Mr02Bn
Charles	10	M	Unknown	15Mr02Bn
John	7	M	Child	15Mr02Bn
Washington	5	M	Child	15Mr02Bn
Mary	3	F	Child	15Mr02Bn
MURPHY, Johanna	33	F	Unknown	15Mr02Bn
Wm.	4	M	Child	15Mr02Bn
Edward	12	M	Unknown	15Mr02Bn
SHEA, Daniel	45	M	Unknown	15Mr02Bn
John	12	M	Unknown	15Mr02Bn
SULLIVAN, Batt	3	M	Child	15Mr02Bn
MCDERMOT, Thos.	30	M	Unknown	15Mr02Bn
DUFFEY, Benj.	30	M	Unknown	15Mr02Bn
COYLE, Cath.	35	F	Unknown	15Mr02Bn
Mary	9	F	Child	15Mr02Bn
Dennis	7	M	Child	15Mr02Bn
Mick	6	M	Child	15Mr02Bn
John	3	M	Child	15Mr02Bn
Ann	.00	F	Infant	15Mr02Bn
COSGROVE, Henry	18	M	Unknown	15Mr02Bn
SMITH, James	19	M	Unknown	15Mr02Bn
FARLEY, Peter	20	M	Unknown	15Mr02Bn
KELLEY, John	40	M	Unknown	15Mr02Bn
CUNISKY, Ben	19	M	Unknown	15Mr02Bn
MCCABE, Judy	36	F	Unknown	15Mr02Bn
SMITH, Mary	25	F	Unknown	15Mr02Bn
BERANS, Jim	30	M	Unknown	15Mr02Bn
RYAN, Mick	30	M	Unknown	15Mr02Bn
MCBRIDE, Thos.	20	M	Unknown	15Mr02Bn
Anthony	20	M	Unknown	15Mr02Bn
Rose	20	F	Unknown	15Mr02Bn
Daniel	20	M	Unknown	15Mr02Bn
Peter	11	M	Unknown	15Mr02Bn
Catherine	10	F	Unknown	15Mr02Bn
HUGHES, Edward	20	M	Unknown	15Mr02Bn
OBRIEN, Maria	16	F	Unknown	15Mr02Bn
MCKENNON, Pat	20	M	Unknown	15Mr02Bn
CLARKE, James	18	M	Unknown	15Mr02Bn
Ann	19	F	Unknown	15Mr02Bn
Alice	18	F	Unknown	15Mr02Bn
MCMAHON, Sam.	20	M	Unknown	15Mr02Bn
PURCEL, Mary	31	F	Unknown	15Mr02Bn
DOYLE, Ellen	14	F	Unknown	15Mr02Bn
BURKE, Pat	25	M	Unknown	15Mr02Bn
DORY, John	20	M	Unknown	15Mr02Bn
SCOTT, Wm.	25	M	Unknown	15Mr02Bn
MCGARLIN, Frances	19	F	Unknown	15Mr02Bn
MURPHY, John	36	M	Unknown	15Mr02Bn
MCDONALD, Mick	30	M	Unknown	15Mr02Bn
NOAH, Martin	25	M	Unknown	15Mr02Bn
BRANIN, John	25	M	Unknown	15Mr02Bn
SPENCER, Sarah	24	F	Unknown	15Mr02Bn
CLARKE, James	20	M	Unknown	15Mr02Bn
ROACHE, Miles	50	M	Unknown	15Mr02Bn
BRADWICK, Ann	20	F	Unknown	15Mr02Bn
THOMPSON, Minerva	20	F	Unknown	15Mr02Bn
TYLER, Mick	40	M	Unknown	15Mr02Bn
Mary	35	F	Unknown	15Mr02Bn
Pat	12	M	Unknown	15Mr02Bn
RYAN, Wm.	20	M	Unknown	15Mr02Bn
Mary	18	F	Unknown	15Mr02Bn
MORAN, Margt.	24	F	Unknown	15Mr02Bn
MCGOVERN, Thos.	30	M	Unknown	15Mr02Bn
U-Mrs.	40	F	Unknown	15Mr02Bn
REILLY, John	9	M	Child	15Mr02Bn
Hugh	32	M	Unknown	15Mr02Bn
GOVERN, Richard	25	M	Unknown	15Mr02Bn
U, U	.00	M	Infant	15Mr02Bn
Born-At-Sea	Died-At-Sea			
DOYLE, Mick	27	M	Unknown	15Mr02Bn
ARMSTRONG, Ann	16	F	Unknown	15Mr02Bn

KATE-HUNTER 16 MARCH 1850

From Liverpool

NAMES OF PASSENGERS	AGE	SEX	OCCUPATIONS	DATE PORT SHIP
BANLEY, John	34	M	Servant	16Mr02Fp
BOLGER, Mary	23	F	Unknown	16Mr02Fp
DOHERTY, Philip	28	M	Unknown	16Mr02Fp
Mary	23	F	Unknown	16Mr02Fp
RYAN, George	25	M	Laborer	16Mr02Fp
COFFY, Pat	28	M	Unknown	16Mr02Fp
Catherine	25	F	Unknown	16Mr02Fp
Ellen	.07	F	Infant	16Mr02Fp
BROWN, Catherine	13	F	Servant	16Mr02Fp
ONEIL, Mary	6	F	Child	16Mr02Fp
MARTIN, Pat	22	M	Unknown	16Mr02Fp
MULLEN, James	18	M	Unknown	16Mr02Fp
CONDONN, Michael	52	M	Unknown	16Mr02Fp
Ann	48	F	Unknown	16Mr02Fp
MURPHY, Catherine	13	F	Unknown	16Mr02Fp
CONDON, John	5	M	Child	16Mr02Fp
Michael	7	M	Child	16Mr02Fp
DEANNE, James	22	M	Unknown	16Mr02Fp
FINNEGAN, James	22	M	Unknown	16Mr02Fp
HOLTON, Bridget	20	F	Unknown	16Mr02Fp
HANNY, Bridget	18	F	Unknown	16Mr02Fp
COWARD, Thomas	26	M	Unknown	16Mr02Fp
REED, Thomas	26	M	Unknown	16Mr02Fp
BINTEN, Sophia	23	F	Unknown	16Mr02Fp
John	20	M	Unknown	16Mr02Fp
GARRET, John	34	M	Unknown	16Mr02Fp
Sarah	30	F	Unknown	16Mr02Fp
PALMER, Jane	17	F	Unknown	16Mr02Fp
Edward	8	M	Child	16Mr02Fp
WALKER, James	23	M	Mechanic	16Mr02Fp
CALWELL, Phillip	38	M	Unknown	16Mr02Fp
Catherine	8	F	Child	16Mr02Fp
TURNEY, Bridget	30	F	Unknown	16Mr02Fp
Catherine	13	F	Unknown	16Mr02Fp
Pat	9	M	Child	16Mr02Fp
Francis	.09	M	Infant	16Mr02Fp
OHARA, James	35	M	Unknown	16Mr02Fp
MURPHY, Dennis	20	M	Unknown	16Mr02Fp
STRANLAND, Bridget	23	F	Laborer	16Mr02Fp
KEATING, Michael	22	M	Unknown	16Mr02Fp
RYAN, Wm.	20	M	Unknown	16Mr02Fp
FOGERTY, Johannah	18	F	Unknown	16Mr02Fp
CONNELL, John	20	M	Unknown	16Mr02Fp
SHERWOOD, Biddy	19	F	Servant	16Mr02Fp
MCGALL, Margret	19	F	Servant	16Mr02Fp
REYNOLDS, Patrick	27	M	Laborer	16Mr02Fp
WYLER, Ann	20	F	Servant	16Mr02Fp
POWELL, Thomas	35	M	Laborer	16Mr02Fp
MCGOVERAN, Biddy	26	F	Servant	16Mr02Fp
NANGLE, James	20	M	Laborer	16Mr02Fp
TUNNY, Michael	50	M	Laborer	16Mr02Fp
Mary	40	F	Laborer	16Mr02Fp
Patrick	13	M	Laborer	16Mr02Fp
Mary	11	F	Laborer	16Mr02Fp
COUGLAN, James	16	M	Laborer	16Mr02Fp
KELLY, Biddy	15	F	Servant	16Mr02Fp
MCDONNELL, Biddy	13	F	Servant	16Mr02Fp
EGAN, Eliza	20	F	Servant	16Mr02Fp
LUDLOW, Thomas	50	M	Farmer	16Mr02Fp

NAMES OF PASSENGERS	AGE	SEX	OCCUPATIONS	DATE PORT SHIP
LUDLOW, James	25	M	Farmer	16Mr02Fp
Margret	18	F	Farmer	16Mr02Fp
William	16	M	Farmer	16Mr02Fp
George	23	M	Shoemaker	16Mr02Fp
BERRY, James	35	M	Laborer	16Mr02Fp
Mary	30	F	Laborer	16Mr02Fp
REID, John	22	M	Laborer	16Mr02Fp
HANLY, Susan	18	F	Servant	16Mr02Fp
MCCAINE, Jane	19	F	Servant	16Mr02Fp
TRACY, Patrick	32	M	Laborer	16Mr02Fp
SHAREN, Owen	40	M	Laborer	16Mr02Fp
John	11	M	Laborer	16Mr02Fp
Bridget	9	F	Child	16Mr02Fp
Patrick	7	M	Child	16Mr02Fp
CUNNINGHAM, Maria	30	F	Servant	16Mr02Fp
Mary	13	F	Servant	16Mr02Fp
John	5	M	Child	16Mr02Fp
Margret	.00	F	Infant	16Mr02Fp
KANE, Mary	22	F	Servant	16Mr02Fp
MARTIN, Peter	18	M	Laborer	16Mr02Fp
JOHNSTON, Catherine	26	F	Servant	16Mr02Fp
CLARK, Ann	18	F	Servant	16Mr02Fp
SMITH, Patt	20	M	Laborer	16Mr02Fp
John	16	M	Laborer	16Mr02Fp
MCCONNELL, Matthew	30	M	Laborer	16Mr02Fp
REILY, Michael	25	M	Laborer	16Mr02Fp
OBRIEN, George	20	M	Laborer	16Mr02Fp
WALLACE, James	19	M	Laborer	16Mr02Fp
MCCONNELL, Elizabeth	36	F	Farmer	16Mr02Fp
Sarah	9	F	Child	16Mr02Fp
James	7	M	Child	16Mr02Fp
Arthur	5	M	Child	16Mr02Fp
DUGGAN, Martin	32	M	Laborer	16Mr02Fp
KEFFE, Martin	29	M	Laborer	16Mr02Fp
DAMPLY, Henry	27	M	Laborer	16Mr02Fp
WALL, Michael	20	M	Laborer	16Mr02Fp
COSTIGAN, Pattk.	23	M	Laborer	16Mr02Fp
BERGEN, Daniel	60	M	Laborer	16Mr02Fp
DUGAN, Ann	37	F	Servant	16Mr02Fp
ELLIOTT, John	24	M	Laborer	16Mr02Fp
FITZGERALD, Archibald	30	M	Laborer	16Mr02Fp
HANNIGAN, Margret	40	F	Servant	16Mr02Fp
BURNS, Owen	19	M	Laborer	16Mr02Fp
SKEELY, Matthew	30	M	Laborer	16Mr02Fp
Emilie	25	F	Laborer	16Mr02Fp
Johanna	2	F	Child	16Mr02Fp
Carol	.00	F	Infant	16Mr02Fp
BROWN, William	49	M	Plumber	16Mr02Fp
HAGEN, Thomas	45	M	Laborer	16Mr02Fp
PENDERGRAST, Catherine	20	F	Laborer	16Mr02Fp
Elizabeth	18	F	Servant	16Mr02Fp
MCGUIRE, Edmund	25	M	Servant	16Mr02Fp
Mary	21	F	Farmer	16Mr02Fp
MCKENNA, Margret	18	F	Farmer	16Mr02Fp
LEARY, John	25	M	Farmer	16Mr02Fp
Margret	22	F	Farmer	16Mr02Fp
Ann	50	F	Farmer	16Mr02Fp
Philip	25	M	Farmer	16Mr02Fp
LOUGHLIN, Catherine	22	F	Farmer	16Mr02Fp
John	.00	M	Infant	16Mr02Fp
KEAN, Margret	20	F	Servant	16Mr02Fp
BROPHY, Mary	26	F	Servant	16Mr02Fp
CONNELLY, Margret	20	F	Servant	16Mr02Fp
DEMPSEY, James	26	M	Laborer	16Mr02Fp
GILLIGAN, Andrew	26	M	Laborer	16Mr02Fp
MCRORY, Hugh	21	M	Laborer	16Mr02Fp
STITCHER, John	30	M	Laborer	16Mr02Fp
James	18	M	Laborer	16Mr02Fp
DAFFY, Mary	37	F	Farmer	16Mr02Fp
Bridget	9	F	Child	16Mr02Fp
Thomas	7	M	Child	16Mr02Fp
Ann	5	F	Child	16Mr02Fp
Michael	3	M	Child	16Mr02Fp
KILMARTIN, John	40	M	Laborer	16Mr02Fp
MALONEY, Catherine	23	F	Servant	16Mr02Fp
MURPHY, Mary	25	F	Servant	16Mr02Fp
LANE, Thomas	50	M	Farmer	16Mr02Fp
Jane	50	F	Farmer	16Mr02Fp
Mary	27	M	Farmer	16Mr02Fp
Norma	21	F	Farmer	16Mr02Fp
Johanna	20	F	Farmer	16Mr02Fp
John	18	M	Farmer	16Mr02Fp
Thomas	14	M	Farmer	16Mr02Fp
Thomas	11	M	Farmer	16Mr02Fp
SMYTH, John	21	M	Laborer	16Mr02Fp
CALLIGAN, Mary	21	F	Servant	16Mr02Fp
John	22	M	Servant	16Mr02Fp
MASON, Richard	24	M	Laborer	16Mr02Fp
Mary	20	F	Laborer	16Mr02Fp
TURNER, Joseph	19	M	Laborer	16Mr02Fp
LYNCH, Bridget	20	F	Servant	16Mr02Fp
MALONEY, Elizabeth	24	F	Servant	16Mr02Fp
RILEY, Peggy	22	F	Servant	16Mr02Fp
MCGOVERNAN, Peter	27	M	Laborer	16Mr02Fp
HANNAGHAN, Patrick	24	M	Laborer	16Mr02Fp
HESLIN, Catherine	28	F	Servant	16Mr02Fp
DOLAN, Susan	10	F	Servant	16Mr02Fp
DIVINE, Arthur	19	M	Laborer	16Mr02Fp
Mary	21	F	Laborer	16Mr02Fp
FAYNE, Thomas	20	M	Laborer	16Mr02Fp
MOORE, Charles	27	M	Laborer	16Mr02Fp
MADDEN, Patrick	27	M	Farmer	16Mr02Fp
Margret	30	F	Farmer	16Mr02Fp
Rose	20	F	Farmer	16Mr02Fp
Patrick	3	M	Child	16Mr02Fp
BURKE, Patrick	20	M	Laborer	16Mr02Fp
SHERRIDAN, Sylvester	12	M	Laborer	16Mr02Fp
BRENNAN, Thomas	21	M	Laborer	16Mr02Fp
MCGRATH, John	20	M	Laborer	16Mr02Fp
DEVIN, Owen	21	M	Laborer	16Mr02Fp
HUGH, Catherine	24	F	Servant	16Mr02Fp
CLARK, William	20	M	Servant	16Mr02Fp
BARLOW, Robert	30	M	Laborer	16Mr02Fp
DELANY, Keran	32	M	Laborer	16Mr02Fp
Judy	22	F	Laborer	16Mr02Fp
William	30	M	Laborer	16Mr02Fp
John	19	M	Laborer	16Mr02Fp
RYAN, John	30	M	Farmer	16Mr02Fp
HARRONN, James	29	M	Farmer	16Mr02Fp
Jane	2	F	Child	16Mr02Fp
CHAMPION, Michael	.00	M	Infant	16Mr02Fp
Bridget	26	F	Laborer	16Mr02Fp
LOUGHLIN, John	22	M	Laborer	16Mr02Fp
KNOWLES, John	20	M	Laborer	16Mr02Fp
PERRY, John	19	M	Laborer	16Mr02Fp
William	20	M	Laborer	16Mr02Fp
Mary	19	F	Laborer	16Mr02Fp
DALTON, James	20	M	Farmer	16Mr02Fp
WESTROPP, George	27	M	Farmer	16Mr02Fp
CLARK, Thomas	24	M	Farmer	16Mr02Fp
MURPHY, Bernard	.00	M	Infant	16Mr02Fp
HART, Patrick	24	M	Laborer	16Mr02Fp
OWENS, Joseph	22	M	Laborer	16Mr02Fp
HIGGINS, Thomas	24	M	Laborer	16Mr02Fp
MOSS, James	23	M	Laborer	16Mr02Fp
James	26	M	Laborer	16Mr02Fp
HALL, William	46	M	Laborer	16Mr02Fp
GUNNER, William	25	M	Laborer	16Mr02Fp
Mary	25	F	Laborer	16Mr02Fp
Eliza	.00	F	Infant	16Mr02Fp
IRISH, Samuel	59	M	Laborer	16Mr02Fp
MCGILL, Thomas	29	M	Laborer	16Mr02Fp
ELLIOTT, George	29	M	Laborer	16Mr02Fp
Mary	50	F	Laborer	16Mr02Fp
PARKER, Mary-Jane	24	F	Servant	16Mr02Fp
Samuel	7	M	Child	16Mr02Fp
MCDONNELL, Margret	20	F	Servant	16Mr02Fp
RIGREY, Mary	22	F	Servant	16Mr02Fp
COUGHLIN, Betty	21	F	Servant	16Mr02Fp
BUSHEY, John	22	M	Laborer	16Mr02Fp

NAMES OF PASSENGERS	AGE	SEX	OCCUPATIONS	DATE PORT SHIP
ROBERTS, Thomas	20	M	Laborer	16Mr02Fp
STEWART, William	24	M	Laborer	16Mr02Fp
DOUGHTY, William	30	M	Laborer	16Mr02Fp
GILLIGHAM, James	16	M	Laborer	16Mr02Fp
MATHEWS, Edward	43	M	Laborer	16Mr02Fp
John	13	M	Laborer	16Mr02Fp
William	11	M	Laborer	16Mr02Fp
FARREL, John	35	M	Ship Mate	16Mr02Fp
Julia	19	F	Servant	16Mr02Fp
STCLAIR, Ellen	19	F	Servant	16Mr02Fp
SHARCOTT, Honor	19	F	Servant	16Mr02Fp
DEMPSEY, Betsey	28	M	Laborer	16Mr02Fp
FINLAY, John	24	M	Laborer	16Mr02Fp
DROLEY, Cormack	20	M	Laborer	16Mr02Fp
HORAN, John	28	M	Servant	16Mr02Fp
REGIN, Michael	11	M	Laborer	16Mr02Fp
MALLEY, Mary	36	F	Farmer	16Mr02Fp
FITZPATRICK, Mary	.00	F	Infant	16Mr02Fp
MCGOUGH, Nancy	22	F	Laborer	16Mr02Fp
BROPHY, Michael	20	M	Laborer	16Mr02Fp
BURKE, Edward	30	M	Laborer	16Mr02Fp
Catherine	19	F	Laborer	16Mr02Fp
WOGLE, Bridget	20	F	Laborer	16Mr02Fp
KELLY, Hugh	17	M	Laborer	16Mr02Fp
LONG, Stephen	22	M	Laborer	16Mr02Fp
DEVANY, John	17	M	Laborer	16Mr02Fp
Margret	22	F	Unknown	16Mr02Fp
Mary	26	F	Unknown	16Mr02Fp
SHANNON, Ann	23	F	Servant	16Mr02Fp
CLARK, Mary	.00	F	Infant	16Mr02Fp
John	20	M	Servant	16Mr02Fp
HARRIGAN, James	20	M	Laborer	16Mr02Fp
GIMMIN, Grace	20	F	Servant	16Mr02Fp
MARS, William	40	M	Laborer	16Mr02Fp
MCNALLY, Peter	21	M	Laborer	16Mr02Fp
DAVIS, Mary-Ann	30	F	Servant	16Mr02Fp
COATES, Thos.	30	M	Laborer	16Mr02Fp

JOHN-CURRIER 16 MARCH 1850

From Liverpool

NAMES OF PASSENGERS	AGE	SEX	OCCUPATIONS	DATE PORT SHIP
LARNEY, Ann	17	F	Fsvnt	16Mr02Fo
SMITH, Wm.	22	M	Farmer	16Mr02Fo
CARROLL, James	20	M	Farmer	16Mr02Fo
BATTES, John	19	M	Farmer	16Mr02Fo
Bridgt.	18	F	Farmer	16Mr02Fo
MULLRAN, John	18	M	Farmer	16Mr02Fo
MCMURRAY, Bartle	17	M	Farmer	16Mr02Fo
MITCHEL, Jo.	24	M	Farmer	16Mr02Fo
SCHOFIELD, John	24	M	Farmer	16Mr02Fo
NUGENT, Bridget	24	F	Unknown	16Mr02Fo
KELLY, Geo.	20	M	Farmer	16Mr02Fo
EAGAN, John	24	M	Farmer	16Mr02Fo
CARNALL, Jas.	28	M	Farmer	16Mr02Fo
GAUNT, Mary	27	F	Unknown	16Mr02Fo
Solina	12	F	Unknown	16Mr02Fo
Louisa	9	F	Child	16Mr02Fo
John	6	M	Child	16Mr02Fo
Caroline	4	F	Child	16Mr02Fo
QUINN, Pat	18	M	Farmer	16Mr02Fo
FLEMING, Michl.	19	M	Farmer	16Mr02Fo
REARDON, Pat	20	M	Farmer	16Mr02Fo
Cathe.	22	F	Unknown	16Mr02Fo
REILY, Peter	30	M	Farmer	16Mr02Fo
Cathe.	28	F	Unknown	16Mr02Fo
Pat	22	M	Farmer	16Mr02Fo
Martin	21	M	Farmer	16Mr02Fo
MCCABE, John	11	M	Farmer	16Mr02Fo

NAMES OF PASSENGERS	AGE	SEX	OCCUPATIONS	DATE PORT SHIP
MCCABE, Mick	11	M	Farmer	16Mr02Fo
MULRONEY, Martin	35	M	Farmer	16Mr02Fo
BOUCHER, Mary	40	F	Farmer	16Mr02Fo
Brid.	15	F	Farmer	16Mr02Fo
Jno.	12	M	Farmer	16Mr02Fo
Ann	11	F	Farmer	16Mr02Fo
Mary	6	F	Child	16Mr02Fo
HAYES, John	24	M	Farmer	16Mr02Fo
DOWNEY, Jno.	32	M	Farmer	16Mr02Fo
Jno.	46	M	Farmer	16Mr02Fo
Bessy	46	F	Farmer	16Mr02Fo
Conner	13	M	Farmer	16Mr02Fo
Jno.	3	M	Child	16Mr02Fo
DEVINE, Pat	24	M	Farmer	16Mr02Fo
OAKES, Mary	24	F	Farmer	16Mr02Fo
GALLEGAN, Pat	18	M	Farmer	16Mr02Fo
Mary	20	F	Farmer	16Mr02Fo
DUFFY, Jane	21	F	Farmer	16Mr02Fo
MALONE, Simon	19	M	Farmer	16Mr02Fo
MANN, Mary	48	F	Farmer	16Mr02Fo
Susan	19	F	Farmer	16Mr02Fo
ENNIS, Jas.	24	M	Farmer	16Mr02Fo
BYRNE, Jas.	33	M	Farmer	16Mr02Fo
U-Mrs.	28	F	Farmer	16Mr02Fo
CASEY, Cathe.	25	F	Farmer	16Mr02Fo
RAY, Mick	30	M	Farmer	16Mr02Fo
CORBET, Margt.	23	F	Farmer	16Mr02Fo
SWEENY, Brd.	25	F	Farmer	16Mr02Fo
Geo.	4	M	Child	16Mr02Fo
Robt.	3	M	Child	16Mr02Fo
John	.00	M	Infant	16Mr02Fo
CARMODERS, Mick	20	M	Farmer	16Mr02Fo
DOYLE, Pat	24	M	Farmer	16Mr02Fo
U-Mrs.	25	F	Farmer	16Mr02Fo
CAVANAH, Jas.	25	M	Farmer	16Mr02Fo
CASSIDY, Andrew	30	M	Farmer	16Mr02Fo
U-Mrs.	25	F	Farmer	16Mr02Fo
Jas.	.00	M	Infant	16Mr02Fo
MANALAFTY, Hugh	21	M	Farmer	16Mr02Fo
MURRAY, Jas.	40	M	Farmer	16Mr02Fo
MANALAFTY, U-Mrs.	21	F	Farmer	16Mr02Fo
SHERMON, Jo.	26	M	Farmer	16Mr02Fo
LYNCH, Ann	28	F	Farmer	16Mr02Fo
SEXTON, Pat	20	M	Farmer	16Mr02Fo
ENGLISH, Toby	28	M	Farmer	16Mr02Fo
Mary	28	F	Farmer	16Mr02Fo
Brid.	3	F	Child	16Mr02Fo
Bessy	.00	F	Infant	16Mr02Fo
DAVERN, Sally	45	F	Farmer	16Mr02Fo
Bridt.	18	F	Farmer	16Mr02Fo
Nancy	20	F	Farmer	16Mr02Fo
Pat	18	M	Farmer	16Mr02Fo
Emma	17	F	Farmer	16Mr02Fo
DOUGHERTY, Pat	18	M	Farmer	16Mr02Fo
Mary	30	F	Farmer	16Mr02Fo
RYAN, Jas.	14	M	Farmer	16Mr02Fo
BRYAN, Michl.	20	M	Farmer	16Mr02Fo
AUSTIN, Sally	7	F	Child	16Mr02Fo
FLOOD, Jas.	20	M	Farmer	16Mr02Fo
Ann	21	F	Farmer	16Mr02Fo
Bryan	6	M	Child	16Mr02Fo
CAHILL, John	23	M	Farmer	16Mr02Fo
Brid.	22	F	Farmer	16Mr02Fo
Owen	.00	M	Infant	16Mr02Fo
COYLE, Thos.	30	M	Farmer	16Mr02Fo
MURRAY, Jas.	25	M	Farmer	16Mr02Fo
COYLE, Ann	24	F	Farmer	16Mr02Fo
QUINN, Pat	18	M	Farmer	16Mr02Fo
BRADY, Jas.	20	M	Farmer	16Mr02Fo
DAILY, Denis	40	M	Farmer	16Mr02Fo
U-Mrs.	36	F	Farmer	16Mr02Fo
Mary	11	F	Farmer	16Mr02Fo
Margret	8	F	Child	16Mr02Fo
Brid.	5	F	Child	16Mr02Fo
Ann	.00	F	Infant	16Mr02Fo

NAMES OF PASSENGERS	AGE	SEX	OCCUPATIONS	DATE PORT SHIP
BARRY, Thos.	40	M	Farmer	16Mr02Fo
U-Mrs.	36	F	Farmer	16Mr02Fo
Thos.	12	M	Farmer	16Mr02Fo
Michl.	7	M	Child	16Mr02Fo
Pat	5	M	Child	16Mr02Fo
Ellen	.00	F	Infant	16Mr02Fo
SMALLES, Mary	15	F	Farmer	16Mr02Fo
BOUCHER, Thos.	17	M	Farmer	16Mr02Fo
SAVAGE, Jno.	28	M	Farmer	16Mr02Fo
KEGAN, Mick	18	M	Farmer	16Mr02Fo
RILEY, Jas.	18	M	Farmer	16Mr02Fo
KEGAN, Sally	40	F	Farmer	16Mr02Fo
Thos.	10	M	Farmer	16Mr02Fo
Cath.	8	F	Child	16Mr02Fo
Maria	.00	F	Infant	16Mr02Fo
GILL, Mary	20	F	Farmer	16Mr02Fo
BRACKEN, Owen	20	M	Farmer	16Mr02Fo
Cath.	22	F	Farmer	16Mr02Fo
Rose	11	F	Farmer	16Mr02Fo
EAGAN, Pat	18	M	Farmer	16Mr02Fo
Mary	18	F	Farmer	16Mr02Fo
Johan	15	F	Farmer	16Mr02Fo
CASEY, Jas.	15	M	Farmer	16Mr02Fo
WALL, Wm.	18	M	Farmer	16Mr02Fo
SLATERLY, N.	23	M	Farmer	16Mr02Fo
OHARA, Jas.	25	M	Farmer	16Mr02Fo
MYLES, Pat	14	M	Farmer	16Mr02Fo
Pat	14	M	Farmer	16Mr02Fo
Brid.	14	F	Farmer	16Mr02Fo
CAIN, Mary	14	F	Farmer	16Mr02Fo
NOLAN, U-Mrs.	40	F	Farmer	16Mr02Fo
Peter	14	M	Farmer	16Mr02Fo
HUGHES, Jas.	30	M	Farmer	16Mr02Fo
U-Mrs.	25	F	Farmer	16Mr02Fo
Bridgt.	20	F	Farmer	16Mr02Fo
WALSH, Mary	18	F	Farmer	16Mr02Fo
MURPHY, Pat	30	M	Farmer	16Mr02Fo
RILEY, Cath.	14	F	Farmer	16Mr02Fo
U	.00	U	Infant	16Mr02Fo
MURPHY, Thos.	40	M	Farmer	16Mr02Fo
READ, Ester	40	F	Farmer	16Mr02Fo
JUSTICE, Mary	18	F	Farmer	16Mr02Fo
LONDON, Margret	19	F	Farmer	16Mr02Fo
HULAVAN, Honor	21	M	Farmer	16Mr02Fo
COX, Brid.	55	F	Cutler	16Mr02Fo
MULVEY, Cath.	20	F	Cutler	16Mr02Fo
Ann	23	F	Cutler	16Mr02Fo
BROADY, Ann	18	F	Cutler	16Mr02Fo
HUSON, Ann	15	F	Cutler	16Mr02Fo
James	12	M	Cutler	16Mr02Fo
NAUGHTON, Mary	35	F	Cutler	16Mr02Fo
KEYES, Frank	30	M	Farmer	16Mr02Fo
MATHESON, Jno.	18	M	Farmer	16Mr02Fo
LITTLE, Mary	42	F	Farmer	16Mr02Fo
Ann	16	F	Farmer	16Mr02Fo
DALY, Michl.	20	M	Farmer	16Mr02Fo
KELLY, Maria	20	F	Farmer	16Mr02Fo
MULDOON, Tim	21	M	Farmer	16Mr02Fo
GRIMES, Bridgt.	16	F	Farmer	16Mr02Fo
ROCK, Margret	16	F	Farmer	16Mr02Fo
DAILY, Ann	17	F	Farmer	16Mr02Fo
NEIL, Corn.	28	M	Farmer	16Mr02Fo
FARRELL, Mick	36	M	Farmer	16Mr02Fo
NEIL, Corn.	4	M	Child	16Mr02Fo
DOLAN, Ann	10	F	Unknown	16Mr02Fo
Rosy	12	F	Unknown	16Mr02Fo
HICKEY, Mick	25	M	Farmer	16Mr02Fo
JOHNSON, Ellen	20	F	Farmer	16Mr02Fo
DALY, Thos.	35	M	Farmer	16Mr02Fo
KEELY, Pat	20	M	Farmer	16Mr02Fo
TIERNEY, Michl.	10	M	Farmer	16Mr02Fo
GRAY, James	10	M	Farmer	16Mr02Fo
KELLY, Margaret	19	F	Farmer	16Mr02Fo
SAPRELLA, Pray	24	M	Farmer	16Mr02Fo
RYAN, Pat	22	M	Farmer	16Mr02Fo
RYAN, Margt.	20	F	Farmer	16Mr02Fo
MAYHON, Peggy	19	F	Farmer	16Mr02Fo
MAHONY, Brid.	17	F	Farmer	16Mr02Fo
CONROY, Mick	18	M	Farmer	16Mr02Fo
COSS, Pat	36	M	Farmer	16Mr02Fo
SHEHAN, Pat	30	M	Farmer	16Mr02Fo
Margret	30	M	Farmer	16Mr02Fo
Jno.	6	M	Child	16Mr02Fo
Hannah	4	F	Child	16Mr02Fo
MCCOURTNEY, Jno.	37	M	Farmer	16Mr02Fo
FITZGERALD, Michl.	36	M	Farmer	16Mr02Fo
BEATTY, Elish.	30	F	Farmer	16Mr02Fo
Elish.	6	F	Child	16Mr02Fo
HALL, John	25	M	Farmer	16Mr02Fo
MADDEN, Mick	30	M	Farmer	16Mr02Fo
Mary	.00	F	Infant	16Mr02Fo
KEVAN, John	17	M	Farmer	16Mr02Fo
MULLEN, Michl.	40	M	Farmer	16Mr02Fo
Mary	30	F	Unknown	16Mr02Fo
CALLAGAN, Cath.	18	F	Unknown	16Mr02Fo
RIDGE, Michl.	16	M	Unknown	16Mr02Fo
Peter	14	M	Unknown	16Mr02Fo
Bridget	12	F	Unknown	16Mr02Fo
MCGINNIS, Owen	20	M	Farmer	16Mr02Fo
CALLAGAN, Chas.	18	M	Farmer	16Mr02Fo
KELLEY, Owen	24	M	Farmer	16Mr02Fo
OHARA, Alice	23	F	Farmer	16Mr02Fo
DUNDEN, Michl.	22	M	Farmer	16Mr02Fo
Pat	25	M	Farmer	16Mr02Fo
REILY, Luke	22	M	Farmer	16Mr02Fo
DILLON, Fitz	16	M	Farmer	16Mr02Fo
KING, John	27	M	Farmer	16Mr02Fo
Jane	26	F	Farmer	16Mr02Fo
Frank	.00	M	Infant	16Mr02Fo
BYRNE, Jno.	27	M	Farmer	16Mr02Fo
NEIL, Michl.	27	M	Farmer	16Mr02Fo
COUGHLAN, Nancy	30	F	Farmer	16Mr02Fo
DUNN, Pat	11	M	Farmer	16Mr02Fo
Michl.	.00	M	Infant	16Mr02Fo
SULIVAN, Denis Died-At-Sea	60	M	Farmer	16Mr02Fo
KENEDY, Pat	28	M	Farmer	16Mr02Fo
RICE, Ann	21	F	Unknown	16Mr02Fo
Brid.	21	F	Unknown	16Mr02Fo
MEE, Alex	20	M	Farmer	16Mr02Fo
Mary	21	F	Farmer	16Mr02Fo
Mary	46	F	Farmer	16Mr02Fo
Marschel	15	M	Farmer	16Mr02Fo
KERMIS, Jas.	20	M	Farmer	16Mr02Fo
ENNIS, Peter	35	M	Farmer	16Mr02Fo
Mary	11	F	Farmer	16Mr02Fo
Cathe.	22	F	Farmer	16Mr02Fo
DOYLE, Thos.	40	M	Farmer	16Mr02Fo
Robt.	27	M	Farmer	16Mr02Fo
RIELY, Mary	32	F	Farmer	16Mr02Fo
Mary	16	F	Farmer	16Mr02Fo
Jas.	14	M	Farmer	16Mr02Fo
Michl.	13	M	Farmer	16Mr02Fo
Cathe.	21	F	Farmer	16Mr02Fo
GREYSON, Jas.	40	M	Farmer	16Mr02Fo
CARNEY, Bryon	27	M	Farmer	16Mr02Fo
GRAHAM, Mary	21	F	Farmer	16Mr02Fo
CORMACK, Mick	20	M	Farmer	16Mr02Fo
MULLEN, Barney	40	M	Farmer	16Mr02Fo
Barney	10	M	Farmer	16Mr02Fo
Cath.	40	F	Farmer	16Mr02Fo
Ann	30	F	Farmer	16Mr02Fo
U	.00	U	Infant	16Mr02Fo
FITZSIMONS, Pat	50	M	Farmer	16Mr02Fo
Henry	30	M	Farmer	16Mr02Fo
URIDAY, Henry	35	M	Farmer	16Mr02Fo
SPELMAN, Cath.	40	F	Farmer	16Mr02Fo
Mary	20	F	Farmer	16Mr02Fo
U	.00	U	Infant	16Mr02Fo
Maria	18	F	Farmer	16Mr02Fo

NAMES OF PASSENGERS	AGE	SEX	OCCUPATIONS	DATE PORT SHIP
SPELMAN, Michael	14	M	Farmer	16Mr02Fo
Pat	11	M	Farmer	16Mr02Fo
Phil	9	M	Child	16Mr02Fo
Edward	3	M	Child	16Mr02Fo
BROWN, Wm.	31	M	Farmer	16Mr02Fo
PHAGER, Richd.	26	M	Farmer	16Mr02Fo
SPELMAN, Denis	24	M	Farmer	16Mr02Fo
MAGUIRE, Michl.	21	M	Farmer	16Mr02Fo
Pat	17	M	Farmer	16Mr02Fo

JACOB-A.WESTERVELT 20 MARCH 1850

From Liverpool

NAMES OF PASSENGERS	AGE	SEX	OCCUPATIONS	DATE PORT SHIP
FOSTER, Isabella	18	F	Spinster	20Mr02Fs
MOONEY, Eliza	23	F	Spinster	20Mr02Fs
SWANN, George	23	M	Saddler	20Mr02Fs
MOONEY, Barnet	40	M	Saddler	20Mr02Fs
John	12	M	Saddler	20Mr02Fs
COLLINS, Hannah	23	F	Spinster	20Mr02Fs
MARTHA, Alice	17	F	Spinster	20Mr02Fs
John	19	M	Laborer	20Mr02Fs
Luke	21	M	Baker	20Mr02Fs
GLANSIA, Michl.	31	M	Shoemaker	20Mr02Fs
REILLY, Peter	23	M	Tailor	20Mr02Fs
DUFFY, Barney	21	M	Laborer	20Mr02Fs
MCALNEY, Michl.	27	M	Laborer	20Mr02Fs
Hugh	25	M	Laborer	20Mr02Fs
HENRY, Pat	24	M	Shoemaker	20Mr02Fs
HUNTER, John	20	M	Laborer	20Mr02Fs
CAULDWELL, James	20	M	Baker	20Mr02Fs
MULLEN, James	19	M	Baker	20Mr02Fs
TRAINER, Eliza	24	F	Baker	20Mr02Fs
Amelia	.00	F	Infant	20Mr02Fs
MCVEY, Cathe.	22	F	Spinster	20Mr02Fs
FLINN, Cathe.	22	F	Spinster	20Mr02Fs
FLEMING, Thos.	25	M	Laborer	20Mr02Fs
FLINN, Thos.	.00	M	Infant	20Mr02Fs
FARREL, Michl.	25	M	Laborer	20Mr02Fs
GAHAGAN, Thos.	18	M	Laborer	20Mr02Fs
MCCLUSTER, Bridget	12	F	Laborer	20Mr02Fs
Mary	7	F	Child	20Mr02Fs
Ellen	5	F	Child	20Mr02Fs
James	9	M	Child	20Mr02Fs
DUNN, Bridget	24	F	Spinster	20Mr02Fs
Winny	17	F	Spinster	20Mr02Fs
GOLDRICK, Mary	17	F	Spinster	20Mr02Fs
Hugh	21	M	Laborer	20Mr02Fs
MANNING, John	30	M	Laborer	20Mr02Fs
CONNOR, John	22	M	Laborer	20Mr02Fs
MULLIGAN, James	12	M	Laborer	20Mr02Fs
KENEDY, Thomas	40	M	Schm	20Mr02Fs
FAHEY, James	22	M	Laborer	20Mr02Fs
HAYES, Judy	25	F	Spinster	20Mr02Fs
CARROLL, Edmund	20	M	Tailor	20Mr02Fs
Judy	22	F	Unknown	20Mr02Fs
RYAN, Biddy	22	F	Spinster	20Mr02Fs
TULLY, Hugh	22	M	Laborer	20Mr02Fs
Mary	16	F	Spinster	20Mr02Fs
BRADY, Sarah	20	F	Spinster	20Mr02Fs
TIERNEY, Edmund	42	M	Laborer	20Mr02Fs
Margt.	15	F	Unknown	20Mr02Fs
HENRY, John	24	M	Laborer	20Mr02Fs
Ann	64	F	Wi	20Mr02Fs
Rose	40	F	Spinster	20Mr02Fs
GIVIN, Sarah	19	F	Spinster	20Mr02Fs
NUGENT, Joseph	19	M	Laborer	20Mr02Fs
MCCORMICK, Nicholas	19	M	Laborer	20Mr02Fs
DAVIES, Margt.	18	F	Spinster	20Mr02Fs

NAMES OF PASSENGERS	AGE	SEX	OCCUPATIONS	DATE PORT SHIP
CULLEN, Chistopher	30	M	Farmer	20Mr02Fs
Margt.	18	F	Farmer	20Mr02Fs
HICKEY, Pat	50	M	Farmer	20Mr02Fs
Margt.	45	F	Farmer	20Mr02Fs
Morris	22	M	Farmer	20Mr02Fs
Ellen	18	F	Spinster	20Mr02Fs
Judith	13	F	Spinster	20Mr02Fs
Mary	12	F	Spinster	20Mr02Fs
Cathe.	10	F	Spinster	20Mr02Fs
Julian	7	M	Child	20Mr02Fs
BURKE, Olivia	20	F	Spinster	20Mr02Fs
HALLORAN, Julia	22	F	Spinster	20Mr02Fs
RYAN, Mick	22	M	Laborer	20Mr02Fs
Honora	15	F	Spinster	20Mr02Fs
HICKEY, William	50	M	Farmer	20Mr02Fs
Mary	45	F	Farmer	20Mr02Fs
Patrick	23	M	Farmer	20Mr02Fs
Mary	22	F	Spinster	20Mr02Fs
Ellen	22	F	Spinster	20Mr02Fs
Michl.	20	M	Laborer	20Mr02Fs
William	19	M	Laborer	20Mr02Fs
Mary	13	F	Laborer	20Mr02Fs
Richard	11	M	Laborer	20Mr02Fs
LANDROGAN, William	22	M	Laborer	20Mr02Fs
Julian	21	F	Unknown	20Mr02Fs
MURPHY, Thos.	22	M	Smith	20Mr02Fs
REED, Cristy	22	F	Spinster	20Mr02Fs
CONLIN, Peter	14	M	Unknown	20Mr02Fs
BEATTY, Matthew	22	M	Unknown	20Mr02Fs
MCGORR, Cathe.	20	F	Spinster	20Mr02Fs
Hannah	22	F	Spinster	20Mr02Fs
MURRAY, Mary	22	F	Spinster	20Mr02Fs
KELLY, Bridget	22	F	Spinster	20Mr02Fs
CARROLL, Mary	30	F	Spinster	20Mr02Fs
COUGHLIN, Maria	17	F	Spinster	20Mr02Fs
CORCORAN, John	30	M	Laborer	20Mr02Fs
Bridget	28	F	Laborer	20Mr02Fs
Martin	6	M	Child	20Mr02Fs
Bernard	5	M	Child	20Mr02Fs
Michl.	3	M	Child	20Mr02Fs
Died-At-Sea				
Cathe.	2	F	Child	20Mr02Fs
READY, Ann	18	F	Spinster	20Mr02Fs
STONE, Michl.	19	M	Laborer	20Mr02Fs
HELAND, Henry	40	M	Laborer	20Mr02Fs
DONOGHUE, James	20	M	Laborer	20Mr02Fs
HELLAND, Hannah	18	F	Spinster	20Mr02Fs
MAHON, James	20	M	Laborer	20Mr02Fs
BUTLER, Michl.	20	M	Laborer	20Mr02Fs
REILLY, Daniel	25	M	Laborer	20Mr02Fs
DOHERTY, Pat	22	M	Laborer	20Mr02Fs
BULLEN, James	21	M	Laborer	20Mr02Fs
DEMPSEY, Pat	20	M	Laborer	20Mr02Fs
EMPEROR, Pat	15	M	Laborer	20Mr02Fs
QUIRK, Michl.	23	M	Laborer	20Mr02Fs
EMPEROR, John	15	M	Laborer	20Mr02Fs
COSTIGAN, Dennis	20	M	Laborer	20Mr02Fs
HENRY, Bridget	40	F	Laborer	20Mr02Fs
FOLEY, Hannah	12	F	Laborer	20Mr02Fs
CULLEN, Cathe.	24	F	Spinster	20Mr02Fs
GANNON, Cathe.	30	F	Spinster	20Mr02Fs
MORGAN, Owen	40	M	Laborer	20Mr02Fs
NICHOLSON, John	30	M	Laborer	20Mr02Fs
KEEFE, John	36	M	Laborer	20Mr02Fs
Pat	7	M	Child	20Mr02Fs
HARPER, Ann	30	F	Unknown	20Mr02Fs
CANNAH, Mary	26	F	Unknown	20Mr02Fs
CABRAH, Eliza	21	F	Spinster	20Mr02Fs
BEGNEY, Michl.	20	M	Laborer	20Mr02Fs
FARREN, Martha	25	F	Spinster	20Mr02Fs
MARTIN, Wm.	25	M	Laborer	20Mr02Fs
LYNCH, Robt.	40	M	Mason	20Mr02Fs
MARTHASON, Ann	20	F	Unknown	20Mr02Fs
Mary	.00	F	Infant	20Mr02Fs
BYRNES, Pat	33	M	Laborer	20Mr02Fs

NAMES OF PASSENGERS	AGE	SEX	OCCUPATIONS	DATE PORT SHIP
FLOOD, Ann	20	F	Spinster	20Mr02Fs
FARLAIN, Michl.	22	M	Laborer	20Mr02Fs
KELLY, Thos.	22	M	Laborer	20Mr02Fs
HEANNAN, Pat	24	M	Laborer	20Mr02Fs
CARNEY, Pat	27	M	Laborer	20Mr02Fs
RUSSELL, Jno.	25	M	Laborer	20Mr02Fs
KENNEY, Mary	20	M	Laborer	20Mr02Fs
MORAN, Ann	20	F	Spinster	20Mr02Fs
HANLEY, Ann	20	F	Spinster	20Mr02Fs
FARRELL, Mary	19	F	Spinster	20Mr02Fs
RYAN, Thos.	36	M	Laborer	20Mr02Fs
Margt.	65	F	Wi	20Mr02Fs
Ellen	15	F	Spinster	20Mr02Fs
MARSH, Wm.	20	M	Laborer	20Mr02Fs
BROUDER, Sarah	52	F	Wi	20Mr02Fs
Mary	22	F	Spinster	20Mr02Fs
BARMADICK, Mary	10	F	Unknown	20Mr02Fs
Cathe.	5	F	Child	20Mr02Fs
LAG, Ambrose	19	M	Laborer	20Mr02Fs
CAVANAH, Cathe.	24	F	Spinster	20Mr02Fs
MALONEY, Edward	22	M	Laborer	20Mr02Fs
MCCARRICK, James	35	M	Laborer	20Mr02Fs
Mary	32	F	Unknown	20Mr02Fs
James	3	M	Child	20Mr02Fs
Ann	2	F	Child	20Mr02Fs
Bernard	.00	M	Infant	20Mr02Fs
Cathe.	.00	F	Infant	20Mr02Fs
COLEMAN, Margt.	18	F	Spinster	20Mr02Fs
CONNERTON, Peter	17	M	Laborer	20Mr02Fs
MCINNINNY, Ed	17	M	Laborer	20Mr02Fs
CONNOR, Margt.	21	F	Spinster	20Mr02Fs
JOHNSON, Mary	19	F	Spinster	20Mr02Fs
HEANEY, James	20	M	Laborer	20Mr02Fs
DUFFY, James	20	M	Laborer	20Mr02Fs
JOHNSON, Wm.	17	M	Laborer	20Mr02Fs
FLOODY, James	28	M	Laborer	20Mr02Fs
VINCENT, John	44	M	Farmer	20Mr02Fs
Wm.	15	M	Unknown	20Mr02Fs
Eliza	7	F	Child	20Mr02Fs
Margt.	17	F	Unknown	20Mr02Fs
PHEARY, Dennis	18	M	Laborer	20Mr02Fs
RYAN, Pat	18	M	Laborer	20Mr02Fs
SKELLY, James	20	M	Laborer	20Mr02Fs
MURPHY, Michl.	36	M	Laborer	20Mr02Fs
OBRIAN, Jerry	18	M	Laborer	20Mr02Fs
DUGAN, James	29	M	Laborer	20Mr02Fs
CONCHLIN, Daniel	22	M	Laborer	20Mr02Fs
DOHERTY, Pat	35	M	Laborer	20Mr02Fs
Ellen	24	F	Unknown	20Mr02Fs
Michl.	3	M	Child	20Mr02Fs
Dennis	.00	M	Infant	20Mr02Fs
Michl.	20	M	Unknown	20Mr02Fs
LARKIN, Mary	50	F	Wi	20Mr02Fs
DUNNIGAN, Robt.	10	M	Unknown	20Mr02Fs
CONLEY, Bridget	18	F	Spinster	20Mr02Fs
MITCHELL, Cathe.	20	F	Spinster	20Mr02Fs
MALONE, Peggy	20	F	Spinster	20Mr02Fs
DODDY, Eliza	50	F	Wi	20Mr02Fs
FRENCH, Peggy	18	F	Spinster	20Mr02Fs
BAAGHAN, Margt.	50	F	Wi	20Mr02Fs
MAHAREN, John	34	M	Laborer	20Mr02Fs
MARTIN, Ellen	25	F	Unknown	20Mr02Fs
MORAN, Thos.	30	M	Laborer	20Mr02Fs
Ellen	27	F	Unknown	20Mr02Fs
Peter	.00	M	Infant	20Mr02Fs
LEE, Thos.	20	M	Laborer	20Mr02Fs
KELLY, Bridget	20	F	Spinster	20Mr02Fs
OMEALY, Biddy	20	F	Spinster	20Mr02Fs
GILFOIL, Sarah	18	F	Spinster	20Mr02Fs
LEATON, Ann	17	F	Spinster	20Mr02Fs
MITCHELL, Mary	12	F	Spinster	20Mr02Fs
GRADY, Fanney	20	F	Spinster	20Mr02Fs
Marcella	26	F	Spinster	20Mr02Fs
JOSEPH, Francis	24	M	Laborer	20Mr02Fs
OGLE, John	21	M	Laborer	20Mr02Fs
HONTAGE, Thos.	26	M	Laborer	20Mr02Fs
CURLEY, John	16	M	Laborer	20Mr02Fs
BURKE, Michl.	17	M	Laborer	20Mr02Fs
BERRINE, Pat	24	M	Laborer	20Mr02Fs
KENNEY, Edward	22	M	Laborer	20Mr02Fs
Michl.	7	M	Child	20Mr02Fs
SULLIVAN, Martin	20	M	Carpenter	20Mr02Fs
BOWARS, Pat	30	M	Laborer	20Mr02Fs
SHANNON, Edmund	20	M	Shoemaker	20Mr02Fs
HANLALAN, Andrew	18	M	Shoemaker	20Mr02Fs
KNOX, Pat	30	M	Shoemaker	20Mr02Fs
SAVAGE, Thos.	20	M	Shoemaker	20Mr02Fs
LAWRENCE, Michl.	19	M	Butcher	20Mr02Fs
HANAHAR, Johanna	19	F	Spinster	20Mr02Fs
DELANCY, Cathe.	18	F	Spinster	20Mr02Fs
MCCABE, Owen	20	M	Laborer	20Mr02Fs
GARVEY, Pat	22	M	Laborer	20Mr02Fs
BYRNES, James	22	M	Laborer	20Mr02Fs
WARD, Alice	20	F	Spinster	20Mr02Fs
TOOLE, Pat	29	M	Plasterer	20Mr02Fs
OGORMAN, Judy	21	F	Spinster	20Mr02Fs
CONROY, Maria	30	F	Unknown	20Mr02Fs
Cathe.	7	F	Child	20Mr02Fs
Margt.	.00	F	Infant	20Mr02Fs
DOOLEY, John	55	M	Butcher	20Mr02Fs
Thomas	25	M	Butcher	20Mr02Fs
Henry	12	M	Unknown	20Mr02Fs
MANUEL, John	35	M	Laborer	20Mr02Fs
CORRIGAN, James	30	M	Laborer	20Mr02Fs
CASEY, Hannah	50	F	Wi	20Mr02Fs
WHEELAN, Bridget	30	F	Unknown	20Mr02Fs
GANNON, Mary-Anne	35	F	Unknown	20Mr02Fs
WHEELAN, Mary	30	F	Spinster	20Mr02Fs
DAVIES, John	21	M	Laborer	20Mr02Fs
JENNINGS, Edward	40	M	Laborer	20Mr02Fs
Pat	15	M	Laborer	20Mr02Fs
TULLY, Pat	27	M	Laborer	20Mr02Fs
MCDONALD, James	18	M	Laborer	20Mr02Fs
BRADY, Phillip	25	M	Laborer	20Mr02Fs
KEARNAN, Jno.	56	M	Laborer	20Mr02Fs
CAVANAGH, Michl.	50	M	Laborer	20Mr02Fs
LEARY, Keady	30	M	Laborer	20Mr02Fs
FINGER, Luke	21	M	Laborer	20Mr02Fs
DONELLY, Edward	65	M	Laborer	20Mr02Fs
John	40	M	Laborer	20Mr02Fs
Edward	30	M	Laborer	20Mr02Fs
REILLY, Mary	18	F	Laborer	20Mr02Fs
HANLAHAN, Wm.	40	M	Laborer	20Mr02Fs
James	11	M	Laborer	20Mr02Fs
Ellen	9	F	Child	20Mr02Fs
GORASK, James	30	M	Laborer	20Mr02Fs
Mary	30	F	Unknown	20Mr02Fs
WATSON, Jno.	60	M	Laborer	20Mr02Fs
Eliza	14	F	Unknown	20Mr02Fs
BREEN, James	40	M	Laborer	20Mr02Fs
MAHAR, Timothy	30	M	Laborer	20Mr02Fs
Timothy	12	M	Laborer	20Mr02Fs
GANNON, Ellen	20	F	Spinster	20Mr02Fs
MAHAR, Judy	26	F	Spinster	20Mr02Fs
HANLAHAN, Mary	25	F	Spinster	20Mr02Fs
MADDEN, Margt.	20	F	Spinster	20Mr02Fs
MCKAY, Phillip	24	M	Laborer	20Mr02Fs
Mary	19	F	Spinster	20Mr02Fs
RYAN, John	28	M	Laborer	20Mr02Fs
Pat	22	M	Laborer	20Mr02Fs
Catherine	9	F	Child	20Mr02Fs
MCINTEE, Terry	40	M	Coachman	20Mr02Fs
Catherine	13	F	Unknown	20Mr02Fs
CONNER, Mary	25	F	Unknown	20Mr02Fs
FINN, Peter	25	M	Laborer	20Mr02Fs
STANTON, Hugh	21	M	Laborer	20Mr02Fs
KENNEDY, Margt.	24	F	Spinster	20Mr02Fs
Johanna	19	F	Spinster	20Mr02Fs
RUSSELL, Eliza	18	F	Spinster	20Mr02Fs
DEMPSY, John	22	M	Laborer	20Mr02Fs

NAMES OF PASSENGERS	AGE	SEX	OCCUPATIONS	DATE PORT SHIP
MCGINNIS, Margt.	22	F	Spinster	20Mr02Fs
CAMPBELL, Elizth.	23	F	Spinster	20Mr02Fs
GRADY, Biddy	33	F	Spinster	20Mr02Fs
BRYAN, Ann	28	F	Spinster	20Mr02Fs
COSGROVE, Edward	52	M	Farmer	20Mr02Fs
Edward	14	M	Farmer	20Mr02Fs
SULLIVAN, John	18	M	Laborer	20Mr02Fs
RAGAN, Cathe.	21	F	Unknown	20Mr02Fs
WELSH, Deborah	20	F	Unknown	20Mr02Fs
John	21	M	Unknown	20Mr02Fs
CONBAR, Pat	22	M	Unknown	20Mr02Fs
Mary	30	F	Unknown	20Mr02Fs
SHANAHAN, Edward	25	M	Laborer	20Mr02Fs
Mary	26	F	Unknown	20Mr02Fs
MAHAR, James	26	M	Laborer	20Mr02Fs
CORCORAN, Richd.	16	M	Laborer	20Mr02Fs
WELSH, Richard	30	M	Carpenter	20Mr02Fs
Mary	30	F	Unknown	20Mr02Fs
Michl.	2	M	Child	20Mr02Fs
John	.00	M	Infant	20Mr02Fs
Margt.	1	F	Child	20Mr02Fs
JENNINGS, John	50	M	Farmer	20Mr02Fs
Cathe.	50	F	Farmer	20Mr02Fs
Dennis	26	M	Laborer	20Mr02Fs
Judy	22	F	Spinster	20Mr02Fs
James	20	M	Laborer	20Mr02Fs
Margt.	18	F	Spinster	20Mr02Fs
Bridget	16	F	Spinster	20Mr02Fs
Henry	40	M	Farmer	20Mr02Fs
KENNEDY, Dennis	25	M	Laborer	20Mr02Fs
CUNNINGHAM, Pat	28	M	Laborer	20Mr02Fs
Mary	25	F	Unknown	20Mr02Fs
ROCKFORT, Thos.	25	M	Laborer	20Mr02Fs
Mary	18	F	Unknown	20Mr02Fs
REEVAN, Thomas	20	M	Laborer	20Mr02Fs
Mary	18	F	Unknown	20Mr02Fs
BOURKE, Thomas	20	M	Laborer	20Mr02Fs
CONNOR, Pat	33	M	Laborer	20Mr02Fs
HANAHAN, Henry	24	M	Laborer	20Mr02Fs
Bridget	20	F	Laborer	20Mr02Fs
MAHAR, Johannah	23	F	Spinster	20Mr02Fs
BROPHY, Cathe.	9	F	Child	20Mr02Fs
NORWOOD, Ellen	30	F	Spinster	20Mr02Fs
SHANNON, Richd.	35	M	Unknown	20Mr02Fs
CURRAN, Lawrence	30	M	Laborer	20Mr02Fs
REARDON, Danl.	25	M	Currier	20Mr02Fs
WATERS, Wm.	39	M	Laborer	20Mr02Fs
Mary	23	F	Spinster	20Mr02Fs
PARDY, John	30	M	Laborer	20Mr02Fs
HALL, John	19	M	Laborer	20Mr02Fs
MCINTYRE, Thos.	36	M	Laborer	20Mr02Fs
William	11	M	Laborer	20Mr02Fs
James	9	M	Child	20Mr02Fs
MEHAN, Andrew	30	M	Laborer	20Mr02Fs
SCULLY, Thomas	21	M	Laborer	20Mr02Fs
HANLIN, Martin	35	M	Laborer	20Mr02Fs
SHAW, Lawrence	30	M	Laborer	20Mr02Fs
DONOGHUE, Thos.	22	M	Laborer	20Mr02Fs
MASTERSON, Abraham	38	M	Laborer	20Mr02Fs
REED, Robt.	50	M	Laborer	20Mr02Fs
READY, Biddy	28	F	Spinster	20Mr02Fs
MCCAN, Ellen	20	F	Spinster	20Mr02Fs
MCCALL, Mary	22	F	Spinster	20Mr02Fs
CONWAY, Edward	25	M	Laborer	20Mr02Fs
Cathe.	25	F	Unknown	20Mr02Fs
Jacob-A.Westervelt	.00	M	Infant	20Mr02Fs
CANNY, James	20	M	Laborer	20Mr02Fs
ROACH, James	30	M	Laborer	20Mr02Fs
William	32	M	Laborer	20Mr02Fs
MORAN, John	34	M	Laborer	20Mr02Fs
Margt.	23	F	Unknown	20Mr02Fs
Mary	19	F	Spinster	20Mr02Fs
REYNOLDS, Martin	17	M	Laborer	20Mr02Fs
Ellen	19	F	Unknown	20Mr02Fs
PATTON, Pat-M.	20	M	Laborer	20Mr02Fs

NAMES OF PASSENGERS	AGE	SEX	OCCUPATIONS	DATE PORT SHIP
HARKINS, Michl.	21	M	Laborer	20Mr02Fs
JENKINS, Andrew	40	M	Laborer	20Mr02Fs
Catherine	50	F	Unknown	20Mr02Fs
CALBERT, Morris	30	M	Laborer	20Mr02Fs
WELSH, Frank	25	M	Laborer	20Mr02Fs
HENRY, Hannah	20	F	Spinster	20Mr02Fs
Matthew	7	M	Child	20Mr02Fs
Michl.	3	M	Child	20Mr02Fs
ROBINSON, Eliza	20	F	Spinster	20Mr02Fs
GULLIGAN, Barney	24	M	Laborer	20Mr02Fs
DOVER, John	19	M	Laborer	20Mr02Fs
BIRRELL, Edward	20	M	Laborer	20Mr02Fs
LYONS, Thos.	23	M	Gdnr	20Mr02Fs
CONROY, Peter	25	M	Laborer	20Mr02Fs
REILLY, Peter	28	M	Laborer	20Mr02Fs
Stephen	2	M	Child	20Mr02Fs
James	1	M	Child	20Mr02Fs
POWERS, Edward	30	M	Laborer	20Mr02Fs
MCGAFFAGAN, Jno.	25	M	Laborer	20Mr02Fs
WHEELAN, Michl.	26	M	Watchmaker	20Mr02Fs
RUSK, Samuel	20	M	Laborer	20Mr02Fs
RODGERS, John	19	M	Laborer	20Mr02Fs
DOHERTY, James	20	M	Laborer	20Mr02Fs
OHARE, Pat	25	M	Laborer	20Mr02Fs
Mary	35	F	Unknown	20Mr02Fs
John	7	M	Child	20Mr02Fs
James	.00	M	Infant	20Mr02Fs
WELDON, Peter	45	M	Butcher	20Mr02Fs
Alice	28	F	Unknown	20Mr02Fs
Margt.	10	F	Unknown	20Mr02Fs
Pat	8	M	Child	20Mr02Fs
Catherine	5	F	Child	20Mr02Fs
James	.00	M	Infant	20Mr02Fs
MULDOWN, Thos.	20	M	Laborer	20Mr02Fs
Mary	13	F	Unknown	20Mr02Fs
Cathe.	11	F	Unknown	20Mr02Fs
DANIELS, Elizth.	12	F	Unknown	20Mr02Fs
MURPHY, John	30	M	Unknown	20Mr02Fs
BRYANS, James	24	M	Carpenter	20Mr02Fs
MARRON, Owen	28	M	Laborer	20Mr02Fs
CAULEY, Pat	40	M	Laborer	20Mr02Fs
Cathe.	26	F	Unknown	20Mr02Fs
Pat	10	M	Unknown	20Mr02Fs
HARVEY, John	23	M	Laborer	20Mr02Fs
NOBLE, Wm.	25	M	Laborer	20Mr02Fs
MCCLUSKER, Elizth.	27	F	Spinster	20Mr02Fs
KENNEDY, Pat	25	M	Laborer	20Mr02Fs
Mary	20	F	Unknown	20Mr02Fs
SULLIVAN, John	26	M	Laborer	20Mr02Fs
DOYLE, Mike	20	M	Laborer	20Mr02Fs
SULLIVAN, Marty	16	M	Laborer	20Mr02Fs
MURPHY, Wm.	25	M	Laborer	20Mr02Fs
Mary	26	F	Unknown	20Mr02Fs
Margt.	20	F	Unknown	20Mr02Fs
NOLAN, John	24	M	Laborer	20Mr02Fs
James	26	M	Laborer	20Mr02Fs
Mary	24	F	Laborer	20Mr02Fs
William	.00	M	Infant	20Mr02Fs
Margt.	3	F	Child	20Mr02Fs
MCKEW, Margt.	34	F	Unknown	20Mr02Fs
Margt.	.00	F	Infant	20Mr02Fs
HERITY, Bridget	20	F	Unknown	20Mr02Fs
John	64	M	Laborer	20Mr02Fs
OSHAUGHNESSY, Pat	20	M	Laborer	20Mr02Fs
DRISCOLL, Martin	19	M	Laborer	20Mr02Fs
FARLEY, John	25	M	Laborer	20Mr02Fs
Margt.	25	F	Laborer	20Mr02Fs
Mary	.00	F	Infant	20Mr02Fs
VASS, Henry	20	M	Laborer	20Mr02Fs
WOOD, William	20	M	Laborer	20Mr02Fs
DOODY, Thos.	40	M	Laborer	20Mr02Fs
Jane	40	F	Unknown	20Mr02Fs
DUNN, Michl.	20	M	Laborer	20Mr02Fs
CONLAN, Peter	23	M	Farmer	20Mr02Fs
Margt.	22	F	Unknown	20Mr02Fs

NAMES OF PASSENGERS	AGE	SEX	OCCUPATIONS	DATE PORT SHIP
MULHOLLAND, Owen	30	M	Laborer	20Mr02Fs

WM.H.HARBECK 20 MARCH 1850

From Liverpool

NAMES OF PASSENGERS	AGE	SEX	OCCUPATIONS	DATE PORT SHIP
MCCAFFREY, Catherine	40	F	Unknown	20Mr02Co
James	19	M	Laborer	20Mr02Co
John	12	M	Laborer	20Mr02Co
Andrew	10	M	Laborer	20Mr02Co
MCMANUS, Bridget	16	F	Laborer	20Mr02Co
GINBERT, Joseph	18	M	Laborer	20Mr02Co
CRAWFORD, Frederick	30	M	Clerk	20Mr02Co
MONAGHAN, Pat	24	M	Clerk	20Mr02Co
MARTIN, Christopher	22	M	Farmer	20Mr02Co
MCGOWAN, James	20	M	Unknown	20Mr02Co
CAVANOGH, Michael	20	M	Unknown	20Mr02Co
CAVANAGH, Rose	17	F	Seamstress	20Mr02Co
Bridget	16	F	Seamstress	20Mr02Co
LYNCH, Owen	18	M	Farmer	20Mr02Co
FEGAN, Bessy	30	F	Farmer	20Mr02Co
John	12	M	Farmer	20Mr02Co
Margt.	13	F	Farmer	20Mr02Co
Mary	10	F	Farmer	20Mr02Co
Julia	9	F	Child	20Mr02Co
Ellen	5	F	Child	20Mr02Co
William	.00	M	Infant	20Mr02Co
KELLY, John	26	M	Laborer	20Mr02Co
JORDON, Thomas	23	M	Laborer	20Mr02Co
CONDRON, James	24	M	Laborer	20Mr02Co
Charley	17	M	Laborer	20Mr02Co
MCFEE, Mary	25	F	Laborer	20Mr02Co
WILLIAMS, Margret	25	F	Laborer	20Mr02Co
Anne	6	F	Child	20Mr02Co
Mary	6	F	Child	20Mr02Co
Margt.	25	F	Servant	20Mr02Co
MCENRY, Samuel	30	M	Carpenter	20Mr02Co
KELLY, Mathew	38	M	Carpenter	20Mr02Co
John	13	M	Laborer	20Mr02Co
GAFFNEY, Michael	27	M	Laborer	20Mr02Co
MANGAN, Patrick	19	M	Laborer	20Mr02Co
Bernard	20	M	Laborer	20Mr02Co
John	18	M	Laborer	20Mr02Co
HOLWELL, Anne	10	F	Seamstress	20Mr02Co
LAMB, Catherine	17	F	Seamstress	20Mr02Co
CARROLL, William	25	M	Unknown	20Mr02Co
Margt.	19	F	Unknown	20Mr02Co
MCKERRILE, Hugh	26	M	Unknown	20Mr02Co
Owen	28	M	Unknown	20Mr02Co
BYRNE, Edward	25	M	Unknown	20Mr02Co
MCKEVITT, Mary	25	F	Unknown	20Mr02Co
MOORE, Patrick	24	M	Unknown	20Mr02Co
Alice	21	F	Unknown	20Mr02Co
SYMTH, Edward	30	M	Unknown	20Mr02Co
SMITH, Francis	20	M	Unknown	20Mr02Co
Abbey	24	F	Unknown	20Mr02Co
Mary	50	F	Unknown	20Mr02Co
CARROLL, James	22	M	Unknown	20Mr02Co
VANCE, Martin	24	M	Unknown	20Mr02Co
MCKINNEEN, Margret	22	F	Unknown	20Mr02Co
FROTTER, Margt.	18	F	Unknown	20Mr02Co
HETHERINGTON, Anne	23	F	Unknown	20Mr02Co
POLLOCK, William	26	M	Unknown	20Mr02Co
GORMAN, James	30	M	Unknown	20Mr02Fs
GILTHROP, Samual	25	M	Unknown	20Mr02Co
LALOR, Edward	21	M	Unknown	20Mr02Co
CASEY, John	25	M	Unknown	20Mr02Co
MCMAHON, Eliza	21	F	Unknown	20Mr02Co
Margret	11	F	Unknown	20Mr02Co

NAMES OF PASSENGERS	AGE	SEX	OCCUPATIONS	DATE PORT SHIP
GEDDIS, Joseph	30	M	Unknown	20Mr02Co
DUFF, John	25	M	Unknown	20Mr02Co
DANTON, Richard	12	M	Unknown	20Mr02Co
GRAHAM, William	30	M	Unknown	20Mr02Co
William	25	M	Unknown	20Mr02Co
TRAVERS, Michael	30	M	Unknown	20Mr02Co
MCGUIRE, Margret	21	F	Unknown	20Mr02Co
JOHNSTON, Robt.	50	M	Unknown	20Mr02Co
Wm.	46	M	Unknown	20Mr02Co
James	17	M	Unknown	20Mr02Co
Sarah	15	F	Unknown	20Mr02Co
Anne	13	F	Unknown	20Mr02Co
Michl.	9	M	Child	20Mr02Co
David	7	M	Child	20Mr02Co
Eliza	5	F	Child	20Mr02Co
John	3	M	Child	20Mr02Co
Richard	.00	M	Infant	20Mr02Co
DWYER, Michl.	21	M	Painter	20Mr02Co
BLYTHE, John	21	M	Painter	20Mr02Co
Patrick	19	M	Painter	20Mr02Co
NEELAN, Edward	20	M	Laborer	20Mr02Co
DOYLE, James	21	M	Laborer	20Mr02Co
MULVEIGH, John	21	M	Laborer	20Mr02Co
FAY, Mary	30	F	Servant	20Mr02Co
Catherine	.00	F	Infant	20Mr02Co
SYMTH, Rose	19	F	Servant	20Mr02Co
SULLIVAN, Pat	30	M	Laborer	20Mr02Co
MCGUIRE, Pat	27	M	Laborer	20Mr02Co
FLEMING, James	20	M	Engraver	20Mr02Co
FEGAN, Alice	19	F	Servant	20Mr02Co
BORLAN, Ellen	18	F	Servant	20Mr02Co
MURTAGH, Edward	40	M	Farmer	20Mr02Co
Mary	37	F	Farmer	20Mr02Co
Edward	17	M	Farmer	20Mr02Co
SHERIDAN, Bartte	22	M	Laborer	20Mr02Co
Michl.	19	M	Laborer	20Mr02Co
Mary	20	F	Servant	20Mr02Co
Catherine	12	F	Servant	20Mr02Co
SMITH, Mary	18	F	Servant	20Mr02Co
GIBNEY, Mary	20	F	Servant	20Mr02Co
GILSHANNON, Bridget	24	F	Servant	20Mr02Co
MARTIN, Sarah	13	F	Servant	20Mr02Co
KELLY, William	21	M	Laborer	20Mr02Co
MASTERSON, John	18	M	Weaver	20Mr02Co
GIBBONS, Lawrence	20	M	Laborer	20Mr02Co
Bess	19	F	Servant	20Mr02Co
SYMTH, Joseph	21	M	Joiner	20Mr02Co
Robert	21	M	Joiner	20Mr02Co
FEGAN, William	30	M	Joiner	20Mr02Co
Thomas	18	M	Joiner	20Mr02Co
ARMSTRONG, Jane	18	F	Joiner	20Mr02Co
FARNLY, Michael	28	M	Joiner	20Mr02Co
Catherine	30	F	Servant	20Mr02Co
SYMTH, Catherine	30	M	Laborer	20Mr02Co
REILY, Thomas	21	M	Laborer	20Mr02Co
FEGAN, Honora	21	F	Laborer	20Mr02Co
DIAS, Thomas	20	M	Laborer	20Mr02Co
JAY, Walter	23	M	Laborer	20Mr02Co
KELLY, James	22	M	Laborer	20Mr02Co
LAW, John	20	M	Laborer	20Mr02Co
SMITH, William	20	M	Carpenter	20Mr02Co
QUINN, Pat	22	M	Laborer	20Mr02Co
MONAGHAN, James	22	M	Laborer	20Mr02Co
RICHARD, John	24	M	Painter	20Mr02Co
U-Mrs.	21	F	Servant	20Mr02Co
DAVIES, John	40	M	Servant	20Mr02Co
COLGAN, Michael	35	M	Laborer	20Mr02Co
HANLON, Michael	38	M	Laborer	20Mr02Co
MCCOY, Edward	21	M	Laborer	20Mr02Co
Emily	18	F	Servant	20Mr02Co
NOUD, Ellen	23	F	Servant	20Mr02Co
Julia	20	F	Servant	20Mr02Co
PEAT, Ellen	20	F	Servant	20Mr02Co
Catherine	18	F	Servant	20Mr02Co
CRAWFORD, John	22	M	Laborer	20Mr02Co

NAMES OF PASSENGERS	AGE	SEX	OCCUPATIONS	DATE PORT SHIP
DOHERTY, William	20	M	Laborer	20Mr02Co
William	24	M	Laborer	20Mr02Co
Catherine	21	F	Servant	20Mr02Co
CARROLL, Peter	19	M	Laborer	20Mr02Co
KING, John	21	M	Joiner	20Mr02Co
CAROLINE, James	21	M	Tailor	20Mr02Co
BYRNE, John	20	M	Laborer	20Mr02Co
NOLAN, James	24	M	Farmer	20Mr02Co
MILANOW, Michael	36	M	Farmer	20Mr02Co
U-Mrs.	25	F	Farmer	20Mr02Co
Thomas	60	M	Farmer	20Mr02Co
MCGOCEY, Peter	24	M	Farmer	20Mr02Co
REILY, Mary	26	F	Servant	20Mr02Co
MILANOW, Margret	18	F	Servant	20Mr02Co
Eliza	50	F	Servant	20Mr02Co
Margret	.00	F	Infant	20Mr02Co
MCGARNEY, John	20	M	Laborer	20Mr02Co
MCGOCEY, Anna	20	F	Servant	20Mr02Co
JANELL, Lawrence	18	M	Servant	20Mr02Co
Catherine	10	F	Servant	20Mr02Co
EGAN, Michael	25	M	Servant	20Mr02Co
JURY, Peter	20	M	Laborer	20Mr02Co
FANELL, James	20	M	Laborer	20Mr02Co
Anne	12	F	Servant	20Mr02Co
HEASTER, Mathew	35	M	Laborer	20Mr02Co
CASSIN, Patrick	25	M	Laborer	20Mr02Co
NEIL, Patrick	20	M	Laborer	20Mr02Co
SYMTH, Margret	23	F	Servant	20Mr02Co
LEE, William	20	M	Servant	20Mr02Co
HANIGAN, Edward	19	M	Farmer	20Mr02Co
AHEIL, James	20	M	Farmer	20Mr02Co
BROWNE, Thomas	35	M	Farmer	20Mr02Co
John	30	M	Farmer	20Mr02Co
Mary	27	F	Farmer	20Mr02Co
KEEGAN, John	17	M	Cooper	20Mr02Co
FITZPATRICK, Bridget	30	F	Servant	20Mr02Co
Michael	15	M	Laborer	20Mr02Co
SYMTH, Michael	36	M	Stctr	20Mr02Co
REEVES, William	30	M	Actor	20Mr02Co
SMYTH, Mary	22	F	Laborer	20Mr02Co
Margret	50	F	Seamstress	20Mr02Co
MCFARLON, James	20	M	Tailor	20Mr02Co
SMITH, John	30	M	Plumber	20Mr02Co
GRAIL, Mary	26	F	Servant	20Mr02Co
FANNER, Edward	20	M	Farmer	20Mr02Co
Jane	19	F	Farmer	20Mr02Co
OBRIEN, Mary	19	F	Servant	20Mr02Co
MCDANIEL, Michael	50	M	Farmer	20Mr02Co
Catherine	49	F	Farmer	20Mr02Co
Mary	19	F	Farmer	20Mr02Co
Anne	16	F	Farmer	20Mr02Co
Allan	14	M	Farmer	20Mr02Co
Catherine	12	F	Farmer	20Mr02Co
James	10	M	Farmer	20Mr02Co
John	7	M	Child	20Mr02Co
Johanna	5	F	Child	20Mr02Co
Margret	2	F	Child	20Mr02Co
DANIEL, John	52	M	Farmer	20Mr02Co
Hanora	53	F	Farmer	20Mr02Co
Bryan	20	M	Farmer	20Mr02Co
James	18	M	Farmer	20Mr02Co
Edward	16	M	Farmer	20Mr02Co
Margret	14	F	Farmer	20Mr02Co
KELLY, James	60	M	Farmer	20Mr02Co
Mary	60	F	Farmer	20Mr02Co
John	30	M	Farmer	20Mr02Co
Thomas	20	M	Farmer	20Mr02Co
Pat	9	M	Child	20Mr02Co
Judy	13	F	Farmer	20Mr02Co
Anty	8	F	Child	20Mr02Co
MURPHY, James	42	M	Laborer	20Mr02Co
Mary	38	F	Servant	20Mr02Co
Richard	8	M	Laborer	20Mr02Co
Catherine	6	F	Servant	20Mr02Co
Pat	4	M	Laborer	20Mr02Co

NAMES OF PASSENGERS	AGE	SEX	OCCUPATIONS	DATE PORT SHIP
MURPHY, John	.00	M	Infant	20Mr02Co
DORAN, John	20	M	Laborer	20Mr02Co
SHANAHAN, Michael	21	M	Farmer	20Mr02Co
REILY, John	20	M	Farmer	20Mr02Co
DWYER, Richard	20	M	Farmer	20Mr02Co
MAHER, John	17	M	Farmer	20Mr02Co
MCGEOGHAN, Mary	20	F	Servant	20Mr02Co
MARKEY, Margret	16	F	Servant	20Mr02Co
GUILLEN, Sally	27	F	Servant	20Mr02Co
BUCHANAN, George	17	M	Laborer	20Mr02Co
BUNTING, William	22	M	Laborer	20Mr02Co
BANISTER, Hugh	30	M	Farmer	20Mr02Co
DUNNE, John	25	M	Farmer	20Mr02Co
FRACEY, Maurice	22	M	Laborer	20Mr02Co
MCRORY, Joseph	30	M	Plasterer	20Mr02Co
LYNCH, John	30	M	Farmer	20Mr02Co
Thomas	25	M	Farmer	20Mr02Co
FANELLY, Nicholas	25	M	Farmer	20Mr02Co
REILY, Anne	24	F	Servant	20Mr02Co
WHITEFIELD, Maria	21	F	Servant	20Mr02Co
BROWNE, Andrew	35	M	Farmer	20Mr02Co
U-Mrs.	30	F	Unknown	20Mr02Co
James	17	M	Unknown	20Mr02Co
Robert	14	M	Unknown	20Mr02Co
John	9	M	Child	20Mr02Co
Andrew	6	M	Child	20Mr02Co
Mary	4	F	Child	20Mr02Co
Hugh	1	M	Child	20Mr02Co
MOORE, Hugh	25	M	Laborer	20Mr02Co
CARTY, Michael	25	M	Farmer	20Mr02Co
HOGAN, Ellen	24	F	Servant	20Mr02Co
Catherine	28	F	Servant	20Mr02Co
FALLON, Edward	24	M	Laborer	20Mr02Co
MCCAHY, Pat	30	M	Laborer	20Mr02Co
MURPHY, Hanora	30	F	Laborer	20Mr02Co
MOYNAHAN, Humphry	16	M	Laborer	20Mr02Co
MALLON, Mil	21	M	Mason	20Mr02Co
FEGAN, Wm.	21	M	Bricklayer	20Mr02Co
BRIEN, Laurence	24	M	Bricklayer	20Mr02Co
BOGEN, Owen	21	M	Bricklayer	20Mr02Co
DORAN, Eliza	25	F	Servant	20Mr02Co
DEMPSEY, Mary	30	F	Servant	20Mr02Co
Judy	26	F	Laborer	20Mr02Co
HOWARTH, John	20	M	Laborer	20Mr02Co
BRYAN, Ellen	25	F	Servant	20Mr02Co
Mary	5	F	Child	20Mr02Co
HUNT, James	20	M	Laborer	20Mr02Co
DUNNE, Bridget	21	F	Servant	20Mr02Co
WHITE, John	27	M	Farmer	20Mr02Co
BRADY, Peter	22	M	Farmer	20Mr02Co
CONNOR, Cornelius	40	M	Farmer	20Mr02Co
Mary	30	F	Servant	20Mr02Co
John	13	M	Laborer	20Mr02Co
Nora	5	F	Servant	20Mr02Co
Mary	2	F	Child	20Mr02Co
LONG, Patrick	36	M	Unknown	20Mr02Co
Catherine	30	F	Unknown	20Mr02Co
U	7	F	Child	20Mr02Co
U	5	F	Child	20Mr02Co
U	3	F	Child	20Mr02Co
U	.00	F	Infant	20Mr02Co
CONNOR, John	34	M	Farmer	20Mr02Co
HERLIHY, Margret	21	F	Servant	20Mr02Co
CONNOR, Mary	20	F	Servant	20Mr02Co
DOODY, Daniel	25	M	Laborer	20Mr02Co
CALLAGHAN, John	27	M	Laborer	20Mr02Co
BROWNE, Denis	50	M	Farmer	20Mr02Co
U-Mrs.	50	F	Servant	20Mr02Co
Mary	13	F	Servant	20Mr02Co
Catherine	12	F	Servant	20Mr02Co
John	9	M	Child	20Mr02Co
James	7	M	Child	20Mr02Co
Judy	4	F	Child	20Mr02Co
MCCARTHY, Tim	27	M	Unknown	20Mr02Co
Dan	18	M	Laborer	20Mr02Co

NAMES OF PASSENGERS	AGE	SEX	OCCUPATIONS	DATE PORT SHIP
MURPHY, Malachy	30	M	Unknown	20Mr02Co
MCCARTHY, John	20	M	Unknown	20Mr02Co
COMISKEY, Patrick	26	M	Unknown	20Mr02Co
LEARLICH, Thomas	25	M	Unknown	20Mr02Co
Patrick	23	M	Unknown	20Mr02Co
HEANY, Patk.	26	M	Carpenter	20Mr02Co
FAMAN, James	25	M	Constable	20Mr02Co
Margret (W)	24	F	Wife	20Mr02Co
MOLONEY, Joseph	20	M	Farmer	20Mr02Co
Michael	18	M	Farmer	20Mr02Co
Nora	10	F	Servant	20Mr02Co
CAROLINE, Catherine	26	F	Stitcher	20Mr02Co
George	3	M	Laborer	20Mr02Co
BAGNALL, George	19	M	Tailor	20Mr02Co
CARROLL, John	25	M	Laborer	20Mr02Co
William	26	M	Farmer	20Mr02Co
EDGEWORTH, Mary	40	F	Servant	20Mr02Co
MARKEY, Margret	40	F	Unknown	20Mr02Co
Mary	15	F	Unknown	20Mr02Co
Mathew	17	M	Laborer	20Mr02Co
KENEDY, Ellen	40	F	Servant	20Mr02Co
CASH, Catherine	22	F	Seamstress	20Mr02Co

MARMION 20 MARCH 1850

From Liverpool

NAMES OF PASSENGERS	AGE	SEX	OCCUPATIONS	DATE PORT SHIP
CONROY, Margaret	40	F	Unknown	20Mr02Ct
Bessy	19	F	Servant	20Mr02Ct
Ellen	17	F	Servant	20Mr02Ct
Mary	16	F	Servant	20Mr02Ct
Daniel	13	M	Servant	20Mr02Ct
Margaret	15	F	Servant	20Mr02Ct
WALLS, William	26	M	Laborer	20Mr02Ct
MARA, Michael	26	M	Laborer	20Mr02Ct
John	26	M	Laborer	20Mr02Ct
Patrick	27	M	Laborer	20Mr02Ct
HICKEY, Patrick	20	M	Laborer	20Mr02Ct
OBRYAN, T.	29	M	Laborer	20Mr02Ct
MCKENNA, Patrick	24	M	Laborer	20Mr02Ct
Bryan	20	M	Laborer	20Mr02Ct
CLEARY, William	16	M	Servant	20Mr02Ct
Margaret	28	F	Unknown	20Mr02Ct
CARNEY, Falmouth	19	M	Laborer	20Mr02Ct
SWAINCOTT, Margt.	27	F	Unknown	20Mr02Ct
HARVEY, Walter	30	M	Laborer	20Mr02Ct
GREENE, James	35	M	Seaman	20Mr02Ct
CARROLL, Willm.	30	M	Mason	20Mr02Ct
GAFFNEY, Hugh	26	M	Laborer	20Mr02Ct
Mary	22	F	Unknown	20Mr02Ct
ROONEY, John	25	M	Laborer	20Mr02Ct
MORRIS, James	39	M	Miller	20Mr02Ct
MACK, Francis	20	M	Laborer	20Mr02Ct
MCCORMICK, Mary	35	F	Unknown	20Mr02Ct
MORRIS, Bridget	16	F	Servant	20Mr02Ct
BYRNE, Mary	35	F	Servant	20Mr02Ct
GILL, Mary	10	F	Servant	20Mr02Ct
KENEDY, Mary	15	F	Servant	20Mr02Ct
KIMOILY, Ellen	16	F	Servant	20Mr02Ct
TADION, Oeny	16	F	Servant	20Mr02Ct
FARRELL, Edwd.	26	M	Laborer	20Mr02Ct
GRAHAM, Willm.	26	M	Cbtmkr	20Mr02Ct
CUNNINGHAM, Thos.	22	M	Carpenter	20Mr02Ct
CARROLL, Patk.	26	M	Laborer	20Mr02Ct
FOGARTY, Jas.	25	M	Laborer	20Mr02Ct
Patk.	16	M	Laborer	20Mr02Ct
BOWE, Willm.	32	M	Laborer	20Mr02Ct
Margaret	27	F	Unknown	20Mr02Ct
Mary	.00	F	Infant	20Mr02Ct

NAMES OF PASSENGERS	AGE	SEX	OCCUPATIONS	DATE PORT SHIP
DORAN, Ellen	18	F	Servant	20Mr02Ct
PROPHY, Catherine	20	F	Servant	20Mr02Ct
RYAN, Judy	22	F	Servant	20Mr02Ct
ROURKE, John	25	M	Laborer	20Mr02Ct
James	24	M	Laborer	20Mr02Ct
Margaret	24	F	Laborer	20Mr02Ct
Eliza	4	F	Child	20Mr02Ct
Johanna	2	F	Child	20Mr02Ct
Honora	.10	F	Infant	20Mr02Ct
DOOLAN, Patrick	22	M	Laborer	20Mr02Ct
SKELAN, Jas.	30	M	Laborer	20Mr02Ct
CARROLL, John	24	M	Laborer	20Mr02Ct
MAHER, Phillip	20	M	Laborer	20Mr02Ct
BERGIN, Jeremiah	25	M	Laborer	20Mr02Ct
Elanor	35	F	Servant	20Mr02Ct
TRAIEY, Martin	20	M	Laborer	20Mr02Ct
Catherine	18	F	Servant	20Mr02Ct
ARMOND, John	21	M	Laborer	20Mr02Ct
HUME, Andrew	22	M	Laborer	20Mr02Ct
HEGARTY, Mary	30	F	Servant	20Mr02Ct
John	13	M	Unknown	20Mr02Ct
Thomas	11	M	Unknown	20Mr02Ct
KELLY, Celia	25	F	Servant	20Mr02Ct
KNARESBORO, Martin	22	M	Laborer	20Mr02Ct
BUTLER, James	18	M	Laborer	20Mr02Ct
BIENNAN, Martin	18	M	Carpenter	20Mr02Ct
GAFFE, James	45	M	Laborer	20Mr02Ct
Mary	30	F	Unknown	20Mr02Ct
Patrick	10	M	Unknown	20Mr02Ct
James	6	M	Child	20Mr02Ct
Michael	4	M	Child	20Mr02Ct
Margaret	1	F	Child	20Mr02Ct
PHELAN, Margt.	18	F	Servant	20Mr02Ct
ROURKE, John	20	M	Mason	20Mr02Ct
GATELEY, Thos.	40	M	Laborer	20Mr02Ct
Eleanor	35	F	Unknown	20Mr02Ct
CUNIFF, Ellen	26	F	Servant	20Mr02Ct
Michael	.00	M	Infant	20Mr02Ct
LARKIN, Patrick	27	M	Laborer	20Mr02Ct
HUILEY, Michael	24	M	Saddler	20Mr02Ct
MCGINTY, John	30	M	Laborer	20Mr02Ct
ODONNELL, James	24	M	Laborer	20Mr02Ct
ANDERSON, James	68	M	Farmer	20Mr02Ct
Died-At-Sea				
James	24	M	Farmer	20Mr02Ct
Mary	18	F	Unknown	20Mr02Ct
David	18	M	Servant	20Mr02Ct
KILLIAN, Michael	19	M	Laborer	20Mr02Ct
Margaret	15	F	Servant	20Mr02Ct
CARROLL, Lawrence	30	M	Printer	20Mr02Ct
DEMPSEY, John	26	M	Butcher	20Mr02Ct
MOLINEAUX, Willm.J.	17	M	Laborer	20Mr02Ct
FOGARTY, Cathe.	20	F	Unknown	20Mr02Ct
MALONE, Simon	30	M	Laborer	20Mr02Ct
PRESTON, James	24	M	Laborer	20Mr02Ct
Margaret	25	F	Unknown	20Mr02Ct
HANNAH, James	27	M	Laborer	20Mr02Ct
Mary-Ann	26	F	Unknown	20Mr02Ct
Thomas	4	M	Child	20Mr02Ct
John	2	M	Child	20Mr02Ct
Margaret	.11	F	Infant	20Mr02Ct
WARD, Bridget	26	F	Unknown	20Mr02Ct
Ellen	3	F	Child	20Mr02Ct
Catherine	.00	F	Infant	20Mr02Ct
MONAGHAN, Ceilia	21	F	Servant	20Mr02Ct
FARRELLY, Thos.	27	M	Tailor	20Mr02Ct
Christy	24	M	Laborer	20Mr02Ct
LOVETT, Pat	23	M	Laborer	20Mr02Ct
BALL, James	22	M	Laborer	20Mr02Ct
MCDONNELL, Pat	30	M	Shoemaker	20Mr02Ct
WHOLOHAN, John	30	M	Laborer	20Mr02Ct
Andrew	26	M	Laborer	20Mr02Ct
MANLY, Richard	27	M	Laborer	20Mr02Ct
ORSON, George	22	M	Laborer	20Mr02Ct
Maria	19	F	Unknown	20Mr02Ct

NAMES OF PASSENGERS	AGE	SEX	OCCUPATIONS	DATE PORT SHIP
NOTT, Catherine	25	F	Unknown	20Mr02Ct
MATTHEWS, Stephen	24	M	Laborer	20Mr02Ct
MCMAHON, Patt	24	M	Laborer	20Mr02Ct
Phillip	23	M	Laborer	20Mr02Ct
James	22	M	Laborer	20Mr02Ct
CLARKE, Michael	30	M	Mason	20Mr02Ct
KERWIN, John	25	M	Laborer	20Mr02Ct
Patrick	21	M	Laborer	20Mr02Ct
SHANAHAN, John	28	M	Laborer	20Mr02Ct
COSTELLO, Timothy	25	M	Laborer	20Mr02Ct
MANGING, Thomas	23	M	Laborer	20Mr02Ct
RYAN, Catherine	20	F	Servant	20Mr02Ct
RABBITT, Pat	20	M	Laborer	20Mr02Ct
MCDONNELL, Barthn.	27	M	Teacher	20Mr02Ct
REEL, William	21	M	Laborer	20Mr02Ct
HOPKINS, Daniel	22	M	Laborer	20Mr02Ct
MCMULLEN, Susanna	30	F	Unknown	20Mr02Ct
Ernest	11	M	Unknown	20Mr02Ct
Elisabeth	9	F	Child	20Mr02Ct
William	6	M	Child	20Mr02Ct
PLUNKETT, Mary	18	F	Servant	20Mr02Ct
HANLON, Thos.	18	M	Laborer	20Mr02Ct
FORD, Stephen	21	M	Laborer	20Mr02Ct
KERRIGAN, John	20	M	Laborer	20Mr02Ct
JONES, Benjamin	24	M	Laborer	20Mr02Ct
Henry	21	M	Laborer	20Mr02Ct
Rebecca	35	F	Unknown	20Mr02Ct
William	10	M	Unknown	20Mr02Ct
Joseph	8	M	Child	20Mr02Ct
Richard	3	M	Child	20Mr02Ct
Christy	1	M	Child	20Mr02Ct
FLYNN, John	26	M	Tailor	20Mr02Ct
TOOLE, Catherine	28	F	Servant	20Mr02Ct
LEARY, John	25	M	Laborer	20Mr02Ct
Richard	20	M	Laborer	20Mr02Ct
MURPHY, John	24	M	Laborer	20Mr02Ct
WALSH, John	18	M	Laborer	20Mr02Ct
Mary	22	F	Servant	20Mr02Ct
BARRON, Bridget	16	F	Servant	20Mr02Ct
HOGAN, Daniel	30	M	Laborer	20Mr02Ct
Mary	25	F	Unknown	20Mr02Ct
HOLDEN, Edward	24	M	Laborer	20Mr02Ct
James	20	M	Laborer	20Mr02Ct
Mary	22	F	Servant	20Mr02Ct
BURROWS, James	24	M	Laborer	20Mr02Ct
CAITY, Judy	45	F	Unknown	20Mr02Ct
COLLINS, Dennis	28	M	Laborer	20Mr02Ct
Patrick	20	M	Laborer	20Mr02Ct
Michael	21	M	Laborer	20Mr02Ct
BRIEN, John	23	M	Laborer	20Mr02Ct
FAGAN, Lawrence	35	M	Laborer	20Mr02Ct
WILLIS, Edwd.	21	M	Laborer	20Mr02Ct
COSTELLO, Dennis	18	M	Laborer	20Mr02Ct
LONDON, William	20	M	Laborer	20Mr02Ct
DONEGAN, Honora	44	F	Unknown	20Mr02Ct
Mary	20	F	Unknown	20Mr02Ct
Margaret	14	F	Unknown	20Mr02Ct
Johanna	11	F	Unknown	20Mr02Ct
Julia	13	F	Unknown	20Mr02Ct
Daniel	9	M	Child	20Mr02Ct
Honora	5	F	Child	20Mr02Ct
CALLAHAN, John	30	M	Laborer	20Mr02Ct
MCDERMOT, Patt	25	M	Laborer	20Mr02Ct
MCGUIRE, Mary	16	F	Servant	20Mr02Ct
MURPHY, John	21	M	Laborer	20Mr02Ct
DALY, James	22	M	Laborer	20Mr02Ct
CLEMENTS, Francis	21	M	Saddler	20Mr02Ct
CUNNINGHAM, Edwd.	24	M	Laborer	20Mr02Ct
HESLAND, Terence	28	M	Laborer	20Mr02Ct
COLLINS, John	22	M	Laborer	20Mr02Ct
HUGHES, Owen	25	M	Bricklayer	20Mr02Ct
KALEY, Judith	21	F	Unknown	20Mr02Ct
COLWELL, Mary	29	F	Servant	20Mr02Ct
CASEY, Thomas	30	M	Laborer	20Mr02Ct
Catherine	26	F	Unknown	20Mr02Ct
CASEY, Cornelius	2	M	Child	20Mr02Ct
Cornelius	28	M	Laborer	20Mr02Ct
Johanna	24	F	Unknown	20Mr02Ct
Thomas	.00	M	Infant	20Mr02Ct
HEALEY, James	33	M	Laborer	20Mr02Ct
Mary	25	F	Unknown	20Mr02Ct
John	28	M	Clerk	20Mr02Ct
Bridget	24	F	Servant	20Mr02Ct
CASEY, John	25	M	Laborer	20Mr02Ct
NOONAN, Willm.	26	M	Laborer	20Mr02Ct
MCGIVERN, John	26	M	Laborer	20Mr02Ct
SHAW, James	21	M	Watchmaker	20Mr02Ct
MEEHAN, Mary	28	F	Servant	20Mr02Ct
FARRELL, Peter	20	M	Laborer	20Mr02Ct
HUTCHINS, Michael	20	M	Laborer	20Mr02Ct
Mary	18	F	Servant	20Mr02Ct
NEARY, John	17	M	Saddler	20Mr02Ct
KELLY, Patt	26	M	Laborer	20Mr02Ct
MCNALLY, John	28	M	Laborer	20Mr02Ct
KENNEY, John	26	M	Laborer	20Mr02Ct
CRANNEY, Patt	26	M	Laborer	20Mr02Ct
MULHALL, Michael	24	M	Laborer	20Mr02Ct
MALONE, Edmund	22	M	Laborer	20Mr02Ct
HENESSY, Richard	26	M	Laborer	20Mr02Ct
BIENNAN, Martin	36	M	Laborer	20Mr02Ct
KEAN, Catherine	20	F	Servant	20Mr02Ct
HAGGARTY, Dennis	26	M	Servant	20Mr02Ct
Johanna	25	F	Unknown	20Mr02Ct
LARKIN, Eliza	25	F	Servant	20Mr02Ct
Ellen	19	F	Servant	20Mr02Ct
KENNEY, Edward	40	M	Laborer	20Mr02Ct
CORIGAN, Thomas	20	M	Laborer	20Mr02Ct
FEALEY, Thomas	20	M	Laborer	20Mr02Ct
HALLORAN, Johanna	40	F	Unknown	20Mr02Ct
Patrick	21	M	Laborer	20Mr02Ct
Patrick	22	M	Laborer	20Mr02Ct
Martin	20	M	Laborer	20Mr02Ct
DOBBIN, Edward	20	M	Laborer	20Mr02Ct
Catherine	12	F	Unknown	20Mr02Ct
SULLIVAN, Timothy	30	M	Laborer	20Mr02Ct
Mary	24	F	Unknown	20Mr02Ct
Mary	5	F	Child	20Mr02Ct
MARTIN, William	50	M	Gdnr	20Mr02Ct
Mary	50	F	Unknown	20Mr02Ct
MULLOWNY, Mary	30	F	Unknown	20Mr02Ct
MARTIN, John	16	M	Gdnr	20Mr02Ct
Michael	6	M	Child	20Mr02Ct
Ellen	.00	F	Infant	20Mr02Ct
DRISCOLL, Jeremiah	21	M	Laborer	20Mr02Ct
Margaret	28	F	Unknown	20Mr02Ct
Bridget	.00	F	Infant	20Mr02Ct
SULLIVAN, Ellen	25	F	Servant	20Mr02Ct
HALLORIN, Catherine	17	F	Servant	20Mr02Ct
NOLAN, John	25	M	Laborer	20Mr02Ct
MONSTER, Mary	30	F	Unknown	20Mr02Ct
Mary	13	F	Unknown	20Mr02Ct
Matt	10	M	Unknown	20Mr02Ct
Patt	8	M	Child	20Mr02Ct
Francis	6	M	Child	20Mr02Ct
John	2	M	Child	20Mr02Ct
DOWES, Margaret	34	F	Unknown	20Mr02Ct
DELANY, Mary	20	F	Servant	20Mr02Ct
BOWES, Mary	11	F	Unknown	20Mr02Ct
Hannah	9	F	Child	20Mr02Ct
Patrick	6	M	Child	20Mr02Ct
William	4	M	Child	20Mr02Ct
Kierin	2	M	Child	20Mr02Ct
Fanny	.00	F	Infant	20Mr02Ct
WARD, Michael	40	M	Laborer	20Mr02Ct
DIMOND, Margaret	00	F	Servant	20Mr02Ct
WALLS, Ann	00	F	Servant	20Mr02Ct

RHEIN 22 MARCH 1850

From Liverpool

NAMES OF PASSENGERS	AGE	SEX	OCCUPATIONS	DATE PORT SHIP
CONWAY, Martin	24	M	Stctr	22Mr02Fu
CRAIG, Thos.	25	M	Unknown	22Mr02Fu
CONNOR, Ann	28	F	Unknown	22Mr02Fu
Thomas	9	M	Child	22Mr02Fu
Pat	6	M	Child	22Mr02Fu
Ann	3	F	Child	22Mr02Fu
MCGILLIGAN, Mary	19	F	Dressmaker	22Mr02Fu
BRICE, Pat	25	M	Laborer	22Mr02Fu
Ann	40	F	Unknown	22Mr02Fu
Thomas	15	M	Unknown	22Mr02Fu
Cath.	20	F	Spinster	22Mr02Fu
FLYNN, Thos.	18	M	Laborer	22Mr02Fu
MCCOY, Peter	28	M	Unknown	22Mr02Fu
MCNAMEE, Bernd.	25	M	Unknown	22Mr02Fu
SHERIDAN, Michl.	40	M	Unknown	22Mr02Fu
KENNY, Thos.	27	M	Unknown	22Mr02Fu
DALTON, James	30	M	Unknown	22Mr02Fu
OCONNOR, Roger	20	M	Unknown	22Mr02Fu
MCGLOUGHLIN, Thos.	15	M	Unknown	22Mr02Fu
DEVINE, Andw.	14	M	Unknown	22Mr02Fu
CUNNINGHAM, Thos.	31	M	Unknown	22Mr02Fu
CORRIGAN, Hugh	38	M	Unknown	22Mr02Fu
BOYLAN, James	23	M	Unknown	22Mr02Fu
CLARKSON, James	47	M	Unknown	22Mr02Fu
Ann	24	F	Unknown	22Mr02Fu
Edward	.00	M	Infant	22Mr02Fu
MORAN, James	30	M	Unknown	22Mr02Fu
Margt.	30	F	Wife	22Mr02Fu
Elizth.	7	F	Child	22Mr02Fu
Mary	.00	F	Infant	22Mr02Fu
MCCULLOUGH, John	20	M	Laborer	22Mr02Fu
MEAGHER, Jeremiah	25	M	Laborer	22Mr02Fu
John	30	M	Unknown	22Mr02Fu
Neddy	20	M	Laborer	22Mr02Fu
FEARY, Mary	25	F	Spinster	22Mr02Fu
GALLAGHER, Thomas	22	M	Unknown	22Mr02Fu
GAVERTY, Francis	26	M	Unknown	22Mr02Fu
MCGRATH, P.	23	M	Unknown	22Mr02Fu
MURRAY, John	24	M	Unknown	22Mr02Fu
MCDONNELL, Eliza	23	F	Wife	22Mr02Fu
COX, Margt.	22	F	Wife	22Mr02Fu
SHANNON, Pat	30	M	Farmer	22Mr02Fu
EGAN, Kate	22	F	Spinster	22Mr02Fu
DUNN, John	30	M	Unknown	22Mr02Fu
KELLY, Michl.	40	M	Laborer	22Mr02Fu
RYAN, John	40	M	Unknown	22Mr02Fu
COX, Thomas	28	M	Unknown	22Mr02Fu
LUCKMAN, Mary	30	F	Unknown	22Mr02Fu
JOYCE, Bridgt.	28	F	Unknown	22Mr02Fu
FLANNERY, Kate	21	F	Unknown	22Mr02Fu
ROLLING, John	40	M	Unknown	22Mr02Fu
Ann	42	F	Wife	22Mr02Fu
Hugh	20	M	Unknown	22Mr02Fu
Mary	13	F	Unknown	22Mr02Fu
Ellen	.00	F	Infant	22Mr02Fu
Ann	8	F	Child	22Mr02Fu
Margt.	57	F	Unknown	22Mr02Fu
Wm.	7	M	Child	22Mr02Fu
Thomas	.00	M	Infant	22Mr02Fu
SEALLY, Michl.	20	M	Farmer	22Mr02Fu
HAWKSHAW, Robt.	22	M	Unknown	22Mr02Fu
LINDSAY, Mary	22	F	Spinster	22Mr02Fu
MCMAHON, Edwd.	10	M	Unknown	22Mr02Fu
Judy	8	F	Child	22Mr02Fu
LARKIN, Michl.	19	M	Unknown	22Mr02Fu
LARKIN, Mary	21	F	Spinster	22Mr02Fu
MORAN, Wm.	29	M	Laborer	22Mr02Fu
CLANCEY, Michl.	23	M	Unknown	22Mr02Fu
Margt.	20	F	Wife	22Mr02Fu
CORCORAN, Johanna	30	F	Unknown	22Mr02Fu
Mary	7	F	Child	22Mr02Fu
Michl.	.00	M	Infant	22Mr02Fu
ROGERS, Michl.	14	M	Laborer	22Mr02Fu
Ann	18	F	Unknown	22Mr02Fu
HAYES, Norah	16	F	Spinster	22Mr02Fu
TOOHY, Mary	17	F	Spinster	22Mr02Fu
FEENY, Francis	20	M	Laborer	22Mr02Fu
KELLY, John	20	M	Unknown	22Mr02Fu
HEAD, Michl.	19	M	Laborer	22Mr02Fu
DELANEY, Kate	30	F	Spinster	22Mr02Fu
Con.	7	M	Child	22Mr02Fu
George	12	M	Unknown	22Mr02Fu
Mary	51	F	Unknown	22Mr02Fu
Ellen Died-At-Sea	.00	F	Infant	22Mr02Fu
WALSH, Ellen	27	F	Spinster	22Mr02Fu
Michl.	.00	M	Infant	22Mr02Fu
MORRIS, Mary	28	F	Unknown	22Mr02Fu
Bridgt.	18	F	Unknown	22Mr02Fu
Ann	13	F	Unknown	22Mr02Fu
MARTIN, Michl.	38	M	Farmer	22Mr02Fu
Winifred	36	F	Wife	22Mr02Fu
John	.00	M	Infant	22Mr02Fu
ENRIGHT, Thomas	36	M	Unknown	22Mr02Fu
RAMSEY, Patterson	35	M	Laborer	22Mr02Fu
Jane	35	F	Wife	22Mr02Fu
ANSON, Sarah	24	M	Unknown	22Mr02Fu
MOORE, Thos.	27	M	Laborer	22Mr02Fu
Ellen	25	F	Wife	22Mr02Fu
ROONEY, Thomas	25	M	Laborer	22Mr02Fu
Wm.	16	M	Unknown	22Mr02Fu
WRIGHT, John	56	M	Unknown	22Mr02Fu
Dorothy	58	F	Wife	22Mr02Fu
James	9	M	Child	22Mr02Fu
John	7	M	Child	22Mr02Fu
Dorothea	5	F	Child	22Mr02Fu
Wm.	5	M	Child	22Mr02Fu
Thomas	.00	M	Infant	22Mr02Fu
MEENY, Margt.	25	F	Unknown	22Mr02Fu
RYAN, Ellen	17	F	Unknown	22Mr02Fu
LEIGH, Mary	17	F	Unknown	22Mr02Fu
RYAN, Bridgt.	23	F	Unknown	22Mr02Fu
HALLOR, Jas.	19	M	Laborer	22Mr02Fu
MAE, Neil	20	M	Laborer	22Mr02Fu
CARTON, Cornelius	25	M	Unknown	22Mr02Fu
BURNES, Wm.	23	M	Unknown	22Mr02Fu
LEIGH, Michl.	22	M	Unknown	22Mr02Fu
GLEESON, Thos.	30	M	Unknown	22Mr02Fu
WHEELAN, John	25	M	Unknown	22Mr02Fu
PRATT, John	24	M	Unknown	22Mr02Fu
BUTLER, Thos.	24	M	Unknown	22Mr02Fu
PETERS, John	23	M	Unknown	22Mr02Fu
SMITH, Michl.	22	M	Unknown	22Mr02Fu
Mary	21	F	Spinster	22Mr02Fu
MORAN, John	19	M	Laborer	22Mr02Fu
BAYLEY, Ann	14	F	Unknown	22Mr02Fu
GAMPHIA, Richd.	26	M	Unknown	22Mr02Fu
Johanna	22	F	Wife	22Mr02Fu
KELLY, Thos.	20	M	Laborer	22Mr02Fu
Mary	17	F	Spinster	22Mr02Fu
DEVINE, John	38	M	Laborer	22Mr02Fu
Ellen	18	F	Spinster	22Mr02Fu
Phillips	.00	M	Infant	22Mr02Fu
GANGAM, Peter	20	M	Unknown	22Mr02Fu
MONAGHAN, Mary	24	F	Wife	22Mr02Fu
MAGELLAH, Jas.	14	M	Servant	22Mr02Fu
HALLIP, John	31	M	Laborer	22Mr02Fu
BENNETT, Wm.	34	M	Laborer	22Mr02Fu
WILSON, Thos.	15	M	Laborer	22Mr02Fu
ANLON, Jas.	28	M	Laborer	22Mr02Fu

NAMES OF PASSENGERS	AGE	SEX	OCCUPATIONS	DATE PORT SHIP
BRANAN, John	24	M	Laborer	22Mr02Fu
Mary	30	F	Wife	22Mr02Fu
MULHAL, Patrick	17	M	Laborer	22Mr02Fu
WALSH, Mary	35	M	Laborer	22Mr02Fu
Thomas	8	M	Child	22Mr02Fu
James	.00	M	Infant	22Mr02Fu
Bridget	6	F	Child	22Mr02Fu
BURNS, Ellen	23	F	Wife	22Mr02Fu
WALSH, Kate	20	F	Wife	22Mr02Fu
COGHLAN, Margt.	56	F	Unknown	22Mr02Fu
Mary	18	F	Spinster	22Mr02Fu
CAHIL, Winifred	20	F	Spinster	22Mr02Fu
LOWRY, Thomas	30	M	Laborer	22Mr02Fu
CONORTON, Michael	28	M	Unknown	22Mr02Fu
DELAHUNTY, Pat	55	M	Unknown	22Mr02Fu
RUDDEN, Andrew	60	M	Unknown	22Mr02Fu
MCKENNA, Peter	42	M	Unknown	22Mr02Fu
KELLY, Bernard-T.	19	M	Unknown	22Mr02Fu
LAIHY, Thomas	45	M	Unknown	22Mr02Fu
BAUGH, James	40	M	Unknown	22Mr02Fu
KENNEDY, Pat	29	M	Unknown	22Mr02Fu
MAGUIRE, Jas.	30	M	Unknown	22Mr02Fu
BROUGHALL, Anne	19	F	Wife	22Mr02Fu
Anne	.00	F	Infant	22Mr02Fu
Christopher	.00	M	Infant	22Mr02Fu
MALONY, Michael	29	M	Laborer	22Mr02Fu
DONOGHUE, Pat	13	M	Unknown	22Mr02Fu
OBRIEN, Bryan	22	M	Unknown	22Mr02Fu
DEGNAN, Owen	17	M	Laborer	22Mr02Fu
DOYLE, Mary	32	F	Wife	22Mr02Fu
WATERS, Ellen	28	F	Unknown	22Mr02Fu
Peter	.00	M	Infant	22Mr02Fu
MORKEN, Pat	20	M	Farmer	22Mr02Fu
Kate	22	F	Wife	22Mr02Fu
BERGIN, Mary	46	F	Unknown	22Mr02Fu
MCDONNELL, John	17	M	Laborer	22Mr02Fu
Michael	15	M	Unknown	22Mr02Fu
Daniel	12	M	Unknown	22Mr02Fu
Bridget	10	F	Unknown	22Mr02Fu
Valentine	.00	M	Infant	22Mr02Fu
KEHOE, Michael	35	M	Laborer	22Mr02Fu
Ellen	22	F	Wife	22Mr02Fu
MARTIN, John	22	M	Carpenter	22Mr02Fu
BEATY, Margt.	30	F	Servant	22Mr02Fu
CONOLLY, Mary	22	F	Unknown	22Mr02Fu
CALLAHAN, Peter	40	M	Laborer	22Mr02Fu
Mary	10	F	Unknown	22Mr02Fu
William	4	M	Child	22Mr02Fu
Ellen	.00	F	Infant	22Mr02Fu
MANGAN, Pat	45	M	Farmer	22Mr02Fu
TOOLE, Mary	55	F	Wife	22Mr02Fu
KEEFE, Bridget	22	F	Spinster	22Mr02Fu
BOYLE, Biddy	34	F	Unknown	22Mr02Fu
Mary	10	F	Unknown	22Mr02Fu
Pat	8	M	Child	22Mr02Fu
Kate	4	F	Child	22Mr02Fu
Thomas	.00	F	Infant	22Mr02Fu
CONOLY, Edwd.	20	M	Laborer	22Mr02Fu
ROWAN, John	21	M	Laborer	22Mr02Fu
DEGNAN, Mary	13	F	Spinster	22Mr02Fu
REILLY, Anne	16	F	Unknown	22Mr02Fu
Mary	5	F	Child	22Mr02Fu
GIBONS, Ellen	20	F	Unknown	22Mr02Fu
BRADY, Anne	50	F	Unknown	22Mr02Fu
DIGNAN, Edward	15	M	Unknown	22Mr02Fu
Anne	11	F	Unknown	22Mr02Fu
Margaret	9	F	Child	22Mr02Fu
Kate	.00	F	Infant	22Mr02Fu
REDDY, Pat	20	M	Laborer	22Mr02Fu
FARRAY, Pat	23	M	Unknown	22Mr02Fu
WATERS, Pat	21	M	Unknown	22Mr02Fu
MCMAHON, John	28	M	Unknown	22Mr02Fu
THOMPSON, Margaret	30	F	Wife	22Mr02Fu
OCONNOR, Cecily	38	F	Servant	22Mr02Fu
BYRNE, Mary	17	F	Spinster	22Mr02Fu

NAMES OF PASSENGERS	AGE	SEX	OCCUPATIONS	DATE PORT SHIP
MCENERNEY, Pat	30	M	Laborer	22Mr02Fu
MCDONNELL, James	50	M	Unknown	22Mr02Fu
Bridget	38	F	Wife	22Mr02Fu
DILLON, John	35	M	Farmer	22Mr02Fu
Kate	26	F	Wife	22Mr02Fu
John	4	M	Child	22Mr02Fu
Mary	.00	F	Infant	22Mr02Fu
GRENNIS, Ellen	40	F	Wife	22Mr02Fu
Paddy	6	M	Child	22Mr02Fu
MCKINSTRY, Ellen	45	M	Unknown	22Mr02Fu
William	20	M	Laborer	22Mr02Fu
Alice	.00	F	Infant	22Mr02Fu
MALONE, Mary	25	F	Servant	22Mr02Fu
CONWAY, Augustus	23	M	Laborer	22Mr02Fu
MULHAL, Con.	20	M	Laborer	22Mr02Fu
NOWLAN, Stephenson	27	M	Unknown	22Mr02Fu
KEEFE, Michael	9	M	Child	22Mr02Fu
BOWE, Ross	23	M	Unknown	22Mr02Fu
KENNY, Ann	19	F	Spinster	22Mr02Fu
SHEARON, Francis	27	M	Laborer	22Mr02Fu
SCULLY, Michael	29	M	Unknown	22Mr02Fu
MARTIN, Thomas	26	M	Unknown	22Mr02Fu
COLEMAN, James	18	M	Unknown	22Mr02Fu
CAMPBELL, Anne	37	F	Wife	22Mr02Fu
Kate	20	F	Spinster	22Mr02Fu
MCGRATH, Kate	30	F	Unknown	22Mr02Fu
Johanna	27	F	Unknown	22Mr02Fu
GORDON, John	28	M	Laborer	22Mr02Fu
FRAZER, William	34	M	Unknown	22Mr02Fu
BROWN, Richard	22	M	Unknown	22Mr02Fu
CRAWFORD, George	23	M	Unknown	22Mr02Fu
MEAGHER, James	21	M	Unknown	22Mr02Fu
Bridget	40	F	Wife	22Mr02Fu
FORD, Pat	20	M	Unknown	22Mr02Fu
BROUGHTON, Emekial	30	M	Architect	22Mr02Fu
Cath.	25	F	Wife	22Mr02Fu
HODGKINSON, B.	34	M	Farmer	22Mr02Fu
ARMSTROTTER, U-Mrs.	50	F	Wife	22Mr02Fu
U-Miss	23	F	Spinster	22Mr02Fu
John-Wm.	18	M	Farmer	22Mr02Fu
Georgianna	15	F	Spinster	22Mr02Fu
MASON, Margt.	32	F	Unknown	22Mr02Fu
BELL, Robert	30	M	Schm	22Mr02Fu
Maria	23	F	Wife	22Mr02Fu
DRYSDALE, Henry	30	M	Laborer	22Mr02Fu
Henry	30	M	Schm	22Mr02Fu
Rebecca-Mrs.	24	F	Unknown	22Mr02Fu
Harriet	.00	F	Infant	22Mr02Fu
WILSON, George	26	M	Bookkeeper	22Mr02Fu
WALL, Peggy	27	F	Spinster	22Mr02Fu
LARKIN, Michl.	00	M	Unknown	22Mr02Fu
U, John	00	M	Unknown	22Mr02Fu
John	00	M	Unknown	22Mr02Fu

AMERICAN-EAGLE 23 MARCH 1850

From London

NAMES OF PASSENGERS	AGE	SEX	OCCUPATIONS	DATE PORT SHIP
DALLECKY, Marcus	29	M	Gentleman	23Mr06Cl
CANTON, William	25	M	Tailor	23Mr06Cl
Catherine	25	F	Unknown	23Mr06Cl
Catherine	2	F	Child	23Mr06Cl
LYONS, Catherine	19	F	Unknown	23Mr06Cl

OHIO 26 MARCH 1850

From Chagres And Havana

NAMES OF PASSENGERS	AGE	SEX	OCCUPATIONS	DATE PORT SHIP
HILL, Da-Rosa	00	U	Unknown	26Mr47Ds

ROSANNA 01 APRIL 1850

From St.Kites

NAMES OF PASSENGERS	AGE	SEX	OCCUPATIONS	DATE PORT SHIP
THWAITE, James-H.	48	M	Planter	01Ap48Ga
U-Mrs.	28	F	Planter	01Ap48Ga
Peter	8	M	Child	01Ap48Ga
Joshiah	7	M	Child	01Ap48Ga
U-Miss	6	F	Child	01Ap48Ga
Charles	4	M	Child	01Ap48Ga
KENNEDY, Saml.Scott	22	M	Merchant	01Ap48Ga
HARRY, Albert	24	M	Merchant	01Ap48Ga

LIVERPOOL 03 APRIL 1850

From Liverpool

NAMES OF PASSENGERS	AGE	SEX	OCCUPATIONS	DATE PORT SHIP
MCCARTY, Margeret	14	F	Unknown	03Ap02Bx
Daniel	6	M	Child	03Ap02Bx
WALSH, Mike	25	M	Laborer	03Ap02Bx
U, U	30	M	Laborer	03Ap02Bx
MULLEN, U	20	M	Laborer	03Ap02Bx
Mary	23	F	Wife	03Ap02Bx
FLAHERTY, Mary	23	F	Servant	03Ap02Bx
MYERS, Martin	40	M	Laborer	03Ap02Bx
Mary	32	F	Wife	03Ap02Bx
Jane	3	F	Child	03Ap02Bx
Bridget	.05	F	Infant	03Ap02Bx
Pat.	50	M	Laborer	03Ap02Bx
PURCELL, John	20	M	Laborer	03Ap02Bx
OROHO, My.	30	U	Servant	03Ap02Bx
FARRELL, Peter	20	M	Laborer	03Ap02Bx
Ann	20	F	Servant	03Ap02Bx
MURDOCK, Pat.	22	M	Laborer	03Ap02Bx
CROWLEY, Richd.	35	M	Mechanic	03Ap02Bx
BRENNAN, Peter	30	M	Brick Maker	03Ap02Bx
HENRY, Thos.	28	M	Laborer	03Ap02Bx
DUCK, Thos.	35	M	Laborer	03Ap02Bx
WARD, Mick	18	M	Laborer	03Ap02Bx
JACKSON, Jno.	18	M	Laborer	03Ap02Bx
KING, Cath.	18	F	Servant	03Ap02Bx
CUNNIFF, Mary	22	F	Servant	03Ap02Bx
DUCK, Cath.	20	F	Servant	03Ap02Bx
TIERNAN, Honor	25	F	Servant	03Ap02Bx
COONEY, Ann	24	F	Servant	03Ap02Bx
FURY, Celia	24	F	Servant	03Ap02Bx
COAN, Mary	12	F	Servant	03Ap02Bx
BRENNAN, Jane	12	F	Servant	03Ap02Bx
COSTELLO, Jas.	20	M	Clerk	03Ap02Bx
COYLE, Pat	40	M	Laborer	03Ap02Bx
BYRNE, Pat.	33	M	Laborer	03Ap02Bx
GLENAHAN, John	18	M	Laborer	03Ap02Bx
THILCREASE, Thos.	20	M	Laborer	03Ap02Bx
FLYNN, Bridgt.	25	F	Servant	03Ap02Bx
MAHER, Bridgt.	20	F	Servant	03Ap02Bx
CORMICK, Danl.	26	M	Laborer	03Ap02Bx
Bridgt.	25	F	Wife	03Ap02Bx
RYAN, Cath.	23	F	Servant	03Ap02Bx
HOWARD, John	40	M	Laborer	03Ap02Bx
BUSH, Honor	21	F	Servant	03Ap02Bx
GLASGOW, Edwd.	50	M	Tailor	03Ap02Bx
Jno.	25	M	Tailor	03Ap02Bx
Mary	28	F	Servant	03Ap02Bx
Marcella	21	F	Servant	03Ap02Bx
MCANDREW, Peter	19	M	Laborer	03Ap02Bx
Pat	40	M	Laborer	03Ap02Bx
CADEN, Mary	20	F	Servant	03Ap02Bx
COUGHLIN, Mick	20	M	Laborer	03Ap02Bx
NALLIN, Wm.	25	M	Laborer	03Ap02Bx
Pat	13	M	Laborer	03Ap02Bx
FLYNN, Mick	8	M	Child	03Ap02Bx
Bridt.	20	F	Servant	03Ap02Bx
Margt.	18	F	Servant	03Ap02Bx
OHARA, Martin	30	M	Laborer	03Ap02Bx
CLARKE, Cath.	24	F	Servant	03Ap02Bx
POWER, Jno.	25	M	Cooper	03Ap02Bx
FALLON, Pat	28	M	Laborer	03Ap02Bx
Ann	6	F	Child	03Ap02Bx
MARA, Mary	21	F	Servant	03Ap02Bx
MCCOY, Cormick	20	M	Laborer	03Ap02Bx
Nancy	4	F	Child	03Ap02Bx
Pat	3	M	Child	03Ap02Bx
WALSH, Mary	15	F	Servant	03Ap02Bx
Cath.	12	F	Servant	03Ap02Bx
RYAN, John	15	M	Laborer	03Ap02Bx
Willm.	14	M	Laborer	03Ap02Bx
Margt.	35	F	Servant	03Ap02Bx
Thos.	11	M	Laborer	03Ap02Bx
ONEILL, Margt.	30	F	Servant	03Ap02Bx
Eliza	10	F	Servant	03Ap02Bx
Margt.	8	F	Child	03Ap02Bx
John	4	M	Child	03Ap02Bx
Jas.	.04	M	Infant	03Ap02Bx
KENNEY, Margt.	35	F	Servant	03Ap02Bx
CASEY, David	43	M	Laborer	03Ap02Bx
MCCARTY, Corn	16	M	Laborer	03Ap02Bx
DONNELLY, Cath.	28	F	Servant	03Ap02Bx
Mary	.07	F	Infant	03Ap02Bx
CAHILL, Peter	17	M	Laborer	03Ap02Bx
MCLOGHLIN, John	18	M	Laborer	03Ap02Bx
NULTY, Bridgt.	25	F	Servant	03Ap02Bx
CASEY, Jas.	24	M	Laborer	03Ap02Bx
CARR, Peter	11	M	Laborer	03Ap02Bx
Cath.	9	F	Child	03Ap02Bx
MCANDREW, Pat	35	M	Carpenter	03Ap02Bx
Edwd.	10	M	Unknown	03Ap02Bx
Cath.	8	F	Child	03Ap02Bx
MCWENAHAN, Mary	48	F	Servant	03Ap02Bx
LAVAN, Mick	25	M	Laborer	03Ap02Bx
ODONNELL, Jas.	18	M	Butcher	03Ap02Bx
LYNCH, Jas.	19	M	Laborer	03Ap02Bx
FRINEGAN, Pat	17	M	Laborer	03Ap02Bx
DUNN, Anty	27	M	Milliner	03Ap02Bx
John	14	M	Laborer	03Ap02Bx
John	25	M	Laborer	03Ap02Bx
DONOHUE, Pat	20	M	Laborer	03Ap02Bx
LOWRY, Pat	20	M	Laborer	03Ap02Bx
FAYNE, Honor	17	F	Laborer	03Ap02Bx
KANE, Ellen	18	F	Servant	03Ap02Bx
DOWLING, Dan	22	M	Laborer	03Ap02Bx
MASTERSON, John	30	M	Surveyor	03Ap02Bx
DOWLING, Jane	22	F	Laborer	03Ap02Bx
SWEHAN, Honor	20	F	Dressmaker	03Ap02Bx
Jane	16	F	Dressmaker	03Ap02Bx
MULLAHY, Mick	18	M	Laborer	03Ap02Bx
FARRELL, Pat	40	M	Farmer	03Ap02Bx

NAMES OF PASSENGERS	AGE	SEX	OCCUPATIONS	DATE PORT SHIP
FARRELL, Cath.	25	F	Servant	03Ap02Bx
Pat	.08	M	Infant	03Ap02Bx
IRWIN, Mary	40	F	Servant	03Ap02Bx
Geo.	12	M	Servant	03Ap02Bx
Bessy	10	F	Servant	03Ap02Bx
Mary	.03	F	Infant	03Ap02Bx
PENFIELD, Mary	25	F	Servant	03Ap02Bx
BYRNE, Mary	21	F	Servant	03Ap02Bx
GAFFEY, Ann	20	F	Servant	03Ap02Bx
MCBREN, Cath.	20	F	Servant	03Ap02Bx
HAMITT, Judy	26	F	Servant	03Ap02Bx
KILBRIDE, Edw.	28	M	Laborer	03Ap02Bx
Mary	21	F	Servant	03Ap02Bx
Jas.	45	M	Laborer	03Ap02Bx
Jas.	18	M	Laborer	03Ap02Bx
Mary	16	F	Servant	03Ap02Bx
Owen	13	M	Laborer	03Ap02Bx
Rose	10	F	Servant	03Ap02Bx
Frank	8	M	Child	03Ap02Bx
HARRIS, Johan	21	M	Servant	03Ap02Bx
HICKEY, Ellen	20	F	Servant	03Ap02Bx
DAVIES, Mick	21	M	Laborer	03Ap02Bx
Jas.	20	M	Laborer	03Ap02Bx
WELSH, Thos.	21	M	Laborer	03Ap02Bx
DUNN, David	21	M	Farmer	03Ap02Bx
READY, Richd.	23	M	Farmer	03Ap02Bx
CONWAY, John	30	M	Farmer	03Ap02Bx
PEMBROKE, John	21	M	Shoemaker	03Ap02Bx
CARROLL, Willm.	21	M	Tailor	03Ap02Bx
RICE, Willm.	24	M	Laborer	03Ap02Bx
WHITE, Mary	25	F	Servant	03Ap02Bx
COGHLAN, Rose	30	F	Servant	03Ap02Bx
LACEY, Mary	20	F	Servant	03Ap02Bx
BOYSON, Willm.	60	M	Laborer	03Ap02Bx
Martin	19	M	Laborer	03Ap02Bx
John	16	M	Laborer	03Ap02Bx
Mary	20	F	Servant	03Ap02Bx
Judy	20	F	Servant	03Ap02Bx
Sally	9	F	Child	03Ap02Bx
Peggy	6	F	Child	03Ap02Bx
MCDONNELL, Bridgt.	19	F	Servant	03Ap02Bx
HANLEY, Jas.	20	M	Laborer	03Ap02Bx
MORRISEY, Tim	30	M	Laborer	03Ap02Bx
MEHAN, Pat	22	M	Laborer	03Ap02Bx
MCKENE, Pat	25	M	Miner	03Ap02Bx
Jno.	18	M	Laborer	03Ap02Bx
CAMPBELL, Thos.	6	M	Child	03Ap02Bx
RYAN, Kearn	40	M	Laborer	03Ap02Bx
Mary	35	F	Wife	03Ap02Bx
Ellen	3	F	Child	03Ap02Bx
Thos.	.07	M	Infant	03Ap02Bx
HUGHES, Richd.	28	M	Laborer	03Ap02Bx
CULLINAN, Jas.	27	M	Laborer	03Ap02Bx
HYLAND, Peggy	23	F	Servant	03Ap02Bx
MALLOY, Bridgt.	30	F	Servant	03Ap02Bx
SCANLON, Felix	50	M	Laborer	03Ap02Bx
Bridgt.	50	F	Wife	03Ap02Bx
Pat	11	M	None	03Ap02Bx
Michl.	9	M	Child	03Ap02Bx
COLLIGAN, John	24	M	Laborer	03Ap02Bx
MCAVOY, Mary	18	F	Servant	03Ap02Bx
DWYER, Cath.	40	F	Servant	03Ap02Bx
John	20	M	Laborer	03Ap02Bx
Mary	11	F	None	03Ap02Bx
LYNCH, Ann	19	F	Servant	03Ap02Bx
Owen	16	M	Laborer	03Ap02Bx
Edwd.	12	M	Laborer	03Ap02Bx
CAMPBELL, Robert	40	M	Laborer	03Ap02Bx
Margt.	40	F	Wife	03Ap02Bx
Robt.	13	M	Laborer	03Ap02Bx
HEFFERNAN, Jane	30	F	Servant	03Ap02Bx
FRINNAN, Margt.	28	F	Servant	03Ap02Bx
KELLEY, Bryan	24	M	Laborer	03Ap02Bx
DOLAN, James	18	M	Laborer	03Ap02Bx
HENNESSEY, James	22	M	Wmcht	03Ap02Bx

NAMES OF PASSENGERS	AGE	SEX	OCCUPATIONS	DATE PORT SHIP
GORWAN, Peter	25	M	Laborer	03Ap02Bx
Mary	25	F	Wife	03Ap02Bx
Ellen	.09	F	Infant	03Ap02Bx
SPAIN, Bernd.	26	M	Laborer	03Ap02Bx
Betty	21	F	Wife	03Ap02Bx
Died-At-Sea				
MURRAY, Pat.	25	M	Laborer	03Ap02Bx
DELANCEY, Loughlin	50	M	Laborer	03Ap02Bx
Judy	40	F	Wife	03Ap02Bx
MCCARTHEY, Lewis	28	M	Blacksmith	03Ap02Bx
TRACEY, John	20	M	Laborer	03Ap02Bx
HIGGINS, Mary	25	F	Servant	03Ap02Bx
KENNEDY, Jno.	24	M	Laborer	03Ap02Bx
Cath.	17	F	Servant	03Ap02Bx
BERGEN, Fanny	27	F	Servant	03Ap02Bx
Pat	16	M	Laborer	03Ap02Bx
Pat	.04	M	Infant	03Ap02Bx
GLUIN, Honor	40	F	Servant	03Ap02Bx
Margt.	45	F	Servant	03Ap02Bx
Edwd.	12	M	None	03Ap02Bx
Jno.	10	M	None	03Ap02Bx
Mary	8	F	Child	03Ap02Bx
DOOLIN, John	26	M	Laborer	03Ap02Bx
Julia	24	F	Servant	03Ap02Bx
FALLON, Bernd.	20	M	Laborer	03Ap02Bx
MACKE, Mich.	26	M	Laborer	03Ap02Bx
MAHER, Mich.	13	M	None	03Ap02Bx
Willm.	10	M	None	03Ap02Bx
HOBAN, Mary	8	F	Child	03Ap02Bx
BYRNE, Judy	25	F	Servant	03Ap02Bx
FITSIMMON, Pat	18	M	Laborer	03Ap02Bx
Chas.	15	M	Laborer	03Ap02Bx
EARLY, George	35	M	Laborer	03Ap02Bx
LAYCOCK, Mary	11	F	Servant	03Ap02Bx
Eliza	10	F	Servant	03Ap02Bx
NAVIN, Eliza	15	F	Servant	03Ap02Bx
MCGRAW, Mary	24	F	Servant	03Ap02Bx
GARGAN, Pat.	25	M	Laborer	03Ap02Bx
Mary	19	F	Servant	03Ap02Bx
MORRISS, Elleanor	20	F	Servant	03Ap02Bx
SMITH, Mary	20	F	Servant	03Ap02Bx
MCGOWRAN, Rose	23	F	Servant	03Ap02Bx
COX, Rose	45	F	Servant	03Ap02Bx
Julia	9	F	Child	03Ap02Bx
WILKINSON, Richd.	21	M	Laborer	03Ap02Bx
POUGH, Mary	30	F	Servant	03Ap02Bx
Jno.	.05	M	Infant	03Ap02Bx
MULLHALL, Ellen	17	F	Servant	03Ap02Bx
LEIGH, James	40	M	Laborer	03Ap02Bx
Ann-Mrs.	40	F	Wife	03Ap02Bx
COLEMAN, Eliza	18	F	Servant	03Ap02Bx
WHALEN, Cath.	40	F	Servant	03Ap02Bx
Cath.	13	F	Servant	03Ap02Bx
Jno.	10	M	Laborer	03Ap02Bx
Willm	8	M	Child	03Ap02Bx
HICKEY, Michl.	33	M	Laborer	03Ap02Bx
Pat	35	M	Laborer	03Ap02Bx
Ellen	25	F	Servant	03Ap02Bx
Eliza	.06	F	Infant	03Ap02Bx
Died-At-Sea				
MCDONNELL, Michl.	22	M	Laborer	03Ap02Bx
SMITH, David	23	M	Laborer	03Ap02Bx
LOUGHAN, Pat	20	M	Laborer	03Ap02Bx
MCGRATH, Pat	18	M	Laborer	03Ap02Bx
NAVIN, Mary	20	F	Servant	03Ap02Bx
BERGEN, Margt.	22	F	Servant	03Ap02Bx
COLLIER, Pat	55	M	Laborer	03Ap02Bx
Mary	50	F	Wife	03Ap02Bx
Jno.	25	M	Laborer	03Ap02Bx
Pat	22	M	Laborer	03Ap02Bx
Edwd.	19	M	Laborer	03Ap02Bx
Michl.	16	M	Laborer	03Ap02Bx
BURKE, Margt.	30	F	Servant	03Ap02Bx
LOUNDRIGAN, Mary	20	F	Servant	03Ap02Bx
Nancy	16	F	Servant	03Ap02Bx

NAMES OF PASSENGERS	AGE	SEX	OCCUPATIONS	DATE PORT SHIP
LOUNDRIGAN, Michl.	21	M	Laborer	03Ap02Bx
LEIGH, Ann	14	F	Servant	03Ap02Bx
MCGOWAN, Ellen	18	F	Servant	03Ap02Bx
REYNOLDS, Edwd.	35	M	Laborer	03Ap02Bx
NALTY, James	22	M	Laborer	03Ap02Bx
Ann	35	F	Servant	03Ap02Bx
MOONAN, James	23	M	Laborer	03Ap02Bx
WALL, Pat	36	M	Laborer	03Ap02Bx
NARRY, Margt.	45	F	Servant	03Ap02Bx
Cath.	18	F	Servant	03Ap02Bx
Eliza	16	F	Servant	03Ap02Bx
HUGHES, Michl.	20	M	Baker	03Ap02Bx
FALLON, Luke	22	M	Laborer	03Ap02Bx
FOX, Bridgt.	17	F	Servant	03Ap02Bx
KELLY, Bridgt.	40	F	Servant	03Ap02Bx
Thos.	18	M	Laborer	03Ap02Bx
James	20	M	Laborer	03Ap02Bx
MAHON, Michl.	37	M	Laborer	03Ap02Bx
U-Mrs.	37	F	Wife	03Ap02Bx
Jno.	.08	M	Infant	03Ap02Bx
TIEGUE, Jas.	12	M	Laborer	03Ap02Bx
MAHON, Margt.	40	F	Servant	03Ap02Bx
Cath.	4	F	Child	03Ap02Bx
Martin	.09	M	Infant	03Ap02Bx
BERGEN, Mary	20	F	Servant	03Ap02Bx
RYAN, Bridgt.	30	F	Servant	03Ap02Bx
Ellen	.07	F	Infant	03Ap02Bx
CASEY, Jno.	30	M	Laborer	03Ap02Bx
Margt.	25	F	Wife	03Ap02Bx
Michl.	.09	M	Infant	03Ap02Bx
ROCKE, Jno.	18	M	Laborer	03Ap02Bx
GILMOUR, Edwd.	25	M	Laborer	03Ap02Bx
BURNS, Jas.	18	M	Farmer	03Ap02Bx
ROWAN, John	25	M	Laborer	03Ap02Bx
CROWLEY, Ann	19	F	Servant	03Ap02Bx
MAHON, Michl.	.06	M	Infant	03Ap02Bx
LACEY, Ann	24	F	Unknown	03Ap02Bx
BURKE, Margt.	20	F	Unknown	03Ap02Bx
DOYLE, Maria	24	F	Unknown	03Ap02Bx

SIDDONS 04 APRIL 1850

From Liverpool

NAMES OF PASSENGERS	AGE	SEX	OCCUPATIONS	DATE PORT SHIP
HIGGINS, Mark	60	M	Ctldlr	04Ap02Cd
STERLING, Robert	28	M	Silk Mercer	04Ap02Cd
Jane	25	F	Unknown	04Ap02Cd
Robert	.07	M	Infant	04Ap02Cd
BIDDY, John	18	M	Laborer	04Ap02Cd
FITZSIMMONS, Matthew	18	M	Laborer	04Ap02Cd
FARRELL, John	42	M	Laborer	04Ap02Cd
Biddy	17	F	Servant	04Ap02Cd
Larry	12	M	Unknown	04Ap02Cd
KEENAN, Thomas	30	M	Laborer	04Ap02Cd
SHIRRAN, Thomas	37	M	Laborer	04Ap02Cd
BELSHAW, Alexr.	16	M	Tailor	04Ap02Cd
MAGENIS, Mary	27	F	Servant	04Ap02Cd
DAULTON, Morris	21	M	Laborer	04Ap02Cd
James	49	M	Laborer	04Ap02Cd
Nancy	17	F	Servant	04Ap02Cd
Joseph	12	M	Unknown	04Ap02Cd
Joseph	45	M	Farmer	04Ap02Cd
READY, John	28	M	Laborer	04Ap02Cd
Norris	29	M	Laborer	04Ap02Cd
HUSSEY, James	28	M	Cord Winder	04Ap02Cd
WYEN, Bridget	20	F	Milliner	04Ap02Cd
QUAIN, John	18	M	Distiller	04Ap02Cd
CONNERY, Cathne.	28	F	Unknown	04Ap02Cd
Michl.	26	M	Farmer	04Ap02Cd
FOLEY, James	30	M	Laborer	04Ap02Cd
MURPHY, Susan	26	F	Servant	04Ap02Cd
HEGARTY, Wm.	30	M	Laborer	04Ap02Cd
CURTIN, Jeremiah	25	M	Laborer	04Ap02Cd
DINEEN, William	30	M	Laborer	04Ap02Cd
BUCKLEY, John	26	M	Laborer	04Ap02Cd
CASEY, James	28	M	Laborer	04Ap02Cd
Bridget	28	F	Unknown	04Ap02Cd
Anne	4	F	Child	04Ap02Cd
John	2	M	Child	04Ap02Cd
U	.00	U	Infant	04Ap02Cd
Danl.	22	M	Cord Winder	04Ap02Cd
WELLSOP, Eliza	20	F	Teacher	04Ap02Cd
CONNERY, Michl.	28	M	Laborer	04Ap02Cd
Ellen	26	F	Unknown	04Ap02Cd
Hannah	15	F	Unknown	04Ap02Cd
Ellen	12	F	Unknown	04Ap02Cd
Cath.	10	F	Unknown	04Ap02Cd
John	4	M	Child	04Ap02Cd
U	.00	U	Infant	04Ap02Cd
WILSON, John	45	M	Unknown	04Ap02Cd
KERR, Bernard	25	M	Clerk	04Ap02Cd
BREEN, Bridget	26	F	Servant	04Ap02Cd
MULHOLLAND, Mary	21	F	Servant	04Ap02Cd
BOYLAN, Nancy	20	F	Servant	04Ap02Cd
KEENAN, Eliza	20	F	Servant	04Ap02Cd
ONEAL, John	36	M	Laborer	04Ap02Cd
Died-At-Sea				
DOOLEY, Edwd.	38	M	Ldstwt	04Ap02Cd
MCGLINN, Patk.	25	M	Unknown	04Ap02Cd
DOOLEY, Danl.	18	M	Unknown	04Ap02Cd
HAMILTON, Beatrice	30	F	Housekeeper	04Ap02Cd
Beatrice	12	F	Unknown	04Ap02Cd
Wm.	11	M	Unknown	04Ap02Cd
Claudius	7	M	Child	04Ap02Cd
Thomas	5	M	Child	04Ap02Cd
Maria	3	F	Child	04Ap02Cd
U	.00	F	Infant	04Ap02Cd
ELLIS, Rose	20	F	Milliner	04Ap02Cd
DELANY, James	22	F	Milliner	04Ap02Cd
MARA, Mary	23	F	Unknown	04Ap02Cd
Danl.	.00	M	Infant	04Ap02Cd
Died-At-Sea				
KELLY, Mat	24	M	Clerk	04Ap02Cd
CONLAN, Andw.	28	M	Laborer	04Ap02Cd
CASSIDY, Ann	23	F	Milliner	04Ap02Cd
BARRETT, John	40	M	Joiner	04Ap02Cd
Mary	40	F	Unknown	04Ap02Cd
Danl.	.00	M	Infant	04Ap02Cd
HICKEY, John	23	M	Mason	04Ap02Cd
LEARY, Thomas	22	M	Tailor	04Ap02Cd
DOYLE, Thomas	21	M	Laborer	04Ap02Cd
CULLIN, Joseph	21	M	Unknown	04Ap02Cd
Died-At-Sea				
DEMPSEY, Peter	25	M	Farmer	04Ap02Cd
Teresa	19	F	Unknown	04Ap02Cd
DOOLAN, James	34	M	Unknown	04Ap02Cd
Died-At-Sea				
MARAN, Pat	24	M	Farmer	04Ap02Cd
John	22	M	Farmer	04Ap02Cd
DOYLE, Peter	23	M	Farmer	04Ap02Cd
SKELLY, Cath.	20	F	Servant	04Ap02Cd
RYAN, Mary	20	F	Servant	04Ap02Cd
MULHANEY, Mary	20	F	Servant	04Ap02Cd
MAHON, Mary	21	F	Servant	04Ap02Cd
BROWN, Martin	22	M	Laborer	04Ap02Cd
HOEY, Michl.	16	M	Cord Winder	04Ap02Cd
MURPHY, Wm.	34	M	Farmer	04Ap02Cd
Sarah	24	F	Unknown	04Ap02Cd
Pat	4	M	Child	04Ap02Cd
Martha	.00	F	Infant	04Ap02Cd
Ann	.00	F	Infant	04Ap02Cd
CRANEY, Betsy	15	F	Servant	04Ap02Cd
James	50	M	Laborer	04Ap02Cd
MÓRRISON, Maxwell	30	M	Farmer	04Ap02Cd

NAMES OF PASSENGERS	AGE	SEX	OCCUPATIONS	DATE PORT SHIP
MORRISON, Mary	20	F	Unknown	04Ap02Cd
HUNTER, James	30	M	Farmer	04Ap02Cd
Ellen	30	F	Unknown	04Ap02Cd
James	10	M	Unknown	04Ap02Cd
Alexr.	7	M	Child	04Ap02Cd
Elisa	6	F	Child	04Ap02Cd
Mary	3	F	Child	04Ap02Cd
William	.00	M	Infant	04Ap02Cd
ANDERSON, Agnes	50	F	Unknown	04Ap02Cd
Isabella	24	F	Unknown	04Ap02Cd
James	21	M	Ldstwt	04Ap02Cd
John	19	M	Teacher	04Ap02Cd
Wm.	17	M	Clerk	04Ap02Cd
Jane	11	F	Unknown	04Ap02Cd
Elisa	5	F	Child	04Ap02Cd
COINEBLE, Sarah	17	F	Servant	04Ap02Cd
ANDERSON, Peter	.00	M	Infant	04Ap02Cd
Died-At-Sea				
Robt.	.00	M	Infant	04Ap02Cd
ONEILL, Bernd.	21	M	Laborer	04Ap02Cd
TROY, Mary	40	F	Unknown	04Ap02Cd
John	16	M	Laborer	04Ap02Cd
Pat	15	M	Laborer	04Ap02Cd
Mary	13	F	Servant	04Ap02Cd
Honora	9	F	Child	04Ap02Cd
Margt.	7	F	Child	04Ap02Cd
Died-At-Sea				
MCCARTHY, Ellen	20	F	Servant	04Ap02Cd
SHEA, Maurice	23	M	Laborer	04Ap02Cd
ROCHE, Cath.	23	F	Unknown	04Ap02Cd
HULCHY, Mary	30	F	Servant	04Ap02Cd
Mary	8	F	Child	04Ap02Cd
John	.00	M	Infant	04Ap02Cd
PHELAN, John	50	M	Farmer	04Ap02Cd
Judy	50	F	Unknown	04Ap02Cd
James	22	M	Clerk	04Ap02Cd
Thomas	24	M	Clerk	04Ap02Cd
Pat	19	M	Farmer	04Ap02Cd
John	27	M	Farmer	04Ap02Cd
Wm.	12	M	Unknown	04Ap02Cd
Martin	8	M	Child	04Ap02Cd
Mary	19	F	Unknown	04Ap02Cd
Cathne.	6	F	Child	04Ap02Cd
SCOTT, Martin	48	M	Laborer	04Ap02Cd
M.	42	F	Unknown	04Ap02Cd
Bridget	18	F	Servant	04Ap02Cd
John	16	M	Laborer	04Ap02Cd
Michl.	14	M	Unknown	04Ap02Cd
Anastatia	12	F	Unknown	04Ap02Cd
Wm.	10	M	Unknown	04Ap02Cd
Thomas	8	M	Child	04Ap02Cd
Robert	6	M	Child	04Ap02Cd
Nicholas	4	M	Child	04Ap02Cd
Died-At-Sea				
Alice	2	F	Child	04Ap02Cd
Died-At-Sea				
MCGILL, Ellen	20	F	Servant	04Ap02Cd
Isabella	16	F	Servant	04Ap02Cd
RUCKTON, Peter	15	M	Laborer	04Ap02Cd
CONNOR, Mary	40	F	Unknown	04Ap02Cd
Bridget	5	F	Child	04Ap02Cd
Mary	.00	F	Infant	04Ap02Cd
Died-At-Sea				
ROUGHTON, Martin	20	M	Laborer	04Ap02Cd
CUNNINGHAM, Hernfd.	19	F	Servant	04Ap02Cd
BRENNAN, Martin	21	M	Miner	04Ap02Cd
WALSH, John	25	M	Laborer	04Ap02Cd
Mary	22	F	Servant	04Ap02Cd
HARVEY, Thomas	25	M	Miller	04Ap02Cd
HOULAGHAN, Pat	28	M	Laborer	04Ap02Cd
HOSEY, Peter	12	M	Servant	04Ap02Cd
RODGERS, Matthew	25	M	Tbcmnftr	04Ap02Cd
MULLAN, John	38	M	Laborer	04Ap02Cd
Edwd.	18	M	Laborer	04Ap02Cd
MCCABE, Thos.	16	M	Laborer	04Ap02Cd

NAMES OF PASSENGERS	AGE	SEX	OCCUPATIONS	DATE PORT SHIP
CLYNES, John	29	M	Servant	04Ap02Cd
Mary	20	F	Unknown	04Ap02Cd
MURTAGH, John	25	M	Laborer	04Ap02Cd
CALDWELL, Cath.	30	F	Unknown	04Ap02Cd
Ann	2	F	Child	04Ap02Cd
Died-At-Sea				
Pat	.00	M	Infant	04Ap02Cd
REILLY, Wm.	35	M	Laborer	04Ap02Cd
MEARY, Julia	25	F	Servant	04Ap02Cd
FITZPATRICK, Bernd.	20	M	Millwright	04Ap02Cd
RABBITT, James	47	M	Farmer	04Ap02Cd
DILLON, Mary	15	F	Servant	04Ap02Cd
Rose-Ann	13	F	Servant	04Ap02Cd
Biddy	11	F	Servant	04Ap02Cd
QUILAN, Mary	21	F	Servant	04Ap02Cd
Biddy	20	F	Servant	04Ap02Cd
MCGURKE, Michl.	30	M	Laborer	04Ap02Cd
Thomas	30	M	Laborer	04Ap02Cd
Rose	27	F	Unknown	04Ap02Cd
Hugh	.00	M	Infant	04Ap02Cd
EAGAN, Peter	40	M	Laborer	04Ap02Cd
Died-At-Sea				
Michl.	18	M	Laborer	04Ap02Cd
WARD, Peter	24	M	Laborer	04Ap02Cd
James	22	M	Laborer	04Ap02Cd
Bridget	20	F	Unknown	04Ap02Cd
MCGRATH, Francis	18	M	Laborer	04Ap02Cd
Cath.	20	F	Unknown	04Ap02Cd
Died-At-Sea				
MARTIN, Elice	18	F	Servant	04Ap02Cd
KING, Peter	40	M	Seaman	04Ap02Cd
HOWELL, Saml.	25	M	Laborer	04Ap02Cd
MITCHELL, James	12	M	Unknown	04Ap02Cd
MCGINN, Larry	28	F	Laborer	04Ap02Cd
Mary	20	F	Servant	04Ap02Cd
CALLAGHAN, Bridget	17	F	Servant	04Ap02Cd
MCGINN, Mary	25	F	Servant	04Ap02Cd
KELLY, Margt.	18	F	Servant	04Ap02Cd
MILLIGAN, Michl.	20	M	Servant	04Ap02Cd
MARKEY, Mary	20	F	Servant	04Ap02Cd
FLANAGAN, Francis	30	M	Laborer	04Ap02Cd
Ann	30	F	Unknown	04Ap02Cd
MCQUIN, Margt.	18	F	Servant	04Ap02Cd
OGORMAN, Michl.	20	M	Butcher	04Ap02Cd
CAHILL, Michl.	23	M	Cord Winder	04Ap02Cd
DAVIN, Ellen	50	F	Unknown	04Ap02Cd
GARVEY, David	25	M	Laborer	04Ap02Cd
REGGAN, Pat	45	M	Laborer	04Ap02Cd
SHEA, John	20	M	Laborer	04Ap02Cd
MACK, James	20	M	Laborer	04Ap02Cd
SHEA, Pat	20	M	Servant	04Ap02Cd
KELLY, Michl.	24	M	Victualler	04Ap02Cd
WALSTEN, Pat	22	M	Coachman	04Ap02Cd
BOYLE, John	17	M	Laborer	04Ap02Cd
RODGERS, James	20	M	Laborer	04Ap02Cd
MCLEARY, Francis	23	M	Farmer	04Ap02Cd
BOYLE, Edwd.	40	M	Clerk	04Ap02Cd
James	16	M	Clerk	04Ap02Cd
MCKANNA, John	27	M	Barber	04Ap02Cd
HICKEY, Oliver	21	M	Laborer	04Ap02Cd
REILLY, Barney	40	M	Farmer	04Ap02Cd
Robert	20	M	Farmer	04Ap02Cd
BREEN, Pat	22	M	Servant	04Ap02Cd
Mary	25	F	Servant	04Ap02Cd
ROURKE, Pat	47	M	Farmer	04Ap02Cd
Eliza	20	F	Unknown	04Ap02Cd
SCOTT, George	30	M	Currier	04Ap02Cd
MOORE, Thomas	25	M	Sawer	04Ap02Cd
Margt.	22	F	Unknown	04Ap02Cd
Elizth.	.00	F	Infant	04Ap02Cd
MCDONNELL, Edwd.	25	M	Laborer	04Ap02Cd
Cath.	27	F	Unknown	04Ap02Cd
Died-At-Sea				
SCOTT, Evan	27	M	Laborer	04Ap02Cd
FINN, Pat	20	M	Laborer	04Ap02Cd

NAMES OF PASSENGERS	AGE	SEX	OCCUPATIONS	DATE PORT SHIP
DOYLE, Thos.	30	M	Laborer	04Ap02Cd
John	25	M	Laborer	04Ap02Cd
Martin	20	M	Laborer	04Ap02Cd
Michl.	18	M	Laborer	04Ap02Cd
NOWLAN, Cathne.	18	F	Servant	04Ap02Cd
Michl.	.00	M	Infant	04Ap02Cd
BRYAN, Alice	25	F	Servant	04Ap02Cd
BYRNE, Pat	25	M	Laborer	04Ap02Cd
TOOLE, Pat	21	M	Laborer	04Ap02Cd
FOLEY, John	20	M	Laborer	04Ap02Cd
BYRNE, Thos.	28	M	Laborer	04Ap02Cd
Ellen	21	F	Unknown	04Ap02Cd
Pat	.00	M	Infant	04Ap02Cd
LYNOCK, Bridget	40	F	Unknown	04Ap02Cd
PAGE, James	21	M	Laborer	04Ap02Cd
WHELAN, Pat	22	M	Laborer	04Ap02Cd
DREW, James	21	M	Victualler	04Ap02Cd
GOLDING, Julia	17	F	Servant	04Ap02Cd
COOLAHAN, James	19	M	Laborer	04Ap02Cd
FLEMING, Mary	30	F	Servant	04Ap02Cd
REYNOLDS, John	20	M	Mason	04Ap02Cd
Hannah	18	F	Milliner	04Ap02Cd
FARRELLY, Thos.	21	M	Laborer	04Ap02Cd
Bridget	18	F	Unknown	04Ap02Cd
MCGILLICK, Pat	16	M	Laborer	04Ap02Cd
LYNCH, Mary-Ann	21	F	Unknown	04Ap02Cd
HOGAN, Phil	24	M	Servant	04Ap02Cd
CLEARY, Margt.	30	F	Servant	04Ap02Cd
RILEY, Edwd.	16	M	Servant	04Ap02Cd
CLEARY, Pat	18	M	Servant	04Ap02Cd
CROWLEY, John	22	M	Carpenter	04Ap02Cd
Mary	26	F	Unknown	04Ap02Cd
STANNTON, John	24	M	Laborer	04Ap02Cd
WALSH, John	18	M	Laborer	04Ap02Cd
DALEY, Wm.	40	M	Jailer	04Ap02Cd
Thos.	12	M	Unknown	04Ap02Cd
Cath.	5	F	Child	04Ap02Cd
James	3	M	Child	04Ap02Cd
MCCORMICK, John	40	M	Laborer	04Ap02Cd
Mary	32	F	Servant	04Ap02Cd
PHELAN, James	50	M	Bacmcht	04Ap02Cd
KENNY, Lucy	25	F	Unknown	04Ap02Cd
ATKINSON, Mary	20	F	Unknown	04Ap02Cd
GRAY, Wm.	20	M	Laborer	04Ap02Cd
VAUGHAN, Chas.	50	M	Laborer	04Ap02Cd
BUTLER, David	20	M	Whitesmith	04Ap02Cd
Rose	20	F	Unknown	04Ap02Cd
Died-At-Sea				
BARNS, John	21	M	Mason	04Ap02Cd
Ellija	20	F	Servant	04Ap02Cd
RYAN, James	23	M	Laborer	04Ap02Cd
CAHILL, Jim	28	M	Laborer	04Ap02Cd
Ned	30	M	Laborer	04Ap02Cd
KENEDY, Pat	35	M	Farmer	04Ap02Cd
Ellen	26	F	Unknown	04Ap02Cd
HEENHAN, James	30	M	Farmer	04Ap02Cd
BROWN, Mary	25	F	Unknown	04Ap02Cd
KENEDY, Margt.	7	F	Child	04Ap02Cd
CONWAY, Martin	28	M	Laborer	04Ap02Cd
Mary	17	F	Servant	04Ap02Cd
DOYLE, John	13	M	Laborer	04Ap02Cd
Cath.	12	F	Unknown	04Ap02Cd
WALSH, Bridget	18	F	Servant	04Ap02Cd
Bridget	18	F	Servant	04Ap02Cd
MURPHY, Biddy	18	F	Servant	04Ap02Cd
Michl.	26	M	Laborer	04Ap02Cd
James	22	M	Laborer	04Ap02Cd
KELLY, Mathw.	22	M	Laborer	04Ap02Cd
DOYLE, Pat	23	M	Laborer	04Ap02Cd
MULRON, John	26	M	Laborer	04Ap02Cd
HORAN, Martin	40	M	Laborer	04Ap02Cd
ARNOLD, David	20	M	Seaman	04Ap02Cd
DOYLE, Timothy	35	M	Laborer	04Ap02Cd
Alice	30	F	Unknown	04Ap02Cd
Lawr.	17	M	Laborer	04Ap02Cd
DOYLE, James	10	M	Unknown	04Ap02Cd
Died-At-Sea				
KELLY, James	26	M	Unknown	04Ap02Cd
WALSH, Walter	40	M	Laborer	04Ap02Cd
Honora	35	F	Unknown	04Ap02Cd
Bridget	.00	F	Infant	04Ap02Cd
RYAN, Mary	25	F	Servant	04Ap02Cd
JORDAN, Cath.	22	F	Servant	04Ap02Cd
CARTY, Wm.	35	M	Laborer	04Ap02Cd
Died-At-Sea				
DONNELLY, Ellenor	30	F	Unknown	04Ap02Cd
Mary	6	F	Child	04Ap02Cd
Bridget	4	F	Child	04Ap02Cd
Robt.	.00	M	Infant	04Ap02Cd
MCJARRY, George	00	M	Farmer	04Ap02Cd
OCONNOR, Bridget	18	F	Milliner	04Ap02Cd
Ann	19	F	Servant	04Ap02Cd
Mary	16	F	Servant	04Ap02Cd
STAPLETON, Danl.	40	M	Blacksmith	04Ap02Cd
BRYAN, John	35	M	Laborer	04Ap02Cd
Bridget	6	F	Child	04Ap02Cd
KELLY, Thos.	24	M	Laborer	04Ap02Cd

COLUMBIA 05 APRIL 1850

From Liverpool

NAMES OF PASSENGERS	AGE	SEX	OCCUPATIONS	DATE PORT SHIP
Edward	18	M	Laborer	05Ap02Fk
MALONEY, Margt.	24	F	Unknown	05Ap02Fk
Patrick	2	M	Child	05Ap02Fk
CRAWLEY, Patrick	29	M	Unknown	05Ap02Fk
DORAY, Mary	22	F	Unknown	05Ap02Fk
DRISCOLL, Margt.	23	F	Unknown	05Ap02Fk
CRAWLEY, Wanl.	24	U	Unknown	05Ap02Fk
MURTAGH, U-Mrs.	36	F	Unknown	05Ap02Fk
Mary	4	F	Child	05Ap02Fk
Michael	6	M	Child	05Ap02Fk
John	1	M	Child	05Ap02Fk
CUNNINGHAM, Patt	36	M	Unknown	05Ap02Fk
MICINAGH, Michl.	24	M	Unknown	05Ap02Fk
BRADY, John	56	M	Unknown	05Ap02Fk
RISARDOW, John	20	M	Unknown	05Ap02Fk
CAMPBELL, John	20	M	Unknown	05Ap02Fk
CUNNINGHAM, Margaret	18	F	Unknown	05Ap02Fk
NORTON, Ellen	18	F	Unknown	05Ap02Fk
Thomas	20	M	Unknown	05Ap02Fk
COACKLEY, John	24	M	Unknown	05Ap02Fk
HELBERD, Ellen	22	F	Unknown	05Ap02Fk
AUSTIN, Mary	22	F	Unknown	05Ap02Fk
John	24	M	Unknown	05Ap02Fk
James	2	M	Child	05Ap02Fk
MARTIN, James	20	M	Unknown	05Ap02Fk
MURPHY, Walter	21	M	Unknown	05Ap02Fk
DUFFEY, Thomas	20	M	Unknown	05Ap02Fk
Died-At-Sea				
Charles	17	M	Unknown	05Ap02Fk
MCCABE, Jerimiah	40	M	Unknown	05Ap02Fk
MCKENNA, Cathn.	16	F	Unknown	05Ap02Fk
GERRAGHTY, Michl.	13	M	Unknown	05Ap02Fk
MURPHY, Margt.	20	F	Unknown	05Ap02Fk
Margt.	00	F	Unknown	05Ap02Fk
Cate	19	F	Unknown	05Ap02Fk
CORCORAN, Cate	22	F	Unknown	05Ap02Fk
BURNE, Patt	20	M	Unknown	05Ap02Fk
ODONNELL, James	14	M	Unknown	05Ap02Fk
Margt.	12	F	Unknown	05Ap02Fk
John	19	M	Unknown	05Ap02Fk
PRATT, Thomas	17	M	Unknown	05Ap02Fk
GILLIGAN, Margt.	44	F	Unknown	05Ap02Fk

NAMES OF PASSENGERS	AGE	SEX	OCCUPATIONS	DATE PORT SHIP
GILLIGAN, Bridget	19	F	Unknown	05Ap02Fk
MCDONNALD, Cathn.	19	F	Unknown	05Ap02Fk
MADYART, Rose	20	F	Unknown	05Ap02Fk
MCALARA, U	19	U	Unknown	05Ap02Fk
MARAN, Rose	25	F	Unknown	05Ap02Fk
CURRAN, Michl.	28	M	Unknown	05Ap02Fk
KAVANGH, Eliza	26	F	Unknown	05Ap02Fk
SIMPSON, Peter	18	M	Unknown	05Ap02Fk
Mary	16	F	Unknown	05Ap02Fk
Bridget	15	F	Unknown	05Ap02Fk
KINDENEY, Edwd.	21	M	Unknown	05Ap02Fk
WARD, Thomas	47	M	Unknown	05Ap02Fk
MCCARTY, Thomas	21	M	Unknown	05Ap02Fk
MCDERMOTT, Ann	17	F	Unknown	05Ap02Fk
DUCK, Alice	20	F	Unknown	05Ap02Fk
GERRAGHTY, James	26	M	Unknown	05Ap02Fk
SMYTH, Bridget	22	F	Unknown	05Ap02Fk
BRADY, Hugh	20	M	Unknown	05Ap02Fk
RILEY, Patt	57	M	Unknown	05Ap02Fk
Edwd.	20	M	Unknown	05Ap02Fk
Bryan	17	M	Unknown	05Ap02Fk
LEAP, Mary	17	F	Unknown	05Ap02Fk
GAFFNEY, Patt	25	M	Unknown	05Ap02Fk
CAFFREY, James	24	M	Unknown	05Ap02Fk
ARNOLT, George	20	M	Unknown	05Ap02Fk
MCLAUGHLIN, Honora	18	F	Unknown	05Ap02Fk
LEE, John	27	M	Unknown	05Ap02Fk
MCMIL, Anne	29	F	Unknown	05Ap02Fk
HAMILTON, Patt	17	M	Unknown	05Ap02Fk
BRENAN, Nicholas	23	M	Unknown	05Ap02Fk
CONRY, John	24	M	Unknown	05Ap02Fk
CABE, Thomas	11	M	Unknown	05Ap02Fk
Bernard	9	M	Child	05Ap02Fk
Leady	7	F	Child	05Ap02Fk
CONCANNON, Winafred	19	U	Unknown	05Ap02Fk
MCCORNNA, Hanoria	7	F	Child	05Ap02Fk
DIXON, Julia	40	F	Unknown	05Ap02Fk
Sarah	10	F	Unknown	05Ap02Fk
William	8	M	Child	05Ap02Fk
Bridget	6	M	Child	05Ap02Fk
CAMPBELL, Edw.	2	M	Child	05Ap02Fk
SADLER, U-Mrs.	60	F	Unknown	05Ap02Fk
Thomas	56	M	Unknown	05Ap02Fk
William	20	M	Unknown	05Ap02Fk
James	19	M	Unknown	05Ap02Fk
Jane	16	F	Unknown	05Ap02Fk
WATERS, James	24	M	Unknown	05Ap02Fk
KENNY, John	24	M	Unknown	05Ap02Fk
Anne	20	F	Unknown	05Ap02Fk
VESSEY, Maria	12	F	Unknown	05Ap02Fk
FARRELL, Bridget	17	F	Unknown	05Ap02Fk
WALSH, John	44	M	Unknown	05Ap02Fk
NOWLAN, Bridget	26	F	Unknown	05Ap02Fk
RYAN, Mathew	20	M	Unknown	05Ap02Fk
DOLAN, John	23	M	Unknown	05Ap02Fk
Michl.	18	M	Unknown	05Ap02Fk
Bridget	17	F	Unknown	05Ap02Fk
DWYER, Patt	14	M	Unknown	05Ap02Fk
DELANCY, Patt	28	M	Unknown	05Ap02Fk
GALBRAITH, Samuel	30	M	Unknown	05Ap02Fk
Mary-Anne	12	F	Unknown	05Ap02Fk
BUSLAND, Martin	28	M	Unknown	05Ap02Fk
SMYTH, Edwd.	19	M	Unknown	05Ap02Fk
DERMOODY, William	20	M	Unknown	05Ap02Fk
MURTAGH, Michl.	26	M	Unknown	05Ap02Fk
POLAN, James	18	M	Unknown	05Ap02Fk
Alice	22	F	Unknown	05Ap02Fk
FLANAGAN, Anne	13	F	Unknown	05Ap02Fk
MCGOVERAN, Anne	22	F	Unknown	05Ap02Fk
Bridget	23	F	Unknown	05Ap02Fk
MCCARRON, Peter	28	M	Unknown	05Ap02Fk
Anne	20	F	Unknown	05Ap02Fk
MAHER, John	26	M	Unknown	05Ap02Fk
CRONIN, Timothy	17	M	Unknown	05Ap02Fk
FITZPATRICK, Ellen	27	F	Unknown	05Ap02Fk

NAMES OF PASSENGERS	AGE	SEX	OCCUPATIONS	DATE PORT SHIP
FITZSIMMONS, Peter	19	M	Unknown	05Ap02Fk
MCLAUGHLIN, Cath.	18	F	Unknown	05Ap02Fk
SCALLY, Mary	18	F	Unknown	05Ap02Fk
MURPHY, John	18	M	Unknown	05Ap02Fk
SMYTH, James	35	M	Unknown	05Ap02Fk
RODGERS, Cate	19	F	Unknown	05Ap02Fk
DUFFEY, Bridget	18	F	Unknown	05Ap02Fk
FETHERSTON, James	33	M	Dyer	05Ap02Fk
George	19	M	Dyer	05Ap02Fk
KELLY, Cate	19	F	Laborer	05Ap02Fk
MCCARTY, Johangh	20	U	Unknown	05Ap02Fk
Eliza	21	F	Unknown	05Ap02Fk
BURNS, John	27	M	Unknown	05Ap02Fk
Edwd.	21	M	Unknown	05Ap02Fk
Mary	19	F	Unknown	05Ap02Fk
JOHNSTON, Ellen	23	F	Unknown	05Ap02Fk
MCSHANE, Margt.	19	F	Unknown	05Ap02Fk
MCGRUGAN, Mary	28	F	Unknown	05Ap02Fk
DUFFEY, Mary	21	F	Unknown	05Ap02Fk
COOKE, Michl.	24	M	Unknown	05Ap02Fk
WILSON, John	23	M	Unknown	05Ap02Fk
WHITEY, James	28	M	Unknown	05Ap02Fk
RUTHERAL, William	20	M	Unknown	05Ap02Fk
FURLEY, Margt.	20	F	Unknown	05Ap02Fk
LEONARD, Bernard	19	M	Unknown	05Ap02Fk
CLEEGAN, Margt.	19	F	Unknown	05Ap02Fk
Catherine	20	F	Unknown	05Ap02Fk
NEVIL, Thomas	19	M	Unknown	05Ap02Fk
DUCK, Ethan	19	M	Unknown	05Ap02Fk
GRUNNIN, Catherine	00	F	Unknown	05Ap02Fk
KENEDY, Mary	34	F	Unknown	05Ap02Fk
RYAN, Eliza	19	F	Unknown	05Ap02Fk
Margt.	21	F	Unknown	05Ap02Fk
MURRAY, Rose	17	F	Unknown	05Ap02Fk
SWEENEY, Patrick	22	M	Unknown	05Ap02Fk
SMYTH, Patrick	19	M	Unknown	05Ap02Fk
DONELY, John	22	M	Unknown	05Ap02Fk
LAHEY, James	30	M	Unknown	05Ap02Fk
U-Mrs.	28	F	Unknown	05Ap02Fk
John	12	M	Unknown	05Ap02Fk
William	8	M	Child	05Ap02Fk
George	6	M	Child	05Ap02Fk
Marian	5	F	Child	05Ap02Fk
U	.00	U	Infant	05Ap02Fk
WILSON, Maria	21	F	Unknown	05Ap02Fk
DIGNAN, Patt	25	M	Unknown	05Ap02Fk
CROGHAN, Bartley	17	M	Unknown	05Ap02Fk
COGHAN, James	19	M	Painter	05Ap02Fk
FLEMMING, Henrietta	19	F	Unknown	05Ap02Fk
Wilhimena	17	F	Unknown	05Ap02Fk
LINAN, William	20	M	Unknown	05Ap02Fk
WOORE, James	69	M	Unknown	05Ap02Fk
KENNEY, John	20	M	Unknown	05Ap02Fk
DEVINE, John	27	M	Unknown	05Ap02Fk
Owen	28	M	Unknown	05Ap02Fk
SALMON, Anne	30	F	Unknown	05Ap02Fk
MITCHELL, Alice	19	F	Unknown	05Ap02Fk
Bessey	18	F	Unknown	05Ap02Fk
BRAWNE, Anne	19	F	Unknown	05Ap02Fk
MONKS, Patt	23	M	Unknown	05Ap02Fk
Ann	19	F	Unknown	05Ap02Fk
MCMANUS, John	29	M	Unknown	05Ap02Fk
WILSON, Mary	20	F	Unknown	05Ap02Fk
BUTLER, Bridget	25	F	Unknown	05Ap02Fk
BURNE, Patt	24	M	Unknown	05Ap02Fk
FIELD, Richard	19	M	Unknown	05Ap02Fk
BURKETT, Eliza	18	F	Unknown	05Ap02Fk
BREASELE, Ann	20	F	Unknown	05Ap02Fk
CAURAN, Edwd.	52	M	Unknown	05Ap02Fk
James	27	M	Unknown	05Ap02Fk
Michl.	12	M	Unknown	05Ap02Fk
Anne	27	F	Unknown	05Ap02Fk
Anne	16	F	Unknown	05Ap02Fk
U	.00	U	Infant	05Ap02Fk
RONAN, Mary	19	F	Unknown	05Ap02Fk

NAMES OF PASSENGERS	AGE	SEX	OCCUPATIONS	DATE PORT SHIP
RONAN, U	.00	U	Infant	05Ap02Fk
CARMON, Bessey	18	F	Unknown	05Ap02Fk
KELLY, Cate	20	F	Unknown	05Ap02Fk
U	.00	U	Infant	05Ap02Fk
CAREY, Judy	21	F	Unknown	05Ap02Fk
MCDONNELL, Jane	28	F	Unknown	05Ap02Fk
U	.00	U	Infant	05Ap02Fk
Julia	27	F	Unknown	05Ap02Fk
RELEKER, John	30	M	Unknown	05Ap02Fk
MINEHAN, Danl.	30	M	Unknown	05Ap02Fk
REEORDAN, Owen	20	M	Unknown	05Ap02Fk
MURPHY, James	18	M	Unknown	05Ap02Fk
COLLINS, Danl.	21	M	Unknown	05Ap02Fk
MCMAHEN, Denis	29	M	Unknown	05Ap02Fk
BARRY, Patt	30	M	Unknown	05Ap02Fk
Morry	25	U	Unknown	05Ap02Fk
TRACY, Michl.	29	M	Unknown	05Ap02Fk
MACKET, John	24	M	Unknown	05Ap02Fk
U-Mrs.	20	F	Unknown	05Ap02Fk
U	.00	U	Infant	05Ap02Fk
COLEAGHAN, Denis	20	M	Unknown	05Ap02Fk
SULLIVAN, Thomas	21	M	Unknown	05Ap02Fk
MOONAN, Margaret	24	F	Unknown	05Ap02Fk
CONWAY, Mary	30	F	Unknown	05Ap02Fk
DELANEY, Bessey	24	F	Unknown	05Ap02Fk
LOONEY, Margt.	19	F	Unknown	05Ap02Fk
REARDON, John	37	M	Unknown	05Ap02Fk
LOONAN, Patt	20	M	Unknown	05Ap02Fk
DALEY, Mary	21	F	Unknown	05Ap02Fk
GALEAGHER, Bridget	18	F	Unknown	05Ap02Fk
MULUREY, Ellen	24	F	Unknown	05Ap02Fk
WARD, Michl.	24	M	Unknown	05Ap02Fk
Mary	19	F	Unknown	05Ap02Fk
TIMONDS, John	24	M	Unknown	05Ap02Fk
PLUNKETT, Mary	19	F	Unknown	05Ap02Fk
PINE, Michl.	25	M	Unknown	05Ap02Fk
NEVINS, Michl.	33	M	Unknown	05Ap02Fk
MULLAY, Mathew	57	M	Unknown	05Ap02Fk
Anne	47	F	Unknown	05Ap02Fk
DAY, Samuel	20	M	Unknown	05Ap02Fk
Mary	19	F	Unknown	05Ap02Fk
Honoria	21	F	Unknown	05Ap02Fk
DUNNE, Margt.	20	F	Unknown	05Ap02Fk
BENSON, Ellen	30	F	Unknown	05Ap02Fk
U	.00	U	Infant	05Ap02Fk
BARTLEY, Mary	19	F	Unknown	05Ap02Fk
Margt.	4	F	Child	05Ap02Fk
U	.00	U	Infant	05Ap02Fk
KENEDY, Michl.	27	M	Unknown	05Ap02Fk
LOBER, Danl.	25	M	Unknown	05Ap02Fk
Anne	19	F	Unknown	05Ap02Fk
CARR, Cath.	15	F	Unknown	05Ap02Fk
CURTY, Mary	11	F	Unknown	05Ap02Fk
ROWEN, Mary	63	F	Unknown	05Ap02Fk
Cath	16	F	Unknown	05Ap02Fk
Bridget	7	F	Child	05Ap02Fk
Michl.	16	M	Unknown	05Ap02Fk
PERSEY, James	20	M	Unknown	05Ap02Fk
Samuel	20	M	Unknown	05Ap02Fk
PIGOT, Mary	27	F	Unknown	05Ap02Fk
Morris	9	M	Child	05Ap02Fk
COOLOGHAN, Patt	21	M	Unknown	05Ap02Fk
CARLLANDS, William	24	M	Unknown	05Ap02Fk
MCCAFFREY, Margt.	7	F	Child	05Ap02Fk
LYNCH, Bernard	20	M	Unknown	05Ap02Fk
Rose	00	F	Unknown	05Ap02Fk
U	.00	U	Infant	05Ap02Fk
Died-At-Sea				
BRENAN, Margt.	27	F	Unknown	05Ap02Fk
HAMILTON, Thomas	22	M	Unknown	05Ap02Fk
U, Bridgit	30	F	Unknown	05Ap02Fk
Robert	7	M	Child	05Ap02Fk
Charley	5	M	Child	05Ap02Fk
HARNETT, Michl.	24	M	Unknown	05Ap02Fk

NAMES OF PASSENGERS	AGE	SEX	OCCUPATIONS	DATE PORT SHIP
TULLY, Nancy	36	F	Unknown	05Ap02Fk
Died-At-Sea				
Margt.	15	F	Unknown	05Ap02Fk
John	10	M	Unknown	05Ap02Fk
CARNEY, John	51	M	Unknown	05Ap02Fk
GRAY, John	30	M	Unknown	05Ap02Fk
MARRISSY, Margt.	20	F	Unknown	05Ap02Fk
CASEY, Mary	31	F	Unknown	05Ap02Fk
CARTY, Denis	35	M	Unknown	05Ap02Fk
HEARTERRY, James	19	M	Unknown	05Ap02Fk
MURPHY, Anne	22	F	Unknown	05Ap02Fk
U	.00	U	Infant	05Ap02Fk
DUNNE, Ellen	20	F	Unknown	05Ap02Fk
CARNEY, Anne	23	F	Unknown	05Ap02Fk
Thomas	24	M	Unknown	05Ap02Fk
DONAHOE, Rose	26	F	Unknown	05Ap02Fk
MCLAUGHLIN, Patt	28	M	Unknown	05Ap02Fk
Ellen	22	F	Unknown	05Ap02Fk
U	.00	U	Infant	05Ap02Fk
James	7	M	Child	05Ap02Fk
Patrick	4	M	Child	05Ap02Fk
Michael	3	M	Child	05Ap02Fk
Catherine	2	F	Child	05Ap02Fk
GARDINER, James	60	M	Unknown	05Ap02Fk
Mary	50	F	Unknown	05Ap02Fk
Biddy	19	F	Unknown	05Ap02Fk
MASTERMAN, Bernard	30	M	Unknown	05Ap02Fk
Mary	4	F	Child	05Ap02Fk
Patt	10	M	Unknown	05Ap02Fk
SHERIDAN, Michl.	26	M	Unknown	05Ap02Fk
U-Mrs.	24	F	Unknown	05Ap02Fk
U	.00	U	Infant	05Ap02Fk
Died-At-Sea				
HICKEY, John	24	M	Unknown	05Ap02Fk
NAUGHTON, Bridget	20	F	Unknown	05Ap02Fk
Mary	18	F	Unknown	05Ap02Fk
KELLY, Mary	17	F	Unknown	05Ap02Fk
BOYLE, John	21	M	Unknown	05Ap02Fk
WALSH, U-Mrs.	49	F	Unknown	05Ap02Fk
U-Miss	19	F	Unknown	05Ap02Fk
GAFFREY, Laurence	17	M	Unknown	05Ap02Fk
VILDENS, Michl.	24	M	Unknown	05Ap02Fk
GRIMES, William	20	M	Unknown	05Ap02Fk
Mary	19	F	Unknown	05Ap02Fk
NIRTNEY, Patt	24	M	Unknown	05Ap02Fk
BURCENT, William	22	M	Unknown	05Ap02Fk
CAMPBELL, John	26	M	Unknown	05Ap02Fk
Anne	17	F	Unknown	05Ap02Fk
OBKIN, John	25	M	Unknown	05Ap02Fk
DALEY, Richard	21	M	Unknown	05Ap02Fk
Mary	22	F	Unknown	05Ap02Fk
DAVYS, John	20	M	Unknown	05Ap02Fk
EVANS, Thomas	29	M	Unknown	05Ap02Fk
Catherine	19	F	Unknown	05Ap02Fk
SANREY, Charles	21	M	Unknown	05Ap02Fk
MCCORMAC, Timothy	19	M	Unknown	05Ap02Fk
Danl.	12	M	Unknown	05Ap02Fk
GERRAGHTY, Margt.	17	F	Unknown	05Ap02Fk

JAMES-WRIGHT 05 APRIL 1850

From Liverpool

NAMES OF PASSENGERS	AGE	SEX	OCCUPATIONS	DATE PORT SHIP
QUILLY, Nick	21	M	Laborer	05Ap02Fw
CONNELL, Dennis	24	M	Laborer	05Ap02Fw
GERMAN, Edwd.	19	M	Laborer	05Ap02Fw
St.GEORGE, Patt	12	M	None	05Ap02Fw
John	10	M	None	05Ap02Fw
DAGNALL, James	22	M	Laborer	05Ap02Fw

NAMES OF PASSENGERS	AGE	SEX	OCCUPATIONS	DATE PORT SHIP
DUMPHY, Patt	20	M	Laborer	05Ap02Fw
GAFFNEY, Mary	55	F	Wi	05Ap02Fw
FINNAND, John	20	M	Laborer	05Ap02Fw
Mary	16	F	Servant	05Ap02Fw
MONEGHAN, Bridgt.	19	F	Servant	05Ap02Fw
BOUMAN, Mary	10	F	Servant	05Ap02Fw
MORRIS. Patt	20	M	Servant	05Ap02Fw
Cathe.	19	F	Servant	05Ap02Fw
MCGAHIN, John	20	M	Laborer	05Ap02Fw
SHIELDS, Arthur	15	M	Laborer	05Ap02Fw
BRADY, Patt	22	M	Laborer	05Ap02Fw
CORCAN, Peter	50	M	Trade Man	05Ap02Fw
Ann	45	F	Trade Man	05Ap02Fw
James	19	M	Trade Man	05Ap02Fw
Elizh.	17	F	Trade Man	05Ap02Fw
Jane	12	F	Trade Man	05Ap02Fw
Maria	10	F	Trade Man	05Ap02Fw
LYNCH, Ann	20	F	Servant	05Ap02Fw
MCGLOUGHLIN. James	30	M	Laborer	05Ap02Fw
KENNY, Michl.	19	M	Laborer	05Ap02Fw
WALDRON, Martin	18	M	Laborer	05Ap02Fw
ROONEY, Cathe.	4	F	Child	05Ap02Fw
Died-At-Sea				
DUFFY, Susan	30	F	Unknown	05Ap02Fw
Bridgt.	10	F	None	05Ap02Fw
Cathe.	7	F	Child	05Ap02Fw
Michl.	5	M	Child	05Ap02Fw
Dennis	2	M	Child	05Ap02Fw
KILLIAN, Bridgt.	40	F	Wife	05Ap02Fw
Ellen	12	F	None	05Ap02Fw
Mary	9	F	Child	05Ap02Fw
SALTS, John	25	M	Laborer	05Ap02Fw
MCCORMICK, Cathe.	34	F	Servant	05Ap02Fw
BRADLY, James	38	M	Laborer	05Ap02Fw
FITZGERRALD, Patt	22	M	Laborer	05Ap02Fw
Cathe.	18	F	Servant	05Ap02Fw
KENNY, James	24	M	Laborer	05Ap02Fw
LAVIN, Bridgt.	20	F	Servant	05Ap02Fw
Thomas	11	M	None	05Ap02Fw
ROGERS, Patt	22	M	Servant	05Ap02Fw
MCPORTLAM, Mary	21	M	Servant	05Ap02Fw
Jane	19	F	Servant	05Ap02Fw
MORAN, Patt	22	M	Servant	05Ap02Fw
SKEVINGTON, Patt	20	M	Servant	05Ap02Fw
CASSIDY, Bridgt.	38	F	Wife	05Ap02Fw
Mary	10	F	None	05Ap02Fw
Brian	.00	M	Infant	05Ap02Fw
HEALEY, James	38	M	Laborer	05Ap02Fw
STREET, John	37	M	Laborer	05Ap02Fw
OLIVER. Wm.	29	M	Laborer	05Ap02Fw
GRUNDY, James	24	M	Laborer	05Ap02Fw
FORD, Bridgt.	21	F	Servant	05Ap02Fw
FETHERSTONE, Michl.	24	M	Servant	05Ap02Fw
KEATING, Michl.	35	M	Farmer	05Ap02Fw
RIFF, Mary	18	F	Servant	05Ap02Fw
CARR, Michl.	24	M	Servant	05Ap02Fw
MCDONALD, Margt.	20	F	Servant	05Ap02Fw
MCQUILIN, Ellen	20	F	Servant	05Ap02Fw
CONVEY, Peter	19	M	Servant	05Ap02Fw
ADMALIKE, Mary	24	F	Servant	05Ap02Fw
BURKE, Patt	26	M	Laborer	05Ap02Fw
GILLAN, Patt	22	M	Laborer	05Ap02Fw
BRADY, Danl.	30	M	Laborer	05Ap02Fw
GREEN, Mary	20	F	Servant	05Ap02Fw
ALLEN, Bridgt.	20	F	Servant	05Ap02Fw
BURNS, Phillip	23	M	Laborer	05Ap02Fw
REDMAN, Edwd.	25	M	Laborer	05Ap02Fw
MILLER, Andw.	21	M	Laborer	05Ap02Fw
MOORE, Thomas	20	M	Waiter	05Ap02Fw
Patt	18	M	Waiter	05Ap02Fw
DALY, Ann	18	F	Waitress	05Ap02Fw
DEMPSY, Margt.	30	F	Wife	05Ap02Fw
Cathe.	6	F	Child	05Ap02Fw
John	.00	M	Infant	05Ap02Fw
MCINTOSH, John	25	M	Laborer	05Ap02Fw
VINCENT, Francis	27	M	Laborer	05Ap02Fw
SHERRIDAN, Bernd.	20	M	Laborer	05Ap02Fw
MCKENNA, Edwd.	18	M	Laborer	05Ap02Fw
CONLON, John	45	M	Farmer	05Ap02Fw
Cathe.	45	F	Farmer	05Ap02Fw
James	20	M	Farmer	05Ap02Fw
John	18	M	Farmer	05Ap02Fw
Michl.	16	M	Farmer	05Ap02Fw
Mary	22	F	Farmer	05Ap02Fw
FOX, Thomas	35	M	Farmer	05Ap02Fw
Mary	30	F	Farmer	05Ap02Fw
Mary	7	F	Child	05Ap02Fw
Thomas	5	M	Child	05Ap02Fw
Willm.	3	M	Child	05Ap02Fw
Patt	.00	M	Infant	05Ap02Fw
REDDEN, Thomas	30	M	Laborer	05Ap02Fw
John	20	M	Laborer	05Ap02Fw
Bridgt.	18	F	Servant	05Ap02Fw
Ann	20	F	Servant	05Ap02Fw
GANNIN, Bridgt.	18	F	Servant	05Ap02Fw
DAY, David	40	M	Farmer	05Ap02Fw
MCCANN, Michl.	20	M	Laborer	05Ap02Fw
Hugh	15	M	Laborer	05Ap02Fw
OBRIAN, Allen	18	M	Laborer	05Ap02Fw
Mary	16	F	Waitress	05Ap02Fw
QUINN, Mary	28	F	Servant	05Ap02Fw
CARR, Stephen	20	M	Servant	05Ap02Fw
PILE, Robt.	18	M	Servant	05Ap02Fw
MCGIMISS, Ann	40	F	Nurse	05Ap02Fw
Bridgt.	20	F	Servant	05Ap02Fw
BOYLAN, Ellen	20	F	Servant	05Ap02Fw
SHANAHAN, Morris	18	M	Laborer	05Ap02Fw
SULLIVAN, Michl.	20	M	Laborer	05Ap02Fw
MULCAHY, Timothy	40	M	Laborer	05Ap02Fw
PATTERSON, Thomas	24	M	Laborer	05Ap02Fw
MURPHY, Thomas	20	M	Laborer	05Ap02Fw
MCELROY, John	23	M	Laborer	05Ap02Fw
MCENEARY, Patt	16	M	Laborer	05Ap02Fw
Francis	14	M	Laborer	05Ap02Fw
MURTAGH, Peter	19	M	Laborer	05Ap02Fw
ROBINSON, Gilbert	24	M	Laborer	05Ap02Fw
STEPHENSON, James	21	M	Laborer	05Ap02Fw
PONTER, Mary-Jane	17	F	Servant	05Ap02Fw
GARRY, Hugh	21	M	Servant	05Ap02Fw
RADICAN, John	24	M	Laborer	05Ap02Fw
MULLIAN, Mary	35	F	Wife	05Ap02Fw
Cathe.	9	F	Child	05Ap02Fw
Hugh	7	M	Child	05Ap02Fw
GALLAHER, Cathe.	24	F	Unknown	05Ap02Fw
John	3	M	Child	05Ap02Fw
DOONAN, Cathe.	24	F	Servant	05Ap02Fw
LOMBARD, Elizh.	25	F	Servant	05Ap02Fw
KIERNAN, Alice	19	F	Servant	05Ap02Fw
LYNCH, Thomas	18	M	Servant	05Ap02Fw
SMITH, Michl.	15	M	Waiter	05Ap02Fw
Ann	20	F	Waitress	05Ap02Fw
John	18	M	Waiter	05Ap02Fw
Rose	22	F	Waitress	05Ap02Fw
MCGOHAN, Cathe.	18	F	Waitress	05Ap02Fw
MCLADY, Mary-A.	28	F	Servant	05Ap02Fw
WILSON, James	18	M	Servant	05Ap02Fw
Ann	17	F	Servant	05Ap02Fw
MALINE, John	20	M	Servant	05Ap02Fw
SMITH, Mathw.	18	M	Servant	05Ap02Fw
LEA, John	18	M	Servant	05Ap02Fw
MONAGHAN, John	20	M	Laborer	05Ap02Fw
Patt	18	M	Laborer	05Ap02Fw
HALTON, Bridgt.	18	F	Servant	05Ap02Fw
DONOUGH, Ellen	13	F	Servant	05Ap02Fw

ELIZA-HELEN 06 APRIL 1850

From Falmouth

NAMES OF PASSENGERS	AGE	SEX	OCCUPATIONS	DATE PORT SHIP
MCBURNEY, Robert	23	M	Gdnr	06Ap49Fx
THOMPSON, Andrew	27	M	Clerk	06Ap49Fx

EUROPA 06 APRIL 1850

From Liverpool

NAMES OF PASSENGERS	AGE	SEX	OCCUPATIONS	DATE PORT SHIP
HENLEY, U-Mrs.	26	F	Unknown	06Ap02Fe
U	3	M	Child	06Ap02Fe
MATHERS, U	30	M	Soldier	06Ap02Fe
ONEILL, P.	37	M	Merchant	06Ap02Fe
EGAN, J.	39	M	Merchant	06Ap02Fe
DOHERTY, U	32	M	Merchant	06Ap02Fe
BRYANT, U	38	M	Merchant	06Ap02Fe
HIGGINS, U	31	M	Merchant	06Ap02Fe

SAMUEL-CAMPBELL 06 APRIL 1850

From St.Martins

NAMES OF PASSENGERS	AGE	SEX	OCCUPATIONS	DATE PORT SHIP
WOOD, Alexander	30	M	Unknown	06Ap50Fy
Elizabeth	27	F	Lady	06Ap50Fy
Janette	4	F	Child	06Ap50Fy
Catharine	2	F	Child	06Ap50Fy

GUY-MANNERING 08 APRIL 1850

From Liverpool

NAMES OF PASSENGERS	AGE	SEX	OCCUPATIONS	DATE PORT SHIP
RODDEN, Epenetus	16	M	Merchant	08Ap02Ax
WILLEY, John-M.	30	M	Doctor	08Ap02Ax
DUKE, James	26	M	Gdnr	08Ap02Ax
FOLEY, Michael	26	M	Farmer	08Ap02Ax
Mary-A.	20	F	Farmer	08Ap02Ax
HALE, Bridget	22	F	Farmer	08Ap02Ax
VALE, Nancy	22	F	Farmer	08Ap02Ax
BURANE, John	30	M	Farmer	08Ap02Ax
ANNESLEY, William	26	M	Farmer	08Ap02Ax
CODY, Patrick	24	M	Unknown	08Ap02Ax
OCONNOR, Biddy	21	F	Spinner	08Ap02Ax
DOWLING, Patk.	23	M	Farmer	08Ap02Ax
Murtagh	22	M	Farmer	08Ap02Ax
Anne	20	F	Farmer	08Ap02Ax
PETERS, Patk.	25	M	Farmer	08Ap02Ax
READ, William	23	M	Servant	08Ap02Ax
SMALL, Francis	20	M	Laborer	08Ap02Ax
QUILLAN, Thomas	26	M	Laborer	08Ap02Ax
QUILLAN, Betsy	28	M	Laborer	08Ap02Ax
GILLIGAN, Margt.	20	F	Laborer	08Ap02Ax
BRADY, Rose	19	F	Laborer	08Ap02Ax
SMITH, Bernard	26	M	Laborer	08Ap02Ax
Patk.	20	M	Laborer	08Ap02Ax
MINER, Patk.	25	M	Laborer	08Ap02Ax
GRIMES, Cathr.	18	F	Laborer	08Ap02Ax
BRENNAN, James	20	M	Laborer	08Ap02Ax
MCCANN, Mary	18	F	Laborer	08Ap02Ax
LOGAN, James	30	M	Laborer	08Ap02Ax
THOMPSON, James	24	M	Weaver	08Ap02Ax
RUTH, Patrk.	34	M	Farmer	08Ap02Ax
Patrk.	8	M	Child	08Ap02Ax
Kate	7	F	Child	08Ap02Ax
POWER, Martin	20	M	Laborer	08Ap02Ax
BRIEN, Walter	26	M	Laborer	08Ap02Ax
KELLY, Patk.	26	M	Farmer	08Ap02Ax
Bridget	24	F	Farmer	08Ap02Ax
Thos.	.00	M	Infant	08Ap02Ax
Bridget	18	F	Farmer	08Ap02Ax
Cathne.	19	F	Farmer	08Ap02Ax
MOYNE, Mary	22	F	Servant	08Ap02Ax
BRIEN, John	27	M	Laborer	08Ap02Ax
DWYRE, Michl.	30	M	Butcher	08Ap02Ax
CANE, James	30	M	Shoemaker	08Ap02Ax
DEMERY, James	26	M	Farmer	08Ap02Ax
Richd.	21	M	Farmer	08Ap02Ax
CONNOLLY, John	28	M	Farmer	08Ap02Ax
Catherine	20	F	Unknown	08Ap02Ax
GAVIN, Catherine	20	F	Unknown	08Ap02Ax
CONLAN, Margaret	18	F	Unknown	08Ap02Ax
Patk.	14	M	Unknown	08Ap02Ax
CORBALLY, Catherine	30	F	Unknown	08Ap02Ax
James	20	M	Laborer	08Ap02Ax
Maria	18	F	Unknown	08Ap02Ax
CHRISTIE, Jane	17	F	Unknown	08Ap02Ax
DONNELLY, Bernard	50	M	Laborer	08Ap02Ax
Rose	45	F	Unknown	08Ap02Ax
CRAVEN, Anne	25	F	Unknown	08Ap02Ax
BRADY, James	18	M	Laborer	08Ap02Ax
CONNOLLY, Michl.	19	M	Laborer	08Ap02Ax
Bernard	16	M	Laborer	08Ap02Ax
Frances	13	M	Laborer	08Ap02Ax
James	11	M	Laborer	08Ap02Ax
Peter	9	M	Child	08Ap02Ax
Maria	7	F	Child	08Ap02Ax
CARROLL, Catherine	25	F	Unknown	08Ap02Ax
James	15	M	Unknown	08Ap02Ax
REYNOLDS, Mary	30	F	Unknown	08Ap02Ax
MINNAUGH, Michl.	60	M	Shoemaker	08Ap02Ax
Catherine	55	F	Unknown	08Ap02Ax
Arthur	15	M	Unknown	08Ap02Ax
MAHONEY, John	40	M	Laborer	08Ap02Ax
MCMURREY, David	27	M	Laborer	08Ap02Ax
MULCARNEY, Thos.	23	M	Laborer	08Ap02Ax
KELLY, Thos.	19	M	Laborer	08Ap02Ax
MCDONNELL, Patk.	24	M	Laborer	08Ap02Ax
Biddy	22	F	Unknown	08Ap02Ax
SYNEY, Patk.	22	M	Laborer	08Ap02Ax
NUNN, James	26	M	Laborer	08Ap02Ax
DALEY, Margt.	20	F	Servant	08Ap02Ax
KEARNEY, Kate	20	F	Servant	08Ap02Ax
CLARKE, Michl.	20	M	Merchant	08Ap02Ax
NULTY, Christopher	30	M	Laborer	08Ap02Ax
Mary	20	F	Dressmaker	08Ap02Ax
FARRELLY, Mary	20	F	Servant	08Ap02Ax
DUNN, Hugh	17	M	Engineer	08Ap02Ax
Edward	18	M	Farmer	08Ap02Ax
GARRICK, John	25	M	Laborer	08Ap02Ax
CLIFFORD, Michl.	16	M	Laborer	08Ap02Ax
DANAHY, Denis	30	M	Farmer	08Ap02Ax
Margt.	50	F	Farmer	08Ap02Ax
Margt.	22	F	Farmer	08Ap02Ax
Thos.	16	M	Farmer	08Ap02Ax
Elisabeth	45	F	Farmer	08Ap02Ax

NAMES OF PASSENGERS	AGE	SEX	OCCUPATIONS	DATE PORT SHIP
KELLY, Dennis	25	M	Farmer	08Ap02Ax
CLIFFORD, Patk.	25	M	Farmer	08Ap02Ax
JEFFERS, Francis	23	M	Servant	08Ap02Ax
HALLION, Michl.	35	M	Laborer	08Ap02Ax
CLARKE, James	40	M	Laborer	08Ap02Ax
CONNALLY, Michl.	38	M	Laborer	08Ap02Ax
FLEMING, Thos.	29	M	Groom	08Ap02Ax
Bridget	27	F	Unknown	08Ap02Ax
Ellen	24	F	Unknown	08Ap02Ax
GILLIGAN, Wineford	22	F	Unknown	08Ap02Ax
FOLEY, James	35	M	Laborer	08Ap02Ax
Nancy	28	F	Laborer	08Ap02Ax
James	5	M	Child	08Ap02Ax
Ellen	2	F	Child	08Ap02Ax
KILEY, William	28	M	Laborer	08Ap02Ax
HILLIARD, John	32	M	Farmer	08Ap02Ax
Sarah	24	F	Farmer	08Ap02Ax
Elisabeth	.00	F	Infant	08Ap02Ax
Guy	35	M	Farmer	08Ap02Ax
MCMAHON, Wm.	21	M	Joiner	08Ap02Ax
MURRAY, James	23	M	Farmer	08Ap02Ax
PATERSON, Elisabeth	24	F	Unknown	08Ap02Ax
TOOLEY, Thomas	29	M	Farmer	08Ap02Ax
Johanna	20	F	Farmer	08Ap02Ax
Thos.	1	M	Child	08Ap02Ax
Ellen	.00	F	Infant	08Ap02Ax
MOCKLEN, Wm.	18	M	Farmer	08Ap02Ax
DOOLAN, Bridgt.	50	F	Farmer	08Ap02Ax
Mary	22	F	Farmer	08Ap02Ax
Anne	19	F	Farmer	08Ap02Ax
John	20	M	Farmer	08Ap02Ax
Peter	15	M	Farmer	08Ap02Ax
REILLY, Anne	20	F	Lad	08Ap02Ax
SMITH, Andrew	66	M	Farmer	08Ap02Ax
Cathr.	50	F	Farmer	08Ap02Ax
Thos.	28	M	Farmer	08Ap02Ax
Mary	26	F	Unknown	08Ap02Ax
Elisa	24	F	Unknown	08Ap02Ax
Cathr.	21	F	Unknown	08Ap02Ax
Bridget	18	F	Unknown	08Ap02Ax
MCGUIRE, Charles	22	M	Farmer	08Ap02Ax
Mary	24	F	Servant	08Ap02Ax
Cathne.	23	F	Servant	08Ap02Ax
NELLY, John	26	M	Farmer	08Ap02Ax
Mary	25	F	Farmer	08Ap02Ax
Bridget	2	F	Child	08Ap02Ax
CONNOR, Bridget	12	F	Unknown	08Ap02Ax
BRADY, Nancy	22	F	Unknown	08Ap02Ax
GRAHAM, Cathn.	21	F	Servant	08Ap02Ax
RYAN, Mary	25	F	Servant	08Ap02Ax
Martin	19	M	Servant	08Ap02Ax
NOWLAN, Mary	21	F	Servant	08Ap02Ax
CURHAM, John	48	M	Farmer	08Ap02Ax
Julia	40	F	Farmer	08Ap02Ax
Mary	13	F	Farmer	08Ap02Ax
Julia	10	F	Farmer	08Ap02Ax
Theresa	6	F	Child	08Ap02Ax
CURRAN, Mary	40	F	Farmer	08Ap02Ax
Michl.	15	M	Farmer	08Ap02Ax
Johanna	13	F	Farmer	08Ap02Ax
John	11	M	Farmer	08Ap02Ax
Danl.	2	M	Child	08Ap02Ax
TIERNEY, Nora	40	F	Farmer	08Ap02Ax
Mary	18	F	Farmer	08Ap02Ax
Cathn.	9	F	Child	08Ap02Ax
STACKE, Sarah	19	F	Farmer	08Ap02Ax
WHEELIN, Thos.	20	M	Laborer	08Ap02Ax
HOGAN, Julia	22	F	Laborer	08Ap02Ax
MORAN, Mary	22	F	Laborer	08Ap02Ax
Patrick	.00	M	Infant	08Ap02Ax
MCDERMAT, Bryan	20	M	Servant	08Ap02Ax
MATHEWS, Honora	11	F	Servant	08Ap02Ax
Pat	9	M	Child	08Ap02Ax
MURPHY, Bridgt.	18	F	Servant	08Ap02Ax
DOYLE, Danl.	24	M	Servant	08Ap02Ax
OLIHAM, William	33	M	Laborer	08Ap02Ax
MORAN, John	50	M	Farmer	08Ap02Ax
Mary	48	F	Farmer	08Ap02Ax
Michael	8	M	Child	08Ap02Ax
Ellen	6	F	Child	08Ap02Ax
BOHEN, Mary	18	F	Servant	08Ap02Ax
WEIREN, Cathn.	20	F	Servant	08Ap02Ax
MCBRIDE, James	29	M	Painter	08Ap02Ax
Elisa	29	F	Painter	08Ap02Ax
Henry	6	M	Child	08Ap02Ax
Carthy	4	M	Child	08Ap02Ax
FARRINTON, Thos.	25	M	Tailor	08Ap02Ax
John	17	M	Tailor	08Ap02Ax
MAHON, Michl.	16	M	Tailor	08Ap02Ax
CASS, Thomas	20	M	Laborer	08Ap02Ax
HAYES, Michl.	18	M	Laborer	08Ap02Ax
MAHON, James	26	M	Carpenter	08Ap02Ax
TREEHY, Mary	20	F	Unknown	08Ap02Ax
BRIEN, James	25	M	Carpenter	08Ap02Ax
FINLAN, Sarah	24	F	Unknown	08Ap02Ax
REILLEY, Owen	35	M	Laborer	08Ap02Ax
DIGNAN, Ellen	19	F	Laborer	08Ap02Ax
TEERY, Mary	16	F	Laborer	08Ap02Ax
ABRAHAM, Elisa	24	F	Servant	08Ap02Ax
REINE, Cathn.	20	F	Servant	08Ap02Ax
DUGGAN, Thos.	48	M	Contractor	08Ap02Ax
CASEY, Bernard	20	M	Laborer	08Ap02Ax
NEELY, Michl.	23	M	Carpenter	08Ap02Ax
Mary	20	F	Carpenter	08Ap02Ax
HENONSY, Edwd.	24	M	Carpenter	08Ap02Ax
BRIEN, Wm.	23	M	Carpenter	08Ap02Ax
Bridget	20	F	Unknown	08Ap02Ax
HAGAN, Judy	20	F	Servant	08Ap02Ax
MURPHY, Thos.	10	M	Unknown	08Ap02Ax
KELLY, Michl.	24	M	Servant	08Ap02Ax
SHADE, Patk.	19	M	Servant	08Ap02Ax
Bridget	16	F	Servant	08Ap02Ax
DUFFY, Mary	30	F	Unknown	08Ap02Ax
Peter	16	M	Unknown	08Ap02Ax
Anne	14	F	Unknown	08Ap02Ax
Charlotte	12	F	Unknown	08Ap02Ax
Peter	9	M	Child	08Ap02Ax
Wm.	8	M	Child	08Ap02Ax
Mary	6	F	Child	08Ap02Ax
Patk.	4	M	Child	08Ap02Ax
Anne	2	F	Child	08Ap02Ax
John	.00	M	Infant	08Ap02Ax
DUGGAN, Michl.	23	M	Laborer	08Ap02Ax
HOGARTY, Catherine	22	F	Unknown	08Ap02Ax
CLARKE, Patk.	50	M	Laborer	08Ap02Ax
Mary	40	F	Unknown	08Ap02Ax
John	18	M	Unknown	08Ap02Ax
Rose	24	F	Unknown	08Ap02Ax
Biddy	17	F	Unknown	08Ap02Ax
Anne	15	F	Unknown	08Ap02Ax
Mary	14	F	Unknown	08Ap02Ax
FARELY, Kitty	3	F	Child	08Ap02Ax
KINCADE, Mary	17	F	Unknown	08Ap02Ax
ONEIL, Patk.	17	M	Laborer	08Ap02Ax
REILLY, Patk.	20	M	Laborer	08Ap02Ax
Michl.	20	M	Laborer	08Ap02Ax
Brien	20	M	Laborer	08Ap02Ax
BELLEW, Peter	25	M	Laborer	08Ap02Ax
BREREDON, Mary	18	F	Dressmaker	08Ap02Ax
MCCOY, John	20	M	Laborer	08Ap02Ax
SHED, Mary	21	F	Unknown	08Ap02Ax
SHEA, Michl.	22	M	Laborer	08Ap02Ax
LEHY, John	24	M	Laborer	08Ap02Ax
BYRON, Mary-A.	30	F	Servant	08Ap02Ax
John	13	M	Unknown	08Ap02Ax
Mary-A.	6	F	Child	08Ap02Ax
WALLACE, Eliza	5	F	Child	08Ap02Ax
Michl.	2	M	Child	08Ap02Ax
RILEY, Bridget	16	F	Servant	08Ap02Ax
SMITH, Ellen	21	F	Servant	08Ap02Ax

NAMES OF PASSENGERS	AGE	SEX	OCCUPATIONS	DATE PORT SHIP
GAINER, Barnard	22	M	Laborer	08Ap02Ax
WALLACE, Philip	21	M	Laborer	08Ap02Ax
NOONAN, Julia	26	F	Unknown	08Ap02Ax
Maurice	6	M	Child	08Ap02Ax
HENNESY, Michl.	18	M	Unknown	08Ap02Ax
FITZGERALD, Patk.	22	M	Laborer	08Ap02Ax
MCMENONEY, Patk.	30	M	Laborer	08Ap02Ax
Bridget	25	F	Unknown	08Ap02Ax
CLEARY, Wm.	20	M	Laborer	08Ap02Ax
COCHRANE, James	21	M	Laborer	08Ap02Ax
CARLEY, Owen	22	M	Laborer	08Ap02Ax
James	24	M	Laborer	08Ap02Ax
Mary	23	F	Unknown	08Ap02Ax
FLANNAGAN, Anne	20	F	Unknown	08Ap02Ax
DUFFY, Catherine	18	F	Unknown	08Ap02Ax
ATRIDGE, Thos.	22	M	Laborer	08Ap02Ax
YOMING, Wm.	20	M	Laborer	08Ap02Ax
HARRIGAN, Danl.	26	M	Laborer	08Ap02Ax
Catherine	22	F	Unknown	08Ap02Ax
CARROLL, Barnard	24	M	Laborer	08Ap02Ax
Mary	21	F	Unknown	08Ap02Ax
FOSTER, John	30	M	Laborer	08Ap02Ax
A.J.	30	F	Unknown	08Ap02Ax
Wm.	.00	M	Infant	08Ap02Ax
Died-At-Sea				
CLARKE, Patk.	20	M	Laborer	08Ap02Ax
Mary	20	F	Unknown	08Ap02Ax
SHERIDAN, James	18	M	Laborer	08Ap02Ax
SEXTON, Timothy	40	M	Laborer	08Ap02Ax
DOLAN, Rose	40	F	Unknown	08Ap02Ax
NEIL, Bridget	40	F	Unknown	08Ap02Ax
Mary	17	F	Unknown	08Ap02Ax
Catherine	16	F	Unknown	08Ap02Ax
John	11	M	Unknown	08Ap02Ax
Biddy	9	F	Child	08Ap02Ax
Thos.	8	M	Child	08Ap02Ax
Martha	7	F	Child	08Ap02Ax
Joseph	5	M	Child	08Ap02Ax
HINLAN, Margt.	16	F	Unknown	08Ap02Ax
NEIL, Patk.	26	M	Laborer	08Ap02Ax
HIGGENBOTHAN, Edwd.	22	M	Laborer	08Ap02Ax
NOOLAR, Patk.	22	M	Laborer	08Ap02Ax
MEAGHER, John	21	M	Laborer	08Ap02Ax
Rosanna	20	F	Unknown	08Ap02Ax
ROONEY, Edwd.	23	M	Laborer	08Ap02Ax
CASHELL, Lawrence	22	M	Laborer	08Ap02Ax
ROACH, Wm.	18	M	Laborer	08Ap02Ax
GILTRAP, Anne	19	F	Unknown	08Ap02Ax
HAYDEN, James	25	M	Laborer	08Ap02Ax
BRENNAN, Anne	20	F	Servant	08Ap02Ax
HALEY, Catherine	50	F	Unknown	08Ap02Ax
Danl.	18	M	Unknown	08Ap02Ax
Ellen	12	F	Unknown	08Ap02Ax
MCKURNEN, Bridget	18	F	Servant	08Ap02Ax
CURRAN, Mary	13	F	Unknown	08Ap02Ax
SWEETMAN, Michl.	47	M	Laborer	08Ap02Ax
Julia	30	F	Unknown	08Ap02Ax
Catherine	8	F	Child	08Ap02Ax
Anne	7	F	Child	08Ap02Ax
John	6	M	Child	08Ap02Ax
Jane	4	F	Child	08Ap02Ax
Elisha	2	M	Child	08Ap02Ax
James	.00	M	Infant	08Ap02Ax
DUNN, Patk.	21	M	Laborer	08Ap02Ax
DEARY, Christopher	20	M	Laborer	08Ap02Ax
Terrisa	21	F	Unknown	08Ap02Ax
DOYLE, Bridget	20	F	Unknown	08Ap02Ax
COLEMAN, Bridget	20	F	Unknown	08Ap02Ax
BROGAN, Patk.	30	M	Shoemaker	08Ap02Ax
KENWICK, James	26	M	Laborer	08Ap02Ax
MURTAGH, Peter	21	M	Laborer	08Ap02Ax
Eliza	25	F	Unknown	08Ap02Ax
FARELY, Eliza	5	F	Child	08Ap02Ax
KEEGAN, James	11	M	Unknown	08Ap02Ax
Mary	7	F	Child	08Ap02Ax
CONKRY, Danl.	25	M	Laborer	08Ap02Ax
SUIMARD, Johanna	18	F	Unknown	08Ap02Ax
MCCORMACK, Bridget	25	F	Unknown	08Ap02Ax
AHAREN, Danl.	24	M	Laborer	08Ap02Ax
DONEVAN, Wm.	20	M	Laborer	08Ap02Ax
HALEY, Patk.	37	M	Laborer	08Ap02Ax
LLOYD, William	23	M	Overseer	08Ap02Ax
Cathr.	16	F	Overseer	08Ap02Ax
SWANWICK, Cathr.	26	F	Overseer	08Ap02Ax
MOLLOY, Bridget	16	F	Overseer	08Ap02Ax
NAEGLE, Margt.	50	F	Overseer	08Ap02Ax
Julia	22	F	Overseer	08Ap02Ax
Margt.	5	F	Child	08Ap02Ax
TIGHE, John	21	M	Overseer	08Ap02Ax
Bridget	20	F	Overseer	08Ap02Ax
FINNEGAN, Aptk.	26	M	Laborer	08Ap02Ax
GERRATY, Cath.	18	F	Laborer	08Ap02Ax
SHEA, Patk.	28	M	Laborer	08Ap02Ax
Mary	35	F	Laborer	08Ap02Ax
Mary	6	F	Child	08Ap02Ax
CONNOR, Daniel	30	M	Laborer	08Ap02Ax
SHEA, Florence	22	F	Laborer	08Ap02Ax
REILLY, Daniel	25	M	Laborer	08Ap02Ax
Honora	25	F	Laborer	08Ap02Ax
SULLIVAN, Biddy	24	F	Laborer	08Ap02Ax
KENNEDY, Mary	24	F	Laborer	08Ap02Ax
BERRY, John	34	M	Laborer	08Ap02Ax
Ellen	24	F	Laborer	08Ap02Ax
Ellen	2	F	Child	08Ap02Ax
Paddy	.00	M	Infant	08Ap02Ax
HENERAN, Michl.	28	M	Carpenter	08Ap02Ax
GRIFFIN, John	40	M	Laborer	08Ap02Ax
Edwd.	28	M	Laborer	08Ap02Ax
Lawrence	16	M	Laborer	08Ap02Ax
John	30	M	Laborer	08Ap02Ax
DONE, Michl.	26	M	Laborer	08Ap02Ax
WINNEY, Geo.	26	M	Farmer	08Ap02Ax
Richard	20	M	Farmer	08Ap02Ax
Sarah	21	F	Farmer	08Ap02Ax
BLACK, Charles	20	M	Farmer	08Ap02Ax
KEARNEY, Hannah	25	F	Seaman	08Ap02Ax
SULLIVAN, Margt.	18	F	Servant	08Ap02Ax
KELAHAN, Stephen	18	M	Laborer	08Ap02Ax
WALSH, James	32	M	Laborer	08Ap02Ax
MARTIN, Thomas	50	M	Laborer	08Ap02Ax
Peggy	35	F	Laborer	08Ap02Ax
Denis	.00	M	Infant	08Ap02Ax
MONARTY, Denis	21	M	Laborer	08Ap02Ax
COURTNEY, John	23	M	Laborer	08Ap02Ax
MONARTY, Bridget	18	F	Servant	08Ap02Ax
DYAS, Thomas	20	M	Laborer	08Ap02Ax
KENNEDY, Thos.	21	M	Laborer	08Ap02Ax
ASPEN, Patk.	28	M	Groom	08Ap02Ax
SLOAN, Henry	18	M	Stctr	08Ap02Ax
CLARKE, Patk.	20	M	Laborer	08Ap02Ax
Phillip	18	M	Laborer	08Ap02Ax
Elisabeth	19	F	Laborer	08Ap02Ax
CAROLINE, Mary	18	F	Laborer	08Ap02Ax
CUNNINGHAM, Dennis	33	M	Overseer	08Ap02Ax
BYRNE, James	49	M	Weaver	08Ap02Ax
Cathn.	16	F	Weaver	08Ap02Ax
Hugh	13	M	Weaver	08Ap02Ax
Mary	11	F	Weaver	08Ap02Ax
MCATTER, Thos.	18	M	Butcher	08Ap02Ax
WOODS, Patk.	18	M	Butcher	08Ap02Ax
MCANINY, Bernard	40	M	Poulterer	08Ap02Ax
MARTHES, Margt.	18	F	Servant	08Ap02Ax
MCANINEY, Francis	20	M	Servant	08Ap02Ax
GALLOGHLEY, Anne	20	F	Servant	08Ap02Ax
Mary	15	F	Servant	08Ap02Ax
CAMPBELL, Geo.	15	M	Servant	08Ap02Ax
GROGHAN, John	35	M	Saddler	08Ap02Ax
HELLAGHY, Jerry	18	M	Laborer	08Ap02Ax
BROHY, Patk.	19	M	Laborer	08Ap02Ax
CARR, Dennis	22	M	Laborer	08Ap02Ax

NAMES OF PASSENGERS	AGE	SEX	OCCUPATIONS	DATE PORT SHIP
CARR, Elizabeth	50	F	Servant	08Ap02Ax
SMITH, Bridget	24	F	Servant	08Ap02Ax
GARRAHAN, Mary	23	F	Servant	08Ap02Ax
RENILLON, Cathr.	18	F	Servant	08Ap02Ax
CAFFERTY, Mary	18	F	Servant	08Ap02Ax
CONWAY, John	20	M	Butcher	08Ap02Ax
MALLAY, John	17	M	Laborer	08Ap02Ax
Patk.	11	M	Laborer	08Ap02Ax
John	9	M	Child	08Ap02Ax
Cathn.	7	F	Child	08Ap02Ax
DALY, Peter	26	M	Laborer	08Ap02Ax
DONEVAN, Peter	24	M	Laborer	08Ap02Ax
MCGUINNESS, Cathr.	40	F	Laborer	08Ap02Ax
LYNCH, James	6	M	Child	08Ap02Ax
Hugh	4	M	Child	08Ap02Ax
Anne	2	F	Child	08Ap02Ax
READ, Anne	20	F	Laborer	08Ap02Ax
MOLLOY, Mary	30	F	Laborer	08Ap02Ax
Maria	11	F	Laborer	08Ap02Ax
Barthlm.	5	M	Child	08Ap02Ax
John	2	M	Child	08Ap02Ax
NUGENT, Michael	27	M	Draper	08Ap02Ax
OLEARY, James	14	M	Draper	08Ap02Ax
NUGENT, John	46	M	Draper	08Ap02Ax
DEMPSY, Katie	9	F	Child	08Ap02Ax
ROGARS, John	20	M	Laborer	08Ap02Ax
CASSIDY, Patk.	18	M	Laborer	08Ap02Ax
Mary	20	F	Laborer	08Ap02Ax
MCGREAVY, Dennis	23	M	Laborer	08Ap02Ax
MCCARTAN, Michl.	30	M	Carpenter	08Ap02Ax
SWANN, Charles	26	M	Brsml	08Ap02Ax
WALSH, Anne	21	F	Unknown	08Ap02Ax
HALOHAN, Cornls.	30	M	Laborer	08Ap02Ax
Margt.	12	F	Laborer	08Ap02Ax
LEAGHY, Ellen	40	F	Laborer	08Ap02Ax
Ellen	3	F	Child	08Ap02Ax
BRENNAN, Rose	20	F	Laborer	08Ap02Ax
SMITH, Mary	60	F	Unknown	08Ap02Ax
KELLY, John	30	M	Servant	08Ap02Ax
MOONEY, William	31	M	Carpenter	08Ap02Ax

WASHINGTON 08 APRIL 1850

From Liverpool

NAMES OF PASSENGERS	AGE	SEX	OCCUPATIONS	DATE PORT SHIP
DUNNE, Michael	20	M	Laborer	08Ap02Gc
MURPHY, Charles	22	M	Laborer	08Ap02Gc
John	20	M	Laborer	08Ap02Gc
DOYLE, Michael	00	M	Laborer	08Ap02Gc
CARROLE, Margaret	00	F	Laborer	08Ap02Gc
DONNELLAN, Richard	25	M	Tailor	08Ap02Gc
KEIFE, Peter	24	M	Joiner	08Ap02Gc
CORRIGAN, Anne	26	F	Servant	08Ap02Gc
CARROLE, Anne	24	F	Servant	08Ap02Gc
FEGAN, Mary	19	F	Servant	08Ap02Gc
DALY, John	29	M	Laborer	08Ap02Gc
MURRAY, James	22	M	Laborer	08Ap02Gc
CREA, Hugh	48	M	Laborer	08Ap02Gc
BEATY, Philip	26	M	Laborer	08Ap02Gc
Judy	25	F	Laborer	08Ap02Gc
Thomas	.06	M	Infant	08Ap02Gc
Died-At-Sea				
REILY, Patt	30	M	Laborer	08Ap02Gc
Mary	29	F	Laborer	08Ap02Gc
KIERNAN, Bridget	14	F	Nurse	08Ap02Gc
REILY, Bridget	15	F	Laborer	08Ap02Gc
FITZSIMMONS, Patt	26	M	Butcher	08Ap02Gc
Margaret	25	F	Unknown	08Ap02Gc
Anne	.07	F	Infant	08Ap02Gc
MCKENNA, Betty	18	F	Unknown	08Ap02Gc
U, U	25	F	Unknown	08Ap02Gc
REILLY, James	24	M	Laborer	08Ap02Gc
CONLIN, Catherine	20	F	Servant	08Ap02Gc
DALY, Joseph	19	M	Groom	08Ap02Gc
VERNON, Anne	20	F	Servant	08Ap02Gc
DUGAN, James	47	M	Farmer	08Ap02Gc
Mary	50	F	Farmer	08Ap02Gc
FITZPATRICK, James	27	M	Mariner	08Ap02Gc
DALY, John	30	M	Farmer	08Ap02Gc
Catherine	.06	F	Infant	08Ap02Gc
Thomas	10	M	Unknown	08Ap02Gc
BARRY, Johanna	35	F	Servant	08Ap02Gc
MCMANUS, Bridget	25	F	Servant	08Ap02Gc
TITHELL, D.	25	M	Laborer	08Ap02Gc
Mary	22	F	Laborer	08Ap02Gc
CRONAN, John	26	M	Laborer	08Ap02Gc
RIORDEN, Ellen	28	F	Servant	08Ap02Gc
COONEY, Patrick	22	M	Laborer	08Ap02Gc
FINEGAN, Thomas	60	M	Laborer	08Ap02Gc
BERGAN, Mary	26	F	Nurse	08Ap02Gc
MCGEE, James	18	M	Laborer	08Ap02Gc
SULLIVAN, Marty	32	M	Laborer	08Ap02Gc
VELLY, Dennis	23	M	Laborer	08Ap02Gc
NAUGHIN, Philip	31	M	Laborer	08Ap02Gc
Jeremiah	21	M	Laborer	08Ap02Gc
CONNELL, Dennis	25	M	Laborer	08Ap02Gc
CURRAN, Rose	22	F	Servant	08Ap02Gc
SMITH, Charles	26	M	Laborer	08Ap02Gc
CAMPION, Bridget	22	F	Nurse	08Ap02Gc
FITZPATRICK, Catharine	17	F	Nurse	08Ap02Gc
SHEA, John	19	M	Tailor	08Ap02Gc
DALY, Anne	40	F	Farmer	08Ap02Gc
Kate	20	F	Farmer	08Ap02Gc
John	12	M	Farmer	08Ap02Gc
Mary	25	F	Farmer	08Ap02Gc
U, Thomas	.08	M	Infant	08Ap02Gc
DOLLARD, John	49	M	Farmer	08Ap02Gc
Margaret	48	F	Farmer	08Ap02Gc
Judy	20	F	Farmer	08Ap02Gc
Mary	18	F	Farmer	08Ap02Gc
Margaret	15	F	Farmer	08Ap02Gc
Anty	13	M	Farmer	08Ap02Gc
Michael	11	M	Farmer	08Ap02Gc
Catherine	9	F	Child	08Ap02Gc
Anne	6	F	Child	08Ap02Gc
CONWAY, James	17	M	Laborer	08Ap02Gc
HYNES, Dennis	40	M	Unknown	08Ap02Gc
GOGHEGAN, John	14	M	Unknown	08Ap02Gc
ODONNELL, Patrick	18	M	Sweeper	08Ap02Gc
MCCOOLE, James	20	M	Smith	08Ap02Gc
BRENNAN, Thomas	30	M	Millwright	08Ap02Gc
MULVEY, Mary	20	F	Servant	08Ap02Gc
HANLEY, Thomas	20	M	Servant	08Ap02Gc
HALPIN, John	19	M	Servant	08Ap02Gc
BYRNES, Phillip	21	M	Servant	08Ap02Gc
DELANY, Timothy	22	M	Laborer	08Ap02Gc
DOHERTY, Daniel	27	M	Laborer	08Ap02Gc
KELLY, James	20	M	Servant	08Ap02Gc
Maria	18	F	Servant	08Ap02Gc
WHELAN, John	50	M	Farmer	08Ap02Gc
Bridget	45	F	Farmer	08Ap02Gc
Margaret	20	F	Farmer	08Ap02Gc
Nancy	18	F	Farmer	08Ap02Gc
Mary	16	F	Farmer	08Ap02Gc
SHEA, Nancy	22	F	Farmer	08Ap02Gc
Michael	14	M	Farmer	08Ap02Gc
Judy	14	M	Farmer	08Ap02Gc
Bridget	8	F	Child	08Ap02Gc
Ellen	5	F	Child	08Ap02Gc
LAHY, James	23	M	Smith	08Ap02Gc
HANRAHAN, Michael	24	M	Farmer	08Ap02Gc
TIMMONS, Owen	22	M	Laborer	08Ap02Gc
Thomas	20	M	Laborer	08Ap02Gc
RYAN, Bernard	22	M	Laborer	08Ap02Gc

NAMES OF PASSENGERS	AGE	SEX	OCCUPATIONS	DATE PORT SHIP	NAMES OF PASSENGERS	AGE	SEX	OCCUPATIONS	DATE PORT SHIP
RYAN, John	28	M	Laborer	08Ap02Gc	MORAN, Peter	5	M	Child	08Ap02Gc
Michael	24	M	Laborer	08Ap02Gc	Michael	4	M	Child	08Ap02Gc
Elizabeth	48	F	Laborer	08Ap02Gc	John	2	M	Child	08Ap02Gc
George	22	M	Laborer	08Ap02Gc	Patrick	.09	M	Infant	08Ap02Gc
Edith	22	F	Laborer	08Ap02Gc	U, Eliza	25	F	Servant	08Ap02Gc
Thomas	18	M	Laborer	08Ap02Gc	CONLAN, Mary	25	F	Servant	08Ap02Gc
Octavius	12	M	Laborer	08Ap02Gc	U	.00	U	Infant	08Ap02Gc
William	10	M	Laborer	08Ap02Gc	FARRELL, Ellen	22	F	Servant	08Ap02Gc
Henry	9	M	Child	08Ap02Gc	FLOOD, Patrick	20	M	Fish Monger	08Ap02Gc
Betsey	20	F	Laborer	08Ap02Gc	KELLY, Garret	30	M	Publican	08Ap02Gc
RAYNOR, John	24	M	Laborer	08Ap02Gc	Bridget	20	F	Unknown	08Ap02Gc
SMITH, John	20	M	Laborer	08Ap02Gc	CARNEY, Margaret	15	F	Servant	08Ap02Gc
JONES, William	22	M	Laborer	08Ap02Gc	DONEGAN, Mary	13	F	Servant	08Ap02Gc
THORPE, Joseph	40	M	Laborer	08Ap02Gc	BRENNAN, Honora	19	F	Servant	08Ap02Gc
Walter	7	M	Child	08Ap02Gc	COONEY, Margaret	20	F	Servant	08Ap02Gc
Sarah	11	F	Laborer	08Ap02Gc	BLACKBURN, Benjamin	30	M	Laborer	08Ap02Gc
Joseph	6	M	Child	08Ap02Gc	KEAN, John	27	M	Laborer	08Ap02Gc
FARRELL, John	24	M	Butcher	08Ap02Gc	Anne	23	F	Laborer	08Ap02Gc
Anne	22	F	Unknown	08Ap02Gc	Mary	2	F	Child	08Ap02Gc
BAIRD, John	26	M	Laborer	08Ap02Gc	Margaret	.05	F	Infant	08Ap02Gc
Mary	24	F	Laborer	08Ap02Gc	HUSSEY, Mary	16	F	Servant	08Ap02Gc
GILMOUR, Daniel	50	M	Laborer	08Ap02Gc	MEE, Martin	20	M	Servant	08Ap02Gc
Catherine	12	F	Laborer	08Ap02Gc	Timothy	14	M	Servant	08Ap02Gc
MANGLE, Edward	30	M	Laborer	08Ap02Gc	MURRAY, Clement	22	M	Laborer	08Ap02Gc
SHAW, Bridget	20	F	Washer	08Ap02Gc	DEGNAN, Joseph	30	M	Farmer	08Ap02Gc
Catherine	18	F	Washer	08Ap02Gc	Catharine	22	F	Farmer	08Ap02Gc
LEAVY, Bryan	20	M	Traveller	08Ap02Gc	Thomas	13	M	Farmer	08Ap02Gc
SHERIDAN, Mary	27	F	Innkeeper	08Ap02Gc	FOX, John	52	M	Farmer	08Ap02Gc
James	9	M	Child	08Ap02Gc	Mary	35	F	Farmer	08Ap02Gc
KELLY, John	23	M	Storekeeper	08Ap02Gc	Michael	14	M	Farmer	08Ap02Gc
Bridget	22	F	Storekeeper	08Ap02Gc	Catharine	12	F	Farmer	08Ap02Gc
BLUET, Patrick	20	M	Ruler	08Ap02Gc	Eliza	9	F	Child	08Ap02Gc
HALPIN, Michael	22	M	Farmer	08Ap02Gc	BYRNE, Timothy	10	M	None	08Ap02Gc
HAMILTON, Thomas	20	M	Farmer	08Ap02Gc	Rosanna	8	F	Child	08Ap02Gc
MCNERNEY, Michael	30	M	Farmer	08Ap02Gc	MCDONALD, James	35	M	Laborer	08Ap02Gc
Mary	25	F	Farmer	08Ap02Gc	KANE, Michael	21	M	Laborer	08Ap02Gc
MALONE, Michael	25	M	Farmer	08Ap02Gc	Margaret	19	F	Laborer	08Ap02Gc
BRIEN, Edward	34	M	Farmer	08Ap02Gc	LUCY, Abbey	20	F	Servant	08Ap02Gc
CARNEY, Michael	27	M	Laborer	08Ap02Gc	CASEY, William	22	M	Servant	08Ap02Gc
MURPHY, Michael	36	M	Laborer	08Ap02Gc	LUCY, Jeremiah	21	M	Servant	08Ap02Gc
BRIEN, Michael	36	M	Laborer	08Ap02Gc	COTTER, James	25	M	Draper	08Ap02Gc
PEAT, Thomas	25	M	Schm	08Ap02Gc	CORCORAN, Abby	24	F	Nurse	08Ap02Gc
BRIEN, Mary	20	F	Prof-Mus	08Ap02Gc	FOLEY, Richard	25	M	Farmer	08Ap02Gc
WALSH, Edward	30	M	Chemist	08Ap02Gc	KEEFE, Cornelius	21	M	Tailor	08Ap02Gc
COOK, Samuel	25	M	Farmer	08Ap02Gc	FOLEY, John	20	M	Farmer	08Ap02Gc
Letita	26	F	Farmer	08Ap02Gc	Ellen	23	F	Farmer	08Ap02Gc
HOBAN, Michael	28	M	Farmer	08Ap02Gc	HEARLEHY, Patrick	20	M	Laborer	08Ap02Gc
Catherine	20	F	Farmer	08Ap02Gc	FOLEY, Michael	22	M	Farmer	08Ap02Gc
ROGERS, Patrick	20	M	Servant	08Ap02Gc	HEARLEHY, Ellen	23	F	Farmer	08Ap02Gc
KIERNAN, John	22	M	Farmer	08Ap02Gc	COONEY, Michael	32	M	Grocer	08Ap02Gc
Michael	20	M	Farmer	08Ap02Gc	MAHONEY, John	21	M	Gdnr	08Ap02Gc
Mary	23	F	Farmer	08Ap02Gc	Catharine	23	F	Gdnr	08Ap02Gc
RYAN, John	38	M	Servant	08Ap02Gc	HANRAHAN, Ellen	25	F	Servant	08Ap02Gc
DUGAN, Joseph	30	M	Farmer	08Ap02Gc	COSGROVE, Judy	22	F	Servant	08Ap02Gc
HORRIGAN, David	25	M	Laborer	08Ap02Gc	MURRAY, Mary	25	F	Servant	08Ap02Gc
HORAGAN, Catherine	27	F	Servant	08Ap02Gc	KILEHER, Catharine	25	F	Servant	08Ap02Gc
Eliza	24	F	Servant	08Ap02Gc	ROULSTONE, Thomas	20	M	Groom	08Ap02Gc
RYAN, Wiliam	60	M	Laborer	08Ap02Gc	GALE, John	20	M	Painter	08Ap02Gc
Anne	35	F	Servant	08Ap02Gc	Thos.	20	M	Painter	08Ap02Gc
Honora	13	F	Servant	08Ap02Gc	COX, Esther	17	F	Servant	08Ap02Gc
TULLY, Biddy	19	F	Servant	08Ap02Gc	KERNAN, Dennis	20	M	Laborer	08Ap02Gc
PRIOR, Margaret	26	F	Servant	08Ap02Gc	HIGARTY, Timothy	27	M	Laborer	08Ap02Gc
CONNOR, Thomas	18	M	Laborer	08Ap02Gc	KENNEDY, James	22	M	Laborer	08Ap02Gc
William	18	M	Shoemaker	08Ap02Gc	DOYLE, Philip	34	M	Grocer	08Ap02Gc
John	16	M	Shoemaker	08Ap02Gc	Rose	18	F	Grocer	08Ap02Gc
CONNELL, Patrick	20	M	Laborer	08Ap02Gc	Judy	16	F	Grocer	08Ap02Gc
STAUNTON, Patrick	20	M	Laborer	08Ap02Gc	KINCILLA, Mary	20	F	Dressmaker	08Ap02Gc
DEVEREAUX, John	22	M	Laborer	08Ap02Gc	SCANLAN, John	40	M	Tile Maker	08Ap02Gc
Judy	14	F	Laborer	08Ap02Gc	DANIEL, Biddy	28	F	Bomkr	08Ap02Gc
Mary	18	F	Laborer	08Ap02Gc	DUNNE, John	24	M	Hatter	08Ap02Gc
Annie	17	F	Laborer	08Ap02Gc	CALLARTY, John	20	M	Glazier	08Ap02Gc
MORAN, Peter	25	M	Farmer	08Ap02Gc	BURKE, Thomas	20	M	Farmer	08Ap02Gc
Anne	25	F	Farmer	08Ap02Gc	WALSH, Ellen	21	F	Dyer	08Ap02Gc
Biddy	9	F	Child	08Ap02Gc	HAGAN, Bess	12	F	Poulterer	08Ap02Gc
Mary	7	F	Child	08Ap02Gc	LENNAN, Mary	20	F	Servant	08Ap02Gc

NAMES OF PASSENGERS	AGE	SEX	OCCUPATIONS	DATE PORT SHIP
GLEESON, Margaret	23	F	Fish Monger	08Ap02Gc
BROPHY, Martin	30	M	Farmer	08Ap02Gc
Mary	32	F	Farmer	08Ap02Gc
Anthony	21	M	Farmer	08Ap02Gc
HOLAHAN, Pat	26	M	Farmer	08Ap02Gc
MOONEY, Peter	19	M	Tinker	08Ap02Gc
MAHON, John	26	M	Coach Maker	08Ap02Gc
Ellen	40	F	Unknown	08Ap02Gc
Margaret	50	F	Unknown	08Ap02Gc
BELLAMY, Mick	18	M	Laborer	08Ap02Gc
Anne	30	F	Laborer	08Ap02Gc
Mary	3	F	Child	08Ap02Gc
Kate	.08	F	Infant	08Ap02Gc
MARALER, Mick	19	M	Laborer	08Ap02Gc
CRONLEY, Mary	19	F	Servant	08Ap02Gc
WALSH, Eliza	22	F	Milliner	08Ap02Gc
Ellen	20	F	Milliner	08Ap02Gc
KENA, Mary	25	F	Servant	08Ap02Gc
NEAL, James	31	M	Laborer	08Ap02Gc
Eliza	26	F	Laborer	08Ap02Gc
Kate	50	F	Laborer	08Ap02Gc
Kate	.09	F	Infant	08Ap02Gc
WALSH, Edward	25	M	Laborer	08Ap02Gc
COLLINS, Catharine	24	F	Servant	08Ap02Gc
Mary	26	F	Servant	08Ap02Gc
MURPHY, William	20	M	Laborer	08Ap02Gc
KEENY, Anthony	20	M	Groom	08Ap02Gc
CAHILL, Mary	18	F	Servant	08Ap02Gc
HEALY, Ellen	18	F	Servant	08Ap02Gc
DOWLING, Mick	22	M	Laborer	08Ap02Gc
MAHER, Peter	30	M	Farmer	08Ap02Gc
Anthony	30	M	Farmer	08Ap02Gc
Mary	10	F	Farmer	08Ap02Gc
Catharine	5	F	Child	08Ap02Gc
Bridget	3	F	Child	08Ap02Gc
Thomas	20	M	Farmer	08Ap02Gc
Mary	18	F	Farmer	08Ap02Gc
Catharine	60	F	Farmer	08Ap02Gc
HENRY, James	20	M	Laborer	08Ap02Gc
BYRNE, Dennis	25	M	Laborer	08Ap02Gc
MORTON, Thomas	22	M	Laborer	08Ap02Gc
DELANEY, Edmund	25	M	Laborer	08Ap02Gc
WOOD, John	21	M	Laborer	08Ap02Gc
FRIPERLY, Mary	21	F	Servant	08Ap02Gc
BYRNES, Mary	50	F	Farmer	08Ap02Gc
Michael	18	M	Farmer	08Ap02Gc
Bernard	17	M	Farmer	08Ap02Gc
Margaret	20	F	Farmer	08Ap02Gc
GANLEY, Catharine	25	F	Servant	08Ap02Gc
CLEARY, Mary	17	F	Servant	08Ap02Gc
ALLEN, Anne	25	F	Servant	08Ap02Gc
GRENNAN, William	22	M	Laborer	08Ap02Gc
FANNING, Anne-Allen	65	F	Farmer	08Ap02Gc
Ambrose	18	M	Farmer	08Ap02Gc
DOORIS, Michael	22	M	Laborer	08Ap02Gc
Ellen	18	F	Laborer	08Ap02Gc
EGAN, Honora	20	F	Servant	08Ap02Gc
CROAK, Judy	18	F	Servant	08Ap02Gc
DELANTY, James	10	M	None	08Ap02Gc
Jane	9	F	Child	08Ap02Gc
MCDONOUGH, Michael	20	M	Joiner	08Ap02Gc
Julia	20	F	Unknown	08Ap02Gc
KEANE, Catherine	22	F	Servant	08Ap02Gc
ROURKE, Mary	18	F	Servant	08Ap02Gc
James	8	M	Child	08Ap02Gc
HARRIGAN, Hannah	20	F	Servant	08Ap02Gc
MALONE, Betty	22	F	Farmer	08Ap02Gc
Mary	23	F	Farmer	08Ap02Gc
FITZPATRICK, Patt	24	M	Farmer	08Ap02Gc
James	23	M	Farmer	08Ap02Gc
COONEY, Frank	16	M	Student	08Ap02Gc
CROSBY, Patt	26	M	Laborer	08Ap02Gc
STEPHENS, Patt	25	M	Laborer	08Ap02Gc
DONNELLY, Patrick	25	M	Laborer	08Ap02Gc
Catherine	19	M	Laborer	08Ap02Gc
MCKENNA, Rose	20	F	Servant	08Ap02Gc
GAITLAND, Bridget	40	F	Laborer	08Ap02Gc
Julia	12	F	Laborer	08Ap02Gc
ANDREWS, William	38	M	Draper	08Ap02Gc
WALL, Thomas	20	M	Shoemaker	08Ap02Gc
Mary-Anne	25	F	Washer	08Ap02Gc
HARTNELL, Daniel	20	M	Laborer	08Ap02Gc
CORCORAN, John	22	M	Laborer	08Ap02Gc
DARBY, James	22	M	Laborer	08Ap02Gc
MURPHY, Patrick	20	M	Laborer	08Ap02Gc
FITZPATRICK, Patrick	25	M	Laborer	08Ap02Gc
CARTY, Timothy	27	M	Laborer	08Ap02Gc
FARREL, Julia	22	F	Servant	08Ap02Gc
DARBY, Julia	22	F	Servant	08Ap02Gc
FITZPATRICK, Christian	27	F	Servant	08Ap02Gc
Mary-Anne	24	F	Servant	08Ap02Gc
HOFRAN, Bridget	23	F	Servant	08Ap02Gc
CASS, James	22	M	Laborer	08Ap02Gc
GOODFELLOW, John	21	M	Laborer	08Ap02Gc
DOWD, Mary	30	F	Servant	08Ap02Gc
Michael	16	M	Servant	08Ap02Gc
FOWLER, Patrick	30	M	Draper	08Ap02Gc
FAVERS, Margaret	18	F	Cook	08Ap02Gc
MCCANN, John	25	M	Laborer	08Ap02Gc
KEARY, Patrick	26	M	Farmer	08Ap02Gc
Bryan	28	M	Farmer	08Ap02Gc
BRADY, James	28	M	Farmer	08Ap02Gc
KEARY, Ellen	23	F	Farmer	08Ap02Gc
STANLEY, Mary	26	F	Servant	08Ap02Gc
Lucy	27	F	Servant	08Ap02Gc
DOLAN, Eliza	22	F	Servant	08Ap02Gc
CROOK, Peter	36	M	Farmer	08Ap02Gc
SHARPE, Patt	18	M	Laborer	08Ap02Gc
BOYLE, Margaret	22	F	Servant	08Ap02Gc
NOCTIN, Sally	33	F	Servant	08Ap02Gc
Thomas	.04	M	Infant	08Ap02Gc
SCULLY, Patrick	22	M	Servant	08Ap02Gc
SAUNDERS, Henry	16	M	Servant	08Ap02Gc
KENNY, Thomas	25	M	Servant	08Ap02Gc
Christopher	22	M	Servant	08Ap02Gc
Catherine	26	F	Servant	08Ap02Gc
KEARNEY, Michael	40	M	Farmer	08Ap02Gc
KIND, Thomas	25	M	Farmer	08Ap02Gc
OBRIEN, Michael	41	M	Farmer	08Ap02Gc
Honora	31	F	Farmer	08Ap02Gc
James	13	M	Farmer	08Ap02Gc
William	11	M	Farmer	08Ap02Gc
Anne	9	F	Child	08Ap02Gc
Mary	5	F	Child	08Ap02Gc
Michael	3	M	Child	08Ap02Gc
Catherine	.05	F	Infant	08Ap02Gc
LONG, Edmond	60	M	Farmer	08Ap02Gc
Margaret	50	F	Farmer	08Ap02Gc
Edward	3	M	Child	08Ap02Gc
CLYNE, Peter	28	M	Laborer	08Ap02Gc
Thomas	30	M	Laborer	08Ap02Gc
Margaret	22	F	Laborer	08Ap02Gc
Bridget	18	F	Laborer	08Ap02Gc
HARRISON, John	24	M	Laborer	08Ap02Gc
NAUGHTON, James	26	M	Laborer	08Ap02Gc
Bridget	24	F	Laborer	08Ap02Gc
Thomas	.07	M	Infant	08Ap02Gc
MCGONNELL, Patt	35	M	Farmer	08Ap02Gc
GLASS, Margaret	19	F	Servant	08Ap02Gc
JONES, Richard	21	M	Servant	08Ap02Gc
U, Adelaide	7	F	Child	08Ap02Gc
CHAPMAN, Robert	30	M	Mechanic	08Ap02Gc
John	26	M	Mechanic	08Ap02Gc
POTTERS, Richard	21	M	Mechanic	08Ap02Gc
CURRY, Christina	20	F	Dressmaker	08Ap02Gc
SANDERS, Joseph	34	M	Smith	08Ap02Gc
BRENNAN, Hugh	24	M	Tinker	08Ap02Gc
Rose	21	F	Unknown	08Ap02Gc
HYNES, Dennis	21	M	Laborer	08Ap02Gc
GEOUGHIGAN, John	24	M	Laborer	08Ap02Gc

NAMES OF PASSENGERS	AGE	SEX	OCCUPATIONS	DATE PORT SHIP
CONWAY, James	19	M	Laborer	08Ap02Gc
MCQUADE, Francis	20	M	Farmer	08Ap02Gc
FARRELL, Patrick	32	M	Laborer	08Ap02Gc
KELLY, Dennis	20	M	Laborer	08Ap02Gc
DUON, John	40	M	Unknown	08Ap02Gc
BRADY, Mary	30	F	Servant	08Ap02Gc
CARROY, Thomas	20	M	Groom	08Ap02Gc
NOLAN, James	30	M	Pouterer	08Ap02Gc
TOOLE, Thomas	40	M	Laborer	08Ap02Gc
John	20	M	Laborer	08Ap02Gc
BEATTY, Thomas	23	M	Laborer	08Ap02Gc
MCLEAN, Neal	20	M	Laborer	08Ap02Gc
MARTNEY, Thomas	35	M	Laborer	08Ap02Gc
Patrick	11	M	Laborer	08Ap02Gc
LYNCH, John	22	M	Farmer	08Ap02Gc
Ellen	20	F	Farmer	08Ap02Gc
MCANALLY, Philip	25	M	Farmer	08Ap02Gc
Bridget	21	F	Farmer	08Ap02Gc
Bridget	.09	F	Infant	08Ap02Gc
BUTLER, Patrick	25	M	Dealer	08Ap02Gc
FOGARTY, Mary	20	F	Milliner	08Ap02Gc
Anne	18	F	Milliner	08Ap02Gc
NOWLAN, Jasper	13	M	Laborer	08Ap02Gc
CURRAN, Clara	30	F	Servant	08Ap02Gc
DUGAN, Michael	13	M	Groom	08Ap02Gc
OBRIEN, Patrick	13	M	Groom	08Ap02Gc
FARRELLY, Catherine	19	F	Servant	08Ap02Gc
MCDERMOT, Catherine	18	F	Servant	08Ap02Gc
CONNOLLY, Thomas	22	M	Laborer	08Ap02Gc
Michael	20	M	Laborer	08Ap02Gc
DOHERTY, Biddy	33	F	Servant	08Ap02Gc
FINNEGAN, Mary	19	F	Servant	08Ap02Gc
MOONEY, William	35	M	Laborer	08Ap02Gc
BYRNE, James	19	M	Farmer	08Ap02Gc
BROUGHLY, Loughlin	54	M	Laborer	08Ap02Gc
BROPHY, William	23	M	Laborer	08Ap02Gc
Mary	22	F	Laborer	08Ap02Gc
Anthony	19	M	Laborer	08Ap02Gc
LAMBERT, Nicholas	46	M	Laborer	08Ap02Gc
Mary	46	F	Laborer	08Ap02Gc
LAHY, Bridget	20	F	Nurse	08Ap02Gc
STAPLETON, Michael	30	M	Gdnr	08Ap02Gc
MCGRATH, Anthony	22	M	Laborer	08Ap02Gc
FINNERTY, Michael	26	M	Laborer	08Ap02Gc
MURPHY, James	20	M	Laborer	08Ap02Gc
MORETON, Michael	20	M	Laborer	08Ap02Gc
BURK, Mary	19	F	Servant	08Ap02Gc
LOWRY, Robert-R.	23	M	Farmer	08Ap02Gc
Hannah	25	F	Farmer	08Ap02Gc
KERR, John	32	M	Farmer	08Ap02Gc
DONNEL, James	26	M	Laborer	08Ap02Gc
BARRON, James	27	M	Laborer	08Ap02Gc
CANNON, Barney	35	M	Laborer	08Ap02Gc
BROWNE, William	19	M	Farmer	08Ap02Gc
HAMILTON, Andrew	20	M	Farmer	08Ap02Gc
KOUGH, Patrick	50	M	Farmer	08Ap02Gc
Mary	50	F	Farmer	08Ap02Gc
James	30	M	Farmer	08Ap02Gc
Mary	27	F	Farmer	08Ap02Gc
Martin	25	M	Farmer	08Ap02Gc
Patrick	17	M	Farmer	08Ap02Gc
Robert	19	M	Farmer	08Ap02Gc
DORAN, Thomas	29	M	Farmer	08Ap02Gc
Eliza	28	F	Servant	08Ap02Gc
DOYLE, Patrick	24	M	Laborer	08Ap02Gc
Bridget	20	F	Laborer	08Ap02Gc
James	19	M	Laborer	08Ap02Gc
Mary	16	F	Laborer	08Ap02Gc
TRACEY, Michael	32	M	Gdnr	08Ap02Gc
Biddy	22	F	Gdnr	08Ap02Gc
Michael	.00	M	Infant	08Ap02Gc
MORRISSY, Patrick	12	M	Student	08Ap02Gc
Catherine	10	F	Student	08Ap02Gc
MCCLUSKY, Patrick	55	M	Farmer	08Ap02Gc
Margaret	50	F	Farmer	08Ap02Gc
MCCLUSKY, Patrick	12	M	Farmer	08Ap02Gc
Charles	9	M	Child	08Ap02Gc
Robert	7	M	Child	08Ap02Gc
Nancy	6	F	Child	08Ap02Gc
MORAN, Michael	20	M	Laborer	08Ap02Gc
HANNEY, Darby	45	M	Farmer	08Ap02Gc
Mary	45	F	Farmer	08Ap02Gc
Daniel	20	M	Farmer	08Ap02Gc
Bridget	19	F	Farmer	08Ap02Gc
Catherine	17	F	Farmer	08Ap02Gc
Thomas	11	M	Farmer	08Ap02Gc
Patrick	9	M	Child	08Ap02Gc
Rody	3	F	Child	08Ap02Gc
KELLY, Anne-Victoria Born-At-Sea	.00	F	Infant	08Ap02Gc
VULLY, Mary-Washington Born-At-Sea	.00	F	Infant	08Ap02Gc
FITZPATRICK, Thomas	28	M	Laborer	08Ap02Gc

WESTMINSTER 08 APRIL 1850

From London

NAMES OF PASSENGERS	AGE	SEX	OCCUPATIONS	DATE PORT SHIP
GREIG, Phillip	54	M	Laborer	08Ap06Cy
TRACY, John	38	M	Laborer	08Ap06Cy
Thos.	10	M	None	08Ap06Cy
EPPENING, Margaret	24	F	None	08Ap06Cy
Patrick	.00	M	Infant	08Ap06Cy
REGAN, John	43	M	Laborer	08Ap06Cy
HARROGAN, Dennis	23	M	Plasterer	08Ap06Cy
KEARNEY, Peter	27	M	Plasterer	08Ap06Cy
Ellen	26	F	None	08Ap06Cy
ROACH, James	23	M	Bookkeeper	08Ap06Cy
CALLAHAN, Margaret	31	F	None	08Ap06Cy
NEALE, Bridget	20	F	None	08Ap06Cy
DONOVAN, Dennis	26	M	Laborer	08Ap06Cy
Ellen	24	F	None	08Ap06Cy
DUNNE, John	30	M	Farmer	08Ap06Cy
Ellen	34	F	None	08Ap06Cy
MCCORMICK, James	36	M	Gasfitter	08Ap06Cy
Ellen	30	F	None	08Ap06Cy
Mary-Ann	9	F	Child	08Ap06Cy

TICONDEROGA 08 APRIL 1850

From Liverpool

NAMES OF PASSENGERS	AGE	SEX	OCCUPATIONS	DATE PORT SHIP
COOK, Mathew	26	M	Servant	08Ap02Gd
Mary (W)	24	F	Wife	08Ap02Gd
FITZGERALD, Mary	22	F	Spinster	08Ap02Gd
HOLMES, John	24	M	Miller	08Ap02Gd
OSTERN, William	31	M	Farmer	08Ap02Gd
BROWN, Honora	30	F	Unknown	08Ap02Gd
Mary	14	F	Unknown	08Ap02Gd
Marcella	11	F	Unknown	08Ap02Gd
Margret	9	F	Child	08Ap02Gd
Edwin	7	M	Child	08Ap02Gd
Thomas	6	M	Child	08Ap02Gd
Anne	4	F	Child	08Ap02Gd
William	2	M	Child	08Ap02Gd
Robert	.09	M	Infant	08Ap02Gd
CARRY, Anne	40	F	Wife	08Ap02Gd
MOFFATT, Samuel-B.	33	M	Clerk	08Ap02Gd

NAMES OF PASSENGERS		AGE	SEX	OCCUPATIONS	DATE PORT SHIP
VAUGHAN, Maryanne		38	F	Wife	08Ap02Gd
Elizabeth		16	F	Unknown	08Ap02Gd
Anna-Maria		14	F	Unknown	08Ap02Gd
James		13	M	Unknown	08Ap02Gd
Fanny		6	F	Child	08Ap02Gd
Clarissa		.04	F	Infant	08Ap02Gd
Jane		8	F	Child	08Ap02Gd
ANDERSON, Alexander		35	M	Gdnr	08Ap02Gd
Helen-Jane		30	F	Spinster	08Ap02Gd
Margaret		25	F	Spinster	08Ap02Gd
Jane		14	F	Spinster	08Ap02Gd
YOUNG, Christopher		24	M	Grocer	08Ap02Gd
Henry		20	M	Shoemaker	08Ap02Gd
OREILY, Pat		25	M	Clerk	08Ap02Gd
Bridget		40	F	Spinster	08Ap02Gd
Jane		20	F	Spinster	08Ap02Gd
Rose		18	F	Spinster	08Ap02Gd
James		15	M	Clerk	08Ap02Gd
CARLOSS, William		24	M	Laborer	08Ap02Gd
MCWATERS, Rosanna		30	F	Spinster	08Ap02Gd
Sophia		25	F	Spinster	08Ap02Gd
ELLIOTT, James		30	M	Farmer	08Ap02Gd
Mary	(W)	40	F	Wife	08Ap02Gd
BEATTY, Margret		15	F	Daughter	08Ap02Gd
ELLIOTT, John		22	M	Carpenter	08Ap02Gd
GRANT, Elizabeth		18	F	Spinster	08Ap02Gd
HARVEY, Pat		24	M	Laborer	08Ap02Gd
MCARTLIN, Charles		18	M	Laborer	08Ap02Gd
HARVEY, Mary		21	F	Spinster	08Ap02Gd
MCARTLIN, Thomas		24	M	Laborer	08Ap02Gd
Mary	(W)	25	F	Wife	08Ap02Gd
Mary	(D)	.03	F	Infant	08Ap02Gd
DUNNE, Paul		38	M	Laborer	08Ap02Gd
Feramagh		17	M	Laborer	08Ap02Gd
Sally	(D)	10	F	Unknown	08Ap02Gd
WRIGHT, Pat		21	M	Blacksmith	08Ap02Gd
STANTON, Richard		22	M	Laborer	08Ap02Gd
MCQUADE, Arther		20	M	Laborer	08Ap02Gd
LALLY, Anthony		24	M	Laborer	08Ap02Gd
HEFFERNAN, David		18	M	Laborer	08Ap02Gd
Mary		19	F	Spinster	08Ap02Gd
FLEMMING, Pat		30	M	Laborer	08Ap02Gd
Anne	(W)	23	F	Wife	08Ap02Gd
Mary	(D)	.02	F	Infant	08Ap02Gd
LENARD, Roger		25	M	Laborer	08Ap02Gd
CADEN, Pat		18	M	Laborer	08Ap02Gd
MIGINNIS, Pat		35	M	Laborer	08Ap02Gd
HART, Margret		30	F	Spinster	08Ap02Gd
FLOOD, John		26	M	Clerk	08Ap02Gd
LYONS, John		36	M	Teacher	08Ap02Gd
Margret	(W)	25	F	Wife	08Ap02Gd
Bessy	(D)	.02	F	Infant	08Ap02Gd
HART, Mary		26	F	Unknown	08Ap02Gd
John	(S)	6	M	Child	08Ap02Gd
Patt	(S)	4	M	Child	08Ap02Gd
Anne	(D)	2	F	Child	08Ap02Gd
FINLY, William		20	M	Laborer	08Ap02Gd
KEATING, Mary		20	F	Spinster	08Ap02Gd
BRAHAN, John		23	M	Laborer	08Ap02Gd
James		20	M	Laborer	08Ap02Gd
SUTTON, Nichlos		21	M	Laborer	08Ap02Gd
MORISSEY, Thomas		21	M	Laborer	08Ap02Gd
Pat		20	M	Laborer	08Ap02Gd
GALLAGHER, Michael		29	M	Laborer	08Ap02Gd
SHELLY, Bernard		25	M	Laborer	08Ap02Gd
COURTNEY, David		20	M	Laborer	08Ap02Gd
SULLIVAN, Michael		32	M	Laborer	08Ap02Gd
LAWLOR, John		24	M	Laborer	08Ap02Gd
MCCLOSKEY, Pat		25	M	Laborer	08Ap02Gd
Henry		21	M	Laborer	08Ap02Gd
Rodey		6	M	Child	08Ap02Gd
Owen		20	M	Laborer	08Ap02Gd
Pat		25	M	Laborer	08Ap02Gd
Nancy		19	F	Spinster	08Ap02Gd
Betty		25	F	Spinster	08Ap02Gd

NAMES OF PASSENGERS		AGE	SEX	OCCUPATIONS	DATE PORT SHIP
MCCLOSKEY, Catherine		25	F	Spinster	08Ap02Gd
MCGILLIGAN, Betty		18	F	Spinster	08Ap02Gd
GARYINE, Nancy		21	F	Spinster	08Ap02Gd
KANE, James		22	M	Laborer	08Ap02Gd
MCIVER, John		22	M	Laborer	08Ap02Gd
MCCLOSKEY, Edward		22	M	Laborer	08Ap02Gd
CASEY, Francis		35	M	Laborer	08Ap02Gd
WATERS, Thomas		24	M	Shoemaker	08Ap02Gd
HALL, Kieran		25	M	Laborer	08Ap02Gd
Anne	(T)	23	F	Sister	08Ap02Gd
DOHERTY, Jane		24	F	Spinster	08Ap02Gd
OHARRA, James		24	M	Laborer	08Ap02Gd
MCRODEY, John		30	M	Laborer	08Ap02Gd
ODONNELL, Mary		20	F	Spinster	08Ap02Gd
REED, Arthur		22	M	Shoemaker	08Ap02Gd
James		21	M	Laborer	08Ap02Gd
LENARD, Michael		16	M	Laborer	08Ap02Gd
BRANNON, Owen		40	M	Laborer	08Ap02Gd
Catherine	(W)	32	F	Wife	08Ap02Gd
James	(S)	9	M	Child	08Ap02Gd
Mary	(D)	7	F	Child	08Ap02Gd
Pat	(S)	5	M	Child	08Ap02Gd
BYRNE, John		24	M	Laborer	08Ap02Gd
ROWLAND, Philip		18	M	Shoemaker	08Ap02Gd
Margret	(T)	30	F	Sister	08Ap02Gd
Essy	(D)	6	F	Child	08Ap02Gd
John	(S)	1	M	Child	08Ap02Gd
FITZPATRICK, John		26	M	Farmer	08Ap02Gd
Ellen	(W)	20	F	Wife	08Ap02Gd
Margret		25	F	Spinster	08Ap02Gd
FINIAN, Mary		20	F	Spinster	08Ap02Gd
NORTON, Sylvester		28	M	Farmer	08Ap02Gd
RIDDLE, John		21	M	Farmer	08Ap02Gd
Debra	(T)	19	F	Sister	08Ap02Gd
Matilda	(W)	18	F	Wife	08Ap02Gd
MCCAUL, Robert		18	M	Farmer	08Ap02Gd
Mary	(T)	18	F	Sister	08Ap02Gd
RILEY, Charles		24	M	Laborer	08Ap02Gd
Miles		20	M	Laborer	08Ap02Gd
Farrell		24	M	Laborer	08Ap02Gd
Peter		20	M	Laborer	08Ap02Gd
Patt		20	M	Laborer	08Ap02Gd
Edward		22	M	Laborer	08Ap02Gd
Bernard		36	M	Laborer	08Ap02Gd
COSGROVE, James		20	M	Laborer	08Ap02Gd
MEEHS, John		20	M	Laborer	08Ap02Gd
HOGAN, Arther		20	M	Laborer	08Ap02Gd
PAUL, John		24	M	Laborer	08Ap02Gd
Joseph		25	M	Laborer	08Ap02Gd
FITZPATRICK, Michael		26	M	Laborer	08Ap02Gd
CALLAGHAN, Bessy		18	F	Spinster	08Ap02Gd
SULLIVAN, Eugene-G.		20	M	Laborer	08Ap02Gd
Margret		13	F	Spinster	08Ap02Gd
Cathrine		22	F	Spinster	08Ap02Gd
CALLAGHAN, Johanna		30	F	Wi	08Ap02Gd
FITZGERALD, Michael	(S)	4	M	Child	08Ap02Gd
MOORE, Rose		35	F	Wi	08Ap02Gd
COLEMAN, Thomas		32	M	Plasterer	08Ap02Gd
Patt		36	M	Plasterer	08Ap02Gd
Catherine	(W)	30	F	Wife	08Ap02Gd
James	(S)	8	M	Child	08Ap02Gd
Mary	(D)	4	F	Child	08Ap02Gd
CAREY, James		26	M	Laborer	08Ap02Gd
Ellen	(T)	24	F	Sister	08Ap02Gd
LYNCH, Michael		30	M	Laborer	08Ap02Gd
KILLROY, Sarah		20	F	Spinster	08Ap02Gd
REYNOLDS, Bridget		30	F	Spinster	08Ap02Gd
HACKETT, Mary		18	F	Spinster	08Ap02Gd
Winefred		12	F	Spinster	08Ap02Gd
Mary		6	F	Child	08Ap02Gd
MCFARLANE, Cathrine		40	F	Wi	08Ap02Gd
James	(S)	7	M	Child	08Ap02Gd
CALLAGHAN, Peggy		20	F	Spinster	08Ap02Gd
WALSH, Philip		24	M	Shoemaker	08Ap02Gd
Mary	(T)	20	F	Sister	08Ap02Gd

NAMES OF PASSENGERS		AGE	SEX	OCCUPATIONS	DATE PORT SHIP
KENNY, Cathrine		20	F	Spinster	08Ap02Gd
Anne	(T)	16	F	Sister	08Ap02Gd
LAWLOR, Ellen		30	F	Spinster	08Ap02Gd
DORAN, Abey		35	F	Wi	08Ap02Gd
Martin	(S)	16	M	Unknown	08Ap02Gd
John	(S)	7	M	Child	08Ap02Gd
Charles	(S)	1	M	Child	08Ap02Gd
LAW, Charles		50	M	Laborer	08Ap02Gd
LARKIN, Martin		20	M	Laborer	08Ap02Gd
PENDERGRAST, Edward		21	M	Laborer	08Ap02Gd
QUIN, Miles		21	M	Laborer	08Ap02Gd
Jane	(W)	19	F	Wife	08Ap02Gd
MANNION, James		30	M	Laborer	08Ap02Gd
RYAN, Edward		25	M	Laborer	08Ap02Gd
Betty	(W)	24	F	Wife	08Ap02Gd
MORAN, Pat		30	M	Laborer	08Ap02Gd
CARROLL, Thomas		28	M	Laborer	08Ap02Gd
MURPHY, Daniel		25	M	Laborer	08Ap02Gd
RIARDON, Margret		35	F	Unknown	08Ap02Gd
SHEELY, Eliza		17	F	Spinster	08Ap02Gd
RIARDON, Mary	(D)	8	F	Child	08Ap02Gd
John	(S)	5	M	Child	08Ap02Gd
Margret	(D)	3	F	Child	08Ap02Gd
Michael	(S)	1	M	Child	08Ap02Gd
MCGUIN, Thomas		21	M	Laborer	08Ap02Gd
DONOHUE, James		19	M	Laborer	08Ap02Gd
SMITH, Bridget		26	F	Spinster	08Ap02Gd
BRYERLY, Catherine		22	F	Spinster	08Ap02Gd
CONNOR, Ellen		20	F	Spinster	08Ap02Gd
MCCLUSKY, James		19	M	Laborer	08Ap02Gd
MACKIN, James		22	M	Shoemaker	08Ap02Gd
DOWNEY, Christopher		24	M	Weaver	08Ap02Gd
KELLY, Cathrine		30	F	Spinster	08Ap02Gd
SHARON, Catharine		20	F	Spinster	08Ap02Gd
MCGRATH, Nicholas		30	M	Laborer	08Ap02Gd
Anne	(M)	60	F	Unknown	08Ap02Gd
GALVIN, Dennis		24	M	Surveyor	08Ap02Gd
Mary	(W)	24	F	Wife	08Ap02Gd
Ellen	(D)	2	F	Child	08Ap02Gd
Johanna	(T)	18	F	Sister	08Ap02Gd
LENNIHAN, Dennis		20	M	Shoemaker	08Ap02Gd
FARRELL, William		13	M	Laborer	08Ap02Gd
DWYER, John		32	M	Laborer	08Ap02Gd
HARLY, Margret		22	F	Spinster	08Ap02Gd
DWYER, Anne		36	F	Wife	08Ap02Gd
Mary	(D)	00	F	Child	08Ap02Gd
James	(S)	.00	M	Infant	08Ap02Gd
Martha	(D)	.11	F	Infant	08Ap02Gd
Bridget		26	F	Spinster	08Ap02Gd
MARRIN, John		17	M	Farmer	08Ap02Gd
Catherine	(T)	14	F	Sister	08Ap02Gd
FINEGAN, Philip		34	M	Farmer	08Ap02Gd
BRENNAN, Peter		40	M	Baker	08Ap02Gd
FINNIGAN, Joseph		36	M	Tailor	08Ap02Gd
LOWRY, Martin		30	M	Farmer	08Ap02Gd
MURRY, Pat		22	M	Bricklayer	08Ap02Gd
QUARY, Pat		30	M	Laborer	08Ap02Gd
GANNON, Wm.		30	M	Laborer	08Ap02Gd
MCGURN, Hugh		22	M	Cooper	08Ap02Gd
Mary	(W)	22	F	Wife	08Ap02Gd
Mary	(D)	.03	F	Infant	08Ap02Gd
Died-At-Sea					
HUNTER, William		18	M	Farmer	08Ap02Gd
STEWARD, Thomas		25	M	Farmer	08Ap02Gd
MCGURN, Mary		24	F	Spinster	08Ap02Gd
MONTGOMERY, Robert		30	M	Farmer	08Ap02Gd
SHERON, Michael		21	M	Laborer	08Ap02Gd
Peter		22	M	Laborer	08Ap02Gd
Susan		20	F	Spinster	08Ap02Gd
CAIN, Mary		22	F	Spinster	08Ap02Gd
CONWAY, Pat		23	M	Laborer	08Ap02Gd
FARRELL, Ruth		16	F	Servant	08Ap02Gd
NELSON, Maryanne		21	F	Servant	08Ap02Gd
WALES, Walter		20	M	Laborer	08Ap02Gd
Pat		18	M	Laborer	08Ap02Gd

NAMES OF PASSENGERS		AGE	SEX	OCCUPATIONS	DATE PORT SHIP
WALES, Bridget	(T)	15	F	Sister	08Ap02Gd
FINLY, Martin		11	M	Laborer	08Ap02Gd
CROAK, Anthony		20	M	Spinster	08Ap02Gd
CRONY, John		25	M	Unknown	08Ap02Gd
HAFFAN, Michael		35	M	Laborer	08Ap02Gd
DOLLARD, John		40	M	Laborer	08Ap02Gd
LAFFAN, Catherine		35	F	Wife	08Ap02Gd
COYLE, Philip		40	M	Grocer	08Ap02Gd
Maria	(W)	36	F	Wife	08Ap02Gd
John	(S)	12	M	Unknown	08Ap02Gd
Matilda	(D)	10	F	Unknown	08Ap02Gd
Hugh	(S)	7	M	Child	08Ap02Gd
Peter	(S)	5	M	Child	08Ap02Gd
Maria	(D)	3	F	Child	08Ap02Gd
DENNING, Ambrose		20	M	Laborer	08Ap02Gd
Eliza	(T)	25	F	Sister	08Ap02Gd
CASS, Pat		20	M	Laborer	08Ap02Gd
LARKIN, Thomas		20	M	Laborer	08Ap02Gd
FARRELL, John		20	M	Laborer	08Ap02Gd
Catherine	(T)	21	F	Sister	08Ap02Gd
Thomas	(B)	11	M	Brother	08Ap02Gd
RUSSELL, Pat		35	M	Laborer	08Ap02Gd
Nancy	(W)	30	F	Wife	08Ap02Gd
James	(S)	3	M	Child	08Ap02Gd
RYAN, Bridget		18	F	Spinster	08Ap02Gd
CRONNIN, Thomas		30	M	Laborer	08Ap02Gd
HAYS, Garrett		35	M	Laborer	08Ap02Gd
MCKENNEY, Francis		22	M	Laborer	08Ap02Gd
COLEMAN, John		18	M	Laborer	08Ap02Gd
HENRY, Pat		28	M	Laborer	08Ap02Gd
Bridget		16	F	Spinster	08Ap02Gd
WARD, Margret		16	F	Spinster	08Ap02Gd
DOLAN, Mary		26	F	Spinster	08Ap02Gd
DORAN, Anne		24	F	Spinster	08Ap02Gd
KILDUFF, Bernard		30	M	Laborer	08Ap02Gd
Mary	(W)	30	F	Wife	08Ap02Gd
Pat	(S)	10	M	Unknown	08Ap02Gd
WARD, Pat		26	M	Laborer	08Ap02Gd
Bridget	(M)	34	F	Unknown	08Ap02Gd
Anne	(D)	8	F	Child	08Ap02Gd
BUCKLY, Dennis		27	M	Farmer	08Ap02Gd
John		21	M	Farmer	08Ap02Gd
FARRELL, James		33	M	Laborer	08Ap02Gd
Margaret	(W)	30	F	Wife	08Ap02Gd
HEANY, John		18	M	Laborer	08Ap02Gd
Anne	(W)	50	F	Wife	08Ap02Gd
Jane	(D)	8	F	Child	08Ap02Gd
Sarah	(D)	5	F	Child	08Ap02Gd
PIERCE, Pat		21	M	Laborer	08Ap02Gd
SULLIVAN, John		30	M	Laborer	08Ap02Gd
FLAHERTY, Thimothy		24	M	Laborer	08Ap02Gd
CONNER, Thimothy		30	M	Laborer	08Ap02Gd
RILEY, Thimothy		30	M	Laborer	08Ap02Gd
Mary	(D)	10	F	Unknown	08Ap02Gd
Bridget	(D)	8	F	Child	08Ap02Gd
Dennis	(S)	4	M	Child	08Ap02Gd
MCLOUGHLIN, Thomas		20	M	Laborer	08Ap02Gd
MCDERMOTT, Pat		21	M	Laborer	08Ap02Gd
BRADLEY, James		21	M	Laborer	08Ap02Gd
Patt		17	M	Laborer	08Ap02Gd
TYRRELL, William		25	M	Laborer	08Ap02Gd
MCCORMICK, James		26	M	Laborer	08Ap02Gd
Margret		20	F	Seamstress	08Ap02Gd
LEAHY, Bridget		20	F	Spinster	08Ap02Gd
CONNERY, Richard		26	M	Laborer	08Ap02Gd
SWEENY, William		35	M	Tailor	08Ap02Gd
Bridget	(M)	55	F	Unknown	08Ap02Gd
John		38	M	Shoemaker	08Ap02Gd
John	(S)	12	M	Unknown	08Ap02Gd
William	(S)	11	M	Unknown	08Ap02Gd
Alexander	(S)	8	M	Child	08Ap02Gd
CONNOR, John		20	M	Laborer	08Ap02Gd
FARRELL, Michael		35	M	Laborer	08Ap02Gd
Honora	(W)	35	F	Wife	08Ap02Gd
Mary	(D)	3	F	Child	08Ap02Gd

NAMES OF PASSENGERS		AGE	SEX	OCCUPATIONS	DATE PORT SHIP
LYNCH, John		25	M	Laborer	08Ap02Gd
HOPKINS, Mary		20	F	Spinster	08Ap02Gd
CAFFREY, Mary		50	F	Spinster	08Ap02Gd
Pat		18	M	Laborer	08Ap02Gd
James		20	M	Laborer	08Ap02Gd
Bryan		13	M	Laborer	08Ap02Gd
Anne	(T)	12	F	Sister	08Ap02Gd
Michael		10	M	Laborer	08Ap02Gd
KING, James		18	M	Laborer	08Ap02Gd
Francis		16	M	Clerk	08Ap02Gd
Jane	(T)	18	F	Sister	08Ap02Gd
FLINN, Bridget		14	F	Unknown	08Ap02Gd
RILEY, James		12	M	Unknown	08Ap02Gd
LORD, John		18	M	Laborer	08Ap02Gd
WADE, Anne		18	F	Spinster	08Ap02Gd
RYAN, Patt		19	M	Laborer	08Ap02Gd
Winefred	(T)	16	F	Sister	08Ap02Gd
KENNEDY, Bryan		15	M	Laborer	08Ap02Gd
Mary		12	F	Unknown	08Ap02Gd
HALL, James		30	M	Laborer	08Ap02Gd
MONAHAN, Peter		19	M	Laborer	08Ap02Gd
WALSH, David		26	M	Bootmaker	08Ap02Gd
DONAHUE, Michael		30	M	Laborer	08Ap02Gd
Pat		28	M	Laborer	08Ap02Gd
Elenor	(T)	26	F	Sister	08Ap02Gd
Alice	(T)	24	F	Sister	08Ap02Gd
MURPHY, John		28	M	Laborer	08Ap02Gd
LACY, Charles		34	M	Laborer	08Ap02Gd
CROW, Judy		26	M	Laborer	08Ap02Gd
Catherine	(T)	23	F	Sister	08Ap02Gd
MCVEIGH, John		37	M	Laborer	08Ap02Gd
FARRELL, Thomas		26	M	Laborer	08Ap02Gd
MCABLE, Peter		28	M	Laborer	08Ap02Gd
Mary	(T)	18	F	Sister	08Ap02Gd
MONAHAN, Alice		24	F	Spinster	08Ap02Gd
Rose		19	F	Spinster	08Ap02Gd
MCGARRY, Mary		9	F	Child	08Ap02Gd
MURRY, Pat		20	M	Laborer	08Ap02Gd
KEEGAN, Mary		19	F	Spinster	08Ap02Gd
MURPHY, John		30	M	Laborer	08Ap02Gd
CAFFY, Michael		35	M	Laborer	08Ap02Gd
Honora	(D)	16	F	Unknown	08Ap02Gd
HALLON, Anne		18	F	Unknown	08Ap02Gd
RYAN, Ellen		19	F	Spinster	08Ap02Gd
MORAN, Catherine		23	F	Spinster	08Ap02Gd
HUGHES, James		20	M	Potter	08Ap02Gd
SULLIVAN, Patrick		22	M	Farmer	08Ap02Gd
Mary	(W)	21	F	Wife	08Ap02Gd
Bridget		13	F	Unknown	08Ap02Gd
CONNELL, Timothy		20	M	Farmer	08Ap02Gd
Ellen	(W)	20	F	Wife	08Ap02Gd
John		25	M	Laborer	08Ap02Gd
Ellen		20	F	Spinster	08Ap02Gd
JONES, Mathew		18	M	Laborer	08Ap02Gd
MCAULIFF, Pat		30	M	Laborer	08Ap02Gd
HANRAHAN, Andrew		26	M	Laborer	08Ap02Gd

COLONIST 08 APRIL 1850

From Liverpool

NAMES OF PASSENGERS	AGE	SEX	OCCUPATIONS	DATE PORT SHIP
OCONNOR, James	24	M	Bookbinder	08Ap02Fz
MULLAN, James	18	M	Laborer	08Ap02Fz
MOYRAHAM, John	22	M	Whitesmith	08Ap02Fz
DULAN, Mary	22	F	Servant	08Ap02Fz
PENDERGRASS, Bridget	20	F	Servant	08Ap02Fz
Mary	18	F	Servant	08Ap02Fz
CULLIN, James	26	M	Servant	08Ap02Fz
Mathew	22	M	Servant	08Ap02Fz
CULLIN, Laurence	28	M	Servant	08Ap02Fz
PATON, Charles	25	M	Sdlmkr	08Ap02Fz
Helen	20	F	Wife	08Ap02Fz
PENDERGRASS, Luke	23	M	Laborer	08Ap02Fz
Cecilia	20	F	Servant	08Ap02Fz
CAIN, Catherine	44	F	Servant	08Ap02Fz
Mary	13	F	Servant	08Ap02Fz
Catherine	11	F	Servant	08Ap02Fz
Thomas	8	M	Child	08Ap02Fz
Ann	6	F	Child	08Ap02Fz
LEACH, Ann	20	F	Servant	08Ap02Fz
MURRAY, Thomas	35	M	Servant	08Ap02Fz
EVANS, Laurence	22	M	Laborer	08Ap02Fz
James	18	M	Laborer	08Ap02Fz
PENDERGRAST, Pat	30	M	Laborer	08Ap02Fz
MICHILL, Owen	20	M	Laborer	08Ap02Fz
GANKIN, Boston	20	M	Laborer	08Ap02Fz
BIRMINGHAM, William	20	M	Laborer	08Ap02Fz
GLYNN, Ann	20	F	Servant	08Ap02Fz
KEAN, John	40	M	Laborer	08Ap02Fz
Judy	36	F	Laborer	08Ap02Fz
Anthony	35	M	Laborer	08Ap02Fz
Peter	17	M	Laborer	08Ap02Fz
Martin	13	M	Laborer	08Ap02Fz
Andrew	12	M	Laborer	08Ap02Fz
Ellen	11	F	Laborer	08Ap02Fz
John	7	M	Child	08Ap02Fz
CAHILL, Thomas	39	M	Laborer	08Ap02Fz
COONAN, John	24	M	Laborer	08Ap02Fz
DUGGIN, John	25	M	Laborer	08Ap02Fz
MCEVOY, John	40	M	Blacksmith	08Ap02Fz
SPILLANE, Jerry	36	M	Laborer	08Ap02Fz
Mary	50	F	None	08Ap02Fz
Catherine	50	F	None	08Ap02Fz
BENNET, James	25	M	None	08Ap02Fz
CARTHY, Honor	30	F	Servant	08Ap02Fz
SPILLANE, Andy	3	M	Child	08Ap02Fz
Mary	4	F	Child	08Ap02Fz
Nelly	.06	F	Infant	08Ap02Fz
DONOVAN, Nelly	20	F	Servant	08Ap02Fz
DONEGAN, Patrick	27	M	Laborer	08Ap02Fz
MURPHY, Margt.	24	F	Servant	08Ap02Fz
TRACHY, Thomas	45	M	Laborer	08Ap02Fz
CROWLEY, John	40	M	Laborer	08Ap02Fz
SWANTON, James	24	M	Laborer	08Ap02Fz
RAHILLY, Thomas	30	M	Laborer	08Ap02Fz
Biddy	22	F	Servant	08Ap02Fz
Mary	20	F	Servant	08Ap02Fz
MOYNAHAN, Danl.	30	M	Laborer	08Ap02Fz
Mary	25	F	None	08Ap02Fz
Andrew	3	M	Child	08Ap02Fz
Dennis	.04	M	Infant	08Ap02Fz
DOGHERTY, Thomas	28	M	Laborer	08Ap02Fz
MOYNAHAN, Francis	22	M	Laborer	08Ap02Fz
Catherine	19	F	None	08Ap02Fz
HETHERTON, Dennis	22	M	Carpenter	08Ap02Fz
CASEY, John	30	M	Laborer	08Ap02Fz
AHERN, John	30	M	Laborer	08Ap02Fz
WALSH, John	22	M	Laborer	08Ap02Fz
CULLAGHAN, Michl.	24	M	Laborer	08Ap02Fz
MCMAHON, Bryan	20	M	Laborer	08Ap02Fz
JORDAN, Catherine	17	F	Servant	08Ap02Fz
DUFFY, Mary	18	F	Servant	08Ap02Fz
LAMB, Philip	21	M	Laborer	08Ap02Fz
Eliza	20	F	Wife	08Ap02Fz
BLAKE, Daniel	20	M	Laborer	08Ap02Fz
Thomas	28	M	Laborer	08Ap02Fz
Bridget	30	F	Servant	08Ap02Fz
TACKEY, Margt.	18	F	Servant	08Ap02Fz
HESTER, John	20	M	Laborer	08Ap02Fz
Felix	24	M	Carpenter	08Ap02Fz
COONEY, Mary	18	F	Servant	08Ap02Fz
REILLY, Peter	27	M	Tailor	08Ap02Fz
MCLEAN, Joseph	18	M	Laborer	08Ap02Fz
BURKE, John	47	M	Blacksmith	08Ap02Fz

NAMES OF PASSENGERS	AGE	SEX	OCCUPATIONS	DATE PORT SHIP
BURKE, Ann	45	F	None	08Ap02Fz
Marcella	18	F	None	08Ap02Fz
Mary	11	F	None	08Ap02Fz
William	8	M	Child	08Ap02Fz
Laurence	6	M	Child	08Ap02Fz
Ann	3	F	Child	08Ap02Fz
MARTIN, Mary	25	F	Servant	08Ap02Fz
WENNIE, Roger	31	M	Laborer	08Ap02Fz
Margaret	22	F	Wife	08Ap02Fz
CONNELL, John	28	M	None	08Ap02Fz
Catherine	22	F	None	08Ap02Fz
QUEARY, John	16	M	None	08Ap02Fz
SHANAHAN, Mary	48	F	None	08Ap02Fz
Mary	16	F	None	08Ap02Fz
Mary	9	F	Child	08Ap02Fz
Patrick	12	M	None	08Ap02Fz
Ellen	7	F	Child	08Ap02Fz
MCGUINESS, John	19	M	None	08Ap02Fz
FOLEY, Eliza	20	F	Servant	08Ap02Fz
Catherine	15	F	Servant	08Ap02Fz
MULLAN, Pat	26	M	Laborer	08Ap02Fz
Mary	18	F	Servant	08Ap02Fz
Michael	22	M	Laborer	08Ap02Fz
GILHOOL, Dennis	36	M	Laborer	08Ap02Fz
Patrick	50	M	Laborer	08Ap02Fz
WHITE, Sally	40	F	Spinster	08Ap02Fz
Luke	12	M	None	08Ap02Fz
MULLIGAN, Michl.	30	M	Laborer	08Ap02Fz
Bridget	25	F	Servant	08Ap02Fz
MARTHA, Edward	30	M	Laborer	08Ap02Fz
JUDGE, Dominick	24	M	Laborer	08Ap02Fz
MARKAY, Richd.	20	M	Laborer	08Ap02Fz
COMERFORD, Thomas	21	M	Laborer	08Ap02Fz
BRADY, Luke	20	M	Laborer	08Ap02Fz
DENNOTT, Michl.	25	M	Laborer	08Ap02Fz
DONAGHY, Michl.	35	M	Laborer	08Ap02Fz
Ann	25	F	Servant	08Ap02Fz
Bernard	8	M	Child	08Ap02Fz
Catherine	.05	F	Infant	08Ap02Fz
OCONNOR, Peter	40	M	Farmer	08Ap02Fz
Peter	18	M	Farmer	08Ap02Fz
Biddy	16	F	Farmer	08Ap02Fz
Peggy	40	F	Farmer	08Ap02Fz
Andrew	14	M	Farmer	08Ap02Fz
Patrick	12	M	Farmer	08Ap02Fz
James	10	M	Farmer	08Ap02Fz
Mary	8	F	Child	08Ap02Fz
MCMAHON, James	20	M	Farmer	08Ap02Fz
DOWD, Nancy	20	F	Farmer	08Ap02Fz
FORBES, John	40	M	Farmer	08Ap02Fz
Patrick	19	M	Farmer	08Ap02Fz
Mary	13	F	Farmer	08Ap02Fz
GAIMES, Michl.	30	M	Farmer	08Ap02Fz
MARA, John	35	M	Laborer	08Ap02Fz
HACKETT, Jerry	22	M	Laborer	08Ap02Fz
RYAN, Tom	18	M	Laborer	08Ap02Fz
Tim	24	M	Laborer	08Ap02Fz
MCCANN, Patrick	20	M	Laborer	08Ap02Fz
DEVLIN, Bridget	16	F	Servant	08Ap02Fz
MCCORMAC, Robert	20	M	Laborer	08Ap02Fz
James	18	M	Laborer	08Ap02Fz
CROSSAN, Nancy	30	F	Servant	08Ap02Fz
GANNON, Matt	30	M	Laborer	08Ap02Fz
COOT, Thomas	40	M	Laborer	08Ap02Fz
HOPKINS, Mary	20	F	Servant	08Ap02Fz
CARTY, Michael	25	M	Carpenter	08Ap02Fz
LEINAN, John	30	F	Servant	08Ap02Fz
CONLEY, John	40	M	Laborer	08Ap02Fz
CLARK, Peter	20	M	Laborer	08Ap02Fz
KINLAND, Pat	19	M	Laborer	08Ap02Fz
FARRELLY, James	25	M	Laborer	08Ap02Fz
MINOCK, P.	30	M	Farmer	08Ap02Fz
Rose	30	F	None	08Ap02Fz
Michael	18	M	None	08Ap02Fz
John	12	M	None	08Ap02Fz

NAMES OF PASSENGERS	AGE	SEX	OCCUPATIONS	DATE PORT SHIP
MINOCK, Bridget	10	F	None	08Ap02Fz
DORAN, William	27	M	Baker	08Ap02Fz
BYRNE, Catherine	15	F	Servant	08Ap02Fz
Bessy	14	F	Servant	08Ap02Fz
FAGAN, John	24	M	Laborer	08Ap02Fz
WILLIS, James	26	M	Laborer	08Ap02Fz
LARKIN, William	25	M	Laborer	08Ap02Fz
Margaret	23	F	Spinster	08Ap02Fz
CLARY, John	35	M	Laborer	08Ap02Fz
Ellen	35	F	Servant	08Ap02Fz
Thomas	6	M	Child	08Ap02Fz
Judy	.00	F	Infant	08Ap02Fz
QUIN, John	18	M	Laborer	08Ap02Fz
PEARSALL, John	31	M	Laborer	08Ap02Fz
Grace	32	F	Servant	08Ap02Fz
BROUNEY, John	23	M	Laborer	08Ap02Fz
KILVARNEY, John	24	M	Laborer	08Ap02Fz
Ellen	40	F	Laborer	08Ap02Fz
FOGARTY, James	36	M	Laborer	08Ap02Fz
Eliza	46	F	Wi	08Ap02Fz
Catherine	25	F	Servant	08Ap02Fz
TOOLY, Bridget	35	F	Servant	08Ap02Fz
CANAVAN, John	39	M	Laborer	08Ap02Fz
BEVENS, Thomas	36	M	Laborer	08Ap02Fz
Margaret	30	F	Wife	08Ap02Fz
Mary	.09	F	Infant	08Ap02Fz
ROCK, Catherine	20	F	Servant	08Ap02Fz
Catherine	20	F	Servant	08Ap02Fz
MORRISON, Catherine	20	F	Servant	08Ap02Fz
SHEEN, Martin	16	M	Laborer	08Ap02Fz
Nora	15	F	Servant	08Ap02Fz
MURPHY, Bridget	18	F	Servant	08Ap02Fz
PHILBAN, Michl.	20	M	Laborer	08Ap02Fz
William	18	M	Laborer	08Ap02Fz
Bridget	16	F	Servant	08Ap02Fz
COURTNEY, John	20	M	Laborer	08Ap02Fz
KIDDRICK, Maria	16	F	Servant	08Ap02Fz
LYNCH, Margaret	24	F	Servant	08Ap02Fz
OROURKE, Timothy	37	M	Laborer	08Ap02Fz
Ann	40	F	Laborer	08Ap02Fz
MAYER, Joseph	17	M	Laborer	08Ap02Fz
CONNEL, Michl.	21	M	Laborer	08Ap02Fz
MINOCK, William	13	M	Laborer	08Ap02Fz

EMPIRE-CITY 08 APRIL 1850

From Chagres And Kingston

BORME, A.	35	U	Lawyer	08Ap36Gb
MCFADEN, P.	28	U	Laborer	08Ap36Gb
HONAN, J.	32	U	Laborer	08Ap36Gb
MCNEILL, M.	34	U	Laborer	08Ap36Gb
SULLIVAN, W.	18	U	Laborer	08Ap36Gb
DOUGHERTY, John	40	M	Laborer	08Ap36Gb
GUSHAIL, J.C.	40	U	Laborer	08Ap36Gb
MCKEWEN, R.	38	U	Merchant	08Ap36Gb
BASSFORD, G.W.	40	U	Merchant	08Ap36Gb

PATRICK-HENRY 08 APRIL 1850

From Liverpool

NAMES OF PASSENGERS	AGE	SEX	OCCUPATIONS	DATE PORT SHIP
CORCORAN, Francis	24	M	Laborer	08Ap02Cw
MEALEY, Bridget	27	F	Laborer	08Ap02Cw
RAINOR, Thos.	25	M	Laborer	08Ap02Cw
MARSHALL, Michl.	30	M	Corn Dealer	08Ap02Cw
Ellen	30	F	None	08Ap02Cw
Mary	9	F	Child	08Ap02Cw
Michl.	7	M	Child	08Ap02Cw
Ellen	5	F	Child	08Ap02Cw
Ann	3	F	Child	08Ap02Cw
Thos.	.00	F	Infant	08Ap02Cw
CONAWAY, Mick	30	M	Corn Dealer	08Ap02Cw
Mary	30	F	None	08Ap02Cw
Denis	4	M	Child	08Ap02Cw
Thos.	2	M	Child	08Ap02Cw
Ellen	.00	F	Infant	08Ap02Cw
CLUNEY, James	20	M	Laborer	08Ap02Cw
Biddy	25	F	Laborer	08Ap02Cw
COSGROVE, John	16	M	Shopman	08Ap02Cw
GILES, John	20	M	Servant	08Ap02Cw
MCARDLE, Owen	24	M	Stctr	08Ap02Cw
Bridget	21	F	None	08Ap02Cw
FRANKLIN, James	29	M	Brick Maker	08Ap02Cw
Mary	24	F	Brick Maker	08Ap02Cw
Ge.	22	U	Brick Maker	08Ap02Cw
TASKER, Richd.	23	M	Brick Maker	08Ap02Cw
GRINNON, John	20	M	Servant	08Ap02Cw
COSTELLO, Danl.	23	M	Servant	08Ap02Cw
SMITH, Bernard	16	M	Servant	08Ap02Cw
BYRNE, James	60	M	Farmer	08Ap02Cw
Pat	30	M	Farmer	08Ap02Cw
Ellen	20	F	Farmer	08Ap02Cw
HART, Bridget	20	F	Farmer	08Ap02Cw
DOREGAN, Margt.	20	F	Farmer	08Ap02Cw
YOUNG, Peter	24	M	Farmer	08Ap02Cw
James	16	M	Farmer	08Ap02Cw
Cath.	15	F	Farmer	08Ap02Cw
MURPHY, John	20	M	Farmer	08Ap02Cw
WILSON, John	20	M	Farmer	08Ap02Cw
NUGENT, Owen	28	M	Farmer	08Ap02Cw
Bridget	25	F	Farmer	08Ap02Cw
Mary	60	F	Farmer	08Ap02Cw
Margt.	30	F	Farmer	08Ap02Cw
BUCHANAN, Susan	20	F	Dressmaker	08Ap02Cw
GARNER, Mary	30	F	None	08Ap02Cw
Margt.	30	F	None	08Ap02Cw
Dennis	.00	M	Infant	08Ap02Cw
HUGHES, Mary	30	F	None	08Ap02Cw
LEWIS, Mary	23	F	Seamstress	08Ap02Cw
POWER, Richd.	23	M	Reporter	08Ap02Cw
HEALY, John	32	M	Blacksmith	08Ap02Cw
CRAMPTON, Anthony	38	M	Farmer	08Ap02Cw
Susanna	36	F	None	08Ap02Cw
John	10	M	None	08Ap02Cw
Joseph	8	M	Child	08Ap02Cw
Jane	6	F	Child	08Ap02Cw
Richd.	3	M	Child	08Ap02Cw
COOPER, Edwd.	60	M	Farmer	08Ap02Cw
Eliza	50	F	None	08Ap02Cw
Francis	24	M	None	08Ap02Cw
Thomas	22	M	None	08Ap02Cw
John	18	M	None	08Ap02Cw
Jane	20	F	None	08Ap02Cw
Margt.	17	F	None	08Ap02Cw
Willm.	9	M	Child	08Ap02Cw
Edwd.	7	M	Child	08Ap02Cw

NAMES OF PASSENGERS	AGE	SEX	OCCUPATIONS	DATE PORT SHIP
BYRNE, Lawrence	35	M	Laborer	08Ap02Cw
DOOLEY, John	34	M	Laborer	08Ap02Cw
BYRNE, Chas.	29	M	Laborer	08Ap02Cw
FINLAND, John	27	M	Laborer	08Ap02Cw
Eliza	23	F	None	08Ap02Cw
Anastasia	21	F	None	08Ap02Cw
Cath.	20	F	None	08Ap02Cw
BYRNE, Betty	19	F	None	08Ap02Cw
MULLIGAN, Margt.	20	F	None	08Ap02Cw
KITNICK, Betsy	20	F	None	08Ap02Cw
HOGAN, Maurice	24	M	Laborer	08Ap02Cw
Pat	22	M	Laborer	08Ap02Cw
Mary	20	M	Laborer	08Ap02Cw
Thos.	12	M	Laborer	08Ap02Cw
Christy	13	M	Laborer	08Ap02Cw
DALY, Michael	20	M	Laborer	08Ap02Cw
CARBIN, Edwd.	35	M	Butler	08Ap02Cw
James	30	M	Butler	08Ap02Cw
Sarah	40	F	None	08Ap02Cw
James	7	M	Child	08Ap02Cw
SHEA, Thomas	26	M	None	08Ap02Cw
Annie	26	F	Farmer	08Ap02Cw
Jane	22	F	Farmer	08Ap02Cw
DOOLAN, Martin	28	M	Farmer	08Ap02Cw
BRENNAN, Wm.	28	M	Farmer	08Ap02Cw
Cath.	21	F	None	08Ap02Cw
CROKE, Cath.	22	F	None	08Ap02Cw
ROURKE, John	28	M	Shopkeeper	08Ap02Cw
Pat	7	M	Child	08Ap02Cw
SHEA, Bridget	5	F	Child	08Ap02Cw
James	3	F	Child	08Ap02Cw
John	.00	M	Infant	08Ap02Cw
MCGREE, Nicholas	27	M	Gdnr	08Ap02Cw
CARNEY, John	24	M	Gdnr	08Ap02Cw
HANRAHAN, Pat	18	M	Gdnr	08Ap02Cw
GALL, Edmd.	23	M	Gdnr	08Ap02Cw
BURKE, Pat	46	M	Gdnr	08Ap02Cw
Lawrence	13	M	Gdnr	08Ap02Cw
HARRIS, John	26	M	Laborer	08Ap02Cw
BUTLER, Pat	25	M	Laborer	08Ap02Cw
COLLINS, Ellinor	30	F	None	08Ap02Cw
Cath.	7	F	Child	08Ap02Cw
SULLIVAN, Bridget	20	F	None	08Ap02Cw
MAGRATH, Phillip	19	M	Butcher	08Ap02Cw
NOWLAND, Thos.	21	M	Butler	08Ap02Cw
MCANDLES, John-A.	18	M	Weaver	08Ap02Cw
BUCHANAN, James	50	M	None	08Ap02Cw
Joseph	18	M	None	08Ap02Cw
Patrick	6	M	None	08Ap02Cw
Jane	11	F	None	08Ap02Cw
NOTLY, Belinda	17	F	Dressmaker	08Ap02Cw
Alisia	15	F	Dressmaker	08Ap02Cw
BLACKBURNE, Jas.	26	M	Carpenter	08Ap02Cw
TIVERDALE, Michl.	23	M	Laborer	08Ap02Cw
KENNADY, Jas.	20	M	Laborer	08Ap02Cw
JACK, George	21	M	Lnmftr	08Ap02Cw
Margt.	19	F	None	08Ap02Cw
NULTY, Michl.	50	M	Jobber	08Ap02Cw
Mary	45	F	None	08Ap02Cw
Rose	16	F	None	08Ap02Cw
Cath.	13	F	None	08Ap02Cw
Margt.	11	F	None	08Ap02Cw
SHEEHAN, Thos.	22	M	Laborer	08Ap02Cw
BERGIN, Jas.	22	M	Laborer	08Ap02Cw
CORKIN, James	22	M	Laborer	08Ap02Cw
FITZPATRICK, Pat	22	M	Laborer	08Ap02Cw
HURDFORD, Ann	22	F	None	08Ap02Cw
POWER, Ann	21	F	None	08Ap02Cw
MORAN, Mary	33	F	None	08Ap02Cw
Stephen	13	M	None	08Ap02Cw
Michael	13	M	None	08Ap02Cw
Nathan	12	M	None	08Ap02Cw
Kate	10	F	None	08Ap02Cw
Ann	8	F	Child	08Ap02Cw
Mary	6	F	Child	08Ap02Cw

NAMES OF PASSENGERS	AGE	SEX	OCCUPATIONS	DATE PORT SHIP
MORAN, Thos.	3	M	Child	08Ap02Cw
Eliza	.00	F	Infant	08Ap02Cw
BAYLEY, Mary	30	F	None	08Ap02Cw
MCNAMARA, Denis	19	M	Clerk	08Ap02Cw
COYNE, Wm.	19	M	Farmer	08Ap02Cw
Michl.	45	M	Baker	08Ap02Cw
BEHAN, John	20	M	Laborer	08Ap02Cw
Sarah	21	F	Dressmaker	08Ap02Cw
HEYLAND, Mary	21	F	Dressmaker	08Ap02Cw
Maria	6	F	Child	08Ap02Cw
MOONEY, Cath.	20	F	Dressmaker	08Ap02Cw
Bridget	45	F	Dressmaker	08Ap02Cw
Wm.	10	M	None	08Ap02Cw
MAHER, John	20	M	Laborer	08Ap02Cw
POWELL, Ann	21	F	Dressmaker	08Ap02Cw
KENNA, Pat	20	M	Laborer	08Ap02Cw
ALLEN, Thos.	26	M	Laborer	08Ap02Cw
Ann	24	F	None	08Ap02Cw
CONNELLY, John	24	M	Laborer	08Ap02Cw
COFFEY, John	45	M	Farmer	08Ap02Cw
John	20	M	None	08Ap02Cw
James	22	M	None	08Ap02Cw
DINSMORE, Henry	30	M	Plasterer	08Ap02Cw
NOLAN, Mary	20	F	Dressmaker	08Ap02Cw
Ann	20	F	Dressmaker	08Ap02Cw
MARTIN, Thos.	21	M	Carpenter	08Ap02Cw
Thos.	21	M	Carpenter	08Ap02Cw
BURKE, Martin	21	M	Carpenter	08Ap02Cw
WARD, James	15	M	None	08Ap02Cw
GAREGIN, Mathew	40	M	Laborer	08Ap02Cw
HARDMAN, Ann	19	F	None	08Ap02Cw
GARGIN, Mary	6	F	Child	08Ap02Cw
TRACEY, Cath.	21	F	None	08Ap02Cw
GARGIN, Denis	8	M	Child	08Ap02Cw
MURRAY, Michl.	23	M	Laborer	08Ap02Cw
LEWIS, Winifred	28	F	None	08Ap02Cw
Matilda	.00	F	Infant	08Ap02Cw
CONNORS, Lawrence	20	M	Laborer	08Ap02Cw
WALSH, Mary	20	F	None	08Ap02Cw
SHERIDAN, Mary	10	F	None	08Ap02Cw
BYRNE, Dominick	33	M	Laborer	08Ap02Cw
MCDERMOTT, Winifred	19	F	Dressmaker	08Ap02Cw
BEATY, Richd.	20	M	Laborer	08Ap02Cw
KELLY, Michl.	40	M	Laborer	08Ap02Cw
TURNER, James	32	M	Shoemaker	08Ap02Cw
NOWLAN, John	24	M	Unknown	08Ap02Cw
COCHRANE, Thos.	27	M	Unknown	08Ap02Cw
FARRELL, Pat	25	M	Unknown	08Ap02Cw
DOYLE, Pat	22	M	Unknown	08Ap02Cw
KIERNAN, Michl.	36	M	Unknown	08Ap02Cw
REAGAN, Mary	25	F	Unknown	08Ap02Cw
CAVANAH, Pat	23	M	Unknown	08Ap02Cw
WALSH, James	26	M	Unknown	08Ap02Cw
HOOLAGHAN, Denis	26	M	Unknown	08Ap02Cw
NEARY, Pat	26	M	Unknown	08Ap02Cw
CONWAY, Ellen	24	F	Unknown	08Ap02Cw
DRUMGOOL, John	14	M	None	08Ap02Cw
KANE, Michl.	40	M	Laborer	08Ap02Cw
MADDEN, Eliza	16	F	None	08Ap02Cw
KANE, Maria	14	F	None	08Ap02Cw
Ellen	12	F	None	08Ap02Cw
COCHLAN, Honora	24	F	Servant	08Ap02Cw
TARPHEY, Bridget	10	F	None	08Ap02Cw
John	9	M	Child	08Ap02Cw
LANGAN, Thos.	21	M	None	08Ap02Cw
James	18	M	None	08Ap02Cw
HOLLORAN, Denis	20	M	Tailor	08Ap02Cw
Thos.	24	M	Tailor	08Ap02Cw
ROURKE, James	21	M	Laborer	08Ap02Cw
NORMAN, Danl.	20	M	Laborer	08Ap02Cw
BRIAN, Mick	12	M	Laborer	08Ap02Cw
GARRAGAN, John	50	M	Laborer	08Ap02Cw
Timothy	25	M	Laborer	08Ap02Cw
Mary	24	F	Servant	08Ap02Cw
Margt.	20	F	Servant	08Ap02Cw
GARRAGAN, Marcella	18	F	Servant	08Ap02Cw
Pat	14	M	Laborer	08Ap02Cw
Wm.	12	M	Laborer	08Ap02Cw
DALEY, Thos.	25	M	Laborer	08Ap02Cw
FITZGERALD, Jas.	30	M	Laborer	08Ap02Cw
DENRIN, Ann	26	F	None	08Ap02Cw
RILEY, John	21	M	Laborer	08Ap02Cw
Daphne	23	F	None	08Ap02Cw
SMITH, Mary	21	F	None	08Ap02Cw
FALOONA, James	25	M	Laborer	08Ap02Cw
HORTY, Michael	18	M	Laborer	08Ap02Cw
Pat.	17	M	Laborer	08Ap02Cw
MCKIVERIN, Ann	25	F	None	08Ap02Cw
BRENNAN, James	40	M	Laborer	08Ap02Cw
Johanna	35	F	None	08Ap02Cw
Mary	8	F	Child	08Ap02Cw
EAGAN, Mary	25	F	Dressmaker	08Ap02Cw
KELLY, Mary	18	F	None	08Ap02Cw
Lawrence	17	M	None	08Ap02Cw
Stephen	9	M	Child	08Ap02Cw
Bridget	6	F	Child	08Ap02Cw
HART, John	26	M	Engineer	08Ap02Cw
WILSON, Saml.	25	M	Carpenter	08Ap02Cw
SPOTT, Mary	12	F	None	08Ap02Cw
HANLON, Margt.	22	F	None	08Ap02Cw
HOPE, Michl.	35	M	Tanner	08Ap02Cw
DYAS, Robt.	50	M	Farmer	08Ap02Cw
U (W)	40	F	None	08Ap02Cw
Mary-Eliza	24	F	None	08Ap02Cw
Essy	19	F	None	08Ap02Cw
Robertina	15	F	None	08Ap02Cw
WARING, Robt.	17	M	None	08Ap02Cw
FITZGERALD, Michl.	30	M	Laborer	08Ap02Cw
Michl.	26	M	None	08Ap02Cw
MCCABE, Elizth.	30	F	None	08Ap02Cw
Ann	10	F	None	08Ap02Cw
KINSELLA, Thos.	30	M	Laborer	08Ap02Cw
Bridget	20	F	None	08Ap02Cw
HALL, Henry	25	M	None	08Ap02Cw
Ally	20	F	None	08Ap02Cw
COLLINS, Timothy	22	M	Laborer	08Ap02Cw
DEVITT, Wm.	26	M	Laborer	08Ap02Cw
HALL, John	24	M	Laborer	08Ap02Cw
MORAN, Kerran	30	M	Laborer	08Ap02Cw
Bridget	24	F	None	08Ap02Cw
FARRELL, John	35	M	Groom	08Ap02Cw
BEEHAN, Mary	19	F	None	08Ap02Cw
CONNOR, Kitty	25	F	None	08Ap02Cw
MORAN, Pat	19	M	Butler	08Ap02Cw
LARKIN, Martin	25	M	Laborer	08Ap02Cw
Cath.	20	F	None	08Ap02Cw
Mary	3	F	Child	08Ap02Cw
Ellen	.00	F	Infant	08Ap02Cw
FARRELL, Mary	16	F	None	08Ap02Cw
CARPENTER, John	26	M	Laborer	08Ap02Cw
NOONAN, Ann	23	F	Servant	08Ap02Cw
MCQUILLAN, Lawrence	25	M	Cooper	08Ap02Cw
Denis	20	M	Laborer	08Ap02Cw
KENNIDY, James	20	M	Laborer	08Ap02Cw

WATERLOO 08 APRIL 1850

From Liverpool

NAMES OF PASSENGERS	AGE	SEX	OCCUPATIONS	DATE PORT SHIP
RIDGEWAY, Saml.	30	M	Gentleman	08Ap02Cs
COCKRANE, Jerry	23	M	Laborer	08Ap02Cs
FRAWLEY, Catharine	20	F	Laborer	08Ap02Cs
WALSH, Michl.	24	M	Laborer	08Ap02Cs
LARRAHAM, Dennis	26	M	Laborer	08Ap02Cs

NAMES OF PASSENGERS	AGE	SEX	OCCUPATIONS	DATE PORT SHIP
JOHNSTON, Bridget	24	F	Laborer	08Ap02Cs
BROWN, William	30	M	Laborer	08Ap02Cs
WILLIAMSON, Thomas	45	M	Laborer	08Ap02Cs
Margt.Jane	22	F	Laborer	08Ap02Cs
THOMPSON, Wm.	60	M	Laborer	08Ap02Cs
Sarah	60	F	Laborer	08Ap02Cs
George	22	M	Laborer	08Ap02Cs
Elizth.	18	F	Laborer	08Ap02Cs
Anthony	30	M	Laborer	08Ap02Cs
Matilda	26	F	Laborer	08Ap02Cs
Sarah	24	F	Laborer	08Ap02Cs
DONAGHY, Ellen	25	F	Laborer	08Ap02Cs
CARUTHERS, John	20	M	Laborer	08Ap02Cs
SLOAN, Bernard	22	M	Laborer	08Ap02Cs
CAHILL, Mary	26	F	Laborer	08Ap02Cs
HOGAN, Sarah	18	F	Laborer	08Ap02Cs
BURKE, Edmond	24	M	Laborer	08Ap02Cs
MANGIN, John	32	M	Laborer	08Ap02Cs
MCKEE, Mary-Ann	19	F	Laborer	08Ap02Cs
HOLMES, Sarah	21	F	Laborer	08Ap02Cs
LAHEY, Margt.	22	F	Laborer	08Ap02Cs
FOLEY, John	32	M	Laborer	08Ap02Cs
MOORE, Mary	11	F	Laborer	08Ap02Cs
John	10	M	Laborer	08Ap02Cs
REARDON, John	27	M	Laborer	08Ap02Cs
MCADLE, Michl.	24	M	Laborer	08Ap02Cs
DEMPSY, Timothy	40	M	Laborer	08Ap02Cs
HART, Margt.	19	F	Laborer	08Ap02Cs
OMEARA, Timothy	13	M	Laborer	08Ap02Cs
GANNON, Michl.	30	M	Laborer	08Ap02Cs
Ellen	25	F	Laborer	08Ap02Cs
HERON, Thomas	16	M	Laborer	08Ap02Cs
Mary	2	F	Child	08Ap02Cs
Elisha	.00	M	Infant	08Ap02Cs
MACKAY, Bridget	14	F	Laborer	08Ap02Cs
DARCY, Mary	10	F	Laborer	08Ap02Cs
KELLY, Ann	13	F	Laborer	08Ap02Cs
KENNY, Jane	50	F	Laborer	08Ap02Cs
Rose	19	F	Laborer	08Ap02Cs
Peter	17	M	Laborer	08Ap02Cs
Christopher	11	M	Laborer	08Ap02Cs
Jane	9	F	Child	08Ap02Cs
HUMPHRY, John	20	M	Laborer	08Ap02Cs
KANE, Bernard	18	M	Laborer	08Ap02Cs
BELL, James	28	M	Laborer	08Ap02Cs
Hugh	34	M	Laborer	08Ap02Cs
MCNEALLY, Saml.	19	M	Laborer	08Ap02Cs
MCDONALD, Margt.	20	F	Laborer	08Ap02Cs
KENT, Stephen	16	M	Laborer	08Ap02Cs
Eliza	24	F	Laborer	08Ap02Cs
BOYLE, John	19	M	Laborer	08Ap02Cs
KELLY, Pat	20	M	Laborer	08Ap02Cs
BURNE, John	19	M	Laborer	08Ap02Cs
ANTHONY, John	20	M	Laborer	08Ap02Cs
Mary	22	F	Laborer	08Ap02Cs
LOGAN, James	23	M	Laborer	08Ap02Cs
HANLEY, Timothy	45	M	Laborer	08Ap02Cs
Ann	11	F	Unknown	08Ap02Cs
KANE, Robert	28	M	Laborer	08Ap02Cs
Margt.	28	F	Unknown	08Ap02Cs
Marsella	9	F	Child	08Ap02Cs
James	7	M	Child	08Ap02Cs
Wm.Henry	5	M	Child	08Ap02Cs
ROGAN, John	22	M	Laborer	08Ap02Cs
CONNER, Lawrence	40	M	Laborer	08Ap02Cs
BRIDGEWOOD, Robt.	16	M	Laborer	08Ap02Cs
Margt.	40	F	Unknown	08Ap02Cs
Catherine	16	F	Unknown	08Ap02Cs
William	12	M	Unknown	08Ap02Cs
SMITH, Catherine	20	F	Laborer	08Ap02Cs
Margt.	25	F	Laborer	08Ap02Cs
Hugh	6	M	Child	08Ap02Cs
COLVIN, Ann	18	F	Laborer	08Ap02Cs
GEHERTY, Catherine	16	F	Laborer	08Ap02Cs
SCANLON, Bridget	26	F	Laborer	08Ap02Cs

NAMES OF PASSENGERS	AGE	SEX	OCCUPATIONS	DATE PORT SHIP
FINLAN, Wm.	28	M	Laborer	08Ap02Cs
BERTS, Joseph	24	M	Laborer	08Ap02Cs
SMITH, Luke	30	M	Laborer	08Ap02Cs
Mary	24	F	Unknown	08Ap02Cs
Ann	.00	F	Infant	08Ap02Cs
DONOHOE, Rose	20	F	Laborer	08Ap02Cs
REILLY, Ann	18	F	Laborer	08Ap02Cs
Catherine	12	F	Unknown	08Ap02Cs
MULDOON, Fanny	50	F	Unknown	08Ap02Cs
William	20	M	Laborer	08Ap02Cs
Ann-Daly	15	F	Laborer	08Ap02Cs
BURKE, Margt.	20	F	Laborer	08Ap02Cs
DOYLE, Margt.	19	F	Laborer	08Ap02Cs
GREEN, Margt.	16	F	Laborer	08Ap02Cs
Ann	19	F	Laborer	08Ap02Cs
SHANAGHAN, Pat	21	M	Laborer	08Ap02Cs
MCKEY, Wm.	24	M	Laborer	08Ap02Cs
BURKE, Catherine	18	F	Laborer	08Ap02Cs
CONNELLY, Andrew	28	M	Laborer	08Ap02Cs
MONRICK, Thomas	18	M	Laborer	08Ap02Cs
SHANAGHAN, Thomas	27	M	Laborer	08Ap02Cs
RYAN, John	27	M	Laborer	08Ap02Cs
Judy	21	F	Laborer	08Ap02Cs
BARRY, Mary	20	F	Laborer	08Ap02Cs
GAVIN, Catherine	20	F	Laborer	08Ap02Cs
FLANAGAN, Michl.	23	M	Laborer	08Ap02Cs
FOGARTY, Nancy	21	F	Laborer	08Ap02Cs
DONNELLY, James	22	F	Laborer	08Ap02Cs
STOKES, Mary	20	F	Laborer	08Ap02Cs
DONNELLY, Mary	20	F	Laborer	08Ap02Cs
LEAHY, Pat	27	M	Laborer	08Ap02Cs
STOKES, James	28	M	Laborer	08Ap02Cs
BURKE, Mary-Martin	35	F	Unknown	08Ap02Cs
Bridget-Martin	9	F	Child	08Ap02Cs
Winifred-Martin	7	M	Child	08Ap02Cs
James-Martin	5	M	Child	08Ap02Cs
DONNELLY, John	19	M	Laborer	08Ap02Cs
MAHER, John	19	M	Laborer	08Ap02Cs
BRYAN, Patrick	27	M	Laborer	08Ap02Cs
GILLIGAN, Johana	23	F	Laborer	08Ap02Cs
MCCLAUGHEY, Alexn.	24	M	Laborer	08Ap02Cs
HART, James	17	M	Laborer	08Ap02Cs
KEENAN, John	16	M	Laborer	08Ap02Cs
REILLY, Ann	30	F	Laborer	08Ap02Cs
Bridget	10	F	Unknown	08Ap02Cs
Catherine	7	F	Child	08Ap02Cs
Patrick	6	M	Child	08Ap02Cs
KERNAN, Bernard	30	M	Laborer	08Ap02Cs
Ann	13	F	Unknown	08Ap02Cs
John	20	M	Laborer	08Ap02Cs
REILLY, Mary	30	F	Laborer	08Ap02Cs
Catherine	3	F	Child	08Ap02Cs
CODY, John	26	M	Laborer	08Ap02Cs
Margt.	26	F	Unknown	08Ap02Cs
Richard	.00	M	Infant	08Ap02Cs
JONES, Jane	35	F	Laborer	08Ap02Cs
PAGE, James	13	M	Unknown	08Ap02Cs
Eliza	12	F	Unknown	08Ap02Cs
MONONGE, John	30	M	Laborer	08Ap02Cs
Ellen	30	F	Unknown	08Ap02Cs
Philip	5	M	Child	08Ap02Cs
MURRAY, John	35	M	Laborer	08Ap02Cs
MORRIS, Bridget	35	F	Laborer	08Ap02Cs
Catherine	20	F	Laborer	08Ap02Cs
COSGROVE, Pat	20	M	Laborer	08Ap02Cs
RYAN, Mortimer	19	M	Laborer	08Ap02Cs
CAHAN, James	30	M	Laborer	08Ap02Cs
LAWSON, Robt.	21	M	Laborer	08Ap02Cs
SHAW, John	14	M	Laborer	08Ap02Cs
WARWICK, Hugh	20	M	Laborer	08Ap02Cs
MASON, Wm.	24	M	Laborer	08Ap02Cs
SIMMONS, Catherine	24	F	Laborer	08Ap02Cs
MAGRATH, Denis	25	M	Laborer	08Ap02Cs
Honora	20	F	Unknown	08Ap02Cs
OBRIEN, Honora	30	F	Laborer	08Ap02Cs

NAMES OF PASSENGERS	AGE	SEX	OCCUPATIONS	DATE PORT SHIP
DOGHERTY, Wm.	22	M	Laborer	08Ap02Cs
CONNERS, Patrick	24	M	Laborer	08Ap02Cs
Deborah	20	F	Laborer	08Ap02Cs
BARRETT, Susan	20	F	Laborer	08Ap02Cs
LINEHAN, Mary	21	F	Laborer	08Ap02Cs
FLANAGAN, Mary	32	F	Laborer	08Ap02Cs
Henry	7	M	Child	08Ap02Cs
Laurence	2	M	Child	08Ap02Cs
ROCKFORD, Pat	19	M	Laborer	08Ap02Cs
James	18	M	Laborer	08Ap02Cs
John	10	M	Unknown	08Ap02Cs
DOWLING, Stephen	19	M	Laborer	08Ap02Cs
FAGAN, Edward	20	M	Laborer	08Ap02Cs
WYLIE, Agnes	25	F	Laborer	08Ap02Cs
James	8	M	Child	08Ap02Cs
John	6	M	Child	08Ap02Cs
INGRAM, Hugh	23	M	Laborer	08Ap02Cs
BRISLANCE, John	22	M	Laborer	08Ap02Cs
ODONNELL, Con.	22	M	Laborer	08Ap02Cs
WARD, Jane	21	F	Laborer	08Ap02Cs
QUIN, Michl.	20	M	Laborer	08Ap02Cs
Mary	18	F	Laborer	08Ap02Cs
KELLY, Susan	50	F	Laborer	08Ap02Cs
HICKEY, Catherine	9	F	Child	08Ap02Cs
PAISLEY, James	22	M	Laborer	08Ap02Cs
HART, Peter	20	M	Laborer	08Ap02Cs
BOHAN, Paul	21	M	Laborer	08Ap02Cs
HART, Patrick	20	M	Laborer	08Ap02Cs
CONLAN, Mary	16	F	Laborer	08Ap02Cs
DEVANE, Bridget	37	F	Laborer	08Ap02Cs
RILEY, Nicholas	25	M	Laborer	08Ap02Cs
CLARKE, Mary	8	F	Child	08Ap02Cs
CAVANAH, John	25	M	Laborer	08Ap02Cs
FORBES, Peter	32	M	Florist	08Ap02Cs
Mary	25	F	Unknown	08Ap02Cs
KENNELLY, William	19	M	Laborer	08Ap02Cs
MALONEY, Darby	21	M	Laborer	08Ap02Cs
CONNELL, Hannah	23	F	Laborer	08Ap02Cs
OMISKIL, John	26	M	Laborer	08Ap02Cs
FLING, John	26	M	Laborer	08Ap02Cs
Richard	50	M	Laborer	08Ap02Cs
MCNABO, Michl.	22	M	Laborer	08Ap02Cs
CAULDFIELD, Cathne.	32	F	Laborer	08Ap02Cs
Honora	3	F	Child	08Ap02Cs
MCKEON, Bridget	16	F	Laborer	08Ap02Cs
MURPHY, James	22	M	Laborer	08Ap02Cs
PHILLIPS, Margt.	18	F	Laborer	08Ap02Cs
Bridget	19	F	Laborer	08Ap02Cs
Ann	25	F	Laborer	08Ap02Cs
James	22	M	Laborer	08Ap02Cs
HENRY, Pat	25	M	Laborer	08Ap02Cs
Honora	23	F	Laborer	08Ap02Cs
MCKENNE, Danl.	30	M	Laborer	08Ap02Cs
LENNARD, Susan	17	F	Laborer	08Ap02Cs
FITZPATRICK, Hugh	25	M	Laborer	08Ap02Cs
James	20	M	Laborer	08Ap02Cs
MCGARVY, John	25	M	Laborer	08Ap02Cs
Mary	30	F	Laborer	08Ap02Cs
Peter	4	M	Child	08Ap02Cs
Thomas	.00	M	Infant	08Ap02Cs
MCGOWN, Honora	25	F	Laborer	08Ap02Cs
RILEY, Mary	20	F	Laborer	08Ap02Cs
STRAFFORD, James	45	M	Laborer	08Ap02Cs
Jane	40	F	Unknown	08Ap02Cs
Alexander	1	M	Child	08Ap02Cs
Henry	13	M	Unknown	08Ap02Cs
John	9	M	Child	08Ap02Cs
James	5	M	Child	08Ap02Cs
KELLETT, Edward	35	M	Laborer	08Ap02Cs
STRAFFORD, Benjn.	30	M	Unknown	08Ap02Cs
Ann	22	F	Laborer	08Ap02Cs
EASTON, George	23	M	Laborer	08Ap02Cs
URELE, Lawrence	24	M	Laborer	08Ap02Cs
ROWE, Eliza	28	F	Laborer	08Ap02Cs
LEDWIDGE, Bridget	20	F	Laborer	08Ap02Cs
VAUGHN, Luke	60	M	Laborer	08Ap02Cs
William	28	M	Laborer	08Ap02Cs
Mary	25	F	Laborer	08Ap02Cs
CAFREY, Bridget	14	F	Laborer	08Ap02Cs
GORREY, John	50	M	Laborer	08Ap02Cs
Thomas	19	M	Laborer	08Ap02Cs
Jane	13	F	Laborer	08Ap02Cs
MALEW, Mary	18	F	Laborer	08Ap02Cs
BIVINE, John	25	M	Laborer	08Ap02Cs
CLEAREY, John	27	M	Laborer	08Ap02Cs
CAIN, David	29	M	Laborer	08Ap02Cs
MAHER, Mary	20	F	Laborer	08Ap02Cs
MURPHY, Mary	18	F	Laborer	08Ap02Cs
PEMBROKE, Mary	30	F	Laborer	08Ap02Cs
Henry	.00	M	Infant	08Ap02Cs
HORN, Jane	20	F	Laborer	08Ap02Cs
MURLEY, Danl.	40	M	Laborer	08Ap02Cs
Biddy	40	F	Unknown	08Ap02Cs
James	6	M	Child	08Ap02Cs
Ellen	4	F	Child	08Ap02Cs
CAGO, Mary	30	F	Laborer	08Ap02Cs
Mick	6	M	Child	08Ap02Cs
Kate	.00	F	Infant	08Ap02Cs
DEHAN, Catherine	21	F	Laborer	08Ap02Cs
LAMBE, Owen	16	M	Laborer	08Ap02Cs
KNOX, Patt	31	M	Laborer	08Ap02Cs
CAVANAGH, James	34	M	Laborer	08Ap02Cs
Catherine	32	F	Unknown	08Ap02Cs
Bernard	9	M	Child	08Ap02Cs
John	7	M	Child	08Ap02Cs
Mary	4	F	Child	08Ap02Cs
Anthony	2	M	Child	08Ap02Cs
Bridget	.00	F	Infant	08Ap02Cs
MORRISS, James	30	M	Laborer	08Ap02Cs
Catherine	.00	F	Infant	08Ap02Cs
Edward	26	M	Laborer	08Ap02Cs
KAVANAGH, Arthur	36	M	Laborer	08Ap02Cs
Matthew	21	M	Laborer	08Ap02Cs
HENRICK, Margt.	16	F	Laborer	08Ap02Cs
MAHER, Stephen	40	M	Laborer	08Ap02Cs
Mary	40	F	Unknown	08Ap02Cs
Patrick	12	M	Unknown	08Ap02Cs
MCVOY, Michl.	30	M	Laborer	08Ap02Cs
Ann	30	F	Unknown	08Ap02Cs
Thomas	7	M	Child	08Ap02Cs
Mary	.00	F	Infant	08Ap02Cs
Edward	30	M	Laborer	08Ap02Cs
Judy	29	F	Unknown	08Ap02Cs
Anne	.00	F	Infant	08Ap02Cs
OBERNARA, Thomas	30	M	Laborer	08Ap02Cs
Johana	25	F	Unknown	08Ap02Cs
Patrick	.00	M	Infant	08Ap02Cs
LEE, Catherine	23	F	Laborer	08Ap02Cs
KENNEDY, Thomas	23	M	Laborer	08Ap02Cs
OBARRY, Margt.	24	F	Laborer	08Ap02Cs
KELLIAGHER, Ellen	22	F	Laborer	08Ap02Cs
RYAN, Margt.	22	F	Laborer	08Ap02Cs
REILLY, Patt	23	M	Laborer	08Ap02Cs
MCMANUS, Thomas	22	M	Laborer	08Ap02Cs
SMITH, Margt.	20	F	Laborer	08Ap02Cs
MCMANY, Mary	25	F	Laborer	08Ap02Cs
LINCH, Bess	25	F	Laborer	08Ap02Cs
MCCARTNEY, Thomas	50	M	Laborer	08Ap02Cs
Bridget	50	F	Unknown	08Ap02Cs
Mary	24	F	Laborer	08Ap02Cs
Anne	20	F	Laborer	08Ap02Cs
Henry	13	M	Laborer	08Ap02Cs
KINDERLAND, James	38	F	Laborer	08Ap02Cs
MAGUIRE, Patt	28	M	Laborer	08Ap02Cs
KERBY, Catherine	24	F	Laborer	08Ap02Cs
CULLEN, Rose	16	F	Laborer	08Ap02Cs
OREILLY, John	20	M	Laborer	08Ap02Cs
GRAY, Davis	25	M	Laborer	08Ap02Cs
REILLY, Mary	21	F	Laborer	08Ap02Cs
BRYAN, Christopher	34	M	Laborer	08Ap02Cs

NAMES OF PASSENGERS	AGE	SEX	OCCUPATIONS	DATE PORT SHIP
SCANLIN, Hugh	20	M	Laborer	08Ap02Cs
Catherine	18	F	Laborer	08Ap02Cs
CROHAN, John	20	M	Laborer	08Ap02Cs
GOLDING, Julia	16	F	Laborer	08Ap02Cs
John	11	M	Laborer	08Ap02Cs
RAY, Ellen	23	F	Laborer	08Ap02Cs
HIGGINS, Edward	24	M	Laborer	08Ap02Cs

NISIDI-STEWART 08 APRIL 1850

From Cork

NAMES OF PASSENGERS	AGE	SEX	OCCUPATIONS	DATE PORT SHIP
MURPHY, Norry	20	M	Laborer	08Ap18Gf
Catherine	5	F	Child	08Ap18Gf
BOUGH, Betty	20	F	Unknown	08Ap18Gf
BRIEN, Johanna	20	F	Unknown	08Ap18Gf
DONOVAN, Mary	24	F	Unknown	08Ap18Gf
COOK, Johanna	24	F	Unknown	08Ap18Gf
CUSHMAN, Ellen	30	F	Unknown	08Ap18Gf
EGAN, Ellen	30	F	Unknown	08Ap18Gf
John	6	M	Child	08Ap18Gf
CARROLL, Catherine	20	F	Unknown	08Ap18Gf
AHERN, Catherine	20	F	Unknown	08Ap18Gf
SHEA, Tom.	24	M	Unknown	08Ap18Gf
Ellen	6	F	Child	08Ap18Gf
BRIEN, Abby	24	F	Unknown	08Ap18Gf
DORGAN, James	20	M	Unknown	08Ap18Gf
CUSHMAN, David	30	M	Unknown	08Ap18Gf
Mary	24	F	Unknown	08Ap18Gf
KELLY, Edward	30	M	Unknown	08Ap18Gf
Mary	26	F	Unknown	08Ap18Gf
Margaret	4	F	Child	08Ap18Gf
Ellen	.06	F	Infant	08Ap18Gf
BRIEN, James	20	M	Unknown	08Ap18Gf
Michael	14	M	Unknown	08Ap18Gf
Ellen	6	F	Child	08Ap18Gf
Norry	8	F	Child	08Ap18Gf
BOLES, Margt.	20	F	Unknown	08Ap18Gf
Anastatia	18	F	Unknown	08Ap18Gf
Norry	16	F	Unknown	08Ap18Gf
Betty	13	F	Unknown	08Ap18Gf
Johanna	10	F	Unknown	08Ap18Gf
George	6	M	Child	08Ap18Gf
Richd.	6	M	Child	08Ap18Gf
WIGMORE, Mary	20	F	Unknown	08Ap18Gf
SHEEHAN, Tom	24	M	Unknown	08Ap18Gf
Bridget	20	F	Unknown	08Ap18Gf
HURLEY, Abby	20	M	Unknown	08Ap18Gf
DESMOND, Norry	20	F	Unknown	08Ap18Gf
Dennis	20	M	Unknown	08Ap18Gf
John	24	M	Unknown	08Ap18Gf
MURPHY, John	20	M	Unknown	08Ap18Gf
HURLY, Conr.	20	M	Unknown	08Ap18Gf
REARDON, Danl.	20	M	Unknown	08Ap18Gf
NAGLE, Julia	26	F	Unknown	08Ap18Gf
Ellen	.03	F	Infant	08Ap18Gf
CADOGAN, Jenny	40	F	Unknown	08Ap18Gf
MURPHY, James	18	M	Unknown	08Ap18Gf
DONOHUE, Mary	30	F	Unknown	08Ap18Gf
John	10	M	Unknown	08Ap18Gf
HANKARD, John	20	M	Unknown	08Ap18Gf
POWER, Patt	25	M	Unknown	08Ap18Gf
CALLAGHAN, Timothy	20	M	Unknown	08Ap18Gf
Anne	18	F	Unknown	08Ap18Gf
Mary	25	F	Unknown	08Ap18Gf
Ellen	18	F	Unknown	08Ap18Gf
Peggy	23	F	Unknown	08Ap18Gf
DESMOND, Ellen	20	F	Unknown	08Ap18Gf
SULLIVAN, Anty	50	M	Unknown	08Ap18Gf
SULLIVAN, Thomas	28	M	Unknown	08Ap18Gf
Mary	16	F	Unknown	08Ap18Gf
Patrick	8	M	Child	08Ap18Gf
Michael	6	M	Child	08Ap18Gf
HENNESSEY, Michael	20	M	Unknown	08Ap18Gf
CARY, Catherine	10	F	Unknown	08Ap18Gf
Mary	14	F	Unknown	08Ap18Gf
Bridget	7	F	Child	08Ap18Gf
WALSH, Kate	25	F	Unknown	08Ap18Gf
Ellen	20	F	Unknown	08Ap18Gf
SULLIVAN, Norry	24	F	Unknown	08Ap18Gf
COURMANE, Mary	20	F	Unknown	08Ap18Gf
CONNOR, Mary	20	F	Unknown	08Ap18Gf
HOARE, Ellen	20	F	Unknown	08Ap18Gf
FRANCIS, Catherine	20	F	Unknown	08Ap18Gf
CLAVANE, Norry	40	F	Unknown	08Ap18Gf
Norry	13	F	Unknown	08Ap18Gf
Kate	8	F	Child	08Ap18Gf
FINEGHTY, Ellen	40	F	Unknown	08Ap18Gf
KENNEDY, Ellen	16	F	Unknown	08Ap18Gf
MANNING, Mary	40	F	Unknown	08Ap18Gf
Pat	9	M	Child	08Ap18Gf
Kate	6	F	Child	08Ap18Gf
Betty	35	F	Unknown	08Ap18Gf
Michael	7	M	Child	08Ap18Gf
HANNEFER, Kate	30	F	Unknown	08Ap18Gf
KAVANAGH, Bridget	28	F	Unknown	08Ap18Gf
DUANE, Bridget	20	F	Unknown	08Ap18Gf
BAYLEY, Michael	20	M	Unknown	08Ap18Gf
HANNAFAR, Norry	16	F	Unknown	08Ap18Gf
Michael	3	M	Child	08Ap18Gf
SULLIVAN, John	40	M	Unknown	08Ap18Gf
Timothy	16	M	Unknown	08Ap18Gf
Mary	50	F	Unknown	08Ap18Gf
Bridget	20	F	Unknown	08Ap18Gf
Kate	12	F	Unknown	08Ap18Gf
DUFFIN, Pat	20	M	Unknown	08Ap18Gf
CONNOR, John	35	M	Unknown	08Ap18Gf
KENNEDY, Betty	30	F	Unknown	08Ap18Gf
CONNOR, John	20	M	Unknown	08Ap18Gf
Bridget	18	F	Unknown	08Ap18Gf
MCFELIN, John	21	M	Unknown	08Ap18Gf
CASEY, John	26	M	Unknown	08Ap18Gf
CONNELL, Catherine	26	F	Unknown	08Ap18Gf
MANNING, Margaret	40	F	Unknown	08Ap18Gf
John	12	M	Unknown	08Ap18Gf
Catherine	4	F	Child	08Ap18Gf
PRENDERGAST, Ellen	20	F	Unknown	08Ap18Gf
Mary	16	F	Unknown	08Ap18Gf
HANNIFAN, Mary	25	F	Unknown	08Ap18Gf
BRIDE, Nelly	20	F	Unknown	08Ap18Gf
MCCARTHY, John	28	M	Stctr	08Ap18Gf
DONOVAN, Mary	20	F	Laborer	08Ap18Gf
WIGMORE, Ellen	30	F	Laborer	08Ap18Gf
Kate	3	F	Child	08Ap18Gf
James	.09	M	Infant	08Ap18Gf
CURTIS, Michael	20	M	Laborer	08Ap18Gf
BOYLE, Margaret	20	F	Laborer	08Ap18Gf
Eliza	20	F	Laborer	08Ap18Gf
CURTIS, Betty	20	F	Laborer	08Ap18Gf
AHEARNE, Pat	20	M	Laborer	08Ap18Gf
FORD, Margt.	20	F	Laborer	08Ap18Gf
DEADY, John	18	M	Laborer	08Ap18Gf
AHEARN, Dennis	40	M	Laborer	08Ap18Gf
DUANE, Ellen	20	F	Laborer	08Ap18Gf
COLLINS, Dennis	20	M	Laborer	08Ap18Gf
Johanna	20	F	Laborer	08Ap18Gf
COOKE, Robt.	55	M	Laborer	08Ap18Gf
Margt.	30	F	Laborer	08Ap18Gf
Robt.	18	M	Laborer	08Ap18Gf
Catherine	16	F	Laborer	08Ap18Gf
John	10	M	Laborer	08Ap18Gf
Richd.	.10	M	Infant	08Ap18Gf
SULLIVAN, Patk.	40	M	Laborer	08Ap18Gf
Mary	13	F	Laborer	08Ap18Gf

NAMES OF PASSENGERS	AGE	SEX	OCCUPATIONS	DATE PORT SHIP
SULLIVAN, John	12	M	Laborer	08Ap18Gf
Pat	8	M	Child	08Ap18Gf
Mary	20	F	Laborer	08Ap18Gf
Murdock	26	M	Laborer	08Ap18Gf
John	20	M	Laborer	08Ap18Gf
Betty	25	F	Laborer	08Ap18Gf
CALLAGHAN, John	20	M	Laborer	08Ap18Gf
CAVANAGH, Johanna	26	F	Laborer	08Ap18Gf
MANNON, Daniel	26	M	Laborer	08Ap18Gf
Michael	20	M	Laborer	08Ap18Gf
COLEMAN, Patt	17	M	Laborer	08Ap18Gf
Anne	13	F	Laborer	08Ap18Gf
TWOREMEY, Ellen	30	F	Laborer	08Ap18Gf
Thomas	5	M	Child	08Ap18Gf
Willm.	4	M	Child	08Ap18Gf
Danl.	.01	M	Infant	08Ap18Gf
RONAN, Maurice	20	M	Laborer	08Ap18Gf
PIGOTTI, Mary	20	F	Laborer	08Ap18Gf
LEARY, Catherine	20	F	Laborer	08Ap18Gf
FORD, Ellen	20	F	Laborer	08Ap18Gf
WILLIAMS, Patt	24	M	Laborer	08Ap18Gf
Mary	20	F	Laborer	08Ap18Gf
MURPHY, Richard	26	M	Laborer	08Ap18Gf
Johanna	26	F	Laborer	08Ap18Gf
Mary	.11	F	Infant	08Ap18Gf
KESKIN, Catherine	20	F	Laborer	08Ap18Gf
BARRY, Ellen	20	F	Laborer	08Ap18Gf
FITZPATRICK, James	20	M	Laborer	08Ap18Gf
LINEHAN, Corns.	30	M	Laborer	08Ap18Gf
Peggy	26	F	Laborer	08Ap18Gf
Tom	2	M	Child	08Ap18Gf
Mary	.09	F	Infant	08Ap18Gf
DOYLE, John	18	M	Laborer	08Ap18Gf
CUNOAN, Michael	20	M	Laborer	08Ap18Gf
COGAN, David	30	M	Laborer	08Ap18Gf
MCCARTHY, Daniel	20	M	Laborer	08Ap18Gf
WALSH, Patt	16	M	Laborer	08Ap18Gf
MAHONEY, Daniel	20	M	Laborer	08Ap18Gf
COUGHLAN, Mary	20	F	Laborer	08Ap18Gf
PRENDERGAST, Patt	40	M	Laborer	08Ap18Gf
Tom	8	M	Child	08Ap18Gf
James	7	M	Child	08Ap18Gf
John	6	M	Child	08Ap18Gf
Johanna	5	F	Child	08Ap18Gf
DUGGAN, Nicholas	20	M	Laborer	08Ap18Gf
Catherine	26	F	Laborer	08Ap18Gf
CUNEEN, David	34	M	Laborer	08Ap18Gf
HEALY, Thomas	40	M	Laborer	08Ap18Gf
Catherine	45	F	Laborer	08Ap18Gf
Dennis	19	M	Laborer	08Ap18Gf
Margt.	17	F	Laborer	08Ap18Gf
Mary	15	F	Laborer	08Ap18Gf
Ellen	13	F	Laborer	08Ap18Gf
KENALLY, John	40	M	Laborer	08Ap18Gf
Julia	40	F	Laborer	08Ap18Gf
SWEENEY, Corn.	25	M	Laborer	08Ap18Gf
MAHONEY, John	25	M	Laborer	08Ap18Gf
MULCHALLEY, John	32	M	Laborer	08Ap18Gf
MOURMANE, Pat	40	M	Laborer	08Ap18Gf
MURRAY, Michael	23	M	Laborer	08Ap18Gf
FITZGERALD, Edwd.	21	M	Laborer	08Ap18Gf
MORMANE, James	9	M	Child	08Ap18Gf
Michael	20	M	Laborer	08Ap18Gf
FLANNIGAN, Mary	25	F	Laborer	08Ap18Gf
TAYLOR, Nora	26	F	Laborer	08Ap18Gf
BEARDON, Ellen	50	F	Laborer	08Ap18Gf
SAYLOR, Wm.	.06	M	Infant	08Ap18Gf
Ellen	2	F	Child	08Ap18Gf
CONNOR, Ellen	11	F	Laborer	08Ap18Gf
DONOVAN, Mary	20	F	Laborer	08Ap18Gf
NUGENT, Patt	20	M	Laborer	08Ap18Gf
Catherine	20	F	Laborer	08Ap18Gf
SEATON, Timothy	20	M	Laborer	08Ap18Gf
MINEHAN, Daniel	26	M	Laborer	08Ap18Gf
Mary	24	F	Laborer	08Ap18Gf
MINEHAN, Johanna	.10	F	Infant	08Ap18Gf
HAGUE, Ellen	20	F	Laborer	08Ap18Gf
MURPHY, John	30	M	Laborer	08Ap18Gf
Mary	20	F	Laborer	08Ap18Gf
Timothy	20	M	Laborer	08Ap18Gf
Mary	6	F	Child	08Ap18Gf
John	6	M	Child	08Ap18Gf
CONNER, Charles	20	M	Laborer	08Ap18Gf
CREED, Corns.	30	M	Laborer	08Ap18Gf
Ellen	20	F	Laborer	08Ap18Gf
DONAHUE, Corns.	40	M	Laborer	08Ap18Gf
DUGGAN, James	26	M	Laborer	08Ap18Gf
Timothy	28	M	Laborer	08Ap18Gf
HICKY, Julia	22	F	Laborer	08Ap18Gf
DRISCOLL, Mary	20	F	Laborer	08Ap18Gf
Leney	22	M	Laborer	08Ap18Gf
HALLOWAY, John	20	M	Laborer	08Ap18Gf
LYNCH, Henry	35	M	Laborer	08Ap18Gf
Timothy	13	M	Laborer	08Ap18Gf
WELLEHER, Bridget	20	F	Laborer	08Ap18Gf
CROWLEY, Daniel	20	M	Laborer	08Ap18Gf
DONOHUE, Timothy	20	M	Laborer	08Ap18Gf
MURPHY, Julia	21	F	Laborer	08Ap18Gf
SCRIVEN, Thomas	18	M	Laborer	08Ap18Gf
DUNCEN, Jerry	60	M	Laborer	08Ap18Gf
Danl.	35	M	Laborer	08Ap18Gf
Catherine	16	F	Laborer	08Ap18Gf
Hannah	60	F	Laborer	08Ap18Gf
LELAND, Jerry	20	M	Laborer	08Ap18Gf
SHEA, Catherine	20	F	Unknown	08Ap18Gf
EVENS, Catherine	20	F	Unknown	08Ap18Gf
COLEMAN, Eliza	20	F	Unknown	08Ap18Gf
SHEA, Ellen	20	F	Unknown	08Ap18Gf

JOHN-HANCOCK 09 APRIL 1850

From Liverpool

NAMES OF PASSENGERS	AGE	SEX	OCCUPATIONS	DATE PORT SHIP
CONNOLLY, Thos.	2	M	Child	09Ap02Gn
OBRIEN, Margaret	25	F	Servant	09Ap02Gn
MCKENNA, Owen	25	M	Laborer	09Ap02Gn
HENESSY, John	35	M	Sawer	09Ap02Gn
Wini	32	F	Wife	09Ap02Gn
Andrew	7	F	Child	09Ap02Gn
Ann	4	F	Child	09Ap02Gn
David	.00	M	Infant	09Ap02Gn
ANDERSON, Mich	18	M	Laborer	09Ap02Gn
RYAN, Margaret	15	F	None	09Ap02Gn
BRYAN, Martin	30	M	Shoemaker	09Ap02Gn
GRAHAM, David	21	M	Laborer	09Ap02Gn
KENNEDY, Mich	36	M	Laborer	09Ap02Gn
KENNY, Margt.	33	F	Servant	09Ap02Gn
CLARK, Mich	30	M	Laborer	09Ap02Gn
CARTER, John	27	M	Laborer	09Ap02Gn
Emma	21	F	Servant	09Ap02Gn
Thomas	.00	M	Infant	09Ap02Gn
CRAIGS, William	19	M	Laborer	09Ap02Gn
WELSH, Owen	22	M	Stone Mason	09Ap02Gn
FITZSTEPHENS, Peter	22	M	Unknown	09Ap02Gn
FLOOD, Mich	29	M	Laborer	09Ap02Gn
CONNLEY, Mat	40	M	Laborer	09Ap02Gn
CONWAY, Pat	25	M	Laborer	09Ap02Gn
REILLY, Sam	20	M	Laborer	09Ap02Gn
BRYAN, John	21	M	Laborer	09Ap02Gn
LYONS, Mary	30	F	Servant	09Ap02Gn
GRIMES, Robt.	20	M	Laborer	09Ap02Gn
BROWN, Mich	30	M	Laborer	09Ap02Gn
CAVANAGH, Edwd.	28	M	Laborer	09Ap02Gn
MCDALLY, Pat	35	M	Laborer	09Ap02Gn

NAMES OF PASSENGERS	AGE	SEX	OCCUPATIONS	DATE PORT SHIP
DOLAN, Judy	30	F	Servant	09Ap02Gn
BOYLE, Anne	20	F	Servant	09Ap02Gn
FANNARY, Anne	20	F	Servant	09Ap02Gn
GALAGHER, James	20	M	Laborer	09Ap02Gn
John	26	M	Laborer	09Ap02Gn
CRAWFORD, Anne	21	F	Servant	09Ap02Gn
HALPIN, Ellen	25	F	Servant	09Ap02Gn
RISPIN, Eliza	40	F	Servant	09Ap02Gn
Anne	17	F	Servant	09Ap02Gn
FLOOD, Bridget	24	F	Servant	09Ap02Gn
MCDONALD, John	24	M	Laborer	09Ap02Gn
CONNOR, John	22	M	Laborer	09Ap02Gn
ENWRIGHT, John	29	M	Plasterer	09Ap02Gn
IGOE, Thos.	36	M	Laborer	09Ap02Gn
DOYLE, Cathn.	26	F	Servant	09Ap02Gn
HARLEY, Pat	27	M	Laborer	09Ap02Gn
CAHILL, John	35	M	Unknown	09Ap02Gn
BUTTERWORTH, Sarah	50	F	Servant	09Ap02Gn
RADCLIFF, Rebec.	20	F	Servant	09Ap02Gn
Sarah	.00	F	Infant	09Ap02Gn
MCMAHAN, James	28	M	Shpc	09Ap02Gn
Mary	21	F	Servant	09Ap02Gn
Rose	19	F	Servant	09Ap02Gn
FITZSIMON, James	32	M	Shpc	09Ap02Gn
Ellen	26	F	Servant	09Ap02Gn
HILL, Robt.	29	M	Shpc	09Ap02Gn
SHEILDS, John	37	M	Laborer	09Ap02Gn
MCMAHON, William	14	M	Laborer	09Ap02Gn
MCMAHAN, Susan	37	F	Servant	09Ap02Gn
BOWES, Margaret	17	F	Servant	09Ap02Gn
GRACE, John	00	M	Tailor	09Ap02Gn
WRIGHT, Bridgt.	22	F	Servant	09Ap02Gn
KENNEDY, Danl.	20	M	Farmer	09Ap02Gn
Bridgt.	17	F	Servant	09Ap02Gn
Thos.	9	M	Child	09Ap02Gn
Anne	5	F	Child	09Ap02Gn
Ellen	3	F	Child	09Ap02Gn
HEALY, Mick	30	M	Baker	09Ap02Gn
MARTIN, James	7	M	Child	09Ap02Gn
DONOHUE, Margt.	34	F	Servant	09Ap02Gn
Pat	6	M	Child	09Ap02Gn
Margt.	2	F	Child	09Ap02Gn
BURNIE, Thos.	30	M	Servant	09Ap02Gn
DONOHUE, Jno.	20	M	Laborer	09Ap02Gn
BURNE, Mary	20	F	Servant	09Ap02Gn
POLLARD, Joseph	32	M	Laborer	09Ap02Gn
Hannah	30	F	Wife	09Ap02Gn
Thos.	2	M	Child	09Ap02Gn
John	1	M	Child	09Ap02Gn
Jane	.00	F	Infant	09Ap02Gn
DOLAN, John	25	M	Servant	09Ap02Gn
TWITT, Cath.	45	F	Servant	09Ap02Gn
Jane	16	F	Servant	09Ap02Gn
Anne	9	F	Child	09Ap02Gn
RAMSDEN, John	30	M	Laborer	09Ap02Gn
U, William	45	M	Laborer	09Ap02Gn
TAYLOR, Ellen	32	F	None	09Ap02Gn
Thos.	2	M	Child	09Ap02Gn
DONOVAN, Bridget	21	F	Unknown	09Ap02Gn
COLNAN, Mat	22	M	Laborer	09Ap02Gn
John	18	M	Laborer	09Ap02Gn
DYER, Cath.	16	F	Servant	09Ap02Gn
FLANIGAN, Mary	16	F	Servant	09Ap02Gn
Susan	11	F	Servant	09Ap02Gn
LEARY, Danl.	20	M	Laborer	09Ap02Gn
FOGARTY, Mich	18	M	Laborer	09Ap02Gn
MCDONALD, Danl.	19	M	Laborer	09Ap02Gn
MAHON, Margaret	25	F	Servant	09Ap02Gn
MASTERSON, Pat	18	M	Laborer	09Ap02Gn
BROWN, Mary	28	F	Servant	09Ap02Gn
BIRMINGHAM, Margaret	40	F	Servant	09Ap02Gn
Mich	15	M	Servant	09Ap02Gn
Margaret	12	F	Servant	09Ap02Gn
Ellen	9	F	Child	09Ap02Gn
GREEN, Thos.	21	M	Laborer	09Ap02Gn
FRENNIGAN, Thos.	20	M	Laborer	09Ap02Gn
QUIGLEY, Bridget	24	F	Servant	09Ap02Gn
CROTTRY, David	25	M	Laborer	09Ap02Gn
KANE, John	9	M	Child	09Ap02Gn
CONNOLLY, John	17	M	Servant	09Ap02Gn
Mary	13	F	Servant	09Ap02Gn
MCLAUGHLIN, Mary	17	F	Servant	09Ap02Gn
HANRAGHAN, Jas.	22	M	Laborer	09Ap02Gn
MAY, Mary	18	F	Servant	09Ap02Gn
NIHAN, Ellen	26	F	Servant	09Ap02Gn
WALSH, Wm.	30	M	Laborer	09Ap02Gn
U-Mrs.	24	F	Unknown	09Ap02Gn
Wini	21	F	Servant	09Ap02Gn
Thos.	30	M	Servant	09Ap02Gn
Mich	18	M	Servant	09Ap02Gn
Edw.	18	M	Servant	09Ap02Gn
HESSION, Pat	20	M	Laborer	09Ap02Gn
WALSH, John	25	M	Laborer	09Ap02Gn
U-Mrs.	20	F	Unknown	09Ap02Gn
BUTLER, Pat	25	M	Laborer	09Ap02Gn
FOX, Jane	25	F	Servant	09Ap02Gn
HYNES, John	20	M	Laborer	09Ap02Gn
HART, Bridget	18	F	Servant	09Ap02Gn
EVANS, Margaret	18	F	Servant	09Ap02Gn
FAHY, Thos.	20	M	Servant	09Ap02Gn
John	30	M	Servant	09Ap02Gn
U-Mrs.	25	F	Unknown	09Ap02Gn
James	2	M	Child	09Ap02Gn
DOLAN, Pat	20	M	Servant	09Ap02Gn
REILLY, Pat	20	M	Servant	09Ap02Gn
Ellen	18	F	Servant	09Ap02Gn
CORLESS, Ellen	18	F	Servant	09Ap02Gn
LUNSKY, Mary	20	F	Servant	09Ap02Gn
DUNBAR, Cath.	20	F	Servant	09Ap02Gn
FINNAUGHTY, Peter	25	M	Laborer	09Ap02Gn
CAMPBELL, Ellen	5	F	Child	09Ap02Gn
HORAN, Pat	11	M	None	09Ap02Gn
DAVIS, Jas.	19	M	Servant	09Ap02Gn
MCCAVE, Mary	39	F	Servant	09Ap02Gn
JONES, Sam	24	M	Laborer	09Ap02Gn
Sarah	24	F	Servant	09Ap02Gn
KINGSTON, Sally	24	F	Servant	09Ap02Gn
RANDALL, Peter	50	M	Laborer	09Ap02Gn
Mary	40	F	Wife	09Ap02Gn
Francis	16	M	None	09Ap02Gn
Mary	13	F	None	09Ap02Gn
Anne	7	F	Child	09Ap02Gn
Peter	5	M	Child	09Ap02Gn
Bridget	3	F	Child	09Ap02Gn
William	.00	M	Infant	09Ap02Gn
NAGLES, John	22	M	Laborer	09Ap02Gn
BUSTER, Michael	17	M	Laborer	09Ap02Gn
KELLY, Ste.	24	M	Laborer	09Ap02Gn
CAVANAGH, Bridget	18	F	Servant	09Ap02Gn
Thomas	14	M	None	09Ap02Gn
WATSON, Thomas	27	M	Plumber	09Ap02Gn
GARR, Michael	22	M	Laborer	09Ap02Gn
LYNOCH, William	18	M	Laborer	09Ap02Gn
BURROW, William	18	M	Laborer	09Ap02Gn
BERGAN, John	23	M	Laborer	09Ap02Gn
WHALIN, William	36	M	Stone Mason	09Ap02Gn
Mary	25	F	Servant	09Ap02Gn
Eliza	2	F	Child	09Ap02Gn
DRENNAN, Martin	40	M	Laborer	09Ap02Gn
DELANY, James	26	M	Laborer	09Ap02Gn
KILCULLEN, Mary	33	F	Servant	09Ap02Gn
Mary	14	F	Servant	09Ap02Gn
John	12	M	None	09Ap02Gn
James	10	M	None	09Ap02Gn
Owen	8	M	Child	09Ap02Gn
Thomas	4	M	Child	09Ap02Gn
Bridget	.00	F	Infant	09Ap02Gn
GURNEY, Thomas	22	M	Laborer	09Ap02Gn
FLITCROFT, James	23	M	Laborer	09Ap02Gn
GARR, Pat	22	M	Laborer	09Ap02Gn

NAMES OF PASSENGERS	AGE	SEX	OCCUPATIONS	DATE PORT SHIP
MITCHELL, James	21	M	Laborer	09Ap02Gn
GEOGHAN, Peter	21	M	Blacksmith	09Ap02Gn
Mary	26	F	Servant	09Ap02Gn
DRYNAN, John	26	M	Laborer	09Ap02Gn
FITZGERALD, Mary	19	F	Servant	09Ap02Gn
PILKINGTON, Michael	30	M	Laborer	09Ap02Gn
Eliza	20	F	Servant	09Ap02Gn
FOGARTY, James	30	M	Laborer	09Ap02Gn
Mary	28	F	Servant	09Ap02Gn
Danl.	2	M	Child	09Ap02Gn
MARA, James	45	M	Laborer	09Ap02Gn
MCBRIDE, Francis	25	M	Laborer	09Ap02Gn
FLINN, Catherine	19	F	Dressmaker	09Ap02Gn
John	16	M	None	09Ap02Gn
DORIAN, Edwd.	54	M	Shpc	09Ap02Gn
U-Mrs.	49	F	Unknown	09Ap02Gn
LAKEY, James	17	M	None	09Ap02Gn
CRAWFORD, Edwd.	33	M	Shoemaker	09Ap02Gn
U-Mrs.	26	F	Unknown	09Ap02Gn
Mary	4	F	Child	09Ap02Gn
Pat	2	M	Child	09Ap02Gn
Eliza	.00	F	Infant	09Ap02Gn
CAIR, U-Mrs.	25	F	Unknown	09Ap02Gn
John	.00	M	Infant	09Ap02Gn
KELLY, John	20	M	Laborer	09Ap02Gn
FLANNERY, Mark	22	M	Laborer	09Ap02Gn
EGAN, Catherine	20	F	Servant	09Ap02Gn
MADDEN, Anne	30	F	Servant	09Ap02Gn
BERRY, Joseph	15	M	None	09Ap02Gn
Betty	16	F	Servant	09Ap02Gn
HUGHS, Eliza	18	F	Servant	09Ap02Gn
SIMPSON, John	60	M	Laborer	09Ap02Gn
U	25	M	Laborer	09Ap02Gn
John	4	M	Child	09Ap02Gn
Maria	3	F	Child	09Ap02Gn
Died-At-Sea				
Sarah	.00	F	Infant	09Ap02Gn
CASEY, Betsey	18	F	Servant	09Ap02Gn
DONNELLY, Maurice	17	M	Servant	09Ap02Gn
Thos.	14	M	Servant	09Ap02Gn
COLLIVAN, Susan	13	F	Servant	09Ap02Gn
CLEARY, John	23	M	Laborer	09Ap02Gn
WINN, Denis	21	M	Laborer	09Ap02Gn
HORAN, Mich	24	M	Shoemaker	09Ap02Gn
NUGENT, Thos.	30	M	Laborer	09Ap02Gn
NAUGHTON, Thos.	33	M	Laborer	09Ap02Gn
Edwd.	7	M	Child	09Ap02Gn
Catherine	3	F	Child	09Ap02Gn
REILLY, Mary	18	F	Servant	09Ap02Gn
MARTIN, John	24	M	Laborer	09Ap02Gn
Pat	10	M	None	09Ap02Gn
HAYES, John	20	M	Laborer	09Ap02Gn
Wm.	18	M	Laborer	09Ap02Gn
JONES, James	40	M	Laborer	09Ap02Gn
FOGARTY, Maria	17	F	Servant	09Ap02Gn
MCCLUSKEY, S.	25	M	Laborer	09Ap02Gn
BYRNE, Catherine	18	F	Servant	09Ap02Gn
KENNEDY, Mary	50	F	Servant	09Ap02Gn
Danl.	27	M	Laborer	09Ap02Gn
Mich	22	M	Laborer	09Ap02Gn
Mary	24	F	Servant	09Ap02Gn
Catherine	20	F	Servant	09Ap02Gn
Thos.	17	M	Servant	09Ap02Gn
Pat	13	M	Servant	09Ap02Gn
James	9	M	Child	09Ap02Gn
Mary	22	F	Servant	09Ap02Gn
Pat	18	M	Laborer	09Ap02Gn
FLEMING, Pat	18	M	Laborer	09Ap02Gn
CLARE, Anne	20	F	Servant	09Ap02Gn
RYAN, Tim	30	F	Laborer	09Ap02Gn
WATSON, John	22	M	Cver	09Ap02Gn
TAYLOR, Mary	21	F	Servant	09Ap02Gn
MAHER, Mary	19	F	Servant	09Ap02Gn
PETERS, Pat	16	M	Laborer	09Ap02Gn
CONNOLLY, Bobby	25	M	Laborer	09Ap02Gn

AMERICA 09 APRIL 1850

From Liverpool

NAMES OF PASSENGERS	AGE	SEX	OCCUPATIONS	DATE PORT SHIP
STEPHENSON, Robt.	21	M	Unknown	09Ap02Cg
Patience	18	F	Unknown	09Ap02Cg
Ann	64	F	Unknown	09Ap02Cg
MAHEN, Margt.	32	F	Spinster	09Ap02Cg
PRENDERGAST, Cathne.	22	F	Spinster	09Ap02Cg
MELIN, Honoria	22	F	Spinster	09Ap02Cg
LYNCH, Mary	18	F	Spinster	09Ap02Cg
CARROLL, John	22	M	Laborer	09Ap02Cg
CULARTON, Peter	20	M	Laborer	09Ap02Cg
SHERLOCK, Ellen	24	F	Spinster	09Ap02Cg
CUNNINGHAM, Sarah	50	F	Spinster	09Ap02Cg
DOUGHERTY, Mary	20	F	Spinster	09Ap02Cg
DOLAN, John	40	M	Laborer	09Ap02Cg
FARRELL, John	11	M	Laborer	09Ap02Cg
James	10	M	Laborer	09Ap02Cg
GORLICK, Patt	15	M	Laborer	09Ap02Cg
MULLINEN, Josh.	30	M	Laborer	09Ap02Cg
DARCY, Ellen	30	F	Spinster	09Ap02Cg
FLYNN, Michl.	20	M	Laborer	09Ap02Cg
Elizth.	20	F	Spinster	09Ap02Cg
HERBERT, Mary	40	F	Spinster	09Ap02Cg
HARRIS, Caroline	15	F	Spinster	09Ap02Cg
Christr.	13	M	Unknown	09Ap02Cg
OHARE, Patt	26	M	Laborer	09Ap02Cg
BROWNE, Alexr.	00	M	Laborer	09Ap02Cg
FALLON, Mary	00	F	Unknown	09Ap02Cg
CARBEN, Ann	17	F	Unknown	09Ap02Cg
MCPARLAN, Chas.	25	M	Laborer	09Ap02Cg
LANE, John	25	M	Laborer	09Ap02Cg
BATES, John	45	M	Clergyman	09Ap02Cg
Sarah	41	F	Unknown	09Ap02Cg
Saml.	12	M	Unknown	09Ap02Cg
Jane	10	F	Unknown	09Ap02Cg
John	7	M	Child	09Ap02Cg
Mary	4	F	Child	09Ap02Cg
Josh.	1	M	Child	09Ap02Cg
GILMORE, Robt.	38	M	Clerk	09Ap02Cg
Mary-A.	37	F	Unknown	09Ap02Cg
Robt.	3	M	Child	09Ap02Cg
Ann	36	F	Unknown	09Ap02Cg
Ellen	30	F	Unknown	09Ap02Cg
HISCOCK, Lazarus	44	M	Farmer	09Ap02Cg
Mary	40	F	Unknown	09Ap02Cg
Hannah	15	F	Unknown	09Ap02Cg
Edmd.	12	M	Unknown	09Ap02Cg
Edwd.	10	M	Unknown	09Ap02Cg
Elijah	9	M	Child	09Ap02Cg
John	5	M	Child	09Ap02Cg
Arthur	1	M	Child	09Ap02Cg
BRICKLE, John	23	M	Farmer	09Ap02Cg
Mary	18	F	Unknown	09Ap02Cg
RIBBICK, Silverster	25	M	Laborer	09Ap02Cg
Ann	23	F	Unknown	09Ap02Cg
MCNANCE, Michl.	23	M	Laborer	09Ap02Cg
Bessy	16	F	Unknown	09Ap02Cg
DAILY, Ann	40	F	Unknown	09Ap02Cg
Bernd.	7	M	Child	09Ap02Cg
DEVITT, Daniel	20	M	Laborer	09Ap02Cg
CONNOLLY, Peter	20	M	Laborer	09Ap02Cg
CONNISKY, Terrence	20	M	Laborer	09Ap02Cg
MCKEERNAN, Margt.	16	F	Laborer	09Ap02Cg
RILEY, Henry	26	M	Laborer	09Ap02Cg
Mary	22	F	Unknown	09Ap02Cg
Ann	18	F	Unknown	09Ap02Cg
LEE, Rose	20	F	Unknown	09Ap02Cg

NAMES OF PASSENGERS	AGE	SEX	OCCUPATIONS	DATE PORT SHIP
RUDDY, Cathne.	20	F	Unknown	09Ap02Cg
MASTRESON, James	20	M	Farmer	09Ap02Cg
Patt	12	M	Farmer	09Ap02Cg
KAINE, John	24	M	Farmer	09Ap02Cg
KILBRIDE, Hugh	26	M	Laborer	09Ap02Cg
DOUGHERTY, Cathe.	9	F	Child	09Ap02Cg
Biddy	7	F	Child	09Ap02Cg
Peter	30	M	Unknown	09Ap02Cg
CARNEY, Bridgt.	26	F	Unknown	09Ap02Cg
BOOKEN, Mary	30	F	Unknown	09Ap02Cg
Francis	9	M	Child	09Ap02Cg
Mary	7	F	Child	09Ap02Cg
PATTERSON, Barbara	27	F	Unknown	09Ap02Cg
TATE, James	22	M	Unknown	09Ap02Cg
PLUNKETT, Bridgt.	20	F	Unknown	09Ap02Cg
LYNCH, Patt	6	M	Laborer	09Ap02Cg
CASCART, John	50	M	Laborer	09Ap02Cg
Robt.	18	M	Unknown	09Ap02Cg
Jane	10	F	Unknown	09Ap02Cg
Ann	23	F	Unknown	09Ap02Cg
TINSTALL, James	19	M	Laborer	09Ap02Cg
KELLY, Patt	38	M	Farmer	09Ap02Cg
Betsy	30	F	Spinster	09Ap02Cg
Mary	5	F	Child	09Ap02Cg
Michl.	30	M	Unknown	09Ap02Cg
DAILEY, James	39	M	Gentleman	09Ap02Cg
FARRELL, Mary	50	F	Spinster	09Ap02Cg
Thomas	17	M	Unknown	09Ap02Cg
John	12	M	Unknown	09Ap02Cg
Michl.	10	M	Unknown	09Ap02Cg
Margt.	40	F	Spinster	09Ap02Cg
Cathe.	17	F	Unknown	09Ap02Cg
Cathe.	15	F	Unknown	09Ap02Cg
Martin	22	M	Laborer	09Ap02Cg
FOX, Margt.	13	F	Spinster	09Ap02Cg
Mary	10	F	Spinster	09Ap02Cg
SULLIVAN, Danl.	24	M	Laborer	09Ap02Cg
PARKER, Andw.	20	M	Laborer	09Ap02Cg
Eliza	16	F	Unknown	09Ap02Cg
CASSIDY, James	23	M	Laborer	09Ap02Cg
CURRY, Ann	20	F	Unknown	09Ap02Cg
PENDER, Wm.	22	M	Laborer	09Ap02Cg
HARROWIN, Margt.	21	F	Unknown	09Ap02Cg
MCNAME, James	30	M	Laborer	09Ap02Cg
MAGURIE, Hugh	26	M	Laborer	09Ap02Cg
DOLAN, Judy	21	F	Unknown	09Ap02Cg
HANLEY, Dennis	28	M	Unknown	09Ap02Cg
DUNNAN, Jerry	25	M	Laborer	09Ap02Cg
KITCHNER, James	22	M	Laborer	09Ap02Cg
FAHY, Jane	18	F	Unknown	09Ap02Cg
DRUDY, John	25	M	Laborer	09Ap02Cg
James	20	M	Laborer	09Ap02Cg
WILSON, Francis	24	M	Laborer	09Ap02Cg
JACKSON, Wm.	22	M	Laborer	09Ap02Cg
RYAN, Wm.	21	M	Laborer	09Ap02Cg
MURRAY, Cathe.	50	F	Spinster	09Ap02Cg
Ellen	11	F	Spinster	09Ap02Cg
James	7	M	Child	09Ap02Cg
NOON, Cathe.	20	F	Spinster	09Ap02Cg
DOYLE, Cathe.	18	F	Spinster	09Ap02Cg
DONOGHUE, Agnes	6	F	Child	09Ap02Cg
Bernard	14	M	Unknown	09Ap02Cg
FITZSIMMONS, Patt	25	M	Laborer	09Ap02Cg
CURLY, Lalia	34	F	Unknown	09Ap02Cg
Cathe.	18	F	Unknown	09Ap02Cg
CARROLL, Rose	35	F	Unknown	09Ap02Cg
Charles	14	M	Unknown	09Ap02Cg
CORBETT, Mary	24	F	Unknown	09Ap02Cg
MCGARRY, Bridgt.	20	F	Unknown	09Ap02Cg
GALVIN, Bridgt.	23	F	Unknown	09Ap02Cg
KELLY, Patt	39	M	Laborer	09Ap02Cg
GORMAN, Christ.	14	M	Laborer	09Ap02Cg
CARROLL, Patt	15	M	Laborer	09Ap02Cg
KILNER, Cathe.	21	F	Spinster	09Ap02Cg
MULLIGAN, John	48	M	Laborer	09Ap02Cg
MULLORY, Michl.	12	M	Laborer	09Ap02Cg
CLAFFY, Rosey	25	F	Spinster	09Ap02Cg
Thomas	2	M	Child	09Ap02Cg
TULLY, Eleaner	20	F	Unknown	09Ap02Cg
GALLAGHER, Wm.	45	M	Laborer	09Ap02Cg
WEER, Elizth.	26	F	Spinster	09Ap02Cg
MCKIERNAN, John	20	M	Laborer	09Ap02Cg
WARD, Michl.	21	M	Laborer	09Ap02Cg
DWYRE, Michl.	20	M	Laborer	09Ap02Cg
MCCABE, Margt.	20	F	Spinster	09Ap02Cg
SEXTON, Bridgt.	25	F	Spinster	09Ap02Cg
Thomas	20	M	Laborer	09Ap02Cg
Brian	23	M	Laborer	09Ap02Cg
LYNCH, John	22	M	Laborer	09Ap02Cg
CONNAUGHTON, Rose	30	F	Spinster	09Ap02Cg
John	8	M	Child	09Ap02Cg
REILLY, Elizth.	20	F	Spinster	09Ap02Cg
DOWDEN, John	20	M	Laborer	09Ap02Cg
Mary	20	F	Spinster	09Ap02Cg
MCKENNER, Mary	40	F	Spinster	09Ap02Cg
BANKER, James	26	M	Laborer	09Ap02Cg
KILLARD, Mary	20	F	Unknown	09Ap02Cg
TONKERD, Margt.	20	F	Unknown	09Ap02Cg
LYNCH, Mary	30	F	Unknown	09Ap02Cg
MCGRATH, Richd.	40	M	Unknown	09Ap02Cg
Biddy	35	F	Unknown	09Ap02Cg
John	14	M	Unknown	09Ap02Cg
Patt	12	M	Unknown	09Ap02Cg
Honora	5	F	Child	09Ap02Cg
Mary	.00	F	Infant	09Ap02Cg
CONNOLLY, Patt	25	M	Laborer	09Ap02Cg
Mary	30	F	Unknown	09Ap02Cg
Margt.	28	F	Unknown	09Ap02Cg
Honora	22	F	Unknown	09Ap02Cg
KENNEDY, Michl.	45	M	Laborer	09Ap02Cg
Ellen	40	F	Unknown	09Ap02Cg
Bridgt.	25	F	Unknown	09Ap02Cg
Ellen	22	F	Unknown	09Ap02Cg
Mary	19	F	Unknown	09Ap02Cg
Ann	17	F	Unknown	09Ap02Cg
Nichls.	15	M	Unknown	09Ap02Cg
John	12	M	Unknown	09Ap02Cg
James	10	M	Unknown	09Ap02Cg
MULCHAY, Ann	23	F	Unknown	09Ap02Cg
COYLE, Margt.	18	F	Unknown	09Ap02Cg
SWIFT, Danl.	23	M	Laborer	09Ap02Cg
GIBNEY, Bridgt.	45	F	Unknown	09Ap02Cg
Patt	13	M	Unknown	09Ap02Cg
Lawrence	11	M	Unknown	09Ap02Cg
Bridgt.	7	F	Child	09Ap02Cg
Cathe.	4	F	Child	09Ap02Cg
BROWNLEE, Josh.	35	M	Laborer	09Ap02Cg
Nathl.	29	M	Laborer	09Ap02Cg
Mary	16	F	Unknown	09Ap02Cg
LYNCH, Barney	29	M	Laborer	09Ap02Cg
MCNAMARA, Bridgt.	34	F	Unknown	09Ap02Cg
Mary	22	F	Unknown	09Ap02Cg
MCGLINN, Peggy	40	F	Unknown	09Ap02Cg
Martin	12	M	Unknown	09Ap02Cg
Willm.	7	M	Child	09Ap02Cg
Walter	5	M	Child	09Ap02Cg
MURTAGH, Michl.	26	M	Laborer	09Ap02Cg
HOGAN, Johanna	25	F	Unknown	09Ap02Cg
RYAN, Teddy	26	M	Unknown	09Ap02Cg
MCGLINN, Thos.	20	M	Unknown	09Ap02Cg
KAYD, Kearan	18	M	Unknown	09Ap02Cg
DILLON, Peter	18	M	Laborer	09Ap02Cg
MEARA, Ann	20	F	Unknown	09Ap02Cg
MCNAMARA, Thos.	25	M	Unknown	09Ap02Cg
PONCE, Robt.	24	M	Wheelwright	09Ap02Cg
JACKSON, Wm.	21	M	Unknown	09Ap02Cg
Joseph	29	M	Unknown	09Ap02Cg
Jane	22	F	Unknown	09Ap02Cg
TURNER, George	25	M	Tailor	09Ap02Cg
MCGRATH, Wm.	50	M	Unknown	09Ap02Cg

NAMES OF PASSENGERS	AGE	SEX	OCCUPATIONS	DATE PORT SHIP	NAMES OF PASSENGERS	AGE	SEX	OCCUPATIONS	DATE PORT SHIP
MCGRATH, Norry	28	F	Unknown	09Ap02Cg	TRAINOR, Michl.	20	M	Laborer	09Ap02Cg
John	26	M	Unknown	09Ap02Cg	DONALDSON, Josh.	24	M	Laborer	09Ap02Cg
RYAN, Patt	24	M	Laborer	09Ap02Cg	CALLAGHAN, Michl.	13	M	Laborer	09Ap02Cg
MCGRATH, Mary	22	F	Unknown	09Ap02Cg	TRAINOR, Eliza	30	F	Unknown	09Ap02Cg
Edwd.	20	M	Unknown	09Ap02Cg	Rose	47	F	Unknown	09Ap02Cg
Phillip	17	M	Unknown	09Ap02Cg	WILLIAMSON, Anna	5	F	Child	09Ap02Cg
WELSH, Mick	30	M	Laborer	09Ap02Cg	MCGUIRE, Phillip	25	M	Laborer	09Ap02Cg
CUNNINGHAM, Cathe.	50	F	Unknown	09Ap02Cg	Elizth.	50	F	Unknown	09Ap02Cg
Wm.	17	M	Unknown	09Ap02Cg	Phillip	50	M	Unknown	09Ap02Cg
WHALEN, Wm.	30	M	Laborer	09Ap02Cg	MCCAFFREY, Mary	11	F	Unknown	09Ap02Cg
MCCORMICK, Dennis	28	M	Laborer	09Ap02Cg	SMITH, James	22	M	Laborer	09Ap02Cg
CRODDICK, Richd.	22	M	Unknown	09Ap02Cg	MCGUIRE, John	6	M	Child	09Ap02Cg
Michl.	17	M	Unknown	09Ap02Cg	BRENNAN, Andw.	50	M	Laborer	09Ap02Cg
CAVANAGH, Thos.	28	M	Unknown	09Ap02Cg	Ann	50	F	Unknown	09Ap02Cg
Eliza	19	F	Unknown	09Ap02Cg	ROSS, Mary	30	F	Unknown	09Ap02Cg
DENNIS, James	30	M	Unknown	09Ap02Cg	Richd.	5	M	Child	09Ap02Cg
Honnor	27	F	Unknown	09Ap02Cg	Mary-A.	3	F	Child	09Ap02Cg
Eliza	7	F	Child	09Ap02Cg	SMITH, Betsy	20	F	Unknown	09Ap02Cg
CARNEY, James	40	M	Laborer	09Ap02Cg	MCGUSKIN, Mary-A.	22	F	Unknown	09Ap02Cg
Patt	30	M	Laborer	09Ap02Cg	CASHEN, Martha	41	F	Unknown	09Ap02Cg
WHYTE, Michl.	20	M	Farmer	09Ap02Cg	BUTLER, Ellen	50	F	Unknown	09Ap02Cg
Patt	22	M	Farmer	09Ap02Cg	Patt	30	M	Unknown	09Ap02Cg
TRESSEY, Thomas	19	M	Farmer	09Ap02Cg	Ellen	25	F	Unknown	09Ap02Cg
Dennis	15	M	Farmer	09Ap02Cg	Jane	15	F	Unknown	09Ap02Cg
MCKENNA, Cathe.	17	F	Spinster	09Ap02Cg	NOWLAN, Patt	22	M	Farmer	09Ap02Cg
CARNEY, Thomas	20	M	Laborer	09Ap02Cg	Ann	18	F	Unknown	09Ap02Cg
FINLEY, Owen	30	M	Laborer	09Ap02Cg	Thomas	35	M	Unknown	09Ap02Cg
KELLY, Mary	16	F	Spinster	09Ap02Cg	DOOLAN, Michl.	22	M	Unknown	09Ap02Cg
SHEELY, Honora	30	F	Spinster	09Ap02Cg	BRITT, John	23	M	Laborer	09Ap02Cg
CUMMISKY, Rose	35	F	Spinster	09Ap02Cg	WADE, Elizth.	40	F	Unknown	09Ap02Cg
LEE, Bryan	9	M	Child	09Ap02Cg	OBRIEN, Dennis	7	M	Child	09Ap02Cg
COLLWELL, Thos.	4	M	Child	09Ap02Cg	Mary	30	F	Unknown	09Ap02Cg
BRINES, Sarah	20	F	Spinster	09Ap02Cg	KENNEDY, Ann	16	F	Unknown	09Ap02Cg
KINKALL, Lucy	18	F	Unknown	09Ap02Cg	FALKNER, James	24	M	Laborer	09Ap02Cg
BLACK, Elizth.	20	F	Unknown	09Ap02Cg	John	30	M	Laborer	09Ap02Cg
LISTON, Ellen	13	F	Unknown	09Ap02Cg	HYSON, Edwd.	22	M	Musician	09Ap02Cg
DENNAN, Wm.	33	M	Laborer	09Ap02Cg	Letitia	20	F	Unknown	09Ap02Cg
MCCARTY, Hannah	30	F	Spinster	09Ap02Cg	Ferrizzin	1	M	Child	09Ap02Cg
John	12	M	Unknown	09Ap02Cg	FINNIGAN, Wm.	22	M	Laborer	09Ap02Cg
Danl.	6	M	Child	09Ap02Cg	REILLY, James	24	M	Laborer	09Ap02Cg
Patt	.00	M	Infant	09Ap02Cg	WHALEN, Patt	20	M	Laborer	09Ap02Cg
DEVLIN, Arthur	18	M	Trade Man	09Ap02Cg	QUINLAN, Margt.	39	F	Unknown	09Ap02Cg
MCKENNA, Patt	16	M	Unknown	09Ap02Cg	John	10	M	Laborer	09Ap02Cg
Ellen	50	F	Unknown	09Ap02Cg	REDMAN, Henry	20	M	Unknown	09Ap02Cg
EARLY, Celia	19	F	Unknown	09Ap02Cg	KERNS, Cathe.	20	F	Unknown	09Ap02Cg
HEVER, Cathe.	20	F	Unknown	09Ap02Cg	WHITEHEAD, Zacharia	20	M	Unknown	09Ap02Cg
DOOLIN, Ann	20	F	Unknown	09Ap02Cg	BELL, Henry	30	M	Unknown	09Ap02Cg
MURPHY, Wm.	50	M	Carpenter	09Ap02Cg	LYONS, Mary	18	F	Unknown	09Ap02Cg
Ellen	45	F	Unknown	09Ap02Cg	MATTHEWMAN, Pat	23	M	Mnftr	09Ap02Cg
WHITE, Cathe.	18	F	Unknown	09Ap02Cg	MCGOWAN, Michl.	27	M	Laborer	09Ap02Cg
QUINLAN, Walter	22	M	Laborer	09Ap02Cg	HICKEY, Ann	22	F	Spinster	09Ap02Cg
John	18	M	Laborer	09Ap02Cg	TRAINER, Cathe.	17	F	Spinster	09Ap02Cg
BUTLER, Edwd.	23	M	Laborer	09Ap02Cg	LENNAN, Thos.	21	M	Laborer	09Ap02Cg
NAGLE, Margt.	17	F	Unknown	09Ap02Cg	James	22	M	Laborer	09Ap02Cg
FOLEY, Michl.	26	M	Laborer	09Ap02Cg	Michl.	18	M	Laborer	09Ap02Cg
REERDON, Johanna	20	F	Unknown	09Ap02Cg	MCCANN, Alley	50	F	Laborer	09Ap02Cg
Bessey	22	F	Unknown	09Ap02Cg	ARMSTRONG, Richd.	27	M	Unknown	09Ap02Cg
RINE, Mary	22	F	Unknown	09Ap02Cg	Jane	28	F	Unknown	09Ap02Cg
KELLY, Owen	17	M	Shoemaker	09Ap02Cg	Ann	17	F	Unknown	09Ap02Cg
CANNEN, Ann	20	F	Unknown	09Ap02Cg	Ann	2	F	Child	09Ap02Cg
HURLEY, Danl.	30	M	Laborer	09Ap02Cg	James	.00	M	Infant	09Ap02Cg
DENNIS, John	30	M	Laborer	09Ap02Cg	BROWN, Robt.	26	M	Unknown	09Ap02Cg
ODONOVAN, Morgan	25	M	Shoemaker	09Ap02Cg	Thos.	22	M	Unknown	09Ap02Cg
CAVANAGH, John	20	M	Laborer	09Ap02Cg	DWYER, Wm.	27	M	Laborer	09Ap02Cg
SALMEN, James	30	M	Laborer	09Ap02Cg	CAULFIELD, Thos.	20	M	Laborer	09Ap02Cg
DALOHERY, Jeremiah	17	M	Farmer	09Ap02Cg	HARDWICK, Cathe.	46	F	Unknown	09Ap02Cg
ARTHUR, Thomas	30	M	Farmer	09Ap02Cg	James	22	M	Unknown	09Ap02Cg
Elizth.	30	F	Unknown	09Ap02Cg	Lawrence	20	M	Unknown	09Ap02Cg
Thomas	.00	M	Infant	09Ap02Cg	Ann	15	F	Unknown	09Ap02Cg
HANNETTY, Owen	50	M	Farmer	09Ap02Cg	Ellen	16	F	Unknown	09Ap02Cg
Mary	22	F	Unknown	09Ap02Cg	Thomas	18	M	Unknown	09Ap02Cg
HANNEN, John	40	M	Farmer	09Ap02Cg	Cathe.	8	F	Child	09Ap02Cg
DONOHOE, Margt.	23	F	Unknown	09Ap02Cg	John	6	M	Child	09Ap02Cg
Margt.	4	F	Child	09Ap02Cg	Thomas	27	M	Unknown	09Ap02Cg
FALVEY, Mary	55	F	Spinster	09Ap02Cg	Bridget	20	F	Unknown	09Ap02Cg

NAMES OF PASSENGERS	AGE	SEX	OCCUPATIONS	DATE PORT SHIP
HARDWICK, Darby	.00	M	Infant	09Ap02Cg
Cathe.	.00	F	Infant	09Ap02Cg
Eliza	15	F	Unknown	09Ap02Cg
CARROLL, John	21	M	Tailor	09Ap02Cg
BUCHER, Pat	60	M	Laborer	09Ap02Cg
Margt.	60	F	Unknown	09Ap02Cg
James	20	M	Unknown	09Ap02Cg
Pat	22	M	Unknown	09Ap02Cg
Mary	16	F	Unknown	09Ap02Cg
Michl.	20	M	Unknown	09Ap02Cg
HERTLEY, Bridget	30	F	Unknown	09Ap02Cg
Mary	12	F	Unknown	09Ap02Cg
MCCARTHY, Danl.	24	M	Unknown	09Ap02Cg
Cathe.	22	F	Unknown	09Ap02Cg
Mary	.00	F	Infant	09Ap02Cg
SMITH, Matthew	24	M	Unknown	09Ap02Cg
KENNA, Susan	40	F	Unknown	09Ap02Cg
Alice	18	F	Unknown	09Ap02Cg
FILMONY, James	18	M	Unknown	09Ap02Cg
FITZGERALD, Pat	35	M	Unknown	09Ap02Cg
SHAW, Thomas	24	M	Unknown	09Ap02Cg
Ellen	18	F	Unknown	09Ap02Cg
GRAVES, Henry	22	M	Unknown	09Ap02Cg
Rachel	22	F	Unknown	09Ap02Cg
FARMER, Bridget	30	F	Unknown	09Ap02Cg
GOOLEY, Angus	60	M	Blacksmith	09Ap02Cg
Mary	60	F	Unknown	09Ap02Cg
Angus	28	M	Unknown	09Ap02Cg
Maria	20	F	Unknown	09Ap02Cg
Esther	18	F	Unknown	09Ap02Cg
HORN, Benjm.	21	M	Laborer	09Ap02Cg
HUNTER, Saml.	20	M	Laborer	09Ap02Cg
Wm.	22	M	Laborer	09Ap02Cg
JOHNSON, Wm.	21	M	Laborer	09Ap02Cg
HUNT, John	25	M	Laborer	09Ap02Cg
HOWLY, Joseph	30	M	Laborer	09Ap02Cg
HARE, Henry	15	M	Laborer	09Ap02Cg
KELLY, Michl.	27	M	Laborer	09Ap02Cg
RAYNER, John	47	M	Weaver	09Ap02Cg
NASH, Thos.	22	M	Laborer	09Ap02Cg
THUDDLE, Geo.	19	M	Laborer	09Ap02Cg
MINCHAN, Thos.	23	M	Laborer	09Ap02Cg
LANE, Thos.	21	M	Laborer	09Ap02Cg
SIENNER, John	22	M	Laborer	09Ap02Cg
GUNN, Chas.	29	M	Laborer	09Ap02Cg
George	16	M	Laborer	09Ap02Cg
FITZPATRICK, Jas.	16	M	Laborer	09Ap02Cg
GRIFFIN, Danl.	24	M	Laborer	09Ap02Cg
MURPHY, Ann	31	F	Unknown	09Ap02Cg
HALE, Chas.	33	M	Laborer	09Ap02Cg
ELLIS, Wm.	27	M	Mariner	09Ap02Cg
Sophia	30	F	Unknown	09Ap02Cg
HIGGINS, John	60	M	Unknown	09Ap02Cg
Judy	50	F	Unknown	09Ap02Cg
Julia	20	F	Unknown	09Ap02Cg
Edward	18	M	Unknown	09Ap02Cg
COLNEY, James	23	M	Unknown	09Ap02Cg
POPE, Thos.L.	27	M	Gentleman	09Ap02Cg
KIDSTON, Thomas	22	M	Gentleman	09Ap02Cg
CARNERON, John-G.	21	M	Gentleman	09Ap02Cg
GLEADOW, Robert	22	M	Gentleman	09Ap02Cg
OHARE, Cathe.	22	F	Unknown	09Ap02Cg

MANHATTAN 09 APRIL 1850

From Liverpool

NAMES OF PASSENGERS	AGE	SEX	OCCUPATIONS	DATE PORT SHIP
LONGWORTH, Danl.	50	M	Farmer	09Ap02Hd
Henry	22	M	Unknown	09Ap02Hd
LONGWORTH, Margaret	37	F	Unknown	09Ap02Hd
Ann	7	F	Child	09Ap02Hd
Michael	5	M	Child	09Ap02Hd
Catherine	2	F	Child	09Ap02Hd
MARTIN, Catherine	25	F	Unknown	09Ap02Hd
KILMONERY, Jno.	30	M	Unknown	09Ap02Hd
Catherine	28	F	Unknown	09Ap02Hd
Michael	18	M	Unknown	09Ap02Hd
Patrick	16	M	Unknown	09Ap02Hd
Thomas	11	M	Unknown	09Ap02Hd
MILLER, Pat	20	M	Unknown	09Ap02Hd
Catherine	21	F	Unknown	09Ap02Hd
KILDAY, Margt.	18	F	Unknown	09Ap02Hd
FOX, Ellen	25	F	Unknown	09Ap02Hd
U	.00	U	Infant	09Ap02Hd
CORNISH, Thos.	35	M	Laborer	09Ap02Hd
Mary	6	F	Child	09Ap02Hd
Catherine	5	F	Child	09Ap02Hd
MCGRATH, Catherine	21	F	Unknown	09Ap02Hd
HUGHES, Owen	19	M	Farmer	09Ap02Hd
GAGHAN, Ellen	24	F	Unknown	09Ap02Hd
ROWE, Thos.	13	M	Unknown	09Ap02Hd
BRENNAN, Mary	30	F	Unknown	09Ap02Hd
MCCARTY, Ellen	26	F	Unknown	09Ap02Hd
LYNNE, Patrick	24	M	Laborer	09Ap02Hd
CROWE, Pat	21	M	Unknown	09Ap02Hd
CAFFREY, Margt.	18	F	Unknown	09Ap02Hd
CONNEL, Mary	19	F	Unknown	09Ap02Hd
BALEY, Ela	20	F	Unknown	09Ap02Hd
SHEEAN, Martin	25	M	Laborer	09Ap02Hd
HART, John	40	M	Mechanic	09Ap02Hd
James	17	M	Mechanic	09Ap02Hd
Ron	13	M	Mechanic	09Ap02Hd
Phillip	11	M	Unknown	09Ap02Hd
John	7	M	Child	09Ap02Hd
Owen	5	M	Child	09Ap02Hd
Thoms.	3	M	Child	09Ap02Hd
RIELLY, James	26	M	Laborer	09Ap02Hd
NEILL, Thomas	19	M	Laborer	09Ap02Hd
Mary	20	F	Unknown	09Ap02Hd
BUCKHERRY, Thomas	20	M	Carpenter	09Ap02Hd
FARR, James	30	M	Laborer	09Ap02Hd
NARAN, Pat	24	M	Laborer	09Ap02Hd
Ann	18	F	Unknown	09Ap02Hd
FARMER, Margaret	22	F	Unknown	09Ap02Hd
GALLAGHAN, Bridget	20	F	Unknown	09Ap02Hd
Edward	18	M	Laborer	09Ap02Hd
John	10	M	Unknown	09Ap02Hd
HEALEY, Jno.	21	M	Farmer	09Ap02Hd
Daniel	19	M	Farmer	09Ap02Hd
JAMES, Ellen	20	F	Unknown	09Ap02Hd
FAGAN, Christopher	21	M	Laborer	09Ap02Hd
BAKER, Wm.	21	M	Carpenter	09Ap02Hd
KELLAHER, Peter	36	M	Shoemaker	09Ap02Hd
Mary	34	F	Unknown	09Ap02Hd
Arthur	19	M	Unknown	09Ap02Hd
Ann	18	F	Unknown	09Ap02Hd
Thomas	17	M	Unknown	09Ap02Hd
COVINGTONS, Bridget	20	F	Unknown	09Ap02Hd
MCMAHEN, Cathern	16	F	Unknown	09Ap02Hd
BRANNIGAN, Biddy	18	F	Unknown	09Ap02Hd
MCKEENY, Mary	30	F	Unknown	09Ap02Hd
GODFRY, Thomas	28	M	Coach Maker	09Ap02Hd
CALLY, Fredk.	35	M	Gun Maker	09Ap02Hd
FITZPATRICK, Thomas	25	M	Farmer	09Ap02Hd
BRADY, Catherine	21	F	Unknown	09Ap02Hd
CAUGLAN, Dennis	25	M	Laborer	09Ap02Hd
CONWAY, Thomas	19	M	Laborer	09Ap02Hd
FITZGERALD, Thomas	21	M	Laborer	09Ap02Hd
GREEN, Barthy	50	M	Laborer	09Ap02Hd
Bridget	40	F	Unknown	09Ap02Hd
Catherine	70	F	Unknown	09Ap02Hd
GOUGHAN, Bessy	20	F	Unknown	09Ap02Hd
OBRIEN, Jane	25	F	Unknown	09Ap02Hd
Bridget	19	F	Unknown	09Ap02Hd

NAMES OF PASSENGERS	AGE	SEX	OCCUPATIONS	DATE PORT SHIP
FITZGERALD, Thomas	25	M	Farmer	09Ap02Hd
DESMOND, Jno.	19	M	Farmer	09Ap02Hd
Patrick	17	M	Farmer	09Ap02Hd
CALLAHAN, Abby	19	M	Unknown	09Ap02Hd
FARLEY, Patrick	13	M	Unknown	09Ap02Hd
LOUGHLIN, Teddy	20	M	Laborer	09Ap02Hd
CAMEFORD, James	35	M	Laborer	09Ap02Hd
BRANNAN, Thomas	29	M	Laborer	09Ap02Hd
LYONS, Thomas	40	M	Laborer	09Ap02Hd
FAY, Edward	50	M	Laborer	09Ap02Hd
EAGAN, Pat	36	M	Laborer	09Ap02Hd
Margaret	30	F	Unknown	09Ap02Hd
Corberry	20	M	Laborer	09Ap02Hd
FITZGERALD, Maurice	21	M	Laborer	09Ap02Hd
TEARN, Owen	19	M	Laborer	09Ap02Hd
MCKEOGH, Jno.	25	M	Laborer	09Ap02Hd
TORGHAN, James	29	M	Laborer	09Ap02Hd
Ann	21	F	Unknown	09Ap02Hd
QUIRK, Julia	18	F	Unknown	09Ap02Hd
GOGGIN, Pat	17	M	Laborer	09Ap02Hd
Jno.	15	M	Laborer	09Ap02Hd
RYAN, Edward	26	M	Laborer	09Ap02Hd
GOGGIN, Mary	23	F	Unknown	09Ap02Hd
Biddy	20	F	Unknown	09Ap02Hd
Nancy	12	F	Unknown	09Ap02Hd
BRESTRUCHER, Pat	38	M	Laborer	09Ap02Hd
Edward	25	M	Carpenter	09Ap02Hd
Daniel	16	M	Unknown	09Ap02Hd
HINKEY, John	21	M	Mechanic	09Ap02Hd
BAGLEY, Edward	19	M	Mechanic	09Ap02Hd
BLEHAN, Pat	20	M	Mechanic	09Ap02Hd
WHELAN, Edward	19	M	Carpenter	09Ap02Hd
BRENNAN, John	25	M	Laborer	09Ap02Hd
CONNOR, Betty	20	F	Unknown	09Ap02Hd
NAUGHTON, Mary	18	F	Unknown	09Ap02Hd
ROURKE, Margaret	19	F	Unknown	09Ap02Hd
TRACY, Thomas	25	M	Laborer	09Ap02Hd
SHENAN, Thomas	20	M	Laborer	09Ap02Hd
KELLY, Hugh	19	M	Laborer	09Ap02Hd
GODRICK, Alice	18	F	Unknown	09Ap02Hd
DARCY, Bridget	25	F	Unknown	09Ap02Hd
Ellen	10	F	Unknown	09Ap02Hd
KIRBY, Maurice	30	M	Farmer	09Ap02Hd
John	7	M	Child	09Ap02Hd
Michael	5	M	Child	09Ap02Hd
CARLEY, Cathern	20	F	Unknown	09Ap02Hd
MURPHY, Pat	21	M	Laborer	09Ap02Hd
GARTLAND, Mary	28	F	Unknown	09Ap02Hd
CONROY, Mathew	25	M	Unknown	09Ap02Hd
SAVANAH, Thoms.	21	M	Unknown	09Ap02Hd
Mark	19	M	Unknown	09Ap02Hd
WALSH, James	20	M	Unknown	09Ap02Hd
Michael	18	M	Unknown	09Ap02Hd
Bessey	16	F	Unknown	09Ap02Hd
CRAVEN, Jno.	30	M	Farmer	09Ap02Hd
Margaret	25	F	Unknown	09Ap02Hd
Edward	3	M	Child	09Ap02Hd
Margaret	10	F	Unknown	09Ap02Hd
Bridget	6	F	Child	09Ap02Hd
MALLONY, Bridget	30	F	Unknown	09Ap02Hd
KILFOYLE, Thomas	36	M	Laborer	09Ap02Hd
Mary	30	F	Unknown	09Ap02Hd
MCGEE, Mary	20	F	Unknown	09Ap02Hd
MCCARTY, Robt.	30	M	Farmer	09Ap02Hd
KEARNAN, Edward	35	M	Farmer	09Ap02Hd
Margaret	30	F	Unknown	09Ap02Hd
Mary	13	F	Unknown	09Ap02Hd
Biddy	9	F	Child	09Ap02Hd
Ann	9	F	Child	09Ap02Hd
Owen	7	M	Child	09Ap02Hd
James	5	M	Child	09Ap02Hd
Julia	3	F	Child	09Ap02Hd
Mary	1	F	Child	09Ap02Hd
MEALEY, Margaret	18	F	Unknown	09Ap02Hd
MARKEY, Edward	20	M	Laborer	09Ap02Hd

NAMES OF PASSENGERS	AGE	SEX	OCCUPATIONS	DATE PORT SHIP
BEDDOES, Francis	30	M	Laborer	09Ap02Hd
RYAN, Timothy	35	M	Laborer	09Ap02Hd
GORAN, Margaret	40	F	Unknown	09Ap02Hd
FEENEY, Bridget	37	F	Unknown	09Ap02Hd
DANFORT, Jane	19	F	Unknown	09Ap02Hd
Mathew	17	M	Laborer	09Ap02Hd
KEANNEY, Ellen	20	F	Unknown	09Ap02Hd
SMITH, Ann	19	F	Unknown	09Ap02Hd
MCCARNEY, Margaret	19	F	Unknown	09Ap02Hd
COOK, Lucien	30	M	Laborer	09Ap02Hd
MCKEOGH, John	30	M	Farmer	09Ap02Hd
Margaret	28	F	Unknown	09Ap02Hd
FAGAN, Frank	30	M	Farmer	09Ap02Hd
Mary	28	F	Unknown	09Ap02Hd
BELLAR, Henry	21	M	Laborer	09Ap02Hd
MCCARTY, Jeremiah	25	M	Clothier	09Ap02Hd
PARROTT, Charles	22	M	Mariner	09Ap02Hd
Henry	50	M	Gentleman	09Ap02Hd
Henry-Jr.	30	M	Surgeon	09Ap02Hd
Cathern	20	F	Unknown	09Ap02Hd
BRADY, Bryan	35	M	Laborer	09Ap02Hd
MCDONNELL, Edward	30	M	Laborer	09Ap02Hd
Ellen	25	F	Unknown	09Ap02Hd
James	20	M	Unknown	09Ap02Hd
Michael	8	M	Child	09Ap02Hd
John	6	M	Child	09Ap02Hd
Lawrence	4	M	Child	09Ap02Hd
CARNEY, Mary	35	F	Unknown	09Ap02Hd
Anthony	30	M	Laborer	09Ap02Hd
Peggy	11	F	Unknown	09Ap02Hd
Judy	8	F	Child	09Ap02Hd
Andy	5	M	Child	09Ap02Hd
William	4	M	Child	09Ap02Hd
BRYAN, Michael	26	M	Mechanic	09Ap02Hd
LOUTH, James	21	M	Carpenter	09Ap02Hd
Catherine	19	F	Unknown	09Ap02Hd
GREGORY, John	25	M	Laborer	09Ap02Hd
Elisha	22	F	Unknown	09Ap02Hd
KEENAN, Patt	25	M	Farmer	09Ap02Hd
Anty	23	M	Farmer	09Ap02Hd
SAVAGE, John	29	M	Farmer	09Ap02Hd
KELLAHER, Michael	25	M	Farmer	09Ap02Hd
REYNOLDS, Francis	21	M	Farmer	09Ap02Hd
DOYLE, Michael	35	M	Farmer	09Ap02Hd
MALONEY, Edward	36	M	Farmer	09Ap02Hd
WALSH, William	23	M	Laborer	09Ap02Hd
DALY, John	21	M	Laborer	09Ap02Hd
BRENAGAN, Danl.	35	M	Laborer	09Ap02Hd
MCEVOY, Edward	20	M	Laborer	09Ap02Hd
FLYNN, Jno.	19	M	Laborer	09Ap02Hd
MULCAHY, Daniel	30	M	Laborer	09Ap02Hd
John	28	M	Laborer	09Ap02Hd
CONWAY, John	19	M	Laborer	09Ap02Hd
HOBERT, Nancy	30	F	Unknown	09Ap02Hd
OCALLEHAN, Bridget	25	F	Unknown	09Ap02Hd
FLYNN, Michael	17	M	Farmer	09Ap02Hd
WELSH, Honora	19	F	Unknown	09Ap02Hd
HONRAHAN, Cornelius	20	M	Laborer	09Ap02Hd
REA, James	35	M	Laborer	09Ap02Hd
Margaret	35	F	Unknown	09Ap02Hd
Richd.	17	M	Laborer	09Ap02Hd
Jane	13	F	Unknown	09Ap02Hd
Kelter	10	F	Unknown	09Ap02Hd
Michael	9	M	Child	09Ap02Hd
HEALY, Kitty	2	F	Child	09Ap02Hd
LYONS, James	25	M	Mechanic	09Ap02Hd
William	20	M	Shoemaker	09Ap02Hd
WALSH, John	30	M	Unknown	09Ap02Hd
Thomas	18	M	Carpenter	09Ap02Hd
REARDON, Ellen	30	F	Unknown	09Ap02Hd
Nelly	17	F	Unknown	09Ap02Hd
Margaret	16	F	Unknown	09Ap02Hd
BUCKLEY, Mary	20	F	Unknown	09Ap02Hd
BARRY, Mary	18	F	Unknown	09Ap02Hd
Hannah	8	F	Child	09Ap02Hd

NAMES OF PASSENGERS	AGE	SEX	OCCUPATIONS	DATE PORT SHIP
BARRY, Margaret	6	F	Child	09Ap02Hd
Kate	5	M	Child	09Ap02Hd
Mary	3	F	Child	09Ap02Hd
Barthy	2	M	Child	09Ap02Hd
SHEEHAN, Bridget	25	F	Unknown	09Ap02Hd
DONOHUE, Johannah	30	F	Unknown	09Ap02Hd
CAHILL, Catherine	20	F	Unknown	09Ap02Hd
DEVINE, John	25	M	Farmer	09Ap02Hd
COLEMAN, Dennis	20	M	Farmer	09Ap02Hd
CAHILL, Patt	35	M	Farmer	09Ap02Hd
Catherine	30	F	Unknown	09Ap02Hd
William	18	M	Farmer	09Ap02Hd
LOVE, Catherine	30	F	Unknown	09Ap02Hd
TURNIGAN, Mary	20	F	Unknown	09Ap02Hd
SMITH, James	35	M	Laborer	09Ap02Hd
WARD, John	18	M	Laborer	09Ap02Hd
BIENAN, Bridget	20	F	Unknown	09Ap02Hd
WHEELAN, Rose	18	F	Unknown	09Ap02Hd
Ann	17	F	Unknown	09Ap02Hd
FITZPATRICK, Catherine	20	F	Unknown	09Ap02Hd
Jane	18	F	Unknown	09Ap02Hd
WHELAN, Biddy	4	F	Child	09Ap02Hd
FITZPATRICK, Patrick	3	M	Child	09Ap02Hd
WHEELAN, Wm.	4	M	Child	09Ap02Hd
DORAN, Margaret	20	F	Unknown	09Ap02Hd
Bridget	18	F	Unknown	09Ap02Hd
Mary-Ann	16	F	Unknown	09Ap02Hd
CASEY, Mary	20	F	Unknown	09Ap02Hd
Julia	18	F	Unknown	09Ap02Hd
DELATERCE, Mary	16	F	Dressmaker	09Ap02Hd
SMALL, Cathn.	26	F	Dressmaker	09Ap02Hd
LEARNEY, Biddy	21	F	Unknown	09Ap02Hd
Patrick	24	M	Laborer	09Ap02Hd
DAVID, Peter	55	M	None	09Ap02Hd
Jane	40	F	Unknown	09Ap02Hd
William	25	M	Unknown	09Ap02Hd
Sarah	18	F	Unknown	09Ap02Hd
John	18	M	Tailor	09Ap02Hd
Peter	16	M	Printer	09Ap02Hd
James	14	M	Unknown	09Ap02Hd
George	12	M	Unknown	09Ap02Hd
Sarah	10	F	Unknown	09Ap02Hd
Bridget	8	F	Child	09Ap02Hd
RIGGS, George	22	M	Shopman	09Ap02Hd
KINGS, James	20	M	Farmer	09Ap02Hd
CASEY, Hannah	25	F	Unknown	09Ap02Hd
POWER, Margaret	18	F	Unknown	09Ap02Hd
QUIRK, Catherine	20	F	Unknown	09Ap02Hd
John	18	M	Laborer	09Ap02Hd
PARDY, John	30	M	Laborer	09Ap02Hd
KEARNAN, Patrick	40	M	Laborer	09Ap02Hd
Elisabeth	35	F	Unknown	09Ap02Hd
Mary	20	F	Unknown	09Ap02Hd
Honora	18	F	Unknown	09Ap02Hd
John	16	M	Unknown	09Ap02Hd
MCGURNEY, Catherine	25	F	Unknown	09Ap02Hd
Margaret	20	F	Unknown	09Ap02Hd
MADDEN, Edward	30	M	Farmer	09Ap02Hd
KEARNAN, Patrick	30	M	Farmer	09Ap02Hd
DIGNAN, John	20	M	Farmer	09Ap02Hd
CONRY, Mary	20	F	Unknown	09Ap02Hd
Thomas	10	M	Unknown	09Ap02Hd
Margaret	18	F	Unknown	09Ap02Hd
KING, Sarah	18	F	Unknown	09Ap02Hd
ONEILL, Wm.	25	M	Laborer	09Ap02Hd
DOOLY, James	20	M	Laborer	09Ap02Hd
Mary	12	F	Unknown	09Ap02Hd
KEEGAN, William	30	M	Farmer	09Ap02Hd
CLEARY, Bridget	35	F	Unknown	09Ap02Hd
Mary	13	F	Unknown	09Ap02Hd
Ellen	12	F	Unknown	09Ap02Hd
Catherine	8	F	Child	09Ap02Hd
Bridget	6	F	Child	09Ap02Hd
MOONEY, Edward	30	M	Farmer	09Ap02Hd
LEECH, Bridget	20	F	Unknown	09Ap02Hd

NAMES OF PASSENGERS	AGE	SEX	OCCUPATIONS	DATE PORT SHIP
MCCABE, Mary	18	F	Unknown	09Ap02Hd
WOODS, Peter	35	M	Surveyor	09Ap02Hd
DALY, Thomas	30	M	Farmer	09Ap02Hd
Mary	23	F	Unknown	09Ap02Hd
MCLOUGHLAND, Michael	30	M	Laborer	09Ap02Hd
MURPHY, Mathew	25	M	Laborer	09Ap02Hd
DAILEY, Anty	20	M	Laborer	09Ap02Hd
John	18	M	Laborer	09Ap02Hd
CAHILL, Edward	30	M	Laborer	09Ap02Hd
MONAGHAN, James	25	M	Laborer	09Ap02Hd
GLENNON, Judy	26	F	Unknown	09Ap02Hd
Elesa	18	F	Unknown	09Ap02Hd
WELDON, Mary	20	F	Unknown	09Ap02Hd
COFFEE, William	25	M	Farmer	09Ap02Hd
LYNCH, James	36	M	Farmer	09Ap02Hd
Rose	36	F	Unknown	09Ap02Hd
Lawrence	12	M	Unknown	09Ap02Hd
Patrick	7	M	Child	09Ap02Hd
Mary	5	F	Child	09Ap02Hd
BOYLE, Peter	25	M	Farmer	09Ap02Hd
LYNCH, John	30	M	Farmer	09Ap02Hd
Catherine	25	F	Unknown	09Ap02Hd
CAFFERY, John	20	M	Farmer	09Ap02Hd
PLUNKETT, Rose	20	F	Unknown	09Ap02Hd
HARTON, Mary	18	F	Unknown	09Ap02Hd
CRONIN, Mary	22	F	Unknown	09Ap02Hd
Margaret	11	F	Unknown	09Ap02Hd
HUGHES, Daniel	20	M	Farmer	09Ap02Hd
FITZSIMMONS, James	12	M	Unknown	09Ap02Hd
BIRD, Peter	25	M	Laborer	09Ap02Hd
HOPE, Lucy	22	F	Unknown	09Ap02Hd
Michael	20	M	Laborer	09Ap02Hd
Rose	18	F	Unknown	09Ap02Hd
SHANTRY, Christy	70	M	Farmer	09Ap02Hd
BERENDY, Bernard	25	M	Farmer	09Ap02Hd
Edward	20	M	Farmer	09Ap02Hd
KELLY, Thoms.	30	M	Farmer	09Ap02Hd
RIELLY, Elder	30	U	Unknown	09Ap02Hd
CROSSDON, John	50	M	Farmer	09Ap02Hd
Ann	50	F	Unknown	09Ap02Hd
John	18	M	Unknown	09Ap02Hd
James	16	M	Unknown	09Ap02Hd
Michael	12	M	Unknown	09Ap02Hd
CROWSDON, Julia	10	F	Unknown	09Ap02Hd
Marks	8	M	Child	09Ap02Hd
Jane	6	F	Child	09Ap02Hd
Anne	4	F	Child	09Ap02Hd
DOWD, Michael	30	M	Laborer	09Ap02Hd
Bernard	25	M	Laborer	09Ap02Hd
MURGAN, Daniel	22	M	Mechanic	09Ap02Hd
BOHEN, James	30	M	Gdnr	09Ap02Hd
GREENE, Luke	25	M	Gdnr	09Ap02Hd
OATES, Charles	20	M	Laborer	09Ap02Hd
KILROY, Anne	22	F	Unknown	09Ap02Hd
CASEY, Ellen	21	F	Unknown	09Ap02Hd
MOONEY, Edward	30	M	Laborer	09Ap02Hd
John	25	M	Laborer	09Ap02Hd
KELLY, Martin	30	M	Laborer	09Ap02Hd
Thomas	20	M	Laborer	09Ap02Hd
BIERMAN, John	35	M	Laborer	09Ap02Hd
CARTER, Bridget	25	F	Unknown	09Ap02Hd
MORRIS, Alicia	30	F	Unknown	09Ap02Hd
Betty	25	F	Unknown	09Ap02Hd
Maria	20	F	Unknown	09Ap02Hd
ONEIL, John	30	M	Farmer	09Ap02Hd
BYRNES, Patrick	25	M	Farmer	09Ap02Hd
HARDMAN, Eliza	20	F	Unknown	09Ap02Hd
Theresa	18	F	Unknown	09Ap02Hd
BRENNAN, Catharine	25	F	Unknown	09Ap02Hd
REILLY, Matthew	30	M	Farmer	09Ap02Hd
CALDWELL, Jane	30	F	Unknown	09Ap02Hd
U	.00	U	Infant	09Ap02Hd
Eliza	8	F	Child	09Ap02Hd
Jane	3	F	Child	09Ap02Hd
MULLIGAN, Chas.	25	M	Unknown	09Ap02Hd

NAMES OF PASSENGERS	AGE	SEX	OCCUPATIONS	DATE PORT SHIP
MULLIGAN, U	.00	U	Infant	09Ap02Hd
DEVLIN, Arthur	30	M	Laborer	09Ap02Hd
Hugh	25	M	Laborer	09Ap02Hd
CAVANAH, Michl.	50	M	Laborer	09Ap02Hd
Mary	45	F	Unknown	09Ap02Hd
Anne	26	F	Unknown	09Ap02Hd
Mary	9	F	Child	09Ap02Hd
John	18	M	Farmer	09Ap02Hd
Rose-Owens	16	F	Unknown	09Ap02Hd
Patrick	20	M	Tailor	09Ap02Hd
STEVENSON, James	30	M	Shoemaker	09Ap02Hd
CLARKE, Patrick	25	M	Farmer	09Ap02Hd
FANNIN, Ellen	22	F	Unknown	09Ap02Hd
MORRISON, Mary	20	F	Unknown	09Ap02Hd
NOON, Bridget	22	F	Unknown	09Ap02Hd
LOWER, George	25	M	Laborer	09Ap02Hd
WARD, Michl.	30	M	Laborer	09Ap02Hd
BYRNES, Michl.	25	M	Laborer	09Ap02Hd
Bridgt.	30	F	Unknown	09Ap02Hd
U	.00	U	Infant	09Ap02Hd
NOLAN, Anne	22	F	Unknown	09Ap02Hd
KEARNS, Anne	20	F	Unknown	09Ap02Hd
RYAN, Timothy	30	M	Unknown	09Ap02Hd
POWER, James	22	M	Laborer	09Ap02Hd
MANNIN, Sarah	17	F	Unknown	09Ap02Hd
BROWN, James	35	M	Laborer	09Ap02Hd
Margt.	30	F	Unknown	09Ap02Hd
James	20	M	Laborer	09Ap02Hd
Henry	10	M	Unknown	09Ap02Hd
Mary	18	F	Unknown	09Ap02Hd
LAMB, Richd.	30	M	Farmer	09Ap02Hd
LANAGAN, Michl.	50	M	Farmer	09Ap02Hd
Rose	48	F	Unknown	09Ap02Hd
Thos.	18	M	Farmer	09Ap02Hd
Bridget	16	F	Unknown	09Ap02Hd
Margaret	11	F	Unknown	09Ap02Hd
Rose	8	F	Child	09Ap02Hd
Michl.	6	M	Child	09Ap02Hd
Patt	5	M	Child	09Ap02Hd
NEWMAN, Christr.	60	M	Farmer	09Ap02Hd
Mary	60	F	Unknown	09Ap02Hd
Anne	22	F	Unknown	09Ap02Hd
Patt	20	M	Farmer	09Ap02Hd
Christ.	18	M	Farmer	09Ap02Hd
Michl.	16	M	Farmer	09Ap02Hd
CAMPBELL, Mary	25	F	Unknown	09Ap02Hd
WALL, James	30	M	Farmer	09Ap02Hd
MARTIN, Edwd.	26	M	Laborer	09Ap02Hd
DWYER, Cathne.	24	F	Unknown	09Ap02Hd
SULLIVAN, Willm.	23	M	Laborer	09Ap02Hd
GRADY, Denis	30	M	Laborer	09Ap02Hd
BEASEL, Wm.	29	M	Laborer	09Ap02Hd
GRADY, Bridget	25	F	Unknown	09Ap02Hd
MARSH, Norry	22	F	Unknown	09Ap02Hd
SLATTERY, Ellen	24	F	Unknown	09Ap02Hd
David	20	M	Farmer	09Ap02Hd
FAGAN, Patt	18	M	Farmer	09Ap02Hd
FLYNN, Thomas	19	M	Farmer	09Ap02Hd
ROBINSON, Mary	20	F	Unknown	09Ap02Hd
REILLY, William	18	M	Farmer	09Ap02Hd
Margaret	17	F	Unknown	09Ap02Hd
DUGGAN, Michl.	30	M	Laborer	09Ap02Hd
TUITE, Michl.	24	M	Laborer	09Ap02Hd
BRADY, Hugh	24	M	Laborer	09Ap02Hd
Catharine	26	F	Unknown	09Ap02Hd
Mary	11	F	Unknown	09Ap02Hd
Barney	9	M	Child	09Ap02Hd
Francis	5	M	Child	09Ap02Hd
Anne	3	F	Child	09Ap02Hd
Patrick	22	M	Farmer	09Ap02Hd
ROURKE, Ellen	22	F	Unknown	09Ap02Hd
BRYAN, Thomas	29	M	Laborer	09Ap02Hd
LYNCH, Peter	30	M	Laborer	09Ap02Hd
STEVENSON, Jas.	21	M	Laborer	09Ap02Hd
DUNNIVAN, Mary	24	F	Unknown	09Ap02Hd
FLEMING, John	13	M	Laborer	09Ap02Hd
DUNNIVAN, John	18	M	Laborer	09Ap02Hd
MCCORMICK, Michl.	20	M	Laborer	09Ap02Hd
Bridget	23	F	Unknown	09Ap02Hd
GARLAND, Michl.	28	M	Laborer	09Ap02Hd
Ellen	25	F	Unknown	09Ap02Hd
Bridget	18	F	Unknown	09Ap02Hd
CONRY, Mary	20	F	Unknown	09Ap02Hd
James	18	M	Carpenter	09Ap02Hd
MCMAHON, James	30	M	Smith	09Ap02Hd
MALONE, Patrick	25	M	Shoemaker	09Ap02Hd
KIRBY, John	27	M	Laborer	09Ap02Hd
Michael	20	M	Laborer	09Ap02Hd
Mary	24	F	Unknown	09Ap02Hd
BRODERICK, James	26	M	Laborer	09Ap02Hd
RYAN, Mary	30	F	Unknown	09Ap02Hd
Edward	11	M	Unknown	09Ap02Hd
Judy	9	F	Child	09Ap02Hd
Andrew	7	M	Child	09Ap02Hd
Margaret	5	F	Child	09Ap02Hd
Henry	3	M	Child	09Ap02Hd
PURDY, Mary	24	F	Unknown	09Ap02Hd
James	12	M	Laborer	09Ap02Hd
Julia	5	F	Child	09Ap02Hd
Timothy	26	M	Laborer	09Ap02Hd
KERNAN, Michael	27	M	Laborer	09Ap02Hd
SHERRY, James	23	M	Laborer	09Ap02Hd
BRENNAN, Richd.	22	M	Laborer	09Ap02Hd
LIDDY, Michl.	18	M	Laborer	09Ap02Hd
WALKER, Maria	4	F	Child	09Ap02Hd
Patrick	5	M	Child	09Ap02Hd
FEHELY, Ellen	24	F	Unknown	09Ap02Hd
U	.00	U	Infant	09Ap02Hd
Thomas	6	M	Child	09Ap02Hd
Patrick	4	M	Child	09Ap02Hd
Michael	3	M	Child	09Ap02Hd
MCDONNELL, Margt.	30	F	Unknown	09Ap02Hd
SMITH, Edward	26	M	Farmer	09Ap02Hd
CAIN, James	24	M	Farmer	09Ap02Hd
DUNBAR, Bridget	25	F	Unknown	09Ap02Hd
PEEL, Thomas	35	M	Laborer	09Ap02Hd
PATTEN, Susan	31	F	Unknown	09Ap02Hd
KEARMAN, Bridget	23	F	Unknown	09Ap02Hd
HOARE, Robt.	18	M	Laborer	09Ap02Hd
William	18	M	Laborer	09Ap02Hd
CONNELL, Thomas	22	M	Laborer	09Ap02Hd
MCKEON, Catharine	35	F	Unknown	09Ap02Hd
FLANNAGAN, John	60	M	Farmer	09Ap02Hd
GRAY, Wm.	27	M	Farmer	09Ap02Hd
MURPHY, Anne	20	F	Unknown	09Ap02Hd
ROGERS, Michl.	18	M	Tailor	09Ap02Hd
LEONARD, Anne	20	F	Unknown	09Ap02Hd
REYNOLDS, Anne	22	F	Unknown	09Ap02Hd
DEMPSY, Mary	18	F	Unknown	09Ap02Hd
BRICE, Anne	22	F	Unknown	09Ap02Hd
SLAVIN, Ellen	24	F	Unknown	09Ap02Hd
KELLY, John	26	M	Laborer	09Ap02Hd
Dennis	27	M	Laborer	09Ap02Hd
TAYLOR, Patrick	25	M	Laborer	09Ap02Hd
HENRY, Patrick	54	M	Laborer	09Ap02Hd
U-Mrs.	45	F	Unknown	09Ap02Hd
Mary	22	F	Unknown	09Ap02Hd
Bridget	16	F	Unknown	09Ap02Hd
Anne	6	F	Child	09Ap02Hd
Patrick	4	M	Child	09Ap02Hd
HOGAN, Thos.	25	M	Farmer	09Ap02Hd
KEOGH, Thos.	27	M	Friar	09Ap02Hd
MCGOWAN, Patrick	18	M	Laborer	09Ap02Hd
MCNEARNEY, Owen	30	M	Laborer	09Ap02Hd
Patrick	20	M	Laborer	09Ap02Hd
Timothy	18	M	Laborer	09Ap02Hd
MCCARTHY, Julia	29	F	Unknown	09Ap02Hd
HOGAN, Daniel	35	M	Farmer	09Ap02Hd
William	27	M	Farmer	09Ap02Hd
George	40	M	Farmer	09Ap02Hd

NAMES OF PASSENGERS	AGE	SEX	OCCUPATIONS	DATE PORT SHIP	NAMES OF PASSENGERS	AGE	SEX	OCCUPATIONS	DATE PORT SHIP
HOGAN, Mary	35	F	Unknown	09Ap02Hd	MCCAUL, Philip	24	M	Farmer	09Ap02Hd
AHERNE, James	22	M	Farmer	09Ap02Hd	REILLY, Peter	21	M	Farmer	09Ap02Hd
ROGERS, William	21	M	Farmer	09Ap02Hd	MCGUIRE, James	27	M	Farmer	09Ap02Hd
SPELMAN, Bridget	31	F	Unknown	09Ap02Hd	MCAVEENY, Ann	18	F	Unknown	09Ap02Hd
HURLEY, Julia	29	F	Unknown	09Ap02Hd	MAHER, Mary	21	F	Unknown	09Ap02Hd
CARRON, Michael	26	M	Laborer	09Ap02Hd	HAMILTON, Ellen	20	F	Unknown	09Ap02Hd
HANNON, John	24	M	Laborer	09Ap02Hd	MCGUIRE, Mary	16	F	Unknown	09Ap02Hd
DONOVAN, Margt.	24	F	Unknown	09Ap02Hd	CARROLL, Patrick	29	M	Laborer	09Ap02Hd
Ellen	30	F	Unknown	09Ap02Hd	RICE, John	32	M	Laborer	09Ap02Hd
KINSELA, Michl.	19	M	Laborer	09Ap02Hd	Stephen	30	M	Laborer	09Ap02Hd
KEERNAN, Anne	21	F	Unknown	09Ap02Hd	MURPHY, Catharine	22	F	Unknown	09Ap02Hd
ROARKE, Bridget	23	F	Unknown	09Ap02Hd	MCCARTY, Mary	18	F	Unknown	09Ap02Hd
MCGARRELL, Peter	21	M	Farmer	09Ap02Hd	DARGAN, Corns.	26	M	Laborer	09Ap02Hd
DORAN, Susan	36	F	Unknown	09Ap02Hd	FAY, Bridget	27	F	Unknown	09Ap02Hd
Michl.	20	M	Shoemaker	09Ap02Hd	Mary	27	F	Unknown	09Ap02Hd
Margt.	18	F	Unknown	09Ap02Hd	KEATING, Michl.	30	M	Farmer	09Ap02Hd
LEDDY, John	29	M	Tailor	09Ap02Hd	Dennis	28	M	Farmer	09Ap02Hd
STEWART, James	27	M	Tailor	09Ap02Hd	LYNAN, James	23	M	Farmer	09Ap02Hd
MURPHY, Eliza	22	F	Unknown	09Ap02Hd	CONNOLLY, Ellen	19	F	Unknown	09Ap02Hd
MONAGHAN, Mary	31	F	Unknown	09Ap02Hd	ELLIOTT, Eliza	17	F	Unknown	09Ap02Hd
Maria	30	F	Unknown	09Ap02Hd	HIGGINS, Margt.	34	F	Unknown	09Ap02Hd
FOLEY, Bernd.	26	M	Farmer	09Ap02Hd	Mary	16	F	Unknown	09Ap02Hd
BYRNE, Patrick	29	M	Farmer	09Ap02Hd	Simon	14	M	Unknown	09Ap02Hd
John	20	M	Farmer	09Ap02Hd	HILL, Catharine	31	F	Unknown	09Ap02Hd
Mary	17	F	Unknown	09Ap02Hd	DESMOND, Martin	26	M	Laborer	09Ap02Hd
LEYDE, Deborah	20	F	Unknown	09Ap02Hd	MCCARTY, Corns.	32	M	Laborer	09Ap02Hd
MAHON, Mary-Anne	21	F	Unknown	09Ap02Hd	REILLY, Hugh	29	M	Laborer	09Ap02Hd
CORCORAN, Patrick	25	M	Laborer	09Ap02Hd	Bridget	18	F	Unknown	09Ap02Hd
MCELVEE, Ellen	21	F	Unknown	09Ap02Hd	REED, Anne	25	F	Unknown	09Ap02Hd
David	18	M	Laborer	09Ap02Hd	MURPHY, John	22	M	Laborer	09Ap02Hd
FURGUSON, Anne	27	F	Unknown	09Ap02Hd	MCDENNOTT, Winifred	30	F	Unknown	09Ap02Hd
Henry	18	M	Carpenter	09Ap02Hd	HEFFERMAN, John	19	M	Laborer	09Ap02Hd
Catharine	16	F	Unknown	09Ap02Hd	Julia	19	F	Unknown	09Ap02Hd
James	15	M	Unknown	09Ap02Hd	Patrick	15	M	Unknown	09Ap02Hd
SLATTERY, John	27	M	Gdnr	09Ap02Hd	FEENEY, Mary	14	F	Unknown	09Ap02Hd
Mary	25	F	Unknown	09Ap02Hd	James	50	M	Farmer	09Ap02Hd
REILLY, Patrick	26	M	Laborer	09Ap02Hd	SMITH, Patrick	22	M	Farmer	09Ap02Hd
MCCURVEY, Hugh	35	M	Laborer	09Ap02Hd	TODD, Margaret	18	F	Unknown	09Ap02Hd
COX, Michl.	24	M	Laborer	09Ap02Hd	ODONNELL, Terence	32	M	Laborer	09Ap02Hd
ARMSTRONG, William	18	M	Laborer	09Ap02Hd	Catharine	32	F	Unknown	09Ap02Hd
MONAGHAN, Eliza	27	F	Unknown	09Ap02Hd	CASEY, Michl.	26	M	Laborer	09Ap02Hd
TUGMAN, Robert	19	M	Laborer	09Ap02Hd	DOHERTY, Thos.	21	M	Laborer	09Ap02Hd
FRIAREY, Rose	35	F	Unknown	09Ap02Hd	REILLY, Michl.	35	M	Unknown	09Ap02Hd
Bridget	30	F	Unknown	09Ap02Hd	KELLY, Margt.	25	F	Unknown	09Ap02Hd
Patrick	20	M	Laborer	09Ap02Hd	MURTHA, Margt.	25	F	Unknown	09Ap02Hd
Anne	18	F	Unknown	09Ap02Hd	James	21	M	Laborer	09Ap02Hd
Bernd.	16	M	Unknown	09Ap02Hd	GAYNOR, Michl.	25	M	Laborer	09Ap02Hd
Bernd.	30	M	Unknown	09Ap02Hd	CAIN, Ellen	35	F	Unknown	09Ap02Hd
GRAHAM, Maria	27	F	Unknown	09Ap02Hd	BRERETON, James	25	M	Laborer	09Ap02Hd
James	24	M	Laborer	09Ap02Hd	KEEGAN, Willm.	25	M	Laborer	09Ap02Hd
Eliza	18	F	Unknown	09Ap02Hd	FEEGAN, Cathne.	18	F	Laborer	09Ap02Hd
David	16	M	Unknown	09Ap02Hd	MULLOWNEY, Michl.	27	M	Laborer	09Ap02Hd
John	14	M	Unknown	09Ap02Hd	MARTIN, Peter	20	M	Laborer	09Ap02Hd
Fanny	12	F	Unknown	09Ap02Hd	FARRELL, John	50	M	Laborer	09Ap02Hd
GERRATY, James	24	M	Laborer	09Ap02Hd	CUNNINGHAM, Michl.	30	M	Laborer	09Ap02Hd
Terence	18	M	Unknown	09Ap02Hd	MAHON, Mary	27	F	Unknown	09Ap02Hd
MURPHY, Patrick	26	M	Laborer	09Ap02Hd	CLARKE, Mary	19	F	Unknown	09Ap02Hd
MILLS, John	30	M	Laborer	09Ap02Hd	GRENNAN, Mary	17	F	Unknown	09Ap02Hd
FAHEY, Anne	35	F	Unknown	09Ap02Hd	FLANNAGAN, Michl.	22	M	Laborer	09Ap02Hd
KANE, Thos.	26	M	Farmer	09Ap02Hd	Maria	17	F	Unknown	09Ap02Hd
GOGARTY, Anne	21	F	Unknown	09Ap02Hd	CONROY, Ellen	15	F	Unknown	09Ap02Hd
KELLY, Abbey	32	F	Unknown	09Ap02Hd	MCGLYNN, Michl.	17	M	Farmer	09Ap02Hd
MCKEARNEY, Owen	18	M	Laborer	09Ap02Hd	James	15	M	Unknown	09Ap02Hd
Anne	25	F	Unknown	09Ap02Hd	REYNOLDS, Maria	30	F	Unknown	09Ap02Hd
MOONEY, Edwd.	20	M	Laborer	09Ap02Hd	CASEY, Fanny	20	F	Unknown	09Ap02Hd
HALEY, Michl.	18	M	Laborer	09Ap02Hd	REYNOLDS, Patrick	21	M	Laborer	09Ap02Hd
CORRIGAN, Luke	29	M	Laborer	09Ap02Hd	William	19	M	Laborer	09Ap02Hd
GIDDES, Joseph	34	M	Laborer	09Ap02Hd	PATTERSON, Margt.	17	F	Unknown	09Ap02Hd
Mathew	32	M	Laborer	09Ap02Hd	CUSHION, David	40	M	Laborer	09Ap02Hd
MCANALLY, Bridget	30	F	Unknown	09Ap02Hd	HANLEY, Patrick	15	M	Unknown	09Ap02Hd
FARRELLY, Jane	40	F	Unknown	09Ap02Hd	CURLAHAN, Maria	17	F	Unknown	09Ap02Hd
Peter	19	M	Laborer	09Ap02Hd	FLOOD, Eliza	13	F	Unknown	09Ap02Hd
Michael	17	M	Laborer	09Ap02Hd	CAHILL, Maria	20	F	Unknown	09Ap02Hd
James	13	M	Unknown	09Ap02Hd	ONEILL, Ann	35	F	Unknown	09Ap02Hd
Anne	11	F	Unknown	09Ap02Hd	MOORE, Lewis	19	M	Unknown	09Ap02Hd

NAMES OF PASSENGERS	AGE	SEX	OCCUPATIONS	DATE PORT SHIP
MCDONNELL, John	40	M	Unknown	09Ap02Hd
KELLY, Maria	20	F	Unknown	09Ap02Hd
CLOONER, Anne	18	F	Unknown	09Ap02Hd
FARRELL, Patrick	35	M	Laborer	09Ap02Hd
HALLIGAN, Thos.	21	M	Laborer	09Ap02Hd
John	19	M	Laborer	09Ap02Hd
MULORY, John	53	M	Laborer	09Ap02Hd
Ann	53	M	Unknown	09Ap02Hd
Michl.	20	M	Laborer	09Ap02Hd
Catharine	8	F	Child	09Ap02Hd
BEGLAN, Margt.	17	F	Unknown	09Ap02Hd
SCALLAN, Rose	18	F	Unknown	09Ap02Hd
GALLIGAN, Chas.	22	M	Laborer	09Ap02Hd
Peter	21	M	Laborer	09Ap02Hd
GILMARTIN, Willm.	20	M	Unknown	09Ap02Hd
HAY, James	14	M	Unknown	09Ap02Hd
GORDON, Willm.	23	M	Laborer	09Ap02Hd
Mary-Ann	20	F	Unknown	09Ap02Hd
RAFFERTY, Mathew	19	M	Farmer	09Ap02Hd
Eliza	17	F	Unknown	09Ap02Hd
MCGONNELL, Edwd.	25	M	Farmer	09Ap02Hd
FEGAN, Bernd.	30	M	Farmer	09Ap02Hd
FLYNN, Mary	19	F	Farmer	09Ap02Hd
Patrick	17	M	Farmer	09Ap02Hd
CONROY, Thomas	15	M	Unknown	09Ap02Hd
Honor	13	F	Unknown	09Ap02Hd
KIRWAN, Margt.	30	F	Unknown	09Ap02Hd
FARRELL, John	50	M	Laborer	09Ap02Hd
HOLOHAN, Thomas	25	M	Laborer	09Ap02Hd
Roger	21	M	Laborer	09Ap02Hd
William	19	M	Laborer	09Ap02Hd
HUGHES, Anne	17	F	Unknown	09Ap02Hd
NAUGHTEN, Cathne.	19	F	Unknown	09Ap02Hd
MONAGHAN, Bessy	30	F	Unknown	09Ap02Hd
REILLY, Mary	24	F	Unknown	09Ap02Hd
Thomas	17	M	Farmer	09Ap02Hd
MCGUIRE, Bernd.	18	M	Unknown	09Ap02Hd
Eliza	14	F	Unknown	09Ap02Hd
KELLAHER, Cathne.	22	F	Unknown	09Ap02Hd
Michl.	20	M	Farmer	09Ap02Hd
Mary	18	F	Unknown	09Ap02Hd
COOK, Bridget	67	F	Unknown	09Ap02Hd
REILLY, Ann	20	F	Unknown	09Ap02Hd
CROWE, Bridget	19	F	Unknown	09Ap02Hd
CORCORAN, Christy	25	M	Laborer	09Ap02Hd
Patrick	23	M	Laborer	09Ap02Hd
PHILLIPS, Rose	18	F	Unknown	09Ap02Hd
RIGAN, Pat	24	M	Laborer	09Ap02Hd
MCKENGAN, Elisa	25	F	Unknown	09Ap02Hd
William	3	M	Child	09Ap02Hd
Clarance	.11	M	Infant	09Ap02Hd
LOUTH, Mary	.11	F	Infant	09Ap02Hd
EAGAN, John	2	M	Child	09Ap02Hd
FARGHAN, Jno.	1	M	Child	09Ap02Hd
KEARNEN, Patrick	.11	M	Infant	09Ap02Hd
FITZPATRICK, Mary	.08	F	Infant	09Ap02Hd
QUIRK, Michael	.10	M	Infant	09Ap02Hd
KEARNON, Patrick	.11	M	Infant	09Ap02Hd
CLEARY, James	.11	M	Infant	09Ap02Hd
DALY, Mary	.11	F	Infant	09Ap02Hd
CALDWELL, Robt.	2	M	Child	09Ap02Hd
MULLIGAN, Jane	.03	F	Infant	09Ap02Hd
FOTHERY, Catherine	.08	F	Infant	09Ap02Hd
ODONNELL, Ellen	.06	F	Infant	09Ap02Hd
CONWAY, Margaret	.11	F	Infant	09Ap02Hd
HENRY, James	.04	M	Infant	09Ap02Hd
WHELAN, Mary	.05	F	Infant	09Ap02Hd
FITZGERALD, James	.00	M	Infant	09Ap02Hd

WABAN 10 APRIL 1850

From Liverpool

NAMES OF PASSENGERS	AGE	SEX	OCCUPATIONS	DATE PORT SHIP
MONTGOMERY, Dora	20	F	Seamstress	10Ap02He
QUINN, Danl.	42	M	Laborer	10Ap02He
BYRNE, John	17	M	Laborer	10Ap02He
Cath.	15	F	None	10Ap02He
Bridget	13	F	None	10Ap02He
MCDONNELL, Ellen	21	F	None	10Ap02He
MCGUINESS, Bridget	10	F	None	10Ap02He
Tim	4	M	Child	10Ap02He
TOOMEY, Margt.	25	F	None	10Ap02He
CONAUGHT, Rinland	22	M	Laborer	10Ap02He
SWEENEY, Denis	24	M	Laborer	10Ap02He
CHEENEY, John	24	M	Laborer	10Ap02He
LYONS, Thos.	24	M	Laborer	10Ap02He
FLYNN, Wm.	34	M	Laborer	10Ap02He
Cath.	24	F	Laborer	10Ap02He
John	.00	M	Infant	10Ap02He
COCHRANE, Danl.	40	M	Laborer	10Ap02He
Michl.	43	M	Laborer	10Ap02He
PURCELL, Dennis	20	M	Laborer	10Ap02He
CROWLEY, Fanny	25	F	None	10Ap02He
SULLIVAN, Ann	23	F	None	10Ap02He
MCGRATH, Jane	30	F	None	10Ap02He
DUNN, Mary	40	F	None	10Ap02He
Wm.	17	M	Laborer	10Ap02He
Cath.	10	F	Laborer	10Ap02He
Mary	8	F	Child	10Ap02He
GEARY, Johannah	20	F	Laborer	10Ap02He
FITZGERALD, Ellen	20	F	Laborer	10Ap02He
TOBIN, Wm.	30	M	Laborer	10Ap02He
James	20	M	Laborer	10Ap02He
HERBUT, Pat	40	M	Laborer	10Ap02He
LYONS, Danl.	23	M	Laborer	10Ap02He
COLIGAN, John	20	M	Laborer	10Ap02He
MORRIS, Mary	29	F	Laborer	10Ap02He
GALVIN, Lez.	20	F	Laborer	10Ap02He
BUCKLEY, Pat	26	M	Laborer	10Ap02He
Peggy	30	F	Laborer	10Ap02He
BURNS, Peggy	22	F	Laborer	10Ap02He
Mary	24	F	Laborer	10Ap02He
CONOR, Pat	19	M	Laborer	10Ap02He
MCCARTY, Jerry	24	M	Farmer	10Ap02He
James	20	M	Laborer	10Ap02He
CARTER, Mary	34	F	Unknown	10Ap02He
James	2	M	Child	10Ap02He
AGIN, Ant.	24	M	Unknown	10Ap02He
Mary	24	F	Unknown	10Ap02He
CUNNINGHAM, Thos.	23	M	Unknown	10Ap02He
Pat.	7	M	Child	10Ap02He
James	5	M	Child	10Ap02He
MOLONEY, Nora	25	F	Unknown	10Ap02He
HAYES, Tim	12	M	Unknown	10Ap02He
DOWELL, Mary	26	F	Unknown	10Ap02He
NEBIL, Tim	25	M	Unknown	10Ap02He
ABRAHAM, Moses	30	M	Unknown	10Ap02He
TALENT, Henry	30	M	Unknown	10Ap02He
CARSON, Pat	18	M	Unknown	10Ap02He
SMITH, John	21	M	Unknown	10Ap02He
WARD, Peter	22	M	Unknown	10Ap02He
Thos.	11	M	Unknown	10Ap02He
HART, Chris.	46	M	Unknown	10Ap02He
Eliza	42	F	Unknown	10Ap02He
Dorods	19	F	Unknown	10Ap02He
James	16	M	Unknown	10Ap02He
Elizabeth	13	F	Unknown	10Ap02He
Fanny	11	F	Unknown	10Ap02He

NAMES OF PASSENGERS	AGE	SEX	OCCUPATIONS	DATE PORT SHIP
HART, Christopher	9	M	Child	10Ap02He
Martha	6	F	Child	10Ap02He
Rebecca	4	F	Child	10Ap02He
George-H.	.00	M	Infant	10Ap02He
John	23	M	Unknown	10Ap02He
DEVOY, Mick	20	M	Unknown	10Ap02He
DENY, John	18	M	Unknown	10Ap02He
MARK, Danl.	24	M	Unknown	10Ap02He
Eliza	22	F	Unknown	10Ap02He
DEVOY, Biddy	22	F	Unknown	10Ap02He
Mary	20	F	Unknown	10Ap02He
ROACH, Ellen	14	F	Unknown	10Ap02He
MAGUIRE, Martha	40	F	Unknown	10Ap02He
James	20	M	Unknown	10Ap02He
Mick	18	M	Unknown	10Ap02He
Rosey	15	F	Unknown	10Ap02He
Matt	13	M	Unknown	10Ap02He
Peter	10	M	Unknown	10Ap02He
Mary	8	F	Child	10Ap02He
Christ.	5	M	Child	10Ap02He
John	3	M	Child	10Ap02He
HANNAH, Mark	24	M	Unknown	10Ap02He
MAGUIRE, John	22	M	Unknown	10Ap02He
MULLIN, John	23	M	Unknown	10Ap02He
HARE, Pat.	23	M	Unknown	10Ap02He
Sally	24	F	Unknown	10Ap02He
MAGANEY, Danl.	21	M	Unknown	10Ap02He
KING, Phillip	30	M	Unknown	10Ap02He
MCGRANE, Catherine	30	M	Unknown	10Ap02He
Pat	11	M	Unknown	10Ap02He
TOKEY, David	27	M	Unknown	10Ap02He
Mary	40	F	Unknown	10Ap02He
Nancy	38	F	Unknown	10Ap02He
Mary	14	F	Unknown	10Ap02He
MOONEY, Mary	30	M	Unknown	10Ap02He
ENGLISH, John	24	M	Unknown	10Ap02He
COFFEE, Wm.	25	M	Unknown	10Ap02He
RYAN, Margt.	22	F	Unknown	10Ap02He
BARNEY, James	17	M	Unknown	10Ap02He
WILLIAMS, Edwd.	25	M	Unknown	10Ap02He
Henry	25	M	Unknown	10Ap02He
U-Mrs.	20	F	Unknown	10Ap02He
Rebecca	.00	F	Infant	10Ap02He
KEENEY, Margt.	20	F	Unknown	10Ap02He
KOUL, Edwd.	16	M	Unknown	10Ap02He
Margt.	20	F	Unknown	10Ap02He
Honor	18	F	Unknown	10Ap02He
MCGRATH, David	32	M	Unknown	10Ap02He
MULLIN, Martin	19	M	Unknown	10Ap02He
Sarah	16	F	Unknown	10Ap02He
John	12	M	Unknown	10Ap02He
MCKIVEN, Mick	19	M	Unknown	10Ap02He
Peter	15	M	Unknown	10Ap02He
GOFNEY, Thos.	22	M	Unknown	10Ap02He
Cath.	25	F	Unknown	10Ap02He
COYLE, Mary	28	F	Unknown	10Ap02He
Charles	13	M	Unknown	10Ap02He
Rose	9	F	Child	10Ap02He
Patt	4	M	Child	10Ap02He
Cath.	.00	F	Infant	10Ap02He
FEGAN, Matt	20	M	Unknown	10Ap02He
GARRIGAN, Anne	40	F	Unknown	10Ap02He
REILY, Betty	30	F	Unknown	10Ap02He
HALON, James	30	M	Unknown	10Ap02He
FITZGERALD, Mary	30	F	Unknown	10Ap02He
Timy	20	M	Unknown	10Ap02He
COGHLAN, Johanna	18	F	Unknown	10Ap02He
WELLS, Thos.	24	M	Unknown	10Ap02He
DUNYSE, Cor.	50	M	Unknown	10Ap02He
KING, Mary	11	F	Unknown	10Ap02He
WHEEL, Pat	9	M	Child	10Ap02He
Mary	40	F	Unknown	10Ap02He
MURPHY, Anne	18	F	Unknown	10Ap02He
HAINE, James	23	M	Unknown	10Ap02He
CANNON, Pat	16	M	Unknown	10Ap02He

NAMES OF PASSENGERS	AGE	SEX	OCCUPATIONS	DATE PORT SHIP
CANNON, Pat	14	M	Unknown	10Ap02He
Susan	20	F	Unknown	10Ap02He
MCCARRUN, Rose	40	F	Unknown	10Ap02He
Mary	20	F	Unknown	10Ap02He
HENRY, Abraia	43	M	Unknown	10Ap02He
THOMPSON, Charles	22	M	Unknown	10Ap02He
BARKER, Thos.	40	M	Unknown	10Ap02He
Ellen	10	F	Unknown	10Ap02He
QUINN, Anne	20	F	Unknown	10Ap02He
FITZSIMONS, Mark	50	M	Unknown	10Ap02He
Cath.	50	F	Unknown	10Ap02He
Anne	18	F	Unknown	10Ap02He
Ellen	8	F	Child	10Ap02He
THOMPSON, Benjamin	22	M	Unknown	10Ap02He
HAYNE, Pat	15	M	Unknown	10Ap02He
HARRISON, Mary	50	F	Unknown	10Ap02He
CAIN, Sam	25	M	Unknown	10Ap02He
CARILY, Mich	18	M	Unknown	10Ap02He
RADY, Wm.	24	M	Unknown	10Ap02He
MULLIN, Thos.	24	M	Unknown	10Ap02He
ODOYLE, Mary	2	F	Child	10Ap02He
JOYCE, Kercy	22	F	Unknown	10Ap02He
Honora	18	F	Unknown	10Ap02He
Biddy	17	F	Unknown	10Ap02He
John	9	M	Child	10Ap02He
RAYNE, Pat	30	M	Unknown	10Ap02He
CARLLY, Anne	23	F	Unknown	10Ap02He
Mary	22	F	Unknown	10Ap02He
BYRNE, Wm.	25	M	Unknown	10Ap02He
TOBIN, Maurice	29	M	Unknown	10Ap02He
Johannah	26	F	Unknown	10Ap02He
Mary	8	F	Child	10Ap02He
Moris	.00	M	Infant	10Ap02He
DAVIS, Thos.	21	M	Unknown	10Ap02He
Jane	22	F	Unknown	10Ap02He
Fanny	3	F	Child	10Ap02He
VAUGH, John	26	M	Unknown	10Ap02He
MCDONNELL, Richd.	47	M	Unknown	10Ap02He
Dennis	17	M	Unknown	10Ap02He
James	12	M	Unknown	10Ap02He
Fanny	10	F	Unknown	10Ap02He
MCAULIFFE, John	26	M	Unknown	10Ap02He
CLIFFORD, Con.	22	M	Unknown	10Ap02He
LYNCH, Thos.	21	M	Unknown	10Ap02He
GORMAN, Judy	25	F	Unknown	10Ap02He
DANEHAN, Mary	22	F	Unknown	10Ap02He
HAYNE, Thos.	20	M	Unknown	10Ap02He
Margt.	19	F	Unknown	10Ap02He
BURKE, Thos.	14	M	Unknown	10Ap02He
CANT, Thos.	22	M	Unknown	10Ap02He
KEARNAN, Bridget	20	F	Unknown	10Ap02He
HARRIS, Geo.	19	M	Unknown	10Ap02He
EARLY, Peggy	20	F	Unknown	10Ap02He
Hugh	22	M	Unknown	10Ap02He
BOWES, Mick	30	M	Unknown	10Ap02He
CANLIFFE, Thos.	20	M	Unknown	10Ap02He
SMITH, John	20	M	Unknown	10Ap02He
MARTON, Thos.	20	M	Unknown	10Ap02He
MIDNEY, Josh.	20	M	Unknown	10Ap02He
Chas.	20	M	Unknown	10Ap02He
CONOFOR, Pat	24	M	Unknown	10Ap02He
BROPLEY, Mick	21	M	Unknown	10Ap02He
Patt	18	M	Unknown	10Ap02He
MCCAN, Richard	20	M	Unknown	10Ap02He
HOGAN, Mary	45	F	Unknown	10Ap02He
DELANEY, Thos.	20	M	Unknown	10Ap02He
FURLONG, John	20	M	Unknown	10Ap02He
CALDING, Anne	17	F	Unknown	10Ap02He
HEANEY, Thos.	20	M	Unknown	10Ap02He
MCCOY, Thos.	20	M	Unknown	10Ap02He
HARVEY, Mary	20	F	Unknown	10Ap02He
CONLY, Maurice	28	M	Unknown	10Ap02He
HOGAN, James	24	M	Unknown	10Ap02He
ADINSON, Wm.	24	M	Unknown	10Ap02He
FLEMMING, John	21	M	Unknown	10Ap02He

NAMES OF PASSENGERS	AGE	SEX	OCCUPATIONS	DATE PORT SHIP
KERFING, Dan	22	M	Unknown	10Ap02He
STAPLETON, Mary	22	F	Unknown	10Ap02He
CONOLEY, Ellen	17	F	Unknown	10Ap02He
MCCABLE, Mary	17	F	Unknown	10Ap02He
KELLY, Edwd.	36	M	Unknown	10Ap02He
Mary	36	F	Unknown	10Ap02He
Anne	.00	F	Infant	10Ap02He
MCCARTHY, Wm.	28	M	Unknown	10Ap02He
Johannah	28	F	Unknown	10Ap02He
Tim	25	M	Unknown	10Ap02He
Mick	21	M	Unknown	10Ap02He
Ellen	17	F	Unknown	10Ap02He
Johannah	18	F	Unknown	10Ap02He
John	8	M	Child	10Ap02He
MCCORMICK, Wm.	18	M	Unknown	10Ap02He
JEFFERSON, Car.	25	M	Unknown	10Ap02He
Bess	34	F	Unknown	10Ap02He
Mary	28	F	Unknown	10Ap02He
DWYRE, Patt	30	M	Unknown	10Ap02He
CONNOR, Ellen	24	F	Unknown	10Ap02He
GAVIN, Thos.	28	M	Unknown	10Ap02He
John	22	M	Unknown	10Ap02He
Lawrence	19	M	Unknown	10Ap02He
Neddy	24	M	Unknown	10Ap02He
DONNELL, Mary	50	F	Unknown	10Ap02He
Niddy	22	F	Unknown	10Ap02He
Nancy	20	F	Unknown	10Ap02He
Peggy	18	F	Unknown	10Ap02He
Patt	16	M	Unknown	10Ap02He
PAGE, Ann	21	F	Unknown	10Ap02He
FOX, Mary	20	F	Unknown	10Ap02He
CUMMINS, John	20	M	Unknown	10Ap02He
OWENS, Johanna	28	F	Unknown	10Ap02He
MCALLISSER, John	16	M	Unknown	10Ap02He
MUCATARE, Hugh	29	M	Unknown	10Ap02He
Prudence	22	F	Unknown	10Ap02He
John	2	M	Child	10Ap02He
Hugh	.00	M	Infant	10Ap02He
LEMINGS, James	27	M	Unknown	10Ap02He
SULLIVAN, Johannah	25	F	Unknown	10Ap02He
Patt	4	M	Child	10Ap02He
MURPHY, Thos.	27	M	Unknown	10Ap02He
HART, Wm.	40	M	Unknown	10Ap02He
COSGROVE, Jos.	47	M	Unknown	10Ap02He
MURPHY, Ellen	25	F	Unknown	10Ap02He
KEENE, Anne	23	F	Unknown	10Ap02He
OMEALY, Bridget	40	F	Unknown	10Ap02He
Bridget	9	F	Child	10Ap02He
John	7	M	Child	10Ap02He
Ellen	5	F	Child	10Ap02He
Martha	20	F	Unknown	10Ap02He
RYAN, Wm.	22	M	Unknown	10Ap02He
Anne	12	F	Unknown	10Ap02He
HENAN, Henery	22	M	Unknown	10Ap02He
CARR, Thos.	22	M	Unknown	10Ap02He
ARMSTRONG, Lawrence	30	M	Unknown	10Ap02He
CULLAN, Thos.	10	M	Unknown	10Ap02He
BYRNE, Catherine	17	F	Unknown	10Ap02He
HARPER, Mick	20	M	Unknown	10Ap02He
KELLY, Mick	24	M	Unknown	10Ap02He
BURKE, Thos.	24	M	Unknown	10Ap02He
HUDSON, Mark	19	M	Unknown	10Ap02He
WHELAN, John	19	M	Unknown	10Ap02He
DALLY, Allen	22	M	Unknown	10Ap02He
CONLY, Danl.	20	M	Unknown	10Ap02He

WM.D.SEWELL 11 APRIL 1850

From Liverpool

NAMES OF PASSENGERS	AGE	SEX	OCCUPATIONS	DATE PORT SHIP
LOUGHNON, Patrick	20	M	Laborer	11Ap02Hc
ROGERS, John	27	M	Laborer	11Ap02Hc
FEANY, Michel	30	M	Laborer	11Ap02Hc
RYLEY, John	21	M	Tailor	11Ap02Hc
FEANY, James	27	M	Laborer	11Ap02Hc
RHYON, Laurence	22	M	Laborer	11Ap02Hc
DORSEY, Thos.	32	M	Laborer	11Ap02Hc
BURNES, Thos.	30	M	Laborer	11Ap02Hc
CONOR, Dennis	35	M	Laborer	11Ap02Hc
SULLIVAN, John	23	M	Laborer	11Ap02Hc
SOLOVAN, Danl.	20	M	Laborer	11Ap02Hc
LAWRAN, Eliza	28	F	Unknown	11Ap02Hc
DONHOUGH, Patrick	25	M	Laborer	11Ap02Hc
Wm.	22	M	Laborer	11Ap02Hc
Michael	18	M	Laborer	11Ap02Hc
John	14	M	Laborer	11Ap02Hc
Mary	20	F	Laborer	11Ap02Hc
Bridget	12	F	Laborer	11Ap02Hc
LIDDA, Mary	20	F	Unknown	11Ap02Hc
DIGAN, Thos.	45	M	Laborer	11Ap02Hc
Wm.	35	M	Laborer	11Ap02Hc
DUFFEY, Cath.	23	F	Unknown	11Ap02Hc
CASTLE, Susan	18	F	Unknown	11Ap02Hc
PEARSON, Thomas	31	M	Miner	11Ap02Hc
Jane	26	F	Miner	11Ap02Hc
NEVIL, Abraham	45	M	Laborer	11Ap02Hc
Margt.	30	F	Laborer	11Ap02Hc
Mary-Ann	7	F	Child	11Ap02Hc
Bridget	5	F	Child	11Ap02Hc
U	.00	U	Infant	11Ap02Hc
MONY, John	33	M	Laborer	11Ap02Hc
Ellen	50	F	Laborer	11Ap02Hc
Martin	20	M	Laborer	11Ap02Hc
Eliza	17	F	Laborer	11Ap02Hc
Ellen	15	F	Laborer	11Ap02Hc
LYNCH, Allis	23	F	Unknown	11Ap02Hc
U	.00	U	Infant	11Ap02Hc
DAYLEY, Margt.	21	F	Dressmaker	11Ap02Hc
WAYLAND, Michael	26	M	Laborer	11Ap02Hc
CONBOY, Patrick	20	M	Laborer	11Ap02Hc
DULY, Jeremiah	22	M	Laborer	11Ap02Hc
WAYLIN, Bridget	26	F	Unknown	11Ap02Hc
GATHLIN, Peter	21	M	Laborer	11Ap02Hc
John	12	M	Laborer	11Ap02Hc
MICKMAYON, Cath.	50	F	Unknown	11Ap02Hc
Allis	14	F	Unknown	11Ap02Hc
Michael	11	M	Unknown	11Ap02Hc
Darby	5	M	Child	11Ap02Hc
BRAYHONY, Bridget	14	F	Unknown	11Ap02Hc
DRYER, John	20	M	Laborer	11Ap02Hc
BURN, Betsy	19	F	Unknown	11Ap02Hc
Mary	26	F	Unknown	11Ap02Hc
CARL, Thos.	22	M	Laborer	11Ap02Hc
RUNNYHEAD, Michael	20	M	Laborer	11Ap02Hc
GIBLAN, Lawrence	40	M	Cooper	11Ap02Hc
Ellen	12	F	Cooper	11Ap02Hc
CODRICK, Thos.	20	M	Laborer	11Ap02Hc
COUSIN, Danl.	36	M	Laborer	11Ap02Hc
David	36	M	Laborer	11Ap02Hc
Jane	30	F	Laborer	11Ap02Hc
Mary	3	F	Child	11Ap02Hc
U	.00	U	Infant	11Ap02Hc
SHEHENE, Patrick	25	M	Laborer	11Ap02Hc
Edward	28	M	Laborer	11Ap02Hc
BETTLES, John	21	M	Laborer	11Ap02Hc

NAMES OF PASSENGERS	AGE	SEX	OCCUPATIONS	DATE PORT SHIP
BOYD, Wm.	24	M	Laborer	11Ap02Hc
MICKENLEY, Mathew	27	M	Laborer	11Ap02Hc
James	46	M	Laborer	11Ap02Hc
Rosa	42	F	Laborer	11Ap02Hc
Bryan	18	M	Laborer	11Ap02Hc
Mary	16	F	Laborer	11Ap02Hc
Laurence	14	M	Laborer	11Ap02Hc
Thos.	12	M	Laborer	11Ap02Hc
James	5	M	Child	11Ap02Hc
Margaret	20	F	Laborer	11Ap02Hc
BURNES, James	22	M	Laborer	11Ap02Hc
Mary-Jane	22	F	Laborer	11Ap02Hc
U	.00	U	Infant	11Ap02Hc
KELLY, Elizabeth	19	F	Unknown	11Ap02Hc
Arthur	14	M	Unknown	11Ap02Hc
BURNES, Eastern	26	M	Farmer	11Ap02Hc
Martha	27	F	Farmer	11Ap02Hc
U	.00	U	Infant	11Ap02Hc
BYLEY, John	50	M	Farmer	11Ap02Hc
Biddey	45	F	Farmer	11Ap02Hc
Mary	18	F	Farmer	11Ap02Hc
Nancy	16	F	Farmer	11Ap02Hc
Burley	15	M	Farmer	11Ap02Hc
Nancy	11	F	Farmer	11Ap02Hc
ODONNEL, James	35	M	Farmer	11Ap02Hc
Mary	24	F	Farmer	11Ap02Hc
Phillip	3	M	Child	11Ap02Hc
U	.00	U	Infant	11Ap02Hc
DAYLEY, Ann	20	F	Unknown	11Ap02Hc
Cath.	27	F	Unknown	11Ap02Hc
Margt.	19	F	Unknown	11Ap02Hc
BURN, Dennis	22	M	Baker	11Ap02Hc
RAY, James	22	M	Laborer	11Ap02Hc
SMALL, Gibson	25	M	Laborer	11Ap02Hc
CANNADY, Patrick	23	M	Laborer	11Ap02Hc
TOBAN, James	23	M	Laborer	11Ap02Hc
CAPPEY, Nicholas	45	M	Laborer	11Ap02Hc
MAGUYRE, James	20	M	Laborer	11Ap02Hc
DELLAHUNTY, Richard	31	M	Laborer	11Ap02Hc
John	32	M	Tailor	11Ap02Hc
DOLIN, Mary	25	F	Unknown	11Ap02Hc
PADDLE, Julia	17	F	Unknown	11Ap02Hc
PHELAN, Cath.	18	F	Dressmaker	11Ap02Hc
DOLONHANTZ, Patk.	37	M	Laborer	11Ap02Hc
Norry	21	F	Laborer	11Ap02Hc
PURCELL, Patk.	20	M	Spinner	11Ap02Hc
Ellen	19	F	Spinster	11Ap02Hc
DREW, Danl.	48	M	Farmer	11Ap02Hc
Patk.	19	M	Farmer	11Ap02Hc
Mary	18	F	Farmer	11Ap02Hc
Danl.	13	M	Farmer	11Ap02Hc
GILMARTIN, Mary	18	F	Unknown	11Ap02Hc
CONNEL, Patk.	20	M	Laborer	11Ap02Hc
SAXTON, John	23	M	Laborer	11Ap02Hc
MURPHY, John	20	M	Laborer	11Ap02Hc
Jeremiah	16	M	Laborer	11Ap02Hc
ROBERTS, Michael	22	M	Laborer	11Ap02Hc
LONG, John	28	M	Laborer	11Ap02Hc
HALEY, Mary	30	F	Unknown	11Ap02Hc
FITZGERALD, Patk.	40	M	Laborer	11Ap02Hc
GRANT, Ellen	16	F	Unknown	11Ap02Hc
FITZGERALD, Mary	9	F	Child	11Ap02Hc
Ellen	7	F	Child	11Ap02Hc
ONEIL, Patk.	20	M	Laborer	11Ap02Hc
GIBSON, Patk.	21	M	Laborer	11Ap02Hc
MONOHAN, Patk.	14	M	Laborer	11Ap02Hc
SMITH, Thos.	26	M	Laborer	11Ap02Hc
Mary	30	F	Unknown	11Ap02Hc
Betsy	35	F	Unknown	11Ap02Hc
Lawrence	32	M	Laborer	11Ap02Hc
MEGUYON, Mary	25	F	Unknown	11Ap02Hc
HENESSY, Thomas	24	M	Laborer	11Ap02Hc
COLLIN, Julia	26	F	Unknown	11Ap02Hc
John	28	M	Unknown	11Ap02Hc
MAROR, Augan	24	M	Laborer	11Ap02Hc
BURK, John	25	M	Laborer	11Ap02Hc
Betsy	23	F	Unknown	11Ap02Hc
CONNEL, John	24	M	Laborer	11Ap02Hc
BURRY, John	24	M	Laborer	11Ap02Hc
KELLY, Wm.	21	M	Laborer	11Ap02Hc
NORRIS, Michael	27	M	Laborer	11Ap02Hc
Margt.	25	F	Laborer	11Ap02Hc
Mary	4	F	Child	11Ap02Hc
CALIGHAN, Danl.	23	M	Laborer	11Ap02Hc
BURN, Edwd.	25	M	Laborer	11Ap02Hc
Mary	24	F	Laborer	11Ap02Hc
U	.00	U	Infant	11Ap02Hc
Hugh	3	M	Child	11Ap02Hc
NASTIN, Thomas	2	M	Child	11Ap02Hc
KARIN, John	32	M	Laborer	11Ap02Hc
Margt.	24	F	Laborer	11Ap02Hc
U	.00	U	Infant	11Ap02Hc
BRIEN, John	30	M	Laborer	11Ap02Hc
WING, John	25	M	Laborer	11Ap02Hc
CANON, John	24	M	Laborer	11Ap02Hc
MAHON, Rose	18	F	Laborer	11Ap02Hc
Michl.	16	M	Laborer	11Ap02Hc
HAND, Andrew	21	M	Laborer	11Ap02Hc
MACKMAN, Mary	28	F	Unknown	11Ap02Hc
Julia	8	F	Child	11Ap02Hc
George	4	M	Child	11Ap02Hc
SHECKLESON, John	35	M	Laborer	11Ap02Hc
Sophia	30	F	Laborer	11Ap02Hc
Charity	5	F	Child	11Ap02Hc
Hannah-M.	3	F	Child	11Ap02Hc
U	.00	U	Infant	11Ap02Hc
ANDERSON, Margt.	9	F	Child	11Ap02Hc
MACCARTY, Catherine	25	F	Unknown	11Ap02Hc
U	.00	U	Infant	11Ap02Hc
CONLEE, Patk.	26	M	Laborer	11Ap02Hc
WARD, Henry	15	M	Laborer	11Ap02Hc
CONLEY, Catherine	20	F	Unknown	11Ap02Hc
CURY, Mary	30	F	Unknown	11Ap02Hc
DAVISON, John	48	M	Farmer	11Ap02Hc
Marthey	16	F	Farmer	11Ap02Hc
MACCARTY, Thomas	20	M	Laborer	11Ap02Hc
GOLOYBY, Mary	40	F	Unknown	11Ap02Hc
WARD, Catherine	19	F	Unknown	11Ap02Hc
NUNAN, Honora	50	F	Unknown	11Ap02Hc
Edmund	22	M	Laborer	11Ap02Hc
BRAIN, Bridget	26	F	Unknown	11Ap02Hc
LYNCH, Catherine	40	F	Unknown	11Ap02Hc
Simon	17	M	Unknown	11Ap02Hc
Bridget	13	F	Unknown	11Ap02Hc
Ann	18	F	Unknown	11Ap02Hc
KERR, Patk.	46	M	Farmer	11Ap02Hc
Ann	60	F	Unknown	11Ap02Hc
Ellen	30	F	Unknown	11Ap02Hc
Edward	17	M	Unknown	11Ap02Hc
Ann	11	F	Unknown	11Ap02Hc
Owen	28	M	Unknown	11Ap02Hc
MCCABE, Mary	16	F	Unknown	11Ap02Hc
MACKEN, George	50	M	Unknown	11Ap02Hc
NORRIS, Edward	30	M	Unknown	11Ap02Hc
TONN, William	25	M	Unknown	11Ap02Hc
CAHILL, Michael	21	M	Unknown	11Ap02Hc
LOCHNINE, John	60	M	Unknown	11Ap02Hc
Cath.	60	F	Unknown	11Ap02Hc
Michael	26	M	Unknown	11Ap02Hc
Mary	21	F	Unknown	11Ap02Hc
Patrick	12	M	Unknown	11Ap02Hc
MAGUIRE, John	28	M	Unknown	11Ap02Hc
Eliza	22	F	Unknown	11Ap02Hc
Margt.	18	F	Unknown	11Ap02Hc
U	.00	U	Infant	11Ap02Hc
CAHAN, Ellen	19	F	Unknown	11Ap02Hc
AGIN, Marion	19	F	Unknown	11Ap02Hc
COCKLEY, Eliza	16	F	Unknown	11Ap02Hc
BRYAN, Bridget	18	F	Unknown	11Ap02Hc
John	28	M	Unknown	11Ap02Hc

NAMES OF PASSENGERS	AGE	SEX	OCCUPATIONS	DATE PORT SHIP
FELAN, Patrick	19	M	Unknown	11Ap02Hc
CORMER, Thos.	17	M	Unknown	11Ap02Hc
DONNEL, Theodore	30	M	Unknown	11Ap02Hc
DORSEY, Mary	40	F	Unknown	11Ap02Hc
Susan	11	F	Unknown	11Ap02Hc
Patrick	22	M	Unknown	11Ap02Hc
Margt.	14	F	Unknown	11Ap02Hc
DOLAN, Betsy	20	F	Unknown	11Ap02Hc
WALPOOLE, Cath.	20	F	Unknown	11Ap02Hc
CONLEY, Moriah	20	F	Unknown	11Ap02Hc
Margt.	25	F	Unknown	11Ap02Hc
Francis	15	M	Unknown	11Ap02Hc
U	.00	U	Infant	11Ap02Hc
KING, Francis	18	M	Unknown	11Ap02Hc
ROBERTS, Robert	25	M	Unknown	11Ap02Hc
Sarah	22	F	Unknown	11Ap02Hc
U	.00	U	Infant	11Ap02Hc
THOMAS, Robert	27	M	Unknown	11Ap02Hc
Ann	21	F	Unknown	11Ap02Hc
WELSH, Wm.	58	M	Unknown	11Ap02Hc
WADE, Michl.	54	M	Unknown	11Ap02Hc
Mary	40	F	Unknown	11Ap02Hc
Cath.	15	F	Unknown	11Ap02Hc
Jonah	7	M	Child	11Ap02Hc
PENDERGRASS, James	43	M	Unknown	11Ap02Hc
Elizabeth	38	F	Unknown	11Ap02Hc
Jonah	8	M	Child	11Ap02Hc
Thos.	3	M	Child	11Ap02Hc
U	.00	U	Infant	11Ap02Hc
HARRINGTON, Dennis	20	M	Unknown	11Ap02Hc
SULLIVAN, Danl.	23	M	Unknown	11Ap02Hc
BYRNE, Hugh	30	M	Unknown	11Ap02Hc
MCGOVERN, Peter	30	M	Unknown	11Ap02Hc
CURTIS, Cornelius	36	M	Unknown	11Ap02Hc
LANE, Judy	30	F	Unknown	11Ap02Hc
KANE, Michael	20	M	Unknown	11Ap02Hc
BURKE, John	22	M	Unknown	11Ap02Hc
Jerry	20	M	Unknown	11Ap02Hc
Ann	16	F	Unknown	11Ap02Hc
Dennis	17	M	Unknown	11Ap02Hc
RYAN, James	24	M	Unknown	11Ap02Hc
HARRIS, James	30	M	Unknown	11Ap02Hc
Phillip	6	M	Child	11Ap02Hc
Mary	4	F	Child	11Ap02Hc
John	20	M	Unknown	11Ap02Hc
DAGNA, Mary	40	F	Unknown	11Ap02Hc
John	8	M	Child	11Ap02Hc
Edwd.	6	M	Child	11Ap02Hc
Mary	4	F	Child	11Ap02Hc
U	.00	U	Infant	11Ap02Hc
MULDRY, Mary	30	F	Unknown	11Ap02Hc
COSGROVE, Sophia	24	F	Unknown	11Ap02Hc
DOWNEY, Patk.	23	M	Unknown	11Ap02Hc
Thos.	19	M	Unknown	11Ap02Hc
John	25	M	Unknown	11Ap02Hc
GERTY, Eliza	18	F	Unknown	11Ap02Hc
CONNOR, Mary	25	F	Unknown	11Ap02Hc
Margt.	23	F	Unknown	11Ap02Hc
Ellen	20	F	Unknown	11Ap02Hc
FALLIN, Michael	30	M	Unknown	11Ap02Hc
CUDDYHEAD, John	21	M	Unknown	11Ap02Hc
ROYSTER, Richard	35	M	Unknown	11Ap02Hc
LYNCH, Wm.	15	M	Unknown	11Ap02Hc
NEVILE, Samuel	14	M	Unknown	11Ap02Hc
HONSLEY, Saml.	27	M	Unknown	11Ap02Hc

DANUBE 13 APRIL 1850

From Liverpool

NAMES OF PASSENGERS	AGE	SEX	OCCUPATIONS	DATE PORT SHIP
TIMBRELL, Robt.	24	M	Shoemaker	13Ap02Gw
Ann	23	F	Unknown	13Ap02Gw
Emma	2	F	Child	13Ap02Gw
Thoms.	22	M	Laborer	13Ap02Gw
PLUMKETT, Judy	30	F	Unknown	13Ap02Gw
Thoms.	9	M	Child	13Ap02Gw
James	7	M	Child	13Ap02Gw
Mary	5	F	Child	13Ap02Gw
Owen	.00	M	Infant	13Ap02Gw
WHELAN, Pat.	30	M	Laborer	13Ap02Gw
PAUL, Martha	26	F	Unknown	13Ap02Gw
BUCK, Jas.	20	M	Laborer	13Ap02Gw
SHEENAN, Margt.	25	F	Unknown	13Ap02Gw
FERRAGHTY, James	27	M	Laborer	13Ap02Gw
HIGGINS, Bryan	60	M	Farmer	13Ap02Gw
Cathe.	13	F	Unknown	13Ap02Gw
GOUGH, Bud	25	M	Laborer	13Ap02Gw
GALAGHER, Michl.	22	M	Laborer	13Ap02Gw
Mary	20	F	Unknown	13Ap02Gw
MCGRAH, Cathe.	20	F	Unknown	13Ap02Gw
TIERNEY, James	20	M	Laborer	13Ap02Gw
CARTY, Mick	18	M	Laborer	13Ap02Gw
DIVINE, Bessy	21	F	Unknown	13Ap02Gw
Mary	13	F	Unknown	13Ap02Gw
WILLIS, James	21	M	Laborer	13Ap02Gw
WHITE, Ann	23	F	Unknown	13Ap02Gw
DEARDEN, Willm.	50	M	Laborer	13Ap02Gw
SCOLLY, Bud	35	M	Unknown	13Ap02Gw
SHEE, Jno.	5	M	Child	13Ap02Gw
DEVANY, Thos.	22	M	Laborer	13Ap02Gw
MORAN, Ann	20	F	Unknown	13Ap02Gw
LYONS, Martin	20	M	Laborer	13Ap02Gw
HALEY, Pat	32	M	Laborer	13Ap02Gw
EDWARDS, John	27	M	Laborer	13Ap02Gw
DOYLE, Cath.	22	F	Unknown	13Ap02Gw
CATON, Jno.	21	M	Laborer	13Ap02Gw
Susan	22	F	Unknown	13Ap02Gw
COUGHLAN, Jas.	14	M	Laborer	13Ap02Gw
KEEGAN, Ellen	18	F	Unknown	13Ap02Gw
READING, Thos.	24	M	Laborer	13Ap02Gw
LYNCH, Pat	22	M	Laborer	13Ap02Gw
HEFFRON, Honor	26	F	Unknown	13Ap02Gw
LEE, Pat	45	M	Laborer	13Ap02Gw
Ann	14	F	Unknown	13Ap02Gw
Willm.	12	M	Unknown	13Ap02Gw
FERRY, Bridget	24	F	Unknown	13Ap02Gw
GUNN, Mary	34	F	Unknown	13Ap02Gw
Sarah	14	F	Unknown	13Ap02Gw
WARNOCK, Rose	18	F	Unknown	13Ap02Gw
PURCELL, James	19	M	Laborer	13Ap02Gw
GARVEY, Sarah	24	F	Laborer	13Ap02Gw
Sarah	4	F	Child	13Ap02Gw
James	3	M	Child	13Ap02Gw
Pat	.00	M	Infant	13Ap02Gw
MCGINNIS, John	20	M	Laborer	13Ap02Gw
FLINN, Ann	18	F	Unknown	13Ap02Gw
BOYLE, Rose	30	F	Unknown	13Ap02Gw
Bud	23	M	Unknown	13Ap02Gw
CURTIS, Michl.	17	M	Unknown	13Ap02Gw
CLINTON, Cath.	18	F	Unknown	13Ap02Gw
ADAMS, Mary-A.	26	F	Unknown	13Ap02Gw
Mary	.00	F	Infant	13Ap02Gw
CALLAN, Ellen	20	F	Unknown	13Ap02Gw
JENNINGS, James	22	M	Laborer	13Ap02Gw
RING, Thos.	22	M	Laborer	13Ap02Gw

NAMES OF PASSENGERS	A G E	S E X	OCCUPATIONS	DATE PORT SHIP
CUNNINGHAM, Jno.	20	M	Laborer	13Ap02Gw
MCCORMICK, Mick	22	M	Laborer	13Ap02Gw
Edw.	17	M	Laborer	13Ap02Gw
MURRY, Edw.	20	M	Laborer	13Ap02Gw
KELLY, Thoms.	22	M	Laborer	13Ap02Gw
OHARA, Pat	35	M	Laborer	13Ap02Gw
FALLON, Brid.	25	F	Unknown	13Ap02Gw
COOGAN, Mich	20	M	Farmer	13Ap02Gw
ROBINSON, Jno.	20	M	Farmer	13Ap02Gw
DONOHUE, Brid.	20	F	Unknown	13Ap02Gw
Margt.	18	F	Unknown	13Ap02Gw
MURTAGH, Jams.	25	M	Laborer	13Ap02Gw
COYLE, Bern.	22	M	Laborer	13Ap02Gw
KEOGH, Pat	30	M	Laborer	13Ap02Gw
HASLINGTON, Math.	40	M	Laborer	13Ap02Gw
Mary	30	F	Laborer	13Ap02Gw
Mary	8	F	Child	13Ap02Gw
Jane	3	F	Child	13Ap02Gw
MCGAHAN, James	18	M	Laborer	13Ap02Gw
MCGUIRE, Cath.	20	F	Laborer	13Ap02Gw
LEE, Mary	20	F	Laborer	13Ap02Gw
FEERICK, Jno.	20	M	Laborer	13Ap02Gw
HOGAN, Martin	30	M	Laborer	13Ap02Gw
HUGHES, Pat	30	M	Laborer	13Ap02Gw
MORGAN, Mary	35	F	Unknown	13Ap02Gw
PEARSON, Jacob	22	M	Laborer	13Ap02Gw
MCLAREN, Wm.	35	M	Laborer	13Ap02Gw
PRICE, James	29	M	Laborer	13Ap02Gw
RILEY, Mary	22	F	Unknown	13Ap02Gw
BRADY, Cath.	19	F	Unknown	13Ap02Gw
MILLS, Jno.	22	M	Laborer	13Ap02Gw
Dinah	20	F	Unknown	13Ap02Gw
CARROLL, John	25	M	Laborer	13Ap02Gw
OBRIEN, James	22	M	Laborer	13Ap02Gw
CONNER, Michl.	20	M	Laborer	13Ap02Gw
DONOVAN, Cathe.	22	F	Unknown	13Ap02Gw
MULCAHY, John	29	M	Laborer	13Ap02Gw
MURLY, Ann	23	F	Unknown	13Ap02Gw
BOYLAN, Chs.	28	M	Laborer	13Ap02Gw
GREEN, Josh.	20	M	Laborer	13Ap02Gw
John	21	M	Laborer	13Ap02Gw
CORCORAN, Richd.	23	M	Laborer	13Ap02Gw
Ellen	21	F	Unknown	13Ap02Gw
GARVEY, Willm.	32	M	Laborer	13Ap02Gw
LAWLER, Mary	20	F	Unknown	13Ap02Gw
GARVEY, John	18	M	Laborer	13Ap02Gw
Michl.	14	M	Unknown	13Ap02Gw
CLINTON, Pat	35	M	Unknown	13Ap02Gw
MCDONNELL, John	30	M	Unknown	13Ap02Gw
Michl.	5	M	Child	13Ap02Gw
TORMEY, Pat	15	M	Unknown	13Ap02Gw
Mary	12	F	Unknown	13Ap02Gw
NEAL, Pat	30	M	Laborer	13Ap02Gw
DOYLE, Ann	24	F	Unknown	13Ap02Gw
HICKEY, Thoms.	17	M	Laborer	13Ap02Gw
WELSH, Pat	27	M	Laborer	13Ap02Gw
SMITH, Phil	35	M	Laborer	13Ap02Gw
SWEENY, Bridget	20	F	Unknown	13Ap02Gw
TRACY, Sarah	20	F	Unknown	13Ap02Gw
DIGAN, John	27	M	Laborer	13Ap02Gw
WHOLOHAN, Brid.	17	F	Unknown	13Ap02Gw
DONNOLLY, Brid.	20	F	Unknown	13Ap02Gw
HALINN, Thos.	14	M	Laborer	13Ap02Gw
BROWN, Margt.	4	F	Child	13Ap02Gw
Mary	10	F	Unknown	13Ap02Gw
MILLS, Cathe.	30	F	Unknown	13Ap02Gw
Julia	25	F	Unknown	13Ap02Gw
MARTIN, Ann	18	F	Unknown	13Ap02Gw
TAGGART, Hugh	24	M	Laborer	13Ap02Gw
MURPHEY, John	35	M	Laborer	13Ap02Gw
KELLY, Bridgt.	18	F	Unknown	13Ap02Gw
THORNTON, Cath.	37	F	Unknown	13Ap02Gw
John	7	M	Child	13Ap02Gw
Sarah	9	F	Child	13Ap02Gw
SAUNDERS, Lawrence	25	M	Laborer	13Ap02Gw
LYNCH, Pat	17	M	Laborer	13Ap02Gw
KEEGAN, Andrew	28	M	Laborer	13Ap02Gw
GREY, Margt.	20	F	Unknown	13Ap02Gw
QUIRK, John	22	M	Laborer	13Ap02Gw
ONEILL, Mary	21	F	Unknown	13Ap02Gw
Jane	19	F	Unknown	13Ap02Gw
ALLEN, Thomas	12	M	Carpenter	13Ap02Gw
Mary	10	F	Carpenter	13Ap02Gw
MCMAHONE, James	22	M	Laborer	13Ap02Gw
CARROLL, Bernard	25	M	Laborer	13Ap02Gw
ONEIL, Thoms.	17	M	Laborer	13Ap02Gw
MANNIX, Johan	35	M	Laborer	13Ap02Gw
Jeremiah	7	M	Child	13Ap02Gw
CULL, Thoms.	30	M	Laborer	13Ap02Gw
BUTLER, John	19	M	Laborer	13Ap02Gw
KILDAY, Thoms.	30	M	Laborer	13Ap02Gw
MORAN, John	13	M	Laborer	13Ap02Gw
MALLIN, Peter	40	M	Laborer	13Ap02Gw
MCQUADE, Owen	20	M	Laborer	13Ap02Gw
CASSIDY, Maria	10	F	Unknown	13Ap02Gw
BEIRNE, James	18	M	Laborer	13Ap02Gw
Margt.	10	F	Unknown	13Ap02Gw
MCWEENY, Ann	16	F	Unknown	13Ap02Gw
CLINTON, John	22	M	Laborer	13Ap02Gw
FALLON, Brid.	17	F	Unknown	13Ap02Gw
BEATEY, Thoms.	20	M	Laborer	13Ap02Gw
DELANY, Cath.	19	M	Laborer	13Ap02Gw
ONEAL, Mick	19	M	Laborer	13Ap02Gw
LYONS, Sally	20	F	Unknown	13Ap02Gw
CONNELL, Pat	25	M	Laborer	13Ap02Gw
Margt.	20	F	Unknown	13Ap02Gw
MAHONEY, Edward	22	M	Tailor	13Ap02Gw
KEATON, John	21	M	Tailor	13Ap02Gw
DONOVAN, Cath.	25	F	Unknown	13Ap02Gw
KELCHER, Cath.	25	F	Unknown	13Ap02Gw
LOMBARD, Willm.	20	M	Laborer	13Ap02Gw
KELLEY, Willm.	25	M	Laborer	13Ap02Gw
Margaret	20	F	Unknown	13Ap02Gw
FOX, Philip	21	M	Laborer	13Ap02Gw
Mary	18	F	Unknown	13Ap02Gw
SMITH, Benj.	20	M	Dyer	13Ap02Gw
FLYNN, William	21	M	Laborer	13Ap02Gw
John	22	M	Unknown	13Ap02Gw
Cath.	16	F	Unknown	13Ap02Gw
MALOY, Ann	18	F	Unknown	13Ap02Gw
CORMICK, Bridget	21	F	Unknown	13Ap02Gw
HYNES, Margaret	18	F	Unknown	13Ap02Gw
MANNY, Cathe.	19	F	Unknown	13Ap02Gw
Ellen	17	F	Unknown	13Ap02Gw
GIBNEY, Mary	19	F	Unknown	13Ap02Gw
NOWLAN, Tim.	30	M	Laborer	13Ap02Gw
ARTERY, John	21	M	Laborer	13Ap02Gw
CLINTON, Judy	35	F	Unknown	13Ap02Gw
SHERRY, Philip	20	M	Laborer	13Ap02Gw
CAHILL, Mary	35	F	Unknown	13Ap02Gw
John	10	M	Unknown	13Ap02Gw
Honor	9	F	Child	13Ap02Gw
Bridget	7	F	Child	13Ap02Gw
Judy	5	F	Child	13Ap02Gw
JULIAN, Betty	25	F	Unknown	13Ap02Gw
NOWLAN, Garret	25	M	Laborer	13Ap02Gw
Bridget	20	F	Unknown	13Ap02Gw
LAWLER, Mary	17	F	Unknown	13Ap02Gw
FEENEY, Sally	35	F	Unknown	13Ap02Gw
Cath.	7	F	Child	13Ap02Gw
Eliza	4	F	Child	13Ap02Gw
Mary	3	F	Child	13Ap02Gw
Margarett	20	F	Unknown	13Ap02Gw
MCMENOMY, Edward	42	M	Laborer	13Ap02Gw
MCMAKIN, Edw.	23	M	Laborer	13Ap02Gw
BUTLER, Mary	40	F	Unknown	13Ap02Gw
Mick	18	M	Laborer	13Ap02Gw
Ellen	12	F	Laborer	13Ap02Gw
John	9	M	Child	13Ap02Gw
Betsey	8	F	Child	13Ap02Gw

NAMES OF PASSENGERS	AGE	SEX	OCCUPATIONS	DATE PORT SHIP
CONNELLY, Thos.	45	M	Laborer	13Ap02Gw
Eliza	35	F	Unknown	13Ap02Gw
Ann	14	F	Unknown	13Ap02Gw
James	13	M	Unknown	13Ap02Gw
Mary	12	F	Unknown	13Ap02Gw
Owen	9	M	Child	13Ap02Gw
Elisa	7	F	Child	13Ap02Gw
Thomas	4	M	Child	13Ap02Gw
HANGHEY, Mick	13	M	Unknown	13Ap02Gw
RILEY, Mary	20	F	Unknown	13Ap02Gw
Bridget	18	F	Unknown	13Ap02Gw
GAHAGAN, Mary	22	F	Unknown	13Ap02Gw
Pat	.00	M	Infant	13Ap02Gw
DUNN, James	40	M	Farmer	13Ap02Gw
Eliza	30	F	Unknown	13Ap02Gw
Pat	12	M	Unknown	13Ap02Gw
Thomas	10	M	Unknown	13Ap02Gw
John	8	M	Child	13Ap02Gw
Joseph	6	M	Child	13Ap02Gw
Peter	.00	M	Infant	13Ap02Gw
BRAWLEY, Margaret	28	F	Unknown	13Ap02Gw
COADY, William	25	M	Laborer	13Ap02Gw
Cathe.	20	F	Unknown	13Ap02Gw
FARRELL, Mary	25	F	Unknown	13Ap02Gw
BRIEN, Lawrencre	20	M	Laborer	13Ap02Gw
Michl.	21	M	Laborer	13Ap02Gw
SWALWELL, Robt.	30	M	Laborer	13Ap02Gw
Ann	34	F	Unknown	13Ap02Gw
RICK, Margt.	50	F	Unknown	13Ap02Gw
John	20	M	Laborer	13Ap02Gw
Jeremiah	18	M	Unknown	13Ap02Gw
Rich.	16	M	Unknown	13Ap02Gw
Pat	14	M	Unknown	13Ap02Gw
Margt.	12	F	Unknown	13Ap02Gw
Michl.	8	M	Child	13Ap02Gw
HARTY, Dennis	30	M	Laborer	13Ap02Gw
MCCARTY, Michl.	18	M	Unknown	13Ap02Gw
CONWAY, Margt.	21	F	Unknown	13Ap02Gw
Robt.	.00	M	Infant	13Ap02Gw
GRIMES, Cathe.	20	F	Unknown	13Ap02Gw
RILEY, John	20	M	Laborer	13Ap02Gw
WHELAN, Thoms.	16	M	Unknown	13Ap02Gw
Margt.	16	F	Unknown	13Ap02Gw
QUINN, Neil	20	M	Laborer	13Ap02Gw
NEVIN, James	40	M	Unknown	13Ap02Gw
John	26	M	Unknown	13Ap02Gw
HOLMES, William	30	M	Unknown	13Ap02Gw
PARK, John	25	M	Unknown	13Ap02Gw
DOYLE, Willm.	22	M	Unknown	13Ap02Gw
CARNEY, Mark	20	M	Unknown	13Ap02Gw
TAYLOR, Eliza	25	F	Unknown	13Ap02Gw

CENTURION 13 APRIL 1850

From Liverpool

MCCUE, Pat	45	M	Farmer	13Ap02Db
Brid.	50	F	Unknown	13Ap02Db
Pat	17	M	Unknown	13Ap02Db
John	11	M	Unknown	13Ap02Db
TENNESSEY, Michael	45	M	Unknown	13Ap02Db
Brid.	45	F	Unknown	13Ap02Db
Ellen	22	F	Unknown	13Ap02Db
Cath.	18	F	Unknown	13Ap02Db
Pat	12	M	Unknown	13Ap02Db
Mary	7	F	Child	13Ap02Db
Joseph	9	M	Child	13Ap02Db
Ally	2	F	Child	13Ap02Db
MCCONKY, Sarah	28	F	Unknown	13Ap02Db
MCCONKY, Ann	11	F	Unknown	13Ap02Db
Betty	7	F	Child	13Ap02Db
GLEESON, Mary	.00	F	Infant	13Ap02Db
KENNEDY, Mary	18	F	Unknown	13Ap02Db
Alice	12	F	Unknown	13Ap02Db
DELANEY, Ellen	34	F	Unknown	13Ap02Db
Ellen	.00	F	Infant	13Ap02Db
KELLY, James	22	M	Unknown	13Ap02Db
MCGEE, John	21	M	Unknown	13Ap02Db
LAING, Edwd.	21	M	Unknown	13Ap02Db
LITTLE, Margt.	21	F	Unknown	13Ap02Db
OCONNELL, Michl.	18	M	Unknown	13Ap02Db
COTTER, John	20	M	Unknown	13Ap02Db
HARKNESS, Rose	16	F	Unknown	13Ap02Db
HOOLIGAN, Wm.	24	M	Unknown	13Ap02Db
FREELY, Pat	25	M	Unknown	13Ap02Db
Mary	20	F	Unknown	13Ap02Db
LYONS, Cath.	20	F	Unknown	13Ap02Db
DURKIN, Oliver	30	M	Unknown	13Ap02Db
GRAHAM, Margt.	30	F	Unknown	13Ap02Db
HAGAN, Wm.	13	M	Unknown	13Ap02Db
Mary	16	F	Unknown	13Ap02Db
Cath.	22	F	Unknown	13Ap02Db
Ellen	21	F	Unknown	13Ap02Db
Pat	21	M	Unknown	13Ap02Db
Peggy	14	F	Unknown	13Ap02Db
HOLLY, Jere.	21	M	Unknown	13Ap02Db
PRENDERGAST, James	21	M	Unknown	13Ap02Db
QUILLARD, Michl.	22	M	Unknown	13Ap02Db
LINDRIGAN, Alice	16	F	Unknown	13Ap02Db
WHITE, Ellen	23	F	Unknown	13Ap02Db
PRENDERGAST, Jeffery	40	M	Unknown	13Ap02Db
Peggy	13	F	Farmer	13Ap02Db
Michl.	22	M	Unknown	13Ap02Db
William	23	M	Unknown	13Ap02Db
SPELLMAN, Pat	19	M	Unknown	13Ap02Db
TENNESSEY, Richd.	35	M	Unknown	13Ap02Db
FLULLENY, Terrence	23	M	Unknown	13Ap02Db
LYNCH, Edwd.	21	M	Unknown	13Ap02Db
SUTHERLAND, Arthur	20	M	Unknown	13Ap02Db
MCKEVITT, Jane	14	F	Unknown	13Ap02Db
TRACY, Michl.	30	M	Unknown	13Ap02Db
HYSETT, Arthur	21	M	Unknown	13Ap02Db
WOOD, George	25	M	Mason	13Ap02Db
ANDERSON, John	26	M	Laborer	13Ap02Db
Isabella	20	F	Unknown	13Ap02Db
BORGALL, Thos.	24	M	Farmer	13Ap02Db
Cath.	21	F	Unknown	13Ap02Db
MAHONEY, Pat	24	M	Unknown	13Ap02Db
CONNOLS, Cath.	18	F	Unknown	13Ap02Db
KENNEDY, Margt.	20	F	Unknown	13Ap02Db
FOLEY, Luke	21	M	Unknown	13Ap02Db
Cath.	20	F	Unknown	13Ap02Db
WALSH, John	23	M	Unknown	13Ap02Db
Bridget	50	F	Unknown	13Ap02Db
CASSIDY, Cath.	25	F	Unknown	13Ap02Db
CONNOLLY, James	55	M	Unknown	13Ap02Db
NICHOLSON, Wm.	33	M	Unknown	13Ap02Db
Jane	33	F	Unknown	13Ap02Db
Thos.	.00	M	Infant	13Ap02Db
STANGER, Thos.	40	M	Unknown	13Ap02Db
Margt.	28	F	Unknown	13Ap02Db
Thos.	2	M	Child	13Ap02Db
Wm.	.00	M	Infant	13Ap02Db
MAHER, Mary	3	F	Child	13Ap02Db
MCCLEARY, Jno.	20	M	Unknown	13Ap02Db
BRYAN, Terrence	26	M	Unknown	13Ap02Db
DUNNING, Honor	26	F	Unknown	13Ap02Db
GRACE, Cath.	35	F	Unknown	13Ap02Db
Richd.	40	M	Unknown	13Ap02Db
Margt.	.00	F	Infant	13Ap02Db
Ellen	.00	F	Infant	13Ap02Db
FAHY, James	35	M	Unknown	13Ap02Db
FITZGERALD, James	30	M	Unknown	13Ap02Db
MAHEN, John	28	M	Unknown	13Ap02Db

NAMES OF PASSENGERS	AGE	SEX	OCCUPATIONS	DATE PORT SHIP
LYONS, Phil	30	M	Unknown	13Ap02Db
KELLY, Law.	25	M	Unknown	13Ap02Db
HINES, Brid.	19	F	Unknown	13Ap02Db
RYAN, Judy	19	F	Unknown	13Ap02Db
STAFFERN, Ellen	40	F	Unknown	13Ap02Db
Mary	8	F	Child	13Ap02Db
Berret	6	M	Child	13Ap02Db
James	4	M	Child	13Ap02Db
Margt.	.00	F	Infant	13Ap02Db
LAMB, Mary	20	F	Unknown	13Ap02Db
POOLE, Joseph	40	M	Unknown	13Ap02Db
U-Mrs.	30	F	Unknown	13Ap02Db
MCGORRON, Pat	25	M	Unknown	13Ap02Db
Rose	19	F	Unknown	13Ap02Db
Brid.	.00	F	Infant	13Ap02Db
Betsy	18	F	Unknown	13Ap02Db
KELLY, John	20	M	Unknown	13Ap02Db
HAYES, John	28	M	Unknown	13Ap02Db
ORMOND, John	32	M	Weaver	13Ap02Db
John	8	M	Child	13Ap02Db
LILLEY, John	50	M	Unknown	13Ap02Db
MIDGEBY, Andrew	25	M	Unknown	13Ap02Db
U-Mrs.	26	F	Unknown	13Ap02Db
PARKER, Richd.	30	M	Unknown	13Ap02Db
U-Mrs.	31	F	Unknown	13Ap02Db
Rose	3	F	Child	13Ap02Db
LAURENSON, Peter	33	M	Unknown	13Ap02Db
Wm.	21	M	Unknown	13Ap02Db
REAGAN, James	60	M	Unknown	13Ap02Db
Mick	23	M	Unknown	13Ap02Db
BRAIN, David	18	M	Unknown	13Ap02Db
LORAN, Margt.	16	F	Unknown	13Ap02Db
CUNNINGHAM, Lawrence	40	M	Unknown	13Ap02Db
LAWRENCE, Edward	30	M	Laborer	13Ap02Db
Wm.	22	M	Laborer	13Ap02Db
John	20	M	Laborer	13Ap02Db
BOUGHAN, Richd.	34	M	Farmer	13Ap02Db
Eliza	34	F	Unknown	13Ap02Db
GLEESON, Mary	38	F	Unknown	13Ap02Db
Margt.	10	F	Unknown	13Ap02Db
Pat	6	M	Child	13Ap02Db
John	2	M	Child	13Ap02Db
STEPHENSON, Thos.	23	M	Weaver	13Ap02Db
MARSHALL, Henry	23	M	Farmer	13Ap02Db
MITCHELL, John	27	M	Unknown	13Ap02Db
HOYER, John	26	M	Unknown	13Ap02Db
HOLDING, Josh.	24	M	Painter	13Ap02Db
JOHNSON, Chas.	25	M	Unknown	13Ap02Db
TOMLINSON, John	24	M	Cbtmkr	13Ap02Db
WALKER, Martha	31	M	Carpenter	13Ap02Db
Thos.	8	M	Child	13Ap02Db
Mary-A.	6	F	Child	13Ap02Db
James	4	M	Child	13Ap02Db
Alice	2	F	Child	13Ap02Db
KILLINBECK, Jos.	25	M	Blacksmith	13Ap02Db
SHAW, James	30	M	Farmer	13Ap02Db
BUTTERWORTH, James	40	M	Unknown	13Ap02Db
WAREHAM, Thos.	30	M	Unknown	13Ap02Db
LIVE, Robt.	30	M	Unknown	13Ap02Db
U-Mrs.	25	F	Unknown	13Ap02Db
James	4	M	Child	13Ap02Db
KEARNEY, John	35	M	Unknown	13Ap02Db
Betsy	20	F	Unknown	13Ap02Db
Cath.	25	F	Unknown	13Ap02Db
SCANLON, Mary	25	F	Unknown	13Ap02Db
WHITE, Brid	18	F	Unknown	13Ap02Db
MAHER, Rodger	35	M	Unknown	13Ap02Db
Mary	30	F	Unknown	13Ap02Db
LIDDY, John	2	M	Child	13Ap02Db
Kitty	.00	F	Infant	13Ap02Db
BRYAN, John	9	M	Child	13Ap02Db
BOHAN, Mary	30	F	Unknown	13Ap02Db
Biddy	3	F	Child	13Ap02Db
Pat	1	M	Child	13Ap02Db
Died-At-Sea				
QUIN, Nancy	40	F	Unknown	13Ap02Db
Mary	23	F	Unknown	13Ap02Db
James	18	M	Unknown	13Ap02Db
Pat	13	M	Unknown	13Ap02Db
CLARKE, Edwd.	47	M	Unknown	13Ap02Db
Brid.	47	F	Unknown	13Ap02Db
Mary	47	F	Unknown	13Ap02Db
KEINAN, Ann	19	F	Unknown	13Ap02Db
MADDEN, Bernd.	20	M	Unknown	13Ap02Db
Ann	50	F	Unknown	13Ap02Db
James	10	M	Unknown	13Ap02Db
DEVINE, Pat	2	M	Child	13Ap02Db
FORSYTH, Mary	20	F	Unknown	13Ap02Db
GRADY, Johan	30	M	Unknown	13Ap02Db
Ellen	18	F	Unknown	13Ap02Db
MCCARTY, Danl.	19	M	Unknown	13Ap02Db
John	40	M	Unknown	13Ap02Db
CUMMISKY, Margt.	15	F	Unknown	13Ap02Db
GILLISPIE, Danl.	25	M	Unknown	13Ap02Db
KELLY, Thos.	20	M	Unknown	13Ap02Db
CONROY, Danl.	18	M	Unknown	13Ap02Db
COSGROVE, Mary	20	F	Unknown	13Ap02Db
LAWLESS, James	18	M	Unknown	13Ap02Db
CURLEY, John	18	M	Unknown	13Ap02Db
BIRMINGHAM, Ellen	22	F	Unknown	13Ap02Db
CASEY, Margt.	25	F	Unknown	13Ap02Db
BRIEN, Thomas	13	M	Unknown	13Ap02Db
GANLEY, Pat	25	M	Unknown	13Ap02Db
Ann	27	F	Unknown	13Ap02Db
Ann	.00	F	Infant	13Ap02Db
Wm.	2	M	Child	13Ap02Db
Michl.	25	M	Unknown	13Ap02Db
CLONAN, Thos.	23	M	Unknown	13Ap02Db
MOORE, Maria	21	F	Unknown	13Ap02Db
DEAN, Ann	18	F	Unknown	13Ap02Db
KEAN, Honor	22	F	Unknown	13Ap02Db
HANNING, Peter	31	M	Unknown	13Ap02Db
U-Mrs.	22	F	Unknown	13Ap02Db
Wm.	9	M	Child	13Ap02Db
John	7	M	Child	13Ap02Db
Henry	5	M	Child	13Ap02Db
James	.00	M	Infant	13Ap02Db
JOHNSON, Peter	57	M	Unknown	13Ap02Db
U-Mrs.	53	F	Unknown	13Ap02Db
TAYLOR, Robt.	30	M	Unknown	13Ap02Db
U-Mrs.	32	F	Unknown	13Ap02Db
DAWSON, John	.00	M	Infant	13Ap02Db
MOAG, Ann	20	F	Unknown	13Ap02Db
Mary	3	F	Child	13Ap02Db
Jos.	.00	M	Infant	13Ap02Db
POWER, Mick	36	M	Unknown	13Ap02Db
Wm.	25	M	Unknown	13Ap02Db
BRENNAN, Tim	21	M	Unknown	13Ap02Db
KIELY, John	40	M	Unknown	13Ap02Db
REYNOLDS, John	17	M	Unknown	13Ap02Db
BLAKERY, Geo.	18	M	Merchant	13Ap02Db
BRIAN, Denis	31	M	Farmer	13Ap02Db
Margt.	25	F	Unknown	13Ap02Db
Cath.	2	F	Child	13Ap02Db
RYAN, Willm.	25	M	Unknown	13Ap02Db
Sally	40	F	Unknown	13Ap02Db
Nancy	28	F	Unknown	13Ap02Db
John	6	M	Child	13Ap02Db
Ellen	18	F	Unknown	13Ap02Db
CONNELL, Johan	18	F	Unknown	13Ap02Db
DURVEN, John	20	M	Unknown	13Ap02Db
Mary	20	F	Unknown	13Ap02Db
Margt.	19	F	Unknown	13Ap02Db
Hugh	17	M	Unknown	13Ap02Db
John	13	M	Unknown	13Ap02Db
James	12	M	Unknown	13Ap02Db
Pat	5	M	Child	13Ap02Db
Margaret	.06	F	Infant	13Ap02Db
CALLAGHAN, Mary	18	F	Unknown	13Ap02Db
DOWNEY, William	20	M	Unknown	13Ap02Db

NAMES OF PASSENGERS	AGE	SEX	OCCUPATIONS	DATE PORT SHIP
MADDEN, Mick	22	M	Unknown	13Ap02Db
BRODERICK, John	21	M	Unknown	13Ap02Db
FRANCIS, Jane	25	F	Unknown	13Ap02Db
Debby	.00	F	Infant	13Ap02Db
RORCK, Ellen	18	F	Unknown	13Ap02Db
NOWLAN, Martin	21	M	Unknown	13Ap02Db
HARWOOD, John	20	M	Unknown	13Ap02Db
MCKENNA, John	40	M	Unknown	13Ap02Db
Cath.	40	F	Unknown	13Ap02Db
Cath.	60	F	Unknown	13Ap02Db
John	8	M	Child	13Ap02Db
Pat	6	M	Child	13Ap02Db
Brian	2	M	Child	13Ap02Db
GORMAN, Ann	20	F	Unknown	13Ap02Db
FOGARTY, Pat	25	M	Unknown	13Ap02Db
RUAL, Philip	23	M	Unknown	13Ap02Db
FRANNY, Thomas	24	M	Unknown	13Ap02Db
MACKIE, Judy	22	F	Unknown	13Ap02Db
FOGARTY, Anty	12	F	Unknown	13Ap02Db
Cath	4	F	Child	13Ap02Db
Margt.	18	F	Unknown	13Ap02Db
FRANNAN, Biddy	28	F	Unknown	13Ap02Db
GLEESON, Julia	20	F	Unknown	13Ap02Db
BURKE, Julia	20	F	Unknown	13Ap02Db
NOWLAN, Sally	30	F	Unknown	13Ap02Db
SLACK, Luke	28	M	Dressmaker	13Ap02Db
Ann	24	F	Unknown	13Ap02Db
Priscilla	1	F	Child	13Ap02Db
BRENNAN, John	40	M	Farmer	13Ap02Db
James	22	M	Farmer	13Ap02Db
Dennis	16	M	Farmer	13Ap02Db
CAVANAGH, James	60	M	Farmer	13Ap02Db
Catherine	40	F	Farmer	13Ap02Db
Peter	18	M	Farmer	13Ap02Db
James	15	M	Farmer	13Ap02Db
Ellen	13	F	Farmer	13Ap02Db
Rose	11	F	Farmer	13Ap02Db
Morris	10	M	Unknown	13Ap02Db
Mary	6	F	Child	13Ap02Db
Eliza	.00	F	Infant	13Ap02Db
Catherine	20	F	Unknown	13Ap02Db
BURN, John	35	M	Unknown	13Ap02Db
Margt.	25	F	Unknown	13Ap02Db
Mary	6	F	Child	13Ap02Db
Thos.	3	M	Child	13Ap02Db
Cath.	3	F	Child	13Ap02Db
James	.00	M	Infant	13Ap02Db
Died-At-Sea				
Ann	.00	F	Infant	13Ap02Db
DAWSON, Jos.	33	M	Unknown	13Ap02Db
Ann	.00	F	Infant	13Ap02Db
John	33	M	Farmer	13Ap02Db
CULLINER, Owen	32	M	Unknown	13Ap02Db
Alicia	19	F	Unknown	13Ap02Db
Owen	.00	M	Infant	13Ap02Db
WHALEN, John	45	M	Unknown	13Ap02Db
HERRING, Mary	22	F	Unknown	13Ap02Db
BRADY, John	40	M	Unknown	13Ap02Db
Pat	40	M	Unknown	13Ap02Db
Ann	40	F	Unknown	13Ap02Db
Ann	9	F	Child	13Ap02Db
OWENS, Margt.	18	F	Unknown	13Ap02Db
FAIN, Mary	40	F	Unknown	13Ap02Db
Cath.	11	F	Unknown	13Ap02Db
Nich	14	M	Unknown	13Ap02Db
Mary	9	F	Child	13Ap02Db
Thos.	8	M	Child	13Ap02Db
OFARRELL, Wm.	21	M	Unknown	13Ap02Db
U-Mrs.	23	F	Unknown	13Ap02Db
COHEN, Ellen	13	F	Unknown	13Ap02Db
Ann	10	F	Unknown	13Ap02Db
LOVEDAY, William	45	M	Unknown	13Ap02Db
U-Mrs.	37	F	Unknown	13Ap02Db
Julius	15	M	Unknown	13Ap02Db
Douglass	9	M	Child	13Ap02Db

NAMES OF PASSENGERS	AGE	SEX	OCCUPATIONS	DATE PORT SHIP
LOVEDAY, Harry	5	M	Child	13Ap02Db
L.	1	F	Child	13Ap02Db
HIND, Pat	26	M	Unknown	13Ap02Db
GIBBONS, James	24	M	Unknown	13Ap02Db
Martin	20	M	Unknown	13Ap02Db
TOBIN, John	26	M	Farmer	13Ap02Db
FITZGERALD, Michl.	24	M	Unknown	13Ap02Db
CALLEN, Elijah	23	M	Unknown	13Ap02Db
PHILIPPS, Joseph	31	M	Potter	13Ap02Db
U-Mrs.	30	U	Potter	13Ap02Db
MCKENNA, John	20	M	Farmer	13Ap02Db
Margt.	25	F	Unknown	13Ap02Db
SMITH, Ann	14	F	Unknown	13Ap02Db
DOOLAN, Biddy	25	F	Unknown	13Ap02Db
CAFFERY, James	28	M	Unknown	13Ap02Db
CROMPTON, Wm.	25	M	Unknown	13Ap02Db
Francis	27	M	Unknown	13Ap02Db
WICKLIFF, Joseph	26	M	Unknown	13Ap02Db
Margt.	24	F	Unknown	13Ap02Db
ROARKE, Cath.	22	F	Unknown	13Ap02Db
GRAINGER, John	45	M	Unknown	13Ap02Db
U-Mrs.	45	F	Unknown	13Ap02Db
Ann	17	F	Unknown	13Ap02Db
James	12	M	Unknown	13Ap02Db
William	12	M	Unknown	13Ap02Db
Jane	9	F	Child	13Ap02Db
Elizabeth	3	F	Child	13Ap02Db
Ann	.00	F	Infant	13Ap02Db
HOWARD, Mark	26	M	Paper Maker	13Ap02Db
FARROW, Handel	26	M	Spinner	13Ap02Db
U-Mrs.	26	F	Unknown	13Ap02Db
HANDICK, Michl.	30	M	Farmer	13Ap02Db
FARY, Mick	23	M	Unknown	13Ap02Db
MCGUNNIN, Martin	21	M	Unknown	13Ap02Db
FARRELL, Pat	20	M	Unknown	13Ap02Db
John	00	M	Unknown	13Ap02Db
MCHUAIN, Edwd.	20	M	Farmer	13Ap02Db
John	17	M	Unknown	13Ap02Db
CORRIGAN, Isabel	20	F	Unknown	13Ap02Db
OBRIEN, John	20	M	Unknown	13Ap02Db
ARMSTRONG, James	50	M	Unknown	13Ap02Db
Eliz.	14	F	Unknown	13Ap02Db
GRAHAM, Eliz.	22	F	Unknown	13Ap02Db
Margt.	20	F	Unknown	13Ap02Db
LITTLE, Cath.	18	F	Unknown	13Ap02Db
WRIGHT, Martha	29	F	Unknown	13Ap02Db
Mary	14	F	Unknown	13Ap02Db
LAWRENCE, John	8	M	Child	13Ap02Db
Wm.	6	M	Child	13Ap02Db
Thos.	3	M	Child	13Ap02Db
Mary	2	F	Child	13Ap02Db
CLARE, Pierce	20	M	Unknown	13Ap02Db
KELLY, Thos.	36	M	Unknown	13Ap02Db
Kiernan	5	M	Child	13Ap02Db
Mary	3	F	Child	13Ap02Db
MOON, Ann	19	F	Unknown	13Ap02Db
GEOGHEGAN, Biddy	16	F	Unknown	13Ap02Db
FINNEGAN, Owen	23	M	Unknown	13Ap02Db
LIDDY, Ann	30	F	Unknown	13Ap02Db
Pat	11	M	Unknown	13Ap02Db
Wm.	6	M	Child	13Ap02Db
James	4	M	Child	13Ap02Db
NOEL, Mary	00	F	Unknown	13Ap02Db
EVERS, John	57	M	Carpenter	13Ap02Db
Emma	14	F	Unknown	13Ap02Db
RAMSDEN, Isaac	21	M	Laborer	13Ap02Db
CAMPBELL, Han.	26	M	Unknown	13Ap02Db
TOBIAS, Philip	25	M	Unknown	13Ap02Db
HANNELLY, James	30	M	Unknown	13Ap02Db
MCKENNA, Law	25	M	Unknown	13Ap02Db
Chris.	22	F	Unknown	13Ap02Db
Jerrin	14	M	Unknown	13Ap02Db
GORNLY, Wm.	26	M	Unknown	13Ap02Db
Bridgt.	.00	F	Infant	13Ap02Db
BROWN, Brid.	20	F	Unknown	13Ap02Db

NAMES OF PASSENGERS	AGE	SEX	OCCUPATIONS	DATE PORT SHIP
FARLEY, Brid.	20	F	Unknown	13Ap02Db
MCGINNESS, Ann	28	F	Unknown	13Ap02Db
CAFFRIN, Chris	40	F	Unknown	13Ap02Db
CARLEN, Jas.	10	M	Unknown	13Ap02Db
Mary	26	F	Unknown	13Ap02Db
ELLIS, William	28	M	Grocer	13Ap02Db
Mary	29	F	Unknown	13Ap02Db
Mary	.00	F	Infant	13Ap02Db
DIAMOND, Jas.	28	M	Farmer	13Ap02Db
U-Mrs.	28	F	Unknown	13Ap02Db
DURRHAM, U	20	M	Unknown	13Ap02Db
Died-At-Sea				
WERD, U	22	M	Unknown	13Ap02Db
HARDT, U-Miss	20	F	Unknown	13Ap02Db
DEFFERN, Pat	18	M	Unknown	13Ap02Db
BRIEN, Ann	34	F	Unknown	13Ap02Db
GERALD, Geo.	22	M	Carpenter	13Ap02Db
Jane	20	F	Unknown	13Ap02Db
HALL, George	53	M	Farmer	13Ap02Db
TONRPHY, Phil	22	M	Unknown	13Ap02Db
DIGGIDEN, Pat	23	M	Unknown	13Ap02Db
LOWRY, J.	40	M	Unknown	13Ap02Db
Mary	30	F	Unknown	13Ap02Db
Pat	40	M	Unknown	13Ap02Db
GEE, Abra.	28	M	Spinner	13Ap02Db
FERSUSS, U-Mrs.	49	F	Farmer	13Ap02Db
George	13	M	Unknown	13Ap02Db
Anna	10	F	Unknown	13Ap02Db
GLEDHILL, Mary	26	F	Unknown	13Ap02Db
WALWORTH, Joseph	25	M	Minister	13Ap02Db
ARMSTRONG, George	15	M	Unknown	13Ap02Db
LOVEDAY, J.	18	F	Spinster	13Ap02Db
Matilda	13	F	Unknown	13Ap02Db
Clair	11	F	Unknown	13Ap02Db
Annette	7	F	Child	13Ap02Db
GRIFFIS, Willm.	30	M	Sgns	13Ap02Db

QUEEN-OF-THE-WEST 13 APRIL 1850

From Liverpool

NAMES OF PASSENGERS	AGE	SEX	OCCUPATIONS	DATE PORT SHIP
DWYER, Catharine	18	F	Servant	13Ap02Dg
CONNELY, Mick	50	M	Farmer	13Ap02Dg
Bridget	50	F	Farmer	13Ap02Dg
Ann	30	F	Farmer	13Ap02Dg
DOWN, Honor	11	F	Farmer	13Ap02Dg
Miles	9	M	Child	13Ap02Dg
MCGOVERN, Bridget	5	F	Child	13Ap02Dg
HORAN, John	20	M	Servant	13Ap02Dg
GRIFFIN, Mick	12	M	Servant	13Ap02Dg
FLANNAGAN, Edwd.	17	M	Clerk	13Ap02Dg
GIVEN, Cathr.	20	F	Seamstress	13Ap02Dg
SMITH, Hugh	18	M	Servant	13Ap02Dg
LAINEY, Ellen	18	F	Unknown	13Ap02Dg
TORNEY, Chas.	19	M	Unknown	13Ap02Dg
Catharine	19	F	Servant	13Ap02Dg
HENNESSY, Wm.	30	M	Unknown	13Ap02Dg
CONNOR, Ellen	18	F	Unknown	13Ap02Dg
DOYLE, Etty	40	F	Unknown	13Ap02Dg
Pat	.00	M	Infant	13Ap02Dg
P.	4	U	Child	13Ap02Dg
QUINN, Mick	50	M	Unknown	13Ap02Dg
Mary	23	F	Unknown	13Ap02Dg
Julia	18	F	Unknown	13Ap02Dg
Eliza	8	F	Child	13Ap02Dg
DOYLE, Mary	16	F	Unknown	13Ap02Dg
Peter	14	M	Unknown	13Ap02Dg
SALT, Sarah	30	F	Unknown	13Ap02Dg
James	8	M	Child	13Ap02Dg

NAMES OF PASSENGERS	AGE	SEX	OCCUPATIONS	DATE PORT SHIP
PURCELL, Margaret	14	F	Farmer	13Ap02Dg
GUNNING, Harriet	18	F	Seamstress	13Ap02Dg
MILLER, Jas.	25	M	Unknown	13Ap02Dg
MITCHELL, Celia	17	F	Unknown	13Ap02Dg
Maria	20	F	Unknown	13Ap02Dg
Mick	22	M	Unknown	13Ap02Dg
Ann	18	F	Farmer	13Ap02Dg
KEEGAN, John-Jr.	21	M	Trader	13Ap02Dg
BYRNES, Margt.	18	F	Unknown	13Ap02Dg
COYLE, Peter	26	M	Unknown	13Ap02Dg
FLINN, Margt.	16	F	Unknown	13Ap02Dg
SMITH, James	24	M	Farmer	13Ap02Dg
MAGENNIS, Cath.	17	F	Seamstress	13Ap02Dg
Ellen	15	F	Seamstress	13Ap02Dg
MCCABE, Law.	18	M	Unknown	13Ap02Dg
BROPHY, Ellen	18	F	Servant	13Ap02Dg
MCELROY, Mick	17	M	Farmer	13Ap02Dg
PATTENHAME, Wm.	18	M	Laborer	13Ap02Dg
FAULKNER, Cath.	30	F	Seamstress	13Ap02Dg
FINNELLY, Ellen	18	F	Seamstress	13Ap02Dg
CLARKIN, Ann	19	F	Seamstress	13Ap02Dg
Cath.	12	F	Servant	13Ap02Dg
MASTERSON, Margt.	18	F	Servant	13Ap02Dg
TURNER, Ann	22	F	Servant	13Ap02Dg
CRONNIN, Cath.	20	F	Weaver	13Ap02Dg
KIENAN, Peter	50	M	Weaver	13Ap02Dg
KEENAN, Cath.	45	F	Weaver	13Ap02Dg
George	20	M	Weaver	13Ap02Dg
Peter	16	M	Weaver	13Ap02Dg
Ann	13	F	Weaver	13Ap02Dg
Thos.	12	M	Weaver	13Ap02Dg
MCGAUGHEN, Mary	18	F	Weaver	13Ap02Dg
Michl.	16	M	Weaver	13Ap02Dg
REILLY, Phil.	18	M	Weaver	13Ap02Dg
CONNOR, Pat	33	M	Mason	13Ap02Dg
DALTON, Cath.	18	F	Servant	13Ap02Dg
MCGUNN, Jas.	40	M	Servant	13Ap02Dg
Brid.	50	F	Servant	13Ap02Dg
Jas.	18	M	Laborer	13Ap02Dg
WHELAN, Cath.	30	F	Servant	13Ap02Dg
Mary	9	F	Child	13Ap02Dg
Brid.	2	F	Child	13Ap02Dg
Danl.	5	M	Child	13Ap02Dg
Mick	.00	M	Infant	13Ap02Dg
BURKE, Danl.	25	M	Laborer	13Ap02Dg
MORAN, Danl.	18	M	Laborer	13Ap02Dg
CASEY, Maria	18	F	Seamstress	13Ap02Dg
CAREY, F.	18	U	Laborer	13Ap02Dg
PATTERSON, Wm.	30	M	Smith	13Ap02Dg
MOONEY, Cath.	21	F	Servant	13Ap02Dg
Brid.	25	F	Servant	13Ap02Dg
Cath.	16	F	Servant	13Ap02Dg
CAMPBELL, Cath.	18	F	Servant	13Ap02Dg
Fras.	18	M	Servant	13Ap02Dg
BOOMER, Wm.	20	M	Servant	13Ap02Dg
MCCURDLE, Mary	45	F	Servant	13Ap02Dg
Jas.	14	M	Servant	13Ap02Dg
Bridget	12	F	Servant	13Ap02Dg
Rose	10	F	Servant	13Ap02Dg
Mary	8	F	Child	13Ap02Dg
Margt.	6	F	Child	13Ap02Dg
Jno.	5	M	Child	13Ap02Dg
Peter	3	M	Child	13Ap02Dg
FEGAN, Alice	17	F	Servant	13Ap02Dg
CULLEN, Henry	30	M	Servant	13Ap02Dg
FAGAN, Mick	40	M	Servant	13Ap02Dg
Maria	40	F	Servant	13Ap02Dg
Mary-Ann	14	F	Unknown	13Ap02Dg
Law.	12	M	Unknown	13Ap02Dg
Liddy	8	F	Child	13Ap02Dg
Mick	5	M	Child	13Ap02Dg
ADAM, Martha	48	F	Servant	13Ap02Dg
Betty	15	F	Servant	13Ap02Dg
SMITH, Elizabeth	18	F	Servant	13Ap02Dg
Robert	16	M	Servant	13Ap02Dg

NAMES OF PASSENGERS	AGE	SEX	OCCUPATIONS	DATE PORT SHIP
NEWMAN, Hugh	22	M	Laborer	13Ap02Dg
Cath.	20	F	Laborer	13Ap02Dg
BROCK, Simon	27	M	Laborer	13Ap02Dg
ONTY, James	19	M	Laborer	13Ap02Dg
WHELAN, Peter	12	M	Laborer	13Ap02Dg
MCCLAY, Mary	20	F	Laborer	13Ap02Dg
KENAN, Garrett	25	M	Laborer	13Ap02Dg
FEENY, Chas.	45	M	Laborer	13Ap02Dg
HUGHES, Thos.	12	M	Laborer	13Ap02Dg
BYRNE, Frances	25	F	Laborer	13Ap02Dg
LYONS, Pat	20	M	Laborer	13Ap02Dg
CURRAN, Thos.	20	M	Laborer	13Ap02Dg
MURRY, Pat	20	M	Laborer	13Ap02Dg
BURKE, Walter	22	M	Laborer	13Ap02Dg
GILL, Darby	40	M	Farmer	13Ap02Dg
Wm.	40	M	Farmer	13Ap02Dg
Darby	16	M	Farmer	13Ap02Dg
John	14	M	Farmer	13Ap02Dg
Mick	27	M	Farmer	13Ap02Dg
U-Mrs.	25	F	Farmer	13Ap02Dg
Bartle	.00	M	Infant	13Ap02Dg
FITZPATRICK, Mary	18	F	Seamstress	13Ap02Dg
Martin	20	M	Laborer	13Ap02Dg
GELSTON, Jas.	22	M	Laborer	13Ap02Dg
William	25	M	Laborer	13Ap02Dg
CASEY, George	21	M	Laborer	13Ap02Dg
SUNS, Elise	24	F	Laborer	13Ap02Dg
HACKER, Edw.	21	M	Laborer	13Ap02Dg
CHURCHES, Thomas	24	M	Laborer	13Ap02Dg
HOWARTH, Luke	26	M	Laborer	13Ap02Dg
U-Mrs.	24	F	Laborer	13Ap02Dg
HEALY, Jas.	34	M	Servant	13Ap02Dg
Maria	33	M	Servant	13Ap02Dg
Joseph	13	M	Servant	13Ap02Dg
Sarah	11	F	Servant	13Ap02Dg
Eliza	.00	F	Infant	13Ap02Dg
SPENCER, Fanny	27	F	Servant	13Ap02Dg
Jas.	.00	M	Infant	13Ap02Dg
WOOLLEY, Jas.	22	M	Servant	13Ap02Dg
WOOLLY, George	.00	M	Infant	13Ap02Dg
Samuel	.00	M	Infant	13Ap02Dg
SUCHFORD, Hannah	25	F	Servant	13Ap02Dg
Arthur	3	M	Child	13Ap02Dg
Mary	.00	F	Infant	13Ap02Dg
COYLE, Bryan	18	M	Laborer	13Ap02Dg
Honor	28	F	Laborer	13Ap02Dg
GRAYNOR, Ellen	18	F	Laborer	13Ap02Dg
RYAN, Margt.	50	F	Laborer	13Ap02Dg
Jno.	29	M	Laborer	13Ap02Dg
Phil	12	M	Laborer	13Ap02Dg
Wm.	11	M	Laborer	13Ap02Dg
Bessy	8	F	Child	13Ap02Dg
Mary	.00	F	Infant	13Ap02Dg
MCKEON, Ann	30	F	Laborer	13Ap02Dg
Cath.	22	F	Laborer	13Ap02Dg
RAFFERTY, Denis	16	M	Laborer	13Ap02Dg
QUINN, John	28	M	Laborer	13Ap02Dg
Ellen	25	F	Laborer	13Ap02Dg
Pat	.00	M	Infant	13Ap02Dg
Ann	20	F	Laborer	13Ap02Dg
MURPHY, Bessy	19	F	Laborer	13Ap02Dg
LENNON, Jas.	32	M	Laborer	13Ap02Dg
MAGILL, Margt.	00	F	Laborer	13Ap02Dg
Margt.	00	F	Laborer	13Ap02Dg
LEE, John	20	M	Laborer	13Ap02Dg
FLINN, Margt.	18	F	Laborer	13Ap02Dg
BRENNAN, Keinan	24	M	Cooper	13Ap02Dg
FLINN, Rose	15	F	Laborer	13Ap02Dg
REARDON, Moris	24	M	Shoemaker	13Ap02Dg
Margaret	21	F	Shoemaker	13Ap02Dg
BENNETT, Thos.	20	M	Laborer	13Ap02Dg
GRILLS, Thos.	27	M	Laborer	13Ap02Dg
HANLON, Pat	30	M	Laborer	13Ap02Dg
MORGAN, Bryan	24	M	Laborer	13Ap02Dg
BYRNE, Jas.	32	M	Laborer	13Ap02Dg

NAMES OF PASSENGERS	AGE	SEX	OCCUPATIONS	DATE PORT SHIP
MCBRIDE, Luke	25	M	Laborer	13Ap02Dg
DORAN, Mary	18	F	Laborer	13Ap02Dg
Bridget	11	F	Laborer	13Ap02Dg
REDDINGTON, Martin	18	M	Laborer	13Ap02Dg
DOLLARD, Cath.	25	F	Laborer	13Ap02Dg
FENNELY, Keenan	18	M	Laborer	13Ap02Dg
MOORE, Jas.	18	M	Laborer	13Ap02Dg
KEENAN, Pat	40	M	Laborer	13Ap02Dg
Mary	30	F	Laborer	13Ap02Dg
GARRETT, Robt.	22	M	Laborer	13Ap02Dg
SPENCER, Mat.	21	M	Laborer	13Ap02Dg
DONNELLY, Wm.	30	M	Laborer	13Ap02Dg
FEGAN, Pat	30	M	Laborer	13Ap02Dg
Rose	25	F	Laborer	13Ap02Dg
Bridget	22	F	Laborer	13Ap02Dg
MCLAUGHLIN, Conn.	20	M	Laborer	13Ap02Dg
DONNELY, Ann	28	F	Laborer	13Ap02Dg
MCDONNELL, Jas.	30	M	Servant	13Ap02Dg
Mary	30	F	Servant	13Ap02Dg
Ellen	4	F	Child	13Ap02Dg
James	3	M	Child	13Ap02Dg
SMITH, Nancy	60	F	Servant	13Ap02Dg
Sarah	9	F	Child	13Ap02Dg
ROURKE, Jas.	25	M	Servant	13Ap02Dg
MALONEY, Thos.	25	M	Servant	13Ap02Dg
Mary	20	F	Servant	13Ap02Dg
Ann	18	F	Servant	13Ap02Dg
CLINTON, Ann	6	F	Child	13Ap02Dg
MCNAMARA, Wm.	26	M	Unknown	13Ap02Dg
James	4	M	Child	13Ap02Dg
Wm.	2	M	Child	13Ap02Dg
ROURK, Ann	30	F	Servant	13Ap02Dg
KENNEDY, Wm.	25	M	Joiner	13Ap02Dg
HALLIGAN, Pat	25	M	Servant	13Ap02Dg
Thos.	20	M	Servant	13Ap02Dg
Mary	21	F	Servant	13Ap02Dg
Margaret	12	F	Servant	13Ap02Dg
Ann	19	F	Servant	13Ap02Dg
Bridget	15	F	Servant	13Ap02Dg
CROSBY, Rose	21	F	Servant	13Ap02Dg
NELSON, Pat	12	M	Servant	13Ap02Dg
CLARKE, Mary	65	F	Servant	13Ap02Dg
Rose	21	F	Servant	13Ap02Dg
Chs.	30	M	Servant	13Ap02Dg
Mick	24	M	Servant	13Ap02Dg
Pat	18	M	Servant	13Ap02Dg
FITZSIMONS, U-Mrs.	20	F	Servant	13Ap02Dg
PHELAN, James	30	M	Laborer	13Ap02Dg
FITZPATRICK, Terence	12	M	Laborer	13Ap02Dg
DOOLEY, John	30	M	Laborer	13Ap02Dg
SCOTT, Hugh	23	M	Laborer	13Ap02Dg
DOUGHERTY, Jno.	12	M	Laborer	13Ap02Dg
FITZPATRICK, Edwd.	35	M	Farmer	13Ap02Dg
Mary	25	F	Farmer	13Ap02Dg
Mary	.00	F	Infant	13Ap02Dg
Dan	.00	M	Infant	13Ap02Dg
Mick	22	M	Farmer	13Ap02Dg
HANLON, Bernd.	24	M	Farmer	13Ap02Dg
Sarah	26	F	Farmer	13Ap02Dg
DEVAINE, Dan	30	M	Farmer	13Ap02Dg
BROUSE, Jim	22	M	Farmer	13Ap02Dg
GLEESON, Thos.	25	M	Farmer	13Ap02Dg
Margt.	22	M	Farmer	13Ap02Dg
Eliza	23	F	Farmer	13Ap02Dg
NOWLAN, Pat	18	M	Farmer	13Ap02Dg
WHITTEN, Jane	25	F	Farmer	13Ap02Dg
WALLACE, Saml.	20	M	Laborer	13Ap02Dg
MURPHY, Mick	25	M	Unknown	13Ap02Dg
Mat	22	M	Unknown	13Ap02Dg
HEFFERON, Mary-A.	20	F	Unknown	13Ap02Dg
SMITH, Wm.B.	30	M	Servant	13Ap02Dg
Ann	12	F	Unknown	13Ap02Dg
Mary	13	F	Unknown	13Ap02Dg
Jame	.00	M	Infant	13Ap02Dg
Cath.	12	F	Unknown	13Ap02Dg

NAMES OF PASSENGERS	AGE	SEX	OCCUPATIONS	DATE PORT SHIP
SMITH, Pat	8	M	Child	13Ap02Dg
Michl.	6	M	Child	13Ap02Dg
Bridget	.00	F	Infant	13Ap02Dg
MCCAHY, John	20	M	Farmer	13Ap02Dg
REILLY, Jas.	21	M	Farmer	13Ap02Dg
Rose	19	F	Farmer	13Ap02Dg
BIGG, Jas.	30	M	Farmer	13Ap02Dg
KENNEDY, John	32	M	Shoemaker	13Ap02Dg
SHORTELL, Thos.	26	M	Farmer	13Ap02Dg
KEEGAN, Chas.	19	M	Farmer	13Ap02Dg
HAGAN, James	28	M	Farmer	13Ap02Dg
RICE, John	25	M	Farmer	13Ap02Dg
FLINN, Pat	21	M	Farmer	13Ap02Dg
MCAVOY, Edw.	22	M	Farmer	13Ap02Dg
DALTON, Jas.	20	M	Farmer	13Ap02Dg
Cath.	23	F	Farmer	13Ap02Dg
Mary	21	F	Farmer	13Ap02Dg
Ann	12	F	Farmer	13Ap02Dg
CONNER, Cath.	24	F	Farmer	13Ap02Dg
GRAY, Esther	26	F	Farmer	13Ap02Dg
MCDOWELL, Mary	60	F	Farmer	13Ap02Dg
Pat	27	M	Unknown	13Ap02Dg
Wm.	25	M	Unknown	13Ap02Dg
Thos.	23	M	Unknown	13Ap02Dg
Nick	21	M	Unknown	13Ap02Dg
Mary	18	F	Unknown	13Ap02Dg
Martin	14	M	Servant	13Ap02Dg
MCCABE, Mary	25	F	Unknown	13Ap02Dg
HUSSY, Jno.	22	M	Unknown	13Ap02Dg
Ann	40	F	Unknown	13Ap02Dg
HUGHES, Jno.	30	M	Unknown	13Ap02Dg
Jno.	18	M	Unknown	13Ap02Dg
ROURKE, Mary	20	F	Unknown	13Ap02Dg
DUNN, Jane	20	F	Unknown	13Ap02Dg
CRAGHER, Pat	25	M	Unknown	13Ap02Dg
KING, Wm.	20	M	Farmer	13Ap02Dg
DEVINE, James	25	M	Farmer	13Ap02Dg
DOLAN, Mick	25	M	Unknown	13Ap02Dg
DUNN, Thomas	25	M	Unknown	13Ap02Dg
REILLY, Jno.	25	M	Unknown	13Ap02Dg
TRACEY, John	35	M	Servant	13Ap02Dg
Cath.	30	F	Servant	13Ap02Dg
MCDONNOUGH, Pat	20	M	Unknown	13Ap02Dg
Sabina	17	F	Unknown	13Ap02Dg
CAVANAGH, Ann	40	F	Unknown	13Ap02Dg
Mary	35	F	Unknown	13Ap02Dg
Ellen	12	F	Unknown	13Ap02Dg
J.	10	U	Unknown	13Ap02Dg
Catharine	8	F	Child	13Ap02Dg
Saml.	4	M	Child	13Ap02Dg
Wm.	3	M	Child	13Ap02Dg
FARRELL, Frank	20	M	Unknown	13Ap02Dg
CLARKE, Jas.	26	M	Unknown	13Ap02Dg
CAREY, Pat	28	M	Unknown	13Ap02Dg
MCANLLY, Pat	21	M	Unknown	13Ap02Dg
CASEY, Ann	20	F	Unknown	13Ap02Dg
MCGUINESS, Thos.	36	M	Unknown	13Ap02Dg
BEERS, Jas.	22	M	Unknown	13Ap02Dg
KEARNS, Mick	26	M	Unknown	13Ap02Dg
Pat	20	M	Farmer	13Ap02Dg
AGNEW, Thos.	24	M	Unknown	13Ap02Dg
HARRIGAN, Pat	26	M	Unknown	13Ap02Dg
REILLY, Martin	20	M	Unknown	13Ap02Dg
MCCLARY, Bessy	.00	F	Infant	13Ap02Dg
Jas.	24	M	Unknown	13Ap02Dg
J.	24	U	Servant	13Ap02Dg
CARRELL, John	35	M	Unknown	13Ap02Dg
PENTIN, John	20	M	Unknown	13Ap02Dg
KELLY, Jas.	21	M	Unknown	13Ap02Dg
RIELLY, Peter	20	M	Unknown	13Ap02Dg
MOORE, Thos.	26	M	Unknown	13Ap02Dg
MITCHELL, Saml.	21	M	Unknown	13Ap02Dg
REYNOLDS, Brid.	50	F	Unknown	13Ap02Dg
Thos.P.	15	M	Unknown	13Ap02Dg
Michl.	11	M	Unknown	13Ap02Dg
REYNOLDS, Brid.	8	F	Child	13Ap02Dg
Mary	5	F	Child	13Ap02Dg
MURRAY, Bryan	30	M	Unknown	13Ap02Dg
MOORE, Wm.	20	M	Unknown	13Ap02Dg
John	18	M	Unknown	13Ap02Dg
LEONARD, Ellen	12	F	Unknown	13Ap02Dg
CASEY, Michael	20	M	Unknown	13Ap02Dg
QUIGLEY, Owen	25	M	Unknown	13Ap02Dg
WAUGH, Jas.	50	M	Unknown	13Ap02Dg
CALAHAN, Alice	19	F	Unknown	13Ap02Dg
COOK, Ann	32	F	Unknown	13Ap02Dg
U-Mrs.	32	F	Unknown	13Ap02Dg
EDGER, David	20	M	Farmer	13Ap02Dg
MORROW, Chas.	20	M	Farmer	13Ap02Dg
John	26	M	Unknown	13Ap02Dg
CANERSON, John	20	M	Unknown	13Ap02Dg
MURPHY, Thos.	22	M	Farmer	13Ap02Dg
Sarah	25	F	Farmer	13Ap02Dg
HUGSON, Pat	22	M	Farmer	13Ap02Dg
LAUGHLIN, Jas.	20	M	Unknown	13Ap02Dg
SHERRON, Jas.	21	M	Unknown	13Ap02Dg
GOLDBY, Saml.	20	M	Unknown	13Ap02Dg
Thomas	22	M	Unknown	13Ap02Dg
HOWE, Luke	25	M	Unknown	13Ap02Dg
NEWTH, Wm.	22	M	Unknown	13Ap02Dg
HONER, Henry	33	M	Unknown	13Ap02Dg
SPILLER, Jos.	34	M	Unknown	13Ap02Dg
U-Mrs.	34	F	Unknown	13Ap02Dg
William	8	M	Child	13Ap02Dg
STEPHENS, Jas.	29	M	Unknown	13Ap02Dg
MAYS, Mary	12	F	Unknown	13Ap02Dg
FOIX, Rebecca	14	F	Unknown	13Ap02Dg
SMITH, George	18	M	Unknown	13Ap02Dg
KENNEDY, Michl.	20	M	Unknown	13Ap02Dg
Michl.	25	M	Unknown	13Ap02Dg
Jno.	22	M	Unknown	13Ap02Dg
DONNAGAN, Jno.	33	M	Servant	13Ap02Dg
LINNEGAN, Pat	15	M	Unknown	13Ap02Dg
HOGARTY, Eliza	30	F	Unknown	13Ap02Dg
Hog---, Sarah	.00	F	Infant	13Ap02Dg
Burk---, Cath.	24	F	Unknown	13Ap02Dg
TRING, Michael	36	M	Unknown	13Ap02Dg
CLARKE, Phil	28	M	Unknown	13Ap02Dg
Thos.	31	M	Unknown	13Ap02Dg
MILLS, U	25	M	Farmer	13Ap02Dg
TOMLINSON, U	20	M	Unknown	13Ap02Dg
HOLESWORTH, Thos.	18	M	Unknown	13Ap02Dg
HULY, Jas.	25	M	Unknown	13Ap02Dg
U-Mrs.	22	F	Unknown	13Ap02Dg
BOSSOM, Noah	29	M	Servant	13Ap02Dg
BERRINGTON, Thos.	20	M	Unknown	13Ap02Dg
CURNS, James	22	M	Unknown	13Ap02Dg
MITCHELL, Thos.	12	M	Farmer	13Ap02Dg
KELLY, Pat	22	M	Unknown	13Ap02Dg
FLINN, James	37	M	Unknown	13Ap02Dg
Cath.	28	F	Unknown	13Ap02Dg
Charles	13	M	Unknown	13Ap02Dg
Pat	.00	M	Infant	13Ap02Dg
Margt.	12	F	Unknown	13Ap02Dg
MCARDLE, Cath.	37	F	Farmer	13Ap02Dg
HAGAR, Js.	21	M	Unknown	13Ap02Dg
SMITH, Jno.	22	M	Unknown	13Ap02Dg
FINNEGAN, Pat	40	M	Unknown	13Ap02Dg
CRAVEN, Isah.	18	M	Unknown	13Ap02Dg
GREENLAUGH, Richd.	35	M	Unknown	13Ap02Dg
OHANELL, Bernd.	50	M	Unknown	13Ap02Dg
Cath.	40	F	Unknown	13Ap02Dg
Thos.	19	M	Farmer	13Ap02Dg
WETHERALL, James	49	M	Unknown	13Ap02Dg
Rachel	49	F	Unknown	13Ap02Dg
Thomas	21	M	Unknown	13Ap02Dg
FORD, Thos.	28	M	Unknown	13Ap02Dg
PITBLADE, Mary	16	F	Unknown	13Ap02Dg
LARKIN, Danl.	38	M	Servant	13Ap02Dg
MCAVOY, J.	20	U	Unknown	13Ap02Dg

NAMES OF PASSENGERS	AGE	SEX	OCCUPATIONS	DATE PORT SHIP
WHALEN, Jno.	21	M	Unknown	13Ap02Dg
QUINN, James	6	M	Child	13Ap02Dg
MAHER, Cath.	20	F	Seamstress	13Ap02Dg
POWERS, Cath.	21	F	Servant	13Ap02Dg
ALLEN, Henry	22	M	Merchant	13Ap02Dg
SUCHFORD, Mary	23	F	Servant	13Ap02Dg

STAR-OF-THE-WEST 13 APRIL 1850

From Liverpool

NAMES OF PASSENGERS	AGE	SEX	OCCUPATIONS	DATE PORT SHIP
MOLLOY, U-Mr.	42	M	Physician	13Ap02Ge
U-Mrs.	35	F	Unknown	13Ap02Ge
U-Miss	10	F	Unknown	13Ap02Ge
U-Miss	2	F	Child	13Ap02Ge
HARRIS, Samuel	50	M	Farmer	13Ap02Ge
George	45	M	Farmer	13Ap02Ge
Samuel	17	M	Farmer	13Ap02Ge
Dorothea	21	F	Farmer	13Ap02Ge
MURPHY, Mary	25	F	Servant	13Ap02Ge
FINEGAN, Margt.	21	F	Servant	13Ap02Ge
SMITH, Phillip	40	M	Farmer	13Ap02Ge
U-Mrs.	40	F	Farmer	13Ap02Ge
John	17	M	Farmer	13Ap02Ge
Anne	18	F	Farmer	13Ap02Ge
Bessy	12	F	Farmer	13Ap02Ge
KIERNAN, Hugh	20	M	Laborer	13Ap02Ge
SMITH, Terence	18	M	Farmer	13Ap02Ge
Mary	15	F	Farmer	13Ap02Ge
Bridget	20	F	Farmer	13Ap02Ge
BIRD, Anne	18	F	Servant	13Ap02Ge
KING, Mary	18	F	Servant	13Ap02Ge
TREUNIOR, Margt.	24	F	Servant	13Ap02Ge
FITZGIBBONS, Mary	56	F	Servant	13Ap02Ge
BROWN, Julia	44	F	Farmer	13Ap02Ge
Sarah	18	F	Farmer	13Ap02Ge
Hans	17	M	Farmer	13Ap02Ge
William	15	M	Farmer	13Ap02Ge
John	10	M	Farmer	13Ap02Ge
Mary-Jane	8	F	Child	13Ap02Ge
Henry	8	M	Child	13Ap02Ge
HOOLAHAN, Thos.	22	M	Laborer	13Ap02Ge
Mary	18	F	Laborer	13Ap02Ge
GLENNAN, Catharine	25	F	Dressmaker	13Ap02Ge
MURNANE, Thomas	26	M	Farmer	13Ap02Ge
Catharine	30	F	Farmer	13Ap02Ge
CAVANAGH, James	24	M	Farmer	13Ap02Ge
GRANE, John	35	M	Laborer	13Ap02Ge
MCDERMOTT, Bernard	20	M	Farmer	13Ap02Ge
FINEGAN, Dafney	22	F	Farmer	13Ap02Ge
RUDDEN, Anne	18	F	Servant	13Ap02Ge
Catharine	22	F	Servant	13Ap02Ge
Mary	23	F	Servant	13Ap02Ge
BRADY, Mary	20	F	Servant	13Ap02Ge
Mary	21	F	Servant	13Ap02Ge
MCDONNELL, Michael	20	M	Laborer	13Ap02Ge
Catharine	16	F	Laborer	13Ap02Ge
Bridget	21	F	Laborer	13Ap02Ge
CARR, James	30	M	Laborer	13Ap02Ge
CULLAVAN, Ann	28	F	Servant	13Ap02Ge
ODAY, Mary	20	F	Servant	13Ap02Ge
REILLY, Michael	35	M	Farmer	13Ap02Ge
Bridget	30	F	Farmer	13Ap02Ge
James	12	F	Farmer	13Ap02Ge
Mary	10	F	Farmer	13Ap02Ge
Ann	9	F	Child	13Ap02Ge
Bernard	7	M	Child	13Ap02Ge
Patk.	5	M	Child	13Ap02Ge
SELLERS, Mary	18	F	Servant	13Ap02Ge
SWAUNE, Pat	36	M	Farmer	13Ap02Ge
Mary	30	F	Farmer	13Ap02Ge
Edward	4	M	Child	13Ap02Ge
MCCORMICK, Patt	38	M	Laborer	13Ap02Ge
DUFFY, Denis	27	M	Farmer	13Ap02Ge
FALLON, Catharine	18	F	Servant	13Ap02Ge
GALVIN, Catharine	34	F	Servant	13Ap02Ge
Patt	9	M	Child	13Ap02Ge
FARREL, Maria	25	F	Dressmaker	13Ap02Ge
COWELL, Teresa	23	F	Servant	13Ap02Ge
CANNON, Pat	50	M	Carpenter	13Ap02Ge
John	20	M	Carpenter	13Ap02Ge
Mary	21	F	Unknown	13Ap02Ge
GALLAHER, Rosey	20	F	Servant	13Ap02Ge
MCGINLEY, Teague	21	M	Servant	13Ap02Ge
DONEEN, Dan	35	M	Farmer	13Ap02Ge
KENNEDY, James	23	M	Farmer	13Ap02Ge
TROUVEN, Edwd.	25	M	Farmer	13Ap02Ge
WATSON, John	24	M	Laborer	13Ap02Ge
MCNAMEE, Mathew	60	M	Laborer	13Ap02Ge
FORD, Bernard	20	M	Laborer	13Ap02Ge
DOUGHERTY, Catherine	25	F	Servant	13Ap02Ge
CONNERS, James	23	M	Laborer	13Ap02Ge
Anne	19	F	Laborer	13Ap02Ge
MCCORMICK, Laurence	26	M	Laborer	13Ap02Ge
MCELEVEN, John	24	M	Laborer	13Ap02Ge
STEWART, Sarah	44	F	Servant	13Ap02Ge
Mary	17	F	Servant	13Ap02Ge
BOYLE, Pat	30	M	Farmer	13Ap02Ge
John	19	M	Farmer	13Ap02Ge
Patt	19	M	Farmer	13Ap02Ge
CONNOR, Dennis	20	M	Laborer	13Ap02Ge
MCBREIALY, Chas.	20	M	Laborer	13Ap02Ge
FUNNY, Sally	17	F	Servant	13Ap02Ge
DONNELL, Hannah	28	F	Servant	13Ap02Ge
CARTY, Catharine	27	F	Servant	13Ap02Ge
BOYLE, John	6	M	Child	13Ap02Ge
Biddy	2	F	Child	13Ap02Ge
CANNAN, Manus	7	M	Child	13Ap02Ge
LEARY, Laurence	20	M	Farmer	13Ap02Ge
FURY, Anne	20	F	Servant	13Ap02Ge
FOLEY, Margt.	18	F	Servant	13Ap02Ge
ROCHE, James	21	M	Servant	13Ap02Ge
BURKE, Michl.	29	M	Servant	13Ap02Ge
DALTON, Thos.	18	M	Servant	13Ap02Ge
Ellen	20	F	Servant	13Ap02Ge
GUILFOYL, Danl.	26	M	Farmer	13Ap02Ge
HOLTON, Laurence	40	M	Farmer	13Ap02Ge
CAHILL, Edwd.	40	M	Farmer	13Ap02Ge
Bridget	40	F	Farmer	13Ap02Ge
DOOMADY, Pat	13	M	Servant	13Ap02Ge
Martin	12	M	Servant	13Ap02Ge
QUIN, Ann	19	F	Servant	13Ap02Ge
MEREDITH, Mary	19	F	Servant	13Ap02Ge
GRIFFITH, Hannah	18	F	Servant	13Ap02Ge
DOWNEND, Thos.	30	M	Servant	13Ap02Ge
OLIVER, Saml.	30	M	Servant	13Ap02Ge
RYAN, Danl.	30	M	Servant	13Ap02Ge
CASSIDY, John	34	M	Farmer	13Ap02Ge
Peter	25	M	Farmer	13Ap02Ge
RYAN, Margt.	22	F	Servant	13Ap02Ge
BURKE, Thos.	30	M	Servant	13Ap02Ge
Bridget	25	F	Servant	13Ap02Ge
EVERNAN, Anne	33	F	Servant	13Ap02Ge
BURKE, Patt	9	M	Child	13Ap02Ge
Wm.	.00	M	Infant	13Ap02Ge
HENAGHAN, Pat	20	M	Servant	13Ap02Ge
MCCULKIN, Thos.	25	M	Servant	13Ap02Ge
Danl.	17	M	Servant	13Ap02Ge
Bridget	50	F	Servant	13Ap02Ge
Mary	15	F	Servant	13Ap02Ge
Catharine	13	F	Servant	13Ap02Ge
HANLON, Mary	27	F	Servant	13Ap02Ge
Eliza	22	F	Servant	13Ap02Ge
COMMINS, Peter	29	M	Servant	13Ap02Ge

NAMES OF PASSENGERS	AGE	SEX	OCCUPATIONS	DATE PORT SHIP
CAIN, John	20	M	Servant	13Ap02Ge
STEWART, James	45	M	Farmer	13Ap02Ge
Sarah	6	F	Child	13Ap02Ge
Ann	4	F	Child	13Ap02Ge
Andrew	1	M	Child	13Ap02Ge
CAVANAGH, Robt.	50	M	Farmer	13Ap02Ge
Jane	50	F	Farmer	13Ap02Ge
John	22	M	Farmer	13Ap02Ge
Sarah	18	F	Farmer	13Ap02Ge
Richard	12	M	Farmer	13Ap02Ge
CONNELL, Wm.	30	M	Servant	13Ap02Ge
CONLIN, Hugh	20	M	Servant	13Ap02Ge
HAMILL, Bernard	20	M	Servant	13Ap02Ge
FLYNN, Margt.	16	F	Servant	13Ap02Ge
RYAN, Wm.	24	M	Servant	13Ap02Ge
HAGAN, Richard	30	M	Servant	13Ap02Ge
QUINLAN, Jas.	24	M	Servant	13Ap02Ge
Jas.	20	M	Servant	13Ap02Ge
Margt.	24	F	Servant	13Ap02Ge
Judy	20	F	Servant	13Ap02Ge
HOGAN, Ellen	20	F	Servant	13Ap02Ge
BOYLE, Judy	20	F	Servant	13Ap02Ge
NOCKLAN, John	26	M	Servant	13Ap02Ge
CONNELLY, Patt	30	M	Farmer	13Ap02Ge
BARRETT, Anthony	20	M	Shoemaker	13Ap02Ge
NOCKLAN, Danl.	20	M	Grocer	13Ap02Ge
LANGAN, Richd.	24	M	Servant	13Ap02Ge
BURN, Edwd.	44	M	Farmer	13Ap02Ge
Mary	40	F	Farmer	13Ap02Ge
MURPHY, Owen	27	M	Farmer	13Ap02Ge
Fanny	22	F	Farmer	13Ap02Ge
Margt.	20	F	Farmer	13Ap02Ge
DEMPSY, James	21	M	Laborer	13Ap02Ge
FLOOD, Wm.	30	M	Laborer	13Ap02Ge
COOD, James	30	M	Shoemaker	13Ap02Ge
LIVERS, John	23	M	Shoemaker	13Ap02Ge
FORAMY, Pat	29	M	Laborer	13Ap02Ge
MCCARTY, Honora	27	F	Laborer	13Ap02Ge
KELLY, John	22	M	Laborer	13Ap02Ge
MCGUIN, Eleanor	30	F	Servant	13Ap02Ge
DRUM, Pat	20	M	Servant	13Ap02Ge
HEWITT, Wm.	33	M	Farmer	13Ap02Ge
TANELL, Margt.	30	F	Dressmaker	13Ap02Ge
KINGSTON, Wm.	12	M	Servant	13Ap02Ge
DENNEY, Peter	30	M	Servant	13Ap02Ge
NEAL, Thos.	25	M	Servant	13Ap02Ge
REAGAN, Thos.	22	M	Servant	13Ap02Ge
MULREADY, John	23	M	Servant	13Ap02Ge
MCCARTY, John	28	M	Servant	13Ap02Ge
GAINOR, Hugh	18	M	Farmer	13Ap02Ge
MCGLOCKLIN, Peter	20	M	Farmer	13Ap02Ge
FITZPATRICK, Peter	21	M	Laborer	13Ap02Ge
FARRELY, Pat	22	M	Laborer	13Ap02Ge
MCMANNS, John	38	M	Laborer	13Ap02Ge
Alice	18	F	Laborer	13Ap02Ge
Mary	16	F	Laborer	13Ap02Ge
RALPH, Pat	22	M	Farmer	13Ap02Ge
GAHAN, James	35	M	Mason	13Ap02Ge
LANE, Patt	30	M	Mason	13Ap02Ge
BRANEGAN, Margt.	20	F	Servant	13Ap02Ge
OBRIEN, Edwd	21	M	Clerk	13Ap02Ge
MOORE, Wm.	25	M	Servant	13Ap02Ge
Jane	25	F	Servant	13Ap02Ge
KILROY, John	52	M	Farmer	13Ap02Ge
Philip	20	M	Farmer	13Ap02Ge
ELLIS, John	24	M	Farmer	13Ap02Ge
SULLIVAN, Mary	25	F	Servant	13Ap02Ge
DONOVAN, Sarah	26	F	Servant	13Ap02Ge
Mary	.00	F	Infant	13Ap02Ge
HAND, Michael	24	M	Servant	13Ap02Ge
MOLLOY, John	30	M	Farmer	13Ap02Ge
QUIGLEY, Edward	41	M	Farmer	13Ap02Ge
Bridget	39	F	Farmer	13Ap02Ge
MOORE, Mary	21	F	Servant	13Ap02Ge
SHEANY, Pat	41	M	Farmer	13Ap02Ge

NAMES OF PASSENGERS	AGE	SEX	OCCUPATIONS	DATE PORT SHIP
MCGINNIS, James	21	M	Laborer	13Ap02Ge
PENTLAND, Alex	35	M	Laborer	13Ap02Ge
OLOUGHLIN, Michl	30	M	Laborer	13Ap02Ge
Susan	30	F	Laborer	13Ap02Ge
Mary	12	F	Laborer	13Ap02Ge
Susan	3	F	Child	13Ap02Ge
CURTIN, Mary	14	F	Servant	13Ap02Ge
HARLEY, Ann	17	F	Servant	13Ap02Ge
QUINLAN, Lott	22	F	Servant	13Ap02Ge
DONOHUE, Pat	50	M	Farmer	13Ap02Ge
Richd.	26	M	Farmer	13Ap02Ge
JAMES, Eliza	19	F	Servant	13Ap02Ge
ODONOHUE, Michl.	24	M	Laborer	13Ap02Ge
Patt	22	M	Laborer	13Ap02Ge
CONNOLLY, Fanny	24	F	Servant	13Ap02Ge
MCDONALD, Ann	20	F	Servant	13Ap02Ge
CASTLY, Ellen	20	F	Servant	13Ap02Ge
DONOHUE, Ellen	18	F	Servant	13Ap02Ge
DELANY, Anthony	34	M	Farmer	13Ap02Ge
CAIN, Michl.	30	M	Farmer	13Ap02Ge
Margt.	25	F	Farmer	13Ap02Ge
Bridget	4	F	Child	13Ap02Ge
Michl.	.00	M	Infant	13Ap02Ge
BYRNE, Danl.	21	M	Servant	13Ap02Ge
EDWARDS, U	40	M	Clerk	13Ap02Ge
CROMWELL, George	27	M	Clerk	13Ap02Ge
KENNEDY, John	18	M	Servant	13Ap02Ge
MADDEN, Ellen	19	F	Servant	13Ap02Ge
WOODWORTH, Henry	38	M	Farmer	13Ap02Ge
Jane	30	F	Farmer	13Ap02Ge
Chas.	13	M	Farmer	13Ap02Ge
Susan	11	F	Farmer	13Ap02Ge
Eliza	9	F	Child	13Ap02Ge
Jane	7	F	Child	13Ap02Ge
Louisa	5	F	Child	13Ap02Ge
Mary	3	F	Child	13Ap02Ge
Robt.	.00	M	Infant	13Ap02Ge
PURCELL, Bridget	16	F	Servant	13Ap02Ge
MEADE, Sylvester	30	M	Farmer	13Ap02Ge
Anne	25	F	Farmer	13Ap02Ge
John	.00	M	Infant	13Ap02Ge
Patt	3	M	Child	13Ap02Ge
COLLAN, Mary	18	F	Servant	13Ap02Ge
RIDLY, John	21	M	Servant	13Ap02Ge
HUTCHINSON, David	17	M	Servant	13Ap02Ge
MITCHELL, Ann	20	F	Servant	13Ap02Ge
HALY, Michl.	30	M	Farmer	13Ap02Ge
Catharine	25	F	Farmer	13Ap02Ge
Mary	25	F	Servant	13Ap02Ge
NEAL, Ann	20	F	Servant	13Ap02Ge
DOYLE, Sarah	25	F	Servant	13Ap02Ge
WHELAN, Pat	52	F	Farmer	13Ap02Ge
POWER, Jeremia	40	M	Farmer	13Ap02Ge
WHEALON, Margt.	17	F	Servant	13Ap02Ge
POWER, Honora	17	F	Servant	13Ap02Ge
QUINLAN, Johanna	17	F	Servant	13Ap02Ge
POWER, Johanna	34	F	Servant	13Ap02Ge
WHEALON, Pat	7	M	Child	13Ap02Ge
WELSH, Richard	40	M	Farmer	13Ap02Ge
Michl.	36	M	Farmer	13Ap02Ge
PURCEL, James	35	M	Farmer	13Ap02Ge
Maria	21	F	Farmer	13Ap02Ge
BRASIL, Margt.	20	F	Farmer	13Ap02Ge
WELSH, Bridget	7	F	Child	13Ap02Ge
Pat	4	F	Child	13Ap02Ge
Pat	25	M	Farmer	13Ap02Ge
Judith	23	F	Farmer	13Ap02Ge
WHEALON, Pat	35	M	Farmer	13Ap02Ge
MULLEN, Wm.	26	M	Servant	13Ap02Ge
MAHONY, Michl.	19	M	Servant	13Ap02Ge
MARA, Pat	20	M	Servant	13Ap02Ge
DELHUNTY, Jas.	27	M	Servant	13Ap02Ge
FOGERTY, Jas.	18	M	Servant	13Ap02Ge
WALLACE, Hance	16	M	Servant	13Ap02Ge
MORAN, Thomas	29	M	Servant	13Ap02Ge

NAMES OF PASSENGERS	AGE	SEX	OCCUPATIONS	DATE PORT SHIP
MORAN, Mary	25	F	Servant	13Ap02Ge
Mary	.00	F	Infant	13Ap02Ge
Roger	12	M	Servant	13Ap02Ge
Morris	10	M	Servant	13Ap02Ge
Margt.	7	F	Child	13Ap02Ge
Mary	5	F	Child	13Ap02Ge
Bridget	4	F	Child	13Ap02Ge
BRYAN, John	40	M	Farmer	13Ap02Ge
BYRNE, Wm.	17	M	Farmer	13Ap02Ge
CASHELL, Michl.	27	M	Farmer	13Ap02Ge
GRIFFIN, Catharine	31	F	Servant	13Ap02Ge
SMITH, James	43	M	Sawer	13Ap02Ge
MCLEAN, John	24	M	Farmer	13Ap02Ge
RYAN, Ellen	18	F	Servant	13Ap02Ge
GREADY, Margt.	25	F	Servant	13Ap02Ge
BURMINGHAM, Eliza	16	F	Servant	13Ap02Ge
GORMAN, Pat	30	M	Farmer	13Ap02Ge
LEARY, Thomas	19	M	Servant	13Ap02Ge
Ann	26	F	Servant	13Ap02Ge
BLAKE, Bernd.	11	M	Servant	13Ap02Ge
John	8	M	Child	13Ap02Ge
James	6	M	Child	13Ap02Ge
MCGARNEY, Wm.	30	M	Farmer	13Ap02Ge
Pat	11	M	Farmer	13Ap02Ge
Mary	7	F	Child	13Ap02Ge
GANGHAN, Catharine	16	F	Servant	13Ap02Ge
OHARA, James	26	M	Farmer	13Ap02Ge
MCKEOWN, Francis	26	M	Farmer	13Ap02Ge
MCGRATH, James	26	M	Farmer	13Ap02Ge
U-Mrs.	23	F	Farmer	13Ap02Ge
James	10	M	Farmer	13Ap02Ge
Mary	7	F	Child	13Ap02Ge
Catharine	3	F	Child	13Ap02Ge
CODY, Denis	34	M	Farmer	13Ap02Ge
Abby	5	F	Child	13Ap02Ge
GEARY, Owen	27	M	Servant	13Ap02Ge
Margt.	27	F	Servant	13Ap02Ge
Denis	4	M	Child	13Ap02Ge
Mary	1	F	Child	13Ap02Ge
JOYCE, Ellen	19	F	Servant	13Ap02Ge
Johanna	22	F	Servant	13Ap02Ge
MOKLEY, Wm.	25	M	Farmer	13Ap02Ge
SMITH, Thos.	25	M	Laborer	13Ap02Ge
CURRAN, Timothy	33	M	Farmer	13Ap02Ge
CARROL, Catharine	18	F	Servant	13Ap02Ge
BYRNE, Eliza	16	F	Servant	13Ap02Ge
Mary	14	F	Servant	13Ap02Ge
MCLEAN, James	30	M	Painter	13Ap02Ge
HAWKIN, John	25	M	Farmer	13Ap02Ge
MAINS, Alex	20	M	Farmer	13Ap02Ge
CASSIDY, John	30	M	Servant	13Ap02Ge
MANNING, Pat	20	M	Servant	13Ap02Ge
CONNER, Pat	21	F	Servant	13Ap02Ge
WALLACE, Hannah	27	F	Servant	13Ap02Ge
DUGGAN, Margt.	20	F	Unknown	13Ap02Ge
MCDONALD, Bridget	30	F	Unknown	13Ap02Ge
Bill	11	M	Unknown	13Ap02Ge
CODY, Catharine	28	F	Farmer	13Ap02Ge

BELLOND 17 APRIL 1850

From Bristol

NAMES OF PASSENGERS	AGE	SEX	OCCUPATIONS	DATE PORT SHIP
WILLIAMS, Joseph	20	M	Laborer	17Ap34Gi
MAIDMENT, Joseph	21	M	Unknown	17Ap34Gi
SHOUK, Eliza	20	F	Unknown	17Ap34Gi
PRINCE, John	50	M	Unknown	17Ap34Gi
EVANS, Evan	50	M	Unknown	17Ap34Gi
WEBB, Henry	33	M	Unknown	17Ap34Gi
WHITE, Thos.	29	M	Unknown	17Ap34Gi
Caroline	19	F	Unknown	17Ap34Gi
HAZLEYNONE, John	21	M	Unknown	17Ap34Gi
WELSH, John	16	M	Unknown	17Ap34Gi
BURKE, Susan	26	F	Unknown	17Ap34Gi
MURPHY, Ellen	23	F	Unknown	17Ap34Gi
PEARCE, Fred	16	M	Unknown	17Ap34Gi
PHEBEY, James	38	M	Unknown	17Ap34Gi
GOULD, James	32	M	Unknown	17Ap34Gi
Mary-Ann	28	F	Laborer	17Ap34Gi
Elizabeth	7	F	Child	17Ap34Gi
James	6	M	Child	17Ap34Gi
Albert	4	M	Child	17Ap34Gi
EDWARDS, Ann	36	F	Unknown	17Ap34Gi
Mary	21	F	Unknown	17Ap34Gi
John	12	M	Unknown	17Ap34Gi
Margt.	10	F	Unknown	17Ap34Gi
Ann	8	F	Child	17Ap34Gi
Jane	6	F	Child	17Ap34Gi
Martha	4	F	Child	17Ap34Gi
Elizabeth	.08	F	Infant	17Ap34Gi
Mary-Ann	2	F	Child	17Ap34Gi
John	.03	M	Infant	17Ap34Gi
STOCK, Wm.	29	M	Unknown	17Ap34Gi
BIDDICK, Wm.	40	M	Unknown	17Ap34Gi
Nancy	35	F	Unknown	17Ap34Gi
MONNSTEPHEN, Samuel	30	M	Unknown	17Ap34Gi
FAY, Peter	19	M	Unknown	17Ap34Gi
John	36	M	Unknown	17Ap34Gi
TONKIN, Samuel	51	M	Unknown	17Ap34Gi

INDUSTRY 19 APRIL 1850

From Dublin

NAMES OF PASSENGERS	AGE	SEX	OCCUPATIONS	DATE PORT SHIP
DOYLE, Michael	33	M	Unknown	19Ap05Gj
Catherine	55	F	Unknown	19Ap05Gj
Mary	28	F	Unknown	19Ap05Gj
Anty	24	F	Unknown	19Ap05Gj
Patt	17	M	Unknown	19Ap05Gj
Catherine	13	F	Unknown	19Ap05Gj
TOOLE, Thomas	20	M	Unknown	19Ap05Gj
Bridget	19	F	Unknown	19Ap05Gj
GONNAN, Thomas	28	M	Unknown	19Ap05Gj
Mary	26	F	Unknown	19Ap05Gj
Martha	1	F	Child	19Ap05Gj
CARRIGAN, Lawrence	40	M	Unknown	19Ap05Gj
Biddy	30	F	Unknown	19Ap05Gj
Biddy	12	F	Unknown	19Ap05Gj
Thomas	8	M	Child	19Ap05Gj
James	6	M	Child	19Ap05Gj
FORLY, Bitty	14	F	Unknown	19Ap05Gj
BYRNE, Peter	30	M	Unknown	19Ap05Gj
BUCKLEY, Peter	20	M	Unknown	19Ap05Gj
DOYLES, James	25	M	Unknown	19Ap05Gj
U-Mrs.	22	F	Unknown	19Ap05Gj
Maria	2	F	Child	19Ap05Gj
Eliza	.00	F	Infant	19Ap05Gj
POWER, James	24	M	Unknown	19Ap05Gj
CONNOLLY, Michl.	20	M	Unknown	19Ap05Gj
MULVANY, U-Mrs.	20	F	Unknown	19Ap05Gj
FARRELL, Wm.	20	M	Unknown	19Ap05Gj
COFFY, Patt	50	M	Unknown	19Ap05Gj
Cath.	45	F	Unknown	19Ap05Gj
Ellen	13	F	Unknown	19Ap05Gj
Mary	12	F	Unknown	19Ap05Gj
Ann	11	F	Unknown	19Ap05Gj
COLLY, Marcella	11	F	Unknown	19Ap05Gj
Cath.	4	F	Unknown	19Ap05Gj

NAMES OF PASSENGERS	AGE	SEX	OCCUPATIONS	DATE PORT SHIP
CULLEN, Daniel	25	M	Unknown	19Ap05Gj
MURRAY, Nicholas	21	M	Unknown	19Ap05Gj
NEAL, Mary	18	F	Unknown	19Ap05Gj
GARVEY, John	22	M	Unknown	19Ap05Gj
BEHAN, Mary	35	F	Unknown	19Ap05Gj
John	5	M	Child	19Ap05Gj
James	4	M	Child	19Ap05Gj
BEALES, Patrick	14	M	Unknown	19Ap05Gj
REDMOND, Michl.	18	M	Unknown	19Ap05Gj
STONY, U-Mrs.	30	F	Unknown	19Ap05Gj
John	3	M	Child	19Ap05Gj
John	.00	M	Infant	19Ap05Gj
BYRNE, John	21	M	Unknown	19Ap05Gj
MURNA, William	34	M	Unknown	19Ap05Gj
Catherine	28	F	Unknown	19Ap05Gj
John	.00	M	Infant	19Ap05Gj
DOYLE, R.	20	M	Unknown	19Ap05Gj
KELLY, Catherine	41	F	Unknown	19Ap05Gj
REYNOLDS, James	24	M	Unknown	19Ap05Gj
MCGUIN, James	30	M	Unknown	19Ap05Gj
BRADY, Thos.	24	M	Unknown	19Ap05Gj
SULLIVAN, Peter	25	M	Unknown	19Ap05Gj
POOLE, Elizabeth	22	F	Unknown	19Ap05Gj
WARD, Patt	25	M	Unknown	19Ap05Gj
FITZSIMMONS, Margaret	28	F	Unknown	19Ap05Gj
Anna	15	F	Unknown	19Ap05Gj
ELLISS, U-Mrs.	00	F	Unknown	19Ap05Gj
GRAY, Mary-A.	56	F	Unknown	19Ap05Gj
SHERIDAN, Phillip	20	M	Unknown	19Ap05Gj
KEARNEY, Patt	18	M	Unknown	19Ap05Gj
Thomas	25	M	Unknown	19Ap05Gj
Peter	18	M	Unknown	19Ap05Gj
Julia	.00	F	Infant	19Ap05Gj
GAFFEY, Edwd.	22	M	Unknown	19Ap05Gj
LOWRY, John	20	M	Unknown	19Ap05Gj
DORAN, Sarah	20	F	Unknown	19Ap05Gj
BARRETT, Leonard	18	M	Unknown	19Ap05Gj
M.Mrs.	24	F	Unknown	19Ap05Gj
RIELLY, John	20	M	Unknown	19Ap05Gj
Bridget	26	F	Unknown	19Ap05Gj
James	.00	M	Infant	19Ap05Gj
MOONEY, John	17	M	Unknown	19Ap05Gj
BURKE, John	47	M	Unknown	19Ap05Gj
Anne	45	F	Unknown	19Ap05Gj
Marcella	18	M	Unknown	19Ap05Gj
Mary	16	F	Unknown	19Ap05Gj
John	13	M	Unknown	19Ap05Gj
Judith	11	F	Unknown	19Ap05Gj
Wm.	8	M	Child	19Ap05Gj
Lawrence	6	M	Child	19Ap05Gj
Anne	.00	F	Infant	19Ap05Gj
DERHAN, Edward	24	M	Unknown	19Ap05Gj
U-Mrs.	22	F	Unknown	19Ap05Gj
Carolina	.00	F	Infant	19Ap05Gj
CASE, John	60	M	Unknown	19Ap05Gj
Biddy	58	F	Unknown	19Ap05Gj
Comfort	26	F	Unknown	19Ap05Gj
Thomas	24	M	Unknown	19Ap05Gj
John	20	M	Unknown	19Ap05Gj
Mark	17	M	Unknown	19Ap05Gj
James	14	M	Unknown	19Ap05Gj
Jxinton (F)	.00	F	Infant	19Ap05Gj
COYLE, Patt (F)	26	M	Unknown	19Ap05Gj
Judith	22	M	Unknown	19Ap05Gj
GOREY, Michael	64	M	Unknown	19Ap05Gj
Patt	21	M	Unknown	19Ap05Gj
Bridget	42	F	Unknown	19Ap05Gj
Mary	19	F	Unknown	19Ap05Gj
Patt	17	M	Unknown	19Ap05Gj
Anna	15	F	Unknown	19Ap05Gj
Biddy	13	F	Unknown	19Ap05Gj
James	11	M	Unknown	19Ap05Gj
Michael	6	M	Child	19Ap05Gj
Elicca	.00	F	Infant	19Ap05Gj
ROOHAN, John	30	M	Unknown	19Ap05Gj
ROOHAN, Mary	28	F	Unknown	19Ap05Gj
Bridget	6	F	Child	19Ap05Gj
Thomas	4	M	Child	19Ap05Gj
Eliza	.00	F	Infant	19Ap05Gj
CARNEY, James	20	M	Unknown	19Ap05Gj
KEEFE, Margaret	50	F	Unknown	19Ap05Gj
Martin	37	M	Unknown	19Ap05Gj
Pierce	35	M	Unknown	19Ap05Gj
Maria	30	F	Unknown	19Ap05Gj
John	28	M	Unknown	19Ap05Gj
Margaret	20	F	Unknown	19Ap05Gj
Thomas	18	M	Unknown	19Ap05Gj
Biddy	16	F	Unknown	19Ap05Gj
Jeremia	12	M	Unknown	19Ap05Gj
Michael	16	M	Unknown	19Ap05Gj
Alley	40	F	Unknown	19Ap05Gj
CASE, John	40	M	Unknown	19Ap05Gj
Mary	36	F	Unknown	19Ap05Gj
Dina	13	F	Unknown	19Ap05Gj
Betty	11	F	Unknown	19Ap05Gj
William	9	M	Child	19Ap05Gj
George	5	M	Child	19Ap05Gj
JOHNSTON, Anne	20	F	Unknown	19Ap05Gj
WALLACE, Biddy	19	F	Unknown	19Ap05Gj
Ellen	17	F	Unknown	19Ap05Gj
KAVANAGH, Walter	56	M	Unknown	19Ap05Gj
Mary	57	F	Unknown	19Ap05Gj
Judy	17	F	Unknown	19Ap05Gj
Mary	13	F	Unknown	19Ap05Gj
Garrett	7	M	Child	19Ap05Gj
FAY, Patt	22	M	Unknown	19Ap05Gj
CLANCY, Edward	50	M	Unknown	19Ap05Gj
Catherine	40	F	Unknown	19Ap05Gj
Edward	19	M	Unknown	19Ap05Gj
Ellen	17	F	Unknown	19Ap05Gj
James	15	M	Unknown	19Ap05Gj
John	13	M	Unknown	19Ap05Gj
Mary	11	F	Unknown	19Ap05Gj
Michael	10	M	Unknown	19Ap05Gj
George	8	M	Child	19Ap05Gj
Ann	6	F	Child	19Ap05Gj
Martin	.00	F	Infant	19Ap05Gj
FARRELL, Catherine	20	F	Unknown	19Ap05Gj
ROGERS, Catherine	20	F	Unknown	19Ap05Gj
FAY, Lawrence	20	M	Unknown	19Ap05Gj
MCGOWICK, Patt	22	M	Unknown	19Ap05Gj
DELANCY, James	22	M	Unknown	19Ap05Gj
ENGLISH, Richard	22	M	Unknown	19Ap05Gj
LAMAX, James	30	M	Unknown	19Ap05Gj
Margret	26	F	Unknown	19Ap05Gj
Christy	8	M	Child	19Ap05Gj
James	5	M	Child	19Ap05Gj
Anne	.00	F	Infant	19Ap05Gj
FITZGERALD, James	24	M	Unknown	19Ap05Gj
CLANCY, Patt	22	M	Unknown	19Ap05Gj
MASTERSON, Mary	20	F	Unknown	19Ap05Gj
ENGLISH, Mat	25	M	Unknown	19Ap05Gj
LALOR, Daniel	30	M	Unknown	19Ap05Gj
U-Mrs.	28	F	Unknown	19Ap05Gj
Daniel	5	M	Child	19Ap05Gj
James	3	M	Child	19Ap05Gj
Pat	2	M	Child	19Ap05Gj
Michl.	.00	M	Infant	19Ap05Gj
BURKE, Robt.	20	M	Unknown	19Ap05Gj
FERGASON, James	25	M	Unknown	19Ap05Gj
GERAGHTY, Lawrence	50	M	Unknown	19Ap05Gj
NOLAN, Danl.	20	M	Unknown	19Ap05Gj
KELLY, Bess	20	F	Unknown	19Ap05Gj
TRACY, Margaret	25	F	Unknown	19Ap05Gj
DUNNE, Anne	22	F	Unknown	19Ap05Gj
BRANNON, Patt	33	M	Unknown	19Ap05Gj
U-Mrs.	33	F	Unknown	19Ap05Gj
John	16	M	Unknown	19Ap05Gj
Alice	13	F	Unknown	19Ap05Gj
Kate	9	M	Child	19Ap05Gj

NAMES OF PASSENGERS	AGE	SEX	OCCUPATIONS	DATE PORT SHIP
BRANNON, Mary	6	F	Child	19Ap05Gj
Edward	4	M	Child	19Ap05Gj
Peter	.00	M	Infant	19Ap05Gj
QUINN, Mick	30	M	Unknown	19Ap05Gj
Wm.	18	M	Unknown	19Ap05Gj
Thomas	2	M	Child	19Ap05Gj
Pat	13	M	Unknown	19Ap05Gj
Bridget	12	F	Unknown	19Ap05Gj
CARRIGAN, Patt	25	M	Unknown	19Ap05Gj
MAGINN, Ann	20	F	Unknown	19Ap05Gj
SHIRRAN, Wm.	20	M	Unknown	19Ap05Gj
CONROY, Robert	16	M	Unknown	19Ap05Gj
John	13	M	Unknown	19Ap05Gj
HADDEN, Mary-Ann	20	F	Unknown	19Ap05Gj
CLANCY, Edward	21	M	Unknown	19Ap05Gj
Mary	20	F	Unknown	19Ap05Gj
DOYLE, George	20	M	Unknown	19Ap05Gj
CUREN, Edward	20	M	Unknown	19Ap05Gj
Mary	20	F	Unknown	19Ap05Gj
BROWN, Edward	24	M	Unknown	19Ap05Gj
Cathe.	22	F	Unknown	19Ap05Gj
Ellen	.00	F	Infant	19Ap05Gj
ORIELLY, Phillip	22	M	Unknown	19Ap05Gj
CAVANAGH, Daniel	40	M	Unknown	19Ap05Gj
Mary	40	F	Unknown	19Ap05Gj
John	12	M	Unknown	19Ap05Gj
James	10	M	Unknown	19Ap05Gj
Cath.	9	F	Child	19Ap05Gj
Eliza	8	F	Child	19Ap05Gj
Mary	4	F	Child	19Ap05Gj
CONOOT, John	36	M	Unknown	19Ap05Gj
Margaret	35	F	Unknown	19Ap05Gj
Mary	12	F	Unknown	19Ap05Gj
Patt	10	M	Unknown	19Ap05Gj
FRY, Wm.	30	M	Unknown	19Ap05Gj
RICHARDSON, U-Miss	24	F	Unknown	19Ap05Gj
OBRIAN, Wm.	24	F	Unknown	19Ap05Gj
U	19	M	Unknown	19Ap05Gj
TOOLE, U	30	M	Unknown	19Ap05Gj
ROBINSON, U	26	M	Unknown	19Ap05Gj
COFFY, U	24	M	Unknown	19Ap05Gj
Uu-Miss	5	F	Child	19Ap05Gj

PRINCETON 19 APRIL 1850

From Liverpool

NAMES OF PASSENGERS	AGE	SEX	OCCUPATIONS	DATE PORT SHIP
KELLEY, Mary	30	F	Domestic	19Ap02Gh
COUGHREN, Catherine	26	F	Cook	19Ap02Gh
BROWN, Julia	20	F	Domestic	19Ap02Gh
BROWDERICK, Julia	23	F	Domestic	19Ap02Gh
SIMOTT, William	30	M	Farmer	19Ap02Gh
LEARY, Margaret	25	F	Dairymaid	19Ap02Gh
HUGHES, Catherine	19	F	Lad	19Ap02Gh
ODONNELL, John	26	M	Weaver	19Ap02Gh
HALEY, Margaret	25	F	Domestic	19Ap02Gh
MCCULLOCK, Margaret	21	F	Embroiderer	19Ap02Gh
HIGHLAND, Catherine	21	F	Dressmaker	19Ap02Gh
Margaret	12	F	Unknown	19Ap02Gh
Johanna	5	F	Child	19Ap02Gh
MCGINLEY, Grace	30	F	Housekeeper	19Ap02Gh
GALOGHER, Sarah	20	F	Domestic	19Ap02Gh
CLOCKLIN, John	20	M	Tanner	19Ap02Gh
DOHERTY, Charles	23	M	Laborer	19Ap02Gh
MCCULLAGH, John	21	M	Laborer	19Ap02Gh
MCCULLOGH, Peter	18	M	Clerk	19Ap02Gh
MCGILLON, William	21	M	Shoemaker	19Ap02Gh
FOLAND, Mary	28	F	Lad	19Ap02Gh
NEAGLE, Ellen	20	F	Domestic	19Ap02Gh
CASADY, Ann	25	F	Domestic	19Ap02Gh
Margaret	20	F	Domestic	19Ap02Gh
BURNE, Martin	19	M	Laborer	19Ap02Gh
William	17	M	Laborer	19Ap02Gh
Mathew	13	M	Laborer	19Ap02Gh
Flora	50	F	Housekeeper	19Ap02Gh
Ellen	16	F	Domestic	19Ap02Gh
FURLONG, James	21	M	Laborer	19Ap02Gh
PENDERGRAST, Margaret	21	F	Domestic	19Ap02Gh
Ann	18	F	Domestic	19Ap02Gh
BOURNE, Betsy	17	F	Domestic	19Ap02Gh
Sally	20	F	Domestic	19Ap02Gh
BERRY, Ann	22	F	Domestic	19Ap02Gh
HALIGAN, Catharine	20	F	Domestic	19Ap02Gh
MCMULLEN, Henry	20	M	Laborer	19Ap02Gh
ELLIOT, Thomas	24	M	Laborer	19Ap02Gh
CONNOR, Nicholas	54	M	Steward	19Ap02Gh
KING, James	20	M	Laborer	19Ap02Gh
Margaret	17	F	Domestic	19Ap02Gh
MCCONN, Dason	18	F	Housekeeper	19Ap02Gh
Betty	16	F	Housekeeper	19Ap02Gh
LOUGHLIN, Thomas	20	M	Laborer	19Ap02Gh
DEWAR, Patrick	27	M	Laborer	19Ap02Gh
STARKEY, John	24	M	Laborer	19Ap02Gh
FITZPATRICK, James	24	M	Laborer	19Ap02Gh
TAGGARD, Ann	30	F	Housekeeper	19Ap02Gh
STARKEY, Sarah	19	F	Dressmaker	19Ap02Gh
MARMION, Patrick	25	M	Laborer	19Ap02Gh
MCCARTY, James	45	M	Laborer	19Ap02Gh
FITZSIMONS, Jane	30	F	Housekeeper	19Ap02Gh
Kate	25	F	Housekeeper	19Ap02Gh
MCMURRAY, William	30	M	Laborer	19Ap02Gh
Ellen	4	F	Child	19Ap02Gh
Eliza	25	F	Housekeeper	19Ap02Gh
Elizabeth	6	F	Child	19Ap02Gh
James	2	M	Child	19Ap02Gh
William	.00	M	Infant	19Ap02Gh
FINN, Biddy	20	F	Dressmaker	19Ap02Gh
Nancy	18	F	Domestic	19Ap02Gh
MANGIN, James	30	M	Laborer	19Ap02Gh
CRAWLEY, Timothy	35	M	Laborer	19Ap02Gh
KENNESFICK, Ellen	24	F	Domestic	19Ap02Gh
BRIEN, Mary	24	F	Domestic	19Ap02Gh
COLLINS, Anna	20	F	Domestic	19Ap02Gh
RYAN, Cornelius	27	M	Laborer	19Ap02Gh
HIPFARNAN, Edmund	26	M	Laborer	19Ap02Gh
CURRY, William	30	M	Laborer	19Ap02Gh
Silvertine	8	M	Child	19Ap02Gh
CAREY, Dennis	26	M	Laborer	19Ap02Gh
HIPFAMAN, John	27	M	Laborer	19Ap02Gh
LOOLEY, Michael	27	M	Laborer	19Ap02Gh
DUNYAR, Patrick	25	M	Laborer	19Ap02Gh
HANEY, Patrick	25	M	Laborer	19Ap02Gh
HIPFAMAN, Jane	25	F	Domestic	19Ap02Gh
MURPHY, Agnes	22	F	Domestic	19Ap02Gh
Bridget	20	F	Domestic	19Ap02Gh
WALL, James	20	M	Joiner	19Ap02Gh
Bridget	22	F	Domestic	19Ap02Gh
KELLEY, Patrick	20	M	Laborer	19Ap02Gh
OLAUGHLIN, John	20	M	Laborer	19Ap02Gh
KELLEY, Patrick	56	M	Laborer	19Ap02Gh
William	16	M	Laborer	19Ap02Gh
MANDEN, Daniel	18	M	Laborer	19Ap02Gh
SHIELD, Thomas	24	M	Laborer	19Ap02Gh
Mary	23	F	Unknown	19Ap02Gh
Patrick	.00	M	Infant	19Ap02Gh
DUNN, Patrick	22	M	Laborer	19Ap02Gh
Michael	15	M	Laborer	19Ap02Gh
James	19	M	Laborer	19Ap02Gh
Alley	17	F	Domestic	19Ap02Gh
MULLANEY, Margaret	22	F	Domestic	19Ap02Gh
MOONEY, Dennis	20	M	Laborer	19Ap02Gh
KARLEY, John	26	M	Laborer	19Ap02Gh
CARPENTER, Thomas	18	M	Laborer	19Ap02Gh
CULLEN, Richard	23	M	Laborer	19Ap02Gh

NAMES OF PASSENGERS	AGE	SEX	OCCUPATIONS	DATE PORT SHIP	NAMES OF PASSENGERS	AGE	SEX	OCCUPATIONS	DATE PORT SHIP
CALLEN, Elizabeth	14	F	Domestic	19Ap02Gh	LYNCH, Ellen	18	F	Domestic	19Ap02Gh
CRAWFORD, John	20	M	Shoemaker	19Ap02Gh	BAGLEY, Catherine	17	F	Domestic	19Ap02Gh
KELBY, Ellen	31	F	Domestic	19Ap02Gh	REILY, Mary	22	F	Domestic	19Ap02Gh
DOYLE, Catherine	21	F	Domestic	19Ap02Gh	BAGLEY, Betsy	23	F	Domestic	19Ap02Gh
MANNON, Thomas	22	M	Laborer	19Ap02Gh	DILLON, Susan	40	F	Domestic	19Ap02Gh
Elizabeth	23	F	Domestic	19Ap02Gh	CANTWELL, Thomas	10	M	Child	19Ap02Gh
TOOHAY, Hannah	22	F	Domestic	19Ap02Gh	James	25	M	Laborer	19Ap02Gh
LAFFLIN, Mary	42	F	Domestic	19Ap02Gh	FITZGERALD, John	20	M	Laborer	19Ap02Gh
RAFFERTY, Mary	18	F	Domestic	19Ap02Gh	NARNAY, Michael	20	M	Laborer	19Ap02Gh
CUMMING, Elizabeth	13	F	Domestic	19Ap02Gh	DORR, Michael	20	M	Laborer	19Ap02Gh
RYAN, Julia	25	F	Domestic	19Ap02Gh	CANTWELL, Ante	40	F	Domestic	19Ap02Gh
NOONAN, John	32	M	Laborer	19Ap02Gh	Bridget	12	F	Domestic	19Ap02Gh
TOOTHY, Jeremiah	23	M	Laborer	19Ap02Gh	Patrick	8	M	Child	19Ap02Gh
GIFFORD, James	30	M	Laborer	19Ap02Gh	Mary	7	F	Child	19Ap02Gh
MARTIN, Thomas	19	M	Laborer	19Ap02Gh	GREENMAN, John	16	M	Laborer	19Ap02Gh
CONNOR, Michael	18	M	Laborer	19Ap02Gh	MALANEY, John	60	M	Laborer	19Ap02Gh
CONNERLY, Mary	20	F	Domestic	19Ap02Gh	William	19	M	Laborer	19Ap02Gh
DAVEY, Mary	30	F	Domestic	19Ap02Gh	John	22	M	Laborer	19Ap02Gh
John	3	M	Child	19Ap02Gh	DORR, Bridget	20	F	Domestic	19Ap02Gh
MALLON, Theresa	14	F	Domestic	19Ap02Gh	MAHON, Sabina	20	F	Domestic	19Ap02Gh
COMMERFORD, John	20	M	Laborer	19Ap02Gh	FALLEY, Mary	16	F	Domestic	19Ap02Gh
GRAY, William	18	M	Laborer	19Ap02Gh	GALLIGAN, Sarah	16	F	Domestic	19Ap02Gh
MAYERMACK, Edward	22	M	Laborer	19Ap02Gh	COFFEE, Daniel	30	M	Laborer	19Ap02Gh
CONAFRED, Bridget	21	F	Domestic	19Ap02Gh	HAGGARTY, John	19	M	Laborer	19Ap02Gh
DORIMM, Catherine	17	F	Domestic	19Ap02Gh	TROTEY, Thomas	22	M	Laborer	19Ap02Gh
NASH, Catherine	40	F	Domestic	19Ap02Gh	SHAR, Cornelius	60	M	Laborer	19Ap02Gh
Richard	10	M	Unknown	19Ap02Gh	James	25	M	Laborer	19Ap02Gh
MANNING, Michael	32	M	Stctr	19Ap02Gh	Cornelius	25	M	Laborer	19Ap02Gh
NASH, Mary	11	F	Unknown	19Ap02Gh	Catherine	25	F	Domestic	19Ap02Gh
MANNING, Bridget	39	F	Domestic	19Ap02Gh	GRENNAN, John	23	M	Laborer	19Ap02Gh
DOWD, James	20	M	Laborer	19Ap02Gh	Patrick	23	M	Laborer	19Ap02Gh
READ, George	20	M	Tailor	19Ap02Gh	SIMONS, Catherine	18	F	Domestic	19Ap02Gh
Isabella	19	F	Domestic	19Ap02Gh	CRAREY, Barney	19	M	Laborer	19Ap02Gh
Maria	17	F	Domestic	19Ap02Gh	QUINLAN, Patrick	20	M	Laborer	19Ap02Gh
Eliza	.00	F	Infant	19Ap02Gh	MCCANNON, John	17	M	Laborer	19Ap02Gh
MASTER, Julia	16	F	Domestic	19Ap02Gh	BRACKLIN, Biddy	35	F	Domestic	19Ap02Gh
HARRAGAN, Patrick	35	M	Laborer	19Ap02Gh	SHERIDAN, Biddy	18	F	Domestic	19Ap02Gh
Johanna	32	F	Domestic	19Ap02Gh	FARREL, Elizabeth	23	F	Domestic	19Ap02Gh
Daniel	6	M	Child	19Ap02Gh	CARROLL, Johanna	45	F	Domestic	19Ap02Gh
James	4	M	Child	19Ap02Gh	QUINLAN, Joseph	17	M	Laborer	19Ap02Gh
Michael	.00	M	Infant	19Ap02Gh	Mary	35	F	Domestic	19Ap02Gh
FITZPATRICK, Mary	30	F	Domestic	19Ap02Gh	CARROLL, Catherine	16	F	Domestic	19Ap02Gh
Jerry	5	M	Child	19Ap02Gh	Mary	15	F	Domestic	19Ap02Gh
ROACH, Margaret	22	F	Domestic	19Ap02Gh	Timothy	12	M	Laborer	19Ap02Gh
WHITE, Margaret	23	F	Domestic	19Ap02Gh	Thomas	10	M	Laborer	19Ap02Gh
COLLINS, Jerry	25	M	Laborer	19Ap02Gh	AGEN, Ellen	44	F	Domestic	19Ap02Gh
KIDNEY, Michael	40	M	Laborer	19Ap02Gh	Mary	16	F	Domestic	19Ap02Gh
TAYLOR, William	50	M	Laborer	19Ap02Gh	Bridget	14	F	Domestic	19Ap02Gh
Mary-Ann	50	F	Wife	19Ap02Gh	Catherine	12	F	Domestic	19Ap02Gh
MCGUIRE, Hannah	19	F	Domestic	19Ap02Gh	Patrick	5	M	Child	19Ap02Gh
CASTELLO, Rosa	16	F	Domestic	19Ap02Gh	Ellen	3	F	Child	19Ap02Gh
MALLER, Catherine	20	F	Domestic	19Ap02Gh	John	35	M	Laborer	19Ap02Gh
FINNAGEN, Michael	20	M	Laborer	19Ap02Gh	James	28	M	Laborer	19Ap02Gh
Patrick	45	M	Laborer	19Ap02Gh	Phillimor	10	M	Unknown	19Ap02Gh
MCGUIRE, John	16	M	Laborer	19Ap02Gh	David	8	M	Child	19Ap02Gh
FINNAGEN, Peter	16	M	Laborer	19Ap02Gh	COLLINS, Richard	35	M	Laborer	19Ap02Gh
MORNE, Charles	25	M	Laborer	19Ap02Gh	MARNAY, Mary	40	F	Domestic	19Ap02Gh
KINNEY, Rose	17	F	Domestic	19Ap02Gh	Mary	15	F	Domestic	19Ap02Gh
SMITH, Ann	24	F	Domestic	19Ap02Gh	Edward	11	M	Unknown	19Ap02Gh
Rose	16	F	Domestic	19Ap02Gh	HENESY, Thadeus	7	M	Child	19Ap02Gh
Martha	3	F	Child	19Ap02Gh	Margaret	5	F	Child	19Ap02Gh
Patrick	.00	M	Infant	19Ap02Gh	Ellen	4	F	Child	19Ap02Gh
HANNAGAN, Patrick	19	M	Laborer	19Ap02Gh	Julia	2	F	Child	19Ap02Gh
OLVANEY, James	30	M	Laborer	19Ap02Gh	Jerry	30	M	Laborer	19Ap02Gh
FARLEY, Owen	33	M	Laborer	19Ap02Gh	Ellen	30	F	Wife	19Ap02Gh
Philip	13	M	Laborer	19Ap02Gh	FARLEY, Johanna	27	F	Domestic	19Ap02Gh
BRADY, James	21	M	Laborer	19Ap02Gh	Mary	6	F	Child	19Ap02Gh
MCCLOCHLIN, Daniel	35	M	Laborer	19Ap02Gh	James	4	M	Child	19Ap02Gh
Ann	40	F	Domestic	19Ap02Gh	Mary	40	F	Domestic	19Ap02Gh
MCFARLIN, George	40	M	Laborer	19Ap02Gh	Bridget	11	F	Domestic	19Ap02Gh
Theresa	31	F	Domestic	19Ap02Gh	DOWNEY, Ellen	25	F	Domestic	19Ap02Gh
HERREN, Michael	42	M	Laborer	19Ap02Gh	Mary	25	F	Domestic	19Ap02Gh
LAWLOR, George	22	M	Laborer	19Ap02Gh	REDDY, James	30	M	Laborer	19Ap02Gh
FITZGERALD, Patrick	21	M	Laborer	19Ap02Gh	Mary	30	F	Domestic	19Ap02Gh
MARKEY, Larry	28	M	Laborer	19Ap02Gh	BRASLES, Miles	26	M	Laborer	19Ap02Gh

NAMES OF PASSENGERS	AGE	SEX	OCCUPATIONS	DATE PORT SHIP
BOMMES, James	27	M	Laborer	19Ap02Gh
CARTHAN, Hugh	23	M	Laborer	19Ap02Gh
LENNON, Hesther	24	F	Laborer	19Ap02Gh
BURNES, John	30	M	Laborer	19Ap02Gh
Eliza	27	F	Domestic	19Ap02Gh
WOODS, Owen	53	M	Laborer	19Ap02Gh
SKELLY, Edward	52	M	Laborer	19Ap02Gh
James	11	M	Unknown	19Ap02Gh
Ann	9	F	Child	19Ap02Gh
Patrick	13	M	Child	19Ap02Gh
MANAHAN, Margaret	40	F	Domestic	19Ap02Gh
Rose	14	F	Domestic	19Ap02Gh
Ann	10	F	Unknown	19Ap02Gh
Margaret	8	F	Child	19Ap02Gh
Patrick	20	M	Laborer	19Ap02Gh
Hugh	18	M	Laborer	19Ap02Gh
Robert	16	M	Laborer	19Ap02Gh
Peter	12	M	Laborer	19Ap02Gh
MURRAY, Judy	40	F	Domestic	19Ap02Gh
Frank	14	M	Laborer	19Ap02Gh
FAWLEY, Owen	60	M	Laborer	19Ap02Gh
Bridget	60	F	Domestic	19Ap02Gh
Patrick	25	M	Laborer	19Ap02Gh
CARTEY, Thomas	22	M	Laborer	19Ap02Gh
SMITH, Rose	19	F	Domestic	19Ap02Gh
Mary	21	F	Domestic	19Ap02Gh
CALLAGHAN, Mary	18	F	Domestic	19Ap02Gh
MOONE, Alley	.00	F	Infant	19Ap02Gh
SHERIDAN, Ann	17	F	Domestic	19Ap02Gh
FINNEY, Peter	25	M	Laborer	19Ap02Gh
James	23	M	Laborer	19Ap02Gh
CARTEY, Brian	25	M	Laborer	19Ap02Gh
CALLAGAN, Barton	22	M	Laborer	19Ap02Gh
Charles	20	M	Laborer	19Ap02Gh
Henry	21	M	Laborer	19Ap02Gh
John	14	M	Laborer	19Ap02Gh
RUTTERS, Anna	13	F	Domestic	19Ap02Gh
Martin	4	M	Child	19Ap02Gh
Margaret	2	F	Child	19Ap02Gh
Mary	18	F	Domestic	19Ap02Gh
Barney	28	M	Laborer	19Ap02Gh
NORTON, Mary	25	F	Domestic	19Ap02Gh
Mike	5	M	Child	19Ap02Gh
Patrick	3	M	Child	19Ap02Gh
Ann	.00	F	Infant	19Ap02Gh
Died-At-Sea				
FITZSIMMONS, Hugh	35	M	Laborer	19Ap02Gh
Rose	28	F	Domestic	19Ap02Gh
Patrick	10	M	Child	19Ap02Gh
Henry	8	M	Child	19Ap02Gh
Hugh	.00	M	Infant	19Ap02Gh
MCELROY, Hugh	24	M	Laborer	19Ap02Gh
HACKET, Barney	23	M	Laborer	19Ap02Gh
MCELROY, Owen	22	M	Laborer	19Ap02Gh
HAVEN, Mary	20	F	Domestic	19Ap02Gh
CASHMAN, Mary	19	F	Domestic	19Ap02Gh
John	14	M	Laborer	19Ap02Gh
MCCANN, Bridget	20	F	Domestic	19Ap02Gh
Margaret	16	F	Domestic	19Ap02Gh
Ellen	18	F	Domestic	19Ap02Gh
BYRON, Bridget	22	F	Domestic	19Ap02Gh
Michael	2	M	Child	19Ap02Gh
CONWAY, Michael	30	M	Laborer	19Ap02Gh
Jane	28	F	Wife	19Ap02Gh
George	5	M	Child	19Ap02Gh
Fanny	7	F	Child	19Ap02Gh
Edward	2	M	Child	19Ap02Gh
CASHER, John	58	M	Laborer	19Ap02Gh
John	18	M	Laborer	19Ap02Gh
MARSHALL, Henry	21	M	Shoemaker	19Ap02Gh
FREEMAN, John	29	M	Laborer	19Ap02Gh
HORNE, Mary	24	F	Domestic	19Ap02Gh
FLANNAGAN, Biddy	25	F	Domestic	19Ap02Gh
BRADY, Mary	21	F	Domestic	19Ap02Gh
CASHIN, Mary	21	F	Domestic	19Ap02Gh
MALONE, Edward	21	M	Laborer	19Ap02Gh
HOLDEN, John	25	M	Laborer	19Ap02Gh
RILEY, John	18	M	Laborer	19Ap02Gh
TAGGET, James	19	M	Laborer	19Ap02Gh
KINNAGIN, Mary	20	F	Domestic	19Ap02Gh
KAGIN, Nancy	25	F	Domestic	19Ap02Gh
HICKS, Bridget	16	F	Domestic	19Ap02Gh
James	10	M	Unknown	19Ap02Gh
Michael	7	M	Child	19Ap02Gh
MALONE, Bridget	17	F	Domestic	19Ap02Gh
DORIN, John	23	M	Laborer	19Ap02Gh
GARDENER, Nancy	24	F	Domestic	19Ap02Gh
Barby	21	F	Domestic	19Ap02Gh
DORIN, Grace	19	F	Domestic	19Ap02Gh
FURAY, Bridget	8	F	Child	19Ap02Gh
MARTIN, Francis	45	M	Laborer	19Ap02Gh
Mary	43	F	Domestic	19Ap02Gh
GALLAGHER, Susan	21	F	Domestic	19Ap02Gh
DORSEY, Eliza	12	F	Domestic	19Ap02Gh
ROGERS, Henry	23	M	Laborer	19Ap02Gh
MALDEN, James	23	M	Laborer	19Ap02Gh
DOHERTY, Rose	26	F	Domestic	19Ap02Gh
Margaret	19	F	Domestic	19Ap02Gh
ORMAN, William	50	M	Laborer	19Ap02Gh
John	7	M	Child	19Ap02Gh
Mary	5	F	Child	19Ap02Gh
Kitty	.00	F	Infant	19Ap02Gh
Margaret	26	F	Domestic	19Ap02Gh
RODDY, Luke	28	M	Laborer	19Ap02Gh
MCCANNA, Patrick	25	M	Laborer	19Ap02Gh
GRIFFITH, Philip	22	M	Carpenter	19Ap02Gh
SPEAR, Mary	15	F	Domestic	19Ap02Gh
MCCULLIGAN, Mary	22	F	Domestic	19Ap02Gh
BRADY, Edward	16	M	Laborer	19Ap02Gh
MONAHAN, Margaret	17	F	Domestic	19Ap02Gh
MCDONNELL, Bridget	16	F	Domestic	19Ap02Gh
GRIFFITHS, Margaret	20	F	Domestic	19Ap02Gh
POTTERS, Jane	16	F	Domestic	19Ap02Gh
Mary-Ann	12	F	Domestic	19Ap02Gh
MONAGHAN, Catherine	45	F	Domestic	19Ap02Gh
Alice	6	F	Child	19Ap02Gh
COUREY, James	27	M	Laborer	19Ap02Gh
KINANCY, John	27	M	Laborer	19Ap02Gh
DANIEL, John	20	M	Laborer	19Ap02Gh
CONERY, Mary	20	F	Domestic	19Ap02Gh
ROSS, Alexander	40	M	Laborer	19Ap02Gh
COFFEE, Daniel	40	M	Laborer	19Ap02Gh
KETTERSON, John	19	M	Laborer	19Ap02Gh
COLLAN, James	27	M	Laborer	19Ap02Gh
KENNEDY, Henry	20	M	Laborer	19Ap02Gh
Ann	22	F	Domestic	19Ap02Gh
John	.00	M	Infant	19Ap02Gh
BURNEY, Ann	22	F	Domestic	19Ap02Gh
SUMMERS, Patrick	18	M	Laborer	19Ap02Gh
HICKEY, James	35	M	Laborer	19Ap02Gh
Mary	33	F	Domestic	19Ap02Gh
Laurana	11	F	Domestic	19Ap02Gh
COLLAN, Mary	16	F	Domestic	19Ap02Gh
COONAN, Catherine	25	F	Domestic	19Ap02Gh
Bridget	22	F	Domestic	19Ap02Gh
Margaret	20	F	Domestic	19Ap02Gh
RYAN, Alley	25	F	Domestic	19Ap02Gh
CARROLL, Catherine	16	F	Domestic	19Ap02Gh
KENNA, Mary	18	F	Domestic	19Ap02Gh
MARTIN, Rose	20	F	Domestic	19Ap02Gh
DUFF, Mary	19	F	Domestic	19Ap02Gh
MCCLUSKEY, Mary	50	F	Domestic	19Ap02Gh
Rose	14	F	Domestic	19Ap02Gh
Catherine	8	F	Child	19Ap02Gh
Mary	6	F	Child	19Ap02Gh
John	18	M	Laborer	19Ap02Gh
Henry	12	M	Laborer	19Ap02Gh
WATSON, Margaret	25	F	Domestic	19Ap02Gh
BRYAN, John	35	M	Domestic	19Ap02Gh
MCDONNELL, Rose	28	F	Domestic	19Ap02Gh

NAMES OF PASSENGERS	AGE	SEX	OCCUPATIONS	DATE PORT SHIP
FITZGERALD, Catherine	30	F	Domestic	19Ap02Gh
FINNELL, Mary	20	F	Domestic	19Ap02Gh
FITZGERALD, Mary	12	F	Domestic	19Ap02Gh
Patrick	10	M	Unknown	19Ap02Gh
Michael	7	M	Child	19Ap02Gh
Edmond	.00	M	Infant	19Ap02Gh
DONNELY, Charles	18	M	Laborer	19Ap02Gh
Frank	18	M	Laborer	19Ap02Gh
MCALLEAR, John	26	M	Laborer	19Ap02Gh
CALLAN, James	22	M	Laborer	19Ap02Gh
FITZGERALD, John	5	M	Child	19Ap02Gh
GOUTH, Mary	20	F	Domestic	19Ap02Gh
DONNELY, Margaret	19	F	Domestic	19Ap02Gh
FLINN, Jane	16	F	Domestic	19Ap02Gh
CANCY, Catherine	20	F	Domestic	19Ap02Gh
KENNAN, -----	20	F	Domestic	19Ap02Gh
BURKE, John	28	M	Domestic	19Ap02Gh
CUNNINGHAM, Patrick	20	M	Domestic	19Ap02Gh
HALLAN, Patrick	20	M	Domestic	19Ap02Gh
KILMARTIN, James	22	M	Domestic	19Ap02Gh
CONWAY, James	30	M	Domestic	19Ap02Gh
CRAVEN, Mathew	26	M	Domestic	19Ap02Gh
HIGGINS, Ann	19	F	Domestic	19Ap02Gh
Mary	16	F	Domestic	19Ap02Gh
DOWAN, Patrick	20	M	Laborer	19Ap02Gh
John	14	M	Laborer	19Ap02Gh
Ann	10	F	Unknown	19Ap02Gh
Thomas	8	M	Child	19Ap02Gh
KELLEY, Michael	20	M	Laborer	19Ap02Gh
MOONEY, Dennis	60	M	Laborer	19Ap02Gh
FOLEY, Thomas	36	M	Laborer	19Ap02Gh
GARVAN, Franklin	25	M	Laborer	19Ap02Gh
MCCANN, Richard	19	M	Laborer	19Ap02Gh
BYRAN, Margaret	20	F	Domestic	19Ap02Gh

MISSISSIPPI 20 APRIL 1850

From London

NAMES OF PASSENGERS	AGE	SEX	OCCUPATIONS	DATE PORT SHIP
SMITH, James	36	M	Carpenter	20Ap06Gp
Henry	30	M	Unknown	20Ap06Gp
Ann	28	F	Unknown	20Ap06Gp
Lydia	35	F	Unknown	20Ap06Gp
Ann	1	F	Child	20Ap06Gp
HONTON, Francis	30	M	Blacksmith	20Ap06Gp
FROST, John	20	M	Unknown	20Ap06Gp
BARTLETT, William	50	M	Unknown	20Ap06Gp
PENN, John	30	M	Unknown	20Ap06Gp
Mary	30	F	Unknown	20Ap06Gp
Mary-Ann	.00	F	Infant	20Ap06Gp
OVERSTON, Thomas	49	M	Bootmaker	20Ap06Gp
MCCOY, Patrick	46	M	Unknown	20Ap06Gp
BULLMAN, James	30	M	Unknown	20Ap06Gp
MACKEY, George	27	M	Unknown	20Ap06Gp
Mary-Ann	22	F	Unknown	20Ap06Gp
ROLEY, Elizabeth	32	F	Unknown	20Ap06Gp
TRACY, Catherine	27	F	Unknown	20Ap06Gp
JARRATT, Elias	28	M	Gdnr	20Ap06Gp
Sarah	27	F	Unknown	20Ap06Gp
Emma	7	F	Child	20Ap06Gp
Thomas	4	M	Child	20Ap06Gp
Rosetta	.00	F	Infant	20Ap06Gp
LOWN, Martin	30	M	Mason	20Ap06Gp
Sarah	30	F	Unknown	20Ap06Gp
James	.11	M	Infant	20Ap06Gp
WINCH, Daniel	36	M	Farmer	20Ap06Gp
Mary	36	F	Unknown	20Ap06Gp
Man	16	U	Unknown	20Ap06Gp
Daniel	13	M	Unknown	20Ap06Gp

NAMES OF PASSENGERS	AGE	SEX	OCCUPATIONS	DATE PORT SHIP
LEPPER, Frederick	19	M	Tanner	20Ap06Gp
SULLIVAN, Stephen	39	M	Unknown	20Ap06Gp
Ann	36	F	Unknown	20Ap06Gp
MONAGHAN, John	30	M	Shoemaker	20Ap06Gp
MULLIN, John	22	M	Unknown	20Ap06Gp
Catharine	22	F	Unknown	20Ap06Gp
James	19	M	Unknown	20Ap06Gp
Michael	13	M	Unknown	20Ap06Gp
Margaret	.06	F	Infant	20Ap06Gp
HOLMES, Richard	21	M	Brf	20Ap06Gp
PEARCE, William	22	M	Unknown	20Ap06Gp
PURDINE, Frederick	27	M	Unknown	20Ap06Gp
Edward	26	M	Unknown	20Ap06Gp
TONJEUR, Robert	56	M	Trunk Maker	20Ap06Gp
SULLEY, John	17	M	Unknown	20Ap06Gp
Ann	10	F	Unknown	20Ap06Gp
Mary	7	F	Child	20Ap06Gp
HEFFENER, Michael	23	M	Unknown	20Ap06Gp
RUBEY, George	25	M	Gdnr	20Ap06Gp
BASS, Mary	23	F	Unknown	20Ap06Gp
WILKS, Sarah	21	F	Unknown	20Ap06Gp
PRIER, Henry	26	M	Brf	20Ap06Gp
Charlotte	34	F	Unknown	20Ap06Gp
BUCK, James	30	M	Unknown	20Ap06Gp
Mary	30	F	Unknown	20Ap06Gp
WALKER, Samuel	30	M	Unknown	20Ap06Gp
Timothy	30	M	Farmer	20Ap06Gp
Robert	3	M	Child	20Ap06Gp
LESSENDEN, John	38	M	Unknown	20Ap06Gp
John	12	M	Gdnr	20Ap06Gp
George	10	M	Child	20Ap06Gp
William	8	M	Child	20Ap06Gp
Elizabeth	.00	F	Infant	20Ap06Gp
Cahrles-N.	22	M	Unknown	20Ap06Gp
FARRIETT, William	26	M	Unknown	20Ap06Gp
LONG, Thomas	28	M	Carpenter	20Ap06Gp
FULLIGIN, William	21	M	Unknown	20Ap06Gp
WICKHAM, James	24	M	Blacksmith	20Ap06Gp
Stephen	21	M	Unknown	20Ap06Gp
William	23	M	Unknown	20Ap06Gp
SULLIWOULD, George	19	M	Unknown	20Ap06Gp
MATHOUSE, William	23	M	Unknown	20Ap06Gp
STUART, William	33	M	Unknown	20Ap06Gp
RURD, William	34	M	Laborer	20Ap06Gp
JACKSON, Jujar	40	U	Unknown	20Ap06Gp
LARDNER, John	45	M	Unknown	20Ap06Gp
Eliza	38	F	Unknown	20Ap06Gp
William	13	M	Unknown	20Ap06Gp
George	11	M	Unknown	20Ap06Gp
John	7	M	Child	20Ap06Gp
Eliza	4	F	Child	20Ap06Gp
LALOR, James	32	U	Child	20Ap06Gp
Mary-Ann	30	F	Unknown	20Ap06Gp
PRIDHAM, George	17	M	Unknown	20Ap06Gp
KINNY, William	17	M	Unknown	20Ap06Gp
GILLS, George	20	M	Unknown	20Ap06Gp
BARTRAM, William	20	M	Unknown	20Ap06Gp
JOINER, Edward	21	M	Unknown	20Ap06Gp
CHEESEWRIGHT, Hannah	25	F	Seamstress	20Ap06Gp
HAMRAN, John	38	M	Unknown	20Ap06Gp
Catharine	25	F	Unknown	20Ap06Gp
Catharine	.08	F	Infant	20Ap06Gp
SCOTT, Michael	21	M	Unknown	20Ap06Gp
HENNARD, William	18	M	Laborer	20Ap06Gp
CONNELL, James	19	M	Unknown	20Ap06Gp
BLISS, John	17	M	Unknown	20Ap06Gp
GRAY, Joshua	35	M	Unknown	20Ap06Gp
Elizabeth	28	F	Unknown	20Ap06Gp
KEMPT, John	25	M	Unknown	20Ap06Gp
George	22	M	Unknown	20Ap06Gp
KENDALL, Sarah	18	F	Unknown	20Ap06Gp
GRAY, William	13	M	Unknown	20Ap06Gp
Maria	11	F	Unknown	20Ap06Gp
Mary-Ann	9	F	Child	20Ap06Gp
Elizabeth	6	F	Child	20Ap06Gp

NAMES OF PASSENGERS	AGE	SEX	OCCUPATIONS	DATE PORT SHIP
GRAY, John	3	M	Child	20Ap06Gp
James	.01	M	Infant	20Ap06Gp
GARE, Charles	30	M	Unknown	20Ap06Gp
Hannah	28	F	Unknown	20Ap06Gp
John	7	M	Child	20Ap06Gp
Eliza	2	F	Child	20Ap06Gp
BARTLETT, Henry	21	M	Farmer	20Ap06Gp
Charlotte	57	F	Unknown	20Ap06Gp
John	17	M	Unknown	20Ap06Gp
SMITH, Isaac	40	M	Unknown	20Ap06Gp
GILLEY, John	27	M	Shipwright	20Ap06Gp
HARRINGTON, Patrick	28	M	Unknown	20Ap06Gp
CALLIHAN, Smith	30	M	Unknown	20Ap06Gp
WHEEDEN, John	29	M	Tailor	20Ap06Gp
SMITH, John	19	M	Unknown	20Ap06Gp
William	21	M	Unknown	20Ap06Gp
Elizabeth	13	M	Unknown	20Ap06Gp
Allen	10	M	Unknown	20Ap06Gp
WATSON, William	30	M	Bootmaker	20Ap06Gp
HENRY, William	19	M	Unknown	20Ap06Gp
MERSCHAFF, Pruley	27	M	Unknown	20Ap06Gp
FLIMING, Margaret	21	F	Seamstress	20Ap06Gp
Johana	21	F	Unknown	20Ap06Gp
COOPER, Balinda	34	F	Unknown	20Ap06Gp
COOPPER, George	2	M	Child	20Ap06Gp
FARRALL, Alix	60	M	Gunsmith	20Ap06Gp
REDING, Henry	19	M	Stctr	20Ap06Gp
OKEIFFER, Johanna	36	F	Unknown	20Ap06Gp
Johanna	8	F	Child	20Ap06Gp
Ellen	6	F	Child	20Ap06Gp
William	4	M	Child	20Ap06Gp
HAZAR, William	25	M	Blacksmith	20Ap06Gp
KELLY, Henry	33	M	Tailor	20Ap06Gp
FOSTER, Ruben	29	M	Laborer	20Ap06Gp
OARS, William	26	M	Unknown	20Ap06Gp
DAVIS, William	19	M	Unknown	20Ap06Gp
BRADY, Joseph	15	M	Unknown	20Ap06Gp

ASHLAND 20 APRIL 1850

From Cork

NAMES OF PASSENGERS	AGE	SEX	OCCUPATIONS	DATE PORT SHIP
LYNCH, Owen	27	M	Laborer	20Ap18Hf
Ellen	25	F	Wife	20Ap18Hf
John	57	M	Unknown	20Ap18Hf
Johana	57	F	Wife	20Ap18Hf
SHEA, Jerry	23	M	Laborer	20Ap18Hf
FOLEY, Pat	28	M	Laborer	20Ap18Hf
Michael	25	M	Laborer	20Ap18Hf
Jeremiah	23	M	Laborer	20Ap18Hf
WALLACE, Ned	21	M	Laborer	20Ap18Hf
BRENAN, Bess	21	F	Servant	20Ap18Hf
CARROL, Ellen	22	F	Servant	20Ap18Hf
GALEN, Eliza	21	F	Servant	20Ap18Hf
SULIVAN, Cornelius	20	M	Laborer	20Ap18Hf
Catherine	30	F	Wife	20Ap18Hf
Mary	13	F	Unknown	20Ap18Hf
SULLIVAN, Catherine	11	F	Unknown	20Ap18Hf
WALSH, John	29	M	Servant	20Ap18Hf
DESMOND, Pat	18	M	Servant	20Ap18Hf
Johanah	13	F	Servant	20Ap18Hf
CONLY, David	26	M	Laborer	20Ap18Hf
NEAGLE, Edmund	19	M	Laborer	20Ap18Hf
WALLACE, Pat	25	M	Farmer	20Ap18Hf
Cath.	20	F	Wife	20Ap18Hf
MCMARION, Pat	25	M	Laborer	20Ap18Hf
HAMSTER, U-Revd.	40	M	Priest	20Ap18Hf
FITZGERALD, Pat	19	M	Laborer	20Ap18Hf
BRIAN, John	17	M	Carpenter	20Ap18Hf
ROCHE, Morris	15	M	Laborer	20Ap18Hf
SULLIVAN, Mary	20	F	Servant	20Ap18Hf
MARTIN, Bess	23	F	Wife	20Ap18Hf
Jane	20	F	Wife	20Ap18Hf
WALLACE, Mary	25	F	Servant	20Ap18Hf
REGAN, Jas.	23	M	Laborer	20Ap18Hf
PADEN, Geo.	50	M	Farmer	20Ap18Hf
Susan	50	F	Wife	20Ap18Hf
Mary	25	F	Servant	20Ap18Hf
Susan	11	F	Unknown	20Ap18Hf
MORGAN, P.C.	19	F	Servant	20Ap18Hf
PADDEN, Richard	11	M	Son	20Ap18Hf
HENELY, Ellen	22	F	Servant	20Ap18Hf
HULY, Margt.	20	F	Servant	20Ap18Hf
HOWLIN, Mary-Ann	22	F	Servant	20Ap18Hf
BARROW, John	29	M	Laborer	20Ap18Hf
MEAHAN, Wm.	24	M	Laborer	20Ap18Hf
BRIAN, Mary	20	F	Servant	20Ap18Hf
DOWNEY, Ellen	20	F	Servant	20Ap18Hf
FITZGERALD, Thos.	22	M	Laborer	20Ap18Hf
Catherine	22	F	Wife	20Ap18Hf
GRIFFIN, Jos.	23	M	Laborer	20Ap18Hf
DURRIGAN, Mary	34	F	Wi	20Ap18Hf
Mary-Ann	11	F	Unknown	20Ap18Hf
Bridget	.00	F	Infant	20Ap18Hf
ROCHE, Kate	22	F	Servant	20Ap18Hf
RYLEY, Mary	22	F	Servant	20Ap18Hf
HARTY, Michael	22	M	Laborer	20Ap18Hf
BEANE, Michael	22	M	Laborer	20Ap18Hf
CONELL, David	27	M	Laborer	20Ap18Hf
MALONEY, John	30	M	Laborer	20Ap18Hf
CARROLL, Michael	40	M	Laborer	20Ap18Hf
COLEMAN, John	40	M	Laborer	20Ap18Hf
GALVIN, John	26	M	Laborer	20Ap18Hf
MILES, Wm.	20	M	Laborer	20Ap18Hf
CURTAIN, Jas.	24	M	Laborer	20Ap18Hf
REGGAN, Thos.	20	M	Laborer	20Ap18Hf
MAHAN, Thos.	20	M	Laborer	20Ap18Hf
CONEY, Mary	28	F	Servant	20Ap18Hf
MCGREEN, Anthy.	25	M	Servant	20Ap18Hf
DALY, Mary	23	F	Servant	20Ap18Hf
CONERS, Betsey	5	F	Child	20Ap18Hf
Margaret	3	F	Child	20Ap18Hf
AMBROSE, Johana	25	F	Unknown	20Ap18Hf
Margaret	22	F	Servant	20Ap18Hf
MURPHY, Jerry	23	M	Laborer	20Ap18Hf
VALE, Catherine	30	F	Servant	20Ap18Hf
KLUCHEN, Hannah	18	F	Servant	20Ap18Hf
GROGAN, Betty	24	F	Servant	20Ap18Hf
KELEHAN, Michael	24	M	Laborer	20Ap18Hf
HARDING, Robert	30	M	Poet	20Ap18Hf
SULLIVAN, John	28	M	Laborer	20Ap18Hf
Betty	20	F	Wife	20Ap18Hf
CLIFFORD, Johana	17	F	Servant	20Ap18Hf
SULLIVAN, Catherine	.00	F	Infant	20Ap18Hf
Jerry	43	M	Laborer	20Ap18Hf
Pat	17	M	Laborer	20Ap18Hf
BRYAN, Martin	34	M	Laborer	20Ap18Hf
WELCH, John	28	M	Miller	20Ap18Hf
CAGENY, Michael	30	M	Laborer	20Ap18Hf
KEIFE, Pat	30	M	Laborer	20Ap18Hf
BRIAN, Tim	30	M	Laborer	20Ap18Hf
John	20	M	Laborer	20Ap18Hf
Peggy	40	F	Unknown	20Ap18Hf
John	40	M	Laborer	20Ap18Hf
COMBS, Wm.	26	M	Laborer	20Ap18Hf
DRISCOL, Deny	26	M	Laborer	20Ap18Hf
MCCARTY, Bart.	23	M	Laborer	20Ap18Hf
Michael	20	M	Laborer	20Ap18Hf
SHEALY, John	24	M	Laborer	20Ap18Hf
DALY, Tim	22	M	Laborer	20Ap18Hf
LUCNEY, Mary	25	F	Servant	20Ap18Hf
Michael	3	M	Child	20Ap18Hf
COFFE, Nancy	25	F	Servant	20Ap18Hf
DORALY, Peg	5	F	Child	20Ap18Hf

NAMES OF PASSENGERS	AGE	SEX	OCCUPATIONS	DATE PORT SHIP
DORALY, Biddy	4	F	Child	20Ap18Hf
CUSAN, Winy	40	F	Unknown	20Ap18Hf
Peggy	12	F	Unknown	20Ap18Hf
Michael	10	M	Unknown	20Ap18Hf
Pat	8	M	Child	20Ap18Hf
Mary	6	F	Child	20Ap18Hf
John	.00	M	Infant	20Ap18Hf
MCCURTY, Nancy	25	F	Servant	20Ap18Hf
CONDEN, Ellen	18	F	Servant	20Ap18Hf
COFFEE, Peggy	20	F	Servant	20Ap18Hf
CONDON, John	20	M	Laborer	20Ap18Hf
Mary	21	F	Servant	20Ap18Hf
QUINLAN, John	24	M	Laborer	20Ap18Hf
Martin	26	M	Laborer	20Ap18Hf
David	17	M	Laborer	20Ap18Hf
Margaret	55	F	Unknown	20Ap18Hf
SHEA, Abey	25	F	Servant	20Ap18Hf
SEAHAN, Peg	35	F	Servant	20Ap18Hf
David	30	M	Farmer	20Ap18Hf
Wm.	10	M	Unknown	20Ap18Hf
Catherine	9	F	Child	20Ap18Hf
Pat	3	M	Child	20Ap18Hf
BURNS, Mary	35	F	Servant	20Ap18Hf
HOGAN, Edward	39	M	Laborer	20Ap18Hf
Michael	.00	M	Infant	20Ap18Hf
FROST, Pat	33	M	Laborer	20Ap18Hf
Biddy	23	F	Wife	20Ap18Hf
CALLIHAN, Pat	40	M	Laborer	20Ap18Hf
MCDONALD, Wm.	24	M	Laborer	20Ap18Hf
RYLEY, Mary	22	F	Servant	20Ap18Hf
HAYS, David	35	M	Smith	20Ap18Hf
LONG, Johanah	25	F	Servant	20Ap18Hf
HEIFFE, Jas.	21	M	Servant	20Ap18Hf
FOLEY, Pat	20	M	Laborer	20Ap18Hf
LONG, Michael	60	M	Laborer	20Ap18Hf
DONERAY, Michael	24	M	Boatman	20Ap18Hf
NEILL, Pat	40	M	Laborer	20Ap18Hf
LADON, John	31	M	Laborer	20Ap18Hf
Daniel	16	M	Laborer	20Ap18Hf
ROCHE, John	30	M	Laborer	20Ap18Hf
WELCH, Bartholomew	35	M	Unknown	20Ap18Hf
SHEY, Michael	18	M	Unknown	20Ap18Hf
HANIFSTER, M.	30	M	Unknown	20Ap18Hf
CAHILL, John	11	M	Unknown	20Ap18Hf
Ellen	6	F	Child	20Ap18Hf
NAGLE, John	35	M	Unknown	20Ap18Hf
SMITH, Thos.	18	M	Unknown	20Ap18Hf

CHAOS 22 APRIL 1850

From Liverpool

NAMES OF PASSENGERS	AGE	SEX	OCCUPATIONS	DATE PORT SHIP
HALL, Catherine	18	F	Milliner	22Ap02Bq
BOOSE, Margrett	20	F	Milliner	22Ap02Bq
CORRIGAN, Patk.	22	M	Laborer	22Ap02Bq
Ann	20	F	Bomkr	22Ap02Bq
MALOY, Bernard	20	M	Laborer	22Ap02Bq
CONNELL, Bridget	18	F	Dressmaker	22Ap02Bq
CORRIGAN, James	18	M	Laborer	22Ap02Bq
Francis	33	M	Laborer	22Ap02Bq
KELLY, Bridget	20	F	Dressmaker	22Ap02Bq
CORRIGAN, Mary	20	F	Dressmaker	22Ap02Bq
WARD, Mary	17	F	Dressmaker	22Ap02Bq
MILTON, Winford	20	F	Dressmaker	22Ap02Bq
CONY, William	22	M	Laborer	22Ap02Bq
BARKINSON, Bridget	18	F	Dressmaker	22Ap02Bq
MCKEVER, John	30	M	Weaver	22Ap02Bq
CASEY, Honour	18	F	Servant	22Ap02Bq
LAMUR, Patrick	26	M	Servant	22Ap02Bq
GRAHAM, Patrick	26	M	Servant	22Ap02Bq
REILY, Mary	30	F	Servant	22Ap02Bq
Bridget	13	F	Servant	22Ap02Bq
Catherine	11	F	Servant	22Ap02Bq
QUINLIN, John	60	M	Farmer	22Ap02Bq
Ellen	48	F	Farmer	22Ap02Bq
Jeremia	24	M	Laborer	22Ap02Bq
Wineferd	18	F	Servant	22Ap02Bq
Patk	13	M	Servant	22Ap02Bq
Mickle	11	M	Servant	22Ap02Bq
John	9	M	Child	22Ap02Bq
William	6	M	Child	22Ap02Bq
Ellen	.00	F	Infant	22Ap02Bq
OSULLIVAN, John	30	M	Laborer	22Ap02Bq
WINN, James	32	M	Laborer	22Ap02Bq
KILROY, Thos.	22	M	Farmer	22Ap02Bq
MULDOON, Mickle	45	M	Servant	22Ap02Bq
SHEA, James	25	M	Laborer	22Ap02Bq
Bridget	21	F	Wife	22Ap02Bq
WADE, Patk.	25	M	Laborer	22Ap02Bq
SIEVERS, Peter	22	M	Laborer	22Ap02Bq
Bridget	25	F	Servant	22Ap02Bq
DAILY, John	28	M	Farmer	22Ap02Bq
BUCKLEY, Barth.	28	M	Blacksmith	22Ap02Bq
DAILY, Mary	22	F	Servant	22Ap02Bq
REILEY, William	18	M	Hrsm	22Ap02Bq
PURCEL, Ellen	20	F	Dressmaker	22Ap02Bq
SARSFIELD, Mary	17	F	Servant	22Ap02Bq
FAY, John	25	M	Laborer	22Ap02Bq
RAHELLY, Phillip	55	M	Laborer	22Ap02Bq
John	50	M	Laborer	22Ap02Bq
Morgan	13	M	Laborer	22Ap02Bq
Daniel	11	M	Laborer	22Ap02Bq
Ellen	9	F	Child	22Ap02Bq
Phillip	5	M	Child	22Ap02Bq
BRANNON, Judy	28	F	Laborer	22Ap02Bq
Ann	.00	F	Infant	22Ap02Bq
LAWLER, Mickle	40	M	Farmer	22Ap02Bq
Elizabeth	33	F	Wife	22Ap02Bq
STAGNEANS, Chatherine	24	F	Servant	22Ap02Bq
KELLY, Thomas	40	M	Farmer	22Ap02Bq
Mary	40	F	Wife	22Ap02Bq
MARTIN, B.	40	M	Farmer	22Ap02Bq
Mary	60	F	Wife	22Ap02Bq
Margrett	17	F	Servant	22Ap02Bq
John	11	M	Miner	22Ap02Bq
OHARE, Thos.	13	M	Laborer	22Ap02Bq
COMESKY, Patk.	29	M	Laborer	22Ap02Bq
Philip	28	M	Tailor	22Ap02Bq
MCCOWEN, James	44	M	Laborer	22Ap02Bq
MCGUIRE, Mary	20	F	Servant	22Ap02Bq
COMESKEY, Ann	20	F	Servant	22Ap02Bq
MCGUIRE, Rose	16	F	Servant	22Ap02Bq
MCGAUL, Ann	10	F	Servant	22Ap02Bq
Catherine	16	F	Servant	22Ap02Bq
MORRIS, Catherine	18	F	Servant	22Ap02Bq
DEVIER, Thos.	24	M	Cbtmkr	22Ap02Bq
CLARK, Mikle	34	M	Laborer	22Ap02Bq
GALVIN, Ann	20	F	Servant	22Ap02Bq
CLARK, Mary	33	F	Servant	22Ap02Bq
COLE, Mary	11	F	Servant	22Ap02Bq
DORNEY, Catherine	20	F	Servant	22Ap02Bq
Ann	19	F	Servant	22Ap02Bq
SHEVIN, Winni	46	F	Dressmaker	22Ap02Bq
Winni	16	F	Dressmaker	22Ap02Bq
DUFFY, Wini	20	F	Dressmaker	22Ap02Bq
LAWLERS, James	45	M	Laborer	22Ap02Bq
Anthony	18	F	Servant	22Ap02Bq
Edwards	16	F	Servant	22Ap02Bq
Catherine	14	F	Servant	22Ap02Bq
Mary	20	F	Servant	22Ap02Bq
James	12	M	Servant	22Ap02Bq
Teresa	10	F	Servant	22Ap02Bq
Edward	40	M	Servant	22Ap02Bq
DONNE, Mickle	30	M	Servant	22Ap02Bq

NAMES OF PASSENGERS	AGE	SEX	OCCUPATIONS	DATE PORT SHIP
GROOM, James	55	M	Laborer	22Ap02Bq
Rose	55	F	Wife	22Ap02Bq
Catherine	6	F	Child	22Ap02Bq
John	4	M	Child	22Ap02Bq
CONE, Mary	24	F	Servant	22Ap02Bq
DEMPSEY, Catherine	24	F	Servant	22Ap02Bq
MCEVOY, Michl.	26	M	Carter	22Ap02Bq
Catherine	20	F	Carter	22Ap02Bq
MURPHY, Denis	20	M	Mason	22Ap02Bq
FITZGERALD, Donald	20	M	Laborer	22Ap02Bq
PRICE, Patk.	20	M	Shoemaker	22Ap02Bq
DONOLY, Patk.	26	M	Laborer	22Ap02Bq
SULLIVAN, Daniel	50	M	Carpenter	22Ap02Bq
MULVEY, Mary	30	F	Servant	22Ap02Bq
DONNELON, Simeon	25	M	Laborer	22Ap02Bq
REYNOLDS, Dan	40	M	Laborer	22Ap02Bq
ONEIL, Eliza	16	F	Dressmaker	22Ap02Bq
DENN, Eliza	15	F	Servant	22Ap02Bq
DARCEY, Edward	23	M	Laborer	22Ap02Bq
KENEDY, Dennis	22	M	Laborer	22Ap02Bq
DELANEY, John	22	M	Laborer	22Ap02Bq
LAWLER, Eliza	25	F	Servant	22Ap02Bq
MORDEN, Bridget	37	F	Servant	22Ap02Bq
HAVANAGH, Mickl.	28	M	Laborer	22Ap02Bq
MORAN, Margret	30	F	Servant	22Ap02Bq
WALLACE, Thomas	27	M	Carpenter	22Ap02Bq
Richard	23	M	Laborer	22Ap02Bq
Smith	21	M	Laborer	22Ap02Bq
CHAPMAN, Frank	30	M	Laborer	22Ap02Bq
Mary	30	F	Wife	22Ap02Bq
HYMS, Ann	30	F	Servant	22Ap02Bq
KERNAN, Frank	20	M	Laborer	22Ap02Bq
CONNOR, Robby	20	M	Servant	22Ap02Bq
MONAGHAN, Malachi	20	M	Clerk	22Ap02Bq
EAGAN, Betsy	14	F	Servant	22Ap02Bq
BRODRICK, Martin	22	M	Laborer	22Ap02Bq
RONLAN, John	30	M	Laborer	22Ap02Bq
Catherine	25	F	Wife	22Ap02Bq
PEMBROOK, Ann	29	F	Servant	22Ap02Bq
HARRINGTON, Jeremia	18	M	Servant	22Ap02Bq
MCDONALL, Margrett	25	F	Cap Maker	22Ap02Bq
MURPHY, Phillip	20	M	Miner	22Ap02Bq
DOODY, Mary	20	F	Servant	22Ap02Bq
DONNELY, Bryan	21	M	Laborer	22Ap02Bq
AHERN, Mary	20	F	Dressmaker	22Ap02Bq
Fanny	22	F	Dressmaker	22Ap02Bq
RICHEY, Patk.	40	M	Laborer	22Ap02Bq
Martha	30	F	Wife	22Ap02Bq
Bridget	20	F	Servant	22Ap02Bq
HOBAN, Honor	20	F	Servant	22Ap02Bq
LALLY, John	20	M	Laborer	22Ap02Bq
MCCERDELL, Ann	20	F	Servant	22Ap02Bq
BYRNE, Thomas	19	M	Laborer	22Ap02Bq
DOBBINS, Henry	33	M	Mason	22Ap02Bq
KENEDY, John	33	M	Laborer	22Ap02Bq
KELLY, Ann	15	F	Servant	22Ap02Bq
BROGAN, Margrett	9	F	Child	22Ap02Bq
FOLEY, Mary	40	F	Cook	22Ap02Bq
John (S)	11	M	Unknown	22Ap02Bq
William (S)	9	M	Child	22Ap02Bq
Patk. (S)	7	M	Child	22Ap02Bq
ONEILL, Ann	20	F	Dressmaker	22Ap02Bq
RODGERS, John	16	M	Laborer	22Ap02Bq
LEAHY, Ellen	25	F	Servant	22Ap02Bq
JEFFRED, Mary	10	F	Servant	22Ap02Bq
HOGAN, Thos.	19	M	Carpenter	22Ap02Bq
ONEILL, Mick	25	M	Laborer	22Ap02Bq
KELCH, John	25	M	Laborer	22Ap02Bq
CONNOR, Mary	20	F	Servant	22Ap02Bq
BARRY, Gaven	19	M	Servant	22Ap02Bq
Catherine	25	F	Servant	22Ap02Bq
Margrett	22	F	Servant	22Ap02Bq
FLINN, Ellen	50	F	Cook	22Ap02Bq
TOBIN, Catherine	14	F	Servant	22Ap02Bq
SULLIVAN, Ellen	40	F	Servant	22Ap02Bq
BRYAN, Julia	4	F	Child	22Ap02Bq
SULLIVAN, Jerh.	40	M	Laborer	22Ap02Bq
Ellen	40	F	Wife	22Ap02Bq
KELCHER, Mick	32	M	Laborer	22Ap02Bq
CRAWLEY, Patt	50	M	Farmer	22Ap02Bq
LORDON, Cornelius	23	M	Farmer	22Ap02Bq
DRISCOLL, Margrett	22	F	Servant	22Ap02Bq
CROWLEY, Mary	34	F	Servant	22Ap02Bq
LEARY, Julia	26	F	Servant	22Ap02Bq
Charles	2	M	Child	22Ap02Bq
Ellen	.00	F	Infant	22Ap02Bq
CONNOLY, Denis	19	M	Laborer	22Ap02Bq
ONEILL, Mary	25	F	Servant	22Ap02Bq
SULLIVAN, Bridgett	17	F	Dressmaker	22Ap02Bq
RUSSELL, Mickle	30	M	Farmer	22Ap02Bq
Honour	30	F	Wife	22Ap02Bq
LEAHY, James	25	M	Laborer	22Ap02Bq
OBRYAN, Mick	20	M	Gdnr	22Ap02Bq
GALVIN, John	35	M	Laborer	22Ap02Bq
SHEA, John	20	M	Laborer	22Ap02Bq
AHEARN, Ellen	30	F	Servant	22Ap02Bq
CASEY, Patk	30	M	Farmer	22Ap02Bq
Ellen	28	F	Wife	22Ap02Bq
DITIS, Johanna	30	F	Cook	22Ap02Bq
PRESTON, Thomas	36	M	Farmer	22Ap02Bq
Stephen	28	M	Gdnr	22Ap02Bq
Mickle	26	M	Farmer	22Ap02Bq
WALL, Ann	15	F	Unknown	22Ap02Bq
Died-At-Sea				
HEALEY, Chaos-Savannah	.00	U	Infant	22Ap02Bq
Born-At-Sea Died-At-Sea				
HILL, John	28	M	Unknown	22Ap02Bq
CHAMBERS, U-Mrs.	20	F	Unknown	22Ap02Bq

GLADIATOR 22 APRIL 1850

From London

NAMES OF PASSENGERS	AGE	SEX	OCCUPATIONS	DATE PORT SHIP
COENEY, Margaret	28	F	Unknown	22Ap06Hg
OKEEFE, John	28	M	Unknown	22Ap06Hg

JOSEPHINE 22 APRIL 1850

From Liverpool

NAMES OF PASSENGERS	AGE	SEX	OCCUPATIONS	DATE PORT SHIP
BERRY, Patk.	20	M	Laborer	22Ap02Cp
DWYER, Judith	20	F	Servant	22Ap02Cp
RYANS, Ellen	20	F	Servant	22Ap02Cp
OBRYAN, Winifred	20	F	Servant	22Ap02Cp
COURIES, Patk.	7	M	Child	22Ap02Cp
QUILLY, William	20	M	Laborer	22Ap02Cp
Thomas	18	M	Laborer	22Ap02Cp
MCGAW, Alexander	28	M	Laborer	22Ap02Cp
ROSS, Hugh	28	M	Laborer	22Ap02Cp
RILLY, Alexander	18	M	Laborer	22Ap02Cp
Jane	19	F	Servant	22Ap02Cp
DAVISON, Elizabeth	21	F	Servant	22Ap02Cp
CONOLLY, Mary	14	F	Servant	22Ap02Cp
CROSSIN, John	20	M	Laborer	22Ap02Cp
MULHOLLAND, Betty	20	F	Servant	22Ap02Cp
CONALLY, Thos.	20	M	Laborer	22Ap02Cp
MAHONEY, Jas.	40	M	Laborer	22Ap02Cp
FITZGERALD, Cath.	20	F	Servant	22Ap02Cp

NAMES OF PASSENGERS		AGE	SEX	OCCUPATIONS	DATE PORT SHIP
RUGLETAN, Jeremiah		40	M	Laborer	22Ap02Cp
RYAN, John		24	M	Laborer	22Ap02Cp
Mary		24	F	Servant	22Ap02Cp
Mary		45	F	Servant	22Ap02Cp
Peggy		8	F	Child	22Ap02Cp
Margaret		.00	F	Infant	22Ap02Cp
BYRNE, Eliza		24	F	Servant	22Ap02Cp
MCNAMA, John		20	M	Farmer	22Ap02Cp
FLEMING, Eliza		18	F	Seamstress	22Ap02Cp
LUIS, Jas.		35	M	Weaver	22Ap02Cp
Anne	(W)	25	F	Unknown	22Ap02Cp
SHARK, Mary		20	F	Dressmaker	22Ap02Cp
Mary-Anne		20	F	Dressmaker	22Ap02Cp
CANTLIN, William		26	M	Weaver	22Ap02Cp
John		25	M	Laborer	22Ap02Cp
Patk.		24	M	Laborer	22Ap02Cp
Bridget		24	F	Servant	22Ap02Cp
Ellen		22	F	Servant	22Ap02Cp
Catherine		18	F	Servant	22Ap02Cp
Mary		21	F	Servant	22Ap02Cp
DAOLIN, Bridget		18	F	Servant	22Ap02Cp
PURCELL, Mary		16	F	Servant	22Ap02Cp
COSTELLO, Mary		17	F	Servant	22Ap02Cp
U, Julia		5	F	Child	22Ap02Cp
FITZGERALD, Edward		50	M	Farmer	22Ap02Cp
Ellen	(W)	45	F	Unknown	22Ap02Cp
Hannah		20	F	Servant	22Ap02Cp
Mary		18	F	Servant	22Ap02Cp
Margaret		9	F	Child	22Ap02Cp
James		12	M	Laborer	22Ap02Cp
Edwin		5	M	Child	22Ap02Cp
RATCHARD, Ellen-L.		.00	F	Infant	22Ap02Cp
EGAN, Thomas		13	M	Unknown	22Ap02Cp
DOOLAN, John		40	M	Unknown	22Ap02Cp
UNIACK, Richd.		35	M	Unknown	22Ap02Cp
FLINN, Timothy		14	M	Laborer	22Ap02Cp
CASTELLO, John		50	M	Farmer	22Ap02Cp
Bridget	(W)	40	F	Unknown	22Ap02Cp
James		24	M	Farmer	22Ap02Cp
Bridget		13	F	Servant	22Ap02Cp
Ellen		11	F	Unknown	22Ap02Cp
Hannah		6	F	Child	22Ap02Cp
BURKE, Jame		33	M	Unknown	22Ap02Cp
FINEGAN, Patk.		24	M	Laborer	22Ap02Cp
LOHAN, Martin		18	M	Unknown	22Ap02Cp
RYAN, Ellen		14	F	Servant	22Ap02Cp
TORPY, Biddy		50	F	Unknown	22Ap02Cp
John		6	M	Child	22Ap02Cp
MADDEN, Jas.		33	M	Farmer	22Ap02Cp
MITCHELL, Jas.		20	M	Laborer	22Ap02Cp
JOYCE, Mary		20	F	Servant	22Ap02Cp
MAHONEY, Thos.		35	M	Farmer	22Ap02Cp
Johanna	(D)	17	F	Unknown	22Ap02Cp
Thomas	(S)	13	M	Unknown	22Ap02Cp
James	(S)	13	M	Unknown	22Ap02Cp
John	(S)	3	M	Child	22Ap02Cp
ANDERSON, Catherine		48	F	Shoemaker	22Ap02Cp
John		27	M	Unknown	22Ap02Cp
Thomas		25	M	Shoemaker	22Ap02Cp
William		23	M	Shoemaker	22Ap02Cp
Margaret		13	F	Servant	22Ap02Cp
Patk.		20	M	Laborer	22Ap02Cp
Julia		9	F	Servant	22Ap02Cp
BAMANE, Judith		50	F	Servant	22Ap02Cp
Mary		27	F	Servant	22Ap02Cp
Margaret		23	F	Servant	22Ap02Cp
Eliza		17	F	Servant	22Ap02Cp
Laurence		12	M	Servant	22Ap02Cp
Patk.		10	M	Servant	22Ap02Cp
RYAN, Patk.		21	M	Laborer	22Ap02Cp
HALLORAN, Johanna		23	F	House Maid	22Ap02Cp
MOORRE, Patk.		33	M	Laborer	22Ap02Cp
Mary	(W)	26	F	Unknown	22Ap02Cp
John	(S)	4	M	Child	22Ap02Cp
Mary		3	F	Child	22Ap02Cp

NAMES OF PASSENGERS		AGE	SEX	OCCUPATIONS	DATE PORT SHIP
MOORRE, Ellen		.00	F	Infant	22Ap02Cp
GRADY, Daniell		36	M	Laborer	22Ap02Cp
Peggy	(W)	26	U	Unknown	22Ap02Cp
Bridget	(D)	5	F	Child	22Ap02Cp
Michl.	(S)	3	M	Husband	22Ap02Cp
John		.00	M	Infant	22Ap02Cp
CAYNE, Mary		20	F	Servant	22Ap02Cp
RALPH, Bessy		16	F	Servant	22Ap02Cp
MCGANDER, Catherine		16	F	Servant	22Ap02Cp
CAYNE, Winifred		18	F	Servant	22Ap02Cp
CANNON, Biddy		60	F	Servant	22Ap02Cp
MORAN, Cath.		18	F	Servant	22Ap02Cp
MCNULLY, Bridget		20	F	Servant	22Ap02Cp
MORAN, Danial		29	M	Laborer	22Ap02Cp
RYAN, Biddy		17	F	Servant	22Ap02Cp
DWYER, John		40	M	Farmer	22Ap02Cp
RYAN, Edmond		30	M	Laborer	22Ap02Cp
DOWNING, Patk. Died-At-Sea		35	M	Unknown	22Ap02Cp
MULIGAN, Felix		30	M	Shoemaker	22Ap02Cp
COLE, Michl.		20	M	Farmer	22Ap02Cp
HICKEY, Edward		17	M	Laborer	22Ap02Cp
FITZGERALD, James		20	M	Laborer	22Ap02Cp
SWANNEY, James		25	M	Laborer	22Ap02Cp
Catherine		23	F	Laborer	22Ap02Cp
FITZGERALD, Margt.		26	F	Servant	22Ap02Cp
CAVANAGH, Tim		19	M	Laborer	22Ap02Cp
BARREN, Richd.		20	M	Clerk	22Ap02Cp
RIELY, Cath.		18	F	Servant	22Ap02Cp
Michl.		20	M	Farmer	22Ap02Cp
CARROLL, Patk.		20	M	Stone Mason	22Ap02Cp
RIELY, Patk.		18	M	Farmer	22Ap02Cp
RYAN, Michl.		18	M	Laborer	22Ap02Cp
ODONNELL, James		30	M	Tailor	22Ap02Cp
SULLIVAN, Tedey		23	M	Stone Mason	22Ap02Cp
GOGGIN, John		24	M	Laborer	22Ap02Cp
Michl.		28	M	Laborer	22Ap02Cp
SHEA, Michl.		25	M	Tailor	22Ap02Cp
WHELIN, Jeremiah		36	M	Shoemaker	22Ap02Cp
Mary	(W)	30	F	Unknown	22Ap02Cp
GRIFFIN, Margt.	(M)	50	F	Unknown	22Ap02Cp
ORGAN, Paul		19	M	Stableman	22Ap02Cp
MCCRAITH, Patk.		35	M	Farmer	22Ap02Cp
Peggy	(W)	30	F	Unknown	22Ap02Cp
Mary	(D)	.00	F	Infant	22Ap02Cp
KEEFE, Pierce		35	M	Shoemaker	22Ap02Cp
U-Mrs.		35	F	Unknown	22Ap02Cp
Margaret	(D)	6	F	Child	22Ap02Cp
Catherine	(D)	4	F	Child	22Ap02Cp
Bridget		3	F	Child	22Ap02Cp
SMITH, Patk.		30	M	Shoemaker	22Ap02Cp
U-Mrs.		25	F	Unknown	22Ap02Cp
Jas.		.00	M	Infant	22Ap02Cp
MCCARTHY, Jerry		35	M	Laborer	22Ap02Cp
Julia	(W)	25	F	Unknown	22Ap02Cp
Ellen		5	F	Child	22Ap02Cp
Dennis		2	M	Child	22Ap02Cp
Mary		.00	F	Infant	22Ap02Cp
HICKEY, Betty		30	F	Servant	22Ap02Cp
HANRAHAN, John		25	M	Laborer	22Ap02Cp
Anne	(W)	19	F	Unknown	22Ap02Cp
FAGAN, Matt		30	M	Farmer	22Ap02Cp
U-Mrs.		30	F	Unknown	22Ap02Cp
Catherine	(D)	9	F	Child	22Ap02Cp
Matt		.00	M	Infant	22Ap02Cp
MURPHY, Danl.		23	M	Laborer	22Ap02Cp
FOGARTY, James		38	M	Laborer	22Ap02Cp
SULLIVAN, Johanna		31	F	Servant	22Ap02Cp
Catherine		30	F	Servant	22Ap02Cp
CONOLLY, Edwd.		20	M	Miller	22Ap02Cp
Margt.		18	F	Servant	22Ap02Cp
MAHON, Margt.		12	F	Servant	22Ap02Cp
DOOLEY, John		25	M	Blacksmith	22Ap02Cp
HADNETT, Andrew		26	M	Laborer	22Ap02Cp
CAREY, Mary		20	F	Servant	22Ap02Cp

NAMES OF PASSENGERS	AGE	SEX	OCCUPATIONS	DATE PORT SHIP
SHEA, Margaret	25	F	Servant	22Ap02Cp
CAMPBELL, Mary	25	F	Servant	22Ap02Cp
DWYER, Jeremiah	22	M	Laborer	22Ap02Cp
FITZGERALD, Richd.	36	M	Laborer	22Ap02Cp
SULLIVAN, Bridget	22	F	Servant	22Ap02Cp
John	19	M	Laborer	22Ap02Cp
MORIARTY, Mary	19	F	Servant	22Ap02Cp
CONOLLY, Patk.	22	M	Laborer	22Ap02Cp
EARLEHY, Danl.	21	M	Laborer	22Ap02Cp
CONNOR, Ellen	19	F	Servant	22Ap02Cp
KENNY, John	22	M	Farmer	22Ap02Cp
Catherine (W)	20	F	Unknown	22Ap02Cp
COLBERT, Margt.	17	F	Servant	22Ap02Cp
HANLAN, Patk.	30	M	Stevedore	22Ap02Cp
FENNTY, Thos.	20	M	Laborer	22Ap02Cp
Maurice	24	M	Laborer	22Ap02Cp
SHEEHAM, Patk.	39	M	Laborer	22Ap02Cp
CONLAN, Cath.	18	F	Servant	22Ap02Cp
WHELIN, John	30	M	Gdnr	22Ap02Cp
MELLON, Luke	30	M	Laborer	22Ap02Cp
GILBEN, Peter	28	M	Farmer	22Ap02Cp
WHITE, Margt.	23	F	Seamstress	22Ap02Cp
Eliza	30	F	Seamstress	22Ap02Cp
FLATTERY, John	23	M	Laborer	22Ap02Cp
LAUGHLIN, Jas.	30	M	Farmer	22Ap02Cp

CORA-LINN 22 APRIL 1850

From Glasgow

NAMES OF PASSENGERS	AGE	SEX	OCCUPATIONS	DATE PORT SHIP
MCMAHON, Hugh	16	M	Servant	22Ap21Cj
ONIEL, Terence	24	M	Laborer	22Ap21Cj
MCDADE, Rose	24	F	Servant	22Ap21Cj
CRAWFORD, Margt.	30	F	Wife	22Ap21Cj
John	3	M	Child	22Ap21Cj
Margt.	.08	F	Infant	22Ap21Cj
FINNIE, John	27	M	Carpenter	22Ap21Cj
KENAN, John	45	M	Laborer	22Ap21Cj
DUFFY, Francis	48	M	Broker	22Ap21Cj
GILSHIN, Michael	32	M	Laborer	22Ap21Cj
SWAINE, William	20	M	Laborer	22Ap21Cj
FITZPATRICK, John	22	M	Laborer	22Ap21Cj
STEWART, John	25	M	Merchant	22Ap21Cj
MCMAHON, John	18	M	Laborer	22Ap21Cj
BELTON, Ann	30	F	Wife	22Ap21Cj
Mary-Ann	6	F	Child	22Ap21Cj
MCGOVERN, John	37	M	Laborer	22Ap21Cj
DONAHOE, Peter	37	M	Laborer	22Ap21Cj

LONDON 22 APRIL 1850

From Sligo

NAMES OF PASSENGERS	AGE	SEX	OCCUPATIONS	DATE PORT SHIP
MITCHEL, Patrick	22	M	Farmer	22Ap09Au
Edward	20	M	Farmer	22Ap09Au
ARMSTRONG, George	18	M	Farmer	22Ap09Au
Mary	12	F	Unknown	22Ap09Au
Bridget	9	F	Child	22Ap09Au
COONEY, Michael	26	M	Farmer	22Ap09Au
FEENEY, Rose	20	F	Spinster	22Ap09Au
KERNS, Mary	18	F	Spinster	22Ap09Au
HANGHAN, Bridget	22	F	Spinster	22Ap09Au
KIENAN, Michael	30	M	Farmer	22Ap09Au
MEEHAN, Patrick	23	M	Servant	22Ap09Au
CLARKE, Bridget	20	F	Servant	22Ap09Au
FENARTY, William	20	M	Laborer	22Ap09Au
DUNN, Mary	23	F	Spinster	22Ap09Au
KELLY, Mary	20	F	Servant	22Ap09Au
CAFFERTY, Michael	22	M	Farmer	22Ap09Au
Libby	50	F	Matron	22Ap09Au
Mary	20	F	Spinster	22Ap09Au
Catherine	18	F	Spinster	22Ap09Au
Patrick	12	M	Unknown	22Ap09Au
FERRINS, James	30	M	Servant	22Ap09Au
Margaret	29	F	Matron	22Ap09Au
George	.01	M	Infant	22Ap09Au
WALKER, Bridget	20	F	Matron	22Ap09Au
John	22	M	Teacher	22Ap09Au
George	.01	M	Infant	22Ap09Au
FENNIGAN, Jane	20	F	Spinster	22Ap09Au
MCMOROW, Michael	30	M	Farmer	22Ap09Au
MEEHAN, Mary	20	F	Spinster	22Ap09Au
MCHUGH, Bridget	20	F	Spinster	22Ap09Au
ARMSTRONG, Thomas	32	M	Laborer	22Ap09Au
SCANLAN, John	35	M	Laborer	22Ap09Au
LANEY, George	20	M	Servant	22Ap09Au
DOWNIE, Jane	21	F	Matron	22Ap09Au
KELLY, Jane	24	F	Spinster	22Ap09Au
SMYTH, Bernard	24	M	Farmer	22Ap09Au
CONNELLY, John	32	M	Laborer	22Ap09Au
KILCULLEN, Thomas	25	M	Farmer	22Ap09Au
Mary	23	F	Matron	22Ap09Au
GILGAN, Hugh	20	M	Laborer	22Ap09Au
BURNS, Martin	25	M	Farmer	22Ap09Au
TEIRNAN, Michael	24	M	Farmer	22Ap09Au
MCGUIRE, Michael	36	M	Farmer	22Ap09Au
PARKS, John	40	M	Farmer	22Ap09Au
MCGOWN, John	33	M	Farmer	22Ap09Au
Thomas	20	M	Farmer	22Ap09Au
MEARN, Patrick	25	M	Farmer	22Ap09Au
TEIRNAN, John	20	M	Farmer	22Ap09Au
BRENNAN, Catherine	20	F	Spinster	22Ap09Au
DOHERTY, Peter	18	M	Laborer	22Ap09Au
DOWNIE, Francis	25	M	Farmer	22Ap09Au
KEENEY, Francis	35	M	Farmer	22Ap09Au
BURNS, Michael	25	M	Farmer	22Ap09Au
KEENEY, William	14	M	Farmer	22Ap09Au
CONNER, Eliza	16	F	Spinster	22Ap09Au
HANNAN, Michael	22	M	Laborer	22Ap09Au
MULLANY, Denis	24	M	Laborer	22Ap09Au
KILCANLEY, Thomas	24	M	Laborer	22Ap09Au
FARNY, Mary	35	F	Matron	22Ap09Au
John	13	M	Unknown	22Ap09Au
CONBOY, Mary	20	F	Spinster	22Ap09Au
POWER, Joseph	20	M	Shoemaker	22Ap09Au
HADDOCK, Jane	17	F	Spinster	22Ap09Au
Robert	14	M	Unknown	22Ap09Au
MURRAY, Cormac	40	M	Farmer	22Ap09Au
Mary	30	F	Matron	22Ap09Au
Mary	17	F	Spinster	22Ap09Au
FINN, Anne	30	F	Matron	22Ap09Au
Jane	13	F	Unknown	22Ap09Au
WHITE, Denis	20	M	Laborer	22Ap09Au
DEVITT, Henry	19	M	Laborer	22Ap09Au
GORMAN, James	30	M	Laborer	22Ap09Au
FLYNNE, John	19	M	Laborer	22Ap09Au
HEALY, Thomas	18	M	Laborer	22Ap09Au
Mary	17	F	Spinster	22Ap09Au
MCGOWN, Libby	20	F	Spinster	22Ap09Au
HANNON, Patrick	48	M	Farmer	22Ap09Au
SCANLON, John	45	M	Farmer	22Ap09Au
GRAY, Bridget	22	F	Spinster	22Ap09Au
MCSHARRY, Thomas	18	M	Laborer	22Ap09Au
Mary	16	F	Spinster	22Ap09Au
Margaret	13	F	Unknown	22Ap09Au
James	9	M	Child	22Ap09Au
Bridget	7	F	Child	22Ap09Au
COONEY, Michael	26	M	Laborer	22Ap09Au

NAMES OF PASSENGERS	AGE	SEX	OCCUPATIONS	DATE PORT SHIP
COONEY, Patrick	19	M	Laborer	22Ap09Au
FOWLEY, Michael	30	M	Laborer	22Ap09Au
Mary	23	F	Matron	22Ap09Au
SCANLON, Bartley	34	M	Laborer	22Ap09Au
Mary	32	F	Matron	22Ap09Au
Martin	.01	M	Infant	22Ap09Au
JOHNSTON, Mary	33	F	Spinster	22Ap09Au
COGGINS, John	18	M	Laborer	22Ap09Au
Patrick	2	M	Child	22Ap09Au
Mary	4	F	Child	22Ap09Au
GILGAN, Terence	21	M	Laborer	22Ap09Au
GRAY, Mary	20	F	Spinster	22Ap09Au
LANGAN, Michael	30	M	Laborer	22Ap09Au
Mary	28	F	Matron	22Ap09Au
SCAHILL, Thomas	33	M	Laborer	22Ap09Au
Mary	30	F	Matron	22Ap09Au
Ann	9	F	Child	22Ap09Au
Sarah	6	F	Child	22Ap09Au
Margaret	3	F	Child	22Ap09Au
Ellen	.01	F	Infant	22Ap09Au
CAUFIELD, Martin	28	M	Laborer	22Ap09Au
Eliza	26	F	Matron	22Ap09Au
Martin	1	M	Child	22Ap09Au
COLLENY, Patrick	34	M	Laborer	22Ap09Au
COLLERY, Edward	28	M	Laborer	22Ap09Au
COLLENY, John	19	M	Laborer	22Ap09Au
Anne	18	F	Spinster	22Ap09Au
COLLERY, Jane	11	F	Spinster	22Ap09Au
STEWART, George	17	M	Laborer	22Ap09Au
NEILLY, Ellen	20	F	Spinster	22Ap09Au
HARRISON, Thomas	20	M	Laborer	22Ap09Au
LOUGHLIN, James	30	M	Laborer	22Ap09Au
GOLDEN, Honora	36	F	Matron	22Ap09Au
Mary	28	F	Matron	22Ap09Au
Catherine	8	F	Child	22Ap09Au
Patrick	6	M	Child	22Ap09Au
Owen	4	M	Child	22Ap09Au
CUMAN, Margret	20	F	Spinster	22Ap09Au
KERRANE, Thomas	34	M	Laborer	22Ap09Au
REDHAIN, Thomas	18	M	Laborer	22Ap09Au
KILCULLEN, Bridget	30	F	Spinster	22Ap09Au
ROONANE, Bridget	25	F	Matron	22Ap09Au
Winifred	.01	F	Infant	22Ap09Au
MEEHAN, Bridget	30	F	Matron	22Ap09Au
Patk.	5	M	Child	22Ap09Au
COGAN, Jane	20	F	Unknown	22Ap09Au
MCCAULEY, Anne	24	F	Unknown	22Ap09Au
MURN, Patrick	28	M	Unknown	22Ap09Au
BRENNAN, Patrick	22	M	Unknown	22Ap09Au
James	20	M	Unknown	22Ap09Au
WILSON, James	18	M	Unknown	22Ap09Au
KIRKPATRICK, John	00	M	Captain	22Ap09Au
GILLAN, John	00	M	First Mate	22Ap09Au
MCGANRAN, Thomas	00	M	Second Mate	22Ap09Au
BARRY, Andrew	00	M	Unknown	22Ap09Au
HART, Bernard	00	M	Unknown	22Ap09Au
GATEN, Henry	00	M	Unknown	22Ap09Au
WARD, Richard	00	M	Ck-Stwd	22Ap09Au
KIRKPATRICK, James	00	M	Unknown	22Ap09Au
DAVIS, William	00	M	Unknown	22Ap09Au
GILLAN, Michael	00	M	Unknown	22Ap09Au
FETHERSTON, Bartholome	00	M	Apprentice	22Ap09Au
KENNY, Patrick	00	M	Apprentice	22Ap09Au

ADAM-CARR 22 APRIL 1850

From Glasgow

NAMES OF PASSENGERS	AGE	SEX	OCCUPATIONS	DATE PORT SHIP
EWING, William	28	M	Laborer	22Ap21Gt
Flora	50	F	Unknown	22Ap21Gt
Mary	25	F	Unknown	22Ap21Gt
BUTLER, Flora	20	F	Unknown	22Ap21Gt
CRAWFORD, Robert	60	M	Farmer	22Ap21Gt
Nell	50	F	Unknown	22Ap21Gt
John	16	M	Unknown	22Ap21Gt
Mary-Jane	15	F	Unknown	22Ap21Gt
DOGHERTY, Thomas	19	M	Laborer	22Ap21Gt
SMITH, James	25	M	Laborer	22Ap21Gt
MCGAGHY, Bessy	20	F	Spinster	22Ap21Gt
TURNER, William	22	M	Laborer	22Ap21Gt
John	21	M	Laborer	22Ap21Gt
KYLE, Robert	21	M	Laborer	22Ap21Gt
GREER, Alexander	25	M	Laborer	22Ap21Gt
Agness	21	F	Unknown	22Ap21Gt
MURDOCK, Andrew	30	M	Laborer	22Ap21Gt
LEWIES, James	19	M	Unknown	22Ap21Gt
HUGHES, Frances	20	M	Unknown	22Ap21Gt
Janet	8	F	Child	22Ap21Gt
QUINN, Mary	32	F	Unknown	22Ap21Gt
COCKRAN, Hugh	33	M	Farmer	22Ap21Gt
Eliza	29	F	Unknown	22Ap21Gt
John	6	M	Child	22Ap21Gt
James	4	M	Child	22Ap21Gt
Anne-Jane	2	F	Child	22Ap21Gt
Hugh	.01	M	Infant	22Ap21Gt
David	19	M	Laborer	22Ap21Gt
TAYLOR, Christiane	40	F	None	22Ap21Gt
Mary-Anne	25	F	Unknown	22Ap21Gt
MCCLELLAND, Alexander	33	M	Carpenter	22Ap21Gt
SANHARTY, Helen	27	F	Wife	22Ap21Gt
Mary	4	F	Child	22Ap21Gt
CLELLAND, Mathew	35	M	Laborer	22Ap21Gt
HENRY, Martin	19	M	Laborer	22Ap21Gt
CONNELL, John	35	M	Laborer	22Ap21Gt
COOPER, Samuel	19	M	Laborer	22Ap21Gt
WOODS, Nancy	18	F	Spinster	22Ap21Gt
Mary	9	F	Child	22Ap21Gt
CUNNINGHAM, Wm.	19	M	Laborer	22Ap21Gt
MCCACHRY, William	42	M	Laborer	22Ap21Gt
DOGHERTY, Marg.	20	F	Spinster	22Ap21Gt
MCKANE, Bridget	35	F	Spinster	22Ap21Gt
DEVELIN, Alice	20	F	Spinster	22Ap21Gt
Mary	18	F	Spinster	22Ap21Gt
GIVEN, John	16	M	Laborer	22Ap21Gt
DOCHERTY, Bridget	22	F	Spinster	22Ap21Gt
KEENAN, Thomas	19	M	Laborer	22Ap21Gt
Issabella	15	F	Spinster	22Ap21Gt
BEAGLEY, John	24	M	Laborer	22Ap21Gt
Ellen	22	F	Spinster	22Ap21Gt
Rose	19	F	Spinster	22Ap21Gt
Margaret	15	F	Spinster	22Ap21Gt
SMALL, Francis	18	F	Spinster	22Ap21Gt
WALKER, John	19	M	Laborer	22Ap21Gt
BURNS, Alexander	19	M	Laborer	22Ap21Gt
MCNAFFY, Susan	30	F	None	22Ap21Gt
Frances	.09	M	Infant	22Ap21Gt
IRVINE, Samuel	30	F	Laborer	22Ap21Gt
FEENEY, Catherine	27	F	Spinster	22Ap21Gt
CONNOR, John	24	M	Laborer	22Ap21Gt
BROLLY, Rachel	24	F	Spinster	22Ap21Gt
ROBB, Isabella	20	F	Spinster	22Ap21Gt
MOORE, Lewis	21	M	Laborer	22Ap21Gt
DONAZHY, Stephen	20	M	Laborer	22Ap21Gt

NAMES OF PASSENGERS	AGE	SEX	OCCUPATIONS	DATE PORT SHIP
SCOTT, Thomas	38	M	Laborer	22Ap21Gt
MCHUGH, Hugh	33	M	Laborer	22Ap21Gt
PEOPLES, William	26	M	Laborer	22Ap21Gt
Jane	22	F	Unknown	22Ap21Gt
John	19	M	Laborer	22Ap21Gt
Aron	15	M	Laborer	22Ap21Gt
Arch.	30	M	Laborer	22Ap21Gt
CAMPBELL, Jane	18	F	Spinster	22Ap21Gt
COPELAND, Amelia	11	F	None	22Ap21Gt
LINDSAY, William	38	M	Laborer	22Ap21Gt
Jane	34	F	Unknown	22Ap21Gt
Anne	.06	F	Infant	22Ap21Gt
BROWN, George	22	M	Unknown	22Ap21Gt
Maria	19	F	None	22Ap21Gt
Elizabeth	.08	F	Infant	22Ap21Gt
BRITAIN, Biddy	30	F	Unknown	22Ap21Gt
WALLS, James	12	M	Unknown	22Ap21Gt
Thomas	9	M	Child	22Ap21Gt
Ellen	29	F	Spinster	22Ap21Gt
DOUGAN, Anthony	18	M	Laborer	22Ap21Gt
IRVINE, Anne	22	F	None	22Ap21Gt
PURDERAUX, Peter	25	M	Laborer	22Ap21Gt
LYNCH, Eliza	21	F	Spinster	22Ap21Gt
GORDON, George	32	M	Laborer	22Ap21Gt
Charles	20	M	Laborer	22Ap21Gt
Jane	15	F	None	22Ap21Gt
WATSON, William	23	M	Laborer	22Ap21Gt
SKIVINGTON, James	28	M	Laborer	22Ap21Gt
KYLE, Mary	18	F	Unknown	22Ap21Gt
MCKEENA, Charles	40	M	Laborer	22Ap21Gt
Margaret	36	F	Unknown	22Ap21Gt
Mary	12	F	Unknown	22Ap21Gt
MCMULLEN, Elizabeth	21	F	Unknown	22Ap21Gt
MCKENNA, Margery	20	F	Unknown	22Ap21Gt
JOHNSTON, George	15	M	Unknown	22Ap21Gt
MCGOWN, Bridget	33	F	Unknown	22Ap21Gt
CONAGHAN, Mary	16	F	Unknown	22Ap21Gt
James	12	M	Unknown	22Ap21Gt
TAITE, Alexander	35	F	Laborer	22Ap21Gt
Margaret	40	F	Laborer	22Ap21Gt
CRAWFORD, William	50	M	Laborer	22Ap21Gt
QUINN, John	20	M	Laborer	22Ap21Gt
DARRAGH, John	43	M	Laborer	22Ap21Gt
SMITH, Edward	40	M	Laborer	22Ap21Gt
COPELAND, John	50	M	Laborer	22Ap21Gt

PHILADELPHIA 23 APRIL 1850

From Liverpool

NAMES OF PASSENGERS	AGE	SEX	OCCUPATIONS	DATE PORT SHIP
KENNY, U-Mrs.	34	F	Unknown	23Ap02Dd
Bridget	8	F	Child	23Ap02Dd
Thos.	7	M	Child	23Ap02Dd
Margaret	5	F	Child	23Ap02Dd
Michael	2	M	Child	23Ap02Dd
CAMPBELL, Robert	21	M	Laborer	23Ap02Dd
MULLIGAN, John	20	M	Unknown	23Ap02Dd
CONLAN, Felix	40	M	Unknown	23Ap02Dd
Ellen	50	F	Unknown	23Ap02Dd
Jno.	10	M	Unknown	23Ap02Dd
MCGINNESS, Margt.	19	F	Unknown	23Ap02Dd
SWEENEY, Martha	29	F	Unknown	23Ap02Dd
MCCOAM, Sarah	20	F	Unknown	23Ap02Dd
ROSBURGH, Joseph	20	M	Unknown	23Ap02Dd
GLASS, Mary-Anne	19	F	Unknown	23Ap02Dd
STEWART, Anne	19	F	Unknown	23Ap02Dd
WHITE, Jno.	30	M	Unknown	23Ap02Dd
REED, Jas.	21	M	Unknown	23Ap02Dd
CONGHAY, Alexander	19	M	Unknown	23Ap02Dd
ARCHYBOLD, Jno.	19	M	Unknown	23Ap02Dd
KENNEDY, Mary	20	F	Unknown	23Ap02Dd
Mary	12	F	Unknown	23Ap02Dd
CONNOLLY, Christopher	28	M	Unknown	23Ap02Dd
SHERBROOK, John	21	M	Bookmaker	23Ap02Dd
Robert	23	M	Unknown	23Ap02Dd
COURTNEY, Anne	18	F	Unknown	23Ap02Dd
MEGAN, Anne	28	F	Unknown	23Ap02Dd
BAKER, Anne	16	F	Unknown	23Ap02Dd
Biddy	14	F	Unknown	23Ap02Dd
ANDREW, Bernard	50	F	Farmer	23Ap02Dd
Margaret	50	F	Unknown	23Ap02Dd
Bernard	20	M	Unknown	23Ap02Dd
Alexander	18	M	Unknown	23Ap02Dd
Margaret	15	F	Unknown	23Ap02Dd
SMITH, Anne	17	F	Unknown	23Ap02Dd
MCCOUGHLIN, Owen	33	M	Farmer	23Ap02Dd
U-Mrs.	30	F	Unknown	23Ap02Dd
Christopher	19	M	Unknown	23Ap02Dd
MCLOUGHLIN, Mary	17	F	Unknown	23Ap02Dd
Margaret	12	F	Unknown	23Ap02Dd
Patrick	11	M	Unknown	23Ap02Dd
John	8	M	Child	23Ap02Dd
Owen	6	M	Child	23Ap02Dd
James	4	M	Child	23Ap02Dd
Anne	2	F	Child	23Ap02Dd
KANE, Peter	21	M	Laborer	23Ap02Dd
KERNIN, Patrick	35	M	Unknown	23Ap02Dd
William	17	M	Unknown	23Ap02Dd
MCKAFFRY, Patrick	22	M	Unknown	23Ap02Dd
Rose	28	F	Unknown	23Ap02Dd
MCANORRY, Thos.	20	M	Unknown	23Ap02Dd
CARSHER, Alice	20	F	Unknown	23Ap02Dd
BYRNE, Sally	35	F	Unknown	23Ap02Dd
William	14	M	Unknown	23Ap02Dd
Sally	10	F	Unknown	23Ap02Dd
Ellen	8	F	Child	23Ap02Dd
Margaret	6	F	Child	23Ap02Dd
Catherine	4	F	Child	23Ap02Dd
U	.00	U	Infant	23Ap02Dd
MURPHY, Sally	14	F	Unknown	23Ap02Dd
MCKENNA, Francis	21	M	Laborer	23Ap02Dd
Sarah	20	F	Unknown	23Ap02Dd
U	.00	U	Infant	23Ap02Dd
Born-At-Sea				
SHERIDAN, Patrick	22	M	Unknown	23Ap02Dd
HAND, Anne	60	F	Unknown	23Ap02Dd
Susan	18	F	Unknown	23Ap02Dd
Peter	22	M	Unknown	23Ap02Dd
David	20	M	Unknown	23Ap02Dd
MONTGOMERY, Pat	30	M	Unknown	23Ap02Dd
MACLIN, George	22	M	Shoemaker	23Ap02Dd
HARRISSON, Peter	21	M	Unknown	23Ap02Dd
NIBLOCK, Joseph	17	M	Unknown	23Ap02Dd
BRENNAN, Catherine	40	F	Unknown	23Ap02Dd
CARROLL, Peter	21	M	Unknown	23Ap02Dd
Bridget	50	F	Unknown	23Ap02Dd
Mary	18	F	Unknown	23Ap02Dd
Anne	14	F	Unknown	23Ap02Dd
TORMEY, Mary	18	F	Unknown	23Ap02Dd
CLARK, Catherine	19	F	Unknown	23Ap02Dd
CALLAN, Thos.	26	M	Unknown	23Ap02Dd
Dennis	24	M	Unknown	23Ap02Dd
TURNEY, Patrick	26	M	Unknown	23Ap02Dd
TORNLEY, John	20	M	Unknown	23Ap02Dd
DONNEGAN, John	20	M	Unknown	23Ap02Dd
BRADY, John	30	M	Laborer	23Ap02Dd
Betty	20	F	Unknown	23Ap02Dd
CONNOR, Patrick	26	M	Unknown	23Ap02Dd
HERBERT, Michael	21	M	Carpenter	23Ap02Dd
MCMAHON, Stephen	26	M	Unknown	23Ap02Dd
Mary	20	F	Unknown	23Ap02Dd
KEATING, John	26	M	Unknown	23Ap02Dd
MANN, Rody	20	M	Unknown	23Ap02Dd
Honora	18	F	Unknown	23Ap02Dd

NAMES OF PASSENGERS	AGE	SEX	OCCUPATIONS	DATE PORT SHIP
PURCELL, Mary	42	F	Unknown	23Ap02Dd
HOGG, Jas.	26	M	Unknown	23Ap02Dd
DIORCUS, Michael	25	M	Joiner	23Ap02Dd
Mary	20	F	Unknown	23Ap02Dd
Catherine	.00	F	Infant	23Ap02Dd
BARRELL, Patrick	20	M	Unknown	23Ap02Dd
FITZPATRICK, Thos.	30	M	Laborer	23Ap02Dd
BURKE, Jas.	15	M	Unknown	23Ap02Dd
DONAHUE, John	30	M	Carpenter	23Ap02Dd
LONGHAM, Mary	15	F	Unknown	23Ap02Dd
R.	11	M	Unknown	23Ap02Dd
GREENAN, Hugh	25	M	Unknown	23Ap02Dd
Bridget	24	F	Unknown	23Ap02Dd
Mary-Anne	.00	F	Infant	23Ap02Dd
FITZPATRICK, Henry	20	M	Unknown	23Ap02Dd
HUGHES, Catherine	18	F	Unknown	23Ap02Dd
CALDWELL, Bernard	34	M	Laborer	23Ap02Dd
MULLAN, William	35	M	Unknown	23Ap02Dd
MCCARTY, John	32	M	Nailer	23Ap02Dd
CARROLL, Jas.	40	M	Unknown	23Ap02Dd
CONNOR, Thos.	20	M	Unknown	23Ap02Dd
TRACY, Catherine	52	F	Unknown	23Ap02Dd
Anne	25	F	Unknown	23Ap02Dd
Thos.	20	M	Unknown	23Ap02Dd
COOK, Patrick	21	M	Unknown	23Ap02Dd
MONAHAN, Catherine	17	F	Unknown	23Ap02Dd
ELLIOTT, John	34	M	Unknown	23Ap02Dd
Mary	26	F	Unknown	23Ap02Dd
HYNN, Thos.	22	M	Laborer	23Ap02Dd
MURRAY, Jas.	25	M	Butcher	23Ap02Dd
CLARK, Elizabeth	20	F	Unknown	23Ap02Dd
BRADY, Catherine	20	F	Unknown	23Ap02Dd
REILLY, Edward	36	M	Farmer	23Ap02Dd
Mary	30	F	Unknown	23Ap02Dd
CLENDINNING, Margt.	22	F	Unknown	23Ap02Dd
Catherine	18	F	Unknown	23Ap02Dd
RUTHERFORD, Joseph	20	M	Unknown	23Ap02Dd
MCNULTY, Mary	22	F	Unknown	23Ap02Dd
MORRESSY, Thos.	45	M	Unknown	23Ap02Dd
Ellen	40	F	Unknown	23Ap02Dd
John	15	M	Unknown	23Ap02Dd
Mary	8	F	Child	23Ap02Dd
Jno.	5	M	Child	23Ap02Dd
Catherine	2	F	Child	23Ap02Dd
WALSH, Patk.	26	M	Unknown	23Ap02Dd
Biddy	23	F	Unknown	23Ap02Dd
Jas.	.00	M	Infant	23Ap02Dd
TOOLS, Patrick	20	M	Unknown	23Ap02Dd
Biddy	22	F	Unknown	23Ap02Dd
Magt.	19	F	Unknown	23Ap02Dd
FINLAN, Patrick	20	M	Laborer	23Ap02Dd
Owen	21	M	Unknown	23Ap02Dd
SINGLETON, Thos.	24	M	Unknown	23Ap02Dd
DOYLE, Patrick	24	M	Unknown	23Ap02Dd
MURPHY, John	26	M	Unknown	23Ap02Dd
MCGRATH, U-Mrs.	22	F	Unknown	23Ap02Dd
Peggy	22	F	Unknown	23Ap02Dd
U	18	M	Unknown	23Ap02Dd
GRIFFIN, Anthony	20	M	Unknown	23Ap02Dd
MURPHY, Pat	29	M	Unknown	23Ap02Dd
Jas.	12	M	Unknown	23Ap02Dd
KENNY, Michael	42	M	Unknown	23Ap02Dd
Mary-Anne	32	F	Unknown	23Ap02Dd
Wm.	10	M	Unknown	23Ap02Dd
Maria	8	F	Child	23Ap02Dd
Fanny	6	F	Child	23Ap02Dd
Patrick	4	M	Child	23Ap02Dd
Margaret	7	F	Child	23Ap02Dd
Fedelia	2	F	Child	23Ap02Dd
Julia	.00	F	Infant	23Ap02Dd
MURRY, Margaret	25	F	Unknown	23Ap02Dd
Mary	22	F	Unknown	23Ap02Dd
WARD, Thos.	35	M	Unknown	23Ap02Dd
Hannah	32	F	Unknown	23Ap02Dd
Bridget	14	F	Unknown	23Ap02Dd
WARD, Patrick	12	M	Laborer	23Ap02Dd
Wm.	6	M	Child	23Ap02Dd
COYLE, Wm.	50	M	Unknown	23Ap02Dd
Anne	48	F	Unknown	23Ap02Dd
James	24	M	Unknown	23Ap02Dd
Henry	20	M	Unknown	23Ap02Dd
John	18	M	Unknown	23Ap02Dd
Mary	15	F	Unknown	23Ap02Dd
Catherine	12	F	Unknown	23Ap02Dd
William	10	M	Unknown	23Ap02Dd
RILEY, Edward	20	M	Unknown	23Ap02Dd
CRUISE, Michael	20	M	Unknown	23Ap02Dd
MCMAHON, Bernard	32	M	Unknown	23Ap02Dd
DOYLE, Patrick	30	M	Unknown	23Ap02Dd
BURKE, Patrick	35	M	Unknown	23Ap02Dd
DALTON, Martha	32	F	Unknown	23Ap02Dd
CONNOLLY, Michael	45	M	Unknown	23Ap02Dd
Ellen	6	F	Child	23Ap02Dd
Lawrence	4	M	Child	23Ap02Dd
Alice	3	F	Child	23Ap02Dd
Johanna	.00	F	Infant	23Ap02Dd
NASH, Mary	30	F	Unknown	23Ap02Dd
FARNELLY, Owen	50	M	Unknown	23Ap02Dd
Mary	46	F	Unknown	23Ap02Dd
Catherine	18	F	Unknown	23Ap02Dd
MAHER, Mary	30	F	Unknown	23Ap02Dd
FENNELLY, Julia	17	F	Unknown	23Ap02Dd
Thos.	15	M	Unknown	23Ap02Dd
Martha	14	F	Unknown	23Ap02Dd
Mary	12	F	Unknown	23Ap02Dd
Ellen	10	F	Unknown	23Ap02Dd
Anthony	7	M	Child	23Ap02Dd
BANON, Thos.	30	M	Unknown	23Ap02Dd
FENNELLY, Owen	36	M	Unknown	23Ap02Dd
Julia	40	F	Unknown	23Ap02Dd
Margaret	30	F	Unknown	23Ap02Dd
Betty	20	F	Unknown	23Ap02Dd
Catherine	7	F	Child	23Ap02Dd
Bridget	5	F	Child	23Ap02Dd
FARRELL, Samuel	35	M	Unknown	23Ap02Dd
Michael	24	F	Unknown	23Ap02Dd
Catherine	20	F	Unknown	23Ap02Dd
WALSH, Thos.	26	M	Unknown	23Ap02Dd
FITZGERALD, Wm.	28	M	Unknown	23Ap02Dd
BURNS, Edward	26	M	Unknown	23Ap02Dd
Anastasia	20	F	Unknown	23Ap02Dd
TOBIN, Betty	19	F	Unknown	23Ap02Dd
CANON, Martha	18	F	Unknown	23Ap02Dd
BURN, John	22	M	Unknown	23Ap02Dd
DOYLE, Peter	20	M	Unknown	23Ap02Dd
LENNAN, Michael	19	M	Laborer	23Ap02Dd
Ellen	18	F	Laborer	23Ap02Dd
Thos.	8	M	Child	23Ap02Dd
DOLLARD, Thos.	20	M	Laborer	23Ap02Dd
Margt.	18	F	Laborer	23Ap02Dd
MURPHY, Jas.	45	M	Laborer	23Ap02Dd
FOLEY, Michael	21	M	Laborer	23Ap02Dd
GORMAN, John	26	M	Laborer	23Ap02Dd
RING, Michael	20	M	Laborer	23Ap02Dd
Bridget	28	F	Laborer	23Ap02Dd
HENNESSY, Morgan	40	M	Laborer	23Ap02Dd
Bridget	18	F	Laborer	23Ap02Dd
COLEMAN, Andy	20	M	Laborer	23Ap02Dd
DOYLE, John	21	M	Laborer	23Ap02Dd
BRYAN, George	35	M	Laborer	23Ap02Dd
Charles	12	M	Laborer	23Ap02Dd
CORY, Michael	24	M	Laborer	23Ap02Dd
CODY, Anne	24	F	Laborer	23Ap02Dd
Mary	10	F	Laborer	23Ap02Dd
Anne	8	F	Child	23Ap02Dd
Johanna	6	F	Child	23Ap02Dd
Michael	4	M	Child	23Ap02Dd
DONNELY, Patrick	36	M	Laborer	23Ap02Dd
MARTIN, Jas.	21	M	Laborer	23Ap02Dd
MCALISTER, A.	21	M	Laborer	23Ap02Dd

NAMES OF PASSENGERS	AGE	SEX	OCCUPATIONS	DATE PORT SHIP
SANDERSTON, E.	24	M	Laborer	23Ap02Dd
MCGERNON, U-Captain	25	M	Laborer	23Ap02Dd
LIONHARD, Wm.	24	M	Laborer	23Ap02Dd
FINNAN, Mary	30	F	Laborer	23Ap02Dd
Honora	25	F	Laborer	23Ap02Dd
Patrick	6	M	Child	23Ap02Dd
Thos.	.00	M	Infant	23Ap02Dd
CULMAN, Pierce	30	M	Laborer	23Ap02Dd
POWER, Pierce	20	M	Laborer	23Ap02Dd
HURLEY, John	30	M	Laborer	23Ap02Dd
Johanna	30	F	Laborer	23Ap02Dd
William	18	M	Laborer	23Ap02Dd
Honora	22	F	Laborer	23Ap02Dd
GRANT, Wm.	25	M	Unknown	23Ap02Dd
Catherine	23	F	Unknown	23Ap02Dd
RUSSEN, Catherine	21	F	Unknown	23Ap02Dd
BYRNE, Patrick	56	M	Unknown	23Ap02Dd
Bridget	50	F	Unknown	23Ap02Dd
Christopher	23	M	Unknown	23Ap02Dd
FINN, Margaret	3	F	Child	23Ap02Dd
BYRNE, Margaret	21	F	Laborer	23Ap02Dd
Jas.	17	M	Laborer	23Ap02Dd
Patrick	15	M	Laborer	23Ap02Dd
DEANE, Patrick	35	M	Laborer	23Ap02Dd
Bridget	34	F	Laborer	23Ap02Dd
Anne	10	F	Laborer	23Ap02Dd
Mary	8	F	Child	23Ap02Dd
Catherine	8	F	Child	23Ap02Dd
William	5	M	Child	23Ap02Dd
CLEARY, John	25	M	Laborer	23Ap02Dd
DOWLING, Thos.	30	M	Laborer	23Ap02Dd
FLINN, Wm.	35	M	Laborer	23Ap02Dd
KELLY, Thos.	32	M	Laborer	23Ap02Dd
FOLEY, Mary	28	F	Laborer	23Ap02Dd
MULCASHY, Mary	24	F	Laborer	23Ap02Dd
ARMON, Bridget	26	F	Laborer	23Ap02Dd
CHRISTOPHER, John	46	M	Laborer	23Ap02Dd
HARTY, Thos.	36	M	Laborer	23Ap02Dd
U-Mrs.	32	F	Laborer	23Ap02Dd
Michael	12	M	Laborer	23Ap02Dd
William	10	M	Laborer	23Ap02Dd
Ellen	5	F	Child	23Ap02Dd
Thos.	.00	M	Infant	23Ap02Dd
Ellen	25	F	Laborer	23Ap02Dd
BRODULL, Michael	34	M	Laborer	23Ap02Dd
U-Mrs.	36	F	Laborer	23Ap02Dd
REANY, U-Mrs.	25	F	Unknown	23Ap02Dd
CONLAN, Jas.	17	M	Laborer	23Ap02Dd
CRONAN, Joseph	21	M	Laborer	23Ap02Dd
James	20	M	Laborer	23Ap02Dd
ROCHE, James	28	M	Laborer	23Ap02Dd
Mary	26	F	Laborer	23Ap02Dd
Patrick	5	M	Child	23Ap02Dd
Jas.	.00	M	Infant	23Ap02Dd
PATTERSON, David	36	M	Laborer	23Ap02Dd
Esther	34	F	Laborer	23Ap02Dd
Jas.	18	M	Laborer	23Ap02Dd
Martha	10	F	Laborer	23Ap02Dd
Joseph	.00	M	Infant	23Ap02Dd
KEATING, Edward	30	M	Laborer	23Ap02Dd
Honora	30	F	Laborer	23Ap02Dd
Mary	10	F	Laborer	23Ap02Dd
Nicholas	8	M	Child	23Ap02Dd
John	5	M	Child	23Ap02Dd
James	3	M	Child	23Ap02Dd
Michael	.00	M	Infant	23Ap02Dd
MCLOUGHTON, Hugh	28	M	Laborer	23Ap02Dd
Mary	24	F	Laborer	23Ap02Dd
Dennis	.00	M	Infant	23Ap02Dd
CARR, Jas.	38	M	Laborer	23Ap02Dd
HORN, Stephen	27	M	Laborer	23Ap02Dd
CORNALLS, John	30	M	Unknown	23Ap02Dd
GORMAN, Eliza	16	F	Unknown	23Ap02Dd
MURPHY, Arthur	21	M	Unknown	23Ap02Dd
Mary	20	F	Unknown	23Ap02Dd
LEONARD, Jas.	23	M	Unknown	23Ap02Dd
HAYES, John	30	M	Unknown	23Ap02Dd
Bridget	30	F	Unknown	23Ap02Dd
Mary	7	F	Child	23Ap02Dd
Thos.	5	M	Child	23Ap02Dd
John	.00	M	Infant	23Ap02Dd
SHEEHAN, Cornelius	28	M	Unknown	23Ap02Dd
BROWN, Margaret	30	F	Unknown	23Ap02Dd
RUSSELL, Sydney	45	M	Laborer	23Ap02Dd
Leonard	43	M	Unknown	23Ap02Dd
REILLEY, Mary	20	F	Unknown	23Ap02Dd
BOWAM, John	40	M	Unknown	23Ap02Dd
Martha	40	F	Unknown	23Ap02Dd
FOX, Mary	8	F	Child	23Ap02Dd
DRAGAN, John	20	M	Unknown	23Ap02Dd
CUNNINGHAM, Peter	20	M	Unknown	23Ap02Dd
KENNEDY, Patrick	25	M	Shoemaker	23Ap02Dd
U-Mrs.	50	F	Unknown	23Ap02Dd
HICKEY, Mary	18	F	Unknown	23Ap02Dd
Margaret	12	F	Unknown	23Ap02Dd
HANORAN, Michael	30	M	Laborer	23Ap02Dd
NASSON, June	19	F	Unknown	23Ap02Dd
PHELAN, John	19	M	Unknown	23Ap02Dd
EGAN, Patrick	21	M	Unknown	23Ap02Dd
FAN, Jam.	25	M	Unknown	23Ap02Dd
CAHILL, U-Mrs.	23	F	Unknown	23Ap02Dd
BANAHAN, Marty	24	M	Unknown	23Ap02Dd
CAHILL, Michael	30	M	Unknown	23Ap02Dd
CARR, Patrick	20	M	Unknown	23Ap02Dd
EGAN, U-Mrs.	21	F	Unknown	23Ap02Dd
Mary-Anne	.00	F	Infant	23Ap02Dd
MCDERMOTT, Catherine	22	F	Unknown	23Ap02Dd
BRENNAN, Mary	18	F	Unknown	23Ap02Dd
DUFFY, Anne	16	F	Unknown	23Ap02Dd
CARTER, Henry	40	M	Unknown	23Ap02Dd
John	30	M	Unknown	23Ap02Dd
BURKE, Jas.	35	M	Unknown	23Ap02Dd
MCKENNA, U-Mrs.	20	F	Unknown	23Ap02Dd
John	20	M	Unknown	23Ap02Dd
Catherine	19	F	Unknown	23Ap02Dd
DUFFY, John	56	M	Unknown	23Ap02Dd
U-Mrs.	40	F	Unknown	23Ap02Dd
Michael	21	M	Unknown	23Ap02Dd
Mary	19	F	Unknown	23Ap02Dd
Catherine	17	F	Unknown	23Ap02Dd
Margaret	15	F	Unknown	23Ap02Dd
Anne	13	F	Unknown	23Ap02Dd
John	9	M	Child	23Ap02Dd
Susan	4	F	Child	23Ap02Dd
Patrick	2	M	Child	23Ap02Dd
GLENN, Biddy	20	F	Unknown	23Ap02Dd
Biddy	18	F	Unknown	23Ap02Dd
DONAHUE, Patrick	30	M	Laborer	23Ap02Dd
MCNAMARRA, Bridget	25	F	Laborer	23Ap02Dd
Jas.	21	M	Laborer	23Ap02Dd
BUTLER, Jas.	19	M	Laborer	23Ap02Dd
Biddy	22	F	Laborer	23Ap02Dd
DONAHUE, Patrick	30	M	Laborer	23Ap02Dd
MCNAMARA, Bridget	25	F	Laborer	23Ap02Dd
Jas.	21	M	Laborer	23Ap02Dd
BUTLER, Jas.	19	F	Laborer	23Ap02Dd
Biddy	22	F	Laborer	23Ap02Dd
MCMAHON, Mary	22	F	Laborer	23Ap02Dd
SULLIVAN, Biddy	30	F	Laborer	23Ap02Dd
BEDNEY, Anne	25	F	Laborer	23Ap02Dd
MOON, Charlotte	30	F	Laborer	23Ap02Dd
Mary	6	F	Child	23Ap02Dd
Patrick	.00	M	Infant	23Ap02Dd
MAHON, Wm.	54	M	Laborer	23Ap02Dd
Margt.	40	F	Laborer	23Ap02Dd
Francis	20	M	Laborer	23Ap02Dd
CUSACK, Patrick	50	M	Laborer	23Ap02Dd
Winifred	50	F	Laborer	23Ap02Dd
SHARKEY, Thos.	36	M	Laborer	23Ap02Dd
BESLICK, Thos.	27	M	Laborer	23Ap02Dd

NAMES OF PASSENGERS	AGE	SEX	OCCUPATIONS	DATE PORT SHIP
FERNAN, Pat	30	M	Laborer	23Ap02Dd
PRENDIRGASS, Chris	35	M	Laborer	23Ap02Dd
FARRELL, John	23	M	Laborer	23Ap02Dd
Michael	21	M	Laborer	23Ap02Dd
Marcela	23	F	Laborer	23Ap02Dd
John	.00	M	Infant	23Ap02Dd
POWER, Michael	50	M	Laborer	23Ap02Dd
Mary	48	F	Laborer	23Ap02Dd
Joseph	22	M	Laborer	23Ap02Dd
James	17	M	Laborer	23Ap02Dd
Mary-Anne	12	F	Laborer	23Ap02Dd
John	10	M	Laborer	23Ap02Dd
BOWDEN, William	18	M	Laborer	23Ap02Dd
KUSHLAN, Rebecca	17	F	Laborer	23Ap02Dd
KEOUGH, Michael	25	M	Laborer	23Ap02Dd
MURPHY, Bridget	20	F	Laborer	23Ap02Dd
POWDERLY, Mary	19	F	Laborer	23Ap02Dd
WIDON, Patrick	28	M	Laborer	23Ap02Dd
MCGROELLAN, Jas.	28	M	Laborer	23Ap02Dd
FINNARGHY, Martin	24	M	Laborer	23Ap02Dd
U-Mrs.	24	F	Laborer	23Ap02Dd
KELLY, Jno.	20	M	Laborer	23Ap02Dd
WALSH, Michael	28	M	Laborer	23Ap02Dd
DUNCAN, John	18	M	Laborer	23Ap02Dd
BUCKLY, Timothy	23	M	Laborer	23Ap02Dd
Mary	24	F	Laborer	23Ap02Dd
CONNORS, John	23	M	Laborer	23Ap02Dd
U-Mrs.	25	F	Laborer	23Ap02Dd
HOLLAND, John	21	M	Laborer	23Ap02Dd
Mary	18	F	Laborer	23Ap02Dd
SWEENEY, Ellen	19	F	Laborer	23Ap02Dd
MURPHY, Jerry	20	M	Laborer	23Ap02Dd
FOLEY, Cornelius	40	M	Laborer	23Ap02Dd
Ellen	23	F	Laborer	23Ap02Dd
FINESTY, Margaret	19	F	Laborer	23Ap02Dd
CLIFFORD, Thos.	23	M	Unknown	23Ap02Dd
Eliza	20	F	Unknown	23Ap02Dd
CLUSSON, Edmund	11	M	Unknown	23Ap02Dd
WALSH, John	40	M	Unknown	23Ap02Dd
U-Mrs.	40	F	Unknown	23Ap02Dd
Thomas	16	M	Unknown	23Ap02Dd
Redmond	13	M	Unknown	23Ap02Dd
Edmund	12	M	Unknown	23Ap02Dd
Elizabeth	3	F	Child	23Ap02Dd
SEXTON, William	30	M	Unknown	23Ap02Dd
MURPHY, William	28	F	Unknown	23Ap02Dd
Mary	20	F	Unknown	23Ap02Dd
Catherine	22	F	Unknown	23Ap02Dd
SULLIVAN, Daniel	32	M	Unknown	23Ap02Dd
CONNER, Margaret	46	F	Unknown	23Ap02Dd
MAKHAM, Edward	28	M	Unknown	23Ap02Dd
Mary	26	F	Unknown	23Ap02Dd
FLEMMING, Mary	20	F	Unknown	23Ap02Dd
HUSSY, John	20	M	Unknown	23Ap02Dd
ALLEN, Michael	25	M	Unknown	23Ap02Dd
Richard	18	M	Unknown	23Ap02Dd
Julia	26	F	Unknown	23Ap02Dd
LEAHY, Mary	39	F	Unknown	23Ap02Dd
BRIAN, Richard	26	M	Unknown	23Ap02Dd
HAND, Thos.	30	M	Unknown	23Ap02Dd
DEVLIN, Connor	30	M	Unknown	23Ap02Dd
U-Mrs.	30	F	Unknown	23Ap02Dd
Edward	9	M	Child	23Ap02Dd
HANLON, Mathew	40	M	Unknown	23Ap02Dd
U-Mrs.	40	F	Unknown	23Ap02Dd
Honora	.00	F	Infant	23Ap02Dd
CONAHAN, Daniel	30	M	Unknown	23Ap02Dd
John	20	M	Unknown	23Ap02Dd
Mary	20	F	Unknown	23Ap02Dd
Honora	60	F	Unknown	23Ap02Dd
DRAKE, Margt.	20	F	Unknown	23Ap02Dd
Mary	13	F	Unknown	23Ap02Dd
ODONNELL, Robt.	26	M	Unknown	23Ap02Dd
FOX, Mary	30	F	Unknown	23Ap02Dd
DARGAN, Cornelius	30	M	Unknown	23Ap02Dd
DARGAN, Julia	30	F	Unknown	23Ap02Dd
HOLLAND, Norry	26	F	Unknown	23Ap02Dd
MCCARTHY, Dennis	25	M	Unknown	23Ap02Dd
Callahan	28	M	Unknown	23Ap02Dd
U-Mrs.	29	F	Unknown	23Ap02Dd
KEOHANE, Patrick	25	M	Unknown	23Ap02Dd
Daniel	25	M	Unknown	23Ap02Dd
BUCKLEY, David	33	M	Unknown	23Ap02Dd
WHITE, John	17	M	Unknown	23Ap02Dd
B--Y, John	24	M	Unknown	23Ap02Dd
U-Mrs.	20	F	Unknown	23Ap02Dd
KEDCHEN, Dennis	30	M	Unknown	23Ap02Dd
U-Mrs.	60	F	Unknown	23Ap02Dd
REGAN, Catherine	23	F	Unknown	23Ap02Dd
FEHELY, Margaret	30	F	Unknown	23Ap02Dd
AULIFFE, Timothy	25	M	Unknown	23Ap02Dd
Mary	20	F	Unknown	23Ap02Dd
KOSGROVE, Mary	20	F	Unknown	23Ap02Dd
John	.00	M	Infant	23Ap02Dd
MCVAIGH, Henry	24	M	Unknown	23Ap02Dd
DONOVAN, William	28	M	Unknown	23Ap02Dd
HACKETT, Margaret	30	F	Unknown	23Ap02Dd
GUNSLAN, Anne	37	F	Unknown	23Ap02Dd
John	11	M	Unknown	23Ap02Dd
June	8	F	Child	23Ap02Dd
Michael	5	M	Child	23Ap02Dd
Mary	2	F	Child	23Ap02Dd
HARIN, Jas.	21	M	Unknown	23Ap02Dd
Francis	19	M	Unknown	23Ap02Dd
DONNELLY, Jane	26	F	Unknown	23Ap02Dd
Catherine	.00	F	Infant	23Ap02Dd
FOX, Anne	26	F	Unknown	23Ap02Dd
MCGERRAN, John	20	M	Unknown	23Ap02Dd
Ellen	21	F	Unknown	23Ap02Dd
DOOLAN, Jane	15	F	Unknown	23Ap02Dd
Bridget	20	F	Unknown	23Ap02Dd
MCMULLIN, Catherine	18	F	Unknown	23Ap02Dd
BURN, Anne	18	F	Unknown	23Ap02Dd
LYNCH, Michael	16	M	Unknown	23Ap02Dd
FOLEY, Jeremiah	50	M	Unknown	23Ap02Dd
Margaret	50	F	Unknown	23Ap02Dd
John	24	M	Unknown	23Ap02Dd
Bartholemew	20	M	Unknown	23Ap02Dd
HAMAN, Margaret	21	F	Unknown	23Ap02Dd
MCCURRAN, John	18	M	Unknown	23Ap02Dd
GATELY, Catherine	40	F	Unknown	23Ap02Dd
Patrick	27	M	Unknown	23Ap02Dd
REDDING, Dennis	35	M	Unknown	23Ap02Dd
GATELY, Catherine	20	F	Unknown	23Ap02Dd

CELESTE 23 APRIL 1850

From Limerick

NAMES OF PASSENGERS	AGE	SEX	OCCUPATIONS	DATE PORT SHIP
JONES, Chas.	36	M	Shoemaker	23Ap10Hk
MACK, John	12	M	None	23Ap10Hk
Hannah	.00	F	Infant	23Ap10Hk
ALLEN, Ann	20	F	Servant	23Ap10Hk
SULLIVAN, Bridget	25	F	Servant	23Ap10Hk
LEONARD, John	30	M	Laborer	23Ap10Hk
CAREY, Michl.	18	M	Laborer	23Ap10Hk
Peter	20	M	Laborer	23Ap10Hk
FOX, Thomas	40	M	Laborer	23Ap10Hk
John	.00	M	Infant	23Ap10Hk
MCCARTHY, Johanna	15	F	Servant	23Ap10Hk
DOWLING, Cathr.	25	F	Servant	23Ap10Hk
RIORDAN, John	.00	M	Infant	23Ap10Hk
LYNCH, Ann	16	F	Servant	23Ap10Hk
SCALLY, John	20	M	Laborer	23Ap10Hk

NAMES OF PASSENGERS	AGE	SEX	OCCUPATIONS	DATE PORT SHIP
Nea--ON, Michl.	28	M	Smith	23Ap10Hk
Mary	28	F	Wife	23Ap10Hk
Johanna	6	F	Child	23Ap10Hk
John	2	M	Child	23Ap10Hk
James	.00	M	Infant	23Ap10Hk
GERRALD, John-F.	22	M	Laborer	23Ap10Hk
CLIFFORD, Cathn.	22	F	Servant	23Ap10Hk
MOSS, Eliza	24	F	Servant	23Ap10Hk
OMEALY, Michael	27	M	Laborer	23Ap10Hk
CONNORS, John	26	M	Laborer	23Ap10Hk
Ellen	16	F	Servant	23Ap10Hk
Cathn.	14	F	Servant	23Ap10Hk
Norry	.00	F	Infant	23Ap10Hk
LANDRIGAN, Cathn.	27	F	Servant	23Ap10Hk
SHEA, John	22	M	Laborer	23Ap10Hk
GERALD, Michael	35	M	Laborer	23Ap10Hk
Hannah	.00	F	Infant	23Ap10Hk
CUSACK, Ellen	24	F	Servant	23Ap10Hk
Mary	.00	F	Infant	23Ap10Hk
ROCHFORD, Ellen	22	F	Servant	23Ap10Hk
HOARE, James	23	M	Laborer	23Ap10Hk
MALONE, John	24	M	Laborer	23Ap10Hk
ALLEN, Ann	22	F	Servant	23Ap10Hk
Mary	.00	F	Infant	23Ap10Hk
KINNELLY, Thomas	22	M	Laborer	23Ap10Hk
John	25	M	Laborer	23Ap10Hk
Hannah	20	F	Servant	23Ap10Hk
FITZGERRALD, John	19	M	Laborer	23Ap10Hk
SULLIVAN, Cathn.	20	F	Servant	23Ap10Hk
Thomas	.00	M	Infant	23Ap10Hk
RYAN, Michael	30	M	Laborer	23Ap10Hk
LYNCH, Mary	16	F	Servant	23Ap10Hk
OBRIEN, Mary	25	F	Servant	23Ap10Hk
Ellen	20	F	Servant	23Ap10Hk
DOOLEY, Hannah	29	F	Servant	23Ap10Hk
GERRALD, Hannah	57	F	Servant	23Ap10Hk
Norry	18	F	Servant	23Ap10Hk
BACKMAN, Ellen	27	F	Servant	23Ap10Hk
BOLAND, Michael	40	M	Laborer	23Ap10Hk
RYAN, William	56	M	Laborer	23Ap10Hk
BURN, Michl.	30	M	Laborer	23Ap10Hk
MACK, Michael	20	M	Laborer	23Ap10Hk
CARROLL, Martin	22	M	Laborer	23Ap10Hk
LYNAN, Robt.	20	M	Laborer	23Ap10Hk
RIORDAN, Jer.	11	M	None	23Ap10Hk
HEFFERNAN, Margt.	20	F	Servant	23Ap10Hk
MACK, Patrick	23	M	Laborer	23Ap10Hk
BOURKE, John	20	M	Laborer	23Ap10Hk
BENSKE, Mary	50	F	Servant	23Ap10Hk
MALONE, James	30	M	Laborer	23Ap10Hk
ROSS, Michael	20	M	Laborer	23Ap10Hk
AHERN, John	35	M	Laborer	23Ap10Hk
RYAN, Malachy	38	M	Laborer	23Ap10Hk
BARRY, Patrick	30	M	Laborer	23Ap10Hk
Johanna	30	F	Servant	23Ap10Hk
Mary-Ann	6	F	Child	23Ap10Hk
Johanna	2	F	Child	23Ap10Hk
Honora	.00	F	Infant	23Ap10Hk
LISTER, John	45	M	Laborer	23Ap10Hk
Johanna	20	F	Wife	23Ap10Hk
ELLIOTT, James	26	M	Laborer	23Ap10Hk
BREEN, Thos.	40	M	Laborer	23Ap10Hk
CANE, Denis	30	M	Laborer	23Ap10Hk
SAVAGE, Ellen	40	F	Servant	23Ap10Hk
William	.00	M	Infant	23Ap10Hk
Michl.	8	M	Child	23Ap10Hk
MCMAHON, Mary	19	F	Servant	23Ap10Hk
RYAN, Dan	24	M	Laborer	23Ap10Hk
DOWLING, John	30	M	Laborer	23Ap10Hk
MADIGAN, James	20	M	Laborer	23Ap10Hk
HOLORAN, Mary	44	F	Servant	23Ap10Hk
Frank	23	M	Unknown	23Ap10Hk
Dan	20	M	Unknown	23Ap10Hk
Mary	18	F	Servant	23Ap10Hk
Michael	.00	M	Infant	23Ap10Hk
CORBETT, Danl.	39	M	Laborer	23Ap10Hk
MANGAN, Pat	21	M	Laborer	23Ap10Hk
QUINN, Margt.	22	F	Servant	23Ap10Hk
Mary-Ann	20	F	Servant	23Ap10Hk
HAYES, John	24	M	Laborer	23Ap10Hk
PRATT, Thos.	30	M	Laborer	23Ap10Hk
BARTLEY, Pat	30	M	Laborer	23Ap10Hk
OLOUGHLAN, Pat	18	M	Laborer	23Ap10Hk
COLLINS, Margt.	23	F	Servant	23Ap10Hk
Pat	.00	M	Infant	23Ap10Hk
MULCAHY, Cath.	35	F	Servant	23Ap10Hk
CASEY, Mary-Ann	20	F	Servant	23Ap10Hk
FRAHILL, Wm.	20	M	Laborer	23Ap10Hk
Hannah	19	F	Servant	23Ap10Hk
HAYES, Thos.	20	M	Laborer	23Ap10Hk
FROST, Robt.	30	M	Laborer	23Ap10Hk
Thos.	20	M	Laborer	23Ap10Hk
LUCAS, John	30	M	Laborer	23Ap10Hk
GALVIN, John	20	M	Laborer	23Ap10Hk
MANNING, John	33	M	Laborer	23Ap10Hk
MULCAHY, Johannah	5	F	Child	23Ap10Hk
DWYER, Danl.	19	M	Laborer	23Ap10Hk
DOYLE, Terence	30	M	Laborer	23Ap10Hk
CLIFFORD, Pat	18	M	Laborer	23Ap10Hk
CULL, Michael	24	M	Laborer	23Ap10Hk
HOGAN, Anty.	45	M	Laborer	23Ap10Hk
FINN, Bridget	18	F	Servant	23Ap10Hk
MCGRATH, Michl.	25	M	Laborer	23Ap10Hk
NEALON, William	25	M	Laborer	23Ap10Hk
Matilda	.00	F	Infant	23Ap10Hk
OBRIEN, Margaret	22	F	Servant	23Ap10Hk

OHIO 24 APRIL 1850

From Havana

NAMES OF PASSENGERS	AGE	SEX	OCCUPATIONS	DATE PORT SHIP
STEVENSON, G.W.	22	M	Clerk	24Ap32Ds

MARY-MORRIS 24 APRIL 1850

From Glasgow

NAMES OF PASSENGERS	AGE	SEX	OCCUPATIONS	DATE PORT SHIP
MCLAUGHLAN, Pat	31	M	Laborer	24Ap21Gl
MCGHEE, Jas.	20	M	Laborer	24Ap21Gl
DUNLANEY, Jas.	34	M	Laborer	24Ap21Gl
SWEENEY, Thos.	25	M	Laborer	24Ap21Gl
MCGUIRE, Hugh	20	M	Laborer	24Ap21Gl
Edward	27	M	Laborer	24Ap21Gl
FANLIE, Jas.	27	M	Laborer	24Ap21Gl
BRADLY, Dennis	13	M	Laborer	24Ap21Gl
KERRIGAN, Mick	35	M	Laborer	24Ap21Gl
MCNAIR, Wm.	30	M	Laborer	24Ap21Gl
BECK, Rob	32	M	Farmer	24Ap21Gl
OROURKE, Thos.	15	M	Laborer	24Ap21Gl
TRACEY, Wm.	30	M	Laborer	24Ap21Gl
BOYLES, John	19	M	Mariner	24Ap21Gl

NEW-HAMPSHIRE 25 APRIL 1850

From Liverpool

NAMES OF PASSENGERS	AGE	SEX	OCCUPATIONS	DATE PORT SHIP
GORREN, Hannah	18	F	Servant	25Ap02Hi
SMITH, Mary	17	F	Unknown	25Ap02Hi
HORLEY, Mary	14	F	Unknown	25Ap02Hi
Ann	8	F	Child	25Ap02Hi
MILLARD, Joseph	22	M	Laborer	25Ap02Hi
HARNEY, Charles	22	M	Unknown	25Ap02Hi
LOWLER, Martin	21	M	Unknown	25Ap02Hi
FENON, John	19	M	Laborer	25Ap02Hi
FLOOD, Mary	18	F	Servant	25Ap02Hi
EDWARDS, Maria	19	F	Shoemaker	25Ap02Hi
WELCH, Bridget	45	F	Unknown	25Ap02Hi
HENNEY, Jones	23	M	Shoemaker	25Ap02Hi
Isaac	19	M	Unknown	25Ap02Hi
CONLON, Patt	32	M	Unknown	25Ap02Hi
U-Mrs.	35	F	Unknown	25Ap02Hi
WELCH, Patk.	21	M	Unknown	25Ap02Hi
CONLON, Charles	20	M	Unknown	25Ap02Hi
James	16	M	Unknown	25Ap02Hi
PORLING, Samuel	25	M	Unknown	25Ap02Hi
U-Mrs.	26	F	Unknown	25Ap02Hi
DOOLEY, Mark	34	M	Unknown	25Ap02Hi
LOWLER, James	22	M	Unknown	25Ap02Hi
CLARKSON, George	35	M	Unknown	25Ap02Hi
CONLEY, John	26	M	Unknown	25Ap02Hi
DEAN, Dennis	34	M	Unknown	25Ap02Hi
KENNEDY, Jane	28	F	Unknown	25Ap02Hi
William	.00	M	Infant	25Ap02Hi
TENNISON, James	20	M	Unknown	25Ap02Hi
COMBS, James	30	M	Unknown	25Ap02Hi
LOOLER, Michael	20	M	Unknown	25Ap02Hi
Bridget	13	F	Unknown	25Ap02Hi
MURTAGH, Michael	20	M	Unknown	25Ap02Hi
DONNELLY, Catherine	20	F	Unknown	25Ap02Hi
SMITH, Shean	19	M	Unknown	25Ap02Hi
HUGHES, James	30	M	Unknown	25Ap02Hi
Thomas	35	M	Unknown	25Ap02Hi
Pat	38	M	Unknown	25Ap02Hi
Thomas	25	M	Unknown	25Ap02Hi
Catherine	23	F	Unknown	25Ap02Hi
MOLE, John	23	M	Unknown	25Ap02Hi
ROLISON, Edmond	21	M	Unknown	25Ap02Hi
AULDUFF, George	21	M	Unknown	25Ap02Hi
CONOLON, Thomas	42	M	Unknown	25Ap02Hi
Jno.	28	M	Unknown	25Ap02Hi
Thomas	22	M	Unknown	25Ap02Hi
Anty	55	F	Unknown	25Ap02Hi
MURPHY, Pat	23	M	Unknown	25Ap02Hi
BURKE, Michael	26	M	Unknown	25Ap02Hi
FOLEY, Ellen	15	F	Unknown	25Ap02Hi
NEALE, John	24	M	Unknown	25Ap02Hi
Catherine	22	F	Unknown	25Ap02Hi
CLARKE, William	21	M	Unknown	25Ap02Hi
ROSKEL, Michael	20	M	Unknown	25Ap02Hi
HEART, William	45	M	Unknown	25Ap02Hi
DOYER, Thomas	28	M	Unknown	25Ap02Hi
WOOLLOCK, Michael	28	M	Unknown	25Ap02Hi
Joan	26	F	Unknown	25Ap02Hi
DWYER, Margarett	26	F	Unknown	25Ap02Hi
RYAN, Daniel	25	M	Unknown	25Ap02Hi
COURNEY, William	20	M	Unknown	25Ap02Hi
FITZGERALD, William	22	M	Unknown	25Ap02Hi
CASY, John	18	M	Unknown	25Ap02Hi
MOCK, John	24	M	Unknown	25Ap02Hi
RYAN, Michael	21	M	Unknown	25Ap02Hi
LYNCH, Oliver	22	M	Unknown	25Ap02Hi

NAMES OF PASSENGERS	AGE	SEX	OCCUPATIONS	DATE PORT SHIP
LYNCH, Honor	20	F	Unknown	25Ap02Hi
CORININ, Owen	26	M	Unknown	25Ap02Hi
FLYNN, Ellen	25	F	Unknown	25Ap02Hi
SHORELAND, Mary	20	F	Unknown	25Ap02Hi
William	19	M	Unknown	25Ap02Hi
BOILSON, Daniel	25	M	Unknown	25Ap02Hi
Patk.	20	M	Unknown	25Ap02Hi
Mary	20	F	Unknown	25Ap02Hi
Joan	10	F	Unknown	25Ap02Hi
CONNORS, Mary	10	F	Unknown	25Ap02Hi
Judy	21	F	Unknown	25Ap02Hi
FOWLEY, John	27	M	Unknown	25Ap02Hi
RYAN, Sally	21	F	Unknown	25Ap02Hi
KING, John	18	M	Unknown	25Ap02Hi
STOKES, John	35	M	Unknown	25Ap02Hi
CAHILL, Judy	45	F	Unknown	25Ap02Hi
Ellen	20	F	Unknown	25Ap02Hi
Mary	26	F	Unknown	25Ap02Hi
John	21	M	Unknown	25Ap02Hi
Bridget	16	F	Unknown	25Ap02Hi
DWYER, Thomas	20	M	Unknown	25Ap02Hi
MCCAHILL, Catherine	18	F	Unknown	25Ap02Hi
MURPHY, John	16	M	Unknown	25Ap02Hi
HART, John	36	M	Unknown	25Ap02Hi
Ruth	34	F	Unknown	25Ap02Hi
Mary	6	F	Child	25Ap02Hi
Nancy	3	F	Child	25Ap02Hi
WILLIAMS, Catherine	20	F	Unknown	25Ap02Hi
Pierce	.00	M	Infant	25Ap02Hi
MCANOLE, James	50	M	Unknown	25Ap02Hi
Sarah	14	F	Unknown	25Ap02Hi
GALLAGHER, Pat	16	M	Unknown	25Ap02Hi
HEFFEREN, John	27	M	Unknown	25Ap02Hi
ELLIOTT, Jane	29	F	Unknown	25Ap02Hi
MCGIRNEY, Mary	49	F	Unknown	25Ap02Hi
BOYLAN, Thomas	17	M	Unknown	25Ap02Hi
CALLERING, Catherine	16	F	Unknown	25Ap02Hi
Margarett	16	F	Unknown	25Ap02Hi
GLEAHE, Ellen	39	F	Unknown	25Ap02Hi
MORSE, James	29	M	Unknown	25Ap02Hi
Mary	17	F	Unknown	25Ap02Hi
MCCORMICK, Dennis	25	M	Unknown	25Ap02Hi
MCCHUKEY, James	29	M	Unknown	25Ap02Hi
READ, Ann	39	F	Unknown	25Ap02Hi
Ann	.00	F	Infant	25Ap02Hi
HENRY, Bridget	20	F	Unknown	25Ap02Hi
GANRINGS, Rob	18	M	Unknown	25Ap02Hi
REILLY, Mary	29	F	Unknown	25Ap02Hi
READ, Pat	18	M	Unknown	25Ap02Hi
MARA, James	39	M	Unknown	25Ap02Hi
KENEDY, Michael	30	M	Unknown	25Ap02Hi
Michael	30	M	Unknown	25Ap02Hi
Patk.	.00	M	Infant	25Ap02Hi
RYAN, Michael	39	M	Unknown	25Ap02Hi
STEAD, Ann	30	F	Unknown	25Ap02Hi
HARTAGAN, Thomas	16	M	Unknown	25Ap02Hi
FOLEY, Daniel	21	M	Unknown	25Ap02Hi
FORREST, Ellen	26	F	Unknown	25Ap02Hi
MCDONALD, Mary	48	F	Unknown	25Ap02Hi
SCULLY, Joseph	40	M	Unknown	25Ap02Hi
Brid.	39	F	Unknown	25Ap02Hi
Thomas	.00	M	Infant	25Ap02Hi
Jno.	30	M	Unknown	25Ap02Hi
MAHONEY, Edmond	22	M	Unknown	25Ap02Hi
SHEALING, S.G.	26	M	Unknown	25Ap02Hi
DONELL, John	18	M	Unknown	25Ap02Hi
WALSH, Thomas	40	M	Unknown	25Ap02Hi
U-Mrs.	40	F	Unknown	25Ap02Hi
William	14	M	Unknown	25Ap02Hi
Mary	10	F	Unknown	25Ap02Hi
James	12	M	Unknown	25Ap02Hi
WALL, William	35	M	Unknown	25Ap02Hi
U-Mrs.	30	F	Unknown	25Ap02Hi
William	4	M	Child	25Ap02Hi
Rose	3	F	Child	25Ap02Hi

NAMES OF PASSENGERS	AGE	SEX	OCCUPATIONS	DATE PORT SHIP
WALL, Michael	.00	M	Infant	25Ap02Hi
CARE, William	28	M	Unknown	25Ap02Hi
BUTT, Andrew	24	M	Unknown	25Ap02Hi
SIMON, Bridget	46	F	Unknown	25Ap02Hi
Thomas	16	M	Unknown	25Ap02Hi
James	15	M	Unknown	25Ap02Hi
Mary	12	F	Unknown	25Ap02Hi
Pat	10	M	Unknown	25Ap02Hi
John	7	M	Child	25Ap02Hi
Edward	5	M	Child	25Ap02Hi
BOYD, Marion	25	F	Unknown	25Ap02Hi
RYAN, Edmond	35	M	Unknown	25Ap02Hi
RORY, John	19	M	Unknown	25Ap02Hi
WARRON, Ann	40	F	Unknown	25Ap02Hi
Margarett	10	F	Unknown	25Ap02Hi
Bridgt.	5	F	Child	25Ap02Hi
Mary	8	F	Child	25Ap02Hi
DAILEY, Michael	8	M	Child	25Ap02Hi
Andrew	22	M	Unknown	25Ap02Hi
HORAN, Michael	22	M	Unknown	25Ap02Hi
Pat	21	M	Unknown	25Ap02Hi
Ellen	25	F	Unknown	25Ap02Hi
KANE, James	16	M	Unknown	25Ap02Hi
MANY, Sarah	20	F	Unknown	25Ap02Hi
Julia	.00	F	Infant	25Ap02Hi
Mary	10	F	Unknown	25Ap02Hi
Margaret	8	F	Child	25Ap02Hi
Andrew	6	M	Child	25Ap02Hi
James	4	M	Child	25Ap02Hi
SMITH, Ellen	20	F	Unknown	25Ap02Hi
HORRIGAN, Julia	20	F	Unknown	25Ap02Hi
ROUNDALL, Owen	28	M	Unknown	25Ap02Hi
EARLE, John	11	M	Unknown	25Ap02Hi
Emma	14	F	Unknown	25Ap02Hi
Rosa	18	F	Unknown	25Ap02Hi
Ellisia	46	F	Unknown	25Ap02Hi
DONOHUE, Michael	16	M	Unknown	25Ap02Hi
FITZPATRICK, Andrew	27	M	Unknown	25Ap02Hi
Margarett	26	F	Unknown	25Ap02Hi
Margarett	.00	F	Infant	25Ap02Hi
KILLBRIDE, Pat	16	M	Unknown	25Ap02Hi
MCCAVAN, Mary	15	F	Unknown	25Ap02Hi
MCMEE, Pat	25	M	Unknown	25Ap02Hi
GALLAGHER, Joan	40	F	Unknown	25Ap02Hi
Mary	20	F	Unknown	25Ap02Hi
GALGAN, John	18	M	Unknown	25Ap02Hi
MOYER, James	12	M	Unknown	25Ap02Hi
RASTROGE, Charlotte	38	F	Unknown	25Ap02Hi
Calub	8	M	Child	25Ap02Hi
William	6	M	Child	25Ap02Hi
John	.00	M	Infant	25Ap02Hi
Susan	4	F	Child	25Ap02Hi
REILLY, Peter	22	M	Unknown	25Ap02Hi
MAINOR, Mary	40	F	Unknown	25Ap02Hi
Mary	15	F	Unknown	25Ap02Hi
Richard	11	M	Unknown	25Ap02Hi
DRAKE, John	26	M	Unknown	25Ap02Hi
KNOWLON, Ann	19	F	Servant	25Ap02Hi
MCGARRET, Michael	19	M	Blacksmith	25Ap02Hi
MCINTYRE, Peter	21	M	Unknown	25Ap02Hi
MCGAGHON, Pat	19	M	Laborer	25Ap02Hi
NORREY, Thomas	21	M	Unknown	25Ap02Hi
Ann	22	F	Unknown	25Ap02Hi
CARSON, Martin	24	M	Unknown	25Ap02Hi
Joan	22	F	Unknown	25Ap02Hi
SYKES, John	27	M	Unknown	25Ap02Hi
CHAPELL, Robt.	24	M	Unknown	25Ap02Hi
DENNON, John	25	M	Unknown	25Ap02Hi
COFFERY, Owen	29	M	Unknown	25Ap02Hi
LYNCH, John	24	M	Unknown	25Ap02Hi
DONOHUE, Mary	20	F	Unknown	25Ap02Hi
HOGAN, Michael	20	M	Unknown	25Ap02Hi
KILINGSON, Michael	25	M	Unknown	25Ap02Hi
CONTERN, Michael	17	M	Unknown	25Ap02Hi
LEONARD, Margarett	30	F	Unknown	25Ap02Hi

NAMES OF PASSENGERS	AGE	SEX	OCCUPATIONS	DATE PORT SHIP
MCAVY, Martin	40	M	Unknown	25Ap02Hi
MAHER, James	25	M	Unknown	25Ap02Hi
CULLEN, John	25	M	Unknown	25Ap02Hi
PHELAN, Bridg.	18	F	Unknown	25Ap02Hi
DUNN, Anthony	22	M	Unknown	25Ap02Hi
SHOUGHLEY, Pat	21	M	Unknown	25Ap02Hi
MCCARRON, John	25	M	Unknown	25Ap02Hi
Ann	4	F	Unknown	25Ap02Hi
Mary	3	F	Child	25Ap02Hi
Ann	50	F	Unknown	25Ap02Hi
MULLIGAN, Richard	24	M	Unknown	25Ap02Hi
Sarah	16	F	Unknown	25Ap02Hi
WELLS, Jane	17	F	Unknown	25Ap02Hi
HANLEY, Sam	29	M	Unknown	25Ap02Hi
ROCHE, Catherine	20	F	Unknown	25Ap02Hi
KERNEY, Geo.	19	M	Unknown	25Ap02Hi
MARTIN, John	19	M	Unknown	25Ap02Hi
MCQUADE, Pat	36	M	Unknown	25Ap02Hi
GORMLY, James	22	M	Unknown	25Ap02Hi
Bernard	12	M	Unknown	25Ap02Hi
MCQUADE, Charles	36	M	Unknown	25Ap02Hi
SAMPSON, George	32	M	Unknown	25Ap02Hi
U-Mrs.	32	F	Unknown	25Ap02Hi
ARMSTRONG, Robt.	21	M	Unknown	25Ap02Hi
U-Mrs.	22	F	Unknown	25Ap02Hi
Eliza	.00	F	Infant	25Ap02Hi
GIBSON, U-Miss	20	F	Unknown	25Ap02Hi
ARNOLD, John	21	M	Unknown	25Ap02Hi
CARLIN, Margarett	14	F	Unknown	25Ap02Hi
MARGERALH, Jane	22	F	Unknown	25Ap02Hi
Pat	20	M	Unknown	25Ap02Hi
HICKLEY, D.	30	M	Unknown	25Ap02Hi
BRISTONAL, Hugh	21	M	Unknown	25Ap02Hi
FOLEY, Denis	25	M	Unknown	25Ap02Hi

EMIGRANT 25 APRIL 1850

From Liverpool

NAMES OF PASSENGERS	AGE	SEX	OCCUPATIONS	DATE PORT SHIP
LYONS, John	32	M	Carpenter	25Ap02Gu
CALLAGHAN, Judy	40	F	Farmer	25Ap02Gu
MCCARTY, Charles	22	M	Farmer	25Ap02Gu
Ellen	20	F	Farmer	25Ap02Gu
Owen	18	M	Farmer	25Ap02Gu
Daniel	15	M	Farmer	25Ap02Gu
Mary	14	F	Farmer	25Ap02Gu
Judy	10	F	Farmer	25Ap02Gu
Catharine	8	F	Child	25Ap02Gu
Dennis	6	M	Child	25Ap02Gu
Elisabeth	.00	F	Infant	25Ap02Gu
RYAN, Patty	30	M	Farmer	25Ap02Gu
Mary	27	F	Farmer	25Ap02Gu
Ellen	25	F	Farmer	25Ap02Gu
BURKE, Mary	19	F	Farmer	25Ap02Gu
RYAN, Allice	7	F	Child	25Ap02Gu
John	4	M	Child	25Ap02Gu
James	3	M	Child	25Ap02Gu
Michael	.00	M	Infant	25Ap02Gu
Patrick	30	M	Farmer	25Ap02Gu
Margaret	30	F	Farmer	25Ap02Gu
Annie	10	F	Farmer	25Ap02Gu
Bernard	.00	M	Infant	25Ap02Gu
Michael	29	M	Farmer	25Ap02Gu
SHANNAGHAN, John	21	M	Laborer	25Ap02Gu
MAHARSER, John	50	M	Farmer	25Ap02Gu
BURKE, Patrick	40	M	Laborer	25Ap02Gu
Mary	17	F	Laborer	25Ap02Gu
Ellen	15	F	Laborer	25Ap02Gu
Dennis	12	M	Laborer	25Ap02Gu

NAMES OF PASSENGERS	AGE	SEX	OCCUPATIONS	DATE PORT SHIP
BURKE, Michael	7	M	Child	25Ap02Gu
Patrick	.00	M	Infant	25Ap02Gu
MCDANNA, Julia	15	F	Laborer	25Ap02Gu
DUFFY, Elisabeth	20	F	Laborer	25Ap02Gu
CLEMENS, Anna	20	F	Laborer	25Ap02Gu
ROURKE, Bernard	35	M	Laborer	25Ap02Gu
Catharine	27	F	Laborer	25Ap02Gu
ROURKES, John	5	M	Child	25Ap02Gu
Turn--, Michael	26	M	Unknown	25Ap02Gu
ROCKETT, Mary	30	F	Trader	25Ap02Gu
Pat	8	M	Child	25Ap02Gu
THOMSON, Mary	20	F	Servant	25Ap02Gu
DULAN, Ann	24	F	Farmer	25Ap02Gu
GOGAN, Catherine	20	F	Farmer	25Ap02Gu
LOLA, Mary	22	F	Servant	25Ap02Gu
CARANNA, Anna	20	F	Servant	25Ap02Gu
KELLY, Michael	8	M	Child	25Ap02Gu
Pat	6	M	Child	25Ap02Gu
FINN, Bridget	16	F	Servant	25Ap02Gu
COOK, John	15	M	Laborer	25Ap02Gu
Ann	8	F	Child	25Ap02Gu
FOGGERTY, Maria	25	F	Farmer	25Ap02Gu
COOK, James	9	M	Child	25Ap02Gu
FARRELL, Thomas	25	M	Laborer	25Ap02Gu
Eliza	25	F	Laborer	25Ap02Gu
ELLIS, Margt.	32	F	Weaver	25Ap02Gu
Louise	5	F	Child	25Ap02Gu
Rebecca	4	F	Child	25Ap02Gu
HICKY, John	26	M	Farmer	25Ap02Gu
MOORE, Thos.	26	M	Farmer	25Ap02Gu
NEIL, Mary	25	F	Farmer	25Ap02Gu
MCDONNELL, Mary	24	F	Servant	25Ap02Gu
James	7	M	Child	25Ap02Gu
MCMAHON, Edward	21	M	Laborer	25Ap02Gu
BLANEY, Thos.	25	M	Tailor	25Ap02Gu
GINNCHY, Hugh	21	M	Laborer	25Ap02Gu
M----, Thos.	18	M	Unknown	25Ap02Gu
Cath.	15	F	Servant	25Ap02Gu
ROSE, Mary	20	F	Servant	25Ap02Gu
MCDERMOTT, Ann	20	F	Servant	25Ap02Gu
HAGAN, Peggy	9	F	Child	25Ap02Gu
BLITHE, Jane	20	F	Servant	25Ap02Gu
MURPHY, John	16	M	Servant	25Ap02Gu
MILES, Biddy	20	F	Servant	25Ap02Gu
MORPHET, Ann	24	F	Servant	25Ap02Gu
DYER, Patrick	6	M	Child	25Ap02Gu
HUGHES, John	20	M	Servant	25Ap02Gu
Mary	15	F	Servant	25Ap02Gu
GILLESPIE, Peter	15	M	Laborer	25Ap02Gu
HUGHES, Thos.	60	M	Laborer	25Ap02Gu
RICKABY, Henry	32	F	Servant	25Ap02Gu
HALEY, Patrick	22	M	Boatman	25Ap02Gu
MCNAMARA, John	22	M	Butcher	25Ap02Gu
NEVIN, Peter	38	M	Laborer	25Ap02Gu
BURKE, Thos.	20	M	Laborer	25Ap02Gu
TINOCHTY, Bartley	20	M	Laborer	25Ap02Gu
ODONNELL, Mannis	24	M	Laborer	25Ap02Gu
MARTIN, Elizabeth	20	F	Servant	25Ap02Gu
HENRY, Mary	18	F	Servant	25Ap02Gu
MCDONAUGH, Mary	35	F	Servant	25Ap02Gu
FINNERTY, Bridget	65	F	Farmer	25Ap02Gu
BRADFORD, Thomas	20	M	Servant	25Ap02Gu
SWAN, Turn	32	M	Laborer	25Ap02Gu
FOLEY, Pat	28	M	Laborer	25Ap02Gu
MOURNE, Michael	35	M	Laborer	25Ap02Gu
Edward	35	M	Laborer	25Ap02Gu
Judy	32	F	Laborer	25Ap02Gu
James	4	M	Child	25Ap02Gu
Ann	.00	F	Infant	25Ap02Gu
KING, Alice	20	F	Servant	25Ap02Gu
FOLEY, Mary	20	F	Servant	25Ap02Gu
MCGLINN, Biddy	30	F	Servant	25Ap02Gu
Pat	9	M	Child	25Ap02Gu
Mary	5	F	Child	25Ap02Gu
Mary	30	F	Servant	25Ap02Gu

NAMES OF PASSENGERS	AGE	SEX	OCCUPATIONS	DATE PORT SHIP
MCGLINN, Mary	9	F	Child	25Ap02Gu
Biddy	7	F	Child	25Ap02Gu
Cath.	5	F	Child	25Ap02Gu
Daniel	3	M	Child	25Ap02Gu
Magey	.00	M	Infant	25Ap02Gu
DONNELL, Unity	25	M	Servant	25Ap02Gu
GORMAN, Martin	25	M	Laborer	25Ap02Gu
BRACKIN, John	23	M	Laborer	25Ap02Gu
SMITH, Geo.	26	M	Laborer	25Ap02Gu
MCLOY, Henry	25	M	Laborer	25Ap02Gu
DROWEY, John	26	M	Laborer	25Ap02Gu
SMITH, John	30	M	Clerk	25Ap02Gu
MALOY, Pat	21	M	Farmer	25Ap02Gu
OMALOY, Wm.	21	M	Farmer	25Ap02Gu
FLINN, Anthony	52	M	Farmer	25Ap02Gu
Bridget	22	F	Farmer	25Ap02Gu
WELSCH, Nelly	45	F	Farmer	25Ap02Gu
Lachy	22	F	Farmer	25Ap02Gu
FLINN, Ellen	13	F	Farmer	25Ap02Gu
John	14	M	Farmer	25Ap02Gu
WELSCH, Mary	22	F	Farmer	25Ap02Gu
CARLEY, Pat	21	M	Laborer	25Ap02Gu
MCGUIRE, Lanly	21	M	Laborer	25Ap02Gu
CUNNINGHAM, Morris	57	M	Farmer	25Ap02Gu
CLUELAN, Edward	14	M	Laborer	25Ap02Gu
MEEHAN, Pat	55	M	Farmer	25Ap02Gu
FOLEY, Owen	25	M	Farmer	25Ap02Gu
FARRELL, Paddy	62	M	Stctr	25Ap02Gu
HANEY, Bridget	21	F	Servant	25Ap02Gu
DALEY, Mary	21	F	Servant	25Ap02Gu
GARRY, Joseph	11	M	Servant	25Ap02Gu
Pat	10	M	Servant	25Ap02Gu
Margaret	8	F	Child	25Ap02Gu
Peter	6	M	Child	25Ap02Gu
Mary	4	M	Child	25Ap02Gu
WALLIS, Catherine	20	F	Servant	25Ap02Gu
CONLIN, Mary	18	F	Servant	25Ap02Gu
RONEY, Mary	25	F	Servant	25Ap02Gu
SKELLY, Mick	18	M	Laborer	25Ap02Gu
Patrick	22	M	Laborer	25Ap02Gu
James	11	M	Servant	25Ap02Gu
SHORT, John	44	M	Laborer	25Ap02Gu
RUCKETT, Chr.	56	M	Laborer	25Ap02Gu
FAGAN, Matty	20	M	Laborer	25Ap02Gu
MULLIN, Biddy	23	F	Servant	25Ap02Gu
LICHY, Biddy	23	F	Servant	25Ap02Gu
CORNER, Mary	24	F	Servant	25Ap02Gu
HUGHES, John	20	M	Shoemaker	25Ap02Gu
DONNAGEN, John-Bern.	24	M	Laborer	25Ap02Gu
MALGROVE, Peter	18	M	Servant	25Ap02Gu
NOLTE, James	18	M	Laborer	25Ap02Gu
FINNAGAN, John	25	M	Laborer	25Ap02Gu
BRADY, Margt.	50	F	Laborer	25Ap02Gu
Bridget	14	F	Servant	25Ap02Gu
James	12	M	Servant	25Ap02Gu
KANE, Mary	60	F	Servant	25Ap02Gu
Died-At-Sea				
WERTY, Pat	25	M	Baker	25Ap02Gu
HEARTY, Thos.	22	M	Engineer	25Ap02Gu
KORN, James	21	M	Mason	25Ap02Gu
DILLON, John	21	M	Laborer	25Ap02Gu
MYNE, Cath.	35	F	Dressmaker	25Ap02Gu
BRAILEY, Mary	18	F	Servant	25Ap02Gu
FITZPATRICK, Mary	12	F	Servant	25Ap02Gu
Peter	10	M	Servant	25Ap02Gu
ARCH, James	12	M	Servant	25Ap02Gu
DUFFY, Thos.	30	M	Laborer	25Ap02Gu
CAFFREY, John	22	M	Laborer	25Ap02Gu
MALLIN, Pat	18	M	Laborer	25Ap02Gu
MCNOY, Jas.	20	M	Farmer	25Ap02Gu
DONNAHUE, Margt.	20	F	Servant	25Ap02Gu
RILEY, Mary	20	F	Servant	25Ap02Gu
GOLDIN, Rose	35	F	Servant	25Ap02Gu
ENGLISH, Thomas	42	M	Laborer	25Ap02Gu
HALL, John	20	M	Laborer	25Ap02Gu

NAMES OF PASSENGERS	AGE	SEX	OCCUPATIONS	DATE PORT SHIP
PATTERSON, Biddy	13	F	Servant	25Ap02Gu
CARLE, Margt.	40	F	Farmer	25Ap02Gu
MCBURNS, Ellen	36	M	Farmer	25Ap02Gu
Ellen	7	F	Child	25Ap02Gu
SMITH, Bridget	20	F	Farmer	25Ap02Gu
Mary	17	F	Farmer	25Ap02Gu
Cath.	15	F	Farmer	25Ap02Gu
CLARK, Judy	17	F	Farmer	25Ap02Gu
HAYES, Thos.	35	M	Farmer	25Ap02Gu
Mick	14	F	Farmer	25Ap02Gu
Philip	12	M	Farmer	25Ap02Gu
John	10	M	Farmer	25Ap02Gu
Margt.	8	F	Child	25Ap02Gu
Ellen	30	F	Farmer	25Ap02Gu
Mary	16	F	Farmer	25Ap02Gu
Tom	6	M	Child	25Ap02Gu
Jane	4	F	Child	25Ap02Gu
Ellen	.00	F	Infant	25Ap02Gu
John	35	M	Farmer	25Ap02Gu
Annora	30	F	Farmer	25Ap02Gu
Margt.	16	F	Farmer	25Ap02Gu
Bridget	13	F	Farmer	25Ap02Gu
Michael	12	M	Farmer	25Ap02Gu
Margt.	9	F	Child	25Ap02Gu
John	5	M	Child	25Ap02Gu

AFGHAN 25 APRIL 1850

From Liverpool

NAMES OF PASSENGERS	AGE	SEX	OCCUPATIONS	DATE PORT SHIP
CURRY, Edward	27	M	Laborer	25Ap02If
MURRAY, Anne	50	F	Spinster	25Ap02If
Mary	23	F	Spinster	25Ap02If
Biddy	13	F	Spinster	25Ap02If
MCEVERY, Mary	20	F	Spinster	25Ap02If
CLARKE, Ch.	18	F	Spinster	25Ap02If
June	17	F	Spinster	25Ap02If
CONLEY, Bridget	24	F	Spinster	25Ap02If
Nancy	13	F	Spinster	25Ap02If
Cathn.	7	F	Child	25Ap02If
Anne	5	F	Child	25Ap02If
Ellen	3	F	Child	25Ap02If
John	.00	M	Infant	25Ap02If
KELLY, Timothy	25	M	Laborer	25Ap02If
ARTHUR, Julia	19	F	Spinster	25Ap02If
MALOWNEY, John	36	M	Laborer	25Ap02If
Bridget	30	F	Spinster	25Ap02If
DEMSEY, Michael	18	M	Laborer	25Ap02If
CAROUGHTON, Martin	40	M	Laborer	25Ap02If
OLALON, Pat	30	M	Laborer	25Ap02If
Ellen	24	M	Spinster	25Ap02If
RYAN, James	26	M	Laborer	25Ap02If
Mary	20	F	Spinster	25Ap02If
Eliza	18	F	Spinster	25Ap02If
Biddy	18	F	Spinster	25Ap02If
HAYES, Daniel	24	M	Laborer	25Ap02If
LAMB, Rose	20	F	Spinster	25Ap02If
CLARKE, Owen	54	M	Laborer	25Ap02If
John	26	M	Laborer	25Ap02If
FINNON, Lawrence	30	M	Laborer	25Ap02If
GILLIGAN, Anne	20	F	Spinster	25Ap02If
HUNTER, Willm.	20	M	Laborer	25Ap02If
Susan	23	F	Unknown	25Ap02If
CARROLL, Thomas	26	M	Laborer	25Ap02If
RUSH, William	33	M	Farmer	25Ap02If
Margaret	27	F	Unknown	25Ap02If
Robert	2	M	Child	25Ap02If
Frances	.08	F	Infant	25Ap02If
Died-At-Sea				

NAMES OF PASSENGERS	AGE	SEX	OCCUPATIONS	DATE PORT SHIP
MCFADDEN, Jane	40	F	Unknown	25Ap02If
George	17	M	Laborer	25Ap02If
BYRNES, Pat	23	M	Laborer	25Ap02If
MCNIVANE, Andrew	17	M	Laborer	25Ap02If
Matthew	14	M	Laborer	25Ap02If
CURRIN, Pat	26	M	Laborer	25Ap02If
CHAMPLINE, Pat	29	M	Laborer	25Ap02If
KEYES, Daniel	33	M	Laborer	25Ap02If
BROPHY, Willm.	33	M	Laborer	25Ap02If
Dan	32	M	Laborer	25Ap02If
Ellen	30	F	Laborer	25Ap02If
MCDONNELL, Edward	28	M	Laborer	25Ap02If
COLLMAN, Daniel	21	M	Laborer	25Ap02If
MCDONALD, John	22	M	Laborer	25Ap02If
WELSH, James	22	M	Laborer	25Ap02If
HUSKEY, Thomas	35	M	Laborer	25Ap02If
Cathn.	30	F	Unknown	25Ap02If
John	4	M	Child	25Ap02If
Owen	.00	M	Infant	25Ap02If
MORROW, Michael	30	M	Laborer	25Ap02If
MCCANN, John	55	M	Laborer	25Ap02If
HYMES, James	60	M	Laborer	25Ap02If
MCCANN, Thomas	23	M	Laborer	25Ap02If
John	21	M	Laborer	25Ap02If
Owen	20	M	Laborer	25Ap02If
Cathn.	19	F	Unknown	25Ap02If
Kerven	16	M	Laborer	25Ap02If
Margaret	6	F	Child	25Ap02If
Cathn.	4	F	Child	25Ap02If
ADAMS, Henry	55	M	Laborer	25Ap02If
Margaret	20	F	Unknown	25Ap02If
CANAGAN, Phillip	50	M	Laborer	25Ap02If
Susan	40	F	Unknown	25Ap02If
ENNIS, Michael	24	M	Laborer	25Ap02If
DEGAN, Ellen	49	F	Unknown	25Ap02If
James	32	F	Unknown	25Ap02If
James	26	F	Unknown	25Ap02If
Anne	26	F	Unknown	25Ap02If
MURPHY, James	20	M	Laborer	25Ap02If
RIDDY, Reas	20	M	Laborer	25Ap02If
KIRNEY, Anne	40	F	Unknown	25Ap02If
Daniel	16	M	Laborer	25Ap02If
JOICE, Henry	26	M	Laborer	25Ap02If
RILLEY, Edmond	25	M	Laborer	25Ap02If
BULGAR, John	55	M	Laborer	25Ap02If
James	20	M	Laborer	25Ap02If
Mary	18	F	Laborer	25Ap02If
PARRY, Peter	40	M	Laborer	25Ap02If
Eliza	35	F	Unknown	25Ap02If
Maryanne	10	F	Unknown	25Ap02If
John	8	M	Child	25Ap02If
Willm.	7	M	Child	25Ap02If
Eliza	7	F	Child	25Ap02If
Cathn.	4	F	Child	25Ap02If
MADDEN, Thomas	24	M	Laborer	25Ap02If
NEILL, Cathn.	15	F	Laborer	25Ap02If
WELSH, Willm.	18	M	Laborer	25Ap02If
DONLAN, Cathn.	17	F	Unknown	25Ap02If
KEARNEY, Dan	23	M	Laborer	25Ap02If
Ellen	22	F	Unknown	25Ap02If
NEILL, Larry	18	M	Laborer	25Ap02If
WELSH, James	24	M	Laborer	25Ap02If
Julia	28	F	Unknown	25Ap02If
Cathn.	21	F	Unknown	25Ap02If
KINAGH, Michael	24	M	Laborer	25Ap02If
SARSENAGH, Julia	19	F	None	25Ap02If
BRYAN, Margaret	25	F	None	25Ap02If
GORMAN, Michael	25	M	Laborer	25Ap02If
FOGARTY, Willm.	25	M	Laborer	25Ap02If
Cathn.	22	F	None	25Ap02If
CROOKS, Michael	35	M	Laborer	25Ap02If
BURKE, Pat	20	M	Laborer	25Ap02If
BOOTH, Timothy	27	M	Laborer	25Ap02If
WHITE, Thomas	22	M	Laborer	25Ap02If
Maryann	23	F	Unknown	25Ap02If

NAMES OF PASSENGERS	AGE	SEX	OCCUPATIONS	DATE PORT SHIP
WHITE, Eliza	.00	F	Infant	25Ap02If
ELLISON, Michael	36	M	Laborer	25Ap02If
CONDON, Willm.	46	M	Laborer	25Ap02If
LANE, Pat	45	M	Laborer	25Ap02If
NONNAN, Dan	34	M	Laborer	25Ap02If
Ellen	27	F	Unknown	25Ap02If
WILLIAMS, Margaret	24	F	Unknown	25Ap02If
Thomas	24	M	Laborer	25Ap02If
RUSSELL, Bridget	22	F	Unknown	25Ap02If
WELSH, John	27	M	Laborer	25Ap02If
Winney	24	F	Unknown	25Ap02If
MAUGHAN, James	24	M	Laborer	25Ap02If
MALLEY, Thomas	28	M	Laborer	25Ap02If
DELANEY, John	45	M	Laborer	25Ap02If
HOYE, Pat	26	M	Laborer	25Ap02If
WALLER, Isabella	20	F	Unknown	25Ap02If
CONELLY, James	20	M	Laborer	25Ap02If
CARROLL, Peggy	19	F	Unknown	25Ap02If
Honor	15	F	Unknown	25Ap02If
Ellen	17	F	Unknown	25Ap02If
KENNEDY, Maryann	19	F	Unknown	25Ap02If
SLATTERY, Dan	30	M	Laborer	25Ap02If
MORAN, John	24	M	Laborer	25Ap02If
Johanna	22	F	Unknown	25Ap02If
MAYLA, John	30	M	Laborer	25Ap02If
Eliza	26	F	Unknown	25Ap02If
Willm.	3	M	Child	25Ap02If
Dan	2	M	Child	25Ap02If
Lawrence	.00	M	Infant	25Ap02If
CONDON, Pat	32	M	Laborer	25Ap02If
Johanna	25	F	Unknown	25Ap02If
Honora	4	F	Child	25Ap02If
Mary	2	F	Child	25Ap02If
Cathn.	.00	F	Infant	25Ap02If
SHEEN, Willm.	22	M	Laborer	25Ap02If
LENNON, John	27	M	Laborer	25Ap02If
Mary	27	F	Unknown	25Ap02If
HALEY, Dennis	20	M	Laborer	25Ap02If
QUIRK, Pat	25	M	Laborer	25Ap02If
RUSSELL, John	26	M	Laborer	25Ap02If
Mary	22	F	Unknown	25Ap02If
ADAMSON, Henry	14	M	Laborer	25Ap02If
Biddy	18	F	Unknown	25Ap02If
DIXON, Jane	22	F	Unknown	25Ap02If
DOLAN, Maria	20	F	Unknown	25Ap02If
MCCORMICK, Pat	22	M	Laborer	25Ap02If
MULDERRY, Thomas	24	M	Laborer	25Ap02If
Rose	24	F	Unknown	25Ap02If
MURPHY, Bridget	45	F	Unknown	25Ap02If
James	21	M	Laborer	25Ap02If
FORISTON, Anne	40	F	Unknown	25Ap02If
ONEILL, Sarah	26	F	Unknown	25Ap02If
CARROLL, James	25	M	Laborer	25Ap02If
Cathn.	21	F	Unknown	25Ap02If
MCDONNELL, Edward	20	M	Laborer	25Ap02If
GALEGHER, Michael	35	M	Laborer	25Ap02If
Thomas	24	M	Laborer	25Ap02If
TOPHY, Dan	20	M	Laborer	25Ap02If
WISEMAN, John	19	M	Laborer	25Ap02If
OSHEA, Nathan	33	M	Laborer	25Ap02If
DUNCAN, Eliza	26	F	Unknown	25Ap02If
RYAN, Eliza	33	F	Unknown	25Ap02If
Margaret	20	F	Unknown	25Ap02If
Ellen	18	F	Unknown	25Ap02If
Thomas	17	M	Laborer	25Ap02If
John	12	M	Unknown	25Ap02If
Bess	10	F	Unknown	25Ap02If
CORCORAN, Thomas	25	M	Laborer	25Ap02If
Jerry	20	M	Laborer	25Ap02If
WISEMAN, Dennis	30	M	Laborer	25Ap02If
Thomas	28	M	Laborer	25Ap02If
Cathn.	22	F	Unknown	25Ap02If
LUGAN, James	18	M	Laborer	25Ap02If
OCONNOR, Conn	18	M	Laborer	25Ap02If
LUGAN, Nane	17	F	Unknown	25Ap02If

NAMES OF PASSENGERS	AGE	SEX	OCCUPATIONS	DATE PORT SHIP
FLYNE, Dennis	28	M	Laborer	25Ap02If
LAMB, John	28	M	Laborer	25Ap02If
QUINN, Willm.	40	M	Laborer	25Ap02If
Mary	12	F	Unknown	25Ap02If
Tim	10	M	Unknown	25Ap02If
MURPHY, Dennis	30	M	Laborer	25Ap02If
GOULD, Pat	21	M	Laborer	25Ap02If
LYONS, Bridget	22	F	Unknown	25Ap02If
COSLAN, Manraer	6	M	Child	25Ap02If
DUGAN, Betty	23	F	Unknown	25Ap02If
Mary	8	F	Child	25Ap02If
Margaret	4	F	Child	25Ap02If
HAYES, Mary	9	F	Child	25Ap02If
John	5	M	Child	25Ap02If
OBRINE, Jerry	25	M	Laborer	25Ap02If
Betty	25	F	Unknown	25Ap02If
Anne	2	F	Child	25Ap02If
MAHONEY, Pat	25	M	Laborer	25Ap02If
HOUTCHEN, John	25	M	Laborer	25Ap02If
BRAHAN, Bridget	20	F	Unknown	25Ap02If
SHEA, Mary	20	F	Unknown	25Ap02If
SAXTON, Michael	40	M	Laborer	25Ap02If
John	12	M	Unknown	25Ap02If
HAYES, Jeremiah	40	M	Laborer	25Ap02If
Cathn.	36	F	Unknown	25Ap02If
Margaret	13	F	Unknown	25Ap02If
Pat	11	M	Unknown	25Ap02If
Mary	11	F	Unknown	25Ap02If
Anne	9	F	Child	25Ap02If
Ellen	6	F	Child	25Ap02If
John	4	M	Child	25Ap02If
Fanny	2	F	Child	25Ap02If
Kate	.00	F	Infant	25Ap02If
MULLEN, Cathn.	22	F	Unknown	25Ap02If
CROWLEY, Michael	24	M	Laborer	25Ap02If
BARRY, Ellen	21	F	Unknown	25Ap02If
DUNIVAN, Ellen	19	F	Unknown	25Ap02If
Mary	21	F	Unknown	25Ap02If

MONTEZUMA 25 APRIL 1850

From St.Thomas

NAMES OF PASSENGERS	AGE	SEX	OCCUPATIONS	DATE PORT SHIP
PORTER, U	37	M	Planter	25Ap51BI
U (W)	24	F	Lady	25Ap51BI
U, U	22	F	Servant	25Ap51BI
DONNALD, U-Mrs.	38	F	Lady	25Ap51BI
RIDLEY, K.	40	M	Planter	25Ap51BI
NEAL, G.W.	37	M	None	25Ap51BI
WATSON, T.	33	M	Merchant	25Ap51BI
BEVAN, T.	36	M	Merchant	25Ap51BI
BELL, U-Rev.	41	M	Clergyman	25Ap51BI
HUTTON, E.H.	10	M	None	25Ap51BI

HAITI 25 APRIL 1850

From Port-Au-Prince

NAMES OF PASSENGERS	AGE	SEX	OCCUPATIONS	DATE PORT SHIP
BARRY, John	45	M	Merchant	25Ap30Hj

DROMAHAIR 26 APRIL 1850

From Sligo

NAMES OF PASSENGERS	AGE	SEX	OCCUPATIONS	DATE PORT SHIP
SHEERAN, Thomas	36	M	Laborer	26Ap09AI
RORKE, Hugh	19	M	Unknown	26Ap09AI
BRENNAN, B.	23	M	Unknown	26Ap09AI
Mary	19	F	Unknown	26Ap09AI
WYNNE, Ann	20	F	Unknown	26Ap09AI
CARVEY, Jno.	26	M	Unknown	26Ap09AI
Hugh	30	M	Unknown	26Ap09AI
Jane	27	F	Unknown	26Ap09AI
Margt.	24	F	Unknown	26Ap09AI
MCGOWAN, Ann	30	F	Unknown	26Ap09AI
Pat	35	M	Unknown	26Ap09AI
Bessy	8	F	Child	26Ap09AI
Maria	6	F	Child	26Ap09AI
KIVEHAN, Pat	16	M	Unknown	26Ap09AI
HEALY, Owen	40	M	Unknown	26Ap09AI
Biddy	30	F	Unknown	26Ap09AI
Thomas	1	M	Child	26Ap09AI
HARGADON, Ann	20	F	Unknown	26Ap09AI
DEVILLE, James	22	M	Unknown	26Ap09AI
CURNAN, Winifred	17	F	Unknown	26Ap09AI
Michl.	15	M	Unknown	26Ap09AI
KELLELEA, Bryan	23	M	Unknown	26Ap09AI
GAFFANY, Owen	38	M	Unknown	26Ap09AI
Mary	28	F	Unknown	26Ap09AI
Ann	5	F	Child	26Ap09AI
Catherine	3	F	Child	26Ap09AI
Mary	.00	F	Infant	26Ap09AI
MCLOUGHLIN, Jno.	26	M	Unknown	26Ap09AI
Jno.	6	M	Child	26Ap09AI
Catherine	3	F	Child	26Ap09AI
MCNIFF, Hugh	20	M	Unknown	26Ap09AI
MCLOUGHLAN, Barbara	50	F	Unknown	26Ap09AI
James	16	M	Unknown	26Ap09AI
Catherine	18	F	Unknown	26Ap09AI
MCSEREMAN, Bryant	25	M	Unknown	26Ap09AI
Alice	24	F	Unknown	26Ap09AI
MCDERMOTT, Kurney	40	U	Unknown	26Ap09AI
WHITE, Jno.	22	M	Unknown	26Ap09AI
MCDERMOTT, Thomas	24	M	Unknown	26Ap09AI
CARNEY, Honor	25	F	Unknown	26Ap09AI
MONAGHAN, Pat	30	M	Unknown	26Ap09AI
GILMARTIN, Thomas	17	M	Unknown	26Ap09AI
HINNEGAN, C.	30	U	Unknown	26Ap09AI
MULLANY, C.	30	U	Unknown	26Ap09AI
Bridget	25	F	Laborer	26Ap09AI
Mary	1	F	Child	26Ap09AI
KELLY, Pat	20	M	Unknown	26Ap09AI
WELSH, Thomas	23	M	Unknown	26Ap09AI
HAMILTON, James	24	M	Unknown	26Ap09AI
MAY, Susan	18	F	Unknown	26Ap09AI
NELSON, Mary	20	F	Unknown	26Ap09AI
BURNS, Catherine	28	F	Unknown	26Ap09AI
DEVANEY, Pat	20	M	Unknown	26Ap09AI
OCONNOR, Jno.	21	M	Unknown	26Ap09AI
KILFEATHER, Mary	20	F	Unknown	26Ap09AI
MCHUGH, Michl.	20	M	Unknown	26Ap09AI
COGHLIN, Catherine	25	F	Unknown	26Ap09AI
MCGLINN, Mary	23	F	Unknown	26Ap09AI
CARTHY, James	20	M	Unknown	26Ap09AI
NICELSON, Pat	20	M	Unknown	26Ap09AI
OBOYLE, Bridget	25	F	Unknown	26Ap09AI
CASSADY, Jno.	40	M	Unknown	26Ap09AI
GIBBIN, Jno.	20	M	Unknown	26Ap09AI
CONLAIN, Pat	26	M	Unknown	26Ap09AI
Catharine	21	F	Unknown	26Ap09AI
RORKE, Ann	16	F	Unknown	26Ap09AI
MITCHELL, Jno.	20	M	Unknown	26Ap09AI
Biddy	18	F	Unknown	26Ap09AI
Jas.	3	M	Child	26Ap09AI
MORRISON, Jas.	17	M	Unknown	26Ap09AI
CULLEN, Margt.	16	F	Unknown	26Ap09AI
CONILAN, Jon	21	M	Unknown	26Ap09AI
Bridget	26	F	Unknown	26Ap09AI
Ann	14	F	Unknown	26Ap09AI
MULLIGAN, Winifred	18	F	Unknown	26Ap09AI
LAVAN, Bridget	15	F	Unknown	26Ap09AI
OHARA, Ellen	22	F	Unknown	26Ap09AI
MURPHY, Ellen	20	F	Unknown	26Ap09AI
MCLOUGHLIN, Mary	19	F	Unknown	26Ap09AI
MORRISON, Richard	27	M	Unknown	26Ap09AI
Mary-Ann	22	F	Unknown	26Ap09AI
Mary-Ann	.00	F	Infant	26Ap09AI
MCCORMACK, Mary	18	F	Unknown	26Ap09AI
MULLANY, Mary	8	F	Child	26Ap09AI
LYNCH, Jane	20	F	Unknown	26Ap09AI
SIMON, Mary	17	F	Unknown	26Ap09AI
GILHALY, Mary	22	F	Unknown	26Ap09AI
MCCAFFREY, Peter	24	M	Unknown	26Ap09AI
Catherine	16	F	Laborer	26Ap09AI
MCPARTLANE, Michl.	25	M	Unknown	26Ap09AI
Ann	22	F	Unknown	26Ap09AI
MCCAHAL, Fanel	30	U	Unknown	26Ap09AI
EARLY, Catherine	24	F	Unknown	26Ap09AI
GILRAN, Michael	30	M	Unknown	26Ap09AI
Ann	27	F	Unknown	26Ap09AI
GALLAGHER, James	28	M	Unknown	26Ap09AI
Margt.	23	F	Unknown	26Ap09AI
Pat	.00	M	Infant	26Ap09AI
MCNIFF, Pat	26	M	Unknown	26Ap09AI
Kinny	24	U	Unknown	26Ap09AI
Catherine	.00	F	Infant	26Ap09AI
MAC, Margaret	20	F	Unknown	26Ap09AI
CUNNISKY, Jno.	28	M	Unknown	26Ap09AI
GILGAN, Ann	24	F	Unknown	26Ap09AI
Ellen	20	F	Unknown	26Ap09AI
KELLY, Eleanor	18	F	Unknown	26Ap09AI
Eliza	.00	F	Infant	26Ap09AI
BLACK, Thomas	22	M	Unknown	26Ap09AI
FARRY, Jas.	60	M	Unknown	26Ap09AI
Bridget	49	F	Unknown	26Ap09AI
Michl.	18	M	Unknown	26Ap09AI
MCGOWAN, Pat	20	M	Unknown	26Ap09AI
GLOVE, Catherine	30	F	Unknown	26Ap09AI
FORD, Jno.	25	M	Unknown	26Ap09AI
SCOLON, Andrew	26	M	Unknown	26Ap09AI
SCANLON, Betty	24	F	Unknown	26Ap09AI
MCPADDEN, Michl.	20	M	Unknown	26Ap09AI
KILROY, Bryan	32	M	Unknown	26Ap09AI
MCAVEY, Jno.	24	M	Unknown	26Ap09AI
NANGLE, Jno.	40	M	Unknown	26Ap09AI
BATTLE, Thomas	23	M	Unknown	26Ap09AI
GELLAN, Pat	18	M	Unknown	26Ap09AI
GANLEY, Peter	17	M	Unknown	26Ap09AI
NANGLE, Ellen	20	F	Unknown	26Ap09AI
ROONEY, Kenny	20	M	Unknown	26Ap09AI
HART, Cicely	20	F	Unknown	26Ap09AI
TUNEY, Kinney	15	M	Unknown	26Ap09AI
MCPARTLANE, Bridget	17	F	Unknown	26Ap09AI
Ellen	15	F	Unknown	26Ap09AI
MCGOWAN, Michl.	20	M	Unknown	26Ap09AI
Peter	18	M	Unknown	26Ap09AI
Chas.	18	M	Unknown	26Ap09AI
KEIGHRON, Jno.	21	M	Laborer	26Ap09AI
MCGARRY, Mary	20	F	Unknown	26Ap09AI
MCDERMOTT, Bridget	50	F	Unknown	26Ap09AI
BUCHARD, Jno.	45	M	Unknown	26Ap09AI
Ann	44	F	Unknown	26Ap09AI
Eliza-Jane	14	F	Unknown	26Ap09AI
Rebecca	10	F	Unknown	26Ap09AI
MCCANN, Thomas	21	M	Unknown	26Ap09AI

NAMES OF PASSENGERS	AGE	SEX	OCCUPATIONS	DATE PORT SHIP
MCDERMOTT, Bridget	14	F	Unknown	26Ap09Al
CLARK, Mary	35	F	Unknown	26Ap09Al
BURNS, Pat	16	M	Unknown	26Ap09Al
MCLOUGHLIN, Mary	60	F	Unknown	26Ap09Al
HARN, Mary	20	F	Unknown	26Ap09Al
MCLOUGHLIN, Ann	20	F	Unknown	26Ap09Al
MULLANY, Jno.	.00	M	Infant	26Ap09Al
HENRY, Thomas-F.	14	M	Unknown	26Ap09Al
PYNE, William	15	M	Unknown	26Ap09Al
GRADY, Jno.	23	M	Unknown	26Ap09Al

UNDINE 26 APRIL 1850

From Limerick

NAMES OF PASSENGERS	AGE	SEX	OCCUPATIONS	DATE PORT SHIP
CONLIHAN, Michl.J.	30	M	Farmer	26Ap10Ho
Pat	26	M	Unknown	26Ap10Ho
CUSARK, Bridget	20	F	Unknown	26Ap10Ho
Ellen	16	F	Unknown	26Ap10Ho
GALONE, John	18	M	Unknown	26Ap10Ho
Lucas	25	M	Unknown	26Ap10Ho
CONWAY, Thos.	60	M	Unknown	26Ap10Ho
Mary	56	F	Unknown	26Ap10Ho
Anne	26	F	Unknown	26Ap10Ho
John	15	M	Unknown	26Ap10Ho
Bridget	10	F	Unknown	26Ap10Ho
NASH, Edmd.	22	M	Unknown	26Ap10Ho
Michl.	19	M	Unknown	26Ap10Ho
Mary	17	F	Unknown	26Ap10Ho
NEALY, Edmd.J.	40	M	Unknown	26Ap10Ho
Patt.	21	M	Unknown	26Ap10Ho
John	17	M	Unknown	26Ap10Ho
Edmd.	14	M	Unknown	26Ap10Ho
Wm.	12	M	Unknown	26Ap10Ho
Dennis	8	M	Child	26Ap10Ho
Thomas	6	M	Child	26Ap10Ho
RYAN, Wm.	24	M	Unknown	26Ap10Ho
Cath.	21	F	Unknown	26Ap10Ho
CULLIHANE, John	20	M	Unknown	26Ap10Ho
CORBETT, Patt.	24	M	Unknown	26Ap10Ho
Bridget	22	F	Unknown	26Ap10Ho
ENRIGHT, Wm.	24	M	Unknown	26Ap10Ho
HOGAN, John	26	M	Unknown	26Ap10Ho
MCDONALD, Hannah	26	F	Unknown	26Ap10Ho
HOWARD, Garrett	36	M	Unknown	26Ap10Ho
CONNORS, Thos.	24	M	Unknown	26Ap10Ho
GRADY, Brdgt.	26	F	Unknown	26Ap10Ho
BRAZILL, Margt.	22	F	Unknown	26Ap10Ho
Bridget	20	F	Unknown	26Ap10Ho
CAGNEY, Wm.	24	M	Unknown	26Ap10Ho
MCMAHON, Thos.	23	M	Unknown	26Ap10Ho
ROURKE, Margt.	16	F	Unknown	26Ap10Ho
Celia	15	F	Unknown	26Ap10Ho
MEEHAN, John	21	M	Unknown	26Ap10Ho
Danl.	18	M	Unknown	26Ap10Ho
Ellen	50	F	Unknown	26Ap10Ho
Susan	15	F	Unknown	26Ap10Ho
Matthius	10	M	Unknown	26Ap10Ho
SLATTENY, John	42	M	Farmer	26Ap10Ho
RUNIS, Michl.	40	M	Unknown	26Ap10Ho
GUORE, Margt.	33	F	Unknown	26Ap10Ho
HEDERMAN, Cath.	17	F	Unknown	26Ap10Ho
MURPHY, Cath.	20	F	Unknown	26Ap10Ho
CLANCHY, John	40	M	Unknown	26Ap10Ho
Michl.	52	M	Unknown	26Ap10Ho
James	30	M	Unknown	26Ap10Ho
Cath.	40	F	Unknown	26Ap10Ho
RIORDAN, James	26	M	Unknown	26Ap10Ho
BREMAN, Mary	19	F	Unknown	26Ap10Ho
CASEY, Mary	21	F	Unknown	26Ap10Ho
VAUGHAN, Cath.	38	F	Unknown	26Ap10Ho
Mary	9	F	Child	26Ap10Ho
CULLIHANE, Mary	26	F	Unknown	26Ap10Ho
KELLY, Patt.	45	M	Unknown	26Ap10Ho
Cath.	46	F	Unknown	26Ap10Ho
Patt.	21	M	Unknown	26Ap10Ho
Mary	20	F	Unknown	26Ap10Ho
John	18	M	Unknown	26Ap10Ho
James	16	M	Unknown	26Ap10Ho
Susan	14	F	Unknown	26Ap10Ho
Thomas	11	M	Unknown	26Ap10Ho
CROWLEY, John	21	M	Unknown	26Ap10Ho
Patt.	18	M	Unknown	26Ap10Ho
CARMODY, Margt.	20	F	Unknown	26Ap10Ho
WARRANS, Michl.	24	M	Unknown	26Ap10Ho
MCNAMARA, Cath.	24	F	Unknown	26Ap10Ho
FAHY, Margt.	16	F	Unknown	26Ap10Ho
SCULLY, James	24	M	Unknown	26Ap10Ho
SENTON, Margt.	16	F	Unknown	26Ap10Ho
GLEESON, Thomas	21	M	Unknown	26Ap10Ho
FAHY, Margt.	18	F	Unknown	26Ap10Ho
QUINN, Margt.	25	F	Unknown	26Ap10Ho
MCMAHON, Thos.	23	M	Unknown	26Ap10Ho
HAWKINS, Ann	22	F	Unknown	26Ap10Ho
WARRANS, Maria	17	F	Unknown	26Ap10Ho
HANAHAN, Wm.	40	M	Unknown	26Ap10Ho
BUCKLY, John	40	M	Unknown	26Ap10Ho
RYAN, Thomas	26	M	Unknown	26Ap10Ho
Thomas	5	M	Child	26Ap10Ho
Cath.	40	F	Unknown	26Ap10Ho
CASEY, Nelly	50	F	Unknown	26Ap10Ho
DOYLE, James	24	M	Unknown	26Ap10Ho
Biddy	20	F	Unknown	26Ap10Ho
MEEHAN, Wm.	6	M	Child	26Ap10Ho
ARTHUR, Margt.	55	F	Unknown	26Ap10Ho
Jane	27	F	Unknown	26Ap10Ho
Harrietta	25	F	Unknown	26Ap10Ho
Margt.	24	F	Unknown	26Ap10Ho
Charlotte	24	F	Unknown	26Ap10Ho
David	22	M	Unknown	26Ap10Ho
Mary-Emily	18	F	Unknown	26Ap10Ho
SHEA, Mary	22	F	Unknown	26Ap10Ho
LANGLEY, Wm.	17	M	Unknown	26Ap10Ho

CORNELIA 27 APRIL 1850

From Liverpool

NAMES OF PASSENGERS	AGE	SEX	OCCUPATIONS	DATE PORT SHIP
MCMAHON, Robert	8	M	Child	27Ap02Hh
Thomas	4	M	Child	27Ap02Hh
Bridget	6	F	Child	27Ap02Hh
Daniel	.03	M	Infant	27Ap02Hh
SUTTON, John	19	M	Laborer	27Ap02Hh
DONOHUE, Johanna	20	F	Servant	27Ap02Hh
SHEEHAN, Margaret	20	F	Servant	27Ap02Hh
BURK, William	31	M	Laborer	27Ap02Hh
Peter	21	M	Laborer	27Ap02Hh
MAHON, Ellen	27	F	Servant	27Ap02Hh
BURNS, Ann	22	F	Servant	27Ap02Hh
FORD, James	20	M	Laborer	27Ap02Hh
GARDNER, John	33	M	Mechanic	27Ap02Hh
HUTTON, James	25	M	Laborer	27Ap02Hh
GILL, Owen	19	M	Laborer	27Ap02Hh
FELLON, Peter	23	M	Laborer	27Ap02Hh
REA, Ann	45	F	Unknown	27Ap02Hh
William	15	M	Laborer	27Ap02Hh
Rose	10	F	Unknown	27Ap02Hh
Richard	8	M	Child	27Ap02Hh

NAMES OF PASSENGERS	AGE	SEX	OCCUPATIONS	DATE PORT SHIP
REA, Christopher	2	M	Child	27Ap02Hh
DWYER, Thady	35	M	Laborer	27Ap02Hh
Johanna	35	F	Servant	27Ap02Hh
HARONS, Thomas	18	M	Laborer	27Ap02Hh
DELARNERE, Margaret	18	F	Servant	27Ap02Hh
KEOGH, James	24	M	Laborer	27Ap02Hh
MAHER, John	28	M	Laborer	27Ap02Hh
MCMAHON, Danl.	36	M	Laborer	27Ap02Hh
ROCH, Mary	28	F	Servant	27Ap02Hh
MCMAHON, Mary	11	F	Servant	27Ap02Hh
MCCARTIN, Peter	21	M	Laborer	27Ap02Hh
MCGARRAGAN, Phebe	19	F	Servant	27Ap02Hh
SHAUGHNESS, Ellen	18	F	Servant	27Ap02Hh
HEART, Mary	64	F	Servant	27Ap02Hh
BUTLER, Pat	24	M	Laborer	27Ap02Hh
SLATTERY, Michl.	23	M	Foundryman	27Ap02Hh
EAGAN, Patrick	21	M	Laborer	27Ap02Hh
LARKIN, John	21	M	Laborer	27Ap02Hh
FITZGERALD, John	18	M	Laborer	27Ap02Hh
HOUNDLAN, Johanna	20	F	Servant	27Ap02Hh
SULLIVAN, Michl.	36	M	Laborer	27Ap02Hh
Catherine	16	F	Servant	27Ap02Hh
TERRILL, Mary	18	F	Servant	27Ap02Hh
BURNS, Margt.	20	F	Servant	27Ap02Hh
MORELAND, James	18	M	Laborer	27Ap02Hh
HUGHES, Andrew	14	M	Laborer	27Ap02Hh
Hugh	12	M	Laborer	27Ap02Hh
Edward	10	M	Laborer	27Ap02Hh
BRADSHAW, Robert	28	M	Laborer	27Ap02Hh
FERRELL, Pat	18	M	Laborer	27Ap02Hh
CODIGAN, David	18	M	Laborer	27Ap02Hh
HARWOOD, Catherine	19	F	Dressmaker	27Ap02Hh
Johanna	16	F	Servant	27Ap02Hh
FOY, Michl.	20	M	Tailor	27Ap02Hh
Stephen	18	M	Laborer	27Ap02Hh
SMITH, Mary	20	F	Servant	27Ap02Hh
GALLAHN, Wm.	15	M	Laborer	27Ap02Hh
James	10	M	Laborer	27Ap02Hh
REYNOLDS, Ann	12	F	Servant	27Ap02Hh
HENEY, Bernard	21	M	Laborer	27Ap02Hh
MCCANN, Owen	34	M	Laborer	27Ap02Hh
Catherine	18	F	Servant	27Ap02Hh
Michl.	8	M	Child	27Ap02Hh
RODGERS, Patrick	56	M	Laborer	27Ap02Hh
CUNNINGHAM, Michl.	22	M	Blacksmith	27Ap02Hh
BURK, Wm.	27	M	Laborer	27Ap02Hh
Catherine	20	F	Servant	27Ap02Hh
WILDON, Pat	22	M	Laborer	27Ap02Hh
MURPHY, James	24	M	Laborer	27Ap02Hh
KERNEY, William	22	M	Laborer	27Ap02Hh
LANNON, Pat	36	M	Laborer	27Ap02Hh
Mary	32	F	Servant	27Ap02Hh
BROPHY, Wm.Caounagh	19	M	Farmer	27Ap02Hh
BOWERS, Edwards	52	M	Laborer	27Ap02Hh
James	22	M	Laborer	27Ap02Hh
Thomas	19	M	Laborer	27Ap02Hh
John	14	M	Laborer	27Ap02Hh
Catherine	36	F	Servant	27Ap02Hh
CUDDIHY, Pat	22	M	Laborer	27Ap02Hh
Mary	22	F	Servant	27Ap02Hh
MURRY, Thomas	29	M	Laborer	27Ap02Hh
LEONARD, Michl.	55	M	Farmer	27Ap02Hh
Died-At-Sea				
SULLIVAN, John	22	M	Laborer	27Ap02Hh
LEONARD, Mary	25	F	Servant	27Ap02Hh
Alley	22	F	Servant	27Ap02Hh
Ellen	20	F	Servant	27Ap02Hh
FITZPATRICK, Mary	20	F	Servant	27Ap02Hh
BANNON, Johanna	20	F	Servant	27Ap02Hh
MOHER, Catherine	19	F	Servant	27Ap02Hh
MURDLY, Pat	20	M	Laborer	27Ap02Hh
FLEY, Michl.	26	M	Laborer	27Ap02Hh
COYLE, Owen	20	M	Laborer	27Ap02Hh
CLINSY, Pat	22	M	Laborer	27Ap02Hh
MCGUIRE, Bridget	20	F	Servant	27Ap02Hh
FOSSET, Dolly	20	F	Servant	27Ap02Hh
COYLE, Anne	21	F	Servant	27Ap02Hh
REILLY, Mary-Ann	8	F	Child	27Ap02Hh
TULLY, Catherine	30	F	Servant	27Ap02Hh
John	12	M	Unknown	27Ap02Hh
Thomas	7	M	Child	27Ap02Hh
James	5	M	Child	27Ap02Hh
GANNON, Fanny	20	F	Unknown	27Ap02Hh
Eliza	17	F	Unknown	27Ap02Hh
WHELIAR, Ann	14	F	Servant	27Ap02Hh
FEENY, Mickell	30	M	Laborer	27Ap02Hh
MCEVERY, Mary	28	F	Unknown	27Ap02Hh
CONNAR, Pat	18	M	Laborer	27Ap02Hh
Honor	30	F	Servant	27Ap02Hh
MONAGHAN, Charles	24	M	Laborer	27Ap02Hh
Ellen	18	F	Servant	27Ap02Hh
SMITH, Charles	45	M	Laborer	27Ap02Hh
Ann	26	F	Servant	27Ap02Hh
Mary	13	F	Servant	27Ap02Hh
Ellen	11	F	Servant	27Ap02Hh
LOWRY, Martin	24	M	Laborer	27Ap02Hh
BRISLAN, Dennis	12	M	Laborer	27Ap02Hh
SHARRY, Pat	38	M	Tailor	27Ap02Hh
GOORAN, Celin	33	F	Servant	27Ap02Hh
DORAN, Bridget	19	F	Servant	27Ap02Hh
DOOLIN, Maria	16	F	Servant	27Ap02Hh
HANLEY, Bridget	52	F	Servant	27Ap02Hh
John	19	M	Laborer	27Ap02Hh
Patt	14	M	Laborer	27Ap02Hh
Thomas	12	M	Laborer	27Ap02Hh
James	10	M	Laborer	27Ap02Hh
COWAN, James	32	M	Laborer	27Ap02Hh
Catherine	16	F	Servant	27Ap02Hh
KELLY, Thomas	23	M	Laborer	27Ap02Hh
CALLAGHER, James	21	M	Laborer	27Ap02Hh
SWEENY, Bryan	20	M	Laborer	27Ap02Hh
DONOVAN, William	17	M	Laborer	27Ap02Hh
FANNON, Patrick	22	M	Laborer	27Ap02Hh
TAYLOR, Thomas	20	M	Laborer	27Ap02Hh
SLAVIN, John	20	M	Laborer	27Ap02Hh
LEHOVAN, Mary	20	F	Servant	27Ap02Hh
SHERRIDAN, Michl.	48	M	Laborer	27Ap02Hh
Mary	42	F	Unknown	27Ap02Hh
Margaret	20	F	Servant	27Ap02Hh
Thomas	18	M	Laborer	27Ap02Hh
Patrick	14	M	Laborer	27Ap02Hh
Michael	12	M	Laborer	27Ap02Hh
John	8	M	Child	27Ap02Hh
Laurance	6	M	Child	27Ap02Hh
Mary	4	F	Child	27Ap02Hh
DUFFY, Michael	33	M	Laborer	27Ap02Hh
Jane	33	F	Servant	27Ap02Hh
Patt	14	M	Laborer	27Ap02Hh
Michael	8	M	Child	27Ap02Hh
John	5	M	Child	27Ap02Hh
HOGAN, Dennis	27	M	Laborer	27Ap02Hh
Ellen	27	F	Unknown	27Ap02Hh
Pat	3	M	Child	27Ap02Hh
Bryan	.06	M	Infant	27Ap02Hh
MORAN, James	25	M	Shoemaker	27Ap02Hh
ODONNELL, James	25	M	Shoemaker	27Ap02Hh
CROWE, Patt	35	M	Smith	27Ap02Hh
Michael	25	M	Smith	27Ap02Hh
FITZGERALD, Richard	60	M	Laborer	27Ap02Hh
Catherine	30	F	Servant	27Ap02Hh
Mary	10	F	Servant	27Ap02Hh
LINCOLN, Fred	40	M	Laborer	27Ap02Hh
KENNY, Bridget	50	F	Servant	27Ap02Hh
James	12	M	Unknown	27Ap02Hh
HARLABY, Cornelious	21	M	Laborer	27Ap02Hh
BOLORN, Mary	25	F	Servant	27Ap02Hh
MAXWELL, James	28	M	Laborer	27Ap02Hh
DWYRE, William	10	M	Laborer	27Ap02Hh
CORRAN, Mary	12	F	Laborer	27Ap02Hh
SHERRIDAN, James	22	M	Laborer	27Ap02Hh

SWITZERLAND 29 APRIL 1850

From Liverpool

NAMES OF PASSENGERS	AGE	SEX	OCCUPATIONS	DATE PORT SHIP
AMORUS, Mary	24	F	Servant	29Ap02Fj
MCMAHON, Daniel	25	M	Clerk	29Ap02Fj
GALVIN, Pat	28	M	Laborer	29Ap02Fj
CONNELL, Cathe.	22	F	Servant	29Ap02Fj
KELLY, Anne	50	F	Servant	29Ap02Fj
MCCARTHY, John	22	M	Servant	29Ap02Fj
GOODWILL, Will	22	M	Servant	29Ap02Fj
BURNHAM, James	25	M	Servant	29Ap02Fj
MCAUNLIFF, Simon	22	M	Farmer	29Ap02Fj
DEARY, Davis	22	M	Farmer	29Ap02Fj
HAYS, John	40	M	Farmer	29Ap02Fj
NOONAN, David	30	M	Tailor	29Ap02Fj
COMARS, Thomas	46	M	Farmer	29Ap02Fj
Catherine	40	F	Farmer	29Ap02Fj
William	12	M	Farmer	29Ap02Fj
Catherine	9	F	Child	29Ap02Fj
DUNNAN, Cons.	42	M	Laborer	29Ap02Fj
BEGLEY, Lon	22	M	Laborer	29Ap02Fj
Margaret	20	F	Laborer	29Ap02Fj
DUNEL, Denis	22	M	Laborer	29Ap02Fj
FOX, Farrel	30	M	Farmer	29Ap02Fj
GALLIGAN, Mary	18	F	Servant	29Ap02Fj
FINEGAN, Peter	13	M	Servant	29Ap02Fj
Mary	17	F	Servant	29Ap02Fj
FARLAND, Will	18	M	Servant	29Ap02Fj
Betsy	16	F	Servant	29Ap02Fj
Biddy	13	F	Servant	29Ap02Fj
GIBBONS, Ellen	22	F	Unknown	29Ap02Fj
CUNE, Mary	28	F	Laborer	29Ap02Fj
OBRIEN, Wm.	19	M	Mason	29Ap02Fj
CARROLL, Pat	20	M	Mason	29Ap02Fj
RUNTY, Peter	20	M	Mason	29Ap02Fj
HARDITY, Will	24	M	Unknown	29Ap02Fj
Eliza	22	F	Unknown	29Ap02Fj
CLARY, Thom.	35	M	Unknown	29Ap02Fj
Ann	35	F	Unknown	29Ap02Fj
LAINE, Thom.	28	M	Laborer	29Ap02Fj
MAHONE, Pat	17	M	Laborer	29Ap02Fj
KENESICK, Philip	31	M	Mason	29Ap02Fj
OBRIEN, Pat	18	M	Tailor	29Ap02Fj
MURRAY, Bryan	40	M	Tailor	29Ap02Fj
Richd.	35	M	Laborer	29Ap02Fj
HINES, Michl.	30	M	Laborer	29Ap02Fj
KELLY, Thomas	15	M	Laborer	29Ap02Fj
Joseph	4	M	Child	29Ap02Fj
CARY, Jane	11	F	Servant	29Ap02Fj
HINES, Wm.	27	M	Servant	29Ap02Fj
CONNAN, Biddy	17	F	Servant	29Ap02Fj
KING, Ann	20	F	Servant	29Ap02Fj
Betsy	19	F	Servant	29Ap02Fj
NOONY, Biddy	18	F	Servant	29Ap02Fj
MCGRATH, Eliza	17	F	Servant	29Ap02Fj
RUTHERLIGE, John	19	M	Clerk	29Ap02Fj
Patk.	20	F	Servant	29Ap02Fj
HAREHAN, Peter	19	M	Servant	29Ap02Fj
Sam	12	M	Servant	29Ap02Fj
CALAHAN, Richard	18	M	Servant	29Ap02Fj
Briget	40	F	Servant	29Ap02Fj
DORDY, Ann	48	F	Servant	29Ap02Fj
Mary	10	F	Servant	29Ap02Fj
Mona	7	M	Child	29Ap02Fj
DOOLY, Wm.	16	M	Unknown	29Ap02Fj
DAILY, Mary	20	F	Unknown	29Ap02Fj
LYNCH, John	16	M	Unknown	29Ap02Fj
Jane	18	F	Unknown	29Ap02Fj

NAMES OF PASSENGERS	AGE	SEX	OCCUPATIONS	DATE PORT SHIP
BLAKE, Pat	20	M	Laborer	29Ap02Fj
OBRIEN, Andrew	20	M	Laborer	29Ap02Fj
Biddy	16	F	Servant	29Ap02Fj
DAGEN, Catherine	16	F	Servant	29Ap02Fj
DUNN, Honora	21	F	Unknown	29Ap02Fj
CATERY, Pat	30	M	Bricklayer	29Ap02Fj
MCGINNIS, Peter	18	M	Bricklayer	29Ap02Fj
CLARK, Hugh	18	M	Bricklayer	29Ap02Fj
FLORD, Rose	24	F	Bricklayer	29Ap02Fj
Thomas	.08	M	Infant	29Ap02Fj
RUTELEGE, Cathe.	32	F	Servant	29Ap02Fj
James	3	M	Child	29Ap02Fj
Ann	20	F	Unknown	29Ap02Fj
MAUGHTON, Sarah	17	F	Servant	29Ap02Fj
TALEY, Peter	22	M	Servant	29Ap02Fj
Abby	30	F	Servant	29Ap02Fj
Margaret	26	F	Servant	29Ap02Fj
Catherine	6	M	Child	29Ap02Fj
KENEDY, Thomas	22	M	Unknown	29Ap02Fj
FLANAGAN, John	22	M	Bookbinder	29Ap02Fj
Alice	20	F	Bookbinder	29Ap02Fj
Thomas	12	M	Unknown	29Ap02Fj
TOFFY, Christopher	28	M	Bookbinder	29Ap02Fj
Ellen	28	F	Servant	29Ap02Fj
Eliza	27	F	Servant	29Ap02Fj
COLBERT, John	20	M	Mason	29Ap02Fj
CARROL, Mary	34	F	Servant	29Ap02Fj
James	8	M	Child	29Ap02Fj
Pat	5	M	Child	29Ap02Fj
Mary	3	F	Child	29Ap02Fj
CARRY, Bridget	17	F	Unknown	29Ap02Fj
DURRY, Eliza	15	F	Servant	29Ap02Fj
Eliza	12	F	Unknown	29Ap02Fj
HARREREN, Margaret	20	F	Servant	29Ap02Fj
KING, Mary	46	F	Servant	29Ap02Fj
Rose	4	F	Child	29Ap02Fj
KILLON, Mary	21	F	Servant	29Ap02Fj
RILEY, Mary	37	F	Servant	29Ap02Fj
Bernd.	12	M	Unknown	29Ap02Fj
John	4	M	Child	29Ap02Fj
Cathne.	2	F	Child	29Ap02Fj
Hugh	44	M	Unknown	29Ap02Fj
Cathe.	9	F	Child	29Ap02Fj
MCDONNALL, Mary	18	F	Unknown	29Ap02Fj
CARRY, Jane	32	F	Servant	29Ap02Fj
Mike	11	M	Unknown	29Ap02Fj
Mary	8	F	Child	29Ap02Fj
DUNN, Betty	18	F	Servant	29Ap02Fj
ROONY, Dunhill	35	M	Servant	29Ap02Fj
KILLINGER, Ann	17	F	Servant	29Ap02Fj
MURPHY, Ron	17	M	Servant	29Ap02Fj
RIELLY, Ann	30	F	Servant	29Ap02Fj
MAHONEY, Dan	30	M	Farmer	29Ap02Fj
Dennis	11	M	Farmer	29Ap02Fj
Cath.	7	F	Child	29Ap02Fj
Margaret	7	F	Child	29Ap02Fj
MCCARTHY, Patt	36	M	Unknown	29Ap02Fj
Ellen	32	F	Servant	29Ap02Fj
Cath.	20	F	Servant	29Ap02Fj
Mary	2	F	Child	29Ap02Fj
LEARY, Jerry	26	M	Servant	29Ap02Fj
Owen	32	M	Unknown	29Ap02Fj
DONAGHY, Catherine	25	F	Unknown	29Ap02Fj
July	24	F	Unknown	29Ap02Fj
CONELLY, Edwd.	25	M	Laborer	29Ap02Fj
KENNY, John	25	M	Unknown	29Ap02Fj
LANDERS, Bridget	20	F	Unknown	29Ap02Fj
GALLIMAN, Jas.	16	M	Unknown	29Ap02Fj
BATTLEBURY, Edwd.	46	M	Laborer	29Ap02Fj
Lucy	32	F	Unknown	29Ap02Fj
John	13	M	Unknown	29Ap02Fj
Ellen	11	F	Unknown	29Ap02Fj
Thomas	4	M	Child	29Ap02Fj
Rich.	.00	M	Infant	29Ap02Fj
CARTY, Denis	20	M	Unknown	29Ap02Fj

NAMES OF PASSENGERS	AGE	SEX	OCCUPATIONS	DATE PORT SHIP
KELLY, Pat	21	M	Unknown	29Ap02Fj
Mary	20	F	Unknown	29Ap02Fj
John	2	M	Child	29Ap02Fj
OBRIEN, Thomas	30	M	Unknown	29Ap02Fj
HAMMOND, John	40	M	Laborer	29Ap02Fj
DONEHUE, Mark	19	M	Unknown	29Ap02Fj
BLAKE, Ellen	55	F	Unknown	29Ap02Fj
DEVERLIN, John	18	M	Unknown	29Ap02Fj
GORMAN, Thomas	55	M	Laborer	29Ap02Fj
WELCH, John	18	M	Unknown	29Ap02Fj
CONNEL, Mark	30	M	Unknown	29Ap02Fj
SHEA, Thomas	26	M	Laborer	29Ap02Fj
Daniel	24	M	Laborer	29Ap02Fj
BERRY, Robert	30	M	Unknown	29Ap02Fj
John	20	M	Laborer	29Ap02Fj
WILLS, Henry	24	M	Laborer	29Ap02Fj
SULLIVEN, Daniel	24	M	Laborer	29Ap02Fj
DELANY, Jerry	5	M	Child	29Ap02Fj
SHANAHAN, Robert	19	M	Laborer	29Ap02Fj
SHEHAN, John	24	M	Laborer	29Ap02Fj
HAND, Mary	30	F	Unknown	29Ap02Fj
GLAND, John	24	M	Laborer	29Ap02Fj
BARRY, Bridget	30	F	Unknown	29Ap02Fj
GROMMING, John	20	M	Laborer	29Ap02Fj
LONG, John	25	M	Unknown	29Ap02Fj
Richard	20	M	Laborer	29Ap02Fj
HAYS, James	20	M	Laborer	29Ap02Fj
SULINA, Mickl.	23	M	Laborer	29Ap02Fj
GIBBONS, Austin	45	M	Clerk	29Ap02Fj
FONRON, Henry	27	M	Clerk	29Ap02Fj
LAMBERS, Ellen	25	F	Unknown	29Ap02Fj
Margt.	9	F	Child	29Ap02Fj
John	5	M	Child	29Ap02Fj
MURTAGH, Rose	12	F	Unknown	29Ap02Fj
MCGINNIS, Bridget	10	F	Unknown	29Ap02Fj
John	14	M	Unknown	29Ap02Fj
NUGENT, Mary	23	F	Clerk	29Ap02Fj
QUINN, John	21	M	Laborer	29Ap02Fj
KELLY, John	26	M	Laborer	29Ap02Fj
SULLY, John	25	M	Laborer	29Ap02Fj
Elizth.	25	F	Unknown	29Ap02Fj
GIBBONS, Mary	26	F	Unknown	29Ap02Fj
ALLEN, Thomas	22	M	Shoemaker	29Ap02Fj
FORD, Alice	28	F	Unknown	29Ap02Fj
Mary	4	F	Child	29Ap02Fj
Pat	26	M	Unknown	29Ap02Fj
Ellen	16	F	Unknown	29Ap02Fj
MATHEWS, John	26	M	Unknown	29Ap02Fj
SMITH, James	25	M	Unknown	29Ap02Fj
BROWN, James	13	M	Shoemaker	29Ap02Fj
MCMAHONE, Rose	18	F	Unknown	29Ap02Fj
Mark	16	M	Shoemaker	29Ap02Fj
HAND, Andw.	20	M	Shoemaker	29Ap02Fj
MUNDE, Henry	13	M	Shoemaker	29Ap02Fj
Catherine	19	F	Unknown	29Ap02Fj
DANLON, John	40	M	Unknown	29Ap02Fj
Mathew	16	M	Shoemaker	29Ap02Fj
MCARTHUR, Thomas	20	M	Shoemaker	29Ap02Fj
GROSS, Mary	28	F	Servant	29Ap02Fj
CONE, Wm.	26	M	Servant	29Ap02Fj
Sarah	24	F	Unknown	29Ap02Fj
Ruth	24	F	Unknown	29Ap02Fj
Qued.	.06	U	Infant	29Ap02Fj
MCGINNIS, Sam	30	M	Servant	29Ap02Fj
HARNAN, Bridget	26	F	Unknown	29Ap02Fj

NEW-YORK 30 APRIL 1850

From Liverpool

NAMES OF PASSENGERS	AGE	SEX	OCCUPATIONS	DATE PORT SHIP
CAHILL, Pat	22	M	Laborer	30Ap02Cx
MISSET, Jas.	20	M	Laborer	30Ap02Cx
FOX, Wm.	22	M	Laborer	30Ap02Cx
DALTON, Jno.	22	M	Laborer	30Ap02Cx
MORAN, Jas.	23	M	Laborer	30Ap02Cx
MAHON, Jno.	19	M	Laborer	30Ap02Cx
SULHIAN, Denis	16	M	Laborer	30Ap02Cx
Ellen	11	F	Spinster	30Ap02Cx
Jno.	6	M	Child	30Ap02Cx
OKEEFE, Alice	21	F	Spinster	30Ap02Cx
FOGARTY, Mick	28	M	Spinner	30Ap02Cx
BRACKEN, Mary	22	F	Spinster	30Ap02Cx
HAGERTY, Cath.	19	F	Spinster	30Ap02Cx
KAIN, Jno.	18	M	Spinner	30Ap02Cx
FOHY, Wm.	60	M	Spinner	30Ap02Cx
Wm.	18	M	Spinner	30Ap02Cx
OBRIEN, Mick	14	M	Mason	30Ap02Cx
Mary	11	F	Unknown	30Ap02Cx
Jno.	9	M	Child	30Ap02Cx
M.	7	F	Child	30Ap02Cx
MAHONY, Pat	14	M	Laborer	30Ap02Cx
Cath.	20	F	Unknown	30Ap02Cx
KEEFE, Wm.	17	M	Joiner	30Ap02Cx
SCANLON, Jno.	21	M	Laborer	30Ap02Cx
Cath.	24	F	Unknown	30Ap02Cx
SLAIN, Miles	20	M	Laborer	30Ap02Cx
Mary	13	F	Servant	30Ap02Cx
LONG, Denis	11	M	Servant	30Ap02Cx
DILLON, Honer	19	F	Servant	30Ap02Cx
MAHONY, Mick	35	M	Laborer	30Ap02Cx
CROWLY, Margt.	2	F	Child	30Ap02Cx
MATHEW, Ann	22	F	Spinster	30Ap02Cx
GANNON, Martha	6	F	Child	30Ap02Cx
MCCANN, Jno.	36	M	Laborer	30Ap02Cx
CANN, Jno.	28	M	Laborer	30Ap02Cx
Geo.	24	M	Laborer	30Ap02Cx
RYAN, Jno.	29	M	Laborer	30Ap02Cx
KENT, Pat	25	M	Laborer	30Ap02Cx
NUGENT, Norry	16	M	Laborer	30Ap02Cx
MCGOVAN, Pat	20	M	Laborer	30Ap02Cx
Cath.	21	F	Spinster	30Ap02Cx
Mary	19	F	Spinster	30Ap02Cx
CLOAK, Jas.	18	M	Laborer	30Ap02Cx
Mary	14	F	Unknown	30Ap02Cx
BULGER, Mick	20	M	Laborer	30Ap02Cx
CALLAN, Pat	20	M	Laborer	30Ap02Cx
WARD, Jim	35	M	Laborer	30Ap02Cx
DENOVAN, Nancy	30	F	Spinster	30Ap02Cx
COUGHLAN, Mary-A.	12	F	Spinster	30Ap02Cx
KENNY, Cath.	20	F	Spinster	30Ap02Cx
KELLY, Fras.	16	M	Spinner	30Ap02Cx
CALHGAN, Mary	18	F	Spinster	30Ap02Cx
Ann	20	F	Spinster	30Ap02Cx
OCODY, David	30	M	Laborer	30Ap02Cx
Abby	23	M	Laborer	30Ap02Cx
SISTER, Alex	16	M	Laborer	30Ap02Cx
DONNELLY, Jno.	18	M	Laborer	30Ap02Cx
RYAN, Jas.	30	M	Laborer	30Ap02Cx
MOCKLER, Mick	22	M	Laborer	30Ap02Cx
DARGAN, Margt.	20	F	Spinster	30Ap02Cx
CINCOXARN, Mick	17	M	Laborer	30Ap02Cx
REITTY, Cath.	18	F	Spinster	30Ap02Cx
MCGUINESS, Mary	15	F	Spinster	30Ap02Cx
DUNN, Mary	21	F	Spinster	30Ap02Cx
MILLER, Eliza	22	F	Spinster	30Ap02Cx

NAMES OF PASSENGERS	AGE	SEX	OCCUPATIONS	DATE PORT SHIP	NAMES OF PASSENGERS	AGE	SEX	OCCUPATIONS	DATE PORT SHIP
SCALLY, Cath.	22	F	Spinster	30Ap02Cx	GANLEY, Ellen	20	F	Spinster	30Ap02Cx
LONGAN, Jno.	18	M	Laborer	30Ap02Cx	Jas.	23	M	Laborer	30Ap02Cx
KEENAN, Jno.	21	M	Laborer	30Ap02Cx	KELLY, Jno.	10	M	Laborer	30Ap02Cx
MARTIN, Jno.	22	M	Laborer	30Ap02Cx	Ann	8	F	Child	30Ap02Cx
DUFFY, Brid.	30	F	Laborer	30Ap02Cx	MAHON, Mick	17	M	Laborer	30Ap02Cx
EVENS, Juilia	20	F	Spinster	30Ap02Cx	TYRRELL, Jane	22	F	Spinster	30Ap02Cx
CURNEY, Thos.	7	M	Child	30Ap02Cx	MURPHY, Bnd.	21	M	Laborer	30Ap02Cx
Julia	4	F	Child	30Ap02Cx	MCGARRELL, Jno.	18	M	Laborer	30Ap02Cx
Mick	.00	M	Infant	30Ap02Cx	BRADY, Ann	20	F	Spinster	30Ap02Cx
BRADY, Pat	20	M	Unknown	30Ap02Cx	GRADY, Mat	23	M	Laborer	30Ap02Cx
GAHERTY, Terence	20	M	Unknown	30Ap02Cx	KANE, John	25	M	Laborer	30Ap02Cx
SMITH, Bryan	35	M	Unknown	30Ap02Cx	QUINN, Jno.	21	M	Laborer	30Ap02Cx
Mary	35	F	Unknown	30Ap02Cx	ASTRACAN, Mary	22	F	Spinster	30Ap02Cx
Brid.	11	F	Unknown	30Ap02Cx	DONOHUE, M.A.	7	F	Child	30Ap02Cx
Mary	9	F	Child	30Ap02Cx	FITZGERALD, Ellen	25	F	Spinster	30Ap02Cx
Cath.	5	F	Child	30Ap02Cx	Jas.	7	M	Child	30Ap02Cx
Pat	3	M	Child	30Ap02Cx	Mary	5	F	Child	30Ap02Cx
Bessy	.00	F	Infant	30Ap02Cx	Thos.	4	M	Child	30Ap02Cx
BRADY, Mick	20	M	Laborer	30Ap02Cx	RYAN, Cath.	25	F	Spinster	30Ap02Cx
PHALEN, Mary	20	F	Unknown	30Ap02Cx	MANN, Brid.	23	F	Spinster	30Ap02Cx
Jno.	18	M	Laborer	30Ap02Cx	ROBERTS, Allen	18	M	Spinner	30Ap02Cx
HOLSHAN, Syl.	22	M	Laborer	30Ap02Cx	HANLEY, Brid.	20	F	Laborer	30Ap02Cx
WINTERS, Cath.	18	F	Unknown	30Ap02Cx	SMITH, Mary	20	F	Spinster	30Ap02Cx
KENEDY, Thos.	35	M	Laborer	30Ap02Cx	Rose	12	F	Spinster	30Ap02Cx
Cath.	16	F	Unknown	30Ap02Cx	MCCONNELL, Pat	14	M	Laborer	30Ap02Cx
GERAGHTY, Mary	17	F	Unknown	30Ap02Cx	DUNN, Jas.	13	M	Laborer	30Ap02Cx
Jas.	11	M	Laborer	30Ap02Cx	FINNEGAN, Pat	8	M	Laborer	30Ap02Cx
MOCKLAN, Anty	20	F	Unknown	30Ap02Cx	Edwd.	13	M	Laborer	30Ap02Cx
FLEMING, David	14	M	Laborer	30Ap02Cx	BOYLAN, Cath.	21	F	Spinster	30Ap02Cx
MCGUINESS, Dan	19	M	Laborer	30Ap02Cx	DOLAN, Brid.	20	F	Laborer	30Ap02Cx
PRIOR, Mary	20	F	Spinster	30Ap02Cx	MAGUIRE, Jno.	21	M	Laborer	30Ap02Cx
HERBERT, Mary	21	F	Spinster	30Ap02Cx	HADDEN, Ann	45	F	Spinster	30Ap02Cx
BAERY, Margt.	17	F	Spinster	30Ap02Cx	Wm.	20	M	Laborer	30Ap02Cx
CONNER, Brid.	50	F	Spinster	30Ap02Cx	Ann	17	F	Spinster	30Ap02Cx
Winny	20	F	Spinster	30Ap02Cx	Eliz.	14	F	Unknown	30Ap02Cx
Jno.	8	M	Child	30Ap02Cx	ROONEY, Mary	16	F	Spinster	30Ap02Cx
Cath.	10	F	Spinster	30Ap02Cx	Mary	.00	F	Infant	30Ap02Cx
CARROLL, Mick	21	M	Laborer	30Ap02Cx	MCDONOGH, Ellen	30	F	Spinster	30Ap02Cx
ODONNELL, Cath.	16	F	Unknown	30Ap02Cx	MELVIN, Jas.	30	M	Laborer	30Ap02Cx
LINN, Mick	21	M	Laborer	30Ap02Cx	Brid.	28	F	Laborer	30Ap02Cx
GUFNEY, Mary	24	F	Spinster	30Ap02Cx	Margt.	17	F	Laborer	30Ap02Cx
CARAGHEN, Thos.	30	M	Laborer	30Ap02Cx	CULLEN, Rose	45	F	Spinster	30Ap02Cx
GWANE, Pat	16	M	Laborer	30Ap02Cx	Mick	20	M	Laborer	30Ap02Cx
Mat	18	M	Laborer	30Ap02Cx	Mary	12	F	Unknown	30Ap02Cx
HACKET, Alex	20	M	Laborer	30Ap02Cx	Bessy	16	F	Spinster	30Ap02Cx
James	18	M	Laborer	30Ap02Cx	Thomas	9	M	Child	30Ap02Cx
COLLIER, Julia	30	F	Spinster	30Ap02Cx	MARTIN, Mary	35	F	Spinster	30Ap02Cx
Cath.	15	F	Spinster	30Ap02Cx	Thomas	9	M	Child	30Ap02Cx
COWMAN, James	35	M	Laborer	30Ap02Cx	Ann	6	F	Child	30Ap02Cx
TULLY, Peter	21	M	Laborer	30Ap02Cx	Chas.	5	M	Child	30Ap02Cx
SMITH, Mick	50	M	Laborer	30Ap02Cx	James	3	M	Child	30Ap02Cx
KEARNS, Fra.	12	M	Unknown	30Ap02Cx	LAHEY, Dan	20	M	Laborer	30Ap02Cx
Pat	10	M	Unknown	30Ap02Cx	MCCABE, Terence	50	M	Laborer	30Ap02Cx
DALY, Ellen	27	F	Spinster	30Ap02Cx	Jas.	26	M	Laborer	30Ap02Cx
MONTGOMORY, Jno.	22	M	Laborer	30Ap02Cx	SMITH, Mick	17	M	Laborer	30Ap02Cx
BRINES, Jno.	26	M	Laborer	30Ap02Cx	COYLE, Chs.	14	M	Laborer	30Ap02Cx
ENNIS, Pat	30	M	Laborer	30Ap02Cx	KEOGH, Thos.	22	M	Laborer	30Ap02Cx
HUSSEY, Jas.	20	M	Laborer	30Ap02Cx	Ann	20	F	Spinster	30Ap02Cx
CUNINGHAM, Winny	16	M	Unknown	30Ap02Cx	MAGUIN, Mat	16	M	Laborer	30Ap02Cx
WILSON, Thos.	18	M	Laborer	30Ap02Cx	Pat	14	M	Laborer	30Ap02Cx
KILCREASE, Ann	20	F	Spinster	30Ap02Cx	NUGENT, Jno.	26	M	Laborer	30Ap02Cx
FANNING, James	16	M	Spinner	30Ap02Cx	WOOD, Peter	16	M	Laborer	30Ap02Cx
Fras.	9	M	Child	30Ap02Cx	COLLIGAN, Jas.	23	M	Laborer	30Ap02Cx
LANGAN, Pat	26	M	Laborer	30Ap02Cx	AGNEW, Maria	20	F	Spinster	30Ap02Cx
HOGAN, Ellen	20	F	Spinster	30Ap02Cx	HAYDEN, Wm.	40	M	Laborer	30Ap02Cx
HICKEY, Wm.	20	M	Laborer	30Ap02Cx	HONNER, Susan	18	F	Laborer	30Ap02Cx
Edwd.	22	M	Laborer	30Ap02Cx	FITZPATRICK, Thos.	18	M	Spinner	30Ap02Cx
MCSOGHLIN, Wm.	20	M	Laborer	30Ap02Cx	MURRAY, Thos.	22	M	Laborer	30Ap02Cx
CAREY, Cath.	20	F	Spinster	30Ap02Cx	Pat	15	M	Laborer	30Ap02Cx
REYNOLDS, Hugh	17	M	Laborer	30Ap02Cx	SMITH, Pat	20	M	Laborer	30Ap02Cx
Jas.	13	M	Laborer	30Ap02Cx	SHERIDAN, Pat	32	M	Laborer	30Ap02Cx
FLOOD, Jno.	20	M	Laborer	30Ap02Cx	RILEY, Rose	30	F	Spinster	30Ap02Cx
MCGUIRE, Pat	22	M	Laborer	30Ap02Cx	Pat	20	M	Laborer	30Ap02Cx
CONNER, Thos.	18	M	Laborer	30Ap02Cx	FARRELL, Edwd.	25	M	Laborer	30Ap02Cx
HANNON, Thos.	18	M	Laborer	30Ap02Cx	BRADY, Barney	22	M	Laborer	30Ap02Cx

NAMES OF PASSENGERS	AGE	SEX	OCCUPATIONS	DATE PORT SHIP
BOYD, James	23	M	Laborer	30Ap02Cx
RILEY, Ann	16	F	Spinster	30Ap02Cx
ODONNELL, Edwd.	25	M	Laborer	30Ap02Cx
MINEHAN, Mary	36	F	Spinster	30Ap02Cx
Brid.	25	F	Spinster	30Ap02Cx
Phil	37	M	Laborer	30Ap02Cx
HIGGINS, Margt.	23	F	Spinster	30Ap02Cx
SCANLON, Pat	16	M	Laborer	30Ap02Cx
Michl.	11	M	Laborer	30Ap02Cx
DONOHUE, Wid.S.	50	M	Laborer	30Ap02Cx
JONES, Mary	20	F	Spinster	30Ap02Cx
MCENY, Alice	35	F	Spinster	30Ap02Cx
MURRY, Bessy	30	F	Spinster	30Ap02Cx
HEFFERNAN, Judy	28	F	Spinster	30Ap02Cx
Cirus	.00	M	Infant	30Ap02Cx
HERAN, Sarah	23	F	Spinster	30Ap02Cx
KELLY, Cath.	24	F	Spinster	30Ap02Cx
DREW, Jno.	56	M	Laborer	30Ap02Cx
Cath.	14	F	Spinster	30Ap02Cx
FITZGERALD, Mary	18	F	Spinster	30Ap02Cx
HANLEY, Honer	28	F	Spinster	30Ap02Cx
HICKEY, Brid.	18	F	Spinster	30Ap02Cx
OBRIEN, Cath.	18	F	Spinster	30Ap02Cx
HART, Mary	20	F	Spinster	30Ap02Cx
CARLTON, Jane	.00	F	Infant	30Ap02Cx
KENNEDY, Mary	24	F	Spinster	30Ap02Cx
MOONEY, Mary	20	F	Spinster	30Ap02Cx
MCGORRIGAN, Ann	20	F	Spinster	30Ap02Cx
MCCONNELLE, Rose	20	F	Spinster	30Ap02Cx
RILEY, Pat	22	M	Laborer	30Ap02Cx
BOLAN, Jno.	30	M	Laborer	30Ap02Cx
Ann	30	F	Spinster	30Ap02Cx
READY, Pat	42	M	Laborer	30Ap02Cx
MALONE, Pat	25	M	Laborer	30Ap02Cx
U-Mrs.	30	F	Spinster	30Ap02Cx
Ann	13	F	Spinster	30Ap02Cx
Jno.	9	M	Child	30Ap02Cx
GODFREY, Jno.	20	M	Laborer	30Ap02Cx
COBURN, Jno.	22	M	Laborer	30Ap02Cx
WALLACE, Jas.	23	M	Laborer	30Ap02Cx
DUFFY, Mary	29	F	Spinster	30Ap02Cx
MCGUIRE, Thos.	20	M	Laborer	30Ap02Cx
EVERS, Mary	48	F	Spinster	30Ap02Cx
Thos.	20	M	Laborer	30Ap02Cx
S.	11	F	Spinster	30Ap02Cx
GRENNAN, Hannah	20	F	Spinster	30Ap02Cx
MOCKLAR, Jas.	25	M	Laborer	30Ap02Cx
BURNE, Phil	25	M	Laborer	30Ap02Cx
FOGARTY, Mary	23	F	Spinster	30Ap02Cx
CODY, Margt.	25	F	Spinster	30Ap02Cx
Ann	.00	F	Infant	30Ap02Cx
WELSH, Johan	13	M	Laborer	30Ap02Cx
MCKENNA, James	25	M	Laborer	30Ap02Cx
REILLY, Jas.	20	M	Laborer	30Ap02Cx
SINCH, Ellen	28	F	Spinster	30Ap02Cx
Jas.	.00	M	Infant	30Ap02Cx
WEBB, Wm.	30	M	Laborer	30Ap02Cx
RILEY, Ann	20	F	Spinster	30Ap02Cx
CARLON, Mary	15	F	Spinster	30Ap02Cx
SANCH, Margt.	12	F	Spinster	30Ap02Cx
WHELAN, Jerold	25	M	Laborer	30Ap02Cx
MCGINNIS, Mary	22	F	Spinster	30Ap02Cx
FLANAGAN, Ann	25	F	Spinster	30Ap02Cx
SMITH, Jas.	12	M	Laborer	30Ap02Cx
ANDERSON, Rich	18	M	Laborer	30Ap02Cx
MCDONNELL, Michl.	24	M	Laborer	30Ap02Cx
LENNON, Pat	26	M	Laborer	30Ap02Cx
Brid.	21	F	Spinster	30Ap02Cx
DEVET, Manns	27	F	Spinster	30Ap02Cx
MCKEOGH, Mary	22	F	Spinster	30Ap02Cx
MCCARREL, Bryan	26	M	Laborer	30Ap02Cx
WADE, Michl.	26	M	Joiner	30Ap02Cx
MCMAHON, Owen	20	M	Laborer	30Ap02Cx
Cath.	19	F	Laborer	30Ap02Cx
MALEY, Geo.	22	M	Laborer	30Ap02Cx

NAMES OF PASSENGERS	AGE	SEX	OCCUPATIONS	DATE PORT SHIP
SMITH, Susan	20	F	Unknown	30Ap02Cx
MCCARROLL, Edwd.	19	M	Laborer	30Ap02Cx
MCGUE, Pat	19	M	Laborer	30Ap02Cx
TRAINER, Owen	19	M	Laborer	30Ap02Cx
WOOD, Pat	19	M	Laborer	30Ap02Cx
Brid.	19	F	Laborer	30Ap02Cx
KELLY, Pat	50	M	Laborer	30Ap02Cx
HICKY, Pat	18	M	Laborer	30Ap02Cx
DUFFY, Peter	24	M	Laborer	30Ap02Cx
FLEMING, Jas.	30	M	Laborer	30Ap02Cx
GIVAN, Mary	30	F	Laborer	30Ap02Cx
FANNING, Maria	20	F	Laborer	30Ap02Cx
DOOLIN, Jas.	20	M	Laborer	30Ap02Cx
Brid.	30	F	Laborer	30Ap02Cx
Anty	6	F	Child	30Ap02Cx
HANNAH, Mary	24	F	Laborer	30Ap02Cx
GILL, Michl.	27	M	Laborer	30Ap02Cx
Cath.	20	F	Laborer	30Ap02Cx
MCGINNIS, Dan	11	M	Laborer	30Ap02Cx
MCARDLE, Brid.	28	F	Laborer	30Ap02Cx
KENNEN, Mary	2	F	Child	30Ap02Cx
DUFFY, Jas.	19	M	Laborer	30Ap02Cx
Terrence	18	M	Laborer	30Ap02Cx
MILLICHANZ, Sarah-A.	21	F	Laborer	30Ap02Cx
Sarah	.00	F	Infant	30Ap02Cx
Eliz.	2	F	Child	30Ap02Cx
GRAY, Mary	11	F	Laborer	30Ap02Cx
MCCARTY, Margt.	25	F	Laborer	30Ap02Cx
ROGERS, James	20	M	Laborer	30Ap02Cx
CALENTH, Alex	22	M	Laborer	30Ap02Cx
Francis	18	M	Laborer	30Ap02Cx
BUTLER, Edw.	25	M	Laborer	30Ap02Cx
EDWARDS, Saml.	50	M	Laborer	30Ap02Cx
George	16	M	Laborer	30Ap02Cx
SINN, Jas.	26	M	Laborer	30Ap02Cx
COX, Henry	32	M	Laborer	30Ap02Cx
U-Mrs.	29	F	Laborer	30Ap02Cx
Jonth.	6	M	Child	30Ap02Cx
Henry	5	M	Child	30Ap02Cx
Chs.	4	M	Child	30Ap02Cx
Julia	.00	F	Infant	30Ap02Cx
ROY, James	16	M	Laborer	30Ap02Cx
LONG, Pat	26	M	Laborer	30Ap02Cx
TROY, Jno.	30	M	Laborer	30Ap02Cx
U-Mrs.	25	F	Laborer	30Ap02Cx
GILBERT, Pat	19	M	Laborer	30Ap02Cx
MCCABE, Peter	20	M	Laborer	30Ap02Cx
MCMAHON, Phil	28	M	Laborer	30Ap02Cx
SMITH, Thos.	24	M	Laborer	30Ap02Cx
MCLELLAN, Wm.	32	M	Laborer	30Ap02Cx
Cath.	30	F	Unknown	30Ap02Cx
Jno.	4	M	Child	30Ap02Cx
Alex.	.00	M	Infant	30Ap02Cx
GLOGLIN, Eliz.	30	F	Spinster	30Ap02Cx
Cath.	6	F	Child	30Ap02Cx
Margt.	4	F	Child	30Ap02Cx
Pat	2	M	Child	30Ap02Cx
HASTINGS, U-Mrs.	23	F	Unknown	30Ap02Cx

INDUSTRY 30 APRIL 1850

From Sligo

NAMES OF PASSENGERS	AGE	SEX	OCCUPATIONS	DATE PORT SHIP
MCHUGH, Jas.	50	M	Laborer	30Ap09Gj
Catherine	40	F	Unknown	30Ap09Gj
Thomas	16	M	Unknown	30Ap09Gj
Jno.	14	M	Unknown	30Ap09Gj
Mary	6	F	Child	30Ap09Gj
CONVEY, Ellen	20	F	Unknown	30Ap09Gj

NAMES OF PASSENGERS	AGE	SEX	OCCUPATIONS	DATE PORT SHIP
DAVEY, Jno.	28	M	Unknown	30Ap09Gj
Winefred	24	F	Unknown	30Ap09Gj
MCMORROW, Owen	20	M	Unknown	30Ap09Gj
Ann	12	F	Unknown	30Ap09Gj
Bridget	14	F	Unknown	30Ap09Gj
MULLOWNEY, Ann	20	F	Unknown	30Ap09Gj
CAMPBELL, Robt.	25	M	Unknown	30Ap09Gj
OBRIEN, Denis	28	M	Unknown	30Ap09Gj
KENIGAN, Pat	20	M	Unknown	30Ap09Gj
MCGOWN, Mary	25	F	Unknown	30Ap09Gj
Nancy	25	F	Unknown	30Ap09Gj
ELLIOT, Catherine	35	F	Unknown	30Ap09Gj
Alexander	16	M	Unknown	30Ap09Gj
Thomas	12	M	Unknown	30Ap09Gj
MCCALMENT, Thomas	25	M	Unknown	30Ap09Gj
WHITE, Mary	20	F	Unknown	30Ap09Gj
CALLAGHER, Owen	26	M	Unknown	30Ap09Gj
DEMPSEY, Peter	25	M	Unknown	30Ap09Gj
JORDAN, Mary	22	F	Unknown	30Ap09Gj
KELLY, Bridget	20	F	Unknown	30Ap09Gj
MCGOWAN, Ann	17	F	Unknown	30Ap09Gj
Denis	13	M	Unknown	30Ap09Gj
Alice	11	F	Unknown	30Ap09Gj
OCONNOR, Margt.	30	F	Unknown	30Ap09Gj
MCGARRY, Mary	27	F	Unknown	30Ap09Gj
HIRTLE, Francis	18	M	Unknown	30Ap09Gj
GAINN, William	23	M	Unknown	30Ap09Gj
KILCULLEN, Geo.	21	M	Unknown	30Ap09Gj
Ann	21	F	Unknown	30Ap09Gj
Honora	.00	F	Infant	30Ap09Gj
KELLY, Michl.	30	M	Unknown	30Ap09Gj
DAVEY, Michael	30	M	Unknown	30Ap09Gj
MURPHY, Thomas	14	M	Unknown	30Ap09Gj
ELLIS, Thomas	23	M	Unknown	30Ap09Gj
Bridget	21	F	Unknown	30Ap09Gj
Catherine	26	F	Unknown	30Ap09Gj
MIDDLETON, John	21	M	Unknown	30Ap09Gj
LONGHEAD, Jane	20	F	Unknown	30Ap09Gj
MCLOUGHLIN, Owen	30	M	Laborer	30Ap09Gj
HARTT, Martin	40	M	Unknown	30Ap09Gj
Catherine	40	F	Unknown	30Ap09Gj
Bessie	18	F	Unknown	30Ap09Gj
GORMAN, Sarah	18	F	Unknown	30Ap09Gj
LACKAN, Hugh	30	M	Unknown	30Ap09Gj
MCCEEVER, Pat	30	M	Unknown	30Ap09Gj
Hannah	28	F	Unknown	30Ap09Gj
MULHOUSE, Ann	27	F	Unknown	30Ap09Gj
GRUMES, Judy	24	F	Unknown	30Ap09Gj
MCNULLY, Bridget	18	F	Unknown	30Ap09Gj
BOURKE, Mathew	25	M	Unknown	30Ap09Gj
Maria	8	F	Child	30Ap09Gj
DONOHY, Owen	52	M	Unknown	30Ap09Gj
Edward	20	M	Unknown	30Ap09Gj
ODONNELL, Roger	24	M	Unknown	30Ap09Gj
DALY, Pat	20	M	Unknown	30Ap09Gj
MULVANEY, Mary	30	F	Unknown	30Ap09Gj
Bridget	13	F	Unknown	30Ap09Gj
Patrick	10	M	Unknown	30Ap09Gj
BURNS, Bridget	28	F	Unknown	30Ap09Gj
HART, Michl.	25	M	Unknown	30Ap09Gj
MCANNEW, Bridget	20	F	Unknown	30Ap09Gj
KUANE, Honora	30	F	Unknown	30Ap09Gj
Catherine	23	F	Unknown	30Ap09Gj
Mary	20	F	Unknown	30Ap09Gj
Patrick	.00	M	Infant	30Ap09Gj
SAVALLE, Margt.	22	F	Unknown	30Ap09Gj
CONNELLY, Alice	25	F	Unknown	30Ap09Gj
COWLEY, William	50	M	Unknown	30Ap09Gj
Bridget	40	F	Unknown	30Ap09Gj
William	20	M	Unknown	30Ap09Gj
Margaret	16	F	Unknown	30Ap09Gj
Mary	14	F	Unknown	30Ap09Gj
HART, Pat	20	M	Unknown	30Ap09Gj
Catherine	13	F	Unknown	30Ap09Gj
CAVANAGH, Chas.	30	M	Unknown	30Ap09Gj
CAVANAGH, Ann	24	F	Unknown	30Ap09Gj
Michl.	35	M	Unknown	30Ap09Gj
Michl.	24	M	Unknown	30Ap09Gj
JORDAN, Mary	20	F	Unknown	30Ap09Gj
KELLY, Pat	25	M	Unknown	30Ap09Gj
Peter	28	M	Unknown	30Ap09Gj
LONGHEAD, Ellen	21	F	Laborer	30Ap09Gj
BRENNAN, Bridget	19	F	Laborer	30Ap09Gj
MCGOWN, Michl.	25	M	Laborer	30Ap09Gj
QUINN, Margt.	40	F	Unknown	30Ap09Gj
Michl.	12	M	Unknown	30Ap09Gj
HEALY, Jno.	25	M	Unknown	30Ap09Gj
Honora	25	F	Unknown	30Ap09Gj
Ann	.00	F	Infant	30Ap09Gj
CONNELL, Mary	30	F	Unknown	30Ap09Gj
Pat	10	M	Unknown	30Ap09Gj
DONOHER, Catherine	21	F	Unknown	30Ap09Gj
GWIL, Jno.	22	M	Unknown	30Ap09Gj
CULLEN, Thomas	25	M	Unknown	30Ap09Gj
Mick	23	M	Unknown	30Ap09Gj
FRY, Margt.	17	F	Unknown	30Ap09Gj
FEMAN, Jno.	30	M	Unknown	30Ap09Gj
BRIEN, Mary	23	F	Unknown	30Ap09Gj
DOWNS, Edward	20	M	Unknown	30Ap09Gj
NUTTY, Hugh	20	M	Unknown	30Ap09Gj
Mary	22	F	Unknown	30Ap09Gj
GRAHAM, Francis	38	M	Unknown	30Ap09Gj
GANAHAN, Bridget	30	F	Unknown	30Ap09Gj
GIBLIN, Henry	24	M	Unknown	30Ap09Gj
GILLISPIE, Pat	21	M	Unknown	30Ap09Gj
HANNIGAN, Pat	25	M	Unknown	30Ap09Gj
MULLOY, Bridget	20	F	Unknown	30Ap09Gj
MCKANE, Bessy	25	F	Unknown	30Ap09Gj
BRENNAN, Mary	2	F	Child	30Ap09Gj
ROCHE, Thomas	28	M	Unknown	30Ap09Gj
HANNOW, Mary	20	F	Unknown	30Ap09Gj
DALY, Bridget	16	F	Unknown	30Ap09Gj
DARCY, Thady	20	M	Unknown	30Ap09Gj
MALCOM, Martin	24	M	Unknown	30Ap09Gj
Mary	23	F	Unknown	30Ap09Gj
COWLEY, Michael	24	M	Unknown	30Ap09Gj
WALTON, Thomas	20	M	Unknown	30Ap09Gj
Ann	16	F	Unknown	30Ap09Gj
Jane	15	F	Unknown	30Ap09Gj
LUNDY, Daniel	25	M	Unknown	30Ap09Gj
DORHERTY, Barbara	40	F	Unknown	30Ap09Gj
Sarah	18	F	Unknown	30Ap09Gj
MOFFITT, Sarah	18	F	Unknown	30Ap09Gj
BARTLETT, Set-M.	24	M	Unknown	30Ap09Gj
MILLER, Sarah	30	F	Unknown	30Ap09Gj
Geo.	3	M	Child	30Ap09Gj
MCHUGH, Bridget	30	F	Unknown	30Ap09Gj

MARGARET 01 MAY 1850

From YARMOUTH, N.S.

NAMES OF PASSENGERS	AGE	SEX	OCCUPATIONS	DATE PORT SHIP
RAMSAY, Saml.	45	M	Gentleman	01Ma53Bw
Rebecca	40	F	Unknown	01Ma53Bw
Anna	20	F	Unknown	01Ma53Bw
Sarah	18	F	Unknown	01Ma53Bw
Emily	16	F	Unknown	01Ma53Bw
George	14	M	Unknown	01Ma53Bw
Susan	13	F	Unknown	01Ma53Bw
Pam	12	F	Unknown	01Ma53Bw
William	3	M	Child	01Ma53Bw
WELSH, Jane	30	F	Servant	01Ma53Bw
Bridget	8	F	Child	01Ma53Bw
Edwd.	.00	M	Infant	01Ma53Bw

NAMES OF PASSENGERS	AGE	SEX	OCCUPATIONS	DATE PORT SHIP
WEBB, Esther	65	F	Unknown	01Ma53Bw

ANNA-TIFT 01 MAY 1850

From Liverpool

NAMES OF PASSENGERS	AGE	SEX	OCCUPATIONS	DATE PORT SHIP
MURTAGH, John	28	M	Tailor	01Ma02Je
SHARKEY, John	18	M	Laborer	01Ma02Je
SCANLON, Margaret	48	F	Servant	01Ma02Je
MOLONEY, Mary	20	F	Servant	01Ma02Je
DERVIN, Catherine	18	F	Servant	01Ma02Je
MCMAHON, Michael	30	M	Laborer	01Ma02Je
MERRIGAN, Thomas	30	M	Laborer	01Ma02Je
Patrick	4	M	Child	01Ma02Je
John	2	M	Child	01Ma02Je
Catherine	25	F	Servant	01Ma02Je
Anne	.02	F	Infant	01Ma02Je
FENNERTY, Catherine	20	F	Servant	01Ma02Je
EAGAN, Mary	20	F	Servant	01Ma02Je
DOLAN, Anne	16	F	Servant	01Ma02Je
MCDONALD, Michael	40	M	Laborer	01Ma02Je
NEARY, John	34	M	Stone Mason	01Ma02Je
SKELLY, James	24	M	Laborer	01Ma02Je
MCDONALD, Elizabeth	60	F	Unknown	01Ma02Je
STEVENS, Elizabeth	16	F	Servant	01Ma02Je
EARLY, Margaret	19	F	Servant	01Ma02Je
BUCKLEY, Julia	20	F	Servant	01Ma02Je
MCNALLY, Mary	26	F	Servant	01Ma02Je
Rosanna	16	F	Servant	01Ma02Je
ROLEY, Francis	35	M	Laborer	01Ma02Je
Patrick	5	M	Child	01Ma02Je
Mary	35	F	Unknown	01Ma02Je
Bridget	7	F	Child	01Ma02Je
COCHLAN, Anne	20	F	Servant	01Ma02Je
HANRATTY, Margaret	23	F	Servant	01Ma02Je
DOLAN, Bridget	25	F	Servant	01Ma02Je
LARKIN, Mathew	57	M	Servant	01Ma02Je
CONROY, Timothy	20	M	Servant	01Ma02Je
EAGAN, Lawrence	17	M	Servant	01Ma02Je
MEALY, John	19	M	Servant	01Ma02Je
ROISTON, Michael	14	M	Servant	01Ma02Je
Jane	12	F	Servant	01Ma02Je
RIGNY, Patrick	12	M	Servant	01Ma02Je
NORRIS, John	26	M	Cooper	01Ma02Je
Mary	26	F	Cooper	01Ma02Je
Mary	60	F	Cooper	01Ma02Je
DANAHER, Patrick	27	M	Laborer	01Ma02Je
MCMANAWAY, John	30	M	Laborer	01Ma02Je
Thomas	9	M	Child	01Ma02Je
BURKE, Thomas	25	M	Laborer	01Ma02Je
COX, Anne	25	F	Servant	01Ma02Je
KEENAN, Catherine	26	F	Servant	01Ma02Je
GRANNON, Bridget	20	F	Servant	01Ma02Je
HALAHAN, Michael	30	M	Laborer	01Ma02Je
MCMAHON, Ellen	16	F	Servant	01Ma02Je
QUIGLY, Catherine	19	F	Servant	01Ma02Je
SEARY, Ellen	22	F	Servant	01Ma02Je
CLARKE, Ellen	19	F	Servant	01Ma02Je
REED, Mathew	18	M	Weaver	01Ma02Je
Bridget	23	F	Servant	01Ma02Je
CORMACK, Margaret	17	F	Servant	01Ma02Je
RYAN, Michael	35	M	Herd	01Ma02Je
Thomas	14	M	Herd	01Ma02Je
FALLON, Dennis	16	M	Shoemaker	01Ma02Je
SULLIVAN, Ellen	58	F	Servant	01Ma02Je
Dennis	23	M	Laborer	01Ma02Je
Daniel	21	M	Laborer	01Ma02Je
Honora	30	F	Servant	01Ma02Je
Dennis	4	M	Child	01Ma02Je

NAMES OF PASSENGERS	AGE	SEX	OCCUPATIONS	DATE PORT SHIP
SULLIVAN, Daniel Died-At-Sea	.09	M	Infant	01Ma02Je
TOOHY, John	45	M	Farmer	01Ma02Je
Thomas	42	M	Farmer	01Ma02Je
DELANY, Ellen	8	F	Child	01Ma02Je
CASSIN, Catherine	22	F	Servant	01Ma02Je
Bridget	22	F	Servant	01Ma02Je
TOOHY, Bridget	17	F	Servant	01Ma02Je
CARMOLLY, Mary	16	F	Servant	01Ma02Je
Ellen	14	F	Servant	01Ma02Je
John	24	M	Laborer	01Ma02Je
TOOHY, Martin	25	M	Laborer	01Ma02Je
CASSIN, William	36	M	Cooper	01Ma02Je
KELLY, Bridget	23	F	Servant	01Ma02Je
Mary	17	F	Servant	01Ma02Je
DOLAN, Patrick	23	M	Laborer	01Ma02Je
Thomas	22	M	Laborer	01Ma02Je
John	16	M	Laborer	01Ma02Je
Terrance	13	M	Laborer	01Ma02Je
Bridget	50	F	Unknown	01Ma02Je
Margaret	20	F	Unknown	01Ma02Je
Catherine	14	F	Unknown	01Ma02Je
Rebecca	27	F	Unknown	01Ma02Je
Catherine	16	F	Unknown	01Ma02Je
MCHUGH, Edward	23	M	Laborer	01Ma02Je
MCGOURAN, Margaret	16	F	Servant	01Ma02Je
DOLAN, John	55	M	Farmer	01Ma02Je
Mary	50	F	Unknown	01Ma02Je
Bryan	11	M	Unknown	01Ma02Je
QUIN, James	25	M	Laborer	01Ma02Je
MULFALL, Charles	20	M	Laborer	01Ma02Je
Patrick	18	M	Laborer	01Ma02Je
MCCORMACK, Thomas	54	M	Laborer	01Ma02Je
Thomas	16	M	Laborer	01Ma02Je
FARRELL, Patrick	26	M	Laborer	01Ma02Je
MCCORMACK, Mary	30	F	Servant	01Ma02Je
CLINTON, Catherine	20	F	Servant	01Ma02Je
BARRY, James	40	M	Farmer	01Ma02Je
Honora	36	F	Unknown	01Ma02Je
Mathew	9	M	Child	01Ma02Je
Garret	7	M	Child	01Ma02Je
William	.11	M	Infant	01Ma02Je
MAHONY, Isabella	52	F	Servant	01Ma02Je
CONNOLL, Elizabeth	10	F	Unknown	01Ma02Je
John	24	M	Laborer	01Ma02Je
HIERLAHY, Margaret	31	F	Servant	01Ma02Je
MCCARTHY, Catherine	20	F	Servant	01Ma02Je
John	25	M	Carpenter	01Ma02Je
SULLIVAN, Daniel	26	M	Laborer	01Ma02Je
DALTON, Patrick	15	M	Laborer	01Ma02Je
William	14	M	Laborer	01Ma02Je
Bridget	20	F	Servant	01Ma02Je
Ellen	17	F	Servant	01Ma02Je
Alicia	16	F	Servant	01Ma02Je
HARRINGTON, Daniel	70	M	Unknown	01Ma02Je
SULLIVAN, Daniel	22	M	Laborer	01Ma02Je
GREGORY, Thomas	22	M	Laborer	01Ma02Je
MCCARTHY, Margaret	16	F	Servant	01Ma02Je
MCNABOLIN, Catherine	18	F	Servant	01Ma02Je
Ellen	15	F	Servant	01Ma02Je
DALTON, Ellen	18	F	Servant	01Ma02Je
KIRK, Anne	22	F	Dressmaker	01Ma02Je
OBRIEN, Johanna	32	F	Servant	01Ma02Je
MOURN, Margaret	35	F	Dressmaker	01Ma02Je
Catherine	32	F	Dressmaker	01Ma02Je
TALOR, Elizabeth	3	F	Child	01Ma02Je
MOURN, Joseph	40	M	Ldghkpr	01Ma02Je
Hugh	30	M	Farmer	01Ma02Je
Edward	5	M	Child	01Ma02Je
CARY, Mary	16	F	Dressmaker	01Ma02Je
CARR, Anne	20	F	Servant	01Ma02Je
BRIEN, Bridget	23	F	Dressmaker	01Ma02Je
CODY, Mary	10	F	Unknown	01Ma02Je
DEVINE, Patrick	20	M	Laborer	01Ma02Je
BROWN, Patrick	24	M	Laborer	01Ma02Je

NAMES OF PASSENGERS	AGE	SEX	OCCUPATIONS	DATE PORT SHIP
CARTER, Michael	22	M	Laborer	01Ma02Je
DEVINE, Louis	31	M	Laborer	01Ma02Je
TAYLOR, Catherine	65	F	Unknown	01Ma02Je
Patrick	25	M	Laborer	01Ma02Je
HOGG, Edward	50	M	Servant	01Ma02Je
BOSE, Dennis	20	M	Servant	01Ma02Je
GAFFREY, Mary	30	F	Unknown	01Ma02Je
MARTIN, Michael	5	M	Child	01Ma02Je
LYNCH, John	18	M	Shoemaker	01Ma02Je
DAVY, William	20	M	Laborer	01Ma02Je
KELLY, John	25	M	Cook	01Ma02Je
MAGEE, John	19	M	Laborer	01Ma02Je
SHANLY, John	35	M	Laborer	01Ma02Je
MARTIN, John	22	M	Laborer	01Ma02Je
DURNEY, Daniel	22	M	Laborer	01Ma02Je
Mary	20	F	Servant	01Ma02Je
IVERS, Thomas	20	M	Laborer	01Ma02Je
CONROY, Dennis	20	M	Laborer	01Ma02Je
HUGHES, Patrick	20	M	Laborer	01Ma02Je
GANNON, Patrick	20	M	Laborer	01Ma02Je
WALSH, Martin	25	M	Laborer	01Ma02Je
CLARKE, William	19	M	Laborer	01Ma02Je
KENNEY, Thomas	25	M	Laborer	01Ma02Je
LALLY, Michael	32	M	Laborer	01Ma02Je
Catherine	32	F	Servant	01Ma02Je
GLYNN, Anne	25	F	Servant	01Ma02Je
Catherine	5	F	Child	01Ma02Je
Thomas	3	M	Child	01Ma02Je
CUNNINGHAM, Bridget	40	F	Servant	01Ma02Je
OBRIEN, Timothy	30	M	Laborer	01Ma02Je
Honora	30	F	Unknown	01Ma02Je
William	.07	M	Infant	01Ma02Je
MAHERN, Julia	23	F	Servant	01Ma02Je
MOLOY, Mary	30	F	Servant	01Ma02Je
Maria	9	F	Child	01Ma02Je
Patrick	11	M	Unknown	01Ma02Je
MCEVOY, Andrew	40	M	Laborer	01Ma02Je
DOOLAN, Loughlin	28	M	Laborer	01Ma02Je
HARTY, Ellen	22	F	Servant	01Ma02Je
GREEN, Margaret	22	F	Servant	01Ma02Je
DOOLAN, Michael	25	M	Laborer	01Ma02Je
Mary	28	F	Unknown	01Ma02Je
Margaret	9	F	Child	01Ma02Je
Michael	7	M	Child	01Ma02Je
Anne	5	F	Child	01Ma02Je
Mary	3	F	Child	01Ma02Je
BUTLER, Maria	20	F	Servant	01Ma02Je
Margaret	18	F	Servant	01Ma02Je
TAHY, Patrick	30	M	Servant	01Ma02Je
Anne	12	F	Unknown	01Ma02Je
WHITE, Catherine	17	F	Unknown	01Ma02Je
JENNINGS, Honora	30	F	Unknown	01Ma02Je
Mathew	.06	M	Infant	01Ma02Je
EAGAN, Anne	17	F	Servant	01Ma02Je
Winifred	19	F	Servant	01Ma02Je
HALL, Anne	18	F	Servant	01Ma02Je
MAGAN, Bridget	20	F	Servant	01Ma02Je
CORDON, Michael	30	M	Weaver	01Ma02Je
PELLY, Francis	25	M	Laborer	01Ma02Je
MCBRIEN, Thomas	29	M	Bricklayer	01Ma02Je
CURLY, Patrick	10	M	Unknown	01Ma02Je
MCGRANE, John	20	M	Servant	01Ma02Je
MURTAGH, Bridget	14	F	Servant	01Ma02Je
BOYLE, Owen	50	M	Laborer	01Ma02Je
Daniel	30	M	Laborer	01Ma02Je
Michael	12	M	Laborer	01Ma02Je
Patrick	.03	M	Infant	01Ma02Je
Mary	50	F	Servant	01Ma02Je
Catherine	22	F	Servant	01Ma02Je
Bridget	30	F	Servant	01Ma02Je
Ellen	8	F	Child	01Ma02Je
NORTON, William	44	M	Clerk	01Ma02Je
Mary	36	F	Unknown	01Ma02Je
Patrick	17	M	Clerk	01Ma02Je
Daniel	13	M	Unknown	01Ma02Je
NORTON, Catherine	5	F	Child	01Ma02Je
William	.11	M	Infant	01Ma02Je
KELLY, James	30	M	Blacksmith	01Ma02Je
TRAVERS, Robin	26	M	Laborer	01Ma02Je
MAHER, Timothy	26	M	Laborer	01Ma02Je
KELLY, Timothy	21	M	Butcher	01Ma02Je
WHELAN, Anne	26	F	Servant	01Ma02Je
MAHER, Mary	21	F	Servant	01Ma02Je
DOOGAN, Thomas	24	M	Laborer	01Ma02Je
HENRY, Michael	11	M	Unknown	01Ma02Je
ROLEY, Bridget	40	F	Servant	01Ma02Je
Michael	4	M	Child	01Ma02Je
Anne	.02	F	Infant	01Ma02Je
MCGARTHY, Catherine	18	F	Servant	01Ma02Je
GILHOOLY, Peter	25	M	Laborer	01Ma02Je
FITZPATRICK, Mary	9	F	Child	01Ma02Je
BANNON, Anne	20	F	Servant	01Ma02Je
RUDDEN, Mary	30	F	Servant	01Ma02Je
MCGUIRE, Catherine	17	F	Servant	01Ma02Je
KEENAN, Peter	22	M	Laborer	01Ma02Je
SMYTH, Patrick	19	M	Laborer	01Ma02Je
Bridget	16	F	Servant	01Ma02Je
GILLAGAN, Rosa	16	F	Servant	01Ma02Je
DOOLY, Dennis	23	M	Laborer	01Ma02Je
HAYS, Thomas	30	M	Laborer	01Ma02Je
Julia	14	F	Servant	01Ma02Je
DUNN, Margaret	22	F	Servant	01Ma02Je
GLEESON, Margaret	20	F	Servant	01Ma02Je
LALER, Catherine	20	F	Servant	01Ma02Je
DAY, Patrick	25	M	Laborer	01Ma02Je
BROPHY, Michael	30	M	Laborer	01Ma02Je
DOWAN, Bernard	19	M	Servant	01Ma02Je
BALMER, Richard	20	M	Laborer	01Ma02Je
BRADY, Edward	19	M	Laborer	01Ma02Je
FITZPATRICK, John	19	M	Servant	01Ma02Je
FITZSIMMONS, Rose	25	F	Servant	01Ma02Je
MCGEE, Margaret	20	F	Servant	01Ma02Je
LINDSEY, John	50	M	Farmer	01Ma02Je
BLESSON, Terrance	30	M	Laborer	01Ma02Je
WARD, Mary	37	F	Servant	01Ma02Je
Catherine	10	F	Servant	01Ma02Je
MCDERMOTT, Rose	14	F	Unknown	01Ma02Je
FITZPATRICK, Anne	17	F	Servant	01Ma02Je
BRENNON, Bridget	18	F	Servant	01Ma02Je
MCCARTHY, Bridget	20	F	Servant	01Ma02Je
DWIGNAN, Anne	20	F	Servant	01Ma02Je
DONOHOE, Catherine	19	F	Servant	01Ma02Je
GARVY, Margaret	20	F	Servant	01Ma02Je
CURLY, Mary	13	F	Servant	01Ma02Je
REYNOLDS, Owen	30	M	Laborer	01Ma02Je
Catherine	30	F	Unknown	01Ma02Je
Michael	12	M	Unknown	01Ma02Je
Bridget	9	F	Child	01Ma02Je
Patrick	7	M	Child	01Ma02Je
Peter	.06	M	Infant	01Ma02Je
CANNON, Catherine	16	F	Servant	01Ma02Je
GAFNEY, Catherine	20	F	Servant	01Ma02Je
LAMB, Patrick	60	M	Farmer	01Ma02Je
Catherine	17	F	Unknown	01Ma02Je
Terrance	14	M	Unknown	01Ma02Je
Philip	12	M	Unknown	01Ma02Je
KERR, Richard	17	M	Laborer	01Ma02Je
NORTON, David	20	M	Laborer	01Ma02Je
SHORT, John	17	M	Unknown	01Ma02Je
REYNOLDS, James	3	M	Child	01Ma02Je
KELLY, J.Doctor	00	M	Unknown	01Ma02Je
U	00	F	Lady	01Ma02Je

EDWARD 01 MAY 1850

From Cork

NAMES OF PASSENGERS	AGE	SEX	OCCUPATIONS	DATE PORT SHIP
MAYE, Michael	28	M	Farmer	01Ma18Hn
Mary	26	F	Unknown	01Ma18Hn
William	.00	M	Infant	01Ma18Hn
LEAHY, James	23	M	Unknown	01Ma18Hn
COURBURY, John	21	M	Unknown	01Ma18Hn
NEENAN, Abby	20	F	Unknown	01Ma18Hn
COINWIN, Aron	.00	M	Infant	01Ma18Hn
Peggy	35	F	Unknown	01Ma18Hn
MACKEY, James	24	M	Unknown	01Ma18Hn
FROY, Ellen	28	M	Unknown	01Ma18Hn
SULLIVAN, Michael	25	M	Unknown	01Ma18Hn
James	30	M	Unknown	01Ma18Hn
Mary	54	F	Unknown	01Ma18Hn
HARRINGTON, Timothy	23	M	Unknown	01Ma18Hn
DONOVAN, Thomas	22	M	Unknown	01Ma18Hn
FLYING, Thombly	26	M	Unknown	01Ma18Hn
FOOLING, Timothy	26	M	Unknown	01Ma18Hn
RYALL, Margaret	26	F	Unknown	01Ma18Hn
HAYES, James	.00	M	Infant	01Ma18Hn
Mary	25	F	Unknown	01Ma18Hn
CAHALANE, Moris	26	M	Unknown	01Ma18Hn
FITZGERRALD, Thomas	24	M	Unknown	01Ma18Hn
SULLIVAN, Julia	24	F	Unknown	01Ma18Hn
COLEMAN, Abby	18	F	Unknown	01Ma18Hn
CLIFFORD, William	24	M	Unknown	01Ma18Hn
COLLINS, Mary	18	F	Unknown	01Ma18Hn
SPILLANE, Jeremiah	23	M	Unknown	01Ma18Hn
FOLEY, Johanna	26	M	Unknown	01Ma18Hn
LEARY, Jerry	20	M	Unknown	01Ma18Hn
Denis	20	M	Unknown	01Ma18Hn
CROWLEY, Mary	40	F	Unknown	01Ma18Hn
COUGHLAN, Andrew	.00	M	Infant	01Ma18Hn
Ann	24	F	Unknown	01Ma18Hn
Mary	22	F	Unknown	01Ma18Hn
Johanna	26	F	Unknown	01Ma18Hn
LEARY, Mary	21	F	Unknown	01Ma18Hn
Johanna	.00	F	Infant	01Ma18Hn
MCCARTHY, James	22	M	Unknown	01Ma18Hn
HANREHAN, Patrick	28	M	Unknown	01Ma18Hn
CARTHY, Patrick	30	M	Unknown	01Ma18Hn
BEARY, William	24	M	Unknown	01Ma18Hn
KEHNASTEN, Pat	22	M	Unknown	01Ma18Hn
CORONAN, Bridget	28	F	Unknown	01Ma18Hn
HENNESSY, Honora	26	F	Unknown	01Ma18Hn
Ellen	22	F	Unknown	01Ma18Hn
Eliza	20	F	Unknown	01Ma18Hn
WALSH, Mary	34	F	Unknown	01Ma18Hn
DRISCOLL, John	26	M	Unknown	01Ma18Hn
DONOVAN, James	28	M	Unknown	01Ma18Hn
WALSH, Pattrick	30	M	Unknown	01Ma18Hn
DONAN, Ellen	23	F	Unknown	01Ma18Hn
COLBERT, David	39	M	Unknown	01Ma18Hn
FLYNN, Mary	22	F	Unknown	01Ma18Hn
Fanney	.00	F	Infant	01Ma18Hn
CONNOR, Betty	32	F	Unknown	01Ma18Hn
NORRIS, Patt	.00	M	Infant	01Ma18Hn
Ellen	26	F	Unknown	01Ma18Hn
BARRY, Thomas	43	M	Unknown	01Ma18Hn
WALSH, Edward	22	M	Unknown	01Ma18Hn
BEATSH, Jerry	42	M	Unknown	01Ma18Hn
CONNOR, Michael	20	M	Unknown	01Ma18Hn
MORRARTY, Biddy	20	F	Unknown	01Ma18Hn
KENNEDY, Biddy	19	F	Unknown	01Ma18Hn
DUANE, Johanna	40	F	Unknown	01Ma18Hn
SULLIVAN, Bridget	25	F	Unknown	01Ma18Hn
SULLIVAN, Ellen	.00	F	Infant	01Ma18Hn
SHEA, Johanna	22	F	Unknown	01Ma18Hn
BOLSTER, Thomas	25	M	Unknown	01Ma18Hn
SHEA, James	22	M	Unknown	01Ma18Hn
SULLIVAN, John	.00	M	Infant	01Ma18Hn
DAUNT, William-B.	21	M	Unknown	01Ma18Hn
BIRD, Ellen	18	F	Unknown	01Ma18Hn
FERRIS, Sarah	23	F	Unknown	01Ma18Hn
Timothy	.00	M	Infant	01Ma18Hn
WARNER, Thomas	25	M	Unknown	01Ma18Hn
Mary	23	F	Unknown	01Ma18Hn
CUE, Eliza	20	F	Unknown	01Ma18Hn
SHEA, Timothy	24	M	Unknown	01Ma18Hn
CASEY, Daniel	24	M	Unknown	01Ma18Hn
CONNOR, Peggy	21	F	Unknown	01Ma18Hn
SHEA, Honora	25	F	Unknown	01Ma18Hn
SULLIVAN, Honora	25	F	Unknown	01Ma18Hn
MORIARTY, Bridget	26	F	Unknown	01Ma18Hn
CRUMMEN, Mary	20	F	Unknown	01Ma18Hn
SULLIVAN, Mary	.00	F	Infant	01Ma18Hn
GLAVIN, Patrick	10	M	Unknown	01Ma18Hn
NUGENT, Morris	10	F	Unknown	01Ma18Hn
CONNELL, John	13	M	Unknown	01Ma18Hn
BUCKLEY, Margaret	13	F	Unknown	01Ma18Hn
CROWLEY, Jerry	.00	M	Infant	01Ma18Hn
Johanna	25	F	Unknown	01Ma18Hn
WALSH, James	25	M	Unknown	01Ma18Hn
GLARANE, John	50	M	Unknown	01Ma18Hn
HENNESSY, Maurice	30	M	Unknown	01Ma18Hn
KANE, Johanna	24	F	Unknown	01Ma18Hn
GRIFFIN, Cathrn.	24	F	Unknown	01Ma18Hn
NUGENT, Patty	40	F	Unknown	01Ma18Hn
SHEA, Daniel	.00	M	Infant	01Ma18Hn
Bridget	32	F	Unknown	01Ma18Hn
CAHALANE, Johanna	20	F	Unknown	01Ma18Hn
CARNEY, Patrick	47	M	Unknown	01Ma18Hn
Ellen	16	F	Unknown	01Ma18Hn
GISS, Ellen	17	F	Unknown	01Ma18Hn
CONNOLLY, John	25	M	Unknown	01Ma18Hn
COLLINS, Tim	25	M	Unknown	01Ma18Hn
CONNOLLY, Johanna	25	F	Unknown	01Ma18Hn
WALSH, Mary	24	F	Unknown	01Ma18Hn
JAY, Mary	24	F	Unknown	01Ma18Hn
COLLINS, Jerry	27	F	Unknown	01Ma18Hn
CONNELL, Andrew	48	M	Unknown	01Ma18Hn
MCCARTHEY, Daniel	.00	M	Infant	01Ma18Hn
Mary	22	F	Unknown	01Ma18Hn
SHEEHAN, Daniel	15	M	Unknown	01Ma18Hn
BROWN, Patt	.00	M	Infant	01Ma18Hn
Julia	32	F	Unknown	01Ma18Hn
AHERN, Susan	24	F	Unknown	01Ma18Hn
MORRISON, Mary	26	F	Unknown	01Ma18Hn
WALSH, William	22	M	Unknown	01Ma18Hn
Mary	11	F	Unknown	01Ma18Hn
Kate	.00	F	Infant	01Ma18Hn
CRUMMEN, Pat	.00	M	Infant	01Ma18Hn
SULLIVAN, Ellen	.00	F	Infant	01Ma18Hn
WALSH, John	.00	M	Infant	01Ma18Hn
Ellen	.00	F	Infant	01Ma18Hn

FANNY 01 MAY 1850

From Londonderry

NAMES OF PASSENGERS	AGE	SEX	OCCUPATIONS	DATE PORT SHIP
MOUNTERE, Isabella	24	F	Servant	01Ma01Ja
POLLOCK, Joseph	21	M	Servant	01Ma01Ja
FUNSON, Henry	21	M	Servant	01Ma01Ja
CARLAND, Mary	19	F	Servant	01Ma01Ja
SANDERSON, James	22	M	Laborer	01Ma01Ja

NAMES OF PASSENGERS	AGE	SEX	OCCUPATIONS	DATE PORT SHIP
SANDERSON, David	18	M	Laborer	01Ma01Ja
MCCLOCKEY, Peter	20	M	Laborer	01Ma01Ja
Sarah	18	F	Servant	01Ma01Ja
THOMPSON, William	21	M	Laborer	01Ma01Ja
HASLET, John	22	M	Laborer	01Ma01Ja
GALLAGHER, Mary	18	F	Servant	01Ma01Ja
John	14	M	Laborer	01Ma01Ja
MCLOUGHLIN, John	21	M	Laborer	01Ma01Ja
Mary	21	F	Servant	01Ma01Ja
KYLE, Luis	21	M	Servant	01Ma01Ja
BOYLE, Anne	18	F	Servant	01Ma01Ja
Catherine	16	F	Servant	01Ma01Ja
LIMERICK, Letitia	19	F	Servant	01Ma01Ja
HATTRICK, George	18	M	Laborer	01Ma01Ja
QUINN, William	18	M	Laborer	01Ma01Ja
MCCAY, Mary	19	F	Servant	01Ma01Ja
COGHRAN, Nancy	21	F	Servant	01Ma01Ja
MCGRATH, Andrew	20	M	Laborer	01Ma01Ja
Mary	19	F	Laborer	01Ma01Ja
MCKNIGHT, Jane	40	F	Servant	01Ma01Ja
CORMER, James	20	M	Servant	01Ma01Ja
DOGHERTY, Martha	20	F	Servant	01Ma01Ja
MCVEY, Sally	21	F	Servant	01Ma01Ja
PHILLIPS, Michael	30	M	Servant	01Ma01Ja
Anne	31	F	Servant	01Ma01Ja
CRAY, John	19	M	Farmer	01Ma01Ja
ONEIL, Patrick	28	M	Farmer	01Ma01Ja
Barney	22	M	Farmer	01Ma01Ja
HARKIN, James	20	M	Laborer	01Ma01Ja
John	21	M	Laborer	01Ma01Ja
KEY, Jane	20	F	Servant	01Ma01Ja
DEVINE, Andrew	24	M	Laborer	01Ma01Ja
MCMENOMY, Sally	15	F	Servant	01Ma01Ja
Anne	13	F	Servant	01Ma01Ja
CORRIGAN, Catherine	21	F	Servant	01Ma01Ja
ALEXANDER, Rebecca	18	F	Servant	01Ma01Ja
Galla----, Patrick	60	M	Laborer	01Ma01Ja
KENEDY, Eliza	20	F	Servant	01Ma01Ja
CORNWORTH, Margaret	21	F	Servant	01Ma01Ja
GILLEHAND, Mary-A.	17	F	Servant	01Ma01Ja
MCCLOSKEY, Sally	60	F	Servant	01Ma01Ja
Mary	28	F	Farmer	01Ma01Ja
Hannah	25	F	Farmer	01Ma01Ja
Henry	21	M	Farmer	01Ma01Ja
TREASY, Cornelius	20	M	Farmer	01Ma01Ja
James	9	M	Child	01Ma01Ja
MCCLOSKEY, John	16	M	Farmer	01Ma01Ja
Patrick	70	M	Farmer	01Ma01Ja
James	19	M	Farmer	01Ma01Ja
BRADLY, Margaret	24	F	Servant	01Ma01Ja
Anne	22	F	Servant	01Ma01Ja
HENRY, Margaret-N.	25	F	Servant	01Ma01Ja
REILY, Jane	22	F	Servant	01Ma01Ja
MUNTIELLE, Eliza	20	F	Servant	01Ma01Ja
LOGUE, Andrew	21	M	Laborer	01Ma01Ja
MCKENNY, Alexander	19	M	Laborer	01Ma01Ja
PORTER, Jane	20	F	Servant	01Ma01Ja
FARGUAHER, Robert	20	M	Laborer	01Ma01Ja
HAMILTON, Eliza	17	F	Servant	01Ma01Ja
HUCHISON, John	47	M	Farmer	01Ma01Ja
Jane	19	F	Farmer	01Ma01Ja
WENSTON, Thomas	20	M	Servant	01Ma01Ja
Essy	18	F	Servant	01Ma01Ja
WILSON, John	17	M	Laborer	01Ma01Ja
MCGUIRE, Mary	21	F	Servant	01Ma01Ja
SHANNON, John	18	M	Laborer	01Ma01Ja
SHIELS, Letty	35	F	Servant	01Ma01Ja
COYLE, Sarah	30	F	Servant	01Ma01Ja
QUIGLEY, Bridget	20	F	Servant	01Ma01Ja
HALY, John	13	M	Laborer	01Ma01Ja
Ralph	11	M	Laborer	01Ma01Ja
MCALLANY, Mary	18	F	Servant	01Ma01Ja
EVANS, Mary	19	F	Servant	01Ma01Ja
HIGGINS, John	21	M	Laborer	01Ma01Ja
PLOCTOR, Joseph-S.	21	M	Laborer	01Ma01Ja
LOGAN, Eliza	6	F	Child	01Ma01Ja
Catherine	5	F	Child	01Ma01Ja
MOORHEAD, John	26	M	Laborer	01Ma01Ja
DOGHERTY, John	50	M	Laborer	01Ma01Ja
Mary	13	F	Servant	01Ma01Ja
LAWN, James	24	M	Mason	01Ma01Ja
Alice	18	F	Servant	01Ma01Ja
BROWN, William	17	M	Laborer	01Ma01Ja
HEARALD, William	40	M	Laborer	01Ma01Ja
MCMUN, Andrew	22	M	Laborer	01Ma01Ja
William	26	M	Laborer	01Ma01Ja
MCFADDEN, Alice	15	M	Servant	01Ma01Ja
DUGAN, James	21	M	Laborer	01Ma01Ja
MCLOUGHLIN, Robert	21	M	Laborer	01Ma01Ja
BOTHWELL, Jane	21	M	Servant	01Ma01Ja
DOGHERTY, Patrick	30	M	Laborer	01Ma01Ja
ONEIL, James	23	M	Laborer	01Ma01Ja
MCCLOSKEY, Mary	16	F	Servant	01Ma01Ja
MCSHEE, William	24	M	Laborer	01Ma01Ja
MCINTIRE, Peter	20	M	Laborer	01Ma01Ja
MCSHEA, Denny	25	M	Laborer	01Ma01Ja
Biddy	60	F	Unknown	01Ma01Ja
Unity	31	F	Servant	01Ma01Ja
DOGHERTY, John	24	M	Laborer	01Ma01Ja
Mary	26	F	Servant	01Ma01Ja
John	18	M	Laborer	01Ma01Ja
Anne	20	F	Servant	01Ma01Ja
HEANY, Rose	20	F	Servant	01Ma01Ja
MCCALVEY, Charles	22	M	Laborer	01Ma01Ja
William	18	M	Laborer	01Ma01Ja
OKANE, Phelix	16	M	Laborer	01Ma01Ja
CROSSEN, Ellen	18	F	Servant	01Ma01Ja
COYLE, James	20	M	Laborer	01Ma01Ja
Mary	19	F	Unknown	01Ma01Ja
MCGARIGLE, William	25	M	Laborer	01Ma01Ja
MCGEE, Paddy	30	M	Laborer	01Ma01Ja
DOGHERTY, Barney	24	M	Laborer	01Ma01Ja
WALLACE, Alexander	21	M	Laborer	01Ma01Ja
MCCOOL, Ellen	24	F	Servant	01Ma01Ja
KEARNEY, Thomas	26	M	Laborer	01Ma01Ja
DOGHERTY, Dominick	24	M	Laborer	01Ma01Ja
MCGARIGLE, Michael	22	M	Laborer	01Ma01Ja
LAFFERTY, James	25	M	Laborer	01Ma01Ja
KIRKLAND, Andrew	24	M	Laborer	01Ma01Ja
Elizabeth	21	F	Servant	01Ma01Ja
CROSSEN, Catherine	30	F	Farmer	01Ma01Ja
Susan	28	F	Farmer	01Ma01Ja
Biddy	24	F	Farmer	01Ma01Ja
Patrick	22	M	Farmer	01Ma01Ja
Kerpatrick	21	F	Farmer	01Ma01Ja
Cornelius	11	M	Farmer	01Ma01Ja
John	9	M	Child	01Ma01Ja
GALASBIE, John	24	M	Laborer	01Ma01Ja
MCGEE, Margaret	24	F	Servant	01Ma01Ja
MCFEELY, Daniel	26	M	Laborer	01Ma01Ja
FARREN, Michael	28	M	Laborer	01Ma01Ja
MCGONIGLE, Joseph	30	M	Laborer	01Ma01Ja
BRADLEY, Mary	21	F	Servant	01Ma01Ja
LYLE, Sarah	18	F	Servant	01Ma01Ja
BOYD, Florence	21	F	Servant	01Ma01Ja
KEARNEY, Jane	21	F	Servant	01Ma01Ja
SWEENEY, George	20	M	Laborer	01Ma01Ja
WILSON, Robert	18	M	Laborer	01Ma01Ja
YOUNG, Catherine	19	F	Servant	01Ma01Ja
MCLOUGHLIN, William	50	M	Laborer	01Ma01Ja
Michael	30	M	Laborer	01Ma01Ja
MCNICOL, Daniel	24	M	Laborer	01Ma01Ja
Ellen	20	F	Unknown	01Ma01Ja
MCLOUGHLIN, Catherine	50	F	Unknown	01Ma01Ja
MCCOOL, Mary	19	F	Servant	01Ma01Ja
GAMBLE, Catherine	35	F	Servant	01Ma01Ja
STEWARD, Mary	19	F	Servant	01Ma01Ja
UNDERWOOD, Jane	40	F	Servant	01Ma01Ja
DOGHERTY, Daniel	20	M	Laborer	01Ma01Ja
Catherine	19	F	Servant	01Ma01Ja

NAMES OF PASSENGERS	AGE	SEX	OCCUPATIONS	DATE PORT SHIP
LAFFERTY, Margaret	25	F	Servant	01Ma01Ja
KENEDY, Mary	.00	F	Infant	01Ma01Ja
DOGHERTY, George	.00	M	Infant	01Ma01Ja
MCLAREN, John	40	M	Baker	01Ma01Ja
Belle	44	F	Wife	01Ma01Ja
John-Jr.	7	M	Child	01Ma01Ja
SMITH, Frances	21	F	Lady	01Ma01Ja
Margaret	28	F	Governess	01Ma01Ja

BROTHERS 02 MAY 1850

From Santo Domingo

NAMES OF PASSENGERS	AGE	SEX	OCCUPATIONS	DATE PORT SHIP
COSGROVE, Joseph	34	M	Carpenter	02Ma54Am

CAMBRIA 02 MAY 1850

From Liverpool

NAMES OF PASSENGERS	AGE	SEX	OCCUPATIONS	DATE PORT SHIP
DOHERTY, James	00	M	Unknown	02Ma02Hm
ARBUCKLE, John	39	M	Contractor	02Ma02Hm
Hugh	37	M	Contractor	02Ma02Hm
CULLMAN, Michl.	24	M	Student	02Ma02Hm
FITZGERALD, Anne	19	F	Unknown	02Ma02Hm
John	11	M	Unknown	02Ma02Hm
REID, Wm.	45	M	Merchant	02Ma02Hm
OBRIEN, Edward	55	M	Barrister	02Ma02Hm
Edward	18	M	None	02Ma02Hm
Richard	16	M	None	02Ma02Hm
Catherine	42	F	None	02Ma02Hm
Mary	20	F	None	02Ma02Hm
Catherine	19	F	None	02Ma02Hm
Elizabeth	14	F	None	02Ma02Hm
Ellinor	8	F	Child	02Ma02Hm

HARMONIA 04 MAY 1850

From Glasgow

NAMES OF PASSENGERS	AGE	SEX	OCCUPATIONS	DATE PORT SHIP
CAVENDUFF, James	35	M	Laborer	04Ma21Cq
MCKINNON, Hugh	48	M	Laborer	04Ma21Cq
U-Mrs.	48	F	Unknown	04Ma21Cq
Ellen	26	F	Unknown	04Ma21Cq
Owen	13	M	Unknown	04Ma21Cq
Patrick	10	M	Unknown	04Ma21Cq
James-Hart	.09	M	Infant	04Ma21Cq
MCMAVIN, Margaret	18	F	Unknown	04Ma21Cq
CAMPBELL, John	00	M	Unknown	04Ma21Cq
Wm.	00	M	Unknown	04Ma21Cq
TAYLOR, Mathew	00	M	Unknown	04Ma21Cq

CHINA 04 MAY 1850

From Liverpool

NAMES OF PASSENGERS	AGE	SEX	OCCUPATIONS	DATE PORT SHIP
HANLON, James	11	M	Unknown	04Ma02Hz
Patrick	9	M	Child	04Ma02Hz
Michael	4	M	Child	04Ma02Hz
MALONE, Rose	22	F	Servant	04Ma02Hz
BARRISE, Isaac	24	M	Farmer	04Ma02Hz
MADDEN, Patrick	25	M	Laborer	04Ma02Hz
WILIE, Wm.	25	M	Joiner	04Ma02Hz
COLEMAN, Patrick	23	M	Joiner	04Ma02Hz
John	20	M	Farmer	04Ma02Hz
BARRY, Michael	27	M	Farmer	04Ma02Hz
Mary	30	F	Matron	04Ma02Hz
Michael	8	M	Child	04Ma02Hz
John	6	M	Child	04Ma02Hz
Catherine	9	F	Child	04Ma02Hz
Ellen	3	F	Child	04Ma02Hz
MULLAD, Catherine	19	F	Dressmaker	04Ma02Hz
GILL, Margaret	45	F	Matron	04Ma02Hz
Mary	20	F	Servant	04Ma02Hz
Patrick	17	M	Laborer	04Ma02Hz
BLAND, Henry	40	M	Farmer	04Ma02Hz
Mary	50	F	Matron	04Ma02Hz
TROY, Mary	38	F	Matron	04Ma02Hz
CULLEN, Thomas	20	M	Tailor	04Ma02Hz
TROY, Patrick	20	M	Joiner	04Ma02Hz
REDMOND, Michael	24	M	Shoemaker	04Ma02Hz
HANLEY, Thomas	18	M	Blacksmith	04Ma02Hz
Mary	28	F	Spinster	04Ma02Hz
BACON, John	22	M	Laborer	04Ma02Hz
RIELY, Patrick	18	M	Laborer	04Ma02Hz
Hugh	23	M	Laborer	04Ma02Hz
TYNE, Wm.	34	M	Laborer	04Ma02Hz
TIENE, Mary	25	F	Servant	04Ma02Hz
Mary	2	F	Child	04Ma02Hz
MCGEE, Ann	18	F	Servant	04Ma02Hz
MCMAHON, Michael	26	M	Joiner	04Ma02Hz
MCVORN, Patrick	39	M	Farmer	04Ma02Hz
Bridget	18	F	Servant	04Ma02Hz
MCNEHORN, John	28	M	Farmer	04Ma02Hz
Betsey	30	F	Matron	04Ma02Hz
John	1	M	Child	04Ma02Hz
HALL, Elizabeth	30	F	Matron	04Ma02Hz
Maria	18	F	Dressmaker	04Ma02Hz
Joseph	5	M	Child	04Ma02Hz
CAMPBELL, Rose	50	F	Matron	04Ma02Hz
Patrick	17	M	Gentleman	04Ma02Hz
E.	16	F	Dressmaker	04Ma02Hz
MCCORMICK, Rose	13	F	Dressmaker	04Ma02Hz
Hugh	9	M	Child	04Ma02Hz
CLUSKY, Richard	35	M	Laborer	04Ma02Hz
COSSE, Joseph	40	M	Unknown	04Ma02Hz
BURKE, Patrick	36	M	Farmer	04Ma02Hz
MCDONALD, Edward	30	M	Farmer	04Ma02Hz
Johanna	30	F	Spinster	04Ma02Hz
Hannah	26	F	Dressmaker	04Ma02Hz
Ellen	16	F	Dressmaker	04Ma02Hz
David	15	M	Laborer	04Ma02Hz
Patrick	12	M	Unknown	04Ma02Hz
John	10	M	Unknown	04Ma02Hz
Joseph	8	M	Child	04Ma02Hz
Maria	6	F	Child	04Ma02Hz
Edward	5	M	Child	04Ma02Hz
James	3	M	Child	04Ma02Hz
BROTHERTON, Wm.	30	M	Draper	04Ma02Hz
Mary	25	F	Matron	04Ma02Hz
Charles	5	M	Child	04Ma02Hz

NAMES OF PASSENGERS	AGE	SEX	OCCUPATIONS	DATE PORT SHIP
BROTHERTON, Mary	.07	F	Infant	04Ma02Hz
TAYLOR, Wm.	22	M	Tailor	04Ma02Hz
HUTCHESON, John	30	M	Sawer	04Ma02Hz
FITZGERALD, David	29	M	Tailor	04Ma02Hz
Bridget	25	F	Matron	04Ma02Hz
Ellen	.07	F	Infant	04Ma02Hz
WHEELAN, John	40	M	Farmer	04Ma02Hz
Michael	26	M	Farmer	04Ma02Hz
Ann	22	F	Servant	04Ma02Hz
Mary	20	F	Servant	04Ma02Hz
SHERIDAN, Francis	18	M	Laborer	04Ma02Hz
COMBS, Mary	34	F	Matron	04Ma02Hz
Geo.	11	M	Unknown	04Ma02Hz
James	11	M	Unknown	04Ma02Hz
ENNIS, James	60	M	Farmer	04Ma02Hz
MULLIGAN, James	40	M	Farmer	04Ma02Hz
Mary	40	F	Matron	04Ma02Hz
James	23	M	Farmer	04Ma02Hz
Wm.	20	M	Farmer	04Ma02Hz
Sarah	18	F	Dressmaker	04Ma02Hz
John	16	M	Farmer	04Ma02Hz
Thomas	13	M	Farmer	04Ma02Hz
Joseph	11	M	Unknown	04Ma02Hz
Robert	9	M	Child	04Ma02Hz
Hugh	7	M	Child	04Ma02Hz
CREENA, Timothy	37	M	Laborer	04Ma02Hz
Mary	2	F	Child	04Ma02Hz
TYRELL, Alice	35	F	Spinster	04Ma02Hz
Thomas	15	M	Shoemaker	04Ma02Hz
Bridget	8	F	Child	04Ma02Hz
SWIFT, Mary	50	F	Matron	04Ma02Hz
Peter	10	M	Unknown	04Ma02Hz
MORRIS, Mary	22	F	Servant	04Ma02Hz
Catherine	26	F	Servant	04Ma02Hz
NEVIN, Michael	24	M	Laborer	04Ma02Hz
KELLY, James	18	M	Sawer	04Ma02Hz
CONWAY, Michael	30	M	Farmer	04Ma02Hz
TOOLE, Wm.	50	M	Tinker	04Ma02Hz
HOGANS, Ann	19	F	Servant	04Ma02Hz
MCINTYRE, Mary	24	F	Servant	04Ma02Hz
BOGAN, Thomas	30	M	Farmer	04Ma02Hz
QUEANE, James	19	M	Laborer	04Ma02Hz
TARNEY, John	20	M	Laborer	04Ma02Hz
MEYERS, Ellen	22	F	Servant	04Ma02Hz
TIERNEY, Mary	16	F	Servant	04Ma02Hz
LEAHY, Bridget	23	F	Dressmaker	04Ma02Hz
MEAGHER, James	26	M	Farmer	04Ma02Hz
SWEENY, Michael	28	M	Weaver	04Ma02Hz
Margt.	17	F	Servant	04Ma02Hz
HAYDEN, John	28	M	Cbtmkr	04Ma02Hz
MARTIN, Wm.	40	M	Joiner	04Ma02Hz
Mary	60	F	Matron	04Ma02Hz
Mary	7	F	Child	04Ma02Hz
KEENE, James	20	M	Laborer	04Ma02Hz
FERGAS, Catherine	18	F	Servant	04Ma02Hz
VINTER, Thomas	20	M	Weaver	04Ma02Hz
DESMOND, Martin	30	M	Tailor	04Ma02Hz
Nancy	50	F	Matron	04Ma02Hz
KAVANAGH, John	37	M	Farmer	04Ma02Hz
CONNOR, Dennis	60	M	Farmer	04Ma02Hz
Andrew	25	M	Farmer	04Ma02Hz
Patrick	20	M	Farmer	04Ma02Hz
Bridget	22	F	Servant	04Ma02Hz
Michael	19	M	Farmer	04Ma02Hz
Daniel	7	M	Child	04Ma02Hz
MEAGHER, Dennis	23	M	Sawer	04Ma02Hz
Michael	20	M	Sawer	04Ma02Hz
Bridget	16	F	Servant	04Ma02Hz
BUTLER, Edmund	36	M	Tailor	04Ma02Hz
KENNEDY, James	28	M	Shoemaker	04Ma02Hz
Mary	30	F	Matron	04Ma02Hz
DELANY, Jeremiah	24	M	Joiner	04Ma02Hz
James	26	M	Joiner	04Ma02Hz
RILEY, Timothy	27	M	Laborer	04Ma02Hz
BRYAN, James	32	M	Laborer	04Ma02Hz
CROLY, Ann	40	F	Matron	04Ma02Hz
MCLOUGHLON, Michael	18	M	Laborer	04Ma02Hz
HEANE, Patrick	22	M	Laborer	04Ma02Hz
LOUGHLAN, Thomas	19	F	Servant	04Ma02Hz
KELLY, Mary	19	F	Servant	04Ma02Hz
Margaret	18	F	Servant	04Ma02Hz
STANTON, Bridget	20	F	Dressmaker	04Ma02Hz
GALLAGHER, Nelly	30	F	Bomkr	04Ma02Hz
GAVIN, Nelly	37	F	Servant	04Ma02Hz
ENNIS, Joseph	45	M	Farmer	04Ma02Hz
DOYLE, Patrick	20	M	Laborer	04Ma02Hz
RYAN, Michael	28	M	Laborer	04Ma02Hz
Ellen	23	F	Servant	04Ma02Hz
Edward	16	M	Laborer	04Ma02Hz
Bridget	12	F	Unknown	04Ma02Hz
John	35	M	Farmer	04Ma02Hz
HAYES, Patrick	26	M	Farmer	04Ma02Hz
John	28	M	Farmer	04Ma02Hz
QUEALE, Daniel	30	M	Farmer	04Ma02Hz
BYRNE, Edward	56	M	Farmer	04Ma02Hz
John	30	M	Farmer	04Ma02Hz
ROACH, Thomas	25	M	Blacksmith	04Ma02Hz
FOX, Patrick	34	M	Sawer	04Ma02Hz
DADY, Richard	25	M	Laborer	04Ma02Hz
BEHAN, David	25	M	Laborer	04Ma02Hz
CONOLLY, Mary	22	F	Dressmaker	04Ma02Hz
LYNCH, Mary	50	F	Matron	04Ma02Hz
BOYLE, Catherine	15	F	Servant	04Ma02Hz
LACEY, Patrick	26	M	Laborer	04Ma02Hz
STEWART, John	17	M	Laborer	04Ma02Hz
FLOOD, Bridget	25	F	Servant	04Ma02Hz
Bridget	20	F	Servant	04Ma02Hz
CLARKE, Bridget	22	F	Servant	04Ma02Hz
CRONAN, John	35	M	Farmer	04Ma02Hz
Jermh.	9	M	Child	04Ma02Hz
John	30	M	Farmer	04Ma02Hz
Mary	25	F	Spinster	04Ma02Hz
Dennis	21	M	Farmer	04Ma02Hz
GOLDEN, Martin	25	M	Farmer	04Ma02Hz
Catherine	20	F	Dressmaker	04Ma02Hz
CUMMINGS, Edward	24	M	Farmer	04Ma02Hz
Andrew	12	M	Farmer	04Ma02Hz
CONNOR, Maurice	25	M	Farmer	04Ma02Hz
HANLY, Patrick	16	M	Farmer	04Ma02Hz
Mary	10	F	Unknown	04Ma02Hz
TILLEY, Mary	23	F	Lad	04Ma02Hz
MCCOY, Wm.	14	M	Farmer	04Ma02Hz
DEENAN, Bridget	22	F	Servant	04Ma02Hz
LYONS, Mary	19	F	Servant	04Ma02Hz
KEVIRNEY, Wm.	30	M	Farmer	04Ma02Hz
Mary	37	F	Matron	04Ma02Hz
HANLEY, Bridget	20	F	Servant	04Ma02Hz
CONNAL, Charles	40	M	Laborer	04Ma02Hz
GERARD, Philip	25	M	Laborer	04Ma02Hz
Honora	30	F	Matron	04Ma02Hz
Mary	.11	F	Infant	04Ma02Hz
John	3	M	Child	04Ma02Hz
KINNEY, John	28	M	Laborer	04Ma02Hz
HICKEY, Anthony	28	M	Unknown	04Ma02Hz
CARTHY, Michael	26	M	Laborer	04Ma02Hz
Margaret	26	F	Matron	04Ma02Hz
Catherine	12	F	Unknown	04Ma02Hz
Johanna	.02	F	Infant	04Ma02Hz
NIER, James	30	M	Laborer	04Ma02Hz
Judith	21	F	Matron	04Ma02Hz
DONELLY, Patrick	19	M	Laborer	04Ma02Hz
TIERNEY, John	16	M	Laborer	04Ma02Hz
CONNOR, Edward	21	M	Farmer	04Ma02Hz
THOMSON, Wm.	24	M	Farmer	04Ma02Hz
DINNY, Michael	25	M	Sawer	04Ma02Hz
CARROLL, John	24	M	Sawer	04Ma02Hz
MARA, Elizia	26	F	Servant	04Ma02Hz
REARDON, Catherine	30	F	Matron	04Ma02Hz
Roger	6	M	Child	04Ma02Hz
James	4	M	Child	04Ma02Hz

NAMES OF PASSENGERS	AGE	SEX	OCCUPATIONS	DATE PORT SHIP
REARDON, John	2	M	Child	04Ma02Hz
HANLON, Michael	50	M	Farmer	04Ma02Hz
Honora	40	F	Matron	04Ma02Hz
John	19	M	Farmer	04Ma02Hz
Michael	15	M	Farmer	04Ma02Hz
Nicholas	13	M	Farmer	04Ma02Hz
DUGGAN, Patrick	22	M	Shoemaker	04Ma02Hz
FOX, Patrick	42	M	Tailor	04Ma02Hz
Anna	38	F	Matron	04Ma02Hz
Thomas	15	M	Tailor	04Ma02Hz
Mary	10	F	Unknown	04Ma02Hz
Catherine	8	F	Child	04Ma02Hz
Ann	3	F	Child	04Ma02Hz
HANLEY, Mary	40	F	Matron	04Ma02Hz
MORGAN, Julia	20	F	Dressmaker	04Ma02Hz
BURCHILL, Margaret	25	F	Dressmaker	04Ma02Hz
COLLINS, Thomas	12	M	Unknown	04Ma02Hz

NESTORIAN 04 MAY 1850

From Liverpool

NAMES OF PASSENGERS	AGE	SEX	OCCUPATIONS	DATE PORT SHIP
WILSON, Cathe.	13	F	Weaver	04Ma02Iz
Jane	2	F	Child	04Ma02Iz
TOBIN, James	27	M	Laborer	04Ma02Iz
MCKELSY, Charles	25	M	Shoemaker	04Ma02Iz
CATING, Michael	28	M	Laborer	04Ma02Iz
BAILEY, Peter	26	M	Laborer	04Ma02Iz
PECKER, Thomas	23	M	Miner	04Ma02Iz
DALTON, Richd.	28	M	Laborer	04Ma02Iz
Bridget	28	F	Laborer	04Ma02Iz
CONNORS, Stephen	24	M	Shepherd	04Ma02Iz
GOAGHAN, Patrick	24	M	Shepherd	04Ma02Iz
ATKINSON, Jacob	21	M	Laborer	04Ma02Iz
FIERNEY, John	28	M	Goldsmith	04Ma02Iz
GARRY, George	26	M	Paper Maker	04Ma02Iz
BROADGALE, Saml.	28	M	Stone Mason	04Ma02Iz
Margt.	28	F	Unknown	04Ma02Iz
Mary-Ann	6	F	Child	04Ma02Iz
COLLINS, Patrick	21	M	Laborer	04Ma02Iz
POWER, Walter	24	M	Laborer	04Ma02Iz
FLYNN, John	21	M	Laborer	04Ma02Iz
WALSH, Willm.	24	M	Laborer	04Ma02Iz
FEEHAN, Edwd.	25	M	Laborer	04Ma02Iz
CONDON, Lawrence	26	M	Gdnr	04Ma02Iz
LYONS, Dennis	27	M	Tinker	04Ma02Iz
BROWNE, Philip	25	M	Silversmith	04Ma02Iz
KEEFE, John	23	M	Laborer	04Ma02Iz
BREWITT, Biddy	20	F	Servant	04Ma02Iz
SWEENEY, Ellen	24	F	Servant	04Ma02Iz
FARRELL, Ellen	20	F	Servant	04Ma02Iz
DONOHUE, Edwd.	21	M	Joiner	04Ma02Iz
WALLACE, Willm.	30	M	Farmer	04Ma02Iz
FLYNN, John	27	M	Farmer	04Ma02Iz
ODONNELL, Michl.	20	M	Farmer	04Ma02Iz
Margt.	20	F	Farmer	04Ma02Iz
REILY, Philip	30	M	Servant	04Ma02Iz
HENNESSY, Ellen	22	F	Servant	04Ma02Iz
MCCABE, Philip	17	M	Servant	04Ma02Iz
KEELY, Mary	20	F	Servant	04Ma02Iz
ELLISON, Hugh	37	M	Laborer	04Ma02Iz
Jane	28	F	Laborer	04Ma02Iz
BRADLEY, Thomas	40	M	Laborer	04Ma02Iz
Ann	40	F	Laborer	04Ma02Iz
Patrick	10	M	Laborer	04Ma02Iz
Michael	8	M	Child	04Ma02Iz
MAHAR, Thomas	21	M	Laborer	04Ma02Iz
CUNNINGHAM, Simon	18	M	Laborer	04Ma02Iz
Mary	16	F	Unknown	04Ma02Iz

NAMES OF PASSENGERS	AGE	SEX	OCCUPATIONS	DATE PORT SHIP
MCNAMARA, Martin	20	M	Laborer	04Ma02Iz
AKIN, Elisa	25	F	Laborer	04Ma02Iz
Mary	23	F	Laborer	04Ma02Iz
SMITH, Jane	28	F	Servant	04Ma02Iz
RIAL, Michael	30	M	Laborer	04Ma02Iz
HYNES, Michael	25	M	Laborer	04Ma02Iz
DUNN, Mary	20	F	Laborer	04Ma02Iz
HESDMAN, Dolly	20	F	Laborer	04Ma02Iz
BRENNIN, John	25	M	Laborer	04Ma02Iz
Cathe.	18	F	Unknown	04Ma02Iz
COSTALEN, Thoms.	24	M	Laborer	04Ma02Iz
DONOVAN, John	40	M	Farmer	04Ma02Iz
Alice	32	F	Farmer	04Ma02Iz
Mary-Crook	12	F	Farmer	04Ma02Iz
Timothy	7	M	Child	04Ma02Iz
James	.00	M	Infant	04Ma02Iz
MCMANNETS, Rodolphus	20	M	Farmer	04Ma02Iz
Catherine	18	F	Farmer	04Ma02Iz
MCCUTTY, Francis	14	M	Farmer	04Ma02Iz
TAYLOR, Jane	16	F	Servant	04Ma02Iz
CASSEDY, Bridget	25	F	Servant	04Ma02Iz
Ann	10	F	Unknown	04Ma02Iz
COX, Mary	17	F	Unknown	04Ma02Iz
SMITH, Kevin	20	M	Watchmaker	04Ma02Iz
THRUSTON, Nathan	20	M	Laborer	04Ma02Iz
MONK, John	24	M	Laborer	04Ma02Iz
Cathe.	55	F	Unknown	04Ma02Iz
James	15	M	Unknown	04Ma02Iz
SPRATT, John	26	M	Laborer	04Ma02Iz
LENO, John	25	M	Laborer	04Ma02Iz
SHERRY, Christe.	35	M	Unknown	04Ma02Iz
SHEERLOCK, Philip	23	M	Unknown	04Ma02Iz
MCCARTNEY, James	21	M	Laborer	04Ma02Iz
Johanna	19	F	Servant	04Ma02Iz
FLEMMING, Patrick	24	M	Laborer	04Ma02Iz
CUNNINGHAM, Magt.	25	F	Servant	04Ma02Iz
HIERLY, Cathe.	24	F	Servant	04Ma02Iz
Willm.	19	M	Servant	04Ma02Iz
LUNDY, James	19	M	Servant	04Ma02Iz
MORRIS, Eliza	23	F	Servant	04Ma02Iz
HENNIGAN, Patrick	34	M	Farmer	04Ma02Iz
James	3	M	Child	04Ma02Iz
Bridget	2	F	Child	04Ma02Iz
Ellen	27	F	Farmer	04Ma02Iz
KELLEY, Magt.	60	F	Farmer	04Ma02Iz
John	23	M	Farmer	04Ma02Iz
Willm.	20	M	Farmer	04Ma02Iz
Margt.	22	F	Farmer	04Ma02Iz
Mary	20	F	Farmer	04Ma02Iz
James	12	M	Farmer	04Ma02Iz
Ellen	23	F	Farmer	04Ma02Iz
Toney	35	F	Farmer	04Ma02Iz
Winnefred	30	F	Farmer	04Ma02Iz
James	38	M	Farmer	04Ma02Iz
Biddy	4	F	Child	04Ma02Iz
Cathe.	3	F	Child	04Ma02Iz
Jeremh.	.00	M	Infant	04Ma02Iz
MADDIN, Thomas	33	M	Farmer	04Ma02Iz
Judith	25	F	Farmer	04Ma02Iz
RUSSELL, Richd.	24	M	Farmer	04Ma02Iz
WILSON, Margt.	40	F	Farmer	04Ma02Iz
Jane	12	F	Farmer	04Ma02Iz
James	7	M	Child	04Ma02Iz
Maria	5	F	Child	04Ma02Iz
RAMSEY, Willm.	20	M	Weaver	04Ma02Iz
GAYLEY, Willm.	20	M	Weaver	04Ma02Iz
WILSON, Robt.	30	M	Weaver	04Ma02Iz
Magt.	30	F	Weaver	04Ma02Iz
HOGG, Moses	40	M	Farmer	04Ma02Iz
Rose	45	F	Farmer	04Ma02Iz
William	19	M	Farmer	04Ma02Iz
Mary	12	F	Farmer	04Ma02Iz
David	7	M	Child	04Ma02Iz
JOHNSON, John	19	M	Farmer	04Ma02Iz
LYNN, Robert	31	M	Farmer	04Ma02Iz

NAMES OF PASSENGERS	AGE	SEX	OCCUPATIONS	DATE PORT SHIP
MCLAUGHLIN, Daniel	40	M	Farmer	04Ma02Iz
Mary	40	F	Farmer	04Ma02Iz
PINKERTON, John	16	M	Farmer	04Ma02Iz
SMITH, Ann	20	F	Farmer	04Ma02Iz
WELCH, James	30	M	Farmer	04Ma02Iz
COWEN, Sarah	35	F	Spinster	04Ma02Iz
FARRELL, James	30	M	Farmer	04Ma02Iz
BYRNE, John	35	M	Farmer	04Ma02Iz
FISHER, George	19	M	Farmer	04Ma02Iz
WALKER, Daniel	19	M	Farmer	04Ma02Iz
MURRAY, Celia	30	F	Servant	04Ma02Iz
COSGROVE, Sarah	30	F	Fsvnt	04Ma02Iz
Anna	8	F	Child	04Ma02Iz
Charles	7	M	Child	04Ma02Iz
Henry	.00	M	Infant	04Ma02Iz
COOPER, James	18	M	Laborer	04Ma02Iz
YOUNG, William	21	M	Laborer	04Ma02Iz
MCFALE, Felix	20	M	Laborer	04Ma02Iz
CASSADY, Mary	20	F	Servant	04Ma02Iz
ELLIOTT, Thomas	22	M	Farmer	04Ma02Iz
John	23	M	Farmer	04Ma02Iz
Alexander	22	M	Farmer	04Ma02Iz
JOHNSON, Helen	18	F	Servant	04Ma02Iz
RUDDY, John	43	M	Laborer	04Ma02Iz
Bridget	30	F	Unknown	04Ma02Iz
DUFFY, James	50	M	Farmer	04Ma02Iz
Catherine	30	F	Farmer	04Ma02Iz
Christopher	13	M	Farmer	04Ma02Iz
Ann	9	F	Child	04Ma02Iz
Catherine	6	F	Child	04Ma02Iz
James	5	M	Child	04Ma02Iz
Patrick	.00	M	Infant	04Ma02Iz
MCLAUGHLIN, Ann	26	F	Servant	04Ma02Iz
MOLANY, Thomas	22	M	Laborer	04Ma02Iz
Bridget	20	F	Servant	04Ma02Iz
NAUGHTON, John	22	M	Servant	04Ma02Iz
DOWLING, William	21	M	Farmer	04Ma02Iz
Michael	18	M	Farmer	04Ma02Iz
Mary	50	F	Farmer	04Ma02Iz
Peter	11	M	Farmer	04Ma02Iz
Alice	13	F	Farmer	04Ma02Iz
MCKOWN, John	16	M	Laborer	04Ma02Iz
MCMAHON, Michael	23	M	Laborer	04Ma02Iz
KELLY, Thomas	30	M	Farmer	04Ma02Iz
James	23	M	Farmer	04Ma02Iz
Honora	20	F	Farmer	04Ma02Iz
Margaret	18	F	Farmer	04Ma02Iz
Mary	17	F	Farmer	04Ma02Iz
John	23	M	Farmer	04Ma02Iz
BYRNE, Lawrence	23	M	Laborer	04Ma02Iz
TOOLE, John	21	M	Laborer	04Ma02Iz
Patrick	20	M	Unknown	04Ma02Iz
CABANEGH, Catherine	24	F	Servant	04Ma02Iz
KINSLEY, Hugh	58	M	Farmer	04Ma02Iz
Mary-Ann	16	F	Farmer	04Ma02Iz
Elisa	14	F	Farmer	04Ma02Iz
Hugh	6	M	Child	04Ma02Iz
KELLY, John	40	M	Farmer	04Ma02Iz
DOYLE, Mary	25	F	Farmer	04Ma02Iz
KEEFE, Elisa	28	F	Farmer	04Ma02Iz
Peggy	26	F	Farmer	04Ma02Iz
KINSLEY, James	12	M	Farmer	04Ma02Iz
DOYLE, Patrick	35	M	Farmer	04Ma02Iz
FURLONG, Johanna	30	F	Farmer	04Ma02Iz
FITZGERALD, Walter	47	M	Laborer	04Ma02Iz
Anty	37	F	Unknown	04Ma02Iz
CAVANAGH, Michael	24	M	Farmer	04Ma02Iz
REDMOND, John	21	M	Farmer	04Ma02Iz
MOYANHAN, Cornelius	26	M	Laborer	04Ma02Iz
Nancy	30	F	Laborer	04Ma02Iz
Michael	.00	M	Infant	04Ma02Iz
MCHENRY, William	36	M	Laborer	04Ma02Iz
DESMOND, Mary	25	F	Servant	04Ma02Iz
KENNEDY, Mary	40	F	Servant	04Ma02Iz
Margaret	.00	F	Infant	04Ma02Iz

NAMES OF PASSENGERS	AGE	SEX	OCCUPATIONS	DATE PORT SHIP
KENNEDY, Mary	25	F	Servant	04Ma02Iz
BOHAN, Thomas	16	M	Laborer	04Ma02Iz
CONNER, James	16	M	Servant	04Ma02Iz
Bridget	13	F	Servant	04Ma02Iz
GLYNN, Patrick	25	M	Servant	04Ma02Iz
MCNULT, Joseph	26	M	Servant	04Ma02Iz
MITCHELL, Jane	30	F	Servant	04Ma02Iz
HAMMELL, Patrick	26	M	Servant	04Ma02Iz
DERFF, Margaret	21	F	Servant	04Ma02Iz
ROCHE, Thomas	25	M	Laborer	04Ma02Iz
KEATON, Patrick	22	M	Laborer	04Ma02Iz
FOLEY, James	30	M	Laborer	04Ma02Iz
MOORE, Darby	30	M	Laborer	04Ma02Iz
REYNOLDS, Charles	31	M	Laborer	04Ma02Iz
CANNON, Margaret	30	F	Servant	04Ma02Iz
FOSTER, John	50	M	Agrc	04Ma02Iz
Susannah	50	F	Unknown	04Ma02Iz
Jane	28	F	Unknown	04Ma02Iz
Sarah	26	F	Unknown	04Ma02Iz
Alexander	24	M	Unknown	04Ma02Iz
Eliza	22	F	Unknown	04Ma02Iz
Susan	20	F	Unknown	04Ma02Iz
Mary	18	F	Unknown	04Ma02Iz
Nancy	16	F	Unknown	04Ma02Iz
Matilda	14	F	Unknown	04Ma02Iz
Robert	11	M	Unknown	04Ma02Iz
William	9	M	Child	04Ma02Iz
MACKEY, Hamilton	25	M	Shoemaker	04Ma02Iz
REA, Thomas	27	M	Farmer	04Ma02Iz
Margaret	26	F	Farmer	04Ma02Iz
Jane	5	F	Child	04Ma02Iz
Ann	3	F	Child	04Ma02Iz
Elisa	3	F	Child	04Ma02Iz
John	.00	M	Infant	04Ma02Iz

CITY-OF-GLASGOW 04 MAY 1850

From Glasgow

NAMES OF PASSENGERS	AGE	SEX	OCCUPATIONS	DATE PORT SHIP
BROOMER, E.Mrs.	20	F	Lady	04Ma21Gm
ARMSTRONG, U-Mrs.	31	F	Lady	04Ma21Gm
U	7	U	Child	04Ma21Gm
U	5	U	Child	04Ma21Gm
HARPER, James	27	M	Minister	04Ma21Gm
CUNE, James	50	M	Farmer	04Ma21Gm
U-Mrs.	30	F	Lady	04Ma21Gm
U	5	U	Child	04Ma21Gm
U	4	U	Child	04Ma21Gm
U	2	U	Child	04Ma21Gm
MCCONN, David	35	M	Clerk	04Ma21Gm
MARTIN, George	32	M	Merchant	04Ma21Gm
BILLHOUSE, U	28	M	Merchant	04Ma21Gm
DARTING, David	24	M	Merchant	04Ma21Gm
MCCOLL, John	22	M	Merchant	04Ma21Gm
COLLEY, George	35	M	Merchant	04Ma21Gm
HATTON, J.G.	21	M	Merchant	04Ma21Gm
U-Mrs.	21	F	Lady	04Ma21Gm
MANN, Alex.	28	M	Merchant	04Ma21Gm
Patrick	21	M	Merchant	04Ma21Gm
TERNE, Adam	74	M	Gentleman	04Ma21Gm
SMITH, David	33	M	Merchant	04Ma21Gm
MORGAN, James	46	M	Merchant	04Ma21Gm
GUNSHIELD, W.G.	30	M	Merchant	04Ma21Gm
KERR, Thos.	24	M	Merchant	04Ma21Gm
SHANKS, Andrew	18	M	Engineer	04Ma21Gm
MORELAND, M.	40	M	Merchant	04Ma21Gm
GLASGOW, J.G.	40	M	Merchant	04Ma21Gm
ELWELL, U	19	M	Merchant	04Ma21Gm
CARMICHELL, J.H.	22	M	Merchant	04Ma21Gm

NAMES OF PASSENGERS	AGE	SEX	OCCUPATIONS	DATE PORT SHIP
HERON, U	32	M	Merchant	04Ma21Gm
DERNCOMBE, U-Dr.	32	M	Merchant	04Ma21Gm
BROWN, Richd.	34	M	Merchant	04Ma21Gm
GRENSHIELD, Thos.	33	M	Merchant	04Ma21Gm
BROWN, U-Mrs.	27	F	Lady	04Ma21Gm
U	.00	U	Infant	04Ma21Gm
U	4	U	Child	04Ma21Gm
U	2	U	Child	04Ma21Gm
DONALD, U-Mrs.	53	F	Lady	04Ma21Gm
BUSH, U-Mrs.	25	F	Lady	04Ma21Gm
ARMSTRONG, James	32	M	Laborer	04Ma21Gm
U-Mrs.	32	F	Lady	04Ma21Gm
U	10	U	Child	04Ma21Gm
U	8	U	Child	04Ma21Gm
U	4	U	Child	04Ma21Gm
U	2	U	Child	04Ma21Gm
MOWATT, Jane	19	F	Unknown	04Ma21Gm
BUNE, U-Mrs.	30	F	Lady	04Ma21Gm
MAIN, Manor	20	F	Lady	04Ma21Gm
PETERS, J.W.	31	M	Farmer	04Ma21Gm
HOWARD, John	26	M	Clerk	04Ma21Gm
MCNUTTE, James	35	M	Laborer	04Ma21Gm
MCFARLANE, Duncan	21	M	Clerk	04Ma21Gm
MURDOCK, U	38	M	Machinist	04Ma21Gm
RUTHWELL, U	45	M	Chemist	04Ma21Gm
LAWSON, Andrew	45	M	Laborer	04Ma21Gm
BURNE, William	31	M	Merchant	04Ma21Gm
DAMOCHE, Edward	46	M	Clergyman	04Ma21Gm
CARNS, William	32	M	Founder	04Ma21Gm
MCANNELL, John	23	M	Farmer	04Ma21Gm
GODDES, Alex	49	M	Farmer	04Ma21Gm
PARRY, Robt.	42	M	Baker	04Ma21Gm
WILSON, Saml.	30	M	Doctor	04Ma21Gm
CUST, Owen	29	M	Mariner	04Ma21Gm
WRIGHT, J.E.	38	M	Clerk	04Ma21Gm
Edward	16	M	Clerk	04Ma21Gm
ROACH, M.	22	M	Laborer	04Ma21Gm
QURSTON, M.M.	14	M	Laborer	04Ma21Gm
RILLACH, John-R.	20	M	Unknown	04Ma21Gm
SINCLAIR, George	20	M	Merchant	04Ma21Gm
SLINTHEN, Robert	36	M	Lawyer	04Ma21Gm
CLADNECH, U	36	M	Agent	04Ma21Gm
FORSYTH, James	32	M	Merchant	04Ma21Gm
CUCHTON, William	64	M	Planter	04Ma21Gm
MCCREDIE, Thos.	32	M	Surgeon	04Ma21Gm
LESTER, James	27	M	Agent	04Ma21Gm
WATERS, Thomas	29	M	Steward	04Ma21Gm
MAXWELL, U	21	M	Steward	04Ma21Gm
HILL, John	18	M	Steward	04Ma21Gm
HENDISON, U-Mrs.	30	F	Lady	04Ma21Gm
U	11	U	Unknown	04Ma21Gm
U	7	U	Child	04Ma21Gm
U	5	U	Child	04Ma21Gm
U	3	U	Child	04Ma21Gm
CHADWICK, U	25	F	Lady	04Ma21Gm
WRIGHT, U-Mrs.	26	F	Lady	04Ma21Gm
Eliza-Jane	11	F	Lady	04Ma21Gm
William-H.	8	M	Child	04Ma21Gm
Fanny	5	F	Child	04Ma21Gm
Henry	3	M	Child	04Ma21Gm
LESTER, U-Mrs.	25	F	Lady	04Ma21Gm
BROWN, U-Mrs.	20	F	Lady	04Ma21Gm
ROBB, U-Miss	25	F	Lady	04Ma21Gm
CRUCKSHANK, U-Miss	21	F	Lady	04Ma21Gm
FINAY, N.	25	U	None	04Ma21Gm
U	19	U	None	04Ma21Gm
BROWN, W.S.	29	U	Chemist	04Ma21Gm
FARLAND, U	47	M	Merchant	04Ma21Gm
COOK, Thomas	40	M	Farmer	04Ma21Gm
LANDELLON, James	31	M	Merchant	04Ma21Gm
HOWARD, Fanny	13	F	Servant	04Ma21Gm

JAMES-FAGAN 06 MAY 1850

From Dublin

NAMES OF PASSENGERS	AGE	SEX	OCCUPATIONS	DATE PORT SHIP
MOLLOY, Sally	20	F	Laborer	06Ma05Hy
Mary	19	F	Unknown	06Ma05Hy
MCGANG, Jane	30	F	Unknown	06Ma05Hy
RUPELL, U-Mr.	24	M	Unknown	06Ma05Hy
MCEVOY, James	22	M	Unknown	06Ma05Hy
CONNOR, Jay	25	M	Unknown	06Ma05Hy
LUDDOW, Wm.	45	M	Unknown	06Ma05Hy
Isabella	40	F	Unknown	06Ma05Hy
John	16	M	Unknown	06Ma05Hy
George	13	M	Unknown	06Ma05Hy
JONES, James	35	M	Unknown	06Ma05Hy
E.Mrs.	30	F	Unknown	06Ma05Hy
Charles	11	M	Unknown	06Ma05Hy
Ada	10	F	Unknown	06Ma05Hy
Ferdwall	8	M	Child	06Ma05Hy
Wm.	6	M	Child	06Ma05Hy
Isaac	4	M	Child	06Ma05Hy
Jesse	.00	M	Infant	06Ma05Hy
DAVIS, James	24	M	Unknown	06Ma05Hy
Mary-Ann	22	F	Unknown	06Ma05Hy
Mary	.00	F	Infant	06Ma05Hy
LAWLESS, James	20	M	Unknown	06Ma05Hy
U-Mrs.	24	F	Unknown	06Ma05Hy
JONES, Eliza	22	F	Unknown	06Ma05Hy
KEEGAN, Patt	20	M	Unknown	06Ma05Hy
Margaret	24	F	Unknown	06Ma05Hy
SWENY, U-Mr.	22	M	Unknown	06Ma05Hy
HARDING, Thos.	20	M	Unknown	06Ma05Hy
WARD, Cath.	20	F	Unknown	06Ma05Hy
Patt	24	M	Unknown	06Ma05Hy
Bridget	21	F	Unknown	06Ma05Hy
John	19	M	Unknown	06Ma05Hy
FOBER, Marg.	15	F	Unknown	06Ma05Hy
ELLIOTT, Alice	20	F	Unknown	06Ma05Hy
DUNN, Margaret	20	F	Unknown	06Ma05Hy
BRENNAN, U-Mr.	30	M	Unknown	06Ma05Hy
U-Mr.	40	M	Unknown	06Ma05Hy
Cath.	15	F	Unknown	06Ma05Hy
John	12	M	Unknown	06Ma05Hy
CARROLL, Wm.	40	M	Unknown	06Ma05Hy
Thomas	19	M	Unknown	06Ma05Hy
Mary	20	F	Unknown	06Ma05Hy
Bridget	.00	F	Infant	06Ma05Hy
Margaret	16	F	Unknown	06Ma05Hy
Catherine	4	F	Child	06Ma05Hy
DOYLE, Betty	25	F	Unknown	06Ma05Hy
JORDAN, Patt	24	M	Unknown	06Ma05Hy
GEMARN, James	28	M	Unknown	06Ma05Hy
Mary	26	F	Unknown	06Ma05Hy
Ellen	18	F	Unknown	06Ma05Hy
Margaret	16	F	Unknown	06Ma05Hy
Joseph	.00	M	Infant	06Ma05Hy
SEXTON, Sal.	28	F	Unknown	06Ma05Hy
CALLEN, Eliza	30	F	Unknown	06Ma05Hy
MURPHY, Edward	25	M	Unknown	06Ma05Hy
LYONS, John	30	M	Unknown	06Ma05Hy
FARRELL, Edward	25	M	Unknown	06Ma05Hy
TRACY, Ann	20	F	Unknown	06Ma05Hy
DEWDAN, Ann	20	F	Unknown	06Ma05Hy
DOOLEY, Eliza	20	F	Unknown	06Ma05Hy
CARPENTER, Jane	30	F	Unknown	06Ma05Hy
Michael	20	M	Unknown	06Ma05Hy
CARPUALED, Day.	30	M	Unknown	06Ma05Hy
Margaret	.00	F	Infant	06Ma05Hy
ACHISON, Joseph	4	M	Child	06Ma05Hy

NAMES OF PASSENGERS	AGE	SEX	OCCUPATIONS	DATE PORT SHIP
ACHISON, Mary	3	F	Child	06Ma05Hy
Mary	30	F	Unknown	06Ma05Hy
Joseph	28	M	Unknown	06Ma05Hy
FANNECAN, James	20	M	Unknown	06Ma05Hy
SMITH, Eliza	20	F	Unknown	06Ma05Hy
MULLIGAN, Robert	28	M	Unknown	06Ma05Hy
SPARKS, U-Mr.	40	M	Unknown	06Ma05Hy
CONOLLEY, Mary	20	F	Unknown	06Ma05Hy
CLARKE, Jane	40	F	Unknown	06Ma05Hy
BOCBELL, Mary	18	F	Unknown	06Ma05Hy
REDMUND, Bryan	22	M	Unknown	06Ma05Hy
ROTH, John	35	M	Unknown	06Ma05Hy
HADEN, Miles	21	M	Unknown	06Ma05Hy
SHETE, Edward	20	M	Unknown	06Ma05Hy
WHITE, Wm.	24	M	Unknown	06Ma05Hy
DANE, George	30	M	Unknown	06Ma05Hy
GAHAN, John	30	M	Unknown	06Ma05Hy
MCGUIRE, Joseph	30	M	Unknown	06Ma05Hy
Sarah	30	F	Unknown	06Ma05Hy
John	2	M	Child	06Ma05Hy
Margaret	.00	F	Infant	06Ma05Hy
HYLAN, Rosanna	20	F	Unknown	06Ma05Hy
MORAN, Peter	22	M	Unknown	06Ma05Hy
Mary	40	F	Unknown	06Ma05Hy
Ellen	18	F	Unknown	06Ma05Hy
Mary	.00	F	Infant	06Ma05Hy
Michael	4	M	Child	06Ma05Hy
SMITH, Thomas	20	M	Unknown	06Ma05Hy
DEVAS, Allen	16	M	Unknown	06Ma05Hy
BYRNE, May--	22	M	Unknown	06Ma05Hy
DOYLE, Denis	24	M	Unknown	06Ma05Hy
JORDAN, Mary	20	F	Unknown	06Ma05Hy
NOLAN, John	24	M	Unknown	06Ma05Hy
MULDOWNY, Johanna	20	F	Unknown	06Ma05Hy
LEARY, Mose	22	M	Unknown	06Ma05Hy
HANDRULL, Miles	30	M	Unknown	06Ma05Hy
CARLAN, Wm.	30	M	Unknown	06Ma05Hy
MCEVOY, U-Mr.	21	M	Unknown	06Ma05Hy
BULGER, Thomas	22	M	Unknown	06Ma05Hy
CORLEN, Betty	21	M	Unknown	06Ma05Hy
KEVANAUGH, Margaret	19	F	Unknown	06Ma05Hy
THOMPSON, John	20	M	Unknown	06Ma05Hy
CRONLEY, John	20	M	Unknown	06Ma05Hy
FILITCHE, Thomas	17	M	Unknown	06Ma05Hy
Margaret	16	F	Unknown	06Ma05Hy
Eliza	16	F	Unknown	06Ma05Hy
Hamick	.00	M	Infant	06Ma05Hy
SEALES, U-Mr.	25	M	Unknown	06Ma05Hy
U-Miss	20	F	Unknown	06Ma05Hy
TELLY, Pat	15	M	Unknown	06Ma05Hy
RUNSHAW, U-Mr.	30	M	Unknown	06Ma05Hy
NOLAN, Esther	17	F	Unknown	06Ma05Hy
Mary	15	F	Unknown	06Ma05Hy
Cath.	14	F	Unknown	06Ma05Hy
GORMAN, U-Mr.	25	M	Unknown	06Ma05Hy
FLENN, Thomas	30	M	Unknown	06Ma05Hy
BAYNALL, Jas.	25	M	Unknown	06Ma05Hy
Thomas	13	M	Unknown	06Ma05Hy
RORKE, Jane	28	F	Unknown	06Ma05Hy
Mary	26	F	Unknown	06Ma05Hy
Betty	.00	F	Infant	06Ma05Hy
MAHAN, Ellen	20	F	Unknown	06Ma05Hy
RYAN, Charles	22	M	Unknown	06Ma05Hy
Ellen	20	F	Unknown	06Ma05Hy
KENNAY, Jarlen	27	M	Unknown	06Ma05Hy
DYLAN, Jas.	20	M	Unknown	06Ma05Hy
NEALY, Cath.	20	F	Unknown	06Ma05Hy
MCDERMOTT, Wm.	30	M	Unknown	06Ma05Hy
Mary	27	F	Unknown	06Ma05Hy
CARTELL, Ann	30	F	Unknown	06Ma05Hy
Nichol.	6	M	Child	06Ma05Hy
Wm.	4	M	Child	06Ma05Hy
John	.00	M	Infant	06Ma05Hy
HARLAN, Robert	20	M	Unknown	06Ma05Hy
SHENLAN, James	20	M	Unknown	06Ma05Hy
COLLEN, Edward	20	M	Unknown	06Ma05Hy
LYONS, Jas.	27	M	Unknown	06Ma05Hy
U-Mr.	24	M	Unknown	06Ma05Hy
BURK, John	30	M	Unknown	06Ma05Hy
Ann	35	F	Unknown	06Ma05Hy
Elly	10	F	Unknown	06Ma05Hy
Mary-Ann	8	F	Child	06Ma05Hy
Robert	4	M	Child	06Ma05Hy
Joseph	.00	M	Infant	06Ma05Hy
CRIMAN, Margaret	30	F	Unknown	06Ma05Hy
Cathn.	11	F	Unknown	06Ma05Hy
WALAN, James	43	M	Unknown	06Ma05Hy
Cath.	40	F	Unknown	06Ma05Hy
Mary	17	F	Unknown	06Ma05Hy
John	15	M	Unknown	06Ma05Hy
James	13	M	Unknown	06Ma05Hy
Cart.	11	F	Unknown	06Ma05Hy
Wm.	9	M	Child	06Ma05Hy
Edward	7	M	Child	06Ma05Hy
Steph.	19	M	Unknown	06Ma05Hy
Thomas	.00	M	Infant	06Ma05Hy
BUCKLY, U-Miss	20	F	Unknown	06Ma05Hy
CONNOLLY, Ann	20	F	Unknown	06Ma05Hy
Edward	30	M	Unknown	06Ma05Hy
WILEY, U-Miss	20	F	Unknown	06Ma05Hy
MCGRATH, P.	26	M	Unknown	06Ma05Hy
U-Mr.	20	M	Unknown	06Ma05Hy
CATHBUT, Joseph	30	M	Unknown	06Ma05Hy
FLETCHER, Wm.	22	M	Unknown	06Ma05Hy
CATHBUT, Jane	20	F	Unknown	06Ma05Hy
RYAN, Margaret	22	F	Unknown	06Ma05Hy
Mary	21	F	Unknown	06Ma05Hy
Johanna	12	F	Unknown	06Ma05Hy
Johan	.00	M	Infant	06Ma05Hy
Bridget	17	F	Unknown	06Ma05Hy
Pat	28	M	Unknown	06Ma05Hy
Miles	23	M	Unknown	06Ma05Hy
Michael	25	M	Unknown	06Ma05Hy
John	16	M	Unknown	06Ma05Hy
QUINNLAND, John	30	M	Unknown	06Ma05Hy
DRUMS, John	21	M	Unknown	06Ma05Hy
CADE, Patt	22	M	Unknown	06Ma05Hy
KANE, Susan	21	F	Unknown	06Ma05Hy
Bridget	20	F	Unknown	06Ma05Hy
Margr.	18	F	Unknown	06Ma05Hy
LANNING, Ellen	24	F	Unknown	06Ma05Hy
COUGHLAN, Bridget	20	F	Unknown	06Ma05Hy
MARTIN, Bridg.	20	F	Unknown	06Ma05Hy
SMITH, John	25	M	Unknown	06Ma05Hy
DENNAN, U	20	M	Unknown	06Ma05Hy
DALY, Jane	22	F	Unknown	06Ma05Hy
ARRON, Mary	20	F	Unknown	06Ma05Hy
LAKE, Mary	28	F	Unknown	06Ma05Hy
Margaret	26	F	Unknown	06Ma05Hy
HAMILTON, Alexander	25	M	Unknown	06Ma05Hy
SPARKS, U-Miss	20	F	Unknown	06Ma05Hy
U-Miss	18	F	Unknown	06Ma05Hy
CULLEN, U-Mr.	45	M	Unknown	06Ma05Hy
Wm.	18	M	Unknown	06Ma05Hy
Patt	16	M	Unknown	06Ma05Hy
MURPHY, J.	21	M	Unknown	06Ma05Hy
BEGAN, C.	22	M	Unknown	06Ma05Hy
HAYDEN, J.	22	M	Unknown	06Ma05Hy
U-Mrs.	22	F	Unknown	06Ma05Hy
DARCY, Cath.	20	F	Unknown	06Ma05Hy
John	18	M	Unknown	06Ma05Hy
Martin	15	M	Unknown	06Ma05Hy
DUNNE, John	38	M	Unknown	06Ma05Hy
Wm.	22	M	Unknown	06Ma05Hy
WEBSTER, U-Mr.	20	M	Unknown	06Ma05Hy
RAFT, Br.	21	M	Unknown	06Ma05Hy
MOLAR, Michael	26	M	Unknown	06Ma05Hy
RILLY, Thomas	21	M	Unknown	06Ma05Hy
CARTON, U	50	M	Unknown	06Ma05Hy
U-Mrs.	45	F	Unknown	06Ma05Hy

NAMES OF PASSENGERS	AGE	SEX	OCCUPATIONS	DATE PORT SHIP
CARTON, Wm.	26	M	Unknown	06Ma05Hy
Ann	24	F	Unknown	06Ma05Hy
John	21	M	Unknown	06Ma05Hy
Patt	19	M	Unknown	06Ma05Hy
Cather.	16	F	Unknown	06Ma05Hy
Edward	.00	M	Infant	06Ma05Hy
GUROSEN, John	16	M	Unknown	06Ma05Hy
U-Mr.	35	M	Unknown	06Ma05Hy
WOMACK, C.	20	M	Unknown	06Ma05Hy
U-Mr.	25	M	Unknown	06Ma05Hy
NOLAN, W.	14	M	Unknown	06Ma05Hy
ONEILL, U-Miss	35	F	Unknown	06Ma05Hy
SHAW, John	25	M	Unknown	06Ma05Hy
PRIOR, G.	20	M	Unknown	06Ma05Hy
MITCHELL, John	25	M	Unknown	06Ma05Hy
WHITE, N.	28	M	Unknown	06Ma05Hy
THOMPSON, J.	27	M	Unknown	06Ma05Hy
Wm.	00	M	Unknown	06Ma05Hy

GRACE-MCNEA 07 MAY 1850

From Liverpool

NAMES OF PASSENGERS	AGE	SEX	OCCUPATIONS	DATE PORT SHIP
FITZPATRICK, Mick	25	M	Laborer	07Ma02Jg
BROWNE, James	35	M	Unknown	07Ma02Jg
U-Mrs.	35	F	Unknown	07Ma02Jg
MCLANE, Johannah	28	F	Unknown	07Ma02Jg
MULCADDY, John	24	M	Unknown	07Ma02Jg
BRENNAN, Pat	20	M	Unknown	07Ma02Jg
JELOCO, Robt.	30	M	Unknown	07Ma02Jg
TREANOR, Jane	16	F	Unknown	07Ma02Jg
John	.00	M	Infant	07Ma02Jg
FRASER, Eliza	18	F	Unknown	07Ma02Jg
BYRNE, Garnett	20	F	Unknown	07Ma02Jg
MCANEY, John	26	M	Unknown	07Ma02Jg
BREEN, John	23	M	Unknown	07Ma02Jg
PHELAN, Thomas	12	M	Farmer	07Ma02Jg
MCAVOY, Cath.	22	F	Unknown	07Ma02Jg
Mary	61	F	Unknown	07Ma02Jg
Conjures	22	M	Unknown	07Ma02Jg
KELLY, Thomas	12	M	Unknown	07Ma02Jg
To--LINSON, John	23	M	Unknown	07Ma02Jg
Anna	42	F	Unknown	07Ma02Jg
Francis	16	M	Unknown	07Ma02Jg
DUGAN, Dennis	40	M	Unknown	07Ma02Jg
CUSSAC, Pattk.	23	M	Unknown	07Ma02Jg
James	41	M	Unknown	07Ma02Jg
Anne	63	F	Unknown	07Ma02Jg
Johanna	25	F	Unknown	07Ma02Jg
CONLON, John	41	M	Shoemaker	07Ma02Jg
SCANLAN, Mary	37	F	Spinster	07Ma02Jg
GOLDRICK, Patt	58	M	Farmer	07Ma02Jg
HENNINSON, John	21	M	Unknown	07Ma02Jg
Ellen	20	F	Unknown	07Ma02Jg
Mary	32	F	Unknown	07Ma02Jg
KELLY, Mick	40	M	Unknown	07Ma02Jg
Cath.	35	F	Unknown	07Ma02Jg
Johannah	27	F	Unknown	07Ma02Jg
Cath.	32	F	Unknown	07Ma02Jg
Mary	41	F	Unknown	07Ma02Jg
QUINLAN, Thomas	20	M	Unknown	07Ma02Jg
Patt	26	M	Unknown	07Ma02Jg
James	12	M	Unknown	07Ma02Jg
KENNEDY, Patt	50	M	Laborer	07Ma02Jg
James	23	M	Unknown	07Ma02Jg
DOYLE, John	32	M	Unknown	07Ma02Jg
SHEA, Dennis	40	M	Unknown	07Ma02Jg
NIEL, George	45	M	Unknown	07Ma02Jg
Anne	23	F	Unknown	07Ma02Jg

NAMES OF PASSENGERS	AGE	SEX	OCCUPATIONS	DATE PORT SHIP
NIEL, John	15	M	Unknown	07Ma02Jg
Edward	12	M	Unknown	07Ma02Jg
Anne	6	F	Child	07Ma02Jg
Elizabeth	4	F	Child	07Ma02Jg
George	2	M	Child	07Ma02Jg
CONDIAN, Francis	20	M	Unknown	07Ma02Jg
HEALIN, Ellen	35	F	Unknown	07Ma02Jg
CONNAWELL, Maurice	42	M	Unknown	07Ma02Jg
KEELY, Maurice	61	M	Unknown	07Ma02Jg
SARGE, Margaret	70	F	Unknown	07Ma02Jg
COOK, Matthew	20	M	Unknown	07Ma02Jg
Mary	15	F	Unknown	07Ma02Jg
FITZGERALD, Margaret	50	F	Wi	07Ma02Jg
PREEGAN, Issabella	35	F	Spinster	07Ma02Jg
BRIAN, Cath.	42	F	Unknown	07Ma02Jg
PRICE, Edward	50	M	Laborer	07Ma02Jg
BURKE, Mick	35	M	Unknown	07Ma02Jg
Johannah	15	F	Unknown	07Ma02Jg
KELLY, Thomas	32	M	Unknown	07Ma02Jg
Mary	30	F	Unknown	07Ma02Jg
LYAN, Mick	27	M	Unknown	07Ma02Jg
KELLY, U-Mrs.	32	F	Unknown	07Ma02Jg
POLLOCK, John	40	M	Unknown	07Ma02Jg
Jane	25	F	Unknown	07Ma02Jg
MCHATTON, George	19	M	Unknown	07Ma02Jg
CONWAY, Bryan	18	M	Unknown	07Ma02Jg
Peggy	14	F	Unknown	07Ma02Jg
QUIN, William	12	M	Unknown	07Ma02Jg
BESTING, John	15	M	Unknown	07Ma02Jg
PENDERGRAS, William	40	M	Unknown	07Ma02Jg
MARTIN, Margaret	45	F	Spinster	07Ma02Jg
CONNOR, Johanna	46	F	Spinster	07Ma02Jg
DAWSON, James	48	M	Laborer	07Ma02Jg
Ellen	50	F	Unknown	07Ma02Jg
SWEENEY, John	23	M	Unknown	07Ma02Jg
Cath.	34	F	Unknown	07Ma02Jg
Bridget	61	F	Unknown	07Ma02Jg
Edward	50	M	Unknown	07Ma02Jg
William	42	M	Unknown	07Ma02Jg
FOGARTY, Wm.	51	M	Unknown	07Ma02Jg
BANNON, Margt.	32	F	Unknown	07Ma02Jg
COUGHLAN, Patt	40	M	Unknown	07Ma02Jg
CANAGAN, James	32	M	Unknown	07Ma02Jg
THOMPSON, Joseph	41	M	Unknown	07Ma02Jg
MULDOWNY, James	53	M	Unknown	07Ma02Jg
Mary	61	F	Unknown	07Ma02Jg
GUIR, Margaret	72	F	Unknown	07Ma02Jg
FOLEY, Corns.	27	M	Unknown	07Ma02Jg
REILLY, John	54	M	Unknown	07Ma02Jg
Hugh	32	M	Unknown	07Ma02Jg
CONAGAN, Patt	61	M	Unknown	07Ma02Jg
WEBSTER, Mary	25	F	Unknown	07Ma02Jg
STOKES, William	32	M	Unknown	07Ma02Jg
Bridget	15	F	Unknown	07Ma02Jg
Thomas	13	M	Unknown	07Ma02Jg
John	11	M	Unknown	07Ma02Jg
Winney	8	F	Child	07Ma02Jg
William	6	M	Child	07Ma02Jg
Mary	2	F	Child	07Ma02Jg
DAYNE, Edward	53	M	Farmer	07Ma02Jg
John	45	M	Farmer	07Ma02Jg
HOWLEY, Margt.	27	F	Unknown	07Ma02Jg
TAYLOR, Margt.	31	F	Unknown	07Ma02Jg
SYNCHAN, Thomas	42	M	Unknown	07Ma02Jg
BEATTY, Thomas	48	M	Unknown	07Ma02Jg
CLINTON, Thomas	50	M	Unknown	07Ma02Jg
BRIAN, Cath.	60	F	Unknown	07Ma02Jg
RYAN, Mick	45	M	Unknown	07Ma02Jg
Sylvester	37	M	Unknown	07Ma02Jg
STAPLETON, Mick	32	M	Unknown	07Ma02Jg
MAHER, Bridgt.	36	F	Unknown	07Ma02Jg
REYNOLDS, Mary	50	F	Unknown	07Ma02Jg
BRADLEY, Mary	43	F	Unknown	07Ma02Jg
Mary	38	F	Unknown	07Ma02Jg
Bridget	42	F	Unknown	07Ma02Jg

NAMES OF PASSENGERS	AGE	SEX	OCCUPATIONS	DATE PORT SHIP
BRADLEY, Michael	53	M	Laborer	07Ma02Jg
BYRNES, Thomas	51	M	Unknown	07Ma02Jg
Judy	27	F	Unknown	07Ma02Jg
SCULLY, Richard	52	M	Unknown	07Ma02Jg
Anne	63	F	Unknown	07Ma02Jg
FENTON, Mary	27	F	Unknown	07Ma02Jg
YOUNG, David	31	M	Unknown	07Ma02Jg
Margaret	42	F	Unknown	07Ma02Jg
Margt.	56	F	Unknown	07Ma02Jg
BARRETT, John	27	M	Unknown	07Ma02Jg
BUMLEY, John	34	M	Unknown	07Ma02Jg
LENNAN, Edward	51	M	Unknown	07Ma02Jg
Mary	32	F	Unknown	07Ma02Jg
Catherine	36	F	Unknown	07Ma02Jg
Barney	50	M	Unknown	07Ma02Jg
COYLE, Charles	27	M	Unknown	07Ma02Jg
MCCAWLEY, Francis	16	M	Unknown	07Ma02Jg
JOHNSON, William	45	M	Unknown	07Ma02Jg
U-Mrs.	40	F	Unknown	07Ma02Jg
Mary-Jane	18	F	Unknown	07Ma02Jg
Charlotte	16	F	Unknown	07Ma02Jg
SIMPSON, U-Mrs.	50	F	Wi	07Ma02Jg
GASKIN, Henry	26	M	Farmer	07Ma02Jg
DYSON, Robt.	31	M	Farmer	07Ma02Jg
BYRNE, Margaret	15	F	Unknown	07Ma02Jg
Anne	12	F	Unknown	07Ma02Jg
BONNEN, Stewart	52	M	Unknown	07Ma02Jg
Catherine	20	F	Unknown	07Ma02Jg
PORTER, Margaret	31	F	Unknown	07Ma02Jg
BONNEN, John	50	M	Unknown	07Ma02Jg
MCCOBE, Andw.	27	M	Unknown	07Ma02Jg
Sally	20	F	Unknown	07Ma02Jg
RYAN, Thomas	32	M	Unknown	07Ma02Jg
Martha	36	F	Unknown	07Ma02Jg
Mary	28	F	Unknown	07Ma02Jg
ADPIN, David	30	M	Unknown	07Ma02Jg
LAINE, Thomas	42	M	Unknown	07Ma02Jg
PHELAN, Pat	53	M	Unknown	07Ma02Jg
DOUGHERTY, David	12	M	Unknown	07Ma02Jg
CONOLY, Mick	13	M	Unknown	07Ma02Jg
Mary	15	F	Unknown	07Ma02Jg
DOONAN, Malcedy	58	F	Spinster	07Ma02Jg
Honor	20	M	Unknown	07Ma02Jg
Margt.	18	F	Unknown	07Ma02Jg
Bridget	16	F	Unknown	07Ma02Jg
Anne	14	F	Unknown	07Ma02Jg
LALIN, Mick	21	M	Laborer	07Ma02Jg
JOHNSON, James	30	M	Unknown	07Ma02Jg
TROHY, William	43	M	Unknown	07Ma02Jg
CAREY, Pat	60	M	Unknown	07Ma02Jg
Mick	54	M	Unknown	07Ma02Jg
MURRAY, Pat	32	M	Unknown	07Ma02Jg
FOGARTY, Merryl	28	F	Unknown	07Ma02Jg
Martha	13	F	Unknown	07Ma02Jg
Thomas	10	M	Unknown	07Ma02Jg
John	8	M	Child	07Ma02Jg
FENNEY, John	43	M	Unknown	07Ma02Jg
NOLIN, Edward	27	M	Unknown	07Ma02Jg
HASTIE, Alex.	41	M	Unknown	07Ma02Jg
Jennett	12	F	Unknown	07Ma02Jg
Bridget	15	F	Unknown	07Ma02Jg
Martin	10	M	Unknown	07Ma02Jg
Martin	8	M	Child	07Ma02Jg
KELLY, Mary	11	F	Unknown	07Ma02Jg
BOTLEE, Bridget	20	F	Unknown	07Ma02Jg
GLEESON, Thomas	31	M	Unknown	07Ma02Jg
FLANAGAN, Thomas	42	M	Unknown	07Ma02Jg
MCBULGER, Osborne	18	M	Unknown	07Ma02Jg
GAFFERY, Bridget	16	F	Unknown	07Ma02Jg
ONEILL, Hugh	12	M	Unknown	07Ma02Jg
CANNON, Tom	54	M	Farmer	07Ma02Jg
James	21	M	Unknown	07Ma02Jg
Ellen	28	F	Unknown	07Ma02Jg
DONDE, Ellen	29	F	Unknown	07Ma02Jg
NAUGHTON, Catherine	33	F	Unknown	07Ma02Jg

NAMES OF PASSENGERS	AGE	SEX	OCCUPATIONS	DATE PORT SHIP
CAIN, Hugh	41	M	Unknown	07Ma02Jg
CRAIN, James	60	M	Unknown	07Ma02Jg
DONNDELEY, Owen	71	M	Unknown	07Ma02Jg
HAGERTY, Honor	43	F	Unknown	07Ma02Jg
Catherine	33	F	Unknown	07Ma02Jg
Mary	28	F	Unknown	07Ma02Jg
Anne	19	F	Unknown	07Ma02Jg
MCDONALD, Mary	30	F	Unknown	07Ma02Jg
MCNAMARA, Corns.	29	M	Unknown	07Ma02Jg
Libby	15	F	Unknown	07Ma02Jg
CONROY, Bridget	16	F	Unknown	07Ma02Jg
MCANDREWS, Honor	12	F	Unknown	07Ma02Jg
RYAN, James	31	M	Unknown	07Ma02Jg
James	14	M	Unknown	07Ma02Jg
Mary	12	F	Unknown	07Ma02Jg
MCDENDIEAN, Hannah	34	F	Spinster	07Ma02Jg
Thomas	12	M	Unknown	07Ma02Jg
Patt	15	M	Unknown	07Ma02Jg
John	12	M	Unknown	07Ma02Jg
MARTIN, Eliza	10	F	Unknown	07Ma02Jg
Sarah	14	F	Unknown	07Ma02Jg
LOUGHLAN, Anne	19	F	Unknown	07Ma02Jg
FINANE, John	27	M	Laborer	07Ma02Jg
MARTIN, Edward	31	M	Unknown	07Ma02Jg
John	22	M	Unknown	07Ma02Jg
James	10	M	Unknown	07Ma02Jg
Robert	8	M	Child	07Ma02Jg
Eliza	6	F	Child	07Ma02Jg
MAHONY, John	30	M	Unknown	07Ma02Jg
GRENNAN, Austin	15	M	Unknown	07Ma02Jg
DOYLE, Patt	20	M	Unknown	07Ma02Jg
HIGGINS, Mick	31	M	Unknown	07Ma02Jg
James	15	M	Unknown	07Ma02Jg
HAGERTY, John	42	M	Unknown	07Ma02Jg
Bridget	13	F	Unknown	07Ma02Jg
DOCKEY, Margt.	56	F	Unknown	07Ma02Jg
GRACE, John	61	M	Unknown	07Ma02Jg
OCONNELL, Richard	63	M	Unknown	07Ma02Jg
James	42	M	Unknown	07Ma02Jg
Ellen	38	F	Unknown	07Ma02Jg
CARDWELL, Mick	19	M	Unknown	07Ma02Jg
FARRELL, Eliza	27	F	Unknown	07Ma02Jg
Eliza	6	F	Child	07Ma02Jg
RYAN, John	23	M	Unknown	07Ma02Jg
MARTIN, James	42	M	Farmer	07Ma02Jg
LONGEVAN, James	18	M	Unknown	07Ma02Jg
NOLAN, Ed.	28	M	Unknown	07Ma02Jg
TULDRAFF, Mick	31	M	Unknown	07Ma02Jg
CORDELLY, Pat	28	M	Unknown	07Ma02Jg
REGAN, John	32	M	Unknown	07Ma02Jg
MARTIN, James	36	M	Unknown	07Ma02Jg
CANNY, Edward	28	M	Unknown	07Ma02Jg
FINIAN, Patt	19	M	Unknown	07Ma02Jg
KIDWICK, Maria	32	F	Unknown	07Ma02Jg
HENRY, Mick	43	M	Unknown	07Ma02Jg
John	12	M	Unknown	07Ma02Jg
HAMILTON, Jenny	00	F	Unknown	07Ma02Jg
MALENNY, John	00	M	Unknown	07Ma02Jg
HASTINGS, U	00	M	Unknown	07Ma02Jg
U-Mrs.	00	F	Unknown	07Ma02Jg
SWEENEY, Michael	32	M	Unknown	07Ma02Jg
PREEGAN, Mary	40	F	Unknown	07Ma02Jg

ABBY-LAND 07 MAY 1850

From Liverpool

NAMES OF PASSENGERS	AGE	SEX	OCCUPATIONS	DATE PORT SHIP
EDWARDS, Wm.	28	M	Clerk	07Ma02ll
ITELAN, Thos.	27	M	Farmer	07Ma02ll

NAMES OF PASSENGERS	AGE	SEX	OCCUPATIONS	DATE PORT SHIP
ITELAN, Margt.	20	F	Farmer	07Ma0211
DUFFY, Cusin	20	F	Laborer	07Ma0211
MCDERMOTT, Ellen	20	F	Spinster	07Ma0211
DAVIES, Thos.	28	M	Laborer	07Ma0211
EVANS, Elizth.	24	F	Spinster	07Ma0211
GILLIGAN, Chas.	25	M	Laborer	07Ma0211
HALEY, Thos.	30	M	Laborer	07Ma0211
KIMMER, Henry	24	M	Laborer	07Ma0211
MCCORKENDLIN, Wm.	30	M	Laborer	07Ma0211
Eliza	30	F	Laborer	07Ma0211
Robert	12	M	Laborer	07Ma0211
Maryanne	8	F	Child	07Ma0211
Wm.	4	M	Child	07Ma0211
Elizabeth	.00	F	Infant	07Ma0211
Died-At-Sea				
MCDONALD, Ronald	20	M	Laborer	07Ma0211
LAVERTY, Hugh	20	M	Laborer	07Ma0211
CONNER, John	24	M	Laborer	07Ma0211
COLOPSY, Jas.	28	M	Laborer	07Ma0211
John	22	M	Laborer	07Ma0211
Pat	40	M	Laborer	07Ma0211
Tim	24	M	Laborer	07Ma0211
Cath.	20	F	Laborer	07Ma0211
DILLIN, Michl.	20	M	Laborer	07Ma0211
COLOPSY, Julia	28	F	Spinster	07Ma0211
LAMBOURNE, Ann	40	F	Spinster	07Ma0211
Charlotte	.00	F	Infant	07Ma0211
Eliza	3	F	Child	07Ma0211
Ellen	5	F	Child	07Ma0211
David	7	M	Child	07Ma0211
Maryanne	9	F	Child	07Ma0211
Michl.George	15	M	Laborer	07Ma0211
Emma	17	F	Spinster	07Ma0211
Jane	19	F	Spinster	07Ma0211
HOCKSEN, Mary	36	F	Spinster	07Ma0211
KERNAN, Pat	36	M	Laborer	07Ma0211
Ann	21	F	Laborer	07Ma0211
GILLICK, John	20	M	Laborer	07Ma0211
BRADY, Tim	40	M	Laborer	07Ma0211
WALSH, Thos.	35	M	Laborer	07Ma0211
Rose	35	F	Laborer	07Ma0211
James	7	M	Child	07Ma0211
Alice	5	F	Child	07Ma0211
Jas.Fex.	20	M	Laborer	07Ma0211
FLANNEGAN, Thos.	22	M	Laborer	07Ma0211
Terrance	24	F	Laborer	07Ma0211
JORDAN, John	20	M	Laborer	07Ma0211
DORAN, Mick.	17	M	Laborer	07Ma0211
DERAN, Rose	19	F	Spinster	07Ma0211
HANLEY, John	22	M	Laborer	07Ma0211
Margt.	29	F	Laborer	07Ma0211
Caroline	3	F	Child	07Ma0211
CLISTEN, John	22	M	Laborer	07Ma0211
CARNEY, Jas.	22	M	Laborer	07Ma0211
GILL, Maria	20	F	Laborer	07Ma0211
FOX, Cath.	20	F	Laborer	07Ma0211
SULLIVAN, Michl.	20	M	Laborer	07Ma0211
CARLEY, Jas.	25	M	Laborer	07Ma0211
BUCKLEY, Ellen	21	F	Spinster	07Ma0211
St.LAURENCE, Jas.	40	M	Laborer	07Ma0211
PREDICK, Jas.	25	M	Laborer	07Ma0211
BYRNES, Jno.	25	M	Laborer	07Ma0211
Bessy	16	F	Spinster	07Ma0211
Bryan	26	M	Laborer	07Ma0211
LUCE, Cath.	16	F	Laborer	07Ma0211
COCHRAN, Jas.	36	M	Laborer	07Ma0211
John	10	M	Laborer	07Ma0211
George	8	M	Child	07Ma0211
QUINN, John	20	M	Laborer	07Ma0211
KIRCIN, Pat	25	M	Laborer	07Ma0211
GUIVIN, Pat	50	M	Laborer	07Ma0211
GOULD, Darby	23	M	Laborer	07Ma0211
STENSON, Ann	18	F	Laborer	07Ma0211
MEARN, Ellen	18	F	Laborer	07Ma0211
DERRICK, Dan	30	M	Laborer	07Ma0211
DERRICK, Mary	45	F	Laborer	07Ma0211
MULLIGAN, Phil	30	M	Laborer	07Ma0211
Laurence	27	M	Laborer	07Ma0211
CONNELL, Stephen	23	M	Laborer	07Ma0211
Thos.	20	M	Laborer	07Ma0211
CATHEEN, James	22	M	Laborer	07Ma0211
REGLAN, Pat	31	M	Laborer	07Ma0211
CARR, Laverty	30	M	Laborer	07Ma0211
Charles	3	M	Child	07Ma0211
CARTY, James	.00	M	Infant	07Ma0211
Margt.	20	F	Laborer	07Ma0211
GLEEN, Cath.	35	F	Laborer	07Ma0211
CATHEN, Sinnin	22	M	Laborer	07Ma0211
ARMSTRONG, Julia	23	F	Laborer	07Ma0211
GIBBINS, Michl.	20	M	Laborer	07Ma0211
Austin	22	M	Laborer	07Ma0211
Anne	24	F	Laborer	07Ma0211
Mary	.00	F	Infant	07Ma0211
GALLOP, Robert	50	M	Laborer	07Ma0211
Johanna	20	F	Laborer	07Ma0211
Mary	18	F	Spinster	07Ma0211
Ann	16	F	Unknown	07Ma0211
CAVANAGH, James	24	M	Laborer	07Ma0211
CORCORAN, James	40	M	Laborer	07Ma0211
WISKELA, Wm.	40	M	Laborer	07Ma0211
MURPHY, Thos.	22	M	Laborer	07Ma0211
DOYLE, Richd.	40	M	Laborer	07Ma0211
MISKELD, Bridget	18	F	Laborer	07Ma0211
Cath.	13	F	Laborer	07Ma0211
DOYLE, Deborah	12	F	Laborer	07Ma0211
Thos.	9	M	Child	07Ma0211
Richd.	50	M	Laborer	07Ma0211
KELLY, Gregory	47	M	Laborer	07Ma0211
Johanna	40	F	Laborer	07Ma0211
Johanna	.00	F	Infant	07Ma0211
Died-At-Sea				
Alice	4	F	Child	07Ma0211
Ann	7	F	Child	07Ma0211
Eliza	11	F	Laborer	07Ma0211
Myles	13	M	Laborer	07Ma0211
Mary	12	F	Laborer	07Ma0211
Gregory	9	M	Child	07Ma0211
Ellen	18	F	Laborer	07Ma0211
DERRY, Patk.	24	M	Laborer	07Ma0211
FARRELL, John	20	M	Unknown	07Ma0211
TOBEN, John	28	M	Unknown	07Ma0211
GORMAN, Mary	13	F	Unknown	07Ma0211
MURPHY, Bridget	13	F	Unknown	07Ma0211
BURNS, Wm.	24	M	Unknown	07Ma0211
REILLEY, Martin	40	M	Unknown	07Ma0211
John	30	M	Unknown	07Ma0211
BURNES, James	20	M	Laborer	07Ma0211
KEILLY, Elijah	20	M	Laborer	07Ma0211
MCCABE, Cath.	20	F	Laborer	07Ma0211
Cath.	20	F	Laborer	07Ma0211
MULVERY, Cath.	20	F	Laborer	07Ma0211
MCKEEN, Richd.	20	M	Laborer	07Ma0211
CONLAY, James	20	M	Laborer	07Ma0211
WINNE, Bridget	20	F	Laborer	07Ma0211
NEARY, Pat	28	M	Laborer	07Ma0211
CARR, Lucinda	50	F	Laborer	07Ma0211
Dorothy	52	F	Laborer	07Ma0211
HIGGINS, Peter	35	M	Laborer	07Ma0211
U-Mrs.	35	F	Laborer	07Ma0211
NICHOLSON, John	21	M	Laborer	07Ma0211
Cath.	30	F	Laborer	07Ma0211
MAKEN, Mary	25	F	Laborer	07Ma0211
NESON, Arthur	25	M	Laborer	07Ma0211
FORGE, Jos.	20	M	Laborer	07Ma0211
HEVITTE, Robt.	45	M	Laborer	07Ma0211
Jane	18	F	Laborer	07Ma0211
DUNN, Michl.	18	M	Laborer	07Ma0211
Bridget	16	F	Laborer	07Ma0211
GUAGHTY, Pat	50	M	Laborer	07Ma0211
U-Mrs.	50	F	Laborer	07Ma0211

NAMES OF PASSENGERS	AGE	SEX	OCCUPATIONS	DATE PORT SHIP
GUAGHTY, Bessy	50	F	Laborer	07Ma02II
Pat	16	M	Laborer	07Ma02II
Lawrence	12	M	Laborer	07Ma02II
MOLLOY, John	10	M	Laborer	07Ma02II
Charles	22	M	Laborer	07Ma02II
Ellen	19	F	Laborer	07Ma02II
FOULTER, Patt.	40	M	Laborer	07Ma02II
CAIN, Eliza	21	F	Laborer	07Ma02II
KANE, Peter	26	M	Laborer	07Ma02II
Francis	30	M	Laborer	07Ma02II
FUGAN, Wm.	26	M	Laborer	07Ma02II
KEAREN, Bartley	24	M	Laborer	07Ma02II
Biddy	20	F	Laborer	07Ma02II
COLECY, Michl.	30	M	Laborer	07Ma02II
PARK, Francis	21	M	Unknown	07Ma02II
BOOTH, Robt.	22	M	Unknown	07Ma02II
STARK, John	34	M	Unknown	07Ma02II
RIDSON, John	19	M	Unknown	07Ma02II
FITZGERALD, Matthew	36	M	Unknown	07Ma02II
TOOLE, Pat	35	M	Unknown	07Ma02II
Margt.	30	F	Unknown	07Ma02II
Lawrence	.00	M	Infant	07Ma02II
Anne	2	F	Child	07Ma02II
MURPHY, John	35	M	Laborer	07Ma02II
BYRNES, James	40	M	Laborer	07Ma02II
Eliza	28	F	Laborer	07Ma02II
WELSH, Robt.	18	M	Laborer	07Ma02II
Lawrence	14	M	Laborer	07Ma02II
SHEAL, Morris	16	M	Laborer	07Ma02II
COMMINS, Mary	23	F	Laborer	07Ma02II
CAVANA, Philip	21	M	Laborer	07Ma02II
CARTY, Martin	30	M	Laborer	07Ma02II
Margt.	26	F	Laborer	07Ma02II
Richd.	4	M	Child	07Ma02II
MURRY, Charles	20	M	Laborer	07Ma02II
MURPHY, James	22	M	Laborer	07Ma02II
Cath.	17	F	Laborer	07Ma02II
RYAN, Martin	25	M	Laborer	07Ma02II
Peggy	27	F	Laborer	07Ma02II
Margaret	.00	F	Infant	07Ma02II
NOONAN, James	27	M	Laborer	07Ma02II
TROY, Maurice	24	M	Laborer	07Ma02II
KELLY, Jerry	26	M	Laborer	07Ma02II
Johanna	13	F	Laborer	07Ma02II
Julia	12	F	Laborer	07Ma02II
SULLIVAN, Mary	40	F	Laborer	07Ma02II
U	20	F	Laborer	07Ma02II
U	24	F	Laborer	07Ma02II
CLANCY, James	35	M	Laborer	07Ma02II
FLYNN, Ann	25	F	Laborer	07Ma02II
WYNNE, Patt	28	M	Laborer	07Ma02II
Honor	40	F	Laborer	07Ma02II
LONDON, Margt.	5	F	Child	07Ma02II
GLEESON, Thos.	25	M	Laborer	07Ma02II
Thos.	40	M	Laborer	07Ma02II
TROY, Ned	13	M	Laborer	07Ma02II
Honora	22	F	Laborer	07Ma02II
Honora	25	F	Laborer	07Ma02II
OWENS, Jno.	23	M	Laborer	07Ma02II
BONNAN, Mary	28	F	Laborer	07Ma02II

NORWAY 08 MAY 1850

From Liverpool

NAMES OF PASSENGERS	AGE	SEX	OCCUPATIONS	DATE PORT SHIP
BROPHY, Patrick	25	M	Laborer	08Ma02Ib
TOBIN, Catherine	40	F	Spinster	08Ma02Ib
KEEF, Mary	30	F	Spinster	08Ma02Ib
BROPHY, John	32	M	Laborer	08Ma02Ib
BROPHY, Catherine	28	F	Spinster	08Ma02Ib
Catherine	.07	F	Infant	08Ma02Ib
Andrew	00	M	Child	08Ma02Ib
Catherine	20	F	Spinster	08Ma02Ib
BREMAN, James	20	M	Laborer	08Ma02Ib
GAVIN, Martin	25	M	Laborer	08Ma02Ib
Biddy	20	F	Matron	08Ma02Ib
MCDONALD, Richard	20	M	Laborer	08Ma02Ib
Ellen	30	F	Matron	08Ma02Ib
SMITH, Richard	23	M	Laborer	08Ma02Ib
Mary	22	F	Matron	08Ma02Ib
Christy	.00	F	Infant	08Ma02Ib
Adam	.00	M	Infant	08Ma02Ib
LAHEE, Ellen	17	F	Spinster	08Ma02Ib
HERDMAN, Mary	35	F	Unknown	08Ma02Ib
Eleanor	19	F	Unknown	08Ma02Ib
Annie	17	F	Unknown	08Ma02Ib
Mary-Eliza	13	F	Unknown	08Ma02Ib
John	11	M	Unknown	08Ma02Ib
James	8	M	Child	08Ma02Ib
John	40	M	Unknown	08Ma02Ib
MOHAN, James	40	M	Laborer	08Ma02Ib
CARTY, Bridget	30	F	Laborer	08Ma02Ib
BRODIGAN, Patrick	9	M	Child	08Ma02Ib
Catherine	3	F	Child	08Ma02Ib
Ann	.00	F	Infant	08Ma02Ib
FRAYNE, James	23	M	Laborer	08Ma02Ib
MURPHY, C.	4	F	Child	08Ma02Ib
CORKERAN, Dennis	25	M	Laborer	08Ma02Ib
PURCELL, P.	19	M	Laborer	08Ma02Ib
QUINTIN, P.	19	M	Laborer	08Ma02Ib
RYAN, M.	30	F	Spinster	08Ma02Ib
Catherine	20	F	Spinster	08Ma02Ib
FITZPATRICK, Mary	18	F	Spinster	08Ma02Ib
REENE, Patrick	24	M	Laborer	08Ma02Ib
COYNE, John	27	M	Laborer	08Ma02Ib
RODGERS, John	23	M	Laborer	08Ma02Ib
Magt.	17	F	Matron	08Ma02Ib
CONCKLIN, Patrick	25	M	Laborer	08Ma02Ib
Bridget	25	F	Matron	08Ma02Ib
Honora	2	F	Child	08Ma02Ib
John	6	M	Child	08Ma02Ib
Bridget	.00	F	Infant	08Ma02Ib
NORTON, Thomas	30	M	Laborer	08Ma02Ib
Hannah	26	F	Matron	08Ma02Ib
Catherine	.00	F	Infant	08Ma02Ib
FOX, Ann	50	F	Matron	08Ma02Ib
Wm.	19	M	Laborer	08Ma02Ib
M.	13	M	Laborer	08Ma02Ib
J.	9	M	Child	08Ma02Ib
T.	20	M	Laborer	08Ma02Ib
F.	17	M	Laborer	08Ma02Ib
Mary-Ann	12	F	Unknown	08Ma02Ib
FOGARTY, Mary	20	F	Spinster	08Ma02Ib
RYAN, Lucy	22	F	Spinster	08Ma02Ib
LANCHAIK, Mary	30	F	Matron	08Ma02Ib
Kitty	3	F	Child	08Ma02Ib
Richard	.00	M	Infant	08Ma02Ib
FITZPATRICK, Mary	25	F	Spinster	08Ma02Ib
HOY, Michael	1	M	Child	08Ma02Ib
CALLINAN, Mike	23	M	Laborer	08Ma02Ib
MCGOWAN, John	25	M	Laborer	08Ma02Ib
PYE, Robt.	25	M	Laborer	08Ma02Ib
MCGOWAN, Andrew	20	M	Laborer	08Ma02Ib
FINNAN, Jas.	30	M	Laborer	08Ma02Ib
ASHFORD, Wm.	30	M	Laborer	08Ma02Ib
RALPH, Honora	25	F	Matron	08Ma02Ib
Bridget	3	F	Child	08Ma02Ib
BRADY, Cormack	21	M	Laborer	08Ma02Ib
Alice	20	F	Matron	08Ma02Ib
IRWIN, C.	30	F	Matron	08Ma02Ib
Annie	2	F	Child	08Ma02Ib
LANNEN, John	.02	M	Infant	08Ma02Ib
Mary	25	F	Spinster	08Ma02Ib
LEE, Christy	20	F	Spinster	08Ma02Ib

NAMES OF PASSENGERS	AGE	SEX	OCCUPATIONS	DATE PORT SHIP
LYNAM, John	20	M	Laborer	08Ma02Ib
GALLAGHER, Wm.	60	M	Laborer	08Ma02Ib
Thos.	1	M	Child	08Ma02Ib
HENRY, John	50	M	Laborer	08Ma02Ib
Patrick	30	M	Laborer	08Ma02Ib
James	18	M	Laborer	08Ma02Ib
Biddy	20	F	Spinster	08Ma02Ib
Annie	60	F	Matron	08Ma02Ib
Biddy	20	F	Spinster	08Ma02Ib
CONWAY, Michael	30	M	Laborer	08Ma02Ib
DAVIS, James	28	M	Laborer	08Ma02Ib
Rose	21	F	Spinster	08Ma02Ib
Mary	20	F	Spinster	08Ma02Ib
KELLY, Biddy	20	F	Spinster	08Ma02Ib
C.	.09	F	Infant	08Ma02Ib
DUNN, Arthur	25	M	Laborer	08Ma02Ib
ROALSTON, Joseph	25	M	Laborer	08Ma02Ib
MCLEAN, James	16	M	Laborer	08Ma02Ib
Arthur	18	M	Laborer	08Ma02Ib
OBRIEN, Hugh	18	M	Laborer	08Ma02Ib
FINNEGAN, P.	30	M	Laborer	08Ma02Ib
LANNERS, M.	30	M	Laborer	08Ma02Ib
U-Mrs.	30	F	Matron	08Ma02Ib
REAMS, John	24	M	Laborer	08Ma02Ib
ROURKE, M.	22	M	Laborer	08Ma02Ib
JOHNSTONE, J.	24	M	Laborer	08Ma02Ib
DOLAN, Anne	40	F	Matron	08Ma02Ib
Nabby	17	F	Spinster	08Ma02Ib
Ann	15	F	Spinster	08Ma02Ib
Felix	1	M	Child	08Ma02Ib
FARRELL, Ellen	20	F	Spinster	08Ma02Ib
Margt.	.11	F	Infant	08Ma02Ib
HILL, Robt.	18	M	Laborer	08Ma02Ib
AHERNE, John	15	M	Laborer	08Ma02Ib
LOUGHNAN, M.	25	M	Laborer	08Ma02Ib
CARROLL, Mary	20	F	Spinster	08Ma02Ib
BRANNON, Biddy	20	F	Spinster	08Ma02Ib
ROLLAND, Honora	30	F	Spinster	08Ma02Ib
BRANNAN, Thos.	28	M	Laborer	08Ma02Ib
BURKE, M.	27	M	Laborer	08Ma02Ib
J.	22	M	Laborer	08Ma02Ib
LYNCH, C.	30	F	Spinster	08Ma02Ib
WALSH, P.	25	M	Spinner	08Ma02Ib
M.	20	M	Spinner	08Ma02Ib
M.	28	M	Spinner	08Ma02Ib
BERRY, M.	25	M	Laborer	08Ma02Ib
John	22	M	Laborer	08Ma02Ib
Mary	17	F	Laborer	08Ma02Ib
Mike	22	M	Laborer	08Ma02Ib
SHANAHAN, Nancy	20	F	Spinster	08Ma02Ib
Mary	14	F	Spinster	08Ma02Ib
QUINTIN, John	15	M	Laborer	08Ma02Ib
Wm.	7	M	Child	08Ma02Ib
GOLD, Michael	30	M	Laborer	08Ma02Ib
Catherine	24	F	Matron	08Ma02Ib
M.	7	M	Child	08Ma02Ib
J.	4	M	Child	08Ma02Ib
B.	2	F	Child	08Ma02Ib
A.	.00	F	Infant	08Ma02Ib
Michael	30	M	Unknown	08Ma02Ib
CONNOR, John	30	M	Laborer	08Ma02Ib
RYAN, Roddy	40	M	Laborer	08Ma02Ib
Bridget	40	F	Matron	08Ma02Ib

HESPERUS 08 MAY 1850

From Belfast

NAMES OF PASSENGERS	AGE	SEX	OCCUPATIONS	DATE PORT SHIP
MERCER, Mary	30	F	Laborer	08Ma17II
Eliza	22	F	Unknown	08Ma17II
MATHEWS, Margaret	30	F	Unknown	08Ma17II
MCGREAVEY, Jane	31	F	Unknown	08Ma17II
BLAIR, William	44	M	Unknown	08Ma17II
NELSON, William	24	M	Unknown	08Ma17II
Robert	34	M	Unknown	08Ma17II
DENOUGH, Nancy	30	F	Unknown	08Ma17II
Susana	17	F	Unknown	08Ma17II
Margaret	13	F	Unknown	08Ma17II
MCQUADE, Alley	55	F	Unknown	08Ma17II
KEENAN, James	31	M	Unknown	08Ma17II
GARDANER, Teresa	20	F	Unknown	08Ma17II
Margt.	17	F	Unknown	08Ma17II
MOONEY, Isabella	28	F	Unknown	08Ma17II
MONEHEAD, Thomas	26	M	Unknown	08Ma17II
Margt.	27	F	Unknown	08Ma17II
MCKIBBAN, Hugh	18	M	Unknown	08Ma17II
LEAVETT, Maryanne	18	F	Unknown	08Ma17II
MCCULLOUGH, Samuel	18	M	Unknown	08Ma17II
David	11	M	Unknown	08Ma17II
MCTAGGART, John	50	M	Unknown	08Ma17II
Rosey	50	F	Unknown	08Ma17II
Patt	16	M	Unknown	08Ma17II
Susan	14	F	Unknown	08Ma17II
Margt.	12	F	Unknown	08Ma17II
Bridgt.	10	F	Unknown	08Ma17II
Lanty	6	U	Child	08Ma17II
DAWLEY, Pat	18	M	Unknown	08Ma17II
CLEAR, Cath.	18	F	Unknown	08Ma17II
DOYLE, Mary-Ann	16	F	Unknown	08Ma17II
HALLS, John	23	M	Unknown	08Ma17II
Anne	22	F	Unknown	08Ma17II
Margt.	12	F	Unknown	08Ma17II
HAUGHERY, George	25	M	Unknown	08Ma17II
BROWN, Robert	30	M	Unknown	08Ma17II
Jane	27	F	Unknown	08Ma17II
Mary	5	F	Child	08Ma17II
John	3	M	Child	08Ma17II
MCMAHON, Eliza	20	F	Unknown	08Ma17II
KNOX, William	28	M	Laborer	08Ma17II
MCMURTY, Andrew	20	M	Unknown	08Ma17II
HANLY, Robert	18	M	Unknown	08Ma17II
MOORE, John	22	M	Unknown	08Ma17II
Margaret	20	F	Unknown	08Ma17II
MCMURTY, Eliza	15	F	Unknown	08Ma17II
HARNE, Thomas	27	M	Unknown	08Ma17II
Rose-Mary	3	F	Child	08Ma17II
Susan	.00	F	Infant	08Ma17II
MCKINTY, Pat	20	M	Unknown	08Ma17II
COWAN, William	20	M	Unknown	08Ma17II
MCKUSTER, Anthony	20	M	Unknown	08Ma17II
Anne	18	F	Unknown	08Ma17II
SCOTT, Margt.	20	F	Unknown	08Ma17II
MAGIVIN, Edward	20	M	Unknown	08Ma17II
LUND, William	50	M	Unknown	08Ma17II
Anne	44	F	Unknown	08Ma17II
Anne	20	F	Unknown	08Ma17II
George	17	M	Unknown	08Ma17II
William	13	M	Unknown	08Ma17II
MCKELVEY, Cath.	40	F	Unknown	08Ma17II
CARRIGAN, Ellen	20	F	Unknown	08Ma17II
MCCALLEN, Ann	27	F	Unknown	08Ma17II
HENRY, Bridgt.	18	F	Unknown	08Ma17II
WALKER, Hannah	50	F	Unknown	08Ma17II

NAMES OF PASSENGERS	AGE	SEX	OCCUPATIONS	DATE PORT SHIP
WALKER, James	22	M	Unknown	08Ma17ll
HANNA, Margt.	18	F	Unknown	08Ma17ll
FLANAGAN, Sanuel	19	M	Unknown	08Ma17ll
SHERIDAN, John	17	M	Unknown	08Ma17ll
CRAIG, Eliza	18	F	Unknown	08Ma17ll
FULTON, Sloane	28	M	Unknown	08Ma17ll
KELLY, Eliza	26	F	Unknown	08Ma17ll
GORMAN, James	40	M	Unknown	08Ma17ll
SMITH, William	18	M	Unknown	08Ma17ll
ROBINSON, William	24	M	Unknown	08Ma17ll
Anne	20	F	Unknown	08Ma17ll
CRAWFORD, James	50	M	Unknown	08Ma17ll
Mary-Anne	46	F	Unknown	08Ma17ll
William	36	M	Unknown	08Ma17ll
John	13	M	Unknown	08Ma17ll
Joseph	11	M	Unknown	08Ma17ll
Mary-Anne	8	F	Child	08Ma17ll
Jane	6	F	Child	08Ma17ll
KENT, George	22	M	Unknown	08Ma17ll
Eliza	20	F	Unknown	08Ma17ll
BROWNLEE, K.	21	U	Unknown	08Ma17ll
NEAL, James	20	M	Unknown	08Ma17ll
FANNIGAN, William	20	M	Unknown	08Ma17ll
OWENS, Cath.	18	F	Unknown	08Ma17ll
LAVERY, Pat	34	M	Unknown	08Ma17ll
SONENS, Thomas	17	M	Laborer	08Ma17ll
KENEDY, John	25	M	Unknown	08Ma17ll
CARSON, James	20	M	Unknown	08Ma17ll
KERNCHEN, Eliza-C.	37	F	Unknown	08Ma17ll
Robert	13	M	Unknown	08Ma17ll
MCKINTY, John	22	M	Unknown	08Ma17ll
CUNDY, Sarah	20	F	Unknown	08Ma17ll
CUSH, Cath.	20	F	Unknown	08Ma17ll
MCCORMACK, Anne	20	F	Unknown	08Ma17ll
MCKANE, Thomas	26	M	Unknown	08Ma17ll
BREATHWENT, W.J.	20	M	Unknown	08Ma17ll
BARTLETT, Robert	18	M	Unknown	08Ma17ll
Eliza	16	F	Unknown	08Ma17ll
FLEMING, Joseph	17	M	Unknown	08Ma17ll
STEWART, William	20	M	Unknown	08Ma17ll
LAMOUNT, Alex.	20	M	Unknown	08Ma17ll
LYTHE, Andrew	20	M	Unknown	08Ma17ll
DOYLE, Hugh	24	M	Unknown	08Ma17ll
DEVLIN, John	26	M	Unknown	08Ma17ll
HANAH, Mary	46	F	Unknown	08Ma17ll
FORSYTH, Agnes	20	F	Unknown	08Ma17ll
Mary-Jane	18	F	Unknown	08Ma17ll
ONEIL, Hugh	23	M	Unknown	08Ma17ll
Mary	20	F	Unknown	08Ma17ll
WOOD, Martin	20	M	Unknown	08Ma17ll
Mary-Ann	18	F	Unknown	08Ma17ll
SPENCER, William	20	M	Unknown	08Ma17ll
Anne	19	F	Unknown	08Ma17ll
MCCANN, Alex	25	M	Unknown	08Ma17ll
ROURKE, Mary	21	F	Unknown	08Ma17ll
MCHAINE, Susan	22	F	Unknown	08Ma17ll
KNOX, James	36	M	Unknown	08Ma17ll
MOWOOD, Thomas	18	M	Unknown	08Ma17ll
MCKUTHY, William	28	M	Unknown	08Ma17ll
FRANCIS, Joseph	25	M	Unknown	08Ma17ll
Elizth.	20	F	Unknown	08Ma17ll
MORGAN, Henry	34	M	Unknown	08Ma17ll
Margt.	28	F	Unknown	08Ma17ll
Biddy	8	F	Child	08Ma17ll
Cath.	6	F	Child	08Ma17ll
James	32	M	Unknown	08Ma17ll
AGNEW, Hugh	25	M	Unknown	08Ma17ll
WARD, Bessy	20	F	Unknown	08Ma17ll
FUNK, James	20	M	Unknown	08Ma17ll
CAMPBELL, Thomas	20	M	Unknown	08Ma17ll
ARTHUR, William	22	M	Unknown	08Ma17ll
Mary	25	F	Unknown	08Ma17ll
Pat	.00	M	Infant	08Ma17ll
KENNEN, John	25	M	Unknown	08Ma17ll
FLEMING, William	20	M	Unknown	08Ma17ll
PIERCE, Martha	20	F	Laborer	08Ma17ll
RODGERS, Michael	25	M	Unknown	08Ma17ll
GAMBLE, Andrew	21	M	Unknown	08Ma17ll
HUBBLESON, John	19	M	Unknown	08Ma17ll
STEWART, Samuel	30	M	Unknown	08Ma17ll
MAHEE, James	30	M	Unknown	08Ma17ll
CONVEY, Francis	30	M	Unknown	08Ma17ll

EUGENIA 08 MAY 1850

From Vera Cruz

NAMES OF PASSENGERS	AGE	SEX	OCCUPATIONS	DATE PORT SHIP
GRANT, Alexr.	41	M	Merchant	08Ma27lk
James	4	M	Child	08Ma27lk
EVANS, S.L.	45	F	Unknown	08Ma27lk

NIAGARA 09 MAY 1850

From Liverpool

NAMES OF PASSENGERS	AGE	SEX	OCCUPATIONS	DATE PORT SHIP
EVITT, U-Mrs.	35	F	Unknown	09Ma02Bg
CLARKE, U-Mrs.	28	F	Unknown	09Ma02Bg
COWAN, Ann	28	F	Servant	09Ma02Bg
BESINET, Henry	30	M	Unknown	09Ma02Bg
MAYER, U	27	M	Merchant	09Ma02Bg
CALDWELL, John	23	M	Merchant	09Ma02Bg
SCHRIEBER, U	43	M	Merchant	09Ma02Bg
U-Jr.	19	M	Gentleman	09Ma02Bg
LANDICK, U	34	M	Merchant	09Ma02Bg
U-Jr.	15	M	Gentleman	09Ma02Bg
SPARROW, Robt.	24	M	Merchant	09Ma02Bg
SHARPLE, Mary-Ann	40	F	Servant	09Ma02Bg
KEARNEY, James	42	M	Merchant	09Ma02Bg
MITCHELL, John	29	M	Merchant	09Ma02Bg
KENNEDY, John	46	M	Merchant	09Ma02Bg
John-Jr.	18	M	Gentleman	09Ma02Bg
KELLY, John	43	M	Gentleman	09Ma02Bg
ADDISON, Samuel	30	M	Gentleman	09Ma02Bg

ADONIA 09 MAY 1850

From Windsor

NAMES OF PASSENGERS	AGE	SEX	OCCUPATIONS	DATE PORT SHIP
WILKINSON, Wm.	45	M	Shoemaker	09Ma52lh

ALBERT-GALLATIN 10 MAY 1850

From Liverpool

NAMES OF PASSENGERS	AGE	SEX	OCCUPATIONS	DATE PORT SHIP
HINTON, John	46	M	Farmer	10Ma02Fb
Margaret	36	F	Unknown	10Ma02Fb

NAMES OF PASSENGERS	AGE	SEX	OCCUPATIONS	DATE PORT SHIP
HINTON, William	11	M	Unknown	10Ma02Fb
Jane	9	F	Child	10Ma02Fb
Elleanor	8	F	Child	10Ma02Fb
John	6	M	Child	10Ma02Fb
Robert	4	M	Child	10Ma02Fb
HOPKINS, William	45	M	Farmer	10Ma02Fb
Henrietta	30	F	Unknown	10Ma02Fb
William	.00	M	Infant	10Ma02Fb
Died-At-Sea				
TUMERTY, Patrick	20	M	Laborer	10Ma02Fb
SWALLDICK, Bessy	20	F	Unknown	10Ma02Fb
BLYTHE, Catharine	20	F	Milliner	10Ma02Fb
WALSH, Thomas	23	M	Laborer	10Ma02Fb
HAMERTY, Margaret	20	F	Unknown	10Ma02Fb
Ellen	.00	F	Infant	10Ma02Fb
KELLY, Pat	40	M	Unknown	10Ma02Fb
Margaret	60	F	Unknown	10Ma02Fb
William	11	M	Unknown	10Ma02Fb
Margt.	9	F	Child	10Ma02Fb
Mick	7	M	Child	10Ma02Fb
James	35	M	Carpenter	10Ma02Fb
FAGAN, James	18	M	Laborer	10Ma02Fb
PETE, Robert	43	M	Laborer	10Ma02Fb
Harriet	29	F	Unknown	10Ma02Fb
NAHER, Honora	20	F	Unknown	10Ma02Fb
Grace	25	F	Unknown	10Ma02Fb
HOGAN, Michael	18	M	Laborer	10Ma02Fb
KEOGH, Thomas	30	M	Unknown	10Ma02Fb
Mary	25	F	Unknown	10Ma02Fb
DOOGIN, Elisabeth	26	F	Unknown	10Ma02Fb
LENNON, Margaret	20	F	Unknown	10Ma02Fb
CUNDER, Bridget	20	F	Unknown	10Ma02Fb
GALLAGHER, Jane	48	F	Unknown	10Ma02Fb
HOLEAN, Thomas	40	M	Laborer	10Ma02Fb
Mary	30	F	Unknown	10Ma02Fb
FINNEGAN, Bridget	20	F	Unknown	10Ma02Fb
MAHER, Pat	26	M	Laborer	10Ma02Fb
SMITH, Pat	27	M	Carpenter	10Ma02Fb
Ann	20	F	Unknown	10Ma02Fb
Elisabeth	.00	F	Infant	10Ma02Fb
FALLOW, Jane	16	F	Milliner	10Ma02Fb
Bridget	14	F	Milliner	10Ma02Fb
Pat	25	M	Carpenter	10Ma02Fb
TRAINOR, James	20	M	Laborer	10Ma02Fb
REED, Michael	22	M	Laborer	10Ma02Fb
FONESTY, Pat	25	M	Laborer	10Ma02Fb
FOGARTY, Betty	20	F	Unknown	10Ma02Fb
DUGNALL, Margt.	25	F	Unknown	10Ma02Fb
Thomas	.00	M	Infant	10Ma02Fb
FLANAGAN, Tim	20	M	Laborer	10Ma02Fb
MCDERMOT, Charles	20	M	Clerk	10Ma02Fb
CAHILL, Bridget	20	F	Unknown	10Ma02Fb
FANGHEY, Catherine	20	F	Unknown	10Ma02Fb
Honora	20	F	Milliner	10Ma02Fb
Thomas	4	M	Child	10Ma02Fb
KEOGH, Edward	26	M	Laborer	10Ma02Fb
RYAN, Kitty	24	F	Unknown	10Ma02Fb
FANNING, Pat	22	M	Laborer	10Ma02Fb
HARRINGTON, Nancy	18	F	Unknown	10Ma02Fb
RYAN, Martin	23	M	Laborer	10Ma02Fb
Ellen	18	F	Unknown	10Ma02Fb
Julia	17	F	Unknown	10Ma02Fb
GLEESON, Catharine	18	F	Unknown	10Ma02Fb
Mary	17	F	Unknown	10Ma02Fb
CONNORS, Thomas	20	M	Laborer	10Ma02Fb
FITZPATRICK, Wm.	21	M	Laborer	10Ma02Fb
Barney	23	M	Laborer	10Ma02Fb
Mary	20	F	Unknown	10Ma02Fb
CASH, James	22	M	Laborer	10Ma02Fb
BOMECUM, Ned	30	M	Laborer	10Ma02Fb
CULLEN, Honora	20	F	Unknown	10Ma02Fb
HENESSY, Catharine	17	F	Unknown	10Ma02Fb
FOGARTY, Catharine	18	F	Unknown	10Ma02Fb
Judy	20	F	Unknown	10Ma02Fb
MULLEN, Thomas	26	M	Laborer	10Ma02Fb

NAMES OF PASSENGERS	AGE	SEX	OCCUPATIONS	DATE PORT SHIP
HANLON, Pat	26	M	Laborer	10Ma02Fb
MCDONALD, Edward	26	M	Unknown	10Ma02Fb
BYRNE, Peter	40	M	Laborer	10Ma02Fb
John	11	M	Unknown	10Ma02Fb
DOYLE, Hugh	40	M	Laborer	10Ma02Fb
Charles	13	M	Unknown	10Ma02Fb
Ellen	20	F	Unknown	10Ma02Fb
JACKSON, William	20	M	Laborer	10Ma02Fb
Agnes	21	F	Unknown	10Ma02Fb
BOYLE, Margaret	36	F	Unknown	10Ma02Fb
DUFFY, Catherine	24	F	Unknown	10Ma02Fb
MCENTAGGART, John	21	M	Farmer	10Ma02Fb
BARNEY, Andrew	30	M	Clerk	10Ma02Fb
Margret	24	F	Unknown	10Ma02Fb
Ellen	.00	F	Infant	10Ma02Fb
DONOHOE, Kitty	28	F	Unknown	10Ma02Fb
Margaret	25	F	Unknown	10Ma02Fb
Mick	26	M	Mason	10Ma02Fb
SHANAHER, Mick	22	M	Laborer	10Ma02Fb
BURKE, Mick	26	M	Mason	10Ma02Fb
GOUGH, Thomas	30	M	Laborer	10Ma02Fb
Honora	28	F	Unknown	10Ma02Fb
BYRNE, Catharine	50	F	Unknown	10Ma02Fb
Betty	20	F	Milliner	10Ma02Fb
KEOGH, Pat	32	M	Farmer	10Ma02Fb
MCCOY, Thomas	21	M	Farmer	10Ma02Fb
Lawrence	17	M	Farmer	10Ma02Fb
DELANCEY, Darby	50	M	Farmer	10Ma02Fb
Thomas	50	M	Farmer	10Ma02Fb
ELLIS, Elizabeth	8	F	Child	10Ma02Fb
CAUFEE, U-Mrs.	28	F	Unknown	10Ma02Fb
U	.00	U	Infant	10Ma02Fb
Sally	10	F	Unknown	10Ma02Fb
Thomas	3	M	Child	10Ma02Fb
BURNES, Alice	30	F	Unknown	10Ma02Fb
EGAN, Pat	21	M	Laborer	10Ma02Fb
CARR, Peter	43	M	Farmer	10Ma02Fb
Ann	50	F	Unknown	10Ma02Fb
Peter	12	M	Unknown	10Ma02Fb
CLANCY, Bridget	18	F	Unknown	10Ma02Fb
MCCANN, Sarah	38	F	Unknown	10Ma02Fb
TAYLOR, Francis	24	M	Mason	10Ma02Fb
U-Mrs.	24	F	Unknown	10Ma02Fb
U	.00	U	Infant	10Ma02Fb
William	6	M	Child	10Ma02Fb
Albert	4	M	Child	10Ma02Fb
Joseph	2	M	Child	10Ma02Fb
BARR, Anne	34	F	Unknown	10Ma02Fb
William	.00	M	Infant	10Ma02Fb
Elisa	13	F	Unknown	10Ma02Fb
Ann	12	F	Unknown	10Ma02Fb
James	10	M	Unknown	10Ma02Fb
John	3	M	Child	10Ma02Fb
KELLY, Catharine	38	F	Unknown	10Ma02Fb
Margaret	17	F	Unknown	10Ma02Fb
BOWES, William	27	M	Laborer	10Ma02Fb
DELANCY, Edward	30	M	Laborer	10Ma02Fb
MAHONEY, Karnes	34	M	Laborer	10Ma02Fb
Mary	28	F	Unknown	10Ma02Fb
Mary	.00	F	Infant	10Ma02Fb
Maria	2	F	Child	10Ma02Fb
DOYLE, Lawrence	24	M	Laborer	10Ma02Fb
HUGHES, Betty	20	F	Unknown	10Ma02Fb
CAUFEE, John	34	M	Laborer	10Ma02Fb
DELANCEY, Mary	20	F	Unknown	10Ma02Fb
KEOGH, Patrick	22	M	Unknown	10Ma02Fb
HOEY, James	40	M	Laborer	10Ma02Fb
LAWREY, John	30	M	Carpenter	10Ma02Fb
Catherine	30	F	Carpenter	10Ma02Fb
Nancy	12	F	Carpenter	10Ma02Fb
Thomas	10	M	Unknown	10Ma02Fb
Margaret	7	F	Child	10Ma02Fb
Rebecca	5	F	Child	10Ma02Fb
FITZGERALD, Judy	40	F	Unknown	10Ma02Fb
DWYER, John	38	M	Printer	10Ma02Fb

NAMES OF PASSENGERS	AGE	SEX	OCCUPATIONS	DATE PORT SHIP
HURST, Charles	73	M	Laborer	10Ma02Fb
Anne	26	F	Unknown	10Ma02Fb
MARLIN, Sarah	15	F	Unknown	10Ma02Fb
WILSON, Mary	28	F	Unknown	10Ma02Fb
Anne	6	F	Child	10Ma02Fb
James	.00	M	Infant	10Ma02Fb
GROOM, Bridget	30	F	Unknown	10Ma02Fb
John	24	M	Laborer	10Ma02Fb
Roga	20	F	Laborer	10Ma02Fb
Roga	20	F	Laborer	10Ma02Fb
EGAN, Bridget	19	F	Unknown	10Ma02Fb
SLOAN, Elisa	50	F	Unknown	10Ma02Fb
Margaret	20	F	Unknown	10Ma02Fb
MCNAMAN, Herney	30	M	Laborer	10Ma02Fb
HAY, Bridget	20	F	Unknown	10Ma02Fb
MURPHY, Thomas	20	M	Laborer	10Ma02Fb
James	22	M	Laborer	10Ma02Fb
MCHAMAN, Michl.	26	M	Farmer	10Ma02Fb
Thomas	21	M	Farmer	10Ma02Fb
Mary	30	F	Unknown	10Ma02Fb
Ann	14	F	Unknown	10Ma02Fb
Ellen	16	F	Unknown	10Ma02Fb
Patrick	29	M	Farmer	10Ma02Fb
Elisa	25	F	Unknown	10Ma02Fb
Honora	3	F	Child	10Ma02Fb
Elisa	2	F	Child	10Ma02Fb
Phillip	.00	M	Infant	10Ma02Fb
HAYS, Michael	30	M	Farmer	10Ma02Fb
Deborah	30	F	Unknown	10Ma02Fb
William	3	M	Child	10Ma02Fb
Alice	2	F	Child	10Ma02Fb
Michael	.00	M	Infant	10Ma02Fb
RYAN, Richard	30	M	Laborer	10Ma02Fb
ORMAND, Johanna	23	F	Unknown	10Ma02Fb
LEONARD, Peggy	24	F	Unknown	10Ma02Fb
ORMAND, Bridget	7	F	Child	10Ma02Fb
WALL, Norry	30	F	Unknown	10Ma02Fb
DRUMOND, Mary	30	F	Unknown	10Ma02Fb
Jane	25	F	Unknown	10Ma02Fb
CANEY, James	20	M	Laborer	10Ma02Fb
John	30	M	Laborer	10Ma02Fb
BEATTY, Joseph	45	M	Farmer	10Ma02Fb
ELLIS, Alfred	31	M	Laborer	10Ma02Fb
Elisa	27	F	Laborer	10Ma02Fb
U	.00	F	Infant	10Ma02Fb
Born-At-Sea				
Maria	6	F	Child	10Ma02Fb
William	3	M	Child	10Ma02Fb
SOUTHERLAND, Francis	24	M	Sawer	10Ma02Fb
KELLY, Hannah	25	F	Unknown	10Ma02Fb
DELANCY, Michael	29	M	Laborer	10Ma02Fb
PORTER, Jane	40	F	Seamstress	10Ma02Fb
Joseph	2	M	Child	10Ma02Fb
Martha	.00	F	Infant	10Ma02Fb
STEWART, Isabella	30	F	Unknown	10Ma02Fb
DUGGIN, Anthony	30	M	Laborer	10Ma02Fb
BEATTY, Matilda	40	F	Unknown	10Ma02Fb
Elisa	20	F	Unknown	10Ma02Fb
William	18	M	Unknown	10Ma02Fb
James	14	M	Unknown	10Ma02Fb
Mary	11	F	Unknown	10Ma02Fb
Joseph	9	M	Child	10Ma02Fb
Bella	6	F	Child	10Ma02Fb
Matilda	4	F	Child	10Ma02Fb
CREIGHTON, John	16	M	Laborer	10Ma02Fb
William	14	M	Unknown	10Ma02Fb
Matilda	20	F	Unknown	10Ma02Fb
CARSON, Margaret	22	F	Unknown	10Ma02Fb
Mary-Jane	20	F	Unknown	10Ma02Fb
WRIGHT, Elisa	20	F	Unknown	10Ma02Fb
FLOOD, Michael	24	M	Laborer	10Ma02Fb
Edward	22	M	Laborer	10Ma02Fb
KELLY, Thomas	22	M	Laborer	10Ma02Fb
STANLEY, John	20	M	Laborer	10Ma02Fb
BRYAN, Patrick	22	M	Tinsmith	10Ma02Fb

NAMES OF PASSENGERS	AGE	SEX	OCCUPATIONS	DATE PORT SHIP
WALSH, Catharine	24	F	Unknown	10Ma02Fb
WOODS, Peter	20	M	Laborer	10Ma02Fb
TURNER, John	18	M	Laborer	10Ma02Fb
BRINNER, John	19	M	Farmer	10Ma02Fb
MURPHY, Ann	19	F	Unknown	10Ma02Fb
MCCATER, Hugh	35	M	Laborer	10Ma02Fb
ROCK, Patrick	23	M	Laborer	10Ma02Fb
BRANNON, William	18	M	Laborer	10Ma02Fb
DALTON, James	40	M	Laborer	10Ma02Fb
SWEENEY, Mathew	30	M	Laborer	10Ma02Fb
Margaret	20	F	Unknown	10Ma02Fb
FLYNN, Peter	30	M	Laborer	10Ma02Fb
Catharine	4	F	Child	10Ma02Fb
MCCOY, Charles	21	M	Cbtmkr	10Ma02Fb
Samuel	22	M	Laborer	10Ma02Fb
Anne	23	F	Unknown	10Ma02Fb
MCELHATTON, John	26	M	Laborer	10Ma02Fb
BORLAND, Wm.	25	M	Laborer	10Ma02Fb
WILSON, Robert	19	M	Laborer	10Ma02Fb
MCCOOKE, Elisabeth	17	F	Milliner	10Ma02Fb
Wm.John	.00	M	Infant	10Ma02Fb
FALTON, Mary-Ann	24	F	Unknown	10Ma02Fb
MURPHY, Patrick	40	M	Laborer	10Ma02Fb
CORSE, James	44	M	Bricklayer	10Ma02Fb
Jemima	20	F	Unknown	10Ma02Fb
KENDLE, William	23	M	Mason	10Ma02Fb
FAY, John	28	M	Laborer	10Ma02Fb
MCGUIRE, Patrick	48	M	Laborer	10Ma02Fb
FITZPATRICK, Owen	30	M	Laborer	10Ma02Fb
MOONAN, James	31	M	Laborer	10Ma02Fb
MOHAN, Peter	20	M	Laborer	10Ma02Fb
BOHAN, Pat	30	M	Laborer	10Ma02Fb
Jane	21	F	Unknown	10Ma02Fb
Bridget	.00	F	Infant	10Ma02Fb
Died-At-Sea				
BUCHALL, Henry	30	M	Laborer	10Ma02Fb
Jane	30	F	Unknown	10Ma02Fb
Johnson	5	M	Child	10Ma02Fb
Arthur	.00	M	Infant	10Ma02Fb
DOLMAGH, Jacob	30	M	Laborer	10Ma02Fb
Anne	50	F	Unknown	10Ma02Fb
Maria	20	F	Unknown	10Ma02Fb
Anne	18	F	Unknown	10Ma02Fb
Ellen	12	F	Unknown	10Ma02Fb
NEARY, Charles	26	M	Laborer	10Ma02Fb
FEENEY, Phillip	40	M	Laborer	10Ma02Fb
DEVANEY, Miche.	26	M	Laborer	10Ma02Fb
BURNES, John	22	M	Laborer	10Ma02Fb
MCAMILTY, John	20	M	Laborer	10Ma02Fb
SMITH, Emma	20	F	Unknown	10Ma02Fb
LEEMINGS, James	18	M	Laborer	10Ma02Fb
RYAN, John	32	M	Laborer	10Ma02Fb
MADDEN, James	25	M	Laborer	10Ma02Fb
POWER, Michael	22	M	Laborer	10Ma02Fb
DWYER, Mary	24	F	Unknown	10Ma02Fb
MATHEWS, James	28	M	Clerk	10Ma02Fb
MCAULEY, Patrick	21	M	Laborer	10Ma02Fb
KEARNEY, Sarah	20	F	Unknown	10Ma02Fb
FALLOOND, Jane	45	F	Unknown	10Ma02Fb
CAHILL, Edward	21	M	Farmer	10Ma02Fb
LANCY, Ellen	20	F	Unknown	10Ma02Fb
Margaret	20	F	Unknown	10Ma02Fb
MAHER, James	22	M	Laborer	10Ma02Fb
HACKETT, John	20	M	Laborer	10Ma02Fb
HEALEY, Daniel	26	M	Laborer	10Ma02Fb
MORTON, John	21	M	Laborer	10Ma02Fb
BAINES, John	50	M	Laborer	10Ma02Fb
Hannah	40	F	Unknown	10Ma02Fb
William	12	M	Unknown	10Ma02Fb
Anthony	8	M	Child	10Ma02Fb
Maria	6	F	Child	10Ma02Fb
U	.00	U	Infant	10Ma02Fb
CONNOLLY, Thomas	35	M	Laborer	10Ma02Fb
Johanna	35	F	Unknown	10Ma02Fb
CLANCY, William	21	M	Laborer	10Ma02Fb

NAMES OF PASSENGERS	AGE	SEX	OCCUPATIONS	DATE PORT SHIP
DWYER, Lawrence	50	M	Laborer	10Ma02Fb
Denis	22	M	Laborer	10Ma02Fb
HICKEY, Patrick	35	M	Laborer	10Ma02Fb
WARD, Patk.	23	M	Farmer	10Ma02Fb
HOULAHAN, James	21	M	Carpenter	10Ma02Fb
CONNERS, Michael	22	M	Laborer	10Ma02Fb
MULACKEY, Mathew	25	M	Laborer	10Ma02Fb
CUMMINGS, Ann	21	F	Unknown	10Ma02Fb
Ellen	22	F	Unknown	10Ma02Fb
BRENNON, Mick	24	M	Laborer	10Ma02Fb
LARKIN, Mary	30	F	Unknown	10Ma02Fb
John	9	M	Child	10Ma02Fb
Bridget	7	F	Child	10Ma02Fb
Johanna	4	F	Child	10Ma02Fb
Thomas	.00	M	Infant	10Ma02Fb
FINNEGAN, Judy	25	F	Milliner	10Ma02Fb
Thomas	23	M	Laborer	10Ma02Fb
MOORE, Joseph	70	M	Weaver	10Ma02Fb
Died-At-Sea				
Elisabeth	50	F	Unknown	10Ma02Fb
John	20	M	Weaver	10Ma02Fb
Arthur	25	M	Weaver	10Ma02Fb
Elisabeth	30	F	Unknown	10Ma02Fb
THOMPSON, Samuel	25	M	Laborer	10Ma02Fb
CUNNINGHAM, Ann	20	F	Unknown	10Ma02Fb
MCCABE, Thomas	19	M	Laborer	10Ma02Fb
GOOD, Thomas	15	M	Tailor	10Ma02Fb
BRADIE, William	20	M	Laborer	10Ma02Fb
KEENA, John	23	M	Laborer	10Ma02Fb
Margaret	45	F	Unknown	10Ma02Fb
Mary	21	F	Unknown	10Ma02Fb
Michael	26	M	Unknown	10Ma02Fb
MASTERSON, Owen	23	M	Laborer	10Ma02Fb
KENATY, Mary	17	F	Unknown	10Ma02Fb
MULHOLLAND, Jane	23	F	Unknown	10Ma02Fb
MUNAGH, Michael	30	M	Laborer	10Ma02Fb
Elisa	30	F	Unknown	10Ma02Fb
MCKEON, James	19	M	Molder	10Ma02Fb
MURPHY, Phillip	18	M	Laborer	10Ma02Fb
FRANEY, James	28	M	Bricklayer	10Ma02Fb
BYRNE, Mary	15	F	Unknown	10Ma02Fb
SLEIGHT, Wm.	26	M	Laborer	10Ma02Fb
Ann	24	F	Unknown	10Ma02Fb
HARE, Thomas	20	M	Baker	10Ma02Fb
MULLAY, Thomas	20	M	Laborer	10Ma02Fb
DOYLE, Lawrence	30	M	Tailor	10Ma02Fb
BYRNE, Bryan	12	M	Unknown	10Ma02Fb
MCCORMICK, Francis	34	M	Barber	10Ma02Fb
FAY, Mary	18	F	Unknown	10Ma02Fb
MCBRIDE, Peter	63	M	Laborer	10Ma02Fb
SINGLETON, Richard	26	M	Joiner	10Ma02Fb
Mary	28	F	Joiner	10Ma02Fb
MAHON, James	18	M	Mason	10Ma02Fb
Anne	16	F	Unknown	10Ma02Fb
KELLY, James	18	M	Blacksmith	10Ma02Fb
DOYLE, Patrick	18	M	Mason	10Ma02Fb
COMAS, Peggy	26	F	Unknown	10Ma02Fb
Peggy	.00	F	Infant	10Ma02Fb
Mary	.00	F	Infant	10Ma02Fb
CURRAN, Julia	24	F	Unknown	10Ma02Fb
FALKNER, James	40	M	Laborer	10Ma02Fb
Patt	26	M	Unknown	10Ma02Fb
Ann	40	F	Unknown	10Ma02Fb
Margaret	20	F	Unknown	10Ma02Fb
Thomas	18	M	Unknown	10Ma02Fb
BURN, Margaret	20	F	Unknown	10Ma02Fb
QUIGLY, Bridget	22	F	Unknown	10Ma02Fb
CONLON, John	19	M	Laborer	10Ma02Fb
HAGAN, John	20	M	Laborer	10Ma02Fb
Thomas	22	M	Laborer	10Ma02Fb
SMITH, Thomas	19	M	Laborer	10Ma02Fb
CLARK, Henry	20	M	Laborer	10Ma02Fb
MCGINN, Michael	23	M	Laborer	10Ma02Fb
SMITH, Michael	23	M	Laborer	10Ma02Fb
HUGHES, Ann	20	F	Unknown	10Ma02Fb
CALLAN, Margt.	20	F	Unknown	10Ma02Fb
GARTLAND, Wm.	20	M	Laborer	10Ma02Fb
Mary	28	F	Unknown	10Ma02Fb
MANDY, Bryan	21	M	Laborer	10Ma02Fb
CALLAN, Bridget	32	F	Unknown	10Ma02Fb
WHEATLEY, Margaret	16	F	Unknown	10Ma02Fb
Michael	20	M	Laborer	10Ma02Fb
ROGERS, Mary	18	F	Milliner	10Ma02Fb
Margt.	20	F	Milliner	10Ma02Fb
DOOLEY, Bridget	27	F	Milliner	10Ma02Fb
GREEN, Sally	20	F	Milliner	10Ma02Fb
Elisa	17	F	Milliner	10Ma02Fb
CASSIDY, Ann	17	F	Unknown	10Ma02Fb
Catherine	13	F	Unknown	10Ma02Fb
KEEGAN, Ann	21	F	Unknown	10Ma02Fb
HARMAN, Elisa	40	F	Unknown	10Ma02Fb
MARTIN, Ann	24	F	Unknown	10Ma02Fb
MAGUIRE, Thomas	8	M	Child	10Ma02Fb
Margaret	6	F	Child	10Ma02Fb
John	4	M	Child	10Ma02Fb
HARTLEY, Bridget	20	M	Shoemaker	10Ma02Fb
Margt.	11	F	Unknown	10Ma02Fb
Maria	8	F	Child	10Ma02Fb
CAMPBELL, Peter	36	M	Shopman	10Ma02Fb
Margt.	32	F	Unknown	10Ma02Fb
Bridget	18	F	Unknown	10Ma02Fb
James	2	M	Child	10Ma02Fb
Peter	.00	M	Infant	10Ma02Fb
LYNCH, Peter	16	M	Laborer	10Ma02Fb
CUMMINS, Thomas	28	M	Laborer	10Ma02Fb
Denis	4	M	Child	10Ma02Fb
CUNNINGHAM, Pat	26	M	Laborer	10Ma02Fb
HARDY, Catherine	24	F	Unknown	10Ma02Fb
James	.00	M	Infant	10Ma02Fb
DOWDALL, Ann	21	F	Unknown	10Ma02Fb
FRANER, James	22	M	Baker	10Ma02Fb
SPINDER, John	20	M	Laborer	10Ma02Fb
MONAGHAN, Mary	20	F	Unknown	10Ma02Fb
CONNOR, James	25	M	Laborer	10Ma02Fb
ROGERS, Thomas	30	M	Laborer	10Ma02Fb
MURPHY, Margaret	20	F	Unknown	10Ma02Fb
LYONS, John	37	M	Musician	10Ma02Fb
MCGUIN, Michael	40	M	Laborer	10Ma02Fb
John	22	M	Laborer	10Ma02Fb
Phillip	13	M	Unknown	10Ma02Fb
FITZMAURICE, Thomas	25	M	Laborer	10Ma02Fb
Mary	18	F	Unknown	10Ma02Fb
WALSH, Mary	13	F	Unknown	10Ma02Fb
RILEY, Catherine	45	F	Unknown	10Ma02Fb
Francis	20	M	Laborer	10Ma02Fb
Catherine	17	F	Unknown	10Ma02Fb
Pat	15	M	Unknown	10Ma02Fb
Bridget	13	F	Unknown	10Ma02Fb
Joseph	11	M	Unknown	10Ma02Fb
Mary	9	F	Child	10Ma02Fb
KELLY, Francis	50	M	Laborer	10Ma02Fb
GANNATY, Edward	30	M	Laborer	10Ma02Fb
FOLEY, Martin	25	M	Laborer	10Ma02Fb
GANNATY, Bartly	25	M	Laborer	10Ma02Fb
FINERTY, Michael	25	M	Laborer	10Ma02Fb
DOGHERTY, James	25	M	Laborer	10Ma02Fb
DOWNES, William	30	M	Laborer	10Ma02Fb
GANNATY, Sarah	18	F	Unknown	10Ma02Fb
MAHONY, Lawrence	28	M	Laborer	10Ma02Fb
Bridget	27	F	Unknown	10Ma02Fb
Bridget	4	F	Child	10Ma02Fb
Michael	2	M	Child	10Ma02Fb
John	.00	M	Infant	10Ma02Fb
ROCHE, William	19	M	Laborer	10Ma02Fb
Mary	25	F	Unknown	10Ma02Fb
David	.00	M	Infant	10Ma02Fb
Edward	13	M	Unknown	10Ma02Fb
Michael	26	M	Laborer	10Ma02Fb
NELSON, Thomas	26	M	Shoemaker	10Ma02Fb
Ellen	23	F	Unknown	10Ma02Fb

NAMES OF PASSENGERS	AGE	SEX	OCCUPATIONS	DATE PORT SHIP
NELSON, Mary	.00	F	Infant	10Ma02Fb
Died-At-Sea				
U	.00	M	Infant	10Ma02Fb
Born-At-Sea				
LUND, Ellen	40	F	Unknown	10Ma02Fb
JENKINS, James	29	M	Unknown	10Ma02Fb
DUME, Mick	30	M	Laborer	10Ma02Fb
Dan	22	M	Laborer	10Ma02Fb
MALONY, Pat	25	M	Farmer	10Ma02Fb
Ellen	25	F	Unknown	10Ma02Fb
Kate	20	F	Unknown	10Ma02Fb
Ellen	10	F	Unknown	10Ma02Fb
Margaret	8	F	Child	10Ma02Fb
Rodger	7	M	Child	10Ma02Fb
CUSAC, John	23	M	Farmer	10Ma02Fb
Kate	27	F	Unknown	10Ma02Fb
Patrick	.00	M	Infant	10Ma02Fb
ODEA, Mick	20	M	Farmer	10Ma02Fb
MILLEN, Pat	23	M	Laborer	10Ma02Fb
CARROLL, John	25	M	Laborer	10Ma02Fb
KERBY, Mary	17	F	Unknown	10Ma02Fb
Honora	22	F	Unknown	10Ma02Fb
WALSH, John	22	M	Unknown	10Ma02Fb
DOGERTY, Joseph	22	M	Blacksmith	10Ma02Fb
MCCARTNEY, James	30	M	Carpenter	10Ma02Fb
Francis	11	M	Unknown	10Ma02Fb
DONOVAN, Martin	36	M	Laborer	10Ma02Fb
BURKE, James	22	M	Farmer	10Ma02Fb
SCULLY, James	25	M	Farmer	10Ma02Fb
HALLORAN, Denis	28	M	Farmer	10Ma02Fb
BURKE, Catherine	26	F	Unknown	10Ma02Fb
U	.00	U	Infant	10Ma02Fb
BURNS, Edward	23	M	Tailor	10Ma02Fb
HORGAN, Pat	30	M	Laborer	10Ma02Fb
REARDON, James	26	M	Laborer	10Ma02Fb
PENNEFATHER, Nathaniel	45	M	Laborer	10Ma02Fb
Elleanor	35	F	Unknown	10Ma02Fb
John	14	M	Laborer	10Ma02Fb
Johanna	12	F	Unknown	10Ma02Fb
Anne	10	F	Unknown	10Ma02Fb
Thomas	7	M	Child	10Ma02Fb
U	.00	U	Infant	10Ma02Fb
GALLAGHER, Elisa	20	F	Unknown	10Ma02Fb
SULLIVAN, John	25	M	Laborer	10Ma02Fb
Bridget	27	F	Unknown	10Ma02Fb
FOLEY, John	24	M	Laborer	10Ma02Fb
Mary	20	F	Unknown	10Ma02Fb
ROCHE, John	25	M	Laborer	10Ma02Fb
ODONNELL, Patrick	30	M	Laborer	10Ma02Fb
Betsey	25	F	Unknown	10Ma02Fb
Lissey	.00	F	Infant	10Ma02Fb
QUINN, Thomas	30	M	Laborer	10Ma02Fb
FLOOD, Thomas	20	M	Farmer	10Ma02Fb
OWEN, John	40	M	Laborer	10Ma02Fb
HART, Michael	20	M	Laborer	10Ma02Fb
FITZPATRICK, Thomas	18	M	Laborer	10Ma02Fb
JORDAN, Michael	22	M	Laborer	10Ma02Fb
Kitty	23	F	Unknown	10Ma02Fb
Shelby	50	F	Unknown	10Ma02Fb
Biddy	23	F	Unknown	10Ma02Fb
Maria	.00	F	Infant	10Ma02Fb
Thomas	23	M	Laborer	10Ma02Fb
HANLEY, Michael	21	M	Laborer	10Ma02Fb
KELLY, Thomas	24	M	Laborer	10Ma02Fb
LANCING, Michael	15	M	Laborer	10Ma02Fb
FEENERTY, Catherine	23	F	Unknown	10Ma02Fb
MCGUIRE, Martin	20	M	Glazier	10Ma02Fb
GAVIN, Miche.	30	M	Unknown	10Ma02Fb
REILLY, Pat	50	M	Laborer	10Ma02Fb
Anne	45	F	Unknown	10Ma02Fb
MALLET, Honora	20	F	Unknown	10Ma02Fb
REILLY, Joseph	20	M	Laborer	10Ma02Fb
Hain--, Mary	22	F	Unknown	10Ma02Fb
STEWART, Mary	14	F	Unknown	10Ma02Fb
HACKETT, George	5	M	Child	10Ma02Fb
CAMPBELL, James	15	M	Carpenter	10Ma02Fb
GRAHAM, Wm.	30	M	Laborer	10Ma02Fb
SLEITH, Thomas	41	M	Weaver	10Ma02Fb
Margaret	41	F	Unknown	10Ma02Fb
Sarah	21	F	Unknown	10Ma02Fb
Richard	18	M	Unknown	10Ma02Fb
OBRIEN, Bridget	15	F	Unknown	10Ma02Fb
DUNNE, Mary	32	F	Unknown	10Ma02Fb
Margaret	11	F	Unknown	10Ma02Fb
Thomas	6	M	Child	10Ma02Fb
James	3	M	Child	10Ma02Fb
Died-At-Sea				
PORTER, Wm.	27	M	Weaver	10Ma02Fb
BARCLAY, Thomas	46	M	Laborer	10Ma02Fb
Elisabeth	46	F	Unknown	10Ma02Fb
John	13	M	Unknown	10Ma02Fb
ARMSTRONG, Thomas-S.	11	M	Unknown	10Ma02Fb
ARTHUR, Mick	30	M	Laborer	10Ma02Fb
DUNNAN, Pat	60	M	Weaver	10Ma02Fb
Pat	16	M	Unknown	10Ma02Fb
Margaret	13	F	Unknown	10Ma02Fb
Hugh	12	M	Unknown	10Ma02Fb
Ann	10	F	Unknown	10Ma02Fb
WEST, James	30	M	Carpenter	10Ma02Fb
SMITH, Julia	24	F	Unknown	10Ma02Fb
DALTON, Michael	17	M	Laborer	10Ma02Fb
RYAN, Thomas	25	M	Laborer	10Ma02Fb
MCCABE, Mary	20	F	Unknown	10Ma02Fb
LOWRY, Mary-Jane	42	F	Unknown	10Ma02Fb
Susan	21	F	Unknown	10Ma02Fb
Denis	19	M	Unknown	10Ma02Fb
Jane	17	F	Unknown	10Ma02Fb
Alexander	13	M	Unknown	10Ma02Fb
James	3	M	Child	10Ma02Fb
MCGARRY, Elisa	20	F	Unknown	10Ma02Fb
Mary-Ann	18	F	Unknown	10Ma02Fb
HORAN, John	20	M	Laborer	10Ma02Fb
BROOKS, John	15	M	Laborer	10Ma02Fb
KING, Bridget	20	F	Unknown	10Ma02Fb
MALDON, Timothy	29	M	Laborer	10Ma02Fb
DUNN, Martin	33	M	Laborer	10Ma02Fb
BURKE, James	30	M	Tailor	10Ma02Fb
HOGAN, Michael	24	M	Farmer	10Ma02Fb
John	19	M	Farmer	10Ma02Fb
Bridget	25	F	Unknown	10Ma02Fb
RYAN, Mary	16	F	Unknown	10Ma02Fb
Margaret	15	F	Unknown	10Ma02Fb
DUNN, Mary	20	F	Unknown	10Ma02Fb
FLANAGAN, James	30	M	Laborer	10Ma02Fb
Teresa	25	F	Unknown	10Ma02Fb
DELANCY, Thomas	20	M	Laborer	10Ma02Fb
KEALEY, James	25	M	Laborer	10Ma02Fb
DOER, John	22	M	Farmer	10Ma02Fb
DWYER, Mary	24	F	Unknown	10Ma02Fb
Ann	26	F	Unknown	10Ma02Fb
BREWSHIHAN, John	25	M	Farmer	10Ma02Fb
SLATTERY, Honora	22	F	Unknown	10Ma02Fb
PILKINGTON, Richard	57	M	Farmer	10Ma02Fb
Catherine	48	F	Unknown	10Ma02Fb
Elisa	24	F	Unknown	10Ma02Fb
Maria	22	F	Unknown	10Ma02Fb
John	20	M	Unknown	10Ma02Fb
Joseph	19	M	Unknown	10Ma02Fb
Susan	17	F	Unknown	10Ma02Fb
MOORE, James	30	M	Farmer	10Ma02Fb
U-Mrs.	30	F	Unknown	10Ma02Fb
John	3	M	Child	10Ma02Fb
GRINAN, James	32	M	Laborer	10Ma02Fb
John	30	M	Laborer	10Ma02Fb
Maurice	24	M	Unknown	10Ma02Fb
Thomas	22	M	Laborer	10Ma02Fb
William	19	M	Laborer	10Ma02Fb
Mary-Ann	26	F	Unknown	10Ma02Fb
COLEMAN, Jeremiah	30	M	Laborer	10Ma02Fb
MORNAN, Cornelius	25	M	Laborer	10Ma02Fb

NAMES OF PASSENGERS	AGE	SEX	OCCUPATIONS	DATE PORT SHIP
MARKAHAN, Ellen	29	F	Unknown	10Ma02Fb
Margaret	.00	F	Infant	10Ma02Fb
MCCORKEY, Elisabeth	44	F	Unknown	10Ma02Fb
Margt.Anne	18	F	Unknown	10Ma02Fb
Elisabeth	16	F	Unknown	10Ma02Fb
Edward	12	M	Unknown	10Ma02Fb
John	9	M	Child	10Ma02Fb
Sarah-Jane	6	F	Child	10Ma02Fb
U	.00	M	Infant	10Ma02Fb
Born-At-Sea				
HUNT, George	30	M	Gdnr	10Ma02Fb
Mary-Ann	26	F	Unknown	10Ma02Fb
William	1	M	Child	10Ma02Fb
WYRE, James	30	M	Laborer	10Ma02Fb
GOOHAGAN, James	11	M	Laborer	10Ma02Fb
NUGENT, Bridget	20	F	Unknown	10Ma02Fb
TIERNAN, Mary	50	F	Unknown	10Ma02Fb
John	30	M	Laborer	10Ma02Fb
Mary-Ann	16	F	Unknown	10Ma02Fb
Simon	13	M	Unknown	10Ma02Fb
Edward	12	M	Unknown	10Ma02Fb
MCMALLEN, Alexander	20	M	Laborer	10Ma02Fb
CLARK, Joseph	20	M	Butcher	10Ma02Fb
MCNEILE, Wm.	50	M	Farmer	10Ma02Fb
Margaret	50	F	Unknown	10Ma02Fb
John	16	M	Unknown	10Ma02Fb
William	9	M	Child	10Ma02Fb
GARNON, Mark	30	M	Laborer	10Ma02Fb
CASEY, John	17	M	Farmer	10Ma02Fb
Mary	15	F	Unknown	10Ma02Fb
Catharine	13	F	Unknown	10Ma02Fb
Ann	11	F	Unknown	10Ma02Fb
Margaret	6	F	Child	10Ma02Fb
Rose	3	F	Child	10Ma02Fb
Thomas	.00	M	Infant	10Ma02Fb
MCCORMAC, Ann	20	F	Unknown	10Ma02Fb
MCKINLEY, John	30	M	Laborer	10Ma02Fb
MCCAMEFRY, John	35	M	Laborer	10Ma02Fb
BERGIN, Jeremiah	18	M	Laborer	10Ma02Fb
Catharine	17	F	Unknown	10Ma02Fb
GRIFFIN, Thomas	50	M	Hatter	10Ma02Fb
CONNOLLY, Andrew	34	M	Clerk	10Ma02Fb
Catharine	27	F	Unknown	10Ma02Fb
Mary	50	F	Unknown	10Ma02Fb
U	.00	M	Infant	10Ma02Fb
Born-At-Sea				
WALSH, Jeremiah	30	M	Laborer	10Ma02Fb
William	18	M	Unknown	10Ma02Fb
Margaret	21	F	Unknown	10Ma02Fb
MCCABE, Ann	30	F	Unknown	10Ma02Fb
ROGAN, Bridget	35	F	Unknown	10Ma02Fb
John	15	M	Laborer	10Ma02Fb
Ann	11	F	Unknown	10Ma02Fb
Bridget	8	F	Child	10Ma02Fb
CORDIDE, Mick	20	M	Laborer	10Ma02Fb
Biddy	18	F	Unknown	10Ma02Fb
KARNEY, John	20	M	Laborer	10Ma02Fb
CUMMINGS, Mick	35	M	Laborer	10Ma02Fb
Sally	35	F	Unknown	10Ma02Fb
Biddy	13	F	Unknown	10Ma02Fb
CARROLL, Catherine	18	F	Unknown	10Ma02Fb
MOORE, Honor	42	F	Unknown	10Ma02Fb
Pat	17	M	Farmer	10Ma02Fb
Edward	13	M	Unknown	10Ma02Fb
Norty	12	M	Unknown	10Ma02Fb
John	10	M	Unknown	10Ma02Fb
CASSINE, James	24	M	Farmer	10Ma02Fb
BURKE, Anthony	30	M	Farmer	10Ma02Fb
HEALY, Nicholas	40	M	Farmer	10Ma02Fb
Bess	24	F	Unknown	10Ma02Fb
Alley	18	F	Unknown	10Ma02Fb
Margaret	15	F	Unknown	10Ma02Fb
Nicholas	11	M	Unknown	10Ma02Fb
Mary	8	F	Child	10Ma02Fb
Nick	2	M	Child	10Ma02Fb

NAMES OF PASSENGERS	AGE	SEX	OCCUPATIONS	DATE PORT SHIP
HANLON, Walter	25	M	Laborer	10Ma02Fb
HOLLAND, Mary	20	F	Unknown	10Ma02Fb
CASEY, Daniel	45	M	Farmer	10Ma02Fb
Ann	40	F	Unknown	10Ma02Fb
NOLAN, Anty	20	M	Laborer	10Ma02Fb
MACKESSY, Pat	20	M	Laborer	10Ma02Fb
CARROLL, Minny	20	F	Unknown	10Ma02Fb
DONNEGAN, Mary-A.	24	F	Unknown	10Ma02Fb
HALL, Margaret	22	F	Unknown	10Ma02Fb
Elisa	18	F	Unknown	10Ma02Fb
FLYNN, Jane	12	F	Unknown	10Ma02Fb
DUNEGAN, John	6	M	Child	10Ma02Fb
Margaret	3	F	Child	10Ma02Fb
AGNELLE, Miles	20	M	Laborer	10Ma02Fb
MCENTEER, Alex	45	M	Unknown	10Ma02Fb
Owen	13	M	Unknown	10Ma02Fb
Paul	11	M	Unknown	10Ma02Fb
Kate	9	F	Child	10Ma02Fb
MADDEN, James	18	M	Laborer	10Ma02Fb
CONNERS, Pat	35	M	Laborer	10Ma02Fb
Nancy	35	F	Unknown	10Ma02Fb
Thomas	8	M	Child	10Ma02Fb
Mary	.00	F	Infant	10Ma02Fb
FITZGERALD, Ellen	18	F	Unknown	10Ma02Fb
Biddy	16	F	Unknown	10Ma02Fb
MAURY, Biddy	18	F	Unknown	10Ma02Fb
RYAN, Mary	21	F	Unknown	10Ma02Fb
Kate	4	F	Child	10Ma02Fb
HIGGINS, Thomas	21	M	Laborer	10Ma02Fb
Thomas	22	M	Laborer	10Ma02Fb
LOUDON, John	12	M	Laborer	10Ma02Fb
KENNEDY, Mick	30	M	Laborer	10Ma02Fb
CARR, Ann-Maria	11	F	Unknown	10Ma02Fb
HOWELL, William	28	M	Farmer	10Ma02Fb
Elisa	26	F	Unknown	10Ma02Fb
Frank	2	M	Child	10Ma02Fb
Thomas	.00	M	Infant	10Ma02Fb
PRENDERGAST, John	26	M	Clergyman	10Ma02Fb
Peter	32	M	Merchant	10Ma02Fb
Mary	22	F	Unknown	10Ma02Fb
CARNEY, Cushin-Mrs.	22	F	Unknown	10Ma02Fb
SPRING, Wm.	30	M	Laborer	10Ma02Fb
EMERSON, John	40	M	Printer	10Ma02Fb
PHILLIPS, Alexander	18	M	Laborer	10Ma02Fb
WILLIAMS, George-Gibbi	38	M	Merchant	10Ma02Fb
GRAY, William	26	M	Unknown	10Ma02Fb

SOUTHAMPTON 11 MAY 1850

From London

MAHER, Lucy	24	F	Servant	11Ma06Do

CONSTITUTION 11 MAY 1850

From Liverpool

KELCHER, Jere.	25	M	Farmer	11Ma02Dl
TOOHEY, Michael	25	M	Farmer	11Ma02Dl
FITZPATRICK, James	21	M	Farmer	11Ma02Dl
Ann	19	F	Servant	11Ma02Dl
MULLIN, John	25	M	Laborer	11Ma02Dl
CALHOON, James	23	M	Laborer	11Ma02Dl

NAMES OF PASSENGERS	AGE	SEX	OCCUPATIONS	DATE PORT SHIP
CALHOON, Ann	27	F	Servant	11Ma02DI
MCMANNUS, John	61	M	Laborer	11Ma02DI
Ann	56	F	Servant	11Ma02DI
John	20	M	Laborer	11Ma02DI
William	18	M	Laborer	11Ma02DI
Ann	16	F	Servant	11Ma02DI
James	13	M	Servant	11Ma02DI
Mary	9	F	Child	11Ma02DI
KELLY, Mary	30	F	Servant	11Ma02DI
U, Mary	35	F	Servant	11Ma02DI
DUFFY, Mary	18	F	Servant	11Ma02DI
MCDONALD, James	18	M	Farmer	11Ma02DI
DUFFY, Catherine	20	F	Servant	11Ma02DI
BURNES, Sally	18	F	Servant	11Ma02DI
CROSSLEY, Margaret	50	F	Servant	11Ma02DI
Peter	25	M	Servant	11Ma02DI
Mary	20	F	Servant	11Ma02DI
FITZPATRICK, Mary	16	F	Servant	11Ma02DI
RILEY, Biddy	40	F	Servant	11Ma02DI
GREGG, Judy	50	F	Servant	11Ma02DI
Michael	17	M	Servant	11Ma02DI
Margaret	12	F	Servant	11Ma02DI
Martin	11	M	Servant	11Ma02DI
SEELY, Mary	20	F	Servant	11Ma02DI
Catherine	18	F	Servant	11Ma02DI
SCULLION, John	17	M	Servant	11Ma02DI
WEST, George	30	M	Servant	11Ma02DI
CABBLE, Edward	25	M	Servant	11Ma02DI
COX, Biddy	20	F	Servant	11Ma02DI
OROOKE, Maria	10	F	Servant	11Ma02DI
QUINN, John	22	M	Servant	11Ma02DI
MAYO, Amelia	21	F	Servant	11Ma02DI
BANAGHER, Margaret	20	F	Servant	11Ma02DI
DONELY, Pat	20	M	Servant	11Ma02DI
MCDERMOTT, Mary	23	F	Servant	11Ma02DI
PAYTON, John	18	M	Farmer	11Ma02DI
Henry	16	M	Farmer	11Ma02DI
BONNER, Mary	44	F	Farmer	11Ma02DI
Barney	15	M	Farmer	11Ma02DI
Hugh	10	M	Farmer	11Ma02DI
Ellen	7	F	Child	11Ma02DI
Mary-A.	3	F	Child	11Ma02DI
HILL, Emma	24	F	Farmer	11Ma02DI
Eliza	2	F	Child	11Ma02DI
Charles	.01	M	Infant	11Ma02DI
KEMP, Betty	46	F	Farmer	11Ma02DI
Robert	35	M	Farmer	11Ma02DI
Jane	11	F	Farmer	11Ma02DI
HAUGHTON, James	59	M	Farmer	11Ma02DI
Sarah	53	F	Farmer	11Ma02DI
Jane	18	F	Farmer	11Ma02DI
Mary	14	F	Farmer	11Ma02DI
OWEN, William	28	M	Laborer	11Ma02DI
CARROLL, Pat	35	M	Laborer	11Ma02DI
Catherine	9	F	Child	11Ma02DI
Henry	7	M	Child	11Ma02DI
William	4	M	Child	11Ma02DI
KELLY, Ann	18	F	Laborer	11Ma02DI
DONALDSON, Ann	22	F	Laborer	11Ma02DI
BRYAN, Peter	35	M	Laborer	11Ma02DI
Mary	34	F	Laborer	11Ma02DI
Johan	8	M	Child	11Ma02DI
Mary	6	F	Child	11Ma02DI
John	4	M	Child	11Ma02DI
Margaret	.01	F	Infant	11Ma02DI
GRIFFIN, Michael	28	M	Farmer	11Ma02DI
CASIDY, Thomas	44	M	Farmer	11Ma02DI
Rose	35	F	Farmer	11Ma02DI
Peter	14	M	Farmer	11Ma02DI
Pat	12	M	Farmer	11Ma02DI
Henry	11	M	Farmer	11Ma02DI
Edward	8	M	Child	11Ma02DI
RENSHAW, Amos	21	M	Farmer	11Ma02DI
PRINCE, Mary	21	F	Weaver	11Ma02DI
Hannah	18	F	Weaver	11Ma02DI

NAMES OF PASSENGERS	AGE	SEX	OCCUPATIONS	DATE PORT SHIP
BOOTH, Martha	24	F	Weaver	11Ma02DI
Robert	4	M	Child	11Ma02DI
Robert	.00	M	Infant	11Ma02DI
SPROTES, William	36	M	Farmer	11Ma02DI
Margaret	34	F	Farmer	11Ma02DI
William	11	M	Farmer	11Ma02DI
Jane	8	F	Child	11Ma02DI
Margaret	4	F	Child	11Ma02DI
PEEL, William	21	M	Farmer	11Ma02DI
Roger	16	M	Farmer	11Ma02DI
PETERS, Ann	51	F	Farmer	11Ma02DI
John	23	M	Farmer	11Ma02DI
Ann	20	F	Farmer	11Ma02DI
Susan	13	F	Farmer	11Ma02DI
HOWARTH, William	35	M	Farmer	11Ma02DI
SATCHILLE, William	25	M	Farmer	11Ma02DI
SMITH, William	30	M	Farmer	11Ma02DI
WATSON, John	24	M	Farmer	11Ma02DI
BELL, John	24	M	Farmer	11Ma02DI
ROBISON, M.	35	M	Farmer	11Ma02DI
U-Mrs.	40	F	Farmer	11Ma02DI
John	4	M	Child	11Ma02DI
William	2	M	Child	11Ma02DI
U	.00	M	Infant	11Ma02DI
EGAN, Andy	20	M	Farmer	11Ma02DI
MCMULLEN, John	19	M	Farmer	11Ma02DI
MULDOON, Andy	19	M	Farmer	11Ma02DI
GOURKE, Richard	18	M	Farmer	11Ma02DI
Catherine	17	F	Farmer	11Ma02DI
DEVERY, James	20	M	Farmer	11Ma02DI
MARTIN, Law.	25	M	Farmer	11Ma02DI
MURPHY, Biddy	24	F	Farmer	11Ma02DI
Catherine	23	F	Farmer	11Ma02DI
DOGHERTY, Pat	36	M	Farmer	11Ma02DI
--Ry	20	F	Servant	11Ma02DI
ROBISON, Catherine	27	F	Servant	11Ma02DI
Maria	9	F	Child	11Ma02DI
Bridget	7	F	Child	11Ma02DI
DOGHERTY, Wm.	40	M	Servant	11Ma02DI
Pat	12	M	Servant	11Ma02DI
Michael	10	M	Servant	11Ma02DI
John	2	M	Child	11Ma02DI
RICKERBY, Thomas	55	M	Servant	11Ma02DI
Isab	54	M	Servant	11Ma02DI
John	16	M	Servant	11Ma02DI
Ann	14	F	Servant	11Ma02DI
Sarah	12	F	Servant	11Ma02DI
BAILEY, James	50	M	Merchant	11Ma02DI
Mary	46	F	Merchant	11Ma02DI
Mary	40	F	Merchant	11Ma02DI
John	16	M	Merchant	11Ma02DI
William	8	M	Child	11Ma02DI
U-Miss	18	F	Merchant	11Ma02DI
SUTTON, J.	45	F	Merchant	11Ma02DI
Hannah	43	F	Merchant	11Ma02DI
Ann	17	F	Merchant	11Ma02DI
Eliza	15	F	Merchant	11Ma02DI
Beth	12	F	Merchant	11Ma02DI
Hannah	10	F	Merchant	11Ma02DI
Edward	8	M	Child	11Ma02DI
Charles	6	M	Child	11Ma02DI
John	4	M	Child	11Ma02DI
MONDAY, Daniel	35	M	Farmer	11Ma02DI
WASTAL, L.	32	M	Farmer	11Ma02DI
JOHNOCK, William	31	M	Farmer	11Ma02DI
Henry	30	M	Farmer	11Ma02DI
HANSLOW, George	34	M	Farmer	11Ma02DI
Mary	36	F	Farmer	11Ma02DI
Henry	13	M	Farmer	11Ma02DI
George	11	M	Farmer	11Ma02DI
Matilda	10	F	Farmer	11Ma02DI
Ann	7	F	Child	11Ma02DI
Mary	5	F	Child	11Ma02DI
John	3	M	Child	11Ma02DI
Jm.	.00	M	Infant	11Ma02DI

NAMES OF PASSENGERS	AGE	SEX	OCCUPATIONS	DATE PORT SHIP
RALPH, Henry	21	M	Tailor	11Ma02DI
Jane	23	M	Tailor	11Ma02DI
FASTER, Charles	25	M	Blacksmith	11Ma02DI
Cath.	21	F	Blacksmith	11Ma02DI
R.	27	M	Blacksmith	11Ma02DI
Harry	21	M	Blacksmith	11Ma02DI
PEELS, Henry	29	M	Blacksmith	11Ma02DI
Jane	30	F	Blacksmith	11Ma02DI
JARDINE, And.	21	M	Blacksmith	11Ma02DI
Gill	21	M	Laborer	11Ma02DI
ARNOLD, Thomas	27	M	Laborer	11Ma02DI
Eliza	26	F	Laborer	11Ma02DI
Thomas	7	M	Child	11Ma02DI
William	5	M	Child	11Ma02DI
Matilda	2	F	Child	11Ma02DI
Charles	2	M	Child	11Ma02DI
FOOTE, Augusta	44	F	Laborer	11Ma02DI
PALMER, Isriel	72	M	Laborer	11Ma02DI
John	21	M	Laborer	11Ma02DI
PARKER, William	12	M	Laborer	11Ma02DI
Thomas	12	M	Laborer	11Ma02DI
TYMAN, Ben	12	M	Laborer	11Ma02DI
BROWN, Asar	40	M	Laborer	11Ma02DI
WARNEY, John	18	M	Laborer	11Ma02DI
LOVELOCK, William	30	M	Farmer	11Ma02DI
BUCKBRIDGE, John	40	M	Farmer	11Ma02DI
MCGRAW, Henry	30	M	Farmer	11Ma02DI
WERNHAM, John	30	M	Weaver	11Ma02DI
WIKWORTH, James	40	M	Farmer	11Ma02DI
GRIFFIN, George	14	M	Laborer	11Ma02DI
John	15	M	Laborer	11Ma02DI
WOODLEY, Andrew	27	M	Laborer	11Ma02DI
William	25	M	Laborer	11Ma02DI
Andrew	3	M	Child	11Ma02DI
Andrew	.00	M	Infant	11Ma02DI
JACKSON, Edward	19	M	Farmer	11Ma02DI
BRAZEBRICK, Robert	23	M	Weaver	11Ma02DI
BURNS, John	27	M	Farmer	11Ma02DI
WILDS, Edward	26	M	Laborer	11Ma02DI
BROUGHTON, John	30	M	Farmer	11Ma02DI
Eliza	26	F	Farmer	11Ma02DI
Ruben	2	M	Child	11Ma02DI
PARKIN, Thomas	30	M	Laborer	11Ma02DI
Amos	32	M	Laborer	11Ma02DI
HAPE, William	24	M	Gdnr	11Ma02DI
HIGHAN, John	41	M	Gdnr	11Ma02DI
Margaret	44	F	Laborer	11Ma02DI
GEE, Thomas	35	M	Laborer	11Ma02DI
BURGESS, Samuel	34	M	Laborer	11Ma02DI
GREEN, Jane	27	F	Servant	11Ma02DI
John	3	M	Child	11Ma02DI
HUMPHRIES, Ebenezer	22	M	Laborer	11Ma02DI
Harriet	20	F	Laborer	11Ma02DI
Mary	65	F	Laborer	11Ma02DI
DUNN, Wm.	30	M	Farmer	11Ma02DI
Sarah	28	F	Farmer	11Ma02DI
ELLIS, Daniel	28	M	Laborer	11Ma02DI
U-Mrs.	32	F	Laborer	11Ma02DI
MORRIS, Richard	34	M	Weaver	11Ma02DI
JONES, Thomas	27	M	Farmer	11Ma02DI
HEALD, Nathan	45	M	Farmer	11Ma02DI
Mary	45	F	Farmer	11Ma02DI
Jane	16	F	Farmer	11Ma02DI
Henry	15	M	Farmer	11Ma02DI
Nathan	14	M	Farmer	11Ma02DI
Ann	13	F	Farmer	11Ma02DI
George	12	M	Farmer	11Ma02DI
William	10	M	Farmer	11Ma02DI
Eliza	9	F	Child	11Ma02DI
Mary	8	F	Child	11Ma02DI
John	5	M	Child	11Ma02DI
Sarah	2	F	Child	11Ma02DI
Harriet	.00	F	Infant	11Ma02DI
HALLOWAY, William	20	M	Farmer	11Ma02DI
HODGES, Charles	28	M	Farmer	11Ma02DI
JONES, Mary	29	F	Farmer	11Ma02DI
Charles	6	M	Child	11Ma02DI
Mary	2	F	Child	11Ma02DI
John	.00	M	Infant	11Ma02DI
CURLEY, Catherine	24	F	Dressmaker	11Ma02DI
TOOLE, Louisa	00	F	Dressmaker	11Ma02DI
EGAN, Mary	00	F	Dressmaker	11Ma02DI
CUNNINGHAM, Catherine	00	F	Dressmaker	11Ma02DI
ELLIS, Charles	24	M	Laborer	11Ma02DI
COWLSEN, Thomas	20	M	Laborer	11Ma02DI
ROBINSON, Edward	23	M	Laborer	11Ma02DI
AMPRON, Charles	30	M	Laborer	11Ma02DI
RUSTING, Thomas	24	M	Laborer	11Ma02DI
SCOTEY, Richard	25	M	Laborer	11Ma02DI
WHITE, John	28	M	Laborer	11Ma02DI
RICE, Robert	45	M	Painter	11Ma02DI
Eliza	19	F	Painter	11Ma02DI
DAVEY, Sarah	20	F	Painter	11Ma02DI
GILLINGHAM, James	23	M	Laborer	11Ma02DI
SALTER, George	22	M	Laborer	11Ma02DI
SYMES, Alfred	23	M	Shoemaker	11Ma02DI
SHAW, Pat	43	M	Farmer	11Ma02DI
Thomas	13	M	Farmer	11Ma02DI
Martha	11	F	Farmer	11Ma02DI
David	5	M	Child	11Ma02DI
Alf.	.00	M	Infant	11Ma02DI
FOSTER, William	47	M	Blacksmith	11Ma02DI
U-Mrs.	48	F	Unknown	11Ma02DI
Thomas	17	M	Blacksmith	11Ma02DI
AUGHALHEN, John	18	M	Laborer	11Ma02DI
CUTHBERT, William	30	M	Weaver	11Ma02DI
WARD, William	27	M	Weaver	11Ma02DI
KIRK, Thomas	27	M	Laborer	11Ma02DI
NEAL, Thomas	24	M	Laborer	11Ma02DI
William	17	M	Laborer	11Ma02DI
CONLETT, Ann	22	F	Milliner	11Ma02DI
Jane	20	F	Milliner	11Ma02DI
LOVE, Robert	19	M	Laborer	11Ma02DI
REVEN, Bridget	22	F	Laborer	11Ma02DI
QUIRK, Jane	17	F	Laborer	11Ma02DI
SCHOOLEY, Thomas	23	M	Farmer	11Ma02DI
U-Mrs.	22	F	Farmer	11Ma02DI
Emily	.00	F	Infant	11Ma02DI
LANE, Richard	43	M	Farmer	11Ma02DI
TOOMEY, Richard	23	M	Farmer	11Ma02DI
U-Mrs.	23	F	Farmer	11Ma02DI
HUGHS, John	28	M	Farmer	11Ma02DI
DANE, William	48	M	Farmer	11Ma02DI
U-Mrs.	46	F	Farmer	11Ma02DI
William	7	M	Child	11Ma02DI
Thomas	5	M	Child	11Ma02DI
KEAN, Fanny	20	F	Laborer	11Ma02DI
WAKER, John	23	M	Laborer	11Ma02DI
PREAST, Mary	23	F	Laborer	11Ma02DI
ONEAL, Mary	21	F	Milliner	11Ma02DI
Rebecca	19	F	Milliner	11Ma02DI
CAROWAN, Margaret	21	F	Milliner	11Ma02DI
TAYLOR, Henry	17	M	Laborer	11Ma02DI
THOMAS, John	57	M	Laborer	11Ma02DI
William	23	M	Laborer	11Ma02DI
Jane	30	F	Laborer	11Ma02DI
Eliza	5	F	Child	11Ma02DI
JONES, Isaac	27	M	Bootmaker	11Ma02DI
ASPILL, Pat	30	M	Bootmaker	11Ma02DI
DONOHOE, Michael	26	M	Laborer	11Ma02DI
SANDERS, Daniel	60	M	Laborer	11Ma02DI
U-Mrs.	60	F	Laborer	11Ma02DI
KINCAID, William	22	M	Laborer	11Ma02DI
MOORE, John	26	M	Laborer	11Ma02DI
Edward	24	M	Laborer	11Ma02DI
PARKINSON, William	40	M	Laborer	11Ma02DI
GILL, Margaret	40	F	Laborer	11Ma02DI
BRYNE, Pat	22	M	Tailor	11Ma02DI
James	20	M	Tailor	11Ma02DI
KILLAN, Michael	26	M	Laborer	11Ma02DI

NAMES OF PASSENGERS	AGE	SEX	OCCUPATIONS	DATE PORT SHIP
NOWLAN, William	26	M	Laborer	11Ma02DI
PALMER, Andrew	18	M	Laborer	11Ma02DI
BEAUMONT, John	30	M	Engineer	11Ma02DI
U-Mrs.	23	F	Unknown	11Ma02DI
BURROWS, Abbi	30	F	Dressmaker	11Ma02DI
SMITH, Ann	27	F	Dressmaker	11Ma02DI
ROUTLEDGE, Thomas	20	M	Laborer	11Ma02DI
SMITH, Samuel	.00	M	Infant	11Ma02DI
MADDEN, Daniel	35	M	Laborer	11Ma02DI
Mary	25	F	Laborer	11Ma02DI
Bridget	.00	F	Infant	11Ma02DI
KENNEDY, Thomas	19	M	Laborer	11Ma02DI
SPRING, Joseph	20	M	Laborer	11Ma02DI
BARRETT, Alex.	22	M	Weaver	11Ma02DI
WARREN, James	22	M	Weaver	11Ma02DI
STEPHENS, J.	30	M	Farmer	11Ma02DI
Sarah	4	F	Child	11Ma02DI
Sophia	2	F	Child	11Ma02DI
Mary	.00	F	Infant	11Ma02DI
DONNER, Sophia	26	F	Farmer	11Ma02DI
William	.00	M	Infant	11Ma02DI
BROWN, Michael	25	M	Laborer	11Ma02DI
Pat	20	M	Laborer	11Ma02DI
KEALY, Thomas	30	M	Laborer	11Ma02DI
CASHEL, Eliza	50	F	Laborer	11Ma02DI
Mary	9	F	Child	11Ma02DI
CARROLL, James	18	M	Laborer	11Ma02DI
COCHRAN, Mary	21	F	Laborer	11Ma02DI
FLANNAGAN, Margaret	20	F	Laborer	11Ma02DI
ROURKE, Pat	21	M	Laborer	11Ma02DI
DAILEY, Dennis	21	M	Laborer	11Ma02DI
CASEY, John	25	M	Farmer	11Ma02DI
Bridget	35	F	Farmer	11Ma02DI
Ann	3	F	Child	11Ma02DI
Michael	2	M	Child	11Ma02DI
Pat	.00	M	Infant	11Ma02DI
DARCY, Thomas	17	M	Laborer	11Ma02DI
James	13	M	Laborer	11Ma02DI
LAVY, Bridget	13	F	Laborer	11Ma02DI
FARREN, Thomas	24	M	Laborer	11Ma02DI
JAMES, U-Mrs.	26	F	Dressmaker	11Ma02DI
Ellen	.00	F	Infant	11Ma02DI
NEW, Teresa	20	F	Laborer	11Ma02DI
BOYD, George	52	M	Laborer	11Ma02DI
Henry	21	M	Laborer	11Ma02DI
Eliza	52	F	Laborer	11Ma02DI
CHARLTON, Mary	27	F	Laborer	11Ma02DI
MERRYWEATHER, John	25	M	Laborer	11Ma02DI
U-Mrs.	24	F	Laborer	11Ma02DI
GEORGE, H.	31	M	Laborer	11Ma02DI
DUNN, Ann	30	F	Laborer	11Ma02DI
DOOK, Robert	45	M	Carpenter	11Ma02DI
Rebecca	40	F	Carpenter	11Ma02DI
SYLVESTER, Martha	35	F	Milliner	11Ma02DI
Mary	11	F	Milliner	11Ma02DI
Eliza	10	F	Milliner	11Ma02DI
Margaret	9	F	Child	11Ma02DI
Martha	7	F	Child	11Ma02DI
Susan	3	F	Child	11Ma02DI
TOMLINSON, Thomas	32	M	Laborer	11Ma02DI
MADALL, James	21	M	Laborer	11Ma02DI
CASEY, John	24	M	Laborer	11Ma02DI
DONNELL, George	27	M	Farmer	11Ma02DI
U-Mrs.	27	F	Farmer	11Ma02DI
Edward	5	M	Child	11Ma02DI
Mary	3	F	Child	11Ma02DI
COYNE, Henry	20	M	Laborer	11Ma02DI
MCARDLE, Phillip	22	M	Laborer	11Ma02DI
Bridget	19	F	Laborer	11Ma02DI
Mary	16	F	Laborer	11Ma02DI
Catherine	14	F	Laborer	11Ma02DI
Michael	40	M	Laborer	11Ma02DI
CARROLL, Bridget	21	F	Laborer	11Ma02DI
MCLOUGHLIN, John	30	M	Laborer	11Ma02DI
DUFFY, Pat	20	M	Laborer	11Ma02DI
OATES, Mat	23	M	Laborer	11Ma02DI
WARD, Catherine	32	F	Milliner	11Ma02DI
Ann	60	F	Milliner	11Ma02DI
CARY, Catherine	30	F	Dressmaker	11Ma02DI
LOWE, Samuel	50	M	Laborer	11Ma02DI
CROFTS, John	19	M	Laborer	11Ma02DI
GRANT, James	45	M	Farmer	11Ma02DI
Ann	20	F	Farmer	11Ma02DI
Mary	18	F	Farmer	11Ma02DI
WALKLIN, James	46	M	Farmer	11Ma02DI
Edwin	17	M	Farmer	11Ma02DI
MCGUIRE, Mary	20	F	Servant	11Ma02DI
GOOD, Michael	22	M	Laborer	11Ma02DI
Mary	23	F	Laborer	11Ma02DI
CONNER, Dennis	18	M	Laborer	11Ma02DI
OLEARY, Henry	17	M	Laborer	11Ma02DI
DOLTON, Eliza	22	F	Laborer	11Ma02DI
U-Mrs.	30	F	Laborer	11Ma02DI
JONES, Mary	1	F	Child	11Ma02DI
BUCK, Daniel	40	M	Gdnr	11Ma02DI
U-Mrs.	37	F	Gdnr	11Ma02DI
John	16	M	Gdnr	11Ma02DI
Jane	14	F	Gdnr	11Ma02DI
Daniel	11	M	Gdnr	11Ma02DI
William	7	M	Child	11Ma02DI
Sarah	3	F	Child	11Ma02DI
BELL, James	25	M	Laborer	11Ma02DI
PADGET, Richard	45	M	Laborer	11Ma02DI
Ellen	21	F	Laborer	11Ma02DI
THOMAS, David	24	M	Laborer	11Ma02DI
WILLIAMS, David	25	M	Laborer	11Ma02DI
CLAY, John	58	M	Farmer	11Ma02DI
U-Mrs.	62	F	Farmer	11Ma02DI
E.	30	F	Farmer	11Ma02DI
Eliza	26	F	Farmer	11Ma02DI
Ann	.00	F	Infant	11Ma02DI
CALLEY, Eli	40	M	Farmer	11Ma02DI
U-Mrs.	30	F	Farmer	11Ma02DI
LEE, William	21	M	Laborer	11Ma02DI
CAYLESS, Jane	48	F	Laborer	11Ma02DI
BATES, Henry	16	M	Laborer	11Ma02DI
ROBINSON, John	34	M	Farmer	11Ma02DI
Ann	36	F	Farmer	11Ma02DI
Eliza	12	F	Farmer	11Ma02DI
Mary	9	F	Child	11Ma02DI
Hannah	6	F	Child	11Ma02DI
William	4	M	Child	11Ma02DI
Richard	1	M	Child	11Ma02DI
Jane	.00	F	Infant	11Ma02DI
GRUNSWELL, John	42	M	Farmer	11Ma02DI
Martha	38	F	Farmer	11Ma02DI
Ann	16	F	Farmer	11Ma02DI
James	14	M	Farmer	11Ma02DI
Mary	10	F	Farmer	11Ma02DI
William	8	M	Child	11Ma02DI
Eliza	5	F	Child	11Ma02DI
John	3	M	Child	11Ma02DI
And.	.00	M	Infant	11Ma02DI
George	44	M	Farmer	11Ma02DI
MORRIS, John	24	M	Laborer	11Ma02DI
Lydia	23	F	Laborer	11Ma02DI
NUTT, Isaiah	26	M	Laborer	11Ma02DI
PERKINS, James	26	M	Laborer	11Ma02DI
Sarah	26	F	Laborer	11Ma02DI
BURDEN, Stephen	26	M	Farmer	11Ma02DI
U-Mrs.	20	F	Farmer	11Ma02DI
HOWARD, U-Mrs.	40	F	Farmer	11Ma02DI
HILL, Thomas	23	M	Laborer	11Ma02DI
MEANS, William	19	M	Laborer	11Ma02DI
ALCOCK, John	22	M	Laborer	11Ma02DI
CONLAN, John	24	M	Laborer	11Ma02DI
CONNOLLY, William	23	M	Laborer	11Ma02DI
Mary	20	F	Laborer	11Ma02DI
Margaret	.00	F	Infant	11Ma02DI
DOOLEY, Martin	24	M	Laborer	11Ma02DI

NAMES OF PASSENGERS	AGE	SEX	OCCUPATIONS	DATE PORT SHIP
PARKINSON, Mary	21	F	Laborer	11Ma02DI
HOLDEN, Thomas	21	M	Laborer	11Ma02DI
James	25	M	Laborer	11Ma02DI
Ralph	18	M	Laborer	11Ma02DI
QUINN, Pat	20	M	Laborer	11Ma02DI
BROOKS, John	44	M	Shoemaker	11Ma02DI
ROBINSON, William	44	M	Farmer	11Ma02DI
Ann	34	F	Farmer	11Ma02DI
George	4	M	Child	11Ma02DI
A.	.00	U	Infant	11Ma02DI
TAYLOR, Mary	22	F	Servant	11Ma02DI
Jane	20	F	Servant	11Ma02DI
FLANAGAN, Bridget	22	F	Servant	11Ma02DI
MCGRAIN, Bernd.	33	M	Laborer	11Ma02DI
Margaret	30	F	Laborer	11Ma02DI
KINSLEY, Pat	22	M	Laborer	11Ma02DI
DOWD, Thomas	20	M	Laborer	11Ma02DI
Mary	16	F	Laborer	11Ma02DI
JONES, John	24	M	Laborer	11Ma02DI
FITZPATRICK, James	16	M	Laborer	11Ma02DI
SHORE, James	22	M	Laborer	11Ma02DI
Alfred	17	M	Laborer	11Ma02DI
MAHONEY, Mary	20	F	Laborer	11Ma02DI
John	40	M	Farmer	11Ma02DI
Mary	35	F	Farmer	11Ma02DI
Thomas	23	M	Farmer	11Ma02DI
REGAN, Mary	17	F	Servant	11Ma02DI
BONNER, Dennis	23	F	Servant	11Ma02DI
Sarah	26	F	Servant	11Ma02DI
WILD, John	39	M	Blacksmith	11Ma02DI
MAXWELL, Samuel	22	M	Laborer	11Ma02DI
LIVINGSTON, James	30	M	Laborer	11Ma02DI
FORSYTH, William	25	M	Laborer	11Ma02DI
BAIRD, Adam	20	M	Laborer	11Ma02DI
THOMPSON, Robert	23	M	Laborer	11Ma02DI
James	26	M	Laborer	11Ma02DI
MILLIGAN, Robert	21	M	Laborer	11Ma02DI
DOOTSON, John	26	M	Laborer	11Ma02DI
WHITEHEAD, James	30	M	Gdnr	11Ma02DI
HAMPTON, Arthur	20	M	Laborer	11Ma02DI
MINCHEN, Fred	23	M	Laborer	11Ma02DI
Agnes	24	F	Laborer	11Ma02DI
MCANENY, Eliza	60	F	Laborer	11Ma02DI
Michael	22	M	Laborer	11Ma02DI
SHEEHEY, William	26	M	Laborer	11Ma02DI
Thomas	21	M	Laborer	11Ma02DI
John	20	M	Laborer	11Ma02DI
ROURKE, James	24	M	Laborer	11Ma02DI
LEE, Pat	20	M	Laborer	11Ma02DI
DONOHUE, Owen	19	M	Laborer	11Ma02DI
KEARY, James	25	M	Tailor	11Ma02DI
WHITE, John	24	M	Laborer	11Ma02DI
TOOHEY, Margaret	20	F	Laborer	11Ma02DI
COSTELLO, James	28	M	Laborer	11Ma02DI
JONES, John	21	M	Laborer	11Ma02DI
BRYAN, John	27	M	Laborer	11Ma02DI
MEAD, James	25	M	Laborer	11Ma02DI
LONGDEN, J.	60	M	Farmer	11Ma02DI
U-Mrs.	36	F	Farmer	11Ma02DI
HAMILTON, James	21	M	Laborer	11Ma02DI
YOUNG, Ellen	40	F	Servant	11Ma02DI
Sarah	17	F	Servant	11Ma02DI
Mary	16	F	Servant	11Ma02DI
Robert	14	M	Servant	11Ma02DI
James	13	M	Servant	11Ma02DI
Margaret	8	F	Child	11Ma02DI
DUNN, Thomas	46	M	Painter	11Ma02DI
Jane	11	F	Painter	11Ma02DI
DENNISTOWN, James	24	M	Laborer	11Ma02DI
Alexander	22	M	Laborer	11Ma02DI
JACKSON, Jas.	39	M	Farmer	11Ma02DI
GIBSON, Fra.	30	M	Farmer	11Ma02DI
JACKSON, U-Mrs.	29	F	Farmer	11Ma02DI
Samuel	37	M	Farmer	11Ma02DI
Mary	6	F	Child	11Ma02DI
JACKSON, Joseph	4	M	Child	11Ma02DI
Louisa	.00	F	Infant	11Ma02DI
DIVINE, Catherine	40	F	Servant	11Ma02DI
John	20	M	Laborer	11Ma02DI
Jere.	15	M	Laborer	11Ma02DI
Mary	11	F	Laborer	11Ma02DI
Ellen	8	F	Child	11Ma02DI
SLATTERY, Ann	15	F	Laborer	11Ma02DI
BRYAN, Dennis	22	M	Laborer	11Ma02DI
RYAN, Brid.	27	F	Laborer	11Ma02DI
Pat	.00	M	Infant	11Ma02DI
GAY, John	00	M	Laborer	11Ma02DI
HELLSBY, Samuel	28	M	Farmer	11Ma02DI
U-Mrs.	28	F	Farmer	11Ma02DI
Mary-A.	.00	F	Infant	11Ma02DI
SYSAGHT, M.	40	M	Farmer	11Ma02DI
U-Mrs.	40	F	Farmer	11Ma02DI
KENEDY, Thomas	35	M	Farmer	11Ma02DI
U-Mrs.	35	F	Farmer	11Ma02DI
MURPHY, John	30	M	Laborer	11Ma02DI
BRAY, John	30	M	Laborer	11Ma02DI
JACKSON, Henry	27	M	Laborer	11Ma02DI
ASHWORTH, James	21	M	Laborer	11Ma02DI
SMITH, Thomas	30	M	Blacksmith	11Ma02DI
Catherine	30	F	Blacksmith	11Ma02DI
CALLARY, Richard	22	M	Laborer	11Ma02DI
DONNELLY, Peter	25	M	Laborer	11Ma02DI
U-Mr.	25	M	Laborer	11Ma02DI
MELLON, Catherine	22	F	Laborer	11Ma02DI
BRENNAN, Thomas	20	M	Laborer	11Ma02DI
FLANNAGAN, Charles	24	M	Laborer	11Ma02DI
Mary	30	F	Laborer	11Ma02DI
Amelia	21	F	Laborer	11Ma02DI
Isab	18	M	Laborer	11Ma02DI
FLETCHER, Jane	26	F	Servant	11Ma02DI
RILEY, P.O.Rev.	20	M	Clergyman	11Ma02DI
SCOLLARD, John-Rev.	31	M	Clergyman	11Ma02DI
BENNETT, Edward	29	M	Farmer	11Ma02DI
U-Mrs.	19	F	Farmer	11Ma02DI
PARKINSON, John	32	M	Farmer	11Ma02DI
U-Mrs.	24	F	Farmer	11Ma02DI
Ann	5	F	Child	11Ma02DI
John	3	M	Child	11Ma02DI
John	.00	M	Infant	11Ma02DI
HERRINGSHAN, John	21	M	Laborer	11Ma02DI
George	60	M	Laborer	11Ma02DI
GILBERT, John	36	M	Laborer	11Ma02DI
Mary	30	F	Laborer	11Ma02DI
BENSON, J.	26	M	Tailor	11Ma02DI
BARRETT, James	29	M	Laborer	11Ma02DI
HUGHS, Mary	32	F	Laborer	11Ma02DI
KELLY, Mary	32	F	Laborer	11Ma02DI
Eliza	4	F	Child	11Ma02DI
KIRVIN, Margaret	22	F	Laborer	11Ma02DI
BUTLER, James	27	M	Watchmaker	11Ma02DI
BRITT, Thomas	22	M	Laborer	11Ma02DI
DELANY, Margaret	23	F	Laborer	11Ma02DI
HOGAN, Martin	19	M	Laborer	11Ma02DI
DEMPSEY, Margaret	19	F	Laborer	11Ma02DI
HENNESSY, Judy	23	F	Laborer	11Ma02DI
SANKIN, Dennis	19	M	Laborer	11Ma02DI
CONNELLY, Thomas	50	M	Laborer	11Ma02DI
BYRNE, Ann	12	F	Laborer	11Ma02DI
TOBIN, Ann	36	F	Laborer	11Ma02DI
MCGURY, Mary	13	F	Laborer	11Ma02DI
FARLEY, Ann	20	F	Laborer	11Ma02DI
CHEEDY, Ellen	21	F	Servant	11Ma02DI
BURK, James	17	M	Laborer	11Ma02DI
RUSSELL, U-Mrs.	00	F	Farmer	11Ma02DI
U	00	M	Farmer	11Ma02DI
MERIDITH, U	00	M	Farmer	11Ma02DI
U-Mrs.	00	F	Farmer	11Ma02DI
WOODS, Owen	35	M	Laborer	11Ma02DI
MCKETTRY, Thomas	30	M	Laborer	11Ma02DI
Catherine	20	F	Laborer	11Ma02DI

NAMES OF PASSENGERS	AGE	SEX	OCCUPATIONS	DATE PORT SHIP
DUFFY, Nancy	20	F	Laborer	11Ma02DI
REDDY, Owen	30	M	Weaver	11Ma02DI
MCSHEEHAN, Felix	32	M	Farmer	11Ma02DI
WEBSTER, George	35	M	Farmer	11Ma02DI
U-Mrs.	40	F	Farmer	11Ma02DI
Rachael	13	F	Farmer	11Ma02DI
Phebe	11	F	Farmer	11Ma02DI
Charles	8	M	Child	11Ma02DI
LEDGER, Mary	27	F	Dressmaker	11Ma02DI
Rachael	5	F	Child	11Ma02DI
Jane	3	F	Child	11Ma02DI
BUNLEY, James	30	M	Farmer	11Ma02DI
Mary	30	F	Farmer	11Ma02DI
PEARSON, John	25	M	Farmer	11Ma02DI
Sarah	23	F	Farmer	11Ma02DI
William	.00	M	Infant	11Ma02DI
WEBSTER, Robert	25	M	Laborer	11Ma02DI
John	22	M	Laborer	11Ma02DI
Wm.	25	M	Laborer	11Ma02DI
GREENHAUGH, Samuel	22	M	Laborer	11Ma02DI
ATKINSON, John	21	M	Laborer	11Ma02DI
THOMPSON, Walter	21	M	Laborer	11Ma02DI

FIDELIA 11 MAY 1850

From Liverpool

NAMES OF PASSENGERS	AGE	SEX	OCCUPATIONS	DATE PORT SHIP
KILRON, Pat	22	M	Laborer	11Ma02Eh
COFFEY, Christy	14	M	Laborer	11Ma02Eh
FARRELL, Ann	16	F	Servant	11Ma02Eh
BARN, John	15	M	Servant	11Ma02Eh
KNOCTON, James	20	M	Laborer	11Ma02Eh
LEE, Owen	35	M	Laborer	11Ma02Eh
Pat	15	M	Laborer	11Ma02Eh
MCDERMOT, James	13	M	Laborer	11Ma02Eh
Phil.	10	M	Laborer	11Ma02Eh
CONNERLY, Cornelius	30	M	Laborer	11Ma02Eh
DUFFY, John	17	M	Laborer	11Ma02Eh
CARRIGAN, Thomas	21	M	Laborer	11Ma02Eh
JONES, Michael	36	M	Laborer	11Ma02Eh
KELLY, Thomas	15	M	Laborer	11Ma02Eh
HOYLE, Patrick	33	M	Laborer	11Ma02Eh
GASEY, Thomas	21	M	Laborer	11Ma02Eh
FARRELL, James	21	M	Laborer	11Ma02Eh
OBRIEN, Andrew	18	M	Laborer	11Ma02Eh
HIGGINS, James	18	M	Laborer	11Ma02Eh
MCGINNESS, Pat	20	M	Laborer	11Ma02Eh
RILEY, Ann	18	F	Laborer	11Ma02Eh
COSGROVE, Pat	18	M	Laborer	11Ma02Eh
FINNEY, John	18	M	Laborer	11Ma02Eh
DUFFY, Mary	45	F	Servant	11Ma02Eh
MCDONALD, Julia	16	F	Servant	11Ma02Eh
LOCKWOOD, Richard	23	M	Servant	11Ma02Eh
MARTER, Pat	23	M	Servant	11Ma02Eh
HANNON, Pat	40	M	Servant	11Ma02Eh
MCCARNEY, Michael	19	M	Servant	11Ma02Eh
DUNN, Pat	18	M	Servant	11Ma02Eh
MURPHY, Michael	20	M	Servant	11Ma02Eh
HANDLY, John	18	M	Servant	11Ma02Eh
SKENLON, Pat	16	M	Servant	11Ma02Eh
Matt	14	M	Servant	11Ma02Eh
COFFEY, Mary	50	F	Servant	11Ma02Eh
James	10	M	Servant	11Ma02Eh
Mary	12	F	Servant	11Ma02Eh
BRIEN, John	19	M	Servant	11Ma02Eh
KENYAN, Terence	18	M	Servant	11Ma02Eh
MURPHY, Mathew	70	M	Servant	11Ma02Eh
Died-At-Sea				
TRACY, Michael	18	M	Laborer	11Ma02Eh

NAMES OF PASSENGERS	AGE	SEX	OCCUPATIONS	DATE PORT SHIP
MACKLEY, Bridget	15	F	Servant	11Ma02Eh
CLANCY, William	40	M	Farmer	11Ma02Eh
Mary	30	F	Unknown	11Ma02Eh
Mary	8	F	Child	11Ma02Eh
KELLY, Mary	13	F	Unknown	11Ma02Eh
RUSSELL, Mary	16	F	Servant	11Ma02Eh
DANEY, Fanny	18	F	Servant	11Ma02Eh
CANVEY, Julia	35	F	Servant	11Ma02Eh
CONNOR, Susan	50	F	Servant	11Ma02Eh
ONEIL, Elizabeth	35	F	Servant	11Ma02Eh
KELFRY, James	50	M	Laborer	11Ma02Eh
WALEN, Timothy	24	M	Laborer	11Ma02Eh
HANDEN, Catherine	23	F	Servant	11Ma02Eh
MCMEAN, Thomas	20	M	Servant	11Ma02Eh
MURPHY, Henry	12	M	Servant	11Ma02Eh
JENKINS, John	60	M	Laborer	11Ma02Eh
MADDEN, Thomas	18	M	Laborer	11Ma02Eh
MCDONALD, John	19	M	Laborer	11Ma02Eh
GALEY, Tim	48	M	Laborer	11Ma02Eh
MULLIGAN, James	20	M	Laborer	11Ma02Eh
JENKINS, John	17	M	Laborer	11Ma02Eh
DUFF, Thomas	35	M	Laborer	11Ma02Eh
GAFFNEY, James	34	M	Laborer	11Ma02Eh
DIGLIN, Barnard	30	M	Laborer	11Ma02Eh
CUFFNEY, Tim	12	M	Laborer	11Ma02Eh
RYAN, Bridget	32	F	Servant	11Ma02Eh
Biddy	7	F	Child	11Ma02Eh
Margaret	6	F	Child	11Ma02Eh
HEYS, Sally	17	F	Unknown	11Ma02Eh
MCLOUGHLIN, Dennis	30	M	Laborer	11Ma02Eh
RYAN, Bernard	2	M	Child	11Ma02Eh
HICKEY, Patrick	6	M	Child	11Ma02Eh
James	9	M	Child	11Ma02Eh
SKILLY, John	30	M	Laborer	11Ma02Eh
RADIGAN, Richard	22	M	Laborer	11Ma02Eh
KELLY, Lawrence	50	M	Laborer	11Ma02Eh
DENNY, Patrick	27	M	Laborer	11Ma02Eh
SKELLY, Catherine	20	F	Servant	11Ma02Eh
DALEY, Margaret	35	F	Servant	11Ma02Eh
HILINESS, Ann	39	F	Servant	11Ma02Eh
GARVEY, Catherine	30	F	Servant	11Ma02Eh
PEARSON, John	27	M	Laborer	11Ma02Eh
GARVEY, Pat	27	M	Laborer	11Ma02Eh
SHEY, Tim	8	M	Child	11Ma02Eh
CURRAN, Tim	35	M	Laborer	11Ma02Eh
John	5	M	Child	11Ma02Eh
Cornelius	70	M	Unknown	11Ma02Eh
SPRAT, William	23	M	Laborer	11Ma02Eh
BRADY, Catherine	18	F	Servant	11Ma02Eh
BLANEY, Thomas	35	M	Laborer	11Ma02Eh
Henry	25	M	Laborer	11Ma02Eh
SWILL, Samuel	24	M	Laborer	11Ma02Eh
OCONNOR, Thomas	37	M	Laborer	11Ma02Eh
OBRIEN, Charles	15	M	Laborer	11Ma02Eh
QUINN, Ann	21	F	Servant	11Ma02Eh
OBRIEN, Catherine	12	F	Servant	11Ma02Eh
BOSTER, Pat	28	M	Laborer	11Ma02Eh
STEEL, Isabella	28	F	Servant	11Ma02Eh
ROCK, Matt	8	M	Child	11Ma02Eh
Mary	37	F	Unknown	11Ma02Eh
Tim	7	M	Child	11Ma02Eh
Pat	6	M	Child	11Ma02Eh
DALY, Mary	25	F	Servant	11Ma02Eh
CLANCY, Margret	17	F	Servant	11Ma02Eh
LOWE, Bridget	10	F	Servant	11Ma02Eh
GENTLY, Robert	35	M	Laborer	11Ma02Eh
WALON, Edward	30	M	Laborer	11Ma02Eh
MCLOUTHER, Michael	22	M	Laborer	11Ma02Eh
KUFF, Pat	30	M	Laborer	11Ma02Eh
Bridget	21	F	Servant	11Ma02Eh
ODONNELL, Mary	18	F	Servant	11Ma02Eh
Catherine	16	F	Servant	11Ma02Eh
KALEY, Ann	21	F	Servant	11Ma02Eh
FLINN, John	35	M	Laborer	11Ma02Eh
JENKINS, William	22	M	Laborer	11Ma02Eh

NAMES OF PASSENGERS	AGE	SEX	OCCUPATIONS	DATE PORT SHIP	NAMES OF PASSENGERS	AGE	SEX	OCCUPATIONS	DATE PORT SHIP
WARD, Thomas	14	M	Laborer	11Ma02Eh	CARTNEY, Mary	7	F	Child	11Ma02Eh
HIGGINS, William	20	M	Laborer	11Ma02Eh	Helen	8	F	Child	11Ma02Eh
RILEY, Hugh	19	M	Laborer	11Ma02Eh	Catherine	9	F	Child	11Ma02Eh
WARDEN, Pat	28	M	Laborer	11Ma02Eh	CONNELL, Ann	12	F	Unknown	11Ma02Eh
HOGAN, Martin	25	M	Laborer	11Ma02Eh	AUNLIFE, James	50	M	Laborer	11Ma02Eh
MALOY, John	18	M	Laborer	11Ma02Eh	James	4	M	Child	11Ma02Eh
PATRICK, Thomas	19	M	Laborer	11Ma02Eh	Pat	8	M	Child	11Ma02Eh
CARLE, Peter	27	M	Laborer	11Ma02Eh	John	10	M	Unknown	11Ma02Eh
LACEY, Tim	30	M	Laborer	11Ma02Eh	Mary	50	F	Unknown	11Ma02Eh
BRADY, John	18	M	Laborer	11Ma02Eh	MCDERMOT, Margaret	16	F	Servant	11Ma02Eh
WHITE, Andrew	18	M	Laborer	11Ma02Eh	GLYNN, Ann	22	F	Servant	11Ma02Eh
CANNON, Richard	21	M	Laborer	11Ma02Eh	MCCANN, Ann	40	F	Servant	11Ma02Eh
MASTERSON, Thomas	26	M	Laborer	11Ma02Eh	Lawrence	12	M	Unknown	11Ma02Eh
GOTT, James	19	M	Laborer	11Ma02Eh	RILEY, James	20	M	Laborer	11Ma02Eh
CONNELL, Sarah	60	F	Unknown	11Ma02Eh	MCCANEY, Margaret	20	F	Servant	11Ma02Eh
KILPATRICK, Robert	14	M	Unknown	11Ma02Eh	MICKLEY, Margaret	4	F	Child	11Ma02Eh
MCKEY, Ann	16	F	Unknown	11Ma02Eh	Mary	6	F	Child	11Ma02Eh
KILPATRICK, Rachael	15	F	Unknown	11Ma02Eh	Eliza	26	F	Unknown	11Ma02Eh
FITZGERALD, Ellen	19	F	Servant	11Ma02Eh	Nancy	2	F	Child	11Ma02Eh
BRIEN, Michael	4	M	Child	11Ma02Eh	MCMACKLE, Rosey	19	F	Servant	11Ma02Eh
HALE, Catherine	16	F	Servant	11Ma02Eh	MCMEA, Pat	20	M	Laborer	11Ma02Eh
FUNNAN, Helen	16	F	Servant	11Ma02Eh	MURPHY, Phill.	20	M	Laborer	11Ma02Eh
FAY, Ann	40	F	Servant	11Ma02Eh	SMITH, Pat	35	M	Laborer	11Ma02Eh
James	20	M	Laborer	11Ma02Eh	GIBS, Christopher	24	M	Laborer	11Ma02Eh
WELSH, William	20	M	Laborer	11Ma02Eh	BRADY, Pat	20	M	Laborer	11Ma02Eh
CORNELL, Sally	60	F	Unknown	11Ma02Eh	GILESHENON, Pat	23	M	Laborer	11Ma02Eh
KIRKPATRICK, Margaret	52	F	Unknown	11Ma02Eh	LYON, Michael	16	M	Laborer	11Ma02Eh
CONNELL, Pat	28	M	Laborer	11Ma02Eh	BRADY, Ann	3	F	Child	11Ma02Eh
MCDULEL, Michael	32	M	Laborer	11Ma02Eh	MCCARTNEY, Sam	27	M	Laborer	11Ma02Eh
LITTLER, Catherine	24	F	Servant	11Ma02Eh	MURPHY, Mathew	7	M	Child	11Ma02Eh
CONNOR, Ann	40	F	Servant	11Ma02Eh	Mary	60	F	Unknown	11Ma02Eh
MURPHY, Margaret	18	F	Servant	11Ma02Eh	Mary	23	F	Unknown	11Ma02Eh
FINNEGAN, Ann	33	F	Servant	11Ma02Eh	DUGAL, Mary	14	F	Unknown	11Ma02Eh
CLARKE, Nora	18	F	Servant	11Ma02Eh	MCDONALD, Mary	50	F	Unknown	11Ma02Eh
KILFOY, James	17	M	Laborer	11Ma02Eh	Bridget	25	F	Servant	11Ma02Eh
LAWSON, William	18	M	Laborer	11Ma02Eh	Michael	70	M	Unknown	11Ma02Eh
Michael	17	M	Laborer	11Ma02Eh	MCKEE, Mary	16	F	Unknown	11Ma02Eh
MOONEY, Pat	18	M	Laborer	11Ma02Eh	RILEY, Catherine	24	F	Servant	11Ma02Eh
HENNEY, Joseph	17	M	Laborer	11Ma02Eh	ARMAGHUE, Helen	17	F	Servant	11Ma02Eh
FAY, John	25	M	Laborer	11Ma02Eh	MULLIGAN, Thomas	50	M	Laborer	11Ma02Eh
HILL, John	26	M	Laborer	11Ma02Eh	CONRAN, Margaret	40	F	Servant	11Ma02Eh
HART, Thomas	22	M	Laborer	11Ma02Eh	Lawrence	4	M	Child	11Ma02Eh
Mary	15	F	Servant	11Ma02Eh	Mary	10	F	Unknown	11Ma02Eh
Mary-Ann	11	F	Unknown	11Ma02Eh	MOONEY, James	28	M	Laborer	11Ma02Eh
Eliza	9	F	Child	11Ma02Eh	Rose	3	F	Child	11Ma02Eh
MURPHY, Edwd.	11	M	Unknown	11Ma02Eh	Julia	24	F	Unknown	11Ma02Eh
ARMSTRONG, Isabella	20	F	Servant	11Ma02Eh	Mary	7	F	Child	11Ma02Eh
FLANAGAN, Ellen	18	F	Servant	11Ma02Eh	Rose	50	F	Unknown	11Ma02Eh
ELLIOT, Rebecca	40	F	Servant	11Ma02Eh	LYNAN, Andrew	45	M	Laborer	11Ma02Eh
CASNEY, Rose	36	F	Servant	11Ma02Eh	CORNAN, James	19	M	Laborer	11Ma02Eh
Scisley	10	F	Servant	11Ma02Eh	FITZGERALD, Joseph	70	M	Unknown	11Ma02Eh
Rose	6	F	Child	11Ma02Eh	Anna	70	F	Unknown	11Ma02Eh
John	8	M	Child	11Ma02Eh	CORTIGAN, Mary	61	F	Unknown	11Ma02Eh
BRANAGAN, Luke	40	M	Laborer	11Ma02Eh	CONLAN, John	15	M	Unknown	11Ma02Eh
LYON, Dennis	8	M	Child	11Ma02Eh	DAWS, Mary	19	F	Servant	11Ma02Eh
COSTERLY, Thomas	27	M	Laborer	11Ma02Eh	DONOUGH, Pat	11	M	Laborer	11Ma02Eh
MURRAY, James	50	M	Laborer	11Ma02Eh	FINNIGAN, Charley	66	M	Laborer	11Ma02Eh
Edward	14	M	Laborer	11Ma02Eh	Margaret	30	F	Servant	11Ma02Eh
John	16	M	Laborer	11Ma02Eh	Mary	28	F	Servant	11Ma02Eh
Michael	12	M	Laborer	11Ma02Eh	MCDONALD, Catherine	12	F	Servant	11Ma02Eh
Catherine	7	F	Child	11Ma02Eh	MCGORVAN, Ann	60	F	Servant	11Ma02Eh
Mary	40	F	Unknown	11Ma02Eh	GOLDAN, Mary-Ann	4	F	Child	11Ma02Eh
DONAHUGH, Margaret	40	F	Unknown	11Ma02Eh	CANFRY, Pat	12	M	Servant	11Ma02Eh
MOONEY, Peter	23	M	Laborer	11Ma02Eh	ROONEY, Pat	40	M	Servant	11Ma02Eh
DONAHUGH, John	12	M	Laborer	11Ma02Eh	Pat	50	M	Servant	11Ma02Eh
Pat	14	M	Laborer	11Ma02Eh	GREEN, Pat	23	M	Servant	11Ma02Eh
Mary	16	F	Unknown	11Ma02Eh	MCDERMOT, Mary	19	F	Servant	11Ma02Eh
ROGAN, Heley	40	F	Servant	11Ma02Eh	WALON, Catherine	25	F	Servant	11Ma02Eh
Oney	8	F	Child	11Ma02Eh	CONNOR, Pat	10	M	Servant	11Ma02Eh
Michael	9	M	Child	11Ma02Eh	Ann	14	F	Unknown	11Ma02Eh
MURPHY, James	20	M	Unknown	11Ma02Eh	OBRIEN, Mary	20	F	Servant	11Ma02Eh
KENNAN, Margaret	23	F	Servant	11Ma02Eh	Michael	18	M	Laborer	11Ma02Eh
WOODS, Ann	24	F	Servant	11Ma02Eh	PROCTOR, John	29	M	Laborer	11Ma02Eh
HARDY, Mary	16	F	Servant	11Ma02Eh	Thomas	3	M	Child	11Ma02Eh
CARTNEY, Bridget	17	F	Servant	11Ma02Eh	Ann	29	F	Unknown	11Ma02Eh

NAMES OF PASSENGERS	AGE	SEX	OCCUPATIONS	DATE PORT SHIP
LOCK, Mary	30	F	Servant	11Ma02Eh
NOLAN, Bridget	5	F	Child	11Ma02Eh
HAYS, Mathew	20	M	Laborer	11Ma02Eh
HAND, James	18	M	Laborer	11Ma02Eh
CARRELL, Ann	15	F	Laborer	11Ma02Eh
BIGOT, Michael	21	M	Laborer	11Ma02Eh
BROOM, Margaret	10	F	Unknown	11Ma02Eh
BRAIN, Christopher	25	M	Laborer	11Ma02Eh
LANE, Julia	16	F	Servant	11Ma02Eh
Ann	7	F	Child	11Ma02Eh
BUTLER, Bridget	38	F	Unknown	11Ma02Eh
BRAUN, William	23	M	Laborer	11Ma02Eh
MCMURRY, Ann	25	F	Servant	11Ma02Eh
RIGAN, Ellen	56	F	Servant	11Ma02Eh
BROWN, Matthew	20	M	Laborer	11Ma02Eh
MARTIN, Nancy	20	F	Servant	11Ma02Eh
GARRETY, Mary	18	F	Servant	11Ma02Eh
MCCARTNEY, Ann	35	F	Servant	11Ma02Eh
Catherine	12	F	Servant	11Ma02Eh
SANDERSON, Mary-Ann	12	F	Unknown	11Ma02Eh
RILEY, Catherine	12	F	Unknown	11Ma02Eh
MADDEN, James	19	M	Laborer	11Ma02Eh
Alice	25	F	Servant	11Ma02Eh
VINCENT, Mary	12	F	Servant	11Ma02Eh
BRANNON, Pat	40	M	Laborer	11Ma02Eh
GROGAN, Matt	30	M	Laborer	11Ma02Eh
DOYLE, John	28	M	Laborer	11Ma02Eh
LANEY, William	23	M	Laborer	11Ma02Eh
KINSELER, Mary	60	F	Unknown	11Ma02Eh
FARRELL, Peter	14	M	Unknown	11Ma02Eh
RYAN, Peter	10	M	Unknown	11Ma02Eh
OGRADY, John	50	M	Laborer	11Ma02Eh
Thomas	7	M	Child	11Ma02Eh
GUFFY, Catherine	8	F	Child	11Ma02Eh
OGRADY, Catherine	4	F	Child	11Ma02Eh
Catherine	16	F	Unknown	11Ma02Eh
Margaret	13	F	Unknown	11Ma02Eh
MCGANAN, Mary	18	F	Servant	11Ma02Eh
GALLIGAN, Lawrence	20	M	Laborer	11Ma02Eh
HIGGINS, Mary	13	F	Servant	11Ma02Eh
GROGAN, Margaret	19	F	Servant	11Ma02Eh
CUNNINGHAM, Rose-Ann	18	F	Servant	11Ma02Eh
HAYS, Ellen	8	F	Child	11Ma02Eh
RODGERS, Mary	20	F	Servant	11Ma02Eh
WILLIAMS, Bridget	30	F	Servant	11Ma02Eh
MCGUFFY, Mary	14	F	Servant	11Ma02Eh
FLOOD, Biddy	25	F	Servant	11Ma02Eh
CLARK, Mary	16	F	Servant	11Ma02Eh
CALLIGAN, Margaret	18	F	Servant	11Ma02Eh
BARNES, Thomas	38	M	Farmer	11Ma02Eh
Catherine	38	F	Unknown	11Ma02Eh
Mary	17	F	Unknown	11Ma02Eh
Joseph	3	M	Child	11Ma02Eh
Lucy	8	F	Child	11Ma02Eh
Pat	11	M	Unknown	11Ma02Eh
Dennis	18	M	Unknown	11Ma02Eh
Catherine	12	F	Unknown	11Ma02Eh
MULLIN, Christy	13	M	Unknown	11Ma02Eh
RICE, Ann	16	F	Unknown	11Ma02Eh
MCDERMOT, Maria	15	F	Unknown	11Ma02Eh
SAFER, Essy	22	F	Servant	11Ma02Eh
MADDON, Marcelery	13	F	Unknown	11Ma02Eh
GORT, John	24	M	Laborer	11Ma02Eh
CARROLL, Bridget	43	F	Servant	11Ma02Eh
SHARE, Johana	40	F	Servant	11Ma02Eh
Margaret	13	F	Servant	11Ma02Eh
Amelia	10	F	Servant	11Ma02Eh
KEEF, Eliza	20	F	Servant	11Ma02Eh
GOFFNEY, Bridget	20	F	Servant	11Ma02Eh
MCTICKEY, Ellen	50	F	Servant	11Ma02Eh
GARNEY, Elizabeth	36	F	Servant	11Ma02Eh
MORLEY, Biddy	7	F	Child	11Ma02Eh
Bessy	3	F	Child	11Ma02Eh
MCKENLON, Mary	50	F	Unknown	11Ma02Eh
DRISTON, Eliza	50	F	Unknown	11Ma02Eh

NAMES OF PASSENGERS	AGE	SEX	OCCUPATIONS	DATE PORT SHIP
MURPHY, Matt	55	M	Unknown	11Ma02Eh
DRISTON, Mary	56	F	Unknown	11Ma02Eh
MURPHY, Ann	15	F	Unknown	11Ma02Eh
CONNOR, Thomas	16	M	Unknown	11Ma02Eh
WARD, Eliza	11	F	Unknown	11Ma02Eh
John	25	M	Laborer	11Ma02Eh
John	7	M	Child	11Ma02Eh
MCCALLEY, Edward	29	M	Hrsm	11Ma02Eh
MCCLUSKEY, John	19	M	Clerk	11Ma02Eh
Philip	19	M	Clerk	11Ma02Eh
Bernard	16	M	Clerk	11Ma02Eh
Margaret	17	F	Unknown	11Ma02Eh
Bridget	15	F	Unknown	11Ma02Eh
ELLIS, Abraham	30	M	Printer	11Ma02Eh
Catherine	28	F	Unknown	11Ma02Eh
CREHEAN, Catherine	16	F	Unknown	11Ma02Eh
Mary	18	F	Unknown	11Ma02Eh
MCCORMICK, Ann	19	F	Servant	11Ma02Eh
GILLICK, Ann	20	F	Servant	11Ma02Eh
FINNIGAN, Thomas	35	M	Laborer	11Ma02Eh
HUTCHINSON, James	00	M	Unknown	11Ma02Eh
PORTAS, Thomas-H.	00	M	Unknown	11Ma02Eh
Helen	00	F	Unknown	11Ma02Eh
Thomas-H.	00	M	Unknown	11Ma02Eh
WILSON, Mary	00	F	Unknown	11Ma02Eh
MURPHY, Ann-Jane	00	F	Unknown	11Ma02Eh

ENTERPRIZE 13 MAY 1850

From Liverpool

NAMES OF PASSENGERS	AGE	SEX	OCCUPATIONS	DATE PORT SHIP
CONNORS, Edward	30	M	Farmer	13Ma02Ab
U-Mrs.	26	F	Farmer	13Ma02Ab
Margaret	.06	F	Infant	13Ma02Ab
LOUGHLEN, Cornelius	30	M	Farmer	13Ma02Ab
MCHALE, A.	22	F	Farmer	13Ma02Ab
THEDOSINE, M.	34	F	Farmer	13Ma02Ab
Frederick	19	M	Farmer	13Ma02Ab
HAMILL, Thomas	28	M	Farmer	13Ma02Ab
Ann	23	F	Farmer	13Ma02Ab
MCCOMB, John	21	M	Farmer	13Ma02Ab
Mary	24	F	Farmer	13Ma02Ab
HENRY, Patrick	24	M	Farmer	13Ma02Ab
HENNESSY, Edmond	15	M	Farmer	13Ma02Ab
FINEGAN, Miles	24	M	Farmer	13Ma02Ab
FLANIGAN, Michael	22	M	Farmer	13Ma02Ab
Mary	20	F	Farmer	13Ma02Ab
DILLON, Maria	25	F	Farmer	13Ma02Ab
REARDON, Dennis	17	M	Farmer	13Ma02Ab
SULLIVAN, Catherine	24	F	Farmer	13Ma02Ab
SCULLY, James	30	M	Farmer	13Ma02Ab
MILLENICK, Patrick	24	M	Farmer	13Ma02Ab
Ellen	20	F	Farmer	13Ma02Ab
HANNAN, James	25	M	Farmer	13Ma02Ab
HENRY, John	.09	M	Infant	13Ma02Ab
DALTON, Margaret	21	F	Farmer	13Ma02Ab
AHEARN, John	19	M	Farmer	13Ma02Ab
KEEFE, Bridget	30	F	Farmer	13Ma02Ab
HANNAN, Daniel	26	M	Farmer	13Ma02Ab
Patrick	20	M	Farmer	13Ma02Ab
POWER, Maurice	21	M	Farmer	13Ma02Ab
DONOVAN, James	30	M	Farmer	13Ma02Ab
U-Mrs.	30	F	Farmer	13Ma02Ab
Anne	.09	F	Infant	13Ma02Ab
BARRY, John	27	M	Infant	13Ma02Ab
MURPHY, Martin	30	M	Farmer	13Ma02Ab
BRISNAHOW, Honora	30	F	Farmer	13Ma02Ab
CONNELL, Mary	20	F	Farmer	13Ma02Ab
CONNORS, Margaret	35	F	Farmer	13Ma02Ab

NAMES OF PASSENGERS	AGE	SEX	OCCUPATIONS	DATE PORT SHIP
CASEY, David	15	M	Farmer	13Ma02Ab
SHEEHAN, Daniel	25	M	Farmer	13Ma02Ab
STACK, Richard	32	M	Farmer	13Ma02Ab
Cherry	24	F	Farmer	13Ma02Ab
REARDON, Thomas	29	M	Farmer	13Ma02Ab
KEARNEY, Johanna	25	F	Farmer	13Ma02Ab
Ellen	15	F	Farmer	13Ma02Ab
Mary	3	F	Child	13Ma02Ab
Thomas	.09	M	Infant	13Ma02Ab
Died-At-Sea				
STACK, Michael	30	M	Farmer	13Ma02Ab
U-Mrs.	30	F	Farmer	13Ma02Ab
Johanna	3	F	Child	13Ma02Ab
MOYNTHAN, Timothy	18	M	Farmer	13Ma02Ab
CARROLL, John	22	M	Farmer	13Ma02Ab
DOODY, John	23	M	Farmer	13Ma02Ab
KELLY, U-Mrs.	50	F	Farmer	13Ma02Ab
Mary	28	F	Farmer	13Ma02Ab
Thomas	24	M	Farmer	13Ma02Ab
OBRIEN, Thomas	24	M	Farmer	13Ma02Ab
LEAHY, James	24	M	Farmer	13Ma02Ab
WALSH, William	22	M	Farmer	13Ma02Ab
CLARK, James	28	M	Farmer	13Ma02Ab
BARRETT, Edmond	16	M	Farmer	13Ma02Ab
HILL, Mary	21	F	Farmer	13Ma02Ab
CONNELL, William	21	M	Farmer	13Ma02Ab
DWYER, Catherine	20	F	Farmer	13Ma02Ab
CROSS, Mary	29	F	Farmer	13Ma02Ab
BARMAN, Thomas	23	M	Farmer	13Ma02Ab
Mary	20	F	Farmer	13Ma02Ab
BYRNE, Michael	19	M	Farmer	13Ma02Ab
CROLLY, John	28	M	Farmer	13Ma02Ab
COLBERT, Daniel	34	M	Farmer	13Ma02Ab
BARRY, Michael	19	M	Farmer	13Ma02Ab
KEEF, Mary	22	F	Farmer	13Ma02Ab
Margaret	20	F	Farmer	13Ma02Ab
WALSH, Mary	19	F	Farmer	13Ma02Ab
NEWMAN, James	22	M	Farmer	13Ma02Ab
MALONEY, Thomas	60	M	Farmer	13Ma02Ab
John	30	M	Farmer	13Ma02Ab
Patrick	25	M	Farmer	13Ma02Ab
Michael	20	M	Farmer	13Ma02Ab
Bridget	50	F	Farmer	13Ma02Ab
Margaret	14	F	Farmer	13Ma02Ab
Hannah	9	F	Child	13Ma02Ab
DALEY, John	25	M	Farmer	13Ma02Ab
Hannah	20	F	Farmer	13Ma02Ab
EGAN, Matthew	25	M	Farmer	13Ma02Ab
John	20	M	Farmer	13Ma02Ab
Patrick	23	M	Farmer	13Ma02Ab
Hannah	23	F	Farmer	13Ma02Ab
MCCADDEN, John	22	M	Farmer	13Ma02Ab
WILLIAMS, Thomas	21	M	Farmer	13Ma02Ab
Ann	22	F	Farmer	13Ma02Ab
BROGAN, John	20	M	Farmer	13Ma02Ab
MEENAN, Susan	19	F	Farmer	13Ma02Ab
FLANIGAN, Patrick	21	M	Farmer	13Ma02Ab
MCCOY, Joseph	50	M	Farmer	13Ma02Ab
U-Mrs.	40	F	Farmer	13Ma02Ab
James	13	M	Farmer	13Ma02Ab
Eliza	11	F	Farmer	13Ma02Ab
William	9	M	Child	13Ma02Ab
Robert	6	M	Child	13Ma02Ab
Jane	4	F	Child	13Ma02Ab
SHALS, Barney	20	M	Farmer	13Ma02Ab
EWEN, Thomas	50	M	Farmer	13Ma02Ab
REYNOLDS, Richard	18	M	Farmer	13Ma02Ab
Patrick	20	M	Farmer	13Ma02Ab
Mary	12	F	Farmer	13Ma02Ab
BRADY, Margaret	7	F	Child	13Ma02Ab
MURPHY, Patrick	20	M	Farmer	13Ma02Ab
GAFFNEY, Luke	20	M	Farmer	13Ma02Ab
Mary	24	F	Farmer	13Ma02Ab
RYAN, Patrick	26	M	Farmer	13Ma02Ab
Alice	27	F	Farmer	13Ma02Ab

NAMES OF PASSENGERS	AGE	SEX	OCCUPATIONS	DATE PORT SHIP
RYAN, Nancy	24	F	Farmer	13Ma02Ab
CASEY, Bridget	20	F	Farmer	13Ma02Ab
CORMICK, Richard	32	M	Farmer	13Ma02Ab
Michael	25	M	Farmer	13Ma02Ab
MAHER, Lawrence	26	M	Farmer	13Ma02Ab
BRENNAN, Thomas	22	M	Farmer	13Ma02Ab
Mary	20	F	Farmer	13Ma02Ab
RYAN, Michael	18	M	Farmer	13Ma02Ab
QUINN, Timothy	58	M	Farmer	13Ma02Ab
Margaret	50	F	Farmer	13Ma02Ab
Patrick	28	M	Farmer	13Ma02Ab
Michael	26	M	Farmer	13Ma02Ab
Richard	21	M	Farmer	13Ma02Ab
James	19	M	Farmer	13Ma02Ab
Morgan	17	M	Farmer	13Ma02Ab
Ellen	16	F	Farmer	13Ma02Ab
Timothy	11	M	Farmer	13Ma02Ab
POWER, William	30	M	Farmer	13Ma02Ab
Catherine	26	F	Farmer	13Ma02Ab
James	5	M	Child	13Ma02Ab
Margaret	3	F	Child	13Ma02Ab
Alice	.06	F	Infant	13Ma02Ab
CORBETT, Catherine	26	F	Farmer	13Ma02Ab
GAIREY, John	29	M	Farmer	13Ma02Ab
DWYER, Dennis	20	M	Farmer	13Ma02Ab
HENNESSY, Edmond	32	M	Farmer	13Ma02Ab
QUIRK, John	25	M	Farmer	13Ma02Ab
MAHONEY, John	23	M	Farmer	13Ma02Ab
Margaret	18	M	Farmer	13Ma02Ab
CROSS, Thomas	19	M	Farmer	13Ma02Ab
MCNERRY, Barth.	20	M	Farmer	13Ma02Ab
CASEY, Mary	17	F	Farmer	13Ma02Ab
ROWLES, George	24	M	Farmer	13Ma02Ab
BENTEN, Nicholas	23	M	Farmer	13Ma02Ab
Mary	21	F	Farmer	13Ma02Ab
MAHER, Ann	22	F	Farmer	13Ma02Ab
MCGUIRE, Barney	24	M	Farmer	13Ma02Ab
MCARDLE, Ellen	18	F	Farmer	13Ma02Ab
BANIGAN, Francis	20	M	Farmer	13Ma02Ab
PEACOCK, John	32	M	Farmer	13Ma02Ab
Thomas	30	M	Farmer	13Ma02Ab
Francis	25	M	Farmer	13Ma02Ab
AGNEW, Thomas	45	M	Farmer	13Ma02Ab
Thomas	7	M	Child	13Ma02Ab
Died-At-Sea				
KEELAN, Peter	21	M	Farmer	13Ma02Ab
MOLLOY, Daniel	22	M	Farmer	13Ma02Ab
HANNAH, John	25	M	Farmer	13Ma02Ab
DUNLOP, Sarah	20	M	Farmer	13Ma02Ab
DOUGLASS, Robert	26	M	Farmer	13Ma02Ab
MCELLROY, Andrew	24	M	Farmer	13Ma02Ab
DALEY, Carrett	50	M	Farmer	13Ma02Ab
Fanny	48	F	Farmer	13Ma02Ab
James	27	M	Farmer	13Ma02Ab
Peter	18	M	Farmer	13Ma02Ab
Michael	14	M	Farmer	13Ma02Ab
Mary	13	F	Farmer	13Ma02Ab
Alice	10	F	Farmer	13Ma02Ab
Rose	12	F	Farmer	13Ma02Ab
Catherine	18	F	Farmer	13Ma02Ab
FLOOD, James	20	M	Farmer	13Ma02Ab
Bessy	18	F	Farmer	13Ma02Ab
MCDEY, Cornelius	20	M	Farmer	13Ma02Ab
HUTTEN, Judy	20	F	Farmer	13Ma02Ab
MCGINNESS, Ann	18	F	Farmer	13Ma02Ab
MCNAMA, James	30	M	Farmer	13Ma02Ab
Margaret	29	F	Farmer	13Ma02Ab
Peter	11	M	Farmer	13Ma02Ab
MCGILL, Jane	30	F	Farmer	13Ma02Ab
COLORAN, Catherine	35	F	Farmer	13Ma02Ab
William	12	M	Farmer	13Ma02Ab
Honora	10	F	Farmer	13Ma02Ab
Ellen	8	F	Child	13Ma02Ab
GILLAN, James	23	M	Farmer	13Ma02Ab
REILLY, Thomas	21	M	Farmer	13Ma02Ab

NAMES OF PASSENGERS	AGE	SEX	OCCUPATIONS	DATE PORT SHIP
WHELAN, Thomas	20	M	Farmer	13Ma02Ab
HAMILL, John	19	M	Farmer	13Ma02Ab
FITZGERALD, James	25	M	Farmer	13Ma02Ab
KINEVAN, Michael	30	M	Farmer	13Ma02Ab
Ellen	25	F	Farmer	13Ma02Ab
James	.06	M	Infant	13Ma02Ab
Mary	25	F	Farmer	13Ma02Ab
Mary	30	F	Farmer	13Ma02Ab
MCNIMY, John	25	M	Farmer	13Ma02Ab
Thomas	24	M	Farmer	13Ma02Ab
IVERS, Lucius	24	M	Farmer	13Ma02Ab
FLANIGAN, James	25	M	Farmer	13Ma02Ab
RYAN, Edmond	20	M	Farmer	13Ma02Ab
CAMRON, John	34	M	Farmer	13Ma02Ab
James	26	M	Farmer	13Ma02Ab
Bridget	26	F	Farmer	13Ma02Ab
MCNANY, Margaret	45	F	Farmer	13Ma02Ab
ROBINSON, Thomas	22	M	Farmer	13Ma02Ab
HANNAH, Philip	20	M	Farmer	13Ma02Ab
CROWE, Philip	25	M	Farmer	13Ma02Ab
CARRELL, Charles	25	M	Farmer	13Ma02Ab
COFFEY, Mary	20	F	Farmer	13Ma02Ab
CALDWELL, Bernard	21	M	Farmer	13Ma02Ab
LEE, Margaret	19	F	Farmer	13Ma02Ab
OCONNOR, James	26	M	Farmer	13Ma02Ab
Mary	20	F	Farmer	13Ma02Ab
TIERNEY, Matthew	30	M	Farmer	13Ma02Ab
John	8	M	Child	13Ma02Ab
MALONEY, Bridget	21	F	Farmer	13Ma02Ab
REILLY, Richard	18	M	Farmer	13Ma02Ab
GOGARTY, Ann	18	F	Farmer	13Ma02Ab
SWIFT, Rose	20	F	Farmer	13Ma02Ab
CARDER, James	25	M	Farmer	13Ma02Ab
Thomas	23	M	Farmer	13Ma02Ab
Joseph	20	M	Farmer	13Ma02Ab
FEE, Arthur	23	M	Farmer	13Ma02Ab
MCGUIRE, John	19	M	Farmer	13Ma02Ab
Bernard	14	M	Farmer	13Ma02Ab
MCBRIEN, Joseph	20	M	Farmer	13Ma02Ab
FANNAN, Edward	20	M	Farmer	13Ma02Ab
KANE, Peggy	19	F	Farmer	13Ma02Ab
MCEVOY, Margaret	50	F	Farmer	13Ma02Ab
BARRETT, Betsy	19	F	Farmer	13Ma02Ab
MURPHY, Patrick	21	M	Farmer	13Ma02Ab
Wm.	36	M	Farmer	13Ma02Ab
GUINAN, U-Mrs.	30	F	Farmer	13Ma02Ab
Patrick	34	M	Farmer	13Ma02Ab
John	7	M	Child	13Ma02Ab
Patrick	4	M	Child	13Ma02Ab
Mary	5	F	Child	13Ma02Ab
Ellen	2	F	Child	13Ma02Ab
Catherine	.06	F	Infant	13Ma02Ab
WALSH, Thomas	50	M	Farmer	13Ma02Ab
U-Mrs.	40	F	Farmer	13Ma02Ab
Catherine	18	F	Farmer	13Ma02Ab
John	12	M	Farmer	13Ma02Ab
Thomas	10	M	Farmer	13Ma02Ab
James	7	M	Child	13Ma02Ab
Mary	5	F	Child	13Ma02Ab
Julia	.06	F	Infant	13Ma02Ab
BUCKLEY, Tim	40	M	Farmer	13Ma02Ab
DUGGAN, Tim	32	M	Farmer	13Ma02Ab
MURPHY, Pat	30	M	Farmer	13Ma02Ab
Michael	35	M	Farmer	13Ma02Ab
LANE, Joseph	26	M	Farmer	13Ma02Ab
CASEY, Jeremiah	26	M	Farmer	13Ma02Ab
SHANAHAN, John	27	M	Farmer	13Ma02Ab
LOVEJOY, Stephen	18	M	Farmer	13Ma02Ab
SULLIVAN, Daniel	20	M	Farmer	13Ma02Ab
SHANAHAN, Mary	20	F	Farmer	13Ma02Ab
LOVEJOY, Mary	12	F	Farmer	13Ma02Ab
SHANAHAN, Mary	.06	F	Infant	13Ma02Ab
GILLBY, Thomas	60	M	Farmer	13Ma02Ab
U-Mrs.	55	F	Farmer	13Ma02Ab
Luke	20	M	Farmer	13Ma02Ab
GILLBY, Margaret	18	F	Farmer	13Ma02Ab
Mary	13	F	Farmer	13Ma02Ab
Catherine	11	F	Farmer	13Ma02Ab
James	8	M	Child	13Ma02Ab
MALONE, Ann	20	F	Farmer	13Ma02Ab
KELLY, Mary-Ann	20	F	Farmer	13Ma02Ab
FITZGERALD, John	20	M	Farmer	13Ma02Ab
Patrick	18	M	Farmer	13Ma02Ab
MARTIN, Joseph	40	M	Farmer	13Ma02Ab
EGAN, Maurice	30	M	Farmer	13Ma02Ab
COUGHLEN, Thomas	30	M	Farmer	13Ma02Ab

ROSCIUS 13 MAY 1850

From Liverpool

NAMES OF PASSENGERS	AGE	SEX	OCCUPATIONS	DATE PORT SHIP
MCAULIFFE, Margt.	11	F	Unknown	13Ma02At
ALLEN, Ellen	25	F	Unknown	13Ma02At
MCAVOY, Ann	48	F	Unknown	13Ma02At
Ann	18	F	Unknown	13Ma02At
Sarah	20	F	Unknown	13Ma02At
Dan	12	M	Unknown	13Ma02At
BELLEW, Thomas	20	M	Stone Mason	13Ma02At
William	18	M	Stone Mason	13Ma02At
BYRNE, John	22	M	Laborer	13Ma02At
BURKE, John	27	M	Laborer	13Ma02At
BROPHY, John	24	M	Laborer	13Ma02At
Sarah	21	F	Unknown	13Ma02At
John	25	M	Laborer	13Ma02At
BARRETT, Thomas	30	M	Laborer	13Ma02At
BODEN, Alice	40	F	Unknown	13Ma02At
Peter	16	M	Laborer	13Ma02At
BUCKLEY, James	00	M	Mason	13Ma02At
CARROLL, Anty	50	M	Laborer	13Ma02At
Pat	20	M	Turner	13Ma02At
Ann	20	F	Unknown	13Ma02At
Margaret	18	F	Unknown	13Ma02At
CORCORAN, Eliza	18	F	Unknown	13Ma02At
CARBURY, John	27	M	Carpenter	13Ma02At
COLLOGAN, Ann	20	F	Unknown	13Ma02At
CORCORAN, John	11	M	Laborer	13Ma02At
CUDDY, Maria	21	F	Unknown	13Ma02At
Mat.	16	M	Unknown	13Ma02At
Johan	18	M	Unknown	13Ma02At
COONAN, Ann	17	F	Unknown	13Ma02At
CASSIDY, Cath.	28	F	Unknown	13Ma02At
CONNER, Margaret	20	F	Unknown	13Ma02At
COOPER, Eliza	15	F	Unknown	13Ma02At
CARBERRY, Jane	22	F	Unknown	13Ma02At
MCCORMACK, George	22	M	Laborer	13Ma02At
CALDWELL, Robert	22	M	Farmer	13Ma02At
Eliza	21	F	Unknown	13Ma02At
CONNELL, James	30	M	Laborer	13Ma02At
CARLIN, Pat	30	M	Unknown	13Ma02At
Mary	28	F	Unknown	13Ma02At
Michl.	21	M	Laborer	13Ma02At
Josh.	.00	M	Infant	13Ma02At
CARTHEY, Murray	10	M	Unknown	13Ma02At
CANNELL, Owen	40	M	Unknown	13Ma02At
Catharine	38	F	Unknown	13Ma02At
CONDALL, John	26	M	Clerk	13Ma02At
U-Mrs.	60	F	Unknown	13Ma02At
COLLINS, Michl.	30	M	Mason	13Ma02At
COYLE, James	20	M	Laborer	13Ma02At
CARBERRY, Sarah	20	F	Unknown	13Ma02At
DOLAN, Bryan	25	M	Laborer	13Ma02At
DONOHUE, Mary	12	F	Unknown	13Ma02At
ODONNELL, Richd.	22	M	Surveyor	13Ma02At
DUNN, Ellen	16	F	Unknown	13Ma02At

NAMES OF PASSENGERS	AGE	SEX	OCCUPATIONS	DATE PORT SHIP
DIAMOND, George	21	M	Farmer	13Ma02At
DELANCY, Pat	27	M	Clerk	13Ma02At
DEVOY, James	35	M	Laborer	13Ma02At
DRYNAN, James	40	M	Auctioneer	13Ma02At
U-Mrs.	23	F	Unknown	13Ma02At
Eliza	5	F	Child	13Ma02At
DALEY, Pat	29	M	Dealer	13Ma02At
DONOVAN, U	32	M	Farmer	13Ma02At
DOYLE, Mary	21	F	Unknown	13Ma02At
DIAMOND, Eliza	21	F	Unknown	13Ma02At
DEVOY, Michl.	20	M	Laborer	13Ma02At
DONOVAN, U-Mrs.	28	F	Unknown	13Ma02At
FANNON, Mary	40	F	Unknown	13Ma02At
Ellen	5	F	Child	13Ma02At
Thomas	3	M	Child	13Ma02At
Catherine	.00	F	Infant	13Ma02At
FOX, Francis	00	M	Mechanic	13Ma02At
FARRELL, Pat	25	M	Laborer	13Ma02At
FALLON, Hughes	25	M	Farmer	13Ma02At
Mary	45	F	Unknown	13Ma02At
Margt.	3	F	Child	13Ma02At
FINNERAN, Mary	20	F	Unknown	13Ma02At
FANNON, Thomas	22	F	Carpenter	13Ma02At
FETHERTON, Ann	9	F	Child	13Ma02At
FINNERN, Bridgt.	22	F	Unknown	13Ma02At
FINNON, Job	18	M	Unknown	13Ma02At
GOFF, James	30	M	Laborer	13Ma02At
Mary	33	F	Unknown	13Ma02At
Esther	7	F	Child	13Ma02At
Robert	11	M	Unknown	13Ma02At
GUBBINS, J.W.	40	M	Farmer	13Ma02At
GATCHELL, Alice	27	F	Unknown	13Ma02At
Mary-J.	3	F	Child	13Ma02At
John	.00	M	Infant	13Ma02At
GRUBB, Matilda	20	F	Unknown	13Ma02At
MCGEE, James	27	M	Laborer	13Ma02At
MCGREGOR, Robt.	28	M	Laborer	13Ma02At
GALLAHER, Owen	35	M	Laborer	13Ma02At
MCGEE, Sally	26	F	Unknown	13Ma02At
HARKIN, Pat	20	M	Laborer	13Ma02At
HUGHES, John	17	M	Unknown	13Ma02At
HYLAND, Margt.	50	F	Unknown	13Ma02At
HARKIN, Kate	20	F	Unknown	13Ma02At
U-Mrs.	40	F	Unknown	13Ma02At
Thomas	12	M	Unknown	13Ma02At
George	13	M	Unknown	13Ma02At
HOLMES, John	35	M	Unknown	13Ma02At
HYLAND, Thomas	24	M	Unknown	13Ma02At
HIGGINS, Thomas	22	M	Storekeeper	13Ma02At
HARDWICK, Saml.	39	M	Laborer	13Ma02At
HOUGHTON, Willm.	23	M	Laborer	13Ma02At
HAND, U	45	M	Farmer	13Ma02At
Mary	30	F	Unknown	13Ma02At
HOLMES, Bessey	25	F	Unknown	13Ma02At
Robt.	.00	M	Infant	13Ma02At
HIGGINS, James	14	M	Unknown	13Ma02At
IREY, Cath.	18	F	Unknown	13Ma02At
JUSTIN, Thomas	25	M	Weaver	13Ma02At
Alice	17	F	Unknown	13Ma02At
JUDY, John	26	M	Laborer	13Ma02At
KEENE, Rose	25	F	Unknown	13Ma02At
KEGAN, Thomas	25	M	Laborer	13Ma02At
KELLY, William	16	M	Laborer	13Ma02At
KIRBEY, D.	29	M	Laborer	13Ma02At
Tim	34	M	Laborer	13Ma02At
KILLCULLEN, Han.	17	F	Unknown	13Ma02At
KELLY, Dennis	22	M	Mason	13Ma02At
MCKEON, Jane	28	F	Unknown	13Ma02At
KING, John	24	M	Laborer	13Ma02At
KNOWLES, Cathr.	20	F	Unknown	13Ma02At
KANE, Pat	30	M	Unknown	13Ma02At
KENNEDY, Pat	27	M	Laborer	13Ma02At
Cath.	25	F	Unknown	13Ma02At
KEON, Cath.	14	F	Unknown	13Ma02At
George	12	M	Unknown	13Ma02At
KILSHULLAN, Edwd.	19	M	Unknown	13Ma02At
Jeremiah	9	M	Child	13Ma02At
LESTRANGE, Pat	30	M	Laborer	13Ma02At
MADDEN, Pat	20	M	Stctr	13Ma02At
Cath.	24	F	Unknown	13Ma02At
Nicholas	6	M	Child	13Ma02At
James	.00	M	Infant	13Ma02At
MARTIN, James	21	M	Blacksmith	13Ma02At
MURPHY, Han.	30	F	Unknown	13Ma02At
Michael	22	M	Laborer	13Ma02At
MADDEN, Bridget	22	F	Unknown	13Ma02At
John	17	M	Unknown	13Ma02At
MONRAN, Maria	21	F	Unknown	13Ma02At
MURRY, Ann	6	F	Child	13Ma02At
MACKAVOY, Pat	50	M	Laborer	13Ma02At
Pat	25	M	Laborer	13Ma02At
Eliza	50	F	Unknown	13Ma02At
Thomas	18	M	Laborer	13Ma02At
Christ.	7	M	Child	13Ma02At
Ellen	22	F	Unknown	13Ma02At
MARTIN, Bernard	60	M	Farmer	13Ma02At
Judy	45	F	Unknown	13Ma02At
Law.	22	M	Unknown	13Ma02At
Bridget	20	F	Unknown	13Ma02At
Maria	13	F	Unknown	13Ma02At
Judy	10	F	Unknown	13Ma02At
Ann	8	F	Child	13Ma02At
James	6	M	Child	13Ma02At
Essey	16	F	Unknown	13Ma02At
Pat	24	M	Laborer	13Ma02At
MURRAY, Pat	23	M	Laborer	13Ma02At
NEAL, James	20	M	Unknown	13Ma02At
NOONAN, Tim.	23	M	Laborer	13Ma02At
NEAL, U	50	M	Farmer	13Ma02At
U-Mrs.	45	F	Unknown	13Ma02At
Richard	24	M	Farmer	13Ma02At
Emiley	20	F	Unknown	13Ma02At
Whilhelmina	22	F	Unknown	13Ma02At
Alfred-Will.	14	M	Unknown	13Ma02At
Louise	7	F	Child	13Ma02At
James-Henry	5	M	Child	13Ma02At
ONEAL, Bryan	56	M	Coach Maker	13Ma02At
NEVIN, Thomas	25	M	Laborer	13Ma02At
MCNALLY, George	40	M	Weaver	13Ma02At
George	10	M	Unknown	13Ma02At
PETTOT, John	25	M	Shoemaker	13Ma02At
Mary	13	F	Unknown	13Ma02At
PARK, Judy	40	F	Unknown	13Ma02At
Thomas	9	M	Child	13Ma02At
Martha	11	F	Unknown	13Ma02At
RUXTON, Betty	16	F	Unknown	13Ma02At
RICHARDS, Eliza	34	F	Unknown	13Ma02At
Helen	12	F	Unknown	13Ma02At
Mary	10	F	Unknown	13Ma02At
Michael	7	M	Child	13Ma02At
ROACH, Cath.	18	F	Unknown	13Ma02At
REYNOLDS, Ann	18	F	Unknown	13Ma02At
ROCHE, John	21	M	Laborer	13Ma02At
Ellen	29	F	Unknown	13Ma02At
Michael	.00	M	Infant	13Ma02At
REARDON, Wm.	30	M	Laborer	13Ma02At
RYAN, Pat	30	M	Laborer	13Ma02At
Martin	30	M	Laborer	13Ma02At
Dennis	25	M	Laborer	13Ma02At
Julia	20	F	Unknown	13Ma02At
ROSS, Sally	20	F	Unknown	13Ma02At
RYAN, Mary	40	F	Unknown	13Ma02At
Lawrence	10	M	Unknown	13Ma02At
Pat	8	M	Child	13Ma02At
Martin	6	M	Child	13Ma02At
Edward	3	M	Child	13Ma02At
Michael	.00	M	Infant	13Ma02At
Lawrence	24	M	Laborer	13Ma02At
RAMSAY, Robt.	16	M	Clerk	13Ma02At
ROCHE, U-Miss	25	F	Unknown	13Ma02At

NAMES OF PASSENGERS	AGE	SEX	OCCUPATIONS	DATE PORT SHIP
REDMAN, Pat	22	M	Laborer	13Ma02At
Ann	22	F	Unknown	13Ma02At
ROAK, Ann	35	F	Unknown	13Ma02At
John	14	M	Unknown	13Ma02At
Pat	11	M	Unknown	13Ma02At
Michael	6	M	Child	13Ma02At
Bridget	8	F	Child	13Ma02At
SMITH, Margt.	30	F	Unknown	13Ma02At
SULLIVAN, Terrance	22	M	Laborer	13Ma02At
Dan.	30	M	Unknown	13Ma02At
SHERIDAN, Wm.	16	M	Tailor	13Ma02At
SHAGAN, John	25	M	Farmer	13Ma02At
Margt.	20	F	Unknown	13Ma02At
STAPLETON, Bridget	30	F	Unknown	13Ma02At
SHAW, Margt.	22	F	Unknown	13Ma02At
SHANKS, Eliza	22	F	Unknown	13Ma02At
Eliza	.00	U	Infant	13Ma02At
SWEETMAN, Henry	14	M	Laborer	13Ma02At
SUAHEN, Pat.	24	M	Laborer	13Ma02At
TIERNAN, Pat.	55	M	Laborer	13Ma02At
Ann	50	F	Unknown	13Ma02At
Ann	13	F	Unknown	13Ma02At
Catharine	10	F	Unknown	13Ma02At
Pat	8	M	Child	13Ma02At
TINONEY, Pat	40	M	Sawer	13Ma02At
TAYLOR, Jane	19	F	Unknown	13Ma02At
TOOHEY, John	40	M	Priest	13Ma02At
WHITTY, Michael	25	M	Laborer	13Ma02At
VINCENT, George	30	M	Farmer	13Ma02At
VICKERS, George	18	M	Stone Mason	13Ma02At
WHITTAKER, William	66	M	Unknown	13Ma02At
Ellen	66	F	Unknown	13Ma02At
James	32	M	Blacksmith	13Ma02At
Mary	35	F	Unknown	13Ma02At
Isab.	11	F	Unknown	13Ma02At
Maryann	3	F	Child	13Ma02At
Wm.Henry	.00	M	Infant	13Ma02At
WHITE, William	40	M	Blacksmith	13Ma02At
U-Mrs.	30	F	Unknown	13Ma02At
Mary	11	F	Unknown	13Ma02At
Ellen	5	F	Child	13Ma02At
Hugh	7	M	Child	13Ma02At
Jane	9	F	Child	13Ma02At
WARD, John	32	M	Laborer	13Ma02At
Mary	31	F	Unknown	13Ma02At
Mary	00	F	Unknown	13Ma02At
Isab.	9	F	Child	13Ma02At
Elinor	6	F	Child	13Ma02At
Eliza	3	F	Child	13Ma02At
Ann	.00	F	Infant	13Ma02At
WILLIAMS, John	45	M	Laborer	13Ma02At
James	13	M	Unknown	13Ma02At
WALL, Francis	13	M	Shoemaker	13Ma02At
WHOLOHAM, Michl.	18	M	Laborer	13Ma02At
WOODCOCK, Robert	21	M	Laborer	13Ma02At
John	19	M	Laborer	13Ma02At
WINE, William	18	M	Farmer	13Ma02At
Mary	20	F	Unknown	13Ma02At
WILKINSON, Robt.	28	M	Unknown	13Ma02At
WHELAN, Terance	23	M	Unknown	13Ma02At

MASONIC 13 MAY 1850

From Liverpool

NAMES OF PASSENGERS	AGE	SEX	OCCUPATIONS	DATE PORT SHIP
CONNER, Ellen	22	F	Unknown	13Ma02Jd
TYNAN, John	17	M	Laborer	13Ma02Jd
Mary	13	F	Unknown	13Ma02Jd
DONNELLY, Margaret	18	F	Unknown	13Ma02Jd
CORSEED, Anna	17	F	Unknown	13Ma02Jd
HANLEY, Thos.	22	M	Laborer	13Ma02Jd
MCCLUSKY, Geo.	22	M	Laborer	13Ma02Jd
Arthur	20	M	Laborer	13Ma02Jd
Nathan	20	M	Laborer	13Ma02Jd
Mary	18	F	Unknown	13Ma02Jd
MULLIGAN, Thos.	22	M	Laborer	13Ma02Jd
WINKOTT, Owen	18	M	Laborer	13Ma02Jd
GALLIGHAN, John	21	M	Laborer	13Ma02Jd
MCEVRIE, John	26	M	Laborer	13Ma02Jd
QUIN, John	40	M	Laborer	13Ma02Jd
MCMANUS, Bernard	50	M	Laborer	13Ma02Jd
KILLBRIDE, Patrick	40	M	Laborer	13Ma02Jd
HART, Mary	36	F	Unknown	13Ma02Jd
CARRID, Michael	26	M	Laborer	13Ma02Jd
DOGAN, John	60	M	Laborer	13Ma02Jd
Rose	60	F	Laborer	13Ma02Jd
Anna	20	F	Unknown	13Ma02Jd
MERRY, Biddy	7	F	Child	13Ma02Jd
Mary	32	F	Unknown	13Ma02Jd
Anna	11	F	Unknown	13Ma02Jd
Mary	9	F	Child	13Ma02Jd
John	6	M	Child	13Ma02Jd
HARELY, Thos.	18	M	Laborer	13Ma02Jd
MCLAUGHLIN, James	20	M	Laborer	13Ma02Jd
U-Mrs.	20	F	Unknown	13Ma02Jd
MCKELLEY, John	20	M	Laborer	13Ma02Jd
Phillip	21	M	Laborer	13Ma02Jd
LANGEN, James	22	M	Laborer	13Ma02Jd
KEARNEY, Hugh	22	M	Laborer	13Ma02Jd
CONNER, John	15	M	Laborer	13Ma02Jd
MCCORMICK, John	17	M	Laborer	13Ma02Jd
HENNESSY, James	25	M	Baker	13Ma02Jd
Hannah	30	F	Unknown	13Ma02Jd
ERVIN, Thos.	20	M	Laborer	13Ma02Jd
GUBBINS, John	20	M	Laborer	13Ma02Jd
DUGGIN, James	23	M	Laborer	13Ma02Jd
MASON, James	20	M	Laborer	13Ma02Jd
MCNICHOL, Geo.	30	M	Shoemaker	13Ma02Jd
KELLY, Lawrence	27	M	Laborer	13Ma02Jd
KELLEY, Anthy.	22	M	Laborer	13Ma02Jd
NUGENT, John	50	M	Farmer	13Ma02Jd
U-Mrs.	50	F	Unknown	13Ma02Jd
Michael	28	M	Farmer	13Ma02Jd
William	22	M	Farmer	13Ma02Jd
David	18	M	Farmer	13Ma02Jd
Catherine	24	F	Unknown	13Ma02Jd
Mary	22	F	Unknown	13Ma02Jd
Mary	6	F	Child	13Ma02Jd
GALLIGHER, Hugh	20	M	Laborer	13Ma02Jd
DONNELLY, Felix	20	M	Laborer	13Ma02Jd
Catherine	20	F	Unknown	13Ma02Jd
DONEGHEY, B.	36	M	Laborer	13Ma02Jd
Mary	20	F	Unknown	13Ma02Jd
MCCULLUGH, Neal	30	M	Laborer	13Ma02Jd
WALKER, Adrian	20	M	Laborer	13Ma02Jd
Sarah	20	F	Unknown	13Ma02Jd
Jane	40	F	Unknown	13Ma02Jd
Margaret	20	F	Unknown	13Ma02Jd
CROWLEY, Michael	30	M	Laborer	13Ma02Jd
KELLEY, Michael	30	M	Laborer	13Ma02Jd
CROWLEY, Tim	22	M	Laborer	13Ma02Jd
KEEFE, Dan	35	M	Laborer	13Ma02Jd
GAUGHAN, William	22	M	Laborer	13Ma02Jd
James	25	M	Laborer	13Ma02Jd
MCCARTY, Ellen	11	F	Unknown	13Ma02Jd
CURLY, Pat	30	M	Laborer	13Ma02Jd
NIELLET, John	23	M	Laborer	13Ma02Jd
WRIGHT, Joseph	35	M	Surveyor	13Ma02Jd
Mary	35	F	Unknown	13Ma02Jd
Mary-Jane	.00	F	Infant	13Ma02Jd
FARBURN, Mary	34	F	Unknown	13Ma02Jd
WRIGHT, Anna	35	F	Unknown	13Ma02Jd
Sarah	12	F	Unknown	13Ma02Jd
John	19	M	Laborer	13Ma02Jd

NAMES OF PASSENGERS	AGE	SEX	OCCUPATIONS	DATE PORT SHIP
BROWN, John	20	M	Laborer	13Ma02Jd
LOUD, James	22	M	Laborer	13Ma02Jd
DOWN, John	38	M	Laborer	13Ma02Jd
DOLAN, Patrick	7	M	Child	13Ma02Jd
JUDGE, Pat	23	M	Laborer	13Ma02Jd
RYAN, Kitty	22	F	Unknown	13Ma02Jd
COLLINS, James	27	M	Laborer	13Ma02Jd
MCDONALD, Mary	21	F	Unknown	13Ma02Jd
GRADY, Mary	25	F	Unknown	13Ma02Jd
KEEFE, John	30	M	Laborer	13Ma02Jd
Pat	44	M	Laborer	13Ma02Jd
Mary	30	F	Unknown	13Ma02Jd
TYNAN, Mary	36	F	Unknown	13Ma02Jd
Ellen	35	F	Unknown	13Ma02Jd
Teaoshey	29	F	Unknown	13Ma02Jd
John	14	M	Unknown	13Ma02Jd
Thos.	9	M	Child	13Ma02Jd
Peggy	10	F	Unknown	13Ma02Jd
Edmund	6	M	Child	13Ma02Jd
DWIRE, Pat	22	M	Laborer	13Ma02Jd
BLAKE, Mary	18	F	Unknown	13Ma02Jd
DONNELL, Ellen	30	F	Unknown	13Ma02Jd
Pat	8	M	Child	13Ma02Jd
RONEY, John	25	M	Policeman	13Ma02Jd
Catherine	18	F	Unknown	13Ma02Jd
FARRELL, James	31	M	Farmer	13Ma02Jd
Edmund	31	M	Farmer	13Ma02Jd
Mary	24	F	Unknown	13Ma02Jd
Bridget	22	F	Unknown	13Ma02Jd
FOLEY, John	60	M	Laborer	13Ma02Jd
Mary	60	F	Unknown	13Ma02Jd
Martin	27	M	Laborer	13Ma02Jd
Bridget	22	F	Unknown	13Ma02Jd
Mary	30	F	Unknown	13Ma02Jd
Judy	16	F	Unknown	13Ma02Jd
William	12	M	Unknown	13Ma02Jd
Thos.	10	M	Unknown	13Ma02Jd
Lawrence	19	M	Laborer	13Ma02Jd
KELLEY, Michael	23	M	Laborer	13Ma02Jd
OBERTON, Mary	16	F	Unknown	13Ma02Jd
KELLEY, Anne	18	F	Unknown	13Ma02Jd
CAHILL, Catherine	25	F	Unknown	13Ma02Jd
LEAN, Joseph	37	M	Unknown	13Ma02Jd
Rose	35	F	Unknown	13Ma02Jd
WRIGHT, William	6	M	Child	13Ma02Jd
Margaret	3	F	Child	13Ma02Jd
Mary	.00	F	Infant	13Ma02Jd
DELLEY, Anna	30	F	Unknown	13Ma02Jd
FITZGERALD, Michael	35	M	Laborer	13Ma02Jd
BENNET, James	30	M	Laborer	13Ma02Jd
MARTEN, Robt.	18	M	Laborer	13Ma02Jd
WRIGHT, Geo.	6	M	Child	13Ma02Jd
MURRAY, Phillip	18	M	Laborer	13Ma02Jd
KELLEY, Catherine	60	F	Unknown	13Ma02Jd
Esther	26	F	Unknown	13Ma02Jd
EARLY, Michael	29	M	Laborer	13Ma02Jd
Mary	50	F	Unknown	13Ma02Jd
Kate	35	F	Unknown	13Ma02Jd
CAYLE, Michael	30	M	Laborer	13Ma02Jd
Johanna	25	F	Unknown	13Ma02Jd
GILLIGHAN, Johanna	36	M	Laborer	13Ma02Jd
Mary	22	F	Unknown	13Ma02Jd
Margaret	37	F	Unknown	13Ma02Jd
Pat	5	M	Child	13Ma02Jd
Michael	.00	M	Infant	13Ma02Jd
JUDGE, Bridget	23	F	Unknown	13Ma02Jd
MONROE, Bridget	30	F	Unknown	13Ma02Jd
FLANNING, Mary	25	F	Unknown	13Ma02Jd
PRENTIGAN, Mary	40	F	Unknown	13Ma02Jd
QUIGLEY, Bridget	22	F	Unknown	13Ma02Jd
MCGLUE, Ann	28	F	Unknown	13Ma02Jd
MCWADE, Catherine	18	F	Unknown	13Ma02Jd
Anna	14	F	Unknown	13Ma02Jd
QUINAN, Catherine	18	F	Unknown	13Ma02Jd
GALIGHER, Pat	21	M	Laborer	13Ma02Jd
GALIGHER, Margaret	18	F	Unknown	13Ma02Jd
OWENS, Ellen	50	F	Unknown	13Ma02Jd
Frances	18	F	Unknown	13Ma02Jd
James	16	M	Unknown	13Ma02Jd
MCWADE, Anna	30	F	Unknown	13Ma02Jd
ARCHDALE, Alexander	50	M	Laborer	13Ma02Jd
MCDERMIT, James	36	M	Laborer	13Ma02Jd
MCQUADE, Catherine	21	F	Unknown	13Ma02Jd
MCGIVIN, Anne	15	F	Unknown	13Ma02Jd
MONAGHAN, Pat	4	M	Child	13Ma02Jd
KEARNEY, Thos.	30	M	Laborer	13Ma02Jd
KENNERY, Kitty	25	F	Unknown	13Ma02Jd
Biddy	.00	F	Infant	13Ma02Jd
Mary	.00	F	Infant	13Ma02Jd

DELAWARE 13 MAY 1850

From Liverpool

NAMES OF PASSENGERS	AGE	SEX	OCCUPATIONS	DATE PORT SHIP
HOUSTON, Jane	25	F	None	13Ma02Jf
Barbara	2	F	Child	13Ma02Jf
Mary	.10	F	Infant	13Ma02Jf
HIGGANBOTTOM, Thomas	30	M	Farmer	13Ma02Jf
Elizabeth	23	F	None	13Ma02Jf
Elizabeth	.11	F	Infant	13Ma02Jf
BARTMAN, George	36	M	Farmer	13Ma02Jf
Jane	26	F	None	13Ma02Jf
Mary	2	F	Child	13Ma02Jf
Anna	.11	F	Infant	13Ma02Jf
THOMAS, James	35	M	Farmer	13Ma02Jf
Ann	38	F	None	13Ma02Jf
HICKERLY, Geo.	40	M	Tinman	13Ma02Jf
Thomas	38	M	Mason	13Ma02Jf
JOHNSON, Tobias	24	M	None	13Ma02Jf
Maria	19	F	None	13Ma02Jf
Mary	8	F	Child	13Ma02Jf
PARKER, Joseph	41	M	Mason	13Ma02Jf
WALKER, Joseph	30	M	Mason	13Ma02Jf
BROWN, Wm.	40	M	Hatter	13Ma02Jf
HUTCHINSON, Robt.	38	M	Mason	13Ma02Jf
HAMELTON, Wm.	25	M	Turner	13Ma02Jf
HODGSON, Wm.	42	M	Blacksmith	13Ma02Jf
BROWN, Chas.	32	M	Blacksmith	13Ma02Jf
Eliza	31	F	Unknown	13Ma02Jf
BREMNER, James	23	M	Laborer	13Ma02Jf
CARLIN, Martha	21	F	None	13Ma02Jf
BOODY, Mary	24	F	None	13Ma02Jf
DALTON, Catherine	12	F	None	13Ma02Jf
Ellen	8	F	Child	13Ma02Jf
HANDIMAN, Jno.	21	M	Tailor	13Ma02Jf
Mary	12	F	Unknown	13Ma02Jf
DUNN, Davis	20	M	Clerk	13Ma02Jf
KAVANAGH, Nat.	21	M	Farmer	13Ma02Jf
Ellen	52	F	Unknown	13Ma02Jf

IVANHOE 13 MAY 1850

From Liverpool

NAMES OF PASSENGERS	AGE	SEX	OCCUPATIONS	DATE PORT SHIP
ROY, William-S.	56	M	Professor	13Ma02Bt
GARIGAN, Eliza	21	F	Servant	13Ma02Bt
DUNNE, Rody	20	M	Laborer	13Ma02Bt
Mary	22	F	Servant	13Ma02Bt

NAMES OF PASSENGERS	AGE	SEX	OCCUPATIONS	DATE PORT SHIP
MOCKLER, Thomas	20	M	Laborer	13Ma02Bt
HARAHAN, Patt	20	M	Laborer	13Ma02Bt
QUIRCK, Bridget	20	F	Servant	13Ma02Bt
GARVEY, Patt	24	M	Laborer	13Ma02Bt
COONEY, Mary	23	F	Servant	13Ma02Bt
HARRIS, William	25	M	Farmer	13Ma02Bt
Eliza	24	F	Servant	13Ma02Bt
James	3	M	Child	13Ma02Bt
MCREEL, Margaret	20	F	Servant	13Ma02Bt
Mary-Anne	18	F	Laborer	13Ma02Bt
David	20	M	Servant	13Ma02Bt
MCCREEDY, David	20	M	Laborer	13Ma02Bt
WILLIAMSON, David	16	M	Laborer	13Ma02Bt
NELSON, Margaret	20	F	Servant	13Ma02Bt
BARNETT, Eliza	16	F	Servant	13Ma02Bt
DUGGAN, Mary	18	F	Servant	13Ma02Bt
BALLAGH, Jane	40	F	Farmer	13Ma02Bt
Alexander	20	M	Servant	13Ma02Bt
Jane	18	F	Servant	13Ma02Bt
Margaret-Jane	10	F	Servant	13Ma02Bt
REGAN, Michael	46	M	Laborer	13Ma02Bt
Margaret	40	F	Unknown	13Ma02Bt
Michael	25	M	Unknown	13Ma02Bt
Patrick	18	M	Unknown	13Ma02Bt
Katherine	14	F	Unknown	13Ma02Bt
Margaret	10	F	Unknown	13Ma02Bt
Charles	5	M	Child	13Ma02Bt
HEALY, John	25	M	Laborer	13Ma02Bt
CUMMINS, Michael	26	M	Laborer	13Ma02Bt
NEIL, Michael	25	M	Laborer	13Ma02Bt
Bridget	26	F	Servant	13Ma02Bt
WOODS, Jane	40	F	Servant	13Ma02Bt
Margaret	13	F	Servant	13Ma02Bt
William	7	M	Child	13Ma02Bt
DACHERTY, Michael	46	M	Laborer	13Ma02Bt
Michael	15	U	Laborer	13Ma02Bt
Matthew	14	U	Laborer	13Ma02Bt
BROADWICK, Jeremiah	35	M	Laborer	13Ma02Bt
Mary	30	F	Unknown	13Ma02Bt
John	6	M	Child	13Ma02Bt
KELTY, Honora	20	F	Servant	13Ma02Bt
ROCHE, Ellen	25	F	Servant	13Ma02Bt
Anne	30	F	Servant	13Ma02Bt
MACDONELL, Alexander	18	M	Farmer	13Ma02Bt
Judith	14	F	Servant	13Ma02Bt
MCDONALD, Anne	18	F	Servant	13Ma02Bt
OROURKE, Thomas	25	M	Laborer	13Ma02Bt
Anne	30	F	Servant	13Ma02Bt
PURFIELD, James	19	M	Laborer	13Ma02Bt
CANNING, Maria	15	F	Servant	13Ma02Bt
MURRAY, Susan	17	F	Servant	13Ma02Bt
Anne-Maria	15	F	Servant	13Ma02Bt
Caroline	13	F	Servant	13Ma02Bt
Fanny	11	F	Unknown	13Ma02Bt
CUSACK, Mary	18	F	Servant	13Ma02Bt
HANNAN, Dennis	42	M	Laborer	13Ma02Bt
Honora	35	F	Servant	13Ma02Bt
John	9	M	Child	13Ma02Bt
Dennis	7	M	Child	13Ma02Bt
GLEESON, Catherine	16	F	Servant	13Ma02Bt
CASEY, Johanna	20	F	Servant	13Ma02Bt
TWOMEY, Timothy	26	M	Weaver	13Ma02Bt
COLEMAN, Connor	38	M	Laborer	13Ma02Bt
MEAD, James	35	M	Shoemaker	13Ma02Bt
LEARY, Mary	22	F	Servant	13Ma02Bt
BRENNAN, Norry	18	F	Servant	13Ma02Bt
GOODMAN, Margaret	22	F	Dressmaker	13Ma02Bt
Mary-Anne	18	F	Dressmaker	13Ma02Bt
QUINN, Richard	32	M	Laborer	13Ma02Bt
William	25	M	Blacksmith	13Ma02Bt
BRIDGELAND, Thomas	35	M	Farmer	13Ma02Bt
Mary	30	F	Unknown	13Ma02Bt
Bridget	15	F	Unknown	13Ma02Bt
Anne	.00	F	Infant	13Ma02Bt
DONELLAN, Maria	18	F	Servant	13Ma02Bt
FARRELL, Anne	20	F	Servant	13Ma02Bt
COLEMAN, Peter	19	M	Laborer	13Ma02Bt
CASEY, John	35	M	Laborer	13Ma02Bt
FARRELL, Catherine	25	F	Servant	13Ma02Bt
LYNCH, Laurence	26	M	Laborer	13Ma02Bt
KENNA, Peter	25	M	Miller	13Ma02Bt
HOOLAHAN, Wm.	26	M	Butcher	13Ma02Bt
LAWLER, Margaret	25	F	Servant	13Ma02Bt
SYNOTT, Thomas	21	M	Grocer	13Ma02Bt
Mary-Anne	23	F	Servant	13Ma02Bt
James	.00	M	Infant	13Ma02Bt
BRIEN, Katherine	24	F	Servant	13Ma02Bt
DAY, Eliza	18	F	Unknown	13Ma02Bt
TUNKARD, Katherine	50	F	Servant	13Ma02Bt
Nancy	42	F	Servant	13Ma02Bt
FINNERTY, John	30	M	Farmer	13Ma02Bt
FOLEY, Thomas	30	M	Farmer	13Ma02Bt
Mary	30	F	Unknown	13Ma02Bt
William	1	M	Child	13Ma02Bt
VANDEN, Robert	18	M	Laborer	13Ma02Bt
Anne	17	F	Unknown	13Ma02Bt
Anne	16	F	Unknown	13Ma02Bt
William	9	M	Child	13Ma02Bt
LYNNE, John	26	M	Unknown	13Ma02Bt
KELLY, Ellen	21	F	Nurse	13Ma02Bt
DOGHERTY, Catherine	25	F	Servant	13Ma02Bt
KELLY, Ellen	20	F	Servant	13Ma02Bt
SEMPLE, Wm.	52	M	Farmer	13Ma02Bt
Esther	50	F	Unknown	13Ma02Bt
Sarah	25	F	Unknown	13Ma02Bt
Samuel	23	M	Unknown	13Ma02Bt
Mary-Anne	19	F	Unknown	13Ma02Bt
FULLER, Michael	.00	M	Infant	13Ma02Bt
WALSH, John	22	M	Laborer	13Ma02Bt
SMITH, Betty	35	F	Servant	13Ma02Bt
Anne	12	F	Servant	13Ma02Bt
Eliza	7	F	Child	13Ma02Bt
MEELIE, Michael	18	M	Gdnr	13Ma02Bt
DOWD, Ann	35	F	Servant	13Ma02Bt
Mary	2	F	Child	13Ma02Bt
DUNCAN, James	18	M	Laborer	13Ma02Bt
WARD, Patt	53	M	Stctr	13Ma02Bt
CATEN, Andrew	26	M	Laborer	13Ma02Bt
CAVANAGH, Anne	23	M	Servant	13Ma02Bt
WHITE, Richard	26	M	Laborer	13Ma02Bt
Judy	20	F	None	13Ma02Bt
HUGHES, Edwd.	25	M	Laborer	13Ma02Bt
FINAGAN, Andrew	20	M	Grocer	13Ma02Bt
DOYLE, Patrick	30	M	Tailor	13Ma02Bt
Mary-Anne	22	F	Wife	13Ma02Bt
CLUSKEY, James	22	M	Laborer	13Ma02Bt
Mary	18	F	Servant	13Ma02Bt
Margaret	11	F	Servant	13Ma02Bt
REYNOLDS, Michael	23	M	Farmer	13Ma02Bt
Anne	18	F	Farmer	13Ma02Bt
TRACY, Bridget	25	F	Servant	13Ma02Bt
RILEY, Farrell	23	M	Laborer	13Ma02Bt
SHERRIDAN, Edwd.	25	M	Farmer	13Ma02Bt
Bridget	25	F	Farmer	13Ma02Bt
Patrick	00	M	Farmer	13Ma02Bt
CONNOR, John	2	M	Child	13Ma02Bt
THACKERAY, Richd.	37	M	Laborer	13Ma02Bt
COLLINS, Maria	30	F	Servant	13Ma02Bt
DALEY, John	24	M	Laborer	13Ma02Bt
THORPE, Philip	18	M	Laborer	13Ma02Bt
BROPHY, Peter	20	M	Laborer	13Ma02Bt
MCKENNY, Patt	20	M	Laborer	13Ma02Bt
CANTIN, James	25	M	Laborer	13Ma02Bt
Biddy	21	F	Laborer	13Ma02Bt
CONWAY, Patt	20	M	Laborer	13Ma02Bt
Biddy	16	F	Laborer	13Ma02Bt
PEREDINE, Patrick	34	M	Laborer	13Ma02Bt
Johanna	34	F	Laborer	13Ma02Bt
John	6	M	Child	13Ma02Bt
DELANE, Honora	30	F	Laborer	13Ma02Bt

NAMES OF PASSENGERS	AGE	SEX	OCCUPATIONS	DATE PORT SHIP
DELANE, Jeremiah	9	M	Child	13Ma02Bt
KENNETH, Nancy	20	F	Laborer	13Ma02Bt
HUBBARD, Mary	20	F	Laborer	13Ma02Bt
STACK, Ellen	20	F	Laborer	13Ma02Bt
KILLIGAT, Daniel	13	M	Laborer	13Ma02Bt
WALSH, Thomas	40	M	Laborer	13Ma02Bt
CONNORS, Honora	32	F	Laborer	13Ma02Bt
MCGORMAN, Patrick	20	M	Laborer	13Ma02Bt
HIGGINS, Mary	22	M	Dressmaker	13Ma02Bt
Ellen	21	M	Dressmaker	13Ma02Bt
HAYS, Morris	18	M	Tailor	13Ma02Bt
Michael	18	M	Laborer	13Ma02Bt
KELBY, Patrick	50	M	Farmer	13Ma02Bt
John	30	M	Farmer	13Ma02Bt
Daniel	26	M	Farmer	13Ma02Bt
James	20	M	Farmer	13Ma02Bt
DONNELLY, James	28	M	Laborer	13Ma02Bt
BOYLE, John	40	M	Laborer	13Ma02Bt
KELLY, Mary	24	F	Laborer	13Ma02Bt
Marg.	22	F	Laborer	13Ma02Bt
KILLAN, Patrick	24	M	Laborer	13Ma02Bt
MCCOURT, Wm.	24	M	Laborer	13Ma02Bt
HOGAN, Sally	20	F	Servant	13Ma02Bt
HASKELL, Bridget	20	F	Servant	13Ma02Bt
MULLEN, Michael	22	M	Weaver	13Ma02Bt
CONWAY, Thos.	24	M	Laborer	13Ma02Bt
HAMILTON, Saml.	27	M	Laborer	13Ma02Bt
James	24	M	Farmer	13Ma02Bt
James	24	M	Farmer	13Ma02Bt
WILLIAMSON, James	24	M	Weaver	13Ma02Bt
KENNEDY, Charles	27	M	Unknown	13Ma02Bt
MEEHAN, Michael	17	M	Laborer	13Ma02Bt
SWEENEY, Catherine	30	F	Servant	13Ma02Bt
BRENNAN, Martin	30	M	Laborer	13Ma02Bt
GAVIN, Patrick	26	M	Laborer	13Ma02Bt
MACKEY, James	21	M	Laborer	13Ma02Bt
CLYNE, Peter	20	M	Laborer	13Ma02Bt
REYNOLDS, Bridget	16	F	Servant	13Ma02Bt
GILCHRIST, Thomas	24	M	Laborer	13Ma02Bt
REYNOLDS, Mary	20	F	Dressmaker	13Ma02Bt
Michael	20	M	Laborer	13Ma02Bt
HEAD, Bridget	27	F	Servant	13Ma02Bt
Michael	.00	M	Infant	13Ma02Bt
CAHILL, Morris	27	M	Laborer	13Ma02Bt
CADDEN, Ellen	23	F	Unknown	13Ma02Bt
FARRELLY, Patt	40	M	Farmer	13Ma02Bt
Thomas	12	M	Farmer	13Ma02Bt
Mary	10	F	Farmer	13Ma02Bt
Betsy	8	F	Child	13Ma02Bt
Andrew	6	M	Child	13Ma02Bt
FITZSIMONS, Mary	17	F	Servant	13Ma02Bt
FARRELLY, Patt	22	M	Laborer	13Ma02Bt
DEMPSEY, John	18	M	Mason	13Ma02Bt
FERGUSON, Margaret	18	F	Servant	13Ma02Bt
WARD, John	19	M	Laborer	13Ma02Bt
FALLEN, Ellen	14	F	Servant	13Ma02Bt
Bridget	60	F	Servant	13Ma02Bt
MCMANUS, Michael	20	M	Laborer	13Ma02Bt
COWLEY, Mary-Burke	45	F	Servant	13Ma02Bt
Esther	18	F	Unknown	13Ma02Bt
David	16	M	Unknown	13Ma02Bt
PEACOCK, Martin	18	M	Servant	13Ma02Bt
MCCLELLAN, Wm.	25	M	Cmagt	13Ma02Bt
JAMES, Charles	26	M	Farmer	13Ma02Bt
MCKEE, John	26	M	Farmer	13Ma02Bt
Margaret	21	F	Wife	13Ma02Bt
RILEY, Ann	20	F	Servant	13Ma02Bt
BRADY, Katherine	18	F	Servant	13Ma02Bt
DOYLE, Mathew	35	M	Carpenter	13Ma02Bt
Margaret	25	F	Wife	13Ma02Bt
RILEY, Robert	25	M	Clerk	13Ma02Bt
ANGLIN, Margaret	22	F	Servant	13Ma02Bt
CASTLE, John	24	M	Laborer	13Ma02Bt
BLANSFIELD, Bridget	22	F	Servant	13Ma02Bt
Cath.	20	F	Servant	13Ma02Bt
HUGHES, Betty	16	F	Servant	13Ma02Bt
BRADLY, Owen	23	M	Laborer	13Ma02Bt
MADDEN, John	25	M	Laborer	13Ma02Bt
KILLANE, Julia	50	F	Servant	13Ma02Bt
Luke	20	M	Laborer	13Ma02Bt
HANNILL, Patt	25	M	Laborer	13Ma02Bt
CORBETT, Patt	20	M	Laborer	13Ma02Bt
Michael	20	M	Laborer	13Ma02Bt
ORORKE, John	21	M	Laborer	13Ma02Bt
BOWDEN, Michael	20	M	Laborer	13Ma02Bt
Anastasia	18	F	Servant	13Ma02Bt
HUGHES, Sarah	20	F	Servant	13Ma02Bt
MCQUILLIAN, Michael	17	M	Laborer	13Ma02Bt
Peter	15	M	Unknown	13Ma02Bt
SEGG, Alex	18	M	None	13Ma02Bt
MCNALTY, Thomas	21	M	Stone Mason	13Ma02Bt
HOWARD, Alfred	20	M	Laborer	13Ma02Bt
HALLON, John	25	M	Farmer	13Ma02Bt
Anne	32	F	Unknown	13Ma02Bt
James	28	M	Unknown	13Ma02Bt
BURROWS, James	25	M	Laborer	13Ma02Bt
TYRELL, Anne	19	M	Servant	13Ma02Bt
Margaret	17	F	Servant	13Ma02Bt
BROUGHELL, John	24	M	Laborer	13Ma02Bt
DARGAN, Catherine	24	F	Servant	13Ma02Bt
DELMORE, Jane	50	F	Servant	13Ma02Bt
WEBB, Eliza	45	F	Servant	13Ma02Bt
Mary-Anne	17	F	Servant	13Ma02Bt
Eliza	13	F	Servant	13Ma02Bt
Robert	11	M	Servant	13Ma02Bt
HAWTHORN, John	25	M	Farmer	13Ma02Bt
Jane	26	F	Wife	13Ma02Bt
Jane	30	F	Dairymaid	13Ma02Bt
JAMES, Robert	16	M	Clerk	13Ma02Bt
KELLY, Thomas	38	M	Farmer	13Ma02Bt
BRIAN, James	31	M	Farmer	13Ma02Bt
KELLY, William	16	M	Farmer	13Ma02Bt
CRINIAN, John	43	M	Farmer	13Ma02Bt
COLLAN, Peter	17	M	Grocer	13Ma02Bt
OSBORNE, Eliza	17	F	Servant	13Ma02Bt
DOYLE, Michael	34	M	Unknown	13Ma02Bt
CONNOR, Thomas	35	M	Farmer	13Ma02Bt
Margaret	30	F	Unknown	13Ma02Bt
CULLEN, Walter	20	M	Joiner	13Ma02Bt
FALLEN, James	20	M	Laborer	13Ma02Bt
Catherine	20	F	Wife	13Ma02Bt
MCCORMICK, Mary	20	F	Servant	13Ma02Bt
HIGGIN, Michael	30	M	Laborer	13Ma02Bt
TIMOTHY, John	15	M	Laborer	13Ma02Bt
Bridget	25	F	Laborer	13Ma02Bt
Bridget	23	F	Laborer	13Ma02Bt
Margaret	23	F	Laborer	13Ma02Bt
HENNEHIN, Mary	30	F	Laborer	13Ma02Bt
Patrick	5	M	Child	13Ma02Bt
Ann	2	F	Child	13Ma02Bt
GILHOOLY, Bridget	18	F	Laborer	13Ma02Bt
PRENDERGAST, Michael	19	M	Laborer	13Ma02Bt
MAHER, Elizth.	22	F	Servant	13Ma02Bt
DALY, Mary	17	F	Servant	13Ma02Bt
ROACH, Pat	21	M	Laborer	13Ma02Bt
CONDON, John	22	M	Laborer	13Ma02Bt
STEAKAM, Wm.	21	M	Laborer	13Ma02Bt
BRODY, Ann	15	F	Servant	13Ma02Bt
Ellen	14	F	Servant	13Ma02Bt
CROWLEY, Daniel	33	M	Laborer	13Ma02Bt
Catherine (W)	36	F	Wife	13Ma02Bt
CAMPBELL, William	21	M	Farmer	13Ma02Bt
Ann (W)	21	F	Wife	13Ma02Bt
MAHON, John	15	M	Blacksmith	13Ma02Bt
MURPHY, Pat	25	M	Laborer	13Ma02Bt
HALLS, William	18	M	Unknown	13Ma02Bt
BOGLAND, Chas.	13	M	Unknown	13Ma02Bt

ATALANTA 13 MAY 1850

From Liverpool

NAMES OF PASSENGERS r	AGE	SEX	OCCUPATIONS	DATE PORT SHIP
MCKEEVER, Mary	22	F	Lad	13Ma02Jr
SHORTALL, Richard	30	M	Farmer	13Ma02Jr
MURPHY, Maria	30	F	Farmer	13Ma02Jr
DALEY, Eliza	22	F	Dressmaker	13Ma02Jr
RILEY, Pat	25	M	Schm	13Ma02Jr
GAFNEY, Mary	5	F	Child	13Ma02Jr
Rose	5	F	Child	13Ma02Jr
BRADY, Anne	20	F	Servant	13Ma02Jr
KERRICK, Dennis	17	M	Laborer	13Ma02Jr
HEALY, Ann	20	F	Laborer	13Ma02Jr
Michl.	2	M	Child	13Ma02Jr
OBRIEN, Brid.	27	F	Servant	13Ma02Jr
MCGUIRE, Brid.	28	F	Servant	13Ma02Jr
MCGEE, Mary	5	F	Child	13Ma02Jr
MARTIN, Jno.	55	M	Laborer	13Ma02Jr
MURRAY, Pat	24	M	Laborer	13Ma02Jr
U, U	25	M	Laborer	13Ma02Jr
GARVEY, Johanna	24	F	Servant	13Ma02Jr
Pat	.10	M	Infant	13Ma02Jr
CAFFREY, Peter	14	M	Laborer	13Ma02Jr
MCCABE, Thos.	20	M	Nailer	13Ma02Jr
SHIELDS, James	22	M	Weaver	13Ma02Jr
HUGHES, Jno.	20	M	Laborer	13Ma02Jr
GROGAN, Pat	33	M	Tailor	13Ma02Jr
CONNOLLY, Jas.	20	M	Tailor	13Ma02Jr
MCCAFFERTY, Cath.	20	F	Dressmaker	13Ma02Jr
LOW, Moses	40	M	Laborer	13Ma02Jr
LOGHAM, John	20	M	Baker	13Ma02Jr
CLANCEY, Jno.	19	M	Sawer	13Ma02Jr
COGGY, Ellen	17	M	Servant	13Ma02Jr
FERRY, Dan	23	M	Laborer	13Ma02Jr
MATHEWS, Thos.	20	M	Blacksmith	13Ma02Jr
Anne	20	F	Unknown	13Ma02Jr
Jno.	.11	M	Infant	13Ma02Jr
Died-At-Sea				
Jno.	14	M	Unknown	13Ma02Jr
James	10	M	Unknown	13Ma02Jr
EWITT, James	24	M	Laborer	13Ma02Jr
MCCABE, Mary	50	F	Lad	13Ma02Jr
FLOOD, Brid.	16	F	Lad	13Ma02Jr
MCCABE, Edwd.	12	M	Lad	13Ma02Jr
LAWLOR, Mich.	20	M	Laborer	13Ma02Jr
MADDEN, Anne	18	F	Servant	13Ma02Jr
STAPLETON, Cath.	35	F	Servant	13Ma02Jr
Biddy	8	F	Child	13Ma02Jr
Nora	5	F	Child	13Ma02Jr
WHITE, Margt.	17	F	Dressmaker	13Ma02Jr
BEATON, Margt.	16	F	Dressmaker	13Ma02Jr
MCELROY, James	30	M	Clerk	13Ma02Jr
DALY, Mary	20	F	Servant	13Ma02Jr
SWEENEY, Jno.	20	M	Laborer	13Ma02Jr
TRIMBLE, Jno.	20	M	Shoemaker	13Ma02Jr
CARROLL, Pat	27	M	Laborer	13Ma02Jr
WALSH, Pat	35	M	Coach Maker	13Ma02Jr
MAGUIRE, Edwd.	25	M	Blacksmith	13Ma02Jr
NULL, James	23	M	Laborer	13Ma02Jr
BRIAN, Martin	23	M	Laborer	13Ma02Jr
BYRNES, Arthur	40	M	Laborer	13Ma02Jr
BARRY, Jno.	21	M	Carpenter	13Ma02Jr
DONOVAN, Jas.	30	M	Carpenter	13Ma02Jr
DWANE, Jere.	25	M	Bootmaker	13Ma02Jr
BROOKS, Henry	26	M	Carpenter	13Ma02Jr
rCALLEN, Owen	42	M	Butcher	13Ma02Jr
RICE, Rose	30	F	Servant	13Ma02Jr
Anne	7	F	Child	13Ma02Jr
DUGAN, Cath.	22	F	Servant	13Ma02Jr
SHORTALL, Mich.	25	M	Mason	13Ma02Jr
WHALEN, Mary	18	F	Servant	13Ma02Jr
MOYLAN, Johan.	30	F	Servant	13Ma02Jr
SHANNON, Robert	50	M	Weaver	13Ma02Jr
Jno.	20	M	Laborer	13Ma02Jr
CARROLL, Pat	35	M	Farmer	13Ma02Jr
John	32	M	Farmer	13Ma02Jr
Will	30	M	Farmer	13Ma02Jr
James	28	M	Farmer	13Ma02Jr
Anne	14	F	Farmer	13Ma02Jr
Ellen	5	F	Child	13Ma02Jr
Mary	16	F	Farmer	13Ma02Jr
Cath.	6	F	Child	13Ma02Jr
Pat	9	M	Child	13Ma02Jr
MCMANUS, Owen	20	M	Laborer	13Ma02Jr
Rose	19	F	Laborer	13Ma02Jr
OWENS, Thos.	55	M	Laborer	13Ma02Jr
Anne	55	F	Laborer	13Ma02Jr
Margt.	30	F	Laborer	13Ma02Jr
Thos.	23	M	Laborer	13Ma02Jr
Thos.	28	M	Laborer	13Ma02Jr
Fras.	27	M	Laborer	13Ma02Jr
WELSH, Wm.	25	M	Laborer	13Ma02Jr
Jane	23	F	Laborer	13Ma02Jr
CONLAN, Jno.	25	M	Carpenter	13Ma02Jr
LAWLOR, U-Miss	23	M	Dressmaker	13Ma02Jr
Mary	24	M	Dressmaker	13Ma02Jr
CORCORAN, Thos.	19	M	Clerk	13Ma02Jr
GANTLEY, Wm.	23	M	Laborer	13Ma02Jr
TIARNAY, Andy	22	M	Laborer	13Ma02Jr
ASPLE, Jno.	26	M	Laborer	13Ma02Jr
CLARKE, Margt.	18	F	Laborer	13Ma02Jr
Archer	19	M	Laborer	13Ma02Jr
Peter	20	M	Laborer	13Ma02Jr
LARKIN, Mich.	30	M	Laborer	13Ma02Jr
Margt.	23	F	Unknown	13Ma02Jr
Biddy	2	F	Child	13Ma02Jr
Jno.	.11	M	Infant	13Ma02Jr
Brid.	50	F	Unknown	13Ma02Jr
James	24	M	Unknown	13Ma02Jr
Pat	19	M	Unknown	13Ma02Jr
Judy	23	F	Unknown	13Ma02Jr
KILMARTIN, Malachi	25	M	Farmer	13Ma02Jr
WHITE, Mich.	27	M	Laborer	13Ma02Jr
Margt.	25	F	Laborer	13Ma02Jr
MOLONEY, Margt.	20	F	Servant	13Ma02Jr
SHANAHAN, Margt.	18	F	Servant	13Ma02Jr
KINARLLY, Pat	24	M	Laborer	13Ma02Jr
TURTLE, John	40	M	Farmer	13Ma02Jr
Pat	9	M	Child	13Ma02Jr
MCDONELL, Thos.	28	M	Laborer	13Ma02Jr
FLEMMING, Edwd.	25	M	Laborer	13Ma02Jr
Cath.	25	F	Laborer	13Ma02Jr
MAHON, Jno.	30	M	Laborer	13Ma02Jr
BRANNON, Thos.	30	M	Laborer	13Ma02Jr
Margt.	25	M	Laborer	13Ma02Jr
MORAN, Mary	25	F	Laborer	13Ma02Jr
MAHON, Thos.	36	M	Laborer	13Ma02Jr
Ellen	34	F	Laborer	13Ma02Jr
SILK, Pat	34	M	Smith	13Ma02Jr
DAW, Geo.	40	M	Infant	13Ma02Jr
Margt.	38	F	Infant	13Ma02Jr
Margt.	2	F	Child	13Ma02Jr
HIGGINS, Eliza	20	F	Servant	13Ma02Jr
REILLY, Thos.	22	M	Laborer	13Ma02Jr
MURPHY, Margt.	19	F	Laborer	13Ma02Jr
MAHON, Margt.	20	F	Servant	13Ma02Jr
BRENNAN, Jas.	25	M	Laborer	13Ma02Jr
Peter	50	M	Laborer	13Ma02Jr
Margt.	50	F	Laborer	13Ma02Jr
Brid.	25	F	Laborer	13Ma02Jr
Betty	28	F	Laborer	13Ma02Jr
MCANDLE, Mick	20	M	Laborer	13Ma02Jr
MCALLISTER, Mary	20	F	Dressmaker	13Ma02Jr

NAMES OF PASSENGERS	AGE	SEX	OCCUPATIONS	DATE PORT SHIP
WALLACE, Margt.	15	F	Servant	13Ma02Jr
SPICER, Edw.	22	M	Laborer	13Ma02Jr
AGNEW, Felix	19	M	Farmer	13Ma02Jr
LARKIN, Pat	26	M	Farmer	13Ma02Jr
HOGAN, Pat	22	M	Farmer	13Ma02Jr
BRADY, Ann	18	F	Farmer	13Ma02Jr
MCGEE, John	30	M	Pltwkr	13Ma02Jr
MURTAGH, Bernd.	30	M	Stctr	13Ma02Jr
Garrett	16	M	Stctr	13Ma02Jr
Ann	25	F	Stctr	13Ma02Jr
Ann	2	F	Child	13Ma02Jr
Wm.	.09	M	Infant	13Ma02Jr
Jno.	.09	M	Infant	13Ma02Jr
DORLIN, Jos.	28	M	Tinner	13Ma02Jr
REILLY, Thos.	18	M	Tailor	13Ma02Jr
FREEBORN, Jno.	40	M	Farmer	13Ma02Jr
EGAN, Brid.	50	F	Servant	13Ma02Jr
Mick	17	M	Servant	13Ma02Jr
Jno.	15	M	Servant	13Ma02Jr
Brid.	10	F	Servant	13Ma02Jr
Peter	8	M	Child	13Ma02Jr
Thos.	5	M	Child	13Ma02Jr
MORGAN, Mick	50	M	Farmer	13Ma02Jr
Jno.	18	M	Weaver	13Ma02Jr
Brid.	17	F	Weaver	13Ma02Jr
Ellen	15	F	Weaver	13Ma02Jr
DOYLE, Henry	18	M	Weaver	13Ma02Jr
WHITE, Wm.	20	M	Weaver	13Ma02Jr
Mary-A.	17	F	Weaver	13Ma02Jr
FARRELL, Ellen	20	F	Lad	13Ma02Jr
KINGHAM, John	21	M	Laborer	13Ma02Jr
WHITE, Wm.	20	M	Laborer	13Ma02Jr
RYAN, Jas.	30	M	Laborer	13Ma02Jr
Mary	24	F	Laborer	13Ma02Jr
WHOLAHAN, Mick	30	M	Laborer	13Ma02Jr
GROGAN, Jno.	26	M	Laborer	13Ma02Jr
GETTINGS, Jos.	22	M	Laborer	13Ma02Jr
CLARKE, Brid.	20	F	Lad	13Ma02Jr
CHUTE, Anne	17	F	Chbrmd	13Ma02Jr
GETTINGS, Ann	20	F	Servant	13Ma02Jr
LYNCH, Cath.	18	F	Servant	13Ma02Jr
Mary	.09	F	Infant	13Ma02Jr
COLEMAN, Jane	60	F	Farmer	13Ma02Jr
BRANNON, Brid.	30	F	Farmer	13Ma02Jr
RYANS, Cath.	25	F	Farmer	13Ma02Jr
Margt.	3	F	Child	13Ma02Jr
Thos.	4	M	Child	13Ma02Jr
RYAN, Cath.	.11	F	Infant	13Ma02Jr
BRANNON, John	4	M	Child	13Ma02Jr
Mary	6	F	Child	13Ma02Jr
KEANE, Mick	20	M	Laborer	13Ma02Jr
KEARNEY, Pat	20	M	Laborer	13Ma02Jr
BRANNON, Mick	20	M	Laborer	13Ma02Jr
MCANNY, Ann	20	F	Servant	13Ma02Jr
ASH, Jane	20	F	Servant	13Ma02Jr
ENGLISH, Mary	20	F	Servant	13Ma02Jr
CARROLL, Rose	20	F	Servant	13Ma02Jr
BRENNAN, Jas.	60	M	Servant	13Ma02Jr
RYAN, Larry	8	M	Child	13Ma02Jr
BRENNAN, Cath.	.11	F	Infant	13Ma02Jr
LANGAN, Thos.	60	M	Laborer	13Ma02Jr
HARRINGTON, Pat	20	M	Laborer	13Ma02Jr
HOLLAND, John	21	M	Clerk	13Ma02Jr
U-Mrs. (W)	20	F	Unknown	13Ma02Jr
Anne	.10	F	Infant	13Ma02Jr
MOFFATT, Cath.	23	F	Unknown	13Ma02Jr
DONNEGAN, Ellen	32	F	Unknown	13Ma02Jr
MCGIVVON, Phil	35	M	Laborer	13Ma02Jr
MULLIGAN, Richd.	26	M	Shoemaker	13Ma02Jr
DABBITH, Jas.	45	M	Steward	13Ma02Jr
Pat	20	M	Shoemaker	13Ma02Jr
Honor	16	F	Unknown	13Ma02Jr
Jas.	15	M	Unknown	13Ma02Jr
Mary-A.	10	F	Unknown	13Ma02Jr
Thos.	8	M	Child	13Ma02Jr

NAMES OF PASSENGERS	AGE	SEX	OCCUPATIONS	DATE PORT SHIP
MARTIN, Mich.	27	M	Puddler	13Ma02Jr
MCGEE, Jno.	30	M	Laborer	13Ma02Jr
NOONAN, Wm.	26	M	Laborer	13Ma02Jr
SHEEHAN, John	30	M	Farmer	13Ma02Jr
NOONAN, Cath.	25	F	Laborer	13Ma02Jr

CHARLES-CROOKER 14 MAY 1850

From Liverpool

NAMES OF PASSENGERS	AGE	SEX	OCCUPATIONS	DATE PORT SHIP
KELLY, Thos.	31	M	Laborer	14Ma02ly
MARTIN, Bridget	20	F	Nurse	14Ma02ly
BUCKLEY, Jno.	30	M	Farmer	14Ma02ly
BEATTY, Wm.	28	M	Laborer	14Ma02ly
MURPHY, Hugh	30	M	Laborer	14Ma02ly
James	26	M	Laborer	14Ma02ly
LAW, Sarah	25	F	Nurse	14Ma02ly
DAVIES, Mary	19	F	Nurse	14Ma02ly
MCKIMATIN, James	19	M	Farmer	14Ma02ly
FOX, Sarah	30	F	Servant	14Ma02ly
Eliza	28	F	Servant	14Ma02ly
REIDY, James	48	M	Farmer	14Ma02ly
Mary	30	F	Unknown	14Ma02ly
Jno.	6	M	Child	14Ma02ly
Richard	4	M	Child	14Ma02ly
James	.00	M	Infant	14Ma02ly
TENHEY, Jno.	28	M	Laborer	14Ma02ly
Taddy	26	F	Unknown	14Ma02ly
Cathne.	24	F	Unknown	14Ma02ly
PINDES, James	25	M	Laborer	14Ma02ly
MAHON, Roger	22	M	Laborer	14Ma02ly
BYRNE, Wm.	23	M	Laborer	14Ma02ly
Jno.	22	M	Tailor	14Ma02ly
KENNY, Jno.	20	M	Mason	14Ma02ly
Margt.	25	F	Unknown	14Ma02ly
GERRAGHTY, Jno.	20	M	Joiner	14Ma02ly
CUNNINGHAM, Maurice	11	M	Unknown	14Ma02ly
ODONNEL, Worry	30	M	Servant	14Ma02ly
Jno.	6	M	Child	14Ma02ly
Edward	.00	M	Infant	14Ma02ly
Mary	.00	F	Infant	14Ma02ly
MANORYE, Bridget	34	F	Servant	14Ma02ly
Bridget	.00	F	Infant	14Ma02ly
MCMAHON, Jno.	28	M	Laborer	14Ma02ly
Bridget	26	F	Unknown	14Ma02ly
MCNAMARA, Thos.	12	M	Laborer	14Ma02ly
SHEEHAN, John	22	M	Laborer	14Ma02ly
Cornl.	20	M	Laborer	14Ma02ly
Ellen	25	F	Nurse	14Ma02ly
RUSSEL, Jno.	35	M	Laborer	14Ma02ly
FOLLEY, Honora	17	F	Laborer	14Ma02ly
FHINING, Johanna	17	F	Nurse	14Ma02ly
Margt.	15	F	Nurse	14Ma02ly
James	13	M	Unknown	14Ma02ly
MCKIBBIN, Henry	22	M	Tailor	14Ma02ly
FAMERAN, Jno.	25	M	Tailor	14Ma02ly
BARRY, Kevin	46	M	Laborer	14Ma02ly
Cathne.	46	F	Unknown	14Ma02ly
Michl.	15	M	Unknown	14Ma02ly
Bridget	12	F	Unknown	14Ma02ly
James	50	M	Unknown	14Ma02ly
Ann	50	F	Unknown	14Ma02ly
Thomas	18	M	Unknown	14Ma02ly
James	14	M	Unknown	14Ma02ly
Watt.	11	M	Unknown	14Ma02ly
Ellen	10	F	Unknown	14Ma02ly
Bridget	7	F	Child	14Ma02ly
BYRNE, Matt.	23	M	Laborer	14Ma02ly
NEILL, Bridget	50	F	Wife	14Ma02ly

NAMES OF PASSENGERS	AGE	SEX	OCCUPATIONS	DATE PORT SHIP
NEILL, Jno.	26	M	Laborer	14Ma02ly
Bridget	24	F	Laborer	14Ma02ly
Ellen	22	F	Laborer	14Ma02ly
Bridget	20	F	Laborer	14Ma02ly
Cathne.	18	F	Laborer	14Ma02ly
Patt	16	M	Laborer	14Ma02ly
Michl.	12	M	Unknown	14Ma02ly
James	9	M	Child	14Ma02ly
GOSS, Ann	20	F	Unknown	14Ma02ly
DOYLE, Mary	34	F	Servant	14Ma02ly
KEILY, Laurence	45	M	Farmer	14Ma02ly
Rose	40	F	Unknown	14Ma02ly
Mary	15	F	Unknown	14Ma02ly
David	10	M	Unknown	14Ma02ly
Anne	2	F	Child	14Ma02ly
GRADY, Eliza	23	F	Servant	14Ma02ly
Philip	27	M	Laborer	14Ma02ly
Laurence	60	M	Laborer	14Ma02ly
GLENN, Bridget	40	F	Servant	14Ma02ly
MURRAY, Bridget	30	F	Servant	14Ma02ly
Joseph	6	M	Child	14Ma02ly
TAMSEY, Pat	22	M	Laborer	14Ma02ly
MANKS, Jos.	22	M	Laborer	14Ma02ly
DONOVAN, Jerh.	40	M	Mason	14Ma02ly
Hannah	35	F	Unknown	14Ma02ly
Michl.	16	M	Mason	14Ma02ly
Peter	14	M	Unknown	14Ma02ly
John	8	M	Child	14Ma02ly
Jerh.	4	M	Child	14Ma02ly
KELLY, Robt.	15	M	Unknown	14Ma02ly
DONOHUE, Thos.	23	M	Farmer	14Ma02ly
OBRIEN, U	4	M	Unknown	14Ma02ly
U	15	F	Unknown	14Ma02ly
SMITH, Pat	22	M	Laborer	14Ma02ly
BRADY, Jno.	22	M	Laborer	14Ma02ly
DAVIES, Jane	19	F	Nurse	14Ma02ly
DOYLE, Margt.	18	F	Nurse	14Ma02ly
MCKEAVIN, Sarah	37	F	Nurse	14Ma02ly
Sarah	11	F	Unknown	14Ma02ly
MCMULLAN, Jas.	22	M	Farmer	14Ma02ly
MAHONEY, Jno.	25	M	Farmer	14Ma02ly
HARNEY, Michl.	20	M	Farmer	14Ma02ly
Philip	25	M	Farmer	14Ma02ly
MCDONALD, Edward	22	M	Farmer	14Ma02ly
MCGRACE, Jno.	20	M	Laborer	14Ma02ly
DUFFY, Neice	20	F	Nurse	14Ma02ly
MCARDLE, Pat	20	M	Laborer	14Ma02ly
CONNOLLY, Owen	22	M	Laborer	14Ma02ly
GILMARTIN, Philip	20	M	Laborer	14Ma02ly
MCCUE, Peter	20	M	Laborer	14Ma02ly
FLANAGAN, Matthew	21	M	Laborer	14Ma02ly
MCGOWAN, Bridget	20	F	Servant	14Ma02ly
Michl.	18	M	Joiner	14Ma02ly
Winney	17	F	Unknown	14Ma02ly
COYLE, Owen	40	M	Farmer	14Ma02ly
OBRIEN, Thos.	30	M	Farmer	14Ma02ly
Pat	25	M	Farmer	14Ma02ly
MCINIES, Jno.	18	M	Farmer	14Ma02ly
Mary	16	F	Unknown	14Ma02ly
HINOUGH, Ann	13	F	Unknown	14Ma02ly
Pat	10	M	Unknown	14Ma02ly
MALLEY, Margt.	11	F	Unknown	14Ma02ly
FISH, Wm.	21	M	Butcher	14Ma02ly
PURCELL, Walter	35	M	Laborer	14Ma02ly
Cathne.	28	F	Unknown	14Ma02ly
BUTLER, Edmund	24	M	Laborer	14Ma02ly
RYAN, James	24	M	Laborer	14Ma02ly
HENRY, George	40	M	Miller	14Ma02ly
MOURNE, Wm.	20	M	Clerk	14Ma02ly
CORCORAN, Mary	30	F	Servant	14Ma02ly
SMITH, Thos.	21	M	Joiner	14Ma02ly
KENNY, Laurence	21	M	Laborer	14Ma02ly
Peter	23	M	Laborer	14Ma02ly
DUFF, Francis	25	M	Laborer	14Ma02ly
Peggy	23	F	Nurse	14Ma02ly

NAMES OF PASSENGERS	AGE	SEX	OCCUPATIONS	DATE PORT SHIP
FOLEY, John	40	M	Bricklayer	14Ma02ly
Alice	30	F	Unknown	14Ma02ly
John	.00	M	Infant	14Ma02ly
MCKEVIN, Daniel	30	M	Clerk	14Ma02ly
LAURENCE, Thos.	35	M	Clerk	14Ma02ly
DOYLE, James	20	M	Unknown	14Ma02ly
WOOD, Agnes	25	F	Nurse	14Ma02ly
CALLAM, Ellen	25	F	Nurse	14Ma02ly
PHILAN, Richard	30	M	Farmer	14Ma02ly
Bridget	29	F	Unknown	14Ma02ly
Catherine	6	F	Child	14Ma02ly
Mary	5	F	Child	14Ma02ly
Aestitia	4	F	Child	14Ma02ly
Ellen	2	F	Child	14Ma02ly
Andrew	.00	M	Infant	14Ma02ly
SMALLIN, Edward	18	M	Laborer	14Ma02ly
FITZSIMMONS, Thos.	27	M	Laborer	14Ma02ly
NOLAN, Jno.	26	M	Laborer	14Ma02ly
LINNESET, Thos.	25	M	Laborer	14Ma02ly
MCLAUGHTON, Jns.	20	M	Laborer	14Ma02ly
MCGARTH, Christy	19	M	Laborer	14Ma02ly
MCCAFFY, Bess	18	F	Servant	14Ma02ly
DONHUE, Biddy	19	F	Servant	14Ma02ly
GAINOR, Mary	19	F	Nurse	14Ma02ly
FITZGERALD, James	25	M	Farmer	14Ma02ly
FRANKLAND, Thos.	22	M	Farmer	14Ma02ly
Margt.	20	F	Farmer	14Ma02ly
BRUMAN, Thos.	16	M	Farmer	14Ma02ly
Margt.	18	F	Unknown	14Ma02ly
FILLIAN, Biddy	20	F	Nurse	14Ma02ly
COTTDOWN, Margt.	20	F	Nurse	14Ma02ly
WALSH, Jane	19	F	Nurse	14Ma02ly
Bridget	18	F	Nurse	14Ma02ly
DUNN, Thos.	30	M	Laborer	14Ma02ly
BRIEN, Thos.	25	M	Laborer	14Ma02ly
WALSH, Ellen	50	F	Wife	14Ma02ly
Mary	20	F	Unknown	14Ma02ly
DELANY, Wm.	40	M	Mason	14Ma02ly
U-Mrs.	44	F	Unknown	14Ma02ly
Ellen	25	F	Unknown	14Ma02ly
Thos.	20	M	Unknown	14Ma02ly
Richard	12	M	Unknown	14Ma02ly
James	10	M	Unknown	14Ma02ly
Pat	7	M	Child	14Ma02ly
HOOLAHAN, Wm.	15	M	Mason	14Ma02ly
DOHONEY, Pat	26	M	Mason	14Ma02ly
Bridget	23	F	Unknown	14Ma02ly
REGAN, James	17	M	Joiner	14Ma02ly
Ellen	19	F	Unknown	14Ma02ly
Wm.	13	M	Unknown	14Ma02ly
David	9	M	Child	14Ma02ly
NEWMAN, Dennis	25	M	Joiner	14Ma02ly
Margt.	25	F	Unknown	14Ma02ly
Ann	.00	F	Infant	14Ma02ly
GARLEY, Pat	20	M	Joiner	14Ma02ly
MCANLEY, Pat	24	M	Joiner	14Ma02ly
DAVIES, Sally	18	F	Servant	14Ma02ly
LENNY, Cathne.	18	F	Servant	14Ma02ly
DINNEN, Hugh	22	M	Laborer	14Ma02ly
Philip	20	M	Laborer	14Ma02ly
Margt.	20	F	Laborer	14Ma02ly
Pat	.00	M	Infant	14Ma02ly
WARREN, Pat	32	M	Laborer	14Ma02ly
DUNN, Pat	17	M	Laborer	14Ma02ly
Margt.	26	F	Unknown	14Ma02ly
Ann	24	F	Unknown	14Ma02ly
MORN, Agnes-Cath.	20	F	Unknown	14Ma02ly
MAGUIRE, Thos.	26	M	Laborer	14Ma02ly
JOHNSTON, James	22	M	Wheelwright	14Ma02ly
KELLY, James	30	M	Wheelwright	14Ma02ly
MACKRAY, Judy	20	F	Servant	14Ma02ly
NEWHAM, Cathne.	21	F	Nurse	14Ma02ly
CREAGH, Michl.	25	M	Laborer	14Ma02ly
Michl.	18	M	Laborer	14Ma02ly
WOLLETT, Wm.	20	M	Laborer	14Ma02ly

NAMES OF PASSENGERS	AGE	SEX	OCCUPATIONS	DATE PORT SHIP
ALLEN, Jno.	20	M	Laborer	14Ma02ly
EMON, Wm.	20	M	Mason	14Ma02ly
ENNIS, Mary	35	F	Dressmaker	14Ma02ly
David-Mary	20	U	Unknown	14Ma02ly
LULLY, Thos.	25	M	Tailor	14Ma02ly
HENRY, John	22	M	Tailor	14Ma02ly
CAUVILLE, Ann	20	F	Servant	14Ma02ly
DOUGHERTY, Rose	19	F	Servant	14Ma02ly
MILADY, Cathne.	20	F	Servant	14Ma02ly
JORDAN, Jane	20	F	Servant	14Ma02ly
GRACE, Pat	25	M	Farmer	14Ma02ly
HICKEY, Pat	25	M	Farmer	14Ma02ly
MURPHY, Tom	25	M	Farmer	14Ma02ly
FARRELL, Biddy	20	F	Farmer	14Ma02ly
DUDLEY, Ann	20	F	Farmer	14Ma02ly
KELLY, Pat	30	M	Farmer	14Ma02ly
Rose	30	F	Unknown	14Ma02ly
Kate	20	F	Unknown	14Ma02ly
GRIFFIN, Biddy	30	F	Servant	14Ma02ly
Michael	11	M	Unknown	14Ma02ly
John	8	M	Child	14Ma02ly
Kate	6	F	Child	14Ma02ly
Mary	3	F	Child	14Ma02ly
Susan	22	F	Servant	14Ma02ly
BRADY, Johanna	50	F	Servant	14Ma02ly
Thos.	1	M	Child	14Ma02ly
FINLAY, Mary	20	F	Nurse	14Ma02ly
LILLAS, Laurence	22	M	Farmer	14Ma02ly
KEAVIN, Biddy	21	F	Servant	14Ma02ly
MCGRATH, Ellen	15	F	Nurse	14Ma02ly
Mary	12	F	Nurse	14Ma02ly
KENNEDY, Ellen	18	F	Nurse	14Ma02ly
KELLY, Honor	20	F	Nurse	14Ma02ly
COLLINS, Mary	30	F	Shopkeeper	14Ma02ly
Michl.	25	M	Shopkeeper	14Ma02ly
Stephen	3	M	Child	14Ma02ly
GRIFFIN, Cath.	26	F	Milliner	14Ma02ly
CAREY, Pat	26	M	Laborer	14Ma02ly
MAGUIRE, John	22	M	Laborer	14Ma02ly
MULLON, Pat	20	M	Laborer	14Ma02ly
MCCAFFY, Pat	25	M	Laborer	14Ma02ly
Sally	18	F	Unknown	14Ma02ly
TAYLOR, Eliza	30	F	Servant	14Ma02ly
Wm.	2	M	Child	14Ma02ly
MCCUNNINGHAM, Jno.	19	M	Farmer	14Ma02ly
Wm.	19	M	Farmer	14Ma02ly
MCELLREY, Pat	20	M	Farmer	14Ma02ly
MAHONEY, Pat	20	M	Farmer	14Ma02ly
MCGINTY, Mary	19	F	Nurse	14Ma02ly
OROURKE, Laurence	20	M	Laborer	14Ma02ly
LAUD, Ellen	20	F	Servant	14Ma02ly
LEECH, Jno.	25	M	Butcher	14Ma02ly
Jno.	27	M	Butcher	14Ma02ly
DELANY, James	20	M	Farmer	14Ma02ly
LEONARD, Margt.	20	F	Servant	14Ma02ly
Cathne.	18	F	Servant	14Ma02ly
RYAN, Jno.	40	M	Farmer	14Ma02ly
Jerry	30	M	Unknown	14Ma02ly
BRADLEY, Mick	25	M	Laborer	14Ma02ly
RESPIE, Eliza	22	F	Nurse	14Ma02ly
BRENAN, James	20	M	Farmer	14Ma02ly
CASSIDEY, Ann	20	F	Servant	14Ma02ly
PHILAN, Jno.	25	M	Laborer	14Ma02ly
HARE, Jno.	20	M	Laborer	14Ma02ly
DORAN, Wm.	20	M	Laborer	14Ma02ly
HANESSEY, Matt	30	M	Laborer	14Ma02ly
CARRY, Wm.	20	M	Laborer	14Ma02ly
OCONNELL, Chas.	35	M	Laborer	14Ma02ly
SHEEHAN, Wm.	40	M	Shopkeeper	14Ma02ly
Cathne.	40	F	Shopkeeper	14Ma02ly
Mary	22	F	Shopkeeper	14Ma02ly
Bridget	20	F	Shopkeeper	14Ma02ly
Kate	18	F	Unknown	14Ma02ly
Francis	13	F	Unknown	14Ma02ly
Jane	11	F	Unknown	14Ma02ly
SHEEHAN, Ellen	9	F	Child	14Ma02ly
Nancy	7	F	Child	14Ma02ly
POWER, Ellen	20	F	Dairymaid	14Ma02ly
FLYNN, Esther	30	F	Nurse	14Ma02ly
WILSON, Richd.	30	M	Clergyman	14Ma02ly
U-Mrs.	24	F	Unknown	14Ma02ly
BANFORD, John	22	M	Mechanic	14Ma02ly
HILL, James	22	M	Unknown	14Ma02ly
CRAWFORD, Mary	20	F	Servant	14Ma02ly
DIGGON, Margt.	20	F	Servant	14Ma02ly
CRAWFORD, Margt.	20	F	Servant	14Ma02ly
BEFFY, Edward	40	M	Farmer	14Ma02ly
QUINN, Margt.	23	F	Nurse	14Ma02ly
LITY, Michl.	28	M	Laborer	14Ma02ly
KENNEDY, Pat	26	M	Gdnr	14Ma02ly
LITY, U-Mrs.	28	F	Unknown	14Ma02ly
MURPHY, Anthony	26	M	Gdnr	14Ma02ly
RYAN, Nicholas	26	M	Tailor	14Ma02ly
MILLE, Michl.	26	M	Farmer	14Ma02ly
READ, James	30	M	Gdnr	14Ma02ly
KELLY, Robt.	36	M	Gdnr	14Ma02ly
Bridget	36	F	Unknown	14Ma02ly
WALSH, U-Mrs.	25	F	Wife	14Ma02ly
John	5	M	Child	14Ma02ly
Mary	2	F	Child	14Ma02ly
KEVIN, Edward	25	M	Farmer	14Ma02ly
Mick-Bowman	25	M	Farmer	14Ma02ly
LONDRYAN, John	25	M	Farmer	14Ma02ly
RIORDAN, May	19	F	Nurse	14Ma02ly
DUGGON, Jno.	30	M	Laborer	14Ma02ly
HYNES, Jno.	34	M	Laborer	14Ma02ly
FORRELL, U-Mr.	25	M	Mason	14Ma02ly
U-Mrs.	25	F	Unknown	14Ma02ly
Peter	5	M	Child	14Ma02ly
Jno.	3	M	Child	14Ma02ly
Thos.	.00	M	Infant	14Ma02ly
CAHOLE, May	20	F	Unknown	14Ma02ly

KATE-HOWE 14 MAY 1850

From Liverpool

NAMES OF PASSENGERS	AGE	SEX	OCCUPATIONS	DATE PORT SHIP
PEWRY, Pat	30	M	Laborer	14Ma02lo
Ellen	35	F	Laborer	14Ma02lo
Cath.	3	F	Child	14Ma02lo
Maria	.00	F	Infant	14Ma02lo
KENNEDY, Owen	24	M	Laborer	14Ma02lo
LAMBERT, James	22	M	Laborer	14Ma02lo
SCANLIN, John	19	M	Laborer	14Ma02lo
TRAVIN, Edward	57	M	Laborer	14Ma02lo
FERNEY, Thos.	23	M	Laborer	14Ma02lo
MCGUIRE, Patrick	13	M	Laborer	14Ma02lo
HARGEN, May	35	F	Servant	14Ma02lo
John	13	M	Servant	14Ma02lo
CARNEY, Ambrose	12	M	Laborer	14Ma02lo
Charles	26	M	Laborer	14Ma02lo
Margaret	19	F	Laborer	14Ma02lo
NORMAN, Margaret	38	F	Servant	14Ma02lo
SWEENEY, Francis	16	M	Laborer	14Ma02lo
FARIRIREUL, Con.	20	M	Laborer	14Ma02lo
CALAGEN, Anne	20	F	Servant	14Ma02lo
BORRIS, Chas.	23	M	Laborer	14Ma02lo
Bridget	20	F	Laborer	14Ma02lo
Honora	18	F	Laborer	14Ma02lo
Judy	20	F	Laborer	14Ma02lo
Richard	16	M	Laborer	14Ma02lo
Cath.	6	F	Child	14Ma02lo
Margt.	4	F	Child	14Ma02lo
John	.00	M	Infant	14Ma02lo

NAMES OF PASSENGERS	AGE	SEX	OCCUPATIONS	DATE PORT SHIP
FOX, Farrell	18	M	Laborer	14Ma02lo
Cath.	17	F	Servant	14Ma02lo
HERAN, John	20	M	Laborer	14Ma02lo
KELLY, Richd.	20	M	Laborer	14Ma02lo
GERE, Cath.	21	F	Servant	14Ma02lo
HINSHELLA, Ann	21	F	Servant	14Ma02lo
DOOLAN, Ann	19	F	Servant	14Ma02lo
MONAGEN, John	34	M	Mason	14Ma02lo
Ann	28	F	Unknown	14Ma02lo
Cath.	3	F	Child	14Ma02lo
Hugh	.00	M	Infant	14Ma02lo
MURPHY, James	29	M	Laborer	14Ma02lo
RILEY, Bernard	19	M	Laborer	14Ma02lo
GRADY, Wm.	20	M	Laborer	14Ma02lo
Jeremiah	12	M	Unknown	14Ma02lo
Margt.	6	F	Child	14Ma02lo
MURPHY, Mary	24	F	Unknown	14Ma02lo
Pat	3	M	Child	14Ma02lo
CURRSIS, Ed.	22	M	Laborer	14Ma02lo
NEVILLE, Don-George	22	M	Laborer	14Ma02lo
DONLOE, John	16	M	Laborer	14Ma02lo
GNATT, Margt.	19	F	Laborer	14Ma02lo
HEFFERMAN, John	20	M	Laborer	14Ma02lo
ROACH, Thos.	18	M	Laborer	14Ma02lo
MCBRIDE, Thos.	30	M	Laborer	14Ma02lo
B.	23	F	Laborer	14Ma02lo
David	2	M	Child	14Ma02lo
Henry	.00	M	Infant	14Ma02lo
CARLY, John	40	M	Laborer	14Ma02lo
BRADY, Thos.	35	M	Laborer	14Ma02lo
DRAKE, Margt.	45	F	Unknown	14Ma02lo
MURPHY, John	10	M	Unknown	14Ma02lo
ROCHE, Thos.	34	M	Cooper	14Ma02lo
LOURY, David	60	M	Gentleman	14Ma02lo
CLARKE, Pat	20	M	Cbtmkr	14Ma02lo
CARTY, Dora	18	F	Servant	14Ma02lo
CURRO, Martin	23	M	Laborer	14Ma02lo
GRAHAM, George	22	M	Laborer	14Ma02lo
FITZSIMMONS, Ellen	28	F	Servant	14Ma02lo
KELLY, John	20	M	Laborer	14Ma02lo
HOPKINS, Wm.	23	M	Laborer	14Ma02lo
BINNIS, Wm.	33	M	Laborer	14Ma02lo
Briges	50	M	Laborer	14Ma02lo
John	50	M	Laborer	14Ma02lo
Margt.	24	F	Laborer	14Ma02lo
Ellen	30	F	Laborer	14Ma02lo
Bridget	.00	F	Infant	14Ma02lo
BRADY, John	18	M	Laborer	14Ma02lo
SHAMENSBURY, Danl.	18	M	Laborer	14Ma02lo
HART, Cath.	24	F	Servant	14Ma02lo
RILEY, Thos.	45	M	Carpenter	14Ma02lo
RORCH, Cath.	20	F	Servant	14Ma02lo
CONNELL, Bridget	11	F	Servant	14Ma02lo
SMITH, Pat.	50	M	Laborer	14Ma02lo
Margt.	11	F	Laborer	14Ma02lo
Pat	9	M	Child	14Ma02lo
HARD, Charles	18	M	Cbtmkr	14Ma02lo
HARTNANE, Bridget	20	F	Dressmaker	14Ma02lo
BRADY, Thos.	45	M	Laborer	14Ma02lo
Ellen	40	F	Laborer	14Ma02lo
Peter	17	M	Laborer	14Ma02lo
Pat	16	M	Laborer	14Ma02lo
John	12	M	Laborer	14Ma02lo
James	10	M	Laborer	14Ma02lo
May	8	F	Child	14Ma02lo
Charles	4	M	Child	14Ma02lo
Thos.	2	M	Child	14Ma02lo
RILEY, Luke	21	M	Laborer	14Ma02lo
KINSELLA, Miles	21	M	Laborer	14Ma02lo
MULLER, John	16	M	Unknown	14Ma02lo
CANN, Thos.	15	M	Unknown	14Ma02lo
MCCANE, Ellen	40	F	Servant	14Ma02lo
Mof., Hannah	18	F	Servant	14Ma02lo
CARROL, Ann	12	F	Servant	14Ma02lo
BURK, Josh.	27	M	Farmer	14Ma02lo
CARROLL, Mich.	15	M	Farmer	14Ma02lo
KEARNEY, P.	20	M	Laborer	14Ma02lo
JOHNSTONE, Wm.	23	M	Laborer	14Ma02lo
Joseph	16	M	Clerk	14Ma02lo
SOMMERVILLE, Alexd.	16	M	Clerk	14Ma02lo
FARRELL, Robert	30	M	Mason	14Ma02lo
MCCONNELL, Robt.	22	M	Carpenter	14Ma02lo
SULLIVAN, Pat	20	M	Cooper	14Ma02lo
BELL, Pat	20	M	Butcher	14Ma02lo
MORGEN, Margt.	14	F	Unknown	14Ma02lo

WILLIAM-RATHBONE 14 MAY 1850

From Liverpool

NAMES OF PASSENGERS	AGE	SEX	OCCUPATIONS	DATE PORT SHIP
MCGRATH, Mary	18	F	Servant	14Ma02lp
DEMPSEY, Patt	18	M	Laborer	14Ma02lp
Ellen	20	F	Laborer	14Ma02lp
CROTTY, Catherine	24	F	Laborer	14Ma02lp
LAWLOR, John	18	M	Laborer	14Ma02lp
KOUGH, Patrick	25	M	Laborer	14Ma02lp
KEARY, Martin	21	M	Laborer	14Ma02lp
FOGARTY, Anne	19	F	Laborer	14Ma02lp
FEGAN, Patrick	30	M	Mason	14Ma02lp
Biddy	24	F	Unknown	14Ma02lp
Mary	12	F	Unknown	14Ma02lp
Michael	3	M	Child	14Ma02lp
Peter	.03	M	Infant	14Ma02lp
SHERWOOD, John	29	M	Tailor	14Ma02lp
CARNEY, James	20	M	Tailor	14Ma02lp
SCHERWOOD, Thomas	18	M	Mechanic	14Ma02lp
CRANE, Richard	40	M	Tailor	14Ma02lp
MAGNER, John	22	M	Mechanic	14Ma02lp
David	20	M	Mechanic	14Ma02lp
BURKE, James	21	M	Laborer	14Ma02lp
Johanna	18	F	Laborer	14Ma02lp
KYLEY, Roger	24	M	Laborer	14Ma02lp
Honora	20	F	Unknown	14Ma02lp
CONWAY, Bridget	18	F	Unknown	14Ma02lp
HENRAHAN, Margaret	20	F	Unknown	14Ma02lp
AHEARN, Morris	20	M	Laborer	14Ma02lp
Mary	25	F	Unknown	14Ma02lp
LORDEN, Daniel	22	M	Laborer	14Ma02lp
MCCARTHY, Angel	16	F	Unknown	14Ma02lp
HENESSY, Arthur	35	M	Laborer	14Ma02lp
Mary	27	F	Unknown	14Ma02lp
Thomas	9	M	Child	14Ma02lp
Timothy	5	M	Child	14Ma02lp
John	2	M	Child	14Ma02lp
MCGENNIS, David	29	M	Mechanic	14Ma02lp
WHITTAM, George	25	M	Unknown	14Ma02lp
GUNNELL, Henry	20	M	Unknown	14Ma02lp
WOOD, John	25	M	Laborer	14Ma02lp
Mary	25	F	Unknown	14Ma02lp
PALMER, James	25	M	Unknown	14Ma02lp
Jessy	24	F	Unknown	14Ma02lp
RUNSIMON, William	22	M	Unknown	14Ma02lp
COCKBURN, Robert	27	M	Unknown	14Ma02lp
HASTEY, Elizabeth	24	F	Unknown	14Ma02lp
IVERS, Michael	21	M	Gunsmith	14Ma02lp
MCNAB, John	25	M	Unknown	14Ma02lp
Jane	25	F	Unknown	14Ma02lp
Samuel	.00	M	Infant	14Ma02lp
MCCAUGHAN, James	50	M	Laborer	14Ma02lp
William	30	M	Unknown	14Ma02lp
FORGREAVE, Thomas	25	M	Laborer	14Ma02lp
MCCOOK, Alex	21	M	Unknown	14Ma02lp
WOODEND, John	25	M	Butcher	14Ma02lp
MOORE, Hugh	25	M	Laborer	14Ma02lp

NAMES OF PASSENGERS	AGE	SEX	OCCUPATIONS	DATE PORT SHIP
BELL, Ellen	20	F	Unknown	14Ma02lp
MCANERRY, Jane	20	F	Unknown	14Ma02lp
BROOKES, Peggy	20	F	Unknown	14Ma02lp
DAVIS, Jane	16	F	Unknown	14Ma02lp
JONES, Henry	19	M	Miller	14Ma02lp
GRIGG, Henry	18	M	Farmer	14Ma02lp
TILLY, Nathan	15	M	Gdnr	14Ma02lp
SYONS, Patt	26	M	Shoemaker	14Ma02lp
MOLONEY, John	24	M	Unknown	14Ma02lp
Mary	21	F	Unknown	14Ma02lp
Bridget	18	F	Servant	14Ma02lp
MCGRATH, Anne	30	F	Unknown	14Ma02lp
John	12	M	Unknown	14Ma02lp
Michael	9	M	Child	14Ma02lp
POTTINGER, Samuel	45	M	Mechanic	14Ma02lp
Mary	45	F	Unknown	14Ma02lp
Samuel	22	M	Mechanic	14Ma02lp
Fanny	24	F	Unknown	14Ma02lp
John	16	M	Clerk	14Ma02lp
Sylvia	9	F	Child	14Ma02lp
Anna	7	F	Child	14Ma02lp
FOWLER, Samuel	21	M	Farmer	14Ma02lp
Mary	20	F	Unknown	14Ma02lp
HUESTON, John	40	M	Laborer	14Ma02lp
Isabella	35	F	Unknown	14Ma02lp
Hannah	7	F	Child	14Ma02lp
Ellen-Jane	2	F	Child	14Ma02lp
James	.06	M	Infant	14Ma02lp
YOUNG, Hugh	26	M	Laborer	14Ma02lp
Martha	22	F	Unknown	14Ma02lp
WALLACE, Anne	18	F	Servant	14Ma02lp
WOODBURN, Isabella	17	F	Servant	14Ma02lp
STUART, Anna	21	F	Servant	14Ma02lp
BOYCE, Hugh	48	M	Laborer	14Ma02lp
Mary	35	F	Laborer	14Ma02lp
Hugh	14	M	Unknown	14Ma02lp
Matthew	8	M	Child	14Ma02lp
James	7	M	Child	14Ma02lp
Mary-Eliza	4	F	Child	14Ma02lp
MOONEY, Luke	20	M	Laborer	14Ma02lp
SHEA, Thomas	21	M	Laborer	14Ma02lp
Michael	25	M	Laborer	14Ma02lp
Margaret	22	F	Unknown	14Ma02lp
Thomas	.07	M	Infant	14Ma02lp
Died-At-Sea				
FLEMING, Thomas	20	M	Unknown	14Ma02lp
MCDERMOT, Patt	20	M	Laborer	14Ma02lp
FARRELL, James	23	M	Laborer	14Ma02lp
MURPHY, James	22	M	Laborer	14Ma02lp
HOOLDHAN, Bridget	20	F	Unknown	14Ma02lp
Margaret	25	F	Servant	14Ma02lp
HOOGAN, Thomas	22	M	Unknown	14Ma02lp
BURTON, William	20	M	Wright	14Ma02lp
BOULTON, Thomas	25	M	Laborer	14Ma02lp
OLDREDSE, William	22	M	Laborer	14Ma02lp
TRACEY, Margt.	21	F	Unknown	14Ma02lp
HAGERTY, James	24	M	Laborer	14Ma02lp
MCDERMOT, Francis	11	M	Laborer	14Ma02lp
MCCRACKEN, William	20	M	Laborer	14Ma02lp
WRIGHT, George	21	M	Farmer	14Ma02lp
MCFARLANE, John	20	M	Farmer	14Ma02lp
BARKER, Joseph	45	M	Farmer	14Ma02lp
THREADGOLD, George	55	M	Laborer	14Ma02lp
U-Mrs.	45	F	Unknown	14Ma02lp
Andrew	23	M	Unknown	14Ma02lp
Jane	22	F	Unknown	14Ma02lp
Hannah	17	F	Unknown	14Ma02lp
Mary	11	F	Unknown	14Ma02lp
Francis	8	M	Child	14Ma02lp
Anne	2	F	Child	14Ma02lp
GAMBLE, John	19	M	Unknown	14Ma02lp
HAWCROFT, George	24	M	Shoemaker	14Ma02lp
Adam	21	M	Unknown	14Ma02lp
CHARLESWORTH, John	25	M	Tailor	14Ma02lp
BACLEY, Henry	26	M	Unknown	14Ma02lp
LEE, Thomas	22	M	Unknown	14Ma02lp
CHARLESWORTH, Mary	21	F	Unknown	14Ma02lp
IRELAND, John	35	M	Unknown	14Ma02lp
LATCHAM, Charles	40	M	Unknown	14Ma02lp
BEERELL, Joseph	35	M	Shoemaker	14Ma02lp
ARMSTRONG, James	50	M	Gunsmith	14Ma02lp
Mary	50	F	Unknown	14Ma02lp
James	18	M	Unknown	14Ma02lp
Samuel	14	M	Unknown	14Ma02lp
William	12	M	Unknown	14Ma02lp
MCGLIMM, Bernard	22	M	Farmer	14Ma02lp
Rose	40	F	Unknown	14Ma02lp
Bridget	30	F	Unknown	14Ma02lp
Catherine	.06	F	Infant	14Ma02lp
REYNOLDS, Bernard	30	M	Unknown	14Ma02lp
Catherine	24	F	Unknown	14Ma02lp
Bridget	.04	F	Infant	14Ma02lp
MCGIBNAY, Anne	16	F	Unknown	14Ma02lp
FEGAN, Michael	40	M	Farmer	14Ma02lp
Isabella	35	F	Unknown	14Ma02lp
Maria	18	F	Unknown	14Ma02lp
James	16	M	Unknown	14Ma02lp
Patrick	14	M	Unknown	14Ma02lp
Eliza	12	F	Unknown	14Ma02lp
Bridget	8	F	Child	14Ma02lp
Mary	7	F	Child	14Ma02lp
Isabella	.10	F	Infant	14Ma02lp
MONOHAY, Nicholas	18	M	Unknown	14Ma02lp
HIGGENS, Thomas	21	M	Ploughman	14Ma02lp
KAIN, John	20	M	Unknown	14Ma02lp
FLAHERTY, Bernard	48	M	Laborer	14Ma02lp
Owen	22	M	Unknown	14Ma02lp
CLAYTON, Thomas	28	M	Unknown	14Ma02lp
WALKER, George	22	M	Unknown	14Ma02lp
ASHTON, Edward	22	M	Mechanic	14Ma02lp
ELLIOTT, George	30	M	Mechanic	14Ma02lp
MORSLEY, William	21	M	Unknown	14Ma02lp
PEACOCK, George	21	M	Shoemaker	14Ma02lp
MCGUIRE, Luke	25	M	Unknown	14Ma02lp
STEVENSON, William	40	M	Laborer	14Ma02lp
JAMES, Joseah	27	M	Unknown	14Ma02lp
GRAINGER, Jane	30	F	Unknown	14Ma02lp
Emma-Jane	6	F	Child	14Ma02lp
Alice	2	F	Child	14Ma02lp
BROWNE, Frederick	36	M	Laborer	14Ma02lp
Mary	34	F	Unknown	14Ma02lp
MCGOVERN, Christian	16	M	Laborer	14Ma02lp
ROGERS, Thomas	22	M	Unknown	14Ma02lp
DALY, Thomas	25	M	Unknown	14Ma02lp
MUNDAY, Martin	23	M	Unknown	14Ma02lp
CHARTERS, David	50	M	Farmer	14Ma02lp
HAMLET, Thomas	20	M	Unknown	14Ma02lp
LEE, James	21	M	Wright	14Ma02lp
CLUNSEN, G.	32	M	Shoemaker	14Ma02lp
Ad	35	F	Unknown	14Ma02lp
Louisa	11	F	Unknown	14Ma02lp
Clara	3	F	Child	14Ma02lp
Celina	.06	F	Infant	14Ma02lp
KELLY, Patt	28	M	Unknown	14Ma02lp
BRINNAN, Thomas	21	M	Unknown	14Ma02lp
DELANY, Mary	19	F	Unknown	14Ma02lp
MCGUIRE, Mary	20	F	Unknown	14Ma02lp
FITZPATRICK, Bridget	19	F	Unknown	14Ma02lp
MAHER, Mary	19	F	Unknown	14Ma02lp
CUMMINGS, John	26	M	Wright	14Ma02lp
Mary	22	F	Unknown	14Ma02lp
Mary	2	F	Child	14Ma02lp
METCALFE, Michael	24	M	Blacksmith	14Ma02lp
SIBBALD, David	24	M	Currier	14Ma02lp
THOMAS, David	54	M	Laborer	14Ma02lp
Jane	52	F	Unknown	14Ma02lp
Richard	13	M	Unknown	14Ma02lp
Josiah	11	M	Unknown	14Ma02lp
Jane	17	F	Unknown	14Ma02lp
WILLIAMS, David	27	M	Unknown	14Ma02lp

NAMES OF PASSENGERS	AGE	SEX	OCCUPATIONS	DATE PORT SHIP
WILLIAMS, Anne	21	F	Unknown	14Ma02lp
Thomas	25	M	Unknown	14Ma02lp
Elizabeth	23	F	Unknown	14Ma02lp
EVANS, John	19	M	Laborer	14Ma02lp
Mary	60	F	Unknown	14Ma02lp
JONES, Mary	52	F	Unknown	14Ma02lp
ATKINSON, John	23	M	Farmer	14Ma02lp
Sarah	22	F	Unknown	14Ma02lp
REID, James	22	M	Unknown	14Ma02lp
DOAK, Samuel	23	M	Laborer	14Ma02lp
David	19	M	Unknown	14Ma02lp
BASSET, Thomas	25	M	Unknown	14Ma02lp
SKELTON, Richard	25	M	Unknown	14Ma02lp
TAYLOR, John	33	M	Unknown	14Ma02lp
SHUTCLIFFE, George	32	M	Blacksmith	14Ma02lp
GRANTON, Richard	35	M	Unknown	14Ma02lp
MCCORMICK, Hugh	21	M	Unknown	14Ma02lp
CAPPS, Thomas	26	M	Unknown	14Ma02lp
Richard	21	M	Unknown	14Ma02lp
Hannah	21	F	Unknown	14Ma02lp
BELL, Michael	22	M	Laborer	14Ma02lp
John	28	M	Laborer	14Ma02lp
Catherine	50	F	Unknown	14Ma02lp
Anne	11	F	Unknown	14Ma02lp
FARRELLY, Dinnes	24	M	Unknown	14Ma02lp
FOLEY, Mary	20	F	Unknown	14Ma02lp
FARRELL, James	21	M	Unknown	14Ma02lp
GATELEY, Onney	20	F	Unknown	14Ma02lp
LEADMORE, Thomas	32	M	Laborer	14Ma02lp
Fanny	28	F	Unknown	14Ma02lp
Charles-James	1	M	Child	14Ma02lp
THACKAWAY, Henry	28	M	Unknown	14Ma02lp
LETCHEM, James	40	M	Miller	14Ma02lp
DUNNE, Margt.	18	F	Unknown	14Ma02lp
COLLASH, William	28	M	Unknown	14Ma02lp
MORRISON, Peter	26	M	Unknown	14Ma02lp
LAMBERT, William	15	M	Laborer	14Ma02lp
CAREY, Rody	20	F	Unknown	14Ma02lp
RYAN, Pierce	26	M	Laborer	14Ma02lp
SLOAN, Michael	26	M	Laborer	14Ma02lp
DUNLEVY, Charles	26	M	Unknown	14Ma02lp
Mary-Anne	24	F	Unknown	14Ma02lp
John	3	M	Child	14Ma02lp
William	.00	M	Infant	14Ma02lp
MCKINSAY, Margaret	19	F	Unknown	14Ma02lp
Mary-Anne	24	F	Unknown	14Ma02lp
COUGHLEN, Michael	26	M	Laborer	14Ma02lp
GIOEIGHIGAN, Honora	25	F	Unknown	14Ma02lp
COWLEY, John	27	M	Unknown	14Ma02lp
BRADY, U-Mr.	17	M	Unknown	14Ma02lp
SMITH, Anne	23	F	Unknown	14Ma02lp
Anne	5	F	Child	14Ma02lp
COWEN, William	20	M	Miller	14Ma02lp
HASARD, Robert	45	M	Unknown	14Ma02lp
WARD, Cathr.	18	F	Laborer	14Ma02lp
SHEA, John	18	M	Unknown	14Ma02lp
RYAN, James	28	M	Unknown	14Ma02lp
HART, Bryan	29	M	Unknown	14Ma02lp
MEAD, John	20	M	Laborer	14Ma02lp
Edward	22	M	Laborer	14Ma02lp
COYLE, Bessy	19	F	Laborer	14Ma02lp
Margt.	22	F	Laborer	14Ma02lp
PARRY, John	30	M	Laborer	14Ma02lp
RYAN, Peter	30	M	Unknown	14Ma02lp
MCENRO, William	23	M	Farmer	14Ma02lp
WILSON, George	26	M	Unknown	14Ma02lp
Henry	20	M	Unknown	14Ma02lp
EOKERDT, Gustav	17	M	Unknown	14Ma02lp
CONSADINE, Jane	15	F	Unknown	14Ma02lp
DEVINE, Patrick	28	M	Unknown	14Ma02lp
BYRNES, Julia	18	F	Unknown	14Ma02lp
John	17	M	Unknown	14Ma02lp
DOONAN, Anne-Jane	20	F	Servant	14Ma02lp
Eliza	18	F	Servant	14Ma02lp
MURPHY, Dennis	28	M	Laborer	14Ma02lp

NAMES OF PASSENGERS	AGE	SEX	OCCUPATIONS	DATE PORT SHIP
MURPHY, William	22	M	Laborer	14Ma02lp
Honora	20	F	Unknown	14Ma02lp
John	13	M	Unknown	14Ma02lp
LUCY, Ellen	18	F	Unknown	14Ma02lp
MURPHY, Robert	22	M	Unknown	14Ma02lp
Nancy	20	F	Unknown	14Ma02lp
Sally	16	F	Unknown	14Ma02lp
Susan	11	F	Unknown	14Ma02lp
BARRETT, Honora	20	F	Unknown	14Ma02lp
DONOHEN, Michael	30	M	Laborer	14Ma02lp
U-Miss	25	F	Unknown	14Ma02lp
HARTNETT, Stephen	30	M	Unknown	14Ma02lp
DOOLING, Timth.	35	M	Unknown	14Ma02lp
MCNAMARD, James	35	M	Unknown	14Ma02lp
Anne	22	F	Unknown	14Ma02lp
LEONARD, John	40	M	Unknown	14Ma02lp
COSTELLO, Michael	25	M	Unknown	14Ma02lp
Alice	24	F	Unknown	14Ma02lp
BOYLE, Daniel	18	M	Unknown	14Ma02lp
BRUMAN, Mary	60	F	Unknown	14Ma02lp
Roger	21	M	Unknown	14Ma02lp
John	30	M	Unknown	14Ma02lp
Mary	6	F	Child	14Ma02lp
MALONE, Patrick	15	M	Laborer	14Ma02lp
HOLDEN, Bridget	31	F	Servant	14Ma02lp
FLYNNE, Thomas	14	M	Unknown	14Ma02lp
DONDHIRE, Andrew	18	M	Unknown	14Ma02lp
Charles	16	M	Unknown	14Ma02lp
Anne	14	F	Unknown	14Ma02lp
RYAN, Anne	20	F	Unknown	14Ma02lp
GIBBONS, Nabby	18	F	Unknown	14Ma02lp
Bridget	9	F	Child	14Ma02lp
RATICAN, Margt.	10	F	Unknown	14Ma02lp
COX, Thomas	20	M	Unknown	14Ma02lp
ROURKE, Edward	21	M	Farmer	14Ma02lp
GAYNOR, Margt.	18	F	Unknown	14Ma02lp
SLYMAN, Thomas	23	M	Unknown	14Ma02lp
MCMAHON, Mary	20	F	Unknown	14Ma02lp
DUNNE, Bridget	10	F	Unknown	14Ma02lp
BRUMAN, Anne	17	F	Unknown	14Ma02lp
HARRIS, Alice	30	F	Unknown	14Ma02lp
Bernard	7	M	Child	14Ma02lp
COGAN, Edward	30	M	Laborer	14Ma02lp
HARRISON, Margt.	7	F	Child	14Ma02lp
Julia	4	F	Child	14Ma02lp
GIBBONS, Bridget	40	F	Child	14Ma02lp
Patrick	10	M	Child	14Ma02lp
Maria	8	F	Child	14Ma02lp
Peter	4	M	Child	14Ma02lp
FLANAGAN, Ellen	20	F	Unknown	14Ma02lp
FILBEN, John	28	M	Laborer	14Ma02lp
Michael	25	M	Unknown	14Ma02lp
LESTRANGE, Mary	19	F	Unknown	14Ma02lp
COYLE, Philip	12	M	Laborer	14Ma02lp
MCCOY, Anne	21	F	Unknown	14Ma02lp
FARRELL, John	22	M	Wool Dyer	14Ma02lp
DONLAN, Rose	18	F	Servant	14Ma02lp
NUMAN, Patrick	21	M	Wool Dyer	14Ma02lp
CURREN, Ellen	19	F	Unknown	14Ma02lp
DELANE, Sarah	20	F	Unknown	14Ma02lp
MANSFIELD, Norry	29	F	Unknown	14Ma02lp
Mary	20	F	Unknown	14Ma02lp
CORNELLY, Mary	26	F	Unknown	14Ma02lp
HANNON, Margt.	55	F	Unknown	14Ma02lp
NEWS, Jane	24	F	Unknown	14Ma02lp
Anne	20	F	Unknown	14Ma02lp
ONEILL, John	16	M	Shoemaker	14Ma02lp
LYNCH, James	18	M	Unknown	14Ma02lp
Bessy	20	F	Unknown	14Ma02lp
DUNNE, John	50	M	Laborer	14Ma02lp
Died-At-Sea				
Patrick	19	M	Unknown	14Ma02lp
Julia	50	F	Unknown	14Ma02lp
GAVEN, Catherina	20	F	Unknown	14Ma02lp
SHEA, James	40	M	Carpenter	14Ma02lp

NAMES OF PASSENGERS	AGE	SEX	OCCUPATIONS	DATE PORT SHIP
SHEA, Catherine	37	F	Unknown	14Ma02Ip
Michael	12	M	Unknown	14Ma02Ip
William	10	M	Unknown	14Ma02Ip
Richard	5	M	Child	14Ma02Ip
Bridget	4	F	Child	14Ma02Ip
James	3	M	Child	14Ma02Ip

NIAGARA 14 MAY 1850

From Liverpool

NAMES OF PASSENGERS	AGE	SEX	OCCUPATIONS	DATE PORT SHIP
PULLMAN, U	26	M	Merchant	14Ma02Bg
Anna	23	F	Unknown	14Ma02Bg
Benjm.	12	M	Unknown	14Ma02Bg
Joseph	9	M	Child	14Ma02Bg
BOLTON, Eliza	22	F	Unknown	14Ma02Bg
FAGAN, Jane	24	F	Unknown	14Ma02Bg
ARMSTRONG, Eliza	21	F	Unknown	14Ma02Bg
CAFFREY, John	25	M	Mason	14Ma02Bg
KELLY, John	19	M	Unknown	14Ma02Bg
GRIFFIN, John	20	M	Farmer	14Ma02Bg
Wm.	19	M	Unknown	14Ma02Bg
THORN, Julia	26	F	Unknown	14Ma02Bg
ELLIS, Mary	20	F	Unknown	14Ma02Bg
FINNERTY, Patt	50	M	Laborer	14Ma02Bg
BRAHANY, Margt.	45	F	Unknown	14Ma02Bg
DONNELLY, Mary	9	F	Child	14Ma02Bg
Margt.	7	F	Child	14Ma02Bg
CONBOY, Judy	28	F	Unknown	14Ma02Bg
James	3	M	Child	14Ma02Bg
Celia	21	F	Unknown	14Ma02Bg
MULLIGAN, Margt.	22	F	Unknown	14Ma02Bg
BAXTER, Patt	22	M	Laborer	14Ma02Bg
Bridgt.	15	F	Unknown	14Ma02Bg
Margt.	12	F	Unknown	14Ma02Bg
James	9	M	Child	14Ma02Bg
BEARN, Chas.	45	M	Unknown	14Ma02Bg
MCKERMAN, Patt	18	M	Laborer	14Ma02Bg
James	16	M	Laborer	14Ma02Bg
Mary	12	F	Unknown	14Ma02Bg
WATSON, John	15	M	Unknown	14Ma02Bg
CORKILL, Margt.	35	F	Unknown	14Ma02Bg
Mary	8	F	Child	14Ma02Bg
Susan	.00	F	Infant	14Ma02Bg
Biddy	.00	F	Infant	14Ma02Bg
KILLANE, Thos.	20	M	Laborer	14Ma02Bg
KEHERN, Patt	30	M	Laborer	14Ma02Bg
Kitty	4	F	Child	14Ma02Bg
MCKINE, Mathw.	40	M	Laborer	14Ma02Bg
Mary	35	F	Unknown	14Ma02Bg
Mick	21	M	Unknown	14Ma02Bg
Thomas	9	M	Child	14Ma02Bg
Rose	11	F	Unknown	14Ma02Bg
GARRELLY, John	30	M	Unknown	14Ma02Bg
Margt.	24	F	Unknown	14Ma02Bg
ROBINSON, Thos.	22	M	Painter	14Ma02Bg
COINE, Mary	12	F	Unknown	14Ma02Bg
PULLMAN, Elizth.	29	F	Unknown	14Ma02Bg
CAFFREY, Margt.	23	F	Unknown	14Ma02Bg
WATSON, Lawre.	27	M	Laborer	14Ma02Bg
Cathe.	25	F	Unknown	14Ma02Bg
REYNOLDS, Wm.	27	M	Blacksmith	14Ma02Bg
LESTON, John	30	M	Laborer	14Ma02Bg
DALEY, Honor	16	F	Unknown	14Ma02Bg
Ann	18	F	Unknown	14Ma02Bg
MOLLOY, Ellen	14	F	Unknown	14Ma02Bg
OHARA, James	21	M	Laborer	14Ma02Bg
RYAN, Ann	17	F	Laborer	14Ma02Bg
FANNON, James	20	M	Laborer	14Ma02Bg

NAMES OF PASSENGERS	AGE	SEX	OCCUPATIONS	DATE PORT SHIP
RYAN, John	50	M	Laborer	14Ma02Bg
Michl.	24	M	Laborer	14Ma02Bg
DONOUGHOE, Hugh	23	M	Laborer	14Ma02Bg
Mary	20	F	Unknown	14Ma02Bg
MAGUIRE, Martin	12	M	Laborer	14Ma02Bg
Eliza	9	F	Child	14Ma02Bg
DELANY, Dennis	25	M	Laborer	14Ma02Bg
Patt	24	M	Laborer	14Ma02Bg
Margt.	20	F	Unknown	14Ma02Bg
Bessy	10	F	Unknown	14Ma02Bg
FARRELLY, Patt	22	M	Laborer	14Ma02Bg
Mary	25	F	Unknown	14Ma02Bg
Mary	7	F	Child	14Ma02Bg
HORE, Mary	20	F	Unknown	14Ma02Bg
CORR, Ann	12	F	Unknown	14Ma02Bg
GRAY, Jackson	22	M	Laborer	14Ma02Bg
CATON, Betty	30	F	Unknown	14Ma02Bg
KELLY, Mat	5	M	Child	14Ma02Bg
HICKEY, Patt	27	M	Laborer	14Ma02Bg
MITCHELL, Mary	30	F	Unknown	14Ma02Bg
PAGE, John	4	M	Child	14Ma02Bg
MCMARROW, Thos.	60	M	Laborer	14Ma02Bg
Honor	80	F	Unknown	14Ma02Bg
Ann	34	F	Unknown	14Ma02Bg
Mary	10	F	Unknown	14Ma02Bg
Thomas	9	M	Child	14Ma02Bg
Cathe.	7	F	Child	14Ma02Bg
Patt	6	M	Child	14Ma02Bg
Ann	4	M	Child	14Ma02Bg
TOBIN, Michl.	50	M	Laborer	14Ma02Bg
MAHER, Patt	25	M	Laborer	14Ma02Bg
Thos.	23	M	Laborer	14Ma02Bg
Wm.	18	M	Laborer	14Ma02Bg
Margt.	27	F	Unknown	14Ma02Bg
RYAN, Wm.	26	M	Laborer	14Ma02Bg
Thos.	28	M	Laborer	14Ma02Bg
DELANEY, Patt	26	M	Farmer	14Ma02Bg
CANNELL, Phil.	27	M	Farmer	14Ma02Bg
MEHAN, Dennis	24	M	Farmer	14Ma02Bg
MASTERSON, Peter	20	M	Farmer	14Ma02Bg
GREEN, Wm.	18	M	Farmer	14Ma02Bg
WELLWOOD, Jane	22	F	Unknown	14Ma02Bg
Mary-A.	20	F	Unknown	14Ma02Bg
BOGHAM, Michl.	30	M	Laborer	14Ma02Bg
CARRIGAN, Ann	17	F	Unknown	14Ma02Bg
DONNELLY, Thos.	30	M	Laborer	14Ma02Bg
Bridgt.	32	F	Unknown	14Ma02Bg
Nabby	31	F	Unknown	14Ma02Bg
CAIN, Ann	21	F	Unknown	14Ma02Bg
WARD, John	18	M	Blacksmith	14Ma02Bg
CONNELLY, John	26	M	Laborer	14Ma02Bg
MULVEY, Patt	21	M	Laborer	14Ma02Bg
WALSH, Thos.	30	M	Laborer	14Ma02Bg
BURKE, Mary	10	F	Unknown	14Ma02Bg
MCDERMOTT, Paul	20	M	Mason	14Ma02Bg
MCGLINCHIE, Andw.	20	M	Laborer	14Ma02Bg
DWYRE, Patt	20	M	Laborer	14Ma02Bg
Died-At-Sea				
ALLEN, Jane	45	F	Unknown	14Ma02Bg
Margt.	14	F	Unknown	14Ma02Bg
MANNION, Patt	25	M	Laborer	14Ma02Bg
Bridgt.	45	F	Unknown	14Ma02Bg
Michl.	4	M	Child	14Ma02Bg
BURKE, Wm.	22	M	Laborer	14Ma02Bg
Henry	18	M	Laborer	14Ma02Bg
Ann	16	F	Unknown	14Ma02Bg
TANGAN, John	29	M	Laborer	14Ma02Bg
Cathe.	29	F	Unknown	14Ma02Bg
Sarah	25	F	Unknown	14Ma02Bg
Patt	10	M	Unknown	14Ma02Bg
Ann	7	F	Child	14Ma02Bg
Bridgt.	.00	F	Infant	14Ma02Bg
SULLIVAN, Michl.	22	M	Laborer	14Ma02Bg
CORDON, Bernd.	22	M	Laborer	14Ma02Bg
BENNETT, Rose	15	F	Unknown	14Ma02Bg

NAMES OF PASSENGERS	AGE	SEX	OCCUPATIONS	DATE PORT SHIP
MCMANUS, Mary	8	F	Child	14Ma02Bg
Mary	8	F	Child	14Ma02Bg
FLOOD, Cathe.	19	F	Unknown	14Ma02Bg
MCSHARRY, Bryan	30	M	Laborer	14Ma02Bg
MCGEVER, Mary	18	F	Unknown	14Ma02Bg
BRADY, Michl.	24	M	Laborer	14Ma02Bg
Cathe.	20	F	Unknown	14Ma02Bg
MURE, Cathe.	22	F	Unknown	14Ma02Bg
ODONNELL, Ellen	54	F	Unknown	14Ma02Bg
Ellen	23	F	Unknown	14Ma02Bg
HARRISON, Edwd.	40	M	Laborer	14Ma02Bg
Patt	20	M	Laborer	14Ma02Bg
DONOUGHOE, Robt.	24	M	Laborer	14Ma02Bg
WILSON, James	25	M	Bootmaker	14Ma02Bg
MALONEY, John	27	M	Mason	14Ma02Bg
WATERSON, John	40	M	Laborer	14Ma02Bg
KEENAN, Danl.	38	M	Farmer	14Ma02Bg
LUBE, John	40	M	Unknown	14Ma02Bg
MILAN, Ellen	13	F	Unknown	14Ma02Bg
LALOR, Edwd.	30	M	Laborer	14Ma02Bg
Ellen	27	F	Unknown	14Ma02Bg
KNAVESBORN, Judith	50	F	Unknown	14Ma02Bg
Catherine	10	F	Unknown	14Ma02Bg
LALOR, Catherine	6	F	Child	14Ma02Bg
James	.00	M	Infant	14Ma02Bg
Died-At-Sea				
RYAN, Michael	50	M	Tailor	14Ma02Bg
MAHER, Bridget	20	F	Unknown	14Ma02Bg
ODONNELL, Catherine	30	F	Unknown	14Ma02Bg
LUNDY, Valentine	46	M	Laborer	14Ma02Bg
MCMANUS, Thomas	40	M	Laborer	14Ma02Bg
Jane	40	F	Unknown	14Ma02Bg
Thomas	20	M	Unknown	14Ma02Bg
Owen	16	M	Unknown	14Ma02Bg
Jane	11	F	Unknown	14Ma02Bg
ALLEN, James	23	M	Laborer	14Ma02Bg
Ellen	16	F	Unknown	14Ma02Bg
AUCHINERTY, A.W.	28	M	Cver	14Ma02Bg
MULGILHILL, John	31	M	Laborer	14Ma02Bg
KEEGAN, John	18	M	Unknown	14Ma02Bg
CRAMER, Michael	50	M	Laborer	14Ma02Bg
Elizabeth	50	F	Unknown	14Ma02Bg
Dennis	15	M	Unknown	14Ma02Bg
WYNNE, Bridget	22	F	Unknown	14Ma02Bg
MCMAHON, John	20	M	Laborer	14Ma02Bg
KEGAN, Winney	16	F	Unknown	14Ma02Bg
MAHONEY, Bridget	35	F	Unknown	14Ma02Bg
Margaret	7	F	Child	14Ma02Bg
KEEFE, Bridget	40	F	Unknown	14Ma02Bg
Thomas	12	M	Unknown	14Ma02Bg
Patrick	4	M	Child	14Ma02Bg
RODGERS, Bridget	25	F	Unknown	14Ma02Bg
BYRNE, Pat	25	M	Herd	14Ma02Bg
DEVERY, Peter	22	M	Unknown	14Ma02Bg
KENNEY, Mary	20	F	Unknown	14Ma02Bg
MCCARN, Thomas	28	M	Laborer	14Ma02Bg
RODGERS, Pat	27	M	Nailer	14Ma02Bg
DUFF, Christopher	35	M	Weaver	14Ma02Bg
Catherine	36	F	Unknown	14Ma02Bg
LUNDY, Catherine	40	F	Unknown	14Ma02Bg
James	17	M	Unknown	14Ma02Bg
Patt	16	M	Unknown	14Ma02Bg
Ann	15	F	Unknown	14Ma02Bg
Rosy	14	F	Unknown	14Ma02Bg
John	12	M	Unknown	14Ma02Bg
MCGILLA, Eliza	40	F	Unknown	14Ma02Bg
DOLAN, Terens	27	M	Laborer	14Ma02Bg
Pat	3	M	Child	14Ma02Bg
CURTIS, Frances	22	F	Unknown	14Ma02Bg
QUINN, Hugh	20	M	Laborer	14Ma02Bg
MCLARREN, Sally	19	F	Unknown	14Ma02Bg
MULLONEY, Catherine	30	F	Unknown	14Ma02Bg
GARLAND, Mary	26	F	Unknown	14Ma02Bg
Jane	13	F	Unknown	14Ma02Bg
Berland	11	M	Unknown	14Ma02Bg
GARLAND, Edward	1	M	Child	14Ma02Bg
MURPHY, Pat	29	M	Cbtmkr	14Ma02Bg
LARKIN, John	22	M	Laborer	14Ma02Bg
Catherine	20	F	Unknown	14Ma02Bg
DUNER, Mary	20	F	Unknown	14Ma02Bg
TIERNEY, John	20	M	Laborer	14Ma02Bg
SOLAN, Mary	25	F	Unknown	14Ma02Bg
JENNINGS, James	20	M	Laborer	14Ma02Bg
DYER, Ellen	30	F	Unknown	14Ma02Bg
Edward	14	M	Unknown	14Ma02Bg
Bridget	8	F	Child	14Ma02Bg
Johanna	2	F	Child	14Ma02Bg
Thomas	.00	M	Infant	14Ma02Bg
ONEIL, Margaret	35	F	Unknown	14Ma02Bg
HARRINGTON, Ann	35	F	Unknown	14Ma02Bg
Michael	35	M	Unknown	14Ma02Bg
Patrick	8	M	Child	14Ma02Bg
John	6	M	Child	14Ma02Bg
James	.00	M	Infant	14Ma02Bg
JENNINGS, Catherine	16	F	Unknown	14Ma02Bg
RYAN, Michael	23	M	Laborer	14Ma02Bg
COLEMAN, Roger	15	M	Unknown	14Ma02Bg
DALEY, James	32	M	Unknown	14Ma02Bg
MCGUINESS, Ann	25	F	Unknown	14Ma02Bg
BYRNE, Michl.	24	M	Unknown	14Ma02Bg
CADDLE, Patrick	30	M	Printer	14Ma02Bg
NORTON, Charles	20	M	Clerk	14Ma02Bg
JENKINSON, James	24	M	Clerk	14Ma02Bg
BOYNE, William	40	M	Laborer	14Ma02Bg
Peggy	40	F	Unknown	14Ma02Bg
MANION, Connor	58	M	Laborer	14Ma02Bg
WHELAN, Robert	26	M	Laborer	14Ma02Bg
Patrick	20	M	Laborer	14Ma02Bg
MANION, Catherine	54	F	Unknown	14Ma02Bg
Kitty	16	F	Unknown	14Ma02Bg
Ann	14	F	Unknown	14Ma02Bg
Ally	9	F	Child	14Ma02Bg
Mary	11	F	Unknown	14Ma02Bg
DICKSON, William	30	M	Laborer	14Ma02Bg
Mary	20	F	Unknown	14Ma02Bg
BYRNES, Bernard	18	M	Carpenter	14Ma02Bg
Thomas	13	M	Unknown	14Ma02Bg
MCDONOUGH, Bernard	37	M	Bootmaker	14Ma02Bg
James	30	M	Bootmaker	14Ma02Bg
MCGLEAN, William	48	M	Laborer	14Ma02Bg
Ellen	14	F	Unknown	14Ma02Bg
MCDONOUGH, Betsy	26	F	Unknown	14Ma02Bg
MCGEE, Thomas	10	M	Unknown	14Ma02Bg
James	8	M	Child	14Ma02Bg
HILL, James	32	M	Farmer	14Ma02Bg

LIVING-AGE 14 MAY 1850

From Liverpool

NAMES OF PASSENGERS	AGE	SEX	OCCUPATIONS	DATE PORT SHIP
WOODS, Peter	25	M	Unknown	14Ma02Jk
Julia	21	F	Unknown	14Ma02Jk
KING, Patt	32	M	Unknown	14Ma02Jk
Ann	28	F	Unknown	14Ma02Jk
NORTON, Michl.	20	M	Unknown	14Ma02Jk
FOGGART, Jas.	20	M	Unknown	14Ma02Jk
BEYLAN, Michl.	26	M	Unknown	14Ma02Jk
HOLMES, Richd.	28	M	Unknown	14Ma02Jk
HOUGHTON, Geo.	18	M	Unknown	14Ma02Jk
CARREAR, Thos.	19	M	Unknown	14Ma02Jk
Robt.	22	M	Unknown	14Ma02Jk
LANGTEAR, Jane	19	F	Unknown	14Ma02Jk
MCRENARD, Owen	20	M	Unknown	14Ma02Jk
REESLET, Thos.	30	M	Unknown	14Ma02Jk

NAMES OF PASSENGERS	AGE	SEX	OCCUPATIONS	DATE PORT SHIP
DEWITT, Michl.	20	M	Unknown	14Ma02Jk
MCKERNAN, Andy	27	M	Unknown	14Ma02Jk
ROGAN, Winey	18	M	Unknown	14Ma02Jk
MCMURRAY, Michl.	20	M	Unknown	14Ma02Jk
REEGAN, Jas.	30	M	Unknown	14Ma02Jk
Winy	26	F	Unknown	14Ma02Jk
Mary	7	F	Child	14Ma02Jk
Michl.	4	M	Child	14Ma02Jk
Charles	.00	M	Infant	14Ma02Jk
MARTIN, Mark	30	M	Unknown	14Ma02Jk
Cath.	25	F	Unknown	14Ma02Jk
MCENTEN, Thos.	21	M	Unknown	14Ma02Jk
KELLY, Mick	40	M	Unknown	14Ma02Jk
QUINLAN, Ellen	12	F	Unknown	14Ma02Jk
MCGEARY, James	29	M	Unknown	14Ma02Jk
MCDONAGH, Cath.	14	F	Unknown	14Ma02Jk
FRISSAL, Jno.	16	M	Unknown	14Ma02Jk
Mick	18	M	Unknown	14Ma02Jk
KORAN, Danl.	25	M	Unknown	14Ma02Jk
TRACY, Tim	24	M	Unknown	14Ma02Jk
RUSSELL, Jno.	30	M	Unknown	14Ma02Jk
Ellen	20	F	Unknown	14Ma02Jk
COMOND, Jas.	30	M	Unknown	14Ma02Jk
CARNEY, Margt.	22	F	Unknown	14Ma02Jk
Jeffrey	13	M	Unknown	14Ma02Jk
DAVIS, Ellen	25	F	Unknown	14Ma02Jk
KENNEDY, Margt.	25	F	Unknown	14Ma02Jk
SOLAN, John	25	F	Unknown	14Ma02Jk
CARNEY, Mick	25	M	Unknown	14Ma02Jk
CONNELLY, Thos.	18	M	Unknown	14Ma02Jk
Bridget	20	F	Unknown	14Ma02Jk
BURKE, Betsey	35	F	Unknown	14Ma02Jk
Phillip	4	M	Child	14Ma02Jk
Mary	.00	F	Infant	14Ma02Jk
Ellen	.00	F	Infant	14Ma02Jk
CONNELLY, Margt.	21	F	Unknown	14Ma02Jk
CASEY, Lawrence	40	M	Unknown	14Ma02Jk
Margt.	13	F	Unknown	14Ma02Jk
John	10	M	Unknown	14Ma02Jk
WHITEHOUSE, Jas.	23	M	Unknown	14Ma02Jk
Matilda	21	F	Unknown	14Ma02Jk
Joseph	.00	M	Infant	14Ma02Jk
TIMMONS, Bernard	34	M	Unknown	14Ma02Jk
FOLEY, Jno.	17	M	Unknown	14Ma02Jk
Honora	18	F	Unknown	14Ma02Jk
MCKENNA, Wm.	40	M	Unknown	14Ma02Jk
MORRIS, Patt	14	M	Unknown	14Ma02Jk
FERRALL, Jno.	10	M	Unknown	14Ma02Jk
James	6	M	Child	14Ma02Jk
Ellen	4	F	Child	14Ma02Jk
Mary	.00	F	Infant	14Ma02Jk
CALLAGHAN, Ellen	22	F	Unknown	14Ma02Jk
FIFE, Edward	20	M	Unknown	14Ma02Jk
Cath.	19	F	Unknown	14Ma02Jk
COLLOGHER, Bridget	28	F	Unknown	14Ma02Jk
MORRIS, Pat	25	M	Unknown	14Ma02Jk
KEARY, Ed.	24	M	Unknown	14Ma02Jk
RYAN, Thomas	21	M	Unknown	14Ma02Jk
Wm.	18	M	Unknown	14Ma02Jk
DRYER, Tim	18	M	Unknown	14Ma02Jk
MAHER, Ellen	18	F	Unknown	14Ma02Jk
DOYLE, James	18	M	Unknown	14Ma02Jk
RYAN, Thomas	16	M	Unknown	14Ma02Jk
Mick	15	M	Unknown	14Ma02Jk
KELLY, Mick	40	M	Unknown	14Ma02Jk
HEWITT, Barney	37	M	Unknown	14Ma02Jk
Sally	30	F	Unknown	14Ma02Jk
POWER, Lawrence	47	M	Unknown	14Ma02Jk
HEWITT, Richd.	5	M	Child	14Ma02Jk
Margt.	2	F	Child	14Ma02Jk
John	.00	M	Infant	14Ma02Jk
RYAN, Mick	17	M	Unknown	14Ma02Jk
MADDIN, Ann	20	F	Unknown	14Ma02Jk
Bridget	7	F	Child	14Ma02Jk
Mick	4	M	Child	14Ma02Jk
MADDIN, Thomas	.00	M	Infant	14Ma02Jk
DANODY, Maria	30	F	Unknown	14Ma02Jk
WOODS, Maria	20	F	Unknown	14Ma02Jk
HANFORD, Mary	20	F	Unknown	14Ma02Jk
DARCY, Cath.	20	F	Unknown	14Ma02Jk
MARTIN, Cath.	51	F	Unknown	14Ma02Jk
Mick	21	M	Unknown	14Ma02Jk
CARRY, Jane-F.	22	M	Unknown	14Ma02Jk
LEE, John	24	M	Unknown	14Ma02Jk
BRADY, Berd.	26	M	Unknown	14Ma02Jk
COOPER, Saml.	30	M	Unknown	14Ma02Jk
IRVING, Jno.	45	M	Unknown	14Ma02Jk
Cath.	16	F	Unknown	14Ma02Jk
LEEDIN, Jos.	21	M	Unknown	14Ma02Jk
THOMPSON, Ann	24	F	Unknown	14Ma02Jk
Jane	.00	F	Infant	14Ma02Jk
CORCORAN, Thos.	50	M	Unknown	14Ma02Jk
Mary	45	F	Unknown	14Ma02Jk
James	18	M	Unknown	14Ma02Jk
Bessy	20	F	Unknown	14Ma02Jk
COYLE, James	20	M	Unknown	14Ma02Jk
COSTIGAN, Mary	20	F	Unknown	14Ma02Jk
PEARDEN, Patt	54	M	Unknown	14Ma02Jk
Patt	20	M	Unknown	14Ma02Jk
MAHONEY, Tim	25	M	Unknown	14Ma02Jk
REARDON, Jas.	18	M	Unknown	14Ma02Jk
Maria	22	F	Unknown	14Ma02Jk
Cath.	20	F	Unknown	14Ma02Jk
HARRIS, Norah	45	F	Unknown	14Ma02Jk
COLNE, Mary	40	F	Unknown	14Ma02Jk
BRIDGWATER, Mary	38	F	Unknown	14Ma02Jk
Ann	7	F	Child	14Ma02Jk
CONNER, Jno.	36	M	Unknown	14Ma02Jk
U-Mrs.	32	F	Unknown	14Ma02Jk
Wm.	2	M	Child	14Ma02Jk
Ellen	.00	F	Infant	14Ma02Jk
WHITELSEY, Jno.	21	M	Unknown	14Ma02Jk
Elleanor	18	F	Unknown	14Ma02Jk
Mary-Ann	16	F	Unknown	14Ma02Jk
TYRELL, John	25	M	Unknown	14Ma02Jk
Ann	24	F	Unknown	14Ma02Jk
ROGERS, Andrew	21	M	Unknown	14Ma02Jk
DOCKERTY, Jno.	23	M	Unknown	14Ma02Jk
WILLIAMS, Walter	24	M	Unknown	14Ma02Jk
MANDEVILLE, Thos.	20	M	Unknown	14Ma02Jk
FIELDS, Richd.	55	M	Unknown	14Ma02Jk
Wm.	26	M	Unknown	14Ma02Jk
Bridget	54	F	Unknown	14Ma02Jk
CLARKE, Wm.	26	M	Unknown	14Ma02Jk
Margt.	17	F	Unknown	14Ma02Jk
FORR, Michl.	22	M	Unknown	14Ma02Jk
HYLANDS, Michl.	35	M	Unknown	14Ma02Jk
LEONARD, Mary	20	F	Unknown	14Ma02Jk
MARTIN, Wm.	9	M	Child	14Ma02Jk
Martin	7	M	Child	14Ma02Jk
GOLDWATER, Mary	5	F	Child	14Ma02Jk
MCMARA, James	25	F	Unknown	14Ma02Jk
CONNER, Cath.	30	F	Unknown	14Ma02Jk
BANNON, Thos.	21	M	Unknown	14Ma02Jk
COOKE, Jacob	30	M	Unknown	14Ma02Jk
KILLCARRY, Bridget	20	F	Unknown	14Ma02Jk
Honora	18	F	Unknown	14Ma02Jk
LEMBEDS, Robt.	40	M	Unknown	14Ma02Jk
LUKE, Ann	20	F	Unknown	14Ma02Jk
HAMMILL, Patt	18	M	Unknown	14Ma02Jk
Rose	15	F	Unknown	14Ma02Jk
PERRALL, Nickolas	40	M	Unknown	14Ma02Jk
Mary	35	F	Unknown	14Ma02Jk
Anne	12	F	Unknown	14Ma02Jk
DOLARD, Wm.	21	M	Unknown	14Ma02Jk
HARRINGTON, Cornelius	30	M	Unknown	14Ma02Jk
MURPHY, John	20	M	Unknown	14Ma02Jk
Bridget	24	F	Unknown	14Ma02Jk
MCCARTY, C.	22	U	Unknown	14Ma02Jk
CULLINS, Jas.	24	M	Unknown	14Ma02Jk

NAMES OF PASSENGERS	AGE	SEX	OCCUPATIONS	DATE PORT SHIP
CULLINS, Margt.	24	F	Unknown	14Ma02Jk
Wm.	.00	M	Infant	14Ma02Jk
SHIELDS, Ed.	40	M	Unknown	14Ma02Jk
Mary-Ann	35	F	Unknown	14Ma02Jk
Matilda	7	F	Child	14Ma02Jk
Wm.	5	M	Child	14Ma02Jk
Arthur	.00	M	Infant	14Ma02Jk
BRIDGEWATER, Thos.	47	M	Unknown	14Ma02Jk
Mary	12	F	Unknown	14Ma02Jk
Mick	8	M	Child	14Ma02Jk
GALLAGHER, Mary	21	F	Unknown	14Ma02Jk
SMITH, Myles	41	M	Unknown	14Ma02Jk
JOHNSON, Martin	23	M	Unknown	14Ma02Jk
GRIMM, Jno.	20	M	Unknown	14Ma02Jk
LANDRIGAN, Thos.	20	M	Unknown	14Ma02Jk
Norah	22	F	Unknown	14Ma02Jk
BANNON, Jas.	30	M	Unknown	14Ma02Jk
MURPHY, Larry	26	M	Unknown	14Ma02Jk
MULDOON, Michl.	16	M	Unknown	14Ma02Jk
John	20	M	Unknown	14Ma02Jk
Mary	22	F	Unknown	14Ma02Jk
Cath.	45	F	Unknown	14Ma02Jk
Judith	40	F	Unknown	14Ma02Jk
RYAN, Dennis	45	M	Unknown	14Ma02Jk
FIRMANLAN, U-Mrs.	45	F	Unknown	14Ma02Jk
Wm.	17	M	Unknown	14Ma02Jk
Michl.	15	M	Unknown	14Ma02Jk
Patt	12	M	Unknown	14Ma02Jk
Dan	8	M	Child	14Ma02Jk
Mary	10	F	Unknown	14Ma02Jk
James	3	M	Child	14Ma02Jk
KENNEDY, Cath.	50	F	Unknown	14Ma02Jk
Mathw.	24	M	Unknown	14Ma02Jk
James	20	M	Unknown	14Ma02Jk
Biddy	22	F	Unknown	14Ma02Jk
John	13	M	Unknown	14Ma02Jk
Margt.	12	F	Unknown	14Ma02Jk
Dan	7	M	Child	14Ma02Jk
Patt	16	M	Unknown	14Ma02Jk
Thos.	3	M	Child	14Ma02Jk
Cath.	6	F	Child	14Ma02Jk
ONEIL, Mary	19	F	Unknown	14Ma02Jk
DONOHOE, Mary	21	F	Unknown	14Ma02Jk
DELAHANTY, Cath.	14	F	Unknown	14Ma02Jk
DOYLE, Patt	17	M	Unknown	14Ma02Jk
FREAL, Ann	20	F	Unknown	14Ma02Jk
FLANNAGAN, Honor	20	F	Unknown	14Ma02Jk
CUNNINGHAM, Jos.	25	M	Unknown	14Ma02Jk
Margt.	25	F	Unknown	14Ma02Jk
Ann	18	F	Unknown	14Ma02Jk
MILES, Martin	35	M	Unknown	14Ma02Jk
SWEENEY, Hugh	54	M	Unknown	14Ma02Jk
Hannah	36	F	Unknown	14Ma02Jk
Hugh	12	M	Unknown	14Ma02Jk
Peter	10	M	Unknown	14Ma02Jk
Ann	8	F	Child	14Ma02Jk
Ellen	6	F	Child	14Ma02Jk
Edward	.00	M	Infant	14Ma02Jk
KELLY, Mary	20	F	Unknown	14Ma02Jk
KAIN, Ellen	22	F	Unknown	14Ma02Jk
HANNAN, Sarah	20	F	Unknown	14Ma02Jk
HAKLAN, Pierce	27	M	Unknown	14Ma02Jk
CREAGHAN, Margt.	24	F	Unknown	14Ma02Jk
Cath.	9	F	Child	14Ma02Jk
Margt.	7	F	Child	14Ma02Jk
Teresa	.00	F	Infant	14Ma02Jk
RUSHTON, Francis	37	M	Unknown	14Ma02Jk
U-Mrs.	56	F	Unknown	14Ma02Jk
Sarah	18	F	Unknown	14Ma02Jk
Francis	17	M	Unknown	14Ma02Jk
Richd.	11	M	Unknown	14Ma02Jk
Susan	9	F	Child	14Ma02Jk
ROWAN, Johanna	30	F	Unknown	14Ma02Jk
Mary	13	F	Unknown	14Ma02Jk
Jno.	11	M	Unknown	14Ma02Jk
ROWAN, Bridget	9	F	Child	14Ma02Jk
CONNORS, Luke	36	M	Unknown	14Ma02Jk
BUCKLEY, Mary	20	F	Unknown	14Ma02Jk
DARRAN, James	35	M	Unknown	14Ma02Jk
James	18	M	Unknown	14Ma02Jk
BURKE, Thomas	24	M	Unknown	14Ma02Jk
FARRILL, Thomas	18	M	Unknown	14Ma02Jk
CUNNINGHAM, Mick	2	M	Child	14Ma02Jk
Mary	.00	M	Infant	14Ma02Jk
HAKLAN, Cath.	20	F	Unknown	14Ma02Jk
MAHER, Michl.	20	M	Unknown	14Ma02Jk
VALE, Thomas	25	M	Unknown	14Ma02Jk
James	20	M	Unknown	14Ma02Jk
HOLLAND, Margt.	26	F	Unknown	14Ma02Jk
DUNNE, Nancy	20	F	Unknown	14Ma02Jk
MCGEE, Pat	30	M	Unknown	14Ma02Jk
KING, Mary	20	F	Unknown	14Ma02Jk
FARRILL, Ann	20	F	Unknown	14Ma02Jk
GARVEY, Ann	20	F	Unknown	14Ma02Jk
DONOHOE, Jno.	12	M	Unknown	14Ma02Jk
SALLS, Ed.	32	M	Unknown	14Ma02Jk
MCCOY, Fred.	25	M	Unknown	14Ma02Jk
SULLIVAN, Ellen	25	F	Unknown	14Ma02Jk
DAINY, Wm.	12	M	Unknown	14Ma02Jk
QUEEN, Owen	25	M	Unknown	14Ma02Jk
GREENFIELD, John	28	M	Unknown	14Ma02Jk
Wm.S.	25	M	Unknown	14Ma02Jk
U-Mrs.	63	F	Unknown	14Ma02Jk
NICHOLS, Wm.	22	M	Unknown	14Ma02Jk
MCDERMOTT, Ellen	24	F	Unknown	14Ma02Jk
Winifred	19	M	Unknown	14Ma02Jk
ARMSTRONG, James	60	M	Unknown	14Ma02Jk
John	24	M	Unknown	14Ma02Jk
Ann-Jane	50	F	Unknown	14Ma02Jk
Archibald	10	M	Unknown	14Ma02Jk
William	8	M	Child	14Ma02Jk
Eliza	22	F	Unknown	14Ma02Jk
Amelia	15	F	Unknown	14Ma02Jk
Susan	19	F	Unknown	14Ma02Jk
Isabella	13	F	Unknown	14Ma02Jk
JOHNSON, U-Mrs.	21	F	Unknown	14Ma02Jk
SIM, Jos.	37	M	Unknown	14Ma02Jk
Jane	36	F	Unknown	14Ma02Jk
Mary	12	F	Unknown	14Ma02Jk
Daniel	10	M	Unknown	14Ma02Jk
Joshua	8	M	Child	14Ma02Jk
Jos.Wm.	5	M	Child	14Ma02Jk
John	3	M	Child	14Ma02Jk
LYAN, Jno.	33	M	Unknown	14Ma02Jk
CARROLL, Jno.	16	M	Unknown	14Ma02Jk

OPHELIA 14 MAY 1850

From Liverpool

NAMES OF PASSENGERS	AGE	SEX	OCCUPATIONS	DATE PORT SHIP
RYAN, Patt	24	M	Unknown	14Ma02Jl
DUNNEEN, Ellen	20	F	Unknown	14Ma02Jl
CURNS, Honora	19	F	Unknown	14Ma02Jl
COLLENS, Mary	23	F	Unknown	14Ma02Jl
CROWLEY, James	28	M	Unknown	14Ma02Jl
Mary	21	F	Unknown	14Ma02Jl
CHAMBERS, George	20	M	Unknown	14Ma02Jl
HARLEY, Ellen	24	F	Unknown	14Ma02Jl
Ellen	.00	F	Infant	14Ma02Jl
SULLIVAN, Catharine	34	F	Unknown	14Ma02Jl
HEGARTY, Daniel	27	M	Unknown	14Ma02Jl
QUAIN, Mary-A.	32	F	Unknown	14Ma02Jl
Margt.	17	F	Unknown	14Ma02Jl
OBRIEN, Corns.	20	M	Unknown	14Ma02Jl

NAMES OF PASSENGERS	AGE	SEX	OCCUPATIONS	DATE PORT SHIP
PINDER, Thomas	30	M	Unknown	14Ma02JI
Jane	28	F	Unknown	14Ma02JI
Ann	.00	F	Infant	14Ma02JI
BURREN, James	20	M	Unknown	14Ma02JI
LAHORTY, Catherine	25	F	Unknown	14Ma02JI
SMITH, Bridget	25	F	Unknown	14Ma02JI
BLYTH, U-Mrs.	38	F	Unknown	14Ma02JI
James	11	M	Unknown	14Ma02JI
Martin	9	M	Child	14Ma02JI
Patt	8	M	Child	14Ma02JI
Mary	5	F	Child	14Ma02JI
FLEMING, Edward	30	M	Unknown	14Ma02JI
RILEY, Patt	18	M	Unknown	14Ma02JI
BURK, Ellen	38	F	Unknown	14Ma02JI
Patt	10	M	Unknown	14Ma02JI
James	8	M	Child	14Ma02JI
Richard	6	M	Child	14Ma02JI
John	4	M	Child	14Ma02JI
SHAHAN, Maria	15	F	Unknown	14Ma02JI
BOSTER, Wm.	21	M	Unknown	14Ma02JI
Catharine	20	F	Unknown	14Ma02JI
MUBVILL, George	30	M	Unknown	14Ma02JI
Ann	22	F	Unknown	14Ma02JI
MAHON, Margt.	16	F	Unknown	14Ma02JI
Mary	10	F	Unknown	14Ma02JI
Patt	12	M	Unknown	14Ma02JI
REED, Michael	17	M	Unknown	14Ma02JI
Mark	20	M	Unknown	14Ma02JI
Cath.	15	F	Unknown	14Ma02JI
Mary	13	F	Unknown	14Ma02JI
Ellen	11	F	Unknown	14Ma02JI
EARL, James	45	M	Unknown	14Ma02JI
Rachel	45	F	Unknown	14Ma02JI
Robert	26	M	Unknown	14Ma02JI
David	23	M	Unknown	14Ma02JI
James	20	M	Unknown	14Ma02JI
Peggy-Ann	17	F	Unknown	14Ma02JI
Ellen	15	M	Unknown	14Ma02JI
Wm.George	10	M	Unknown	14Ma02JI
Martin	20	M	Unknown	14Ma02JI
MCCLAYON, James	20	M	Unknown	14Ma02JI
ARMSTRONG, David	55	M	Unknown	14Ma02JI
James	20	M	Unknown	14Ma02JI
SHEPHARD, John	40	M	Unknown	14Ma02JI
Betsy	39	F	Unknown	14Ma02JI
Mary	16	F	Unknown	14Ma02JI
Thomas	4	M	Child	14Ma02JI
Francis	.00	M	Infant	14Ma02JI
EINS, Catharine	16	F	Unknown	14Ma02JI
HALL, John	18	M	Unknown	14Ma02JI
FERGUSON, Wm.	24	M	Unknown	14Ma02JI
MULLALY, John	50	M	Unknown	14Ma02JI
Judy	20	F	Unknown	14Ma02JI
Lalley	18	F	Unknown	14Ma02JI
Mark	13	M	Unknown	14Ma02JI
Wm.	11	M	Unknown	14Ma02JI
Eliza	9	F	Child	14Ma02JI
Joanah	7	F	Child	14Ma02JI
Patt	5	M	Child	14Ma02JI
James	.00	M	Infant	14Ma02JI
MCLAYTON, Maria	16	F	Unknown	14Ma02JI
SIMMONS, Edward	32	M	Unknown	14Ma02JI
LEWIS, Edward	30	M	Unknown	14Ma02JI
HALEY, Mc.	30	M	Unknown	14Ma02JI
James	13	M	Unknown	14Ma02JI
CORBET, John	32	M	Unknown	14Ma02JI
Mary	12	F	Unknown	14Ma02JI
CARTELL, Mary	22	F	Unknown	14Ma02JI
OBRIEN, Maria	20	F	Unknown	14Ma02JI
CARTY, Olive	40	F	Unknown	14Ma02JI
Cate	13	F	Unknown	14Ma02JI
Mary	12	F	Unknown	14Ma02JI
John	11	M	Unknown	14Ma02JI
Thomas	8	M	Child	14Ma02JI
COWELL, Thomas	21	M	Unknown	14Ma02JI

NAMES OF PASSENGERS	AGE	SEX	OCCUPATIONS	DATE PORT SHIP
COWELL, U-Mrs.	21	F	Unknown	14Ma02JI
HUGHES, Patt	25	M	Unknown	14Ma02JI
OHARA, John	20	M	Unknown	14Ma02JI
BARNETT, Maria	22	F	Unknown	14Ma02JI
MCDERMOTT, Cath.	18	F	Unknown	14Ma02JI
GURTREY, Michl.	20	M	Unknown	14Ma02JI
CONROY, Maurice	20	M	Unknown	14Ma02JI
CLANCY, John	20	M	Unknown	14Ma02JI
MALONE, Patt	25	M	Unknown	14Ma02JI
CLARE, John	22	M	Unknown	14Ma02JI
MCMAHON, John	25	M	Unknown	14Ma02JI
SLATTERY, U-Mrs.	48	F	Unknown	14Ma02JI
HEWEY, Bernard	36	M	Unknown	14Ma02JI
CAINE, Michael	25	M	Unknown	14Ma02JI
GORMAN, Bridget	22	F	Unknown	14Ma02JI
HENWAY, James	19	M	Unknown	14Ma02JI
Margt.	19	F	Unknown	14Ma02JI
Cate	13	F	Unknown	14Ma02JI
Bridget	7	F	Child	14Ma02JI
Patt	10	M	Unknown	14Ma02JI
Bernard	8	M	Child	14Ma02JI
MEANRY, Bridget	38	F	Unknown	14Ma02JI
Bridget	4	F	Child	14Ma02JI
Michael	.00	M	Infant	14Ma02JI
BARNEY, James	30	M	Unknown	14Ma02JI
Wm.	28	M	Unknown	14Ma02JI
Mary	24	F	Unknown	14Ma02JI
Sally	24	F	Unknown	14Ma02JI
MCCONNELL, Patt	18	M	Unknown	14Ma02JI
COLLIGAN, Thomas	30	M	Unknown	14Ma02JI
Bridget	24	F	Unknown	14Ma02JI
MUDDY, Catharine	30	F	Unknown	14Ma02JI
Cate	4	F	Child	14Ma02JI
John	.00	M	Infant	14Ma02JI
CONNOLLY, Michl.	34	M	Unknown	14Ma02JI
DONNEGAN, Mick	30	M	Unknown	14Ma02JI
COWLAN, John	22	M	Unknown	14Ma02JI
ONEILL, Owen	21	M	Unknown	14Ma02JI
REGAN, John	28	M	Unknown	14Ma02JI
Jeremiah	24	M	Unknown	14Ma02JI
LACKFOY, John	21	M	Unknown	14Ma02JI
HUYRE, John	24	M	Unknown	14Ma02JI
REGAN, Mary	19	F	Unknown	14Ma02JI
FAHEY, Ellen	19	F	Unknown	14Ma02JI
BURKE, Dennis	30	M	Unknown	14Ma02JI
Julia	26	F	Unknown	14Ma02JI
TUCKER, Wm.	22	M	Unknown	14Ma02JI
LARGE, Thomas	19	M	Unknown	14Ma02JI
KENNEDY, John	24	M	Unknown	14Ma02JI
WALSH, John	20	M	Unknown	14Ma02JI
Judy	24	F	Unknown	14Ma02JI
Hannah	22	F	Unknown	14Ma02JI
Anne	19	F	Unknown	14Ma02JI
KESSHAN, Elisa	40	F	Unknown	14Ma02JI
AMOND, Wm.	34	M	Unknown	14Ma02JI
WHELAND, James	26	M	Unknown	14Ma02JI
GLENNAN, John	24	M	Unknown	14Ma02JI
FARRELL, Mary-Ann	18	F	Unknown	14Ma02JI
CONNOR, Martin	24	M	Unknown	14Ma02JI
Mary	17	F	Unknown	14Ma02JI
MURPHY, Margaret	20	F	Unknown	14Ma02JI
WHELAND, Sally	20	F	Unknown	14Ma02JI
FASSETT, Christy	20	M	Unknown	14Ma02JI
BURK, Wm.	30	M	Unknown	14Ma02JI
DOONAN, John	22	M	Unknown	14Ma02JI
HANTON, James	18	M	Unknown	14Ma02JI
MCCLOSKEY, James	21	M	Unknown	14Ma02JI
HILL, Wm.	50	M	Unknown	14Ma02JI
U-Mrs.	45	F	Unknown	14Ma02JI
Moses	20	M	Unknown	14Ma02JI
Abraham	17	M	Unknown	14Ma02JI
Jane	13	F	Unknown	14Ma02JI
Sarah	8	F	Child	14Ma02JI
Bess	6	F	Child	14Ma02JI
KANE, Ann-M.	12	F	Unknown	14Ma02JI

NAMES OF PASSENGERS	AGE	SEX	OCCUPATIONS	DATE PORT SHIP
MEE, John	22	M	Unknown	14Ma02Jl
Biddy	20	F	Unknown	14Ma02Jl
KINDLAND, Margt.	20	F	Unknown	14Ma02Jl
MCKENNA, Mathew	20	M	Unknown	14Ma02Jl
WILSON, Robert	30	M	Unknown	14Ma02Jl
Sarah	30	F	Unknown	14Ma02Jl
Ann	26	F	Unknown	14Ma02Jl
MARSHALL, Thomas	20	M	Unknown	14Ma02Jl
HATTON, Joseph	24	M	Unknown	14Ma02Jl
Matilda	23	F	Unknown	14Ma02Jl
MCCLUSKEY, Paul	50	M	Unknown	14Ma02Jl
Mary	45	F	Unknown	14Ma02Jl
Peggy	18	F	Unknown	14Ma02Jl
John	13	M	Unknown	14Ma02Jl
Mary	18	F	Unknown	14Ma02Jl
James	11	M	Unknown	14Ma02Jl
MCLOUGHLAN, James	20	M	Unknown	14Ma02Jl
Manny	21	M	Unknown	14Ma02Jl
Mary	21	F	Unknown	14Ma02Jl
HASSON, Jane	15	F	Unknown	14Ma02Jl
NALLY, Christy	26	M	Unknown	14Ma02Jl
Mary	40	F	Unknown	14Ma02Jl
Luke	16	M	Unknown	14Ma02Jl
Christy	9	M	Child	14Ma02Jl
Mary	7	F	Child	14Ma02Jl
James	2	M	Child	14Ma02Jl
MCCALL, Bridget	30	F	Unknown	14Ma02Jl
FINNEGAN, Thomas	30	M	Unknown	14Ma02Jl
MARCE, Patt	22	M	Unknown	14Ma02Jl
BREEN, Ann	21	F	Unknown	14Ma02Jl
REGAN, Micke	26	M	Unknown	14Ma02Jl
KELLEY, John	20	M	Unknown	14Ma02Jl
FURY, Biddy	20	F	Unknown	14Ma02Jl
MCCORMAC, John	40	M	Unknown	14Ma02Jl
John	13	M	Unknown	14Ma02Jl
Ellen	20	F	Unknown	14Ma02Jl
Kate	22	F	Unknown	14Ma02Jl
Bessey	24	F	Unknown	14Ma02Jl
HANNERY, John	22	M	Unknown	14Ma02Jl
LAWLESS, Mark	35	M	Unknown	14Ma02Jl
MINSEY, Ann	18	F	Unknown	14Ma02Jl
KING, John	26	M	Unknown	14Ma02Jl
Stephen	14	M	Unknown	14Ma02Jl
James	22	M	Unknown	14Ma02Jl
Patt	22	M	Unknown	14Ma02Jl
Mary	18	F	Unknown	14Ma02Jl
Ann	3	F	Child	14Ma02Jl
Margt.	2	F	Child	14Ma02Jl
MCKEE, John	17	M	Unknown	14Ma02Jl
Joseph	15	M	Unknown	14Ma02Jl
SHARP, Rose	50	F	Unknown	14Ma02Jl
MCAUDE, Cath.	18	F	Unknown	14Ma02Jl
SHARP, Bridget	20	F	Unknown	14Ma02Jl
Peter	12	M	Unknown	14Ma02Jl
Hannah	8	F	Child	14Ma02Jl
Mary	30	F	Unknown	14Ma02Jl
GALLAGHER, Peter	30	M	Unknown	14Ma02Jl
HUGHES, John	23	M	Unknown	14Ma02Jl
FOGARTY, Patt	25	M	Unknown	14Ma02Jl
EVANS, John	21	M	Unknown	14Ma02Jl
REGAN, Patt	28	M	Unknown	14Ma02Jl
Owen	24	M	Unknown	14Ma02Jl
Judy	27	F	Unknown	14Ma02Jl
Norah	3	F	Child	14Ma02Jl
DAWSON, Jeremiah	23	M	Unknown	14Ma02Jl
HARLAN, James	14	M	Unknown	14Ma02Jl
CAMPION, John	23	M	Unknown	14Ma02Jl
REGAN, David	22	M	Unknown	14Ma02Jl
FINLAND, John	26	M	Unknown	14Ma02Jl
HASSETT, Mary	22	F	Unknown	14Ma02Jl

AMBASSADRESS 14 MAY 1850

From Liverpool

NAMES OF PASSENGERS	AGE	SEX	OCCUPATIONS	DATE PORT SHIP
SPALDING, Alex.	57	M	Farmer	14Ma02Js
Mary	50	F	Wife	14Ma02Js
Robt.	24	M	Farmer	14Ma02Js
Jane	22	F	Spinster	14Ma02Js
Thos.	20	M	Farmer	14Ma02Js
Elizth.	20	F	Spinster	14Ma02Js
Margt.	18	F	Spinster	14Ma02Js
Alexr.	16	M	Unknown	14Ma02Js
Jas.	14	M	Unknown	14Ma02Js
John	12	M	Unknown	14Ma02Js
Isabella	10	F	Spinster	14Ma02Js
MALONE, D.	25	M	Surgeon	14Ma02Js
MCCABE, Mat	40	M	Laborer	14Ma02Js
Mary	30	F	Wife	14Ma02Js
Sarah	30	F	Spinster	14Ma02Js
Mary	12	F	Spinster	14Ma02Js
KENNEDY, Jas.	26	M	Laborer	14Ma02Js
WALSH, Thos.	23	M	Laborer	14Ma02Js
FOY, John	46	M	Laborer	14Ma02Js
Bridgt.	46	F	Wife	14Ma02Js
Pat	22	M	Laborer	14Ma02Js
Susannah	22	F	Spinster	14Ma02Js
Nancy	20	F	Spinster	14Ma02Js
Mary	18	F	Spinster	14Ma02Js
Bernard	13	M	Unknown	14Ma02Js
MORAN, Jno.	21	M	Laborer	14Ma02Js
RADIGHAN, Farrel	20	M	Laborer	14Ma02Js
CAMPBELL, Pat	21	M	Laborer	14Ma02Js
BOLAND, Michl.	40	M	Laborer	14Ma02Js
CLIFFORD, Jas.	22	M	Laborer	14Ma02Js
GALLAGHER, Pat	30	M	Laborer	14Ma02Js
WAGNER, Pat	30	M	Laborer	14Ma02Js
WARD, Cath.	26	F	Spinster	14Ma02Js
FITZPATRICK, Corn.	22	M	Laborer	14Ma02Js
Jno.	20	M	Laborer	14Ma02Js
DONNELLY, Michl.	20	M	Laborer	14Ma02Js
RIELLY, Hugh	24	M	Laborer	14Ma02Js
Mary	19	F	Spinster	14Ma02Js
MCDERMOTT, Cath.	25	F	Wife	14Ma02Js
Elizth.	.08	F	Infant	14Ma02Js
Rod.	14	M	Unknown	14Ma02Js
Thos.	10	M	Unknown	14Ma02Js
Bridgt.	.06	F	Infant	14Ma02Js
ROCHE, Mary	45	F	None	14Ma02Js
Wm.	15	M	Laborer	14Ma02Js
GREARY, Jno.	20	M	Laborer	14Ma02Js
KEOGH, Owen	20	M	Laborer	14Ma02Js
JAYNEY, Jas.	24	M	Laborer	14Ma02Js
Hugh	22	M	Laborer	14Ma02Js
MCMAHON, Mary	20	F	Spinster	14Ma02Js
MURPHY, Jos.	18	M	Laborer	14Ma02Js
RISPIN, Jno.	59	M	Laborer	14Ma02Js
Jno.Jr.	27	M	Laborer	14Ma02Js
Jas.	13	M	Unknown	14Ma02Js
Jno.	9	M	Child	14Ma02Js
Ann	50	F	None	14Ma02Js
Ann	11	F	Spinster	14Ma02Js
QUINNEN, Mary	50	F	Wi	14Ma02Js
Geo.	22	M	Laborer	14Ma02Js
MCCODY, L.	22	M	Laborer	14Ma02Js
MALLY, J.	50	M	Laborer	14Ma02Js
Mary	40	F	Wife	14Ma02Js
Jno.	25	M	Laborer	14Ma02Js
Brig.	40	F	Wife	14Ma02Js
Arthur	.09	M	Infant	14Ma02Js

NAMES OF PASSENGERS	AGE	SEX	OCCUPATIONS	DATE PORT SHIP
MALLY, Mary	12	F	Unknown	14Ma02Js
CARNON, Pat	24	M	Laborer	14Ma02Js
Mary	16	F	Spinster	14Ma02Js
NEIL, Corn.	13	M	Unknown	14Ma02Js
MALLY, Henry	12	M	Unknown	14Ma02Js
KEAN, Aly	12	F	Unknown	14Ma02Js
LAILLICH, Ann	16	F	Spinster	14Ma02Js
MEALLY, Ella	16	F	Spinster	14Ma02Js
REILLY, Hon.	20	F	Spinster	14Ma02Js
BOURKE, Hugh	40	M	Laborer	14Ma02Js
Mary	28	F	Wife	14Ma02Js
Peter	.08	M	Infant	14Ma02Js
JOHNSON, Saml.	30	M	Laborer	14Ma02Js
Letitia	32	F	Wife	14Ma02Js
HUGHES, Geo.	22	M	Laborer	14Ma02Js
Harriet	22	F	Wife	14Ma02Js
Roy	20	M	Laborer	14Ma02Js
POPE, Edwd.	18	M	Laborer	14Ma02Js
RYAN, Bernard	25	M	Laborer	14Ma02Js
MITCHELL, Thos.	25	M	Laborer	14Ma02Js
MORAN, Danl.	23	M	Laborer	14Ma02Js
GONLAN, Mary	18	F	Spinster	14Ma02Js
REGAN, Cath.	20	F	Spinster	14Ma02Js
WRIGHT, Mgt.	30	F	Wife	14Ma02Js
Thos.	.06	M	Infant	14Ma02Js
HASTINGS, Wm.	33	M	Laborer	14Ma02Js
HARSLY, Mary	22	F	Wife	14Ma02Js
DINNON, Jas.	24	M	Laborer	14Ma02Js
Cath.	18	F	Spinster	14Ma02Js
RONEY, Jno.	30	M	Laborer	14Ma02Js
SHERIDAN, Jas.	25	M	Laborer	14Ma02Js
Cath.	30	F	Wife	14Ma02Js
RISCON, Benj.	40	M	Shoemaker	14Ma02Js
SMITH, Jno.	22	M	Laborer	14Ma02Js
FARN, Jas.	19	M	Tailor	14Ma02Js
DAFFY, Mary	18	F	Spinster	14Ma02Js
BROOKER, Wm.	50	M	Farmer	14Ma02Js
Charlotte	45	F	Wife	14Ma02Js
Charlotte	19	F	Spinster	14Ma02Js
Ann	16	F	Spinster	14Ma02Js
Wm.	14	M	Unknown	14Ma02Js
Harriet	12	F	Unknown	14Ma02Js
MALY, Jno.	30	M	Laborer	14Ma02Js
MCCANN, Sarah	50	F	None	14Ma02Js
Mary	20	F	Spinster	14Ma02Js
MORAN, Jereme	50	M	Laborer	14Ma02Js
MCGRATH, Ann	20	F	Spinster	14Ma02Js
WOODLY, Wm.	40	M	Laborer	14Ma02Js
Jane	30	F	Wife	14Ma02Js
John	7	M	Child	14Ma02Js
Jane	.05	F	Infant	14Ma02Js
MCKER, Jas.	40	M	Laborer	14Ma02Js
BRIMAN, Pat	35	M	Laborer	14Ma02Js
BRENNAN, Alice	30	F	Wife	14Ma02Js
Edwd.	.06	M	Infant	14Ma02Js
WALSH, Mat.	35	M	Laborer	14Ma02Js
MCGENRAN, Margt.	20	F	Spinster	14Ma02Js
MCGORMAN, Jane	20	F	Spinster	14Ma02Js
HUNTER, Jno.	25	M	Laborer	14Ma02Js
MARTIN, Joseph	68	M	Laborer	14Ma02Js
HEFFERMAN, Danl.	20	M	Laborer	14Ma02Js
STENSON, Sam	30	M	Farmer	14Ma02Js
Amy	22	F	Wife	14Ma02Js
Mary	.06	F	Infant	14Ma02Js
BERKSHIRE, Josh.	21	M	Hatter	14Ma02Js
WRIGHT, David	40	M	Laborer	14Ma02Js
Jane	30	F	Wife	14Ma02Js
Jno.	26	M	Laborer	14Ma02Js
Wm.	18	M	Laborer	14Ma02Js
Elizth.	25	F	Spinster	14Ma02Js
SCOTT, Jas.	50	M	Printer	14Ma02Js
MCCORMICK, Danl.	20	M	Laborer	14Ma02Js
NULTY, Michl.	50	M	Laborer	14Ma02Js
Julia	18	F	Spinster	14Ma02Js
Pat	12	M	Unknown	14Ma02Js
PALMER, Terry	25	M	Laborer	14Ma02Js
LARKIN, Ann	32	F	Spinster	14Ma02Js
MCCABE, James	20	M	Laborer	14Ma02Js
MCGALLY, Mary	30	F	Spinster	14Ma02Js
MAY, Pat	32	M	Laborer	14Ma02Js
SIMMS, Ellen	37	F	Spinster	14Ma02Js
NEIL, Jno.	30	M	Laborer	14Ma02Js
MCNEIL, Ann	30	F	Wife	14Ma02Js
BROWNE, Jas.	28	M	Laborer	14Ma02Js
CASPER, Eliza	25	F	Spinster	14Ma02Js
MCDOWL, Jane	30	F	Spinster	14Ma02Js
QUIGLEY, Bridg.	66	F	None	14Ma02Js
BRANNEN, Jas.	28	M	Laborer	14Ma02Js
Mary	28	F	Wife	14Ma02Js
HARTNELL, Ann	50	F	Wi	14Ma02Js
Jane	23	F	Spinster	14Ma02Js
Anne	20	F	Spinster	14Ma02Js
BUCKLEY, Mary	17	F	Spinster	14Ma02Js
ONEIL, Thos.	14	M	Unknown	14Ma02Js
Jas.	12	M	Unknown	14Ma02Js
Jno.	10	M	Unknown	14Ma02Js
GATES, Jas.	23	M	Laborer	14Ma02Js
HAGAN, Eliza	20	F	Wife	14Ma02Js
KINSAL, Cath.	22	F	Spinster	14Ma02Js
MCLEAN, Thos.	16	M	Laborer	14Ma02Js
Jno.	12	M	Unknown	14Ma02Js
PRICE, Margt.	20	M	Spinster	14Ma02Js
HUNTER, Pat	36	M	Laborer	14Ma02Js
EAGAN, Jno.	40	M	Laborer	14Ma02Js
Anne	18	F	Spinster	14Ma02Js
PHILLIPS, John	50	M	Laborer	14Ma02Js
Bridgt.	45	F	Wife	14Ma02Js
Pat	12	M	Unknown	14Ma02Js
Peter	4	M	Child	14Ma02Js
John	.06	M	Infant	14Ma02Js
MATHEWS, Mary	22	F	Spinster	14Ma02Js
STANLY, Eliz.	23	F	Spinster	14Ma02Js
MARTIN, Michl.	30	M	Laborer	14Ma02Js
CONDON, Mary	20	F	Spinster	14Ma02Js
DANBRY, Pat	27	M	Laborer	14Ma02Js
CRAILY, Richd.	25	M	Laborer	14Ma02Js
MCCALLY, Peter	28	M	Laborer	14Ma02Js
MCCABE, Margt.	20	F	Spinster	14Ma02Js
WINDLE, John	39	M	Laborer	14Ma02Js
Harriet	28	F	Wife	14Ma02Js
Sarah	.06	F	Infant	14Ma02Js
Jno.	.06	M	Infant	14Ma02Js
RALLEAGH, Jno.	28	M	Laborer	14Ma02Js
GRIFFIN, Pat	40	M	Laborer	14Ma02Js
Cath.	40	F	Wife	14Ma02Js
FINN, Thos.	20	M	Laborer	14Ma02Js
REILLY, Michl.	40	M	Laborer	14Ma02Js
MCDOWL, Pat	40	M	Laborer	14Ma02Js
Bernard	40	M	Laborer	14Ma02Js
MCCARTIN, Jas.	25	M	Laborer	14Ma02Js
John	19	M	Laborer	14Ma02Js
GARATY, Thos.	23	M	Laborer	14Ma02Js
SHARPE, Margt.	20	F	Spinster	14Ma02Js
KILPATRICK, Michl.	17	M	Laborer	14Ma02Js
WALSH, Pat	20	M	Laborer	14Ma02Js
BRADY, D.	20	M	Laborer	14Ma02Js
IRVIN, Jno.	20	M	Laborer	14Ma02Js
GLENN, Thos.	20	M	Laborer	14Ma02Js
ONEAL, Jane	21	F	Spinster	14Ma02Js
LIPPY, Thos.	23	M	Laborer	14Ma02Js
Catherine	27	F	Wife	14Ma02Js
Edwd.	.06	M	Infant	14Ma02Js
PARKE, Robt.	20	M	Laborer	14Ma02Js
Matilda	21	F	Wife	14Ma02Js
HARPER, Wm.	25	M	Laborer	14Ma02Js
LAYNE, Adam	35	M	Laborer	14Ma02Js
BALINSE, Rachel	18	F	Spinster	14Ma02Js
FINN, M.	40	M	Farmer	14Ma02Js
Ellen	30	F	Wife	14Ma02Js
Michl.	.08	M	Infant	14Ma02Js

NAMES OF PASSENGERS	AGE	SEX	OCCUPATIONS	DATE PORT SHIP
DUGGAN, Jas.	19	M	Tailor	14Ma02Js
COLLINS, Susan	18	F	Spinster	14Ma02Js
MCENNOR, Bridgt.	20	F	Spinster	14Ma02Js
SMITH, Jas.	26	M	Laborer	14Ma02Js
LENNON, Jas.	35	M	Laborer	14Ma02Js
KIRK, Henry	31	M	Laborer	14Ma02Js
COULTON, Margt.	50	F	Wi	14Ma02Js
Alex.	30	M	Laborer	14Ma02Js
MANLEY, Cath.	30	F	Wife	14Ma02Js
Margt.	.09	F	Infant	14Ma02Js
Mary	3	F	Child	14Ma02Js
BRENNON, Ann	21	F	Spinster	14Ma02Js
CLARKE, Mary	20	F	Spinster	14Ma02Js
DUFFY, Ellen	40	F	Wife	14Ma02Js
Rose	.08	F	Infant	14Ma02Js
Died-At-Sea				
MURREY, Mary	28	F	Spinster	14Ma02Js
Margt.	23	F	Spinster	14Ma02Js
MCCARDLE, Cath.	28	F	Spinster	14Ma02Js
DUFFY, Jno.	3	M	Child	14Ma02Js
BOYLE, Mary	30	F	Spinster	14Ma02Js
MCGRATH, Pat	19	M	Laborer	14Ma02Js
Honora	24	F	Spinster	14Ma02Js
MARA, Jno.	40	M	Laborer	14Ma02Js
Mary	40	F	Wife	14Ma02Js
Wm.	12	M	Unknown	14Ma02Js
Thos.	8	M	Child	14Ma02Js
Joseph	.09	M	Infant	14Ma02Js
Mary	5	F	Child	14Ma02Js
Susan	11	F	Unknown	14Ma02Js
SAPHINSON, Peter	36	M	Laborer	14Ma02Js
RYDER, Jno.	26	M	Laborer	14Ma02Js
HURSTON, Chr.	34	M	Servant	14Ma02Js
Ann	31	F	Wife	14Ma02Js
Richd.	.08	M	Infant	14Ma02Js
MIDDLETON, Hy.	26	M	Teacher	14Ma02Js
Emma	24	F	Wife	14Ma02Js
HEFFERMAN, Hy.	22	M	Laborer	14Ma02Js
Corn.	20	M	Laborer	14Ma02Js
John	18	M	Laborer	14Ma02Js
BRENNAN, Bridgt.	30	F	Spinster	14Ma02Js
SPILLAND, Mat.	50	M	Laborer	14Ma02Js
MURPHY, Anne	30	F	Spinster	14Ma02Js
MCCOY, Rose	40	F	None	14Ma02Js
Pat	11	M	Unknown	14Ma02Js
Mary	6	F	Child	14Ma02Js
GRAY, Wm.	20	M	Laborer	14Ma02Js
RUSSELL, Tim.	35	M	Farmer	14Ma02Js
RONTER, Jas.	30	M	Laborer	14Ma02Js
KERNY, Michl.	24	M	Laborer	14Ma02Js
Lara	16	F	Laborer	14Ma02Js
ELLIS, Isabella	17	F	Spinster	14Ma02Js
Dib.	13	M	Spinner	14Ma02Js
Hy.	11	M	Spinner	14Ma02Js
RYAN, Cath.	18	F	Spinster	14Ma02Js
HINDER, Alex.	18	M	Laborer	14Ma02Js
DAFFRY, Jas.	30	M	Laborer	14Ma02Js
MEALY, Edw.	22	M	Laborer	14Ma02Js
WOODKIN, Thos.	30	M	Laborer	14Ma02Js
TONER, Jno.	36	M	Laborer	14Ma02Js
Wm.	33	M	Laborer	14Ma02Js
HONONAH, Hugh	20	M	Laborer	14Ma02Js
MCLEAN, Michl.	30	M	Laborer	14Ma02Js
CONNELL, Mar.	28	M	Laborer	14Ma02Js
DALEY, Cath.	20	F	Spinster	14Ma02Js
FROST, Anthy.	40	M	Laborer	14Ma02Js
SYKES, Anna	25	F	Spinster	14Ma02Js
Eliza	23	F	Spinster	14Ma02Js
FINN, Jas.	20	M	Laborer	14Ma02Js
MARE, Maren	20	F	Spinster	14Ma02Js
CUNNINGHAM, Michl.	23	M	Laborer	14Ma02Js
PATTEN, Edwd.	18	M	Laborer	14Ma02Js
CONNOLLY, Mat.	22	M	Laborer	14Ma02Js
CARROLL, Aby	22	M	Laborer	14Ma02Js
GORMAN, Jno.	22	M	Laborer	14Ma02Js
CALLAGH, Michl.	20	M	Victualler	14Ma02Js
NAUGHTON, Bryan	20	M	Laborer	14Ma02Js
SWEENY, Mary	20	F	Spinster	14Ma02Js
MCKERR, Jno.	34	M	Carpenter	14Ma02Js
HICKEY, Edwd.	30	M	Laborer	14Ma02Js
HALEY, And.	12	M	Unknown	14Ma02Js
BOURKE, Mary	36	F	Spinster	14Ma02Js
HALEY, Jno.	56	M	Laborer	14Ma02Js
MCGRATH, Pat	18	M	Laborer	14Ma02Js
FINLAY, Jas.	26	M	Laborer	14Ma02Js
FANHOTH, J.	19	M	Laborer	14Ma02Js
MCLEAN, Chs.	26	M	Laborer	14Ma02Js
DUFFY, Pat	50	M	Laborer	14Ma02Js
Died-At-Sea				
ARMSTRONG, Robt.	17	M	Laborer	14Ma02Js
Mgt.	.09	F	Infant	14Ma02Js
MARTIN, Jas.	26	M	Laborer	14Ma02Js
MCQUIGLEY, John	26	M	Laborer	14Ma02Js
BURKES, Thos.	24	M	Laborer	14Ma02Js

HUGUENOT 14 MAY 1850

From Liverpool

NAMES OF PASSENGERS	AGE	SEX	OCCUPATIONS	DATE PORT SHIP
KERNEY, John	40	M	Laborer	14Ma02Jm
BRIEN, Denis	18	M	Farmer	14Ma02Jm
HICKS, George	40	M	Imkr	14Ma02Jm
FITZSIMMONS, Cathn.	24	F	Servant	14Ma02Jm
Bridget	22	F	Servant	14Ma02Jm
WRITE, Joseph	26	M	Farmer	14Ma02Jm
Jam.	24	M	Farmer	14Ma02Jm
Wm.	22	M	Farmer	14Ma02Jm
DRISCOLL, Wm.	21	M	Farmer	14Ma02Jm
TESSE, Margt.	26	F	Servant	14Ma02Jm
KOCH, Margt.	14	F	Servant	14Ma02Jm
BERGAN, Mary	28	F	Servant	14Ma02Jm
Patrick	22	M	Farmer	14Ma02Jm
Johanna	23	F	Servant	14Ma02Jm
FOGARTY, Johanna	22	F	Servant	14Ma02Jm
CLARA, Mary	32	F	Servant	14Ma02Jm
Wm.	6	M	Child	14Ma02Jm
Ellen	.09	F	Infant	14Ma02Jm
FITZGERRALD, Charles	27	M	Farmer	14Ma02Jm
RUSSELL, Edwd	24	M	Hrsdlr	14Ma02Jm
GARMON, John	31	M	Farmer	14Ma02Jm
BRYAN, Pat	20	M	Shoemaker	14Ma02Jm
BINDON, Richard	20	M	Tailor	14Ma02Jm
DAILSTON, Michl.	34	M	Farmer	14Ma02Jm
LONDRIGAN, Richd.	20	M	Farmer	14Ma02Jm
BRENNAN, Thomas	24	M	Laborer	14Ma02Jm
COGLIN, John	30	M	Laborer	14Ma02Jm
PHELAN, Ellen	25	F	Servant	14Ma02Jm
Catherine	21	F	Servant	14Ma02Jm
SMITHY, Ellen	28	F	Servant	14Ma02Jm
ODONALLE, Wm.	32	M	Farmer	14Ma02Jm
Winifred	27	F	Farmer	14Ma02Jm
HONNOLEY, Ellen	30	F	Dressmaker	14Ma02Jm
Margt.	.04	F	Infant	14Ma02Jm
FITZGIBBONS, Winifred	20	F	Servant	14Ma02Jm
COX, Richd.	20	M	Mechanic	14Ma02Jm
Catherine	20	F	Mechanic	14Ma02Jm
KERNAN, John	18	M	Farmer	14Ma02Jm
BOWE, Richd.	30	M	Farmer	14Ma02Jm
Biddy	40	F	Farmer	14Ma02Jm
Mary	38	F	Farmer	14Ma02Jm
WALSH, John	20	M	Tailor	14Ma02Jm
CARROLL, John	20	M	Groom	14Ma02Jm
BERGAN, Dennis	32	M	Fsvnt	14Ma02Jm
DOLLORD, Catharine	20	F	Fsvnt	14Ma02Jm

NAMES OF PASSENGERS	AGE	SEX	OCCUPATIONS	DATE PORT SHIP
DOUGHTY, Ann	45	F	Farmer	14Ma02Jm
Geo.	20	M	Farmer	14Ma02Jm
Bess	20	F	Farmer	14Ma02Jm
Henry	16	M	Farmer	14Ma02Jm
LEVY, Thomas	40	M	Farmer	14Ma02Jm
James	8	M	Child	14Ma02Jm
Jno.	6	M	Child	14Ma02Jm
HORAN, Dan	45	M	Farmer	14Ma02Jm
Catharine	12	F	Farmer	14Ma02Jm
KROUGH, Johanna	15	F	Servant	14Ma02Jm
Sarah	13	F	Servant	14Ma02Jm
HORRAN, Margt.	21	F	Servant	14Ma02Jm
FLYNN, Mickl.	16	M	Servant	14Ma02Jm
CORAN, Thos.	50	M	Farmer	14Ma02Jm
Jeremh.	13	M	Farmer	14Ma02Jm
Honora	11	F	Farmer	14Ma02Jm
Mary	50	F	Farmer	14Ma02Jm
Julia	16	F	Farmer	14Ma02Jm
HORAN, David	23	M	Farmer	14Ma02Jm
LELAND, Mary	4	F	Child	14Ma02Jm
MCCARTY, John	24	M	Laborer	14Ma02Jm
POWER, Wm.	23	M	Shoemaker	14Ma02Jm
Mary	25	F	Shoemaker	14Ma02Jm
LEONARD, Nat	21	M	Laborer	14Ma02Jm
RORA, Thomas	28	M	Tailor	14Ma02Jm
Mary	20	F	Tailor	14Ma02Jm
Margaret	22	F	Servant	14Ma02Jm
MCDONALD, Bridget	20	F	Servant	14Ma02Jm
MONOHON, Margt.	20	F	Servant	14Ma02Jm
MCGEE, Robert	20	M	Farmer	14Ma02Jm
John	18	M	Farmer	14Ma02Jm
GOODWIN, Arnold	30	M	Bookmaker	14Ma02Jm
Frances-Ann	22	F	Bookmaker	14Ma02Jm
Sarah-Ann	30	F	Bookmaker	14Ma02Jm
Eliza-Jane	.08	F	Infant	14Ma02Jm
SMITH, Mary-Ann	18	F	Spinster	14Ma02Jm
WILSON, Richd.	32	M	Clerk	14Ma02Jm
Eliza	28	F	Servant	14Ma02Jm
Letty	24	F	Servant	14Ma02Jm
Ann	18	F	Servant	14Ma02Jm
NICKLE, Maria	20	F	Servant	14Ma02Jm
GRIFFITHS, Thomas	20	M	Laborer	14Ma02Jm
HEATH, Francis	20	M	Flabr	14Ma02Jm
Eliza	18	F	Flabr	14Ma02Jm
KERNEY, Hannah	18	F	Servant	14Ma02Jm
JOHNSTONE, Jane	16	F	Servant	14Ma02Jm
MOONEY, Mary	16	F	Dressmaker	14Ma02Jm
STOKES, Mary	16	F	Dressmaker	14Ma02Jm
MCGILL, Thomas	27	M	Farmer	14Ma02Jm
Mary	27	F	Farmer	14Ma02Jm
John	4	M	Child	14Ma02Jm
HOWARD, Michl.	18	M	Laborer	14Ma02Jm
MCGUINESS, Mary	20	F	Seamstress	14Ma02Jm
BUTLER, Ellen	21	F	Seamstress	14Ma02Jm
Thomas	16	M	Joiner	14Ma02Jm
MCMANUS, James	30	M	Farmer	14Ma02Jm
Ellen	30	F	Farmer	14Ma02Jm
Elizh.	17	F	Farmer	14Ma02Jm
TRAY, William	32	M	Farmer	14Ma02Jm
FRAY, Eliza	40	F	Farmer	14Ma02Jm
KEAN, Patrick	22	M	Servant	14Ma02Jm
Catherine	22	F	Servant	14Ma02Jm
KELLY, Mary	22	F	Servant	14Ma02Jm
ALPIN, John	22	M	Manservant	14Ma02Jm
MAHOONEY, Margt.	22	F	Servant	14Ma02Jm
BYERS, James	25	M	Farmer	14Ma02Jm
Jos.	20	M	Farmer	14Ma02Jm
Mary	17	F	Farmer	14Ma02Jm
HICKEN, Pat	35	M	Farmer	14Ma02Jm
Johanna	32	F	Farmer	14Ma02Jm
Jane	4	F	Child	14Ma02Jm
Catharine	2	F	Child	14Ma02Jm
Hannah	.06	F	Infant	14Ma02Jm
Died-At-Sea				
WALSH, Pat.	22	M	Farmer	14Ma02Jm

NAMES OF PASSENGERS	AGE	SEX	OCCUPATIONS	DATE PORT SHIP
WALSH, Jane	22	F	Farmer	14Ma02Jm
GLEASON, Wm.	50	M	Farmer	14Ma02Jm
Ellen	21	F	Farmer	14Ma02Jm
Mick	16	M	Farmer	14Ma02Jm
Kate	15	F	Farmer	14Ma02Jm
Willm.	10	M	Farmer	14Ma02Jm
Dennis	8	M	Child	14Ma02Jm
Margaret	13	F	Farmer	14Ma02Jm
John	3	M	Child	14Ma02Jm
Mary	45	F	Farmer	14Ma02Jm
Mary	8	F	Child	14Ma02Jm
REAL, John	34	M	Farmer	14Ma02Jm
Pat.	12	M	Farmer	14Ma02Jm
MAROONEY, Kate	35	F	Servant	14Ma02Jm
SHERIDAN, Catherine	23	F	Servant	14Ma02Jm
Alice	17	F	Servant	14Ma02Jm
NOLIN, Pat.	20	M	Laborer	14Ma02Jm
MURPHY, Mich.	20	M	Laborer	14Ma02Jm
CULLEN, David	38	M	Laborer	14Ma02Jm
Catherine	37	F	Laborer	14Ma02Jm
Ellen	12	F	Laborer	14Ma02Jm
Margaret	10	F	Laborer	14Ma02Jm
Michl.	8	M	Child	14Ma02Jm
Dennis	6	M	Child	14Ma02Jm
William	5	M	Child	14Ma02Jm
LANTREY, Michl.	25	M	Joiner	14Ma02Jm
ODONNELL, Nappy	20	F	Lad	14Ma02Jm
BOYLE, Catherine	25	F	Lad	14Ma02Jm
GRADY, Lacky	60	M	Laborer	14Ma02Jm
Biddy	60	F	Laborer	14Ma02Jm
Matthew	13	M	Laborer	14Ma02Jm
Lacky	11	M	Laborer	14Ma02Jm
Mattw.	9	M	Child	14Ma02Jm
HAGGERTY, Ann	40	F	Servant	14Ma02Jm
Mary	13	F	Servant	14Ma02Jm
Peggy	13	F	Servant	14Ma02Jm
Biddy	11	F	Servant	14Ma02Jm
Mary	50	F	Servant	14Ma02Jm
John	18	M	Manservant	14Ma02Jm
MCCONNIGLE, John	18	M	Stone Mason	14Ma02Jm
CARNEY, Michl.	12	M	Stone Mason	14Ma02Jm
MCGRATH, Biddy	15	F	Unknown	14Ma02Jm
DRISCOLL, Timothy	23	M	Farmer	14Ma02Jm
Cornelius	24	M	Farmer	14Ma02Jm
GORGAN, Mary	24	F	Seamstress	14Ma02Jm
DEMPY, Betty	20	F	Seamstress	14Ma02Jm
MCGANGLE, Terence	30	M	Farmer	14Ma02Jm
Biddy	30	F	Farmer	14Ma02Jm
Horan	.08	M	Infant	14Ma02Jm
Died-At-Sea				
MCELVINE, Rebecca	18	F	Servant	14Ma02Jm
KERNEY, Biddy	20	F	Servant	14Ma02Jm
KELLEY, James	30	M	Farmer	14Ma02Jm
Margaret	70	F	Farmer	14Ma02Jm
WISHAM, Mary	23	F	Seamstress	14Ma02Jm
KELLY, Martha	20	F	Seamstress	14Ma02Jm
FASLEY, David	23	M	Fsvnt	14Ma02Jm
WELSH, Mary	40	F	Fsvnt	14Ma02Jm
Anthony	10	M	Fsvnt	14Ma02Jm
Catherine	8	F	Child	14Ma02Jm
Ellen	4	F	Child	14Ma02Jm
JADWOOD, Blythe	32	M	Fsvnt	14Ma02Jm
KEEGAN, James	24	M	Farmer	14Ma02Jm
MONAHON, Michl.	20	M	Manservant	14Ma02Jm
MEEGAN, John	24	M	Manservant	14Ma02Jm
BROGAN, James	20	M	Laborer	14Ma02Jm
MCCONNIGLE, Charles	25	M	Fsvnt	14Ma02Jm
DWANE, Ann	20	F	Dressmaker	14Ma02Jm
MORRISON, Ellen	21	F	Servant	14Ma02Jm
SULLIVAN, Peter	33	M	Ewd	14Ma02Jm
WALLAHON, John	24	M	Shoemaker	14Ma02Jm
MCGILLIS, Corn.	30	M	Laborer	14Ma02Jm
Catherine	22	F	Laborer	14Ma02Jm
AIKEN, Bridget	22	F	Servant	14Ma02Jm
MCCUE, Nappy	22	F	Servant	14Ma02Jm

NAMES OF PASSENGERS	AGE	SEX	OCCUPATIONS	DATE PORT SHIP
KILHUHU, Cornelius	35	M	Laborer	14Ma02Jm
MCCAUL, Sally	45	F	Farmer	14Ma02Jm
Sarah	22	F	Farmer	14Ma02Jm
James	20	M	Farmer	14Ma02Jm
GREEN, U-Mr.	27	M	Farmer	14Ma02Jm
U-Mrs.	24	F	Farmer	14Ma02Jm
U-Miss	20	F	Farmer	14Ma02Jm
BARRY, Ellen	28	F	Servant	14Ma02Jm
Margaret	24	F	Servant	14Ma02Jm
MOONEY, John	10	M	Servant	14Ma02Jm
MONAHON, Thomas	30	M	Laborer	14Ma02Jm
Hugh	22	M	Laborer	14Ma02Jm
DOWD, Michl.	30	M	Laborer	14Ma02Jm
MCNIFF, Ann	28	F	Servant	14Ma02Jm
ONEILL, Patk.	23	M	Farmer	14Ma02Jm
Cathe.	22	F	Farmer	14Ma02Jm
John-James	.06	M	Infant	14Ma02Jm
LACHRAN, Sarah	20	F	Servant	14Ma02Jm
Ann	16	F	Servant	14Ma02Jm
MCKINN, Mary	30	F	Servant	14Ma02Jm
DONOVAN, John	23	M	Laborer	14Ma02Jm
Timothy	23	M	Laborer	14Ma02Jm
RYAN, Pat	30	M	Farmer	14Ma02Jm
Winifred	28	F	Farmer	14Ma02Jm
Catherine	.08	F	Infant	14Ma02Jm
Pat	8	M	Child	14Ma02Jm
Nedddy	3	M	Child	14Ma02Jm
Peggy	6	F	Child	14Ma02Jm
DOLLORY, Dennis	34	M	Farmer	14Ma02Jm
HOGARMY, Ellen	15	F	Farmer	14Ma02Jm
Margaret	11	F	Farmer	14Ma02Jm
BULGER, Lydia	40	F	Servant	14Ma02Jm
Ellen	12	F	Servant	14Ma02Jm
James	10	M	Servant	14Ma02Jm
WITH, Mary	24	F	Dressmaker	14Ma02Jm
MARTIN, Patk.	60	M	Laborer	14Ma02Jm
Bessy	55	F	Laborer	14Ma02Jm
MURRAY, Bridget	20	F	Servant	14Ma02Jm
OCONNOR, Patrick	8	M	Child	14Ma02Jm
ODONNELL, Nancy	24	F	Seamstress	14Ma02Jm
MCKINNEY, Eliza	18	F	Seamstress	14Ma02Jm
Mary	17	F	Seamstress	14Ma02Jm
CURRAN, Pat	56	M	Farmer	14Ma02Jm
Rose	22	F	Farmer	14Ma02Jm
HANLON, Pat	38	M	Laborer	14Ma02Jm
FLEMING, John	26	M	Laborer	14Ma02Jm
FITZGERROLD, James	20	M	Farmer	14Ma02Jm
Maria	25	F	Farmer	14Ma02Jm
Bridget	22	F	Farmer	14Ma02Jm
EGAN, Patrick	18	M	Farmer	14Ma02Jm
HUGHES, Sarah	26	F	Servant	14Ma02Jm
Elizh.	17	F	Servant	14Ma02Jm
Elizh.	18	F	Servant	14Ma02Jm
Charles	.02	M	Infant	14Ma02Jm
Died-At-Sea				
CULLEN, Ellen	19	F	Servant	14Ma02Jm
DONELLY, Pat.	17	M	Farmer	14Ma02Jm
John	15	M	Farmer	14Ma02Jm
ENNIS, James	18	M	Farmer	14Ma02Jm
WALSH, Mattw.	27	M	Farmer	14Ma02Jm
LACY, Josh.	17	M	Farmer	14Ma02Jm
FINLONG, Willm.	17	M	Farmer	14Ma02Jm
CULLEN, Ellen	5	F	Child	14Ma02Jm
James	2	M	Child	14Ma02Jm
Mary	.03	F	Infant	14Ma02Jm
MURPHY, Nicholas	30	M	Farmer	14Ma02Jm
Mary	30	F	Farmer	14Ma02Jm
BURT, John	27	M	Farmer	14Ma02Jm
Sarah	23	F	Farmer	14Ma02Jm
Charles	4	M	Child	14Ma02Jm
William	3	M	Child	14Ma02Jm
HASSEY, Ann	24	F	Servant	14Ma02Jm
FITZSIMMONS, Patk.	18	M	Shoemaker	14Ma02Jm
GANNON, John	19	M	Joiner	14Ma02Jm
LANGSTER, Eliza	30	F	Joiner	14Ma02Jm

NAMES OF PASSENGERS	AGE	SEX	OCCUPATIONS	DATE PORT SHIP
SIMPSON, Peter	00	M	Unknown	14Ma02Jm
MARTIN, Bridget	00	F	Unknown	14Ma02Jm
HUGHES, Francis	00	M	Unknown	14Ma02Jm

MARCHIONESS-OF-BUTE 15 MAY 1850

From Newry

NAMES OF PASSENGERS	AGE	SEX	OCCUPATIONS	DATE PORT SHIP
HALLIGAN, Rosanna	22	F	Milliner	15Ma04Im
Eliza	25	F	Governess	15Ma04Im
WILSON, James	21	M	Clerk	15Ma04Im
TODD, Samuel	14	M	Clerk	15Ma04Im
MAGONE, Michael	24	M	Farmer	15Ma04Im
CASSIDY, Edward	50	M	Ploughman	15Ma04Im
Patrick	48	M	Farmer	15Ma04Im
Eleann	30	F	Spinster	15Ma04Im
Catharine	.00	F	Infant	15Ma04Im
DUNN, Anne	26	F	Spinster	15Ma04Im
QUINN, John	30	M	Laborer	15Ma04Im
CONNOR, Peter	11	M	Servant	15Ma04Im
Arthur	9	M	Child	15Ma04Im
Mary-Jane	2	F	Child	15Ma04Im
Died-At-Sea				
MCSHANE, James	23	M	Laborer	15Ma04Im
MCKEOWN, Peter	22	M	Laborer	15Ma04Im
GARVEY, Rose	40	F	Spinster	15Ma04Im
Christy	17	M	Unknown	15Ma04Im
Mary	15	F	Unknown	15Ma04Im
Rose-Ann	12	F	Unknown	15Ma04Im
Biddy	10	F	Unknown	15Ma04Im
Elizabeth	7	F	Child	15Ma04Im
James	4	M	Child	15Ma04Im
John	21	M	Unknown	15Ma04Im
KENNEDY, William	25	M	Laborer	15Ma04Im
CRANNEY, Elizabeth	24	F	Servant	15Ma04Im
HAMILTON, Jane	30	F	Servant	15Ma04Im
DEVLIN, James	24	M	Laborer	15Ma04Im
FARREL, Bridget	28	F	Servant	15Ma04Im
MCDONNELL, Patt	50	M	Ploughman	15Ma04Im
GARVEY, Susan	18	F	Spinster	15Ma04Im
CASSIDY, Alice	21	F	Servant	15Ma04Im
MARLIN, James	45	M	Farmer	15Ma04Im
Thomas	20	M	Unknown	15Ma04Im
James	18	M	Unknown	15Ma04Im
Agnes	24	F	Unknown	15Ma04Im
John	18	M	Unknown	15Ma04Im
SINCLAIR, Margaret	24	F	Spinster	15Ma04Im
SIMMS, Alice	65	F	Spinster	15Ma04Im
DEACAN, Margaret	25	F	Servant	15Ma04Im
DELANY, William	50	M	Ploughman	15Ma04Im
Mary	22	F	Spinster	15Ma04Im
Peter	14	M	Servant	15Ma04Im
MUGAN, Patrick	40	M	Tailor	15Ma04Im
GOLLOPHY, Ann	18	F	Servant	15Ma04Im
MCBRIDE, Thomas	21	M	Mason	15Ma04Im
MILLS, William	24	M	Servant	15Ma04Im
SLOAN, Stephen	32	M	Laborer	15Ma04Im
DIGNY, Patrick	21	M	Servant	15Ma04Im
MURNAGHAN, Betty	23	F	Spinster	15Ma04Im
TOAL, Margaret	22	F	Servant	15Ma04Im
GOLLOPHY, Matthew	40	M	Farmer	15Ma04Im
Mary	17	F	Spinster	15Ma04Im
MCCONVILL, John	22	M	Servant	15Ma04Im
HANRATTY, John	14	M	Laborer	15Ma04Im
HANLON, Catherine	26	F	Spinster	15Ma04Im
Agnes	23	F	Seamstress	15Ma04Im
DONAGHY, Michael	38	M	Laborer	15Ma04Im
MANEELY, John	23	M	Laborer	15Ma04Im
CARSON, Robert	26	M	Ploughman	15Ma04Im

NAMES OF PASSENGERS	AGE	SEX	OCCUPATIONS	DATE PORT SHIP
MCVEIGH, Alice	20	F	Spinster	15Ma04Im
MORGAN, Mary	30	F	Servant	15Ma04Im
Rose-Ann	5	F	Child	15Ma04Im
James	3	M	Child	15Ma04Im
Terence	.00	M	Infant	15Ma04Im
DORAN, Margaret	22	F	Spinster	15Ma04Im
COLLINS, Ann	22	F	Servant	15Ma04Im
Alice	3	F	Child	15Ma04Im
MCGATNEY, Biddy	15	F	Spinster	15Ma04Im
John	13	M	Unknown	15Ma04Im
Sarah	8	F	Child	15Ma04Im
CULL, Rose	40	F	Spinster	15Ma04Im
Mary	18	F	Unknown	15Ma04Im
Rose	17	F	Unknown	15Ma04Im
John	14	M	Unknown	15Ma04Im
Thomas	12	M	Unknown	15Ma04Im
Francis	11	M	Unknown	15Ma04Im
Daniel	9	M	Child	15Ma04Im
Ann	7	F	Child	15Ma04Im
Ellen	5	F	Child	15Ma04Im
SMALL, Joseph	21	M	Laborer	15Ma04Im
KELLY, Hugh	25	M	Farmer	15Ma04Im
CALLAN, Mary-Ann	20	F	Spinster	15Ma04Im
Margaret	18	F	Spinster	15Ma04Im
STEPHENS, Francis	25	M	Farmer	15Ma04Im
Mary	30	F	Spinster	15Ma04Im
William	20	M	Laborer	15Ma04Im
GORDON, Joseph	24	M	Farmer	15Ma04Im
DELAH, Biddy	10	F	Unknown	15Ma04Im
MAGENNIS, Hugh	24	M	Farmer	15Ma04Im
Robert	20	M	Farmer	15Ma04Im
MCANNLTY, Thomas	35	M	Ploughman	15Ma04Im
Jane	28	F	Servant	15Ma04Im
Patt	.00	M	Infant	15Ma04Im
WRIGHT, James	25	M	Servant	15Ma04Im
Daniel	27	M	Servant	15Ma04Im
STEPHENS, Susan	20	F	Spinster	15Ma04Im
DUNLOP, Catherine	6	F	Child	15Ma04Im
MCDONNELL, Edward	30	M	Farmer	15Ma04Im
Anne	27	F	Wife	15Ma04Im
Michael	6	M	Child	15Ma04Im
Catherine	4	F	Child	15Ma04Im
Bridget	2	F	Child	15Ma04Im
HARD, John	36	M	Servant	15Ma04Im
Agnes	27	F	Spinster	15Ma04Im
Elizabeth	8	F	Child	15Ma04Im
William	6	M	Child	15Ma04Im
Jane	4	F	Child	15Ma04Im
Joseph	3	M	Child	15Ma04Im
Margaret	.00	F	Infant	15Ma04Im
HERRIN, David	40	M	Farmer	15Ma04Im
Jane	30	F	Wife	15Ma04Im
Mary	15	F	Unknown	15Ma04Im
Margaret	12	F	Unknown	15Ma04Im
William	10	M	Unknown	15Ma04Im
Jane	8	F	Child	15Ma04Im
John	6	M	Child	15Ma04Im
James	3	M	Child	15Ma04Im
Sarah-Anne	.00	F	Infant	15Ma04Im
IRVIN, George	16	M	Servant	15Ma04Im
MORGAN, John	30	M	Boatman	15Ma04Im
MCKEVITT, Elizabeth	20	F	Spinster	15Ma04Im
BOYLE, John	50	M	Ploughman	15Ma04Im
Arthur	22	M	Servant	15Ma04Im
Anne	11	F	Spinster	15Ma04Im
CARVILL, Anne	40	F	Servant	15Ma04Im
RYAN, Owen	22	M	Servant	15Ma04Im
DONNOLLY, Bridget	21	F	Spinster	15Ma04Im
Michael	19	M	Laborer	15Ma04Im
John	17	M	Laborer	15Ma04Im
James	11	M	Servant	15Ma04Im
MCDONNELL, John	50	M	Ploughman	15Ma04Im
Anne	50	F	Wife	15Ma04Im
Anne	20	F	Unknown	15Ma04Im
Rose	18	F	Unknown	15Ma04Im
MCDONNELL, Thomas	12	M	Unknown	15Ma04Im
Mary	6	F	Child	15Ma04Im
Catharine	4	F	Child	15Ma04Im
RONEY, Anne	22	F	Servant	15Ma04Im
MORGAN, Michael	20	M	Wood Ranger	15Ma04Im
RORKE, Charles	24	M	Servant	15Ma04Im
MAGEOWN, Henry	25	M	Laborer	15Ma04Im
KELLY, Mary	28	F	Spinster	15Ma04Im
Patrick	3	M	Child	15Ma04Im
HANLON, Thomas	30	M	Farmer	15Ma04Im
Catharine	28	F	Wife	15Ma04Im
CAMPBELL, Margaret	40	F	Spinster	15Ma04Im
Mary	10	F	Spinster	15Ma04Im
HANLON, Margaret	3	F	Child	15Ma04Im
Edward	2	M	Child	15Ma04Im
Mary	.00	F	Infant	15Ma04Im
RICE, Anne	20	F	Spinster	15Ma04Im
MAGEE, Thomas	35	M	Laborer	15Ma04Im
HANLON, Felix	23	M	Laborer	15Ma04Im
MCKEEVER, James	23	M	Farmer	15Ma04Im
TRAINOR, Anne	25	F	Spinster	15Ma04Im
Mary	6	F	Child	15Ma04Im
MALAN, Patrick	24	M	Farmer	15Ma04Im
MAGRAN, Stephen	30	M	Farmer	15Ma04Im
RICE, Stephen	20	M	Laborer	15Ma04Im
MCASTAVE, Thomas	19	M	Laborer	15Ma04Im
CORY, Anne	20	F	Spinster	15Ma04Im
MCKEOWN, Anne	25	F	Servant	15Ma04Im
MCDONNELL, Margaret	40	F	Servant	15Ma04Im
MAGENNIS, Rose	35	F	Spinster	15Ma04Im
Michael	.00	M	Infant	15Ma04Im
MCQUADE, Michael	22	M	Laborer	15Ma04Im
BOYLE, Joseph	24	M	Laborer	15Ma04Im
John	14	M	Servant	15Ma04Im
KELLY, James	30	M	Farmer	15Ma04Im
Mary	18	F	Servant	15Ma04Im
COYLE, Catharine	18	F	Spinster	15Ma04Im
FERGUSON, Daniel	20	M	Laborer	15Ma04Im
LEVY, Francis	25	M	Farmer	15Ma04Im
COMISKY, Bridget	16	F	Servant	15Ma04Im
MAGEE, Biddy	20	F	Spinster	15Ma04Im
Richard	17	M	Farmer	15Ma04Im
Michael	20	M	Servant	15Ma04Im
RICE, John	50	M	Farmer	15Ma04Im
Anne	45	F	Wife	15Ma04Im
Anne	22	F	Unknown	15Ma04Im
James	18	M	Unknown	15Ma04Im
Biddy	15	F	Unknown	15Ma04Im
Margaret	12	F	Unknown	15Ma04Im
Elizabeth	10	F	Unknown	15Ma04Im
Sarah	8	F	Child	15Ma04Im
Daniel	4	M	Child	15Ma04Im
MAGRA, James	34	M	Laborer	15Ma04Im
RONEY, Thomas	39	M	Laborer	15Ma04Im
Rose	40	F	Servant	15Ma04Im
Biddy	12	F	Unknown	15Ma04Im
Mary	9	F	Child	15Ma04Im
MAGRAND, Andrew	30	M	Laborer	15Ma04Im
MURPHY, Arthur	50	M	Laborer	15Ma04Im
Mary	50	F	Spinster	15Ma04Im
James	25	M	Laborer	15Ma04Im
John	18	M	Servant	15Ma04Im
Anne	15	F	Spinster	15Ma04Im
FITZSIMMONS, John	45	M	Laborer	15Ma04Im
Peter	19	M	Servant	15Ma04Im
FINIGAN, Jane	27	F	Spinster	15Ma04Im
BOYLE, Jane	18	F	Servant	15Ma04Im
Elizabeth	18	F	Spinster	15Ma04Im
FINIGAN, James	7	M	Child	15Ma04Im
Stephen	5	M	Child	15Ma04Im
Patrick	.00	M	Infant	15Ma04Im
MURPHY, Peter	40	M	Servant	15Ma04Im
MCPARLAND, Elizabeth	20	F	Spinster	15Ma04Im
Margaret	28	F	Wife	15Ma04Im
Ellen	21	F	Sister	15Ma04Im

NAMES OF PASSENGERS	AGE	SEX	OCCUPATIONS	DATE PORT SHIP
MURPHY, Patrick	20	M	Farmer	15Ma04Im
Francis	40	M	Ploughman	15Ma04Im
MCKEVITT, Stephen	40	M	Farmer	15Ma04Im
DOGHERTY, Anne	50	F	Spinster	15Ma04Im
CARAHER, Patrick	22	M	Farmer	15Ma04Im
RUDDY, Matthew	50	M	Ploughman	15Ma04Im
Ann	19	F	Spinster	15Ma04Im
COMISKY, Thomas	41	M	Farmer	15Ma04Im
MATEER, Margaret	28	F	Spinster	15Ma04Im
HAMATTY, Edward	40	M	Laborer	15Ma04Im
HAROLD, Peter	32	M	Farmer	15Ma04Im
MACKEN, Thomas	45	M	Laborer	15Ma04Im
Ann	20	F	Spinster	15Ma04Im
MCKEWN, Patrick	25	M	Laborer	15Ma04Im
MCKEOWN, Elizabeth	20	F	Spinster	15Ma04Im
FEEHAN, Owen	37	M	Laborer	15Ma04Im
MAGRATH, Thomas	22	M	Tailor	15Ma04Im
MCCRUM, William	18	M	Laborer	15Ma04Im
MCDONELL, Susan	27	F	Spinster	15Ma04Im
MORGAN, Patrick	30	M	Farmer	15Ma04Im
MCKEEVER, Bridget	24	F	Spinster	15Ma04Im
CARVILL, Bryan	40	M	Farmer	15Ma04Im
Owen	11	M	Unknown	15Ma04Im
John	4	M	Child	15Ma04Im
HUNTER, Robert	35	M	Carpenter	15Ma04Im
OHARE, Bernard	50	M	Farmer	15Ma04Im
Bridget	48	F	Wife	15Ma04Im
GRACIE, Joshua	21	M	Shoemaker	15Ma04Im
MCKEWN, John	31	M	Laborer	15Ma04Im
Mary	40	F	Spinster	15Ma04Im
Henry	13	M	Unknown	15Ma04Im
Ellen	3	F	Child	15Ma04Im
Sarah	.00	F	Infant	15Ma04Im
CANAVAN, James	15	M	Shoemaker	15Ma04Im
Ellen	13	F	Spinster	15Ma04Im
Matthew	22	M	Clerk	15Ma04Im
DOGHERTY, Ann	10	F	Unknown	15Ma04Im
CARRON, Patrick	13	M	Servant	15Ma04Im

DEVON 15 MAY 1850

From Liverpool

NAMES OF PASSENGERS	AGE	SEX	OCCUPATIONS	DATE PORT SHIP
THORNTON, John	49	M	Laborer	15Ma02Jw
Jane	46	F	Laborer	15Ma02Jw
Christy	21	M	Laborer	15Ma02Jw
James	17	M	Laborer	15Ma02Jw
Cathe.	19	F	Laborer	15Ma02Jw
John	12	M	Laborer	15Ma02Jw
Ann	.09	F	Infant	15Ma02Jw
CHALMERS, Jas.	35	M	Laborer	15Ma02Jw
MCGIVENI, Hooks	20	M	Laborer	15Ma02Jw
RALSTONE, Williams	23	M	Laborer	15Ma02Jw
NEILL, Matt	24	M	Laborer	15Ma02Jw
CONNAY, John	19	M	Laborer	15Ma02Jw
BANNON, Biddy	13	F	Laborer	15Ma02Jw
MURPHY, Cathl.	13	F	Unknown	15Ma02Jw
Patk.	30	M	Unknown	15Ma02Jw
Judy	30	F	Unknown	15Ma02Jw
Margt.	.00	F	Infant	15Ma02Jw
CULLEN, Biddy	30	F	Unknown	15Ma02Jw
Mary	.06	F	Infant	15Ma02Jw
COTTRELL, A.	11	M	Unknown	15Ma02Jw
CULLEN, Dennis	.00	M	Infant	15Ma02Jw
CUMMING, Ellen	21	F	Unknown	15Ma02Jw
MAHONEY, Thomas	26	M	Unknown	15Ma02Jw
KEENAN, Sarah	24	F	Unknown	15Ma02Jw
FEENY, John	25	M	Unknown	15Ma02Jw
MAHER, Bridgt.	20	F	Unknown	15Ma02Jw

NAMES OF PASSENGERS	AGE	SEX	OCCUPATIONS	DATE PORT SHIP
DIERY, Andrew	24	M	Unknown	15Ma02Jw
Margt.	24	F	Unknown	15Ma02Jw
KINEHAN, Margt.	24	F	Unknown	15Ma02Jw
WALSH, Mary	32	F	Unknown	15Ma02Jw
SCULLY, Rose	20	F	Unknown	15Ma02Jw
Michl.	19	M	Unknown	15Ma02Jw
John	17	M	Unknown	15Ma02Jw
Biddy	12	F	Unknown	15Ma02Jw
Sarah	.10	F	Infant	15Ma02Jw
CONNELLY, John	22	M	Unknown	15Ma02Jw
CARTY, Margt.	50	F	Unknown	15Ma02Jw
LAHEY, James	24	M	Unknown	15Ma02Jw
BARRETT, Michl.	24	M	Unknown	15Ma02Jw
SHADY, Ellen	23	F	Unknown	15Ma02Jw
BARRETT, John	24	M	Unknown	15Ma02Jw
LEERY, Daniel	17	M	Unknown	15Ma02Jw
Dinah	12	F	Unknown	15Ma02Jw
RIORDAN, Andy	30	M	Unknown	15Ma02Jw
Johana	12	F	Unknown	15Ma02Jw
MAHONEY, Mary	16	F	Unknown	15Ma02Jw
FENTON, Mary	25	F	Unknown	15Ma02Jw
John	.03	M	Infant	15Ma02Jw
HANLY, Mary	20	F	Unknown	15Ma02Jw
JERRYMAN, Michl.	16	M	Unknown	15Ma02Jw
John	20	M	Unknown	15Ma02Jw
HENDERSON, James	26	M	Unknown	15Ma02Jw
MOORE, Martin	45	M	Unknown	15Ma02Jw
Andrew	22	M	Unknown	15Ma02Jw
Bridget	18	F	Unknown	15Ma02Jw
Joseph	13	M	Unknown	15Ma02Jw
CONNER, Jerry	20	M	Unknown	15Ma02Jw
STRANY, James	20	M	Unknown	15Ma02Jw
Rose	22	F	Unknown	15Ma02Jw
KILLIMICK, John	17	M	Unknown	15Ma02Jw
Biddy	27	F	Unknown	15Ma02Jw
BURNS, Phillip	17	M	Unknown	15Ma02Jw
HYNES, Jno.	50	M	Unknown	15Ma02Jw
Mary	47	F	Unknown	15Ma02Jw
Cathe.	6	F	Child	15Ma02Jw
Ann	.05	F	Infant	15Ma02Jw
DILLION, Peter	25	M	Unknown	15Ma02Jw
FERRIS, Mary	24	F	Unknown	15Ma02Jw
OBRIEN, Richard	27	M	Unknown	15Ma02Jw
Margt.	25	F	Unknown	15Ma02Jw
John	.00	M	Infant	15Ma02Jw
MCCOONY, Betty	16	F	Unknown	15Ma02Jw
Kate	18	F	Unknown	15Ma02Jw
GORMAN, Eliza	16	F	Unknown	15Ma02Jw
HELPENTIN, Mary	20	F	Unknown	15Ma02Jw
MOONEY, Biddy	19	F	Unknown	15Ma02Jw
Margt.	20	F	Unknown	15Ma02Jw
BEYSTONE, Wm.	29	M	Unknown	15Ma02Jw
Samuel	22	M	Unknown	15Ma02Jw
DUNN, Edward	18	M	Unknown	15Ma02Jw
DIXON, Margt.	35	F	Unknown	15Ma02Jw
Patk.	23	M	Unknown	15Ma02Jw
Bridgt.	21	F	Unknown	15Ma02Jw
Mary	19	F	Unknown	15Ma02Jw
Morris	17	F	Unknown	15Ma02Jw
PLUNKET, Bridgt.	16	F	Unknown	15Ma02Jw
BRID, Thomas	30	M	Unknown	15Ma02Jw
Christian	27	F	Unknown	15Ma02Jw
Joseph	.00	M	Infant	15Ma02Jw
SHERLOCK, Pat	20	M	Unknown	15Ma02Jw
BERRY, James	23	M	Unknown	15Ma02Jw
GOORMAN, John	23	M	Unknown	15Ma02Jw
GALLIGHER, Michl.	20	M	Unknown	15Ma02Jw
DUFFY, Charles	25	M	Unknown	15Ma02Jw
HOGAN, Ann	18	F	Unknown	15Ma02Jw
RYAN, Mary	19	F	Unknown	15Ma02Jw
LENNON, Darby	22	M	Unknown	15Ma02Jw
MCGEE, John	20	M	Unknown	15Ma02Jw
ROCK, John	17	M	Unknown	15Ma02Jw
MCGEE, Ann	31	F	Unknown	15Ma02Jw
Owen	11	M	Unknown	15Ma02Jw

NAMES OF PASSENGERS	AGE	SEX	OCCUPATIONS	DATE PORT SHIP
MCGEE, Betty	5	F	Child	15Ma02Jw
James	3	M	Child	15Ma02Jw
Mary	.00	F	Infant	15Ma02Jw
CALL, Johana	21	F	Unknown	15Ma02Jw
PRITCHON, William	22	M	Unknown	15Ma02Jw
HUGHES, Charles	22	M	Unknown	15Ma02Jw
CLARKE, Pat	23	M	Unknown	15Ma02Jw
Charles	22	M	Unknown	15Ma02Jw
CARTON, Pat	20	M	Unknown	15Ma02Jw
TULLY, John	20	M	Unknown	15Ma02Jw
FEENY, Cathn.	21	F	Unknown	15Ma02Jw
Ann	18	F	Unknown	15Ma02Jw
MCPHILIP, Cathe.	22	F	Unknown	15Ma02Jw
DECONY, Jane	25	F	Unknown	15Ma02Jw
Mary	.00	F	Infant	15Ma02Jw
REILLY, Ann	30	F	Unknown	15Ma02Jw
GALLAGHER, Margt.	26	F	Unknown	15Ma02Jw
GALVIN, Biddy	27	F	Unknown	15Ma02Jw
Biddy	.00	F	Infant	15Ma02Jw
SOLIN, Margt.	17	F	Unknown	15Ma02Jw
KENNEDY, John	19	M	Unknown	15Ma02Jw
FEEING, Phoebe	16	F	Unknown	15Ma02Jw
RYAN, Pat	55	M	Unknown	15Ma02Jw
William	17	M	Unknown	15Ma02Jw
Patk.	15	M	Unknown	15Ma02Jw
Margt.	12	F	Unknown	15Ma02Jw
William	50	M	Unknown	15Ma02Jw
BRANNON, Patt	21	M	Unknown	15Ma02Jw
IRVING, Sam	28	M	Unknown	15Ma02Jw
HODY, Ellen	16	F	Unknown	15Ma02Jw
SMITH, Margt.	20	F	Unknown	15Ma02Jw
SULLIVAN, Cathe.	45	F	Unknown	15Ma02Jw
James	23	M	Unknown	15Ma02Jw
Christy	20	M	Unknown	15Ma02Jw
Terence	15	M	Unknown	15Ma02Jw
WALSH, Michl.	21	M	Unknown	15Ma02Jw
MCMEANY, James	47	M	Unknown	15Ma02Jw
Bridgt.	27	F	Unknown	15Ma02Jw
Patk.	.00	M	Infant	15Ma02Jw
BROWNE, Bridgt.	24	F	Unknown	15Ma02Jw
CONNOLLEY, Mary	13	F	Unknown	15Ma02Jw
CONLON, Edward	13	M	Unknown	15Ma02Jw
CLANCY, John	40	M	Unknown	15Ma02Jw
Bessy	40	F	Unknown	15Ma02Jw
Cathle.	22	F	Unknown	15Ma02Jw
Patk.	23	M	Unknown	15Ma02Jw
COMACK, James	24	M	Unknown	15Ma02Jw
Mary	23	F	Unknown	15Ma02Jw
DEVATT, Margt.	24	F	Unknown	15Ma02Jw
MCCUE, Margt.	23	F	Unknown	15Ma02Jw
CLANCY, James	18	M	Unknown	15Ma02Jw
HUGHES, Owen	30	M	Unknown	15Ma02Jw
Ellen	30	F	Unknown	15Ma02Jw
EVANS, William	.06	M	Infant	15Ma02Jw
MCCARTY, Michl.	20	M	Unknown	15Ma02Jw
Michl.	.04	M	Infant	15Ma02Jw
SMITH, Philip	50	M	Unknown	15Ma02Jw
COPENHAGEN, Jas.	27	M	Unknown	15Ma02Jw
CLARKE, Pat	20	M	Unknown	15Ma02Jw
TRAYNOR, Biddy	20	F	Unknown	15Ma02Jw
OHARA, Mary	23	F	Unknown	15Ma02Jw
R.Ann	4	F	Child	15Ma02Jw
GALLAGHER, Biddy	20	F	Unknown	15Ma02Jw
CARNEY, Mary	20	F	Unknown	15Ma02Jw
MCLOUGHLEY, Mary-A.	20	F	Unknown	15Ma02Jw
Kate	20	F	Unknown	15Ma02Jw
MULLEN, James	40	M	Unknown	15Ma02Jw
Bridgt.	7	F	Child	15Ma02Jw
Tobias	.09	M	Infant	15Ma02Jw
GALLAGHER, Ann	30	F	Unknown	15Ma02Jw
DOUGHERTY, Ann	16	F	Unknown	15Ma02Jw
GALLAGHER, John	15	M	Unknown	15Ma02Jw
Ann	6	F	Child	15Ma02Jw
Michl.	4	M	Child	15Ma02Jw
Cathe.	.02	F	Infant	15Ma02Jw
WYNN, Denis	29	M	Unknown	15Ma02Jw
SWEENEY, Thos.	45	M	Unknown	15Ma02Jw
WILSON, William	50	M	Unknown	15Ma02Jw
MULLIN, Dennis	24	M	Laborer	15Ma02Jw
Ellen	20	F	Unknown	15Ma02Jw
NICKLESON, Mary	20	F	Unknown	15Ma02Jw
THOMPSON, Jos.	45	M	Unknown	15Ma02Jw
Phebe	38	F	Unknown	15Ma02Jw
Joseph	15	M	Unknown	15Ma02Jw
Ann	20	F	Unknown	15Ma02Jw
Henry	13	M	Unknown	15Ma02Jw
Fanny	9	F	Child	15Ma02Jw
Phoebe-A.	.00	F	Infant	15Ma02Jw
GOWAN, William	30	M	Unknown	15Ma02Jw
Eliza	30	F	Unknown	15Ma02Jw
CONLAN, Pat	19	M	Unknown	15Ma02Jw
MARTIN, Benjm.	44	M	Unknown	15Ma02Jw
MULLIGAN, Martin	20	M	Unknown	15Ma02Jw
CALERY, Pat	25	M	Unknown	15Ma02Jw
Mary	22	F	Unknown	15Ma02Jw
Biddy	.00	F	Infant	15Ma02Jw
WHITTEN, Jos.	23	M	Unknown	15Ma02Jw
George	21	M	Unknown	15Ma02Jw
KELLY, James	45	M	Unknown	15Ma02Jw
Cathe.	31	F	Unknown	15Ma02Jw
Henrietta	25	F	Unknown	15Ma02Jw
Ellen	20	F	Unknown	15Ma02Jw
Nell	20	F	Unknown	15Ma02Jw
Bridget	9	F	Child	15Ma02Jw
Patk.	7	M	Child	15Ma02Jw
Mary	5	F	Child	15Ma02Jw
Martin	.00	M	Infant	15Ma02Jw
John	3	M	Child	15Ma02Jw
MCCANLEY, Hugh	28	M	Unknown	15Ma02Jw
SHEEHAN, Timothy	19	M	Unknown	15Ma02Jw
FISHER, Raphael	21	M	Unknown	15Ma02Jw
BROMBERG, Abraham	21	M	Unknown	15Ma02Jw
MEYER, Solomon	21	M	Unknown	15Ma02Jw
DWYER, John	27	M	Unknown	15Ma02Jw
Margt.	26	F	Unknown	15Ma02Jw
James	.00	M	Infant	15Ma02Jw
REILLY, James	20	M	Unknown	15Ma02Jw
CUNNINGHAM, Margt.	17	F	Unknown	15Ma02Jw
BARRETT, Richd.	22	M	Unknown	15Ma02Jw
KEEFE, Biddy	20	F	Unknown	15Ma02Jw
Kate	2	F	Child	15Ma02Jw
Ellen	.00	F	Infant	15Ma02Jw
JONES, Thos.	20	M	Unknown	15Ma02Jw
CHARLOTTE, Jas.	25	M	Unknown	15Ma02Jw
Cathe.	23	F	Unknown	15Ma02Jw
LEERY, John	17	M	Unknown	15Ma02Jw
Brid.	.00	F	Infant	15Ma02Jw
Died-At-Sea				
KAYE, Carrol	26	M	Unknown	15Ma02Jw
Susan	37	F	Unknown	15Ma02Jw
Susan	7	F	Child	15Ma02Jw
John	5	M	Child	15Ma02Jw
Eliza	.04	F	Infant	15Ma02Jw
PINDER, Francis	37	M	Unknown	15Ma02Jw
Mary	38	F	Unknown	15Ma02Jw
Ann	10	F	Unknown	15Ma02Jw
Charles	7	M	Child	15Ma02Jw
William	5	M	Child	15Ma02Jw
Francis	2	M	Child	15Ma02Jw
Susan	.00	F	Infant	15Ma02Jw
RODES, Samuel	38	M	Unknown	15Ma02Jw
Elizt.	38	F	Unknown	15Ma02Jw
Elizt.	14	F	Unknown	15Ma02Jw
Henry	12	M	Unknown	15Ma02Jw
Sarah-J.	10	F	Unknown	15Ma02Jw
William	9	M	Child	15Ma02Jw
John-F.	7	M	Child	15Ma02Jw
Mary-A.	.05	F	Infant	15Ma02Jw
FERRIS, Henry	63	M	Unknown	15Ma02Jw
Cath.	62	F	Unknown	15Ma02Jw

NAMES OF PASSENGERS	AGE	SEX	OCCUPATIONS	DATE PORT SHIP
POTTER, Wm.	38	M	Unknown	15Ma02Jw
Ann	14	F	Unknown	15Ma02Jw
Cathe.	12	F	Unknown	15Ma02Jw
Eliza	.08	F	Infant	15Ma02Jw
BIRD, Charles	31	M	Unknown	15Ma02Jw
Martha	31	F	Unknown	15Ma02Jw
George	10	M	Unknown	15Ma02Jw
Joshua	7	M	Child	15Ma02Jw
Charles	5	M	Child	15Ma02Jw
Martha	.03	F	Infant	15Ma02Jw

EL-DORADO 16 MAY 1850

From London

NAMES OF PASSENGERS	AGE	SEX	OCCUPATIONS	DATE PORT SHIP
WARD, Mary	19	F	Servant	16Ma06It
Peter	7	M	Child	16Ma06It
Richd.	2	M	Child	16Ma06It
John	.00	M	Infant	16Ma06It
COLLINS, Margt.	19	F	Servant	16Ma06It
ROURKE, Joseph	24	M	Laborer	16Ma06It
Johanna	25	F	Unknown	16Ma06It
Mary	.00	F	Infant	16Ma06It
RAGAN, Mary	31	F	Servant	16Ma06It
HAYES, Corns.	59	M	Weaver	16Ma06It
DALEY, Jane	23	F	Servant	16Ma06It
Catherine	3	F	Child	16Ma06It
Mary	.00	F	Infant	16Ma06It
MCARTY, Ann	22	F	Servant	16Ma06It
DALEY, Willm.	22	M	Laborer	16Ma06It
MEONA, Ellen	25	F	Servant	16Ma06It
KINGSTON, John	29	M	Laborer	16Ma06It
HARRINGTON, Dennis	32	M	Farmer	16Ma06It
COSGRAVE, Margt.	21	F	None	16Ma06It
John	.00	M	Infant	16Ma06It
MAHONEY, Dennis	20	M	Laborer	16Ma06It
SULLIVAN, Ann	35	F	Unknown	16Ma06It
THOMPSON, Hannah (W)	25	F	Wife	16Ma06It
MCKEVETT, Willm.	35	M	Ship Master	16Ma06It
MABLEY, Richd.	30	M	First Mate	16Ma06It
MCKEVETT, Hugh	22	M	Second Mate	16Ma06It
LINDEN, Peter	23	M	Shpc	16Ma06It
MACGUIRE, Owen	30	M	Boatswain	16Ma06It
FEARSON, Laurence	20	M	Steward	16Ma06It
HAGAN, John	60	M	Cook	16Ma06It
MURPHY, Danl.	28	M	Seaman	16Ma06It
SHIELS, Michl.	28	M	Seaman	16Ma06It
HAGAN, John-Jr.	18	M	Seaman	16Ma06It
BROWN, Richd.	46	M	Seaman	16Ma06It
MCCANN, Michl.	28	M	Seaman	16Ma06It
SLOAN, Peter	25	M	Seaman	16Ma06It
REYNOLDS, Patk.	19	M	Seaman	16Ma06It
KERNEY, John	16	M	Seaman	16Ma06It
MORAN, Jas.	45	M	Seaman	16Ma06It
CARVELL, Owen	28	M	Seaman	16Ma06It
MCCANN, John	17	M	Apprentice	16Ma06It
MURPHY, Joseph	12	M	Cabin Boy	16Ma06It
JENNINGS, F.	20	M	Unknown	16Ma06It
SMITH, John	20	M	Unknown	16Ma06It
GEORGE, Matthew	23	M	Unknown	16Ma06It
GRIMES, Francis	19	M	Unknown	16Ma06It
MEAGHAN, Thos.	28	M	Unknown	16Ma06It
Mary	27	F	Unknown	16Ma06It
Owen	18	M	Unknown	16Ma06It
Ann	18	F	Unknown	16Ma06It
Patk.	17	M	Unknown	16Ma06It
F.	10	U	Unknown	16Ma06It
KING, Rose	25	M	Unknown	16Ma06It
MORTAIRE, Home	35	M	Unknown	16Ma06It
MORTAIRE, Jerry	30	M	Unknown	16Ma06It
Owen	2	M	Child	16Ma06It
OHAGAN, J.	50	U	Unknown	16Ma06It
BERNAN, Patk.	23	M	Unknown	16Ma06It
Mary	20	F	Unknown	16Ma06It
MILLIGHAN, Hugh	20	M	Unknown	16Ma06It
CAMMELL, Bridgt.	53	F	Unknown	16Ma06It
Patk.	23	M	Unknown	16Ma06It
Ann	22	F	Unknown	16Ma06It
Peter	19	M	Unknown	16Ma06It
Cathe.	19	F	Unknown	16Ma06It
Aler.	20	M	Unknown	16Ma06It
J.	12	U	Unknown	16Ma06It
Mary	9	F	Child	16Ma06It
Mary	7	F	Child	16Ma06It
MURRAY, Bridgt.	15	F	Unknown	16Ma06It
B.	1	U	Child	16Ma06It
Mary	8	F	Child	16Ma06It
Alex.	1	M	Child	16Ma06It
Peter	30	M	Unknown	16Ma06It
Bg.	50	F	Unknown	16Ma06It
Cathe.	32	F	Unknown	16Ma06It
Ellen	3	F	Child	16Ma06It
Biddy	1	F	Child	16Ma06It
CARNEY, Mary	56	F	Unknown	16Ma06It
Cathe.	16	F	Unknown	16Ma06It
MURRAY, Pat	5	M	Child	16Ma06It
CARNEY, Laurence	15	M	Unknown	16Ma06It
TRENNER, Owen	30	M	Unknown	16Ma06It
FARREN, Sarah	19	F	Unknown	16Ma06It
Elizabeth	20	F	Unknown	16Ma06It
CUNNINGHAM, Sarah	20	F	Unknown	16Ma06It
CLARK, Stephn.	30	M	Unknown	16Ma06It
MCBRIDE, Terren.	18	M	Unknown	16Ma06It
LOWE, Geoe.	25	M	Unknown	16Ma06It
KELLY, Henry	21	M	Unknown	16Ma06It
FINNINGHAM, Thos.	21	M	Unknown	16Ma06It
ROURKE, Cathe.	18	F	Unknown	16Ma06It
MCDOWER, Cathe.	16	F	Unknown	16Ma06It
WILSON, John	15	M	Unknown	16Ma06It
Elizabeth	16	F	Unknown	16Ma06It
OWEN, F.	15	U	Unknown	16Ma06It
I.	10	U	Unknown	16Ma06It
FLANAGHAN, Patk.	21	M	Unknown	16Ma06It
Edwd.	20	M	Unknown	16Ma06It
PREEDY, Moses	21	M	Unknown	16Ma06It
IRWIN, Robt.	21	M	Unknown	16Ma06It
MOCKAGHAN, Thos.	12	M	Unknown	16Ma06It
Ann	50	F	Unknown	16Ma06It
Pat	7	M	Child	16Ma06It
Ann	17	F	Unknown	16Ma06It
MCANOTTY, Pat	28	M	Unknown	16Ma06It
KEAGHAN, J.	22	U	Unknown	16Ma06It
Pat	18	M	Unknown	16Ma06It
SHIELS, Elizth.	21	F	Unknown	16Ma06It

ANDREW-FOSTER 16 MAY 1850

From Liverpool

NAMES OF PASSENGERS	AGE	SEX	OCCUPATIONS	DATE PORT SHIP
MCELROY, Hugh	22	M	Farmer	16Ma02Dt
KAIN, Mick	26	M	Laborer	16Ma02Dt
DONNELL, Wm.	24	M	Laborer	16Ma02Dt
GINAN, Mary	20	F	None	16Ma02Dt
IVERS, Sarah	20	F	None	16Ma02Dt
STONES, Mary	20	F	None	16Ma02Dt
Ellen	18	F	None	16Ma02Dt
GANLEY, Richard	22	M	Laborer	16Ma02Dt
MALOY, Thos.	2	M	Child	16Ma02Dt

NAMES OF PASSENGERS	AGE	SEX	OCCUPATIONS	DATE PORT SHIP
IRWIN, Saml.	25	M	Farmer	16Ma02Dt
MCMANUS, Mary	30	F	None	16Ma02Dt
Mary	3	F	Child	16Ma02Dt
Ann	.06	F	Infant	16Ma02Dt
BROWN, Andy	28	M	Laborer	16Ma02Dt
CASLEY, Thos.	20	M	Laborer	16Ma02Dt
DAVLIN, Hugh	36	M	Laborer	16Ma02Dt
GOOEN, Wm.	39	M	Laborer	16Ma02Dt
Julia	18	F	None	16Ma02Dt
Catherine	16	F	None	16Ma02Dt
CARROLL, Mary	19	F	None	16Ma02Dt
MULLAWAY, Ellen	13	F	None	16Ma02Dt
NUGENT, Richard	54	M	Laborer	16Ma02Dt
Margaret	55	F	Laborer	16Ma02Dt
Andy	23	M	Laborer	16Ma02Dt
GAMMON, Thos.	22	M	Laborer	16Ma02Dt
Margaret	17	F	None	16Ma02Dt
HARALD, Margaret	22	F	None	16Ma02Dt
Pat	17	M	Laborer	16Ma02Dt
MCLOUGHLIN, John	20	M	Laborer	16Ma02Dt
MORROW, John	30	M	Laborer	16Ma02Dt
MURRAY, Margaret	22	F	None	16Ma02Dt
CAHILL, Nickolas	21	M	Laborer	16Ma02Dt
MORROW, James	8	M	Child	16Ma02Dt
MCGRATH, Michl.	22	M	Laborer	16Ma02Dt
BELL, John	21	M	Laborer	16Ma02Dt
MOLEY, Margaret	25	F	Laborer	16Ma02Dt
DOOLAN, John	21	M	Laborer	16Ma02Dt
CARROLL, Pat	30	M	Laborer	16Ma02Dt
John	26	M	Laborer	16Ma02Dt
Margaret	23	F	Laborer	16Ma02Dt
MCCARTHY, Pat	22	M	Laborer	16Ma02Dt
MCRALSEA, Wm.	25	M	Laborer	16Ma02Dt
MCNICKLES, Pat	25	M	Laborer	16Ma02Dt
Ann	20	F	Laborer	16Ma02Dt
NESAN, Pat	24	M	Laborer	16Ma02Dt
Charles	24	M	Laborer	16Ma02Dt
MCCLUST, John	22	M	Laborer	16Ma02Dt
GREOGAN, Chas.	40	M	Laborer	16Ma02Dt
Betty	30	F	Laborer	16Ma02Dt
Jane	40	F	Laborer	16Ma02Dt
James	20	M	Laborer	16Ma02Dt
Betty	40	F	Laborer	16Ma02Dt
BACHER, Wm.	36	M	Farmer	16Ma02Dt
Betsey	30	F	Farmer	16Ma02Dt
LLUNA, James	25	M	Laborer	16Ma02Dt
CARR, Richard	48	M	Laborer	16Ma02Dt
MULANE, Pat	50	M	Laborer	16Ma02Dt
Judy	45	F	Laborer	16Ma02Dt
John	19	M	Laborer	16Ma02Dt
Ellen	12	F	Laborer	16Ma02Dt
Kate	17	F	Laborer	16Ma02Dt
LEE, John	20	M	Laborer	16Ma02Dt
Margt.	18	F	Laborer	16Ma02Dt
BRENNAN, John	24	M	Laborer	16Ma02Dt
MAYHUN, John	26	M	Laborer	16Ma02Dt
FOX, John	24	M	Laborer	16Ma02Dt
ROACHE, Thos.	25	M	Laborer	16Ma02Dt
Kearine	22	F	None	16Ma02Dt
MADEN, Margt.	20	F	None	16Ma02Dt
PURDY, John	41	M	Farmer	16Ma02Dt
BALANE, Wm.	30	M	Farmer	16Ma02Dt
COLE, John	30	M	Farmer	16Ma02Dt
MCCAGAN, Thos.	31	M	Laborer	16Ma02Dt
CULLEROU, John	23	M	Laborer	16Ma02Dt
REMEDY, Stephen	52	M	Laborer	16Ma02Dt
Bridget	50	F	Laborer	16Ma02Dt
Mary	26	F	Laborer	16Ma02Dt
Pat	27	M	Laborer	16Ma02Dt
Catherine	25	F	Laborer	16Ma02Dt
Peter	13	M	Laborer	16Ma02Dt
Mick	11	M	Laborer	16Ma02Dt
Bridget	8	F	Child	16Ma02Dt
LYNCH, Jane	26	F	None	16Ma02Dt
COWEY, Ned	25	M	Laborer	16Ma02Dt
COWEY, James	18	M	Laborer	16Ma02Dt
MULANE, Bridget	50	F	None	16Ma02Dt
Wm.	24	M	Laborer	16Ma02Dt
James	18	M	Laborer	16Ma02Dt
Bridget	13	F	Laborer	16Ma02Dt
Margaret	7	F	Child	16Ma02Dt
HINCHAN, Mike	30	M	Laborer	16Ma02Dt
Martin	22	M	Laborer	16Ma02Dt
NARY, Thos.	22	M	Laborer	16Ma02Dt
EAGAN, Nickolas	19	M	Laborer	16Ma02Dt
BRYDEN, Thos.	19	M	Laborer	16Ma02Dt
EAGAN, Wm.	20	M	Laborer	16Ma02Dt
KIRK, John	20	M	Laborer	16Ma02Dt
MULLIGAN, Thos.	25	M	Laborer	16Ma02Dt
FARRELL, Edward	25	M	Laborer	16Ma02Dt
BURKE, James	28	M	Laborer	16Ma02Dt
DEVLIN, Jane	21	F	Laborer	16Ma02Dt
MCKEOWN, Ann	21	F	Laborer	16Ma02Dt
BARNEY, John	32	M	Laborer	16Ma02Dt
COGAN, Peter	28	M	Laborer	16Ma02Dt
Wm.	22	M	Laborer	16Ma02Dt
KEHOE, Pat	22	M	Laborer	16Ma02Dt
NICKELSON, Thos.	36	M	Laborer	16Ma02Dt
RICE, Thos.	30	M	Laborer	16Ma02Dt
Catherine	22	F	Laborer	16Ma02Dt
Ellen	20	F	Laborer	16Ma02Dt
MOONEY, John	26	M	Laborer	16Ma02Dt
GREEN, Edward	28	M	Laborer	16Ma02Dt
Bartlett	26	M	Laborer	16Ma02Dt
BYRNE, Eliza	23	F	Laborer	16Ma02Dt
LUNT, Catherine	20	F	Laborer	16Ma02Dt
NEIL, Nathaniel	28	M	Farmer	16Ma02Dt
Mary	24	F	Farmer	16Ma02Dt
Harriet	3	F	Child	16Ma02Dt
Esther	.09	F	Infant	16Ma02Dt
MCALLISON, John	22	M	Laborer	16Ma02Dt
Jane	22	F	Laborer	16Ma02Dt
WHEELAN, Margaret	50	F	None	16Ma02Dt
Joseph	10	M	None	16Ma02Dt
Bridget	13	F	None	16Ma02Dt
CONNELLY, Judy	27	F	None	16Ma02Dt
BLUEIN, Jane	50	F	None	16Ma02Dt
Thomas	12	M	None	16Ma02Dt
FURMAY, James	26	M	Laborer	16Ma02Dt
ROLAND, Robert	23	M	Laborer	16Ma02Dt
CARR, Michl.	26	M	Laborer	16Ma02Dt
COYLE, Wm.	27	M	Laborer	16Ma02Dt
MURPHY, Joseph	24	M	Laborer	16Ma02Dt
DEMPSEY, Peter	40	M	Laborer	16Ma02Dt
Margaret	24	F	Laborer	16Ma02Dt
James	.10	M	Infant	16Ma02Dt
HESLIN, Mathew	26	M	Laborer	16Ma02Dt
PERRY, Peter	22	M	Laborer	16Ma02Dt
BARRY, James	19	M	Laborer	16Ma02Dt
Ellen	24	F	Laborer	16Ma02Dt
KAVANAGH, Michl.	25	M	Farmer	16Ma02Dt
Mary	22	F	Farmer	16Ma02Dt
JOHNSTONE, Arthur	23	M	Laborer	16Ma02Dt
KEHOE, Lawrence	28	M	Laborer	16Ma02Dt
TYNAN, Catherine	16	F	Laborer	16Ma02Dt
LAWLER, John	30	M	Laborer	16Ma02Dt
Bridget	50	F	Laborer	16Ma02Dt
Margt.	20	F	Laborer	16Ma02Dt
MCGRAHAM, Sarah	20	F	Laborer	16Ma02Dt
SCALLAN, Wm.	20	M	Laborer	16Ma02Dt
MCKENNON, Francis	25	M	Laborer	16Ma02Dt
Pat	20	M	Laborer	16Ma02Dt
Mary	2	F	Child	16Ma02Dt
RILEY, Joseph	20	M	Laborer	16Ma02Dt
GRIFFETH, John	18	M	Laborer	16Ma02Dt
GRADY, Mary	24	F	None	16Ma02Dt
TURPAY, Rose	19	F	None	16Ma02Dt
CARNEY, Pat	18	M	Laborer	16Ma02Dt
Bridget	11	F	None	16Ma02Dt
Mary	9	F	Child	16Ma02Dt

NAMES OF PASSENGERS	AGE	SEX	OCCUPATIONS	DATE PORT SHIP
CARNEY, Margaret	5	F	Child	16Ma02Dt
DYKES, John	28	M	Laborer	16Ma02Dt
Margaret	30	F	Laborer	16Ma02Dt
Lucy	3	F	Child	16Ma02Dt
George	2	M	Child	16Ma02Dt
GOOSE, Thomas	29	M	Tailor	16Ma02Dt
MCCAIN, Michl.	32	M	Laborer	16Ma02Dt
MELDOM, Richard	21	M	Laborer	16Ma02Dt
HENRY, Elizabeth	18	F	Laborer	16Ma02Dt
Betsey	20	F	Laborer	16Ma02Dt
HARROW, David	15	M	Farmer	16Ma02Dt
BARRY, Davy	20	M	Farmer	16Ma02Dt
GRADY, Judy	18	F	Farmer	16Ma02Dt
DALEY, John	27	M	Laborer	16Ma02Dt
REID, John	27	M	Laborer	16Ma02Dt
BURGEN, Jessy	29	F	Laborer	16Ma02Dt
John	29	M	Laborer	16Ma02Dt
GOWMAN, Daniel	17	M	Laborer	16Ma02Dt
KING, Catherine	41	F	Laborer	16Ma02Dt
RORKE, Michl.	27	M	Laborer	16Ma02Dt
Rose	45	F	Laborer	16Ma02Dt
John	13	M	Laborer	16Ma02Dt
Edward	21	M	Laborer	16Ma02Dt
LANAN, John	24	M	Joiner	16Ma02Dt
ROACHE, Mary	19	F	Joiner	16Ma02Dt
QUINN, Michl.	51	M	Laborer	16Ma02Dt
MCKENNA, Peter	22	M	Laborer	16Ma02Dt
KEAN, James	23	M	Laborer	16Ma02Dt
Jane	21	F	Laborer	16Ma02Dt
CONNELL, Nickolas	24	M	Laborer	16Ma02Dt
Kate	22	F	None	16Ma02Dt
Mary	20	F	None	16Ma02Dt
Ellen	18	F	None	16Ma02Dt
CONNOR, Ann	18	F	None	16Ma02Dt
ROONEY, John	28	M	Laborer	16Ma02Dt
GILLICK, John	34	M	Laborer	16Ma02Dt
PLUNKETT, Phillip	21	M	Laborer	16Ma02Dt
Ann-Jane	22	F	None	16Ma02Dt
DALEY, Thos.	30	M	Laborer	16Ma02Dt
Mary	24	F	None	16Ma02Dt
GOUGH, Pat	26	M	Laborer	16Ma02Dt
BRADY, Michl.	40	M	Laborer	16Ma02Dt
ONEIL, Michl.	26	M	Laborer	16Ma02Dt
BRODRICK, Honoria	13	F	Laborer	16Ma02Dt
ASKEW, Thos.	24	M	Laborer	16Ma02Dt
BEUTHAM, John	30	M	Laborer	16Ma02Dt
BUETHEM, Mary	25	F	None	16Ma02Dt
Thomas	6	M	Child	16Ma02Dt
Eliza	3	F	Child	16Ma02Dt
Hewey	.05	M	Infant	16Ma02Dt
ORMSTEN, Michl.	28	M	Laborer	16Ma02Dt
CORRYDON, Michl.	50	M	Laborer	16Ma02Dt
BRYAN, Hugh	40	M	Laborer	16Ma02Dt
HAMSTHEY, Rosa	20	F	Laborer	16Ma02Dt
JENNINGS, Thos.	20	M	Laborer	16Ma02Dt
STEBBINS, Jas.	21	M	Laborer	16Ma02Dt
William	20	M	Laborer	16Ma02Dt
ATKINSON, Jas.	25	M	Laborer	16Ma02Dt
MOORE, Jabez	25	M	Laborer	16Ma02Dt
GREGORY, Robert	23	M	Laborer	16Ma02Dt
MOONEY, Jas.	42	M	Laborer	16Ma02Dt
Wm.	38	M	Laborer	16Ma02Dt
MCDERMITT, Sarah	30	F	None	16Ma02Dt
CONNELLY, Bridget	50	F	None	16Ma02Dt
KEARNY, Sarah	30	F	None	16Ma02Dt
Winney	6	F	Child	16Ma02Dt
Mary	4	F	Child	16Ma02Dt
Levina	2	F	Child	16Ma02Dt
Arthur	.06	M	Infant	16Ma02Dt
MCGURRAY, Thos.	25	M	Laborer	16Ma02Dt
NEANY, Michl.	27	M	Laborer	16Ma02Dt
Mary	20	F	None	16Ma02Dt
CULLEN, Ellen	25	F	None	16Ma02Dt
DARLEY, John	31	M	Laborer	16Ma02Dt
MCCONNELL, Pat	30	M	Laborer	16Ma02Dt

NAMES OF PASSENGERS	AGE	SEX	OCCUPATIONS	DATE PORT SHIP
MCCONNELL, Andrew	27	M	Laborer	16Ma02Dt
MAHON, Stephen	32	M	Laborer	16Ma02Dt
GORMAN, John	22	M	Laborer	16Ma02Dt
BRUN, Peter	35	M	Laborer	16Ma02Dt
CARROLL, Michl.	50	M	Laborer	16Ma02Dt
Sarah	50	F	Laborer	16Ma02Dt
LELLAN, Wm.	18	M	Laborer	16Ma02Dt
CORROGAN, Jos.	29	M	Laborer	16Ma02Dt
MCGUINNIS, John	19	M	Laborer	16Ma02Dt
SMITH, Wm.	17	M	Laborer	16Ma02Dt
BURNS, John	18	M	Laborer	16Ma02Dt
TAGGART, Martin	26	M	Laborer	16Ma02Dt
FEAKIN, Andrew	20	M	Laborer	16Ma02Dt
MAHON, Catherine	21	F	Laborer	16Ma02Dt
Anne	23	F	None	16Ma02Dt
FAGERTY, Anne	24	F	None	16Ma02Dt
MAHON, Nickolas	20	M	Laborer	16Ma02Dt
CONNELLY, Pat	28	M	Laborer	16Ma02Dt
STRAINER, Wm.	26	M	Laborer	16Ma02Dt
MCBRIDE, Jerry	24	M	Laborer	16Ma02Dt
MURPHY, Henry	21	M	Laborer	16Ma02Dt
Mary	19	F	None	16Ma02Dt
CANTWELL, John	24	M	Laborer	16Ma02Dt
Kate	22	F	None	16Ma02Dt
JACOB, Margt.	60	F	None	16Ma02Dt
DELANEY, Pat	28	M	Laborer	16Ma02Dt
CAHILL, John	28	M	Laborer	16Ma02Dt
HOGAN, Edward	28	M	Laborer	16Ma02Dt
DELANCY, Martin	24	M	Laborer	16Ma02Dt
Bridget	26	F	None	16Ma02Dt
Catherine	27	F	None	16Ma02Dt
KISWICH, Pat	29	M	Laborer	16Ma02Dt
DOOLON, Ann	29	F	None	16Ma02Dt
BRODERICK, John	21	M	Laborer	16Ma02Dt
FURY, Daniel	29	M	Laborer	16Ma02Dt
LEWLO, Wm.	25	M	Laborer	16Ma02Dt
TINNAY, John	20	M	Laborer	16Ma02Dt
MCGEAHY, Stewart	55	M	Gdnr	16Ma02Dt
Jane	50	F	Gdnr	16Ma02Dt
John	21	M	Gdnr	16Ma02Dt
Robert	18	M	Gdnr	16Ma02Dt
Elizabeth	15	F	Gdnr	16Ma02Dt
Martha	12	F	Gdnr	16Ma02Dt
William	7	M	Child	16Ma02Dt
BRACKMAN, Patrick	20	M	Laborer	16Ma02Dt
MOORE, Joseph	16	M	Laborer	16Ma02Dt
DOOLON, John	18	M	Laborer	16Ma02Dt
ADAMS, Robert	20	M	Laborer	16Ma02Dt
HANLEY, James	26	M	Laborer	16Ma02Dt

WATERFORD 16 MAY 1850

From Waterford

NAMES OF PASSENGERS	AGE	SEX	OCCUPATIONS	DATE PORT SHIP
MCCARTHY, Thos.	54	M	Laborer	16Ma35Is
Mary	50	F	Unknown	16Ma35Is
John	23	M	Unknown	16Ma35Is
Michael	12	M	Unknown	16Ma35Is
Mary	20	F	Unknown	16Ma35Is
Thomas	11	M	Unknown	16Ma35Is
Bridget	.00	F	Infant	16Ma35Is
CAMPELL, Edward	20	M	Unknown	16Ma35Is
Bridget	23	F	Unknown	16Ma35Is
DWYER, William	20	M	Unknown	16Ma35Is
HOGAN, Patt	30	M	Unknown	16Ma35Is
Eliza	28	F	Unknown	16Ma35Is
MCMALIN, Mary	40	F	Unknown	16Ma35Is
Ann	7	F	Child	16Ma35Is
John	5	M	Child	16Ma35Is

NAMES OF PASSENGERS	AGE	SEX	OCCUPATIONS	DATE PORT SHIP
MCMALIN, Patt	.00	M	Infant	16Ma35Is
SHEEHY, James	45	M	Unknown	16Ma35Is
Jane	18	F	Unknown	16Ma35Is
MADIGAN, Thomas	16	M	Unknown	16Ma35Is
EGAN, Simon	23	M	Unknown	16Ma35Is
CARNNODY, Michael	22	M	Unknown	16Ma35Is
FRANE, Darby	35	F	Unknown	16Ma35Is
OBRIAN, Michael	26	M	Unknown	16Ma35Is
LAWLA, James	26	M	Unknown	16Ma35Is
MORAN, Patt	20	M	Unknown	16Ma35Is
David	12	M	Unknown	16Ma35Is
Ann	40	F	Unknown	16Ma35Is
Margaret	18	F	Unknown	16Ma35Is
MCNAMARA, Jo.	18	M	Unknown	16Ma35Is
KENAN, Thomas	27	M	Unknown	16Ma35Is
HERNE, Owen-A.	30	M	Unknown	16Ma35Is
MULCAHEY, Jno.	35	M	Unknown	16Ma35Is
Kate	30	F	Unknown	16Ma35Is
MORRIS, Margaret	30	F	Unknown	16Ma35Is
Denis	7	M	Child	16Ma35Is
Ellen	4	F	Child	16Ma35Is
Kitty	.00	F	Infant	16Ma35Is
BUCKLY, Con.	25	M	Unknown	16Ma35Is
PARKER, F.N.	25	M	Unknown	16Ma35Is
U-Mrs.	25	F	Unknown	16Ma35Is
Francis	5	M	Child	16Ma35Is
ENRIGHT, Kitty	13	F	Unknown	16Ma35Is
Henrietta	.00	F	Infant	16Ma35Is
PARKER, A.	25	F	Laborer	16Ma35Is
J.B.	33	M	Unknown	16Ma35Is
ENRIGHT, Patt	45	M	Unknown	16Ma35Is
LYNCH, James	28	M	Unknown	16Ma35Is
Michael	20	M	Unknown	16Ma35Is
CARROLL, Cornls.	22	M	Unknown	16Ma35Is
Bridget	24	F	Unknown	16Ma35Is
VALLORAN, Mary	24	F	Unknown	16Ma35Is
LINNANE, Patrick	30	M	Unknown	16Ma35Is
DOHERTY, Martin	30	M	Unknown	16Ma35Is
SHEAN, Michael	30	M	Unknown	16Ma35Is
MULCONY, Andrew	24	M	Unknown	16Ma35Is
Ally	25	M	Unknown	16Ma35Is
John	.00	M	Infant	16Ma35Is
SHEAN, Denis	22	M	Unknown	16Ma35Is
Margaret	26	F	Unknown	16Ma35Is
MINKAN, Bridget	22	F	Unknown	16Ma35Is
KENNADY, James	24	M	Unknown	16Ma35Is
FLANAGAN, John	35	M	Unknown	16Ma35Is
PARKER, Rd.	23	M	Unknown	16Ma35Is
MANNING, John	28	M	Unknown	16Ma35Is
HALLORAN, John	34	M	Unknown	16Ma35Is
Mary	27	F	Unknown	16Ma35Is
CARROLL, Mary	25	F	Unknown	16Ma35Is
MCNAMARA, Mary	24	F	Unknown	16Ma35Is
Bridget	22	F	Unknown	16Ma35Is
MCMAHON, Ann	21	F	Unknown	16Ma35Is
Patt	30	M	Unknown	16Ma35Is
Kate	30	F	Unknown	16Ma35Is
WALSH, Mary	35	F	Unknown	16Ma35Is
Michael	.00	M	Infant	16Ma35Is
James	4	M	Child	16Ma35Is
Patt	2	M	Child	16Ma35Is
HURLEY, Thomas	30	M	Unknown	16Ma35Is
Ellen	24	F	Unknown	16Ma35Is
Anne	24	F	Unknown	16Ma35Is
MOLONY, Mary	30	F	Unknown	16Ma35Is
Anne	20	F	Unknown	16Ma35Is
Margaret	18	F	Unknown	16Ma35Is
John	6	M	Child	16Ma35Is
KEANE, Michael	40	M	Unknown	16Ma35Is
Sarah	16	F	Unknown	16Ma35Is
FERRAY, Michael	26	M	Unknown	16Ma35Is
ODONNALL, Bridget	20	F	Unknown	16Ma35Is
Margaret	21	F	Unknown	16Ma35Is
ENGLISH, Thomas	40	M	Unknown	16Ma35Is
Bridget	40	F	Unknown	16Ma35Is
MORAN, Patt	20	M	Laborer	16Ma35Is
SHANAHAN, Patt	20	M	Unknown	16Ma35Is
OMARA, Mary	20	F	Unknown	16Ma35Is
HARTINGS, Mary	20	F	Unknown	16Ma35Is
MCFEGAN, Michael	56	M	Unknown	16Ma35Is
Ellen	50	F	Unknown	16Ma35Is
Denis	7	M	Child	16Ma35Is
Margaret	6	F	Child	16Ma35Is
Simon	.00	M	Infant	16Ma35Is
YALTY, Patt	26	M	Unknown	16Ma35Is
MORONY, Michael	40	M	Unknown	16Ma35Is
Mary	16	F	Unknown	16Ma35Is
HYNES, James	17	M	Unknown	16Ma35Is
HOWARD, Michael	33	M	Unknown	16Ma35Is
FITZGIBBONS, John	24	M	Unknown	16Ma35Is
Thomas	22	M	Unknown	16Ma35Is
MCGAN, Catherine	18	F	Unknown	16Ma35Is
GALLAGHER, Peter	30	M	Unknown	16Ma35Is
WALSH, Margaret	26	F	Unknown	16Ma35Is
GALLAGHER, Mary	30	F	Unknown	16Ma35Is
DELLORE, Michael	34	M	Unknown	16Ma35Is
LYNCH, James	20	M	Unknown	16Ma35Is
FOSTER, James	22	M	Unknown	16Ma35Is
BROWNE, Ellen	23	F	Unknown	16Ma35Is
ENRIGHT, John	21	M	Unknown	16Ma35Is
Mary	19	F	Unknown	16Ma35Is
CARROLL, John	24	M	Unknown	16Ma35Is
Lucy	22	F	Unknown	16Ma35Is
BAGAN, Patt	25	M	Unknown	16Ma35Is
Died-At-Sea				

YORKTOWN 17 MAY 1850

From London

NAMES OF PASSENGERS	AGE	SEX	OCCUPATIONS	DATE PORT SHIP
QUAID, James	28	M	None	17Ma06Dr
CALLAN, Catherine	20	F	None	17Ma06Dr

DOWNES 17 MAY 1850

From Waterford

NAMES OF PASSENGERS	AGE	SEX	OCCUPATIONS	DATE PORT SHIP
HAYES, Edward	24	M	Laborer	17Ma35Jn
POWER, Mary	24	F	Spinster	17Ma35Jn
GLASCOTT, Thomas	39	M	Laborer	17Ma35Jn
Ann	30	F	Wife	17Ma35Jn
Ann-Jr.	10	F	Unknown	17Ma35Jn
Jane	8	F	Child	17Ma35Jn
Bridget	7	F	Child	17Ma35Jn
Patrick	6	M	Child	17Ma35Jn
Mary	5	F	Child	17Ma35Jn
John	3	M	Child	17Ma35Jn
Eliza	.00	F	Infant	17Ma35Jn
Died-At-Sea				
HART, Michl.	30	M	Laborer	17Ma35Jn
DALTON, John	42	M	Laborer	17Ma35Jn
U	40	F	Wife	17Ma35Jn
SPRATT, Jas.	26	M	Unknown	17Ma35Jn
SHEA, John	27	M	Laborer	17Ma35Jn
CHRISTIAN, Denis	18	M	Laborer	17Ma35Jn
EVANS, John	50	M	Laborer	17Ma35Jn
Johanna	45	F	Wife	17Ma35Jn
James	22	M	Laborer	17Ma35Jn

NAMES OF PASSENGERS	AGE	SEX	OCCUPATIONS	DATE PORT SHIP
EVANS. Michl.	18	M	Laborer	17Ma35Jn
Mary	14	F	Wife	17Ma35Jn
Patrick	12	M	Unknown	17Ma35Jn
CULLITON. John	25	M	Laborer	17Ma35Jn
Eliza	22	F	Spinster	17Ma35Jn
William	5	M	Child	17Ma35Jn
Johanna	3	F	Child	17Ma35Jn
Patrick	.00	M	Infant	17Ma35Jn
Wm.	40	M	Laborer	17Ma35Jn
WALSH, Francis	35	M	Laborer	17Ma35Jn
Mary	30	F	Spinster	17Ma35Jn
John	22	M	Laborer	17Ma35Jn
Cathe.	20	F	Spinster	17Ma35Jn
Johanna	17	F	Spinster	17Ma35Jn
Mary	15	F	Spinster	17Ma35Jn
Bridget	12	F	Unknown	17Ma35Jn
Ellen	10	F	Unknown	17Ma35Jn
Mary	.00	F	Infant	17Ma35Jn
SMYTH, Bridget	20	F	Spinster	17Ma35Jn
HASSETT. David	23	M	Laborer	17Ma35Jn
MOLIERY, James	30	M	Laborer	17Ma35Jn
CASEY, Edmd.	32	M	Laborer	17Ma35Jn
QUAN, Maurce.	18	M	Laborer	17Ma35Jn
LINNOTT, Michls.	22	M	Carpenter	17Ma35Jn
BROWN, Math.	24	M	Laborer	17Ma35Jn
Thoms.	24	M	Laborer	17Ma35Jn
SMYTH, Ann	19	F	Spinster	17Ma35Jn
KELLY. Judy	20	F	Spinster	17Ma35Jn
MARA. Jno.	20	M	Shoemaker	17Ma35Jn
KELLY, Bridget	20	F	Spinster	17Ma35Jn
KEEFFE, Bridget	19	F	Spinster	17Ma35Jn
Patrick	17	M	Laborer	17Ma35Jn
QUINLON, Andw.	21	M	Laborer	17Ma35Jn
Margt.	19	F	Spinster	17Ma35Jn
KEARNEY. Thoms.	20	M	Laborer	17Ma35Jn
MURPHY, John	25	M	Laborer	17Ma35Jn
WALSH. Michl.	21	M	Laborer	17Ma35Jn
PURCELL, Joha.	21	F	Spinster	17Ma35Jn
BUTLER. Jams.	24	M	Laborer	17Ma35Jn
BROPHY. Thomas	26	M	Laborer	17Ma35Jn
BOYAN. James	23	M	Laborer	17Ma35Jn
CONDON, Patrick	21	M	Laborer	17Ma35Jn
Bridget	15	F	Spinster	17Ma35Jn
Cathr.	22	F	Spinster	17Ma35Jn
BOYAN, Jane	24	F	Spinster	17Ma35Jn
HEFFERMAN. David	30	M	Laborer	17Ma35Jn
DOHERTY. Pierce	14	M	None	17Ma35Jn
DUNPHY. James	7	M	Child	17Ma35Jn
CORMICK, Thos.	18	M	Laborer	17Ma35Jn
BREFN. Mary	20	F	Spinster	17Ma35Jn
KARRINAN, Martin	22	M	Laborer	17Ma35Jn
DEMPSY. Mary	20	F	Spinster	17Ma35Jn
WILLIAMS, Margt.	21	F	Spinster	17Ma35Jn
BUTLER. Cathe.	19	F	Spinster	17Ma35Jn
POWER. Wm.	25	M	Laborer	17Ma35Jn
CARROLL, Michl.	24	M	Laborer	17Ma35Jn
Bridget	18	F	Spinster	17Ma35Jn
WALLIS, Mat.	16	M	Laborer	17Ma35Jn
BENDERGAST. John	32	M	Laborer	17Ma35Jn
FITZGERALD. James	22	M	Laborer	17Ma35Jn
RENDE, Wm.	24	M	Laborer	17Ma35Jn
WALSH. Margt.	20	F	Spinster	17Ma35Jn
PHELAN, James	19	M	Laborer	17Ma35Jn
CASEY. James	25	M	Laborer	17Ma35Jn
MURPHY. Margt.	17	F	Spinster	17Ma35Jn
BUCKLEY. Danl.	20	M	Printer	17Ma35Jn
DUNN. John	20	M	Laborer	17Ma35Jn
Michl.	19	M	Laborer	17Ma35Jn
SHEA. Ann	20	F	Spinster	17Ma35Jn
DEMPSY. Thos.	24	M	Laborer	17Ma35Jn
Ellen	22	F	Spinster	17Ma35Jn
ROURKE, Margt.	20	F	Spinster	17Ma35Jn
DWYER. John	21	M	Laborer	17Ma35Jn
POWERS, Margt.	20	F	Spinster	17Ma35Jn
ROOKE. Edwd.	26	M	Laborer	17Ma35Jn
CURRAY. John	27	M	Laborer	17Ma35Jn
RYAN, Margt.	20	F	Spinster	17Ma35Jn
DWYER, Thos.	17	M	Laborer	17Ma35Jn

ATALANTA 17 MAY 1850

From Wexford

NAMES OF PASSENGERS	AGE	SEX	OCCUPATIONS	DATE PORT SHIP
BYRNE, Patk.	22	M	Laborer	17Ma57Jr
CARDIFF, Patk.	22	M	Cooper	17Ma57Jr
ROCHE. Edwd.	30	M	Carpenter	17Ma57Jr
SINNOTT, Mary	21	F	Servant	17Ma57Jr
Richd.	17	M	Laborer	17Ma57Jr
PIERCE. Mary	25	F	Servant	17Ma57Jr
MCCABE. Mary	24	F	Servant	17Ma57Jr
SINNOTT. John	27	M	Laborer	17Ma57Jr
Jane	21	F	Servant	17Ma57Jr
BUCKLEY. Mary	18	F	Servant	17Ma57Jr
CONNOR, Eliza	18	F	Servant	17Ma57Jr
MURPHY. Anne	27	F	Servant	17Ma57Jr
POWER. William	22	M	Laborer	17Ma57Jr
BRIEN, Nicholas	17	M	Laborer	17Ma57Jr
DEMPSEY. Elizabeth	25	F	Servant	17Ma57Jr
ROCHE. Judy	24	F	Servant	17Ma57Jr
DANBY, James	60	M	Laborer	17Ma57Jr
Mary	20	F	Servant	17Ma57Jr
Anne	17	F	Servant	17Ma57Jr
Michael	4	M	Child	17Ma57Jr
RONAN, Patrick	21	M	Laborer	17Ma57Jr
WHITLY, Patk.	26	M	Laborer	17Ma57Jr
MEYLER. Margt.	42	F	Servant	17Ma57Jr
SINNOTT, Patk.	6	M	Child	17Ma57Jr
HAGAN, John	40	M	Smith	17Ma57Jr
MONAGHAN, Timothy	24	M	Laborer	17Ma57Jr
Patrick	20	M	Laborer	17Ma57Jr
Elizabeth	25	F	Servant	17Ma57Jr
KAVANAGH, M.	18	M	Laborer	17Ma57Jr
DEMPSEY. Myles	21	M	Laborer	17Ma57Jr
NOWLAN, Michl.	27	M	Laborer	17Ma57Jr
FIELDING, Thos.	16	M	Laborer	17Ma57Jr
MURPHY. Chas.	27	M	Laborer	17Ma57Jr
Mary	25	F	Servant	17Ma57Jr
Thos.	26	M	Laborer	17Ma57Jr
Robert	22	M	Laborer	17Ma57Jr
BRENAN, Catharine	18	F	Servant	17Ma57Jr
WALSH, John	40	M	Laborer	17Ma57Jr
SINNOTT, Mary	18	F	Servant	17Ma57Jr
KAVANAGH. Catharine	18	F	Servant	17Ma57Jr
HANLON. Patk.	33	M	Laborer	17Ma57Jr
MURPHY. James	24	M	Laborer	17Ma57Jr
SHERLOCK, James	21	M	Laborer	17Ma57Jr
CREMINE. Lawce.	30	M	Laborer	17Ma57Jr
BRIEN. Thomas	20	M	Laborer	17Ma57Jr
NOWLAN, Kate	22	F	Servant	17Ma57Jr
SINNOTT. Anne	15	F	Servant	17Ma57Jr
Myles	24	M	Laborer	17Ma57Jr
Mary	22	F	Servant	17Ma57Jr
Catharine	20	F	Servant	17Ma57Jr
Thomas	18	M	Farmer	17Ma57Jr
Ellen	8	F	Child	17Ma57Jr
Patrick	24	M	Farmer	17Ma57Jr
Anne	54	F	Servant	17Ma57Jr
DOYLE. John	19	M	Blacksmith	17Ma57Jr
Margt.	25	F	Servant	17Ma57Jr
MONAHAN. Lawce.	35	M	Laborer	17Ma57Jr
SHANNON, Anne	27	F	Servant	17Ma57Jr
FOLEY. John	16	M	Laborer	17Ma57Jr
DOYLE, Anne	24	F	Servant	17Ma57Jr
BRIEN. Margaret	18	F	Servant	17Ma57Jr

NAMES OF PASSENGERS	AGE	SEX	OCCUPATIONS	DATE PORT SHIP
BUTLER. Mary	21	F	Servant	17Ma57Jr
HOGAN. Fanny	20	F	Servant	17Ma57Jr
DOYLE. Catharine	50	F	Servant	17Ma57Jr
Mary	25	F	Servant	17Ma57Jr
ROSSITER. Elizabeth	60	F	Servant	17Ma57Jr
DOYLE, James	20	M	Laborer	17Ma57Jr
SINNOTT. Margaret	27	F	Servant	17Ma57Jr
KEHOE. John	18	M	Tailor	17Ma57Jr
Mary	16	F	Servant	17Ma57Jr
GAHAN, Catharine	27	F	Servant	17Ma57Jr
HAYDEN. John	30	M	Laborer	17Ma57Jr
Mary	22	F	Servant	17Ma57Jr
MULLET. Mary	24	F	Servant	17Ma57Jr
NEVIN. Johanna	16	F	Servant	17Ma57Jr
Margaret	18	F	Servant	17Ma57Jr
Theresa	20	F	Servant	17Ma57Jr
John	12	M	Laborer	17Ma57Jr
Kate	10	F	Servant	17Ma57Jr
Mary-Anne	6	F	Child	17Ma57Jr
Patrick	4	M	Child	17Ma57Jr
James	2	M	Child	17Ma57Jr
Johanna	16	F	Laborer	17Ma57Jr
BOLGER. John	20	M	Servant	17Ma57Jr
GRANNELL, Mary	26	F	Laborer	17Ma57Jr
DEMPSEY. Catharine	54	F	Servant	17Ma57Jr
Dennis	24	M	Servant	17Ma57Jr
Mary	.00	F	Infant	17Ma57Jr
BOLGER. Mary	24	F	Servant	17Ma57Jr
ROSSITER. John	19	M	Laborer	17Ma57Jr
CREMINE. Bridget	21	F	Servant	17Ma57Jr
COGLEY. Anty.	33	F	Servant	17Ma57Jr
DEMPSEY. Susan	19	F	Servant	17Ma57Jr
Owen	24	M	Laborer	17Ma57Jr
Dorah	18	F	Servant	17Ma57Jr
Mary	16	F	Servant	17Ma57Jr
CROWLY. Catharine	19	F	Servant	17Ma57Jr
CONNOR. Margaret	00	F	Servant	17Ma57Jr
KEARIN, John	30	M	Laborer	17Ma57Jr
KEHOE. Hanna	19	F	Servant	17Ma57Jr
DOYLE. John	19	M	Laborer	17Ma57Jr
BREFNE. Thomas	30	M	Laborer	17Ma57Jr
MCINTYRE. Patk.	50	M	Steward	17Ma57Jr
Thomas	17	M	Steward	17Ma57Jr
Richd.	14	M	Steward	17Ma57Jr
Mary	9	F	Child	17Ma57Jr
Eliza	11	F	Servant	17Ma57Jr
COYLE. Jane	24	F	Servant	17Ma57Jr
RUDD. Thomas	27	M	Laborer	17Ma57Jr
FENLIN. Margt.	25	F	Servant	17Ma57Jr
FITZPATRICK. Patrick	22	M	Laborer	17Ma57Jr
Eliza	20	F	Servant	17Ma57Jr
Mary	19	F	Servant	17Ma57Jr
REDMOND. Gregory	25	M	Laborer	17Ma57Jr
BRIEN. Ellen	38	F	Servant	17Ma57Jr
Michael	19	M	Laborer	17Ma57Jr
Catharine	50	F	Servant	17Ma57Jr
Richard	21	M	Laborer	17Ma57Jr
NEVIN, Ellen	8	F	Child	17Ma57Jr
NAGLE. James	21	M	Laborer	17Ma57Jr
DOYLE. Mary	24	F	Servant	17Ma57Jr
KELLY. Martin	22	M	Farmer	17Ma57Jr
John	20	M	Farmer	17Ma57Jr
LAFFAR. Thos.	20	M	Cbtmkr	17Ma57Jr
SIMONDE, Richd.E.	20	M	Cbtmkr	17Ma57Jr
QUIRK, Philip	30	M	Laborer	17Ma57Jr
NEVIN, John	24	M	Laborer	17Ma57Jr
GRANNILL, Edwd.	32	M	Laborer	17Ma57Jr
CONNOR. Thos.	33	M	Laborer	17Ma57Jr

CAMBRIDGE 17 MAY 1850

From Liverpool

NAMES OF PASSENGERS	AGE	SEX	OCCUPATIONS	DATE PORT SHIP
MULVERY, Ann	25	F	Servant	17Ma02Dm
NOWLAN, Susan	18	F	Servant	17Ma02Dm
LEE. James	20	M	Laborer	17Ma02Dm
HEFFERAN, Jane	20	F	Servant	17Ma02Dm
MORGAN, Bridget	24	F	Servant	17Ma02Dm
HORAN, Francis	24	M	Laborer	17Ma02Dm
NUGENT. Mathew	25	M	Laborer	17Ma02Dm
MILLS. Thomas	30	M	Laborer	17Ma02Dm
Mary	26	F	Servant	17Ma02Dm
MILLAR, Robert	22	M	Farmer	17Ma02Dm
RUSSELE, Christopher	21	M	Farmer	17Ma02Dm
John	20	M	Farmer	17Ma02Dm
HADDENS, William	30	M	Laborer	17Ma02Dm
BURKE, Patrick	26	M	Laborer	17Ma02Dm
ROCK, Daniel	26	M	Laborer	17Ma02Dm
HEAD. Thomas	20	M	Laborer	17Ma02Dm
Catherine	16	F	Laborer	17Ma02Dm
QUINN. Patrick	18	M	Laborer	17Ma02Dm
Mary	17	F	Laborer	17Ma02Dm
ELLIOTT. Robert	23	M	Laborer	17Ma02Dm
Ellen	20	F	Laborer	17Ma02Dm
GALLAGHER, Felix	20	M	Laborer	17Ma02Dm
FITZPATRICK, James	32	M	Laborer	17Ma02Dm
DUFFY, James	28	M	Laborer	17Ma02Dm
BURK, Cornelius	20	M	Laborer	17Ma02Dm
EALCORT. Luke	24	M	Laborer	17Ma02Dm
QUINNLOW, Edward	27	M	Laborer	17Ma02Dm
HADFIELD, Andrew	25	M	Weaver	17Ma02Dm
Mary	3	F	Child	17Ma02Dm
DONOHOE. Michael	17	M	Laborer	17Ma02Dm
CAIN, Jane	50	M	Servant	17Ma02Dm
Bernard	11	M	None	17Ma02Dm
LANDERS, Margaret	28	F	Servant	17Ma02Dm
Mary	8	F	Child	17Ma02Dm
Michael	6	M	Child	17Ma02Dm
Ann	.00	F	Infant	17Ma02Dm
SUITE, Mick	40	M	Laborer	17Ma02Dm
Eliza	35	F	None	17Ma02Dm
Bridget	9	F	Child	17Ma02Dm
Thomas	7	M	Child	17Ma02Dm
Simon	5	M	Child	17Ma02Dm
Mary	.00	F	Infant	17Ma02Dm
CONNOR, Mary	12	F	None	17Ma02Dm
GUNNER. Cornelius	22	M	Laborer	17Ma02Dm
Bridget	32	F	Servant	17Ma02Dm
Hannah	20	F	Servant	17Ma02Dm
Margaret	18	F	Servant	17Ma02Dm
KEILLY, Ann	22	F	Servant	17Ma02Dm
GILHEARY, Mary	17	F	Servant	17Ma02Dm
KENNAN, Ann	22	F	Servant	17Ma02Dm
FLEISHER. Mary	20	F	Servant	17Ma02Dm
GALVIN, Michael	30	M	Laborer	17Ma02Dm
John	11	M	None	17Ma02Dm
HANLY, Mary	60	F	Servant	17Ma02Dm
Mary	20	F	Servant	17Ma02Dm
BROADLEY. James	30	M	Laborer	17Ma02Dm
Patrick	10	M	None	17Ma02Dm
MARTIN, Ann	18	F	Servant	17Ma02Dm
PHILIPS, Ann	55	F	Servant	17Ma02Dm
CLARK, Ann	19	F	Servant	17Ma02Dm
DUNN. James	24	M	Laborer	17Ma02Dm
MCENTER. James	21	M	Laborer	17Ma02Dm
MCCARRON. Catherine	40	F	Servant	17Ma02Dm
Ann	11	F	None	17Ma02Dm
Eliza	9	F	Child	17Ma02Dm

NAMES OF PASSENGERS	AGE	SEX	OCCUPATIONS	DATE PORT SHIP
MCCARRON. Bridget	6	F	Child	17Ma02Dm
DUFFY. Biddy	25	F	Servant	17Ma02Dm
HISTIN, Daniel	25	M	Laborer	17Ma02Dm
WALTERS, Roger	24	M	Laborer	17Ma02Dm
HANELLY, Martin	26	M	Laborer	17Ma02Dm
BECKETT. Sarah	21	F	Servant	17Ma02Dm
MORAN, Marcella	18	F	Servant	17Ma02Dm
FLESHIN, Rose	24	F	Servant	17Ma02Dm
REYNOLDS, Bernard	18	M	Laborer	17Ma02Dm
Mary	16	F	None	17Ma02Dm
DUNIGAN, James	20	M	Laborer	17Ma02Dm
POWER. William	22	M	Laborer	17Ma02Dm
KEELEY. Mark	26	M	Laborer	17Ma02Dm
MANION. Thomas	21	M	Laborer	17Ma02Dm
Michael	20	M	Laborer	17Ma02Dm
MANLAN. William	21	M	Laborer	17Ma02Dm
CONNOR. Michael	18	M	Laborer	17Ma02Dm
CASEY. James	15	M	Laborer	17Ma02Dm
WOODS. Mary-A.	22	F	Servant	17Ma02Dm
RYAN. Mary	13	F	Servant	17Ma02Dm
MCPEAKE. Bridget	20	F	Servant	17Ma02Dm
NICHOLS. Catherine	30	M	Servant	17Ma02Dm
Essy	6	F	Child	17Ma02Dm
MCGOVERN. Mary	44	F	Servant	17Ma02Dm
Patrick	22	M	Laborer	17Ma02Dm
Bridget	18	F	Laborer	17Ma02Dm
Hannah	16	F	Laborer	17Ma02Dm
Peter	11	M	Laborer	17Ma02Dm
DEGIRAN. Michael	35	M	Laborer	17Ma02Dm
Ann	28	F	Servant	17Ma02Dm
Owen	6	M	Child	17Ma02Dm
Thomas	4	M	Child	17Ma02Dm
SMITH. Mathew	14	M	Servant	17Ma02Dm
Peter	11	M	Servant	17Ma02Dm
James	7	M	Child	17Ma02Dm
Catherine	5	F	Child	17Ma02Dm
Ann	.00	F	Infant	17Ma02Dm
FINNEGAN. Peter	20	M	Servant	17Ma02Dm
GARRAGAN. Philip	24	M	Laborer	17Ma02Dm
Judith	20	F	Laborer	17Ma02Dm
MCPHERSON. Ellen	36	F	Servant	17Ma02Dm
GRACE. Winifred	50	F	Servant	17Ma02Dm
Bridget	18	F	Servant	17Ma02Dm
MCDONALD. Bridget	30	F	Servant	17Ma02Dm
PHELAN. Martin	52	M	Laborer	17Ma02Dm
Peggy	42	F	Laborer	17Ma02Dm
Peggy	10	F	Laborer	17Ma02Dm
MOOLY. Thomas	10	M	Laborer	17Ma02Dm
GAFFNEY, Bernard	30	M	Laborer	17Ma02Dm
MARTIN. Michael	20	M	Laborer	17Ma02Dm
BARRELL, Mary	20	F	Servant	17Ma02Dm
WALSH. Judith	30	F	Servant	17Ma02Dm
Richard	4	M	Child	17Ma02Dm
Ellen	.00	F	Infant	17Ma02Dm
FLYNN. Maria	9	F	Child	17Ma02Dm
Elisha	7	M	Child	17Ma02Dm
OCONNOR, Margaret	30	F	Servant	17Ma02Dm
Charles	13	M	Servant	17Ma02Dm
Margaret	12	F	Servant	17Ma02Dm
Randall	7	M	Child	17Ma02Dm
Mary	5	F	Child	17Ma02Dm
Mathew	.00	M	Infant	17Ma02Dm
KENNY, John	18	M	Laborer	17Ma02Dm
WILLIAMS, Robert	21	M	Laborer	17Ma02Dm
COLINSHIN. Peter	20	M	Laborer	17Ma02Dm
COOLY. Catherine	28	F	Servant	17Ma02Dm
Peter	11	M	Servant	17Ma02Dm
GILLS. Ann	23	F	Servant	17Ma02Dm
DIGNAN, Thomas	8	M	Child	17Ma02Dm
CODY. Richard	40	M	Laborer	17Ma02Dm
KILLEADY. Ann	24	F	Servant	17Ma02Dm
Ann	60	F	Servant	17Ma02Dm
Thomas	24	M	Laborer	17Ma02Dm
Patrick	16	M	Laborer	17Ma02Dm
CODY. Eleanor	24	F	Servant	17Ma02Dm

NAMES OF PASSENGERS	AGE	SEX	OCCUPATIONS	DATE PORT SHIP
SHERIDAN, Rose	30	F	Servant	17Ma02Dm
DOWD, Bridget	11	F	Servant	17Ma02Dm
CLASSICK. Margaret	17	F	Servant	17Ma02Dm
OWEN. Catherine	16	F	Servant	17Ma02Dm
CLASSICK, Mary	50	F	Servant	17Ma02Dm
Michael	9	M	Child	17Ma02Dm
Mary	6	F	Child	17Ma02Dm
GALLAGHER. Honor	30	F	Servant	17Ma02Dm
HYNES, Ann	20	F	Servant	17Ma02Dm
OBRIEN. Margaret	20	F	Servant	17Ma02Dm
John	14	M	None	17Ma02Dm
NOONAN, Catherine	20	F	Servant	17Ma02Dm
Margaret	18	F	Servant	17Ma02Dm
BYRNE, Bryan	18	M	Laborer	17Ma02Dm
MCBREATY. Edward	20	M	Laborer	17Ma02Dm
MORAN, John	16	M	Laborer	17Ma02Dm
DEVENY, Henry	20	M	Laborer	17Ma02Dm
MCDERMOTT. James	20	M	Laborer	17Ma02Dm
HENSTER. James	20	M	Laborer	17Ma02Dm
BRISLAND. Catherine	28	F	Servant	17Ma02Dm
PATTERSON. Eliza	17	F	Servant	17Ma02Dm
DOLAN, Ann	20	F	Servant	17Ma02Dm
MCFADIN, Catherine	21	F	Servant	17Ma02Dm
NESTOR, Margaret	17	F	Servant	17Ma02Dm
CURLEY. Kerwin	20	M	Laborer	17Ma02Dm
FITZPATRICK, Lawrence	22	M	Laborer	17Ma02Dm
CURLEY, Michael	21	M	Laborer	17Ma02Dm
WALKER, Mary	20	F	Servant	17Ma02Dm
HOYAN. Julia	28	F	Servant	17Ma02Dm
Hetty	27	F	Servant	17Ma02Dm
RYAN, Catherine	24	F	Servant	17Ma02Dm
DONOHOE, Margaret	20	F	Servant	17Ma02Dm
MARTIN, Sarah	18	F	Servant	17Ma02Dm
MCDERMOTT, Rose	15	F	Servant	17Ma02Dm
SHELIN, Mary	30	F	Servant	17Ma02Dm
Catherine	5	F	Child	17Ma02Dm
Daniel	.00	M	Infant	17Ma02Dm
MOORE, Timothy	20	M	Laborer	17Ma02Dm
MURRY. James	27	M	Laborer	17Ma02Dm
DRISCOLL, William	22	M	Laborer	17Ma02Dm
Catherine	24	F	Servant	17Ma02Dm
KEEGAN, Bridget	30	F	Servant	17Ma02Dm
Mary	3	F	Child	17Ma02Dm
Edward	.00	M	Infant	17Ma02Dm
LOGUR, William	21	M	Laborer	17Ma02Dm
MCGRIDDY, John	22	M	Laborer	17Ma02Dm
MCCUSKY, Bessy	20	F	Spinster	17Ma02Dm
GAIRAN. William	26	M	Laborer	17Ma02Dm
MCKEON, Thomas	14	M	Farmer	17Ma02Dm
Mary	16	F	None	17Ma02Dm
BROADLY, James	30	M	Farmer	17Ma02Dm
Patrick	22	M	Farmer	17Ma02Dm
MURRY. Ann	40	F	Servant	17Ma02Dm
Mathew	13	M	None	17Ma02Dm
Patrick	7	M	Child	17Ma02Dm
John	4	M	Child	17Ma02Dm
Thomas	.00	M	Infant	17Ma02Dm
DROINE. John	26	M	Laborer	17Ma02Dm
BUSHE. John	17	M	Laborer	17Ma02Dm
CONROY. Thomas	50	M	Laborer	17Ma02Dm
Catherine	50	F	None	17Ma02Dm
James	14	M	None	17Ma02Dm
Richard	11	M	None	17Ma02Dm
Michael	8	M	Child	17Ma02Dm
Thomas	18	M	None	17Ma02Dm
BUTLER. Margaret	20	F	Servant	17Ma02Dm
MAHER, Mary	8	F	Child	17Ma02Dm
HESLIN, Rose	21	F	Servant	17Ma02Dm
MURRY, Catherine	28	F	Servant	17Ma02Dm
William	28	M	Laborer	17Ma02Dm
ROCHE, William	20	M	Laborer	17Ma02Dm
MONAGHAN, Mary	48	F	Servant	17Ma02Dm
Martin	18	M	Laborer	17Ma02Dm
Dennis	15	M	Laborer	17Ma02Dm
Honora	16	F	None	17Ma02Dm

NAMES OF PASSENGERS	AGE	SEX	OCCUPATIONS	DATE PORT SHIP
MONAGHAN, Catherine	11	F	None	17Ma02Dm
KEEFE, Richard	19	M	Laborer	17Ma02Dm
RYAN, Margaret	30	F	Servant	17Ma02Dm
DOHERTY, Patrick	27	M	Servant	17Ma02Dm
MCCARTY, Thomas	24	M	Laborer	17Ma02Dm
HARLY, James	18	M	Laborer	17Ma02Dm
GEARY, Abby	20	F	Servant	17Ma02Dm
MONAGHAN, John	18	M	Laborer	17Ma02Dm
Mary	24	F	Servant	17Ma02Dm
ONEILE, Jane	21	F	Servant	17Ma02Dm
WINTER, Daniel	22	M	Laborer	17Ma02Dm
Isaac	20	M	Laborer	17Ma02Dm
KEATING, John	30	M	Laborer	17Ma02Dm
Mary	5	F	Child	17Ma02Dm
MONAGHAN, Ann	20	F	Servant	17Ma02Dm
DOYLE, Patrick	11	M	Laborer	17Ma02Dm
KORKE, John	21	M	Laborer	17Ma02Dm
James	11	M	Laborer	17Ma02Dm
Patrick	9	M	Child	17Ma02Dm
MULLIN, Thomas	26	M	Laborer	17Ma02Dm
FITZPATRICK, Maria	22	F	Servant	17Ma02Dm
COLLINS, Thomas	25	M	Laborer	17Ma02Dm
COINER, Rose	25	F	Servant	17Ma02Dm
DILLON, Catherine	20	F	Servant	17Ma02Dm
COUGHLIN, Catherine	20	F	Servant	17Ma02Dm
Catherine	30	F	Servant	17Ma02Dm
MCTAIGHE, Ann	45	F	Servant	17Ma02Dm
Mary	16	F	Servant	17Ma02Dm
Catherine	17	F	Servant	17Ma02Dm
Ann	10	F	Servant	17Ma02Dm
Patrick	9	M	Child	17Ma02Dm
John	8	M	Child	17Ma02Dm
Biddy	7	F	Child	17Ma02Dm
Margaret	3	F	Child	17Ma02Dm
Peter	4	M	Child	17Ma02Dm
Luke	.00	M	Infant	17Ma02Dm
Francis	5	M	Child	17Ma02Dm
FITZSIMONS, John	30	M	Laborer	17Ma02Dm
LEONARD, John	21	M	Laborer	17Ma02Dm
Mary	6	F	Child	17Ma02Dm
Eliza	4	F	Child	17Ma02Dm
KING, Ellen	18	F	Servant	17Ma02Dm
MCKERN, John	26	M	Laborer	17Ma02Dm
BARCLAY, James	16	M	Laborer	17Ma02Dm
BANNET, Margaret	21	F	Servant	17Ma02Dm
KENNY, Jane	18	F	Servant	17Ma02Dm
BRISLANE, Ann	18	F	Servant	17Ma02Dm
HIGGINS, Mary	28	F	Servant	17Ma02Dm
REILY, Ann	21	F	Servant	17Ma02Dm
BENSON, Margaret	18	F	Servant	17Ma02Dm
HORAN, Mary	40	F	Servant	17Ma02Dm
Margaret	15	F	Servant	17Ma02Dm
Mary	15	F	Servant	17Ma02Dm
Sarah	9	F	Child	17Ma02Dm
Ann	4	F	Child	17Ma02Dm
Johannah	2	F	Child	17Ma02Dm
CARGERY, John	22	M	Tailor	17Ma02Dm
NUGENT, Michael	22	M	Tailor	17Ma02Dm
Bridget	18	F	None	17Ma02Dm
SMITH, Catherine	40	F	Servant	17Ma02Dm
Ann	36	F	Servant	17Ma02Dm
KING, Bridget	14	F	Servant	17Ma02Dm
LANDERS, Marshal	25	M	Servant	17Ma02Dm
DUNN, Patrick	15	M	Carpenter	17Ma02Dm
KENNEDY, Mary	15	F	Servant	17Ma02Dm
EWING, George	12	M	Farm Hand	17Ma02Dm
Robert	10	M	Farm Hand	17Ma02Dm
MCCANLEY, Bridget	17	M	Servant	17Ma02Dm
WEINY, George-A.	25	M	Shoemaker	17Ma02Dm
ARMSTRONG, Robert	20	M	Shoemaker	17Ma02Dm
KENNY, Bridget	14	F	Servant	17Ma02Dm
OKEEFFE, John	21	M	Farmer	17Ma02Dm
DONOVAN, William	12	M	None	17Ma02Dm
Timothy	10	M	None	17Ma02Dm
KENNARY, Eliza	22	F	Servant	17Ma02Dm

NAMES OF PASSENGERS	AGE	SEX	OCCUPATIONS	DATE PORT SHIP
CARTY, James	15	M	Tailor	17Ma02Dm
REILLY, Michael	25	M	Tailor	17Ma02Dm
MCPHERSON, David	10	M	None	17Ma02Dm
Mary-Ann	8	F	Child	17Ma02Dm
James	2	M	Child	17Ma02Dm
Robert	23	M	None	17Ma02Dm
Rachel	20	F	None	17Ma02Dm
ELCHER, Eliza	20	F	Servant	17Ma02Dm
LOANE, Eliza	20	F	Servant	17Ma02Dm
HALL, Bridget	24	F	Servant	17Ma02Dm
Catherine	20	F	Servant	17Ma02Dm
DUNIGAN, Charles	25	M	Shoemaker	17Ma02Dm

A.Z. 17 MAY 1850

From Liverpool

NAMES OF PASSENGERS	AGE	SEX	OCCUPATIONS	DATE PORT SHIP
QUINN, Ann	18	F	Servant	17Ma02Ed
BANICK, Edward	18	M	Shoemaker	17Ma02Ed
HOYNES, Sally	21	F	Servant	17Ma02Ed
GARDEN, John	30	M	Laborer	17Ma02Ed
John	4	M	Child	17Ma02Ed
SHERIDAN, Mary	25	F	Servant	17Ma02Ed
Bridget	3	F	Child	17Ma02Ed
MCNELLY, Jane	21	F	Servant	17Ma02Ed
MATHEWS, Ben	30	M	Laborer	17Ma02Ed
Pat	25	M	Laborer	17Ma02Ed
Rose	60	F	Servant	17Ma02Ed
MOLHOLEM, Bet.	20	F	Servant	17Ma02Ed
Jane	16	F	Servant	17Ma02Ed
Olney	15	M	Laborer	17Ma02Ed
BURNS, Eliza	20	F	Dressmaker	17Ma02Ed
MCINTEE, James	22	M	Laborer	17Ma02Ed
Rebeca	40	F	Servant	17Ma02Ed
CALIGAN, Rose	28	F	Servant	17Ma02Ed
George	14	M	Servant	17Ma02Ed
Margret	9	F	Child	17Ma02Ed
CONISKY, Terence	20	M	Laborer	17Ma02Ed
BRADY, Eliza	19	F	Servant	17Ma02Ed
FITZGERALD, John	19	M	Pipe Maker	17Ma02Ed
James	17	M	Pipe Maker	17Ma02Ed
Nicolas	15	M	Pipe Maker	17Ma02Ed
Pat	14	M	Pipe Maker	17Ma02Ed
Maria	22	F	Servant	17Ma02Ed
Cath.	28	F	Servant	17Ma02Ed
DUFFY, Bridget	24	F	Servant	17Ma02Ed
CARNEY, Catherine	16	F	Servant	17Ma02Ed
LUNNEMAN, Catherine	22	F	Servant	17Ma02Ed
STICKEY, Mat.	16	M	Laborer	17Ma02Ed
DWIRE, Mary	40	F	Unknown	17Ma02Ed
NUGENT, W.	23	M	Laborer	17Ma02Ed
Thomas	16	M	Shoemaker	17Ma02Ed
RAY, Sam	23	M	Gdnr	17Ma02Ed
Eliza	60	F	Unknown	17Ma02Ed
Eliza	24	F	Unknown	17Ma02Ed
WILLSON, Charles	17	M	Servant	17Ma02Ed
DUGAN, Allice	36	F	Servant	17Ma02Ed
Bridt.	18	F	Servant	17Ma02Ed
Edward	16	M	Servant	17Ma02Ed
James	14	M	Servant	17Ma02Ed
Judeth	12	F	Servant	17Ma02Ed
Cathren	10	F	Servant	17Ma02Ed
Margret	8	F	Child	17Ma02Ed
Julia	6	F	Child	17Ma02Ed
Dennis	4	M	Child	17Ma02Ed
Mary	3	F	Child	17Ma02Ed
Ellen	.00	F	Infant	17Ma02Ed
Allice	2	F	Child	17Ma02Ed
SULIVAN, Michael	25	M	Servant	17Ma02Ed

NAMES OF PASSENGERS	AGE	SEX	OCCUPATIONS	DATE PORT SHIP
RYAN, Mary	14	F	Servant	17Ma02Ed
Pat	28	M	Carpenter	17Ma02Ed
Bridget	24	F	Unknown	17Ma02Ed
Will	22	M	Unknown	17Ma02Ed
Nora	20	F	Unknown	17Ma02Ed
CURK, Allice	18	F	Unknown	17Ma02Ed
Bridget	16	F	Unknown	17Ma02Ed
DURIN, Pat	20	M	Unknown	17Ma02Ed
Johanna	19	F	Unknown	17Ma02Ed
DESMAN, Pat	35	M	Fisherman	17Ma02Ed
Corn.	40	M	Fisherman	17Ma02Ed
DUGAN, William	35	M	Farmer	17Ma02Ed
Margret	30	F	Unknown	17Ma02Ed
Ellen	9	F	Child	17Ma02Ed
Mary	6	F	Child	17Ma02Ed
Cathren	.00	F	Infant	17Ma02Ed
NEAL, Michael	23	M	Unknown	17Ma02Ed
GAILAN, John	47	M	Farmer	17Ma02Ed
Thomas	40	M	Farmer	17Ma02Ed
William	28	M	Unknown	17Ma02Ed
Thomas	18	M	Unknown	17Ma02Ed
Bridget	40	F	Unknown	17Ma02Ed
Mary	25	F	Unknown	17Ma02Ed
MAHER, Dan	29	M	Farmer	17Ma02Ed
Betty	27	F	Unknown	17Ma02Ed
Thomas	7	M	Child	17Ma02Ed
Fill	5	M	Child	17Ma02Ed
Pat	2	M	Child	17Ma02Ed
Bridget	.00	F	Infant	17Ma02Ed
MULLEN, H.	40	M	Laborer	17Ma02Ed
U-Mrs.	40	F	Unknown	17Ma02Ed
Thomas	49	M	Unknown	17Ma02Ed
Mary	17	F	Unknown	17Ma02Ed
Rose	10	F	Unknown	17Ma02Ed
LITTLE, Pat	26	M	Mason	17Ma02Ed
James	26	M	None	17Ma02Ed
Allice	22	F	None	17Ma02Ed
Mary	22	F	None	17Ma02Ed
Thomas	.00	M	Infant	17Ma02Ed
MCVAY, Michael	35	M	Farmer	17Ma02Ed
J.	20	M	None	17Ma02Ed
Sally	22	F	None	17Ma02Ed
SLATERY, Bridget	22	F	None	17Ma02Ed
CLARNEY, Sally	55	F	None	17Ma02Ed
REARDEN, Mat.	13	M	None	17Ma02Ed
ROGERS, Rose	22	F	Servant	17Ma02Ed
COSGROVE, Libe	25	F	Servant	17Ma02Ed
FENEY, William	35	M	Laborer	17Ma02Ed
CUNNINGHAM, John	29	M	Laborer	17Ma02Ed
GRENON, Michael	26	M	Laborer	17Ma02Ed
CLIMES, James	20	M	Laborer	17Ma02Ed
DOUGERTY, Ellen	18	F	Dressmaker	17Ma02Ed
WARD, Charles	20	M	Tailor	17Ma02Ed
MONEGAN, Martin	32	M	Laborer	17Ma02Ed
Eliza	20	F	None	17Ma02Ed
DALEY, Thomas	26	M	None	17Ma02Ed
Dan.	38	M	None	17Ma02Ed
Owen	32	M	None	17Ma02Ed
Ann	14	F	None	17Ma02Ed
MCCLOGOGO, John	25	M	None	17Ma02Ed
Mary	26	F	None	17Ma02Ed
COLGAN, Margaret	22	F	Laborer	17Ma02Ed
KENNEDY, Pat	19	M	None	17Ma02Ed
SPANE, Ann	15	F	None	17Ma02Ed
Michael	18	M	None	17Ma02Ed
MONEGAN, Bridget	20	F	None	17Ma02Ed
RYAN, Martin	30	M	None	17Ma02Ed
CANE, Mary	23	F	None	17Ma02Ed
MCGOUGH, Pat	38	M	None	17Ma02Ed
Mary	38	F	None	17Ma02Ed
Ann	5	F	Child	17Ma02Ed
SHALE, Terrence	63	M	Farmer	17Ma02Ed
Mary	60	F	None	17Ma02Ed
Criss	21	M	None	17Ma02Ed
James	19	M	None	17Ma02Ed
SHALE, Ann	14	F	None	17Ma02Ed
Catherine	10	F	None	17Ma02Ed
KILLNONEY, Pat	32	M	None	17Ma02Ed
DULLEY, Ellen	22	F	Unknown	17Ma02Ed
RILLEY, James	30	M	None	17Ma02Ed
SMITH, George	18	M	None	17Ma02Ed
LENNON, Michael	21	M	None	17Ma02Ed
OHARE, Ann	21	F	None	17Ma02Ed

NEW-WORLD 17 MAY 1850

From Liverpool

NAMES OF PASSENGERS	AGE	SEX	OCCUPATIONS	DATE PORT SHIP
LITTLE, Eliz.	22	F	Servant	17Ma02Ec
Cath.	18	F	Servant	17Ma02Ec
HENRY, Eliz.	20	F	Servant	17Ma02Ec
HUNTER, Henry	25	M	Joiner	17Ma02Ec
PRICE, Joseph	30	F	Smith	17Ma02Ec
SHANNON, James	20	M	Smith	17Ma02Ec
MCKELVEY, John	58	M	Bookkeeper	17Ma02Ec
U-Mrs.	58	F	Wife	17Ma02Ec
Mary	21	F	Servant	17Ma02Ec
Joseph	33	M	Grocer	17Ma02Ec
M.	28	U	Servant	17Ma02Ec
Jno.	7	M	Child	17Ma02Ec
Thos.	5	M	Child	17Ma02Ec
Margt.	4	F	Child	17Ma02Ec
Mary	2	F	Child	17Ma02Ec
Martha	.00	F	Infant	17Ma02Ec
MADDOCK, Ann	12	F	Servant	17Ma02Ec
THOMPSON, William	22	M	Farmer	17Ma02Ec
MULHOLLAND, Hugh	22	M	Farmer	17Ma02Ec
EVERETT, John	47	M	Farmer	17Ma02Ec
Sarah	44	F	Servant	17Ma02Ec
Mary	21	F	Servant	17Ma02Ec
Charles	19	M	Laborer	17Ma02Ec
Rachael	17	F	Servant	17Ma02Ec
Alice	7	F	Child	17Ma02Ec
Elinor	5	F	Child	17Ma02Ec
R-Ch	17	U	Servant	17Ma02Ec
LEGRACE, Thos.	22	M	Watchmaker	17Ma02Ec
CLARK, Thomas	30	M	Laborer	17Ma02Ec
Cath.	28	F	Servant	17Ma02Ec
DUNN, Thos.	30	M	Laborer	17Ma02Ec
CLARK, D.	20	U	Farmer	17Ma02Ec
Julia	18	F	Servant	17Ma02Ec
COYNE, U	20	M	Shoemaker	17Ma02Ec
Mary	18	F	Servant	17Ma02Ec
WALLACE, Mary	18	F	Servant	17Ma02Ec
TURLEY, Thos.	20	M	Clerk	17Ma02Ec
John	14	M	Servant	17Ma02Ec
MCDONNEL, Brid.	40	F	Servant	17Ma02Ec
Mary	20	F	Servant	17Ma02Ec
HARMON, Patrick	31	M	Servant	17Ma02Ec
Mary	25	F	Servant	17Ma02Ec
Ann	21	F	Servant	17Ma02Ec
Bridget	22	F	Servant	17Ma02Ec
MALONE, James	18	M	Silversmith	17Ma02Ec
MCAVERY, Ann	25	F	Servant	17Ma02Ec
Mary	17	F	Servant	17Ma02Ec
LAWLESS, Michael	20	M	Laborer	17Ma02Ec
STANKARD, Thos.	20	M	Laborer	17Ma02Ec
HILL, Pat.	26	M	Tailor	17Ma02Ec
U-Mrs.	25	F	Wife	17Ma02Ec
HARRELL, Ellen	24	F	Servant	17Ma02Ec
CURRY, U	35	U	Servant	17Ma02Ec
CORCORAN, Thos.	27	M	Servant	17Ma02Ec
MAIN, Mary	27	M	Servant	17Ma02Ec
ODONNELL, Luke	40	M	Wheelwright	17Ma02Ec

NAMES OF PASSENGERS	AGE	SEX	OCCUPATIONS	DATE PORT SHIP
ODONNELL, Margaret	40	F	Servant	17Ma02Ec
FETHERSTONE, Susan	35	F	Servant	17Ma02Ec
Susan	15	F	Servant	17Ma02Ec
Will.	11	M	Servant	17Ma02Ec
Luke	9	M	Child	17Ma02Ec
Robert	5	M	Child	17Ma02Ec
John	3	M	Child	17Ma02Ec
Charles	.00	M	Infant	17Ma02Ec
BAILEY, Mary	13	F	Unknown	17Ma02Ec
ROCKITT, Jno.	25	M	Farmer	17Ma02Ec
MOORE, Robt.	50	M	Surveyor	17Ma02Ec
Nancy	48	F	Wife	17Ma02Ec
MAR, Jane	23	F	Servant	17Ma02Ec
And.	21	M	Servant	17Ma02Ec
RILEY, Ann	23	F	Servant	17Ma02Ec
James	21	M	Servant	17Ma02Ec
Mary	19	F	Servant	17Ma02Ec
CANDY, Owen	38	M	Laborer	17Ma02Ec
DOYLE, Pat	50	M	Farmer	17Ma02Ec
Ann	45	F	Servant	17Ma02Ec
Eliza	24	F	Servant	17Ma02Ec
Mary	22	F	Servant	17Ma02Ec
James	20	M	Servant	17Ma02Ec
Richard	13	M	Servant	17Ma02Ec
Margaret	12	F	Servant	17Ma02Ec
Judy	10	F	Servant	17Ma02Ec
Ann	7	F	Child	17Ma02Ec
CLAFF, U	23	U	Laborer	17Ma02Ec
BURROWES, Phil.	28	M	Farmer	17Ma02Ec
U-Mrs.	22	F	Wife	17Ma02Ec
John	24	M	Farmer	17Ma02Ec
U	.00	U	Infant	17Ma02Ec
BENNETT, Mary	20	F	Servant	17Ma02Ec
MARTIN, Thos.	25	M	Farmer	17Ma02Ec
GALLIGAN, Matthew	30	M	Farmer	17Ma02Ec
KENNEDY, Mary	16	F	Servant	17Ma02Ec
REYNOLDS, John	41	M	Farmer	17Ma02Ec
DEGNAN, James	35	M	Laborer	17Ma02Ec
Wm.	12	M	Laborer	17Ma02Ec
James	6	M	Child	17Ma02Ec
HOLOHAN, Pat.	22	M	Baker	17Ma02Ec
Mrs.	20	F	Servant	17Ma02Ec
SCRIMAGE, James	22	M	Laborer	17Ma02Ec
BYRNE, Mich.	22	M	Laborer	17Ma02Ec
MOLLEY, Thos.	24	M	Laborer	17Ma02Ec
CLAYTON, John	14	M	Laborer	17Ma02Ec
YORK, Mich.	25	M	Laborer	17Ma02Ec
REGAN, James	23	M	Laborer	17Ma02Ec
MORAN, Jane	24	F	Laborer	17Ma02Ec
Mich.	20	M	Laborer	17Ma02Ec
Marcella	16	F	Laborer	17Ma02Ec
MANEY, Eliza	18	F	Servant	17Ma02Ec
MCLAUGHLIN, Thos.	18	M	Servant	17Ma02Ec
Ellen	22	F	Servant	17Ma02Ec
Brid.	12	F	Servant	17Ma02Ec
FOLEY, Ann	22	F	Servant	17Ma02Ec
RAHER, Pat	30	M	Laborer	17Ma02Ec
Jeremiah	17	M	Laborer	17Ma02Ec
REGAN, Mich.	12	M	Laborer	17Ma02Ec
TOOHEY, Mich.	37	M	Laborer	17Ma02Ec
MURPHY, Alice	11	F	Servant	17Ma02Ec
BURGESS, John	40	M	Laborer	17Ma02Ec
DIXON, James	35	M	Laborer	17Ma02Ec
HARTNESS, Andrew	18	M	Laborer	17Ma02Ec
BURGESS, John	16	M	Laborer	17Ma02Ec
GLENDINAN, John	20	M	Laborer	17Ma02Ec
DIXON, Mary	30	F	Servant	17Ma02Ec
THOMPSON, U	20	U	Servant	17Ma02Ec
MATTHEWS, Theresa	27	F	Laborer	17Ma02Ec
KELLY, Ann	17	F	Servant	17Ma02Ec
CALLAN, James	38	M	Servant	17Ma02Ec
Betty	28	F	Servant	17Ma02Ec
Bridget	2	F	Child	17Ma02Ec
CASEY, John	28	M	Baker	17Ma02Ec
DOUGHERTY, James	23	M	Laborer	17Ma02Ec
MULHOLLAND, David	20	M	Laborer	17Ma02Ec
CROWLEY, John	20	M	Laborer	17Ma02Ec
MILLIGAN, Ann	20	F	Servant	17Ma02Ec
CARROLL, Wm.	30	M	Farmer	17Ma02Ec
WOODS, Jas.	26	M	Farmer	17Ma02Ec
HARMAN, Jas.	30	M	Farmer	17Ma02Ec
MCCABE, Margt.	15	F	Servant	17Ma02Ec
CARTY, Jas.	35	M	Servant	17Ma02Ec
GAVAN, Ellen	19	F	Servant	17Ma02Ec
HARRISON, Thomas	.00	M	Infant	17Ma02Ec
MONAGHAN, Cath.	34	F	Servant	17Ma02Ec
DOWDALE, Barth.	8	M	Child	17Ma02Ec
WELSH, Pat	19	M	Laborer	17Ma02Ec
REYNOLDS, John	22	M	Laborer	17Ma02Ec
MCGUIRE, James	19	M	Farmer	17Ma02Ec
DUFF, John	35	M	Farmer	17Ma02Ec
FALLON, Bryan	28	M	Engineer	17Ma02Ec
DONAGH, Felin	60	M	Laborer	17Ma02Ec
Thos.	17	M	Laborer	17Ma02Ec
JNANE, Joseph	16	M	Laborer	17Ma02Ec
FORD, John	26	M	Laborer	17Ma02Ec
U-Mrs.	24	F	Servant	17Ma02Ec
CATTERAL, U-Mrs.	30	F	Servant	17Ma02Ec
FORREST, Pat.	33	M	Laborer	17Ma02Ec
MCCABE, Mat	50	M	Laborer	17Ma02Ec
SEXTON, Thos.	26	M	Farmer	17Ma02Ec
GLEESON, Mich.	28	M	Farmer	17Ma02Ec
DROYER, Judy	21	F	Servant	17Ma02Ec
DWYER, Kitty	11	F	Servant	17Ma02Ec
HACKETT, Mary	11	F	Servant	17Ma02Ec
BROWN, Sam	40	M	Servant	17Ma02Ec
Rebec.	34	F	Servant	17Ma02Ec
My	15	U	Servant	17Ma02Ec
Susan	13	F	Servant	17Ma02Ec
John	13	M	Servant	17Ma02Ec
Margt.	8	F	Child	17Ma02Ec
Rebec.	6	F	Child	17Ma02Ec
HUNT, Henry	24	M	Laborer	17Ma02Ec
U	25	U	Laborer	17Ma02Ec
CROW, Thos.	30	M	Laborer	17Ma02Ec
Thos.	3	M	Child	17Ma02Ec
PEARSON, Samuel	27	M	Laborer	17Ma02Ec
MURPHY, John	22	M	Laborer	17Ma02Ec
Walter	16	M	Servant	17Ma02Ec
Bridget	19	F	Servant	17Ma02Ec
TOBIN, Bridget	25	F	Servant	17Ma02Ec
MCDONNELL, Ann	20	F	Servant	17Ma02Ec
CASEY, Anty	55	F	Servant	17Ma02Ec
Mary	50	F	Servant	17Ma02Ec
Hugh	20	M	Servant	17Ma02Ec
BURNS, Sarah	4	F	Child	17Ma02Ec
HAMMOND, Thos.	24	M	Laborer	17Ma02Ec
MCDONNELL, L.	20	U	Laborer	17Ma02Ec
MCCABE, Mat	30	M	Laborer	17Ma02Ec
LYNN, Michael	32	M	Laborer	17Ma02Ec
WYBRUNT, Chas.	26	M	Laborer	17Ma02Ec
SHAW, James	30	M	Laborer	17Ma02Ec
BRODAGAN, James	20	M	Laborer	17Ma02Ec
BRANAN, Mich.	16	M	Laborer	17Ma02Ec
FANNELLY, Wm.	26	M	Laborer	17Ma02Ec
Comb., M.M.	22	M	Laborer	17Ma02Ec
HENSHAW, U	22	M	Tailor	17Ma02Ec
REAGAN, John	48	M	Laborer	17Ma02Ec
CONROY, U	25	M	Laborer	17Ma02Ec
NOLAN, Owen	26	M	Laborer	17Ma02Ec
FETTERSON, Jas.	32	M	Laborer	17Ma02Ec
GLEASON, Pat.	20	M	Laborer	17Ma02Ec
KELLY, Jo.	26	M	Laborer	17Ma02Ec
TRACEY, Eliza	25	F	Servant	17Ma02Ec
MCGUIRE, Pat.	25	M	Servant	17Ma02Ec
CUNNINGHAM, James	24	M	Servant	17Ma02Ec
INGRAM, Sarah	25	F	Servant	17Ma02Ec
KANE, Martha	26	F	Servant	17Ma02Ec
Margt.	24	F	Servant	17Ma02Ec
MCCORMICK, John	26	M	Laborer	17Ma02Ec

NAMES OF PASSENGERS	AGE	SEX	OCCUPATIONS	DATE PORT SHIP
HUGHES, Mary	20	F	Unknown	17Ma02Ec
EARLY, Ann	20	F	Unknown	17Ma02Ec
BYRNES, Pat	11	M	Laborer	17Ma02Ec
James	10	M	Laborer	17Ma02Ec
NOWLAN, Bridget	36	F	Servant	17Ma02Ec
WALL, Mary	18	F	Servant	17Ma02Ec
OCALLAGHAN, Henry	20	M	Laborer	17Ma02Ec
FITZGERALD, James	35	M	Laborer	17Ma02Ec
COUGHLAN, Dan	22	M	Laborer	17Ma02Ec
U-Mrs.	22	F	Unknown	17Ma02Ec
Mary	18	F	Unknown	17Ma02Ec
KITTRICK, Simon	23	M	Laborer	17Ma02Ec
DONAHUE, Law.	23	M	Laborer	17Ma02Ec
TOOLE, Ann	20	F	Servant	17Ma02Ec
KENNEDY, John	29	M	Servant	17Ma02Ec
COLLINS, Tom	21	M	Servant	17Ma02Ec
FOSTER, Sam.	19	M	Servant	17Ma02Ec
LYMAN, James	33	M	Servant	17Ma02Ec
QUINN, Arthur	30	M	Servant	17Ma02Ec
U-Mrs.	30	F	Unknown	17Ma02Ec
BRADY, Mary	25	F	Servant	17Ma02Ec
MAHER, Richard	20	M	Laborer	17Ma02Ec
MEAD, Law.	32	M	Laborer	17Ma02Ec
HANLOW, Ellen	21	F	Unknown	17Ma02Ec
MADDIGAN, Pat	28	M	Laborer	17Ma02Ec
John	22	M	Laborer	17Ma02Ec
Johann	18	M	Laborer	17Ma02Ec
KANE, Mary	20	F	Servant	17Ma02Ec
BRENNAN, Mich.	24	M	Servant	17Ma02Ec
BROADFOOT, John	18	M	Servant	17Ma02Ec
BURKE, Pat	26	M	Laborer	17Ma02Ec
Hannah	26	F	Servant	17Ma02Ec
CAMPBELL, Madgy	20	F	Servant	17Ma02Ec
DUGAN, Ellen	20	F	Servant	17Ma02Ec
JOHNSON, Ann	19	F	Servant	17Ma02Ec
MITCHELL, Peter	34	M	Laborer	17Ma02Ec
Ann	17	F	Servant	17Ma02Ec
FLYNN, James	14	M	Servant	17Ma02Ec
Mary	28	F	Servant	17Ma02Ec
Ann	17	F	Servant	17Ma02Ec
CORRS, Thos.	20	M	Servant	17Ma02Ec
Richard	18	M	Servant	17Ma02Ec
Ann	60	F	Servant	17Ma02Ec
HAUGHEY, Cornelius	20	M	Servant	17Ma02Ec
SMITH, Ann	26	F	Servant	17Ma02Ec
John	7	M	Child	17Ma02Ec
Eliz.	5	F	Child	17Ma02Ec
Maria	3	F	Child	17Ma02Ec
MCDONNELL, Peter	18	M	Laborer	17Ma02Ec
MACK, Cath.	20	F	Servant	17Ma02Ec
WALL, John	11	M	Servant	17Ma02Ec
Hugh	8	M	Child	17Ma02Ec
MADDEN, Mary	13	F	Servant	17Ma02Ec
REILLY, Mary	20	F	Servant	17Ma02Ec
NESBIT, Jane	40	F	Servant	17Ma02Ec
Ann	13	F	Servant	17Ma02Ec
John	4	M	Child	17Ma02Ec
DIADIN, Chris	20	M	Laborer	17Ma02Ec
COLLINS, Martha	17	F	Laborer	17Ma02Ec
BANNON, Pat	18	M	Laborer	17Ma02Ec
LADDY, Bridget	54	F	Servant	17Ma02Ec
Bridget	14	F	Servant	17Ma02Ec
Bernard	48	M	Servant	17Ma02Ec
MITCHELL, Mary	24	F	Servant	17Ma02Ec
FARRELL, Cath.	22	F	Servant	17Ma02Ec
BEGLUS, Honor	20	F	Servant	17Ma02Ec
CONNOR, John	20	M	Laborer	17Ma02Ec
Thomas	10	M	Laborer	17Ma02Ec
John	11	M	Laborer	17Ma02Ec
Mary	9	F	Child	17Ma02Ec
LANE, Morris	22	M	Servant	17Ma02Ec
OBRIEN, Pat.	22	M	Servant	17Ma02Ec
SHEEHAN, Mich.	30	M	Servant	17Ma02Ec
OBRIEN, Pat.	22	M	Servant	17Ma02Ec
SHEEHAN, Mich.	30	M	Servant	17Ma02Ec

NAMES OF PASSENGERS	AGE	SEX	OCCUPATIONS	DATE PORT SHIP
SHEEHAN, Mary	5	F	Child	17Ma02Ec
KING, Margt.	22	F	Servant	17Ma02Ec
SULLIVAN, Mary	25	F	Servant	17Ma02Ec
LEONARD, Dennis	29	M	Laborer	17Ma02Ec
MULLIGAN, Dennis	34	M	Laborer	17Ma02Ec
HERN, Honora	14	F	Servant	17Ma02Ec
Jerry	22	M	Servant	17Ma02Ec
COONAHAN, Margt.	26	F	Servant	17Ma02Ec
BYRNES, Bessy	14	F	Servant	17Ma02Ec
HAGGERTY, Dennis	22	M	Laborer	17Ma02Ec
OKEEFFE, Dan	22	M	Laborer	17Ma02Ec
KELLY, Bernard	30	M	Laborer	17Ma02Ec
ANDREWS, Margt.M.	25	F	Servant	17Ma02Ec
MAGAR, John	20	M	Laborer	17Ma02Ec
HICKEY, Mary	18	F	Servant	17Ma02Ec
RYAN, Cath.	20	F	Servant	17Ma02Ec
DOUGLASS, Rose	24	F	Servant	17Ma02Ec
HAYDEN, Cath.	20	F	Servant	17Ma02Ec
AHERN, Mary	20	F	Servant	17Ma02Ec
MURPHY, Ann	20	F	Servant	17Ma02Ec
CARROLL, Cath.	20	F	Servant	17Ma02Ec
CLANCEY, John	24	M	Laborer	17Ma02Ec
TUMPRIT, John	27	M	Laborer	17Ma02Ec
Julia	24	F	Servant	17Ma02Ec
OCONNOR, John	20	M	Servant	17Ma02Ec
Isabella	17	F	Servant	17Ma02Ec
ROACHE, Wm.	22	M	Servant	17Ma02Ec
DRISCOLL, Mary	12	F	Servant	17Ma02Ec
ROACHE, James	30	M	Servant	17Ma02Ec
DOWLING, John	19	M	Laborer	17Ma02Ec
VAUGHAN, Phil.	20	M	Laborer	17Ma02Ec
CALLAGHAN, Margt.	25	F	Servant	17Ma02Ec
HAYES, Eliza	21	F	Servant	17Ma02Ec
TURNIS, Ann	45	F	Servant	17Ma02Ec
MCDERMOTT, Isabella	14	F	Servant	17Ma02Ec
William	13	M	Servant	17Ma02Ec
ONEIL, Pat.	00	M	Laborer	17Ma02Ec
MURRAN, Law.	35	M	Laborer	17Ma02Ec
CURRAN, Ellen	28	F	Servant	17Ma02Ec
LEOD, Mary	18	F	Servant	17Ma02Ec
PLUNKETT, James	28	M	Laborer	17Ma02Ec
NALLY, John	40	M	Laborer	17Ma02Ec
Rose	8	F	Child	17Ma02Ec
Brid.	6	F	Child	17Ma02Ec
MEE, Mat.	24	M	Servant	17Ma02Ec
THIBBS, Geo.	35	M	Laborer	17Ma02Ec
REILLY, Pat.	40	M	Laborer	17Ma02Ec
Margt.	35	F	Servant	17Ma02Ec
Pat	10	M	Laborer	17Ma02Ec
James	10	M	Child	17Ma02Ec
Ellen	3	F	Child	17Ma02Ec
Rose	.00	F	Infant	17Ma02Ec
Bridget	21	F	Servant	17Ma02Ec
MULLIGAN, James	28	M	Laborer	17Ma02Ec
SMITH, Charles	25	M	Laborer	17Ma02Ec
James	10	M	Laborer	17Ma02Ec
Mary	8	F	Servant	17Ma02Ec
MCQUADE, Sarah	26	F	Servant	17Ma02Ec
DOHENY, Pat.	24	M	Laborer	17Ma02Ec
DUNFY, Cath.	25	F	Servant	17Ma02Ec
MURRAY, Rose	50	F	Servant	17Ma02Ec
Pat	20	M	Laborer	17Ma02Ec
LIVINGSTON, Mary-R.	18	F	Servant	17Ma02Ec
Sarah-L.	20	F	Servant	17Ma02Ec
ARMSTRONG, Edwd.	45	M	Laborer	17Ma02Ec
ODONNELL, Ann	18	F	Servant	17Ma02Ec
Mary	10	F	Servant	17Ma02Ec
Margt.	8	F	Child	17Ma02Ec
BROPHY, Cath.	30	F	Wife	17Ma02Ec
Ellen	20	F	Unknown	17Ma02Ec
Julia	16	F	Unknown	17Ma02Ec
Mary	14	F	Unknown	17Ma02Ec
Bridget	10	F	Unknown	17Ma02Ec
John	8	M	Child	17Ma02Ec
DOYLE, Patk.	40	M	Lmnftr	17Ma02Ec

NAMES OF PASSENGERS	AGE	SEX	OCCUPATIONS	DATE PORT SHIP
DOYLE, Mary	25	F	Wife	17Ma02Ec
Nick.Jos.	4	M	Child	17Ma02Ec
James	2	M	Child	17Ma02Ec
Mary	.00	F	Infant	17Ma02Ec
FRYAR, Mary	60	F	Servant	17Ma02Ec
DWYER, Ann	25	F	Servant	17Ma02Ec
Kate	23	F	Servant	17Ma02Ec
FARIN, Mary	21	F	Servant	17Ma02Ec
IRVINN, U	28	F	Wife	17Ma02Ec
Eliz.	4	F	Child	17Ma02Ec
William	2	M	Child	17Ma02Ec
WARNIG, Thos.C.	30	M	Farmer	17Ma02Ec
U-Mrs.	25	F	Wife	17Ma02Ec

ANNIE 17 MAY 1850

From Belfast

NAMES OF PASSENGERS	AGE	SEX	OCCUPATIONS	DATE PORT SHIP
JOHNSTON, Hugh	52	M	Laborer	17Ma17Ia
Martha	55	F	Unknown	17Ma17Ia
David	20	M	Unknown	17Ma17Ia
MCDOWELL, Robt.	25	M	Unknown	17Ma17Ia
Eliza	24	F	Unknown	17Ma17Ia
William	30	M	Unknown	17Ma17Ia
Ann	40	F	Unknown	17Ma17Ia
James	3	M	Child	17Ma17Ia
Jane	.00	F	Infant	17Ma17Ia
WARD, Robert	30	M	Unknown	17Ma17Ia
Johnson	28	M	Unknown	17Ma17Ia
Sarah	23	F	Unknown	17Ma17Ia
PATTERSON, Isabella	30	F	Unknown	17Ma17Ia
CALVERT, William	25	M	Unknown	17Ma17Ia
MAHON, Wm.	28	M	Unknown	17Ma17Ia
Jane	28	F	Unknown	17Ma17Ia
Jonah	16	M	Unknown	17Ma17Ia
ROE, Thomas	26	M	Unknown	17Ma17Ia
HARISK, Daniel	20	M	Unknown	17Ma17Ia
FIRTH, Jane	20	F	Unknown	17Ma17Ia
MCCRACKEN, Agnes	35	F	Unknown	17Ma17Ia
Robert	16	M	Unknown	17Ma17Ia
Agnes	7	F	Child	17Ma17Ia
Elizabeth	5	F	Child	17Ma17Ia
Maria	3	F	Child	17Ma17Ia
Margt.	9	F	Child	17Ma17Ia
HERINGTON, Clement	22	M	Unknown	17Ma17Ia
Sarah	20	F	Unknown	17Ma17Ia
WATSON, Adam	16	M	Unknown	17Ma17Ia
MCKEE, Saml.	50	M	Unknown	17Ma17Ia
Mary	40	F	Unknown	17Ma17Ia
James	21	M	Unknown	17Ma17Ia
John	12	M	Unknown	17Ma17Ia
Alexander	7	M	Child	17Ma17Ia
MCANERNY, Thos.	22	M	Unknown	17Ma17Ia
Margt.	19	F	Unknown	17Ma17Ia
BROWNE, George	30	M	Unknown	17Ma17Ia
BROWN, John	20	M	Unknown	17Ma17Ia
DONNELLY, Eleanor	30	F	Unknown	17Ma17Ia
KINNEAL, Martha	40	F	Unknown	17Ma17Ia
Robert	20	M	Unknown	17Ma17Ia
CLAGSTONE, Hugh	24	M	Unknown	17Ma17Ia
JOHNSTON, Samuel	28	M	Unknown	17Ma17Ia
GALWAY, John	26	M	Unknown	17Ma17Ia
JAMISON, Saml.	30	M	Unknown	17Ma17Ia
Margt.	30	F	Unknown	17Ma17Ia
David	.00	M	Infant	17Ma17Ia
Margt.	20	F	Unknown	17Ma17Ia
MCDOWELL, Jane	22	F	Unknown	17Ma17Ia
Robt.	17	M	Unknown	17Ma17Ia
MCMULLEN, Mary	20	F	Unknown	17Ma17Ia

NAMES OF PASSENGERS	AGE	SEX	OCCUPATIONS	DATE PORT SHIP
SMYTH, Margt.	25	F	Unknown	17Ma17Ia
JONES, John	36	M	Unknown	17Ma17Ia
GRAHAM, Catharine	18	F	Unknown	17Ma17Ia
KERNAN, Saml.	28	M	Unknown	17Ma17Ia
Fanny	23	F	Unknown	17Ma17Ia
Saml.	.00	M	Infant	17Ma17Ia
MCCALLEN, Owned	18	M	Unknown	17Ma17Ia
Peter	16	M	Unknown	17Ma17Ia
Bridget	13	F	Unknown	17Ma17Ia
BYERS, Robt.	18	M	Unknown	17Ma17Ia
MCWHEIK, Eliza	25	F	Unknown	17Ma17Ia
CORSKERY, Robt.	29	M	Unknown	17Ma17Ia
Hannah	26	F	Unknown	17Ma17Ia
WALLACE, John	22	M	Unknown	17Ma17Ia
Hugh	16	M	Unknown	17Ma17Ia
MCCREERY, John	40	M	Unknown	17Ma17Ia
Elizabeth	35	F	Unknown	17Ma17Ia
STEWART, Wm.	13	M	Unknown	17Ma17Ia
John	11	M	Unknown	17Ma17Ia
Saml.	6	M	Child	17Ma17Ia
Mary	3	F	Child	17Ma17Ia
Jane	.00	F	Infant	17Ma17Ia
BELL, John	40	M	Unknown	17Ma17Ia
Jane	36	F	Unknown	17Ma17Ia
PATTISON, James	35	M	Unknown	17Ma17Ia
AUSTIN, Jane	23	F	Unknown	17Ma17Ia
PATTERSON, Mary	6	F	Child	17Ma17Ia
REA, Rebecca	7	F	Child	17Ma17Ia
MCKINTY, Jane	17	F	Unknown	17Ma17Ia
MCMULLAN, Patrick	26	M	Unknown	17Ma17Ia
LUCAS, John	15	M	Unknown	17Ma17Ia
Margaret	12	F	Unknown	17Ma17Ia
VERNER, Robt.	65	M	Unknown	17Ma17Ia
Sarah	54	F	Unknown	17Ma17Ia
Francis	19	M	Unknown	17Ma17Ia
Ann	16	F	Unknown	17Ma17Ia
Robt.	14	M	Unknown	17Ma17Ia
LUNDY, Wm.	22	M	Unknown	17Ma17Ia
TROTTER, Margaret	21	F	Unknown	17Ma17Ia
BELL, Matthew	22	M	Unknown	17Ma17Ia
MCGREADY, Danl.	18	M	Laborer	17Ma17Ia
Adelaide	16	F	Unknown	17Ma17Ia
MURRAY, Hugh	30	M	Unknown	17Ma17Ia
Bridget	23	F	Unknown	17Ma17Ia
Margaret	2	F	Child	17Ma17Ia
KELLY, Elizabeth	50	F	Unknown	17Ma17Ia
MCWHIN, Mary	34	F	Unknown	17Ma17Ia
Margt.	11	F	Unknown	17Ma17Ia
Catharine	9	F	Child	17Ma17Ia
Roseann	7	F	Child	17Ma17Ia
Robert	3	M	Child	17Ma17Ia
Margt.Jane	2	F	Child	17Ma17Ia
RONEY, Ellen	25	F	Unknown	17Ma17Ia
MCMAHON, David	19	M	Unknown	17Ma17Ia
Jane	21	F	Unknown	17Ma17Ia
NEILL, Wm.	40	M	Unknown	17Ma17Ia
JOHNSTON, Sarah	20	F	Unknown	17Ma17Ia
BURNS, Ellen	20	F	Unknown	17Ma17Ia
SHANNON, Saml.	21	M	Unknown	17Ma17Ia
MURPHY, Henry	19	M	Unknown	17Ma17Ia
MCMULLAN, David	35	M	Unknown	17Ma17Ia
Daniel	26	M	Unknown	17Ma17Ia
CRAWFORD, John	20	M	Unknown	17Ma17Ia
TAGGERT, Danl.	26	M	Unknown	17Ma17Ia
MCKAY, Cath.	16	F	Unknown	17Ma17Ia
ROBINSON, Mary	19	F	Unknown	17Ma17Ia
MOORE, Wm.	22	M	Unknown	17Ma17Ia
KELLY, Peter	18	M	Unknown	17Ma17Ia
Mary	16	F	Unknown	17Ma17Ia
FRENCH, Jos.	32	M	Unknown	17Ma17Ia
Martha	32	M	Unknown	17Ma17Ia
George	7	M	Child	17Ma17Ia
Sarah	6	F	Child	17Ma17Ia
Mary	2	F	Child	17Ma17Ia
James	.00	M	Infant	17Ma17Ia

NAMES OF PASSENGERS	AGE	SEX	OCCUPATIONS	DATE PORT SHIP
MARTIN, Adam	23	M	Unknown	17Ma17Ia
DONLEY, Wm.	22	M	Unknown	17Ma17Ia
DONAGHY, Hugh	21	M	Unknown	17Ma17Ia
MCMULLAN, Ellen	17	F	Unknown	17Ma17Ia
SMITH, Martha	20	F	Unknown	17Ma17Ia
LAVERY, Ann	18	F	Unknown	17Ma17Ia
Margt.	20	F	Unknown	17Ma17Ia
HASLETT, Jas.	17	M	Unknown	17Ma17Ia
MALCOMSON, Jane	25	F	Unknown	17Ma17Ia
HERON, Mary	60	F	Unknown	17Ma17Ia
James	32	M	Unknown	17Ma17Ia
Sarah	28	F	Unknown	17Ma17Ia
Robert	26	M	Unknown	17Ma17Ia
Thomas	24	M	Unknown	17Ma17Ia
Jane	22	F	Laborer	17Ma17Ia
David	20	M	Unknown	17Ma17Ia
John	18	M	Unknown	17Ma17Ia
Wm.	16	M	Unknown	17Ma17Ia
Hugh	14	M	Unknown	17Ma17Ia
MCMULLAN, Margt.	40	F	Unknown	17Ma17Ia
John	18	M	Unknown	17Ma17Ia
Joseph	16	M	Unknown	17Ma17Ia
Andrew	15	M	Unknown	17Ma17Ia
WRIGHT, Andrew	18	M	Unknown	17Ma17Ia
DOWNEY, Margt.	60	F	Unknown	17Ma17Ia
Mary	22	F	Unknown	17Ma17Ia
Cath.	14	F	Unknown	17Ma17Ia
FLANNIGAN, Jas.	30	M	Unknown	17Ma17Ia
DICKSON, John	23	M	Unknown	17Ma17Ia
WOODS, Wm.	24	M	Unknown	17Ma17Ia
MCMASTER, Wm.	24	M	Unknown	17Ma17Ia
MORLAND, Wm.	21	M	Unknown	17Ma17Ia
REID, Robt.	22	M	Unknown	17Ma17Ia
Mary	20	F	Unknown	17Ma17Ia
ARMSTRONG, Andw.	25	M	Unknown	17Ma17Ia
TAYLOR, Jos.	32	M	Unknown	17Ma17Ia
MCLAMIR, Ellen	35	F	Unknown	17Ma17Ia
Eliza	21	F	Unknown	17Ma17Ia
Ann	16	F	Unknown	17Ma17Ia
Jane	16	F	Unknown	17Ma17Ia
Mary	12	F	Unknown	17Ma17Ia
HOWELL, Jas.	30	M	Unknown	17Ma17Ia
Elizabeth	28	F	Unknown	17Ma17Ia
RAMSEY, Jane	60	F	Unknown	17Ma17Ia
Wm.	25	M	Unknown	17Ma17Ia
John	23	M	Unknown	17Ma17Ia
Jane	21	F	Unknown	17Ma17Ia
MCNEILL, Helena	24	F	Unknown	17Ma17Ia
FERRIER, Matilda	22	F	Unknown	17Ma17Ia
MULHOLLAND, Susan	22	F	Unknown	17Ma17Ia
MCADARY, John	55	M	Unknown	17Ma17Ia
Sarah	40	F	Unknown	17Ma17Ia
Mary	20	M	Unknown	17Ma17Ia
Rose	18	F	Unknown	17Ma17Ia
Jane	16	F	Unknown	17Ma17Ia
LYLE, Jas.	21	M	Unknown	17Ma17Ia
HORNER, Saml.	21	M	Unknown	17Ma17Ia
CONER, Jane	28	F	Unknown	17Ma17Ia
MCCULLIN, Owen	20	M	Unknown	17Ma17Ia
IRVIN, Robert	17	M	Unknown	17Ma17Ia
GARRET, Robert	18	M	Unknown	17Ma17Ia
STEVENSON, Arthur	19	M	Unknown	17Ma17Ia
DUN, Ann	16	F	Unknown	17Ma17Ia
MCCOSKAR, Jas.	20	M	Unknown	17Ma17Ia
CLARKE, Cath.	23	F	Laborer	17Ma17Ia
GILMORE, Elizabeth	24	F	Unknown	17Ma17Ia
PATTERSON, Saml.	18	M	Unknown	17Ma17Ia
ANDERSON, Jas.	26	M	Unknown	17Ma17Ia
WATSON, Rob.	25	M	Unknown	17Ma17Ia
DEMSTER, Matilda	22	F	Unknown	17Ma17Ia
Fanny	20	F	Unknown	17Ma17Ia
SCOTT, Wm.	20	M	Unknown	17Ma17Ia
ANDERSON, Marg.	20	F	Unknown	17Ma17Ia
SCOTT, Wm.	19	M	Unknown	17Ma17Ia
BELL, Susanna	22	F	Unknown	17Ma17Ia
ALLEN, Martha	20	F	Unknown	17Ma17Ia
JAMISON, Ann	20	F	Unknown	17Ma17Ia
Alexr.	19	M	Unknown	17Ma17Ia
MORRISON, Robt.	20	M	Unknown	17Ma17Ia
AGNEW, Wm.	18	M	Unknown	17Ma17Ia
MCMULLAN, Henry	25	M	Unknown	17Ma17Ia
CONLEY, Mary	20	F	Unknown	17Ma17Ia
IRWIN, David	20	M	Unknown	17Ma17Ia
MCFARLAND, Robt.	23	M	Unknown	17Ma17Ia
FARE, Jane	22	F	Unknown	17Ma17Ia
CROOKERY, Margaret-Jr.	00	F	Unknown	17Ma17Ia
CORBITT, Jas.	20	M	Unknown	17Ma17Ia
THOMSON, John	25	M	Unknown	17Ma17Ia
GORMAN, Felix	30	M	Unknown	17Ma17Ia
SLOAN, Thomas	19	M	Unknown	17Ma17Ia
DALLON, Bridget	52	F	Matron	17Ma17Ia
George	21	M	Unknown	17Ma17Ia
Francis	17	M	Unknown	17Ma17Ia
MOORE, Wm.	6	M	Child	17Ma17Ia
STEVENS, John	38	M	Clerk	17Ma17Ia
U-Mrs.	35	F	Matron	17Ma17Ia
Margt.	13	F	Unknown	17Ma17Ia
Mary	12	F	Unknown	17Ma17Ia
Edward	11	M	Unknown	17Ma17Ia
John	7	M	Child	17Ma17Ia
William	5	M	Child	17Ma17Ia
Thomas	23	M	Clerk	17Ma17Ia
GREENFIELD, Jas.	28	M	Merchant	17Ma17Ia
DOWNING, Wm.	21	M	Clerk	17Ma17Ia
GALLAGHER, Margt.	26	F	Servant	17Ma17Ia
DAVIS, Alexander	30	M	Mariner	17Ma17Ia

ELIZA 17 MAY 1850

From Waterford

NAMES OF PASSENGERS	AGE	SEX	OCCUPATIONS	DATE PORT SHIP
TARP, Mary	24	F	Spinster	17Ma35HI
WALSH, Thomas	22	M	Laborer	17Ma35HI
FLOOD, John	22	M	Laborer	17Ma35HI
MURPHY, Peter	20	M	Laborer	17Ma35HI
WILKINSON, Ellen	20	F	Spinster	17Ma35HI
PHEALAN, Jane	24	F	Wi	17Ma35HI
Anne	.08	F	Infant	17Ma35HI
KELLY, John	22	M	Laborer	17Ma35HI
KAVEMACH, Mary	20	F	Spinster	17Ma35HI
MURRAY, Ellen	20	F	Spinster	17Ma35HI
MURPHY, Mary	37	F	None	17Ma35HI
Thomas (S)	10	M	Son	17Ma35HI
John (S)	3	M	Child	17Ma35HI
Michael (S)	.09	M	Infant	17Ma35HI
CULLUN, Bridget	27	F	Spinster	17Ma35HI
Michael	5	M	Child	17Ma35HI
Judy	4	F	Child	17Ma35HI
MURRAY, Mary	24	F	Spinster	17Ma35HI
BOWDEN, Michael	40	M	Laborer	17Ma35HI
Patrick	13	M	Son	17Ma35HI
William	13	M	Son	17Ma35HI
POWER, James	27	M	Laborer	17Ma35HI
HEAN, Mary	21	F	Spinster	17Ma35HI
Ann	23	F	Spinster	17Ma35HI
MCGINNIS, Anne	26	F	Spinster	17Ma35HI
HICKEY, Patrick	28	M	Laborer	17Ma35HI
HUTCHISON, Thos.	13	M	None	17Ma35HI
TOBIN, Margaret	30	F	Spinster	17Ma35HI
Catherine	24	F	Unknown	17Ma35HI
DROHIM, John	23	M	Laborer	17Ma35HI
PURCELL, William	35	M	Smith	17Ma35HI
MCGRATH, Catherine	30	F	Spinster	17Ma35HI
Michael	6	M	Child	17Ma35HI

NAMES OF PASSENGERS		AGE	SEX	OCCUPATIONS	DATE PORT SHIP
WALSH, Honora		26	F	Spinster	17Ma35HI
HICKEY, Michael		22	M	Laborer	17Ma35HI
NEIL, Anne		21	F	Spinster	17Ma35HI
HICKEY, Mary		20	F	Spinster	17Ma35HI
Catherine		19	F	Spinster	17Ma35HI
RYAN, J.		35	M	Laborer	17Ma35HI
Mary		30	F	Spinster	17Ma35HI
DUGAN, Morice		42	M	Farmer	17Ma35HI
Mary	(W)	35	F	Wife	17Ma35HI
Mary	(D)	12	F	Daughter	17Ma35HI
Ellen	(D)	11	F	Daughter	17Ma35HI
Johanna	(D)	.09	F	Infant	17Ma35HI
WILL, Michael		6	M	Child	17Ma35HI
MCGRATH, Michael		30	M	Laborer	17Ma35HI
MACKEY, Margaret		40	F	Spinster	17Ma35HI
KIRBY, Bridget		30	F	Spinster	17Ma35HI
WELSH, Ellen		27	F	None	17Ma35HI
Eliza		.10	F	Infant	17Ma35HI
HENSBERRY, Mary		18	F	Spinster	17Ma35HI
SAVAGE, Nicholas		25	M	Laborer	17Ma35HI
MCCAVIN, D.		18	M	Laborer	17Ma35HI
KENNY, Ellen		22	F	Spinster	17Ma35HI
FOLEY, Edmond		23	M	Laborer	17Ma35HI
Catherine		29	F	Spinster	17Ma35HI
CROKE, J.		27	M	Farmer	17Ma35HI
Anty	(W)	30	F	Wife	17Ma35HI
Mary		30	F	Spinster	17Ma35HI
Thomas		.08	M	Infant	17Ma35HI
BYRNE, James		22	M	Laborer	17Ma35HI
CORBETT, James		52	M	Laborer	17Ma35HI
Thomas		18	M	Laborer	17Ma35HI
KEATING, William		30	M	Laborer	17Ma35HI
BYRNE, Bridget		23	F	Spinster	17Ma35HI
HEFFERMAN, Catherine		16	F	Spinster	17Ma35HI
MAHER, James		18	M	None	17Ma35HI
DUNN, Patrick		35	M	Laborer	17Ma35HI
BRYAN, Mary		50	F	Spinster	17Ma35HI
FINN, Ellen		39	F	None	17Ma35HI
Margaret		.10	F	Infant	17Ma35HI
Morris		19	M	Laborer	17Ma35HI
KELLY, Patrick		30	M	Laborer	17Ma35HI
CORMICK, Patrick		26	M	Laborer	17Ma35HI
HEAN, Michael		18	M	Laborer	17Ma35HI
DILLON, John		27	M	Laborer	17Ma35HI
MULLINS, Ellen		24	F	Spinster	17Ma35HI
Alice		20	F	Spinster	17Ma35HI
BROWN, Johanna		28	F	Spinster	17Ma35HI
PEARD, Ellen		36	F	Wi	17Ma35HI
Mary	(D)	13	F	Daughter	17Ma35HI
Jane	(D)	11	F	Daughter	17Ma35HI
Hannah	(D)	.10	F	Infant	17Ma35HI

ELIZABETH 17 MAY 1850

From Dublin

NAMES OF PASSENGERS	AGE	SEX	OCCUPATIONS	DATE PORT SHIP
CONROY, John	20	M	Laborer	17Ma05Jj
BYRNES, U	25	M	Laborer	17Ma05Jj
rROONEY, U	25	M	Laborer	17Ma05Jj
BRADY, Mary	8	F	Child	17Ma05Jj
MORTON, Wm.	20	M	Laborer	17Ma05Jj
LEAVY, John	18	M	Laborer	17Ma05Jj
Ann	16	F	Laborer	17Ma05Jj
SIMS, Wm.	30	M	Laborer	17Ma05Jj
COX, Mathew	22	M	Laborer	17Ma05Jj
MCCARTHY, James	40	M	Laborer	17Ma05Jj
U-Mrs.	30	F	Laborer	17Ma05Jj
Miles	10	M	Laborer	17Ma05Jj
Bridgt.	8	F	Child	17Ma05Jj

NAMES OF PASSENGERS	AGE	SEX	OCCUPATIONS	DATE PORT SHIP
MCCARTHY, James	6	M	Child	17Ma05Jj
Hugo	3	M	Child	17Ma05Jj
Mary	.00	F	Infant	17Ma05Jj
JERVIS, Richd.	20	M	Laborer	17Ma05Jj
ONEILL, John	45	M	Laborer	17Ma05Jj
John	16	M	Laborer	17Ma05Jj
Ann	50	F	Laborer	17Ma05Jj
Teresa	24	F	Laborer	17Ma05Jj
Margt.	23	F	Laborer	17Ma05Jj
Eliza	21	F	Laborer	17Ma05Jj
Celia	17	F	Laborer	17Ma05Jj
CLARKE, Cathn.	21	F	Laborer	17Ma05Jj
ENNISS, John	13	M	Laborer	17Ma05Jj
ROBINSON, Winny	20	M	Laborer	17Ma05Jj
KELLY, Cathn.	20	F	Laborer	17Ma05Jj
BRENNAN, Rosanna	21	F	Laborer	17Ma05Jj
NEILL, Patt	47	M	Laborer	17Ma05Jj
Mary	40	F	Laborer	17Ma05Jj
Winifred	22	M	Laborer	17Ma05Jj
Michl.	20	M	Laborer	17Ma05Jj
Ellen	18	F	Laborer	17Ma05Jj
Honor	16	F	Laborer	17Ma05Jj
Mary	14	F	Laborer	17Ma05Jj
Bridget	10	F	Laborer	17Ma05Jj
Cathn.	8	F	Child	17Ma05Jj
Margt.	4	F	Child	17Ma05Jj
Edwd.	.00	M	Infant	17Ma05Jj
DWYER, Winifred	26	M	Unknown	17Ma05Jj
CROUGH, Judith	24	F	Unknown	17Ma05Jj
Honor	22	F	Unknown	17Ma05Jj
Cathn.	27	F	Unknown	17Ma05Jj
HEWETT, Timothy	50	M	Laborer	17Ma05Jj
Tim	22	M	Unknown	17Ma05Jj
John	20	M	Unknown	17Ma05Jj
Edmond	15	M	Unknown	17Ma05Jj
Cornelius	13	M	Unknown	17Ma05Jj
Michl.	9	M	Child	17Ma05Jj
Daniel	.00	M	Infant	17Ma05Jj
Alice	18	F	Unknown	17Ma05Jj
Margt.	16	F	Unknown	17Ma05Jj
Joanna	14	F	Unknown	17Ma05Jj
Cathn.	11	F	Unknown	17Ma05Jj
Mary	8	F	Child	17Ma05Jj
Ellen	.00	F	Infant	17Ma05Jj
ONEILL, Amelia	17	F	Unknown	17Ma05Jj
WILKINSON, Edwd.	17	M	Unknown	17Ma05Jj
Ellen	20	F	Unknown	17Ma05Jj
JOHNSTON, U-Mrs.	20	F	Unknown	17Ma05Jj
FITZPATRICK, Andy	25	M	Unknown	17Ma05Jj
WILKINS, David	40	M	Unknown	17Ma05Jj
CASSELLS, Mary	20	F	Unknown	17Ma05Jj
WALSH, Cathn.	20	F	Unknown	17Ma05Jj
NAVAN, Cathn.	20	F	Unknown	17Ma05Jj
LAWLOR, Joanna	26	F	Unknown	17Ma05Jj
HARE, Thos.	22	M	Unknown	17Ma05Jj
WILSON, James	24	M	Unknown	17Ma05Jj
FLYNN, John	35	M	Unknown	17Ma05Jj
Mary	30	F	Unknown	17Ma05Jj
Patrick	7	M	Child	17Ma05Jj
Phillip	.00	M	Infant	17Ma05Jj
FILNITER, Wm.	24	M	Unknown	17Ma05Jj
HASSET, Pat	25	M	Unknown	17Ma05Jj
Hugh	12	M	Unknown	17Ma05Jj
Ellen	16	F	Unknown	17Ma05Jj
Judith	14	F	Unknown	17Ma05J
Margt.	.00	F	Infant	17Ma05Jj
Phelan	18	M	Laborer	17Ma05Jj
MCCORMICK, Pat	40	M	Unknown	17Ma05Jj
Peggy	40	F	Unknown	17Ma05Jj
Felix	18	M	Unknown	17Ma05Jj
Ann	16	F	Unknown	17Ma05Jj
Tom	13	M	Unknown	17Ma05Jj
John	11	M	Unknown	17Ma05Jj
Mary	9	F	Child	17Ma05Jj
Bessy	7	F	Child	17Ma05Jj

NAMES OF PASSENGERS	AGE	SEX	OCCUPATIONS	DATE PORT SHIP
MCCORMICK, Peggy	.00	F	Infant	17Ma05Jj
WHITE, Peter	24	M	Unknown	17Ma05Jj
U-Miss	22	F	Unknown	17Ma05Jj
GAFFNEY, A.Miss	20	F	Unknown	17Ma05Jj
M.Miss	18	F	Unknown	17Ma05Jj
MURPHY, U	30	M	Unknown	17Ma05Jj
U-Mrs.	30	F	Unknown	17Ma05Jj
John	.00	M	Infant	17Ma05Jj
Cathn.	5	F	Child	17Ma05Jj
FLANAGAN, Margt.	45	F	Unknown	17Ma05Jj
Maria	16	F	Unknown	17Ma05Jj
Kate	14	F	Unknown	17Ma05Jj
Wm.	11	M	Unknown	17Ma05Jj
Michl.	7	M	Child	17Ma05Jj
James	4	M	Child	17Ma05Jj
Susan	.00	F	Infant	17Ma05Jj
Margt.	22	F	Unknown	17Ma05Jj
MCNAMARA, Letitia	18	F	Unknown	17Ma05Jj
RYAN, Michl.	20	M	Unknown	17Ma05Jj
WALSH, John	20	M	Unknown	17Ma05Jj
CARROLL, Ellen	24	F	Unknown	17Ma05Jj
DOHERTY, Mary	20	F	Unknown	17Ma05Jj
SHERRAN, Mat.	18	M	Unknown	17Ma05Jj
CONNOR, Pat	21	M	Unknown	17Ma05Jj
GAVIS, Larry	20	M	Unknown	17Ma05Jj
Cathn.	20	F	Unknown	17Ma05Jj
RYAN, Wm.	20	M	Unknown	17Ma05Jj
BANFIELD, Thos.	22	M	Unknown	17Ma05Jj
John	20	M	Unknown	17Ma05Jj
Kennedy	18	M	Unknown	17Ma05Jj
SHANAGHAN, Stephen	20	M	Unknown	17Ma05Jj
MCROACHE, U-Revd.	30	M	Priest	17Ma05Jj
WELDON, U	18	M	Gentleman	17Ma05Jj
KEOGH, U	26	M	Gentleman	17Ma05Jj

WATTROW 17 MAY 1850

From Cork

NAMES OF PASSENGERS	AGE	SEX	OCCUPATIONS	DATE PORT SHIP
BROSSAHAN, Michael	40	M	Agrc	17Ma18lq
Margaret	30	F	Unknown	17Ma18lq
Mary	9	F	Child	17Ma18lq
Catherine	7	F	Child	17Ma18lq
MULLANE, Philip	24	M	Unknown	17Ma18lq
DONOHUE, Mary	19	F	Unknown	17Ma18lq
MCCARTHY, Ellen	21	F	Unknown	17Ma18lq
BRUTHER, James	20	M	Unknown	17Ma18lq
BURN, Mary	20	F	Unknown	17Ma18lq
CROWLY, Denis	22	M	Unknown	17Ma18lq
Johanna	17	F	Unknown	17Ma18lq
Julia	70	F	Unknown	17Ma18lq
DONOVAN, Patrick	18	M	Unknown	17Ma18lq
Catherine	17	F	Unknown	17Ma18lq
GRACE, Mary	18	F	Unknown	17Ma18lq
CARROLL, Daniel	30	M	Unknown	17Ma18lq
Johanna	22	F	Unknown	17Ma18lq
CALLAGHAN, Johanna	46	F	Unknown	17Ma18lq
John	13	M	Unknown	17Ma18lq
Johanna	11	F	Unknown	17Ma18lq
Timothy	9	M	Child	17Ma18lq
DONOVAN, Timothy	50	M	Unknown	17Ma18lq
COLLINS, Cornelius	22	M	Unknown	17Ma18lq
CASEY, John	30	M	Unknown	17Ma18lq
SULLIVAN, Dennis	20	M	Unknown	17Ma18lq
John	18	M	Unknown	17Ma18lq
Anne	11	F	Unknown	17Ma18lq
KEMP, Fanny	28	F	Unknown	17Ma18lq
Mary	.00	F	Infant	17Ma18lq
MAHONEY, Daniel	24	M	Unknown	17Ma18lq
BRADFIELD, Thomas	30	M	Unknown	17Ma18lq
FARRELL, Margaret	20	F	Unknown	17Ma18lq
BUCKLEY, Timothy	25	M	Unknown	17Ma18lq
Eliza	22	F	Unknown	17Ma18lq
Margaret	3	F	Child	17Ma18lq
ODONELL, Mary	50	F	Unknown	17Ma18lq
Peggy	20	F	Unknown	17Ma18lq
LEARY, Daniel	20	M	Unknown	17Ma18lq
Daniel	50	M	Unknown	17Ma18lq
Humphrey	60	M	Unknown	17Ma18lq
PANE, Robert	26	M	Unknown	17Ma18lq
FITZGERALD, Edward	40	M	Unknown	17Ma18lq
CROWLEY, James	35	M	Unknown	17Ma18lq
Catherine	34	F	Unknown	17Ma18lq
HURLEY, Margaret	30	F	Unknown	17Ma18lq
CROWLEY, Catherine	7	F	Child	17Ma18lq
MURPHY, John	27	M	Unknown	17Ma18lq
MAHONEY, Ann	24	F	Unknown	17Ma18lq
DESMOND, Mary	22	F	Unknown	17Ma18lq
CARROLL, Mary	18	F	Unknown	17Ma18lq
HENLEY, John	25	M	Unknown	17Ma18lq
LUDDY, Patrick	22	M	Unknown	17Ma18lq
William	19	M	Unknown	17Ma18lq
Johanna	20	F	Unknown	17Ma18lq
Margaret	16	F	Unknown	17Ma18lq
HICKEY, Maurice	28	M	Unknown	17Ma18lq
CUNNINGHAM, Mary	24	F	Unknown	17Ma18lq
Johanna	22	F	Unknown	17Ma18lq
MILLER, Catherine	22	F	Unknown	17Ma18lq
RYAN, William	18	M	Unknown	17Ma18lq
William	45	M	Unknown	17Ma18lq
Margaret	28	F	Unknown	17Ma18lq
NEILL, Mary	25	F	Unknown	17Ma18lq
DONOVAN, Margaret	18	F	Unknown	17Ma18lq
THOMPSON, William	58	M	Unknown	17Ma18lq
CAHILL, Michael	20	M	Unknown	17Ma18lq
Mary	20	F	Unknown	17Ma18lq
DELAY, Johanna	19	F	Unknown	17Ma18lq
KEOHANE, Timothy	25	M	Unknown	17Ma18lq
DONOHUE, Johanna	25	F	Unknown	17Ma18lq
SULLIVAN, Dennis	28	M	Unknown	17Ma18lq
RYAN, Mary	40	F	Unknown	17Ma18lq
Margaret	15	F	Unknown	17Ma18lq
Michael	13	M	Unknown	17Ma18lq
PARKER, Edward	24	M	Unknown	17Ma18lq
FLANNEGAN, Ellen	25	F	Unknown	17Ma18lq
PINE, Thomas	26	M	Unknown	17Ma18lq
Hanora	22	F	Unknown	17Ma18lq
William	.06	M	Infant	17Ma18lq
BRADLEY, Dennis	30	M	Unknown	17Ma18lq
Johanna	25	F	Unknown	17Ma18lq
Mary	.00	F	Infant	17Ma18lq
CARROLL, Julia	20	F	Unknown	17Ma18lq
Ellen	13	F	Unknown	17Ma18lq
BARRY, Bess	26	F	Unknown	17Ma18lq
Mary	.00	F	Infant	17Ma18lq
OCONNELL, Michael	30	M	Unknown	17Ma18lq
COLLIS, Mary	20	F	Unknown	17Ma18lq
BRICK, Mary	20	F	Unknown	17Ma18lq
SULLIVAN, Roger	28	M	Unknown	17Ma18lq
DENAHY, John	25	M	Unknown	17Ma18lq
SHEEHAN, James	13	M	Unknown	17Ma18lq
Margaret	60	F	Unknown	17Ma18lq
BARNETT, John	25	M	Unknown	17Ma18lq
MCCARTHEY, Johanna	55	F	Unknown	17Ma18lq
OFARREL, James	40	M	Unknown	17Ma18lq
Margaret	30	F	Unknown	17Ma18lq
John	3	M	Child	17Ma18lq
Patrick	7	M	Child	17Ma18lq
Falacia	.00	F	Infant	17Ma18lq
RYAN, Patrick	28	M	Unknown	17Ma18lq
HIGGINS, John	13	M	Unknown	17Ma18lq
MULLANE, Jenney	6	F	Child	17Ma18lq
COURTNEY, Dennis	20	M	Unknown	17Ma18lq
RIORDEN, Michael	24	M	Unknown	17Ma18lq

NAMES OF PASSENGERS	AGE	SEX	OCCUPATIONS	DATE PORT SHIP
MURPHY, Darby	25	M	Unknown	17Ma18Iq
BROWN, Martin	17	M	Unknown	17Ma18Iq
DEVEINE, Daniel	40	M	Unknown	17Ma18Iq
SHEEHAN, Daniel	30	M	Unknown	17Ma18Iq
Abby	26	F	Unknown	17Ma18Iq
John	4	M	Child	17Ma18Iq
William	2	M	Child	17Ma18Iq
NEILL, Mary	22	F	Unknown	17Ma18Iq
SULLIVAN, Catherine	25	F	Unknown	17Ma18Iq
CONNELL, John	52	M	Unknown	17Ma18Iq
Jeffrey	9	M	Child	17Ma18Iq
John	9	M	Child	17Ma18Iq
MCGOWEN, John	22	M	Merchant	17Ma18Iq

BROOKSBY 17 MAY 1850

From Glasgow

NAMES OF PASSENGERS	AGE	SEX	OCCUPATIONS	DATE PORT SHIP
BARR, Walter	28	M	Laborer	17Ma21Du
Mary	29	F	Unknown	17Ma21Du
Elizabeth	7	F	Child	17Ma21Du
Agnes	.00	F	Infant	17Ma21Du
HAMILTON, Agusta-Ann	23	F	Unknown	17Ma21Du
WALKER, Samuel	28	M	Unknown	17Ma21Du
Mary	20	F	Unknown	17Ma21Du
FULLER, James	21	M	Unknown	17Ma21Du
BALMAN, James	67	M	Unknown	17Ma21Du
George	40	M	Unknown	17Ma21Du
ELEANOR, Ann	37	F	Unknown	17Ma21Du
Mary	8	F	Child	17Ma21Du
Elisabeth	5	F	Child	17Ma21Du
George	3	M	Child	17Ma21Du
Eleanor	1	F	Child	17Ma21Du
HALYBENTON, John	71	M	Unknown	17Ma21Du
Hannah	72	F	Unknown	17Ma21Du
Charles	30	M	Unknown	17Ma21Du
Rebecca	30	F	Unknown	17Ma21Du
FORD, Sarah	76	F	Unknown	17Ma21Du
LEWIS, Sophia	21	F	Unknown	17Ma21Du
LEIGHTON, Marion	17	F	Unknown	17Ma21Du
HALYBENTON, Thos.Charl	6	M	Child	17Ma21Du
Rebecca	1	F	Child	17Ma21Du
BARR, Amelia	17	F	Unknown	17Ma21Du
CRICHTON, James	45	M	Unknown	17Ma21Du
Isabella	44	F	Unknown	17Ma21Du
Wm.	17	M	Unknown	17Ma21Du
John	15	M	Unknown	17Ma21Du
Ellen	14	F	Unknown	17Ma21Du
Isabella	12	F	Unknown	17Ma21Du
Fanny	10	F	Unknown	17Ma21Du
James	8	M	Child	17Ma21Du
Mary	6	F	Child	17Ma21Du
Rose	2	F	Child	17Ma21Du
KILLACH, Andrew	27	M	Unknown	17Ma21Du
Agnes	25	F	Unknown	17Ma21Du
CLINKER, James	36	M	Unknown	17Ma21Du
Agnes	36	F	Unknown	17Ma21Du
James	10	M	Unknown	17Ma21Du
CLARK, Wm.	7	M	Child	17Ma21Du
Jarles	2	M	Child	17Ma21Du
Nicholas	25	M	Unknown	17Ma21Du
MCCALLISTEN, Margt.	50	F	Unknown	17Ma21Du
FARRELL, Patrick	26	M	Unknown	17Ma21Du
BENDEN, Wm.	50	M	Unknown	17Ma21Du
Elizabeth	50	F	Unknown	17Ma21Du
Janet	28	F	Unknown	17Ma21Du
Catherine	25	F	Unknown	17Ma21Du
Mary	22	F	Unknown	17Ma21Du
John	9	M	Child	17Ma21Du
BENDEN, Ann	6	F	Child	17Ma21Du
CARMICHAL, Archibald	22	M	Unknown	17Ma21Du
Mary	19	F	Unknown	17Ma21Du
BURNS, Mary	50	F	Unknown	17Ma21Du
James	22	M	Unknown	17Ma21Du
MORRISON, Wm.	49	M	Unknown	17Ma21Du
Helen	51	F	Unknown	17Ma21Du
Thomas	16	M	Unknown	17Ma21Du
Ontram	13	M	Unknown	17Ma21Du
WORKMAN, Ann-Mrs.	30	F	Unknown	17Ma21Du
THOMSON, Andrew	30	M	Unknown	17Ma21Du
Jane	20	F	Unknown	17Ma21Du
MARSHALL, John	50	M	Unknown	17Ma21Du
Margaret	48	F	Unknown	17Ma21Du
Eliza	22	F	Unknown	17Ma21Du
Marvin	20	M	Unknown	17Ma21Du
Janet	18	F	Unknown	17Ma21Du
Jane	15	F	Unknown	17Ma21Du
John	13	M	Unknown	17Ma21Du
ROBERTSON, John	26	M	Unknown	17Ma21Du
Agnes	20	F	Unknown	17Ma21Du
MINGLE, Janet	22	F	Unknown	17Ma21Du
MCPHARON, Wm.	31	M	Unknown	17Ma21Du
Isabella	32	F	Unknown	17Ma21Du
Margaret	60	F	Unknown	17Ma21Du
Janet	32	F	Unknown	17Ma21Du
WHYTE, Wm.	29	M	Unknown	17Ma21Du
Margt.	16	F	Unknown	17Ma21Du
MCKAY, Wm.	22	M	Unknown	17Ma21Du
ADAMS, James	28	M	Unknown	17Ma21Du
CRAWFORD, John	33	M	Unknown	17Ma21Du
HIAM, Isaac	20	M	Unknown	17Ma21Du
TAYLOR, Thomas	40	M	Unknown	17Ma21Du
Mary-Ann	30	F	Unknown	17Ma21Du
Elizabeth	11	F	Unknown	17Ma21Du
Emi.	8	F	Child	17Ma21Du
Ann	4	F	Child	17Ma21Du
MONTGOMERY, John	20	M	Unknown	17Ma21Du
MAHEY, James	60	M	Unknown	17Ma21Du
WERTEL, Elizabeth	55	F	Unknown	17Ma21Du
Wm.	36	M	Unknown	17Ma21Du
John	34	M	Unknown	17Ma21Du
Arthur	18	M	Unknown	17Ma21Du
Jane	25	F	Unknown	17Ma21Du
Matthew	16	M	Unknown	17Ma21Du
BRYSON, James	50	M	Unknown	17Ma21Du
Ann	44	F	Unknown	17Ma21Du
James	18	M	Unknown	17Ma21Du
Sarah	15	F	Unknown	17Ma21Du
William	13	M	Unknown	17Ma21Du
Margt.	11	F	Unknown	17Ma21Du
Daniel	9	M	Child	17Ma21Du
Martha	7	F	Child	17Ma21Du
Matthew	2	M	Child	17Ma21Du
GIBSON, Samuel	18	M	Unknown	17Ma21Du
SERVICE, Wm.John	20	M	Unknown	17Ma21Du
CLARKE, Isabella	40	F	Unknown	17Ma21Du
Ann	25	F	Unknown	17Ma21Du
GRIMES, Mary	2	F	Child	17Ma21Du
PONY, Alexander	30	M	Unknown	17Ma21Du
Mary	30	F	Unknown	17Ma21Du
John	11	M	Unknown	17Ma21Du
Elizabeth	8	F	Child	17Ma21Du
Mary-Jane	6	F	Child	17Ma21Du
Rebecca	3	F	Child	17Ma21Du
MCCOUCH, Hugh	18	M	Unknown	17Ma21Du
Ann	20	F	Unknown	17Ma21Du
STEWART, Andrew	20	M	Unknown	17Ma21Du
DAVIDSON, John	26	M	Unknown	17Ma21Du
GALLEY, Wm.	21	M	Unknown	17Ma21Du
CHRYSTAL, Wm.	26	M	Unknown	17Ma21Du
George	18	M	Unknown	17Ma21Du
DUNN, Thomas	25	M	Unknown	17Ma21Du
BOLESTON, Alexander	27	M	Unknown	17Ma21Du
DODD, Archibald	24	M	Unknown	17Ma21Du

NAMES OF PASSENGERS	AGE	SEX	OCCUPATIONS	DATE PORT SHIP
ARMSTRONG, Mary-Ann	30	F	Unknown	17Ma21Du
Robert	11	M	Unknown	17Ma21Du
Archibald	9	M	Child	17Ma21Du
Margt.	7	F	Child	17Ma21Du
Christopher	4	M	Child	17Ma21Du
Jane	.00	F	Infant	17Ma21Du
FOSTER, Ellen	18	F	Unknown	17Ma21Du
QUINN, James	16	M	Unknown	17Ma21Du
CARNS, James	43	M	Unknown	17Ma21Du
Mary	43	F	Unknown	17Ma21Du
BOYD, Elizth.	24	F	Unknown	17Ma21Du
Ann	19	F	Unknown	17Ma21Du
Elizth.	.00	F	Infant	17Ma21Du
NELSON, James	19	M	Unknown	17Ma21Du
CALLIEDIR, Peter	20	M	Unknown	17Ma21Du
BEGG, Alexander	28	M	Unknown	17Ma21Du
MCNEILL, John	30	M	Unknown	17Ma21Du
SANSON, John	21	M	Unknown	17Ma21Du
LESSELS, John	28	M	Unknown	17Ma21Du
CAHILL, Wm.	28	M	Unknown	17Ma21Du
MILLER, Walter	24	M	Unknown	17Ma21Du
DODGE, Archibald	26	M	Unknown	17Ma21Du
CATHETT, Hugh	23	M	Unknown	17Ma21Du
MCGERMMEL, James	30	M	Unknown	17Ma21Du
Ange	25	F	Unknown	17Ma21Du
John	25	M	Unknown	17Ma21Du
Hugh	18	M	Unknown	17Ma21Du
CARTON, John	25	M	Unknown	17Ma21Du
Mary-Ann	25	F	Unknown	17Ma21Du
KILLAN, Hugh	23	M	Unknown	17Ma21Du
James	21	M	Unknown	17Ma21Du
Hellen	19	F	Unknown	17Ma21Du
DARLIN, Simon	40	M	Unknown	17Ma21Du
Simon	14	M	Unknown	17Ma21Du
Betty	18	F	Unknown	17Ma21Du
Rose	20	F	Unknown	17Ma21Du
MCCAFFEE, James	25	M	Unknown	17Ma21Du
BELL, Elizabeth	19	F	Unknown	17Ma21Du
MORRIS, Catherine	20	F	Unknown	17Ma21Du
Margt.	18	F	Unknown	17Ma21Du
MATTHEWS, Henry	27	M	Unknown	17Ma21Du
QUINN, Hugh	29	M	Unknown	17Ma21Du
MONTGOMERY, John	25	M	Unknown	17Ma21Du
FRAZER, John	46	M	Unknown	17Ma21Du
Elizabeth	46	F	Unknown	17Ma21Du
Mary-Jane	12	F	Unknown	17Ma21Du
EWING, John	40	M	Unknown	17Ma21Du
MONTCURE, Thomas	21	M	Unknown	17Ma21Du
KOSTUCH, Andreas	38	M	Unknown	17Ma21Du
C.	42	F	Unknown	17Ma21Du
Conrad	22	M	Unknown	17Ma21Du
Catherine	20	F	Unknown	17Ma21Du
Aloins	15	M	Unknown	17Ma21Du
Trony	7	M	Child	17Ma21Du
BRATTORICH, Alouis	40	M	Unknown	17Ma21Du
NANDISH, Betty	24	F	Unknown	17Ma21Du
Betty	.00	F	Infant	17Ma21Du
SCHUSTER, Talian	57	M	Unknown	17Ma21Du
Marion	36	F	Unknown	17Ma21Du
Leopoldin	7	M	Child	17Ma21Du
Johann	.00	M	Infant	17Ma21Du
MANHAIT, Jancy	32	F	Unknown	17Ma21Du
Jancy	3	M	Child	17Ma21Du
Johanna	.00	F	Infant	17Ma21Du
WOODWARD, James	24	M	Unknown	17Ma21Du
Margarey	24	F	Unknown	17Ma21Du
Elizabeth	.00	F	Infant	17Ma21Du
MCCLELLAND, Wm.	26	M	Unknown	17Ma21Du
COLLARD, Thomas	30	M	Unknown	17Ma21Du
Rebecca	29	F	Unknown	17Ma21Du
Sarah	18	F	Unknown	17Ma21Du
Elizabeth	20	F	Unknown	17Ma21Du
KIRKWOOD, Peter	14	M	Unknown	17Ma21Du
KILDAY, Patrick	24	M	Unknown	17Ma21Du
CLARKE, Robt.	50	M	Unknown	17Ma21Du

NAMES OF PASSENGERS	AGE	SEX	OCCUPATIONS	DATE PORT SHIP
CLARKE, Jim	40	M	Unknown	17Ma21Du
Elizabeth	5	F	Child	17Ma21Du
CHALTON, James	25	M	Unknown	17Ma21Du
Sarah	22	F	Unknown	17Ma21Du
Andrew	22	M	Unknown	17Ma21Du
John	.00	M	Infant	17Ma21Du
MCBRIDE, Isabella	40	F	Unknown	17Ma21Du
Isabella	13	F	Unknown	17Ma21Du
Thomas	10	M	Unknown	17Ma21Du
Charles	8	M	Child	17Ma21Du
Mary	6	F	Child	17Ma21Du
MCPHERSON, James	9	M	Child	17Ma21Du
Margt.	.00	F	Infant	17Ma21Du
WHYTE, Wm.	16	M	Unknown	17Ma21Du
John-M.	5	M	Child	17Ma21Du
Eliza-M.	2	F	Child	17Ma21Du
MURPHY, Helen	12	F	Unknown	17Ma21Du
LYNCH, Sarah	45	F	Unknown	17Ma21Du
Mary	19	F	Unknown	17Ma21Du
Margaret	20	F	Unknown	17Ma21Du
KERR, John	40	M	Unknown	17Ma21Du
BROLLY, Clark	20	M	Unknown	17Ma21Du
John	18	M	Unknown	17Ma21Du
MCMANNUS, Wm.	20	M	Unknown	17Ma21Du
WILHOMDON, Samuel	15	M	Unknown	17Ma21Du
MCNALL, John	18	M	Unknown	17Ma21Du
DOCHERTY, Wm.	21	M	Unknown	17Ma21Du
MCGILL, Michael	24	M	Unknown	17Ma21Du
MCLANGLILAND, Wm.	23	M	Unknown	17Ma21Du
ORR, Margaret	18	F	Unknown	17Ma21Du
CARTEN, Patrick	23	M	Unknown	17Ma21Du
DONAGHY, Philip	23	M	Unknown	17Ma21Du
MCGLINFE, Mary-Jane	22	F	Unknown	17Ma21Du
James	22	M	Unknown	17Ma21Du
MCGARVEY, Daniel	25	M	Unknown	17Ma21Du
JACKSON, Wm.	24	M	Unknown	17Ma21Du

ACME 18 MAY 1850

From Liverpool

NAMES OF PASSENGERS	AGE	SEX	OCCUPATIONS	DATE PORT SHIP
REYNOLDS, Henry	40	M	Laborer	18Ma02Jy
STRONG, Jno.	18	M	Laborer	18Ma02Jy
REILEY, Bernard	21	M	Laborer	18Ma02Jy
MARTIN, Pat	16	M	Laborer	18Ma02Jy
BREEN, Mary	17	F	Spinster	18Ma02Jy
WHELAN, Peter	24	M	Laborer	18Ma02Jy
MCKOVE, Jas.	30	M	Laborer	18Ma02Jy
MADDEN, Mary	40	F	Unknown	18Ma02Jy
Honor	12	F	Laborer	18Ma02Jy
GILSHANNON, Pat	15	M	Laborer	18Ma02Jy
Wm.	10	M	Laborer	18Ma02Jy
CLEIVEN, Thos.	17	M	Laborer	18Ma02Jy
GREEN, Mary	22	F	Laborer	18Ma02Jy
HAYDEN, Bryan	40	M	Laborer	18Ma02Jy
MANION, Cathe.	22	F	Laborer	18Ma02Jy
COREY, Mary	38	F	Laborer	18Ma02Jy
Mary	7	F	Child	18Ma02Jy
Pat	12	M	Laborer	18Ma02Jy
CLARKE, Jno.	25	M	Laborer	18Ma02Jy
BOUGH, Jno.	25	M	Laborer	18Ma02Jy
MCMAHON, Rose	23	F	Laborer	18Ma02Jy
Mary	23	F	Laborer	18Ma02Jy
MEHAN, Edwd.	19	M	Laborer	18Ma02Jy
Ellen	25	F	Laborer	18Ma02Jy
LAWLER, Jas.	20	M	Unknown	18Ma02Jy
FOY, Edwd.	40	M	Unknown	18Ma02Jy
Cathe.	40	F	Unknown	18Ma02Jy
John	6	M	Child	18Ma02Jy

NAMES OF PASSENGERS	AGE	SEX	OCCUPATIONS	DATE PORT SHIP
FOY, Mary	4	F	Child	18Ma02Jy
Margt.	.00	F	Infant	18Ma02Jy
REILLY, Andrew	22	M	Unknown	18Ma02Jy
NOLAN, Mary	20	F	Unknown	18Ma02Jy
Bernard	14	M	Unknown	18Ma02Jy
CAROLAN, Owen	23	M	Unknown	18Ma02Jy
Jas.	14	M	Unknown	18Ma02Jy
MCCABE, Alexr.	22	M	Unknown	18Ma02Jy
Cathe.	40	F	Wife	18Ma02Jy
CLARKE, Jas.	20	M	Laborer	18Ma02Jy
KELLY, Michl.	18	M	Laborer	18Ma02Jy
Jno.	18	M	Unknown	18Ma02Jy
Mary	14	F	Unknown	18Ma02Jy
MCAULIFF, Archd.	30	M	Unknown	18Ma02Jy
HAYES, Jno.	30	M	Unknown	18Ma02Jy
WALSH, John	30	M	Unknown	18Ma02Jy
Bernard	25	M	Laborer	18Ma02Jy
Thos.	7	M	Child	18Ma02Jy
Bernard	5	M	Child	18Ma02Jy
Kate	3	F	Child	18Ma02Jy
DONOHUE, Cathe.	25	F	Unknown	18Ma02Jy
SKOLLY, John	28	M	Unknown	18Ma02Jy
Eliza	13	F	Unknown	18Ma02Jy
BURKE, Cathe.	40	F	Unknown	18Ma02Jy
SILLAS, Ellen	00	F	Unknown	18Ma02Jy
Cathe.	00	F	Unknown	18Ma02Jy
POWER, Jas.	00	M	Unknown	18Ma02Jy
Mary	00	F	Unknown	18Ma02Jy
Jno.	.00	M	Infant	18Ma02Jy
MULLIGAN, Eliza	00	F	Unknown	18Ma02Jy
MCGOWAN, Mary	00	F	Unknown	18Ma02Jy
POSSAN, Margt.	00	F	Unknown	18Ma02Jy
FENIN, Cathe.	00	F	Unknown	18Ma02Jy
FORD, Michl.	00	M	Unknown	18Ma02Jy
Sarah	00	F	Unknown	18Ma02Jy
Mary	00	F	Unknown	18Ma02Jy
MURPHY, Ellen	00	F	Unknown	18Ma02Jy
DENETRY, Jerry	00	M	Unknown	18Ma02Jy
Mary	00	F	Unknown	18Ma02Jy
CONNELL, Jno.	00	M	Unknown	18Ma02Jy
CROCOLLY, Jno.	00	M	Unknown	18Ma02Jy
CALLAGHAN, Jno.	00	M	Unknown	18Ma02Jy
MADDEN, Martin	30	M	Laborer	18Ma02Jy
WATERS, U	21	M	Laborer	18Ma02Jy
MCCARTY, Denis	26	M	Laborer	18Ma02Jy
Jno.	32	M	Laborer	18Ma02Jy
Ellen	18	F	Laborer	18Ma02Jy
BOYLE, Margt.	36	F	Laborer	18Ma02Jy
REILLY, Phil	30	M	Laborer	18Ma02Jy
CRONAN, Mary	11	F	Laborer	18Ma02Jy
HOPKINS, Martin	16	M	Laborer	18Ma02Jy
Jno.	36	M	Laborer	18Ma02Jy
Mary	13	F	Laborer	18Ma02Jy
Mary	6	F	Child	18Ma02Jy
Hugh	3	M	Child	18Ma02Jy
DAILY, Jno.	19	M	Laborer	18Ma02Jy
GARRAGHAN, Wm.	18	M	Laborer	18Ma02Jy
BERGAN, Mary	10	F	Laborer	18Ma02Jy
Bernard	8	M	Child	18Ma02Jy
FITZPATRICK, Eleanor	30	F	Laborer	18Ma02Jy
Honor	32	F	Laborer	18Ma02Jy
DONOHUE, Honor	22	F	Laborer	18Ma02Jy
HEFFERAN, Jno.	5	M	Child	18Ma02Jy
BRYAN, Geo.	17	M	Laborer	18Ma02Jy
MCPHILLIPS, Mat.	27	M	Laborer	18Ma02Jy
Cath.	7	F	Child	18Ma02Jy
SMITH, Mary	20	F	Laborer	18Ma02Jy
CONNERS, Thos.	18	M	Laborer	18Ma02Jy
HEW, Jes.	30	M	Laborer	18Ma02Jy
Ellen	20	F	Laborer	18Ma02Jy
John	.00	M	Infant	18Ma02Jy
MCDONALD, Mary	60	F	Laborer	18Ma02Jy
Julia	24	F	Laborer	18Ma02Jy
Mary	22	F	Laborer	18Ma02Jy
Edward	20	M	Laborer	18Ma02Jy

NAMES OF PASSENGERS	AGE	SEX	OCCUPATIONS	DATE PORT SHIP
MCDONALD, Cath.	18	F	Laborer	18Ma02Jy
Ellen	16	F	Laborer	18Ma02Jy
MCDONNELL, Chas.	20	M	Laborer	18Ma02Jy
Michl.	20	M	Laborer	18Ma02Jy
KEANNERY, Edwd.	45	M	Laborer	18Ma02Jy
Thos.	30	M	Laborer	18Ma02Jy
Mary	28	F	Laborer	18Ma02Jy
Michl.	20	M	Laborer	18Ma02Jy
CONNELL, Pat	21	M	Laborer	18Ma02Jy
MCNAMARA, John	24	M	Laborer	18Ma02Jy
MCGIVIER, Pat	29	M	Laborer	18Ma02Jy
MANION, Abigal	21	F	Laborer	18Ma02Jy
HORRIGAN, Bernard	25	M	Laborer	18Ma02Jy
HANANE, Jas.	23	M	Laborer	18Ma02Jy
KEEFE, Bridget	22	F	Laborer	18Ma02Jy
FUNN, Cathe.	16	F	Laborer	18Ma02Jy
FOLEY, Mary	16	F	Laborer	18Ma02Jy
Edwd.	10	M	Laborer	18Ma02Jy
CORKEY, Tim	20	M	Laborer	18Ma02Jy
Mary	20	F	Laborer	18Ma02Jy
KEELEY, Pat	34	M	Laborer	18Ma02Jy
Mary	30	F	Laborer	18Ma02Jy
Cathe.	29	F	Laborer	18Ma02Jy
MURPHY, Cathe.	.00	F	Infant	18Ma02Jy
MCCLURE, Jas.	28	M	Laborer	18Ma02Jy
COTTER, Bernard	18	M	Laborer	18Ma02Jy
WHELAN, Wm.	60	M	Laborer	18Ma02Jy
STACK, Mary	20	F	Laborer	18Ma02Jy
Cathe.	15	F	Laborer	18Ma02Jy
COOK, Andrew	18	M	Laborer	18Ma02Jy
Margt.	15	F	Laborer	18Ma02Jy
CLANCY, Margt.	30	F	Laborer	18Ma02Jy
MURPHY, Margt.	28	F	Laborer	18Ma02Jy
Sarah	25	F	Laborer	18Ma02Jy
ODOWELL, Margt.	18	F	Laborer	18Ma02Jy
Thos.	24	M	Laborer	18Ma02Jy
HEALY, Michl.	23	M	Laborer	18Ma02Jy
Bernard	20	M	Laborer	18Ma02Jy
SWEENEY, Thos.	20	M	Laborer	18Ma02Jy
QUELLEN, Pat	22	M	Laborer	18Ma02Jy
LYNCH, Bernard	18	M	Laborer	18Ma02Jy
BRAY, Mary	18	F	Laborer	18Ma02Jy
THORP, Jas.	28	M	Laborer	18Ma02Jy
JENKINSON, Jas.	16	M	Laborer	18Ma02Jy
Mary	26	F	Laborer	18Ma02Jy
MANION, Margt.	19	F	Laborer	18Ma02Jy
HURLEY, Ellen	35	F	Laborer	18Ma02Jy
Mary	20	F	Laborer	18Ma02Jy
Peggy	.00	F	Infant	18Ma02Jy
HART, John	30	M	Laborer	18Ma02Jy
MALLERAN, Mary	22	F	Laborer	18Ma02Jy
GRIFFIN, Ellen	25	F	Laborer	18Ma02Jy
SAVAGE, Ann	7	F	Child	18Ma02Jy
POWER, John	27	M	Laborer	18Ma02Jy
BASHFELD, L.	24	M	Laborer	18Ma02Jy
U-Mrs.	22	F	Laborer	18Ma02Jy
Mary	.00	F	Infant	18Ma02Jy
HORLUAGE, Chas.	28	M	Laborer	18Ma02Jy
Harriet	24	F	Laborer	18Ma02Jy
Susan	.00	F	Infant	18Ma02Jy
WILLIS, Geo.	24	M	Laborer	18Ma02Jy
U-Mrs.	24	F	Laborer	18Ma02Jy
Caroline	.00	F	Infant	18Ma02Jy
JONES, Thos.	23	M	Laborer	18Ma02Jy
DALTON, John	20	M	Laborer	18Ma02Jy
DERRICK, Edwd.	37	M	Laborer	18Ma02Jy
U-Mrs.	32	F	Laborer	18Ma02Jy
Edwd.	11	M	Laborer	18Ma02Jy
Hannah	4	F	Child	18Ma02Jy
SYNNES, Chas.	24	M	Laborer	18Ma02Jy
George	26	M	Laborer	18Ma02Jy
BARTLET, Bernard	28	M	Laborer	18Ma02Jy
Ann	26	F	Wife	18Ma02Jy
Jos.	30	M	Laborer	18Ma02Jy
Ann	.00	F	Infant	18Ma02Jy

NAMES OF PASSENGERS	AGE	SEX	OCCUPATIONS	DATE PORT SHIP
HEBBERT, Judy	20	F	Laborer	18Ma02Jy
COOK, Mary	15	F	Laborer	18Ma02Jy
KELLALOGH, Cathe.	16	F	Laborer	18Ma02Jy
KELLY, Martin	30	M	Laborer	18Ma02Jy
Cathe.	28	F	Laborer	18Ma02Jy
EGAN, Edwd.	30	M	Laborer	18Ma02Jy
FITZSIMMONS, Miles	28	M	Laborer	18Ma02Jy
Bernard	24	M	Laborer	18Ma02Jy
ROSELAN, Thos.	49	M	Laborer	18Ma02Jy
BROWNIMARD, Jas.	21	M	Laborer	18Ma02Jy
ALTHERRON, Atty	60	M	Laborer	18Ma02Jy
Isabella	60	F	Laborer	18Ma02Jy
HODGSOR, Ed	23	M	Laborer	18Ma02Jy
SIMPSON, Ralph	23	M	Laborer	18Ma02Jy
ELLIOTT, Jas.	20	M	Laborer	18Ma02Jy
CARTER, Jas.	30	M	Laborer	18Ma02Jy
SWEENY, Cathe.	14	F	Laborer	18Ma02Jy
TROY, Ann	25	F	Laborer	18Ma02Jy
Mary	20	F	Laborer	18Ma02Jy
BUCKLEY, Pat	26	M	Laborer	18Ma02Jy
NOWLAN, Ann	18	F	Laborer	18Ma02Jy
ASHER, Jas.	40	M	Laborer	18Ma02Jy
FULLY, Cathe.	20	F	Laborer	18Ma02Jy
RODDY, Ann	20	F	Laborer	18Ma02Jy
MCPARTIN, Cathe.	21	F	Laborer	18Ma02Jy
CORCORAN, Mary	30	F	Laborer	18Ma02Jy
John	5	M	Child	18Ma02Jy
Margt.	.00	F	Infant	18Ma02Jy
CLAREY, Ann	21	F	Laborer	18Ma02Jy
STATETON, Michl.	18	M	Laborer	18Ma02Jy
CRAGG, Mary-A.	33	F	Laborer	18Ma02Jy
Eliza	5	F	Child	18Ma02Jy
Margt.	.00	F	Infant	18Ma02Jy
KALENE, John	29	M	Laborer	18Ma02Jy
MCWILLIAMS, Jas.	21	M	Laborer	18Ma02Jy
BRADLEY, Jas.	14	M	Laborer	18Ma02Jy
WOOD, Wm.	28	M	Laborer	18Ma02Jy
ELLIOTT, Geo.	38	M	Laborer	18Ma02Jy
U-Mrs.	29	F	Laborer	18Ma02Jy
BANNING, Tim	21	M	Laborer	18Ma02Jy
BOLAN, Ellen	22	F	Laborer	18Ma02Jy
Johane	25	F	Laborer	18Ma02Jy
Pat	6	M	Child	18Ma02Jy
GRIFFIN, Mary	15	F	Laborer	18Ma02Jy
SELLERS, Michl.	18	M	Laborer	18Ma02Jy
Mary	16	F	Laborer	18Ma02Jy
Peter	14	M	Laborer	18Ma02Jy
Jno.	10	M	Laborer	18Ma02Jy
Thos.	8	M	Child	18Ma02Jy
Cealy	6	F	Child	18Ma02Jy
MAHER, Mary	30	F	Laborer	18Ma02Jy
Bridget	20	F	Laborer	18Ma02Jy
Johan	18	F	Laborer	18Ma02Jy
BRIDGET, Martin	25	M	Laborer	18Ma02Jy
KEEFFE, Thos.	22	M	Laborer	18Ma02Jy
Jas.	18	M	Laborer	18Ma02Jy
SWANN, Jno.	63	M	Laborer	18Ma02Jy
U-Mrs.	50	F	Laborer	18Ma02Jy
Alf	23	M	Laborer	18Ma02Jy
U-Mrs.	20	F	Laborer	18Ma02Jy
Susan	21	F	Laborer	18Ma02Jy
Eliza	19	F	Laborer	18Ma02Jy
OGDEN, Jno.	21	M	Laborer	18Ma02Jy
FULCHES, Jas.	47	M	Laborer	18Ma02Jy
U-Mrs.	45	F	Laborer	18Ma02Jy
Sarah	16	F	Laborer	18Ma02Jy
Mary	12	F	Laborer	18Ma02Jy
Jas.	7	M	Child	18Ma02Jy
Ann	3	F	Child	18Ma02Jy
Emma	.00	F	Infant	18Ma02Jy
LEECH, Wm.	22	M	Laborer	18Ma02Jy
U-Mrs.	32	F	Laborer	18Ma02Jy
Kate	2	F	Child	18Ma02Jy
Jane	18	F	Laborer	18Ma02Jy
Robt.	16	M	Laborer	18Ma02Jy

NAMES OF PASSENGERS	AGE	SEX	OCCUPATIONS	DATE PORT SHIP
SCOTT, Geo.	32	M	Laborer	18Ma02Jy
POWERS, M.	20	M	Laborer	18Ma02Jy
TOWNES, Jno.	24	M	Laborer	18Ma02Jy
ROBINSON, Jno.	32	M	Laborer	18Ma02Jy
U-Mrs.	26	F	Laborer	18Ma02Jy
ROW, Mary	32	F	Laborer	18Ma02Jy
WILLIAMSON, Robt.	22	M	Laborer	18Ma02Jy
TAYLOR, Sarah	26	F	Laborer	18Ma02Jy
Emma	2	F	Child	18Ma02Jy
HEWITT, Matthew	25	M	Laborer	18Ma02Jy
Jos.	3	M	Child	18Ma02Jy
Thosella	.00	F	Infant	18Ma02Jy
NEWTON, Thos.	25	M	Laborer	18Ma02Jy
GRAYSON, Geo.	26	M	Laborer	18Ma02Jy
Jno.	28	M	Laborer	18Ma02Jy
RAY, Jas.	15	M	Laborer	18Ma02Jy
Robt.	19	M	Laborer	18Ma02Jy
Jos.	16	M	Laborer	18Ma02Jy
GLEESON, Jas.	35	M	Laborer	18Ma02Jy
U-Mrs.	30	F	Laborer	18Ma02Jy
Pat	11	M	Laborer	18Ma02Jy
Michl.	10	M	Laborer	18Ma02Jy
Cathe.	12	F	Laborer	18Ma02Jy
DONOVAN, Michl.	27	M	Laborer	18Ma02Jy
GREEN, John	44	M	Laborer	18Ma02Jy
KEOGH, Esther	19	F	Laborer	18Ma02Jy
BYRNES, Eliz.	20	F	Laborer	18Ma02Jy
Mary	20	F	Laborer	18Ma02Jy
DEMPSEY, Thos.	18	M	Laborer	18Ma02Jy
MOWEER, Wm.	50	M	Laborer	18Ma02Jy
U-Mrs.	45	F	Laborer	18Ma02Jy
Jno.	21	M	Laborer	18Ma02Jy
Kelly	19	F	Laborer	18Ma02Jy
Ann	18	F	Unknown	18Ma02Jy
Wm.	14	M	Unknown	18Ma02Jy
Margt.	13	F	Unknown	18Ma02Jy
Thos.	10	M	Unknown	18Ma02Jy
Jas.	5	M	Child	18Ma02Jy
Jno.Neal	21	M	Unknown	18Ma02Jy
Chas.	3	M	Child	18Ma02Jy
HERMEEN, Cathe.	21	F	Unknown	18Ma02Jy
Wm.	26	M	Unknown	18Ma02Jy
U-Mrs.	23	F	Unknown	18Ma02Jy
Jno.	21	M	Unknown	18Ma02Jy
Ann	.00	F	Infant	18Ma02Jy
QUILL, Cathe.	18	F	Unknown	18Ma02Jy
CHASE, Rob	30	M	Unknown	18Ma02Jy
SHERMAN, Jno.	19	M	Unknown	18Ma02Jy
CLARKE, David	39	M	Unknown	18Ma02Jy
Nancy	5	F	Child	18Ma02Jy
Mary	38	F	Unknown	18Ma02Jy
Jas.	8	M	Child	18Ma02Jy
Hannah	13	F	Unknown	18Ma02Jy
Emma	.00	F	Infant	18Ma02Jy
SHIELDS, Jos.	30	M	Unknown	18Ma02Jy
U-Mrs.	24	F	Unknown	18Ma02Jy
DOHERTY, Cathe.	27	F	Unknown	18Ma02Jy
CAVANAGH, Edwd.	25	M	Unknown	18Ma02Jy
Bridget	45	F	Unknown	18Ma02Jy
Ann	19	F	Unknown	18Ma02Jy
Wm.	8	M	Child	18Ma02Jy
FLOOD, Esther	35	F	Unknown	18Ma02Jy
Kelly	30	F	Unknown	18Ma02Jy
BOLAN, Jas.	40	M	Unknown	18Ma02Jy
MCDOWELL, Wm.	23	M	Unknown	18Ma02Jy
CUGH, John	37	M	Unknown	18Ma02Jy
KEINE, Thos.	32	M	Unknown	18Ma02Jy
U-Mrs.	40	F	Unknown	18Ma02Jy
Matthew	21	M	Unknown	18Ma02Jy
Dorothy	18	F	Unknown	18Ma02Jy
B.	7	U	Child	18Ma02Jy
KINSHELA, Michl.	30	M	Child	18Ma02Jy
WHITE, Dave	66	M	Child	18Ma02Jy
Ann	56	F	Child	18Ma02Jy
Pat	30	M	Unknown	18Ma02Jy

NAMES OF PASSENGERS	AGE	SEX	OCCUPATIONS	DATE PORT SHIP
OBRIEN, Martin	40	M	Unknown	18Ma02Jy
RYAN, Mary	11	F	Unknown	18Ma02Jy
SULLIVAN, Danl.	24	M	Unknown	18Ma02Jy
MURDOCK, Alexr.	26	M	Unknown	18Ma02Jy
U-Mrs.	21	F	Unknown	18Ma02Jy
Jane	.00	F	Infant	18Ma02Jy
NELSON, Jno.	38	M	Unknown	18Ma02Jy
U-Mrs.	38	F	Unknown	18Ma02Jy
Jno.	8	M	Child	18Ma02Jy
CONNELLY, Alexr.	28	M	Unknown	18Ma02Jy
U-Mrs.	26	F	Unknown	18Ma02Jy
TAYLOR, Mary	25	F	Unknown	18Ma02Jy
FREN, Thos.	22	M	Unknown	18Ma02Jy
BLACK, John	24	M	Unknown	18Ma02Jy
U-Mrs.	24	F	Unknown	18Ma02Jy
TWOLON, Jno.	24	M	Unknown	18Ma02Jy
U-Mrs.	24	F	Unknown	18Ma02Jy
HURSLEY, U-Mrs.	60	F	Unknown	18Ma02Jy
ROY, Jno.	24	M	Unknown	18Ma02Jy
Geo.	20	M	Unknown	18Ma02Jy
DOUGHERTY, John	31	M	Unknown	18Ma02Jy
COLLINGWOOD, Roger	31	M	Unknown	18Ma02Jy
Jacob	29	M	Unknown	18Ma02Jy
BALL, Ann	9	F	Child	18Ma02Jy
Ralph	6	M	Child	18Ma02Jy
Eliza	4	F	Child	18Ma02Jy
Jane	.00	F	Infant	18Ma02Jy
PARKINSON, Jno.	21	M	Unknown	18Ma02Jy
HANEY, Rob	40	M	Unknown	18Ma02Jy
Ann-C.	40	F	Unknown	18Ma02Jy
Mary	5	F	Child	18Ma02Jy
WEEKSHEAD, Leigle	26	U	Unknown	18Ma02Jy
Henry	4	M	Child	18Ma02Jy
Wm.	.00	M	Infant	18Ma02Jy
GRIFFIN, Pat	30	M	Unknown	18Ma02Jy
BROWN, Jas.	15	M	Unknown	18Ma02Jy
Cathe.	9	F	Child	18Ma02Jy
Ellen	35	F	Unknown	18Ma02Jy
John	14	M	Unknown	18Ma02Jy
HANLINS, Andrew	5	M	Child	18Ma02Jy
Bridget	3	F	Child	18Ma02Jy
BYRNE, Jno.	45	M	Unknown	18Ma02Jy
Alice	30	F	Unknown	18Ma02Jy
Ann	18	F	Unknown	18Ma02Jy
Jno.	14	M	Unknown	18Ma02Jy
WALLACE, Elias	14	M	Unknown	18Ma02Jy
KEY, U	45	M	Unknown	18Ma02Jy
U-Mrs.	40	F	Unknown	18Ma02Jy
U (D)	10	F	Unknown	18Ma02Jy
U (S)	7	M	Child	18Ma02Jy
BAXTER, U	25	M	Unknown	18Ma02Jy
BUTLER, U	19	M	Unknown	18Ma02Jy
POSSAN, Mary	00	F	Unknown	18Ma02Jy

MOUNTAINEER 18 MAY 1850

From Penzance

NAMES OF PASSENGERS	AGE	SEX	OCCUPATIONS	DATE PORT SHIP
KEMPTHOME, Jacob	45	M	Farmer	18Ma16Ae
Mary	46	F	Unknown	18Ma16Ae
James	18	M	Unknown	18Ma16Ae
Cathl.	11	F	Unknown	18Ma16Ae
Charles	9	M	Child	18Ma16Ae
Josiah	7	M	Child	18Ma16Ae
WALKEY, Richd.	21	M	Unknown	18Ma16Ae
PHILLIPS, Jenefer	34	F	Unknown	18Ma16Ae
James	7	M	Child	18Ma16Ae
John	5	M	Child	18Ma16Ae
Elizabeth	6	F	Child	18Ma16Ae
PHILLIPS, Lucy	4	F	Child	18Ma16Ae
U	.00	U	Infant	18Ma16Ae
CLARK, James	25	M	Unknown	18Ma16Ae
Caroline	22	F	Unknown	18Ma16Ae
U	.00	U	Infant	18Ma16Ae
Died-At-Sea				
MITCHELL, Henry	23	M	Unknown	18Ma16Ae
Lewellyn	15	M	Unknown	18Ma16Ae
Rufas	12	M	Unknown	18Ma16Ae
Gordon	9	M	Child	18Ma16Ae
Charles	3	M	Child	18Ma16Ae
LARTY, Jane-Orchard	22	F	Unknown	18Ma16Ae
John	2	M	Child	18Ma16Ae
U	.00	U	Infant	18Ma16Ae
WILLIAMS, Martin	21	M	Unknown	18Ma16Ae
CARTER, Robert	28	M	Unknown	18Ma16Ae
Thos.	26	M	Unknown	18Ma16Ae
STEVENS, Henry	25	M	Unknown	18Ma16Ae
BURNS, Richd.	18	M	Unknown	18Ma16Ae
RICHARDS, John	17	M	Unknown	18Ma16Ae
ROWE, Wm.	17	M	Unknown	18Ma16Ae
CHAMPION, Elizth.	43	F	Unknown	18Ma16Ae
Eliza-Ann	11	F	Unknown	18Ma16Ae
John	13	M	Unknown	18Ma16Ae
WEST, Jane	26	F	Unknown	18Ma16Ae
Sophia	5	F	Child	18Ma16Ae
Baonet	3	M	Child	18Ma16Ae
CHADWICK, Gordon	35	M	Teacher	18Ma16Ae
HARVEY, Wm.	26	M	Miner	18Ma16Ae
HENDALL, Richd.	28	M	Butcher	18Ma16Ae
THOMAS, Henry	28	M	Miner	18Ma16Ae
Joseph	36	M	Unknown	18Ma16Ae
PERRY, Anne	20	F	Unknown	18Ma16Ae
EUSTICE, Maroy	37	M	Unknown	18Ma16Ae
MATTHEWS, Thos.	29	M	Unknown	18Ma16Ae
PETERS, Nicholas	40	M	Unknown	18Ma16Ae
WILLIAMS, Joshua	35	M	Grocer	18Ma16Ae
FINNEGAN, Thos.	58	M	Farmer	18Ma16Ae
Eliza	21	F	Farmer	18Ma16Ae
BOWDEN, Charles	31	M	Engineer	18Ma16Ae
ROBERTS, Henry	20	M	Farmer	18Ma16Ae
John	17	M	Unknown	18Ma16Ae
ELLIS, Richard	34	M	Unknown	18Ma16Ae
Johanna	32	F	Unknown	18Ma16Ae
Thos.	6	M	Child	18Ma16Ae
Richard	4	M	Child	18Ma16Ae
Mary	3	F	Child	18Ma16Ae
EARLE, James	32	M	Unknown	18Ma16Ae
HARRIS, Simon	23	M	Unknown	18Ma16Ae
EARLE, Johanna	32	F	Unknown	18Ma16Ae
James	6	M	Child	18Ma16Ae
Elizth.	4	F	Child	18Ma16Ae
John	3	M	Child	18Ma16Ae
ROWE, Eliza	22	F	Servant	18Ma16Ae
FARRELL, Mary	44	F	Unknown	18Ma16Ae
Thos.	19	M	Unknown	18Ma16Ae
Richd.	13	M	Unknown	18Ma16Ae
Eliza	12	F	Unknown	18Ma16Ae
John	10	M	Unknown	18Ma16Ae
Jane	8	F	Child	18Ma16Ae
Ann	6	F	Child	18Ma16Ae
Wm.	4	M	Child	18Ma16Ae
James	.00	M	Infant	18Ma16Ae
JEWALL, Thos.	34	M	Unknown	18Ma16Ae
John	43	M	Unknown	18Ma16Ae
Jane	39	F	Unknown	18Ma16Ae
John	4	M	Child	18Ma16Ae
Thomas	5	M	Child	18Ma16Ae
MANN, James	44	M	Laborer	18Ma16Ae
Grace	39	F	Laborer	18Ma16Ae
HENRY, Wm.	13	M	Unknown	18Ma16Ae
James	12	M	Unknown	18Ma16Ae
Thos.Chs.	5	M	Child	18Ma16Ae
EDWARDS, David	38	M	Carpenter	18Ma16Ae
Charlotte	38	F	Unknown	18Ma16Ae

NAMES OF PASSENGERS	AGE	SEX	OCCUPATIONS	DATE PORT SHIP
EDWARDS, Elizth.Ann	13	F	Unknown	18Ma16Ae
Mary-Jane	12	F	Unknown	18Ma16Ae
Amelia	11	F	Unknown	18Ma16Ae
Alfred	8	M	Child	18Ma16Ae
Eliza	6	F	Child	18Ma16Ae
Rinseilla	5	F	Child	18Ma16Ae
Ellen	3	F	Child	18Ma16Ae
BILKEY, Wm.Hy.	37	M	Farmer	18Ma16Ae
RICH, Cathr.	37	F	Unknown	18Ma16Ae
Elizth.	11	F	Unknown	18Ma16Ae
PENBERTHY, Mary	52	F	Unknown	18Ma16Ae
Cath.	24	F	Unknown	18Ma16Ae
Jane	16	F	Unknown	18Ma16Ae
GROSS, Jane	29	F	Unknown	18Ma16Ae
Jane	9	F	Child	18Ma16Ae
Elizth.	6	F	Child	18Ma16Ae
James	6	M	Child	18Ma16Ae
Thos.	2	M	Child	18Ma16Ae
ROWE, Ann	69	F	Unknown	18Ma16Ae
JAMES, Wm.	22	M	Miner	18Ma16Ae
HODGES, Lawrence	19	F	Servant	18Ma16Ae
RICHARD, Mary	62	F	Unknown	18Ma16Ae
Wm.Hy.	17	M	Miner	18Ma16Ae
HODGE, Wm.	25	M	Farmer	18Ma16Ae
MATTHEWS, Hy.	29	M	Farmer	18Ma16Ae
Grace	28	F	Unknown	18Ma16Ae
WILLOWS, Anne	33	F	Unknown	18Ma16Ae
POWLING, Thos.	63	M	Unknown	18Ma16Ae
Mary	56	F	Unknown	18Ma16Ae
Joseph	18	M	Printer	18Ma16Ae
MITCHELL, Phillip	49	M	Farmer	18Ma16Ae
Philip	18	M	Unknown	18Ma16Ae
James	14	M	Unknown	18Ma16Ae
HOOKING, Eliza	24	F	Unknown	18Ma16Ae
FREDERICK, Eliza	25	F	Unknown	18Ma16Ae
PEARBERTY, Saml.	29	M	Unknown	18Ma16Ae
Wilmot	26	F	Unknown	18Ma16Ae
Saml.	.00	M	Infant	18Ma16Ae
REARSE, Emily	51	F	Unknown	18Ma16Ae
BEAVER, Emily	51	F	Farmer	18Ma16Ae
Christian	23	F	Unknown	18Ma16Ae
THOMAS, James	22	M	Unknown	18Ma16Ae
TURNER, Sophia	33	F	Unknown	18Ma16Ae
John	7	M	Child	18Ma16Ae
Sophia	3	F	Child	18Ma16Ae
MAJOR, John	24	M	Unknown	18Ma16Ae
Chas.	20	M	Unknown	18Ma16Ae
Mary	26	F	Unknown	18Ma16Ae
John	.00	M	Infant	18Ma16Ae
LAY, Wm.	27	M	Unknown	18Ma16Ae
WHITE, Jenifer	32	F	Unknown	18Ma16Ae
Thos.	5	M	Child	18Ma16Ae
Maria	2	F	Child	18Ma16Ae
BROWNE, Amelia	25	F	Unknown	18Ma16Ae
DINGLE, John	28	M	Unknown	18Ma16Ae
DREW, Edward	20	M	Unknown	18Ma16Ae
WILLIAMS, John	69	M	Unknown	18Ma16Ae
Mary	68	F	Unknown	18Ma16Ae
ADDY, Hart	65	M	Unknown	18Ma16Ae
Hart-Jr.	23	M	Unknown	18Ma16Ae
ELVANS, Betsey	63	F	Unknown	18Ma16Ae
M.E.	13	F	Unknown	18Ma16Ae
George	11	M	Unknown	18Ma16Ae
ONEIL, Richard	54	M	Unknown	18Ma16Ae
Thomasine	52	F	Unknown	18Ma16Ae
PAUL, Henry	27	M	Unknown	18Ma16Ae
Jane	25	F	Unknown	18Ma16Ae
James	19	M	Unknown	18Ma16Ae
Jane	19	F	Unknown	18Ma16Ae
LYNN, Philip	60	M	Unknown	18Ma16Ae
JAY, John	20	M	Unknown	18Ma16Ae

COLUMBINE 18 MAY 1850

From London

NAMES OF PASSENGERS	AGE	SEX	OCCUPATIONS	DATE PORT SHIP
DARVILL, Richard	45	M	Watchmaker	18Ma06Aa
Maria	43	F	Watchmaker	18Ma06Aa
Mary-Ann	21	F	Watchmaker	18Ma06Aa
John	17	M	Watchmaker	18Ma06Aa
Richard	13	M	Watchmaker	18Ma06Aa
Ann	12	F	Watchmaker	18Ma06Aa
Sarah	5	F	Child	18Ma06Aa
William	3	M	Child	18Ma06Aa
Eleanor	2	F	Child	18Ma06Aa
Reuben	.07	M	Infant	18Ma06Aa
BARLING, Alfred	33	M	Talch	18Ma06Aa
Charlotte	29	F	Unknown	18Ma06Aa
Watler	11	M	Unknown	18Ma06Aa
Francis	8	M	Child	18Ma06Aa
John	5	M	Child	18Ma06Aa
Joseph	3	M	Child	18Ma06Aa
Charles	.00	M	Infant	18Ma06Aa
Died-At-Sea				
RUSSELL, William	42	M	Glazier	18Ma06Aa
Elizabeth	42	F	Unknown	18Ma06Aa
Sophia	21	F	Unknown	18Ma06Aa
Charles	18	M	Unknown	18Ma06Aa
William	12	M	Unknown	18Ma06Aa
Alfred	7	M	Child	18Ma06Aa
John	9	M	Child	18Ma06Aa
Christopher	5	M	Child	18Ma06Aa
Alfred-Ford	2	M	Child	18Ma06Aa
Mary	.00	F	Infant	18Ma06Aa
Joseph	33	M	Glazier	18Ma06Aa
Mary	33	F	Unknown	18Ma06Aa
CROCKER, William	35	M	Mechanic	18Ma06Aa
Mary-Ann	33	F	Unknown	18Ma06Aa
Charles	12	M	Unknown	18Ma06Aa
Mary-Ann	11	F	Unknown	18Ma06Aa
Mark	10	M	Unknown	18Ma06Aa
Eliza	9	F	Child	18Ma06Aa
John	2	M	Child	18Ma06Aa
William	5	M	Child	18Ma06Aa
Fanny	4	F	Child	18Ma06Aa
Indine	3	U	Child	18Ma06Aa
Emily	.00	F	Infant	18Ma06Aa
HOLLOWAY, Sarah	21	F	Unknown	18Ma06Aa
CHAPMAN, Susan	45	F	Unknown	18Ma06Aa
Charles	12	M	Unknown	18Ma06Aa
Mary-Ann	10	F	Unknown	18Ma06Aa
TUTTLE, John	39	M	Unknown	18Ma06Aa
Maria	40	F	Unknown	18Ma06Aa
Mary-Ann	9	F	Child	18Ma06Aa
Emily	6	F	Child	18Ma06Aa
Agnes	3	F	Child	18Ma06Aa
PIETZEL, Frederic	31	M	Unknown	18Ma06Aa
PLATH, Martin	47	M	Unknown	18Ma06Aa
GERNER, George	22	M	Unknown	18Ma06Aa
MARTIN, Edward	32	M	Unknown	18Ma06Aa
CROUCH, Richard	21	M	Unknown	18Ma06Aa
Margaret	21	F	Unknown	18Ma06Aa
LEAHY, Patrick	35	M	Unknown	18Ma06Aa
DAWSON, Mary-Anne	24	F	Unknown	18Ma06Aa
Jane	20	F	Unknown	18Ma06Aa
MUNTLOW, Elizabeth	33	F	Unknown	18Ma06Aa
CONLEY, John	53	M	Unknown	18Ma06Aa
Harriett	43	F	Unknown	18Ma06Aa
Died-At-Sea				
Harriett	17	F	Unknown	18Ma06Aa
Amelia	6	F	Child	18Ma06Aa

NAMES OF PASSENGERS	AGE	SEX	OCCUPATIONS	DATE PORT SHIP
MUNTLOW, Edward	4	M	Child	18Ma06Aa
Joseph	2	M	Child	18Ma06Aa
NEALE, William	23	M	Schm	18Ma06Aa
Susan	21	F	Unknown	18Ma06Aa
MAILE, John	38	M	Unknown	18Ma06Aa
Mary	42	F	Unknown	18Ma06Aa
Ann	15	F	Unknown	18Ma06Aa
Sarah-Ann	10	F	Unknown	18Ma06Aa
John-L.	6	M	Child	18Ma06Aa
James	2	M	Child	18Ma06Aa
BARKER, William	24	M	None	18Ma06Aa
Catharine	21	F	Unknown	18Ma06Aa
Catharine	2	F	Child	18Ma06Aa
Ingle	16	U	Unknown	18Ma06Aa
WADE, Matthew	29	M	Unknown	18Ma06Aa
Mahome	30	U	Unknown	18Ma06Aa
Joseph	4	M	Child	18Ma06Aa
Ann	2	F	Child	18Ma06Aa
Ralph	34	M	None	18Ma06Aa
ROBERTS, Angelina-T.	25	F	Servant	18Ma06Aa
CONCORAN, John	52	M	Hatter	18Ma06Aa
GURNHAM, James	50	M	Unknown	18Ma06Aa
MACKAY, Michael	18	M	Bomkr	18Ma06Aa
THOMAS, James	25	M	Bomkr	18Ma06Aa
Elizabeth	25	F	Unknown	18Ma06Aa
ELLIS, Ezra	22	M	Furrier	18Ma06Aa
Victoria	23	F	Furrier	18Ma06Aa
FULLAGAN, James	22	M	Carpenter	18Ma06Aa
BURNS, Owen	30	M	Laborer	18Ma06Aa
Mary	22	F	Laborer	18Ma06Aa
RILEY, Jeremiah	22	M	Unknown	18Ma06Aa
Bridget	22	F	Unknown	18Ma06Aa
John	3	M	Child	18Ma06Aa
Jeremiah	.00	M	Infant	18Ma06Aa
Patrick	.00	M	Infant	18Ma06Aa
DONAHOE, Jeremiah	20	M	Laborer	18Ma06Aa
Patrick	16	M	Laborer	18Ma06Aa
REYNOLDS, William	24	M	Laborer	18Ma06Aa
BROWNING, Thomas	23	M	Stone Mason	18Ma06Aa
TREADWELL, Thomas	29	M	Furrier	18Ma06Aa
Caroline	30	F	Furrier	18Ma06Aa
DUNHENE, Henry	43	M	Laborer	18Ma06Aa
SMITH, Henry	34	M	Carpenter	18Ma06Aa
LUCY, Jeremiah	29	M	Laborer	18Ma06Aa
Mary	22	F	Unknown	18Ma06Aa
MACARTY, Jas.	26	M	Unknown	18Ma06Aa
DIXON, Edward	27	M	Unknown	18Ma06Aa
SULLIVAN, Dennis	25	M	Unknown	18Ma06Aa
Mary	24	F	Unknown	18Ma06Aa
HEFFERMAN, Thomas	35	M	Unknown	18Ma06Aa
Maria	32	F	Unknown	18Ma06Aa
ROOKES, William	35	M	Unknown	18Ma06Aa
BLOCKE, Aaron	28	M	Unknown	18Ma06Aa
VIENSKENPAN, Alfred	27	M	Unknown	18Ma06Aa
Emma	27	F	Unknown	18Ma06Aa
Alfred	6	M	Child	18Ma06Aa
Samuel	.08	M	Infant	18Ma06Aa
MAHONEY, Mary	35	F	None	18Ma06Aa
Margaret	12	F	None	18Ma06Aa
Daniel	8	M	Child	18Ma06Aa
John	6	M	Child	18Ma06Aa
Ellen	.04	F	Infant	18Ma06Aa
ELLIS, Henry	23	M	None	18Ma06Aa
LEARY, John	22	M	Agrc	18Ma06Aa
BURMAGE, George	36	M	Agrc	18Ma06Aa
MURPHY, Margaret	24	F	Unknown	18Ma06Aa
KELLY, John	30	M	Unknown	18Ma06Aa
FAMING, Mary	28	F	Unknown	18Ma06Aa
WELCH, John	40	M	Unknown	18Ma06Aa
WILDEY, Edward	17	M	Unknown	18Ma06Aa
ASKEW, John	49	M	Unknown	18Ma06Aa
Frederick	19	M	Unknown	18Ma06Aa
James	8	M	Child	18Ma06Aa
Benjamin	12	M	Unknown	18Ma06Aa
Elizabeth	16	F	Unknown	18Ma06Aa
ASKEW, Lydia	52	F	Unknown	18Ma06Aa
OBRIEN, Patrick	29	M	Unknown	18Ma06Aa
MCGAW, James	30	M	Unknown	18Ma06Aa
Thomas	25	M	Unknown	18Ma06Aa
DIVER, John	31	M	Unknown	18Ma06Aa
EVANS, Roger	40	M	Unknown	18Ma06Aa
Mary-Ann	30	F	Unknown	18Ma06Aa
WIGGINS, Reuben	31	M	Unknown	18Ma06Aa
CASEY, William	32	M	Unknown	18Ma06Aa
CHARTOST, Cornelius	22	M	Unknown	18Ma06Aa
DONAGUE, John	22	M	Unknown	18Ma06Aa
ADAMS, James	32	M	Unknown	18Ma06Aa
Ann	27	F	Unknown	18Ma06Aa
WILKINS, James	20	M	Unknown	18Ma06Aa
COLLINS, John	50	M	Unknown	18Ma06Aa
LYNCH, Thomas	23	M	Unknown	18Ma06Aa
WELLS, Susannah	64	F	Unknown	18Ma06Aa
PRAEGER, Emily	21	F	Unknown	18Ma06Aa
BRAND, James	18	M	Unknown	18Ma06Aa
SMITH, John	18	M	Agrc	18Ma06Aa
FREEBOUND, Francis	17	M	Agrc	18Ma06Aa
CHURCH, James	16	M	Unknown	18Ma06Aa
CANE, John	45	M	Unknown	18Ma06Aa
CRAIG, Henry	33	M	Unknown	18Ma06Aa
Lydia	34	F	Unknown	18Ma06Aa
Elizabeth	10	F	Unknown	18Ma06Aa
Jane	8	M	Child	18Ma06Aa
JOHNSON, John	32	M	Unknown	18Ma06Aa
Fanny	30	F	Unknown	18Ma06Aa
John	3	M	Child	18Ma06Aa
Ann	1	F	Child	18Ma06Aa
FRIEND, William	44	M	Unknown	18Ma06Aa
Martha	51	F	Unknown	18Ma06Aa
Sarah	22	F	Unknown	18Ma06Aa
Esther	20	F	Unknown	18Ma06Aa
Nimrod	16	M	Unknown	18Ma06Aa
Ann	14	F	Unknown	18Ma06Aa
William	13	M	Agrc	18Ma06Aa
FAGGE, James	23	M	Unknown	18Ma06Aa
BRISLEY, Stephen	35	M	Unknown	18Ma06Aa
JOINER, Thomas	26	M	Unknown	18Ma06Aa
FOORD, Henry	37	M	Unknown	18Ma06Aa
Eliza	28	F	Unknown	18Ma06Aa
Mary-Ann	6	F	Child	18Ma06Aa
Henry	2	M	Child	18Ma06Aa
Sarah	.00	F	Infant	18Ma06Aa
BULINGER, James	21	M	Unknown	18Ma06Aa
BLOXAM, Thomas	28	M	Unknown	18Ma06Aa
Ann	24	F	Unknown	18Ma06Aa
WHITEHEAD, Richard	35	M	Unknown	18Ma06Aa
Catherine	37	F	Unknown	18Ma06Aa
Charles	11	M	Unknown	18Ma06Aa
Jane	9	F	Child	18Ma06Aa
Henry	6	M	Child	18Ma06Aa
Thomas	4	M	Child	18Ma06Aa
Catherine	3	F	Child	18Ma06Aa
Sarah	.00	F	Infant	18Ma06Aa
Died-At-Sea				
BUSLEY, George	32	M	Unknown	18Ma06Aa
FIELD, Lydia	45	F	Unknown	18Ma06Aa
James	17	M	Unknown	18Ma06Aa
William	13	M	Unknown	18Ma06Aa
Edward	12	M	Unknown	18Ma06Aa
Thomas	10	M	Unknown	18Ma06Aa
GOLDER, John	30	M	Unknown	18Ma06Aa
PARKER, John	30	M	Unknown	18Ma06Aa
BAKER, Gabriel	19	F	Unknown	18Ma06Aa
MUSTELL, Joseph	50	M	Laborer	18Ma06Aa
JOHNSON, Charles	20	M	Laborer	18Ma06Aa
REYNOLDS, William	21	M	Laborer	18Ma06Aa
RILEY, Catherine	30	F	Laborer	18Ma06Aa
BEATUS, John	32	M	Smith	18Ma06Aa
WADE, William	38	M	Smith	18Ma06Aa
MCCONNELL, Hugh	33	M	None	18Ma06Aa
HERSEY, George	22	M	Agrc	18Ma06Aa

NAMES OF PASSENGERS	AGE	SEX	OCCUPATIONS	DATE PORT SHIP
GELSDOWSKY, Julius	29	M	Agrc	18Ma06Aa
BROWN, Garrett	30	M	Agrc	18Ma06Aa
HOWELL, Elizabeth	30	F	Unknown	18Ma06Aa
SUNS, Ellen	21	F	Unknown	18Ma06Aa
HOWELL, Robert	24	M	Unknown	18Ma06Aa
CHARWOOD, William	17	M	Unknown	18Ma06Aa
ODONE, William	16	M	Unknown	18Ma06Aa
MCCARTY, Jeremiah	22	M	Unknown	18Ma06Aa
POWELL, Ricahrd	25	M	Unknown	18Ma06Aa
CAHERTON, George	43	M	Unknown	18Ma06Aa
WOOL, Bartholomew	34	M	Unknown	18Ma06Aa
CLAY, Alfred-Wm.	16	M	Unknown	18Ma06Aa
NEWMAN, George	29	M	Unknown	18Ma06Aa
Caroline	29	F	Unknown	18Ma06Aa
George	7	M	Child	18Ma06Aa
Sarah	3	F	Child	18Ma06Aa
Thomas	.00	M	Infant	18Ma06Aa
GRAGEN, Jane	40	F	Unknown	18Ma06Aa
Anora	12	F	Unknown	18Ma06Aa
Albe	11	U	Unknown	18Ma06Aa
John	9	M	Child	18Ma06Aa
MEAL, Ellen	26	F	Unknown	18Ma06Aa
FOREMAN, John	48	M	Unknown	18Ma06Aa
SAKELL, Joseph	30	M	Unknown	18Ma06Aa
HEWETT, James	28	M	Unknown	18Ma06Aa
WAGNER, William	38	M	Unknown	18Ma06Aa
PARTTEN, Bradley	40	M	Unknown	18Ma06Aa
ILBERY, J.	26	M	Unknown	18Ma06Aa
U-Mrs.	24	F	Unknown	18Ma06Aa

BRITISH-QUEEN 18 MAY 1850

From Londonderry

NAMES OF PASSENGERS	AGE	SEX	OCCUPATIONS	DATE PORT SHIP
MCCLENOHON, Robert	25	M	Flabr	18Ma01Bp
Mary	26	F	Flabr	18Ma01Bp
James	2	M	Child	18Ma01Bp
David	.04	M	Infant	18Ma01Bp
MCCLELLOND, William	26	M	Flabr	18Ma01Bp
Catherine	25	F	Flabr	18Ma01Bp
Alexander	16	M	Flabr	18Ma01Bp
KINCAID, Ann	20	F	Spinster	18Ma01Bp
DEANS, Samuel	20	M	Flabr	18Ma01Bp
FARRING, Fanny	20	F	Spinster	18Ma01Bp
MCDOUGH, James	21	M	Flabr	18Ma01Bp
Ellen	18	F	Spinster	18Ma01Bp
PEOPLES, Robert	40	M	Flabr	18Ma01Bp
Ann	40	F	Flabr	18Ma01Bp
Florenda	10	F	Flabr	18Ma01Bp
Rebeca	7	F	Child	18Ma01Bp
Hellen	.09	F	Infant	18Ma01Bp
BLACKBURN, Jane	20	F	Spinster	18Ma01Bp
DUDDY, Fanny	21	F	Spinster	18Ma01Bp
ELLIS, John	19	M	Laborer	18Ma01Bp
FRIEL, Cathrn.	34	F	Wi	18Ma01Bp
Patrick	5	M	Child	18Ma01Bp
Cathn.	3	F	Child	18Ma01Bp
ROSA, Rachael	20	F	Spinster	18Ma01Bp
MORRON, John	26	M	Flabr	18Ma01Bp
MCGINLY, Ann	20	F	Spinster	18Ma01Bp
MILLAN, John	19	M	Flabr	18Ma01Bp
DENLIN, Owen	50	M	Flabr	18Ma01Bp
ANDERSON, James	20	M	Flabr	18Ma01Bp
CAIN, Mary	20	F	Spinster	18Ma01Bp
MCELHINNEY, Nancy	20	F	Spinster	18Ma01Bp
DOUGHERTY, Thomas	14	M	None	18Ma01Bp
Michael	12	M	None	18Ma01Bp
CASSIDY, Docca	20	F	Spinster	18Ma01Bp
MCLOUGHLIN, Ann	40	F	Unknown	18Ma01Bp
MCLOUGHLIN, Thomas	16	M	Unknown	18Ma01Bp
James	14	M	Unknown	18Ma01Bp
Daniel	12	M	Unknown	18Ma01Bp
Isabella	10	F	Unknown	18Ma01Bp
William	8	M	Child	18Ma01Bp
Charles	6	M	Child	18Ma01Bp
Mary	.10	F	Infant	18Ma01Bp
WELLINGTON, Jane	30	F	None	18Ma01Bp
Jane	4	F	Child	18Ma01Bp
CARGILL, Henry	19	M	Laborer	18Ma01Bp
HAMILTON, Susan	20	F	Spinster	18Ma01Bp
MOORE, Robert	20	M	None	18Ma01Bp
STENSON, Martha	50	F	Spinster	18Ma01Bp
William	20	M	None	18Ma01Bp
Eliza	5	F	Child	18Ma01Bp
MCGUGAN, Charles	19	M	Laborer	18Ma01Bp
MCLOUGHLIN, Martha	25	F	None	18Ma01Bp
MCELSNER, Michael	20	M	Laborer	18Ma01Bp
SPROAL, Hanah	20	F	Spinster	18Ma01Bp
Eliza	18	F	Spinster	18Ma01Bp
FUSTON, Margt.	20	F	Spinster	18Ma01Bp
WOODS, Catherine	20	F	Spinster	18Ma01Bp
VANCE, Sarah	20	F	Spinster	18Ma01Bp
BLONEY, Mary	19	F	Spinster	18Ma01Bp
WOODS, William	20	M	Laborer	18Ma01Bp
HAMILTON, Samuel	20	M	Laborer	18Ma01Bp
LYNCH, Sally	21	F	Milliner	18Ma01Bp
HUTCHISON, Charles	20	M	Servant	18Ma01Bp
MCINTIRE, Thomas	20	M	Carpenter	18Ma01Bp
ANDERSON, Jacob	17	M	Laborer	18Ma01Bp
CAMPBELL, Sarah	18	F	Spinster	18Ma01Bp
Margaret	12	F	Spinster	18Ma01Bp
MCCOURT, James	20	M	Weaver	18Ma01Bp
Mary	22	F	Spinster	18Ma01Bp
MCWILLIAMS, John	50	M	Cooper	18Ma01Bp
Dominick	20	M	Laborer	18Ma01Bp
Denis	18	M	Unknown	18Ma01Bp
Biddy	21	F	Unknown	18Ma01Bp
Geo.	11	M	Unknown	18Ma01Bp
Cathn.	10	F	Unknown	18Ma01Bp
MCDERMOT, Bridget	30	F	Spinster	18Ma01Bp
SMYTH, Cornelius	60	M	Flabr	18Ma01Bp
Hannah	30	F	Unknown	18Ma01Bp
Mary	18	F	Unknown	18Ma01Bp
Ann	16	F	Unknown	18Ma01Bp
John	14	M	Unknown	18Ma01Bp
Susan	10	F	Unknown	18Ma01Bp
Peter	8	M	Child	18Ma01Bp
Rosey	6	F	Child	18Ma01Bp
Cosmos	4	M	Child	18Ma01Bp
QUIGBY, Margaret	40	F	Wi	18Ma01Bp
Ellen (D)	18	F	None	18Ma01Bp
John (S)	19	M	None	18Ma01Bp
Rosana (D)	8	F	Child	18Ma01Bp
Mary (D)	6	F	Child	18Ma01Bp
DUFFY, Mary	20	F	Spinster	18Ma01Bp
MCCORMICK, Pat	20	M	Laborer	18Ma01Bp
SWEENEY, Edwd.	12	M	Unknown	18Ma01Bp
CARNEY, Ellen	26	F	Unknown	18Ma01Bp
James	5	M	Child	18Ma01Bp
John	.00	M	Infant	18Ma01Bp

SIR-HARRY-SMITH 18 MAY 1850

From Glasgow

NAMES OF PASSENGERS	AGE	SEX	OCCUPATIONS	DATE PORT SHIP
MARTIN, Catherine	22	F	Servant	18Ma21Iw
MCGRANACHAN, Wm.	30	M	Btlmkr	18Ma21Iw
Ann	30	F	Btlmkr	18Ma21Iw

NAMES OF PASSENGERS	AGE	SEX	OCCUPATIONS	DATE PORT SHIP
MCGRANACHAN, Bernard	6	M	Child	18Ma21Iw
William	4	M	Child	18Ma21Iw
Ellen	2	F	Child	18Ma21Iw
Died-At-Sea				
ALFORD, Charles	33	M	Btlmkr	18Ma21Iw
Catherine	30	F	Btlmkr	18Ma21Iw
Rosana	6	F	Child	18Ma21Iw
John	4	M	Child	18Ma21Iw
William	.00	M	Infant	18Ma21Iw
OHARA, Peter	10	M	Laborer	18Ma21Iw
Thomas	19	M	Unknown	18Ma21Iw
KENT, Thomas	60	M	Farmer	18Ma21Iw
Nancy	56	F	Farmer	18Ma21Iw
Thomas	18	M	Farmer	18Ma21Iw
Ann	13	F	Farmer	18Ma21Iw
Thomas	9	M	Child	18Ma21Iw
MCKEE, John	14	M	Laborer	18Ma21Iw
KENT, Mary	70	F	Farmer	18Ma21Iw

VICTORIA 18 MAY 1850

From London

NAMES OF PASSENGERS	AGE	SEX	OCCUPATIONS	DATE PORT SHIP
LANE, Ellen	27	F	Domestic	18Ma06Aj
CARMODY, Catherine	30	F	Wi	18Ma06Aj
John (S)	8	M	Child	18Ma06Aj
Thos. (S)	6	M	Child	18Ma06Aj
Mary (D)	4	F	Child	18Ma06Aj
Mary (D)	2	F	Child	18Ma06Aj
DOHERTY, Daniel	45	M	Gentleman	18Ma06Aj
Mary	37	F	Lady	18Ma06Aj
Mary-Ann	20	F	Lady	18Ma06Aj
Johannah	18	F	Lady	18Ma06Aj
Frances-E.	7	F	Child	18Ma06Aj
Richd.F.M.	1	M	Child	18Ma06Aj

ANN-MOORE 18 MAY 1850

From Limerick

NAMES OF PASSENGERS	AGE	SEX	OCCUPATIONS	DATE PORT SHIP
OSHEA, Denis	27	M	Laborer	18Ma10Jq
GARDINER, Michl.	25	M	Laborer	18Ma10Jq
MULLINS, John	15	M	Laborer	18Ma10Jq
BEHAN, John	24	M	Laborer	18Ma10Jq
COONEY, Matthew	21	M	Laborer	18Ma10Jq
LYONS, Mary	21	F	Laborer	18Ma10Jq
DOWNES, Thos.	40	M	Laborer	18Ma10Jq
Catherine	35	F	Laborer	18Ma10Jq
CARROL, Michl.	19	M	Laborer	18Ma10Jq
WILLIAMS, Jane	20	F	Laborer	18Ma10Jq
Sarah	23	F	Laborer	18Ma10Jq
DUGGAN, Pat	13	M	Laborer	18Ma10Jq
HANRAHAN, Ellen	15	F	Laborer	18Ma10Jq
GALLAGHER, Mary	20	F	Laborer	18Ma10Jq
Eliza	14	F	Laborer	18Ma10Jq
Jane	14	F	Laborer	18Ma10Jq
BRENNAN, Thos.	20	M	Laborer	18Ma10Jq
JAMESON, Brdgt.	20	F	Laborer	18Ma10Jq
MCMAHON, Thos.	40	M	Laborer	18Ma10Jq
ODONNELL, Mary	30	F	Laborer	18Ma10Jq
James	11	M	Laborer	18Ma10Jq
William	8	M	Child	18Ma10Jq
Mary	5	F	Child	18Ma10Jq
ODONNELL, Robert	3	M	Child	18Ma10Jq
Eliza	2	F	Child	18Ma10Jq
CULLINAN, John	40	M	Laborer	18Ma10Jq
HENNDER, Mary	33	F	Laborer	18Ma10Jq
FITZPATRICK, Daniel	26	M	Laborer	18Ma10Jq
CRAWFORD, Margt.	24	F	Laborer	18Ma10Jq
Patrick	12	M	Laborer	18Ma10Jq
DONOVAN, Anthony	24	M	Laborer	18Ma10Jq
Mary	11	F	Laborer	18Ma10Jq
Ellen	7	F	Child	18Ma10Jq
James	6	M	Child	18Ma10Jq
MCKAY, Brdgt.	35	F	Laborer	18Ma10Jq
Ann	6	F	Child	18Ma10Jq
Michl.	3	M	Child	18Ma10Jq
Ellen	2	F	Child	18Ma10Jq
CARNEY, Matt	26	M	Laborer	18Ma10Jq
MCMULANEY, Patt	18	M	Laborer	18Ma10Jq
MACK, Mary	30	F	Laborer	18Ma10Jq
HARRIS, Richard	35	M	Laborer	18Ma10Jq
PINKER, Michl.	58	M	Laborer	18Ma10Jq
Esther	56	F	Laborer	18Ma10Jq
CUSSACK, John	25	M	Laborer	18Ma10Jq
KEOGH, Margt.	13	F	Laborer	18Ma10Jq
MULQUEEN, Jerry	20	M	Laborer	18Ma10Jq
Buddy	9	M	Child	18Ma10Jq
MAGINIS, Biddy	15	F	Laborer	18Ma10Jq
CLOUGHESEY, Cath.	20	F	Laborer	18Ma10Jq
COONEY, Michl.	25	M	Laborer	18Ma10Jq
KEOGH, John	30	M	Laborer	18Ma10Jq
HENRY, Patt	30	M	Laborer	18Ma10Jq
BOLAND, Patt	20	M	Laborer	18Ma10Jq
MINTER, Biddy	11	F	Laborer	18Ma10Jq
HOLLAND, Alice	20	F	Laborer	18Ma10Jq
MEEHAN, Norry	16	F	Laborer	18Ma10Jq
COLLOE, Margt.	20	F	Laborer	18Ma10Jq
SHEEHY, Maurice	24	M	Laborer	18Ma10Jq
SHANNAHAN, Ellen	24	F	Laborer	18Ma10Jq
HEELEAD, Lawrence	40	M	Laborer	18Ma10Jq
CULLINANE, Biddy	20	F	Laborer	18Ma10Jq
HOWARD, Sally	18	F	Laborer	18Ma10Jq
MOHONEY, John	75	M	Laborer	18Ma10Jq
MULLALLY, Thos.	34	M	Laborer	18Ma10Jq
Biddy	30	F	Laborer	18Ma10Jq
Margt.	6	F	Child	18Ma10Jq
Biddy	7	F	Child	18Ma10Jq
Edward	30	M	Laborer	18Ma10Jq
Mary	28	F	Laborer	18Ma10Jq
Margt.	54	F	Laborer	18Ma10Jq
MOLONEY, Michl.	27	M	Laborer	18Ma10Jq
Biddy	23	F	Laborer	18Ma10Jq
RIORDAN, James	20	M	Laborer	18Ma10Jq
FITZGERALD, Mary-A.	26	F	Laborer	18Ma10Jq
Honora	32	F	Laborer	18Ma10Jq
MCMERTNEY, Michl.	20	M	Laborer	18Ma10Jq
MEDE, Sally	21	F	Laborer	18Ma10Jq
KELLY, James	30	M	Laborer	18Ma10Jq
Ellen	18	F	Laborer	18Ma10Jq
LENIHAN, Thos.	50	M	Laborer	18Ma10Jq
Mary	45	F	Laborer	18Ma10Jq
Ellen	17	F	Laborer	18Ma10Jq
Cath.	14	F	Laborer	18Ma10Jq
Ann	12	F	Laborer	18Ma10Jq
BROWNE, Eliza	24	F	Laborer	18Ma10Jq
HOLIHAN, Michl.	40	M	Laborer	18Ma10Jq
Thos.	22	M	Laborer	18Ma10Jq
Kate	25	F	Laborer	18Ma10Jq
SHEEHAN, James	21	M	Laborer	18Ma10Jq
CAREY, Ellen	24	F	Laborer	18Ma10Jq
MAHONEY, Mary	.00	F	Infant	18Ma10Jq
CAREY, Margt.	22	F	Laborer	18Ma10Jq
Bridgt.	22	F	Laborer	18Ma10Jq
DENNEY, Michl.	20	M	Laborer	18Ma10Jq
VAUGHAN, Martin	20	M	Laborer	18Ma10Jq
COONEY, Michl.	24	M	Laborer	18Ma10Jq
Nancy	20	F	Laborer	18Ma10Jq

NAMES OF PASSENGERS	AGE	SEX	OCCUPATIONS	DATE PORT SHIP
COONEY. Ellen	20	F	Laborer	18Ma10Jq
LYNCH, Daniel	12	M	Laborer	18Ma10Jq
Pat	11	M	Laborer	18Ma10Jq
DONNELL, Michl.	.00	M	Infant	18Ma10Jq
WARREN. S.	00	U	Unknown	18Ma10Jq
OBRIEN. Ellen	00	F	Unknown	18Ma10Jq
HEADLY. Ellen	00	F	Unknown	18Ma10Jq
BAKER. Ann	00	F	Unknown	18Ma10Jq
FERGUSON. Anne	00	F	Unknown	18Ma10Jq
BOURKE. Patt	26	M	Laborer	18Ma10Jq
FITZGERALD, Bridget	50	F	Laborer	18Ma10Jq
Johana	15	F	Laborer	18Ma10Jq

NO RECORD OF SHIP

From Madeira

NAMES OF PASSENGERS	AGE	SEX	OCCUPATIONS	DATE PORT SHIP
PARK. Archd.	30	M	Merchant	18Ma56

GIPSEY 18 MAY 1850

From Liverpool

NAMES OF PASSENGERS	AGE	SEX	OCCUPATIONS	DATE PORT SHIP
CRAWLEY, Chas.	48	M	Laborer	18Ma02Hq
Bridget	48	F	Unknown	18Ma02Hq
Mary	19	F	Unknown	18Ma02Hq
Bridget	12	F	Unknown	18Ma02Hq
Catherine	10	F	Unknown	18Ma02Hq
Betty	8	F	Child	18Ma02Hq
Mary	20	F	Unknown	18Ma02Hq
DARCY, Kate	20	F	Unknown	18Ma02Hq
HIGGINS. Thos.	22	M	Unknown	18Ma02Hq
John	24	M	Unknown	18Ma02Hq
HENRY. Patrick	26	M	Unknown	18Ma02Hq
John	24	M	Unknown	18Ma02Hq
Honor	20	F	Unknown	18Ma02Hq
Catherine	20	F	Unknown	18Ma02Hq
James	5	M	Child	18Ma02Hq
GILLIN, Pat	10	M	Unknown	18Ma02Hq
Ann	6	F	Child	18Ma02Hq
GEELESTER. Michl.	8	M	Child	18Ma02Hq
PLEACY. James	50	M	Unknown	18Ma02Hq
Margt.	50	F	Unknown	18Ma02Hq
Michl.	22	M	Unknown	18Ma02Hq
Bridget	19	F	Unknown	18Ma02Hq
Mary	17	F	Unknown	18Ma02Hq
Margt.	13	F	Unknown	18Ma02Hq
John	11	M	Unknown	18Ma02Hq
Anne	9	F	Child	18Ma02Hq
Jane	6	F	Child	18Ma02Hq
Thomas	4	M	Child	18Ma02Hq
GALLAHER, James	17	M	Unknown	18Ma02Hq
HONORAN, Thos.	10	M	Unknown	18Ma02Hq
HANKS. Margt.	20	F	Unknown	18Ma02Hq
WATTS. James	50	M	Unknown	18Ma02Hq
Margt.	60	F	Unknown	18Ma02Hq
Roger	20	M	Unknown	18Ma02Hq
Anne	18	F	Unknown	18Ma02Hq
Matt	12	M	Unknown	18Ma02Hq
Bridget	10	F	Unknown	18Ma02Hq
Cumoin	8	F	Child	18Ma02Hq
Martin	5	M	Child	18Ma02Hq
RYAN. Wm.	20	M	Unknown	18Ma02Hq

NAMES OF PASSENGERS	AGE	SEX	OCCUPATIONS	DATE PORT SHIP
IRVIN, John	25	M	Unknown	18Ma02Hq
Margaret	26	F	Unknown	18Ma02Hq
MCGUIRE. Margt.A.	21	F	Unknown	18Ma02Hq
REBIN, James	54	M	Unknown	18Ma02Hq
James	15	M	Unknown	18Ma02Hq
ELLIS. Wm.	20	M	Unknown	18Ma02Hq
CARROLL, Ronny	20	M	Unknown	18Ma02Hq
TUIRNEY, Francis	20	M	Unknown	18Ma02Hq
GLEESON, John	20	M	Unknown	18Ma02Hq
BLUES. James	20	M	Unknown	18Ma02Hq
GLEESON. Cathn.	22	F	Unknown	18Ma02Hq
GILLMAN, John	24	M	Unknown	18Ma02Hq
STEVENSON, W.H.	30	M	Unknown	18Ma02Hq
Margt.	30	F	Unknown	18Ma02Hq
Margt.	11	F	Unknown	18Ma02Hq
Eliza	11	F	Unknown	18Ma02Hq
MURPHY. John	30	M	Unknown	18Ma02Hq
Margt.	27	F	Unknown	18Ma02Hq
Wm.	3	M	Child	18Ma02Hq
BOND. Wm.	7	M	Child	18Ma02Hq
MURPHY. Mory	9	F	Child	18Ma02Hq
Cathn.	6	F	Child	18Ma02Hq
Maria	20	F	Unknown	18Ma02Hq
Richard	9	M	Child	18Ma02Hq
FAULCLOUGH, Thos.	19	M	Unknown	18Ma02Hq
QUIRCK, Edwd.	26	M	Unknown	18Ma02Hq
HOOLOHAN, Tim	32	M	Unknown	18Ma02Hq
GAHEN, Tim	20	M	Unknown	18Ma02Hq
GRAHAM, James	50	M	Unknown	18Ma02Hq
Eliza	40	F	Unknown	18Ma02Hq
James	18	M	Unknown	18Ma02Hq
Willm.	15	M	Unknown	18Ma02Hq
Alex.	13	M	Unknown	18Ma02Hq
Thos.	9	M	Child	18Ma02Hq
David	7	M	Child	18Ma02Hq
Eliza	5	F	Child	18Ma02Hq
GLIMLY. Catherine	14	F	Unknown	18Ma02Hq
HUNCH, Saml.	17	M	Unknown	18Ma02Hq
JOHNSON, John	20	M	Unknown	18Ma02Hq
Maria	17	F	Unknown	18Ma02Hq
FENDLE. James	30	M	Unknown	18Ma02Hq
CUSIN, John	20	M	Unknown	18Ma02Hq
DELANY. Darby	50	M	Unknown	18Ma02Hq
Thomas	45	M	Unknown	18Ma02Hq
Mary	20	F	Unknown	18Ma02Hq
CARMAN, Biddy	20	F	Unknown	18Ma02Hq
RYAN, Darby	50	M	Unknown	18Ma02Hq
Danl.	45	M	Unknown	18Ma02Hq
Mary	30	F	Unknown	18Ma02Hq
Margt.	.00	F	Infant	18Ma02Hq
SHEA. Margt.	20	F	Unknown	18Ma02Hq
Bridgt.	20	F	Unknown	18Ma02Hq
CASEY. Hannah	25	F	Unknown	18Ma02Hq
DOYLE, Mary	20	F	Unknown	18Ma02Hq
FOLEY. Margt.	20	F	Unknown	18Ma02Hq
MCCARTHY. Chas.	21	M	Unknown	18Ma02Hq
CRAIG, Abrah.	50	M	Unknown	18Ma02Hq
TRAINOR. Jane	32	F	Unknown	18Ma02Hq
TURNER. Adam	25	M	Unknown	18Ma02Hq
CRAIG, Nancy	30	F	Unknown	18Ma02Hq
Thos.	28	M	Unknown	18Ma02Hq
Ellen	24	F	Unknown	18Ma02Hq
Helen	26	F	Unknown	18Ma02Hq
Margt.	22	F	Unknown	18Ma02Hq
Sarah	22	F	Unknown	18Ma02Hq
James	17	M	Unknown	18Ma02Hq
Abrah.	15	M	Unknown	18Ma02Hq
Maria	12	F	Unknown	18Ma02Hq
Henry	10	M	Unknown	18Ma02Hq
CONNOR, John	22	M	Unknown	18Ma02Hq
MCGUINNESS, Thos.	22	M	Unknown	18Ma02Hq
Mary	39	F	Unknown	18Ma02Hq
MCMAHON, Owen	49	M	Unknown	18Ma02Hq
Nancy	35	F	Unknown	18Ma02Hq
Patrick	18	M	Unknown	18Ma02Hq

NAMES OF PASSENGERS	AGE	SEX	OCCUPATIONS	DATE PORT SHIP	NAMES OF PASSENGERS	AGE	SEX	OCCUPATIONS	DATE PORT SHIP
MCMAHON. Owen	16	M	Unknown	18Ma02Hq	SHAY. George	22	M	Unknown	18Ma02Hq
Owen	13	M	Unknown	18Ma02Hq	Bridget	21	F	Unknown	18Ma02Hq
Alia	12	F	Unknown	18Ma02Hq	BEALE. Hugh	31	M	Unknown	18Ma02Hq
Catherine	8	F	Child	18Ma02Hq	Margt.	31	F	Unknown	18Ma02Hq
Rosey	3	F	Child	18Ma02Hq	James	13	M	Unknown	18Ma02Hq
Betsey	.00	F	Infant	18Ma02Hq	TALLARIN, Jas.	18	M	Unknown	18Ma02Hq
HUGHES. Owen	21	M	Unknown	18Ma02Hq	Bridget	17	F	Unknown	18Ma02Hq
TRAINER. Bernard	20	M	Unknown	18Ma02Hq	GALLAHER, Ann	17	F	Unknown	18Ma02Hq
MACKEY, Owen	40	M	Unknown	18Ma02Hq	HUGHES. James	17	M	Unknown	18Ma02Hq
BARRY, John	24	M	Unknown	18Ma02Hq	Cath.	30	F	Unknown	18Ma02Hq
COLLINGS. Ellen	20	F	Unknown	18Ma02Hq	John	30	M	Unknown	18Ma02Hq
NUGENT. Johannah	25	F	Unknown	18Ma02Hq	MCLAUGHLIN. Thos.	6	M	Child	18Ma02Hq
HUGHES. John	28	M	Unknown	18Ma02Hq	Pat	20	M	Unknown	18Ma02Hq
Mary	18	F	Unknown	18Ma02Hq	Nancy	40	F	Unknown	18Ma02Hq
HUDSON. Alex.	21	M	Unknown	18Ma02Hq	HENISY, Janis	40	F	Unknown	18Ma02Hq
BATTY. Richd.	25	M	Unknown	18Ma02Hq	POWER, Ann	30	F	Unknown	18Ma02Hq
Cath.	8	F	Child	18Ma02Hq	HANAGHAN, Pat	20	M	Unknown	18Ma02Hq
DALTON. George	25	M	Unknown	18Ma02Hq	BARRETT, Ml.	30	M	Unknown	18Ma02Hq
Sarah	23	F	Unknown	18Ma02Hq	MCCREARRY. Rd.	25	M	Unknown	18Ma02Hq
James	.00	M	Infant	18Ma02Hq	John	32	M	Unknown	18Ma02Hq
HOFTEND. Thos.	30	M	Unknown	18Ma02Hq	OKEEFE. Wm.	24	M	Unknown	18Ma02Hq
MCADAMS, Pat	20	M	Unknown	18Ma02Hq	Mary	27	F	Unknown	18Ma02Hq
BYRNES. Pat	22	M	Unknown	18Ma02Hq	PIGOTT. Jas.	28	M	Unknown	18Ma02Hq
MCGUIRE. Ellen	20	F	Unknown	18Ma02Hq	Margt.	45	F	Unknown	18Ma02Hq
SMITH. Anne	20	F	Unknown	18Ma02Hq	Margt.	15	F	Unknown	18Ma02Hq
MURPHY. Eliza	26	F	Unknown	18Ma02Hq	Maria	20	F	Unknown	18Ma02Hq
SMITH. Wm.	30	M	Unknown	18Ma02Hq	MURPHY. John	35	M	Unknown	18Ma02Hq
MOFFATT. Wm.	21	M	Unknown	18Ma02Hq	PIGOTT, John	10	M	Unknown	18Ma02Hq
MCKNIGHT. Thos.	35	M	Unknown	18Ma02Hq	FAIR, George	30	M	Unknown	18Ma02Hq
Judy	35	F	Unknown	18Ma02Hq	DOWNEY. John	45	M	Unknown	18Ma02Hq
KELLY. Michl.	20	M	Unknown	18Ma02Hq	Allen	27	M	Unknown	18Ma02Hq
Mary	18	F	Unknown	18Ma02Hq	MURRY. Thos.	23	M	Unknown	18Ma02Hq
CASEY. John	25	M	Unknown	18Ma02Hq	DOWNEY. Eal.	.00	M	Infant	18Ma02Hq
CONNOR, Mat	30	M	Unknown	18Ma02Hq	FARRELL, Richd.	20	M	Unknown	18Ma02Hq
Bridgt.	20	F	Unknown	18Ma02Hq	FOWLER. John	18	M	Unknown	18Ma02Hq
COGAN. Ann	20	F	Unknown	18Ma02Hq	STEVENS. John	50	M	Unknown	18Ma02Hq
Anthony	26	M	Unknown	18Ma02Hq	Thos.	40	M	Unknown	18Ma02Hq
Peter	20	M	Unknown	18Ma02Hq	HOOLAHAN, Marg.	40	M	Unknown	18Ma02Hq
ENNIS. Pat	20	M	Unknown	18Ma02Hq	RYAN. U-Mrs.	30	F	Unknown	18Ma02Hq
BOGNEY. Eliza	20	F	Unknown	18Ma02Hq	Margt.	10	F	Unknown	18Ma02Hq
DWYER. Margt.	17	F	Unknown	18Ma02Hq	Michl.	26	M	Unknown	18Ma02Hq
LAWLER. Jane	20	F	Unknown	18Ma02Hq	Cathn.	20	F	Unknown	18Ma02Hq
BARRETT. John	20	M	Unknown	18Ma02Hq	FITZGERALD, Pat	23	M	Unknown	18Ma02Hq
Honora	40	F	Unknown	18Ma02Hq	MORRISEY. Mary	17	F	Unknown	18Ma02Hq
Wm.	40	M	Unknown	18Ma02Hq	GARVIN, Ellen	24	F	Unknown	18Ma02Hq
Anthony	12	M	Unknown	18Ma02Hq	GLEESON, Robert	20	M	Unknown	18Ma02Hq
Maria	8	F	Child	18Ma02Hq	CHRISTY. Mgt.	25	F	Unknown	18Ma02Hq
GRADY. John	6	M	Child	18Ma02Hq	MIXSON, Janet	20	F	Unknown	18Ma02Hq
MCDONNELL, Andw.	35	M	Unknown	18Ma02Hq	VANDERGRIST. Garret	20	M	Unknown	18Ma02Hq
MURRY. Ellas.	20	F	Unknown	18Ma02Hq	HAMMOND. John	40	M	Unknown	18Ma02Hq
MAHON. Ellen	13	F	Unknown	18Ma02Hq	MCMANDA, John	32	M	Unknown	18Ma02Hq
Margt.	20	F	Unknown	18Ma02Hq	MURPHY, Andrew	32	M	Unknown	18Ma02Hq
DANLAN. Michl.	.00	M	Infant	18Ma02Hq	ARMSTRONG, William	40	M	Unknown	18Ma02Hq
DONOVAN. John	24	M	Unknown	18Ma02Hq	U-Mrs.	32	F	Unknown	18Ma02Hq
MURPHY. Honora	16	F	Unknown	18Ma02Hq	Ann	20	F	Unknown	18Ma02Hq
MCGONEN. Silas	20	M	Unknown	18Ma02Hq	David	.00	M	Infant	18Ma02Hq
CONNOLLY. M.	28	M	Unknown	18Ma02Hq	REILY. James	40	M	Unknown	18Ma02Hq
GRIFFIN, James	28	M	Unknown	18Ma02Hq	Chas.	15	M	Unknown	18Ma02Hq
Chas.	27	M	Unknown	18Ma02Hq	James	15	M	Unknown	18Ma02Hq
COLLINS. John	26	M	Unknown	18Ma02Hq	Eliza	13	F	Unknown	18Ma02Hq
Dennis	27	M	Unknown	18Ma02Hq	Anne	11	F	Unknown	18Ma02Hq
Bridgt.	35	F	Unknown	18Ma02Hq	Mary	9	F	Child	18Ma02Hq
Martin	23	M	Unknown	18Ma02Hq	George	.00	M	Infant	18Ma02Hq
Mary	27	F	Unknown	18Ma02Hq	MCDONALD, Pat	25	M	Unknown	18Ma02Hq
MAHONY, John	24	M	Unknown	18Ma02Hq	U	2	F	Child	18Ma02Hq
CLEA. David	26	M	Unknown	18Ma02Hq	ROVER. Peter	21	M	Unknown	18Ma02Hq
BUTLER. Maria	24	F	Unknown	18Ma02Hq	WHITESIDE, Wm.	20	M	Unknown	18Ma02Hq
CASEY. Pat	25	M	Unknown	18Ma02Hq	DALY. Peter	20	M	Unknown	18Ma02Hq
CONLAN. Wm.	20	M	Unknown	18Ma02Hq	DEE, Thos.	20	M	Unknown	18Ma02Hq
CASEY. James	20	M	Unknown	18Ma02Hq	U-Mrs.	31	F	Unknown	18Ma02Hq
CARR. Dennis	20	M	Unknown	18Ma02Hq	HANRAHAN, Michl.	13	M	Unknown	18Ma02Hq
RICE. James	36	M	Unknown	18Ma02Hq	MARSHALL, Biddy	10	F	Unknown	18Ma02Hq
MCGLAN. Terance	34	M	Unknown	18Ma02Hq	SULLIVAN, Henry	6	M	Unknown	18Ma02Hq
FENNY. James	28	M	Unknown	18Ma02Hq	RYAN, Morriss	40	M	Unknown	18Ma02Hq
KEMP. A.	36	M	Unknown	18Ma02Hq	MEARDLE. Pat	21	M	Unknown	18Ma02Hq

NAMES OF PASSENGERS	AGE	SEX	OCCUPATIONS	DATE PORT SHIP
EGAN. Michl.	21	M	Unknown	18Ma02Hq
U-Mrs.	20	F	Unknown	18Ma02Hq
CRONIN. Michl.	23	M	Unknown	18Ma02Hq
W.	23	M	Unknown	18Ma02Hq
DONNELLY. Margt.	40	F	Unknown	18Ma02Hq
MCARDLE. Pat	23	M	Unknown	18Ma02Hq
U-Mrs.	45	F	Unknown	18Ma02Hq
Kate	20	F	Unknown	18Ma02Hq
Emily	25	F	Unknown	18Ma02Hq
Bridget	23	F	Unknown	18Ma02Hq
LATHIM. Wm.	20	M	Unknown	18Ma02Hq
DONOGHUE. Simon	30	M	Unknown	18Ma02Hq
FENNY. Rose	20	F	Unknown	18Ma02Hq
RILY. Pat	26	M	Unknown	18Ma02Hq
SULLIVAN. Mary	30	F	Unknown	18Ma02Hq
FITZGIBBON. Dennis	29	M	Unknown	18Ma02Hq
Mary	20	F	Unknown	18Ma02Hq
GEPMAN. U-Mrs.	23	F	Unknown	18Ma02Hq
RADEY. Martin	22	M	Unknown	18Ma02Hq
Mary	20	F	Unknown	18Ma02Hq
RYAN. Pat	6	M	Child	18Ma02Hq
Judy	4	F	Child	18Ma02Hq
SULLIVAN. Pat	20	M	Unknown	18Ma02Hq
Anne	18	F	Unknown	18Ma02Hq
MCALLESTER. Alex.	20	M	Unknown	18Ma02Hq
WELDEN. Alfred	27	M	Unknown	18Ma02Hq
EDLOW, John	31	M	Unknown	18Ma02Hq
MEARNAN. Richd.	24	M	Unknown	18Ma02Hq
Dennis	25	M	Unknown	18Ma02Hq
ROONEY. Mary	27	F	Unknown	18Ma02Hq
Bryan	18	M	Unknown	18Ma02Hq
SAYSE. Richd.	28	M	Unknown	18Ma02Hq
DOWLING, Margt.	20	F	Unknown	18Ma02Hq
James	6	M	Child	18Ma02Hq
MORRISON. Martin	20	M	Unknown	18Ma02Hq
Bridgt.	16	F	Unknown	18Ma02Hq
WADE. Nancy	20	F	Unknown	18Ma02Hq
MURRAY. Ellen	13	F	Unknown	18Ma02Hq
CALAM. Bridgt.	30	M	Unknown	18Ma02Hq
MORRE. Michl.	26	M	Unknown	18Ma02Hq
ROBERTSON. G.B.Mrs.	00	F	Unknown	18Ma02Hq
U	00	F	Unknown	18Ma02Hq
Archibald	00	M	Unknown	18Ma02Hq
Ellen	00	F	Unknown	18Ma02Hq
DAVIS. Jas.Mrs.	00	F	Unknown	18Ma02Hq
U	.00	U	Infant	18Ma02Hq
U. U	.00	U	Infant	18Ma02Hq
Born-At-Sea				
U	.00	U	Infant	18Ma02Hq
Born-At-Sea				
U	.00	U	Infant	18Ma02Hq
Born-At-Sea Died-At-Sea				
U	.00	U	Infant	18Ma02Hq
Born-At-Sea Died-At-Sea				

BRITISH-QUEEN 18 MAY 1850

From Dublin

NAMES OF PASSENGERS	AGE	SEX	OCCUPATIONS	DATE PORT SHIP
MALONE. James	23	M	Laborer	18Ma05Bp
MCGILLANUN. John	40	M	Laborer	18Ma05Bp
William	16	M	Unknown	18Ma05Bp
MALONE. Mary	18	F	Spinster	18Ma05Bp
HOGG, James	28	M	Laborer	18Ma05Bp
TOFFE. John	38	M	Laborer	18Ma05Bp
HALPIN. James	30	M	Laborer	18Ma05Bp
DIDLON, Thomas	26	M	Laborer	18Ma05Bp
TOFFE. Alice	40	F	Spinster	18Ma05Bp
CARROLL, Patrick	28	M	Laborer	18Ma05Bp
WITHERS, William	34	M	Laborer	18Ma05Bp
RYAN, John	30	M	Laborer	18Ma05Bp
Mary-Ann	26	F	Unknown	18Ma05Bp
Eleanor	.11	F	Infant	18Ma05Bp
Bridget	.01	F	Infant	18Ma05Bp
CREIGHTON. Mary	22	F	Matron	18Ma05Bp
NOWLAN. James	29	M	Laborer	18Ma05Bp
Ann	28	F	Spinster	18Ma05Bp
Mary-Ann	.09	F	Infant	18Ma05Bp
MURPHY. Michael	21	M	Laborer	18Ma05Bp
ENNIS, Hugh	21	M	Laborer	18Ma05Bp
COURISE. Eliza	25	F	Spinster	18Ma05Bp
CAFFIN, Christopher	40	M	Laborer	18Ma05Bp
Christopher	19	M	Laborer	18Ma05Bp
POOLE, Ellen	24	F	Spinster	18Ma05Bp
BYRNF. Thomas	33	M	Laborer	18Ma05Bp
DERECOY. Hugh	29	M	Laborer	18Ma05Bp
HINEY. Ann	20	F	Spinster	18Ma05Bp
CULIAGHEN, Thomas	21	M	Laborer	18Ma05Bp
CARINGTON, Christopher	34	M	Laborer	18Ma05Bp
Bridget	30	F	Spinster	18Ma05Bp
James	26	M	Laborer	18Ma05Bp
Thomas	.11	M	Infant	18Ma05Bp
Myles	34	M	Laborer	18Ma05Bp
Michael	.01	M	Infant	18Ma05Bp
KELLY. Mary	21	F	Spinster	18Ma05Bp
MILEY, Wm.	18	M	Laborer	18Ma05Bp
SMITH, Henry	33	M	Laborer	18Ma05Bp
MUGHTEN, John	28	M	Laborer	18Ma05Bp
Mary	30	F	Spinster	18Ma05Bp
TOOLE. James	24	M	Laborer	18Ma05Bp
FORD. John	20	M	Laborer	18Ma05Bp
ARNOLD. James	24	M	Laborer	18Ma05Bp
REILLY, Patrick	23	M	Laborer	18Ma05Bp
BRENNAN, Charles	28	M	Laborer	18Ma05Bp
KEATING, John	28	M	Laborer	18Ma05Bp
FEHAN, Ann	20	F	Spinster	18Ma05Bp
JOHNSTON, Elizabeth	26	F	Matron	18Ma05Bp
KEEFE, Joseph	24	M	Laborer	18Ma05Bp
TOBIN, Thomas	24	M	Laborer	18Ma05Bp
MCGRATH, Joseph	21	M	Laborer	18Ma05Bp
DALY, Bartholemew	40	M	Laborer	18Ma05Bp
GOVERNEY. James	29	M	Laborer	18Ma05Bp
NOWLAN. Hugh	26	M	Laborer	18Ma05Bp
KELLY, John	24	M	Laborer	18Ma05Bp
HAVARD. John	22	M	Laborer	18Ma05Bp
FLEMING, James	26	M	Laborer	18Ma05Bp
JONES. Wm.	48	M	Laborer	18Ma05Bp
Jim	20	M	Laborer	18Ma05Bp
RUNNIGEN. Ann	23	F	Spinster	18Ma05Bp
HENLY. Thomas	35	M	Laborer	18Ma05Bp
Eliza	35	F	Spinster	18Ma05Bp
Marin	.11	F	Infant	18Ma05Bp
Francis	6	M	Child	18Ma05Bp
Rose	4	F	Child	18Ma05Bp
Ann	.03	F	Infant	18Ma05Bp
SHANNON. Thomas	28	M	Laborer	18Ma05Bp
ONEILL, Mary	50	F	Spinster	18Ma05Bp
Mary	16	F	Spinster	18Ma05Bp
Michael	21	M	Laborer	18Ma05Bp
Christopher	18	M	Laborer	18Ma05Bp
GREHAN. Patrick	35	M	Laborer	18Ma05Bp
COURTNEY. Mary	48	F	Spinster	18Ma05Bp
BYRNE. John	20	M	Laborer	18Ma05Bp
RANKIN, Hugh	45	M	Laborer	18Ma05Bp
Jane	45	F	Wife	18Ma05Bp
William	10	M	Unknown	18Ma05Bp
Simon	9	M	Child	18Ma05Bp
Margaret	8	F	Child	18Ma05Bp
Mary	5	F	Child	18Ma05Bp
James	3	M	Child	18Ma05Bp
David	.11	M	Infant	18Ma05Bp
George	.11	M	Infant	18Ma05Bp
BYRNE. James	62	M	Laborer	18Ma05Bp
Patrick	35	M	Laborer	18Ma05Bp

NAMES OF PASSENGERS	AGE	SEX	OCCUPATIONS	DATE PORT SHIP
BYRNE. Mary	20	F	Spinster	18Ma05Bp
Julia	16	F	Spinster	18Ma05Bp
FITZGERALD, George	25	M	Laborer	18Ma05Bp
Sarah	27	F	Spinster	18Ma05Bp
GRAHAM, Thomas	26	M	Laborer	18Ma05Bp
PERCY, Mary	17	F	Spinster	18Ma05Bp
DUFFY. Bernard	45	M	Laborer	18Ma05Bp
Bridget	60	F	Spinster	18Ma05Bp
MOONEY. Edmund	30	M	Laborer	18Ma05Bp
Bridget	22	F	Wife	18Ma05Bp
Joanne	23	F	Spinster	18Ma05Bp
Philip	.01	M	Infant	18Ma05Bp
Thomas	.11	M	Infant	18Ma05Bp
Peter	29	M	Laborer	18Ma05Bp
HICKEY. Charles	33	M	Laborer	18Ma05Bp
Margaret	33	F	Spinster	18Ma05Bp
FRAWLEY. Patrick	15	M	Laborer	18Ma05Bp
BRENNAN. James	57	M	Laborer	18Ma05Bp
James	23	M	Laborer	18Ma05Bp
Judith	18	F	Spinster	18Ma05Bp
BYRNE. Gerald	22	M	Laborer	18Ma05Bp
HEYFORD, John	60	M	Laborer	18Ma05Bp
John	17	M	Laborer	18Ma05Bp
LOWRY. John	45	M	Laborer	18Ma05Bp
Mary	40	F	Spinster	18Ma05Bp
Ann	.10	F	Infant	18Ma05Bp
MADDEN. Margaret	16	F	Spinster	18Ma05Bp
CORCORAN, John	17	M	Laborer	18Ma05Bp
Margaret	12	F	Spinster	18Ma05Bp
MCDERMOTT. Mary	20	F	Spinster	18Ma05Bp
Eliza	19	F	Spinster	18Ma05Bp
MURPHY. Daniel	70	M	Laborer	18Ma05Bp
Thomas	24	M	Laborer	18Ma05Bp
Luke	17	M	Laborer	18Ma05Bp
KEARNS. John	33	M	Laborer	18Ma05Bp
ELIFFE. Mary	27	F	Spinster	18Ma05Bp
PLUNKET. Ellen	20	F	Spinster	18Ma05Bp
POOLE. John	40	M	Laborer	18Ma05Bp
Marin	30	F	Spinster	18Ma05Bp
William	19	M	Laborer	18Ma05Bp
John	12	M	Unknown	18Ma05Bp
WHELAN, John	32	M	Laborer	18Ma05Bp
Mary	32	F	Wife	18Ma05Bp
Ann	.08	F	Infant	18Ma05Bp
LEMON. James	34	M	Laborer	18Ma05Bp
Bridget	21	F	Spinster	18Ma05Bp
LEVI. Bryan	24	M	Laborer	18Ma05Bp
Cornelius	24	M	Laborer	18Ma05Bp
NOWLAN, Patrick	24	M	Laborer	18Ma05Bp
Bridget	25	F	Spinster	18Ma05Bp
John	.10	M	Infant	18Ma05Bp
BRENNAN. Daniel	26	M	Laborer	18Ma05Bp
BYRNE. Mary	36	F	Spinster	18Ma05Bp
Mary-Ann	15	F	Spinster	18Ma05Bp
CORCORAN, Ellen	21	F	Spinster	18Ma05Bp
Margaret	.07	F	Infant	18Ma05Bp
Bridget	9	F	Child	18Ma05Bp
KENLY, James	40	M	Laborer	18Ma05Bp
Mary	35	F	Spinster	18Ma05Bp
Catherine	11	F	Unknown	18Ma05Bp
Mary-Ann	9	F	Child	18Ma05Bp
John	7	M	Child	18Ma05Bp
Thomas	5	M	Child	18Ma05Bp
Daniel	3	M	Child	18Ma05Bp
Eliza	.11	F	Infant	18Ma05Bp
Ann	.11	F	Infant	18Ma05Bp
DUNNIGAN, Margaret	19	F	Spinster	18Ma05Bp
CONWAY, Alley	30	F	Spinster	18Ma05Bp
LEE. Richard	19	M	Laborer	18Ma05Bp
KELLY, James	22	M	Laborer	18Ma05Bp
Mary	18	F	Spinster	18Ma05Bp
SWORDS. Patrick	40	M	Laborer	18Ma05Bp
MACDONALD, Rose	24	F	Spinster	18Ma05Bp
MAHER. John	30	M	Laborer	18Ma05Bp
Darby	.09	M	Infant	18Ma05Bp
MAHER. Winifred	24	F	Spinster	18Ma05Bp
KINSELLA. Jessy	19	F	Spinster	18Ma05Bp
GAHAN. Eliza	21	F	Spinster	18Ma05Bp
Martha	.10	F	Infant	18Ma05Bp
CARROLL, Mary	19	F	Spinster	18Ma05Bp
Catherine	.07	F	Infant	18Ma05Bp
EVANS. John	22	M	Laborer	18Ma05Bp
HANLON. Michael	23	M	Laborer	18Ma05Bp
CLASKEY. Margaret	22	F	Spinster	18Ma05Bp
STEPHON, Catherine	21	F	Spinster	18Ma05Bp
MAGUIRE. Jane	26	F	Spinster	18Ma05Bp
BERGIN, William	18	M	Laborer	18Ma05Bp
CANNIAN. Michael	31	M	Laborer	18Ma05Bp
Margaret	23	F	Spinster	18Ma05Bp
DONAHOE. Eliza	18	F	Spinster	18Ma05Bp
CANNIAN, Bridget	00	F	Spinster	18Ma05Bp
Catherine	.11	F	Infant	18Ma05Bp
William	25	M	Laborer	18Ma05Bp
KENLY, Mary	60	F	Spinster	18Ma05Bp
James	28	M	Laborer	18Ma05Bp
John	26	M	Laborer	18Ma05Bp
KEOUGH, James	25	M	Laborer	18Ma05Bp
CURTY. Bridget	15	F	Spinster	18Ma05Bp
BOLAND, Patrick	21	M	Laborer	18Ma05Bp
BRENNAN, John	31	M	Laborer	18Ma05Bp
SLATFR. James	18	M	Laborer	18Ma05Bp
RYAN, Jeremiah	17	M	Laborer	18Ma05Bp
MORRISEY. Denis	27	M	Laborer	18Ma05Bp
Margaret	3	F	Spinster	18Ma05Bp
QUIRK. Thomas	18	M	Laborer	18Ma05Bp
PURCELL, Margaret	24	F	Spinster	18Ma05Bp
KILDUFF, Timothy	44	M	Laborer	18Ma05Bp
LARKIN, Thomas	40	M	Laborer	18Ma05Bp
DUNNE, Essey	25	F	Spinster	18Ma05Bp
BURTON, Jane	25	F	Spinster	18Ma05Bp
RYAN, Ellen	22	F	Spinster	18Ma05Bp
MONLAN, John	26	M	Laborer	18Ma05Bp
James	22	M	Laborer	18Ma05Bp
Daniel	18	M	Laborer	18Ma05Bp
Mary	20	F	Spinster	18Ma05Bp
Catherine	.11	F	Infant	18Ma05Bp
Bridget	00	F	Child	18Ma05Bp
TURNER, Timothy	27	M	Laborer	18Ma05Bp
BUCKLEY, James	24	M	Laborer	18Ma05Bp
TURNER, James	20	M	Laborer	18Ma05Bp
MURPHY. Ellen	31	F	Spinster	18Ma05Bp
Michael	16	M	Laborer	18Ma05Bp
REYNOLDS, Thomas	21	M	Laborer	18Ma05Bp
PHELAN, John	29	M	Laborer	18Ma05Bp
GAVERN, Catherine	19	F	Spinster	18Ma05Bp
CONNELLY. Philip	19	M	Laborer	18Ma05Bp
QUIGLEY. James	18	M	Laborer	18Ma05Bp
MCCABE. Edward	29	M	Laborer	18Ma05Bp
Jane	18	F	Spinster	18Ma05Bp
MANEN. Ann	20	F	Spinster	18Ma05Bp
CARPENTER. Rosamund	66	F	Spinster	18Ma05Bp
Johanna	24	F	Spinster	18Ma05Bp
John	.11	M	Infant	18Ma05Bp
Ann	1	F	Infant	18Ma05Bp
FLYNNE. Edward	26	M	Laborer	18Ma05Bp
CONTES, Michael	28	M	Laborer	18Ma05Bp
FEGAN, Francis	30	M	Laborer	18Ma05Bp
BENTLY, Christopher	17	M	Laborer	18Ma05Bp
STUMILLER. Mary	15	F	Spinster	18Ma05Bp
PHELAN. Timothy	22	M	Laborer	18Ma05Bp
SAUNDERS. Michael	25	M	Laborer	18Ma05Bp
NEALE. John	25	M	Laborer	18Ma05Bp
BYRNE. Denis	38	M	Laborer	18Ma05Bp
CALLAMAN, John	25	M	Laborer	18Ma05Bp
Michael	25	M	Laborer	18Ma05Bp
ROURKE, Mary	23	F	Spinster	18Ma05Bp
SHAN. Wm.	25	M	Laborer	18Ma05Bp
KELLY, Anne	25	F	Spinster	18Ma05Bp
LENAHAN. Michael	20	M	Laborer	18Ma05Bp
QUINN, Catherine	65	F	Spinster	18Ma05Bp

NAMES OF PASSENGERS	AGE	SEX	OCCUPATIONS	DATE PORT SHIP
FLYNNE, John	21	M	Laborer	18Ma05Bp
HOGAN, Wm.	16	M	Laborer	18Ma05Bp
SANDERS, James	28	M	Laborer	18Ma05Bp
LYNIHALL, Thomas	32	M	Block Maker	18Ma05Bp
Agnes	21	F	Wife	18Ma05Bp
SLEVIN, Winifred	34	F	Matron	18Ma05Bp
RILEY, Eugene	18	M	Clerk	18Ma05Bp
HICKEY, Catherine	26	F	Spinster	18Ma05Bp
GIBBEN, Francis	24	M	Clerk	18Ma05Bp
CAMPBELL, William	22	M	Laborer	18Ma05Bp
REDMOND, Bartle	27	M	Farmer	18Ma05Bp
Mary-Ann	22	F	Wife	18Ma05Bp
BRENNAN, Richard	27	M	Painter	18Ma05Bp
Catherine	26	F	Wife	18Ma05Bp
BLIGH, Wm.	19	M	Gentleman	18Ma05Bp

EMPIRE-STATE 18 MAY 1850

From Liverpool

NAMES OF PASSENGERS	AGE	SEX	OCCUPATIONS	DATE PORT SHIP
HAMMOND, Hugh	52	M	Farmer	18Ma02Fc
Maria	53	F	Unknown	18Ma02Fc
John	14	M	Farmer	18Ma02Fc
Frank	16	M	Farmer	18Ma02Fc
Edward	22	M	Farmer	18Ma02Fc
Arthur	25	M	Farmer	18Ma02Fc
Margt.H.	23	F	Unknown	18Ma02Fc
Hugh	18	M	Farmer	18Ma02Fc
WISCOTT, Susan	27	F	Unknown	18Ma02Fc
HAMMOND, Mary	20	F	Unknown	18Ma02Fc
Ellen	12	F	Unknown	18Ma02Fc
Emma	19	F	Unknown	18Ma02Fc
Sarah	16	F	Unknown	18Ma02Fc
Rebecca	15	F	Unknown	18Ma02Fc
PATT, George	35	M	Farmer	18Ma02Fc
Mary	32	F	Farmer	18Ma02Fc
HARRIS, James	10	M	Farmer	18Ma02Fc
BOYLE, Richd.	25	M	Farmer	18Ma02Fc
GROOM, John	30	M	Farmer	18Ma02Fc
LEA, John	29	M	Farmer	18Ma02Fc
Henry	25	M	Farmer	18Ma02Fc
GRINSHAW, Sarah	70	F	Farmer	18Ma02Fc
POOLE, Mary	45	F	Farmer	18Ma02Fc
BARLEY, Cathe.	16	F	Farmer	18Ma02Fc
BROOKS, Jane	13	F	Farmer	18Ma02Fc
NEAL, Wm.	00	M	Farmer	18Ma02Fc
U-Mrs.	00	F	Farmer	18Ma02Fc
Isaac	6	M	Child	18Ma02Fc
Mary	5	F	Child	18Ma02Fc
Henry	5	M	Child	18Ma02Fc
George	.00	M	Infant	18Ma02Fc
YOUNG, George	00	M	Farmer	18Ma02Fc
LONEGAN, Michl.	34	M	Farmer	18Ma02Fc
Ellen	30	F	Farmer	18Ma02Fc
John	.00	M	Infant	18Ma02Fc
GRIFFIN, Rachl.	22	F	Farmer	18Ma02Fc
CARLOW, Thos.	30	M	Farmer	18Ma02Fc
SMITH, James	32	M	Farmer	18Ma02Fc
CLARKE, Jully	27	F	Farmer	18Ma02Fc
Silvester	22	M	Farmer	18Ma02Fc
Patt	18	M	Farmer	18Ma02Fc
Cathe.	11	F	Laborer	18Ma02Fc
Mary	50	F	Unknown	18Ma02Fc
RYAN, Thos.	26	M	Unknown	18Ma02Fc
FOGERTY, Bridgt.	30	F	Unknown	18Ma02Fc
ENGLISH, Phil.	24	M	Unknown	18Ma02Fc
Thos.	21	M	Unknown	18Ma02Fc
SWEENEY, Danl.	15	M	Unknown	18Ma02Fc
PINTINS, Mary	40	F	Wi	18Ma02Fc
PINTINS, Ann	13	F	Unknown	18Ma02Fc
Wm.	9	M	Child	18Ma02Fc
Saml.	3	M	Child	18Ma02Fc
SHAW, Christn.	40	M	Unknown	18Ma02Fc
Bridgt.	38	F	Unknown	18Ma02Fc
Bedilia	10	F	Unknown	18Ma02Fc
Maria	6	F	Child	18Ma02Fc
NOLAN, Rose	20	F	Unknown	18Ma02Fc
MACKIN, Ann	23	F	Unknown	18Ma02Fc
Mary	2	F	Child	18Ma02Fc
CLARKE, Josh.	23	M	Unknown	18Ma02Fc
SPINK, Richd.	45	M	Unknown	18Ma02Fc
Hannah	40	F	Unknown	18Ma02Fc
Wm.	30	M	Unknown	18Ma02Fc
Hannah	25	F	Unknown	18Ma02Fc
GIDDENS, Thos.	23	M	Unknown	18Ma02Fc
DEFFILY, Patt	28	M	Unknown	18Ma02Fc
Mary	12	F	Unknown	18Ma02Fc
CONNELLY, Thos.	45	M	Unknown	18Ma02Fc
Lawr.	11	M	Unknown	18Ma02Fc
POWELL, John	00	M	Unknown	18Ma02Fc
GRATTAN, Ann	19	F	Unknown	18Ma02Fc
HILL, Alice	32	F	Unknown	18Ma02Fc
Ruth	10	F	Unknown	18Ma02Fc
Mary-A.	.00	F	Infant	18Ma02Fc
MCGREGAN, Margt.	25	F	Unknown	18Ma02Fc
FARRELL, Mary	20	F	Unknown	18Ma02Fc
CHAPMAN, U-Mrs.	50	F	Unknown	18Ma02Fc
Mary-A.	14	F	Unknown	18Ma02Fc
Edwin	18	M	Unknown	18Ma02Fc
Fredk.	10	M	Unknown	18Ma02Fc
LAUNDERS, Vanpult	30	M	Unknown	18Ma02Fc
PATTISON, George	20	M	Unknown	18Ma02Fc
Mary	18	F	Unknown	18Ma02Fc
Margt.	17	F	Unknown	18Ma02Fc
Ann	20	F	Unknown	18Ma02Fc
KELLY, James	18	M	Unknown	18Ma02Fc
SPINK, Susanne	4	F	Child	18Ma02Fc
Sarah	2	F	Child	18Ma02Fc
Mary-A.	.00	F	Infant	18Ma02Fc
MCGUIRE, Mary	20	F	Unknown	18Ma02Fc
LYNCH, Owen	35	M	Unknown	18Ma02Fc
U-Mrs.	30	F	Unknown	18Ma02Fc
Peter	30	M	Unknown	18Ma02Fc
MCGRAN, Susan	20	F	Unknown	18Ma02Fc
SHERIDAN, Wm.	20	M	Unknown	18Ma02Fc
NOLAN, Mary	18	F	Unknown	18Ma02Fc
KELLAHEN, Ellen	20	F	Unknown	18Ma02Fc
BRADY, Peter	21	M	Unknown	18Ma02Fc
CLARKE, Cathe.	20	F	Unknown	18Ma02Fc
MONAGHAN, Mary	20	F	Unknown	18Ma02Fc
RATHBONE, Ann	23	F	Unknown	18Ma02Fc
Margt.	4	F	Child	18Ma02Fc
ADCOCK, John	59	M	Unknown	18Ma02Fc
Elizh.	58	F	Unknown	18Ma02Fc
Edwd.	32	M	Unknown	18Ma02Fc
Ann	37	F	Unknown	18Ma02Fc
John-W.	4	M	Child	18Ma02Fc
Wm.	2	M	Child	18Ma02Fc
Edwd.	.00	M	Infant	18Ma02Fc
DENNIAN, Thos.	40	M	Unknown	18Ma02Fc
Cathe.	32	F	Unknown	18Ma02Fc
Wm.	16	M	Unknown	18Ma02Fc
HASTINGS, Chas.	13	M	Unknown	18Ma02Fc
DENNIAN, George	12	M	Unknown	18Ma02Fc
HASTINGS, Wm.	10	M	Unknown	18Ma02Fc
DENNIAN, Thos.	9	M	Child	18Ma02Fc
HASTINGS, Sarah	8	F	Child	18Ma02Fc
DENNIAN, Josh.	7	M	Child	18Ma02Fc
Henry	.00	M	Infant	18Ma02Fc
HUTCHABARK, James	27	M	Unknown	18Ma02Fc
WILLIAMS, John	29	M	Unknown	18Ma02Fc
Eliza	39	F	Unknown	18Ma02Fc
CHARLES, Wm.	26	M	Unknown	18Ma02Fc
SLEWELLYN, Wm.	39	M	Unknown	18Ma02Fc

NAMES OF PASSENGERS	AGE	SEX	OCCUPATIONS	DATE PORT SHIP
THOMAS, Evan	18	M	Unknown	18Ma02Fc
WILLIAMS, John	28	M	Unknown	18Ma02Fc
Wm.	34	M	Unknown	18Ma02Fc
Rachl.	26	F	Unknown	18Ma02Fc
Hugan	2	M	Child	18Ma02Fc
Wm.	.00	M	Infant	18Ma02Fc
HAGGETT, Barney	40	M	Unknown	18Ma02Fc
Mary	36	F	Unknown	18Ma02Fc
Frances	11	F	Unknown	18Ma02Fc
Mary-A.	10	F	Unknown	18Ma02Fc
DAVIES, G.C.	31	M	Unknown	18Ma02Fc
MCINTYRE, Michl.	36	M	Unknown	18Ma02Fc
SHEENAN, Eliza	26	F	Unknown	18Ma02Fc
Danl.	3	M	Child	18Ma02Fc
MCENTEE, Mary	60	F	Unknown	18Ma02Fc
Robt.	46	M	Unknown	18Ma02Fc
BAXTER, Cathe.	30	F	Unknown	18Ma02Fc
Mary	60	F	Unknown	18Ma02Fc
MILLER, Thos.	22	M	Unknown	18Ma02Fc
MCCULLOCK, Wm.	21	M	Unknown	18Ma02Fc
ALLEN, Alice	25	F	Unknown	18Ma02Fc
HAMLET, John	26	M	Unknown	18Ma02Fc
Cathe.	22	F	Unknown	18Ma02Fc
Saml.	1	M	Child	18Ma02Fc
CARRIKER, Owen	20	M	Unknown	18Ma02Fc
Cathe.	19	F	Unknown	18Ma02Fc
MCKENNA, Owen	47	M	Unknown	18Ma02Fc
Mick	15	M	Unknown	18Ma02Fc
Mick	16	M	Unknown	18Ma02Fc
COVINS, G.	25	M	Unknown	18Ma02Fc
Alfred	.00	M	Infant	18Ma02Fc
HEYNES, Robt.	29	M	Unknown	18Ma02Fc
FAHEY, Chas.	20	M	Unknown	18Ma02Fc
Ann	20	F	Unknown	18Ma02Fc
MCCALL, Bernd.	30	M	Unknown	18Ma02Fc
Mary	45	F	Unknown	18Ma02Fc
Mary	20	F	Unknown	18Ma02Fc
Bridgt.	18	F	Unknown	18Ma02Fc
DUNN, Michl.	30	M	Unknown	18Ma02Fc
HAYNES, Thos.	28	M	Unknown	18Ma02Fc
Ann	24	F	Unknown	18Ma02Fc
Chas.	8	M	Child	18Ma02Fc
Charlotte	1	F	Child	18Ma02Fc
Wm.	26	M	Unknown	18Ma02Fc
Dorothy	24	F	Unknown	18Ma02Fc
Emma	.00	F	Infant	18Ma02Fc
HAMLETT, Wm.	21	M	Unknown	18Ma02Fc
Emma	20	F	Unknown	18Ma02Fc
SIMMS, James	20	M	Unknown	18Ma02Fc
CULLEN, Cathe.	30	F	Unknown	18Ma02Fc
KEENAN, Ann	30	F	Unknown	18Ma02Fc
COMMUNE, Bridgt.	19	F	Unknown	18Ma02Fc
Patt	16	M	Unknown	18Ma02Fc
ARMSTRONG, Chas.	00	M	Unknown	18Ma02Fc
Thos.	00	M	Unknown	18Ma02Fc
DEAN, Elizh.	00	F	Unknown	18Ma02Fc
MURPHY, James	21	M	Unknown	18Ma02Fc
HADDOCK, Jane	27	F	Unknown	18Ma02Fc
Wm.	6	M	Child	18Ma02Fc
Margt.	4	F	Child	18Ma02Fc
Died-At-Sea				
Ann	.00	F	Infant	18Ma02Fc
PIKE, Thos.	23	M	Unknown	18Ma02Fc
John	25	M	Unknown	18Ma02Fc
Elizh.	22	F	Unknown	18Ma02Fc
John	2	M	Child	18Ma02Fc
Thos.	.00	M	Infant	18Ma02Fc
DEX, Wm.	30	M	Unknown	18Ma02Fc
YATES, Thos.	32	M	Unknown	18Ma02Fc
Emma	31	F	Unknown	18Ma02Fc
Alfred	11	M	Unknown	18Ma02Fc
Emma	10	F	Unknown	18Ma02Fc
Cathe.	5	M	Child	18Ma02Fc
Isabella	.00	F	Infant	18Ma02Fc
PIERCE, John	19	M	Unknown	18Ma02Fc
PIERCE, Margt.	27	F	Unknown	18Ma02Fc
ROBERTS, Evan	.00	M	Infant	18Ma02Fc
VICTORY, Mary	19	F	Unknown	18Ma02Fc
CAHILL, Mary	20	F	Unknown	18Ma02Fc
WATERS, Luke	43	M	Unknown	18Ma02Fc
U-Mrs.	43	M	Unknown	18Ma02Fc
WARD, Wm.	25	M	Unknown	18Ma02Fc
U-Mrs.	23	F	Unknown	18Ma02Fc
LEALAND, Robt.	25	M	Unknown	18Ma02Fc
U-Mrs.	25	F	Unknown	18Ma02Fc
Ruth	.00	F	Infant	18Ma02Fc
WATERWORTH, Benjn.	29	M	Unknown	18Ma02Fc
U-Mrs.	25	F	Unknown	18Ma02Fc
WATERS, Wm.	26	M	Unknown	18Ma02Fc
U-Mrs.	22	F	Unknown	18Ma02Fc
ROBINSON, Anthy.	48	M	Unknown	18Ma02Fc
CARROLL, Michl.	15	M	Unknown	18Ma02Fc
Margt.	13	F	Unknown	18Ma02Fc
DINAGAN, Margt.	19	F	Unknown	18Ma02Fc
OBRIEN, John	30	M	Unknown	18Ma02Fc
NOWLAN, John	18	M	Unknown	18Ma02Fc
BURNS, Michl.	26	M	Unknown	18Ma02Fc
DONNELLY, Patt	30	M	Unknown	18Ma02Fc
SHANLEY, John	20	M	Unknown	18Ma02Fc
Mary	15	F	Unknown	18Ma02Fc
BRIEN, Mary	18	F	Unknown	18Ma02Fc
HANNON, John	17	M	Unknown	18Ma02Fc
MCCOGHIN, George	36	M	Unknown	18Ma02Fc
MCHENRY, John	16	M	Unknown	18Ma02Fc
MCGARITY, Michl.	40	M	Unknown	18Ma02Fc
James	12	M	Unknown	18Ma02Fc
Thos.	10	M	Unknown	18Ma02Fc
Mick	8	M	Child	18Ma02Fc
Peter	6	M	Child	18Ma02Fc
REYNOLDS, Margt.	40	F	Unknown	18Ma02Fc
REECE, Mary-Jane	14	F	Unknown	18Ma02Fc
LIMERICK, Matilda	10	F	Unknown	18Ma02Fc
RODGERS, Thos.	28	M	Unknown	18Ma02Fc
HARRINGTON, Anthy.	18	M	Unknown	18Ma02Fc
Mary	8	F	Child	18Ma02Fc
Honor	14	F	Unknown	18Ma02Fc
CALLAGHAN, Thos.	18	M	Unknown	18Ma02Fc
QUALY, Simon	21	M	Unknown	18Ma02Fc
BYRNE, John	15	M	Unknown	18Ma02Fc
GLYNN, Ann	18	F	Unknown	18Ma02Fc
BYRNES, Terrce.	18	M	Unknown	18Ma02Fc
GALBRAITH, Jane	20	M	Unknown	18Ma02Fc
SMITH, Jeremiah	11	M	Unknown	18Ma02Fc
Mary	9	F	Child	18Ma02Fc
GAFFNEY, Mary	18	F	Unknown	18Ma02Fc
SPRING, Julia	30	F	Unknown	18Ma02Fc
Maria	7	F	Child	18Ma02Fc
Josh.	5	M	Child	18Ma02Fc
DUGAN, Ann	18	F	Unknown	18Ma02Fc
FOLAN, Cathe.	14	F	Unknown	18Ma02Fc
Patt	11	M	Unknown	18Ma02Fc
Wm.	7	M	Child	18Ma02Fc
HEFFERNAN, Johanna	45	F	Unknown	18Ma02Fc
Mary	23	F	Unknown	18Ma02Fc
Kate	22	F	Unknown	18Ma02Fc
Ellen	20	F	Unknown	18Ma02Fc
Bridgt.	19	M	Unknown	18Ma02Fc
Johanna	18	F	Unknown	18Ma02Fc
Danl.	17	M	Unknown	18Ma02Fc
James	15	M	Unknown	18Ma02Fc
Eliza	14	F	Unknown	18Ma02Fc
John	12	M	Unknown	18Ma02Fc
Ann	10	F	Unknown	18Ma02Fc
Thos.	7	M	Child	18Ma02Fc
WICKAN, Richd.	19	M	Unknown	18Ma02Fc
James	17	M	Unknown	18Ma02Fc
Cathe.	21	F	Unknown	18Ma02Fc
REDMOND, John	21	M	Unknown	18Ma02Fc
BYRNE, Thos.	25	M	Unknown	18Ma02Fc
Wm.	20	M	Unknown	18Ma02Fc

NAMES OF PASSENGERS	AGE	SEX	OCCUPATIONS	DATE PORT SHIP
BYRNE. Cathe.	16	F	Unknown	18Ma02Fc
Maria	8	F	Child	18Ma02Fc
MAHER. John	50	M	Unknown	18Ma02Fc
Mary	50	F	Unknown	18Ma02Fc
Johanna	20	F	Unknown	18Ma02Fc
Margt.	13	F	Unknown	18Ma02Fc
Bridgt.	11	F	Unknown	18Ma02Fc
WALSH, Thos.	23	M	Unknown	18Ma02Fc
PLUNKETT. Patt	40	M	Unknown	18Ma02Fc
FIFE. Hugh	28	M	Unknown	18Ma02Fc
MURTAGH, Margt.	22	F	Unknown	18Ma02Fc
MEWES. Herbert	30	M	Unknown	18Ma02Fc
CUNNINGHAM. Ann	20	F	Unknown	18Ma02Fc
BREGEN, Ann	18	F	Unknown	18Ma02Fc
SMITH. Ellen	18	F	Unknown	18Ma02Fc
BURKE. Cathe.	18	F	Unknown	18Ma02Fc
MULHALL, Patt	18	M	Unknown	18Ma02Fc
KEHOE. Kate	18	F	Unknown	18Ma02Fc
KERRIGAN. Ann	25	F	Unknown	18Ma02Fc
FARRELLY. Thos.	50	M	Unknown	18Ma02Fc
Ann	48	F	Unknown	18Ma02Fc
John	19	M	Unknown	18Ma02Fc
Mick	9	M	Child	18Ma02Fc
Margt.	7	F	Child	18Ma02Fc
FEENY. Eleanor	50	F	Laborer	18Ma02Fc
Bridgt.	16	F	Unknown	18Ma02Fc
Cannor	20	F	Unknown	18Ma02Fc
HOPKINS. Martin	18	M	Laborer	18Ma02Fc
KERNS. Ruth	20	F	Unknown	18Ma02Fc
Bridgt.	18	F	Unknown	18Ma02Fc
DONAGHER. John	30	M	Laborer	18Ma02Fc
ROALAN. Mary	20	F	Unknown	18Ma02Fc
JAMES. Mary	40	F	Unknown	18Ma02Fc
Sarah	20	F	Unknown	18Ma02Fc
HAULHAN, Wm.	28	M	Laborer	18Ma02Fc
BERRINGHAN. James	32	M	Laborer	18Ma02Fc
Bridgt.	34	F	Unknown	18Ma02Fc
GRACE. Patt	34	M	Laborer	18Ma02Fc
LURAN, Mich	35	M	Laborer	18Ma02Fc
RENNDY, Thoms.	45	M	Laborer	18Ma02Fc
Mary	48	F	Laborer	18Ma02Fc
Phill	20	M	Laborer	18Ma02Fc
Johanne	13	F	Unknown	18Ma02Fc
Mary	11	F	Unknown	18Ma02Fc
MCGRATH. Johanna	19	F	Laborer	18Ma02Fc
POWER. Mary	22	F	Unknown	18Ma02Fc
HIGGINS. Michl.	22	M	Laborer	18Ma02Fc
GALLAGHER. Jas.	16	M	Laborer	18Ma02Fc
MCELHAIZ, Wm.	20	M	Unknown	18Ma02Fc
CUNNINGHAM. Bridgt.	22	F	Laborer	18Ma02Fc
MULHAN, Elizh.	19	F	Unknown	18Ma02Fc
LEDDY. Mary	20	F	Unknown	18Ma02Fc
BEATY. Walter	50	M	Laborer	18Ma02Fc
Ann	35	F	Unknown	18Ma02Fc
Chls.	18	M	Laborer	18Ma02Fc
Adam	16	M	Laborer	18Ma02Fc
John	12	M	Laborer	18Ma02Fc
James	9	M	Child	18Ma02Fc
WOODS. John	22	M	Laborer	18Ma02Fc
MCMAHIN, James	20	M	Laborer	18Ma02Fc
BYRNE. James	22	M	Laborer	18Ma02Fc
HOGAN, Margt.	20	F	Unknown	18Ma02Fc
GANDNER. Cathn.	18	F	Unknown	18Ma02Fc
BARNHOUSE. George	30	M	Laborer	18Ma02Fc
ROACH, John	50	M	Laborer	18Ma02Fc
Ann	45	F	Unknown	18Ma02Fc
Richd.	21	M	Laborer	18Ma02Fc
Sarah	19	F	Unknown	18Ma02Fc
Rebecca	18	F	Unknown	18Ma02Fc
Elisa	17	F	Unknown	18Ma02Fc
Maria	13	F	Unknown	18Ma02Fc
John	12	M	Laborer	18Ma02Fc
Phillip	11	M	Unknown	18Ma02Fc
GOODWIN, Wm.	20	M	Farmer	18Ma02Fc
Ellen	16	F	Unknown	18Ma02Fc
GOODWIN. Alice	30	F	Unknown	18Ma02Fc
MCFARLAN, James	20	M	Farmer	18Ma02Fc
HAMILLTON, Andrew	20	M	Farmer	18Ma02Fc
MCADDIN, John	20	M	Farmer	18Ma02Fc
DALY. Ann	20	F	Farmer	18Ma02Fc
FITZGERRALD. Ellen	18	F	Unknown	18Ma02Fc
PIOOTE. George	25	M	Farmer	18Ma02Fc
FLYNN. Cath.	20	F	Farmer	18Ma02Fc
SHETTIN, Mick	30	M	Unknown	18Ma02Fc
BEATY. Wm.	20	M	Farmer	18Ma02Fc
Mary-A.	21	F	Laborer	18Ma02Fc
Elisa	16	F	Unknown	18Ma02Fc
Margt.	13	F	Unknown	18Ma02Fc
RITTLE. Yeon	31	F	Unknown	18Ma02Fc
Sarah	26	F	Unknown	18Ma02Fc
RYLE, Robt.	30	M	Laborer	18Ma02Fc
FITSPATRICK, Fred.	18	M	Laborer	18Ma02Fc
GAVIN, John	45	M	Laborer	18Ma02Fc
Julia	12	F	Unknown	18Ma02Fc
HUNT, Jas.	24	M	Laborer	18Ma02Fc
Cath.	20	F	Unknown	18Ma02Fc
FAY. John	20	M	Laborer	18Ma02Fc
MENAGHAN. Judith	23	F	Laborer	18Ma02Fc
Wm.	22	M	Laborer	18Ma02Fc
RYAN, Paul	57	M	Laborer	18Ma02Fc
Margt.	7	F	Child	18Ma02Fc
LENAHAN. Danl.	24	M	Laborer	18Ma02Fc
HALLOHAN, Dennis	25	M	Laborer	18Ma02Fc
Patt	35	M	Laborer	18Ma02Fc
Elisa	27	F	Unknown	18Ma02Fc
Patt	5	M	Child	18Ma02Fc
Danl.	4	M	Child	18Ma02Fc
Cath.	7	F	Child	18Ma02Fc
HAY. Ann	20	F	Unknown	18Ma02Fc
CANNITY. Cath.	20	F	Unknown	18Ma02Fc
MCDONALD. Arthur	21	M	Laborer	18Ma02Fc
EMIS. Ellen	42	F	Unknown	18Ma02Fc
Mary	12	F	Unknown	18Ma02Fc
Bridgt.	10	F	Unknown	18Ma02Fc
Catherine	7	F	Child	18Ma02Fc
CARRIGAN. John	18	M	Laborer	18Ma02Fc
Mick	12	M	Laborer	18Ma02Fc
MCLOUGHLIN, Jms.	24	M	Laborer	18Ma02Fc
MCLOUCHE. Isaac	27	M	Laborer	18Ma02Fc
BYRNE, Mich	35	M	Laborer	18Ma02Fc
Honer	35	F	Unknown	18Ma02Fc
Tim	30	M	Laborer	18Ma02Fc
Willm.	8	M	Child	18Ma02Fc
Margt.	6	F	Child	18Ma02Fc
DUNLIN, Michl.	30	M	Laborer	18Ma02Fc
OBRINE. Michl.	18	M	Laborer	18Ma02Fc
WILLONGHLY. Jams.	17	M	Laborer	18Ma02Fc
WALSH, Mary	20	F	Unknown	18Ma02Fc
CARREN, David	16	M	Laborer	18Ma02Fc
CANSSEN. Mary	20	F	Unknown	18Ma02Fc
QUINLAN, Deterh.	20	F	Unknown	18Ma02Fc
BUCKLY. John	60	M	Laborer	18Ma02Fc
Simon	30	M	Unknown	18Ma02Fc
David	23	M	Laborer	18Ma02Fc
CANNELL, Tim	25	M	Laborer	18Ma02Fc
SASSAN, Wm.	22	M	Laborer	18Ma02Fc
SULLIVAN, Stephen	30	M	Laborer	18Ma02Fc
Julia	14	F	Unknown	18Ma02Fc
DOVELY, Jeremiah	22	M	Laborer	18Ma02Fc
OHARRA. Cath.	3	F	Child	18Ma02Fc
RINALY. John	21	M	Unknown	18Ma02Fc
BRANNECK. Bridgt.	16	F	Unknown	18Ma02Fc
PRINNELL, Ann	20	F	Unknown	18Ma02Fc
SULLIVAN, Wm.	20	M	Laborer	18Ma02Fc
Elisa	15	F	Unknown	18Ma02Fc
SCARLIN, John	40	M	Laborer	18Ma02Fc
Margt.	35	F	Unknown	18Ma02Fc
Margt.	12	F	Unknown	18Ma02Fc
MADDEN. Wm.	50	M	Laborer	18Ma02Fc
HOOPER, Patt	20	M	Laborer	18Ma02Fc

NAMES OF PASSENGERS	AGE	SEX	OCCUPATIONS	DATE PORT SHIP
HARBY, Peggy	19	F	Unknown	18Ma02Fc
CARELINE, John	21	M	Unknown	18Ma02Fc
HALLIDAY, John	20	M	Laborer	18Ma02Fc
WALSH, Ellen	54	F	Unknown	18Ma02Fc
Ellen	20	F	Unknown	18Ma02Fc
FOX, Matilda	25	F	Unknown	18Ma02Fc
CUMMINGS, Sarah	19	F	Unknown	18Ma02Fc
REARSY, Margt.	25	F	Unknown	18Ma02Fc
ROURKE, Michl.	20	M	Laborer	18Ma02Fc
GRATON, Peter	25	M	Laborer	18Ma02Fc
BARNSALE, Mary	20	F	Unknown	18Ma02Fc
BOYDE, Margt.	16	F	Unknown	18Ma02Fc
SHINE, Was.	30	M	Laborer	18Ma02Fc
Hannah	30	F	Unknown	18Ma02Fc
U	.06	U	Infant	18Ma02Fc
JOY, J.	16	M	Laborer	18Ma02Fc
Hannah	11	F	Unknown	18Ma02Fc
Patt	8	M	Child	18Ma02Fc
BORRY, Johana	21	F	Unknown	18Ma02Fc
DALY, Math.	30	M	Unknown	18Ma02Fc
COUNCHEY, Ann	17	F	Unknown	18Ma02Fc
HAGAN, Ellen	3	F	Child	18Ma02Fc
SALLIVAN, Hannah	25	F	Unknown	18Ma02Fc
Cathn.	20	F	Unknown	18Ma02Fc
DELANEY, Bridgt.	15	F	Laborer	18Ma02Fc
DANOVEN, James	32	M	Laborer	18Ma02Fc
Cathn.	32	F	Unknown	18Ma02Fc
James	18	M	Laborer	18Ma02Fc
Mary	25	F	Unknown	18Ma02Fc
REILLY, Cathn.	17	F	Unknown	18Ma02Fc
COOBY, Jane	30	F	Laborer	18Ma02Fc
Ann	11	F	Unknown	18Ma02Fc
Jane	8	F	Child	18Ma02Fc
CANLY, Thms.	5	M	Child	18Ma02Fc
Ellen	2	F	Child	18Ma02Fc
HARRISON, John	19	M	Laborer	18Ma02Fc
MCCONNER, John	19	M	Laborer	18Ma02Fc
CROWLEY, John	36	M	Laborer	18Ma02Fc
SHEEHAN, Cathn.	40	F	Laborer	18Ma02Fc
U	.06	U	Infant	18Ma02Fc
Jeremiah	19	M	Unknown	18Ma02Fc
Mary	18	F	Unknown	18Ma02Fc
Cath.	16	F	Laborer	18Ma02Fc
Patt	13	M	Laborer	18Ma02Fc
John	10	M	Laborer	18Ma02Fc
Ellen	9	F	Child	18Ma02Fc
Hannah	4	F	Child	18Ma02Fc
GLYNN, Margt.	50	F	Unknown	18Ma02Fc
Margt.	10	F	Unknown	18Ma02Fc
Margt.	16	F	Unknown	18Ma02Fc
MALINE, Daney	50	F	Unknown	18Ma02Fc
Ann	30	F	Unknown	18Ma02Fc
Mary	25	F	Unknown	18Ma02Fc
Phillip	20	M	Laborer	18Ma02Fc
Phillip	15	M	Laborer	18Ma02Fc
MARTIN, Cath.	11	F	Unknown	18Ma02Fc
Ellen	6	F	Child	18Ma02Fc
John	5	M	Child	18Ma02Fc
LEE, Cath.	19	F	Unknown	18Ma02Fc
BYRNN, Byron	18	M	Unknown	18Ma02Fc
MCKEE, Jane	18	F	Unknown	18Ma02Fc
Eliza	18	F	Laborer	18Ma02Fc
KELLEY, John	32	M	Unknown	18Ma02Fc
WAKEFIELD, Nath.	30	M	Laborer	18Ma02Fc
Mary-A.	28	F	Unknown	18Ma02Fc
HENERFIN, Mary	19	F	Unknown	18Ma02Fc
SHEE, Patt	13	M	Unknown	18Ma02Fc
Hannah	11	F	Unknown	18Ma02Fc
LYNCH, Mary	20	F	Unknown	18Ma02Fc
PURLLY, Mary	50	F	Unknown	18Ma02Fc
KELLEY, Rose	35	F	Laborer	18Ma02Fc
BRAG, John	11	M	Laborer	18Ma02Fc
REILLY, Hugh	16	M	Laborer	18Ma02Fc
Bernard	8	M	Child	18Ma02Fc
Mary	6	F	Child	18Ma02Fc
REILLY, Mary	4	F	Child	18Ma02Fc
John	2	M	Child	18Ma02Fc
BROPHY, Cath.	15	F	Unknown	18Ma02Fc
LYNCH, Sas.	21	M	Unknown	18Ma02Fc
DUFFY, Cathn.	17	F	Unknown	18Ma02Fc
HARDERRY, Ellen	50	F	Unknown	18Ma02Fc
James	6	M	Child	18Ma02Fc
DACTON, Martin	18	M	Unknown	18Ma02Fc
BRADY, Thomas	23	M	Laborer	18Ma02Fc
OBRENE, Denis	25	M	Unknown	18Ma02Fc
KERLY, Ellen	17	F	Unknown	18Ma02Fc
Margt.	14	F	Unknown	18Ma02Fc
OSHANSY, Sarah	20	F	Unknown	18Ma02Fc
MURRY, Ann	40	F	Unknown	18Ma02Fc
Bridgt.	19	F	Unknown	18Ma02Fc
HIGGINS, Bridgt.	11	F	Unknown	18Ma02Fc
Mary	9	F	Child	18Ma02Fc
FINE, James	18	M	Unknown	18Ma02Fc
OBRIEN, Mary	9	F	Child	18Ma02Fc
MCMAYHEN, Allen	18	M	Laborer	18Ma02Fc
STURR, Thos.	20	M	Laborer	18Ma02Fc
U, Thos.	28	M	Laborer	18Ma02Fc
DENT, Elisa	17	F	Unknown	18Ma02Fc
Andrew	7	M	Child	18Ma02Fc
Margt.	5	F	Child	18Ma02Fc
ADAMS, Elisa	18	F	Unknown	18Ma02Fc
GRAY, Bern.	50	M	Unknown	18Ma02Fc
Bridgt.	24	F	Unknown	18Ma02Fc
SEAGRON, Peter	27	M	Laborer	18Ma02Fc
MCEVOY, Margt.	18	F	Unknown	18Ma02Fc
FOX, John	20	M	Unknown	18Ma02Fc
AGAN, Judy	14	F	Unknown	18Ma02Fc
SMITH, Bridgt.	33	F	Unknown	18Ma02Fc
Cath.	14	F	Unknown	18Ma02Fc
Thomas	9	M	Child	18Ma02Fc
Bridg.	7	F	Child	18Ma02Fc
Mary	4	F	Child	18Ma02Fc
DOYLE, Pat	15	M	Laborer	18Ma02Fc
GALLIGAN, John	14	M	Laborer	18Ma02Fc
Mick	10	M	Laborer	18Ma02Fc
FLYNN, Bridgt.	16	F	Unknown	18Ma02Fc
MCGRATY, Willm.	22	M	Laborer	18Ma02Fc
REYNOLDS, Maria	20	F	Unknown	18Ma02Fc
DEMPSEY, Barney	22	M	Unknown	18Ma02Fc
SLATER, John	21	M	Laborer	18Ma02Fc
PLASTON, Dnl.	25	M	Laborer	18Ma02Fc
DUNN, John	27	M	Laborer	18Ma02Fc
Peter	21	M	Laborer	18Ma02Fc
MALONE, Rose	60	F	Unknown	18Ma02Fc
James	26	M	Laborer	18Ma02Fc
KEEGAN, James	18	M	Laborer	18Ma02Fc
Alice	18	F	Unknown	18Ma02Fc
DOOLIN, Mary	24	F	Unknown	18Ma02Fc
MCCARR, Thos.	50	M	Laborer	18Ma02Fc
Margt.	15	F	Unknown	18Ma02Fc
Bern.	11	M	Unknown	18Ma02Fc
Cathn.	9	F	Child	18Ma02Fc
REILLY, Phillip	21	M	Laborer	18Ma02Fc
RYAN, Sarah	14	F	Unknown	18Ma02Fc
FOX, Thomas	20	M	Laborer	18Ma02Fc
PURCELL, Wm.	26	M	Laborer	18Ma02Fc
Bridgt.	24	F	Unknown	18Ma02Fc
U	.04	F	Infant	18Ma02Fc
Bridgt.	20	F	Unknown	18Ma02Fc
Cath.	18	F	Unknown	18Ma02Fc
ALLEN, Michl.	21	M	Laborer	18Ma02Fc
HILL, Mary	31	F	Unknown	18Ma02Fc
CHAMBERS, Lucy	25	F	Unknown	18Ma02Fc
MCEVOY, Thos.	35	M	Unknown	18Ma02Fc
Mary	58	F	Unknown	18Ma02Fc
Margt.	11	F	Unknown	18Ma02Fc
Thos.	8	M	Child	18Ma02Fc
Patt	6	M	Child	18Ma02Fc
ROUGH, James	24	M	Laborer	18Ma02Fc
CARTER, Peter	24	M	Laborer	18Ma02Fc

NAMES OF PASSENGERS	AGE	SEX	OCCUPATIONS	DATE PORT SHIP
NOWLAN, Margt.	24	F	Unknown	18Ma02Fc
RIGBY, John	50	M	Laborer	18Ma02Fc
DUGAN, Thos.	24	M	Laborer	18Ma02Fc
HALL, Thos.	55	M	Laborer	18Ma02Fc
GAMBLE, Frd.	21	M	Laborer	18Ma02Fc
BIGLEY, Cath.	18	F	Unknown	18Ma02Fc
MCAVERY, James	15	M	Laborer	18Ma02Fc
DONNELLY, Ann	18	F	Unknown	18Ma02Fc
DALY, Ellen	25	F	Unknown	18Ma02Fc
JERET, Patt	23	M	Laborer	18Ma02Fc
Thos.	25	M	Laborer	18Ma02Fc
James	22	M	Laborer	18Ma02Fc
Anth.	17	M	Laborer	18Ma02Fc
Mary	16	F	Unknown	18Ma02Fc
MCKEENA, Bridg.	20	F	Unknown	18Ma02Fc
DARDUS, Christ.	22	M	Laborer	18Ma02Fc
CARTY, Ellen	25	F	Unknown	18Ma02Fc
HESLIN, Ann	18	F	Unknown	18Ma02Fc
HODGENS, John	21	M	Laborer	18Ma02Fc
DENT, Thos.	30	M	Laborer	18Ma02Fc
Ann	13	F	Unknown	18Ma02Fc
FLYN, John	30	M	Laborer	18Ma02Fc
Wm.	34	M	Laborer	18Ma02Fc
HICKEY, Edwd.	29	M	Laborer	18Ma02Fc
TAGHEN, James	49	M	Laborer	18Ma02Fc
FITZPATRICK, John	24	M	Laborer	18Ma02Fc
WALSH, Thos.	24	M	Laborer	18Ma02Fc
DUNN, Patt	23	M	Laborer	18Ma02Fc
Ann	16	F	Unknown	18Ma02Fc
Can---, Marcela	20	F	Unknown	18Ma02Fc
DOVAN, John	28	M	Laborer	18Ma02Fc
U	30	F	Unknown	18Ma02Fc
U	.00	U	Infant	18Ma02Fc
Died-At-Sea				
MCDANNELL, R.	50	F	Unknown	18Ma02Fc
Elisa	50	F	Unknown	18Ma02Fc
Johana	22	F	Laborer	18Ma02Fc
DOVAN, Margt.	25	F	Unknown	18Ma02Fc
KELLY, Mary	52	F	Unknown	18Ma02Fc
WHALAN, Mary	22	F	Unknown	18Ma02Fc
BRESEAN, Honor	20	F	Unknown	18Ma02Fc
SALLY, James	30	M	Laborer	18Ma02Fc
MUNING, James	60	M	Laborer	18Ma02Fc
Francis	22	M	Unknown	18Ma02Fc
DUCKANN, Matilda	11	F	Unknown	18Ma02Fc
MCMEHAN, Cathe.	18	F	Unknown	18Ma02Fc
Patt	13	M	Laborer	18Ma02Fc
FARINGTON, A.	21	M	Laborer	18Ma02Fc
HEALEY, Judith	22	F	Unknown	18Ma02Fc
LYNCH, Patt	23	M	Laborer	18Ma02Fc
MULLEN, Patrick	20	M	Laborer	18Ma02Fc
Mary	18	F	Laborer	18Ma02Fc
CUNNINGHAM, Robert	15	M	Laborer	18Ma02Fc
TRAYNOR, Michael	20	M	Laborer	18Ma02Fc
Cathe.	30	F	Laborer	18Ma02Fc
PLATT, James	17	M	Laborer	18Ma02Fc
CAREY, E.	16	M	Laborer	18Ma02Fc
Cathrn.	22	F	Laborer	18Ma02Fc
MOORE, U-Mrs.	30	F	Lady	18Ma02Fc
George	14	M	Unknown	18Ma02Fc
SMITH, Andrew	11	M	Unknown	18Ma02Fc

ELIZA-ANN 18 MAY 1850

From Liverpool

NAMES OF PASSENGERS	AGE	SEX	OCCUPATIONS	DATE PORT SHIP
ROANE, Jon	38	M	Laborer	18Ma02Jz
Brown-OBRIEN, Jas.Timo	30	M	Laborer	18Ma02Jz
Died-At-Sea				
Brown-OBRIEN, U-Mrs.	28	F	Laborer	18Ma02Jz
LOFTIS, John	38	M	Laborer	18Ma02Jz
L.	19	U	Laborer	18Ma02Jz
FARNWICK, Pat	19	M	Laborer	18Ma02Jz
DURKAN, Thos.	20	M	Laborer	18Ma02Jz
James	18	M	Laborer	18Ma02Jz
John	10	M	Laborer	18Ma02Jz
JORDAN, James	40	M	Laborer	18Ma02Jz
James	27	M	Laborer	18Ma02Jz
ROWAN, Luke	38	M	Blacksmith	18Ma02Jz
P.	25	M	Laborer	18Ma02Jz
MCLOUGHLIN, John	27	M	Laborer	18Ma02Jz
BROWN, Michl.	22	M	Laborer	18Ma02Jz
Ellen	20	F	Unknown	18Ma02Jz
MCDEAN, Cathe.	20	F	Unknown	18Ma02Jz
BURNS, Thos.	23	M	Laborer	18Ma02Jz
Cathe.	23	F	Unknown	18Ma02Jz
CRAMPTON, Mary	35	F	Unknown	18Ma02Jz
Henry	8	M	Child	18Ma02Jz
John	6	M	Child	18Ma02Jz
Wm.	4	M	Child	18Ma02Jz
Herbert	3	M	Child	18Ma02Jz
Thomas	.00	M	Infant	18Ma02Jz
SULLIVAN, Pat	15	M	Laborer	18Ma02Jz
JASKAR, Thomas	35	M	Calb	18Ma02Jz
Wm.	28	M	Unknown	18Ma02Jz
ARMSTRONG, Richard	30	M	Calf	18Ma02Jz
FENTON, Margt.	30	F	Dressmaker	18Ma02Jz
Amelia	5	F	Child	18Ma02Jz
Betsey	3	F	Child	18Ma02Jz
Betsey	.00	F	Infant	18Ma02Jz
ROURKE, Margt.	19	F	Seamstress	18Ma02Jz
DUNN, John	18	M	Laborer	18Ma02Jz
COX, Catherine	19	F	Servant	18Ma02Jz
FREELY, Ellen	20	F	Servant	18Ma02Jz
CURMAN, Margt.	20	F	Servant	18Ma02Jz
COAN, Bridget	21	F	Servant	18Ma02Jz
HASLIN, Michl.	15	M	Laborer	18Ma02Jz
BROWN, Cicily	50	F	Spinster	18Ma02Jz
Thos.	20	M	Laborer	18Ma02Jz
DOYLE, Cathe.	30	F	Servant	18Ma02Jz
MCCANN, Thos.	35	M	Ploughman	18Ma02Jz
RICE, Carol	28	F	Laborer	18Ma02Jz
Wm.	7	M	Child	18Ma02Jz
Carol	5	F	Child	18Ma02Jz
Andrew	3	M	Child	18Ma02Jz
Edward	.00	M	Infant	18Ma02Jz
KELLY, Wm.	40	M	Laborer	18Ma02Jz
Mary	10	F	Unknown	18Ma02Jz
LYONS, Rosa	38	F	Unknown	18Ma02Jz
Mary	3	F	Child	18Ma02Jz
DOLAN, Jane	38	F	Unknown	18Ma02Jz
Jas.	10	M	Unknown	18Ma02Jz
Cathe.	6	F	Child	18Ma02Jz
U	4	U	Child	18Ma02Jz
MCCOLLOGH, Peter	25	M	Laborer	18Ma02Jz
BOYLAN, Bridget	30	F	Unknown	18Ma02Jz
Phil	3	M	Child	18Ma02Jz
REILLY, Bridget	10	F	Unknown	18Ma02Jz
LYNCH, Michl.	40	M	Unknown	18Ma02Jz
Cathe.	30	F	Unknown	18Ma02Jz
MCDONALD, Mary	40	F	Unknown	18Ma02Jz
Jas.	40	M	Unknown	18Ma02Jz
Rose	9	F	Child	18Ma02Jz
Pat	7	M	Child	18Ma02Jz
Cathe.	5	F	Child	18Ma02Jz
Bridget	3	F	Child	18Ma02Jz
CALAHAN, John	50	M	Stone Mason	18Ma02Jz
Pat	9	M	Child	18Ma02Jz
Margt.	7	F	Child	18Ma02Jz
OHARA, Sarah	30	F	Unknown	18Ma02Jz
DARCEY, Sarah	18	F	Unknown	18Ma02Jz
BURKE, Edward	40	M	Laborer	18Ma02Jz
MAHER, Michael	18	M	Laborer	18Ma02Jz
Jas.	6	M	Child	18Ma02Jz

NAMES OF PASSENGERS	AGE	SEX	OCCUPATIONS	DATE PORT SHIP
MAHER. Thos.	4	M	Child	18Ma02Jz
FALLON, Mary	25	F	Unknown	18Ma02Jz
Thos.	4	M	Child	18Ma02Jz
GRAHAM, Edward	25	M	Unknown	18Ma02Jz
FINLEY, Adam	53	M	Laborer	18Ma02Jz
Sarah	18	F	Unknown	18Ma02Jz
Margt.	11	F	Unknown	18Ma02Jz
FEENEY. Bridget	22	F	Unknown	18Ma02Jz
WASH. Peter	23	M	Laborer	18Ma02Jz
G.	18	U	Unknown	18Ma02Jz
LEVEY. Mary	18	F	Unknown	18Ma02Jz
BRENAN. Bridget	18	F	Unknown	18Ma02Jz
MCDONALD, Jas.	25	M	Laborer	18Ma02Jz
DROUGHT. Thos.	40	M	Laborer	18Ma02Jz
Thos.	18	M	Laborer	18Ma02Jz
MULCAHY. Mary	25	F	Unknown	18Ma02Jz
CLEARY. Dan	19	M	Laborer	18Ma02Jz
MANION. Jas.	24	M	Laborer	18Ma02Jz
BOYLE. Ellen	20	F	Dressmaker	18Ma02Jz
DERNOTT, E.	12	F	Unknown	18Ma02Jz
BLACK. Geo.	16	M	Laborer	18Ma02Jz
CRAWFORD. Sarah-A.	15	F	Unknown	18Ma02Jz
DEVILL, Hugh	23	M	Laborer	18Ma02Jz
CONVEY. Martha	19	F	Laborer	18Ma02Jz
GALLAGHER. Cathe.	15	F	Unknown	18Ma02Jz
CAHILL, Jas.	20	M	Laborer	18Ma02Jz
Mary	22	F	Unknown	18Ma02Jz
FITZGERALD, Cathe.	22	F	Unknown	18Ma02Jz
Eliza	22	F	Unknown	18Ma02Jz
DUFFY. Eliza	60	F	Unknown	18Ma02Jz
DILLON. Johanna	20	F	Unknown	18Ma02Jz
Thos.	16	M	Unknown	18Ma02Jz
LANDY, Margt.	18	F	Unknown	18Ma02Jz
MALONEY. D.	22	M	Laborer	18Ma02Jz
BURKE, Denis	18	M	Unknown	18Ma02Jz
YOUNG, Margt.	22	F	Unknown	18Ma02Jz
LYNCH, Michael	21	M	Unknown	18Ma02Jz
Mary	18	F	Unknown	18Ma02Jz
HANEY. Mary	20	F	Unknown	18Ma02Jz
Jas.	20	M	Unknown	18Ma02Jz
MULAEY. Jos.	30	M	Laborer	18Ma02Jz
Mary	50	F	Unknown	18Ma02Jz
Ann	25	F	Unknown	18Ma02Jz
Henry	20	M	Unknown	18Ma02Jz
FITZSIMONS. Bridget	20	F	Unknown	18Ma02Jz
FEENEY. Michl.	40	M	Unknown	18Ma02Jz
Margt.	15	F	Unknown	18Ma02Jz
Teresa	11	F	Unknown	18Ma02Jz
Thos.	4	M	Child	18Ma02Jz
GILJOYCE. Michl.	25	M	Unknown	18Ma02Jz
HOLIDAY. Pat	22	M	Unknown	18Ma02Jz
MCLOUGHLIN, Anty.	18	M	Unknown	18Ma02Jz
CAWLEY, Pat	22	M	Unknown	18Ma02Jz
Mary	18	F	Unknown	18Ma02Jz
Johana	16	F	Unknown	18Ma02Jz
OBRIEN. Johana	23	F	Unknown	18Ma02Jz
AHERN. Cathe.	22	F	Unknown	18Ma02Jz
COUGHLAN. Cathe.	9	F	Child	18Ma02Jz
Mary	6	F	Child	18Ma02Jz
MCQUINNAN. Jas.	18	M	Unknown	18Ma02Jz
HANNAGHAN. Ellen	22	F	Unknown	18Ma02Jz
GORDAN. Ellen	25	F	Unknown	18Ma02Jz
Sally	3	F	Child	18Ma02Jz
CALLAN, Maria	18	F	Laborer	18Ma02Jz
BRENNAN, Bridget	22	F	Unknown	18Ma02Jz
MCANDREWS, Margt.	23	F	Unknown	18Ma02Jz
QUINLAN, Martin	14	M	Unknown	18Ma02Jz
Julia	15	F	Unknown	18Ma02Jz
Mary	7	F	Child	18Ma02Jz
DUNN. Bridget	50	F	Unknown	18Ma02Jz
Felica	40	F	Unknown	18Ma02Jz
Cathe.	20	F	Unknown	18Ma02Jz
CARESS. Mary	30	F	Unknown	18Ma02Jz
Wm.	4	M	Child	18Ma02Jz
Winny	.00	F	Infant	18Ma02Jz
CAMBELL, Mary	25	F	Unknown	18Ma02Jz
CANNERY. Cathe.	30	F	Unknown	18Ma02Jz
KENNEDY. Jas.	30	M	Unknown	18Ma02Jz
MOORERS. Pat	24	M	Unknown	18Ma02Jz
DAROLING, Fenton	25	M	Unknown	18Ma02Jz
Eliza	23	F	Unknown	18Ma02Jz
Julia	20	F	Unknown	18Ma02Jz
LAWLER. Cathe.	30	F	Unknown	18Ma02Jz
MCSWEENEY. Julia	18	F	Unknown	18Ma02Jz
DWENT, John	14	M	Unknown	18Ma02Jz
LUDLOWS, Sarah	21	F	Unknown	18Ma02Jz
Ann	40	F	Unknown	18Ma02Jz
WARD. Wm.	43	M	Unknown	18Ma02Jz
SHEA. Richd.	30	M	Unknown	18Ma02Jz
Bridget	14	F	Unknown	18Ma02Jz
SMITH, Ann	57	F	Unknown	18Ma02Jz
WILSON. Isabella	48	F	Unknown	18Ma02Jz
Mary	26	F	Unknown	18Ma02Jz
REGAN, Jno.	34	M	Unknown	18Ma02Jz
WASH. Honor	24	F	Unknown	18Ma02Jz
PALMER. Wm.	33	M	Unknown	18Ma02Jz
TRACY. Wm.	32	M	Unknown	18Ma02Jz
KANE. Ann	30	F	Unknown	18Ma02Jz
MAHON. Michl.	20	M	Laborer	18Ma02Jz
JORDAN. Jno.	24	M	Laborer	18Ma02Jz
STAPLETON. Ned.	26	M	Laborer	18Ma02Jz
Mary	18	F	Unknown	18Ma02Jz
CONNELS, Margt.	26	F	Unknown	18Ma02Jz
Michl.	.00	M	Infant	18Ma02Jz
GARVEY. Cathe.	20	F	Unknown	18Ma02Jz
Mary	20	F	Unknown	18Ma02Jz
Ambrose	13	M	Unknown	18Ma02Jz
MULCAHY. Mary	30	F	Unknown	18Ma02Jz
ABERNATHY. Jas.	27	M	Farmer	18Ma02Jz
Wm.	16	M	Unknown	18Ma02Jz
MCQUADE. Nelly	34	F	Unknown	18Ma02Jz
HALLIGAN, Mary	25	F	Unknown	18Ma02Jz
Cathe.	20	F	Unknown	18Ma02Jz
Jas.	50	F	Unknown	18Ma02Jz
DONNELLY, Pat	20	M	Unknown	18Ma02Jz
SALLOWAY, Rob	31	M	Unknown	18Ma02Jz
MOORE. Wm.	56	M	Unknown	18Ma02Jz
Margt.	51	F	Unknown	18Ma02Jz
Chas.	17	M	Unknown	18Ma02Jz
Henry	13	M	Unknown	18Ma02Jz
Emily	11	F	Unknown	18Ma02Jz
CHAMBERS, Henry	21	M	Unknown	18Ma02Jz
Eliza	21	F	Unknown	18Ma02Jz
Wm.	23	M	Unknown	18Ma02Jz
Ann	22	F	Unknown	18Ma02Jz
MORGAN, Chas.	18	M	Unknown	18Ma02Jz
QUINN. Henry	20	M	Unknown	18Ma02Jz
DUNN. Ellen	30	F	Unknown	18Ma02Jz
DWYER. Cathe.	25	F	Unknown	18Ma02Jz
WARRY. Bernard	27	M	Unknown	18Ma02Jz
Alice	26	F	Unknown	18Ma02Jz
Pat	.00	M	Infant	18Ma02Jz
BRETT, Michl.	30	M	Unknown	18Ma02Jz
FRANEY. Thos.	25	M	Butcher	18Ma02Jz
WALSH, Wm.	24	M	Unknown	18Ma02Jz
KELLY. Jno.	24	M	Unknown	18Ma02Jz
MCKEE. Jno.	20	M	Unknown	18Ma02Jz
DUGDALL, Ann	24	F	Unknown	18Ma02Jz
Jos.	19	M	Unknown	18Ma02Jz
Mary	4	F	Child	18Ma02Jz
TOORNEY. Rob.	22	M	Unknown	18Ma02Jz
BURKE. Michl.	16	M	Unknown	18Ma02Jz
HENREY. Jos.	30	M	Unknown	18Ma02Jz
DONOGHEN, Mary	20	F	Unknown	18Ma02Jz
Margt.	21	F	Unknown	18Ma02Jz
TOOLE. U	17	F	Unknown	18Ma02Jz
JORDAN. John	24	M	Unknown	18Ma02Jz
DOUGLAS. Jno.	35	M	Unknown	18Ma02Jz
BROWN. Michl.	35	M	Unknown	18Ma02Jz
MURPHY. Cathe.	25	F	Unknown	18Ma02Jz

NAMES OF PASSENGERS	AGE	SEX	OCCUPATIONS	DATE PORT SHIP
CONNER, Cathe.	15	F	Unknown	18Ma02Jz
DOWN, Jos.	22	M	Unknown	18Ma02Jz
DOHERTY, Hugh	21	M	Unknown	18Ma02Jz
CALLAGHAN, Mary	35	F	Unknown	18Ma02Jz
Ellen	10	F	Unknown	18Ma02Jz
John	2	M	Child	18Ma02Jz
HENRY, George	46	M	Unknown	18Ma02Jz
RILEY, Mary-A.	25	F	Unknown	18Ma02Jz
LYNCH, Michl.	40	M	Unknown	18Ma02Jz
Ellen	40	F	Unknown	18Ma02Jz
Mary	13	F	Unknown	18Ma02Jz
Cathe.	11	F	Unknown	18Ma02Jz
Ellen	7	F	Child	18Ma02Jz
Michl.	9	M	Child	18Ma02Jz
Bridget	.00	F	Infant	18Ma02Jz

FALCON 18 MAY 1850

From Bermuda

EVANS, U-Mr.	60	M	None	18Ma22Bd
U-Mrs.	45	F	Lady	18Ma22Bd
ADAMS, U-Mr.	25	M	Ay-Off	18Ma22Bd
U-Mrs.	20	F	Lady	18Ma22Bd
MCSWEENEY, U-Rev.Mr.	40	M	Clergyman	18Ma22Bd
BLACK, Francis	35	M	Nvof	18Ma22Bd
SLATER, Thomas	40	M	Nvof	18Ma22Bd
COX, Charles	10	M	None	18Ma22Bd
SMITH, Mary-H.	16	F	Lady	18Ma22Bd
PITT, Eliza	15	F	Lady	18Ma22Bd
Mary	17	F	Lady	18Ma22Bd
ROBINSON, Dorcas	50	F	Servant	18Ma22Bd
ALLEN, John	20	M	Seaman	18Ma22Bd
JOIL, William	10	M	None	18Ma22Bd

MONMOUTH 18 MAY 1850

From Cardiff

RASKLEY, Dorah	22	F	Servant	18Ma31Go

POLLY 18 MAY 1850

From Limerick

MCLEE, Mary	22	F	Laborer	18Ma10Kj
DENT, Pat	31	M	Unknown	18Ma10Kj
BUSSEN, Edward	30	M	Unknown	18Ma10Kj
HEDEMANN, Pat	19	M	Unknown	18Ma10Kj
CLANCHY, John	25	M	Unknown	18Ma10Kj
GRADY, John	17	M	Unknown	18Ma10Kj
FORRESTAL, James	22	M	Unknown	18Ma10Kj
LEE, Margt.	26	F	Unknown	18Ma10Kj
CARRWAY, Patt	20	M	Unknown	18Ma10Kj
BOURKE, Bridgt.	12	F	Unknown	18Ma10Kj
CASEY, John	20	M	Unknown	18Ma10Kj
MCMAHON, Patt	20	M	Unknown	18Ma10Kj

NAMES OF PASSENGERS	AGE	SEX	OCCUPATIONS	DATE PORT SHIP
KEANE, John	26	M	Unknown	18Ma10Kj
HANNIGAN, Patt	26	M	Unknown	18Ma10Kj
FORLEY, Pat	45	M	Unknown	18Ma10Kj
John	15	M	Unknown	18Ma10Kj
Mary	16	F	Unknown	18Ma10Kj
SLATTERY, John	30	M	Unknown	18Ma10Kj
Patt	14	M	Unknown	18Ma10Kj
Anne	40	F	Unknown	18Ma10Kj
Mary	20	F	Unknown	18Ma10Kj
QUILLINAN, James	20	M	Unknown	18Ma10Kj
HENCHY, Ellen	40	F	Unknown	18Ma10Kj
Ellen	11	F	Unknown	18Ma10Kj
Susan	8	F	Child	18Ma10Kj
Michl.	.00	M	Infant	18Ma10Kj
MADIGAN, Bridget	20	F	Unknown	18Ma10Kj
CELINE, Ellen	17	F	Unknown	18Ma10Kj
MCNAMARA, Biddy	20	F	Unknown	18Ma10Kj
FLYNN, Biddy	17	F	Unknown	18Ma10Kj
HILLECE, Mary	21	F	Unknown	18Ma10Kj
FULRIDGE, Martin	22	M	Unknown	18Ma10Kj
Thomas	19	M	Unknown	18Ma10Kj
HONLEHAN, James	26	M	Unknown	18Ma10Kj
EUSTICE, Thomas	21	M	Unknown	18Ma10Kj
GALVIN, Biddy	16	F	Unknown	18Ma10Kj
COLLINS, Stephen	21	M	Unknown	18Ma10Kj
LYNCH, John	19	M	Unknown	18Ma10Kj
Martin	22	M	Unknown	18Ma10Kj
FARRELL, Edmund	26	M	Unknown	18Ma10Kj
GARVEY, James	24	M	Laborer	18Ma10Kj
CONSIDINE, Honor	21	F	Unknown	18Ma10Kj
AUGHIM, Charles	25	M	Unknown	18Ma10Kj
John	22	M	Unknown	18Ma10Kj
Patt	20	M	Unknown	18Ma10Kj
Cath.	20	F	Unknown	18Ma10Kj
ODEA, Thos.	20	M	Unknown	18Ma10Kj
EUSTICE, Bridgt.	19	F	Unknown	18Ma10Kj
Daniel	15	M	Unknown	18Ma10Kj
CONSIDINE, Anne	27	F	Unknown	18Ma10Kj
Nancy	26	F	Unknown	18Ma10Kj
John	26	M	Unknown	18Ma10Kj
HOGAN, Larry	30	M	Unknown	18Ma10Kj
Biddy	28	F	Unknown	18Ma10Kj
Mary	5	F	Child	18Ma10Kj
FITZGIBBON, John	25	M	Unknown	18Ma10Kj
CULHANN, Anne	20	F	Unknown	18Ma10Kj
MALONEY, Patt	21	M	Unknown	18Ma10Kj
SHEAHON, Biddy	23	F	Unknown	18Ma10Kj
NORWELL, Eliza	23	F	Unknown	18Ma10Kj
CROWE, Dennis	17	M	Unknown	18Ma10Kj
RYAN, Mary	40	F	Unknown	18Ma10Kj
Maurice	.00	M	Infant	18Ma10Kj
HOGAN, Michl.	20	M	Unknown	18Ma10Kj
NICHOLS, Mary-A.	27	F	Unknown	18Ma10Kj
HOGAN, Anne	28	F	Unknown	18Ma10Kj
BARTLEY, Jane	20	F	Unknown	18Ma10Kj
Mary	22	F	Unknown	18Ma10Kj
NEWMAN, Edmund	25	M	Unknown	18Ma10Kj
MALONE, John	20	M	Unknown	18Ma10Kj
Honor	23	F	Unknown	18Ma10Kj
DUANE, Biddy	23	F	Unknown	18Ma10Kj
GETTINANE, Michl.	20	M	Unknown	18Ma10Kj
BOGILL, Patt	30	M	Unknown	18Ma10Kj
Ellen	28	F	Unknown	18Ma10Kj
CONNORS, Jere.	19	M	Unknown	18Ma10Kj
BOGILL, Mary	.00	F	Infant	18Ma10Kj
HOLLAND, D.	20	U	Unknown	18Ma10Kj
Honor	30	F	Unknown	18Ma10Kj
Patt	2	M	Child	18Ma10Kj
CORBETT, James	25	M	Unknown	18Ma10Kj
HICKEY, James	19	M	Unknown	18Ma10Kj
MCHANNA, Martin	30	M	Unknown	18Ma10Kj
CRONANE, Thos.	34	M	Unknown	18Ma10Kj
Jeny	18	F	Unknown	18Ma10Kj
Margt.	23	F	Unknown	18Ma10Kj
Mary	48	F	Unknown	18Ma10Kj

NAMES OF PASSENGERS	AGE	SEX	OCCUPATIONS	DATE PORT SHIP
DENHAM, Edward	30	M	Unknown	18Ma10Kj
SHAUGHNESSY. Patt	25	M	Unknown	18Ma10Kj
FITZGERALD, Patt	30	M	Unknown	18Ma10Kj
REYNOLDS. Martin	21	M	Laborer	18Ma10Kj
FLANNAGAN, James	18	M	Unknown	18Ma10Kj
HALLORAN. Mary	44	F	Unknown	18Ma10Kj
Pat	17	M	Unknown	18Ma10Kj
John	13	M	Unknown	18Ma10Kj
BROWNE. Francis	20	M	Unknown	18Ma10Kj
LACY, Mary	20	F	Unknown	18Ma10Kj
LIDDY, Margt.	32	F	Unknown	18Ma10Kj
James	26	M	Unknown	18Ma10Kj
BIDDY. Patt	21	M	Unknown	18Ma10Kj
HOLLAND, Honor	20	F	Unknown	18Ma10Kj
Patt	35	M	Unknown	18Ma10Kj
LINNANE. Patt	40	M	Unknown	18Ma10Kj
Biddy	16	F	Unknown	18Ma10Kj
CURSACH, Thos.	45	M	Unknown	18Ma10Kj
SULLIVAN. S.	40	U	Unknown	18Ma10Kj
Mary	6	F	Child	18Ma10Kj
Patt	.00	M	Infant	18Ma10Kj
FLANERY. Mary	35	F	Unknown	18Ma10Kj
Biddy	15	F	Unknown	18Ma10Kj
Thos.	6	M	Child	18Ma10Kj
GALVIN. Margt.	18	F	Unknown	18Ma10Kj
MANETT. Richard	40	M	Unknown	18Ma10Kj
CONNORS. Mary	18	F	Unknown	18Ma10Kj
John	16	M	Unknown	18Ma10Kj
SMILEY. John	23	M	Unknown	18Ma10Kj
Mary	23	F	Unknown	18Ma10Kj
DONELLAN. Patt	21	M	Unknown	18Ma10Kj
Bridgt.	20	F	Unknown	18Ma10Kj
COLLINS. Bartholomew	25	M	Unknown	18Ma10Kj
Margt.	25	F	Unknown	18Ma10Kj
MANKHAM, Nicholas	30	M	Unknown	18Ma10Kj
Mary	26	F	Unknown	18Ma10Kj
CASTEN. John	23	M	Unknown	18Ma10Kj
STUDDERT. John	22	M	Unknown	18Ma10Kj
Eliza	24	F	Unknown	18Ma10Kj
BOWNE. Margt.	12	F	Unknown	18Ma10Kj
Susan	7	F	Child	18Ma10Kj
John	40	M	Unknown	18Ma10Kj
BONNELL, Susan	22	F	Unknown	18Ma10Kj
Henrietta	25	F	Unknown	18Ma10Kj
BOWNE. Edward	00	M	Unknown	18Ma10Kj

WARREN 18 MAY 1850

From Glasgow

NAMES OF PASSENGERS	AGE	SEX	OCCUPATIONS	DATE PORT SHIP
MCLOUGHLIN, John	50	M	Merchant	18Ma21Jt
GILLIS. Daniel	22	M	Weaver	18Ma21Jt
John	35	M	Weaver	18Ma21Jt
Anne	35	F	Wife	18Ma21Jt
CASSADY, Anne	18	F	Servant	18Ma21Jt
Mary	17	F	Servant	18Ma21Jt
DOCHERTY. Daniel	33	M	Laborer	18Ma21Jt
GALLAGHAN. Neil	24	M	Laborer	18Ma21Jt
MCCOWAN. Janet	17	F	Servant	18Ma21Jt
CLARK, Peter	30	M	Laborer	18Ma21Jt
MURRY, Dennis	20	M	Laborer	18Ma21Jt
CLARK, Bridget	20	F	Servant	18Ma21Jt
MCKEEHER. John	30	M	Laborer	18Ma21Jt
ALLEN. Dennis	22	M	Laborer	18Ma21Jt
LAIRD. John	23	M	Laborer	18Ma21Jt
MCGEE. Margt.	19	F	Servant	18Ma21Jt
DEVINE. Margt.	18	F	Servant	18Ma21Jt
MCTARISH. James	33	M	Laborer	18Ma21Jt
Arther	23	M	Laborer	18Ma21Jt
MCGOVER. Patrick	30	M	Laborer	18Ma21Jt
MCGROTY. Edwd.	22	M	Laborer	18Ma21Jt
Susannah	25	F	Wife	18Ma21Jt
MCDIVIT. Patrick	28	M	Laborer	18Ma21Jt
MCGHOUGHEY. Chs.	18	M	Laborer	18Ma21Jt
MCMILLEN, Jane	22	F	Servant	18Ma21Jt
MCLAUGHLIN, Patrick	39	M	Laborer	18Ma21Jt
SHAY. John	44	M	Laborer	18Ma21Jt
Alice	42	F	Wife	18Ma21Jt
HANOVER. Wm.	28	M	Farmer	18Ma21Jt
Christina	30	F	Wife	18Ma21Jt
James	10	M	None	18Ma21Jt
William	.02	M	Infant	18Ma21Jt
HARVY, James	30	M	Laborer	18Ma21Jt
BROGAN, Cornelius	19	M	Laborer	18Ma21Jt
MCLOUGHLIN, Agnes	22	F	Servant	18Ma21Jt

HELENA 20 MAY 1850

From Bristol

NAMES OF PASSENGERS	AGE	SEX	OCCUPATIONS	DATE PORT SHIP
HALL, George	40	M	Yeoman	20Ma34Jh
Jane-Ann	20	F	Unknown	20Ma34Jh
MINETT, James	31	M	Yeoman	20Ma34Jh
SMITH, Alfred	22	M	Yeoman	20Ma34Jh
BANFIELD. Lewis	21	M	Yeoman	20Ma34Jh
MCGEORGE, Mary-Ann	40	F	Seamstress	20Ma34Jh
Harriet-Ann	18	F	Unknown	20Ma34Jh
Janet-Amelia	16	F	Unknown	20Ma34Jh
Percy-Allen	13	M	Unknown	20Ma34Jh
William	6	M	Child	20Ma34Jh
Wallace	7	M	Child	20Ma34Jh
Joseph	.00	M	Infant	20Ma34Jh
Died-At-Sea				
John-Borris	4	M	Child	20Ma34Jh
ROSSITEN, James	37	M	Yeoman	20Ma34Jh
Ellen	25	F	Unknown	20Ma34Jh
William	27	M	Yeoman	20Ma34Jh
John	25	M	Yeoman	20Ma34Jh
BROWN. Wm.	50	M	Yeoman	20Ma34Jh
Anne	50	F	Unknown	20Ma34Jh
William	21	M	Yeoman	20Ma34Jh
Ann	10	F	Unknown	20Ma34Jh
BILLET. John	30	M	Yeoman	20Ma34Jh
Lydia	22	F	Unknown	20Ma34Jh
Francis	14	M	Yeoman	20Ma34Jh
William	.00	M	Infant	20Ma34Jh
TAYLOR, Charles	50	M	Unknown	20Ma34Jh
Ann	52	F	Unknown	20Ma34Jh
Charles	29	M	Yeoman	20Ma34Jh
Mary-Ann	30	F	Unknown	20Ma34Jh
Ann	25	F	Unknown	20Ma34Jh
Mary	17	F	Unknown	20Ma34Jh
Susan	13	F	Unknown	20Ma34Jh
Hanna	11	F	Unknown	20Ma34Jh
Jemima	8	F	Child	20Ma34Jh
Samuel	16	M	Yeoman	20Ma34Jh
John	.00	M	Infant	20Ma34Jh
COKE. Fred.	17	M	Yeoman	20Ma34Jh
DARBY. Elizabeth	20	F	Seamstress	20Ma34Jh
PARKER. James	42	M	Yeoman	20Ma34Jh
Susanah	33	F	Unknown	20Ma34Jh
Richard	3	M	Child	20Ma34Jh
RICHARDS, Jobe	38	M	Yeoman	20Ma34Jh
DANIELS. James	30	M	Yeoman	20Ma34Jh
BESSNE. Thomas	13	M	Yeoman	20Ma34Jh
PAIRFIT, John	39	M	Yeoman	20Ma34Jh
DIBBLE. W.Geo.	28	M	Yeoman	20Ma34Jh
Maria	22	F	Unknown	20Ma34Jh

NAMES OF PASSENGERS	AGE	SEX	OCCUPATIONS	DATE PORT SHIP
DIBBLE. Mary-M.	.00	F	Infant	20Ma34Jh
Oliver-M.	.00	M	Infant	20Ma34Jh
MILLER. Edward	27	M	Yeoman	20Ma34Jh
Selina	27	F	Yeoman	20Ma34Jh
Robert	5	M	Child	20Ma34Jh
Alfred	1	M	Child	20Ma34Jh
WARREN. John	49	M	Yeoman	20Ma34Jh
Ann	39	F	Unknown	20Ma34Jh
Matilda	17	F	Unknown	20Ma34Jh
Triphena	11	F	Unknown	20Ma34Jh
Joseph	7	M	Child	20Ma34Jh
Phoebe	5	F	Child	20Ma34Jh
James	4	M	Child	20Ma34Jh
John	3	M	Child	20Ma34Jh
William	.00	M	Infant	20Ma34Jh
PITT. Samuel	22	M	Mechanic	20Ma34Jh
ADAMS. Ambrose-T.	18	M	Mechanic	20Ma34Jh
HICKS. William	28	M	Mechanic	20Ma34Jh
Edith	30	F	Mechanic	20Ma34Jh
Jane	6	F	Child	20Ma34Jh
William	28	M	Unknown	20Ma34Jh
MATHEWS. William	40	M	Engineer	20Ma34Jh
Ann	50	F	Unknown	20Ma34Jh
John	19	M	Engineer	20Ma34Jh
Wm.Thomas	12	M	Unknown	20Ma34Jh
ANDREWS. Wm.	25	M	Farmer	20Ma34Jh
PITT. Thomas	23	M	Tailor	20Ma34Jh
CHANCEDOR. Wm.	21	M	Farmer	20Ma34Jh
PINE. James	32	M	Laborer	20Ma34Jh
OTY. Isaac	38	M	Laborer	20Ma34Jh
Thomas	11	M	Laborer	20Ma34Jh
SMITH, John	39	M	Farmer	20Ma34Jh
Maria	30	F	Unknown	20Ma34Jh
John	4	M	Child	20Ma34Jh
Emma	.00	F	Infant	20Ma34Jh
JAMES. Hugh	40	M	Farmer	20Ma34Jh
HAYWARD. Giles	20	M	Farmer	20Ma34Jh
JOHNSON. Wm.	35	M	Farmer	20Ma34Jh
BREWER. James	4	M	Child	20Ma34Jh
BANFIELD. James	30	M	Farmer	20Ma34Jh
FISHER. George	23	M	Farmer	20Ma34Jh
WINDSON. John	20	M	Farmer	20Ma34Jh
JENKINS. Thomas	25	M	Farmer	20Ma34Jh
Ruth	27	F	Farmer	20Ma34Jh
Patience	8	M	Child	20Ma34Jh
Robert	6	M	Child	20Ma34Jh
Samuel	4	M	Child	20Ma34Jh
David	.00	M	Infant	20Ma34Jh
WHITE. Jane	28	F	Dressmaker	20Ma34Jh
Jeannette	3	F	Child	20Ma34Jh
JONES. Joseph	25	M	Farmer	20Ma34Jh
MAPSTONE. John	31	M	Farmer	20Ma34Jh
MILL, James	32	M	Farmer	20Ma34Jh
COCKING, Stephen	22	M	Farmer	20Ma34Jh
WILLET. William	21	M	Farmer	20Ma34Jh
CARTER. James	20	M	Farmer	20Ma34Jh
STONE. William	26	M	Farmer	20Ma34Jh
FITZGERALD, Mary	29	F	Farmer	20Ma34Jh
MESKILL, John	24	M	Farmer	20Ma34Jh
SLOANE. Robt.	30	M	Farmer	20Ma34Jh
CLANCY. Betsey	29	F	Unknown	20Ma34Jh

WEST-POINT 20 MAY 1850

From Liverpool

NAMES OF PASSENGERS	AGE	SEX	OCCUPATIONS	DATE PORT SHIP
HAYES. U-Miss	35	F	Lady	20Ma02Er
HAMILTON. U-Miss	30	F	Lady	20Ma02Er
BARNES. Sarah	20	F	Servant	20Ma02Er
FORD, Margt.	16	F	Servant	20Ma02Er
WALSH, Jas.K.	29	M	Apothecary	20Ma02Er
Ann	34	F	Apothecary	20Ma02Er
Hannah	.00	F	Infant	20Ma02Er
Eliza	28	F	Unknown	20Ma02Er
GOODFELLOW, Mary	20	F	Seamstress	20Ma02Er
MCCABE, Michl.Revd.	50	M	Priest	20Ma02Er
LYONS, D.G.	38	M	Farmer	20Ma02Er
HARMOND. Francis	20	M	Farmer	20Ma02Er
KEO. P.M.	26	M	Ldpr	20Ma02Er
LYNCH, Joseph-Francis	30	M	Architect	20Ma02Er
U-Mrs.	30	F	Unknown	20Ma02Er
LYNANE. John	25	M	Shopkeeper	20Ma02Er
U-Miss	26	F	Unknown	20Ma02Er
RIDER. John	28	M	Unknown	20Ma02Er
U-Mrs.	26	F	Unknown	20Ma02Er
Charles	.00	M	Infant	20Ma02Er
LARKIN, Thos.	23	M	Farmer	20Ma02Er
MOLONEY. Thos.	18	M	Shoemaker	20Ma02Er
MULVANIE. Pat	40	M	Laborer	20Ma02Er
MCMAHON. Sarah	50	F	Servant	20Ma02Er
Bridget	20	F	Servant	20Ma02Er
Thos.	16	M	Servant	20Ma02Er
Michael	11	M	Servant	20Ma02Er
Hugh	9	M	Child	20Ma02Er
James	7	M	Child	20Ma02Er
RUDDEN. Fanny	25	F	Servant	20Ma02Er
DONOHOE. Ann	15	F	Servant	20Ma02Er
GAFFREY. Margt.	16	F	Servant	20Ma02Er
FARRIS. David	25	M	Farmer	20Ma02Er
MCGEE. Bridget	16	F	Servant	20Ma02Er
FINY. John	20	M	Laborer	20Ma02Er
CONDORAN. Richard	30	M	Laborer	20Ma02Er
REILLY, Margt.	21	F	Servant	20Ma02Er
DOYAL, James	23	M	Laborer	20Ma02Er
DUNLOP. John	20	M	Laborer	20Ma02Er
DONOHOE. Thos.	19	M	Laborer	20Ma02Er
KELLY. Ellen	20	F	Servant	20Ma02Er
GILMARTIN, Ellen	25	F	Servant	20Ma02Er
DONOVAN. Jane	18	F	Servant	20Ma02Er
MEEHAN, Pat	28	M	Laborer	20Ma02Er
CURRIER. Thos.	30	M	Laborer	20Ma02Er
CUNEN. James	35	M	Farmer	20Ma02Er
Mary	37	F	Farmer	20Ma02Er
Mary	12	F	Farmer	20Ma02Er
WHITE. Mary	13	F	Farmer	20Ma02Er
SIMPSON, William	25	M	Farmer	20Ma02Er
DOLAN. Pat	19	M	Farmer	20Ma02Er
Eliza	12	F	Farmer	20Ma02Er
Mary	12	F	Farmer	20Ma02Er
BRODY. John	18	M	Farmer	20Ma02Er
DUFFY. Pat	35	M	Farmer	20Ma02Er
DONOHOE. Ellen	22	F	Farmer	20Ma02Er
CUNNINGHAM. James	30	M	Laborer	20Ma02Er
Eliza	16	F	Laborer	20Ma02Er
Mary	5	F	Child	20Ma02Er
SHERIDAN, Cath.	20	F	Servant	20Ma02Er
Bridget	18	F	Servant	20Ma02Er
Lawrence	15	M	Servant	20Ma02Er
MASTERSON, John	35	M	Laborer	20Ma02Er
James	14	M	Laborer	20Ma02Er
Ann	7	F	Child	20Ma02Er
DUNNE. Essy	26	F	Laborer	20Ma02Er
John	5	M	Child	20Ma02Er
Ann	4	F	Child	20Ma02Er
OBRIEN. Thos.	20	M	Laborer	20Ma02Er
MCNAMARA. James	18	M	Laborer	20Ma02Er
KENNEDY, Michael	25	M	Blacksmith	20Ma02Er
FARRELL, Pat	20	M	Laborer	20Ma02Er
JACKSON, Ralph	40	M	Peddler	20Ma02Er
MARA. Ann	25	F	Peddler	20Ma02Er
BYERS, Matthew	26	M	Plasterer	20Ma02Er
Michael	22	M	Laborer	20Ma02Er
BOYLE. Mary-Ann	18	F	Servant	20Ma02Er
MCCOMB, Matthew	22	M	Laborer	20Ma02Er

NAMES OF PASSENGERS	AGE	SEX	OCCUPATIONS	DATE PORT SHIP
MCCOMB, Eliza	18	F	Laborer	20Ma02Er
CLANCY, Margt.	30	F	Laborer	20Ma02Er
HOLLERAN, Thos.	25	M	Farmer	20Ma02Er
BEATTY, Michael	35	M	Farmer	20Ma02Er
FARRELL, Mary	18	F	Servant	20Ma02Er
MCLAUGHLIN, John	22	M	Laborer	20Ma02Er
Maria	20	F	Laborer	20Ma02Er
FANNON, John	23	M	Laborer	20Ma02Er
KELLY, Cath.	40	F	Laborer	20Ma02Er
STOCKDALE, John	30	M	Tailor	20Ma02Er
EARL, James	28	M	Tailor	20Ma02Er
NEWCOMBE, Thos.	35	M	Laborer	20Ma02Er
Pat	20	M	Laborer	20Ma02Er
Margt.	22	F	Laborer	20Ma02Er
Catherine	3	F	Child	20Ma02Er
MCDONNELL, John	25	M	Laborer	20Ma02Er
TAFFE, Michael	24	M	Laborer	20Ma02Er
Bridget	18	F	Laborer	20Ma02Er
Pat	24	M	Laborer	20Ma02Er
EARLY, Pat	30	M	Carpenter	20Ma02Er
TOAL, Pat	22	M	Laborer	20Ma02Er
WARD, Rose	25	F	Servant	20Ma02Er
GUIGEN, Mary	25	F	Servant	20Ma02Er
ONARY, Alice	35	F	Servant	20Ma02Er
MCGUIN, Cath.	30	F	Servant	20Ma02Er
ONARY, Pat	.00	M	Infant	20Ma02Er
CLUSKY, George	30	M	Laborer	20Ma02Er
MARKE, James	40	M	Laborer	20Ma02Er
James	15	M	Laborer	20Ma02Er
NUGENT, Pat	30	M	Laborer	20Ma02Er
MCPAITTIN, John	27	M	Laborer	20Ma02Er
DAWSON, John	25	M	Carpenter	20Ma02Er
RODGERS, John	25	M	Carpenter	20Ma02Er
DAILY, Mary	21	F	Servant	20Ma02Er
GREENE, James	35	M	Servant	20Ma02Er
LEECH, Margt.	20	F	Servant	20Ma02Er
KEOGH, Cath.	20	F	Dressmaker	20Ma02Er
CONNOR, Charles	24	M	Laborer	20Ma02Er
WELSH, James	26	M	Laborer	20Ma02Er
U-Mrs.	22	F	Laborer	20Ma02Er
CASSEN, Cath.	30	F	Laborer	20Ma02Er
Ann	7	F	Child	20Ma02Er
SHIELDS, Cath.	30	F	Laborer	20Ma02Er
Martin	7	M	Child	20Ma02Er
RYAN, Margt.	21	F	Servant	20Ma02Er
BRENAN, Nicholas	24	M	Laborer	20Ma02Er
HOGAN, Thos.	34	M	Mason	20Ma02Er
Mary	30	F	Mason	20Ma02Er
FLANAGAN, Mick	20	M	Laborer	20Ma02Er
RYAN, Dennis	17	M	Laborer	20Ma02Er
John	16	M	Laborer	20Ma02Er
IRVIN, Daniel	19	M	Laborer	20Ma02Er
MCMASTER, Thos.	35	M	Laborer	20Ma02Er
Jane	35	F	Laborer	20Ma02Er
James	13	M	Laborer	20Ma02Er
Ellen	10	F	Laborer	20Ma02Er
Eliza-Jane	8	F	Child	20Ma02Er
Cath.	5	F	Child	20Ma02Er
Robert	14	M	Laborer	20Ma02Er
BRIAN, Mary	25	F	Servant	20Ma02Er
FLOOD, Richard	20	M	Laborer	20Ma02Er
SMITH, John	8	M	Child	20Ma02Er
EGAN, John	20	M	Shoemaker	20Ma02Er
BIRD, Bridget	21	F	Servant	20Ma02Er
MCCRANE, Mary	18	F	Servant	20Ma02Er
Ellen	18	F	Servant	20Ma02Er
PETIT, Catherine	45	F	Wi	20Ma02Er
Mick	22	M	Unknown	20Ma02Er
Thos.	28	M	Unknown	20Ma02Er
Margt.	18	F	Unknown	20Ma02Er
SHANLEY, Margaret	45	F	Unknown	20Ma02Er
Michael	14	M	Unknown	20Ma02Er
Thos.	11	M	Unknown	20Ma02Er

ORONOCO 20 MAY 1850

From Waterford

NAMES OF PASSENGERS	AGE	SEX	OCCUPATIONS	DATE PORT SHIP
SULLIVAN, Richard	20	M	Farmer	20Ma35Iu
FREEMAN, Patrick	19	M	Unknown	20Ma35Iu
Mary	.00	F	Infant	20Ma35Iu
MADIGAN, Patt	39	M	Unknown	20Ma35Iu
James	35	M	Unknown	20Ma35Iu
John	20	M	Unknown	20Ma35Iu
Michael	.00	M	Infant	20Ma35Iu
Margaret	17	F	Unknown	20Ma35Iu
Ellen	6	F	Child	20Ma35Iu
Mary	.00	F	Infant	20Ma35Iu
SULLIVAN, James	20	M	Unknown	20Ma35Iu
HENEBERRY, Anty.	21	M	Unknown	20Ma35Iu
WALSH, Margaret	17	F	Unknown	20Ma35Iu
ANDERSON, Mary	22	F	Unknown	20Ma35Iu
Ellen	.00	F	Infant	20Ma35Iu
HARVEY, Mary	25	F	Unknown	20Ma35Iu
KEEFFE, Patt	22	M	Unknown	20Ma35Iu
PHALAN, Phillip	24	M	Unknown	20Ma35Iu
MOORNY, Maurice	21	M	Unknown	20Ma35Iu
COUDY, Richard	18	M	Unknown	20Ma35Iu
James	9	M	Child	20Ma35Iu
SHANNAHAN, James	35	M	Unknown	20Ma35Iu
CONWAY, Bridget	36	F	Unknown	20Ma35Iu
MURES, Mary	23	F	Unknown	20Ma35Iu
CONWAY, Thomas	16	M	Unknown	20Ma35Iu
Mary	14	F	Unknown	20Ma35Iu
KENNEDY, Michael	24	M	Unknown	20Ma35Iu
RYAN, Michael	36	M	Unknown	20Ma35Iu
QUINN, Thomas	20	M	Unknown	20Ma35Iu
MURPHY, Lawrence	18	M	Unknown	20Ma35Iu
HANRAHAN, Thomas	25	M	Unknown	20Ma35Iu
MORAN, Wm.	34	M	Unknown	20Ma35Iu
RYAN, Edward	27	M	Unknown	20Ma35Iu
Richard	.00	M	Infant	20Ma35Iu
JOYCE, Catherine	25	F	Unknown	20Ma35Iu
Anty.	23	M	Unknown	20Ma35Iu
Catherine	.00	F	Infant	20Ma35Iu
POWER, Judy	17	F	Unknown	20Ma35Iu
WHITE, Bridget	20	F	Unknown	20Ma35Iu
MEARA, John	25	M	Unknown	20Ma35Iu
MACKEY, Mathew	36	M	Unknown	20Ma35Iu
Anty.	.00	M	Infant	20Ma35Iu
KENNEDDY, Ellen	21	F	Unknown	20Ma35Iu
MCNAMARA, Michael	40	M	Unknown	20Ma35Iu
Thomas	38	M	Unknown	20Ma35Iu
Patt	16	M	Unknown	20Ma35Iu
Margaret	14	F	Unknown	20Ma35Iu
Catherine	.00	F	Infant	20Ma35Iu
BARTON, Johanna	17	F	Unknown	20Ma35Iu
COOGAN, Bridget	22	F	Unknown	20Ma35Iu
Patt	.00	M	Infant	20Ma35Iu
DWYER, John	20	M	Unknown	20Ma35Iu
COSTELLOE, Richard	25	M	Unknown	20Ma35Iu
WALSH, Richard	21	M	Unknown	20Ma35Iu
Margaret	20	F	Unknown	20Ma35Iu
Catherine	.00	F	Infant	20Ma35Iu
FLYNN, Peggy	20	F	Unknown	20Ma35Iu
HAURAHAN, Ellen	19	F	Unknown	20Ma35Iu
MURPHY, Nicholas	40	M	Unknown	20Ma35Iu
Andrew	19	M	Unknown	20Ma35Iu
Catherine	35	F	Unknown	20Ma35Iu
Patrick	17	U	Unknown	20Ma35Iu
Anty	14	M	Unknown	20Ma35Iu
Peggy	12	F	Unknown	20Ma35Iu
Ellen	.00	F	Infant	20Ma35Iu

NAMES OF PASSENGERS	AGE	SEX	OCCUPATIONS	DATE PORT SHIP
NOLAN, John	20	M	Unknown	20Ma35Iu
MURPHY, Richard	24	M	Unknown	20Ma35Iu
BLANCHE, Edmond	24	M	Unknown	20Ma35Iu
COODY, Thomas	23	M	Unknown	20Ma35Iu
GOLMAN, Michael	30	M	Unknown	20Ma35Iu
DOYLE, Patrick	27	M	Unknown	20Ma35Iu
RYAN, Judy	23	F	Unknown	20Ma35Iu
DALLON, Edmond	40	M	Unknown	20Ma35Iu
Ellen	37	F	Unknown	20Ma35Iu
Nancy	17	F	Unknown	20Ma35Iu
Ann	14	F	Unknown	20Ma35Iu
Johanna	12	F	Unknown	20Ma35Iu
Peter	.00	M	Infant	20Ma35Iu
POWER, William	23	M	Unknown	20Ma35Iu
WALSH, John	23	M	Unknown	20Ma35Iu
Wm.	20	M	Unknown	20Ma35Iu
MOORE, Mary	25	F	Unknown	20Ma35Iu
FINN, Edward	22	M	Unknown	20Ma35Iu
POWER, John	35	M	Unknown	20Ma35Iu
Peggy	30	F	Unknown	20Ma35Iu
Patrick	.00	M	Infant	20Ma35Iu
Lessy	2	F	Child	20Ma35Iu
RYAN, Thomas	18	M	Unknown	20Ma35Iu
GRACE, John	33	M	Unknown	20Ma35Iu
James	33	M	Unknown	20Ma35Iu
John	13	M	Unknown	20Ma35Iu
Cather.	10	F	Unknown	20Ma35Iu
Betsy	.00	F	Infant	20Ma35Iu
KELLY, Edmond	25	M	Unknown	20Ma35Iu
MCGRATH, Mary	26	F	Unknown	20Ma35Iu
HANRAHAN, Michael	28	F	Unknown	20Ma35Iu
CLARY, Robert	24	M	Unknown	20Ma35Iu
MAHER, Pat	26	M	Unknown	20Ma35Iu
GRIFFIN, Mary	19	F	Unknown	20Ma35Iu
DOODY, John	34	M	Unknown	20Ma35Iu
CONODY, John	27	M	Unknown	20Ma35Iu
PURCELL, Michael	25	M	Unknown	20Ma35Iu
Margaret	23	F	Unknown	20Ma35Iu
Michael	.00	M	Infant	20Ma35Iu
BROPHY, Thomas	27	M	Unknown	20Ma35Iu
WALSH, Michael	23	M	Unknown	20Ma35Iu
DUGGAN, Patrick	25	M	Unknown	20Ma35Iu
WALL, Robert	19	M	Unknown	20Ma35Iu
FARRELL, John	26	M	Unknown	20Ma35Iu
QUINN, Johannah	22	F	Unknown	20Ma35Iu
DUNPHY, Mary	27	F	Unknown	20Ma35Iu
MCGRATH, Anty.	20	F	Unknown	20Ma35Iu
John	17	M	Unknown	20Ma35Iu
FLETCHER, Patrick	27	M	Unknown	20Ma35Iu
MYSTICK, Patrick	20	M	Unknown	20Ma35Iu
FLYNN, Edward	25	M	Unknown	20Ma35Iu
James	13	M	Unknown	20Ma35Iu
Margaret	21	F	Unknown	20Ma35Iu
Mary	.00	F	Infant	20Ma35Iu
GRACE, Edmond	25	M	Unknown	20Ma35Iu
Judy	23	F	Unknown	20Ma35Iu
WREPOND, Wallace	27	M	Unknown	20Ma35Iu
MURPHY, Patrick	26	M	Unknown	20Ma35Iu
Bridget	23	F	Unknown	20Ma35Iu
HOBANN, Margaret	12	F	Unknown	20Ma35Iu
FLEMMING, Michael	23	M	Unknown	20Ma35Iu
KEEFFE, Mary	12	F	Unknown	20Ma35Iu
WALSH, Michael	20	M	Unknown	20Ma35Iu
HARRINGTON, Michael	19	M	Unknown	20Ma35Iu
MORRISSY, John	25	M	Unknown	20Ma35Iu
DEADY, Wm.	32	M	Unknown	20Ma35Iu
KENNEDDY, John	26	M	Unknown	20Ma35Iu
REDDY, Anty.	38	M	Unknown	20Ma35Iu
Johanna	33	F	Unknown	20Ma35Iu
WALSH, John	25	M	Unknown	20Ma35Iu
Anty.	20	M	Unknown	20Ma35Iu
Ellen	.00	F	Infant	20Ma35Iu
CALLEN, John	30	M	Unknown	20Ma35Iu
KELLY, Richard	25	M	Unknown	20Ma35Iu
KNOX, John	22	M	Unknown	20Ma35Iu

NAMES OF PASSENGERS	AGE	SEX	OCCUPATIONS	DATE PORT SHIP
CLANCY, Jeremiah	22	M	Unknown	20Ma35Iu
WALSH, Thomas	27	M	Unknown	20Ma35Iu
HAYES, John	32	M	Unknown	20Ma35Iu
WALL, Phillip	40	M	Unknown	20Ma35Iu
GAULE, Cathrn.	25	F	Unknown	20Ma35Iu
DOOHAN, Anne	20	F	Unknown	20Ma35Iu
RYAN, Mary	23	F	Unknown	20Ma35Iu
LONG, Thomas	35	M	Unknown	20Ma35Iu
Margaret	32	F	Unknown	20Ma35Iu
MOLLOY, Thomas	25	M	Unknown	20Ma35Iu
WALKER, Richard	29	M	Unknown	20Ma35Iu
FOSTER, James	29	M	Unknown	20Ma35Iu
DURNEY, Lawrence	29	M	Unknown	20Ma35Iu
WASLOW, Richard	26	M	Unknown	20Ma35Iu
CONNELL, Margaret	33	F	Unknown	20Ma35Iu
WALSH, Walter	30	M	Unknown	20Ma35Iu
John	26	M	Unknown	20Ma35Iu
ODONNALD, Patrick	22	M	Unknown	20Ma35Iu
MCANY, Michael	27	M	Unknown	20Ma35Iu
DUGGAN, James	20	M	Unknown	20Ma35Iu
FORRESTEL, Thomas	32	M	Unknown	20Ma35Iu
MORRISSY, David	00	M	Unknown	20Ma35Iu
David	34	M	Unknown	20Ma35Iu
KELLY, Peggy	20	F	Unknown	20Ma35Iu
KENNY, Margaret	28	F	Unknown	20Ma35Iu
SULLIVAN, Samuel	25	F	Unknown	20Ma35Iu
KEARNY, James	.00	M	Infant	20Ma35Iu
Margaret	26	F	Unknown	20Ma35Iu
RYAN, Mary	22	F	Unknown	20Ma35Iu
MCGRATH, Cathn.	20	F	Unknown	20Ma35Iu
WALSH, Cathn.	.00	F	Infant	20Ma35Iu
MEAN, Bridget	20	F	Unknown	20Ma35Iu
LARKIN, John	28	M	Unknown	20Ma35Iu
WALSH, Cathrn.	26	F	Unknown	20Ma35Iu
DEE, Norry	26	F	Unknown	20Ma35Iu
FITZGERALD, Michael	20	M	Unknown	20Ma35Iu
Patt	21	M	Unknown	20Ma35Iu
Ellen	.00	F	Infant	20Ma35Iu
LEARY, John	22	M	Unknown	20Ma35Iu
SHANAHAN, John	.00	M	Infant	20Ma35Iu
DANIEL, Patt	13	M	Unknown	20Ma35Iu
WALSH, Bessy	21	F	Unknown	20Ma35Iu
KEEFFE, Edmond	25	M	Unknown	20Ma35Iu
NIXON, William	20	M	Unknown	20Ma35Iu
POWEL, Robert	19	M	Unknown	20Ma35Iu
BURR, Anastasia	.00	F	Infant	20Ma35Iu
CATHRALL, Mary	10	F	Unknown	20Ma35Iu
HEARNE, Patrick	25	M	Unknown	20Ma35Iu
REDDY, Edmond	30	M	Unknown	20Ma35Iu
LUCH, Margaret	26	F	Unknown	20Ma35Iu
MCDONALD, Cathrn.	32	F	Unknown	20Ma35Iu
WALSH, James	29	M	Unknown	20Ma35Iu
FINN, Edmond	34	M	Unknown	20Ma35Iu

ALERT 20 MAY 1850

From Waterford

REDDY, Anty.	20	F	Laborer	20Ma35Ka
WALSH, Mary	18	F	Unknown	20Ma35Ka
GORMAN, Wm	19	M	Unknown	20Ma35Ka
FARMING, Edmund	24	M	Unknown	20Ma35Ka
GRANT, Bridget	30	F	Unknown	20Ma35Ka
DOBBIN, Michaei	25	M	Unknown	20Ma35Ka
DRISCOLL, Mary	17	F	Unknown	20Ma35Ka
JONES, Wm.	19	M	Unknown	20Ma35Ka
TOBIN, Ellen	34	F	Unknown	20Ma35Ka
Thomas	10	M	Unknown	20Ma35Ka
POWER, Thomas	30	M	Unknown	20Ma35Ka

NAMES OF PASSENGERS	AGE	SEX	OCCUPATIONS	DATE PORT SHIP	NAMES OF PASSENGERS	AGE	SEX	OCCUPATIONS	DATE PORT SHIP
TOBIN, Martin	28	M	Unknown	20Ma35Ka	MURPHY, Anty.	31	F	Unknown	20Ma35Ka
SHANAHAN, Walter	23	M	Unknown	20Ma35Ka	Bridget	28	F	Unknown	20Ma35Ka
NOLAN, Margaret	25	F	Unknown	20Ma35Ka	CASHEN, Michl.	27	M	Unknown	20Ma35Ka
Patrick	8	M	Child	20Ma35Ka	BUTLER, John	24	M	Unknown	20Ma35Ka
CARROLL, Margaret	24	F	Unknown	20Ma35Ka	CODY, Hugh	25	M	Unknown	20Ma35Ka
MURRAY, Patrick	22	M	Unknown	20Ma35Ka	Bridget	7	F	Child	20Ma35Ka
QUINLAN, Thomas	18	M	Unknown	20Ma35Ka	WHITE, James	27	M	Unknown	20Ma35Ka
HUNT, Cath.	24	F	Unknown	20Ma35Ka	MOLLONY, Thomas	28	M	Unknown	20Ma35Ka
QUINLAN, Cath.	26	F	Unknown	20Ma35Ka	Martin	29	M	Unknown	20Ma35Ka
BLAKE, John	32	M	Unknown	20Ma35Ka	WALSH, Bridget	24	F	Unknown	20Ma35Ka
WALSH, Cath.	40	F	Unknown	20Ma35Ka	MOLLONY, John	32	M	Unknown	20Ma35Ka
LYNN, Edmund	25	M	Unknown	20Ma35Ka	KELLY, Timothy	34	M	Unknown	20Ma35Ka
WALSH, Michael	18	M	Unknown	20Ma35Ka	PHELAN, Johanna	35	F	Unknown	20Ma35Ka
Mary	22	F	Unknown	20Ma35Ka	POWER, Betty	9	F	Child	20Ma35Ka
GORMAN, Peter	20	M	Unknown	20Ma35Ka	PHELAN, Bridget	6	F	Child	20Ma35Ka
Michl.	26	M	Unknown	20Ma35Ka	Moses	25	M	Unknown	20Ma35Ka
HENNESSY, Bridget	35	F	Unknown	20Ma35Ka	WHITE, Edmund	24	M	Unknown	20Ma35Ka
HYNES, Michael	33	M	Unknown	20Ma35Ka	Martha	30	F	Unknown	20Ma35Ka
GRACE, Robert	32	M	Unknown	20Ma35Ka	Cath.	18	F	Unknown	20Ma35Ka
CORCORAN, Michl.	24	M	Unknown	20Ma35Ka	Anty.	16	F	Unknown	20Ma35Ka
MURPHY, Mary	26	F	Unknown	20Ma35Ka	Peggy	14	F	Unknown	20Ma35Ka
KENNEDY, Thomas	28	M	Unknown	20Ma35Ka	Bridget	.00	F	Infant	20Ma35Ka
DUNN, Michl.	30	M	Unknown	20Ma35Ka	BARRENN, Phillip	20	M	Unknown	20Ma35Ka
MACKAY, Ann	20	F	Unknown	20Ma35Ka	Ellen	21	F	Unknown	20Ma35Ka
NOWLAN, Patrick	21	M	Unknown	20Ma35Ka	WALSH, Michl.	24	M	Unknown	20Ma35Ka
DEVEREUX, Mary	19	F	Unknown	20Ma35Ka	DUNPHY, Walter	25	M	Unknown	20Ma35Ka
BYRNE, Mary	20	F	Unknown	20Ma35Ka	BRIEN, Patrick	24	M	Unknown	20Ma35Ka
TOBIN, Thomas	18	M	Unknown	20Ma35Ka	PHELAN, Mary	23	F	Unknown	20Ma35Ka
DARMODY, Patrick	16	M	Unknown	20Ma35Ka	GALIVAN, Thomas	10	M	Unknown	20Ma35Ka
REDMONDS, George	24	M	Unknown	20Ma35Ka	Cath.	.00	F	Infant	20Ma35Ka
WILSON, Mary	30	F	Unknown	20Ma35Ka	DUNPHY, Mary	20	F	Unknown	20Ma35Ka
Hannah	33	F	Unknown	20Ma35Ka	MORRISSY, Ellen	19	F	Unknown	20Ma35Ka
MILLA, James	25	M	Unknown	20Ma35Ka	FITZMAURICE, Eliza	16	F	Unknown	20Ma35Ka
PHELAN, Nicholas	22	M	Unknown	20Ma35Ka	Thomas	4	M	Child	20Ma35Ka
MURPHY, Pierce	19	M	Unknown	20Ma35Ka	DELANEY, William	18	M	Unknown	20Ma35Ka
POWER, Patrick	15	M	Unknown	20Ma35Ka	CROWLY, Robert	20	M	Unknown	20Ma35Ka
ROCH, Ellen	17	F	Unknown	20Ma35Ka	BOURKE, Michl.	21	M	Unknown	20Ma35Ka
DOWLY, Ellen	43	F	Unknown	20Ma35Ka	PURCELL, Michl.	19	M	Unknown	20Ma35Ka
Cath.	18	F	Unknown	20Ma35Ka	GRANT, James	25	M	Unknown	20Ma35Ka
ROSSETTER, James	35	M	Unknown	20Ma35Ka	POWER, Michl.	25	M	Unknown	20Ma35Ka
John	19	M	Unknown	20Ma35Ka	BURGESS, Mary	27	F	Unknown	20Ma35Ka
Thomas	8	M	Child	20Ma35Ka	KEATING, Mary	28	F	Unknown	20Ma35Ka
Jeremiah	17	M	Unknown	20Ma35Ka	KIRWAN, Edmund	30	M	Unknown	20Ma35Ka
Ellen	15	F	Unknown	20Ma35Ka	LYONS, Cath.	15	F	Unknown	20Ma35Ka
Margaret	7	F	Child	20Ma35Ka	KELLY, Cath.	16	F	Unknown	20Ma35Ka
REDMONDS, Michl.	30	M	Unknown	20Ma35Ka	Mary	18	F	Unknown	20Ma35Ka
Thomas	18	M	Unknown	20Ma35Ka	CLANCY, Mary	21	F	Unknown	20Ma35Ka
James	16	M	Unknown	20Ma35Ka	GORMAN, Ellen	23	F	Unknown	20Ma35Ka
FLAHERTY, Michl.	24	M	Unknown	20Ma35Ka	DARMODY, Patrick	17	M	Unknown	20Ma35Ka
REDMOND, Cath.	25	F	Unknown	20Ma35Ka	CONWAY, Mary	18	F	Unknown	20Ma35Ka
Ellen	15	F	Unknown	20Ma35Ka	GULE, Cath.	19	F	Unknown	20Ma35Ka
QUINN, Mary	18	F	Unknown	20Ma35Ka	BARRENN, Richard	8	M	Child	20Ma35Ka
GANLAN, Cath.	19	F	Unknown	20Ma35Ka	Margaret	5	F	Child	20Ma35Ka
KENT, Cath.	15	F	Unknown	20Ma35Ka	Cath.	4	F	Child	20Ma35Ka
LEHOE, John	20	M	Unknown	20Ma35Ka	Mary	.00	F	Infant	20Ma35Ka
MURPHY, Patrick	30	M	Unknown	20Ma35Ka	BARRY, Ann	15	F	Unknown	20Ma35Ka
WALSH, Bart.	25	M	Unknown	20Ma35Ka	FOWLY, Cath.	17	F	Unknown	20Ma35Ka
Winny	19	F	Unknown	20Ma35Ka	SMITH, Michl.	19	M	Unknown	20Ma35Ka
Ally	17	F	Unknown	20Ma35Ka	GRIFFIN, Mary	20	F	Unknown	20Ma35Ka
MURPHY, Michl.	33	M	Unknown	20Ma35Ka	REILLY, Cath.	18	F	Unknown	20Ma35Ka
WALSH, Cath.	24	F	Unknown	20Ma35Ka	John	.00	M	Infant	20Ma35Ka
Ellen	16	F	Unknown	20Ma35Ka	FANCHON, Mary	16	F	Unknown	20Ma35Ka
John	17	M	Unknown	20Ma35Ka	POWER, Ann	18	F	Unknown	20Ma35Ka
POWER, John	14	M	Unknown	20Ma35Ka	William	.00	M	Infant	20Ma35Ka
CUNNINGHAM, Wm.	19	M	Unknown	20Ma35Ka	HEARN, Mary	19	F	Unknown	20Ma35Ka
DOUGHERTY, Bridget	23	F	Unknown	20Ma35Ka	HENNESSY, John	18	M	Unknown	20Ma35Ka
DOYLE, Thomas	33	M	Unknown	20Ma35Ka	TOBIN, Lawrence	17	M	Unknown	20Ma35Ka
DOOLY, Patrick	25	M	Unknown	20Ma35Ka	Judy	10	F	Unknown	20Ma35Ka
GRACE, Anty.	29	F	Unknown	20Ma35Ka	Cath.	6	F	Child	20Ma35Ka
COSTELLO, Wm.	32	M	Unknown	20Ma35Ka	Mary	4	F	Child	20Ma35Ka
LONGORGAN, Margt.	25	F	Unknown	20Ma35Ka	DOYLE, Patrick	20	M	Unknown	20Ma35Ka
BLAKE, Cath.	24	F	Unknown	20Ma35Ka	MURPHY, Sarah	18	F	Unknown	20Ma35Ka
MORRISON, Walter	25	M	Unknown	20Ma35Ka	Eliza	19	F	Unknown	20Ma35Ka
MURPHY, John	27	M	Unknown	20Ma35Ka	Margaret	16	F	Unknown	20Ma35Ka
POWER, James	29	M	Unknown	20Ma35Ka	Patrick	6	M	Child	20Ma35Ka

NAMES OF PASSENGERS		AGE	SEX	OCCUPATIONS	DATE PORT SHIP
CASEY, Edward		16	M	Unknown	20Ma35Ka
GAULE, John		19	M	Unknown	20Ma35Ka
WALSH, Bridget		20	F	Unknown	20Ma35Ka
Michl.		6	M	Child	20Ma35Ka
Cath.		.00	F	Infant	20Ma35Ka
FITZGERALD, Mary		28	F	Unknown	20Ma35Ka
Anastasia		18	F	Unknown	20Ma35Ka
DUGGAN, Cath.		16	F	Unknown	20Ma35Ka
BYRNE, Judy		14	F	Unknown	20Ma35Ka
TOBIN, Patrick		.00	M	Infant	20Ma35Ka
REDDY, Johanna		.00	F	Infant	20Ma35Ka
ALLIDEN, Richard		24	M	Unknown	20Ma35Ka
Cath.		21	F	Unknown	20Ma35Ka
CASHIN, Wm.		20	M	Unknown	20Ma35Ka
Bridget		18	F	Unknown	20Ma35Ka
Ally		19	F	Unknown	20Ma35Ka
Judy		21	F	Unknown	20Ma35Ka
POWER, John		26	M	Unknown	20Ma35Ka
MAHONY, Hugh		28	M	Unknown	20Ma35Ka
WALSH, William		20	M	Unknown	20Ma35Ka
MAGUIRE, Ann		20	F	Unknown	20Ma35Ka

BROTHERS 20 MAY 1850

From Newry

NAMES OF PASSENGERS		AGE	SEX	OCCUPATIONS	DATE PORT SHIP
BOYD, William		22	M	Clerk	20Ma04Am
WHITE, Eliza	(M)	28	F	Servant	20Ma04Am
James	(S)	8	M	Child	20Ma04Am
Catherine	(D)	6	F	Child	20Ma04Am
William	(S)	4	M	Child	20Ma04Am
George	(S)	.00	M	Infant	20Ma04Am
CRAMER, Matilda		30	F	Governess	20Ma04Am
KENNEY, Peter	(H)	22	M	Shopkeeper	20Ma04Am
Catherine	(W)	20	F	Unknown	20Ma04Am
MCANALLY, Michael		24	M	Carpenter	20Ma04Am
RONEY, Ann		18	F	Spinster	20Ma04Am
COLE, Catherine		23	F	Servant	20Ma04Am
WILSON, John		28	M	Farmer	20Ma04Am
RICHARDSON, Sarah		26	F	Spinster	20Ma04Am
TOMNEY, Michael		24	M	Farmer	20Ma04Am
HANSON, Thomas		24	M	Farmer	20Ma04Am
TUFFTS, William		22	M	Gdnr	20Ma04Am
Mary	(W)	50	F	Unknown	20Ma04Am
Eleanor		23	F	Spinster	20Ma04Am
IRVINE, Archibald	(H)	25	M	Farmer	20Ma04Am
Maria	(W)	20	F	Unknown	20Ma04Am
BENNETT, Hugh	(H)	22	M	Ploughman	20Ma04Am
Charlotte	(W)	22	F	Unknown	20Ma04Am
KNIGHT, William		18	M	Farmer	20Ma04Am
GLASS, Thomas		18	M	Farmer	20Ma04Am
MCCLATCHEY, James		19	M	Ploughman	20Ma04Am
COLLINS, Mary		18	F	Servant	20Ma04Am
FITZPATRICK, Judy		55	F	Spinster	20Ma04Am
James		25	M	Servant	20Ma04Am
Ann		23	F	Servant	20Ma04Am
HANLON, Michael		50	M	Laborer	20Ma04Am
Mary		18	F	Servant	20Ma04Am
Rose		16	F	Servant	20Ma04Am
James		12	M	Unknown	20Ma04Am
FITZPATRICK, John		55	M	Farmer	20Ma04Am
Patt		18	M	Servant	20Ma04Am
Mary		14	F	Spinster	20Ma04Am
INGRAM, Robert		20	M	Blacksmith	20Ma04Am
SHANNON, James		25	M	Shoemaker	20Ma04Am
TOAL, Thomas		24	M	Tailor	20Ma04Am
SMALL, Patt		22	M	Farmer	20Ma04Am
Mary		19	F	Spinster	20Ma04Am
Edward		.00	M	Infant	20Ma04Am

NAMES OF PASSENGERS		AGE	SEX	OCCUPATIONS	DATE PORT SHIP
MOORE, John		19	M	Farmer	20Ma04Am
Mary		21	F	Servant	20Ma04Am
Betty		23	F	Servant	20Ma04Am
MCMANUSS, Rose		36	F	Spinster	20Ma04Am
Mrgaret		.00	F	Infant	20Ma04Am
SLOAN, Patt		28	M	Laborer	20Ma04Am
MCCLORY, Lawrence		42	M	Mason	20Ma04Am
CORBITT, John		24	M	Farmer	20Ma04Am
GIBNEY, William		25	M	Ploughman	20Ma04Am
LENNON, Catherine		26	F	Servant	20Ma04Am
FEGAN, Michael		19	M	Farmer	20Ma04Am
ONEILL, Mary		18	F	Unknown	20Ma04Am
Ann		16	F	Unknown	20Ma04Am
HAUGHEY, Ann		5	F	Child	20Ma04Am
BURNS, James	(H)	45	M	Farmer	20Ma04Am
Mary	(W)	45	F	Unknown	20Ma04Am
Ann	(D)	18	F	Unknown	20Ma04Am
James	(S)	14	M	Unknown	20Ma04Am
MALLON, Bernard	(H)	25	M	Farmer	20Ma04Am
Mary	(W)	30	F	Unknown	20Ma04Am
Bridget	(R)	30	F	Unknown	20Ma04Am
Mary	(R)	25	F	Unknown	20Ma04Am
MCCANN, Thomas		16	M	Boatman	20Ma04Am
MCKEE, Hugh		21	M	Carpenter	20Ma04Am
HUNT, Bridget		26	F	Servant	20Ma04Am
LEWIS, John		26	M	Farmer	20Ma04Am
WILLIS, James		36	M	Clerk	20Ma04Am
Sinclair		27	M	Clerk	20Ma04Am
FEARON, Ann		28	F	Spinster	20Ma04Am
Margaret		28	F	Servant	20Ma04Am
SLOAN, Elizabeth		22	F	Spinster	20Ma04Am
DALY, Bernard		28	M	Gdnr	20Ma04Am
WARD, Roger	(H)	36	M	Laborer	20Ma04Am
Nancy	(W)	34	F	Unknown	20Ma04Am
Daniel	(S)	10	M	Unknown	20Ma04Am
Mary	(D)	8	F	Child	20Ma04Am
Patt	(S)	4	M	Child	20Ma04Am
Margaret	(D)	.00	F	Infant	20Ma04Am
FEGAN, Patt		16	M	Servant	20Ma04Am
Bernard		40	M	Laborer	20Ma04Am
BLAKELY, Mary		40	F	Spinster	20Ma04Am
Margaret		16	F	Servant	20Ma04Am
James		14	M	Butler	20Ma04Am
Maria		7	F	Child	20Ma04Am
CROOP, Mary-Ann	(R)	30	F	Spinster	20Ma04Am
Margaret	(R)	9	F	Child	20Ma04Am
John	(R)	6	M	Child	20Ma04Am
Walter	(R)	3	M	Child	20Ma04Am
Thomas	(R)	.00	M	Infant	20Ma04Am
CARAGHER, Mary		40	F	Spinster	20Ma04Am
James		16	M	Servant	20Ma04Am
KERNAGHAN, Agnes		20	F	Servant	20Ma04Am
Francis		5	M	Child	20Ma04Am
ROONEY, John		15	M	Servant	20Ma04Am
WALSH, Eliza		6	F	Child	20Ma04Am
MCCABE, Henry	(H)	32	M	Ploughman	20Ma04Am
Mary	(W)	37	F	Unknown	20Ma04Am
CONY, Ann		24	F	Spinster	20Ma04Am
MCATEER, Peter		22	M	Clerk	20Ma04Am
John		23	M	Farmer	20Ma04Am
HAREGHEN, John		23	M	Farmer	20Ma04Am
WHIN, Richard		24	M	Farmer	20Ma04Am
MCCAVRA, Thomas		25	M	Ploughman	20Ma04Am
Eliza		22	F	Spinster	20Ma04Am
FEGAN, John	(H)	30	M	Boatman	20Ma04Am
Sarah	(W)	25	F	Unknown	20Ma04Am
MARTIN, William		22	M	Sailor	20Ma04Am
MAGONE, Hugh		20	M	Laborer	20Ma04Am
KERNAGHAN, Catherine		22	F	Spinster	20Ma04Am
ONEILL, Rose		18	F	Servant	20Ma04Am
BECK, William		22	M	Farmer	20Ma04Am
JOHNSTON, Bridget		21	F	Spinster	20Ma04Am
FINNEGAN, Bernard		40	M	Ploughman	20Ma04Am
MARSHALL, Robert		25	M	Gdnr	20Ma04Am
SLOAN, Eliza		19	F	Servant	20Ma04Am

NAMES OF PASSENGERS		AGE	SEX	OCCUPATIONS	DATE PORT SHIP
MCARDLE, Joseph		25	M	Plumber	20Ma04Am
BUCKLEY, Henry		25	M	Tailor	20Ma04Am
LARKIN, Owen		47	M	Farmer	20Ma04Am
CLARK, Owen		25	M	Farmer	20Ma04Am
MALLON, Michael		26	M	Farmer	20Ma04Am
MCSTEIGH, William		22	M	Farmer	20Ma04Am
CONVILL, Hugh		23	M	Unknown	20Ma04Am
TUFTS, Robert		17	M	Ploughman	20Ma04Am
NOBLE, William		22	M	Farmer	20Ma04Am
TOAL, David		25	M	Shoemaker	20Ma04Am
Mary		23	F	Spinster	20Ma04Am
MCCRUM, James		21	M	Sailor	20Ma04Am
AGNEW, Eliza		20	F	Spinster	20Ma04Am
Susannah		18	F	Spinster	20Ma04Am
WILSON, James		20	M	Farmer	20Ma04Am
HUTCHESON, James		28	M	Blacksmith	20Ma04Am
WATSON, John		28	M	Tailor	20Ma04Am
GOODMAN, Patrick		23	M	Farmer	20Ma04Am
Thomas		20	M	Servant	20Ma04Am
Mary		25	F	Spinster	20Ma04Am
MCKEVITT, Arthur		21	M	Laborer	20Ma04Am
WARD, Hugh		23	M	Carpenter	20Ma04Am
KELLY, Mary		25	F	Spinster	20Ma04Am
HEARTY, Thomas		16	M	Gdnr	20Ma04Am
KEARLY, John		15	M	Servant	20Ma04Am
THOMPSON, James		45	M	Plumber	20Ma04Am
Essy		21	F	Spinster	20Ma04Am
MCKEE, James		28	M	Laborer	20Ma04Am
Hugh		23	M	Miller	20Ma04Am
HAUGHEN, Daniel	(H)	31	M	Farmer	20Ma04Am
Catherine	(W)	27	F	Unknown	20Ma04Am
Cecelia	(D)	7	F	Child	20Ma04Am
John	(S)	.00	M	Infant	20Ma04Am
Cecelia		60	F	Spinster	20Ma04Am
Catherine		18	F	Servant	20Ma04Am
Robert		20	M	Farmer	20Ma04Am
RODGERS, Ellen		18	F	Spinster	20Ma04Am
HANNAH, James		26	M	Bleacher	20Ma04Am
FITZPATRICK, Peter		30	M	Fireman	20Ma04Am
ROONEY, John		24	M	Tailor	20Ma04Am
CUNNINGHAM, Arthur		21	F	Servant	20Ma04Am
PRESTON, William		14	M	Boatman	20Ma04Am
MCCULLA, David	(H)	28	M	Farmer	20Ma04Am
Ellen	(W)	34	F	Unknown	20Ma04Am
William	(S)	11	M	Unknown	20Ma04Am
PANE, Matilda		10	F	Unknown	20Ma04Am
Sarah		7	F	Child	20Ma04Am
MCARDLE, James	(H)	30	M	Tailor	20Ma04Am
Mrgaret	(W)	28	F	Unknown	20Ma04Am
Joseph Died-At-Sea	(S)	.00	M	Infant	20Ma04Am
Mary	(D)	.00	F	Infant	20Ma04Am
LAVERY, Mark		25	M	Sawer	20Ma04Am
FEGAN, Hugh		28	M	Gdnr	20Ma04Am
MARTIN, Elizabeth		22	F	Spinster	20Ma04Am
Mary-Jane		18	F	Spinster	20Ma04Am
SIMMS, William		20	M	Farmer	20Ma04Am
Robert		13	M	Servant	20Ma04Am
PORTER, Benjamin		28	M	Laborer	20Ma04Am
HENDERSON, Samuel		14	M	Servant	20Ma04Am
FEGAN, Bernard		20	M	Farmer	20Ma04Am
CAMPBELL, John	(H)	41	M	Laborer	20Ma04Am
Nancy	(W)	45	F	Unknown	20Ma04Am
Thomas		17	M	Servant	20Ma04Am
SHIELDS, John		14	M	Carpenter	20Ma04Am
FAGAN, Edward	(H)	19	M	Farmer	20Ma04Am
Nancy	(W)	20	F	Unknown	20Ma04Am
MURPHY, Patrick		19	M	Sawer	20Ma04Am
CUNNINGHAM, Michael	(H)	23	M	Miller	20Ma04Am
Nancy	(W)	20	F	Unknown	20Ma04Am
GRIMLEY, John		22	M	Millwright	20Ma04Am
DEVLIN, Ann		27	F	Spinster	20Ma04Am
DAVISON, Andrew		20	F	Farmer	20Ma04Am
GORMAN, Michael		26	M	Farmer	20Ma04Am
BEST, Hannah		50	F	Spinster	20Ma04Am

NAMES OF PASSENGERS		AGE	SEX	OCCUPATIONS	DATE PORT SHIP
BEST, William		11	M	Servant	20Ma04Am
Essy		13	F	Servant	20Ma04Am
ROURKE, Mary		24	F	Spinster	20Ma04Am
MCKEON, Owen	(F)	30	M	Farmer	20Ma04Am
Judy	(D)	6	F	Child	20Ma04Am
Jane	(D)	.00	F	Infant	20Ma04Am
KELLY, William		20	M	Farmer	20Ma04Am
CONNOR, John		25	M	Farmer	20Ma04Am
MURPHY, John		35	M	Schm	20Ma04Am
ELPHINSTONE, Jane		25	F	Schms	20Ma04Am
KANE, Mary		20	F	Bomkr	20Ma04Am
BRADY, Mary		18	F	Shopwoman	20Ma04Am
COOGAN, Biddy		30	F	Matron	20Ma04Am

WESTERN-WORLD 20 MAY 1850

From Liverpool

NAMES OF PASSENGERS	AGE	SEX	OCCUPATIONS	DATE PORT SHIP
DUNCAN, Barbara	25	F	Unknown	20Ma02Kg
James	.00	M	Infant	20Ma02Kg
CARNEY, Patt	18	M	Sawer	20Ma02Kg
John	20	M	Sawer	20Ma02Kg
Alice	24	F	Unknown	20Ma02Kg
BOUGHAN, John	20	M	Nailer	20Ma02Kg
FINN, Cath.	19	F	Spinster	20Ma02Kg
HACKETT, Patt	25	M	Laborer	20Ma02Kg
GALLAGHER, Ann	22	F	Servant	20Ma02Kg
Michl.	18	M	Laborer	20Ma02Kg
COONEY, Ann	20	F	Housekeeper	20Ma02Kg
MURRAY, Ellen	20	F	Spinster	20Ma02Kg
MANNING, Ann	25	F	Servant	20Ma02Kg
COULSIN, Wm.	46	M	Merchant	20Ma02Kg
Mary-A.	45	F	Unknown	20Ma02Kg
KELLY, Chas.	55	M	Laborer	20Ma02Kg
Rose	21	F	Unknown	20Ma02Kg
Cathe.	13	F	Unknown	20Ma02Kg
Mary	11	F	Unknown	20Ma02Kg
Hannah	7	F	Child	20Ma02Kg
ENGLISH, Patt	35	M	Laborer	20Ma02Kg
LOUGHNEY, U-Mrs.	28	F	Servant	20Ma02Kg
LOYNE, Peter	42	M	Farmer	20Ma02Kg
James	23	M	Flabr	20Ma02Kg
Francis	18	M	Flabr	20Ma02Kg
Jane	22	F	Spinster	20Ma02Kg
Eliza	12	F	Unknown	20Ma02Kg
Betty	50	F	Unknown	20Ma02Kg
Robt.	16	M	Laborer	20Ma02Kg
MAGUGIN, Frank Died-At-Sea	55	M	Unknown	20Ma02Kg
Ellen	20	F	Unknown	20Ma02Kg
GRAHAM, James	45	M	Farmer	20Ma02Kg
Betty	40	F	Unknown	20Ma02Kg
Edwd.	21	M	Laborer	20Ma02Kg
Mary-A.	17	F	Unknown	20Ma02Kg
Eliza	15	F	Unknown	20Ma02Kg
Jane	13	F	Unknown	20Ma02Kg
HUST, James	30	M	Farmer	20Ma02Kg
GRAHAM, Wm.	6	M	Child	20Ma02Kg
Hugh	9	M	Child	20Ma02Kg
James	7	M	Child	20Ma02Kg
Beck	6	M	Child	20Ma02Kg
LAMBERT, John	37	M	Groom	20Ma02Kg
COULTER, Eliza	22	F	Spinster	20Ma02Kg
MCGOLDRICK, Ellen	16	F	Servant	20Ma02Kg
MOORE, Lewis	20	M	Laborer	20Ma02Kg
GAFFNEY, Mary	26	F	Servant	20Ma02Kg
LEE, Honora	20	F	Spinster	20Ma02Kg
KINNALLY, Patt	29	M	Laborer	20Ma02Kg
POLLIN, Cathe.	30	F	Servant	20Ma02Kg

NAMES OF PASSENGERS	AGE	SEX	OCCUPATIONS	DATE PORT SHIP
DOOLIN, Ann	25	F	Servant	20Ma02Kg
FLYNN, Thos.	60	M	Farmer	20Ma02Kg
GAROIN, Cathe.	20	F	Servant	20Ma02Kg
MCQUIN, Wm.	48	M	Farmer	20Ma02Kg
Alicin	30	F	Unknown	20Ma02Kg
James	13	M	Unknown	20Ma02Kg
Malcolm	10	M	Unknown	20Ma02Kg
Jane	7	F	Child	20Ma02Kg
George	5	M	Child	20Ma02Kg
DONNELLY, John	45	M	Laborer	20Ma02Kg
COSGROVE, Ann	50	F	Spinster	20Ma02Kg
RAFFERTY, Nancy	16	F	Servant	20Ma02Kg
AGNEW, Peter	50	M	Laborer	20Ma02Kg
Ann	50	F	Unknown	20Ma02Kg
STACEY, Mary	16	F	Servant	20Ma02Kg
Mick	5	M	Child	20Ma02Kg
FOX, Ann	50	F	Housekeeper	20Ma02Kg
Biddy	16	F	Unknown	20Ma02Kg
ROBINSON, William	00	M	Unknown	20Ma02Kg
MCCAHEY, Hugh	20	M	Laborer	20Ma02Kg
MCCABE, U-Mr.	25	M	Farmer	20Ma02Kg
U-Mrs.	20	F	Unknown	20Ma02Kg
Ann	16	F	Unknown	20Ma02Kg
TWEEDY, U-Mrs.	20	F	Housekeeper	20Ma02Kg
Wm.	1	M	Child	20Ma02Kg
John	.00	M	Infant	20Ma02Kg
Died-At-Sea				
FARRELLY, Mary	8	F	Sister	20Ma02Kg
CONNELL, John	24	M	Carpenter	20Ma02Kg
BUTLER, Edwd.	33	M	Laborer	20Ma02Kg
LAWLER, Francis	35	M	Farmer	20Ma02Kg
HOARE, Lawce.	21	M	Laborer	20Ma02Kg
AUSTIN, Cathe.	20	F	Servant	20Ma02Kg
HICKEY, Cathe.	20	F	Servant	20Ma02Kg
SHANNEN, Bridgt.	18	F	Spinster	20Ma02Kg
NAUGHTON, Billy	27	M	Laborer	20Ma02Kg
GAFFNEY, Mary	20	F	Spinster	20Ma02Kg
RILEY, Thos.	14	M	Laborer	20Ma02Kg
MCKENNA, Mary	16	F	Spinster	20Ma02Kg
HENRY, Alexr.	22	M	Farmer	20Ma02Kg
Margt.	18	F	Unknown	20Ma02Kg
STEINS, Sarah	18	F	Spinster	20Ma02Kg
HARKINS, Eliza	18	F	Spinster	20Ma02Kg
GALLIGAN, Michl.	25	M	Laborer	20Ma02Kg
Julia	40	F	Spinster	20Ma02Kg
HANNON, Wm.	35	M	Farmer	20Ma02Kg
LEARY, John	30	M	Farmer	20Ma02Kg
Ann	24	F	Farmer	20Ma02Kg
FLYNN, Patt	22	M	Laborer	20Ma02Kg
ROBINSON, Christr.	25	M	Farmer	20Ma02Kg
Died-At-Sea				
REILLY, Robt.	20	M	Farmer	20Ma02Kg
DOYLE, Bridgt.	40	F	Servant	20Ma02Kg
Ann	13	F	Unknown	20Ma02Kg
Thos.	12	M	Unknown	20Ma02Kg
John	9	M	Child	20Ma02Kg
LENNORD, Michl.	24	M	Carpenter	20Ma02Kg
WILLIAMSON, John	43	M	Laborer	20Ma02Kg
TITTER, Thos.	25	M	Laborer	20Ma02Kg
MCCABE, John	40	M	Laborer	20Ma02Kg
FINNEN, Ann	34	F	Laborer	20Ma02Kg
MCNAMARA, James	25	M	Farmer	20Ma02Kg
Ann	22	F	Unknown	20Ma02Kg
FINNEN, Thos.	35	M	Laborer	20Ma02Kg
MCNAMARA, Patt	.00	M	Infant	20Ma02Kg
CASEY, Michl.	20	M	Laborer	20Ma02Kg
Margt.	24	F	Unknown	20Ma02Kg
MCCLERTICK, Alexr.	25	M	Laborer	20Ma02Kg
Mary	60	F	Unknown	20Ma02Kg
TULLY, Wm.	27	M	Laborer	20Ma02Kg
REILLY, Edwd.	19	M	Servant	20Ma02Kg
REEGAN, Margt.	24	F	Servant	20Ma02Kg
MCDERMOTT, Cathe.	13	F	Unknown	20Ma02Kg
WALKER, Henry	12	M	Son	20Ma02Kg
Robt.	10	M	Unknown	20Ma02Kg

NAMES OF PASSENGERS	AGE	SEX	OCCUPATIONS	DATE PORT SHIP
LILLY, George	34	M	Laborer	20Ma02Kg
HARLEY, Patt	18	M	Laborer	20Ma02Kg
MCKENNA, James	20	M	Laborer	20Ma02Kg
Francis	18	M	Laborer	20Ma02Kg
TRACEY, James	28	M	Merchant	20Ma02Kg
KANE, Mary	60	F	Servant	20Ma02Kg
GANNEN, Patt	18	M	Blacksmith	20Ma02Kg
WHITEHEAD, David	30	M	Laborer	20Ma02Kg
Biddy	30	F	Unknown	20Ma02Kg
BROSLEY, Wm.	30	M	Flabr	20Ma02Kg
WHITEHEAD, Ralph	5	M	Child	20Ma02Kg
Mary	4	F	Child	20Ma02Kg
John	2	M	Child	20Ma02Kg
MARTIN, Patt	23	M	Laborer	20Ma02Kg
MACKMONIGH, Margt.	18	F	Servant	20Ma02Kg
MARKEY, Thos.	25	M	Laborer	20Ma02Kg
John	24	M	Laborer	20Ma02Kg
MCDONALD, Ann	15	F	Servant	20Ma02Kg
Mary	20	F	Servant	20Ma02Kg
SUMERVILLE, James	40	M	Farmer	20Ma02Kg
Margt.	40	F	Unknown	20Ma02Kg
Martha	11	F	Unknown	20Ma02Kg
Wm.	8	M	Child	20Ma02Kg
James	6	M	Child	20Ma02Kg
MARTIN, Margt.	21	F	Servant	20Ma02Kg
MCGAHEN, Michl.	24	M	Farmer	20Ma02Kg
GANNON, Martin	23	M	Laborer	20Ma02Kg
OCONNER, Teddy	28	M	Laborer	20Ma02Kg
DUFFY, Michl.	23	M	Laborer	20Ma02Kg
LAWLER, Mary	27	F	Spinster	20Ma02Kg
RAMSBOTTOM, Richd.	60	M	Laborer	20Ma02Kg
John	24	M	Laborer	20Ma02Kg
Cathe.	20	F	Unknown	20Ma02Kg
Ann	18	F	Unknown	20Ma02Kg
BROPHY, Margt.	20	F	Servant	20Ma02Kg
Winifred	18	F	Servant	20Ma02Kg
CARTY, Patt	25	M	Laborer	20Ma02Kg
KELLY, Thos.	21	M	Laborer	20Ma02Kg
ODONNELL, Ann	25	F	Servant	20Ma02Kg
MCGARR, Peter	45	M	Laborer	20Ma02Kg
Sally	50	F	Unknown	20Ma02Kg
Owen	18	M	Laborer	20Ma02Kg
Biddy	18	F	Unknown	20Ma02Kg
Thos.	20	M	Laborer	20Ma02Kg
FITZPATRICK, Margt.	47	F	Housekeeper	20Ma02Kg
Ann	23	F	Housekeeper	20Ma02Kg
DUNN, Timy.	30	M	Laborer	20Ma02Kg
Julia	28	F	Unknown	20Ma02Kg
PHELAN, Maria	16	F	Servant	20Ma02Kg
MARK, Cathe.	30	F	Servant	20Ma02Kg
NOWLAN, U-Mrs.	32	F	Wife	20Ma02Kg
Mary	4	F	Child	20Ma02Kg
Henry	3	M	Child	20Ma02Kg
Teresa	.00	F	Infant	20Ma02Kg
CURLEY, Michl.	25	M	Sawer	20Ma02Kg
MULLEN, Sally	20	F	Servant	20Ma02Kg
HARRISON, Mary	28	F	Servant	20Ma02Kg
LOWRY, Peter	25	M	Laborer	20Ma02Kg
CASEY, Margt.	18	F	Servant	20Ma02Kg
Maria	15	F	Servant	20Ma02Kg
HUSSEY, Bridget	16	F	Servant	20Ma02Kg
MURTOGH, Thos.	30	M	Laborer	20Ma02Kg
SCULLY, Patt	30	M	Laborer	20Ma02Kg
BYRNE, Luke	49	M	Farmer	20Ma02Kg
HARNETT, Thos.	26	M	Farmer	20Ma02Kg
KELLY, Jane	25	F	Servant	20Ma02Kg
MURPHY, Hugh	34	M	Joiner	20Ma02Kg
GARRIGAN, Lawrence	16	M	Laborer	20Ma02Kg
Jos.	13	M	Laborer	20Ma02Kg
Terence	11	M	Laborer	20Ma02Kg
HEANY, Danl.	18	M	Lnbl	20Ma02Kg
Danl.	20	M	Farmer	20Ma02Kg
MCKERNAN, Jas.	18	M	Farmer	20Ma02Kg
BOYLE, Jas.	19	M	Bleacher	20Ma02Kg
KENNY, Jas.	19	M	Farmer	20Ma02Kg

NAMES OF PASSENGERS	AGE	SEX	OCCUPATIONS	DATE PORT SHIP
HODGE, Robt.	25	M	Carpenter	20Ma02Kg
FRANCIS, Saml.	19	M	Laborer	20Ma02Kg
HOOD, Hugh	19	M	Laborer	20Ma02Kg
LUCAS, Hugh	19	M	Schm	20Ma02Kg
GIBB, Jas.	16	M	Laborer	20Ma02Kg
Robt.	21	M	Laborer	20Ma02Kg
KIERNAN, Ann	24	F	Servant	20Ma02Kg
NAUGHTON, Ann	66	F	Housekeeper	20Ma02Kg
FINEN, Patt	6	M	Child	20Ma02Kg
CUNNINGHAM, Michl.	21	M	Laborer	20Ma02Kg
John	19	M	Laborer	20Ma02Kg
PARSONS, Winny	22	F	Servant	20Ma02Kg
OBRADY, Patt	31	M	Merchant	20Ma02Kg
KIERNAN, Ann	28	F	Servant	20Ma02Kg
ROURKE, John	14	M	Laborer	20Ma02Kg
NEIL, Ann	22	F	Wife	20Ma02Kg
Mary	.00	F	Infant	20Ma02Kg
TEENY, Jas.	22	M	Laborer	20Ma02Kg
GUINEN, Michl.	39	M	Laborer	20Ma02Kg
BURN, Bridgt.	18	F	Niece	20Ma02Kg
Eliza	16	F	Unknown	20Ma02Kg
CALHOUN, Jane	20	F	Servant	20Ma02Kg
TOPHAM, Ruth	22	F	Farmer	20Ma02Kg
John	52	M	Unknown	20Ma02Kg
Pheobe	24	F	Unknown	20Ma02Kg
Ann	20	F	Unknown	20Ma02Kg
Jos.	17	M	Unknown	20Ma02Kg
George	14	M	Unknown	20Ma02Kg
TOY, Bernard	28	M	Servant	20Ma02Kg
MURPHY, Ann	18	F	Servant	20Ma02Kg
TEMPLE, Eliza	22	F	Servant	20Ma02Kg
SHIELDS, Cath.	20	F	Servant	20Ma02Kg
John	19	M	Laborer	20Ma02Kg
RONEY, Mary	30	F	Servant	20Ma02Kg
FARRELL, Mary	16	F	Servant	20Ma02Kg
MCALLEN, Jas.	26	M	Shoemaker	20Ma02Kg
Sarah	22	F	Unknown	20Ma02Kg
Rose	20	F	Servant	20Ma02Kg
MCQUADE, Patt	45	M	Laborer	20Ma02Kg
John	49	M	Laborer	20Ma02Kg
MCQUIRE, Chas.	55	M	Carpenter	20Ma02Kg
WARREN, Chas.	30	M	Farmer	20Ma02Kg
Ann	30	F	Unknown	20Ma02Kg
Jas.	3	M	Child	20Ma02Kg
Elesha	.00	F	Infant	20Ma02Kg
BRANNON, Mary-A.	20	F	Dressmaker	20Ma02Kg
TITTER, Jas.	20	M	Laborer	20Ma02Kg
DENNAN, Jas.	22	M	Laborer	20Ma02Kg
NORMELL, Simon	35	M	Laborer	20Ma02Kg
Biddy	10	F	Unknown	20Ma02Kg
TEE, Patt	22	M	Laborer	20Ma02Kg
HALL, Elizth.	35	F	Wife	20Ma02Kg
BRACKEN, Patt	22	M	Laborer	20Ma02Kg
Jas.	19	M	Laborer	20Ma02Kg
Michl.	16	M	Laborer	20Ma02Kg
Ann	14	F	Servant	20Ma02Kg
Cath	23	F	Servant	20Ma02Kg
WILSON, John	28	M	Groom	20Ma02Kg
MORRISON, Wm.	24	M	Joiner	20Ma02Kg
CAIN, John	19	M	Joiner	20Ma02Kg
GILL, Thos.	19	M	Laborer	20Ma02Kg
MANGIN, Julia	24	F	Servant	20Ma02Kg
PERRICK, Mary	18	F	Servant	20Ma02Kg
BRADY, Mary	25	F	Servant	20Ma02Kg
COIL, Chas.	41	M	Laborer	20Ma02Kg
Mary	13	F	Servant	20Ma02Kg
COOKE, Patt	12	M	Servant	20Ma02Kg
MCCOLLIN, Danl.	18	M	Laborer	20Ma02Kg
John	23	M	Laborer	20Ma02Kg
Patt	12	M	Laborer	20Ma02Kg
BIRTHNIGHON, Winny	20	F	Servant	20Ma02Kg
MCLOUGHLIN, Patt	23	M	Laborer	20Ma02Kg
CANNON, Honora	16	F	Servant	20Ma02Kg
CAMPBELL, Robt.	20	M	Laborer	20Ma02Kg
FINN, Mich.	50	M	Laborer	20Ma02Kg

NAMES OF PASSENGERS	AGE	SEX	OCCUPATIONS	DATE PORT SHIP
FINN, Etty	50	F	Unknown	20Ma02Kg
Margt.	24	F	Unknown	20Ma02Kg
Peter	23	M	Unknown	20Ma02Kg
Biddy	20	F	Unknown	20Ma02Kg
Wm.	18	M	Unknown	20Ma02Kg
Henry	17	M	Unknown	20Ma02Kg
Polly	11	F	Unknown	20Ma02Kg
Jas.	4	M	Child	20Ma02Kg
QUIN, R.	52	M	Laborer	20Ma02Kg
KEAGAN, Bridget	19	F	Servant	20Ma02Kg
DONOHOE, Mary	20	F	Servant	20Ma02Kg
Margt.	21	F	Servant	20Ma02Kg
POOLE, Honora	17	F	Servant	20Ma02Kg
MCMAHON, Sylvester	30	M	Cooper	20Ma02Kg
U	30	F	Unknown	20Ma02Kg
Phillip	25	M	Laborer	20Ma02Kg
BURNS, Richd.	22	M	Unknown	20Ma02Kg
Cathn.	21	F	Unknown	20Ma02Kg
CAMPBELL, Cath.	28	F	Servant	20Ma02Kg
MCGRAY, Michl.	26	M	Laborer	20Ma02Kg
Peter	20	M	Laborer	20Ma02Kg
MCMAHON, Biddy	40	F	Servant	20Ma02Kg
Barny	15	M	Servant	20Ma02Kg
MCANANY, Patt	35	M	Laborer	20Ma02Kg
CRAWLEY, Nic	21	M	Laborer	20Ma02Kg
HULL, Betty	20	F	Servant	20Ma02Kg
MCGUINESS, Lawrence	16	M	Laborer	20Ma02Kg
QUINLAN, Jane	30	F	Servant	20Ma02Kg
HUGHES, Mary	40	F	Servant	20Ma02Kg
Eliza	18	F	Servant	20Ma02Kg
Annie	15	F	Servant	20Ma02Kg
John	16	M	Laborer	20Ma02Kg
WELLS, John	24	M	Weaver	20Ma02Kg
ROSS, Wm.	20	M	Weaver	20Ma02Kg
Jas.	26	M	Miller	20Ma02Kg
BAILIE, Hugh	21	M	Merchant	20Ma02Kg
MCCHESNEY, Margt.	22	F	Servant	20Ma02Kg
SHANKS, Margt.	21	F	Servant	20Ma02Kg
NORTON, Mary	18	F	Servant	20Ma02Kg
HUSTON, Martha	18	F	Servant	20Ma02Kg
Elizth.	17	F	Dressmaker	20Ma02Kg
DONOHOE, Thos.	30	M	Laborer	20Ma02Kg
MCENERNY, Cath.	20	F	Servant	20Ma02Kg
RILEY, Patt	18	M	Laborer	20Ma02Kg
MCCORMICK, Elizth.	20	F	Servant	20Ma02Kg
GREG, Abbey	21	F	Servant	20Ma02Kg
OREILLY, Patt	52	M	Farmer	20Ma02Kg
Eliza	32	F	Unknown	20Ma02Kg
Wm.	8	M	Child	20Ma02Kg
Mary	5	F	Child	20Ma02Kg
TAYLOR, Thos.	30	M	Merchant	20Ma02Kg
BRANAN, Cath.	28	F	Wife	20Ma02Kg
Mary-A.	7	F	Child	20Ma02Kg
BLAKE, John	36	M	Laborer	20Ma02Kg
FAY, Bridget	13	F	Servant	20Ma02Kg
FARLEY, Ann	16	F	Servant	20Ma02Kg
MURPHY, Thos.	20	M	Laborer	20Ma02Kg
Mary	40	F	Unknown	20Ma02Kg
Mary	17	F	Unknown	20Ma02Kg
Nic	11	M	Unknown	20Ma02Kg
John	9	M	Child	20Ma02Kg
FITZPATRICK, Susan	20	F	Servant	20Ma02Kg
SMITH, Michl.	20	M	Laborer	20Ma02Kg
MCCAHILL, Wm.	21	M	Laborer	20Ma02Kg
SHERIDAN, Patt	20	M	Laborer	20Ma02Kg
Mary	20	F	Unknown	20Ma02Kg
TIMMONS, Robt.	29	M	Laborer	20Ma02Kg
FAHEN, Jas.	20	M	Laborer	20Ma02Kg
Eliza	30	F	Unknown	20Ma02Kg
Johanna	7	F	Child	20Ma02Kg
HINEY, Michl.	28	M	Laborer	20Ma02Kg
Cath.	16	F	Unknown	20Ma02Kg
BRERETON, Jas.	16	M	Son	20Ma02Kg
Mary	19	F	Daughter	20Ma02Kg
BRYAN, Jas.	21	M	Carpenter	20Ma02Kg

NAMES OF PASSENGERS	AGE	SEX	OCCUPATIONS	DATE PORT SHIP
BRYAN, Mary	18	F	Unknown	20Ma02Kg
Thos.	.00	M	Infant	20Ma02Kg
Bridgt.	29	F	Spinster	20Ma02Kg
EMMET, Patt	25	M	Laborer	20Ma02Kg
BRENNAN, Henry	25	M	Laborer	20Ma02Kg
ROWE, Michl.	24	M	Laborer	20Ma02Kg
NOWLAN, Tim	36	M	Laborer	20Ma02Kg
Margt.	30	F	Unknown	20Ma02Kg
Thos.	40	M	Fsvnt	20Ma02Kg
Michl.	50	M	Fsvnt	20Ma02Kg
LANGAN, Patt	30	M	Laborer	20Ma02Kg
HUTCHINGSON, Elizth.	18	F	Dressmaker	20Ma02Kg
EAGAN, Patt	25	M	Laborer	20Ma02Kg
MOLEY, Michl.	24	M	Laborer	20Ma02Kg
WARD, Jas.	23	M	Laborer	20Ma02Kg
GALLAGHER, Margt.	18	F	Servant	20Ma02Kg
BUTLER, Edwd.	30	M	Laborer	20Ma02Kg
Ann	21	F	Unknown	20Ma02Kg
HUGHS, Francis	30	M	Fsvnt	20Ma02Kg
Michl.	52	M	Laborer	20Ma02Kg
THOMPSON, Ann	13	F	Unknown	20Ma02Kg
CROGAN, Patt	20	M	Laborer	20Ma02Kg
Mary	22	F	Servant	20Ma02Kg
THOMPSON, Mary	13	F	Servant	20Ma02Kg
MCADAM, Margt.	23	F	Servant	20Ma02Kg
GORMAN, Julia	7	F	Child	20Ma02Kg
DOWNEY, John	40	M	Butcher	20Ma02Kg
GARVIN, Norry	40	F	Servant	20Ma02Kg
John	9	M	Child	20Ma02Kg
Patt	5	M	Child	20Ma02Kg
BEGLEY, Ellen	20	F	Servant	20Ma02Kg
Mary	20	F	Servant	20Ma02Kg
BROWN, Mary	16	F	Daughter	20Ma02Kg
Margt.	.06	F	Infant	20Ma02Kg
MCMULLEN, Thos.	18	M	Laborer	20Ma02Kg
MARSHALL, Keron	17	F	Laborer	20Ma02Kg
John	14	M	Laborer	20Ma02Kg
KIERNAN, Cath.	48	F	Housekeeper	20Ma02Kg
Cath.	17	F	Servant	20Ma02Kg
SHEEN, Jas.	22	M	Laborer	20Ma02Kg
FARRELLY, Mic	23	M	Laborer	20Ma02Kg
MASTERSON, John	20	M	Laborer	20Ma02Kg
Patt	10	M	Laborer	20Ma02Kg
KIERNON, Jas.	17	M	Laborer	20Ma02Kg
MULDOWNEY, Margt.	40	F	Housekeeper	20Ma02Kg
Edwd.	9	M	Child	20Ma02Kg
FAHEY, Margt.	16	F	Servant	20Ma02Kg
DAHLY, Jas.	26	M	Laborer	20Ma02Kg
CUMMINS, Martin	20	M	Laborer	20Ma02Kg
Jos.	19	M	Laborer	20Ma02Kg
LOGAN, Peter	14	M	Son	20Ma02Kg
Edwd.	11	M	Son	20Ma02Kg
Cath.	15	F	Servant	20Ma02Kg
FARLEY, Ann	20	F	Servant	20Ma02Kg
Rose	30	F	Servant	20Ma02Kg
Hugh	26	M	Gdnr	20Ma02Kg
Mary	20	F	Servant	20Ma02Kg
BROWN, Johanna	30	F	Servant	20Ma02Kg
Bridget	7	F	Child	20Ma02Kg
Mary	6	F	Child	20Ma02Kg
LEAVY, Chas.	30	M	Laborer	20Ma02Kg
ORR, Jos.	28	M	Farmer	20Ma02Kg
Jos.	19	M	Merchant	20Ma02Kg
SCULLY, Honora	20	F	Dressmaker	20Ma02Kg
FUTHILL, John	20	M	Merchant	20Ma02Kg
MOUNTAIN, Henry	18	M	Laborer	20Ma02Kg
BEGGY, Thos.	16	M	Laborer	20Ma02Kg
QUIN, John	40	M	Laborer	20Ma02Kg
GALLAGHER, Felix	20	M	Laborer	20Ma02Kg
MCNAMARA, Micl.	25	M	Laborer	20Ma02Kg
REGAN, Patt	9	M	Child	20Ma02Kg
NUGENT, Richd.	60	M	Farmer	20Ma02Kg
Cath.	58	F	Unknown	20Ma02Kg
Patt	21	M	Farmer	20Ma02Kg
MCCAFFREY, Betty	18	r	Servant	20Ma02Kg

NAMES OF PASSENGERS	AGE	SEX	OCCUPATIONS	DATE PORT SHIP
CARRIGAN, Margt.	40	F	Servant	20Ma02Kg
MCGRATH, Thos.	32	M	Laborer	20Ma02Kg
COYLE, Micl.	19	M	Laborer	20Ma02Kg
Nic	22	M	Laborer	20Ma02Kg
Bridget	45	F	Housekeeper	20Ma02Kg
BRADY, Ann	19	F	Servant	20Ma02Kg
GROVES, Mary	22	F	Servant	20Ma02Kg
DONOVAN, Jim	25	M	Laborer	20Ma02Kg
Danl.	22	M	Laborer	20Ma02Kg
Jos.	24	M	Laborer	20Ma02Kg
TULLIVAN, Mary	20	F	Servant	20Ma02Kg
TOOKEY, Keron	40	F	Laborer	20Ma02Kg
WELSH, John	24	M	Laborer	20Ma02Kg
MERIDITH, Thos.	25	M	Merchant	20Ma02Kg
GIBSON, Mary-O.	18	F	Shirt Maker	20Ma02Kg
CONNOR, David	29	M	Laborer	20Ma02Kg
Mary	28	F	Unknown	20Ma02Kg
BARRETT, John	24	M	Laborer	20Ma02Kg
CONNOR, Thos.	.00	M	Infant	20Ma02Kg
KIELLY, David	40	M	Laborer	20Ma02Kg
Ansty	40	M	Laborer	20Ma02Kg
PUGOTT, Ellen	13	F	Servant	20Ma02Kg
REILLY, Richd.	80	M	Unknown	20Ma02Kg
Bridget	10	F	Unknown	20Ma02Kg
Mary	6	F	Child	20Ma02Kg
Ellen	4	F	Child	20Ma02Kg
David	.00	M	Infant	20Ma02Kg
HOWARD, Maurice	20	M	Laborer	20Ma02Kg
DUGAN, Ellen	8	F	Servant	20Ma02Kg
CONNOR, Thos.	35	M	Laborer	20Ma02Kg
DONOVAN, Cath.	22	F	Servant	20Ma02Kg
JACKSON, Elizth.	30	F	Housekeeper	20Ma02Kg
HESLOP, Sarah	28	F	Servant	20Ma02Kg
SNELL, Mary	26	F	Servant	20Ma02Kg
KENNY, Con.	21	M	Laborer	20Ma02Kg
REILLY, Danl.	20	M	Peddler	20Ma02Kg
MAYLER, John	22	M	Farmer	20Ma02Kg
BRYANN, Patt	27	M	Miller	20Ma02Kg
CONNOLLY, Michl.	35	M	Laborer	20Ma02Kg
THORNTON, Michl.	22	M	Ploughman	20Ma02Kg
POWER, Danl.	32	M	Laborer	20Ma02Kg
LANIGAN, Cath.	12	F	Servant	20Ma02Kg
GRIFFIN, Rachael	22	F	Unknown	20Ma02Kg
MATHEWS, Henry	15	M	Unknown	20Ma02Kg
HANDY, Wm.	30	M	Solicitor	20Ma02Kg
Rebecca	25	F	Unknown	20Ma02Kg
COLLISS, Fanny	12	F	Unknown	20Ma02Kg
HANDY, Jane	1	F	Child	20Ma02Kg
CLARK, Bessy	25	F	Servant	20Ma02Kg
GOING, Harvey	24	M	Farmer	20Ma02Kg
Fanny	20	F	Unknown	20Ma02Kg
Sarah	19	F	Unknown	20Ma02Kg

ADLER 20 MAY 1850

From Glasgow

NAMES OF PASSENGERS	AGE	SEX	OCCUPATIONS	DATE PORT SHIP
KAIN, John	25	M	Laborer	20Ma21Kk
Catherine	22	F	Unknown	20Ma21Kk
Bridget	20	F	Unknown	20Ma21Kk
Ann	22	F	Unknown	20Ma21Kk
PUCK, John	30	M	Laborer	20Ma21Kk
WELSH, Anna	21	F	Unknown	20Ma21Kk
MCNALLY, Mary	26	F	Unknown	20Ma21Kk
MCBRIDE, James	26	M	Laborer	20Ma21Kk
MCGRUTTAN, Jenkin	50	M	Unknown	20Ma21Kk
Sarah	52	F	Unknown	20Ma21Kk
Sarah	18	F	Unknown	20Ma21Kk
Mary	15	F	Unknown	20Ma21Kk

NAMES OF PASSENGERS	AGE	SEX	OCCUPATIONS	DATE PORT SHIP
MCGRUTTAN, Nancy	10	F	Unknown	20Ma21Kk
Henry	7	M	Child	20Ma21Kk
MCNEALL, Archibald	48	M	Unknown	20Ma21Kk
Rose	50	F	Unknown	20Ma21Kk
Mary	22	F	Unknown	20Ma21Kk
Ann	19	F	Unknown	20Ma21Kk
John	24	M	Unknown	20Ma21Kk
Catherine	24	F	Unknown	20Ma21Kk
MCGEE, Charles	27	M	Unknown	20Ma21Kk
MCDOWELL, Francis	24	M	Unknown	20Ma21Kk
Margaret	60	F	Unknown	20Ma21Kk
MCBRIDE, Rose	19	F	Unknown	20Ma21Kk
MCNEALL, Mary-Ann	18	F	Unknown	20Ma21Kk
FOX, Ann	24	F	Unknown	20Ma21Kk
QUIN, Ned.	37	M	Laborer	20Ma21Kk
OLONE, Michael	20	M	Unknown	20Ma21Kk
John	24	M	Unknown	20Ma21Kk
CONAGHAN, Michael	19	M	Unknown	20Ma21Kk
Pat	24	M	Unknown	20Ma21Kk
MITCHELL, Michael	22	M	Unknown	20Ma21Kk
CAILIN, Catherine	23	M	Unknown	20Ma21Kk
DONALDSON, William	45	M	Unknown	20Ma21Kk
Martha	41	F	Unknown	20Ma21Kk
James	15	M	Unknown	20Ma21Kk
Sarah-Jane	10	F	Unknown	20Ma21Kk
SPROUL, Jonathan	22	M	Unknown	20Ma21Kk
Eliza	18	F	Unknown	20Ma21Kk
PATERSON, Ellen	19	F	Unknown	20Ma21Kk
QUIGG, David	20	M	Unknown	20Ma21Kk
CAIN, Mary	17	F	Unknown	20Ma21Kk
HAGAN, John	20	M	Unknown	20Ma21Kk
Susan	20	F	Unknown	20Ma21Kk
Rose	18	F	Unknown	20Ma21Kk
MCKEEVEN, William	20	M	Laborer	20Ma21Kk
HILL, Rose	16	F	Unknown	20Ma21Kk
ONEIL, John	21	M	Unknown	20Ma21Kk
MCCORMICK, Henry	21	M	Unknown	20Ma21Kk
GALLAGHER, Owen	35	M	Laborer	20Ma21Kk
ODONNEL, Conely	30	M	Laborer	20Ma21Kk
GALLAGHER, Conely	19	M	Laborer	20Ma21Kk
CANNING, James	24	M	Laborer	20Ma21Kk
James	20	M	Laborer	20Ma21Kk
HEARST, Margaret	18	F	Unknown	20Ma21Kk
WORTHINGTON, Eliza	22	F	Unknown	20Ma21Kk
LITTLE, Mary	30	F	Unknown	20Ma21Kk
ODONNELL, Anne	36	F	Unknown	20Ma21Kk
MCALEANY, Jane	20	F	Unknown	20Ma21Kk
LINDSEY, Elenor	60	F	Unknown	20Ma21Kk
Patrick	30	M	Laborer	20Ma21Kk
William	14	M	Unknown	20Ma21Kk
GALLAGHER, Mary	20	F	Unknown	20Ma21Kk
KELLY, John	28	M	Unknown	20Ma21Kk

ABEONA 20 MAY 1850

From Liverpool

NAMES OF PASSENGERS	AGE	SEX	OCCUPATIONS	DATE PORT SHIP
SMITH, Owen	30	M	Laborer	20Ma02Da
MILLS, James	50	M	Laborer	20Ma02Da
PENDLETON, Jane	46	F	Laborer	20Ma02Da
George	10	M	Laborer	20Ma02Da
William	7	M	Child	20Ma02Da
REILLY, Cornelius	22	M	Laborer	20Ma02Da
Catherine	20	F	Laborer	20Ma02Da
POLLOCK, John	23	M	Laborer	20Ma02Da
MITCHELL, Margt.	18	F	Laborer	20Ma02Da
SOMERVILLE, Thomas	12	M	Laborer	20Ma02Da
GORT, Rachael	28	F	Laborer	20Ma02Da
SAVERY, James	21	M	Laborer	20Ma02Da
ADAIR, Sarah	20	F	Laborer	20Ma02Da
SMITH, Barth.	18	M	Laborer	20Ma02Da
Mary	20	F	Unknown	20Ma02Da
HARRIS, Henry	30	M	Unknown	20Ma02Da
Caroline	28	F	Unknown	20Ma02Da
EVANS, George-O.	21	M	Unknown	20Ma02Da
COOK, Richard	40	M	Unknown	20Ma02Da
Mary-Ann	40	F	Unknown	20Ma02Da
Enock	16	M	Unknown	20Ma02Da
Maria	14	F	Unknown	20Ma02Da
Joseph	9	M	Child	20Ma02Da
James-Wm.	5	M	Child	20Ma02Da
John	3	M	Child	20Ma02Da
Sarah-Ann	2	F	Child	20Ma02Da
Cathe.	.00	F	Infant	20Ma02Da
REILLY, Owen	18	M	Unknown	20Ma02Da
HEALY, Patrick	15	M	Unknown	20Ma02Da
JONES, Mary	46	F	Unknown	20Ma02Da
DAVIS, John	21	M	Unknown	20Ma02Da
Ann	20	F	Unknown	20Ma02Da
Mary-A.	.00	F	Infant	20Ma02Da
JONES, Thomas	23	M	Unknown	20Ma02Da
Mary	21	F	Unknown	20Ma02Da
HENRY, John	21	M	Unknown	20Ma02Da
J.	16	M	Unknown	20Ma02Da
George	12	M	Unknown	20Ma02Da
Obedial	10	F	Unknown	20Ma02Da
Richard	8	M	Child	20Ma02Da
Martha	6	F	Child	20Ma02Da
FINEGAN, Patrick	20	M	Unknown	20Ma02Da
HOLMES, Thomas	20	M	Unknown	20Ma02Da
BROWN, Robert	40	M	Unknown	20Ma02Da
RYAN, Edmund	20	M	Laborer	20Ma02Da
Michael	24	M	Unknown	20Ma02Da
William	20	M	Unknown	20Ma02Da
Mary	21	F	Unknown	20Ma02Da
COY, Robert	42	M	Unknown	20Ma02Da
U-Mrs.	35	F	Unknown	20Ma02Da
Thomas	13	M	Unknown	20Ma02Da
Henry	10	M	Unknown	20Ma02Da
William	8	M	Child	20Ma02Da
Samuel	6	M	Child	20Ma02Da
Jane	3	F	Child	20Ma02Da
Francis	2	M	Child	20Ma02Da
WALZ, Connor	55	M	Unknown	20Ma02Da
Elizth.	40	F	Unknown	20Ma02Da
ILL, Frans.	21	F	Unknown	20Ma02Da
KETTLE, James	22	M	Unknown	20Ma02Da
MULLEN, James	26	M	Unknown	20Ma02Da
USHER, Isaih	26	M	Unknown	20Ma02Da
THORN, Edward	22	M	Unknown	20Ma02Da
NORMAN, John	40	M	Unknown	20Ma02Da
Cathe.	40	F	Unknown	20Ma02Da
Mary	15	F	Unknown	20Ma02Da
MERIDITH, John	40	M	Unknown	20Ma02Da
Mary	60	F	Unknown	20Ma02Da
Thomas	40	M	Unknown	20Ma02Da
Ann	25	F	Unknown	20Ma02Da
SHAW, Thomas	24	M	Unknown	20Ma02Da
BALDWICK, Isaac	28	M	Unknown	20Ma02Da
Hannah	25	F	Unknown	20Ma02Da
Fanny	13	F	Unknown	20Ma02Da
E.Jane	5	F	Child	20Ma02Da
Rachael	3	F	Child	20Ma02Da
Henry	2	M	Child	20Ma02Da
LADD, Maria	30	F	Unknown	20Ma02Da
Betsey	14	F	Unknown	20Ma02Da
Jane	7	F	Child	20Ma02Da
Mary-A.	5	F	Child	20Ma02Da
William	3	M	Child	20Ma02Da
Henry	.00	M	Infant	20Ma02Da
MCANALLY, John	30	M	Unknown	20Ma02Da
Mary	30	F	Unknown	20Ma02Da
Judith	30	F	Unknown	20Ma02Da
Joseph	20	M	Unknown	20Ma02Da

NAMES OF PASSENGERS	AGE	SEX	OCCUPATIONS	DATE PORT SHIP
MCANALLY, Thomas	20	M	Unknown	20Ma02Da
DUNNE, Patrick	7	M	Child	20Ma02Da
MCCONALY, Ellen	16	F	Unknown	20Ma02Da
CRAIG, Margt.	12	F	Unknown	20Ma02Da
CARROLL, Patk.	20	M	Unknown	20Ma02Da
GREENBANK, U-Mrs.	29	F	Unknown	20Ma02Da
Nelson	10	M	Unknown	20Ma02Da
RUNKER, William	20	M	Unknown	20Ma02Da
SMITH, John	26	M	Unknown	20Ma02Da
MCARDLE, Henry	21	M	Laborer	20Ma02Da
CURTIS, Patrick	24	M	Unknown	20Ma02Da
WOOLLERY, Samuel	24	M	Unknown	20Ma02Da
HARE, James	18	M	Unknown	20Ma02Da
Jane	40	F	Unknown	20Ma02Da
COURTNEY, Owen	30	M	Unknown	20Ma02Da
CONNOR, James	26	M	Unknown	20Ma02Da
Johanna	24	F	Unknown	20Ma02Da
JONES, William	16	M	Unknown	20Ma02Da
CAPRINDEAD, Jas.	24	M	Unknown	20Ma02Da
HINCHCLIFF, Francis	21	M	Unknown	20Ma02Da
HONLSTON, Joseph	40	M	Unknown	20Ma02Da
Cathe.	15	F	Unknown	20Ma02Da
SWEENY, John	30	M	Unknown	20Ma02Da
JACKSON, Henry	30	M	Unknown	20Ma02Da
Jane	24	F	Unknown	20Ma02Da
WALSH, Thomas	30	M	Unknown	20Ma02Da
NOONAN, Roger	30	M	Unknown	20Ma02Da
FITZPATRICK, William	23	M	Unknown	20Ma02Da
FEGAN, Bryan	40	M	Unknown	20Ma02Da
Thomas	12	M	Unknown	20Ma02Da
FITZPATRICK, Terence	27	M	Unknown	20Ma02Da
JOHNSON, William	29	M	Unknown	20Ma02Da
WATSON, David	28	M	Unknown	20Ma02Da
HENDERSON, Saml.	40	M	Unknown	20Ma02Da
Saml.	12	M	Unknown	20Ma02Da
Jane	25	F	Unknown	20Ma02Da
BYRNE, John	24	M	Unknown	20Ma02Da
DUGAN, Danl.	24	M	Unknown	20Ma02Da
COOGAN, James	24	M	Unknown	20Ma02Da
MURPHY, Ellen	30	F	Unknown	20Ma02Da
HILLARD, Peter	21	M	Unknown	20Ma02Da
ELLIS, Edward	24	M	Unknown	20Ma02Da
WILSON, John	18	M	Unknown	20Ma02Da
GEIGHAN, Philip	27	M	Unknown	20Ma02Da
Jane	26	F	Unknown	20Ma02Da
FEATHERSTIN, Eliza	30	F	Unknown	20Ma02Da
DELANY, Danl.	18	M	Unknown	20Ma02Da
Mary	22	F	Unknown	20Ma02Da
OSHEA, Margt.	28	F	Unknown	20Ma02Da
KILRONY, John	20	M	Unknown	20Ma02Da
SWEENEY, Ellen	22	F	Unknown	20Ma02Da
Ellen	.00	F	Infant	20Ma02Da
GREEN, Elizt.	44	F	Unknown	20Ma02Da
Elizt.	18	F	Unknown	20Ma02Da
CARROLL, John	26	M	Unknown	20Ma02Da
DONNELY, Cathl.	22	F	Unknown	20Ma02Da
NULTY, Pat	23	M	Unknown	20Ma02Da
SHEEHAN, Pat	17	M	Unknown	20Ma02Da
GILLISPIE, Michl.	17	M	Unknown	20Ma02Da
MURRAY, Johanna	18	F	Unknown	20Ma02Da
Margt.	16	F	Unknown	20Ma02Da
SULLIVAN, Cathl.	50	F	Laborer	20Ma02Da
James	22	M	Unknown	20Ma02Da
Denis	20	M	Unknown	20Ma02Da
William	18	M	Unknown	20Ma02Da
Margt.	15	F	Unknown	20Ma02Da
Harriet	17	F	Unknown	20Ma02Da
DONOHOE, Johanna	20	F	Unknown	20Ma02Da
RINDEN, Owen	30	M	Unknown	20Ma02Da
WALL, Thomas	22	M	Unknown	20Ma02Da
U-Miss	23	F	Unknown	20Ma02Da
MAHONY, Mary	25	F	Unknown	20Ma02Da
FITZPATRICK, C.	30	F	Unknown	20Ma02Da
MURPHY, Edw.	22	M	Unknown	20Ma02Da
SCULLY, Honor	19	F	Unknown	20Ma02Da

NAMES OF PASSENGERS	AGE	SEX	OCCUPATIONS	DATE PORT SHIP
MCGRATH, Fras.	17	F	Unknown	20Ma02Da
Bridgt.	54	F	Unknown	20Ma02Da
LIDDY, Bridget	21	F	Unknown	20Ma02Da
CUNNINGHAM, Michl.	20	M	Unknown	20Ma02Da
OCONNOR, Mary-A.	14	F	Unknown	20Ma02Da
CONNOR, James	15	M	Unknown	20Ma02Da
TIERNAN, Lawrence	24	M	Unknown	20Ma02Da
SUMMIMILLER, Thomas	40	M	Unknown	20Ma02Da
Summi., Elizth.	40	F	Unknown	20Ma02Da
Matilda	60	F	Unknown	20Ma02Da
Robert	16	M	Unknown	20Ma02Da
James	10	M	Unknown	20Ma02Da
Joseph	9	M	Child	20Ma02Da
MULVEY, Michl.	26	M	Unknown	20Ma02Da
DONOVAN, John	24	M	Unknown	20Ma02Da
MCLOUGHLAN, Edw.	18	M	Unknown	20Ma02Da
MCELROY, Neil	60	M	Unknown	20Ma02Da
Sally	56	F	Unknown	20Ma02Da
CONLAN, Mary-A.	20	F	Unknown	20Ma02Da
SMITH, Barth.	16	M	Unknown	20Ma02Da
Elizth.	11	F	Unknown	20Ma02Da
John	9	M	Child	20Ma02Da
Thomas	7	M	Child	20Ma02Da
Ann	4	F	Child	20Ma02Da
MAHON, Alice	30	F	Unknown	20Ma02Da
Ellen	11	F	Unknown	20Ma02Da
John	9	M	Child	20Ma02Da
Bridgt.	7	F	Child	20Ma02Da
Dorothy	5	F	Child	20Ma02Da
James	2	M	Child	20Ma02Da
KILBRIDE, Marks	24	M	Unknown	20Ma02Da
DUNNE, Edwd.	22	M	Unknown	20Ma02Da
COSTELLO, Peter	12	M	Unknown	20Ma02Da
William	9	M	Child	20Ma02Da
Richard	6	M	Child	20Ma02Da
CARTY, Thomas	23	M	Unknown	20Ma02Da
Ann	22	F	Unknown	20Ma02Da
GROGORY, Walter	20	M	Unknown	20Ma02Da
BROWNE, John	27	M	Unknown	20Ma02Da
Martha	36	F	Unknown	20Ma02Da
Ann	3	F	Child	20Ma02Da
James	.00	M	Infant	20Ma02Da
MORAN, Bridget	27	F	Unknown	20Ma02Da
GARRAHAN, James	30	M	Unknown	20Ma02Da
MCMAHEN, Michl.	20	M	Laborer	20Ma02Da
LENEHAN, Cathe.	17	F	Unknown	20Ma02Da
LEONARD, Fras.	23	F	Unknown	20Ma02Da
DOYLE, Andrew	35	M	Unknown	20Ma02Da
MCEVERN, John	24	M	Unknown	20Ma02Da
AGNEW, William	20	M	Unknown	20Ma02Da
HEANEY, James	20	M	Unknown	20Ma02Da
MCGINNES, Mary	15	F	Unknown	20Ma02Da
DONAHY, John	28	M	Unknown	20Ma02Da
AHERN, Michael	50	M	Unknown	20Ma02Da
Honora	20	F	Unknown	20Ma02Da
Margt.	16	F	Unknown	20Ma02Da
Meehan	3	F	Child	20Ma02Da
CARROLL, Robt.	20	M	Unknown	20Ma02Da
Susan	22	F	Unknown	20Ma02Da
Margt.	21	F	Unknown	20Ma02Da
Jane	17	F	Unknown	20Ma02Da
Mary	22	F	Unknown	20Ma02Da
MURPHY, Nort.	24	M	Unknown	20Ma02Da
WALSH, Alice	10	F	Unknown	20Ma02Da
KENNEDY, John	44	M	Unknown	20Ma02Da
Edward	8	M	Child	20Ma02Da
John	6	M	Child	20Ma02Da

ANNONDALE 20 MAY 1850

From Liverpool

NAMES OF PASSENGERS	AGE	SEX	OCCUPATIONS	DATE PORT SHIP
CASTLE, Hannah	43	F	Laborer	20Ma02lv
John	12	M	Unknown	20Ma02lv
Hannah-Marnette	10	F	Unknown	20Ma02lv
Ann-Elizabeth	7	F	Child	20Ma02lv
David	5	M	Child	20Ma02lv
Jane	3	F	Child	20Ma02lv
Elizabeth	.00	F	Infant	20Ma02lv
MICHOLS, George	28	M	Carpenter	20Ma02lv
OLIVER, William	30	M	Wheelwright	20Ma02lv
Martha	29	F	Unknown	20Ma02lv
Martha	4	F	Child	20Ma02lv
Sarah	2	F	Child	20Ma02lv
Mary-Ann	.00	F	Infant	20Ma02lv
JACKSON, Edward	20	M	Laborer	20Ma02lv
THOMPSON, William	30	M	Farmer	20Ma02lv
Cherry	26	F	Unknown	20Ma02lv
Elizabeth	3	F	Child	20Ma02lv
Eliza	2	F	Child	20Ma02lv
Abraham	1	M	Child	20Ma02lv
Richard	.00	M	Infant	20Ma02lv
EAST, John	20	M	Tailor	20Ma02lv
HARRIS, Jane	18	F	Servant	20Ma02lv
ATKINSON, William	40	M	Farmer	20Ma02lv
BUE, Henry	25	M	Stctr	20Ma02lv
TAYLOR, Nathan	20	M	Husbandman	20Ma02lv
STUBS, A.	28	M	Husbandman	20Ma02lv
SIMMS, Abram	20	M	Husbandman	20Ma02lv
DRUMMUND, Wm.	35	M	Broker	20Ma02lv
YOUNG, Wm.	22	M	Clerk	20Ma02lv
MIDDLETON, K.C.	20	M	Draper	20Ma02lv
LOCHRANE, J.W.	23	M	Clerk	20Ma02lv
HURBUT, William	48	M	Wood Burner	20Ma02lv
Ann	44	F	Unknown	20Ma02lv
Sarah	18	F	Unknown	20Ma02lv
Eliza	16	F	Unknown	20Ma02lv
Henry	10	M	Unknown	20Ma02lv
Martha	8	F	Child	20Ma02lv
Ann	5	F	Child	20Ma02lv
Elizabeth	2	F	Child	20Ma02lv
George	.00	M	Infant	20Ma02lv
HAYES, John	50	M	Husbandman	20Ma02lv
Darley	17	M	Husbandman	20Ma02lv
HUTCHINGTON, James	30	M	Husbandman	20Ma02lv
REDMAN, Michl.	22	M	Tailor	20Ma02lv
HILL, Joseph	36	M	Laborer	20Ma02lv
Fredrick	18	M	Laborer	20Ma02lv
SHARDOCK, Michl.	26	M	Laborer	20Ma02lv
Ch., Michl.	20	M	Laborer	20Ma02lv
HIND, Wm.	24	M	Laborer	20Ma02lv
COLLINS, Patrick	23	M	Laborer	20Ma02lv
EMIS, John	24	M	Laborer	20Ma02lv
GINNIS, Peter	30	M	Laborer	20Ma02lv
MAGNESS, John	26	M	Laborer	20Ma02lv
James	30	M	Laborer	20Ma02lv
RICE, Mary-Ann	15	F	Unknown	20Ma02lv
MAGUNESS, Cath.	26	F	Unknown	20Ma02lv
Mary	25	F	Unknown	20Ma02lv
Charles	27	M	Laborer	20Ma02lv
Catherine	23	F	Unknown	20Ma02lv
MAGNEN, Andrew	50	M	Laborer	20Ma02lv
Catherine	43	F	Unknown	20Ma02lv
PRENDERGUST, Cath.	24	F	Unknown	20Ma02lv
FLIN, Sarah	21	F	Unknown	20Ma02lv
HACKET, Anas	22	F	Unknown	20Ma02lv
DONNELLY, Cornelius	21	M	Laborer	20Ma02lv

NAMES OF PASSENGERS	AGE	SEX	OCCUPATIONS	DATE PORT SHIP
DONNELLY, Edward	20	M	Laborer	20Ma02lv
Betsey	18	F	Unknown	20Ma02lv
BROWN, Ann	26	F	Unknown	20Ma02lv
GAFNEY, Patrick	18	M	Laborer	20Ma02lv
REILLY, Thomas	20	M	Unknown	20Ma02lv
FAGAN, Rose	21	F	Unknown	20Ma02lv
John	19	M	Laborer	20Ma02lv
FORD, Mary	18	F	Unknown	20Ma02lv
FORREST, Rose	14	F	Unknown	20Ma02lv
Wm.	50	M	Tailor	20Ma02lv
Mary	50	F	Unknown	20Ma02lv
SHERLOCK, Bridget	22	F	Unknown	20Ma02lv
COOK, Ann	20	F	Unknown	20Ma02lv
LEAVERY, Bridget	21	F	Unknown	20Ma02lv
SHERLOCK, Ann	18	F	Unknown	20Ma02lv
LEAVERY, Edward	45	M	Gdnr	20Ma02lv
FORREST, James	20	M	Laborer	20Ma02lv
DOLAN, Mary	33	F	Unknown	20Ma02lv
GALLNEY, Catherine	14	F	Unknown	20Ma02lv
CORD, Luke	20	M	Laborer	20Ma02lv
FORREST, William	15	M	Laborer	20Ma02lv
MCHARDY, Mathew	25	M	Bricklayer	20Ma02lv
GALLAHER, Edward	25	M	Smith	20Ma02lv
ALLEN, Edward	22	M	Farmer	20Ma02lv
MCCULOCK, Robert	24	M	Farmer	20Ma02lv
William	18	M	Farmer	20Ma02lv
MANNERON, Chris	24	M	Butcher	20Ma02lv
GRAY, William	20	M	Farmer	20Ma02lv
MAHON, Bridget	24	F	Unknown	20Ma02lv
Mary	20	F	Unknown	20Ma02lv
MCLESNEY, Essey	20	F	Unknown	20Ma02lv
Sarah	17	F	Unknown	20Ma02lv
MAGLIN, Patrick	36	M	Unknown	20Ma02lv
PLUNKET, Mitch	20	M	Laborer	20Ma02lv
BISSEL, James	70	M	Husbandman	20Ma02lv
HILL, John	40	M	Plasterer	20Ma02lv
BEDOWAN, Thomas	30	M	Laborer	20Ma02lv
MCCARTHY, John	27	M	Shoemaker	20Ma02lv
Mary	18	F	Unknown	20Ma02lv
MONLIN, Richard	25	M	Shoemaker	20Ma02lv
DUFFY, Owen	40	M	Potter	20Ma02lv
BROWN, George	23	M	Laborer	20Ma02lv
MERRYWEATHER, Wm.	26	M	Laborer	20Ma02lv
FRENOLAN, Ann	30	F	Unknown	20Ma02lv
Ann	20	F	Unknown	20Ma02lv
SMITH, George	22	M	Laborer	20Ma02lv
Ann	23	F	Unknown	20Ma02lv
John	28	M	Laborer	20Ma02lv
Charlotte	28	F	Unknown	20Ma02lv
PICWORTH, Jane	18	F	Unknown	20Ma02lv
Rebeca	10	F	Unknown	20Ma02lv
Emma	7	F	Child	20Ma02lv
William	36	M	Laborer	20Ma02lv
Elizabeth	43	F	Unknown	20Ma02lv
Robert	16	M	Unknown	20Ma02lv
John	22	M	Unknown	20Ma02lv
Elizabeth	19	F	Unknown	20Ma02lv
William	.00	M	Infant	20Ma02lv
PARTUS, Thomas	4	M	Child	20Ma02lv
COX, Mary	20	F	Unknown	20Ma02lv
WILTIN, Mary	30	F	Unknown	20Ma02lv
GIBBINS, Mary	17	F	Unknown	20Ma02lv
GRANT, James	25	M	Laborer	20Ma02lv
Ann	26	F	Unknown	20Ma02lv
Maria	2	F	Unknown	20Ma02lv
Magt.	7	F	Child	20Ma02lv
Jane	6	F	Child	20Ma02lv
Charles	3	M	Child	20Ma02lv
Ann	4	F	Child	20Ma02lv
MCCARTHY, Joseph	30	M	Laborer	20Ma02lv
BYAN, John	50	M	Laborer	20Ma02lv
MCHENNA, James	30	M	Laborer	20Ma02lv
MCCORREN, Owen	25	M	Laborer	20Ma02lv
MCHENNA, Ann	5	F	Child	20Ma02lv
FARREL, Patrick	12	M	Unknown	20Ma02lv

NAMES OF PASSENGERS	AGE	SEX	OCCUPATIONS	DATE PORT SHIP
CORCORAN, Andrew	20	M	Laborer	20Ma02lv
HACKET, Bernard	17	M	Shoemaker	20Ma02lv
MCCARTHY, Michl.	25	M	Laborer	20Ma02lv
Jame	17	F	Unknown	20Ma02lv
MCBRIDE, James	11	M	Laborer	20Ma02lv
DONNELLY, Nial.	20	M	Unknown	20Ma02lv
MCBRIDE, Cathn.	20	F	Unknown	20Ma02lv
HAYS, Mary-Jane	17	F	Dressmaker	20Ma02lv
BURKE, Jeremiah	30	M	Laborer	20Ma02lv
MURPHY, Morris	30	M	Farmer	20Ma02lv
WILSON, George	30	M	Laborer	20Ma02lv
CONNOR, Michl.	27	M	Unknown	20Ma02lv
Alice	27	F	Unknown	20Ma02lv
Catherine	17	F	Unknown	20Ma02lv
MCBRIDE, John	26	M	Farmer	20Ma02lv
CONNELLY, Edward	23	M	Farmer	20Ma02lv
MCAULLY, R.	22	M	Stctr	20Ma02lv
DALTON, Ellen	23	F	Unknown	20Ma02lv
MULLERY, Cath.	4	F	Child	20Ma02lv
Magt.	30	F	Unknown	20Ma02lv
DOLLAN, James	25	M	Laborer	20Ma02lv
FLAHARTY, Michl.	30	M	Laborer	20Ma02lv
DALTEN, George	28	M	Joiner	20Ma02lv
MCDONOLLY, Michl.	22	M	Laborer	20Ma02lv
MCGEE, James	23	M	Ploughman	20Ma02lv
John	21	M	Gdnr	20Ma02lv
RAYMOND, Mathew	24	M	Laborer	20Ma02lv
MIDLER, U-Mrs.	60	F	Unknown	20Ma02lv
KING, Ann	20	F	Unknown	20Ma02lv
MIDLER, Thomas	14	M	Unknown	20Ma02lv
William	21	M	Laborer	20Ma02lv
STONEY, James	20	M	Laborer	20Ma02lv
WHEELER, Samuel	24	M	Laborer	20Ma02lv
Jane	26	F	Unknown	20Ma02lv
GRAHAM, Michl.	20	M	Laborer	20Ma02lv
Mary	20	F	Unknown	20Ma02lv
BILDEN, Edward	26	M	Miller	20Ma02lv
KEEGAN, William	20	M	Shoemaker	20Ma02lv
RICHARDSON, Wm.	30	M	Laborer	20Ma02lv
DOILE, Ellen	30	F	Unknown	20Ma02lv
Bridget	25	F	Unknown	20Ma02lv
YOXALL, Moses	23	M	Laborer	20Ma02lv
SULTON, Jonathan	22	M	Unknown	20Ma02lv
MULANY, Michl.	22	M	Laborer	20Ma02lv
LEONARD, John	26	M	Laborer	20Ma02lv
LONGHAM, Thomas	23	M	Laborer	20Ma02lv
GEARY, John	72	M	Laborer	20Ma02lv
ALSTON, John	24	M	Laborer	20Ma02lv
CANNARY, Timmothy	40	M	Laborer	20Ma02lv
Mary	34	F	Unknown	20Ma02lv
John	14	M	Unknown	20Ma02lv
Michl.	13	M	Unknown	20Ma02lv
Magt.	2	F	Child	20Ma02lv
DOUGLASS, James	18	M	Gdnr	20Ma02lv
RUFF, William	24	M	Bricklayer	20Ma02lv
Eliza	24	F	Unknown	20Ma02lv
BURNS, Patrick	27	M	Laborer	20Ma02lv
MCKINLY, Michl.	25	M	Laborer	20Ma02lv
KELVEN, Peter	28	M	Laborer	20Ma02lv
Ellen	24	F	Unknown	20Ma02lv
Mary	.00	F	Infant	20Ma02lv
FARRLIE, John	35	M	Carpenter	20Ma02lv
DONNELLY, John	24	M	Laborer	20Ma02lv
BURK, James	34	M	Laborer	20Ma02lv
FLERVEY, William	33	M	Laborer	20Ma02lv
DONNELLY, Ann	20	F	Unknown	20Ma02lv
MCKNON, Winney	20	F	Unknown	20Ma02lv
RAINSIN, Thomas	34	M	Laborer	20Ma02lv
Emily	27	F	Unknown	20Ma02lv
Emily	8	F	Child	20Ma02lv
George	5	M	Child	20Ma02lv
Isabella	2	F	Child	20Ma02lv
CREAMER, Mary	20	F	Unknown	20Ma02lv
MULAY, Bridget	22	F	Unknown	20Ma02lv
HESLIN, Ann	18	F	Unknown	20Ma02lv

NAMES OF PASSENGERS	AGE	SEX	OCCUPATIONS	DATE PORT SHIP
SMITH, Edmond	20	M	Laborer	20Ma02lv
JACKSON, John	20	M	Bricklayer	20Ma02lv
ROBINSON, Mathew	19	M	Laborer	20Ma02lv
SLUNT, Thomas	25	M	Laborer	20Ma02lv
MITCHELL, John	22	M	Laborer	20Ma02lv
George	18	M	Laborer	20Ma02lv
LOOP, Christopher	20	M	Laborer	20Ma02lv
RONNERS, John	23	M	Laborer	20Ma02lv
LEAVY, John	22	M	Laborer	20Ma02lv
William	24	M	Brewer	20Ma02lv
CONERFORD, John	21	M	Laborer	20Ma02lv
Ann	20	F	Unknown	20Ma02lv
BAXLES, George	38	M	Laborer	20Ma02lv
Ann	33	F	Unknown	20Ma02lv
REILLY, Rose	35	F	Unknown	20Ma02lv
Ann	14	F	Unknown	20Ma02lv
SALVIER, Daniel	20	M	Laborer	20Ma02lv
MCCONNELL, William	24	M	Carpenter	20Ma02lv
HEEP, Patk.	40	M	Baker	20Ma02lv
MAHON, Martin	32	M	Stctr	20Ma02lv
Lawrence	30	M	Laborer	20Ma02lv
MADEN, George	21	M	Unknown	20Ma02lv
PRISTEN, Michl.	28	M	Laborer	20Ma02lv
WATSEN, William	25	M	Laborer	20Ma02lv
NAGLE, Richard	30	M	Laborer	20Ma02lv
Mary	28	F	Unknown	20Ma02lv
CURTIS, Charles	22	M	Unknown	20Ma02lv
Robert	21	M	Laborer	20Ma02lv
THORP, John	22	M	Laborer	20Ma02lv
LEE, George	19	M	Bootmaker	20Ma02lv
QUIN, Patrick	25	M	Builder	20Ma02lv
WINSTLEY, Thomas	30	M	Engftr	20Ma02lv
ORGAN, Cath.	17	F	Servant	20Ma02lv
NEIL, Magt.	24	F	Servant	20Ma02lv
PRESCOT, Mary	22	F	Unknown	20Ma02lv
CARTHENRY, Mary	16	F	Unknown	20Ma02lv
John	50	M	Unknown	20Ma02lv
Ann	50	F	Unknown	20Ma02lv
Mary-A.	3	F	Child	20Ma02lv
Sarah-Eliza	2	F	Child	20Ma02lv
MCDONALD, Bridget	30	F	Unknown	20Ma02lv
Mary	20	F	Unknown	20Ma02lv
Patrick	22	M	Unknown	20Ma02lv
HILLILA, Bridget	50	F	Unknown	20Ma02lv
Mary	19	F	Unknown	20Ma02lv
Ellen	13	F	Unknown	20Ma02lv
Bridget	10	F	Unknown	20Ma02lv
Francis	8	M	Child	20Ma02lv
Eliza	5	F	Child	20Ma02lv
BROWN, James	30	M	Unknown	20Ma02lv
GOODWIN, John	37	M	Laborer	20Ma02lv
GONELY, Michl.	18	M	Laborer	20Ma02lv

GEORGE 20 MAY 1850

From Liverpool

NAMES OF PASSENGERS	AGE	SEX	OCCUPATIONS	DATE PORT SHIP
CAMPBELL, A.	20	U	Laborer	20Ma02KI
GRANT, Elizabeth	26	F	Servant	20Ma02KI
Ann	6	F	Child	20Ma02KI
Hugh	4	M	Child	20Ma02KI
Patrick	30	M	Laborer	20Ma02KI
LINDIGAN, Honora	16	F	Servant	20Ma02KI
Margaret	20	F	Servant	20Ma02KI
KEEFE, John	24	M	Laborer	20Ma02KI
Cath.	16	F	Servant	20Ma02KI
CORRY, Simon	40	M	Servant	20Ma02KI
Pat	31	M	Laborer	20Ma02KI
LINGHTON, Mary	13	F	Servant	20Ma02KI

NAMES OF PASSENGERS	AGE	SEX	OCCUPATIONS	DATE PORT SHIP
LINGHTON, Patrick	11	M	Laborer	20Ma02KI
LEE, Cath.	19	F	Servant	20Ma02KI
FALLON, Maria	55	F	Servant	20Ma02KI
MURPHY, Michael	45	M	Unknown	20Ma02KI
KENNEDRY, Gregory	27	M	Laborer	20Ma02KI
Mary	24	F	Laborer	20Ma02KI
COAKLEY, Thos.	30	M	Piper	20Ma02KI
GRAY, Janet	70	F	Servant	20Ma02KI
Geo.	55	M	Servant	20Ma02KI
Mary	50	F	Servant	20Ma02KI
Thomas	20	M	Servant	20Ma02KI
Elizth.	19	F	Servant	20Ma02KI
Wm.	17	M	Laborer	20Ma02KI
Geo.	11	M	Servant	20Ma02KI
Mary-Ellen	9	F	Laborer	20Ma02KI
John	5	M	Child	20Ma02KI
MCKERVAN, Mary	28	F	Servant	20Ma02KI
SWEETFIN, Dennis	20	M	Laborer	20Ma02KI
CLIFTON, Jas.	20	M	Laborer	20Ma02KI
CERVEN, Jas.	20	M	Laborer	20Ma02KI
GRAHAM, Eliza	21	F	Servant	20Ma02KI
HAGGERTY, Jas.	16	F	Servant	20Ma02KI
KRATINE, Peter	24	M	Servant	20Ma02KI
FINNY, Cath.	30	F	Servant	20Ma02KI
MCNAMARA, Mary	30	F	Servant	20Ma02KI
GANGHAN, Cath.	27	F	Servant	20Ma02KI
Bessy	20	F	Servant	20Ma02KI
BRADY, Bridget	20	F	Servant	20Ma02KI
BRADLEY, Alice	25	F	Servant	20Ma02KI
Rose	10	F	Unknown	20Ma02KI
BRIGGS, Ann	49	F	Servant	20Ma02KI
Patrick	11	M	Laborer	20Ma02KI
John	9	M	Child	20Ma02KI
BOWLAN, Andrew	35	M	Laborer	20Ma02KI
Ann	30	F	Servant	20Ma02KI
Ann	3	F	Child	20Ma02KI
MCWILLIAM, Mary	50	F	Servant	20Ma02KI
Anthony	14	M	Laborer	20Ma02KI
Nancy	12	F	Laborer	20Ma02KI
Edward	8	M	Child	20Ma02KI
CONWAY, Honora	55	F	Servant	20Ma02KI
LYNCH, Jas.	20	M	Servant	20Ma02KI
CALLANAN, Ellen	50	F	Servant	20Ma02KI
DUFFY, Mary	10	F	Unknown	20Ma02KI
WALSH, Mary	14	F	Servant	20Ma02KI
Elle--, Cath.	14	F	Servant	20Ma02KI
KELLEY, Thos.	20	M	Laborer	20Ma02KI
Winnefrd.	16	F	Servant	20Ma02KI
Bridget	20	F	Servant	20Ma02KI
DREVIN, Mary	20	F	Servant	20Ma02KI
KRAVEN, Julia	20	F	Servant	20Ma02KI
KARKERT, Mary	4	F	Child	20Ma02KI
WALSH, Martin	20	F	Tailor	20Ma02KI
MULLEN, Marg.	23	F	Tailor	20Ma02KI
SCALLERY, Mary	29	F	Unknown	20Ma02KI
MCHUGH, Pat	20	M	Laborer	20Ma02KI
GOLDING, Martin	30	M	Laborer	20Ma02KI
CULLEN, Honora	36	F	Servant	20Ma02KI
Sarah	16	F	Servant	20Ma02KI
CAHILL, Cath.	17	F	Servant	20Ma02KI
KELLEY, Martha	20	F	Servant	20Ma02KI
CARNEY, Wm.	20	M	Servant	20Ma02KI
Ellen	17	F	Servant	20Ma02KI
BALES, Ellen	30	F	Unknown	20Ma02KI
Geo.	28	M	Servant	20Ma02KI
HART, Cath.	18	F	Servant	20Ma02KI
MURPHY, Mary	25	F	Servant	20Ma02KI
NORTON, Alice	25	F	Servant	20Ma02KI
Cath.	20	F	Servant	20Ma02KI
SHRILL, Jas.	20	M	Servant	20Ma02KI
Jas.	20	M	Servant	20Ma02KI
Pat	26	M	Servant	20Ma02KI
CULLANAN, Pat	21	M	Laborer	20Ma02KI
HEVAN, Michael	20	M	Laborer	20Ma02KI
SHERIDAN, Ellen	18	F	Laborer	20Ma02KI

NAMES OF PASSENGERS	AGE	SEX	OCCUPATIONS	DATE PORT SHIP
SHERIDAN, Pat	20	M	Laborer	20Ma02KI
James	15	M	Laborer	20Ma02KI
MCDONOHUE, John	22	M	Laborer	20Ma02KI
Bridget	20	F	Servant	20Ma02KI
KELLY, Pat	34	M	Servant	20Ma02KI
Marg.	28	F	Servant	20Ma02KI
Phillip	6	M	Child	20Ma02KI
Cath.	4	F	Child	20Ma02KI
CENNIN, Marg.	15	F	Servant	20Ma02KI
BUCKLY, Cath.	20	F	Servant	20Ma02KI
OBRIEN, Mary	12	F	Servant	20Ma02KI
Marg.	11	F	Servant	20Ma02KI
RYAN, Johana	30	F	Servant	20Ma02KI
John	29	M	Laborer	20Ma02KI
FANNEN, Cath.	8	F	Child	20Ma02KI
GALVIN, Pat	30	M	Laborer	20Ma02KI
GOUGH, Eliz.	32	F	Servant	20Ma02KI
Jas.	11	M	Servant	20Ma02KI
Bessy	9	F	Child	20Ma02KI
John	7	M	Child	20Ma02KI
Michael	5	M	Child	20Ma02KI
ROACH, Mary	22	F	Servant	20Ma02KI
HOGAN, Peter	39	M	Servant	20Ma02KI
KENNEDY, Jas.	20	M	Servant	20Ma02KI
Judy	40	F	Servant	20Ma02KI
HOGAN, Mary	5	F	Child	20Ma02KI
KENNEDY, Bryan	7	M	Child	20Ma02KI
Maurice	5	M	Child	20Ma02KI
Mary	2	F	Child	20Ma02KI
BRYAN, Judy	20	F	Laborer	20Ma02KI
BRENTIN, Alice	18	F	Laborer	20Ma02KI
CONOVAN, Martin	24	M	Unknown	20Ma02KI
WALSH, Mary	19	F	Servant	20Ma02KI
DELANEY, Marg.	20	F	Servant	20Ma02KI
DUNN, Cath.	11	F	Servant	20Ma02KI
CASSIDY, Ellen	20	F	Servant	20Ma02KI
BURN, Julia	20	F	Servant	20Ma02KI
BARDEN, Rose	18	F	Servant	20Ma02KI
MCCALL, Cath.	35	F	Servant	20Ma02KI
Ann	11	F	Unknown	20Ma02KI
Thomas	9	M	Child	20Ma02KI
BURK, John	25	M	Servant	20Ma02KI
Harriet	28	F	Servant	20Ma02KI
Harriet	5	F	Child	20Ma02KI
John	3	M	Child	20Ma02KI
HAYS, Thos.	25	M	Laborer	20Ma02KI
Bridget	25	F	Laborer	20Ma02KI
ORTON, John	26	M	Laborer	20Ma02KI
TOOLE, Pat	21	M	Laborer	20Ma02KI
SCANLON, John	25	M	Laborer	20Ma02KI
DILLON, Martin	22	M	Laborer	20Ma02KI
CULLEN, John	26	M	Laborer	20Ma02KI
CASKILL, Mary	21	F	Unknown	20Ma02KI
BARRY, Marg.	55	F	Laborer	20Ma02KI
Mary	16	F	Laborer	20Ma02KI
MATTHEWS, Marg.	26	F	Laborer	20Ma02KI
HEANEY, Pat	20	M	Laborer	20Ma02KI
WHEELAN, Andy	15	M	Servant	20Ma02KI
John	11	M	Unknown	20Ma02KI
SMITH, Mick	18	M	Laborer	20Ma02KI
JEDINTH, Cath.	15	F	Servant	20Ma02KI
MOORE, Danl.	53	M	Laborer	20Ma02KI
DELANEY, Cath.	20	F	Servant	20Ma02KI
Jas.	22	M	Servant	20Ma02KI
MCKENNA, Ellen	16	F	Servant	20Ma02KI
MCLOBY, Alice	18	F	Servant	20Ma02KI
CUNGARN, Ellen	20	F	Servant	20Ma02KI
FLANNIGAN, Hugh	25	M	Laborer	20Ma02KI
MCKERVAN, Mick	22	M	Laborer	20Ma02KI
Terence	17	M	Laborer	20Ma02KI
CAN, John	40	M	Laborer	20Ma02KI
Mary	40	F	Servant	20Ma02KI
BURK, Pat	20	F	Servant	20Ma02KI
SULLIVAN, Julia	53	F	Servant	20Ma02KI
John	7	M	Child	20Ma02KI

NAMES OF PASSENGERS	AGE	SEX	OCCUPATIONS	DATE PORT SHIP
REARDON, Mary	14	F	Servant	20Ma02KI
COLEMAN, Dan.	35	M	Servant	20Ma02KI
M.	33	U	Servant	20Ma02KI
Jno.	28	M	Servant	20Ma02KI
MURPH, Mary	50	F	Servant	20Ma02KI
GALLAHER, John	25	M	Servant	20Ma02KI
MALONE, Mary	50	F	Servant	20Ma02KI
Ann	3	F	Child	20Ma02KI
Mary	25	F	Servant	20Ma02KI
Phillip	20	M	Laborer	20Ma02KI
Phillip	31	M	Laborer	20Ma02KI
MARTIN, Cath.	11	F	Laborer	20Ma02KI
Ellen	6	F	Child	20Ma02KI
John	5	M	Child	20Ma02KI
MURPHY, John	20	M	Laborer	20Ma02KI
SULLIVAN, John	26	M	Laborer	20Ma02KI
COLLINS, Ellen	52	F	Laborer	20Ma02KI
BRIEN, Bertha	30	F	Laborer	20Ma02KI
HERSEY, Mary	18	F	Laborer	20Ma02KI
MURPHY, John	24	M	Laborer	20Ma02KI
MINARTY, Ellen	18	F	Laborer	20Ma02KI
Eliza	15	F	Servant	20Ma02KI
BREMAN, Mary	19	F	Servant	20Ma02KI
HAMPSON, John	18	M	Laborer	20Ma02KI
SHEEHAN, Cath.	40	F	Laborer	20Ma02KI
Jeremiah	19	M	Laborer	20Ma02KI
Mary	18	F	Laborer	20Ma02KI
Cath.	16	F	Laborer	20Ma02KI
Pat	13	M	Laborer	20Ma02KI
Jno.	10	M	Laborer	20Ma02KI
Hannah	4	F	Child	20Ma02KI
QUINN, Pat	30	M	Servant	20Ma02KI
Ann	20	F	Servant	20Ma02KI
FLYN, Marg.	50	F	Servant	20Ma02KI
Margaret	14	F	Servant	20Ma02KI
Bridget	16	F	Servant	20Ma02KI
WARD, Pat	22	M	Laborer	20Ma02KI
COURTNEY, Jno.	39	M	Laborer	20Ma02KI
BRADY, Jno.	20	M	Laborer	20Ma02KI
WILSON, Eliza	16	F	Servant	20Ma02KI
MCCUSKER, Bennett	40	M	Servant	20Ma02KI
Rosa.	40	F	Servant	20Ma02KI
U	.00	U	Infant	20Ma02KI
Cath.	13	F	Servant	20Ma02KI
Rose	11	F	Servant	20Ma02KI
COOLAN, Pat	27	M	Laborer	20Ma02KI
SMMITH, Jas.	22	M	Laborer	20Ma02KI
CONWAY, Jas.	28	M	Laborer	20Ma02KI
CAVEY, John	24	M	Laborer	20Ma02KI
Cath.	26	F	Laborer	20Ma02KI
PARKER, Bess.	17	F	Laborer	20Ma02KI
Crit--, Ellen	20	F	Laborer	20Ma02KI
CURRAN, Daniel	18	M	Laborer	20Ma02KI
AGNEW, Marg.	30	F	Laborer	20Ma02KI
U	.00	U	Infant	20Ma02KI
COAKLEY, Mary	30	F	Servant	20Ma02KI

INDEPENDENCE 20 MAY 1850

From London

NAMES OF PASSENGERS	AGE	SEX	OCCUPATIONS	DATE PORT SHIP
SHEA, Patrick	32	M	Painter	20Ma06Hv
Patrick	52	M	Painter	20Ma06Hv
CUTITHY, Patrick	22	M	Farmer	20Ma06Hv

JAS.H.SHEPHERD 20 MAY 1850

From Liverpool

NAMES OF PASSENGERS	AGE	SEX	OCCUPATIONS	DATE PORT SHIP
HARREN, Mary	18	F	Servant	20Ma02Ea
QUINN, Bridgt.	25	F	Servant	20Ma02Ea
KIRBY, John	30	M	Farmer	20Ma02Ea
Rose	40	F	Farmer	20Ma02Ea
GAFNY, Jas.	30	M	Unknown	20Ma02Ea
GRIFFIN, Mgt.	50	F	Servant	20Ma02Ea
Danl.	14	M	Servant	20Ma02Ea
Mary	12	F	Servant	20Ma02Ea
Barth.	10	M	Servant	20Ma02Ea
John	8	M	Child	20Ma02Ea
Michl.	6	M	Child	20Ma02Ea
LEE, Chas.	32	M	Farmer	20Ma02Ea
GINNON, Eliz.	18	F	Servant	20Ma02Ea
MASTERSON, Bern.	16	M	Servant	20Ma02Ea
Cath.	18	F	Unknown	20Ma02Ea
ADAMS, Agnes	55	F	Seamstress	20Ma02Ea
Eliza	21	F	Seamstress	20Ma02Ea
Robt.	.00	M	Infant	20Ma02Ea
Wm.	28	M	Unknown	20Ma02Ea
FAGAN, Mgt.	40	F	Unknown	20Ma02Ea
Michl.	20	M	Farmer	20Ma02Ea
Julia	11	F	Unknown	20Ma02Ea
RILEY, Mary	20	F	Unknown	20Ma02Ea
MEGAN, Mary	16	F	Unknown	20Ma02Ea
LINAGH, J.	33	M	Laborer	20Ma02Ea
COOLIGAN, Michl.	22	M	Unknown	20Ma02Ea
MCDERMOTT, F.	24	M	Laborer	20Ma02Ea
PALFREY, W.	30	M	Laborer	20Ma02Ea
MAHEE, Denis	30	M	Laborer	20Ma02Ea
KELLS, John-M.	30	M	Laborer	20Ma02Ea
Bridgt.	25	F	Laborer	20Ma02Ea
Mary	.00	F	Infant	20Ma02Ea
BRINE, Cath.	20	F	Laborer	20Ma02Ea
KEEF, Jerry	50	M	Laborer	20Ma02Ea
Edward	18	M	Laborer	20Ma02Ea
BRADY, Michl.	22	M	Laborer	20Ma02Ea
CLINTON, Mary	34	F	Laborer	20Ma02Ea
COCKRAN, John	24	M	Servant	20Ma02Ea
TIERNY, Nancy	23	F	Servant	20Ma02Ea
MANNUS, Bridgt.	24	F	Servant	20Ma02Ea
MAHON, Michl.	24	M	Laborer	20Ma02Ea
MAGNIS, Michl.	25	M	Laborer	20Ma02Ea
LONG, Alice	24	F	Laborer	20Ma02Ea
CLARKE, Mat	40	M	Laborer	20Ma02Ea
Thos.	40	M	Laborer	20Ma02Ea
Pat	20	M	Laborer	20Ma02Ea
Mary	50	F	Laborer	20Ma02Ea
MARNOT, Thos.	46	M	Laborer	20Ma02Ea
LEECH, Ann	19	F	Unknown	20Ma02Ea
DONOHUE, Ellen	25	F	Unknown	20Ma02Ea
CORMICK, Ellen	25	F	Unknown	20Ma02Ea
James	20	M	Unknown	20Ma02Ea
FLEMMING, Michl.	34	M	Farmer	20Ma02Ea
Mary	25	F	Farmer	20Ma02Ea
BRADY, S.	20	M	Farmer	20Ma02Ea
BURKE, John	40	M	Laborer	20Ma02Ea
Bridget	40	F	Laborer	20Ma02Ea
John	9	M	Child	20Ma02Ea
Mary	6	F	Child	20Ma02Ea
Michl.	.00	M	Infant	20Ma02Ea
BROWN, John	25	M	Laborer	20Ma02Ea
HEFFNER, John	23	M	Tinman	20Ma02Ea
LAWLER, M.	26	M	Tinman	20Ma02Ea
CONNERTY, John	37	M	Tinman	20Ma02Ea
MURPHY, Ellen	55	F	Tinman	20Ma02Ea

NAMES OF PASSENGERS	AGE	SEX	OCCUPATIONS	DATE PORT SHIP
MURPHY, Bridgt.	5	F	Child	20Ma02Ea
Pat	9	M	Child	20Ma02Ea
John	12	M	Tinman	20Ma02Ea
Peggy	.00	F	Infant	20Ma02Ea
KILROY, John	21	M	Tinman	20Ma02Ea
BRYON, Bridgt.	30	F	Unknown	20Ma02Ea
John	30	M	Unknown	20Ma02Ea
Mgt.	.00	F	Infant	20Ma02Ea
Wm.	2	M	Child	20Ma02Ea
Michl.	23	M	Unknown	20Ma02Ea
MARTIN, John	30	M	Shoemaker	20Ma02Ea
SULLIVAN, Tim	24	M	Laborer	20Ma02Ea
Eugene	23	M	Unknown	20Ma02Ea
KEEFE, Wm.	30	M	Unknown	20Ma02Ea
James	4	M	Child	20Ma02Ea
Mary	30	F	Unknown	20Ma02Ea
Ellen	2	F	Child	20Ma02Ea
John	.00	M	Infant	20Ma02Ea
KEEF, Mary	18	F	Unknown	20Ma02Ea
Jane	18	F	Unknown	20Ma02Ea
QUINN, John	24	M	Shoemaker	20Ma02Ea
LYNCH, Wm.	45	M	Farmer	20Ma02Ea
Mary	33	F	Unknown	20Ma02Ea
Pat	9	M	Child	20Ma02Ea
James	7	M	Child	20Ma02Ea
Pat	35	M	Unknown	20Ma02Ea
MCGEE, Bart.	22	M	Unknown	20Ma02Ea
Mgt.	23	F	Unknown	20Ma02Ea
FOX, John	32	M	Bricklayer	20Ma02Ea
Betty	33	F	Unknown	20Ma02Ea
HACHER, Hugh	33	M	Laborer	20Ma02Ea
SMITH, John	22	M	Unknown	20Ma02Ea
GARON, John	26	M	Unknown	20Ma02Ea
MARTIN, James	25	M	Bricklayer	20Ma02Ea
MCKENNIGAN, John	25	M	Laborer	20Ma02Ea
CALLEN, Wm.	15	M	Laborer	20Ma02Ea
Mary	8	F	Child	20Ma02Ea
GAFNY, Pat	25	M	Laborer	20Ma02Ea
CULLIN, Pat	20	M	Laborer	20Ma02Ea
MCGLONE, Thos.	22	M	Laborer	20Ma02Ea
GETTENS, Cath.	30	F	Unknown	20Ma02Ea
CATTLE, Pat	54	M	Unknown	20Ma02Ea
COSTELLO, John	28	M	Laborer	20Ma02Ea
BRADY, Mary	20	F	Unknown	20Ma02Ea
CALLAGHAN, Mary	20	F	Unknown	20Ma02Ea
CAWLY, Farrell	36	M	Unknown	20Ma02Ea
OBRIEN, Thos.	18	M	Unknown	20Ma02Ea
GLEENN, Dan	20	M	Unknown	20Ma02Ea
MONOGHAN, Alice	30	F	Unknown	20Ma02Ea
DEVLIN, Judy	25	F	Unknown	20Ma02Ea
BATES, Robt.	28	M	Laborer	20Ma02Ea
STANTON, Luke	21	M	Laborer	20Ma02Ea
WHALEN, John	35	M	Laborer	20Ma02Ea
BURNS, Mgt.	25	F	Unknown	20Ma02Ea
EGAN, Honor	35	F	Laborer	20Ma02Ea
MURPHY, James	9	M	Child	20Ma02Ea
Mary	7	F	Child	20Ma02Ea
BARNAN, Hugh	25	M	Laborer	20Ma02Ea
WALSH, Wm.	26	M	Unknown	20Ma02Ea
BEHAN, John	25	M	Unknown	20Ma02Ea
CALLAGHAN, Cath.	26	F	Unknown	20Ma02Ea
GURGOTY, James	29	M	Unknown	20Ma02Ea
Mary	24	F	Unknown	20Ma02Ea
FLANIGAN, John	25	M	Unknown	20Ma02Ea
Rose	26	F	Unknown	20Ma02Ea
Rose	.00	F	Infant	20Ma02Ea
MONOGHAN, John	30	M	Unknown	20Ma02Ea
BYRNE, Eliza	18	F	Unknown	20Ma02Ea
GAMMON, Michl.	32	M	Laborer	20Ma02Ea
Cath.	30	F	Unknown	20Ma02Ea
Jane	.00	F	Infant	20Ma02Ea
STONE, Pat	35	M	Laborer	20Ma02Ea
LEE, Mary-A.	30	F	Unknown	20Ma02Ea
Pat	13	M	Laborer	20Ma02Ea
DONOHUE, Cath.	30	F	Unknown	20Ma02Ea
DONOHUE, Bridget	23	F	Unknown	20Ma02Ea
CUMMINGS, Mgt.	32	F	Unknown	20Ma02Ea
RODDY, Martha	20	F	Unknown	20Ma02Ea
RILEY, Ellen	20	F	Unknown	20Ma02Ea
LAHY, Thos.	18	M	Laborer	20Ma02Ea
CAVEY, Wm.	30	M	Unknown	20Ma02Ea
Martin	20	M	Unknown	20Ma02Ea
BURKE, Peter	35	M	Unknown	20Ma02Ea
LYNCH, James	55	M	Unknown	20Ma02Ea
DUNN, Henry	30	M	Unknown	20Ma02Ea
Alice	25	F	Unknown	20Ma02Ea
LALLY, Ann	18	F	Unknown	20Ma02Ea
Jane	16	F	Unknown	20Ma02Ea
CORCORAN, James	25	M	Unknown	20Ma02Ea
DARNY, Danl.	40	M	Unknown	20Ma02Ea

FOREST-QUEEN 21 MAY 1850

From Liverpool

NAMES OF PASSENGERS	AGE	SEX	OCCUPATIONS	DATE PORT SHIP
DUNNA, Wm.	50	M	Farmer	21Ma02Ht
U-Mrs.	40	F	Unknown	21Ma02Ht
Margaret	17	F	Unknown	21Ma02Ht
Eliza	14	F	Unknown	21Ma02Ht
Anna	7	F	Child	21Ma02Ht
Jane	5	F	Child	21Ma02Ht
Cate	3	F	Child	21Ma02Ht
Wm.	13	M	Unknown	21Ma02Ht
Bartolomew	12	M	Unknown	21Ma02Ht
Michael	11	M	Unknown	21Ma02Ht
Patrick	9	M	Child	21Ma02Ht
WELCH, Bridget	20	F	Unknown	21Ma02Ht
DUNNA, John	45	M	Farmer	21Ma02Ht
HOGAN, Margaret	21	F	Unknown	21Ma02Ht
CONNERTY, Thomas	27	M	Laborer	21Ma02Ht
CARR, William	30	M	Laborer	21Ma02Ht
MORRISEY, Sarah	30	F	Unknown	21Ma02Ht
John	10	M	Unknown	21Ma02Ht
REILLY, James	18	M	Laborer	21Ma02Ht
KERNAN, Bridget	60	F	Unknown	21Ma02Ht
REILLY, Mary	10	F	Unknown	21Ma02Ht
Abbey	7	F	Child	21Ma02Ht
Bridget	5	F	Child	21Ma02Ht
John	3	M	Child	21Ma02Ht
MCGIRR, Mary	20	F	Unknown	21Ma02Ht
INGLISBY, Bridget	25	F	Laborer	21Ma02Ht
Catherine	20	F	Unknown	21Ma02Ht
John	21	M	Laborer	21Ma02Ht
WILLIAMS, Mary	18	F	Unknown	21Ma02Ht
GRIFFIN, Dennis	42	M	Laborer	21Ma02Ht
LYONS, Margaret	16	F	Laborer	21Ma02Ht
GRIFFIN, Mary	11	F	Unknown	21Ma02Ht
Catherine	9	F	Child	21Ma02Ht
John	7	M	Child	21Ma02Ht
REILLY, Rose	15	F	Unknown	21Ma02Ht
MCGOVERN, Mary	17	F	Laborer	21Ma02Ht
REILLY, James	24	M	Laborer	21Ma02Ht
REDONT, Thos.	18	M	Painter	21Ma02Ht
Lavinia	16	F	Unknown	21Ma02Ht
MULLREY, Ellen	11	F	Unknown	21Ma02Ht
Sarah	9	F	Child	21Ma02Ht
MURRAY, Bridget	19	F	Painter	21Ma02Ht
MURPHY, Mary	17	F	Unknown	21Ma02Ht
DOWD, Elizabeth	18	F	Unknown	21Ma02Ht
GETHORLY, James	21	M	Shoemaker	21Ma02Ht
Margaret	18	F	Unknown	21Ma02Ht
CONRY, Bridget	20	F	Unknown	21Ma02Ht
MCBRIDE, Birmn.	22	M	Laborer	21Ma02Ht

HANNAH-KERR 21 MAY 1850

From Londonderry

NAMES OF PASSENGERS	AGE	SEX	OCCUPATIONS	DATE PORT SHIP
MCGLIDE, James	40	M	Laborer	21Ma01Kb
Mary	30	F	Unknown	21Ma01Kb
Mary-Anne	.00	F	Infant	21Ma01Kb
MCNALTY, Hannah	30	F	Unknown	21Ma01Kb
MINAGLE, Anne	21	F	Unknown	21Ma01Kb
MCGLIM, Barney	36	M	Unknown	21Ma01Kb
ALISON, Hugh	19	M	Unknown	21Ma01Kb
QUIN, Nancy	18	F	Unknown	21Ma01Kb
Sarah	21	F	Unknown	21Ma01Kb
Thomas	12	M	Unknown	21Ma01Kb
CUMENTHUS, Robert	34	M	Unknown	21Ma01Kb
MCGINLEY, Hugh	29	M	Unknown	21Ma01Kb
STEWART, James	31	M	Unknown	21Ma01Kb
CASHLIN, Eliza	21	F	Unknown	21Ma01Kb
MCAVERS, John	18	M	Unknown	21Ma01Kb
HALTON, Anne	17	F	Unknown	21Ma01Kb
BLANEY, William	23	M	Unknown	21Ma01Kb
MCGANIGLE, Mary	45	F	Unknown	21Ma01Kb
Catherine	19	F	Unknown	21Ma01Kb
Charles	17	M	Unknown	21Ma01Kb
James	14	M	Unknown	21Ma01Kb
Sarah	10	F	Unknown	21Ma01Kb
SIMPSON, Margaret	34	F	Unknown	21Ma01Kb
BELL, Mary-J.	16	F	Unknown	21Ma01Kb
James	18	M	Unknown	21Ma01Kb
Sarah	23	F	Unknown	21Ma01Kb
MCCOLSAN, Mary	36	F	Unknown	21Ma01Kb
DIVER, Patrick	14	M	Unknown	21Ma01Kb
LYTLE, John	26	M	Unknown	21Ma01Kb
QUIG, Benjamin	23	M	Unknown	21Ma01Kb
LYTLE, Catherine	22	F	Unknown	21Ma01Kb
CONWAY, Michle.	35	M	Unknown	21Ma01Kb
FOSH, Benjamin	40	M	Unknown	21Ma01Kb
Rebecca	37	F	Unknown	21Ma01Kb
Mary-J.	18	F	Unknown	21Ma01Kb
STEWART, Isabella	21	F	Unknown	21Ma01Kb
MCLOUGHLIN, James	30	M	Unknown	21Ma01Kb
MCDERIRT, John	40	M	Unknown	21Ma01Kb
LAUREL, Samuel	19	M	Unknown	21Ma01Kb
GONLY, Mary	18	F	Unknown	21Ma01Kb
MCKINSLY, Margaret	46	F	Unknown	21Ma01Kb
MCFELLEARD, Sarah	18	F	Unknown	21Ma01Kb
MCCONNELL, Andrew	25	M	Unknown	21Ma01Kb
ALCOME, William	50	M	Unknown	21Ma01Kb
Jane	45	F	Unknown	21Ma01Kb
Margaret	21	F	Unknown	21Ma01Kb
James	19	M	Unknown	21Ma01Kb
Mary-J.	17	F	Unknown	21Ma01Kb
HAGAN, Jane	27	F	Unknown	21Ma01Kb
HARTY, Jane	23	F	Unknown	21Ma01Kb
MCDOWELL, William	18	M	Unknown	21Ma01Kb
LIPPON, Mary	17	F	Unknown	21Ma01Kb
QUINN, Mary	15	F	Unknown	21Ma01Kb
Annie	18	F	Unknown	21Ma01Kb
CONNOR, John	26	M	Unknown	21Ma01Kb
JONES, James	19	M	Unknown	21Ma01Kb
KENNY, Terrence	22	M	Unknown	21Ma01Kb
COYLE, Biddy	19	F	Unknown	21Ma01Kb
MCGIBAY, Mary	26	F	Unknown	21Ma01Kb
BRADLEY, Mary	18	F	Unknown	21Ma01Kb
MCGUIRE, John	27	M	Unknown	21Ma01Kb
Patrick	30	M	Unknown	21Ma01Kb
DOHERTY, John	18	M	Unknown	21Ma01Kb
GELL, Michael	54	M	Unknown	21Ma01Kb
U-Mrs.	49	F	Unknown	21Ma01Kb
GELL, Peggy	25	F	Unknown	21Ma01Kb
Eleanor	20	F	Unknown	21Ma01Kb
John	18	M	Unknown	21Ma01Kb
WALLACE, Robert	36	M	Unknown	21Ma01Kb
DOHERTY, Hugh	60	M	Unknown	21Ma01Kb
ARNOLD, Mathew	43	M	Unknown	21Ma01Kb
Mary	40	F	Unknown	21Ma01Kb
James	18	M	Unknown	21Ma01Kb
Mathew	16	M	Unknown	21Ma01Kb
James	14	M	Unknown	21Ma01Kb
THOMPSON, John	20	M	Unknown	21Ma01Kb
KEARNY, Catherine	55	F	Unknown	21Ma01Kb
Charles	24	M	Unknown	21Ma01Kb
Michael	21	M	Unknown	21Ma01Kb
Mary	19	F	Unknown	21Ma01Kb
Catherine	15	F	Unknown	21Ma01Kb
DICKENSON, Catherine-J	18	F	Unknown	21Ma01Kb
MCGENNIS, Charles	40	M	Unknown	21Ma01Kb
MCGRAHAM, James	39	M	Unknown	21Ma01Kb
MCADE, Patrick	50	M	Unknown	21Ma01Kb
DOHERTY, Peggy	17	F	Unknown	21Ma01Kb
MORAND, Alexander	40	M	Unknown	21Ma01Kb
Mary	36	F	Unknown	21Ma01Kb
James	20	M	Unknown	21Ma01Kb
Catherine	16	F	Unknown	21Ma01Kb
Mary-J.	14	F	Unknown	21Ma01Kb
BLANEY, Grace	17	F	Unknown	21Ma01Kb
ALLISON, Rebecca	18	F	Unknown	21Ma01Kb
HILLAN, Michle.	30	M	Unknown	21Ma01Kb
REGAN, Nancy	23	F	Unknown	21Ma01Kb
JOY, Joseph	18	M	Unknown	21Ma01Kb
BLANEY, John	32	M	Unknown	21Ma01Kb
SIVINEY, Francis	26	M	Unknown	21Ma01Kb
LOGIE, John	40	M	Unknown	21Ma01Kb
DOHERTY, James	37	M	Unknown	21Ma01Kb
SHIMERDALE, James	33	M	Unknown	21Ma01Kb
MCGUINESS, Patrick	19	M	Unknown	21Ma01Kb
Charles	23	M	Unknown	21Ma01Kb
CARNNHBEE, Elizabeth	48	F	Unknown	21Ma01Kb
Rebecca	20	F	Unknown	21Ma01Kb
LOGAN, Mary	48	F	Unknown	21Ma01Kb
Ann	23	F	Unknown	21Ma01Kb
Maurice	20	M	Unknown	21Ma01Kb
John	18	M	Unknown	21Ma01Kb
Charles	16	M	Unknown	21Ma01Kb
KELLY, Anne	19	F	Unknown	21Ma01Kb
LAIRD, Margaret	21	F	Unknown	21Ma01Kb
BEGLEY, James	30	M	Unknown	21Ma01Kb
Mary-Ann	18	F	Unknown	21Ma01Kb
Ellen	20	F	Unknown	21Ma01Kb
MCAFFEY, Susan	21	F	Unknown	21Ma01Kb
DENAHY, Ellen	19	F	Unknown	21Ma01Kb
KEARNEY, Margaret	18	F	Unknown	21Ma01Kb
MCLONGHTON, Rose	23	F	Unknown	21Ma01Kb
DICKEY, John	26	M	Unknown	21Ma01Kb
SHERRIDAN, John	24	M	Unknown	21Ma01Kb
MCDERETT, Edward	27	M	Unknown	21Ma01Kb
KELGROVE, Eliza	18	F	Unknown	21Ma01Kb
MCCANNON, Catherine	33	F	Unknown	21Ma01Kb
Peggy	16	F	Unknown	21Ma01Kb
Mary	14	F	Unknown	21Ma01Kb
MCLOUGHLAN, Daniel	50	M	Unknown	21Ma01Kb
David	20	M	Unknown	21Ma01Kb
Mary	18	F	Unknown	21Ma01Kb
Mathy	16	F	Unknown	21Ma01Kb
COYLE, Bridget	43	F	Unknown	21Ma01Kb
SCANLON, Peter	37	M	Unknown	21Ma01Kb
DOHERTY, John	25	M	Unknown	21Ma01Kb
HERMEY, Elizabeth	30	F	Unknown	21Ma01Kb
Rachel	23	F	Unknown	21Ma01Kb
MCDEVIT, Henry	29	M	Unknown	21Ma01Kb
MORRISSON, George	35	M	Unknown	21Ma01Kb
HOLMES, U	18	F	Unknown	21Ma01Kb
NESBIT, William	32	M	Unknown	21Ma01Kb
CUNNINGHAM, David	45	M	Unknown	21Ma01Kb

NAMES OF PASSENGERS	AGE	SEX	OCCUPATIONS	DATE PORT SHIP
BRADLEY, Biddy	50	F	Unknown	21Ma01Kb
James	30	M	Unknown	21Ma01Kb
John	28	M	Unknown	21Ma01Kb
Patrick	25	M	Unknown	21Ma01Kb
Mary-A.	18	F	Unknown	21Ma01Kb
Michl.	16	M	Unknown	21Ma01Kb
Peter	12	M	Unknown	21Ma01Kb
Francis	10	M	Unknown	21Ma01Kb
Hugh	8	M	Child	21Ma01Kb
Kitty	5	F	Child	21Ma01Kb
CARR, John	31	M	Unknown	21Ma01Kb
DEWAR, Mary	18	F	Unknown	21Ma01Kb
Kitty	16	F	Unknown	21Ma01Kb
MULLIN, Lawrence	31	M	Unknown	21Ma01Kb
HEGARTY, James	46	M	Unknown	21Ma01Kb
James	21	M	Unknown	21Ma01Kb
Margaret	18	F	Unknown	21Ma01Kb
Rosey	15	F	Unknown	21Ma01Kb
QUINN, Margaret	50	F	Unknown	21Ma01Kb
John	26	M	Unknown	21Ma01Kb
Michael	21	M	Unknown	21Ma01Kb
Kitty	18	F	Unknown	21Ma01Kb
Daniel	15	M	Unknown	21Ma01Kb
Anney	12	F	Unknown	21Ma01Kb
MCGINLY, Peter	36	M	Unknown	21Ma01Kb
MORAN, Anne	18	F	Unknown	21Ma01Kb
MCGARVEY, Ann	27	F	Unknown	21Ma01Kb
DOHERTY, Rose	19	F	Unknown	21Ma01Kb
CAMBLE, George	30	M	Unknown	21Ma01Kb
PORTER, Elizabeth	23	F	Unknown	21Ma01Kb
DUFFY, Nancy	21	F	Unknown	21Ma01Kb
SWEENY, George	23	M	Unknown	21Ma01Kb
Mary	18	F	Unknown	21Ma01Kb
GRIFFIN, Clinty	27	U	Unknown	21Ma01Kb
MILLAR, Mary	18	F	Unknown	21Ma01Kb
HARVEY, Jane	18	F	Unknown	21Ma01Kb
MCAULANE, Mary-A.	18	F	Unknown	21Ma01Kb
ROSS, Anne	19	F	Unknown	21Ma01Kb
HEGARTY, William	34	M	Unknown	21Ma01Kb
MCGINTY, Patrick	40	M	Unknown	21Ma01Kb
MCGUIRE, Ellen	43	F	Unknown	21Ma01Kb
Philip	20	M	Unknown	21Ma01Kb
Thomas	16	M	Unknown	21Ma01Kb
WILLIAMS, Bridget	54	F	Unknown	21Ma01Kb
Mary-Anne	20	F	Unknown	21Ma01Kb
Margaret	17	F	Unknown	21Ma01Kb
Catherine	15	F	Unknown	21Ma01Kb
DOHERTY, Adam	48	M	Unknown	21Ma01Kb
William	20	M	Unknown	21Ma01Kb
Rose	18	F	Unknown	21Ma01Kb
Biddy	15	F	Unknown	21Ma01Kb
QUIG, John	23	M	Unknown	21Ma01Kb
BAXTER, Mary	17	F	Unknown	21Ma01Kb
MCCANNON, Jane	21	F	Unknown	21Ma01Kb
BENSON, John	27	M	Unknown	21Ma01Kb
Michael	24	M	Unknown	21Ma01Kb
MCKEE, Alexander	47	M	Unknown	21Ma01Kb
Margaret	40	F	Unknown	21Ma01Kb
Margaret	20	F	Unknown	21Ma01Kb
KING, Samuel	48	M	Unknown	21Ma01Kb
Margaret	37	F	Unknown	21Ma01Kb
Sarah	20	F	Unknown	21Ma01Kb
John	15	M	Unknown	21Ma01Kb
Robert	12	M	Unknown	21Ma01Kb
Samuel	10	M	Unknown	21Ma01Kb
Elizabeth	6	F	Child	21Ma01Kb
STARS, Mary	24	F	Unknown	21Ma01Kb
DOHERTY, Nancy	19	F	Unknown	21Ma01Kb
LYNCH, George	24	M	Unknown	21Ma01Kb
MCHAGGIN, Daniel	23	M	Unknown	21Ma01Kb
GILBRAITH, U-Mrs.	40	F	Unknown	21Ma01Kb
Jane	20	F	Unknown	21Ma01Kb
Lydia	18	F	Unknown	21Ma01Kb
Martha	16	F	Unknown	21Ma01Kb
Rachel	14	F	Unknown	21Ma01Kb
ROGERS, Julia	19	F	Unknown	21Ma01Kb
MCGINGLE, Patrick	23	M	Unknown	21Ma01Kb
AUNERS, Catherine	21	F	Unknown	21Ma01Kb
HEINOW, Margaret	30	F	Unknown	21Ma01Kb
CLACKEN, Catherine	29	F	Unknown	21Ma01Kb
Cath.	12	F	Unknown	21Ma01Kb
MCCORMICK, William	47	M	Unknown	21Ma01Kb
U-Mrs.	40	F	Unknown	21Ma01Kb
John	18	M	Unknown	21Ma01Kb
George	16	M	Unknown	21Ma01Kb
Charles	12	M	Unknown	21Ma01Kb
MCLOUGHLIN, Biddy	27	F	Unknown	21Ma01Kb
MCCANNON, John	31	M	Unknown	21Ma01Kb
MCLOUGHLIN, Patrick	27	M	Unknown	21Ma01Kb
MORAND, William	18	M	Unknown	21Ma01Kb

HIGHLAND-MARY 21 MAY 1850

From London

NAMES OF PASSENGERS	AGE	SEX	OCCUPATIONS	DATE PORT SHIP
COOK, Joseph	43	M	Shoemaker	21Ma06Kc
Matilda	42	F	Unknown	21Ma06Kc
James	12	M	Unknown	21Ma06Kc
George	10	M	Unknown	21Ma06Kc
Nathaniel	8	M	Child	21Ma06Kc
Emma	6	F	Child	21Ma06Kc
Eliza	4	F	Child	21Ma06Kc
Theresa	.00	F	Infant	21Ma06Kc
DUGDALE, Richard	48	M	None	21Ma06Kc
BARRETT, Richard	27	M	Laborer	21Ma06Kc
Hannah	28	F	Laborer	21Ma06Kc
REARING, Catherine	20	F	Servant	21Ma06Kc
BENTLEY, William	39	M	Shoemaker	21Ma06Kc
Rebecca	43	F	Unknown	21Ma06Kc
Robert	11	M	Unknown	21Ma06Kc
William	10	M	Unknown	21Ma06Kc
Mary	8	F	Child	21Ma06Kc
Louisa	.00	F	Infant	21Ma06Kc
BENHAM, Samuel	15	M	None	21Ma06Kc
ARBER, Charles	39	M	None	21Ma06Kc
Eliza	37	F	None	21Ma06Kc
Henry	8	M	Child	21Ma06Kc
Alfred	.00	M	Infant	21Ma06Kc
COHEN, Dennis	35	M	None	21Ma06Kc
SULLIVAN, James	23	M	Laborer	21Ma06Kc
WOOLCOCK, James	26	M	Laborer	21Ma06Kc
DAVIS, William	21	M	Laborer	21Ma06Kc
RYAN, Thomas	22	M	None	21Ma06Kc
Margaret	23	F	None	21Ma06Kc
BRITTEN, George	20	M	None	21Ma06Kc
SHEEN, Daniel	23	M	None	21Ma06Kc
HERON, Bridget	22	F	None	21Ma06Kc
GRACY, Hannah	20	F	Laborer	21Ma06Kc
SMITH, Nathan-J.	16	M	Laborer	21Ma06Kc
DACEY, William	50	M	Laborer	21Ma06Kc
SULLIVAN, John	31	M	Laborer	21Ma06Kc
ROBINSON, William	23	M	Laborer	21Ma06Kc
PARKISS, Joseph	48	M	Laborer	21Ma06Kc
Sarah	50	F	Laborer	21Ma06Kc
Eliza	20	F	Laborer	21Ma06Kc
BROWN, John	28	M	Laborer	21Ma06Kc
Sarah	27	F	Laborer	21Ma06Kc
Emily	.00	F	Infant	21Ma06Kc
BRYAN, William	18	M	Laborer	21Ma06Kc
Mary	50	F	Laborer	21Ma06Kc
SAMUEL, Jane	32	F	Laborer	21Ma06Kc
BISHOP, William	30	M	Laborer	21Ma06Kc
BAKER, George	30	M	Laborer	21Ma06Kc
HEFFENHAN, Cornelius	25	M	Laborer	21Ma06Kc

NAMES OF PASSENGERS	AGE	SEX	OCCUPATIONS	DATE PORT SHIP
HEFFENHAN, Emma	22	F	Laborer	21Ma06Kc
Catherine	.00	F	Infant	21Ma06Kc
PERSHEN, John	29	M	Laborer	21Ma06Kc
Jemina	30	F	Laborer	21Ma06Kc
Maria	.00	F	Infant	21Ma06Kc
LARTER, James	32	M	Laborer	21Ma06Kc
WIGGINS, Francis	21	M	None	21Ma06Kc
SULLIVAN, Timothy	24	M	None	21Ma06Kc
HUSHEN, Thomas	30	M	Clerk	21Ma06Kc
Sebina	27	M	Laborer	21Ma06Kc
RAYNER, Jeremiah	35	M	Laborer	21Ma06Kc
Mary	35	F	Laborer	21Ma06Kc
Mary-Ann	.00	F	Infant	21Ma06Kc
CONNOLEY, Jerry	21	M	Laborer	21Ma06Kc
BAILEY, Martin	22	M	Laborer	21Ma06Kc
CARROLL, Mary	30	F	None	21Ma06Kc
Mary-Ann	6	F	Child	21Ma06Kc
John	5	M	Child	21Ma06Kc
Catherine	2	F	Child	21Ma06Kc
Thomas	.00	M	Infant	21Ma06Kc
WYGO, Margaret	40	F	Laborer	21Ma06Kc
WRIGHT, Daniel	26	M	Laborer	21Ma06Kc
REGAN, William	32	M	Laborer	21Ma06Kc
SMITH, Michael	26	M	Laborer	21Ma06Kc
STENCER, Carl	31	M	Laborer	21Ma06Kc
CONNER, John	21	M	Laborer	21Ma06Kc
DERSHEN, Mary	36	F	Laborer	21Ma06Kc
Donald	13	M	None	21Ma06Kc
Hannah	23	F	None	21Ma06Kc
Michael	2	M	Child	21Ma06Kc
Margaret	.00	F	Infant	21Ma06Kc
HOAR, Benjamin	24	M	None	21Ma06Kc
OATES, John	35	M	Laborer	21Ma06Kc
Catherine	32	F	Laborer	21Ma06Kc
Salem	6	M	Child	21Ma06Kc
Peter	.00	M	Infant	21Ma06Kc
PIKE, George	34	M	Laborer	21Ma06Kc
Elizabeth	41	F	Laborer	21Ma06Kc
Pike	11	M	Laborer	21Ma06Kc
Frederic	9	M	Child	21Ma06Kc
Herbert	1	M	Child	21Ma06Kc
Sarah	4	F	Child	21Ma06Kc
BOX, James	21	M	Laborer	21Ma06Kc
HART, Catherine	24	F	Laborer	21Ma06Kc
GRANEY, Patric	26	M	Laborer	21Ma06Kc
LONARGER, Dennis	20	M	Laborer	21Ma06Kc
MORAN, William	36	M	Shoemaker	21Ma06Kc
Ann	38	F	Shoemaker	21Ma06Kc
William	2	M	Child	21Ma06Kc
Mary	2	F	Child	21Ma06Kc
Mora	.00	F	Infant	21Ma06Kc
DONAVAN, Daniel	26	M	Surveyor	21Ma06Kc
Catherine	26	F	Surveyor	21Ma06Kc
Peter	.00	M	Infant	21Ma06Kc
BROOK, Charles	32	M	Surveyor	21Ma06Kc
Ann	28	F	Surveyor	21Ma06Kc
Ellen	6	F	Child	21Ma06Kc
Flora	5	F	Child	21Ma06Kc
LAVENDER, Jane	22	F	Surveyor	21Ma06Kc
George	.00	M	Infant	21Ma06Kc
Ellen	36	F	Tailor	21Ma06Kc
Ellen	.00	F	Infant	21Ma06Kc
ABBOT, Harriett	23	F	Tailor	21Ma06Kc
ODONALD, Michael	23	M	Agrc	21Ma06Kc
HAYES, William	52	M	Agrc	21Ma06Kc
Catherine	15	F	Agrc	21Ma06Kc
FROOME, Francis	45	M	Agrc	21Ma06Kc
Mary	35	F	Agrc	21Ma06Kc
John	7	M	Child	21Ma06Kc
William	6	M	Child	21Ma06Kc
James	4	M	Child	21Ma06Kc
Frederic	4	M	Child	21Ma06Kc
Eliza	3	F	Child	21Ma06Kc
HARMAR, George	38	M	Agrc	21Ma06Kc
SERGROVE, John	32	M	Agrc	21Ma06Kc

NAMES OF PASSENGERS	AGE	SEX	OCCUPATIONS	DATE PORT SHIP
AIREY, Elizabeth	24	F	Agrc	21Ma06Kc
DONOVAN, John	38	M	None	21Ma06Kc
JORDAN, Joseph	26	M	None	21Ma06Kc
JOHNSON, John	24	M	None	21Ma06Kc
CLEVEN, Julia	30	F	None	21Ma06Kc
PIRMER, David	47	M	None	21Ma06Kc
SONTER, David	30	M	None	21Ma06Kc
SMITH, James	21	M	Clerk	21Ma06Kc
LANGFORD, Henry	30	M	Shipwright	21Ma06Kc
BRACER, Edmund	29	M	Mariner	21Ma06Kc
RUSSELL, James	21	M	Mariner	21Ma06Kc
Robert	28	M	Mariner	21Ma06Kc
COLLARD, Charles	40	M	Unknown	21Ma06Kc
SMITH, Henry	29	M	Unknown	21Ma06Kc
LEVI, Harriet	30	F	Unknown	21Ma06Kc
Rosa	10	F	Unknown	21Ma06Kc
U	.00	F	Infant	21Ma06Kc

CHARLES-RICHARD 21 MAY 1850

From Limerick

NAMES OF PASSENGERS	AGE	SEX	OCCUPATIONS	DATE PORT SHIP
REDDEE, Andrew	20	M	Laborer	21Ma10Kd
MULLIGAN, John	20	M	Unknown	21Ma10Kd
LYNCH, Mary	30	F	Unknown	21Ma10Kd
Cath.	2	F	Child	21Ma10Kd
DONOHUE, Thomas	32	M	Unknown	21Ma10Kd
Margt.	31	F	Unknown	21Ma10Kd
DESMOND, William	35	M	Unknown	21Ma10Kd
Cath.	30	F	Unknown	21Ma10Kd
Margt.	3	F	Unknown	21Ma10Kd
Kate	.00	F	Infant	21Ma10Kd
OBRIEN, Pat	28	M	Unknown	21Ma10Kd
Margaret	26	F	Unknown	21Ma10Kd
Ellen	.00	F	Infant	21Ma10Kd
DORONEY, James	32	M	Infant	21Ma10Kd
HANOREN, Margt.	18	F	Unknown	21Ma10Kd
Daniel	26	M	Unknown	21Ma10Kd
GLEESON, Daniel	17	M	Unknown	21Ma10Kd
LANAN, Hannah	23	F	Unknown	21Ma10Kd
MALONY, Jeremiah	30	M	Unknown	21Ma10Kd
GLEESON, Mary	28	F	Unknown	21Ma10Kd
John	25	M	Unknown	21Ma10Kd
Kitty	4	F	Child	21Ma10Kd
LYNCH, Mary	26	F	Unknown	21Ma10Kd
CONNORS, Judy	26	F	Unknown	21Ma10Kd
BURNELL, James	25	M	Unknown	21Ma10Kd
AKEIN, Patt	20	M	Unknown	21Ma10Kd
Biddy	20	F	Unknown	21Ma10Kd
RILEY, Cath.	23	F	Unknown	21Ma10Kd
ROBERTS, Joseph	16	M	Unknown	21Ma10Kd
Margt.	15	F	Unknown	21Ma10Kd
MCNAMARA, Patt	23	M	Unknown	21Ma10Kd
James	35	M	Unknown	21Ma10Kd
Cath.	28	F	Unknown	21Ma10Kd
Biddy	28	F	Unknown	21Ma10Kd
C.	.00	F	Infant	21Ma10Kd
HUDDERT, John	27	M	Unknown	21Ma10Kd
Thomas	20	M	Unknown	21Ma10Kd
Eliza	24	F	Unknown	21Ma10Kd
COLLMAN, Thomas	30	M	Unknown	21Ma10Kd
FITZGERALD, Andrew	18	M	Unknown	21Ma10Kd
ODEA, William	26	M	Unknown	21Ma10Kd
Michl.	23	M	Unknown	21Ma10Kd
John	21	M	Unknown	21Ma10Kd
MULLGREEN, Mary	27	F	Unknown	21Ma10Kd
MORIARTY, John	30	M	Unknown	21Ma10Kd
SHANNAHAN, Cornelius	16	M	Unknown	21Ma10Kd
MURPHY, Cath.	20	M	Unknown	21Ma10Kd

NAMES OF PASSENGERS	AGE	SEX	OCCUPATIONS	DATE PORT SHIP
ROCHE, Cath.	20	F	Unknown	21Ma10Kd
MORIARTY, Nancy	20	F	Unknown	21Ma10Kd
CONNELAN, Patt	45	M	Unknown	21Ma10Kd
Tim	38	U	Unknown	21Ma10Kd
MALONEY, Bridget	28	F	Unknown	21Ma10Kd
WELSH, Margt.	20	F	Unknown	21Ma10Kd
RIELY, Thomas	25	M	Unknown	21Ma10Kd
ROURKE, James	40	M	Unknown	21Ma10Kd
Cath.	18	F	Unknown	21Ma10Kd
QUIN, Mary	20	F	Unknown	21Ma10Kd
Ellen	19	F	Unknown	21Ma10Kd
GLEESON, Dennis	40	M	Unknown	21Ma10Kd
Patt	19	F	Unknown	21Ma10Kd
Cath	15	F	Unknown	21Ma10Kd
DARCEY, Corn.	13	M	Unknown	21Ma10Kd
LEDGER, Ann	24	F	Unknown	21Ma10Kd
John	.00	M	Infant	21Ma10Kd
CARNGY, Mathew	24	M	Unknown	21Ma10Kd
CONNOLLY, Mary	44	F	Unknown	21Ma10Kd
Mary	21	F	Unknown	21Ma10Kd
Patt	13	M	Unknown	21Ma10Kd
Cath.	8	F	Child	21Ma10Kd
Patt	5	M	Child	21Ma10Kd
NUGENT, Thos.	21	M	Unknown	21Ma10Kd
CUNNINGHAM, John	30	M	Unknown	21Ma10Kd
SULLIVAN, Michl.	25	M	Unknown	21Ma10Kd
Bridget	20	F	Unknown	21Ma10Kd
Lawrence	.00	M	Infant	21Ma10Kd
ROBERTS, Thos.	22	M	Unknown	21Ma10Kd
OBRIEN, Matt	21	M	Unknown	21Ma10Kd
MOLYNES, Mary	20	F	Unknown	21Ma10Kd
BROWNE, Cath.	40	F	Unknown	21Ma10Kd
Patt	21	M	Unknown	21Ma10Kd
MOLONEY, Michl.	17	M	Unknown	21Ma10Kd
HOGAN, Patt	30	M	Unknown	21Ma10Kd
MULLGREEN, Michl.	30	M	Unknown	21Ma10Kd
COLLINS, Michael	36	M	Unknown	21Ma10Kd
MURAN, James	16	M	Unknown	21Ma10Kd
SPERIN, Maria	35	F	Unknown	21Ma10Kd
Lawrence	35	F	Unknown	21Ma10Kd
Henry	21	M	Unknown	21Ma10Kd
Mary-Ann	12	F	Unknown	21Ma10Kd
Isabella	10	F	Unknown	21Ma10Kd
SHAW, Patrick	3	M	Child	21Ma10Kd
Catherine	.00	F	Infant	21Ma10Kd
HEFFENNER, Patt	28	M	Unknown	21Ma10Kd
Rodger	21	M	Unknown	21Ma10Kd
HANES, Joseph	30	M	Unknown	21Ma10Kd
DALEY, John	40	M	Unknown	21Ma10Kd
Bessy	18	F	Unknown	21Ma10Kd
WHITECOMB, William	40	M	Unknown	21Ma10Kd
WILMETT, James	26	M	Laborer	21Ma10Kd

PRINCESS-VICTORY 21 MAY 1850

From Limerick

NAMES OF PASSENGERS	AGE	SEX	OCCUPATIONS	DATE PORT SHIP
ENWRIGHT, Michael	29	M	Laborer	21Ma10Jx
OSHEA, Michael	21	M	Unknown	21Ma10Jx
ENWRIGHT, Margt.	23	F	Unknown	21Ma10Jx
OSHEA, Michael	22	M	Unknown	21Ma10Jx
HOWARD, John	30	M	Unknown	21Ma10Jx
John	28	M	Unknown	21Ma10Jx
Anne	25	F	Unknown	21Ma10Jx
HOGAN, Cath.	28	F	Unknown	21Ma10Jx
HOWARD, James	7	M	Child	21Ma10Jx
HOLLORAN, Bridgt.	20	F	Unknown	21Ma10Jx
KENE, John	26	M	Unknown	21Ma10Jx
LYONS, Johana	25	F	Unknown	21Ma10Jx
ROACH, Maurice	27	M	Unknown	21Ma10Jx
OBRIEN, Mick	17	M	Unknown	21Ma10Jx
Cath.	23	F	Unknown	21Ma10Jx
RUSSELL, Michael	16	M	Unknown	21Ma10Jx
HEWTON, Winney	40	F	Unknown	21Ma10Jx
Thomas	9	M	Child	21Ma10Jx
ROYAL, John	23	M	Unknown	21Ma10Jx
Eliza	21	F	Unknown	21Ma10Jx
OBRIEN, Mary	32	F	Unknown	21Ma10Jx
LONG, Sally	18	F	Unknown	21Ma10Jx
GARVEY, Francis	20	M	Unknown	21Ma10Jx
COSTELLO, Timothy	21	M	Unknown	21Ma10Jx
GREEN, Johana	20	F	Unknown	21Ma10Jx
BRADLEY, Margaret	20	F	Unknown	21Ma10Jx
MCCARTHY, Ellen	20	F	Unknown	21Ma10Jx
FINNERY, Margaret	22	F	Unknown	21Ma10Jx
BEHANE, Mary	12	F	Unknown	21Ma10Jx
Hannah	15	F	Unknown	21Ma10Jx
KEANE, Johana	17	F	Unknown	21Ma10Jx
SHANAHAN, Edward	36	M	Unknown	21Ma10Jx
KERBY, Daniel	24	M	Unknown	21Ma10Jx
Patt	25	M	Unknown	21Ma10Jx
MCNALLY, Thos.	35	M	Unknown	21Ma10Jx
DELEANE, Biddy	18	F	Unknown	21Ma10Jx
FOWLEY, Bridgt.	24	F	Unknown	21Ma10Jx
Hannah	24	F	Unknown	21Ma10Jx
Judy	22	F	Unknown	21Ma10Jx
MCMAHON, Margt.	25	F	Unknown	21Ma10Jx
BURKE, William	22	M	Unknown	21Ma10Jx
Cath.	14	F	Unknown	21Ma10Jx
RYAN, John	25	M	Unknown	21Ma10Jx
Mary	20	F	Unknown	21Ma10Jx
FARRELL, Satt.	30	F	Unknown	21Ma10Jx
RYAN, Patt	35	M	Unknown	21Ma10Jx
MEARY, Bridgt.	34	F	Unknown	21Ma10Jx
Mary	2	F	Child	21Ma10Jx
John	.00	M	Infant	21Ma10Jx
CONNORS, David	21	M	Unknown	21Ma10Jx
Mary	30	F	Unknown	21Ma10Jx
EGAN, Mary	20	F	Unknown	21Ma10Jx
SMITH, John	35	M	Unknown	21Ma10Jx
Mary	30	F	Unknown	21Ma10Jx
Mary	9	F	Child	21Ma10Jx
William	7	M	Child	21Ma10Jx
John	.00	M	Infant	21Ma10Jx
George	.00	M	Infant	21Ma10Jx
KELLY, Pat	30	M	Unknown	21Ma10Jx
CRONNER, James	30	M	Unknown	21Ma10Jx
MERRITT, Michl.	21	M	Unknown	21Ma10Jx
MOLONY, Michl.	40	M	Unknown	21Ma10Jx
DONOHUE, Ellen	25	F	Unknown	21Ma10Jx
GLEESON, John	18	M	Unknown	21Ma10Jx
JORDAN, Bridgt.	22	F	Unknown	21Ma10Jx
Johana	21	F	Unknown	21Ma10Jx
SMITH, Biddy	2	F	Child	21Ma10Jx
HARTLEY, Edmund	23	M	Unknown	21Ma10Jx
MORAN, Michael	25	M	Unknown	21Ma10Jx
John	25	M	Unknown	21Ma10Jx
Mary	20	F	Unknown	21Ma10Jx
SHAN. \N, William	21	M	Unknown	21Ma10Jx
HERBERT, Bridgt.	30	F	Unknown	21Ma10Jx
Mary	45	F	Unknown	21Ma10Jx
DOYLE, James	22	M	Unknown	21Ma10Jx
Cath.	28	F	Unknown	21Ma10Jx
RYAN, Johana	16	F	Unknown	21Ma10Jx
Bridgt.	47	F	Unknown	21Ma10Jx
HOGAN, Stephen	22	M	Unknown	21Ma10Jx
GABBETT, John	19	M	Unknown	21Ma10Jx
OBREEN, Jas.	17	M	Unknown	21Ma10Jx
SHEEHAN, Michl.	20	M	Unknown	21Ma10Jx
John	22	M	Unknown	21Ma10Jx
GIBBON, Thos.F.	40	M	Unknown	21Ma10Jx
LONG, Hannah	20	F	Unknown	21Ma10Jx
SHEEHY, Margt.	15	F	Unknown	21Ma10Jx
Thos.	13	M	Unknown	21Ma10Jx

NAMES OF PASSENGERS	AGE	SEX	OCCUPATIONS	DATE PORT SHIP
SHEEHY, Mary	11	F	Unknown	21Ma10Jx
Bridgt.	9	F	Child	21Ma10Jx
Edward	.00	M	Infant	21Ma10Jx
MCNALLY, Edward	22	M	Merchant	21Ma10Jx
OBRIEN, Mary	21	F	Spinster	21Ma10Jx
Cath.	21	F	Spinster	21Ma10Jx
WEBB, Margt.	21	F	Spinster	21Ma10Jx
MCMAHON, Mary	16	F	Spinster	21Ma10Jx
LEWIS, David	36	M	Unknown	21Ma10Jx

DUKE 21 MAY 1850

From Liverpool

NAMES OF PASSENGERS	AGE	SEX	OCCUPATIONS	DATE PORT SHIP
MCCORMACK, Biddy	20	F	Spinster	21Ma02Hs
WELSH, Cathr.	20	F	Spinster	21Ma02Hs
WADE, Bernd.	18	M	Laborer	21Ma02Hs
MCGREEVY, Denis	20	M	Laborer	21Ma02Hs
FLEMING, Eliza	20	F	Spinster	21Ma02Hs
MCGUINNESS, Margt.	24	F	Wi	21Ma02Hs
James	.00	M	Infant	21Ma02Hs
ROONEY, James	30	M	Laborer	21Ma02Hs
CAHILL, Mary	14	F	Spinster	21Ma02Hs
MULLAN, Wm.	31	M	Laborer	21Ma02Hs
MULVANY, Jas.	30	M	Servant	21Ma02Hs
COYNE, Margt.	22	F	Spinster	21Ma02Hs
CROLLY, Timothy	31	M	Laborer	21Ma02Hs
QUINN, Mary	21	F	Spinster	21Ma02Hs
LUCKLEY, Cathr.	13	F	Spinster	21Ma02Hs
DOOLAN, John	18	M	Laborer	21Ma02Hs
Mary	25	F	Unknown	21Ma02Hs
WHALEN, Michl.	30	M	Unknown	21Ma02Hs
GALLAGHER, Rose	35	F	Wi	21Ma02Hs
Bridget	9	F	Child	21Ma02Hs
Mary	7	F	Child	21Ma02Hs
FORD, James	20	M	Laborer	21Ma02Hs
MCDONALD, Mary	20	F	Unknown	21Ma02Hs
CONNELL, Ann	18	F	Unknown	21Ma02Hs
GLASHAW, John	50	M	Laborer	21Ma02Hs
Winfred	40	F	Unknown	21Ma02Hs
Mary	11	F	Unknown	21Ma02Hs
Winifred	5	F	Child	21Ma02Hs
John	3	M	Child	21Ma02Hs
Martin	.00	M	Infant	21Ma02Hs
Cathr.	40	F	Wi	21Ma02Hs
Thomas	11	M	Unknown	21Ma02Hs
Bridget	11	F	Unknown	21Ma02Hs
OBRIEN, Mich	20	M	Laborer	21Ma02Hs
Thomas	22	M	Laborer	21Ma02Hs
OBRADY, Stanus	18	M	Laborer	21Ma02Hs
MARSHALL, Margt.	16	F	Spinster	21Ma02Hs
NAUGHTON, Richard	40	M	Laborer	21Ma02Hs
CAFFY, Michl.	22	M	Laborer	21Ma02Hs
MANGIN, Ellen	20	F	Spinster	21Ma02Hs
DOWDALL, Mary	50	F	Wi	21Ma02Hs
BOYD, Alexr.	20	M	Laborer	21Ma02Hs
Eliza	24	F	Spinster	21Ma02Hs
BOYSON, Ellen	15	F	Spinster	21Ma02Hs
CAHILL, Peter	40	M	Laborer	21Ma02Hs
BRENNAN, James	40	M	Unknown	21Ma02Hs
Mary	23	F	Unknown	21Ma02Hs
Mary-Ann	2	F	Child	21Ma02Hs
William	.00	M	Infant	21Ma02Hs
ODONNELL, Hugh	37	M	Laborer	21Ma02Hs
KERNAN, Patk.	33	M	Laborer	21Ma02Hs
Margt.	30	F	Unknown	21Ma02Hs
James	.00	M	Infant	21Ma02Hs
FLANIGAN, Wm.	40	M	Laborer	21Ma02Hs
Mary	26	F	Unknown	21Ma02Hs

NAMES OF PASSENGERS	AGE	SEX	OCCUPATIONS	DATE PORT SHIP
FLANIGAN, Timothy	4	M	Child	21Ma02Hs
MULLAN, Thomas	20	M	Unknown	21Ma02Hs
Bridget	13	F	Unknown	21Ma02Hs
Elizabeth	16	F	Unknown	21Ma02Hs
DIGNAN, Mary	20	F	Unknown	21Ma02Hs
GALLAGHER, Christy	26	M	Mechanic	21Ma02Hs
MURPHY, Thomas	45	M	Mechanic	21Ma02Hs
RANDALL, Jas.	20	M	Mechanic	21Ma02Hs
George	18	M	Mechanic	21Ma02Hs
DWYER, Thomas	35	M	Mechanic	21Ma02Hs
Sarah	12	F	Unknown	21Ma02Hs
STYLES, George	12	M	Unknown	21Ma02Hs
CLEMENTS, Saml.	20	M	Mechanic	21Ma02Hs
GIBBS, Emma	39	F	Unknown	21Ma02Hs
Adelaide	18	F	Unknown	21Ma02Hs
Harriet	16	F	Unknown	21Ma02Hs
Joseph	12	M	Mechanic	21Ma02Hs
Edwin	10	M	Mechanic	21Ma02Hs
Mary-A.	8	F	Child	21Ma02Hs
Eliza	6	F	Child	21Ma02Hs
Emma	3	F	Child	21Ma02Hs
CLEMENTS, Peter	44	M	Mechanic	21Ma02Hs
Hannah	54	F	Unknown	21Ma02Hs
William	13	M	Mechanic	21Ma02Hs
Sarah	12	F	Unknown	21Ma02Hs
Thomas	8	M	Child	21Ma02Hs
Margt.	4	F	Child	21Ma02Hs
PERULT, Wm.	60	M	Mechanic	21Ma02Hs
James	15	F	Unknown	21Ma02Hs
BROPHY, Michael	22	M	Unknown	21Ma02Hs
WHELAN, David	26	M	Mechanic	21Ma02Hs
Margt.	21	F	Unknown	21Ma02Hs
CALLAGHAN, Anty	21	M	Mechanic	21Ma02Hs
GREENAN, Edward	41	M	Mechanic	21Ma02Hs
Eliza	41	F	Unknown	21Ma02Hs
Mary	18	F	Unknown	21Ma02Hs
Rose	16	F	Unknown	21Ma02Hs
Eliza	11	F	Unknown	21Ma02Hs
Sarah	9	F	Child	21Ma02Hs
Joseph	8	M	Child	21Ma02Hs
Anne	6	F	Child	21Ma02Hs
Teresa	2	F	Child	21Ma02Hs
Bridget	.00	F	Infant	21Ma02Hs
MARTIN, John	18	M	Mechanic	21Ma02Hs
SHEA, Ellen	18	F	Unknown	21Ma02Hs
DAYLE, Martin	25	M	Laborer	21Ma02Hs
MURPHY, Thos.	12	M	Laborer	21Ma02Hs
Johanna	8	F	Child	21Ma02Hs
DAVIS, Jas.	33	M	Laborer	21Ma02Hs
PHILLIPS, William	25	M	Laborer	21Ma02Hs
Mary-A.	27	F	Unknown	21Ma02Hs
FEEHAN, Eliza	13	F	Unknown	21Ma02Hs
CAMERON, James	60	M	Laborer	21Ma02Hs
Jane	45	F	Unknown	21Ma02Hs
John	26	M	Laborer	21Ma02Hs
Eliza	6	F	Child	21Ma02Hs
CARTIN, Jas.	30	M	Laborer	21Ma02Hs
SWEENEY, Edwd.	24	M	Laborer	21Ma02Hs
FORDE, Danl.	28	M	Laborer	21Ma02Hs
DONLAN, John	20	M	Laborer	21Ma02Hs
Mary	13	F	Unknown	21Ma02Hs
Bess	11	F	Unknown	21Ma02Hs
CARROLL, Margt.	17	F	Unknown	21Ma02Hs
DALTIN, Margt.	12	F	Unknown	21Ma02Hs
KEEGAN, John	21	M	Laborer	21Ma02Hs
TAFT, Margt.	27	F	Unknown	21Ma02Hs
MANSFIELD, Saml.	24	M	Laborer	21Ma02Hs
DENNIS, Danl.	24	M	Laborer	21Ma02Hs
SULLIVAN, Dennis	24	M	Laborer	21Ma02Hs
CABIN, Thomas	30	M	Laborer	21Ma02Hs
JONES, James	30	M	Laborer	21Ma02Hs
James-Jr.	8	M	Child	21Ma02Hs
BONEY, Henry	26	M	Laborer	21Ma02Hs
MAGUIRE, John	62	M	Laborer	21Ma02Hs
GARNEY, Benj.	30	M	Laborer	21Ma02Hs

NAMES OF PASSENGERS	AGE	SEX	OCCUPATIONS	DATE PORT SHIP
GARNEY, U-Mrs.	20	F	Unknown	21Ma02Hs
Emily	.00	F	Infant	21Ma02Hs
Edward	34	M	Laborer	21Ma02Hs
REARDON, Bryan	55	M	Laborer	21Ma02Hs
MCNAMARA, Mary	24	F	Unknown	21Ma02Hs
Timothy	24	M	Laborer	21Ma02Hs
KENNEDY, Margt.	18	F	Unknown	21Ma02Hs
CLARK, Alfred	20	M	Laborer	21Ma02Hs
OBRIEN, Edward	28	M	Laborer	21Ma02Hs
WICHAM, Thomas	26	M	Laborer	21Ma02Hs
FARRELL, John	19	M	Laborer	21Ma02Hs
MITCHELL, Thos.	45	M	Laborer	21Ma02Hs
William	17	M	Laborer	21Ma02Hs
Thos.	12	M	Laborer	21Ma02Hs
FLOOD, Edward	20	M	Laborer	21Ma02Hs
Sarah	40	F	Unknown	21Ma02Hs
GIBBONS, Thos.	31	M	Laborer	21Ma02Hs
Bridget	31	F	Unknown	21Ma02Hs
Mary	.00	F	Infant	21Ma02Hs
FENAUGHTY, John	27	M	Laborer	21Ma02Hs
MULLAGHEY, Mary	24	F	Unknown	21Ma02Hs
John	.00	M	Infant	21Ma02Hs
KING, Cathr.	12	F	Unknown	21Ma02Hs
DUFFIN, James	57	M	Farmer	21Ma02Hs
Mary	50	F	Unknown	21Ma02Hs
Elizabeth	18	F	Spinster	21Ma02Hs
Esther	15	F	Spinster	21Ma02Hs
Ellen	11	F	Spinster	21Ma02Hs
Nancy	7	F	Child	21Ma02Hs
REEVES, Thomas	35	M	Laborer	21Ma02Hs
Mary	28	F	Unknown	21Ma02Hs
Anne	13	F	Unknown	21Ma02Hs
Cathr.	12	F	Unknown	21Ma02Hs
Mary	10	F	Unknown	21Ma02Hs
John	8	M	Child	21Ma02Hs
Patk.	2	M	Child	21Ma02Hs
Sarah	.00	F	Infant	21Ma02Hs
LYON, Anne	26	F	Unknown	21Ma02Hs
Margt.	3	F	Child	21Ma02Hs
REEVES, William	18	M	Laborer	21Ma02Hs
WALTERS, Chas.	20	M	Laborer	21Ma02Hs
BRYAN, James	21	M	Laborer	21Ma02Hs
Christopher	26	F	Laborer	21Ma02Hs
William	10	M	Laborer	21Ma02Hs
John-Lyons	3	M	Child	21Ma02Hs
ANDERSON, Michl.	35	M	Laborer	21Ma02Hs
KELLY, Michl.	21	M	Laborer	21Ma02Hs
DOWLAN, Sally	22	F	Spinster	21Ma02Hs
MCGIRL, Ann	17	F	Spinster	21Ma02Hs
MCLAUGHLIN, Anne	44	F	Wi	21Ma02Hs
PRIER, Michl.	16	M	Painter	21Ma02Hs
Patk.	17	M	Clerk	21Ma02Hs
FAGAN, Thomas	16	M	Clerk	21Ma02Hs
James	10	M	Clerk	21Ma02Hs
SMITH, U	00	M	Unknown	21Ma02Hs
WOOD, U	00	M	Unknown	21Ma02Hs
AUSTIN, U	00	M	Unknown	21Ma02Hs
JONES, U	00	M	Unknown	21Ma02Hs
U-Mrs.	00	F	Unknown	21Ma02Hs
TAITE, U	00	M	Unknown	21Ma02Hs
IRVINE, U-Miss	00	F	Unknown	21Ma02Hs
GRACEY, U-Miss	00	F	Unknown	21Ma02Hs
JOHNSON, U-Miss	00	F	Unknown	21Ma02Hs
FIRTH, U	00	M	Unknown	21Ma02Hs
HOME, U	00	M	Unknown	21Ma02Hs
U-Mrs.	00	F	Unknown	21Ma02Hs
U	.00	U	Infant	21Ma02Hs
DYDE, U	00	M	Unknown	21Ma02Hs
U-Mrs.	00	F	Unknown	21Ma02Hs
HEWSON, U	00	M	Unknown	21Ma02Hs
U-Mrs.	00	F	Unknown	21Ma02Hs

MISSISSIPPI 21 MAY 1850

From Glasgow

NAMES OF PASSENGERS	AGE	SEX	OCCUPATIONS	DATE PORT SHIP
MILLS, Jane	27	F	Unknown	21Ma21Gp
RINMOUTH, John	73	M	Milliner	21Ma21Gp
LAWSON, Janet	19	F	Farmer	21Ma21Gp
BRAND, Ellen	24	F	Unknown	21Ma21Gp
HENDERSON, Alex.	51	M	Unknown	21Ma21Gp
U-Mrs.	50	F	Unknown	21Ma21Gp
John	19	M	Unknown	21Ma21Gp
Mary	9	F	Child	21Ma21Gp
JOHNSTON, James	23	M	Unknown	21Ma21Gp
CARSONS, John	25	M	Unknown	21Ma21Gp
Alizon	23	F	Unknown	21Ma21Gp
ANDERSON, Alex	23	M	Unknown	21Ma21Gp
U-Mrs.	23	F	Unknown	21Ma21Gp
FORSYTH, Mathw.	23	F	Unknown	21Ma21Gp
HAILSTONES, John	23	F	Unknown	21Ma21Gp
SWANSON, Robert	24	F	Unknown	21Ma21Gp
DIVINEY, Owen	23	M	Unknown	21Ma21Gp
ELLIOT, James	19	M	Unknown	21Ma21Gp
SCOTT, William	19	M	Unknown	21Ma21Gp
GARCADDEN, Jane	33	F	Unknown	21Ma21Gp
Margr.	16	F	Unknown	21Ma21Gp
Cath.	10	F	Unknown	21Ma21Gp
John	.06	M	Infant	21Ma21Gp
HERON, Thomas	30	M	Unknown	21Ma21Gp
U-Mrs.	27	F	Unknown	21Ma21Gp
Christina	8	F	Child	21Ma21Gp
James	6	M	Child	21Ma21Gp
Elizabeth	3	F	Child	21Ma21Gp
Margt.	.11	F	Infant	21Ma21Gp
DICKSON, Wm.	29	M	Unknown	21Ma21Gp
U-Mrs.	26	F	Unknown	21Ma21Gp
Joseph	6	M	Child	21Ma21Gp
Arhcr.	00	M	Unknown	21Ma21Gp
GARDENER, Wm.	21	M	Unknown	21Ma21Gp
U-Mrs.	19	F	Unknown	21Ma21Gp
WALLS, Robert	36	M	Unknown	21Ma21Gp
HULTON, Janet	32	F	Unknown	21Ma21Gp
James	7	M	Child	21Ma21Gp
John	4	M	Child	21Ma21Gp
Andrew	2	M	Child	21Ma21Gp
Robert	.09	M	Infant	21Ma21Gp
COWIE, Thomas	25	M	Unknown	21Ma21Gp
MCALVEE, Biddy	11	F	Unknown	21Ma21Gp
MILLAR, Robert	30	M	Unknown	21Ma21Gp
COWIE, Isabella	23	F	Unknown	21Ma21Gp
Elizabeth	2	F	Child	21Ma21Gp
William	.06	M	Infant	21Ma21Gp
BYLE, Alison	23	F	Unknown	21Ma21Gp
KINGHORN, Robert	50	M	Unknown	21Ma21Gp
Ann	50	F	Unknown	21Ma21Gp
Robert	24	M	Unknown	21Ma21Gp
Alex	28	M	Unknown	21Ma21Gp
Janet	26	F	Unknown	21Ma21Gp
SLIGHT, Archd.	21	M	Unknown	21Ma21Gp
SHAW, Clara	23	F	Unknown	21Ma21Gp
U-Mrs.	22	F	Unknown	21Ma21Gp
CANLY, Thomas	24	M	Unknown	21Ma21Gp
U-Mrs.	21	F	Unknown	21Ma21Gp
SHAW, John	.08	M	Infant	21Ma21Gp
DAWINE, John	31	M	Unknown	21Ma21Gp
KENNIS, Andrew	23	M	Unknown	21Ma21Gp
COWANS, Alex	23	M	Unknown	21Ma21Gp
COCKBURN, David	19	M	Unknown	21Ma21Gp
BIRCH, Robert	66	M	Unknown	21Ma21Gp
BANAGHAN, Hugh	28	M	Unknown	21Ma21Gp

NAMES OF PASSENGERS	AGE	SEX	OCCUPATIONS	DATE PORT SHIP
BANAGHAN, U-Mrs.	29	F	Unknown	21Ma21Gp
Margt.	4	F	Child	21Ma21Gp
John	.02	M	Infant	21Ma21Gp
Peter	32	M	Unknown	21Ma21Gp
U-Mrs.	32	F	Unknown	21Ma21Gp
Margt.	5	F	Child	21Ma21Gp
Thomas	3	M	Child	21Ma21Gp
Peter	.09	M	Infant	21Ma21Gp
YOUNG, Willm.	32	M	Unknown	21Ma21Gp
FOSTERER. Robert	25	M	Unknown	21Ma21Gp
RIDER, Jacob	26	M	Unknown	21Ma21Gp
U-Mrs.	23	F	Unknown	21Ma21Gp
HEIN, Peter	13	M	Unknown	21Ma21Gp
KLOSS, Martin	13	M	Unknown	21Ma21Gp
Catherine	13	F	Unknown	21Ma21Gp
KIEL, Elizabeth	12	F	Unknown	21Ma21Gp
RIDER. Christopher	.08	M	Infant	21Ma21Gp
CARFRAY. Edward	40	M	Unknown	21Ma21Gp
Edward	.04	M	Infant	21Ma21Gp
Elizabeth	12	F	Unknown	21Ma21Gp
REID. James	20	M	Unknown	21Ma21Gp
GALLAGHER. Barny	22	M	Unknown	21Ma21Gp
GRAY. Bridget	34	F	Unknown	21Ma21Gp
Mary	16	F	Unknown	21Ma21Gp
Catherine	13	F	Unknown	21Ma21Gp
Ann	6	F	Child	21Ma21Gp
Cecilia	.04	F	Infant	21Ma21Gp
OGILWIE. Willm.	41	M	Unknown	21Ma21Gp
DOWIE. Allan	33	M	Unknown	21Ma21Gp
STRALAN, Charles	33	M	Unknown	21Ma21Gp
MCHAY. Andrew	17	M	Unknown	21Ma21Gp
BOY. Robert	24	M	Unknown	21Ma21Gp
MARTIN. Willm.	25	M	Unknown	21Ma21Gp
Mary	23	F	Unknown	21Ma21Gp
KINGHORN. Allan	2	M	Child	21Ma21Gp
Thomas	.09	M	Infant	21Ma21Gp
Nathaniel	5	M	Child	21Ma21Gp
BONART. Peter	13	M	Unknown	21Ma21Gp
JOHNSTON, William	24	M	Unknown	21Ma21Gp
RAITT. Alex	25	M	Unknown	21Ma21Gp
U-Mrs.	25	F	Unknown	21Ma21Gp
James	.04	M	Infant	21Ma21Gp
CUNNINGHAM. James	22	M	Unknown	21Ma21Gp
HAY. Alexander	22	M	Unknown	21Ma21Gp
MCVAY. Jessie	22	F	Unknown	21Ma21Gp
MCKAY. John	24	M	Unknown	21Ma21Gp
ROSS. William	23	M	Unknown	21Ma21Gp
TIEZZ Catherine	22	F	Unknown	21Ma21Gp
WALLS. John	20	M	Unknown	21Ma21Gp
COONEY. Edward	20	M	Unknown	21Ma21Gp
VALLELY. Patrick	22	M	Unknown	21Ma21Gp
COONEY. Mary	22	F	Unknown	21Ma21Gp
Nancy	24	F	Unknown	21Ma21Gp
DAND. Thomas	26	M	Unknown	21Ma21Gp
Catherine	26	F	Unknown	21Ma21Gp
John	.06	M	Infant	21Ma21Gp
Catherine	.06	F	Infant	21Ma21Gp
GALLAGHER, Nod	20	M	Unknown	21Ma21Gp
Jane	30	F	Unknown	21Ma21Gp
BAIN, John	20	M	Unknown	21Ma21Gp
BUTTERFORD. Willm.	26	M	Unknown	21Ma21Gp
Andrew	23	M	Unknown	21Ma21Gp
James	19	M	Unknown	21Ma21Gp
KERR, Willm.	31	M	Unknown	21Ma21Gp
GOODWIN, Bard	27	M	Unknown	21Ma21Gp
WHITE, Andrew	21	M	Unknown	21Ma21Gp
MCCAFERTY. James	17	M	Unknown	21Ma21Gp
LATHERDALE, Martha	35	F	Unknown	21Ma21Gp
Margt.	13	F	Unknown	21Ma21Gp
Raphael	12	M	Unknown	21Ma21Gp
James	10	M	Unknown	21Ma21Gp
Anna	8	F	Child	21Ma21Gp
Samuel	6	M	Child	21Ma21Gp
Thomas	4	M	Child	21Ma21Gp
John	.11	M	Infant	21Ma21Gp

NAMES OF PASSENGERS	AGE	SEX	OCCUPATIONS	DATE PORT SHIP
IRWINE. John	23	M	Unknown	21Ma21Gp
BROOM. Sarah	23	F	Unknown	21Ma21Gp
MCBROOM. Mathew	20	M	Unknown	21Ma21Gp
Ellen	.08	F	Infant	21Ma21Gp
WHITTER, Sarah	25	F	Unknown	21Ma21Gp
Allis	22	M	Unknown	21Ma21Gp
FULLAN, John	49	M	Unknown	21Ma21Gp
Died-At-Sea				
Martha	40	F	Unknown	21Ma21Gp
John	11	M	Unknown	21Ma21Gp
Patrick	9	M	Child	21Ma21Gp
MCALVEE. Nancy	11	F	Unknown	21Ma21Gp
MCMATH, James	25	M	Unknown	21Ma21Gp
Mary	24	F	Unknown	21Ma21Gp
WORKMAN, Robert	26	M	Unknown	21Ma21Gp
Eliza	21	F	Unknown	21Ma21Gp
DALE. John	20	M	Unknown	21Ma21Gp
SHAW, Sarah	19	F	Unknown	21Ma21Gp
ARTT. David	27	M	Unknown	21Ma21Gp
Robert	21	M	Unknown	21Ma21Gp
Margt.	30	F	Unknown	21Ma21Gp
ILLWINE, James	19	M	Unknown	21Ma21Gp
SCOTT, Wm.J.	28	M	Unknown	21Ma21Gp
MASON, Ellen	15	F	Unknown	21Ma21Gp
Eliza	20	F	Unknown	21Ma21Gp
Jessie	12	M	Unknown	21Ma21Gp
CAMBPELL, Margt.	18	F	Unknown	21Ma21Gp
MCCAVERTY, Mary	11	F	Unknown	21Ma21Gp
CORBITT, John	70	M	Unknown	21Ma21Gp
Jane	50	F	Unknown	21Ma21Gp
Elizabeth	25	F	Unknown	21Ma21Gp
Sarah	20	F	Unknown	21Ma21Gp
Ellen	18	F	Unknown	21Ma21Gp
DICKSON, Hanah	20	F	Unknown	21Ma21Gp
PATERSON. Sarah	28	F	Unknown	21Ma21Gp
TAYLOR, Ann	23	F	Unknown	21Ma21Gp
ALLAN, James-W.	30	M	Unknown	21Ma21Gp
LOUGH, Henry	25	M	Unknown	21Ma21Gp
Catherine	20	F	Unknown	21Ma21Gp
GIBSON, Willm.	28	M	Unknown	21Ma21Gp
BAIN, Robert	20	M	Unknown	21Ma21Gp
COATS. John	46	M	Unknown	21Ma21Gp
Rachael	40	F	Unknown	21Ma21Gp
Sarah	17	F	Unknown	21Ma21Gp
John	15	M	Unknown	21Ma21Gp
Edward	13	M	Unknown	21Ma21Gp
Thomas	11	M	Unknown	21Ma21Gp
Henry	10	M	Unknown	21Ma21Gp
Margt.	8	F	Child	21Ma21Gp
Eliza	6	F	Child	21Ma21Gp
William	.03	M	Infant	21Ma21Gp
HILL, John	20	M	Unknown	21Ma21Gp
SPRATT. John	50	M	Unknown	21Ma21Gp
Ann	36	F	Unknown	21Ma21Gp
Mary	7	F	Child	21Ma21Gp
Ellen	.03	F	Infant	21Ma21Gp
FALCON, Mary	40	F	Unknown	21Ma21Gp
Isabella	15	F	Unknown	21Ma21Gp
James	25	M	Unknown	21Ma21Gp
Hugh	20	M	Unknown	21Ma21Gp
LACHEY. Willm.	32	M	Unknown	21Ma21Gp
Mary	28	F	Unknown	21Ma21Gp
John	4	M	Child	21Ma21Gp
Willm.	.02	M	Infant	21Ma21Gp
MCGARRETY. W.	15	M	Unknown	21Ma21Gp
Hannah	20	F	Unknown	21Ma21Gp
LEMON, Mary	35	F	Unknown	21Ma21Gp
MCCONNELL, Eliza	22	F	Unknown	21Ma21Gp
GRANT. Willm.	18	M	Unknown	21Ma21Gp
MCALLENY. Mary	36	F	Unknown	21Ma21Gp
Hugh	13	M	Unknown	21Ma21Gp
Biddy	11	F	Unknown	21Ma21Gp
Michael	9	M	Child	21Ma21Gp
KELLY. Cecilia	34	F	Unknown	21Ma21Gp
Patrick	15	M	Unknown	21Ma21Gp

NAMES OF PASSENGERS	AGE	SEX	OCCUPATIONS	DATE PORT SHIP
SMITH, Elizabeth	40	F	Unknown	21Ma21Gp
Catherine	13	F	Unknown	21Ma21Gp
Charlotte	10	F	Unknown	21Ma21Gp
Elizabeth	8	F	Child	21Ma21Gp
Michael	.05	M	Infant	21Ma21Gp
Hugh	14	M	Unknown	21Ma21Gp
WALLS, Catherine	24	F	Unknown	21Ma21Gp
MCGUCK, Mathew	50	M	Unknown	21Ma21Gp
Ann	10	F	Unknown	21Ma21Gp
BRADLEY, Michael	9	M	Child	21Ma21Gp
William	.07	M	Infant	21Ma21Gp
MCGRUGGAN, Mary	25	F	Unknown	21Ma21Gp
MCKERNY, Hugh	65	M	Unknown	21Ma21Gp
Catherine	60	F	Unknown	21Ma21Gp
Bernhard	28	M	Unknown	21Ma21Gp
James	20	M	Unknown	21Ma21Gp
MONAGHAN, Catherine	21	F	Unknown	21Ma21Gp
MCHUGH, Mary	19	F	Unknown	21Ma21Gp
COULTER, Ann	24	F	Unknown	21Ma21Gp
DOHERTY, Willm.	20	M	Unknown	21Ma21Gp
HINSHAM, Edward	23	M	Unknown	21Ma21Gp
BROWN, John	23	M	Unknown	21Ma21Gp
Thomas	20	M	Unknown	21Ma21Gp
LITHGOW, George	56	M	Unknown	21Ma21Gp
Elizabeth	20	F	Unknown	21Ma21Gp
John	18	M	Unknown	21Ma21Gp
George	13	M	Unknown	21Ma21Gp
Jane	11	F	Unknown	21Ma21Gp
Eleazor	9	M	Child	21Ma21Gp
Robert	.06	M	Infant	21Ma21Gp
Rebecca	24	F	Unknown	21Ma21Gp
RODGERS, Ann	19	F	Unknown	21Ma21Gp
MCINTYRE, Neal	22	M	Unknown	21Ma21Gp
David	25	M	Unknown	21Ma21Gp
U, U	.00	M	Infant	21Ma21Gp
Born-At-Sea				
STARK, Thomas	20	M	Unknown	21Ma21Gp

NEPTUNIS 22 MAY 1850

From Belfast

NAMES OF PASSENGERS	AGE	SEX	OCCUPATIONS	DATE PORT SHIP
FITZPATRICK, Michael	55	M	Farmer	22Ma17In
CARROLL, Thomas	30	M	Mechanic	22Ma17In
Nancy	00	F	Unknown	22Ma17In
John	9	M	Child	22Ma17In
Mary	8	F	Child	22Ma17In
Elizabeth	1	F	Child	22Ma17In
FERRIS, Joseph	20	M	Unknown	22Ma17In
MAGRATH, Bernard	21	M	Unknown	22Ma17In
MAGIN, John	27	M	Unknown	22Ma17In
Mary	24	F	Unknown	22Ma17In
Bridget	24	F	Unknown	22Ma17In
MCCANA, Peter	27	M	Unknown	22Ma17In
MCCAVRE, Hune	24	M	Farmer	22Ma17In
MAGEE, Mary	24	F	Mechanic	22Ma17In
HORY, Thomas	30	M	Unknown	22Ma17In
MCEVOY, Edwd.	26	M	Unknown	22Ma17In
Bridget	26	F	Unknown	22Ma17In
TWEEDY, Martha	20	F	Unknown	22Ma17In
MAGEE, John	20	M	Unknown	22Ma17In
MCELROY, Margt.	20	F	Unknown	22Ma17In
MCCLELLAND, Margt.	20	F	Unknown	22Ma17In
NINTES, Thomas	27	M	Unknown	22Ma17In
Elizabeth	19	F	Unknown	22Ma17In
Rossanna	25	F	Unknown	22Ma17In
GASS, Sarah	25	F	Unknown	22Ma17In
MCHEAR, Patrick	30	M	Unknown	22Ma17In
MARTIN, Bridget	30	F	Unknown	22Ma17In

NAMES OF PASSENGERS	AGE	SEX	OCCUPATIONS	DATE PORT SHIP
MARTIN, Michael	24	M	Unknown	22Ma17In
Mary	22	F	Unknown	22Ma17In
James	19	M	Unknown	22Ma17In
Frances	12	F	Unknown	22Ma17In
WOODS, Margt.	40	F	Unknown	22Ma17In
Mary	25	F	Unknown	22Ma17In
Thomas	20	M	Unknown	22Ma17In
Rose	18	F	Unknown	22Ma17In
Catherine	13	F	Unknown	22Ma17In
Margaret	12	F	Unknown	22Ma17In
MEGAN, Patrick	18	M	Unknown	22Ma17In
Mary	12	F	Unknown	22Ma17In
James	10	M	Unknown	22Ma17In
TRAYNOR, Mary	20	F	Unknown	22Ma17In
John-N.	12	M	Unknown	22Ma17In
Peter	10	M	Unknown	22Ma17In
MCMAHON, Patrick	19	M	Unknown	22Ma17In
MCCUSKER, James	25	M	Unknown	22Ma17In
MCCANNON, Michael	16	M	Unknown	22Ma17In
MCQUADE, Charles	30	M	Unknown	22Ma17In
Mary	35	F	Unknown	22Ma17In
Susan	5	F	Child	22Ma17In
Anne	37	F	Unknown	22Ma17In
RUDDY, Betty	50	F	Farmer	22Ma17In
Betty	19	F	Mechanic	22Ma17In
William	16	M	Unknown	22Ma17In
MADDEN, John	22	M	Unknown	22Ma17In
MURPHY, Nancy	18	F	Unknown	22Ma17In
DONNELLY, Patrick	20	M	Unknown	22Ma17In
Mary	20	F	Unknown	22Ma17In
YANOW, Mary	20	F	Unknown	22Ma17In
MCGURK, Bridget	18	F	Unknown	22Ma17In
MCKENNA, Anne	13	F	Unknown	22Ma17In
NOPHES, John	21	M	Unknown	22Ma17In
MCCOY, Patrick	20	M	Unknown	22Ma17In
Bernard	17	M	Unknown	22Ma17In
MCCULLOGH, Bridget	20	F	Unknown	22Ma17In
MCGAINTY, Betty	20	F	Unknown	22Ma17In
LOGAN, Betty	20	F	Unknown	22Ma17In
CONWAY, Patrick	24	M	Unknown	22Ma17In
Sarah	2	F	Child	22Ma17In
Charles	13	M	Unknown	22Ma17In
MORGAN, Peter	23	M	Unknown	22Ma17In
CARR, Mary-Anne	26	F	Unknown	22Ma17In
John	13	M	Unknown	22Ma17In
John	18	M	Unknown	22Ma17In
ANDERSON, Mary-Anne	19	F	Unknown	22Ma17In
MCVALLEY, John	13	F	Unknown	22Ma17In
Anne	22	F	Unknown	22Ma17In
STEEL, George	22	M	Unknown	22Ma17In
BOYD, Mary	19	F	Unknown	22Ma17In
HUGHES, Bridget	30	F	Unknown	22Ma17In
MAGEE, Rose	35	F	Unknown	22Ma17In
Cath.	11	F	Unknown	22Ma17In
James	8	M	Child	22Ma17In
John	5	M	Child	22Ma17In
Patrick	8	M	Child	22Ma17In
MCGIVIGAN, John	25	M	Unknown	22Ma17In
TRENOR, Patrick	22	M	Unknown	22Ma17In
Michael	24	M	Farmer	22Ma17In
WILSON, Mary	48	F	Mechanic	22Ma17In
Jane	18	F	Unknown	22Ma17In
TUMES, Rosana	28	F	Unknown	22Ma17In
Anne	.01	F	Infant	22Ma17In
MCCULLOUGH, Bridget	18	F	Unknown	22Ma17In
OBRIEN, Anthony	24	M	Unknown	22Ma17In
CLARKE, Alice	45	F	Unknown	22Ma17In
William	25	M	Unknown	22Ma17In
Mary	16	F	Unknown	22Ma17In
Mary	18	F	Unknown	22Ma17In
MARSHALL, John	18	M	Unknown	22Ma17In
MCCASLAND, Robert	20	M	Unknown	22Ma17In
OREILLY, Eliza	20	F	Unknown	22Ma17In
COCHRAN, William	20	M	Unknown	22Ma17In
BYRNE, Ellen	20	F	Unknown	22Ma17In

NAMES OF PASSENGERS	AGE	SEX	OCCUPATIONS	DATE PORT SHIP
RICE, William	17	M	Unknown	22Ma17In
MONAGHAN, William	23	M	Unknown	22Ma17In
CAULFIELD, Edwd.	30	M	Unknown	22Ma17In
FINNEGAN, Mary	20	F	Unknown	22Ma17In
BOYLE, Eliza	12	F	Unknown	22Ma17In
Jane	10	F	Unknown	22Ma17In
James	7	M	Child	22Ma17In
MURPHY, Anne	20	F	Unknown	22Ma17In
GORMAN, John	30	M	Unknown	22Ma17In
MURPHY, Rose	48	F	Unknown	22Ma17In
Charles	13	M	Unknown	22Ma17In
CABRY, John	34	M	Unknown	22Ma17In
Margt.	32	F	Unknown	22Ma17In
Eliza	3	F	Child	22Ma17In
Wm.John	1	M	Child	22Ma17In
MCVAUNELL, Anne	30	F	Unknown	22Ma17In
Sally	10	F	Unknown	22Ma17In
John	13	M	Unknown	22Ma17In
QUIN, Anne	13	F	Unknown	22Ma17In
Mary	11	F	Unknown	22Ma17In
DENNELES, Mary	21	F	Unknown	22Ma17In
MOON, Micahel	18	M	Farmer	22Ma17In
SHIELD, Francis	20	F	Mechanic	22Ma17In
Alice	19	F	Unknown	22Ma17In
Thomas	1	M	Child	22Ma17In
EVANS, Catherine	27	F	Unknown	22Ma17In
Francis	6	F	Child	22Ma17In
Anne	4	F	Child	22Ma17In
Mary	3	F	Child	22Ma17In
HARVEY, Rosa	40	F	Unknown	22Ma17In
Edwd.	20	M	Unknown	22Ma17In
MCKEOWN, Patrick	7	M	Child	22Ma17In
Mary	8	F	Child	22Ma17In
TRUSAL, Mary	25	F	Unknown	22Ma17In
CONLY, Susan	20	F	Unknown	22Ma17In
EARLES, Margt.	25	F	Unknown	22Ma17In
HARRY, Catherine	30	F	Unknown	22Ma17In
HARVY, Alice	30	F	Unknown	22Ma17In
MCCLEAN, Alice	8	F	Child	22Ma17In
Mary	6	F	Child	22Ma17In
CUNNINGHAM, Thomas	20	M	Unknown	22Ma17In
CASSIDY, Catherine	20	F	Unknown	22Ma17In
LONE, Cath.	16	F	Unknown	22Ma17In
U, U Born-At-Sea	.00	U	Infant	22Ma17In

M.HAWES 22 MAY 1850

From Belfast

NAMES OF PASSENGERS	AGE	SEX	OCCUPATIONS	DATE PORT SHIP
WILSON, U	30	M	Trade Man	22Ma17Jv
U-Mrs.	25	F	Unknown	22Ma17Jv
U	.05	M	Infant	22Ma17Jv
MARTIN, Mary-Ann	28	F	Servant	22Ma17Jv
CLELLAND, U	19	F	Spinster	22Ma17Jv
BLAIR, W.	21	M	Merchant	22Ma17Jv
GREENE, John	19	M	Trade Man	22Ma17Jv
CREEGHTON, Isabella	21	F	Seamstress	22Ma17Jv
SLOAN, Thomas	23	M	Laborer	22Ma17Jv
Marcella	18	F	Milliner	22Ma17Jv
ROGAN, Jane	30	F	Seamstress	22Ma17Jv
BRADSHAW, Jane	30	F	W-Fmr	22Ma17Jv
Ellen (D)	7	F	Child	22Ma17Jv
John (S)	5	M	Child	22Ma17Jv
Isabella (D)	3	F	Child	22Ma17Jv
WARNOCK, John (B)	22	M	Farmer	22Ma17Jv
Sarah (S)	20	F	Farmer	22Ma17Jv
Mary (S)	20	F	Farmer	22Ma17Jv
ADDAMS, David	18	M	Farmer	22Ma17Jv
GAMBLE, Jane	40	F	Seamstress	22Ma17Jv
Mary	25	F	Seamstress	22Ma17Jv
Jane	3	F	Child	22Ma17Jv
DUNN, Anna	20	F	Seamstress	22Ma17Jv
Jane	18	F	Seamstress	22Ma17Jv
KAIN, James	18	M	Carpenter	22Ma17Jv
FORSYTHE, George	20	M	Baker	22Ma17Jv
FLANNIGAN, Thomas	18	M	Laborer	22Ma17Jv
Isabella	20	F	Seamstress	22Ma17Jv
HARVEY, John	24	M	Laborer	22Ma17Jv
SMITH, Henry	36	M	Farmer	22Ma17Jv
John	9	M	Child	22Ma17Jv
Eliza	13	F	Unknown	22Ma17Jv
KERNAGHAN, Andrew	40	M	Farmer	22Ma17Jv
Mary	30	F	Unknown	22Ma17Jv
Mary (S)	30	F	Unknown	22Ma17Jv
Eliza	28	F	Unknown	22Ma17Jv
Thos.	19	M	Unknown	22Ma17Jv
Mary	10	F	Unknown	22Ma17Jv
RICHMOND, John	20	M	Unknown	22Ma17Jv
MCAVOY, Catherine	29	F	Seamstress	22Ma17Jv
John	30	M	Laborer	22Ma17Jv
TURNLEY, Francis	21	M	Clerk	22Ma17Jv
SPENCE, Hugh	18	M	Fisherman	22Ma17Jv
DRAKE, Samuel	40	M	Fisherman	22Ma17Jv
Eliza	40	F	Servant	22Ma17Jv
Richard	19	M	Laborer	22Ma17Jv
HALSE, Eliza	28	F	Servant	22Ma17Jv
Ann	4	F	Child	22Ma17Jv
Richard	2	M	Child	22Ma17Jv
John	.08	M	Infant	22Ma17Jv
JOHNSTON, William	16	M	Clerk	22Ma17Jv
MARTIN, Mathew	50	M	Farmer	22Ma17Jv
Margaret	48	F	Unknown	22Ma17Jv
LOWRY, Archibald	40	M	Farmer	22Ma17Jv
MARTIN, Eliza	20	F	Unknown	22Ma17Jv
Ann	18	F	Unknown	22Ma17Jv
Thomas	16	M	Unknown	22Ma17Jv
Jane	13	F	Unknown	22Ma17Jv
James	12	M	Unknown	22Ma17Jv
Mathew	10	M	Unknown	22Ma17Jv
John	8	M	Child	22Ma17Jv
STEED, James	29	M	Unknown	22Ma17Jv
Eliza	26	F	Unknown	22Ma17Jv
ROSS, James	26	M	Unknown	22Ma17Jv
NEILL, Ann	18	F	Unknown	22Ma17Jv
RANSTON, Robert	18	M	Clerk	22Ma17Jv
MCDONALD, Peter	18	M	Farmer	22Ma17Jv
THOMSON, Joseph	40	M	Farmer	22Ma17Jv
Jane	45	F	Farmer	22Ma17Jv
James	15	M	Farmer	22Ma17Jv
Elizabeth	13	F	Farmer	22Ma17Jv
Eliza	11	F	Farmer	22Ma17Jv
Margaret	9	F	Child	22Ma17Jv
Mary	6	F	Child	22Ma17Jv
Joseph	4	M	Child	22Ma17Jv
SHORT, Robert	25	M	Farmer	22Ma17Jv
MCKEATTIN, Jane	19	F	Servant	22Ma17Jv
MAGEE, Agness	21	F	Farmer	22Ma17Jv
SMITH, Isabella	19	F	Servant	22Ma17Jv
FITSPATRICK, William	45	M	Farmer	22Ma17Jv
Patrick (S)	19	M	Farmer	22Ma17Jv
Mary-Ann	16	F	Farmer	22Ma17Jv
Betty	11	F	Farmer	22Ma17Jv
FITSIMONS, Bernard	19	M	Laborer	22Ma17Jv
JOHNSTON, Henry	60	M	Farmer	22Ma17Jv
Margaret	50	F	Farmer	22Ma17Jv
Agness	25	F	Farmer	22Ma17Jv
Essy-Jane	23	F	Farmer	22Ma17Jv
Martha	20	F	Farmer	22Ma17Jv
James	45	M	Farmer	22Ma17Jv
Margaret	40	F	D-Fmr	22Ma17Jv
FLINN, Patrick	23	M	Laborer	22Ma17Jv
SINGER, Jane	25	F	Spinster	22Ma17Jv
Lambert	30	M	Laborer	22Ma17Jv

NAMES OF PASSENGERS	AGE	SEX	OCCUPATIONS	DATE PORT SHIP
ANDERSON, Letitia	26	F	Farmer	22Ma17Jv
HERBISON, John	15	M	Unknown	22Ma17Jv
HENDERSON, Jane	19	F	Dressmaker	22Ma17Jv
WILSON, Mary-Jane	19	F	Dressmaker	22Ma17Jv
MURRAY, Dennis	18	M	Laborer	22Ma17Jv
George	20	M	Laborer	22Ma17Jv
QUILLAN, James	25	M	Laborer	22Ma17Jv
DARRAGH, Mary-Jane	20	F	Engineer	22Ma17Jv
FOWLER, Mary	20	F	Servant	22Ma17Jv
PALMER, Robert	30	M	Servant	22Ma17Jv
BELL, Catherine	17	F	Farmer	22Ma17Jv
MURRAY, Neal	15	M	Servant	22Ma17Jv
SMITH, Cornelius	17	M	Laborer	22Ma17Jv
James	22	M	Laborer	22Ma17Jv
MCALISTER, John	35	M	Laborer	22Ma17Jv
MADINE, Ellen	18	F	Laborer	22Ma17Jv
SHORT, William	15	M	Servant	22Ma17Jv
YOUNG, Hugh	17	M	Servant	22Ma17Jv
BURNS, Archibald	22	M	Servant	22Ma17Jv
STRANG, Richard	20	M	Servant	22Ma17Jv
SAVAGE, Patrick	18	M	Servant	22Ma17Jv
JOHNSON, Samuel	25	M	Servant	22Ma17Jv
CAIRNS, Samuel	28	M	Carpenter	22Ma17Jv
GASS, Robert	19	M	Clerk	22Ma17Jv
LONG, James	35	M	Farmer	22Ma17Jv
Grace	30	F	Farmer	22Ma17Jv
Robert	7	M	Child	22Ma17Jv
Hugh	5	M	Child	22Ma17Jv
Grace	3	F	Child	22Ma17Jv
Samuel	1	M	Child	22Ma17Jv
KAIN, John	30	M	Farmer	22Ma17Jv
SLOAN, John	16	M	Clerk	22Ma17Jv
Eliza	15	F	Seamstress	22Ma17Jv
JOHNSTON, John	25	M	Farmer	22Ma17Jv
MARTIN, Wm.	15	M	Farmer	22Ma17Jv
James	12	M	Farmer	22Ma17Jv
ONEILL, Charles	21	M	Laborer	22Ma17Jv
BOYD, Eliza	20	F	Servant	22Ma17Jv
FITSPATRICK, Margt.	20	F	Dressmaker	22Ma17Jv
GILMER, John	22	M	Brf	22Ma17Jv
MCWILLIAMS, John	25	M	Farmer	22Ma17Jv
MCGREARY, Patrick	23	M	Shoemaker	22Ma17Jv
GORMAN, Patrick	25	M	Laborer	22Ma17Jv
HANNA, Eleanor	40	F	Fwkr	22Ma17Jv
Mary	20	F	Fwkr	22Ma17Jv
Agness	18	F	Fwkr	22Ma17Jv
Emily	16	F	Fwkr	22Ma17Jv
Margaret	14	F	Fwkr	22Ma17Jv
Andrew	12	M	Fwkr	22Ma17Jv
John	10	M	Fwkr	22Ma17Jv
BOYD, Rose	50	F	Seamstress	22Ma17Jv
Maria	27	F	Seamstress	22Ma17Jv
Margaret	4	F	Child	22Ma17Jv
Thos.	14	M	Farmer	22Ma17Jv
KINAIRD, Maria	20	F	Servant	22Ma17Jv
ADDAMS, John	19	M	Shoemaker	22Ma17Jv
James	12	M	Shoemaker	22Ma17Jv
FERRES, Eliza	25	F	Spinster	22Ma17Jv
HARRIS, Patrick	24	M	Carpenter	22Ma17Jv
Ann	21	F	Carpenter	22Ma17Jv
Jane	15	F	Carpenter	22Ma17Jv
James	13	M	Carpenter	22Ma17Jv
FINLAY, Wm.	23	M	Weaver	22Ma17Jv
TODD, Andrew	21	M	Clerk	22Ma17Jv
LOWRY, Ann	30	F	Farmer	22Ma17Jv

CIRCASSIAN 22 MAY 1850

From Glasgow

NAMES OF PASSENGERS	AGE	SEX	OCCUPATIONS	DATE PORT SHIP
RAE, Ann	50	F	Farmer	22Ma21El
Jemima	19	F	Farmer	22Ma21El
MATHEWS, David	34	M	Farmer	22Ma21El
Margaret	32	F	Farmer	22Ma21El
Jane	12	F	Farmer	22Ma21El
John	10	M	Unknown	22Ma21El
Martha	9	F	Child	22Ma21El
Elizth.	8	F	Child	22Ma21El
Maryann	6	F	Child	22Ma21El
James	.09	M	Infant	22Ma21El
RAE, Samuel	30	M	Laborer	22Ma21El
Jane	40	F	Wife	22Ma21El
James	50	M	Unknown	22Ma21El
BELL, Margaret	18	F	Unknown	22Ma21El
Sarah	13	F	Unknown	22Ma21El
Mary	9	F	Child	22Ma21El
MCARTHUR, William	24	M	Laborer	22Ma21El
Martha	20	F	Sister	22Ma21El
AKINS, Patrick-H.	25	M	Laborer	22Ma21El
MCFEDEGAN, Biddy	38	F	Unknown	22Ma21El
Charles	12	M	Unknown	22Ma21El
Michael	10	M	Unknown	22Ma21El
Margaret	8	F	Child	22Ma21El
Mary	6	F	Child	22Ma21El
James	4	M	Child	22Ma21El
Patrick	.09	M	Infant	22Ma21El
MCSHANE, William	27	M	Laborer	22Ma21El
Ellen	25	F	Laborer	22Ma21El
MCSHANIS, James	.06	M	Infant	22Ma21El
DONAHUE, John	24	M	Laborer	22Ma21El
Mary	22	F	Wife	22Ma21El
MULLAN, Daniel	24	M	Laborer	22Ma21El
MULHOLLAN, Charles	23	M	Laborer	22Ma21El
DOHARTY, John	30	M	Laborer	22Ma21El
HASSAN, Bridget	24	F	Laborer	22Ma21El
Margaret	42	F	Unknown	22Ma21El
CAMPBELL, Bridget	50	F	Laborer	22Ma21El
Mary	26	F	Unknown	22Ma21El
Patrick	24	M	Laborer	22Ma21El
Luke	18	M	Laborer	22Ma21El
BOWAR, James	40	M	Laborer	22Ma21El
Susanna	30	F	Wife	22Ma21El
Neil	9	M	Child	22Ma21El
James	7	M	Child	22Ma21El
Anne	.06	F	Infant	22Ma21El
MCCULLIEN, Patrick	24	M	Laborer	22Ma21El
Patrick	20	M	Laborer	22Ma21El
Anne	22	F	Laborer	22Ma21El
MCSHANE, John	19	M	Laborer	22Ma21El
MCCUE, James	22	M	Laborer	22Ma21El
ROWELEY, Biddy	32	F	Unknown	22Ma21El
KESSAN, Rosa	24	F	Unknown	22Ma21El
Susan	18	F	Unknown	22Ma21El
Ellen	18	F	Unknown	22Ma21El
KERN, Mary	25	F	Unknown	22Ma21El
KESSAN, Ann	30	F	Unknown	22Ma21El
BRISLANE, Barny	22	M	Laborer	22Ma21El
CASSIDY, Michael	21	M	Laborer	22Ma21El
BRADY, Patrick	30	M	Laborer	22Ma21El
CULLEN, Marns	25	U	Laborer	22Ma21El
JOHNSTON, Martha	25	F	Unknown	22Ma21El
MORAN, Michael	26	M	Laborer	22Ma21El
GRAHAM, James	25	M	Laborer	22Ma21El
KASSIN, Thomas	30	M	Laborer	22Ma21El
MCDONNEL, Mary	18	F	Unknown	22Ma21El

NAMES OF PASSENGERS	AGE	SEX	OCCUPATIONS	DATE PORT SHIP
MCFARLANE, Elis	26	M	Unknown	22Ma21EI
Hannah	24	F	Unknown	22Ma21EI
William	20	M	Laborer	22Ma21EI
FASTENS, Maria	20	F	Unknown	22Ma21EI
DONNELLY, John	20	M	Laborer	22Ma21EI
MURPHY, Susan	20	F	Unknown	22Ma21EI
GREEN, John	25	M	Farmer	22Ma21EI
Elisth.	21	F	Unknown	22Ma21EI
YARD, Elis.	50	M	Unknown	22Ma21EI
GIBBONS, Daniel	22	M	Laborer	22Ma21EI
GRAHAM, George	26	M	Laborer	22Ma21EI
Alexr.	24	M	Laborer	22Ma21EI
Died-At-Sea				
JOHNSTON, John	21	M	Laborer	22Ma21EI
MCGUGHAR, James	23	M	Laborer	22Ma21EI
HASSAN, Mary	18	F	Laborer	22Ma21EI
NEILSON, Charles	43	M	Farmer	22Ma21EI
Catherine	42	F	Relative	22Ma21EI
Elenor	13	F	Relative	22Ma21EI
Mary	13	F	Relative	22Ma21EI
Charles	11	M	Relative	22Ma21EI
Catherine	4	F	Child	22Ma21EI
George	2	M	Child	22Ma21EI
Patrick	.10	M	Infant	22Ma21EI
MCDADE, John	30	M	Laborer	22Ma21EI
James	26	M	Relative	22Ma21EI
Sarah	26	F	Relative	22Ma21EI
GALLAGHER, Charles	29	M	Laborer	22Ma21EI
DEVLIN, William	25	M	Laborer	22Ma21EI
KILGAR, Francis	20	M	Laborer	22Ma21EI
BRENNAN, Daniel	28	M	Laborer	22Ma21EI
GALLAGHER, Charles	22	M	Laborer	22Ma21EI
IRVINE, George	20	M	Laborer	22Ma21EI
CULLINS, John	24	M	Laborer	22Ma21EI
CAHILL, Michael	24	M	Laborer	22Ma21EI
ROBERTSON, Thomas	27	M	Laborer	22Ma21EI
ONEIL, Mary	18	F	Laborer	22Ma21EI
DOHERTY, John	55	M	Laborer	22Ma21EI
Bridget	55	F	Wife	22Ma21EI
Peter	20	M	Relative	22Ma21EI
Mary	21	F	Relative	22Ma21EI
Rosa	17	F	Relative	22Ma21EI
HAMITLTON, Ann	28	F	Unknown	22Ma21EI
GALBRAITH, Martha	17	F	Unknown	22Ma21EI
BROWN, James	26	M	Unknown	22Ma21EI
RICHEY, David	24	M	Unknown	22Ma21EI
LUCAS, William	39	M	Unknown	22Ma21EI
KINSTON, William	20	M	Unknown	22Ma21EI
KIPAN, Peter	20	M	Unknown	22Ma21EI
FINLEY, James	26	M	Cver	22Ma21EI

WOLFVILLE 23 MAY 1850

From Belfast

NAMES OF PASSENGERS		AGE	SEX	OCCUPATIONS	DATE PORT SHIP
FITZPATRICK, Patt		31	M	Farmer	23Ma17Ic
Margaret		29	F	Wife	23Ma17Ic
William		.00	M	Infant	23Ma17Ic
REDFATTE, Wm.		35	M	Farmer	23Ma17Ic
Sarah		32	F	Spinster	23Ma17Ic
Jane		30	F	Spinster	23Ma17Ic
Alex		20	M	Weaver	23Ma17Ic
Chas.		18	M	Weaver	23Ma17Ic
Joseph		16	M	Weaver	23Ma17Ic
Waddle		16	M	Weaver	23Ma17Ic
Jane		14	F	Spinster	23Ma17Ic
Martha		12	F	Spinster	23Ma17Ic
Robert		.00	M	Infant	23Ma17Ic
CORRAGH, Hugh		22	M	Weaver	23Ma17Ic
MCWILLIAM, Matthew		17	M	Weaver	23Ma17Ic
JAMISON, Jno.		25	M	Weaver	23Ma17Ic
MCCONFARS, Wm.		20	M	Weaver	23Ma17Ic
BURROWS, Jane		20	F	Spinster	23Ma17Ic
MAXWELL, John		16	M	Weaver	23Ma17Ic
Jane		18	F	Spinster	23Ma17Ic
ATKINSON, Ellen		20	F	Spinster	23Ma17Ic
ROBERTS, Wm.		22	M	Weaver	23Ma17Ic
RODGERS, Johanna		21	F	Spinster	23Ma17Ic
LILEY, Daniel		30	M	Weaver	23Ma17Ic
Hugh		25	M	Weaver	23Ma17Ic
CAMPBELL, Wm.		18	M	Weaver	23Ma17Ic
WRIGHT, Jane		35	F	Spinster	23Ma17Ic
Thos.		15	M	Weaver	23Ma17Ic
SKANKS, John		21	M	Weaver	23Ma17Ic
MCCOUCH, Anne		45	F	Wi	23Ma17Ic
Saml.	(S)	20	M	Son	23Ma17Ic
Anne	(D)	13	F	Daughter	23Ma17Ic
Mary	(D)	11	F	Daughter	23Ma17Ic
DUFF, Wm.		25	M	Weaver	23Ma17Ic
Sarah		31	F	Spinster	23Ma17Ic
Anne		.00	F	Infant	23Ma17Ic
LONGRIDGE, Margaret		25	F	Spinster	23Ma17Ic
BECK, Ellen		24	F	Spinster	23Ma17Ic
GRAY, Robert		21	M	Weaver	23Ma17Ic
SCOTT, Archy		19	M	Weaver	23Ma17Ic
KERNAGHAN, Wm.		50	M	Unknown	23Ma17Ic
Ellen		48	F	Spinster	23Ma17Ic
Archy		23	M	Son	23Ma17Ic
Wm.	(S)	20	M	Son	23Ma17Ic
Mary	(D)	18	F	Son	23Ma17Ic
Margaret	(D)	16	F	Son	23Ma17Ic
MCKNIGHT, Sarah		24	F	Spinster	23Ma17Ic
KANE, Jacob		18	M	Weaver	23Ma17Ic
Eliza		20	F	Spinster	23Ma17Ic
ARCKSON, Wm.		30	M	Weaver	23Ma17Ic
Mathew		40	M	Farmer	23Ma17Ic
Mary		40	F	Wife	23Ma17Ic
Wm.		14	M	Unknown	23Ma17Ic
Mary		12	F	Unknown	23Ma17Ic
POLAND, Jas.		35	M	Farmer	23Ma17Ic
Ellen		35	F	Wife	23Ma17Ic
Peggy		30	F	Spinster	23Ma17Ic
Cicily		32	F	Spinster	23Ma17Ic
MCGREADY, Ellen		40	F	Spinster	23Ma17Ic
BLEAKLY, Anne		40	F	Spinster	23Ma17Ic
FREANOR, Ursilla		21	F	Spinster	23Ma17Ic
MATTHEWS, Margaret		25	F	Spinster	23Ma17Ic
Anne		.00	F	Infant	23Ma17Ic
MCCLARE, Wm.		20	M	Weaver	23Ma17Ic
MATTHEWS, Andrew		28	M	Weaver	23Ma17Ic
MCGRAW, Jas.		20	M	Weaver	23Ma17Ic
MOORE, Jas.		20	M	Weaver	23Ma17Ic
WADE, Wm.		29	M	Weaver	23Ma17Ic
Jarred		25	F	Spinster	23Ma17Ic
ROBINSON, Jane		30	F	Spinster	23Ma17Ic
Racheal		12	F	Spinster	23Ma17Ic
MCALLISTER, Jno.		18	M	Weaver	23Ma17Ic
Rachel		20	F	Spinster	23Ma17Ic
TAYLOR, Sarah		19	F	Spinster	23Ma17Ic
Anne		17	F	Spinster	23Ma17Ic
Margaret		11	F	Spinster	23Ma17Ic
Geo.		.00	M	Infant	23Ma17Ic
GREEN, Thos.		21	M	Weaver	23Ma17Ic
SHAW, Robinson		21	M	Weaver	23Ma17Ic
LOWRIE, Eliza		26	F	Spinster	23Ma17Ic
MCCLUSKY, Teressa		13	F	Spinster	23Ma17Ic
NICHOLS, Jno.		20	M	Weaver	23Ma17Ic
HANNA, Jno.		28	M	Weaver	23Ma17Ic
PHILSON, Robt.		13	M	Weaver	23Ma17Ic
MULLEN, Jane		21	F	Spinster	23Ma17Ic
ROBB, David		20	M	Weaver	23Ma17Ic
TODD, Eliza		45	F	Spinster	23Ma17Ic
Jno.		18	M	Weaver	23Ma17Ic
Eliza	(D)	12	F	Daughter	23Ma17Ic

NAMES OF PASSENGERS	AGE	SEX	OCCUPATIONS	DATE PORT SHIP
HAMILTON, Geo.	29	M	Farmer	23Ma17Ic
COMB, Margaret	18	F	Spinster	23Ma17Ic
COLLAGHAN, Ellen	18	F	Spinster	23Ma17Ic
TOPPING, Jane	20	F	Spinster	23Ma17Ic
MCCANILL, Henry	.00	M	Infant	23Ma17Ic
MCKIBBON, Chas.	30	M	Weaver	23Ma17Ic
HAWTHORN, Robt.	29	M	Weaver	23Ma17Ic
JUDGE, Peggy	18	F	Spinster	23Ma17Ic
MCFADDEN, Maria	29	F	Spinster	23Ma17Ic
Jane	.00	F	Infant	23Ma17Ic
GALLESPIE, Wm.	40	M	Farmer	23Ma17Ic
Susan	25	F	Spinster	23Ma17Ic
James	24	M	Weaver	23Ma17Ic
Edward	22	M	Weaver	23Ma17Ic
Jane	20	F	Spinster	23Ma17Ic
Eliza	17	F	Spinster	23Ma17Ic
Robt.	.00	F	Infant	23Ma17Ic
Wm.	40	M	Weaver	23Ma17Ic
Joseph	22	M	Weaver	23Ma17Ic
BROWN, Henry	26	M	Weaver	23Ma17Ic
CAMPBELL, Elenor	21	F	Spinster	23Ma17Ic
MCELROY, Jane	29	F	Spinster	23Ma17Ic
ADGAR, Jno.	28	M	Weaver	23Ma17Ic
Mary	25	F	Spinster	23Ma17Ic
Wm.	.00	M	Infant	23Ma17Ic
CRUGHLEY, Robt.	30	M	Farmer	23Ma17Ic
CULLY, Wm.	21	M	Weaver	23Ma17Ic
GRIMLY, Jno.	30	M	Farmer	23Ma17Ic
Catherine	30	F	Wife	23Ma17Ic
LIPPIEL, Ally	21	F	Spinster	23Ma17Ic
Jane	20	F	Spinster	23Ma17Ic
MCCOY, Patt	21	M	Weaver	23Ma17Ic
Rose	19	F	Spinster	23Ma17Ic
MCGILL, Mary	21	F	Spinster	23Ma17Ic
MOFFATT, Matilda	20	F	Spinster	23Ma17Ic
Hopewell	18	M	Weaver	23Ma17Ic
Robt.	.00	M	Infant	23Ma17Ic
Died-At-Sea				
MCCRACKEN, Sarah	21	F	Spinster	23Ma17Ic
MCMURRAY, Wm.	21	F	Farmer	23Ma17Ic
WARDEN, David	29	F	Weaver	23Ma17Ic
FLETCHER, Alex	21	M	Farmer	23Ma17Ic
MCMANUS, Ellen	18	F	Spinster	23Ma17Ic
ADAMS, Andrew	29	M	Weaver	23Ma17Ic
GRANT, James	29	M	Weaver	23Ma17Ic
ANDREWS, Geo.	28	M	Weaver	23Ma17Ic
NEVIN, Thos.	40	M	Farmer	23Ma17Ic
Anne	34	F	Wife	23Ma17Ic
Jane	20	F	Unknown	23Ma17Ic
Mary	11	F	Unknown	23Ma17Ic
Margaret	7	F	Child	23Ma17Ic
Magdaline	.00	F	Infant	23Ma17Ic
MULLIGAN, Jno.	21	M	Weaver	23Ma17Ic
BAIRD, Margaret	21	F	Spinster	23Ma17Ic
DUNCAN, David	50	M	Farmer	23Ma17Ic
Margaret	48	F	Wife	23Ma17Ic
Wm.	13	M	Unknown	23Ma17Ic
Ellen	11	F	Unknown	23Ma17Ic
Isabella	.00	F	Infant	23Ma17Ic
MCKEE, Wm.	21	M	Weaver	23Ma17Ic
GILKISON, Saml.	21	M	Weaver	23Ma17Ic
Mary	21	F	Wife	23Ma17Ic
MACAVOY, James	29	M	Unknown	23Ma17Ic
MCADAMS, Sarah	29	F	Spinster	23Ma17Ic
NEELY, Ellen	22	F	Spinster	23Ma17Ic
LENDRENCE, Geo.	35	M	Weaver	23Ma17Ic
LYNCH, Michael	20	M	Weaver	23Ma17Ic
MURDOCK, Michael	24	M	Weaver	23Ma17Ic
MCELROY, Jane	24	F	Spinster	23Ma17Ic
MCBARRIE, Catherine	30	F	Spinster	23Ma17Ic
NORRIS, Robt.	21	M	Weaver	23Ma17Ic
LINDSAY, Maria	25	F	Spinster	23Ma17Ic
HANNA, Jno.	29	M	Weaver	23Ma17Ic
NEWVRAY, Jno.	31	M	Weaver	23Ma17Ic
Jane	31	F	Wife	23Ma17Ic

NAMES OF PASSENGERS	AGE	SEX	OCCUPATIONS	DATE PORT SHIP
SPIERS, Saml.	21	M	Weaver	23Ma17Ic
MCADAMS, Sarah	20	F	Spinster	23Ma17Ic
MCKILLOCK, Robt.	20	M	Weaver	23Ma17Ic
GABIC, Ellen	40	F	Spinster	23Ma17Ic
MCCOY, Margaret	20	F	Spinster	23Ma17Ic

CLARENCE 23 MAY 1850

From Galway

NAMES OF PASSENGERS	AGE	SEX	OCCUPATIONS	DATE PORT SHIP
BROWN, Mary	40	F	Farmer	23Ma42Da
William	9	M	Child	23Ma42Da
Mary	7	F	Child	23Ma42Da
Sally	.00	F	Infant	23Ma42Da
KELLY, Sally	2	F	Child	23Ma42Da
Pat	.00	M	Infant	23Ma42Da
OBRIEN, Terence	28	M	Farmer	23Ma42Da
DAVORAN, Dominick	26	M	Farmer	23Ma42Da
William	19	M	Farmer	23Ma42Da
OBRYAN, Cornelius	26	M	Farmer	23Ma42Da
OLAUGHLAN, John	00	M	Farmer	23Ma42Da
Mary	30	F	Farmer	23Ma42Da
DEVIRAN, Bridget	20	F	Farmer	23Ma42Da
BRODERICK, Hugh	20	M	Farmer	23Ma42Da
COLEMAN, John	18	M	Farmer	23Ma42Da
DUGGAN, Bidelin	18	M	Farmer	23Ma42Da
FLAHERTY, Ann	20	F	Farmer	23Ma42Da
Honora	20	F	Farmer	23Ma42Da
CLOONAN, John	.00	M	Infant	23Ma42Da
BARGIN, Catherine	.00	F	Infant	23Ma42Da
ODONNELL, Coleman	24	M	Farmer	23Ma42Da
MURRAY, Margaret	18	F	Farmer	23Ma42Da
LOGHAN, John	35	M	Farmer	23Ma42Da
DONOHUE, Mary	20	F	Farmer	23Ma42Da
LYDON, Michael	20	M	Farmer	23Ma42Da
HORAN, Peter	21	M	Farmer	23Ma42Da
WARD, Teddy	22	M	Farmer	23Ma42Da
RAFFERTY, Honora	30	F	Farmer	23Ma42Da
GRADY, Catherine	25	F	Farmer	23Ma42Da
FEHERTY, Michael	22	M	Farmer	23Ma42Da
CROSBERY, Michael	25	M	Farmer	23Ma42Da
GILERMON, Cathern.	40	F	Farmer	23Ma42Da
Anne-G.	19	F	Farmer	23Ma42Da
William	18	M	Farmer	23Ma42Da
Patt	17	M	Farmer	23Ma42Da
John	17	M	Farmer	23Ma42Da
SILVER, Thomas	27	M	Farmer	23Ma42Da
MOONEY, Bridget	18	F	Farmer	23Ma42Da
GIBBONS, James	30	M	Farmer	23Ma42Da
CLASBY, Cathern.	18	F	Farmer	23Ma42Da
MALLEY, James	22	M	Farmer	23Ma42Da
ADAMS, Julia	18	F	Farmer	23Ma42Da
HANNAHAN, Kelly	30	F	Farmer	23Ma42Da
LINANE, Cathri.	20	F	Farmer	23Ma42Da
MCMAHON, James	24	M	Farmer	23Ma42Da
Michael	10	M	Farmer	23Ma42Da
Martin	8	M	Child	23Ma42Da
Thomas	6	M	Child	23Ma42Da
Thomas	24	M	Farmer	23Ma42Da
John	17	M	Farmer	23Ma42Da
William	.00	M	Infant	23Ma42Da
GILLIGAN, Patt	21	M	Farmer	23Ma42Da
MALLEY, John	25	M	Farmer	23Ma42Da
LYDEN, July	20	F	Farmer	23Ma42Da
Biddy	13	F	Farmer	23Ma42Da
CULLUNE, Bridget	30	F	Farmer	23Ma42Da
DUMPHRY, Timothy	32	M	Farmer	23Ma42Da
Michael	21	M	Farmer	23Ma42Da
WHELAN, Thomas	27	M	Farmer	23Ma42Da

NAMES OF PASSENGERS	AGE	SEX	OCCUPATIONS	DATE PORT SHIP
FARRELL, Michael	20	M	Farmer	23Ma42Da
Bridget	25	F	Farmer	23Ma42Da
RYAN, James	24	F	Farmer	23Ma42Da
Mary	.00	F	Infant	23Ma42Da
FARRELL, Thomas	30	M	Farmer	23Ma42Da
Cathrn.	.00	F	Infant	23Ma42Da
HALEY, Mary	16	F	Farmer	23Ma42Da
FOLEY, John	20	M	Farmer	23Ma42Da
MEE, Biddy	35	F	Farmer	23Ma42Da
Tally	13	M	Farmer	23Ma42Da
Thomas	16	M	Farmer	23Ma42Da
Mary	.00	F	Infant	23Ma42Da
MALLORY, Bridget	20	F	Farmer	23Ma42Da
KIRGAN, Judy	13	F	Farmer	23Ma42Da
GERARY, Margaret	30	F	Farmer	23Ma42Da
Patt	3	M	Child	23Ma42Da
Margaret	.00	F	Infant	23Ma42Da
KILLELEA, Thomas	18	M	Farmer	23Ma42Da
FORD, Martin	22	M	Farmer	23Ma42Da
RAFFERTY, Nally	30	M	Farmer	23Ma42Da
Sally	18	F	Farmer	23Ma42Da
Biddy	8	F	Child	23Ma42Da
Mary	14	F	Farmer	23Ma42Da
Thomas	.00	M	Infant	23Ma42Da
DEVANY, John	39	M	Farmer	23Ma42Da
MULLEN, Thomas	50	M	Farmer	23Ma42Da
Mary	40	F	Farmer	23Ma42Da
BROWN, James	24	M	Farmer	23Ma42Da
MULLEN, John	21	M	Farmer	23Ma42Da
Nancy	21	F	Farmer	23Ma42Da
Matthew	20	M	Farmer	23Ma42Da
Thomas	13	M	Farmer	23Ma42Da
George	9	M	Child	23Ma42Da
Margaret	.00	F	Infant	23Ma42Da
BALKIN, James	25	M	Farmer	23Ma42Da
MOUSSY, Patt	20	M	Farmer	23Ma42Da
Cathn.	20	F	Farmer	23Ma42Da
FURY, James	26	M	Farmer	23Ma42Da
Peter	26	M	Farmer	23Ma42Da
Michael	20	M	Farmer	23Ma42Da
SHANNAHAN, Patt	24	M	Farmer	23Ma42Da
MANNION, Mary	12	F	Farmer	23Ma42Da
FORD, Ella	20	F	Farmer	23Ma42Da
SINNAN, Ann	20	F	Farmer	23Ma42Da
COHAN, Patt	20	M	Farmer	23Ma42Da
FAHEY, Mary	16	F	Farmer	23Ma42Da
Honora	15	F	Farmer	23Ma42Da
MORAN, Bridget	21	F	Farmer	23Ma42Da
FAHEY, Andy	21	F	Farmer	23Ma42Da
Mary	18	F	Farmer	23Ma42Da
GOGHAN, Bathw.	17	M	Farmer	23Ma42Da
MCLAUGHIN, Briddy	18	F	Farmer	23Ma42Da
GREOLY, Hugh	26	M	Farmer	23Ma42Da
KELLY, John	30	M	Farmer	23Ma42Da
SWEENEY, Eliza	17	F	Unknown	23Ma42Da
B.	13	M	Unknown	23Ma42Da
CAVANAGH, Michael	23	M	Unknown	23Ma42Da
Patt	20	M	Unknown	23Ma42Da
U-Mrs.	20	F	Unknown	23Ma42Da
BURK, Cather.	40	F	Unknown	23Ma42Da
CAVANAGH, William	.00	M	Infant	23Ma42Da
FAUHY, Mary	6	F	Child	23Ma42Da
YOMEY, James	20	M	Unknown	23Ma42Da
MARCHAL, George	00	M	Unknown	23Ma42Da
Jane	30	F	Unknown	23Ma42Da
ALKINSON, Ellen	16	F	Unknown	23Ma42Da
DONOHUE, Bridget	20	F	Farmer	23Ma42Da
GREDICH, Peggy	18	F	Farmer	23Ma42Da
EGAN, Peggy	18	F	Farmer	23Ma42Da
CLASBY, Mary	18	F	Farmer	23Ma42Da
GRIALISH, Peggy	20	F	Farmer	23Ma42Da
MULLINS, Honor	23	F	Farmer	23Ma42Da

HYNDEFORD 23 MAY 1850

From Glasgow

NAMES OF PASSENGERS	AGE	SEX	OCCUPATIONS	DATE PORT SHIP
DEVINE, Samuel	36	M	Laborer	23Ma21Ee
MCKELVIE, Robert	22	M	Laborer	23Ma21Ee
ELLIS, George	20	M	Laborer	23Ma21Ee
MALLAND, Michael	32	M	Laborer	23Ma21Ee
WARD, Patrick	23	M	Laborer	23Ma21Ee
Ann	21	F	Wife	23Ma21Ee
MCKAY, Joseph	20	M	Laborer	23Ma21Ee
JOHNSTON, Patrick	50	M	Laborer	23Ma21Ee
Ann	6	F	Child	23Ma21Ee
MCKAKEN, Robert	22	M	Laborer	23Ma21Ee
Agness	17	F	Laborer	23Ma21Ee
DOUGLAS, James	30	M	Laborer	23Ma21Ee
Jane	26	F	Laborer	23Ma21Ee
Robert	2	M	Child	23Ma21Ee
Margaret	.03	F	Infant	23Ma21Ee
BROWNLEE, James	29	M	Laborer	23Ma21Ee
HUNTER, John	30	M	Laborer	23Ma21Ee
MONTGOMERY, James	16	M	Laborer	23Ma21Ee
ROBINSON, John	30	M	Laborer	23Ma21Ee
Sarah	19	F	Laborer	23Ma21Ee
KENEDY, Edward	19	M	Laborer	23Ma21Ee
CARLETON, Hugh	22	M	Laborer	23Ma21Ee
THOMSON, William	23	M	Laborer	23Ma21Ee
CAFFERTY, William	23	M	Laborer	23Ma21Ee
FEENEY, James	20	M	Laborer	23Ma21Ee
MCCORMACH, Matilda	20	F	Servant	23Ma21Ee
CONNOR, Margaret	20	F	Servant	23Ma21Ee
MCHENRY, William	20	M	Laborer	23Ma21Ee
Margaret	18	F	Servant	23Ma21Ee
MCCLUSKY, Eliza	22	F	Servant	23Ma21Ee
MURPHY, Michael	22	M	Laborer	23Ma21Ee
GRAHAM, John	22	M	Laborer	23Ma21Ee
KILPATRICK, James	23	M	Laborer	23Ma21Ee
HUNTER, George	23	M	Laborer	23Ma21Ee
LEAKIE, William	43	M	Laborer	23Ma21Ee
DICK, Wm. (R)	45	M	Laborer	23Ma21Ee
Mary (R)	44	F	Wife	23Ma21Ee
Margaret (R)	16	F	Unknown	23Ma21Ee
Jane (R)	14	F	Unknown	23Ma21Ee
Mary-Ann (R)	12	F	Unknown	23Ma21Ee
Thomas (R)	10	M	Unknown	23Ma21Ee
William (R)	8	M	Child	23Ma21Ee
Isabella (R)	6	F	Child	23Ma21Ee
Eliza (R)	2	F	Child	23Ma21Ee
Died-At-Sea				
WHITECROSS, William	26	M	Laborer	23Ma21Ee
FLYN, Dominic	20	M	Laborer	23Ma21Ee
LOGAN, Archibald	20	M	Laborer	23Ma21Ee
GLEN, James	19	M	Laborer	23Ma21Ee
GILLESPIE, David	21	M	Laborer	23Ma21Ee
MCTUCHAIN, Robt.	24	M	Laborer	23Ma21Ee
MCAULES, Abram	17	M	Laborer	23Ma21Ee
KENEDY, Phillip	27	M	Laborer	23Ma21Ee
CAMPBELL, Isabella	20	F	Servant	23Ma21Ee
FALLON, Robt.	22	M	Laborer	23Ma21Ee
MILLS, George	25	M	Laborer	23Ma21Ee
BAILIE, Elizabeth	30	F	Servant	23Ma21Ee
BURSE, Alexd.	35	M	Laborer	23Ma21Ee
JENNINGTON, Elizabeth-	29	F	Servant	23Ma21Ee
Ellen	8	F	Child	23Ma21Ee
Robert	3	M	Child	23Ma21Ee
Eliza	.10	F	Infant	23Ma21Ee
MILEY, William	20	M	Laborer	23Ma21Ee
BOODLY, U-Mrs.	45	F	Unknown	23Ma21Ee
HUTCHINSON, Eleanor(R)	13	F	Servant	23Ma21Ee

NAMES OF PASSENGERS	AGE	SEX	OCCUPATIONS	DATE PORT SHIP
DANAH, Mary	20	F	Servant	23Ma21Ee
MUGHAN, Connie	24	M	Laborer	23Ma21Ee
MONTGOMERY, Michael	22	M	Laborer	23Ma21Ee
BYRNE, William	17	M	Laborer	23Ma21Ee
LEUNE, Ellen	22	F	Servant	23Ma21Ee
WALMSLEY, Jane	30	F	Wife	23Ma21Ee
Jane	13	F	Servant	23Ma21Ee
William	11	M	Unknown	23Ma21Ee
Joseph	9	M	Child	23Ma21Ee
Catherine	7	F	Child	23Ma21Ee
Isabella	4	F	Child	23Ma21Ee
Dennis	.09	M	Infant	23Ma21Ee
KEYS, Jane	15	F	Servant	23Ma21Ee
MULDSOON, Jane	30	F	Servant	23Ma21Ee
FINNUS, Phillip	32	M	Laborer	23Ma21Ee
MCDONALD, Andrew	20	M	Laborer	23Ma21Ee

FORESTAL 23 MAY 1850

From Waterford

NAMES OF PASSENGERS	AGE	SEX	OCCUPATIONS	DATE PORT SHIP
LUENS, James	34	M	Farmer	23Ma35Jl
MOORE, Richard	27	M	Unknown	23Ma35Jl
Bridget	27	F	Unknown	23Ma35Jl
Thomas	2	M	Child	23Ma35Jl
MURPHY, Stephen	29	M	Unknown	23Ma35Jl
Patrick	24	M	Unknown	23Ma35Jl
Mary	20	F	Unknown	23Ma35Jl
Maria	20	F	Unknown	23Ma35Jl
KEEFE, John	33	M	Unknown	23Ma35Jl
DEADY, John	22	M	Unknown	23Ma35Jl
POWER, John	35	M	Unknown	23Ma35Jl
Bridget	14	F	Unknown	23Ma35Jl
CONNORS, Patrick	23	M	Unknown	23Ma35Jl
Mary	15	F	Unknown	23Ma35Jl
ROCHE, Mary	30	F	Unknown	23Ma35Jl
HOARE, John	19	M	Unknown	23Ma35Jl
DELANCY, Catherine	22	F	Unknown	23Ma35Jl
SCANLON, Teresa	24	F	Unknown	23Ma35Jl
MORISON, Ellen	25	F	Unknown	23Ma35Jl
FLAHERTY, James	14	M	Unknown	23Ma35Jl
NOWLAN, James	30	M	Unknown	23Ma35Jl
HOARE, Margaret	23	F	Unknown	23Ma35Jl
DOYLE, Martin	26	M	Unknown	23Ma35Jl
PHELAN, Lawrence	40	M	Unknown	23Ma35Jl
Bridget	40	F	Unknown	23Ma35Jl
Mary	16	F	Unknown	23Ma35Jl
LONDRAGON, Cath.	50	F	Unknown	23Ma35Jl
PRYDE, Margt.	19	F	Unknown	23Ma35Jl
COSTELLO, Nancy	18	F	Unknown	23Ma35Jl
MCGRATH, Thomas	35	M	Unknown	23Ma35Jl
Cath.	36	F	Unknown	23Ma35Jl
John	9	M	Child	23Ma35Jl
Anne	8	F	Child	23Ma35Jl
LINNOTT, James	23	M	Unknown	23Ma35Jl
CARTHY, James	26	M	Unknown	23Ma35Jl
GRIFFIN, Phillip	30	M	Unknown	23Ma35Jl
HEARNE, Wm.	24	M	Unknown	23Ma35Jl
Bridget	20	F	Unknown	23Ma35Jl
VEALE, Robert	36	M	Unknown	23Ma35Jl
Mary	50	F	Unknown	23Ma35Jl
HEADEN, Alice	24	F	Unknown	23Ma35Jl
MANNING, Cath.	22	F	Unknown	23Ma35Jl
PHELAN, Patrick	23	M	Unknown	23Ma35Jl
LINNOTT, Patrick	17	M	Unknown	23Ma35Jl
ROCHE, John	30	M	Unknown	23Ma35Jl
DORRILL, Michl.	30	M	Unknown	23Ma35Jl
DOUNILL, Con.	32	M	Unknown	23Ma35Jl
DORRILL, Ally	28	F	Unknown	23Ma35Jl
LONDRAGON, Pat	30	M	Unknown	23Ma35Jl
DANIEL, Mary	7	F	Child	23Ma35Jl
BUTLER, Michl.	25	M	Unknown	23Ma35Jl
Anty.	30	F	Unknown	23Ma35Jl
REDDY, Betty	26	F	Unknown	23Ma35Jl
BLANCH, James	35	M	Unknown	23Ma35Jl
Bridget	25	F	Unknown	23Ma35Jl
SKEANE, Henry	20	M	Unknown	23Ma35Jl
LONDRAGAN, Mary	4	F	Child	23Ma35Jl
HALFPENNY, Patt	25	M	Unknown	23Ma35Jl
MULLINS, Mary	21	F	Unknown	23Ma35Jl
POWER, Patt	30	M	Unknown	23Ma35Jl
FORTUNE, Garret	50	M	Unknown	23Ma35Jl
EARL, Margt.	17	F	Unknown	23Ma35Jl
Allen	16	M	Unknown	23Ma35Jl
Henry	35	M	Unknown	23Ma35Jl
POWER, Lawrence	25	M	Unknown	23Ma35Jl
OWEN, Richard	21	M	Unknown	23Ma35Jl
Jane	21	F	Unknown	23Ma35Jl
DONOVAN, Thomas	28	M	Unknown	23Ma35Jl
FLYNN, Mary	30	F	Unknown	23Ma35Jl
WALSH, Margt.	21	F	Unknown	23Ma35Jl
ROCHE, Patt	16	M	Unknown	23Ma35Jl
Francis	14	M	Unknown	23Ma35Jl
HART, Cath.	24	F	Unknown	23Ma35Jl
KIERSEY, Michl.	27	M	Unknown	23Ma35Jl
Mary	25	F	Unknown	23Ma35Jl
POWER, James	21	M	Unknown	23Ma35Jl
CROWE, Dennis	28	M	Unknown	23Ma35Jl
POWER, Mary	28	F	Unknown	23Ma35Jl
FLEMMING, Anne	.00	F	Infant	23Ma35Jl
HERBERT, Ellen	20	F	Unknown	23Ma35Jl
TIMMONS, Margt.	20	F	Unknown	23Ma35Jl
MAHER, Mary	23	F	Unknown	23Ma35Jl
LONDRIGAN, Margt.	.00	F	Infant	23Ma35Jl
BATES, Eliza	21	F	Unknown	23Ma35Jl
COONEY, Margt.	22	F	Unknown	23Ma35Jl
KENNY, Edward	20	M	Unknown	23Ma35Jl
KINSALA, Francis	18	M	Unknown	23Ma35Jl
Christiana	19	F	Unknown	23Ma35Jl
OBRIEN, Stephen	24	M	Unknown	23Ma35Jl
SULLIVAN, Wm.	25	M	Unknown	23Ma35Jl
Mary	25	F	Unknown	23Ma35Jl
FARRELL, Wm.	24	M	Unknown	23Ma35Jl
STEPHENS, Mary	28	F	Unknown	23Ma35Jl
HATTON, Mary	29	F	Unknown	23Ma35Jl

POLYNESIA 23 MAY 1850

From Limerick

NAMES OF PASSENGERS	AGE	SEX	OCCUPATIONS	DATE PORT SHIP
OMORREN, Johanna	20	F	Laborer	23Ma10Km
HALLMAN, Edmund	25	M	Unknown	23Ma10Km
CLANCHY, Daniel	80	M	Unknown	23Ma10Km
Cath.	20	F	Unknown	23Ma10Km
HEALY, Michl.	16	M	Unknown	23Ma10Km
PERRYMAN, John	30	M	Unknown	23Ma10Km
MCCARTHY, Michl.	28	M	Unknown	23Ma10Km
LYNDON, Patt	20	M	Unknown	23Ma10Km
Cath.	18	F	Unknown	23Ma10Km
DUNK, William	23	M	Unknown	23Ma10Km
Cath.	19	F	Unknown	23Ma10Km
BORDON, Mary	20	F	Unknown	23Ma10Km
OBRIEN, John	30	M	Unknown	23Ma10Km
HANNEN, Henry	25	M	Unknown	23Ma10Km
COTTEREL, John	21	M	Unknown	23Ma10Km
MILLGREEN, Patt	21	M	Unknown	23Ma10Km
HEFFERNAN, Wm.	50	M	Unknown	23Ma10Km
James	24	M	Unknown	23Ma10Km

NAMES OF PASSENGERS	AGE	SEX	OCCUPATIONS	DATE PORT SHIP
HEFFERNAN, Connor	20	M	Unknown	23Ma10Km
Thos.	16	M	Unknown	23Ma10Km
Robt.	7	M	Child	23Ma10Km
Mary	11	F	Unknown	23Ma10Km
ROURK, Margt.	24	F	Unknown	23Ma10Km
MASH, Mary	50	F	Unknown	23Ma10Km
RILLER, Mary	30	M	Unknown	23Ma10Km
FITZGERALD, James	24	M	Unknown	23Ma10Km
LYNCH, Mary	22	F	Unknown	23Ma10Km
BYRNES, John	30	M	Unknown	23Ma10Km
Edmund	22	M	Unknown	23Ma10Km
Hannah	60	F	Unknown	23Ma10Km
Michael	5	M	Child	23Ma10Km
MCMAHON, Thos.	25	M	Unknown	23Ma10Km
MCNAMARA, Cath.	28	F	Unknown	23Ma10Km
DUNAGAN, Cath.	14	F	Unknown	23Ma10Km
HANNAN, Patt	22	M	Unknown	23Ma10Km
CONNOR, Michl.	21	M	Unknown	23Ma10Km
SHEAHAN, Terence	23	M	Unknown	23Ma10Km
CLOUGHESSY, Bridgt.	20	F	Unknown	23Ma10Km
MALLTON, John	25	M	Unknown	23Ma10Km
WARD, Mary-Ann	11	F	Unknown	23Ma10Km
JOHNSON, Mary	13	F	Unknown	23Ma10Km
FLANGAN, James	25	M	Unknown	23Ma10Km
OBRIEN, Edmund	21	M	Unknown	23Ma10Km
Mary	26	F	Unknown	23Ma10Km
DOYLE, Cath.	25	F	Unknown	23Ma10Km
Mary	.00	F	Infant	23Ma10Km
PURCELL, Johanna	25	F	Unknown	23Ma10Km
COLLINS, Jane	30	F	Unknown	23Ma10Km
FITZGERALD, Maurice	36	M	Unknown	23Ma10Km
Mary	30	F	Unknown	23Ma10Km
Ellen	20	F	Unknown	23Ma10Km
WELSH, Ellen	8	F	Child	23Ma10Km
Bridgt.	2	F	Child	23Ma10Km
FITZGERALD, James	.00	M	Infant	23Ma10Km
GRIFFIN, Daniel	24	M	Unknown	23Ma10Km
GREEN, Michael	20	M	Unknown	23Ma10Km
MOLONY, Winifred	17	M	Unknown	23Ma10Km
DOWNES, Ellen	18	F	Unknown	23Ma10Km
CROWLEY, John	21	M	Unknown	23Ma10Km
MCGRATH, Michl.	24	M	Unknown	23Ma10Km
MORONEY, Michl.	29	M	Unknown	23Ma10Km
Anthony	27	M	Unknown	23Ma10Km
R.	19	M	Unknown	23Ma10Km
Biddy	25	F	Unknown	23Ma10Km
ROWLEY, William	19	M	Unknown	23Ma10Km
COUGHLAN, James	24	M	Unknown	23Ma10Km
LYNCH, Michl.	25	M	Unknown	23Ma10Km
PIGOT, John	20	M	Unknown	23Ma10Km
Sarah	20	F	Unknown	23Ma10Km
REFFARD, John	25	M	Unknown	23Ma10Km
Margt.	22	F	Unknown	23Ma10Km
MURPHY, Michl.	23	M	Unknown	23Ma10Km
BRAZILL, Ellen	33	F	Unknown	23Ma10Km
DUNN, Patt	27	M	Unknown	23Ma10Km
WELSH, Michl.	24	M	Unknown	23Ma10Km
Michl.	26	M	Unknown	23Ma10Km
JERITY, Michl.	34	M	Unknown	23Ma10Km
SHEEHY, James	35	M	Unknown	23Ma10Km
Mary	35	F	Unknown	23Ma10Km
ROURK, John	25	M	Unknown	23Ma10Km
Thomas	20	M	Unknown	23Ma10Km
Margt.	11	F	Unknown	23Ma10Km
Sally	20	F	Unknown	23Ma10Km
SMALL, Thomas	22	M	Unknown	23Ma10Km
BRIEN, John	18	M	Unknown	23Ma10Km
BOURKE, Patt	21	M	Unknown	23Ma10Km
William	22	M	Unknown	23Ma10Km
Cath.	23	F	Unknown	23Ma10Km
MULLINS, Mary	20	F	Unknown	23Ma10Km
DONOHUE, James	26	M	Unknown	23Ma10Km
Patt	40	M	Unknown	23Ma10Km
Martin	28	M	Unknown	23Ma10Km
Mary	50	F	Unknown	23Ma10Km
DONOHUE, Biddy	.00	F	Infant	23Ma10Km
AUGHER, Patt	20	M	Unknown	23Ma10Km
CLUNE, Ellen	50	F	Unknown	23Ma10Km
BUCKLEY, Margt.	35	F	Unknown	23Ma10Km
KELLY, James	19	M	Unknown	23Ma10Km
HYNES, John	19	M	Unknown	23Ma10Km
KELLY, Mary	21	F	Unknown	23Ma10Km
GUNN, Mary	17	F	Unknown	23Ma10Km
MONSELL, William	25	M	Unknown	23Ma10Km
Margt.	20	F	Unknown	23Ma10Km
SHEEHAN, John	24	M	Unknown	23Ma10Km
CONNERY, James	25	M	Unknown	23Ma10Km
RYAN, Patt	25	M	Unknown	23Ma10Km
MCCARTHY, Daniel	20	M	Unknown	23Ma10Km
DOWNEY, Mary	15	F	Unknown	23Ma10Km
OKEEFE, Bridgt.	17	F	Unknown	23Ma10Km
DUARD, Michl.	24	M	Unknown	23Ma10Km
Patt	15	M	Unknown	23Ma10Km
Cath.	.00	F	Infant	23Ma10Km
BOURKE, Thos.	24	M	Unknown	23Ma10Km
FINN, James	22	M	Unknown	23Ma10Km
Mary	20	F	Unknown	23Ma10Km
Biddy	.00	F	Infant	23Ma10Km
KEANE, William	26	M	Unknown	23Ma10Km
Michl.	23	M	Unknown	23Ma10Km
GREALLY, Michl.	30	M	Unknown	23Ma10Km
Daniel	24	M	Unknown	23Ma10Km
KENE, John	21	M	Unknown	23Ma10Km
Michael	20	M	Unknown	23Ma10Km
Nancy	19	F	Unknown	23Ma10Km
BUCKLEY, Simon	21	M	Unknown	23Ma10Km
BLAKE, John	24	M	Unknown	23Ma10Km
ODONNELL, Mary	18	F	Unknown	23Ma10Km
BLAKE, Ellen	19	F	Unknown	23Ma10Km
ODONNELL, Richard	19	M	Unknown	23Ma10Km
MANGAN, Patt	18	M	Unknown	23Ma10Km
DULLMAN, Anne	20	F	Unknown	23Ma10Km
LYDDY, William	.00	M	Infant	23Ma10Km

MARY-WARD 23 MAY 1850

From Liverpool

NAMES OF PASSENGERS	AGE	SEX	OCCUPATIONS	DATE PORT SHIP
WRIGHT, John	40	M	Baker	23Ma02Jp
Mary	41	F	Unknown	23Ma02Jp
John	17	M	Unknown	23Ma02Jp
Eliza	11	F	Unknown	23Ma02Jp
Ellen	7	F	Child	23Ma02Jp
Martha	5	F	Child	23Ma02Jp
Agnes	3	F	Child	23Ma02Jp
ONEILL, James	22	M	Farmer	23Ma02Jp
CARTY, Mathew	21	M	Laborer	23Ma02Jp
CULLEN, Patrick	22	M	Laborer	23Ma02Jp
MANEY, Mary	20	F	Unknown	23Ma02Jp
GRAY, Bridget	20	F	Unknown	23Ma02Jp
Honora	22	F	Unknown	23Ma02Jp
CODEY, Catherine	18	F	Unknown	23Ma02Jp
WOODS, Ann	40	F	Unknown	23Ma02Jp
Bernard	10	M	Unknown	23Ma02Jp
MCCOWL, Phillip	47	M	Unknown	23Ma02Jp
Bridget	45	F	Unknown	23Ma02Jp
CALWELL, John	20	M	Baker	23Ma02Jp
BRYAN, Robt.	23	M	Painter	23Ma02Jp
U-Mrs.	23	F	Unknown	23Ma02Jp
WALSH, Patrick	20	M	Laborer	23Ma02Jp
GILL, Geo.	40	M	Farmer	23Ma02Jp
Francis	20	M	Farmer	23Ma02Jp
John	16	M	Laborer	23Ma02Jp
MARTIN, Mary	38	F	Unknown	23Ma02Jp

NAMES OF PASSENGERS	AGE	SEX	OCCUPATIONS	DATE PORT SHIP
MARTIN, Mathew	12	M	Unknown	23Ma02Jp
Mary	10	F	Unknown	23Ma02Jp
Francis	.00	M	Infant	23Ma02Jp
BAGLEY, Thos.	40	M	Mariner	23Ma02Jp
Mary	31	F	Unknown	23Ma02Jp
GAY, Wm.	22	M	Miner	23Ma02Jp
READY, John	22	M	Laborer	23Ma02Jp
Sarah	16	F	Unknown	23Ma02Jp
BERGEN, Michl.	40	M	Unknown	23Ma02Jp
DERMODY, John	30	M	Unknown	23Ma02Jp
BRENAN, Citty	22	F	Unknown	23Ma02Jp
Judy	.00	F	Infant	23Ma02Jp
ROBISON, Thos.	24	M	Unknown	23Ma02Jp
MIGSWORTH, Mary	18	F	Unknown	23Ma02Jp
KERNAN, Pat.	20	M	Farmer	23Ma02Jp
Hugh	30	M	Farmer	23Ma02Jp
Biddy	30	F	Unknown	23Ma02Jp
Michl.	20	M	Unknown	23Ma02Jp
Catherine	20	F	Unknown	23Ma02Jp
Margaret	20	F	Unknown	23Ma02Jp
CONOLLY, Terence	20	M	Painter	23Ma02Jp
WHALAN, James	30	M	Laborer	23Ma02Jp
MCCONNER, Rose	13	F	Unknown	23Ma02Jp
YATES, John	20	M	Unknown	23Ma02Jp
LANIGAN, John	26	M	Unknown	23Ma02Jp
John	12	M	Unknown	23Ma02Jp
Ann	21	F	Unknown	23Ma02Jp
Wm.	2	M	Child	23Ma02Jp
RYAN, Luke	30	M	Laborer	23Ma02Jp
Biddy	24	F	Unknown	23Ma02Jp
CANACH, Patt	23	M	Laborer	23Ma02Jp
GAKIN, John	39	M	Trader	23Ma02Jp
MCDONALD, Alex.	25	M	Servant	23Ma02Jp
WALLACE, John	28	M	Farmer	23Ma02Jp
DUFFY, Cath.	18	F	Unknown	23Ma02Jp
TOBING, Patt	28	M	Carpenter	23Ma02Jp
NOLEN, Michl.	22	M	Laborer	23Ma02Jp
Edward	18	M	Unknown	23Ma02Jp
Margaret	45	F	Unknown	23Ma02Jp
Mary	19	F	Unknown	23Ma02Jp
HILL, Margaret	22	F	Unknown	23Ma02Jp
WALSH, Robt.	26	M	Farmer	23Ma02Jp
Alice	23	F	Unknown	23Ma02Jp
Alice	.00	F	Infant	23Ma02Jp
Died-At-Sea				
Richd.	18	M	Farmer	23Ma02Jp
LONG, John	28	M	Farmer	23Ma02Jp
Mary	24	F	Unknown	23Ma02Jp
Eliza	.00	F	Infant	23Ma02Jp
Richd.	52	M	Unknown	23Ma02Jp
Cath.	50	F	Unknown	23Ma02Jp
Robt.	20	M	Unknown	23Ma02Jp
Mary	20	F	Unknown	23Ma02Jp
Nancy	.00	F	Infant	23Ma02Jp
COSTELLO, Edmund	20	M	Farmer	23Ma02Jp
Alice	18	F	Unknown	23Ma02Jp
James	.00	M	Infant	23Ma02Jp
Mary	22	F	Unknown	23Ma02Jp
Thos.	19	M	Unknown	23Ma02Jp
Robt.	.00	M	Infant	23Ma02Jp
LONG, Mary	13	F	Unknown	23Ma02Jp
MCEVOY, Dennis	24	M	Carpenter	23Ma02Jp
BULGER, Wm.	50	M	Farmer	23Ma02Jp
John	12	M	Unknown	23Ma02Jp
Mary	8	F	Child	23Ma02Jp
MARTHA, Biddy	26	F	Unknown	23Ma02Jp
MACKIN, Thos.	34	M	Miller	23Ma02Jp
Eliza	36	F	Unknown	23Ma02Jp
MANEY, Dennis	30	M	Laborer	23Ma02Jp
DUGGIN, Margt.	24	F	Laborer	23Ma02Jp
HOOLAHIN, Martin	13	M	Laborer	23Ma02Jp
TORPEY, Ellen	17	F	Laborer	23Ma02Jp
Ann	25	F	Laborer	23Ma02Jp
Bridget	19	F	Laborer	23Ma02Jp
DOYLE, Mary	20	F	Laborer	23Ma02Jp
CASEY, Thos.	24	M	Laborer	23Ma02Jp
HURY, Thos.	24	M	Carpenter	23Ma02Jp
CROM, Michl.	24	M	Laborer	23Ma02Jp
MCCORMACK, Pat.	30	M	Laborer	23Ma02Jp
DALTON, Wm.	33	M	Laborer	23Ma02Jp
FOLEY, Maurice	20	M	Laborer	23Ma02Jp
LEARY, Pat.	45	M	Laborer	23Ma02Jp
Bridget	40	F	Laborer	23Ma02Jp
Ann	24	F	Laborer	23Ma02Jp
KELLY, Martin	45	M	Laborer	23Ma02Jp
Mary	35	F	Unknown	23Ma02Jp
DOYLE, Pat	27	M	Unknown	23Ma02Jp
HUGH, Mary	25	F	Unknown	23Ma02Jp
GILLESPIE, John	20	M	Unknown	23Ma02Jp
Ann	21	F	Unknown	23Ma02Jp
LYONS, Bridget	17	F	Unknown	23Ma02Jp
BRADY, Ellen	20	F	Unknown	23Ma02Jp
FEANY, John	19	M	Unknown	23Ma02Jp
Rose	25	F	Unknown	23Ma02Jp
WARE, Mary	28	F	Unknown	23Ma02Jp
HAMILTON, John	14	M	Unknown	23Ma02Jp
KERGAN, Mary-A.	18	F	Unknown	23Ma02Jp
JACKSON, Ellen	16	F	Unknown	23Ma02Jp
KELLY, Martin	20	M	Unknown	23Ma02Jp
RYAN, Ann	24	F	Unknown	23Ma02Jp
Bridget	20	F	Unknown	23Ma02Jp
KING, James	30	M	Bricklayer	23Ma02Jp
WILLHERNAN, E.	30	M	Joiner	23Ma02Jp
MULLEN, U	30	M	Stctr	23Ma02Jp
MORRIS, Thos.	22	M	Laborer	23Ma02Jp
DUDDY, Bridget	18	F	Unknown	23Ma02Jp
LOOSKIN, Michl.	20	M	Laborer	23Ma02Jp
Biddy	18	F	Laborer	23Ma02Jp
MCTEGH, John	25	M	Laborer	23Ma02Jp
Bridget	20	F	Laborer	23Ma02Jp
FLANAGAN, Cath.	18	F	Laborer	23Ma02Jp
EAGAN, Cath.	20	F	Unknown	23Ma02Jp
THANTY, Connor	60	M	Unknown	23Ma02Jp
Died-At-Sea				
Margt.	50	F	Unknown	23Ma02Jp
Bernard	22	M	Unknown	23Ma02Jp
Jane	12	F	Unknown	23Ma02Jp
Francis	9	M	Child	23Ma02Jp
CONYERS, Cath.	6	F	Child	23Ma02Jp
WHELAN, Edwd.	50	M	Farmer	23Ma02Jp
FLOOD, Ann	12	F	Farmer	23Ma02Jp
KEHAN, Cath.	16	F	Unknown	23Ma02Jp
WOGAN, Mary	33	F	Unknown	23Ma02Jp
Martin	.00	M	Infant	23Ma02Jp
Wm.	5	M	Child	23Ma02Jp
Eliza	3	F	Child	23Ma02Jp
BARRY, Thos.	12	M	Unknown	23Ma02Jp
Eliza	9	F	Child	23Ma02Jp
Ellen	7	F	Child	23Ma02Jp
MCEVOY, Jesse	23	M	Unknown	23Ma02Jp
Cath.	.00	F	Infant	23Ma02Jp
PENDERGRASS, Janet	56	F	Seamstress	23Ma02Jp
Ellen	55	F	Unknown	23Ma02Jp
Michl.	26	M	Unknown	23Ma02Jp
Eliza	12	F	Unknown	23Ma02Jp
Thos.	10	M	Unknown	23Ma02Jp
HALLISEY, Ellen	20	F	Unknown	23Ma02Jp
LYNCH, Thos.	24	M	Carpenter	23Ma02Jp
John	22	M	Unknown	23Ma02Jp
ARNOLD, Wm.	13	M	Unknown	23Ma02Jp
Agnes	11	F	Unknown	23Ma02Jp
MCCLARE, Andrew	25	M	Laborer	23Ma02Jp
Mary	22	F	Unknown	23Ma02Jp
FARRELL, Laura	10	F	Unknown	23Ma02Jp
DUFFY, Lawrence	50	M	Unknown	23Ma02Jp
Bridget	50	F	Unknown	23Ma02Jp
Pat	23	M	Unknown	23Ma02Jp
CONNER, John	12	M	Unknown	23Ma02Jp
Thos.	7	M	Child	23Ma02Jp
Patt	5	M	Child	23Ma02Jp

NAMES OF PASSENGERS	AGE	SEX	OCCUPATIONS	DATE PORT SHIP
JERDAN, Honora	28	F	Unknown	23Ma02Jp
Pat.	25	M	Unknown	23Ma02Jp
Jessy	14	M	Unknown	23Ma02Jp
DUNROORTH, James	23	M	Unknown	23Ma02Jp
BRUNICK, Johan	20	M	Unknown	23Ma02Jp
SHEA, Bryan	14	M	Unknown	23Ma02Jp
Patt	12	M	Unknown	23Ma02Jp
GLEESON, John	20	M	Unknown	23Ma02Jp
HEFFERMAN, Michl.	8	M	Child	23Ma02Jp
MCQUAID, Michl.	40	M	Unknown	23Ma02Jp
Mary	35	F	Unknown	23Ma02Jp
CUNNINGHAM, Jas.	20	M	Tailor	23Ma02Jp
Cicily	22	F	Unknown	23Ma02Jp
DEHAIN, Bridget	25	F	Unknown	23Ma02Jp
*zRT, John	25	M	Laborer	23Ma02Jp
NAUGHTON, Peggy	30	F	Unknown	23Ma02Jp
Thos.	6	M	Child	23Ma02Jp
James	4	M	Child	23Ma02Jp
Ellen	.00	F	Infant	23Ma02Jp
MULVEINE, John	28	M	Unknown	23Ma02Jp
BOYLE, Maria	17	F	Unknown	23Ma02Jp
Jas.	16	M	Farmer	23Ma02Jp
KING, Cath.	28	F	Unknown	23Ma02Jp
CONNAUGHT, Bridget	19	F	Unknown	23Ma02Jp
MCGUIRE, Bridget	20	F	Unknown	23Ma02Jp
James	12	M	Unknown	23Ma02Jp
ILES, John	38	M	Mason	23Ma02Jp
Sarah	37	F	Unknown	23Ma02Jp
John	11	M	Unknown	23Ma02Jp
Ellen	9	F	Child	23Ma02Jp
Chas.	6	M	Child	23Ma02Jp
Jane	3	F	Child	23Ma02Jp
Tasslin	.00	U	Infant	23Ma02Jp
TELWOOD, Richd.	20	M	Laborer	23Ma02Jp
Mary	20	F	Laborer	23Ma02Jp
Ann-Maria	.00	F	Infant	23Ma02Jp
RUDMAN, M.	26	M	Blacksmith	23Ma02Jp
Eliza	25	F	Unknown	23Ma02Jp
LOW, Chas.	22	M	Laborer	23Ma02Jp
Jane	22	F	Unknown	23Ma02Jp
Chas.	.00	F	Infant	23Ma02Jp
KING, Wm.	21	M	Unknown	23Ma02Jp
HUNT, John	16	M	Unknown	23Ma02Jp
RICKS, John	43	M	Unknown	23Ma02Jp
Sarah	43	F	Unknown	23Ma02Jp
Caroline	12	F	Unknown	23Ma02Jp
NIFE, Henry	28	M	Unknown	23Ma02Jp
Sarah	27	F	Unknown	23Ma02Jp
Sarah	.00	F	Infant	23Ma02Jp
KENNETT, M.	25	U	Unknown	23Ma02Jp
MORAN, Richd.	23	M	Unknown	23Ma02Jp
MARSKILL, Ellen	20	F	Unknown	23Ma02Jp
RYAN, Danl.	29	M	Farmer	23Ma02Jp
RUGENT, Jno.	19	M	Cooper	23Ma02Jp
FITZGERALD, Michl.	22	M	Farmer	23Ma02Jp
Pat.	25	M	Unknown	23Ma02Jp
MARONY, Pat.	29	M	Unknown	23Ma02Jp
CUMMINGS, Edward	28	M	Unknown	23Ma02Jp
HALASY, Margaret	14	F	Unknown	23Ma02Jp
GRIFFIN, Michl.	28	M	Laborer	23Ma02Jp
Honora	28	F	Unknown	23Ma02Jp
HALPIN, Michl.	36	M	Farmer	23Ma02Jp
Pat.	16	M	Unknown	23Ma02Jp
DORELL, Pat.	30	M	Laborer	23Ma02Jp
GORMAN, Terence	25	M	Unknown	23Ma02Jp
FILLING, Henry	21	M	Unknown	23Ma02Jp
PIERCE, James	23	M	Unknown	23Ma02Jp
SHEEHAN, Mary	17	F	Unknown	23Ma02Jp
DENNIKER, A.	35	M	Merchant	23Ma02Jp
BURKE, Mary	24	F	Unknown	23Ma02Jp
BRYAN, Cath.	24	F	Laborer	23Ma02Jp
MCDONNELL, Henry	17	M	Unknown	23Ma02Jp
Francis	31	M	Laborer	23Ma02Jp
REDY, John	21	M	Unknown	23Ma02Jp
SULLIVAN, Jas.	25	M	Unknown	23Ma02Jp
TWIG, David	23	M	Unknown	23Ma02Jp
GORMAN, Cath.	25	F	Unknown	23Ma02Jp
William	6	M	Child	23Ma02Jp
Richd.	3	M	Child	23Ma02Jp
James	.00	M	Infant	23Ma02Jp
FURLONG, Richard	25	M	Unknown	23Ma02Jp
MASTERSON, John	25	M	Gdnr	23Ma02Jp
Ann	25	F	Unknown	23Ma02Jp
CARBERRY, Ellen	14	F	Unknown	23Ma02Jp
GELASSY, Pat.	13	M	Unknown	23Ma02Jp
WALSH, Alice	00	F	Unknown	23Ma02Jp
COSTELLO, Rosan	20	F	Unknown	23Ma02Jp

ABEONA 23 MAY 1850

From Liverpool

NAMES OF PASSENGERS	AGE	SEX	OCCUPATIONS	DATE PORT SHIP
MOULTRY, Edmund	25	M	Farmer	23Ma02Da
Mary	25	F	Farmer	23Ma02Da
SPEARS, John	17	M	Farmer	23Ma02Da
CALLAGHAN, Eliza	25	F	Farmer	23Ma02Da
BAXTER, Adelaide	21	F	Farmer	23Ma02Da
REID, Adam	25	M	Farmer	23Ma02Da
MAINES, James	27	M	Surveyor	23Ma02Da
Maria	23	F	Surveyor	23Ma02Da
KILPATRICK, John	38	M	Mason	23Ma02Da
MCBRIDE, John	24	M	Grocer	23Ma02Da
Mary-Ann	22	F	Grocer	23Ma02Da
Mary	50	F	Farmer	23Ma02Da
MACKAY, James	20	M	Farmer	23Ma02Da
JOICE, Mary	21	F	Governess	23Ma02Da
Rachael	18	F	Governess	23Ma02Da
PORTER, Hannah	16	F	Servant	23Ma02Da
CUMMINS, Dennis	56	M	Farmer	23Ma02Da
Michael	28	M	Farmer	23Ma02Da
Ann	26	F	Farmer	23Ma02Da
John	3	M	Child	23Ma02Da
John	26	M	Farmer	23Ma02Da
Thomas	20	M	Farmer	23Ma02Da
MAHER, Sally	40	F	Spinster	23Ma02Da
HACKET, Peter	26	M	Printer	23Ma02Da
BRADY, James	18	M	Laborer	23Ma02Da
Ann	13	F	Servant	23Ma02Da
WARD, Patrick	50	M	Gdnr	23Ma02Da
Alice	40	F	Gdnr	23Ma02Da
RANEFORD, Henry	20	M	Bricklayer	23Ma02Da
DILLON, Sherry	20	M	Miller	23Ma02Da
Thomas	16	M	Cnf	23Ma02Da
WARD, Essy	9	F	Child	23Ma02Da
Margaret	11	F	Spinster	23Ma02Da
SHORT, Christian	35	M	Spinster	23Ma02Da
SMITH, James	20	M	Laborer	23Ma02Da
BRAY, Lawrence	15	M	Laborer	23Ma02Da
Rose	10	F	Laborer	23Ma02Da
MCMAHON, Hugh	26	M	Laborer	23Ma02Da
Ann	21	F	Laborer	23Ma02Da
GLEESON, Daniel	27	M	Farmer	23Ma02Da
Mary	27	F	Farmer	23Ma02Da
HOWLEY, Mary	20	F	Servant	23Ma02Da
MALONE, Timothy	24	M	Laborer	23Ma02Da
ENGLISH, James	40	M	Gdnr	23Ma02Da
SLATTERY, Mary	18	F	Servant	23Ma02Da
GRIFFIN, Mary	25	F	Servant	23Ma02Da
HICK, John	50	M	Preacher	23Ma02Da
Ann	50	F	Wife	23Ma02Da
Biddy	12	F	Spinster	23Ma02Da
DICKENSON, James	22	M	Servant	23Ma02Da
ROSS, Charles	32	M	Weaver	23Ma02Da
Sarah	8	F	Child	23Ma02Da

NAMES OF PASSENGERS	AGE	SEX	OCCUPATIONS	DATE PORT SHIP
HORNBY, Richard	31	M	None	23Ma02Da
BRADON, Hugh	27	M	Carpenter	23Ma02Da
CULLEN, James	24	M	Laborer	23Ma02Da
Margaret	22	F	Laborer	23Ma02Da
LAWLESS, Timothy	40	M	Laborer	23Ma02Da
Catherine	40	F	Farmer	23Ma02Da
Judy	13	F	Farmer	23Ma02Da
Lawrence	11	M	Farmer	23Ma02Da
Patrick	9	M	Child	23Ma02Da
James	6	M	Child	23Ma02Da
Mary	3	F	Child	23Ma02Da
MOLOUGHLY, Daniel	30	M	Baker	23Ma02Da
Margaret	35	F	Baker	23Ma02Da
Mary	30	F	Baker	23Ma02Da
Catherine	27	F	Baker	23Ma02Da
Jane	9	F	Child	23Ma02Da
RYAN, James	35	M	Ostler	23Ma02Da
Ellen	35	F	Ostler	23Ma02Da
James	10	M	Ostler	23Ma02Da
Thomas	8	M	Child	23Ma02Da
BOLAND, John	21	M	Laborer	23Ma02Da
FARRELL, Patrick	18	M	Servant	23Ma02Da
DOYLE, John	25	M	Laborer	23Ma02Da
Martin	22	M	Laborer	23Ma02Da
CULLEN, James	25	M	Laborer	23Ma02Da
Mary	23	F	Laborer	23Ma02Da
DUNN, John	40	M	Laborer	23Ma02Da
Catherine	36	F	Laborer	23Ma02Da
HAWKINS, Dora	23	F	Servant	23Ma02Da
HOULAHERN, Anmity	20	F	Servant	23Ma02Da
LENNON, Patrick	20	M	Servant	23Ma02Da
OHERN, Ann	26	F	Servant	23Ma02Da
PATTERSON, Mary	30	F	Servant	23Ma02Da
TURNER, Edward	23	M	Servant	23Ma02Da
SHANLEY, Patrick	20	M	Gdnr	23Ma02Da
BURN, Charles	20	M	Farmer	23Ma02Da
KENNEY, Mary	15	F	Farmer	23Ma02Da
MCCOLRICK, John	20	M	Smith	23Ma02Da
MCCANN, John	35	M	Unknown	23Ma02Da
KILTER, Barney	29	M	Farmer	23Ma02Da
Susan	23	F	Farmer	23Ma02Da
Sarah	65	F	Farmer	23Ma02Da
LYNCH, Sarah	20	F	Farmer	23Ma02Da
DALEY, Mary	18	F	Farmer	23Ma02Da
MCCANN, Mary-Ann	20	F	Farmer	23Ma02Da
MONTGOMERRY, William	23	M	Bootmaker	23Ma02Da
HAZELTON, Margaret	17	F	Spinster	23Ma02Da
Isabella	17	F	Spinster	23Ma02Da
WELSH, Sarah	30	F	Governess	23Ma02Da
HOWARD, Arthur	25	M	Cbtmkr	23Ma02Da
OBLUNDER, Valentine	29	M	Farmer	23Ma02Da
FARRELL, Mary	54	F	Farmer	23Ma02Da
Ann	30	F	Farmer	23Ma02Da
Mary	12	F	Farmer	23Ma02Da
MURPHY, John	21	M	Servant	23Ma02Da
JONES, Matthew	35	M	Farmer	23Ma02Da
CRITCHLY, Patrick	36	M	Coachman	23Ma02Da
BRADLEY, William	24	M	Butler	23Ma02Da
BRENNAN, John	23	M	Brush Maker	23Ma02Da
MCKENNA, Michael	41	M	Laborer	23Ma02Da
HARWIN, James	15	M	Laborer	23Ma02Da
MCCUDDY, James	35	M	Laborer	23Ma02Da
Johanna	30	F	Laborer	23Ma02Da
Thomas	34	M	Laborer	23Ma02Da
MCGRATH, Margaret	20	F	Laborer	23Ma02Da
MCCUDDY, Mary	8	F	Child	23Ma02Da
Bridget	6	F	Child	23Ma02Da
Michael	3	M	Child	23Ma02Da
DENNY, Margaret	20	F	Servant	23Ma02Da
FOGARTY, Thomas	20	M	Servant	23Ma02Da
DOYLE, Richard	50	M	Farmer	23Ma02Da
Biddy	50	F	Farmer	23Ma02Da
Phillip	25	M	Farmer	23Ma02Da
James	18	M	Farmer	23Ma02Da
Richard	11	M	Farmer	23Ma02Da
KELLY, James	60	M	Farmer	23Ma02Da
Bridget	50	F	Farmer	23Ma02Da
Kate	23	F	Farmer	23Ma02Da
John	20	M	Farmer	23Ma02Da
Thomas	18	M	Farmer	23Ma02Da
Biddy	16	F	Farmer	23Ma02Da
Johanna	15	F	Farmer	23Ma02Da
Ellen	13	F	Farmer	23Ma02Da
William	13	M	Farmer	23Ma02Da
MURPHY, Michael	23	M	Farmer	23Ma02Da
WHEELAN, Edward	22	M	Farmer	23Ma02Da
DOYLE, Arthur	20	M	Farmer	23Ma02Da
OBRIAN, Daniel	26	M	Farmer	23Ma02Da
Bridget	20	F	Farmer	23Ma02Da
MCQUINN, Daniel	20	M	Farmer	23Ma02Da
CONDON, John	20	M	Farmer	23Ma02Da
HICKEY, Michael	34	M	Farmer	23Ma02Da
Margaret	50	F	Farmer	23Ma02Da
CARROLL, I.	30	M	Farmer	23Ma02Da
STONEY, James	24	M	Schm	23Ma02Da
ARCHER, James	33	M	Builder	23Ma02Da
Eliza	28	F	None	23Ma02Da
Ann	8	F	Child	23Ma02Da
Sarah	6	F	Child	23Ma02Da
Eliza	4	F	Child	23Ma02Da
MCGIONAN, John	21	M	Saddler	23Ma02Da
PATTERSON, Alexander	18	M	Tailor	23Ma02Da
HUGHES, Edward	25	M	Carpenter	23Ma02Da
Ellen	25	F	None	23Ma02Da
BLOOMER, Ellen	17	F	Servant	23Ma02Da
MCQUAIDE, Ellen	47	F	Egg Dealer	23Ma02Da
WILKINS, Mary	16	F	Servant	23Ma02Da
Sarah	12	F	Servant	23Ma02Da
HIGGINS, Rose	17	F	Servant	23Ma02Da
HACKET, Martin	28	M	Laborer	23Ma02Da
CONNER, Patrick	22	M	Laborer	23Ma02Da
LYONS, Mary	20	F	Servant	23Ma02Da
ODONNELL, John	50	M	Farmer	23Ma02Da
Mary	36	F	Farmer	23Ma02Da
John	4	M	Child	23Ma02Da
Michael	2	M	Child	23Ma02Da
MANSFIELD, Michael	50	M	Farmer	23Ma02Da
Mary	50	F	Farmer	23Ma02Da
Ellen	4	F	Child	23Ma02Da
GRILEY, Patrick	20	M	Laborer	23Ma02Da
GOOLAHAN, Daniel	50	M	Shoemaker	23Ma02Da
William	12	M	Shoemaker	23Ma02Da
Ann	50	F	Servant	23Ma02Da
MCELROY, Daniel	25	M	Laborer	23Ma02Da
Fanny	18	F	Servant	23Ma02Da
COLL, Ann	17	F	Servant	23Ma02Da
MEENON, John	21	M	Fisherman	23Ma02Da
GALLAGHER, Cormac	26	M	Laborer	23Ma02Da
COYLE, Mary	22	F	Servant	23Ma02Da
CARROLL, Bridget	30	F	Servant	23Ma02Da
BRADY, Michael	30	M	Laborer	23Ma02Da
Edward	28	M	Laborer	23Ma02Da
Catherine	48	F	Servant	23Ma02Da
Mary	18	F	Servant	23Ma02Da
QUINLAN, Patrick	30	M	Laborer	23Ma02Da
MOLONEY, Andrew	24	M	Laborer	23Ma02Da
Margaret	30	F	Servant	23Ma02Da
DALEY, Margaret	16	F	Servant	23Ma02Da
HOPKINS, James	50	M	Clerk	23Ma02Da
Mary	45	F	Clerk	23Ma02Da
Edward	12	M	Clerk	23Ma02Da
Margaret-Ann	10	F	Clerk	23Ma02Da
Margaret	7	F	Child	23Ma02Da
Thomas	4	M	Child	23Ma02Da
Mary	50	F	Clerk	23Ma02Da
James	12	M	Clerk	23Ma02Da
DONOHUE, Michael	20	M	Laborer	23Ma02Da
Ann	10	F	Servant	23Ma02Da
MCKORY, Alice	17	F	Servant	23Ma02Da
KELLY, Biddy	22	F	Servant	23Ma02Da

NAMES OF PASSENGERS	AGE	SEX	OCCUPATIONS	DATE PORT SHIP
NEILL, Jane	17	F	Servant	23Ma02Da
HOGAN, Ellen	22	F	Servant	23Ma02Da
Mary	24	F	Servant	23Ma02Da
DOGHERTY. Judy	50	F	Servant	23Ma02Da
BURKE. David	40	M	Farmer	23Ma02Da
FITZPATRICK. Margaret	55	F	Farmer	23Ma02Da
BURKE. Jessie	40	F	Farmer	23Ma02Da
Grace	11	F	Farmer	23Ma02Da
Patrick	9	M	Child	23Ma02Da
Nora	5	F	Child	23Ma02Da
LOOBY. Mary	40	F	Farmer	23Ma02Da
Michael	12	M	Farmer	23Ma02Da
John	10	M	Farmer	23Ma02Da
Edmund	7	M	Child	23Ma02Da
Catherine	4	F	Child	23Ma02Da
FITZPATRICK. John	30	M	Farmer	23Ma02Da
William	12	M	Unknown	23Ma02Da
WEST. Richard	40	M	Cutler	23Ma02Da
Eliza	35	F	None	23Ma02Da
FINNIGAN, Michael	25	M	Laborer	23Ma02Da
MOLONEY. Edward	24	M	Laborer	23Ma02Da
SLATTERY. Lawrence	25	M	Unknown	23Ma02Da
LYNCH, Johanna	25	F	Servant	23Ma02Da
Ellen	18	F	Servant	23Ma02Da
MULLER. John	40	M	Laborer	23Ma02Da
HADIN, Edward	30	M	Laborer	23Ma02Da
DOLON, Margaret	18	F	Servant	23Ma02Da
DUFFY. Catherine	20	F	Servant	23Ma02Da
KELLY. Ann	18	F	Servant	23Ma02Da
MURPHY. William	18	M	Clerk	23Ma02Da
DUNELL, John	18	M	Servant	23Ma02Da
MOULDONEY. Bridget	18	F	Servant	23Ma02Da
Margaret	16	F	Servant	23Ma02Da
CALLAGHAN. Patrick	24	M	Fisherman	23Ma02Da
THOMPSON. James	26	M	Tailor	23Ma02Da
WOODS. Patrick	30	M	Laborer	23Ma02Da
MATTHEWS. Catherine	22	F	Servant	23Ma02Da
HAMROCK. James	20	M	Servant	23Ma02Da
MCCARTHY. John	18	M	Baker	23Ma02Da
GLEENON, Thomas	20	M	Gdnr	23Ma02Da
SMITH, Michael	27	M	Gdnr	23Ma02Da
BUTLER. Michael	24	M	Shoemaker	23Ma02Da
FORD. Patrick	36	M	Laborer	23Ma02Da
Rose	60	F	Unknown	23Ma02Da
Died-At-Sea				
MCGRATH. James	34	M	Laborer	23Ma02Da
FRIANE, Edward	63	M	Publican	23Ma02Da
KENE, William-S.	41	M	Laborer	23Ma02Da
Catherine	25	F	Servant	23Ma02Da
RYAN, Johanna	16	F	Servant	23Ma02Da
ONEILL, Patrick	42	M	Unknown	23Ma02Da
ODONNELL, John	43	M	Farmer	23Ma02Da
Julia	40	F	Farmer	23Ma02Da
Margaret	20	F	Farmer	23Ma02Da
Jeremiah	21	M	Farmer	23Ma02Da
HOGAN, William	21	M	Farmer	23Ma02Da
HEALY. Johanna	20	F	Farmer	23Ma02Da
Ellen	18	F	Farmer	23Ma02Da
COLEMAN. Mary	20	F	Farmer	23Ma02Da
HUFFERNAN. John	22	M	Laborer	23Ma02Da
WHEELAN, Margaret	16	F	Farmer	23Ma02Da
BUTLER. William	.09	M	Infant	23Ma02Da
CUMMINS. Ellen	.11	F	Infant	23Ma02Da
KIRK. David	.11	M	Infant	23Ma02Da
Died-At-Sea				
MCMAHON. Essy	.11	F	Infant	23Ma02Da
CULLEN. Margaret	.04	F	Infant	23Ma02Da
MCLOUGHLY. Thomas	.06	M	Infant	23Ma02Da
NELSON. Mary	.11	F	Infant	23Ma02Da
CUDDY. Richard	.11	M	Infant	23Ma02Da
DENNY. Margaret	.02	F	Infant	23Ma02Da
FARRELL, Biddy	.02	F	Infant	23Ma02Da
HOPKINS, John	.04	M	Infant	23Ma02Da
FAIR. Patrick	.11	M	Infant	23Ma02Da
BURKE. Honora	.11	F	Infant	23Ma02Da

NAMES OF PASSENGERS	AGE	SEX	OCCUPATIONS	DATE PORT SHIP
MEDICROFT. Robert	.10	M	Infant	23Ma02Da
BUTLER. William-Revd.	30	M	Minister	23Ma02Da
NEALY. Ann	21	F	None	23Ma02Da
HAZLETON. Mary	55	F	Unknown	23Ma02Da
CUPPAGE, Thomas	25	M	Surgeon	23Ma02Da
FULHAM. Patrick	20	M	Hairdresser	23Ma02Da
PENDERGAST. Mary	29	F	Laborer	23Ma02Da

EUROPA 23 MAY 1850

From Liverpool

COTTON. Charles	18	M	Unknown	23Ma02Fe
MULVANY. M.	26	F	Unknown	23Ma02Fe
BOURKE. U	47	M	Farmer	23Ma02Fe
NAGLE. D.	26	M	Farmer	23Ma02Fe
RYAN, Jno.W.	30	M	Farmer	23Ma02Fe
CULLEN, Bernard	45	M	Cver	23Ma02Fe

LETITIA-HYNE 24 MAY 1850

From Liverpool

MCCASKEY. John	30	M	Farmer	24Ma02Hp
Jane	30	F	Unknown	24Ma02Hp
Patt	7	M	Child	24Ma02Hp
Rose	5	F	Child	24Ma02Hp
Ann	.00	F	Infant	24Ma02Hp
MESEN. Wm.	45	M	Unknown	24Ma02Hp
U-Mrs.	40	F	Unknown	24Ma02Hp
John	13	M	Unknown	24Ma02Hp
Mary	8	F	Child	24Ma02Hp
William	6	M	Child	24Ma02Hp
Thomas	3	M	Child	24Ma02Hp
George	.00	M	Infant	24Ma02Hp
SPENCE. Will	45	M	Unknown	24Ma02Hp
Ann	40	F	Unknown	24Ma02Hp
AUSTIN, John	30	M	Unknown	24Ma02Hp
Ellen	26	F	Unknown	24Ma02Hp
George	5	M	Child	24Ma02Hp
Lewis	3	M	Child	24Ma02Hp
Dan	.00	M	Infant	24Ma02Hp
GORDAN, George	26	M	Unknown	24Ma02Hp
Amelia	23	F	Unknown	24Ma02Hp
BELL, Wm.	28	M	Unknown	24Ma02Hp
Matthew	24	M	Unknown	24Ma02Hp
Lewis	3	M	Child	24Ma02Hp
DREW, Henry	24	M	Unknown	24Ma02Hp
Ann	21	F	Unknown	24Ma02Hp
Henry	3	M	Child	24Ma02Hp
LEE. Sophia	22	F	Unknown	24Ma02Hp
MCENTIRE. Owen	40	M	Unknown	24Ma02Hp
U-Mrs.	30	F	Unknown	24Ma02Hp
John	10	M	Unknown	24Ma02Hp
Richard	8	M	Child	24Ma02Hp
Mary-Ann	6	F	Child	24Ma02Hp
Owen	4	M	Child	24Ma02Hp
Cathrn.	2	F	Child	24Ma02Hp
Thomas	.00	M	Infant	24Ma02Hp
MASON. Sarah	00	F	Unknown	24Ma02Hp
Died-At-Sea				

ANNA-MARIA 24 MAY 1850

From Limerick

NAMES OF PASSENGERS	AGE	SEX	OCCUPATIONS	DATE PORT SHIP
BARROW, Eliza	30	F	Laborer	24Ma10Ix
Honora	8	F	Child	24Ma10Ix
Mary	6	F	Child	24Ma10Ix
CONNERS, Alice	38	F	Unknown	24Ma10Ix
Bridget	18	F	Unknown	24Ma10Ix
CARROLL, Pat	28	M	Unknown	24Ma10Ix
Elizabeth	24	F	Unknown	24Ma10Ix
Bridget	25	F	Unknown	24Ma10Ix
HENNESSEY, Mary	18	F	Unknown	24Ma10Ix
MURPHY, Johanna	35	F	Unknown	24Ma10Ix
Jas.	10	M	Unknown	24Ma10Ix
Mary	12	F	Unknown	24Ma10Ix
TIERNEY, Mary	30	F	Unknown	24Ma10Ix
MADAGAN, Mary	20	F	Unknown	24Ma10Ix
HOUGH, Michl.	28	M	Unknown	24Ma10Ix
DONEGAN, Mary	31	F	Unknown	24Ma10Ix
GALPIN, Catherine	32	F	Unknown	24Ma10Ix
GASS, Mary	38	F	Unknown	24Ma10Ix
Mary	6	F	Child	24Ma10Ix
Pat	.00	M	Infant	24Ma10Ix
WALSH, Mary	25	F	Unknown	24Ma10Ix
Richard	.00	M	Infant	24Ma10Ix
MURPHY, Peggy	19	F	Unknown	24Ma10Ix
ONEILL, Mary	50	F	Unknown	24Ma10Ix
Michl.	16	M	Unknown	24Ma10Ix
TOOMEY, Catherine	20	F	Unknown	24Ma10Ix
MAHON, Michael	20	M	Unknown	24Ma10Ix
HOGAN, Jno.	22	M	Unknown	24Ma10Ix
MAGAN, Mary	22	F	Unknown	24Ma10Ix
SHEELY, Michl.	18	M	Unknown	24Ma10Ix
Mary	28	F	Unknown	24Ma10Ix
HAYES, Pat	20	M	Unknown	24Ma10Ix
MURPHY, James	33	M	Unknown	24Ma10Ix
Catherine	33	F	Unknown	24Ma10Ix
Pat	3	M	Child	24Ma10Ix
GRADY, David	15	M	Unknown	24Ma10Ix
COFFEY, Jno.	30	M	Unknown	24Ma10Ix
RYAN, Jno.	26	M	Unknown	24Ma10Ix
SCULLY, Pat	23	M	Unknown	24Ma10Ix
GATHRY, Margt.	19	F	Unknown	24Ma10Ix
Susan	16	F	Unknown	24Ma10Ix
NUNAN, Simon	35	M	Unknown	24Ma10Ix
Mary	35	F	Unknown	24Ma10Ix
KANE, Jno.	23	M	Unknown	24Ma10Ix
Mary	15	F	Unknown	24Ma10Ix
DOWNES, Mary	19	F	Unknown	24Ma10Ix
MCMAHON, Michl.	36	M	Unknown	24Ma10Ix
Mary	28	F	Unknown	24Ma10Ix
Wm.	9	M	Child	24Ma10Ix
Chas.	8	M	Child	24Ma10Ix
Martin	.00	M	Infant	24Ma10Ix
MALONEY, Mary	40	F	Unknown	24Ma10Ix
Thomas	12	M	Unknown	24Ma10Ix
Richard	5	M	Child	24Ma10Ix
COLLINS, Billy	28	M	Unknown	24Ma10Ix
Nancy	26	F	Unknown	24Ma10Ix
Anthony	12	M	Unknown	24Ma10Ix
HOUGH, Pat	23	M	Unknown	24Ma10Ix
FURNY, Patk.	21	M	Unknown	24Ma10Ix
SHEA, Bridget	28	F	Unknown	24Ma10Ix
COLLINS, Thomas	30	M	Unknown	24Ma10Ix
CASTELLOE, Ann	18	F	Unknown	24Ma10Ix
ONEILL, Michl.	20	M	Unknown	24Ma10Ix
LEENEY, Mary	20	F	Unknown	24Ma10Ix
Michl.	7	M	Child	24Ma10Ix
LEENEY, William	3	M	Child	24Ma10Ix
Bridget	4	F	Child	24Ma10Ix
KENNEDY, Mary	32	F	Unknown	24Ma10Ix
William	2	M	Child	24Ma10Ix
CRONIN, Margt.	26	F	Unknown	24Ma10Ix
LEENEY, Catherine	26	F	Unknown	24Ma10Ix
FITZPATRICK, Danl.	26	M	Unknown	24Ma10Ix
James	28	M	Unknown	24Ma10Ix
CONNELL, Pat	19	M	Unknown	24Ma10Ix
LEADEN, Bridget	20	F	Unknown	24Ma10Ix
CONNELL, Susan	20	F	Unknown	24Ma10Ix
KENNEDY, Mag	30	F	Unknown	24Ma10Ix
COLEMAN, Thomas	33	M	Unknown	24Ma10Ix

MARY-HALE 24 MAY 1850

From Liverpool

NAMES OF PASSENGERS	AGE	SEX	OCCUPATIONS	DATE PORT SHIP
DOWNEY, Mary-A.	18	F	Weaver	24Ma02Ks
Sylvester	13	M	Unknown	24Ma02Ks
Joseph	11	M	Unknown	24Ma02Ks
MCGURK, Hercules	24	M	Farmer	24Ma02Ks
Eliza	22	F	Unknown	24Ma02Ks
Mary-Jane	.04	F	Infant	24Ma02Ks
John	18	M	Unknown	24Ma02Ks
John	20	M	Unknown	24Ma02Ks
Mary-Anne	.10	F	Infant	24Ma02Ks
MCTHAW, Francis	24	M	Unknown	24Ma02Ks
DUGAN, Anne	24	F	Unknown	24Ma02Ks
Eliza	18	F	Unknown	24Ma02Ks
MCGLENN, Peter	24	M	Unknown	24Ma02Ks
Ellen	50	F	Unknown	24Ma02Ks
Ellen	20	F	Unknown	24Ma02Ks
GALLAGHER, Mary	16	F	Unknown	24Ma02Ks
MORAN, Honora	34	F	Unknown	24Ma02Ks
Eliza	9	F	Child	24Ma02Ks
James	4	M	Child	24Ma02Ks
RILEY, Pat	25	M	Unknown	24Ma02Ks
BRYAN, Patt	18	M	Unknown	24Ma02Ks
CARTY, Patt	20	M	Unknown	24Ma02Ks
MCNALLY, Thoms.	16	M	Unknown	24Ma02Ks
Mary	18	F	Unknown	24Ma02Ks
Patt	4	M	Child	24Ma02Ks
CAHILL, James	28	M	Unknown	24Ma02Ks
CUSAC, Thos.	18	M	Unknown	24Ma02Ks
Kate	15	F	Unknown	24Ma02Ks
Mary	12	F	Unknown	24Ma02Ks
DEVANEY, Gilbert	20	M	Unknown	24Ma02Ks
KEENAN, Bernard	22	M	Unknown	24Ma02Ks
LYNCH, John	30	M	Unknown	24Ma02Ks
Richard	20	M	Unknown	24Ma02Ks
FAGAN, Peter	25	M	Unknown	24Ma02Ks
ROONEY, Mich.	24	M	Unknown	24Ma02Ks
POWDER, Margaret	18	F	Unknown	24Ma02Ks
Ellen	17	F	Unknown	24Ma02Ks
DELANY, Mary	22	F	Unknown	24Ma02Ks
John	34	M	Unknown	24Ma02Ks
Mary	19	F	Unknown	24Ma02Ks
COTTLE, John	18	M	Unknown	24Ma02Ks
Celia	13	F	Unknown	24Ma02Ks
MCKEOWN, Patt	26	M	Unknown	24Ma02Ks
HUGHES, Felix	23	M	Laborer	24Ma02Ks
MCGOVERN, Patt	23	M	Unknown	24Ma02Ks
DUMNER, Cicely	21	F	Unknown	24Ma02Ks
DELANY, Margaret	23	F	Unknown	24Ma02Ks
CARROLL, James	24	M	Unknown	24Ma02Ks
CONNELL, Catherine	38	F	Unknown	24Ma02Ks
SWEENY, Jeremiah	40	M	Unknown	24Ma02Ks
DIGNAN, Andrew	26	M	Unknown	24Ma02Ks

NAMES OF PASSENGERS	AGE	SEX	OCCUPATIONS	DATE PORT SHIP
MONNEY, Will	40	M	Unknown	24Ma02Ks
GURTY, Francis	22	M	Unknown	24Ma02Ks
TUITE, Ann	18	F	Unknown	24Ma02Ks
ONEILL, John	30	M	Unknown	24Ma02Ks
Mary	28	F	Unknown	24Ma02Ks
Betty	24	F	Unknown	24Ma02Ks
HUGHES, Eleanor	55	F	Unknown	24Ma02Ks
Bernard	35	M	Unknown	24Ma02Ks
John	30	M	Unknown	24Ma02Ks
Richard	28	M	Unknown	24Ma02Ks
Peter	19	M	Unknown	24Ma02Ks
Margaret	25	F	Unknown	24Ma02Ks
KEEFE, Margaret	28	F	Unknown	24Ma02Ks
Andrew	19	M	Unknown	24Ma02Ks
CAVANAGH, James	28	M	Unknown	24Ma02Ks
Eliza	24	F	Unknown	24Ma02Ks
MCLOUGHLIN, Mich.	18	M	Unknown	24Ma02Ks
LACKEY, Joseph	20	M	Unknown	24Ma02Ks
BIRD, Sarah	50	F	Unknown	24Ma02Ks
Jane	24	F	Unknown	24Ma02Ks
Thomas	35	M	Unknown	24Ma02Ks
Archy	19	M	Unknown	24Ma02Ks
Anne	18	F	Unknown	24Ma02Ks
NISSE, John	20	M	Unknown	24Ma02Ks
Margaret	.11	F	Infant	24Ma02Ks
IRWIN, Andy	18	M	Unknown	24Ma02Ks
FERGUSON, Margaret	25	F	Unknown	24Ma02Ks
REGNEY, Wm.	22	M	Unknown	24Ma02Ks
GORMAN, Patt	22	M	Unknown	24Ma02Ks
MOORTY, Thos.	37	M	Unknown	24Ma02Ks
RYAN, Patt	46	M	Unknown	24Ma02Ks
Ellen	56	F	Unknown	24Ma02Ks
KEELY, John	16	M	Unknown	24Ma02Ks
Margaret	12	F	Unknown	24Ma02Ks
NEILL, Peter	24	M	Unknown	24Ma02Ks
MURRAY, John	22	M	Unknown	24Ma02Ks
WYLOS, Wm.	29	M	Unknown	24Ma02Ks
U-Mrs.	25	F	Unknown	24Ma02Ks
BRUMMETT, Bennett	34	M	Unknown	24Ma02Ks
John	27	M	Unknown	24Ma02Ks
BUCKLEY, Joseph	27	M	Unknown	24Ma02Ks
PENEMORE, Francis	23	M	Unknown	24Ma02Ks
MYERS, James	23	M	Unknown	24Ma02Ks
CUMORE, Anthony	17	M	Unknown	24Ma02Ks
CUNNINGHAM, Martin	24	M	Unknown	24Ma02Ks
Judy	22	F	Unknown	24Ma02Ks
Betsy	20	F	Unknown	24Ma02Ks
BRANOCKS, John	22	M	Unknown	24Ma02Ks
HILL, Mary	27	F	Unknown	24Ma02Ks
NISSE, Margaret	50	F	Unknown	24Ma02Ks
John	3	M	Child	24Ma02Ks
MANAGUE, James	25	M	Farmer	24Ma02Ks
Mary	20	F	Unknown	24Ma02Ks
POWER, Mary	22	F	Unknown	24Ma02Ks
KALEY, Jeremiah	11	M	Unknown	24Ma02Ks
DUNN, John	50	M	Unknown	24Ma02Ks
Margaret	36	F	Unknown	24Ma02Ks
Walter	22	M	Unknown	24Ma02Ks
Jane	3	F	Child	24Ma02Ks
Eliza	.00	F	Infant	24Ma02Ks
MCCLURE, Bridget	23	F	Unknown	24Ma02Ks
Patrick	.00	M	Infant	24Ma02Ks
BORGAN, Christopher	50	M	Unknown	24Ma02Ks
CORRIGAN, John	40	M	Unknown	24Ma02Ks
Elisha	30	F	Unknown	24Ma02Ks
Susan	.00	F	Infant	24Ma02Ks
HICKSEY, Jas.	50	M	Unknown	24Ma02Ks
SHEHAN, Catherine	20	F	Unknown	24Ma02Ks
Ellen	21	F	Unknown	24Ma02Ks
GRACE, John	20	M	Unknown	24Ma02Ks
RICHIE, Mary	26	F	Unknown	24Ma02Ks
Anne	25	F	Unknown	24Ma02Ks
MINNOCK, Henry	40	M	Unknown	24Ma02Ks
Catherine	25	F	Unknown	24Ma02Ks
Alice	25	F	Unknown	24Ma02Ks

NAMES OF PASSENGERS	AGE	SEX	OCCUPATIONS	DATE PORT SHIP
MINNOCK, Maria	12	F	Unknown	24Ma02Ks
Catherine	11	F	Unknown	24Ma02Ks
Matthew	9	M	Child	24Ma02Ks
Margaret	3	F	Child	24Ma02Ks
Bernard	.00	M	Infant	24Ma02Ks
LINDSEY, Patt	21	M	Unknown	24Ma02Ks
Margaret	23	F	Unknown	24Ma02Ks
CARROLL, Margaret	24	F	Weaver	24Ma02Ks
BINGHAM, Richard	25	M	Unknown	24Ma02Ks
WILLOW, William	19	M	Unknown	24Ma02Ks
Jane	22	F	Unknown	24Ma02Ks
SELKIRK, John	30	M	Unknown	24Ma02Ks
Eliza	28	F	Unknown	24Ma02Ks
CARTY, John	23	M	Unknown	24Ma02Ks
Ellen	24	F	Unknown	24Ma02Ks
BRODERS, Mary	26	F	Unknown	24Ma02Ks
BRENNAN, Daly	20	M	Unknown	24Ma02Ks
CARTY, Richard	.00	M	Infant	24Ma02Ks
COSTELLO, John	18	M	Unknown	24Ma02Ks
QUINN, Denis	36	M	Unknown	24Ma02Ks
Margaret	33	F	Unknown	24Ma02Ks
Mary	13	F	Unknown	24Ma02Ks
John	12	M	Unknown	24Ma02Ks
Edmund	8	M	Child	24Ma02Ks
SHEEDY, John	18	M	Unknown	24Ma02Ks
Margaret	26	F	Unknown	24Ma02Ks
HOCKET, Bridget	21	F	Unknown	24Ma02Ks
BURKE, Thomas	45	M	Unknown	24Ma02Ks
Thomas	17	M	Unknown	24Ma02Ks
MCGRATH, Denis	35	M	Unknown	24Ma02Ks
Ellen	35	F	Unknown	24Ma02Ks
Johannah	7	F	Child	24Ma02Ks
Daniel	4	M	Child	24Ma02Ks
Ellen	.00	F	Infant	24Ma02Ks
MAHER, James	23	M	Unknown	24Ma02Ks
CLANCEY, Edward	48	M	Unknown	24Ma02Ks
Judy	48	F	Unknown	24Ma02Ks
Johanna	16	F	Unknown	24Ma02Ks
Mary	14	F	Unknown	24Ma02Ks
SWEENY, Honora	42	F	Unknown	24Ma02Ks
BURKE, Thomas	20	M	Unknown	24Ma02Ks
CROWLEY, Mary	26	F	Unknown	24Ma02Ks
MAHONEY, Daniel	26	M	Unknown	24Ma02Ks
DEVINE, Catherine	22	F	Unknown	24Ma02Ks
Rose	18	F	Unknown	24Ma02Ks
GOUGIN, James	21	M	Unknown	24Ma02Ks
BYRNES, John	14	M	Unknown	24Ma02Ks
Michl.	13	M	Unknown	24Ma02Ks
CRENNAN, Mich.D.	29	M	Laborer	24Ma02Ks
DUGAN, Edward	29	M	Unknown	24Ma02Ks
CORGAN, Timothy	27	M	Unknown	24Ma02Ks
DUNN, Martin	24	M	Unknown	24Ma02Ks
COMERFORD, Margaret	20	F	Unknown	24Ma02Ks
STEWART, Patrick	25	M	Unknown	24Ma02Ks
WORK, Thos.	42	M	Unknown	24Ma02Ks
CUMMINS, John	35	M	Unknown	24Ma02Ks

SIR-WM.MOLESWORTH 25 MAY 1850

From Glasgow

NAMES OF PASSENGERS	AGE	SEX	OCCUPATIONS	DATE PORT SHIP
MCGIBBON, Moses	45	M	Farmer	25Ma21Eb
Ann	40	F	Farmer	25Ma21Eb
Isabella	20	F	Farmer	25Ma21Eb
John	11	M	Farmer	25Ma21Eb
Elizabeth	9	F	Child	25Ma21Eb
Ann	5	F	Child	25Ma21Eb
Margaret	3	F	Child	25Ma21Eb
William	.04	M	Infant	25Ma21Eb

NAMES OF PASSENGERS	AGE	SEX	OCCUPATIONS	DATE PORT SHIP
MCGIBBON, Ann	13	F	Farmer	25Ma21Eb
SCOTT, John	25	M	Farmer	25Ma21Eb
THOMPSON, Joseph	34	M	Farmer	25Ma21Eb
Isabella	40	F	Farmer	25Ma21Eb
James	4	M	Child	25Ma21Eb
William	2	M	Child	25Ma21Eb
Sarah	.02	F	Infant	25Ma21Eb
MASON, Samuel	22	M	Mason	25Ma21Eb
DOYLE, Alex	20	M	Mason	25Ma21Eb
MCCANN, James	24	M	Laborer	25Ma21Eb
MCARAN, Ann	20	F	Laborer	25Ma21Eb
GREEN, Mary	24	F	Laborer	25Ma21Eb
CORRY, Mary	19	F	Spinster	25Ma21Eb
MCQUESTON, Mary	26	F	Spinster	25Ma21Eb
Ann	22	F	Spinster	25Ma21Eb
LOW, John	27	M	Farmer	25Ma21Eb
Margaret	24	F	Farmer	25Ma21Eb
John	.03	M	Infant	25Ma21Eb
James	3	M	Child	25Ma21Eb
MCCONELL, Magt.	20	F	Farmer	25Ma21Eb
Mary	17	F	Farmer	25Ma21Eb
BAXTER, Wm.	26	M	Farmer	25Ma21Eb
Ann	25	F	Farmer	25Ma21Eb
MAN, John	24	M	Farmer	25Ma21Eb
GRAHAM, Wm.	40	M	Farmer	25Ma21Eb
Ann	40	F	Farmer	25Ma21Eb
MCLANYORD, Hamilton	23	M	Farmer	25Ma21Eb
COTTINGTON, Mary	21	F	Farmer	25Ma21Eb
MCGUINISS, Hugh	40	M	Farmer	25Ma21Eb
Ann	45	F	Farmer	25Ma21Eb
John	25	M	Farmer	25Ma21Eb
Ann	25	F	Farmer	25Ma21Eb
WINCY, Geo.	22	M	Farmer	25Ma21Eb
RINGLAN, Jas.	30	M	Farmer	25Ma21Eb
PORRELL, Thos.	42	M	Farmer	25Ma21Eb
MASON, John	.09	M	Infant	25Ma21Eb
KELLY, William	38	M	Farmer	25Ma21Eb
Agnes	37	F	Farmer	25Ma21Eb
Grace	16	F	Farmer	25Ma21Eb
Mary	17	F	Farmer	25Ma21Eb
Agnes	12	F	Farmer	25Ma21Eb
Samuel	.10	M	Infant	25Ma21Eb
Elizabeth	.10	F	Infant	25Ma21Eb
CARROLL, Wm.	20	M	Farmer	25Ma21Eb
MCHAILAND, John	25	M	Farmer	25Ma21Eb
MCKEE, Sam.	20	M	Farmer	25Ma21Eb
CATHERWOOD, John	24	M	Farmer	25Ma21Eb
RUNNEY, Dan	30	M	Farmer	25Ma21Eb
MCBRIDE, James	42	M	Farmer	25Ma21Eb
Denis	17	M	Farmer	25Ma21Eb
Ann	15	F	Farmer	25Ma21Eb
Mary	.09	F	Infant	25Ma21Eb
MCCULLAND, Rodger	40	M	Farmer	25Ma21Eb
Mary	38	F	Farmer	25Ma21Eb
Ann	9	F	Child	25Ma21Eb
John	7	M	Child	25Ma21Eb
Patt	4	M	Child	25Ma21Eb
Edwd.	.06	M	Infant	25Ma21Eb
WASTE, Sarah	22	M	Spinster	25Ma21Eb
CUNINGHAM, Patt	27	M	Laborer	25Ma21Eb
QUINN, John	25	M	Laborer	25Ma21Eb
SMALL, John	20	M	Laborer	25Ma21Eb
MURPHY, Owen	34	M	Laborer	25Ma21Eb
Catherine	30	F	Laborer	25Ma21Eb
Edward	.03	M	Infant	25Ma21Eb
MCGAUCHIE, Phelix	39	M	Laborer	25Ma21Eb
MULLIN, Owen	25	M	Laborer	25Ma21Eb
MCQUISTON, Mary-Jane	24	F	Farmer	25Ma21Eb
Bell	20	F	Farmer	25Ma21Eb
Owen	18	M	Farmer	25Ma21Eb
MCGAUCHIE, Mary	27	F	Spinster	25Ma21Eb
Catherine	12	F	Spinster	25Ma21Eb
Anna-Maria	.03	F	Infant	25Ma21Eb
SURGEON, Mary	18	F	Spinster	25Ma21Eb
DOCHERTY, Elizabeth	33	F	Dressmaker	25Ma21Eb
MCQUISTON, Jas.	23	M	Tailor	25Ma21Eb

WAVE 25 MAY 1850

From Dublin

NAMES OF PASSENGERS	AGE	SEX	OCCUPATIONS	DATE PORT SHIP
KELLY, James	20	M	Farmer	25Ma05Hb
NEAL, Patt	30	M	Unknown	25Ma05Hb
Mary	30	F	Unknown	25Ma05Hb
John	.00	M	Infant	25Ma05Hb
FAGAN, Bridget	20	F	Unknown	25Ma05Hb
PARROTT, Patt	22	M	Unknown	25Ma05Hb
FLAHERTY, Patt	21	M	Unknown	25Ma05Hb
MATTHEW, Catherine	22	F	Unknown	25Ma05Hb
Eliza	20	F	Unknown	25Ma05Hb
KELLY, Ellen	20	F	Unknown	25Ma05Hb
HENDERSON, Susan	26	F	Unknown	25Ma05Hb
CALLY, James	25	M	Unknown	25Ma05Hb
MORAN, Wm.	24	M	Unknown	25Ma05Hb
PURCELL, Mary	20	F	Unknown	25Ma05Hb
DOHERTY, Margaret	20	F	Unknown	25Ma05Hb
HENDER, Joseph	19	M	Unknown	25Ma05Hb
HUGHES, Patt	18	M	Unknown	25Ma05Hb
MOLLAY, Patt	18	M	Unknown	25Ma05Hb
Margaret	28	F	Unknown	25Ma05Hb
BROWN, Michael	26	M	Unknown	25Ma05Hb
U-Mrs.	40	F	Unknown	25Ma05Hb
Joseph	36	M	Unknown	25Ma05Hb
Henry	40	M	Unknown	25Ma05Hb
James	13	M	Unknown	25Ma05Hb
Mary	12	F	Unknown	25Ma05Hb
Eliza	9	F	Child	25Ma05Hb
Margaret	11	F	Unknown	25Ma05Hb
Francis	7	M	Child	25Ma05Hb
Ann	6	F	Child	25Ma05Hb
Agnes	.00	F	Infant	25Ma05Hb
Fanny	20	F	Unknown	25Ma05Hb
PHILLIPS, William	24	M	Unknown	25Ma05Hb
HOLORAN, Wm.	36	M	Unknown	25Ma05Hb
U-Mrs.	36	F	Unknown	25Ma05Hb
Dennis	16	M	Unknown	25Ma05Hb
Margret	20	F	Unknown	25Ma05Hb
Eliza	14	F	Unknown	25Ma05Hb
Ann	12	F	Unknown	25Ma05Hb
Mary	.00	F	Infant	25Ma05Hb
Catherine	.00	F	Infant	25Ma05Hb
HENDERSON, Joseph	15	M	Unknown	25Ma05Hb
HEGERTY, John	28	M	Unknown	25Ma05Hb
Bridget	24	F	Unknown	25Ma05Hb
MAXWELL, Rose	16	F	Unknown	25Ma05Hb
MURTAGH, Terence	26	M	Unknown	25Ma05Hb
GAFFNEY, U-Mrs.	34	F	Unknown	25Ma05Hb
Kate	5	F	Child	25Ma05Hb
John	.00	M	Infant	25Ma05Hb
REDMOND, David	28	M	Unknown	25Ma05Hb
James	24	M	Unknown	25Ma05Hb
RODGERS, Eliza	20	F	Unknown	25Ma05Hb
KENNEDY, Charles	40	M	Unknown	25Ma05Hb
U-Mrs.	40	F	Unknown	25Ma05Hb
GARRY, Terry	22	M	Unknown	25Ma05Hb
RYAN, John	20	M	Unknown	25Ma05Hb
FITZSIMMONS, Patt	20	M	Unknown	25Ma05Hb
FOX, Joe	23	M	Unknown	25Ma05Hb
COLLINS, A.	20	F	Unknown	25Ma05Hb
CANNON, Bernard	35	M	Unknown	25Ma05Hb
Thomas	11	M	Unknown	25Ma05Hb
MORAN, Mary-A.	40	F	Unknown	25Ma05Hb
Patt	12	M	Unknown	25Ma05Hb
Christy	11	M	Unknown	25Ma05Hb

NAMES OF PASSENGERS	AGE	SEX	OCCUPATIONS	DATE PORT SHIP
MORAN, James	9	M	Child	25Ma05Hb
John	.00	M	Infant	25Ma05Hb
Catherine	5	F	Child	25Ma05Hb
BROWN, Ignatius	28	M	Unknown	25Ma05Hb
Catherine	26	F	Unknown	25Ma05Hb
BELL, Andrew	19	M	Unknown	25Ma05Hb
EGAN, Ellen	19	F	Unknown	25Ma05Hb
DORNEL, Edward	25	M	Unknown	25Ma05Hb
COSGRAVE, Catherine	30	F	Unknown	25Ma05Hb
MCQUADE, Hugh	21	M	Unknown	25Ma05Hb
CLARENDON, Geo.	50	M	Unknown	25Ma05Hb
Rebecca	45	F	Unknown	25Ma05Hb
Judith	17	F	Unknown	25Ma05Hb
Mat	13	M	Unknown	25Ma05Hb
Cathn.	11	F	Unknown	25Ma05Hb
Ann	9	F	Child	25Ma05Hb
Wilhemina	.00	F	Infant	25Ma05Hb
FARRELL, Mary-A.	20	F	Unknown	25Ma05Hb
RYDING, Wm.	20	M	Unknown	25Ma05Hb
SHERRY, John	25	M	Unknown	25Ma05Hb
U-Mrs.	24	F	Unknown	25Ma05Hb
BANCE, John	35	M	Unknown	25Ma05Hb
James	.00	M	Infant	25Ma05Hb
John	12	M	Unknown	25Ma05Hb
DARCY, Kate	18	F	Unknown	25Ma05Hb
KELLY, Thomas	25	M	Unknown	25Ma05Hb
Bridget	25	F	Unknown	25Ma05Hb
BROWN, Mary	40	F	Unknown	25Ma05Hb
Sarah	14	F	Unknown	25Ma05Hb
William	9	M	Child	25Ma05Hb
KELLY, John	40	M	Unknown	25Ma05Hb
SUTTON, Essy	20	F	Unknown	25Ma05Hb
Mary	25	F	Unknown	25Ma05Hb
SACULL, John	14	M	Unknown	25Ma05Hb
MCEVOY, U	20	M	Unknown	25Ma05Hb
FLYNN, Sarah	17	F	Unknown	25Ma05Hb
SHANNON, Pat	22	M	Unknown	25Ma05Hb
LYONS, Mary	20	F	Unknown	25Ma05Hb
U	24	M	Unknown	25Ma05Hb
ADAMSON, Geo.	30	M	Unknown	25Ma05Hb
U-Mrs.	20	F	Unknown	25Ma05Hb
John	.00	M	Infant	25Ma05Hb
MOLLAY, Biddy	15	F	Unknown	25Ma05Hb
John	35	M	Unknown	25Ma05Hb
QUIGLEY, Mat	26	M	Unknown	25Ma05Hb
COSGROVE, Eliza	20	F	Unknown	25Ma05Hb
MURTAGH, Thomas	50	M	Unknown	25Ma05Hb
Thomas	23	M	Unknown	25Ma05Hb
Mary	22	F	Unknown	25Ma05Hb
Margret	24	F	Unknown	25Ma05Hb
MCNULTY, Anne	16	F	Unknown	25Ma05Hb
MAGRATH, Peter	25	M	Unknown	25Ma05Hb
DRYNAL, Kit	24	F	Unknown	25Ma05Hb
THOMPSON, U-Mrs.	50	F	Unknown	25Ma05Hb
Barthlmw.	18	M	Unknown	25Ma05Hb
John	30	M	Unknown	25Ma05Hb
ONEILL, John	20	M	Unknown	25Ma05Hb
SHORTALL, John	12	M	Unknown	25Ma05Hb
James	10	M	Unknown	25Ma05Hb
RANKIN, Charles	10	M	Unknown	25Ma05Hb
HALEY, Patt	21	M	Unknown	25Ma05Hb
ROC, Thomas	21	M	Unknown	25Ma05Hb
FLYNNE, Thomas	21	M	Unknown	25Ma05Hb
BRISN, Mary	20	F	Unknown	25Ma05Hb
LAMBE, Ellen	20	F	Unknown	25Ma05Hb
STRAW, Ellen	24	F	Unknown	25Ma05Hb
James	2	M	Child	25Ma05Hb
BRADY, Michael	38	M	Unknown	25Ma05Hb
Ellen	28	F	Unknown	25Ma05Hb
James	.00	M	Infant	25Ma05Hb
TOOLE, Michael	20	M	Unknown	25Ma05Hb
CUMMINS, Pat	26	M	Unknown	25Ma05Hb
Mat	20	M	Unknown	25Ma05Hb
Ellen	16	F	Unknown	25Ma05Hb
FINIGAN, John	20	M	Unknown	25Ma05Hb

NAMES OF PASSENGERS	AGE	SEX	OCCUPATIONS	DATE PORT SHIP
WOODWARD, M.	30	M	Unknown	25Ma05Hb
Edwin	25	M	Unknown	25Ma05Hb
John	13	M	Unknown	25Ma05Hb
CUSACK, Pat	17	M	Unknown	25Ma05Hb
ONEILL, Eliza	20	F	Unknown	25Ma05Hb
LODGE, John	28	M	Unknown	25Ma05Hb
HARREY, Peter	23	M	Unknown	25Ma05Hb
BRENNAN, M.	20	F	Unknown	25Ma05Hb
MAHAN, Bridget	20	F	Unknown	25Ma05Hb
CONNOR, Irvin	20	M	Unknown	25Ma05Hb
Mat	20	M	Unknown	25Ma05Hb
DUMPHRY, Bridget	20	F	Unknown	25Ma05Hb
MONAGHAN, Patt	20	M	Unknown	25Ma05Hb
CAULFIELD, John	18	M	Unknown	25Ma05Hb
CONNOR, Peter	20	M	Unknown	25Ma05Hb
CUMINSKY, Michael	20	M	Unknown	25Ma05Hb
FAGAN, Hugh	20	M	Unknown	25Ma05Hb
MARTIN, Margaret	14	F	Unknown	25Ma05Hb
Ann	30	F	Unknown	25Ma05Hb
SINGLETON, Maria	20	F	Unknown	25Ma05Hb
LANION, Peter	21	M	Unknown	25Ma05Hb
SHANNAHAN, Anne	13	F	Unknown	25Ma05Hb
BOLAND, James	20	M	Unknown	25Ma05Hb
TOOLE, U-Mrs.	45	F	Unknown	25Ma05Hb
Catherine	20	F	Unknown	25Ma05Hb
MOLLOY, Anne	30	F	Unknown	25Ma05Hb
RULLY, Garret	22	M	Unknown	25Ma05Hb
HEALY, Mary	20	F	Unknown	25Ma05Hb
Margaret	48	F	Unknown	25Ma05Hb
NOLAN, Johanna	20	F	Unknown	25Ma05Hb
PURCELL, Judy	20	F	Unknown	25Ma05Hb
BRENNAN, Jas.	20	M	Unknown	25Ma05Hb
HATEY, Martin	20	M	Unknown	25Ma05Hb
WHELAHAN, Eliza	18	F	Unknown	25Ma05Hb
Anne	16	F	Unknown	25Ma05Hb
KING, Kate	16	F	Unknown	25Ma05Hb
HAYDEN, Margaret	20	F	Unknown	25Ma05Hb
BRENNA, Catherine	20	F	Unknown	25Ma05Hb
HAYS, Margt.	20	F	Unknown	25Ma05Hb
MCDONNELL, Joanna	20	F	Unknown	25Ma05Hb
FOX, Wm.	25	M	Unknown	25Ma05Hb
MCKENNA, Patt	20	M	Unknown	25Ma05Hb
MULVAY, John	25	M	Unknown	25Ma05Hb
BEHAN, John	36	M	Unknown	25Ma05Hb
U-Mrs.	30	F	Unknown	25Ma05Hb
Ellen	11	F	Unknown	25Ma05Hb
Eliza	8	F	Child	25Ma05Hb
James	4	M	Child	25Ma05Hb
John	.00	M	Infant	25Ma05Hb
SHERIDAN, U-Mrs.	26	F	Unknown	25Ma05Hb
LEONARD, Cathr.	24	F	Unknown	25Ma05Hb
Lucinda	20	F	Unknown	25Ma05Hb
CRANY, James	24	M	Unknown	25Ma05Hb
DENIS, Patt	24	M	Unknown	25Ma05Hb
DOOLY, Alicia	26	F	Unknown	25Ma05Hb
MCCABE, Pat	28	M	Unknown	25Ma05Hb
U-Mrs.	24	F	Unknown	25Ma05Hb
HANLA, Pat	00	M	Unknown	25Ma05Hb
FLOOD, Mat	22	M	Unknown	25Ma05Hb
MAGER, Thomas	26	M	Unknown	25Ma05Hb
TIGHE, Mick	20	M	Unknown	25Ma05Hb
SHANNEN, Cath.	20	F	Unknown	25Ma05Hb
DONNEY, Mary	20	F	Unknown	25Ma05Hb
SCALLY, Mary	20	F	Unknown	25Ma05Hb
HOGAN, James	25	M	Unknown	25Ma05Hb
FALLAN, Michael	24	M	Unknown	25Ma05Hb
Mary	22	F	Unknown	25Ma05Hb
Bridget	.00	F	Infant	25Ma05Hb
JACKSON, Thomas	25	M	Unknown	25Ma05Hb
SMITH, Chas.	24	M	Unknown	25Ma05Hb
KERAN, James	20	M	Unknown	25Ma05Hb
BELAN, Ann	26	F	Unknown	25Ma05Hb
KINCELLY, Thomas	24	M	Unknown	25Ma05Hb
SCULLY, Thomas	24	M	Unknown	25Ma05Hb
SWONE, Biddy	25	F	Unknown	25Ma05Hb

NAMES OF PASSENGERS	AGE	SEX	OCCUPATIONS	DATE PORT SHIP
CONNOR, John	20	M	Unknown	25Ma05Hb
SWEENEY, John	19	M	Unknown	25Ma05Hb
TURBET, Samuel	34	M	Unknown	25Ma05Hb
ALLEN, George	20	M	Unknown	25Ma05Hb
MURGHEN, Jane	22	F	Unknown	25Ma05Hb
Eliza	2	F	Child	25Ma05Hb
FARREL, Wm.	21	M	Unknown	25Ma05Hb
COLLINS, Wm.	36	M	Unknown	25Ma05Hb
U-Mrs.	30	F	Unknown	25Ma05Hb
Henry	12	M	Unknown	25Ma05Hb
John	8	M	Child	25Ma05Hb
EDGAN, James	24	M	Unknown	25Ma05Hb
JAMES, Susan	20	F	Unknown	25Ma05Hb
KELLY, Edward	28	M	Unknown	25Ma05Hb
U-Miss	18	F	Unknown	25Ma05Hb
MURPHY, U	30	M	Unknown	25Ma05Hb
TROM, Jacob	16	M	Unknown	25Ma05Hb
EARLY, U-Mrs.	28	F	Unknown	25Ma05Hb
SAREN, Robert	19	M	Unknown	25Ma05Hb

SCOTLAND 25 MAY 1850

From Liverpool

NAMES OF PASSENGERS	AGE	SEX	OCCUPATIONS	DATE PORT SHIP
GREGORY, George	24	M	Laborer	25Ma02Kp
DUTTON, Joseph	22	M	Laborer	25Ma02Kp
FORSTER, Thos.	60	M	Laborer	25Ma02Kp
Wm.	23	M	Laborer	25Ma02Kp
LAFFEN, James	21	M	Laborer	25Ma02Kp
DALEY, Thos.	37	M	Laborer	25Ma02Kp
Harriet	27	F	Laborer	25Ma02Kp
WEBB, Geoe.	20	M	Laborer	25Ma02Kp
WALSH, John	22	M	Laborer	25Ma02Kp
Bridgt.	20	F	Laborer	25Ma02Kp
Ellen	.00	F	Infant	25Ma02Kp
Michl.	25	M	Laborer	25Ma02Kp
Jessie	30	F	Laborer	25Ma02Kp
MARCH, Henry	19	M	Laborer	25Ma02Kp
WALSH, William	21	M	Laborer	25Ma02Kp
PORTER, James	17	M	Laborer	25Ma02Kp
ELVERY, Mary	22	F	Dressmaker	25Ma02Kp
MACKEY, Hugh	26	M	Laborer	25Ma02Kp
STOCK, Thos.	50	M	Laborer	25Ma02Kp
Eliza	35	F	Wife	25Ma02Kp
Levi	22	M	Unknown	25Ma02Kp
WILKINSON, Wm.	28	M	Laborer	25Ma02Kp
MITCHELL, John-C.	30	M	Laborer	25Ma02Kp
MCLENNAHAN, Eliza	.00	F	Infant	25Ma02Kp
DICKSON, John	28	M	Laborer	25Ma02Kp
Mary	23	F	Wife	25Ma02Kp
Ann	.00	F	Infant	25Ma02Kp
Arthur	23	M	Laborer	25Ma02Kp
KERTERSTON, George	51	M	Laborer	25Ma02Kp
Sarah	37	F	Laborer	25Ma02Kp
Sarah	6	F	Child	25Ma02Kp
Fanny	3	F	Child	25Ma02Kp
Jane	.00	M	Infant	25Ma02Kp
George	21	M	Laborer	25Ma02Kp
WALSTEN, Saml.	30	M	Laborer	25Ma02Kp
MALE, Henry	24	M	Laborer	25Ma02Kp
Ann	26	F	Laborer	25Ma02Kp
Henry	.00	M	Infant	25Ma02Kp
Jessie	20	F	Laborer	25Ma02Kp
BUCKERSTRATE, Hugh	36	M	Laborer	25Ma02Kp
PRENS, E.	38	M	Laborer	25Ma02Kp
KRANTER, William	29	M	Laborer	25Ma02Kp
U-Mrs. (W)	29	F	Wife	25Ma02Kp
Eleanor	.00	F	Infant	25Ma02Kp
GROH, Chrisr.	39	M	Laborer	25Ma02Kp
GROH, U-Mrs. (W)	39	F	None	25Ma02Kp
AUBBE, H.	40	F	Unknown	25Ma02Kp
Margt.	38	F	Unknown	25Ma02Kp
Elizth.	24	F	Unknown	25Ma02Kp
KENNEDY, James	44	M	Laborer	25Ma02Kp
William	6	M	Child	25Ma02Kp
James	10	M	Unknown	25Ma02Kp
STANTON, Pat	20	M	Laborer	25Ma02Kp
Cath.	18	F	Spinster	25Ma02Kp
CONNOR, Mary	40	F	Unknown	25Ma02Kp
FLYNN, Mary	30	F	Unknown	25Ma02Kp
BEATES, Joseph	21	M	Laborer	25Ma02Kp
CORMACK, James	47	M	Laborer	25Ma02Kp
Cath.	36	F	Wife	25Ma02Kp
Cath.	16	F	Unknown	25Ma02Kp
Mary-Ann	14	F	Unknown	25Ma02Kp
William	11	M	None	25Ma02Kp
Thomas	10	M	None	25Ma02Kp
Ann	7	F	Child	25Ma02Kp
James	5	M	Child	25Ma02Kp
Anastasia	.00	F	Infant	25Ma02Kp
KATING, James	30	M	Unknown	25Ma02Kp
DEAKIN, Thomas	15	M	Unknown	25Ma02Kp
Margt.	17	F	Spinster	25Ma02Kp
CANNON, Pat	22	M	Laborer	25Ma02Kp
GARVEY, John	20	M	Laborer	25Ma02Kp
HIGHLAND, Mary	20	F	Spinster	25Ma02Kp
Cath.	.00	F	Infant	25Ma02Kp
GRIFFERN, Thos.	20	M	Laborer	25Ma02Kp
FINNERTY, Michl.	30	M	Laborer	25Ma02Kp
Rose	29	F	Spinster	25Ma02Kp
Mary	5	F	Child	25Ma02Kp
RYAN, Larry	30	M	Laborer	25Ma02Kp
Sally	24	F	Spinster	25Ma02Kp
Andy	30	M	Laborer	25Ma02Kp
Neil	38	M	Laborer	25Ma02Kp
MOYHAN, James	23	M	Laborer	25Ma02Kp
John	25	M	Laborer	25Ma02Kp
Pat	20	M	Laborer	25Ma02Kp
James	22	M	Laborer	25Ma02Kp
Margt.	17	F	Spinster	25Ma02Kp
MAHER, Mary	22	F	Unknown	25Ma02Kp
STAPLETON, Michl.	20	M	Laborer	25Ma02Kp
Andy	24	M	Laborer	25Ma02Kp
WALLACE, Pat	45	M	Laborer	25Ma02Kp
Margt.	35	F	Wife	25Ma02Kp
William	21	M	Unknown	25Ma02Kp
Robert	12	M	Unknown	25Ma02Kp
Thomas	10	M	Unknown	25Ma02Kp
John	6	M	Child	25Ma02Kp
Joshua	2	M	Child	25Ma02Kp
Margt.	.00	F	Infant	25Ma02Kp
MCLOUGHLIN, Fanny	18	F	Unknown	25Ma02Kp
Minay-MURRAY, Robert	23	M	Laborer	25Ma02Kp
RYAN, John	30	M	Laborer	25Ma02Kp
Cath.	27	F	Wife	25Ma02Kp
MALE, William	6	M	Child	25Ma02Kp
WHELAN, Josh.	22	M	Laborer	25Ma02Kp
RYAN, Dennis	13	M	Unknown	25Ma02Kp
Honora	12	F	None	25Ma02Kp
Pat	.00	M	Infant	25Ma02Kp
FIRKINS, Wm.	23	M	Laborer	25Ma02Kp
Mary (W)	20	F	Wife	25Ma02Kp
HASKALE, Susannah	46	F	Unknown	25Ma02Kp
John	20	M	Farmer	25Ma02Kp
Elizth.	8	F	Child	25Ma02Kp
Saml.	6	M	Child	25Ma02Kp
Wm.	.00	M	Infant	25Ma02Kp
GURLEY, John	50	M	Laborer	25Ma02Kp
SCOTT, John	24	M	Laborer	25Ma02Kp
RORKE, John	30	M	Laborer	25Ma02Kp
Margt. (W)	30	F	Wife	25Ma02Kp
Mary	25	F	Unknown	25Ma02Kp
Ann	.00	F	Infant	25Ma02Kp
Margt.	.00	F	Infant	25Ma02Kp

NAMES OF PASSENGERS	AGE	SEX	OCCUPATIONS	DATE PORT SHIP
GALLAGHER, Danl.	16	M	Laborer	25Ma02Kp
MONTGOMERY, Thos.	21	M	Laborer	25Ma02Kp
ANTIKER, Wm.	20	M	Laborer	25Ma02Kp
BEATTY, Thos.	16	M	Laborer	25Ma02Kp
GRIFFIN, Rachael	22	F	Spinster	25Ma02Kp
HARRISON, Henry	27	M	Laborer	25Ma02Kp
COHEN, William	22	M	Laborer	25Ma02Kp
GOODMAN, Edwd.	45	M	Laborer	25Ma02Kp
IRVIN, Ann	36	F	Laborer	25Ma02Kp
Martha	30	F	Wife	25Ma02Kp
Eliza	24	F	Unknown	25Ma02Kp
Charlotte	20	F	Unknown	25Ma02Kp
Honora-Adelaide	17	F	Unknown	25Ma02Kp
DAVIS, Thos.J.	25	M	Laborer	25Ma02Kp
Ann-Jane	22	F	Laborer	25Ma02Kp
MONAGHAN, Thos.	40	M	Laborer	25Ma02Kp
DONOHUE, Philip	35	M	Laborer	25Ma02Kp
Cath.	45	F	Laborer	25Ma02Kp
Philip	15	M	Laborer	25Ma02Kp
Margt.	12	F	None	25Ma02Kp
HARRINGTON, Julia	20	F	Laborer	25Ma02Kp
CROMIE, James	31	M	Laborer	25Ma02Kp
PHALEN, U-Mrs.	22	F	Laborer	25Ma02Kp
Michl.	.00	M	Infant	25Ma02Kp
RONAN, Margt.	18	F	Unknown	25Ma02Kp
ROBERT, Jno.	36	M	Farmer	25Ma02Kp
FORDE, Cath.	35	F	Unknown	25Ma02Kp
Benjn.	12	M	None	25Ma02Kp
John	10	M	None	25Ma02Kp
Elizth.	8	F	Child	25Ma02Kp
Michl.	6	M	Child	25Ma02Kp
Margt.	4	F	Child	25Ma02Kp
Pat	.00	M	Infant	25Ma02Kp
MCDONOUGH, Winney	9	F	Child	25Ma02Kp
MCCUE, Bridgt.	16	F	Unknown	25Ma02Kp
CONNOR, Ann	16	F	Spinster	25Ma02Kp
Jane	25	F	Spinster	25Ma02Kp
COLEMAN, Margt.	45	F	Spinster	25Ma02Kp
FLANNERY, Julia	20	F	Spinster	25Ma02Kp
CARROLL, Michl.	18	M	Laborer	25Ma02Kp
BYRNE, Thomas	25	M	Laborer	25Ma02Kp
Cath.	18	F	Laborer	25Ma02Kp
Bessey	16	F	Laborer	25Ma02Kp
SHEEHY, Ann	22	F	Laborer	25Ma02Kp
Thomas	15	M	Laborer	25Ma02Kp
Edward	15	M	Laborer	25Ma02Kp
FINN, Michl.	25	M	Laborer	25Ma02Kp
Pat.	22	M	Laborer	25Ma02Kp
LONG, Thomas	17	M	Laborer	25Ma02Kp
CARROLL, Thomas	25	M	Laborer	25Ma02Kp
FINN, Mary	18	F	Dressmaker	25Ma02Kp
LONG, John	22	M	Laborer	25Ma02Kp
MOORE, Louis	37	F	Laborer	25Ma02Kp
Louisa	16	F	Laborer	25Ma02Kp
Mary-Ann	7	F	Child	25Ma02Kp
Eliza	6	F	Child	25Ma02Kp
ONEILL, James	27	M	Laborer	25Ma02Kp
Died-At-Sea				
Eliza	19	F	Laborer	25Ma02Kp
BOWNE, Andw.	23	M	Laborer	25Ma02Kp
Ellen	24	F	Laborer	25Ma02Kp
RICE, John	18	M	Laborer	25Ma02Kp
COOPER, U-Mrs.	40	F	Laborer	25Ma02Kp
U-Miss	26	F	Laborer	25Ma02Kp
U-Miss	24	F	Dressmaker	25Ma02Kp
U-Miss	9	F	Child	25Ma02Kp
Luke	23	M	Laborer	25Ma02Kp
Saml.	22	M	Laborer	25Ma02Kp
William	18	M	Laborer	25Ma02Kp
John-Edwd.	12	M	Laborer	25Ma02Kp
LESTER, Wm.	45	M	Laborer	25Ma02Kp
GOUGH, William	16	M	Laborer	25Ma02Kp
DILLON, James	20	M	Laborer	25Ma02Kp
MURPHY, Mary	30	F	Spinster	25Ma02Kp
MOONEY, Eliza	10	F	Spinster	25Ma02Kp

NAMES OF PASSENGERS	AGE	SEX	OCCUPATIONS	DATE PORT SHIP
PADDEN, Anty.	12	M	Unknown	25Ma02Kp
Mary	53	F	Unknown	25Ma02Kp
Danl.	50	M	Farmer	25Ma02Kp
Mick	30	M	Farmer	25Ma02Kp
Honor	17	F	Spinster	25Ma02Kp
Anty.	45	M	Unknown	25Ma02Kp
Danl.	7	M	Child	25Ma02Kp
Bridgt.	14	F	Unknown	25Ma02Kp
DEVINE, David	24	M	Unknown	25Ma02Kp
TIGHE, Michl.	22	M	Unknown	25Ma02Kp
HAMILL, Pat	33	M	Unknown	25Ma02Kp
Cath. (W)	21	F	Wife	25Ma02Kp
James	34	M	Unknown	25Ma02Kp
Ann	20	F	Unknown	25Ma02Kp
Margt.	18	F	Unknown	25Ma02Kp
BYRNE, Mick	30	M	Laborer	25Ma02Kp
Rose	25	F	Laborer	25Ma02Kp
John	.00	M	Infant	25Ma02Kp
Mick	.00	M	Infant	25Ma02Kp
BURKE, Rose	20	F	Laborer	25Ma02Kp
MCDERMOTT, Pat	18	M	Laborer	25Ma02Kp
Mary	16	F	Spinster	25Ma02Kp
FERGUSON, Thomas	28	M	Farmer	25Ma02Kp
COLEMAN, Cath.	16	F	Spinster	25Ma02Kp
FERGUSON, Penelope	28	F	Farmer	25Ma02Kp
Pat	.00	M	Infant	25Ma02Kp
CLARKE, John	26	M	Farmer	25Ma02Kp
CONWAY, Thos.	54	M	Farmer	25Ma02Kp
Mary (W)	59	F	Wife	25Ma02Kp
Jathelam	30	U	Unknown	25Ma02Kp
James	27	M	Laborer	25Ma02Kp
MAHONEY, Margt.	21	F	Laborer	25Ma02Kp
HOGAN, Michl.	21	M	Laborer	25Ma02Kp
MORRIS, Ellen	18	F	Laborer	25Ma02Kp
Ann	20	F	Laborer	25Ma02Kp
GLYNN, Eliza	12	F	Laborer	25Ma02Kp
John	10	M	Laborer	25Ma02Kp
ELLIOTT, David	21	M	Laborer	25Ma02Kp
KEEGAN, John	21	M	Laborer	25Ma02Kp
GERRATY, James	30	M	Laborer	25Ma02Kp
DOWDELL, Mary	22	F	Laborer	25Ma02Kp
GORMAN, Ann	50	F	Laborer	25Ma02Kp
FINNERTY, Pat	50	M	Laborer	25Ma02Kp
Rose (W)	50	F	Wife	25Ma02Kp
Mary	16	F	Laborer	25Ma02Kp
Stephen	13	M	None	25Ma02Kp
Cath.	7	F	Child	25Ma02Kp
WALSH, Matt	40	M	Farmer	25Ma02Kp
Bridgt. (W)	36	F	Wife	25Ma02Kp
DUNN, Lewis	50	M	Unknown	25Ma02Kp
Pat	14	M	Unknown	25Ma02Kp
Peter	10	M	None	25Ma02Kp
Ann	6	F	Child	25Ma02Kp
DONNELLY, Sarah	20	F	Wife	25Ma02Kp
John	18	M	Laborer	25Ma02Kp
Jane	26	F	Laborer	25Ma02Kp
BYRON, Mattw.	32	M	Laborer	25Ma02Kp
Elizth. (W)	20	F	Wife	25Ma02Kp
Haney-HAWES, Pat	21	M	Laborer	25Ma02Kp
KANE, Pat	35	M	Laborer	25Ma02Kp
CARROLL, Jane	35	F	Laborer	25Ma02Kp
William	.00	M	Infant	25Ma02Kp
HALEY, Bernd.	19	M	Laborer	25Ma02Kp
Margt.	14	F	Spinster	25Ma02Kp
ALLEY, Will	18	M	Laborer	25Ma02Kp
SHAW, John	21	M	Laborer	25Ma02Kp
CLEARY, James	30	M	Laborer	25Ma02Kp
Eliza	25	F	Laborer	25Ma02Kp
Dennis	11	M	None	25Ma02Kp
Pat	9	M	Child	25Ma02Kp
William	7	M	Child	25Ma02Kp
TRAVERS, Michl.	26	M	Farmer	25Ma02Kp
MCCORMICK, Ann	20	F	Farmer	25Ma02Kp
DOHENY, John	22	M	Farmer	25Ma02Kp
LYNCH, Thos.	28	M	Farmer	25Ma02Kp

NAMES OF PASSENGERS	AGE	SEX	OCCUPATIONS	DATE PORT SHIP
MAHEY, Michl.	25	M	Farmer	25Ma02Kp
John	60	M	Farmer	25Ma02Kp
Bridgt. (W)	50	F	Wife	25Ma02Kp
Michl.	25	M	Laborer	25Ma02Kp
CAVANAGH, John	23	M	Laborer	25Ma02Kp
REID, John	21	M	Laborer	25Ma02Kp
MCHENDRY, Charlotte	18	F	Laborer	25Ma02Kp
STINGER, Sarah	20	F	Spinster	25Ma02Kp
John	12	M	Unknown	25Ma02Kp
KILBRIDE, Francis	20	M	Unknown	25Ma02Kp
MAGUIRE, Judy	20	F	Spinster	25Ma02Kp
MURPHY, Dennis	30	M	Laborer	25Ma02Kp
WRIGHT, Allen	20	M	Laborer	25Ma02Kp
U-Mrs.	40	F	Wife	25Ma02Kp
Eliza	23	F	Unknown	25Ma02Kp
Sarah	.00	F	Infant	25Ma02Kp
TAYLOR, Joshua	30	M	Laborer	25Ma02Kp
MCDONALD, Bridgt.	34	F	Spinster	25Ma02Kp
BARRETT, Ann	20	F	Spinster	25Ma02Kp
CONNOR, Pat	36	M	Laborer	25Ma02Kp
BULGER, Lawn.	24	M	Laborer	25Ma02Kp
STAFFORD, Will	17	M	Laborer	25Ma02Kp
BRYAN, Martha	10	F	None	25Ma02Kp
Honor	16	F	Spinster	25Ma02Kp
MULLEN, Pat	20	M	Unknown	25Ma02Kp
Michl.	14	M	Servant	25Ma02Kp
OCONNOR, Wm.	30	M	Servant	25Ma02Kp
MALEY, Edwd.	20	M	Servant	25Ma02Kp
BOHAN, Jas.	28	M	Servant	25Ma02Kp
QUINTER, Edwd.	32	M	Servant	25Ma02Kp
Mary (W)	30	F	Wife	25Ma02Kp
NOLAN, Edwd.	30	M	Laborer	25Ma02Kp
REDMOND, Wm.	52	M	Laborer	25Ma02Kp
Jane (W)	49	F	Wife	25Ma02Kp
Jane	14	F	Unknown	25Ma02Kp
Will	18	M	Unknown	25Ma02Kp
Susan	10	F	None	25Ma02Kp
Thomas	12	M	None	25Ma02Kp
Jessey	7	F	Child	25Ma02Kp
Mary	4	F	Child	25Ma02Kp
HUNTLEY, M.	30	F	Wife	25Ma02Kp
Benjn.	4	M	Child	25Ma02Kp
KINSLEY, Ann	36	F	Wife	25Ma02Kp
Wm.	41	M	Laborer	25Ma02Kp
Susan	8	F	Child	25Ma02Kp
Mary-Ann	12	F	None	25Ma02Kp
Sarah	10	F	None	25Ma02Kp
Ruth	5	F	Child	25Ma02Kp
Jane	4	F	Child	25Ma02Kp
Henry	30	M	Farmer	25Ma02Kp
WRIGHT, John	40	M	Farmer	25Ma02Kp
DEMPSEY, Cath.	27	F	Wife	25Ma02Kp
U-Mrs.	24	F	Unknown	25Ma02Kp
Pat	19	M	Laborer	25Ma02Kp
Eliza	16	F	Laborer	25Ma02Kp
SCOTT, John	20	M	Laborer	25Ma02Kp
SUTTON, Joseph	20	M	Laborer	25Ma02Kp
SAUNDERS, William	34	M	Laborer	25Ma02Kp
DEBURNETT, Wm.	20	M	Laborer	25Ma02Kp
GIBSON, Henry	26	M	Laborer	25Ma02Kp
Ann	3	F	Child	25Ma02Kp
KEARNEY, James	24	M	Laborer	25Ma02Kp
Hugh	23	M	Laborer	25Ma02Kp
SPEARMAN, Simon	20	M	Laborer	25Ma02Kp
WOODE, Pat	22	M	Laborer	25Ma02Kp
BYRNE, John	20	M	Laborer	25Ma02Kp
WHITE, John	23	M	Laborer	25Ma02Kp
Mary (W)	30	F	Wife	25Ma02Kp
MCILLONEAL, Edwd.	20	M	Laborer	25Ma02Kp
James	19	M	Laborer	25Ma02Kp
Cathr.	18	F	Spinster	25Ma02Kp
MULLOY, Bryan	30	M	Laborer	25Ma02Kp
MACKIN, Mary	22	F	Laborer	25Ma02Kp
MALONE, William	19	M	Laborer	25Ma02Kp
KELLY, Pat	28	M	Laborer	25Ma02Kp

NAMES OF PASSENGERS	AGE	SEX	OCCUPATIONS	DATE PORT SHIP
KELLY, Cathr. (W)	30	F	Wife	25Ma02Kp
BLAKE, Peter	40	M	Laborer	25Ma02Kp
WARREN, G.	17	M	Laborer	25Ma02Kp
PURCELL, John	30	M	Laborer	25Ma02Kp
Margt. (W)	40	F	Wife	25Ma02Kp
Bridgt.	20	F	Unknown	25Ma02Kp
Margt.	18	F	Unknown	25Ma02Kp
Jane	4	F	Child	25Ma02Kp
DALEY, Ann	20	F	Unknown	25Ma02Kp
WALL, John	24	M	Farmer	25Ma02Kp
Wm.	26	M	Farmer	25Ma02Kp
MCGLENEE, Michl.	19	M	Farmer	25Ma02Kp
OSBORNE, Wm.	26	M	Farmer	25Ma02Kp
BROWNE, Thos.	23	M	Farmer	25Ma02Kp
CORRISH, James	21	M	Farmer	25Ma02Kp
MCDERMOTT, Michl.	20	M	Farmer	25Ma02Kp
COHEN, Besselter	20	M	Farmer	25Ma02Kp
U-Mrs. (W)	19	F	Wife	25Ma02Kp
MCGINN, John	25	M	Laborer	25Ma02Kp
BRISTACH, William	18	M	Laborer	25Ma02Kp
PIERSON, Thos.	33	M	Laborer	25Ma02Kp
KEENAN, Bridgt.	23	F	Laborer	25Ma02Kp
KALAHER, Mary	35	F	Laborer	25Ma02Kp
WALSH, Nicholas	24	M	Laborer	25Ma02Kp
BROWN, Thos.	36	M	Laborer	25Ma02Kp
COMPIN, Margt.	20	F	Spinster	25Ma02Kp
FOE, Mathias	30	M	Unknown	25Ma02Kp
MCKEEGAN, Cath.	19	F	Spinster	25Ma02Kp
DUFFY, John	19	M	Laborer	25Ma02Kp
MCQUEENY, Eliza	00	F	Spinster	25Ma02Kp
MCDONALD, Margt.	21	F	Dressmaker	25Ma02Kp
Rose-Ann	23	F	Dressmaker	25Ma02Kp
REILLY, Jas.	20	M	Unknown	25Ma02Kp
MCCONNELL, Geoe.	20	M	Unknown	25Ma02Kp
COOK, James	19	M	Unknown	25Ma02Kp
MCKEEGAN, Cathr.	19	F	Unknown	25Ma02Kp
KELCHER, Bridgt.	8	F	Child	25Ma02Kp

HERCULES 25 MAY 1850

From Liverpool

NAMES OF PASSENGERS	AGE	SEX	OCCUPATIONS	DATE PORT SHIP
MCACHULLY, Jas.	18	M	Laborer	25Ma02Kt
MALLORY, Mary	20	F	Laborer	25Ma02Kt
Margt.	14	F	Laborer	25Ma02Kt
HABON, Phillip	25	M	Laborer	25Ma02Kt
CLARK, Jno.	18	M	Laborer	25Ma02Kt
Margt.	12	F	Laborer	25Ma02Kt
Ann	10	F	Laborer	25Ma02Kt
Rose	8	F	Child	25Ma02Kt
Patk.	6	M	Child	25Ma02Kt
MENKEY, Mary	12	F	Laborer	25Ma02Kt
REILLY, Strange	20	F	Laborer	25Ma02Kt
Mary	18	F	Laborer	25Ma02Kt
BUSTIN, Irvan	58	M	Laborer	25Ma02Kt
HEWISON, G.	18	F	Laborer	25Ma02Kt
GILMAN, Eliza	20	F	Laborer	25Ma02Kt
NIXON, Margt.	30	F	Laborer	25Ma02Kt
CRAWFORD, Judy	22	F	Laborer	25Ma02Kt
NANGESON, Timothy	25	M	Laborer	25Ma02Kt
CONWAY, Bridget	18	F	Laborer	25Ma02Kt
FARRELL, Richd.	30	M	Laborer	25Ma02Kt
NOLAN, Sarah	30	F	Laborer	25Ma02Kt
Conls.	18	M	Laborer	25Ma02Kt
Hugh	14	M	Laborer	25Ma02Kt
Thos.	8	M	Child	25Ma02Kt
Sarah	11	F	Laborer	25Ma02Kt
MEATH, Cathr.	25	F	Laborer	25Ma02Kt
MONSING, Pattk.	23	M	Laborer	25Ma02Kt

NAMES OF PASSENGERS	AGE	SEX	OCCUPATIONS	DATE PORT SHIP
KILLITEER, Rose	23	F	Laborer	25Ma02K+
Patk.	22	M	Laborer	25Ma02K+
MCGRAW, Edwd.	22	M	Laborer	25Ma02K+
CAHILL, Mary	18	F	Laborer	25Ma02K+
MCKENNA, Lawr.	23	M	Laborer	25Ma02K+
CLARK, Ann	18	F	Laborer	25Ma02K+
ROBINSON, Mary	38	F	Laborer	25Ma02K+
John	6	M	Child	25Ma02K+
LEE, John	3	M	Child	25Ma02K+
MCGRUGH, Felix	22	M	Laborer	25Ma02K+
LAWLER, Cath.	33	F	Laborer	25Ma02K+
DUFFY, Felix	22	M	Laborer	25Ma02K+
DOWD, Susan	10	F	Unknown	25Ma02K+
DROWAY, Patk.	8	M	Child	25Ma02K+
MULONEY, Chas.	20	M	Laborer	25Ma02K+
Mary	60	F	Laborer	25Ma02K+
Mary	20	F	Laborer	25Ma02K+
Cathr.	10	F	Laborer	25Ma02K+
BOSSAN, Peter	25	M	Laborer	25Ma02K+
KILROY, Mary	12	F	Laborer	25Ma02K+
BRADY, Patk.	13	M	Laborer	25Ma02K+
HORNE, Ellen	20	F	Laborer	25Ma02K+
LEGAN, Daniel	28	M	Laborer	25Ma02K+
RIELLY, Jane	20	F	Laborer	25Ma02K+
REGAN, Sarah	20	F	Laborer	25Ma02K+
MCDERMOTT, Ann	18	F	Laborer	25Ma02K+
LOCISE, Michl.	24	M	Laborer	25Ma02K+
GALVIN, Mick	21	M	Laborer	25Ma02K+
TWINMAN, Margt.	21	F	Laborer	25Ma02K+
GRIFFITH, Sarah	22	F	Laborer	25Ma02K+
Humphrey	25	M	Laborer	25Ma02K+
SAULS, Mary	45	F	Laborer	25Ma02K+
John	16	M	Laborer	25Ma02K+
Ellen	11	F	Laborer	25Ma02K+
Thos.	5	M	Child	25Ma02K+
Teresa	9	F	Child	25Ma02K+
FLANEGAN, John	11	M	Laborer	25Ma02K+
HENNESSY, Peter	26	M	Laborer	25Ma02K+
HINES, Cathr.	24	F	Laborer	25Ma02K+
MURREY, Bridgt.	18	F	Laborer	25Ma02K+
FAHEY, Cathr.	20	F	Laborer	25Ma02K+
John	20	M	Laborer	25Ma02K+
DUNN, Mary	21	F	Laborer	25Ma02K+
HONEY, Nancy	20	F	Laborer	25Ma02K+
DREW, James	26	M	Laborer	25Ma02K+
GARVIN, U	56	M	Laborer	25Ma02K+
HOGAN, Mary	56	F	Laborer	25Ma02K+
Ann	19	F	Laborer	25Ma02K+
Eliza	15	F	Laborer	25Ma02K+
DOYLE, Luke	20	M	Laborer	25Ma02K+
JACKSON, Robt.	28	M	Laborer	25Ma02K+
Jas.	28	M	Laborer	25Ma02K+
U-Mrs.	25	F	Laborer	25Ma02K+
Isabella	3	F	Child	25Ma02K+
John	.00	M	Infant	25Ma02K+
WITHERALL, Geo.	25	M	Laborer	25Ma02K+
U-Mrs.	22	F	Laborer	25Ma02K+
KIRK, John	40	M	Laborer	25Ma02K+
SHAW, Mathw.	21	M	Laborer	25Ma02K+
BENDEN, Michl.	20	F	Laborer	25Ma02K+
DAVIDSON, John	32	M	Laborer	25Ma02K+
WHYTE, James	26	M	Laborer	25Ma02K+
FARRINGTON, Patk.	20	M	Laborer	25Ma02K+
GALVIN, Michl.	35	M	Laborer	25Ma02K+
MCNAUGHTON, U	50	M	Laborer	25Ma02K+
MCMAHON, John	30	M	Laborer	25Ma02K+
Johanna	30	F	Laborer	25Ma02K+
Dennis	7	M	Child	25Ma02K+
Patk.	.00	M	Infant	25Ma02K+
WILSON, Bridget	21	F	Laborer	25Ma02K+
DWYER, John	30	M	Laborer	25Ma02K+
Ann	30	F	Laborer	25Ma02K+
Patk.	2	M	Child	25Ma02K+
Died-At-Sea				
Bridget	50	F	Laborer	25Ma02K+
DWYER, Peter	.00	M	Infant	25Ma02K+
Honor	16	F	Laborer	25Ma02K+
COONAN, John	30	M	Laborer	25Ma02K+
CASHEN, Thos.	32	M	Laborer	25Ma02K+
HOGAN, Sarah	40	F	Laborer	25Ma02K+
HUGHES, Bridget	25	F	Laborer	25Ma02K+
CORBETT, Michl.	18	M	Laborer	25Ma02K+
CORNEY, Cathr.	18	F	Laborer	25Ma02K+
BRYSEN, Dennis	35	M	Laborer	25Ma02K+
MURPHY, Anthy.	22	M	Laborer	25Ma02K+
HAGGERTY, Wm.	19	M	Laborer	25Ma02K+
CARBYSHORE, John	29	M	Laborer	25Ma02K+
U-Mrs.	20	F	Laborer	25Ma02K+
LYNCH, Cathr.	12	F	Laborer	25Ma02K+
WALTER, Timothy	26	M	Laborer	25Ma02K+
MCCLARK, John	28	M	Laborer	25Ma02K+
HUDSON, Wm.	20	M	Laborer	25Ma02K+
John	18	M	Unknown	25Ma02K+
Mary	16	F	Unknown	25Ma02K+
CASEY, Cathr.	18	F	Unknown	25Ma02K+
MCDERMOTT, Jas.	45	M	Unknown	25Ma02K+
FOX, Jas.	50	M	Unknown	25Ma02K+
Marcella	45	F	Unknown	25Ma02K+
J.	15	F	Unknown	25Ma02K+
CORNELL, Cathr.	20	F	Unknown	25Ma02K+
CASEY, Wm.	28	M	Unknown	25Ma02K+
HOLLORN, Patk.	25	M	Unknown	25Ma02K+
BRODERICK, Anthy.	35	M	Unknown	25Ma02K+
BARRETT, Mary	35	F	Unknown	25Ma02K+
WART, John	31	M	Unknown	25Ma02K+
HODGE, Jas.	30	M	Unknown	25Ma02K+
DOYLE, Hugh	33	M	Unknown	25Ma02K+
DUFFY, Patt	24	M	Unknown	25Ma02K+
DOUGLAS, Thos.	24	M	Unknown	25Ma02K+
BRAXHAM, Wm.	31	M	Unknown	25Ma02K+
SPENCE, Geo.	21	M	Unknown	25Ma02K+
Daniel	25	M	Unknown	25Ma02K+
Cathr.	7	F	Child	25Ma02K+
John	8	M	Child	25Ma02K+
TAYSON, Wm.	38	M	Unknown	25Ma02K+
MCELROY, John	18	M	Unknown	25Ma02K+
Mary	20	F	Unknown	25Ma02K+
KEOGH, Sarah	33	F	Unknown	25Ma02K+
Wm.	6	M	Child	25Ma02K+
Thos.	3	M	Child	25Ma02K+
Died-At-Sea				
Jas.	.00	M	Infant	25Ma02K+
DOGHERTY, Wm.	26	M	Unknown	25Ma02K+
ELLIOTT, John	40	M	Unknown	25Ma02K+
Wm.	40	F	Unknown	25Ma02K+
Geo.	13	M	Unknown	25Ma02K+
Thos.	11	M	Unknown	25Ma02K+
Hannah	6	F	Child	25Ma02K+
HALEY, Wm.	19	M	Unknown	25Ma02K+
MCNALLY, Wm.	25	M	Unknown	25Ma02K+
FLASK, Robert	20	M	Unknown	25Ma02K+
HANSEN, Patk.	13	M	Unknown	25Ma02K+
BYRNES, Palen	28	M	Unknown	25Ma02K+
CHALLSON, John	16	M	Unknown	25Ma02K+
GALAVIN, Wm.	32	M	Unknown	25Ma02K+
OLEARY, Timothy	18	M	Unknown	25Ma02K+
CLANCY, Patk.	20	M	Unknown	25Ma02K+
BLESSING, Hugh	30	M	Unknown	25Ma02K+
BROWN, James	50	M	Unknown	25Ma02K+
WALSH, Mary	40	F	Unknown	25Ma02K+
Cathr.	8	F	Child	25Ma02K+
Jas.	6	M	Child	25Ma02K+
Bridget	4	F	Child	25Ma02K+
BARKLEY, Pheobe	50	F	Unknown	25Ma02K+
Michl.	2	M	Child	25Ma02K+
DICKSON, Thos.	22	M	Unknown	25Ma02K+
RADCLIFF, Wm.	20	M	Unknown	25Ma02K+
QUADE, John	20	M	Unknown	25Ma02K+
GREEN, Thos.	15	M	Unknown	25Ma02K+
SAVLIN, Ann	20	F	Unknown	25Ma02K+

NAMES OF PASSENGERS	AGE	SEX	OCCUPATIONS	DATE PORT SHIP
RYDER. John	40	M	Unknown	25Ma02Kt
John	9	M	Child	25Ma02Kt
BOYLAN. Jas.	22	M	Unknown	25Ma02Kt
WELSEY. Henry	24	M	Unknown	25Ma02Kt
Julia	23	F	Unknown	25Ma02Kt
HELLERNEY. Patk.	15	M	Unknown	25Ma02Kt
KERNAY. Mary	50	F	Unknown	25Ma02Kt
COUGHLAN, Patk.	23	M	Unknown	25Ma02Kt
Michl.	30	M	Unknown	25Ma02Kt
RIELLY. Mickey	30	M	Unknown	25Ma02Kt
MULLOCK. James	25	M	Unknown	25Ma02Kt
ASHLEY. James	20	M	Unknown	25Ma02Kt
KINOVAN. Jas.	35	M	Unknown	25Ma02Kt
BOLAND. Thos.	27	M	Unknown	25Ma02Kt
QUIN, Elizath.	23	F	Unknown	25Ma02Kt
DEVLIN. Ellen	22	F	Unknown	25Ma02Kt
Mary	24	F	Unknown	25Ma02Kt
SPENCE. Edw.	24	M	Unknown	25Ma02Kt
KIRNAN, James	30	M	Unknown	25Ma02Kt
CASS. Patk.	18	M	Unknown	25Ma02Kt
HAYES. Thos.	32	M	Unknown	25Ma02Kt
MURREY. Martin	32	M	Unknown	25Ma02Kt
HALEY. Thos.	23	U	Unknown	25Ma02Kt
RYAN, John	22	U	Unknown	25Ma02Kt
CLARK. Bernard	21	M	Unknown	25Ma02Kt
RIELLY. Thos.	18	M	Unknown	25Ma02Kt
HANALEN. Thos.	27	M	Unknown	25Ma02Kt
Mary	30	F	Unknown	25Ma02Kt
HIGGINBOTTOM. John	25	M	Unknown	25Ma02Kt
GREEN. Jabiz	44	M	Unknown	25Ma02Kt
DOYLE. John	24	M	Unknown	25Ma02Kt
MCCUSE. John	.00	M	Infant	25Ma02Kt
BRABLEY. Michl.	16	M	Unknown	25Ma02Kt
Cathr.	12	F	Unknown	25Ma02Kt
CAFFREY. John	21	M	Unknown	25Ma02Kt
ALLEN, Bridget	20	F	Unknown	25Ma02Kt
TORNEY. Cathr.	20	F	Unknown	25Ma02Kt
HEALEY. C.	4	U	Child	25Ma02Kt
Cathr.	3	F	Child	25Ma02Kt
IRWIN, Patk.	60	M	Unknown	25Ma02Kt
Patk.	14	M	Unknown	25Ma02Kt
Thos.	18	M	Unknown	25Ma02Kt
Honora	16	F	Unknown	25Ma02Kt
Mary	5	F	Child	25Ma02Kt
DESMOND. Jane	25	F	Unknown	25Ma02Kt
MURPHY. Margt.	21	F	Unknown	25Ma02Kt
Hannah	18	F	Unknown	25Ma02Kt
Danl.	28	M	Unknown	25Ma02Kt
PATT. Chas.	25	M	Unknown	25Ma02Kt
Mons.	27	M	Unknown	25Ma02Kt
FRAME. Thos.	40	M	Unknown	25Ma02Kt
U-Mrs.	40	F	Unknown	25Ma02Kt
Herbert	15	M	Unknown	25Ma02Kt
WILSON. Wm.	27	M	Unknown	25Ma02Kt
HICKS. Saml.	20	M	Unknown	25Ma02Kt
WILKINS. John	33	M	Unknown	25Ma02Kt
HYSLOP. Robt.	27	M	Unknown	25Ma02Kt
Susan	27	F	Unknown	25Ma02Kt
AMASON, Wm.	35	M	Unknown	25Ma02Kt
WEBB. John	28	M	Unknown	25Ma02Kt
GRAVES. John	30	M	Unknown	25Ma02Kt
Ann	26	F	Unknown	25Ma02Kt
Robt.	6	M	Child	25Ma02Kt
Isabella	4	M	Child	25Ma02Kt
Thos.	.00	M	Infant	25Ma02Kt
Mary	24	F	Unknown	25Ma02Kt
Geo.	24	M	Unknown	25Ma02Kt
WHYTE. Bessey	22	F	Unknown	25Ma02Kt
Jane	38	M	Unknown	25Ma02Kt
LAING, Thos.	21	M	Unknown	25Ma02Kt
Ann	29	F	Unknown	25Ma02Kt
Eben	19	M	Unknown	25Ma02Kt
Mary	17	F	Unknown	25Ma02Kt
Geo.	13	M	Unknown	25Ma02Kt
WHYTE. Jessey	11	F	Unknown	25Ma02Kt

NAMES OF PASSENGERS	AGE	SEX	OCCUPATIONS	DATE PORT SHIP
WHYTE, Jane	9	F	Child	25Ma02K
James	7	M	Child	25Ma02K
Patk.	5	M	Child	25Ma02K
Einphem	3	F	Child	25Ma02K
Mary	.00	F	Infant	25Ma02K
Andrew	.00	M	Infant	25Ma02K
SCOTT. Jessy	18	F	Unknown	25Ma02K
CRAWFORD. Thos.	25	M	Laborer	25Ma02K

ISAAC-WEBB 25 MAY 1850

From Liverpool

NAMES OF PASSENGERS	AGE	SEX	OCCUPATIONS	DATE PORT SHIP
WHITLAW, Anne	30	F	Unknown	25Ma02H
Thomas	7	M	Child	25Ma02H
James	3	M	Child	25Ma02H
CORKERAN. Jane	20	F	Servant	25Ma02H
FARLEY. Biddy	20	F	Servant	25Ma02H
FLOOD. Ellen	10	F	Unknown	25Ma02H
SMITH, Mary	22	F	Servant	25Ma02H
REILY. Edward	23	M	Laborer	25Ma02H
LYNCH, Charles	25	M	Laborer	25Ma02H
MACKINRON. Henry	22	M	Laborer	25Ma02H
FLOOD. Phillip	40	M	Laborer	25Ma02H
NEILLY. Michl.	25	M	Laborer	25Ma02H
REILY. Cath.	60	F	Unknown	25Ma02H
SMITH. Ellen	18	F	Servant	25Ma02H
Pat	17	M	Laborer	25Ma02H
MACKURRY. Michael	22	M	Mechanic	25Ma02H
MULLINS. Thomas	20	M	Laborer	25Ma02H
MACKURRY. James	18	M	Mechanic	25Ma02H
Mary	50	F	Unknown	25Ma02H
Mary	20	F	Servant	25Ma02H
MULLINS, Anne	20	F	Servant	25Ma02H
LYNCH, Cath.	50	F	None	25Ma02H
MURRAY. James	60	M	Laborer	25Ma02H
JONES. William	24	M	Laborer	25Ma02H
MURRAY. Frank	23	M	Laborer	25Ma02H
DOOLEY. James	26	M	Laborer	25Ma02H
MOLONE. Michl.	45	M	Farmer	25Ma02H
Mary	45	F	None	25Ma02H
Mary	8	F	Child	25Ma02H
Eliza	6	F	Child	25Ma02H
Pat	2	M	Child	25Ma02H
LUKE, Thomas	40	M	Laborer	25Ma02H
GROGAN. Pat	25	M	Laborer	25Ma02H
Thomas	40	M	Laborer	25Ma02H
NEILY. Anne	26	F	Servant	25Ma02H
KIRLY, Bitty	20	F	Servant	25Ma02H
HAMMOND. Lizy	20	F	Servant	25Ma02H
DIXON, Matilda	12	F	Servant	25Ma02H
CARROLL, Peter	16	M	Laborer	25Ma02H
COLBY. Thomas	14	M	Laborer	25Ma02H
NEWMAN, Hugh	44	M	Laborer	25Ma02H
FLANNAGAN. Larry	18	M	Laborer	25Ma02H
DARCEY. John	18	M	Laborer	25Ma02H
CONNELLY. Sarah	18	F	Servant	25Ma02H
GALLAGHER. Margt.	20	F	Servant	25Ma02H
JUDGE, Sarah	20	F	Servant	25Ma02H
DUFFY. Anne	20	F	Servant	25Ma02H
MCANLIFFE, Jury	30	M	Laborer	25Ma02H
Mary	26	F	Servant	25Ma02H
COONAN, Darby	49	M	Laborer	25Ma02H
Anne	40	F	Unknown	25Ma02H
SHEVLIN, David	23	M	Laborer	25Ma02H
TOBIN, Thomas	24	M	Laborer	25Ma02H
PHELAN. Danl.	20	M	Mechanic	25Ma02H
TOBIN, Hanna	60	F	Unknown	25Ma02H
Ellen	25	F	Servant	25Ma02H

NAMES OF PASSENGERS	AGE	SEX	OCCUPATIONS	DATE PORT SHIP
TOBIN, Hanna	18	F	Servant	25Ma02Ha
BUTLER, Margt.	30	F	Servant	25Ma02Ha
COFFRY, Jas.	40	M	Unknown	25Ma02Ha
Margt.	15	F	Unknown	25Ma02Ha
Judy	7	F	Child	25Ma02Ha
Thomas	3	M	Child	25Ma02Ha
BOG, Simean	27	M	Laborer	25Ma02Ha
Bridget	16	F	Servant	25Ma02Ha
WHITE, Maria	18	F	Servant	25Ma02Ha
PHELAN, Judy	22	F	Servant	25Ma02Ha
HYMES, Honnora	56	F	Servant	25Ma02Ha
DELANY, Judy	22	F	Servant	25Ma02Ha
MCBRIEN, Suzan	24	F	Servant	25Ma02Ha
ROURKE, Anne	23	F	Servant	25Ma02Ha
BUCKLEY, Cathe.	25	F	Servant	25Ma02Ha
Ellen	11	F	Unknown	25Ma02Ha
Mary	7	F	Child	25Ma02Ha
Daniel	5	M	Child	25Ma02Ha
TURNER, Margt.	19	F	Servant	25Ma02Ha
MCGUELLAN, Danl.	29	M	Mechanic	25Ma02Ha
Anne	20	F	Unknown	25Ma02Ha
Thomas	.11	M	Infant	25Ma02Ha
SKENE, John	30	M	Laborer	25Ma02Ha
Mry	28	F	Unknown	25Ma02Ha
Dennis	35	M	Laborer	25Ma02Ha
DUNN, James	20	M	Laborer	25Ma02Ha
DONNELL, Michl.	30	M	Laborer	25Ma02Ha
MULLOGHERY, Thomas	17	M	Laborer	25Ma02Ha
CLARY, Thomas	17	M	Laborer	25Ma02Ha
BURKE, Edmond	18	M	Laborer	25Ma02Ha
DOOLAN, Mary	30	F	Servant	25Ma02Ha
Michael	3	M	Child	25Ma02Ha
HICKEY, John	20	M	Laborer	25Ma02Ha
DOOLAN, Pat	30	M	Laborer	25Ma02Ha
Bridgt.	20	F	Unknown	25Ma02Ha
Michael	29	M	Laborer	25Ma02Ha
Cath.	21	F	Servant	25Ma02Ha
COFFEE, Bridgt.	28	F	Servant	25Ma02Ha
Andrew	26	M	Laborer	25Ma02Ha
MCDONOGHUE, John	26	M	Laborer	25Ma02Ha
HANLY, Mary	32	F	Servant	25Ma02Ha
CONNOLLY, Bridgt.	27	F	Servant	25Ma02Ha
HANLY, Bridgt.	.10	F	Infant	25Ma02Ha
John	28	M	Laborer	25Ma02Ha
MCDONOGH, Michl.	25	M	Laborer	25Ma02Ha
HANLY, John	4	M	Child	25Ma02Ha
STRICK, James	50	M	Laborer	25Ma02Ha
TRACY, Patk.	23	M	Laborer	25Ma02Ha
POWER, John	26	M	Laborer	25Ma02Ha
RYAN, John	26	M	Laborer	25Ma02Ha
TRACY, Bridgt.	25	F	Servant	25Ma02Ha
RYAN, John	30	F	Servant	25Ma02Ha
STRICK, Mary	26	F	Servant	25Ma02Ha
GRADY, Thomas	30	M	Mechanic	25Ma02Ha
Cath.	35	F	Unknown	25Ma02Ha
Sally	30	F	Servant	25Ma02Ha
Mary	6	F	Child	25Ma02Ha
WILLIAMS, John	42	M	Laborer	25Ma02Ha
LANE, Thomas	35	M	Laborer	25Ma02Ha
WILLIAMS, William	16	M	Laborer	25Ma02Ha
Michael	14	M	Laborer	25Ma02Ha
Mary	40	F	Unknown	25Ma02Ha
John	13	M	Unknown	25Ma02Ha
Honora	10	F	Unknown	25Ma02Ha
Johna.	9	F	Child	25Ma02Ha
Mary	1	F	Child	25Ma02Ha
DICK, Saml.	30	M	Laborer	25Ma02Ha
CUNNINGHAM, Thos.	32	M	Laborer	25Ma02Ha
DIXON, Ellen	20	F	Servant	25Ma02Ha
MCDERMOTT, Alley	20	F	Servant	25Ma02Ha
Mary	20	F	None	25Ma02Ha
COUGHLAN, Mary	23	F	Servant	25Ma02Ha
MCDERMOTT, James	4	F	Child	25Ma02Ha
MOORE, Cathn.	24	F	Servant	25Ma02Ha
GATLIN, Alley	25	F	Servant	25Ma02Ha
KELLY, Anne	16	F	Servant	25Ma02Ha
RODAN, Pat	35	M	Laborer	25Ma02Ha
David	14	M	Laborer	25Ma02Ha
MCGAVRAN, Jas.	20	M	Laborer	25Ma02Ha
MURRAY, Garrett	25	M	Laborer	25Ma02Ha
CULLEN, Biddy	22	F	Servant	25Ma02Ha
Nancy	20	F	Servant	25Ma02Ha
BANNIN, Bridgt.	20	F	Servant	25Ma02Ha
Mry	22	F	Servant	25Ma02Ha
HORRIGAN, Ellen	25	F	Servant	25Ma02Ha
Johan.	20	F	Servant	25Ma02Ha
NUGENT, Cath.	21	F	Servant	25Ma02Ha
COSTELLO, Bridgt.	20	F	Servant	25Ma02Ha
WALSH, John	22	M	Laborer	25Ma02Ha
CONROY, Michl.	34	M	Laborer	25Ma02Ha
GREY, Joseph	17	M	Laborer	25Ma02Ha
Robt.	42	M	Laborer	25Ma02Ha
MCCAFFRY, Thomas	40	M	Mechanic	25Ma02Ha
Margt.	40	F	Unknown	25Ma02Ha
Frank	22	M	Servant	25Ma02Ha
Eliza	12	F	Unknown	25Ma02Ha
Anne	11	F	Unknown	25Ma02Ha
CRANFORD, William	25	M	Laborer	25Ma02Ha
WHITE, Thomas	45	M	Mechanic	25Ma02Ha
NEIL, John	20	M	Laborer	25Ma02Ha
COONAN, James	17	M	Laborer	25Ma02Ha
ERWIN, Willm.	25	M	Laborer	25Ma02Ha
Hannah	20	F	Unknown	25Ma02Ha
PARSENS, Frank	28	M	Laborer	25Ma02Ha
Richard	19	M	Laborer	25Ma02Ha
DELANY, Joseph	16	M	Laborer	25Ma02Ha
ODONNELL, Peter	20	M	Laborer	25Ma02Ha
MAGRUY, Pat	30	M	Laborer	25Ma02Ha
Thomas	15	M	Laborer	25Ma02Ha
MARTIN, Pat	20	M	Laborer	25Ma02Ha
Bessy	18	F	Servant	25Ma02Ha
REILY, Anne	16	F	Servant	25Ma02Ha
DOYLE, James	20	M	Laborer	25Ma02Ha
WHITTLE, John	22	M	Laborer	25Ma02Ha
Mary	18	F	Servant	25Ma02Ha
MCCORMAN, Owen	30	M	Laborer	25Ma02Ha
Margt.	24	F	Unknown	25Ma02Ha
Pat	6	M	Child	25Ma02Ha
Thomas	4	M	Child	25Ma02Ha
Mary	8	F	Child	25Ma02Ha
DODD, Charles	20	M	Mechanic	25Ma02Ha
CARROLL, James	18	M	Mechanic	25Ma02Ha
HAGERTY, Larry	18	M	Mechanic	25Ma02Ha
SMITH, Tho.	41	M	Laborer	25Ma02Ha
Bernard	18	M	Laborer	25Ma02Ha
HURST, Henry	19	M	Laborer	25Ma02Ha
HENRY, Edward	19	M	Laborer	25Ma02Ha
TIERNAN, Pat	20	M	Laborer	25Ma02Ha
Thomas	9	M	Child	25Ma02Ha
Mrgt.	20	F	Unknown	25Ma02Ha
SHANNAHAN, Ellen	18	F	Servant	25Ma02Ha
FARRELL, Lawrence	27	M	Laborer	25Ma02Ha
RAFFERTY, James	20	M	Laborer	25Ma02Ha
MCGUIRE, James	48	M	Laborer	25Ma02Ha
MCCAY, Anne	21	F	Servant	25Ma02Ha
DRALY, Anne	22	F	Servant	25Ma02Ha
EGAN, Mary	21	F	Servant	25Ma02Ha
CHRISTIAN, Rose	30	F	Servant	25Ma02Ha
FLANNERY, Biddy	35	F	Servant	25Ma02Ha
FARRELL, Margt.	23	F	Servant	25Ma02Ha
WILLSON, Henry	22	M	Laborer	25Ma02Ha
POTTS, Lewis	24	M	Laborer	25Ma02Ha
TIMON, Timothy	56	M	Laborer	25Ma02Ha
KERNS, Pat	24	M	Laborer	25Ma02Ha
TIGHE, John	35	M	Carpenter	25Ma02Ha
Eliza	34	F	Unknown	25Ma02Ha
Thos.	12	M	Unknown	25Ma02Ha
Margt.	10	F	Unknown	25Ma02Ha
Winny	6	F	Child	25Ma02Ha
Ellen	3	F	Child	25Ma02Ha

NAMES OF PASSENGERS	AGE	SEX	OCCUPATIONS	DATE PORT SHIP
TIGHE. Jane	9	F	Child	25Ma02Ha
ENGLISH, Phillip	24	M	Laborer	25Ma02Ha
Patk.	18	M	Laborer	25Ma02Ha
QUINN. Matt	28	M	Laborer	25Ma02Ha
SKELLY. John	22	M	Laborer	25Ma02Ha
GOULDING, Cath.	16	F	Servant	25Ma02Ha
SKELLY. Mary	20	F	Servant	25Ma02Ha
CANNY. Ellen	17	F	Servant	25Ma02Ha
NORMAN, Mary	60	F	Unknown	25Ma02Ha
Teresa	30	F	Unknown	25Ma02Ha
Anny	3	F	Child	25Ma02Ha
Thos.	.10	M	Infant	25Ma02Ha
Ben	40	M	Laborer	25Ma02Ha
John	23	M	Laborer	25Ma02Ha
DOYLE. Willm.	40	M	Laborer	25Ma02Ha
Cath.	40	F	Unknown	25Ma02Ha
Dan	12	M	Unknown	25Ma02Ha
Wm.	13	M	Unknown	25Ma02Ha
Peter	11	M	Unknown	25Ma02Ha
Pat	6	M	Child	25Ma02Ha
MURR. Thos.	37	M	Laborer	25Ma02Ha
MARR. Jane	30	F	Unknown	25Ma02Ha
Margt.	7	F	Child	25Ma02Ha
Pat	3	M	Child	25Ma02Ha
Eliza	50	F	Unknown	25Ma02Ha
MARNELL, Thos.	30	M	Laborer	25Ma02Ha
FITZGERALD. Mary	29	F	Servant	25Ma02Ha
NARY. Ellen	29	F	Servant	25Ma02Ha
MARNELL, Ellen	3	F	Child	25Ma02Ha
GRACE. Pierce	32	M	Laborer	25Ma02Ha
Ellen	31	F	Unknown	25Ma02Ha
KENNY. Cath.	29	F	Servant	25Ma02Ha
LARENS. Cath.	12	F	Unknown	25Ma02Ha
GRACE. Anty	3	F	Child	25Ma02Ha
John	.05	M	Infant	25Ma02Ha
MARROSSE. Richd.	32	M	Laborer	25Ma02Ha
LANNAGAN, Mary	17	F	Laborer	25Ma02Ha
TRACEY. Martin	60	M	Unknown	25Ma02Ha
FAGAN. John	38	M	Mechanic	25Ma02Ha
WALSH, Hester	30	F	Servant	25Ma02Ha
COSTELO. Eliza	20	F	Servant	25Ma02Ha
DONOHUE. Margt.	22	F	Servant	25Ma02Ha
REILY. Margt.	33	F	Unknown	25Ma02Ha
Phil.	1	M	Child	25Ma02Ha
GANLEY. Jas.	34	M	Laborer	25Ma02Ha
Jane	30	F	Unknown	25Ma02Ha
Richard	7	M	Child	25Ma02Ha
Ellen	10	F	Unknown	25Ma02Ha
James	.11	M	Infant	25Ma02Ha
CLARK. Hugh	41	M	Carpenter	25Ma02Ha
John	21	M	Carpenter	25Ma02Ha
John	19	M	Carpenter	25Ma02Ha
CHAMBERLAIN. Richard	24	M	Laborer	25Ma02Ha
John	21	M	Laborer	25Ma02Ha
FLYNN, Christ.	26	M	Laborer	25Ma02Ha
GANNAN. John	24	M	Laborer	25Ma02Ha
KERNAN, Margt.	18	F	Servant	25Ma02Ha
QUINN, Bridgt.	18	F	Servant	25Ma02Ha
GREY. Anne	17	F	Servant	25Ma02Ha
CONNER. Margt.	18	F	Servant	25Ma02Ha
MOLONY. John	16	M	Laborer	25Ma02Ha
COUGHLAN. James	20	M	Laborer	25Ma02Ha
Cath.	18	F	Servant	25Ma02Ha
SMITH, F.K.	26	M	Mechanic	25Ma02Ha
DILLON, Pat	45	M	Laborer	25Ma02Ha
Cath.	45	F	Servant	25Ma02Ha
Ellen	2	F	Unknown	25Ma02Ha
Cath.	4	F	Child	25Ma02Ha
BROWN. Joha.	16	F	Servant	25Ma02Ha
BARRY. Joha.	28	F	Servant	25Ma02Ha
KEDDIGAN, Eliza	4	F	Child	25Ma02Ha
WHITE. Bridgt.	25	F	Servant	25Ma02Ha
KERNEFALY. Mary	20	F	Servant	25Ma02Ha
TWOONY. Tim.	20	M	Laborer	25Ma02Ha
BENLER. Cath.	30	F	Unknown	25Ma02Ha

NAMES OF PASSENGERS	AGE	SEX	OCCUPATIONS	DATE PORT SHIP
BENLER, Pat	6	M	Child	25Ma02Ha
HALL, Willm.	23	M	Laborer	25Ma02Ha
Saml.	18	M	Laborer	25Ma02Ha
John	14	M	Laborer	25Ma02Ha
HENNESSY. Martin	23	M	Laborer	25Ma02Ha
DONOHUE. Michl.	14	M	Laborer	25Ma02Ha
HALL, Betty	45	F	Unknown	25Ma02Ha
Mary	13	F	Unknown	25Ma02Ha
George	9	M	Child	25Ma02Ha
Eliza	5	F	Child	25Ma02Ha
Thos.	.06	M	Infant	25Ma02Ha
FARRELL, Willm.	36	M	Laborer	25Ma02Ha
HENRY. Pat.	30	M	Laborer	25Ma02Ha
ODONNELL, Willm.	18	M	Laborer	25Ma02Ha
CAW, Jane	20	F	Servant	25Ma02Ha
DAVIS, Mary	18	F	Servant	25Ma02Ha
DEMPSTER. Cath.	16	F	Servant	25Ma02Ha
HALLAHAN, Ellen	18	F	Servant	25Ma02Ha
BURNS, Margt.	17	F	Servant	25Ma02Ha
CARROLL, Bridgt.	30	F	Servant	25Ma02Ha
CARESSY. Ellen	12	F	Unknown	25Ma02Ha
Jas.	10	M	Unknown	25Ma02Ha
DUNLEVY. Mary	17	F	Servant	25Ma02Ha
JENNINGS, Mary	11	F	Unknown	25Ma02Ha
GORMAN, Anne	24	F	Servant	25Ma02Ha
HELAN, Bridgt.	20	F	Servant	25Ma02Ha
FAGAN, Hessy	20	F	Servant	25Ma02Ha
JORDAN, Cath.	14	F	Servant	25Ma02Ha
CASEY. Biddy	9	F	Child	25Ma02Ha
MEAGHER, Biddy	4	F	Child	25Ma02Ha
HYMES. Biddy	15	F	Unknown	25Ma02Ha
CASEY. Michl.	22	M	Laborer	25Ma02Ha
Peter	20	M	Laborer	25Ma02Ha
MEAGHER. Thos.	28	M	Laborer	25Ma02Ha
SMITH, Pat	24	M	Laborer	25Ma02Ha
GRANT. Jas.	45	M	Laborer	25Ma02Ha
Anne	30	F	Unknown	25Ma02Ha
Cath.	4	F	Child	25Ma02Ha
Mary	3	F	Child	25Ma02Ha
Michl.	.09	M	Infant	25Ma02Ha
MATHEWS. Peter	36	M	Laborer	25Ma02Ha
Margt.	36	F	Unknown	25Ma02Ha
Biddy	3	F	Child	25Ma02Ha
Anne	.10	F	Infant	25Ma02Ha
CONNELL. Michl.	23	M	Mechanic	25Ma02Ha
DINNEAN, Joha.	23	F	Unknown	25Ma02Ha
CUNNINGHAM. John	32	M	Laborer	25Ma02Ha
QUIGLY. James	36	M	Laborer	25Ma02Ha
FINN, Michl.	28	M	Laborer	25Ma02Ha
FLURNTON, Jas.	26	M	Laborer	25Ma02Ha
QUINN, Mary	18	F	Servant	25Ma02Ha
FEE. Hugh	25	M	Laborer	25Ma02Ha
QUIGLY. Alley	18	F	Servant	25Ma02Ha
MURPHY. Mary	25	F	Servant	25Ma02Ha
FINN, Anne	19	F	Servant	25Ma02Ha
BRADLY. Jas.	30	M	Laborer	25Ma02Ha
Mary	8	F	Child	25Ma02Ha
Cath.	5	F	Child	25Ma02Ha
IGO. Jas.	22	M	Laborer	25Ma02Ha
FITZPATRICK. Terence	28	M	Laborer	25Ma02Ha
FLAHERTY. John	30	M	Laborer	25Ma02Ha
SULLIVAN. Julia	20	F	Servant	25Ma02Ha
Pat	6	M	Child	25Ma02Ha
FLYNN, Tho.	26	M	Laborer	25Ma02Ha
MURPHY. James	20	M	Laborer	25Ma02Ha
NALLY. Jas.	24	M	Laborer	25Ma02Ha
WARD. Thos.	17	M	Laborer	25Ma02Ha
Ellen	26	F	Servant	25Ma02Ha
MARSLEY. Ellen	22	F	Servant	25Ma02Ha
WARD. Bridgt.	22	F	Unknown	25Ma02Ha
DAWSON. Anne	18	F	Servant	25Ma02Ha
LEYDEN. Cathn.	20	F	Servant	25Ma02Ha
SKINNES. Mary	20	F	Servant	25Ma02Ha
Mary	2	F	Child	25Ma02Ha
TRULEY. Joha.	18	F	Servant	25Ma02Ha

NAMES OF PASSENGERS	AGE	SEX	OCCUPATIONS	DATE PORT SHIP
DORAN, Margt.	20	F	Unknown	25Ma02Ha
ROONEY, James	4	M	Child	25Ma02Ha
Margt.	3	F	Child	25Ma02Ha
BRITT, John	28	M	Laborer	25Ma02Ha
Wm.	28	M	Laborer	25Ma02Ha
DUMPHY, Michl.	23	M	Laborer	25Ma02Ha
COMAN, Thomas	24	M	Laborer	25Ma02Ha
MAHER, John	26	M	Laborer	25Ma02Ha
LYNCH, Andy	60	M	Laborer	25Ma02Ha
Mary	30	F	Unknown	25Ma02Ha
DUFFY, Judy	10	F	Unknown	25Ma02Ha
Mary	15	F	Unknown	25Ma02Ha
CUSAC, Mary	17	F	Servant	25Ma02Ha
Anne	19	F	Servant	25Ma02Ha
Norry	30	F	Servant	25Ma02Ha
BRITT, Cath.	19	F	Servant	25Ma02Ha
DUMPHY, Mary	30	F	Servant	25Ma02Ha
COMAN, Honora	60	F	Unknown	25Ma02Ha
Margt.	30	F	Servant	25Ma02Ha
BRITT, Bridgt.	13	F	Servant	25Ma02Ha
ROCHE, Jas.	21	M	Laborer	25Ma02Ha
Mary	26	F	Unknown	25Ma02Ha
OBRIEN, Jane	50	F	Unknown	25Ma02Ha
Felix	18	M	Laborer	25Ma02Ha
Andy	14	M	Laborer	25Ma02Ha
Pat	12	M	Unknown	25Ma02Ha
MCCANN, John	25	M	Laborer	25Ma02Ha
BOYLAN, Pat	25	M	Laborer	25Ma02Ha
GREEN, Terence	40	M	Laborer	25Ma02Ha
MCDERMOTT, Anne	20	F	Servant	25Ma02Ha
MURTY, Martha	18	F	Servant	25Ma02Ha
Anny	17	F	Servant	25Ma02Ha
SEDLARD, Cath.	22	F	Servant	25Ma02Ha
MCKERRY, Mary-A.	22	F	Unknown	25Ma02Ha
Pat	7	M	Child	25Ma02Ha
Teresa	5	F	Child	25Ma02Ha
BROOKS, Bridgt.	50	F	Unknown	25Ma02Ha
Patk.	33	M	Laborer	25Ma02Ha
MCNALLY, Pat	13	M	Unknown	25Ma02Ha
MCCABE, Anne	20	F	Servant	25Ma02Ha
TALCHRIST, Christn.	31	M	Laborer	25Ma02Ha
WALSH, Pat	33	M	Laborer	25Ma02Ha
DODD, Mary	16	F	Servant	25Ma02Ha
THOMAS, Ed.	36	M	Laborer	25Ma02Ha
Ellen	36	F	Unknown	25Ma02Ha
Anne	9	F	Child	25Ma02Ha
Hugh	2	M	Child	25Ma02Ha
REYNOLDS, Bernard	22	M	Laborer	25Ma02Ha
LEAHY, John	12	M	Unknown	25Ma02Ha
Thos.	10	M	Unknown	25Ma02Ha
Jas.	8	M	Child	25Ma02Ha
WOODS, Cath.	30	F	Servant	25Ma02Ha
LEAHY, Joha.	33	F	Servant	25Ma02Ha
TARBEST, Pat	6	M	Child	25Ma02Ha
BURNS, Biddy	18	F	Servant	25Ma02Ha
FITZMORRIS, Jas.	23	M	Laborer	25Ma02Ha
DUNN, Danl.	23	M	Laborer	25Ma02Ha
LEEN, Maurice	20	M	Laborer	25Ma02Ha
David	24	M	Laborer	25Ma02Ha
BURNS, Cath.	12	F	Unknown	25Ma02Ha
Pat	18	M	Servant	25Ma02Ha
MURPHY, John	50	M	Laborer	25Ma02Ha
MEAGHER, Con.	20	M	Laborer	25Ma02Ha
HASSETT, Thos.	32	M	Laborer	25Ma02Ha
BRENNAN, Joseph	25	M	Laborer	25Ma02Ha
DELAHUNTY, Rose	28	F	Servant	25Ma02Ha
BRADDLE, Honor	27	F	Servant	25Ma02Ha
MURPHY, Mary	13	F	Servant	25Ma02Ha
BRADDLE, Thos.	8	M	Child	25Ma02Ha
SWEENY, Charles	18	M	Servant	25Ma02Ha
GALLAHER, John	16	M	Servant	25Ma02Ha
HORRIGAN, Michl.	19	M	Laborer	25Ma02Ha
MORAN, Cath.	50	F	Unknown	25Ma02Ha
FARRELL, Mary	18	F	Servant	25Ma02Ha
KEEFFE, Anne	16	F	Servant	25Ma02Ha

NAMES OF PASSENGERS	AGE	SEX	OCCUPATIONS	DATE PORT SHIP
KEEFFE, Ellen	14	F	Servant	25Ma02Ha
BRENNAN, Thos.	20	M	Laborer	25Ma02Ha
FARRELL, Peter	20	M	Laborer	25Ma02Ha
LEEN, Thos.	24	M	Laborer	25Ma02Ha
MAHONEY, Cath.	30	F	Servant	25Ma02Ha
CLERK, Mary	8	F	Child	25Ma02Ha
MCCARTHY, John	28	M	Laborer	25Ma02Ha
HENESSY, Danl.	29	M	Laborer	25Ma02Ha
DONOVAN, Michl.	27	M	Laborer	25Ma02Ha
CLARY, Ellen	25	F	Servant	25Ma02Ha
FLYNN, Judy	19	F	Servant	25Ma02Ha
FOLEY, Jas.	35	M	Laborer	25Ma02Ha
SULLIVAN, Danl.	20	M	Laborer	25Ma02Ha
HALLERAN, Jas.	20	M	Laborer	25Ma02Ha
DASY, Mary	16	F	Servant	25Ma02Ha
LAWTON, Mary	20	F	Servant	25Ma02Ha
CULLNANE, Joha.	28	F	Servant	25Ma02Ha
WHITE, Cath.	23	F	Servant	25Ma02Ha
SHIELDS, Frank	25	M	Laborer	25Ma02Ha
MURPHY, Pat	34	M	Laborer	25Ma02Ha
HODGIN, Jas.	12	M	Unknown	25Ma02Ha
Anne	14	F	Unknown	25Ma02Ha
FARREN, Ellen	20	F	Servant	25Ma02Ha
MCIVIE, George	19	M	Laborer	25Ma02Ha
DOAD, Michl.	30	M	Laborer	25Ma02Ha
MULOCHIN, Timty.	22	M	Laborer	25Ma02Ha
CANNING, Edward	36	M	Laborer	25Ma02Ha
ODONNELL, Wm.	26	M	Laborer	25Ma02Ha
COLLINS, Peter	21	M	Laborer	25Ma02Ha
MCGRUTHER, Pat	23	M	Laborer	25Ma02Ha
SHALVY, Pat	28	M	Laborer	25Ma02Ha
SHEVLIN, Owen	50	M	Laborer	25Ma02Ha
MCGARRY, Cath.	34	F	Unknown	25Ma02Ha
Timty.	5	M	Child	25Ma02Ha
CANNING, Cathn.	8	F	Child	25Ma02Ha
Margt.	10	F	Unknown	25Ma02Ha
MERRITY, Julia	24	F	Servant	25Ma02Ha
GRADY, Eliza	18	F	Servant	25Ma02Ha
Mary	20	F	Servant	25Ma02Ha
MOLLNY, Bridgt.	16	F	Servant	25Ma02Ha
BANNIN, Pat	10	M	Unknown	25Ma02Ha
Anne	18	F	Servant	25Ma02Ha
MCGARDY, Anne	20	F	Servant	25Ma02Ha
LOVE, Elgin	18	F	Servant	25Ma02Ha
HAGERTY, Cath.	40	F	Servant	25Ma02Ha
MCCORMAC, Margt.	20	F	Servant	25Ma02Ha
HAGERTY, Mary	14	F	Unknown	25Ma02Ha
Alley	12	F	Unknown	25Ma02Ha
Margt.	10	F	Unknown	25Ma02Ha
MCCALL, Bernard	38	M	Laborer	25Ma02Ha
ADRICE, Thos.	7	M	Child	25Ma02Ha
Mry	11	F	Unknown	25Ma02Ha
DALY, Jas.	46	M	Laborer	25Ma02Ha
SHEKELTON, Thos.	25	M	Laborer	25Ma02Ha
DALY, Thos.	20	M	Laborer	25Ma02Ha
POWER, Mary	19	F	Servant	25Ma02Ha
LANE, Mary	14	F	Servant	25Ma02Ha
Margt.	11	F	Unknown	25Ma02Ha
SHALVY, Rose	20	F	Servant	25Ma02Ha
CONWAY, Darby	34	M	Laborer	25Ma02Ha
TWOOMY, Maurice	22	M	Laborer	25Ma02Ha
HALY, Danl.	22	M	Laborer	25Ma02Ha
CONWAY, Michl.	8	M	Child	25Ma02Ha
MAHONY, Judy	17	F	Servant	25Ma02Ha
KENNY, Biddy	22	F	Servant	25Ma02Ha
MCCARTHY, Margt.	20	F	Servant	25Ma02Ha
CONNELL, Sally	20	F	Servant	25Ma02Ha
GOGGIN, Margt.	22	F	Servant	25Ma02Ha
FORD, Cath.	25	F	Servant	25Ma02Ha
GOGGIN, Sarah	20	F	Servant	25Ma02Ha
FITZPATRICK, Wm.	16	M	Laborer	25Ma02Ha
Winefred	14	F	Unknown	25Ma02Ha
SKEKELTON, Anne	20	F	Servant	25Ma02Ha
QUIGLY, Mary	22	F	Servant	25Ma02Ha
DALTON, Bridgt.	30	F	Servant	25Ma02Ha

NAMES OF PASSENGERS	AGE	SEX	OCCUPATIONS	DATE PORT SHIP
WILLETT, Ellen	49	F	Servant	25Ma02Ha
MOLLONY, Biddy	30	F	Servant	25Ma02Ha
DALY, Ellen	20	F	Servant	25Ma02Ha
FLANNAGAN, Isabella	26	F	Servant	25Ma02Ha
MCEVAN, Rose	42	F	Servant	25Ma02Ha
MAVILLE, Cath.	21	F	Servant	25Ma02Ha
MCEVAN, Anne	22	F	Servant	25Ma02Ha
DALY, Tim	25	M	Laborer	25Ma02Ha
Cath.	20	F	Unknown	25Ma02Ha
Mry	3	F	Child	25Ma02Ha
LYNN, Richd.	27	M	Laborer	25Ma02Ha
CALLAGHAN, Mary	24	F	Servant	25Ma02Ha
CALLAGHER, Timothy	.10	M	Infant	25Ma02Ha
SULLIVAN, David	37	M	Laborer	25Ma02Ha
Pat	11	M	Unknown	25Ma02Ha
Jerry	9	M	Child	25Ma02Ha
Mary	7	F	Child	25Ma02Ha
BENNETT, David	30	M	Laborer	25Ma02Ha
Joha.	25	F	Servant	25Ma02Ha
Judy	20	F	Servant	25Ma02Ha
Mary	22	F	Servant	25Ma02Ha
MCKLERN, Pat	37	M	Laborer	25Ma02Ha
Pat	11	M	Unknown	25Ma02Ha
Thomas	9	M	Child	25Ma02Ha
NEIL, Joseph	26	M	Laborer	25Ma02Ha
PRICE, John	60	M	Laborer	25Ma02Ha
Margt.	44	F	Unknown	25Ma02Ha
MOCOTE, Eliza	44	F	Unknown	25Ma02Ha
Mary	25	F	Servant	25Ma02Ha
MCCARTHY, Wm.	47	M	Farmer	25Ma02Ha
Margt.	45	F	Farmer	25Ma02Ha
Eliza	19	F	Farmer	25Ma02Ha
Margt.	17	F	Farmer	25Ma02Ha
Mary	8	F	Child	25Ma02Ha
Grace	4	F	Child	25Ma02Ha
M.	13	M	Farmer	25Ma02Ha
Isaac	20	M	Laborer	25Ma02Ha
Willm.	10	M	Unknown	25Ma02Ha
Robt.	6	M	Child	25Ma02Ha
PRICE, Robt.	40	M	Laborer	25Ma02Ha
Ellen	24	F	Laborer	25Ma02Ha
Richard	.11	M	Infant	25Ma02Ha
John	16	M	Laborer	25Ma02Ha
Thomas	3	M	Child	25Ma02Ha
DAVIS, Edward	30	M	Laborer	25Ma02Ha
EDWARDS, Jas.	32	M	Laborer	25Ma02Ha
Anny	30	F	Unknown	25Ma02Ha
HALL, Anne	32	F	Unknown	25Ma02Ha
Wm.	7	M	Child	25Ma02Ha
Thos.	4	M	Child	25Ma02Ha
MORGAN, Richd.	37	M	Laborer	25Ma02Ha
FERTH, Charles	40	M	Farmer	25Ma02Ha
Sarah	36	F	Unknown	25Ma02Ha
George	12	M	Unknown	25Ma02Ha
Joseph	10	M	Unknown	25Ma02Ha
Alex.	8	M	Child	25Ma02Ha
Charles	7	M	Child	25Ma02Ha
Isaac	3	M	Child	25Ma02Ha
Mary-A.	14	F	Unknown	25Ma02Ha
Thos.	16	M	Unknown	25Ma02Ha
CLEBORN, Robt.	24	M	Unknown	25Ma02Ha
LLOYD, Gilbert	48	M	Farmer	25Ma02Ha
Maria	11	F	Unknown	25Ma02Ha
Letitia	9	F	Child	25Ma02Ha
Cath.	3	F	Child	25Ma02Ha
Gilbert	.10	M	Infant	25Ma02Ha
FITZGERALD, Cath.	30	F	Servant	25Ma02Ha
LEAHY, Louisa	28	F	Servant	25Ma02Ha
Harriett	30	F	Servant	25Ma02Ha
John-Price	40	M	Farmer	25Ma02Ha
Martha	25	F	Unknown	25Ma02Ha
Bridget	60	F	Unknown	25Ma02Ha
Jane	18	F	Unknown	25Ma02Ha
Anne	10	F	Unknown	25Ma02Ha
Mry	7	F	Child	25Ma02Ha
BOWEN, Anne	25	F	Servant	25Ma02Ha
MCLAUN, Michl.	18	M	Laborer	25Ma02Ha
SCANLAN, Thos.	20	M	Laborer	25Ma02Ha
DUANE, Dennis	25	M	Laborer	25Ma02Ha
QUINN, Pat.	20	M	Laborer	25Ma02Ha
SLATTERY, Martin	50	M	Laborer	25Ma02Ha
John	18	M	Laborer	25Ma02Ha
FATHER, Michl.	24	M	Laborer	25Ma02Ha
WARD, Martin	20	M	Laborer	25Ma02Ha
TOBIN, Julia	20	F	Servant	25Ma02Ha
MORRIS, Bridgt.	20	F	Servant	25Ma02Ha
LANGSTAFF, John	35	M	Laborer	25Ma02Ha
Maria	30	F	Unknown	25Ma02Ha
Matilda	11	F	Unknown	25Ma02Ha
John	2	M	Child	25Ma02Ha
NURNAN, John	35	M	Laborer	25Ma02Ha
DRUMHAN, John	25	M	Laborer	25Ma02Ha
DARGAN, Willm.	30	M	Laborer	25Ma02Ha
BARRY, Garrett	26	M	Laborer	25Ma02Ha
Michl.	25	M	Laborer	25Ma02Ha
John	23	M	Laborer	25Ma02Ha
GALVIN, Michl.	20	M	Laborer	25Ma02Ha
CALLAGHAN, Pat	26	M	Laborer	25Ma02Ha
CURTIN, John	30	M	Laborer	25Ma02Ha
BARRY, Bridgt.	20	F	Servant	25Ma02Ha
CURTIN, Anne	18	F	Servant	25Ma02Ha
REILY, Rose	22	F	Servant	25Ma02Ha
CAVARNY, Mary	20	F	Servant	25Ma02Ha
COSGROVE, Margt.	20	F	Servant	25Ma02Ha
MANN, Sarah	60	F	Servant	25Ma02Ha
Martha	20	F	Servant	25Ma02Ha
LYNAM, Margt.	17	F	Servant	25Ma02Ha
DROUGHTON, Anne	28	F	Servant	25Ma02Ha
MANN, Michl.	18	M	Laborer	25Ma02Ha
Pat	32	M	Laborer	25Ma02Ha
DROAK, Jas.	23	M	Laborer	25Ma02Ha
JUDGE, Robt.	16	M	Laborer	25Ma02Ha
MCCORMAC, Michl.	20	M	Laborer	25Ma02Ha
DALY, Pat	35	M	Laborer	25Ma02Ha
Rose	32	F	Unknown	25Ma02Ha
Bridgt.	7	F	Child	25Ma02Ha
Wm.	5	M	Child	25Ma02Ha
Mary	3	F	Child	25Ma02Ha
Julia	.06	F	Infant	25Ma02Ha
HARNON, James	30	M	Laborer	25Ma02Ha
COLLINS, Dennis	21	M	Laborer	25Ma02Ha
HIERNAN, Dennis	18	M	Laborer	25Ma02Ha
GOLEY, Andw.	35	M	Laborer	25Ma02Ha
DROAK, Margt.	18	F	Servant	25Ma02Ha
JUDGE, Martha	17	F	Servant	25Ma02Ha
GOGGIN, Eliza	21	F	Servant	25Ma02Ha
JUDGE, Eliza	18	F	Servant	25Ma02Ha
CARTER, James	48	M	Laborer	25Ma02Ha
John	9	M	Child	25Ma02Ha
Anne	16	F	Servant	25Ma02Ha
KILECHER, Ellen	40	F	Unknown	25Ma02Ha
Bessy	9	F	Child	25Ma02Ha
Andy	7	M	Child	25Ma02Ha
SMITH, Cath.	50	F	Servant	25Ma02Ha
MULLEN, Bridgt.	18	F	Servant	25Ma02Ha
MURPHY, Ann	18	F	Servant	25Ma02Ha
WHITNEY, Margt.	45	F	Servant	25Ma02Ha
ROWLAN, Mary	40	F	Servant	25Ma02Ha
CLERK, Mary	18	F	Servant	25Ma02Ha
ROWLAN, Ellen	.11	F	Infant	25Ma02Ha
ONEIL, Owen	27	M	Laborer	25Ma02Ha
Mary-Anne	24	F	Unknown	25Ma02Ha
DEMPSEY, Michl.	60	M	Laborer	25Ma02Ha
Julia	50	F	Unknown	25Ma02Ha
Anne	20	F	Servant	25Ma02Ha
Bridgt.	16	F	Servant	25Ma02Ha
Michl.	11	M	Unknown	25Ma02Ha
Cath.	9	F	Child	25Ma02Ha
BENSON, John	45	M	Laborer	25Ma02Ha
Mary	25	F	Servant	25Ma02Ha

NAMES OF PASSENGERS	AGE	SEX	OCCUPATIONS	DATE PORT SHIP
MCLOUGHLAN, Pat	55	M	Laborer	25Ma02Ha
Ellen	22	F	Servant	25Ma02Ha
CARINGS, Mary	20	F	Servant	25Ma02Ha
MCTIERNAN, Ellen	20	F	Servant	25Ma02Ha
LLOYD, Wm.	30	M	Farmer	25Ma02Ha
Sarah	31	F	Unknown	25Ma02Ha
Georgina	.03	F	Infant	25Ma02Ha
Willm.	3	M	Child	25Ma02Ha
COUGHLAN, Mary	21	F	Servant	25Ma02Ha
SKELLY, Mary	20	F	Servant	25Ma02Ha
COAN, Jas.	16	M	Laborer	25Ma02Ha

DEVONIA 25 MAY 1850

From Bristol

NAMES OF PASSENGERS	AGE	SEX	OCCUPATIONS	DATE PORT SHIP
BRAIN, Silas	23	M	Laborer	25Ma34Fi
MOODY, James	19	M	Laborer	25Ma34Fi
GRIFFITH, Joseph	21	M	Laborer	25Ma34Fi
GIBBS, Martha	20	F	Unknown	25Ma34Fi
Joseph	24	M	Farmer	25Ma34Fi
MILLARD, Stephen	50	M	Farmer	25Ma34Fi
Hester	24	F	Unknown	25Ma34Fi
U	.00	U	Infant	25Ma34Fi
Robert	10	M	Unknown	25Ma34Fi
George	4	M	Child	25Ma34Fi
TAYLOR, Sarah	26	F	Unknown	25Ma34Fi
U	.00	U	Infant	25Ma34Fi
Ann	5	F	Child	25Ma34Fi
Ellen	3	F	Child	25Ma34Fi
MILLAN, Elizabeth	2	F	Child	25Ma34Fi
HAM, John	22	M	Farmer	25Ma34Fi
Harriett	20	F	Unknown	25Ma34Fi
John	21	M	Farmer	25Ma34Fi
CORP, Sidney	19	M	Farmer	25Ma34Fi
COWARD, Charles	20	M	Farmer	25Ma34Fi
BURROW, William	26	M	Farmer	25Ma34Fi
HIGGS, James	19	M	Farmer	25Ma34Fi
NICHOLS, Mary	44	F	W-Labr	25Ma34Fi
Eliza	12	F	Unknown	25Ma34Fi
Robert	10	M	Unknown	25Ma34Fi
Mary-Ann	8	F	Child	25Ma34Fi
Emma	7	F	Child	25Ma34Fi
WALL, Robert	27	M	Laborer	25Ma34Fi
Ann	32	F	Unknown	25Ma34Fi
U	.00	U	Infant	25Ma34Fi
John	11	M	Unknown	25Ma34Fi
Ann	8	F	Child	25Ma34Fi
Ruth	6	F	Child	25Ma34Fi
William	2	M	Child	25Ma34Fi
HEBBARD, Stephen	33	M	Laborer	25Ma34Fi
William	26	M	Laborer	25Ma34Fi
CHANT, Fredk.	33	M	Laborer	25Ma34Fi
DOWDING, Mary	50	F	Unknown	25Ma34Fi
John	2	M	Child	25Ma34Fi
MEEHAN, Charles	18	M	Laborer	25Ma34Fi
KEEN, Abraham	28	M	Farmer	25Ma34Fi
Elizabeth	24	F	Unknown	25Ma34Fi
BAKER, Richard	21	M	Farmer	25Ma34Fi
PROSSER, Thomas	39	M	Farmer	25Ma34Fi
Ann	37	F	Unknown	25Ma34Fi
William	10	M	Unknown	25Ma34Fi
Maria	7	F	Child	25Ma34Fi
Betsey	5	F	Child	25Ma34Fi
John	3	M	Child	25Ma34Fi
JAMES, John	40	M	Farmer	25Ma34Fi
Eliza	40	F	Unknown	25Ma34Fi
Henry	13	M	Unknown	25Ma34Fi
William	10	M	Unknown	25Ma34Fi

NAMES OF PASSENGERS	AGE	SEX	OCCUPATIONS	DATE PORT SHIP
SHIPWAY, Thomas	40	M	Farmer	25Ma34Fi
Ann	35	F	Unknown	25Ma34Fi
Mary-Ann	13	F	Unknown	25Ma34Fi
Sarah	11	F	Unknown	25Ma34Fi
Martha	9	F	Child	25Ma34Fi
Ann	8	F	Child	25Ma34Fi
Thomas	5	M	Child	25Ma34Fi
Elizabeth	3	F	Child	25Ma34Fi
BURLETON, Henry	38	M	Ctldlr	25Ma34Fi
George	32	M	Mason	25Ma34Fi
FITZMAURICE, Hannah	25	F	Unknown	25Ma34Fi
WARREN, Jane	30	F	Unknown	25Ma34Fi
U	.00	U	Infant	25Ma34Fi
John	8	M	Child	25Ma34Fi
Francis	6	M	Child	25Ma34Fi
KIMMINS, John	65	M	Farmer	25Ma34Fi
Jane	34	F	Unknown	25Ma34Fi
JEFFERIES, William	26	M	Laborer	25Ma34Fi
REED, James	25	M	Laborer	25Ma34Fi
Thomas	50	M	Blacksmith	25Ma34Fi
Edith	58	F	Unknown	25Ma34Fi
SHEPPARD, Jane	58	F	Unknown	25Ma34Fi
POWELL, John	24	M	Mason	25Ma34Fi
FEE, Ellen	20	F	Unknown	25Ma34Fi
FLOWER, James	23	M	Farmer	25Ma34Fi
GLOVER, Mary	42	F	Unknown	25Ma34Fi
Elizabeth	21	F	Unknown	25Ma34Fi
Joseph	18	M	Unknown	25Ma34Fi
Andrew	11	M	Unknown	25Ma34Fi
Grace	10	F	Unknown	25Ma34Fi
Catherine	7	F	Child	25Ma34Fi
John	5	M	Child	25Ma34Fi
Thomas	2	M	Child	25Ma34Fi
STONEMAN, Phillip	34	M	Farmer	25Ma34Fi
Sarah	35	F	Unknown	25Ma34Fi
U	.00	U	Infant	25Ma34Fi
James	24	M	Laborer	25Ma34Fi
William	6	M	Child	25Ma34Fi
Died-At-Sea				
Mary-Ann	3	F	Child	25Ma34Fi
JOLLIFFE, John	21	M	Laborer	25Ma34Fi
PANNERSTEIN, Robt.	35	M	Laborer	25Ma34Fi
CUPPER, Mary	35	F	Unknown	25Ma34Fi
DART, Michael	60	F	Farmer	25Ma34Fi
Agnes	59	F	Unknown	25Ma34Fi
William	20	M	Laborer	25Ma34Fi
Elizabeth	13	F	Unknown	25Ma34Fi
Margaret	11	F	Unknown	25Ma34Fi
Michael	27	M	Farmer	25Ma34Fi
Elizabeth	40	F	Unknown	25Ma34Fi
Harriett	3	F	Child	25Ma34Fi
William	12	M	Unknown	25Ma34Fi
NICHOLLS, Sarah	42	F	W-Fmr	25Ma34Fi
Harriett	8	F	Child	25Ma34Fi
Mary-Ann	5	F	Child	25Ma34Fi
GULLIFORD, James	22	M	Unknown	25Ma34Fi
John	18	M	Unknown	25Ma34Fi
HAM, Mary-Ann	.00	F	Infant	25Ma34Fi
Died-At-Sea				
THOMAS, Thomas	25	M	Unknown	25Ma34Fi
ATYEO, Isaac	54	M	Farmer	25Ma34Fi
Hannah	50	F	Unknown	25Ma34Fi
U	.00	F	Infant	25Ma34Fi
John	24	M	Farmer	25Ma34Fi
Thizza	23	F	Unknown	25Ma34Fi
William	22	M	Farmer	25Ma34Fi
George	20	M	Farmer	25Ma34Fi
Charlotte	13	F	Unknown	25Ma34Fi
Isaac	11	M	Unknown	25Ma34Fi
James	9	M	Child	25Ma34Fi
Ann	7	F	Child	25Ma34Fi
Mary	2	F	Child	25Ma34Fi
SAWTELL, Thos.	25	M	Farmer	25Ma34Fi
MEAD, Anthony	25	M	Farmer	25Ma34Fi
ALLEN, Joseph	28	M	Unknown	25Ma34Fi

NAMES OF PASSENGERS	AGE	SEX	OCCUPATIONS	DATE PORT SHIP
THOMAS, William	30	M	Unknown	25Ma34Fi

DEWITT-CLINTON 26 MAY 1850

From Liverpool

NAMES OF PASSENGERS	AGE	SEX	OCCUPATIONS	DATE PORT SHIP
MOTLY, Abraham	28	M	Farmer	26Ma02Ar
Maria	26	F	Unknown	26Ma02Ar
REILLY, Robert	23	M	Laborer	26Ma02Ar
Elizabeth	21	F	Unknown	26Ma02Ar
Rebecca	.10	F	Infant	26Ma02Ar
HOLMES, William	55	M	Farmer	26Ma02Ar
Anna	42	F	Unknown	26Ma02Ar
William	20	M	Farmer	26Ma02Ar
William	21	M	Farmer	26Ma02Ar
George	13	M	Farmer	26Ma02Ar
Mary	11	F	Farmer	26Ma02Ar
Thomas	9	M	Child	26Ma02Ar
Anna	2	F	Child	26Ma02Ar
NOLAN, Margaret	30	F	Servant	26Ma02Ar
GORMAN, Daniel	55	M	Farmer	26Ma02Ar
Bridget	45	F	Unknown	26Ma02Ar
Anne	20	F	Servant	26Ma02Ar
James	18	M	Farmer	26Ma02Ar
Daniel	13	M	Unknown	26Ma02Ar
Patrick	11	M	Unknown	26Ma02Ar
Rose	9	F	Child	26Ma02Ar
John	7	M	Child	26Ma02Ar
BOWAN, Thomas	50	M	Laborer	26Ma02Ar
PROSSOR, David	27	M	Laborer	26Ma02Ar
Wninfred	24	F	Seamstress	26Ma02Ar
John	.11	M	Infant	26Ma02Ar
John	35	M	Laborer	26Ma02Ar
SHACKFIELD, Joseph	25	M	Shoemaker	26Ma02Ar
DOYLE, Edward	20	M	Laborer	26Ma02Ar
Elizabeth	23	F	Servant	26Ma02Ar
NOLAN, Margaret	22	F	Servant	26Ma02Ar
HOGAN, Ann	23	F	Servant	26Ma02Ar
CORCORAN, Catherine	24	F	Servant	26Ma02Ar
HOLDEN, Elizabeth	24	F	Servant	26Ma02Ar
JOYCE, Ann	21	F	Servant	26Ma02Ar
FAHEY, Mary	17	F	Servant	26Ma02Ar
DOYLE, Michael	26	M	Farmer	26Ma02Ar
STAUNTON, Sarah	20	F	Seamstress	26Ma02Ar
CLEARY, Patrick	18	M	Laborer	26Ma02Ar
WILEY, Robert	22	M	Laborer	26Ma02Ar
MCGAN, Margaret	21	F	Laborer	26Ma02Ar
MURPHY, James	25	M	Laborer	26Ma02Ar
HARMON, Alexander	26	M	Laborer	26Ma02Ar
Mary	22	F	Servant	26Ma02Ar
Isabella	.08	F	Infant	26Ma02Ar
Isabella	30	F	Seamstress	26Ma02Ar
Elizabeth	12	F	Unknown	26Ma02Ar
KELLY, Eliza	18	F	Servant	26Ma02Ar
FAHY, James	25	M	Laborer	26Ma02Ar
Mary	28	F	Servant	26Ma02Ar
Ellen	20	F	Servant	26Ma02Ar
Bridget	60	F	Seamstress	26Ma02Ar
Catherine	20	F	Servant	26Ma02Ar
James	38	M	Laborer	26Ma02Ar
Edward	21	M	Laborer	26Ma02Ar
MAHER, Kate	18	F	Servant	26Ma02Ar
MURPHY, James	20	M	Laborer	26Ma02Ar
DWAN, Michael	20	M	Laborer	26Ma02Ar
Alice	20	F	Seamstress	26Ma02Ar
HICKERY, John	25	M	Joiner	26Ma02Ar
Bridget	20	F	Joiner	26Ma02Ar
Catherine	18	F	Joiner	26Ma02Ar
BOWES, Mary	15	F	Servant	26Ma02Ar
KANE, Mary	25	F	Servant	26Ma02Ar
WRIGHT, Henry	27	M	Farmer	26Ma02Ar
AMERONEY, Stephen	30	M	Farmer	26Ma02Ar
KANE, Robert	19	M	Laborer	26Ma02Ar
RADCLIFF, Lace	16	F	Seamstress	26Ma02Ar
KIERNAN, Mary	21	F	Seamstress	26Ma02Ar
HEALY, Peter	18	M	Laborer	26Ma02Ar
MCGAULEY, Catherine	54	F	Seamstress	26Ma02Ar
FOX, Bridget	17	F	Servant	26Ma02Ar
GAVIN, Edward	19	M	Laborer	26Ma02Ar
BOYD, James	16	M	Laborer	26Ma02Ar
BOYLE, Mary	20	F	Seamstress	26Ma02Ar
THORBE, Jacob	28	M	Blacksmith	26Ma02Ar
WILLIAMS, John	24	M	Blacksmith	26Ma02Ar
HENNELLY, Richard	40	M	Joiner	26Ma02Ar
KELLY, James	28	M	Joiner	26Ma02Ar
MURPHY, Patt	18	M	Laborer	26Ma02Ar
DALHUNTY, Mary	25	F	Servant	26Ma02Ar
FARRELL, James	30	M	Farmer	26Ma02Ar
MALONEY, Richard	35	M	Farmer	26Ma02Ar
GARITY, Patrick-J.	44	M	Farmer	26Ma02Ar
KELLY, Thomas	40	M	Farmer	26Ma02Ar
John	18	M	Tailor	26Ma02Ar
Mary-Ann	20	F	Seamstress	26Ma02Ar
Ellen	11	F	Unknown	26Ma02Ar
NEEDHAM, Thomas	30	M	Farmer	26Ma02Ar
Bridget	26	F	Unknown	26Ma02Ar
Ellen	4	F	Child	26Ma02Ar
Mary	2	F	Child	26Ma02Ar
KEEFE, Lawrence	24	M	Tailor	26Ma02Ar
HANLY, Patt	20	M	Laborer	26Ma02Ar
Mary	50	F	Seamstress	26Ma02Ar
Margaret	25	F	Seamstress	26Ma02Ar
LONG, Mary	20	F	Seamstress	26Ma02Ar
FOLEY, Thomas	30	M	Laborer	26Ma02Ar
RYAN, Michael	21	M	Laborer	26Ma02Ar
MCGRATH, Patt	24	M	Laborer	26Ma02Ar
BRENNAN, Judy	24	F	Seamstress	26Ma02Ar
RYAN, Bridget	24	F	Servant	26Ma02Ar
Bridget	20	F	Servant	26Ma02Ar
CLEARY, John	30	M	Farmer	26Ma02Ar
RYAN, Patt	28	M	Blacksmith	26Ma02Ar
Bernard	40	M	Farmer	26Ma02Ar
Ellen	30	F	Farmer	26Ma02Ar
Catherine	13	F	Unknown	26Ma02Ar
Ellen	12	F	Unknown	26Ma02Ar
John	10	M	Unknown	26Ma02Ar
Bernard	6	M	Child	26Ma02Ar
Mary	.11	F	Infant	26Ma02Ar
RICE, John	19	M	Laborer	26Ma02Ar
HOGAN, James	24	M	Laborer	26Ma02Ar
GORMON, William	38	M	Farmer	26Ma02Ar
TIMMONS, Martha	26	F	Servant	26Ma02Ar
KELLY, Mary	26	F	Seamstress	26Ma02Ar
William	7	M	Child	26Ma02Ar
John	4	M	Child	26Ma02Ar
James	.06	M	Infant	26Ma02Ar
DOYLE, Alice	23	F	Servant	26Ma02Ar
INGRAHAM, Mary	7	F	Child	26Ma02Ar
TURNBULL, James	25	M	Farmer	26Ma02Ar
Ellen	24	F	Unknown	26Ma02Ar
Mary	4	F	Child	26Ma02Ar
Margaret	.04	F	Infant	26Ma02Ar
BINSON, Mary-A.	20	F	Servant	26Ma02Ar
SHELLEDAY, Agnes	24	F	Servant	26Ma02Ar
Betty	22	F	Servant	26Ma02Ar
NERNY, Thomas	25	M	Tailor	26Ma02Ar
ROCH, Mary	20	F	Servant	26Ma02Ar
GOSS, James	22	M	Laborer	26Ma02Ar
CONNOLLY, Anne	22	F	Servant	26Ma02Ar
DRUNAN, Catherine	24	F	Servant	26Ma02Ar
CRONIN, John	58	M	Farmer	26Ma02Ar
Michael	28	M	Farmer	26Ma02Ar
John	22	M	Farmer	26Ma02Ar
Honora	24	F	Unknown	26Ma02Ar

NAMES OF PASSENGERS	AGE	SEX	OCCUPATIONS	DATE PORT SHIP
CRONIN, Mary	17	F	Unknown	26Ma02Ar
COLLINS, John	34	M	Laborer	26Ma02Ar
Honora	6	F	Child	26Ma02Ar
LESTON, Mary	17	F	Servant	26Ma02Ar
KEATING, Ellen	20	F	Servant	26Ma02Ar
IRVING, Mary	26	F	Servant	26Ma02Ar
AGNESS, Catherine	42	F	Servant	26Ma02Ar
Mary	18	F	Unknown	26Ma02Ar
HARTNETT, John	26	M	Shoemaker	26Ma02Ar
Margaret	19	F	Servant	26Ma02Ar
COLLINS, Honora	27	F	Servant	26Ma02Ar
COWAN, Mary	20	F	Servant	26Ma02Ar
REILLY, Rose	19	F	Servant	26Ma02Ar
GAUGHRAN, Mary	15	F	Servant	26Ma02Ar
Elizabeth	13	F	Servant	26Ma02Ar
Rose-Ann	10	F	Unknown	26Ma02Ar
HUSSY, William	26	M	Laborer	26Ma02Ar
MCGINNIS, John	25	M	Laborer	26Ma02Ar
LANGHAN, Thomas	24	M	Laborer	26Ma02Ar
BOYLE, John	26	M	Laborer	26Ma02Ar
REYNOLDS, John	24	M	Laborer	26Ma02Ar
GARIGAN, Catherine	24	F	Seamstress	26Ma02Ar
MURPHY, George	30	M	Shoemaker	26Ma02Ar
STOEY, Hugh	29	M	Shoemaker	26Ma02Ar
Rose	24	F	Servant	26Ma02Ar
Eliza	.10	F	Infant	26Ma02Ar
HEANY, William	21	M	Laborer	26Ma02Ar
Thomas	19	M	Laborer	26Ma02Ar
CLARK, Catherine	25	F	Servant	26Ma02Ar
MEAD, Catherine	18	F	Servant	26Ma02Ar
Bessy	17	F	Servant	26Ma02Ar
CARR, Margaret	50	F	Farmer	26Ma02Ar
Judith	17	F	Unknown	26Ma02Ar
Michael	12	M	Unknown	26Ma02Ar
Patrick	10	M	Unknown	26Ma02Ar
DONNOLLY, John	28	M	Laborer	26Ma02Ar
MCLAUGHTON, Peter	28	M	Laborer	26Ma02Ar
BANNON, Richard	18	M	Laborer	26Ma02Ar
SMITH, Catherine	17	F	Servant	26Ma02Ar
WEBB, Richard	45	M	Farmer	26Ma02Ar
QUINN, Bernard	26	M	Farmer	26Ma02Ar
DEVOY, Bernard	24	M	Laborer	26Ma02Ar
James	26	M	Laborer	26Ma02Ar
William	23	M	Laborer	26Ma02Ar
CARROLL, Joseph	14	M	Laborer	26Ma02Ar
Mary	23	F	Servant	26Ma02Ar
WALSH, Benedict	21	M	Laborer	26Ma02Ar
COTTER, Michael	25	M	Laborer	26Ma02Ar
Anne	23	F	Servant	26Ma02Ar
Mary	.11	F	Infant	26Ma02Ar
GIBSON, Sarah-Ann	5	F	Child	26Ma02Ar
Eleanor	2	F	Child	26Ma02Ar
MOFFATT, John	22	M	Blacksmith	26Ma02Ar
HARDY, Jane	36	F	Blacksmith	26Ma02Ar
John	5	M	Child	26Ma02Ar
Jacob	.10	M	Infant	26Ma02Ar
OLIVANT, William	24	M	Farmer	26Ma02Ar
Ann	22	F	Farmer	26Ma02Ar
Sarah-Jane	2	F	Child	26Ma02Ar
John	.09	M	Infant	26Ma02Ar
LYNCH, Thomas	40	M	Laborer	26Ma02Ar
Rose	30	F	Seamstress	26Ma02Ar
Anne	10	F	Unknown	26Ma02Ar
Bridget	8	F	Child	26Ma02Ar
Catherine	6	F	Child	26Ma02Ar
Rose	4	F	Child	26Ma02Ar
Margaret	3	F	Child	26Ma02Ar
Thomas	.09	M	Infant	26Ma02Ar
PAYNTON, Thomas	30	M	Stone Mason	26Ma02Ar
SHARKEY, Michael	35	M	Stone Mason	26Ma02Ar
HASKINS, Robert	32	M	Stone Mason	26Ma02Ar
Catherine	21	F	Unknown	26Ma02Ar
TOMKINS, Eliza	25	F	Seamstress	26Ma02Ar
Peter	21	M	Shoemaker	26Ma02Ar
Charles	19	M	Shoemaker	26Ma02Ar

NAMES OF PASSENGERS	AGE	SEX	OCCUPATIONS	DATE PORT SHIP
GORMLY, John	50	M	Farmer	26Ma02Ar
Ann	50	F	Unknown	26Ma02Ar
Eliza	20	F	Unknown	26Ma02Ar
Margaret	16	F	Unknown	26Ma02Ar
KELLY, Luke	20	M	Unknown	26Ma02Ar
TOOLE, Margaret	21	F	Servant	26Ma02Ar
CHESNUT, Samuel	22	M	Laborer	26Ma02Ar
REILLY, John	25	M	Laborer	26Ma02Ar
COWAN, Thomas	24	M	Laborer	26Ma02Ar
HOYLAND, John	50	M	Laborer	26Ma02Ar
Nancy	40	F	Unknown	26Ma02Ar
Jane	27	F	Servant	26Ma02Ar
Anne	18	F	Servant	26Ma02Ar
Lydia	17	F	Servant	26Ma02Ar
Margaret	14	F	Servant	26Ma02Ar
Thomas	11	M	Unknown	26Ma02Ar
Nancy	6	F	Child	26Ma02Ar
Richard	4	M	Child	26Ma02Ar
John	.07	M	Infant	26Ma02Ar
CARROLL, Thomas	18	M	Laborer	26Ma02Ar
MAFRAM, Thomas	35	M	Laborer	26Ma02Ar
FUNNY, Ann	14	F	Servant	26Ma02Ar
HOEY, James	21	M	Laborer	26Ma02Ar
NEILAN, Patt	25	M	Tailor	26Ma02Ar
GILMOUR, Hugh	17	M	Laborer	26Ma02Ar
FAHEY, Honora	18	F	Servant	26Ma02Ar
TRACY, Michael	20	M	Laborer	26Ma02Ar
COUGHLAN, Ellen	20	F	Servant	26Ma02Ar
Judy	14	F	Servant	26Ma02Ar
Catherine	17	F	Servant	26Ma02Ar
MORAN, James	68	M	Farmer	26Ma02Ar
William	23	M	Farmer	26Ma02Ar
Thomas	24	M	Farmer	26Ma02Ar
LEDWITH, Margaret	40	F	Farmer	26Ma02Ar
James	20	M	Farmer	26Ma02Ar
Julia	18	F	Farmer	26Ma02Ar
HEALIN, Mary	18	F	Farmer	26Ma02Ar
WHELAN, John	20	M	Laborer	26Ma02Ar
NALLY, Margaret	17	F	Servant	26Ma02Ar
FOX, Catherine	18	F	Servant	26Ma02Ar
SKELTON, Mary	16	F	Servant	26Ma02Ar
MITCHELL, William	21	M	Laborer	26Ma02Ar
RYAN, Jeremiah	21	M	Laborer	26Ma02Ar
FARRALLY, Sarah-A.	20	F	Servant	26Ma02Ar
BENNITT, Patt	22	M	Blacksmith	26Ma02Ar
SHIELS, Bessy	18	F	Servant	26Ma02Ar
SHANLY, Catherine	30	F	Servant	26Ma02Ar
Frances	20	F	Servant	26Ma02Ar
Ellen	26	F	Servant	26Ma02Ar
Michael	11	M	Unknown	26Ma02Ar
Bridget	13	F	Unknown	26Ma02Ar
CALL, Catherine	15	F	Unknown	26Ma02Ar
Mary	16	F	Unknown	26Ma02Ar
WILLIAMS, Gidion	23	M	Laborer	26Ma02Ar
Anne	28	F	Servant	26Ma02Ar
MCCORMICK, Hugh	22	M	Farmer	26Ma02Ar
Ellen	18	F	Unknown	26Ma02Ar
ONEILL, John	28	M	Laborer	26Ma02Ar
Patrick	16	M	Laborer	26Ma02Ar
DAWSON, Ralph	30	M	Laborer	26Ma02Ar
KICKLY, Thomas	22	M	Laborer	26Ma02Ar
WRIGHT, George	21	M	Laborer	26Ma02Ar
MEDCALF, Christopher	24	M	Laborer	26Ma02Ar
CROWELL, Henry	26	M	Servant	26Ma02Ar
Jane	20	F	Servant	26Ma02Ar
GOUNDY, Thomas	20	M	Laborer	26Ma02Ar
NIXON, Thomas	20	M	Laborer	26Ma02Ar
HAWELL, John	22	M	Laborer	26Ma02Ar
RILEY, Charles	21	M	Laborer	26Ma02Ar
MACKESY, William	18	M	Laborer	26Ma02Ar
WILLOCK, John	13	M	Laborer	26Ma02Ar
SCOLLON, Bridget	31	F	Servant	26Ma02Ar
John	10	M	Unknown	26Ma02Ar
NEEDHAM, Bessy Born-At-Sea	.00	F	Infant	26Ma02Ar

NAMES OF PASSENGERS	AGE	SEX	OCCUPATIONS	DATE PORT SHIP
MCKINLEY, Mary	25	F	Servant	26Ma02Ar
GIBSON, Robert	30	M	Laborer	26Ma02Ar
Ellen	30	F	Seamstress	26Ma02Ar
Mary	.10	F	Infant	26Ma02Ar
OHAGAN, Patrick	25	M	Solicitor	26Ma02Ar

ROLLA 27 MAY 1850

From Dublin

DRUMMOND, James	28	M	Laborer	27Ma05Hr
GREEN, Charles	19	M	Unknown	27Ma05Hr
CARDIFF, Eliza	20	M	Unknown	27Ma05Hr
Bridgt.	18	F	Unknown	27Ma05Hr
DOODY, Phillip	26	M	Unknown	27Ma05Hr
U-Mrs.	20	F	Unknown	27Ma05Hr
Mary	.00	F	Infant	27Ma05Hr
HUGHES, Jos.	40	M	Unknown	27Ma05Hr
U-Mrs.	40	F	Unknown	27Ma05Hr
Betty	21	F	Unknown	27Ma05Hr
Mary	19	F	Unknown	27Ma05Hr
John	16	M	Unknown	27Ma05Hr
Ann	13	F	Unknown	27Ma05Hr
Kate	12	F	Unknown	27Ma05Hr
Edwd.	9	M	Child	27Ma05Hr
Pat	7	M	Child	27Ma05Hr
TRACY, John	40	M	Unknown	27Ma05Hr
BYRNE, Margt.	21	F	Unknown	27Ma05Hr
MOORE, Michl.	24	M	Unknown	27Ma05Hr
John	8	M	Child	27Ma05Hr
MASTERSON, Terance	28	M	Unknown	27Ma05Hr
FARRELL, James	30	M	Unknown	27Ma05Hr
KEEGAN, Ann	50	F	Unknown	27Ma05Hr
Mary	24	F	Unknown	27Ma05Hr
Pat	22	M	Unknown	27Ma05Hr
Ann	20	F	Unknown	27Ma05Hr
Cathn.	17	F	Unknown	27Ma05Hr
MARKIE, Richd.	20	M	Unknown	27Ma05Hr
MOONEY, Wm.	38	M	Unknown	27Ma05Hr
Ellen	28	F	Unknown	27Ma05Hr
Bessy	18	F	Unknown	27Ma05Hr
Bridget	17	F	Unknown	27Ma05Hr
Bernard	14	M	Unknown	27Ma05Hr
James	8	M	Child	27Ma05Hr
Cathn.	.00	F	Infant	27Ma05Hr
BUNFIELD, Jane	21	F	Unknown	27Ma05Hr
MCNALLY, James	22	M	Unknown	27Ma05Hr
CLANSEY, Pat	25	M	Unknown	27Ma05Hr
FARRELL, Wm.	18	M	Unknown	27Ma05Hr
HUTCHUSSON, Robt.	25	M	Unknown	27Ma05Hr
HAUSATTY, Pat	13	M	Unknown	27Ma05Hr
BREEN, Cathn.	30	F	Unknown	27Ma05Hr
BOYLAN, Cathn.	20	F	Unknown	27Ma05Hr
FITZGERRALD, Thos.	22	M	Unknown	27Ma05Hr
Pat	20	M	Unknown	27Ma05Hr
DWYER, Jane	20	F	Unknown	27Ma05Hr
HENRY, John	20	F	Unknown	27Ma05Hr
HARRISON, Wm.	28	M	Unknown	27Ma05Hr
John	50	M	Unknown	27Ma05Hr
James	21	M	Unknown	27Ma05Hr
Jane	16	F	Unknown	27Ma05Hr
Henry	14	M	Unknown	27Ma05Hr
DAW, Mathew	20	M	Unknown	27Ma05Hr
MITCHELL, Daniel	20	M	Unknown	27Ma05Hr
FARRELL, Thos.	50	M	Unknown	27Ma05Hr
U-Mrs.	45	F	Unknown	27Ma05Hr
U	20	F	Unknown	27Ma05Hr
HUGHES, Pat	20	M	Unknown	27Ma05Hr
DONOHOE, John	25	M	Unknown	27Ma05Hr
CROSBY, Pat	21	M	Unknown	27Ma05Hr
MACK, Rose	20	F	Unknown	27Ma05Hr
CONNELLY, Margt.	20	F	Unknown	27Ma05Hr
MACK, Bridget	20	F	Unknown	27Ma05Hr
FOWLER, Thos.	20	M	Unknown	27Ma05Hr
METCALF, U	20	M	Unknown	27Ma05Hr
Cathn.	20	F	Unknown	27Ma05Hr
LAWLOR, John	50	M	Unknown	27Ma05Hr
Mary	19	F	Unknown	27Ma05Hr
Wm.	21	M	Unknown	27Ma05Hr
Honor	17	F	Unknown	27Ma05Hr
Eliza	13	F	Unknown	27Ma05Hr
Eliza	11	F	Unknown	27Ma05Hr
James	8	M	Child	27Ma05Hr
John	.00	M	Infant	27Ma05Hr
HERBERT, John	35	M	Infant	27Ma05Hr
KENNA, Wm.	22	M	Infant	27Ma05Hr
MEHAN, Michl.	23	M	Infant	27Ma05Hr
HARTFORD, Henry	20	M	Infant	27Ma05Hr
LAWRY, Bessy	20	F	Infant	27Ma05Hr
BYRNE, Mary	19	F	Unknown	27Ma05Hr
DOHEEN, Bridget	22	F	Unknown	27Ma05Hr
DUNGAN, Edwd.	30	M	Unknown	27Ma05Hr
U	24	F	Unknown	27Ma05Hr
John	2	M	Child	27Ma05Hr
Mary	.00	F	Infant	27Ma05Hr
NULTY, Patk.	20	M	Unknown	27Ma05Hr
OBRIEN, Mrs.	27	F	Unknown	27Ma05Hr
KENEFICK, Wm.	25	M	Unknown	27Ma05Hr
MCDERMOTT, John	22	M	Unknown	27Ma05Hr
LEWIS, Wm.	30	M	Unknown	27Ma05Hr
SHERIDAN, John	30	M	Unknown	27Ma05Hr
DONNELLY, Joe	13	M	Unknown	27Ma05Hr
BYRNE, Patk.	30	M	Unknown	27Ma05Hr
CROSS, James	45	M	Unknown	27Ma05Hr
Cathn.	50	F	Unknown	27Ma05Hr
Mary	18	F	Unknown	27Ma05Hr
Thos.	15	M	Unknown	27Ma05Hr
Gerald	9	M	Child	27Ma05Hr
Michael	11	M	Child	27Ma05Hr
James	.00	M	Infant	27Ma05Hr
OMORAN, James	20	M	Unknown	27Ma05Hr
FARRELL, Henry	27	M	Unknown	27Ma05Hr
James	24	M	Unknown	27Ma05Hr
Michael	22	M	Unknown	27Ma05Hr
Julia	30	F	Unknown	27Ma05Hr
MULHOLLAND, Rose	20	F	Unknown	27Ma05Hr
Thos.	13	M	Unknown	27Ma05Hr
FERRAGHTY, Margt.	30	F	Unknown	27Ma05Hr
WALSH, Margt.	30	F	Unknown	27Ma05Hr
NIXON, James	24	M	Unknown	27Ma05Hr
MCCANN, Christy	35	M	Unknown	27Ma05Hr
MURRAY, Judy	18	F	Unknown	27Ma05Hr
POWER, Margt.	26	F	Unknown	27Ma05Hr
SIERY, James	30	M	Unknown	27Ma05Hr
Margt.	00	M	Unknown	27Ma05Hr
Pat	50	M	Unknown	27Ma05Hr
Cathn.	50	F	Unknown	27Ma05Hr
Christy	10	M	Unknown	27Ma05Hr
Andrew	8	M	Child	27Ma05Hr
WADE, John	30	M	Child	27Ma05Hr
KELLY, Cathn.	18	F	Child	27Ma05Hr
WADE, Pat	5	M	Child	27Ma05Hr
Mary	3	F	Child	27Ma05Hr
Ann	.00	F	Infant	27Ma05Hr

LADY-COLEBROOKE 27 MAY 1850

From Glasgow

NAMES OF PASSENGERS	AGE	SEX	OCCUPATIONS	DATE PORT SHIP
ROGAN, James	18	M	Weaver	27Ma21Gs
BURKE, Peter	28	M	Laborer	27Ma21Gs
GUNN, James	28	M	Laborer	27Ma21Gs
BROADLY, Patrick	31	M	Laborer	27Ma21Gs
ODONNELL, Mary	17	F	Unknown	27Ma21Gs
MCLUSKEY, Mary-Ann	19	F	Servant	27Ma21Gs
BURNET, Rachel	18	F	Unknown	27Ma21Gs
Isabella	13	F	Unknown	27Ma21Gs
LYNCH, William	29	M	Laborer	27Ma21Gs
Betty	27	F	Unknown	27Ma21Gs
Mary	3	F	Child	27Ma21Gs
Margaret	.10	F	Infant	27Ma21Gs
HIGGINS, James	24	M	Laborer	27Ma21Gs
DILLON, Dinnes	23	M	Laborer	27Ma21Gs
EMACKS, Joseph	40	M	Laborer	27Ma21Gs
BIRNIE, Thomas	18	M	Laborer	27Ma21Gs
John	16	M	Laborer	27Ma21Gs
MCMANAGH, Michael	28	M	Laborer	27Ma21Gs
OMAN, Edward	34	M	Carpenter	27Ma21Gs
CORIGALL, William	28	M	Shoemaker	27Ma21Gs
MORIS, Jane	50	F	Unknown	27Ma21Gs
James	19	M	Laborer	27Ma21Gs
MURPHY, James	22	M	Laborer	27Ma21Gs
KANE, E.J.	45	M	Unknown	27Ma21Gs
Charlotte	20	F	Unknown	27Ma21Gs
Benjamin	17	F	Unknown	27Ma21Gs
Eliza	10	F	Unknown	27Ma21Gs
Robert	1	M	Child	27Ma21Gs
John	14	M	Unknown	27Ma21Gs
William	9	M	Child	27Ma21Gs
Sarah	12	F	Unknown	27Ma21Gs
Thomas	4	M	Child	27Ma21Gs
BROWN, John	40	M	Laborer	27Ma21Gs
Sarah	39	F	Unknown	27Ma21Gs
Thomas	14	M	Unknown	27Ma21Gs
John	11	M	Unknown	27Ma21Gs
James	9	M	Child	27Ma21Gs
Sarah	6	F	Child	27Ma21Gs
Catherine	.11	F	Infant	27Ma21Gs
STEVENSON, Jane	20	F	Unknown	27Ma21Gs
RAFTER, John	32	M	Seaman	27Ma21Gs
CARSON, James	19	M	Laborer	27Ma21Gs
GIBSON, John	50	M	Weaver	27Ma21Gs
MCFARLANE, Peter	22	M	Dealer	27Ma21Gs
Daniel	27	M	Weaver	27Ma21Gs
Ann	24	F	Dressmaker	27Ma21Gs
Susan	27	F	Weaver	27Ma21Gs
COOPER, David	25	M	Laborer	27Ma21Gs
CHALMERS, Robert	21	M	Laborer	27Ma21Gs
DENISTOUN, Jane	18	F	Servant	27Ma21Gs
GRAHAM, John	12	M	Laborer	27Ma21Gs
MCKINLEY, John	17	M	Laborer	27Ma21Gs

MARY-RUSSELL 27 MAY 1850

From Limerick

NAMES OF PASSENGERS	AGE	SEX	OCCUPATIONS	DATE PORT SHIP
CONNORS, William	19	M	Farmer	27Ma10Gk
CHERRY, Honora	16	F	Spinster	27Ma10Gk
HILL, Pierce	40	M	Farmer	27Ma10Gk
Elizabeth	35	F	Wife	27Ma10Gk
William	17	M	Farmer	27Ma10Gk
MCCONNEL, Ann	39	F	Spinster	27Ma10Gk
Eliza	18	F	Spinster	27Ma10Gk
POWER, Michael	26	M	Laborer	27Ma10Gk
MYERS, Patrick	30	M	Laborer	27Ma10Gk
RIORDAN, Bridget	30	F	Spinster	27Ma10Gk
COLLINS, Michael	9	M	Child	27Ma10Gk
John	7	M	Child	27Ma10Gk
MOLONEY, Margaret	20	F	Spinster	27Ma10Gk
DOWLIN, Hannah	21	F	Spinster	27Ma10Gk
ONEIL, Elizabeth	24	F	Spinster	27Ma10Gk
WOODS, Michael	50	M	Laborer	27Ma10Gk
Norry	46	F	Spinster	27Ma10Gk
James	17	M	Laborer	27Ma10Gk
Patrick	14	M	Laborer	27Ma10Gk
Denis	11	M	Laborer	27Ma10Gk
CRONIN, Mary	21	F	Spinster	27Ma10Gk
MURPHY, Michael	28	M	Laborer	27Ma10Gk
MULGREEN, Ellen	18	F	Spinster	27Ma10Gk
KEANE, Thade	25	M	Laborer	27Ma10Gk
SWINEY, John	13	M	Laborer	27Ma10Gk
WALSH, James	25	M	Laborer	27Ma10Gk
NULMASTER, John	30	M	Laborer	27Ma10Gk
Mary	26	F	Wife	27Ma10Gk
Michael	6	M	Child	27Ma10Gk
Kate	4	F	Child	27Ma10Gk
William	2	M	Child	27Ma10Gk
Ellen	.10	F	Infant	27Ma10Gk
KILMARTIN, Mary-Anne	20	F	Spinster	27Ma10Gk
COLEMAN, Owen	24	M	Laborer	27Ma10Gk
Margret	30	F	Spinster	27Ma10Gk
GIBBONS, Mary	16	F	Spinster	27Ma10Gk
COLLOPPY, Thomas	40	M	Laborer	27Ma10Gk
Mary	30	F	Spinster	27Ma10Gk
FITZGIBBON, Edmond	30	M	Laborer	27Ma10Gk
SCANLON, Cornelius	22	M	Laborer	27Ma10Gk
Patrick	16	M	Laborer	27Ma10Gk
James	15	M	Laborer	27Ma10Gk
WALSH, John	40	M	Laborer	27Ma10Gk
Mary	30	F	Spinster	27Ma10Gk
Harry	10	M	None	27Ma10Gk
John	7	M	Child	27Ma10Gk
Michael	4	M	Child	27Ma10Gk
BROUGHTON, Michael	47	M	Laborer	27Ma10Gk
U-Mrs.	45	F	Wife	27Ma10Gk
Patrick	22	M	Farmer	27Ma10Gk
Thomas	21	M	Farmer	27Ma10Gk
John	20	M	Farmer	27Ma10Gk
Bridget	19	F	Spinster	27Ma10Gk
Honora	18	F	Spinster	27Ma10Gk
Mary	15	F	Spinster	27Ma10Gk
Michael	7	M	Child	27Ma10Gk
Johanna	4	F	Child	27Ma10Gk
COUGHLAN, Thomas	50	M	Farmer	27Ma10Gk
James	52	M	Farmer	27Ma10Gk
RIORDAN, Thos.	30	M	Farmer	27Ma10Gk
Ellen	26	F	Spinster	27Ma10Gk
RYAN, Michael	20	M	Spinner	27Ma10Gk
BOLERNO, Michael	24	M	Spinner	27Ma10Gk
Mary	17	F	Spinster	27Ma10Gk
Ellen	20	F	Spinster	27Ma10Gk
CUNNEEN, David	40	M	Farmer	27Ma10Gk
Bridget	26	F	Spinster	27Ma10Gk
Margret	.11	F	Infant	27Ma10Gk
Patrick	.01	M	Infant	27Ma10Gk
SULLIVAN, Joseph	58	M	Farmer	27Ma10Gk
U-Mrs.	50	F	Wife	27Ma10Gk
Margret	25	F	Spinster	27Ma10Gk
Anne	22	F	Spinster	27Ma10Gk
SAVAGE, Thomas	24	M	Farmer	27Ma10Gk
FOLEY, Daniel	24	M	Farmer	27Ma10Gk
Norry	20	F	Spinster	27Ma10Gk
DOWNES, Bridget	19	F	Spinster	27Ma10Gk

NAMES OF PASSENGERS	AGE	SEX	OCCUPATIONS	DATE PORT SHIP
ODEAL, Bridget	18	F	Spinster	27Ma10Gk
KENNEDY. Thomas	22	M	Farmer	27Ma10Gk
NAUGHTEN, Johanna	24	F	Spinster	27Ma10Gk
Honora	22	F	Spinster	27Ma10Gk
ONEIL, Robert	18	M	Farmer	27Ma10Gk
HARRIGAN. Patk.	28	M	Farmer	27Ma10Gk
COUGHLAN. Michael	25	M	Farmer	27Ma10Gk
Margret	20	F	Spinster	27Ma10Gk
William	.03	M	Infant	27Ma10Gk
CONWAY. Bridget	30	F	Matron	27Ma10Gk
Mary	9	F	Child	27Ma10Gk
John	7	M	Child	27Ma10Gk
Margret	5	F	Child	27Ma10Gk
Ellen	1	F	Child	27Ma10Gk
WORTHINGTON, William	21	M	Engineer	27Ma10Gk
U, U	00	U	Unknown	27Ma10Gk

ATLAS 27 MAY 1850

From Liverpool

NAMES OF PASSENGERS	AGE	SEX	OCCUPATIONS	DATE PORT SHIP
COSTELLO. Wm.	18	M	Laborer	27Ma02Gv
Thos.	20	M	Laborer	27Ma02Gv
MEDLA. Hugh	20	M	Laborer	27Ma02Gv
CROSS. Wm.	20	M	Laborer	27Ma02Gv
MILLAR. Teresa	21	F	Laborer	27Ma02Gv
RIELY. Michael	35	M	Laborer	27Ma02Gv
MALONEY. Owen	22	M	Laborer	27Ma02Gv
CLANSKY. E.	17	U	Laborer	27Ma02Gv
MURRY. Anne	18	F	Laborer	27Ma02Gv
MARKEY. Mary	20	F	Laborer	27Ma02Gv
RIELY. Ellen	24	F	Laborer	27Ma02Gv
Mary	22	F	Laborer	27Ma02Gv
Mary	.00	F	Infant	27Ma02Gv
LYNCH, Patt	26	M	Unknown	27Ma02Gv
FRANKLIN, Margaret	30	F	Unknown	27Ma02Gv
HEARNEY. Jas.	18	M	Unknown	27Ma02Gv
MCWILLIAM. Robert	32	M	Unknown	27Ma02Gv
COAPLES. Wm.	21	M	Unknown	27Ma02Gv
HAMILTON, Jas.	23	M	Unknown	27Ma02Gv
Robert	18	M	Unknown	27Ma02Gv
RATCLIFF. Saml.	29	M	Unknown	27Ma02Gv
MCGUINESS. Arthur	40	M	Unknown	27Ma02Gv
MATES. Jos.	20	M	Unknown	27Ma02Gv
BRENAN. Wm.	9	M	Child	27Ma02Gv
MCDERMOTT. Patt	30	M	Unknown	27Ma02Gv
Cathn.	30	F	Unknown	27Ma02Gv
Bee	3	U	Child	27Ma02Gv
John	2	M	Child	27Ma02Gv
Patrick	.02	M	Infant	27Ma02Gv
EGAN, B.	18	U	Unknown	27Ma02Gv
Anne	14	F	Unknown	27Ma02Gv
CASSIDY. Patt	24	M	Unknown	27Ma02Gv
QUINN. Patt	23	M	Unknown	27Ma02Gv
BAXTER, Jas.	35	M	Unknown	27Ma02Gv
MCALOON, Patt	30	M	Unknown	27Ma02Gv
SHORT, Jno.	20	M	Unknown	27Ma02Gv
TOKER, Mary	20	F	Unknown	27Ma02Gv
MAHER. Jas.	35	M	Unknown	27Ma02Gv
Mary	30	F	Unknown	27Ma02Gv
Jos.	5	M	Child	27Ma02Gv
SHERLOCK. Mary	3	F	Child	27Ma02Gv
Ellen	.03	F	Infant	27Ma02Gv
DWYER. Honora	22	F	Unknown	27Ma02Gv
SHARVIN. Jno.	28	M	Unknown	27Ma02Gv
ORNSBY. George	27	M	Unknown	27Ma02Gv
Mgt.Anne	25	F	Unknown	27Ma02Gv
Janet	6	F	Child	27Ma02Gv
Isabella	4	F	Child	27Ma02Gv

NAMES OF PASSENGERS	AGE	SEX	OCCUPATIONS	DATE PORT SHIP
ORNSBY. Thomas	2	M	Child	27Ma02Gv
BELL, Robert	23	M	Unknown	27Ma02Gv
OWENS, Eliza	29	F	Unknown	27Ma02Gv
Anne	28	F	Unknown	27Ma02Gv
BYRNE. Jno.	20	M	Unknown	27Ma02Gv
GRIFFIN, Jas.	30	M	Unknown	27Ma02Gv
Mary	18	F	Unknown	27Ma02Gv
HANSON, Martha	50	F	Mechanic	27Ma02Gv
Peter	16	M	Unknown	27Ma02Gv
COOPER. Patt	35	M	Unknown	27Ma02Gv
KENNEDY. Jno.	10	M	Unknown	27Ma02Gv
GRADY. James	24	M	Laborer	27Ma02Gv
James	26	M	Unknown	27Ma02Gv
BINSHAN, Richd.	30	M	Unknown	27Ma02Gv
PARKER, U-Mrs.	24	F	Unknown	27Ma02Gv
Agnes	23	F	Unknown	27Ma02Gv
MCKAY. Jno.	20	M	Unknown	27Ma02Gv
MCGOUIHAN, Mary	40	F	Unknown	27Ma02Gv
Rose	30	F	Unknown	27Ma02Gv
Cecely	7	F	Child	27Ma02Gv
ROURKE, Jas.	35	M	Unknown	27Ma02Gv
ROGERS, Wm.	30	M	Unknown	27Ma02Gv
KING, Jno.	26	M	Unknown	27Ma02Gv
MAHONY. Thos.	26	M	Unknown	27Ma02Gv
James	24	M	Unknown	27Ma02Gv
James	25	M	Unknown	27Ma02Gv
Honora	28	F	Unknown	27Ma02Gv
Catharine	21	F	Unknown	27Ma02Gv
Patrick	20	M	Unknown	27Ma02Gv
CORBELL, Patt	44	M	Unknown	27Ma02Gv
Mared	15	U	Unknown	27Ma02Gv
DOUDAL, Robert	18	M	Unknown	27Ma02Gv
POWDERLY. Mary	18	F	Unknown	27Ma02Gv
MAHER. Michael	21	M	Unknown	27Ma02Gv
MULLER. Bridget	30	F	Unknown	27Ma02Gv
COSTIGAN. Cornelius	30	M	Unknown	27Ma02Gv
LYNCH, Mathew	40	M	Unknown	27Ma02Gv
James	38	M	Unknown	27Ma02Gv
HUGHS, Sarah	22	F	Unknown	27Ma02Gv
HANWAY, John	20	M	Unknown	27Ma02Gv
Patt	22	M	Unknown	27Ma02Gv
EGAN. Michael	20	M	Unknown	27Ma02Gv
DORAN. Peter	23	M	Unknown	27Ma02Gv
Bridget	56	F	Unknown	27Ma02Gv
COONY. Michael	24	M	Unknown	27Ma02Gv
CONOR. Jno.	19	M	Unknown	27Ma02Gv
SHERLOCK. Patt	27	M	Unknown	27Ma02Gv
Anne	18	F	Unknown	27Ma02Gv
LARKEN. Mary	23	F	Unknown	27Ma02Gv
DORAN, Betty	17	F	Unknown	27Ma02Gv
KENNEDY. Mary	20	F	Unknown	27Ma02Gv
HANNAN, Jno.	30	M	Unknown	27Ma02Gv
MCMULLEN. Jno.	24	M	Unknown	27Ma02Gv
CORAN, Bessy	24	F	Unknown	27Ma02Gv
Cathrn.	20	F	Unknown	27Ma02Gv
KELLY. Martin	30	M	Unknown	27Ma02Gv
Margaret	.00	F	Infant	27Ma02Gv
Margaret	50	F	Unknown	27Ma02Gv
Mary	20	F	Unknown	27Ma02Gv
Margaret	18	F	Unknown	27Ma02Gv
DUNN, Jas.	28	M	Unknown	27Ma02Gv
Mary	24	F	Unknown	27Ma02Gv
ROSS. George	24	M	Unknown	27Ma02Gv
Emma	23	F	Unknown	27Ma02Gv
MCKOWN, Danl.	20	M	Unknown	27Ma02Gv
CANNON, Sally	20	F	Unknown	27Ma02Gv
MARON, Ellen	21	F	Unknown	27Ma02Gv
HOGG, Thos.	24	M	Unknown	27Ma02Gv
GRANT. David	23	M	Unknown	27Ma02Gv
BRIEN. Robert	29	M	Unknown	27Ma02Gv
ELLISON, Jos.	35	M	Unknown	27Ma02Gv
PARIEN. Jas.	24	M	Unknown	27Ma02Gv
HOGDON, Michael	29	M	Unknown	27Ma02Gv
ENNIS. Thos.	25	M	Unknown	27Ma02Gv
Patt	36	M	Unknown	27Ma02Gv

NAMES OF PASSENGERS	AGE	SEX	OCCUPATIONS	DATE PORT SHIP
WALSH, Cathn.	20	F	Unknown	27Ma02Gv
CONNOR, Sarah	20	F	Unknown	27Ma02Gv
DUNN, Thos.	30	M	Unknown	27Ma02Gv
PONNIGER, Wm.D.	20	M	Unknown	27Ma02Gv
MUNY, Jas.	22	M	Unknown	27Ma02Gv
Joseph	11	M	Unknown	27Ma02Gv
MORGAN, Jno.	35	M	Unknown	27Ma02Gv
Thos.	10	M	Unknown	27Ma02Gv
BRYNE, Jno.	28	M	Unknown	27Ma02Gv
Eliza	26	F	Unknown	27Ma02Gv
Patrick	.05	M	Infant	27Ma02Gv
PATON, E.	26	U	Unknown	27Ma02Gv
LANAGAN, Margaret	20	F	Unknown	27Ma02Gv
WALL, Cathn.	21	F	Unknown	27Ma02Gv
MARKLES, Judith	24	F	Unknown	27Ma02Gv
HUGHS, Hayly	26	F	Unknown	27Ma02Gv
Wm.	24	M	Unknown	27Ma02Gv
CULLINS, Susan	30	F	Unknown	27Ma02Gv
Wm.	17	M	Unknown	27Ma02Gv
Anne	13	F	Unknown	27Ma02Gv
Ellen	9	F	Child	27Ma02Gv
MCMANUS, Jno.	20	M	Unknown	27Ma02Gv
MCGOHAN, Jno.	35	M	Unknown	27Ma02Gv
Ellen	50	F	Unknown	27Ma02Gv
Ellen	17	F	Unknown	27Ma02Gv
Patt	8	M	Child	27Ma02Gv
Owen	4	M	Child	27Ma02Gv
Jno.	2	M	Child	27Ma02Gv
Thos.	.06	M	Infant	27Ma02Gv
TIGHE, James	30	M	Unknown	27Ma02Gv
BALF, Thos.	25	M	Unknown	27Ma02Gv
WILLISTON, Henry	35	M	Unknown	27Ma02Gv
Elizabeth	30	F	Unknown	27Ma02Gv
Henry	5	M	Child	27Ma02Gv
Emma	3	F	Child	27Ma02Gv
ANGORE, Jas.	24	M	Unknown	27Ma02Gv
MORRIS, Anne	21	F	Unknown	27Ma02Gv
RICE, Walter	55	M	Unknown	27Ma02Gv
Bridget	55	F	Unknown	27Ma02Gv
Winifred	23	F	Unknown	27Ma02Gv
Bridget	7	F	Child	27Ma02Gv
Joseph	3	M	Child	27Ma02Gv
NEAL, Mary	26	F	Unknown	27Ma02Gv
BRENAN, Jas.	19	M	Unknown	27Ma02Gv
MAHER, Jas.	26	M	Unknown	27Ma02Gv
GAFFNEY, Andrew	34	M	Unknown	27Ma02Gv
Anne	24	F	Unknown	27Ma02Gv
BRIEN, Wm.	26	M	Unknown	27Ma02Gv
HUGHS, Jno.	44	M	Unknown	27Ma02Gv
MULLHALL, Pat	44	M	Unknown	27Ma02Gv
KELLY, Thos.	40	M	Unknown	27Ma02Gv
Thos.	30	M	Unknown	27Ma02Gv
Patt	26	M	Unknown	27Ma02Gv
COMORSE, Jas.	20	M	Unknown	27Ma02Gv
NEAL, Jas.	26	M	Unknown	27Ma02Gv
WHITE, Jno.	30	M	Unknown	27Ma02Gv
SCHOENBURG, A.	32	U	Unknown	27Ma02Gv
Jas.	40	M	Unknown	27Ma02Gv
MISHEL, Ludwig	10	M	Unknown	27Ma02Gv
HYRONIUS, Paul	33	M	Unknown	27Ma02Gv
KELB, Jas.	29	M	Unknown	27Ma02Gv
STYRITER, Joan	27	F	Unknown	27Ma02Gv
FLAHER, Jno.	27	M	Unknown	27Ma02Gv
KRIESER, Earnest	25	M	Unknown	27Ma02Gv
SALEG, Heinrich	26	M	Unknown	27Ma02Gv
Beinhard	24	M	Unknown	27Ma02Gv
HEINAKER, Jno.	39	M	Unknown	27Ma02Gv
HEIHT, Saml.	21	M	Unknown	27Ma02Gv
FERS, Julius	25	M	Unknown	27Ma02Gv
SHOOT, Jno.	33	M	Unknown	27Ma02Gv
George	21	M	Unknown	27Ma02Gv
MCARTHUR, Michael	24	M	Unknown	27Ma02Gv
MERRYGAN, Wm.	30	M	Unknown	27Ma02Gv
Bridget	27	F	Unknown	27Ma02Gv
CASHIN, Sarah	26	F	Unknown	27Ma02Gv
CASHIN, Michael	3	M	Child	27Ma02Gv
Elisha	.07	F	Infant	27Ma02Gv
RYAN, Nicholas	28	F	Unknown	27Ma02Gv
U-Mrs.	27	F	Unknown	27Ma02Gv
DEAN, Michael	28	M	Unknown	27Ma02Gv
Mary	26	F	Unknown	27Ma02Gv
Margaret	.08	F	Infant	27Ma02Gv
DELANY, Elisha	22	F	Unknown	27Ma02Gv
GELLAN, Chas.	20	M	Unknown	27Ma02Gv
MCCONNOLLY, Alexr.	23	M	Unknown	27Ma02Gv
Ellen	21	F	Unknown	27Ma02Gv
Jno.	25	M	Unknown	27Ma02Gv
MCARTAN, Jas.	20	M	Unknown	27Ma02Gv
GORMLY, Wm.	21	M	Unknown	27Ma02Gv
MCGONITS, Jas.	18	M	Unknown	27Ma02Gv
ONEAL, Jas.	20	M	Unknown	27Ma02Gv
MULLIGHAN, Bessy	35	F	Unknown	27Ma02Gv
MONAHAN, Mary	18	F	Unknown	27Ma02Gv
DEADY, Alice	60	F	Unknown	27Ma02Gv
Mary	28	F	Unknown	27Ma02Gv
Margaret	22	F	Unknown	27Ma02Gv
Honora	21	F	Unknown	27Ma02Gv
Bridget	21	F	Unknown	27Ma02Gv
Mary	13	F	Unknown	27Ma02Gv
Pattrick	32	M	Unknown	27Ma02Gv
James	30	M	Unknown	27Ma02Gv
Wm.	20	M	Unknown	27Ma02Gv
ATKINSON, Jno.	32	M	Unknown	27Ma02Gv
BROWN, James	40	M	Unknown	27Ma02Gv
WHITE, U-Mrs.	25	F	Unknown	27Ma02Gv
BROWN, U-Miss	18	F	Unknown	27Ma02Gv
KENEDY, Jas.	22	M	Unknown	27Ma02Gv
MASTISON, Lawrence	27	M	Unknown	27Ma02Gv
Judith	25	F	Unknown	27Ma02Gv
GIBNER, Margaret	26	F	Unknown	27Ma02Gv
CRAVEN, Peter	46	M	Unknown	27Ma02Gv
SIMPSON, E.	26	U	Unknown	27Ma02Gv
PRESTON, Margaret	30	F	Unknown	27Ma02Gv
MARTIN, Bridget	20	F	Unknown	27Ma02Gv
Cathn.	18	F	Unknown	27Ma02Gv
BARTON, Sarah	18	F	Unknown	27Ma02Gv
FARRELL, Anne	30	F	Unknown	27Ma02Gv
James	12	M	Unknown	27Ma02Gv
Mary	11	F	Unknown	27Ma02Gv
MCBRIEN, Jas.	9	M	Child	27Ma02Gv
LIVISTER, George	21	M	Unknown	27Ma02Gv
Margaret	50	F	Unknown	27Ma02Gv
Hugh	25	M	Unknown	27Ma02Gv
Jane	17	F	Unknown	27Ma02Gv
PHILLIPS, Francis	12	M	Unknown	27Ma02Gv
Bridget	42	F	Unknown	27Ma02Gv
James	15	M	Unknown	27Ma02Gv
Jno.	12	M	Unknown	27Ma02Gv
BOYLAN, Rose	8	F	Child	27Ma02Gv
HALL, Robert	6	M	Child	27Ma02Gv
FITZGERALD, David	30	M	Unknown	27Ma02Gv
RYAN, Francis	15	M	Unknown	27Ma02Gv
HOGAN, Thos.	24	M	Unknown	27Ma02Gv
HENESSY, Jas.	21	M	Unknown	27Ma02Gv
U-Mrs.	25	F	Unknown	27Ma02Gv
Richard	35	M	Unknown	27Ma02Gv
Ellen	35	F	Unknown	27Ma02Gv
Cathn.	15	F	Unknown	27Ma02Gv
Jno.	17	M	Unknown	27Ma02Gv
TOBIN, Jas.	20	M	Unknown	27Ma02Gv
MCGRATH, Jno.	23	M	Unknown	27Ma02Gv
POWER, Richard	27	M	Unknown	27Ma02Gv
WHELAN, Mary	17	F	Unknown	27Ma02Gv
LEONARD, Mary	30	F	Unknown	27Ma02Gv
George	12	M	Unknown	27Ma02Gv
MURPHY, Richd.	20	M	Unknown	27Ma02Gv
KELLEHAN, Rose	19	F	Unknown	27Ma02Gv
KELLY, Jas.	28	M	Unknown	27Ma02Gv
CORCORAN, Patt	30	M	Unknown	27Ma02Gv
U-Mrs.	26	F	Unknown	27Ma02Gv

NAMES OF PASSENGERS	AGE	SEX	OCCUPATIONS	DATE PORT SHIP
CORCORAN, Cathn.	.09	F	Infant	27Ma02Gv
CULLEN, Wm.	44	M	Unknown	27Ma02Gv
Mary	43	F	Unknown	27Ma02Gv
James	19	M	Unknown	27Ma02Gv
Wm.	16	M	Unknown	27Ma02Gv
Bernard	13	M	Unknown	27Ma02Gv
Ann	11	F	Unknown	27Ma02Gv
Patt	10	M	Unknown	27Ma02Gv
FARRELL, Jas.	50	M	Unknown	27Ma02Gv
Fanny	40	F	Unknown	27Ma02Gv
Fanny	18	F	Unknown	27Ma02Gv
MCAULEY, Ann	24	F	Unknown	27Ma02Gv
LEE, Margaret	30	F	Unknown	27Ma02Gv
Peter	12	M	Unknown	27Ma02Gv
Bernard	10	M	Unknown	27Ma02Gv
Terrence	5	M	Child	27Ma02Gv
MEALY, Jas.	14	M	Unknown	27Ma02Gv
FEENY, Ann	16	F	Unknown	27Ma02Gv
KEENAN, Patt	16	M	Unknown	27Ma02Gv
BLACKBURN, Mary	40	F	Unknown	27Ma02Gv
MONAHAN, Darby	30	M	Unknown	27Ma02Gv
Mary	30	F	Unknown	27Ma02Gv
Cathn.	4	F	Child	27Ma02Gv
MCGARNES, Mary	40	F	Unknown	27Ma02Gv
Rodger	4	M	Child	27Ma02Gv
Mary	2	F	Child	27Ma02Gv
ODONNEL, Daniel	20	M	Unknown	27Ma02Gv
HARDING, Jno.	20	M	Unknown	27Ma02Gv
Bridget	18	F	Unknown	27Ma02Gv
Mary	16	F	Unknown	27Ma02Gv
MCGRATH, Timothy	35	M	Unknown	27Ma02Gv
SAUCE, James	29	M	Unknown	27Ma02Gv
Ellen	5	F	Child	27Ma02Gv
MAHER, Susan	16	F	Unknown	27Ma02Gv
James	.10	M	Infant	27Ma02Gv
MULLHALL, Mary	21	F	Unknown	27Ma02Gv
CUMMINS, Betty	30	F	Unknown	27Ma02Gv
KELLY, U-Mrs.	46	F	Unknown	27Ma02Gv
BRYAN, Rose	20	F	Unknown	27Ma02Gv

YORKSHIRE 27 MAY 1850

From Liverpool

NAMES OF PASSENGERS	AGE	SEX	OCCUPATIONS	DATE PORT SHIP
DUGAN, Nancy	14	F	Laborer	27Ma02Az
Chas.	11	M	Farmer	27Ma02Az
COLLINS, Margt.	21	F	Farmer	27Ma02Az
MCKEENAN, Ann	30	F	Farmer	27Ma02Az
Jas.	12	M	Farmer	27Ma02Az
Mary	6	F	Child	27Ma02Az
Cathr.	4	F	Child	27Ma02Az
BIRD, Margtt.	14	F	Farmer	27Ma02Az
OBRIAN, Ann	50	F	Farmer	27Ma02Az
Margt.	16	F	Farmer	27Ma02Az
MAGUIRE, Margt.	24	F	Farmer	27Ma02Az
RENDEN, Ellen	2	F	Child	27Ma02Az
MCCLUSKEY, Danl.	22	M	Unknown	27Ma02Az
JORDAN, Maria	13	F	Unknown	27Ma02Az
CASEY, Jas.	30	M	Unknown	27Ma02Az
Jno.	16	M	Unknown	27Ma02Az
Cathr.	12	F	Unknown	27Ma02Az
Tunis	7	F	Child	27Ma02Az
MONAGHAN, Jno.	4	M	Child	27Ma02Az
HOGAN, Ann	16	F	Unknown	27Ma02Az
FLANIGAN, Bridget	5	F	Child	27Ma02Az
FINEGAN, Sarah	28	F	Unknown	27Ma02Az
Jas.	9	M	Child	27Ma02Az
Cathr.	6	F	Child	27Ma02Az
James	5	M	Child	27Ma02Az
CAMPBELL, Eliza	50	F	Unknown	27Ma02Az
U-Mr.	34	M	Unknown	27Ma02Az
U-Mrs.	25	F	Unknown	27Ma02Az
U	.00	F	Infant	27Ma02Az
Jos.	25	M	Unknown	27Ma02Az
Nancy	26	F	Unknown	27Ma02Az
U	.00	F	Infant	27Ma02Az
James	10	M	Unknown	27Ma02Az
Francis	8	M	Child	27Ma02Az
James	3	M	Child	27Ma02Az
DORRAN, Brid.	18	F	Unknown	27Ma02Az
OBRIAN, Mary	12	F	Unknown	27Ma02Az
Cathr.	6	F	Child	27Ma02Az
MCGANLY, Peter	18	M	Unknown	27Ma02Az
Bessey	25	F	Farmer	27Ma02Az
CAZELL, James	25	M	Laborer	27Ma02Az
U-Mrs.	28	F	Unknown	27Ma02Az
DELANEY, Dan	24	M	Unknown	27Ma02Az
U-Mr.	34	M	Unknown	27Ma02Az
FITZGERALD, Wm.	25	M	Unknown	27Ma02Az
KENNY, Marg.	20	F	Unknown	27Ma02Az
BRYAN, Ann	22	F	Unknown	27Ma02Az
MURPHY, J.	21	M	Unknown	27Ma02Az
DANGHAN, Dan	50	M	Unknown	27Ma02Az
Mary	33	F	Unknown	27Ma02Az
Pat	55	M	Unknown	27Ma02Az
Jno.	11	M	Unknown	27Ma02Az
Dennis	9	M	Child	27Ma02Az
Dan	5	M	Child	27Ma02Az
Pat	3	M	Child	27Ma02Az
Mary	9	F	Child	27Ma02Az
Ellen	7	F	Child	27Ma02Az
Margt.	5	F	Child	27Ma02Az
Jno.	3	M	Child	27Ma02Az
Wm.	.00	M	Infant	27Ma02Az
WHETBEARER, U-Mr.	25	M	Unknown	27Ma02Az
WALSH, Jas.	28	M	Unknown	27Ma02Az
BRAIT, Mary-Ann	26	F	Unknown	27Ma02Az
WHETBEARER, U-Mrs.	23	F	Unknown	27Ma02Az
LYNDER, Peter	21	M	Unknown	27Ma02Az
DOONAN, Rich.	25	M	Unknown	27Ma02Az
MCGRANE, Wm.	19	M	Unknown	27Ma02Az
MAHER, Timothy	30	M	Unknown	27Ma02Az
PURCELL, Pat.	29	M	Unknown	27Ma02Az
DORAN, Ann	23	F	Unknown	27Ma02Az
Cathr.	24	F	Unknown	27Ma02Az
TURRCEL, Edwd.	27	M	Unknown	27Ma02Az
Ellen	25	F	Unknown	27Ma02Az
LONGBOTTOM, Martha	60	F	Unknown	27Ma02Az
Jno.	22	M	Unknown	27Ma02Az
Ellen	24	F	Unknown	27Ma02Az
Chas.	19	M	Unknown	27Ma02Az
Saml.	16	M	Unknown	27Ma02Az
DONOHUE, Peter	28	M	Unknown	27Ma02Az
Bridt.	25	F	Unknown	27Ma02Az
KELLY, Michl.	18	M	Unknown	27Ma02Az
Danl.	28	M	Unknown	27Ma02Az
WHALEN, Jas.	20	M	Unknown	27Ma02Az
QUINN, Robt.	45	M	Farmer	27Ma02Az
KEEGAN, Biddy	18	F	Laborer	27Ma02Az
BISHOP, Jno.	26	M	Unknown	27Ma02Az
Theresa	22	F	Unknown	27Ma02Az
OCONNOR, U-Mr.	23	M	Unknown	27Ma02Az
U-Mrs.	23	F	Unknown	27Ma02Az
WALSH, Henry	20	M	Unknown	27Ma02Az
MCGEE, Sarah	25	F	Unknown	27Ma02Az
MALNA, Marg.	18	F	Unknown	27Ma02Az
BYRNE, Denis	6	M	Child	27Ma02Az
MCGAUGHRAN, Martha	30	F	Unknown	27Ma02Az
Jno.	13	M	Unknown	27Ma02Az
IRWAN, Cathr.	17	F	Unknown	27Ma02Az
RYAN, Ellen	18	F	Unknown	27Ma02Az
CUNNINGHAM, Pat	25	M	Unknown	27Ma02Az
Brid.	25	F	Unknown	27Ma02Az
Maria	6	F	Child	27Ma02Az

NAMES OF PASSENGERS	AGE	SEX	OCCUPATIONS	DATE PORT SHIP
CUNNINGHAM, Pat.	4	M	Child	27Ma02Az
Peter	.00	M	Infant	27Ma02Az
COFF, Mary	20	F	Unknown	27Ma02Az
DRAICK, Mary	18	F	Unknown	27Ma02Az
Bridt.	15	F	Unknown	27Ma02Az
Mary	13	F	Unknown	27Ma02Az
Jno.	11	M	Unknown	27Ma02Az
Ellen	4	F	Child	27Ma02Az
CALAGHAN, Cathr.	14	F	Unknown	27Ma02Az
ROHAN, Fras.	20	M	Unknown	27Ma02Az
CARR, Mary	8	F	Child	27Ma02Az
Ann	4	F	Child	27Ma02Az
FRERAN, Winl	50	M	Unknown	27Ma02Az
Mary	12	F	Unknown	27Ma02Az
Betty	10	F	Unknown	27Ma02Az
BURK, Jane	22	F	Unknown	27Ma02Az
GLONER, Mary	5	F	Child	27Ma02Az
MURPHY, Michl.	27	M	Unknown	27Ma02Az
KENDRICKS, Mary	25	F	Unknown	27Ma02Az
NOLAN, Margt.	25	F	Unknown	27Ma02Az
OCONNOR, Pat	13	M	Unknown	27Ma02Az
Mary	11	F	Unknown	27Ma02Az
MCHUGHS, Margt.	18	F	Unknown	27Ma02Az
KILLON, Jas.	14	M	Unknown	27Ma02Az
Tho.	12	M	Unknown	27Ma02Az
KEERNAN, Jas.	15	M	Unknown	27Ma02Az
SHENDAN, Mag.	20	F	Unknown	27Ma02Az
MCCANN, Brid.	20	F	Farmer	27Ma02Az
Michl.	25	M	Laborer	27Ma02Az
MCGRANE, Miles	16	M	Unknown	27Ma02Az
SWEENEY, Wm.	13	M	Unknown	27Ma02Az
BONNENCE, Mary	19	F	Unknown	27Ma02Az
MONTAGUE, Bridgt.	25	F	Unknown	27Ma02Az
Denis	40	M	Unknown	27Ma02Az
DONOHUE, Mary	18	F	Unknown	27Ma02Az
KELKENNY, Jno.	25	M	Unknown	27Ma02Az
KELLY, Cathr.	20	F	Unknown	27Ma02Az
MARTIN, Edwd.	5	M	Child	27Ma02Az
LAW, Ann	14	F	Unknown	27Ma02Az
Wm.	14	M	Unknown	27Ma02Az
RIELLY, Margt.	15	F	Unknown	27Ma02Az
CORBALLY, Margt.	20	F	Unknown	27Ma02Az
Mary	18	F	Unknown	27Ma02Az
Ann	19	F	Unknown	27Ma02Az
Wm.	14	M	Unknown	27Ma02Az
BILL, Fras.	14	M	Unknown	27Ma02Az
EVRENGTON, Anna	25	F	Unknown	27Ma02Az
MADDEN, Jas.	22	M	Unknown	27Ma02Az
ONEAL, U-Mrs.	50	F	Laborer	27Ma02Az
Cathr.	19	F	Farmer	27Ma02Az
Margt.	16	F	Unknown	27Ma02Az
Albert	10	M	Unknown	27Ma02Az
Fanny	6	F	Child	27Ma02Az
WHALAN, Mary	20	F	Unknown	27Ma02Az
GALLEGAN, Cathr.	20	F	Unknown	27Ma02Az
SHAUGHNESSY, Brid.	25	F	Unknown	27Ma02Az
HOLLERAN, Brid.	20	F	Unknown	27Ma02Az
FANNERY, Nabby	18	F	Unknown	27Ma02Az
KILMASTEN, Tho.	25	M	Unknown	27Ma02Az
GEFFNEY, Brid.	18	F	Unknown	27Ma02Az
HAMECE, Cathr.	21	F	Unknown	27Ma02Az
SIMMONS, Alf.W.	25	M	Unknown	27Ma02Az
U-Mrs.	24	F	Unknown	27Ma02Az
CONNERS, Dennis	16	M	Unknown	27Ma02Az
Corn.	18	M	Unknown	27Ma02Az
CATHENGAL, Eliza	26	F	Unknown	27Ma02Az
Jas.	.00	M	Infant	27Ma02Az
MCGEE, Ann	21	F	Unknown	27Ma02Az
COSGRAVE, Cathr.	21	F	Unknown	27Ma02Az
MURPHY, Danl.	30	M	Unknown	27Ma02Az
U-Mrs.	24	F	Unknown	27Ma02Az
CUMMINGS, Mary-A.	25	F	Unknown	27Ma02Az
DONOHUE, Wm.	16	M	Unknown	27Ma02Az
COWLESHOW, Jas.	20	M	Unknown	27Ma02Az
CARRAGAN, Owen	20	M	Unknown	27Ma02Az
MULEHY, John	26	M	Unknown	27Ma02Az
U-Mrs.	26	F	Unknown	27Ma02Az
Mary	60	F	Unknown	27Ma02Az
MAHER, John	28	M	Unknown	27Ma02Az
U-Mrs.	20	F	Unknown	27Ma02Az
Danl.	.00	M	Infant	27Ma02Az
CORKRAN, U-Mr.	24	M	Unknown	27Ma02Az
Margt.	20	F	Unknown	27Ma02Az
HAINES, Cabel	18	M	Unknown	27Ma02Az
LEARY, Jere	18	F	Unknown	27Ma02Az
DUNN, Johan	20	F	Unknown	27Ma02Az
WILLIAMS, Sulma	22	F	Unknown	27Ma02Az
CORMICK, Pat	19	M	Unknown	27Ma02Az
COMERFERD, Edwd.	16	M	Unknown	27Ma02Az
Brid.	20	F	Unknown	27Ma02Az
CONLLEN, Pat	40	M	Unknown	27Ma02Az
NINE, Wm.	20	M	Unknown	27Ma02Az
MCCRONE, Tho.	22	M	Unknown	27Ma02Az
MATHAN, Geo.	27	M	Unknown	27Ma02Az
U-Mrs.	24	F	Unknown	27Ma02Az
KILLELL, Henry	36	M	Unknown	27Ma02Az
Eliza	26	F	Unknown	27Ma02Az
BYRNS, Ann	30	F	Unknown	27Ma02Az
WALKER, Jno.	45	M	Unknown	27Ma02Az
LYON, Jane	40	F	Unknown	27Ma02Az
Martha	18	F	Unknown	27Ma02Az
Turis	13	M	Unknown	27Ma02Az
CARR, Wm.	30	M	Unknown	27Ma02Az
U-Mrs.	28	F	Unknown	27Ma02Az
Tho.	4	M	Child	27Ma02Az
Mary	2	F	Child	27Ma02Az
Alf.	.00	M	Infant	27Ma02Az
Peter	22	M	Unknown	27Ma02Az
Mary	20	F	Unknown	27Ma02Az
BOLANCE, Ann	20	F	Unknown	27Ma02Az
SHEAKER, James	24	M	Unknown	27Ma02Az
Geo.	20	M	Unknown	27Ma02Az
DENLEY, Jno.	24	M	Unknown	27Ma02Az
HARA, Jas.	22	M	Unknown	27Ma02Az
CANNON, Henry	28	M	Farmer	27Ma02Az
U-Mrs.	25	F	Laborer	27Ma02Az
DAIRY, Abrm.	21	M	Unknown	27Ma02Az
POACH, James	32	M	Unknown	27Ma02Az
MIEVS, Jas.	23	M	Unknown	27Ma02Az
U-Mrs.	23	F	Unknown	27Ma02Az
DOLAN, Nancy	50	F	Unknown	27Ma02Az
Jno.	14	M	Unknown	27Ma02Az
MAHER, Ellen	16	F	Unknown	27Ma02Az
RYAN, Nancy	40	F	Unknown	27Ma02Az
SMITH, Mary	23	F	Unknown	27Ma02Az
Pat	24	M	Unknown	27Ma02Az
LOYD, Robt.	22	M	Unknown	27Ma02Az
MCGOVEN, Tho.	20	M	Unknown	27Ma02Az
AKIN, Cathr.	10	F	Unknown	27Ma02Az
GOFFREY, Honer	7	M	Child	27Ma02Az
WELCH, Sam	22	M	Unknown	27Ma02Az
BARNWALL, Rob.	20	M	Unknown	27Ma02Az
RORY, Rochel	52	F	Unknown	27Ma02Az
Cathr.	52	F	Unknown	27Ma02Az
BRADY, Ann	50	F	Unknown	27Ma02Az
BURNS, Pat	19	M	Unknown	27Ma02Az
BRADY, Rose	6	F	Child	27Ma02Az
Ann	4	F	Child	27Ma02Az
MCGUIRE, Margt.	20	F	Unknown	27Ma02Az
Mich.	22	M	Unknown	27Ma02Az
DEVLEN, Jno.	18	M	Unknown	27Ma02Az
MOONEY, Cathr.	18	F	Unknown	27Ma02Az
Jas.	20	M	Unknown	27Ma02Az
SLEVEN, Tho.	20	M	Unknown	27Ma02Az
Rose	18	F	Farmer	27Ma02Az
OBRIEN, Wm.	36	M	Laborer	27Ma02Az
Margt.	30	F	Unknown	27Ma02Az
Wm.	10	M	Unknown	27Ma02Az
Cathr.	7	F	Child	27Ma02Az
Ellen	3	F	Child	27Ma02Az

NAMES OF PASSENGERS	AGE	SEX	OCCUPATIONS	DATE PORT SHIP
BRADY, Ann	16	F	Unknown	27Ma02Az
MCCAFREY, Chas.	30	M	Unknown	27Ma02Az
MCMANNERS, Brid.	18	F	Unknown	27Ma02Az
RIELLY, Jno.	11	M	Unknown	27Ma02Az
BROPHY, Mary	25	F	Unknown	27Ma02Az
GREER, Mrgt.	16	F	Unknown	27Ma02Az
HOGAN, Margt.	18	F	Unknown	27Ma02Az
Jane	17	F	Unknown	27Ma02Az
E.	15	F	Unknown	27Ma02Az
Wm.	13	M	Unknown	27Ma02Az
Mat.	10	M	Unknown	27Ma02Az
Jno.	8	M	Child	27Ma02Az
Alice	5	F	Child	27Ma02Az
LANG, Tho.	35	M	Unknown	27Ma02Az
CORMICK, Pat	26	M	Unknown	27Ma02Az
RIGBY, Alice	30	F	Unknown	27Ma02Az
DONOVAN, Maurice	32	M	Unknown	27Ma02Az
HICKEY, Jno.	20	M	Unknown	27Ma02Az
LYNCH, Ann	15	F	Unknown	27Ma02Az
DUFFY, Cathr.	20	F	Unknown	27Ma02Az
FLANAGAN, Tho.	30	M	Unknown	27Ma02Az
BRADY, Chas.	34	M	Unknown	27Ma02Az
FLANAGAN, Mat.	30	M	Unknown	27Ma02Az
CONEGAN, Jas.	40	M	Unknown	27Ma02Az
Jas.	9	M	Child	27Ma02Az
Bridgt.	17	F	Unknown	27Ma02Az
Thos.	12	M	Unknown	27Ma02Az
TROY, Margt.	18	F	Unknown	27Ma02Az
Jas.	40	M	Unknown	27Ma02Az
RYAN, Wm.	18	M	Unknown	27Ma02Az
MURPHY, Jno.	25	M	Unknown	27Ma02Az
LEGGETT, Jas.	18	M	Unknown	27Ma02Az
DONNELLY, Ann	22	F	Unknown	27Ma02Az
GEFFREY, Brid.	20	F	Unknown	27Ma02Az
ROONS, Wm.	28	M	Unknown	27Ma02Az
MEHAN, Mary	25	F	Unknown	27Ma02Az
Cathr.	.00	F	Infant	27Ma02Az
Ann	3	F	Child	27Ma02Az
BOLAND, Honor	28	M	Unknown	27Ma02Az
REGAN, Mary	26	F	Unknown	27Ma02Az
Mary	.00	F	Infant	27Ma02Az
CONNLLY, U-Mr.	25	M	Merchant	27Ma02Az
ORMSBY, U-Mr.	28	M	Merchant	27Ma02Az
HOPE, U-Mr.	35	M	Merchant	27Ma02Az
KILMARTIN, Margt	7	F	Child	27Ma02Az

VANGUARD 27 MAY 1850

From Liverpool

NAMES OF PASSENGERS	AGE	SEX	OCCUPATIONS	DATE PORT SHIP
SHINLOCK, Sophia	26	F	Unknown	27Ma02Gg
MCGIRVAN, Margt.	20	F	Unknown	27Ma02Gg
CASSIDY, Bridgt.	18	F	Unknown	27Ma02Gg
KIENNAN, Ann	18	F	Unknown	27Ma02Gg
KINDALE, Thos.	18	M	Laborer	27Ma02Gg
Christn.	21	M	Laborer	27Ma02Gg
KELLY, Thos.	30	M	Laborer	27Ma02Gg
KILMURRAY, Michl.	25	M	Laborer	27Ma02Gg
PHILLIPS, Christn.	25	M	Laborer	27Ma02Gg
MCKEIN, Bridgt.	18	F	Unknown	27Ma02Gg
OBRIEN, Mary	40	F	Unknown	27Ma02Gg
Margt.	10	F	Unknown	27Ma02Gg
Ellen	8	F	Child	27Ma02Gg
Patt	.00	M	Infant	27Ma02Gg
ROBERTS, Abrhm.	40	M	Unknown	27Ma02Gg
PINE, Esther	20	F	Lady	27Ma02Gg
ROBERTS, Ann	40	F	Unknown	27Ma02Gg
MULLONY, Mary	30	F	Unknown	27Ma02Gg
PINE, Albert	.00	M	Infant	27Ma02Gg
DONOVAN, Corn.	19	M	Laborer	27Ma02Gg
DRISCOTT, Thos.	19	M	Laborer	27Ma02Gg
MINAGHAN, Sarah	36	F	Seamstress	27Ma02Gg
PEGG, Richd.	20	M	Blacksmith	27Ma02Gg
CLIFFORD, Ann	26	F	Unknown	27Ma02Gg
OWENS, John	22	M	Laborer	27Ma02Gg
GLANCY, John	22	M	Laborer	27Ma02Gg
GALL, Chas.	50	M	Laborer	27Ma02Gg
Margt.	50	F	Unknown	27Ma02Gg
KEELY, Thos.	30	M	Laborer	27Ma02Gg
PIERCE, Cathe.	5	F	Child	27Ma02Gg
MCGEE, Bridgt.	10	F	Unknown	27Ma02Gg
MCGOWAN, Honor	15	F	Unknown	27Ma02Gg
KEIGAN, Mary	19	F	Unknown	27Ma02Gg
KILLAGHER, Mary	24	F	Unknown	27Ma02Gg
Martha	20	F	Unknown	27Ma02Gg
HENAGHTY, Biddy	27	F	Unknown	27Ma02Gg
MORRISON, Wm.	27	M	Unknown	27Ma02Gg
DORAN, Susan	8	F	Child	27Ma02Gg
Hugh	5	M	Child	27Ma02Gg
CARRALD, Hugh	35	M	Trader	27Ma02Gg
Edwd.	28	M	Trader	27Ma02Gg
GOBLING, Susan	40	F	Servant	27Ma02Gg
Rosey	13	F	Unknown	27Ma02Gg
Susan	11	F	Unknown	27Ma02Gg
James	8	M	Child	27Ma02Gg
Patt	6	M	Child	27Ma02Gg
Biddy	.00	F	Infant	27Ma02Gg
LOYNE, Patt	38	M	Laborer	27Ma02Gg
BYRNE, Ann	30	F	Unknown	27Ma02Gg
HOLLEN, Hugh	18	M	Baker	27Ma02Gg
LEE, John	20	M	Unknown	27Ma02Gg
COLLINS, Bridgt.	24	F	Unknown	27Ma02Gg
SMITH, Patt	20	M	Unknown	27Ma02Gg
HURLEY, Ellen	24	F	Unknown	27Ma02Gg
Ann	21	F	Unknown	27Ma02Gg
BASSILE, Mary	30	F	Unknown	27Ma02Gg
Bridgt.	5	F	Child	27Ma02Gg
HERRING, Wm.	54	M	Unknown	27Ma02Gg
HOLMES, Francis	20	M	Unknown	27Ma02Gg
CULBASON, James	20	M	Farmer	27Ma02Gg
Jane	17	F	Unknown	27Ma02Gg
MARON, Peter	26	M	Laborer	27Ma02Gg
Mary	30	F	Unknown	27Ma02Gg
MCCARTNEY, James	25	M	Blacksmith	27Ma02Gg
BAHY, John	24	M	Laborer	27Ma02Gg
MARON, Mary	19	F	Unknown	27Ma02Gg
BYRNE, John	18	M	Plasterer	27Ma02Gg
JORDON, Elizh.	23	F	Dressmaker	27Ma02Gg
WHITFORD, Jane	50	F	Milliner	27Ma02Gg
Jane	25	F	Unknown	27Ma02Gg
Saml.	18	M	Unknown	27Ma02Gg
Mary	17	F	Unknown	27Ma02Gg
CALDWELL, Ann	22	F	Unknown	27Ma02Gg
FLYNN, Honora	5	F	Child	27Ma02Gg
FITZPATRICK, Patt	22	M	Unknown	27Ma02Gg
LEE, Thos.	30	M	Unknown	27Ma02Gg
Rose	35	F	Unknown	27Ma02Gg
Margt.	12	F	Unknown	27Ma02Gg
Patt	9	M	Child	27Ma02Gg
SHORT, Martha	17	F	Child	27Ma02Gg
NESBITT, James	32	M	Schm	27Ma02Gg
DUCY, Margt.	17	F	Unknown	27Ma02Gg
CARR, Timy.	22	M	Unknown	27Ma02Gg
SCULLY, Nancy	24	F	Unknown	27Ma02Gg
MINAGHAN, Patt	24	M	Unknown	27Ma02Gg
KEELY, Elizh.	22	F	Unknown	27Ma02Gg
CASSIDY, John	24	M	Stkw	27Ma02Gg
BROPHY, Ellen	45	F	Unknown	27Ma02Gg
BARNAVILLE, James	13	M	Unknown	27Ma02Gg
Thos.	10	M	Unknown	27Ma02Gg
TROBE, John	30	M	Shepherd	27Ma02Gg
KELLY, Margt.	19	F	Unknown	27Ma02Gg
MANIN, Eliza	19	F	Unknown	27Ma02Gg
LAWLER, Ann	20	F	Unknown	27Ma02Gg

NAMES OF PASSENGERS	AGE	SEX	OCCUPATIONS	DATE PORT SHIP
LAWLER, Thos.	7	M	Child	27Ma02Gg
OCONNELL, Francis	30	M	Engineer	27Ma02Gg
HENRY, Mary	19	F	Unknown	27Ma02Gg
Mary-A.	.00	F	Infant	27Ma02Gg
RAMSEY, Francis	25	M	Unknown	27Ma02Gg
MURPHY, Eliza	25	F	Unknown	27Ma02Gg
GOODWIN, Dennis	20	M	Unknown	27Ma02Gg
Sarah	21	F	Unknown	27Ma02Gg
Rose	18	F	Unknown	27Ma02Gg
MCCANN, Barry	20	M	Unknown	27Ma02Gg
MINAGHAN, Patt	18	M	Unknown	27Ma02Gg
MOORE, Patt	18	M	Unknown	27Ma02Gg
John	16	M	Unknown	27Ma02Gg
Thos.	8	M	Child	27Ma02Gg
CONRY, Francis	50	M	Unknown	27Ma02Gg
Mary	50	F	Unknown	27Ma02Gg
OBRIEN, John	37	M	Unknown	27Ma02Gg
FRENCH, Patt	26	M	Unknown	27Ma02Gg
RYAN, John	30	M	Unknown	27Ma02Gg
Ann	25	F	Unknown	27Ma02Gg
DWYER, Mary	30	F	Unknown	27Ma02Gg
FANNING, Michl.	30	M	Laborer	27Ma02Gg
LOUTH, Michl.	20	M	Currier	27Ma02Gg
MCKENNY, Thos.	20	M	Blacksmith	27Ma02Gg
CASSIDY, John	35	M	Unknown	27Ma02Gg
SHEWELL, Rosey	21	F	Unknown	27Ma02Gg
LOBE, Wm.	26	M	Merchant	27Ma02Gg
GILMORE, Wm.	19	M	Unknown	27Ma02Gg
STEWART, Martha	18	F	Dressmaker	27Ma02Gg
Betty	22	F	Unknown	27Ma02Gg
CARROLL, James	20	M	Laborer	27Ma02Gg
MATTHIAS, James	21	M	Laborer	27Ma02Gg
MARTIN, Mary	19	F	Laborer	27Ma02Gg
ROURKE, Patt	18	M	Laborer	27Ma02Gg
Eliza	20	F	Unknown	27Ma02Gg
FITZPATRICK, John	38	M	Laborer	27Ma02Gg
Margt.	12	F	Unknown	27Ma02Gg
Phil	36	M	Laborer	27Ma02Gg
Cathe.	12	F	Unknown	27Ma02Gg
MCBRIEN, Daffney	16	F	Unknown	27Ma02Gg
Rose	13	F	Unknown	27Ma02Gg
CULVEN, John	34	M	Laborer	27Ma02Gg
Rose	11	F	Unknown	27Ma02Gg
MCCAM, Hugh	40	M	Laborer	27Ma02Gg
Michl.	16	M	Laborer	27Ma02Gg
Cathe.	14	F	Unknown	27Ma02Gg
FARRELLY, Math.	40	M	Laborer	27Ma02Gg
James	11	M	Unknown	27Ma02Gg
Cathe.	9	F	Child	27Ma02Gg
LEE, Michl.	38	M	Laborer	27Ma02Gg
Thos.	40	M	Laborer	27Ma02Gg
KEAN, Margt.	60	F	Unknown	27Ma02Gg
Patt	15	M	Unknown	27Ma02Gg
Frank	11	M	Unknown	27Ma02Gg
Ann	10	F	Unknown	27Ma02Gg
Margt.	7	F	Child	27Ma02Gg
ROCHE, Pierce	26	M	Engineer	27Ma02Gg
DWYRE, Dennis	17	M	Farmer	27Ma02Gg
ROBERTS, Mary	17	F	Dressmaker	27Ma02Gg
LAWLESS, Susan	18	F	Dressmaker	27Ma02Gg
CONNOR, Elizh.	28	F	Unknown	27Ma02Gg
GLASS, Pheobe	23	F	Unknown	27Ma02Gg
Anna	25	F	Unknown	27Ma02Gg
GALLAGHAN, Mary	56	F	Unknown	27Ma02Gg
HAGERTY, Michl.	23	M	Unknown	27Ma02Gg
BUCKLEY, Corn.	20	M	Watchmaker	27Ma02Gg
Margt.	20	F	Dressmaker	27Ma02Gg
FISHER, Dennis	26	M	Dyer	27Ma02Gg
LEAHY, John	16	M	Weaver	27Ma02Gg
BOSWELL, Jane	29	F	Unknown	27Ma02Gg
Patt	2	M	Child	27Ma02Gg
DOOLING, John	25	M	Unknown	27Ma02Gg
Patt	3	M	Child	27Ma02Gg
ONEAL, Patt	2	M	Child	27Ma02Gg
SULLIVAN, Margt.	28	F	Unknown	27Ma02Gg
BRANNIGAN, Hugh	29	M	Shoemaker	27Ma02Gg
BOSWELL, James	30	M	Unknown	27Ma02Gg
SHIELDS, Patt	30	M	Unknown	27Ma02Gg
DONOVAN, Johanna	20	F	Dressmaker	27Ma02Gg
BRIEN, Ellen	20	F	Dressmaker	27Ma02Gg
CARROLL, Michl.	20	M	Laborer	27Ma02Gg
WALSH, Mary	24	F	Unknown	27Ma02Gg
SULLIVAN, Ellen	27	F	Unknown	27Ma02Gg
RYANS, Thos.	26	M	Unknown	27Ma02Gg
MORAN, Margt.	26	F	Unknown	27Ma02Gg
MURPHY, Wm.	23	M	Laborer	27Ma02Gg
SULLIVAN, Michl.	35	M	Roof Maker	27Ma02Gg
Ellen	33	F	Unknown	27Ma02Gg
Mary	7	F	Child	27Ma02Gg
Margt.	35	F	Unknown	27Ma02Gg
Cathe.	11	F	Unknown	27Ma02Gg
Joe	9	M	Child	27Ma02Gg
DRISCOTT, Johanna	26	F	Unknown	27Ma02Gg
BARNEY, Margt.	20	F	Unknown	27Ma02Gg
Patt	15	M	Unknown	27Ma02Gg
SULLIVAN, Margt.	.00	F	Infant	27Ma02Gg
MAHONEY, Hannah	6	F	Child	27Ma02Gg
MOLVY, Wm.	30	M	Unknown	27Ma02Gg
CONNOR, Margt.	20	F	Unknown	27Ma02Gg
Hugh	23	M	Smith	27Ma02Gg
KEARNY, Peter	25	M	Wood Cutter	27Ma02Gg
FARRELL, Bryan	21	M	Shoemaker	27Ma02Gg
SWEENEY, Bridgt.	22	F	Unknown	27Ma02Gg
Margt.	18	F	Unknown	27Ma02Gg
John	32	M	Laborer	27Ma02Gg
WHITE, Bridgt.	30	F	Hatter	27Ma02Gg
ROBINSON, John	38	M	Unknown	27Ma02Gg
Sarah	35	F	Unknown	27Ma02Gg
Cathe.	.00	F	Infant	27Ma02Gg
LEAVY, Edwd.	26	M	Stctr	27Ma02Gg
Mary	26	F	Unknown	27Ma02Gg
MCGUINNESS, Dennis	23	M	Mason	27Ma02Gg
Mary	19	F	Unknown	27Ma02Gg
EVANS, Margt.	26	F	Unknown	27Ma02Gg
Nathl.	25	M	Stctr	27Ma02Gg
LAWLER, Thos.	22	M	Laborer	27Ma02Gg
Mary	22	F	Unknown	27Ma02Gg
DOWNEY, Cathe.	21	F	Unknown	27Ma02Gg
Mary	23	F	Unknown	27Ma02Gg
OWENS, Margt.	35	F	Unknown	27Ma02Gg
HAGGERTY, Bridgt.	23	F	Unknown	27Ma02Gg
Mary	19	F	Unknown	27Ma02Gg
MCHUGH, Thos.	30	M	Weaver	27Ma02Gg
CORCORAN, Wm.	23	M	Laborer	27Ma02Gg
GILLASPIE, Lilly	20	F	Unknown	27Ma02Gg
Mary	14	F	Unknown	27Ma02Gg
CONNOR, John	20	M	Farmer	27Ma02Gg
CAMPBELL, Patt	27	M	Brewer	27Ma02Gg
CASSIDY, Patt	26	M	Maltster	27Ma02Gg
FAUGHY, John	20	M	Mason	27Ma02Gg
Bridgt.	24	F	Unknown	27Ma02Gg
ENGLISHBY, Mary	19	F	Unknown	27Ma02Gg
Margt.	20	F	Unknown	27Ma02Gg
MORGAN, Mary	20	F	Unknown	27Ma02Gg
DOUGHERTY, James	18	M	Laborer	27Ma02Gg
CAMPBELL, John	26	M	Baker	27Ma02Gg
WATT, Thos.	35	M	Shoemaker	27Ma02Gg
LANAN, John	30	M	Laborer	27Ma02Gg
MCCABE, Hugh	20	M	Laborer	27Ma02Gg
MCCUE, Patt	35	M	Laborer	27Ma02Gg
Frank	30	M	Laborer	27Ma02Gg
BOYLE, Wm.	17	M	Turner	27Ma02Gg
LANAN, Cathe.	20	F	Unknown	27Ma02Gg
QUIRK, James	25	M	Turner	27Ma02Gg
AVNICK, Thos.	40	M	Miner	27Ma02Gg
HENRY, James	20	M	Student	27Ma02Gg
Terresa	18	F	Unknown	27Ma02Gg
FITZGERRALD, James	25	M	Laborer	27Ma02Gg
MCCARROW, Mary	18	F	Unknown	27Ma02Gg
COUGHLAN, Mary	20	F	Unknown	27Ma02Gg

NAMES OF PASSENGERS	AGE	SEX	OCCUPATIONS	DATE PORT SHIP
WALLDS, Patt	30	M	Laborer	27Ma02Gg
Ellen	20	F	Unknown	27Ma02Gg
MCCANN, Margt.	32	F	Unknown	27Ma02Gg
Ellen	18	F	Unknown	27Ma02Gg
SMITH, Joseph	18	M	Gentleman	27Ma02Gg
BROWN, Edwin-B.	21	M	Gentleman	27Ma02Gg
POWELL, James	35	M	Gentleman	27Ma02Gg
Elizabeth	34	F	None	27Ma02Gg
Annie	34	F	None	27Ma02Gg
Elizabeth	11	F	None	27Ma02Gg

JOHN-HAMILTON 22 MAY 1850

From Liverpool

NAMES OF PASSENGERS	AGE	SEX	OCCUPATIONS	DATE PORT SHIP
HATCH, Jno.	29	M	Tailor	22Ma02Gq
BAKER, Joseph	29	M	Farmer	22Ma02Gq
Jno.	21	M	Farmer	22Ma02Gq
JAMES, Jno.	30	M	Farmer	22Ma02Gq
Anne	30	F	None	22Ma02Gq
Edward	3	M	Child	22Ma02Gq
George	2	M	Child	22Ma02Gq
HANBURG, John	24	M	Laborer	22Ma02Gq
Anne	20	F	None	22Ma02Gq
Richard	.00	M	Infant	22Ma02Gq
BUNTING, Sarah	26	F	Milliner	22Ma02Gq
MATHEWS, Thomas	30	M	Nailer	22Ma02Gq
NESBITT, Robt.	35	M	Farmer	22Ma02Gq
Selina	30	F	Wife	22Ma02Gq
Jno.	60	M	Farmer	22Ma02Gq
Jane	45	F	Farmer	22Ma02Gq
Mary	30	F	Farmer	22Ma02Gq
Robt.	24	M	Farmer	22Ma02Gq
Dora	23	F	Farmer	22Ma02Gq
Susan	22	F	Farmer	22Ma02Gq
Isaac	20	M	Farmer	22Ma02Gq
James	15	M	Farmer	22Ma02Gq
Charles	13	M	Farmer	22Ma02Gq
Francis	11	M	Farmer	22Ma02Gq
Jane-Anne	8	F	Child	22Ma02Gq
Henry	7	M	Child	22Ma02Gq
Richard	12	M	Farmer	22Ma02Gq
Arthur	9	F	Child	22Ma02Gq
RAFFERTY, Patt	35	M	Servant	22Ma02Gq
INGOLDRICH, Jno.	36	M	Farmer	22Ma02Gq
MCCANN, Jno.	20	M	Grocer	22Ma02Gq
ROONEY, Bernard	30	M	Farmer	22Ma02Gq
Terence	28	M	Farmer	22Ma02Gq
MCNADE, Anne	40	F	Spinster	22Ma02Gq
Mary	12	F	None	22Ma02Gq
Anne	10	F	None	22Ma02Gq
BARKER, Jno.	28	M	Farmer	22Ma02Gq
DRYER, Sally	20	F	Spinster	22Ma02Gq
LAWLOR, Cath.	25	F	Dairymaid	22Ma02Gq
BUTLER, Edmund	24	M	Laborer	22Ma02Gq
Charles	20	M	None	22Ma02Gq
Johanna	60	F	Unknown	22Ma02Gq
Thomas	28	M	Unknown	22Ma02Gq
NEAGLE, Pat	48	M	Farmer	22Ma02Gq
Margt.	35	F	Farmer	22Ma02Gq
Mary	18	F	Farmer	22Ma02Gq
John	14	M	Farmer	22Ma02Gq
Wm.	13	M	Farmer	22Ma02Gq
James	8	M	Child	22Ma02Gq
Anne	6	F	Child	22Ma02Gq
SHEEHAN, Dennis	50	M	Gdnr	22Ma02Gq
SULLIVAN, Jno.	15	M	Laborer	22Ma02Gq
DORAN, Bessy	18	F	Spinster	22Ma02Gq
Patt	17	M	Farmer	22Ma02Gq

NAMES OF PASSENGERS	AGE	SEX	OCCUPATIONS	DATE PORT SHIP
DORAN, Susan	20	F	None	22Ma02Gq
Mary	18	F	None	22Ma02Gq
LOONEY, Wm.	25	M	Molder	22Ma02Gq
FIRTH, John	41	M	Weaver	22Ma02Gq
Mary	23	F	Wife	22Ma02Gq
FLEMING, Mary	22	F	Lad	22Ma02Gq
Margt.	16	F	Lad	22Ma02Gq
LOONEY, Jerry	28	M	Molder	22Ma02Gq
MORGAN, Richd.	49	M	Farmer	22Ma02Gq
Mary	40	F	Farmer	22Ma02Gq
Thomas	13	M	Farmer	22Ma02Gq
Nick	10	M	Farmer	22Ma02Gq
WELSH, Mick	50	M	Farmer	22Ma02Gq
Eliza	45	F	Farmer	22Ma02Gq
Jno.	20	M	Farmer	22Ma02Gq
Bridget	18	F	Farmer	22Ma02Gq
Johanna	16	F	Farmer	22Ma02Gq
Pat	12	M	Farmer	22Ma02Gq
Thomas	10	M	Farmer	22Ma02Gq
Mick	9	M	Child	22Ma02Gq
Robert	7	M	Child	22Ma02Gq
Arthur	2	M	Child	22Ma02Gq
John	26	M	Farmer	22Ma02Gq
Thomas	22	M	Farmer	22Ma02Gq
Johanna	21	F	Farmer	22Ma02Gq
ELOSHAN, Wm.	27	M	Laborer	22Ma02Gq
BERGIN, Nicholas	55	M	Farmer	22Ma02Gq
Ellen	49	F	Farmer	22Ma02Gq
Mick	26	M	Farmer	22Ma02Gq
Mary	24	F	Farmer	22Ma02Gq
Margt.	20	F	Farmer	22Ma02Gq
Wm.	18	M	Farmer	22Ma02Gq
BERIGAN, Cath.	16	F	Farmer	22Ma02Gq
Ellen	15	F	Farmer	22Ma02Gq
Edmond	9	M	Child	22Ma02Gq
Bridget	8	F	Child	22Ma02Gq
Johanna	7	F	Child	22Ma02Gq
Sarah	5	F	Child	22Ma02Gq
Honora	4	F	Child	22Ma02Gq
KIRBY, Thos.	16	M	Farmer	22Ma02Gq
RICHMAN, Bildad	22	M	Gdnr	22Ma02Gq
Bryan	26	M	Gdnr	22Ma02Gq
Anne	26	F	Gdnr	22Ma02Gq
BARNES, David	24	M	Servant	22Ma02Gq
Sarah	20	F	Unknown	22Ma02Gq
DOYLE, Cath.	20	F	Spinster	22Ma02Gq
Mary	20	F	Spinster	22Ma02Gq
BRESNAHAN, John	20	M	Laborer	22Ma02Gq
DILLON, Thos.	20	M	Farmer	22Ma02Gq
James	17	M	Unknown	22Ma02Gq
Richard	16	M	Unknown	22Ma02Gq
SWEENEY, Anne	17	F	Spinster	22Ma02Gq
CREANS, Mary	24	F	Spinster	22Ma02Gq
BANNON, Bernard	30	M	Farmer	22Ma02Gq
MEGEE, Cath.	20	F	Spinster	22Ma02Gq
MAHER, John	24	M	Tailor	22Ma02Gq
HENRY, Thomas	36	M	Farmer	22Ma02Gq
Cath.	36	F	Farmer	22Ma02Gq
Nicholas	13	M	Farmer	22Ma02Gq
Cath.	10	F	Farmer	22Ma02Gq
Jno.	8	M	Child	22Ma02Gq
Margt.	6	F	Child	22Ma02Gq
Thomas	4	M	Child	22Ma02Gq
Andrew	.00	M	Infant	22Ma02Gq
MCCABE, Jno.	40	M	Laborer	22Ma02Gq
BULLWINKLE, Jno.	22	M	Mtldlr	22Ma02Gq
MONTGOMERY, George	25	M	Farmer	22Ma02Gq
TURNER, Alice	31	F	Wife	22Ma02Gq
Mary	6	F	Child	22Ma02Gq
Edmund	10	M	Son	22Ma02Gq
DAVIS, Thos.	25	M	Farmer	22Ma02Gq
Jane	23	F	Farmer	22Ma02Gq
DOGHERTY, James	31	M	Printer	22Ma02Gq
MAGUIRE, Jno.	25	M	Shoemaker	22Ma02Gq
AMES, Sarah	18	F	Milliner	22Ma02Gq

NAMES OF PASSENGERS		AGE	SEX	OCCUPATIONS	DATE PORT SHIP
LONGMAN, Margt.		21	F	Milliner	22Ma02Gq
BOWNIE, Mark		45	M	Carpenter	22Ma02Gq
Dora		40	F	Wife	22Ma02Gq
MANGAN, John		35	M	Carpenter	22Ma02Gq
FIELD, Mick		25	M	Carpenter	22Ma02Gq
CAVANAGH, Margt.		19	F	Spinster	22Ma02Gq
RYAN, Margt.		20	F	Spinster	22Ma02Gq
KENNEDY, Sarah		23	F	Spinster	22Ma02Gq
BYRNE, Thos.		19	M	Laborer	22Ma02Gq
Margt.		17	F	Laborer	22Ma02Gq
HOLLAND, Jos.		24	M	Unknown	22Ma02Gq
BLACKEN, Henry		19	M	Farmer	22Ma02Gq
FENTON, John		22	M	Corn Miller	22Ma02Gq
CAVANAGH, James		30	M	Laborer	22Ma02Gq
Jno.		20	M	Laborer	22Ma02Gq
Bridget		26	F	Dairymaid	22Ma02Gq
Cath.		25	F	Dairymaid	22Ma02Gq
FEGAN, Andrew		30	M	Laborer	22Ma02Gq
BOWDEN, Mick		33	M	Laborer	22Ma02Gq
BEATTY, Anne		50	F	House Maid	22Ma02Gq
Sarah		26	F	House Maid	22Ma02Gq
Robert		.00	M	Infant	22Ma02Gq
CUNNINGHAM, Milty		26	M	Baker	22Ma02Gq
LONG, Nathl.		31	M	Laborer	22Ma02Gq
Emery		28	M	Laborer	22Ma02Gq
Jno.		.00	M	Infant	22Ma02Gq
Jno.A.		38	M	Unknown	22Ma02Gq
BOWDON, Sarah		48	F	Spinster	22Ma02Gq
Susanna		21	F	Spinster	22Ma02Gq
Henry		24	M	Unknown	22Ma02Gq
Anne		12	F	Unknown	22Ma02Gq
GALLON, Margt.		25	F	Spinster	22Ma02Gq
Nathanl.		5	M	Child	22Ma02Gq
Francis		.00	M	Infant	22Ma02Gq
EMERY, Jno.		30	M	Laborer	22Ma02Gq
EVANS, Jno.		21	M	Laborer	22Ma02Gq
Ellen		21	F	Spinster	22Ma02Gq
YATES, John		12	M	Unknown	22Ma02Gq
JONES, Ellen		21	F	Spinster	22Ma02Gq
WALKER, George		45	M	Irnmldr	22Ma02Gq
U	(W)	40	F	None	22Ma02Gq
WATSON, Joseph		43	M	Laborer	22Ma02Gq
BAKER, Thomas		28	M	Laborer	22Ma02Gq
HOLDEN, Thomas		72	M	Farmer	22Ma02Gq
Evans		25	M	Farmer	22Ma02Gq
James		21	M	Farmer	22Ma02Gq
Eliza		65	F	Farmer	22Ma02Gq
Ellen		19	F	Farmer	22Ma02Gq
FLYNN, Festus		20	M	Laborer	22Ma02Gq
Thomas		5	M	Child	22Ma02Gq
LETTY, Leonard		50	M	Farmer	22Ma02Gq
U	(W)	46	F	Farmer	22Ma02Gq
Leonard		20	M	Farmer	22Ma02Gq
Anne		18	F	Farmer	22Ma02Gq
Mary		15	F	Farmer	22Ma02Gq
John		13	M	Farmer	22Ma02Gq
George		11	M	Farmer	22Ma02Gq
Brid.		8	F	Child	22Ma02Gq
Nathan		6	M	Child	22Ma02Gq
Jane		.00	F	Infant	22Ma02Gq
MOORE, Keran		26	M	Farmer	22Ma02Gq
FITZPATRICK, Thos.		20	M	Farmer	22Ma02Gq
PHELAN, Pat		30	M	Farmer	22Ma02Gq
ALLEN, George		26	M	Farmer	22Ma02Gq
FROUNES, Mary		27	F	Spinster	22Ma02Gq
MCCANN, James		25	M	Laborer	22Ma02Gq
REILLY, Christie		20	M	Butcher	22Ma02Gq
GREY, Thos.		27	M	Farmer	22Ma02Gq
PLOWEY, Henry		28	M	Farmer	22Ma02Gq
HANSTOR, George		20	M	Farmer	22Ma02Gq
U	(W)	21	F	Farmer	22Ma02Gq
JOHNSON, John		30	M	Laborer	22Ma02Gq
U	(W)	22	F	Laborer	22Ma02Gq
Mary-Anne		7	F	Child	22Ma02Gq
Wm.		5	M	Child	22Ma02Gq

NAMES OF PASSENGERS		AGE	SEX	OCCUPATIONS	DATE PORT SHIP
MATHER, Jno.		30	M	Laborer	22Ma02Gq
HILL, U		35	M	Farmer	22Ma02Gq
U	(W)	35	F	Farmer	22Ma02Gq
Jane		10	F	Farmer	22Ma02Gq
John		8	M	Child	22Ma02Gq
Thomas		6	M	Child	22Ma02Gq
Anne		4	F	Child	22Ma02Gq
KEAT, Thos.		50	M	Farmer	22Ma02Gq
U	(W)	50	F	Farmer	22Ma02Gq
Thomas		20	M	Farmer	22Ma02Gq
MONLAN, Thos.		60	M	Farmer	22Ma02Gq
U	(W)	50	F	Farmer	22Ma02Gq
Thomas		15	M	Farmer	22Ma02Gq
Bessy		12	F	Farmer	22Ma02Gq
Anne		8	F	Child	22Ma02Gq
Susanna		3	F	Child	22Ma02Gq
Margt.		11	F	Farmer	22Ma02Gq
CAITHIN, Me.		30	M	Farmer	22Ma02Gq
Mary-Bess		30	F	Farmer	22Ma02Gq
U		.00	U	Infant	22Ma02Gq
GABRIEL, Hymes		40	M	Tailor	22Ma02Gq
BOWEN, Lyans		29	M	Joiner	22Ma02Gq
SYLVESTONE, U-Mrs.		34	F	Tailor	22Ma02Gq
Morris		6	M	Child	22Ma02Gq
William		2	M	Child	22Ma02Gq
CARNELL, Thos.		33	M	Cbtmkr	22Ma02Gq
GOGGIN, Dan		24	M	Gdnr	22Ma02Gq
Jane		25	F	Servant	22Ma02Gq
HILL, James		24	M	Laborer	22Ma02Gq
LEAVERS, Patt		15	M	Laborer	22Ma02Gq
MURPHY, Martin		20	M	Laborer	22Ma02Gq
Alice		21	F	Spinster	22Ma02Gq
Bridgett		18	F	Laborer	22Ma02Gq
GRADY, Thos.		26	M	Laborer	22Ma02Gq
WHELAN, U-Mrs.		17	F	Spinster	22Ma02Gq
DEAN, Lewis		50	M	Farmer	22Ma02Gq
Patt		24	M	Farmer	22Ma02Gq
Peter		10	M	Farmer	22Ma02Gq
Mary		6	F	Child	22Ma02Gq
MURPHY, Peter		30	M	Farmer	22Ma02Gq
Cath.		35	F	Farmer	22Ma02Gq
BYRNE, Mary		40	F	Farmer	22Ma02Gq
MORGAN, Anne		12	F	Farmer	22Ma02Gq
Sarah		6	F	Child	22Ma02Gq
CANFIELD, Mary		18	F	Farmer	22Ma02Gq
Jas.		39	M	Farmer	22Ma02Gq
MCCANE, Bryan		31	M	Farmer	22Ma02Gq
GIBBIN, U		20	M	Farmer	22Ma02Gq
BRENNAN, Jas.		30	M	Butcher	22Ma02Gq
Eliza		30	F	Butcher	22Ma02Gq
Patt		.00	M	Infant	22Ma02Gq
WOODS, Cath.		30	F	Butcher	22Ma02Gq
John		7	M	Child	22Ma02Gq
Michael		5	M	Child	22Ma02Gq
MCLOUGHLAN, Rose		45	F	Butcher	22Ma02Gq
Owen		25	M	Butcher	22Ma02Gq
Ellen		12	F	Unknown	22Ma02Gq
Patt		5	M	Child	22Ma02Gq
LEARY, Biddy		20	F	Spinster	22Ma02Gq
HARNEAH, Ellen		50	F	Spinster	22Ma02Gq
William		13	M	Farmer	22Ma02Gq
LEAN, Margt.		20	F	Spinster	22Ma02Gq
HANSEN, Jas.		12	M	Spinner	22Ma02Gq
DALY, Barney		18	M	Laborer	22Ma02Gq
Rose		22	F	Laborer	22Ma02Gq
Biddy		14	F	Laborer	22Ma02Gq
Mary		12	F	Laborer	22Ma02Gq
MCCALLEN, Jas.		18	M	Laborer	22Ma02Gq
MCEWIN, Hugh		25	M	Unknown	22Ma02Gq
FINN, Jas.		30	M	Unknown	22Ma02Gq
Thos.		23	M	Unknown	22Ma02Gq
MANY, Patt		16	M	Unknown	22Ma02Gq
Mary		18	F	Spinster	22Ma02Gq
DALEY, Ann		41	F	Spinster	22Ma02Gq
Patt		22	M	Shoemaker	22Ma02Gq

NAMES OF PASSENGERS	AGE	SEX	OCCUPATIONS	DATE PORT SHIP
DALEY, Mick	20	M	Shoemaker	22Ma02Gq
Anne	18	F	Shoemaker	22Ma02Gq
Susan	10	F	Shoemaker	22Ma02Gq
Edwd.	9	M	Child	22Ma02Gq
BREEN, Robt.	22	M	Farmer	22Ma02Gq
BROWN, Florence	23	F	Laborer	22Ma02Gq
ELLIOTT, Robt.	20	M	Farmer	22Ma02Gq
Wm.	18	M	Farmer	22Ma02Gq
GORMAN, Mary	24	F	Spinster	22Ma02Gq
Mary	50	F	Spinster	22Ma02Gq
NOOK, James	24	M	Laborer	22Ma02Gq
CAMPBELL, Jno.	22	M	Laborer	22Ma02Gq
NEWLAND, Mi.	26	M	Laborer	22Ma02Gq
BOOTS, James	12	M	Laborer	22Ma02Gq
Robt.	9	M	Child	22Ma02Gq
Mary	6	F	Child	22Ma02Gq
Jeanett	3	F	Child	22Ma02Gq
John	.00	M	Infant	22Ma02Gq
TAYLOR, Jeffry	40	M	Bleacher	22Ma02Gq
James	34	M	Baker	22Ma02Gq
Sarah	30	F	Baker	22Ma02Gq
MCMAHON, Bernd.	20	M	Laborer	22Ma02Gq
MCALOON, Michl.	20	M	None	22Ma02Gq
KANE, Thos.	21	M	Shoemaker	22Ma02Gq
MCGUILLAN, Dennis	20	M	Laborer	22Ma02Gq
ROONEY, Thos.	25	M	Carpenter	22Ma02Gq
COULON, M.	25	M	Shoemaker	22Ma02Gq
Ellen (W)	22	F	Wife	22Ma02Gq
FANIENT, Mary	20	F	Spinster	22Ma02Gq
LEADEN, Rose	20	F	Spinster	22Ma02Gq
John	.00	M	Infant	22Ma02Gq
MORGAN, Mary	20	F	Spinster	22Ma02Gq
MANLY, Charlotte	20	F	Spinster	22Ma02Gq
John	.00	M	Infant	22Ma02Gq
MORGAN, Mick	24	M	Carpenter	22Ma02Gq
Patt	9	M	Child	22Ma02Gq
FENNELL, Eliza	20	F	Spinster	22Ma02Gq
DIGNAN, Cath.	18	F	Unknown	22Ma02Gq
BELL, Mary	30	F	Unknown	22Ma02Gq
Patt	.00	M	Infant	22Ma02Gq
MAGUIRE, Tobias	23	M	Farmer	22Ma02Gq
CALLIN, Wm.	21	M	Laborer	22Ma02Gq
MULLIGAN, And.	24	M	None	22Ma02Gq
CLESSY, Mick	30	M	Farmer	22Ma02Gq
FRANEY, Mick	25	M	Laborer	22Ma02Gq
BUGERTIN, Pat.	23	M	Laborer	22Ma02Gq
MARTIN, Pat.	10	M	Laborer	22Ma02Gq
Wm.	6	M	Child	22Ma02Gq
Samuel	2	M	Child	22Ma02Gq

HENRY 27 MAY 1850

From London

NAMES OF PASSENGERS	AGE	SEX	OCCUPATIONS	DATE PORT SHIP
UGLOW, William	23	M	Unknown	27Ma06Gr
Jane	23	F	Baker	27Ma06Gr
LEGG, John	22	M	None	27Ma06Gr
ROBERTS, Robert	30	M	Unknown	27Ma06Gr
Eliza	26	F	None	27Ma06Gr
APTED, James	44	M	Unknown	27Ma06Gr
Elizabeth	45	F	Unknown	27Ma06Gr
WOODHAMS, Edgar	18	M	Unknown	27Ma06Gr
APTED, Sarah	18	F	Unknown	27Ma06Gr
John	15	M	Unknown	27Ma06Gr
William	13	M	Unknown	27Ma06Gr
Henrietta	11	F	Tailor	27Ma06Gr
Fanny	10	F	Tailor	27Ma06Gr
Emily	8	F	Child	27Ma06Gr
Albert	7	M	Child	27Ma06Gr
APTED, Mary	4	F	Child	27Ma06Gr
OLIVER, Dorothy	60	F	Unknown	27Ma06Gr
Elizabeth	21	F	Unknown	27Ma06Gr
JOSEPH, Thomas	18	M	Mariner	27Ma06Gr
MURPHY, Alice	28	F	None	27Ma06Gr
SLADE, George	24	M	Unknown	27Ma06Gr
Frederick	17	M	Engd	27Ma06Gr
LOFKIN, William	32	M	Unknown	27Ma06Gr
Anne	33	F	Miner	27Ma06Gr
William	8	M	Child	27Ma06Gr
PAGE, William	20	M	Laborer	27Ma06Gr
PLACE, Robert	34	M	Unknown	27Ma06Gr
Sarah	34	F	Laborer	27Ma06Gr
ASPLAN, James	10	M	Laborer	27Ma06Gr
PLACE, Robert	.00	M	Infant	27Ma06Gr
CHAPMAN, Wm.	30	M	Unknown	27Ma06Gr
KENT, George	20	M	Carpenter	27Ma06Gr
Mary	20	F	Unknown	27Ma06Gr
HURVILLE, Theresa	25	F	Unknown	27Ma06Gr
Walter	.00	M	Infant	27Ma06Gr
HUTCHINSON, George	41	M	Unknown	27Ma06Gr
SLOAN, James	28	M	None	27Ma06Gr
Eliza	23	F	Unknown	27Ma06Gr
CARMICHAEL, Selina	28	F	None	27Ma06Gr
Abbe	10	F	Unknown	27Ma06Gr
HAYWARD, Geo.	22	M	Unknown	27Ma06Gr
PRY, Robert	33	M	Unknown	27Ma06Gr
GIFFREY, George	21	M	Unknown	27Ma06Gr
GURPIN, Joseph	25	M	Unknown	27Ma06Gr
MCCARTY, Dennis	33	M	Unknown	27Ma06Gr
Margaret	24	F	Unknown	27Ma06Gr
Jeremiah	6	M	Child	27Ma06Gr
John	3	M	Child	27Ma06Gr
Catherine	.00	F	Infant	27Ma06Gr
LEE, Catherine	48	F	Unknown	27Ma06Gr
Richard	12	M	Unknown	27Ma06Gr
Henry	9	M	Child	27Ma06Gr
Elizabeth	7	F	Child	27Ma06Gr
SMITH, Francis	32	F	Unknown	27Ma06Gr
Thebe	39	F	Unknown	27Ma06Gr
Charlotte	10	F	Unknown	27Ma06Gr
Frederick	7	M	Child	27Ma06Gr
Alfred	5	M	Child	27Ma06Gr
GILLS, John	25	M	Unknown	27Ma06Gr
Ann	24	F	Unknown	27Ma06Gr
George	.00	M	Infant	27Ma06Gr
EDWARDS, William	20	M	Unknown	27Ma06Gr
RUMNEY, James	57	M	None	27Ma06Gr
Mary	47	F	Unknown	27Ma06Gr
Robert	19	M	Unknown	27Ma06Gr
William	15	M	Unknown	27Ma06Gr
Martha	10	F	Unknown	27Ma06Gr
Ann	5	F	Child	27Ma06Gr
WOOD, John	32	M	Unknown	27Ma06Gr
TADMAN, James	30	M	Unknown	27Ma06Gr
William	21	M	Unknown	27Ma06Gr
LLOYD, John	21	M	Unknown	27Ma06Gr
MANBY, Job	21	M	Unknown	27Ma06Gr
MUNN, William	35	M	Unknown	27Ma06Gr
Jane	30	F	Unknown	27Ma06Gr
Elizabeth-Jane	7	F	Child	27Ma06Gr
Costine	5	F	Child	27Ma06Gr
Alice	3	F	Child	27Ma06Gr
Maria	.00	F	Infant	27Ma06Gr
LOVEY, Martha	27	F	Unknown	27Ma06Gr
Sarah	9	F	Child	27Ma06Gr
BERMNOS, Peter	22	M	Unknown	27Ma06Gr
GIVYCROSS, Charles	30	M	Unknown	27Ma06Gr
KNIGHT, Arthur	30	M	Unknown	27Ma06Gr
Mary	28	F	Unknown	27Ma06Gr
GEER, William	25	M	Unknown	27Ma06Gr
BENNETT, Mary	24	F	Unknown	27Ma06Gr
Isaac	.00	M	Infant	27Ma06Gr
MCCARTY, Peter	25	M	Unknown	27Ma06Gr
BROWN, James	30	M	Unknown	27Ma06Gr

NAMES OF PASSENGERS	AGE	SEX	OCCUPATIONS	DATE PORT SHIP
BROWN, Elizabeth	24	F	Unknown	27Ma06Gr
Seth	13	M	Unknown	27Ma06Gr
CHURCHES, James	36	M	Unknown	27Ma06Gr
Samuel	13	M	Unknown	27Ma06Gr
Edith	31	F	Unknown	27Ma06Gr
Catherine	12	F	Unknown	27Ma06Gr
Ellen	11	F	Unknown	27Ma06Gr
James	9	M	Child	27Ma06Gr
Ann	7	F	Child	27Ma06Gr
John	1	M	Child	27Ma06Gr
WATTS. John	20	M	Unknown	27Ma06Gr
PEISER. Samuel	30	M	Unknown	27Ma06Gr
PILKINSON. George	20	M	Unknown	27Ma06Gr
REDWARD. George	50	M	Unknown	27Ma06Gr
WATSS. Robert	45	M	Unknown	27Ma06Gr
WATTS. Matilda	35	F	Unknown	27Ma06Gr
James	17	M	Unknown	27Ma06Gr
Mary-Ann	16	F	Unknown	27Ma06Gr
Robert	13	M	Unknown	27Ma06Gr
William	12	M	Unknown	27Ma06Gr
LEACH, John	45	M	Unknown	27Ma06Gr
UNDERDOWN, William	36	M	Unknown	27Ma06Gr
Elizabeth	38	F	Unknown	27Ma06Gr
Matilda	12	F	Unknown	27Ma06Gr
William	8	M	Child	27Ma06Gr
Mary-Ann	4	F	Child	27Ma06Gr
WATTS, Mary	36	F	Unknown	27Ma06Gr
WALKER, Joseph	30	M	Unknown	27Ma06Gr
Jane	25	F	Unknown	27Ma06Gr
ABRAHAM. Ellen	18	F	Unknown	27Ma06Gr
STEAD, Charles	30	M	Unknown	27Ma06Gr
MAHONEY. Catherine	20	F	Unknown	27Ma06Gr
CRAWLEY. Johannah	26	F	Unknown	27Ma06Gr
WATLEY. Mary-Ann	30	F	Unknown	27Ma06Gr
Robert	8	M	Child	27Ma06Gr
ROSE. William	27	M	Unknown	27Ma06Gr
Edward	30	M	Unknown	27Ma06Gr
Elizabeth	22	F	None	27Ma06Gr
BERRICK. Charles	22	M	Unknown	27Ma06Gr
TYLER, Frederick	21	M	Unknown	27Ma06Gr
STOUB, Philip	22	M	Unknown	27Ma06Gr
Martha	21	F	Unknown	27Ma06Gr
NIGHTINGALE. William	55	M	Unknown	27Ma06Gr
Elizabeth	51	F	Unknown	27Ma06Gr
David	21	M	Unknown	27Ma06Gr
Job	21	M	Unknown	27Ma06Gr
Aaron	16	M	Farmer	27Ma06Gr
Jane	14	F	Unknown	27Ma06Gr
Emma	11	F	Unknown	27Ma06Gr
Elizabeth	9	F	Child	27Ma06Gr
Moses	7	M	Child	27Ma06Gr
WOOLMAN. Frederick	26	M	Unknown	27Ma06Gr
BLANCKE. Henry	22	M	Unknown	27Ma06Gr
BOWLING, Henry	25	M	Unknown	27Ma06Gr
GANTE. Frederick	27	M	Unknown	27Ma06Gr
SMITH. Charles	30	M	Unknown	27Ma06Gr
Mary-Ann	34	F	Unknown	27Ma06Gr
John	8	M	Child	27Ma06Gr
Elizabeth	6	F	Child	27Ma06Gr
FERGUSON, Thomas	28	M	Unknown	27Ma06Gr
SWAINE. Edward	21	M	Unknown	27Ma06Gr
LANE. Mary	21	F	Unknown	27Ma06Gr
CONLEY. Elizabeth	23	F	None	27Ma06Gr
COOK, Wm.	45	M	Unknown	27Ma06Gr
CASTELLO. Daniel	25	M	Unknown	27Ma06Gr
Bridget	26	F	Unknown	27Ma06Gr
PEISER. Jacob	19	M	Unknown	27Ma06Gr
ONESS, John	36	M	Unknown	27Ma06Gr
Harriette	13	F	Unknown	27Ma06Gr
John	12	M	Unknown	27Ma06Gr
William	8	M	Child	27Ma06Gr
Elizabeth	8	F	Child	27Ma06Gr
Lister	.04	U	Infant	27Ma06Gr
Harriet	.00	F	Infant	27Ma06Gr
SMITH. George	13	M	Unknown	27Ma06Gr
SALRIDGE, Ann	15	F	Unknown	27Ma06Gr
MCLANGBLOTHE. Ann	27	F	Unknown	27Ma06Gr
SULLIVAN, James	24	M	Unknown	27Ma06Gr
Honora	24	F	Servant	27Ma06Gr
Sophia	.00	F	Infant	27Ma06Gr
BERRY. George	21	M	Unknown	27Ma06Gr
Mary	60	F	Unknown	27Ma06Gr
DANE. James	50	M	Unknown	27Ma06Gr
HEGERTY. Mathew	30	M	Unknown	27Ma06Gr
Anatasia	35	F	Unknown	27Ma06Gr
FREHERNE, John	47	M	Unknown	27Ma06Gr
Elizabeth	37	F	Unknown	27Ma06Gr
Charles	16	M	Unknown	27Ma06Gr
Sarah	13	M	Unknown	27Ma06Gr
LOVEY. Martha	29	F	Unknown	27Ma06Gr
Sarah	9	F	Child	27Ma06Gr
REMNISCH, Elizabeth	28	F	None	27Ma06Gr
Joseph	2	M	Child	27Ma06Gr
HAYES. George	24	M	Unknown	27Ma06Gr
GILBERT. William	40	M	Unknown	27Ma06Gr
Sarah	40	F	Unknown	27Ma06Gr
Emily	13	F	Unknown	27Ma06Gr
Mary-Ann	12	F	Unknown	27Ma06Gr
Maria	.00	F	Infant	27Ma06Gr
George	7	M	Child	27Ma06Gr
WHITE. Walter	28	M	Unknown	27Ma06Gr
BARDWELL, Wm.	19	M	Unknown	27Ma06Gr
SEDGWICKE, Emily	21	F	Unknown	27Ma06Gr

NAOMI 27 MAY 1850

From Liverpool

NAMES OF PASSENGERS	AGE	SEX	OCCUPATIONS	DATE PORT SHIP
CONACOR, Catherine	20	F	Spinster	27Ma02Ev
TRACY. Michael	20	M	Laborer	27Ma02Ev
CUMMIN. John	29	M	Laborer	27Ma02Ev
SHEEHAN, Thomas	22	M	Unknown	27Ma02Ev
FLANIGAN. Anthony	44	M	Unknown	27Ma02Ev
Pat	20	M	Unknown	27Ma02Ev
Margaret	40	M	Unknown	27Ma02Ev
Catherine	18	F	Unknown	27Ma02Ev
Dominick	11	M	Unknown	27Ma02Ev
Bridget	13	F	Unknown	27Ma02Ev
Peter	9	M	Child	27Ma02Ev
John	23	M	Unknown	27Ma02Ev
Martin	30	M	Unknown	27Ma02Ev
Mary	30	F	Unknown	27Ma02Ev
Catherine	26	F	Unknown	27Ma02Ev
DALY. Elizabeth	20	F	Unknown	27Ma02Ev
MCDOUGH, Wm.	22	M	Unknown	27Ma02Ev
CORMICK, Bridget	40	F	Unknown	27Ma02Ev
Eliza	13	F	Unknown	27Ma02Ev
Mary	6	F	Child	27Ma02Ev
Bridget	.10	F	Infant	27Ma02Ev
MCDOUGH, Wm.	22	M	Unknown	27Ma02Ev
OSBORNE. Phillip	20	M	Unknown	27Ma02Ev
Pat	22	M	Unknown	27Ma02Ev
Ann	23	F	Unknown	27Ma02Ev
Mary	18	F	Unknown	27Ma02Ev
Bridget	13	F	Unknown	27Ma02Ev
Rosa	4	F	Child	27Ma02Ev
Catherine	.08	F	Infant	27Ma02Ev
HARKINS. Bridget	30	F	Unknown	27Ma02Ev
Pat	11	M	Unknown	27Ma02Ev
Catherine	9	F	Child	27Ma02Ev
Rosa	7	F	Child	27Ma02Ev
James	.05	M	Infant	27Ma02Ev
MCGILL, Thos.	20	M	Unknown	27Ma02Ev
Died-At-Sea				

NAMES OF PASSENGERS	AGE	SEX	OCCUPATIONS	DATE PORT SHIP
MCGILL, Joseph	10	M	Servant	27Ma02Ev
GALVIN, Richard	20	M	Servant	27Ma02Ev
PARNEL, John	23	M	Servant	27Ma02Ev
David	26	M	Servant	27Ma02Ev
QUINTIN, Jeremiah	22	M	Servant	27Ma02Ev
GUNNEL, Charles	33	M	Servant	27Ma02Ev
Hannah	32	F	Servant	27Ma02Ev
Henry	7	M	Child	27Ma02Ev
John	6	M	Child	27Ma02Ev
Edward	4	M	Child	27Ma02Ev
Anthony	2	M	Child	27Ma02Ev
Mary	.06	F	Infant	27Ma02Ev
EDWARDS, James	30	M	Unknown	27Ma02Ev
Mary-A.	27	F	Unknown	27Ma02Ev
HANLEY, John	25	M	Unknown	27Ma02Ev
Mary	28	F	Unknown	27Ma02Ev
RYAN, Julia	50	F	Unknown	27Ma02Ev
William	.10	M	Infant	27Ma02Ev
MANAHAN, Bridget	18	F	Unknown	27Ma02Ev
RATTIGAN, John	18	M	Unknown	27Ma02Ev
TRACY, Catherine	22	F	Unknown	27Ma02Ev
FAHEY, Thomas	40	M	Unknown	27Ma02Ev
Peter	29	M	Laborer	27Ma02Ev
Mary	30	F	Unknown	27Ma02Ev
MADDEN, Thomas	10	M	Unknown	27Ma02Ev
GILCHRIST, Malachi	29	M	Unknown	27Ma02Ev
Pat-Loler	19	M	Unknown	27Ma02Ev
WATSON, Mary	15	F	Unknown	27Ma02Ev
HENERY, Pat	23	M	Unknown	27Ma02Ev
GIBSON, Wm.	21	M	Unknown	27Ma02Ev
WOON, Francis	29	M	Unknown	27Ma02Ev
BRADY, Thomas	20	M	Unknown	27Ma02Ev
BARNARD, Elizabeth	20	F	Unknown	27Ma02Ev
CALDER, Mary-Ann	20	F	Unknown	27Ma02Ev
KELLY, Ellen	16	F	Unknown	27Ma02Ev
DIGMAN, Mary	24	F	Unknown	27Ma02Ev
MURRAY, Catherine	18	F	Unknown	27Ma02Ev
ONEILL, Ann	13	F	Unknown	27Ma02Ev
WALKER, Danl.	23	M	Unknown	27Ma02Ev
GETTINS, Mary	64	F	Unknown	27Ma02Ev
Bridget	42	F	Unknown	27Ma02Ev
OBRIEN, Daniel	26	M	Unknown	27Ma02Ev
MURRAY, William	31	M	Unknown	27Ma02Ev
NASISS, John	20	M	Unknown	27Ma02Ev
MALADY, Peter	22	M	Unknown	27Ma02Ev
MURRAY, Michael	18	M	Unknown	27Ma02Ev
MORAN, Pat	28	M	Unknown	27Ma02Ev
Kitty	22	F	Unknown	27Ma02Ev
SWEENY, Patrick	30	M	Unknown	27Ma02Ev
CAVANAH, James	35	M	Unknown	27Ma02Ev
Mary	26	F	Unknown	27Ma02Ev
DALEY, Bridget	37	F	Unknown	27Ma02Ev
Cath.	10	F	Unknown	27Ma02Ev
Phillip	8	M	Child	27Ma02Ev
Owen	6	M	Child	27Ma02Ev
BRESLAN, Pat	21	M	Unknown	27Ma02Ev
MARTIN, John	21	M	Unknown	27Ma02Ev
FITZSIMMONS, John	21	M	Unknown	27Ma02Ev
TULLY, Pat	17	M	Unknown	27Ma02Ev
LAY, Thomas	25	M	Unknown	27Ma02Ev
WALKIN, Thomas	24	M	Unknown	27Ma02Ev
DIXON, John	23	M	Unknown	27Ma02Ev
JOHNSTON, Wm.	20	M	Unknown	27Ma02Ev
NOBLE, John	15	M	Unknown	27Ma02Ev
SKELLY, Thomas	24	M	Unknown	27Ma02Ev
HAYNES, Peter	20	M	Unknown	27Ma02Ev
SHAUGHNESSEY, Thomas	20	M	Unknown	27Ma02Ev
CORWIN, Mary	36	F	Unknown	27Ma02Ev
Mary	12	F	Unknown	27Ma02Ev
ONEILL, James	25	M	Unknown	27Ma02Ev
Margret	21	F	Unknown	27Ma02Ev
Cath.	.09	F	Infant	27Ma02Ev
COONAN, Wm.	21	M	Unknown	27Ma02Ev
CAHILL, Bridget	36	F	Unknown	27Ma02Ev
Thomas	12	M	Unknown	27Ma02Ev
HICKEY, Ann	34	F	Unknown	27Ma02Ev
Ann	9	F	Child	27Ma02Ev
Bridget	13	F	Unknown	27Ma02Ev
HOGAN, John	35	M	Unknown	27Ma02Ev
Mary	30	F	Unknown	27Ma02Ev
Catherine	13	F	Unknown	27Ma02Ev
Martin	11	M	Unknown	27Ma02Ev
Pat	9	M	Child	27Ma02Ev
SMITH, Mary	28	F	Unknown	27Ma02Ev
HANNAN, Wm.	46	M	Laborer	27Ma02Ev
Mary	21	F	Unknown	27Ma02Ev
Ellen	17	F	Unknown	27Ma02Ev
William	12	M	Unknown	27Ma02Ev
MADDEN, Ann	27	F	Servant	27Ma02Ev
WHELAN, John	20	M	Unknown	27Ma02Ev
Margaret	22	F	Unknown	27Ma02Ev
Mary	18	F	Unknown	27Ma02Ev
KELLY, Esther	20	F	Unknown	27Ma02Ev
TEEFY, Thomas	42	M	Unknown	27Ma02Ev
Pat	18	M	Unknown	27Ma02Ev
Margaret	16	F	Unknown	27Ma02Ev
KELLY, Thady	40	M	Unknown	27Ma02Ev
Bridget	21	F	Unknown	27Ma02Ev
John	32	M	Unknown	27Ma02Ev
TEEFY, Cath.	35	F	Unknown	27Ma02Ev
Michael	.10	M	Infant	27Ma02Ev
DONNELAN, John	21	M	Unknown	27Ma02Ev
WELDON, Ricd.	18	M	Unknown	27Ma02Ev
CURLEY, Thomas	28	M	Laborer	27Ma02Ev
SCULLY, Bridget	13	F	Unknown	27Ma02Ev
MURPHY, Barnd.	18	M	Unknown	27Ma02Ev
MCCANNA, James	15	M	Unknown	27Ma02Ev
BARRY, Johanna	20	F	Unknown	27Ma02Ev
GAFFY, Lawrence	28	M	Unknown	27Ma02Ev
SIMPSON, Bridget	20	F	Unknown	27Ma02Ev
CLAVIN, Michael	20	M	Unknown	27Ma02Ev
Catherine	18	F	Unknown	27Ma02Ev
MCCALL, Thomas	20	M	Unknown	27Ma02Ev
WALSH, Bridget	17	F	Unknown	27Ma02Ev
REARDEN, Pat	27	M	Unknown	27Ma02Ev
SHERIDAN, Ellen	30	F	Unknown	27Ma02Ev
James	.07	M	Infant	27Ma02Ev
PELLY, Rose	35	F	Unknown	27Ma02Ev
ENGLISH, James	20	M	Unknown	27Ma02Ev
Bridget	18	F	Unknown	27Ma02Ev
SHILLETOR, Amos	26	M	Unknown	27Ma02Ev
Mary	28	F	Unknown	27Ma02Ev
Betty	70	F	Unknown	27Ma02Ev
John	4	M	Child	27Ma02Ev
Frank	1	M	Child	27Ma02Ev
Died-At-Sea				
Eliza	.04	F	Infant	27Ma02Ev
MELLOY, James	30	M	Unknown	27Ma02Ev
BROWN, Charley	23	M	Unknown	27Ma02Ev
BURKE, Edward	28	M	Unknown	27Ma02Ev
OHARA, Alice	20	F	Unknown	27Ma02Ev
WHELAN, Bridget	19	F	Unknown	27Ma02Ev
WILSON, Ann	24	F	Unknown	27Ma02Ev
FURKUM, Patrick	12	M	Unknown	27Ma02Ev
Bridget	11	F	Unknown	27Ma02Ev
Jane	10	F	Unknown	27Ma02Ev
ARMSDEN, Josiah	20	M	Servant	27Ma02Ev
LUDLAN, James	18	M	Unknown	27Ma02Ev
SWEENY, Daniel	24	M	Unknown	27Ma02Ev
PYNE, Cath.	25	F	Unknown	27Ma02Ev
HIERN, Margaret	28	F	Unknown	27Ma02Ev
NORRIS, Catherine	30	F	Unknown	27Ma02Ev
DUNN, Mary	50	F	Unknown	27Ma02Ev
Joseph	10	M	Unknown	27Ma02Ev
FAGAN, Anne	16	F	Unknown	27Ma02Ev
BOHEN, Martin	25	M	Unknown	27Ma02Ev
Thomas	20	M	Unknown	27Ma02Ev
HUNTER, Thomas	19	M	Unknown	27Ma02Ev
FLYNN, Michael	22	M	Unknown	27Ma02Ev
KELLY, Anne	16	F	Unknown	27Ma02Ev

NAMES OF PASSENGERS	AGE	SEX	OCCUPATIONS	DATE PORT SHIP
MOORE, Anne	22	F	Unknown	27Ma02Ev
FLETCHER, Peter	30	M	Mechanic	27Ma02Ev
BROWN, Hugh	23	M	Unknown	27Ma02Ev
COYNE, Thomas	25	M	Unknown	27Ma02Ev
Bridget	23	F	Unknown	27Ma02Ev
Honor	21	M	Laborer	27Ma02Ev
BROWN, Cath.	30	F	Unknown	27Ma02Ev
WILLIAMS, Thomas	20	M	Unknown	27Ma02Ev
LALLY, Mary	14	F	Unknown	27Ma02Ev
Cath.	10	F	Unknown	27Ma02Ev
OHARA, Dennis	23	M	Unknown	27Ma02Ev
KING, Mary	23	F	Unknown	27Ma02Ev
Mary	5	F	Child	27Ma02Ev
Dennis	.11	M	Infant	27Ma02Ev
GLEMLY, Wm.	11	M	Unknown	27Ma02Ev
RENHAN, Lees	27	M	Unknown	27Ma02Ev
U-Mrs.	22	F	Unknown	27Ma02Ev
Andrew	3	M	Child	27Ma02Ev
Benjamin	.08	M	Infant	27Ma02Ev
CLEARY, Anthony	40	M	Unknown	27Ma02Ev
Richd.	21	M	Unknown	27Ma02Ev
Judith	19	F	Unknown	27Ma02Ev
Mary	17	F	Unknown	27Ma02Ev
Alice	16	F	Unknown	27Ma02Ev
Thomas	13	M	Unknown	27Ma02Ev
Margaret	11	M	Unknown	27Ma02Ev
Catherine	9	F	Child	27Ma02Ev
MAHER, Richd.	30	M	Servant	27Ma02Ev
Alice	28	F	Unknown	27Ma02Ev
Thomas	24	M	Laborer	27Ma02Ev
Nicholas	21	M	Unknown	27Ma02Ev
Honora	18	F	Unknown	27Ma02Ev
Margaret	15	F	Unknown	27Ma02Ev
CADDILY, Joseph	55	M	Unknown	27Ma02Ev
Edward	27	M	Unknown	27Ma02Ev
Pat	24	M	Unknown	27Ma02Ev
Mary	22	F	Servant	27Ma02Ev
Joseph	20	M	Unknown	27Ma02Ev
Lucy	18	F	Unknown	27Ma02Ev
Catherine	15	F	Unknown	27Ma02Ev
Thomas	11	M	Unknown	27Ma02Ev
CLEARY, Catherine	30	F	Unknown	27Ma02Ev
Edward	10	M	Unknown	27Ma02Ev
Michael	8	M	Child	27Ma02Ev
Pat	6	M	Child	27Ma02Ev
Andrew	.10	M	Infant	27Ma02Ev
NUGENT, Norry	36	F	Unknown	27Ma02Ev
Cath.	11	F	Unknown	27Ma02Ev
Thomas	16	M	Unknown	27Ma02Ev
FERNAN, Matthew	28	M	Unknown	27Ma02Ev
Ellen	25	F	Laborer	27Ma02Ev
Cath.	.06	F	Infant	27Ma02Ev
SOMES, U	50	F	Wi	27Ma02Ev
Patt	21	M	Unknown	27Ma02Ev
Judith	23	F	Unknown	27Ma02Ev
Margaret	18	F	Unknown	27Ma02Ev
Mary	17	F	Unknown	27Ma02Ev
OSBORNE, Thomas	10	M	Unknown	27Ma02Ev
OHARA, Patrick	30	M	Unknown	27Ma02Ev
MORGAN, Thomas	23	M	Unknown	27Ma02Ev
DALY, Owen	25	M	Unknown	27Ma02Ev
HAHN, U-Mr.	28	M	Unknown	27Ma02Ev
U-Mrs.	24	F	Unknown	27Ma02Ev
BUTTERLY, U-Miss	25	F	Unknown	27Ma02Ev
CARROL, U-Mrs.	36	F	Unknown	27Ma02Ev
U	7	M	Child	27Ma02Ev
Jane	.10	F	Infant	27Ma02Ev
GEOUGIN, U-Miss	20	F	Unknown	27Ma02Ev
JAMES, Daniel	26	M	Unknown	27Ma02Ev
U-Mrs.	25	F	Unknown	27Ma02Ev
LIFF, Wm.	22	M	Unknown	27Ma02Ev
HOECKLAND, Henry	20	M	Unknown	27Ma02Ev
JAMES, Josh	22	M	Unknown	27Ma02Ev
U-Mrs.	19	F	Unknown	27Ma02Ev
Nicholas	.09	M	Infant	27Ma02Ev
KEIGH, John	22	M	Unknown	27Ma02Ev
ROBINSON, Edward	30	M	Unknown	27Ma02Ev
U-Mrs.	46	F	Unknown	27Ma02Ev
Arthur	19	M	Unknown	27Ma02Ev

GUY-MANNERING 28 MAY 1850

From Liverpool

NAMES OF PASSENGERS	AGE	SEX	OCCUPATIONS	DATE PORT SHIP
WRIGHT, Richard	23	M	Farmer	28Ma02Ax
BLACKMORE, Richard	11	M	Farmer	28Ma02Ax
SHERRIDON, Mary	30	F	Unknown	28Ma02Ax
MCDERMONT, Mary	25	F	Servant	28Ma02Ax
RILEY, Peter	50	M	Mason	28Ma02Ax
Bridget	48	F	Unknown	28Ma02Ax
Mary	15	F	Unknown	28Ma02Ax
GATLAND, Mary	20	F	Servant	28Ma02Ax
GORMAN, Wm.	40	M	Laborer	28Ma02Ax
HURSE, Wm.	23	M	Laborer	28Ma02Ax
Anne	24	F	Unknown	28Ma02Ax
MCDONNAGH, Bridget	24	F	Unknown	28Ma02Ax
SWEENEY, Ann	6	F	Child	28Ma02Ax
MACKAY, Patrick	26	M	Farmer	28Ma02Ax
Patrick	20	M	Unknown	28Ma02Ax
Mary	18	F	Unknown	28Ma02Ax
RYAN, Ellen	23	F	Unknown	28Ma02Ax
NOLAN, Nicholas	29	M	Gdnr	28Ma02Ax
DUNNE, Bridget	22	F	Unknown	28Ma02Ax
LAYNE, Thomas	24	M	Farmer	28Ma02Ax
CULNANE, Mary	22	F	Unknown	28Ma02Ax
Eliza	19	F	Unknown	28Ma02Ax
HEARE, John	23	M	Merchant	28Ma02Ax
Mary	19	F	Unknown	28Ma02Ax
Michael	.00	M	Infant	28Ma02Ax
Biddy	14	F	Unknown	28Ma02Ax
GAHERN, Rose	40	F	Unknown	28Ma02Ax
Ellen	6	F	Child	28Ma02Ax
Anne	4	F	Child	28Ma02Ax
Jane	2	F	Child	28Ma02Ax
Margaret	.00	F	Infant	28Ma02Ax
TORMY, Bridget	45	F	Servant	28Ma02Ax
CORCORAN, Eliza	18	F	Unknown	28Ma02Ax
FARELLEY, Anne	18	F	Unknown	28Ma02Ax
LEARY, Wm.	40	M	Laborer	28Ma02Ax
Mary	20	F	Unknown	28Ma02Ax
RIDES, Eliza	40	F	Stay Maker	28Ma02Ax
Jane	16	F	Unknown	28Ma02Ax
Anette	13	F	Unknown	28Ma02Ax
Benjamen	8	M	Child	28Ma02Ax
BRIEN, W.J.	30	M	Merchant	28Ma02Ax
KINEALY, Edward	36	M	Blacksmith	28Ma02Ax
MOORE, Joseph	26	M	Gentleman	28Ma02Ax
Margaret	22	F	Unknown	28Ma02Ax
CORCORAN, Hugh	26	M	Farmer	28Ma02Ax
BROGAN, Michael	18	M	Laborer	28Ma02Ax
MANNING, Thomas	24	M	Laborer	28Ma02Ax
MONAGAN, Patt	29	M	Laborer	28Ma02Ax
BYRNE, Michael	26	M	Forester	28Ma02Ax
DOWLING, Margaret	50	F	Agrc	28Ma02Ax
COLLINS, John	25	M	Laborer	28Ma02Ax
Patt	25	M	Laborer	28Ma02Ax
KEEFE, Norry	53	F	Unknown	28Ma02Ax
Winifred	24	F	Unknown	28Ma02Ax
Alice	17	F	Unknown	28Ma02Ax
Thomas	22	M	Unknown	28Ma02Ax
Ellen	15	F	Unknown	28Ma02Ax
MCCORMICK, Kate	55	F	Unknown	28Ma02Ax
RYNES, James	24	M	Unknown	28Ma02Ax
FOLEY, Fanny	22	F	Unknown	28Ma02Ax

NAMES OF PASSENGERS	AGE	SEX	OCCUPATIONS	DATE PORT SHIP
COFFEJ, Maria	29	F	Unknown	28Ma02Ax
DEVAN, Patrick	22	M	Laborer	28Ma02Ax
Bridget	16	F	Unknown	28Ma02Ax
MOLLAY, Patt	33	M	Laborer	28Ma02Ax
Mary	30	F	Unknown	28Ma02Ax
Thomas	8	M	Child	28Ma02Ax
Cathrine	6	F	Child	28Ma02Ax
Lawrence	4	M	Child	28Ma02Ax
Anne	2	F	Child	28Ma02Ax
FERNS, William	50	M	Servant	28Ma02Ax
Catherine	45	F	Unknown	28Ma02Ax
Mary	17	F	Unknown	28Ma02Ax
Michael	13	M	Unknown	28Ma02Ax
OBRIEN, Michael	16	M	Unknown	28Ma02Ax
Joseph	12	M	Unknown	28Ma02Ax
KEALING, Ellen	17	F	Servant	28Ma02Ax
CROTY, Cathrine	17	F	Servant	28Ma02Ax
KEALING, Bridget	20	F	Servant	28Ma02Ax
COX, John	60	M	Cooper	28Ma02Ax
Ellen	22	F	Unknown	28Ma02Ax
Anne	58	F	Unknown	28Ma02Ax
MULLIGAN, Patrick	27	M	Laborer	28Ma02Ax
DONNELLY, Thomas	29	M	Carpenter	28Ma02Ax
DEEL, Edmund	32	M	Farmer	28Ma02Ax
Anne	28	F	Unknown	28Ma02Ax
CALAGHAN, Thomas	25	M	Farmer	28Ma02Ax
DRISCOLL, David	25	M	Farmer	28Ma02Ax
HERLAGHY, Denis	20	M	Farmer	28Ma02Ax
DRISCOLL, William	20	M	Farmer	28Ma02Ax
BRAWN, Mary-Ann	18	F	Servant	28Ma02Ax
CASSELL, Margaret	50	F	Servant	28Ma02Ax
Anne	50	F	Servant	28Ma02Ax
ODONNELL, Mathew	18	M	Farmer	28Ma02Ax
Margaret	50	F	Unknown	28Ma02Ax
Cathrine	13	F	Unknown	28Ma02Ax
GRADY, Margaret	10	F	Unknown	28Ma02Ax
Thomas	10	M	Unknown	28Ma02Ax
Michael	22	M	Unknown	28Ma02Ax
MURREY, Mary	18	F	Unknown	28Ma02Ax
MAHER, Flourance	22	M	Laborer	28Ma02Ax
BURKE, Honora	30	F	Unknown	28Ma02Ax
DONOHOE, John	20	M	Laborer	28Ma02Ax
Margaret	30	F	Unknown	28Ma02Ax
COSTELLA, Margaret	30	F	Unknown	28Ma02Ax
LAUGHEN, Sarah	35	F	Servant	28Ma02Ax
MCOWOY, Mary	18	F	Servant	28Ma02Ax
LESTER, Eliza	20	F	Servant	28Ma02Ax
MCGARVEY, Rose	20	F	Servant	28Ma02Ax
MULLIN, Bridget	22	F	Servant	28Ma02Ax
BRENAN, Cathrine	26	F	Servant	28Ma02Ax
Mary	22	F	Servant	28Ma02Ax
HACKETT, John	36	M	Laborer	28Ma02Ax
Mary	22	F	Unknown	28Ma02Ax
Bessy	22	F	Servant	28Ma02Ax
Michael	18	M	Unknown	28Ma02Ax
Cathrine	24	F	Unknown	28Ma02Ax
FOGARTY, Mary	26	F	Unknown	28Ma02Ax
DRISCOLL, David	25	M	Laborer	28Ma02Ax
NOLAN, James	23	M	Laborer	28Ma02Ax
John	24	M	Laborer	28Ma02Ax
Charles	22	M	Laborer	28Ma02Ax
Charles	24	M	Laborer	28Ma02Ax
Mary	20	F	Servant	28Ma02Ax
GINTY, Dines	24	M	Laborer	28Ma02Ax
RIELEY, John	20	M	Laborer	28Ma02Ax
CAHILL, Michael	30	M	Carpenter	28Ma02Ax
HINLY, Patt	30	M	Laborer	28Ma02Ax
Bridget	20	F	Unknown	28Ma02Ax
GURREN, Ellen	18	F	Unknown	28Ma02Ax
MARA, Anthony	24	M	Farmer	28Ma02Ax
SHEA, Cathrine	20	F	Unknown	28Ma02Ax
BOGHAN, Alice	16	F	Unknown	28Ma02Ax
SULLIVAN, Jane	30	F	Unknown	28Ma02Ax
MCNAMARA, John	27	M	Shoemaker	28Ma02Ax
Aleina	20	F	Unknown	28Ma02Ax
MCCABE, Henry	21	M	Laborer	28Ma02Ax
Francis	11	M	Unknown	28Ma02Ax
KEEFE, Mary	16	F	Unknown	28Ma02Ax
HARRINGTON, Mary	30	F	Unknown	28Ma02Ax
MAXWELL, Alley	18	F	Servant	28Ma02Ax
HANOLAN, Clara	18	F	Servant	28Ma02Ax
GARVEY, Bridget	18	F	Servant	28Ma02Ax
FLANNARY, Maria	21	F	Servant	28Ma02Ax
MAHON, Thomas	40	M	Laborer	28Ma02Ax
Bridget	32	F	Unknown	28Ma02Ax
Mary	13	F	Unknown	28Ma02Ax
Biddy	11	F	Unknown	28Ma02Ax
Michael	9	M	Child	28Ma02Ax
Margaret	7	F	Child	28Ma02Ax
Anne	5	F	Child	28Ma02Ax
Cathrine	3	F	Child	28Ma02Ax
Patrick	.00	M	Infant	28Ma02Ax
KENNY, Ellen	26	F	Unknown	28Ma02Ax
DANIEL, John	35	M	Laborer	28Ma02Ax
Margaret	4	F	Child	28Ma02Ax
MULLANY, Patt	20	M	Laborer	28Ma02Ax
MORRISON, Peter	21	M	Laborer	28Ma02Ax
HAMILTON, James	22	M	Laborer	28Ma02Ax
DANIELL, Mary	30	F	Unknown	28Ma02Ax
Cathrine	.00	F	Infant	28Ma02Ax
Johannah	40	F	Unknown	28Ma02Ax
GILLIGAN, Biddy	21	F	Unknown	28Ma02Ax
RONEY, Bess	20	F	Unknown	28Ma02Ax
MCGOOGHEY, Mary	35	F	Unknown	28Ma02Ax
Cathrine	11	F	Unknown	28Ma02Ax
Mary	9	F	Child	28Ma02Ax
John	7	M	Child	28Ma02Ax
Mathew	5	M	Child	28Ma02Ax
Ellen	2	F	Child	28Ma02Ax
MCGLONE, Dennis	22	M	Laborer	28Ma02Ax
MCNAULTY, Peter	22	M	Laborer	28Ma02Ax
Ellen	20	F	Unknown	28Ma02Ax
Hugh	22	M	Unknown	28Ma02Ax
MCGEEL, Tarry	40	M	Laborer	28Ma02Ax
MCNAULTY, Mary	20	F	Servant	28Ma02Ax
GODSON, William	23	M	Laborer	28Ma02Ax
BULKLEY, Timothy	28	M	Laborer	28Ma02Ax
MOORE, John	21	M	Laborer	28Ma02Ax
MONOGAN, Cathrine	21	F	Servant	28Ma02Ax
CARROLL, Biddy	22	F	Servant	28Ma02Ax
MAHONEY, Ellen	18	F	Servant	28Ma02Ax
MORAN, Cathrine	19	F	Servant	28Ma02Ax
PRENDERGASE, Bridget	20	F	Servant	28Ma02Ax
MCLIA, Mary-A.	21	F	Unknown	28Ma02Ax
MALONE, Margaret	21	F	Unknown	28Ma02Ax
KIRLEY, James	25	M	Laborer	28Ma02Ax
KEOGH, John	30	M	Clerk	28Ma02Ax
PRENDERGASEE, Martin	25	M	Brguskr	28Ma02Ax
ALYWARD, Johanna	25	F	Servant	28Ma02Ax
CONWAY, Mary	50	F	Servant	28Ma02Ax
Patrick	25	M	Laborer	28Ma02Ax
Mary	26	F	Servant	28Ma02Ax
KELLY, Barthm.	21	M	Laborer	28Ma02Ax
DOWNES, Mary	45	F	Unknown	28Ma02Ax
Bridget	18	F	Unknown	28Ma02Ax
Edward	16	M	Unknown	28Ma02Ax
NOLAN, Bridget	15	F	Unknown	28Ma02Ax
DOWNES, Thomas	11	M	Unknown	28Ma02Ax
Anne	8	F	Child	28Ma02Ax
Margaret	6	F	Child	28Ma02Ax
THOMPSON, William	18	M	Child	28Ma02Ax
MURPHY, Peter	35	M	Laborer	28Ma02Ax
MATHEW, Anne	55	F	Unknown	28Ma02Ax
CONNOR, Andrew	25	M	Laborer	28Ma02Ax
COLEMAN, Bridget	30	F	Unknown	28Ma02Ax
SUTTON, Thomas	30	M	Farmer	28Ma02Ax
NEIL, Thomas	40	M	Laborer	28Ma02Ax
MARTIN, John	38	M	Laborer	28Ma02Ax
KINEALLY, Patrick	30	M	Cooper	28Ma02Ax
GORMAN, William	28	M	Laborer	28Ma02Ax

NAMES OF PASSENGERS	AGE	SEX	OCCUPATIONS	DATE PORT SHIP	NAMES OF PASSENGERS	AGE	SEX	OCCUPATIONS	DATE PORT SHIP
KINEALLY, Thomas	30	M	Unknown	28Ma02Ax	SULLIVAN, Dennis	6	M	Child	28Ma02Ax
GORMAN, Honora	27	F	Laborer	28Ma02Ax	DUNN, William	40	M	Laborer	28Ma02Ax
CONNELLY, Mary	22	F	Servant	28Ma02Ax	Anne	40	F	Unknown	28Ma02Ax
REILLY, Mary	40	F	Unknown	28Ma02Ax	Madge	16	F	Unknown	28Ma02Ax
Ellen	20	F	Unknown	28Ma02Ax	John	13	M	Unknown	28Ma02Ax
Michael	18	M	Unknown	28Ma02Ax	Thomas	10	M	Unknown	28Ma02Ax
Elizabeth	11	F	Unknown	28Ma02Ax	William	5	M	Child	28Ma02Ax
Thomas	9	M	Child	28Ma02Ax	MCMANNS, Margaret	24	F	Dressmaker	28Ma02Ax
James	7	M	Child	28Ma02Ax	Anne	21	F	Dressmaker	28Ma02Ax
CARLAS, Thomas	28	M	Laborer	28Ma02Ax	Mary	20	F	Dressmaker	28Ma02Ax
RHINA, Dennis	20	M	Laborer	28Ma02Ax	GILLAN, Cathrine	25	F	Dressmaker	28Ma02Ax
Bridget	20	f	Unknown	28Ma02Ax	KEARNEY, Margaret	50	F	Unknown	28Ma02Ax
Patrick	25	M	Laborer	28Ma02Ax	James	20	M	Laborer	28Ma02Ax
Cathrine	50	F	Unknown	28Ma02Ax	Kate	16	F	Dressmaker	28Ma02Ax
MCGOWAN, William	26	M	Laborer	28Ma02Ax	Mary	13	F	Dressmaker	28Ma02Ax
Margaret	19	F	Unknown	28Ma02Ax	Sarah	11	F	Unknown	28Ma02Ax
MCMAHON, John	50	M	Farmer	28Ma02Ax	Margaret	9	F	Child	28Ma02Ax
LEONARD, Francis	42	M	Gdnr	28Ma02Ax	Charles	7	M	Child	28Ma02Ax
HARTNETT, David	25	M	Laborer	28Ma02Ax	DERMOND, James	17	M	Laborer	28Ma02Ax
SHEA, Timothy	19	M	Laborer	28Ma02Ax	OCONNOR, Cathrine	20	F	Servant	28Ma02Ax
CROOK, William	12	M	Laborer	28Ma02Ax	HOGAN, Mary	34	F	Servant	28Ma02Ax
Daniel	47	M	Laborer	28Ma02Ax	Mary-J.	18	F	Servant	28Ma02Ax
LEONARD, Francis	30	M	Laborer	28Ma02Ax	Daniel	13	F	Unknown	28Ma02Ax
MITCHELL, Brien	22	M	Farmer	28Ma02Ax	Maria	11	F	Unknown	28Ma02Ax
CLANCEY, Patt	23	M	Farmer	28Ma02Ax	BARNELL, Bridget	15	F	Unknown	28Ma02Ax
ROMEY, Thomas	21	M	Farmer	28Ma02Ax	DWYER, Michael	24	M	Laborer	28Ma02Ax
MITCHELL, Peggy	22	F	Unknown	28Ma02Ax	CASTELLA, John	24	M	Laborer	28Ma02Ax
REDDY, Patrick	22	M	Farmer	28Ma02Ax	AHERNE, William	30	M	Laborer	28Ma02Ax
MCKEAUGH, Mary	20	F	Unknown	28Ma02Ax	HENESSEY, Patrick	30	M	Laborer	28Ma02Ax
MCGARVAN, Rose	20	F	Unknown	28Ma02Ax	CASEY, Maurice	40	M	Laborer	28Ma02Ax
Sally	19	F	Unknown	28Ma02Ax	Dennis	30	M	Laborer	28Ma02Ax
ROWNEY, Bridget	18	F	Unknown	28Ma02Ax	Francis	25	M	Laborer	28Ma02Ax
HIGHEE, Margaret	20	F	Unknown	28Ma02Ax	SINNOD, Patrick	50	M	Laborer	28Ma02Ax
MCCLUE, Cathrine	20	F	Dressmaker	28Ma02Ax	Mary	48	F	Unknown	28Ma02Ax
KANE, Bernard	18	M	Dressmaker	28Ma02Ax	Moses	14	M	Unknown	28Ma02Ax
GORMAN, Cathrine	24	F	Unknown	28Ma02Ax	Mary	9	F	Child	28Ma02Ax
DEVAN, James	28	M	Servant	28Ma02Ax	HEFFERAN, Mathew	23	M	Laborer	28Ma02Ax
Anne	28	F	Servant	28Ma02Ax	OLIVER, James	19	M	Laborer	28Ma02Ax
Michael	5	M	Child	28Ma02Ax	MORROW, William	22	M	Laborer	28Ma02Ax
James	2	M	Child	28Ma02Ax	William	22	M	Laborer	28Ma02Ax
CONNOR, Edward	27	M	Laborer	28Ma02Ax	QUILLION, James	21	M	Laborer	28Ma02Ax
JOYCE, Julia	25	F	Unknown	28Ma02Ax	MORROW, Margaret	17	F	Unknown	28Ma02Ax
SALINON, Essy	20	F	Unknown	28Ma02Ax	Honora	20	F	Unknown	28Ma02Ax
LAWLOR, Essy	26	F	Servant	28Ma02Ax	MCQUILLAN, James	20	M	Shoemaker	28Ma02Ax
DOOLEY, Johanna	20	F	Servant	28Ma02Ax	Cathrine	17	F	Unknown	28Ma02Ax
Mary-A.	19	F	Servant	28Ma02Ax	HARDEN, Jane	22	F	Servant	28Ma02Ax
FITZPATRICK, John	21	M	Laborer	28Ma02Ax	SMITH, Patrick	30	M	Baker	28Ma02Ax
BRIEN, Mary	36	F	Unknown	28Ma02Ax	Ellen	17	F	Dressmaker	28Ma02Ax
Patt	11	M	Unknown	28Ma02Ax	MASON, Edward	26	M	Printer	28Ma02Ax
Michael	8	M	Child	28Ma02Ax	LAWRENCE, William	26	M	Unknown	28Ma02Ax
MORMAN, Daniel	11	M	Unknown	28Ma02Ax	MURPHY, James	29	M	Laborer	28Ma02Ax
BUCKLEY, Mary	20	F	Unknown	28Ma02Ax	HUGHS, Daniel	20	M	Unknown	28Ma02Ax
GORMAN, Susanna	18	F	Unknown	28Ma02Ax	MCDONALD, Mary	17	F	Unknown	28Ma02Ax
MCDERMOT, John	23	M	Laborer	28Ma02Ax	Mary	20	F	Unknown	28Ma02Ax
Michael	19	M	Servant	28Ma02Ax	REYNOLDS, George	20	M	Unknown	28Ma02Ax
CALKIN, Patrick	20	M	Laborer	28Ma02Ax	WALSH, James	50	M	Unknown	28Ma02Ax
CALL, Mary	20	F	Unknown	28Ma02Ax	DUGGAN, Patt	50	M	Unknown	28Ma02Ax
BRIEN, Dennis	26	M	Laborer	28Ma02Ax	Mary	50	F	Unknown	28Ma02Ax
BURGESS, Maria	22	F	Servant	28Ma02Ax	James	15	F	Unknown	28Ma02Ax
CALHOUN, Samuel	25	M	Laborer	28Ma02Ax	Bridget	20	F	Unknown	28Ma02Ax
Eliza	9	F	Child	28Ma02Ax	GALLAHER, Patt	26	M	Unknown	28Ma02Ax
Cathrine	7	F	Child	28Ma02Ax	John	15	M	Unknown	28Ma02Ax
George	3	M	Child	28Ma02Ax	REID, Thomas	21	M	Laborer	28Ma02Ax
LEO, John	18	M	Laborer	28Ma02Ax	KANE, Hugh	15	M	Baker	28Ma02Ax
MALLEY, James	28	M	Gdnr	28Ma02Ax	CASH, Honora	22	F	Servant	28Ma02Ax
NOLAN, Bridget	24	F	Unknown	28Ma02Ax	MEEHAN, Ellen	22	F	Dressmaker	28Ma02Ax
SHEEHAN, Johanna	26	F	Servant	28Ma02Ax	RIELEY, Ann	18	F	Servant	28Ma02Ax
CONNELL, Dennis	29	M	Laborer	28Ma02Ax	KEATING, Wm.	12	M	Unknown	28Ma02Ax
Margaret	24	F	Unknown	28Ma02Ax	Nora	10	F	Unknown	28Ma02Ax
MCAULIFFE, Ellen	19	F	Unknown	28Ma02Ax	PRONNTY, Cathrine	21	F	Unknown	28Ma02Ax
Florence	18	F	Unknown	28Ma02Ax	INGLESLY, Cathrine	13	F	Unknown	28Ma02Ax
MCCARTHY, Mary	26	F	Unknown	28Ma02Ax	WYLIE, Jane	40	F	Unknown	28Ma02Ax
SULLIVAN, John	40	M	Laborer	28Ma02Ax	Sarah	16	F	Unknown	28Ma02Ax
Timothy	8	M	Child	28Ma02Ax	Elizabeth	13	F	Unknown	28Ma02Ax
Maria	10	F	Unknown	28Ma02Ax	MCKANE, Biddy	22	F	Unknown	28Ma02Ax

NAMES OF PASSENGERS	AGE	SEX	OCCUPATIONS	DATE PORT SHIP
MCCAULEY, Alexd.	30	M	Farmer	28Ma02Ax
Cathrine	26	F	Unknown	28Ma02Ax
John	4	M	Child	28Ma02Ax
Cathrine	2	F	Child	28Ma02Ax
Mary	.00	F	Infant	28Ma02Ax
LYNCH, Daniel	35	M	Laborer	28Ma02Ax
Winifred	20	F	Unknown	28Ma02Ax
ROGER, Margaret	20	F	Unknown	28Ma02Ax
QUIN, Margaret	12	F	Unknown	28Ma02Ax
John	7	M	Child	28Ma02Ax
SHINNERS, Patt	19	M	Unknown	28Ma02Ax
Cathrine	18	F	Unknown	28Ma02Ax
WALSH, Bridget	40	F	Unknown	28Ma02Ax
BRENNOCK, Ann	35	F	Unknown	28Ma02Ax
John	20	M	Servant	28Ma02Ax
Martin	10	M	Unknown	28Ma02Ax
Patt	8	M	Child	28Ma02Ax
Thomas	5	M	Child	28Ma02Ax
John	3	M	Child	28Ma02Ax
Maria	.00	F	Infant	28Ma02Ax
Died-At-Sea				
WALSH, John	18	M	Unknown	28Ma02Ax
DODD, Richard	7	M	Child	28Ma02Ax
Michael	6	M	Child	28Ma02Ax
Patt	40	M	Laborer	28Ma02Ax
GUIREY, Timothy	26	M	Laborer	28Ma02Ax
HOLLOWAY, James	22	M	Laborer	28Ma02Ax
TORMEY, Charles	30	M	Carpenter	28Ma02Ax
Bridget	26	M	Unknown	28Ma02Ax
Michael	4	M	Child	28Ma02Ax
FLYNE, Elizabeth	17	F	Unknown	28Ma02Ax
Bridget	9	F	Child	28Ma02Ax
MCILVENIAL, John	18	M	Clerk	28Ma02Ax
MILES, James	36	M	Farmer	28Ma02Ax
STAPLETON, Sarah	26	F	Servant	28Ma02Ax
NEVILLEL, Anne	25	F	Servant	28Ma02Ax
CARRIDON, Timothy	15	M	Unknown	28Ma02Ax
Ellen	18	F	Unknown	28Ma02Ax
MCGAUGHRAN, Cathrine	20	F	Unknown	28Ma02Ax
DEVON, Johanna	30	F	Unknown	28Ma02Ax
MASON, Mary	20	F	Servant	28Ma02Ax
Bridget	.00	F	Infant	28Ma02Ax
BURNES, Norry	30	F	Unknown	28Ma02Ax
John	7	M	Child	28Ma02Ax
Mary	.00	F	Infant	28Ma02Ax
GRADY, Honora	48	F	Unknown	28Ma02Ax
Ellen	26	F	Unknown	28Ma02Ax
KELLY, Mary	46	F	Unknown	28Ma02Ax
LAMB, Mary	20	F	Unknown	28Ma02Ax
TEEHAN, Bessy	18	F	Unknown	28Ma02Ax
OCONNOR, Daniel	23	M	Laborer	28Ma02Ax
DALBY, Cathrine	18	F	Unknown	28Ma02Ax
FITZPATRICK, Cathrine	16	F	Unknown	28Ma02Ax
DELANEY, John	22	M	Clerk	28Ma02Ax
DRAPER, Joseph	22	M	Farmer	28Ma02Ax
Sarah	50	F	Unknown	28Ma02Ax
BURKE, James	13	M	Unknown	28Ma02Ax
HAINES, Michael	23	M	Laborer	28Ma02Ax
MCGEE, Henry	24	M	Servant	28Ma02Ax
WILSON, George	25	M	Weaver	28Ma02Ax
BROWN, Ellen	22	F	Servant	28Ma02Ax
SIMPSON, Judy	25	F	Servant	28Ma02Ax
DENAHEY, Thomas	16	M	Unknown	28Ma02Ax
Ellen	17	F	Unknown	28Ma02Ax
MURPHY, Honora	24	F	Unknown	28Ma02Ax
MANAHAN, Michael	20	M	Unknown	28Ma02Ax
LYNCH, Ellen	18	F	Unknown	28Ma02Ax
FLANAGAN, Charles	29	M	Shopkeeper	28Ma02Ax
KEIRMAN, Mary	14	F	Unknown	28Ma02Ax
JACKABERRY, James	21	M	Carpenter	28Ma02Ax
BARRETT, Edmund	36	M	Servant	28Ma02Ax
BURKE, James	13	M	Unknown	28Ma02Ax
KEATING, Cornelius	24	M	Tailor	28Ma02Ax
KEALEHAR, Cathrine	23	F	Unknown	28Ma02Ax
Timothy	10	M	Unknown	28Ma02Ax

NAMES OF PASSENGERS	AGE	SEX	OCCUPATIONS	DATE PORT SHIP
KEALEHAR, Johanna	8	F	Child	28Ma02Ax
Cathrine	6	F	Child	28Ma02Ax
Mary	4	F	Child	28Ma02Ax
TODD, Francis	20	M	Laborer	28Ma02Ax
TEENEY, Thomas	17	M	Laborer	28Ma02Ax
ALBERT, Edmund	18	M	Laborer	28Ma02Ax
ROCHE, Patrick	27	M	Hrstnr	28Ma02Ax
Mary	25	F	Unknown	28Ma02Ax
MCCLAIG, James	21	M	Servant	28Ma02Ax
HOGAN, Edward	45	M	Stone Mason	28Ma02Ax
Joseph	14	M	Unknown	28Ma02Ax
DONNELLY, James	26	M	Stone Mason	28Ma02Ax
Bridget	26	F	Unknown	28Ma02Ax
CAMPION, Patrick	22	M	Farmer	28Ma02Ax
George	17	M	Farmer	28Ma02Ax
GAY, David	22	M	Farmer	28Ma02Ax
HOGORTY, Bridget	25	F	Unknown	28Ma02Ax
Bridget	8	F	Child	28Ma02Ax
Martin	4	M	Child	28Ma02Ax
Patt	.00	M	Infant	28Ma02Ax
Died-At-Sea				
BYRNES, Cathrine	25	F	Servant	28Ma02Ax
CROKER, John	18	M	Laborer	28Ma02Ax
MCMANUS, Thomas	30	M	Laborer	28Ma02Ax
Francis	28	M	Laborer	28Ma02Ax
Jerry	23	M	Laborer	28Ma02Ax
QUINN, Cathr.	35	F	Unknown	28Ma02Ax
Ellen	7	F	Child	28Ma02Ax
James	4	M	Child	28Ma02Ax
Mary	2	F	Child	28Ma02Ax
MEEHAN, Patk.	45	M	Laborer	28Ma02Ax
HENDERSON, James	18	M	Unknown	28Ma02Ax
FLYNN, Chas.	35	M	Farmer	28Ma02Ax
Bessy	32	F	Unknown	28Ma02Ax
Bridget	12	F	Unknown	28Ma02Ax
John	8	M	Child	28Ma02Ax
Mary	6	F	Child	28Ma02Ax
Alice	4	F	Child	28Ma02Ax
Gertrude	3	F	Child	28Ma02Ax
Thos.	.00	M	Infant	28Ma02Ax
FARRELL, Margt.	18	F	Unknown	28Ma02Ax
MORRISEY, Nicha.	26	M	Carpenter	28Ma02Ax
KEASFOOL, John	28	M	Laborer	28Ma02Ax
CONNOR, John	23	M	Hatter	28Ma02Ax
DALY, Richd.	20	M	Painter	28Ma02Ax
DONOGHUE, Mary	20	F	Unknown	28Ma02Ax
Michl.	20	M	Laborer	28Ma02Ax
FORDE, Cathr.	40	F	Spinner	28Ma02Ax
Cathr.	7	F	Child	28Ma02Ax
DUFFY, Margt.	38	F	Unknown	28Ma02Ax
ANDERSON, William	16	M	Unknown	28Ma02Ax
John	50	M	Farmer	28Ma02Ax
SULLIVAN, Patt	17	M	Laborer	28Ma02Ax
Mary	15	F	Unknown	28Ma02Ax
GORMAN, Edmd.	36	M	Laborer	28Ma02Ax
GRACE, Michl.	35	M	Painter	28Ma02Ax
WALSH, John	25	M	Laborer	28Ma02Ax
MCGINNIS, James	21	M	Laborer	28Ma02Ax
WALSH, Mary	21	F	Unknown	28Ma02Ax
RICE, John	22	M	Weaver	28Ma02Ax
LAFFAN, John	24	M	Laborer	28Ma02Ax
DOOLY, John	20	M	Laborer	28Ma02Ax
RONANE, John	24	M	Laborer	28Ma02Ax
Bridgt.	25	F	Laborer	28Ma02Ax
SHEEHAN, Thos.	27	M	Servant	28Ma02Ax
Honora	35	F	Servant	28Ma02Ax
MAHER, Michl.	17	M	Plasterer	28Ma02Ax
RYAN, Anne	20	F	Unknown	28Ma02Ax
MULDAWNEY, Bridgt.	20	F	Servant	28Ma02Ax
CONOLLY, Nelly	20	F	Servant	28Ma02Ax
CALHOUN, Sarah	21	F	Servant	28Ma02Ax
MCCABE, Bernd.	18	M	Laborer	28Ma02Ax
PATERSON, Margt.	43	F	Servant	28Ma02Ax
PACKHILL, Margt.	21	F	Servant	28Ma02Ax
BACKER, Jane	16	F	Servant	28Ma02Ax

NAMES OF PASSENGERS	AGE	SEX	OCCUPATIONS	DATE PORT SHIP
JOHNSON, Grace	25	F	Unknown	28Ma02Ax
Anne	5	F	Child	28Ma02Ax
MAHER, John	22	M	Laborer	28Ma02Ax
HULREY, Julia	18	F	Servant	28Ma02Ax
DONOVAN, Cathn.	20	F	Servant	28Ma02Ax
MAHONY, Timothy	28	M	Laborer	28Ma02Ax
CRONAN, Timothy	25	M	Unknown	28Ma02Ax
SULLIVAN, Jerry	46	M	Laborer	28Ma02Ax
HAYES, Rodger	54	M	Farmer	28Ma02Ax
GRIFFIN, Cathr.	36	F	Unknown	28Ma02Ax
John	13	M	Unknown	28Ma02Ax
Mary	13	F	Unknown	28Ma02Ax
TAGNEY, John	21	M	Shoemaker	28Ma02Ax
SULLIVAN, Anne	22	F	Servant	28Ma02Ax
Honora	26	F	Unknown	28Ma02Ax
HUGHES, David	32	M	Iron Monger	28Ma02Ax
Anne	26	F	Unknown	28Ma02Ax
WALSH, Paul	28	M	Carpenter	28Ma02Ax
HEFFERAN, Edwd.	12	M	Unknown	28Ma02Ax
FITZPATRICK, Isabella	30	F	Housekeeper	28Ma02Ax
RODGERS, Peter	23	M	Laborer	28Ma02Ax
BENNETT, John	35	M	Laborer	28Ma02Ax
Mary	28	F	Unknown	28Ma02Ax
Michael	.00	M	Infant	28Ma02Ax
CONNELL, Johanna	13	F	Unknown	28Ma02Ax
Honora	12	F	Unknown	28Ma02Ax
BENNETT, James	18	M	Unknown	28Ma02Ax
MCAULIFFE, Brian	32	M	Laborer	28Ma02Ax
FOLEY, Patk.	20	M	Unknown	28Ma02Ax
QUINN, Johanna	19	F	Unknown	28Ma02Ax
KEATING, John	22	M	Unknown	28Ma02Ax
MCANELLY, Jane	21	F	Servant	28Ma02Ax
BURNS, Cathr.	55	F	Spinner	28Ma02Ax
SMITH, Rose	46	F	Spinner	28Ma02Ax
MARTIN, Ellen	12	F	Unknown	28Ma02Ax
MAHONY, Mary	20	F	Servant	28Ma02Ax
LANE, Harry	24	M	Laborer	28Ma02Ax
MCDONALD, Nancy	20	F	Servant	28Ma02Ax
GALVIN, Julia	20	F	Servant	28Ma02Ax
MAHONY, Cathr.	23	F	Servant	28Ma02Ax
CONNORS, Mary	23	F	Servant	28Ma02Ax
BROWN, John	20	M	Laborer	28Ma02Ax
Honora	22	F	Unknown	28Ma02Ax
CONDON, Mary	20	F	Servant	28Ma02Ax
SLOANE, Sarah	43	F	Servant	28Ma02Ax
David	21	M	Servant	28Ma02Ax
MCMAHON, Patk.	20	M	Laborer	28Ma02Ax
Sarah	21	F	Unknown	28Ma02Ax
POTTER, Thos.	60	M	Farmer	28Ma02Ax
Mary-A.	30	F	Unknown	28Ma02Ax
Alexr.	16	M	Unknown	28Ma02Ax
RYAN, John	30	M	Laborer	28Ma02Ax
Judy	30	F	Unknown	28Ma02Ax
Brigt.	6	F	Child	28Ma02Ax
Michl.	4	M	Child	28Ma02Ax
John	.00	M	Infant	28Ma02Ax
CARMODY, Ned	23	M	Tailor	28Ma02Ax
Judy	30	F	Unknown	28Ma02Ax
James	10	M	Unknown	28Ma02Ax
Judy	7	F	Child	28Ma02Ax
LAHES, Michael	17	M	Laborer	28Ma02Ax
DUFFY, Michl.	18	M	Tailor	28Ma02Ax
Anne	13	F	Unknown	28Ma02Ax
MULVEY, Mary	22	F	Servant	28Ma02Ax
BYRNE, Bridgt.	24	F	Servant	28Ma02Ax
RYAN, Mary	23	F	Servant	28Ma02Ax
CAVANNAH, Bridgt.	25	F	Servant	28Ma02Ax
SULLIVAN, Denis	20	M	Laborer	28Ma02Ax
Mary	18	F	Unknown	28Ma02Ax
BUCKLEY, Patk.	27	M	Laborer	28Ma02Ax
Michl.	26	M	Laborer	28Ma02Ax
Daniel	27	M	Laborer	28Ma02Ax
BARRETT, Michl.	25	M	Laborer	28Ma02Ax
COUGHLAN, James	24	M	Laborer	28Ma02Ax
HUSSEY, Michl.	24	M	Laborer	28Ma02Ax
AICKEN, Thos.	60	M	Farmer	28Ma02Ax
John	30	M	Farmer	28Ma02Ax
Hannah	12	F	Unknown	28Ma02Ax
David	10	M	Unknown	28Ma02Ax
Robert	7	M	Child	28Ma02Ax
BROWN, Bridget	20	F	Dressmaker	28Ma02Ax
FANAN, Michl.	22	M	Laborer	28Ma02Ax
FEELEY, Cathr.	50	F	Unknown	28Ma02Ax
John	24	M	Farmer	28Ma02Ax
RAYMOND, John	22	M	Laborer	28Ma02Ax
FORAN, Sylvester	26	M	Laborer	28Ma02Ax
SLICK, Wm.	30	M	Laborer	28Ma02Ax
BYRNE, Michl.	22	M	Laborer	28Ma02Ax
BUCKLEY, John	20	M	Laborer	28Ma02Ax
Jane	18	F	Unknown	28Ma02Ax
SLACK, Margt.	27	F	Unknown	28Ma02Ax
CURLING, Margt.	35	F	Unknown	28Ma02Ax
John	15	M	Unknown	28Ma02Ax
Margt.	11	F	Unknown	28Ma02Ax
Mary	9	F	Child	28Ma02Ax
Wm.	5	M	Child	28Ma02Ax
Robert	3	M	Child	28Ma02Ax
CARLIN, Mary	30	F	Unknown	28Ma02Ax
Bridget	12	F	Unknown	28Ma02Ax
Martin	11	M	Unknown	28Ma02Ax
Michl.	10	M	Unknown	28Ma02Ax
HICKEY, Honora	20	F	Unknown	28Ma02Ax
CARLIN, John	5	M	Child	28Ma02Ax
LESTER, Patk.	50	M	Laborer	28Ma02Ax
John	11	M	Unknown	28Ma02Ax
FLEMMING, Michl.	21	M	Laborer	28Ma02Ax
CARNY, Martin	11	M	Unknown	28Ma02Ax
Mary	21	F	Servant	28Ma02Ax
MOORE, Anne	26	F	Servant	28Ma02Ax
REILLEY, Margt.	20	F	Servant	28Ma02Ax
REGAN, Wm.	25	M	Laborer	28Ma02Ax
Julia	23	F	Unknown	28Ma02Ax
Mary	17	F	Unknown	28Ma02Ax
PIERSON, Patk.	25	M	Laborer	28Ma02Ax
Rosanna	20	F	Unknown	28Ma02Ax
BULYEN, Edwd.	35	M	Farmer	28Ma02Ax
Margt.	33	F	Unknown	28Ma02Ax
Michl.	8	M	Child	28Ma02Ax
Cathr.	6	F	Child	28Ma02Ax
Robt.	.00	M	Infant	28Ma02Ax
RANE, John	45	M	Cooper	28Ma02Ax
DONOGHUE, Margt.	58	F	Unknown	28Ma02Ax
Margt.	19	F	Unknown	28Ma02Ax
John	22	M	Laborer	28Ma02Ax
Mary	23	F	Unknown	28Ma02Ax
HOPKINS, Marcella	17	F	Unknown	28Ma02Ax
Bridget	22	F	Unknown	28Ma02Ax
KEENAN, John	24	M	Unknown	28Ma02Ax
GALLAGHER, Brigt.	18	F	Servant	28Ma02Ax
REIL, Cathr.	19	F	Servant	28Ma02Ax
DODD, John	22	M	Laborer	28Ma02Ax
Pat	23	M	Laborer	28Ma02Ax
CONRAY, Peter	32	M	Farmer	28Ma02Ax
WALSH, Patk.	27	M	Laborer	28Ma02Ax
Bridgt.	27	F	Laborer	28Ma02Ax
Elizabeth	35	F	Unknown	28Ma02Ax
HOLMES, Margt.	20	F	Unknown	28Ma02Ax
CLERK, Jane	28	F	Servant	28Ma02Ax
BRADY, Ellen	18	F	Servant	28Ma02Ax
FANELLY, Michl.	25	M	Laborer	28Ma02Ax
WALSH, Margt.	12	F	Unknown	28Ma02Ax
Richd.	10	M	Unknown	28Ma02Ax
Margt.	7	F	Child	28Ma02Ax
Robert	4	M	Child	28Ma02Ax
Francis	2	M	Child	28Ma02Ax
ARMSTRONG, Eliza	18	F	Schms	28Ma02Ax
Wm.	10	M	Unknown	28Ma02Ax
TUOHY, Honora	23	F	Servant	28Ma02Ax
Michl.	7	M	Child	28Ma02Ax
HULOHIN, James	24	M	Laborer	28Ma02Ax

NAMES OF PASSENGERS	AGE	SEX	OCCUPATIONS	DATE PORT SHIP
TUOHY, Margt.	24	F	Unknown	28Ma02Ax
MARTIN, Ellen	30	F	Unknown	28Ma02Ax
MEEHAN, Michl.	21	M	Laborer	28Ma02Ax
MCMAHAN, Brian	22	M	Laborer	28Ma02Ax
MCDONALD, Patk.	20	M	Unknown	28Ma02Ax
COLLINS, Mary	19	F	Unknown	28Ma02Ax
FINEGAN, Biddy	20	F	Servant	28Ma02Ax
LENEHAN, Johanna	22	F	Servant	28Ma02Ax
MCALAY, Wm.	24	M	Laborer	28Ma02Ax
GRAMES, Patk.	26	M	Carpenter	28Ma02Ax
Wm.	25	M	Blacksmith	28Ma02Ax
RAFFERTY, Mary	24	F	Servant	28Ma02Ax
ENRIGHT, Anne	20	F	Servant	28Ma02Ax
MCNAMARA, Mary	21	F	Servant	28Ma02Ax
DONOVAN, John	40	M	Laborer	28Ma02Ax
FOGARTY, Kate	.00	F	Infant	28Ma02Ax
Born-At-Sea				

ODESSA 28 MAY 1850

From Dublin

NAMES OF PASSENGERS	AGE	SEX	OCCUPATIONS	DATE PORT SHIP
BRANNICKS, Luke	26	M	Unknown	28Ma05Kr
REILLY, Ellen	30	F	Unknown	28Ma05Kr
John	13	M	Unknown	28Ma05Kr
Eliza	10	F	Unknown	28Ma05Kr
Arthur	6	M	Child	28Ma05Kr
Cath.	.00	F	Infant	28Ma05Kr
SMITH, Patrick	15	M	Unknown	28Ma05Kr
CALDWELL, Henry	22	M	Unknown	28Ma05Kr
OGRADY, Thomas	20	M	Unknown	28Ma05Kr
GRIFFORD, U	20	F	Unknown	28Ma05Kr
Cather.	18	F	Unknown	28Ma05Kr
HOLLOWAY, James	34	M	Unknown	28Ma05Kr
Ann	30	F	Unknown	28Ma05Kr
William	6	M	Child	28Ma05Kr
John	4	M	Child	28Ma05Kr
Mary	.00	F	Infant	28Ma05Kr
LEWIS, Wm.	48	M	Unknown	28Ma05Kr
U-Mrs.	30	F	Unknown	28Ma05Kr
John	10	M	Unknown	28Ma05Kr
Richard	6	M	Child	28Ma05Kr
Lucy	4	F	Child	28Ma05Kr
Jane	.00	F	Infant	28Ma05Kr
TALBOT, Montague	17	M	Unknown	28Ma05Kr
GALLAGHER, William	00	M	Unknown	28Ma05Kr
GRACE, Michael	23	M	Unknown	28Ma05Kr
U-Mrs.	30	F	Unknown	28Ma05Kr
Thos.	36	M	Unknown	28Ma05Kr
Mary	.00	F	Infant	28Ma05Kr
MCLOUGHLAN, Richard	24	M	Unknown	28Ma05Kr
DOLAN, Peter	28	M	Unknown	28Ma05Kr
MARWELL, Ellen	20	F	Unknown	28Ma05Kr
MCGEE, Felix	21	M	Unknown	28Ma05Kr
ANDREWS, Joseph	24	M	Unknown	28Ma05Kr
U-Mrs.	21	F	Unknown	28Ma05Kr
Jane	20	F	Unknown	28Ma05Kr
MCKENNA, John	44	M	Unknown	28Ma05Kr
Eliza	44	F	Unknown	28Ma05Kr
John	26	M	Unknown	28Ma05Kr
James	21	M	Unknown	28Ma05Kr
Patrick	13	M	Unknown	28Ma05Kr
Anne	12	F	Unknown	28Ma05Kr
Ellen	20	F	Unknown	28Ma05Kr
Rose	18	F	Unknown	28Ma05Kr
Francis	15	M	Unknown	28Ma05Kr
Terence	9	M	Child	28Ma05Kr
ODONNELL, Maria	20	F	Unknown	28Ma05Kr
WILSON, Maria	20	F	Unknown	28Ma05Kr

NAMES OF PASSENGERS	AGE	SEX	OCCUPATIONS	DATE PORT SHIP
WILSON, Ellen	18	F	Unknown	28Ma05Kr
JOHNSON, Mary-A.	25	F	Unknown	28Ma05Kr
JONES, Elizabeth	18	F	Unknown	28Ma05Kr
YOUNG, U-Mrs.	36	F	Unknown	28Ma05Kr
Anna	18	F	Unknown	28Ma05Kr
Susanne	16	F	Unknown	28Ma05Kr
Harriett	12	F	Unknown	28Ma05Kr
Moses	9	M	Child	28Ma05Kr
Miles	.00	M	Infant	28Ma05Kr
Florinda	5	F	Child	28Ma05Kr
Francis	20	M	Unknown	28Ma05Kr
Sarah	.00	F	Infant	28Ma05Kr
PERRY, Henry	23	M	Unknown	28Ma05Kr
ROGERS, Dennis	28	M	Unknown	28Ma05Kr
MONKS, Bridget	20	F	Unknown	28Ma05Kr
FOHEN, James	22	M	Unknown	28Ma05Kr
HOLAHAN, Michael	24	M	Unknown	28Ma05Kr
FANNING, Mary	19	F	Unknown	28Ma05Kr
DOWD, Ann	50	F	Unknown	28Ma05Kr
BERMINGHAM, John	50	M	Unknown	28Ma05Kr
John	10	M	Unknown	28Ma05Kr
MOONEY, Pat	22	M	Unknown	28Ma05Kr
Cath.	21	F	Unknown	28Ma05Kr
William	20	M	Unknown	28Ma05Kr
WHELAN, John	25	M	Unknown	28Ma05Kr
James	30	M	Unknown	28Ma05Kr
DOWD, John	26	M	Unknown	28Ma05Kr
KAY, William	20	M	Unknown	28Ma05Kr
KERWAN, James	20	M	Unknown	28Ma05Kr
HAGAN, Ellen	20	F	Unknown	28Ma05Kr
HARATY, Ann	20	F	Unknown	28Ma05Kr
TULHICK, William	30	M	Unknown	28Ma05Kr
U-Mrs.	28	F	Unknown	28Ma05Kr
Mary	16	F	Unknown	28Ma05Kr
NOLAN, James	26	M	Unknown	28Ma05Kr
CASSIDY, John	20	M	Unknown	28Ma05Kr
DUNN, James	26	M	Unknown	28Ma05Kr
KELLY, James	13	M	Unknown	28Ma05Kr
DEVERY, James	20	M	Unknown	28Ma05Kr
FLOOD, John	20	M	Unknown	28Ma05Kr
PHELAN, James	32	M	Unknown	28Ma05Kr
U-Mrs.	20	F	Unknown	28Ma05Kr
Mary	23	F	Unknown	28Ma05Kr
Eliza	.00	F	Infant	28Ma05Kr
SWEENY, Emma	40	F	Unknown	28Ma05Kr
PHELAN, Michael	18	M	Unknown	28Ma05Kr
TURNER, Michael	18	M	Unknown	28Ma05Kr
James	13	M	Unknown	28Ma05Kr
Margaret	12	F	Unknown	28Ma05Kr
Maria	10	F	Unknown	28Ma05Kr
Anne	9	F	Child	28Ma05Kr
Eliza	7	F	Child	28Ma05Kr
Ellen	.00	F	Infant	28Ma05Kr
LYNCH, Patt	24	M	Unknown	28Ma05Kr
Patk.	50	M	Unknown	28Ma05Kr
MCCOWAN, Pat	15	M	Unknown	28Ma05Kr
WEAL, U-Mrs.	28	F	Unknown	28Ma05Kr
Lewis	7	M	Child	28Ma05Kr
Mary	5	F	Child	28Ma05Kr
Isaac	.00	M	Infant	28Ma05Kr
MAHON, Thomas	55	M	Unknown	28Ma05Kr
Eliza	32	F	Unknown	28Ma05Kr
GAFFNEY, Mary	13	F	Unknown	28Ma05Kr
MAHON, Anne	13	F	Unknown	28Ma05Kr
POLLOCK, Ann	20	F	Unknown	28Ma05Kr
SMITH, Patrick	40	M	Unknown	28Ma05Kr
Judy	4	F	Child	28Ma05Kr
James	40	M	Unknown	28Ma05Kr
HAYES, James	45	M	Unknown	28Ma05Kr
LEDWIDGE, Dennis	40	M	Unknown	28Ma05Kr
BYRNE, Michl.	19	M	Unknown	28Ma05Kr
LYNCH, Patrick	20	M	Unknown	28Ma05Kr
FOX, Charles	40	M	Unknown	28Ma05Kr
DALY, John	25	M	Unknown	28Ma05Kr
Phillip	30	M	Unknown	28Ma05Kr

NAMES OF PASSENGERS	AGE	SEX	OCCUPATIONS	DATE PORT SHIP
LYONS, Pat	26	M	Unknown	28Ma05Kr
MCGRATH, John	28	M	Unknown	28Ma05Kr
BEANY, Frank	23	M	Unknown	28Ma05Kr
SHEAL, Massen	23	M	Unknown	28Ma05Kr
Mary	25	F	Unknown	28Ma05Kr
MCLOUGHLIN, Susan	26	F	Unknown	28Ma05Kr
CONROY, Mat	18	M	Unknown	28Ma05Kr
Bridget	24	F	Unknown	28Ma05Kr
FITZPATRICK, Ann	26	F	Unknown	28Ma05Kr
DOULL, R.	24	M	Unknown	28Ma05Kr
BAYLEY, U	20	F	Unknown	28Ma05Kr
KELLY, John	20	M	Unknown	28Ma05Kr
FAY, John	15	M	Unknown	28Ma05Kr
John	13	M	Unknown	28Ma05Kr
John	12	M	Unknown	28Ma05Kr
Bridget	00	F	Unknown	28Ma05Kr
Anne	00	F	Unknown	28Ma05Kr
CALLY, Eliza	00	F	Unknown	28Ma05Kr
MAWE, U	00	M	Unknown	28Ma05Kr
U-Mrs.	00	F	Unknown	28Ma05Kr
Charles	00	M	Unknown	28Ma05Kr
Louisa	00	F	Unknown	28Ma05Kr
RESPIN, John	00	M	Unknown	28Ma05Kr
PRICE, Julia	00	F	Unknown	28Ma05Kr

RIVERDALE 28 MAY 1850

From Liverpool

NAMES OF PASSENGERS	AGE	SEX	OCCUPATIONS	DATE PORT SHIP
EGAN, Patrick	40	M	Farmer	28Ma02Hu
Honora	38	F	Farmer	28Ma02Hu
Thomas	20	M	Farmer	28Ma02Hu
MURPHY, Thomas	30	M	Laborer	28Ma02Hu
Alice	28	F	Servant	28Ma02Hu
Eliza	18	F	Servant	28Ma02Hu
CONLEY, Rachel	28	F	Servant	28Ma02Hu
Ellen	9	F	Child	28Ma02Hu
Elizabeth	7	F	Child	28Ma02Hu
Mary	5	F	Child	28Ma02Hu
Rose-Anne	3	F	Child	28Ma02Hu
Catherine	.11	F	Infant	28Ma02Hu
MANGIN, Patrick	22	M	Farmer	28Ma02Hu
KELLY, Bridget	21	F	Spinster	28Ma02Hu
COLEMAN, Catherine	28	F	Spinster	28Ma02Hu
OBYLE, Mary	18	F	Spinster	28Ma02Hu
HAMILTON, James	25	M	Laborer	28Ma02Hu
COLEORAN, Ellen	27	F	Spinster	28Ma02Hu
WARD, Mary	22	F	Spinster	28Ma02Hu
KENNEY, Patrick	18	M	Laborer	28Ma02Hu
MURPHY, Anne	18	F	Spinster	28Ma02Hu
ALBERTON, John	18	M	Servant	28Ma02Hu
MCARTHUR, Catherine	26	F	Servant	28Ma02Hu
KENNEY, Ann	18	F	Servant	28Ma02Hu
MCONVOY, Margaret	18	F	Servant	28Ma02Hu
FITZSIMONS, Margaret	16	F	Servant	28Ma02Hu
FENANTY, Michael	40	M	Farmer	28Ma02Hu
Bridget	46	F	Farmer	28Ma02Hu
Michael	8	M	Child	28Ma02Hu
Mary	5	F	Child	28Ma02Hu
Catherine	2	F	Child	28Ma02Hu
MCGIVEREN, Catherine	21	F	Servant	28Ma02Hu
BURNS, Samuel	28	M	Blacksmith	28Ma02Hu
EVANS, David	30	M	Farmer	28Ma02Hu
Mary	31	F	Farmer	28Ma02Hu
Catherine	7	F	Child	28Ma02Hu
Mary	4	F	Child	28Ma02Hu
Margaret	2	F	Child	28Ma02Hu
Hugh	.07	M	Infant	28Ma02Hu
JONES, William	40	M	Farmer	28Ma02Hu
JONES, Mary	36	F	Farmer	28Ma02Hu
Catherine	12	F	Farmer	28Ma02Hu
Robert	10	M	Farmer	28Ma02Hu
Margaret	8	F	Child	28Ma02Hu
John	6	M	Child	28Ma02Hu
Mary	4	F	Child	28Ma02Hu
Patrick	3	M	Child	28Ma02Hu
OATS, Thomas	28	M	Joiner	28Ma02Hu
FINLAY, John	17	M	Joiner	28Ma02Hu
MCNALLY, James	46	M	Cartwright	28Ma02Hu
Catherine	30	F	Laborer	28Ma02Hu
OBRIEN, Michael	20	M	Carpenter	28Ma02Hu
MCCARTHY, James	22	M	Carpenter	28Ma02Hu
BEGLEY, Mary	20	F	Servant	28Ma02Hu
FARRELL, Honora	18	F	Servant	28Ma02Hu
KANE, Donly	26	M	Mason	28Ma02Hu
SANDY, Thomas	26	M	Mason	28Ma02Hu
Christian	27	F	Servant	28Ma02Hu
John	6	M	Child	28Ma02Hu
Emily	4	F	Child	28Ma02Hu
Thomas	.11	M	Infant	28Ma02Hu
BURNS, John	30	M	Laborer	28Ma02Hu
HAYES, Benjamin	26	M	Laborer	28Ma02Hu
STERLING, Alexander	28	M	Laborer	28Ma02Hu
Martha	40	F	Wi	28Ma02Hu
WALSH, Thomas	19	M	Shoemaker	28Ma02Hu
MORGAN, Julia	20	F	Servant	28Ma02Hu
WALSH, Julia	19	F	Servant	28Ma02Hu
KENNEDDY, John	20	M	Shoemaker	28Ma02Hu
FIELDS, Joseph	22	M	Tailor	28Ma02Hu
ANDERSON, James	19	M	Tailor	28Ma02Hu
INGRIM, James	18	M	Tailor	28Ma02Hu
JOHNSTON, William	24	M	Shoemaker	28Ma02Hu
Margaret	20	F	Seamstress	28Ma02Hu
ADAMS, James	18	M	Gdnr	28Ma02Hu
Catherine	26	F	Servant	28Ma02Hu
Mary	20	F	Servant	28Ma02Hu
FARRELL, Anne	18	F	Servant	28Ma02Hu
MCNAMARA, Mary	16	F	Servant	28Ma02Hu
FITZGERALD, Michael	22	M	Sawer	28Ma02Hu
CONWAY, James	18	M	Sawer	28Ma02Hu
KENEDY, Winifred	24	M	Shoemaker	28Ma02Hu
GLEESON, Anne	20	F	Stay Maker	28Ma02Hu
LANIGAN, Marian	45	F	Stay Maker	28Ma02Hu
HORTELE, Nancy	9	F	Child	28Ma02Hu
Bridget	7	F	Child	28Ma02Hu
THESEDIAM, Thomas	30	M	Joiner	28Ma02Hu
CHRISTIAN, Robert	40	M	Blacksmith	28Ma02Hu
Margaret	35	F	Wife	28Ma02Hu
Jane	20	F	Bomkr	28Ma02Hu
Peter	18	M	Joiner	28Ma02Hu
Margaret	20	F	Bomkr	28Ma02Hu
THESEDEAN, Eliza	30	F	Bomkr	28Ma02Hu
PARK, Mary	28	F	Bomkr	28Ma02Hu
Ellen	7	F	Child	28Ma02Hu
Thomas	5	M	Child	28Ma02Hu
MATHEW, John	26	M	Carpenter	28Ma02Hu
REDDINGTON, Thomas	22	M	Carpenter	28Ma02Hu
DOYLE, Robert	28	M	Carpenter	28Ma02Hu
LEWIS, Michael	20	M	Carpenter	28Ma02Hu
CRAFTON, James	16	M	Shoemaker	28Ma02Hu
WHITE, William	20	M	Shoemaker	28Ma02Hu
HANEY, Charles	17	M	Blacksmith	28Ma02Hu
FITZMAURICE, John	27	M	Blacksmith	28Ma02Hu
REYNOLDS, James	19	M	Blacksmith	28Ma02Hu
FULLEN, Barney	30	M	Teamster	28Ma02Hu
DORAN, Barney	26	M	Teamster	28Ma02Hu
KEANE, James	30	M	Shoemaker	28Ma02Hu
Catherine	38	F	Stay Maker	28Ma02Hu
Mary	20	F	Stay Maker	28Ma02Hu
Rose	15	F	Stay Maker	28Ma02Hu
Anne	13	F	Stay Maker	28Ma02Hu
Bridget	10	F	None	28Ma02Hu
Patrick	7	M	Child	28Ma02Hu
John	6	M	Child	28Ma02Hu

NAMES OF PASSENGERS	AGE	SEX	OCCUPATIONS	DATE PORT SHIP
NEWGENT, Michl.	22	M	Laborer	28Ma02Hu
DALY, Andrew	45	M	Laborer	28Ma02Hu
BURNS, Patrick	20	M	Laborer	28Ma02Hu
LYNCH, Bridget	16	F	Servant	28Ma02Hu
MCKENNA, Peter	21	M	Laborer	28Ma02Hu
Felix	14	M	Laborer	28Ma02Hu
Betty	19	F	Servant	28Ma02Hu
Annie	17	F	Servant	28Ma02Hu
MAHONEY, John	35	M	Jeweller	28Ma02Hu
CHRISTOPHER, Michael	26	M	Tailor	28Ma02Hu
Mary	20	F	Seamstress	28Ma02Hu
Peggy	18	F	Seamstress	28Ma02Hu
MORRISSON, Johanna	16	F	Seamstress	28Ma02Hu
CONWAY, John	38	M	Clerk	28Ma02Hu
MULLOWNEY, John	27	M	Mason	28Ma02Hu
FLINK, John	24	M	Servant	28Ma02Hu
MCHIVEE, Edward	22	M	Servant	28Ma02Hu
Neil	18	M	Servant	28Ma02Hu
MCGRAW, Thomas	20	M	Servant	28Ma02Hu
MORRISSON, Johanna	38	F	Servant	28Ma02Hu
James	13	M	Servant	28Ma02Hu
Annie	10	F	None	28Ma02Hu
Catherine	8	F	Child	28Ma02Hu
FOBIN, Michael	30	M	Farmer	28Ma02Hu
PORT, George	30	M	Farmer	28Ma02Hu
TAYLOR, Edward	23	M	Farmer	28Ma02Hu
MCAVOY, Owen	20	M	Farmer	28Ma02Hu
BRENOW, Peter	24	M	Schm	28Ma02Hu
Margaret	20	F	Stay Maker	28Ma02Hu
WESTWORTH, Harriet	22	F	Stay Maker	28Ma02Hu
HOWENTH, Alice	20	F	Stay Maker	28Ma02Hu
DOWNEY, John	22	M	Laborer	28Ma02Hu
DEADY, Patrick	28	M	Laborer	28Ma02Hu
DOHENEY, Edward	28	M	Laborer	28Ma02Hu
MCATRICK, Patrick	20	M	Laborer	28Ma02Hu
Rose	21	F	Servant	28Ma02Hu
MUNEY, Mary	17	F	Servant	28Ma02Hu
Annie	17	F	Servant	28Ma02Hu
KELLY, Catherine	16	F	Servant	28Ma02Hu
Annie	16	F	Servant	28Ma02Hu
BIRCH, Annie	17	F	Servant	28Ma02Hu
CLERK, Hannah	22	F	Servant	28Ma02Hu
CLARY, James	25	M	Shoemaker	28Ma02Hu
DUNFEY, Owen	20	M	Carpenter	28Ma02Hu
CLARY, Tim	18	M	Servant	28Ma02Hu
KELLY, Edward	23	M	Servant	28Ma02Hu
QUINLAN, Mary	31	F	Servant	28Ma02Hu
Bridget	22	F	Servant	28Ma02Hu
KALLY, Betsy	15	F	Servant	28Ma02Hu
Mary	10	F	None	28Ma02Hu
Hannah	8	F	Child	28Ma02Hu
James	6	M	Child	28Ma02Hu
GREY, Peter	18	M	Tailor	28Ma02Hu
Hugh	16	M	Tailor	28Ma02Hu
BOYLE, Michael	24	M	Tailor	28Ma02Hu
JOHNSTON, Dennis	23	M	Tailor	28Ma02Hu
HANIGAN, Michael	24	M	Tailor	28Ma02Hu
Thomas	18	M	Tailor	28Ma02Hu
Rose	16	F	Seamstress	28Ma02Hu
LINEHAN, James	29	M	Tailor	28Ma02Hu
MARTIN, Biddy	12	F	Seamstress	28Ma02Hu
WATERS, Bridget	21	F	Cook	28Ma02Hu
MARTIN, Bridget	20	F	Cook	28Ma02Hu
MCLAUREN, James	30	M	Unknown	28Ma02Hu
RYAN, James	24	M	Grinder	28Ma02Hu
BROWNE, William	24	M	Unknown	28Ma02Hu
BALLY, James	21	M	Unknown	28Ma02Hu
GEORGE, John	26	M	Unknown	28Ma02Hu
CONNELY, James	18	M	Laborer	28Ma02Hu
DAILY, Luke	28	M	Unknown	28Ma02Hu
HANLY, Jane	48	F	Spinster	28Ma02Hu
Bernard	12	M	Servant	28Ma02Hu
Luke	10	M	Servant	28Ma02Hu
Annie	8	F	Child	28Ma02Hu
Mary	6	F	Child	28Ma02Hu

NAMES OF PASSENGERS	AGE	SEX	OCCUPATIONS	DATE PORT SHIP
HANLY, Patrick	3	M	Child	28Ma02Hu
John	2	M	Child	28Ma02Hu
FARRELL, John	24	M	Farmer	28Ma02Hu
JONES, Bridget	23	F	Farmer	28Ma02Hu
MILES, John	21	M	Farmer	28Ma02Hu
CARROLL, Margaret	18	F	Stay Maker	28Ma02Hu
BURNS, Elizabeth	16	F	Stay Maker	28Ma02Hu
RIELY, Mary	18	F	Stay Maker	28Ma02Hu
William	18	M	Servant	28Ma02Hu
Jane	16	F	Servant	28Ma02Hu
Catherine	12	F	Servant	28Ma02Hu
KING, John	20	M	Mason	28Ma02Hu
CANAGHAN, John	18	M	Mason	28Ma02Hu
HUDSON, Thomas	20	M	Ploughman	28Ma02Hu
WATT, John	21	M	Ploughman	28Ma02Hu
RIELY, Patrick	40	M	Ploughman	28Ma02Hu
Margaret	36	F	Dairymaid	28Ma02Hu
Patrick	3	M	Child	28Ma02Hu
Mary	1	F	Child	28Ma02Hu
William	38	M	Shoemaker	28Ma02Hu
Jheophilus	16	M	Shoemaker	28Ma02Hu
Margaret	26	F	Stay Maker	28Ma02Hu
John	15	M	None	28Ma02Hu
William	13	M	None	28Ma02Hu
Sophia	11	F	None	28Ma02Hu
DORSY, Annie	23	F	Servant	28Ma02Hu
ARMSTRONG, John	22	M	Servant	28Ma02Hu
Christine	20	F	Servant	28Ma02Hu
CASSIDY, Michael	35	M	Servant	28Ma02Hu
Annie	20	F	Servant	28Ma02Hu
THOMPSON, Edward	18	M	Servant	28Ma02Hu
BRUNT, James	30	M	Farmer	28Ma02Hu
MISGROVE, John	20	M	Cutler	28Ma02Hu
REVE, William	18	M	Cutler	28Ma02Hu
BRUNT, Mary	16	F	Spinster	28Ma02Hu
BROWNE, Elizabeth	16	F	Spinster	28Ma02Hu
Issabel	16	F	Spinster	28Ma02Hu
CASEY, Patrick	35	M	Farmer	28Ma02Hu
MORAN, Patrick	38	M	Farmer	28Ma02Hu
MALONE, Thomas	30	M	Farmer	28Ma02Hu
Margaret	18	F	Spinster	28Ma02Hu
DUFFEY, Michael	25	M	Farmer	28Ma02Hu
SHANON, Owen	40	M	Farmer	28Ma02Hu
CALLAGHAN, James	42	M	Tailor	28Ma02Hu
CARTER, William	23	M	Servant	28Ma02Hu
MCGOUGH, Catherine	18	F	Servant	28Ma02Hu
CARTER, Caroline	23	F	Servant	28Ma02Hu
DUFFEY, Bridget	16	F	Servant	28Ma02Hu
IRWIN, Michl.	27	M	Servant	28Ma02Hu
Winefred	24	F	Servant	28Ma02Hu
Mary	22	F	Servant	28Ma02Hu
William	10	M	Servant	28Ma02Hu
HITNELL, John	21	M	Farmer	28Ma02Hu
SOLE, George	21	M	Shopman	28Ma02Hu
SMITH, Charles	22	M	Shipwright	28Ma02Hu
HANARTY, John	18	M	Shopman	28Ma02Hu
Robert	28	M	Carpenter	28Ma02Hu
BROWNE, William	34	M	Carpenter	28Ma02Hu
Margaret	30	F	Wife	28Ma02Hu
MOORE, Peter	28	M	Farmer	28Ma02Hu
John	24	M	Farmer	28Ma02Hu
BULLEN, James	23	M	Clerk	28Ma02Hu
TATE, James	20	M	Clerk	28Ma02Hu
HAYES, Mathew	20	M	Clerk	28Ma02Hu
Jane	18	F	Stay Maker	28Ma02Hu
KNOBLE, John	20	M	Farmer	28Ma02Hu
ARCKEENY, Annie	20	F	Seamstress	28Ma02Hu
Elizabeth	20	F	Seamstress	28Ma02Hu
WOOD, Charles	28	M	Clerk	28Ma02Hu
ABRAHAM, Israel	20	M	Pawn Broker	28Ma02Hu
BAYLISS, Eliza	30	F	Dressmaker	28Ma02Hu
Mary-Anne	4	F	Dressmaker	28Ma02Hu
Eliza	.11	F	Infant	28Ma02Hu
CHANLER, Caroline	20	F	Dressmaker	28Ma02Hu
CARROLE, Sarah	21	F	Dressmaker	28Ma02Hu

NAMES OF PASSENGERS	AGE	SEX	OCCUPATIONS	DATE PORT SHIP
TUCKER, Mary-Anne	11	F	None	28Ma02Hu
U, Kitty	24	M	Tailor	28Ma02Hu
SHEER, Carl	23	M	Tailor	28Ma02Hu
VEDUMSKEY, Carl	27	M	Tailor	28Ma02Hu
ANFERT, John	22	M	Tailor	28Ma02Hu
SPERO, Marcus	25	M	Tailor	28Ma02Hu
WIEBUR, U-Madam	23	F	Governess	28Ma02Hu
DALY, Mary	27	F	Servant	28Ma02Hu
DENNING, John	30	M	Servant	28Ma02Hu
BURNS, Mary	29	F	Servant	28Ma02Hu
KNOWNER, John	30	M	Unknown	28Ma02Hu
MCLOUGHLIN, Francis	19	M	Unknown	28Ma02Hu
HANARTY, James	24	M	Shopman	28Ma02Hu
CHRISTIAN, Mary	18	F	Bomkr	28Ma02Hu

WARRIOR 28 MAY 1850

From Belfast

NAMES OF PASSENGERS	AGE	SEX	OCCUPATIONS	DATE PORT SHIP
MAJURY, William	20	M	Unknown	28Ma17Bj
HERON, William	20	M	Unknown	28Ma17Bj
Jane	30	F	Unknown	28Ma17Bj
John	6	M	Child	28Ma17Bj
Robert	3	M	Child	28Ma17Bj
Thomas	.00	M	Infant	28Ma17Bj
SHIRLEY, James	21	M	Unknown	28Ma17Bj
STEWART, Eliza	22	F	Unknown	28Ma17Bj
CRAWFORD, John	30	M	Unknown	28Ma17Bj
MCROBERTS, Hugh	20	M	Unknown	28Ma17Bj
MARTIN, Samuel	20	M	Unknown	28Ma17Bj
SKILLAN, John	20	M	Unknown	28Ma17Bj
FLEMMING, William	24	M	Unknown	28Ma17Bj
Sarah	23	F	Unknown	28Ma17Bj
John	2	M	Child	28Ma17Bj
ALEXANDER, Martha	20	F	Unknown	28Ma17Bj
MAXWELL, William	50	M	Unknown	28Ma17Bj
James	17	M	Unknown	28Ma17Bj
Robert	15	M	Unknown	28Ma17Bj
Esther	13	F	Unknown	28Ma17Bj
Sarah	11	F	Unknown	28Ma17Bj
Joseph	.00	M	Infant	28Ma17Bj
LOVE, Joseph	43	M	Unknown	28Ma17Bj
Jane	43	F	Unknown	28Ma17Bj
Ann	17	F	Unknown	28Ma17Bj
George	15	M	Unknown	28Ma17Bj
Elizabeth	13	F	Unknown	28Ma17Bj
Margaret	11	F	Unknown	28Ma17Bj
Ephraim	8	M	Child	28Ma17Bj
James	6	M	Child	28Ma17Bj
Joseph	.00	M	Infant	28Ma17Bj
ANDREWS, Eliza-J.	30	F	Unknown	28Ma17Bj
Thos.	.00	M	Infant	28Ma17Bj
LICKEY, Mary	47	F	Unknown	28Ma17Bj
HAMILL, Jane	44	F	Unknown	28Ma17Bj
CARLIN, Jane	17	F	Unknown	28Ma17Bj
MOORE, William	20	M	Unknown	28Ma17Bj
Thomas	21	M	Unknown	28Ma17Bj
MCLIMANT, Hance	30	M	Unknown	28Ma17Bj
Agnes	40	M	Unknown	28Ma17Bj
HAMILTON, Andrew	36	M	Unknown	28Ma17Bj
WILSON, John	21	M	Unknown	28Ma17Bj
ARDE, John	15	M	Unknown	28Ma17Bj
Christian	20	M	Unknown	28Ma17Bj
BRUCE, Margt.	48	F	Unknown	28Ma17Bj
Mary-Ann	40	F	Unknown	28Ma17Bj
CRAWFORD, Alexander	18	M	Unknown	28Ma17Bj
Gardner	16	M	Unknown	28Ma17Bj
James	.00	M	Infant	28Ma17Bj
MCGARRILL, Hugh	27	M	Unknown	28Ma17Bj
MCGARRILL, Robert	22	M	Unknown	28Ma17Bj
WATSON, Cath.	20	F	Unknown	28Ma17Bj
JOHNSTON, James	25	M	Unknown	28Ma17Bj
NICHOLL, Mary-Ann	25	F	Unknown	28Ma17Bj
Died-At-Sea				
MCNEILL, John	27	M	Unknown	28Ma17Bj
MCKEE, Rosanna	28	F	Unknown	28Ma17Bj
MCROBERTS, James	21	M	Unknown	28Ma17Bj
REID, Patrick	20	M	Unknown	28Ma17Bj
COLHOON, David	20	M	Unknown	28Ma17Bj
MCKEE, Margt.	16	F	Unknown	28Ma17Bj
MURPHY, James	30	M	Unknown	28Ma17Bj
Agnes	22	F	Unknown	28Ma17Bj
MCDONALD, Eleanor	24	F	Unknown	28Ma17Bj
Margaret	16	F	Unknown	28Ma17Bj
GODFREY, John	45	M	Unknown	28Ma17Bj
William	29	M	Unknown	28Ma17Bj
Robert	22	M	Unknown	28Ma17Bj
Margaret	19	F	Unknown	28Ma17Bj
BALLENTINE, James	35	M	Unknown	28Ma17Bj
MCAFEEL, James	25	M	Unknown	28Ma17Bj
PRINGLE, Anne	49	F	Unknown	28Ma17Bj
Died-At-Sea				
MULLHOLLAND, Anthony	49	M	Unknown	28Ma17Bj
MCCANGHERAN, Alex	17	M	Unknown	28Ma17Bj
MCCALLOW, John	27	M	Unknown	28Ma17Bj
WARD, Thomas	24	M	Unknown	28Ma17Bj
DOUGLAS, Mary	23	F	Unknown	28Ma17Bj
Thos.Jas.	13	M	Unknown	28Ma17Bj
Archibald	12	M	Unknown	28Ma17Bj
James	.00	M	Infant	28Ma17Bj
JOHNSTON, William	23	M	Unknown	28Ma17Bj
Jane	22	F	Unknown	28Ma17Bj
James	.00	M	Infant	28Ma17Bj
MANNING, John	28	M	Unknown	28Ma17Bj
Mary	25	F	Unknown	28Ma17Bj
MCMULLEN, Jane	20	F	Unknown	28Ma17Bj
Mary	28	F	Unknown	28Ma17Bj
Ellen	.00	F	Infant	28Ma17Bj
MICHELL, William	40	M	Unknown	28Ma17Bj
Mary	35	F	Unknown	28Ma17Bj
Maria	16	F	Unknown	28Ma17Bj
John	13	M	Unknown	28Ma17Bj
Ephrian	11	M	Unknown	28Ma17Bj
William	8	M	Child	28Ma17Bj
James	7	M	Child	28Ma17Bj
Mary-Jane	.00	F	Infant	28Ma17Bj
Died-At-Sea				
SATEL, Mary	20	F	Unknown	28Ma17Bj
MCSLAVY, Ros.	20	F	Unknown	28Ma17Bj
CUSSAY, Cathn.	18	F	Unknown	28Ma17Bj

ACADIA 28 MAY 1850

From Liverpool

NAMES OF PASSENGERS	AGE	SEX	OCCUPATIONS	DATE PORT SHIP
FIELDHOUSE, William	28	M	Unknown	28Ma02Kn
KENNEDY, Rose	.00	F	Infant	28Ma02Kn
BRIEN, James	30	M	Unknown	28Ma02Kn
FRADNOD, Owen	23	M	Unknown	28Ma02Kn
MEADLER, Betty	25	F	Unknown	28Ma02Kn
MCDONALD, Ann	20	F	Unknown	28Ma02Kn
CAMPBELL, Bridget	20	F	Unknown	28Ma02Kn
FOLEY, Jno.	26	M	Unknown	28Ma02Kn
Patt	22	M	Unknown	28Ma02Kn
CAVAUNAH, Jno.	19	M	Unknown	28Ma02Kn
Rose	20	F	Unknown	28Ma02Kn
PARKER, Jas.	28	M	Unknown	28Ma02Kn
COUGHAM, Ann	19	F	Unknown	28Ma02Kn

NAMES OF PASSENGERS	AGE	SEX	OCCUPATIONS	DATE PORT SHIP
COUGHAM, Margt.	17	F	Unknown	28Ma02Kn
CULLEN, Pat	24	M	Unknown	28Ma02Kn
CORLETT, Wm.	20	M	Unknown	28Ma02Kn

NANCY 28 MAY 1850

From Galway

NAMES OF PASSENGERS	AGE	SEX	OCCUPATIONS	DATE PORT SHIP
MCGUANN, Barbara	25	F	Laborer	28Ma42Kq
KING, Peter	30	M	Unknown	28Ma42Kq
Honor	25	F	Unknown	28Ma42Kq
Martin	.00	M	Infant	28Ma42Kq
RUAN, Thady.	30	M	Unknown	28Ma42Kq
Margt.	22	F	Unknown	28Ma42Kq
FAHY, Pat	26	M	Unknown	28Ma42Kq
MANNING, John	30	M	Unknown	28Ma42Kq
QUALEY, Thomas	20	M	Unknown	28Ma42Kq
CONNOR, Eliza	38	F	Unknown	28Ma42Kq
BRENTON, John	12	M	Unknown	28Ma42Kq
Mary	9	F	Child	28Ma42Kq
MONAGHAN, Cath.	15	F	Unknown	28Ma42Kq
HYNES, Michl.	35	M	Unknown	28Ma42Kq
Bridget	6	F	Child	28Ma42Kq
WALSH, Bridget	30	F	Unknown	28Ma42Kq
Eliza	13	F	Unknown	28Ma42Kq
MARTIN, Bridget	18	F	Unknown	28Ma42Kq
RYAN, Bridget	6	F	Child	28Ma42Kq
DEVELY, Thomas	12	M	Unknown	28Ma42Kq
WALSH, Martin	30	M	Unknown	28Ma42Kq
James	20	M	Unknown	28Ma42Kq
BROWNSHAW, Mary	32	F	Unknown	28Ma42Kq
COLLINS, Pat	7	M	Child	28Ma42Kq
Thomas	.00	M	Infant	28Ma42Kq
BRENNAN, Bridget	23	F	Unknown	28Ma42Kq
BURKE, Bridget	30	F	Unknown	28Ma42Kq
OBRIAN, Margt.	35	F	Unknown	28Ma42Kq
CUNNINGHAM, Anty	18	F	Unknown	28Ma42Kq
KELLY, Pat	26	M	Unknown	28Ma42Kq
KILKELLY, Francis	36	M	Unknown	28Ma42Kq
Cath.	28	F	Unknown	28Ma42Kq
Bridget	.00	F	Infant	28Ma42Kq
HAYES, Martin	22	M	Unknown	28Ma42Kq
Margt.	20	F	Unknown	28Ma42Kq
MILLER, Bridget	16	F	Unknown	28Ma42Kq
HUGHES, Mary	30	F	Unknown	28Ma42Kq
WARD, Bridget	18	F	Unknown	28Ma42Kq
ROACHE, Margt.	19	F	Unknown	28Ma42Kq
FAHY, Honor	22	F	Unknown	28Ma42Kq
MULLEN, Roger	29	M	Unknown	28Ma42Kq
Winny	18	F	Unknown	28Ma42Kq
Ellen	16	F	Unknown	28Ma42Kq
MANNION, Honor	17	F	Unknown	28Ma42Kq
Mary	18	F	Unknown	28Ma42Kq
Cath.	.00	F	Infant	28Ma42Kq
WALSH, Martin	25	M	Unknown	28Ma42Kq
OFLAHERTY, Pat	29	M	Unknown	28Ma42Kq
BURKE, Honor	22	F	Unknown	28Ma42Kq
ROLAN, Thomas	22	M	Unknown	28Ma42Kq
Bridget	17	F	Unknown	28Ma42Kq
LYNSKEY, Michl.	30	M	Unknown	28Ma42Kq
Mary	19	F	Unknown	28Ma42Kq
GLYNN, John	25	M	Unknown	28Ma42Kq
CONNELL, James	22	M	Unknown	28Ma42Kq
REGAN, Thomas	20	M	Unknown	28Ma42Kq
Mary	18	F	Unknown	28Ma42Kq
CONWAY, Mary	20	M	Unknown	28Ma42Kq
FOX, Patrick	28	M	Unknown	28Ma42Kq
KILLROY, Judy	13	F	Unknown	28Ma42Kq
CONWAY, John	20	M	Unknown	28Ma42Kq
CONWAY, Thomas	18	M	Unknown	28Ma42Kq
KELLY, Thomas	20	M	Unknown	28Ma42Kq
SILK, Mary	40	F	Unknown	28Ma42Kq
Honor	13	F	Unknown	28Ma42Kq
CONNELLY, Martin	28	M	Unknown	28Ma42Kq
Mary	20	F	Unknown	28Ma42Kq
Margt.	18	F	Unknown	28Ma42Kq
SHAUGHNESSY, Mary	50	F	Unknown	28Ma42Kq
LAFFY, Pat	32	M	Unknown	28Ma42Kq
Kitty	26	F	Unknown	28Ma42Kq
RILEY, Kitty	40	F	Unknown	28Ma42Kq
Kitty	15	F	Unknown	28Ma42Kq
Margt.	17	F	Unknown	28Ma42Kq
MELDON, John	18	M	Unknown	28Ma42Kq
MURPHY, Biddy	20	F	Unknown	28Ma42Kq
MCDONOUGH, Honor	16	F	Unknown	28Ma42Kq
GAVIN, Richard	25	M	Unknown	28Ma42Kq
LEONARD, Cath.	21	F	Unknown	28Ma42Kq
SULLIVAN, Francis	22	M	Unknown	28Ma42Kq
MCGUANN, Mary	22	F	Unknown	28Ma42Kq
SWEENY, James	18	M	Unknown	28Ma42Kq
MULLEN, Martin	19	M	Unknown	28Ma42Kq
HART, Honor	19	F	Unknown	28Ma42Kq
Kate	17	F	Unknown	28Ma42Kq
COSTELLO, Mary	20	F	Unknown	28Ma42Kq
RUAN, Cath.	.00	F	Infant	28Ma42Kq
FLAHERTY, Mary	24	F	Unknown	28Ma42Kq
FARRELL, James	25	M	Unknown	28Ma42Kq
Mary	29	F	Unknown	28Ma42Kq
DOOLY, Pat	20	M	Unknown	28Ma42Kq

FRANCONIA 29 MAY 1850

From Glasgow

NAMES OF PASSENGERS	AGE	SEX	OCCUPATIONS	DATE PORT SHIP
MORGAN, Helen	46	F	None	29Ma21Id
Maria	15	F	None	29Ma21Id
Helen	13	F	None	29Ma21Id
William	9	M	Child	29Ma21Id
REILLY, Mary-Ann	26	F	None	29Ma21Id
Mary	63	F	None	29Ma21Id
RYAN, Mary	39	F	None	29Ma21Id
Ann	13	F	None	29Ma21Id
Julia	11	F	None	29Ma21Id
DOOLAN, Dennis	28	M	Smith	29Ma21Id
Ann	28	F	Smith	29Ma21Id
Mary-J.	2	F	Child	29Ma21Id
Cathn.	1	F	Child	29Ma21Id
RICHIE, Robt.	27	M	Farmer	29Ma21Id
MCGHEE, Jane	26	F	Servant	29Ma21Id
DICKINSON, Wm.	30	M	None	29Ma21Id
DENHOLEN, Thos.	26	M	Laborer	29Ma21Id
MCLOOSKIR, Jas.	21	M	Laborer	29Ma21Id
BROOKE, Owen	23	M	Laborer	29Ma21Id
KEELAN, Peter	20	M	Laborer	29Ma21Id
PETRIE, Wm.	21	M	Auctioneer	29Ma21Id
LOVE, Saml.	30	M	None	29Ma21Id
James	28	M	None	29Ma21Id
GARVIN, James	23	M	Laborer	29Ma21Id
SLOAN, Thos.	30	M	Laborer	29Ma21Id
James	8	M	Child	29Ma21Id
DOHERTY, James	20	M	Laborer	29Ma21Id

MARTHA-KINSMAN 29 MAY 1850

From St.JOHNS, P.R.

NAMES OF PASSENGERS	AGE	SEX	OCCUPATIONS	DATE PORT SHIP
MCMULLIN, George	26	M	Coachman	29Ma43Ku
Jane	28	F	Unknown	29Ma43Ku
Jane	5	F	Child	29Ma43Ku
Catherine	3	F	Child	29Ma43Ku
Julia	.08	F	Infant	29Ma43Ku
DONNELY, Agness	18	F	Seamstress	29Ma43Ku

CANADA 30 MAY 1850

From Liverpool

NAMES OF PASSENGERS	AGE	SEX	OCCUPATIONS	DATE PORT SHIP
MCREILLY, Alice	22	F	Spinster	30Ma02Ag
MCSHANE, Owen	18	M	Unknown	30Ma02Ag
MULLEN, Alice	18	F	Unknown	30Ma02Ag
CAMPBELL, Jane	31	F	Unknown	30Ma02Ag
Fanny	6	F	Child	30Ma02Ag
Wm.	4	M	Child	30Ma02Ag
Sarah	2	F	Child	30Ma02Ag
KENNEDY, Patrick	26	M	Unknown	30Ma02Ag
WHUTEN, Owen	40	M	Unknown	30Ma02Ag
Michl.	17	M	Unknown	30Ma02Ag
John	15	M	Unknown	30Ma02Ag
William	11	M	Unknown	30Ma02Ag
Ste.	9	M	Child	30Ma02Ag
Mary	7	F	Child	30Ma02Ag
Catherine	5	F	Child	30Ma02Ag
Dorkas	3	F	Child	30Ma02Ag
TRACEY, Eliza	17	F	Unknown	30Ma02Ag
Rose	15	F	Unknown	30Ma02Ag
Maria	11	F	Unknown	30Ma02Ag
NOWLAN, Thomas	20	M	Unknown	30Ma02Ag
Patrick	18	M	Unknown	30Ma02Ag
CALLAGHAN, Bridget	21	F	Unknown	30Ma02Ag
FOGGAT, Phillip	18	M	Unknown	30Ma02Ag
Wm.	13	M	Unknown	30Ma02Ag
John	7	M	Child	30Ma02Ag
BRADDEN, Cathn.	22	F	Unknown	30Ma02Ag
NOBLE, Thos.	5	M	Child	30Ma02Ag
WELDEN, Mary	20	F	Unknown	30Ma02Ag
Cath.	8	F	Child	30Ma02Ag
Anne	6	F	Child	30Ma02Ag
CEALEY, Thos.	30	M	Unknown	30Ma02Ag
FLEMING, Cath.	7	F	Child	30Ma02Ag
KANE, John	30	M	Unknown	30Ma02Ag
Eliza	3	F	Child	30Ma02Ag
CORCORAN, And.	18	M	Unknown	30Ma02Ag
Mary	15	F	Unknown	30Ma02Ag
Patrick	12	M	Unknown	30Ma02Ag
Mat	11	M	Unknown	30Ma02Ag
Owen	6	M	Child	30Ma02Ag
HART, Margaret	45	F	Unknown	30Ma02Ag
HARVEY, John	20	M	Unknown	30Ma02Ag
BURKE, Mat	13	M	Unknown	30Ma02Ag
John	11	M	Unknown	30Ma02Ag
MACKEY, Bridget	20	F	Unknown	30Ma02Ag
DOLEAN, Hugh	20	M	Unknown	30Ma02Ag
TERMOYLE, Sarah	50	F	Unknown	30Ma02Ag
Mary	28	F	Unknown	30Ma02Ag
Wm.	26	M	Unknown	30Ma02Ag
KEYS, John	20	M	Unknown	30Ma02Ag
MCGRATH, Michl.	20	M	Unknown	30Ma02Ag
GREEN, John	22	M	Unknown	30Ma02Ag
BARRETT, Bridget	25	F	Unknown	30Ma02Ag
DOYLE, Mary	25	F	Unknown	30Ma02Ag
Mary	18	F	Unknown	30Ma02Ag
MURPHY, Henry	20	M	Unknown	30Ma02Ag
NORLIETT, Wm.	20	M	Unknown	30Ma02Ag
ENGLISH, Edwin	20	M	Unknown	30Ma02Ag
Ellen	30	F	Unknown	30Ma02Ag
BUTLER, John	45	M	Unknown	30Ma02Ag
Johanna	45	F	Unknown	30Ma02Ag
Margt.	30	F	Unknown	30Ma02Ag
Wm.	8	M	Child	30Ma02Ag
Johanna	7	F	Child	30Ma02Ag
Jas.	5	M	Child	30Ma02Ag
Pat	3	M	Child	30Ma02Ag
SAWLER, Jane	30	F	Unknown	30Ma02Ag
Mary	.00	F	Infant	30Ma02Ag
BROPHY, Cath.	16	F	Infant	30Ma02Ag
BOWES, Chs.	22	M	Unknown	30Ma02Ag
PETTIGREW, Jno.	29	M	Unknown	30Ma02Ag
Janet	39	F	Unknown	30Ma02Ag
Jno.	.00	M	Infant	30Ma02Ag
Jno.	18	M	Unknown	30Ma02Ag
Geo.	13	M	Unknown	30Ma02Ag
Ann	12	F	Unknown	30Ma02Ag
Ellen	10	F	Unknown	30Ma02Ag
Isab.	9	F	Child	30Ma02Ag
Robt.	6	M	Child	30Ma02Ag
Margt.	4	F	Child	30Ma02Ag
Richd.	.00	M	Infant	30Ma02Ag
HEALY, John	40	M	Unknown	30Ma02Ag
ASTELL, Michl.	21	M	Unknown	30Ma02Ag
HAGERTY, Mary	18	M	Unknown	30Ma02Ag
HUFFORD, Bridget	24	F	Unknown	30Ma02Ag
Margt.	18	F	Unknown	30Ma02Ag
DUFFY, Rose	50	F	Unknown	30Ma02Ag
Pat	13	M	Unknown	30Ma02Ag
Margt.	7	F	Child	30Ma02Ag
Ann	54	F	Unknown	30Ma02Ag
Mary	18	F	Unknown	30Ma02Ag
Jas.	16	M	Unknown	30Ma02Ag
Edwd.	7	M	Child	30Ma02Ag
LABBY, Mary	30	F	Unknown	30Ma02Ag
Michl.	9	M	Child	30Ma02Ag
John	6	M	Child	30Ma02Ag
DOYLE, Mark	18	M	Unknown	30Ma02Ag
Cath.	18	F	Unknown	30Ma02Ag
HAMON, Bryan	34	M	Unknown	30Ma02Ag
KEOGH, Peter	30	M	Unknown	30Ma02Ag
FEGAN, Law.	48	M	Unknown	30Ma02Ag
DALY, Chs.	18	M	Unknown	30Ma02Ag
ONEILL, Jas.	30	M	Unknown	30Ma02Ag
MOSS, Grace	16	F	Unknown	30Ma02Ag
MCDONNELL, Mary	13	F	Unknown	30Ma02Ag
MCCOOSAN, Robt.	30	M	Unknown	30Ma02Ag
WOOD, Chris	50	M	Unknown	30Ma02Ag
OCONNELL, Mary	25	F	Unknown	30Ma02Ag
Ellen	23	F	Unknown	30Ma02Ag
Eliza	16	F	Unknown	30Ma02Ag
Margt.	13	F	Unknown	30Ma02Ag
GRAHAM, Ellen	11	F	Unknown	30Ma02Ag
MAGREN, Bridget	20	F	Unknown	30Ma02Ag
Margt.	16	F	Unknown	30Ma02Ag
MAGUIRE, Patrick	20	M	Unknown	30Ma02Ag
Francis	18	M	Unknown	30Ma02Ag
HINES, Bartle	35	M	Unknown	30Ma02Ag
Bridget	10	F	Unknown	30Ma02Ag
Mary	8	F	Child	30Ma02Ag
BRENNAN, John	20	M	Unknown	30Ma02Ag
FLOOD, John	30	M	Unknown	30Ma02Ag
Peter	26	M	Unknown	30Ma02Ag
MURPHY, Pat	23	M	Unknown	30Ma02Ag
REILLY, Mary	20	F	Unknown	30Ma02Ag

NAMES OF PASSENGERS	AGE	SEX	OCCUPATIONS	DATE PORT SHIP
REILLY, Thos.	35	M	Unknown	30Ma02Ag
FITZPATRICK, Mary	28	F	Unknown	30Ma02Ag
MCMANGLE, Saml.	17	M	Unknown	30Ma02Ag
Jno.	15	M	Unknown	30Ma02Ag
TEASDALE, Bessey	18	F	Unknown	30Ma02Ag
MALONE, Jno.	19	M	Unknown	30Ma02Ag
Wm.	17	M	Unknown	30Ma02Ag
MCCORMICK, Thos.	18	M	Unknown	30Ma02Ag
LADLEY, Ellen	35	F	Unknown	30Ma02Ag
Geo.	12	M	Unknown	30Ma02Ag
Ellen	3	F	Child	30Ma02Ag
DOYLE, Catherine	25	F	Unknown	30Ma02Ag
MCCOY, Matt.	35	M	Unknown	30Ma02Ag
Mary	25	F	Unknown	30Ma02Ag
Jas.	11	M	Unknown	30Ma02Ag
Mary	.00	F	Infant	30Ma02Ag
DOLAN, Cathn.	50	F	Unknown	30Ma02Ag
CONALE, Mary	35	F	Unknown	30Ma02Ag
Phillip	.00	M	Infant	30Ma02Ag
HANNON, Bessy	25	F	Unknown	30Ma02Ag
KERNBLE, John	16	M	Unknown	30Ma02Ag
MOORE, James	50	M	Unknown	30Ma02Ag
NEILLE, Pat	20	M	Unknown	30Ma02Ag
CAREY, Martin	30	M	Unknown	30Ma02Ag
MCAVERY, Jno.	35	M	Unknown	30Ma02Ag
KING, Pat	30	M	Unknown	30Ma02Ag
Judy	30	F	Unknown	30Ma02Ag
Tom	3	M	Child	30Ma02Ag
Terence	.00	M	Infant	30Ma02Ag
MICK, Margt.	50	F	Unknown	30Ma02Ag
CAMPBELL, Ann	40	F	Unknown	30Ma02Ag
WADDELL, Thos.	25	M	Unknown	30Ma02Ag
Janet	25	F	Unknown	30Ma02Ag
LAWLER, Mich	30	M	Unknown	30Ma02Ag
Jno.	2	M	Child	30Ma02Ag
DELANY, Wm.	30	M	Unknown	30Ma02Ag
KNOWLAN, Ja.	21	M	Unknown	30Ma02Ag
KINE, Jas.	27	M	Unknown	30Ma02Ag
HAGARTY, Pat	21	M	Unknown	30Ma02Ag
ROGERS, M.	33	M	Unknown	30Ma02Ag
Bridget	18	F	Unknown	30Ma02Ag
A.	.00	M	Infant	30Ma02Ag
BYRNE, John	25	M	Unknown	30Ma02Ag
TUCKER, Thos.	22	M	Unknown	30Ma02Ag
Bridget	20	F	Unknown	30Ma02Ag
LANGTON, Andr.	21	M	Unknown	30Ma02Ag
DILLON, James	30	M	Unknown	30Ma02Ag
BRADLEY, James	40	M	Unknown	30Ma02Ag
U-Mrs.	40	F	Unknown	30Ma02Ag
U-Mrs.	60	F	Unknown	30Ma02Ag
ROTHWELL, P.	24	M	Unknown	30Ma02Ag
TEAL, Wm.	30	M	Unknown	30Ma02Ag
WALKER, Anne	20	F	Unknown	30Ma02Ag
HORAN, James	20	M	Unknown	30Ma02Ag
MULLONEY, Sarah	20	F	Unknown	30Ma02Ag
BURKE, Owen	18	M	Unknown	30Ma02Ag
MOFFATT, Mary	13	F	Unknown	30Ma02Ag
MURPHY, Ellen	11	F	Unknown	30Ma02Ag
BARRETT, Martin	10	M	Unknown	30Ma02Ag
MCANULTY, Pat	13	M	Unknown	30Ma02Ag
ROSS, Bridget	34	F	Unknown	30Ma02Ag
BOLAN, Sally	60	F	Unknown	30Ma02Ag
Anne	13	F	Unknown	30Ma02Ag
Chrs.	12	M	Unknown	30Ma02Ag
CURRAN, Michl.	16	M	Unknown	30Ma02Ag
ROWAN, Mary	18	F	Unknown	30Ma02Ag
COLLINS, Sally	18	F	Unknown	30Ma02Ag
JUDGE, James	20	M	Unknown	30Ma02Ag
MUNEELY, James	20	M	Unknown	30Ma02Ag
ROACH, Thos.	20	M	Unknown	30Ma02Ag
CUGGAN, Richd.	20	M	Unknown	30Ma02Ag
FORAN, Bridgt.	30	F	Unknown	30Ma02Ag
GODFREY, Margt.	27	F	Unknown	30Ma02Ag
WALSH, Bridgt.	18	F	Unknown	30Ma02Ag
DONOVAN, Pat	20	M	Unknown	30Ma02Ag
FITZPATRICK, Jas.	30	M	Unknown	30Ma02Ag
TOOMEY, Robt.	16	M	Unknown	30Ma02Ag
BARRETT, Edwd.	18	M	Unknown	30Ma02Ag
DOOLEY, Jas.	36	M	Unknown	30Ma02Ag
CAMPBELL, Wm.	40	M	Unknown	30Ma02Ag
DUNNE, Michl.	25	M	Unknown	30Ma02Ag
HENNIGAN, Pat	50	M	Unknown	30Ma02Ag
ODONNELL, Anne	15	F	Unknown	30Ma02Ag
ELLIS, Edw.	39	M	Unknown	30Ma02Ag
JONES, John	50	M	Unknown	30Ma02Ag
Watkin	20	M	Unknown	30Ma02Ag
U-Mrs.	27	F	Unknown	30Ma02Ag
Cathn.	21	F	Unknown	30Ma02Ag
David	12	M	Unknown	30Ma02Ag
Thos.	10	M	Unknown	30Ma02Ag
Jno.	8	M	Child	30Ma02Ag
Margt.	6	F	Child	30Ma02Ag
Eliza	2	F	Child	30Ma02Ag
Mary	.00	F	Infant	30Ma02Ag
Ben	30	M	Unknown	30Ma02Ag
Anne	25	F	Unknown	30Ma02Ag
Evan	7	M	Child	30Ma02Ag
Jno.	4	M	Child	30Ma02Ag
Esther	.00	F	Infant	30Ma02Ag
DWYER, Wm.	45	M	Unknown	30Ma02Ag
Wm.	23	M	Unknown	30Ma02Ag
Eliza	20	F	Unknown	30Ma02Ag
Bridget	19	F	Unknown	30Ma02Ag
Mary-Ann	18	F	Unknown	30Ma02Ag
Johanna	10	M	Unknown	30Ma02Ag
LOGAN, Cath.	26	F	Unknown	30Ma02Ag
REARDON, Mary	16	F	Unknown	30Ma02Ag
LEOREY, Tim	33	M	Unknown	30Ma02Ag
Cath.	13	F	Unknown	30Ma02Ag
Tim	.00	M	Infant	30Ma02Ag
OBRIEN, Sarah	22	F	Unknown	30Ma02Ag
MURPHY, Mary	2	F	Child	30Ma02Ag
Dennis	.00	M	Infant	30Ma02Ag
ODONOHOE, Tim	26	M	Unknown	30Ma02Ag
GORMAN, Jno.	24	M	Unknown	30Ma02Ag
Mary	16	F	Unknown	30Ma02Ag
DESMOND, Andr.	24	M	Unknown	30Ma02Ag
KAVANGH, Anne	18	F	Unknown	30Ma02Ag
TIERNY, Peter	50	M	Unknown	30Ma02Ag
Anne	17	F	Unknown	30Ma02Ag
RYAN, Jane	22	F	Unknown	30Ma02Ag
Michl.	20	M	Unknown	30Ma02Ag
BLANCH, Margt.	23	F	Unknown	30Ma02Ag
ENGLISH, Isabella	25	F	Unknown	30Ma02Ag
Margt.	5	F	Child	30Ma02Ag
Thos.	4	M	Child	30Ma02Ag
GREEN, Mich	22	M	Unknown	30Ma02Ag
DICKSON, Sarah-J.	19	F	Unknown	30Ma02Ag
NOLAN, Thomas	20	M	Unknown	30Ma02Ag
MAHON, Pat	17	M	Unknown	30Ma02Ag
Margt.	7	F	Child	30Ma02Ag
HORTY, Margt.	20	F	Unknown	30Ma02Ag
BUCKLEY, Mary	20	F	Unknown	30Ma02Ag
TARRINGTON, Cath.	14	F	Unknown	30Ma02Ag
MCCARTHY, Ellen	16	F	Unknown	30Ma02Ag
Tim	11	M	Unknown	30Ma02Ag
John	8	M	Child	30Ma02Ag
LEAREY, Honor	22	F	Unknown	30Ma02Ag
MURRAY, Mary	30	F	Unknown	30Ma02Ag
ROWAN, Cathne.	25	F	Unknown	30Ma02Ag
John	9	M	Child	30Ma02Ag
Wm.	7	M	Child	30Ma02Ag
Bridget	4	F	Child	30Ma02Ag
LAMB, Wm.	46	M	Unknown	30Ma02Ag
Ellen	18	F	Unknown	30Ma02Ag
U-Mrs.	46	F	Unknown	30Ma02Ag
Mary	16	F	Unknown	30Ma02Ag
Anne	20	F	Unknown	30Ma02Ag
Joseph	00	M	Unknown	30Ma02Ag

WILLIAM 30 MAY 1850

From Cork And Cardiff

NAMES OF PASSENGERS	AGE	SEX	OCCUPATIONS	DATE PORT SHIP
TOOMY, Kitty	20	F	Servant	30Ma55Ko
FLEYNN, N.	20	F	Servant	30Ma55Ko
OMEARA, Wm.	30	M	Laborer	30Ma55Ko
FORD, Wm.	20	M	Laborer	30Ma55Ko
HALLORAN, Ellen	50	F	Servant	30Ma55Ko
Edwd.	20	M	Laborer	30Ma55Ko
John	9	M	Child	30Ma55Ko
Ellen	13	F	Servant	30Ma55Ko
Mary	20	F	Servant	30Ma55Ko
RICE, Pierce	20	M	Laborer	30Ma55Ko
CONDON, Mary	20	F	Servant	30Ma55Ko
LYON, Timothy	25	M	Laborer	30Ma55Ko
SULLIVAN, Mary	20	F	Servant	30Ma55Ko
Johannah	20	F	Servant	30Ma55Ko
MELIM, Mary	25	F	Servant	30Ma55Ko
FITZMAURICE, Mary	22	F	Servant	30Ma55Ko
JEAN, John	20	M	Laborer	30Ma55Ko
KEEFE, John	25	M	Laborer	30Ma55Ko
Mary	25	F	Servant	30Ma55Ko
LEAN, Mary	20	F	Servant	30Ma55Ko
Mary	60	F	Servant	30Ma55Ko
MCEGAN, John	20	M	Laborer	30Ma55Ko
Michl.	13	M	Laborer	30Ma55Ko
Ellen	20	F	Servant	30Ma55Ko
LEAN, Bryan	5	M	Child	30Ma55Ko
Maurice	.00	M	Infant	30Ma55Ko
LEAHY, Ellen	30	F	Servant	30Ma55Ko
William	8	M	Child	30Ma55Ko
Margaret	6	F	Child	30Ma55Ko
John	5	M	Child	30Ma55Ko
Jaremiah	.00	M	Infant	30Ma55Ko
SCANNELL, Joseph	50	M	Laborer	30Ma55Ko
John	20	M	Laborer	30Ma55Ko
Ellen	11	F	Servant	30Ma55Ko
COLLINS, Cornelius	20	M	Laborer	30Ma55Ko
CONNOR, Thos.	20	M	Laborer	30Ma55Ko
Pat	13	M	Laborer	30Ma55Ko
Norry	40	M	Laborer	30Ma55Ko
Johannah	12	F	Child	30Ma55Ko
KENEDY, Catherine	50	F	Servant	30Ma55Ko
Mary	20	F	Servant	30Ma55Ko
Ellen	10	F	Child	30Ma55Ko
Pat	8	M	Child	30Ma55Ko
Michl.	2	M	Child	30Ma55Ko
MURPHY, Mary	22	F	Servant	30Ma55Ko
CONNOR, Thos.	20	M	Laborer	30Ma55Ko
GALVIN, Thos.	20	M	Laborer	30Ma55Ko
KENEDY, Mary	6	F	Child	30Ma55Ko
ROCHE, Cathrine	20	F	Servant	30Ma55Ko
Mary	21	F	Servant	30Ma55Ko
BRIEN, Catherine	22	F	Servant	30Ma55Ko
Margaret	20	F	Servant	30Ma55Ko
MURPHY, Jerry	25	M	Laborer	30Ma55Ko
Michl.	20	M	Laborer	30Ma55Ko
WALSH, Ellen	20	F	Servant	30Ma55Ko
HIGGINS, Johannah	60	F	Laborer	30Ma55Ko
Stephen	13	M	Laborer	30Ma55Ko
GODLY, Richard	25	M	Laborer	30Ma55Ko
Mary	20	F	Servant	30Ma55Ko
David	.00	M	Infant	30Ma55Ko
GRUMMELL, Mary	20	F	Servant	30Ma55Ko
DOOLIN, Peggy	20	F	Servant	30Ma55Ko
GARVEY, Dennis	25	M	Laborer	30Ma55Ko
LEAN, Thos.	25	M	Laborer	30Ma55Ko
HALLORAN, Stephen	23	M	Laborer	30Ma55Ko

NAMES OF PASSENGERS	AGE	SEX	OCCUPATIONS	DATE PORT SHIP
ROCHE, John	20	M	Laborer	30Ma55Ko
KENNY, Maurice	25	M	Laborer	30Ma55Ko
KIRBY, Thos.	22	M	Laborer	30Ma55Ko
Pat	24	M	Laborer	30Ma55Ko
CARROLL, Pat	25	M	Laborer	30Ma55Ko
GODLY, Cath.	20	F	Servant	30Ma55Ko
GLEASON, Pat	25	M	Laborer	30Ma55Ko
KENNY, Mary	10	F	Servant	30Ma55Ko
HUSSEY, Edwd.	22	M	Laborer	30Ma55Ko
CRONIN, John	25	M	Laborer	30Ma55Ko
Cath.	24	F	Servant	30Ma55Ko
Timothy	20	M	Laborer	30Ma55Ko
DINNEEN, Pat	20	M	Laborer	30Ma55Ko
HIGGINS, John	12	M	Child	30Ma55Ko
BLAIR, John	20	M	Laborer	30Ma55Ko
DALY, Bess	20	F	Servant	30Ma55Ko
Pat	20	M	Laborer	30Ma55Ko
SHEA, Jeremiah	25	M	Laborer	30Ma55Ko
Mary	20	F	Servant	30Ma55Ko
DALY, Bridget	10	F	Servant	30Ma55Ko
Julia	20	F	Servant	30Ma55Ko
Thomas	13	M	Laborer	30Ma55Ko
SHEA, Michl.	20	M	Laborer	30Ma55Ko
SHINE, Patt	25	M	Laborer	30Ma55Ko
Margaret	20	F	Servant	30Ma55Ko
BOWER, Mary-Anne	20	F	Servant	30Ma55Ko
MANNON, Ellen	20	F	Servant	30Ma55Ko
SCANNELL, Mary	13	F	Child	30Ma55Ko
FANNING, Cath.	20	F	Servant	30Ma55Ko
HIGGINS, Mary	26	F	Servant	30Ma55Ko
Daniel	.00	M	Infant	30Ma55Ko
Denis	30	M	Laborer	30Ma55Ko
Morris	20	M	Laborer	30Ma55Ko
LONG, Kate	24	F	Servant	30Ma55Ko
DOYLE, John	50	M	Laborer	30Ma55Ko
John	26	M	Laborer	30Ma55Ko
Maurice	26	M	Laborer	30Ma55Ko
Edmund	28	M	Laborer	30Ma55Ko
Margaret	26	F	Servant	30Ma55Ko
Bridget	24	F	Servant	30Ma55Ko
ROMAYNE, Denis	24	M	Laborer	30Ma55Ko
BRIEN, Johanna	20	F	Servant	30Ma55Ko
CALLAGHAN, Abby	28	F	Servant	30Ma55Ko
RIORDAN, Ellen	24	F	Servant	30Ma55Ko
CROSBY, Ellen	11	F	Servant	30Ma55Ko
MAHONEY, Margaret	20	F	Servant	30Ma55Ko
Eliza	13	F	Servant	30Ma55Ko
SWEENEY, Edmund	20	M	Laborer	30Ma55Ko
SHEA, Mary-A.	20	F	Servant	30Ma55Ko
QUAID, Denis	30	M	Laborer	30Ma55Ko
David	20	M	Laborer	30Ma55Ko
Thomas	21	M	Laborer	30Ma55Ko
Mary	60	F	Servant	30Ma55Ko
Margaret	23	F	Servant	30Ma55Ko
Toney	24	F	Servant	30Ma55Ko
Mary	20	F	Servant	30Ma55Ko
MURPHY, Margt.	1	F	Child	30Ma55Ko
LUREHAN, Wm.	20	M	Laborer	30Ma55Ko
OBRIEN, Michl.	20	M	Laborer	30Ma55Ko
MONAGHAN, Mary	36	F	Servant	30Ma55Ko
COMICHAN, Michl.	25	M	Laborer	30Ma55Ko
Mary	50	F	Servant	30Ma55Ko
Margt.	20	F	Servant	30Ma55Ko
Peggy	20	F	Servant	30Ma55Ko
Francis	11	M	Child	30Ma55Ko
William	9	M	Child	30Ma55Ko
COLLINS, Margt.	20	F	Servant	30Ma55Ko
AHEARN, Margt.	20	F	Servant	30Ma55Ko
DUGGAN, Nancy	20	F	Servant	30Ma55Ko
FINTON, John	30	M	Laborer	30Ma55Ko
Margt.	30	F	Servant	30Ma55Ko
Ellen	.00	F	Infant	30Ma55Ko
Pat	11	M	Child	30Ma55Ko
Norry	9	F	Child	30Ma55Ko
HOBART, U-Miss	20	F	Servant	30Ma55Ko

NAMES OF PASSENGERS	AGE	SEX	OCCUPATIONS	DATE PORT SHIP
SEXTON, Wm.	22	M	Laborer	30Ma55Ko
LOBIN, Wm.	20	M	Laborer	30Ma55Ko
CARLETON, Wm.	20	M	Laborer	30Ma55Ko
Mary	20	F	Servant	30Ma55Ko
SHEA, Mary	22	F	Servant	30Ma55Ko
Johanna	20	F	Servant	30Ma55Ko
WALSH, Norry	20	F	Servant	30Ma55Ko
COLLINS, Michl.	26	M	Laborer	30Ma55Ko
Ellen	22	F	Servant	30Ma55Ko
COUGHLAN, Wm.	25	M	Laborer	30Ma55Ko
LYONS, Cath.	20	F	Servant	30Ma55Ko
LEAVEY, Christopher	25	M	Laborer	30Ma55Ko
REGAN, Catherine	20	F	Servant	30Ma55Ko
DONEGAN, Mary	25	F	Servant	30Ma55Ko
Thomas	20	M	Laborer	30Ma55Ko
REGAN, Tim	20	M	Laborer	30Ma55Ko
DONOVAN, Johanna	20	F	Servant	30Ma55Ko
MCCARTHY, John	25	M	Laborer	30Ma55Ko
DURNLEER, Denis	25	M	Laborer	30Ma55Ko
PAYNE, John	26	M	Laborer	30Ma55Ko
Bridget	20	F	Servant	30Ma55Ko
REGAN, Ellen	20	F	Servant	30Ma55Ko
RYAN, Mary	22	F	Servant	30Ma55Ko
MONAGHAN, Mary	24	F	Servant	30Ma55Ko
BURCHILL, Saml.	26	M	Laborer	30Ma55Ko
MOURNANE, Danl.	20	M	Laborer	30Ma55Ko
WADDLE, George	20	M	Laborer	30Ma55Ko
NICE, Jane	20	F	Servant	30Ma55Ko
CALLAGHAN, Michl.	12	M	None	30Ma55Ko
DONOVAN, John	20	M	Laborer	30Ma55Ko
HORTUFF, Richd.	40	M	Laborer	30Ma55Ko
LEARY, Ellen	26	F	Servant	30Ma55Ko
Mary	22	F	Servant	30Ma55Ko
KIELY, Biddy	20	F	Servant	30Ma55Ko
CAREY, John	20	M	Laborer	30Ma55Ko
Bridget	22	F	Servant	30Ma55Ko
Mary	18	F	Servant	30Ma55Ko
William	16	M	Laborer	30Ma55Ko
CRONIN, Philip	2	M	Child	30Ma55Ko
PAYNE, John	35	M	Farmer	30Ma55Ko
Bridget	32	F	Wife	30Ma55Ko
CURTAYNE, Wm.	35	M	Clerk	30Ma55Ko
HERLIHY, Jess.	20	F	Unknown	30Ma55Ko
CURTAYNE, Charlotte	20	F	Wife	30Ma55Ko
Wm.	3	M	Child	30Ma55Ko
Charlotte	.00	F	Infant	30Ma55Ko
MAHONEY, Mary	25	F	Servant	30Ma55Ko
HUMPHREYS, Mary	25	F	Seamstress	30Ma55Ko
DRISCOL, Daniel	26	M	Plasterer	30Ma55Ko
LAVALLAN, Michael	25	M	Farmer	30Ma55Ko
COGHLIN, John	20	M	Clerk	30Ma55Ko
BASS, Samuel	20	M	Printer	30Ma55Ko
BOWEN, Catherine	22	F	Stewardess	30Ma55Ko
HICKEY, Patt	35	M	Landlord	30Ma55Ko
Johannah	35	F	Wife	30Ma55Ko
Ellen	24	F	Unknown	30Ma55Ko
John	12	M	Unknown	30Ma55Ko
Anne	10	F	Unknown	30Ma55Ko
Patt	8	M	Child	30Ma55Ko
James	6	M	Child	30Ma55Ko
Mary-Anne	4	F	Child	30Ma55Ko
Peter	2	M	Child	30Ma55Ko

QUEEN 30 MAY 1850

From Cork

NAMES OF PASSENGERS	AGE	SEX	OCCUPATIONS	DATE PORT SHIP
HIGGINS, Julia	20	F	Farmer	30Ma18le
MURPHY, Mary	38	F	Unknown	30Ma18le
MURPHY, Anne	12	F	Unknown	30Ma18le
DAVIS, Mary-Ann	20	F	Unknown	30Ma18le
HYDE, Nancy	20	F	Unknown	30Ma18le
HICKEY, Michl.	20	M	Unknown	30Ma18le
David	20	M	Unknown	30Ma18le
CONNOR, Nory	20	F	Unknown	30Ma18le
Cath.	2	F	Child	30Ma18le
Cath.	.00	F	Infant	30Ma18le
DEA, Peggy	20	F	Unknown	30Ma18le
ANDREWS, Margt.	25	F	Unknown	30Ma18le
LIGUE, Charles	32	F	Unknown	30Ma18le
DOOHIG, David	32	M	Unknown	30Ma18le
Ellen	38	F	Unknown	30Ma18le
BARRY, John	20	M	Unknown	30Ma18le
LINCHAN, Margt.	20	F	Unknown	30Ma18le
MURPHY, Margt.	12	F	Unknown	30Ma18le
HIGGINS, Mary	13	F	Unknown	30Ma18le
LOTTER, Johanna	20	F	Unknown	30Ma18le
MACKEY, Peter	25	M	Unknown	30Ma18le
Eliza	23	F	Unknown	30Ma18le
CONNOR, Patt	20	M	Unknown	30Ma18le
AHEARN, Nicholas	20	M	Unknown	30Ma18le
GOGGIN, Michl.	20	M	Unknown	30Ma18le
BROWN, Cath.	25	F	Unknown	30Ma18le
WALSH, William	20	M	Unknown	30Ma18le
MCGRATH, Bridget	20	F	Unknown	30Ma18le
ROCHE, David	13	M	Unknown	30Ma18le
AHEARN, Mary	20	F	Unknown	30Ma18le
CAHILL, Thos.	24	M	Unknown	30Ma18le
Mary	24	F	Unknown	30Ma18le
BRODRICK, Dennis	20	M	Unknown	30Ma18le
OLOUGHLAN, Peter	30	M	Unknown	30Ma18le
Bridget	30	F	Unknown	30Ma18le
Kate	4	F	Child	30Ma18le
Bridget	3	F	Child	30Ma18le
Charles	.00	M	Infant	30Ma18le
DEA, Kate	20	F	Unknown	30Ma18le
LOUGHLIN, Patt	20	M	Unknown	30Ma18le
HENNESSY, Patt	22	M	Unknown	30Ma18le
Mary	20	F	Unknown	30Ma18le
Ned.	22	M	Unknown	30Ma18le
Michl.	24	M	Unknown	30Ma18le
Peggy	.00	F	Infant	30Ma18le
BUCKLEY, Michl.	25	M	Unknown	30Ma18le
BURKE, John	20	M	Unknown	30Ma18le
ODELL, John	20	M	Unknown	30Ma18le
Thos.	20	M	Unknown	30Ma18le
GRIFFIN, Patt	20	M	Unknown	30Ma18le
John	16	M	Unknown	30Ma18le
PIGOTT, Johanna	21	F	Unknown	30Ma18le
Johanna	22	F	Unknown	30Ma18le
Hannah	20	F	Unknown	30Ma18le
DUGGAN, Margt.	22	M	Unknown	30Ma18le
BRYAN, Ellen	12	F	Unknown	30Ma18le
Bess	12	F	Unknown	30Ma18le
WILLIAMS, Anne	20	F	Unknown	30Ma18le
CONNOR, Cath.	20	F	Unknown	30Ma18le
PIGOTT, George	20	M	Unknown	30Ma18le
Agnes	12	F	Unknown	30Ma18le
Julia	.00	F	Infant	30Ma18le
MURPHY, Jerry	30	M	Unknown	30Ma18le
LINCHAN, Margt.	20	F	Unknown	30Ma18le
Mary	20	F	Unknown	30Ma18le
RYAN, Michl.	36	M	Unknown	30Ma18le
CANNING, Michl.	30	M	Unknown	30Ma18le
BALWIN, John	28	M	Unknown	30Ma18le
MURPHY, Michl.	20	M	Unknown	30Ma18le
CONWAY, Michl.	20	M	Unknown	30Ma18le
William	26	M	Unknown	30Ma18le
COLLINS, Eliza	20	F	Unknown	30Ma18le
John	20	M	Unknown	30Ma18le
Eliza	13	F	Unknown	30Ma18le
Ellen	.00	F	Infant	30Ma18le
WORTH, Mary	26	F	Unknown	30Ma18le
Anne	26	F	Unknown	30Ma18le

NAMES OF PASSENGERS	AGE	SEX	OCCUPATIONS	DATE PORT SHIP
WORTH, Isabella	11	F	Unknown	30Ma18le
Henry	5	M	Child	30Ma18le
Albert	.00	M	Infant	30Ma18le
DEALER, Michl.	20	M	Unknown	30Ma18le
Patt	20	M	Unknown	30Ma18le
SANDERS, Ellen	25	F	Unknown	30Ma18le
Biddy	.00	F	Infant	30Ma18le
KERVANE, Ellen	18	F	Unknown	30Ma18le
MCKENNA, Kate	18	F	Unknown	30Ma18le
COLLINS, Kitty	20	F	Unknown	30Ma18le
WALSH, John	20	M	Unknown	30Ma18le
Morry	4	M	Child	30Ma18le
BRENNAN, Kitty	30	F	Infant	30Ma18le
Mary	11	F	Unknown	30Ma18le
SANDERS, Peggy	25	F	Unknown	30Ma18le
RUSSELL, Mary	25	F	Unknown	30Ma18le
ASH, Johanna	20	F	Unknown	30Ma18le
FITZGERALD, Kitty	12	F	Unknown	30Ma18le
Kitty	35	F	Unknown	30Ma18le
KERVANE, Mary	20	F	Unknown	30Ma18le
Paddy	25	F	Unknown	30Ma18le
BOLAND, Nelly	18	F	Unknown	30Ma18le
GRIFFIN, Nancy	20	F	Unknown	30Ma18le
FITZGERALD, U	22	F	Unknown	30Ma18le
THOMAS, John	22	M	Unknown	30Ma18le
Richard	10	M	Unknown	30Ma18le
MCKENNA, Michl.	13	M	Unknown	30Ma18le
SULLIVAN, Kate	13	F	Unknown	30Ma18le
FITZGERALD, Michl.	20	M	Unknown	30Ma18le
KENNEDY, Johanna	20	F	Unknown	30Ma18le
SHEA, Michl.	16	M	Unknown	30Ma18le
DALY, Patt	20	M	Unknown	30Ma18le
Cath.	40	F	Unknown	30Ma18le
GRADY, James	30	M	Unknown	30Ma18le
HERLAHY, Mary	21	F	Unknown	30Ma18le
Kate	.00	F	Infant	30Ma18le

IRWIN 30 MAY 1850

From Galway

NAMES OF PASSENGERS	AGE	SEX	OCCUPATIONS	DATE PORT SHIP
CARTY, Thady	30	F	Laborer	30Ma42Ef
LENNAN, Mary	30	F	Unknown	30Ma42Ef
KENESY, Mary	.00	F	Infant	30Ma42Ef
John	20	M	Unknown	30Ma42Ef
KEEMAN, John	19	M	Unknown	30Ma42Ef
COLLINS, Mary	23	F	Unknown	30Ma42Ef
FAHY, Ellen	23	F	Unknown	30Ma42Ef
MOHAN, Biddy	11	F	Unknown	30Ma42Ef
BENTLY, Catherine	30	F	Unknown	30Ma42Ef
SMITH, Bridget	.00	F	Infant	30Ma42Ef
John	4	M	Child	30Ma42Ef
Michael	40	M	Unknown	30Ma42Ef
SHEEHAN, Peggy	30	F	Unknown	30Ma42Ef
MCHUGH, Judy	20	F	Unknown	30Ma42Ef
CUSACK, Patt	28	M	Unknown	30Ma42Ef
FORD, Margaret	10	F	Unknown	30Ma42Ef
HOWARD, James	24	M	Unknown	30Ma42Ef
Malachy	12	M	Unknown	30Ma42Ef
HARLY, John	30	M	Unknown	30Ma42Ef
DEELY, Patt	22	M	Unknown	30Ma42Ef
SMITH, Patt	22	M	Unknown	30Ma42Ef
MCGRALY, Margaret	22	F	Unknown	30Ma42Ef
HUGHES, Michael	24	M	Unknown	30Ma42Ef
COLEMAN, Michael	26	M	Unknown	30Ma42Ef
LOFTUS, John	30	M	Unknown	30Ma42Ef
EGAN, Martin	30	M	Unknown	30Ma42Ef
Mary	25	F	Unknown	30Ma42Ef
FEEHY, Nappy	30	F	Unknown	30Ma42Ef

NAMES OF PASSENGERS	AGE	SEX	OCCUPATIONS	DATE PORT SHIP
SHOUGHNESSY, John	30	M	Unknown	30Ma42Ef
BUTTER, James	.00	M	Infant	30Ma42Ef
CASSIDY, Mary	20	F	Unknown	30Ma42Ef
Margaret	35	F	Unknown	30Ma42Ef
COTTINGHAM, Bridget	16	F	Unknown	30Ma42Ef
MCDERMOTT, Nancy	26	F	Unknown	30Ma42Ef
SMALL, William	18	M	Unknown	30Ma42Ef
FARRELL, Ellen	18	F	Unknown	30Ma42Ef
DERMODY, James	20	M	Unknown	30Ma42Ef
Maria	18	F	Unknown	30Ma42Ef
James	19	M	Unknown	30Ma42Ef
MCMAHON, Margaret	50	F	Unknown	30Ma42Ef
KELLY, Mary	23	F	Unknown	30Ma42Ef
FALEY, Bridget	6	F	Child	30Ma42Ef
FLAHERTY, Mary	11	F	Unknown	30Ma42Ef
Maria	5	F	Child	30Ma42Ef
Martin	.00	M	Infant	30Ma42Ef
John	6	M	Child	30Ma42Ef
Patt	11	M	Unknown	30Ma42Ef
WHEELAN, Mary	5	F	Child	30Ma42Ef
Biddy	16	F	Unknown	30Ma42Ef
Ann	.00	F	Infant	30Ma42Ef
FORD, Mary	18	F	Unknown	30Ma42Ef
Peggy	20	F	Unknown	30Ma42Ef
HAYS, John	30	M	Unknown	30Ma42Ef
CARTY, Judy	.00	F	Infant	30Ma42Ef
Margaret	20	F	Unknown	30Ma42Ef
HAYS, Kate	15	F	Unknown	30Ma42Ef
Patt	13	M	Unknown	30Ma42Ef
John	.00	M	Infant	30Ma42Ef
HYNES, Bridgt.	24	F	Unknown	30Ma42Ef
SCULLY, John	17	M	Unknown	30Ma42Ef
HYNES, Mary	46	F	Unknown	30Ma42Ef
EARLNEY, Biddy	22	F	Unknown	30Ma42Ef
FLAHERTY, Margaret	19	F	Unknown	30Ma42Ef
CONROY, Michael	28	M	Unknown	30Ma42Ef
BURNS, Mary	28	F	Unknown	30Ma42Ef
CLANCY, Martin	26	M	Unknown	30Ma42Ef
GERATY, Marty	28	M	Unknown	30Ma42Ef
WALSH, Margaret	18	F	Unknown	30Ma42Ef
NEWELE, Bridget	20	F	Unknown	30Ma42Ef
John	.00	M	Infant	30Ma42Ef
SARSFIELD, James	20	M	Unknown	30Ma42Ef
GRIFFIN, Biddy	20	F	Unknown	30Ma42Ef
MORAN, Mary	17	F	Unknown	30Ma42Ef
KAIN, John	20	M	Unknown	30Ma42Ef
MELODY, Patt	28	M	Unknown	30Ma42Ef
GORDON, Honor	30	F	Unknown	30Ma42Ef
BURNS, Michael	19	M	Unknown	30Ma42Ef
WALSH, Honor	38	F	Unknown	30Ma42Ef
John	15	M	Unknown	30Ma42Ef
NEWELE, William	17	M	Unknown	30Ma42Ef
Biddy	.00	F	Infant	30Ma42Ef
KAHILL, Patt	29	M	Unknown	30Ma42Ef
DEELY, Thos.	16	M	Unknown	30Ma42Ef
GILIGAN, Patt	20	M	Unknown	30Ma42Ef
LOGAN, Mary	17	F	Unknown	30Ma42Ef
BRADY, Bridget	46	F	Unknown	30Ma42Ef
CONNELL, Catherine	18	F	Unknown	30Ma42Ef
DOLAN, Rodger	13	M	Unknown	30Ma42Ef
BOHAN, Michael	20	M	Laborer	30Ma42Ef
HALPIN, Bartly	26	M	Unknown	30Ma42Ef
DEVANY, Bridget	24	F	Unknown	30Ma42Ef
John	23	M	Unknown	30Ma42Ef
MONNION, John	30	M	Unknown	30Ma42Ef
Judy	.00	F	Infant	30Ma42Ef
COTTINGHAM, John	20	M	Unknown	30Ma42Ef
MANRION, Patt	25	M	Unknown	30Ma42Ef
KELLY, Bridget	28	F	Unknown	30Ma42Ef
KERNS, Martin	27	M	Unknown	30Ma42Ef
Bridget	20	F	Unknown	30Ma42Ef
Patt	30	M	Unknown	30Ma42Ef
William	.00	M	Infant	30Ma42Ef
RUSH, Biddy	60	F	Unknown	30Ma42Ef
Michael	28	M	Unknown	30Ma42Ef

NAMES OF PASSENGERS	AGE	SEX	OCCUPATIONS	DATE PORT SHIP
GRIFFIN, Biddy	30	F	Unknown	30Ma42Ef
KELLY, Michael	.00	M	Infant	30Ma42Ef
HAMILTON, Peter	20	M	Unknown	30Ma42Ef
CORNICAN, Martin	25	M	Unknown	30Ma42Ef
Biddy	29	F	Unknown	30Ma42Ef
Mary	18	F	Unknown	30Ma42Ef
RURANE, Biddy	20	F	Unknown	30Ma42Ef
CARTY, John	30	M	Unknown	30Ma42Ef
Catherine	28	F	Unknown	30Ma42Ef
HORNER, Margaret	.00	F	Infant	30Ma42Ef
OBRIEN, Mary	21	F	Unknown	30Ma42Ef
John	23	M	Unknown	30Ma42Ef
MCLOUGHLAN, Edward	29	M	Unknown	30Ma42Ef
Martin	.00	M	Infant	30Ma42Ef
Teresa	46	F	Unknown	30Ma42Ef
JENNINGS, Michael	39	M	Unknown	30Ma42Ef
William	19	M	Unknown	30Ma42Ef
Sebina	16	F	Unknown	30Ma42Ef
Mary	30	F	Unknown	30Ma42Ef
KEARNS, Honor	28	F	Unknown	30Ma42Ef
NOON, Mary	11	F	Unknown	30Ma42Ef
FOLCEN, Honor	20	F	Unknown	30Ma42Ef
John	18	M	Unknown	30Ma42Ef
CREGAN, John	18	M	Unknown	30Ma42Ef
Patt	.00	M	Infant	30Ma42Ef
John	17	M	Unknown	30Ma42Ef
FORD, John	26	M	Unknown	30Ma42Ef
OLOUGHLIN, Ellen	29	F	Laborer	30Ma42Ef
MCLEON, Mary	25	F	Unknown	30Ma42Ef
HUGHES, Bartly	26	M	Unknown	30Ma42Ef
Margaret	18	F	Unknown	30Ma42Ef
Mary	20	F	Unknown	30Ma42Ef
BRADY, Larry	.00	M	Infant	30Ma42Ef
Bridget	15	F	Unknown	30Ma42Ef
Richard	25	M	Unknown	30Ma42Ef
CONNELLY, Judy	24	F	Unknown	30Ma42Ef
POWER, Patt	.00	M	Infant	30Ma42Ef
DREWERY, Mary	22	F	Unknown	30Ma42Ef
MITHCELL, Margaret	24	F	Unknown	30Ma42Ef
CALOMAN, Honor	26	F	Unknown	30Ma42Ef
DONOLON, Patt	20	M	Unknown	30Ma42Ef
SHIEL, Mary	19	F	Unknown	30Ma42Ef
HOLAN, Michael	20	M	Unknown	30Ma42Ef
BRADY, Patt	25	M	Unknown	30Ma42Ef
LAWLER, James	24	M	Unknown	30Ma42Ef
Margaret	22	F	Unknown	30Ma42Ef
PAPNAN, Margaret	20	F	Unknown	30Ma42Ef
MORAN, Biddy	.00	F	Infant	30Ma42Ef
JOYCE, Michael	25	M	Unknown	30Ma42Ef
FLAHERTY, Martin	29	M	Unknown	30Ma42Ef
CORNICAN, James	20	M	Unknown	30Ma42Ef
MURPHY, Biddy	21	F	Unknown	30Ma42Ef
BARRETT, John	25	M	Unknown	30Ma42Ef
LOGAN, Ann	27	F	Unknown	30Ma42Ef
CAHILL, John	25	M	Unknown	30Ma42Ef
FAFF, Catherine	24	F	Unknown	30Ma42Ef
REGAN, Thos.	22	M	Unknown	30Ma42Ef
Bridget	20	F	Unknown	30Ma42Ef
CASSIDY, James	18	M	Unknown	30Ma42Ef
KENNEDY, Margaret	19	F	Unknown	30Ma42Ef
Michael	17	M	Unknown	30Ma42Ef
NESTOR, Ann	16	F	Unknown	30Ma42Ef
Bridget	.00	F	Infant	30Ma42Ef
FRANCIS, Stephen	14	M	Unknown	30Ma42Ef
FORD, Sarah	25	F	Unknown	30Ma42Ef
MCCULLOUGH, Mary	27	F	Unknown	30Ma42Ef
Sally	25	F	Unknown	30Ma42Ef
BURKE, Mary	26	F	Unknown	30Ma42Ef
GREALY, Mary	.00	F	Infant	30Ma42Ef
Nappy	20	F	Unknown	30Ma42Ef
Mary	25	F	Unknown	30Ma42Ef
Peter	16	M	Unknown	30Ma42Ef
BODKIN, Biddy	19	F	Unknown	30Ma42Ef
DONOHOE, Nicholas	.00	M	Infant	30Ma42Ef
HALLORAN, Michael	19	M	Unknown	30Ma42Ef
WALSH, Michael	24	M	Unknown	30Ma42Ef
MURPHY, Bridget	23	F	Unknown	30Ma42Ef
MORAN, Nappy	20	F	Unknown	30Ma42Ef
REILLY, Michael	20	M	Unknown	30Ma42Ef
CASY, Michael	21	M	Unknown	30Ma42Ef
JULEY, Hugh	30	M	Unknown	30Ma42Ef
KELLERY, Catherine	30	F	Unknown	30Ma42Ef
TULLY, Mary	34	F	Unknown	30Ma42Ef
ONEIL, Thos.	20	M	Unknown	30Ma42Ef
FRANCIS, Martin	18	M	Unknown	30Ma42Ef
WALSH, Patt	26	M	Unknown	30Ma42Ef
LOFTUS, Thos.	23	M	Unknown	30Ma42Ef
FOLEY, Michael	30	M	Unknown	30Ma42Ef
FALERNY, Sarah	28	F	Unknown	30Ma42Ef
ORMSLEY, Thos.	25	M	Unknown	30Ma42Ef
FINNEGAN, Mary	.00	F	Infant	30Ma42Ef
KING, Thos.	24	M	Unknown	30Ma42Ef
NEWELE, Margaret	20	F	Unknown	30Ma42Ef
BARRETT, Ellen	21	F	Unknown	30Ma42Ef
QUINN, Bridget	26	F	Unknown	30Ma42Ef
RUIRN, Patt	25	M	Unknown	30Ma42Ef
KILLEAN, Thos.	25	M	Unknown	30Ma42Ef
HICKEY, Patt	.00	M	Infant	30Ma42Ef
GOLDING, John	36	M	Unknown	30Ma42Ef
RYAN, Martin	30	M	Unknown	30Ma42Ef
MCHUGH, James	20	M	Unknown	30Ma42Ef
Catherine	21	F	Unknown	30Ma42Ef
HARDINAN, Patt	15	M	Unknown	30Ma42Ef
GREALY, Mary	19	F	Unknown	30Ma42Ef
Biddy	18	F	Unknown	30Ma42Ef
Michael	29	M	Unknown	30Ma42Ef
J.Ann	.00	F	Infant	30Ma42Ef
SHAUGNESSY, Susan	15	F	Unknown	30Ma42Ef
MULLIN, Michael	12	M	Unknown	30Ma42Ef
WALSH, Michael	24	M	Unknown	30Ma42Ef
Mary	26	F	Unknown	30Ma42Ef
Kate	27	F	Unknown	30Ma42Ef
BARRETT, Honor	25	F	Unknown	30Ma42Ef
NOONAN, Bartly	.00	M	Infant	30Ma42Ef
Catherine	25	F	Unknown	30Ma42Ef
SCULLY, Bridget	28	F	Unknown	30Ma42Ef
HICKEY, John	21	M	Unknown	30Ma42Ef
CONHILLY, Honor	.00	F	Infant	30Ma42Ef
NEWELL, John	20	M	Unknown	30Ma42Ef
COLEMAN, Maria	19	F	Laborer	30Ma42Ef
RIERDAN, Mary	19	F	Unknown	30Ma42Ef
Ann	28	F	Unknown	30Ma42Ef
Mary	20	F	Unknown	30Ma42Ef
William	19	M	Unknown	30Ma42Ef
BROTHERNAY, Malacky	18	M	Unknown	30Ma42Ef
Biddy	.00	F	Infant	30Ma42Ef
WHEELAN, Martha	19	F	Unknown	30Ma42Ef
NOONAN, Martin	30	M	Unknown	30Ma42Ef
SHOUGNESSEY, Juddy	24	M	Unknown	30Ma42Ef
WARD, Winefred	18	M	Unknown	30Ma42Ef
FAHY, Thos.	26	M	Unknown	30Ma42Ef
NOLAN, Andrew	19	M	Unknown	30Ma42Ef
CARMADDEY, Patt	22	M	Unknown	30Ma42Ef
MULLAN, Mary	24	F	Unknown	30Ma42Ef
CARR, Philip	49	M	Unknown	30Ma42Ef
SMITH, George	21	M	Unknown	30Ma42Ef
MCHAYS, U-Mrs.	22	F	Unknown	30Ma42Ef
John	17	M	Unknown	30Ma42Ef
George	22	M	Unknown	30Ma42Ef
HINTON, John	22	M	Unknown	30Ma42Ef
Wm.	40	M	Unknown	30Ma42Ef
BLACK, Jane	00	F	Unknown	30Ma42Ef
CRUICE, U-Mrs.	41	F	Unknown	30Ma42Ef
Ellen	15	F	Unknown	30Ma42Ef
John	16	M	Unknown	30Ma42Ef
Robert	11	M	Unknown	30Ma42Ef
STEPHENS, U-Mrs.	35	F	Unknown	30Ma42Ef
Walter	15	M	Unknown	30Ma42Ef
WALSH, Timothy	22	M	Unknown	30Ma42Ef
CONRON, Biddy	17	F	Unknown	30Ma42Ef

NAMES OF PASSENGERS	AGE	SEX	OCCUPATIONS	DATE PORT SHIP
BURKE, John	14	M	Unknown	30Ma42Ef
STARKEY, Dominick	16	M	Unknown	30Ma42Ef
CARUS, Peter	14	M	Unknown	30Ma42Ef

EUPHEMIA 31 MAY 1850

From Liverpool

NAMES OF PASSENGERS	AGE	SEX	OCCUPATIONS	DATE PORT SHIP
DIXON, Robert	47	M	Laborer	31Ma02KV
Mary	.11	F	Infant	31Ma02KV
John	15	M	Unknown	31Ma02KV
David	13	M	Unknown	31Ma02KV
Jane	11	F	Unknown	31Ma02KV
Mary	8	F	Child	31Ma02KV
Janett	5	F	Child	31Ma02KV
Isabella Died-At-Sea	.10	F	Infant	31Ma02KV
HEANEY, Joseph	26	M	Unknown	31Ma02KV
BRIEN, Bridget	18	F	Unknown	31Ma02KV
CARROLL, Ellen	26	F	Unknown	31Ma02KV
LEE, Pat	18	M	Unknown	31Ma02KV
OGORMAN, Mick	25	M	Unknown	31Ma02KV
OKEEFE, Bridget	29	F	Unknown	31Ma02KV
KELLY, Catherine	20	F	Unknown	31Ma02KV
Johanna	18	F	Unknown	31Ma02KV
THOMAS, Robert	23	M	Unknown	31Ma02KV
CARR, Henry	20	M	Unknown	31Ma02KV
MACKEY, Ellen	42	F	Unknown	31Ma02KV
Ellen	14	F	Unknown	31Ma02KV
KELLY, Lydia	18	F	Unknown	31Ma02KV
ASTON, Henry	4	M	Child	31Ma02KV
DODD, John	30	M	Unknown	31Ma02KV
Isaac	20	M	Unknown	31Ma02KV
Thomas	9	M	Child	31Ma02KV
CLEGG, Robert	20	M	Unknown	31Ma02KV
MCGOVERN, Phillip	20	M	Unknown	31Ma02KV
MCCARTY, John	20	M	Unknown	31Ma02KV
REILY, Rose	20	F	Unknown	31Ma02KV
COLIN, Mary	11	F	Unknown	31Ma02KV
FAGAN, Mick	25	M	Unknown	31Ma02KV
DUNNING, Pat	18	M	Unknown	31Ma02KV
OCARREN, Edward	18	M	Unknown	31Ma02KV
Lair--, George	24	M	Unknown	31Ma02KV
SMITH, Alexander	26	M	Unknown	31Ma02KV
Mary	26	F	Unknown	31Ma02KV
MCRIE, Peter	22	M	Unknown	31Ma02KV
James	18	M	Unknown	31Ma02KV
KING, Wm.	26	M	Unknown	31Ma02KV
MCGAWEY, Allen	16	M	Unknown	31Ma02KV
FITZGERALD, Mick	30	M	Unknown	31Ma02KV
Mary	30	F	Unknown	31Ma02KV
Mary	.06	F	Infant	31Ma02KV
James	50	M	Unknown	31Ma02KV
Mary	16	F	Unknown	31Ma02KV
Margaret	12	F	Unknown	31Ma02KV
MICHAN, Johanna	18	F	Unknown	31Ma02KV
PURDY, Catherine	19	F	Unknown	31Ma02KV
COONEN, Mick	7	M	Child	31Ma02KV
John	4	M	Child	31Ma02KV
NEVIN, John	14	M	Unknown	31Ma02KV
TRACY, Charles	20	M	Unknown	31Ma02KV
Mick	18	M	Unknown	31Ma02KV
Ellen	12	F	Unknown	31Ma02KV
MARKEY, Pat	21	M	Unknown	31Ma02KV
REYNOLDS, Pat	28	M	Unknown	31Ma02KV
Allen	26	M	Unknown	31Ma02KV
SUMMERS, Francis	16	M	Unknown	31Ma02KV
Ann	13	F	Unknown	31Ma02KV
Thomas	9	M	Child	31Ma02KV

NAMES OF PASSENGERS	AGE	SEX	OCCUPATIONS	DATE PORT SHIP
REILEY, Margaret	40	F	Unknown	31Ma02KV
Rose	11	F	Unknown	31Ma02KV
John	7	M	Child	31Ma02KV
Mary	5	F	Child	31Ma02KV
Elizabeth	2	F	Child	31Ma02KV
REILY, Phillip	30	M	Unknown	31Ma02KV
WRIGHT, John	5	M	Child	31Ma02KV
COONEY, James	20	M	Unknown	31Ma02KV
Pat	11	M	Unknown	31Ma02KV
Mick	8	M	Child	31Ma02KV
MAHON, John	40	M	Unknown	31Ma02KV
Pat	12	M	Unknown	31Ma02KV
Allen	8	M	Child	31Ma02KV
Ann	6	F	Child	31Ma02KV
MCGWIN, Bridget	5	F	Child	31Ma02KV
CROAK, Tom	28	M	Unknown	31Ma02KV
DERMOD, Tom	31	M	Unknown	31Ma02KV
JUDGE, John	30	M	Unknown	31Ma02KV
PILLOGLY, Jim	21	M	Unknown	31Ma02KV
BYRNE, Jane	24	F	Unknown	31Ma02KV
CLACKIN, Cate.	20	F	Unknown	31Ma02KV
Mary	28	F	Unknown	31Ma02KV
BYRNE, Ann	12	F	Unknown	31Ma02KV
MURPHY, Andrew	26	M	Unknown	31Ma02KV
WALLACE, John	25	M	Unknown	31Ma02KV
ROBINSON, Rachel	15	F	Unknown	31Ma02KV
MCMILLIGAN, Ellen	44	F	Unknown	31Ma02KV
Nicolas	13	M	Unknown	31Ma02KV
Alice	4	F	Child	31Ma02KV
Jane	.11	F	Infant	31Ma02KV
CROAK, Richard	34	M	Unknown	31Ma02KV
WOODS, Ann	18	F	Unknown	31Ma02KV
MURPHY, Mary-A.	18	F	Unknown	31Ma02KV
DIGNAN, Mick	18	M	Unknown	31Ma02KV
HANNIGAN, Mary	30	F	Unknown	31Ma02KV
CASSIDY, Catherine	5	F	Child	31Ma02KV
Margaret	3	F	Child	31Ma02KV
FENTON, John	30	M	Unknown	31Ma02KV
ROURKE, Wm.	20	M	Unknown	31Ma02KV
HOGAN, Pat	11	M	Unknown	31Ma02KV
John	7	M	Child	31Ma02KV
THOMPSON, Clara	40	F	Unknown	31Ma02KV
Elizabeth	18	F	Unknown	31Ma02KV
Rebecca	11	F	Unknown	31Ma02KV
Clara	5	F	Child	31Ma02KV
Sarah	3	F	Child	31Ma02KV
MCDONALD, John	28	M	Unknown	31Ma02KV
RILEY, Pat	19	M	Unknown	31Ma02KV
Thomas	4	M	Child	31Ma02KV
BRADY, Ann	16	F	Unknown	31Ma02KV
GRACE, Edward	13	M	Unknown	31Ma02KV
Thomas	12	M	Unknown	31Ma02KV
PURCELL, John	13	M	Unknown	31Ma02KV
Bridget	11	F	Unknown	31Ma02KV
GRIFFIN, James	30	M	Unknown	31Ma02KV
KEOUGH, Bridget	20	F	Unknown	31Ma02KV
Catherine	18	F	Unknown	31Ma02KV
HOWE, Mick	40	M	Unknown	31Ma02KV
BYRNE, Mary	22	F	Unknown	31Ma02KV
MCGUIRE, Peter	4	M	Child	31Ma02KV
MURRAY, Thomas	20	M	Unknown	31Ma02KV
FLOOD, Ellen	11	F	Unknown	31Ma02KV
Catherine	9	F	Child	31Ma02KV
Rose	7	F	Child	31Ma02KV
Bridget	4	F	Child	31Ma02KV
SHEEHAN, C.	26	F	Unknown	31Ma02KV
John	8	M	Child	31Ma02KV

INDEX